AMERICAN NATIONAL BIOGRAPHY

AMERICAN NATIONAL BIOGRAPHY

Published under the auspices of the
AMERICAN COUNCIL OF LEARNED SOCIETIES

General Editors

John A. Garraty
Mark C. Carnes

VOLUME 3

OXFORD UNIVERSITY PRESS
New York 1999 Oxford

OXFORD UNIVERSITY PRESS

Oxford New York
Athens Auckland Bangkok Bogotá
Buenos Aires Calcutta Cape Town Chennai
Dar es Salaam Delhi Florence Hong Kong Istanbul
Karachi Kuala Lumpur Madrid Melbourne Mexico City
Mumbai Nairobi Paris São Paulo Singapore
Taipei Tokyo Toronto Warsaw
and associated companies in
Berlin Ibadan

Published by Oxford University Press, Inc.,
198 Madison Avenue, New York, New York 10016
http://www.oup-usa.org

Funding for this publication was provided in part by the Andrew W. Mellon Foundation, the Rockefeller Foundation, and the National Endowment for the Humanities, a federal agency.

Library of Congress Cataloging-in-Publication Data

American national biography / general editors, John A. Garraty, Mark C. Carnes
p. cm.
"Published under the auspices of the American Council of Learned Societies."
Includes bibliographical references and index.
1. United States—Biography—Dictionaries. I. Garraty, John Arthur, 1920– . II. Carnes, Mark C. (Mark Christopher), 1950– . III. American Council of Learned Societies.
CT213.A68 1998 98-20826 920.073—dc21 CIP
ISBN 0-19-520635-5 (set)
ISBN 0-19-512782-X (vol. 3)

Printing (last digit): 9 8 7 6 5 4 3 2 1

Printed in the United States of America
on acid-free paper

B

CONTINUED

BLATCHFORD, Richard Milford (23 Apr. 1798–4 Sept. 1875), banking and trust lawyer and politician, was born in Stratford, Connecticut, the son of Samuel Blatchford and Alicia Windeatt, a couple who had come from England in the summer of 1795. His father, a Presbyterian minister, subsequently was in charge of the Lansingburgh Academy and a church at Waterford, New York, and became the first president of Rensselaer Polytechnic Institute in 1824, officiating there until his death in 1828. The ninth of seventeen children, Richard received a bachelor's degree from Union College in 1815 and then moved to New York City, where a brother, also a Union graduate, had won appointment as resident physician of the Greenwich Prison. While studying law, Blatchford served briefly as a fireman in 1817, and taught school in Jamaica, Long Island. In 1819 he married Julia Ann Mumford, daughter of John P. Mumford of New York City, a merchant who had increasingly concentrated on the development of insurance companies. Julia Blatchford died in 1857. Four of their five children survived to adulthood, and their one son, Samuel, became a justice of the U.S. Supreme Court. In 1860 Blatchford married Angelica Hamilton, a daughter of James A. Hamilton. She died in 1868, and in 1870 he married Katherine Hone, a daughter of his friend Philip Hone. His second and third marriages were childless.

Blatchford's legal career, which commenced in 1819, laid some foundations of the Cravath firm of New York City and established him as more than a simple provider of political security for moneyed clients. Made counsel and agent for the Bank of England in 1826, he also served the (Second) Bank of the United States as counsel and settled accounts between the two institutions after the charter of the Bank of the United States expired in 1836. He frequently acted as a receiver for other banks. Concentrating on advising and creating legal instruments for banks, insurance companies, trusts, and English investors, Blatchford left courtroom litigation largely to Edgcumbe H. Blatchford, his youngest brother and partner from 1832 until Edgcumbe's death in 1853. An "office lawyer," Blatchford became essentially a professional trustee. He served businesses needing large infusions of capital by conveying marketable securities to the management of trustees who acted for the joint benefit of investors, a device that anticipated the corporate trust and later investment funds. The result could be messy when the issuing agency failed, creating doubts about the title to the assets that the trustees managed. This happened with the insolvency of the North American Trust & Banking Company, which led to 235 suits between 1841 and 1858. With the help of able and influential counsel, Blatchford's legal arrangements were vindicated. He retired to an advisory role in 1854, as Samuel Blatchford and his associates prepared to carry on the work of the firm.

Blatchford's parallel political career commenced almost as soon as he started to practice as an attorney. Following the pattern of Charles Glidden Haines, a lawyer and backer of De Witt Clinton in state politics, Blatchford combined politics and New York City benevolent causes before attending the 1826 Clintonian nominating convention at Utica. A moderately active supporter of John Quincy Adams, Blatchford began to work aggressively for the Whigs in 1834, becoming a supplier of funds through his ties to English investors, to American banks and insurance companies, and to Manhattan merchants Robert B. Minturn, Moses H. Grinnell, and Simeon Draper, Jr. He provided William H. Seward—like many Blatchford associates, a Union graduate—with credit and financial management that helped Seward live well while governor and afterward recover his finances. Long friendly with Thurlow Weed, and consistently loyal to Seward, in whom he saw a future president, Blatchford characteristically told "the Governor" that "I know no human being out of the circle of my own family whom I love as I do you. Command me at any time and in any way": Seward accepted Samuel Blatchford as his private secretary. Ingratiating, a member of the Hone and Kent clubs, and ever ready to ease the cares of politicians at his country estate near Hell Gate or at Astor House, Richard Blatchford also established a close relationship with Daniel Webster, who had married a daughter of Herman Le Roy of New York City in 1829. Blatchford acted as an executor under Webster's will, and Webster's frequent and friendly letters to him appeared when that senator's son published his father's private correspondence in 1857.

Occasionally, Blatchford hungered for public office, even when it threatened to interrupt his legal and financial work. In early 1840 Governor Seward hesitantly offered him the post of comptroller, but Blatchford turned it down after Seward failed to veto a law designed to intimidate immigrant voters in New York City. Later, having declined the office of secretary of state of New York in November 1841, he expressed dismay that fellow Whigs had argued that he would make an unpopular appointee. Elected to the state assembly in 1855, however, Blatchford worked to return Seward to the U.S. Senate as a Republican. Following the outbreak of the Civil War, with other members of New York City's mercantile elite, Blatchford labored on the Union Defense Committee to furnish troops and to defuse criticism of Republican management of the war. Because of his effort and his financial contributions, Blatchford believed that he deserved a diplomatic post. He would have preferred a brief posting to Vienna but in 1862 went to the Vatican. Reluctant to be distant from his business and legal interests, he stayed only eight months.

Interested in Manhattan real estate on his own behalf and for clients, English and American, Blatchford served as a commissioner of Central Park from 1859 until retired by the city's new charter in 1870. From 1860 to 1863 he presided over the park commission; the Blatchford firm represented it in Albany and managed the acquisition of land for the park. Immediately after the war, more eager to secure salaried posts, Blatchford maneuvered unsuccessfully for a position in the New York Customs Office. Reinstalled as a parks commissioner by Mayor A. Oakey Hall in 1870, he resigned from the reshaped Board of Commissioners of the Department of Public Parks created by the reform charter that went into effect in 1873. His health failing, he died two years later at his son's home in Newport, Rhode Island.

• The largest collection of letters by Blatchford can be found in the papers of William H. Seward in the Rush Rhees Library of the University of Rochester, also available on microfilm. Evidence of many sides of Blatchford's relationship to Webster can be seen in *The Papers of Daniel Webster, Correspondence*, ed. Charles M. Wiltse et al., vols. 4–7 (1980–1986), and *The Papers of Daniel Webster, Legal Papers*, ed. Andrew J. King, vols. 2–3 (1983–1989). Samuel Blatchford, *Blatchford Memorial* (1871), and Eliphalet Wickes Blatchford, *Blatchford Memorial II* (1912), outline the extended connection created by Rev. Samuel Blatchford. Robert T. Swaine, *The Cravath Firm and Its Predecessors, 1819–1947*, vol. 1, *The Predecessor Firms 1819–1906* (1946), provides basic information about Blatchford's legal practice, and Blatchford's *Extract from a Report to the Trustees of the Apalachicola Land Company* (1837) gives an idea of the care with which he looked after investor interests. *Autobiography of Thurlow Weed*, ed. Harriet A. Weed (1883), and Glyndon G. Van Deusen, *William Henry Seward* (1967), suggest the essential elements of Blatchford's political contributions; something of his social style is revealed in Fletcher Webster, *Private Correspondence of Daniel Webster* (1857), and Allan Nevins, *Diary of Philip Hone, 1828–1851* (1927). For traces of Blatchford's later contributions in New York City, see Charles E. Beveridge and David Schuyler, *The Papers of Frederick Law Olmstead*, vol. 3, *Creating Central Park, 1857–1861* (1983); David Schuyler and Jane Turner Censer, *The Years of Olmstead, Vaux & Company, 1865–1874*, vol. 4 (1992); *Minutes of the Proceedings of the Board of Commissioners of the Central Park* (1858–1869); and John A. Stevens, *The Union Defense Committee of New York City* (1885). An obituary is in the *New York Times*, 5 Sept. 1875.

CRAIG HANYAN

BLATCHFORD, Samuel (9 Mar. 1820–7 July 1893), associate justice of the U.S. Supreme Court, was born in New York City, the son of Richard M. Blatchford, a well-connected Whig attorney, and Julia Ann Mumford. He entered Columbia College at the age of thirteen, "signal proof," *Harper's Weekly* later proclaimed, "of a well-spent boyhood not largely wasted in unnecessary vacations." Blatchford graduated at the head of his class in 1837, read law for a year, and in 1839 became private secretary to William H. Seward. He stayed with Seward until the latter's second term as governor of New York expired on 31 December 1842. Blatchford completed his legal education in his father's office and was admitted to the bar in late 1843. Shortly afterward he moved to Auburn, New York, where he began practice as office partner in the firm of Seward & Morgan. In 1844 he married Caroline Appleton of Lowell, Massachusetts.

Blatchford returned to New York City in 1854 and formed a partnership with Clarence A. Seward, the former governor's adopted son, and Burr W. Griswold. The firm quickly established a flourishing commercial practice with a largely Whig, later Republican, clientele. Blatchford's specialty was maritime law. He also made a mark on the profession as a reporter. Beginning in 1852, Blatchford published a volume of admiralty cases decided in the U.S. District Court for the Southern District of New York, a volume of Civil War prize cases from the same jurisdiction, and twenty-four volumes of Second Circuit decisions. He continued to report Second Circuit opinions following his appointment as district judge (1867), circuit judge (1872), and circuit justice (1882).

Blatchford's judicial career began in 1867 when Secretary of State Seward persuaded Andrew Johnson to appoint Blatchford to the New York district court. It culminated with his appointment to the U.S. Supreme Court by Chester A. Arthur in 1882. Blatchford was not Arthur's first choice. Only after Roscoe Conkling, leader of the New York "Stalwart" Republicans, and Senator George F. Edmunds of Vermont, a prominent "Half-Breed" Republican, declined the appointment did Arthur turn to Blatchford, who was confirmed without opposition. Blatchford's colleagues were quick to acknowledge his expertise in admiralty law, patent law, and questions involving the national banking acts; he soon became the Court's workhorse. Blatchford wrote 435 majority opinions during his eleven-year tenure, almost 20 percent more than his share.

Blatchford made modest contributions to American constitutional development. He was singularly uninterested in questions of statecraft, political economy, and philosophy; he was so committed to a collective conception of the judicial function that he dissented less frequently than any justice since the era of John Marshall. These attitudes, coupled with Chief Justice Morrison R. Waite's disinclination to assign him cases involving constitutional interpretation, kept Blatchford out of the limelight during his first eight years on the Court. But his compromising tendency prompted Waite's successor, Melville Fuller, to regard him as the logical spokesman for narrow, unstable majorities in two landmark due process cases.

In *Chicago, Milwaukee & St. Paul Ry. v. Minnesota* (1890) Blatchford spoke for a 6 to 3 majority that struck down a statute authorizing a railroad commission to set "final and conclusive" schedules of maximum rates. "The question of the reasonableness of a rate of charge . . . is eminently a question for judicial investigation, requiring due process of law for its determination," he explained. "If the company is deprived of the power of charging reasonable rates for the use of its property, and such deprivation takes place in the absence of an investigation by judicial machinery, it is deprived of the lawful use of its property, and thus, in substance and effect, of the property itself." Justice Joseph Bradley dissented. "In effect," he complained, the Court had "practically overruled" *Munn v. Illinois* (1877) by now holding "that the judiciary, and not the legislature, is the final arbiter in the regulation of fares and freights." Two years later in *Budd v. New York* (1892), however, Blatchford, again speaking for a 6 to 3 majority, ruled that courts had no authority to review grain-storage prices fixed by the New York legislature. The two cases were "quite distinguishable," he insisted, "for in this instance the rate of charges is fixed directly by the legislature." Blatchford apparently regarded this formulation as an appropriate means of reconciling all previous decisions on the subject. But the distinction between legislative and administrative regulation was so artificial that Justice John Marshall Harlan (1833–1911) simply ignored it in *Smythe v. Ames* (1898), where the Court held that the due process principle mandated judicial review of any government price-fixing measure that threatened to devote private property to public use without providing just compensation for its owners.

Blatchford died in Newport, Rhode Island. At the memorial service in the Supreme Court room on 13 November 1893, Attorney General Richard Olney made some perceptive remarks about Blatchford's approach to judging: "Judge Blatchford would have been the last to claim for himself those extraordinary gifts which have made some men seem to be called the giants of the law. . . . He never undertook by an opinion in one case to settle principles for other anticipated cases. . . . Thus, if he was not brilliant, he was safe; if he did not make large contributions to the science of jurisprudence, he won respect for the law and its administration . . . ." Seymour D. Thompson, editor of the *American Law Review*, was less gracious. "It is no great disparagement of [Blatchford]," he wrote, "to say that he was probably a better reporter than Judge."

• The best account of Blatchford's judicial career is Arnold Paul, "Samuel Blatchford," in *The Justices of the United States Supreme Court, 1789–1969: Their Lives and Major Opinions*, ed. Leon Friedman and Fred L. Israel (1969). For details on his early life and New York practice, see Robert T. Swaine, *The Cravath Firm and Its Predecessors, 1819–1947* (1946). See also "Memorial Service for Samuel Blatchford," *U.S. Reports* 150 (1893).

CHARLES W. MCCURDY

BLATHWAYT, William (1649?–16 Aug. 1717), imperial bureaucrat, was born in London, England, the son of William Blathwayt, a lawyer of the Middle Temple, and Anne Povey, daughter of the auditor of the exchequer Justinian Povey. His father died, broken and bankrupt by the civil wars, when William was less than two years old. He was raised by his uncle Thomas Povey, a connoisseur of Dutch decorative art and colonial administrator under Cromwell and Charles II, who sent him to the Middle Temple, 1665–1668. In 1668 Povey arranged Blathwayt's clerkship with Sir William Temple, ambassador at The Hague and champion of an alliance of the Protestant maritime states, England and the Netherlands, against Catholic France. Blathwayt not only absorbed the ambassador's ideals, he also impressed that influential statesman with his energy (it was said that in any office where Blathwayt worked no one else had anything to do). Blathwayt gained recognition for his method of filing and indexing correspondence (his first official letter was from Edmund Andros, the pioneering governor-general, about raising from the bottom of Ostend Harbor the Cornish tin that financed English espionage in the Netherlands). Blathwayt's facility in French and Dutch made him indispensable to Temple.

In 1672 Temple was recalled, and the third Dutch War began. Blathwayt was assigned to embassies in Denmark and Sweden. In 1673 he visited capital cities and courts in the German states and northern Italy in a semiofficial capacity. Home from his Grand Tour in 1674, Blathwayt sought to capitalize on the Povey investments in Jamaican plantations by becoming the secretary of that colony. In 1675 Blathwayt became the clerk for plantation affairs to Sir Robert Southwell (whose son Edward later married Blathwayt's daughter Anne), head of the new colonial office for the privy council. In 1676 Southwell put all the colonial office affairs in Blathwayt's hands.

In 1677 Blathwayt filed his first policy paper, addressed to the lord treasurer, the earl of Danby. Reflecting that chief minister's imperial assumptions, Blathwayt declared that the colonies must be defended. All other claims on the colonies, whether merchants' or proprietors', were to be subordinated to imperial defense coordinated from Whitehall. For a generation, Blathwayt did more than any other individual to make this policy predominant in imperial administration.

A personal episode, characteristic of court life, won Blathwayt his own place in the empire's central administrative body, the king's privy council. In 1678 Blathwayt came down with a malarial fever, to the concern of his royal master, King Charles II. The clerk was cured, probably by quinine, the American plant product being introduced into English medicine by a Dr. Tabor. King Charles sent clerk and physician posthaste to Paris, where Tabor also cured the king's niece. The grateful monarch then gave way to Southwell's solicitation, and Blathwayt became a clerk in extraordinary of the privy council, with permission to attend the debates of the council committees for trade and for plantations. Also in 1678 he was admitted to the full council's debates as the reward for his American administration. As Blathwayt remarked to his colonial correspondents, governors-general, and royal investigators, he was now at the origin of American policymaking and so able to serve them. They made their gratitude manifest. Blathwayt opened an account with a merchant banker. In 1679 Sir Robert Southwell resigned from the privy council secretariat and left Blathwayt, in effect, colonial secretary. In May 1680 he was commissioned "Surveyor and Auditor General of all His Majesties Revenues in America," with the power to appoint deputy auditors in every province.

Blathwayt's American bureaucracy still lacked one essential element, the army. In his lifetime almost 90 percent of the governors-general were career officers in the royal army. During 1681 Blathwayt had proven his capacity in military administration by allocating the 3,000-man Tangier garrison to crucial English garrisons. In 1683 he won royal permission to purchase the post of secretary at war. Every professional army officer became Blathwayt's client. None advanced to the command of a colony without his good offices. This became clear in 1685 when the secretary of war and of plantations not only administered the repression of Monmouth's revolt against York's accession as King James II but facilitated the new king's commission to Sir Edmund Andros, a cavalry commander in the repression, to replace Colonel Piercy Kirke, formerly governor of Tangier, as commander of the American epitome of Stuart centralization, the Dominion of New England. But Blathwayt shared with the professional soldiers Andros and Kirke—and with the New Englanders—a determined Protestantism, indistinguishable from English patriotism. That made them the enemies of the Catholic King James's program to force England back to Rome and so to perpetuate England's subservience to France both in Europe and in America. In November 1688 Blathwayt's overly permissive orders to Lord Cornbury (later governor-general of New York) made possible the initial desertion to the invading army of William of Orange. The Glorious Revolution meant a change of commanders in chief only, not of administrative personnel or of American policy. Blathwayt himself suffered only a six-week hiatus in one of his offices, the secretaryship of war. Blathwayt's Dutch fluency and his bureaucratic method made "the Elephant" (they never forget) indispensable to William III. As soon as the reconquest of Ireland and the resettlement of Blathwayt's military clients as American executives was complete in the summer of 1692, the new king took Blathwayt with him on his campaigns in Flanders. After redefining Blathwayt's military secretaryship to include America, King William made his "never erring Minister" a secretary of state. Blathwayt had reached the acme of his imperial influence.

In seven to nine months' attendance each year as the only English minister with the king, Blathwayt was at liberty to apply the "blue water," or Tory, theory of empire. The expedition of 1692–1693, aimed at the French Leeward Islands, the French Maritimes, Canada, and Newfoundland, illustrated the scope of Tory imperial ambitions. Its divided command, impoverished finances, and failed communications demonstrated how completely England's imperial reach exceeded its institutional grasp. The identification of "the imperial fixer" himself with the war against France and with the right wing of English conservatism meant that the peace of 1697 and a change of parties crippled Blathwayt's authority and unstrung his American administration.

The royal creation of the Board of Trade in 1696 (to head off parliamentary interference in Atlantic trade and American affairs) and its domination by Whig visionaries such as John Locke sapped Blathwayt's administrative grip. Even though he was a member of the board, his nephew Povey lost control of the colonial office. The disbanding of the army and the recall of the colonels—Edmund Andros from Virginia, James Kendall from Barbados, and Benjamin Fletcher from New York—apparently marked the end of Blathwayt's symbiosis of army with empire. The accession of Queen Anne, the restoration of the Tories, and the renewal of the war with France in 1702, however, emboldened Blathwayt to press the concept of strategic conquests in America on England's chief diplomat, the general of the allied armies, the earl of Marlborough. In the Treaty of Utrecht (1713), Blathwayt's imperial insistence bore fruit in England's recovery of St. Christopher's, Newfoundland, and Hudson Bay, as well as France's cession of Acadia and its admission of British sovereignty over the Five Nations (Iroquois), but Blathwayt himself had long since fallen from power. Neither as diplomat nor as general did Marlborough need Blathwayt's assistance, and he disliked Blathwayt's association with the Tory right. Blathwayt was replaced as secretary of war in April 1704. The fiscal acumen of the lord treasurer, Sidney, earl of Godolphin, cost Auditor General Blathwayt effective control of the American accounts after 1705. He was removed from the Board of Trade in April 1707. He lost his seat in Parliament in 1710.

Blathwayt retired to his great country house, "Dyrham Park," in Gloucestershire, England. It had been built around the Tudor manor that was part of the dowry of Mary Wynter, whom Blathwayt had married in 1686, and who died in 1691. The couple had three children. The new Dyrham Park was built from the spoils of imperial governance (quite literally in the case of staircases of Virginia walnut and South Carolina cedar). Its famous gardens were alive with specimens of American flora. Its archives, in the midst of which Blathwayt died, were crowded with the records of his American administration. These are still being sold by lots to rare book libraries, each sale expanding appreciation of William Blathwayt's eminence in Anglo-American administration.

• Public collections of Blathwayt papers are at the British Public Record Office (see esp. Treasury 64/88, War Office 4/1); the British Library (see esp. Additional Manuscripts 9719–9747); the National Maritime Museum, Greenwich (see esp. Southwell papers 1–18); the Gloucestershire Record Office, Gloucester; Nottingham University Library (Portland MS, Px V 51–61); the Archives of Colonial Williamsburg, Va.; the Huntington Library, San Marino, Calif.; and the Beinecke Library, Yale University. See also Jeanette D. Black, ed., *The Blathwayt Atlas* (1975). Blathwayt's biographer is Gertrude Ann Jacobsen, *William Blathwayt: A Late Seventeenth Century English Administrator* (1932), whose excellent work has been revised as further Blathwayt manuscripts became available by Stephen Saunders Webb in "William Blathwayt, Imperial Fixer: From Popish Plot to Glorious Revolution; Muddling through to Empire," *William and Mary Quarterly*, 3d ser., 25 (1968): 3–21, and 26 (1969): 373–415, and in "William Blathwayt: The 'Never-erring Minister,'" in *The Age of William III & Mary II*, ed. Robert P. Maccubin and Martha Hamilton Phillips (1989); and by Barbara Cresswell Murchison in "William Blathwayt's Empire: Politics and Administration in England and the Atlantic Colonies, 1668–1710" (Ph.D. diss., Univ. of Western Ontario, 1981). Further attention to Blathwayt is given in Webb's *The Governors-General: The English Army and the Definition of the Empire, 1569–1681* (1979; repr. 1987), *1676: The End of American Independence* (1984; repr. 1995), and *Lord Churchill's Coup: The Anglo-American Empire and the Glorious Revolution Reconsidered* (1995).

STEPHEN SAUNDERS WEBB

BLAU, Joseph Leon (6 May 1909–28 Dec. 1986), philosopher and educator, was born in Brooklyn, New York, the son of Joel Leon Blau, a rabbi, and Rachel Woolf. He received his B.A. (1931), M.A. (1933), and Ph.D. degrees (1944) from Columbia University. His dissertation was titled "The Christian Interpretation of the Cabala in the Renaissance." It substantiated the Jewish influence on Christianity during this period. Among those who exerted a special influence on Blau were Salo W. Baron, James Gutmann, and Herbert Schneider, an important mentor in American philosophy. Blau taught philosophy for the bulk of his career at Columbia University in the Departments of Philosophy and Religion from 1944 until 1977, when he retired. His two strongest and most lasting interests were American philosophy and modern Judaism. He was chairman of the Religion Department at Columbia from 1967 to 1976.

Blau began his career as an English teacher in New York City high schools (1932–1946). On 23 June 1940 he married Eleanor S. Weslock, and they had two daughters. He served at Columbia University as lecturer and assistant and associate professor of philosophy before being appointed professor of religion in 1963. Following in the naturalistic/humanistic tradition of John Dewey and his school at Columbia, he wrote *Men and Movements in American Philosophy* (1952). In this book, published in six languages, Blau traces the development of philosophical ideas and systems in the United States from Jonathan Edwards (1703–1758) to Dewey. Identifying ten major movements or schools of American philosophy, Blau shows he is well acquainted with the primary sources.

In his major work, *Modern Varieties of Judaism* (1966), Blau shows how the religion's major branches—reform, neoorthodox, and conservative—reflect emancipation from medievalism and indicate influences of the secular life on each branch. Praised by one critic as "well-documented, skillfully written, and eminently fair," it emphasized that the development of Judaism was nonlinear and strongly influenced throughout its history by cultural factors. In other words, Judaism throughout its long history has never been isolated from cultural changes and often responded in direct ways to them.

For Blau, Charles Darwin had a profound influence on both philosophy and religion with regard to the problems of being, knowing, and doing. For him Darwin's view came into direct conflict with the doctrine of special creation (Genesis), restricted the scope of divine intervention, reduced God to a remote first cause, and cast doubts on the occurrence of miracles and the reliability of biblical chronology and the anthropocentric worldview. In general Blau thinks that a Darwinian approach requires us to rethink our concept of God in terms of process or becoming rather than being. Becoming is no longer to be conceived as inferior or subordinate to being, and supernaturalism is swept aside by naturalism. God is to be conceived as "indeterminate" and adverbial in nature, although not wholly dissociated from the God of the Judaic tradition.

In explaining how American culture has changed Judaism, Blau emphasized the effects of an American distrust of intellectual systems, the stress of pluralism, and the secular emphases of moralism and individualism. Moralism, he explains, involves an evaluation of conduct in terms of human relationships rather than theological concerns and individualism. In a democratic context moralism gives priority to the rights of individuals over those of society. For Blau the idea of democracy is grounded in morality, and it is more of an achievement than a gift. It is a form of social/political organization in which the welfare and self-realization of each person is the concern of all and the communal life of the whole is the concern of each. This is how Blau solves the classical democratic problem of excellence and equality.

In a spirit not out of accord with Dewey, Blau emphasized the importance of scientific method and scientific knowledge and the contribution of democracy as "a social philosophy of altruism." These insights are likely to endure. Whether Darwinism can serve as a substitute for traditional methaphysics remains to be seen. Blau's views were discussed in a lively manner by some of his colleagues, including Justus Buchler, Paul O. Kristeller, Howard B. Radest, Paul Kurtz, and David L. Norton. In personal influence and scholarly impact he contributed heavily to the "Ethical Culture movement" within a revised, modern Judaism. However, he never attempted to reduce any form of religion or humanism to a mere ethical perspective. He died in New York City.

• The papers of Blau (personal and professional) were placed in the Columbia University archives by his wife Eleanor Blau in 1989 and 1990. These include correspondence, manuscripts, course materials, research notes, and letters from Salo Baron, Albert Einstein, and Reinhold Niebuhr. The archives of the Ethical Culture Movement also contain additional papers and materials. Notable works by Blau not mentioned in the article include *Modern Varieties of Judaism* (1966), *Judaism in America* (1976), *The Jews of the United States, 1790–1840: A Documentary History*, with Salo Witt-mayer Baron (3 vols., 1963), and *The Story of Jewish Philosophy* (1962). A bibliography of the complete writings of Blau (through 1979) has been prepared by Sam DeKay, and it is included in the Blau festschrift titled *History, Religion and Spiritual Democracy*, ed. Mauric Wholgelernter (1980), pp. 341–64. Some biographical comments on the teaching career and research of Blau are also available in this book. An obituary appears in the *New York Times*, 1 Jan. 1987.

JOHN HOWIE

BLAUSTEIN, David (5 May 1866–26 Aug. 1912), rabbi, educator, and social worker, was born in Lida, Russian Poland, the son of Isaiah Blaustein and Sarah Natzkovsky. The family was of humble means, and David was eight years old when his father died. Nine years later he ran away from home to the Prussian town of Memel in order to obtain an education. He then journeyed to Schwerin, the capital of Mecklenburg-Schwerin, where he enrolled in a Jewish teacher's preparatory school under the leadership of Dr. Fabian Feilchenfeld. His intention was to be a cantor-shochet-teacher to the German Jews, but Bismarck's ban on Russian Jews in Germany forced him to emigrate to America.

On arrival in Boston in 1886, Blaustein quickly established a modern German and Hebrew school, the first of its kind in America. He also became involved in the organization and promotion of Jewish charitable and educational societies in the city, such as the B'nai Zion Educational Society and the Sheltering Home for Immigrants. Three years after his arrival in Boston, Blaustein enrolled in Harvard College to study Semitics, graduating with a B.A. in 1893. The year prior to this he had been elected rabbi of the Congregation Sons of Israel and David in Providence, Rhode Island, and from that time forth his name was prefixed with the title "Doctor."

In Providence, as in Boston, Blaustein became involved in charitable and social work among the Jewish community as well as the community at large. He was a member of the Rhode Island State Charity Board and of the Executive Board of Organized Charities. In addition to his work as rabbi, Blaustein also served as assistant professor of Semitics at Brown University, receiving an M.A. from that institution in 1898.

In 1898 Blaustein resigned his position in Rhode Island to accept the superintendency of the Educational Alliance in New York City. The Educational Alliance provided educational opportunities for those of New York's East Side ghetto, and in the tradition of late nineteenth-century settlement houses, served as the community's social center. It provided a meeting place in which to learn the English language and American culture and receive lessons in Judaism as well as various job training opportunities.

Blaustein fostered and built the Alliance throughout his ten-year term as superintendent. On assuming his position he found the Alliance to be the focus of community struggles, with orthodox and reformist, socialist and Zionist, and radical and conservative factions battling for control. He attempted to forge a middle path and make the Alliance an institution that could act as a wholesome influence on every possible group on the East Side.

The main cause for concern was how to breach the gap between first-generation immigrants and their native-born children. Blaustein's aim was to stress Americanization as more than the mere acquisition of language and culture skills. Instead he focused on the preservation of the home as a strongly American institution, thus integrating Jewish heritage and new opportunities. Despite his efforts, many of Blaustein's attitudes were seen as patronizing, and radical opposition to him and to the Alliance grew. In 1901 this opposition culminated in the formation of the Educational League, which stated that its organization was effected as a protest against the retrogressive policy of the Alliance. Largely as a result of this conflict, Blaustein resigned in 1907.

For a year he was a bank manager at the Houston Street Branch of the Jefferson Bank before assuming the superintendency of the Chicago Hebrew Institute. There he encountered similar problems with radical groups who were upset with his refusal to let Emma Goldman, a left-wing social reformer, speak at the institute. He resigned in 1910.

After his retirement from active social work Blaustein lectured in Boston in the School of Philanthropy of the Charity Organization Society. He also toured America investigating suitable locations for Jewish farmers. In 1911 he married Miriam Umstader of Norfolk, Virginia; they had no children. Less than a year later he died of apoplexy at the summer camp of the Educational Alliance and of the Young Men's Hebrew Association in Cold Spring, New York. Blaustein established a tradition of trained social work within the American Jewish community. He did much to aid the Jewish immigrants' transition to American life, to build an understanding of the generational tension that developed in Jewish families, and to help people to both assimilate and retain their Jewish identity.

• For additional information see Miriam Blaustein, *Memoirs of David Blaustein* (1913), and Boris D. Bogen, *Jewish Philanthropy* (1917). Also see two articles in *Reform Advocate*, 31 Aug. 1912 and 7 Sept. 1912. Blaustein is mentioned in the *Secretary's Fifth Report*, *Harvard College*, Class of 1893 and in the *Secretary's Sixth Report, Harvard College, Class of 1893*. An obituary is in the *New York Times*, 28 Aug. 1912.

CLAIRE STROM

BLAVATSKY, Helena Petrovna (31 July 1831–8 May 1891), major occult writer and cofounder of the Theosophical Society, was born Helena de Hahn in Ekaterinoslav (later Dnepropetrovsk) in the Ukraine, the daughter of Colonel Peter Hahn and Helena Pavlovna Fadeev. Both parents were of aristocratic stock. Her father, of German descent, was an artillery officer, and her mother was a popular novelist whose stories inevitably turned on the sufferings of women at the hands of callous men. Much of Helena's childhood was spent on the estates of her maternal grandfather, a provincial governor. Helena was a strong-willed, imaginative child who would sometimes hide from household members for hours and on other occasions make up exceedingly elaborate stories.

In 1849 (some sources say 1848), she married a widower more than twice her age, Nikifor Vasilievich Blavatsky, vice-governor of Yerevan, Armenia, but she left him before the end of the honeymoon, making her way to Constantinople. This was the beginning of some twenty years of traveling. According to her own later account, she reached Tibet where she received certain high initiations. She seems to have traveled in Europe and Russia with a Serbian singer, Agardi Metrovitch. She was back in Russia from 1858 to 1864 and perhaps from 1867 to 1871. She was associated about 1858 with the famous medium D. D. Home, who she said converted her to Spiritualism. During these years she often indulged her fascination for Spiritualism and mystical phenomena, becoming adept as an occultist.

In 1871 Blavatsky resided in Cairo, Egypt, where she organized a short-lived Spiritualist society in association with Emma Cutting (later Coulomb). The following year she returned to Russia. In 1873 she went to Paris and then to New York, arriving 7 July. She later said that she came to the United States as a Muslim to Mecca, since it was the homeland of Spiritualism. Arriving almost penniless, she supported herself at various jobs until receiving an inheritance from her father, who died that year.

In October 1874, after seeing an article by the lawyer and journalist Henry Steel Olcott about spirit manifestations at the home of the Eddy brothers near Chittenden, Vermont, she proceeded to their farmstead. There she met Olcott. After returning to New York, the two quickly developed a close relationship. Blavatsky introduced Olcott to "Brahma Vidya," or "Eastern Spiritualism." At the same time, the pair investigated several mediums, and Blavatsky wrote controversial articles about their findings for Spiritualist periodicals.

The following year Blavatsky went to Philadelphia where, in a puzzling incident on 3 April, she "married" an immigrant businessman from Russian Georgia, M. C. Betanelly, despite the fact that N. V. Blavatsky was still alive. She lived with Betanelly only briefly, then returned to New York, where she and Olcott soon attracted a circle of esotericists and seekers.

On 7 September, at a meeting in her rooms at 46 Irving Place, the establishment of a society to promote occult research was broached. This eventuated in the Theosophical Society, formally established with Olcott as the first president on 17 November 1875. In his inaugural address, reflecting Blavatsky's views as well as his own, Olcott alluded to the great controversy of the day, science versus religion, suggesting that both were burdened with excessive dogmatism. To transcend the standoff it would be necessary to recover forgotten wisdom of the ancients, in which the spiritual and material worlds were better harmonized than in modern times.

The 1875 Theosophical Society was not active more than a few months. But Blavatsky, Olcott, and a few others began work on a major publication, summarizing the occult wisdom that Theosophy inculcated. To facilitate the work, in 1876 Olcott and Blavatsky moved into an apartment, the famous "Lamasery," which for two years was a magnet for the city's coterie of seekers and bohemians and the site of discussions and parties described in Olcott's memoirs, *Old Diary Leaves*.

Isis Unveiled (1877) was Blavatsky's first major work. It presents a wide-ranging picture of magic and mystery and explains these marvels in terms of a constituency of three parts: matter, an invisible energizing spirit, and immortal consciousness.

Blavatsky and Olcott were becoming more and more aware of India and Tibet as major reservoirs of the Ancient Wisdom. The Masters, adepts with whom Blavatsky claimed to be in contact, increasingly were of Indian provenance. By 1878, the year Blavatsky became a U.S. citizen, they were ready to move to that subcontinent. In December 1878 they sailed for India, arriving in February 1879. Blavatsky never returned to the United States.

In India, Blavatsky and Olcott traveled and campaigned on behalf of Theosophy. They made British Indian converts, among them A. P. Sinnett, the journalist, and Octavian Hume, a founder of the Indian National Congress. The response to Theosophy from Indian intellectuals was quite positive, no doubt because the two Theosophists, unlike most Westerners, had a high regard for India's religions and culture. They believed Hinduism and Buddhism to be clear channels of the primordial truth behind all religion. Both took *pansil* in Ceylon in 1880, becoming nominal Buddhists. In India, as in Ceylon (now Sri Lanka), Theosophy was a catalyst for the Hindu/Buddhist intellectual and cultural renaissance of the late nineteenth century, which in turn prepared the way for the Indian independence movement.

Blavatsky and Olcott first settled in Bombay. There, they began a magazine, the *Theosophist*, in 1879, and in 1882 they were able to purchase an estate at Adyar, near Madras, which became, and remains, the world headquarters of the Theosophical Society. Here, Blavatsky received letters from her Masters in a cabinet located in a "shrine room." In 1884 she traveled to England, where a report on extraordinary phenomena associated with the Theosophical movement was favorably received by the new Society for Psychical Research. However, a charge of fraud was made by Blavatsky's assistant at Adyar, Emma Cutting Coulomb. The Society for Psychical Research sent Richard Hodgson to India to investigate. His report, published in 1885, was very damaging to Blavatsky and Theosophy. In the course of the upheaval over the charges and the investigation, Blavatsky, now in failing health, returned to Europe in March 1885. Olcott remained at Adyar as president of the Theosophical Society.

Blavatsky first stayed in Würzburg, Germany, with Countess Constance Wachtmeister, then at Ostend, and finally settled in London in 1887, where her major work, *The Secret Doctrine*, was published the following year. *The Secret Doctrine* goes beyond *Isis Unveiled* and develops Theosophical perspectives on the evolution of the universe and humanity. (Blavatsky's other important books include *The Voice of the Silence* [1889] and *The Key to Theosophy* [1889].) In London she also founded the Blavatsky Lodge (1887), edited a magazine, *Lucifer* (established 1887), and taught pupils individually and in small groups. She died in London.

Blavatsky is surely among the most enigmatic and paradoxical figures in human history. While she was capable of egregiously foolish and deceptive behavior, her writings reveal an assiduous and powerful if sometimes undisciplined intellect. Her voluminous publications in English, her editorial work, and her correspondence, all forceful and felicitous in style in a language not native to her, is an impressive accomplishment; she also published well-regarded travel narratives and other pieces in Russian. Her Theosophical movement has played a not insignificant role in the modern spiritual revitalization of several nations, including India, Sri Lanka, and Ireland. Living in an age of feminine subordination, she stands out dramatically as a woman of independence, colorful character, and achievement.

• Virtually all of Blavatsky's published work and a number of her letters can be found in Helena P. Blavatsky, *Collected Writings* (ed. Boris de Zirkov; 15 vols., including index volume, 1966–1991). Invaluable reminiscences by her companion and co-worker are to be found in Henry Steel Olcott, *Old Diary Leaves* (6 vols., 1895–1935; repr. 1941–1975). Mary K. Neff, *Personal Memoirs of H. P. Blavatsky* (1937), an important resource, organizes an account of the subject's life as Blavatsky related it at various times, together with supplemental material. Jean Overton Fuller, *Blavatsky and Her Teachers* (1988), deals with some of the many biographical problems Blavatsky presents from a sympathetic, Theosophical point of view. A new look at the early years of Theosophy, including fresh insights on the sources of Blavatsky's writing, can be found in Michael Gomes, *The Dawning of the Theosophical Movement* (1987). For a critical independent life, see Marion Meade, *Madame Blavatsky* (1980). Sylvia Cranston, *H.P.B.: The Extraordinary Life and Influence of Helena Blavatsky* (1993), is a large-scale sympathetic biography containing much new material and emphasizing the subject's impact on her times and after.

ROBERT S. ELLWOOD

BLEASE, Coleman Livingston (8 Oct. 1868–19 Jan. 1942), governor of South Carolina and U.S. senator, was born near Newberry Courthouse, South Carolina, the son of Henry Horatio Blease, a farmer who later became a hotel and livery stable owner, and Mary Ann Livingston. Cole, or "Coley," lived with his large family in the conviviality of their popular Newberry hotel, which nurtured his gregarious personality and prepared him for a career in popular politics. In 1879 he entered Newberry Academy (later College), where he eventually completed the junior year of the school's collegiate curriculum. In 1887 he enrolled at the law school of South Carolina College but was soon expelled for plagiarism. In 1888 he ran for the state legislature, mounting a campaign that featured white supremacist and anticorporate harangues, but he received little support at the Democratic county convention. Following his defeat, he attended Georgetown University in Washington, D.C., where he earned a bachelor of laws degree in 1889, and later that year he began practicing law in Newberry and Saluda, South Carolina. In 1890 he married Lillie B. Summers, who died in 1934. They had no children.

Although Blease's law practice was extremely successful, politics remained his primary vocation. Capitalizing on his growing reputation as a spellbinding courtroom orator and allying himself with the agrarian insurgency of gubernatorial candidate Benjamin R. Tillman of nearby Edgefield County, he won a seat in the legislature in 1890. Reelected in 1892, he served as Governor Tillman's house floor leader during his second term, gaining notoriety as a passionate Negrophobe and a fervent supporter of a ten-hour day labor bill. When told that the bill would force the closing of every cotton mill in the state, he responded "If we have to buy capital by murdering women and children, for God's sake let it go, let it go!" Newberry County, which boasted several large cotton mills, was not ready for such unvarnished anticorporate radicalism, and in 1894 Blease was defeated for reelection. In 1898, after a brief stint as mayor of Helena, he finally won a third legislative term, running primarily as a supporter of a controversial state liquor dispensary system.

In 1900 and 1902 Blease sought the Democratic nomination for lieutenant governor but finished last in both primaries. In 1904 he won a seat in the state senate, where he served as president pro tempore from 1907 to 1908. He earned a reputation as an impassioned champion of white cotton mill workers and an apologist for corrupt dispensary officials. The dispensary issue doomed his first run for the governorship in 1906, despite a vigorous and unprecedented effort to mobilize the mill worker vote through class and racial appeals. In 1908, using similar tactics, he finished a distant second behind incumbent governor Martin Ansel.

Finally, in 1910 Blease found a successful political formula. Dubbed "Bleaseism" by the press, the new approach paradoxically combined personal identification with downtrodden mill workers and opposition to progressive labor legislation. During the campaign, Blease promised to cut taxes, reduce appropriations, and dismantle much of the state government. At the same time, he accentuated his emotional and symbolic ties to "the damned factory class," as Tillman and other agrarian purists scornfully called them. Making daily forays into the mill villages, Blease courted the mill worker vote with constant attention, flattery, and respect, plus a heavy dose of Negrophobia. Offering his followers a vague sense of power rather than concrete reform measures, he made, as V. O. Key later wrote, "a class appeal without offering a class program." Blease's brand of politics drew bitter criticism from "respectable" South Carolinians, who viewed him as a charlatan and a shameless demagogue. But in a state where politicians rarely offered textile workers anything other than social scorn and the condescending rhetoric of progressive uplift, his flamboyant personal appeal was more than enough to secure the workers' loyalty. In the 1910 primary, buoyed by Senator Tillman's endorsement, he easily defeated C. C. Featherstone, a devout and colorless prohibitionist.

Blease's governorship proved to be politically tumultuous, largely because of his determination to create a personal organization that superseded the traditional relationships that had defined South Carolina politics since the beginning of the Tillman era. Rent by bitter factionalism, which the governor seemed to relish, the state legislature produced little in the way of reform other than the establishment of a state tuberculosis sanatorium, the elimination of an inhumane hosiery mill at the state penitentiary, and the procurement of state funding for the Medical College of South Carolina. To the dismay of conservatives and progressives alike, Blease issued a record number of paroles and pardons, vetoed more bills than any previous governor in the state's history, spoke out in favor of lynching, and presided over a ruthless spoils system that led him to dissolve the state militia and to revoke the commissions of several thousand notaries public. Blease's intemperate style and allegedly immoral character were also controversial, as he made no attempt to hide his fondness for liquor, gambling, and carousing. All of this was too much for Tillman, who publicly repudiated his former lieutenant during the final week of the 1912 primary campaign. Blease won reelection anyway, narrowly defeating Judge Ira Jones in the primary.

Controversy and scandal continued to plague Blease during his second term. Politically isolated and contemptuous of the Wilsonian progressivism that was becoming fashionable among Democratic leaders, he vehemently opposed all reform measures that entailed governmental expansion, even those designed to provide relief for the working class voters whom he professed to champion. Posing as the last bastion of Jeffersonian democracy, he spoke out against factory inspection laws, compulsory education, literacy campaigns, child labor laws, medical examinations for schoolchildren, agricultural demonstration projects, and enforcement of liquor laws. Blease's opposition to reform drew support from conservatives, including several mill owners; however, it also deepened his feud with Tillman and President Woodrow Wilson, who cut off his access to federal patronage. In 1914 Blease made a spirited attempt to unseat Senator Ellison D. "Cotton Ed" Smith, but the combined influence of Tillman and Wilson insured Smith's reelection.

In spite of Blease's defeat, his continuing popularity among mill workers and impoverished white farmers sustained his hopes of replacing Tillman as the primary powerbroker in South Carolina politics. Those hopes were dashed, however, when the controversy over American involvement in World War I exposed his antiwar and pro-German sentiments. In 1916 he lost a close race for the governorship to the incumbent Richard Manning, a paternalistic Wilsonian progressive who had won election in 1914. Two years later he made a second bid for the Senate, hoping to replace the aging Tillman, but his bitter denunciations of Wilson and his lack of enthusiasm for the American war effort resulted in a landslide defeat.

By the early 1920s Blease's career appeared to be in permanent eclipse, and he failed in yet another comeback bid for the governorship in 1922. But in the senatorial campaign of 1924 he won a narrow upset victory over James F. Byrnes by toning down his rhetoric and emphasizing his willingness to cooperate with mill owners and other business leaders. In the Senate, Blease generally was an obstructionist, opposing the McNary-Haugen farm program and the internationalism of the League of Nations and the World Court. On several occasions he drew national attention with inflammatory speeches endorsing white supremacy, black disfranchisement, and lynching. Other than serving as a colorful symbol of southern demagoguery, he exerted little influence in Washington. Blease's exhibitionist diversions were a major issue in the 1930 Democratic primary and contributed to his defeat by Byrnes. For nearly a decade afterward he remained on the political scene as an unsuccessful but potentially dangerous challenger. In a 1932 Senate race, he demonstrated that the mystique of Bleaseism persisted in some mill worker precincts, but in his two final bids for the governorship, in 1934 and 1938, most of the mill worker vote deserted him. In 1939 he married Caroline Floyd, but they separated in 1940. They had no children.

Blease spent his final years in Columbia, where he was often seen in the company of his younger brother Eugene Blease, an associate justice of the state supreme court. He died following abdominal surgery in Columbia; he is buried at Rosemont Cemetery in Newberry.

Blease's rancorous and unproductive career revealed the curious and tragic nature of mass politics in early twentieth-century South Carolina. As an outgrowth of Tillmanism, Bleaseism bore the unmistakable marks of "Solid South" insurgency: personalized invective, populistic rhetoric, and racial demagoguery. But Blease added a new dimension to regional politics when he became as W. J. Cash wrote, "the first of the Southern demagogues to appeal directly and consistently to the cotton mill workers as their peculiar candidate and champion." That many mill workers responded to his appeals with undying devotion, even though he seemed to serve the economic interests of cotton mill owners more faithfully than he served the interests of the workers or the commonweal, testifies not only to Blease's skills as a charismatic leader but also to the limited options afforded by personal factionalism and one-party politics.

• Blease left no personal papers, but the voluminous public correspondence related to his governorship is in the Blease papers at the South Carolina Department of Archives and History in Columbia. The most comprehensive analysis of

Blease's governorship is Ronald D. Burnside, "The Governorship of Coleman Livingston Blease of South Carolina, 1911–1915" (Ph.D. diss., Indiana Univ., 1963). The standard treatments of Blease as a demagogue appear in W. J. Cash, *The Mind of the South* (1941); Rupert B. Vance, "Rebels and Agrarians All: Studies in One-Party Politics," *Southern Review* 4 (Summer 1938): 26–44; and V. O. Key, *Southern Politics in State and Nation* (1949). A lengthy chapter on Blease is in Francis Butler Simkins, *Pitchfork Ben Tillman: South Carolinian* (1944). For insightful, revisionist interpretations of his career, see David Carlton, *Mill and Town in South Carolina 1880–1920* (1982), and Bryant Simon, "The Appeal of Cole Blease of South Carolina: Race, Class, and Sex in the New South," *Journal of Southern History* 62 (Feb. 1996): 57–86. Other useful sources on his governorship and early gubernatorial and senatorial campaigns include Robert M. Burts, *Richard Irvine Manning and the Progressive Movement in South Carolina* (1974); David D. Wallace, History of South Carolina, vols. 3 and 4 (1934); James C. Derieux, "Crawling toward the Promised Land," *Survey* 48 (29 Apr. 1922): 175–80; Clarence Stone, "Bleaseism and the 1912 Election in South Carolina," *North Carolina Historical Review* 40 (1963): 54–74; Burnside, "Racism in the Administrations of Governor Cole Blease," *Proceedings of the South Carolina Historical Association* 34 (1964): 43–57; Daniel W. Hollis, "Cole Blease and the Senate Campaign of 1924," *Proceedings of the South Carolina Historical Association* 48 (1978): 53–68; and Hollis, "Cole Blease: The Years between the Governorship and the Senate, 1915–1924," *South Carolina Historical Magazine* 80 (1979): 1–17. On his senatorial career, see Kenneth W. Mixon, "The Senatorial Career of Coleman Livingston Blease, 1925–31" (M.A. thesis, Univ. of South Carolina, 1970); and Osta L. Warr, "Mr. Blease of South Carolina," *American Mercury* 16 (Jan. 1929): 25–32. A lengthy obituary is in the *Charleston News and Courier*, 20 Jan. 1942.

RAYMOND ARSENAULT

BLECKLEY, Logan Edwin (3 July 1827–6 Mar. 1907), jurist, was born near Clayton, Rabun County, Georgia, the son of James Bleckley and Catherine Lutz, native North Carolinians. Although Bleckley's father came from humble origins, he possessed a keen intellect and wielded considerable influence within his community. Beginning as a sheriff, James Bleckley went on to serve as a clerk for three separate courts and capped his career with a county judgeship. In 1838 he hired his eleven-year-old son to do clerical work in his office. Through this experience Bleckley developed a profound passion for the law. Indeed, at the age of seventeen he borrowed books and without the benefit of an instructor began his legal education in earnest. In 1846, following his admission to the bar, the self-taught eighteen-year-old lawyer established a private practice in Rabun County that lasted almost two years.

In 1847, lacking clients and wanting a more lucrative occupation, Bleckley went to Milledgeville hoping to secure a job with the Georgia legislature. On his way to the capital, Bleckley stopped at Clayton, where he learned that the town sheriff had placed a woman in jail for owing a debt she could not pay. Before the authorities could transfer her to debtor's prison, a generous gentleman paid the debt, and the sheriff discharged the woman. The episode affected Bleckley deeply, and when he reached Milledgeville he drafted a bill to abolish the imprisonment of women for debt. The legislature endorsed the measure, and it became law.

Shortly thereafter, Bleckley accepted a clerkship in a transportation office in Atlanta. In his third year at that job, Governor George W. Towns appointed him as an assistant to the executive. In 1852, following a change in administrations, he resigned the position and opened a law office in Atlanta that enjoyed much success. In 1853 the legislature elected Bleckley solicitor general for the Coweta circuit, which then embraced eight counties and included the city of Atlanta. "The office to which I aspired," Bleckley later recalled, "was believed and reputed to be the best-paying office in the state." He served one four-year term before returning solely to private practice. In 1857 he married Clara Caroline Haralson. Their union produced five children.

With the outbreak of the Civil War in 1861, Bleckley joined the Confederate army. The army discharged Bleckley from active duty because of his poor health and transferred him to its law department in Atlanta. Bleckley handled legal affairs for the Confederacy until 1864, the year he became reporter for the Georgia Supreme Court. Three years later Bleckley quit to resume private practice.

In 1875, by executive appointment, Bleckley became an associate justice of the Georgia Supreme Court. Although "the busy and devoted attorney" initially declined the seat, he ultimately accepted and held that office for five difficult and overworked years. Bleckley resigned in 1880 because of the court's excessive workload. His retirement proved short-lived, for duty summoned him again. In 1887 the governor appointed Bleckley chief justice to the high court, where he presided for the next seven years.

In 1892, fearing that Bleckley would soon step down from the bench, his supporters tried to encourage him to seek another term. To that end, 139 lawyers from all parts of Georgia signed a letter indicating the great respect that the state's bar had for the judge. Bleckley's tenure on the bench, the letter claimed, "furnished proof of patience, industry, intellectual grasp and clearness, and of devotion to truth and justice, to a degree rarely in any judge equaled, and by none excelled." According to his colleague Judge John L. Hopkins, every lawyer in Georgia would have signed the letter if the opportunity had presented itself.

Yet despite his popularity within the legal profession, Bleckley's days on the bench had become numbered. In 1892, following nearly thirty-five years of marriage, Bleckley's wife died. The next year, the 66-year-old widower married Chloe Herring, with whom he would have five more children. Perhaps wishing to spend more time with his new wife and because court business had become far too heavy for three judges to handle adequately, Bleckley resigned his seat permanently in 1894. The remaining years of his life Bleckley spent in semiretirement between his two mountain homes in north Georgia. There he provided intermittent legal work for attorneys and others, who consulted him as "an oracle of the law." Bleckley died in Clarkesville, Georgia.

Precise and perspicacious, Bleckley's judicial opinions embodied sound judgment and correct apprehension of the law. Still they remained, wrote a contemporary, "rich in imagery and metaphor, and scintillant with pure, spontaneous humor, a humor which, though trenchant, never sinks to buffoonery or farce." To be sure, during the years 1884 to 1920, no appellate judge in Georgia took more delight in or proved more adept at dispensing literary gems than Bleckley. As the legal historian George E. Butler II put it: "Humor was not simply a diversion for Bleckley; he used it liberally in his opinions." In doing so, he championed the kind of good-natured, self-deprecating humor that southern lawyers often claim as a birthright. Most lawyers probably best remember Bleckley for his opinion in *Lyons v. Planters' Loan and Savings Bank*. Speaking for the court, Bleckley stated his philosophy in a concise but potent sentence: "Justice is not only one of the cardinal virtues, it is the pontifical virtue."

• Although a 2,000-page manuscript burned in a fire at Bleckley's mountain cottage at Clarksville, an article by him published posthumously survives; see "Joseph Henry Lumpkin: First Chief Justice of Georgia," *The Green Bag* 19 (Nov. 1907): 633–35. In addition, Bleckley's opinions fill a significant portion of the *Reports of Cases Decided in the Supreme Court of the State of Georgia* (*Georgia Reports*) and provide engaging reading. For a collection of opinions that includes samples of Bleckley's legal wit, see Berto Rogers, ed., *Opinions and Stories of and from the Georgia Courts and Bar* (1973). Contemporary assessments of Bleckley include Alfred H. Russell, "Wit and Wisdom of Chief Justice L. E. Bleckley in the Georgia Reports," Georgia Bar Association, *Reports* 15 (1898): 244–78; L. B. Ellis, "Logan E. Bleckley: Former Chief Justice of the Supreme Court of Georgia," *The Green Bag* 15 (Dec. 1903): 555–59; "Two Georgia Judges," *The Green Bag* 21 (Jan. 1909): 20–21; John L. Hopkins et al., "Memorial of Hon. Logan E. Bleckley," *Georgia Reports* 128 (1907). For modern appraisals of Bleckley, see George E. Butler II, "Forward," *Journal of Southern Legal History* 3 (1994): ii–ix; J. Richard Neville, "Appreciating Humor: Anecdotes of the Georgia Judiciary, 1884–1920," *Journal of Southern Legal History* 3 (1994): 241–48. Obituaries are in the *Atlanta Georgian*, 6 Mar. 1907, and the *Augusta Chronicle* and the *New York Times*, both 7 Mar. 1907.

JOHN J. GUTHRIE, JR.

BLEDSOE, Albert Taylor (9 Nov. 1809–8 Dec. 1877), educator and author, was born in Frankfort, Kentucky, the son of Moses Ousley Bledsoe, a newspaper editor, and Sophia Childress Taylor. Graduating from the U.S. Military Academy at West Point in 1830, Bledsoe served two years on the frontier as a brevet second lieutenant in the Seventh U.S. Infantry. Thereafter, he resigned his commission and took up the post of tutor at Kenyon College in Ohio. In 1833–1834 he held the titles of adjunct professor of mathematics and teacher of French at that institution. The following school year he was a professor of mathematics at Miami University, and in 1836 he married Harriet Coxe. The couple had seven children, four of whom survived childhood. He served briefly as an assistant to the Episcopal bishop of Kentucky, but because he could not bring himself to accept the doctrine of baptismal regeneration, he gave up thoughts of an ecclesiastical career and turned instead to the study of law. Moving to Springfield, Illinois, in 1838, he began to practice law alongside the likes of Abraham Lincoln and Stephen A. Douglas. During the ten years that he practiced in the Illinois bar, he continued his interest in theology and in 1845 wrote *Examination of President Edwards' "Inquiry into the Freedom of the Will."*

In 1848 Bledsoe left the North and the practice of law, returning to education as a professor of mathematics at the University of Mississippi. In 1854 he accepted a similar position at the University of Virginia. Despite the fact that his field was mathematics, Bledsoe's writing continued to involve theology, metaphysics, and politics. His *A Theodicy; or, Vindication of the Divine Glory* appeared in 1853, and in 1856 he published *An Essay on Liberty and Slavery* in defense of the South and its "peculiar institution."

As a professor Bledsoe was known for his phenomenal memory, having reputedly once reproduced the entire index of one of his books from memory after the original and only copy was lost on the way to the publisher. University of Virginia students also remarked on his tendency to concentrate so deeply that he was conscious of no disturbance around him unless addressed directly by name. When he was so interrupted, he tended to be irritable, once complaining that "a blow on the head with a hammer . . . would be much more merciful." His son noted, "He would go to his meals, eat them mechanically, and never once come to a sense of where he was or what he was doing."

Yet Bledsoe was aware of the political situation in Virginia in the late 1850s and had very definite ideas about which way he wanted to go. Using his position as a member of the faculty of the University of Virginia, he helped Edmund Ruffin stir up secessionist sentiment in the state. As agitation grew in the South against northern educational institutions as well as everything else northern, southerners made it a point to send their young people to sound southern colleges. The University of Virginia grew from under 200 to over 700 students during the decade of the 1850s. Bledsoe was among the professors who, as the *Kanawha Valley Star* described it, were "uniting the young men of the South together, making them more and more attached to the peculiar institutions." Bledsoe worked eagerly to bring about Virginia's secession and welcomed it when, in April 1861, it came.

Bledsoe immediately began to do what he could to see that the new government placed a proper importance on the state of Virginia. While the capital of the new Confederate States of America was at Montgomery, Alabama, Bledsoe wrote Confederate president Jefferson Davis on 10–11 May 1861, urging him to come to Richmond and take command in person. "Your presence is desired in Richmond," he wrote, "nay, it is longed for, by every man, woman, and child in the State. . . . You would be worth more than

50,000 men to us. . . . Virginia is to be the principal seat of the war. . . . All eyes, and hearts turn to you. . . . *We greatly need a deliverer and we look to you.*" Whether at Bledsoe's urging or on other considerations, of which many existed, Davis and the Confederate Congress did collaborate to move the Confederate capital to Richmond that May.

Meanwhile, Bledsoe had joined the Confederate army in April and, because of his West Point training and two years of regular army experience, was immediately commissioned a colonel. Later that year, Davis intervened to give Bledsoe the more important position of chief of the Bureau of War, a subdivision of the Confederate Department of War. Later the same year, Davis again promoted Bledsoe, this time to assistant secretary of war. On 1 October 1862 Bledsoe resigned this position, and in 1863, apparently once again at the instigation of Davis, he traveled to London to do research in the British Museum for a book he planned to write as a constitutional defense of secession. His mission may also have been intended to influence British public opinion.

The latter purpose became moot with the fall of the Confederacy in 1865. The following year Bledsoe returned to the United States and wrote a defense of the imprisoned former Confederate president entitled *Is Davis a Traitor; or, Was Secession a Constitutional Right*. This 263-page work has proven to be Bledsoe's most significant. Some of his contemporary southerners considered the book one of the main influences preventing a treason indictment against Davis, though this is doubtful. Bledsoe did, however, provide one of the most forceful and succinct statements ever made of the stock southern rights arguments. Beginning with the premise that the recent war had changed the basis of the Union from compact to conquest, he admitted that secession might no longer be a right but maintained that it previously had been. Asserting that his opponents were driven by hate and rage while he was influenced only by dispassionate reason, he devoted the bulk of his book to an attempt to prove that the government formed by the Constitution was a compact created by sovereign states rather than a sovereign nation created by the American people. For this purpose he called to witness such of the founders as seemed to further his case while going to great lengths to label their contrary statements as lies. His conclusion, of course, was that secession was right and, when slave states came to be outnumbered in Congress, also eminently reasonable. Thus Davis and his cohorts were, to Bledsoe, anything but traitors.

In 1867 Bledsoe founded and became the first editor of the quarterly *Southern Review* in Baltimore, Maryland, and in that capacity he continued to advance his virulently prosouthern views. It was a labor of love, dedicated to "the despised, disfranchised, and downtrodden people of the South," and its bulky issues, of which Bledsoe always wrote a substantial part and sometimes nearly the entire issue, celebrated the South. Ever a controversialist, he inveighed continually against democracy, industrialization, the Union, and Thomas Jefferson while championing all that had been peculiar to the South, most especially slavery. His was the quintessential voice of the unreconstructed southerner. Nevertheless, the *Southern Review* did not produce much income. The South was impoverished, and its people apparently were more willing to accept the future than was Bledsoe. Thus during the ten years of his labor as editor, his family was dependent on his daughters' incomes as schoolteachers. Bledsoe's own continued interest in education was reflected in his advocacy of a distinctly southern education for southern young people, avoiding the methods and the textbooks used in the rest of the nation's schools.

Bledsoe also retained his interest in religion throughout his life, and in this realm as well he tended toward controversy. Issues of predestination and baptism kept him at odds with several denominations, so that when he sought the opportunity to preach, only the pulpits of the Southern Methodist denomination were open to him. His success as a preacher was, by all accounts, not very great. Though his sermons were profound and deeply reasoned, they tended to be a bit heavy for popular consumption, and in addition, his enunciation was not pleasing. He died in Alexandria, Virginia.

• Some Bledsoe correspondence is in the Houghton Library, Harvard University. Postwar letters by Bledsoe are held at the University of Virginia. Biographical information about him is in a sketch by his daughter Sophia Bledsoe Herrick in *The Library of Southern Literature*, vol. 1 (1907), and in Philip Alexander Bruce, *History of the University of Virginia, 1819–1919*, vol. 3 (1921). The latter, however, contains some errors in the sequence of Bledsoe's early employment. Henry T. Shanks, *The Secession Movement in Virginia, 1847–1861* (1934), touches on Bledsoe's involvement as a radical southerner in the years leading up to the Civil War and his contributions toward a distinctly southern education during the same period. His literary activities receive attention in James W. Davidson, *Living Writers of the South* (1869).

STEVEN E. WOODWORTH

BLEDSOE, Jules (29 Dec. 1897–14 July 1943), baritone, was born Julius Lorenzo Cobb Bledsoe in Waco, Texas, the son of Henry L. Bledsoe and Jessie Cobb, occupations unknown. Following his parents' separation in 1899, he lived with his maternal grandmother, a midwife and nurse, who encouraged him to appreciate music. Graduating in 1918 magna cum laude from Bishop College, Bledsoe began graduate medical studies at Columbia University, withdrawing after the death of his mother in 1920 to dedicate himself to singing. In 1924 he presented his debut recital at Aeolian Hall in New York.

Bledsoe's first major stage role was as Tizan in the racially mixed *Deep River* by Frank Harling and Laurence Stalling in 1926. That same year, he performed the premiere of Louis Gruenberg's *The Creation* (conducted by Serge Koussevitzky in New York) and worked as an actor at the Provincetown Playhouse. He is best known for creating the role of Joe in 1927 in Jerome Kern's *Show Boat*, which ran for two years at the Ziegfeld Theatre. (He later estimated that he had sung "Old Man River" 20,000 times.) In 1929 Bledsoe recorded "Lonesome Road" and "Old Man River" to be added to the soundtrack of the 1929 silent film of *Show Boat*. On screen he was represented by the black actor and comedian, Stepin Fetchit. In 1925 he appeared at the Gallo Theater in New York as Amonasro in the third act of Verdi's *Aida*, performing with members of the New York Philharmonic. In that year, he also began a two-year tour of *Show Boat*, followed by a Carnegie Hall recital and concerts in Europe.

In 1932 Bledsoe sang in the Cleveland performance of *Tom-Tom*, an opera by Shirley Graham, later the wife of W. E. B. Du Bois. He then returned to the role of Amonasro in Cleveland and New York, with occasional vaudeville and radio engagements. He performed the *Aida* role in Amsterdam the next season and toured Europe in *The Emperor Jones*. Beginning in 1934, Bledsoe performed in New York, adding to his repertoire the major baritone roles of *Carmen, Faust*, and *Boris Godunov*. His recitals and radio broadcasts, however, included spirituals and even blues.

In 1935 Bledsoe participated in charity events in New York, helping to raise money for the Metropolitan Opera (although he was not even considered for employment by that company), for out-of-work actors, and for pacifist causes. He also returned to Europe to work in musicals. By 1936 he composed and performed his own song cycle, *African Suite*, with Amsterdam's Concertgebouw Orchestra, conducted by Willem Mengelberg.

Bledsoe's plans to leave his home in Roxbury, New York, to return to Europe were thwarted by the outbreak of war in 1939. He spent the remainder of his career largely in recitals to benefit patriotic or humanitarian causes, although he did appear in several films: *Safari* (1940), *Santa Fe Trail* (1940), *Western Union* (1941), and *Drums of the Congo* (1942). He died of a cerebral hemorrhage in Hollywood, where he had been promoting the sale of war bonds. His funeral was held the next week at his boyhood church, New Hope Baptist, in Waco, Texas. He never married.

Although cast in opera for several "race" roles in the United States, Bledsoe was also successful in European productions that were not race based. Reviews indicate he was a major vocal talent with an outstanding ability to communicate. One New York critic observed in 1926: "He has a baritone voice of truly exceptional quality. He is a singer who can pick the heart right out of your body—if you don't look out. And in the second act [of *Deep River*] he showed last night that he is a very fine actor as well." A Parisian critic, praising Bledsoe in 1931, said, "If he remained absolutely what he is, he would be unique in the history of song."

Among Bledsoe's compositions, in addition to the *African Suite*, are arrangements of spirituals for voice and piano, *Ode to America* for baritone and chorus (dedicated to Franklin Roosevelt and first performed in a 1941 broadcast hosted by Eleanor Roosevelt), and the opera *Bondage*, after Harriet Beecher Stowe's *Uncle Tom's Cabin* (unproduced).

Bledsoe's career was distinguished by his opera performances, particularly in Europe. American performance opportunities sometimes allied him with figures of the Harlem Renaissance and of vaudeville. Few other black concert artists during this period were able to sustain careers, the major exceptions being Roland Hayes, Marian Anderson, and Paul Robeson (who followed Bledsoe as Joe in *Show Boat*).

In 1939, Bledsoe wrote a former classmate: "I have to be very careful not to injure my prestige. I have had to refuse lesser offers already this year. Most people don't understand that an artist is like a piece of merchandise, which has to be maintained and kept around a certain value, or else . . . the downward grade is begun."

• The Jules Bledsoe Papers are held within the Texas Collection of Baylor University Library. The vertical file of the Schomburg Research Center at the New York Public Library contains newspaper clippings. The major study of his life is Lynnette G. Geary, "Jules Bledsoe: The Original Ol' Man River," in *The Black Perspective in Music*, vol. 17, ed. Eileen Southern (1989), pp. 27–54. An obituary is in the *Waco Tribune*, 21 July 1943.

DOMINIQUE-RENÉ DE LERMA

BLEECKER, Ann Eliza (Oct. 1752–23 Nov. 1783), poet and novelist, was born in New York City, the daughter of Brandt Schuyler, a prosperous merchant from an upper-class New York family, and Margaret Van Wyck. Her father died two months before Ann Eliza's birth, but he left his family of one son and three daughters in comfortable circumstances. In childhood she read widely, wrote verse, and was part of the cultural life of upper-class New York society.

In March 1769, at the age of seventeen, she married John James Bleecker, a lawyer from an established New Rochelle family. After living two years in Poughkeepsie, the couple moved in 1771 to Tomhanick, a frontier community eighteen miles north of Albany, where they established a large farm. They had two children. Her poetry from this period suggests that she lived in an idyllic setting, "painted by a hand divine," and that her marriage and home life were very happy.

This peaceful life was shattered when, in 1777, the British army under General John Burgoyne approached Tomhanick. Like other families in the area, the Bleeckers looked for safety, and in that summer John Bleecker left for Albany to make arrangements for a family move. Left alone, and hearing that Burgoyne's men were near, Ann Eliza Bleecker, with her two daughters and a young female servant, fled Tomhanick. She headed on foot for Albany. It was a mournful retreat according to her daughter Margaretta, who recalled the event years later in a memoir of her mother: "The roads were crowded with carriages loaded with women and children, but none could afford her [Mrs. Bleecker] assistance . . . and no sound but the dismal creaking of burdened wheels and the trampling of horses interrupted the mournful silence." Two days later, John Bleecker met up with the family outside of Albany; fearing that the city would be attacked, the family went down the Hudson River toward Red Hook, New York, where they planned to meet Margaret Schuyler. On the trip, the Bleeckers' younger daughter Abella died of dysentery. Bleecker later wrote to her brother that she had one of her "mahogany dining-tables cut up" to make her daughter's coffin and that she buried "the little angel" on the river bank. Overwhelmed with grief, and ill herself, Bleecker arrived at Red Hook just in time to have her mother die in her arms. She returned to Albany to face more death when, she wrote her brother, "I saw [my] poor sister Caty expire."

After Burgoyne's surrender, the Bleeckers returned to Tomhanick. Deeply depressed, Ann Eliza Bleecker tried to cope with these losses and with constant anxiety "under perpetual alarms from the savages." Her fears of imminent catastrophe were realized when, in August 1781, a party of six Tories captured her husband. Although he was rescued and home within a week, Bleecker later wrote to her brother that it was a "shock I could not support," and "soon after I fell into premature labour and was delivered of a dead child." She observed that "affliction has broken my spirit." She died at Tomhanick the following November.

In the 1790s, Margaretta Bleecker Faugeres published much of her mother's writing in *New-York Magazine*, and in October 1793 she published *The Posthumous Works of Ann Eliza Bleecker in Prose and Verse*. This volume contains most of Ann Eliza Bleecker's surviving work, including most of her poems and letters; a short story, "The Story of Henry and Ann"; and an Indian captivity narrative, *The History of Maria Kittle*.

Bleecker's writing is about her life in Tomhanick and tells of the country's extraordinary natural beauty and equally extraordinary loneliness. Neoclassic in form and preromantic in content, Bleecker's poetry dwells on the death of her child Abella, the beauty of her surroundings in Tomhanick, and the pleasures of rural solitude. Her letters, a counterpoint to the poetry, are not self-consciously literary, as the poems are, but they cover the same material from an unvarnished and personal perspective. Through her letters one can see the toll that the lonely frontier life took on Bleecker's mental health.

Taken together, Bleecker's two pieces of fiction show the promise and the agony of frontier life. "The Story of Henry and Ann" tells of an impoverished young Germanic couple, victims of a tyrannical "Baron," who emigrate to America and find independence, prosperity, and democratic values on their Tomhanick farm. *The History of Maria Kittle* does not tell such an optimistic story, however. Instead, it dwells on the horrors of life in the American wilderness, its highly emotional language and detailed descriptions of the blood and gore of the Indian attacks undoubtedly drawn from Bleecker's own fear of attack when she was left alone, as she often was, on her farm. The plotline also must have been drawn from Bleecker's worst fears. Like her, the heroine of the novel, Maria, is a refined and delicate young mother who lives with her family on a beautiful but isolated Tomhanick estate. Set during the French and Indian Wars, the story begins with a graphic account of an Indian attack on the estate while Maria's husband is away. The Indians gleefully slaughter the family and capture Maria. After a harrowing trek to Canada, Maria is ransomed and returned to her husband but not before she is changed forever. She cannot forget the horrors of the Indian attack, when before her eyes her children were "wrapt in arching sheets of flame."

The History of Maria Kittle is Ann Eliza Bleecker's best-known work. Although it is sentimental and predictable, it exemplifies the captivity narrative genre and is one of the first attempts to make literary use of the French and Indian Wars. Thus, although Ann Eliza Bleecker's work has never had much of an audience, it is a small but notable contribution to literature of the period of the American Revolution.

• *The Posthumous Works of Ann Eliza Bleecker in Prose and Verse* (1793), with a memoir of her life by Margaretta Bleecker Faugeres, is the most accessible source of Ann Eliza Bleecker's work. An introduction and a few of her poems can be found in Rufus Wilmot Griswold, *The Female Poets of America* (1848). An early appraisal appears in Evert A. Duyckinck and George Duyckinck, *Cycle of American Literature*, vol. 1 (1855). Two important articles are Julie Ellison, "Race and Sensibility in the Early Republic: Ann Eliza Bleecker and Sarah Wentworth Morton," *American Literature* 65, no. 3 (1993): 446–71, and Allison Giffen, "'Till Grief Melodious Grow,' The Poems and Letters of Ann Eliza Bleecker," *Early American Literature* 28, no. 3 (1993): 222–41. Also see Kenneth Silverman, *A Cultural History of the American Revolution* (1976), and Mary Beth Norton, *Liberty's Daughters: The Revolutionary Experience of American Women 1750–1800* (1980).

MAUREEN GOLDMAN

BLEGEN, Carl William (27 Jan. 1887–23 Aug. 1971), archaeologist and educator, was born in Minneapolis, Minnesota, the son of John H. Blegen, a university professor, and Anna Bergine Olsen. Blegen earned bachelor's degrees from three institutions: Augsburg Seminary (1904), the University of Minnesota (1907), and Yale University (1908). Following two years of graduate study at Yale, Blegen went to Greece in 1910 as a student at the American School of Classical Studies at Athens. He remained there until 1927, as student, secretary, assistant director, and acting director, with time out from 1918 to 1920 to work with the American Red Cross in Greece. During his years in Greece, Blegen formed close and enduring friendships with Bert Hodge Hill, director of the American school, A. J. B. Wace, director of the British school, and Elizabeth Denny Pierce, fellow archaeologist and professional collaborator, whom he married in 1924.

Blegen's first major excavation was at Korakou (1915–1916), where he established for the first time the chronological sequence of Bronze Age habitation in the area. The results of that excavation, published in 1921, formed his doctoral dissertation, for which he earned a Ph.D. at Yale the same year. The significance of the work lies in its organization of ceramic chronology based on principles of precise stratigraphy. Blegen introduced consistent terminology and proposed a scheme of absolute chronology that related to the rest of the eastern Mediterranean. Through further research at sites like Mycenae, Zygouries, Colophon, Phlius, Nemea, Prosymna, and Corinth, Blegen clarified aspects of his proposed ceramic chronology.

In 1927, Blegen moved to the University of Cincinnati, where for the next thirty years he educated students of archaeology both in the classroom and in the trenches. His first major archaeological enterprise while at Cincinnati was a reinvestigation of Troy from 1932 to 1938. In light of scientific advances and technological improvements, Blegen and his team sought to bring order to the strata discovered in the late nineteenth century by Heinrich Schliemann and his associate Wilhelm Dörpfeld. In the course of successive campaigns at the site, Blegen reassessed the nine major layers recognized by his German predecessors and discovered that each had multiple subdivisions, for a total of forty-nine phases. The resulting clarification of stratigraphy was an enduring contribution to prehistoric studies. Less clear is the issue of levels that were destroyed and their possible relationship to the legendary Trojan War. Many scholars have believed, with Dörpfeld, that Troy VI was the Homeric city destroyed by enemy action. Blegen, however, arguing that its leveling resulted from violent earthquake activity, proposed instead the relatively modest Troy VIIa as Priam's citadel. A more fundamental controversy, which continues today, involved the question of the historicity of the Trojan War and the heroes from the Homeric epic.

Blegen's great undertaking at Pylos, in southwestern Greece, was the crowning achievement of his career. His preliminary field work in 1939 was interrupted by World War II, during which Blegen served with the Office of Strategic Services in Washington (1942–1945) and then as cultural relations attaché at the U.S. embassy in Athens (1945–1946). After the war he spent two years (1948–1949) as acting director of the American School of Classical Studies. In 1950 Blegen became head of the classics department at Cincinnati and resumed his excavations at Pylos. The initial excavation season at Pylos produced sensational results, in the form of a cache of clay tablets covered with Linear B inscriptions, a form of writing known from Crete but not understood; further excavations at Pylos uncovered many more. The source of the tablets was a Mycenaean palace that Blegen associated with King Nestor of Homeric fame. Remarkably well preserved, the palace affords in plan and permanent installations a vivid glimpse into a royal household of the Late Bronze Age. Michael Ventris, an English architect and accomplished linguist, captured worldwide interest by deciphering the Linear B tablets. That the language was in fact Greek proved to have broad ramifications for reconstructing Aegean prehistory. The subject matter of the Pylos tablets is administrative, and from it scholars could draw conclusions about political, social, and religious organization, even though interpretation was difficult and controversial.

Blegen retired from the University of Cincinnati as emeritus in 1957 and was made Distinguished Service Professor Emeritus in 1969. He was a member of numerous scholarly societies, receiving many honors and awards in America and abroad, including the gold medal from the Archaeological Institute of America. He died and was buried in Athens.

Blegen was a pioneer of the third generation of preclassical Greek archaeologists, following in the footsteps of Heinrich Schliemann and Sir Arthur Evans. His precise but cautious observations were instrumental in establishing Bronze Age ceramic chronology based on stratigraphic sequence and in elucidating many other aspects of Bronze Age culture. He was a conscientious writer who recognized the need for factual reporting to provide a basis for future research. In his later field work Blegen employed an increasing number of natural scientists, thus paving the way for the accepted interdisciplinary collaboration of the following generation.

• Blegen's papers are preserved in the archives of the American School of Classical Studies at Athens. His major works include *Korakou, a Prehistoric Settlement near Corinth* (1921); *Zygouries, a Prehistoric Settlement in the Valley of Cleonae* (1928); *Corinth* III,i, *Acrocorinth, Excavations in 1926*, chaps. 1 and 2 (1930); with Elizabeth Pierce Blegen, *Prosymna, the Helladic Settlement Preceding the Argive Heraeum* (1937); with collaborators, *Troy Excavations Conducted by the University of Cincinnati 1932–1938*, vols. 1–4 (1950–1958), and *Supplements*, vols. 1–4 (1951–1982); foreword to E. L. Bennett, Jr., *The Pylos Tablets: Texts of the Inscriptions Found 1939–1954* (1955); *Troy and the Trojans* (1963); *Corinth*, XIII, *The North Cemetery*, part 1 (1964); with collaborators, *The Palace of Nestor at Pylos in Western Messenia*, vols. 1–3 (1966–1973). A complete bibliography of his work appears in *Hesperia* 35 (1966): 287–94. A scholarly assessment of Blegen's archaeological achievements appears in W. A. McDonald and C. G. Thomas, *Progress into the Past: The Rediscovery of Mycenaean Civilization*, 2d ed. (1990). Obituaries are in the *New York Times*, 26 Aug., 1971, *Classical World* 65 (Oct. 1971): 68, and the *American Philosophical Society Yearbook* (1972): 121–25.

STELLA G. MILLER

BLENNERHASSETT, Harman (8 Oct. 1764 or 1765–2 Feb. 1831), lawyer, was born in Hampshire, England, the son of Conway Blennerhassett and his wife (name unknown), Irish gentry who were traveling at the time of his birth. Blennerhassett was an ordinary man blessed with extraordinary advantages. His education was impeccable; he graduated from Westminster School in London and from Trinity College, Dublin, in 1790. Admitted to the Irish bar in 1790, the fortuitous deaths of his older brothers left him owner of the family estates at Castle Conway. Suddenly a gentleman of leisure, Harman devoted himself to the age of revolution. He read Voltaire and Rousseau, attended the first anniversary of the fall of the Bastille in Paris, and dabbled in music and science. Blennerhassett was a salon radical, a sincere man who liked to discuss the ways in which the world might be improved without actually doing much about it. His most direct challenge to conventional mores was his 1796 marriage to his sister Catherine Agnew's nineteen-year-old daughter, Margaret Agnew. The relationship caused a scandal in Ireland. Faced with resultant social ostracism and legal problems, Harman sold his landholdings for $160,000 and left Ireland with Margaret in 1796 for the United States.

Although they were briefly in both New York and Philadelphia, the Blennerhassetts did not stay in the East. Instead, they plunged on to the fringes of Euroamerican society, traveling to Pittsburgh and then down the Ohio River to the new settlement of Marietta in the Northwest Territory. Delighted with the decade-old town, Blennerhassett bought 170 acres for $4,500 on an island in the Ohio about fifteen miles downriver (near present-day Parkersburg, W.V.). The Blennerhassetts spent much of the next decade and the bulk of their fortune remaking the island into their idea of a romantic, wilderness retreat. Their slaves and local workers constructed a two-story white house, complete with wings, outbuildings, and gardens, which the couple furnished with imported paintings, furniture, mirrors, and curtains. Thereafter, Harman conducted scientific experiments (chemistry, astronomy, electricity), played his violin, and hunted (although his nearsightedness made his aim dependent on the instructions of his wife and slaves), while Margaret wrote poetry, rehearsed Shakespearean plays, and rode her horse in a scarlett riding habit.

In the spring of 1805 former vice president Aaron Burr (1756–1836) stopped by the Blennerhassett estate on a trip downriver. Near the end of their money and bored with life on their island, the couple listened eagerly as Burr discussed his vague plans for an enterprise against the Spanish empire in Mexico. Enticed by the prospects for both romantic adventure and financial gain, Harman became a strong supporter of Burr's scheme. In 1806 he made his island a rendezvous for the enterprise, paying to have boats built in Marietta, buying supplies, and housing converts on his island. He also wrote a series of articles in the Marietta *Ohio Gazette* under the name "Querist," which argued that alleged discrimination by the East would eventually lead to the secession of Trans-Appalachia from the United States.

Blennerhassett's activities alarmed his neighbors and raised suspicions of treason. On 11 December 1806 a group of Wood County, Virginia, militiamen moved onto the island and looted the property. Blennerhassett had left his home the previous evening with four boats crammed with supplies and recruits. Federal authorities briefly detained him, in the company of Burr and others, in the Mississippi Territory and then arrested him in Kentucky. He was taken to Richmond, Virginia, to stand trial for treason but was released when the government failed to convict Burr. During his prison sojourn, Blennerhassett kept a journal that reveals his genuine compassion for others, his love of society and erudition, and his devotion to Margaret and their sons. The journal ends with Blennerhassett's pursuit of Burr to Philadelphia, where he unsuccessfully demanded reimbursement and some sort of recognition from the former vice president.

Blennerhassett returned to his island, which was in disrepair, sold some of it, and rented the rest. He joined his family in Natchez and purchased 1,000 acres for a cotton plantation in Claiborne County, Mississippi Territory. Meanwhile, he lobbied Burr's son-in-law, Joseph Alston, for repayment of expenses incurred in supplying Burr's enterprise. He was not above threatening to write an exposé, but he got nowhere with his demands.

The rest of the Blennerhassetts' lives was a series of tribulations. In 1811 a fire destroyed their island mansion. In the mid-1810s they had to sell the failing cotton plantation along with twenty-two slaves. The family moved in 1819 to Montreal, where Harman unsuccessfully practiced law. Desperate for money, he went back to Ireland in 1822 to reclaim some land or obtain a government sinecure. Margaret stayed in Montreal with their three sons, one of whom became an alcoholic and completely disappeared.

A despondent Blennerhassett returned to Canada in 1825 to collect his wife and two remaining sons. The family lived for several years in England, depending on the kindness of relatives. Blennerhassett died on the island of Guernsey. Margaret supported herself and her sons for another decade. In 1842 she sailed to New York in order to petition Congress for money, but she died shortly after her arrival.

At Blennerhassett's trial, his Marietta business partner Dudley Woodbridge astutely remarked that Harman had "more other sense than common sense." Historians have generally followed this tack, writing of Blennerhassett's life as a mixture of farce and tragedy. What they have neglected is the element of romance. The most constant theme in his life was neither the consequences of his seduction by Burr nor his inability to survive in a society that had no place for learned landed gentlemen. Far more important was the remarkable love he shared with Margaret, a passion that both created their troubles and gave them the strength to endure them.

• There are some Blennerhassett papers in the Library of Congress and the Campus Martius Museum in Marietta, Ohio. William H. Safford, *The Blennerhassett Papers* (1864), is an excellent source, containing letters and other documents Safford obtained from Joseph Lewis Blennerhassett, the last surviving son. Just as useful is Raymond E. Fitch, *Breaking with Burr: Harman Blennerhassett's Journal, 1807* (1988), an annotated edition of the prison journal. See also Mary-Jo Kline, ed., *Political Correspondence and Public Papers of Aaron Burr* (1983). Ronald Ray Swick, "Harman Blennerhassett: An Irish Aristocrat on the American Frontier" (Ph.D. diss., Miami Univ. of Ohio, 1978), is a detailed biography.

ANDREW CAYTON

BLESH, Rudi (21 Jan. 1899–25 Aug. 1985), writer, record producer, and broadcaster, was born Rudolph Pickett Blesh in Guthrie, Oklahoma Territory, the son of Abraham Lincoln Blesh, a doctor, and Theodora Bell Pickett, a piano teacher. In 1910 a family visit to

Vienna stimulated Blesh's interest in the arts, and consequently, he learned to play the piano, the violin, and the cello. Although his musical activities were restricted to the classical repertory at home, Blesh was impressed by the ragtime pianists who performed in Guthrie.

Having enrolled at Dartmouth College in 1917, Blesh heard the pioneering Original Dixieland Jazz Band while visiting New York City and immediately developed a love for this music. He made some progress toward a major in English, but he dropped out of Dartmouth in 1920. After the Blesh family moved to Berkeley, he studied at the University of California, gaining a B.S. in architecture in 1924. That same year he embarked on a career as an interior designer in San Francisco. He married Editha Tuttle in February 1925, and they had a daughter; the manner by which this marriage ended is unknown. By the time of Blesh's second marriage, to Barbara Lamont in July 1939, he was working in the San Francisco Bay Area as an industrial, furniture, and architectural designer.

Having collected jazz records since his Dartmouth days, Blesh began thinking about the music's history. On the strength of *This Is Jazz: A Series of Lectures Given at the San Francisco Museum of Art*, which he wrote in the spring of 1943 and published himself, Blesh was asked to become jazz critic for the *San Francisco Chronicle*. His career as a designer ended. He promoted concerts by traditional jazz musicians Bunk Johnson and Kid Ory, and on a visit to New York in 1944 he was commissioned to write a history of jazz.

At this point Blesh met Harriet Grossman Janis, a specialist in modern art. They moved to New York in 1945, and Blesh became a jazz critic for the *New York Herald Tribune*. Blesh and Janis traveled together conducting research and interviews for *Shining Trumpets: A History of Jazz* (1946; rev. ed., 1958; repr. 1975). In January 1946 the two also founded Circle Records. In 1947 Blesh began a three-year stint writing and narrating radio programs on both jazz and American folk music. The most memorable program, titled "This Is Jazz," ran over the Mutual Broadcasting System for thirty-five weeks between 18 January and 4 October 1947. "This Is Jazz" offered national exposure to veterans of early jazz styles, including reed player Sidney Bechet, pianist James P. Johnson, bassist Pops Foster, and drummer Baby Dodds. Excerpts from their performances were issued on Circle Records, as were new sessions made independently of the radio show by Dodds, clarinetist George Lewis, and others. Most significantly, Circle produced the first issue of Jelly Roll Morton's 1938 recordings for the Library of Congress.

During these years Blesh figured prominently in a vicious dispute between fans of traditional jazz and fans of bebop. Gradually coming to recognize bebop alto saxophonist Charlie Parker's genius, Blesh softened his position somewhat. In 1947 he presented Dixieland trumpeter Wild Bill Davison's group in contrast with that of Parker and trumpeter Dizzy Gillespie. At a similar event in March 1949, Parker's group was set against a traditional ensemble led by Bechet.

In 1950, with Janis as coauthor, Blesh published *They All Played Ragtime*; it subsequently went through several editions, the fourth in 1971. From 1956 to his retirement in 1974, Blesh taught jazz history as a member of the music faculty at Queens College and the American arts faculty at New York University. In January 1959 Janis and he founded a new label, Solo Art Records, but for several years during this period Blesh turned his attention away from music to publish various books, including *Modern Art U.S.A.* (1956); *Stuart Davis* (1960); *De Kooning* (1960), with Janis; *Collage: Personalities, Concepts, Techniques* (1962), again with Janis; and on his own, after her death, *Keaton* (1966). In the late 1960s and 1970s, in addition to returning briefly to the radio studio in 1964, he wrote liner notes for ragtime recordings, compiled ragtime piano music collections, and wrote the introductory essay "Scott Joplin: Black-American Classicist" in editor Vera Brodsky Lawrence's *The Collected Works of Scott Joplin* (1971). He also published a biographical volume, *Combo USA: Eight Lives in Jazz* (1971). After a decade in comfortable retirement, he died at his farm, "Hill Forge," in Gilmanton, New Hampshire.

Blesh exemplified the twentieth-century cultivated semiprofessional Renaissance man. Like many such figures, his work was sometimes hampered by the absence of expert research skills, and it was often lopsided, with enthusiasm getting in the way of fact. His history of modern art particularly exemplified these weaknesses, and it received brutal reviews. His history of jazz can be similarly infuriating to anyone who does not share Blesh's dislike of modern jazz, but at least in this area Blesh was reasonably well informed, and his perspective on the genre's first decades is rewarding.

Blesh's finest work is distinguished. His biography of silent film comedian, screenwriter, director, and producer Buster Keaton offers a detailed technical account of Keaton's films while sensibly placing this detail within the context of Keaton's life and the transition from silent films to movies with sound. Likewise, Blesh's collaboration with Janis, *They All Played Ragtime*, is a monumental work. It prompted a general revival of the music, and, more specifically, it led to a rediscovery of composer and pianist Eubie Blake (whom Blesh urged out of retirement) and composer James Lamb. It also revised conceptualizations of ragtime, which thereafter came to be understood as an independent genre, rather than merely a prejazz style.

• A detailed autobiographical letter from Blesh to jazz writer Leonard Feather dated 19 Mar. 1958 is in the files of the Institute of Jazz Studies, Newark, N.J. The essential biographical survey is John Edward Hasse, "Rudi Blesh and the Ragtime Revivalists," in *Ragtime: Its History, Composers, and Music*, ed. Hasse (1985). Blesh's contributions to ragtime are analyzed in Edward A. Berlin, *Ragtime: A Musical and Cultural History* (1980). A detailed guide to the notable radio show, including quotations from Blesh's narration, is Jack Litchfield, *This Is Jazz* (1985). See also "Rudi Blesh Conducts Battle of the Bands, between Old and New Forms of Jazz," *New York Herald Tribune*, 7 Mar. 1949. David Reffkin, "Ragtime Machine," *Mississippi Rag* 11 (June 1984): 7; Feather, *The Jazz Years: Earwitness to an Era* (1986); and "Circle (i)," in *The New Grove Dictionary of Jazz*, ed. Barry Kernfeld (1988), are also helpful. Reviews of Blesh's nonmusical publications include Alfonso Ossorio, "One Man's Art U.S.A.," *Art News* 55 (Oct. 1956): 47–48, and 55 (Nov. 1956): 12; Hilton Kramer, "Books: Modern Art USA," *Arts* 31 (Dec. 1956): 45; Lawrence D. Steefel, Jr., "Harriet Janis and Rudi Blesh: Collage," *Art Journal* 22 (Spring 1963): 212, 214; and Hugh Kenner, "Books: Keaton," *Film Quarterly* 20 (Fall 1966): 60–61. Obituaries are in the *New York Times*, 28 Aug. 1985; the *San Francisco Examiner*, 6 Sept. 1985; and *C. R. C. Newsletter* 11, no. 4 (1985): 2.

BARRY KERNFELD

BLEYER, Willard Grosvenor (27 Aug. 1873–31 Oct. 1935), journalism educator, was born in Milwaukee, Wisconsin, the son of Albert J. Bleyer, a newspaperman, and Elizabeth Groshans. Six of Albert's brothers also worked for newspapers. While an undergraduate at the University of Wisconsin (1892–1896), Bleyer edited the student newspaper, the *Daily Cardinal*, as well as the school yearbook and a literary magazine. He was elected to Phi Beta Kappa and graduated with honors in 1896. After earning an M.A. in English in 1898, Bleyer taught for two years at a Milwaukee public school. He returned to the University of Wisconsin and received a Ph.D. in English in 1904. His department then appointed him assistant professor.

In 1904 Bleyer persuaded university president Charles H. Van Hise to create a press office, which the young professor headed for nine years. Bleyer edited the *University Press Bulletin*, which carried stories on university research and was distributed to newspapers throughout the state and nation. The *University Press Bulletin*, a self-conscious effort to create goodwill for the university, endeavored to sell the university as more than the site of athletic contests and fraternity parties. And with many articles on applied research useful to farmers and others, the *Bulletin* represented an institutionalization of what was dubbed "the Wisconsin Idea," that the university should serve all of the state's citizens.

While organizing the press office, Bleyer aspired to teach courses in journalism. In the late nineteenth century, only a few American colleges and universities had offered journalism classes, none on a permanent basis. Bleyer, in an 1893 *Cardinal* editorial, had urged the university to offer formal instruction in journalism and award college credits for student newspaper work. With the approval of Van Hise, Bleyer in 1905 began teaching a journalism course in the English department. In 1912 Wisconsin established a separate department of journalism, with a two-person faculty consisting of Bleyer and another instructor. During this period, in 1911, Bleyer married Alice Haskell of Providence, Rhode Island; they had no children.

Bleyer's plan for journalism majors limited formal journalism instruction to no more than a quarter of all college credits. And not all journalism courses were of a technical nature; Bleyer developed classes on journalism history, law, and ethics. Much of the work outside of the major was to be in the social sciences. All in all, journalism majors were expected to leave Wisconsin with a broad liberal arts education.

Bleyer tried to shape journalism education nationwide. In 1912 he helped to organize the first federation of journalism instructors, the American Association of Teachers of Journalism (AATJ). Bleyer was the AATJ's first president. He later led efforts to accredit journalism schools, using a variation of the Wisconsin program as a model. Many programs, while claiming to honor the liberal arts ideal of Wisconsin, in fact gave more weight to the technical aspects of journalism education. In and out of AATJ leadership positions for the next twenty years, Bleyer actively promoted faculty research. Journalism faculty, he averred, should be more than instructors in technique. Bleyer himself, in addition to writing several of the field's first textbooks, conducted original historical research and wrote a history of the fourth estate, *Main Currents in the History of American Journalism* (1927). But, as in setting curriculum standards, many rival schools, led by the University of Missouri, resisted Bleyer's faculty research standard.

Bleyer had greater success at Wisconsin. In 1916 the university awarded its first master's degrees in journalism. Eleven years later, journalism became a separate school and Bleyer was its first director. By then, Wisconsin had trained a generation of journalists and journalism educators.

Bleyer's commitment to journalism education flowed from his conviction that newspaper work had become a respectable middle-class profession, no different from law and medicine. And journalists, Bleyer insisted, were no less important to a self-governing people. "Universities have spent millions of dollars on establishing and maintaining medical and law schools," he wrote in 1931. "Are journalists less important to the welfare of society and to the success of democratic government?" ("What Schools of Journalism Are Trying to Do," *Journalism Quarterly* 8 [Mar. 1931]: 35–44). Not everyone accepted Bleyer's arguments. Although more than 200 colleges and universities offered some form of journalism instruction in 1925, many editors and publishers dismissed journalism education as a waste of time. But Bleyer persistently defended journalism schools, which in 1931 he judged "necessary to protect society and government against immature, half-educated, unscrupulous journalists."

Bleyer also fought to improve reporters' status and pay. He urged journalists to form guilds modeled after bar and medical associations and to fight for better wages. He assailed publishers in the early 1930s for inadequately compensating reporters, especially women writers and editors. Self-interest, Bleyer acknowledged, partly explained his position. Wisconsin students were less likely to major in journalism once they learned of the poor pay at many newspapers.

Other trends in newspaper publishing deeply troubled Bleyer. In the 1920s the number of communities served by only one newspaper had risen dramatically, as had the number of newspapers owned by single owners or chains. To Bleyer, this greatly increased the power of individual publishers to mold public opinion. "In the monopolistic character of present-day newspaper publishing," Bleyer wrote in 1934, "lies great danger to the formation of sound opinion." Newspapers, Bleyer had concluded, were "quasi-public" institutions. "The newspaper, obviously, is more than a private business enterprise." Anticipating criticisms of the press in the late 1940s, he urged newspapers to become "socially responsible" by being as objective and fair as possible. Otherwise, some form of government regulation might be warranted ("Freedom of the Press and the New Deal," *Journalism Quarterly* 11 [Mar. 1934]: 22–35).

Bleyer's passions were not easily noticed by Wisconsin students, who uniformly judged him to be a horrendously dull lecturer. Soft-spoken and careful, Bleyer wore galoshes at the slightest hint of rain and always drove the same make of automobile. He was long called "Daddy" Bleyer, though rarely to his face.

He died suddenly of a cerebral hemorrhage in Madison. "It is nothing less than a national loss," Frank Luther Mott, the head of Iowa's journalism school, wrote. "We all looked to Doctor Bleyer as the leader of the forces for education in journalism" (letter to Grant Hyde, 6 Nov. 1935, Univ. of Wisconsin Archives, Madison).

• Bleyer's papers and a biographical file of newspaper clippings and correspondence are at the University of Wisconsin Archives, Madison. Bleyer's textbooks include *Newspaper Writing and Editing* (1913; 2d ed. 1923), *How to Write Special Feature Articles* (1920), and *Types of News Writing* (1916). He also edited a collection of newspaper criticism, *The Profession of Journalism* (1918), and a brief essay, *Journalism* (1929). On Bleyer himself, Donald Keith Ross, "W. G. Bleyer and the Development of Journalism Education" (M.A. thesis, Univ. of Wisconsin, 1952), is thickly detailed; a small portion of Ross's thesis appeared in *Journalism Quarterly* 34 (Fall 1957): 466–74. See also William David Sloan, "Willard Bleyer and Propriety," in *Makers of the Media Mind: Journalism Educators and Their Ideas*, ed. William David Sloan (1990). Obituaries, in addition to those in the Madison dailies, are in the *Capital Times* and the *New York Times*, both 1 Nov. 1935, and the *Milwaukee Journal*, 31 Oct. 1935. Two helpful tributes, among the many that followed Bleyer's death, are Daniel D. Mich, "The Press Roars a Requiem for 'Daddy' Bleyer," *Wisconsin State Journal*, 1 Nov. 1935, and Ralph O. Nafziger, "Willard G. Bleyer, 1875–1935," *Journalism Quarterly* 12 (Dec. 1935): 374–78.

JAMES L. BAUGHMAN

BLICHFELDT, Hans Frederik (9 Jan. 1873–16 Nov. 1945), mathematician, was born in the village of Iller in Grønbaeck Sogn, Denmark, the son of Erhard Christoffer Laurentius Blichfeldt and Nielsine Maria Schøler, farmers. Although not poverty-stricken, the Blichfeldt family lived frugally, and the children worked in their earlier years to help make ends meet. After the family's move to Copenhagen in 1881, Blichfeldt began to demonstrate his mathematical prowess. By the age of fifteen, he had discovered for himself the solutions of the general polynomial equations of the third and fourth degrees. At this same age, he earned the highest honors on a general preliminary state examination held at the University of Copenhagen. A lack of financial resources, however, prevented Blichfeldt from attending the university.

Blichfeldt's opportunity for education came later, six years after he emigrated to the United States in 1888 with his father and older half brother. From 1888 to 1892 he worked with his "hands doing everything, East and West the country across," particularly in the lumber industry in the Northwest (Dickson, p. 882). He spent the years from 1892 to 1894 as a draftsman for the engineering department of the city and county of Whatcom, Washington. Noticing Blichfeldt's mathematical talent, his employers and co-workers in Whatcom encouraged him to pursue mathematics at the newly opened Stanford University, and the county superintendent of schools wrote a letter of support for Blichfeldt's application.

In 1894 Blichfeldt matriculated at Stanford, where he managed to live on his savings and earn a B.A. in 1896 and an M.A. (probably in mathematics) in 1897. Like many promising mathematicians of his day, Blichfeldt traveled to Germany for his doctoral work; Professor Rufus Green, one of two members of the mathematical faculty at Stanford at the time, lent Blichfeldt the necessary funds for his year abroad. Blichfeldt spent the year from 1897 to 1898 studying under one of the premier mathematicians of the day, Sophus Lie, at the University of Leipzig. In 1898 he received his doctorate from Leipzig summa cum laude for his dissertation "On a Certain Class of Groups of Transformation in Space of Three Dimensions."

Following his return to the United States, Blichfeldt began in 1898 his more than forty-year tenure at Stanford University, serving first as an instructor. He became assistant professor of mathematics in 1901, associate professor in 1906, professor in 1913, and professor emeritus in 1938. He chaired the mathematics department from 1927 until his retirement in 1938. During this time, as a reflection of Blichfeldt's keen interest in the international exchange of ideas, a steady stream of prominent European mathematicians, such as Harald Bohr, Edmund Landau, George Polya, and Gabor Szegö, visited Stanford. Blichfeldt himself lectured as a visiting professor at the University of Chicago in the summer of 1911 and at Columbia University in the summers of 1924 and 1925.

Although not a prolific writer, Blichfeldt made significant contributions to both group theory and the geometry of numbers. In group theory, for example, he solved a difficult classical problem, which had eluded at least two eminent Europeans, Felix Klein and Camille Jordan: the complete determination of the finite linear groups in four variables. In the geometry of numbers, he furthered the work of German mathematician Hermann Minkowski and explicitly stated bounds for minima of quadratic forms in six, seven, and eight variables. Blichfeldt wrote "Finite Groups of Linear Homogeneous Transformations," which formed the second part of *Theory and Application of Finite Groups*, coauthored with L. E. Dickson and G. A. Miller, in 1916. In 1917 he published *Finite Collineation Groups*.

Blichfeldt served as vice president of the American Mathematical Society in 1912. In 1918, during World War I, he worked with other mathematicians under the guidance of Oswald Veblen on range-firing and ballistic investigations. He was elected to the National Academy of Sciences in 1920. From 1924 to 1927 Blichfeldt was a member of the National Research Council. He represented the United States at the International Mathematical Congresses in Zurich in 1932 and in Oslo in 1936. In 1938 the King of Denmark made Blichfeldt a knight of the Order of Dannebrog.

Although Blichfeldt never married, he maintained close family ties with relatives in both Denmark and the United States. As a young man, and, later, as long as his health permitted, he enjoyed swimming, bicycling, hiking, and traveling. He died in Palo Alto, California. According to his contemporary, leading group theorist L. E. Dickson, "Blichfeldt was for forty years one of America's leading research men in groups and theory of numbers" (Dickson, p. 882).

• The David Starr Jordan Papers at Stanford University contain a few of Blichfeldt's letters. Among Blichfeldt's works not already mentioned are "On Primitive Linear Homogeneous Groups," *Transactions of the American Mathematical Society* 6 (1905): 230–36; "The Finite Discontinuous Primitive Groups of Collineations in Four Variables," *Mathematische Annalen* 60 (1905): 204–31; "A New Principle in the Geometry of Numbers, with Some Applications," *Transactions of the American Mathematical Society* 15 (1914): 227–35; "The Minimum Value of Quadratic Forms, and the Closest Packing of the Spheres," *Mathematische Annalen* 101 (1929): 605–8; and "The Minimum Values of Positive Quadratic Forms in Six, Seven and Eight Variables," *Mathematische Zeitschrift* 39 (1934): 1–15. On Blichfeldt's life and work, see E. T. Bell, "Hans Frederik Blichfeldt," National Academy of Sciences, *Biographical Memoirs* (1951), which includes a bibliography and brief description of Blichfeldt's mathematical papers, and a photograph of Blichfeldt as a young man; and L. E. Dickson, "Hans Frederik Blichfeldt," *Bulletin of the American Mathematical Society* 53 (1947): 882–83, which also contains a bibliography of Blichfeldt's work. Blichfeldt's influence on the mathematics department at Stanford is treated in Halsey Royden, "A History of Mathematics at Stanford," in *A Century of Mathematics in America*, pt. 2, ed. Peter Duren (1989), pp. 237–77.

DELLA DUMBAUGH FENSTER

BLIND TOM (25 May 1849–13 June 1908), pianist and composer, was born Thomas Grimes in Harris County, Georgia, the son of Mingo Wiggins and Charity, slaves on the Wiley Jones plantation. His first master's teenage daughter named him "Grimes" for an admirer of hers. Blind from birth, he was included when James N. Bethune, a Columbus, Georgia, lawyer-journalist who was referred to as either "Colonel" or "General" Bethune because of his service in the Georgia militia in 1830, purchased Tom's parents in 1850. According to most accounts, Tom demonstrated his aptitude for music at age four, when he slipped into the big house and picked out several tunes on the piano he had heard Bethune's daughters playing. Thereafter he was allowed access to the piano and received informal instruction from Bethune's wife and daughter. When professional performers gave concerts in Columbus, the Bethunes hired them to play for Tom, thus enabling him to increase his repertoire. By his sixth birthday Tom had become a "prized possession," with Bethune's children exhibiting him to their neighbors.

Following his first public performance at Columbus's Temperance Hall on 7 October 1857, Tom was taken to Atlanta, Macon, and Athens, where the editor of the *Southern Watchman* described his University of Georgia concert as "the most remarkable ever witnessed in Athens." Shortly thereafter Tom was hired out to Perry Oliver, a Savannah tobacco planter under a three-year contractual agreement with Bethune, who was paid $15,000 for allowing Tom to be exhibited in other southern cities. After several concerts in Savannah, Oliver exhibited Tom in other proslavery states as the "Musical Prodigy of the Age, a Plantation Negro." By 1861 Tom's reputation was such that he appeared in a private concert at Willard Hall in Washington, D.C., in honor of the first visiting Japanese delegation to the United States. His July 1860 concerts in Baltimore, Maryland, so impressed William Knabe, the famous piano manufacturer, that he gave the ten-year-old slave an elaborately carved rosewood grand piano with a silver plate bearing the inscription "Tribute To Genuis." Tom's compositions *Oliver Galop* and *Virginia Polka* were published that same year by Oliver Ditson.

With the outbreak of the Civil War, Oliver canceled Tom's nonsouthern engagements and returned to Georgia, where Tom was forced to give fundraisers for the Confederate cause. By October 1862 Tom was back with the Bethunes, who continued to use his talent for proslavery activities. Among other works, he performed his own piece, "Battle of Manassas," written after he heard one of Bethune's sons (a member of the Second Georgia Regiment) describe that famous Confederate victory.

Determined to continue his monetary control over Tom's talents in case of a Confederate defeat, Bethune had Tom's parents sign a five-year indenture agreement giving him legal guardianship of Tom. Following the capture of Atlanta in September 1864, Tom was taken by Bethune to Florida, where Bethune's daughters lived. After President Andrew Johnson ended the federal blockade of the South, the Bethunes began to exhibit Tom in the North. On 25 July 1865 in a Cincinnati court, Tabbs Gross—an African American who had purchased his freedom and who is referred to as the "Barnum of the African Race"—challenged the "agreement" by which Tom was placed under Bethune's guardianship. This historic guardianship trial in the Hamilton County Probate Court ended on 31 July 1865 with the judge's decision favoring the Bethunes. From there Tom was taken to several other Ohio cities, and then he made his eastern debut at Philadelphia's Concert Hall on 12 September. Although Professor W. P. Howard, an Atlanta music teacher, accompanied the Bethunes as Tom's full-time music tutor, Tom was still being promoted as a "natural untaught pianist." Though scheduled for one week, the Philadelphia engagement was extended to four weeks and was followed by similar successes in New York and Boston.

Although Tom was only sixteen, his repertoire included many of the most technical and musically demanding works of Bach, Beethoven, Chopin, Liszt, and other European composers. Like other pianists of his day, he demonstrated his improvisational and theoretical skills by performing variations and fantasias on operatic airs and popular ballads of the day.

After a second four-week concert engagement at New York's Irving Hall in April 1866, Tom was taken to Europe, where he was continuously subjected to rigorous tests by noted musicians such as Ignaz Moscheles and Charles Halle, whose testimonial letters were published by the Bethunes in a pamphlet, *The Marvelous Musical Prodigy Blind Tom*. By 1868 the Bethunes had moved to a farm in Warrenton, Virginia. Tom was brought there every summer following his concert season. He continued to tour annually throughout the United States and Canada, with Colonel Bethune's son John G. Bethune serving as his manager. On 25 July 1870 John Bethune had himself appointed Tom's legal guardian in a Virginia probate court, thereby negating the 1865 indentureship agreement. By now the Bethunes were realizing $50,000 yearly from Tom's concerts. They began to schedule concerts in the South and returned to Springer Opera House in Columbus, Georgia, on 10 February 1879.

For nine years Tom lived in New York since his manager had married Eliza Stutzback, owner of the boardinghouse where they stayed. In the summers Tom studied with Joseph Poznansky, who also wrote down many of Tom's compositions. He also studied with Amelia A. Tutien, a student of Franz Liszt, during his Philadelphia concerts in 1886. When John G. Bethune was killed in February 1884 trying to board a train, Colonel Bethune had himself appointed Tom's guardian and continued the concert tours. A three-year court battle between him and Eliza Bethune (who had divorced John Bethune before the accident) over control of Tom's career ended 31 July 1887 when the court granted custody to the widow. During the trial it was revealed that the Bethunes had cleared $3,000 monthly through exhibiting Tom.

Tom continued to perform under the management of Eliza Bethune and her second husband, attorney Albert J. Lerché. In May 1897 Tom was temporarily withdrawn from the stage for health reasons and to learn new compositions. He reappeared later that year in Falls River, Massachusetts. In 1898 his *Marche Timpani*, *Military Waltz*, and *Imitation of a Sewing Machine* were published under the pseudonums J. C. Beckel and François Sexalise.

In December 1903 Tom became a headline feature on the Keith and Orpheum Vaudeville Circuit. After his performances in Boston's Keith Theatre from 18 to 27 April 1905, he made no more public appearances. However, he was heard playing many hours daily by neighbors and friends of the Lerchés until his death at their home near Hoboken, New Jersey. He was buried in Brooklyn, New York, as Thomas Wiggins. Twenty years later his remains were taken to Columbus, Georgia, where a marker was erected near his buriel site by the Georgia Historical Society.

For four decades Blind Tom was a celebrated legend. He composed over 100 piano compositions, and an examination of his works in the Library of Congress gives a clear indication of his virtuosity and expressiveness at the keyboard. They also offer a microcosm of the pianistic and theoretical practices of nineteenth-century parlor pieces and descriptive works. Tom had a profound memory, and he supposedly was able to perform over eighty compositions at any concert. He could duplicate almost flawlessly after one hearing any music played for him. Immortalized by poets and literary personages such as Florence Anderson, Orelia Key Bell, Willa Cather, and James D. Corrothers, Blind Tom remains a musical institution who made fortunes for his owners.

• The best documented writings on Blind Tom are Geneva Southall, *Blind Tom: The Post–Civil War Reenslavement of a Black Musical Genuius* (1979) and *The Continuing Enslavement of Blind Tom, the Black Pianist-Composer, 1865–1887* (1983). This two-volume set chronicles the musical activities and development related to his legal status and follows yearly tours, revealing press releases and numerous musical "tests" he underwent. For contemporary accounts, see Eileen Southern, "Thomas Greene Bethune," *Black Perspective in Music*, July 1976, on European concerts, testimonial letters, and opinion; John A. Becket, "Blind Tom as He Is Today," *Ladies Home Journal*, Sept. 1898; J. Frank Davies, "Blind Tom," *Human Life*, Sept. 1908; Amelia Tytien, "The Phenomenon of Blind Tom," *Etude*, Feb. 1918; and W. C. Woodall, "Blind Tom as Seen by His Mother, Charity Wiggins," *Sunny South*, Oct. 1900. Also see black and white newspapers of the period, including the *New York Clipper* and *New York Dramatic News*. Most important are the legal papers in the New York State Supreme Court.

GENEVA H. SOUTHALL

BLINKS, Lawrence Rogers (22 Apr. 1900–4 Mar. 1989), biologist and botanist, was born in Michigan City, Indiana, the son of Walter Moulton Blinks, a chemist, and Ella Rogers. His interest in biology came from his father as well as from the writings of Henry Thoreau, John Muir, and John Burrows. While attending Kalamazoo College in 1918 and 1919, he spent a summer taking botany courses at a field station run by the University of Michigan. Blinks said that that summer spent in the forest fueled his interest in biology and botany and set him on the path of a career in those areas.

Blinks spent two years at Stanford University (1919–1921) and finally settled at Harvard University, where he completed his B.S. in 1923, his master's degree two years later, and his Ph.D. in 1926. At Harvard Blinks was encouraged further by one of his professors, W. J. V. Osterhout. At his urging Blinks abandoned the idea of becoming a teacher and instead accompanied Osterhout in 1923–1924 to the new Bermuda Biological Station to pursue research on *Valonia*, a giant-celled marine alga.

Blinks's first position after graduation from Harvard was as assistant in general physiology at the Rockefeller Institute in New York City. He spent three years there; each summer he traveled, as a guest investigator of the Carnegie Institution, to do research in the Tortugas and Florida. His work centered on electrical activity in cells and membrane permeability. In 1928 he married Anne Catherine Hof; they had one son.

Blinks moved up the ranks at the Rockefeller Institute in 1929 to become an associate in general physiology. He continued his summer research in 1931, this time as an invited lecturer in plant physiology at the Hopkins Marine Station.

In 1933 Blinks moved to California and took the position of associate professor of plant physiology at Stanford University; he became professor of biology in 1936. Blinks was an important player in the formative years of experimental biology in the United States. During the 1930s he developed instruments to measure the electric properties of plants. With this technology he was able to better understand bioelectric potential in plant cells, and this knowledge was later applied to research on animal nerve action. In the same decade Blinks was one of a group of scientists in the Stanford biology department who received a substantial research grant from the Rockefeller Foundation; the six came to be known as "the Rockefeller Gang," and five of them, including Blinks, were elected to the National Academy of Sciences in 1955 in recognition of their work.

Photosynthesis is the process by which plants use the energy in light to help convert carbon dioxide into organic compounds and create oxygen. During the 1940s Blinks conducted experiments on photosynthesis and showed that when light was flashed at a green leaf, the leaf instantaneously released a burst of oxygen. He and Royce K. Skow went on to develop an electrical method to make the process of photosynthesis visible to the eye.

Blinks is perhaps best known for having served as director of Stanford's Hopkins Marine Station in Pacific Grove, California, for twenty-two years, from 1943 to 1965. One of his specialties was teaching a course on the physiology of algae. As director he was instrumental in getting the funds to establish the oceanographic program; he also persuaded a Portland, Oregon, family to donate their sailing yacht, *Te Vega*, which was renovated to serve as a floating laboratory for a Stanford–National Science Foundation oceanography program.

Blinks also had a role in government service. In 1947 he took part in a resurvey of the Bikini Atoll in the South Pacific as a member of the Scripps Institute's team. The goal was to assess the affects of atomic bomb testing on algae in the atoll. Concurrently, during the 1950s and 1960s Blinks devoted time to consulting and editing journals. He served as editor of the *Journal of General Physiology* (1950–1962), *Biological Bulletin* (1952–1955), *Annual Review of Plant Physiology* (1955–1956), and *Botanica Marina* (from 1959). He was also a staff member of the National Science Foundation from 1951 and was its assistant director, managing an $11 million research budget, in 1954 and 1955. From 1962 to 1966 he was a member of the Committee on Science and Public Policy for the U.S. National Academy of Sciences.

The 1960s were highlighted by Blinks's groundbreaking physiological studies of *Boergesenia*, an Australian alga. In 1965, when he might have retired, Blinks instead chose to change schools. He retained the position of emeritus professor of biology at Stanford and became visiting professor at the new campus of the University of California at Santa Cruz, teaching marine biology. His advice to the administration was credited for the university's developing a strong marine science program. He was the first and only convener of the biology board of study, appointed to coordinate the faculty members annually chosen to serve on the board.

In 1965 Blinks also set sail with the *Te Vega* expedition to Borneo and the Solomon Islands. The research vessel was an integral part of the oceanography research program at Stanford. He went on several voyages to the Indian and Pacific oceans aboard it.

Blinks was twice the recipient of Guggenheim fellowships (1939–1940 and 1949) and was a Fulbright scholar at Cambridge University in 1957. Other honors included election to the National Academy of Sciences and receiving the Stephen Hales Award from the American Society of Plant Physiologists in 1952. His other professional memberships included the American Academy of Arts and Sciences (vice president, 1955), the Society of General Physiologists (president, 1952), the Western Society of Naturalists, and the British Society of Experimental Biologists. He was also an honorary member of the Zoological and Botanical Society, Vienna.

In 1972 Blinks became emeritus professor at Santa Cruz and concentrated the rest of his working life on research at the Hopkins Marine Station. In recognition of his long-standing association with the Hopkins Marine Station, a research laboratory there was named in his honor. (Blinks's fundraising efforts in the 1960s enabled the building to be constructed.)

Blinks was the author of many scientific papers. Among his most important contributions to botany were a study of the action potential of *Nitella*, his years of work on the sea-bottle, and the electrode measurement for oxygen, based on the polarographic method that he and Skow developed in 1938. Blinks and F. T. Haxo built on this oxygen measurement to study, in the late 1940s, the photosynthetic action spectra of marine algae. This study of the relationship of plant pigments to photosynthesis was the second major chapter of his career, following the work on permeability and electrical activity. The third and final chapter was his study of accessory pigments.

During an eighty-fifth birthday celebration for Blinks, held 22 April 1985 at Hopkins Marine Station, his untiring love of his subject was noted, "His enthusiasm for exploring the unknown, asking important questions, and setting up the critical experiment, continues unabated. Visitors are as likely to find him at work in his Hopkins research lab on a weekend or holiday as during the week. This inquisitive mind and drive to understand are important facets of his life." He died in San Jose, California.

• Memoirs written by Blinks in the 1980s are in Special Collections at Stanford University; other documents are in the special collections office at the University of California at Santa Cruz. Much information on his career, particularly at Stanford, is in a memorial resolution in Stanford's *Campus Report*, 28 Feb. 1990. An autobiographical entry, mostly in technical terms about his research, appears in *McGraw-Hill Modern Scientists and Engineers*, vol. 1 (1980). There are obituaries in the *Monterey Herald*, 5 Mar. 1989; *Stanford News*, 7 Mar. 1989; *San Francisco Chronicle*, 8 Mar. 1989; and *San Jose Mercury-News*, 10 Mar. 1989.

MARIANNE FEDUNKIW STEVENS

BLINN, Holbrook (23 Jan. 1872–24 June 1928), actor, was born in San Francisco, California, the son of Charles H. Blinn, a surveyor and customshouse inspector, and Nellie Holbrook, an actress and dramatic coach. After one year at Stanford University (1891–1892), Blinn attained a small role in a West Coast production of *The New South*, and in 1893 he performed in the play in New York. Returning to San Francisco, Blinn appeared with Effie Ellsler's company and in other productions. Early in 1896, hearing news of the Klondike gold rush, the 24-year-old actor organized a theatrical company for a two-month tour of Alaska. Among the troupe was a young actress, Ruth Benson, and the two were married in August 1896.

In 1897, after opening in San Francisco, Blinn gained attention both in New York and London as the lead in *The Cat and the Cherub*, a one-act drama about mysterious Chinatown. For the next few years he alternated between work in Great Britain and the United States. In 1900, during an American road tour of *The Battle of the Strong*, he was wounded in a stage duel with the erratic Maurice Barrymore. In London in 1903 Blinn was widely hailed for his portrayal of Napoleon in *The Duchess of Dantzig*. The play ran for two years in England and moved to New York in 1905 for a year. For the next two years he both acted the lead in and directed *Man and His Angel* (1906), appeared with Arnold Daly in Daly's Theatre Antoine venture, a season of new short plays of high literary quality, and toured with Eleanor Robson in *Salomy Jane* and other plays.

In November 1908 Blinn opened in New York playing opposite Minnie Maddern Fiske in *Salvation Nell*, and he made a strong impression on theatergoers as the brutal Jim Platt. *New York Times* notices (18 and 22 Nov. 1908) acclaimed him as "one of the very best actors at present before the public" and his characterization as "complete . . . big and vital." After the play's New York run, he toured with Fiske's company during the years 1909–1911, scoring in her revival of *The Pillars of Society* and other plays.

Blinn was of medium height, square-jawed, and thickset, with a deep, rich voice. These traits, combined with a commanding stage presence, typecast him for playing men of power and authority, often ruthless to the point of villainy. His portrayal of Jim Platt in *Salvation Nell* was the most successful of a series of menacing roles he had played since beginning his career. He became a star in his next such part, that of Michael Regan in *The Boss* (1911). Reviewers found his performance the play's chief distinction. He toured in the play after its successful New York run.

In an article in the *Green Book Album* (May 1911), Blinn good-naturedly acknowledged that he was usually typecast. A chance to break the commercial theater's bonds came in 1913, however, when he became director of the new, small Princess Theater in New York. He was able there to play a wide range of roles in various one-act plays. Critical reception was favorable, but the series lasted only into the 1914–1915 season.

Blinn returned to a series of Broadway appearances during the next several years. He also made his entry into motion pictures with a film version of *The Boss* (1915). Other movie roles followed through 1917. His stage work included directing two plays and appearing to general praise in revivals of *A Woman of No Importance* with Margaret Anglin in 1916 and *The Lady of the Camellias* with Ethel Barrymore in 1917. He also created the role of Louis XIV in *Molière* (1919), with Henry Miller in the title role. In none of these plays was he the central figure, and in *The Lady of the Camellias*, playing Armand's father, he had only one scene. By the time he opened in *The Challenge* (1919), the *New York Times* critic was noting that though Blinn was advertised as the play's star, he was in a "distinctly secondary part."

In the historic Actors' Equity strike of August 1919, Blinn took the side of the theater managers, resigning from Actors' Equity to join the Actors' Fidelity League. Later he twice became president of the league. His apparent decline into supporting roles was decisively reversed in *The Bad Man* in 1920. Here Blinn played the title role, an affable Mexican bandit named Pancho Lopez who straightens out the lives of some Americans with lovable lawlessness. The *New York Times* review described his performance as "one of the most satisfying achievements in the uneven career of Holbrook Blinn, whose work for the last twelve years has been a varyingly successful attempt to live up to the reputation he made in 'Salvation Nell'" (31 Aug. 1920). A runaway success, the play occupied Blinn for the next three seasons. In his next play, a melodrama titled *The Dove* (1923), he played another Mexican, this time a charming but ruthless oil tycoon. He also costarred with Mary Pickford in the film *Rosita* (1923) and in three films with Marion Davies (1924–1925), playing characters similar to those he had created on stage.

Blinn's final success was a theater comedy, *The Play's the Thing* (1926), in which he was both director and star. He appeared as Sandor Turai, a witty playwright who straightens out a romantic imbroglio for an ardent young man. Yet his film work continued to stereotype him: a review of a 1927 movie, *The Masked Woman*, describes his role as that of a "sophisticated light 'menace.' " (*Variety*, 12 Jan. 1927).

In June 1928 Blinn was on vacation at his country home in Croton-on-Hudson, New York, and while he was riding, he was thrown to the ground by a new horse. He was injured seriously and developed an infection that proved fatal. He died at age fifty-six an extremely accomplished and versatile actor, never out of work, but never for long free of the constraints imposed by the commercial theater. He was considered popular rather than great, though his *New York Times* obituary declared that "producers and other people of the theatre thought his greatest triumphs were ahead of him."

• Copious materials on Blinn's life and career are in the Billy Rose Theatre Collection at the New York Public Library for the Performing Arts, Lincoln Center. An important study of Blinn's work in the theater is Ronald B. Hirsen, "The Stage Career of Holbrook Blinn" (Ph.D. diss., Univ. of Illinois, 1976). A bibliography of articles concerning Blinn as a stage actor is in Stephen Archer, *American Actors and Actresses* (1983). See also Mel Schuster, *Motion Picture Performers* (1971), and John Stewart, *Filmarama*, vols. 1 and 2 (1975, 1977). Portraits of Blinn at various stages of his life and career are in Daniel C. Blum, *Great Stars of the American Stage* (1952). Scenes from his stage performances are in Blum's *Pictorial History of the American Theatre* (1960), and scenes from his films are in Blum's *Pictorial History of the Silent Screen* (1953). An obituary is in the *New York Times*, 25 June 1928.

WILLIAM STEPHENSON

BLISS, Cornelius Newton (13 Apr. 1874–5 Apr. 1949), philanthropist and businessman, was born in New York City, the son of Cornelius Newton Bliss, a wealthy merchant, and Elizabeth M. Plummer. After attending the Cutler School, Bliss entered Harvard College, where he obtained a B.A. in 1897. He then entered his father's wholesale dry-goods commission house, Bliss, Fabyan and Company, becoming a partner two years later. In 1906 he married Zaidee C. Cobb. They had three children. Bliss worked in the family firm for the next twenty-five years, serving as chair of the board from 1928 through 1932, then as a director until the firm went out of business in 1940. He also served on the boards of nearly a dozen banks, insurance companies, and corporations.

In 1916 Bliss was an alternate delegate to the Republican National Convention, and during the presidential campaign that fall he was treasurer of the Republican National Committee, as his father had been in earlier years. However, the Republicans' defeat led to a general reorganization of the committee, and Bliss resigned in 1917. After supporting General Leonard Wood's unsuccessful candidacy for the Republican nomination in 1920, Bliss devoted himself to state politics, becoming treasurer of the New York State Republican Committee in 1923. He was a delegate to the Republican National Convention in 1928.

Besides business and politics, Bliss devoted a growing portion of his time to social welfare. When hard times swept New York City during the winter of 1914–1915, he was chosen to serve on the Mayor's Committee on Unemployment, which raised nearly $200,000 in private contributions and used the funds to operate workshops and services for the unemployed. About the same time Bliss became active in the New York Association for Improving the Condition of the Poor (AICP). After the stock market crash in 1929, the AICP and other charitable organizations found themselves overwhelmed with requests for help. Accordingly, Bliss and the chair of the Charity Organization Society (COS) organized an Emergency Employment Committee, a group of 100 financiers and civic leaders who promised to raise funds every week for distribution by the AICP and COS. These funds also proved insufficient, however, and in 1931 Mayor James J. Walker appointed Bliss as head of a commission to administer a much larger publicly financed relief fund.

Bliss continued to believe that private charities had an important role to play in civic life. He served as AICP president from 1928 to 1935, then as vice president. After the AICP and COS merged to form the Community Service Society of New York in 1939, he stayed on as vice president until 1943. He also worked with the American Red Cross during both world wars and served on the boards of the Milbank Memorial Fund, the Greater New York Fund, the Army Relief Society, and the National Foundation for Infantile Paralysis. In 1909 Bliss succeeded his father on the New York Hospital Board of Governors and served until just before his death, at which time his son Cornelius succeeded him on the board.

Bliss's other great interest was the arts. He was a trustee of the Metropolitan Museum of Art from 1931 to 1949 and the Juilliard School of Music from 1933. He also joined the board of the Museum of Modern Art in 1932, shortly after the death of his sister Lizzie P. Bliss, who had been one of its three founders. But his first love was the Metropolitan Opera. Having inherited a box at the opera from his father, Bliss became a director of the real estate company that owned the opera house in 1926. Then in 1933 he moved to the board of the Metropolitan Opera Association, the organization that ran the opera company.

The association was in desperate financial trouble, and when the Committee for Saving the Metropolitan Opera was formed, Bliss took charge of its fundraising drive, the association's first national effort of this kind. His son later recalled that for months Bliss "virtually lived at the opera house." The success of the campaign marked a new stage in the opera company's history, affirming that it was not merely a New York institution but a national treasure. The generous response from every corner of the country not only saved the opera but produced enough additional funds to pay for the first renovation of the theater in thirty years. Bliss then chaired an administrative committee that supervised the association's operations, hired a new general manager, and enforced many cuts in expenses.

Bliss became chair of the Metropolitan Opera Association board in 1938 and was immediately faced with a new crisis because of the financial problems of the company that owned the opera house. After strenuous lobbying, Bliss persuaded the boxholders who dominated the company to accept the association's rather low purchase offer for the building. He then organized a new fundraising campaign that collected more than $1 million—enough to make the initial payment on the theater, renovate it, and create several new productions. Eleanor Belmont, one of the Met's most faithful supporters, later said that it was Bliss "to whom opera owes, more than to any other individual, the fact of its survival."

After resisting unionization of the opera soloists for several years, Bliss was obliged to sign with their union in 1938, after legal counsel concluded that they were covered by the state's new labor law. He continued as chair of the board through World War II, presiding over the Met's first publication of a detailed financial statement in 1942. In 1946 he stepped down to make room for Charles M. Spofford, whom he believed had much to contribute to the association. Bliss remained on the board until his death; he was succeeded by his son Anthony, who himself built a distinguished career at the Met, becoming president of the association in 1956 and general manager in 1975. In 1966, during Anthony's presidency, the opera company moved to Lincoln Center, where the board room was named for Cornelius Bliss. Bliss died in New York City, where he left a distinguished legacy of philanthropy and public service. Calling him "the able son of an able father," the *New York Times* observed that the city "in its arts and social causes, was enriched by his useful life."

• Bliss appears to have left no papers. Frequent references to his activities appeared in the *New York Times*; see especially 21 Dec. 1917, 23 Oct. 1930, and 14 Feb. 1946. Information on his years with the New York Association for Improving the Condition of the Poor can be found in the AICP Papers, which are at Columbia University. Martin Mayer, *The Met: One Hundred Years of Grand Opera* (1983), gives an excellent account of Bliss's work with the opera company. Obituaries are in the *New York Times*, 6 Apr. 1949, *Musical America* 69 (15 Apr. 1949), and *Newsweek*, 18 Apr. 1949.

SANDRA OPDYCKE

BLISS, Daniel (17 Aug. 1823–27 July 1916), missionary educator and founder and first president of the Syrian Protestant College in Beirut (later the American University), was born in Georgia, Vermont, the son of Loomis Bliss and Susanna Farwell, farmers. When he was a young child, his family moved to a farm in Cambridge, Vermont. His mother died when he was nine years old, and soon thereafter his father moved to a new farm in Jericho, Vermont, moving again to Painesville, Ohio, when Bliss was thirteen and then to Kingsville, Ohio. Bliss attended local schools and was apprenticed by his father to a tanner. In 1844 his master's business failed, and he turned his hand to grafting fruit trees. Two years later he entered Kingsville Academy in Ohio and earned his living by teaching at a local school.

In 1848 Bliss enrolled in Amherst College in Massachusetts, graduating in 1852. He paid his college debts by running a private school in Shrewsbury, Massachusetts. In the fall of 1852 he entered Andover Theological Seminary to study for the ministry. He completed his degree and was ordained a Congregational minister in 1855. That year he married Abby Maria Wood; soon afterward, they sailed for the Middle East under the auspices of the American Board of Foreign Missions.

Bliss's first assignment was in a small Lebanese village, Abeih. He assumed the post on 15 April 1856. He worked with a few hundred Christian and Druze villagers and expanded the Christian school that had been founded by a missionary by the name of Van Dyck in 1843. The local government restricted their work to the Christian contingent because Muslim converts to Christianity were persecuted. During his two and one-half years at Abeih, Bliss concentrated on mastering Arabic. He studied the language five hours a day and finally achieved a high level of proficiency.

In 1858 the Blisses were placed in charge of the Girls' Boarding School in Suq al-Gharb. While there, Bliss preached his first sermon in Arabic and further displayed his competency in missionary work through his ability to reach across cultural boundaries. The Blisses were in Suq al-Gharb during the massacre of thousands of Christians by Druze and Moslem groups in 1860 but survived to continue their work.

During 1861 Bliss became increasingly interested in the possibility of starting a school of higher education for Arabic-speaking peoples in the Middle East. On 27 January 1862, the Syrian Mission, part of the American Board of Foreign Missions, voted to establish such a school and asked Bliss to organize it and act as its first president. That summer Bliss and his family returned to the United States to organize the new school. The Syrian Protestant College was incorporated under the laws of the State of New York early in 1863, and Bliss embarked on the tiring job of publicizing and funding the new project. He managed to acquire a sufficient endowment fund during his two years in America, in the course of which he made 279 public addresses and traveled 16,993 miles. The endowment fund was subsequently augmented during five visits to England and the United States between 1874 and 1899.

The Blisses arrived back in Beirut on 2 March 1866, having been away nearly three and a half years. The college opened its doors on 3 December 1866 with a service of prayer for the first sixteen students. Initially all classes were conducted in Arabic, a practice that was abandoned in the 1880s because of the impossibility of keeping up with textbook translations into that language.

Bliss worked hard to maintain good relations with the Turkish government. When he retired in 1902 after thirty-six years, the college had 626 students and more than forty professors. The campus consisted of twelve buildings spread over a forty-acre site.

Despite a long vacation in the United States, the Blisses remained in Beirut for the rest of their lives, dying within two years of each other. They had four children. Bliss was honored by the Syrian Protestant College with a large marble statue that was erected in 1904 by the school's alumni. He authored two texts in Arabic, *Mental Philosophy* (1874) and *Natural Philosophy* (1874).

During his life, Bliss made a significant contribution to the westernizing of the Middle East—Syria in particular. Through his work, he inculcated Christian values and Western ideals into a large number of the Semitic elite throughout the area. This legacy both facilitated the later interaction of the Middle East with the West and exacerbated the internal tensions that continue to plague the region.

• A complete source on the life of Daniel Bliss is *The Reminiscences of Daniel Bliss* (1920), edited by his eldest son, Frederick Jones Bliss. There is also genealogical information on his ancestors in C. A. Hoppin, *The Bliss Book* (1913), and John H. Bliss, *The Genealogy of the Bliss Family* (1881). Accounts of his work can be found in contemporary issues of *The Missionary Herald*, published by the American Board of Commissioners for Foreign Missions, Boston, Mass. An obituary is in the *New York Times*, 8 Aug. 1916.

CLAIRE STROM

BLISS, Gilbert Ames (9 May 1876–8 May 1951), mathematician, was born in the suburbs of Chicago, Illinois, the son of George Harrison Bliss and Mary Maria Gilbert. Although his father was president of the Chicago Edison Company, the panic of 1893 forced Bliss to pay his own way through college, which he did by earning a scholarship and by playing in a professional mandolin group. His degrees were all earned at the University of Chicago: B.S., 1897; M.S. in mathematical astronomy, 1898; Ph.D. in mathematics, 1900. He studied under Eliakim Hastings Moore, Heinrich Maschke, and Oskar Bolza. Bolza directed his dissertation in the calculus of variations. Bliss proceeded to Göttingen for postdoctoral study under David Hilbert, Felix Klein, and Hermann Minkowski, all famous names in mathematics. After brief appointments in the United States he went to Princeton (1905–1908) as preceptor and associate editor of the *Annals of Mathematics*. Finally he returned to Chicago as associate professor and remained there as professor and then Martin A. Ryerson Distinguished Professor. He was chair of the mathematics department from 1927 to his retirement in 1941.

In 1912 Bliss married Helen Hurd. They had two children before Helen died in the influenza epidemic of 1918. In 1920 he married Olive Hunter. It is a tribute to her that he used to tell love-distraught students that he knew that more than one woman exists who can make a man happy.

Bliss's major mathematical work with his students was to reconstruct in rigorous modern formulation the classical, but flawed, discipline of the calculus of variations, a natural extension of the ordinary calculus in which one seeks to find the arc or surface that minimizes a quantity associated with it. For example, in his dissertation Bliss studied geodesics, the shortest arcs between two points on a curved surface. He succeeded but at the cost of narrowing its scope and expressing the elaborate technicality. This left the subject finished for the time being, but when research begins anew in the general calculus of variations, it will have to build on the work of the Bliss school. He published the results of this work in *Lectures on the Calculus of Variations* (1946). The dissertations of the school appeared in the four-volume *Contributions to the Calculus of Variations* (1930–1941).

It is proof of his art as a teacher that the Bliss school developed a number of mathematicians who later did distinguished work in other fields of mathematics. These included Lawrence M. Graves in functional analysis, Magnus R. Hestenes in optimal control theory, A. S. Householder in numerical analysis, E. James McShane in the general theory of integration and probability theory, and Herman H. Goldstine in pioneering research on the modern computer. But Bliss's own concept of the Ph.D. was broader than that, although he did not agree with those who called for scholarly doctoral degrees without a research component. He argued for retaining the research requirement in it, saying in his "Autobiographical Notes" (1952), "Such a training is invaluable for teaching, or business, or whatever activity may claim the student's future interest" (p. 606).

Even Bliss himself was more influential with wide-ranging research exposition and philosophy of science than with his research in the calculus of variations. This work showed his great intellectual power and versatility. His seminal paper "Mathematical Interpretations of Geometric and Physical Phenomena" (*American Mathematical Monthly* 40 [1933]: 472–80), was a landmark in the quiet revolution in the philosophy of science that displaced the idea of the one true theory of a natural science. Instead, Bliss showed that multiple theories, or mathematical models as we now call them, may be valid and useful. Others of his papers have become necessary reading in their fields. His *Fundamental Existence Theorems* (American Mathematical Society Colloquium Publication, vol. 6 [1913]) remained a basic tool in all branches of analysis. His elementary exposition, *Calculus of Variations*, a Carus monograph (1925), gave thousands their knowledge of the subject. In 1918 he devised more accurate methods of calculating trajectories for American artillery in World War I. In 1919 he recorded his work in the *Journal of the U.S.*

Artillery (50 [1919]: 455–60, and 51 [1919]: 445–49), and in 1944 he published the book *Mathematics for Exterior Ballistics* to make his knowledge available for World War II. In 1925 he received the first Chauvenet Prize of the Mathematical Association of America for his paper on algebraic functions and their divisors, a topic outside his main field of research. He did some brilliant teaching in quantum mechanics in the late 1920s when that subject was just breaking. He summarized this in "Calculus of Variations and the Quantum Theory," his retiring address as vice president of section A of the American Association for the Advancement of Science, later published in the *Bulletin of the American Mathematical Society* (38 [1932]: 201–24).

Bliss was elected to the National Academy of Sciences (1916) and the American Philosophical Society (1926) and was president of the American Mathematical Society (1921–1922). He served as an editor for the *Transactions of the American Mathematical Society* (1908–1916) and on the board of the (then new) National Research Council fellowships (1924–1936). Bliss headed a government commission to construct precise rules for assigning to states seats in the U.S. House of Representatives, under the vague constitutional provisions for proportional representation. He managed the planning and construction of Eckhart Hall as a mathematics-physics research-teaching facility of the University of Chicago (1929–1930). Bliss died in Chicago.

• Gilbert Bliss, "Autobiographical Notes," *American Mathematical Monthly* 59 (1952): 595–606, was published posthumously from a 1938 manuscript. It is particularly significant for Bliss's account of his teachers as well as his statement of his philosophy of graduate education. For a short biography see Ronald S. Calinger, "Gilbert Ames Bliss," *Dictionary of Scientific Biography* (1970). Lawrence M. Graves, "Gilbert Ames Bliss," *Bulletin of the American Mathematical Society* 58 (Mar. 1952): 251–64, is the official obituary with a complete list of his publications. E. James McShane, "Gilbert Ames Bliss," National Academy of Sciences, *Biographical Memoirs* (1958), includes an informed critique of his work in ballistics as well as in the calculus of variations. Also see Saunders MacLane, "Biographical Memoirs: Gilbert Ames Bliss (1876–1951)," *Yearbook* of the American Philosophical Society (1951). W. L. Duren, Jr., "Graduate Student at Chicago in the Twenties," *American Mathematical Monthly* 83 (1967): 243–47, repr. in *A Century of Mathematics in America*, pt. 2, ed. Peter Duren (1989), recalls Bliss and his department from a student's point of view. MacLane, "Mathematics at the University of Chicago," in the same volume, covers the Bliss period in a history of the department.

WILLIAM L. DUREN, JR.

BLISS, Lillie P. (11 Apr. 1864–12 Mar. 1931), art collector, patron, and benefactor, was born Lizzie Plummer Bliss in Boston, Massachusetts, daughter of Cornelius Newton Bliss, a dry goods merchant who was active in Republican Party politics, and Elizabeth Mary Plummer. In 1866 the family moved to the Murray Hill Section of New York City, where as a young girl Bliss was privately educated. She lived there until 1923, when her mother died. Bliss acted as hostess in New York and Washington, D.C., for her father, who served as secretary of the interior (1897–1899) in the cabinet of William McKinley after declining McKinley's offer to run as his vice president; he was also treasurer of the Republican National Committee from 1892 through 1908.

Bliss's life in New York centered on her devotion to promising artists and musicians. Although "in manner she was quiet, . . . the gentlest, and certainly the most modest of women, she was absolutely independent in her taste and courageous as to her method of doing things" (Eleanor Belmont in *Memorial Exhibition* catalog [1931]). She was an accomplished pianist, founded the Kreisel Quartet, and supported the Juilliard Foundation for musical education, performance, and publication.

However, the visual arts overtook even Bliss's passion for music. Her most enthusiastic cultural commitment was to the International Exhibition of Modern Art, known as the Armory Show, which opened at the Sixtieth Regiment Armory on 17 February 1913. Arthur B. Davies, a painter and one of the organizers of the Armory Show, was her mentor and close friend. Attracted to the lyrical quality of his work, Bliss had been purchasing his paintings since 1907. Davies was knowledgeable about European art, and, as a result of their alliance, Bliss began collecting art in earnest by purchasing five paintings and some drawings and prints from the show. In 1921 she was one of those who persuaded the Metropolitan Museum of Art to organize an exhibition of works of the impressionists through Pablo Picasso's pre-cubist period. However, the hostile press reaction to the exhibition caused that museum to avoid another exhibition of the kind for some time.

In spite of her professional interest and support for the arts, Bliss kept most of her purchases out of the sight of her family, who found modern art bizarre and distasteful. On her mother's death in 1923, Bliss purchased the top three floors of an apartment house on Park Avenue, where she could hang all of her pictures freely and entertain her wide circle of friends from the worlds of art, music, and theater.

The great collector of modern art John Quinn died in 1924, and Davies died in 1929; the sales of their collections made it more apparent than ever among progressive New Yorkers that a museum devoted to modern art was needed. In 1929 Bliss, together with two other influential and public-spirited women, Abby Aldrich Rockefeller and Mary Quinn Sullivan (both collectors and part of the New York establishment), founded such an institution. The three knew each other through their visits to art galleries and frequently met for tea at the Cosmopolitan Club. The necessity of founding a museum devoted only to modern art was a subject of great importance to them.

The opening of the Museum of Modern Art on 7 November 1929 was a courageous action that revolutionized the idea of the art museum in the United States; at the time it was unusual to exhibit early twentieth-century art or the work of living artists in an

American museum. With Rockefeller as president, Bliss was an actively engaged vice president of the museum until her death in New York City. However, the new museum did not yet have its own collection of masterpieces. When Bliss died, she provisionally bequeathed to the museum the major part of her important collection on the condition that within three years it raise $1 million to endow its survival as a permanent institution. Because of the depression the estate lowered its price to $600,000, and the necessary funds were raised among the trustees. The terms of the Bliss bequest were met, thus securing a magnificent group of modern paintings that became the cornerstone of the museum's collection. Included were works by Paul Cézanne (twenty-one), Honoré Daumier (one), Edgar Degas (eight), Paul Gauguin (two), Henri Matisse (two), Pablo Picasso (two), Odillon Redon (two), Auguste Renoir (one), Jean Jacques Rousseau (one), and Georges Seurat (nine), and fifty prints.

A significant and generous provision of Bliss's will allowed the museum to sell or exchange works from the Bliss collection to acquire other important or needed objects, such as the 1939 acquisition of Picasso's *Les Demoiselles d'Avignon* in exchange for Degas's *Racecourse* (1884). Hundreds of works in the museum collection are credited as "acquired through the Lillie P. Bliss Bequest." During her lifetime she was known as Lillie, using the name Lizzie only when she signed checks; after her death, Cornelius Newton Bliss, Jr., her brother and executor, had her name legally changed to Lillie when her collection was provisionally bequeathed to the Museum of Modern Art.

Bliss was much beloved, and although her time during the last years of her life was largely spent on museum affairs, many others were generously remembered in her will: the Metropolitan Museum of Art, the Society of the New York Hospital, the Broadway Tabernacle Society, the New York Association for Improving the Condition of the Poor, the Brooklyn Museum of Arts and Science, and several individuals. However, her foresight, courage, and generosity as a collector and patron were most widely noted and acknowledged in the obituaries and tributes that appeared in newspapers and periodicals throughout the world. More personally, her kind and gentle nature was recalled by her friend Eleanor Belmont, who delivered one of the eulogies at the service preceding the opening of the memorial exhibition *The Collection of the Late Lillie P. Bliss* at the Museum of Modern Art on 17 May 1931: "God gave us memory so that we might have roses in December."

• Correspondence and other relevant documentation on Bliss can be found in the Lillie P. Bliss Scrapbook, A. Conger Goodyear Papers, Public Information Scrapbooks, and Elizabeth Bliss Parkinson Cobb Oral History, all in the Museum of Modern Art Archives. Catalogs published by the Museum of Modern Art for exhibitions of the Bliss collection include *Memorial Exhibition: The Collection of the Late Miss Lizzie P. Bliss* (1931) and *The Lillie P. Bliss Collection* (1934), in which her one known piece of writing, "From a Letter to a National Academician," appeared. *Modern Masters from the Collection of Miss Lizzie P. Bliss* (1932) was published by the John Heron Art Institute, Indianapolis, Ind., when her works were shown there. For secondary source material, see Alfred H. Barr, Jr., "Chronicle of the Collection" and "The Lillie P. Bliss Bequest," *Painting and Sculpture in the Museum of Modern Art* (1977), pp. 620–24, 651–53. References to Bliss can be found in Milton W. Brown, *The Story of the Armory Show* (1988); Geoffrey T. Hellman's two-part article "Profiles: Action on West Fifty-Third Street," *New Yorker*, 12 and 19 Dec. 1953; Hellman, "Profile of a Museum," *Art in America* 52 (Feb. 1964); Russell Lynes, *Good Old Modern: An Intimate Portrait of the Museum of Modern Art* (1973); and Aline B. Saarinen, *The Proud Possessors: The Lives, Times and Tastes of Some Adventurous American Art Collections* (1958). Obituaries and editorials are in the *New York Times*, 13 and 16 Mar. 1931.

RONA ROOB

BLISS, Philip Paul (9 July 1838–29 Dec. 1876), hymnodist and musical evangelist, was born in Clearfield County, Pennsylvania, the son of Isaac Bliss and Lydia Doolittle, farmers. As an adolescent, he worked on farms and in lumber camps. Bliss proclaimed his personal conversion to Christ in 1850 and joined a Baptist church. After attending a select school in East Troy, Pennsylvania, in 1855 and working on a farm during the summer, he taught school in Hartsville, New York, during the winter of 1856. The following year he received his first formal instruction in music at J. G. Towner's music school in Towanda, Pennsylvania. During 1858 Bliss taught school in Rome, Pennsylvania, where he boarded with the Young family. In 1859 he married Lucy Young, the oldest daughter of his hosts; the couple had two children. In the early 1860s Bliss taught music at Pennsylvania schools during the winter months, worked on his father-in-law's farm during the summer, and attended occasional normal academies of music in Geneseo, New York.

In 1864 Bliss sent one of his song manuscripts to George F. Root, a music publisher in Chicago, Illinois, who purchased it. Root was known as a "layman's composer" because he wrote and published music primarily for performance by amateur musicians in the home, classroom, and church. Like Root, Bliss composed songs that appealed to the musical tastes and performing abilities of church congregations. In the summer of 1865, the Union army drafted Bliss but discharged him only two weeks later because the Civil War had ended. At the invitation of Root, Bliss moved to Chicago in November 1865 to work as a representative for the music publishing firm of Root and Cady. For nearly a decade he wrote songs, gave concerts, and held musical conventions throughout Illinois and neighboring states. In 1870 he became the director of music for the First Congregational Church in Chicago, where he also served for a time as Sunday school superintendent. His first songbook, *The Charm*, was published in 1871, and several more followed in the next few years. They became especially popular in the growing number of Sunday schools across the nation.

In his songwriting, Bliss sometimes collaborated with Root or Ira D. Sankey, the song leader for the prominent revivalist Dwight L. Moody. Bliss first met Moody in 1869, and occasionally he led the singing at Moody's meetings in Chicago. While in Scotland during the winter of 1873–1874, Moody wrote several letters encouraging the young songwriter to form a revival team with evangelist Daniel Webster Whittle. After a successful trial meeting with Whittle in Waukegan, Illinois, in March 1874, Bliss resigned his position at the First Congregational Church to take up itinerant evangelism. Over the next three years, he and Whittle held twenty-five revival meetings together in the West and the South, while Moody and Sankey toured the North and Great Britain. Music formed an integral part of these revivals, producing the atmosphere in which evangelistic sermons could be most successful. Primarily by correspondence during this period, Bliss and Sankey jointly produced two volumes of gospel songs. These works contained such Bliss classics as "Almost Persuaded," "Let the Lower Lights Be Burning," and "Hold the Fort."

After spending Christmas at his family's home in Pennsylvania in 1876, Bliss and his wife boarded a train for Chicago to join Moody in another revival meeting. As the train neared Ashtabula, Ohio, a railway bridge collapsed, and the train plunged into the icy creek and caught fire. According to some eyewitnesses, Bliss initially survived the crash, but when he returned to the wreckage to rescue his trapped wife, both died in the fire.

Although Bliss wrote ninety-five secular songs early in his career, the 303 gospel hymns that bear his name form his most important contribution to American music. Bliss usually composed both the music and the text, although he sometimes collaborated with others. Among the most enduring of his hymns are "I Will Sing of My Redeemer," "It Is Well with My Soul," "Hallelujah, What a Savior," "Wonderful Words of Life," "Jesus Loves Even Me," and "I Gave My Life for Thee."

Bliss was one of a small group of mid-nineteenth-century composers and musicians who created a new style of gospel music to complement the work of revivalists and Sunday schools. Whether joyous or poignant, the songs were simple, and audiences could learn them quickly. The terms "gospel songs" and "gospel hymns" first appeared in the titles of Bliss's songbooks. His gospel songs represented a compromise between the jubilant camp-meeting spirituals and the more formal hymn style of composers such as Lowell Mason. Drawn from a variety of religious sources, the gospel music style remained popular in Protestant churches in America for more than a century.

• Bliss's other gospel songbooks include *The Song Tree* (1872), *Sunshine for Sunday Schools* (1873), *The Joy* (1873), and *Gospel Songs* (1874). In collaboration with Ira D. Sankey, Bliss produced *Gospel Hymns and Sacred Songs* (1875) and *Gospel Hymns No. 2* (1876). In 1877 Whittle edited the *Memoirs of Philip P. Bliss*, which provides biographical information and tributes by those who knew him, as well as a collection of many of Bliss's hymns and letters. Bobby Joe Neil, "Philip P. Bliss (1838–1876): Gospel Hymn Composer and Compiler" (Ed.D. diss., New Orleans Baptist Theological Seminary, 1977), provided the first modern biography. For Bliss's place in American music history, see David Joseph Smucker, "Philip Paul Bliss and the Musical, Cultural, and Religious Sources of the Gospel Music Tradition in the United States, 1850–1876" (Ph.D. diss., Boston Univ., 1981).

DANIEL W. STOWELL

BLISS, Tasker Howard (31 Dec. 1853–9 Nov. 1930), soldier, scholar, and diplomat, was born in Lewisburg, Pennsylvania, the son of George Ripley Bliss, a Baptist clergyman and professor at Lewisburg Academy (now Bucknell University), and Mary Ann Raymond. After attending Lewisburg Academy for two years, Tasker Bliss was admitted to West Point, where he excelled in foreign languages and finished eighth in his class in 1875. After graduating, he was assigned to the First Artillery in Savannah, Georgia. The next year he returned to West Point for a four-year tour as an instructor in modern languages. His grasp of other tongues included not only his beloved Greek, which he studied relentlessly, but also Latin, French, Spanish, Italian, and Russian. The Custer massacre in 1876 prompted him to request active duty at a frontier post, but Major General John McAllister Schofield, who valued his young officer's teaching abilities, denied the request. Throughout his career, Bliss made his principal military contributions from behind a desk, not in the field.

Bliss's four years teaching at West Point were followed by three years of regimental duty in California and Georgia. In 1882 he married Eleanora E. Anderson, with whom he reared two children. In 1885 he began a three-year stint teaching military science at the new Naval War College in Newport. His performance in the classroom enhanced his growing reputation as a leading military theorist, and he was sent to Europe to study the military education systems in France, Germany, and Great Britain. When General Schofield became commanding general of the army in 1888, he selected Bliss, only thirty-five years old, as an aide-de-camp. Bliss served under Schofield for the next seven years as inspector of small arms and artillery target practice and took advantage of the quiet times on the frontier to indulge in his favorite pastime of reading widely in military history, organization, and administration. The slow pace of military promotion in the post–Civil War decades doomed Bliss to years of service at a low rank. After two decades in uniform, he was still only a captain.

In the late nineteenth and early twentieth centuries, however, Bliss rapidly rose to the very top of the army hierarchy. In 1897 he was assigned as military attaché to Spain. When war with Spain broke out in 1898, he returned to the United States as a major and participated in the Puerto Rico campaign under the command of General James H. Wilson. Early in 1899 Bliss became chief of customs collection for Cuba and the port of Havana, partly because of his Spanish language skills. His ability as an administrator, paying close attention to detail, was highly useful in rectifying the enormous corruption that had developed under Spanish rule. From this assignment he learned about the complex world of tariffs, which he applied as principal negotiator for a treaty of reciprocity with Cuba in 1902.

For his work in Cuba Bliss earned his first star in 1902. During the reorganization of the army under a general staff system, Secretary of War Elihu Root invited Bliss to return to Washington, D.C., to serve on the nascent Army War College Board as an adviser. Bliss then served as the first president of the Army War College from 1903 to 1905. During the first year, when the school had no students, he worked to develop the curriculum and the faculty. Bliss believed that the Army War College should serve as a planning arm of the General Staff, working on various problems and drawing up contingency plans for future use. In 1905 he left the War College to join Secretary of War William Howard Taft's diplomatic mission to Japan. Later that year he posted to the Philippines, where he succeeded General Leonard Wood as military governor of the Moro Province from 1906 to 1908. He sought to calm the turbulent atmosphere after Emilio Aguinaldo's two-year insurrection was defeated in 1901 and to improve the educational system on the islands. His final year in the Philippines, 1908–1909, was spent in command of the Philippine Division.

In 1909, when he returned to the United States, Bliss was only eight years from retirement, yet his most important years of service were ahead. After a brief three-month stint as president of the Army War College, he assumed command of the Department of California. Troubles on the Mexican border occupied much of his time during the next few years. Between 1911 and 1913 he headed the Department of the East, which was followed by a two-year term as commander of the Southern Department. By 1915 he had broadened his administrative experience as commander of three different regional departments, which qualified him for his next appointment as assistant chief of staff and promotion to major general. With his fellow West Point classmate General Hugh L. Scott holding the position of chief of staff, Bliss held little hope of attaining any higher position in the military before retirement.

The nation's entry into World War I dramatically changed Bliss's career prospects. When Scott left on assignment to Russia in May 1917, Bliss became acting chief of staff and, with Scott's retirement, chief of staff with the rank of general in September 1917. Although he was slated for retirement at the end of the year, Congress continued Bliss on active duty. He worked hard to keep Secretary of War Newton Baker's desk from overflowing with unnecessary paperwork and advised the secretary daily during the first hectic months of the war. Bliss and Baker worked closely together organizing the U.S. military machine that would go to France. Bliss was in full accord with General John J. Pershing's demand that as many as 100 divisions would be needed by 1919 to defeat Germany. In January 1918 Bliss went to Europe to serve as the U.S. military representative on the Supreme War Council, which had recently been formed to coordinate the Allied war effort. Early on, Bliss advocated creation of a unified command under French general Ferdinand Foch, which finally occurred with the pressure of the German advance in March 1918. Bliss also backed Pershing's insistence that the U.S. forces fight as separate divisions and not be amalgamated into the Allied armies. As the senior U.S. representative to the Supreme War Council, Bliss had far-reaching diplomatic responsibilities, which required all the tact and powers of persuasion he could muster.

With the war's conclusion, President Woodrow Wilson chose Bliss as one of the five U.S. commissioners leading the delegation to the Paris Peace Conference in 1919. Wilson worked independently of the commissioners during the treaty negotiations, relying a great deal on the advice of his assistant, Colonel Edward House. Bliss stressed the importance of reestablishing a European balance of power with the emergence of a democratic regime in Germany, but his views were buried under the postwar rancor of the Allies. Bliss supported the League of Nations and opposed military intervention in Soviet Russia. Having seen firsthand the ravages of a world war, he became a staunch advocate for the limitation of armaments. He returned to the United States in 1919 and retired as general. From 1920 to 1927 he served as governor of the Soldiers' Home in Washington, D.C. Ever interested in international issues, he helped launch the Council on Foreign Relations and was a member of the editorial board of *Foreign Affairs*, in which he published occasional articles. His final years were spent giving speeches and writing on behalf of U.S. involvement in the World Court and the League of Nations. He died in Washington, D.C.

Over six feet tall and powerfully built, Bliss exuded the calm demeanor of a college professor with his pince-nez spectacles, bald head, and full mustache. His lifelong interest in classical literature provided him with a more sophisticated world perspective than most of his colleagues. Bliss was able to synthesize and summarize enormous amounts of information for those he served. He was also an exceptionally able military administrator.

Bliss's career reflects the changes in the U.S. military as it entered the twentieth century. He made significant contributions as an educator, colonial administrator, diplomat, strategist, and staff officer. As the first president of the Army War College, he influenced the course of U.S. military education and helped the new army prepare intellectually for future warfare. On the Supreme War Council in World War I, he voted to reconcile differences while still pressing for unified Allied command. With organizational skills that matched his tremendous learning, Bliss provided the intelligence and efficiency the new military required to participate successfully in twentieth-century warfare.

• Bliss's papers are in the Library of Congress. Papers from his early career at the U.S. Army Military History Institute, Carlisle Barracks, Pa. Important writings by Bliss include

"The Armistice," *American Journal of International Law* 16 (1922): 509–22; "The Evolution of the Supreme Command," *Foreign Affairs* 1 (1922): 1–30; "European Conditions versus Disarmament," *Foreign Affairs* 1, spec. supp. (1923): ii–xii; and "What Is Disarmament?" *International Conciliation* 220 (1926): 263–79. The only full-length biography is Frederick Palmer, *Bliss, Peacemaker: The Life and Letters of General Tasker Howard Bliss* (1934; repr. 1970). Other aspects of his career are recounted in Harry P. Ball, *Of Responsible Command: A History of the U.S. Army War College* (1983); John D. Wainwright, "Root versus Bliss: The Shaping of the Army War College," *Parameters* 4 (1974): 52–65; Wayne W. Thompson, "Governors of the Moro Province: Wood, Bliss, and Pershing in the Southern Philippines, 1903–1913" (Ph.D. diss., Univ. of California, San Diego, 1975); and David F. Trask, *The United States in the Supreme War Council: American War Aims and Inter-Allied Strategy, 1917–1918* (1961) and "General Tasker Howard Bliss and the 'Sessions of the World,' 1919," *Transactions of the American Philosophical Society*, n.s., 56, pt. 8 (1966): 5–80. An obituary is in the *New York Times*, 9 Nov. 1930.

EDWARD A. GOEDEKEN

BLISS, William Dwight Porter (20 Aug. 1856–8 Oct. 1926), clergyman and reformer, was born in Constantinople (now Istanbul), the son of Edwin Elisha Bliss and Isabella Holmes Porter, Congregationalist missionaries from New England. A graduate of Amherst College (1878) and the Hartford Theological Seminary (1882), he served Congregational churches in Denver, Colorado, and South Natick, Massachusetts, from 1882 until 1885. In 1884 he married Mary Pangalo of Constantinople; they had two children.

Drawn to a study of Anglicanism, he was impressed by its theological breadth and became convinced that its heritage as a national church gave it a continuing sense of responsibility for the well-being of all classes in society. He converted to the Protestant Episcopal church in late 1885 and served as a licensed lay reader in Lee, Massachusetts, before receiving ordination as a priest and taking charge of a mission congregation in South Boston in 1887.

Bliss is best remembered for his efforts to spread the Social Gospel within American Protestantism. Advocates of the Social Gospel insisted that the churches' mission was not to save individual souls from a doomed world, but to aid in establishing the Kingdom of God on earth; to this end they promoted social, economic, and political reforms. For Bliss, the key concept undergirding a social understanding of the Gospel was the doctrine of the Incarnation.

Unlike most proponents of the Social Gospel, Bliss advocated not only reforms within capitalism, but also the eventual implementation of the socialist program of collective ownership of the means of production and distribution. He came to embrace socialism through involvement in the labor movement. An active member of the Knights of Labor in Lee, he was offered (but declined) the Massachusetts Labor party's nomination for lieutenant governor in 1887. By the end of the decade he was convinced that socialism expressed economically the spirit and ethical ideals of Christianity. Thus, he became a charter member of Boston's First Nationalist Club, which was inspired by Edward Bellamy's utopian socialist novel, *Looking Backward* (1888). He also joined the Socialist Labor party and spoke and wrote on its behalf until the fall of 1891, when the section to which he belonged prohibited its members from working on behalf of the People's party.

In 1889 Bliss launched the two ventures for which he would be best remembered among American Christian radicals: the Society of Christian Socialists, whose objectives included persuading churches that the teachings of Christ would best be fulfilled in a socialist reconstruction of society, and the *Dawn*, a religious publication open to a wide range of radical and reformist perspectives. Though neither the society nor the periodical was ever financially stable, and neither attracted more than a small number of adherents in scattered locations across the United States, they were significant for demonstrating that Christian principles and modern socialist ideas could be fused. A third venture illustrates the need Bliss felt to ground his reformist activities in the church: his withdrawal in 1890 from the South Boston mission to organize the Mission (later Church) of the Carpenter, an explicitly Christian Socialist congregation.

Bliss embraced the ideal of a socialist society unequivocally, but he believed that change must come gradually through an informed public. Thus, his means often seemed more moderate than his ends or his rhetoric. He helped found and gave leadership to two Episcopal organizations that were only mildly reformist: the Church Association for the Advancement of the Interests of Labor, or CAIL (1887), and the Christian Social Union (1891). Willing to work with all those who were moving in what he considered the right direction, he sought through these organizations to influence public opinion by disseminating information about a wide array of social problems and proposed remedies. That same purpose guided his *Encyclopedia of Social Reform* (1897; revised as the *New Encyclopedia of Social Reform*, 1908), an unusual compendium of historical and contemporary facts and commentary.

His political choices also reflect a willingness to proceed a step at a time rather than wait for the accomplishment of ultimate aims. He withdrew from the Socialist Labor party in 1891, although he preferred its platform, because he believed that the rising Populist movement would have broader public appeal. His acquaintance with the writings of such British Fabian socialists as Beatrice and Sidney Webb, Graham Wallas, and George Bernard Shaw reinforced his gradualist and educational proclivities, and he helped found and served as the first editor of the *American Fabian* in 1895–1896. In the presidential campaigns of 1896 and 1900 he endorsed William Jennings Bryan in the hope that the Democratic party was experiencing a reformation that might make it the core of a broad-based coalition of workers, farmers, and reformers. Though he continued to proclaim that his goal was socialism, it was not until 1906, when he became prominent in the newly founded Christian Socialist Fellowship, that he tacitly endorsed the Socialist Party of America.

After nearly a decade in Boston, Bliss lived in California from 1897 to 1901 and thereafter in and around New York City. He served several Episcopal parishes in California and New York, but none demanded his full attention. From 1904 to 1915 he conducted surveys, edited publications, and wrote Social Gospel Sunday school lessons for the American Institute for Social Service. The Federal Labor Bureau employed him in 1907–1909 to investigate European unemployment programs and women's trade unions in the United States. During World War I he directed educational programs for the YMCA in Europe. He died in New York City.

Bliss's socialism was always a minority position within American Christianity. In addition, his frenetic pace and a tendency to create and disband organizations with bewildering frequency limited his effectiveness. He had little influence on the political movements with which he identified, but his irenic temperament and unimpeachable piety won for him surprisingly respectful hearings before even conservative religious audiences. If he converted few Christians to socialism, he certainly contributed prolifically to the religious idealism that surged through American society in the years of Progressive reform.

• Bliss left no collection of personal manuscripts, but some of his letters are in the papers of Richard T. Ely and of Henry Demarest Lloyd at the State Historical Society of Wisconsin in Madison. The *Dawn* (1889–1896) is an invaluable record of his pioneering fusion of Christianity and socialism. His *Handbook of Socialism* (1895) and encyclopedias illustrate his reliance on educational strategies for reform. Important sketches of Bliss appear in Peter J. Frederick, *Knights of the Golden Rule: The Intellectual as Christian Social Reformer in the 1890s* (1976); Charles Howard Hopkins, *The Rise of the Social Gospel in American Protestantism, 1865–1915* (1940); Howard H. Quint, *The Forging of American Socialism: Origins of the Modern Movement* (1953); and Christopher L. Webber, "William Dwight Porter Bliss (1856–1926): Priest and Socialist," *Historical Magazine of the Protestant Episcopal Church* 28 (Mar. 1959): 9–39. The best analysis of his socialism is Richard B. Dressner, "William Dwight Porter Bliss's Christian Socialism," *Church History* 47 (Mar. 1978): 66–82. An obituary is in the *New York Times*, 9 Oct. 1926.

JACOB H. DORN

BLITZSTEIN, Marc (2 Mar. 1905–22 Jan. 1964), composer, was born in Philadelphia, Pennsylvania, the son of Samuel Marcus Blitzstein, a banker, and Anna Levitt. Blitzstein was afforded every opportunity for early musical training. He began piano studies at age three and at age seven made his concert debut and began to compose. He attended Philadelphia public schools and the University of Pennsylvania, where he received a full merit scholarship. In 1921 he was the gold medalist in a Philharmonic Society of Philadelphia contest, leading to a performance with the Academy of Music orchestra the following season. In 1922 he left the university without taking a degree and studied piano privately with Alexander Siloti in New York.

In 1924 Blitzstein left the University of Pennsylvania to become one of the first students to enter the newly formed Curtis Institute, where he studied composition with Rosario Scalero. In 1926 he traveled to Paris to study with Nadia Boulanger and subsequently to Berlin to pursue compositional studies with Arnold Schoenberg. It was in Berlin in 1928 that he was first exposed to the Brecht-Weill work *Die Dreigroschenoper*, which he later successfully translated and adapted as *The Threepenny Opera* in 1952. He returned to the United States in 1928 and supported himself as a musician—teaching, performing, and lecturing at both women's music clubs and universities. That summer, Blitzstein was a fellow at the McDowell Colony, where he met novelist Eva Goldbeck, whom he married in 1933. She died in 1936.

Blitzstein's early compositions encompassed many genres, including ballet, chamber music, piano music, and opera. These early works were harmonically dissonant and rhythmic and often experimental in form.

In 1935 Blitzstein attended lectures given by Hanns Eisler at the New School of Social Research in New York. These lectures, titled "The Crisis in Music," led him to examine the role of music in society and helped to shape what became the driving force of his compositions for the next decade: "art for society's sake." In 1935 he composed the song, "The Nickel under My Foot," which became the catalyst for his first critical success, the musical play *The Cradle Will Rock* (1937). *Cradle* was conceived by Blitzstein, who also wrote its music, book, and lyrics. It was produced by the Federal Theater Project of the Works Progress Administration (WPA), with Orson Welles and John Houseman serving as director and producer, respectively. The show's controversial subject matter—the attempt of "the establishment" (business, education, religion, etc.) to silence the voice of the working class, and the workers' eventual triumph—was objectionable to the WPA, who pulled its funding on the day of the opening. The show did open, however, with Blitzstein playing the score for the show from an on-stage piano, while members of the cast performed their parts from the audience. It was a huge success and launched Blitzstein's career as a composer for the theater. *Cradle*'s score consists of many types of songs found in musical theater works, including torch, patter, and parody, and it featured many types of performance styles, such as singing, rhythmic speaking, and *sprechstimme*. These performance styles played an important role in his later compositions for the stage.

During World War II, Blitzstein served in the U.S. Eighth Army Air Force in England, where he composed music for special projects for the military and civilian audiences. During this time, he composed *Freedom Morning* (1943), for orchestra, and the *Airborne Symphony* (1944), for orchestra, male chorus, soloists, and narrator. Blitzstein also wrote the text for the latter, which was political in tone.

Blitzstein's next work for the stage was an opera, *Regina* (1949), a musical adaptation of Lillian Hellman's play *The Little Foxes*. Once again, Blitzstein served as his own librettist. He drew upon all of his musical talents for this innovative score, which fused the tradition of European opera with American popular song. The result was a musical mélange that combined *sprechstimme*, rhythmic speaking, and underscored dialogue with singing. Although it received a short initial run by Broadway standards, it was a critical success and has been revived numerous times by the New York City Opera and other regional companies.

Blitzstein's other two musical plays, *Reuben, Reuben* (1955), an original libretto, and *Juno* (1959), based on Sean O'Casey's *Juno and the Paycock*, were neither critically well received nor commercially successful.

At the time of his death, Blitzstein was working on a score for the Metropolitan Opera Association through a Ford Foundation grant. The subject of this three-act opera was Sacco and Vanzetti. Two one-act operas, *Idiots First* and *The Magic Barrel*, based on short stories by Bernard Malamud, also remained unfinished. Blitzstein was murdered while on vacation in Martinique, West Indies.

Blitzstein's most notable contribution to American music was his success in combining existing styles and techniques from both classical and popular genres to create, in his words, "a fusion." In addition to his works for the stage, Blitzstein composed scores for several films, incidental music for plays, songs, and chamber music.

• Two articles by Blitzstein provide valuable insight into his work: "Notes on the Musical Theatre," *Theatre Arts*, June 1950, pp. 30–31; and "On Words and Music," *Theatre Arts*, Nov. 1950, pp. 52–53. The most thorough chronology of Blitzstein's personal life and career is Eric A. Gordon's biography, *Mark the Music: The Life and Works of Marc Blitzstein* (1989). Other detailed studies include R. J. Dietz, "The Operatic Style of Marc Blitzstein" (Ph.D. diss., Univ. of Iowa, 1970); A. B. Foradori, "Marc Blitzstein's *Regina*: A Pivotal Work in American Musical Theater" (D.M.A. diss., Ohio State Univ., 1994); and P. M. Talley, "Social Criticism in the Original Theatre Librettos of Marc Blitzstein" (Ph.D. diss., Univ. of Wisconsin, 1965). Other sources of interest include Leonard Bernstein's "Prelude to a Musical," *New York Times*, 30 Oct. 1949; and Tommy Krasker's liner notes to the 1992 recording of *Regina* (London 433 812-2).

ANNE BILL FORADORI

BLIVEN, Bruce (27 July 1889–27 May 1977), journalist, was born in Emmetsburg, Iowa, the son of Charles F. Bliven and Lilla C. Ormsby. After graduating from the Emmetsburg public schools, Bliven received his A.B. from Stanford University in 1911. While in college he was the paid Stanford reporter of the San Francisco *Bulletin* and after graduating worked as advertising manager of a Los Angeles department store. In 1913 he married Rose Frances Emery; they had one child. The following year Bliven joined the Department of Journalism at the University of Southern California and was its first director (1914–1916). He then moved to New York and served on the editorial staff of *Printer's Ink* (1917–1918), then joined the editorial board of the New York *Globe* in 1919, becoming its managing editor a year later. He left the *Globe* to become managing editor of the liberal *New Republic* when the *Globe* was merged with the *Evening Sun* by its new owner, Frank Munsey, in 1923. In the same year Bliven became a member of the board of directors of the Twentieth Century Fund, on which he served until 1957.

While with the *New Republic* (1923–1955) Bliven exerted his greatest influence, particularly during the 1930s. His newspaper experience had introduced him to a number of the radicals, reformers, and muckrakers of the Progressive Era, including "Big Bill" Haywood of the Industrial Workers of the World and Lincoln Steffens. The *Globe* was the most liberal newspaper in New York City, without being radical. Bliven's move to the *New Republic* was a natural one, and when its founder and general editor, Herbert Croly, suffered a paralytic stroke in 1928, Bliven succeeded him as general manager in 1930.

Throughout the 1920s Bliven tilted with the conservative Warren G. Harding and Calvin Coolidge administrations, writing some of the best descriptions of the corruption in the former. The *New Republic* was one of the few voices in behalf of liberalism during that decade, championing the causes of academic freedom, freedom of speech, the rights of women and minorities, and conservation of natural resources, while battling restrictive immigration policies, the Ku Klux Klan, censorship, and the stifling effects of religious fundamentalism. Although Bliven had been one of the first to promote Herbert Hoover for the presidency—in an article for the *Independent* in 1920—he spared his fellow Iowan's administration no criticism over what he regarded as Hoover's failure to cope adequately with the depression after the stock market crash of 1929.

Bliven and the *New Republic* welcomed the inauguration of Franklin Delano Roosevelt in 1933. In a 1951 oral history interview, Bliven recalled that the *New Republic* had been for the New Deal long before Roosevelt embraced it. The original members of Roosevelt's brain trust, the Columbia University group that included Rexford Tugwell, Raymond Moley, and Adolf Berle, were New York friends of the *New Republic* staff while Roosevelt was still governor of the state; once the New Deal was launched, the magazine became one of its most devoted supporters. Dedicated, like the early New Dealers, to the concepts of economic planning and federal regulation of the economy, Bliven gained a reputation as an intellectual godfather of the New Deal although he frequently criticized the Roosevelt administration for not going far enough.

While editing the *New Republic*, Bliven contributed a six-days-a-week column to Great Britain's *Manchester Guardian* as its New York correspondent between 1927 and 1947; he also undertook extensive speaking commitments across the country. With the outbreak of war in Europe in 1939, Bliven and the *New Republic* took a position unpopular with many liberals by opposing U.S. intervention until 1941, when the prospect of an Axis victory began to trouble him. Shortly after World War II his contrary positions on a number of issues began to create a small but important gulf between him and many leading liberals. Despite the brief tenure of Henry A. Wallace as nominal editor of the *New Republic* (1946–1948), Bliven and the magazine supported Harry S. Truman for the presidency in 1948 rather than Wallace, the choice of many liberals. Bliven was also one of only a few liberals convinced from the outset of the guilt of Alger Hiss.

In December 1951 Bliven suffered a heart attack that caused him to reduce his activities with the *New Republic*. In 1953 he returned to Stanford University to be near the research facilities of the Hoover Institution on War, Revolution, and Peace, where he concentrated on writing several books while occasionally teaching a journalism course at the university. He developed an interest in writing history and biography, beginning with *The Twentieth Century Unlimited* (1950); there then followed works such as *Preview for Tomorrow* (1953) and *From Pearl Harbor to Okinawa* (1960). In 1970 his autobiography, *Five Million Words Later*, was published.

Bliven died at the Stanford University Medical Center. The *New York Times* hailed him as a "champion of liberalism" in its obituary.

• Most of Bliven's letters were destroyed, but a small collection is held by the Stanford University Library. Besides his autobiography, Bliven's interview for the Columbia Oral History Collection provides details of his early life and of his years with the *New Republic*. Several studies of the *New Republic* have been published, including Charles Forcey, *The Crossroads of Liberalism* (1961), and David W. Levy, *Herbert Croly of the New Republic* (1985), which devote some attention to Bliven. An obituary is in the *New York Times*, 29 May 1977.

GARY DEAN BEST

BLOCH, Claude Charles (12 July 1878–6 Oct. 1967), naval officer, was born in Woodbury, Kentucky, the son of Adolph Bloch, a merchant. His mother's name is unknown. From 1892 to 1895 he attended Ogden College in Kentucky and entered the U.S. Naval Academy in 1895. As a cadet, he served aboard the battleship *Iowa* at the battle of Santiago, Cuba, during the Spanish-American War and received a Specially Meritorious Medal for his rescue of enemy sailors from their burning ships. He completed his education at the Naval Academy in 1899. He served aboard the gunboat *Wheeling* in the Philippine insurrection and, in connection with the Boxer Rebellion, with the international force sent to relieve the legations in Beijing. He was commissioned an ensign in 1901. While captain of the naval station in American Samoa, he in 1903 married Augusta Kent McCausland; they had one child.

Bloch specialized in ordnance work, serving as inspector of powder in 1905 and aboard the battleship *Virginia* from 1906 to 1907. From 1909 to 1911 he saw shore duty at the Naval Proving Ground at Indian Head, Maryland, where he was in charge of gun testing for range and accuracy and against armor plating. For Bloch and other officers, such an assignment served as an important stage in the advancement of their ordnance careers.

After Indian Head, Bloch served aboard the battleships *Delaware* and *Maine*. During 1918 he commanded the *Plattsburg*, which transported troops to Europe, for which he was later awarded the Navy Cross. He also commanded the battleship *Massachusetts* for two months at the end of World War I. From 1918 to 1921 Bloch served as assistant to the chief of the Bureau of Ordnance and was again inspector of ordnance in 1923. He returned to the Indian Head Naval Proving Ground, by then renamed the Naval Powder Factory, briefly in 1923 as commanding officer. In October 1923 he was advanced to the temporary rank of rear admiral and was appointed chief of the Bureau of Ordnance, where he served through 1927.

In 1927 Bloch reverted to captain and commanded the battleship *California*, 1927–1929. In 1930 he was commandant at the Washington Navy Yard, and in 1931 he was promoted to the permanent rank of rear admiral. Through the 1930s he was prominent in naval administration, serving as budget officer for the Navy Department in 1934 and as judge advocate general for the navy from 1934 to 1936. He was a strong advocate of preparedness and, arguing for the thorough fortification of Guam, earned the nickname "Jack Dempsey of the Navy" for remarking that the United States should beat the enemy to the punch. He was regarded as without peer in testifying before congressional committees and as a solid seagoing naval tactician of surface vessels.

In 1936 Bloch assumed command of Battleship Division Two, Battle Force, and in 1937 he became commander of the Battle Force, U.S. Fleet. In 1938–1940 he was commander in chief of the U.S. Fleet based on the West Coast and in 1940 was assigned as commandant of the Fourteenth Naval District at Pearl Harbor, Hawaii, regarded at the time as a routine preretirement assignment in a comfortable tropical port. As Bloch sought to strengthen the defenses of Hawaii, he ran into interference from Admiral Husband E. Kimmel, who took command of the U.S. Fleet after the president transferred its headquarters from California to Hawaii in 1940 as a gesture of American strength in the Pacific. After the Japanese attack on Pearl Harbor, Admiral Kimmel and General Walter Short were both removed from their commands, but Admiral Bloch was cleared of any responsibility for the debacle.

In 1942 Bloch engaged in a dispute with Admiral Chester W. Nimitz as to the conduct of naval operations in the Pacific and returned to Washington, where he presided over the Navy General Board until his retirement later that year. In retirement, he remained active as chairman of the Navy Board for Production Awards until the end of World War II. In 1945 he received the Legion of Merit award for his service during the war. He died in Washington, D.C.

As a Naval Academy graduate, gunnery officer, and ordnance specialist, Bloch brought a surface-vessel, blue-water perspective to the issue of national defense. His service in weapons testing at Indian Head, his later command there, and his appointment as chief of the Bureau of Ordnance demonstrated that orientation and background. His strong advocacy of building a powerful navy based in cruisers and battleships reflected his membership in the faction of the navy informally known as "the gun club" rather than the growing group committed to a heavier reliance on naval air power.

• Bloch's personal papers are in the Manuscripts Division, Library of Congress. See also Samuel Eliot Morison, *History of the United States Naval Operations in World War II*, vol. 3 (1948). An obituary is in the *New York Times*, 7 Oct. 1967.

RODNEY P. CARLISLE

BLOCH, Ernest (24 July 1880–15 July 1959), composer and educator, was born in Geneva, Switzerland, the son of Maurice Bloch, a purveyor of tourist merchandise, and Sophie Brunschwig. Bloch senior, an official of the small Jewish community in Legnau, in the canton of Aargau, provided his family with an Orthodox environment. Bloch exhibited an early interest in music, and during his teenage years he received training in violin from Albert Goss and Louis Etienne-Reyer and in solfège and composition from Émile Jaques-Dalcroze. He left school at the age of fourteen, shortly after his bar mitzvah. From 1896 to 1899 Bloch studied in Brussels, where his teachers included Eugène Ysaÿe, Franz Schörg, and François Rasse. Bloch's compositions from this apprenticeship period reveal the influence of the Russian national school, particularly in matters of fluctuating meters, folk-flavored melodies, irregular rhythms, exotic scalar constructions, a propensity for modality, and coloristic scoring. His *Symphonie orientale* (1896) and *Orientale* (1898), their titles suggestive of the music's orientation, are representative works from this period. In the midst of the fin de siècle atmosphere of Brussels, Bloch also began exploring the Franco-Belgian approach to composition. His *Poème concertante* (1898) and *Concerto* (1899), both for violin and orchestra, reflect the Franco-Belgian style, characterized by elegant and refined melodic contours and harmonic support and cyclical treatment as a means of attaining structural unity in essentially rhapsodic creations. Bloch's evident preference in these works for frequent instrumental solos as opposed to large blocks of sound indicates a shift to the French style of orchestration. Programmatic references are also reduced or avoided.

At age nineteen Bloch went to Frankfurt, where he studied with the revered pedagogue and composer Ivan Knorr. Under Knorr, he retraced his steps and mastered the complexities of counterpoint, fugue, and harmony. Bloch's symphonic poem *Vivre–Aimer* (1900), dedicated to Jaques-Dalcroze, retains the Franco-Belgian traits of Bloch's Brussels juvenilia, but its thematic metamorphoses of various leitmotifs emulate the Lisztian prototype.

Bloch's studies with composer Ludwig Thuille in Munich from 1901 to 1903, though neither systematic nor ongoing, and the influence of the Wagnerian poet Alexander Ritter helped him to synthesize the lessons learned from earlier mentors. Bloch's Symphony in C-sharp Minor (1901–1903), a four-movement opus on a grand scale, exemplifies a Germanic tilt, with its Straussian chromaticism, rich orchestration, and use of leitmotifs. His susceptibility to divergent influences is no better illustrated than in a body of compositions that appear to have been inspired by his brief stay in Paris in 1903–1904. His early masterwork *Hiver–Printemps* (1905), for example, reveals Debussyan traits, such as blurring effects associated with seventh and ninth chords, a lack of harmonic clarity, and a subdued and coloristic orchestral palette. After returning to Geneva in 1904, Bloch entered his father's business but devoted his spare time to the composition of his music drama *Macbeth* (premiered 30 Nov. 1910, Opéra-Comique, Paris). In 1904 he married Margarethe Augusta Schneider of Hamburg; they had three children.

Bloch's song cycles *Historiettes au crépuscule* (based on the poetry of Camille Mauclair, 1904) and *Poèmes d'automne* (based on the poetry of Béatrix Rodès, 1906) exhibit a French orientation. *Macbeth*, however, a lyric drama in seven scenes, reveals a stunning co-mingling of antipodal elements, including Wagnerian leitmotifs, impressionistic color and atmosphere, intensely dramatic character definition, and cyclical treatment of themes. Apart from his daily business chores, Bloch conducted orchestral concerts at Lausanne and Neuchâtel in 1909–1910 and lectured on aesthetics at the Geneva Conservatory from 1911 to 1916.

After much soul-searching on the subject of Judaism and his place within the faith and culture, and influenced by his correspondence on the subject with Edmund Fleg, the *Macbeth* librettist, Bloch arrived at a unique mode of expression so intensely personal that the world of music was forced to take notice. He returned to his Jewish roots and, from that self-examination, created a series of biblically inspired epics resplendent with a rich orchestral garb and charged with surging energy and emotive power. These historic works, known collectively as the "Jewish Cycle," include *Trois poèmes Juifs* (1913), Prelude and Two Psalms (nos. 114 and 137) for soprano and orchestra (1912–1914), *Psalm 22* for baritone and orchestra (1914), the symphony with voices *Israel* (1912–1916), and the Hebraic rhapsody for violoncello and orchestra *Schelomo* (1915–1916). Despite occasional references to Hebraic sources, Bloch's expression is largely his own personal conception of Jewish music, not an attempt at an archaeological reconstruction of ancient melos. But because of the Jewish imprimatur of these compositions, he was promptly hailed—and derided—as "the Jewish composer." His music, nonetheless, spoke to Jews and non-Jews alike, for its communicative power transcended provincialism.

Bloch came to the United States in 1916 as conductor of Maud Allan's dance company. In November 1916, when that organization's tour collapsed, Bloch was rescued by the Flonzaley Quartet, which premiered his String Quartet no. 1 on 31 December 1916. Shortly thereafter, performances of the "Jewish" works in Boston and New York resulted in public and critical acclaim and launched Bloch on a new career in the New World. Bloch accepted teaching engagements at David Mannes's music school in New York and at Joanne Bird Shaw's school in Peterboro, New Hampshire. He also conducted an untrained chorus in works by such Renaissance masters as Josquin Des Prez and Giovanni Pierluigi Palestrina at the Manhattan Trade School, and he received the Coolidge Prize for his Suite for Viola and Piano (1919). All of these achievements served as building blocks in Bloch's career, culminating in his appointment as the first director of the Cleveland Institute of Music, a post he held from 1920 to 1925. During his involvement with academic life in the American Midwest, he continued to compose eclectically. His solo piano compositions have an impressionistic cast, as suggested by their titles, created by harmonically blurred chordal structures and evocative mood changes. They include *Five Sketches in Sepia* (1923), *Nirvana* (1923), and *Poems of the Sea* (1922), the last inspired by the verse of Walt Whitman. Other works from this period include two sonatas for violin and piano, the first (1920) abstract and containing more than a hint of primitivism, and the second, *Poème mystique* (1924), a romantic outpouring with references to Gregorian melodies; Piano Quintet no. 1 (1923), with quarter tones in its outer movements; Concerto Grosso no. 1 for string orchestra with piano obbligato (1924–1925), with a prelude and fugue comprising the outer movements that frame two descriptive interior movements; *Enfantines* (1923), the modally tinged collection of children's cameos for piano; and such Jewish-oriented creations as *Baal Shem* for violin and piano (1923), *From Jewish Life* for violoncello and piano (1924), and *Méditation hébraïque* for violoncello and piano (1924). Bloch became an American citizen in 1924.

As a teacher, Bloch's views were considered radical departures from the expected norms envisioned by the trustees of the Cleveland music school. His abandonment of textbooks and grades in favor of studying music directly from the scores of the great composers was seen as impractical. In 1925, when Ada Clement and Lillian Hodghead offered him an administrative post at their newly created San Francisco Conservatory of Music, Bloch and his family moved to California. There he produced two patriotic works, *America* (1926), an epic rhapsody with a closing choral anthem, and his symphonic fresco *Helvetia* (1928). The former composition, replete with literal quotations of American Indian melodies, sea chanteys, Negro spirituals, and patriotic tunes associated with critical periods in American history, won the *Musical America* prize of $3,000 in 1928. *Helvetia*, an homage to Bloch's native land that is sprinkled with Swiss folk melodies, shared with four other compositions a $25,000 prize awarded by the RCA Victor Company in 1930. Along with the earlier *Israel*, these large-scale efforts are pointed references to the threefold national-religious-cultural allegiance of their creator.

By 1930 Bloch had decided to sever ties with San Francisco and to return to Europe. His decision was helped by the magnanimity of the Rosa and Jacob Stern family, art patrons who established a $100,000 trust, the interest on which would provide Bloch with up to $5,000 per year for a ten-year period. A key proviso required that he devote his energies solely to composition. In addition to this stroke of good fortune, Bloch was commissioned, through the efforts of Cantor Reuben Rinder of San Francisco's Temple Emanuel, to compose a Sabbath morning service based on texts drawn from Reform Judaism's Union Prayer Book. Bloch, freed of the entanglements of academia, returned to his land of birth and set about learning the Hebrew language, something he had done only superficially when preparing for his bar mitzvah. The world premiere of the *Sacred Service*, as it came to be called, took place in Turin on 12 January 1934. This towering choral masterpiece was not performed at Temple Emanuel until March 1938. In this work, Bloch created unity through the employment of a six-note mixolydian motif that recurs at critical points throughout the piece; he achieved a universal mode of expression acceptable to all peoples. The 1930s also produced such disparate works as his abstractionist and virtuosic three-movement Piano Sonata (1935), dedicated to Guido Agosti; the six-movement *Voice in the Wilderness* (1936), a Hebraically spirited set of meditations for violoncello and orchestra; and the three-movement Violin Concerto (1938). Although the last work is based, according to Bloch, on American Indian motifs, some critics, such as Arthur Berger, noted a Jewish flavor.

Before his decade in Europe was ended, Bloch was able to savor the triumph, albeit a brief one, of *Macbeth*, which was given in a revival in March 1938 in Naples. The rise of anti-Semitism and the Mussolini-Hitler alliance limited the number of performances of the opera. In 1939 a London-based Ernest Bloch Society was formed, with Albert Einstein as honorary president.

In 1940 the Stern bequest directed Bloch to assume a teaching post at the University of California, Berkeley. He and his wife settled in Agate Beach, Oregon, and Bloch limited his teaching duties to the summers. Over the next eighteen years he composed a series of works in a variety of genres and for various media. In general the compositions are objective, formally designed, abstract, and devoid of the rhetorical features associated with his earlier compositions. A passacaglia reminiscent of the baroque period, for example, comprises the second movement of the *Suite Symphonique* (1944) and the final movement of the String Quartet no. 2 (1945). Other works composed during this period include the *Sinfonia breve* (1952), with a twelve-tone theme in the second movement; the neoclassical

Concerto Grosso no. 2 (1952); the neoromantic *Concerto Symphonique* (1948) for piano and orchestra, the Symphony in E-flat Major (1954–1955); the Symphony for Trombone and Orchestra (1954); the *Suite Modale* (1956) for flute and string orchestra; the String Quartets nos. 3, 4, and 5 (1952, 1953, 1956); two suites for unaccompanied violin (1958); three suites for unaccompanied violoncello (1956, 1956, 1957); one suite for unaccompanied viola (last movement incomplete, 1958); and the Piano Quintet no. 2 (1957).

Despite his relatively secluded life, Bloch received many honors, among them the first Gold Medal in music from the American Academy of Arts and Letters in 1947 for his String Quartet no. 2; the New York Music Critics Circle Award in 1953 in both orchestral and chamber music for, respectively, his Concerto Grosso no. 2 and String Quartet no. 3; the Stephen Wise Award in 1951 for outstanding contributions to the field of Jewish culture; and the Henry Hadley Medal of the National Association for American Composers and Conductors in 1957 for distinguished service to American music. Bloch died in Portland, Oregon. Although he was neither a trailblazer nor the founder of a particular school of composition, Bloch was aware of and utilized assorted contemporary techniques and devices when they suited his artistic needs. He taught his many students, including Herbert Elwell, Frederick Jacobi, Douglas Moore, Quincy Porter, Leon Kirchner, and Roger Sessions, to develop their innate talents along individual lines and to become their own masters, much as he had become his own master under the guidance of Knorr. While it may appear that Bloch was a voice in the wilderness, his was a strong and original voice, one that did not waver in the face of changing fashions, fetishes, or neoteric exercises. A universal humanism informs his creative achievements. Bloch is among the elite of twentieth-century masters.

• The Library of Congress holds eighty manuscripts of Bloch's published and unpublished compositions, individual parts, sketches, drafts, and proofs, plus scrapbooks, letters, personal notes, memorabilia, and reviews. The University of California at Berkeley holds manuscripts and sketches of works donated during the composer's lifetime by the Jacob and Rosa Stern Musical Fund. The Ernest Bloch Archives includes autograph scores, drafts, and sketches; correspondence and memorabilia (correspondents include Lillian Hodghead, Ada Clement, Albert Elkus, Alfred Hertz, Eugene Goossens, Reuben Rinder); newspaper articles, press critiques, original program notes, periodical articles about Bloch and his music, promotional materials from publishers, photographs of Bloch, medals, and Bloch's (honorary) doctoral hood. The Hebrew-Union College, Jewish Institute of Religion (Cincinnati, OH) includes correspondence between Bloch and Rinder and five photos of Bloch. Eastman School of Music (Rochester, N.Y.) contains a collection of didactic materials, including Bloch's analyses of works by J. S. Bach, Beethoven, Mussorgsky, and Debussy; pedagogical writings reflecting Bloch's approach to teaching harmony, counterpoint, and fugue; notebooks and early manuscripts. The University of Hartford holds forty-eight letters by Bloch, thirty-seven of them to Julius Hartt.

David Z. Kushner's bio-bibliographical study, *Ernest Bloch: A Guide to Research* (1988), includes catalogs of the unpublished and published works, a discography (including 78 RPM recordings), a list of archival and repository holdings, a list of honors and awards received by Bloch, and an annotated bibliography containing 579 items. For other biographical information and discussion about Bloch's music see R. Strassburg, *Ernest Bloch, Voice in the Wilderness* (1977); Suzanne Bloch and Irene Heskes, *Ernest Bloch: Creative Spirit* (1976); and Kushner, "Bloch, Ernest," in the *New Grove Dictionary of American Music*, vol. 1 (1986). Obituaries are in the *New York Times*, 16 July 1959, and *Musical America*, Aug. 1959.

DAVID Z. KUSHNER

BLOCH, Felix (23 Oct. 1905–10 Sept. 1983), physicist, was born in Zurich, Switzerland, the son of Gustav Bloch, a wholesale grain dealer, and Agnes Meyer. He matriculated at Zurich's Federal Institute of Technology in 1924 with the intention of becoming an engineer, but after spending a summer in an iron foundry he opted instead to become a physicist. In 1927 he enrolled at the University of Leipzig in Germany and received his Ph.D. in theoretical physics the next year. His doctoral dissertation made a major contribution to the development of quantum physics by explaining electrical conductivity in metals in terms of the wave behavior of electrons. Known today as the Bloch theorem, this explanation led to the postulation of the band theory, which explains a solid's relative conductivity in terms of the range of electron energy levels or bands that it can accommodate. This theory led by turns to the identification of insulators and semiconductors and the invention of the transistor, the main components of solid-state electronics.

Bloch spent the next four years conducting research at the Federal Institute of Technology and the universities of Utrecht, Haarlem, Rijks, Leipzig, and Copenhagen. During this period he applied quantum theory to the development of several concepts that proved to be fundamentally important to the development of solid-state physics. One of these concepts was the Bloch-Grüneisen relationship, a theoretical explanation for the empirical data compiled by the German physicist Eduard Grüneisen concerning the relationship between a metal's temperature and its ability to conduct electricity. Another was the Bloch T $^{3}/_{2}$ law, which describes the relationship between temperature and magnetization in a ferromagnetic material such as iron. He also described the Bloch wall, the boundary area between two regions of different magnetic orientation in a ferromagnetic substance, such as the one that occurs between the "positive" and "negative" ends of a bar magnet. His research also yielded the Bethe-Bloch expression, a calculation derived largely from the work of the German-American physicist Hans Albrecht Bethe, which addresses the ability of a given element's nucleus to absorb a charged subatomic particle attempting to pass through it.

In 1932 Bloch became a lecturer in theoretical physics at Leipzig but, because he was Jewish, left the next year when the Nazis took control of the German government. He taught at the Institut Henri Poincaré in Paris and conducted research at the University of Rome before accepting a position as associate professor of physics at Stanford University in 1934. He turned his attention to investigating the recently discovered neutron's properties of magnetism, a phenomenon that fascinated him because it could not be explained in terms of electrical charge, as with the electron, because the neutron possesses no such charge. In 1936, the same year he was promoted to full professor, he postulated that the neutron's magnetic moment, a function of its magnetic strength that determines the way it "spins" in the presence of a magnetic field, could be determined experimentally; his method involved beaming relatively slow-moving neutrons at an iron target and then measuring the degree of polarization of the deflected beam, yielding a prediction that was confirmed in the laboratory by other researchers the next year. Two years later he turned away from formulating theories to conducting his own experiments. In 1939 he and Luis W. Alvarez beamed polarized neutrons through a magnetic field with a variable frequency, in the process successfully measuring the neutron's magnetic moment. That same year he became an American citizen, and in 1940 he married Lore C. Misch, with whom he had four children.

Bloch contributed to the American effort during World War II as a member of the Manhattan Project from 1942 to 1944 and then as an associate leader of a group at the Radio Research Laboratory at Harvard that was investigating counter-radar measures. While engaged in this latter endeavor he realized that microwave technology could be used to determine the magnetic moment of a nucleus, and upon his return to Stanford he developed the nuclear induction method. This method, known today as nuclear magnetic resonance (NMR), determines the magnetic moment of the nucleus; by passing a beam of polarized nuclei through a magnetic field, the strength of which is adjusted using microwave radio frequencies. The nuclei reverse their spin at a certain precise frequency, from which the magnetic moment can be extrapolated. Bloch's work in this regard was duplicated independently and simultaneously by the American physicist Edward M. Purcell, and in 1952 both researchers were awarded the Nobel Prize in physics.

The fact that NMR does not harm sample material in any way makes it a particularly useful tool for researchers in a wide range of spectroscopic applications. The most important of these applications involves the use of NMR in computer-assisted tomography (CAT) scanning equipment, developed by Allan Cormack and Godfrey Hounsfield in the 1970s and put into commercial operation in the mid-1980s. This development made possible the observation of chemical reactions inside the human body, establishing the CAT-scan as a powerful medical diagnostic tool.

In 1954 Bloch was appointed director of the newly established European Nuclear Research Center in Geneva, Switzerland, where he devoted his energies to harnessing atomic energy for peacetime applications. The next year he returned to Stanford, where he concentrated on problems involving superconductivity, the phenomenon of electrical conductivity at temperatures approaching absolute zero, and statistical mechanics, the application of probability theory to quantum physics. In 1963 he was appointed Max H. Stein Professor of Physics. He served as president of the American Physical Society from 1965 to 1966 and was elected to the National Academy of Sciences in 1948. He retired in 1971 and returned to Zurich, where he remained until his death there.

Bloch contributed to the development of physics in two major ways. Because of his ability to employ quantum theory to arrive at a more nuanced understanding of the physical principles connected with electrical conductivity and ferromagnetism, he is considered by many to be the "father of solid-state physics." His pioneering work with nuclear magnetic resonance led to revolutionary developments in the fields of spectroscopy and medical diagnostics.

• Bloch's papers are located in the Stanford University Archives and the Niels Bohr Library, Center for the History of Physics, at the American Institute of Physics. A biography, including a selected bibliography, is Robert Hofstadter, "Felix Bloch," National Academy of Sciences, *Biographical Memoirs* 64 (1989): 35–70. A festschrift is Marvin Chodorow et al., eds., *Felix Bloch and Twentieth-Century Physics* (1980). Obituaries are in the *New York Times*, 12 Sept. 1983, and *Time*, 26 Sept. 1983.

CHARLES W. CAREY, JR.

BLODGET, Samuel, Jr. (28 Aug. 1757–11 Apr. 1814), entrepreneur, architect, and economist, was born in Goffstown, New Hampshire, the son of Samuel Blodget and Hannah White. The elder Blodget was a merchant, manufacturer, and canal builder, and also a visionary, having developed machinery for raising sunken ships. The son seems to have inherited the father's versatility and visionary quality.

The younger Blodget served in the New Hampshire militia from 1775 to 1777, then resigned to pursue the mercantile trade in Exeter, New Hampshire, and in Boston, in partnership with Daniel Gilman, a younger son of an Exeter family prominent in New Hampshire politics. Blodget made two trips to Europe, in 1784 and again around 1790. He married Dorothy Folsom in Exeter in 1778; she died in Philadelphia in 1790. Two years later he married Rebecca Smith, the daughter of the provost of the University of Pennsylvania.

In 1789 Blodget moved from Boston to Philadelphia, but he continued to conduct business in Boston. In 1791 he was a founder of the Boston Tontine Association, a life insurance scheme in which individuals purchased a subscription and received an annuity. As each subscriber died his annuity was divided among the survivors, and the last subscriber took all. When the tontine failed to attract sufficient subscribers, the members, including Blodget, used the funds to found the Union Bank in 1792.

In that same year Blodget and former postmaster general Ebenezer Hazard announced another tontine arrangement in Philadelphia. Again sales went poorly, and the subscribers decided to use the funds to organize the Insurance Company of North America. This company underwrote merchants' ships at sea; within a few years, it expanded to offer fire insurance and life insurance. Blodget sold a great deal of the stock himself—40,000 shares were bought within eleven days, the greatest triumph of his entrepreneurial career. He was elected to the board of directors and served until 1799.

Blodget was an early advocate for the new District of Columbia, both as an investor and as an architect. In January 1792, months before the official sale of lots, he purchased 494 acres, known as the Jamaica tract, for $36,000. His first known venture as an amateur architect was a design for the U.S. Capitol, which owed a great deal to conversations with Thomas Jefferson. The building was to have four porticoes and a dome; the columns were based on the Corinthian order of the Maison Carrée at Nîmes and the dome on that of the Halle aux Blés in Paris. All these features Jefferson admired individually, if not in the combination Blodget proposed. The plan, however, was not adopted.

Undeterred, Blodget lobbied for the position of superintendent of buildings. George Washington acknowledged in a letter of 30 November 1792 that Blodget had traveled extensively, claimed to have studied architecture, "and is certainly a projecting Genius," yet he was unsure whether Blodget was the right man for the job. In spite of Washington's reservations, Blodget was appointed early in 1793.

On taking office Blodget proposed a lottery to raise funds for the district. First prize was a hotel worth $50,000, designed by James Hoban, architect of the White House. When the winners were not announced in fall 1793, the capital commissioners declared Blodget personally liable for the lottery, and there his financial problems began. In January 1794 the commissioners informed Blodget that his continued service was impracticable, given that he was not resident in the city and given his involvement in the lottery. In October 1794 the lottery winner, Robert S. Bickley, discovered that the hotel was unfinished, and in 1798 he brought suit against Blodget.

With Benjamin Stoddert, another investor in district lands and later secretary of the navy under John Adams, Blodget founded the Bank of Columbia, the first private bank in the district. The state of Maryland chartered the bank in December 1793, permitting the capital commissioners, acting for the federal government, to subscribe for up to 2,000 shares in the bank, though the commissioners actually purchased 1,053 shares. Blodget served as president for one year, then was succeeded by Stoddert.

The building for which Blodget is remembered as an architect—indeed, his only built work—is the Bank of the United States in Philadelphia (1795). Its exterior was strongly influenced by Thomas Cooley's Royal Exchange in Dublin, but the *Gazette of the United States* observed that the proportions of the portico corresponded to those of the Maison Carrée, and that the six Corinthian columns were ornamented as "at Palmyra and Rome when architecture was at its zenith in the Augustan age." The first-floor banking room featured two rows of Corinthian columns supporting a barrel vault, which ran from front to back. The interior was completely remodeled by James Windrim in 1901, but Blodget's monumental exterior stands largely intact.

In 1802 the Pennsylvania courts ruled that Blodget owed Bickley the title to the unfinished hotel and an additional $21,500 to complete it. Blodget found himself in debtor's prison, and his property was sold off in 1805. However, the proceeds were not even near the required sum of $21,500, and an additional sale of property was held in 1813.

Blodget was an outspoken advocate for building a combined monument to Washington and a national university. In an 1803 memorial to Congress he proposed that Washington's tomb be placed in the center of the complex, encircled with a portico and surrounded with buildings of the college, much like the Timoleonton in Syracuse, as described in Plutarch. Blodget began collecting $5 donations for the project and continued to do so even while in debtor's prison. At his death he had accumulated some $7,000, but, as with so many of his ideas, nothing ever came of it, and the money disappeared.

Besides his work as a gentleman architect, Blodget was also one of the earliest American writers on political economy. His first publication was *Thoughts on the Increasing Wealth and National Economy of the United States of America*, a pamphlet published in Washington in 1801. Not surprisingly, he praised Alexander Hamilton's report on public credit. Blodget argued that cheap and extensive lands in the United States would give a much higher return for labor than in Great Britain; he proposed a policy of mercantile expansionism and urged the government to borrow from other countries and to maintain a constantly increasing money supply.

Blodget's principal written work, *Economica: A Statistical Manual for the United States* (1806), is considered to be the earliest American book on economics. It is a fairly miscellaneous collection of materials, including a lengthy prefatory address, a chronology of American history, notes on agriculture, commerce, and banking, and an appendix devoted to his pet project of a national university. A modern economic historian has characterized Blodget's estimates of 1805 as "a heroic one-man effort with weak statistical underpinnings." A second printing in 1810 added the results of the years 1805 to 1809 and offered "Thoughts on a Plan of Economy (Suited to the Crisis of 1808)."

As a gentleman architect Blodget drew on contemporary European neoclassicism and its ancient sources to create a dignified image for the First Bank. As an entrepreneur and economist he saw banks, insurance companies, and other financial institutions as agents of stability, development, and democracy. He eagerly embraced the industrial and consumer revolutions of the eighteenth century and foresaw the United States as a continental nation. His optimism frequently outran his prudence, for which he ultimately paid a heavy price. He died in a Baltimore hospital.

• *Economica* is a critical primary source on Blodget, as are the papers of Washington, Jefferson, and Madison and a sprinkling of Blodget papers at the Massachusetts Historical Society. On the First Bank, see James O. Wettereau, "The Oldest Bank Building in the United States," in *Historic Philadelphia: From the Founding until the Early Nineteenth Century*, American Philosophical Society *Transactions*, vol. 43, part 1 (1953). On Blodget's business affairs see Marquis James, *Biography of a Business: 1792–1942: Insurance Company of North America* (1942), and John Joseph Walsh, *Early Banks in the District of Columbia, 1792–1818* (1940). On Blodget's activities in Washington see Wilhelmus Bogart Bryan, *A History of the National Capital* (1914). For an assessment by an economic historian, see Alice Hanson Jones, *Wealth of a Nation to Be* (1980), p. 82.

KENNETH HAFERTEPE

BLODGETT, Katharine Burr (10 Jan. 1898–12 Oct. 1979), chemist and inventor, was born in Schenectady, New York, the daughter of George Bedington Blodgett, a patent attorney for the General Electric Company, and Katharine Buchanan Burr. Her father was murdered a few weeks before her birth, a crime never solved. She grew up in reasonably comfortable circumstances in New York City, where her mother worked in child care. She attended Bryn Mawr College, graduating in 1917 with an A.B. and majoring in physics. She then undertook graduate study in chemistry at the University of Chicago, obtaining the M.S. degree in 1918.

In that year, she obtained a job in the research laboratory of the General Electric Company, at the same Schenectady plant where here father had worked. The shortage of personnel due to the war helped her obtain a post as a technician and research assistant to Dr. Irving Langmuir, an unusual position for a woman in industry at that time, but not an unprecedented one (GE had hired its first woman researcher in 1904). Blodgett assisted Langmuir, a subsequent Nobel laureate (1932), in his studies of the physics, chemistry, and technology of incandescent lamps and vacuum tubes, coauthoring papers with him on the flow of electrons in the near-vacuum of those tubes. In addition, in 1919 she carried out some experiments, at his request, on the transfer of films a single molecule thick from liquid to solid surfaces, work that presaged her future major endeavor.

In 1924, at Langmuir's urging and with his recommendation, she became a graduate student at the Cavendish Laboratory of England's University of Cambridge. Two years later she graduated with the first Ph.D. degree in physics awarded to a woman by Cambridge. Her thesis described the determination of the mean free path of electrons in mercury vapor, a result important for the use of electronics for power purposes and later for the development of the fluorescent lamp.

She returned to Schenectady to resume her work with Langmuir. Over the next five years she assisted him with further electrical and electronic studies related to filaments and their interaction with gases and electrons. Her work was characterized by great experimental skill, careful measurement, and thoroughness.

Blodgett's greatest contributions to science and invention began in 1933 when Langmuir asked her to undertake a study of "monomolecular" films of oil on water—that is, films that spread out until they are only one molecule thick. In the course of that work, GE's meter department came to the research laboratory with a request for better bearings. It was conveyed to Langmuir, who asked Blodgett to compare the friction of dry shafts with those covered with monomolecular films of oil. In the course of this work, Blodgett developed for the first time methods of transferring a series of monomolecular films of oil from the surface of water to a solid surface (1934). Because the films were stacked in layers, each one molecule thick, thickness could be controlled with unprecedented accuracy. This technique opened up a field of science and technology that, under the name Langmuir-Blodgett films, has found ever-widening uses both in scientific research and in practical applications ranging from solar energy conversion to integrated circuit manufacture. Her initial paper on the topic, published in the *Journal of the American Chemical Society* in 1934, is the field's founding paper.

In that and a series of subsequent publications she showed that these films could be used as spacers or thickness gauges for thicknesses of less than one ten-millionth of a meter, a realm previously too small for such applications. The films could also be controlled in thickness to within a fraction of the typical wavelength of visible light. This suggested to her a major invention: invisible glass (1938). She pointed out that by properly adjusting the thickness and refractive index of a soap film on glass, light reflected from the underlying glass layer could be "cancelled out" by the interference of light reflected from the top of the film. She went on to develop an ingenious technique for controlling the refractive index of the film (1940). The basic patents she got on these methods are the foundation for the antireflective coatings used to cut glare due to reflection in applications ranging from optical equipment to the exhibition of artwork. The particular materials she used, principally soap films, proved too fragile for everyday use and were supplanted by more durable films invented by others but based on her principles.

She went on to pioneer a range of other uses for Langmuir-Blodgett films, such as "indicator" oil for controlling the thickness of films and the first controlled-thickness X-ray grating. This work continued until 1941, when she shifted her attention to problems related to national defense. She worked on preventing icing of aircraft wings and generating improved types of smoke screens. With Langmuir, Vincent Schaefer, and others, she then participated in pioneering research on cloud physics (1944). Her use of a large analog computer to study the trajectory of fine particles in the vicinity of fibers was one of the first computer simulations in the field of environmental science, and it led to the development of a highly efficient aerosol filter.

Blodgett's achievements were recognized with such awards as the American Chemical Society's Garvan Medal (1951) and the Photographic Society of America's Progress Medal (1972). She never married and lived out her entire life in Schenectady, New York. A colleague described her as "a modest, unassuming person, small of stature, but with a quick wit and a twinkling eye." Her hobbies included gardening, amateur astronomy, and antique collecting. Her contribution to science stemmed from the simplicity and elegance of her experimental work. That work opened up a major field of study, Langmuir-Blodgett films, and provided an armory of tools and techniques to explore those films' fascinating properties and many useful applications.

• No biography of Katharine Blodgett exists. Her laboratory notebooks and a small collection of material about her are at the General Electric Research and Development Center, Schenectady, N.Y. The biographical sketches that best capture her career and its significance are in *Current Biography* (1952), pp. 55–57, and George Gaines, Jr., "In Memoriam: Katharine Burr Blodgett, 1898–1979," *Thin Solid Films* 4 (1980): vii.

GEORGE WISE

BLOEDE, Gertrude (10 Aug. 1845–14 Aug. 1905), poet, was born in Dresden, Germany, the daughter of Dr. Gustavus Bloede, a German Liberal, and Marie Jungnitz, an author of poems in English and German and half-sister of the Silesian poet Friedrich von Sallet. Gustavus Bloede, after imprisonment in Dresden during the revolution of 1848, escaped with his family to the United States, and they settled in Brooklyn, New York. Gertrude was privately educated and demonstrated natural abilities in music and language, speaking French and German fluently and reading Latin, Italian, and Dutch.

Literary gatherings at the Bloede home were frequented by such literary figures as Richard Henry Stoddard, E. C. Stedman, Thomas Aldrich, and Bayard Taylor. One of their pastimes was improvising brilliant imitations of one another's works, which gave rise to Taylor's "Echo Club." These associations provided Gertrude Bloede with a stimulus to try her hand at writing, and in her twenties she began publishing poetry in periodicals under the pseudonym of Stuart Sterne. She used this pen name in all of her published works, claiming as the reason that men's work was considered stronger than women's, and she wished her work to stand or fall on its own merits.

Bloede's collection titled *Poems*, published in 1875, was favorably reviewed in the *New York Times* (10 Jan. 1875) by Richard Grant White, who said of her, "We do not say a great poet, but certainly one of peculiar powers." He also praised the form of her expressions of sorrow over an unrequited love. In gratitude she dedicated to him the manuscript of *Angelo* (a long poem concerning the friendship of Michaelangelo and Vittoria Colonna), and he persuaded a prominent Boston house, Houghton-Mifflin, to publish it. *Angelo* was quite successful, going through sixteen editions from its first appearance in 1878 to 1896. A review in the *Nation* (10 Jan. 1878, p. 18) stated, "The action goes on resolutely to its climax. . . . The most graceful special passages grow directly out of the main narrative. . . . This writer has certainly given evidence of real poetic power."

Subsequent works were *Giorgio* (1881), a long poem about the painter Giorgione and his unhappy love; *Beyond the Shadow and Other Poems* (1888); *Piero da Castiglione* (1890), a story in verse of the struggle between love and vocation during the time of Savonarola; and *The Story of Two Lives* (1891), a novel written chiefly in the form of a journal.

Bloede summed up her work and personality thus: "There is very little to tell. I have published five volumes of poems, and that is all. I live very quietly. I go into society but little, and I do not belong to anything" (*American Women*, p. 98). She enjoyed the companionship of only a few intimate friends who were, like her, interested in intellectual pursuits. Bloede felt that in the city, where she had lived all her life, she could find greater seclusion than in a rural area, and she steadfastly refused to join any women's organizations in Brooklyn, feeling that the work of societies from which men were excluded amounted to little.

From such a secluded life, it is difficult to learn much about the person, other than what may be revealed through the poetry. It is evident from *Poems* that Bloede had experienced an unhappy love relationship; indeed the poems that touch on her personal feelings and sorrows are among the most successful of the short poems. Other poems, especially the longer ones that deal with religious or historical themes, although quite dramatic, seem more conventional in language and phrasing. Contemporary critics found her work full of passion and feeling, with a dramatic instinct, but to the modern eye the old-fashioned language and conventional subject matter of most of the poems have not stood the test of time. Although she enjoyed some popularity in her day, particularly with *Angelo*, her works are not reprinted or readily available today.

Never having married, Bloede lived with her sister in Brooklyn from 1861 until her death while on a summer visit to Baldwin, Long Island.

• Little biographical information is available on Gertrude Bloede other than standard reference sources. An additional source is *American Women: Fifteen Hundred Biographies with Over 1,400 Portraits* (1897). An obituary is in the *Brooklyn Daily Eagle*, 16 Aug. 1905.

ANN PERKINS

BLONDELL, Joan (30 Aug. 1909–25 Dec. 1979), actress, was born Rose Joan Blondell in New York City, the daughter of vaudevillians Eddie Blondell, one of the original Katzenjammer Kids, and Kathryn Cain.

Blondell made her first stage appearance as a "carry-on" in *The Greatest Love* at the age of four months; later, with her parents, brother, and sister, she toured the vaudeville circuit, performing in the United States, Europe, Australia, and China. Her family appearances ended when, at seventeen, she joined a dramatic stock company in Dallas, where she won a Miss Dallas beauty contest.

Blondell went to New York and in 1927 made her Broadway debut in a small part in *The Trial of Mary Dugan*. In 1929 she appeared opposite the yet-unknown James Cagney in the musical *Penny Arcade*. The following year, when Warner Brothers purchased the play and remade it as the movie *Sinner's Holiday* with starring roles for both young actors, Blondell started a productive association with the studio. Frequently teamed with Cagney and with Dick Powell, she appeared in fifty films from 1930 to 1938, making as many as ten pictures a year.

Blondell generally portrayed a feisty, wisecracking blonde with a well-honed knack at looking out for herself, an ability impressively demonstrated in such gangster films as *Blonde Crazy*, in which she beat a group of con artists at their own game, and *Blondie Johnson*, in which she formed her own extortion gang.

Well qualified by her song-and-dance background, she also appeared in many musicals, such as *Footlight Parade* and *Dames*, produced by Warner Brothers. These musicals, which provided a lavish respite from the nation's drab economic reality, also created a new type of heroine: the gold digger, who, using a combination of charm and shrewdness, excelled in the art of survival at the expense of the men she encountered. Blondell performed superbly in such roles. Typically, in *Gold Diggers of 1933*, as a resourceful chorine, she used a clever impersonation of a friend to drain money from a wealthy snob. Even while engaging in sometimes shady acts, however, the Blondell gold digger conveyed the impression that her brassy exterior camouflaged a warmth of heart.

Blondell's films won consistent audience approval; yet she remained a supporting player at Warners, which was reputedly biased in favor of its male stars. In 1939, dissatisfied with her status, she left the studio to free-lance, and within a short time she costarred with Bing Crosby in the Universal film *East Side of Heaven* and with Dick Powell in the comedy *Model Wife*.

In 1943 Blondell ended her lengthy absence from the Broadway stage to appear in the Mike Todd production of Gypsy Rose Lee's comedy *The Naked Genius*. When the play concluded its short run and Blondell returned to Hollywood, her career appeared to be in decline, for the breezy types she personified had dropped in box office appeal. By contrast with her earlier prolific output, she made only thirteen films during the 1940s. With fewer roles, however, came a form of compensation. No longer the model pert young chorus girl, she now appeared in films that enabled her to demonstrate her ability as a character actress in such parts as a hardened carnival queen in *Nightmare Alley*, a burlesque performer turned nurse in *Cry Havoc*, and the incomparable Aunt Cissy in *A Tree Grows in Brooklyn*.

Blondell left Hollywood again in 1948 for another return to the stage and the start of her three-year marriage to Mike Todd. This marriage followed two unsuccessful ones in Hollywood. The first, in 1933 to cameraman George S. Barnes, by whom she had a son, ended in divorce in 1936; the second, in 1936 to Dick Powell, by whom she had a daughter, ended in divorce in 1944.

When she divorced Todd, Blondell again went to Hollywood where her appearance as a fading vaudeville star in *The Blue Veil* earned her an Academy Award nomination in 1951 for best supporting actress. For the remainder of her career, she continued in supporting roles as a character actress: among others, a cynical Girl Friday in *Will Success Spoil Rock Hunter?*; Eleanor Parker's drunken aunt in *Lizzie*; and a wealthy racehorse owner in *The Champ* in 1979. On television, she starred in the series "Here Come the Brides," had feature roles in network movies, and often appeared in the 1970s' series "Banyon."

During her later career, she wrote *Center Door Fancy* (1972), a novel in which the fortunes of the heroine Nora mirrored Blondell's own rise from vaudeville performer to Hollywood celebrity. She died in Santa Monica, California.

• Clippings on Blondell can be found in the New York Public Library for the Performing Arts. See also Robyn Karney, *The Movie Stars' Story* (1984); Marjorie Rosen, *Popcorn Venus* (1973); Karyn Kay and Gerald Peary, *Women and the Cinema* (1977); Thomas W. Bohn and Richard Stromgren, *Light and Shadows* (1975); Ephraim Katz, *The Film Encyclopedia* (1979). An obituary is in the *New York Times*, 26 Dec. 1979.

DOROTHY KISH

BLOOD, Ernest Artel (4 Oct. 1872–5 Feb. 1955), athlete and basketball coach, nicknamed "Prof," was born in Manchester, New Hampshire, the son of farmers. Blood spent most of his youth in New Hampshire and Massachusetts but did not attend college. An all-around athlete, he excelled in basketball, football, baseball, fencing, gymnastics, and tumbling. Short of stature but muscularly developed, he could throw a sixteen-pound shot put into the air and then catch it on the nape of his neck.

Blood learned about basketball during the early 1890s and began coaching the sport in 1895 at the Nashua, New Hampshire, Young Men's Christian Association (YMCA). Subsequently, he coached at YMCAs in Somerville and Springfield, Massachusetts; Rutland and St. Johnsbury, Vermont; Pawtucket, Rhode Island; and Brooklyn, as well as the Young Men's Hebrew Association (YMHA) in Passaic, New Jersey. In 1906 Blood began coaching at the high school level in Potsdam, New York, where he produced several championship teams at the Potsdam Normal and Training High School and Clarkson Technical School.

In 1915 Blood became a physical education instructor at Passaic High School and became the school's basketball coach in 1918. He is known best for his teams at Passaic, which won 188 games and lost just one. The renowned "Wonder Five" teams, as they were called, won 159 consecutive games from 1919 to 1925, a feat unmatched at the time on any level. Blood resigned after the 1924 season in a dispute with the local board of education, which had charged him with placing too much emphasis on winning. At the time he departed, the streak had reached 147 games, and Blood's teams had won four state championships. His only loss at Passaic came in the state championship finals in 1919.

Blood emphasized offensive play; his formula for success consisted of developing: (1) well-conditioned athletes, (2) a short passing game, and (3) a "feeder system" from the city's twelve grammar schools that he nurtured on his weekly visits to each school for the pupils' exercise sessions. He encouraged the more athletic students to take up basketball. His "Wonder Teams" scored more than 100 points on 12 occasions and held their opponents to less than 20 points 74 times. During their 159-game winning streak, the "Wonder Five" teams scored 9,413 points to their opponents 3,237. The 1921–1922 team, which Blood considered his best, won all thirty-three games by an average score of 69 to 19.

Blood's trademark was his pet bear, Zep, which he rescued as a cub on a hunting trip and raised in his cellar. He would often wrestle it at public functions for entertainment, but it was known more as the mascot of the "Wonder Five" teams as it occupied a place on the bench next to the players.

After leaving Passaic, Blood coached briefly at the U.S. Military Academy at West Point before accepting the head basketball post at St. Benedict's Preparatory School in Newark in 1926. He coached at the parochial school until 1949, and his teams there won 421 out of 549 games along with nine prep school titles and two state championships.

In a coaching career spanning fifty-two years, Blood compiled a 1,268–165 record. Upon his retirement from St. Benedict's the mayor of Passaic gave Blood a key to the city and named him honorary mayor. An editorial in the *Passaic-Clifton Herald-News* regarded "Prof" Blood as "the best publicity man the City of Passaic ever had . . . No one before or since brought the city as much fame as this positive little man whose basketball genius produced the Passaic High School Wonder Teams." He was elected to the Basketball Hall of Fame in Springfield, Massachusetts, in 1960. His "Wonder Teams," inducted in 1974, are the only high school basketball teams in the Hall of Fame.

In 1899 or 1900 Blood married Margaret Thomas of England and had three children. His first wife died in 1948, and he married Myrtle Dilley the following year. He spent the remainder of his life in New Smyrna Beach, Florida, where he died.

Blood was one of the early geniuses of basketball. He understood the rules well and knew the value of height. He capitalized on both by recruiting tall players for his teams and whipping them into shape. In Blood's day, there was a center jump after each basket or foul shot. He taught his teams to gain possession with each jump, pass the ball quickly down court, and shoot the ball from close range before their opponents could set up their defense. In this manner Blood's teams outscored the opposition, most of the time by large margins. Eventually, however, the elimination of the center jump and fast-break basketball led to the downfall of his system. Of his many contributions, his most lasting was that of popularizing basketball on the high school level.

• Information on Blood is rather scarce, most having come from local newspapers following his retirement and death. A file on Blood is in the Basketball Hall of Fame, Springfield, Mass. The best source is the *Passaic-Clifton Herald-News*, in the issues of 30 Sept. 1949, 27 Jan. 1950, 7 Feb. 1955, and 8 Feb. 1955. See also the *Newark Star-Ledger*, 7 Feb. 1955. Obituaries are in the *Passaic-Clifton Herald-News*, 7 Feb. 1955, and the *Newark Star-Ledger*, 6 Feb. 1955.

J. THOMAS JABLE

BLOOD, Johnny. *See* McNally, Johnny Blood.

BLOODWORTH, Timothy (1736–24 Aug. 1814), Antifederalist politician, was born in New Hanover County, North Carolina, probably the son of Timothy Bloodworth from Virginia. Two of his brothers, James Bloodworth and Thomas Bloodworth, also were active in state politics. Although Bloodworth lacked formal education, he became a veritable jack-of-all-trades, reportedly working in a variety of occupations, including ordinary keeper, mechanic, preacher, cobbler, wheelwright, ferryman, blacksmith, farmer, teacher, and politician. He was successful in his various enterprises, accumulating over 4,000 acres of land and nine slaves by 1790. His home was located near the present town of Burgaw in Pender County, North Carolina. He married Priscilla (maiden name unknown); they had two children.

In an age when an aristocratic background was assumed for anyone contemplating politics, few of the artisan or working class would rise as Bloodworth did to the U.S. Senate. Bloodworth was characterized by historian Archibald Henderson as a "natural leader and generous-hearted radical" who became the "prototype of the modern political boss" in his leadership of the mechanics and farmers of the Wilmington area. A strong advocate of a common people's democracy throughout the revolutionary and early national periods, he was described by late nineteenth-century historian John H. Wheeler as "intensely radical, almost a red Republican."

Beginning his public life in county politics, in 1775 Bloodworth was an organizer of the New Hanover County and Wilmington Committees of Safety and two years later served as a justice on the county court under the state government. In 1776 he manufactured arms for the Continental army. First elected to the North Carolina General Assembly in 1778, over the next two decades he served ten terms in the House of Commons and one in the state senate. In the session of 1794–1795 he was Speaker of the state house. While treasurer of the Wilmington District in 1780–1783, he vainly sought to protect government stores from destruction by the British. A local tradition credits Bloodworth with designing and using a long-range sniper's rifle during the British occupation of Wilmington. As commissioner of confiscated property for this district he earned a reputation as a relentless persecutor of Loyalists. As early as 1784 he was elected to the Continental Congress but did not serve until 1786. He resigned from Congress in 1787 to oppose the ratification of the federal Constitution, which he believed would establish an "autocratic tyranny or monarchical monarchy" and entrench aristocratic domination of the Republic. A delegate to both state conventions, he soon became one of the leading Antifederalists.

After the Constitution was ratified in November 1789 in Fayetteville, Bloodworth ran for the U.S. Congress, winning a seat in the House of Representatives in the First Congress (1790–1791). As colonel of the county militia he refused to enforce the Federalist-sponsored neutrality proclamation of 1793, believing that the government had sold out its revolutionary ally France in favor of England. Although he had unsuccessfully run in 1789 for the U.S. Senate, he won in 1795, serving an undistinguished term until 1801. After leaving the Senate he was appointed by President Thomas Jefferson as collector of customs for the port of Wilmington. Bloodworth was not an efficient customs officer. When he resigned in 1807 he left an arrears that was still $22,500 at the time of his death in Washington, North Carolina.

• The official papers of Bloodworth are in William L. Saunders, ed., *The Colonial Records of North Carolina*, vols. 9–10 (1890), and Walter J. Clark, ed., *The State Records of North Carolina*, vols. 12–24 (1896–1907). Other sources are Mattie Bloodworth, *History of Pender County, North Carolina* (1947); D. H. Gilpatrick, *Jeffersonian Democracy in North Carolina, 1789–1816* (1931); John H. Wheeler, *Reminiscences and Memoirs of North Carolina and Eminent North Carolinians* (1884); and Archibald Henderson, *North Carolina: The Old North State and the New*, vol. 1 (1941).

LINDLEY S. BUTLER

BLOOM, Allan (14 Sept. 1930–7 Oct. 1992), philosopher, was born Allan David Bloom in Indianapolis, Indiana, the son of Allan Bloom and Malvina Glasner, social workers. The elder Blooms, descendants of German Jewish immigrants, had a strong interest in social and political issues, and their son was brought up in an atmosphere of intellectual ferment. The rise and eventual downfall of Adolf Hitler's Germany occurred during Bloom's childhood, and these events also made a strong impression on him.

Bloom attended local public schools in Indianapolis, then enrolled at the University of Chicago in 1946, shortly after his parents moved to that city, in a program that admitted gifted students in their junior year of high school. The liberal arts curriculum was based on the so-called Great Books, classics of Western literature. At its core was a belief in the existence of universal truths and values that pointed toward a unity in life. As he plunged into the required readings, beginning with the works of Sigmund Freud, Karl Marx, and Max Weber, the sixteen-year-old Bloom realized that he had come to the right place. Years later he wrote of his first weeks at the university that "I somehow sensed that I had discovered my life." After reading Plato's *Republic* that fall, Bloom knew that he wanted to become a philosopher.

Bloom completed the undergraduate program in three years, receiving a B.A. in 1949. He then began graduate work in a division of the university called the Committee on Social Thought, which limited enrollment to a handful of the most talented students and offered seminars that ranged over disciplines in the social sciences and humanities. Bloom was most influenced in this program by one of his tutors, the German political philosopher Leo Strauss. Under Strauss's tutelage Bloom had what he later described as a "transforming" experience, in which he came to believe in what he called "transcultural truth"—the notion that certain truths remain absolute throughout history despite cultural and social change.

After receiving an M.A. from the university in 1953, Bloom attended the University of Paris as a University of Chicago exchange fellow and completed requirements for the Ph.D., which he was awarded in 1955. That fall he joined the faculty of the University of Chicago's undergraduate college as a lecturer in liberal arts. During the 1957–1958 academic year he was also a Rockefeller Fellow in Legal and Political Philosophy at the university. His first book, a translation of Rousseau's *Politics and the Arts: Letter to M. D'Alembert*, was published in 1960.

In 1962 Bloom moved to the political science faculty at Yale University, where he taught for one year, then became an assistant professor of government at Cornell University; he was promoted to associate professor and given tenure following the publication in 1964 of his second book, *Shakespeare's Politics*, a collection of essays coauthored with Harry V. Jaffa. In his introductory essay, Bloom wrote that the book was intended as a step toward "making Shakespeare again the theme of philosophic reflection and a recognized source for the serious study of moral and political problems." Bloom's third book, a translation of Plato's *Republic*, was published in 1968.

In the late 1960s, as student unrest swept many American universities, Bloom became increasingly disheartened with academic life in the United States. His concern reached a climax in 1969, when a group of armed students took over the main administration building at Cornell and forced officials to accede to their demands for curriculum changes. Disturbed by this and similar events at other campuses, which he likened to Nazi invasions of German universities in the 1930s, Bloom spent the academic year of 1969–1970 abroad, teaching first at the University of Tel Aviv and then at the University of Paris. He resigned from the

Cornell faculty in 1970 and that fall became a professor of political science at the University of Toronto.

In 1972 Bloom suffered a heart attack, and during his months of recuperation he worked on a translation of Rousseau's *Émile*, which was published some years later (1979). In the fall of 1979 he left Toronto and returned to the University of Chicago, joining the Committee on Social Thought as a professor. Over the next few years Bloom became increasingly concerned with what he considered the decline of higher education in the United States, a topic he had addressed in several essays published during the 1970s. Bloom located one cause of that decline in the ever-widening split between the sciences and the humanities, and he also decried the politicization of universities in response to student demands for "relevance"; universities, he believed, had relinquished their historical task of teaching students the philosophical basis for dealing with life's fundamental questions, and he called for the readoption of a curriculum based on the Great Books.

In December 1982 Bloom published his strongest attack to date on the universities in an issue of a conservative weekly, the *National Review*, charging that they seemed powerless to deal with the nihilistic views of their students, who believed that all ideas and values had equal worth. The article attracted wide attention and led Bloom to expand his ideas into a book, an effort that was encouraged by his friend Saul Bellow, the Nobel Prize–winning novelist who also taught at the University of Chicago. The result was *The Closing of the American Mind: How Higher Education Has Failed Democracy and Impoverished the Souls of Today's Students*, published in the spring of 1987. The book received enthusiastic reviews in many influential popular magazines and newspapers, including the *New York Times*, which declared in its weekly *Book Review* that it was "essential reading for anyone concerned with the state of liberal education in this country." By June it had reached the top spot on the *New York Times* nonfiction bestseller list, where it remained for ten weeks; it eventually sold more than 1 million copies.

Perhaps not surprisingly, reviewers in academic publications were less enthusiastic about Bloom's book, accusing him of writing from a politically conservative bias and of being insensitive to the needs of black and other minority students. In responding to these critics, Bloom maintained that his book was "firmly in the 'liberal tradition,'" and that instead of defending a conservative point of view, as they charged, he was offering an "accurate description of American life."

Bloom's *Giants and Dwarfs*, a collection of his essays written over the prior three decades, was published in 1990. His last book, *Love and Friendship*, published in 1991, explores different notions of love expressed in literary classics, including the works of Shakespeare and Plato's *Symposium*.

From 1981 until his death Bloom was an adjunct scholar at the American Enterprise Institute in Washington, D.C. He also served as editor of Agora Editions and Agora Paperbacks, published by Cornell University Press. In 1987 he received the Prix Jean-Jacques Rousseau from the city of Geneva in recognition of his scholarly work on the philosopher. At his death he was professor of political philosophy and co-director of the John M. Olin Center for Inquiry into the Theory and Practice of Democracy at the University of Chicago.

A lifelong bachelor, Bloom was a heavy smoker for many years; for relaxation he enjoyed listening to classical music from an extensive personal collection of compact discs. He died in Chicago several weeks after being hospitalized for a bleeding ulcer; his death was attributed to liver failure.

• Biographical information on Allan Bloom can be found in *Current Biography Yearbook 1988*; the *New York Times Magazine*, 3 Jan. 1988; the *Washington Post*, 18 June 1987; and *Publishers Weekly*, 3 July 1987. Bloom also includes autobiographical information in *The Closing of the American Mind*. An obituary is in the *New York Times*, 8 Oct. 1992.

ANN T. KEENE

BLOOMER, Amelia Jenks (27 May 1818–30 Dec. 1894), temperance and women's rights reformer and editor, was born in Homer, New Jersey, the daughter of Ananias Jenks, a clothier, and Lucy Webb. She received a basic education in Homer's district schools and by the age of seventeen was teaching in Clyde, New York. After a year of teaching, Bloomer became a governess and tutor for a Waterloo, New York, family.

In 1840 she married Dexter C. Bloomer, a newspaper editor and attorney. The couple resided in Seneca Falls, New York, where he edited the *Seneca County Courier*. With her husband's encouragement, Amelia Bloomer began to write anonymous reform-minded articles for local papers, including the *Courier*, the *Water Bucket*, a temperance paper, and the *Free Soil Union*.

Bloomer's early reform interest was confined primarily to the temperance movement, but she had long believed in the equality of women and men, striking the promise to obey from her marriage vows and attending the 1848 women's rights convention in Seneca Falls. Like many women involved in the temperance movement, Bloomer was inspired by new opportunities to express her opinions and to advocate change but was frustrated by the limitations placed on these opportunities by male-dominated temperance groups. Desiring to provide a greater voice for the women's temperance movement, in 1849 she founded the *Lily*, a monthly journal. In the *Lily*'s first issue, she wrote: "It is *woman* that speaks through the *Lily*. It is upon an important subject, too, that she comes before the public to be heard. Intemperance is the great foe to her peace and happiness. . . . Surely she has a right to wield the pen for its suppression. . . . It is this which she proposes to do in the columns of the *Lily*" (1 Jan. 1849). Bloomer coupled her work on the *Lily* with her duties as deputy to her husband, who was postmaster of Seneca Falls.

The *Lily* soon began to include articles on woman suffrage, property rights, education, employment, and dress reform. Bloomer wrote many of the journal's articles, but she also received contributions from other women, including Elizabeth Cady Stanton. Although she gradually joined Stanton as an advocate of woman suffrage, Bloomer took a relatively moderate view of the issue, maintaining that the burden for achieving their rights fell upon women. She wrote in the *Lily* in 1853: "We think it all important that woman obtain the right of suffrage; but . . . she must gradually prepare the way for such a step, by showing that she is worthy of receiving, and capable of rightly exercising it. If she do this, prejudice will fast give way, and she gain her cause."

In 1851 Bloomer adopted the style of dress with which her name became linked. She was neither the originator nor the most vigorous advocate of the "Bloomer Costume," a short skirt and full Turkish trousers, but she did promote the new outfit in the *Lily* as a healthy, comfortable, and sanitary garment for women. Bloomer became identified with the costume when her articles received attention in the *New York Tribune* and other papers, making her a national celebrity and increasing the *Lily*'s circulation eightfold.

Bloomer remained adamant that temperance reform must not be slighted in favor of suffrage advocacy and that the fight for a sober home and society was a woman's special calling. In 1853 she was elected corresponding secretary of the New York Woman's Temperance Society, after having argued successfully against a proposal by Stanton, Susan B. Anthony, and others that the society be opened to men. Bloomer also had an active career as a temperance and women's rights lecturer. With other prominent women reformers, she spoke before audiences throughout New York State in 1853. Later that year she lectured on women's rights in several midwestern cities. Although Bloomer's "costume" attracted large crowds to her lectures, she returned to more conventional dress after several years, hoping to focus attention on her reform ideas rather than on her appearance.

In December 1853 Bloomer moved to Mount Vernon, Ohio, where her husband became part-owner of the reform-oriented *Western Home Visitor*. She became assistant editor of the paper, using its pages to advocate reform but retaining her strongest opinions for the *Lily*. Circulation of the *Lily*, now a four-page semimonthly rather than an eight-page monthly, continued to grow, reaching 6,000 during Bloomer's years in Ohio. The Bloomers' 1855 move to Council Bluffs, Iowa, ended her association with the *Lily*. Unable to print or distribute her paper from the frontier town, Bloomer sold it to Mary B. Birdsall of Indiana. Bloomer remained corresponding editor of the *Lily* until January 1856, but the paper did not thrive under Birdsall and ceased publication in December of that year. Bloomer remained active in temperance and suffrage reform in Council Bluffs. In 1856 she helped found a local lodge of the Good Templars, a temperance group to which she had belonged for many years. After 1874 she remained active in the Women's Christian Temperance Union. As a lecturer and frequent contributor to newspapers and reform publications, she lobbied for strict prohibition laws.

By 1870 Bloomer had begun to work particularly vigorously for woman suffrage, now believing it an essential prerequisite to temperance reform. She was the first vice president of the Iowa Woman Suffrage Society in 1870 and became the society's president in 1871. She was a key advocate of an 1873 Iowa law granting married women property rights nearly equivalent to those enjoyed by their husbands. Bloomer retained her ties to national suffrage leaders, representing Iowa to the American Equal Rights Association's 1869 meeting in New York City and contributing a chapter on the state to Stanton's *History of Woman Suffrage* (6 vols., 1881–1922).

Shortly after moving to Council Bluffs, the Bloomers adopted two children. They had no other children. After the early 1870s Bloomer reduced her public activities, although she retained her reform sentiments throughout her life. She died in Council Bluffs.

• Bloomer's files on the *Lily* are held by the New York State Library. Other papers relating to her life and career are held by the Seneca Falls Historical Society and the Council Bluffs Free Public Library. The Sophia Smith Collection at Smith College contains a complete microfilm run of the *Lily*. Dexter C. Bloomer, *Life and Writings of Amelia Bloomer* (1895), is the most complete source on Bloomer's life and contains excerpts from her columns, lectures, and other writings. *Hear Me Patiently: The Reform Speeches of Amelia Jenks Bloomer*, ed. Anne C. Coon (1994), contains many of Bloomer's temperance and women's rights speeches. Margaret Farrand Thorp, *Female Persuasion* (1949), and Paul Fatout, "Amelia Bloomer and Bloomerism," *New York Historical Society Quarterly* 36 (Oct. 1952): 360–74, are also valuable. Linda Steiner, "Finding Community in Nineteenth Century Suffrage Periodicals," *American Journalism* 1 (Summer 1983): 1–16, examines the *Lily* in the context of similar periodicals. An obituary is in the *Iowa State Register*, 1 Jan. 1895.

KATHLEEN FEENEY

BLOOMFIELD, Joseph (18 Oct. 1753–8 Oct. 1823), lawyer, soldier, and politician, was born in Woodbridge, New Jersey, the son of Moses Bloomfield, a physician, and Sarah Ogden. The family was one of the most prominent in colonial New Jersey. His father had received a first-rate medical education in Edinburgh, Scotland, and had a thriving practice in Middlesex County by the time Joseph was born. Joseph's mother was a member of a wealthy and influential family of Elizabethtown, which further assured Joseph's upper-class pedigree. His education and choice of occupation were in line with his social standing. While in his early teens, he attended the Reverend Enoch Green's classical academy in Deerfield, Cumberland County, at the opposite end of the province from Woodbridge. Upon graduation, Bloomfield returned to East Jersey, determined to be a lawyer. He entered the profession at the top, studying in Perth Amboy with Cortlandt Skinner, attorney general of New Jersey, and was admitted to the bar in November

1774. Setting up practice in Bridgeton, Cumberland County, he soon became known and respected in all of New Jersey's southern counties. The future seemed secure, had not the American Revolution intervened.

Although many of Bloomfield's social class remained loyal to the Crown, Bloomfield took the patriotic side. However, the decision was not a rebellion against his family and friends. His father was an equally staunch patriot who served in the New Jersey Provincial Congress in 1776 and spent time as a surgeon in the Continental army. Like many 23-year-old men, Joseph Bloomfield was not content to sit on the sidelines when there was a chance for action, and on 8 February 1776 he was commissioned a captain in the Third New Jersey Regiment. His active service lasted until the autumn of 1778. The regiment was stationed in New York's Mohawk Valley as part of the American effort to keep the Iroquois Indians from aiding the British and then in the Philadelphia area, where it participated in the battles of Brandywine Creek and Monmouth.

For a number of reasons Bloomfield's fighting days were over in 1778. First, he was wounded at Brandywine and had not healed properly. In addition, after Monmouth, New Jersey, ceased to be the "cockpit of the Revolution," and the theater of operations was transferred south. Social stability was returning to the Garden State, providing an encouraging field for a young lawyer of energy and ambition. Finally, in 1778 he married Mary Polly McIlvaine. The couple had no children and lived in Burlington.

From the late 1770s to the late 1790s Bloomfield flourished as a lawyer, businessman, and rising politician, and by the time he approached fifty he was among the most prominent men in the state. In 1797 a Presbyterian parish in Newark, on seceding from its parent parish, named itself "Bloomfield," passing over "Jefferson" and "Randolph." Bloomfield was considered worthy because of "the benevolence of his character, his kindness, and his disposition, as the soldier's friend," according to testimony given at the first meeting of the parish council. In 1812 the parish was incorporated as a township and has continued to bear the name Bloomfield.

In the political context of the 1790s, a man of Bloomfield's social and military background was propelled to the Federalist party. Why then did this natural-born aristocrat emerge by 1800 as a leader of the New Jersey Republicans? No answers are clear, but historians have worked on several possibilities. Apparently Bloomfield's early Federalism was based on admiration for George Washington. The more pro-English the party became, especially after the Jay Treaty of 1795, the less enamored Bloomfield became. Presumably, memories of British destruction of the family home and harsh treatment of his father during the fighting in 1776 got in the way of party loyalty. He was on the sidelines in the presidential election of 1796 and formally declared himself a Republican the next year.

The elections of 1800, state and national, swept the Federalists out of power. The Republican-controlled legislature, acting on its constitutional authority to elect the governor, chose Bloomfield for a one-year term. He was reelected through 1811 except for 1802, when the party was deadlocked. On paper, the New Jersey constitution gave the legislature enormous appointive power and reduced the governor to a figurehead, but Bloomfield, like William Livingston before him, influenced legislative action by virtue of party leadership and personality. Thus, stock dividends of state banks were taxed, arms were twisted in the legislative Republican caucus, and President Thomas Jefferson was cajoled into steering a goodly amount of federal patronage New Jersey's way. Most importantly, the governor directed the legislature toward the 1804 act providing for the gradual abolition of slavery. The greatest test of Bloomfield's leadership came when the New Jersey Republicans almost split over U.S. trade policies with England in the years before the war of 1812. His persuasiveness was largely responsible for the party unity.

After war was declared, President James Madison recalled a number of revolutionary veterans to service, and Governor Bloomfield became a brigadier general. Now fifty-nine years old, he had lost much of his youthful energy. He and his troops waited in Plattsburgh, New York, for an invasion of Canada that never came. When the war ended, he was desk bound in Philadelphia, the major commands having been given to younger men. Bloomfield's active military service ended in 1815, but his political career had a final act. As the elder statesman of New Jersey Republicanism, he served two terms, 1817–1821, in Congress, where his major contribution was to urge legislation providing that benefits for revolutionary war veterans should be based on financial need rather than physical disability alone.

Bloomfield's first wife died in 1818. In 1820 he married Isabella Macomb; they had no children. His last years were devoted to speculation in western lands. While he was inspecting his holdings around Cincinnati, Ohio, his carriage overturned, mortally wounding him. The then-standard medical remedy of bleeding did not work, and he died at his house in Burlington.

Bloomfield was a gentleman in two senses. First, in the social class sense, his adherence to the American Revolution and Jeffersonian Democracy was motivated in large part by noblesse oblige. Like the other leaders of his generation, he felt it was the duty of those who were privileged in birth, education, and wealth to serve the community and be benevolent guides to the less fortunate. He was a gentleman in the broader sense as well, fair in his dealings, loved and respected by those who knew he was worthy of their trust.

• Various collections of documents contain material on Bloomfield, notably the New Jersey Historical Society's holdings of the papers of Bloomfield, Elias Dayton, and Jonathan Dayton and the Ely collection. Other Bloomfield letters are in the Gratz collection, Governors of State, Historical Society of Pennsylvania in Philadelphia; Special Collections, Rutgers University Library; and the Thomas Jefferson Papers, Manuscript Division, Library of Congress. John P.

Butler, *Index: The Papers of the Continental Congress, 1774–1789* (5 vols., 1978), is useful for locating Bloomfield correspondence with that body. The most detailed account of Bloomfield's life is "Gentleman-Republican," in *Citizen Soldier: The Revolutionary War Journal of Joseph Bloomfield*, ed. Mark Lender and James Kirby Martin (1982). Carl E. Prince, "Joseph Bloomfield," in *The Governors of New Jersey, 1664–1974: Biographical Essays*, ed. Paul A. Stellhorn and Michael J. Birkner (1982), should also be consulted, as should William Nelson, *New Jersey Biographical and Genealogical Notes . . .* , Collections of the New Jersey Historical Society, vol. 9 (1916). Lucius Q. C. Elmer, *The Constitution and Government of the Province and State of New Jersey . . .* , Collections of the New Jersey Historical Society, vol. 7 (1872), is useful. Studies that place Bloomfield's activities in their overall setting are Larry Gerlach, *Prologue to Independence: New Jersey in the Coming of the American Revolution* (1976); Lender, *The New Jersey Soldier*, New Jersey's Revolutionary Experience, no. 5 (1975); Richard P. McCormick, *Experiment in Independence: New Jersey in the Critical Period, 1781–1789* (1950); Rudolph J. Pasler and Margaret C. Pasler, *The New Jersey Federalists* (1975); and Prince, *New Jersey's Jeffersonian Republicans: The Genesis of an Early Party Machine, 1789–1817* (1967).

HERMANN K. PLATT

BLOOMFIELD, Leonard (1 Apr. 1887–18 Apr. 1949), linguist, was born in Chicago, the son of Sigmund Bloomfield and Carola Buber, who ran a resort hotel in Elkhart Lake, Wisconsin.

Bloomfield received an A.B. from Harvard College in 1906. He began his graduate studies at the University of Wisconsin, where he also served as assistant in German, a language he spoke natively. Deciding to pursue a career in linguistics, he transferred to the University of Chicago, which awarded him a Ph.D. in 1909 for a dissertation on "A Semasiologic Differentiation in Germanic Secondary Ablaut." Also in 1909 Bloomfield married Alice Sayers. They had no children of their own but adopted two boys.

After serving as instructor in German at the University of Cincinnati (1909–1910) and the University of Illinois (1910–1913), he took leave to pursue advanced linguistic studies at the universities of Leipzig and Göttingen (1913–1914). During these years in Germany, he was able to study with some of the most prominent linguists in the world, including Karl Brugmann, one of the founders of Indo-European comparative linguistics, and August Leskien. He later acknowledged particularly the influence of the Indologist Jacob Wackernagel of the University of Basel in the area of descriptive methodology, as well as of the highly analytical grammar of Sanskrit by the ancient Hindu grammarian Pānini.

Bloomfield's academic posts after returning from his leave were: assistant professor of comparative philology and German, University of Illinois (1914–1921); professor of German and linguistics, Ohio State University (1921–1927); professor of Germanic philology, University of Chicago (1927–1940); Sterling Professor of Linguistics, Yale University (1940–1949).

Bloomfield was at first concerned with problems in Germanic and Indo-European comparative linguistics, and he also published a general survey, *An Introduction to the Study of Language* (1914). After his European leave, and later stimulated by the ideas in Ferdinand de Saussure's *Cours de linguistique générale* (Paris, 1916; available to Bloomfield about 1920), Bloomfield began working on the description of unwritten languages on the basis of fieldwork with native speakers. His first descriptive work (published 1917) was on Tagalog, an Austronesian language of the Philippines, based on work with a speaker found in Urbana, Illinois.

Bloomfield then turned to the study of the Algonquian languages, beginning with a systematic analysis of the published materials on Fox. He conducted intensive fieldwork among the Menominee of Wisconsin in the summers of 1920 and 1921, publishing in 1928 a massive volume of texts that he had taken down from dictation. Over the following years he continually rethought and revised his presentation of Menominee grammar, trying out a number of approaches to the description of the complex vowel alternations of the language and their interplay with its extensive inflectional morphology. Eventually Bloomfield settled on a descriptive approach that set up abstract phonological segments, called morphophonemes, and a series of formulaic rules that converted these segments into various realizations in actual speech. In this he was influenced by ideas that were gaining ground in linguistics in the late 1930s, especially through Morris Swadesh (who worked with Menominee speakers in 1937 and 1938), but he was also coming back to ideas he had pursued earlier based on the method used by Pānini. The final pieces of the analysis fell into place after a brief return to the Menominee in 1939, when he checked details that had been unclear or imprecise in his earlier field notes, and are reflected in the nearly completed drafts of a grammar he left at his death.

In what appears to have been little more than a month of fieldwork in Saskatchewan in the summer of 1925, Bloomfield recorded a vast amount of dictated textual material in Cree for the Victoria Memorial Museum in Ottawa. Two volumes of these texts were published (1930, 1934), and a third remains in manuscript. He also did extensive work with a speaker of Ottawa.

Bloomfield's second general introduction to linguistics, *Language* (1933), entirely different from his earlier book, was widely used as a textbook and established him as a major figure. He adopted a behaviorist approach, which excluded speculation about mental processes and instead regarded the norm of the linguistic community as the objective definition of what language was and as the object to be described by the linguist. Deviations from the norm, which he took to be the observed usage of the best speakers, he referred to with the oxymoronic metaphor "illiterate speech."

Bloomfield applied the insights of linguistics to language teaching and the teaching of reading to children. During the Second World War he had a major influence on the Intensive Language Program organized by the American Council of Learned Societies and helped develop the instructional materials on Dutch and Russian.

At the time of his death, Bloomfield resided in New Haven, Connecticut.

• The obituary by Bernard Bloch (*Language* 25 [1949]: 87–98) is supplemented by the reminiscences and critical essays in Robert A. Hall, ed., *Leonard Bloomfield: Essays on His Life and Work* (1987). Most of his important articles and reviews are reprinted in Charles F. Hockett, ed., *A Leonard Bloomfield Anthology* (1970), with a complete bibliography and other materials. Bloomfield's papers are in the American Philosophical Society, Philadelphia, and the National Anthropological Archives, Department of Anthropology, Smithsonian Institution. His Algonquian grammars, published posthumously, are *The Menomini Language* (1962) and *Eastern Ojibwa: Grammatical Sketch, Texts, and Word List* (1957; describing an Ottawa dialect).

IVES GODDARD

BLOOMFIELD, Maurice (23 Feb. 1855–13 June 1928), philologist, was born in Bielitz, Austria, the son of Solomon Bloomfield and Bertha Jaeger. In 1859 the family emigrated to the United States, took up residence in Milwaukee, Wisconsin, and shortly thereafter moved to Chicago, Illinois. There Bloomfield received his early education and entered the University of Chicago in 1871. After three years he decided to continue his studies at Furman University in Greenville, South Carolina, and earned his B.A. there and then his M.A. in 1877. While attending Furman, Bloomfield became interested in Oriental studies (Indology) while under the sway of biblical scholar Crawford H. Toy, and he subsequently took up Sanskrit and comparative philology at Yale (1877–1878) under William Dwight Whitney. After his year of study there, he was offered a fellowship at Johns Hopkins University in Baltimore, Maryland, where Charles Rockwell Lanman directed his doctoral studies on the Rig-Veda, an ancient collection of verses and hymns. In 1879 he was awarded a Ph.D., having defended a dissertation titled "Noun-Formation in the Rig-Veda." He continued his research for two years in Germany, working at the universities of Berlin and Leipzig in Indo-European philology. In 1881 he was invited to return to Johns Hopkins University to accept a position as professor of Sanskrit and comparative philology. In this capacity he began his long and eminent career as Sanskritist, philologist, and highly esteemed teacher.

Bloomfield made considerable contributions to Indo-European studies: he published some two hundred journal articles, books, and reviews. The greater part of his work treats the history, mythology, sacred literature, and grammatical detail of the ancient languages of the Indian subcontinent. His work may be divided into three sections. His earliest labors include an edition of the *Kauçika-Sutra of the Atharva-Veda* (1890), which discusses the rules regarding ritual and ceremony contained in a collection of verses and hymns attributed to a legendary priestly family, and a translation of the *Hymns of the Atharva-Veda* (1897). A decade of work on the Atharva-Veda concluded with the monograph *The Atharva-Veda*, published in the *Grundriss der indoarischen Philologie und Altertumskunde* (1899), and a reproduction of the Tübingen manuscript of the *Kashmirian Atharva-Veda* (1901), edited in collaboration with the German scholar Richard Garbe. This productive span of years established Bloomfield as an authority on the Atharva-Veda, but the Rig-Veda was his chief interest and focus during the middle years of his research. *A Vedic Concordance . . .* (1906), an index of the Vedic mantras and their variations, stands today as his central and perhaps most valuable work, and students of Sanskrit still profit from a consultation of the *Rig-Veda Repetitions . . .* (1916). The *Religion of the Veda* (1908) contains a series of lectures on the history of the Vedic religion. His latter years were spent researching Hindu fiction, notably the *Life and Stories of the Jaina Savior, Parçvanatha* (1919). This yielded a number of related articles in the *Journal of the American Oriental Society*, for example, "The Śālibhadra Carita, A Story of Conversion to Jaina Monkhood" (1923) and "On False Ascetics and Nuns in Hindu Fiction" (1924).

Bloomfield was no stranger to comparative linguistics. His writings in this field include "On Adaptation of Suffixes in Congeneric Classes of Substantives" in the *Journal of American Philology* (1891) and "On a Case of Suppletive Indo-European Suffixes" in *Language* (1925). The preliminary discoveries of J. A. Knudtzon (1902) and the extensive compilations of B. Hrozný (1915) established Hittite as a member of the Indo-European family of languages. Bloomfield took an immediate interest in the Hittite discoveries, and his research is summarized in "The Hittite Language" in the *Journal of the American Oriental Society* (1921). Bloomfield received honors from many institutions and was a member of several learned societies. He served as director of the American Oriental Society from 1884 to 1928 and, in 1925, was a founding member of the Linguistic Society of America, of which he served as president in 1926.

Bloomfield transmitted his lively interest in literature and comparative linguistics to a generation of students; their great affection and respect is captured in a 1920 Festschrift, *Studies in Honor of Maurice Bloomfield by a Group of His Pupils*. This text is valuable not just as a testament to the kindness and learned enthusiasm Bloomfield imparted to his students, but also as a rich biographical and bibliographical source. By all accounts, he was not recluse; indeed, he enjoyed music, reading, and hiking. He was twice married, first to Rosa Zeisler of Vienna, in 1885; they had two children. She died on their thirty-fifth wedding anniversary in 1920. In 1921 he married Helen Townsend Scott of Baltimore, who had been one of his students at Johns Hopkins. He retired from teaching in 1926 for reasons of health. The following year he moved to San Francisco where his son, Arthur Bloomfield, was director of the Leland Stanford Hospital. Bloomfield enjoyed the cultural diversions of that city for only a year and died there after a brief illness. A final work, *Vedic*

Variants, appeared posthumously in 1930, finished and edited by Franklin Edgerton and Murray Barnson Emeneau.

• Most of Bloomfield's personal correspondence is in the Gilman and Guildersleeve collections at Johns Hopkins University, Baltimore, Md., and in the Norman Brown Collection at the University of Pennsylvania, Philadelphia. Most of Bloomfield's major works exist in both the original editions and reprints, including *A Vedic Concordance, Being an Alphabetic Index of Every Line of Every Stanza of the Published Vedic Literature and to the Liturgical Formulas Thereof; That Is, an Index to the Vedic Mantras Together with an Account of Their Variations in the Different Vedic Books*, Harvard Oriental Series, vol. 10 (1906; repr. 1964). Similarly, Harvard University Press published the *Rig-Veda Repetitions: The Repeated Verses and Distichs and Stanzas of the Rig-Veda in Systematic Presentation and with Critical Discussion*, Harvard Oriental Series, vols. 20 and 24 (1916; repr. 1981). *The Religion of the Veda* (1908) was first published in the series American Lectures on the History of Religion (7th ser.) and was reprinted as *The Religion of the Veda, the Ancient Religion of India* (1969). The key Atharvavedic literature may be found in the *Atharvaveda* (1899), also in English and Hindi reprints as *Atharvaved and the Gopath Brahmana* (1978); see also the *Hymns of the Atharva-Veda, Together with Extracts from the Ritual Books and Commentaries* (1969). *Vedic Variants* appears in a 1930 edition and in reprint (1979). Obituaries are in *Language* 4 (1928): 214–17, which has a valuable bibliography, and in the *Journal of the American Oriental Society* 48 (1928): 193–99.

MARK J. CONNELLY

BLOOMGARDEN, Kermit (15 Dec. 1904–20 Sept. 1976), theater producer, was born in Brooklyn, New York, the son of Samuel Zemad Bloomgarden, a manufacturer of matzos, and Annie Groden. Raised in a prosperous Orthodox Jewish home in Brooklyn, he received art lessons at the Pratt Institute as a boy. However, after his father had suffered a series of strokes, the family's financial situation changed for the worse. After graduating from high school in 1922, Bloomgarden attended evening classes at New York University and supported himself with a full-time office job. He received a bachelor of business science degree in 1926 and then became a certified public accountant.

After working at several accounting firms, including his own, Bloomgarden became financial adviser to Arthur Beckhard in 1932. Beckhard, a concert manager, produced his first Broadway play in that same year. Bloomgarden became his general manager, supervising Beckhard's theatrical enterprises. In 1935 he was hired in the same capacity by Herman Shumlin, a highly successful producer-director. Bloomgarden served as general manager for several Broadway productions, most of them produced by Shumlin but one produced by the Group Theatre, for which Bloomgarden served as a part-time business manager. When Harold Clurman of the Group decided not to present Albert Bein's *Heavenly Express*, he encouraged Bloomgarden to produce it independently. The 1940 production, involving fourteen members of the Group Theatre, was not successful, and Bloomgarden continued working for Shumlin. Despite the failure, Bloomgarden determined from then on to pursue a career as an independent producer. He opened his own office in 1945.

Bloomgarden earned a reputation for producing plays with strong social content, beginning with his 1945 presentation of *Deep Are the Roots* by Arnaud d'Usseau and James Gow (coproduced with George Heller), a play about race relations in the United States. Plays advocating racial tolerance were rare in the mid-1940s; however, despite warnings that it would not find an audience, the production ran for 477 performances, establishing Bloomgarden as both a financial and artistic success. Lillian Hellman, a playwright whose works invariably conveyed her left-wing social and political convictions, began her association with Bloomgarden in 1946 with his production of *Another Part of the Forest*, the first of seven plays that she wrote or adapted and that Bloomgarden produced.

Bloomgarden's most noted success occurred in 1949, when he and Walter Fried presented Arthur Miller's *Death of a Salesman*. This groundbreaking production combined a brilliant play with an outstanding cast and a magnificent set design. Bloomgarden claimed to have persuaded Miller to scrap a revised version of the play he had written at the insistence of the director, Elia Kazan. Bloomgarden also maintained that he had recommended that Mildred Dunnock be cast as Linda Loman despite Miller's and Kazan's opposition, and that he had overturned the original commitment to hire designer Boris Aaronson because, in Bloomgarden's words, "I felt that we needed a 'lighting' man, someone who could both design and light, and I finally persuaded them [Miller and Kazan] to take Jo Mielziner" (quoted in Conrad, p. 53). All three decisions were significant: one of the play's great strengths proved to be its unorthodox dramatic structure; Dunnock gave a superb performance; and Mielziner's set, perhaps the most celebrated single work ever produced by a scenic designer, turned what might have been a cumbersome production into a fluid and haunting one. Even Kazan called it "the single most critically important contribution and the key to the way I directed the play" (Kazan, p. 361). However, two of Bloomgarden's claims regarding his role in the production were disputed. Miller and Kazan maintained that neither of them had ever contemplated significant rewrites, and Bloomgarden's influence in hiring Mielziner is not supported by any of the other participants in the production. Moreover, both playwright and director claimed that Bloomgarden had predicted failure for the production unless its title were changed to something more optimistic. He suggested *Free and Clear*, a proposal that Miller and Kazan firmly rejected.

Bloomgarden's later productions included two more plays by Miller, *The Crucible* (1953), and *A View from the Bridge* (1955), both written in part as Miller's response to McCarthyism. While Bloomgarden, unlike Miller and Hellman, was not subpoenaed to testify before the House Committee on Un-American Activities (although his association with left-wing causes and plays made such a subpoena possible), he was listed in the now-discredited but once-influential *Red Channels*, a supposed compendium of Communists and their sympathizers.

Other than *Death of a Salesman*, the most successful productions (both in artistic and financial terms) produced or coproduced by Bloomgarden were *The Diary of Anne Frank* (1955), *The Lark* (1955, the production of which Bloomgarden claimed to be most proud), *The Most Happy Fella* (1956), *Look Homeward, Angel* (1957), *The Music Man* (1957), *Toys in the Attic* (1960), *The Hot l Baltimore* (1973), and *Equus* (1974). As the dates of these productions indicate, Bloomgarden's most productive years were between 1949 and 1957. He went through a long period afterward during which most of his productions (on Broadway, off-Broadway, and off-off-Broadway) were dismissed by critics and audiences alike. Even *Equus*, his last success, was a bitter experience, as director John Dexter banned Bloomgarden from attending rehearsals and treated him shabbily throughout the rehearsal process.

Bloomgarden believed that the playwright was the most important component in a theatrical venture: "The author is in charge," he once remarked. Speaking of his role as producer he observed, "it's part of the producer's function to keep the author and the director working well as a team" (*Women's Wear Daily*, 28 Jan. 1974).

Bloomgarden married Hattie Richardson, an actress and singer, whose professional name was Linda Lee, in 1939. They had no children. In 1942, in what was either an accident or a suicide, she fell to her death from a window in their high-rise apartment. Bloomgarden married Virginia Kaye, an actress, in 1943. They had two children before their marriage ended in divorce in 1964. Bloomgarden was plagued by various illnesses, including a heart attack in 1957, a leg that required amputation in 1971, and an inoperable brain tumor in 1975, leading to his death in New York City the following year.

Despite having his share of failures, Bloomgarden must be counted among the leading producers of his time. In his book *The Season* (1970), screenwriter and novelist William Goldman lists him as one of the people "responsible for what gets done" on Broadway (p. 411). Andrew B. Harris, author of *Broadway Theatre*, groups Bloomgarden with other "creative producers" who "were committed to the plays they produced because in one way or another they felt that the play reflected them" (*Broadway Theatre*, p. 125). Critic Whitney Bolton, in a 7 May 1956 article in the New York *Morning Telegraph*, notes that Bloomgarden had produced *A View from the Bridge*, *The Diary of Anne Frank*, *The Lark*, and *The Most Happy Fella* all in a single season. "It is not possible to express one's thanks to Mr. Bloomgarden," Bolton writes. "He provided four works of singular distinction and merit, he cast them impeccably, he mounted them with taste and imagination" (quoted in Doherty, p. 117). Lynn Doherty, whose Ph.D. dissertation gives the fullest account of Bloomgarden's career, sums up his contributions by observing, "He combined sound fiscal abilities with a genuine commitment to the artistic worth of his productions" (Doherty, p. 8).

• Bloomgarden's business papers are housed at the State Historical Society of Wisconsin in Madison. The only thorough treatment of Bloomgarden's career is Lynn Doherty, "The Art of Producing: The Life and Work of Kermit Bloomgarden" (Ph.D. diss., City Univ. of New York, 1989). Bloomgarden's tape-recorded recollections, which are limited to discussions on certain clearly defined topics, are published in Christine Conrad, "The Unfinished Memoirs of Kermit Bloomgarden," *American Theatre*, Nov. 1988. Other sources describing various individuals' perspectives on presentations produced by Bloomgarden include Arthur Miller, *Timebends* (1987); Elia Kazan, *A Life* (1988); Otis L. Guernsey, Jr., ed., *Broadway Song & Story* (1985), which contains a transcript of a panel discussion about the original production of *Death of a Salesman*, in which the participants were involved; and an account of the history of *Death of a Salesman* in Andrew B. Harris, *Broadway Theatre* (1994). Howard Kissel, "Kermit Bloomgarden: 'I Know What I Like,'" *Women's Wear Daily*, 28 Jan. 1974, p. 28, is an interview with Bloomgarden. An obituary is in the *New York Times*, 21 Sept. 1976.

JARED BROWN

BLOOMINGDALE, Alfred Schiffer (15 Apr. 1916–20 Aug. 1982), cofounder of Diners Club and adviser to President Ronald Reagan, was born in New York City, the son of Hiram Bloomingdale and Rosalind Schiffer. Alfred Bloomingdale attended Brown University, where he played varsity football, graduating in 1938 after spending a year in a hospital recovering from a football-related back injury. He began his business career working as a salesman at Bloomingdale Brothers, the firm founded by his grandfather Lyman and great-uncle Joseph in 1872. In 1941 he switched careers and became a theatrical agent, producer, and financial backer of Broadway shows and Hollywood movies. Among his clients were Judy Garland, Judy Holliday, and Frank Sinatra; and the *Ziegfeld Follies of 1943*, starring Milton Berle, proved to be one of his more successful ventures. During World War II he ran a New York shipyard and produced shows for U.S. servicepeople. His involvement with the motion picture industry led to an executive position with Columbia Pictures in Hollywood in 1946, and that same year he married Betsy Lee Newling, with whom he had three children.

In 1949 Bloomingdale, his friend Frank McNamara, and McNamara's attorney Ralph Schneider, met for lunch in New York City. McNamara headed an unsuccessful finance company, the Hamilton Credit Corporation, which had $35,000 in uncollected receivables and little else. In discussing McNamara's debt-collection problems, the three men developed the idea that was to become the Diners Club.

To finance the new enterprise, McNamara contributed Hamilton and its debt, while Bloomingdale contributed $5,000 in cash. After Bloomingdale returned to California, McNamara and Schneider launched the new venture. In the first three weeks of operation, they purchased a mailing list of 5,000 sales managers for $75 and found 100 who were interested; they also located about a dozen interested restaurants. The two then borrowed an additional $35,000 from a finance company. Within two months, they requested additional capital from Bloomingdale, who agreed to supply it in exchange for a greater interest in the venture. When the other two demurred, Bloomingdale started a similar business named Dine and Sign in Los Angeles. A month later, the two firms merged, and Bloomingdale was named vice president. A year later, McNamara elected to sell his 70 percent interest in the business to his two partners. Bloomingdale became president in 1955, a position he would hold until 1968. Schneider became chairman of the board, a position Bloomingdale assumed when Schneider died in 1964. The company grew to include a collection agency, a credit-checking firm, and the Fugazy Travel Bureau, thus meeting the competitive challenges of both American Express and Carte Blanche.

When Schneider died, Bloomingdale was unable to raise the funds to purchase the outstanding shares himself, so he arranged for the Continental Insurance Company to acquire the shares. By 1967 a two-year struggle had developed between Bloomingdale and Continental for control of Diners Club, and in 1969 Bloomingdale resigned from the board. Since Continental did not want Bloomingdale joining the competition, it gave him a lifetime contract as a consultant to the firm. Bloomingdale then turned his attention to real estate ventures in California, Florida, and Georgia.

Bloomingdale became active in Republican party causes following the party's 1964 national convention. With Ronald Reagan's election in 1980, Bloomingdale became one of a number of Californians in Reagan's "kitchen cabinet," advising the president on such matters as personnel and policy. Bloomingdale also was a member of the Reagan Coalition Conference, a group of wealthy friends who solicited grass-roots support for Reagan's program to reduce the federal budget. Reagan in turn appointed Bloomingdale to the Foreign Intelligence Advisory Board and the Advisory Commission on Public Diplomacy. Despite these public positions, Bloomingdale remained a very private person. The Bloomingdales were frequent visitors to the White House, and his wife was often described as Nancy Reagan's best friend.

Bloomingdale's death occurred shortly after Vicki Morgan filed a $10 million suit against him for breach of contract. In one of the first highly publicized "palimony" cases, Morgan claimed to have been Bloomingdale's companion for twelve years and alleged that he had promised her lifetime support. After Morgan was slain in 1983 by the man with whom she was then living, a jury awarded her only son $200,000, to be paid from Bloomingdale's estate. (The son had been born before Morgan met Bloomingdale.) A letter with Bloomingdale's signature promising to pay Morgan $240,000 was ruled to be a legally binding agreement. Of this, $40,000 had been paid before his death.

Alfred Bloomingdale retained a lifelong interest in sports, particularly football, and was an ardent fan of the Los Angeles Rams. The year before his death he was named to the Rams advisory board, which also included former president Gerald Ford. He served as a trustee of his alma mater, Brown University, and was a member of the Board of Regents of Loyola Marymount University. He died in Santa Monica, California.

The 1949 lunchtable idea of Bloomingdale, McNamara, and Schneider grew into a multimillion-dollar industry. The number of places that would accept a Diners Club card or one of its competitors grew far beyond restaurants, and the multipurpose credit card became a common feature of everyday life. He did not invent the credit card, but he so expanded its use that the *Washington Post* noted in his obituary that Alfred Bloomingdale was known sometimes as "the father of the credit card."

• Information on Bloomingdale's role in Diners Club is presented in Lewis Mandell, *The Credit Card Industry* (1990). Obituaries are in the *New York Times*, the *Washington Post*, and the *Los Angeles Times*, 24 Aug. 1982.

LOUIS P. CAIN

BLOOR, Ella Reeve (8 July 1862–10 Aug. 1951), radical labor organizer and feminist, was born on Staten Island, New York, the daughter of Charles Reeve, a successful drugstore owner, and Harriet Amanda Disbrow, a community affairs activist. While still a child, Ella moved to Bridgeton, New Jersey, where her family led a conservative, upper-middle-class life. An important counterinfluence was Ella's great-uncle Dan Ware, a former abolitionist, liberal, Unitarian, greenbacker, and general freethinker. After attending local public schools, Ella spent a year at Ivy Hall Seminary, a finishing school she disliked. When she was fourteen, her mother began tutoring her at home.

The eldest child, Ella cared for her home and siblings after her mother died in 1879. Her father forbade her to attend college, but Ella continued her education informally. She enjoyed reading and was especially drawn to women's biographies and Walt Whitman's poetry. Taking an interest in social and political reform, she spent time with Dan Ware, who introduced her to agnostic Robert Ingersoll's works. Ella's father remarried in 1881, and Ella married Ware's son Lucien, her cousin, later the same year. The couple took up several residences before settling in Woodbury, New Jersey, where Dan Ware also lived, and Ella continued to be influenced by her uncle's views.

Influenced as well by Quakers and Unitarians while living in Woodbury, Ella began working for women's rights and equality. She took an interest in suffrage, helping women gain the right to vote in school board elections. Also concerned with prohibition, Ella established the local chapter of the Woman's Christian Temperance Union and became its president. She joined the Ethical Culture Society of Philadelphia and wrote about political issues for local newspapers. With her earnings from writing, Ella hired a tutor to help her with subjects she had wanted to study in college, including the works of Marx and Engels. Growing more interested in labor issues, she participated in a Philadelphia streetcar workers' strike in 1890 and assisted in the workers' unionization efforts.

Ella's unstable marriage to Lucien Ware, which produced six children, ended with divorce in 1896. She then moved to West Philadelphia with her children and attended the University of Pennsylvania, where she studied history, philosophy, and science and took teachers' training courses. Needing to earn money to support her children, she wrote two children's books and various newspaper articles, including a young people's column in the *Social Democrat*, published by the Social Democratic party. When she learned that women weavers earned a fraction of the wages paid to men doing similar work, she joined the weavers' union to organize women.

In 1895 Ella had met socialist leader Eugene V. Debs and then briefly resided in an Arden, Delaware, socialist utopian community. There she met novelist and reformer Upton Sinclair. In 1897 Ella joined Debs's Social Democratic party and married Louis Cohen, an associate of Daniel De Leon in the Socialist Labor party. Ella joined De Leon's group in 1898. She wrote articles for the party journals *Daily People* and *Weekly People* and helped edit socialist writings for publication. Ella and Louis Cohen separated in 1902 after the birth of two sons and were later divorced. She rejoined Debs and his newly formed Socialist party in the same year.

Ella then devoted herself completely to organized labor and women's issues. She became a state labor organizer for Debs's Socialist party in Pennsylvania, working among striking coal miners. She was also a labor organizer for several unions, including garment workers, mine workers, and machinists. In 1905 she took over Socialist party organizing in Connecticut and wrote articles for that state's *Waterbury American* until her exposé of harsh child labor conditions in Connecticut cost her that job.

In 1906 Ella traveled to Illinois to help Sinclair investigate the Chicago meatpacking industry. She was to gather information for a government commission inspecting stockyard conditions in response to Sinclair's book *The Jungle*. Richard Bloor, a young socialist pottery worker, accompanied Ella to protect her. Sinclair worried that the public would disapprove of an unmarried team of investigators, and thus convinced Ella to publish her reports under the alias of "Mrs. Richard Bloor." The reports made Ella nationally famous, so she continued to use the name, while claiming there was no romantic attachment between them. Later in life she became affectionately known as "Mother Bloor."

Concerned with working women and their children, Ella Bloor frequently took her own children with her on travels, to meetings, and to political demonstrations and strikes. She planned cooperative nurseries and kitchens for working women and advocated communal sharing of household duties. In 1910, after an unsuccessful attempt at becoming Connecticut's first female secretary of state, Bloor helped establish the Socialist party's National Women's Committee. At the party's national congress, she proposed that socialist women support the suffrage movement. In 1913 she participated in the Ohio referendum campaign for women's voting rights and joined in the suffragists' mass demonstration at President Woodrow Wilson's inauguration.

Later in 1913 Bloor worked with striking copper miners in Calumet, Michigan. She organized a Christmas Eve party for the strikers' children. The festivities were interrupted when a man, later revealed as a friend of the mine owners, shouted that the wooden building was on fire. In the ensuing rush down the narrow stairs to the door, seventy-two children were crushed to death. Bloor described the tragedy for the newspapers and later testified about it before congressional investigators.

During World War I Bloor helped radical labor activist Elizabeth Gurley Flynn and others establish the Workers' Defense Union, which provided assistance to men and women arrested for antiwar activities. Bloor herself was nearly arrested as a radical during the postwar Red Scare, but she evaded the police. At one point she fled Worcester, Massachusetts, abandoning her belongings in the process.

Bloor deplored many socialists' support for World War I, and she joined in the 1919 creation of the American Communist party. Now firmly in the leftist, radical camp of American socialism, she approved of the Russian Bolshevik Revolution and helped Communist functionary Earl Browder run the *Worker's World*, the Communist papers, while he was in prison. (Browder later led the American Communist party from 1935 to 1945.)

From that point forward Bloor devoted herself to Communist party activism. In 1921 she was a trade union delegate to the Red International of Labor Unions meeting in Moscow. In 1925, at sixty-three years of age, she traveled across the United States recruiting new party members and selling subscriptions to the party's *Daily Worker*. She embarked on a second similar journey in 1927, after joining the unsuccessful effort to free Sacco and Vanzetti and helping organize the United Front Committee of Textile Workers in various cities.

Even in her seventies, Bloor remained active, making speeches, raising funds, and organizing workers for Communist causes. In 1930 she traveled to the Dakotas to oversee the Communist party's election campaign and build mass support for the United Farmers' League. In 1932 she married Andrew Omholt, a North Dakota farmer and Communist candidate for Congress. She led farmers' strikes and was elected the regional secretary for farmers in the Midwest. She also participated in hunger marches on Washington, D.C., when unemployed workers protested their plight during the first years of the Great Depression.

In the later 1930s Bloor worked with the American League against War and Fascism and chaired the commission to grant women equal rights within the Communist party. She also campaigned cross-country for the party's national candidates and assisted with party organizing drives in eastern Pennsylvania. In 1937 the Soviet Union made her an honored guest at the commemoration of the Bolshevik Revolution's twentieth anniversary. A Communist party Central Committee member from 1932 to 1948, Bloor led her last major campaign during World War II, when she traveled to major American cities and argued for international struggle against fascism.

In 1940 Bloor published her autobiography *We Are Many*, which she promoted nationally the next year, recruiting new party members and selling party paper subscriptions in the process. She led the Pennsylvania Communist party from 1941 to 1947 and then retired to a working apple farm in eastern Pennsylvania with her husband Omholt. She died in a Richlandtown, Pennsylvania, convalescent home.

An activist rather than a theoretician, Ella Reeve Bloor dedicated her life to alleviating the oppression of women, children, and the working class. She weathered and supported sudden changes in the Communist party official "line" during the tumultuous years of the Great Depression, World War II, and the early Cold War. Although party policy fluctuated and sometimes contradicted what had gone before, Bloor believed strongly in Communism's constant and unique ability to protect and liberate the proletariat. Her devotion to the party never faltered, even when she endured arrests, harassment, and threats of bodily harm from police and vigilantes. Elizabeth Gurley Flynn summed up her life by recalling Bloor's words that it had been "a privilege and joy to carry the torch for Socialism."

• Bloor's personal papers are stored at Smith College. Some of her correspondence is in the Grace Hutchins Papers and Anna Rochester Papers at the University of Oregon, the Elizabeth Gurley Flynn Papers at New York University's Tamiment Institute Library, the Mary Marvin (Heaton) Vorse Papers at Wayne State University, and the Victor Jeremy Jerome Papers at Yale University. Her children's books are *Three Little Lovers of Nature* (1895) and *Talks about Authors and Their Work* (1899). Her autobiography, *We Are Many* (1940), is informative but occasionally inaccurate. See also her *Women and the Soviet Union* (1938). For biographical sketches, see Ann Barton, *Mother Bloor: The Spirit of '76* (1937), and Elizabeth Gurley Flynn, *Daughters of America: Ella Reeve Bloor and Anita Whitney* (1942). *The Mother Bloor 75th Birthday Souvenir Book* (1937) provides an additional overview of her life. See also articles in the *Communist*, the *Daily Worker*, the *Farmers National Weekly*, the *Party Organizer*, and the *New York Call*. Upton Sinclair's *Autobiography* (1962) describes Bloor's investigation of the meatpacking industry. For her Socialist and Communist party activism, see Theodore Draper, *The Roots of American Communism* (1957) and *American Communism and Soviet Russia* (1960); Joseph Starobin, *American Communism in Crisis, 1943–1957* (1972); and Flynn, *The Rebel Girl* (1973). Thorough obituaries appear in the *Philadelphia Inquirer* and the *New York Times*, both 11 Aug. 1951, the *Daily Worker*, 13 Aug. 1951, and *Time* and *Newsweek* magazines, both 20 Aug. 1951.

VERONICA A. WILSON

BLOSS, William Clough (19 Jan. 1795–18 Apr. 1863), abolitionist and reformer, was born in West Stockbridge, Massachusetts, the son of Joseph Bloss, a Connecticut farmer who served in the American Revolution, and Amy Wentworth Kennedy. Bloss obtained his education through the common schools prior to his family's 1816 move to the town of Brighton, New York, on what was then the outskirts of Rochester. At some point between 1816 and 1823 Bloss taught briefly in Maryland and South Carolina where he acquired, he would later claim, his lifelong hatred for the institution of slavery. Returning to Rochester in 1823, he built a brick tavern on the edge of the Erie Canal and that same year married Mary Bangs Blossom, with whom he had six children.

A Methodist and revivalist, Bloss abandoned tavernkeeping in 1826 by pouring the contents of his bar into the Erie Canal, becoming a lifelong temperance advocate. He served as a Brighton delegate to the county Anti-Masonic convention in October 1829; that same year he signed a petition advocating passage of a federal law banning Sunday postal services. In 1830 he sold his former tavern building and opened a short-lived mercantile business in Rochester. In later years he would be listed in city directories as having no occupation (1838, 1844, 1859), as a "yeoman" (1840, 1841), as a land agent (1851, 1853, 1857), and as an insurance agent (1861).

In the summer of 1833 Bloss promoted a series of antislavery meetings—that were disrupted by hecklers—and signed the call to the first New York State Anti-Slavery Convention to be held in Utica. On 19 November he helped organize the first Monroe County antislavery convention. When local newspapers refused to publish the convention's constitution, Bloss and four other leaders of the Rochester Anti-Slavery Society purchased a printing press and began the *Rights of Man* in 1834. Listed as the newspaper's "traveling agent," Bloss was the central figure in this pioneering abolitionist newspaper whose surviving issues, all from its first volume, date from April to July 1834. Working closely with local "colored leaders" such as Thomas James, the society also fought for "equal rights" for African Americans.

In its 26 April 1834 issue, the *Rights of Man* published a detailed report on the local population of 360 "colored people" and denounced the discriminatory treatment it received in Rochester. In May 1834 eighty local residents—including Bloss's father and brother—signed a call for a 4 July 1834 convention to form a Monroe County Anti-Slavery Society. The next year Bloss and his wife petitioned Congress to end slavery and the slave trade in the nation's capital and signed petitions, in 1837 and 1838, against the annexation of Texas.

A longtime Whig, Bloss first ran for public office in 1841 as one of four candidates for the state assembly nominated by local abolitionists at a 22 September meeting. On 5 March 1842 Bloss, in his capacity as a leader of the state Anti-Slavery Convention, held from 2 March to 4 March in Rochester, wrote to New York state governor William H. Seward, praising him for his "noble stance" against slavery. Seeing no "necessity of forming a [new] political party" to promote abolition, Bloss repeatedly defended the Whigs from attacks by supporters of the Liberty party in 1843 and again in 1844. In November 1844 Bloss was elected to the state assembly on the Whig ticket. During three one-year terms in the legislature, he fought unsuccessfully for an amendment to the state constitution to bar any form of discrimination in voting rights against "persons of color" compared to "white persons."

As an advocate of the Free School Law, Bloss was especially angered by the legal segregation in the public schools that confronted African-American abolitionist Frederick Douglass when he moved to Rochester in 1847. As Douglass recalled in his memoirs, Bloss and a handful of others were strong supporters of his "demand for equal rights" and for free public access to "all places of public resort" in Rochester. Bloss also rejected customary segregation in private life. While in Albany, Bloss, "in rebuke of the caste prejudice of the day," is said to have left his seat among the whites at a communion service and, "seating himself with the separated Blacks, partook of the sacrament with them" (untitled pamphlet, 1893, Rochester Historical Society).

Despite his legislative responsibilities, Bloss continued to be active in reform movements directed against drinking, vice, and masonry. He was an early supporter of woman suffrage, being said by his son to have endorsed this demand in 1838. At a Unitarian church convention on 2 August 1848, Bloss publicly supported the Declaration of Sentiments reached at the Seneca Falls women's rights meeting held earlier that year. For years he also served as a self-appointed chaplain of the county jail. As a former legislator, Bloss addressed a gathering of the Free Soil party on 2 October 1848 as well as a state mechanics' convention in Syracuse on 23 February 1850. With the passage of the Fugitive Slave Law in that year, Bloss intensified his activities with the Underground Railroad, which included sheltering slaves at his Brighton home. In these activities Bloss continued to work closely with Douglass and attended the 5 July 1852 meeting in Rochester, New York, where Douglass presented his famous speech, "What to the Slave Is the Fourth of July?"

In 1855 Bloss emerged as a leading opponent of the Know Nothing party that swept the Rochester municipal elections in March. A supporter of unrestricted immigration, Bloss served as a foreman of a grand jury that split 15 to 5 over alleged election irregularities associated with the Know Nothing agitation. Although unable to prove individual cases of postelection retribution, the majority report nonetheless criticized the use of "oaths and combinations" as a violation of the individual's "free and voluntary choice in casting the ballot."

Bloss's antislavery militancy remained undimmed as the sectional crisis intensified in the decade prior to the Civil War. During the 1856 Fremont campaign, Bloss originated a map showing "the area and aggressions of the Slave Power." Republican politicians distributed thousands of copies, as did Bloss during his campaign trips in the eastern and western states. Far from restricting his activities to the electoral realm, Bloss raised funds to arm members of the Massachusetts colonists en route to Kansas, also providing them with the gift of a Bible and a spelling book "to establish civil and religious liberty in Kansas."

In October 1858 Bloss joined with others in Rochester's vibrant reform community to protest capital punishment in the case of a local man condemned to be hanged for murder. The protesters, Susan B. Anthony recalled, did not doubt the guilt of the individual charged but "were opposed to the principle of what they termed judicial murder." Widely criticized for their unpopular stance, the protesters' 7 October 1858 meeting was mobbed by an unruly crowd, and Anthony, Bloss, and Douglass were forced to escape the hall through the rear.

William Clough Bloss died in Rochester about three months after Abraham Lincoln's Emancipation Proclamation was issued.

• Bloss left no papers, although the surviving 1834 copies of his newspaper, the *Rights of Man*, are in the Rundel branch of the Rochester Public Library, which also houses a useful index of Rochester newspapers published between 1818 and 1897 that contain many references to Bloss. Copies of some miscellaneous materials regarding Bloss and his descendants can be found at the Rochester Historical Society Library. The National Archives contains various petitions signed by Bloss and other antislavery activists in Rochester. In addition, the William C. Seward Collection at the University of Rochester contains at least one letter coauthored by Bloss. References to Bloss appear in *The Life and Times of Frederick Douglass* (1941); John W. Blassingame, ed., *The Frederick Douglass Papers*, 1st ser., vol. 2 (1982); Ida Husted Harper, *Life and Work of Susan B. Anthony* (1899); and *The Autobiography of Reverend Thomas James* (an 1887 work reprinted in *Rochester History* 37 [1975]). Useful information can be found in two *Rochester Historical Society* publications: Amy Hammer Croughton, "Anti-Slavery Days in Rochester," 14 (1936): 113–55, and F. J. Zwielen, "Religious Liberty in Rochester," 6 (1936): 201–5.

JOHN D. FRENCH

BLOSSOM, Henry Martyn, Jr. (6 May 1866–23 Mar. 1919), librettist, lyricist, and playwright, was born in St. Louis, Missouri, the son of Henry Martyn Blossom, an insurance executive, and Susan S. Brigham. He came from a wealthy family and, after graduating from the Stoddard School in St. Louis, chose not to attend college but rather to enter his father's insurance business. He soon became disenchanted with the insurance trade and began his career as an author. Two novels appeared in the 1890s. The first, *Documents in Evidence* (1894), told of a fictional society marriage.

The second, *Checkers: A Hard Luck Story* (1896), was a tale of horse racing. He also wrote a third work, *The Brother of Chuck McGann*.

Blossom eventually moved to New York City to write for the theater. One of his earliest credits was as lyricist for the musical comedy *Fad and Folly* (1902). His first drama, *Checkers*, an adaptation of his novel by the same name, appeared in 1903. Another play, *A Fair Exchange*, opened in 1905.

But it was as a librettist and lyricist for operettas that Blossom made his most significant contributions. His most successful collaborations were with the Irish-born cellist-conductor-composer Victor Herbert. For Herbert, Blossom wrote lyrics and libretti that surpassed those of most of his contemporaries. Blossom's libretti were light, jovial, and witty, while cohesive and dramatically viable. Blossom collaborated with Herbert on eight shows: *Mademoiselle (Mlle.) Modiste* (1905), *The Red Mill* (1906), *The Prima Donna* (1908), *The Only Girl* (1914), *The Princess Pat* (1915), *The Century Girl* (1916), *Eileen* (1917), and *The Velvet Lady* (1919), his final show. As with so many creative teams, the earlier shows of Blossom and Herbert were the most successful; later efforts never achieved the popularity of the initial ones.

Herbert and Blossom wrote *Mlle. Modiste* especially for the Viennese opera singer Fritzi Scheff. Critics generally cited Scheff with a great deal of the operetta's successful run of 202 performances. Blossom's libretto told of a salesgirl in a Paris hat shop who becomes an opera star and eventually marries the man she loves, after winning the approval of his aristocratic uncle. The show's big hit was "Kiss Me Again," a song that became synonymous with Scheff. The lyric was typical for an operetta that concerned a performer as a major character—she describes the various roles she would like to play, but the one she wants the most is that of a real-life lover. Other Herbert-Blossom standards that came from this show included "The Mascot of the Troop," "The Time and the Place and the Girl," and "I Want What I Want When I Want It." The show was revived, with Scheff reprising her leading role, in 1913. Herbert and Blossom wrote two other operettas for Scheff, *The Prima Donna* and *The Duchess*, but neither achieved the success of *Mlle. Modiste*.

Blossom and Herbert wrote *The Red Mill*, their most successful show (with 274 performances in its initial run), for the comic team of Dave Montgomery and Fred Stone. The libretto was more in line with a farce than with an operetta. In the show, Montgomery and Stone played two American tourists in Holland (Kid Conner and Con Kidder) who get involved with the romantic escapades of two Dutch girls, one of whom they rescue from a red windmill. Blossom wrote many comic episodes for the leads, including one where they appear disguised as Sherlock Holmes and Dr. Watson. The libretto was typical of many of the period, in that it portrayed Americans who travel abroad as being somewhat naive and innocent. Because of the many topical references in its libretto, the show remains dated and its subtle humor is difficult for modern audiences to comprehend in its entirety. The songs, however, have remained part of the musical theater repertory. For *The Red Mill*, Blossom and Herbert wrote such gems as "The Streets of New York," "When You're Pretty and the World Is Fair," "Moonbeams," "Every Day Is Ladies' Day with Me," "Because You're You," and "The Isle of Our Dreams."

A number of the most popular musical theater songs from the early decades of the twentieth century were the creations of Blossom and Herbert. In addition to those listed above, other famous Blossom lyrics include "When You're Away" from *The Only Girl* and "The Irish Have a Great Day Tonight" from *Eileen*.

Blossom worked with other composers in addition to Herbert, although none of these collaborations proved to be as successful either commercially or artistically. He collaborated with Alfred G. Robyn on *The Yankee Consul* (1904) and *All for the Ladies* (1912) and assisted John Golden with the music and lyrics for *The Candy Shop* (1909). Other credits for both book and lyrics included *The Slim Princess* (1911, music by Leslie Stuart), *The Man from Cook's* (1912, music by Raymond Hubbell), *A Trip to Washington* (1913, music by Ben Jerome), and *Follow the Girl* (1918, music by Zoel Parenteau). He also prepared the English-language version of Felix Albini's operetta *Baron Trenck* (1912).

Blossom was married to Marjorie Seely; the year of the marriage is not known. He died in New York City. His funeral was attended by more than 500 people. Victor Herbert and John Golden were among the honorary pallbearers.

• Brief entries on Blossom appear in several works: among the most informative are David Ewen, *New Complete Book of the American Musical Theater* (1958), and Gerald Bordman, *Oxford Companion to the American Theatre* (1984). For information about specific shows, see Ewen, *New Complete Book of the American Musical Theater*, Bordman, *American Musical Theatre: A Chronicle* (2d ed., 1992), and Stanley Green, *Broadway Musicals Show by Show* (4th ed., 1994). An obituary is in the *New York Times*, 24 Mar. 1919, and an article about his funeral service is in the *New York Times*, 27 Mar. 1919.

WILLIAM A. EVERETT

BLOUGH, Roger Miles (19 Jan. 1904–8 Oct. 1985), businessman, was born in Riverside, Pennsylvania, the son of Christian E. Blough, a farmer, and Viola Hoffman. Blough was granted an A.B. in 1925 from Susquehanna University in Selinsgrove, Pennsylvania. He taught history for three years at the high school in Hawley, Pennsylvania (1925–1928). He married Helen Martha Decker in 1928; they had twin daughters. He studied law at Yale Law School in New Haven, Connecticut (1928–1931), obtaining his LL.B. in 1931.

Upon graduating from Yale, Blough began a general practice of law with the law firm of White & Case in New York City. He was admitted to the New York bar and the Pennsylvania bar and practiced before the U.S. Supreme Court. During the investigation of the steel industry in the late 1930s and early 1940s, White & Case's Irving S. Olds was appointed special counsel for the U.S. Steel Company. In 1940 Blough acted as associate counsel for U.S. Steel, his first association with the company.

After leaving White & Case in 1942, Blough became a general solicitor in charge of all legal matters for the U.S. Steel Corporation of Delaware until 1951. On 1 January 1951 Blough became executive vice president (law), secretary, and director of the new U.S. Steel Company. In 1952, as President Harry S. Truman invoked a seizure of the steel industry in order to prevent a steel strike over failed wage negotiations, Blough and John W. Davis pleaded the case for U.S. Steel. On 2 June 1952 the Supreme Court ruled that Truman's seizure was unconstitutional, and the mills were to be returned promptly to their owners. Within twenty-four hours of the ruling, 560,000 steelworkers were on strike, and steel production came to a halt in what was the worst strike in steel industry history.

When the position of general counsel to U.S. Steel became vacant in 1953 after the death of former counsel Nathan L. Miller, Blough assumed the position. After Benjamin Fairless, then the chairman of the corporation, retired in the spring of 1955, Blough was elected chairman of the board of directors and chief executive officer of the $2.35 billion steel empire—the world's largest steel producer at the time.

Blough brought to his position a new attitude toward labor-management relations. Unlike his predecessor Fairless, Blough applied the philosophy that management and labor should remain separate entities. While Fairless would bring the United Steel Workers of America (USWA) boss David McDonald to tour the plants in an effort to forge peace between the two groups, Blough was, according to one union leader quoted by *Time* magazine, "a man you don't get to know much about. He stays in his ivory tower."

During the 1959 steel strike, which lasted 116 days, Blough took a tough stance on union demands, claiming that the United States was no longer a "laboristic" society and that union power had to be kept in check if the U.S. steel industry was to remain competitive. Blough argued for cost competitiveness, claiming that "the only practical way to reach foreign markets successfully is to keep our costs—which means, primarily, our wage costs—competitive."

In 1962 Blough locked horns with the Kennedy administration when he sought an increase in steel prices that reflected rising costs, particularly wage costs. The confrontation hinged on a long-standing issue in the American steel industry: the large steelmakers' perceived competitive position both in the United States and the world market. As Blough had indicated in 1959, domestic labor costs were escalating rapidly compared to those of foreign producers. With major steel-producing nations expanding capacity, U.S. firms felt the pressure to expand as well; however, the restraints put on steel prices by the Truman administration hindered efforts to raise the necessary capital for modernization. Industry leaders, particularly U.S. Steel, believed a strategy of price increases was necessary in order to generate these funds.

The 1962 confrontation between the Kennedy administration and the large steel firms over prices began shortly after the steel industry and the USWA reached an agreement for an increase in wages. The modest increase was good news for the Kennedy administration, which was concerned about inflation. Of concern to U.S. Steel was not simply the wage increase scheduled for the following year, but the corporation's decline in profits from $304.2 million in 1960 to $190.2 million in 1961. Subsequently, reinvestment levels declined and the ability of the corporation to modernize was perceived to be in jeopardy. As a result, on 10 April 1962 Blough announced to President Kennedy after a press release that U.S. Steel was increasing the price of steel by 3.5 percent, or $6 per ton.

As reported in the *New York Times* on 12 April 1962, President Kennedy responded angrily at a news conference in Washington, charging that "the American people will find it hard, as I do, to accept a situation in which a tiny handful of steel executives whose pursuit of private power and profit exceeds their sense of public responsibility, can show such utter contempt for the interest of 185,000,000 Americans." Blough responded with his own news conference, during which the *New York Times* reported that he said, "as citizens we must . . . discharge fully our responsibilities to the nation. The action we have taken is designed to meet . . . those responsibilities."

U.S. Steel's competitor Inland Steel then announced it would not increase its prices, and Kaiser Steel followed suit. Bethlehem Steel, America's second largest steel producer, rescinded its price increase sometime after. Realizing that it could not sustain its price increase without the support of other major steel producers, U.S. Steel rescinded on 13 April 1962.

In his thirteen years as head of U.S. Steel, Blough saw his company's share of domestic steel sales drop from 30 percent to 25 percent, as steel imports into the United States rose to 16 percent of the U.S. market in 1968. Steel industry leaders have, in retrospect, faulted Blough for his inability to fully articulate the industry's position on trade and other matters and for his poor handling of industry-government relations during the 1962 steel-price showdown. However, it is clear that Blough's new hard line on labor changed industry-labor relations forever, and this change directly affected the role of steel importing in the industry. During the 1959 wage negotiations between labor and management, imports exceeded exports for the first time, and this relationship would never reverse again.

Blough retired from U.S. Steel in 1969 and promptly returned to White & Case, this time as a partner in the firm until 1976. His career was supplemented with various community and cultural activities. Blough was a trustee of the U.S. Steel Foundation from 1955 to 1976 and was an honorary vice president of the American Iron and Steel Institute. He was a member of the Centre for Inter-American Relations, the Council on Foreign Relations, the New York State Bar Association, and the Academy of Political Science. He was a trustee of the Grand Central Art Galleries and of the Presbyterian Hospital, and he was a founding member of the Business Community for the Arts. He died in Hawley, Pennsylvania.

The *New York Times* described Roger Blough as a "soft spoken man" having a "nimble and well-organized mind." Former U.S. Steel CEO Fairless claimed that "Blough was thorough, tenacious and had the ability to dig below the surface." He was a hardworking man who worked his way up from his poor beginnings to become a powerful and influential business leader.

• William Hogan, *Economic History of the Iron and Steel Industry*, vols. 4 and 5 (1971), sets the historical context for Blough's contribution. Other sources include newspaper and magazine articles on Blough. See especially the *New York Times*, 4 May 1955, 12 Apr. 1962, and 13 Apr. 1962; "Man of Steel," *Time*, 20 July 1959, pp. 70–75; and "A New Boss for Big Steel," *Time*, 27 Dec. 1968, pp. 49–50. An obituary is in the *New York Times*, 13 Oct. 1985.

ROBERT E. ANKLI

BLOUNT, James Henderson (12 Sept. 1837–8 Mar. 1903), lawyer, congressman, and special diplomatic envoy, was born near the village of Clinton, Jones County, Georgia, the son of Thomas Blount and Mary Ricketts, planters. Blount, whose parents died during his childhood, was raised in the household of his older half-brother, David Blount. He attended private schools in Clinton, Georgia, and Tuscaloosa, Alabama, before graduating with honors from the University of Georgia in 1858. He read law and was admitted to the Georgia bar in 1859, and after a brief practice in Clinton, joined the firm of Anderson and Simmons in nearby Macon.

With the outbreak of the Civil War, Blount enlisted in Company C, Second Georgia Battalion, as a private. In 1861 he also married Eugenia Wiley; they had six children, four of whom lived to maturity. Little happened during his first year of service, but according to his daughter he was seriously wounded during the Seven Days' battle near Richmond, Virginia, in July 1862 and was invalided home. Following partial recovery, he helped organize the First Battalion, Georgia Reserve Cavalry, in December 1864 and was elected its lieutenant colonel on 9 January 1865.

With the war over, Blount returned to Clinton and the law and soon became involved in Reconstruction. He was a delegate to the state convention held in 1865 under President Andrew Johnson's Reconstruction plan and represented Jones County as a delegate to Georgia's first postwar state Democratic convention in December 1867. He supported the party's so-called "nonaction policy" of refusing to take part in congressional Reconstruction. Nevertheless, Blount was viewed as a reconciling force in Macon, where in 1872 he had again taken up residence. While he opposed the Ku Klux Klan, he was an advocate of states' rights and a white-dominated South.

Blount was an important Democratic party leader in the House of Representatives. In 1872 he was elected from the Sixth Congressional District of Georgia and was reelected nine times thereafter, serving from the Forty-third through the Fifty-second Congresses. He was not a great speaker, although he played conspicuous parts in various debates. At the time of his retirement he was described as "without graces of oratory, but with directness, sterling honesty, and lack of fear" (*New York Times*, 5 Feb. 1893). In his initial speech to Congress he attacked the Civil Rights Act of 1875, and fifteen years later he was a leader in the fight against Henry Cabot Lodge's unsuccessful Federal Elections Bill. Some writers have considered him a part of the "New South" movement, but his actions during most of the twenty years he spent in Congress belie this attribution. He did serve on the Committee on Manufactures during his first term.

From 1875 to 1881, Blount served on the Committee on Appropriations, where he helped minimize spending. He later said, "For six years of financial depression I struggled to keep down expenditures and to avoid an increase of taxation" (*Congressional Record*, 48th Cong., 1st sess. [16 Apr. 1884]: 3025). Other committee assignments included the Committee on Foreign Affairs, which he chaired for two years; the Ways and Means Committee; the Committee on the Post-Office and Post-Roads, which he chaired for two sessions; the Committee on Expenditures in the Department of Justice; and the Select Committee on the Eleventh Census. Following the death of Representative Samuel J. Randall of Pennsylvania in April 1890, Blount replaced him on the Committee on Rules, where he accepted in silence Republican Speaker Thomas B. Reed's rules revision "outrages." On the floor, however, he joined fellow Democrats in unsuccessfully contending against the alleged arbitrary dictates of "Czar" Reed. His votes during that Congress (1889–1891) were consistent with his overall career. He voted against the McKinley Tariff; the Sherman Silver Purchase Act, which he considered too restrictive; the Dependent Pension and Disability Act; and the Lodge Force Bill. He also opposed the entry of North Dakota, South Dakota, Wyoming, and Washington into the Union and was adverse to the organization of the Oklahoma Territory. He voted for the Sherman Anti-Trust Act.

Blount, a monetary inflationist, opposed the Resumption Act of 1875 and favored the Bland-Allison Act of 1878. On other major legislation, he supported Chinese exclusion, creation of the Interstate Commerce Commission, reclaiming unused government land grants given to railroads, and a national board of arbitration to be used in labor-management disputes. He opposed efforts to ban convict labor, government financing of irrigation projects, national Prohibition, a ban on carrying deadly weapons, and the merit system of civil service.

Blount was also an anti-imperialist, hostile to a large navy and the construction of an isthmian canal. Early in his congressional career he denounced the U.S.

Diplomatic Corps, stating: "If there is any service that is of questionable value to the country it is our diplomatic service. . . . I would gladly see the time come when we could get rid of nearly every diplomatic agent that we have" (*Congressional Record*, 45th Cong., 2d sess. [13 Mar. 1878]: 1733).

Because of Blount's antiexpansionist views, Secretary of State Walter Q. Gresham and other anti-imperialists in President Grover Cleveland's cabinet recommended him as the special commissioner to Hawaii. Cleveland sought a reliable representative who could determine whether the United States had been unjustly involved in the January 1893 revolution that overthrew the Hawaiian monarchy and whether a majority of islanders wanted annexation to the American Union. Blount had just retired from the House and, ironically, now wanted a diplomatic posting in the hope that it would help his future candidacy for the U.S. Senate.

Affairs in Hawaii reached the critical stage on 17 January 1893, when whites overthrew Queen Liliuokalani in a bloodless coup after she had prorogued the islands' parliament and announced a new, undemocratic constitution by royal decree. The revolutionaries established a provisional government headed by Sanford B. Dole and dispatched a five-man delegation to Washington to achieve annexation. Working with Secretary of State John W. Foster, they hastily concluded a treaty of annexation, which was submitted to the Senate in the closing days of the Benjamin Harrison administration.

When Cleveland became president on 4 March 1893, he withdrew the treaty from the Senate. Seven days later he appointed Blount special commissioner to Hawaii and gave him "paramount" authority "in all matters pertaining to the existing government of the islands." Blount arrived in Honolulu on 29 March and began to interview locals in a circumspect and meticulous way. He hoped to answer Cleveland's questions about American complicity in the revolution and whether most Hawaiians wanted the islands annexed. He completed his work on 27 July and mailed a report to Gresham. Then, acting against Cleveland's wishes, he returned to Washington on 8 August. Blount's conclusions were simple and straightforward. He stated that John L. Stevens, U.S. minister to Hawaii and an expansionist, had aided in the overthrow of the queen and that if annexation were put to a vote the islanders would overwhelmingly reject it.

Gresham kept the report until October, when he sent it, with recommendations, on to the president. In December Cleveland, in two messages to Congress, made clear his decision not to return the treaty to the Senate. He added that he would not reinstate the monarchy because the queen refused to grant full amnesty to the revolutionists, and he commended the entire matter to Congress. When he was out of office five years later, the former president said, "Ever since the question of Hawaiian annexation was presented I have been utterly and constantly opposed to it" (Osborne, p. 15). Nevertheless, many scholars believe Blount's report determined President Cleveland's action at the time.

In late 1893 Blount's views were denounced by Stevens and others as inaccurate and biased. His position was likewise criticized by the press, which favored annexation. While a House majority supported his stand, hearings held by the Senate Foreign Relations Committee in 1894 were more critical. Republicans challenged his authority as a special commissioner to Hawaii without the approval of the whole Senate. Blount defended himself and his report at the hearings. Despite the controversy in Washington, Hawaii's provisional government established the Republic of Hawaii on 4 July 1894, and on 12 August 1898, with the support of the William McKinley administration, Congress annexed it by joint resolution.

Blount returned to Georgia and entered society as a former statesman, planter, and lawyer. Despite his earlier intentions, he never ran for the Senate. His later years were spent tending an ample estate in Jones County, where he died.

• Some of Blount's letters are in the Walter Q. Gresham and Grover Cleveland papers, both in the Library of Congress. Information about his military service is in National Archives Microfilms, Southwest Region, Fort Worth, Tex., Rolls M-226, "Index to Georgia Confederate Soldiers"; M-836, "Confederate States Army Casualties"; and T-455, "Reference File Relating to Confederate Organizations from Georgia, 1861–65." His congressional career is in the *Congressional Record*, 1873–1893. Blount's daughter's autobiography, Dolly Blount Lamar, *When All Is Said and Done* (1952), provides a lengthy discussion of him. For his role during Reconstruction see I. W. Avery, *The History of the State of Georgia from 1850 to 1881* (1881), and Alan Conway, *The Reconstruction of Georgia* (1966). On his Hawaiian undertaking, the most useful sources are Tennant S. McWilliams, "James H. Blount, the South, and Hawaiian Annexation," *Pacific Historical Review* 57 (1988): 25–46; Carole E. Scott, "Racism and Southern Anti-imperialists: The Blounts of Georgia," *Atlanta History* 31 (1987): 24–29; Thomas J. Osborne, *"Empire Can Wait," American Opposition to Hawaiian Annexation, 1893–1898* (1981); Merze Tate, *The United States and the Hawaiian Kingdom, A Political History* (1965); and Sylvester K. Stevens, *American Expansion in Hawaii, 1842–1898* (1945). A small but useful compilation of selected documents bearing on the investigation is in J. A. Gillis, *The Hawaiian Incident* (1897). An obituary is in the *New York Times*, 9 Mar. 1903.

ROBERT S. LA FORTE

BLOUNT, William (26 Mar. 1749–21 Mar. 1800), territorial governor and U.S. senator, was born in Bertie County, North Carolina, the son of Jacob Blount, a landowner, and Barbara Gray. While probably not formally schooled, he displayed a keen interest in the promotion of education throughout his career. Blount married Mary Grainger (known as "Molsey") in 1778; they had eight children.

In the early 1780s, Blount and his brothers established John Gray and Thomas Blount, Merchants, with branches throughout North Carolina. The company engaged in merchandising and coastal and overseas commerce. The Blounts also became land speculators on a vast scale in the area of present-day Tennessee and Alabama.

The development of the Blount business was promoted by the brothers' military and political activity during the American Revolution. William Blount served in the North Carolina army as a financial officer. He held a seat in the state legislature from 1780 to 1790 and while there served on legislative committees that dealt with soldiers' claims and land titles. North Carolina during this time developed a plan to pay Carolina soldiers for their revolutionary service with titles to land in uncolonized areas claimed by the state in present-day Tennessee. As a member of the legislative committees that developed and implemented this payment plan, Blount was able to secure private advantage for himself and his associates. He was elected Speaker of the House of Commons in 1784 and then served two terms in the senate. It was during this period that Blount established the foundations of his extensive land speculation in the area west of the Appalachians.

As a partner in his family firm, Blount established an alliance with James Robertson (1742–1814), a founder of the settlement at present-day Nashville in Middle Tennessee. This area lay at the heart of the North Carolina Military District established in 1784 by North Carolina soldiers receiving land grants in lieu of salaries for their service in the Revolution. Blount and Robertson were able to purchase unused military warrants from soldiers. Blount also headed a group involved in land speculation under the name of the Bend of the Tennessee (Muscle Shoals) Company that hoped to establish a separate state in that area of present-day Alabama.

Blount emerged as the linchpin of a growing western land speculation that eventually led to state making and national political activity. The firm of John Gray and Thomas Blount sought to achieve further economic advantage and influence on the national level. William Blount, the firm's political agent, was selected to serve in the Continental Congress in 1782–1783 and again in the critical years of 1786–1787. While in that body, Blount sought to protect the firm's extensive western land investments by calling for expanded national control over the American Indian tribes in the area, and he cultivated good relations with Spanish and other foreign diplomats to protect navigation of the Mississippi River for people in the western lands. Additionally, Blount was in constant motion seeking investors in company lands and developing well-placed friends among the powerful such as George Washington, with whom Blount became acquainted while at the Continental Congress and other national forums.

Blount saw that a stronger central authority could promote and protect his business activities. The turmoil of the Confederation Era jeopardized his holdings in western North Carolina. Giving the Continental Congress a one-year period to accept its western lands into the national domain in 1784, North Carolina retroceded the area in 1785. This action sparked a secessionist or independence effort by the people in the affected area, calling it the state of Franklin.

Blount was chosen as a delegate from North Carolina to the Constitutional Convention of 1787 and served in the North Carolina ratification convention. Following ratification, Blount unsuccessfully sought election to the U.S. Senate. In 1790 President Washington appointed him territorial governor of the territory south of the Ohio River. That position afforded Blount the opportunity to protect his western land investments because the territorial governor also served as superintendent of Indian affairs. He told his brother that he rejoiced in the appointment for "I think it of great importance to our western speculation" (Keith, vol. 2, p. 67).

The position of territorial governor gave Blount an extensive political patronage, well calculated for Blount's viewpoint, as he told future Tennessee governor John Sevier, "It is a principle with me never to . . . stand between a friend and a benefit" (Blount to Sevier, 6 July 1798, Tennessee Historical Society: Miscellaneous Collection). One of the most significant features of Blount's career was the number of leading Tennesseans who achieved prominence because of his patronage, the most noted being Andrew Jackson, whom he appointed attorney general for the Miro District (Middle Tennessee) on 15 February 1791. Jackson became a principal figure within the Blount organization and succeeded Blount as a U.S. senator from Tennessee and leader of the Blount political faction in the state.

Blount's term as territorial governor allowed him the opportunity to build a political organization in what became Tennessee. This organization included Sevier; John Overton; Robertson; Willie Blount, a half-brother; George Roulstone, editor of the territorial newspaper; and others. While protecting his land interests, the governor steered a course that enabled him to control the clashing demands of the frontier for punitive action against the American Indians and the policy of the federal government for a "defensive only" posture toward the tribes.

Blount served as presiding officer at the Constitutional Convention in 1796 that drew up the fundamental document for the state of Tennessee. His particular interests were low taxes on land and the protection of the right of navigation on the Mississippi River, a critical factor in Blount's political and economic career. The legislature chosen under the new state constitution selected Blount as a U.S. senator in 1796.

His political fortunes were on the ascendancy, but economic problems soon brought him down. Blount and his brothers entered the "raging mania of speculation" that swept the nation in the 1790s. They made commitments to purchase millions of acres before western land values collapsed when war broke out between Great Britain and Spain in 1796. Fearing that France would gain control of the Mississippi, Blount entered into a conspiracy that sought to join the western Mississippi area with Britain, a party to the Treaty of 1783 guaranteeing navigation of that river. For a

U.S. senator to enter into a plan that called for a foreign nation to assume sovereignty over territory belonging to the United States or desired by it was at best ill advised. Senator Blount put his design into a letter that fell into the hands of his opponents and was publicly revealed. He resigned his Senate post to avoid impeachment. Returning to Tennessee, he received a hero's welcome and was elected to the state senate and to the Speakership, the state's second highest office. Blount's career ended at Knoxville, where he died of chills and possibly a stroke.

• Major manuscript collections on Blount include the John Gray Blount Manuscripts in the North Carolina Department of Archives and History at Raleigh; the Blount correspondence collection in the McClung collection at the Knoxville Public Library; the Blount letters at Knoxville's Hoskins Library Special Collections; the Blount papers at the Tennessee State Library and Archives; the Blount Family Papers, 1794–1829, in the Historic New Orleans Collection; and the Blount collection at the Library of Congress. Published primary material includes the essential three volumes of Alice B. Keith, ed., *John Gray Blount Papers* (1959), and C. E. Carter, comp. and ed., *Territorial Papers of the U.S.: Territory of the U.S. South of the Ohio, 1790–1796*, vol. 4 (1936). The most complete biography of Blount is William A. Masterson, *William Blount* (1954); a more recent treatment is Walter T. Durham, *Before Tennessee: The Southwest Territory* (1990).

THOMAS H. WINN

BLOUNT, Willie (18 Apr. 1768?–10 Sept. 1835), lawyer and governor of Tennessee, was born in Bertie County, North Carolina, the son of Jacob Blount, a prominent landowner, and Hannah (Salter) Baker, the daughter of the influential settler Edward Salter and widow of William Baker of South Quay, Virginia. Although a member of a leading family, little is known about Willie's (pronounced Wylie) early life and education. He attended both King's College and the College of New Jersey (now Columbia and Princeton Universities, respectively) and subsequently read law with the noted judge John Sitgraves at New Bern, North Carolina.

Blount's financial and political fortunes were closely linked to those of his half brother, William Blount. In 1790 the latter obtained appointment as governor of the new Southwest Territory, and Willie Blount accompanied him as a private secretary. The brothers eventually settled at Knoxville, the territorial seat, where Blount became acquainted with most of the leaders of the area and obtained a license to practice law in 1794. Politics in the territory revolved around two personalities. Blount was a member of his brother's political faction, which included, among others, Andrew Jackson, Archibald Roane, and Joseph McMinn. The other faction was headed by revolutionary war hero John Sevier. The rivalry between these factions shaped politics during the territorial and, after 1796, early statehood years. Accordingly, Sevier became Tennessee's first governor and William Blount one of two U.S. senators. Although the new state legislature elected Willie Blount to the Superior Court of Law and Equity in 1796, he chose not to serve. Thereafter he moved west to Montgomery County, Tennessee, where he practiced law and married Lucinda Baker. The couple had two children.

William Blount's financial reverses, his involvement in an abortive effort to seize control of Louisiana and Florida from Spain, and his expulsion from the Senate, followed by his death in 1800, led to the Blount faction's decline. Sevier served three consecutive two-year terms as governor, the constitutional maximum, waited out the governorship of Blountite Archibald Roane, and then returned to serve another three terms. Throughout this period Willie Blount, who had assumed responsibility for his brother's family and financial affairs, continued his law practice and increased his land holdings. In 1794 he had been named a trustee of Blount College (later the University of Tennessee) and in 1806 a trustee of Nashville's Cumberland College.

Although intimately involved in the organization of his late brother's faction, Blount's first overt political activity was one term in the Tennessee House of Representatives (1807–1809). By that time, he was ready to assume the faction's leadership. In 1809 Blount defeated former U.S. senator William Cocke for the first of what proved to be Blount's three consecutive terms as governor of Tennessee. His election marked a decisive shift in political power from East Tennessee to the more recently settled lands to the west. During his six years in office Blount emphasized policies that would speed the state's settlement and development. A proponent of internal improvements, the governor favored the duty-free navigation of the waterways between Tennessee and Mobile, Alabama, and the construction of roads to surrounding states in order to expedite commerce and communication. His tenure saw the completion of the "turnpike road" between Knoxville and Nashville. Other policies fostered the creation of the first state bank in 1811 and sought to regularize the overlapping and often conflicting land titles issued under the aegis of Tennessee, North Carolina, and Kentucky.

But no greater issue confronted the state's ever increasing white population than Indian land claims. Not only did the Cherokee and Chickasaw nations control significant areas within Tennessee, but the state's Gulf-bound commerce had to pass through areas controlled by two other powerful Indian nations, the Creek and Choctaw. Blount proposed extinguishing Indian land titles and removing the Indian nations from Tennessee to an area west of the Mississippi River. Despite his continued recommendations to the federal government, these policies were not fully adopted until Andrew Jackson's presidency. Blount's early and constant advocacy of this program earns him a large share of responsibility for its final adoption.

The real or perceived threat of Indian uprising shaped American and Tennessean attitudes and policies throughout Blount's governorship. Fear of British exploitation of tensions with the Indian nations fueled sentiment for action against marauding Creeks in 1812 and 1813 and expanded the war with Great Britain to include the so-called Creek War of 1813–1814. Blount is remembered chiefly for securing on his own authority more than $370,000 in financial support for the federalized Tennessee volunteer militia under the command of Major General Andrew Jackson. Credit for Jackson's victory over the Creeks at the battle of Horseshoe Bend in March 1814, therefore, also accrued to Blount. The governor contributed as well, to a lesser extent, to Jackson's victory, as a major general of the regular army, over the British at New Orleans on 8 January 1815.

After leaving office in September 1815, Blount returned to Montgomery County, where he spent the remaining twenty years of his life. His first wife had died, and in 1812 he married Mary White, the widow of Knoxvillian Hugh White. He pursued the law and farming but retained an interest in politics. He and Jackson remained allies, and their correspondence is laced with Blount's acerbic comments. In 1827 Blount lost badly to Sam Houston in a bid to return to the governorship. Blount concluded his public service as a member of the 1834 constitutional convention, where he chaired the committee on internal improvements. The following year he died near Nashville. Blount's historical importance relies more on his proposed policies than on his accomplishments, on his support for the Tennessee volunteers during the War of 1812, and perhaps most significantly on his resuscitation of the political faction whose ablest lieutenant was Andrew Jackson.

• No collection of Blount's papers remains. Some manuscripts are in the Draper manuscripts, Wisconsin Historical Society; the Blount Family Papers are located at the North Carolina State Department of Archives and History. Other correspondence is in the Andrew Jackson Papers, chiefly at the Library of Congress and National Archives. Selected editions of the Jackson papers (containing Blount correspondence) include the *Correspondence of Andrew Jackson*, ed. John S. Bassett (7 vols., 1926–1935), and the multivolume *Papers of Andrew Jackson*, ed. Sam B. Smith et al. (1980–); see also Robert H. White, ed., *Messages of the Governors of Tennessee*, vol. 1 (1952), pp. 274–441, for selected official documents with commentary and overview of Blount's administration. Blount authored one pamphlet of note, *A Catechetical Exposition of the Construction of the State of Tennessee: Intended Principally for the Use of Schools* (1803), had begun a history of Tennessee (now lost), and prepared an (unpublished) defense of his brother William. The latter is reprinted in John Trotwood Moore, *Tennessee: The Volunteer State, 1769–1923* (1923), pp. 285–87. Material about the Blount family can be found in *The Papers of John Gray Blount*, ed. Alice B. Keith (3 vols., 1952–1965), and in William H. Masterson, *William Blount* (1954). A lengthy sketch on Blount appears in Charles W. Crawford, ed., *Governors of Tennessee, 1790–1835* (1979), pp. 79–95; see also Elizabeth H. Peeler, "Policies of Willie Blount as Governor of Tennessee," *Tennessee Historical Quarterly* 1, no. 4 (Dec. 1942): 309–27; and Joshua W. Caldwell, *Sketches of the Bench and Bar of Tennessee* (1898), pp. 30–32.

GEORGE H. HOEMANN

BLOW, Henry Taylor (15 July 1817–11 Sept. 1875), entrepreneur and congressman, was born in Southhampton County, Virginia, the son of Peter Blow, a planter, and Elizabeth Taylor. Depressed conditions in Virginia forced the family to move to northeastern Alabama in 1820. Ten years later they migrated farther west to St. Louis. Henry graduated from St. Louis College (now University) in 1835. He briefly studied law but gave that up to enter the retail drug business in 1836 with Joseph Charless, who had married his older sister. Blow married Minerva Grimsley in 1840; they had 12 children.

Blow took an interest in the production of castor and linseed oil, which the Charless firm sold, and set up several small mills for their manufacture. Since little flax was grown in Missouri at the time, he successfully promoted its culture throughout the state. He dissolved his business partnership with Charless in 1844 and thereafter devoted himself exclusively to manufacturing and mining, amassing a considerable fortune. Blow ultimately formed the Collier White Lead and Oil Company and became a major figure in the commercial and industrial development of St. Louis. With his brother Peter, who was involved in lead mining in Washington County, Missouri, Blow played a leading role in lead mining development in southwest Missouri. Although this enterprise was disrupted by the Civil War, at the end of that conflict the Blow brothers established the Granby Mining and Smelting Company, which was an immediate success.

Blow was also active in promoting transportation facilities for St. Louis, working with James B. Eads and others to improve Mississippi River navigation and assisting in the construction of the St. Louis and Iron Mountain Railroad, which serviced his brother's lead mining interests in Washington County, during the late 1850s. Blow also concerned himself with a variety of civic enterprises in St. Louis. He helped establish the Western Academy of Art, the city's first art gallery, shortly before the Civil War and was a particularly strong supporter of the public school movement following the war. One of his daughters, Susan E. Blow, pioneered the public kindergarten movement in the United States.

Blow took an early interest in the emerging Free Soil movement in the late 1840s. Dred Scott was raised in the Blow family home as a child, and in 1846 Blow and other members of his family helped finance Scott's initial suit for freedom in the Missouri courts. Blow was elected as a Whig to the Missouri Senate in 1854. In the legislature he joined with Frank Blair (1821–1875) and B. Gratz Brown to promote the idea of compensated emancipation of Missouri's slaves and their colonization elsewhere to remove them as competition for free white labor. These three played a leading role in the formation of the Republican party in Missouri.

Blow served as a delegate to the Republican National Convention in Chicago in 1860, initially favoring, with the rest of the Missouri delegation, the candidacy of favorite son Edward Bates. The following year President Abraham Lincoln appointed him minister to Venezuela, but he returned in 1862 to run successfully for Congress as a "Charcoal" Republican, that is one who favored immediate and uncompensated emancipation. The following year Blow joined Charles D. Drake, who had married another of his sisters, and others to establish the Radical Union party of Missouri with a platform of immediate emancipation for Missouri's slaves and the enlistment of free blacks into the armed forces. In 1864 he served as a delegate to the Republican National Convention in Baltimore, where the Missouri delegation, dominated by Radicals, cast their ballots for Ulysses S. Grant, the only votes against Lincoln's renomination.

Blow was reelected to Congress in 1864 and served on the Joint Committee on Reconstruction, where he tended to support the Radical position for a more stringent reconstruction policy toward the South. He retired from Congress in 1866 because of the need to give his full attention to his expanding mining interests. In 1869 President Grant appointed him minister to Brazil, where he served two years. Initially reluctant to accept this post because it would take him away from his business, he did so at the urging of his St. Louis friends, who saw this as an opportunity to open trade between Brazil and the Mississippi Valley. In this Blow made considerable progress. He resumed his business interests in 1871 but was persuaded to act as chair of the Republican State Central Committee the following year. In 1874 Grant appointed him a commissioner for the District of Columbia, which was undergoing a political reorganization. Blow died suddenly, presumably of a heart attack, in Saratoga, New York.

• Henry T. Blow's papers are included with those of his brothers Peter and Taylor and other members of the family in a collection known as the Blow Family Papers in the Missouri Historical Society in St. Louis. He has not received a full-length biographical treatment, but biographical sketches are available in J. Thomas Scharf, *History of Saint Louis City and County* (1883), and L. U. Reavis, *Saint Louis, the Future Great City of the World*, biographical ed. (1875). Blow's role in the formation of the Missouri Radical Union party is discussed in his brother-in-law Charles D. Drake's "Autobiography" in the Drake Papers, State Historical Society of Missouri in Columbia, and in William E. Parrish, *Missouri under Radical Rule, 1865–1870* (1965).

WILLIAM E. PARRISH

BLOW, Susan Elizabeth (7 June 1843–?27 Mar. 1916), educational reformer, was born in Carondelet, a section of St. Louis, Missouri, the daughter of Henry Taylor Blow, a wealthy owner of lead-mining operations, president of the Iron Mountain Railroad, state senator, and minister to Venezuela and Brazil, and Minerva Grimsley, daughter of another prominent manufacturer and local politician. Susan Blow grew up in a large household and an environment of high German culture, business, and government affairs. Her extended family and social network included uncles, cousins, and business associates of her father who were involved in local, state, national, and international politics. Her grandfather Peter Blow had brought slaves with him from Virginia and Alabama. One of them was Dred Scott, who in 1857 unsuccessfully challenged the slavery issue in court. Taylor Blow, her uncle, inherited the Blow family slaves when his father died. He freed Dred Scott and his wife Harriet, and Henry Blow paid for Scott's funeral expenses in 1858. A Whig who later became a "black Republican" over the issue of slavery, Henry Blow served in the U.S. Congress during Reconstruction.

As the eldest daughter in this wealthy and influential German mercantile family, Susan Blow was educated at home by her mother and father, who also employed governesses and private tutors for her. She attended the William McCauley school in New Orleans from ages eight to ten, and at sixteen she enrolled in the New York school of Henrietta Haines. In 1861, classes having been discontinued, she and her sister Nellie returned to St. Louis, where she remained for the duration of the Civil War, tutoring her six younger brothers and sisters and teaching Sunday school at the Carondelet Presbyterian Church, where her father was a trustee.

During the war many young soldiers were stationed at Jefferson Barracks in St. Louis. Blow, at age twenty, fell in love with Colonel William Coyle. However, her parents thought he was not suitable for her. Shortly after she had met and corresponded with him, Coyle was discharged from the army for medical reasons and returned to his home in Kentucky. Henry Blow then took her to Washington, D.C., where he introduced her to another military man he favored. She chose not to marry anyone. After President Ulysses S. Grant appointed her father minister to Brazil in 1869, Blow traveled with him to that country and served as his secretary. She quickly learned Portuguese, which eased trade communications between the United States and Brazil.

Following her fifteen-month sojourn in South America, Blow, her mother, and her siblings traveled to Europe. As an intellectual, Blow studied and read a great deal, including the philosophies of Hegel and the American Transcendentalists. During her year in Europe she also encountered the kindergarten ideas of German educator Friedrich Froebel. Blow was in her late twenties by this time, and her earlier experiences as a teacher were rekindled by Froebel's ideas about cognitive development in children.

Many immigrants who had fled Prussia in 1848 eventually settled in St. Louis, where they served as early school board members and active social reformers in the postwar period, a time when the city was becoming heavily urbanized and industrialized. The common school movement had taken hold, and by 1870 St. Louis could boast of an established system of public schools and private kindergartens. The German leaders favored Froebel's ideas about educating and socializing children during their early growth years. Because she had learned kindergarten methods in Germany, Blow was able to take these ideas and formulate them into a practical plan for establishing a public kindergarten in St. Louis.

William Torrey Harris, superintendent of St. Louis schools, saw the greatest educational problem of the time as children dropping out of school too early and thus initially resisted the idea of kindergarten. The school board, however, supported preprimary classes. Its support, combined with Blow's proposal to direct the kindergarten experiment and her social stature, cultural background, and intellectual abilities persuaded Harris to champion her plan. In 1871 she went to New York City, where she studied for a year with Maria Kraus-Boelte, the "spiritual daughter of Froebel," who established a class for mothers and kindergartners in that city in 1872. Blow became the first American kindergarten teacher to be trained by Boelte. Blow returned to St. Louis in 1873 and opened the nation's first public-school kindergarten in the Des Peres School in her neighborhood of Carondelet. She directed and, along with two assistants, Mary Timberlake and Cynthia Dozier, taught in the school, which enrolled forty-two students. The experiment was a resounding success. The classes were popular with the community and quickly expanded.

Blow next turned to meeting the exploding demand for trained kindergarten teachers. In 1874 she opened a training school in which trainees spent half-days as volunteers in kindergarten classes and the other half of each day, plus weekends, reading and discussing Froebel's theories. Without the unpaid labor of these women, the kindergarten experiment would have faced far greater odds of success. Women took the training as idealists and social reformers but also with the expectation of finding employment in a time of great social and economic change. Graduates of Blow's normal training school taught in kindergartens all over the country and in turn trained the next generation of kindergarten teachers. Through their teaching and the formation of the Kindergarten Association, these women and Blow played a significant part in the history and development of early childhood education. The Froebelian method became widely known in the United States after 1895; when Blow translated Froebel's *Mother Play* for day-to-day use in her classroom and training courses, and many elements of his educational philosophy, such as mothers' meetings, home visits, school gardens, and nature study, continue to be used in preschools and kindergartens. Within three years the kindergarten system in St. Louis enrolled more than a thousand students and employed fifty teachers.

Blow suffered from Graves' disease, a form of hyperthyroidism, which forced her to withdraw from teaching in 1884 and into a period of retirement from 1886 to 1895. That year she began to lecture again in Boston, where she also conducted study classes in the Bible, Homer, Dante, Goethe, and Shakespeare. She spent the last years of her life in New York City, near her sister Nellie, working with the Kindergarten Association and teaching at Teacher's College, Columbia University. She died in New York City. Blow's tombstone in Bellefontaine Cemetery in St. Louis lists her date of death as 27 March 1916, although most reference works say she died on 26 March.

• The Susan Blow Museum and Collection is housed in the Des Peres School, Carondelet Historical Society, St. Louis. Her publications include *Symbolic Education* (1894), *The Mottoes and Commentaries of Friedrich Froebel's Mother Play* (1895), *The Songs and Music of Froebel's Mother Play* (1895), *Letters to a Mother on the Philosophy of Froebel* (1899), *Kindergarten Education* (1900), and *Educational Issues in the Kindergarten* (1908). See also S. J. Van Ausdal, "Case Study in Innovation: The Public Kindergarten in St. Louis, 1870–1890" (Ph.D. diss., Southern Illinois Univ., Edwardsville, 1985), and G. Stanley Hall, *Educational Problems* (1911). An obituary is in the *New York Times*, 29 Mar. 1916.

KATHLEEN S. BROWN

BLUE JACKET (1740?–1808?), Shawnee warrior and diplomat, was probably born in Pennsylvania. Originally called Sepettekenathe (Big Rabbit), he changed his name to Waweyapiersenwa (Whirlpool) before 1778 but was generally known as Blue Jacket. He probably belonged to the Pekowi division of the Shawnee tribe. By 1772 he had become a war chief among the Shawnees of the upper Scioto River, where he had a village on Deer Creek. His influence rested upon his prowess as a warrior and his extensive connections and familiarity with whites.

Blue Jacket supported his people's opposition to the white settlement of Kentucky after the treaty of Fort Stanwix (1768) and was almost certainly a leader of the force defeated by the Virginians at Point Pleasant on 10 October 1774. He was married twice, first to Margaret Moore, a white captive of the Shawnee, and second to the Shawnee daughter of the important French Canadian trader Jacques Dupéront Baby (her name is unknown). Of his five children, at least two of whom (Nancy and Joseph) were by his second wife, one (Mary) married an influential French Canadian trader, Jacques Lacelle, and another (George) was educated in Detroit and, because of his command of the English language, served as an interpreter. Blue Jacket may have been related, through their Shawnee wives, to Alexander McKee and Matthew Elliott, both of whom became key Indian agents in the Crown's service. Such relationships gave Blue Jacket an acquisitive, more European life-style. He lived in substantial, well-equipped houses, raised considerable livestock and crops, and owned a store.

In 1775–1776 Blue Jacket and other chiefs visited Pittsburgh to confer with the representatives of the revolutionary government, but in 1777 he and most of his fellow Shawnee allied with the British and moved west to the Great and Little Miami rivers. Blue Jacket established a new village where Bellefontaine, Ohio, now stands. He served throughout the revolutionary war with distinction, accompanying the British commander of Detroit Henry Hamilton's expedition against Vincennes, Indiana, in 1778–1779 and probably Captain Henry Bird's invasion of Kentucky in 1780.

After the war, Shawnee hopes of peace ended when the United States imposed the treaty of Fort Finney upon them in 1786, claiming territory north of the Ohio and east of the Great Miami. Deteriorating relations caused the Kentuckians under Colonel Benjamin Logan to destroy the Shawnee towns, including Blue Jacket's, in October 1786. Again the Shawnee withdrew, many joining the Miamis at the head of the Maumee River (near present-day Fort Wayne, Indiana), including Blue Jacket. The Shawnee endorsed the Mohawk Joseph Brant's efforts to form a multitribal confederacy to resist U.S. encroachment and launched raids upon settlers in Kentucky and along the Ohio River.

The treaties of Fort Harmar (1789), by which some Indians acknowledged U.S. claims to Ohio, were repudiated by the Shawnee. However, disagreement among tribes over support for the treaties dismantled Brant's confederacy. It was then that Blue Jacket, now the principal Shawnee war chief, began his most important work. With other tribal leaders, including his younger brother Musquaconocah (Red Pole), the head civil chief Kekewepelethy (Great or Tame Hawk, also known as Captain Johnny), and the war leader Ptasua (Captain Snake), he revived Brant's confederacy, initially joining with the Miamis and Delawares at the head of the Maumee. This confederacy was attacked by General Josiah Harmar's force of 1,500 regulars and militia in October 1790. Although several of their towns were destroyed, Blue Jacket, Little Turtle of the Miamis, and other chiefs evacuated their noncombatants, called in their scattered hunters, and counterattacked, costing Harmar's force 183 killed and missing and turning the army's withdrawal to Fort Washington into a rout. The Indians reestablished their villages, and by mid-1791 the confederacy had secured the support of other tribes, including the Potawatomis, Ottawas, Ojibwas, and Wyandots.

In 1791 General Arthur St. Clair led a new army against the confederacy. Instead of waiting for the attack, some one thousand warriors stormed St. Clair's camp on the Wabash River on 4 November, inflicting nearly a thousand casualties. The Indian force was controlled by a council of chiefs, but a commander was appointed to oversee the attack. Although Little Turtle later contended that he had served as commander, contemporary reports from among the confederacy name Blue Jacket. The victory raised Blue Jacket's prestige to unprecedented heights. The British began to call him "General Blue Jacket" and apparently allowed him a stipend, and Americans, including St. Clair's successor, Major General Anthony Wayne, repeatedly referred to him as "the famous Blue Jacket."

In June 1792 the United States made overtures of peace with the Shawnee and other northwestern tribes. That year the confederacy moved its headquarters to "the Glaize" at the junction of the Maumee and the Auglaize rivers in Ohio, closer to British supplies, and circulated calls for unity among the tribes. Blue Jacket toured towns around the western Great Lakes and upper Mississippi River, and Red Pole led an embassy to the Creeks and Cherokees to the south. A congress held at the Glaize from 30 September to 9 October 1792 attracted representatives of tribes from the St. Lawrence River to Missouri and endorsed the Shawnee demand for a boundary along the Ohio.

Peace negotiations with the United States broke down in August 1793. In the spring of 1794 Blue Jacket was again visiting native villages to the west, calling warriors to rendezvous at the foot of the Maumee rapids. In June he led a thousand men against Wayne's communications (the latter was extending a line of forts from Fort Washington roughly northerly toward the head of the Maumee), capturing a convoy outside Fort Recovery but falling back after an unsuccessful attack on the post. The confederacy then abandoned their villages at the Glaize and retired to a defensive position at Fallen Timbers, near the Maumee rapids. There they were defeated by the U.S. Army on 20 August. Blue Jacket saw the failure of the British at nearby Fort Miamis to provide support as confirmation of his suspicions that they were fickle allies, and although his people retired to Swan Creek at the mouth of the Maumee to receive British supplies, he decided to meet the U.S. terms. Blue Jacket visited Wayne at Fort Greenville, representing the Shawnees, Miamis, and Delawares, and concluded preliminary peace articles on 11 February 1795. It was in large part through his efforts that so many of the hostile warriors agreed to meet in Greenville the following summer to cede southern and eastern Ohio in return for a down payment and annuities.

For some years after the war Blue Jacket remained a major spokesman for the Shawnee. The U.S. government built him a house on the St. Marys River, near Fort Wayne, in 1796, and the ensuing winter he was entertained in Philadelphia and met George Washington. About 1800 he established his last town on the Detroit River near present-day Gibraltar, Michigan.

Alone among senior Shawnee chiefs Blue Jacket backed the efforts of Tecumseh and Tenskwatawa to unite Indians behind a reformist religion, from 1806 acting as their principal adviser and spokesman. The religion called upon the Indians to reject contaminating influences of whites, to restore aboriginal customs, and to abandon alcohol and the use of witchcraft. In September 1807 Blue Jacket completed a difficult schedule on behalf of Tecumseh's band, conferrring with the Wyandots at Brownstown, Michigan, and defending the band before the governor of the Michigan Territory in Detroit, emissaries of the governor of Ohio at Greenville, and a large gathering in Chillicothe. A witness to the Chillicothe speech, perhaps his final public address, described him as "an old man, an eminently dignified speaker, and of calm, persuasive eloquence." Blue Jacket apparently died at home the following year.

In his prime Blue Jacket was handsome, tall, and well formed, with a liking for fine clothes, although in old age he grew stout. He had many faults, including vanity and ambition, and he was throughout his life a heavy drinker. But he was also brave, circumspect, kind, generous, and hospitable. His career stands comparison with those of Brant and Tecumseh. He was one of the few Indian leaders to orchestrate and successfully lead multitribal forces and was crucial in establishing the Pan-Indian tradition.

• Of the older works, Benjamin Drake, *Life of Tecumseh* (1841), contains useful, if fragmentary, references to Blue Jacket. John Bennett, *Blue Jacket, War Chief of the Shawnees* (1943), although more complete, perpetuates several inaccuracies, including the story that Blue Jacket was a white man who had been captured by the Shawnee, an influential fiction first attacked by Helen Hornbeck Tanner in "The Glaize in 1792: A Composite Indian Community," *Ethnohistory* 25 (1978): 15–39. The entry on Blue Jacket by Reginald Horsman in *Dictionary of Canadian Biography* 5 (1983): 852–53 itemizes most of the references in printed sources; a complete biography, drawing upon these and scattered manuscript materials, is being prepared by John Sugden.

JOHN SUGDEN

BLUEMNER, Oscar Julius (21 June 1867–12 Jan. 1938), painter, was born in Prenzlau, Germany (Prussia), the son of Hermann Bluemner, a master builder. His mother's name is unknown. After passing his *Abitur* examination in Elberfeld, he entered the Königliche Technische Hochschule in Berlin (Charlottenburg), where he studied architecture under Hermann Ende and Fritz Wolff between 1887 and 1892. Before graduating he designed public buildings in Glewitz and Halle am Saale and was awarded a Royal Academy medal for the painting of an architectural subject.

In October 1892 Bluemner emigrated to the United States, a decision prompted by the prevailing aesthetic conservatism of his homeland and good prospects of employment in Chicago at the World's Columbian Exposition. In a short article for *Camera Work* (Jan. 1915), he recalled, "It seemed as if in America there would exist that all-around liberty . . . under which a new idea, in architecture if not in art, could take form all the better." After serving briefly as a design assistant at the exposition and a two-year stint in New York, where a severe recession limited his work to part-time draftsman, dishwasher, and street peddler, Bluemner settled in Chicago from 1895 to 1900. During this interval he earned a modest income as an architect, married Lina Schumm (1897), who gave birth to the first of their two children the following year, and was granted U.S. citizenship (1899).

In 1900 a building boom drew Bluemner back to New York, where over the next decade he designed several homes and the new Bronx Borough Courthouse, but he grew increasingly dissatisfied with the commercial aspects of architecture. For relief he began to make long sketching trips into rural Long Island and New Jersey, and around 1910 he met Alfred Stieglitz, whose 291 Gallery afforded a sanctuary for avant-garde artists and a context for Bluemner to quit "architekturkram" for painting. In 1912 he revisited Europe, where he held his first solo exhibition at Galerie Fritz Gurlitt in Berlin, which included *March Wind, Passaic River, N.J.* and *Old Canal, Red and Blue (Rockaway River)*, and where he witnessed pioneering displays of modern art at the Sonderbund exhibition in Cologne, the Kahnweiler and Druet galleries in Paris, and Roger Fry's second postimpressionist exhibition in London. Upon his return to New York, Bluemner entered five paintings, including *Hackensack River* and *Morning on Long Island*, in the controversial Armory Show and defended the event in a lengthy essay for *Camera Work* (June 1913), proclaiming that "the new vision of nature and the new synthesis of the pictorial elements are not capricious, but a conscious movement for perfect freedom of artistic individuality and for expression of modern culture." Bluemner's first American solo exhibition, held at 291 in 1915, featured a series of eight landscapes, including *Stanhope (Contemplation in a New Jersey Town)* and *Paterson Centre (Expression of a Silktown)*, whose "synthesis" of local scenery, emotive color, and cubist structure clearly reflected the "new vision." The following year his place among the leaders of early modernism was affirmed by his inclusion in the closely juried Forum Exhibition of Modern American Painters in which he exhibited *Stanhope*, *Paterson Centre*, *Wharton (Space Motive, New Jersey Valley)*, and *Montville (Movement of Space and Form, New Jersey Town)*.

When U.S. entry into World War I closed 291 and heightened anti-German sentiment in New York, Bluemner resettled in New Jersey from 1916 to 1926, at various times living in Bloomfield, Belleville, Irvington, Newark, and Elizabeth. During this difficult decade, his family lived in chronic poverty despite various efforts by dealers, including Stephan Bourgeois, J. B. Neumann, and Aline Liebman, to sell his paintings. Artist Georgia O'Keeffe remembered him as a man "who lived in a house that was half in one county and half in another . . . [so that] when the collector came for the rent, Bluemner would go to the other side." Unable to afford canvas or frames, Bluemner devoted his time to developing a theory of painting based on a fusion of romantic and symbolist ideals, Oriental aesthetics, and the metaphysical tenets of thinkers such as Goethe, Schopenhauer, Bergson, and Spengler. In his 1924 painting diary he declared, "The visible world as a transitory play of elemental force and matter exhibits to us beauty of form and color, and Beauty elevates our minds toward comprehension of Spirit." That same year Bluemner put his theory into practice by launching an ambitious new series, "One Hundred Pure Watercolors." He had painted only fifty-nine of these, including *Glowing Night* and *Flag Station, Elizabeth*, when his wife died in March 1926, and he never completed the series.

Bluemner spent his last years in South Braintree, Massachusetts. During this productive period, he was recognized with three solo New York exhibitions at Stieglitz's Intimate Gallery (1928), the Whitney Studio Galleries (1929), and the Marie Harriman Gallery

(1935). He was also chosen for two major invitational shows organized by the Whitney Museum of American Art: the first *Biennial Exhibition of Contemporary American Painting* (1932) and *Abstract Painting in America* (1935). Despite his participation in the latter, he called for stylistic moderation in an essay for *Art Digest* (Mar. 1935): "Two activities, the abstract and the concrete . . . like ebb and tide, are the constant rhythm of all things throughout history." In the studio, Bluemner concentrated on devising a special casein recipe for large works on paper, and he initiated a final series, "Compositions for Color Themes," whose principal objectives were prescribed in his diary: "To use full pigments like Musical Tones, to see a scene humanly, and to convert it all into a peculiar emotional space-form." Bluemner signed these late paintings "Florianus," a Latin conversion of his own surname that he felt reflected the universal currency of art. In 1936, after a second term with the depression-era Public Works of Art Project, failing eyesight and bleeding ulcers forced Bluemner to stop painting. Unable to work, in poor health, and living in straitened circumstances, he committed suicide at his home in South Braintree, Massachusetts.

Following his death, critic Paul Rosenfeld wrote in *University Review* (Summer 1939) that Bluemner was "one of the talented representatives of the modern art movement in America." That assessment, though only gradually acknowledged, is supported by Bluemner's vigorous colorism, distinctive theory, and steadfast efforts to cultivate public understanding of modernism.

• Bluemner's painting and theory diaries, writings, correspondence, and other papers are in the Archives of American Art, Washington, D.C. His letters to Stieglitz and O'Keeffe are in the Beinecke Rare Book and Manuscript Library, Yale University, New Haven, Conn. For a full biographical and critical study, see Jeffrey R. Hayes, *Oscar Bluemner* (1991). A detailed discussion of a specific collection of paintings and drawings is found in Judith Zilczer, *Oscar Bluemner: The Hirshhorn Museum and Sculpture Garden Collection* (1979). Theory and iconography are addressed in Hayes, "Theory and Practice: Hartley, Bluemner, and the Expressionist Landscape," in *The Expressionist Landscape: North American Modernist Painting, 1920–1947*, organized by Ruth Stevens Appelhof et al. (1988), and in Frank Gettings, "The Human Landscape: Subjective Symbolism in Oscar Bluemner's Painting," *Archives of American Art Journal* 19 (1979): 9–14. An obituary is in the *New York Times*, 13 Jan. 1938.

JEFFREY R. HAYES

BLUHDORN, Charles G. (20 Sept. 1926–19 Feb. 1983), conglomerate entrepreneur, was born in Vienna, Austria, the son of Paul Bluhdorn and Rose (maiden name unknown). Bluhdorn was first educated in his native Austria, but fled after Hitler invaded, and was sent to school in England. In 1942 he came to the United States, where he worked for a cotton broker in New York City and attended the City College of New York. In 1945 Bluhdorn joined the U.S. Army Air Force. When he was released he got a job with an import-export firm and attended Columbia University in the evenings. In 1949 Bluhdorn formed his own importing firm, which specialized in commodities. The venture was very successful, and within five years he was a millionaire. Desiring to find a business less subject to the vicissitudes of the commodities markets, Bluhdorn purchased a controlling interest in Michigan Plating and Stamping, a small auto bumper manufacturer that had an almost worthless contract with Studebaker Motors. The firm was listed on the New York Stock Exchange, however, and provided Bluhdorn with an entrance to the auto parts distribution segment of the rapidly expanding auto industry. The next year he acquired an auto parts replacement firm, Beard and Stone Electric of Houston, Texas. He merged the two businesses to create the Gulf and Western Corporation, a move that began an auto parts distribution network in the southwestern states.

From 1960 to 1965 Bluhdorn enlarged his business interests primarily by purchasing other auto parts companies, but in 1966 he took the first step toward creating a diversified conglomerate when he bought the New Jersey Zinc Company. This was followed a year later with his acquisition of Paramount Pictures. By 1968 Gulf and Western was worth over $1 billion and Bluhdorn had become the boy wonder of a new phenomenon on the American economic scene—the conglomerate—a firm with many nonuniform divisions that make and sell totally or almost totally unrelated products. Throughout the 1970s Bluhdorn continued to add properties in a bewildering number of areas to the Gulf and Western empire. With acquisitions as diverse as sugar plantations in Puerto Rico and the Dominican Republic; Consolidated Cigar Corporation, the world's largest cigar company; E. W. Bliss and Company, maker of steel rolling mills and stamp presses; and Brown and Company, a paper products firm, Bluhdorn soon found it expedient to split Gulf and Western into a number of divisions. The manufacturing division alone was separated into industrial products, systems, precision engineering, and metals-forming. There were also various auto parts companies, plus companies focused on such leisure time activities as motion pictures, television, recordings, and sheet music. Other divisions included its natural resources businesses, especially large holdings of zinc mines in Canada, and the food products affiliate that concentrated mainly on sugar production.

All of this was quite profitable for both Bluhdorn and Gulf and Western by the late 1970s, as he rode the great wave of optimism that accompanied the conglomerate surge during those years. One of the few negative voices raised against Bluhdorn, Gulf and Western, and conglomerates was that of the comic actor and director Mel Brooks. In his *Silent Movie* (1976) he featured a rapacious conglomerate, called Engulf and Devour, headed by a frothing chief executive who was trying to capture a major motion picture company. This was followed by a more serious challenge. In 1979, after a three-and-a-half-year investigation, the Securities and Exchange Commission filed a civil complaint against Gulf and Western and Bluhdorn, charging them with improper financial reporting and "fraudulent courses of conduct." Bluhdorn called the charges "totally unwarranted," but in 1981 he and his firm signed a consent decree in which, without admitting any wrongdoing, they promised not to violate federal laws.

Two years later, while flying home from a business trip to the Dominican Republic, Bluhdorn was stricken with a heart attack aboard his corporate jet. He died in flight, leaving a widow (the former Yvette LeMarreo) and their two children. No one was terribly surprised that he was just fifty-six years old at the time of his death. Bluhdorn was a driven, obsessed corporate executive who acknowledged his compulsiveness: "You know my hobby is business, right? I eat, sleep, dream the business. I get my best ideas at 4 o'clock in the morning," he once told *Forbes*. After Bluhdorn's death, his lieutenant, Martin S. Davis, assumed command of Gulf and Western. Davis immediately began to streamline its operations and then shifted its focus primarily to entertainment, publishing, communications, and consumer and commercial finance, purchasing Prentice-Hall, Simon and Schuster, Silver Burdett, and a number of other concerns. In 1989 Gulf and Western was renamed Paramount Communications, and revenues in the early 1990s were in excess of $5 billion. Although Bluhdorn once proclaimed "I'd like to get some credit for the time I've spent here," there was little evidence of Bluhdorn's legacy in the streamlined Paramount of the 1990s.

• Charles Bluhdorn's papers are not available, nor are company archives open. The *New York Times* did an extensive three-part series on Bluhdorn and Gulf and Western on 17 and 21 Aug. 1979 and 27 Nov. 1979. *Forbes* followed his career closely; see especially 3 Sept. 1979 and 14 Mar. 1983, pp. 41–42. Useful articles on Bluhdorn and Gulf and Western can be found in *Business Week*, 3 Apr. 1983, 29 Aug. 1983, and 24 Oct. 1983. See also *Time*, 3 Dec. 1965, 15 May 1972, 18 July 1977, 25 Feb. 1983, and 29 Aug. 1983; *Newsweek*, 5 Feb. 1968, 28 Feb. 1983, and 14 Mar. 1983. A rare interview is in *Nation's Business*, Mar. 1979; a profile, in *Life*, 10 Mar. 1967; and an investigation of Gulf and Western's sugar plantations, in *Christian Century*, 13 Oct. 1982. The *Wall Street Journal* also provided detailed coverage of the activities of Gulf and Western over the years. An obituary is in the *New York Times*, 20 Feb. 1983.

JOHN N. INGHAM

BLUM, Robert Frederick (9 July 1857–8 June 1903), artist, was born in Cincinnati, Ohio, the son of Frederick Blum, an employee of the German Mutual Insurance Company, and Mary Haller. In the mid-1870s Blum and several colleagues, including Kenyon Cox and Alfred Brennan, broke away from the program of study established by the McMicken School of Design and instead received instruction from Frank Duveneck at the Ohio Mechanics' Institute and spearheaded a minor rebellion at McMicken by organizing an extracurricular class during the 1875–1876 school year. Beginning in 1875 Blum emulated the art of the Spanish virtuoso Mariano Fortuny, studying every locally available example of Fortuny's work, which was known for its depiction of Arab life in Spain as well as Morocco and other nearby locales. While in Philadelphia in 1876 and 1877 Blum continued his study of Fortuny's art but also attended a life class under Christian Schussele at the Pennsylvania Academy of the Fine Arts and developed a great interest in the art of Japan as well.

Blum settled in New York City in 1878 and soon received recognition for his work as an illustrator (for, among other publications, the *Century* and *Scribner's Monthly*) and as a watercolorist. His emulation of Fortuny both impressed and irritated the New York critics, who in the late 1870s labeled him, along with Winslow Homer and Frank Currier, as the leading American "impressionist" watercolorists. Blum's art and his personable nature gained him the friendship of many of the leading and influential young New York artists, and he became a prominent member of the city's progressive artistic circle.

In company with many American artists of his generation, Blum often traveled to Europe in quest of inspiration and artistic subjects. In Venice in 1880 he became friendly with James McNeill Whistler, and the art of the American expatriate influenced Blum's style and aesthetic viewpoint. In his work of the early 1880s Blum sought to reconcile aspects of the art of Fortuny and Whistler that most intrigued him. Both were characterized by "art for art's sake." While Fortuny might not have agreed that his art was primarily a beautifully painted surface, in terms of what the majority of critics and artists admired in his art—his virtuosity and the dazzling effects he created with brush, pen, or etching needle—his work was aligned with the notion of art for art's sake. Under Whistler's inspiration, Blum became an advocate of the increased importance of graphic media. He also began to work in pastel, becoming in 1882 a founding member and then president of the Society of Painters in Pastel.

Blum spent most of the period from 1885 to 1890 living in Venice, where, often painting in oil, he executed his major pictures *Venetian Lace Makers* (Cincinnati Art Museum) and *Venetian Bead Stringers* (private collection). Blum was a slow and deliberate painter in oil and in previous years had favored the greater spontaneity afforded by pen and ink, watercolor, etching, dry point, and pastel. While in Italy, though remaining cognizant of the compositional and coloristic qualities that initially inspired his enthusiasm for the works of Fortuny and Whistler, Blum nevertheless began to develop a more original style and to adopt subject matter favored by Ludwig Passini, Giuseppe Favretto, Ettore Tito, and other artists of the "neo-Venetian" school.

From mid-1890 until late 1892 Blum lived in Japan and was one of the first American artists to visit that country. While there, he depicted the aspects of Japanese life that most impressed him and in the process created several of his major works in oil and pastel, including the paintings *The Ameya* (Metropolitan Museum of Art) and *Flower Market, Tokyo* (private collection). In his Japanese pictures, Blum sought to express the customs, fashions, and architecture of the Japanese, glorifying workers and the beauty of Japanese women. After returning to the United States, he briefly benefited from the patronage of Alfred Corning Clark, who commissioned him to paint the murals *Moods to Music* and *The Vintage Festival* (both at the Brooklyn Museum); Clark also owned more than thirty pictures. This period, from 1893 to 1898, was the high point of Blum's artistic career, and his murals were accorded great critical praise.

After Blum finished *Moods to Music* and *The Vintage Festival*, his health deteriorated, and for his few remaining years he accepted comparatively minor decorative commissions, worked intermittently as an illustrator and art instructor, and abandoned the creation of independent easel pictures. Blum's sudden death in New York City from pneumonia at the age of forty-five was mourned by the leading artists and critics of his time.

Blum was somewhat of an artistic maverick, going his own way and following his own instincts, as, for example, when as a young man he chose not to pursue a formal art education abroad. In terms of quantity, Blum's artistic legacy lies in his pen-and-ink and wash drawings, pastels, and watercolors. During his lifetime he was most widely known for his work as an illustrator, a vocation he pursued at various times in order to make a living, and though his illustrations reveal his graphic style, they are among his most literal efforts. Beginning in the mid-1880s, when Blum was freed for the most part from financial concerns, his art began to transcend the influences of Fortuny and Whistler, and in the late 1880s critics came to view him as one of the major American figurative painters. During his relatively short life, Blum evolved from being an erstwhile student of the principles of decoration to the creator of two of the most widely commended murals of the 1890s. As he matured, he allowed his experience and talent to direct his efforts toward increasingly ambitious undertakings. Through much of his career Blum depicted picturesque and exotic subjects, but later in life he also treated themes based on allegorical subjects as well as his imagination.

At his death Blum's half-sister and sole heir (he never married), Henrietta Haller, selected artist William Baer (a close friend of Blum's) as executor of Blum's estate and charged him to select works from Blum's studio and present them as gifts to various American art institutions. The majority were given to the Cincinnati Art Museum, but the Museum of the Art of Decoration at Cooper Institute (now the Cooper-Hewitt Museum of Decorative Arts and Design), the National Academy of Design, and the Metropolitan Museum of Art received pieces as well. In 1916 Baer divided Blum's sketchbooks equally between the Cincinnati Art Museum and the Cooper Institute so that each institution would have representative drawings from the span of the artist's life. Baer also arranged for Elizabeth Clark, Alfred Corning Clark's widow, to give Blum's *Venetian Lace Makers* and *Study for Moods to Music* to the Cincinnati Art Museum and *The Ameya* to the Metropolitan Museum of Art.

A small memorial exhibition of Blum's work was held in April 1904 at M. Knoedler & Co. in New York City, and the following year the Cincinnati Art Museum displayed the pictures that had been left to that institution. The most comprehensive loan exhibition of Blum's work ever held was organized by Martin Birnbaum for the Berlin Photographic Gallery in New York in 1913. Ten years later an exhibition of forty-two of Blum's pictures was organized by Homer Saint-Gaudens for the Carnegie Institute in Pittsburgh. In 1926 a small exhibition of Blum's art was held at Feragil Galleries in New York City, and in 1966 the Cincinnati Art Museum organized a retrospective exhibition drawn principally from its permanent collection.

Baer also attempted to raise funds for the erection of a Blum memorial in Cincinnati (where he is buried in Spring Grove Cemetery), to establish a Robert Blum Scholarship at the Cincinnati Art Academy, and to have individual sets made of twenty of Blum's etchings for sale to interested parties. His efforts were only partly successful. Scholarships in Blum's name appear to have been disbursed to students for a year or two, and twelve of the printed sets (the total number of sets is unknown) were given to various American museums, but a memorial has yet to be erected to Blum in his hometown.

• The best and most reliable source on Blum is Bruce Weber, "Robert Frederick Blum (1857–1903) and His Milieu" (Ph.D. diss., Graduate School of the City Univ. of New York, 1985). At Blum's death, obituaries and tributes appeared in New York and Cincinnati newspapers, and complimentary articles on his life and career included Robert Bridges, "Robert Frederick Blum," *Lamp* 26 (July 1903): 473–77; "Robert Frederick Blum," *Art Interchange* 51 (July 1903): 2–3; Charles H. Caffin, "Robert Frederick Blum," *International Studio* 21 (Dec. 1903): clxxvii–cxcii; and Charles Mason Fairbanks, "Robert Blum: An Appreciation," *Metropolitan Magazine* 20 (July 1904): 507–19. A brief but fitting tribute to Blum, possibly written by art critic and great Blum admirer Royal Cortissoz, appeared in the editorial section of the *New York Daily Tribune*, 10 June 1903.

BRUCE WEBER

BLUME, Peter (27 Oct. 1906–30 Nov. 1992), artist, was born in Smorgon, Russia, the son of Harry Blume, a clothing cutter, and Rose Gopin. He came to the United States with his family in 1911, settling in Brooklyn, New York, where he attended public schools for the next eight years. At age twelve he began to study art at night classes and support himself by working as a letterer and jewelry designer. In 1921 Blume became a United States citizen and began to study drawing at the Educational Alliance School of Art, a settlement-house project sponsored by wealthy members of New York City's Jewish community. He also received art instruction at the Beaux-Arts Institute of Design and at the Art Students League, both in New York City. By age eighteen he had acquired his own studio, and he was managing to earn a living from his pictures.

In the late 1920s Blume moved to Sherman, Connecticut. At first, he achieved only modest success as an artist. But his career picked up in 1930, when the Daniel Gallery in New York held his first solo exhibition. His painting *Parade*, on which he had worked exclusively for an entire year, was singled out for critical praise, and it was subsequently acquired by the Museum of Modern Art in New York. The painting depicts an outdoor scene that features giant air ventilators, a smokestack belching smoke, and several interlocking machine parts. What prevents it from being just another precisely rendered modern industrial landscape painting is its inclusion of the incongruous image of a solitary man carrying a suit of medieval armor on a stick. Such a bizarre juxtaposition of disparate and unrelated objects associates the painting with surrealism.

Two events of tremendous importance in Blume's life occurred in 1931. On the personal side, he married Grace Douglas Gibbs "Ebie" Craton; they had no children. On the professional side, he completed the painting *South of Scranton*, which three years later won first prize at the Carnegie International Exhibition. At age twenty-eight, Blume was the youngest artist ever to win this prestigious honor. The selection proved controversial and generated much publicity because the dreamlike depiction of coal mines and mountains of waste coal on one side and men apparently flying through the air on the other struck some viewers as random and haphazard, although many critics admired the draftsmanship and the formal arrangement of shapes and colors. The controversy catapulted Blume to a position of public prominence that he had not achieved previously.

In 1932 Blume traveled to Italy on a Guggenheim Fellowship for painting. He stayed for two years, and then returned again in 1936 on a second Guggenheim Fellowship. While in Italy, Blume was horrified by his observations of Italian fascism, and he developed the idea for what became the most celebrated painting of his career, *The Eternal City*, completed, after three years of work, in 1937.

Blume filled this 34-by-48-inch canvas with images of Italy being brought to ruin by the reign of Mussolini. Blume juxtaposed reminders of the glories of Rome's past (as seen, for example, in rows of intricately detailed ancient Roman columns) with images of despair and destruction. Broken fragments of a statue from Rome's classical past, a pathetic-looking old woman begging with her foot in a cast, and Mussolini's soldiers beating people up in the background were all rendered in the precise realism for which Blume was already widely noted. However, the painting's dominant image, and the one that immediately catches the viewer's eye, is not realistic at all and thus seems to clash violently with the rest of the painting. It is a large green-headed representation of Mussolini, depicted as a scowling papier-mâché jack-in-the-box with his eyes bulging out.

The painting immediately attracted a great deal of attention, bringing big crowds each day to the Julien Levy Galleries in New York, where it was first exhibited. The reaction was by no means uniformly favorable. Blume's work was attacked both on strictly aesthetic grounds (the primary objection was to the hideous jack-in-the-box head) and on political grounds (many resented the ferocity of his attack on a foreign leader). Blume himself seemed to sympathize with the former objection, as he admitted that Mussolini's red lips clashed with the green of his head and that the color of the head was "like nothing else in the picture: antithesis, dissonance." He explained: "It hurt me to paint the head, but no compromise was possible. I felt that in doing this picture the question of harmony was superseded by other considerations" (Trapp, p. 65).

The Eternal City made news again in 1939, when it was rejected by the jury for the Biennial Exhibition at the Corcoran Gallery of Art in Washington, D.C. Suspecting that it had been rejected on purely political grounds, especially in light of the Italian diplomatic presence in the nation's capital, some artists' groups protested its exclusion, but to no avail. Blume shrugged off the controversy and continued painting, working in his customary slow, painstaking fashion. It was not until 1948, after seven years' continuous work during which he made more than five hundred preliminary drawings, that Blume completed his next major painting, *The Rock*. It won great critical acclaim, and in 1950 it received the Popular Prize at the Carnegie International Exhibition. The painting is an outdoor scene in which several people are at work on various construction tasks such as digging, chiseling stone, quarrying and excavating manually, and erecting a new building. The central, dominating image is a magnificent jagged rock. Images of death and destruction also appear, most notably ruined buildings and a pile of bones lying at the base of the rock. Completed shortly after World War II, *The Rock* is usually interpreted as depicting a desperate attempt to rebuild a world that had been destroyed, perhaps in a nuclear holocaust.

Blume continued to paint for more than four additional decades, receiving good critical notices and successfully selling his pictures. However, *The Rock* was, in terms of the attention it attracted, the praise it won, and the influence it exerted, his last truly "major" work. He died in New Milford, Connecticut.

Blume shared artistic aims with the precisionists, most notably Charles Sheeler, Charles Demuth, Niles Spencer, and Preston Dickinson, all of whom were associated with the Charles Daniel Gallery, as was Blume. But Blume is not remembered as a member of a particular art movement, though his style also has affinities with surrealism and magic realism. Nor is he known as a producer of a substantial body of work. Rather, he is recognized for having created a rather small number of truly memorable paintings, each of which manifests Blume's unique and distinctive style. *South of Scranton* (Metropolitan Museum of Art, New York), *The Eternal City* (Museum of Modern Art, New York), and *The Rock* (Art Institute of Chicago), in addition to hanging in major museums, are among the most widely reproduced works in twentieth-century American art. They feature all of the elements of Blume's signature style: the juxtaposition of seemingly unrelated objects and figures, the inclusion of bizarre and fantastic items, and the rendering of all of these in clear, minute, and ultra-realistic detail. The latter two paintings also exhibit Blume's enthusiasm for political allegory, a characteristic shared by many of his later works.

• Blume's papers are at the Archives of American Art, Smithsonian Institution, Washington, D.C. A brief statement by Blume, in which he expresses his views on art, is his "After Surrealism," *New Republic*, 31 Oct. 1934. The most comprehensive work on Blume, encompassing both biographical information and an extensive evaluation of his art, is Frank Anderson Trapp, *Peter Blume: Sixty Years of His Art* (1987). An obituary is in the *New York Times*, 1 Dec. 1992.

DAVID DETMER

BLUMENSCHEIN, Ernest L. (26 May 1874–6 June 1960), painter and illustrator, was born Ernest Leonard Blumenschein in Pittsburgh, Pennsylvania, the son of William L. Blumenschein, a highly cultured German-born musician, and Leonora Chapin. After his mother died in childbirth in 1878, the family moved to Dayton, Ohio, where his father accepted the directorship of the Philharmonic Chorus and also served as organist for the Third Presbyterian Church. At seventeen Blumenschein received a scholarship to study violin at the Cincinnati College of Music. During the same year he took a course in illustration at the Cincinnati Art Academy, and the following year he transferred to the Art Students League in New York City. He never completely abandoned the violin for art, and during his student years he earned additional income as a violinist for the New York National Conservatory Orchestra, then under the directorship of Antonín Dvořák. After two years at the Art Students League, Blumenschein left for study in Paris under Jean Paul Laurens, Benjamin Constant, and Raphael Colin at the Académie Julian. Returning to New York in 1896, he shared an illustration studio with Bert G. Phillips, a fellow Académie Julian student.

In 1897 Blumenschein traveled to New Mexico and Arizona as an illustrator for *McClure's Magazine*. The following summer he convinced Phillips to travel with him on a sketching trip from Denver to Mexico. A broken wagon wheel near Taos forced the two to stop at the then remote location, and they decided to stay for the remaining summer. Blumenschein recalled, "The color, the effective character of the landscape, the drama of the vast spaces, the superb beauty and serenity of the hills, stirred me deeply. . . . New Mexico inspired me to a profound degree" (Henning, p. 12). Though Phillips elected to stay at Taos, Blumenschein returned to New York and continued to do illustrations for the leading magazines of the day, including *Century Magazine, Harper's Weekly*, and *Scribner's*.

In 1899 Blumenschein returned to Paris for further study, remaining there until 1909 except for a short trip to New York and Taos in 1901. While he supported his painting study in Paris by working as an illustrator, Blumenschein resented the time and energy illustrations took from painting, which he had resolved would be his foremost occupation. In 1905 he married Mary Shepherd Green, an American painter also working in Paris. The two shared studio space and often worked on commissions together for magazines and books by Booth Tarkington, Stephen Crane, Jack London, and Willa Cather. On Christmas Day 1906 Mary gave birth, but the child died two days later. When she became pregnant again, the couple returned to New York, and in November 1909 their only child, Helen Greene, was born.

Blumenschein opened another illustration studio, and between 1912 and 1915 he taught at the Art Students League. Though he was successful in New York, Taos was never far from his mind. Even during his second stay in Paris, his letters frequently mention his desire to return there. In 1910 Blumenschein began spending summers in Taos with a number of other artists who were also drawn to the area, including Oscar E. Berninghaus, E. Irving Couse, Victor Higgins, Walter Ufer, and W. Herbert Dunton. As Blumenschein explained, "We were ennuied with the hackneyed subject matter of thousands of painters: windmills in Dutch landscape; Brittany peasants and sabots; French roads lined with Normandy poplars; lady in negligee reclining on a sumptuous divan; lady gazing in mirror; lady powdering her nose; etc. We felt the need of a stimulating subject" (quoted in Henning, p. 17). Blumenschein saw in the daily routines of the Taos Indians, the warmth and clarity of the New Mexico light, and the drama of the western landscape just such a stimulating subject.

In 1912 he and five other artists working in Taos founded the Taos Society of Artists to organize and circulate group exhibitions for its members, who would eventually number eleven. Their exhibitions traveled throughout the United States, effectively promoting the group's artistic reputation, and most of the artists also exhibited in the major eastern as well as western art exhibitions. Blumenschein regularly exhibited his works at the Salmagundi Club, the National Academy of Design, the Pan-Pacific Exposition, the Chicago Art Institute, and the National Arts Club. The artist also received commissions for a number of murals, including those for the Missouri State Capitol in the early 1920s. Blumenschein was commissioned to complete three lunettes of scenes from Missouri history and two full-length figures, one of General John Joseph Pershing and the other of Missouri artist and politician George Caleb Bingham.

In 1919 Blumenschein closed his New York studio, refused further illustration commissions, and moved to Taos permanently. During the ensuing decade he produced some of his best work. Blumenschein's modernist sensibilities can be seen most clearly in his intense palette and simplification of forms into solid geometric masses. His color is unmodeled, and space is built through tightly composed, architectonic planes. Blumenschein's success with such compositions not only caused him to be regarded as one of the key figures of the Taos Society of Artists during his own lifetime, but he continues to be considered one of the leading artists of early twentieth-century southwestern modernism. Such sensibilities are foreshadowed as early as 1914 in his essay "The Painting of To-morrow," an enthusiastic response to the 1913 Armory Show published in *Century Magazine*, and continued to be prevalent throughout his career. In a letter to the editor of the *New York Times* on 7 February 1926, he criticized museums and the academic art world for their lack of support and understanding of modern art. He continued his activity in the Taos Society of Artists, serving as the group's president from 1921 to 1923. In 1927, the same year that the society disbanded, Blumenschein was elected to full membership in the National Academy. He received many awards, including the Potter Palmer Gold Medal awarded by the Art Institute of Chicago in 1917 for *The Chief Speaks* (unlocated); the first Altman Prize, awarded by the National Academy of Design in 1921 for *Superstition* (1921, Thomas Gilcrease Institute of American History and Art, Tulsa); the second Altman Prize in 1925 for *Sangre de Cristo Mountains* (1925, Anschutz Collection); and the National Arts Club Medal in 1938 for *Jury for Trial of a Sheepherder for Murder* (1936, Museum of Western Art, Denver).

While modernist tendencies clearly inform his art, it is also affected by the local character and customs of the Taos Indians and the Hispanic community of New Mexico. *Jury for Trial of a Sheepherder for Murder*, his most famous painting and the work he considered his best, is based on the trial of a young shepherd who, while isolated in the hills for several months, killed a hiker who surprised him. With much emotional debate, the jury convicted him. Typical of Blumenschein's work, the painting is a re-creation, part fact and part imagination, of his impressions of the event. The twelve jurors' images were taken from local characters rather than the actual jurors, and the room depicted is his studio rather than the courtroom.

Blumenschein's art of the 1940s and 1950s is often overworked and shows evidence of a lingering melancholy. His periodic depressions were most likely due to his unwillingness to accept advancing age, weakening eyesight, and the pains of arteriosclerosis. In 1958 his wife passed away, and following a prolonged illness Blumenschein died two years later in Albuquerque. His ashes were deposited at the Taos Indian reservation.

• Blumenschein's papers are in the Archives of American Art, Washington, D.C. His house in Taos has been turned into a museum and houses the largest collection of his works. Other museums that hold his works include the Museum of New Mexico, Santa Fe; the Eiteljorg Museum of American Indians and Western Art, Indianapolis; the Museum of Western Art, Denver; the Albuquerque Museum; and the Dayton Art Institute, Dayton, Ohio. His artistic views can be found in "The Painting of To-morrow," *Century Magazine*, Apr. 1914, pp. 845–50; "Blumenschein Regrets Generation Is Educated on Modern Art Ideas," *Albuquerque Journal*, 16 Nov. 1952; and "Blumenschein Explains: What Makes a Painting New," *New Mexican*, 13 Sept. 1953. The artist's biography can be found in several exhibition catalogs, including *A Retrospective Exhibition of the Life Work of Ernest L. Blumenschein* (Museum of New Mexico, 1948) and William T. Henning, Jr., *Ernest L. Blumenschein Retrospective* (Colorado Springs Fine Arts Center, 1978). Blumenschein's daughter, Helen Greene Blumenschein, also compiled a memoir of the family, *Recuerdos: Early Days of the Blumenschein Family* (1979). Publications that discuss the artist and his connection with the Taos Society of Artists include Laura Bickerstaff, *Pioneer Artists of Taos* (1955), and Charles C. Eldredge et al., *Art in New Mexico, 1900–1945: Paths to Taos and Santa Fe* (1986).

M. MELISSA WOLFE

BLUMER, George Alder (25 May 1857–25 Apr. 1940), psychiatrist, was born in Sunderland, England, the son of Luke Blumer, a physician, and Mary Jane Bone. After an excellent education in the classics and foreign languages at schools in England, Germany, and France, he attended the University of Edinburgh as a medical student in 1874–1875 and completed his medical degree at the University of Pennsylvania in 1879. He later returned to Edinburgh for a year of postgraduate training in 1884–1885. In 1880 he obtained a post as assistant physician at the Utica (N.Y.) State Hospital for the Insane, one of the best-known psychiatric asylums in the country. He also joined the staff of the *American Journal of Insanity*, forerunner of the present-day *American Journal of Psychiatry*. Six years later Blumer became Utica's medical superintendent and editor of the *AJI*, a post he held until 1894. In 1886 Blumer married Helen Antoinette Spriggs; they had four children.

Blumer played an important role at a critical time in the history of American psychiatry. Up to the end of the nineteenth century, psychiatry was predominantly a hospital-based medical specialty, and most attention was devoted to matters of asylum management, administration, and construction. But with general medicine's great breakthroughs in fields like surgery and bacteriology, psychiatry was in danger of being left behind if it stuck to its old ideas and practices. The field needed physicians who were receptive to new trends in pathology, diagnosis, and treatment. Like other psychiatrists of the time, Blumer was keenly aware of this, but at the same time he refused to turn his back on psychiatry's traditional humanitarian pledge to the mentally disabled.

Described by a journalist in 1890 as a "medium-sized, slender, scholarly man, who does not look at all capable of coping with lunatics," Blumer nonetheless gained a reputation as one of the brightest young psychiatrists in the Anglo-American world largely because of his reforms of customary asylum practices. By the end of the nineteenth century most asylum physicians had given up hope that many of their institutionalized patients could be cured, and treatment consequently stressed techniques that were designed to restrain and pacify patients rather than eradicate their diseases. Blumer rebelled against this trend, and in his most famous reform at Utica he eliminated use of the notorious "Utica Crib," a wooden, covered bed device used to confine violent patients. This and other changes in the treatment of inmates reflected Blumer's belief that psychiatry had lost sight of the benevolent and optimistic goals of the psychiatrists who had staffed the first asylums back in the early nineteenth century. In his editorials for the *AJI* and other publications, Blumer urged psychiatrists never to forget this dimension of their work.

As editor of the *AJI* Blumer also spoke out against changes that institutional psychiatry was undergoing by the end of the century. As Progressivism increasingly affected more aspects of American life, politicians and public charity officials sought to break down the independence of state asylums and make them more accountable than ever before to statewide standards of care, management, and fiscal efficiency. Most of the medical superintendents of state asylums resented this unprecedented interference in their daily working lives, which, they felt, would adversely affect their ability to provide quality care for their patients. In time Blumer found himself at the center of the growing conflict between state officials and asylum psychiatrists. When New York State tried to wrest legal control over the *AJI* from Utica's board of trustees, Blumer sold it in 1894 to the American Medico-Psychological Association (after 1921, the American Psychiatric Association). As a result, the principal journal for American psychiatrists narrowly missed falling into the hands of New York State, a fate that undoubtedly would have further compromised the independence of the profession.

Blumer's trials of the 1890s in the New York State mental health care bureaucracy persuaded him in 1899 to accept the post of medical superintendent at the Butler Hospital in Providence, Rhode Island. The Butler Hospital tended to serve a more affluent clientele than did Utica, and this consideration definitely influenced Blumer's decision. But he continued to be interested in the Empire State's affairs, and in 1903, in his presidential address at the annual meeting of the American Medico-Psychological Association in Washington, he bitterly denounced trends in New York State mental health care. In this speech Blumer also made one of the most forceful medical arguments in favor of eugenic policies, particularly in terms of immigration restriction and marriage laws. Although he soon discarded these pro-eugenic views, his speech was typical of the dominant psychiatric belief that insanity was primarily a hereditary disease and that the best course of action was to prevent it.

In the years between his move to Providence and his retirement, Blumer became less and less emotionally engaged in New York State matters and emerged as one of the city's most distinguished citizens. As the medical superintendent of a private hospital, Blumer moved in social and cultural circles that suited his own upper middle-class tastes, upbringing, and interests. During his years in Providence, Blumer also contributed to the founding of the Mental Hygiene movement. He was one of the first readers of Clifford Beers's manuscript that would later be published in 1907 as *A Mind That Found Itself*. He was a founding member of both the Rhode Island and national Mental Hygiene Associations, speaking out frequently about the need to prevent mental and nervous illness. But Blumer did not accept all the new theories that surrounded the practice of psychiatry in the early twentieth century. His attitude toward Freudian ideas was, like that of many other psychiatrists, decidedly hostile, both because he disliked Freud's stress on sexuality and because he feared that psychoanalysis would weaken faith in the theory that insanity was a physical disease of the nervous system. This attitude underlines Blumer's chief historical significance: he was a man who, though impressed with some aspects of scientific medicine, was also skeptical of what he thought were faddish or dogmatic ideas. In many ways he saw himself as the conscience of psychiatry at a time when some old-style, yet valuable methods of nineteenth-century psychiatry were in danger of being forgotten.

As his correspondence shows, Blumer was very popular with and well respected by his colleagues, who frequently complimented him on the elegance, humor, and sagacity of his writing. One psychiatrist friend said, "I read his reports for I like what he says; but above all I admire the way he says it." While he did not appreciably affect the history of psychiatric ideas, there is little doubt that most psychiatrists read carefully what he wrote and believed that he added a touch of integrity and grace to a profession whose reputation was in decline at the turn of the century. Blumer retired in 1921 and spent the remainder of his life in Providence, where he died.

• Blumer's personal papers and correspondence are located at the Isaac Ray Historical Library of the Butler Hospital in Providence, R.I. There are no book-length studies of him, but see Ian Dowbiggin, "'Midnight Clerks and Daily Drudges': Hospital Psychiatry in New York State, 1890–1905," *Journal of the History of Medicine and Allied Sciences* 47 (1992): 130–52, and "'An Exodus of Enthusiasm': G. Alder Blumer, Eugenics, and U.S. Psychiatry, 1890–1920," *Medical History* 36 (1992): 379–402. For other biographical details, see "Notes and Comment," *American Journal of Psychiatry* 12 (1932): 374–88.

IAN R. DOWBIGGIN

BLUMER, Herbert George (7 Mar. 1900–13 Apr. 1987), sociologist and teacher, was born in St. Louis, Missouri, the son of Richard George Blumer, a cabinetmaker, and Margaret Marshall. He was married twice, first in 1922 to Marguerite Barnett, with whom he had one daughter. After their divorce, he married Marcia Jackson in 1943. They had two daughters. Blumer earned a B.A. (1921) and an M.A. (1922) from the University of Missouri, and a Ph.D. from the University of Chicago (1928). He supplemented his income during graduate school and in his first years of teaching by playing professional football with the Chicago Cardinals from 1925 to 1933, competing against football greats Red Grange, Bronko Nagurski, Jim

Thorpe, and Ernie Nevers. He taught at the University of Chicago from 1928 to 1951 and at the University of California at Berkeley from 1952 until he retired in 1967; he was an emeritus professor there until 1986.

Blumer was almost certainly introduced to the ideas of both John Dewey and George Herbert Mead that undergird symbolic interactionism by Charles Ellwood, his thesis adviser at Missouri. His master's thesis, "Theory of Social Revolutions" (1922), marked the beginning of a lifelong interest in the social psychological dynamics within and among individuals and groups. Playing the critic, as he did throughout his career, his thesis faulted abstract theorists, including Ellwood, who eschewed close study of social readjustment. At this early stage Blumer's views were also influenced by the ideas of W. I. Thomas, Florian Znaniecki, Robert Park, and Charles Cooley.

At Chicago, Blumer worked closely with George Herbert Mead. When Mead became ill in 1931, Blumer took over his course in advanced social psychology and became regarded as one of the foremost interpreter's of Mead's ideas. In his doctoral dissertation, "Method in Social Psychology" (1928), he examined the work of some two dozen social theorists in order to present a "critical consideration" of social science methodology that failed to test interpretations of a complex and infinitely changing world against the world as observed. His conceptualization of social science, derived from both Dewey and Mead, rejected positivist notions of scientific method, including the quest to discover social laws. He urged social science to "employ techniques adaptable to its particular problems" and suggested "that methods take their form from the peculiar character of the data being investigated."

Because Blumer did not accept prevailing notions of social reality and how to study it, he sparked numerous debates. Those focusing on limitations of quantitative analysis and its positivist assumptions began in the late 1920s with William Ogburn and were later picked up by many, including Samuel Stouffer and George Lundberg. Blumer's attacks on structural-functionalism (especially Talcott Parsons's view), behaviorism, as well as narrowly conceived quantitative analysis, sharpened distinctions between those linking a deterministic model of social action with quantitative and "operationalist" methods, and those who, as he did, favored a nondeterministic view of human action that encouraged the use of qualitative methods, such as interviews and participant observation. He coined the term "symbolic interactionists" in 1937 to classify a group of early twentieth-century sociologists, social psychologists, and philosophers who espoused a unique view of the nature of social life, human social action, and communication.

Blumer caused a furor in the social sciences in 1939 with a methodological critique of Thomas and Znaniecki's *The Polish Peasant in Europe and America* (2 vols., 1927). Though he concurred with the authors' assertion that researchers must understand actors' personal perspectives when explaining individual and collective action, he argued (and Thomas and Znaniecki later agreed) that their theoretical conclusions could not have been developed exclusively from their data. Blumer's assessment brought into focus such major research issues in the social sciences as how to judge the adequacy of research and whether or not social sciences could reveal laws governing relations among social values, attitudes, and action.

Some three decades later, Joan Huber's neopositivist criticism of pragmatism's assumptions and symbolic interactionism's methodology ("Symbolic Interactionism as a Pragmatic Perspective: The Bias of Emergent Theory," *American Sociological Review* 38 [Apr. 1973]) rekindled debate over related issues by claiming they allow investigators' and informants' subjective views to compromise objectivity. Invoking the example of Charles Darwin's methodology in response, Blumer urged social scientists to define problems and to build theory through "flexible" and continuous involvement with the empirical world. Gregory P. Stone et al. ("On Methodology and Craftsmanship in the Criticism of Sociological Perspectives," *American Sociological Review* 39 [June 1974]) sided with Blumer and argued that Huber's "realist" position mistakenly equated the use of a priori theory and distanced the investigator from the research topic with objectivity. Since then, the relevance of Blumer's perspective for establishing fundamental principles of valid ethnographic research has been convincingly argued (Robert Prus, *Symbolic Interaction and Ethnographic Research: Intersubjectivity and the Study of Human Lived Experience* [1996]).

Blumer's interpretation of Mead's pragmatism and social psychology stirred controversy. In 1979 Clark McPhail and Cynthia Rexroat claimed Mead had had a minimal influence in shaping symbolic interactionism and that Blumer's naturalistic methods were not compatible with Mead's views. Blumer refuted their claims with an analysis of Mead's work bolstered by recollections of his discussions with Mead at Chicago. He offered, instead, a view of Mead's pragmatism as a "combination" of both realism and idealism that assumes the simultaneous coexistence and mutual dependence of a world with "obdurate" features, independent of individual definition, and a world comprised of actors' definitions of that world. In 1980 neopositivists J. David Lewis and Richard Smith contended that Blumer's symbolic interactionism was essentially a nominalist-subjectivist perspective while Mead's was that of a realist. They claimed, albeit unconvincingly, that Blumer, therefore, misrepresented Mead's view of society, the self, and social action.

Blumer continued to develop and defend his interpretation of Mead's conception of the self. The "Iowa School" of symbolic interactionism represented by Manford Kuhn depicted the self (particularly Mead's notion of the "I" and the "Me") as a structure with a determinate character. Blumer's "Chicago School" of symbolic interactionism, on the other hand, viewed the self as an active and indeterminate process of symbolic interaction during which definitions of situations are formed and subsequent actions are constructed. So conceived, the self mediates between action and the forces that affect it, such as culture, norms, psychological and biological conditions, and social structure.

Positivists, structuralists, and functionalists are unsympathetic to Blumer's belief that social structure is an ongoing process of symbolic interaction and portray his perspective as "microsociological" and "astructural" even though a review of the full range of his work reveals little basis for such contentions. Blumer not only consistently crafted analyses of "macro" social phenomena but also envisioned them in a society organized through the play of large-scale social processes, including power-based collective conflicts. The many "macro" topics he investigated and on which he published pioneering work include race relations ("The Nature of Race Prejudice," *Social Forces in Hawaii* 5 [1939], and "Race Prejudice as a Sense of Group Position," *Pacific Sociological Review* 1, no. 1 [1958]), fashion ("Fashion," *International Encyclopedia of the Social Sciences*, vol. 5, ed. David L. Sills [1968]), collective behavior ("Collective Behavior," *Principles of Sociology*, ed. A. M. Lee [1951]), public opinion ("Public Opinion and Public Opinion Polling," *American Sociological Review* 13, no. 5 [1948]), social change and industrialization (*Industrialization as an Agent of Social Change*, ed. David Maines and Thomas J. Morrione [1990]), and labor relations ("Sociological Theory in Industrial Relations," *American Sociological Review* 12, no. 3 [1947]).

Regardless of the scale of the action Blumer chose to study, he applied "three simple premises" of symbolic interactionism to the analysis; to wit: "human beings act toward things on the basis of the meanings that the things have for them. . . . The meaning of such things is derived from, or arises out of, the social interaction that one has with one's fellows . . . [and] these meanings are handled in, and modified through an interpretative process used by the person in dealing with the things he encounters" (*Symbolic Interactionism* [1969], p. 2).

Blumer relished opportunities to test his ideas against other views. And, with this in mind as chair at UC Berkeley, he brought together one of the premier faculties in the country. Eschewing orthodoxy, he deliberately hired top sociologists with diverse and sometimes opposing views. He retired from full-time teaching in 1967 but continued working at Berkeley as professor emeritus until a year before his death at his home in Pleasanton, California.

During the course of his career, Blumer garnered numerous awards and held many positions of responsibility both in and outside of academia. He was editor of the *American Journal of Sociology* (1940–1952) and secretary of the American Sociological Society (1930–1935). From 1943 to 1945 he was both principal liaison officer for the Department of State's Office of War Information and public panel chair of the War Labor Board. A charter member of the U.S. Board of Arbitration, he also chaired the board of arbitration for the U.S. Steel Corporation and United Steel Workers of America (1945–1947). He was director of the Institute of Social Sciences (UC Berkeley, 1959–1965), president of the Society for the Study of Social Problems (1954) and of the American Sociological Association (1954), vice president of the International Sociological Association (1962–1966), and president of the Pacific Sociological Association (1971–1972). In 1983 he received the ASA's highest recognition, "The Award for a Career of Distinguished Scholarship."

Blumer was exceptionally generous with his time when students or colleagues requested comments on their work. His extensive and painstakingly detailed reviews of papers and manuscripts evidenced an unselfish dedication to furthering the understanding of human action and social life. The questions he raised and the answers he offered have influenced generations of students, many of them leaders in their fields, including Tamotsu Shibutani, Howard S. Becker, Anselm L. Strauss, Stanford M. Lyman, and Arlene K. Daniels.

Blumer looms large in twentieth-century sociological theory for having codified the theoretical and methodological premises of the sociological perspective known as "symbolic interactionism," and for serving as its major spokesperson for fifty years. Because his methodological and theoretical stance was "ahead of his time" (Shibutani [1970]) and advocated an empiricism grounded in human experience, the relevance of what he said about how best to study collective life, how to unravel the complexities of communication and interaction, how to fathom the relations among the self, identity, social structure, social change, and myriad other social phenomena continues to grow.

• Blumer's interpretation of symbolic interactionism's methodological and theoretical premises and Mead's position may be found in Blumer's most widely read book, *Symbolic Interactionism: Perspective and Method* (1969). Blumer responded to critics and probed what he saw as areas of weakness in the social sciences in "Science without Concepts," *American Journal of Sociology* 36, no. 4 (1931); "Critiques of Research in the Social Sciences: An Appraisal of Thomas and Znaniecki's *The Polish Peasant in Europe and America*," *Social Science Research Council Bulletin* 44 (1939); "Comment on Lewis's 'The Classic American Pragmatists as Forerunners to Symbolic Interactionism,'" *Sociological Quarterly* 18, no. 2 (1977); "Going Astray with a Logical Scheme," *Symbolic Interaction* 6, no. 1 (1983); and "Rejoinder to George A. Lundberg's 'Operational Definitions in the Social Sciences,'" *American Journal of Sociology* 47, no. 5 (1942). He analyzed society and the range of collective activity comprising it in "Social Structure and Power Conflict," *Industrial Conflict*, ed. Arthur Kornhauser et al. (1954); and "Social Problems as Collective Behavior," *Social Problems* 18, no. 3 (1971).

Works on Blumer's career include Kenneth Baugh, Jr., *The Methodology of Herbert Blumer: Critical Interpretation and Repair* (1990); G. David Johnson and Peggy A. Shifflet, "George Herbert Who? A Critique of the Objectivist Reading of Mead," *Symbolic Interaction* (Fall 1981); Stanford M. Lyman and Arthur J. Vidich, *Social Order and the Public Philosophy: An Analysis and Interpretation of the Work of Herbert Blumer* (1988); Clark McPhail and Cynthia Rexroat, "Mead vs. Blumer: The Divergent Methodological Perspectives of Social Behaviorism and Symbolic Interactionism," *American*

Sociological Review 44 (June 1979); J. David Lewis and Richard L. Smith, *American Sociology and Pragmatism: Mead, Chicago Sociology and Symbolic Interaction* (1980); Thomas J. Morrione, "Herbert G. Blumer (1900–1987): A Legacy of Concepts, Criticisms and Contributions," *Symbolic Interaction* 11 (1988); Dimitri Shalin, "Pragmatism and Social Interactionism," *American Sociological Review* 51, no. 1 (Feb. 1986); and Tamotsu Shibutani, ed., *Human Nature and Collective Behavior: Papers in Honor of Herbert Blumer* (1970). See also Lester R. Kurtz, *Evaluating Chicago Sociology: A Guide to the Literature with an Annotated Bibliography* (1984).

THOMAS J. MORRIONE

BLUNT, James Gillpatrick (21 July 1826–25 July 1881), physician, soldier, and politician, was born in Trenton, Hancock County, Maine, the son of John Blunt. Blunt spent his early youth in Ellsworth, Maine, but at age fifteen enlisted as a merchant seaman. Leaving the sea at age twenty, Blunt studied medicine at the Starling Medical College in Columbus, Ohio, earning a medical degree in 1849. He set up a practice in New Madison, Ohio, where he married Nancy Carson Putnam. In 1856 he migrated to the frontier, settling at Greeley, Kansas. There he continued his medical practice but soon became actively interested in politics, becoming deeply involved in the antislavery movement and aiding John Brown in transporting runaway slaves to Canada. Blunt represented Anderson County at the Wyandotte Constitutional Convention in 1859, serving as chairman of the committee on militia.

On 24 July 1861 Blunt was commissioned lieutenant colonel of the Third Kansas Volunteer Cavalry and was assigned to Brigadier General James H. Lane's Kansas Brigade. The first year of the war Blunt participated in several "jayhawking" affairs in Kansas, Missouri, and the Indian Territory, adding to the bitter fratricidal nature of the war in that region by preying on pro-Confederate families. His campaigns were noted for nothing very remarkable except that "our trail was marked by the feathers of 'secesh' poultry and the debris of disloyal beegums," he later wrote. But as an aggressive commander as well as a political radical, he was outspoken in his dissatisfaction with the Union effort in the region. Establishing a pattern that would last through his career, Blunt quarreled with Major General John Charles Frémont, the commander of the Department of Missouri, charging that his failure to take the offensive against the Confederates was a result of general incompetence. Blunt concluded that "no general who parted his hair in the middle was capable of leading an army in the field with success." Thus, Blunt claimed, his command spent the winter of 1861 in camp "where, for the want of anything else to kill, we 'killed time,' in masticating government rations."

When Lane's brigade was mustered into Federal service on 8 April 1862, Blunt was promoted to brigadier general, and one month later, on 5 May 1862, he succeeded Major General David Hunter as commander of the Department of Kansas, serving until 19 September 1862. This assignment was, to Blunt, "an unpleasant and embarrassing position, which I would have gladly avoided if the matter had been left to my own choice." Again he complained of his superiors' misconduct, charging Major General Henry Halleck with "questionable loyalty" and "bitter and hostile feeling towards Kansas" and toward Blunt personally, an indication, perhaps, of the paranoia that would eventually overwhelm him.

Despite his apparent inability to cooperate with his superiors, on 12 October 1862 Blunt was appointed to command of the First Division of Brigadier General John M. Schofield's Army of the Frontier. With his new brigade of Kansans and Cherokees, Blunt defeated Colonel Douglas H. Cooper's 3,000–5,000 Confederate Cherokees and Choctaws at Old Fort Wayne, Indian Territory, on 22 October 1862. On 20 November 1862 an ailing Schofield, whom Blunt accused of "cowardice," "weakness," and "imbecility," turned over to Blunt command of the Army of the Frontier. Seizing the offensive, Blunt attacked Brigadier General John Sappington Marmaduke at Cane Hill, Arkansas, on 28 November 1862 and, with the cooperation of Brigadier General Francis J. Herron, defeated Major General Thomas C. Hindman at nearby Prairie Grove on 7 December 1862. Then, in defiance of orders from Schofield, he captured Van Buren, Arkansas, causing Hindman to fall back fifty miles to the Arkansas River and to abandon his objective of occupying Missouri. In reward, Blunt was promoted to major general of volunteers on 16 March 1863, to rank from 29 November 1862. However, when Schofield returned to the command of the Army of the Frontier in May 1863, he declared that the command had been "demoralized and its efficiency destroyed" and that all of its operations while under Blunt's command were "a series of stupid blunders." Schofield's judgment was perhaps unduly harsh, considering Blunt's victories at Prairie Grove and Van Buren, but certainly Blunt's personal behavior was highly obnoxious, and his dealings with the quartermaster depot at Fort Leavenworth were highly suspect. On 19 June 1863, therefore, he became the commander of the newly constituted District of the Frontier, serving until 6 January 1864, when the district was subsumed under the Department of Arkansas. On 17 July 1863 Blunt's Indian and African American troops again defeated Cooper's Indian brigade at Honey Springs (Elk Creek), the largest battle to take place in Indian Territory.

At Atchison, Kansas, Blunt convened a military tribunal to try "several desperate villains." A number of these men were hanged by the general's order, without recourse to civil law, causing Governor Thomas Carney to accuse Blunt of being "a usurper, a tyrant and a murderer," and to appeal to the Federal government for an end to his "reign of terror." This action Blunt attributed to a conspiracy against him among Carney, Governor Hamilton Rowan Gamble of Missouri, and Senator Thomas Ewing of Ohio, who wished to "gratify personal malice" or to "secure personal or political agridizement [*sic*]."

At Schofield's direction, Blunt's records were audited for evidence of fiscal impropriety, adding to his sense of persecution. Finding evidence of corruption, Schofield determined on 1 October 1863 to remove Blunt from command. Before Schofield could act, however, while Blunt was transferring his headquarters from Fort Scott to Fort Smith, William C. Quantrill's bushwhackers attacked Blunt and his personal retinue at Baxter Springs, Kansas, on 6 October 1863, sending Blunt racing for his life. Ninety of Blunt's men, mostly African Americans, were killed without quarter, constituting what was perhaps the most vicious atrocity of the war. Blunt, however, expressed little sympathy for the victims. "Had the escort stood their ground, as they should have done, instead of becoming panic stricken, all would have been well, and the horrible massacre would not have occurred," Blunt wrote. Thoroughly discredited by the incident, Blunt was thereafter shuttled from one minor administrative post to another, largely being assigned recruiting duty among the former slaves along the Kansas-Missouri frontier.

After Major General Samuel R. Curtis assumed command of the Department of Missouri, despite the fact that his son Major Henry Z. Curtis had been among the slain at Baxter Springs, he elevated Blunt to command of the District of Upper Arkansas on 2 August 1864. This proved to be a grand-sounding title, however, with only 600 soldiers assigned to him with the responsibility of guarding the Platte River frontier against recurring Indian raids, especially by the Cheyennes and the Arapahos. In response to Major General Sterling Price's final attempt to reoccupy Missouri, Blunt was assigned to command of the District of South Kansas on 9 October 1864. Ten days later Price's cavalry drove Blunt out of Lexington, Missouri, and two days after they forced him out of Independence and back onto Curtis's main force at Westport. Blunt had attempted to hold these forward positions despite Curtis's instructions to the contrary; after losing them Blunt accused his superior of "interfering with the disposition of my troops" and of "throwing my command into confusion." At Westport, however, on 28 October he took part in Curtis's defeat of Price's column in one of the biggest battles fought west of the Mississippi River.

After returning to Paola, Kansas, the headquarters of his district, Blunt was chosen by Major General John Pope to lead a cavalry division out of Missouri to attack the army of Lieutenant General Edmund Kirby Smith at Shreveport, Louisiana. The surrender of the Confederate trans-Mississippi department precluded the move. Blunt was mustered out of Federal service on 29 July 1865 to resume his medical practice at Leavenworth, Kansas.

Blunt moved to Washington, D.C., in 1869, where he worked for twelve years as a government solicitor of claims. On 9 April 1873 he was charged with conspiracy to defraud the government and the Cherokee Indians of North Carolina. After two years of investigation the charges were dropped by the U.S. court in North Carolina. On 12 February 1879 Blunt was admitted to St. Elizabeths, the government hospital for the insane in Washington, D.C., with a condition diagnosed as "softening of the brain." There he died two years later.

Although generally unpopular in the army and often referred to as "the fat boy," he was a personal favorite of James Lane and so won early promotion to high command, which he generally exercised with skill and determination. Coarse and licentious, quarrelsome and often insubordinate, Blunt was also an aggressive fighter and fanatically loyal to the Union and the cause of abolition.

• Blunt's own account is published as "General Blunt's Account of His Civil War Experiences," *Kansas Historical Quarterly* 1 (1932): 211–65. See also Alvin M. Josephy, Jr., *The Civil War in the American West* (1991), and Ezra J. Warner, *Generals in Blue: Lives of the Union Commanders* (1964).

THOMAS W. CUTRER

BLUNT, Katharine (28 May 1876–29 July 1954), college administrator, educator, and nutritionist, was born in Philadelphia, Pennsylvania, the daughter of Stanhope English Blunt, an army officer and technical writer, and Fanny Smyth. Little is know about her childhood except that she was first educated at a preparatory school before attending Miss Porter's School in Springfield, Massachusetts. In 1894 she enrolled at Vassar, where she studied chemistry. She graduated Phi Beta Kappa with an A.B. in 1898, then returned home to her family and engaged in service to her church and community for four years.

In 1902 Blunt studied at the Massachusetts Institute of Technology. In 1903 she became an assistant instructor in chemistry at Vassar and in 1905 entered the doctoral program at the University of Chicago, where she received a Ph.D. in organic chemistry in 1907. She taught chemistry at the Pratt Institute in New York City in the Department of Domestic Science in 1907. The following year she went to Vassar, teaching there until 1913 when she joined the University of Chicago home economics staff.

Blunt was among a number of educated women with chemistry degrees who became part of the new field of home economics, one area where it was possible for women to advance in the academic community. Her belief was that women who received their education in this new field not only were stretching the limits of their intellectual capacity and improving their imaginative thinking but were "making a direct contribution to wholesome living."

In 1917 Blunt was granted a leave of absence from Chicago to work as a nutrition expert during World War I. With Florence Powdermaker she produced a number of leaflets on food conservation. Later the leaflets were compiled into a textbook, *Food and the War* (1918).

After her service in the war, Blunt returned to the University of Chicago in 1918 as an associate professor and informal chair of the home economics department. In 1925 she was officially designated department chair, becoming a full professor. When she assumed leadership the two departments merged to form the Department of Home Economics and Household Administration of the College of Arts, Literature, and Sciences. The merger allowed for more budget flexibility and the ability to include more degrees. By 1929 student enrollment at the university had increased substantially and seventeen doctorates and 163 master's degrees had been awarded in the department.

Blunt developed a strong curriculum and enhanced the faculty. Home economists were expected to be technicians in their field. Students learned about food, nutrition, clothing, home electrical equipment, interior decorating, the psychology of dress, and preparation to become a parent.

Established in 1908, the American Home Economics Association (AHEA), helped in furthering the education of women in the science of home economics. A very active member and officer in the organization, Blunt served as president of the Illinois chapter from 1921 to 1922, as national vice president from 1921 to 1924, and president from 1924 to 1926. The AHEA recognized her contributions to the study of basal energy metabolism that showed the effects of poor eating habits, her study on the benefits of calcium and phosphorus in milk, and her research on nutrition.

In 1929 Blunt resigned her university post and accepted the position of president of Connecticut College for Women in New London, becoming the college's third president and the first woman in the position. The college, founded in 1911, developed into a nationally known institution under Blunt's leadership. A very capable administrator and fundraiser, she expanded the faculty, student body, and endowments. Also during her tenure several new buildings were constructed.

Blunt emphasized intellectual self-reliance and citizenship and encouraged women to take a particular interest in public service. In promoting these ideas the college held a variety of specialized schools including a six-week secretarial school, an institute that acted as a clearinghouse for information regarding work opportunities and further education for women. In 1942 it offered an eight-week War Session designed for training secretaries, chemists, statisticians, accountants, and nursery school teachers. In 1943 she retired from the college but was recalled to be president in 1945, finally retiring the next year.

Besides numerous articles on food chemistry and nutrition, Blunt published *Ultra-Violet Light and Vitamin D in Nutrition* (1930), with Ruth Cowan. In her writings she had a flair for expressing the most complex material in simple and easily understood language. In addition to administrating and writing, she served on the Connecticut State Board of Education from 1931 to 1940. Blindness plagued her in later years. Blunt, who never married, died in New London.

A woman who loved travel and enjoyed being outdoors, Blunt had tremendous energy. She encouraged the education of women so that they would be productive members of society and believed that women should be educated in all areas, including politics, labor, and economics.

• Some of Blunt's papers are in the Connecticut College Archives. Other sources with details on her career include American Home Economics Association, *Home Economists: Portraits and Brief Biographies of the Men and Women Prominent in the Home Economics Movement in the United States* (1929); Irene Nye, *Chapters in the History of Connecticut College during the First Three Administrations 1911–1942* (1943); Keturah E. Baldwin, *The AHEA Saga* (1949); Clara Mae Taylor, Grace Macleod, and Mary Swartz Rose, *Foundations of Nutrition*, 5th ed. (1956); Marie Dye, *History of the Department of Home Economics, University of Chicago* (1972); and Harmke Kamminga and Andrew Cunningham, eds., *The Science and Culture of Nutrition, 1840–1940* (1995). Obituaries are in the *New York Times*, 30 July 1954, and the *Journal of Home Economics* 46 (Sept. 1954).

MARILYN ELIZABETH PERRY

BLY, Nellie (5 May 1864–27 Jan. 1922), reporter and manufacturer, was born Elizabeth Jane Cochran in Cochran's Mills, Pennsylvania, the daughter of Michael Cochran, a mill owner and associate justice of Armstrong County, Pennsylvania, and Mary Jane Kennedy Cummings. Judge Cochran, the father of fifteen children by two wives, died suddenly without a will in 1870, leaving Mary Jane with little money. Mary Jane's abusive third marriage to John Jackson Ford ended in divorce in 1878, and "Pink," as Elizabeth Jane was known, at age fifteen, went off to Indiana (Pa.) Normal School, adding a final *e* to Cochran at that time. After only one term her money ran out, and she returned to her mother's home in Apollo, Pennsylvania. She convinced Mary Jane to move to Pittsburgh, where her two older brothers had settled.

Seeing herself responsible for the family's well-being, Pink Cochrane looked for work, finding much less open to her than to her brothers, who had even less education. A newspaper column by Erasmus Wilson, "The Quiet Observer," appeared in the *Pittsburg[h] Dispatch*, decrying the appearance of women in the workforce. Incensed, Cochrane dashed off a long polemic in reply. Signing herself "Lonely Orphan Girl," she demanded a wider definition of "woman's sphere," especially for those with financial responsibility to their families. Editor George Madden saw enough in the letter to think the writer might make a good reporter. He ran a notice on his editorial page asking the "Orphan Girl" to come forward. She did, soon joining the *Dispatch* staff as "Nellie Bly," a misspelling of the popular Stephen Foster song "Nelly Bly." She quickly tired of writing what she considered women's page drivel and quit before completing her first year. She took off for Mexico with her mother as chaperone, reporting for the first five months of 1886. She returned briefly to the *Dispatch* as a culture reporter, but that also left her dissatisfied. "Dear Q.O.," she wrote in a note left on Wilson's desk one day in the spring of 1887, "I'm off for New York. Look out for me. BLY."

It took months to find a job in New York City, so Bly supported herself doing freelance work from New York for her old Pittsburgh newspaper. Her piece on how hard it was for a woman reporter to find work in New York—giving her the chance to interview the great editors of the day—led to her first assignment from the *New York World*: to feign insanity and get herself committed to the Women's Lunatic Asylum on Blackwell's (now Roosevelt) Island. Bly stayed ten days in the "madhouse," taking in the horrendous conditions and keeping her identity secret. Her two-part series in October 1887 was a sensation, effectively launching the decade of "stunt" or "detective" reporting, a clear precursor to investigative journalism and one of Joseph Pulitzer's innovations that helped give "New Journalism" of the 1880s and 1890s its moniker. The employment of "stunt girls" has often been dismissed as a circulation-boosting gimmick of the sensationalist press. However, the genre also provided women with their first collective opportunity to demonstrate that, as a class, they had the skills necessary for the highest level of general reporting. The stunt girls, with Bly as their prototype, were the first women to enter the journalistic mainstream in the twentieth century.

From the insane asylum, Bly went on to almost weekly exposés of New York's social evils, from employment agencies for domestic servants to the baby-buying trade to official corruption in the New York legislature in Albany. Always she assayed the universe through a special lens with her own peculiar tint. It was not her wit or investigative skills but her compassion and social conscience, buttressed by a disarming bluntness, that captivated her audience. There was no mind-splitting intellectual insight or noteworthy literary finesse. Bly simply produced, week after week, an uninhibited display of her delight in being female and fearless and her joy in having such an attention-getting outlet.

In November 1889 Bly left on the journey that made her a legend: a "lightning" trip around the world in the fastest time ever achieved: seventy-two days, six hours, eleven minutes, and fourteen seconds. The *World* covered her journey with day-by-day excitement and a contest, offering a trip to Europe to the person who guessed exactly how long Bly's journey would take. The adventure made her a national celebrity. Yet she was furious at the newspaper for not rewarding her for the effort, and she quit the *World* immediately after her triumphant return. She accepted a lucrative three-year contract to produce serial fiction for N. L. Munro's *New York Family Story Paper*. She showed no promise in fiction. Three years later, in 1893, she returned to the *World*, producing splashy interviews with Emma Goldman and Eugene V. Debs, among others, and covering major stories such as the march of Jacob Coxey's Army on Washington and the Pullman strike in Chicago.

Bly left the *World* again in 1895 to join the staff of the *Chicago Times-Herald* but lasted there only six weeks. Just shy of her thirty-first birthday, she married a wealthy New York businessman, Robert Livingston Seaman, who was some forty years her senior. They had no children. Robert Seaman lived another nine years, during which time Bly took over his iron enamel-ware firm, the Iron Clad Manufacturing Co. She also patented, manufactured, and marketed the steel barrel in the United States. She ran her company as a model of social welfare, replete with health benefits and recreational facilities. But Bly was hopeless at understanding the financial aspects of her business and ultimately lost everything. Unscrupulous employees bilked the firm of hundreds of thousands of dollars, troubles compounded by a protracted and costly bankruptcy litigation.

In an effort to obtain new financing, Bly left for Vienna in August 1914 as war was breaking out. She remained until 1919, writing for the *New York Evening Journal* from the Russian and Serbian fronts in 1914 and appealing for American aid to Austrian war orphans and widows over the next two years. At the war's end she journeyed in a quasi-official capacity to Paris, where President Woodrow Wilson was attending the Paris Peace Conference. Bly appealed for monetary help for the Austrians to help them fend off Bolshevism, though she was not taken seriously. She returned to New York in March 1919, taking a job at the *Evening Journal*. She wrote some attention-getting pieces, such as her coverage of the Jess Willard-Jack Dempsey championship bout, but mostly she ran an editorial page advice column. Bly gave advice in her column and then found practical ways to follow up with the people involved. Her most notable efforts in this period involved placing the children of unwed mothers in good homes and her crusade for American seamen, who were having trouble finding work. Bly died of pneumonia complicated by heart disease at St. Mark's Hospital in New York City. In a published tribute in his *New York Evening Journal* column in the next day's newspaper, Arthur Brisbane remembered her as "the best reporter in America."

• Bly's publications include *Six Months in Mexico* (1886), *Ten Days in a Madhouse* (1887), *The Mystery of Central Park* (1889), and *Nellie Bly's Book: Around the World in Seventy-two Days* (1890). Some 600 newspaper stories appeared in the *Pittsburgh[h] Dispatch* (1885–1887), the *New York World* (1887–1890; 1893–1896), the *Chicago Times-Herald* (Mar.–Apr. 1895), and the *New York Evening Journal* (1914–1916; 1919–1922). Exact citations for these and hundreds of articles about her are in Brooke Kroeger, *Nellie Bly: Daredevil, Reporter, Feminist* (1994). The biography also includes full documentation on all other information included above. The various Young Adult books on the subject include fictionalized material from earlier undocumented books for juvenile audiences.

BROOKE KROEGER

BLYDEN, Edward Wilmot (3 Aug. 1832–12 Feb. 1912), advocate of Pan Africanism, was born on the island of St. Thomas, part of the present-day Virgin Islands, the son of Romeo Blyden, a tailor, and Judith (maiden name unknown), a schoolteacher. The family lived in a predominantly Jewish, English-speaking community in the capital, Charlotte-Amalie. Blyden went to the local primary school but also received private tutoring from his father. In 1842 the Blydens left St. Thomas for Porto Bello, Venezuela, where Blyden showed his facility for learning foreign languages. By 1844 the family had returned home to St. Thomas. Blyden attended school only in the morning, and in the afternoons he served a five-year apprenticeship as a tailor. In 1845 the Blyden family met the Reverend John P. Knox, a famous white American minister who had assumed pastorship of the Dutch Reformed Church in St. Thomas, where the Blydens were members. Knox quickly became Blyden's mentor and encouraged his academic studies and oratorical skills. Because of Knox's influence, Blyden decided to become a clergyman, an aspiration his parents supported.

In May 1850 Blyden accompanied Mrs. John Knox to the United States and attempted to enroll in Rutgers Theological College, which was Reverend Knox's alma mater, but was refused admission because he was black. Blyden's attempts to gain admission to other theological colleges also failed. During this time he met important white Presbyterian clergymen, such as John B. Pinney, Walter Lowrie, and William Coppinger, who became his lifelong supporters. All three men were involved with the American Colonization Society. They convinced Blyden to go to Liberia, which had become an independent nation in 1847.

Blyden left the United States for Liberia on 21 December 1850 and arrived at Monrovia on 26 January 1851. Initially, he worked as a part-time clerk for a merchant and resumed his studies at Alexander High School, a new Presbyterian institution under the principalship of the Reverend D. A. Wilson, a graduate of Princeton Theological Seminary. Blyden's intellectual abilities impressed Wilson who then persuaded Knox to support Blyden as a full-time student. By 1853 Blyden was a lay preacher, and by 1854 he was a tutor at his high school and acted as principal during Wilson's frequent absences due to illness. Blyden published one of the first of many provocative pamphlets on African affairs, *A Voice from Bleeding Africa*, in 1856, the year he married Sarah Yates, the mulatto niece of B. P. Yates, the vice president of Liberia. Their marriage remained an unhappy one. Blyden blamed his marital troubles on his wife's loyalty to what he termed "the mulatto clique" that dominated Liberian politics. However, other important reasons for the marriage's collapse were financial problems due to Blyden's insufficient income and his wife's disinterest in her husband's intellectual pursuits. They had two children. In 1858 he was ordained a Presbyterian minister, succeeding Wilson as principal of Alexander High School.

Throughout the 1860s and 1870s Blyden became intensely involved in the educational and political affairs of Liberia. In 1861 he was appointed Liberian educational commissioner and traveled to the United States and Britain on a lecture and fundraising tour. He encouraged African Americans to immigrate to Liberia, "back home to the Fatherland," where he contended they could live free from slavery and racial inequality. From 1860 to 1871 he taught classics at Liberia College; he was also the Liberian secretary of state (1864–1866). In 1871 Blyden was forced to leave Liberia temporarily for Sierra Leone after a coup d'état against the Edward Roye administration (1870–1871) endangered his life. He returned to Liberia in 1872 to become principal of Alexander High School again, a post he held until 1878. As the Liberian ambassador to the Court of St. James in Britain from 1877 to 1879, Blyden unsuccessfully tried to win financial support for Liberia from Britain. He then served as president of Liberia College (1880–1884) and was minister of the interior (1880–1882). In 1885 he ran unsuccessfully for president of Liberia, though he had left the country to live in Sierra Leone.

From the late 1880s to the early 1900s Blyden wrote his most important work on Pan Africanism and maintained his diplomatic and educational commitments. In 1887 he published his seminal work, *Christianity, Islam, and the Negro Race*. The Liberian government again appointed him ambassador to the Court of St. James in 1892, and he served as a special envoy to London and Paris in 1905. From 1901 to 1906 he was director of Mohammedan education in Sierra Leone. Poor and frail, he underwent an operation for an aneurysm in the knee at the Royal Southern Hospital in Liverpool in 1909. His friends in the Colonial Office in London helped secure for him a small pension in 1910. He died in Sierra Leone two years later. His funeral service represented the unity he tried to forge among Africans during his lifetime: it was a Christian service in which Muslim men bore his coffin from his residence. His long career as an educator, diplomat, and proponent of Pan Africanism attracted scholarly attention from African, Caribbean, and African-American historians, biographers, and political scientists.

• Biographical works on Blyden include A. Deniga, *Blyden: The African Educationalist* (1923), and Julius Ojo Cole, *Edward Wilmont Blyden: An Interpretation* (1935). Hollis Lynch, *Edward Wilmont Blyden: Pan-Negro Patroit* (1967), is a political biography that focuses on the historical evolution of Blyden's Pan-Africanist ideas and educational reform. Works that discuss the legacy of Blyden's ideas and involvement in the development of Pan Africanism are Adekunle Ajala, *Pan Africanism: Evolution, Progress and Prospects* (1973); J. A. Langely, *Pan Africanism and Nationalism in West Africa, 1900 to 1945* (1973); I. Geiss, *The Pan African Movement* (1974); and P. Esedebe, *Pan Africanism: The Idea and the Movement, 1776–1963* (1982). Wilson Moses, *The Golden Age of Black Nationalism, 1850–1925* (1978), examines the significance of Blyden's work on the transformation of Pan-African nationalism within the nineteenth-century African diaspora.

KIMBERLY WELCH

BOARDMAN, George Dana (18 Aug. 1828–28 Apr. 1903), Baptist preacher, was born in Tavoy, Burma, the son of George D. Boardman, Sr., and Sarah Hall, Baptist missionaries. When Boardman was six, his father died and his mother married. Adoniram Judson, a missionary in Burma. In 1834 Boardman was sent to the United States for his education. The nine-month sea voyage from India to Boston, Massachusetts, aboard the *Cashmere* was a tramautic and violent experience for the frail young Boardman. He witnessed the crew of the ship throw his belongings overboard, was tied aloft while his pet goat had its throat slit, was dragged through the sea by a rope, and was made to fire a cannon, which he was told would kill him.

In 1846 Boardman entered Brown University to study law. After his sophomore year, disappointed with school, he went to Missouri, where he tried some mercantile pursuits while continuing to read law. In 1850, as he was about to be admitted to the bar in St. Louis, a cholera epidemic broke loose. After recovering from the sickness, from which he nearly died, Boardman reevaluated his life's goals and decided to enter the vocation of his parents and serve God. He returned to Brown University graduating with a D.D. in 1852. He then studied at Newton Theological Institute and graduated with an LL.D. In August 1855 he married Ella W. Covell. They had no children.

Boardman's first parish was in Barnwell Court House, South Carolina, where he was ordained a Baptist minister in December 1855. After Preston Brooks was hailed as a hero for his brutal assault on the abolitionist senator Charles Sumner, Boardman left the South because he "could not conscientiously live among slave holders." He resettled in Rochester, New York, where he pastored the Second Baptist Church from 1856 to 1864, when he became pastor of the prestigious First Baptist Church of Philadelphia, Pennsylvania, where he remained until retiring in 1895. From 1880 to 1884 he was president of the American Baptist Missionary Union.

Boardman was greatly admired as an intellectual, a pastor, and a civic-minded individual. In addition to his formal pastoral duties, he delivered a number of lectures open to the public including Tuesday noon lectures at the Young Men's Christian Association, a Wednesday night Bible study resulting in 981 lectures, and Sunday afternoon presentations at the University of Pennsylvania.

Boardman was strongly convinced that Christianity must address the needs of society, claiming that it was necessary to "secularize Christianity in order to Christianize secularity." To pursue this goal he, along with fellow Baptist and social gospel pioneer Walter Rauschenbusch and two pastors from New York City, helped create the Brotherhood of the Kingdom.

Boardman believed that the world and humanity were constantly progressing. He understood there to be three stages in humanity's development, and that the world was presently in the third stage. First, there was the "I-istic" or barbarous stage, saying with Cain, "Am I my brother's keeper?" Second, there was the "Other-istic" or civilized stage, saying with St. Paul, "We are members one of another." Third, there was the "Whole-istic" or Christian stage, saying with the Son of Man, "perfected into one."

Boardman took his message of universal unity wherever he could. In 1893 he attended the Parliament of Religions in Chicago, Illinois, which was the first truly international and ecumenical gathering of world religions, and gave the final address, titled, "Christ the Unifier of Mankind." He was also known for a variety of epigrams that underscored his view that the world should become one. Chief among them was: "Chivalry consists in beatitudes; manliness consists in Christliness; righteousness consists in altruism; patriotism consists in internationalism; and that the athletics of the Beatitudes require most sturdy moral muscle."

Boardman's most important contribution was his involvement in the peace movement. He served as president of the American Arbitration and Peace Society and belonged to several American and European peace organizations, including the Pennsylvania Peace Society; the Universal Peace Union; the Boston Peace Society; the British National Peace Society; La Société de la Paix, France; the International Bureau de la Paix, Berne Switzerland; and the International Arbitration and Peace Association.

Boardman sent his 1890 pamphlet, "The Disarmament of Nations," to the czar of Russia, Queen Victoria, and the archbishop of Canterbury. In 1890 as president of the American Arbitration and Peace Society, he addressed a Washington, D.C., audience that included the secretary of State and members of the cabinet and of Congress. He opposed the U.S. annexation of the Philippines as well as the Spanish-American War. He wrote: "I also believe that all war in the closing part of the nineteenth century of Christ's grace is inhuman and unchristian." In 1899 he established an annual lectureship series called the Boardman Foundation in Christian Ethics at the University of Pennsylvania to teach "Christian precepts concerning the international life; for instance, treaties, diplomacy, war, arbitration, tariff, reciprocity." That year he also attended the Hague Conference on peace. Boardman was particularly grieved by the Spanish-American War of 1898. In the aftermath of the war, convinced that militarism and nationalism were outmoded, he wrote a letter to President Theodore Roosevelt, urging him to establish a secretary of peace to be a companion to the secretary of war. When asked to sum up his life's work, Boardman answered, "Eirene" (the Greek word for peace). He died in Atlantic City, New Jersey.

• Boardman's papers are in the American Baptist Historical Society, Rochester, N.Y. His most important writings are *Studies in the Creative Week* (1875), *Studies in the Model Prayer* (1879), *Studies in the Mountain Instruction* (1881), *The Divine Man: From the Nativity to the Temptation* (1887), *The Ten Commandments* (1889), *The Problem of Jesus* (1902), *The Kingdom* (1901), *The Church* (1901), *Our Risen King's Forty Days* (1902), and *Ethics of the Body* (1903). His wife, Ella Covell Boardman, published a collection of his writings and encomia from friends and colleagues in *Life and Light: Thoughts from the Writings of George Dana Boardman, with Memorabilia* (1905). The only complete account of his life is Joseph Ide Mortenson, "The Career of the Reverend George Dana Boardman" (Th.D. diss. Boston Univ., 1966). An essay emphasizing Boardman's contribution to the peace movement is Janet Kerr Morchaine, "George Dana Boardman: Propagandist for Peace," *Foundations* 9 (1966): 145–58. A helpful work, not only on Boardman but on his parents and stepfather as well, is Joan Jacobs Brumberg, *Mission for Life* (1980).

WESLEY SMITH

BOARDMAN, Mabel Thorp (12 Oct. 1860–17 Mar. 1946), Red Cross leader, was born in Cleveland, Ohio, the daughter of William Jarvis Boardman, a wealthy businessman and attorney, and Florence Sheffield. She attended private schools in Cleveland and New York City and then traveled in Europe. From 1889 to 1893 she enjoyed court life in Berlin with her uncle William Walter Phelps, who was minister to Germany. By the time Boardman returned to the United States, her family had moved to Washington, D.C. She joined the board of the Children's Hospital there and also helped recruit army nurses for the Spanish-American War in 1898.

After the war, there was considerable criticism of the way that the nineteen-year-old American Red Cross had performed, and in 1900 it was decided to restructure the society as a congressionally chartered organization. Though Boardman always claimed it was done without her knowledge, her name was included in the list of incorporators, and she soon joined the Red Cross executive committee. Many critics blamed the society's problems on Clara Barton, the aging founder, whose style of management was autocratic and somewhat disorganized. Boardman, who came to share this view, led the fight for a reorganization, but in 1902 Barton's allies on the board defeated Boardman's proposals and made Barton president for life. Boardman then turned for support to political friends such as President Theodore Roosevelt's sister Anna Roosevelt Cowles and Secretary of War William Howard Taft. Within weeks the White House broke off its association with the Red Cross and called for a congressional investigation of Barton's administration. Barton was soon persuaded to resign, and a new group of trustees sympathetic to Boardman's views was elected. Soon thereafter Boardman drafted a new charter that would establish the Red Cross as a quasi-governmental organization, with its chief officers named by the president of the United States and its accounts audited annually by the War Department. The charter became law in 1905.

During the next decade Boardman crisscrossed the country building support for the Red Cross among civic leaders, creating hundreds of state and local chapters, establishing first aid and lifesaving courses, and designing training programs for volunteers. In 1913, with funding from both government and private sources, she launched the construction of a marble headquarters building in Washington, D.C.; it was completed in 1917. Some years later she raised funds for a second, even larger structure. Boardman also raised an endowment fund of nearly $2 million and organized the annual sale of Christmas seals to generate money for the Red Cross and to fight tuberculosis. Officially Boardman remained an unpaid member of the executive committee; she insisted that the chairmanship must be held by a man. Nevertheless, as a colleague later observed, "Miss Boardman was the chief, make no mistake about that." Her friend President Taft explained, "She is not the president—she is not the chairman—she *is* the Red Cross!"

When World War I began in Europe in 1914, Boardman maintained the Red Cross's traditional neutrality by shipping medical supplies to combatants on both sides. But as American sympathy for the Allies grew more pronounced, her policies received less support. At the same time, the organization was expanding exponentially, outgrowing Boardman's administrative skills. At the recommendation of a committee of leading businessmen, a new Red Cross War Council was established under the control of a male trustee; Boardman was given a subordinate role. Even when the War Council disbanded after the war, Boardman was not at first reappointed to the executive committee. Seeking other interests, she served one term on the District of Columbia's Board of Commissioners and devoted several months to inspecting the city's hospitals and welfare agencies.

Boardman reentered the Red Cross in 1921, in time to participate in the debate over whether the organization should continue its focus on emergency assistance or move into providing regular public health and welfare services. Boardman maintained that the Red Cross should concentrate on the emergency services it knew best, rather than trying to break into the vast and complex welfare field. The new chairman, John Barton Payne, supported her views (in part because they would be less costly) and a new "common-sense approach" was endorsed, in which local chapters would continue their existing nursing and family programs and would prepare corps of volunteers to serve in emergencies but would not develop new welfare services.

In 1923 Boardman was named director of the Red Cross Volunteer Special Services program. For the next seventeen years she concentrated on this project, building specialized units such as the Nurses Aides, the Motor Corps, and the Gray Ladies. Under Boardman's leadership these units tended to recruit primarily wealthy society women. The Red Cross chapter in Washington, founded by Boardman in 1905, was also notable for its exclusivity. This stress on social criteria seemed increasingly inappropriate as the depression deepened. Nevertheless, the cachet that Boardman gave to Red Cross work probably helped bring wealthy women into Volunteer Special Services during the difficult years of the 1930s; by 1940 the program had 2.7 million members.

Boardman received many foreign decorations and in 1944 was the first recipient of the Red Cross's Distinguished Service Medal. Tall and erect, she continued to wear the pompadour hairdo and large hats that had been fashionable in her younger days. She often retold the story of the duke of Windsor seeing her across a room and exclaiming, "Good Lord—there's Mother!" Boardman resigned as director of Volunteer Special Services in 1940 but directed various relief projects during World War II. She retired from the District of Columbia Chapter in January 1944 and from the Red Cross central committee that December. Boardman never married. She died in Washington.

Shortly before her retirement, Boardman was presented with a citation that read, in part, "Possessed of many talents, she has devoted her life to one purpose—the American Red Cross." Though she never regained the organizational control that she lost during World War I, Boardman remained a devoted worker for the Red Cross throughout her professional life and could take particular pride in her first decade of service, during which she presided over the difficult transition from Barton's personalized leadership to building the huge and widely respected national organization of later years.

• Boardman's personal papers are in the Library of Congress. Her professional life is documented in the archives of the American Red Cross in Washington, D.C., which include her correspondence, numerous pamphlets and magazine articles by her, and a series of historical monographs on the organization's history from 1881 to 1945. Boardman's *Under the Red Cross Flag at Home and Abroad* (1915) gives some information on her early years with the Red Cross. The most comprehensive biographical sketch appears in Edward T. James et al., eds., *Notable American Women, 1607–1950: A Biographical Dictionary* (1971). See also Foster Rhea Dulles, *The American Red Cross: A History* (1950); Blanche Colton Williams, *Clara Barton: Daughter of Destiny* (1941); and Elizabeth Brown Pryor, *Clara Barton: Professional Angel* (1987).

SANDRA OPDYCKE

BOARDMAN, Sarah Hall (4 Nov. 1803–1 Sept. 1845), Baptist missionary and translator, was born in Alstead, New Hampshire, the daughter of Ralph Hall and Abiah O. Hall (her maiden name). Sarah learned Latin, read widely in Christian apologetics and philosophy, and taught school for a time. She was also a writer and poet, and as the eldest of thirteen children, she helped to raise her siblings. Sarah converted to the Christian faith at age sixteen and was baptized by Lucius Bolles, a Baptist pastor in Salem, Massachusetts. In 1825 she married the Reverend George Dana Boardman; they had three children. The couple then accepted a missionary assignment with the Baptist Board of Foreign Missions in Burma. Temporarily detained in Calcutta, India, because of the Burmese War, they arrived in Moulmain in 1827 and settled in Tavoy in 1828. In 1831 George died, and Boardman was left with her children in Tavoy, which was under military siege.

As a single missionary for three years, Boardman traveled extensively in the Karen wilderness east of Tavoy. She concentrated on the establishment of village schools. In the 1830s the Burmese government used her village plan to build its education system. Although opposed to females taking the place of males in ministry, she was frequently compelled to conduct worship in the Karen assemblies. In 1834 Boardman married the American Baptist missionary, Adoniram Judson. They had eight children. After the birth of her last child, she suffered from chronic dysentery and had to travel to a better climate. En route to England and then to the United States, she died on the island of St. Helena.

Boardman was a gifted linguist. She translated John Bunyan's *Pilgrim's Progress*, a catechism, a devotional work, and several hymns into Burmese. She was a pioneer translator in the Peguan language, superintending a translation of the New Testament from Burmese to Peguan. Her final project was a series of hymns and Sunday school aids for use in Burma.

The life of Boardman became a model for nineteenth-century Christian women, particularly in the evangelical community. The hagiographic saga that Emily Judson, Adoniram Judson's third wife, wrote about Boardman included advice on motherhood, Christian sacrifice, and "how to die as a Christian."

• The correspondence of Boardman is in the files of the American Baptist Foreign Mission Society in the American Baptist Archives, Valley Forge, Pa. She translated six works, of which the most prominent were *The Catechism* (1829) and *Pilgrim's Progress* (1840). Her works include *The Life of Our Lord and Saviour Jesus Christ* (1837) and *Scripture Questions for Sabbath Schools* (1837). Biographical details are found in Emily C. Judson, *Memoir of Sarah B. Judson* (1848), and Clara L. Balfour, *Sketch of Mrs. Ann H. Judson, Mrs. Sarah B. Judson, and Mrs. Emily C. Judson* (1854). Her importance in shaping the ideals of American Christian women is discussed in Joan J. Brumberg, *Mission for Life: The Story of the Family of Adoniram Judson* (1980). An obituary is in the *Baptist Memorial and Monthly Chronicle*, Mar. 1846, pp. 79–83.

WILLIAM H. BRACKNEY

BOAS, Franz (9 July 1858–21 Dec. 1942), anthropologist, was born in Minden, Westphalia, Germany, the son of Meier Boas, a merchant, and Sophie Meyer. His mother founded a local kindergarten and maintained "a lively interest in public matters," he later recalled. To his parents, "the ideals of the revolution of 1848 were a living force." Franz developed an early distaste for authority and was shocked when an associate defended an unquestioning obedience to tradition. Frail in health as a child, he was passionately interested in books and nature; his mother encouraged his interest in botany. The parents were not overtly religious, so he "was spared the struggle against religious dogma that besets the lives of so many young people" (Boas, *The Nation*, 1938, p. 201).

At universities in Bonn, Heidelberg, and Kiel, Boas studied physics, mathematics, and geography. He resented anti-Semitism expressed by other students; he bore facial scars sustained while dueling to defend his ethnic background. Boas came to know the distinguished Theobald Fischer, who got him interested in geography. Another inspiration was the great pathologist Rudolf Virchow. Virchow was politically liberal and intellectually combative, and he scorned speculative hypotheses in science—all traits later associated with Boas. Boas obtained his doctorate in physics at the University of Kiel in 1881.

Boas was intrigued by then-popular theories of geographical determinism that traced cultural traits to regional environments. To investigate such theories, he journeyed in 1883 to Baffin Island in the Northwest Territories of North America, where he studied Eskimos for a year. To his "thorough disillusionment" (Harris, p. 266) he found that the Eskimos were molded more by their social traditions than by their harsh terrain and climate. This early field research "had a profound influence upon the development of my views . . . because it led me away from my former interests and toward the desire to understand what determines the behavior of human beings" (Boas, *The Nation*, 1938, p. 202). It may also account for his subsequent hostility to sweeping theories of human nature and society.

After his Eskimo venture, Boas spent time in New York. In 1885 he returned to Germany, where he served as docent in geography at the University of Berlin. In 1887 he was named assistant editor of *Science* magazine in New York. That year he married Marie Krackowizer; they had six children. In 1888 he began intensive field studies of Northwest Indian tribes; this work would occupy much of his life. In 1891 he became a U.S. citizen. Meanwhile, in 1888–1892 he taught at Clark University. In 1892 he was named curator of anthropology at the Field Museum in Chicago, where he was dismissed because of a personal conflict. In 1899 he became a full professor of anthropology at Columbia University, where he remained until his death more than four decades later.

Boas once observed that his "whole outlook upon social life is determined by the question: How can we recognize the shackles that tradition has laid upon us? For when we recognize them, we are also able to break them" (Kardiner and Preble, p. 139). He scorned sweeping generalizations and speculations, particularly those that had infected the fledgling social sciences of the nineteenth century. That era produced grandiose social theories that were early attempts at a so-called science of man, or anthropology. According to "evolutionary" theories, human society evolved in stages. Some theorists alleged that behavioral, emotional, and intellectual differences among ethnic and national groups were caused by genetic and evolutionary factors. Thus some groups were more advanced on the evolutionary scale than others. In the United States, racists employed such dubious hypotheses to justify the enslavement of, or discrimination against, African Americans.

Such attitudes enraged Boas. He was a firm cultural relativist whose personal experiences with prejudice disinclined him toward theories of ethnic and racial hierarchies. In his view, "Every classification of mankind must be more or less artificial" (Hyatt, p. 117). As early as 1894, he gave a vice presidential speech to the American Association for the Advancement of Science in which he rejected racial theories of intelligence. In a 1906 address at Atlanta University, he compared American discrimination against blacks to European prejudice against Jews. In those days, many Americans feared that the swelling numbers of immigrants included persons of biologically inferior stock who would degrade the national gene pool. Even many scholars of that era assumed that different ethnic groups were different "races" with distinctive biologies and personalities. To counter such anxieties, Boas exposed their pseudoscientific basis. He and thirteen aides studied the heads of 17,821 immigrants and their offspring. He published his results in an article, "Changes in the Bodily Form of Descendants of Immigrants," in *American Anthropologist* in 1912. Head forms of immigrants varied markedly from those of their descendants born in the United States, he found. The longer the descendants had lived in America, the larger the cranial variation. In other words, people of specific cultural backgrounds—he had analyzed Czech, Italian, and Jewish immigrants—did not have hereditary predispositions to particular head shapes. Hence, as human bodies were so plastic, theories of "innate" racial factors were absurd.

Boas's highly influential book *The Mind of Primitive Man* (1911) argued that no racial group is genetically "pure"; that races change physical traits over time; that the inherent differences between races are minor compared to their similarities; and that all races are uniformly capable of developing cultures. Such views challenged then-current warnings that immigration would degrade the United States into a "mongrel nation." As Boas wrote in *Anthropology and Modern Life* (1928), "Some of the most firmly rooted opinions of our times appear from a wider point of view as prejudices, and . . . a knowledge of anthropology enables us to look with greater freedom at the problems confronting our civilization" (Spier, p. 123). He urged social scientists to be more cautious—specifically, to "investigate the truth or fallacy of each theory rather than excite the public mind by indulgence in the fancies of our speculation" (Hyatt, p. 113).

In later years, Boas scoffed at the grandiose psychohistorical hypotheses of the Freudians, who traced the structure of modern society to prehistoric Oedipal guilt. Boas was also skeptical of theories of economic determinism. To him, the age demanded the careful collection of field data on the peoples of earth, not vaporous speculation. Many were puzzled by his seemingly hyper-Baconian research style—collecting mountains of data while delaying indefinitely attempts to synthesize it into theory. But he defended this approach:

> It may seem to the distant observer that American students are engaged in a mass of detailed investigations without much bearing upon the solution of the ultimate problems of a philosophic history of human civilization. I think this interpretation of the American attitude would be unjust because the ultimate questions are as near to out hearts as they are to those of other scholars, only we do not hope to be able to solve an intricate historical problem by a formula. (Wax, p. 64)

Boas took courageous political stands that could have endangered his career. During the First World War he opposed U.S. participation in the war against his native Germany. At that time, Columbia University officials asked students to report possibly disloyal comments by teachers. In response, Boas read to his students a summary of his unorthodox ideas, then offered to let them pass copies to the campus trustees. In a letter to the 20 December 1919 issue of *The Nation*, he attacked anthropologists who "have prostituted science by using it as a cover for their activities as spies."

Boas has been called the father of modern anthropology, partly because he influenced so many outstanding students and associates—among them Margaret Mead, Ruth Benedict, Alfred Kroeber, Robert Lowie, Edward Sapir, Zora Neale Hurston, Melville Herskovits, Leslie Spier, Jules Henry, and Ashley Montagu. Personally, Boas struck others as austere, even forbidding. Lowie recalled "actually dreading meeting him on the way to classes" because of Boas's aloofness (Kardiner and Preble, p. 142). To his best-known student, Mead, Boas was "a surprising and somewhat frightening teacher" (Hyatt, p. 153). Even so, Boas seems to have felt more comfortable with female students. If students worked closely with him, they recognized his "warm personal concern for the training and success of each of us" (Spier, p. 111).

Boas was a pioneer of modern folklore research. He edited the *Journal of American Folklore* from 1908 to 1925. Early in his career, folklorists debated why native tales around the world had so many common themes. Was it because humanity possessed an underlying "psychic unity"? Or was it because stories "diffused" from geographical centers as people migrated? Boas pointed out that if the psychic-unity theory were true, then myths from adjacent and widely dispersed tribes would be equally likely to resemble each other. In fact, his research supported a diffusionist interpretation by showing that myths from adjacent tribes are likelier to have similar content.

Boas had enormous impact on the fledgling science of comparative linguistics. He believed that to grasp fully the meanings of natives' statements, an anthropologist must learn their language in detail rather than merely try to classify their verbal structures according to a language family (for example, Indo-European). His hostility to theorizing could have adverse effects: he reportedly dismissed Kroeber's efforts to show him underlying links between various Native-American tongues.

In the 1930s Boas was repelled by the rise of fascism in his native Germany. Nazis burned his books in 1933 at Kiel, where he had received his doctorate. Despite his advanced age, he threw himself into the fight against Nazi racial doctrines. At the same time, he refused to gloss over the bigotry of American culture, which was still scarred by racial segregation and the lynchings of blacks. "The hysterical claims of the Aryan enthusiasts have never had any scientific background," he declared in 1938. "The crudest form of racial consciousness is at present confined to Germany—although with respect to stronger [racial] divergences, such as those between Negroes or Asiatics and whites, it is almost equally potent in the United States and in England, mitigated by a hypocritical desire to avoid legal recognition of the facts." As the Second World War loomed, he scorned patriotic fervor and nationalism as "the herd instinct in man" (Boas, *The Nation*, 1938, p. 203).

Boas died of a heart attack at a Columbia faculty luncheon. His legacy was debated for decades after his death. On the one hand, detractors complained that he had sent inadequately prepared students into the field; that he hoarded and published huge archives of data with insufficient structure or analysis; and that his extreme cultural relativism implied that anthropologists had little to say about human nature. As some analysts wryly observed, Boas had seemed content "to go on recording information and postponing [theoretical] explanation until that time in the distant future when the patient bookkeeping of generations of anthropologists would reveal sound inductive generalizations about man and society" (Kardiner and Preble, p. 212). On the other hand, that such broad criticisms could be hurled at one man testifies to his historic impact. He championed an antiracist view of humanity long before it was intellectually and socially fashionable; he risked his reputation, and perhaps his career, by taking risky political and ethical stands; and he replaced the often sloppy, ethnocentric speculation of his predecessors with intimidatingly high standards of data collection and analysis. As his former student Spier wrote soon after Boas's death: "So far as anthropology is a science, he made it one" (Spier, p. 108).

• Boas published more than 600 articles. He eloquently summarized his early life, career, and beliefs in "An Anthropologist's Credo," *The Nation*, 27 Aug. 1938. His other books include *Primitive Art* (1927), *General Anthropology* (1938), and a collection of papers, *Race, Language and Culture* (1940). An early biography of Boas is Melville J. Herskovits, *Franz Boas: The Science of Man in the Making* (1953). Also see Herskovits, "Some Further Notes on Franz Boas's Arctic Expedition," *American Anthropologist* (Feb. 1957): 112–16. Another biography is Marshall Hyatt, *Franz Boas: Social Activist* (1990), which depicts Boas's struggle against racism and nativism. See the superb analysis of Boas's work in Abram Kardiner and Edward Preble, *They Studied Man* (1961). Also see Walter Goldschmidt, ed., *The Anthropology of Franz Boas: Essays on the Centennial of His Birth*, American Anthropological Association Memoir no. 89, vol. 61, no. 5, pt. 2 (Oct. 1959); and the intricate and not altogether favorable analysis of Boas in Marvin Harris, *The Rise of Anthropological Theory* (1968). A detailed review of Boas's work also appears in George W. Stocking, Jr., ed., *Volksgeist as Method and Ethic: Essays on Boasian Ethnography and the German Anthropological Tradition* (1996). Other interesting assessments include A. L. Kroeber, "History and Science in Anthropology," *American Anthropologist* (Oct.–Dec. 1935); Leslie Spier, "Franz Boas and Some of His Views," *Acta Americana* (Jan.–Mar. 1943); Robert H. Lowie, "Franz Boas (1858–1942)," *Journal of American Folklore* (Jan.–Mar. 1944); Leslie White, "'Diffusion vs. Evolution': An Anti-evolutionist Fallacy," *American Anthropologist* 47 (1945): 339–56; Murray Wax, "The Limitations of Boas's Anthropology," *American Anthropologist* 58 (1956): 68–74, which praised Boas for attacking "slipshod methods" but accused him of failing to provide "positive leadership"; and Verne F. Ray's review of the Herskovits biography in *American Anthropologist* 57 (1955): 138–

40. A controversial critique of Boas and his impact on his best-known student appears in Derek Freeman, *Margaret Mead and Samoa: The Making and Unmaking of an Anthropological Myth* (1983). An obituary is in the *New York Times*, 22 Dec. 1942.

KEAY DAVIDSON

BOAS, Franziska Marie (8 Jan. 1902–22 Dec. 1988), dancer, percussionist, and dance teacher and therapist, was born in New York City, the daughter and youngest of six children of noted anthropologist Franz Boas and Marie Krackowizer. Educated in public schools in Englewood, New Jersey, Boas received a B.A. degree in zoology and chemistry from Barnard College in 1923. Her undergraduate studies also included dance with Bird Larson, with whom she continued to study from time to time after graduation. Other formal study included drawing and sculpture with Robert Laurent and Boardman Robinson at the Art Students League in New York from 1923 to 1924, and in Breslau, Germany, in 1927. Additional dance studies included working with Mary Wigman in Germany and with Hanya Holm in New York, where she served as Holm's assistant and percussionist until 1933. During that time, in 1928, Boas was married to Nicholas Michelson, a doctor; they had one child, a daughter, before they were divorced in 1942.

In 1933 Boas founded and until 1949 directed the Boas School of Dance, an interracial school with a performing company located at 323 West Twenty-first Street in New York. Among her many notable pupils were Ed Bates, Valerie Bettis, John Cage, Merce Cunningham, Norman Coker, Katherine Dunham, Claude Merchant, and Alwin Nikolais. In 1944 she founded the Boas Summer School of Dance on Lake George in Bolton Landing, New York. Also described in newspaper articles as being an interracial school, the summer school continued under her direction until 1950. A 1945 article in the *Pittsburgh Courier* is a good example of the type of attention she generated. Under the headline "American of Good Will—Franziska Boas Effects Democracy through the Dance," the article goes on to say: "Miss Boas entertains the same belief as that of her father that people should be brought together in order to better understand one another. Without making any attempt at effecting a spirit of brotherhood between the various races, creeds and colors that compose her student body, she encourages freedom of expression in dancing by bringing them together on one plane."

Besides teaching in her own schools, Boas also taught at the Walden School in New York and at Bennington College, Mills College, Columbia University Teachers College, the Horace Mann School, Bank Street College, Bryn Mawr College, Colorado State Teachers College, and the Savage School for Physical Education. In the program notes for a dance demonstration presented at the Savage School, Boas wrote about what she hoped the students would gain from the dance activities. Under the title "Recreational Activities for Social Integration" appears the note: "A social consciousness makes it possible for people to live together harmoniously and stimulates their future development. The strength of a democracy lies in the ability of its people to adapt themselves to each other and to changing situations, in the knowledge that progress comes through the effort of many rather than from the dictatorship of a few." This statement is typical of the thrust of Boas's teaching, which sought to provide social integration through dance and other artistic endeavors. This thrust was taken even farther through her work with schizophrenic children at Bellevue Hospital in New York. There, while working with psychiatrist Laretta Bender, Boas pioneered the use of dance movement in the therapeutic treatment of profoundly disturbed patients. Work at Bellevue continued throughout the 1940s, all of which she did as a volunteer.

In the early 1940s Boas created the first all-percussion orchestra in the West. From 1947 to 1949 she toured the United States giving dance performances, lecture-demonstrations in dance, and percussion performances. These manifested her aesthetic theory that percussion carried the inner line of thought while the dancer outwardly expressed the thought. Sound, to Boas, was a palpable substance in which to dance. During this period she also continued to explore and study dance therapy at numerous institutions, including the Menninger Institute, UCLA, the Langley Porter Institute, the Anna Halprin Studio, Stanford University, the University of Wisconsin, the University of Washington, Wayne State University, the Veterans Administration Hospital, North Texas State College, Indiana University, the Art Students League in New York, the Bolton Music Festival, Scripps College, Fresno State Teachers College, Lake Erie College, and the New School for Social Research, and at various meetings of the American Association for Health, Physical Education, and Recreation (AAHPER). The following program, which was presented at North Texas State, includes the titles of some of the choreographic works she created during these years:

Landscape—Javanese music
Monotony—Colin McPhee
Playful Interlude—percussion
Goyaesque—Meyer Kupferman
Lament—Cola Heiden
Bolton Set—Meyer Kupferman
  The Windbag
  The Drudge
  The Grapevine
  The Bobbie Soxer
  The Tourist

Three other choreographic titles are known: *Soliloque*, *March*, and *Duet*; the last was performed at the Boas School in New York with her daughter, Trudel.

Boas's writings include two groundbreaking articles on dance as therapy: "Creative Dance as Therapy" (*American Journal of Orthopsychiatry*) and "Psychological Aspects in the Practice and Teaching of Dancing" (*Journal of Aesthetics and Art Criticism*), both published in 1941. Probably her most noted work, particularly among dance ethnologists, was *The Function of Dance in Human Society* (1944), the edited volume of the seminar series of the same name that took place at her studio in 1942. Participants included Franz Boas, Harold Courlander, Claire Holt, Gregory Bateson, George Herzog, Cora DeBois, and Geoffrey Gorer. The introduction reflects Boas's global perspective toward dance education: "Dance must be thought of as an expression of communal activity, and its constructive social influence on the individual must be realized and promoted. The possibilities of dance as mental therapy must be explored just as, until now, its uses in physical training have been emphasized. The psychological implications of dance and the methods of using it as a broadening educative medium on a par with the other arts must be widely understood and propagandized."

Personal and economic setbacks forced Boas to leave New York in 1950 and to take the position as head of the dance and physical education department at Shorter College in Rome, Georgia. In 1957, under her direction, the department became the Dance Department, Division of Fine Arts at Shorter College, where Boas remained until 1965. Between 1950 and 1959 she was very active in the Southern Association for Health, Physical Education and Recreation (SAHPER), and in 1955 she organized the Georgia Dance Association. Within the curriculum at Shorter, Boas introduced the concept of culture into her dance history classes and in so doing clearly went beyond the then-accepted historical perspectives on dance. During this time she was also a member of the Georgia Council of Human Relations and a founding member of the Rome (Ga.) Council on Human Relations, an organization devoted to advancing the cause of racial integration.

In 1965 Boas took early retirement from Shorter College and moved to Sandisfield, Massachusetts, where she was active in the Sandisfield Arts Council and taught dance to community residents at the Sandisfield Town Hall. In 1986 she attended the Hunt-Boas family reunion in Alert Bay, British Columbia, which was a celebration of the meeting of Franz Boas and the Kwakiutl Indian informant, George Hunt. The descendants of both men attended; at eighty-four, Franziska Boas was the oldest. Despite suffering from Alzheimer's disease during the last four years of her life, Boas remained active—still dancing in the fall of her last year—until her death in Sandisfield. A memorial service was held at Barnard College in New York on 30 April 1989.

Although she was not a well-known dancer or choreographer, such as Martha Graham, Charles Weidman, or other of her contemporaries, Boas is remembered for the way in which she combined her multiple dance talents with wide-ranging social and professional concerns to create and define many of the subfields of dance that are studied today. Like her father, who was known for his commitment to social activism and his battle to rid the scientific community of racially based theories of intelligence, Franziska Boas was also a committed activist for racial equality and social justice. She worked to teach young people about the value of dance as a means of communication; she pioneered dance as therapy; she encouraged students to expand their own creativity through improvisation; she combined the study of dance with ethnology; and she helped to break down the racial barriers that stood between African Americans and the desire to pursue a career in dance. An obituary written by her granddaughter Valerie Pinsky described her aptly as a "woman of extraordinary grace and vitality, whose life could not have been more rich, and whose sense of humor was never lost."

• Franziska Boas's papers are in the Music Division of the Library of Congress in Washington, D.C. On Boas's work as a dance therapist see Irmgard Bartenieff, "Dance Therapy: A New Profession or a Rediscovery of an Ancient Role of the Dance?" *Dance Scope* 7 (Fall–Winter 1972–1973): 6–18.

MARY E. EDSALL

BOBBITT, Franklin (16 Feb. 1876–7 Mar. 1956), educator, was born John Franklin Bobbitt in English, Indiana, the son of the Reverend James Bobbitt and Martha Smith. His father was superintendent of the Crawford County Schools in Indiana. Franklin Bobbitt, who rarely used his given name, married Sarah Annis of San Diego, California, in 1903. The couple had one child.

Bobbitt taught in Union Township schools in Crawford County, southern Indiana, from 1893 to 1902. He received his A.B. degree from Indiana University in 1901. He was an instructor at the Philippine Normal School in Manila from 1902 to 1907. During this same period, he served on the Commission of Seven, a committee charged with developing a curriculum for the Philippine schools. In 1909 Bobbitt received his Ph.D. in psychology and education from Clark University in Worcester, Massachusetts. He was attracted to Clark because of the work of the psychologist G. Stanley Hall, who was a professor there. His dissertation, patterned after Hall's work, was titled "The Growth of Philippine Children." In 1909 he began his long association with the University of Chicago as an instructor in educational administration becoming, upon his retirement in August 1941, professor emeritus.

Bobbitt pioneered the use of the public school survey as a basis for developing the school curriculum and issued widely circulated reports on surveys conducted in Cleveland, Ohio (1915), San Antonio, Texas (1915), and Denver, Colorado (1916). He was a leading member of the National Education Association Committee on Economy of Time in Education (1911), which concentrated its efforts on eliminating nonessential study from the school curriculum. During leaves of absence from the University of Chicago, Bobbitt also served as assistant superintendent of schools in Los Angeles, California (1922–1923), and Toledo, Ohio (1924).

The surveys conducted by Bobbitt were directed toward the "scientific" analysis of life activities. The results of the surveys were to contribute to the development of curricular objectives based on clearly identified, contemporary adult activities. These curricular objectives were to form the bases for more efficient classroom instruction. Central to these efforts was Bobbitt's belief that education ought to prepare children for those activities likely to characterize their adult lives.

Bobbitt's approach has been widely criticized for its unquestioning acceptance of the societal status quo and its uncritical mixing of industrial, engineering, and scientific metaphors. In a 1933 chapter, "The Underlying Philosophy of Education" (in *The Educational Frontier*, ed. William H. Kilpatrick), John Dewey and John L. Childs observed, quite critically, that the formulation of such specific curricular objectives assumed, "that character, mental life, experience, and the methods of dealing with them, are composed of separable parts, and that there is no whole, no integralness in them, that what seems to be a unity is in reality nothing but an aggregate of parts" (p. 289).

Nevertheless, Bobbitt's work laid the foundation for a new technological approach to curricular planning. Two of his books, *The Curriculum* (1918) and *How to Make a Curriculum* (1924), are considered cornerstones of their field. Although his own work was not generally implemented, Bobbitt undoubtedly influenced one of the most widely accepted approaches to curriculum development, proposed in 1949 by his younger University of Chicago colleague Ralph Tyler.

Bobbitt published an extensive list of works. Among the best known is a chapter, "Some General Principles of Management Applied to the Problems of City-School Systems," published, while he was still an instructor, in the National Society for the Study of Education's Twelfth Yearbook (1913). This work, together with such articles as "The Elimination of Waste in Education" (in *The Elementary School Teacher* [1912]) and his book *What Schools Teach and Might Teach* (1916), set the stage early for his participation in the social efficiency movement. His determination to bring the scientific method to curriculum making was part of a broader effort to increase the efficiency and effectiveness of American schools. This was to be his lifelong endeavor, although in later life, he did appear to moderate his position, moving closer to John Dewey's progressive approach to education. *The Curriculum of Modern Education* (1941) was his last major work.

Sarah and Franklin Bobbitt were divorced in 1937, and Bobbitt married Mabel Deiwert, a nurse from Waldron, Indiana, in 1941. Bobbitt died in Waldron.

• For more on Bobbitt's life see John W. Bobbitt, *The Bobbitt Family in America* (1985). For his career in curriculum see Daniel Tanner and Laurel Tanner, *Curriculum Development: Theory into Practice*, 2d ed. (1980), and Mary Louise Seguel, *The Curriculum Field* (1966).

WILMA S. LONGSTREET

BÔCHER, Maxime (28 Aug. 1867–12 Sept. 1918), mathematician, was born in Boston, Massachusetts, the son of Ferdinand Bôcher and Caroline Little. His father was the first professor of modern languages at the Massachusetts Institute of Technology and later was professor of French at Harvard. Young Bôcher received his early education at the Cambridge Latin School and graduated summa cum laude from Harvard in 1888.

After receiving Harvard, Harris, and Parker fellowships he spent 1888 to 1891 at the University of Göttingen studying with mathematician Felix Klein. His doctorate was awarded in 1891 for a dissertation on classical potential theory, "Ueber die Reihenentwickelungen der Potentialtheorie." This was a literal tour de force of Bôcher's mathematical ability, expressed through a subtle interplay of higher algebra and geometry, analysis, and mathematical physics; each later became essential parts of his mathematical repertoire. Moreover, it received a university prize (Gekrönte Preisschrift), and in 1894 its elaboration, quadrupling its length, was published as his first book under the same title. In July 1891 Bôcher married Marie Niemann of Göttingen, with whom he had three children. Immediately after they were wed, Bôcher returned to Harvard, where he served as an instructor (1891–1894), assistant professor (1894–1904), and finally professor (1904–1918). During the academic year 1913–1914 he was Harvard Exchange Professor at the University of Paris.

Despite a relatively brief 27-year career, Bôcher was widely honored for his remarkable ability and contributions. He was one of the founders of the journal *Transactions of the American Mathematical Society* and served as its editor in chief (1908–1909, 1911–1913). In a 1903 poll of leaders in science in the United States, conducted by *American Men of Science*, Bôcher was rated fourth of eighty in mathematics. He was elected a member of the National Academy of Science in 1909, and during 1909–1910 he served as tenth president of the American Mathematical Society and as one of the organization's first two colloquium lecturers in 1896. In 1923 the American Mathematical Society established its first prize, the Bôcher Prize, in his honor; awarded every five years, one stipulation of the prize is that its recipient be under forty years of age.

Bôcher's mathematical work included some seventy research papers that are essentially concerned with boundary-value problems and ordinary differential equations, with an occasional excursion into higher algebra and geometry. Much of his work in mathematical analysis can be regarded as amplifications and extensions of the ideas of the French mathematician Charles Sturm, which held an especial fascination for him. These include generalizations of the Sturm comparison, oscillation, and separation theorems (1898–1901) and numerous questions relating to Green's functions and differential equations. Bôcher also produced the first explanation of the so-called Gibbs phenomenon in the theory of Fourier series (1906, 1914) and detailed studies of harmonic functions. He was invited to contribute an authoritative survey article, "Randwertaufgaben bei gewöhnlichen Differentialgleichungen," which appeared in the prestigious *Encyklopädie der mathematischen Wissenschaften* (1900).

Bôcher's second book, *Introduction to Higher Algebra* (1907), was a great success and was subsequently translated into German and Russian; for several decades it dominated instruction on matrix theory in American graduate schools. His next book was the Cambridge mathematical tract, *An Introduction to the Study of Integral Equations* (1909), which offered one of the first introductory treatments of the subject. His Paris lectures of 1913–1914 led to his final book, *Leçons sur les méthodes de Sturm dans la théorie des équations différentielles linéaires et leurs développements modernes* (1917), in the celebrated Borel Collection of mathematical monographs. In addition to these advanced texts Bôcher actively collaborated on the publication and revision of several elementary books on analytic geometry and trigonometry.

Bôcher was a lucid lecturer, and together with his colleague William F. Osgood he played a leading role in the reinvigoration of the Harvard mathematics program during the years 1894–1914. While these men never actively collaborated on research, each provided valuable support and stimulus for the other, and together they laid the foundation for Harvard's excellence in the years following the First World War. Bôcher produced seventeen doctoral students, most notably Milton B. Porter, Griffith C. Evans, and Lester R. Ford. Decades later it is difficult to adequately appreciate Bôcher's influence on his time because so much of his work was devoted to perfecting and polishing material rather than to producing striking new results that would bear his name. Nevertheless, his instinct and sense of what was important was impressive, and much of his work became common knowledge although his authorship was largely forgotten. A prime example is his seminal 1900 writings on linear dependence in which he masterfully treats both the algebraic and functional notions in a single paper.

Bôcher's health was never strong, and it began to fail about the time of his Paris lectures. He died following a prolonged illness at his home in Cambridge, Massachusetts. In style and temperament Bôcher was a consummate artist whose loss was keenly felt by both his immediate colleagues and the American mathematical community at large.

• A collection of Bôcher material is in the Harvard University Archives. A biographical sketch by Raymond C. Archibald is in *A Semicentennial History of the American Mathematical Society, 1888–1938* (1938), pp. 161–66. Two appreciations of his work and life, written by his Harvard colleagues George D. Birkhoff and William F. Osgood, were published in the *Bulletin of the American Mathematical Society* 25 (Feb. 1919): 197–215, and 25 (May 1919): 337–50, respectively. His retirement address as president of the American Mathematical Society, "The Published and Unpublished Work of Charles Sturm on Algebraic and Differential Equations," *Bulletin of the American Mathematical Society* 18 (Oct. 1911): 1–18, contains a valuable overview of his predominant mathematical interests. A brief obituary is in the *New York Times*, 13 Sept. 1918.

JOSEPH D. ZUND

BOCHNER, Salomon (20 Aug. 1899–2 May 1982), mathematician, was born in Podgorze, Austria-Hungary, the son of Joseph Bochner, a businessman, and Rude Haber. In 1914 the family moved to Berlin, where Bochner obtained his Gymnasium education. In 1918 he entered the University of Berlin, from which he received a Ph.D. in mathematics in 1921, with the dissertation "Orthogonale Systeme analytischer und harmonischer Funktionen," directed by E. Schmidt. In order to help his family survive the postwar economic difficulties, he worked for several years in the import-export business. He successfully pursued this occupation until being awarded an International Education Board Fellowship, then spent 1924 to 1926 studying successively in Copenhagen (with H. Bohr), Oxford (with G. H. Hardy), and Cambridge (with J. E. Littlewood). From 1927 to 1933 he was a docent at the University of Munich.

Upon the Nazi accession to power Bochner immigrated to the United States, where he joined the faculty of Princeton University as an associate in 1933, assistant professor in 1934, associate professor in 1939, professor in 1946, and as the H. B. Fine Professor (1959–1968). Upon his retirement from Princeton, he became the E. O. Lovett Professor of Mathematics at Rice University from 1968 until his death. From 1969 to 1976 he was chairman of the mathematics department at Rice. In addition, he was a part-time member of the Institute for Advanced Study at Princeton, New Jersey, from 1945 to 1948; a visiting professor at Harvard University (Spring 1947) and at the University of California at Berkeley in the Department of Statistics (Spring 1953); a consultant for the Los Alamos Project at Princeton University (1951–1952); and a consultant to the National Science Foundation and the U.S. Air Force Air Research and Development Command from 1952 onward.

In 1937 Bochner married Naomi Weinberg; they had one child. Bochner became a naturalized U.S. citizen in 1938 and was elected a member of the National Academy of Sciences in 1950. He was the colloquium lecturer of the American Mathematical Society in 1956, served as vice president of that organization (1957–1958), and was the recipient of its Steele Prize in 1979.

Bochner's work displays an unusual versatility combined with truly remarkable depth and insight. In mathematics, his interests ranged freely over the theories of Fourier series, integrals, and transforms; almost periodic functions; functional analysis; probability; complex analysis of one and several variables; and differential geometry. While in Munich he published two papers on X-ray crystallography with the physicist H. Seyfarth (1928); in Princeton he wrote an elegant paper on general relativity (1955). Because the diversity of his mathematical interests do not fall into precise periods of activity, it is convenient to delineate only two general periods of work: the time in Germany (1921–1933) and his American years (1933–1982).

After Bochner's dissertation material was independently undertaken by another mathematician, he boldly struck out in new directions. His first work considered almost periodic functions, originally introduced by Bohr, however Bochner contributed noteworthy new methods (1925–1926) and may be regarded as one of the founders of the theory. His study in England introduced him to the zeta function, which also became a lifelong interest. In an entirely different area, in a paper on Riemann surfaces (1928), he anticipated what was later known as Zorn's Lemma. However, the most striking research of his time in Munich was concerned with Fourier analysis. This ultimately led to his very influential *Vorlesungen über Fouriersche Integrale* (1933), putatively his most important work. The book appeared in an English translation (with a supplement by the author) as *Lectures on Fourier Integrals* (1959) and in a Russian translation (1962). It contained the famous Bochner Theorem on the characterization of Fourier-Stieltjes transforms of positive measures as positive definite functions, which is fundamental in abstract harmonic analysis, as well as material of later importance in the theory of distributions. He also produced a generalization of the Lebesgue integral, known as the Bochner integral (1932).

Bochner's years at Princeton continued to break new ground in startlingly new directions, including functional analysis and group theory. He collaborated with a number of distinguished mathematicians, perhaps most notably J. von Neumann on a theory of almost periodic functions on a group (1935). Bochner found that the Riemann Localization Theorem was not valid for Fourier series of several variables (1935–1936), which led him indirectly to consider functions of several complex variables (1937). He made basic contributions to this theory that included the Bochner-Martinelli Formula (1943), and extensions of the Cauchy Integral Formula (1944). His research was summarized in *Several Complex Variables* (1948), written with W. T. Martin, which was the first American book on the subject. Once again, Bochner's work in several complex variables was later seen to contain rudimentary ideas involving cohomology theory and vector bundles. During the same time he also collaborated with K. Chandrasekharan on *Fourier Transforms* (1949). Bochner had been interested in differential geometry since the early 1940s, and he rounded out the end of the decade with a flurry of publications concerning real and complex global differential geometry. These were later summarized masterly in *Curvature and Betti Numbers* (1953), written with K. Yano. Much of this material has proved to be of great importance in the general theory of complex algebraic and differentiable manifolds. During this time he also became interested in probability theory, particularly stochastic processes (1947, 1949–1950), and this led to his final mathematics book, *Harmonic Analysis and the Theory of Probability* (1955).

Beginning in the 1960s Bochner also became seriously involved in the history and philosophy of science. His active participation in the Princeton program in these areas led to *The Role of Mathematics in the Rise of Science* (1966) and *Eclosion and Synthesis: Perspectives on the History of Knowledge* (1969). Both of these contain fascinating, often piquant and penetrating, observations on mathematics and its diverse practitioners. In addition, he was the only scientific member of the editorial board of the five-volume *Dictionary of the History of Ideas: Studies of Selected Pivotal Ideas* (1973–1974). He died in Houston.

Bochner was a personable individual who had an intense curiosity and seemingly boundless energy. These talents served him well, and he made a remarkable contribution to the mathematical program at Princeton (where he supervised a quarter of the doctorates awarded during his time there) and the American mathematical community at large. His research was highly influential and farsighted.

• Forty of Bochner's most influential research papers appear in *Selected Mathematical Papers of Salomon Bochner* (1969), which was published in connection with a symposium held in Princeton on the occasion of his retirement. This volume includes a portrait, a list of his publications (complete up to June 1969), and a list of his thirty-five Princeton doctoral students together with the titles of their dissertations. Two of his later expository publications of particular interest are "Mathematical Reflections," *American Mathematical Monthly* 81 (Oct. 1974): 827–52; and "Einstein between Centuries," *Rice University Studies* 65 (1979): 1–54. An interesting autobiographical sketch appears in *McGraw Hill Modern Scientists and Engineers*, vol. 1, ed. Sybil P. Parker (1980). An obituary is in the *New York Times*, 5 May 1982.

JOSEPH D. ZUND

BOCOCK, Thomas S. (18 May 1815–5 Aug. 1891), lawyer and politician, was born in Buckingham County (now Appomattox County), Virginia, the son of John Thomas Bocock, a clerk of court and Virginia state legislator, and Mary Flood. After receiving private tutoring in Buckingham County, Bocock entered Hampden-Sydney College in 1837. He graduated with a B.A. in 1838, then spent several months reading law in Buckingham County with his brother Willis P. Bocock (later attorney general of Va.). Following admission to the bar in 1840, he began a private practice in Buckingham County. From 1842 to 1844 Bocock represented the county in the Virginia House of Delegates. Following the formation of Appomattox County in 1845, Bocock was appointed as the county's first prosecuting attorney, a position he held until 1846. In 1846 he married Sarah Patrick Flood; they had one child. Also in 1846 Bocock was elected as a Democrat to the House of Representatives in the Thirtieth Congress and served seven consecutive terms (1847–1861). Known for neither radical views on sectional issues nor for leadership in the key congressional debates of the 1850s, Bocock favored compromise in 1850 but also defended the right of secession. He later favored the Kansas-Nebraska Bill and the Lecompton

Constitution. Bocock served as chair of the Committee on Naval Affairs and was a Democratic candidate for Speaker of the House in the dramatic and pivotal election of 1859–1860.

Many observers realized that the breakdown in the Thirty-sixth Congress between Republicans, diverse factions of Democrats, and those listed as Americans or Whigs would complicate the House Speakership election. Despite the clear dissatisfaction of some anti-Lecompton Democrats, most of the party's congressional delegation caucused before Congress convened to select a candidate. Recognized as a skilled parliamentarian and with a reputation as a moderate supporter of states' rights, Bocock was selected as a candidate who might appeal to southern Democrats, moderate northern Democrats, and possibly even southern opposition members. Stephen A. Douglas (anticipating the 1860 presidential campaign) and other Democratic leaders realized that such a coalition would be necessary for the party to win the Speakership. As expected, when Congress convened on 5 December 1859 (three days after the execution of John Brown), a sectional dispute immediately arose over the Speakership contest. Running against Bocock would be, most significantly, the Republican John Sherman of Ohio. In spite of receiving widespread support, neither Bocock nor Sherman was able to gain the necessary majority. The inability to elect a Speaker through eight weeks of acrimonious debate and indecisive balloting nearly incapacitated the House. Realizing that he would be unable to gain the necessary number of votes, Bocock withdrew after the eleventh ballot. Failing to gain a majority, Sherman also withdrew on 30 January. Finally, William Pennington of New Jersey was nominated by the Republicans and, after several attempts, was elected on the forty-fourth ballot. Bocock left the House at the end of the Thirty-sixth Congress on 3 March 1861.

During the Civil War, Bocock served in the unicameral Provisional Confederate Congress, from 20 July 1861 through its conclusion on 17 February 1862, and as Speaker of the Confederate House of Representatives during both Congresses of the permanent government (18 Feb. 1862–18 Mar. 1865). Without a significant legislative program to push through, Bocock as Speaker primarily was concerned with procedural matters and the parliamentary functioning of the House. In addition to maintaining order and ruling on parliamentary procedure, Bocock often served as a liaison between Congress and the administration. In performing this function, Bocock had a well-documented encounter with President Jefferson Davis in early 1865. In January the Virginia congressional delegation requested that Bocock express to Davis its lack of confidence in his cabinet and request a reorganization. After meeting privately with Davis on 20 January, Bocock further detailed the position of the Virginia delegation the following day by letter. Although generally recognized as a supporter of the administration, Bocock clearly was disturbed by the growing dissatisfaction with the government's handling of the war. In his 21 January letter, Bocock expressed to Davis his view, perhaps overstated, that if a resolution were presented to the Confederate House declaring "that the country wants confidence in the cabinet as an administration," it would receive a three-quarters vote. Fearing the loss of public support for the Confederacy, Bocock wrote that he felt "altogether sure that something must be done . . . to restore confidence and revive hopes or else we may look for the worst result." Davis resented what he perceived to be legislative interference and rejected the suggestion that he make changes in his cabinet, but, largely because of congressional opposition, Secretary of War James A. Seddon resigned. Following Seddon's resignation, both Davis and Bocock, as a representative of the Virginia delegation, took their respective cases to the public through the Richmond press. In the end, perhaps the most significant aspect of this legislative-executive dispute was that it was symptomatic of broader problems that seemed to plague the Confederate government throughout its existence.

After the war, Bocock resumed his private law practice. He was an attorney for various railroads and was active in Conservative and Democratic party politics, serving as a delegate to the Democratic national conventions of 1868, 1876, and 1880. From 1877 to 1879 he again served in the Virginia House of Delegates, representing Appomattox County. Attempting to resolve the troubling issue of the payment of Virginia's war debt, Bocock, as a moderate Conservative delegate, in 1878 cosponsored the compromise Bocock-Fowler Bill. Despite failing health, during his final years Bocock also gave numerous public appearances and served on the University of Virginia Board of Visitors from 1876 to 1882.

Bocock's second marriage, after the death of his first wife, was to Annie Holmes Faulkner, a union that produced five children. Bocock died at his home, "Wildway," near Appomattox Court House.

• The most significant collections of Thomas S. Bocock and Bocock family manuscripts are in the Virginia Historical Society and the Alderman Library of the University of Virginia. The most significant printings of Bocock's speeches came in relation to his service in the U.S. Congress; see the *Congressional Globe*, 1847–1861. Official documents concerning Bocock's service as Speaker of the Confederate House of Representatives are in *The War of the Rebellion: A Compilation of the Official Records of the Union and Confederate Armies* (128 vols., 1880–1901). Additional records along with unofficial published manuscript materials and secondary sources concerning his Civil War activities are contained in various volumes of the *Southern Historical Society Papers*. Published information on Bocock tends to be quite superficial. Thomas Cary Johnson, *The Hon. Thomas S. Bocock* (1891), an eight-page tribute, is more substantive than the obituaries published in newspapers.

ALAN L. GOLDEN

BODE, Boyd Henry (4 Oct. 1873–29 Mar. 1953), professor of philosophy and philosophy of education, was born in Ridott, Illinois, the son of Henry (Hendrik) Bode, a farmer and minister of the First Christian Reformed church, and Gertrude Weinenga. Bode's family, although Dutch, was part of a religious migration of Germans to the United States in 1848. They settled first in Holland, Michigan, and then moved to northern Illinois, where Boyd was born as Boyo Hendrik Bode. In the late 1870s the family purchased farm land and moved to Iowa. Bode was the eldest son in a family of eight children and the only one allowed to pursue an education (as was customary so that he could follow his father into the ministry). His primary and secondary schooling consisted of Christian schools and Calvinist doctrine; however, the family permitted him to attend William Penn College (affiliated with the Friends) in Oskaloosa, Iowa, where he received an A.B. in 1896. Bode took a second A.B. at the University of Michigan in 1897 and then went on to study European philosophy at Cornell University, where he completed his Ph.D. in 1900 with a dissertation titled the "Principle of Gratia Gratum in the Ethics of Saint Thomas Aquinas." In 1903 Bode married Bernice Ballard; they had two children.

Bode served as an instructor and assistant professor of philosophy and psychology at the University of Wisconsin from 1900 to 1909. He was lured away from Madison for a professorship of philosophy at the University of Illinois and was supported for this position by William James, John Dewey, and James Tufts. Bode's first publication, *An Outline of Logic* (1910), received favorable reviews and established him as a creative young scholar in the field of philosophy. Bode stayed at Illinois from 1909 to 1921, becoming involved in the university's department of education by joining his former Cornell classmate William Bagley in the teaching of graduate education seminars.

While Bode was well received by students and many faculty at the University of Illinois, his German-sounding name and liberal point of view caused difficulties for him during the years of World War I. In 1921 Dean George Arps easily persuaded Bode to leave Illinois to accept a professorship in education and head the Department of Principles and Practices of Education at Ohio State University. As Bode stated at the time, "After . . . years of reflection on Appearance and Reality and the relation between Subject and Object, I feel like going out to see the wheels go round." Bode held this professorship until 1944, when he officially retired.

Bode's position within the history of ideas will always be somewhat obscured by the fact that not only was he seen by others as a follower of John Dewey but also that he did not receive as much attention as the self-promoting Deweyian disciple, William Heard Kilpatrick. While Kilpatrick was a self-proclaimed follower, correspondence indicates that Dewey viewed Bode as a fellow philosopher and not simply as a disciple of his philosophy of education. Bode's role in intellectual discourse was typically one of a gadfly and critic; he believed there were no absolutes and no truths. As a leading philosopher for a loose configuration of progressive educators, Bode generated philosophical underpinnings for progressivism as well as some of its harshest criticism. This is best seen in his early successful publication *Modern Educational Theories* (1927), in which he takes to task not only scientific management educators Franklin Bobbitt and W. W. Charters but also child-centered educators such as Kilpatrick.

Bode's perspective revolved around the making of a new social order in America—the move away from an aristocratic and authoritarian order and toward democracy. Education and the schools were to be the institutions that permitted democracy to become a way of life; the wonderfully confusing and amorphous conception of democracy served as Bode's guiding idea for the reform of education. "Democracy as a way of life," according to Bode, provided opportunities for "the common man" to develop capacities and to liberate intelligence for the good of society. The goal of schooling thereby became the development of individual growth that would foster a democratic way of living. Bode's finest statements on the meaning of democracy for the determination of educational purposes are in *Progressive Education at the Crossroads* (1938) and *Democracy as a Way of Life* (1939).

One of Bode's significant contributions to educational thought was his statement on "the conception of needs." Bode addresses the conception of needs in *Progressive Education* (chap. 4), where he questions one of the most fundamental assumptions of progressive education, namely that the curriculum should attend to the needs of students, and thus the determination of needs should determine curricular content. Bode had previously called "needs" a "weasel word" and removed himself from the organizing committee of the Progressive Education Association's renowned Eight Year Study due to these objections. Bode criticized the use of student needs, as well as student interests and/or growth, as a centerpiece for curriculum organization because students—children as well as adults—are not always aware of their own needs. As Bode stated, "We cannot start with needs, because needs must be determined with reference to the way of life which the pupil eventually adopts as his own and the choice that he will make cannot be presupposed from the outset. Instead of using needs as a starting point, we educate people in order that they may discover their needs" (*Progressive Education*, p. 70).

As Bode criticized the child-centered contingent of progressive education for its reliance on student needs, the more radical contingent of the movement entered into an extended debate with Bode in what became known as the Imposition Controversy, or the issue of whether educators should indoctrinate values. George Counts framed the issue of indoctrination as an aspect of education in his famous 1932 address "Dare Progressive Education Be Progressive?" John Childs and Bode debated the key ideas in a series of articles in the *Social Frontier: A Journal of Educational Criticism and Reconstruction* between 1934 and 1939. Childs and Counts, two leading foundations of education professors from Teachers College, Columbia University, argued that because values were embodied in all activities of schools and because teachers were incapable of being neutral, it was a moral act for educators to impose values and ideas that embody the tenets of democracy. Bode argued that while the ends of education were the "extension of genuine democracy," this cannot be achieved through undemocratic means. He ultimately asserted that "belief in democracy commits him [the teacher] to the faith that the democratic ideal will prevail in the long run if it can be given a decent chance to be heard" ("Democratic Education and Conflicting Cultural Values," *Social Frontier* 5 [1939]: 107).

While Bode focused his conception of education on the social ideal of democracy at the philosophical level, his former student and colleague Harold Alberty applied Bode's ideas to actual school situations and settings. The Ohio State University School was primarily organized by Alberty around Bode's concepts of education and democracy. After Bode retired in 1944 he accepted teaching positions at the Graduate Institute for Education in Cairo, Egypt, the University of Tennessee, the University of British Columbia, and, finally, at the University of Florida at Gainesville, where he died.

• Neither archival materials nor collected papers of Boyd H. Bode exist. Some of his correspondence is included in the Max Otto Papers at the Wisconsin Historical Society, the John Dewey Papers at the University of Southern Illinois, and the H. Gordon Hullfish Papers at Ohio State University. Other important works by Bode include *Fundamentals of Education* (1921), *Conflicting Psychologies of Learning* (1929), and *How We Learn* (1940). Critical reviews of Bode's work include J. J. Chambliss, *Boyd H. Bode's Philosophy of Education* (1963); John Childs, *American Pragmatism and Education* (1956), chap. 9; and Norman Woelfel, *Molders of the American Mind* (1933). Outstanding biographical work on Bode has been published by Robert V. Bullough, Jr., *Democracy in Education: Boyd H. Bode* (1981) and "Harold B. Alberty and Boyd H. Bode: Pioneers in Curriculum Theory" (Ph.D. diss., Ohio State Univ., 1976). See also Kenneth Winetrout, "Boyd H. Bode: The Professor and Social Responsibility," in *Teachers and Mentors*, ed. Craig Kridel et al. (1996), chap. 5; and Ralph W. Tyler, "Remembering Boyd Bode," *Curriculum Theory Network* 5, no. 1 (1975): 61–62. An obituary is in the *New York Times*, 30 Mar. 1953.

CRAIG KRIDEL

BODE, Hendrik Wade (24 Dec. 1905–2 June 1982), research engineer and educator, was born in Madison, Wisconsin, the son of Boyd Henry Bode and Bernice Ballard. Bode attended Ohio State University, receiving a B.A. in 1924 and an M.A. in 1926. In 1935 he earned a Ph.D. in physics at Columbia University and was elected a member at Phi Beta Kappa. He started work as an assistant professor of mathematics at Ohio State (1925–1926). He moved in 1926 to Bell Telephone Laboratories, where he remained until 1967. While at Bell Labs he worked on the technical staff, researching electrical network theory. He served as a research mathematician (1944–1952), director of mathematical research (1952–1955), director of research, physical sciences (1955–1958), and vice president of military systems engineering (1958–1967). In 1967 he left Bell Labs to go to Harvard University as Gordon McKay Professor of Systems Engineering, serving in that capacity until his retirement in 1974, when he was made emeritus professor.

According to Prescott C. Mabon, Hendrik Bode, along with other Bell Labs scientists, "developed and refined the basic theory that governs design of the electrical networks used to filter and shape signals in nearly all electronic systems" (*Mission Communications*, p. 31). He personally redesigned the complete feedback loop to compensate for changes in temperature and other variants in transmission lines so that transcontinental telephone lines could overcome loss of volume and prevent distortion of sound. Bode headed a team of mathematicians whose role was to bring mathematical theory to bear on problems in physics, network design, probability, and other areas. This included work on improving weaponry control in electronic systems for gunfire and missile systems during World War II.

Bode wrote an informal mimeographed text on telephony for a course given in the laboratory in 1938. The text was later used as a reference work during World War II. In 1945 he published the work as *Network Analysis and Feedback Amplifier Design*. This respected textbook "set forth the principles for designing transmission systems" as well as being a "treatise on general network theory, material on design of nonfeedback as well as feedback amplifiers (band type) and trans problems arising in wide band systems generally," according to Bode's introduction.

In his second book, *Synergy* (1971), Bode discussed his underlying philosophy. He understood the need for collaboration in scientific research and the maintenance of close relationships among working groups. "Building on the experience and the techniques and skills acquired in the development of the preceding technology is . . . vital," Bode wrote, in order to integrate research, development, and manufacture. He applied his ideas and theories not only to physical systems but also to the management aspect of the research and development process. Through such a partnership, researchers and technicians focused on understanding the concept of the whole project instead of working only on a specific part.

Bode held a number of patents. These include an adjustable attenuation equalizer for wave transmission lines (1937); an amplifier having uniform gain over a frequency range that includes the frequency range of the signals (1938); a design of broad band repeater sections for broad band transmission, comprising an amplifying repeater at each end, each having a stabilizing feedback path (1941); a transformer system connected to provide parallel transmission paths (1942); an electric wave amplifier providing stabilizing feedback (1943); a coupling network (1943); a wave transmission network (1944); a broad band amplifier (1945); an averaging mechanism (1948); and a smoothing network (1949).

Bode married Barbara Lane Poore in 1933. They had two children. Bode received the Presidential Certificate of Merit in 1948 and the Edison Medal of the Institute for Electrical and Electronic Engineers in 1969. He was a member of the National Academy of Sciences (councillor, 1967–1970), the National Academy of Engineers, the American Institute of Aeronautics and Astronautics, the American Mathematical Society, and the American Academy of Arts and Sciences. He died in Cambridge, Massachusetts.

• Among Bode's other writings, "Feedback—The History of an Idea," in *Active Networks and Feedback Systems: Proceedings of the Symposium* (1960), explains his role in the development of the negative feedback amplifier. Bode is the author of several articles in the *Bell System Technical Journal*, including "Relations between Attenuation and Phase in Feedback Amplifier Design," 19 (1940): 421–54; "Variable Equalizers," 17 (1938): 229–44; "A Method of Impedance Correction," 9 (1930): 794–835; "A General Theory of Wave Filters," 14 (1935): 211–14; and "Ideal Wave Filters," with R. L. Dietzold, 14 (1935): 215–52. The most complete account of Bode's work is in Prescott C. Mabon, *Mission Communications: The Story of Bell Laboratories* (1975).

VERONICA JUNE BRUCE

BODENHEIM, Maxwell (26 May 1892–7 Feb. 1954), poet, critic, and novelist, was born in Hermanville, Mississippi, the son of Solomon Bodenheimer and Caroline Herman. An emigrant from Alsace, Solomon Bodenheimer never found financial or professional security; his career included stints as a traveling whiskey salesman and unsuccessful forays into clothing stores and men's haberdashery. The daughter of a distinguished and wealthy surgeon, Caroline Bodenheimer came from a milieu that was vastly different from that of her husband. Indeed, the town of Hermanville itself obtained its name from Caroline Bodenheimer's uncle, M. B. Herman, who had founded the town and established a small mercantile empire there. Caroline's tales of lost prosperity provided a bitter contrast to the impoverished world in which Maxwell Bodenheim was reared.

Bodenheim spent his early youth in Hermanville and in Memphis, Tennessee, but moved to Chicago at age ten. There, the emotional splintering of Bodenheim's family continued; Caroline and Solomon fought frequently over issues of finance and aesthetics, and their mutual dissatisfaction made a lasting impact on their son. Rebellious and mercurial, Bodenheim left home and school long before his eighteenth birthday. A number of Bodenheim's novels—most notably *Blackguard* (1923), *A Virtuous Girl* (1930), and *Ninth Avenue* (1926)—touch on his disenchantment with bourgeois family life and his general rejection of authority.

Ironically, after being expelled from school, in 1909 Bodenheim chose to express his rejection of conventional values by joining the army, where he rejected his Jewish heritage and shortened his name from Bodenheimer to Bodenheim. This choice proved to be disastrous, and in 1911 he was briefly jailed for desertion of duty and then subsequently dishonorably discharged. (A variety of myths later surrounded his military experience; Bodenheim himself was fond of suggesting that he had fought Pancho Villa in Mexico and that he engaged in combat with anti-Semitic officers.) Bodenheim spent the next two years laboring as a migrant worker in the South and Southwest and as a telephone linesman in the Chicago area. He was arrested several times for vagrancy and for stealing cotton. But his return to Chicago proved to be fortuitous, for in the theater and coffeehouses that accompanied the Chicago renaissance of this era, Bodenheim began to find a place for himself within the bohemian literary establishment.

By the time that World War I was breaking out in Europe, Bodenheim was writing poetry, dramas, and essays and engaging in public debate. In 1914 his first poems were published in *Poetry* and in the *Little Review*, and he was befriended and championed by Harriet Monroe, Edgar Lee Masters, Sherwood Anderson, Theodore Dreiser, Ben Hecht, and Carl Sandburg. In 1915 Bodenheim left Chicago for New York City, where he lived for a while with poet and critic Alfred Kreymborg. Feted at literary parties, where he met early modernist luminaries such as Marcel Duchamp, Bodenheim was made editor of *Others*, a small literary magazine. But he became rather quickly disenchanted with the life of the wealthy and well connected. He relocated in Greenwich Village, where he continued to write and also to frequent the offices of the socialist *Catholic Worker*. There he spent time with editor Dorothy Day and Eugene O'Neill as well as with members of the more notorious Hudson Dusters, an underworld gang. In 1918 Bodenheim married Minna Schein and published his first volume of poetry, *Minna and Myself*.

In the years that followed, Bodenheim became a high-profile member of New York's literary and avant-garde community. Widely regarded as brilliant, he also possessed a reputation for eccentricity, violence, and alcoholism. Bodenheim was highly prolific during the 1920s, but his fortunes fell with the nation's during the 1930s. By 1934 he was living as an indigent, trying to sell his poems to passersby on the street in order to buy liquor. In 1938 Minna divorced him. In 1940 the Federal Writers' Project fired Bodenheim and banned him from its rosters because of his alleged involvement in Communist activities. He experienced moments of seeming recovery—he published his *Selected Poems* in 1946—but these periods were interposed with episodes of personal degradation. In 1939 Bodenheim married Grace Finan, who died in 1950 after a long illness. In 1951 Bodenheim married Ruth Fagan.

The last few years of Bodenheim's life were troubled and painful and culminated in his brutal, well-publicized murder in 1954. Ruth and Maxwell Bodenheim were repeatedly arrested for vagrancy and public drunkenness, and during this time they both developed an affection for 25-year-old Harold Weinberg, who was largely regarded as criminally insane. On the night of 6 February 1954, in New York City, a violent argument broke out among the triad; early on the following morning Weinberg shot Maxwell Bodenheim in the heart with a .22 caliber rifle and then stabbed Ruth four times with a hunting knife. Arrested on 10 February, Weinberg bragged, "I ought to get a medal. I killed two Communists."

In the face of his sensationalist lifestyle, it is easy to lose sight of Bodenheim's very real contribution to American letters. Capable of tremendous literary output, Bodenheim had an early premonition of the direction that the American "beat" movement would take. Novels such as *Naked on Roller Skates* (1930) and *Run, Sheep, Run* (1932) place him within the tradition of William Burroughs, Allan Ginsberg, Neal Cassady, and Jack Kerouac, while his poetry, most notably *Bringing Jazz* (1930), sought to bring the marginalized voice of Harlem into the mainstream of American literature.

• Bodenheim's numerous and frequently autobiographical novels, besides those mentioned in the text, include *Crazy Man* (1924), *Replenishing Jessica* (1925), *Ninth Avenue* (1926), *Georgie May* (1928), *Sixty Seconds* (1929), *Duke Herring* (1931), *6 AM: New York* (1932), *New York Madness* (1933), and *Slow Vision* (1934). Bodenheim's poetry was mythic in theme as well as precise and sensual. Poetic works include *Advice* (1920), *Introducing Irony* (1922), *Against This Age* (1923), *The Sardonic Arm* (1923), *Returning to Emotion* (1927), *The King of Spain* (1928), *Lights in the Valley* (1942), and *Seven Poets in Search of an Answer* (1944). Biographical information is in Dorothy Day, *Loaves and Fishes* (1963); Ben Hecht, *A Child of the Century* (1954); Milton Klonsky, "Squash and Stretch," *Esquire*, Dec. 1963; and Jack B. Moore, *Maxwell Bodenheim* (1970).

DEBORAH HATHEWAY

BODLEY, Rachel Littler (7 Dec. 1831–15 June 1888), botanist, chemist, and educator, was born in Cincinnati, Ohio, the daughter of Anthony Prichard Bodley, a carpenter and patternmaker, and Rebecca Wilson Talbott, a teacher. An 1849 graduate in classical studies of Wesleyan Female College in Cincinnati, Rachel Bodley taught there and served as preceptor in higher college studies until 1860, when she decided to pursue her interests in botany and chemistry. She began advanced studies in the natural sciences at the Polytechnic College in Philadelphia in 1860 and returned to Ohio in early 1862 to accept a position as professor of natural sciences at the Cincinnati Female Seminary.

Bodley spent her free time and summer vacations in Cincinnati, classifying and mounting an extensive collection of herbarium specimens that had been bequeathed to the seminary. Her first original scientific work, this demanding research project culminated in an impressive display and the 48-page *Catalogue of Plants Contained in the Herbarium of Joseph Clark, Arranged according to the Natural System* (1865). It was praised by noted Harvard botanist Asa Gray as "very satisfactory."

Both botanist and chemist, Bodley had particular botanical interests in seedless land and sea plants (mosses, algae, fungi, and ferns). She botanized at various land and sea sites around the country, including Longport, New Jersey, during many summers. She shared her interests and expertise with the public in a series of articles on seaweeds for the Philadelphia *Ledger* and in lectures in Philadelphia during the springs of 1867 and 1868.

In 1865 Bodley was appointed professor and chair of chemistry and toxicology at the Female Medical College in Philadelphia (renamed Women's Medical College of Pennsylvania in 1868; now Medical College of Pennsylvania)—the first woman professor of chemistry in the country. Nine years later, in 1874, she was chosen to succeed Emmeline Cleveland as dean of the Women's Medical College. An inspired and admired chemistry professor, Bodley sought to ground laboratory science firmly in the medical curriculum. She introduced new scientific instruments into the laboratory and required precision and accuracy from her students. An able and farsighted dean, she instituted the Progressive Course, which lengthened the medical course to three years and broadened clinical training beyond simply a preceptor system, in which advanced students who had finished the course of formal lectures worked on projects with individual teachers. A new building to house the medical college was dedicated in 1875 and included a surgical amphitheater. Bodley also hired outstanding new faculty, such as Anna Broomall as chair of obstetrics and Clara Marshall, later the Women's Medical College's dean.

The Women's Medical College awarded an honorary doctor of medicine degree to Bodley in 1879. In her valedictory address to the graduating class of 1880 she presented the results of a survey she had conducted of the college's graduates. Published as *The College Story* (1881) and welcomed as the first careful study of the professional life of women, Bodley's survey found that of the 189 women who responded to the mailed questionnaire, 166 were in active medical practice. Most practiced in obstetrics and gynecology; about one-third were or had been institutionally employed; and one-third were involved in medical education. Their average yearly income was substantial for the time, close to $3,000.

Bodley's scientific activities were recognized in her election to membership and active participation in a variety of scientific societies, including the Academy of Natural Sciences in Philadelphia (1871), the Cincinnati Society of Natural History (1873), and the New York Academy of Sciences (1876). At Bodley's suggestion, a planned centennial celebration of Joseph Priestley's discovery of oxygen was held at Priestley's burial site in Northumberland, Pennsylvania, in 1874. Plans for establishing the American Chemical Society were laid at this meeting, and Bodley was elected one of thirteen honorary vice presidents to serve on the interim committee. At the society's inception in 1876 she was named a charter member. Also elected a charter member of the Franklin Institute of Philadelphia in 1880, Bodley was soon afterward invited to deliver a regular course of six lectures on household chemistry for the institute during the early 1880s.

Missionary work was a long-standing interest of Bodley's. As a young girl, only poor health kept her from entering that field. At the Women's Medical College she encouraged medical missionary applicants, kept in touch with graduates doing this work around the globe, and welcomed them for stays in her home when they returned or visited the college. Her active correspondence spread the reputation of the Women's Medical College widely and drew students from abroad, including India and Japan.

Bodley was also active in the Philadelphia community. Elected a member of the Educational Society of Philadelphia in 1882 and shortly thereafter one of the first of two women members of the school board in Philadelphia, she served from 1882 to 1885 and then again from 1887 until her death. She also served, beginning in 1883, on the Women's Committee of the State Board of Public Charities as an inspector of local charitable institutions.

Bodley served the cause of women's medical education as both professor and dean of a very important nineteenth-century women's medical institution. Under her stewardship enrollment increased, and the medical curriculum was expanded. Keenly interested in both botany and chemistry, Bodley found opportunities to join the male-dominated scientific establishments limited; like most women scientists of her day, she was forced to remain on the periphery. Again like most women in professional fields, Bodley carried on her duties in the context of demanding family and household responsibilities. During her years in Philadelphia, for example, she cared for her invalid mother and was host to a continuing stream of visiting graduates and students. Bodley died of a heart attack in Philadelphia.

• Bodley's printed and manuscript materials are in the Archives and Special Collections on Women and Medicine of the Medical College of Pennsylvania, Philadelphia. Her *Annual Session Introductory Lectures* (1868, 1875) and *Valedictory Addresses* (1874, 1881) were published as pamphlets. An important source on her life is *Papers Read at the Memorial Hour Commemorative of the Late Prof. Rachel L. Bodley, M.D.* (1888). For assessment of Bodley's scientific and medical work and its context, the best sources are John Harshberger, *The Botanists of Philadelphia and Their Work* (1899); Margaret W. Rossiter, *Women Scientists in America: Struggles and Strategies to 1940* (1982); Sally Gregory Kohlstedt, "In from the Periphery: American Women in Science, 1830–1880," *SIGNS* 4 (Autumn 1978): 81–98; and Regina Markell Morantz-Sanchez, *Sympathy and Science: Women Physicians in American Medicine* (1985). An obituary is in the *Woman's Journal*, 23 June 1888, and a biographical sketch is in the *Journal of the American Medical Women's Association* 4 (Dec. 1949): 534–36.

JANET CARLISLE BOGDAN

BODMER, Karl (11 Feb. 1809–30 Oct. 1893), artist, was born in Zurich, Switzerland, the son of Heinrich Bodmer, a cotton merchant, and his second wife Elisabeth Meier. After a brief elementary education, Bodmer was apprenticed to his uncle Johann Jakob Meier, from whom he learned sketching, engraving, and watercolor, the medium of his finest works.

In 1828 Bodmer settled in the Rhine and Moselle region of Germany, working as a landscape illustrator for travel albums. There he caught the attention of Prince Maximilian of Wied, a naturalist and explorer from the nearby principality of Neuwied. Maximilian was planning an expedition to North America to collect fauna and observe Indian tribes. Needing an artist to record the Indians especially, and aware of his own limitations as a draftsman, he invited Bodmer to accompany him.

Maximilian and Bodmer arrived in in the United States on 4 July 1832. After spending late July through mid-September in Bethlehem, Pennsylvania, and the winter in New Harmony, Indiana, they headed west in the spring of 1833 to undertake the most important phase of the expedition. After arriving in St. Louis on 24 March, Maximilian made arrangements with the American Fur Company to travel up the Missouri River by steamboat and keelboat as far as Fort McKenzie (about fifty miles from present-day Great Falls, Montana). On 10 April Maximilian and Bodmer left to spend a year in the West. During the journey Maximilian collected specimens of flora and fauna and made copious notes in his diary on natural history, topography, and American Indian ethnography; meanwhile Bodmer painted depictions of landscapes and Indians they encountered on their journey. Spending the harsh winter of 1833–1834 in Fort Clark (near present-day Bismarck, N. Dak.), Bodmer and Maximilian established warm rapport with the Mandan and Hidatsa Indians; their memorable stay at Fort Clark proved to be the climactic point of their journey. Bodmer and Maximilian returned to Europe in July 1834.

Bodmer produced nearly 400 watercolors and sketches, mostly North American landscapes but also numerous American Indian portraits, in which he achieved a level of accuracy and sensitivity that no other artist of the American frontier has ever surpassed. His work is particularly valuable for its detailed rendition of the Indians' ornamentation, attire, and implements. Indeed, Bodmer was far superior to his better-known contemporary George Catlin, whose work lacks the Swiss artist's fidelity and meticulous attention to detail. Nothing better attests to the precision of Bodmer's work than the exact correspondence of the garb depicted in his watercolors with the actual costumes that Prince Maximilian purchased from the artist's subjects. It is a great irony that Bodmer had no previous experience in portraiture. Yet his lack of training proved an advantage: he applied no European ideals of form or beauty to his portraits, conventions that might have distorted his work. The story of Bodmer's journey has a tragic dimension in that just a few years later many of his subjects perished in a smallpox epidemic, brought by white traders and trappers, that virtually destroyed the Mandan culture and decimated other tribes.

After returning to Europe, Maximilian decided to publish a deluxe account of his journey, with illustrations based on Bodmer's watercolors. Bodmer, who moved to Paris in 1836, supervised the preparation of the aquatints; promotion of the work occupied him for most of the next decade. Between 1838 and 1843 Maximilian's account, *Travels in the Interior of North America*, appeared first in German and then in French and English translations, each edition including eighty-one aquatints of American landscapes and Indians. For over a century Bodmer's aquatints have been regarded as one of the most significant contributions to the iconography of the western frontier.

Because of its high price and limited sales, Maximilian's publication venture proved to be a financial failure. For the same reason, Bodmer's own contribution became better known and appreciated only years later after the aquatints were copied and reproduced in less expensive works. Embittered, Bodmer later lamented that the ten years he dedicated to American themes had retarded his creative growth. He devoted the rest of his career to forest scenes and animal portraits, topics more popular and remunerative in his own day, but which today seem trite compared to his far more original American work. American themes rarely figured in Bodmer's later work and, though he later fondly recalled his travels on the frontier, there is no basis for the long-standing legend that he left the United States reluctantly and always longed to return to his beloved Indians. It is ironic that Bodmer's greatest achievement was the result of a brief, unplanned episode in a career that otherwise produced creditable but largely forgotten art.

In the 1850s Bodmer settled outside Paris in the Barbizon forest near Fontainebleau, loosely affiliating himself with the Barbizon school of French painters. He led a somewhat reclusive life. Though he had gotten along well with Maximilian, Bodmer was often headstrong and contentious in his relations with others. Before settling in France, Bodmer had entered into a common-law union with a German peasant girl named Anna-Maria Magdalena Pfeiffer; the marriage was legitimized in 1876, and they had three children. Bodmer gradually abandoned all ties to his homeland. For a time he achieved recognition and success in France. His paintings were frequently exhibited in the Paris salons of the 1850s and 1860s. His engravings of forest scenes and animals were a regular feature of popular illustrated magazines. In 1876 the French government awarded Bodmer the Legion of Honor. In the 1880s, however, his work lost popularity and his fortunes declined; he was forced to sell his house in Barbizon and move into a cramped apartment in Paris. Bodmer's last years were spent in blindness and dire poverty, and he died in Paris in relative obscurity.

During Bodmer's lifetime only a few of his original watercolors were ever exhibited, in Paris in 1836. Maximilian kept Bodmer's paintings, and after the prince's death in 1867 they remained, forgotten, in Neuwied palace. After World War II a German scholar, Josef Roeder, rediscovered Bodmer's watercolors, along with Maximilian's diaries and notebooks. In 1959 Prince Friedrich Wilhelm of Wied sold the Maximilian collection to M. Knoedler and Company in New York. In 1962 the Northern Natural Gas Company of Omaha, Nebraska, purchased the North American material, consisting of the Bodmer watercolors and Maximilian's North American diaries. The company's successor, Enron Corporation, donated the collection to the Joslyn Art Museum in Omaha in 1986, where it had been on permanent loan. The recovery of Bodmer's original watercolors reveal the full range of his work. Exhibitions and publications have since established Bodmer as a premier artist of a now vanished frontier and its once powerful inhabitants.

• Most of Bodmer's American watercolors and Maximilian's North American diaries and manuscripts are in the Joslyn Art Museum in Omaha, Neb. Maximilian's manuscripts also include many letters from Bodmer from the years before and after the expedition, focusing primarily on the publication of Maximilian's travel account and the accompanying aquatint atlas. The definitive publication on Bodmer's life and work is the platebook edited by William H. Goetzmann, *Karl Bodmer's America* (1984). Hans Läng, *Indianer waren meine Freunde* (1976), provides important information on Bodmer's youth and final years. The primary work on the North American expedition is the prince's published narrative, which was reissued in Reuben Gold Thwaites, ed., *Early Western Travels*, vols. 22–25 (1906). A more recent popular account of the journey is Davis Thomas and Karin Ronnefeldt, *People of the First Man* (1976), which includes illustrations from Bodmer's work. See also the exhibition catalog by John C. Ewers et al., *Views of a Vanishing Frontier* (1984), and William J. Orr, "Portraits of the Plains," *FMR* 1, no. 4 (1984): 91–116.

William J. Orr

BOEHLER, Peter (31 Dec. 1712–27 Sept. 1775), Moravian pioneer in the American colonies, was born in Frankfurt on the Main, Germany, son of John Conrad Boehler, an innkeeper and later comptroller of the corn office, and Antoinette Elizabeth Hanf. Peter was sent to school at age four, commenced the study of Latin when he was eight, and soon thereafter entered the Gymnasium at Frankfurt. His family wanted him to study medicine, so he entered the University of Jena on 20 April 1731. On 16 June 1734 he matriculated at the University of Leipzig but soon returned to Jena, where he was given the title *magister legens* (junior professor). He remained at Jena for seven years.

Although reportedly "wild and wicked" as a youth, Boehler was deeply affected by religion during his days at the Gymnasium. At Jena he sought out a circle of friends who were attracted to the Moravian leader August Gottlieb Spangenberg. Spangenberg's religious influence on Boehler was decisive. The young student presently changed course and decided to pursue theological studies. His Moravian contacts, moreover, led to his acquaintance with the founder of the Moravian church, Count Nikolaus Ludwig von Zinzendorf, who visited Jena early in 1732 and asked Boehler to become the English tutor of his son Renatus. Subsequently the count gave him a twofold commission. He asked Boehler, on the one hand, to go to

America in order to become the pastor of the struggling Moravian congregation in Savannah, Georgia. Having been informed of the plight of the slaves in South Carolina by the English Society for the Propagation of the Gospel in Foreign Parts, Zinzendorf commissioned him also to be a missionary to them. In this capacity, therefore, Boehler was to represent both Zinzendorf and the society, his mission having been approved by the archbishop of Canterbury. Accordingly he visited Herrnhut, the center of Moravianism, and on 16 December 1737 was ordained presbyter by Zinzendorf and Moravian bishop John Nitschmann at the fortress of Ronneburg, near Frankfurt.

Early in 1738 Boehler was directed by Zinzendorf to take up his American assignment. On the way he visited Holland and England, establishing contact with various Moravian groups. Quite naturally he met John Wesley, the founder of Methodism, and his brother Charles. The Wesleys and Boehler were attracted to the religious societies that then flourished within the Anglican establishment. Boehler's influence upon the Wesleys and the beginnings of Methodism, although the subject of much discussion, was likely considerable.

On 18 May 1738 Boehler finally embarked for America, arriving in Savannah on 15 October. There he served briefly as pastor of the Moravians, after which Governor James Oglethorpe sent him to South Carolina to do missionary work among the slaves. His stay there was also brief. At the direction of Zinzendorf and Bishop Spangenberg, whom the count had put in charge of the Moravian work in America, Boehler traveled almost constantly as a Moravian missionary.

In January 1741, summoned by Bishop Nitschmann to return to Europe, Boehler embarked for Bristol, England. On 20 February 1742, while still in England, he married Elizabeth Hobson, who was later made a deaconess and then an eldress. As such she assisted him greatly in his work. The couple had seven children.

In June 1742 Boehler landed in Philadelphia, this time as chaplain of a group of Moravian immigrants whom Spangenberg had organized in England as the First Sea Congregation. In Pennsylvania he presided at some of the seven Union Synods called by Zinzendorf in the hope of uniting Christians in what he called a "Congregation of God in the Spirit." Subsequently the count entrusted Boehler with the "itineracy," or the supervision of the Moravian enterprise in Pennsylvania and New York, the Georgia experiment having been abandoned. After Spangenberg's arrival in the colonies in 1745, Boehler left again for Europe. There he served in various capacities, among them the deanship of the Moravian seminary at Ludheim near Marienborn, Germany.

Boehler was consecrated bishop in Herrnhag on 10 January 1748. His episcopal responsibilities extended to England, Ireland, and America. When he arrived once again in the colonies on 9 September 1753 in Spangenberg's absence, the entire American operation of the Moravians was temporarily under his care. Under the circumstances he had to deal with a whole array of economic, religious, and organizational problems related to the Moravian enterprise in the American colonies. When Spangenberg returned in 1754, Boehler assisted him in various capacities until Spangenberg returned to Europe. In 1764 Boehler was asked to come to Marienborn to attend the General Synod, the chief tasks of which were to frame a constitution for the Renewed Moravian church and to name a directory, or central administrative body. Boehler served on the directory, handling, among other things, the American correspondence until 1768. The following year he was elected to his church's elders conference.

As a member of the directory and of the elders conference he continued to act in a supervisory capacity, notably in England, to the end of his life. On his last trip to England, while preparing to participate in a service at the Moravian Fetter Lane Society, he was stricken and died. Although Peter Boehler was overshadowed by Zinzendorf and Spangenberg, whose gifts of leadership exceeded his, Moravianism is greatly indebted to his willingness to work tirelessly and with dedication under their general direction.

• The main depositories for Boehler material are the Moravian Archives in Bethlehem, Pa., and the Library of Congress. An important aid to Boehler study remains J. P. Lockwood, *Memorials of the Life of Peter Boehler, Bishop of the Church of the United Brethren* (1868), which contains a portrait of Boehler. Also useful is Edmund A. de Schweinitz, *Some of the Fathers of the American Moravian Church* (1881). Meticulously researched is Albert J. Jordan, *The Chronicle of Peter Boehler, Who Led John and Charles Wesley to the Full Light of the Gospel* (1977). Clifford W. Towlson, *Moravian and Methodist: Relationships and Influences in the Eighteenth Century* (1957), is a good introduction to Boehler's influence on the Wesleys. For a general history of Moravianism in America see J. Taylor Hamilton and Kenneth G. Hamilton, *History of the Moravian Church, the Renewed Unitas Fratrum, 1722–1957* (1967).

F. ERNEST STOEFFLER

BOEHM, John Philip (25 Nov. 1683–29 Apr. 1749), founder of the German Reformed church in America, was born in Hochstadt near Hanau, in the principality of Hesse-Cassel, the son of Philip Ludwig Boehm, a clergyman, and Maria (maiden name unknown), his first wife. At Hochstadt his father was the pastor of the Reformed church. Little is known about John's youth or education. On 11 March 1708 he was elected to the position of schoolteacher in the Reformed parish at Worms. Before he moved to Worms he married Anna Maria Stehler. They had four children at Worms, two of whom apparently died young. After a protracted controversy he resigned his post in 1715 and accepted a similar position at nearby Lambsheim. His first wife having died, he married another woman, Anna Maria Scherer, and they had four more children. Largely due to the prevailing conditions in the Palatinate, which were the result of raids by Louis XIV of France as well as crop failures, the family immigrated to Pennsylvania. They arrived in Philadelphia in the fall of 1720 and settled in Whitpain, Montgomery County.

Because of hard times large numbers of German-speaking people, notably Swiss and Palatines, left their homeland early in the eighteenth century and sought to establish themselves in Pennsylvania, which had been well advertised on the Continent by William Penn. Among the so-called German church people in Pennsylvania were the German Reformed. Like other German religious groups at the time, they were disorganized and without clerical leadership. For that reason his Reformed neighbors asked Boehm soon after his arrival to become their "reader" at such religious services as could be arranged. He accepted this invitation without compensation. Because no ordained pastors were available, the Reformed settlers eventually, in 1725, asked Boehm to assume the responsibilities of a pastor. He heeded their invitation with great reluctance, aware that such a move would be widely regarded as highly irregular. His first official act in that office was to draw up a constitution for his "charge," consisting of three hitherto informally organized congregations. Each of these then extended to him a regular call. Soon thereafter he administered the sacraments, first at Falkner Swamp (Hannover), then at Skippack, and finally at Whitemarsh. This constitutes the beginning of regular worship among the German Reformed.

In 1727 George Michael Weiss, who two years before had been ordained by the Upper Consistory of the Palatinate, arrived in Philadelphia. He soon began to question Boehm's credentials, thereby provoking a serious controversy. Upon the advice of the Dutch Reformed clergy in New York, the matter was referred to the Classis of Amsterdam. In 1729 the Classis replied that under the circumstances Boehm's administration of baptism and the Lord's supper must be deemed lawful but that he should apply for ordination. Following that advice, he was ordained in New York by Henricus Boel and Gualterius DuBois on 23 November 1729. As a result, the German Reformed work in America was under the supervision of the Classis of Amsterdam until 1792.

Boehm faithfully tended his congregations, but his work was by no means confined to them. He itinerated on horseback over 24,000 miles and is credited with founding at least twelve congregations. He warded off various theological challenges to this work, first by the mystical Rev. John Peter Miller, who eventually joined the Ephrata Society, then by Henry Goetschy, who was inclined toward Pietism, and finally by Nicolaus Ludwig Zinzendorf (Count von Zinzendorf), founder of the Moravian church, or Renewed Unitas Fratrum. Zinzendorf meant to unite all German-speaking Christians in Pennsylvania in a "Congregation of God in the Spirit," which the various religious groups perceived as a threat. Against this attempt Boehm wrote his highly polemical *Faithful Letter of Warning*.

With Michael Schlatter, who arrived in Pennsylvania in 1746, he organized the so-called Coetus, or convention, in 1747, in which twelve of the thirteen German Reformed congregations were represented by four ordained clergymen and twenty-seven elders. Boehm had the honor of serving briefly as its president. The last church that he and Schlatter organized, and which he continued to serve, bears his name. It is located in Whitpain township, Montgomery County. He died at his oldest son's home in Hellertown, Pennsylvania.

• The most helpful depository of sources is the library of Franklin and Marshall College, Lancaster, Pa. The *Constitution of the German Reformed Church in the United States of North America*, written by Boehm for his first congregations, and later adopted by the Coetus, may also be of interest, as may his *Getreuer Warnungsbrief an die Hochteutschen Evangelisch Reformirten Gemeinden* (1742), written against the Moravians. For his other writings see *The Writings of the Rev. John Philip Boehm, Founder of the Reformed Church in Pennsylvania*, ed. and trans. William J. Hinke (1912). By far the best biography of John Philip Boehm is that by Hinke, *Life and Letters of the Rev. John Philip Boehm, 1683–1749* (1916; rep. 1972). Later biographers are often dependent upon Henry S. Dotterer's pamphlet, *Rev. John Philip Boehm* (1890). See also Hinke's *Ministers of the German Reformed Congregations in Pennsylvania and Other Colonies in the Eighteenth Century* (1951).

F. ERNEST STOEFFLER

BOEHM, Martin (30 Nov. 1725–23 Mar. 1812), Mennonite and United Brethren bishop, was born in Conestoga Township, Pennsylvania, the son of Jacob Boehm, an emigrant blacksmith and farmer from the Palatinate. His mother's name is unknown. Boehm was self-taught and read widely in German and English literature. In 1753 he married Eve Steiner; they had eight children.

Although a successful farmer, Boehm's interest was primarily in religious matters, and he was chosen by lot to be a Mennonite preacher in 1756. At first he was reluctant to assume leadership because he felt unworthy. Further, Boehm found the Mennonites excessively formal and sought a more pietistic expression of his emerging faith. While plowing in his fields in 1758, he became so overwrought with his spiritual inadequacy that he cried out to God for help. He recalled being overcome with joy and an assurance of personal salvation. The next year he was elected a Mennonite bishop. During a preaching tour in Maryland and Virginia, Boehm encountered the New Light movement, a transatlantic revival started by George Whitefield, which stressed individual conversion, a devotion to prayer, and study of the Bible; it had a profound influence on his understanding of faith. His home in Lancaster County, Pennsylvania, became an oasis for evangelical preachers of a wide variety of denominations. As opportunities came to share his personal conversion story, what came to be called the "Boehm Revival" spread through the Mennonite churches.

Boehm's New Light beliefs and practices followed many of the trends of the Great Awakening. From the Church of the Brethren he learned and perfected the *Grosse Versammlung*, or great meeting, a religious regional gathering primarily in the German community and held in a barn or grove. Such meetings were ecumenical, multiday preaching events that drew large crowds from many miles. He organized several of these great meetings and was a popular German-language preacher in Pennsylvania, Maryland, and Virginia.

But Boehm found little support for his evangelical practices among the leaders of the Pennsylvania Mennonite community. He was censured for his overly experiential doctrine and preaching methods and his association with people of other denominations. About 1775 Mennonite leaders concluded that he was creating a serious division among Mennonites, and they met to consider appropriate action. Records indicate that five charges were brought against the evangelist, including that he associated with worldly Christians who practiced warfare and oath taking and that he gave too little attention to the ordinances of baptism and communion. Three times he refused to renounce his "errors," and he attempted to present an unwanted self-defense. The result of the conference was to excommunicate him and his followers from "the communion and counsel of the brotherhood." However, his preaching was in great demand, and he traveled throughout Pennsylvania, Maryland, and the valley of Virginia, preaching to great crowds of Lutheran, Reformed Church, and Dunker folk.

Despite the Mennonite criticism, Boehm's broader contacts among other Christians prospered. Probably on Pentecost Day 1767, at one of the great evangelical meetings that he organized at the farm of Isaac Long, about two miles from Neffsville, Pennsylvania, Boehm encountered Philip William Otterbein, a Dutch Reformed minister from York, Pennsylvania. Their friendship proved to be highly influential among German pietists. The famous meeting was recalled in the words "Wir sind Brüder" (We are brethren), uttered by Otterbein following the sermon that Boehm preached on the threshing floor of the barn. The two men were the cofounders of a new sect called the United Brethren in Christ, and they met regularly in Otterbein's parsonage in Baltimore, Maryland, from 1789 until the first formal annual conference was held in 1800. Otterbein and Boehm were chosen the first bishops of the United Brethren in Christ.

Boehm was also a close friend of Methodist preachers, who frequently preached in his barn, and he formed a class meeting, a small group that met for prayer and Bible study, at his house in 1775, with his wife becoming one of the first members. Boehm often expressed appreciation for the published sermons of John Wesley, which he possessed in his library. In 1791 a chapel for the Methodists was built on Boehm's property, and in 1802 he joined this Methodist congregation, while concurrently maintaining leadership in the United Brethren. Francis Asbury, an early Methodist bishop, counted Boehm as a primary leader among German-speaking Methodist adherents.

Called a gentle spirit and a deeply spiritual man, Boehm was one of the best-known clergymen of the Middle States in the eighteenth century. Long after his disassociation from the Mennonites, he wore the plain garb and flowing beard of that community. He died at his Lancaster home following fifty-five years of preaching. Asbury, who preached at Boehm's funeral, referred to him as "Father Boehm" and regretted only that Boehm had not been more authoritative in following the Methodist *Discipline*.

• The only source for details of much of Boehm's life is his son Henry Boehm's *Reminiscences* (1875). There are references in the writings of Francis Asbury and in congregation records at local Mennonite churches in eastern Pennsylvania. John Williamson Nevin, a German Reformed theologian, recorded his observations of Boehm's ministry in *The Anxious Book* (1843). Modern analyses are in F. Ernest Stoeffler, *Continental Pietism and Early American Christianity* (1976), and J. Bruce Behney and Paul H. Eller, *The History of the Evangelical United Brethren Church* (1979).

WILLIAM H. BRACKNEY

BOEING, William Edward (1 Oct. 1881–28 Sept. 1956), aviation industry pioneer, was born in Detroit, Michigan, the son of Wilhelm Boeing and Marie Ortman. His father, a native of Germany, and his mother, born in Vienna, emigrated to the United States with considerable wealth. They invested mainly in tracts of iron-ore and timber lands in Michigan and the rich Mesabi range. His father died when Boeing was just eight years old. His mother, known for her stern values and reserved, aristocratic manner, was the main influence on him. Throughout his life he was private and withdrawn, always shunning publicity. His education included brief study in Switzerland and at the Sheffield Scientific School at Yale University. He gained a footing in mechanical engineering but did not complete his final year and failed to graduate with the class of 1904.

An investment in iron-ore lands near Taconite, Minnesota, produced a lucrative income for Boeing and gave him a strong confidence in his own ability. At twenty-two he went west, hoping to set the course of his life independently and telling friends that he planned to retire as a young man. He settled at Grays Harbor on the mouth of the Chehalis River in Washington State, where he purchased timberland, the first of his many investments in the natural resources of the Pacific Northwest.

In 1908 Boeing moved to Seattle, where he managed his investments and fed his passion for automobiles and power boats and for exploring the forests and fishing the waterways of Oregon, Washington, British Columbia, and Alaska. In banking documents he described himself as a "speculator and financier." He became acquainted with Captain G. C. Westervelt, an engineer starting a career in naval aviation. Beginning in 1910 they attended airshows together, and Boeing cultivated an expertise in the new technology of powered flight, calling it his "hobby."

By 1914 Boeing was a qualified pilot. One of his instructors was Glenn L. Martin, a Los Angeles designer. Boeing bought a Martin seaplane in 1915, reportedly telling his associates, "I think we could build a better one." The first two Boeing aircraft were soon completed, a pair of seaplanes designated B/W after Boeing and Captain Westervelt.

Boeing established the Pacific Aero Products Company in 1916. The firm was capitalized at $100,000, and all but two of its 1,000 shares were owned by Boeing. Work began in a refurbished shipyard on the Duwamish Waterway where Boeing kept his yacht, *Taconite.* Boeing's long-term hope was to build aircraft for sport and commercial air transport. His immediate aim was to supply seaplanes to the U.S. Navy. The war in Europe revealed the promise of airpower, and Congress was spending large sums on military aviation. Boeing avidly promoted airpower. He dropped paper "bombs" in mock air raids over Seattle, hoping to foster sentiment for war preparedness.

The navy accepted a Boeing design for a seaplane trainer in 1917 and ordered fifty of the craft. Boeing changed the firm's name to Boeing Airplane Company and hired two young engineers from the University of Washington—C. L. Egtvedt and P. G. Johnson—who were the company's key executives through the 1950s. Boeing received a contract to build fifty patrol planes, but the order was cut to twenty-five when the war ended.

The small number of marginally profitable wartime orders for his company, in comparison to the huge contracts let to eastern manufacturers, led Boeing to doubt the impartiality of the military-contracting process and to believe in an East Coast "aviation establishment" bent on cornering the new aircraft market. This misplaced resentment, together with his deep commitment to aviation, prompted Boeing to use his personal funds to sustain the firm—its designers and craftsmen—through the unprofitable postwar years.

The firm remained active, filling minor military contracts and even building furniture, until mid-1921 when it won a national price-bidding war for the production of 200 Thomas-Morse army fighters. A small profit was eked out but reinvested in new military and commercial designs. "Our job," Boeing said, "is to keep everlastingly at research and experiment." His manner and bearing seemed ideal for overseeing the complex processes of financing, designing, and producing advanced aircraft. To his associates and employees, Boeing was a reserved, even shy, individual who took advice and delegated decisions. Yet Boeing was a tall, strapping man who exuded an authority and evenhanded fairness that compelled dedication and commitment to thoroughness and success. The result was one of the nation's most innovative and competitive aircraft firms. The company produced a series of fighter craft, culminating in the classic P-26 "Peashooter" of the early 1930s. Larger designs also were pursued as markets emerged for bombers and commercial airliners. Boeing was as much a pioneer of the airline industry as he was of aircraft manufacture. As early as 1919 Boeing planes carried mail between Seattle and Victoria, British Columbia, often with Boeing at the controls. In 1927 Boeing Air Transport was formed to fly the mail between Chicago and San Francisco.

Boeing shaped the so-called Golden Age of Aviation of the late 1920s and was well placed to take advantage of it. There seemed no limit to the new technology or to the public's desire to invest in it. Of the many aviation firms that emerged, Boeing formed one of the largest, most imaginative, and most successful—the United Aircraft and Transport Corporation. He bought out other airlines and manufacturers with the goal of creating a fully integrated company. With Boeing as chairman of the board and Boeing Airplane at the center, the company assembled into a complementary whole such firms as Pratt & Whitney, the engine maker; Hamilton-Standard Propeller; the diverse aircraft designers and builders Igor Sikorsky, Chance Vought, and Lloyd Stearman of Wichita; and air transport companies that together became United Airlines.

While other aviation companies folded or suffered huge losses during the first years of the Great Depression, Boeing's company remained profitable. By 1934 a radically new transport craft was in service, and a multiengine, long-range bomber was being designed. However, sound, measured management practices could not save the firm from the harsh attacks of congressmen and the press during the early New Deal years. Aviation industries unfairly became lightning rods for popular resentment against Wall Street, "big business," and the "trusts," which were widely assumed to have caused the depression. Military and airmail contracts were scrutinized and, despite little evidence of profiteering or malfeasance, were held in abeyance by Congress until holding companies like United were broken up.

Boeing deeply resented such exposure, which violated his sense of fair play. In 1934 he unrepentantly testified before senators who focused their investigations on profits he and others had made during the great run-up in the value of aviation stocks during 1928–1929. Indignant and bitter, he resigned his company positions in 1934 and sold nearly all his aviation holdings, including his shares of Boeing Airplane. Ironically, in the same year Boeing was awarded the coveted Daniel Guggenheim Medal "for successful pioneering and achievement in aircraft manufacturing and air transport."

The Boeing name remains one of the most illustrious in aircraft and aerospace manufacture. Yet Boeing's participation in the industry, apart from a brief advisory role to the company during World War II, ended in 1934. He spent the rest of his years in early retirement and carefully cultivated obscurity in the Seattle area. With his wife, Bertha Potter Paschell, whom he had married in 1921, Boeing cruised the region's waterways aboard the *Taconite* and his personal seaplanes. The couple had three children, two of whom were Boeing's stepsons. He became a renowned fly fisherman. It was said that Boeing's sense of decorum and proper form compelled him to shave and wear a coat and tie even at fish fries in the wilderness.

Boeing developed an interest in breeding Hereford cattle and thoroughbred horses, which he entered in competitions and races in the East. In 1942, after donating his estate in the Highlands district of Seattle to the Children's Orthopedic Hospital, he purchased and moved to a large ranch east of Seattle called "Aldarra Farms." There he pursued his many interests and developed the ranch into a model cattle producer. His neighbors recalled the sight of the tall Boeing striding about his ranch, inspecting it acre by acre, with a dog named General Motors in train and an unnecessary cane in hand.

Boeing's health began failing in 1955. He died in Puget Sound aboard his beloved yacht, *Taconite*. Before he died, Boeing witnessed his corporate progeny's steps into the age of the jet airliner as the Boeing 707, forerunner to the great Boeing 700 series, made its first flight from Renton Municipal Airport on 15 July 1954.

• Further information on Boeing is in H. Mansfield, *Vision: A Saga of the Sky* (1956), and the *Boeing Magazine* (Nov. 1956). An obituary is in the *Seattle Post-Intelligencer,* 29 Sept. 1956.

JACOB VANDER MEULEN

BOGAN, Louise (11 Aug. 1897–4 Feb. 1970), poet and critic, was born Louise Marie Bogan in Livermore Falls, Maine, the daughter of Daniel Joseph Bogan, a superintendent in a paper mill, and Mary Helen Murphy Shields. She grew up in various mill towns in the Northeast, moving often with her parents and brother. Her parents' marriage was volatile, and her mother's affairs haunted Bogan for much of her life.

Although Bogan attended Boston University for only one year in 1915–1916, her early education at Boston Girls' Latin School gave her a rigorous foundation. She was already writing poetry and reading *Poetry: A Magazine of Verse* in its first issues in 1912. While modernism in literature and the arts was gaining in momentum and shape, Bogan was quietly mastering metrics and defining her style. She later wrote passionately about her artistic awakening, describing a visit to her mother in the hospital. There in the room she saw a vase of marigolds: "Suddenly I *recognized* something at once simple and full of the utmost richness of design and contrast that was mine." Design and contrast are at the heart of her formal poetry, and the style that she crafted early did not vary much throughout her later years.

She married Curt Alexander in 1916, but the marriage was not a happy one. They had one daughter, born just a year later. By 1920 Bogan was a widow (she had earlier separated from her husband), left with a child to care for and without a reliable income. After moving to New York City, where she would live for the rest of her life, Bogan started to piece together the life of a working writer. She soon met other writers in the city's thriving literary community: William Carlos Williams, Malcolm Cowley, Lola Ridge, John Reed (1887–1920), Marianne Moore, and, most important, Edmund Wilson, who became her early mentor. Wilson, already a man of reputation, urged her to write reviews of literature for periodicals, and this eventually became a steady source of income.

A year after modernism peaked in 1922 with T. S. Eliot's *The Waste Land*, Bogan published her first book, *Body of This Death*. In contrast to Eliot's expansive, associative, free verse, Bogan's lyrics were brief, limited in theme, and highly formal. The volume, which was well received although many reviewers found the poetry obscure, speaks eloquently about love and grief, Bogan's twin themes. At this time she was seeing a psychiatrist to help her battle the depressions that relentlessly beset her and occasionally hospitalized her. Her life and her lyrics are intimately intertwined, although Bogan would be the last person to elucidate the connection. She was intensely private; for years many of her friends did not know she had a daughter.

Bogan had married again in 1925, this time to the writer Raymond Holden. This marriage, like the first, was troubled and did not last. Despite the personal turmoil, the 1920s and 1930s were Bogan's most productive poetic years. She published *Dark Summer* in 1929 and her third volume, *The Sleeping Fury*, in 1937. Other books that followed mainly collected previously published work and added a few new poems. The writing process for Bogan was painful and exacting; poems came rarely and at a cost. Her poem "The Daemon" depicts her muse as a monster demanding revelations again and again. Much of her work, in fact, draws upon the themes of silence and language as well as upon the failure of love.

During the 1930s, when many of her writer friends turned to the left, Bogan fought a lonely battle for literary purity. She was adamant that politics had no place in poetry; art called for something grander and more honest. Additionally, she saw the temporary defection of her friends (Edmund Wilson, Rolfe Humphries, Léonie Adams) as evidence of intellectual and emotional weakness and as a betrayal of the authority of the self.

During this decade she began reviewing poetry for the *New Yorker*, a job she held for thirty-eight years. Many of these reviews, as well as others, are collected in *A Poet's Alphabet: Reflections on the Literary Art and Vocation* (1970). Her prose is direct, nonacademic, and sharp. The series of articles on her two favorite poets, William Butler Yeats and Rainer Maria Rilke, is particularly insightful. The poet W. H. Auden thought she was the best critic of poetry in America.

Her occasional teaching stints, which began in the 1940s, were another, more direct way to influence the minds of young people. As the strain of writing poetry increased, Bogan turned more and more to criticism and education. In 1951 she was commissioned to write a short history of American poetry, eventually published as *Achievement in American Poetry, 1900–1950*, in which she does not once mention herself. She also translated poetry and prose and worked with younger writers (William Maxwell, for example) to help them distill beauty and truth from their writing.

The reviews of her last collections were admiring, if quietly so. Her second collection, *Collected Poems, 1923–1953* (*Poems and New Poems* had come out in 1941), won a shared Bollingen Prize in 1955. Nonetheless, for most of her writing life she felt invisible in the literary world. Late in her life financial burdens eased somewhat, helped in large part by a monetary award from the Academy of American Poets in 1959 and another from the National Endowment for the Arts in 1967. Her final and most complete collection, *The Blue Estuaries: Poems 1923–1968* (1968), contains only 103 poems. She died alone in her New York apartment, fighting the familiar depression she had wrestled with all her life.

Interest from feminist circles in the hidden lives of women writers has prompted new assessments of Bogan. The "mosaic" of her autobiographical pieces, *Journey around My Room* (1980), and the Pulitzer Prize–winning biography by Elizabeth Frank, *Louise Bogan: A Portrait* (1985), have introduced her to the general public. Yet Bogan remains a poet's poet, yielding beauty to those whose ear, mind, and heart are open to the demands of her poetry. Her work is particularly important in light of her place in the company of other modernists. In a time of experimentation, of a general loosening of structures and subjects, she held the line for formal poetry and for the precise blend of emotion and intellect to enliven that poetry.

• Bogan's papers, including manuscripts for many of the poems, are held at Amherst College Special Collections, Amherst, Mass. The most helpful source is Claire E. Knox's annotated bibliography, *Louise Bogan: A Reference Source* (1990). For a taste of Bogan's wit, her spirited letters, *What the Woman Lived: Selected Letters of Louise Bogan, 1920–1970*, ed. Ruth Limmer (1973), should not be missed. Important reviews are collected in Martha Collins, *Critical Essays on Louise Bogan* (1984). The only full-length studies are Jacqueline Ridgeway's general introduction, *Louise Bogan* (1984), and Gloria Bowles's feminist reading, *Louise Bogan's Aesthetic of Limitation* (1987). Obituaries are in the *New York Times*, 5 Feb. 1970, and the *New Yorker*, 14 Feb. 1970.

WENDY HIRSCH

BOGARDUS, Emory Stephen (21 Feb. 1882–21 Aug. 1973), sociologist and university administrator, was born near Belvidere, Illinois, the son of Henry Brown Bogardus, a farmer of Dutch descent, and Eliza Stevenson. Growing up in a rural household, with no mail delivery or daily paper, Bogardus learned of the outside world through publications such as the *Youth's Companion*, *Farm and Fireside*, and a weekly Sunday-school paper. Although rural isolation fostered intellectual self-reliance, his childhood, he later commented, was also dominated by the "authoritative voices" of adults; his parents were over forty when he was born, and his two brothers sixteen and ten years older (*Much Have I Learned*, p. 4).

After graduating from high school, torn between choosing a career in "money-making" or "human values," Bogardus sought a compromise as cub reporter for the *Belvidere Standard*. But he soon returned to farming for five years to earn money for college. Entering Northwestern, he received a B.A. in 1908 and an M.A. in 1909, both in philosophy and psychology, before obtaining his doctorate at the University of Chicago (1911) for a thesis on "The Relation of Fatigue to Industrial Accidents." To finance his first year of graduate study, he obtained a fellowship at the Northwestern University Settlement on Chicago's North Side, where he developed a lifelong interest in the relations of immigrant groups. At Chicago he was especially influenced by the sociology of Albion Small, Charles Henderson, and William I. Thomas and the social psychology of George H. Mead, James R. Angell, and Harvey W. Carr. Avowedly eclectic, Bogardus sidestepped the methodological debates of his time. "Interview, life history, participant observation, and statistical methods," he once wrote, "are all needed . . . in order that one may understand a human relations problem" (*Much Have I Learned*, p. 63).

Appointed assistant professor of sociology and economics at the University of Southern California in 1911, Bogardus headed the newly created sociology department from 1915 until 1946, gaining for it a reputation as one of the finest on the West Coast. He also served as director of the Division of Social Work from 1920 to 1937 and as acting dean (1926–1927) and later dean of the Graduate School (1945–1949). A prodigious writer, he published more than twenty-four books, including revisions of the textbooks for which he was most widely known. Among them were *Social Psychology* (1918), *A History of Social Thought* (1922), *Sociology* (1922), and *Contemporary Sociology* (1931), each of which appeared in several editions. He also addressed contemporary issues in *Essentials of Americanization* (1919), *The Mexican in the United States* (1934), and *Leaders and Leadership* (1934). In addition, he wrote some 275 articles, which, with a characteristic enthusiasm for quantification, he later classified as 12 percent each treating social theory, race, and immigration, 10 percent measuring "social distance," and the remainder dealing with cooperative movements, research methods, world organization, public opinion, and democracy.

In his research and teaching, Bogardus contributed to the interwar drive to make sociology more rigorously "scientific," though not without regard to social welfare. In the early 1920s he organized at USC a "Social Research Clinic," where graduate students could bring problems to clinic members serving as "doctors" to diagnose "research impasses" (*Much Have I Learned*, p. 61). In 1924 he formulated the first of the "social distance" scales for which he was best known. Developed initially when he was director of the Pacific Coast Race Relations survey (assisted by Robert E. Park), the "Bogardus scales" charted the psychological-social distance separating individuals in different racial and nationality groups by measuring willingness to accept social intimacy, as expressed in attitudes ranging from exclusion from the country to admission to family membership through marriage. Published in leading sociological journals, his findings were collected in revised form in *Social Distance* (1959) and applied in countries such as South Africa, Ethiopia, and Thailand.

As editor of *Sociology and Social Research* (founded in 1915) from 1916 to 1961 and as editor emeritus until 1967, Bogardus earned the journal national stature. Although less prestigious than the *American Journal of Sociology*, *Social Forces*, or the *American Sociological Review*, it provided a forum for discussion of "applied" sociology and contemporary issues at a time when such interests were increasingly unfashionable within the profession. Commenting, for example, on Benito Mussolini in 1933, when the Italian dictator was still admired in many quarters, Bogardus predicted that fascism contained the "seeds of its own destruction in its autocracy."

Bogardus was extremely active in the professional and civic organizations that mushroomed in the interwar years. In 1920 he founded Alpha Kappa Delta, the sociological honor society. In 1929 he helped found the Pacific Sociological Society, serving as its first president from 1929 to 1931, and in 1931 was elected president of the American Sociological Society. In Los Angeles, he worked with organizations concerned with race relations and the problems of young people, the latter the subject of *The Boy in Los Angeles* (1925). For his professional contributions and public activities he received honorary degrees from USC and several other universities.

Despite his many professional activities, Bogardus found time for a rich personal life. Married in 1911 to Edith Mildred Pritchard, with whom he had one child, he enjoyed more than thirty-seven years of what he termed "genuine marital happiness" before his wife's death in 1949. An avid world traveler, he kept double-entry notebooks of his adventures: one page contained pre-trip notes, the second, impressions from his travels, the most memorable of which he published as *The Traveler* (1956) and *Explorer* (1961). Some impressions took the form of sonnets, which he also regularly composed and published on a variety of subjects. His visits to cooperatives across the world formed the basis of his *Problems of Cooperation* (1960). He probably died in Glendale, California; he is buried there.

Although the "social distance scale" won Bogardus a footnote in the history of American sociology, he never quite enjoyed the reputation of William F. Ogburn, F. Stuart Chapin, and other leaders of sociology's "second generation," who dominated the profession in the interwar years. But, in conjunction with other institution builders of this generation, he played an important part in securing for the discipline a permanent place within the nation's universities.

• Bogardus described his early life and career in *Much Have I Learned* (1962) and the development of sociology at his university in *A History of Sociology at the University of Southern California* (1972). An earlier unpublished autobiographical sketch is in the Luther Lee Bernard Papers at Penn State. Additional books by Bogardus include *An Introduction to the Social Sciences* (1913), *Essentials of Social Psychology* (1918), *Methods of Training Social Workers* (1921), *Fundamentals of Social Psychology* (1924), *Making Social Science Studies* (1925), *The New Social Research* (1926), *Immigration and Race Attitudes* (1928), *Introduction to Social Research* (1936), and *The Making of Public Opinion* (1951). Bogardus's role in the history of American sociology is discussed briefly in Howard Odum, *American Sociology* (1951), and his opposition to fascism is in Robert Bannister, "Principle, Politics, Profession: American Sociology and Fascism, 1930s–1950s" in *Sociology Responds to Fascism*, ed. Stephen Turner and Dirk Käsler (1992). An obituary and tribute appear in *Sociological Inquiry* 44 (1973): 3–5.

ROBERT C. BANNISTER

BOGARDUS, Everardus (1607–27 Sept. 1647), minister, was born at Woerden, the Netherlands, the son of Willem Bogardus. The occupation of his father and the name of his mother are unknown. He attended Leiden University from 1627 until 1630, but his studies were interrupted when he was sent by the Consistory of Amsterdam to act as a comforter of the sick in Guinea. Bogardus served faithfully in that capacity until 1632. Upon his return to the Netherlands, he was examined and ordained to the ministry. On 15 July 1632 he was accepted for service as the new minister for New Netherland. His pastorship included both New Amsterdam (now New York) and Fort Orange (now Albany), 150 miles apart.

Bogardus sailed aboard the *Soutberg* with the new director of the colony, Wouter van Twiller. They arrived at New Amsterdam in April 1633, and Bogardus began to preach in a small wooden building on present-day Pearl Street in Manhattan. Van Twiller soon acquired a reputation for drunkenness and incompetence, and Bogardus was among those who turned against him. At one point he denounced the director as a "child of the Devil." Van Twiller was indeed inept, but he hardly deserved the abuse that Bogardus heaped on him. The dispute grew so bitter that on one occasion citizens of New Amsterdam were treated to the sight of van Twiller, sword in hand, pursuing Bogardus through the streets. Bogardus escaped without injury.

It was apparent that Bogardus saw himself not only as the defender of the faithful but also as the chastiser of faulty government. He achieved a measure of success in another rivalry with the public prosecutor Lubbert van Dincklage. Bogardus excommunicated van Dincklage, who returned to the Netherlands and protested in vain against the pastor. In 1638 Bogardus married Anneke Jansz, a wealthy widow who owned a 62-acre farm on Manhattan. They had four children.

Bogardus may well have been pleased when van Twiller was replaced as director of the colony by Willem Kieft in 1638. However, Kieft's administration proved even more vexing for the minister and other residents of New Netherland. It initially appeared that relations between Bogardus and the new director might proceed amicably. In 1642, at the wedding of Bogardus's stepdaughter, Kieft raised money from the half-drunken citizens to build a new stone church within the walls of the fort on Manhattan Island. However, any goodwill that existed between the two evaporated when Kieft led the colony into a disastrous war with Indians in the vicinity that began in 1643 and dragged on for more than two years. Bogardus denounced Kieft for running a murderous and corrupt administration and at one point asked his parishioners, "What else are the greatest in the land but vessels of wrath and fountains of evil?"

After Bogardus delivered a particularly scathing sermon, Kieft threatened in 1646 to prosecute him for "conduct [that] stirs the people to mutiny and rebellion." Kieft also accused Bogardus of frequently being drunk in both private and public and offered as evidence a list he had compiled of the minister's transgressions. The two reached a partial reconciliation later that year. In 1647 Kieft was replaced as director by Peter Stuyvesant, and Bogardus resigned his post as minister. Each man was determined to return to Amsterdam and clear his name of charges made by the other. A major showdown loomed ahead, but it was prevented when the ship bearing both men, the *Princess*, sank off the coast of Wales. Bogardus and Kieft both died in the wreck, and most of their papers were lost.

Bogardus was a true "fighting pastor" in the tradition of the Dutch Reformed church. At times he doubtless felt that his opposition to van Twiller and Kieft recalled that of the ministers and leaders of the Netherlands who resisted the tyranny of Philip II of Spain. In addition, Bogardus's activities echoed those of other ministers in colonial North America. Though he is less well known than Cotton Mather, John Davenport, Roger Williams, and other English ministers, Bogardus was similar to these men in his courage. He used the power of the pulpit to attack what he saw as the inept and unjust government of New Netherland. It is unfortunate that so few of his speeches and writings survive; they were probably full of eloquence and passion. Nonetheless, he often displayed more courage than judgment in his attacks on the civil authorities. He contributed to making church-state relations difficult in the new colony, and that difficulty was one of the many problems that thwarted the development of New Netherland.

• The sources for Bogardus's life and career are few, and most of his papers were lost. One primary source for his pastorship is E. B. O'Callaghan, *Documents Relative to the Colonial History of the State of New York*, vol. 1 (1856). Information on Bogardus is in parts of a number of other books. The most prominent are Henri van der Zee and Barbara van der Zee, *A Sweet and Alien Land: The Story of Dutch New York* (1978); Ellis Lawrence Raesly, *Portrait of New Netherland* (1965); William R. Shepherd, *The Story of New Amsterdam* (1926); Alexander C. Flick, ed., *History of the State of New York*, vol. 2 (1933); J. H. Innes, *New Amsterdam and Its People* (1902); and O'Callaghan, *History of New Netherland*, vol. 1 (1945).

SAMUEL WILLARD CROMPTON

BOGARDUS, James (14 Mar. 1800–13 Apr. 1874), inventor and builder, was born near Catskill, New York, the son of John Bogardus and Sara Stockens, farmers. Apprenticed when he was fourteen years old to the local watchmaker, he became skilled in work with precision instruments, die sinking, and engraving. In 1820, "desiring to see something of the world," he went to Savannah, Georgia, where he worked at engraving. By 1823 he was back in Catskill, with his own clock and engraving business. He emerged as an inventor in 1828, exhibiting a new type of three-wheeled, eight-day clock that won the highest premium at the first fair (1828) of the American Institute of New York.

The aspiring inventor moved to New York City in 1828 or 1829. There in 1831 he married Margaret Maclay, a painter of miniature portraits and daughter of the prominent Baptist clergyman Archibald Maclay, a founder of New York University, joining the well-educated and influential Maclay household. Bogardus is reported to have been an amiable but shy man; he avoided public life even after he was widely known. He and Margaret, childless, reared her niece, Harriet Hogg.

Bogardus's inventions won many medals from the American Institute and eventually provided an ample income. He was granted thirteen U.S. patents. Two (1832 and 1841) were for his highly original eccentric mill, capable of grinding substances as diverse as sugar, paint pigments, grains, and coal. Its two wheels turned in the same direction, one on an off-center pivot, producing a wrenching effect, and it was considered "of that class of inventions of which but few are made in centuries" (*Franklin Journal*, May 1846). Bogardus's brother-in-law Congressman William Maclay helped extend the life of the remunerative 1832 patent by special act of Congress in 1846. Other patents included two for clocks (1830, 1832), a "ring flyer" for textile spinning (1830), a mechanical pencil (1833), a device to separate gold from its ore (1834), a dry gas meter (1834) to measure the newly introduced illuminating gas, a diaphragm meter for measuring fluids (1837), devices for cutting and corrugating India rubber (both 1845), a gear system to increase horsepower (1848), and his best-known patent, Number 7337 (1850), for "construction of the frame, roof and floor of iron buildings." His one British patent was for a type of postage stamp (1839). Inventions for engraving, awarded medals but not patented, included an extremely accurate machine for delicate engraving in high relief and a transferring machine for banknote engraving (both 1831). Other inventions were a machine to press glass, a pyrometer, a dynamometer, and finally, at the end of the 1860s, an apparatus for deep-sea soundings.

Seeking to protect his gas meter patent rights abroad, Bogardus went to England in October 1836. Although unable to salvage his inventor's claim in London, he profitably marketed his engraving machine to the proprietor of the *Public Ledger* in 1837 and also modified it to engrave from high-relief medals; the modified machine was used in 1837 to engrave the likeness of the teenaged Queen Victoria. In 1838 Margaret joined James in London, where in 1839 she exhibited miniatures at the Royal Academy. Bogardus entered an 1839 British competition for a postage-stamp system. None of the 2,600 submissions was adopted, but Bogardus's was adjudged one of the four best, winning a £100 prize.

In England Bogardus observed many examples of cast-iron bridges, market interiors, and other construction uses of the newly available metal. While touring Italy in 1840, he was seized by a vision of reproducing Renaissance designs with mass-produced cast iron building elements. He returned home convinced that metal construction could bring fire-resistant architecture to American cities, many of which had experienced tragic urban conflagrations, and its potential for speedy construction could establish a new building industry.

Despite public derision and assertions that iron buildings would attract lightning or collapse of their own weight, Bogardus introduced iron-walled buildings in New York by erecting on Duane Street (1848–1849) a totally iron factory for manufacturing his eccentric grinding mills. Opposition withered and commissions came, first for an ornamented iron front to update Dr. John Milhau's old brick pharmacy on Broadway (1848, facade removed 1934), and for Edgar Laing's row of five stores (1849, razed 1971). California's 1849 gold rush opened a market for portable, prefabricated cast-iron houses, which Bogardus helped supply.

The decade of the 1850s was Bogardus's most productive period as constructor of large cast-iron commercial buildings. It began when Baltimore publisher Arunah Abell commissioned him and architect Robert Hatfield to erect a richly ornamented, five-story, iron-framed, iron-front plant as headquarters for the *Sun* newspaper (1850–1851). Orders followed quickly: three iron-front commercial buildings in Washington (Adams Express, 1850; Shanks, 1851; Coyle Warehouse, 1852); and two in Baltimore (Shoemaker, 1852; Larrabee, 1853). In 1853–1854 he built three iron fronts in New York City: 82 Beekman Street (Tatham Lead), 61 Barclay Street (Hopkins Brothers), and 338 Broadway (Sperry Clocks). Bogardus had a major role in rebuilding Harper Brothers' big fire-ravaged publishing plant at Franklin Square (1854, razed 1925), employing a fireproof system that combined cast-iron bowstring girders with America's first lengthy, seven-inch wrought-iron floor beams, rolled at Peter Cooper's Trenton foundry. For printer George Bruce he constructed a four-story building at Canal and Lafayette streets, having iron fronts on two sides totalling 178 feet (1856). With associates he erected for New York City the block-square three-story Tompkins Market (1857–1860, razed 1911) on Third Avenue, replacing a wooden market and also providing an armory for the Seventh Regiment. In 1857 he built a four-story iron front at 50 Murray Street for Blunt and Syms (razed 1958) and in 1858 an identical front on Chestnut Street in Philadelphia for William Swain, publisher of the *Ledger*, employing for both the casting patterns used for the *Baltimore Sun* in 1851 and reused for Harper's in 1854. Early in 1858 he completed a second building for Hopkins at 75 Murray Street and a four-story office in Albany for stove maker Samuel Ransom (razed 1931). By 1858 he had also erected four iron structures in Chicago for various businessmen (Burley, Page, Tuttle, and Burch) and at least another nine in New York City, including one on Fulton Street for druggists McKesson and Robbins and another for the Emigrants' Savings Bank. In 1857–1860 he erected the 600-foot-long, two-story Santa Catalina sugar warehouse on the harbor of Havana, Cuba (destroyed by hurricane in 1906).

Also in the 1850s Bogardus was a pioneer in building suspended roofs and very tall towers. His entry in the 1852 competition for the New York Crystal Palace, though not a winner, proposed a four-story circular building of iron and glass 1,200 feet in circumference, covered by a metal roof suspended from a 300-foot-high metal tower. He actually constructed a suspended roof system in his "Rotunda" pavilion for the Astor Hotel (1852, razed 1913) and again in the "Exchange" of South Carolina's Charleston Hotel (1853). Of more lasting import were four austere skeletal iron towers erected in Manhattan. The first (1851, 100 feet tall) and second (1853, 125 feet), were watchtowers for New York's fire department, demolished by 1885, by which time the telegraph had made them obsolete. The third tower, the 175-foot-tall McCullough shot tower (1855), and the fourth, the 217-foot-tall Tatham shot tower (1857), were for producing gunshot from melted lead. The very tall shot towers, with brick infill panels in the iron skeletons to keep molten shot from blowing away, are now recognized as precursors of the skyscraper (both razed 1907).

In 1856 Bogardus and long-time aide John W. Thomson published a seminal sixteen-page pamphlet, *Cast Iron Buildings, Their Construction and Advantages*, reissued in 1858. Use of cast iron for exterior walls was scorned by British taste-maker William Morris and by conventional builders but championed by such avant-garde architects as Richard Morris Hunt and soon became nationally accepted for architectural purposes.

In the 1860s Bogardus scaled back his own work. The widening of Duane Street in 1859 forced him to dismantle his all-iron factory and move his shop to nearby White and Elm streets. In the 1860s he built only two cast-iron structures: 85 Leonard Street (1861) for Manhattan silk merchants and the elegant Iron Clad Building (1862–1863) in Cooperstown, New York. In 1865 Bogardus delegated to John Thomson management of the eccentric mill business. He died at his home in New York City.

Bogardus was a creative mechanic-inventor of the expansive years of the mid-nineteenth century and a pioneer of iron construction who played a leading role in establishing metal architecture in America. His work stands midway between the late eighteenth-century British innovative uses of cast iron for bridges and interior columns in cotton mills and the late nineteenth century's reliance on steel skeletal systems and vast engineering structures, including the skyscraper. Highly regarded by his contemporaries, Bogardus's reputation was eclipsed as cast-iron architecture lost favor. Now, with revived appreciation of America's early metal buildings and intense efforts to preserve surviving examples, Bogardus's prominence has been restored.

• Bogardus left behind only a few papers, preserved in the Newington-Cropsey Foundation Archives, Hastings-on-Hudson, N.Y. Contemporary views can be found in the journals of the American Institute (New York City) and the Franklin Institute (Philadelphia). More recent accounts are Sigfried Giedion, *Space, Time and Architecture* (1941; 5th ed., 1967), and Carl W. Condit, *Macmillan Encyclopedia of Architects*, vol. 1 (1982). The most important study of Bogardus's architectural work is Turpin C. Bannister's two-part article, "Bogardus Revisited," *Journal of the Society of Architectural Historians* 15, no. 4 (1956), "The Iron Fronts," and 16, no. 1 (1957), "The Iron Towers." Bogardus's inventions are covered in Barbara A. Baxter's unpublished paper, "The Inventive Career of James Bogardus" (1989). Obituaries are in the *New York Herald*, 14 Apr. 1874; *Scientific American*, 2 May 1874; and *Annual American Cyclopaedia of the U.S.*, vol. 14 (1877), p. 681.

MARGOT GAYLE

BOGART, Humphrey (23 Jan. 1899–14 Jan. 1957), film and stage actor, was born Humphrey DeForest Bogart in New York City, the son of Belmont DeForest Bogart, a prominent doctor, and Maud Humphrey, a successful illustrator. As a boy, Bogart lived on Manhattan's well-to-do Upper West Side and summered at the family's country home on Canandaigua Lake, New York, where he developed a lifelong love of sailing. In preparation for an Ivy League education, he attended Trinity School in New York and Phillips Academy in Massachusetts; at Phillips, he showed little interest in his studies and was expelled in 1918. He immediately enlisted in the navy and served aboard the *Leviathan*. While on duty, he injured his upper lip, causing him to have a firmly set mouth and slight, graveled lisp, both of which became his most identifiable physical characteristics.

On his discharge, Bogart became a runner on Wall Street until theatrical producer William A. Brady, a family friend, made him assistant stage manager for one of his plays. Bogart also did small jobs at Brady's World Film Corporation in New York. Bogart turned to acting and had a bit part in *Drifting* (1922); by the end of that year he was playing the second lead in *Swiftly*, a comedy that quickly folded. In 1923 he acted alongside Mary Boland and Clifton Webb in *Meet the Wife*, but it was not until *Cradle Snatchers*, which had the 1925–1926 Broadway season's longest run, that he had any notable success. During thirteen years of stage acting, in all, he only occasionally achieved more than steady work in unremarkable roles. The critic Alexander Woollcott said of his early performance in *Swiftly* that it was "what is usually and mercifully described as inadequate," a comment that Bogart often repeated.

In 1926 he married Helen Menken, an actress; they were divorced eighteen months later. Shortly thereafter, he married another actress, Mary Phillips, and their turbulent relationship lasted almost ten years, ending in divorce.

In 1928 Bogart had his first film role in a two-reeler made in New York, *The Dancing Town*, starring Helen Hayes, and in 1930 he traveled to Hollywood for a short, *Broadway's Like That*, which led to a role in *A Devil with Women*. He then was in *Up the River* (1930), directed by John Ford, a picture that also had Spencer Tracy in the cast. Tracy gave him the nickname "Bogey," and the two actors became close friends.

After making seven more movies over the next few years, Bogart returned to New York to experience one of the low periods in his life. In 1934 his father died, leaving debts, and his own career seemed headed downhill. But later that year he got an important break: the role of Duke Mantee in Robert E. Sherwood's Broadway drama, *The Petrified Forest*, starring Leslie Howard. Warner Bros. bought the film rights to the play, intending to offer the role of Mantee to Edward G. Robinson, but Howard firmly insisted that Bogart be given the part. Some film critics now consider *The Petrified Forest* (1936) to be a preachy melodrama in which Duke Mantee stands as a symbol of rugged outlaw individualism in the midst of a spiritually dead society, but Bogart's dynamic portrayal earned him critical and popular acclaim. He signed a long-term contract with Warner Bros. and assumed the obligations—and opportunities—of a studio actor's career.

From 1936 through 1940 Bogart made twenty-eight films, perhaps half of them routine, while in a dozen or more, especially *Marked Woman*, *Black Legion*, and *Dead End* (all 1937), *Angels with Dirty Faces* (1938), and *They Drive by Night* (1940), he made a strong impression in the sort of realistic, socially conscious pictures that Warner Bros. did better than any other studio. A pivotal role came with *High Sierra* (1941), in which he played Roy Earle, another outlaw individualist who comes to a tragic end. As private eye Sam Spade in the film classic *The Maltese Falcon* (1941), Bogart further displayed the unusual physical characteristics—off-center smile, distinctive voice, staccato delivery, sardonic sense of humor, and assured self-control—that became his hallmarks over the next fifteen years.

These traits appealed to movie audiences to an even greater degree in what was to be his best-known role, that of Rick Blaine, the American expatriate nightclub owner in *Casablanca* (1943). Bogart's role as Rick, some of the lines he delivered ("Here's looking at you, kid") and one that he didn't ("Play it again, Sam"), the outstanding supporting cast, and moviegoers' enthusiastic response to the film, which won an Academy Award for best picture, all became part of Hollywood mythology.

In all, Bogart made eighty-one films in a career that extended over nearly three decades. Among his best pictures, some of them recognized by film historians and critics as classics, were *To Have and Have Not* (1944), *The Big Sleep* (1946), *The Treasure of the Sierra Madre* (1948), *Key Largo* (1948), *In a Lonely Place* (1950), *The African Queen* (1951), *Beat the Devil*, *The Barefoot Contessa*, and *The Caine Mutiny* (all 1954). He won Academy Awards as best actor in *The African Queen* and *The Caine Mutiny*.

Starting in 1943 with his popularity in *Casablanca* and continuing each year throughout the 1940s, Bogart was one of the ten leading box office stars in Hollywood, outranking all but four others (Bing Crosby, Betty Grable, Bob Hope, and Gary Cooper) during that span. Bogart appeared once again on the theater operators' list of top ten in 1955.

While filming *To Have and Have Not* in 1944, Bogart began an affair with his young costar, Lauren Bacall, that led to his divorcing actress Mayo Methot, his wife since 1938. He and Bacall were married in 1945; they had two children.

In 1947 Bogart was prominent among a delegation of motion picture professionals who formed the Committee for the First Amendment and traveled to Washington, D.C., to protest hearings held by the House Committee on Un-American Activities (HUAC) into the activities of a group of leftist screenwriters and a director who became known as the Hollywood Ten. Confronted by assertions from right-wing newspapers and commentators that he and his colleagues were communists or communist dupes, Bogart and the others beat a hurried retreat. Publicly stating that he detested communism, Bogart renounced his anti-HUAC trip as "ill-advised, even foolish."

The cancer that eventually overwhelmed Bogart became apparent in 1954 while he was filming his role as Captain Queeg in *The Caine Mutiny*. From 1954 until 1956 he made a half-dozen other films, but after completing *The Harder They Fall* (1956), his last picture, the cancer operation he underwent proved unsuccessful. Ten months later he died in Beverly Hills.

In the years since his death, Bogart has become a kind of institutional—or archetypal—figure in American and international film history and celebrity legend. Clips from his movies, particularly the airport farewell scene with Ingrid Bergman in *Casablanca*, have been shown countless times in other movies and on television. Like Charlie Chaplin, W. C. Fields, John Wayne, or Marilyn Monroe, Bogart, often pictured in trench coat and expertly creased snap-brim, is instantly recognizable to many millions of people, a great number of whom have never seen his films. In the 1940s and 1950s, Bogart made his mark on American movies and American culture, an imprint that will last well into another century.

• The best of many Bogart biographies is Jonathan Coe, *Humphrey Bogart: Take It and Like It* (1991); personal accounts by Nathaniel Benchley, *Humphrey Bogart* (1975), and Louise Brooks, *Lulu in Hollywood* (1982), are of special interest. An interesting scholarly work comparing three Hollywood tough guys, James Cagney, Bogart, and John Garfield, is Robert Sklar, *City Boys* (1992). An obituary is in the *New York Times*, 15 Jan. 1957.

NORMAN S. COHEN

BOGGS, Dock (7 Feb. 1898–7 Feb. 1971), folk singer and banjoist, was born Moran Lee Boggs in West Norton, Virginia. His father worked as a blacksmith and carpenter. He grew up in a family of musicians; three of his older brothers played the banjo and sang, two sisters were excellent singers, and his father could even read music and sing "written" music. Dock grew up attending typical Appalachian music-making events—square dances, molasses stir-offs, barn raisings, pie suppers—but the area's mining and railroading enterprises also put him in touch with a large number of African-American folk musicians, from whom he learned the blues and other types of popular songs. In his own work later he sought to combine the two styles, the black and the white, creating a unique strain of "mountain blues."

For much of Boggs's early life, however, music remained a hobby. In 1910, when he was only twelve, he went to work in the local coal mines as a "trapper" for seven cents an hour. For the next ten years the coal industry was booming in southwest Virginia, and it provided him with a modest livelihood. Even after he married a local woman, Sara (maiden name unknown), in 1918, he continued to play music informally. For a time Boggs had a contract job in the mines, but in the early 1920s a depression settled over the industry and the young couple had trouble making ends meet. Boggs found himself forced to turn to bootlegging, and his life was soon filled with gunfights, scrapes with the local sheriffs, speakeasy brawls, and family feuds. He later admitted that at one time he beat up some in-laws so badly that he feared the family would seek retribution.

By 1927 Boggs had decided it might be possible to make money playing his music; record companies were sending talent scouts to roam throughout his part of the mountains, signing contracts with some of his friends and fellow musicians. Unlike many of these musicians, who were rather passive about recording, Boggs took the initiative and wrote some of the companies himself, offering his services. One, Victor, wrote back offering him a chance to record, but he was unable to borrow the money to travel to the recording site. Then he heard of auditions held by the Brunswick Phonograph Company in Norton; he tried out and was invited to travel to New York City to record. In March 1927 he and a local string band, Dykes Magic City Trio, journeyed to New York by train, and Boggs recorded eight selections.

The "high lonesome" sound and modal patterns of mountain lyric songs fused naturally with black blues styles on these classic recordings, creating a unique hybrid called "mountain blues." The titles, all released in the next year on the Brunswick label, included "Down South Blues," which he had learned from an earlier blues recording, and "Country Blues," learned from a fellow mountain singer in about 1914; they became very popular and influential on younger musicians, both in the 1930s and later in the 1960s. His other songs included some traditional ballads, as well as some stark lyrics such as "Sammie, Where You Been So Long?" By now Boggs knew exactly what he wanted to do with his music. "I put so much of myself into some pieces that I very nearly broke down emotionally," he recalled in later years.

Boggs returned to his life in the mines and got caught up in the sometimes violent struggle to unionize the workers. But he saw too many of his friends killed in the mines or shot to death on mountain trails, so once again he tried to capitalize on his success with Brunswick and develop his recording career. By then, however, the Great Depression had all but wrecked the music industry. He recorded a couple of releases for a local West Virginia label, but the company failed, and Boggs gave up his dreams. For several years he gave up music completely. He and Sara were unable to have children, and they moved often around the little coal-mining towns of Kentucky, West Virginia, and Virginia.

In 1954 the mine Boggs had been working in closed down, and his coal-mining career was over. He managed to survive until he qualified for Social Security, expecting to live his life in quiet obscurity. Then in 1963 folklorist and musician Mike Seeger, who had learned some of his own style from Boggs's old records, tracked him down and encouraged him to continue playing the banjo. To Boggs's surprise, he regained much of his old skill, and Seeger persuaded him to record the first in a series of four LPs for Folkways Records. As the folk revival movement spread, Boggs was invited to do concerts at festivals in Chicago, Illinois, Asheville, North Carolina, and New York City, and at the famed Newport Folk Festival in Rhode Island. He sometimes performed with another rediscovered traditional musician, black guitarist Mississippi John Hurt—an artist Boggs had always admired.

Boggs's comeback brought new joys, but also new frustrations, and in his later days he was tormented by the question of what he might have become had he been luckier earlier in his career. A generation of young banjoists, however, and an audience that was possibly larger than his original one applauded his new LPs and cherished his music. He died in Norton.

• The most detailed account of Dock Boggs's recordings and career is a booklet by Barry O'Connel designed to accompany the Folkways LP, *Dock Boggs—His Twelve Original Recordings*, RBF 654 (1983). An account of his work as a white bluesman is in Charles Wolfe's chapter "White Country Blues" in *Nothing but the Blues*, ed. Larry Cohn (1993), pp. 233–64.

CHARLES K. WOLFE

BOGGS, Lilburn W. (14 Dec. 1796–11 Mar. 1860), governor of Missouri and California pioneer, was born in Lexington, Kentucky, the son of John M. Boggs and Martha Oliver. After graduating from the local public schools at age fifteen, he became a bookkeeper at the Insurance Bank of Kentucky in Lexington. Following the outbreak of the War of 1812, Boggs enlisted with a force of Kentucky volunteers who, under the command of Governor Isaac Shelby, helped William Henry Harrison defeat the British and their American Indian allies led by chief Tecumseh at the battle of the Thames in October 1813. Boggs returned to his bank post at the end of the war but soon resigned to move west and enter the fur trade.

Settling in St. Louis in the spring of 1816, Boggs opened a dry goods store in partnership with Thomas Hanley. The two quickly went bankrupt, but Boggs landed on his feet by securing a position as the first cashier of the newly incorporated Bank of Missouri in September 1816. Boggs assured his prominence in Missouri society in 1817 when he married Julia Ann Bent, the daughter of territorial judge Silas Bent and sister of William Bent and Charles Bent, builders of the famous Bent's Fort trading post on the Arkansas River and Santa Fe Trail. The couple had two children before Julia died in 1820.

In the meantime, renewed financial setbacks forced Boggs to relocate in the summer of 1818 to Howard County, where he opened a new store in Franklin. Two years later, in June 1820, Boggs received a federal appointment as the assistant factor at Fort Osage, a U.S. Army post on the Missouri frontier. Boggs held this position until the fort was closed in the fall of 1822, whereupon he moved to the nearby town of Sibley and opened another store. For the next four years Boggs peddled goods to white and Osage Indian customers throughout the area that would soon comprise Jackson County.

In July 1823 Boggs married Panthea Grant Boone, a granddaughter of the legendary frontiersman Daniel Boone. Boggs and his new bride had ten children. In 1826 Boggs entered politics and won election to the Missouri State Senate as a Democrat and pledged supporter of U.S. senator Thomas Hart Benton. The following year Boggs accepted an appointment as the first county clerk of newly created Jackson County. Moving his family to the county seat of Independence, Boggs served as clerk for seven months and established a new store that he operated with his wife and eldest sons. Reelected to the state senate in 1828 and 1830, the fast-rising Boggs became president pro tempore and, in 1832, was swept into the lieutenant governor's office as the successful running mate of Governor Daniel Dunklin.

Four years later, in 1836, Boggs ran for governor and narrowly defeated Congressman William H. Ashley, the popular and well-known Rocky Mountain fur trader. Though his own term did not begin until November, Boggs took an early oath of office in September 1836 after Governor Dunklin resigned to accept a federal surveyorship.

During his four years as governor, Boggs presided over the incorporation of the Missouri state bank and the construction of a new state capitol in Jefferson City. Vigorously asserting his executive authority,

Boggs created an internal improvements board to promote the building of roads, bridges, canals, and railroads. He also signed into law a comprehensive education bill that authorized a statewide system of public elementary schools, academies, and colleges supported by a permanent school fund and administered by a state superintendent. To crown the system, the landmark legislation provided for the establishment of a state university. In July 1840 construction began at the new University of Missouri campus at Columbia.

Despite these achievements, Boggs's administration was plagued by controversy and hard times. Shortly after Boggs took office, the panic of 1837 struck the nation, and Missouri remained financially depressed for the rest of his term. Huge cost overruns on the capitol building project compounded his difficulties, as did a series of armed conflicts that compelled him to call out the militia three times within two years. In November 1837 Boggs, at the urging of Senator Benton, volunteered the services of 600 militiamen to help suppress the Seminole Indians in southern Florida. Led by Colonel Richard Gentry, the Missourians participated in Colonel Zachary Taylor's victory over the Seminoles at Lake Okeechobee, where Gentry was killed in action. Two years later, in the so-called Honey War, Boggs dispatched the militia to Clark County to resolve a border dispute with authorities in the Iowa Territory.

Boggs's most famous and controversial use of the militia, however, occurred during the Missouri Mormon War of 1838, when he issued his infamous "extermination order." Capping eight years of mounting social tension, the Mormon War had its roots in Joseph Smith's decision to establish a new "Zion" on the western frontier. In 1831 the Mormon prophet sent a group of his followers from his headquarters in Kirtland, Ohio, to Jackson County. Two years later violence erupted between Smith's rapidly expanding colony and its increasingly fearful neighbors. In November 1833 local officials mobilized the Jackson County militia to put down the Mormons and restore order. Boggs, then still lieutenant governor, supported the move and personally intervened to negotiate a settlement that resulted in a complete Mormon surrender. Smith's followers agreed to give up their arms and evacuate across the Missouri River to Clay and Ray counties.

For the next several years, the refugees dwelled peacefully in northern Missouri, and in 1836 the state legislature created the new county of Caldwell as a special Mormon enclave. Unfortunately, the arrival of Smith in January 1838 quickly revived anti-Mormon fears and sentiments. Fleeing financial troubles in Kirtland, the prophet and his complete Ohio entourage settled in Far West, the Caldwell county seat. Violence broke out again in August, and by October open warfare and terrorism engulfed much of northwestern Missouri. Seeking to end the "Mormon problem" once and for all, Boggs, now governor, called out five divisions of the state militia on 27 October and declared, "The Mormons must be treated as enemies, and *must be exterminated or driven from the state* if necessary for the public peace—their outrages are beyond all description" (Gayler, p. 23). After quickly surrounding Far West, the militia succeeded in arresting Smith on 31 October and forcing a complete capitulation the following day. This time the Mormons were ordered to leave Missouri altogether. By the spring of 1839 Smith's entire flock had fled to Illinois.

Though constitutionally barred from succeeding himself as governor in 1840, Boggs forever remained a demon in the eyes of the Mormon church. When an unknown assailant shot and nearly killed him at his home in Independence on 6 May 1842, suspicion quickly fell upon the Mormons and particularly upon Smith's notorious bodyguard, Orrin Porter Rockwell. Neither Rockwell nor anyone else, however, was ever convicted of the crime. The assassination attempt failed to prevent the former governor from making a successful political comeback. Though severely wounded, Boggs managed to win reelection to his old state senate seat in 1842.

Unfortunately, any plans Boggs may have had for a return to higher office were ruined in 1845, when his business failed, and he lost his home and savings. Moving his family to a farm outside of town, Boggs decided to leave Missouri and revive his fortunes in the Mexican territory of California. Joining and later heading a large wagon train of westward bound emigrants over the Oregon and California trails, Boggs set out from St. Joseph on 10 May 1846, just two days after the outbreak of the Mexican War. Six months later he arrived at Sutter's Fort to find California occupied by American troops. Proceeding at once to Sonoma, Boggs opened a new store and post office there in the spring of 1847. In April he accepted an appointment from General Stephen Watts Kearny as alcalde for the Northern District of California. The onset of the California gold rush the following year dramatically improved Boggs's financial affairs. Taking full advantage of his position as a merchant, Boggs outfitted gold-seeking expeditions into the Mother Lode region and began to double as a banker and moneylender. His business thrived, and Boggs swiftly made a fortune, which he invested in farmland acquisitions. In 1849 Sonoma voters selected Boggs as one of their delegates to the state constitutional convention that met in Monterey in September and October. Boggs's failure to attend did not prevent his subsequent election to the state assembly, where he represented Sonoma County in 1852. Later that year Boggs purchased a ranch in the Napa Valley, where he retired to raise cattle. He died at his Napa estate.

• Most of Boggs's personal papers, which he carefully stored in four barrels, were destroyed by his heirs. Boggs's gubernatorial papers, along with the Mormon War Papers collection, are housed at the Missouri State Archives in Jefferson City. The Western Historical Manuscript Collection, jointly maintained by the University of Missouri and the State Historical Society of Missouri, contains six separate collections of Boggs's papers, all located in the Ellis Library on the university's main campus at Columbia. Additional Boggs materials are at the Missouri Historical Society archives in St. Louis.

The most complete sources on Boggs remain Joseph F. Gordon, "The Public Career of Lilburn W. Boggs" (M.A. thesis, Univ. of Missouri-Columbia, 1949); and L. Dean Marriott, "Lilburn W. Boggs: Interaction with Mormons Following Their Expulsion from Missouri" (Ed.D. diss., Brigham Young Univ., 1979). Brief biographical profiles are contained in C. A. Menefee, *Historical and Descriptive Sketch Book of Napa, Sonoma, Lake, and Mendocino Counties* (1873), and the *History of Napa and Lake Counties, California* (1881). Also helpful are William M. Boggs, "A Short Biographical Sketch of Lilburn W. Boggs, by His Son," *Missouri Historical Review* 4 (Jan. 1910): 106–10; Gordon, "The Political Career of Lilburn W. Boggs," *Missouri Historical Review* 52 (Jan. 1958): 111–22; and Monte McLaws, "The Attempted Assassination of Missouri's Ex-Governor, Lilburn W. Boggs," *Missouri Historical Review* 60 (Oct. 1965): 50–62. The extensive literature on the Mormons in Mo. also contains many references to Boggs. This literature is well summarized by Stephen C. LeSueur, *The 1838 Mormon War in Missouri* (1987).

MICHAEL MAGLIARI

BOGLE, Sarah Comly Norris (17 Nov. 1870–11 Jan. 1932), librarian, educator, and administrator, was born in White Deer Mills, Union County, Pennsylvania, the daughter of John Armstrong Bogle, a chemical engineer, and Emma Ridgway Norris. Bogle's early years were typical of those expected of a young woman of her comfortable status. She and her brother John grew up in Milton, Pennsylvania. Bogle was privately tutored until age fourteen when she attended Miss Steven's School in Germantown. Bogle attended the University College of the University of Chicago but did not finish her undergraduate degree. In 1904 she earned a certificate from the library school at Drexel Institute. According to Harrison Craver, "the pleasure of society was no longer sufficient," and she decided to find "more satisfying employment" (Craver, p. 489). Bogle received an M.A. (field unknown) from Juniata College, Huntingdon, Pennsylvania in 1917.

Following her graduation from Drexel, Bogle became the director of the Juniata College Library. She reorganized the library and supervised its move into a new, Carnegie-funded building. Her personal contact with philanthropist Andrew Carnegie and the success of her efforts at Juniata foreshadowed her long and equally successful relationship in the 1920s and the early 1930s with Frederick P. Keppel and the Carnegie Corporation of New York, Carnegie's institutional successors. Bogle left Juniata College in 1907. She worked at the Queens Borough (N.Y.) Public Library in 1909. Recruited by Craver, she joined the Carnegie Library of Pittsburgh (CLP) staff in 1910. Bogle was quickly moved into the dual position of supervisor of children's services and director of the library school at CLP following the forced resignation in 1911 of the school's first director, Frances Jenkins Olcott. Bogle served as the director of the Carnegie Training School for Children's Librarians from 1911 to 1920.

Bogle's work at CLP changed the education of children's and school librarians. The most important change made was Bogle's expectation that applicants have a college degree. By requiring a college education, a condition she could not meet herself, Bogle set an admission criterion that changed the applicant pools significantly. The earlier apprenticeship methods of library education used by the male directors of academic and public libraries had effectively shut out many women. The degree requirement also added credibility to the children's and youth services movement. Women quickly moved into positions of leadership in that developing specialty.

Bogle remained in Pennsylvania until 1920, when at age fifty she finally left the state for the American Library Association (ALA) headquarters in Chicago. But she never really left home. Her widowed mother lived with her as she had done in Pittsburgh. They often vacationed at her brother's home in White Plains, New York. She served as the president of the Association of American Library Schools (AALS) from 1917 to 1918, secretary of the American Library Association's Board of Education for Librarianship from 1923 to 1932, the director and principal fundraiser of ALA's Paris Library School from 1923 to 1929, the ALA liaison member on the University of Chicago Graduate Library School's library curriculum study, and the principal investigator in a study of southern library schools (1930). She was also elected to the ALA Council while at CLP (1917–1920). Unlike her close friends William Warner Bishop and Margaret Mann, Bogle was never an elected officer of the ALA. Assuming the association's assistant secretary position in 1920 preempted any ALA political ambition she may have entertained. Her job as second in command to Carl H. Milam frequently included representing ALA in work with the Carnegie Corporation of New York.

Bogle created and supervised the Paris Library School, which opened in 1923. This American-style library school continued the work started by Jessie M. Carson and the American Committee for Devastated France (CARD), which provided funds and training to assist French public libraries after World War I. The school was the first formal education program for librarians in France; librarians had previously been scholars, archivists, or men of letters. The school closed in 1929 but left a legacy that included an expanded role for women in French libraries; the significant improvement in public library services in France, especially for children; and the importation into the European world of the American "library spirit" characterized by idealism, enthusiasm, and unshakable belief in the far-ranging mission of libraries.

Bogle was the first secretary of the Board of Education for Librarianship (BEL). The BEL, created by the ALA following the Williamson Report (1923), was charged with the evaluation and reorganization of library training, library service, and library certification. Accreditation of library schools, previously done by their own AALS, now shifted to the largest professional association for librarians, the ALA.

Bogle had a significant role in the establishment of the Graduate Library School (GLS) at the University of Chicago (1926) and in the placement and funding of a library school at Hampton University (1925). The Hampton program, under Bogle colleague Florence Rising Curtis, was the first established to offer library education to "Negro librarians." The Southern Study, led by Bogle in 1930, improved training for both black and white librarians. Bogle's work with the GLS textbook/curriculum project included shepherding to print Margaret Mann's milestone, *Introduction to Cataloging and the Classification of Books* (1930).

The complexity and essence of Bogle's personality remain largely undocumented. Louis Round Wilson, University of North Carolina library director, characterized her as "the most able person I've met in librarianship" (Holley, p. 26). Bogle was demanding and expected much from her students, her staff, her colleagues, and her friends. Sarah Vann has suggested that Bogle "would not tolerate any objections to her point of view" (Johnson, p. 339). She provoked strong responses from her contemporaries, both enmity and great admiration. She gave much in return: a humorous touch, a calming intercession, and a professional expertise and dedication that kept her on the job while quietly battling terminal cancer. Bogle died in White Plains, New York. She never married. A driving force in library science education, Bogle guided library schools internationally to higher professional standards.

• Bogle's papers are scattered among several collections, most notably the archives of the American Library Association at the University of Illinois and the William Warner Bishop papers at the Bentley Historical Library, The University of Michigan. Bogle's articles in the library press were generally formally written and are without the humor that decorates her correspondence. "Trends and Tendencies in Education for Librarianship," *Library Journal* 56, no. 22 (15 Dec. 1931): 1029–36, the text of a speech given just months before her death, sums up the profession as she entered it, the many changes in library science education during her lifetime, and her recommendations for the future. Two important biographical sketches are Sarah Vann's in *Notable American Women, 1607–1950* (1971), and Peggy Sullivan's in *Dictionary of American Library Biography* (1978). See Nancy Becker Johnson, "Sarah C. N. Bogle: Librarian at Large" (Ph.D. diss., Univ. of Michigan, 1991) for a more complete treatment. Harrison Craver's extensive memorial remarks appear in *Bulletin of the American Library Association* 26, no. 8 (Aug. 1932): 489–90. Also important in understanding Bogle's contribution are John Richardson, *The Spirit of Inquiry: The Graduate Library School at Chicago, 1921–1951* (1982); Peggy Sullivan, *Carl H. Milam and the American Library Association* (1976); and Edward Holley, "One Hundred Years of Progress: The Growth and Development of Library Education," *ALA Yearbook of Library and Information Services* (1986). An obituary is in the *New York Times*, 12 Jan. 1932.

NANCY BECKER JOHNSON

BOGY, Lewis Vital (9 Apr. 1813–20 Sept. 1877), lawyer and U.S. senator, was born at Ste. Genevieve, Missouri Territory, the son of Joseph Bogy, a lawyer, and Marie Beauvais. He was educated in the common schools and then in 1832 began reading law with Judge Nathaniel Pope in Kaskaskia, Illinois. He served briefly as a private in the Black Hawk War and then enrolled in Transylvania University; he graduated in 1835. He then moved to St. Louis and built an extensive law practice. In 1839 Bogy traveled through Indian Territory, observing the various tribes, and went as far as the Comanche Nation on the Mexican border. From then on he took a keen interest in Indian affairs and primarily sided with those who sought to bring the tribes into the mainstream of American life.

Bogy was elected as a Democrat to the St. Louis Board of Aldermen in 1838 and then to the lower house of the Missouri legislature in 1840, where he served for a single term. In the late 1840s he became heavily involved in developing the iron ore deposits in the Pilot Knob region of the Iron Mountains southwest of St. Louis, and he helped establish the St. Louis and Iron Mountain Railroad to service the area. He returned to Ste. Genevieve in 1849 and joined the anti-Benton wing of the Missouri Democratic party, which overthrew Senator Thomas Hart Benton (1782–1858) because of his opposition to the extension of slavery into new territories. Three years later Bogy opposed Benton unsuccessfully in a contest for the U.S. House of Representatives. Not one to be daunted by defeat, he ran successfully for the Missouri House of Representatives in 1854. By the late 1850s he was back in St. Louis where he ran unsuccessfully for mayor in 1859.

Although he sympathized with the southern cause, Bogy did not actively participate in the movements to take Missouri into the Confederacy at the outbreak of the Civil War. He ran for Congress in 1862 on the Democratic ticket but finished a poor third. In the aftermath of the war, Bogy worked with Francis Preston Blair (1821–1875) and others to revive the Democratic party in opposition to the dominant Radical Republican element, which had established a stringent disfranchisement of ex-Confederates and southern sympathizers. President Andrew Johnson appointed him Commissioner of Indian Affairs in 1867. He served six months with little in the way of accomplishment, and he relinquished the office after he failed to receive Senate confirmation.

With the return of the Democrats to power in Missouri in the early 1870s, Bogy moved to the forefront of the prosouthern, ex-Confederate element within the party. He was elected to the U.S. Senate in 1872 to succeed Blair, following a vigorous contest in the party caucus. In the Senate he was a strong advocate of western interests. He supported legislation to improve the western rivers, including the improvement of the mouth of the Mississippi by the jetty system, and he pushed through Congress a bill to compel the Union Pacific Railroad to prorate its fares with the Kansas Pacific, thus improving traffic through Missouri to St. Louis. He opposed the resumption of specie payment, championing instead the appreciation of paper currency and its acceptance for payment of import duties. He staunchly opposed the continuation of the Republican program of Reconstruction, and he supported the movements to overthrow Radical governments in the

South. He was married to Pelagie Pratte; they had three children. He died at his home in St. Louis.

• No body of Bogy papers is known to exist, nor is there a full-length biography. The best biographical sketches are in L. U. Reavis, *St. Louis, the Future Great City of the World* (1875), and W. V. N. Bay, *Bench and Bar of Missouri* (1878). Additional information can be obtained from the eulogies delivered in the Senate and the House of Representatives at the time of Senator Bogy's death, published in the *Congressional Record*, 45th Cong., 2d sess., 1878, vol. 7, pp. 354–58.

WILLIAM E. PARRISH

BOHLEN, Charles Eustis (30 Aug. 1904–1 Jan. 1974), diplomat, was born in Clayton, New York, the son of Charles Bohlen, a banker, and Celestine Eustis. His mother, the daughter of a U.S. senator and ambassador to France, came from a prominent New Orleans family. Bohlen made frequent boyhood visits to Europe and grew up first in Aitken, South Carolina, and later near Boston. After private schooling he attended Harvard University and graduated in 1927 with a bachelor's degree in European history. Following a period of soul-searching he entered the Foreign Service in March 1929. In an unusual decision, Bohlen chose the Soviet Union as a special field. Initially posted in Prague, he then trained for two and a half years in Russian language and culture in Paris and, for two summers, in Estonia. In February 1934 he joined the staff of the first American embassy to the Soviet Union under William C. Bullitt. Occupied mainly with the task of news analysis, he used the opportunities for travel and social intercourse that were still available in the brief interlude between the disastrous famine and the Communist party purges.

In 1935 Bohlen was transferred to Washington and shortly thereafter married Avis Thayer; they had three children. Two years of diverse assignments followed, first in the office of the undersecretary of state, then in the Division of East European Affairs. He participated in the Brussels conference of 1937, which was held to discuss Japan's invasion of China. In 1938 he was again posted to Moscow, where the purge trials now dominated the scene. The former comparative freedom of movement and association was gone, and Bohlen saw a more ruthless generation of leaders emerging under Joseph Stalin. From May 1939 he was repeatedly approached by a friendly German colleague who revealed, well before its consummation in August, the unfolding German-Soviet rapprochement. Secretary of State Cordell Hull conveyed this information to the British and French governments, but to no effect. At the end of 1940 Bohlen was transferred to Tokyo, where the embassy required a Soviet specialist. He was interned after Pearl Harbor until his repatriation in mid-1942.

In late 1943 Hull chose Bohlen as his interpreter and adviser on Soviet affairs for the Foreign Ministers' conference at Moscow. This led to his selection as President Franklin D. Roosevelt's interpreter for the summit conference at Teheran in November 1943. His performance there impressed Harry Hopkins, the president's principal aide, who arranged Bohlen's appointment as chief of the Division of East European Affairs. He now became the main liaison between the White House and the State Department, a role made necessary by both the growing accumulation of diplomatic business and the continuing inability of Roosevelt and Hull to work together effectively. "Through the accident of fate," Bohlen later recalled, "my career had been fundamentally altered. I had leaped over the barrier that insulated the State Department from decision-making at the White House." He again interpreted for Roosevelt at the Yalta conference in February 1945. He had by now modified his hitherto critical views of Soviet conduct to conform to the more hopeful White House outlook. He approved the president's aims at Yalta and, despite reservations about the Far Eastern and United Nations membership arrangements made there, generally defended the agreements and blamed Stalin for violating them. Between Yalta and Roosevelt's death on 12 April, Bohlen composed the first drafts of most if not all the president's correspondence with Stalin and Winston Churchill.

He continued to play an important role in the early Cold War years. He accompanied Hopkins to Moscow in May 1945 on the latter's mission of conciliation. He interpreted for President Harry S. Truman at the ensuing Potsdam conference and was a key adviser of secretaries of state James F. Byrnes, George C. Marshall, and Dean Acheson. Bohlen became increasingly critical of the Soviets, but through late 1945, reflecting perhaps a continuing Rooseveltian optimism and the neo-accommodationist thinking of Secretary Byrnes, he suggested that the United States might accept a Soviet nonexclusive, "open" sphere of influence in Eastern Europe, a stratagem Arthur J. Schlesinger, Jr., has aptly called "the Bohlen plan of trying diplomacy first." In early 1946, however, he adapted to the emerging, more confrontational line that was being pressed by his colleague George F. Kennan. Promoted to counselor in 1947, Bohlen attended nearly all the significant postwar conferences. He was one of the principal architects of the Marshall Plan, and he headed the departmental committee that monitored the Berlin crisis in 1948. Less close to Acheson than to Marshall, Bohlen nevertheless remained influential during Truman's second term. He served first as Minister in the Paris embassy and then returned in mid-1951 to Washington, where he was closely involved with the diplomacy of the Korean War.

Bohlen's 1953 nomination by President Dwight D. Eisenhower as U.S. ambassador to the Soviet Union brought him into a turbulent public arena. His appointment was vigorously opposed by Senator Joseph R. McCarthy and other conservative senators, who portrayed him as the symbol of "Yalta appeasement." Secretary of State John Foster Dulles, himself the protagonist of a tougher line with Moscow, offered only lukewarm support. Eisenhower's firm commitment and Bohlen's sturdy defense of Roosevelt's conduct at Yalta prevailed, however, in what was widely seen as a substantial check to McCarthy's dominance.

From Moscow Bohlen interpreted the events of the post-Stalin era with prescience, though he failed to anticipate the rise of Nikita Khrushchev or the Soviet decision in 1956 to suppress the Hungarian uprising. Bohlen's ambassadorship was, arguably, a period when U.S.-Soviet relations might have undergone a substantial improvement. Khrushchev characterized Bohlen as "a shameless reactionary"—a revealing counterpoint to McCarthy's attack from the right. In fact, of course, Dulles set the tone of American diplomacy. On several occasions, moreover, Bohlen urged a conciliatory gesture. In 1955 he successfully urged Eisenhower, over Dulles's objections, to meet with Khrushchev. It remains true, however, that Bohlen regarded the Soviets as "implacably hostile" and was generally pessimistic about their intentions.

In 1957 Dulles, after falsely representing to Eisenhower that Bohlen wished to devote himself to writing, succeeded in transferring him to the ambassadorial post in Manila—a comparative backwater. Upon Dulles's death in 1959, however, Secretary of State Christian A. Herter (1895–1966) recalled Bohlen to Washington as his principal Soviet adviser, a role that he continued to occupy in the Kennedy administration. President John F. Kennedy consulted him frequently. He attended the Vienna summit meeting in 1961 and was deeply involved in the tense confrontation over Berlin that followed. He was also a prominent actor in the Cuban missile crisis of late 1962, as the first to advocate the "blockade" strategy.

In the midst of this confrontation Bohlen assumed his last foreign post as ambassador to France, where he remained until February 1968 and made the best of a difficult task. In this role he had to contend with President Charles de Gaulle's robust effort to diminish American influence in Europe, which culminated in the French withdrawal from the military structure of the North Atlantic Treaty Organization in 1966. Bohlen concluded his career with a short term as deputy undersecretary of state for political affairs from 1967 to 1969. He finally retired in early 1969 and spent much of his time thereafter lecturing and writing his memoirs. He died in Washington, D.C.

Identified by a poll of professional colleagues in the late 1960s as "the ideal diplomat," Bohlen was more consistently associated with the great issues of American foreign relations between 1943 and 1968 than any other man. He characterized himself simply as a "witness" to history. Yet he was consulted and trusted by every president in this period and by all but one secretary of state. The scope and character of his influence is hard to establish precisely. It undoubtedly owed much to his unusually pleasing personality and the affectionate regard in which he was widely held, and much also to what his friend and colleague George F. Kennan called his reluctance "to fight the prevailing trends." That reticence perhaps reflected a certain temperamental placidity, but it sprang too from a traditional conception of the diplomat's role as that of adviser rather than policy formulator and from the fact that he fully shared the prevailing ethos of his time. His ultimate significance derives from his ability to serve a postwar generation of American leaders whose fundamental opposition to Soviet expansionism and communism he helped, within the deepest recesses of government, to encourage, shape, and translate into policy.

• Bohlen's papers are located in the Library of Congress. A collection of his correspondence and memoranda is in the State Department records in the National Archives, and an oral history interview is in the Columbia University Library. His two publications are *The Transformation of American Foreign Policy* (1969), based on lectures given at Columbia University in April 1969, and a memoir, *Witness to History, 1929–1969* (1973). T. Michael Ruddy, *The Cautious Diplomat: Charles E. Bohlen and the Soviet Union, 1929–1969* (1986), treats his professional career. There are many accounts of Bohlen in the memoirs of contemporaries and in historical works such as Daniel Yergin, *Shattered Peace* (1977), and Walter Isaacson and Evan Thomas, *The Wise Men* (1986). An obituary is in the *New York Times*, 2 Jan. 1974.

FRASER J. HARBUTT

BOIES, Horace (7 Dec. 1827–4 Apr. 1923), governor of Iowa, was born near Aurora in Erie County, New York, the son of Eber Boies and Esther Henshaw, farmers. Educated irregularly in country schools, Boies went west to Wisconsin Territory when he was sixteen and worked as a farm laborer. He returned to New York in 1847 and in 1848 married Adella King, a childhood sweetheart. They had one daughter. Adella encouraged him to read law, and after he was admitted to the bar in 1852, he practiced in the village of Hamburg and in Buffalo. Adella died in 1855, and in 1858 Boies married Versalia Barber; they had three children.

Boies was originally a Whig, but in 1857 he was elected as a Republican to the New York legislature. Redistricting apparently checked his political aspirations, and in 1859 he returned to the law. In 1867 he again went west, this time to Waterloo, Iowa, where his second wife's parents had moved. His very successful legal practice in Waterloo allowed him to purchase hundreds of acres of rich farmlands in adjacent counties, which led to the rather bogus sobriquet of "Farmer Boies " in later political contests. Boies's unseamed appearance belied such a tag. A conservative, lawyerly style marked his political career, and a modest manner distinguished his character.

When moralistic Iowa Republicans pushed through a constitutional amendment that made the state "dry" in 1882, Boies entered Iowa politics as a Democrat. In numerous public addresses he argued that the amendment invaded individual rights and took private property without compensation. The amendment was declared unconstitutional by the Iowa Supreme Court on the technicality that the Iowa House and Iowa Senate had approved different versions. Republicans then passed a prohibitory law. Democrats welcomed prohibition as an issue and in 1889 nominated Boies for governor. Ethnocultural influences, especially in heavily Irish and German Mississippi River cities, best explain his election in 1889. Boies belonged to a temperance society, but as governor he advocated local option and license laws. He said in his first inaugural message, "He who strives for this is not the foe of temperance, but is the friend of a state too grand in its natural advantages, too broad in the diversity of its interests, too widely at variance in the education, habits, and customs of its people to be appropriated by any single class or sect." Republicans kept control of the general assembly, and Boies failed to secure a local option law. In other respects, his governorship was uneventful. No agrarian radical, he said in his second inaugural message,"I cannot avoid the conclusion that we legislate too much." He did balance the state's budget.

As the first Democratic governor since the Civil War of one of the citadels of Republicanism, Boies became something of a spokesman for western farmers. In 1890 he attacked protective tariffs in a New York speech on "What Our Farmers Have a Right to Demand," insisting that tariffs lowered farm prices and increased farm costs and that farmers had a right to demand impartial legislation. After his reelection as governor in 1891, Boies was heralded by some as a contender for the Democratic presidential nomination, and his name was placed in nomination at the 1892 convention. Former president Grover Cleveland won the nomination and the November election. Boies declined Cleveland's offer to become secretary of agriculture and instead remained governor of Iowa. His 1893 bid for a third term failed after Iowa Republicans dropped prohibition and accepted local option.

Boies remained politically active, but his conservative sensibilities were evident in an 1894 address at the Iowa State Democratic Convention, in which he attacked Eugene V. Debs's leadership of the American Railway Union's strike against the Pullman company. The strike led to a boycott against Pullman cars and tied up all midwestern railroads. Boies's name was again placed before the Democratic National Convention in 1896, but his equivocal views on "free silver" were displaced by the "cross of gold" rhetoric of William Jennings Bryan. In addition, Illinois governor John Peter Altgeld, a supporter of the Pullman strikers, dismissed Boies as antilabor. Boies appeared increasingly detached from the 1890s world of financial panic, populist uprising, and labor conflict. Like Cleveland and other moderate Democrats, Boies was uncomfortable in the new urban-industrial society and he retired from politics. He died at his winter home in Long Beach, California.

• The State Historical Society of Iowa has small collections of Boies's correspondence and letter books in its libraries in Iowa City and Des Moines. His messages as governor are in Benjamin Shambaugh, ed., *The Messages and Proclamations of the Governors of Iowa*, vol. 6 (1904). Boies's importance in Iowa politics is discussed in Jean B. Kern, "The Political Career of Horace Boies," *Iowa Journal of History* 47 (1949): 215–46. Richard J. Jensen, *The Winning of the Midwest: Social and Political Conflict, 1888–1896* (1971), deals with the issue of prohibition in Iowa and places Boies in the context of ethnocultural politics and moralistic Republicanism. Jeffrey Ostler, *Prairie Populism: The Fate of Agrarian Radicalism in Kansas, Nebraska, and Iowa, 1880–1892* (1993), does not make a populist or a radical out of Boies. An obituary is in the *Waterloo Courier*, 5 Apr. 1923.

ALAN R. JONES

BOISEN, Anton Theophilus (29 Oct. 1876–1 Oct. 1965), educator and Presbyterian minister, was born in Bloomington, Indiana, the son of Hermann B. Boisen and Louise Wylie. Because his father was a university professor and his maternal grandfather a Presbyterian pastor and university professor, Boisen was steeped in both academic and ecclesiastical traditions. His mother was the first woman to enroll at Indiana University, from which she graduated in 1871. Boisen's middle name stemmed from his maternal grandfather, Theophilus Wiley, chairman of the Department of Pure Mathematics at Indiana University and a Scotch-Irish Reformed Presbyterian minister, into whose home the family moved after Hermann Boisen died at age thirty-eight.

Extremely shy, Anton Boisen was brilliant and intense. He graduated in 1897 from Indiana University, and, although he felt called to the ministry, he taught German and French, first in high school and then as a tutor at Indiana University. During this period he suffered the first of several psychotic episodes. When given the chance for further study, he turned to forestry, graduating in 1905 from the Yale University School of Forestry.

After working for the U.S. Forest Service—and after a second psychotic episode—he entered Union Theological Seminary in New York City, from which he graduated in 1911. At Union he absorbed the theological liberalism of William Adams Brown and George Albert Coe, thus beginning a lifelong interest in science and in a theology amenable to empirical verification and correction. Yet he never lost the Calvinist concern with sin and salvation.

Transferring from the Presbyterian to the Congregational church, Boisen labored for the next ten years in rural church survey work, in rural pastorates in Kansas and Maine, and for two years during World War I with the YMCA in Europe. Returning from Europe in 1917, he again suffered a breakdown, but when he accepted an offer to join the Interchurch World Movement and moved to North Dakota to conduct a rural survey for this Protestant ecumenical effort, his symptoms disappeared.

When the Interchurch World Movement collapsed in 1920, Boisen again fell victim to psychosis, and his family had him hospitalized at Westboro State Hospital. It took him fifteen months to recover. During this time, he recorded the symptoms of his illness and the progress of his recovery in letters to friends, and the experience convinced him that some mental illnesses were problem-solving experiences, attempts at reorganization in times of crisis. He eventually attributed his own illness to a complex of events linked to his feelings of guilt about sex, of inferiority, of grief at the early loss of his father, and of pain for the unrequited love of his lifelong friend, Alice Batchelder, but he also theorized that mental breakdowns, including his own, could have a religious dimension.

After his release, Boisen began studies in the psychology of religion at Andover Theological Seminary, an affiliate of Harvard Divinity School, where he remained from 1922 to 1924 working especially with the physician and ethicist Richard Cabot. In 1924 William Bryan of the Worcester (Mass.) State Hospital invited Boisen to become a hospital chaplain, and the following year, encouraged by Cabot, he inaugurated at the hospital a program in the clinical training of theological students. At the same time, he began a five-year stint lecturing each fall quarter to students in the social ethics department of Chicago Theological Seminary. Although his emerging theories alienated Cabot, he began to explore more deeply the notion that mental illness often represented a crisis brought about by the failure to grow into higher social loyalties, including loyalty to God, and by the effort to overcome that failure. Some cases of mental illness were attempts by people to reorganize their sense of the world. In these cases, mental illness was purposive, and the curative powers of religion could facilitate its cure.

Boisen's program of clinical training taught students that by studying the "living human documents" whom they found in the mental hospital, they could learn something about both health and religious experience. In 1930 he joined with others in forming the Council for the Clinical Training of Theological Students, which would expose students for extended periods to people suffering illness and crisis, mainly in mental hospitals. In the same year, however, the death of his mother helped to precipitate still another brief period of mental illness.

In 1932 Boisen became chaplain at Elgin State Hospital near Chicago. While there he also organized a Chicago Council for the Clinical Training of Theological Students, functioning effectively until he learned in 1935 that his friend Alice Batchelder was dying of cancer. The discovery resulted in his brief hospitalization in Baltimore, Maryland, but in December 1935 he returned to his chaplaincy post at Elgin. In 1936 he published his ideas about religion and mental health in his influential *Exploration of the Inner World.* He subsequently remained free of symptoms and worked as the chaplain—and then chaplain emeritus—at Elgin until his death.

Influenced by such psychologists as William James, Carl Jung, and Harry Stack Sullivan, on the one hand, and by such philosophers as George Herbert Mead, Josiah Royce, and William Ernest Hocking, on the other, Boisen came to think of the church as a social group of imperfect persons that could serve a therapeutic purpose. He explicated his religious views in countless articles and several other books, notably *Religion in Crisis and Custom* (1955) and *Out of the Depths* (1960), his autobiography. He died in Chicago.

Boisen's most noteworthy achievement was his program in clinical training, which became a prominent part of ministerial education in seminaries and clinical education centers throughout the United States. He exercised influence on the early development of mental health counseling, on the appropriation of psychology by theological schools, and on the burgeoning conversation between leaders in religion and in mental health. No other single person had greater influence on the efforts of Protestant churches to incorporate the insights of psychology into their ministries.

• Boisen's *Out of the Depths* (1960) remains the best source about his life. See also Edward E. Thornton, *Professional Education for Ministry: A History of Clinical Pastoral Education* (1970); E. Brooks Holifield, *A History of Pastoral Care in America* (1983); Robert C. Powell, *CPE: Fifty Years of Learning through Supervised Encounter with Living Human Documents* (1975); and Hugh W. Sanborn, *Mental-Spiritual Health Models: An Analysis of the Models of Boisen, Hiltner, and Clinebell* (1979).

MARSEILLE M. PRIDE

BOISSEVAIN, Inez Milholland (6 Aug. 1886–25 Nov. 1916), lawyer, feminist, and suffrage activist, was born in Brooklyn, New York, the daughter of John Elmer Milholland, a reporter and editorial writer, and Jean Torrey. Her father supported many reforms, among them world peace, civil rights, and woman suffrage. It was probably through his influence that Inez acquired her sense of moral justice and her activist stance.

Boissevain was educated in New York City, London, and Berlin and attended Vassar College from 1905 through 1909. An athletic young woman, she was the captain of the hockey team and a member of the 1909 track team; she also set a record in the basketball throw. Athletics were not the only extracurricular activities that appealed to her. She delivered speeches to students on socialism and women's rights, which drew criticism from faculty members. To prove her points she employed dramatic measures, once demonstrating the ridiculousness of women wearing their hair long by growing hers so long that she could sit on it.

Boissevain's appearance caused student audiences to gasp "at her goddess-like beauty" when she delivered her lectures on "the Social Problem and the College Girl." Taking the platform for woman suffrage, she delivered dynamic speeches, through which she convinced two-thirds of Vassar's students to join her suffrage club. Subsequently she and around forty students assembled in a cemetery to hear suffragist Harriot Stanton Blatch when she visited the campus and was forbidden from holding a meeting on school grounds.

After receiving a B.A. from Vassar in 1909, Boissevain entered the Law School of New York University, one of the few major law schools allowing women to enroll. Her reform campaigns continued while she attended law school. Parading down Fifth Avenue with a megaphone, she called for "votes for women!" Arguing for woman suffrage in 1912, she reasoned, "Women are the mothers of the race, and as such are admittedly more concerned than anyone else with all that goes to protect life" (quoted in Banner, p. 114). She took up the cause of labor reform, picketing with women shirtwaist workers during their strike, for which she was arrested with fourteen other women.

Boissevain received her LL.B. in 1912. Admitted to the bar, she joined the New York law firm of Osborne, Lamb, and Garvan and handled criminal and divorce cases. In one of her first assignments, she investigated conditions at Sing Sing prison. Although female contact with male prisoners was frowned upon, Boissevain talked personally to the men to uncover the horrendous conditions. She prepared the documentation that went into a report exposing the poor prison conditions.

While championing the rights of others, Boissevain dreamed that others might one day have "at least as much as" she had. Her causes were far-reaching: in addition to prison reform, she sought world peace and worked for equality for African Americans. She was a socialist and a member of the National Association for the Advancement of Colored People, the Women's Trade Union League, the Equality League of Self Supporting Women in New York (later the Women's Political Union), the National Child Labor Committee, and England's Fabian Society. For a brief period in 1913 she edited the "Department for Women" for *McClure's Magazine* and contributed a number of articles to the publication.

Her interest in suffrage led Boissevain in 1913 to join the militant Congressional Union, later called the National Woman's Party (NWP). Called the "American Joan of Arc," she marched in parades carrying a banner inscribed with the slogan "Forward Out of Darkness, Forward into Light." The NWP eventually used the phrase for its official slogan. She gained much public attention for suffrage when she appeared in a parade wearing a white Cossack robe and riding astride a white horse named "Gray Dawn."

In 1903 Boissevain had been romantically linked to Guglielmo Marconi, the inventor of the wireless. Although he proposed marriage, the engagement was short. Ten years later her reform endeavors brought her into contact with the colorful artists and radicals living in Greenwich Village, one of whom was Max Eastman, the editor of *Masses* magazine. She aided Eastman, who shared her radical vision, in raising funds for the magazine, and she participated in its defense during a 1913 libel suit. Their shared passions led to romance. However, that summer she met Eugen Jan Boissevain, a New York importer, aboard a ship. They married in July 1913 in London, England; they had no children. She admitted to proposing to Boissevain first, and she referred to this initiative as being a woman's "new freedom."

At the start of World War I, Boissevain traveled overseas as a war correspondent for a Canadian newspaper to gain access to the front lines. From that vantage point she composed pacifist articles, which led to her censure by the Italian government, which finally ousted her from the country. In another effort to bring about world peace, Boissevain sailed on Henry Ford's "Peace Ship," but she left the ship in Stockholm because the venture was unorganized and dissension had ensued between passengers.

In 1916 Boissevain was appointed by the NWP as a special flying envoy, commissioned to convince enfranchised women in twelve western states with equal suffrage to endorse a federal suffrage amendment. "Together we shall stand shoulder to shoulder for the greatest principle the world has known, the right of self-government," she said at a rally that year. Her battle cry as she crossed the states was that women had to stand up for one another "until the fight is won." Despite the admonitions of her family, who were concerned about her deteriorating health and her lingering case of pernicious anemia, Boissevain maintained a full schedule of travel and speechmaking until she collapsed during an appearance and speech in Los Angeles. Ten weeks later she died in a Los Angeles hospital after a series of blood transfusions, recoveries, and setbacks.

Boissevain, who was only thirty years old at the time of her death, became a martyr for the cause of suffrage, particularly because she died while working for the vote. Suffragists gathered in the Capitol in Washington, D.C., on Christmas Day and Inauguration Day. Their plea to President Woodrow Wilson was on a banner penned with Boissevain's final words, "Mr. President, how long must women wait for liberty?" In a tribute to Boissevain, Mount Discovery in the Adirondacks was renamed Mount Inez.

An idealist filled with aspirations to "liberate humanity," Boissevain declared that she could not "be happy while others are not." Her radical viewpoints were dramatized by her abilities as a speaker, which were enhanced by her striking beauty. In life she brought attention to societal ills in need of reform and to the cause of woman suffrage; in her death she became a hero for women who yearned to move forward in liberty.

• Information on Boissevain can be found in Harriot Stanton Blatch and Alma Lutz, *Challenging Years: The Memoirs of Harriot Stanton Blatch* (1940); Max Eastman, *Enjoyment of Living* (1948); Allen Churchill, *The Improper Bohemians: A Re-creation of Greenwich Village in Its Heyday* (1959); Degna Marconi, *My Father Marconi* (1962); S. Josephine Baker, *Fighting for Life* (1939; repr. 1974); Lois W. Banner, *Women in Modern America: A Brief History* (1974); Electra Clark, *Leading Ladies: An Affectionate Look at American Women of the Twentieth Century* (1976); Lynn Sherr, *The American Women's Gazetteer* (1976); Inez Haynes Irwin, *The Story of Alice Paul and the National Women's Party* (1977); Alan Covey, ed., *A Century of Women* (1994); Ellen Carol DuBois, "Working Women, Class Relations, and Suffrage Militance," in *One Woman, One Vote: Rediscovering the Woman Suffrage Movement*, ed. Marjorie Spruill Wheeler (1995); and Doris Stevens, *Jailed for Freedom: American Women Win the Vote*, rev. ed. (1995). An obituary is in the *New York Times*, 27 Nov. 1916.

MARILYN ELIZABETH PERRY

BOIT, Elizabeth Eaton (9 July 1849–14 Nov. 1932), textile manufacturer, was born in Newton, Massachusetts, the daughter of James Henry Boit, a janitor and sexton, and Amanda Church Berry. Boit attended Newton public schools and completed two years at Lasell Seminary in Auburndale, Massachusetts. At eighteen she was hired as a timekeeper in the finishing department at Dudley Hosiery Knitting Mill in Newton. She was rewarded for her leadership skills by promotion to assistant forewoman of the finishing department and by 1872 to forewoman. In 1883 the agent of the mill, H. B. Scudder, hired Boit to superintend the manufacturing of children's scarlet-wool goods and hosiery at his newly established Allston Mills, a position that was normally held by a man.

After five years the mill was sold, and in 1888 Boit became the first woman to establish proprietorship in the textile industry. She founded Winship, Boit & Co. in partnership with Charles N. Winship, the head of the knitting department at Allston Mills. In 1888 the firm established the Harvard Knitting Mill in Cambridge, Massachusetts, for the manufacture of women's undergarments. Their initial investment, combined with their knowledge of textile manufacturing, guaranteed their success. Boit was general superintendent of the finishing department and managed the finances, while Winship supervised the knitting departments. They produced approximately twenty dozen garments per day, with three knitting machines, five finishing machines, and a work force of twenty-five seamstresses.

In 1889 the company moved to the growing suburban town of Wakefield, Massachusetts, where they could draw from a larger pool of female employees. By 1896 the firm employed 160 persons in the mill and an additional 200 pieceworkers to produce 300 dozen garments a day of men's, women's, and children's wear. The following year profits reached $250,000 annually, and expansion was imminent. A new Harvard Knitting Mill was erected in 1897, furnished with state-of-the-art machinery and appliances. The mill produced top-quality merchandise, particularly women's underwear, made of cotton, silk, and wool, which was sold under the brand names "Merode" and "Forest Mills." The merchandise was distributed, first by William Iselin & Company of New York City and then by Lord and Taylor of New York and Brown, Durrell of Boston.

Winship and Boit's allegiance to producing quality knit goods led to consistently increased sales, expansions of the plant in 1901, 1903, 1907, and 1911, and elevation of the standards of the American textile industry in general. At the height of production the mill covered 8.5 acres of floor space and employed 850 workers, who worked on 500 knitting and 500 sewing machines to produce 2,000 garments daily. In 1910 it was the fifth largest knitting mill in Massachusetts (by number of employees). Winship, Boit & Co. provided thousands of undergarments for the U.S. Army and Navy during World War I and World War II and grew to have a volume of over $1 million. In the late 1920s, though she continued to visit the mill daily, Boit turned the business over to the Winship family. From 1934 to 1956 Walter B. Winship was president and Charles N. Winship was treasurer.

Boit's success had a great deal to do with how much she invested in her employees, both monetarily and personally. She improved the quality of life of her female employees by improving working conditions, supporting high moral standards, and establishing an employee savings program. It was not unusual for Boit to arrange for streetcars to transport her employees home when it rained. Her company was known throughout the manufacturing industry for offering to its employees a fifty-fifty profit-sharing plan, which began in 1920. By 1927 $228,000 of company profits had been distributed to employees.

Boit's philanthropic interests went beyond the walls of her mill and extended to the community. As director of the Wakefield Cooperative Bank, she had the opportunity to spread her ideas on thrift for the economic betterment of the community. The bank was organized in 1887 to provide a "means of systematic savings" and to "provide an easy method for a person to pay for his home" (Eaton, p. 182). In 1894 she funded the erection of the Wakefield Home for Aged Women and served as its treasurer. The furnished home sheltered aging Protestant women who had been residents of the town of Wakefield for not less than ten years. Boit remained involved in the home until her death. In 1921 the board of managers recommended "that the name of the Wakefield Home for Aged Women be changed to the Elizabeth E. Boit Home for Aged Women in recognition of Miss Boit's great generosity to the Home since the foundation, and of her faithful assistance in the management of the affairs of the Home" (Eaton, p. 229).

Boit contributed to other charities, such as the Ladies' Aid Society of Massachusetts, and served as treasurer of the Kosmos Club, a literary organization that worked "to broaden and strengthen the moral, social, and intellectual life of its members and through them to make itself a power for good in the community" (Eaton, p. 214). In 1905 the club established a fund from which selected Wakefield high school students could borrow money for their college education. Boit was a benefactor to many local churches besides her own, the First Baptist Church of Wakefield. She never married. She was considered a generous hostess and entertained in her built-to-order stucco house, where she lived with companion Emma May Bartlett. She died in Wakefield.

• Biographical information on Boit appears in Julia Ward Howe, *Sketches of Representative Women of New England* (1904). Edwin P. Conklin, *Middlesex County and Its People* (1927), includes an entry on Charles Winship in addition to an entry on Boit. For information on the history of Wakefield, see William E. Eaton, *History of Wakefield (Middlesex County) Massachusetts* (1944), and *Proceedings of the 250th Anniversary of the Ancient Town of Redding* (1896). Information about Boit's firm may be found in textile directories, *Davison's Textile Blue Book* and *Official American Textile Directory*.

Obituaries are in the *Wakefield Daily Item*, 15, 16, and 17 Nov. 1932; the *Boston Globe*, 15 Nov. 1932; and the *New York Times*, 15 Nov. 1932.

BARBARA L. CICCARELLI

BÓJNOWSKI, Lucyan (5 Feb. 1868–28 July 1960), priest of the Roman Catholic church, was born in the village of Świerzbutowo, county of Sokólka, province of Grodno, in the Russian-dominated part of partitioned Poland. His parents, Stanisław Bójnowski and Aleksandra Maciejewska, were of Polish *szlachta* or petty landowning noble rank. After graduation from a traditional European Gymnasium (1888) in the town of Suwałki, near his birthplace, Bójnowski decided to join the wave of Polish immigrants to the New World.

Bójnowski arrived in New York City in 1888 almost penniless. He spent one year working as a farmhand in Glastonbury, Connecticut, in order to achieve the financial means for a choice of career or vocation. It is not known when he decided to become a priest. In 1889 he entered the Seminary of SS. Cyril and Methodius, founded in Detroit, Michigan, in 1885 to prepare Polish-speaking priests for service in Polish immigrant parishes.

Little is known of his record in the seminary (1889–1894). He completed his preparation for the priesthood at St. John's Seminary, Brighton, Massachusetts, in 1895 and was ordained a priest in Hartford, Connecticut, in 1895. After briefly holding two positions as a curate, he was assigned on 10 September 1895 as pastor of the recently organized parish of St. Casimir the Prince, renamed in 1896 the parish of the Sacred Heart of Jesus, New Britain, Connecticut, where he spent the rest of his life.

The Polish immigrant community of New Britain was in many ways similar to immigrant communities throughout the United States. Bewildered, disorganized, lacking an intelligentsia to lead them, these peasants turned factory workers looked to the local pastor for guidance. Father Bójnowski took command of this growing community and, through sheer authoritarian will, raised it to extraordinary heights of religious and community achievement.

The most visible problem faced by Polish immigrants was the taunts of both American nativists and Irish immigrants to forgo their "foreignness" and become Americans as soon as possible. Bójnowski instinctively recognized the danger in such acculturation, which could divide the community into young "Americanizers" and an older generation of traditionalists. Such a generational division could lead to rootlessness and family disintegration. As an antidote, he taught them to value their Polish background while at the same time educating themselves to become American citizens by learning the English language and participating in the political life of the wider New Britain community. He envisioned a bilingual and bicultural community in which both Polish and American values could ultimately merge into a new culture.

Bójnowski adopted a slogan from the leadership of the failed Polish insurrection of 1863: work, study, prayer, emulation. He counseled his parishioners to work and study to improve themselves, to pray for divine guidance, and to emulate those, like the Irish, who were gradually overcoming the handicaps of their foreign background. His grand vision entailed a "cradle-to-grave" plan to build the institutions that a community needs to satisfy human wants. Aside from the church as the first priority, he established a school (1896) and staffed it with a new religious order of nuns—the Daughters of the Immaculate Conception—founded by himself (1904); he established a weekly newspaper, *Przewodnik Katolicki* (*Catholic Leader*), to inform and educate his parishioners (1907); he established an orphanage staffed by his nuns (1904); he built St. Lucian's Home for the Aged (1925); he rescued St. Joseph's Immigrant Home in New York City from bankruptcy (1925) then used it as a home for working girls; and finally, he planned a hospital for the Polish community, for which he began to gather funds as early as 1921, but this part of his vision remained a blueprint, undoubtedly beyond the financial ability of his parish to achieve.

Father Bójnowski scolded and shamed and drove his parishioners in his sermons and in his newspaper to the point that a minority revolted against him. Underlying the confrontation between Bójnowski and the dissidents before World War I was the movement of independency, which had spread to many Polish immigrant communities and which resulted in the formation of the schismatic Polish National Catholic church (1907). Both ownership of parish properties and the right of the laity to choose the clergy of the parish were the major issues, suggesting the impact of American Protestant cultural values.

After World War I another, more serious challenge awaited him. This was the "crisis of 1927" when the first-generation children of Polish immigrants revolted against his "undemocratic, un-American ways." This struggle drew the concern of the entire city, for Father Bójnowski was known to have influenced his parishioners to maintain labor peace, and it was feared that turmoil in the parish might lead to industrial unrest.

The result of this "crisis" was the founding of New Britain's second Polish parish, Holy Cross Church. Although Father Bójnowski's influence in New Britain had diminished, he continued to play an influential role in all the issues that dominated the life of Polish-American communities in the first half of the twentieth century. Among these were the "equality of right" campaign by the Polish-American clergy to achieve an honorable representation of Polish bishops in the American hierarchy; the creation of a Polish-American army in World War I; the political debate over the Józef Pilsudski dictatorship in Poland (1926–1939); and the struggle to maintain Poland's honor and independence against her Nazi and Soviet oppressors during and after World War II. His position in all these issues was guided by loyalty to his church and his Polish-American patriotism.

Father Bójnowski was awarded the title of "right reverend monsignor" by Pope Pius XII in 1945. The last decade of his active pastorate was spent trying to extend his charitable activity beyond New Britain. He founded Sancta Maria Hospital in Cambridge, Massachusetts, and a mission school in cooperation with the Jesuit fathers in Lusaka, Northern Rhodesia.

Bójnowski died in the rectory of Sacred Heart of Jesus Church in New Britain. His parishioners always referred to him simply as "Father B." To his opponents he was "the tsar of Broad Street." Outside the community that he helped to build, the eulogies were an encomium to unsung greatness, as the diocesan newspaper, the *Catholic Leader*, summarized with the epitaph: *Exegi monumentum, aere perennius* (I have created a monument more enduring than bronze).

• The principal unpublished sources on Rev. Msgr. Lucyan Bójnowski are at the rectory of the Church of the Sacred Heart of Jesus, New Britain, Conn., and at the Motherhouse of the Daughters of the Immaculate Conception, New Britain, Conn. Among them is a daily diary of his journey in 1931 to South America, Palestine, Rome, Germany, and Poland. Msgr. Bójnowski's published writings are twofold: his *Historja Parafji polskich w Diecezji Hartfordskiej, w stanie Connecticut, w Stanach Zjednoczonych* [A history of Polish parishes in the Hartford diocese, state of Connecticut, U.S.A.] (1939), which is really an *apologia pro vita sua*; and his weekly newspaper published from 1907 to 1957, available, with some lacunae, at the Center for Research Libraries, Chicago, Ill. The only biography is by Daniel S. Buczek, *Immigrant Pastor: The Life of the Right Rev. Msgr. Lucyan Bójnowski* (1974). A comparison of his work with that of two other priests has been written by Buczek, "Three Generations of the Polish Immigrant Church: Changing Styles of Pastoral Leadership," in *Pastor of the Poles: Polish American Essays*, ed. S. A. Blejwas and M. B. Biskupski (1982). Of related interest is Blejwas, *A Polish Community in Transition: The Origins and Evolution of Holy Cross Parish, New Britain, Connecticut* (1977, 1978), which presents the "crisis of 1927" from the perspective of the dissidents. Obituaries are in the *Catholic Leader*, 12 Aug. 1960, and *Catholic Transcript*, 4 Aug. 1960.

DANIEL S. BUCZEK

BOK, Bart Jan (28 Apr. 1906–5 Aug. 1983), astronomer, was born Bartholomeus Jan Bok in Hoorn, Holland, the son of Jan Bok, a soldier, and Gesina Annetta Van Der Lee. He grew up in Haarlem and The Hague and completed undergraduate studies in astronomy at the University of Leiden in 1927. He then entered graduate school at the University of Groningen, from which he received a Ph.D. in 1932. While at Leiden, he was inspired by the work of Harvard University astronomer Harlow Shapley, who had proved that the solar system is located well away from the center of the Milky Way galaxy. Studies of the Milky Way galaxy were the focus of Bok's career. During the meetings of the International Astronomical Union held in Leiden in 1928, Bok met Shapley and was invited to take up a fellowship at Harvard. He also met American astronomer Priscilla Fairfield, ten years his senior, who worked for Shapley, and when Bok went to Boston in 1929, they were married. They had two children.

At Shapley's suggestion, Bok chose the star Eta Carinae as the topic of his doctoral thesis. The star and its neighbors are surrounded by an extensive cloud of interstellar gas, and Bok realized that this nebulosity offered an opportunity to study the distribution of young, hot stars in the galaxy. This research expanded to include the stability of star clusters and their eventual disintegration and other consequences of the rotation of the Milky Way galaxy. In the late 1940s, together with Edith Reilly, he identified and photographed about 200 extremely dark clouds in the Sun's sector of the Milky Way galaxy. Thousands of these nebulae, typically a light year across, became known as "Bok globules" and are thought to represent a special stage in the evolution of stars. To pursue these projects, Bok developed considerable skill as an observer, and his enthusiasm for telescopes and any method or technique that could be turned to the night sky was well known. His work contributed to the modern conception of the Milky Way galaxy as a flattened pinwheel, with billions of stars streaming out in spiral arms.

Bok was assistant professor at Harvard from 1933 to 1939, then associate professor until 1946 and professor until 1957. He became a naturalized U.S. citizen in 1938 and shortened his first name. Bok and his wife coauthored *The Milky Way* in 1941. This description of the discoveries about the Milky Way galaxy underwent several editions and is considered a classic introduction to the subject.

In 1950–1951 Bok spent eighteen months in South Africa, involved in the management and operation of Harvard's observing station near Bloemfontein. Bok was also active in promoting science in the political arena, and he championed international cooperation and contacts in astronomy. A letter Bok co-wrote with chemist Isadore Amdur in 1945 helped convince the United Nations to include science in the mandate of what became the United Nations Educational, Scientific and Cultural Organization. He maintained friendships with many astronomers around the world regardless of political barriers, notably with Soviet astronomer Viktor Ambartsumian. Late in Bok's life, he encouraged the Iraqi government to set up a national observatory, even though Iraq was then a pariah among nations. It is likely that he was passed over for the directorship of the Harvard Observatory following the retirement of Shapley in 1952 partly because Bok had supported Shapley when Shapley's name was mentioned by the House Committee on Un-American Activities.

For this reason and also because he did not think Harvard would continue to support fully his research concerning the Milky Way, Bok and his wife determined to leave Harvard. In 1957 Bok accepted the directorship of Mount Stromlo Observatory in Canberra, Australia, along with a professorship at Australian National University. Because from southerly latitudes the richest star fields of the Milky Way galaxy can more easily be studied, the location was an advantage for Bok's work. Eta Carinae, in particular, cannot be observed from northerly latitudes such as Boston's. The appointment also gave Bok the opportunity to play a key role in the development in Australia of astronomical research and graduate astronomy education in the early 1960s. He was also involved in popular education, broadcasting about astronomy on Australian television.

In 1966 Bok returned to the United States and became head of the Department of Astronomy at the University of Arizona in Tucson. He relinquished that position in 1970 but continued as professor in the department until 1974 and then was professor emeritus until his death. He was elected to membership in the National Academy of Sciences in 1968. At the University of Arizona, as in Australia, he again advanced the status of the department. He influenced the development of Kitt Peak National Observatory by fostering the university's participation, which included the funding and construction (1966–1969) of a 90-inch telescope. He served as vice president of the International Astronomical Union from 1970 to 1974 and as president of the American Astronomical Society from 1972 to 1974. Bok was a vocal supporter of the space telescope project, believing that ground-based observatories would eventually be relegated to a supporting role in astronomical research. He also campaigned to discourage public acceptance of astrology, and this brought him considerable notoriety within the astronomical community and in the public eye.

Bok was a member or honorary member of many astronomical societies and scientific academies around the world and was a member of the board of directors of the Astronomical Society of the Pacific from 1977 to 1980. He was awarded the society's Catherine Wolfe-Bruce Gold Medal in 1977. Particularly after the death of his wife in 1975, he traveled and lectured widely. He always demonstrated "an exuberance for the art of astronomy." He was a friendly but outspoken person, kind but strict, an energetic leader, and a capable, if demanding, administrator. The force of Bok's personality caused some heated professional conflicts over the years with colleagues such as H. H. Plaskett, Piet van Rhijn, Edwin Hubble, and Leo Goldberg. He always relished a glass of sherry, he delighted in the company of his grandchildren, and, until his wife died, he enjoyed playing the mandolin. Somewhat constrained by several mild attacks of angina and edema in his last years, Bok died at his home in Tucson.

• Bok's papers are in the archives of Harvard University and the University of Arizona. Bok's final summary of his field of research is *The Milky Way*, with Priscilla F. Bok, 5th ed. (1981). Related articles by Bok are "The Milky Way Galaxy," *Scientific American* 244 (Mar. 1981): 92–120; "Our Bigger and Better Galaxy," *Mercury* 10, no. 5 (Sept.–Oct. 1981): 130–33, 158; and an earlier review, "The Milky Way," *Scientific American* 182 (Feb. 1950): 30–39. For a review of his life and contributions, see David Levy, "Bart Bok at 75," *Astronomy* 10 (Feb. 1982): 24–28, and Raymond E. White, "Bart J. Bok (1906–1983): A Personal Memoir from a 'Grandson'," *Sky & Telescope* 66, no. 4 (Oct. 1983): 303–6. See also J. A. Graham et al., "Bart J. Bok," National Academy of Sciences, *Biographical Memoirs* 64 (1994): 73–97. A thorough biography is David Levy, *The Man Who Sold the Milky Way: A Biography of Bart Bok* (1993), which contains a comprehensive list of Bok's publications. An obituary is in the *New York Times*, 11 Aug. 1983.

PETER JEDICKE

BOK, Edward William (9 Oct. 1863–9 Jan. 1930), editor, philanthropist, and peace advocate, was born in den Helder, Holland, the son of William John Hidde Bok and Sieke Gertrude van Herwerden, who, having lost their inherited fortune through unwise investments, immigrated to the United States in 1870. They settled in Brooklyn, where Bok and his older brother learned English in public school. With his father at first unable to find steady employment, Bok delivered newspapers, worked in a bakery, and wrote up childrens' parties for the *Brooklyn Eagle*. When he was thirteen he left school to be an office boy in Manhattan for the Western Union Telegraph Company, where his father had obtained a job as a translator. Bok had already started an autograph collection, which would become famous after it was written up in several newspapers. He was determined to buy *Appletons' Annual Cyclopaedia* to prepare fitting questions to ask the important people whose signatures he sought.

Bok bettered his day job by studying shorthand at night, after which he did evening reporting for the *Brooklyn Eagle*. When he fell behind in his first verbatim assignment—a rapid-fire speech by President Rutherford B. Hayes—Bok asked him for a copy and spent the next evening with the president and his wife. They were captivated by him, as were other political and literary luminaries whom he met through his autograph collecting. The fact that Bok was so ambitious and hardworking at such an early age impressed these famous people, as did his knowledge of them and what they had written.

In 1881 Bok's father died. The next year Bok began working for the publisher Henry Holt and two years later for Charles Scribner, who made him head of his advertising department in 1887. Bok's evenings were as busy as his days. He started the booklet-shaped theater playbill and edited the *Brooklyn Magazine*, which in 1884 grew out of the organ of the Philomathean Society, a debating club of which he was president at Henry Ward Beecher's Plymouth Church. Besides publishing sermons of Beecher and his fellow Brooklyn minister T. De Witt Talmage, Bok ran articles written by celebrities with whom he had become acquainted through his autograph collecting. Among these were William Dean Howells, William T. Sherman, and Phillips Brooks. In 1886 Bok sold the *Brooklyn Magazine* (which later became *Cosmopolitan Magazine*) and started the Bok Syndicate Press, the country's third syndicate (which listed his brother as its head), to which 137 newspapers subscribed. Its weekly letter on women's topics, written by journalist Ella Wheeler Wilcox, grew to an entire women's page. Bok also syndicated a letter, "Literary Leaves," to which forty-five newspapers subscribed.

In 1889 Cyrus H. K. Curtis, who had read some of Bok's syndicated material, enticed him to edit the six-year-old *Ladies' Home Journal*, whose circulation was 440,000. A 26-year-old bachelor who knew little about women had suddenly become the youngest and highest-paid magazine editor in the country and the butt of numerous jokes by gossip columnists or paragraphers, as they were then called. Undisturbed, he secured material from world-famous writers for his magazine and offered his new readers prizes for the best suggestions on improving it. By 1892 he was vice president of the Curtis Publishing Company, and four years later he married Mary Louise Curtis, his boss's only child. They had two children.

Bok inspired *Ladies' Home Journal* readers to join him in his numerous reform efforts. Together they embarked on crusades to banish the germ-passing public drinking cup, to substitute more useful rooms for the stuffy Victorian parlor, to reduce excessive decoration on clothes and home furnishings, to include music in public education, to prevent power companies from ruining Niagara Falls, and to stop the erection of a gigantic billboard on the Grand Canyon. Even though 25,000 of his readers canceled their subscriptions when he pioneered sex education and advertisers were outraged when he discredited the claims of patent medicine manufacturers, Bok advocated these risky reforms anyway. Bok and his supporters helped pass the Food and Drug Act (1906) and launch sex education. In 1906, following his first editorial on that subject, Bok hired a male and a female expert to answer his readers' queries and courageously arranged for qualified individuals to write a series of small books on sex-related topics. Called the *Edward Bok Books*, they sold for twenty-five cents each. Always innovative, Bok was the first magazine editor to mix advertisements and text on the same pages and the first one to help young people pay for their education by offering them scholarships for selling magazine subscriptions.

With 2 million subscribers to the *Ladies' Home Journal*, Bok bragged to George Bernard Shaw that his editorials were the world's "largest . . . pulpit" (Steinberg, p. 52). But besides preaching to his readers, he listened to them, and his staff answered every one of their letters (which by 1918 reached nearly a million annually). To meet his subscribers' needs he designed departments and columns, such as "Heart to Heart Talks." In one department, started in 1909, mothers could register their babies and receive expert mail-order advice on their care. Nine years later 60,000 babies were enrolled. Aided by thirty-five editors and a host of specialists and other staff members, Bok made his magazine a gigantic clearinghouse of information. The personal services it offered gave the *Journal* "so firm and unique a hold" on its readers that they continued to subscribe despite financial panics (Bok, *Americanization*, p. 179).

Bok also used his magazine to beautify urban areas. To convince his readers that their homes should look good and be comfortable, beginning in 1895 he ran, for twenty-five years, plans for well-designed houses costing between $1,500 and $5,000. When thousands of these homes were built, the renowned architect Stanford White exclaimed, "Edward Bok has more completely influenced American domestic architecture for the better than any man in this generation" (*Americanization*, p. 243). By publishing pictures of the ugliest areas in a number of American cities, Bok shamed them (as well as other cities fearful of being singled out) into improving their worse sections.

With help from his readers, Bok reshaped the ideal Victorian woman—frail, dependent, and idle—into a busy, lively, sturdy, intellectually assured woman. But he refused to believe she was ready for the vote. Although he usually presented both sides of the issue and in 1910 ran a major article by Jane Addams endorsing woman suffrage, two years later he actively opposed it, even though he thought supporting it would gain him 100,000 subscribers. He defended his opposition, insisting that his research indicated that most women did not want the vote.

Bok, who had made it a policy to have presidents and former presidents write for the *Ladies' Home Journal*, virtually turned it over to President Woodrow Wilson and his cabinet when the United States entered World War I. A year earlier he had established an editorial office in Washington, D.C., to start preparing American women for involvement in the war effort. His magazine soon proved "the most effective vehicle . . . for organizing the homefront" and keeping up morale (Schell, p. 23). The *Ladies' Home Journal* was also the third most popular magazine among American servicemen overseas.

In 1919 Bok resigned from his editorship, having completed thirty years of service. The war had made answering nearly a million letters less feasible and had ended his great personal involvement with his readers. He became disillusioned when they proved less enthusiastic than he was in welcoming war refugees and when his efforts to stop the killing of nesting herons for aigrette feathers had actually increased women's desire to wear this "hallmark of torture" (*Americanization*, p. 334).

In 1923 Bok—who as vice president of the Belgian Relief Fund had seen the effects of war firsthand—announced a $100,000 American Peace Award. Half of the amount would be given for the "best practicable" plan for U.S. cooperation in world peace and the other half would be awarded if the plan were enacted. The next year, after 22,165 peace plans had been submitted, the prize was presented to Charles H. Levermore, retired president of Adelphi College, who called for backing the Permanent Court of International Justice and the League of Nations. When, despite an unparalleled advertising blitz, Bok could not pressure the Senate into enacting the winning plan, he endowed the American Foundation, which pushed unsuccessfully to secure U.S. entrance into the World Court. In 1926 he established the Woodrow Wilson Professorship of Literature at Princeton; three years later he endowed a Wilson chair in government at Williams, and he also was a founder of the Walter Hines Page School at Johns Hopkins.

Bok died at "Mountain Lake Park," his estate near Lake Wales, Florida, which was landscaped by Frederick Law Olmsted. At its center is a 14½-acre bird sanctuary, open to the public and featuring a Singing Tower with a carillon of bells.

• The Historical Society of Pennsylvania has the letterbooks of Edward Bok and Cyrus Curtis, 1889 to 1908, and Bok letters in several collections. There is also pertinent material in the Charles Coolidge Parlin Papers in the Rare Books Division of the University of Pennsylvania Library. For detailed information on Bok's life and work, see his two autobiographies, *The Americanization of Edward Bok: The Autobiography of a Dutch Boy Fifty Years After* (1920), which became a bestseller and won a Pulitzer Prize, and *Twice Thirty: Some Short and Simple Annals of the Road* (1925), and his twenty other books. The best single work on Bok is Salme Harju Steinberg, *Reformer in the Marketplace: Edward W. Bok and the "Ladies' Home Journal"* (1979). See also Ernest Schell, "Edward Bok and the *Ladies' Home Journal*," *American History Illustrated* 16 (Feb. 1982): 16–29; David Shi, "Edward Bok and the Simple Life," *American Heritage* 36 (Dec. 1984): 100–109; Esta Seaton, "The Pragmatic Woman in Edward Bok's *Ladies' Home Journal*," *San Jose Studies* 5 (1979): 31–45; Charles DeBenedetti, "The $100,000 American Peace Award of 1924," *Pennsylvania Magazine of History and Biography* 98 (1974): 224–49; and Edward W. Bok, "America's Taj Mahal," *Scribner's* 85 (Feb. 1929): 155–62. Obituaries are in the *New York Times*, 10 Jan. 1930; *Editor and Publisher*, 11 Jan. 1930; and the *Ladies' Home Journal*, Mar. 1930.

OLIVE HOOGENBOOM

BOKER, George Henry (6 Oct. 1823–2 Jan. 1890), playwright and diplomat, was born in Philadelphia, Pennsylvania, the son of Lydia Stewart and Charles S. Boker, a banker and merchant. Boker's wealthy father provided him with an education at the College of New Jersey (now Princeton) and a lavish lifestyle, including extensive travel abroad, leaving the son free to pursue a career in letters and diplomacy without the usual economic worries that plagued writers. Boker's only obligation was to study law, which he read in the office of John Sergeant in Philadelphia from 1842 to 1844, but his father soon recognized that this pursuit was the wrong profession for his literary son.

In 1844 Boker married Julia Mandeville Riggs; they had three children. His wife joined him on his grand tour of Europe in preparation for his career as a poet, and continued to provide him with the social support that he needed to cultivate the literati of the day and compose poetry and plays. In 1848 he published his first volume of verse, *A Lesson of Life*, and saw his first play, *Calaynos*, produced in London's Sadler's Wells Theatre. James E. Murdoch, an actor chiefly associated with the Walnut Street Theatre in Philadelphia, made the play one of his specialties, performing in it over fifty times.

Although Boker went on to become a fairly prolific and very skilled playwright and poet, his fame rests almost solely on one play, which opened at the Broadway Theatre in New York City on September 26, 1855. Set in seventeenth-century Italy, the theme of the drama is the illicit love affair made immortal in the fifth canto of Dante's *Inferno*. A drama in the tragic, romantic mode, it is written in verse. Although revivals secured for the play and Boker a place in theater history, *Francesca da Rimini* had an initial run of only eight nights.

The lukewarm reception given Boker by the contemporary theatergoing public caused him to turn most of his efforts to the writing of poetry, much of which was inspired by the Civil War. Between 1865 and 1870 he toured the United States, giving readings of his own verse. At a time when many writers and actors were going on the circuit to read works of their own and of others, Boker's power as a performer prompted Edwin Forrest, one of the nineteenth century's foremost actors, to say that Boker was the finest reader in America.

In 1871, having relinquished all hope of success as a playwright and feeling discouraged by a protracted trial to clear his father's name of a charge of fraud, Boker entered the foreign service as minister to Turkey. This was followed in 1875 by a post in Russia; he returned to Philadelphia in 1878.

In 1882 Boker published a book-length account of the long legal battle he had waged to clear his father's name. *The Book of the Dead* celebrates the character of his father, who had, as his son had proven, saved rather than destroyed the financial institution for which he had worked. Boker took up two other causes upon his return from Russia—his work with the Union League of Philadelphia, which he helped found in 1862 and had served as president, and his efforts to restore Philadelphia as a center of the literary arts. To this end, he worked closely with that city's *Lippincott Magazine* to encourage American writers.

In 1882 Lawrence Barrett, actor and producer, mounted what would be the first of several revivals of Boker's *Francesca da Rimini*. With the help of William Winter, well-known drama critic of the day, Barrett cut much of the original drama, rearranged scenes, quickened the pace, and, in general, heightened the dramatic effect of the play. The Philadelphia opening was received with wild enthusiasm and was followed by other highly successful runs in Chicago and New York City. It is this reworked 1882 version that received success. For Boker, the unexpected successes were bittersweet since they came too late for him to pick up the career in the theater that he had abandoned for lack of encouragement. To Barrett he wrote, "Why didn't I receive this encouragement years ago? Then I might have done something." His joy was also tempered by his bitter fight with Barrett over his share of the income from the many performances. Boker's place in American drama, resting solely on *Francesca da Rimini*, has far outdistanced the success he found in the theater in his own lifetime. Many critics of America's early drama are in agreement that the play is the finest literary achievement by a nineteenth-century American playwright. Ironically, it is one of the few original plays by an American that does not deal with an American setting or uniquely American issues. George C. D. Odell, famous chronicler of the New

York stage, records well-received New York performances as late as 1888 and calls Boker and Barrett the "high priests of the production."

Two years later Boker died in Philadelphia. The next year Lawrence Barrett died. Boker would scarcely have been pleased that the actor whom he despised for altering his play and supposedly cheating him of his profits was also the individual most responsible for Boker's fame. For it is unlikely that Boker would be remembered at all had it not been for Barrett's revival of *Francesca da Rimini*. For ten years it appeared that Boker's play had died with Barrett. Then, in 1901 Otis Skinner, who had played a major role in Barrett's revival of the play, took the lead in a second revival. Again, the production was a stunning success, playing for fifty-six performances.

On the strength of this one play, Boker is often regarded as the first superior dramatist of the American stage and the only tragedian of quality until the twentieth century. His enduring reputation rests on his dual abilities as poet and dramatist.

• Collections of Boker's work published in his lifetime include *Plays and Poems* (1856), *Poems of the War* (1864), and *Königsmark, the Legend of the Hounds and Other Poems* (1869). Edward Sculley Bradley published a posthumous collection, *Sonnets: A Sequence on Profane Love* (1929), comprising 314 of Boker's sonnets. The standard book on Boker and his work is Bradley, *George Henry Boker* (1927). An obituary is in the Philadelphia *Evening Telegraph*, 2 Jan. 1890.

CLAUDIA DURST JOHNSON

BOLDEN, Buddy (6 Sept. 1877–4 Nov. 1931), jazz musician, was born Charles Joseph Bolden in New Orleans, Louisiana, the son of Westmore Bolden, a drayman, and Alice Harrison. A cornetist and bandleader, Bolden is one of the earliest known figures in the development of jazz in New Orleans and was active from 1895 until 1906—the formative period in jazz's early history.

Little factual information about Bolden was known, however, until the publication of Donald M. Marquis's *In Search of Buddy Bolden* (1978). In this admirable piece of investigative research, Marquis dispels much of the rumor that had grown around Bolden's life in New Orleans and establishes him as an important member of the founding generation of jazz musicians. Marquis confirms that Bolden was not a barber and did not own a barbershop, as popularly believed, although he apparently spent considerable time at barber shops, which served as musicians' meeting places, where information on jobs could be exchanged. Nor did he edit a "scandal sheet" called the *Cricket*. He did drink a lot, played a loud cornet, and was eventually committed to an asylum for erratic behavior resulting from chronic alcoholism.

Like most other New Orleans musicians of that period, Bolden's career performing jazz (then called ragtime) was a part-time pursuit. Not until 1902 did city directories begin listing him as a "musician." Before that year he was identified as a "plasterer" and resided in his family's uptown home on First Street in New Orleans. Sufficient documentation and testimony exist to verify that about 1895 Bolden became active as a cornetist and bandleader at various indoor and outdoor locations in New Orleans, including Lincoln and Johnson parks, Longshoreman's Hall, and Tulane University in the uptown area, the Milneburg and West End resorts on Lake Pontchartrain, the Masonic Hall in Algiers, the Fairgrounds Race Track, and a number of "social clubs" whose halls lined the Perdido–South Rampart Street area. The period from 1897 until 1906 marked the prime of Bolden's tenure as a jazz musician—a time when he enjoyed a sort of preeminence among other players for his boldness, audacity, and the barrelhouse nature of his music.

Essentially an "uptown" musician, Bolden had limited contact with the more learned downtown musicians and performed primarily for black audiences. As an untutored musician with little if any formal education, and as one who played mostly by ear, he made music of the "rough blues" variety used to accompany the "slow drag" and other enticing dances of prostitutes. The downtown Creoles called it "honky tonk" music, and Bolden's repertoire was reputed to be especially coarse. According to Marquis, it appealed "especially to a liberated, post–Civil War generation of young blacks." One number in particular, "Buddy Bolden's Blues," also known as "Funky Butt," was popular enough to cause Union Sons Hall (a location that Bolden's band frequently played) to be commonly referred to as Funky Butt Hall in his honor.

The principal difficulty in assessing the musical contributions of Bolden stems from the total absence of audio recordings. Although he was active during a period when early recordings were being made, no cylinders or records of his playing are known to exist. The search for a cylinder allegedly made by Bolden and his band in the late 1890s, and first reported by Willie Cornish to *Jazzmen* editor Charles Edward Smith in 1939, proved fruitless. The only photograph (the original now lost) of Bolden shows him with a six-piece ensemble that included cornet, trombone, two clarinets, guitar, and string bass. Consequently, legendary accounts abound of his playing, bandleading, and even his lifestyle. As his celebrity as a cornetist and bandleader grew, so did his appetite for high living. Even as early as 1895 he had become a "ladies' man," known to have consorted with the sporting crowd and prostitutes, one of whom, Hattie Oliver, gave birth to his illegitimate son. Their common-law marriage lasted only a few years, and in 1902 Bolden met Nora Bass and entered into a second common-law marriage that produced his only daughter. The Boldens' domestic environment was anything but tranquil, as contemporary police records and testimony from family members attest. Early in 1906 Bolden began suffering severe headaches, fits of depression, and episodes of violent behavior—all apparently related to his excessive drinking. An attack on his mother-in-law on 27 March, during which he struck her in the head with a water pitcher, led to his arrest and detainment by police, initiating the only apparent newspaper coverage he was to receive during his lifetime. Continued episodes of depression and violent behavior left him in a deranged state that placed him in conflict with many of his former musical cohorts as well as members of his family. Finally, in April 1907, having been confined to the house of detention, Bolden was moved to the state hospital for the insane in Jackson, Louisiana. There he lived out the remaining twenty-four years of his life, separated from his family and largely forgotten for the role he played as one of the earliest identifiable jazz pioneers.

• Marquis in his book on Bolden relies on primary sources and interviews with individuals who actually knew Bolden, and he separates fact from fiction while he explores the many legends of Bolden, his family, his relationships with fellow musicians, and the period during which Bolden lived. Discussion of the particulars of Bolden's music is scant. A colorful although somewhat more fanciful account of Bolden and the places he played is in Danny Barker, "A Memory of King Bolden," *Evergreen*, no. 37, Sept. 1965, pp. 66–74. As proof that the Bolden band existed, at least in 1903, see Paige Van Vorst, "Jazz Expert Discovers Bolden Band Proof," *Mississippi Rag*, Mar. 1974, p. 2, which describes an invitation card discovered with "Bolden's Orchestra" listed as the entertainment. Other sources of information include Bob Austin, "Buddy Bolden's Blues," *Storyville Notes*, vol. 1 (May–June 1987), pp. 23–24; and Len Page, "Thought I Heard Buddy Bolden Play," *Footnote* 18 (Apr.–May 1987): 20–25.

CHARLES BLANCQ

BOLDT, George Hugo (28 Dec. 1903–18 Mar. 1984), federal judge, was born in Chicago, Illinois, the son of George F. Boldt and Christine Carstensen. Boldt graduated from high school in Stevensville, Montana, in 1921. He attended the University of Montana, where he received his bachelor's degree in 1925 and his law degree the following year. After a year in private practice with the firm of W. D. Rankin in Helena, Montana, he relocated to Seattle and became a partner in the firm of Ballinger, Hutson and Boldt. In 1928 he married Eloise Baird; they had three children.

During World War II Boldt worked in military intelligence in the China-Burma-India theater, reaching the rank of lieutenant colonel. At the war's end he became a partner in the firm of Metzger, Blair, Gardner and Boldt in Tacoma, Washington. In 1953 President Dwight D. Eisenhower appointed Boldt, a Republican, to the bench of the U.S. District Court of Western Washington. Two years later he was an American delegate to the United Nations congress on prevention of crime and treatment of offenders.

As a district judge Boldt tried a number of cases that garnered national attention, including the 1959 income tax evasion case of former union leader Dave Beck, whom Boldt sentenced to five years in prison. In 1970 Boldt presided over the conspiracy trial of the Seattle Seven, protesters charged with violations of a federal antiriot law. Determined to prevent the trial from degenerating into a media circus, he was lenient toward the accused, who disrupted court proceedings with shouts and heckling. His restrained handling of the case earned him praise from both the media and some of the defendants. However, when the defendants allegedly made violent threats, which included assassinating the judge, Boldt found them guilty of contempt of court. He later declared a mistrial in the conspiracy case.

In 1971 Boldt became chief judge of the Western Washington District. Later that year President Richard M. Nixon appointed him chairman of the newly created Pay Board of the Economic Stabilization Program. Nixon's ninety-day wage and price freeze was coming to a close, and the Pay Board was charged with the difficult task of deciding policy concerning wage hikes. The problem was compounded by the composition of the Pay Board, which was made up of labor, business, and public officials who had decidedly different views. Though Nixon chose Boldt for his ideological neutrality and his abilities as a "harmonizer," Boldt found himself heading a contentious committee. The Pay Board was dissolved in 1973.

Boldt rendered his most important decision in 1974 in the case of *United States v. Washington*. Thirteen American Indian tribes filed suit in federal court claiming that the state of Washington used its regulatory powers to limit Indian fishing in violation of a number of treaties signed in 1854 and 1855. Hoping that his decision in the case would end the numerous disputes over Indian fishing rights in the Pacific Northwest, Boldt studied the issue exhaustively. He divided the case into two phases, the first to consider the rights of Indians to fish off-reservation, the second to examine the question of artificially bred fish and environmental protection. He heard almost fifty witnesses and held court six days a week. After several months of deliberation, he offered his decision in February 1974. Boldt concluded that the Indians were entitled to 50 percent of the harvest that passed through their traditional fishing grounds, and he set forth strict guidelines for state conservation policies.

The Boldt decision, as the ruling was commonly known, created a furor in Washington that lasted for years. Commercial fishermen, many of whom faced the loss of their livelihood, protested. Much of their animosity was directed toward Boldt, who was burned in effigy in 1977. However, the case was not yet over. In 1976 the U.S. Supreme Court refused to hear the state's appeal. Two years later, angered by violations of his ruling and the state's failure to enforce his decision, Boldt took over management of the state's fishery. In 1979 the Supreme Court agreed to review the original case and affirmed Boldt's decision with only minor revisions. Boldt's involvement with the case ended when he retired from the bench in 1979. He lived in retirement in Tacoma, Washington, and died in a hospital near Lakewood, Washington.

Boldt is remembered largely for the 1974 decision that bears his name. Although he recognized the legitimacy of Indian treaties, he created no significant legal precedent. His decision was based on previous court rulings. Receiving national attention, the Boldt decision in some cases created resentment and a backlash against Native Americans. Nonetheless, Boldt reaffirmed the responsibility of the federal government to recognize its obligations to Native Americans, even in the face of significant opposition.

• A brief but useful biographical sketch of Boldt is in the *New York Times*, 23 Oct. 1971. Fay G. Cohen, *Treaties on Trial* (1986), includes a laudatory account of the Boldt decision. An obituary is in the *New York Times*, 21 Mar. 1984.

THOMAS CLARKIN

BOLESLAVSKY, Richard Valentinovich (4 Feb. 1889–17 Jan. 1937), acting teacher, stage and film director, actor, and author, was born Boleslaw Ryszard Srzednicki in Plock, Poland, the son of Valentine Srzednicki, a landowner, and Pani (maiden name unknown). When the family estate was lost, the Srzednickis relocated to South Bessarabia and then to Odessa, where Boleslaw received his education at the Polytechnic Institute of Odessa and the University of Odessa. He joined an amateur theater group in Odessa called the Polish Hearth, which he administered during his college days, in addition to performing leading roles. His first professional acting engagement was with a Russian troupe, sometime around 1904; his career began to flourish in 1908, when he was fully accepted as a student at the Moscow Art Theatre (MAT) and almost immediately was admitted into the acting company. Richard Valentinovich Boleslavsky was his stage name, and he retained it when he immigrated to the United States in 1922.

The MAT, founded by Konstantin Stanislavsky and Vladimir Nemirovich-Danchenko in 1898, was the home of the Stanislavsky "system," the earliest and most celebrated attempt to codify and teach an approach to acting. Stanislavsky did not consider it fully formed until 1918 (and even then he continued to shape and redefine it), after he had tested it on the MAT company in productions like the 1908 *A Month in the Country* (by Ivan Turgenev), in which Boleslavsky appeared. The system departed from the more declamatory style of performance popular on the stages of Europe in the nineteenth century: it placed a premium on meticulous research and realistic detail, required an intricate and structured approach to working through a role, strove to achieve consistent ensemble playing, and vehemently opposed any kind of stage fakery. Most famously, it encouraged the actor to look within himself or herself for the character—an approach that generated fierce debate when, on American shores, the system became the "Method."

Boleslavsky was one of Stanislavsky's most gifted students and one of the company's prime movers. He quickly became its leading juvenile and a Moscow matinee idol as well as a director in the MAT's smaller theater space, the First Studio, which he eventually administered. At the same time he began to act in and direct motion pictures. His burgeoning career was interrupted by a stint in the army, between 1915 and 1917, at which time his marriage to MAT actress Maria Yefremova fell apart. (They had married in 1913.) His Russian films include *Khleb* (Bread), a Bolshevik propaganda film released in 1918, which he codirected with Boris Suskevich. In 1919 he returned to Poland, ironically, to fight against the Bolshevik forces and to supervise the film coverage of the Polish campaigns. The result was a semidocumentary, *The Miracle of the Vistula*, released in 1920.

As a director, Boleslavsky was more of a minimalist than Stanislavsky, more concerned with creating mood through visual and aural effects, more excited about exploring new theatrical styles. Inevitably, he and his teacher quarreled. Feeling the need to establish himself independent of the MAT and impatient with the artistic restrictions imposed by the Bolsheviks, Boleslavsky fled Russia with his second wife, actress and singer Natasha Platonova (whom he had married in 1918), for Warsaw, Paris, Berlin (where he played Fedja in Carl Dreyer's 1922 film *Die Gezeichneten*), and finally New York (in 1922), where they traveled with a revue. Boleslavsky remained in the United States to assist Stanislavsky on the MAT's 1923 American tour, during which he began to lecture on the system—first at the Princess Theatre and later at Bryn Mawr and the Provincetown Playhouse. When the company returned to Russia, Boleslavsky found himself the leading interpreter in the United States of Stanislavsky's approach to acting. In June 1923 he established the Laboratory Theatre (the "Lab"), which became known as the American Laboratory Theatre in 1925, the first American school of Stanislavskian acting. Boleslavsky's "laboratory" strategies—his acknowledgment of the importance of continued education and experimentation for professional actors—were the inspiration behind both the Group Theatre (1931–1941) and the Actors Studio (which opened in 1947), the respective homes of the first and second generations of American Method actors. Harold Clurman and Lee Strasberg, two of the Group's founders, and Stella Adler, its leading actress, all attended Boleslavsky's lectures at the Lab. By the 1950s Strasberg and Adler were the most famous and influential acting teachers in America.

Like Stanislavsky, Boleslavsky believed that talent could not be taught, only cultivated, and that actors were essentially at the service of the visions of playwrights and directors. With the assistance of another MAT graduate, Maria Ouspenskaya, who joined him at the Lab in 1924, he tried to teach his students how they could best prepare themselves to convey those visions—by developing mind and body, discipline, and the powers of observation and imagination. Boleslavsky paralleled Stanislavsky in shifting the focus of his approach from the rekindling of genuine emotion to the creation of dramatic action on the stage, and that shift may have helped to foster the controversy over "emotion memory" (a technique Stanislavsky pioneered to reproduce emotional states in performance), which continued to rage as long as Strasberg, its chief proponent, and Adler, its chief debunker, were alive.

The Lab started to give public performances in 1925, and, concurrently, Boleslavsky picked up his professional directing career in New York, staging, among other plays, the Broadway production of Rudolf Friml's operetta *The Vagabond King* (1925). He moved to Hollywood in 1929, just after divorcing Natasha and marrying Norma Drury; their son was born there in 1935. Boleslavsky directed his first American motion picture, *The Last of the Lone Wolf*, in 1930. His fifteen subsequent movies include *Rasputin and the Empress* (1932); *Storm at Daybreak* (1933), which contains a reconstruction of the assassination of the archduke at Sarajevo in 1914; the film version of the Group Theatre's Broadway success *Men in White* (1934); *The Painted Veil* (1934), with Greta Garbo; *Les Miserables* (1935), with Fredric March; *Theodora Goes Wild* (1936), with Irene Dunne; and *The Garden of Allah* (1936), with Marlene Dietrich. Of these, only the screwball comedy *Theodora Goes Wild* is notable as a film, although *Rasputin and the Empress* is at least of historic value, since it established Boleslavsky as a major director and it was the only time Ethel, Lionel, and John Barrymore appeared together on screen. Ethel Barrymore specifically requested that Boleslavsky replace the original director, Charles Brabin, because of his Russian background, but there was so much squabbling on the set that the movie earned the nickname "Disputin' and the Empress," and the results, except at the box office, were disastrous. Boleslavsky died suddenly in Los Angeles, California, of a heart attack, while in midproduction of *The Last of Mrs. Cheyney*, which George Fitzmaurice completed.

As a stage director Boleslavsky was famous for his handling of crowd scenes, but neither that skill nor his apparently profound influence over actors comes across in most of his screen work. A flamboyant and domineering personality is evident, however, in his 1933 book *Acting: The First Six Lessons*, a charmingly idiosyncratic collection of articles he wrote for *Theatre Arts Magazine* between 1929 and 1932.

• Boleslavsky's papers are in the Bobbs-Merrill Collection, Lilly Library, Indiana University, which includes correspondence and assorted records, and the Billy Rose Theatre Collection at the New York Public Library for the Performing Arts, Lincoln Center, which includes a transcription of his unpublished article "The Creative Theatre." The American Laboratory Theatre files are in the possession of Ronald A. Willis at the University of Kansas, Lawrence. Boleslavsky wrote two novels, *Lances Down* and *Way of the Lancer* (both 1932), with Helen Woodward, based on his experiences with the Polish Lancers during the First World War. A valuable full-length study of Boleslavsky is J. W. Roberts, *Richard Boleslavsky: His Life and Work in the Theatre* (1981). The most engaging account of Boleslavsky's influence on the founding of the Group Theatre is found in Harold Clurman, *The Fervent Years: The Story of the Group Theatre and the Thirties* (1945).

STEVE VINEBERG

BOLGER, Ray (10 Jan. 1904–15 Jan. 1987), comedy-actor and dancer, was born Raymond Wallace Bolger in Dorchester, near Boston, Massachusetts, the son of James Edward Bolger, a painter, and Anne Wallace. After he graduated from Dorchester High School in 1920, Bolger initially was employed in office work, including positions with First National Bank of Boston, New England Mutual Life Insurance Company, and Kelly Peanut Company. His involvement with performing had been at the amateur level, and he found his way into a ballet school run by Senia Rusakoff (Roussakoff) because the institution required someone with bookkeeping knowledge and offered him free dancing lessons in return. Training in ballet and tap led to Bolger's first stage appearance in 1922 as a soloist in Rusakoff's dance recital, followed by a couple of years touring with the Bob Ott Musical Comedy Repertoire Company. This experience enabled Bolger to develop his craft in various musicals. He acquired skills in comedy and acting while continuing to broaden his range of dancing.

Teaming up with Ralph Sanford to perform on the vaudeville circuit as "A Pair of Nifties" at the Central Theatre in Cambridge, Massachusetts (1925), Bolger subsequently appeared as a dancing comedian at New York's Rialto Theatre (1925), in *The Merry World* (Imperial Theatre, 1926), and in the second edition of *A Night in Paris* (Forty-fourth Street Theatre, 1926). He also played in Gus Edwards's *Ritz-Carlton Nights* (Palace Theatre, 1926), with which he toured the Keith-Albee and Orpheum circuits in 1927–1928, and appeared in small-scale revues throughout the United States in 1928–1929. Also in 1929 Bolger married Gwen Rickard.

The next decade provided Bolger with his first important roles, notably as principal dancer in *George White's Scandals of 1931* at the Apollo Theatre, as one of the stars of *Life Begins at 8:40* (Winter Garden, 1934), and as Phil Dolan III in the Rodgers and Hart musical *On Your Toes* (Imperial Theatre, 1936). It was the ballet in this show, "Slaughter on Tenth Avenue," that clearly demonstrated to Broadway audiences the actor-dancer's talent and inventiveness. The choreography was by George Balanchine, and the plot concerned the adventures of Phil, the son of veteran vaudeville hoofers who sets his sights on becoming a music teacher. He becomes interested in ballet and falls in love with a member of the Russian Ballet, Tamara Geva (Vera Barnova). Phil joins the dance company that mounts "Slaughter on Tenth Avenue" as it attempts to avoid bankruptcy. The segment was a spoof on a movie about a dancer and his moll who run away from gangsters and hide in a café located on Tenth Avenue. It had a running time of eleven minutes and made Bolger a star. Critics called him "the foremost eccentric dancer on our stage" and said "the show is his from curtain rise to curtain fall" (Thomas, p. 132).

Broadway triumph was followed by success in Hollywood. Bolger made his screen debut in *The Great Ziegfeld* (MGM, 1936), appearing in one number, "You Gotta Pull Strings," tapping, spinning, and skidding. He was surrounded by glamorous chorus girls, which contrasted with his physical appearance—comprising long legs, slim build, large ears, and a parrot-like nose. Seymour Felix, the choreographer, exploited the performer's loose-limbed eccentricities. The number had been filmed before the opening of *On Your Toes*, and the show's acclaim led to Bolger receiving further invitations from Hollywood and an MGM contract.

Bolger next played in *Rosalie* (MGM, 1937), with Nelson Eddy and Eleanor Powell, which was followed by the Jeanette MacDonald–Nelson Eddy musical *Sweethearts* (MGM, 1938). In the spring of 1938 *The Wizard of Oz* (MGM, 1939) project commenced. The Tin Woodman was the role originally offered to Bolger, but he protested that the metal suit would restrict his mobility and hamper his dancing style. The studio relented, giving him the role of the Scarecrow, which was the ideal vehicle to display his gift for characterization as he stumbled unforgettably along "The Yellow Brick Road" with Dorothy (Judy Garland).

In 1942 Bolger returned to the New York stage in a Rodgers and Hart musical, *By Jupiter*, at the Shubert Theatre. The show was based on the Julian F. Thompson play *The Warrior's Husband* and focused on Amazon women at war with the men of ancient Greece. Bolger portrayed Sapiens, husband of Queen Hippolyta. Spectators commented on his seeming lack of dancing in the show; Bolger responded by declaring, "In *By Jupiter* I am dancing all the time. Every gesture, the body line of every pose, the way I get from place to place, the movement in the acting—it's all dance. None of it would be the way it is if I weren't a dancer" (Beiswanger, p. 89). For Bolger the psychology of the character was a supreme influence on the composition of movement, each gesture serving to reveal the personality of whom he portrayed.

Reinterpreting dance steps such as a tapping version of the lindy hop, incorporating a slipping, almost falling action in the breakaway also highlighted Bolger's trademark of combining humor with dancing skill. This entertained troops during World War II. For USO tours he developed the character of Sad Sack, a dim private who finds it difficult to cope with military life. The character appears in the film *Stage Door Canteen* (United Artists, 1943) and performs an acclaimed tap dancing number.

Throughout the 1940s Bolger's film and stage career developed. *The Harvey Girls* (MGM, 1946) renewed his association with Garland. In "The Atcheson, Topeka, and the Santa Fe" number Bolger leads a group of dancers in an imitation of a moving train, jumping into high-strut steps, undulating his body in a rhythm akin to the turning wheels of a train. Unfortunately, much of Bolger's contribution to the film was cut.

It was not until 1948 that Bolger was more fully able to utilize his talents, appearing in *Where's Charley?* (St. James Theater), a musical version of *Charley's Aunt* (1892) by Brandon Thomas. Bolger played an Oxford University undergraduate, Charley Wykeham, who along with his friend Jack Chesney (Byron Palmer) wishes to entertain some young ladies. Social etiquette necessitates a chaperone and Charley has to disguise himself as his own rich aunt. Choreographed by Balanchine, Bolger appeared in five dance numbers, including a solo soft-shoe and tap routine to "Once in Love with Amy." In reviewing the work, Arthur Todd in *Dance Magazine* (Jan. 1949, p. 24) commented on Bolger's wonderful sense of projection and split-second timing. The affinity he had with his audiences was to prove an important component of his success. It was reported that during a performance of "Once in Love with Amy" Bolger noticed a young girl singing along at the front of the theater. He encouraged her to sing and then asked the audience to join in. This audience participation became a regular feature of the show, which ran for more than two years, and Bolger's performance was rewarded with a Tony Award. A filmed version starring Bolger was released by Warner Brothers in 1952. His other films included *April in Paris* (Warner Brothers, 1952) and *Babes in Toyland* (Buena Vista, 1961).

During the rest of his career Bolger appeared on television, in nightclubs, and in other stage musicals, including *All America* as Professor Fodorski (Winter Garden, 1962) and *Come Summer* as Phineas Sharp (Lunt-Fontanne Theater, 1969). Frequent TV showings of *The Wizard of Oz* continued to maintain his public profile. In 1984 Bolger was invited to act as a linking host for the film dance compilation *That's Dancing!* (MGM-UA), produced by Jack Haley, Jr., and David Niven, Jr. Among the dance segments was a routine that had been cut from the original *Wizard of Oz* in which Bolger as the Scarecrow hops around the road, bounces off fences, and, aided by wires, flies through the air. This and other recordings document his delightful performances.

Bolger died in a Los Angeles nursing home. In one of his last interviews he had commented, "long after I am gone I will still be remembered as the Scarecrow. How many people on this earth can say that after they die they will still be remembered by people all over the world?" (*Standard*, 16 Jan. 1987).

• Recordings of Bolger's work and other pertinent resources are available in the Dance Collection, the New York Public Library for the Performing Arts at Lincoln Center. Additional details and comments on his life and stage performances can be found in George Beiswanger, "Ray Bolger—All-Out Theatre Man," *Theatre Arts* (1942), pp. 85–90; Arthur Todd, "A Brace of Musicals," *Dance Magazine*, Jan. 1949, pp. 24, 37, 43–44; Iva Kitchell, "Satire in the Dance," *Dance Magazine*, May 1949, pp. 18–20; David Ewen, *Complete Book of the American Musical Theater* (1959); Abe Laufe, *Broadway's Greatest Musicals* (1977); and Gerald Bordman, *American Musical Theatre: A Chronicle* (1986). For Bolger's career in the context of the history of popular dance forms in performance, see Jean Stearns and Marshall Stearns, *Jazz Dance: The Story of American Vernacular Dance* (1968; rev. ed. 1994). His film career is considered in general film musical texts, including Tony Thomas, *That's Dancing! A Glorious Celebration of Dance in the Hollywood Musical* (1984), and Thomas G. Aylesworth, *Broadway to Hollywood: Musicals from Stage to Screen* (1985). Obituaries are in the *New York Times* and the *Standard* (London), both 16 Jan. 1987.

MELANIE TRIFONA CHRISTOUDIA

BOLL, Jacob (29 May 1828–29 Sept. 1880), naturalist and geologist, was born at Dieticon, Bremgarten, Canton Aargau, Switzerland, the son of Henry Boll and Magdalena Peier. The family was moderately wealthy, so Jacob was able to attend a Gymnasium, where he soon developed a passion for natural history. Apparently while enrolled there he met Louis Agassiz, the eminent naturalist, who was teaching at the College of Neuchatel. This further stimulated Boll's enthusiasm for biology and formed the basis for his later professional association with Agassiz in the United States. Boll subsequently attended the University of Jena for two years, studying chemistry, pharmacy, and natural history, but he left in 1853 without receiving a degree.

Returning to Bremgarten, Boll opened an apothecary shop in 1854 and married Henriette Humbel the same year; they had three children. Boll soon began devoting his spare time to a careful survey of the biota of his home region. He also served as professor of natural history in the college at Bremgarten. He wrote several papers on the natural history of the area, and in 1869 he published a 127-page book on the flora of Canton Aargau. Boll suffered serious financial losses in the late 1860s, culminating in the bankruptcy of his apothecary business in 1869, and his wife developed psychological problems so severe that she had to be confined to a sanitarium. Faced with these personal disasters, Boll decided to move to America. His parents and brothers were living in Dallas, Texas, at the time, having emigrated to the Fourieristic colony at La Reunion.

Boll arrived in the United States late in 1869. Before proceeding to Texas, he visited Cambridge and Boston to renew his contact with Agassiz, who was now at the center of the scientific establishment at Harvard. Agassiz welcomed Boll, introduced him to the academic community, and requested that he collect specimens in Texas for the Museum of Comparative Zoology at Harvard. Boll proved to be an obliging collector, sending a large number of specimens to the museum during 1869 and 1870. He provided Agassiz with material of high quality from all branches of natural history, including birds, crustaceans, arachnids, reptiles, fossil invertebrates, and more than 15,000 insects. Boll returned to Cambridge and spent the winter of 1870–1871 at the museum as an assistant to Agassiz and to the entomologist Hermann A. Hagen.

In the spring of 1871 Boll returned to Switzerland to settle business matters and to conduct research for the Canton Aargau government. Agassiz offered Boll a formal appointment at the museum in May 1871, but Boll was unable to return to accept the position until October. The brief appointment was one of the most intense and satisfying periods of Boll's life; he traveled widely in New England to collect insects, organized the museum's entomological collections, had his materials on public exhibit, and began raising lepidopterous insects from larvae. In January 1872 he was elected a member of the Boston Society of Natural History.

News of his wife's illness in March 1872 forced another return to Switzerland, where Boll remained until her death in August 1873. Not to be distracted from his natural history work, he took a huge collection of lepidoptera cocoons with him to Europe and raised some 600 specimens. In March 1873 he was honored by election to membership in the prestigious Academia Caesaraea Leopoldino-Carolina Naturae Curiosorum of Germany. He found time to collaborate with his friend, Heinrich Frey of the University of Zurich, conducting botanical fieldwork and completing a number of publications based on Boll's American collections.

His affairs finally in order, Boll departed Switzerland for the last time, returned to the United States in January 1874, and made his way to Cambridge, where he intended to accept Agassiz's earlier offer of a reappointment at the museum. Upon learning that Agassiz had died in December 1873, Boll instead went to Texas, where he spent his remaining years exploring and collecting. He studied not only the living flora and fauna during this period but also the geology and paleontology of the region. Much of his work was conducted under extremely harsh conditions in remote and rugged areas of frontier Texas. Nevertheless, his pioneering investigation of the Permian rocks of Texas yielded an array of important new fossils, and his work laid the foundation for a state geological survey. Most of his fieldwork was in the eastern part of the state, but he extended his explorations as far as northwest Texas in 1876.

Perhaps the most important event in Boll's career occurred in 1877, when he met the paleontologist Edward D. Cope, who was visiting Dallas to secure the services of a local collector. Excited by the fossils Boll showed him, Cope contracted with Boll to collect both fossils and living vertebrates for him. From 1878 until his death in 1880 Boll worked for Cope, providing an array of living and fossil reptiles, amphibians, and fish. His most important collections were from the Big and Little Wichita rivers. Cope moved aggressively to publish descriptions of the new species that Boll unearthed, but before Boll's death, Cope avoided identifying the source of these specimens in order to prevent Othniel C. Marsh of Yale from gaining any advantage in the battle for primacy in American paleontology by hiring or spying on Boll. Cope presented Boll's discoveries in a series of papers from 1878 through 1883 and in a monograph, *On the Zoological Position of Texas* (1880). Of the fifty-seven new Permian vertebrate species and genera described by Cope, thirty-two had been collected by Boll.

After Boll's death, Cope credited him for his contributions by naming a number of species in his honor and by acknowledging, "He discovered numerous remarkable extinct vertebrates, which . . . have thrown great light on the nature of vertebrate life at that early period" (Geiser, *Naturalists of the Frontier*, p. 26). Boll's Permian fossils revealed a new and extraordinarily rich fauna of primitive reptiles and amphibians "differing widely from any previously known."

Boll also continued his entomological studies during his Texas years, acquiring a particularly large collection of microlepidoptera. In 1874 his cantonal government in Switzerland requested that he provide specimens of the Colorado potato beetle, seeds of various woody plants, and samples of freshwater and marine mollusks from Texas for agricultural research and study by biology students. From 1877 to 1880 he worked with the U.S. Entomological Commission on a study of the Rocky Mountain locust, and representatives of the French silk industry paid him to research the possibility of introducing hardy American silkworm species into Europe. Boll provided specimens to many European museums, and his data were important for E. T. Cresson's *Hymenoptera Texana* (1872) and for A. S. Packard's *Monograph of the Geometrid Moths* (1876).

Described as modest and unassuming, Boll was highly respected by scientists of his day, both for the quality and quantity of his work and for his devotion to science. His name was commemorated in the names of species of insects, fish, a clam, a lizard, and reptilian fossils. He died of appendicitis at his campsite in Wilbarger County, Texas, near the confluence of the Pease River and the Red River, while on a collecting trip in search of fossils for Cope.

• Noteworthy collections of Boll's papers are in the Cope Collection of the American Museum of Natural History, the Boll Papers at the Academy of Natural Sciences in Philadelphia, and the Library of the Museum of Comparative Zoology at Harvard University. Many of Boll's fossils are on display and in the study collections of the American Museum of Natural History in New York City. Studies of Boll's life include Samuel Wood Geiser, "Professor Jacob Boll and the Natural History of the Southwest," *American Midland Naturalist* 11 (1929): 439–52, and *Naturalists of the Frontier* (1948), pp. 19–29; the latter includes an extensive bibliography and list of manuscript resources. See also R. T. Hill, "Present Condition of Knowledge of the Geology of Texas," *Bulletin XLV of the United States Geological Survey* (1887). Boll's two U.S. publications were "Texas in Its Geognostic and Agricultural Aspect," *American Naturalist* 13 (1879): 375–84, and "Geological Examinations in Texas," *American Naturalist* 14 (1880): 684–86, which identified Permian rocks of northwest Texas. Boll's data were also published by E. D. Cope, "On the Zoological Position of Texas," U.S. National Museum, *Bulletin 17* (1880).

MARCUS B. SIMPSON, JR.

BOLLAN, William (1710?–1782), colonial agent and lawyer, was born in England and emigrated from there to America while a teenager. He pursued a legal career by studying as an apprentice under the tutelage of Massachusetts attorney Robert Auchmuty. Little is known of Bollan's early life and career. However, by 1733 he had begun to gain prominence as an attorney, as evidenced by his acquisition of Harvard College and Boston's Anglican parish, King's Chapel, as clients. Bollan was an Anglican, which placed him in a religious minority in Congregational-dominated Boston. By the mid-1730s he had begun to venture into land speculation in both Massachusetts and Rhode Island.

Beginning in the early 1740s Bollan pursued a political career. In 1743 he married Frances Shirley, the daughter of Massachusetts governor William Shirley. (His wife died in childbirth two years later, leaving a surviving daughter.) Late in 1745 Bollan was sent by Governor Shirley to London as a colonial agent to seek reimbursement for Massachusetts of £183,649 the colony had expended during King George's War (1744–1748) for the capture of the fortress at Louisburg in Canada. After three years of negotiation, Bollan won his case when Parliament agreed to send £200,000 in silver to Massachusetts.

By 1748 Bollan had emerged as one of only two full-time career colonial agents, the other being Pennsylvania's Robert Charles, prior to the Revolution. From 1745 to 1762 Bollan singlemindedly pursued Massachusetts colonial interests within the fractured London bureaucracy of the British empire. He quickly developed a reputation as an officious agent and tireless lobbyist who offered policy advice to the king's representatives from prime ministers to minor civil servants. In negotiation Bollan emphasized the mutual economic interests of Massachusetts and England but always maintained the subordinate political and legal status of the colony to Parliament and the Crown.

In order to function effectively, Bollan maintained residences in London and Boston, but he lived mostly in London. Bollan proved an effective lobbyist for Massachusetts's commercial interests. He gained recognition in the inner political circles of Massachusetts for his repeated opposition to British impressment of Massachusetts residents, his campaign against Parliament's anti–paper money bill of 1751, his battle against the enforcement in Massachusetts ports of the prohibitory duties passed in 1733 on foreign molasses, and his uncanny ability to secure parliamentary reimbursements for Massachusetts's wartime expenses.

Bollan, however, angered many Massachusetts politicians outside the Shirley camp by his constant complaints that he was overworked and underpaid. After the arrival of Thomas Pownall in 1757 to replace Bollan's father-in-law as governor, Bollan was compelled to fight for his political life. Governor Pownall immediately sought to replace Bollan with his own brother, John Pownall, and joined in an alliance with the faction led by the Boston lawyer and merchant James Otis to achieve those ends. Pownall's blatant nepotism aroused the wrath of Lieutenant Governor Thomas Hutchinson, who refused to abandon Bollan. The contest over Bollan's fate as a colonial agent developed severe political ramifications as it spawned a decade-long battle between Hutchinson and the Otis family that played a key role in the coming of the American Revolution by placing the Otises and other Massachusetts lawyers in the vanguard of the anti-imperial forces. Thus, Bollan continued as a colonial agent until 1762 owing to the ability of his patron Hutchinson to influence the Massachusetts assembly.

In 1762, however, Bollan became a political casualty in the Hutchinson-Otis contest. He was removed as a colonial agent in an effort by the Otis faction to weaken Hutchinson's base of support in London. Otis and his followers portrayed Bollan as a sycophant of Governor Shirley at the expense to the rest of the colony, a self-interested agent who put personal financial gain above the common good by padding his personal expense accounts and a weak-willed hypochondriac.

Bollan was unaware of Hutchinson's rapidly fading political power in Massachusetts and blamed his patron for his sudden misfortunes. He openly broke ranks with Hutchinson by promoting the anti-imperialist cause in 1766 and continued to seek reinstatement as colonial agent. His new strategy was to abandon the corridors of Westminster in favor of a career as a patriotic pamphleteer, offering numerous solutions to restore harmony between England and its American colonies. From 1762 to 1774 Bollan authored no fewer than thirteen separate pamphlets on the constitutional issues of the imperial crisis and how to reconcile the interests of the two contestants. In these pamphlets, Bollan clearly advanced an ideological position that relied on classic English libertarian beliefs as championed in the writings of John Trenchard and Thomas Gordon. He put forth the view that a corrupt and ineffective group of ministerial advisers were abandoning basic English rights and liberties in favor of tyrannical despotism. Despite these beliefs, Bollan was steadfast in his dismissal of any talk of American independence from the British empire.

In 1769 Bollan's attacks on the British ministry were rewarded when he was rehired by the Massachusetts council as a colonial agent. The council was engaged in a life or death struggle with Hutchinson for control of the colony and recognized Bollan's conservatism. Parliament, on the advice of Hutchinson who feared the political damage Bollan could cause in London, refused to acknowledge the appointment and withheld Bollan's sorely needed salary of £300. To extract his revenge on Hutchinson and promote the radical cause, Bollan forwarded to Boston's radicals a series of thirty-three private letters between Governor Francis Bernard and General Thomas Gage that seemingly advocated military despotism in Massachusetts. The letters greatly inflamed the radical cause in America.

Bollan never again served Massachusetts as an agent and never returned to the colony, having sold his Boston home and furnishings in 1765. He devoted his remaining years to ending the imperial crisis through his petitions to Parliament and his increasingly pro-American pamphlets. By 1774 Bollan foresaw the inevitability of the Revolution and in an eleventh hour appeal for compromise called for a British empire of equal and independent political units joined only by a common culture and the British monarchy. Bollan died in London on the eve of the achievement of the American independence he had sought so desperately to avoid.

• Personal manuscript collections for Bollan are located in the New York Public Library, the Massachusetts State Archives, the Massachusetts Historical Society, and the New England Historical and Genealogical Society, as well as in the official published records of the Massachusetts General Court and Parliament. A detailed listing of Bollan's published writings is offered in Michael Kammen, *A Rope Of Sand* (1968), pp. 334–35, which is among the more complete modern appraisals of Bollan's career as a colonial agent; other useful assessments include Malcolm Freiburg, "William Bollan: Agent of Massachusetts," *More Books* 23 (1948): 178–80; and Joel Myerson, "The Private Revolution of William Bollan," *New England Quarterly* 41 (Dec. 1968): 536–59. For two insightful studies that discuss Bollan's place in Massachusetts political history see William Pencak, *War, Politics, and Revolution* (1981), and Robert Zemsky, *Merchants, Farmers, and River Gods* (1971).

RONALD LETTIERI

BOLLES, Frank (31 Oct. 1856–10 Jan. 1894), writer and university secretary, was born in Winchester, Massachusetts, the son of John A. Bolles, a lawyer and former secretary of the commonwealth of Massachusetts, and Catherine Dix. His early years were spent in Winchester, where he developed a love and an appreciation of nature that never left him. He moved with his family to Baltimore, Maryland, in 1866, when his father became solicitor of the U.S. Navy. In the following year the family moved again, this time to Washington, D.C., where Bolles attended Young's private academy. While at the school he formed a club with eleven other classmates (including President Ulysses S. Grant's son, Jesse) called the K.F.R. (it is not known what the initials represented). A literary and debating society, the club also published a monthly journal to which Bolles contributed. At this time he also contributed prose and poetry to *Oliver Optic's Magazine* and other periodicals. Fearing that Washington contained too many social distractions, Bolles requested that he be sent to Dean Academy in Franklin, Massachusetts. His wish was granted, and he spent two years at that institution.

Bolles returned to Washington eager to pursue journalism as a career but instead deferred to his father's wishes that he become a lawyer. Entering the law department at Columbian University (now George Washington University) in 1877, he subsequently graduated with an LL.B. with high honors in 1879. His father died in the spring of 1878, and again acceding to his wishes (that he complete his education at a New England college) Bolles entered Harvard Law School in 1879.

While at Harvard Bolles became advertising manager and editor of the *Echo*, the first daily paper established at the school. He also founded and served as the first president of the Harvard Coöperative Society, an organization that provided books, clothing, and other necessities to students at reduced prices. His writings at Harvard proved noteworthy; he won the Bowdoin prize for an essay called "Arbitration as a Means of Settling International Disputes," compiled a genealogy of his mother's family, and published (with Edmund M. Parker and Edmund L. Baylies) *A Collection of Important English Statutes* (1880). He later published two larger editions of the work on his own.

After graduating with an LL.D. in 1882, Bolles remained in Cambridge and took additional classes in law, literature, history, and economics. Deciding that his first interest, literature, was his true calling, he rejected the idea of establishing a legal practice in Rumney, New Hampshire, and became a correspondent of the *Boston Advertiser* in 1882. His contributions were so noteworthy that he was offered the position of associate editor, which he accepted in July 1883. With his newfound employment, he was able to marry Elizabeth Quincy Swan of Cambridge in October 1884. They had four children.

Although Bolles enjoyed editorial work, the long night hours it required affected his health. He also found himself disaffected by the paper's shift in political stance (probably toward a more partisan viewpoint) following the 1884 election. He resigned and on 1 April 1886 assumed the duties of secretary to the president of Harvard University, becoming secretary of the university in the following year.

Bolles threw himself into his new duties with vigor. Interested in all facets of operations at the university, he turned his position (hardly more than bookkeeper at his acceptance) into one of wide-ranging influence. He founded an employment bureau that enabled students who needed jobs to meet prospective employers. Blessed with remarkable powers of observation and a powerful memory, Bolles took great pride in assisting students, whether rich or poor, in all facets of their lives at Harvard. He lobbied extensively for the erection of a new dining hall and helped to found an association that loaned furniture to students at reduced prices. He also arranged numerous loans for students in financial difficulties.

Harvard grew in size and complexity under Bolles's superior, President Charles W. Eliot, and Bolles aided this development. He streamlined the operations of the secretary's office, issuing circulars that were used to answer standard written inquiries. He also wrote pamphlets that dealt with various aspects of the "new" Harvard—including one that listed the yearly budgets of recent graduates, with the goal of demonstrating that even students of modest means could successfully attend Harvard. Perhaps his most lasting contribution was the founding in 1893 of the quarterly *Harvard Graduates Magazine*, which helped alumni around the world keep in touch with their alma mater.

Bolles's other passion in life—dating from his childhood—was nature. He spent a great deal of time at Mount Chocorua in New Hampshire, where he could observe all forms of flora and fauna at his leisure. Bolles wrote of his impressions in a series of letters to the *Boston Post*, which he signed "O.W.L." Encouraged by many, including James Russell Lowell, he published a set of the sketches in *The Land of the Lingering Snow* (1891) and *At the North of Bearcamp Water* (1893). He died of pneumonia in Cambridge; *From Blomidon to Smoky, and Other Papers* (1894) and *Chocorua's Tenants* (1895) were published posthumously.

Bolles's early death cut short a budding literary career and a successful tenure as a progressive university administrator. He was among the first to implement many of the support services that are today standard features at all large colleges and universities.

• The Harvard University Archives in Cambridge, Mass., contain a very limited amount of Bolles's papers. Information on his life and career is scarce. The best source is William Thayer, "Frank Bolles," *Harvard Graduates Magazine* 6 (Mar. 1894): 366–72. Obituaries are in the *Boston Advertiser*, *Journal*, and *Transcript*, all 11 Jan. 1894.

EDWARD L. LACH, JR.

BOLLING, George Melville (13 Apr. 1871–2 June 1963), classical philologist and linguist, was born in Baltimore, Maryland, the son of William Nicholls Bolling and Hannah Lamb Bonham. Bolling's teacher, master Hellenist Basil L. Gildersleeve, described him as "a gentleman by birth and breeding." The Bollings and Lambs traced their ancestors back to seventeenth-century Virginia.

After graduation in 1891 from Loyola College of Baltimore, Bolling took his Ph.D. in classics from the Johns Hopkins University in 1896 with a dissertation, directed by Gildersleeve, on *The Participle in Hesiod* (published in the *Catholic University Bulletin* 3 [1897]: 421–71). From 1895 to 1913 he taught Greek, Sanskrit, and comparative philology at Catholic University of America in Washington, D.C. In 1898 he married Irene Johnson; they had no children. At Hopkins he had studied Sanskrit with Maurice Bloomfield and in 1909 published a critical edition of the *Parisistas of the Atharvaveda*, with Julius von Negelein. Feeling academically frustrated, Bolling left his post at Catholic University. Gildersleeve arranged for his appointment as Henry E. Johnston, Jr., scholar at Johns Hopkins for 1913–1914 and then recommended him for the Greek chair at Ohio State University, which Bolling held from 1914 until his retirement in 1939. During World War I President Woodrow Wilson, a relative and fellow southern democrat, officially consulted him on the history and ethnic complexion of Thrace. For his services the Greek government awarded Bolling the Gold Cross of the Knights of the Redeemer in 1919.

Bolling was an active and important Indo-European linguist, cofounder of the Linguistic Society of America and its president in 1932. Bolling, the linguist Leonard Bloomfield (a member of Ohio State's German department from 1921 to 1927), and classicist Edgar H. Sturtevant of Yale comprised the organizing committee that mailed out the call that led to the society's founding (1924). Bolling edited the first fifteen volumes of the society's journal *Language* (1925–1939). His wife died soon after his retirement, and in 1943 he moved to the Nassau Club in Princeton, New Jersey, near some relatives. There he continued his Homeric researches, using Princeton undergraduates as research assistants. On his ninetieth birthday the Linguistic Society sent its congratulations to him "as the youngest in spirit of Homeric scholars and the best-loved member of the Linguistic Society," while the American Oriental Society dedicated to him a number of its journal.

It was Bolling's desire to develop a sound textual basis for scientific study of the language of Homer that helped him to become, along with Milman Parry, one of America's two most important Homeric scholars. His books on Homer, supplemented by his articles and those of his students, include *The External Evidence for Interpolation in Homer* (1925), *The Athetized Lines of the Iliad* (1944), and *Ilias Atheniensium: The Athenian Iliad of the Sixth Century B.C.* (1950). Bolling had a linguist's fascination with the details of Homeric language and syntax, on which he wrote throughout his life. He wrote, "Our first effort must be to recover with all possible exactness the form of the poems as they existed at the beginning of our tradition. Until that is accomplished . . . we are like archaeologists who would discuss the style and authorship of a vase-painting before cleansing it" (*External Evidence*, pp. 1–2).

Bolling took observations made by others and formed them into a coherent and testable theory. It had long been known that the printed vulgate of Homer included nearly 100 lines of quotations not found in any manuscript. The medieval manuscripts contained weakly attested lines. Although the earliest Alexandrian papyri, from the third and early second centuries, B.C., contained many lines not elsewhere attested, later ancient texts, from c. 150 B.C. to c. A.D. 700, had few lines not present in the consensus of medieval manuscripts. The English papyrologists Bernard Pyne Grenfell and Arthur Surridge Hunt, in making this last observation, attributed the new consensus in number of lines (not in readings) to the authoritative text of the great Alexandrian critic Aristarchus. Since Karl Lachmann, many scholars have agreed that the Alexandrian text was derived from the one the Athenians used in the sixth century, B.C., for performance in the Panathenaic Festival. In *External Evidence*, Bolling sought to begin to recover the sixth-century Athenian text by successively removing each layer of interpolation, beginning with quotations found in no manuscript, then lines weakly attested in medieval manuscripts, and, finally, lines omitted from the texts of Alexandrian scholars of the third and second centuries, B.C. He predicted that, if the later ancient tradition, post 150 B.C., represents the text of Aristarchus, newly discovered papyri will contain all lines known from the scholia to have formed part of Aristarchus's text and will usually not contain lines weakly attested in medieval manuscripts. Later research by Bolling, his students, and others has tended to confirm this prediction.

In *Athetized Lines*, Bolling continued to approach the sixth-century B.C. text that stood at the beginning of our written tradition by assuming that lines athetized, that is, included in the text but condemned by a marginal sign, by third- and second-century Alexandrian scholars were weakly attested in the written sources known to them. A gradual growth in the tradition seemed to be indicated by a number of lines omitted by Zenodotus and then athetized by Aristarchus a century later, as well as by the parallel expansion of the tradition of the Indian epic *Mahabharata*. In 1950 he concluded his work with an *Iliad* text that omitted all lines noted in the scholia as omitted or athetized by any Alexandrian scholar, omitted in the secondary tradition, or weakly attested in the medieval manuscripts. One can debate individual decisions, e.g., the omission of the "Shield of Achilles" from *Iliad* XVIII, but the presentation of the evidence of the ancient scholia gives a clear picture of the basis of Homeric scholarship in the third and second centuries, B.C.

Bolling is a key figure in the development of linguistics as an academic discipline in the United States. He also formulated an important issue in Homeric studies in a form that convinced some important European scholars and provoked others to active debate. Despite lack of appreciation from fellow American classicists, Bolling's work continues to excite debate and new research in Homeric studies. Bolling died in Princeton, New Jersey.

• A complete bibliography of Bolling's works in *Language* 40 (1964): 333–36, following the lively obituary on pp. 329–33 by Henry M. Hoenigswald of the University of Pennsylvania, who was left in possession of Bolling's unpublished writings from his later years. Bolling's work, largely ignored by American classicists, has attracted considerable notice from Europeans, both in dissent (Hermann Fränkel, Giorgio Pasquali, Klaus Nickau) and in agreement (D. L. Page, Rudolf Pfeiffer, Stephanie West); see E. Christian Kopff's footnote 93 in *Wilamowitz nach 50 Jahren* (1985), p. 578. Gildersleeve's letter of recommendation is in *The Letters of Basil Lanneau Gildersleeve*, ed. Ward W. Briggs, Jr. (1987), p. 315. An obituary is in the *New York Times*, 3 June 1963.

E. CHRISTIAN KOPFF

BOLLING, Robert (17 Aug. 1738–21 July 1775), Virginia burgess and poet, was born in Varina, Henrico (new Chesterfield) County, Virginia, the son of John Bolling II, burgess and planter, and Elizabeth Blair. He was the third of their eight children who lived to adulthood. Through his father's side, he was a great, great, great-grandson of Pocahontas and John Rolfe. From 1751 to 1755 he attended the Grammar School of Queen Elizabeth in Wakefield, Yorkshire, England. Returning to Virginia, he studied law in Williamsburg.

After his father died in 1757, Bolling moved to the family plantation at Cobbs, Chesterfield County, until mid-1760, when he built a home at his plantation in Buckingham County. From January to September 1760 Bolling courted Anne Miller, his second, half cousin. The affair ended when she sailed to Scotland with her father. "A Circumstantial Account," his narrative about the relationship (drafted in late 1760), gives the best extant view of courtship among the eighteenth-century Virginia gentry.

With the most votes from Buckingham County, Bolling was elected to Virginia's House of Burgesses in 1761. He married Mary Burton, the daughter of William Burton III, of Northampton County, on 5 June 1763. Bolling's wife died in 1764, two days after the birth of their daughter. On 31 May 1765, thirteen months after the death of his first wife, he posted a marriage bond in Amherst County and evidently married Susanna Watson shortly thereafter. They were to have four children. Bolling had attended the Virginia assembly of 1761–1765 regularly until late May 1765, when, thinking that the session's most important business was over, he left to be married. Consequently, he missed the meeting of the House of Burgesses on 29 May 1765 when Patrick Henry presented the Virginia Resolves against the Stamp Act. Bolling was a leader of the Virginia revolutionaries, writing poems like "The Bramin at Atchin" against the Stamp Act.

Bolling himself became embroiled in other controversies. When Rev. George Whitefield preached at the Anglican Bristol Parish, Blandford, in April 1765, Bolling, a latitudinarian Anglican, heard him and wrote a letter satirizing his revivalistic preaching. In Purdie and Dixon's *Virginia Gazette,* 20 June 1766, Bolling precipitated a major crisis by questioning whether three members of the General Court had shown partiality in bailing their friend Colonel John Chiswell, who stood accused of murder. For several months, writers hotly debated the question in the Virginia newspapers. Then William Byrd III, a judge who allowed Chiswell bail, sued Bolling for libel; and John Wayles, whose deposition Bolling called a "mockery," sued both Bolling and the newspapers' printers. On 16 October 1766, Virginia governor Francis Fauquier charged a grand jury to "punish the Licentiousness of the Press." The grand jury, however, "returned the said Indictments, NOT TRUE BILLS." Byrd subsequently challenged Bolling to a duel. At 2 A.M., a few hours before the duel was to take place, the two were arrested. Later that day, after being bound over to keep the peace, they were released.

Against his wishes, Bolling was appointed Buckingham County sheriff for 1765 and 1766. He served on the Buckingham County Court from its creation in 1760, and in the last list of the justices of the peace taken during his life, 27 June 1774, he was the second-ranking member. Since he was called "Colonel" in the 1773 list of tithes as well as in his obituary, evidently by 1773 he had become one of the three colonels of the Buckingham County militia.

In 1770 Bolling's younger brother Edward Bolling died, leaving Bolling his Buffalo Lick plantation. His youngest brother, Archibald Bolling, thought he should receive that year's crop from Buffalo Lick and sued Bolling, hiring George Wythe as his attorney. Bolling employed Thomas Jefferson. On 13 September 1771 Bolling paid Jefferson £9.17 for acting as his attorney and another £5 for a transcription of the complex arguments in the case. Although it is not known who won the case, the record provides the best single example of Jefferson's abilities as a lawyer.

Perhaps the greatest student of Italian literature in colonial America, Bolling wrote poetry in Italian, French, and Latin, as well as English, and appears to have been the most prolific American poet from 1759 to his death in 1775. His work was published frequently in English magazines and dominated the Virginia gazettes. One of his typical poems appeared in the *London Magazine* for February 1764:

The FLAMERS.

SEE, from Stella's sloe-black eyes,
How the forked light'ning flies!
Arrows wound in every glance,
Every look a dagger plants!
Yet such melting graces join,
Stung to death, we scarce repine;
For that softness seems to cure
All the harm, they did before.
Yet, in truth, it doth not heal;
Witness, Love, I suffer still!

His verse ranged through the usual occasional genres of eighteenth-century popular poetry but also included some extraordinary pieces, such as the grotesque poem "Neanthe" (c. 1763) describing a disgusting fight over a revolting harlot, which reflected Italian anti-Petrarchan traditions, colonial Virginia folklore, and English Hudibrastic poetry. In the earliest appreciation of Bolling's poetry, appearing in the *Columbian Magazine* (Apr. 1788), Pierre Etienne Du Ponceau extravagantly judged him "one of the greatest poetical geniuses that ever existed."

Bolling again ran for public office in 1775, this time for the Third Virginia Convention. As in 1761, he won with the most votes from Buckingham County and was in Richmond on 17 July 1775 for the convention's opening. He died in Richmond a few days later, perhaps of a heart attack. George Gilmer wrote Thomas Jefferson the news: "Poor Bob Bolling has run his race, adieu to Burgundy, died suddenly at Richmond." Although his friend and executor, Theodorick Bland, Jr., intended to publish a collection of Bolling's writings, he died before doing so, and Bolling's poetry and prose remained largely unknown from his death to the late twentieth century.

• The Huntington Library, San Marino, Calif., possesses Bolling's manuscript volume on vineyards and wine making as well as two volumes of belletristic materials and several letters to Robert Pleasants. The microfilm of a privately owned manuscript volume of poetry is at the University of Virginia Library. Bolling himself wrote of his genealogy and early years in *A Memoir of a Portion of the Bolling Family in England and Virginia* (1868). Philip Slaughter, *History of Bristol Parish, Va.,* 2d ed. (1879), prints Bolling's letter satirizing Whitefield. J. A. Leo Lemay, "Robert Bolling and the Bailment of Colonel Chiswell," *Early American Literature* 6 (1971): 99–142, prints several poems and supplements and corrects Carl Bridenbaugh's account, "Violence and Virtue in Virginia, 1766; or, The Importance of the Trivial," *Proceedings of the Massachusetts Historical Society* 76 (1964): 1–29. For the court case of 1771 featuring the arguments of Jefferson versus Wythe, see Edward Dumbauld, *Thomas Jefferson and the Law* (1978). Bolling's poetry to 1766 is cataloged in J. A. Leo Lemay, "A Calendar of American Poetry in the Colonial Newspapers and Magazines and in the Major English Magazines through 1765," *Proceedings of the American Anti-*

quarian Society 79 (1969): 291–392, and 80 (1970): 71–222, 353–469. His most extraordinary poem is edited, with an appreciation, in Lemay, "Southern Colonial Grotesque: Robert Bolling's 'Neanthe,'" *Mississippi Quarterly* 35 (1982): 97–126. Lemay's *Robert Bolling Woos Anne Miller: Love and Courtship in Colonial Virginia* (1990) prints his courtship journal and seventeen poems about the courtship, together with a biography and full bibliographical references. Robert D. Arner edits two of Bolling's occasional poems in "The Muse of History: Robert Bolling's Verses on the Norfolk Inoculation Riots of 1768–1769," in *Early American Literature and Culture: Essays Honoring Harrison T. Meserole,* ed. Kathryn Zabelle Derounian-Stodola (1992). Pinckney's *Virginia Gazette* of 27 July 1775, Purdie's of 28 July 1775, and Dixon's of 29 July 1775 all noted his death.

J. A. LEO LEMAY

BOLM, Adolph (25 Sept. 1884–15 Apr. 1951), dancer, teacher, and choreographer, was born Adol'f Rudol'fovich Bolm in Saint Petersburg, Russia, the son of Rudolf Bolm, a concertmaster and assistant conductor of the Mikhailovsky Imperial Theater Orchestra. His mother's name is unknown. Among his four brothers, he was called "little bear" because of his ungainliness. Their home was filled with music and their father's artist friends. By all accounts, these years formed Bolm's love of all the arts as well as his inordinate vigor and sense of adventure.

This ambience also gave opportunity and support to the superb technical developments of his body's particularity, its strengths, and eventually his choreography. His father's good friend was the famous Russian dancer Platon Karsavin, who taught ballet in the Imperial Theater School in Saint Petersburg. Through Karsavin's influence, Rudolf Bolm put his clumsy son to the rigors of the Imperial school, where he flourished. Adolf Bolm graduated in 1903 with honors in dance as well as the academic courses, which included music, art, and literature. Later, in Serge Diaghilev's Ballets Russes company, he partnered Karsavin's daughter, Tamara Karsavina, a 1902 graduate and one of the great ballerinas of the twentieth century. Bolm made the "grand tour" of Europe following his graduation, then in 1904 became a member of the Maryinsky Ballet. At that time the company also included two other important graduates, Michel Fokine and Anna Pavlova. In the same year that Bolm joined the company, Fokine announced his unorthodox thoughts on choreographic reforms. He wanted ballets to have artistic unity; all elements of a composition should be interrelated and have a logic that supported and furthered the story and emotional content. The next year Fokine began to compose dances for the company that realized some of the harmony to which he aspired. Bolm witnessed these new ideas. Further, through Pavlova's influence, Bolm studied in Turin in 1906 with the revered Italian teacher Enrico Cecchetti. Both he and Cecchetti then returned to Russia.

Lessons with Cecchetti brought to Bolm's schooling Italian technical refinements and a rich store of ballet's mime tradition. At the Maryinsky, Nikolai Legat, an able caricaturist as well as excellent dancer and partner, expanded Bolm's understanding of the dramatic and character roles. From Legat and Karsavin, then Cecchetti, Bolm cultivated technical achievements with a body whose unusual proportions never failed to generate comment. Fokine wrote in his *Memoirs* that Bolm had "heavy feet and a rounded back." Fokine nevertheless used its "attributes and shortcomings" to shape Bolm's best-known role, the Chief Warrior in the *Polovtsian Dances* from Aleksandr Borodin's opera *Prince Igor*, one of the stellar events in the first Paris season of Diaghilev's Ballets Russes in May 1909. Bolm's "fire and spirit," wrote dancer Bronislava Nijinska, created one of the season's most memorable dances, and Bolm was "forever unsurpassed" in the role. Moreover, Bolm's dancing embodied energies and dimensions that helped to further new choreography and prominence for the male dancer.

Early in 1911 Bolm resigned from the Maryinsky Ballet and joined Diaghilev's Ballets Russes. His success continued; programs noted him as *danseur classique*. English critic Cyril Beaumont wrote about the first time he saw Bolm perform, in June 1912, in the role of the Stranger in Fokine's *Thamar*. One had to "imagine him as a dominating personality with a big head, large mouth, determined nose, and dark piercing eyes. He had a strange head, half warrior, half musician, the embodiment of action and intelligence" (Beaumont, p. 7). The ballet was set in the Caucasus and included Georgian and Circassian folk dances. Bolm was equally arresting in the mystery he made in the opening scenes of *The Firebird*. "Ever absorbed" in his art, the dancer always impressed Beaumont with his "fire and enthusiam" for reading and study.

Other contemporary critics also observed Bolm's exploration of each role for its multiple dramatic possibilities. Bolm created Darkon in the Fokine ballet *Daphnis et Chloë* in Paris on 8 June 1912, and on 2 June 1914 he first danced the title role of *Midas*. One must also imagine Bolm's "action and intelligence," as Beaumont noted, in roles danced first by Fokine himself: Amoun in *Cléopâtre*, King Dodon in *Le Coq d'Or*, Ivan Tsarevich in *The Firebird*, and Pierrot in *Le Carnaval*. In these ballets Bolm partnered all the era's great ballerinas: Anna Pavlova, Lydia Kyasht, Tamara Karsavina, Serafina Astafieva, and Lydia Lopokova.

In 1912 in Monte Carlo, Bolm choreographed Jean-Philippe Rameau's *La Fête d'Hébé* for a Monte Carlo Opera gala and partnered Carlotta Zambelli. Later in the year Diaghilev asked Bolm to be the company's *régisseur* in place of Serge Grigoriev, who had returned to Russia. Around the same time he accompanied Diaghilev to Hellerau, where he became acquainted with Émile Jaques-Dalcroze and his system of eurythmics. Bolm always included Dalcroze eurythmics—instruction in translating sounds into physical movements—in his studio course work. Bolm announced in 1913 that he had secretly married Beata Krebs Alanova, mother of two children. Eventually they had a son.

Although his experiences choreographing were limited, Bolm acted as Diaghilev's choreographer during World War I when Fokine returned to Russia. During this period Bolm created the ballet *Sadko* (1916), based on a Russian legend and set to a score taken from the Nikolai Rimsky-Korsakov opera of the same title. He also staged at this time the dances in two operas, Rimsky-Korsakov's *La Nuit de Mai* and the Mussogorsky–Rimsky-Korsakov *Khovanshchina*, with "a subtlety before unknown in operatic ballets" (Deakin, p. 109). Bolm's time with Diaghilev occurred during the period of the latter's early collaborative activities, which defined the form of twentieth-century ballet.

Bolm's own enterprising nature had been evident in his early career in the 1908 and 1909 tours he led from Saint Petersburg to Europe with dancers from both the Maryinsky and the Bolshoi; his brother Otto Bolm was conductor. Diaghilev knew these qualities and the character of Bolm's dancing when he asked him to join his Ballets Russes. Thus Bolm's talents were for eight years a vital part of the economic and artistic adventure from which emerged the modern one-act ballet of highly integrated design. Fokine's 1904 ideas had matured and were realized in many parts of the Diaghilev adventure. No one observed more closely than Adolph Bolm.

Early in 1917, during the second transcontinental tour of the Ballets Russes, Bolm was injured onstage in Salt Lake City. This accident prompted him to leave the Ballets Russes to pursue his career in the United States. The same vitality, curiosity, and artistry that had served Bolm so well in the Ballets Russes easily pointed the dancer into a new career in a new country. His activities from 1917, in which he found performance opportunities in many venues, taught, and choreographed, reached into the other arts and set standards for modern ballet's development in America. Bolm's ballets (more than forty) always reflected his excitement about music, art, and literature. Many represented singular collaborations. Further, Bolm passed on to his students a strong sense of discipline, excellence, and drama, traditions in which he had been schooled.

Bolm organized almost immediately a small group of dancers called Ballet Intime to perform in New York and Washington, D.C. The dancers included Michio Ito and his wife and partner, Tulle Lindahl; Ratan Devi; Roshanara; and a former dancer in Pavlova's company, Rita Zalmani. Another young dancer, Ruth Page, came—directly at Pavlova's bidding—to daily class in Bolm's newly established New York school. Those lessons began the long artistic association between Bolm and Page.

On 20 August 1917 at the Booth Theater in New York City, Bolm gave the first performance of his libretto and choreography for *Danse Macabre*, which used a score by Camille Saint-Saëns. He partnered Page, and Marshall Hail danced Death. In 1922 Bolm produced a film of the ballet, directed by Dudley Murphy and photographed by Francis Brugière, in which he again partnered Page; Olin Howland danced the role of Death. Bolm also did the choreography for a Charles Dillingham and Florenz Ziegfeld show, *Miss 1917*, in which he and Page danced the Wind in "Autumn Leaves."

Otto Kahn, chair of the board at the Metropolitan Opera, invited Bolm to mount Fokine's *Le Coq d'Or* for the company. The opera was produced in 1918, with Bolm as King Dodon and Rosina Galli as the Queen of Shemakhan. This was the first of Bolm's many restagings of Fokine's ballets originally produced by Diaghilev's Ballets Russes. Bolm set Fokine's *Petrouchka* for the Metropolitan Opera the following year and danced the title role, with Galli as the Ballerina. In New York Bolm also composed short prologues for the feature films that Hugo Riesenfeld showed in his movie houses, the Rivoli and the Rialto. Page recalled the group's dependence on these "little dances" for money.

In 1919 Bolm began an extended association with Chicago composer John Alden Carpenter and the Chicago Opera Company. He choreographed Oscar Wilde's story *The Birthday of the Infanta* to Carpenter's 27-minute score during the first season the Chicago Opera and introduced short ballet works that were not part of an opera into its programs. On the Auditorium Theater stage, Bolm danced the Grotesque role, and Page performed that of the twelve-year-old Infanta. During the 1919–1920 season Bolm also was *premier danseur* of the Chicago Opera and shared the ballet's direction with two former members of Pavlova's company, Serge Oukrainsky and Andreas Pavley.

In 1920 Bolm again collaborated with Carpenter on setting his jazz score *Krazy Kat*. George Herriman did the scenario and costumes for this dance of "unrequited passion" based on his popular comic strip, introducing a particularly American topic into ballet. *Krazy Kat* was performed in January 1922 at Town Hall in New York City with Bolm in the title role.

When Bolm became sole ballet master of the Chicago Opera for the 1922–1923 and 1923–1924 seasons he opened a school. He continued to choreograph and to tour with groups variously called Adolph Bolm Ballet and Ballet Intime, whose dancers included Harriet Lundgren, Jorg Fasting, and Edna McRae; Page remained principal dancer.

Bolm helped found another arts organization in 1924. Its committee of artists included designer Nicholas Remisoff and conductor Eric De Lamarter. Directed by Carpenter and called Chicago Allied Arts, its *premiere danseuse* was Ruth Page. Carpenter, respected for his business acumen, found money to produce modern ballets and modern music. Late in 1924 Bolm's Ballet Intime featured Tamara Karsavina, with Page and Caird Leslie in *Foyer de la Danse*. In 1925 Bolm returned to New York to restage *Petrouchka* for the Metropolitan Opera, on the occasion of Igor Stravinsky's first visit to the United States. Under Allied Arts auspices, Bolm eventually choreographed at least twelve works using scores by contemporary composers such as Manuel de Falla, Ralph Vaughan Williams, Erik Satie, Karol Szymanowski, Alexander Tansman, and American black composer William

Grant Still. In 1926 Bolm gave the first stage performance of Arnold Schoenberg's *Pierrot Lunaire*.

In 1926 Bolm went to Buenos Aires for six months as choreographer for the Teatro Colón opera company, with Page as *premiere danseuse*. The June-to-September season included performances of *Coq d'Or* and *Petrouchka*. Later that year he collaborated on another American topic with Carpenter, *Skyscrapers*, produced by Chicago Allied Arts. In 1928 Bolm was invited to choreograph Stravinsky's *Apollon Musagète* for the Chamber Music Society at the Library of Congress. The premiere took place in late April with Bolm as Apollo, Page as Terpsichore, Elise Reiman as Calliope, and Berenice Holmes as Polyhymnia. (In early June, George Balanchine created for the Ballets Russes his ballet to the same score.) In the autumn Agnes de Mille was Ballet Intime's guest soloist, replacing Page in its Midwest tour; Louis Horst conducted its small orchestra.

Bolm spent his final twenty years in California. He taught at Norma Gould's Los Angeles studio in 1930. He created a ballet, *The Spirit of the Factory*, to the score by Aleksandr Mosolov, for a John Barrymore movie, *The Mad Genius* (1931). The same year he mounted *The Spirit of the Factory* at the Hollywood Bowl and the following year *Ballet Mécanique*. Los Angeles audiences were thrilled with his movement conceptions of flywheels, pistons, dynamos, and switches. In 1932 Bolm became ballet master of the San Francisco Opera and founded its school. The following year the opera produced its first all-ballet evening, including *The Spirit of the Factory*, in which Bolm and Reiman danced. In these years he also became involved in plans for various dance projects for the 1933 Chicago World's Fair. In 1935 he choreographed his *Bach Cycle* for San Francisco, then mounted it later that season at the Hollywood Bowl. He staged another Bowl evening in 1936 that included the *Bach Cycle* and Fokine's *Schéhérazade*. He directed the dances for Max Reinhardt's 1938 California Festival production of *Faust* and in 1939 produced another Hollywood Bowl program.

Later in 1939 Bolm went to New York to help prepare Ballet Theatre's first season, beginning in January 1940. For that company Bolm set *Peter and the Wolf* to Prokofiev's score and restaged his own *The Spirit of the Factory*. Fokine had been asked to mount *Le Carnaval*, which he agreed to do only if Bolm danced the Pierrot role. In that year, the Adolph Bolm Ballet again performed at the Hollywood Bowl in Bolm's staging of *The Firebird*, with Nana Gollner in the title role.

In the 1942–1943 season Bolm became ballet master for Ballet Theatre. He gave his last performance in the role of the Moor in its production of *Petrouchka* in the summer of 1943. He staged *The Firebird* for them, with Alicia Markova and Anton Dolin in the principal roles, in 1945. Bolm's last choreography was the two-scene *Mephisto*, to a score by Franz Liszt.

Adolph Bolm's experimental and evolving spirit were at the center of twentieth-century ballet's development in the United States. Bolm's experiences of Fokine and the Ballets Russes continued in his own ballets, that is, in his use of untried subject matter as well as in the collaborations through which he realized them. Much rich American dance developed from the directions Bolm imprinted on his students and their professional lives. He died in Hollywood.

• The Adolph Bolm Papers, including programs, letters, photographs, brochures, and clippings, are in the George Arents Research Library, Syracuse University; see also the Adolph Bolm Collection and the Ruth Page Collection of the Dance Collection of the New York Public Library; the Adolph Bolm Papers in the University Research Library, University of California, Los Angeles; the Walter Camryn, the Edna McRae, and the Ann Barzel papers in the Newberry Library, Chicago, Ill.; and the Diaghilev Collection of Butler University Library, Indianapolis. The Los Angeles Public Library and the Pasadena Historical Society contain clippings and programs on Bolm's Hollywood Bowl activities. George Amberg, *Ballet in America: The Emergence of an American Art* (1949), is an important source on Bolm's American choreography. See also Cyril Beaumont, *The Diaghilev Ballet in London* (1951), for an assessment of Bolm's role in the Ballets Russes, as well as Michel Fokine, *Memoirs of a Ballet Master* (1961). Irving Deakin, husband of Bolm's stepdaughter, Kyra Alanova, has written fully about both the man and his work in "Adolph Rudolphovich Bolm," in *Ballet Profile* (1936). Lynn Garafola, *Diaghilev's Ballets Russes* (1989); S. L. Grigoriev, *The Diaghilev Ballet, 1909–1929* (1953); and Bronislava Nijinska, *Nijinska: Early Memoirs* (1981), sketch other dimensions. Ruth Page, *Class* (1984) and *Page by Page* (1978), are valuable resources on Bolm's Chicago years as are the author's unpublished conversations (1980–1984) with Walter Camryn, Ruth Page, and Edna McRae. Obituaries are in the *Chicago Sun-Times*, the *Chicago Tribune*, and the *New York Times*, all 17 Apr. 1951.

ELIZABETH WEIGAND

BOLOTOWSKY, Ilya (1 July 1907–22 Nov. 1981), painter, was born in St. Petersburg, Russia, the son of Jules J. Bolotowsky, a law student, and Anastasia Shapiro, a commercial artist with university training in the natural sciences. When Ilya was still very young the family moved to Baku, Azerbaijan, where his father began a law practice. Baku offered a tumultuous boyhood in the closing years of World War I, as the city was successively besieged or occupied by Bolshevik, Ottoman, and British troops before ultimately falling to the Red Army in 1920. With this second arrival of the Bolsheviks, the family fled the city, making a difficult journey to the neighboring country of Georgia, where Jules Bolotowsky became involved with an import-export company. In 1921 the Bolotowskys left Georgia for Constantinople, Turkey. They lived there for two and a half years as part of a large colony of Russian expatriates, and in the fall of 1923 they moved again, this time to settle permanently in New York City.

Shortly after the family's arrival in New York, Bolotowsky began attending evening drawing classes at the National Academy of Design. He had shown a talent for drawing at an early age, encouraged by his mother's artistic efforts and an active group of Moscow and

St. Petersburg artists seeking refuge from the war in Baku. The academy was his first formal art training, however, and he excelled there, winning first prize for drawing in 1925 with other honors following. In 1926 he began attending the academy full-time during the day to study painting; he remained there for the next four years. Despite the fact that he found the school to be rigidly traditional in its teaching, particularly discouraging his inclination to experiment with color, he stayed on because it offered inexpensive access to studio space and a model from which to paint at a time when his family was struggling to make ends meet.

Upon leaving the academy in 1930 Bolotowsky found work as a textile designer at a batik studio. By the end of 1931 he had saved enough money to take a ten-month trip to Europe. There, under the influence of William Henry Johnson, a fellow National Academy of Design student then living in Denmark, his work began to shift away from "academic impressionism," as he described his early work, to a bolder, fauve-like style. After his return to New York, this new freedom led to experiments with cubist and expressionist distortions. He turned to abstract art in 1933, greatly influenced by the simple geometric forms of Russian suprematist Kasimir Malevich, whose work he had seen in New York in 1930. (See *White Abstraction* [1934–1935].)

The genesis of Bolotowsky's mature style began when he encountered the work of Piet Mondrian at A. E. Gallatin's Gallery of Living Art in New York in 1933. Although his first reaction was "shock and even anger," he soon gained a lasting admiration for Mondrian and his philosophy of neoplasticism, which sought a harmonious balance of visual tensions created on the surface of a painting by subtle arrangements of right-angle shapes and primary colors. That same year Bolotowsky saw the work of Joan Miro, whose biomorphic shapes instantly attracted him. (See *Construction in a Square* [1940].) It was another decade before he pared down his style to exclude all forms extraneous to the vertical and horizontal lines of Mondrian's neoplasticism (see *Arctic Diamond* [1948]).

Abstract art was not well received by the museum establishment or the American public in the 1930s, the heyday of regionalism and social realism in American art. Exhibition opportunities were rare, inspiring a group of artists with a shared interest in nonrepresentational art to found the American Abstract Artists group in 1936 as a forum for the exchange of ideas and the promotion of group exhibitions. Bolotowsky, who had already participated in the exhibiting group known as "The Ten" (which also included Mark Rothko and Adolph Gottlieb), was one of the new group's founding members. Many of the participating artists had come to know each other through the government-sponsored art programs of the depression era. Most of these programs—such as the PWAP easel painting project that Bolotowsky first joined—commissioned realistic scenes, but the Works Progress Administration mural project he later took part in provided opportunities for abstract art. Headed in New York by Burgoyne Diller, himself a devoted follower of Mondrian, the mural project produced some of the world's first abstract murals. Among them were Bolotowsky's 1936–1937 mural at the Willimsburg Housing Project in Brooklyn; a mural in the Hall of Medicine and Public Health at the New York World's Fair from 1939 to 1940; and a mural in the Chronic Diseases Hospital on Welfare Island in 1941.

Meetings of the American Abstract Artists were often characterized by vigorous debate over the definition of the word "abstract." Bolotowsky was an energetic advocate of the view that abstract art should rely solely on relationships of form and color within a work of art, in contrast to the view that abstraction could include styles, such as cubism, that were derived from nature. The group was never able to agree on a single definition of "abstract," but Bolotowsky recalled the "friction" of their arguments as "very healthy and good." Indeed, many commentators have given credit to the American Abstract Artist for developing an awareness of abstract art in the American art community that fostered the emergence of the abstract expressionists in the 1940s.

Bolotowsky's painting and his vociferous participation in these arguments were interrupted from 1942 to 1945, when he served as a draftee in the U.S. Army Air Force. Stationed in Nome, Alaska, he acted as a liaison with Soviet troops engaged in the transfer of American aircraft to Russia. This position, which followed an assignment in New York for the War Department writing a Russian-English military dictionary, kept Bolotowsky far from the epicenter of American abstraction. Through correspondence with Esphyr Slobodkina, a fellow member of the American Abstract Artists whom he had married in 1933 but separated from in 1937, he at least kept abreast of the arguments within the group and participated in exhibitions, even selling some work during this period. He was far too busy with military duties, however, to produce new artwork, with the exception of some sketches of fellow soldiers and local Eskimos.

Upon demobilization Bolotowsky returned to New York and resumed painting "as if I had left only to go for a walk," now fully absorbed by the tenets of neoplasticism. All biomorphic forms had been eliminated before he was drafted, and he soon abandoned suprematist diagonals—although he "hated to give them up"—because the suggestion of depth they inevitably produced was incompatible with neoplastic concern for the "tense flatness" of the picture plane. (See *City Rectangle* [1949].) Bolotowsky's career rebounded with similar alacrity. In 1946 J. B. Neumann presented the artist's first significant one-man show at his New Art Circle. The work displayed there, most of it produced since his leaving the army the year before, elicited generally positive reviews, as did subsequent one-man shows—chiefly at the Grace Borgenicht Gallery—and a multitude of group exhibitions over the next several decades. Through Neumann, Bolotowsky met Josef Albers, who selected him to be his replacement as head of the art department at Black Mountain

College in North Carolina while Albers took a two-year sabbatical. Bolotowsky's successes extended to his personal life as well; in 1947 he married Meta Cohen. The couple had one child.

Black Mountain College was the first in a succession of teaching appointments for Bolotowsky. From North Carolina, he went to the University of Wyoming at Laramie, where he remained until 1957, apart from a leave of absence from 1954 to 1956 that he spent in New York teaching at Brooklyn College and serving as president of the American Abstract Artists. He returned to the New York area in 1957, teaching at the State Teachers College in New Paltz until 1965 and then at Southampton College on Long Island until shortly before his death. He also served as a visiting professor at a number of other institutions.

As his career progressed, Bolotowsky's interpretation of neoplasticism developed beyond Mondrian's example. He expanded a palette limited to primary colors to include secondary and tertiary colors and dropped Mondrian's characteristic use of black lines in the formation of his colored rectangles (see *Red Key* [1952]). In the early 1950s he began to explore shaped canvases—tondos, triangles, ellipses—fascinated by the visual tensions produced between the canvas edges and the straight lines on its surface (see *White Circle* [1955], *Red and Black Tondo* [1962], and Deep Blue Diamond [1973]). In 1961 he produced the first of a series of free-standing "columns" with three, four, or eight sides, an attempt to put neoplastic architectural theories into practice. The sides of a column each stand alone but must also work together "like the walls of a room" as the viewer changes position. (See *Dark Red Column* [1966].)

Bolotowsky's creative outlets expanded as well. In 1953, with a grant from the University of Wyoming, he began to make experimental films, one of which, *Metanoia* (1961), won first prize at the Midwest Film Festival at the University of Chicago in 1963. He also began writing plays in the early 1960s. Both filmmaking and playwriting—where "literary elements, psychology, drama, myths, and familiar images are right and proper"—offered opportunities for Bolotowsky to incorporate interests banished from his strictly abstract paintings.

Nevertheless, neoplasticism remained the artist's most deeply satisfying creative outlet until his death in 1981, when he accidentally fell into the shaft of the antiquated elevator system in his apartment building in New York City. As he explained to an interviewer in 1968, "It's a feeling of perfect balance, as if you suddenly have discovered the final solution, which of course is nothing but an illusion, but there is a spiritual feeling of a solution."

The style of neoplasticism—decidedly unfashionable in the 1950s, gaining in acceptance with the interest in geometricity of the 1960s and 1970s—never attracted the critical enthusiasm that other abstract movements have. Nevertheless, critics throughout Bolotowsky's career consistently acknowledged his skill and integrity as an artist. A retrospective of his work at the Guggenheim Museum in 1974, his first one-man show in a New York museum, confirmed his stature as an important innovator of abstraction in America and a dedicated practitioner of neoplasticism. Bolotowsky's contributions to American art are incontrovertible.

• The Archives of American Art holds a small collection of Bolotowsky's papers, including the unpublished manuscripts of five plays. Also at the Archives of American Art is an extensive and unusually engaging interview with Bolotowsky conducted by Paul Cummings in 1968 for the archives' Oral History Program. The artist's "On Neo-Plasticism and My Own Work: A Memoir," in *Leonardo* 2 (1969), is an excellent account of his artistic development. The catalog for the Guggenheim Museum's 1974 retrospective exhibition of the artist's work is an important resource for reproductions of his work, and Hayden Herrera's review of the show in *ARTnews* (Nov. 1974) gives an eloquent assessment of Bolotowsky's career. John Elderfield, "American Geometric Abstraction in the Late Thirties," *Artforum* (Dec. 1972), provides a broad description of the era in which Bolotowsky came of age as an artist. Sandra Kraskin, "Ilya Bolotowsky: A Study of His Painting and an Examination of His Relationship to the Development of Abstract Art in the United States" (Ph.D. diss., Univ. of Minnesota, 1993), offers a detailed analysis of his career. An obituary is in the *New York Times*, 24 Nov. 1981.

DIANA NUNLEY JOHNSON

BOLTON, Elmer Keiser (23 June 1886–30 July 1968), chemist and industrial research director, was born in Philadelphia, Pennsylvania, the son of George Bolton, the owner of a men's clothing store, and Jane Holt. After attending Philadelphia's prestigious Central High School and obtaining a B.A. from Bucknell University in 1908, Bolton undertook graduate studies at Harvard University. There, he received an A.M. in 1910 and a Ph.D. in organic chemistry in 1913 under Charles L. Jackson, on the chemistry of octoiodoparaquinhydrone. A Sheldon fellowship from Harvard enabled Bolton to spend the next two years doing postdoctoral research with Richard Willstätter at the Kaiser Wilhelm Institute for Chemistry in Berlin, where he identified the anthocyanin pigments in red geraniums, scarlet sage, and dark red chrysanthemums.

In August 1915 Bolton joined the Chemical Department of E. I. Du Pont Company in Wilmington, Delaware, as a chemist. His first project was to synthesize glycerol, but within a year he was appointed leader of a group set up to develop manufacturing processes for dyes. There was then little knowledge of dye manufacture in the United States, and in December 1916 Bolton was sent to England to study British technology in the field, particularly concerning indigo. When he returned, he became Du Pont's adviser for dyes and intermediates and in 1918 was transferred to the Dyestuffs Department as assistant general manager of the Lodi, New Jersey, dye plant. He had married Marguerite L. Duncan in 1916; they had three children. In 1919 he returned to the Chemical Department as manager of its Organic Division, one function of which was dye research.

By 1920 Bolton had formulated three principles of research management, which he would insist on throughout his career: first, search the literature thoroughly and develop a full understanding of the problem before starting work; second, design projects for new processes to give maximum results in the shortest time at minimum cost; and third, use only pure chemicals in experimental work to eliminate the confusing effects caused by impurities and then adapt laboratory processes for commercial use using the raw materials available in the market.

After Bolton became director of research of the Dyestuffs Department in 1921, he began to explore other products besides dyes that might be made from dye intermediates. By 1923 he had begun projects on rubber accelerators, ore flotation agents, insecticides, seed disinfectants, and large-scale manufacture of tetraethyl lead, then the preferred anti-knock compound for gasoline. As new products emerged from these programs, the department's business was broadened substantially. In 1925 he launched research on the polymerization of butadiene, the goal being to make synthetic rubber, an idea that had intrigued him for more than a decade.

In 1929 Bolton was appointed assistant director of the Chemical Department and in 1930 became its director, a post he held until his retirement in 1951. By design, this department (later the Central Research Department) was wholly independent of manufacturing, reported directly to the president and executive committee, and was free to investigate any aspect of the entire field of chemistry. The director was also an adviser to all manufacturing departments on research matters.

Bolton saw research as a big gamble with success depending on wisdom, luck, and judgment in selecting areas of investigation. He always opposed following side issues that could waste time. He knew that the results of careful, painstaking investigations became of value only when they were translated into something useful to society. As director, it was his job "to pick the winners." Colleagues attributed his great success in large part to his comprehensive knowledge of organic chemistry, his broad vision, and his uncanny ability to keep investigators focused on their objectives. Once a laboratory discovery had been targeted for development, his most frequent advice to his staff was "Keep your eye on the ball."

Bolton had a passion for providing his scientists with every service that would conserve their time: analytical chemists, technicians, glassblowers, machinists, cabinetmakers, patent searchers, translators, and librarians. He was also a strong advocate of hiring the best minds in academia as consultants at a time when the practice was not yet in vogue.

In 1945 Bolton attributed the Du Pont Company's success to five aspects of corporate research policy, much of which he had formulated: a focus on research as a major activity in an atmosphere of appreciation, encouragement, liberality, and patience; a commitment to long-range investigations, the primary concern being future businesses; program continuity and funding in bad times as well as good; having the best qualified personnel available; and, finally, teamwork, namely, the close cooperation of research, manufacturing, and sales. Among the thousands of chemical products being manufactured by Du Pont in 1945, Bolton listed dyes and intermediates; neoprene, the first general-purpose synthetic rubber; ammonia and other products of high-pressure synthesis; moisture-proof cellophane; nitrocellular lacquers; and nylon as outstanding examples of the fruits of company research.

Bolton's guiding hand on all of these programs is best illustrated by a critical, farsighted decision he made in 1935 during the development of nylon. In 1928, the year before Bolton became assistant director of the Chemical Department, Du Pont had hired Wallace H. Carothers, an instructor at Harvard, to head a group to do fundamental research on synthetic polymers. Du Pont was already making rayon and acetate from cellulose, a natural polymer, so Carothers aimed his work toward making fibers from a totally synthetic polymer—a polyester. When all of the polyester candidates proved to be only of theoretical interest, the fiber project was shelved. Bolton did not forget it though, and in early 1934 he suggested that Carothers consider polyamides. Out of eighty-one potential fiber-forming polyamides studied over the next several months, the one Carothers and his managers chose for further development was based on castor oil. Bolton, however, totally rejected their choice, reasoning that the world supply of castor oil, an agricultural product, would not sustain a commercial venture of the magnitude he envisioned. Instead, he ordered that work proceed with a new polyamide to be made by reacting hexamethylenediamine and adipic acid, both of which could be made from benzene, of which there was a virtually limitless supply from cheap coal tar. Bolton also guided the development of many other leading Du Pont products, including polyvinyl fluoride film, high molecular weight polyethylene, tetrafluoroethylene fluorocarbon polymers and fibers, urea herbicides, and photosensitive polymer printing plates.

Bolton had an abiding interest in his scientists and knew them by name as well as by accomplishment. The morale of his staff was high, and the people genuinely respected him. Most of his associates addressed him as "Dr. Bolton"; only a few of his closest friends called him "Elmer." To keep in touch, he met twice weekly with his managers and supervisors to review the progress of their projects and to hear first-line chemists give a brief talk about their work.

Bolton's overarching modesty was an outstanding character trait. He was adamant that the scientists who made discoveries be given credit for them. For that reason his own contributions to the many projects that were brought to fruition under his guidance are largely unknown. He published only twelve articles (ten before 1917), but received, throughout his career, twenty-one patents on far-ranging subjects such as ore concentration, insecticides, dye and pigment manufacture, photographic emulsions, and synthetic resins, rubber, and polymers.

Bolton thoroughly enjoyed chemistry, and his life seems to have revolved around his work. His evenings were frequently spent poring through the latest chemical journals, and he fully expected his scientists to do the same. Even in retirement, he kept a strong interest in Du Pont's research and, at his own request, continued to receive abstracts of company reports, which he followed closely. Outside of his work, he enjoyed opera, organ music, and good literature but had little or no interest in politics or religion. Golf with the same four cronies every Saturday seems to have been his only diversion.

Bolton was a member of the Visiting Committee of the Chemistry Department at Massachusetts Institute of Technology in 1938–1939 and at Harvard University in 1940–1941. He was also a member of the advisory board of the Rutgers University Research Council for more than ten years, president of the Elizabeth Storch Kraemer Memorial Foundation for Cancer Research, a member of the board of managers of the Wilmington Institute Free Library, a trustee of Bucknell University, and a member of the technical advisory panel on materials for the U.S. Department of Defense.

Bolton was a member of Sigma XI, Phi Kappa Psi, and Alpha Chi Sigma fraternities, the American Institute of Chemical Engineers, the American Association for Advancement of Science, the Society for Chemical Industry, and the American Chemical Society. He was a regional director of ACS from 1936 to 1938 and director at large from 1940 to 1943. He also was a member of the advisory board of *Industrial and Engineering Chemistry* in 1947. The American Section of the Society of Chemical Industry awarded him its Chemical Industry Medal (1941) and Perkin Medal (1945). He was elected to the National Academy of Sciences in 1946. In 1952 he was elected an honorary member of Phi Lambda Upsilon, the national honorary chemical society. In 1954 he received the Willard Gibbs Medal from the Chicago Section of the ACS, which listed him as one of the top ten industrial chemists in the United States. Posthumously, in 1990, he was among the first recipients of the Du Pont Company's prestigious Lavoisier Medal awarded to those select employees whose technical achievements have contributed most to corporate growth and success. He died in Wilmington, Delaware.

• Bolton's business correspondence is at the Hagley Museum and Library, Wilmington, Del. For his insights on successful research, see his Perkin Medal Address in *Industrial and Engineering Chemistry* 37, no. 2 (1945): 106–15. See also the clippings files at the Wilmington Institute Free Library. A memoir by Robert M. Joyce in the National Academy of Sciences, *Biographical Memoirs* 54 (1983): 51–72, the best overall source of information about Bolton, contains a late photograph of him and a list of his patents and publications. Bolton's role in research at Du Pont is covered in detail in David A. Hounshell and John Kenly Smith, Jr., *Science and Corporate Strategy, Du Pont R&D, 1902–1980* (1988). His day-to-day role in the development of nylon is best covered by Matthew Hermes, *Enough for One Lifetime: Wallace Carothers, Inventor of Nylon* (1996). See also, by Bolton, "Development of Nylon," *Industrial and Engineering Chemistry* 34 (1942): 53–58; Audrey D. McFadyen, "An American Contemporary: Elmer K. Bolton," *Chemical and Engineering News* 25 (27 Oct. 1947): 3145; and two unsigned articles, "Bolton, Crone, Curme, Hildebrand Win Phi Lambda Upsilon Accolades," *Chemical and Engineering News* 30 (6 Oct. 1952): 4143; and "Research a Risky Business," *Chemical and Engineering News* 32 (31 May 1954): 2196–98. William S. Haynes, *American Chemical Industry: A History*, 3, 4, and 5 (1945, 1948, 1954), gives details of Bolton's early work not covered elsewhere. H. Clay Reed, *Delaware: A History of the First State*, vol. 3 (1947), pp. 251–52, contains family information. An obituary is in the *Morning News* (Wilmington, Del.), 31 July 1968.

HERBERT T. PRATT

BOLTON, Frances Payne (29 Mar. 1885–9 Mar. 1977), congresswoman and nursing advocate, was born Frances Payne Bingham in Cleveland, Ohio, the daughter of Charles W. Bingham, a leading businessman and industrialist, and Mary Perry Payne. Frances Bingham attended private high schools in Cleveland and New York City. An accomplished vocalist, she was also fluent in German and French.

After graduating from Miss Speuce's School for Girls in 1904, Bingham joined a group of young women who volunteered time to help the visiting nurses in Cleveland attend the poor. There she was exposed to a side of urban living she had never seen before and to the daunting challenges the nurses faced every day. Based on that experience, she remained committed to the support of the nursing profession for her entire life.

Frances Bingham married Chester Castle Bolton in 1907; they had three sons. During World War I, Frances Payne Bolton, as she came to be known, was instrumental in convincing the secretary of war to create an army school of nursing. In 1923 she donated more than $1 million of her own inherited wealth to establish a school of nursing at Western Reserve University. Named in her honor, the Frances Payne Bolton School of Nursing was the first in the nation to be affiliated with a university. The program provided nursing students a more formal education than the training they received at a hospital school.

After a successful business career, Chester Bolton entered politics. In 1929 he was elected to Congress as a Republican representative for the Twenty-second Congressional District of Ohio. When he died suddenly in 1939, Frances Payne Bolton was chosen to fill his unexpired term in a special election and became the first woman to serve in Congress from Ohio. The next year she won the seat on her own. As a member of the House Foreign Affairs Committee, Bolton spoke out and voted against the selective service and lend-lease bills in 1941. Nevertheless, once it was clear that the United States would be drawn into the war, she supported the buildup of the military and aid for the Allies. At the same time, recognizing that there would be a greater demand for nurses, she worked to encourage more women to enter nursing. The Bolton bill, which passed in 1943, authorized federal funds to provide financial aid to nursing students and schools and established the Cadet Nurse Corps. Shortly afterward Bolton secured regular officers' commissions for nurses in the military. The following year she traveled at her own expense to the European theater of war, where she visited hospitals to observe the treatment of wounded soldiers.

Bolton continued to win reelection to her seat in Congress. As a Republican she supported in 1947 the passage of the Taft-Hartley bill and legislation to limit the terms of the president but voted independent of the party's line on such other issues as public housing and an amendment (which she opposed) to the Taft-Hartley bill that outlawed union and closed shops. She also traveled to Europe and visited the Soviet Union in 1947 to discuss worldwide nursing issues and was the first woman to direct a congressional study abroad.

In 1952 Oliver Payne Bolton joined his mother in Congress as the representative from the Eleventh Congressional District of Ohio. Together they achieved the unique position as the first mother and son to serve in the same Congress. During that term, President Dwight D. Eisenhower appointed Frances Payne Bolton as a congressional delegate to the United Nations General Assembly.

Bolton continued to serve as a member of the House Foreign Affairs Committee, eventually reaching the position of ranking Republican. During the early part of the Cold War, she traveled overseas to gain a clearer perspective on such issues as economic development with no-interest loans for the construction of dams, irrigation systems, power plants, and transportation facilities. One trip to Africa lasted ninety-nine days and included a visit to the newly established country of Israel.

In 1968 Bolton lost her reelection bid for Congress. She had served fourteen terms. After her retirement from public life, she remained active as a trustee or board member for various colleges, societies, and institutes. Although she never studied at the college or university level, Bolton received numerous honorary degrees for her public service. Throughout her life she had donated generously her time, energy, and financial support to causes that she believed would improve the human condition. Although recognized chiefly for her support of the nursing profession, Frances Payne Bolton also helped pave the way for later generations of women to serve in politics. She died in Lyndhurst, Ohio.

• Frances Payne Bolton's papers are at the Western Reserve Historical Society in Cleveland, Ohio. David Loth, *A Long Way Forward: The Biography of Congresswoman Frances Payne Bolton* (1957), written while she was still a member of Congress, provides a noncritical examination of her life to that point. An obituary is in the *New York Times*, 10 Mar. 1977.

JUDITH R. JOHNSON

BOLTON, Guy Reginald (23 Nov. 1884–5 Sept. 1979), writer, was born in England, the son of American parents Reginald Pelham Bolton and Katherine Behenna. Bolton's father was a consulting engineer, which may have helped to determine Bolton's initial decision to become an architect. After studying at the Pratt Institute in Brooklyn and the Atelier Masquerey in France, he designed some houses in Manhattan, worked at West Point, and helped design the Soldier's and Sailor's Monument on Riverside Drive. He married four times: to Julie Alexander Currie in 1910 (two children), Marguerite Namara in 1917 (one child), Marion Redford in 1927 (one child), and Virginia de Lanty in 1939. He became an American citizen in 1956.

At nineteen Bolton began writing short stories and then plays; his first Broadway production, *The Drone* (1911), was written in collaboration with Douglas J. Wood. During the rest of his life he wrote more than one hundred plays and librettos for musicals (most in collaboration), over ten screenplays, one book of reminiscences (with P. G. Wodehouse—*Bring on the Girls* [1953]), and three novels. His big breakthrough came with the Princess Theatre shows. The Princess Theatre was a 299-seat house on Thirty-ninth Street, east of Broadway. In part, the size of the house forced changes in the form of musical comedy—few sets, small chorus, tight book. The Princess Theatre shows dealt with humorous contemporary situations, where the songs defined character and helped to carry the story forward; the characters were somewhat believable, as were the situations, and the productions were mounted with charm. Bolton wrote *Nobody Home* and *Very Good Eddie* (both in 1915, with music by Jerome Kern) for the Princess Theatre. In 1917 Bolton began collaborating with P. G. Wodehouse (whose early work was largely in the theater before he achieved fame with his Jeeves novels); Bolton wrote the librettos to their musical comedies and Wodehouse the lyrics. Wodehouse and Bolton became lifelong friends. Bolton's show *Oh, Boy!* (1917, still with Kern) was especially successful, and the trio's next, *Oh, Lady, Lady* (1918), even more so. One critic burst out in verse:

> This is the trio of musical fame
> Bolton and Wodehouse and Kern:
> Better than anyone else you can name,
> Bolton and Wodehouse and Kern.

Dorothy Parker wrote: "Every time these three gather together, the Princess Theatre is sold out for months in advance. You can get a seat for *Oh, Lady, Lady* somewhere around the middle of August for just about the price of one on the stock exchange." At one point the show played in two theaters only a couple of hundred yards apart.

After twelve shows with Kern, Bolton and Wodehouse started working with other composers, including seven shows with George Gershwin and one with Cole Porter. Altogether, Bolton and Wodehouse collaborated on twenty-three shows. Bolton said, "Writing musicals is like eating almonds—you can always manage one more." Indeed, at one point in 1917 he had six shows running on Broadway: five musicals (*Oh, Boy!*; *Leave It to Jane*; *The Rose of China*; *The Riviera Girl*; *Miss 1917*) and one straight play, *Polly with a Past*, in collaboration with George Middleton. Other Bolton hits include *Sally* (1920), *Oh, Kay!* (1926), *Rio Rita* (1927), *Rosalie* (1928), *Girl Crazy* (1930), *Anything Goes* (1934), and *Anya* (1965). Although he claimed to have written more musicals than anyone else, he was pleased with some of his nonmusical plays, especially *Polly with a Past* (1917), *Anastasia* (1954), and *A Man and His Wife* (1970). Almost every major name in the American theater appeared in a Bolton show: Viveca Lindfors, Marilyn Miller, Ethel Merman, Ina Claire, Ed Wynn, Fred Astaire, Adele Astaire, Ginger Rogers, Gertrude Lawrence, and Jackie Gleason, to name but a few.

Bolton and Wodehouse and Kern helped bring the American musical to maturity as they attempted to make the libretto, the book of the show, independently strong and to integrate the music and lyrics and dance so as to further both plot and character. Bolton was proud of his role in helping to change musical comedy. He wrote, "No longer is the 'musical' regarded as something to be given no more than patronizing notice. If it was once the frisky youngster tagging behind a sedate parent, it has now reached a man's estate." Bolton's literate, witty, cohesive librettos, far advanced for their time, helped move the American musical to maturity.

While Bolton's output slowed down as he got older, no decade passed until the time of his death without several of his plays and film scripts being produced. In the year before he died he spoke of his new works and of his temperament: "I never lose my temper. I don't believe in arguing with people—except over something in connection with my work." He was lively and sophisticated, qualities that were reflected in all his work.

Bolton spent his last years living in Remsenburg, Long Island, New York, though he continued to travel frequently to England. He was still writing plays at age ninety-five, and he died in England (at Goring-on-Thames, near London), nearly ninety-six years old. "I'm against retiring," he said. "It's fatal."

• Bolton's papers are in the possession of Lee Davis, Westhampton, New York. Information about Bolton may be found in *Who's Who in the Theatre* (1972); *Notable Names in the American Theatre* (1976); David Jasen, *P. G. Wodehouse: A Portrait of a Master* (1974); Stanley Green, *Encyclopedia of the Musical Theatre* (1976); and Gerald Bordman, *Concise Oxford Companion to American Theatre* (1987). An interview with Bolton appeared in "Talk of the Town," *New Yorker*, 30 Jan. 1978, pp. 25–26. Some autobiographical information is contained in P. G. Wodehouse and Guy Bolton, *Bring on the Girls* (1953). An obituary is in the *New York Times*, 6 Sept. 1979.

JULIAN MATES

BOLTON, Henry Carrington (28 Jan. 1843–19 Nov. 1903), chemist and historian, was born in New York City, the only child of Jackson Bolton, a physician, and Anna Hinman North. Bolton graduated from Columbia College in 1862 after showing aptitude in mathematics and chemistry. Over the next four years he studied chemistry with some of the best minds in Europe: Jean-Baptiste-André Dumas at the Sorbonne and Charles-Adolphe Wurtz of the École de Médicine in Paris; Robert Wilhelm Bunsen, Hermann Franz Moritz Kopp, and Gustav Robert Kirchhoff at the University of Heidelberg; Friedrich Wöhler at Göttingen; and August Wilhelm von Hofmann of the University of Berlin. In 1866, the year his father died, he was awarded a Ph.D. at the University of Göttingen for his work "On the Fluorine Compounds of Uranium." Throughout his stay in Europe, Bolton traveled the whole of the Continent, particularly in Switzerland, where he became an expert alpine climber.

On his return to the United States in late 1867, Bolton toured Canada and Mexico before settling in 1868 in New York City, where he opened a private chemical research laboratory and accepted a few students. Meanwhile, his pen was seldom idle. His *Index to the Literature of Uranium* and an article in the *American Chemist*, "Historical Notes on the Defunct Elements," both published in 1870, were portents of the work that would win him great distinction in bibliography and chemical history over the next quarter century. From 1872 to 1875 he had charge of the laboratory for analytical chemistry at the School of Mines, Columbia College, under Charles F. Chandler. In what was perhaps his most important chemical work, Bolton published in 1873, with Henry Morton of the Stevens Institute of Technology, work on the fluorescent and absorption spectra of uranium salts.

Bolton was the first to suggest, in 1874, that American chemists should celebrate the centennial of Joseph Priestley's discovery of oxygen. The meeting in July of that year at Priestley's home in Northumberland, Pennsylvania, led to the founding of the American Chemical Society in 1876. From 1875 to 1877 Bolton was professor of chemistry at the Woman's Medical College of the New York Infirmary. Starting in 1877 he taught chemistry at Trinity College in Hartford, Connecticut, and over the next decade opened its new chemical laboratory, built an outstanding 3,000-piece mineral collection, published *The Student's Guide in Quantitative Analysis* (1882), and published three papers on the use of organic acids in the identification of minerals. His *Catalogue of Scientific and Technical Periodicals, 1665–1882* was published in 1885. The second edition (1897) includes the full titles of 8,603 journals in twenty languages, together with chronological tables showing the year of issue for each volume of 500 of the publications and a check list of libraries holding them. After finding himself with a substantial income following the death of his mother in 1887, he gave up teaching and returned to New York City to devote all of his time to research and publication.

In 1893 Bolton published *A Select Bibliography of Chemistry, 1492–1892*, whose 1,212 pages contain 12,031 titles arranged topically in seven sections: bibliography, dictionaries, history, biography, chemistry pure and applied, alchemy, and periodicals, as well as a subject index. The enormity of his task can be judged by the fact that proofreading alone required twelve months to complete. Supplements in 1899 and 1904 added 3,803 more titles. An eighth section (1901), devoted exclusively to more than 3,000 academic dissertations in chemistry, is indexed both by author and by subject.

Just as Bolton's bibliographies are an enduring monument to the depth of his scholarship and his dedication to a task, so a sampling of topics covered by his more than 300 monographs, journal articles, and addresses reveal the breadth of his interests: action of light on uranium, counting-out rhymes for children, Russian transliteration, Chinese alchemy, glaciers, the early medical practice of women, microscopic crystals in the vertebrae of toads, Bolton family genealogy, humor in chemistry, fortune telling, Hawaiian pastimes, evolution of the thermometer, divination with mirrors, physics and faith, language used in talking to domesticated animals, and musical notes emitted by certain beach sands when they are stepped on. It seems he felt comfortable approaching all subjects.

In 1892 George Washington University appointed Bolton nonresident lecturer on the history of chemistry. Although he was not the first to teach the subject in this country, he was the first to approach it equipped as a professional. Fluent, humorous, and charming, he was always in great demand as a speaker.

Colleagues speculated that Bolton was a member of more scientific societies than any other American of his day. Among those in which he held office were the New York Academy of Sciences (secretary, vice president, president, and patron), the American Chemical Society (charter member and president), the American Association for the Advancement of Science (vice president, founder of the section on chemical bibliography), the Washington Chemical Society (president), and the Council of the Scientific Alliance (treasurer). He was also founder of the American Folk-lore Society (a council member and president of the New York City branch), a member of the District of Columbia Library Association (president), and secretary of the Literary Society of Washington, which counted among its members Alexander Graham Bell, John Wesley Powell, and President Theodore Roosevelt.

In 1893 Bolton married Henrietta Irving, a great-grandniece of author Washington Irving. In 1896 the Boltons moved from New York to Washington, D.C., presumably to take advantage of Washington's splendid libraries. Their attractive home became a social center for the city's scientific elite. Amiable and deeply religious (Episcopalian), Bolton was admired for his geniality, culture, kindly spirit, and encyclopedic knowledge. His untimely death in Washington, D.C., came at the height of his creative abilities. His collection of 600 or so early books in alchemy and chemistry, one of the finest of its kind at the time, was donated by his wife to the Library of Congress.

Close friend and fellow chemist Frank Wigglesworth Clarke eulogized Bolton as "honest, faithful, straightforward, a delightful friend and companion . . . who was universally beloved. Higher praise than this cannot be given any man."

• A box of Bolton's papers, from 1873 to 1887, are in the Manuscript Division of the Library of Congress. The fullest accounts of Bolton's life are given in *Popular Science Monthly* 43 (Sept. 1893): 688–95, and by C. A. Browne in *Journal of Chemical Education* 17, no. 10 (Oct. 1940): 457–61, which is mostly an elaboration on Bolton's publications. Details of his involvement in founding the American Chemical Society are in Charles Albert Browne and Mary Elvira Weeks, *A History of the American Chemical Society: Seventy-five Eventful Years* (1952). Statistics on the contents of his *Select Bibliography of Chemistry, 1492–1892* (1893) are given in the preface of that work. See also Wyndham D. Miles in the *Capitol Chemist* 17 (Apr. 1967): 86–87, and in *American Chemists and Chemical Engineers* (1976): 40–41. Obituaries are in the *New York Times*, 20 Nov. 1903, and by Frank Wigglesworth Clarke in *Proceedings of the American Chemical Society* (1904): 6–8.

HERBERT T. PRATT

BOLTON, Herbert Eugene (20 July 1870–30 Jan. 1953), historian, was born near Tomah, Wisconsin, the son of Edwin Latham Bolton and Rosaline Cady, farmers. He graduated from Milwaukee State Normal School (now the University of Wisconsin at Milwaukee) in 1891 and taught school, sometimes as principal, from time to time during the next few years. He entered the University of Wisconsin in 1893, shortly after a young member of the history faculty there, Frederick Jackson Turner, presented a paper on "The Significance of the Frontier in American History." After graduating in 1895, Bolton married Gertrude Janes. They had seven children. He did graduate work in history at the University of Wisconsin and then earned a Ph.D. in 1899 from the University of Pennsylvania with a dissertation on "The Free Negro in the South before the Civil War," under the direction of John Bach McMaster. Then he returned to Wisconsin and taught for two years at Milwaukee Normal.

Bolton began to discover his life's work only after moving in 1901 to the University of Texas, where he edited the state historical journal. He became interested in the southwestern frontier and embarked on the study of Spanish so he could research it. His teaching and research over the next fifty years explored what he termed the "Spanish Borderlands," the region of northern New Spain as well as Spanish Florida, areas previously neglected by historians of Latin America and the United States alike.

Shifting operations to California, Bolton taught at Stanford University from 1909 to 1911 and then moved to Berkeley and the University of California. His most popular course, "History of the Americas," took the view that the Spanish presence was as central to American history as was the French or the British and, moreover, that the study and teaching of American history should be not merely national or continental but, rather, hemispheric. He saw the colonial era beginning long before Jamestown and far distant from it. Attracting large numbers of graduate students, he directed 104 dissertations and 323 master's theses. He taught at Berkeley until his mandatory retirement in 1940 at the age of seventy, though he was called back to teaching—always his "favorite sport"—for a time after World War II broke out. Retired again in 1944, he continued his research—much of it on horseback—for still more books.

Bolton was a prolific and influential scholar. Two of his more enduring professional papers were "The Mission as a Frontier Institution in the Spanish-American Colonies" (*American Historical Review* 23 [Oct. 1917]: 42–61) and "The Epic of Greater America" (*American Historical Review* 38 [Apr. 1933]: 448–74). As he once explained, "Unless I use my vacations for work I will never get anything done" (Bannon, p. 96). His many books include *The Spanish Borderlands: A Chronicle of Old Florida and the Southwest* (1921), *History of the Americas: A Syllabus with Maps* (1928), *Outpost of Empire: The Story of the Founding of San Francisco* (1931), *Rim of Christendom: A Biography of Eusebio Francisco Kino, Pacific Coast Pioneer* (1936), and *Wider Horizons of American History* (1939).

Bolton contributed to the historical profession in many ways, and he received various honors. In 1916 he became curator of the Bancroft Library, the great research library that had brought him to Berkeley in the first place. Beginning in 1917 he chaired the history department. He initiated publication of the *Hispanic American Historical Review* as a member of the council of the American Historical Association, to which he was elected in 1917. The king of Spain knighted him in 1926, and the king of Italy decorated him in 1931. In 1932 he was chosen president of the American Historical Association. Eight universities in the United States and Canada awarded him honorary degrees. His final book, *Coronado on the Turquoise Trail: Knight of Pueblos and Plains* (1949), won the Bancroft Prize in 1950.

Bolton's emphasis on the Spanish role in North American history paralleled Francis Parkman's earlier emphasis on the importance of the French. Bolton resembled Parkman, too, when he rode by horse or mule to trace old trails of exploration. He unearthed the documents, and processed them in articles and books, that opened up a vast new area of inquiry. His writing style attracted a popular audience as well as an academic one. He died at his home in Berkeley.

Throughout his long life Bolton had only limited success in convincing historians to reconceive the history of the Americas, yet by the 1990s his impact had increased in studies of the western United States, indeed of "the Borderlands." Building upon Bolton's work was a major book by David J. Weber, *The Spanish Frontier in North America* (1992). At the same time exemplifying significant shifts from Bolton's approach, Weber extended the region's history well beyond the colonial period, and he gave less emphasis to celebrating Spanish triumphs and more to the roles Indians played in the encounter and the costs they incurred from it.

• Bolton's papers are in the Bancroft Library at the University of California at Berkeley. The fullest account of him and his work is a book by one of his leading students, John Francis Bannon, *Herbert Eugene Bolton: The Historian and the Man, 1870–1953* (1978). Other significant assessments are Adele Ogden, ed., *Greater America: Essays in Honor of Herbert Eugene Bolton* (1945); Lewis Hanke, ed., *Do the Americas Have a Common History? A Critique of the Bolton Theory* (1964); John W. Caughey, "Herbert Eugene Bolton," in *Turner, Bolton, and Webb: Three Historians of the American Frontier*, Wilbur R. Jacobs et al. (1965); Amy Bushnell, "Herbert E. Bolton," *Dictionary of Literary Biography*, vol. 17, *Twentieth-Century American Historians* (1983), pp. 74–78; David J. Weber, "Turner, the Boltonians, and the Borderlands," *American Historical Review* 91 (Feb. 1986): 66–81; Weber, "Herbert Eugene Bolton: The Making of a Western Historian," in *Writing Western History: Essays on Major Western Historians*, ed. Richard W. Etulain (1991); Albert L. Hurtado, "Herbert E. Bolton, Racism, and American History," *Pacific Historical Review* 62 (May 1993): 127–42; and James A. Sandos, "From 'Boltonlands' to 'Weberlands': The Borderlands Enter American History," *American Quarterly* 46 (Dec. 1994): 595–604. Obituaries are in the *New York Times*, 31 Jan. 1953; *Mississippi Valley Historical Review* 46 (Jan. 1953): 185–86; *American Historical Review* 58 (Apr. 1953): 791–92; *The Americas* 9 (Apr. 1953): 391–98; and *Hispanic American Historical Review* 33 (May 1953): 184–86.

PETER WALLENSTEIN

BOLTON, Sarah Knowles (15 Sept. 1841–20 Feb. 1916), writer and reform activist, was born in Farmington, Connecticut, the daughter of John Segar Knowles and Elizabeth Miller, farmers. Bolton was a descendant, on her father's side, of Joseph Jenckes, a governor of Rhode Island (1772–1732), and on her mother's side, a descendant of Nathaniel Stanley, a treasurer of the Connecticut Colony.

Bolton spent her early childhood in Farmington, Connecticut, where she developed a lifelong passion for animal welfare. When she was eleven, her father died, leaving her mother to raise three children alone. The family went to live with an uncle, Samuel Miller, and later with another uncle, Colonel H. L. Miller, an attorney in Hartford. Through circumstance she was able to become acquainted with Lydia Sigourney and Harriet Beecher Stowe, and during this period she began writing. At age fifteen she published her first piece in *Waverly Magazine*, under the pseudonym Alice Merton.

Bolton graduated from the Hartford Female Seminary in 1860 and moved to Fayette, Mississippi, to teach at a private school. In 1861, at the outbreak of the Civil War, she returned to Meriden, Connecticut, to teach in a safer environment. Leaving her teaching, she traveled to Farmington to gather forty-four poems for a book. Though she experienced difficulties in finding a publisher, D. Appleton and Company eventually published *Orlean Lamar and Other Poems* in 1863. The volume had only modest success.

Determined to have a writing career, Bolton wrote *Wellesley*, a novel that was published in the *Literary*

Recorder in 1865 rather than in book form. Seeking to write a third book, in 1864 Bolton moved to Amherst, Massachusetts, to have access to the university library. In 1866 she met and married Charles E. Bolton, a student and active temperance advocate. The couple made their home in Cleveland, Ohio, where they had one child. Bolton joined the temperance movement in 1871. Extremely active in the movement, Bolton published in 1874 a temperance tract, *The Present Problem*, which had limited sales. These and other temperance activities were funded by Charles Bolton's successful career as vice president of the Cleveland Machine Company.

Beginning in 1878, Bolton became associate editor of the *Congregationalist*, forcing a temporary move to Boston, where she met Bronson Alcott, Elizabeth Peabody, Ralph Waldo Emerson, and other renowned intellectuals. These experiences led to Bolton's later biographical writings. In 1885 she published *How Success Is Won*, a series of biographical sketches of successful men such as John Greenleaf Whittier, Johns Hopkins, and Alexander Stephens. Following this work, a veritable flood of biographical books appeared, including *Lives of Poor Boys Who Became Famous* (1885) and *Lives of Girls Who Became Famous*, a book that addressed Maria Mitchell, Mary Lyon, and Florence Nightingale. Other biographical accounts included *Famous American Statesmen* (1888), *Famous Men of Science* (1889), *Famous European Artists* (1890), *Famous English Authors of the Nineteenth Century* (1890), *Famous English Statesmen of Queen Victoria's Reign* (1891), *Famous Types of Womanhood* (1892), *Famous Voyagers and Explorers* (1893), *Famous Leaders among Men* (1894), and *Famous Leaders among Women* (1895).

After her tenure in Boston, Bolton spent several years in Europe studying women's higher education and improvement of working conditions. She also served as secretary of the Woman's Christian Association and assistant corresponding secretary in the Woman's Christian Temperance Union.

In 1887 she published a volume of poetry in collaboration with her son, *From Heart and Nature*, and followed it with *The Inevitable and Other Poems* (1895). Her later years were steeped in her lifelong interest in animal rights, which eventually led to the book *Our Devoted Friend, the Dog* (1901). She was also responsible for the ban on pigeon hunting, later an Ohio law, and on many occasions successfully intervened with the Cleveland City Council on behalf of dogs. She died at her home in Elmoak, in East Cleveland, Ohio.

Though little recognized today, Bolton pursued with dogged determination her career as a writer and activist. An assertive leader in the women's temperance movement and a pioneering animal activist, Bolton bolstered these movements in their infant stages, paving the way for future female leaders.

• Archival sources on Bolton are in the Schlesinger Library at Harvard University, which holds Bolton's diaries from 1881 to 1882 and 1894 to 1915. The Bolton-Stanwood Family Papers are at the American Antiquarian Society in Worchester, Mass., and contain some of Bolton's correspondence and journal selections, edited by her son Charles Knowles Bolton. The best biographical source is *Sarah K. Bolton: Pages from an Intimate Autobiography* (1923), an autobiographical narrative heavily edited by her son. See also Charles Bolton, *The Boltons in Old and New England* (1890).

SHERRIE A. INNESS

BOLTWOOD, Bertram Borden (27 July 1870–14/15 Aug. 1927), radiochemist, was born in Amherst, Massachusetts, the son of Thomas Kast Boltwood, an attorney, and Margaret Mathilda Van Hoesen. Despite his father's death when Boltwood was two years old and the family's relatively modest circumstances, his mother's social position impelled him to be a student at Yale. Upon completion of the three-year course in chemistry at Yale's Sheffield Scientific School (1889–1892), Boltwood spent two years in Munich studying analytical procedures and the special chemistry of rare earth elements. He returned to Yale for the doctoral degree, which he received in 1897.

After three years as an instructor in analytical and physical chemistry at "Sheff," Boltwood joined Joseph Hyde Pratt, a former schoolmate, to establish a mining engineering and chemistry consulting company. Pratt sent ore samples from the Carolinas, many of which contained rare earths as well as uranium and thorium, to Boltwood's private laboratory in New Haven. Although these elements had been known for some time, the phenomenon of radioactivity had been discovered only in 1896, so Boltwood's attention and special expertise were directed to a subject of some current interest.

When Boltwood commenced his radioactivity research in 1904, Marie and Pierre Curie had become famous (and Nobel laureates) for their discovery of radium, and Ernest Rutherford and Frederick Soddy, working in Montreal, had recently provided an intriguing explanation for radioactivity. They argued that some atoms were unstable; these spontaneously disintegrated, transforming themselves into atoms of a different element; the alpha, beta, and gamma radiations observed were indications of the transmutations.

Most research to that time had concentrated on the physical character of the radiations, and chemical confirmation was now needed. Boltwood reasoned that old minerals, unaltered by weathering, must show an almost constant ratio of uranium to radium if one decayed into the other. The quantity of radium present in most uranium minerals was too small to separate and measure, but radium itself decayed into a gaseous product called emanation, now known as radon, whose presence is easily detected. Within a few months, he showed a direct relationship between the radioactivity of emanation and the amount of uranium in each of his samples. Buoyed by this success, and by the encouragement of Rutherford, with whom he was in contact, Boltwood decided to directly prove the genetic relationship by "growing" radium in a sample of uranium.

This proved to be more difficult than anticipated. While in collaboration with Rutherford he determined the amount of radium in equilibrium with a gram of uranium, a discovery of great importance; the formation of radium was apparently slowed by a decay product of long lifetime between the two elements. The search for this "parent of radium" was itself slowed as Boltwood assumed the duties of an assistant professor of physics at Yale in 1906. In 1907, however, he isolated a new substance that produced radium. It had chemical properties similar to thorium, but different physical properties (the half-life). This was the first element discovered in America, a radioelement he named ionium.

One outgrowth of this work was a better method for the determination of radium's half-life, a value upon which other radioactive constants depended. Another was the growing recognition that a number of radioelements could not be separated chemically because they possessed different radiations and half-lives. This led Kasimir Fajans and subsequently Frederick Soddy in 1913 to declare them chemically identical—isotopes—and to explain the decay series by the group displacement laws. Still another consequence of Boltwood's research between 1904 and 1907 came from his recognition that lead invariably was associated with uranium and that the older samples contained more lead; he suggested that it was the inactive end product of the decay series. Indeed, in 1907 he offered the first radioactive dating of a geological sample, Ceylonese thorianite, by the lead method, claiming a billion-year span at a time when most geologists were willing to allow only tens of millions of years for the age of the earth.

Aside from a year (1909–1910) spent working with Rutherford, by then in Manchester, Boltwood remained at Yale for the rest of his career. He was appointed professor of radiochemistry in 1910. Heavy academic duties, such as supervising construction of new physics and chemistry laboratories, drained his strength. His usual buoyant personality gave way to periods of deep depression, during one of which he committed suicide.

Boltwood's stature as America's leading radiochemist brought him election to the National Academy of Sciences in 1911. He influenced the field through his publications, personal contacts, and extensive correspondence, but not especially through his research students, of whom he had few. His contact with Rutherford directed his career in important ways, but like such other associates of Rutherford as Soddy, Fajans, Georg von Hevesy, and Otto Hahn, Boltwood had his own spark of genius.

• Boltwood's unpublished papers are preserved in the Yale University Library. Most of his published articles are listed in the sketch of his life by Alois Kovarik in *Biographical Memoirs of the National Academy of Sciences* 14 (1930): 69–96. His extensive correspondence with Rutherford, describing not only matters of radioactivity, but items of general scientific interest, is edited by Lawrence Badash, *Rutherford and Boltwood: Letters on Radioactivity* (1969). See also the sketch by Badash in *Dictionary of Scientific Biography*, vol. 2 (1970), pp. 257–60; Badash, "Rutherford, Boltwood, and the Age of the Earth: The Origin of Radioactive Dating Techniques," *Proceedings of the American Philosophical Society* 112 (1968): 157–69; Badash, "The Age-of-the-Earth Debate," *Scientific American* 260 (1989): 90–96; and Badash, *Radioactivity in America: Growth and Decay of a Science* (1979). An obituary is in *Nature* 121 (1928): 64–65.

LAWRENCE BADASH

BOLTZIUS, Johann Martin (15 Dec. 1703–19 Nov. 1765), Lutheran minister, was born in Forst, a small Lusatian town in Saxony, to a well-established artisan family. His name was also spelled Bolzius. Boltzius was introduced by an uncle, Johann Müller, to the influential network of Halle Pietism, an evangelical movement of religious and social reform. Baron von Burgdorf, a member of the nobility supporting Pietist reform, offered Boltzius a stipend to Friedrich University at Halle. He studied theology from 1727 to 1731 under two eminent Pietist teachers, Paul Anton and Joachim Justus Breithaupt. He was guided by the Pietist search for salvation and by the model of an active and searching Christian life set by August Hermann Francke; like most Pietists, he experienced an emotionally intense conversion.

Suffering ill health, Boltzius traveled in the border areas of his home province, which provided churches of refuge for Protestants persecuted in Catholic Silesia and became a center of evangelical revival. In 1730 he was appointed a senior supervisor at the Latin School of the Halle Orphanage. There he attended daily conferences at which both the orphanage founder, August Hermann Francke, who died in 1727, and his son, Gotthilf August Francke, communicated with the numerous supervisory staff of the educational, medical, and commercial branches of the foundations. Boltzius was thus well prepared by religious training, administrative and secular experience, and awareness of the Pietist mission by the time he was chosen to lead a flock of Salzburger Protestants to settle in the new American colony of Georgia in 1733.

The choice of Boltzius had been made by Samuel Urlsperger, senior of the Protestant ministry of Augsburg and the sponsor of the refugees from the Catholic Archbishopric of Salzburg. With the help of Michael Friedrich Ziegenhagen, Lutheran court preacher in London, he negotiated with the Georgia Trustees and the Society for Promoting Christian Knowledge (SPCK) for the provision, status, and reimbursement of a pastor and a vicar. The Georgia Trustees in England granted the Salzburger Protestants freedom of their Lutheran confession and accorded Boltzius, his vicar, and their successors the same status as Anglican clergy. This included an annual stipend through a fund provided by the SPCK, which had been closely associated with Halle since the beginning of the century. The stipend was paid until the American Revolution.

Boltzius served as the senior minister of the Salzburger settlement at Ebenezer, Georgia, until his death. In 1735 he married Katharina Kroehr, daughter of one of the refugees from Salzburg; they had four children. Boltzius escaped the diseases that ravaged the colony and killed two of his children; he suffered only occasional attacks of malaria and a prolonged eye ailment in his fifties. He firmly subscribed to the medical regime of exercise, bleeding, diet, and moderation taught at the Halle University. He encouraged the use and sale of the famous Halle Orphanage medications both within his congregation and in neighboring communities.

The career of Boltzius in Ebenezer belies the Pietist rhetoric of humility and modest ambition that pervades his detailed diaries and correspondence. His training as a Lutheran minister defined his views of church government and his responsibility for a congregation that included a number of Reformed members. He stood in the Pietist tradition of repentance and the enduring fight for salvation, and he maintained congregational peace despite the absence of a formal chain of synodal authority reaching back to Europe. He deflected enthusiasm, perceived sectarian tendencies on the part of his flock, and the influence of the Herrnhuters—a competing evangelical group under Count Nikolaus von Zinzendorf. Supported by rich supplies of bibles, hymnals, and similar materials sent regularly from Europe, he laid the American foundation for Lutheran practices of internal piety and church music. Despite several concessions with regard to Anglican marriage and baptism ceremonials, he maintained a careful doctrinal distance from the Anglican church and from Presbyterianism. The thin demographic base of Georgia before the Revolution ensured that his spiritual leadership was not challenged by other ministers, nor was it effectively challenged by the Georgia Lutheran congregations, who knew that their ministers depended not on them so much as on support from London, Halle, and Augsburg.

The Georgia Trustees bestowed considerable self-governance on the Salzburger settlement. Within his congregation—which by the end of the 1750s numbered three parishes, three pastors, and roughly 3,000 people—Boltzius exercised tight church discipline. Of his parishioners he required intense preparation for communion, regular attendance at multiple Sunday sermons and weekly edification and repetition hours, and abstention from intoxication, swearing, coarseness, and contentiousness. Ebenezer was not a theocracy, as it has occasionally been called; instead, it was intended to emulate the Halle model of a Christian community. According to a letter from G. A. Francke in 1744, it was to become a "City on the Hill" and a shining light to other evangelical communities in North America.

Boltzius maintained the reformist mission of the Halle Orphanage, including the provision of free social and medical services and, above all, a Christian education for both children and adults. A modest orphanage was established in Ebenezer in 1737, three years before the building of the town's first church and two years before the English evangelist George Whitfield built his orphanage outside Savannah. The Ebenezer orphanage from the outset transcended its charitable function and became a center of economic enterprise. As its head, Boltzius initiated and completed the public works that laid the basis for prosperity, most notably a series of gristmills and sawmills and a silk manufacture. The success of these ventures, against some local opposition by farmers insisting on the right to their own labor, required financial backing from European donors and early support from the trustees and their Georgia emissary, James Edward Oglethorpe. They survived, however, through the indefatigable zeal of Boltzius and the Halle spirit of Christian enterprise. Boltzius assumed considerable financial risk, borrowing against his annual stipend when donations from Europe were delayed and losing funds in the lumber trade with the Caribbean. The community's success in the production of silk, which reached a peak in the 1750s, would have been impossible without Boltzius's perseverance. To this must be added the skills of his wife, who despite much opposition from Savannah, became a skilled reeler of silk and supervised the silk-making in Ebenezer.

Boltzius is also remembered for his battle against slavery, which was waged with much publicity in Savannah, reported throughout Protestant Europe in the printed mission diaries. Boltzius based his argument not on abolitionist doctrine but on the original position of the Georgia Trustees. In the 1720s the new philanthropists around Dr. Thomas Bray and Lord Egmont in London and at the orphanage in Halle had shared assumptions about the labor of the common man as part of a good Christian life. Slavery, Boltzius argued—most explicitly in a 1746 letter to Whitefield, who used slaves bought with charity funds to run his orphanage—would defeat this purpose and at the same time threaten the financial independence of his capital-poor flock. Against the argument of the British missionary societies that the conversion of African slaves to a Christian life justified their bondage, he found reason in the scriptures to doubt "if a Christian can buy them in good conscience and maintain them in constant slavery" (23 Aug. 1750).

Until the end of the trusteeship in 1752, the Lutheran settlers and their ministers made Ebenezer the most successful and stable, and probably the most devout and literate, community in Georgia. It remained united in the Lutheran faith until the Revolution, despite considerable social stratification and the formation of factions. This stability was remarkable in the face of a physically and socially difficult environment, friction with the authorities in Savannah, and the lack of continuous immigration. Ebenezer's success must be credited in large part to the tactical skill, economic initiative, and single-minded perseverance of Boltzius. He died in Ebenezer.

• A substantial collection of Boltzius's correspondence is held in Missions-Archiv Series 5A to 5E, Archives of the Franckesche Stiftungen in Halle, Germany. A brief autobiography by Boltzius is in *Detailed Reports of the Salzburger Emigrants Who Settled in America*, vol. 17 (1991); the eighteen volumes of this series (1976–1995) are English translations of the diaries of Pietist ministers in Ebenezer. See also Hermann Winde, *Die Frühgeschichte der Lutherischen Kirche in Georgia* (diss., Martin-Luther Univ., Halle-Wittenberg, 1960). For the European and colonial American context of Boltzius's career, see George F. Jones, *The Georgia Dutch* (1992), and two articles by Renate Wilson, "Continental Protestant Refugees and Their Protectors in Germany and London: Commercial and Denominational Networks," *Pietismus und Neuzeit* 20 (1994): 101–18, and "Piety and Commerce in Colonial Georgia," *Georgia Historical Quarterly* 77 (Summer 1993): 336–66.

RENATE WILSON
GEORGE FENWICK JONES

BOLZA, Oskar (12 May 1857–5 July 1942), mathematician, was born in Bergzabern in the Rhenish Palatinate, the son of Moritz Bolza, a civil servant in the judicial branch, and Luise Koenig. Bolza's father's position took the family to various towns in the south of Germany early in Bolza's life, but in 1873 the family settled permanently in Freiburg, the city to which Bolza would feel great attachment for the rest of his life. After pursuing his secondary studies in Neuchâtel and Freiburg, Bolza passed his university qualifying examination in the summer of 1875. That fall he enrolled in both the University of Berlin (for a liberal education) and the Berlin Gewerbeakademie or trade school (for his technical training). When this proved too ambitious a program, Bolza concentrated on physics at the university, where from 1876 to 1878 he studied principally under Gustav Kirchhoff and Hermann von Helmholtz. In the summer semester of 1878 he worked in the laboratory of August Kundt in Strasbourg with an eye toward writing a doctoral dissertation under Kundt's guidance. Bolza quickly realized that his strength did not lie in laboratory work. He abandoned physics for pure mathematics and studied through the summer of 1880 under Elwin Bruno Cristoffel and Theodore Reye in Strassburg, Karl Weierstrass in Berlin, and Hermann Amandus Schwarz in Göttingen. No closer to a dissertation topic after this period of concentrated study, Bolza decided to take the state teachers' examination and prepare himself for a career in secondary education. In 1882 he successfully passed the test, and by 1883 he had completed the mandatory year of student teaching.

In spite of this preparation, Bolza opted not to teach and spent two years in Freiburg privately working on research that he hoped would earn him the doctoral degree. In 1885 he thought that he had succeeded when he demonstrated which hyperelliptic integrals were reducible to elliptic integrals via third-degree transformations. Unfortunately, French mathematician Édouard Goursat had just superseded this work by publishing a stronger result. Undaunted, Bolza turned to the analogous problem for fourth-degree transformations and solved it as well. This success spurred Bolza to return for further study to the University of Berlin, where he worked with Leopold Kronecker and Lazarus Fuchs. Bolza also communicated his results to Felix Klein, a professor of mathematics at Göttingen and a leading international mathematical figure. In 1886, Bolza finally took his Ph.D. from Göttingen under Klein's supervision.

The next year Bolza and his longtime friend Heinrich Maschke engaged in postgraduate study under Klein. In addition to attending Klein's regularly scheduled lecture course on algebraic equations and his concurrent seminar, both young men also met weekly in a private seminar held at Klein's home. While this experience proved rewarding for Maschke, it caused Bolza to doubt his mathematical ability and despair of his chances of securing a university position in Germany.

Bolza decided to follow the lead of another of his longtime friends, the physicist Franz Schulze-Berge, and seek a post in the United States. He spent the fall and winter of 1887–1888 in England honing his spoken English and then traveled to Baltimore, where, armed with a letter of recommendation from Klein, he hoped for a job at Johns Hopkins University. There, with the help of professor of mathematics and astronomy Simon Newcomb, Bolza got an unsalaried appointment as a reader in mathematics and gave a series of twenty lectures on the theory of substitutions in the spring of 1889. Six months later, he accepted a salaried, three-year appointment at the newly founded Clark University in Worcester, Massachusetts.

After three years, the internal political situation at Clark drove nine of eleven faculty members, including Bolza, to resign. Although Bolza had decided to return to Germany, the mathematician E. H. Moore encouraged him to consider a position at the newly forming University of Chicago. Bolza not only accepted an associate professorship there but also managed to secure an assistant professorship for Maschke, who had decided to try his luck in the United States. When the university opened in the fall of 1892, Moore, Bolza, and Maschke formed one of the strongest departments of mathematics the country had yet known. Together, they worked to train future mathematical researchers and to establish a mathematical research community in America. Bolza, who was promoted to the rank of professor in 1894, helped to organize the Mathematical Congress that was held in conjunction with the 1893 World's Columbian Exposition in Chicago, participated vigorously in the Chicago Section of the American Mathematical Society, and served as AMS vice president from 1903 to 1904. Invited in 1901 to be one of the keynote speakers at the third summer colloquium of the AMS, he fulfilled the goal of the colloquia, namely, the broader diffusion of then-current mathematical research, through his lectures on the calculus of variations. These lectures, which appeared in expanded form as *Lectures on the Calculus of Variations* (1904), effectively redirected his own active research interests from the interrelations between hyperelliptic and elliptic integrals into this area. In 1898 he married Anna Neckel; they had no children.

After Maschke died in 1908, Bolza left the University of Chicago to return to Freiburg with his wife in 1910. At Chicago, nine graduate students had benefited from his fast-paced but compassionate teaching style to earn their doctoral degrees under his supervision. At the time of his departure, Bolza's colleagues officially acknowledged his commitment and contributions to the institution with the title that he held until his death, "Nonresident Professor of Mathematics."

In 1910 Bolza accepted the post of honorary professor at the University of Freiburg and continued both to lecture in mathematics and to conduct his own mathematical research. He returned for the summer quarter of 1913 to the University of Chicago, where he lectured on function theory and the theory of integral equations. That same year he did some of his most influential work in the calculus of variations by formulating the key generalization that would come to be called "Bolza's Problem."

The First World War permanently turned Bolza's interests from this and other promising lines of mathematical research to religious psychology, languages (especially Sanskrit), and the religions of India. He continued to teach until 1926 and then resumed his courses from 1929 to 1933. During this period he produced *Glaubenlose Religion* (Religion without belief), which was published in 1930 under the pseudonym F. H. Marneck, and an autobiography, *Aus meinem Leben* (1936). He died in Freiburg.

Bolza made important and lasting contributions to the calculus of variations and fundamentally influenced the first generation of American research-level mathematicians who were trained on American shores. In particular, his student Gilbert Ames Bliss perpetuated the strong program in the calculus of variations that Bolza had established at Chicago. Largely through the efforts of the Chicago school, in which Bolza played an integral part, a self-sustaining community of mathematical researchers developed in the United States at the turn of the twentieth century.

• Correspondence between Bolza and Felix Klein may be found in the Klein Nachlaß at the Niedersächsische Staats- und Universitätsbibliothek, Göttingen. The E. H. Moore Papers in the Joseph Regenstein Library at the University of Chicago contain several letters from Bolza to Moore. Among Bolza's most important works are "On the Theory of Substitution Groups and Its Application to Algebraic Equations," *American Journal of Mathematics* 13 (1891): 59–144; *Mathematical Papers Read at the International Mathematical Congress Held in Connection with the World's Columbian Exposition Chicago 1893*, ed. E. H. Moore et al. (1896); "New Proof of a Theorem of Osgood in the Calculus of Variations," *Transactions of the American Mathematical Society* 2 (1901): 422–27; *Vorlesungen über Variationsrechnung* (1908); and "über den 'Anormalen Fall' beim Lagrangeschen und Meyerschen Problem mit gemischten Bedingungen und variablen Endpunkten," *Mathematische Annalen* 74 (1913): 430–46. The chief source of information on Bolza's life is his aforementioned autobiography. See also Gilbert A. Bliss, "Oskar Bolza—in Memoriam," *Bulletin of the American Mathematical Society* 50 (1944): 478–89; and Lothar Heffter, "Oskar Bolza," *Jahresbericht der Deutschen Mathematiker-Vereinigung* 53 (1943): 2–13, which contain complete bibliographies of Bolza's works. Bolza's role in American mathematics is detailed in Karen Hunger Parshall and David E. Rowe, *The Emergence of the American Mathematical Research Community 1876–1900: J. J. Sylvester, Felix Klein, and E. H. Moore* (1994). His work in the calculus of variations, and particularly his formulation of "Bolza's Problem," is placed in historical perspective in Herman H. Goldstine, *A History of the Calculus of Variations from the 17th through the 19th Century* (1980).

KAREN HUNGER PARSHALL

BOMBERGER, John Henry Augustus (13 Jan. 1817–19 Aug. 1890), pastor and theologian, was born in Lancaster, Pennsylvania, the son of George H. Bomberger, a tailor, clothing merchant, and clerk of the orphan's court, and Mary Hoffmeier. Bomberger's maternal grandfather was the Reverend John Henry Hoffmeier, who had come to the United States from Köthen in the Anhalt of Germany and served as pastor of the First Reformed Church in Lancaster. John Henry Augustus was his only grandchild and the special concern of the grandfather, who dedicated the boy for service in the ministry.

Hoffmeier's pastorate in Lancaster was the scene of controversy over the Americanization of the German Reformed church and the use of German in the worship services. Bomberger's closeness to his grandfather and the struggle over Americanization were to shape the contours of Bomberger's later work as a theologian of the Reformed church in the United States.

In 1828 young John Henry Augustus began a three-year course of study at Lancaster County Academy, then went on to the Reformed church's *hochschule* in York and eventually to Marshall College, the new classical school of the denomination located in Mercersburg. In 1837 Bomberger was the first and only graduate of the short-lived college. His valedictory address on "The Moral Liberty of Man" received denominational attention and was published in the December issue of the *Messenger*. At Mercersburg he had been active in the work of the temperance societies, one of the many voluntary associations linked to the evangelicalism that was rapidly becoming the dominant force in American religion. Bomberger's evangelical activities stemmed partly from the influence of Pietism in the Reformed church of his day, but he was also convinced early on that the Reformed church had to adapt to the American scene in order to survive. At this point in his life, he did not recognize the tension between this attitude and his increasing devotion to the classical orthodoxy of the sixteenth-century Reformed tradition of Switzerland and the German Palatinate.

After graduating from Marshall College, Bomberger took on intensive study of theology under the direction of Frederick A. Rauch, who was president of the college, there being as yet no theological seminary in Mercersburg. Bomberger finished theological studies in 1838 and was licensed and ordained that same year. For about twenty months he served a three-congregation mission in the vicinity of Lewistown, Pennsylvania. He had no interest in perpetuating the bilingual (German-English) ministry required for this pastorate, because he was already committed to the idea of nonethnic Christianity in America. In 1839 Bomberger married Marian Elizabeth Huston; they had eight children, two of whom became ministers in the Reformed church. Several years after Marian Elizabeth's death in 1863, Bomberger married Julia Aymer Wright of Philadelphia.

In July 1840 Bomberger was called to the pastorate of the Waynesboro, Pennsylvania, charge, consisting of two congregations in Pennsylvania and two across the border in Cavetown and Leitersburg, Maryland. Bomberger quickly rose to prominence in ecclesiastical circles; in 1843 and 1844 he was a delegate to the meeting of the Eastern Synod at the beginning of the Mercersburg controversy. This controversy was generated by the efforts of John Williamson Nevin and Phillip Schaff to reclaim the pre–sixteenth-century heritage of Christianity as a continuing factor in historical development. Nevin and Schaff sought to bring the insights of German historians, philosophers, and theologians to bear upon the task of shaping an evangelical catholicism that would be richer liturgically and theologically than the American Christianity being fashioned by revivalistic evangelicalism. Bomberger, having been nurtured by Rauch, a precursor of the Mercersburg theology, rose to the support of Nevin and Schaff in the synodical deliberations.

However, Bomberger saw little conflict between the evangelical catholicism represented by the Mercersburg theology and American evangelicalism. His vision of the church was strongly influenced by the voluntarism of the benevolent reform associations and the activistic character of the evangelical empire. He found theological and historical support for the emerging devotion to the democratic piety and moral policy of American Christianity in an increased study of what he called the "Old Reformed" heritage of Heidelberg and the Palatinate of Germany. Bomberger's understanding of the Reformed tradition was shaped by evangelical American ideas and by his commitment to Americanization itself. He thus failed to confront the sense of dilemma and paradox that was implicit in the theology of Nevin.

Bomberger's early support for the theological, historical, and liturgical concerns of the Mercersburg movement began to wane in the face of what he saw as the increasingly academic, speculative, and ritualistic direction of "Nevinism." Bomberger was a scholarly pastor, studying and publishing polemical writings, textbooks, translations, and edited works. He published articles in the *Mercersburg Review* between 1849 and 1860, supporting liturgy while setting forth certain principles of pastoral concern and scriptural authority. He prepared a "Youth's Catechism" and became an editor and translator of Johann Herzog's *Encyclopedia of Religious Knowledge*. Bomberger objected to the Mercersburg theologians because he thought they appealed to history for proof of doctrine, ritual, and polity. In good American fashion, Bomberger sought to judge the past by its fruits—scholarship should look to history for evidence of charitable work, not for intellectual vindication. He was much impressed with the social reform program of American evangelicalism.

Bomberger's increasing loyalty to an "Old Reformed" tradition that was congenial to the spirit of American evangelicalism was developed during pastorates in Easton and Philadelphia, where in 1854 he succeeded the Reverend Joseph Berg as pastor of the Race Street (First) Church. His dissatisfaction with the Mercersburg movement led to the founding in 1869 of Ursinus College, located in what was to become Collegeville, Pennsylvania, adjacent to the village of Trappe. The Ursinus School of Theology was later (1873) a companion to the collegiate institution. Bomberger became the first president of Ursinus, resigning his Race Street pastorate in 1870 and becoming pastor of St. Luke's Church in Trappe, a congregation he continued to serve along with his duties at Ursinus until 1884. He remained as president of the latter institution until his death at "Zwingli Hof," his home in Trappe. The college and its theology department had served as a center of opposition to the work of Nevin and Schaff, a controversy with no obvious winner. The Mercersburg theologians produced interesting works of scholarship for future generations of Americans and had significant influence on a segment of the Reformed church and its heirs. Their concerns linger on in the work of the Mercersburg Society. However, it must be admitted that Bomberger's "Old Reformed" notions were more in harmony with the developing Americanization of Christianity.

Although a very controversial figure in the Reformed church, Bomberger was often unjustly vilified. The Mercersburg theologians sought to avoid schism; they sought conciliation. Bomberger's stature in the ecclesiastical judicatories of the denomination was eventually restored; he was president of the General Synod of the church for two years prior to his death.

• Many of Bomberger's writings are available in the archives of the Historical Society of the Evangelical and Reformed Church and the United Church of Christ at Lancaster Seminary in Pa. Bomberger's publications include *The Revised Liturgy: A History and Criticism of the Ritualistic Movement in the German Reformed Church* (1867), *Reformed, Not Ritualistic: Apostolic, Not Patristic* (1867), and *Infant Salvation in Its Relation to Infant Depravity, Infant Regeneration, and Infant Baptism* (1859). Many of his hundreds of articles are in the *Mercersburg Review* (1849–1860), the *Reformed Messenger* (1845–1869), and his own *Reformed Church Monthly* (1868–1876). A rather extended analysis of Bomberger and his work is in Gerald Hahn Hinkle, "The Theology of the Ursinus Movement: Its Origins and Influence in the German Reformed Church" (Ph.D. diss., Yale Univ., 1964). Attention to the Mercersburg-Ursinus controversy was rekindled by the publication of James Hastings Nichols, *Romanticism in American Theology: Nevin and Schaff at Mercersburg* (1961). In 1917 a festschrift appeared, edited on behalf of Ursinus College by George L. Omwake, *John H. A. Bomberger: Centenary Volume*. Richard Wentz touches on Bomberger's significance in *John Williamson Nevin: American Theologian* (1997).

RICHARD WENTZ

BOMFORD, George (c. 1780–25 Mar. 1848), soldier, was born in New York City. Little information about his parents is known other than that his father was a military officer during the American Revolution, though it is not clear on which side. George officially became a cadet of the U.S. Military Academy on 24

October 1804, one of a class of three. He graduated only eight months later, on 1 July 1805, and was appointed second lieutenant of engineers. He received promotion to first lieutenant on 30 October 1806 and to captain 23 February 1808.

Bomford was initially assigned to forts in New York harbor, then to those on Chesapeake Bay beginning in 1808. He returned to New York City in 1810 and oversaw construction of Castle Williams on Governors' Island. Through his service at these forts and by diligent study, he developed an expertise in ordnance and eventually became one of the few Americans of his era skilled in the manufacture of ordnance and ordnance stores. On 14 May 1812 Congress created an Ordnance Department, with Colonel Decius Wadsworth as chief and Bomford as his assistant. Promotion to major came in the summer of 1812. Bomford had no opportunity to gather glory on the battlefield but, instead, spent most of the war that began that year at an arsenal in Albany, New York, distributing weapons, manufacturing ammunition and gun carriages, and repairing damaged guns. In 1815 he became lieutenant colonel in the Ordnance Department.

Little is known of the Ordnance Department in the six years after the War of 1812, but it was radically altered in 1821 by being merged with the artillery. Only four trained ordnance men were retained, the department being expected to use artillery officers. Bomford, now lieutenant colonel of the First Artillery Regiment, argued that ordnance, being more concerned with ballistics and metallurgy, was too technically oriented to be merged successfully with the line of the army. His argument was rejected. Nevertheless, as ranking ordnance officer, Bomford effectively controlled the federal arsenals. He reported in the 1820s that they furnished ordnance for both the army and the navy of higher quality than they could get from other sources and that they were capable of producing more cannon than the country needed. In 1832 Congress heeded Bomford's earlier arguments and separated the artillery from ordnance. Bomford, who had been colonel by brevet since 1825, became chief of ordnance.

By this time Bomford ranked as the foremost ordnance expert in the United States. He was vigorous, highly intelligent, and had fine organizational ability. His official papers were models of clarity, allowing him to communicate effectively with Congress and with administrators in the executive branch. High social standing helped, too. He had married Clara Baldwin, the niece of poet and diplomat Joel Barlow. The Bomfords purchased Barlow's luxurious Washington estate, "Kalorama," where important people gathered. Among Bomford's good friends were Stephen Decatur, Sylvanus Thayer, and even Andrew Jackson.

Bomford is remembered primarily for inventing (1809–1811) cannon known as Columbiads, presumably named for Barlow's poem. This gun bulged at the breech to handle the higher explosive pressures there. The first Columbiads were 50- and 100-pounders. Eighteen of the latter did service in the War of 1812, generally being mounted in forts or on large warships. In spite of the great weight of these pieces—15,400 pounds—the limited metallurgy of the time rendered them liable to premature explosions, so they were discontinued. Bomford introduced a second generation of Columbiads in the 1830s.

The 8- and 10-inch versions of the Columbiads were a combination of gun, howitzer, and mortar, capable of firing solid shot horizontally (like guns) or explosive shells at an angle (like mortars and howitzers) or horizontally. Unlike other heavy guns, which could elevate only about 15 degrees, Bomford's Columbiads, by means of a crank and toothed wheels, could fire shot or shell at any elevation up to 40 degrees. Although credit for creating a gun that could fire hollow shot horizontally has gone to a Frenchman, Henri Paixhans, Bomford preceded him by ten years. Moreover, his Columbiads achieved greater range with less powder than other guns. In 1840 a Columbiad broke existing records by throwing a 140-pound solid shot 6,160 yards or about 3½ miles, using twenty pounds of powder. The principal features of the Columbiad were carried into the Civil War as Rodman guns.

Bomford also pressed uniformity of production at the arsenals, particularly in the case of a rifle developed by John H. Hall. In 1819 he established Hall at Harpers Ferry arsenal to make the guns, the first regulation army breech-loading shoulder arm. Hall received one-fifth of whatever sum was appropriated for the arsenal. The local junto that controlled Harpers Ferry insisted that Bomford had no right to allow an independent contractor to do his manufacturing on federal premises. But Hall remained, and by 1825 1,000 rifles had been completed. Bomford encouraged the development of machines that would make interchangeable parts for Hall's rifles, and subsequently they were manufactured much more quickly. Though production was discontinued in 1840, these rifles were employed both in the Mexican War and the Civil War.

In 1841 Bomford instituted several controversial changes at the arsenals. Wishing to diminish the impact of patronage politics on the facilities, he demanded a change from civilian superintendents to military officers. He also insisted workers punch the clock. Though the arsenal workers were used to laboring for the stipulated ten hours, they viewed themselves as craftsmen who would be reduced to mere employees by a requirement to punch in and out. In 1842 all walked out for a time. But, in the end, the shift was made to military superintendents and to the clocked ten-hour day.

After a decade as chief of ordnance, Bomford in 1842 gave way to Lieutenant Colonel George Talcott but remained colonel of ordnance, charged with inspecting arsenals, ordnance, arms, and munitions. He died in Boston during an inspection tour. Failed investments in a cotton mill and real estate had forced the sale of Kalorama before his death. Bomford had a son who likewise became a military officer.

• For a useful primary source, see *Reports and Other Important Papers Relating to the Ordnance Department* (4 vols.,

1878–1890). George W. Cullum, *Biographical Register of the Officers and Graduates of the United States Military Academy*, vol. 1, 1830–1840 (1868); Theophilus F. Rodenbough and William L. Hawkins, eds., *The Army of the United States: Historical Sketches of Staff and Line* (1896); and Roger Spiller and Joseph G. Dawson III, eds., *Dictionary of American Military Biography* (3 vols., 1984), contain biographical data. See also Frank E. Comparato, *The Age of Great Guns* (1965); Emanuel E. Lewis, *Seacoast Fortifications of the United States* (1979); and Merritt Roe Smith, *Harpers Ferry Armory and the New Technology: The Challenge of Change* (1977).

JOHN K. MAHON

BONANO, Sharkey (9 Apr. 1902–27 Mar. 1972), jazz trumpeter and singer, was born Joseph Gustaf Bonano in the Milneburg section of New Orleans, Louisiana. His father was a classical flutist. He was given his nickname after the professional boxer "Sailor" Tom Sharkey. Using an instrument bought from black cornetist Buddy Petit, Bonano began playing while in his midteens, gaining some experience in local bands before working briefly in early 1920 in trombonist Eddie Edwards's Jazz Orchestra in New York City. After returning to New Orleans, around 1921 he worked at a dance hall in the Lake Pontchartrain resort area in a band led by tubaist and bassist Chink Martin and then in pianist Freddie Newman's group at the Ringside Club.

In October 1924, acting on a recommendation by Paul Mares, leader of the New Orleans Rhythm Kings, Bonano traveled to New York in the hope of taking cornetist Bix Beiderbecke's place in the Wolverines. However, Bonano was unfamiliar with the popular midwestern band's repertoire and style and apparently could not readily assimilate. He was unable to learn the material, much less emulate the required Beiderbecke tone and phrasing.

After playing briefly with Jimmy Durante's Original New Orleans Jazz Band, Bonano returned to New Orleans to resume work with pianist Norman Brownlee's orchestra and in January 1925 made his first records with that band. His simple, full-toned direct lead is evident on "Peculiar" and "Dirty Rag." In the mid-1920s Bonano led a band on a Mississippi riverboat, the SS *Island Queen* and in 1927 played briefly in one of Jean Goldkette's Detroit-area orchestras and for a longer period with the New Orleans Rhythm Masters at the Ringside Club. In April 1928 Bonano recorded the old rag standard "Panama" and King Oliver's "Dipper Mouth Blues" with pianist Johnny Miller's New Orleans Frolickers, a seven-piece band that included former New Orleans Rhythm Masters clarinetist Sidney Arodin and saxman Hal Jordy. In December he was featured, again with Arodin and Jordy, on drummer Monk Hazel's Bienville Roof Orchestra's "Sizzling the Blues," "High Society," "Git wit It," and "Ideas." After a 1929 trip to Hollywood with Larry Shields's band, in 1930 Bonano co-led a ten-piece orchestra with trumpeter Leon Prima, older brother of the more widely known Louis Prima. While working on riverboats, at the Little Club and the Club Forrest, and broadcasting over WSMB, the Prima-Sharkey Melody Makers included the young and later renowned clarinetist Irving Fazola, trombonist Charlie Hartman, and tenorman Nino Picone.

Bonano remained in New Orleans during the early 1930s, working outside of music but also playing at various local venues. In mid-1936, after the worst years of the depression, a slight resurgence of job opportunities for jazz musicians led Bonano to join a new group assembled by former New Orleans Rhythm Kings drummer and one-time successful bandleader Ben Pollack. Before that, though, in March 1936, using all–New Orleanian personnel, Bonano had recorded "Everybody Loves My Baby" and "Yes, She Do—No, She Don't," on which he both sang and played in a style obviously influenced by Louis Armstrong, thereby establishing the pattern he would follow throughout his career. By the fall, he was settled in New York, where he recorded with similarly structured jazz groups drawn from the personnels of Pollack's big band and Joe Marsala and Eddie Condon's small ad hoc groups. Between October 1936 and January 1937, under the name of Sharkey and His Sharks of Rhythm, he recorded twelve titles in three sessions, using men such as trombonists Santo Pecora, Moe Zudecoff (later known as Buddy Morrow), and George Brunies, clarinetists Irving Fazola and Joe Marsala, pianists Clyde Hart and Joe Bushkin, guitarist Condon, bassist Artie Shapiro, and drummers Pollack and George Wettling. Of the twelve titles recorded only "High Society" does not feature a novelty vocal chorus by Bonano.

After a December 1937 opening with his own band at Nick's in Greenwich Village, in February 1938 Bonano replaced Nick La Rocca for a commercial recording date under the direction of the revived O.D.J.B.'s (Original Dixieland Jazz Band) trombonist/leader Eddie Edwards, but in 1939 he returned to New Orleans, where he played in residence at the Moulin Rouge. With U.S. entry into the war, Bonano enlisted in the Coast Guard. After his discharge in the spring of 1945 he resumed his career in local clubs. From early 1949 on he once again led his own band, which, like so many other latter-day "dixieland" groups, proved to be a popular tourist attraction in the gaudy clubs lining Bourbon Street. During the 1950s he also toured overseas with the band and played longer engagements in Chicago and New York. Bonano continued to perform in New Orleans through the 1960s and appeared at the New Orleans Jazz Festival in June 1969. He died in New Orleans.

Between May 1949 and January 1960 Bonano recorded extensively, using many of the same musicians he had worked with since the 1920s and 1930s. These included trombonists Pecora and Julian Laine, clarinetists Leonard "Bujie" Centobie, Harry Shields, and Lester Bouchon, pianists Armand Hug and Jeff Riddick, bassists Chink Martin, Arnold Loyacano, and Joe Loyacano, and drummers Hazel and Abbie Brunies. But he also used younger New Orleans jazzmen such as trombonists Jack Delaney and Bob Havens, clarinetist Pete Fountain, and pianist Stan Mendelson.

Throughout the last two decades of his career, Bonano maintained the same musical format he had been associated with all his life—a traditional front line instrumentation of trumpet, trombone, and clarinet, a three-piece rhythm section, and a style and repertoire patterned after the early dixieland bands. This essentially conservative approach was made even more commercially acceptable by his showmanship, vocals, and consistently assertive—if not particularly original or imaginative—trumpet playing. He invariably displayed good taste in his choice of sidemen, among whom were some of the best white New Orleans musicians then working.

• Some oral history material on Bonano is at Tulane University. Because of the low regard in which commercialized "dixieland" has been held by serious jazz historians and critics, comparatively little has been written about either Bonano or his bands. Historical interest that has been shown in his career rests on his earlier activities in New Orleans, and even this tends to focus more on his colleagues than on Bonano himself. Accordingly, his name is rarely mentioned in histories and never in works of a more theoretical or analytical nature. However, Al Rose and Edmond Souchon, *New Orleans Jazz: A Family Album* (1967), offer some material on Bonano's early years and associations.

JACK SOHMER

BONAPARTE, Charles Joseph (9 June 1851–28 June 1921), lawyer and politician, was born in Baltimore, Maryland, the son of Jerome Bonaparte, a wealthy property owner, and Susan Mary Williams. His grandfather, Jerome Bonaparte, was Napoleon Bonaparte's brother, and his grandmother, Elizabeth Patterson Bonaparte, was involved in a bitter dispute with Napoleon over her marriage. Growing up in wealthy circumstances, Charles had private tutors before he entered Harvard. A gifted student, he graduated in 1872, completed Harvard Law School in 1874, and was admitted to the Maryland bar that same year. He married Ellen Channing Day of Boston on 1 September 1875; they had no children. A Roman Catholic, Bonaparte took a great interest in the role of his church in American life.

Bonaparte did not have to earn a living and thus devoted his law practice to his family's properties and cases that appealed to him. "A stocky little man," he was known for a perpetual smile that one reporter called "a smile of fascination" (Goldman, p. 11). He gained a reputation as a potent orator who could flay opponents; his enemies in Baltimore called him "the Peacock of Park Avenue" (Goldman, p. 16). Bonaparte's major political goal was civil service reform, and he was among the organizers of the National Civil Service Reform League in 1881. In Maryland, he was an ardent foe of Isaac Rasin, the Democratic boss of Baltimore, and the state's other leading Democrat, Senator Arthur Pue Gorman.

Bonaparte was appointed to the board of election supervisors in Baltimore in 1895 because of a popular clamor for his selection. Although he argued that "very few innocent men are lynched" (Goldman, p. 32), he wrote and spoke out against Democratic efforts to disfranchise African-American voters in Maryland from 1899 to 1908.

Bonaparte's reform work brought him to the attention of Theodore Roosevelt (1858–1919), and the two men became friends during the 1890s when Roosevelt was on the Civil Service Commission. After Roosevelt entered the White House in 1901, the new president named Bonaparte to the Board of Indian Commissioners to examine the situation in the Indian Territory. In that position, Bonaparte was successful in helping Catholics receive more equitable access to contracts for religious schools devoted to Native Americans. In 1903, after Roosevelt enlisted Bonaparte to probe charges of corruption in the Post Office Department, he was able to root out some wrongdoers without political embarrassment to the president. When Roosevelt reshuffled his cabinet during the summer of 1905, he appointed Bonaparte to be secretary of the navy to replace Paul Morton. The plan was to have Bonaparte hold the navy post until Attorney General William H. Moody retired a year later. Roosevelt was also aware of the political advantages of having a Catholic member of the cabinet. Recognizing what Bonaparte had accomplished as a troubleshooter for the administration, the president asserted that his friend had "the most forceful mind of the country" (Goldman, p. 91).

Because Roosevelt acted as his own secretary of the navy, Bonaparte did not play a large role in the operations of the department during the year that followed. In public speeches, he echoed the president's call for greater naval appropriations. "While we prize peace," Bonaparte said, "we do not fear and have no reason to fear war" (Goldman, p. 104). When Moody was nominated to the U.S. Supreme Court in late 1906, Bonaparte became attorney general. In that capacity, Bonaparte served as the leading agent in implementing Roosevelt's regulatory policies toward large corporations.

Although one reporter predicted that Bonaparte would prove to be "a terror to every trust magnate in the country" (Goldman, p. 130), most critics perceived him as cool toward an energetic enforcement of the Sherman Antitrust Act. To quiet such fears, Bonaparte launched an investigation of the International Harvester Company as a possible target of an antitrust prosecution. He soon discovered that Roosevelt had reached private understandings with the company's officers through the Bureau of Corporations not to proceed with antitrust indictments in return for corporate behavior that was agreeable to the White House. In September 1907 the president instructed Bonaparte not to proceed further with the inquiry. The attorney general did, however, begin the antitrust prosecution of the American Tobacco Company, which eventually brought about the firm's dissolution in 1911. For the most part, Bonaparte found himself in time-consuming turf fights with the Bureau of Corporations over which agency should take the lead in carrying out Roosevelt's policies toward big business.

Although he was less accessible to reporters and less of an activist than Moody had been, Bonaparte had greater zeal as a prosecutor. He expanded the power of the Justice Department in naturalization proceedings and pursued anarchists such as Emma Goldman. His most lasting institutional legacy was the establishment of a bureau of investigation within his department to end its reliance on the Secret Service. The bureau was needed, Bonaparte warned, in order to combat the spread of more sophisticated criminal activities. Congress endeavored to block his proposal in 1909 before Roosevelt left office, but the new Bureau of Investigation survived and later evolved into the Federal Bureau of Investigation.

Bonaparte's term ended in March 1909 with the beginning of William Howard Taft's presidency. He supported Roosevelt and the Progressive party in 1912 and remained loyal to the former president when Roosevelt sought the Republican nomination in 1916. He argued for preparedness before World War I and opposed Woodrow Wilson's League of Nations. He died at his home outside of Baltimore.

Bonaparte was a significant force in the civil service reform movement and in the turbulent politics of Maryland. As a cabinet officer, he followed the broad lines of policy that Roosevelt had established; neither at the Navy Department nor in the Department of Justice did he leave a distinct personal mark on policy making. In many ways he was typical of second-level politicians of the era of progressive reform at the opening of the twentieth century.

• A rich collection of Bonaparte papers is at the Library of Congress. Other collections at the Library of Congress with Bonaparte materials include the Theodore Roosevelt, William Howard Taft, and Elihu Root papers. The records of the Department of the Navy and the Department of Justice at the National Archives also are useful for Bonaparte's official career. Bonaparte wrote extensively for a number of causes. Two representative examples are "Two Years of a Government That Does Things," *Outlook*, Mar. 1907, pp. 599–603, and "Experiences of a Cabinet Officer under Roosevelt," *Century*, Mar. 1910, pp. 752–58. The only complete biography is Joseph Bucklin Bishop, *Charles Joseph Bonaparte: His Life and Public Services* (1922). Eric F. Goldman, *Charles J. Bonaparte: Patrician Reformer, His Earlier Career* (1943), is a published doctoral dissertation that was intended to be a fuller account. A. Walker Rumble, "Rectitude and Reform: Charles J. Bonaparte and the Politics of Gentility, 1851–1921" (Ph.D. diss., Univ. of Maryland, 1970), is the most modern treatment. A contemporary assessment is Willard French, "Promotions in the Cabinet," *World Today*, Jan. 1907, pp. 82–85. For his role in Maryland politics, see James B. Crooks, *Politics & Progress: The Rise of Urban Progressivism in Baltimore, 1895–1911* (1968). An excellent treatment of Bonaparte's work in the Justice Department is in Thomas R. Wessel, "Republican Justice: The Department of Justice under Roosevelt and Taft, 1901–1913" (Ph.D. diss., Univ. of Maryland, 1972). A full obituary is in *The New York Times*, 29 June 1921.

LEWIS L. GOULD

BONAPARTE, Charles Lucien Jules Laurent (24 May 1803–29 July 1857), ornithologist, was born in Paris, France, the son of Lucien Bonaparte, a younger brother of Napoleon Bonaparte and a senator and president of the Council of Five Hundred during the Directorate, and Alexandrine de Bleschamps. His early life was full of turmoil since Napoleon bitterly opposed his father's marriage considering it insufficiently elevated for the brother of a future emperor. Lucien, an ardent republican who disapproved of Napoleon's empire, refused to divorce his wife. In 1804 he left France for Rome, where he placed himself under the protection of Pope Pius VII. His eldest son, Charles, banned by Napoleon from the line of succession, nevertheless spent a childhood surrounded by luxury until Napoleon's break with the pope forced his father to flee in 1810. Lucien planned to emigrate to the United States, but he and his family were captured by the British off Sardinia and taken to England. During the next four years, Charles was privately tutored. He concentrated on his favorite subject, natural history, and learned English. In 1814, after Napoleon's exile to Elba, Lucien and his family returned to Rome, where Pope Pius VII granted Lucien the title of prince of Canino and named Charles prince of Musignano. Charles continued to study plants, insects, and vertebrate animals (including birds) in Rome and at Lucien's estates in Frascati and Canino; he also commenced a natural history of the birds of Rome.

In 1822 Charles married his cousin Zenaide Laetitia Julie, the eldest daughter of his uncle Joseph Bonaparte, the former king of Spain under Napoleon's empire; they had twelve children, four of whom died in infancy or early childhood. The following year Charles and his wife went to the United States to stay with Joseph in Philadelphia and at his estate, "Point Breeze," in Bordentown, New Jersey, to which he had relocated after Napoleon's downfall. In 1824 Charles joined the American Philosophical Society and the Academy of Natural Sciences of Philadelphia, and in 1827 he joined the Maclurian Lyceum of Arts and Sciences. He published a major series of papers in 1824 and 1825 in the *Journal of the Academy of Natural Sciences* titled "Observations on the Nomenclature of Wilson's Ornithology," in which he used new information concerning the transformation of bird plumage due to age or moulting to revise the naming of certain species by Alexander Wilson, a Scottish immigrant who wrote and illustrated the first book on American birds, *American Ornithology*. He also sorted out the females and young of various species.

Bonaparte's most important work in America was *American Ornithology; or, The Natural History of Birds Inhabiting the United States Not Given by Wilson* (1825–1833), illustrated by Titian Ramsay Peale and Alexander Rider. Bonaparte had thought of using illustrator John James Audubon, whom he had met in Philadelphia in 1824, but the engraver Alexander Lawson refused to engrave Audubon's drawings. One drawing, nevertheless, was included: Audubon's first published work, the "Great Crow Blackbird" (now called the boat-tailed grackle). Bonaparte continued an intense, often stormy relationship with Audubon for many years.

In *American Ornithology* Bonaparte described birds that had been discovered since Wilson's early death in 1813, most of which had been collected by Thomas Say—Bonaparte's close friend and mentor in America for whom he named Say's phoebe, *Sayornis saya*—on the government-sponsored Long Expedition to the Rocky Mountains of 1819–1820. He also incorporated the changes in nomenclature noted in his earlier articles.

At the end of 1826, Bonaparte went to Europe to pursue a survey of the genera of the world's birds, the libraries and museums of the United States being then inadequate for his project. He attended meetings of the Linnaean Society of London and was elected to foreign membership in May 1826. He traveled to Leiden, Holland, to meet Coenraad Jacob Temminck, whose *Manual d'Ornithologie* (1815) had so influenced him, and then he traveled on to Italy. It was on this journey that he published a *Specchio comparativo delle ornitologie di Roma e di Filadelfia* (1827) in Pisa, making a significant contribution to zoogeography (the study of the geographical distribution of animals) by comparing the birds of two cities on opposite sides of the Atlantic.

In February 1828 Bonaparte and his family left America and moved to Italy. He left the New Yorker William Cooper (for whom he named the Cooper's hawk, *Accipiter cooperii*) the task of seeing his last three volumes through the press. Back in Rome, he and Zenaide lived in the Villa Paolina, inherited from their mutual aunt, Pauline Borghese.

In 1838 Bonaparte published *A Geographical and Comparative List of the Birds of Europe and North America* in England, an expansion of his earlier study of the birds of Philadelphia and Rome. But his major work between 1832 and 1841 was his comprehensive *Iconografia della fauna italica per le quattro classi degli Animali Vertebrati*, covering in three volumes the mammals, birds, amphibians, reptiles, and fish of Italy. He also wrote papers for professional journals and corresponded and exchanged specimens with naturalists in America and on the continent.

Fervently interested in republican politics—a legacy from his father, who died in 1840, bequeathing him the additional title of prince of Canino—Bonaparte was instrumental in organizing scientific congresses held in various Italian cities from 1839 to 1847. Still in touch with the United States, where democratic ideals had strengthened his convictions, he wrote to the American Philosophical Society for permission to represent them at these meetings. Although nominally scientific, most of these gatherings had political undertones for those members, like Bonaparte, who advocated Italian unification.

In Rome Bonaparte openly supported the independence party and was named vice president of the legislative council in February 1849 after Pope Pius IX fled the Vatican. But the French president, Bonaparte's cousin Louis Napoleon, squashed the revolt against the repressive clergy, and Bonaparte secretly left Italy. He was prohibited from landing in France, and after a sojourn in England and Scotland he spent the next six months with his colleague Hermann Schlegel in Holland before being permitted by Louis Napoleon to live in Paris in 1850. By then he was separated from Zenaide; the separation was made legal in 1854 by decree of his cousin French emperor Louis Napoleon. Some of Bonaparte's children occasionally stayed with him in Paris.

Bonaparte was enthusiastic and warmhearted, yet fiery, pompous, difficult, and often at cross-purposes with his intentions. He bore a striking physical resemblance to Napoleon, and in his single-minded drive to put the nomenclature and classification of birds on a solid footing he recalled the prodigious energy and determination of his famous uncle.

His friendship in Paris with the eminent zoologist Isadore Geoffroy Saint-Hilaire provided a valuable stimulus to his work, and under Saint-Hilaire's influence, "Bonaparte foreshadowed the theory of evolution" (Stresemann, p. 163). His last great work, *Conspectus generum avium* (2 vols., 1850–1857), written in Latin to emphasize its international significance, was intended to include all of the world's known species of birds. But it was unfinished at his premature death in Paris. He was buried in the Bonaparte chapel at Ajaccio, Corsica, the home of his paternal ancestors.

For his contributions to ornithology in the United States, Bonaparte has been described as the "Father of Systematic Ornithology in America" (William Howard Ball, note on the location of Bonaparte's grave *Auk* [1930], p. 462). Through his careful study of species in many museums on two continents and his numerous publications in four languages, his achievements in the classification of birds of the world "ensure him an outstanding place in history" (Stresemann, p. 168). In America he made it possible for his colleagues to place their indigenous fauna in a more universal context.

• Bonaparte's letters from American scientists are in the library of the Muséum National d'Histoire Naturelle à Paris and on microfilm at the American Philosophical Society in Philadelphia. Several Bonaparte letters and manuscripts for his journal articles are at the Academy of Natural Sciences of Philadelphia, and the Houghton Library of Harvard University has some of his correspondence with Louis Agassiz. At the Natural History Museum and the Linnaean Society of London are letters to English naturalists, and the Fondazioni Primoli in Rome has a large collection of family correspondence. Another of his major works is *Iconographie des pigeons non figures par Madame Knip [Mlle. Pauline de Courcelles]* (2 vols., 1857). Among his most important articles for scientific journals in the United States are "Catalogue of the Birds of the United States, Systematically Arranged in Orders, Families, Genera, and Subgenera," *Contributions of the Maclurian Lyceum of Arts and Science* 1 (1827); and "The Genera of North American Birds and a Synopsis of the Species Found within the Territory of the United States; Systematically Arranged in Orders and Families," *Annals of the Lyceum of Natural History of New York* 2 (1828). An article on Bonaparte's work, with biographical details, is Michael J. Brodhead, "The Work of Charles Lucien Bonaparte in America," *Proceedings of the American Philosophical Society* 122, no. 4 (18 Aug. 1978): 198–203. His relationship with Thomas Say and other naturalists in Philadelphia is discussed in Patricia Tyson Stroud, *Thomas Say: New World Naturalist* (1992). There are chapters on Bonaparte in Erwin Stresemann, *Ornithology from Aristotle to the Present* (1975). An obituary is in the *Proceedings of the Linnaean Society of London* 3 (1859).

PATRICIA TYSON STROUD

BONAPARTE, Elizabeth Patterson (6 Feb. 1785–4 Apr. 1879), celebrity, was born in Baltimore, Maryland, the daughter of William Patterson, a wealthy shipper and real estate investor, and Dorcas Spear, daughter of a well-to-do merchant. Elizabeth was the eldest daughter in a family of thirteen children. She was known as "Betsy" and received her education from her mother and at a French school in Baltimore. Famed for her beauty as a young woman, she was known as "The belle of Baltimore" (Mitchell, p. 35). She was also ambitious and willful and hungered for a life of excitement and adventure.

Betsy Patterson met Jerome Bonaparte, Napoleon Bonaparte's youngest brother, in Baltimore in 1803. He was serving in the French navy and was on his way back to France. A womanizer and a spendthrift, he was "the most seductive, the most brilliant in the drawing room" of all his family (Mitchell, p. 24). Patterson fell in love with him immediately and thought how "she was to be a member of the family whose name was echoing through two worlds" (Mitchell, p. 36). The couple planned to be married before Jerome Bonaparte went home. Their prospective union faced significant legal obstacles. Jerome was only nineteen, and in France parental consent was required until the age of twenty-five. The marriage also had to be registered with French officials to be legal in that country. Most important, marriage to an American woman did not fit Napoleon's dynastic plans for his brother. With plans to have himself declared emperor of France, Napoleon had no intention of recognizing the legality of the wedding.

Despite these concerns, Jerome Bonaparte and Betsy Patterson were married in a Roman Catholic ceremony by Bishop John Carroll on 24 December 1803. Her father had opposed the wedding, but finding "that nothing short of violence could prevent their union" (Mitchell, p. 44), he finally yielded. He sought to protect his Presbyterian daughter with a marriage in her husband's church and a legal contract. By the time the couple sailed for Europe on 10 March 1805, Betsy Bonaparte was pregnant.

William Patterson's precautions about his daughter's future proved inadequate. Napoleon had begun to exercise his power to end the marriage. He tried without success to have the Vatican issue an annulment. In France he decreed that the union could not be legally registered, and a French ecclesiastical court declared the marriage annulled on 6 October 1806. When the Bonapartes reached Europe, she was denied entry into areas that the French controlled. She went to England where her son, Jerome, was born on 7 July 1805. She then returned to the United States in September 1805. Meanwhile, Napoleon arranged for Jerome to marry Princess Catherine of Württemberg in August 1807. Although Jerome was genuinely in love with Betsy, he did not have the strength of will to resist the demands of his brother. In 1813 the Maryland legislature granted Elizabeth Patterson Bonaparte a divorce. Jerome and Betsy never saw each other again except for a chance and embarrassing encounter in a Florence museum some years later.

For the next two decades, Betsy Patterson Bonaparte lived in Europe most of the time and sought to have her son achieve legitimacy and a good European marriage. These endeavors failed. The Bonapartes never considered Jerome's first marriage legal. In 1829 Betsy Bonaparte's son married into a wealthy Baltimore family. He had two sons, one of whom was Charles Joseph Bonaparte, a member of Theodore Roosevelt's (1858–1919) cabinet.

After the fall of Napoleon, Betsy Bonaparte—who enjoyed notoriety and European society—lost the pension that the emperor had provided for her. She did not take lovers and never remarried. "How fortunate it is I have never repeated the experience of marrying," she wrote in 1823, "which, indeed, the dread of laying up trouble for my old age in a family of children has prevented me from" (Mitchell, p. 181).

Betsy Bonaparte came back to the United States in 1834 when her father died. He left her only a small amount of money because "she has caused me more anxiety and trouble than all my other children put together" (Mitchell, p. 191). The episode caused a permanent personal split with her brothers. She devoted herself to real estate holdings in Baltimore and grew quite prosperous. In 1854 Napoleon III received her son and grandson as part of the family and even granted them titles, which were refused. After Jerome Bonaparte died in 1860, Betsy Bonaparte sued in French court to be declared his widow, but the ruling went against her claims in 1861.

Although her business affairs remained lucrative over the next eighteen years, she lived in a boardinghouse in "squalid seclusion" (*New York Tribune*, 5 Apr. 1879). Her relations with her son and grandsons became distant and formal, confined largely to the business matters that occupied most of her time. Toward the end of her life she commented, "Once I had everything but money. Now I have nothing but money" (Mitchell, p. 197). Her connection with the Bonapartes, said one editorial writer when she died in Baltimore, was "short-lived and almost accidental" (*New York Tribune*, 5 Apr. 1879). Nonetheless, it made her a famous woman. She became a forerunner of other daughters of wealthy Americans who married into the European aristocracy with mixed results in the decades after her death.

• The Elizabeth Patterson Bonaparte Papers, the Jerome Napoleon Bonaparte Papers, and the Jerome Bonaparte Papers at the Maryland Historical Society, Baltimore, are basic sources for her life. The Charles J. Bonaparte Papers, Library of Congress, have other materials. The Archives of the Ministry of Foreign Affairs and the Archives Nationale, Paris, document the French side of the Bonaparte-Patterson marriage. There is no modern biography of Elizabeth Patterson Bonaparte. William Saffell, *The Bonaparte-Patterson Marriage* (1873), and Eugene L. Didier, *The Life and Letters of Madame Bonaparte* (1879), have been attacked by later authorities on her life. Dorothy Mackay Quynn began a full treatment but did not complete it before her death. A manuscript biography, which her husband finished, is housed at the Maryland Historical Society as the "Elisabeth Patterson Bonaparte Biography." Quynn wrote, with Frank F. White, "Jerome and Betsy Cross the Atlantic," *Maryland Historical Magazine*, Sept. 1953, pp. 204–14. Sidney Mitchell, *A Family Lawsuit: The Story of Elisabeth Patterson and Jerome Bonaparte* (1958), reprints French documents and offers an incisive interpretation of her life. The *New York Tribune*, 5 Apr. 1879, contains a perceptive editorial obituary.

LEWIS L. GOULD

BOND, Carrie Jacobs (11 Aug. 1861–28 Dec. 1946), songwriter and music publisher, was born Carrie Minetta Jacobs in Janesville, Wisconsin, the daughter of Hannibal Cyrus Jacobs, a grain dealer and amateur flutist, and Mary Emogene Davis. By the age of four she was playing the piano by ear and then began to study with local teachers. In 1880 she married E. J. Smith and bore one son, Frederic Bond Smith, but the couple separated in 1887 and later divorced. In 1889 she married Dr. Frank Lewis Bond, a physician who encouraged her to compose. An economic downturn curtailed his practice, so she traveled to Chicago to try to sell her songs to publishers. On being told that only children's songs would sell, she immediately wrote one, "Is My Dolly Dead?" which became her first published work (1894).

In 1895 Frank Bond died in a freak accident, and to support herself and her young son Carrie Bond moved to Chicago. At first she barely scraped by, taking in boarders and painting china by hand, but she continued to compose. Realizing that she needed a well-known singer to popularize her songs, she approached the contralto Jessie Bartlett Davis, who helped finance her first collection, *Seven Songs as Unpretentious as the Wild Rose* (1901). Two were to be among her most popular, "Just A-wearyin' For You" and "I Love You Truly."

For most of her songs Bond wrote both words and music and also drew the sheet music covers. Lacking formal training in composition or harmony, she generally had to dictate what she composed at the piano to a music printer. Nevertheless, her music displays a fine lyrical gift and considerable craftsmanship. Probably most important was her remarkable ability to convey genuine emotion, which is what gave her songs their enduring popularity.

Although she disliked public performance, to publicize her songs Bond frequently gave little recitals, either singing herself or accompanying a singer. However, her work did not sell very well, and about 1901 she decided to set up her own music company, the Bond Shop, into which she eventually took her son. At first the business occupied her dining room, but, moving to ever larger quarters, in ten years it expanded enough to employ seventeen assistants and send out 400,000 sheets of music a month.

By 1905 she had published twelve books of songs. Her efforts at publicity were greatly assisted by the well-known baritone David Bispham, who sang fifteen of her songs in a recital at Chicago's Studebaker Hall. By far her most popular composition, "A Perfect Day" (originally called "The End of a Perfect Day"), for which she wrote both words and music, was published in 1910. In her autobiography, Bond gave the background for this song. To improve poor health, doctors had advised her to seek a warmer winter climate. She could not afford such a journey, but then the Santa Fe Railroad offered to transport artists to California free if they would perform for passengers in its club cars on the way. Bond took up the offer, and on one such trip a beautiful southern California mountain sunset prompted her to write "A Perfect Day."

This song made her fortune, for it became one of the most successful songs ever written by an American. Introduced by Bispham in a New York recital, it was soon heard in concert halls, vaudeville shows, weddings and funerals; barrooms and churches, and throughout World War I in soldiers' camps. There were some sixty different arrangements, including renditions for ukulele, banjo, guitar, accordion, organ, male and female voices, mixed voices, quartets, trios, piano, and military band. The sheet music sale passed the eight million mark, and some fifty different recordings were made.

Bond herself performed twice at the White House, once for President Theodore Roosevelt (1858–1919) and once for President Warren Harding, with whom she became particularly friendly. ("A Perfect Day" was performed at Harding's funeral.) During World War I she also appeared in numerous benefits for soldiers.

The climate of California proved so beneficial that Bond began spending all her winters there, earning her keep by giving musicales at a Hollywood hotel. In 1920 she finally could afford to leave Chicago permanently and moved her publishing enterprise and its sales outlet, the Bond Shop, to Hollywood. Soon afterward, however, she gave over publication and distribution of her music to G. Schirmer, and although the Bond Shop stayed open, she spent most of her time in a mountain retreat she built in Grossmont. She made friends with numerous film stars and musicians, including the opera star Ernestine Schumann-Heink, who particularly liked "His Lullaby" and Bond's only war song, "My Son." In 1927 she published her autobiography, *The Roads of Melody*.

Bond's remaining years were not without tragedy. In 1928 her son committed suicide. Nevertheless, she continued to compose songs and piano pieces until her death in California. Her total output includes some 400 compositions, although only about 170 were published. Among the most successful, besides those mentioned, were the children's song "I'm the Captain of the Broomstick Cavalry" and "Poor Little Lamb" (lyric by Paul Laurence Dunbar).

Bond's output represents the last flowering of the sentimental nineteenth-century parlor song. After 1920 this style of American popular music began to decline, due partly to increased audience sophistication and also to more general cynicism and disillusionment during the postwar period. Nevertheless, Bond's lyrical gift helped some of her songs to survive to this day, in spite rather than because of their oversentimental texts.

• The largest collection of Bond material (programs, letters, and music manuscripts, including original of "A Perfect Day") is in the Rock County Historical Society, Janesville, Wis. Other repositories of music, press clippings, and memorabilia are in the Illinois State Historical Library; Miami County Historical Museum, Peru, Ind.; Transylvania University, Lexington, Ky. (38 items); New York Public Library Music Division (manuscripts); Port Townsend, Wash. (30 items of sheet music); and Boston Public Library Music Division. Bond's autobiography, *The Roads of Melody* (1927), gives a good picture of her life but is sketchy on dates and other details. Phyllis Bruce's M.A. thesis, "From Rags to Roses: The Life and Times of Carrie Jacobs Bond" (Wesleyan Univ., 1980), is more reliable.

CHRISTINE AMMER

BOND, George Phillips (20 May 1825–17 Feb. 1865), astronomer, was born in Dorchester, Massachusetts, the son of William Cranch Bond, a clockmaker and astronomer, and Selina Cranch. A member of Harvard's class of 1845, Bond became assistant astronomer at the school's observatory, where his father was director, upon graduation. Using the Harvard College Observatory's 15-inch refracting telescope, Bond and his father worked so closely together that they usually made joint announcements of their discoveries. He assisted his father with observations of Saturn, that resulted in the discovery of the planet's satellite Hyperion in 1848 and, two years later, of the planet's crepe ring. Now officially known as Ring C, this ring was also discovered independently in England by W. R. Dawes whose friend W. Lassell named it the "crepe ring." Bond's monograph on Donati's Comet of 1858 (published in 1862), which included exceptional drawings by Bond, earned him international recognition. The most prestigious award for this work came in 1865, when the Royal Astronomical Society awarded him its gold medal, the first to go to an American.

Bond shared his father's interest in experiments with applying photography to astronomy. The notes on daguerreotyping and collodion photography found in the record books for the Harvard refracting telescope are mostly in George Bond's handwriting. With Boston photographers John A. Whipple and William B. Jones, the Bonds shot about seventy daguerreotypes of the moon and the stars. On the night of 16–17 July 1850 the team got the first successful photograph of a star. The subject was first-magnitude α Lyrae; the exposure, 100 seconds. In 1857 Whipple and another assistant, James Black, introduced the Bonds to wet-plate photography, and the team went on to produce between 200 and 300 collodion plates of celestial bodies. They raised the magnitude of photographable stars from first (brightest) to sixth (faintest) magnitude and made preliminary attempts to measure stellar distances and intensity based on the images on the plates. Their photographs of the sun, moon, and planets led to Bond's research on their relative brightness. Although widespread use of photography as a research tool for astronomy came in the 1880s, when more sensitive dry plates became common, Bond nevertheless saw great promise in the new technology, and he predicted a day when the clear air of mountaintop observatories would make photography truly workable for astronomy. Bond married Harriet Gardner Harris in 1853; they had three children.

In 1859 Bond lost his father, his wife, and his youngest daughter within a few months of each other. After his father's death a contest for the observatory's directorship with Harvard professor Benjamin Peirce left Bond the winner, but Peirce's standing in the American astronomical community and Bond's own bitterness over the affair meant that Bond was thereafter ostracized. Despite international recognition of his accomplishments, the rivalry cost Bond membership in the newly formed National Academy of Sciences in 1863. The Civil War left the observatory short of assistants and funding as able-bodied students left to serve in the army, and the lucrative federal contracts for longitude work were discontinued. Bond began work on the nebula of Orion, which he and his father first observed at Harvard in 1847, but his work was published posthumously. He contracted tuberculosis and died in Cambridge, Massachusetts.

• Bond's papers relating to work at the Harvard College Observatory are in the Harvard University Archives. Family memorabilia and papers relating to the firm of William Bond & Son are in the Collection of Historical Scientific Instruments at Harvard. Two large collections of Bond artifacts survive at the Collection of Historical Scientific Instruments and at the National Museum of American History, Smithsonian Institution. Excerpts from Bond papers are in Edward S. Holden, *Memorials of William Cranch Bond and His Son George Phillips Bond* (1897). Bond's extensive writings include "Account of the Great Comet of 1858," *Annals of the Harvard College Observatory* 3 (1862): 1–372; and "Observations upon the Great Nebula of Orion," *Annals of the Harvard College Observatory* 5 (1867): 1–189. The Bonds' astronomy and their administrative contributions to the observatory are described in Bessie Zaban Jones and Lyle Gifford Boyd, *The Harvard Observatory: The First Four Directorships, 1839–1919* (1971), and in Solon I. Bailey, *The History and Work of Harvard Observatory, 1839–1927* (1931). The Bonds' photographic experiments are discussed in Dorrit Hoffleit, *Some Firsts in Astronomical Photography* (1950), and their work on time and longitude is in Carlene E. Stephens, "'The Most Reliable Time': William Bond, the New England Railroads, and Time Awareness in 19th-Century America," *Technology and Culture* 30 (Jan. 1989): 1–24.

CARLENE E. STEPHENS

BOND, Horace Mann (8 Nov. 1904–21 Dec. 1972), college professor and administrator, was born in Nashville, Tennessee, the son of James Bond, a Congregationalist minister, and Jane Alice Browne, a graduate of Oberlin College and a schoolteacher. Horace Bond's paternal grandmother, Jane Arthur Bond, was a slave who raised two sons by herself. These two sons, Horace's father and his uncle Henry, both earned college degrees and embarked on professional careers. Three of Horace's four siblings earned college degrees, and his cousins on his father's side also distinguished themselves academically. This family achievement was important to Horace Bond because it exemplified the way in which numerous scholars of his generation were nurtured within the African-American community. He published a book on the family origins of African-American scholars near the end of his life, *Black American Scholars: A Study of Their Beginnings* (1972).

Bond was an intellectually precocious child. He was educated at schools attached to colleges and universities in towns where his father served as a minister, Talladega, Alabama, and Atlanta, Georgia. He finished high school at the age of fourteen at the Lincoln Institute in Shelbyville, Kentucky. He attended Lincoln University (Pa.) and was graduated, at the age of eighteen, in the class of 1923. He stayed on at Lincoln for a year as a teaching assistant, attended graduate school for a summer at the Pennsylvania State College (now university), and earned master's (1926) and doctoral (1936) degrees from the University of Chicago.

Bond's major field was education, and he specialized in both the history of education and the sociology of education in his graduate studies. He served on the faculties of Langston University (Okla., 1926–1928), Alabama State College (Montgomery, 1928–1929), Fisk University (Nashville, 1929–1931), and Dillard University (New Orleans, 1932–1935). He also was chairman of the education department at Fisk and the founding academic dean at Dillard. In the first two decades of his academic career he was closely associated with the Julius Rosenwald Fund and its president, Edwin Embree. In part, because of this relationship, he was chosen as president of Fort Valley (Ga.) State College in 1939. He served in that position until 1945, when he became president of his alma mater, Lincoln University. Bond remained as president of Lincoln until 1957, when he resigned amid controversy over a plan to increase the number of white students at the institution; his relations with older, white faculty, many of whom had taught him as an undergraduate and had difficulty seeing their former student as their superior; and his frequent trips away from campus. He then moved to Atlanta University, where he served as dean of the School of Education for five years and then as director of its Bureau of Educational and Social Research. He retired in 1971 and died in Atlanta one year later.

Bond was the author of six books and numerous articles. In the 1920s he published articles critical of the racial bias in Intelligence Quotient (IQ) tests. His two most enduring books were published in the 1930s, *The Education of the Negro in the American Social Order* (1934), a study of the inferior conditions in black schools and colleges, and *Negro Education in Alabama: A Study in Cotton and Steel* (1939), an economic interpretation of educational conditions for blacks in Alabama. His articles from the 1930s until the end of his life were published in both academic and popular journals, and he made numerous speeches to black church and civic groups in his later years. His scholarly output was a lifelong concern for Bond, but it diminished in the 1940s and 1950s as he took on the duties of a college president. Bond worked as a historian for the National Association for the Advancement of Colored People as it prepared a brief answering historical questions asked by the U.S. Supreme Court in deliberating the famous *Brown v. Board of Education* (1954) school desegregation case.

Bond became particularly interested in Africa and Africans in the late 1940s, and he took nearly twenty trips to that continent in the 1940s and 1950s. He was a founder of the American Society for African Culture (AMSAC) and was active in numerous groups that advocated cooperation between Africans and African Americans. He developed the Institute for African Studies at Lincoln University and made sure that African students were welcome at Lincoln and supported financially where possible. In this regard he built on a long-standing commitment of Lincoln to Africa and Africans. Bond was especially interested in Liberia, Nigeria, and Ghana. During Bond's presidency, the Gold Coast (later Ghana) political leader and Lincoln alumnus, Kwame Nkrumah, was awarded an honorary doctorate from Lincoln.

Bond married Julia Washington in 1929; they had three children. Bond's second child, Julian, became famous as a member of the student civil rights movement in the 1960s and served as a Georgia state legislator.

During his career Bond carefully balanced concern for personal survival and professional advancement with the pursuit of social and political activism on behalf of his race that often risked reprisals. He was a representative of the middle generation of African-American intellectuals that followed the W. E. B. Du Bois–Booker T. Washington generation of the early twentieth century and preceded the civil rights activists of the 1960s. He was one of the first of his race to be recognized for his professional academic accomplishments and also was one of the first to head an institution of higher learning.

• Bond's papers are in the Archives and Manuscripts Division, University of Massachusetts (Amherst) Library. He also was the author of *Education for Production* (1944), *The Search for Talent* (1959), and *Education for Freedom: A History of Lincoln University* (1976). His most notable articles include "Intelligence Tests and Propaganda," *The Crisis*, June 1924, pp. 61–64; "Two Racial Islands in Alabama," *American Journal of Sociology* 36 (1931): 552–67; "A Negro Looks at His South," *Harper's*, June 1931, pp. 98–108; "The Evolution and Present Status of Negro Higher Education in the United

States," *Journal of Negro Education* 17 (1948): 224–35; "Observations on Education in British West Africa," *Educational Record* 31 (1950): 129–40; and "Some Major Problems in Africa South of the Sahara," *Journal of Negro Education* 30 (1961): 358–64.

A full biography is Wayne J. Urban, *Black Scholar: Horace Mann Bond, 1904–1972* (1992). Also by Urban, see "The Black Scholar and Intelligence Testing: The Case of Horace Mann Bond," *Journal of the History of the Behavioral Sciences* 25 (1989): 323–34, and "Philanthropy and the Black Scholar: The Case of Horace Mann Bond," *Journal of Negro Education* 58 (1989): 478–93. Horace Bond and the rest of his family are profiled in Roger Williams, *The Bonds: An American Family* (1971). Also see Michael Fultz, "A 'Quintessential' American: Horace Mann Bond, 1924–1939," *Harvard Educational Review* 55 (1985): 416–42.

WAYNE J. URBAN

BOND, Hugh Lennox (16 Dec. 1828–24 Oct. 1893), lawyer and judge, was born in Baltimore, Maryland, the son of Thomas E. Bond, a doctor and clergyman, and Christina Birckhead. Having been sent to New York at a very young age, Bond enrolled at the University of the City of New York, where he received his undergraduate degree in 1848. Bond's family was firmly rooted in Maryland, and he soon returned to Baltimore, where his father had established the city's first medical school. Bond chose to pursue a career in law, and by 1851 he had been admitted to the state bar. Two years later he married Anne Griffith Penniman, also of Baltimore.

After only nine years as a barrister, Bond was appointed to the bench by Governor Thomas H. Hicks in 1860 and was elected by popular vote the following year. Maryland was then a paradoxical state, refusing to officially secede while simultaneously sympathizing with the Confederacy. Although Henry Winter Davis and the Unionist legislature were able to abolish slavery and disfranchise secessionists between 1863 to 1865, by 1867 conservatives had denied the vote to blacks and repealed the act that disfranchised Confederate sympathizers. During his seven-year stint as a criminal court judge, Bond, less radical than Davis, proved loyal to the Union in the midst of these dramas, despite the often tangible resistance of conservatives.

Bond's first encounter with Maryland's turbulent divisions came in 1861. When the Sixth Massachusetts Regiment reached Baltimore en route to defend the capital, a violent mob, armed with paving stones, firearms, and even kitchen utensils, descended upon the troops with a fury that prompted one soldier to comment, "I had rather, any time, face the enemy in the open field than go through such a scene as that was in the streets of Baltimore" (Watson, p. 38). Exhibiting both his commitment to the Union and his uncompromising sense of justice, Bond instructed a grand jury that those who participated in the riot were guilty of murder, an unpopular charge given the fact that many public officials had supported the attack.

Also characteristic of Bond's persistence in matters of national allegiance was his release on writs of habeas corpus of seventy-five Unionists who had been detained for displaying an American flag, an act that was legal in a state still technically loyal to the Union. Similarly, in 1864, after conservative slaveholders attempted to apprentice the children of blacks who had been freed under the Thirteenth Amendment by employing an old provision in the "Black Code" of state laws, Bond again issued writs of habeas corpus to release the children, who, in some cases, had been taken without their parents' consent.

As a judge Bond also persuaded many nonslaveholding whites to support emancipation by helping to increase black enlistments. Initially only free blacks were eligible for military service, but after Bond issued a levy "from the slave population, in order that Union men might have the free colored population to hire," many poor whites in plantation counties who had been at the mercy of slaveholders for generations began to support emancipation, as "every slave enlisted was a poor white man's substitute" (Steiner, p. 274). While Bond's decision was based on political and economic reasoning, the levy did more for the support of emancipation in the state of Maryland than perhaps many more noble abolition attempts.

Despite his obvious loyalty to the Union and emancipation, however, Bond never lost sight of his obligation to uphold the laws of the state. Consequently, ignoring his disdain for secessionists, Bond urged the grand jury to indict the military commissioners who had, under orders of the national government, tried Maryland inhabitants for crimes against the United States. By Bond's estimate, Maryland was not under martial law, and therefore the United States had no jurisdiction over such offenses.

In 1867 a new state constitution was drafted, reorganizing the courts. Bond stepped down from the bench, entering into private practice for the next three years. Bond continued in his support of the advancement of blacks, endorsing an educational plan that was eventually transformed into the "Association for the Improvement of Colored People." Largely because of Bond's contributions and the achievements of this organization, Baltimore was able not only to establish black schools in 1868 but also to aid other schools along the eastern shore.

In 1870 President Ulysses S. Grant appointed Bond judge of the newly established Fourth U.S. Circuit Court with jurisdiction over Maryland, Virginia, West Virginia, and the Carolinas. Within a year of the appointment, he presided over the South Carolina Ku Klux Klan trials. Shortly following the election of 1870, Klan activity in South Carolina had become pervasive. Still, Grant remained unwilling to put an end to the violence by engaging federal soldiers until the spring of 1871, after a winter of bloody bullying by the Klan. Soon after sending a small detachment of federal troops, Congress passed the Ku Klux Act. Armed with this particular piece of legislation and meticulous data that had been gathered against the Klan in South Carolina, Grant finally declared martial law and employed the army to break up the Klan, suspending the writ of habeas corpus in nine counties.

Unfortunately, justice was neither swift nor substantial. Although almost 500 men awaited trial before Bond in November, at the close of the term early the next year only fifty-four had been convicted and sentenced, nearly all after pleading guilty. Although thirty cases were thrown out, there were 278 carryover cases for the court to hear during its April term, a problem that raised the obvious question of how stringent of an example could be set given the seemingly slow results. In addition, the federal prosecutors had to charge defendants with "conspiracy to deprive a citizen of his right to vote on account of race and color," a federal crime, rather than murder, a state crime. Consequently, Bond was forced to hand down mild sentences, ranging generally from six to eighteen months, with fines of $10 to $100.

Although Grant's crackdown in South Carolina was ultimately ineffective, as many leaders escaped punishment, Bond's remarks concerning the defendants indicate the mixture of sorrow and contempt he felt for men who were little more than pawns. "You have, as it appears from your statements to the Court, been brought up in the most deplorable ignorance. At the age of manhood, but one or two of you can either read or write. . . . But what is quite as appalling to the Court as the horrible nature of these offenses is the utter absence, on your part . . . of any sense or feeling, that you have done anything very wrong in your confessed participation in outrages which are unexampled outside of the Indian territory." Still, Bond recognized that their actions were ultimately inexcusable, stating "You and your confederates must make up your minds either to resist the Ku Klux conspiracy or the laws of the United States. They cannot both exist together."

Five years after the Ku Klux Klan trials, Bond rendered the decision that propelled Rutherford Hayes to the executive office. Once again releasing individuals on writs of habeas corpus, Bond sided with the Republicans on the South Carolina state board of canvassers whom he believed had been unjustly imprisoned by the state supreme court in an attempt to sway the state for Samuel Tilden, the Democratic presidential candidate. Bond's objectivity is suspect, however, since during his Columbia term he was living with Daniel Chamberlain, who was running for governor as a Republican incumbent.

Although he continued to serve as judge for the fourth circuit for the next twenty-five years in both criminal and civil cases, including the Virginia Coupon cases of 1886 and the Navassa Island murder cases, Bond's earlier decisions were more renowned, particularly for their unswerving allegiance to the law above personal ideological considerations. As a jurist, Bond was both fair and even-handed, capable of meting out justice to citizens whose loyalties often ran the gamut of the national political spectrum.

• For a complete transcription of the South Carolina Ku Klux Klan trials, including Bond's remarks after sentencing, see *Proceedings in the Ku Klux Trials at Columbia, South Carolina, in the U.S. Circuit Court, November Term, 1871* (1872). More recent information and commentary about those proceedings appears in Lou Falkner Williams, *The Great South Carolina Ku Klux Klan Trials, 1871–1872* (1996). Brief information concerning Bond's life and decisions are in Bernard Steiner, *Life of Henry Winter Davis (1817–1865)* (1916). The circumstances surrounding the attack on the Sixth Massachusetts Regiment are recorded in an oration given by Colonel B. E. Watson on the twenty-fifth anniversary of the events entitled *Old Sixth Mass* (1886). For facts concerning M.D. and S.C. during Reconstruction, see Hans L. Trefousse, *Historical Dictionary of Reconstruction* (1991). For specific information about the turbulent affairs in South Carolina, including the Klan activity mentioned in the text, see Richard Zuczek, *State of Rebellion: Reconstruction in South Carolina* (1996). Information concerning the advances of African Americans in Maryland can be found in Jeffrey R. Brackett, "Notes on the Progress of the Colored People of Maryland since the War," *Johns Hopkins University Studies in Historical and Political Science* 7–9 (July–Sept. 1890): 5–95. Obituaries are in the *Baltimore Sun*, 26 Oct. 1893, the *Baltimore Weekly Sun*, 28 Oct. 1893, and the *Baltimore American*, 25–27 Oct. 1893.

DONNA GREAR PARKER

BOND, Johnny (1 June 1915–12 June 1978), songwriter, musician, and writer, was born Cyrus Whitfield Bond in Enville, Oklahoma, the son of Rufus Thomas Bond, a storekeeper and cotton gin operator, and Anna May Camp. While the family had little money, they did own a Victrola player that Bond found fascinating. Inspired by Jimmie Rodgers's recordings and his performances on radio, Bond focused on the idea of playing and writing music and making phonograph records. In 1933 he bought a 98-cent ukelele from a Montgomery Ward catalog, borrowed a guitar, and taught himself to play both instruments. After graduation from high school in 1934, he moved to Oklahoma City, hoping to work in radio. Bond later attended the University of Oklahoma for one year while pursuing his musical goals.

Bond auditioned for the local stations and in 1934 was hired by KFXR (Oklahoma City) to perform a daily fifteen-minute spot. He met singer Jimmy Wakely in 1936, and the next year, joined by Scotty Harrel, the three formed a western group, the Bell Boys. Named after their sponsor, the Bell Clothing Company, they performed daily on WKY in Oklahoma City. Once a week, the trio drove to Tulsa to record six fifteen-minute shows for KVOO. In addition to their radio broadcasts, the Bell Boys made personal appearances around the state. Bond, now known as Johnny Bond, selected and arranged songs for the trio and began to compose original music. His first attempt yielded a classic, the much recorded "Cimarron (Roll On)," in 1938. He married Dorothy Louise Murcer in 1939; they had three children.

The Bell Boys traveled to Hollywood in 1939 and appeared in the Roy Rogers film *Saga of Death Valley* (1939). This was the first of many such appearances for Bond, who worked in thirty-seven movies between 1940 and 1947, most of them westerns. Some of his original compositions were featured in these films. The group, renamed the Jimmy Wakely Trio, returned home after making the film, but the prospects in Hollywood remained attractive. Bond, Wakely, and Dick Reinhart, standing in for Harrel, migrated west in the spring of 1940 and became cast members of Gene Autry's "Melody Ranch" CBS radio series. Bond performed the introduction to the theme song, "Back in the Saddle Again," and provided the distinctive guitar runs heard on many of Autry's records through 1962. He appeared on most of Autry's tours in the 1940s and 1950s as a musician and comedian and stayed with the radio show until it ended in 1956. Autry describes Bond as "a great talent, very intelligent, and a good friend of mine" (G. Autry letter to M. Felchin, 9 Feb. 1996).

Bond took advantage of the many opportunities available to western musicians in southern California during the 1940s. Already working in radio and film, touring with Autry, and performing locally, he and the trio signed with Decca Records and recorded several Bond compositions, including "I Wonder Where You Are Tonight" (1941). Wakely, Reinhart, and Bond were also recording as solo artists. In 1941 Bond signed with producer Art Satherley, spending sixteen years with OKeh and Columbia Records. Most of his success on the record charts came with novelties like "Der Fuehrer's Face" (1942), rather than his own compositions. In the 1950s Bond became known for drinking songs, such as "Sick, Sober and Sorry" (1951). During his Columbia years (1941–1957), the most popular and enduring recordings of his original compositions were made by other artists. These include "Tomorrow Never Comes" (1943), "I'll Step Aside" (1945), "Glad Rags" (1950), and "Your Old Love Letters" (1951). By 1943 the Jimmy Wakely Trio had disbanded because Wakely wanted to pursue a film career. With Autry in military service, the "Melody Ranch" series was on hold, and Bond joined CBS radio's "Hollywood Barn Dance." He was featured as a comedian on the show from 1943 to 1947.

Changing programming trends in radio and the advent of television brought new opportunities to Bond in the late 1940s. He became active in other aspects of the music business, starting his own publishing company, Red River Songs, in 1949. He also produced innovative recordings in his home studio, repeatedly overdubbing his voice and guitar to form a quartet. In 1953 he joined "Town Hall Party," a combination live music and dance show broadcast locally on radio and television and kinescoped for military distribution overseas. Hired to perform and write the scripts, Bond was a regular during the show's 1953–1961 run. In 1958 filmed segments were syndicated and televised as "Ranch Party." Recognizing that the wealth of talent he met through "Town Hall Party" could provide a valuable music catalog, Bond formed Vidor Publications in 1955 with Tex Ritter, singing star of musical westerns in the 1930s and 1940s. Vidor published the first compositions by the country songwriting great Harlan Howard.

Bond left Columbia Records in 1957 but continued to compose and record. A versatile artist, he experimented with new styles, like western swing or early rock. "Hot Rod Lincoln" (1960), released on Autry's Republic Records was a crossover hit on both country and pop charts. The next year Starday released Bond's first album, *That Wild, Wicked but Wonderful West*, featuring original songs. "Ten Little Bottles" (1964), a stage routine Bond had performed for years, became his first and only number one hit on the country charts. On *Something Old, New, Patriotic and Blue* (1970), Bond produced updated versions of his classics. Several albums of past hits, released in the mid-1970s, successfully captured the sounds of the western music Bond had created earlier.

Bond's long association with Autry continued when he was hired to write scripts and perform for the "Melody Ranch" TV series, broadcast weekly from 1964 to 1970. No longer touring or appearing regularly on television, Bond turned his creative energies to writing about music in 1972. Though his biography of Autry has never appeared, two of his other books, *Reflections: The Autobiography of Johnny Bond* and *The Tex Ritter Story*, were published in 1976. He also published *The Recordings of Jimmie Rodgers: An Annotated Discography* (1978). Bond died in Burbank, California.

Bond was a talented songwriter whose classics are still recorded. A gifted and creative musician, he was involved deeply in the music business. He is known not only as a guitar player but also as a composer, performer, and arranger of songs; a scriptwriter for radio and television; and a country music historian. He adapted successfully to changes in style, taste, and technology and was a major figure in western music for more than four decades. An intelligent, humble, and well-respected man, he was always grateful for the admiration he received. Commenting in *Reflections* on his career, Bond modestly said, "I'm just going along with the crowd—that is as long as they'll let me."

• *Reflections: The Autobiography of Johnny Bond* (1976) contains reproductions of photographs, clippings, and scripts from Bond's personal collection, as well as a discography, a filmography, and a list of his original compositions performed by other artists. A detailed and thorough article is Jonathan Guyot Smith, "Johnny Bond: An Appreciation," *DISCoveries* 63 (1993): 22–28. Bill C. Malone, *Country Music U.S.A.* (1985), is a well-documented study that places Bond in the cultural and historical context of country music. For an insightful obituary see western music historian Ken Griffis's, "I Remember Johnny Bond," *JEMF Quarterly* 14 (1978): 110–12.

MARVA R. FELCHIN

BOND, Shadrach (14 Nov. 1773–12 Apr. 1832), first governor of the state of Illinois, was born in Baltimore County, Maryland, the son of Nicodemus Bond and Rachel Stevenson, prosperous farmers. He was the sixth of ten children, and economic opportunity was limited for the Bond offspring. Shadrach's father, a man known for his piety, manumitted his four slaves before his death in 1804.

In 1794 Bond moved to Illinois, then a part of the Northwest Territory, to join an uncle of the same name. The elder Bond had come west with George

Rogers Clark and his gallant band of Kentucky and Virginia riflemen during the revolutionary war. The two Bonds, uncle and nephew, became successful farmers and active land speculators in the New Design community near Kaskaskia. To their credit, neither of their names is connected with the extensive federal investigation of land-grant frauds in early nineteenth-century Illinois.

The careers of the two Bonds were intertwined throughout the territorial period, leading to some confusion. Both of them held public office when Illinois became part of the new Indiana Territory. Following service in the St. Clair County militia (where he rose to the rank of lieutenant colonel), the younger Bond was elected (1806) to the seat in the Indiana territorial legislature previously held by his uncle. In the following year he replaced the elder Bond in the legislative council, and in 1808 he replaced his uncle as the presiding judge of the court of common pleas for St. Clair County.

When Illinois became a separate territory in 1809, Bond did not immediately seek elective office. One of the paramount principles of his public life was his determination to avoid involvement in the personal cliques and petty partisanship that characterized territorial and early statehood politics. In 1810 he traveled to Nashville, Tennessee, where he married a distant cousin, Achsah Bond. They had seven children.

In 1812 the territorial legislature selected the younger Bond as its first delegate to Congress. The War of 1812 had broken out, and territorial governor Ninian Edwards (1775–1833) also appointed him one of his four aides-de-camp. Before Edwards's campaign against the Indian tribes around Peoria could begin, however, Bond was on his way to Washington and saw no service during the War of 1812.

Bond represented the territory with vigor and insight. With the support of an Ohio congressman he secured the passage of an act that broadened the preemption rights of Illinois squatters to cover up to 160 acres of land. This enabled settlers who had lived on land for a number of years and made improvements on it to have the first opportunity to purchase it once land offices were opened. With the war on, he urged the creation of additional units of mounted rangers to better protect the frontier from marauding Indian bands, and he sought federal reimbursement for the expenses of the Illinois militia.

Bond did not seek reelection as territorial delegate, preferring instead to accept appointment by President James Madison as the receiver of public moneys for the Kaskaskia land office. In that position he exhibited impartiality in responsibly resolving land claims in southern Illinois. As his personal landholdings increased he moved nearer to Kaskaskia, where he built a substantial two-story brick home. To cultivate his extensive lands, he owned and employed slaves, as did many of his Illinois neighbors. The census of 1820 shows him owning fourteen slaves.

When statehood for Illinois approached (1818), Bond remained silent as the question of slavery agitated the constitutional convention. He first announced for the fledgling state's only congressional seat, but as the election drew near, he was persuaded instead to become a candidate for governor. Having refused to align himself with either of the dominant factions in Illinois politics, those headed by Edwards and Jesse B. Thomas (1777–1853), Bond possessed a degree of independence that no other candidate could match. Sound practical judgment and unquestioned integrity were the basis of his popular appeal. Though the official returns have been lost, Bond was elected almost unanimously, only a few hundred votes being cast in opposition.

In spite of an empty treasury and a constitution that sharply curtailed executive power, Bond had more success than some other early governors in dealing with the general assembly. Urging fiscal responsibility, he succeeded in persuading the legislature to borrow money initially rather than resorting to unpopular taxes to fund essential capital improvements. The entire expenditure of the state government for the biennial period, 1821–1822, was less than $50,000. He strongly recommended a revision of the territorial criminal code, looking toward more humane treatment of criminals. Nevertheless, he did sign the state's first "Black Code," which placed harsh and restrictive limitations on the state's resident Negroes. The construction of the first penitentiary in Illinois began during his term. The state's first experiment with a lottery, which it was hoped would finance river improvements and drainage projects, was a failure, and the unwise chartering of the State Bank of Illinois with branches muddled state finances for years.

Bond proved to be a reputable and unassuming administrator. A future governor, Thomas Ford, who was a member of the first general assembly, described him as "a substantial, farmer-like man of strong, plain common sense, with but little pretentions to learning or general information. He was a well-made, well-set, sturdy gentleman" (Ford, p. 19). Early in Bond's term, the state's capital was removed from Kaskaskia to Vandalia, where it remained for twenty years before moving permanently to Springfield. Bond became the first of six successive governors to strongly recommend the construction of a canal connecting Lake Michigan with the Illinois River, first suggested by Louis Jolliet and Jacques Marquette in the seventeenth century. The Illinois and Michigan Canal remained as the centerpiece of the state's internal improvements planning for the next thirty years.

Soon after his gubernatorial term ended in 1822 (governors under the early Illinois constitutions were not eligible for immediate reelection), Bond was appointed by President James Monroe as registrar and receiver of the Kaskaskia land office; President John Quincy Adams reappointed him four years later. The former governor ran unsuccessfully for the state's only congressional seat in 1826 and was passed over once again when a Senate vacancy was being filled in 1830. He was honored as the first grand master of the initial Masonic Lodge in Illinois and had the satisfaction of being appointed by the general assembly to prestigious boards and commissions planning significant public improvements for the state of Illinois.

Still serving in the land office position, Bond died of pneumonia at his home near Kaskaskia. An inventory of his estate included, in addition to spacious lands and livestock, nine slaves. Though not a commanding figure, Bond was a good representative of the sturdy pioneer class who transformed eighteenth-century French Illinois into a thoroughly American commonwealth in the nineteenth century.

• The sources for Bond's life and public career are skimpy and scattered. Robert P. Howard's useful paper, "Myths after Shadrach Bond," *Transactions of the Illinois State Historical Society* (1989), corrects many of the legends and inaccuracies that have grown up around the first governor. Howard's *Mostly Good and Competent Men: Illinois Governors, 1818–1988* (1988), provides a basic introduction. See also Evarts Boutell Greene and Clarence W. Alvord, eds., *The Governors' Letter-Books, 1818–1834*, vol. 4, Collections of the Illinois State Historical Library (1909), and John Francis Snyder, *Adam W. Snyder and His Period in Illinois History, 1817–1842* (1906). The Bond years are covered adequately in several nineteenth-century state histories, including Henry Brown, *The History of Illinois from Its First Discovery and Settlement to the Present Time* (1844); Alexander Davidson and Bernard Stave, *A Complete History of Illinois from 1673 to 1873* (1874); Thomas Ford, *A History of Illinois from Its Commencement as a State in 1818 to 1847* (1854); and John Moses, *Illinois Historical and Statistical* (2 vols., 1889).

ROBERT M. SUTTON

BOND, Thomas (3 May 1713–26 Mar. 1784), physician and surgeon, was born in Calvert County, Maryland, the son of Richard Bond, a planter, and Elizabeth Benson Chew, the widow of Benjamin Chew. A birthright Quaker, Bond drifted away from the Society of Friends, was "dealt with . . . for taking an oath," and was disowned, probably by 1742.

Bond read medicine with John Hamilton of Calvert County and then continued his studies in Philadelphia with his half-brother Samuel Chew, whose partner in medical practice he was in 1734. In 1738 Bond went to Europe for formal instruction in medicine. He carried with him turtle eggs, insects, plants and flowers, and letters of introduction from the seedsman John Bartram to the English horticulturist Peter Collinson. In London he met the young Quaker physician John Fothergill, who later became a friend of Benjamin Franklin and the patron of several Philadelphia institutions. In Paris he studied anatomy, medicine, and botany at the Hôtel-Dieu and the Jardin des Plantes—"the most diligently I ever did in my life." He carried away a lasting affection for France and a respect for French science and medicine. He neither sought nor received an M.D. degree.

Back in Philadelphia in 1739, Bond was appointed one of the port physicians in 1741 and in 1743 formed a professional partnership with his younger brother Phineas that lasted until the latter's death in 1773. A member of Franklin's circle, Bond subscribed to the Library Company of Philadelphia in 1741, was an original member of the American Philosophical Society in 1743, and in 1749 became one of the first trustees of the Academy and College of Philadelphia. He was elected to the Philadelphia Common Council in 1745.

As a physician Bond rejected systems in medicine, preferring to be guided by observation and experience. Though not averse to bleeding, he advocated mild measures, including hot, cold, and vapor baths. His reputation as a surgeon soon spread beyond Philadelphia. The young Robert Treat Paine (later a signer of the Declaration of Independence) came to him from Boston in 1751 to be inoculated against smallpox, and Caesar Rodney of Delaware and Richard Stockton of New Jersey, both of whom were also later signers of the Declaration of Independence, were patients for the surgical removal of cancers. Bond was especially successful as a lithotomist, removing stones from the bladder; he performed the operation at least as early as 1756.

During nearly half a century Bond repeatedly expressed concern about smallpox. In 1737 he joined other physicians in publicly recommending inoculation, and in 1774 he was a physician of the Society for the Inoculation of the Poor Gratis. In 1779 he wrote a defense of inoculation. This paper, or a version of it, was read to the American Philosophical Society; Bond gave a copy to the French minister to the United States; and it was published in French at Strasbourg in 1784 (*Défense de l'inoculation, et relation des progrès qu'elle a faits à Philadelphie en 1758*) and in a German translation at Nürnberg in 1787. An English translation was never published.

Bond was perhaps the first to propose a hospital for Philadelphia, but his advocacy was unsuccessful until Franklin joined him. The episode, related in the latter's autobiography, is well known. The Pennsylvania Hospital was opened for patients in 1752. Bond was one of the original managers, but he resigned to become an attending physician. It was his custom to take his apprentices on his rounds; with the opening of a school of medicine in Philadelphia in 1765, he formalized the practice. In an address to the hospital managers in 1766, repeated to the doctors and medical students, he explained the role of the clinical professor, who "comes into the Aid of Speculation and demonstrates the Truth of Theory by Facts." Attendance at Bond's lectures was made a requirement for the M.D. degree. A few years later, as physician to the Almshouse, Bond also lectured and demonstrated on midwifery. The opportunities thus afforded medical students to observe sick and injured patients in a hospital—unequaled elsewhere in America before 1820—were a principal reason why Philadelphia was for more than half a century the largest and most influential center for medical study in the colonies and the United States.

In 1767 Bond took a leading part in reviving the American Philosophical Society, which had not met since 1745 or 1746. As its vice president after 1769, during years that Franklin was in London and Paris, Bond was in effect its president. Too old to take an active part in the Revolution, he nevertheless volunteered his services occasionally to treat soldiers in hospitals near Philadelphia and to examine candidates for appointment as military surgeons and mates. He tried to keep up his teaching but was limited in this, he complained, because so few patients were in the hospital.

Bond took a prominent part in reorganizing the American Philosophical Society after the war and in its annual oration, which he delivered in 1782, expressed a vision for the new nation: "The Fame of America must rest on a broader Basis than that of Arms alone. . . . our Consequence abroad, depends on our preserving a noble, generous and *unspotted Character* at Home."

Bond was married twice. His first wife, whom he wed in 1735, was Susannah Roberts, daughter of Edward Roberts, who became mayor of Philadelphia; she died of complications following the birth of their second child in 1737. In 1742 Bond married Sarah Weyman, daughter of Robert Weyman, rector of the Anglican church in Burlington, New Jersey. They had seven children. Three of Bond's sons studied medicine; but of these, one died young, one gave up the study, and only Thomas, Jr., entered practice. Bond died in Philadelphia and was buried there, in Christ Church cemetery.

Like other prominent physicians of his time, Bond owed his reputation not to discoveries, for he made none, or to authorship, for he wrote little, but to cautious but successful practice over many years, skill in some surgical operations, and character and personality. He owes his place in American medical history almost entirely to his address at the Pennsylvania Hospital on the usefulness of clinical instruction.

• Elizabeth H. Thomson, "Thomas Bond, 1713–84: First Professor of Clinical Medicine in the American Colonies," *Journal of Medical Education* 33 (1958): 614–24, established Bond's birth date from the manuscript minutes of Herring Creek Monthly Meeting in the archives of Baltimore Yearly Meeting, Society of Friends. See also J. Alison Scott, "A Sketch of the Life of Thomas Bond, Clinician and Surgeon," *University of Pennsylvania Medical Bulletin* 18 (1905–1906): 306–18. Letters to and from Bond and references to him may be found in William Darlington, *Memorials of John Bartram and Humphry Marshall* (1849); Leonard W. Labaree, ed., *The Papers of Benjamin Franklin* (1959–); Thomas G. Morton and Frank Woodbury, *History of the Pennsylvania Hospital* (1895); and Caspar Morris, "Contributions to the Medical History of Pennsylvania," Historical Society of Pennsylvania, *Memoirs* 1, pt. 2 (1826): 337–50. The text of Bond's lecture "On the Utility of Clinical Lectures" is in Morton and Woodbury, pp. 462–67, and, as edited by Carl Bridenbaugh, in *Journal of the History of Medicine and Allied Sciences* 2 (1947): 10–19. Two cases were reported by Bond and published in London: *Medical Observations & Inquiries* 1 (1757): 67–80 and 2 (1762): 265–68.

WHITFIELD J. BELL, JR.

BOND, Ward (9 Apr. 1903–5 Nov. 1960), film and television actor, was born in Bendelmen, Nebraska. Information is unavailable on Bond's parents or his early life. In 1923 he briefly attended the Colorado School of Mines, then left college to work for several years. About 1927 he enrolled at the University of Southern California, where he played tackle on the football team coached by Howard Jones. Bond graduated from USC in 1931.

One of Bond's Southern Cal teammates was Marion "Duke" Morrison, who as a rising movie star a few years later changed his name to John Wayne. Starting on the playing field, Bond and Wayne became lifelong friends. A third man who came to share that friendship, motion picture director John Ford, hired them for small parts in *Salute* (1929), a picture about football-playing midshipmen at Annapolis. The neophyte actors next performed together in *The Big Trail* (1930), before going their separate on-screen ways for ten years.

After 1932 Bond was firmly established in films as a supporting actor. From a handful of films that year, his assignments nearly doubled in 1933, then doubled again the following year before leveling off to an average of sixteen films per year through the rest of the 1930s. In just an eight-year span, he made more than 100 motion pictures—an astonishing total, even for an actor in smaller roles. During this period of his life (in 1936), Bond married Doris Sellers; they divorced during World War II.

Most of Bond's earliest movies were rapidly made, low-budget westerns. To land parts in those films, he became a capable horseman, and he developed the skills to carry out his own stunts. A tall, powerfully built, heavy-featured actor, on the screen he usually wore a stern, even a fierce, expression. With such characteristics, he could impersonate either brutal heavies or stoical, hard-knuckled good guys. Each year his range of film work broadened, until by the mid-1930s he was alternating cowboy parts with characterizations of cops and crooks.

Yet among those run-of-the-mill program fillers, Bond managed to land occasional parts in a number of respected pictures that were directed by some of the best studio filmmakers of the era: William A. Wellman's *Wild Boys of the Road* (1933), Frank Capra's classic *It Happened One Night* (1934), Ford's *The Informer* (1935), and Fritz Lang's *You Only Live Once* and William Wyler's *Dead End* (both 1937).

The year 1939 was a banner one for Bond, as it was for the entire Hollywood film industry. He earned supporting credits in sixteen pictures, which included two of John Garfield's earliest starring roles; pictures opposite James Cagney, Errol Flynn, Henry Fonda, Carole Lombard, Randolph Scott, and Humphrey Bogart; and even a part as one of Scarlett O'Hara's many admirers in *Gone with the Wind*. Bond was cast in two other films that year, *Drums along the Mohawk* and *Young Mr. Lincoln*, which were among the best that Ford directed during the 1930s. Roles in those pictures seemed to mark Bond's initiation into Ford's unofficial stock company of actors who recurrently appeared in his films.

Bond's hectic working pace slowed to an almost normal tempo during the 1940s, over the course of which he made some forty-five films. The quality of those films significantly improved, as did the importance of his roles. In 1940, for example, he was seen in Ford's *The Grapes of Wrath* and *The Long Voyage Home* (reunited with Wayne) and in Frank Borzage's *The Mortal Storm*. In 1941 he acted in Ford's *Tobacco Road*, Howard Hawks's *Sergeant York*, Jean Renoir's *Swamp Water* (the great French director's first American venture), and John Huston's *The Maltese Falcon*. As the dying seaman, Yank, in *The Long Voyage Home* and as heavyweight champion John L. Sullivan in Raoul Walsh's *Gentleman Jim* (1942), Bond achieved some of his finest screen moments.

In the mid-1940s, Bond, a fervent anticommunist, became a prominent officer in the Motion Picture Alliance for the Preservation of American Ideals (MPA), a group of right-wing film industry figures that included Charles Coburn, Gary Cooper, Walt Disney, Adolphe Menjou, Robert Taylor, and MPA founder Sam Wood. Dedicated to thwarting what they perceived as the infusion of communist propaganda into studio films, Bond and other MPA officers fully cooperated with the U.S. House Committee on Un-American Activities during the committee's hearings on Hollywood "subversives" in 1947. With the motion picture industry's creation of the blacklist that same year, Bond made every effort until well into the 1950s to see that employment was denied to actors, screenwriters, and other film workers suspected of communist backgrounds or left-wing sympathies.

In his own film work, Bond's attention increasingly focused on pictures directed by Ford. Some of Bond's best postwar acting occurred in *They Were Expendable* (1945), *My Darling Clementine* (1946), *The Fugitive* (1947), *Fort Apache* (1948), *Wagontrain* (1950), *The Quiet Man* (1952), and *The Searchers* (1956). In *The Wings of Eagles* (1957), he played movie director "John Dodge," Ford's sharply satirical parody of himself. Bond's work with other directors after 1945 was highlighted by such supporting roles as the accordion-playing Bedford Falls policeman, Bert, in Capra's memorable *It's a Wonderful Life* (1946), as a villain in Nicholas Ray's *Johnny Guitar* (1954), and as a wagon master in Bond's final of a dozen films with Wayne, *Rio Bravo* (1959).

In 1954 Bond married his second wife, Mary Lou May. The number of children, if any, from both of his marriages is not known.

At the same time that he was making his final Hollywood films, Bond was transforming his status from supporting actor to star. On 18 September 1957 he introduced the part of Major Seth Adams to many millions of Americans in the first episode of one of television's best and most popular western series, "Wagon Train." Based on Ford's earlier film, *Wagonmaster*, in which Bond played a fanatic Mormon elder, "Wagon Train" in its second season reached the Top 10 in audience ratings, and in 1959 it was the second most popular TV show in the country, close behind the perennial leader, "Gunsmoke." Bond himself was a special audience favorite: no longer the gruff, stone-faced sidekick of his Hollywood feature films, his character in "Wagon Train" came across as a wise, kindly uncle.

Bond's newfound success lasted for three full seasons, then unexpectedly ended when he died of a heart attack in Dallas, Texas, where he was scheduled to be honored at a Cowboys' football game.

• Most standard film reference works give his birthplace as Denver, but that is contradicted by his *New York Times* obituary. The consensus among apparently misinformed reference books, however, suggests that he possibly grew up and was educated in Denver, especially since he attended the Colorado School of Mines. Many—but not most—film reference books offer concise biographical entries on Bond along with selected filmographies; however, no easily available filmography is close to complete. For basic information on Bond, see Ephraim Katz, *The Film Encyclopedia*, 2d ed. (1994), *Films in Review* 13 (1962): 547–51, and *Leonard Maltin's Movie Encyclopedia* (1994). Helpful on individual pictures are J. A. Place, *The Western Films of John Ford* (1974) and *The Non-Western Films of John Ford* (1979). On TV's "Wagon Master," see Archie P. McDonald, ed., *Shooting Stars: Heroes and Heroines of Western Film* (1987). Bond's political activities are briefly mentioned in Eric Bentley, ed., *Thirty Years of Treason* (1971), and Victor S. Navasky, *Naming Names* (1980). An obituary is in the *New York Times*, 6 Nov. 1960.

ROBERT MIRANDON

BOND, William Cranch (9 Sept. 1789–29 Jan. 1859), clockmaker and astronomer, was born in Falmouth (now Portland), Maine, the son of Cornish immigrant William Bond, a silversmith and watchmaker, and Hannah Cranch. The elder Bond began a lumber business in Falmouth in 1786. Four years later, when a ship carrying the entire season's cuttings went down and ruined the business, Bond moved his penniless family to Boston. In 1793 he set up a watch and jewelry business on Marlboro Street, which continued until 1977 as the firm of William Bond & Son.

Set to work with his father before he finished formal schooling, William Cranch Bond was largely a self-taught astronomer, although he received some instruction from Harvard's mathematics professor John Farrar and from New England's most famous self-taught astronomer, Nathaniel Bowditch. Bond's observations of the comet of 1811 impressed Farrar, and when Bond scheduled a trip to England in 1815 for firm and family business, Farrar recommended that Harvard ask him to survey British observatories with a view to building one on campus. Bond returned with details about structures and instruments, but, for lack of funds, the college dropped the matter.

Bond married his cousin Selina Cranch in 1819, and they had six children. Selina died in 1831, and Bond married her sister Mary Roope Cranch; no children were born of this marriage.

About that time, the firm of William Bond & Son expanded from the watch and jewelry trade to include marine chronometers. Beginning in 1834 a series of contracts with the U.S. Navy gave Bond the opportunity to rate, clean, repair, insure, and deliver chronometers for ships in the ports of Boston and Portsmouth. From 1838 to 1842 he received his first professional job as an astronomer, another contract with the navy to provide meteorological and astronomical observations for the U.S. Exploring Expedition under Charles Wilkes.

Harvard's president Josiah Quincy (1772–1864) noted Bond's work for the Wilkes Expedition and, late in 1839, convinced him to become the school's astronomer. Bond did not receive a salary, but living quarters and space for instruments were provided free in Dana House. When his instruments proved inadequate for revealing the details of the dazzling comet of 1843, the wealthy citizens of Boston pooled their resources to build a formidable new observatory for the college and to equip it with a telescope equal to the world's largest at the Pulkovo Observatory, Russia. In 1848 a $100,000-bequest to the observatory allowed Bond to become Phillips Professor of Practical Astronomy. (Both he and his son George, who worked closely with him, had received modest salaries since 1842.) Together they contributed new information about the physical features of planets, comets, and nebulae. The Bonds received international acclaim for their discoveries, which included a satellite of Saturn and the planet's crape ring, the third ring to be observed at the time of its discovery.

During his twenty-year tenure as director at Harvard's observatory (1839–1859), Bond's determination to make the observatory useful to a broad public and his interest in longitude determinations resulted in numerous U.S. government contracts for astronomical work. In addition to his early work with the navy, he worked with the U.S. Topographical Engineers on international boundary surveys and the Great Lakes Survey. For the U.S. Coast Survey he conducted numerous longitude campaigns, including transatlantic chronometer expeditions and the first international telegraphic determination between Halifax, Nova Scotia, and Boston (1851).

Bond had considerable success applying new technologies to astronomy. With his son George and Boston daguerreotypists John A. Whipple and William B. Jones he helped pioneer celestial photography. The team took the first photograph ever made of a star in 1850. Under contract to the U.S. Coast Survey, Bond and his sons Richard and George improved devices for use with the new American telegraph to determine longitude: a break-circuit device for attachment to the escapement of the clock and a drum chronograph for recording the instant of an astronomical event in a time scale. This technology made the everyday operations of longitude expeditions significantly easier and, for the first time, gave astronomers a way of recording all sorts of observations with electricity. The Bonds promoted the apparatus they made for the Coast Survey at home and abroad, and at the London Crystal Palace Exhibition in 1851 they won a Council Medal, the exhibition's highest award. In December 1851 Bond started the world's first public time service based on clock beats telegraphed from Harvard's observatory. His principal clients for the service, which established a standard time in the region, were New England's railroads. Bond died in Cambridge, Massachusetts.

• William Cranch Bond's papers relating to work at Harvard College Observatory are in the Harvard University Archives. Family memorabilia and papers relating to the firm of William Bond & Son are in the Collection of Historical Scientific Instruments, Harvard University. Two large collections of Bond artifacts survive at the Collection of Historical Scientific Instruments and at the National Museum of American History, Smithsonian Institution. Excerpts from Bond papers are in Edward S. Holden, *Memorials of William Cranch Bond, Director of the Harvard College Observatory, 1840–1859, and his Son, George Phillips Bond, Director of the Harvard College Observatory, 1859–1865,* (1897). William Cranch Bond's writings include "History and Description of the Astronomical Observatory of Harvard College," *Annals of the Harvard College Observatory* 1 (1856): i–cxci. Bond's contributions, both administrative and scientific, to the observatory are described in Bessie Zaban Jones and Lyle Gifford Boyd, *The Harvard Observatory: The First Four Directorships, 1839–1919* (1971), and in Solon I. Bailey, *The History and Work of Harvard Observatory, 1839–1927* (1931). His photographic experiments with his son are discussed in Dorrit Hoffleit, *Some Firsts in Astronomical Photography* (1950), and his work on time and longitude is discussed in Carlene E. Stephens, "'The Most Reliable Time': William Bond, The New England Railroads, and Time Awareness in 19th-Century America," *Technology and Culture* 30 (Jan. 1989): 1–24.

CARLENE E. STEPHENS

BONDS, Margaret Jeannette Allison (3 Mar. 1913–26 Apr. 1972), composer, pianist, and teacher, was born in Chicago, Illinois, the daughter of Dr. Monroe Alpheus Majors, a pioneering black physician, medical researcher, and author, and Estelle C. Bonds, a music teacher and organist. Although legally born Majors, she used her mother's maiden name (Bonds) in her youth and throughout her professional life. She grew up in intellectually stimulating surroundings; her mother held Sunday afternoon salons at which young black Chicago musicians, writers, and artists gathered and where visiting musicians and artists were always welcomed. Bonds first displayed musical talent in her piano composition "Marquette Street Blues," written at the age of five. She then began studying piano with local teachers and by the time she was in high school was taking lessons in piano and composition with Florence B. Price and William Dawson, two of the first black American symphonic composers, who were both professionally active in Chicago. Bonds remarked that through her mother's circle she had "actual contact with all the living composers of African descent." As a young girl she served as the pianist at the Berean Baptist Church, where her mother was organist. One of several black Chicago churches that fostered performances of classical music, Berean Baptist was the home of a black community orchestra led by Harrison Farrell.

When Bonds was a teenager, singer Abbie Mitchell introduced her to the European art song and to songs by American black composers, especially those of Henry T. Burleigh. At about the same time Bonds ran across the first published poem of Langston Hughes, "The Negro Speaks of Rivers," which made a great impact on her and which she later set to music. She set many of his texts and collaborated with him in theater works, such as *Shakespeare in Harlem* (1959).

Bonds studied with Emily Boettscher Bogue at Northwestern University, where she received B.M. and M.M. degrees (1933, 1934). While still a student, she received the Wanamaker Foundation Prize for her song "Sea Ghost" (1932). In 1933 she became the first black American soloist to perform with the Chicago Symphony, playing John Alden Carpenter's *Concertino*. She was also the soloist in a performance of Florence Price's Piano Concerto at the 1933 World's Fair. During the 1930s she performed frequently in the United States and Canada, and she also founded and taught at the Allied Arts Academy in Chicago, an institution devoted to the teaching of ballet and music to black children.

In 1939 Bonds moved to New York City, where she became more active as a composer and arranger and where she served as an editor in the Clarence Williams music publishing firm. For a time she composed pop music; her most famous hits were collaborations—with Andy Razafar for "Peachtree Street" (1939) and with Hal Dickinson for "Spring Will Be So Sad" (1940). Her popular songs were recorded by Glenn Miller, Charley Spivak, and Woody Hermann. In New York she studied both piano (with Djane Herz) and composition (with Robert Starer) at the Juilliard School of Music. She also studied composition with Roy Harris. She made her Town Hall debut as a pianist in 1952. Bonds taught at the American Music Wing in New York and was music director for such theaters as the East Side Settlement House, the White Barn Theater, and the Stage of Youth. She promoted work of black American musicians and composers by organizing a chamber music society and establishing a sight-singing program at Harlem's Mount Calvary Baptist Church. She married Lawrence Richardson in 1940, and the couple had one child. In 1968 she moved to Los Angeles, where she taught at the Inner City Institute and Repertory Theater and worked as an arranger for the Los Angeles Jubilee Singers.

John Lovell, Jr., in *Black Song: The Forge and the Flame* (1972), described Bonds as one of the most significant twentieth-century arrangers of traditional spirituals, along with Burleigh and Will Marion Cook, all of whose arrangements cultivated widespread appreciation of the repertory. She arranged spirituals throughout her career, many for solo voice and piano, and some as choral pieces; singer Leontyne Price commissioned and recorded Bonds's arrangement of "He's Got the Whole World in His Hands." Other compositions of Bonds's, such as the piano piece *Troubled Water* (1967, also set later for cello and piano), were often strongly steeped in the spiritual idiom.

Bonds's forty-two art songs include "The Pasture" (1958) and "Stopping by the Woods on a Snowy Evening" (1963), both set to texts of Robert Frost, and, perhaps her best-known songs, "Three Dream Portraits" (1959) and "To a Brown Girl, Dead" (1956), both settings of Langston Hughes poems. Her major choral works include the *Ballad of the Brown King* (1954, to text by Hughes), which has been performed annually in many black churches, and a Mass in D Minor for chorus and orchestra or organ (1959). The *Montgomery Variations*, dedicated to Martin Luther King, Jr. and composed at the time of the march on Montgomery in 1965, was her most successful orchestral piece. Her last work, Credo for baritone, chorus and orchestra (text by W. E. B. Du Bois), was performed the month after her death by the Los Angeles Philharmonic, conducted by Zubin Mehta. She died in Los Angeles.

Bonds was recognized during her lifetime with many commissions and awards, including a Distinguished Alumna Award from Northwestern University (1967). Although much of her music is still in manuscript, there is a renewed interest in making it more available for performance, especially her piano music and songs. However, some of her most significant works were her modern Shakespearean musical theater works (*Shakespeare in Harlem* and *Romey and Julie*) as well as other dramatic musicals and ballets, which brought her music to a broad audience. These important works were not published, however, and the manuscripts remain in the hands of the family. Her close friendship and collaboration with Langston Hughes, as well as her many settings of his poems (from "The Negro Speaks of Rivers" to the 1964 choral work "Fields of Wonder") resulted in a very significant body of work that exemplifies the close mutual interaction of poet and composer in expressing the Afro-American ethnic identity. Bonds's many programmatic works for piano and for orchestra also speak of the black experience through their use of spiritual materials, jazz harmonies and rhythms, and social themes. Her music fuses European musical Romanticism with the varied strands of her Afro-American heritage to form a distinctive musical corpus, although since her death access to her most extended works has been limited.

• Bonds's papers and manuscripts are owned and held by her daughter, Djane Richardson, in New York. Bonds's own account of her musical development is in "A Reminiscence," *International Library of Negro Life and History: The Negro in Music and Art* (1967), pp. 190–93. Lists of her works are found in Alice Tischler, *Fifteen Black American Composers with a Bibliography of Their Works* (1981), and in the *New Grove Dictionary of American Music* (1986). Her mass is discussed by Andre Jerome Thomas in "A Study of the Selected Masses of Twentieth-Century Black Composers: Margaret Bonds, Robert Ray, George Walker, and David Baker" (D.M.A. diss., Univ. of Illinois, Champaign-Urbana, 1983). A biographical study and analysis of some of Bonds's music is found in Mildred D. Green, *Black Women Composers: A Genesis* (1983). Bonds's collaboration with Langston Hughes is covered in F. Berry, *Langston Hughes: Before and Beyond Harlem* (1983). The Chicago period of her life is covered in Rae Linda Brown, "Florence B. Price and Margaret Bonds: The Chicago Years," *Black Music Research Bulletin* 12, no. 2 (1990): 11–14, and Helen Walker-Hill, "Black Women Composers in Chicago: Then and Now," *Black Music Research Journal* 12 (Spring 1992): 1–23. Walker-Hill's anthology *Black Women Composers: A Century of Piano Music (1893–1990)* (1992) includes music by Bonds. Two 1980s recordings include her "Three Dream Portraits": *Art Songs by Black American Composers* (Univ. of Michigan, 1981) and *Focus on Women in the Arts: Women in Song* (Smith College, 1982). Obituaries are in the *New York Times*, 29 Apr. 1972; *Variety*, 10 May 1972; *Jet*, 18 May 1972, *Chicago Defender*, 13 Jan. 1973, and *The Black Perspective in Music* 1 (1973): 197.

BARBARA G. JACKSON

BONFANTI, Maria (16 Feb. 1847–25 Jan. 1921), ballerina and teacher, also known as Marie and as Marietta, was born in Milan, Italy, the daughter of Gaetano Bonfanti, an army veteran, and Graziosa Geroni. Bonfanti received her dance training from Carlo Blasis, the ballet master of the La Scala Opera House, in his private school in Milan. In January 1860 she made her debut in Vercelli, Italy, and the following fall was featured at La Scala in Meyerbeer's *Roberto il Diavolo*. During the 1861–1862 season Bonfanti was engaged as a principal dancer at both La Scala and the Teatro Canobbiana, also in Milan. She left Italy in 1864 for engagements in Lyons and Paris and then went to London, where she became one of the featured dancers in London's Covent Garden Opera House.

While in London in the summer of 1866, American theater managers Henry C. Jarrett and A. M. Palmer engaged Bonfanti to appear as prima ballerina assoluta in *The Black Crook* at Niblo's Garden Theatre in New York City. Best known of all nineteenth-century theatrical spectacles, Charles Barras's *The Black Crook* is a loosely structured musical melodrama based on the Faust legend. The production, which opened at Niblo's on 12 September 1866, featured Italian ballerinas and included variety acts, elaborate changing scenery, and marching armies of supernumeraries. Dances of all sorts were featured in the production: cancans, acrobatic specialties, and large-scale ballets, with well-trained ballerinas surrounded by minimally trained and scantily clad American ballet girls.

The first production of *The Black Crook* ran a record-breaking 474 performances, and the show was revived frequently from 1870 to 1909. Throughout her career, Bonfanti's name was closely associated with *The Black Crook*; she performed in at least fourteen revivals in theaters from New York to San Francisco. Although most of the variety acts and dances in the initial *Black Crook* were changed frequently to attract returning audiences, Bonfanti remained for the entire first run. Jarrett and Palmer then renewed her contract for *The White Fawn*, a musical spectacle based on the Sleeping Beauty fairy tale, which opened on 18 January 1868. Bonfanti, considered a matinee idol in New York City, inspired poetical praise:

Her step so light, Her brow so fair, She moveth like a thing of air, Or fairy in her wanton play, Or Naiad on the moonlight spray, Like gossamer on wings of light, She floats before our entranced sight, Let us gaze no more, Nor speak nor stir, Lest we fall down and worship her (Bonfanti clipping file, anonymous poem, Chicago, 1868).

Critics hailed Bonfanti's dancing style as "in accordance with the elegance of her person; it is full of grace, buoyant and elastic, and avoiding all forced exertions of other artists . . . " (*New York Clipper*, 11 July 1868, p. 110).

Bonfanti left Niblo's in June 1868, moving to Crosby's Opera House in Chicago and later to Philadelphia to appear in Jarrett and Palmer's touring production of *The White Fawn* and in another spectacle titled *Undine*. On 4 January 1869 Jarrett and Palmer's newly named troupe, the Royal Alhambra Company, starring Bonfanti, made its first appearance at the Tammany entertainment center in Manhattan.

Bonfanti remained at the Tammany until February 1869, when she struck out on her own. She began what became a lifelong pattern of touring the United States and dancing in New York City, interspersed with visits to her home in Italy. There she studied at La Scala and purchased costumes and shoes unavailable in New York City. She was usually accompanied on these trips by her sister Olimpia.

In December 1869 Bonfanti made her first cross-country tour, appearing at Tom Maguire's California Theater in San Francisco in *The Black Crook* with rival Rita Sangalli. During this trip Bonfanti also visited silver and gold mining towns in Nevada and California. In 1872 she toured the southern United States, visiting New Orleans, Louisiana, and Galveston, Texas. It was on this trip that Bonfanti met her future husband, George Curtiss Hoffman, the young son of a wealthy and socially prominent New York family. Although liaisons between ballerinas and members of the aristocracy were common in Europe, Bonfanti was the first dancer to marry into New York's exclusive Four Hundred, the socially elite New York high society founded by Caroline Schemmerhorn Astor. Bonfanti and Hoffman were married in Paris in 1872, and they moved to London, where Bonfanti performed until 1873; they had one child. Although Hoffman's family had initially disapproved of his marriage, following his death in 1876 they embraced Bonfanti, urging her to leave the theater and make her home with them. For nine months she engaged in social and philanthropic activities, became an active member of Sorosis, an early feminist organization, and formed what became a lifelong friendship with Caroline Soule, an author and editor who worked in support of the temperance movement and the Association for the Advancement of Women.

At age twenty-nine, Bonfanti returned to the theater to perform in Augustin Daly's play *Life* at the Fifth Avenue Theatre in October 1876. For the next fourteen years she alternated between performing in New York and taking long, exhausting cross-country tours comprised of one-night stands with various combination companies (touring troupes organized around a star performer). During this period she also visited Europe occasionally. In all her professional contracts

Bonfanti insisted on top billing. She starred at the newly built Metropolitan Opera House in New York in the 1884–1885 and 1885–1886 seasons. Bonfanti concluded her career as a performer with two long tours, appearing first in *The Arabian Nights, or Aladdin's Wonderful Lamp* in 1887–1888, followed by *The Twelve Temptations* during the 1888–1890 seasons.

After a long European vacation that began in 1890, Bonfanti returned to the United States in 1897 to open her own dance school in New York City. She taught strict, uncompromising Blasis (Italian school) ballet technique to a new generation of American dancers. Among her students were Ruth St. Denis, a founder of American modern dance, and society women whom she had met through her in-laws, including Emelyn Roosevelt, Lady Cunard, Mrs. Cornelius Vanderbilt, and Edith Whitney. In 1916 Bonfanti retired from teaching and lived quietly in New York until her death there.

Bonfanti represented the best Italian training and dance traditions. Throughout her career she maintained an exhausting schedule, often performing in productions that catered to popular audiences. In the large-scale musical spectacles of the late nineteenth century, produced in small towns and large cities across the United States, Bonfanti performed with uncompromising artistic integrity the dance technique she had learned in Europe's greatest ballet school.

• Bonfanti's correspondence, contracts, sheet music, and clipping and photographic scrapbooks are in the Dance Collection, the New York Public Library for the Performing Arts, Lincoln Center. For information on Bonfanti, see Barbara Barker, *Ballet or Ballyhoo: The American Careers of Maria Bonfanti, Rita Sangalli, and Giuseppina Morlacchi* (1984).

BARBARA BARKER

BONFILS, Frederick Gilmer (31 Dec. 1860–2 Feb. 1933), and **Harry Heye Tammen** (6 Mar. 1856–19 July 1924), newspaper publishers, were born, respectively, in Lincoln County near Troy, Missouri, and Baltimore, Maryland. Bonfils was the son of Henrietta Lewis and Eugene Napoleon Bonfils, a judge whose Corsican family claimed kinship to Napoleon Bonaparte. Tammen was the son of Heye Heinrich Tammen, a pharmacist, and Caroline Henriette Piepenbrinker. Although Bonfils would later stress his early poverty, his family actually seems to have lived quite comfortably. Bonfils entered the U.S. Military Academy at West Point in 1878. After resigning in 1881 without graduating, he worked briefly in a New York City bank and then returned to Troy to work in his father's new insurance business. He married Belle Barton in 1882; they had two daughters. Immediately after marrying, the couple moved to Cañon City, Colorado, where Bonfils taught tactics and mathematics in a military school. A few months later, reportedly because of his wife's ill health, Bonfils moved back to Missouri. There, after brief stints working for his father, a local newspaper, and the state legislature, Bonfils embarked on a career of land speculation. He gained little from his first venture selling Texas land, but in 1889 he struck it rich in Oklahoma, where Indian territory had just been opened to white settlers; in the subsequent real estate boom, Bonfils made thousands of dollars, some of it clearly through fraud. Moving on to Kansas City, Kansas, he invested his new wealth in a crooked lottery, running it under various aliases until 1894, when reformers closed it down.

Looking for new opportunities, he moved his family to Denver, Colorado, and there met his future partner, Harry Tammen. The death of Tammen's father in 1870 had forced the boy to go to work, first in a print shop in Philadelphia and then as a bartender. In 1880 he moved to Denver, where he again found work as a bartender; in later years, he would boast that he had been "the best booze-juggler in the world." The following year he married Elizabeth Evans; they had no children. Fascinated with Colorado's mineral wealth, Tammen organized the H. H. Tammen Curio Company, which sold mineral specimens as well as a variety of unlikely souvenirs, including multiple scalps of the Indian chief Geronimo. In 1886 he began publishing a monthly, *The Great Divide*, describing life in the West; he also began marketing colored pictures of western scenes. Tammen's wife died in 1890, and two years later he married Agnes Reid. The couple remained childless. Meanwhile, his curio business continued to expand, adding both wholesale and mail-order divisions.

Tammen was wiped out by the 1893 depression, and in 1895 he persuaded Bonfils to join him in taking over the Denver *Evening Post*. Just three years old, this eight-page publication had a circulation of 4,000, the smallest of the city's four papers. In October 1895 the two men launched the renamed *Denver Evening Post*, operating as equal partners despite the fact that Bonfils had contributed the $12,500 purchase price. (The word "Evening" was dropped from the title in 1901.) Bonfils looked like a handsome gambler with his loud clothes and sharp black mustache, but he emerged as the disciplined businessman of the team, while the portly and ebullient Tammen invented most of the *Post*'s innumerable stunts and contests. The team functioned well, and the *Post*'s sensational stories, ferocious crusades, bold type, and sizzling headlines offered a lively alternative to the city's sedate morning paper, the *Rocky Mountain News*. Explaining the *Post*'s criterion for news, Bonfils observed: "A dogfight on Sixteenth Street is a better story than a war in Timbuktu." Tammen urged the staff to take a lesson from vaudeville: "It's got every sort of act—laughs, tears, wonder, thrills, melodrama, tragedy, comedy, love, and hate. That's what I want you to give our readers." Crime stories abounded; when critics accused the paper of sensationalism, the *Post* responded by adding a tag on each story: "Crime Never Pays." The paper also offered voluminous feature material, columns, pictures, and comic strips.

Bonfils and Tammen carried on a succession of crusades, many initiated under the banner, "So the People May Know." Using scare headlines and blistering language, the paper denounced the community's largest utilities, most of its public officials (particularly Senator Thomas Patterson, who owned the *News*), its preachers, and almost everyone else in a position of power. Billing itself "the people's champion," "Your Big Brother," and "The Paper with a Heart and a Soul," the *Post* weathered innumerable fights and libel suits. On one occasion, its building was ransacked by a mob after it opposed a street-railway strike; another time, the paper's effort to get a pardon for a man serving time for cannibalism led to gunfire, with both Bonfils and Tammen wounded in the encounter. But the *Post* persisted; Bonfils even went into the coal business briefly to force the local monopoly to cut its prices. Besides its colorful news coverage, the *Post* launched an avalanche of promotions: cross-country roller-skating contests, ladies' wrestling matches, high-wire acts over Denver's business district, outdoor concerts, kite-flying contests, competitions to name the new elephant in the city zoo, and hundreds of other events, an average of about one a week. Between 1904 and 1921 the paper also owned the Sells-Floto Circus, Tammen's particular delight.

The *Post*'s blend of populism, sensation, and entertainment proved very successful; by 1901 it had become the largest paper in Colorado. In 1907 the organization moved into a handsome new building; locals dubbed the partners' red-walled office "The Bucket of Blood." The following year, for the very first time, Bonfils allowed himself and Tammen to draw salaries: $1,000 per week. In 1909 the two men bought the *Kansas City Post*, hoping to replicate their Denver success; Bonfils also relished challenging the *Kansas City Star*, which had led the fight to close down his lottery in 1894. But after fierce battles on the newsstands and in court, the partners decided to retreat from the field. They sold out in 1922 for about eight times what they had originally paid. Meanwhile, their Denver operation continued to flourish; by 1923 each man was earning more than $1 million a year.

During the summer of 1922 the *Post* ran some of the country's earliest stories on the so-called Teapot Dome scandal, raising the possibility that private oil companies had used bribery to obtain valuable oil leases on federal land. Then after a few months, with the story still unfolding, the *Post* suddenly dropped all mention of the subject. Two years later a Senate investigating committee established that in September 1922 Bonfils teamed up with John Leo Stack, a Colorado oilman whose own claim to a share of the profits had been passed over. Together, they persuaded Harry Sinclair, president of one of the companies involved, to give them cash and securities amounting to $1 million. Bonfils always denied that Sinclair was buying the *Post*'s silence. No legal action was taken against him, but many observers questioned his explanation, and in 1927 he was forced to resign from the American Society of Newspaper Editors.

Harry Tammen died in Denver as the Teapot Dome case was unfolding. In his will, he left thousands of dollars to the *Post*'s employees and $300,000 to endow a wing on the Denver Children's Hospital. Not long after, Bonfils was swept into another circulation war, when the new Scripps-Howard chain bought up two local papers and made an aggressive play for the *Post*'s afternoon readership. In retribution, the *Post* started a morning paper in January 1927. For two years the rivals poured out their resources in an orgy of promotions and giveaways; at one point, the papers were offering five gallons of gas to anyone who placed a 20¢ ad in their Sunday editions. Finally in November 1928 a truce was declared: Scripps-Howard withdrew from the afternoon field, and the *Post* discontinued its morning paper.

When Bonfils died a few years later in Denver, he left a sizable portion of his more than $8 million estate to the Frederick G. Bonfils Foundation, which he had established in 1927. Contentious to the last, he died in the midst of a libel suit against his old rival, the *Rocky Mountain News*, which had published a local politician's description of him as "a public enemy [who] has left the trail of a slimy serpent across Colorado for 30 years." Bonfils, by contrast, liked to describe himself as "the champion of every good and pure and holy and righteous cause." Both he and Tammen were guilty of many sins in the course of their long partnership, yet one cannot but recognize the many occasions on which they did speak for the ordinary citizens of Denver, and the zest and color that they added to the life of their community over a period of nearly four decades.

• The files of the *Denver Post* and the *Rocky Mountain News* provide an extensive record of Bonfils's and Tammen's professional activities. The most thorough secondary account of their careers is Bill Hosokawa, *Thunder in the Rockies: The Incredible Denver Post* (1976). The two were also the subject of Gene Fowler's *Timber Line: A Story of Bonfils and Tammen* (1933). Briefer descriptions appear in Silas Bent, *Ballyhoo: The Voice of the Press* (1927); Edwin Emery and Michael Emery, *The Press in America* (1978); and Frank Luther Mott, *American Journalism* (1962). An obituary for Tammen is in the *New York Times*, 20 July 1924, and for Bonfils, 3 Feb. 1933.

SANDRA OPDYCKE

BONFILS, Winifred. *See* Black, Winifred Sweet.

BONHAM, Milledge Luke (25 Dec. 1813–27 Aug. 1890), governor, congressman, and soldier, was born in South Carolina's Edgefield District, the son of James Bonham and Sophie Smith, planters. His father died when he was two, and his mother saw to his education. Bonham attended private academies before graduating from South Carolina College in 1834. He entered the legal profession, engaged in local politics, and became prominent in state military affairs, rising to the rank of major general of militia. He led a brigade of Palmetto State volunteers in the Seminole War of 1836, a position that helped win him a stint in the state house of representatives (1840–1844). In 1845 he married Ann Griffin; they had fourteen children.

At the outset of the Mexican War, President James Polk tendered Bonham a regular army commission as lieutenant colonel of the Twelfth U.S. Infantry. After seeing intermittent action below the Rio Grande, the lawyer-turned-soldier governed an occupied province as peace talks dragged on between the warring governments. In 1848 he returned to his legal practice in Edgefield, then served for almost a decade as solicitor of the southern district of his state. In 1857 he was elected to complete the congressional term of his deceased cousin, Preston S. Brooks, the celebrated assailant of Senator Charles Sumner. Bonham remained in the House of Representatives until his state declared itself out of the Union in December 1860—a decision he applauded, as befitted an ardent secessionist.

When South Carolina formed an independent army, Bonham's military experience recommended him for the major generalship of state volunteers. Early in 1861 he took command of troops and facilities at Charleston, a position in which he remained after the Confederate States Army (CSA) was formed. Resentful of the claims to preference of professional soldiers, he protested Confederate president Jefferson Davis's policy of reserving high rank for officers who had served in the peacetime U.S. Army. At the request of his friend, Governor Francis W. Pickens, Bonham grudgingly waived his seniority to serve under Brigadier General Pierre G. T. Beauregard, CSA.

After the bombardment of Fort Sumter, Bonham was sent to northeastern Virginia to command troops forming a defensive position along Bull Run; there, on 31 May, he was again superseded by Beauregard. By early July Bonham's brigade of approximately 3,500 South Carolinians held an exposed position around Fairfax Court House, eight miles in advance of the main Confederate line. In mid-July his command staged a careful retreat upon the approach of Brigadier General Irvin McDowell's Union army. On 21 July Bonham's men held the right center of Beauregard's line, seeing only intermittent action at First Manassas (Bull Run).

Disappointed with his failure to rise above brigade command, Bonham resigned his commission early in 1862 to wage a successful campaign for a seat in the Confederate House of Representatives. Later that year he emerged as a dark horse in the race to select Governor Pickens's successor. When the leading candidates deadlocked, Bonham was elected. During his two-year term, he generally supported the war aims of the Davis administration, despite his personal antipathy toward the president. While dedicated to upholding the sovereignty of South Carolina, he appeared more conciliatory toward the central government, and more understanding of the problems it faced, than neighboring governors Joseph E. Brown of Georgia and Zebulon Vance of North Carolina. Bonham was disposed to compromise on such contentious issues as draft exemptions for state and local officials and the impressment of slaves to work on government military projects. Only in the last months of his term, with William T. Sherman's army poised to invade his state, did Bonham act to restrict the number of draft-age constituents and laborers available for duty beyond South Carolina's borders.

When his term of office ended late in 1864, Bonham reentered the Confederate army, serving as a brigadier general of cavalry during General Joseph E. Johnston's futile effort to curtail Sherman's foray through the Carolinas. During Reconstruction he resumed his law practice in Edgefield, served in the legislature as a Democrat, and after Wade Hampton's election as governor in 1876, worked avidly to restore white supremacy to the state government. Appointed railroad commissioner by Hampton, he worked to rebuild rail transportation. The task was so difficult and taxing that it hastened his death at White Sulphur Springs, Virginia, a spa he was visiting in a futile attempt to regain his health.

In the role of both politician and soldier, Bonham was a man of commanding presence, his appearance highlighted by gray-streaked hair, steely eyes, and an immaculately kept beard. His forceful personality was somewhat weakened by a difficult temper and a tendency to mood swings. From his twenties to the end of his public life he struck observers such as James Henry Hammond as "not of an equable temperament, being either full of hope or plunged in despair." High-minded and generous, he could also be condescending, imperious, and abrupt to the point of rudeness; during his Civil War military service, his staff referred to him behind his back as "the Dictator." His frequent squabbling with regular army and West Point–trained superiors such as Beauregard and his acute sensitivity to matters of seniority betrayed the worst traits of the citizen-soldier.

• Bonham's papers are in the South Caroliniana Library, University of South Carolina, Columbia. A large collection of his letters to his predecessor as governor can be found in the Francis W. Pickens Collection at Duke University, while Bonham's correspondence with Hammond reposes in the James Henry Hammond Papers, South Caroliniana Library. The best source on Bonham's gubernatorial career is Charles E. Cauthen, *South Carolina Goes to War, 1860–1865* (1950), while his term as a Confederate legislator receives some attention in William B. Yearns, *The Confederate Congress* (1960). Bonham's brief stint in Civil War military command is covered in *The War of the Rebellion: A Compilation of the Official Records of the Union and Confederate Armies* (128 vols., 1880–1901), especially ser. 1, vol. 2; William C. Davis, *Battle at Bull Run: A History of the First Major Campaign of the Civil War* (1977); and the 1861 letters of two of Bonham's officers, Edward G. Longacre, ed., "A South Carolinian Awaits 'Abraham's Forces,'" *Manuscripts* 30 (1978): 21–29, and "On the Staff of the 'Dictator,'" *Manuscripts* 36 (1984): 224–27.

EDWARD G. LONGACRE

BONI, Albert (21 Oct. 1892–31 July 1981), publisher, was born in New York City, the son of Charles Boni, an insurance executive, and Bertha Seltzer. Educated at Harvard and Cornell Universities, he later conceived and executed some of the most creative publishing ventures of the twentieth century. In 1913 Boni, with his brother Charles, opened the Washington Square Book Shop at 137 McDougal Street in New York's Greenwich Village, where many of the city's bohemian artists often gathered. In a back room of the bookshop the following year, Lawrence Langner, Max Eastman, Mary Heaton Vorse, and John Reed helped found the Washington Square Players, a small theater troupe that evolved into the Theatre Guild; later, a splinter group of the guild, calling itself the Provincetown Players, performed plays by Theodore Dreiser and Eugene O'Neill.

The first book published by the Bonis was Robert Blatchford's *Not Guilty* (1914), whose sale of fifty thousand copies allowed the brothers to publish Alfred Kreymborg's new literary magazine, the *Glebe*. The first and most important number of the *Glebe*'s short run, *Des Imagistes: An Anthology* (Feb. 1914), included poems by Ezra Pound, Amy Lowell, Ford Madox Ford, Hilda Doolittle, and William Carlos Williams, among others. The Bonis founded the Little Leather Library, which produced small volumes bound in lambskin. Among its first titles were *The 50 Best American Poems* and *The 50 Best English Poems*. These attractive volumes, selling nearly one million copies the first year, evolved into the Book-of-the-Month Club.

By the end of 1915, financial difficulties caused the Bonis to close. Albert, in an effort to gain more business experience, joined an uptown advertising agency for a short period. A deft persuasiveness and salty tenacity aided him in his return to publishing as he told Horace Liveright, who was then manufacturing and selling household products, about his idea for a select series of reprints consisting of only modern European classics. This idea began the partnership that led to the birth of the Modern Library, whose first volumes were announced by the firm of Boni & Liveright in the spring of 1917.

Boni's selections for publication reflected the bohemian tastes of the Washington Square Book Club crowd, featuring works from authors such as Oscar Wilde, August Strindberg, Henrik Ibsen, and Guy de Maupassant. Inexpensive and handsomely bound, the Modern Library became one of the most popular series in the history of American book publishing and thus the center of the firm's business as its most lucrative property. Differences developed, however, between Boni and Liveright as a result of Boni's focus on European socialist and pacifist writers during these World War I years. These works generally did not do well; some, such as Henri Barbusse's *The Inferno* (1918), did not find an American audience, and though Leon Trotsky's *The Bolsheviki and World Peace* (1918) initially sold twenty thousand copies in the United States, sales were abruptly halted by the Red Scare, which arose soon after. The firm itself was under military surveillance to ensure that it would obey a ban against the publication of Andreas Latzko's *Men in War*. Nevertheless, Boni gave increasing attention to these writers, and Liveright, while sympathetic, preferred to publish works by unknowns from the Greenwich Village set as well as works by well-known writers. Since neither partner was willing to sell his interest, the sole control of the firm hinged on a simple coin toss—which Liveright won. The firm remained Boni & Liveright, however, retaining Boni's name through its most successful years.

Boni then left the United States to tour Europe; drawn by the excitement of the Russian Revolution, he visited the USSR, where he was arrested on charges of espionage. He rejoined his brother Charles after his release in 1923 and founded a new publishing venture, Albert and Charles Boni. In 1925 the new firm played a role in the inauguration of the Harlem Renaissance by publishing its intellectual manifesto, *The New Negro: An Anthology*, edited by Alain LeRoy Locke. By 1927 Boni began publishing radical European and American writers. Several novels by Upton Sinclair and historical and philosophical treatises by Max Eastman made the lists, and the addition of Marcel Proust's works was also an important event. By far, however, the firm's most significant discovery was of the unknown novelist Thornton Wilder, whose *Bridge of San Luis Rey* (1927) sold 240,000 copies in its first year and won the Pulitzer Prize in 1928.

The stock market crash would shortly alter these new fortunes; after Charles left the firm in 1930 to develop new ventures in modern art, Boni worked alone during the depression years to publish titles by Proust, Colette, Mark Van Doren, and John Huston. The lists were impressive, though not enough to sustain the firm, and Albert and Charles Boni was finally forced to close in 1939. Toward the end of the thirties, Boni began to experiment with the microfilming of books. Early results of poor quality proved frustrating, and in 1942 he abandoned the project. He returned to it in 1945 and by 1950 had perfected a process whereby entire books could be reduced onto cards and read through a machine that magnified the cards and projected them onto a screen. The result, the Readex Microprint Corporation, became highly popular with researchers and librarians, and in the first fifteen years of its existence issued more than 500,000 titles. This would be Boni's last enterprise; with its success, he retired in 1974. His son William then assumed control and inherited a legacy of innovation in both publishing and American intellectual culture that had spanned the previous six decades. Boni died in Ormond Beach, Florida.

• A discussion of the Bonis, including the early years of the Washington Square Book Shop, is in Walker Gilmer's *Horace Liveright: Publisher of the Twenties* (1970). See also Charles Lee, *The Hidden Public: The Story of the Book-of-the-Month Club* (1958). A more detailed treatment of Albert Boni and his contributions is found in his obituary in *Publishers Weekly*, 14 Aug. 1981, pp. 13, 16.

NATHAN L. GRANT

BONNELL, John Sutherland (10 Jan. 1893–23 Feb. 1992), Presbyterian clergyman, was born in Dover, Prince Edward Island, Canada, the son of Abraham Bonnell, a hospital superintendent, and Catherine Cameron. Beginning at the age of ten, he often accompanied his father on daily rounds at Falconwood, an institution for the mentally ill in Charlottetown, the provincial capital.

In 1916 Bonnell interrupted his tutorials in preparation for collegiate studies to join the Canadian army. As part of the Fifth Canadian Siege Battery he rose from the rank of private soldier to that of senior sergeant; after being wounded twice and gassed, he returned home before war's end. In 1919 he graduated with a B.A. from Dalhousie University in Halifax, Nova Scotia. In 1922 he was ordained a Presbyterian minister. Between 1923 and 1929 he served as pastor of St. Andrew's Church in St. John, New Brunswick, while pursuing formal theological training at Pine Hill Hall in Halifax. In 1923 he married Bessie Louise Caruthers; they had four children. After graduating from seminary in 1927, he served as minister of Westminster Church in Winnipeg from 1929 to 1935, when he accepted an invitation from the Fifth Avenue Presbyterian Church in New York City to be pastor. He remained in this capacity until his retirement in 1962.

In New York, Bonnell's direct, sincere preaching drew large audiences, and his sermons were regularly reported in local newspapers. In 1943 he began radio sermons for the American Broadcasting Company, attracting over three million listeners. Always one to utilize modern technology for ministerial purposes, Bonnell was one of the first to inaugurate a "dial-a-prayer" service for telephone use. He was also a part-time lecturer at Princeton Theological Seminary between the years 1938 and 1960.

In July 1953 Bonnell was one of the three leaders in the National Conference of Christians and Jews who publicly denounced Joseph McCarthy. When the junior senator from Wisconsin claimed that Protestant clergy were a major source of support for Communist activities, Bonnell protested in a public telegram to President Dwight D. Eisenhower. In 1957 he welcomed Billy Graham's first evangelical crusade in New York, while urging fellow ministers to continue speaking out on social and economic issues. However, while serving as interim president of Union Seminary (1966–1969), he warned against "go-go theology," which he said consisted of views that allowed social and political causes to obviate the need for evangelism.

But Bonnell's most innovative ministerial contribution lay in another sphere, one rarely approached in those days and seldom explored. Drawing on experiences with his father regarding mental illness, he became a pioneer in blending spiritual counseling and psychiatry. As early as 1935 he had established a clinic in his church for those who sought psychological and religious advice. Soon more than one thousand people visited the clinic each year, and in 1938 he wrote *Pastoral Psychiatry*. Although he made no claim to be a psychiatrist in the medical sense of the term, he believed that people could be helped by physicians of the soul. All around him he saw instances of divorce, suicide, nervous breakdowns, and other types of functional disorders. His response was that emotional difficulties such as anxiety, insecurity, and guilt pertained to the human soul as well as the mind. Consequently, there could be spiritual prescriptions for mental problems, and calling on God for help could buttress psychotherapy. He urged his ministerial colleagues to be alert to distress signals in counseling sessions, to listen sympathetically, and then to make use of latent strengths that are in everyone. For him providing an understanding environment and stimulating basic spiritual impulses were tangible manifestations of Christian helpfulness. Through his ground-breaking work and writing, the synthesis of religion and psychology became better known. Many churches copied his idea of erecting consulting clinics, and soon many seminaries began offering courses in this field. He died in Roseburg, Oregon.

• Other works of Bonnell include *Fifth Avenue Sermons* (1936), *Pastoral Psychiatry* (1938), *Psychology for Pastor and People: A Book on Spiritual Counseling* (1948), *The Practice and Power of Prayer* (1954), *I Believe in Immortality* (1959), *Certainties for Uncertain Times* (1961), and *Do You Want To Be Healed?* (1968). An obituary is in the *New York Times*, 26 Feb. 1992.

HENRY WARNER BOWDEN

BONNER, Campbell (30 Jan. 1876–12 July 1954), classical scholar, was born in Nashville, Tennessee, the son of Willis Bonner, a judge, and Frances Campbell. He earned an A.B. at Vanderbilt in 1896 and an A.M. there the next year. He took a second A.M. at Harvard in 1898 and a Ph.D. there in 1900 with a dissertation *de Danaidibus commentatio*, published as "A Study of the Danaid Myth" in *Harvard Studies in Classical Philology* (1902). In 1901 he studied in Berlin, where he improved his German and heard the lectures of the greatest classical scholars of his time. In 1901–1902 he traveled and studied in Italy and Greece. In 1903 he married Ethel Howell; the number of their children, if any, is unknown.

His first professional post was university professor of Greek at Peabody College for teachers at the University of Nashville (1901–1907). In 1907 he was appointed junior professor of Greek at the University of Michigan at Ann Arbor. He would devote the rest of his professional life to that institution, becoming full professor of Greek language and literature there in 1912, a post he held until his retirement in 1946. The esteem in which his colleagues held him is proven by three posts awarded to him. He was president of the Classical Association of the Midwest and South 1918–1919, annual professor at the American School of Classical Studies in Athens 1927–1928, and president of the American Philological Association in 1932–1933. His election as Corresponding Fellow of the British Academy best attests his achievement.

Through the excellence and number of his publications, Bonner contributed decisively to securing national recognition for Michigan classics. He was the first Michigan classical scholar to write articles necessarily read with care by European scholars. He chose early on not to gain a provincial reputation in central subjects such as Homer or tragedy, where he could not compete with continental scholars. He preferred to secure a lasting international reputation in two peripheral but important subjects, which he could thoroughly control. These were papyrology and ancient magic. Through the initiative of Francis W. Kelsey, his senior colleague at the University of Michigan, the school had purchased, as had Yale and Columbia, considerable papyri, much of them excavated by the British at Oxyrhynchus in Egypt. Bonner edited these accurately and promptly. They were often new texts or considerably older versions of preserved texts. In either case, quite apart from details of interpretation, Bonner's editions of new material became indispensable on publication. He also, at a time when attention to the subject was unfashionable, became an authority in the field of ancient magic, more specifically magical amulets of the Roman period. The paradox became that although his work was exemplary, he detested the subject of his work. His closest colleague, H. C. Youtie, observed: "Bonner appreciated the great minds of classical Athens, but the timid and superstitious folk of the decadence repelled him" (Youtie, p. 303). This limited his contribution, in that he could not see ancient magic in context and evaluate it historically. He was unable for the sake of his research "to be a believer." He followed more the evolutionary approach of religion of the English than the historical approach of the Germans.

Bonner was never a popularizer. His lucid, factual articles regularly appeared in learned journals intended for specialists. He wrote four books of lasting importance: *A Papyrus Codex of the Shepherd of Hermas* (1933); *The Last Chapters of Enoch in Greek*, with H. C. Youtie (1937); *The Homily on the Passion by Melito, Bishop of Sardis* (1940); and *Studies in Magical Amulets Chiefly Greco-Egyptian* (1950). These books are models of precise erudition, careful documentation, and cautious commentary. The first three are used by all serious historians of early Christianity. The last is one of the most enduring books written by an American on the history of Greco-Roman religion. Bonner typified the successful scholar of his generation: he was loyal to one institution throughout his life and wisely chose specialized areas where he could make permanent contributions.

• There is no known repository of Bonner's papers. The published sources for his life are Morton Smith, *Biographical Dictionary of North American Classicists*, ed. Ward W. Briggs, Jr. (1944), pp. 53–55, which includes a bibliography of Bonner's published articles; and Henry A. Sanders, *Yearbook APhS* (1954), pp. 403–6. Herbert C. Youtie, *Gnomon* 27 (1955): 301–3 is best for a description of the man. There is an obituary in the *New York Times*, 13 July 1954.

WILLIAM M. CALDER III

BONNER, Marita Odette (16 June 1898–6 Dec. 1971), educator and author, was born in Boston, Massachusetts, the daughter of Joseph Bonner, a machinist and laborer, and Mary A. Nowell. Educated in the Brookline, Massachusetts, public schools, she applied to Radcliffe College at the urging of her high school faculty adviser and was one of the few African-American students accepted for admission. She majored in English and comparative literature and founded the Radcliffe chapter of Delta Sigma Theta, a black sorority. A gifted pianist and student of musical composition, she won the Radcliffe song competition in 1918 and 1922. Bonner also studied German, a language in which she became fluent. During her last year in college she taught English at a Cambridge high school. After graduating with a B.A. in 1922, she taught at the Bluefield Colored Institute in Bluefield, Virginia, until 1924 and at Armstrong High School in Washington, D.C., from 1924 to 1930, when she married William Almy Occomy, a Brown graduate. The couple moved to Chicago, where they raised three children.

Bonner began writing in high school, contributing pieces to the student magazine, the *Sagamore*. At Radcliffe, she was selected to study writing under Charles Townsend Copeland. Copeland, who encouraged her to write fiction, also gave Bonner what she considered the clichéd advice that she not be "bitter," advice she ignored. During her literary career she published short stories, essays, and plays, most of which examined the debilitating effects of economic, racial, and sexual prejudice on black Americans. Bonner's first publication came in August 1925, a short story, "The Hands," in *Opportunity*, and her award-winning essay "On Being Young—A Woman—and Colored" was published in December of that year in *Crisis*; these two magazines continued to publish her work. In her essay, she examines the triple jeopardy facing black women writers and answers Copeland when she addresses "white friends who have never had to draw breath in a Jim-Crow train. Who never had petty putrid insult dragged over them."

She continues these themes in her other writings. In her 1928 essay "The Young Blood Hungers" a haunting refrain captures the anger and despair of a generation facing economic slavery and brutal racism. In her short story "Nothing New" she introduces Frye Street, a fictional neighborhood in Chicago that she describes as running "from freckled-face tow heads to yellow Orientals; from broad Italy to broad Georgia; from hooked noses to square black noses. . . . Like muddy water in a brook" (*Crisis* [1926]). She later returned to this neighborhood for many of her stories. Although multiethnic, black Frye Street does not have the same opportunities as white Frye Street.

While living in Washington, D.C., Bonner wrote and published several works that won awards from *Crisis*, including "Drab Rambles" (1927) and "The Young Blood Hungers" (1928). She was also an active member of the S Street literary salon of black writers established by poet and playwright Georgia Douglas Johnson. During this time Bonner wrote and published three plays: *The Pot-Maker: A Play to Be Read* (1927), *The Purple Flower* (1928), and *Exit an Illusion* (1929); the latter two also won *Crisis* awards. In her introduction to *Nine Plays by Black Women* (1986), Margaret Wilkerson calls Bonner's *The Purple Flower* a black quest for freedom and happiness in a racist society and "perhaps the most provocative play" of the first half of this century.

After her marriage and subsequent move to Chicago, Bonner took a three-year break from publishing, and when she returned devoted herself exclusively to fiction, publishing her stories under her married name. These stories offer a vivid portrait of black Chicago and its strained interactions with other minorities and a racist white society. Her first work was a three-part narrative titled "A Possible Triad on Black Notes," published in the July, August, and September 1933 issues of *Opportunity*. "Tin Can," a two-part narrative, won the 1933 *Opportunity* literary prize for fiction and was published in the July and August 1934 issues of that magazine. These stories and the eight that followed all show the destructiveness of the urban environment on a people suffering from economic slavery and enforced poverty. All set on Frye Street in Chicago, these stories work together, as critics have noted, much the same way as James Joyce's *Dubliners*; Bonner may have intended this, as shown by the heading to her story "Corner Store:" "Three Tales of Living: From 'The Black Map' (A book Entirely Unwritten)" (*Opportunity* [1933]).

Bonner's literary career ended in 1941, the year she and her husband joined the First Church of Christ, Scientist. Although the church tenets did not conflict with her writing, Bonner nonetheless devoted her intellectual energy to the church rather than a literary career. After her children were all in school, Bonner resumed teaching. The Chicago Board of Education, dismissing both her Radcliffe degree and prior teaching experience, required that she take education classes that she passed easily. From 1944 to 1949 she taught at Phillips High School and from 1950 to 1963 at the Dolittle School, where she taught mentally and educationally disadvantaged students. Joyce Occomy Stricklin remembers her mother, a woman who approached everything she did "with every fiber of her being," frequently spending her evenings calling students' parents to offer encouragement and advice: "She believed in her students and was convinced that lack of love and attention were the most serious handicaps they faced" (*Frye Street*, p. ix).

Bonner died due to complications after a fire in her Chicago apartment. She left behind a notebook containing six completed but unpublished stories. All her works have since been collected in one volume, *Frye Street and Environs: The Collected Works of Marita Bonner* (1987), by Joyce Flynn and Joyce Occomy Stricklin. In her introduction, Flynn writes, "Bonner's works offer the perspective of an educated black female consciousness on a rapidly changing America between the world wars." Bonner was a thematic associate of Jessie Faust, Nella Larsen, and Zora Neale Hurston and the literary foremother of many black writers, including Richard Wright, Alice Walker, and Toni Morrison.

• A notebook of previously unpublished stories and Bonner's letters are in the Arthur and Elizabeth Schlesinger Library at Radcliffe College. Joyce Flynn and Joyce Occomy Stricklin, eds., *Frye Street and Environs: The Collected Works of Marita Bonner* (1987), includes two stories published under pseudonyms: "One Boy's Story," as Joseph Maree Andrew, and "Hate Is Nothing," as Joyce N. Reed. For a discussion of Bonner's works, see Doris Abramson, "Angelina Weld Grimké, Mary T. Burrill, Georgia Douglas Johnson, and Marita O. Bonner: An Analysis of Their Plays," *Sage* 2 (Spring 1985): 9–13; Lorraine Elena Roses and Ruth Elizabeth Randolph, "Marita Bonner: In Search of Other Mothers' Gardens," *Black American Literature Forum* 21 (Spring–Summer 1987): 165–83, and their *Harlem Renaissance and Beyond* (1990); and Bernard L. Peterson, Jr., *Early Black American Playwrights and Dramatic Writers* (1990).

ALTHEA E. RHODES

BONNER, Robert (28 Apr. 1824–6 July 1899), newspaper publisher and horseman, was born in Ramelton, Northern Ireland, the son of Scotch-Irish parents who schooled him in the strict Presbyterian tenets of abstinence, hard work, and faith in the Scriptures. At age fifteen he evidently came to the United States with an older brother and soon found work as a printer's devil for the *Hartford (Conn.) Courant*. In 1844 he moved to New York City, where he took a job with a campaign newspaper, the *American Republican*. After the 1844 election he found a job with the *New York Evening Mirror*. There Bonner grew as an editor and writer. He soon saved enough money to acquire a press and to begin job printing. In 1846 Bonner began printing the *New York Merchant's Ledger*, which contained little news and featured numerous classified advertisements and financial and business information. Bonner continued working for the *Evening Mirror*; he saved $500, and in 1851 he purchased the *Ledger* and its circulation of 3,000.

The physical format of the *New York Ledger* never changed under Bonner's ownership. It was a single-fold, four-page sheet about twenty-two by fourteen inches, with five columns to a page, a simple design, and a clean typography. Bonner's great innovation, however, was to transform its contents, as he gradually (so as not to offend existing subscribers) added short stories, poems, correspondence, editorials, and, above all, serialized fiction. He also lowered the subscription rate from one dollar to fifty cents and added illustrations as the stories and other features of the publication gradually displaced the financial and mercantile contents. He also created a family story weekly. With the issue of 14 April 1855, the word "Merchant's" was quietly dropped from the masthead as the *Ledger's* circulation surged.

Bonner began to form a group of writers (which included several women) whose serialized fiction propelled the Ledger to become the highest-circulating newspaper in the United States. In 1854 Bonner recruited the poet Lydia H. Sigourney, whose affiliation Bonner often publicized in other newspapers by the iterative advertising technique of repeating many times in succession: "Mrs. Lydia H. Sigourney writes exclusively for the *New York Ledger*." Soon afterward, Bonner signed—for the then-unprecedented sum of $100 per column—Sara Payson Willis Parton, who used the nom de plume, "Fanny Fern." Bonner soon published her serialized story "Fanny Ford: A Story of Every Day Life" and advertised his new writer in several other newspapers, using the same technique he had used with Sigourney. Bonner also took the unusual step in the spring and summer of 1855 of purchasing entire pages in rival newspapers, publishing a single page of a serial story, and then announcing that the balance might be read in the pages of the *Ledger*. Later advertisements would announce, "The *Ledger* is out."

Bonner's business practices were as irritating to his competitors as they were visionary. In 1856 he enraged and very likely doomed his chief competitor Maturin Ballou (the publisher of the story paper, *Flag of Our Nation*) by signing Ballou's most popular writer, Sylvanus Cobb, Jr. Cobb went on to write for the *Ledger* for more than thirty years, producing more than 100 serialized stories and more than 800 short stories. His first serialized fiction for the *Ledger*, "The Gunmaker of Moscow," was a sensation on which Bonner quickly capitalized by arranging a 100-gun salute in New York's City Hall Park. The celebration also announced that the *Ledger* had attained a circulation of 100,000. Bonner was unabashed in his effort to publicize his paper, even suggesting that the likes of Queen Victoria, Secretary of State William Marcy, the Swedish singer Jenny Lind, and the Empress Eugenie were all enthusiastic readers of the *Ledger*. Bonner's fledging efforts in the area of display advertising helped boost the circulation of the *Ledger* to over 300,000 by 1858.

Bonner's efforts to publicize the *Ledger* were accompanied by his recruitment of a remarkable group of nineteenth-century writers, including E. D. E. N. Southworth, historians George Bancroft and James Parton, and poets Louisa May Alcott and William Cullen Bryant. The only story that Charles Dickens ever wrote for an American publication was "Hunted Down," published in the *Ledger* on 20 August 1859. Bonner's payments were also stunning. He once paid Alfred Lord Tennyson $5,000 for a single poem, and he paid $10,000 to Edward Everett for a series of articles titled "The Mount Vernon Papers." Henry Ward Beecher was paid $30,000 for "Norwood," his only novel. Bonner was generous and loyal to his writers, and they reciprocated by dedicating much of their output to his pages. In a letter to Bonner, Beecher once wrote: "I cannot help contrasting the shrewd and close bargaining which has elsewhere been dealt out to me, with the great generosity which you have shown, and continue to show" (9 Aug. 1867, Bonner Papers). Bonner's reliance on professional writers played no small role in the development of the profession of authorship in mid-nineteenth-century America. His innovative advertising boosted their careers and the circulation of the *Ledger*.

Bonner was abstemious and uncomplicated in his personal habits. He did not drink, smoke, gamble, or use offensive language. If he was aggressive in recruiting writers for his newspaper, he also prided himself on always paying cash and being free of debt.

Bonner developed an abiding interest in horses in 1857 when a doctor ordered him to take daily drives through Central Park as a means of improving his health. Bonner soon became fascinated by his horses and developed a desire to own the fastest in America. He created a sensation by purchasing the famous Maud S. for $40,000 from Commodore Cornelius Vanderbilt and then paying $38,000 for the trotter, Dexter. Both horses were immortalized in lithographs produced by Currier and Ives. As Bonner would not tolerate gambling, he retired the many horses he owned from racing to the chagrin and anger of many aficionados of the sport, and he bred trotting horses at his farm near Tarrytown, New York.

Bonner's engagement in his work gradually diminished, particularly after the deaths of his sixteen-year-old daughter, Mary, and his wife, Jane McCanlis, within a week of each other in 1878. (He and his wife had six children.) Competing newspapers, particularly the *Family Story Paper* and the *New York Weekly*, began making inroads on the *Ledger*, while Bonner's prices paid to contributors were no longer breathtaking. The circulation of his paper began to falter in the face of the competition. Bonner retired from the *Ledger* in 1887, leaving it to three of his sons. After making the *Ledger* a monthly in 1898 and enduring several more years of declining revenues, his sons finally closed the paper in 1903. Bonner died in New York City, leaving an estate of $6 million. His passing was front-page news.

Bonner offered his readers stories of romance and escape and unrequited love, mixed in with history and politics and other serious subjects, a combination that created an enormous circulation and that anticipated the later success of popular magazines such as the *Saturday Evening Post*. The *Ledger* appealed to unity and nationality during the height of its popularity from the 1850s to the 1870s. Celebrating Bonner's nationalism, a contributor observed that in the *Ledger* "any man, be he red-hot Rebel, or dyed-in-the-wool Union, will read the story fully assured that it was written by his friend" (Sylvanus Cobb to Robert Bonner, 27 Nov. 1873, Bonner Papers). Similarly, Bonner's effort to expand circulation through direct and aggressive advertising anticipated successful publishing practice in the twentieth century.

• The Bonner Papers are located in the New York Public Library. The fullest written assessment is Ralph Admari, "Bonner and the *Ledger*," in *The American Book Collector*, vol. 6 (1935); there is also useful information contained in Stanwood Cobb, *The Magnificent Partnership* (1954). See also the editorials on Bonner's career as a journalist and publisher in the *New York Times*, and the *New York Sun*, both 7 July 1899, and the letter from "an Old Friend" in the *New York Sun*, 8 July 1899, which outlines his views on horse racing.

WILLIAM L. JOYCE

BONNER, Robert Johnson (24 Oct. 1868–23 Jan. 1946), classical scholar, was born in New Hamburg, Ontario, Canada, the son of John Bonner and Nancy Turnbull. After graduating with honors in classics from the University of Toronto (1890) and taking a law degree from Ontario Law School (1893), he joined the Ontario bar. In 1894 he married Annie Wilson, with whom he had three children. The following year his preference for the classics and a life of teaching led him to accept a position as classical master at the Collegiate Institute in Collingswood, Ontario. He remained there until 1899, when he began graduate work in Greek at the University of Chicago under Paul Shorey. The next year he left to become professor of Latin at John B. Stetson University in DeLand, Florida, but in 1903 he returned to graduate school at Chicago and received his Ph.D. in 1904. Bonner then began a distinguished career of teaching and scholarship at Chicago, as instructor of Greek in 1904, professor in 1913, and chairman of the Department of Greek from 1927 until his retirement in 1934.

During his long and distinguished career Bonner attained a worldwide reputation not only for his own scholarly work but also for that of his many pupils, including George M. Calhoun, John O. Lofberg, Gertrude Smith, and others, whose dissertations and subsequent works on Greek law led scholars to talk of "the Bonner school." He worked tirelessly with his students, and after his death Smith noted that "he often seemed far prouder of his students' achievements than of his own." He was also known for his devotion to elementary Greek, which he taught regularly. He wrote two Greek textbooks and gave strong support to two organizations primarily serving high school teachers, the Classical Association of the Middle West and South, of which he was president in 1928–1929, and the Chicago Classical Club. He was a founder of the national undergraduate classics society, Eta Sigma Phi.

Bonner's dissertation, *Evidence in Athenian Courts* (1905), immediately established him as the leading American scholar on ancient Greek law by offering a comprehensive and sensible treatment of evidence using the language and categories of Anglo-American common law rather than those of Roman law, which were (and still are) commonly used by the Continental scholars who dominated the field. Bonner realized that modern parallels are often inexact but used them nonetheless to help his readers "appreciate more clearly both the excellences and the shortcomings of the Athenian system." *Evidence* remains the best single treatment of the subject. Another important work, *Lawyers and Litigants in Ancient Athens* (1927), conveys clearly to nonspecialist readers the workings of the Athenian legal system. Bonner also wrote some two dozen articles on aspects of Greek law, many of which are still consulted today. In 1932 he was selected to give the Sather Lectures at Berkeley, an honor conferred only on the world's most distinguished classical scholars. The book that resulted from these lectures, *Aspects of Athenian Democracy* (1933), is directed at the general reader rather than classical scholars.

The work that earned Bonner his greatest renown was *Administration of Justice from Homer to Aristotle* (2 vols., 1930–1938), written with his Chicago colleague and former pupil Gertrude Smith. "Bonner and Smith" constitutes the most important and influential American work to date in the field of Greek law, notable both for its broad scope and its use of literary and documentary evidence. The work had an immediate impact in Europe, where it drew praise from some of the leading authorities in the field despite its challenge to mainstream European views. Whereas the Europeans, drawing on comparative evidence, tended to postulate an evolution of the Greek legal system parallel to that of early Germanic law, Bonner and Smith limited their conclusions to what could be supported by the historical evidence from Greece itself. They put considerably more weight on practical considerations—the community's efforts to contain violence and regulate self-help—than on religious factors such as trial by ordeal or the ritual "pollution" of a killer, and thus produced a more realistic picture of the growth of a legal system rather than the grand evolutionary schema favored by Continental scholars. Bonner and Smith's approach is characteristically American and owes much to American legal scholarship—especially to the "realist" school of Oliver Wendell Holmes (1845–1935), Karl Llewellyn (who taught at Chicago during this period), and others. A third volume of *Administration of Justice*, on legal systems of cities other than Athens, remained unfinished at Bonner's death, though parts of it were published as articles.

Bonner continued to teach and write in Chicago until he had a stroke in 1942; thereafter he lived with his daughter in Maryland but returned frequently to Chicago until his death in Aberdeen, Maryland.

The American contribution to the study of ancient Greek law has not yet matched that of European scholars, but in the first half of the twentieth century the Bonner school showed the potential that exists in this country for understanding Greek law in the context of Greek history and society. His distinctively American perspective, focusing on the actual operation of law in society, is gaining ground as Anglo-American classical scholars take greater interest in ancient Greek law.

• There is no archive of Bonner's papers. The fullest obituary notice is by Gertrude Smith in the *Classical Journal* 41 (1945–1946): 360–62.

MICHAEL GAGARIN

BONNER, Sherwood (26 Feb. 1849–22 July 1883), author, was born Katherine Sherwood Bonner in Holly Springs, Mississippi, the daughter of Charles Bonner, a physician, and Mary Wilson, daughter of a southern plantation owner. Although the Bonners were among the most wealthy and aristocratic families of Holly Springs, and although many of her contemporaries went to colleges and universities throughout the South, practically all of Bonner's formal instruction was received in local schools. She did attend the Holly Springs Female Institute for two years, but the Civil War and her early marriage at age twenty-one put an end to her formal education.

Her marriage to Edward McDowell, also of Holly Springs, lasted only two years; they had one child. Bonner moved to Boston in the fall of 1873. Almost immediately she wrote the then 67-year-old patriarch of American literature, Henry Wadsworth Longfellow, requesting a meeting. Bonner's career as an essayist, short story writer, and novelist was launched under his protection and with his financial support and professional encouragement. Longfellow employed her in the mid-1870s as his editorial assistant on his multivolume *Poems of Places* (1876–1879). This work and their increasingly intimate relationship put her in contact with editors and publishers who afforded her opportunities to advance her own work. It was also during 1876 that Bonner, accompanied by the well-known novelist Louise Chandler Moulton, toured England and Europe for approximately ten months and wrote more than a dozen travel articles that were published simultaneously in the Boston *Times* and the Memphis, Tennessee, *Avalanche*. Numerous short stories placed in such magazines as *Lippincott's*, *Harper's Young People*, and *Youth's Companion* finally brought her a contract for her only novel, *Like unto Like* (1878). But her joy was short-lived; within three months of its publication Holly Springs was devastated by a yellow fever epidemic. Among the victims were Bonner's father and brother, who had deliberately chosen to stay in the stricken area to provide medical care for the populace.

Bonner spent the remaining five years of her life writing the short stories, both local color and realistic fiction, that her two collections, *Dialect Tales* (1883) and *Suwanee River Tales* (1884), would comprise. In the spring of 1882 Bonner went to New Orleans for a medical checkup and was informed that she had advanced breast cancer, with at best only a year to live. She died in Holly Springs at the age of thirty-four.

Of the eleven stories that make up *Dialect Tales*, most had been published in periodical form. The stories are of varying lengths and range from the purely humorous, such as "Aunt Anniky's Teeth," to those of illicit love, murder, and revenge, such as "Lame Jerry." All, however, possess plot, various regional dialects, and a unique character, sometimes the protagonist, as in "Sister Weeden's Prayer," or sometimes an observer, as in "Jack and the Mountain Pink." Not only is Bonner's ear for dialect sensitive, but her powers of observation and description are keen, as when she describes Sincerity Hicks: "Her eyes had the melancholy of a cow's, without the ruminative expression that gives sufficient intellectuality to a cow's sad gaze. . . . Her dress of whitish linsey was skimpy in its cut, and she wriggled in it as if it were a loose skin she was trying to get out of."

Despite the uneven execution of some of the tales, they have considerable substance. Measured against the prevailing fictional currents of her time, Bonner's stories in *Dialect Tales* mark a genuine advance in the movement of the short story from sketches of local color to the realistic fiction that was soon to come from William Dean Howells, Hamlin Garland, and Henry James (1843–1916). The collection, therefore, reveals a shifting of subject matter and a developing attitude toward life that points toward realism and naturalism. Bonner is able to distinguish among her short-story characters by dramatically changing the setting, content, and level of language from one story to the next. A reader of Bonner's fiction, except for the "Gran'mammy" stories, meets an enormous range of characters, from high and low society and from points as distant as the Mississippi Delta, the southern Illinois plains, and the mountains of western Tennessee. Thus she is able to suggest individuals rather than types, whereas in the fiction of other local color writers such as Bret Harte, neither the locale nor the cast of characters changes a great deal. Undoubtedly the literary environment of Boston and the emphasis on realism in the fiction of Howells and James, with which she was familiar, stimulated Bonner to attempt to transcend the limits of the local colorists.

The stories in *Suwanee River Tales* are grouped in three sections: the first, "Gran'mammy," contains six tales based largely on Bonner's reminiscences of her childhood; the second section, "Four Sweet Girls of Dixie," consists of autobiographical stories set in the Civil War and the Reconstruction era; the third section is "A Ring of Tales for Younger Folks." The "Gran'mammy" stories possess genuine literary merit, revealing especially Bonner's adept and skillful handling of Negro dialect. They were the first such stories to appear in a northern journal and predated Joel Chandler Harris's first dialect story by three years. Although Bonner had an accurate eye for detail, she frequently allowed an excess of details to get in the way of a story. Her chief weakness, particularly in the longer stories, is a tendency to invent irrelevant subplots or implausible connectives between legitimate incidents in the story. Nevertheless, the stories and sketches that make up *Suwanee River Tales* compare favorably with the better-known work of Harte, even if they are considerably less worthy than the work of James and Mark Twain.

All sources agree that *Like unto Like*, Bonner's only published novel, is at least semiautobiographical; some consider it wholly autobiographical. *Like unto Like* succeeds primarily as a novel of character, the principal characters being most assuredly southern and representing the southern view toward life. Despite the occasional bitterness of several of its characters, and its relatively slight plot, *Like unto Like* is as delightful and entertaining a tale as the majority of Bonner's other stories. Although not as profuse as in the Gran'mammy tales, the Negro dialect is evident and just as accurate and appealing. Satire is not one of the novel's strongest elements, but Bonner makes gentle fun of both northern and southern points of view.

Bonner was constantly trying to improve her writing, willingly accepting suggestions and criticism. Unlike Bret Harte and Hamlin Garland, she was not content to repeat her earlier successes. By reading her work in the order of its publication, one has the genuine pleasure of following, over a relatively brief period of time, Bonner's development from a mediocre author of children's tales to an accomplished author of stories in the realistic and early naturalistic style that was to be dominant in American literature for nearly one hundred years.

• Since the inclusion of Bonner's short story "A Volcanic Interlude" in Claude Simpson's short-story anthology *The Local Colorists* (1960), there has been growing interest in Bonner's fiction. W. L. Frank, *Sherwood Bonner* (1976), in Twayne's United States Authors Series, provides a general introduction to her life and fiction and contains a lengthy bibliography. Hubert H. McAlexander, *The Prodigal Daughter: A Biography of Sherwood Bonner* (1981), has the most comprehensive bibliographic listing. Jean Nosser Biglane, "Sherwood Bonner: A Bibliography of Primary and Secondary Materials," *American Literary Realism, 1870–1910* 5 (Winter 1972): 39–60, is the most heavily annotated bibliography.

WILLIAM L. FRANK

BONNER, Tom Wilkerson (19 Oct. 1910–6 Dec. 1961), physicist, was born in Greenville, Texas, the son of Medona Bonner, a lawyer, and Bessie Spears. He went to high school in Dallas, Texas, and upon graduation he entered Southern Methodist University, where he received his B.S. in physics in 1931. He then attended the Rice Institute (now Rice University) in Houston, Texas, where he was awarded an A.M. in 1932 and a Ph.D. in 1934; his dissertation, "Collisions of Neutrons with Atomic Nuclei," was directed by Harold A. Wilson. A National Research Council fellow at the California Institute of Technology during the years 1934–1936, he worked with Charles C. Lauritsen and his nuclear physics group. He then spent the remainder of his academic life at Rice as an instructor (1936–1938); an assistant professor (1938–1941); an associate professor (1941–1945); and professor from 1945 until his death and head of the physics department from 1947 until his death.

On 7 September 1937 Bonner married Jarmila Prasilova, and they had three children. For the 1938–1939 academic year Bonner worked at the Cavendish Laboratory at the University of Cambridge under a Guggenheim memorial fellowship. During World War II he served as associate head of the Airborne Division of the Radiation Laboratory at the Massachusetts Institute of Technology, which won him a Presidential Certificate of Merit in 1946. He was elected a member of the National Academy of Sciences in 1959.

Bonner's research included the technique of using high-pressure cloud chambers for demonstrating the energy spectra of the reactions first employed in producing neutrons during the years 1933–1935. In the 1940s he invented a neutron-counter technique to determine the thresholds of endothermic nuclear reactions in which neutrons were emitted. This used a polyethylene sphere surrounding a lithium detector to yield a neutron detector of known spectral sensitivity. Using this technique, Bonner discovered a previously undetected high-energy tail of the neutron spectrum from fission reactions. An adaption of this equipment was for a time employed in medical biophysics to provide a highly accurate simulation of the biological effect of neutrons on the human body.

In his research Bonner chose generally to use already available equipment rather than to embark on the construction of larger, more elaborate and expensive equipment. This wise choice made his adaptations and modifications useful to other experimental physicists, who had relatively limited resources. Thus his most significant contributions were in his techniques and instrumentation, which were used extensively worldwide. These often had the genius of simplicity and rested on a deep physical understanding of the processes involved in the experiments. He had a seemingly uncanny ability to make things work, and this, coupled with his patience and unperturbed demeanor, allowed him to get the most out of both his machines and his people. To some he seemed shy, but this belied a completely unassuming simplicity, a warm friendliness, and a quick sense of humor. He was singularly devoted to his work and his students, and he had a seemingly unbounded enthusiasm for physics.

An internationally recognized authority on low energy nuclear physics, especially neutron physics, Bonner served on numerous advisory boards and committees. He became a consultant to the Los Alamos Scientific Laboratory in 1946, a member of the council of the Oak Ridge Institute of Nuclear Studies in 1949, and a member of the Nuclear Cross Section Advisory Group to the Atomic Energy Commission in 1951; he was active in all of these areas until his death. In addition, he was an associate editor of both the *Review of Scientific Instruments* (1946–1949 and 1952–1955), and the *Physical Review* (1951). He also was a member of the U.S. national committee of the International Union of Pure and Applied Physics (1957–1961) and a fellow of the American Physical Society. Bonner's reputation with the Atomic Energy Commission was such that they chose to locate one of the new commercial 6 MeV Van der Graaf generators at Rice in 1953; and in 1961 the commission placed a 12 MeV tandem type accelerator there.

Bonner died unexpectedly of a heart attack at his home in Houston. In February 1963 an international conference on fast neutron physics was held at Rice in memory of Bonner. On this occasion the Nuclear Physics Laboratory, which had been completed under Bonner's direction in 1952, was renamed the Bonner Nuclear Laboratories. It was demolished in 1994 in order to construct a Computational Engineering Building. In 1964 the American Physical Society established a Tom W. Bonner Prize in Nuclear Physics, given annually to recognize and encourage outstanding experimental research in nuclear physics, including the development of a method, technique, or device that significantly contributes in a general way to research in nuclear physics. Normally awarded to experimental physicists, the prize has also been given for outstanding theoretical research.

• The archives at the Rice University Library has a collection of material related to Bonner and his career. An obituary notice is in National Academy of Sciences, *Biographical Memoirs* 38 (1965): 16–32; this contains a portrait and a complete list of his publications. Obituaries are also in *Physics Today*, Feb. 1952, p. 72; *Nuclear Physics* 32 (1962), pp. 1–4; and the *Houston Chronicle*, 6 Dec. 1961.

JOSEPH D. ZUND

BONNEVILLE, Benjamin Louis Eulalie de (14 Apr. 1796–12 June 1878), explorer and army officer, was born in or near Paris, France, the son of Nicolas de Bonneville, a writer-editor, and Margaret Brazier. During the French Revolution Bonneville's father was prominent in the *Cercle Social*, a political club that published several newspapers, and a member of the Girondins. He was also a close friend of Thomas Paine, who resided in the Bonnevilles' Paris home for several years. After Nicolas came under Napoleon's disfavor, Mrs. Bonneville, Benjamin, and younger brother Thomas fled France in 1803 and joined Paine in New Rochelle, New York. Nicolas remained under government surveillance until he rejoined his family, probably in 1815. Despite petty frictions between Mrs. Bonneville and Paine, the two remained close friends until Paine's death in 1809. Paine's will provided for the Bonneville children's education.

Bonneville entered the U.S. Military Academy in 1813 and graduated as a brevet second lieutenant in 1815. He served in New England and in recruiting service before his assignment to military road construction in Mississippi in 1820. The following year Bonneville joined the Seventh Infantry at Fort Smith, Arkansas Territory. After serving in Arkansas and at Fort Gibson, Indian Territory, he escorted the marquis de Lafayette, a family friend, during his triumphant tour of the United States in 1825. Bonneville accompanied Lafayette to France and remained there several months. By late 1826, Bonneville had returned to Fort Gibson where, except for a few months in St. Louis, he remained until 1831. Long interested in frontier enterprises, Bonneville's meeting with Joseph Reddeford Walker, an experienced fur trapper and Santa Fe trader, at Fort Gibson in early 1831 very likely led to Bonneville's decision to enter the western fur trade. He justified his request for a two-year leave of absence from the army by promising to gather geographical information about the Far West and its Indian inhabitants. After winning approval in July, Bonneville visited New York City and arranged financing through Alfred Seton, who owned a fur store and was a former resident of Astoria, John Jacob Astor's fur trading post at the mouth of the Columbia River. Circumstantial evidence indicates that Astor also may have been a backer.

On 1 May 1832 Bonneville left Fort Osage, Missouri, in charge of a large fur trapping expedition that proceeded up the Oregon Trail. He is credited as being the first person to take wagons through South Pass. He spent nearly three years in the northern Rockies during the heyday of the fur trade, but because of employee desertions, problems with Indians, and cutthroat competition with rival fur companies he earned little or no profits. Bonneville took little direct role in trapping operations. Instead, he dispatched brigades of trappers under such lieutenants as Walker and Michel Cerré to conduct field operations. Walker's expedition to the Great Salt Lake and across the Sierras into California in 1833 and 1834 was an important exploration, but Walker, much to Bonneville's disgust, returned without furs. Abandoning the fur trade, Bonneville returned to Independence, Missouri, in August 1835 and learned that the army had dropped him from the rolls in 1834. During Bonneville's efforts to win reinstatement, he unsuccessfully attempted to publish the journal of his western experiences. In early 1836 he sold a rewritten version to Washington Irving, who published *The Adventures of Captain Bonneville* in 1837.

After regaining his commission, Bonneville briefly returned to Fort Gibson, served at Fort Smith, participated in the second Seminole War, and was stationed at several southern posts. As a member of the Sixth Infantry during the Mexican War, he fought in General Winfield Scott's campaign to capture Mexico City. Bonneville won citations for meritorious service at the battles of Contretas and Churubusco, but a later court-martial found him guilty of three counts of "misbehavior before the enemy." He afterward held several commands, mostly in the West, including four years as head of the Department of New Mexico (1856–1860). He retired for health reasons in September 1861 but reentered the army later that same year because of the Civil War. He served as recruiting officer for Missouri and commanded Benton Barracks and Jefferson Barracks at St. Louis before retiring as brevet brigadier general on 15 October 1866. He spent the remainder of life at Fort Smith, where he earlier had purchased land.

Information on Bonneville's family life is somewhat sketchy. He married Anne (or Ann) Callender Lewis of Monroe County, Virginia, at Carlisle, Pennsylvania, on 12 December 1842. Sources indicate that the marriage produced a daughter and a son, who died in infancy. The daughter and her mother died during a yellow fever epidemic at St. Louis in August 1862. On 30 November 1871, at Fort Smith, Bonneville married Susan Neis, who survived his death there.

Bonneville's historical significance is clouded by two issues. Although some scholars consider his maps of the West and Walker's expedition to California in 1834–1835 as important contributions to western exploration and geographical knowledge, his fame rests largely on the skillful pen of Washington Irving. The romantic style Irving employed in *The Adventures of Captain Bonneville* saved Bonneville from almost certain obscurity and (along with Irving's *A Tour of the Prairies* and *Astoria*) greatly influenced popular fictional and nonfictional depictions of the fur trade.

The second issue deals with the possibility that Bonneville was a government agent sent to spy on the British in Oregon. Such an interpretation rests on circumstantial evidence such as the army's willingness to grant Bonneville a leave of absence to engage in the fur trade, the ease of his reinstatement, and various statements Bonneville made to his superiors in letters. Several writers have supported this view, but others have argued that Bonneville's true motive was commercial success and that he justified a questionable leave of absence by promising to provide scientific information about the Far West and Indians. Until more conclusive evidence can be found, the issue cannot be resolved. Unfortunately, Bonneville's private papers, which might have provided a definitive answer about his purpose, were destroyed in a warehouse fire in St. Louis. Neither the original copy of his journal nor the rewritten version that he sold to Irving have been located.

• The best summary of Bonneville's career is Edgeley W. Todd, "Benjamin L. E. Bonneville," in *The Mountain Men and the Fur Trade of the Far West*, ed. LeRoy R. Hafen, vol. 5 (1968), pp. 45–63. Todd also wrote the introduction to a reissue of Washington Irving, *The Adventures of Captain Bonneville, U.S.A., in the Rocky Mountains and the Far West* (1961). Despite a frustrating lack of context, the best source on the relations between the Bonnevilles and Thomas Paine remains Moncure Daniel Conway, *The Life of Thomas Paine* (1908). For a discussion of Bonneville's involvement with Irving, see John Francis McDermott, "Washington Irving and the Journal of Captain Bonneville," *Mississippi Valley Historical Review* 43 (Dec. 1956): 459–67. Bonneville's service record is outlined in George W. Cullum, *Biographical Register of the Officers and Graduates of the U.S. Military Academy*, vol. 1 (1868), pp. 156–57. Hiram M. Chittenden, *The American Fur Trade of the Far West*, vol. 1 (1954), pp. 396–433, denounces Bonneville as a "history-made man" and denigrates his importance in the fur trade. For a more positive treatment that also argues that Bonneville was a government agent, see Bernard DeVoto, *Across the Wide Missouri* (1947), especially pp. 51–61.

DONALD L. PARMAN

BONNEY, Mary Lucinda (8 June 1816–24 July 1900), educator and reformer, was born in Hamilton, New York, the daughter of Benjamin Bonney and Lucinda Wilder, farmers. Her father, a veteran of the War of 1812, was an officer in the New York State Militia. Her mother had been a schoolteacher until marriage in 1808. Bonney and her brother, Benjamin, grew up in a home marked by the characteristics of "intelligence, integrity, and piety" (Fairbanks, p. 138).

When Bonney was less than ten years old, she was sent from the family farm into a nearby village to live and study in the private school of a local minister and his wife. She continued her education at the Hamilton Academy and then studied for almost two years at Troy Female Seminary, Emma Willard's institution. She graduated from Troy in 1835.

Bonney taught in a number of schools in the East. Those who observed her teaching commented on her "intellectual grasp, her masterful judgment, her deep conscientiousness, and her quick sympathies" (Fairbanks, p. 138). She worked in Jersey City, New York City, and DeRuyter, New York, then returned to Troy Female Seminary. In 1842 she moved to South Carolina, teaching at Beaufort and Robertville. Her next teaching assignment was in Providence, Rhode Island, and, finally, she taught at Miss Phelps' school in Philadelphia.

In 1850 Bonney and Harriette A. Dillaye founded the Chestnut Street Female Seminary in Philadelphia. Later the school was moved to the suburb of Ogontz and was renamed the Ogontz School for Young Ladies. Bonney remained at the school as principal for thirty-eight years, retiring in 1888. She was remembered as one who "taught her pupils how to think. With clear perceptions, logical processes, and conclusions that could be firmly held and vigorously pushed she not only impressed her own strong nature on her pupils, but equipped them with her methods, to go out into the world as independent thinkers and actors" (*Indian's Friend*, Aug. 1900, p. 8).

Bonney's own life was a paradigm for the type of activity she encouraged in her students. Her involvements included many philanthropic enterprises, often centered around Christian endeavors. She provided financial support for the training of both African-American and white men for the ministry. In addition, she was involved in the development of the Women's Union Missionary Society. In 1879 Bonney joined with Amelia S. Quinton to protest the further encroachment of white settlers on land set aside for Native Americans. A petition was drawn up that also addressed the binding obligation of treaties between the United States and American-Indian nations. After circulation in fifteen states, the petition, containing thousands of signatures, was presented to President Rutherford B. Hayes at the White House and in the U.S. House of Representatives in 1880, marking the beginning of the Women's National Indian Association (WNIA). Bonney provided for all its expenses in the early stages and served as the organization's first president from 1881 to 1884. Shortly thereafter she was appointed honorary president, a post she maintained until her death.

Bonney's work with the WNIA was propelled by a sense of outrage toward the federal government's relations with Native-American nations. "How great a debt to the Indian has our nation contracted by all these crimes against his natural rights, his manhood, his humanity! And many of these wrongs still exist" (*Indian's Friend*, Jan. 1893, p. 36). In addition to the 1880 petition, the WNIA worked for lands in severalty, universal education, U.S. citizenship, and equal protection for Native Americans under U.S. laws. The organization was influential in bringing about the Dawes Act of 1887, which addressed a number of these issues. Senator Henry L. Dawes remarked that the newly adopted federal policy toward Native Americans "was born of and nursed by the women of this Association" (*Indian's Friend*, Jan. 1893, p. 3).

The philosophy of the WNIA, which was reflected in national policy, called for assimilation of Native-American people rather than preservation of their cultures and was clearly articulated in a statement of purpose for the Missionary Department of the WNIA, added in 1884. Some of the objectives of workers in this department were to teach Native Americans "to respect work and to become self-supporting; to influence and to help them to learn the English language; and above all and constantly to teach them the truths of the gospel, and to seek their conversion to genuine and practical Christianity" (*Indian's Friend*, Jan. 1893, p. 4).

In 1888 Bonney attended the Centenary Conference on the Protestant Missions of the World in London. Here she crossed paths with a childhood friend, Thomas Rambaut, a Baptist minister and the retired president of William Jewell College in Missouri. In 1888, at age seventy-two, she married Rambaut, and they moved to Hamilton, New York. He died two years later.

Bonney lived a life motivated by missionary zeal. She displayed her energies in two of the few approved arenas for nineteenth-century American women: schools for young women and the reformer's circle. She died in Hamilton.

• Bonney's manuscript ledger, 1878–1888, is at the American Baptist Historical Society, Rochester, N.Y. For biographical information consult Frances E. Willard and Mary A. Livermore, eds., *A Woman of the Century* (1893), and Mary J. Fairbanks, ed., *Emma Willard and Her Pupils* (1898). Information on her activities in the WNIA can be found in *Annual Reports* of the Women's National Indian Association, 1883–1900; Mary E. Dewey, *Historical Sketch of the Formation and Achievements of the Women's National Indian Association in the United States* (1900); and issues of the *Indian's Friend*, a WNIA periodical, cited in the text. Other data is available from William W. Keen, ed., *The Bi-Centennial Celebration of the Founding of the First Baptist Church of the City of Philadelphia* (1899), and Charles L. Bonney, *The Bonney Family*, 2d ed. (1898). Obituaries are in the *Indian's Friend*, Aug. 1900; the *Hamilton Republican*, 26 July 1900; and the *New York Times*, 26 July 1900.

KAREN L. GRAVES

BONNEY, William H. *See* Billy the Kid.

BONNIE AND CLYDE. *See* Barrow, Clyde Chestnut, and Bonnie Parker.

BONNIN, Gertrude Simmons (22 Feb. 1876–26 Jan. 1938), author and activist, was born on the Yankton Sioux reservation in Dakota Territory, the daughter of Ellen Tate'Iyohiwin Simmons. Bonnin's father, about whom little is known other than that he was named Felker and was white, had left the family before Bonnin's birth. Bonnin, who later became known as Zitkala-Sa or Red Bird, lived with her mother on the reservation until the age of eight, when she attended White's Indiana Labor Institute, a boarding school for Native American children providing instruction in English and manual labor. These early experiences of indoctrination into European-American culture and the separation from her mother would inform Bonnin's later writings and her commitment to Native American self-determination.

From 1895 to 1897 Bonnin attended Earlham College, where she distinguished herself as a gifted orator by winning second place in the Indiana State Oratorical Contest in 1896. After a short stint as a teacher at the Carlisle Indian School, she studied as a violinist at the New England Conservatory of Music and then toured Europe in 1900 with the Carlisle Indian Band. She also started publishing essays and short stories in 1900 with the appearance of "Impressions of an Indian Childhood," "The School Days of an Indian Girl," and "An Indian Teacher among Indians" in the *Atlantic Monthly*. She followed with the controversial essay "Why I Am a Pagan" in the *Atlantic Monthly* and several short stories in *Harper's Magazine* and *Everybody's Magazine*. These would appear later in a book titled *American Indian Stories* published in 1921. In 1901 she authored *Old Indian Legends*, a collection of stories she had heard as a child and translated into English for publication.

After this burst of literary production, Bonnin turned her skills to organizing on behalf of Native Americans. In 1902 she married Raymond Bonnin, also Siouan, and moved to the Uintah and Ouray reservation in Utah, where he worked as an agent for the Bureau of Indian Affairs. During her residence in Utah, Gertrude Bonnin gave birth to her only child in 1903, taught school, directed community service programs, and started a children's band. She also collaborated with William Hanson on the composition of an opera titled *The Sun Dance*, which was performed in Vernal, Utah, in 1913 and in New York in 1938 by the New York Light Opera Guild. In 1916 she became secretary of the Society of the American Indian, a pan-Indian activist group, and moved to Washington, D.C.

From 1916 on, Bonnin worked as a lecturer, writer, lobbyist, and organizer for a variety of issues affecting Native Americans. She fought for Indian citizenship (won in 1924), criticized the Bureau of Indian Affairs for hindering tribal self-determination and for hiring few Native Americans, spoke against unfairness in land claim settlement, led an unsuccessful campaign against the use of peyote (she found it similar in its social effects to alcohol), and advocated changes in Native American health care and education. In addition, she served as the editor of the Society of the American Indian journal, the *American Indian Magazine*, in 1918 and 1919. When the society dissolved in 1920, Bonnin lectured for the General Federation of Women's Clubs and formed an Indian Welfare Committee under the auspices of that organization. In 1924 she coauthored a report called *Oklahoma's Poor Rich Indians, an Orgy of Graft and Exploitation of the Five Civilized Tribes, Legalized Robbery*, which exposed the corrupted practice of "legal guardianship" of Indian land by non-Indians for the purpose of oil and gas extraction. In 1926 Bonnin founded the National Council of American Indians and continued her activism as president of the organization until her death. It focused on a broad range of reforms including efforts toward gaining tribal independence from the government and providing Indian voter education. Deborah Welch notes that Bonnin's activism responded to the changing demographics of Native American communities, for as "increasing numbers of Indian peoples were compelled to live apart from the reservations," Bonnin "fought to establish and preserve the strength of tribal identities and responsibilities . . . even as she fought to protect the Indian land base as a perpetual cultural homeland" (*Reader's Companion*, p. 122).

In her literary work, Bonnin focused much of her attention on publicizing the trauma of assimilation. In "The School Days of an Indian Girl" she described the transition from reservation life to boarding school as one of shock, for out of "happy dreams of Western rolling lands and unlassoed freedom we tumbled out upon bare floors back again into a paleface day." She likened her school life to the "iron routine" of a "civilizing machine." Yet after some time away from the reservation, she found herself discontent with her previous life: "Even nature seemed to have no place for me. I was neither a wee girl nor a tall one; neither a wild Indian nor a tame one. This deplorable situation was the effect of my brief course in the East, and the unsatisfactory 'teenth' in a girl's years." As a teacher at Carlisle, she recognized fully what she had exchanged for assimilation, and she recorded her feelings in "An Indian Teacher among Indians": "For the white man's papers I had given up my faith in the Great Spirit. For these same papers I had forgotten the healing in trees and brooks. On account of my mother's simple view of life, and my lack of any, I gave her up, also. I made no friends among the race of people I loathed. Like a slender tree, I had been uprooted from my mother, nature and God." By confronting in literature the issues inherent in her cultural duality, she brought awareness to the difficulty Native Americans faced in assimilation into a hostile environment. Through her activism she sought to provide Native Americans with the skills needed for self-determination in that same environment. In both projects, she exhibited an amazing fearlessness and an intense determination. She once told a friend, "I fear no man—sometimes I think I do not even fear God" (Johnson and Wilson, p. 38).

Gertrude Bonnin died in Washington, D.C., and was buried in Arlington National Cemetery. As one of the most influential Native American activists of the twentieth century, she left an articulated theory of Indian resistance and a model for reform. Her activism forced crucial changes in education, health care, and legal standing for Native Americans, and her literature brought a marginalized viewpoint to the center of national attention.

• A complete list of Bonnin's published writings can be found in Daniel Littlefield and James Parin, *Biobibliography of Native American Writers, 1772–1924* (1981). Some of Bonnin's correspondence is in the Carlos Montezuma Papers in the Division of Archives and Manuscripts of the State Historical Society of Wisconsin. See also Record Group 75 (Indian Affairs) of the National Archives in Washington, D.C. Several articles and dissertations examine portions of Bonnin's life. Dexter Fisher, "Zitkala Sa: The Evolution of a Writer," *American Indian Quarterly* 5, no. 3 (1979): 229–38, and Deborah Welch, "Zitkala-Sa: An American Indian Leader, 1876–1938" (Ph.D. diss., Univ. of Wyoming, 1985) and "Gertrude Bonnin" in *Reader's Companion to American History* (1991), treat Bonnin's work broadly. See also Mary Stout, "Zitkala-Sa: The Literature of Politics" in *Coyote Was Here* (1984), and two articles by William Willar in the *Wicazo Sa Review*: "Zitkala Sa: A Woman Who Would Be Heard!" 1, no. 1 (1985): 11–16, and "The First Amendment, Anglo-Conformity and American Indian Religious Freedom" 7, no. 1 (1991): 25–41. Two useful articles that focus on the literature are Dorthea M. Susag, "Zitkala-Sa (Gertrude Simmons Bonnin), A Power(full) Literary Voice," *Studies in American Indian Literatures* 5, no. 4 (1993): 3–24, and Laura Wexler, "Tender Violence: Literary Eavesdropping, Domestic Fiction, and Educational Reform," *Yale Journal of Criticism* 5, no. 1 (1991): 151–87. David Johnson and Raymond Wilson examine Bonnin's activism in "Gertrude Simmons Bonnin, 1876–1938: 'Americanize the First American,'" *American Indian Quarterly* 12, no. 1 (Winter 1988): 27–40. Also informative are Janet Witalec, ed., *Native North American Literature* (1994), and Sharon Malinowski, ed., *Notable Native Americans* (1995). Obituaries are in the *New York Times* and the *Washington Post*, 27 Jan. 1938.

TAMMY STONE

BONSTELLE, Jessie (19 Nov. 1871–14 Oct. 1932), actress and director-manager, was born Laura Justine Bonesteele, in Greece, New York, the daughter of Joseph Frederick Bonesteele, an attorney turned farmer, and Helen Louisa Norton. Justine was called "Jessie" by her family and early in her career chose Bonstelle as her stage name. Under her mother's tutelage, she was trained in theatrical skills as a toddler and was frequently taken to the theater in Rochester, New York.

Around the age of nine Bonstelle joined a touring company of *Bertha, The Beautiful Sewing Machine Girl* in Rochester. Following the tour's end in California, she returned home to attend the Nazareth Convent School, which was the only formal education that she is known to have had. In 1886 she toured in a one-woman act under the management of Edward D. Stair.

When both of her parents died in 1890, Bonstelle headed for New York City and sought out a childhood idol, the actress Fanny Janauschek, whom she had seen perform in Rochester. She was accepted into Janauschek's company, and in 1893 she married its leading actor, Alexander Hamilton Stuart; they had no children. That year both Bonstelle and her husband joined the Forepaugh Stock Company in Philadelphia. While playing secondary roles in the Forepaugh repertory, Jessie Bonstelle often made appearances in smaller theaters in more substantial roles, such as Juliet, Margaret Gautier, and Lady Teazle. During the 1898–1899 season she was the leading lady of the Standard Theatre Stock Company in Philadelphia.

When, shortly after the turn of the century Jacob J. Shubert handed over to Bonstelle the management of one of the brothers' syndicate theaters in Rochester, she still performed in stock in New York and Philadelphia and toured in Canada.

In 1906 Bonstelle took on the management of the Star Theatre in Buffalo. The addition to her management schedule of the Garrick Theatre in Detroit in 1910 would prove to be crucial to her later career and to her most significant contribution to American theater: the concept and realization of a civic theater in 1928. As early as 1914 an editorial in a Detroit newspaper lauded her: "The following which Miss Bonstelle has built for herself in this city, is a more effective tribute than mere words at once to her own talents and the conscientiousness with which she applies them to staging her productions."

Throughout her career Bonstelle interspersed her managerial commitments with performing engagements, not only in her own companies but on Broadway. In 1908 she was featured in Frederick Pauling's *The Great Question* and in 1909, *The Faith Healer* by William Vaughn Moody.

In 1911 she conceived of and produced a stage adaptation of Louisa May Alcott's *Little Women*, adapted by Marion de Forest, coproduced by William Brady, and codirected by Bertram Harrison. Four national companies toured it across the country for a year, after which it opened for a long and successful run on Broadway. In 1919 a London production opened headed by Katherine Cornell, one of Bonstelle's protégés who went on to stardom.

During the years she spent managing stock companies, Bonstelle discovered many actors, directors, and scenic designers who later went on to fame. Dubbed by colleagues "The Star Maker," Bonstelle in a 1926 interview in *The Drama* claimed, "The value of stock to the actor is immeasurable. It is the only real training school when he is beginning, and the only postgraduate course for him after he has arrived and wants to keep out of the rut induced by long runs and type-casting."

In 1912, again with Bertram Harrison as codirector, Bonstelle managed the first municipal theater in the United States, in Northampton, Massachusetts. This thousand-seat theater was founded and funded by a philanthropic merchant who donated it to the city. The weekly change of bills featured commercial Broadway fare. This tenure lasted until 1917, during which time Bonstelle attempted to establish a national Women's Theatre but was unable to raise sufficient financial support.

The Detroit Civic Theatre was to be based on fiscal, social, and artistic principles entirely different from those of the Northampton theater. Utilizing the respect she had gained over the years from the Detroit business community, Bonstelle easily found support. In 1925 the Bonstelle Playhouse opened; after three full seasons it became the Detroit Civic Theatre. Large investors were responsible for $200,000 of the subscriptions, but subscriptions as low as one dollar accounted for $50,000. Operating a noncommercial theater with profits going into a sustaining fund, the "petticoated Belasco" (as she was sometimes called) was free to explore a more experimental repertory. She founded the Bonstelle Theatre Guild and presented plays by Ferenc Molnar, Eugene O'Neill, and Edna St. Vincent Millay. In addition, she mounted modern-dress productions of *Hamlet* and *Romeo and Juliet*. Bonstelle endeavored to involve the Civic Theatre with all cultural aspects of the community. The theater offered classes in acting, directing, and stagecraft in addition to the productions. Extracurricular activities included suppers served on the mezzanine, after-performance dancing on the stage, art exhibits, and interdenominational religious services.

In 1932 Bonstelle visited Hollywood, apparently aiming to scout a site for a stock company and to discuss directing films. While there she became ill; she returned to Detroit, where she died. She was buried in Mount Hope Cemetery in Rochester, New York, next to her husband, who had passed away in 1911. After her death the Detroit Civic Theatre continued for only one season.

The significance of Bonstelle's career in acting, directing, and managing, while not negligible in itself, is enhanced by her launching of the careers of scores of theater artists of note and by her great experiment—the Detroit Civic Theatre.

• A series of articles by Helen G. Bennett in *McCall's*, Sept. 1928–Feb. 1929, takes the form of an autobiographical narrative with photographs. The Billy Rose Theatre Collection at the New York Public Library for the Performing Arts, Lincoln Center, contains scrapbooks and clippings in portfolios. Weldon B. Durham, ed., *American Theatre Companies* (1987), contains entries on the Forepaugh Stock Company and the Standard Theatre Stock Company by Mari Kathleen Fielder. Also see William Luther Dean, "A Biographical Study of Miss Laura Justine Bonstelle Stuart" (Ph.D. diss., Univ. of Michigan, 1954).

CONSTANCE CLARK

BONTEMPS, Arna Wendell (13 Oct. 1902–4 June 1973), writer, was born in Alexandria, Louisiana, the son of Paul Bismark Bontemps, a bricklayer, and Maria Carolina Pembroke, a schoolteacher. He was reared in Los Angeles, where his family moved when he was three. He graduated from Pacific Union College in Angwin, California, in 1923.

Bontemps then moved to New York's Harlem, where the "Harlem Renaissance" had already attracted the attention of West Coast intellectuals. He found a teaching job at the Harlem Academy in 1924 and began to publish poetry. He won the Alexander Pushkin Prize of *Opportunity*, a journal published by the National Urban League, in 1926 and 1927 and the *Crisis* (official journal of the NAACP) Poetry Prize in 1926. His career soon intersected that of the poet Langston Hughes, with whom he became a close friend and sometime collaborator. In Harlem Bontemps also came to know Countee Cullen, W. E. B. Du Bois, Zora Neale Hurston, James Weldon Johnson, Claude McKay, and Jean Toomer.

In 1926 Bontemps married Alberta Johnson; they had six children. In 1931, as the depression deepened, Bontemps left the Harlem Academy and moved to Huntsville, Alabama, where he taught for three years at Oakwood Junior College. By the early 1930s Bontemps had begun to publish fiction as well as poetry. His first novel, *God Sends Sunday*, was published in 1931, and an early short story, "A Summer Tragedy," won the *Opportunity* Short Story Prize in 1932. *God Sends Sunday* is typical of the Harlem Renaissance movement. Little Augie, a black jockey, earns money easily and spends it recklessly. When his luck as a jockey runs out, he drifts through the black sporting world. Slight in plot, the novel is most appreciated for its poetic style, its re-creation of the black idiom, and the depth of its characterization. While most reviewers praised it, W. E. B. Du Bois found it "sordid" and compared it with other "decadent" books of the Harlem Renaissance such as Carl Van Vechten's *Nigger Heaven* (1926) and Claude McKay's *Home to Harlem* (1928). But Bontemps thought enough of the basic story to collaborate with Countee Cullen on *St. Louis Woman* (1946), a dramatic adaptation of the book.

Bontemps's next novel would be on a much more serious theme, but he first attempted another genre. In collaboration with Langston Hughes, he wrote *Popo and Fifina* (1932), the first of his many children's books. A travel book for children, it introduced readers to Haitian life by describing the lives of a boy named Popo and his sister Fifina. Bontemps followed his initial success in the new field with *You Can't Pet a Possum* (1934), a story of a boy and his dog in rural Alabama.

Northern Alabama in the early 1930s proved to be inhospitable to an African-American writer and intellectual. The Scottsboro boys were being tried at Decatur, just thirty miles from Huntsville. Friends visited Bontemps on their way to protest the trial, and a combination of his out-of-state visitors and the fact that he was ordering books by mail worried the administration of the school. Bontemps claimed in later years that he was ordered to demonstrate his break with the world of radical politics by burning a number of books from his private library—works by James Weldon Johnson, W. E. B. Du Bois, and Frederick Douglass. Bontemps refused. Instead he resigned and moved back to California, where he and his family moved in with his parents.

In 1936 he published *Black Thunder*, his finest work in any genre. Based on historical research, *Black Thunder* tells the story of Gabriel Prosser's rebellion near Richmond, Virginia, in 1800. Gabriel, an uneducated field worker and coachman, planned to lead a slave army equipped with makeshift weapons on a raid against the armory in Richmond. Once armed with real muskets, the rebels would defend themselves against all attackers. Betrayed by another slave and hampered by a freak storm, the rebels were crushed, and Gabriel was hanged, but in Bontemps's version of the affair, whites won a Pyrrhic victory. They were forced to recognize the human potential of slaves.

Although *Black Thunder* was well reviewed by both black and mainstream journals such as the *Saturday Review of Literature*, the royalties were not sufficient to support Bontemps's family in Chicago, where they had moved just before publication. He taught briefly in Chicago at the Shiloh Academy and then accepted a job with the WPA Illinois Writers' Project. In 1938, after publishing another children's book, *Sad-Faced Boy* (1937), he received a Rosenwald fellowship to work on what became his last novel, *Drums at Dusk* (1939), based on the Haitian rebellion led by Toussaint L'Ouverture. Although the book was more widely reviewed than his previous novels, the critics were divided, some seeing it as suffering from a sensational and melodramatic plot, others praising its characterizations.

The disappointing reception of the book and the poor royalties that it earned convinced Bontemps that "it was fruitless for a Negro in the United States to address serious writing to my generation, and . . . to consider the alternative of trying to reach young readers not yet hardened or grown insensitive to man's inhumanity to man" (1968, p. x). Henceforth, Bontemps addressed most of his books to youthful audiences. *The Fast Sooner Hound* (1942), was written in collaboration with Jack Conroy, whom he had met on the Illinois Writers' Project.

In 1943 Bontemps earned his master's degree in library science from the University of Chicago. The necessity of earning a living then took him to Fisk University, where he became head librarian, a post he held until 1964. Thereafter he returned to Fisk from time to time. He also accepted positions at the Chicago Circle campus of the University of Illinois and at Yale University, where he served as curator of the James Weldon Johnson Collection of Negro Arts and Letters.

During these years Bontemps produced an astonishing variety and number of books. His children's books included *Slappy Hooper* (1946) and *Sam Patch* (1951), which he wrote in collaboration with Conroy, as well as *Lonesome Boy* (1955) and *Mr. Kelso's Lion* (1970). At the same time, he wrote biographies of George Washington Carver, Frederick Douglass, and Booker T. Washington for teenage readers; *Golden Slippers* (1941), an anthology of poetry for young readers; *Famous Negro Athletes* (1964); *Chariot in the Sky* (1951), the story of the Fisk Jubilee Singers; and *The Story of the Negro* (1948).

For adults, he and Hughes edited *The Poetry of the Negro* (1949) and *The Book of Negro Folklore* (1958). With Conroy he wrote *They Seek a City* (1945), a history of African-American migration in the United States, which they revised and published in 1966 as *Anyplace But Here*. Bontemps's historical interests also led him to write *100 Years of Negro Freedom* (1961) and to edit *Great Slave Narratives* (1969) and *The Harlem Renaissance Remembered* (1972). He also edited a popular anthology, *American Negro Poetry* (1963), just in time for the black reawakening of the 1960s.

Bontemps had been forced by the reception of his work to put his more creative writing on hold after 1939, but the 1960s encouraged him to return to it. He collected his poetry in a slim volume, *Personals* (1963), and wrote an introduction for *Black Thunder* when it was republished in 1968 in a paperback edition. At the time of his death, he was completing the collection of his short fiction in *The Old South* (1973). Bontemps died at his home in Nashville.

Arna Bontemps excelled in no single literary genre. A noteworthy poet, he published only one volume of his verse. As a writer of fiction, he is best known for a single novel, written in midcareer and rediscovered in his old age. Yet the impact of his work as poet, novelist, historian, children's writer, editor, and librarian is far greater than the sum of its parts. He played a major role in shaping modern African-American literature and had a wide-ranging influence on African-American culture of the latter half of the twentieth century.

• The major collections of Arna Bontemps's papers are at Fisk University; the George Arents Research Library, Syracuse University; and the James Weldon Johnson Collection, Beinecke Rare Book Room and Manuscript Library, Yale University. No book-length biography exists, but Bontemps wrote several autobiographical essays: Introduction to *Black Thunder* (1968), Preface to *Personals* (1963), and "Why I Returned," in *The Old South* (1973). An interview appears in John O'Brien, *Interviews with Black Writers* (1973). A bibliography is Robert E. Fleming, *James Weldon Johnson and Arna Wendell Bontemps: A Reference Guide* (1978). See also Minrose C. Gwin, "Arna Bontemps," *American Poets, 1880–1945* (1986), and Kirkland C. Jones, "Arna Bontemps," *Afro-American Writers from the Harlem Renaissance to 1940* (1987).

ROBERT E. FLEMING

BOOLE, Ella Alexander (26 July 1858–13 Mar. 1952), temperance reformer, was born in Van Wert, Ohio, the daughter of Isaac Newton Alexander, a lawyer, and Rebecca Alban. Both parents were born in Ohio and were committed Presbyterians and social reformers. Ella attended the Van Wert public schools and the College of Wooster, where she received A.B. and A.M. degrees in classics. She graduated second in her class and taught in the local high school for five years after college. On 3 July 1883 she married William H. Boole, a twice-widowed, prominent Methodist minister and cofounder of the Prohibition party. After her marriage she joined the Methodist church and moved to her husband's pastorate in Brooklyn, New York. There she had one daughter and raised two stepdaughters from her husband's previous marriages.

Boole dated her sympathy for the temperance cause from the Woman's Crusade of the early 1870s, which occurred when she was still a girl. These early convictions, based on a strong sense of responsibility inherited from both of her parents, led to one of the longest records of service to the temperance movement. Soon after her marriage she joined the Woman's Christian Temperance Union (WCTU) in Brooklyn and became active along with her husband in mission work among the city's alcoholics. She was elected state corresponding secretary at the first WCTU convention she attended in 1886. An effective speaker and a keen organizer, Boole used the WCTU as the means to further temperance as well as other related concerns, including child labor reform, woman suffrage, and international peace.

Boole was president of the New York State WCTU from 1898 to 1903 and again from 1909 to 1926. As a temperance reformer in a state where the liquor traffic was probably more deeply entrenched than in any other state, Boole increased WCTU membership and formed an efficient organization. She traveled widely throughout New York, testifying at many legislative hearings for the temperance cause. "Few men or women are as gifted in oratorical talent as Mrs. Boole," wrote one New York newspaper, "she holds her audience in profound attention."

Under Boole's direction, the New York WCTU advocated for separate courts for juvenile offenders, protective legislation for women and children in industry, and woman suffrage. During her presidency of the New York WCTU the state ratified the Eighteenth Amendment on national prohibition and promoted better law enforcement through the Mullen-Gage Law Enforcement Act. Boole was elected vice president of the national WCTU in 1914 and took a leading role in gaining the support of women's groups for constitutional prohibition. In 1920 she was a candidate for the U.S. Senate on the Prohibition ticket; though not elected, she received more votes than any woman for public office up to that time.

Boole assumed the presidency of the national WCTU in 1925 and defined her mission as the enforcement of the Eighteenth Amendment. Her devotion to prohibition, which she believed to be the best method to solve alcohol-related problems, gained her the respect of those within and without the temperance movement. As president of the national WCTU, Boole traveled to every state and to Great Britain and Europe. She worked successfully to remove alcohol from all military installations, American Indian reservations, and government buildings.

Boole's hopes for the Eighteenth Amendment are described in her book, *Give Prohibition Its Chance* (1929). Though the book was immensely popular, Boole was unable to counteract the gradual decline in public support for the temperance cause. On the defensive, she became inflexible and refused to allow any changes in prohibition legislation, a strategy that brought criticism from those who opposed prohibition as well as from within the movement itself. Openly ridiculed at a meeting of the Women's National Republican Club in 1930, Boole became further disheartened by the blows the temperance cause suffered in the election in 1932 and in the repeal of prohibition in 1933.

During these difficult years for the temperance movement, Boole continued to receive consolation from the continuing support of temperance workers who credited her with holding their organization together. She was elected president of the world WCTU in 1931 and served in that capacity until 1947, retaining emeritus status for the rest of her life. Despite the increasing unpopularity for the temperance cause within the United States, under Boole's leadership the world WCTU expanded to fifty-six countries. Boole also worked to expand the organization's mandate to include peace and disarmament, the abolition of the international drug traffic, and the status and condition of women throughout the world. Under her leadership the world WCTU was one of eight women's organizations often consulted by the nongovernmental section of the United Nations.

In addition to her lifelong dedication to the temperance cause, Boole worked actively in her church and in other organizations. Shortly after her husband's death, she reaffiliated with the Presbyterian church and served as secretary of the Woman's Board of Home Missions from 1903 to 1909. During her tenure, contributions for mission work increased as did the number of local missionary societies within the Presbyterian church. Always strongly motivated by her religious faith, she was eventually ordained as a Presbyterian deaconess. Boole also served as a director of the National Kindergarten Association, a first vice president of the National Council of Women of the United States, and a member of the executive committee of the Women's National Radio Committee.

A woman deeply committed to moral reform in all forms, Boole worked for the betterment of conditions for women and children throughout the world. She was an indefatigable organizer and a skilled lobbyist. Ella Boole died of a stroke in her Brooklyn home, having given more than sixty years to the temperance movement.

• Sources related to Boole's early life are at the Ohio State Historical Society, Columbus, and the archives of the College of Wooster. The WCTU papers are the primary source for Boole's temperance work and are located in the Frances Willard Library, WCTU Headquarters, Evanston, Ill. The papers of the New York State WCTU are in the organization's headquarters in Syracuse. See also WCTU, *The Temperance and Prohibition Papers*, microfilm. Papers related to Boole's work with the Presbyterian church are at the Presbyterian Historical Society, Philadelphia. *The Reminiscences of Ella A. Boole* (1950) was a project of the Oral History Collection, Columbia University. Helpful secondary sources include Ian Tyrrell, *Woman's World, Woman's Empire: The WCTU in International Perspective, 1880–1930* (1991), and Frances W. Graham, *Sixty Years of Action: A History of Sixty Years' Work of the WCTU of the State of New York* (1934). An obituary is in the *New York Times*, 14 Mar. 1952.

SHERYL A. KUJAWA

BOONE, Daniel (2 Nov. 1734–26 Sept. 1820), pioneer and early settler of Kentucky, was born in Berks County, Pennsylvania, on what was then the western perimeter of English colonial settlement in America, the son of Sarah Morgan and Squire Boone, a weaver, land speculator, and farmer. Daniel Boone's formal education is a much-disputed matter. He always insisted to his children that he never went to school a day in his life. A tale survives, however, that has young Daniel spiking his schoolteacher's hidden bottle of whiskey with a potent tartar emetic. His older brother Samuel's wife, Sarah Day, is said to have taught him the rudiments of the three R's, but a glance at his letters confirms that he never mastered grammar and spelling. In 1750 Squire Boone moved his large family to the wild frontier country along the Yadkin River in North Carolina, and five years later Daniel, an accomplished backwoodsman, enlisted as a volunteer in the American militia to aid General Edward Braddock's attempted capture of Fort Duquesne, now Pittsburgh, in the French and Indian Wars. Surprised in an ambush and routed, Braddock's English troops and Boone and the other wagon drivers fled for their lives. Boone had, however, made an acquaintance who was later to alter his life. John Findley (or Finley), another wagoner, spun tales to Boone of his trip to a hunter's paradise beyond the Appalachian Mountains called Kentucky and how it could be reached through the Cumberland Gap and the Warriors' Path.

Back on the Yadkin, Boone married Rebecca Bryan in 1756, with whom he eventually had ten children. Always one who preferred hunting, trapping, exploring, and land speculating to civilization and farming, in 1765 Boone traveled as far south as Pensacola, Florida, in search of a new home. He purchased a house and a town lot and was eligible to receive the 100 acres of free land offered to each new Protestant immigrant by the British government to encourage quick settlement of the territory recently ceded by Spain. This was the only time Rebecca refused to move. Florida was just too far from family and friends. Two years later, still enamored of Findley's descriptions of a dozen years earlier, Boone and two companions crossed the Cumberland Mountains and kept winter camp ten miles west of the present-day town of Prestonsburg, Kentucky, but they returned home in the spring because of the rugged terrain still to the west. He did not realize that he had reached Kentucky and that an additional few days' journey would have brought him to the fertile plains of bluegrass and cane that Findley had described.

In the winter of 1768–1769 Findley came to Boone's cabin seeking his help in finding the Warriors' Path. They set out on 1 May 1769 with four other men and, after crossing the Blue Ridge and passing through the Cumberland Gap, reached on 7 June what must have seemed to Boone the promised land. Sometimes with a companion and sometimes alone, he explored and hunted for two years before returning to North Carolina. In 1773 Boone led a group of family and friends to settle Kentucky, but the expedition turned back against Boone's wishes when his son James and another boy were captured, tortured, and killed by Indians. He finally succeeded in settling in Kentucky in 1775. Under the aegis of Richard Henderson's Transylvania Company, an enterprise that hoped to establish a new American colony, Boone and thirty other backwoodsmen cut the Wilderness Road. He then brought his family to settle in Boonesborough.

Although the British were encouraging their Indian allies to attack these frontier stations, 1776 had been quiet until 14 July, when Jemima Boone and Betsy and Fanny Callaway were captured by a war party. Boone and a band of rescuers overtook them three days later. He directed a surprise attack, killed one of the braves, and rescued the girls. The event caused a sensation on the frontier and raised Boone's reputation as the frontiersman par excellence. Years later, James Fenimore Cooper used the adventure in *The Last of the Mohicans*, and the main character of his Leatherstocking Tales always bore a resemblance to Boone.

On 7 February 1778 Boone and his force of thirty salt makers were captured by a large band of Shawnee Indians. Along with sixteen of his men, he was adopted into the tribe; the others were sold to the British at Detroit. Given the name "Shel-tow-ee" or "Big Turtle" by his "father," Chief Blackfish, Boone pretended to love his new life but prepared for escape. When he learned of an impending attack on Boonesborough, he could wait no longer; he escaped and made the 160-mile trip home in four days. On 7 September Blackfish brought over 400 warriors against the settlement, which had only 40 able-bodied fighting men. Surrounded and outnumbered, the settlers withstood the attacks and the siege, and Blackfish and his braves withdrew after eleven days. Four years later, Boone's son Israel was killed at the battle of Blue Licks, and the settlers lost the last major battle of the revolutionary war. And although peace talks began that November, Indian attacks on the frontier continued until 1794.

Boone's international fame was secured with the publication of "The Adventures of Col. Daniel Boon" in John Filson's *Discovery, Settlement and Present State of Kentucke* in 1784 and its subsequent translation and reprinting in France and Germany the next year. At this time in addition, he achieved some degree of political eminence in Kentucky. Beginning as magistrate in the area of Boonesborough under the authority of the Transylvania Company in 1776, in the 1780s and 1790s he served as the sheriff, coroner, and county lieutenant of Fayette County, deputy surveyor, lieutenant colonel of the militia, county representative to the Virginia state assembly, and trustee of Maysville. Boone was also one of the wealthiest men in Kentucky, with nearly 100,000 acres of land under claim. However, in 1775 he had begun a fight he was ill prepared to win. Lawyers sued him and proved he had failed to get proper title to the lands he claimed. It was an all-too-common occurrence on the frontier. By 1798 he had lost nearly all his land and gladly accepted the invitation he received the next year from the Spanish governor of Missouri to settle in the Femme Osage district, about sixty miles from present-day St. Louis. For this he received 850 acres of land and was appointed the syndic (magistrate) of the district. The Spanish authorities offered Boone 8,500 additional acres if he could bring 100 new families to settle in Missouri. He succeeded and received the land, but he lost it all again when the territory became part of the United States under the Louisiana Purchase because he had proper Spanish but not American title. In 1814 Congress awarded him 850 acres for his services in opening the trans-Appalachian and the trans-Mississippi West, but he sold it to pay off the last of his debts from the Kentucky lawsuits. He was free of debt for the first time in thirty years and was penniless.

Even at his advanced age, Boone continued to hunt and explore. When his eyesight weakened to the point where he could not shoot accurately, he set traps. He died at the home of his son Nathan.

Boone's significance to American history and culture is hard to overestimate, for in a very real sense, it is impossible to discuss the frontier without discussing Boone. Historically and imaginatively, perhaps no single individual is more central to the frontier experience. Nearly seventy of his eighty-six years were involved with the exploration and settlement of the frontier. Born on the western perimeter of English settlement, at the age of thirty-one, he ventured as far south as Pensacola, Florida. Four years later, after a thirty-seven-day trek that he called "a long and fatiguing journey through a mountainous wilderness," he first "saw with pleasure the beautiful level of Kentucke" (John Filson, *The Discovery, Settlement, and Present State of Kentucke* [1784]). When he died, he was living on the western boundary of American settlement in St. Charles County, Missouri, one of the outposts for fitting out expeditions to explore the Rocky Mountains. Boone constantly placed himself on the cutting edge of the frontier and did so with evident relish.

Imaginatively, Boone is the prototype of the frontier hero. His life formed a general pattern that was reenacted with certain variations by the next three major heroes of the westering frontier of the nineteenth century—Davy Crockett, Kit Carson (a distant relative of Boone), and "Buffalo Bill" Cody. And like the frontier, he remained an invaluable spiritual constant. Boone exemplified the American way of life, the ideal of frontier independence and virtue. In a country whose history has been dominated by continuing migration, the majority of early Americans believed themselves to be pioneers to some extent and, as such, identified with Boone as their hero. Dan Beard, the founder of the Boy Scouts of America, described his conception of the organization as "a society of scouts to be identified with the greatest of all Scouts, Daniel Boone, and to be known as the Sons of Daniel Boone."

• A large volume of material on Boone, including important interviews with his son Nathan Boone and Nathan's wife, is in the Lyman Copeland Draper Manuscript Collection of the State Historical Society of Wisconsin. Two useful biographies of Boone are John Bakeless, *Daniel Boone: Master of the Wilderness* (1939; repr. 1965), and Michael A. Lofaro, *The Life and Adventures of Daniel Boone*, 2d ed. (1986). Boone figures prominently in relevant sections of Richard Slotkin, *Regeneration through Violence: The Mythology of the American Frontier, 1600–1860* (1973).

MICHAEL A. LOFARO

BOONE, Richard (18 June 1917–10 Jan. 1981), motion picture, stage, and television actor, was born Richard Allen Boone in Los Angeles, California, the son of Kirk Boone, a corporation lawyer, and Cecile Beckerman. Boone graduated from the San Diego Army and Navy Academy in 1932 and enrolled at Stanford University two years later. He worked on fishing boats during the summers. At Stanford he studied art and became a member of the boxing team, winning amateur light heavyweight championships in 1936 and 1937. He was expelled from Stanford after becoming involved in a prank that resulted in an injury to the wife of former U.S. president Herbert Hoover.

Boone worked for a time as a roustabout and truck driver in the California oil fields, then moved to an artist's colony in Carmel, California, after marrying Jane Hopper in 1937. Childless, they divorced in 1940. In Carmel he studied painting and writing, but he achieved little success. He joined the navy when the United States entered World War II and served three and one-half years as an aerial gunner in a torpedo plane squadron, mostly aboard the aircraft carriers *Intrepid*, *Enterprise*, and *Hancock* in the South Pacific.

After the war Boone used his G.I. Bill benefits to join the Neighborhood Playhouse in New York to study acting with Sanford Meisner; later he studied acting with Elia Kazan at the Actors Studio and modern dance with Martha Graham, and he joined Nina Fonaroff's dance company. Boone's first role on Broadway came in 1947 in *Medea*. In 1948 he appeared in Michael Redgrave's *Macbeth* and in *The Man* in 1950. Boone married singer Mimi Kelly in 1949, but they divorced the following year.

While still at the Actors Studio, Boone assisted a fellow student in a screen test for Twentieth Century–Fox by reading lines off camera. His voice so impressed director Lewis Milestone that he won a part in Milestone's *The Halls of Montezuma* (1951). He rose to first lead or prominent character roles in films released through the 1970s, including *Kangaroo* (1952); *Way of the Gaucho*, *Man on a Tightrope*, and *The Robe* (1953); *Dragnet* (1954); *Man without a Star* (1955); *Battle Stations* and *Away All Boats* (1956); *The Alamo* (1960); *Rio Conchos* (1964); and *The Shootist* (1976). Boone appeared in forty-nine feature films. His last film appearance was in *Winter Kills* (1979).

Beginning in 1955, Boone began a two-year appearance as Dr. Konrad Styner in "Medic," a weekly television drama broadcast by NBC. He was twice nominated for an Emmy for this role and developed a loyal following, especially among women viewers, despite his having a face often described as "craggy." His rough appearance and precise speech appealed to men as well, especially in his role as Paladin in the western series "Have Gun—Will Travel," which began in 1957 and ran for six seasons. Boone quickly tired of continuing roles; he voluntarily left "Medic" for the role of Paladin, and he tried to leave that program after five years but was persuaded to stay for a sixth season by a salary that exceeded $1 million. Paladin, a mysterious gunfighter who always dressed in black when working, carried business cards that read "Have Gun—Will Travel, Wire Paladin, San Francisco." When not working, Paladin lived in a San Francisco hotel, read poetry, and enjoyed the good life made possible by his mercenary activities. Boone married Claire McAloon in 1951; they had one child.

While still appearing in "Have Gun—Will Travel," Boone took roles in episodes of "Playhouse 90" and "United States Steel Hour," and in 1959 he returned to Broadway in *The Rivalry*, in which he portrayed Abraham Lincoln. While playing the part, he was invited to read the Gettysburg Address at the Lincoln Memorial on the 150th anniversary of the sixteenth president's birth.

In 1964 Boone pioneered repertory theater on television in "The Richard Boone Show" on CBS. The show's format, which featured regular players cast in different roles in each episode, gave him the vehicle for versatility that he had always sought. He told an interviewer, "I just won't accept the precept that the public is a big baggling idiot. If you give the people good exciting shows, they will watch." He believed that the rush to complete weekly episodes harmed the product. "Lack of preparation in television," he said, "results in too much surface playing. Actors, meet, say 'How do you do?' and start acting right off with little or no rehearsal." The repertory concept would correct this, he believed. His hopes proved wrong when CBS canceled the show after one season of twenty-five programs. Boone moved to Hawaii, but he continued to appear in theatrical and made-for-television films. He eventually settled in St. Augustine, Florida, and returned to painting. At the time of his death in St. Augustine he was serving as "cultural ambassador" for the state of Florida.

• A good review of Boone's career may be found in the *Current Biography Yearbook* for 1964. See also *Variety Obituaries, 1905–1986* (1988) and *The International Dictionary of Films and Filmmakers*, vol. 3: *Actors and Actresses* (1984). For Boone's opinions on television, see the interview with John Waugh in the *Christian Science Monitor*, 25 May 1963.

ARCHIE P. MCDONALD

BOOTH, Edwin Thomas (13 Nov. 1833–7 June 1893), actor and theatrical manager, was born near Bel Air, Maryland, the son of Junius Brutus Booth, an actor, and Mary Ann Holmes. Edwin's formal education ended at age thirteen, when he began to accompany his father on theatrical tours. The elder Booth, a brilliant actor but an alcoholic, attempted to discourage his children from entering the theatrical profession (he advised Edwin to become a cabinetmaker), but Edwin gained an invaluable theatrical education while accompanying his father. Although Edwin had appeared at age fourteen on a Baltimore stage, he considered his first real performance to be in 1849 as Tressel in *Richard III* at the Boston Museum in support of his father. He continued to play similar small roles until 1851 when the elder Booth refused to appear as Richard, and his son substituted for him. Edwin later maintained that his father had planned the whole event ahead of time with the theater manager.

The next year Edwin and his older brother, Junius, Jr., accompanied their father to California, where they performed in San Francisco and Sacramento during a financial depression. On his return east alone via New Orleans, their father died while journeying on the

Mississippi River. Edwin followed his mother's advice and remained in California, acting in mining camps while spending his free time drinking, gambling, and womanizing. He appeared as Hamlet for the first time in 1853 in San Francisco. Catherine Sinclair, the divorced wife of actor Edwin Forrest, hired him to play major supporting roles, often opposite renowned actress Laura Keene, in Sinclair's San Francisco theatrical company. In 1854 he toured Australia and Honolulu, where business was poor, then after some California successes decided to return to the East Coast in 1856. Managed by Benjamin A. Baker, Booth opened in Baltimore, then toured the South. In Richmond, Virginia, he met the actress Mary Devlin, to whom he was immediately attracted.

Booth began to attract favorable national attention after his 1857 performances in Boston as Sir Giles Overreach in *A New Way to Pay Old Debts*, one of his father's more successful roles. He also won acclaim in the title roles of *Richelieu* and *Richard III* during the same engagement. Contemporary accounts describe him as "a slight, pale youth with black flowing hair, soft brown eyes full of tenderness and gentle timidity, and a manner mixed with shyness and quiet repose." In 1860 he married Mary Devlin after her retirement from the stage. Having acted with most of the major performers of the day, Devlin greatly assisted Booth in developing a more natural style. About the same time, Adam Badeau, then a freelance theater critic and later a general on Ulysses S. Grant's staff, began to assist Booth with his intellectual studies, including deeper analyses of his roles.

In 1861 Booth departed for London and a lackluster engagement at the Haymarket Theatre. He performed in Manchester and Liverpool but returned to London for the birth of his and Mary's first and only child, Edwina, in December 1861. The family returned to the United States and moved to New York City. In 1863, however, Mary Booth died suddenly. Her premature death plunged Booth into melancholy. He gave up drinking almost entirely, and his grief later enriched some of his performances.

Booth's career continued. In 1864 the three Booth brothers appeared for the only time together in *Julius Caesar* at New York City's Winter Garden Theatre. The next night Edwin opened in *Hamlet* at the same theatre; the run extended to 100 consecutive performances, at the time a record for a Shakespearean play in the United States. Booth had become the leading U.S. actor, his only rival being Edwin Forrest, ironically one of the two men for whom he was named, the other being actor Thomas Flynn.

Booth retired temporarily from the stage after his brother John Wilkes Booth assassinated President Abraham Lincoln at Ford's Theatre in Washington, D.C., on 14 April 1865. In early 1866 he returned to, as he put it, "the only profession for which God has suited me." For the remainder of his life, however, he refused invitations to perform in Washington, D.C. Audiences attached no blame to Booth for his brother's crime. Drama critic William Winter described his return to the stage: "Nine cheers hailed the melancholy Dane upon his first entrance. The spectators rose and waved their hats and handkerchiefs. Bouquets fell in a shower upon the stage, and there was a tempest of applause, wherever he appeared." Booth continued his career with almost universal acclaim. In 1867, however, after a production of *Brutus*, the Winter Garden Theatre burned to the ground, destroying Booth's entire stock of costumes, properties, and scripts, many of which had belonged to his father.

Turning adversity into advantage, Booth raised enormous sums of money and in 1869 opened his own theater at Sixth Avenue and Twenty-third Street in New York City. That year he married another actress, Mary McVicker; at Booth's request she retired from the stage. The next year a son was born to them but died during the birth. In 1876 Booth revisited California, twenty years after leaving it. Back in New York City, Booth's managerial attempts led him to bankruptcy, and he was forced to abandon his theater. By touring extensively he was able to pay off his debts. He and his wife then traveled to London, where he had a theatrical engagement in 1880. There, following a cool reception for his performance as Hamlet and in other roles, he met with great success in *King Lear*. British actor Henry Irving suggested that the two actors alternate playing Iago and Othello at the Lyceum Theatre, with Ellen Terry as Desdemona. The engagement succeeded brilliantly, but Mary Booth's decline into madness and tuberculosis forced their return in June 1881 to the United States, where they separated. She died that November.

Among Booth's other contributions to his profession were his "prompt-books," detailed treatments of his productions. Beginning with *Richard III* in 1877, sixteen treatments appeared during the next decade. Booth also began to use Shakespeare's text for *Richard III*, abandoning the Colley Cibber version that had held the stage for over a century. Similarly, he restored to the stage Shakespeare's *King Lear*, replacing the version by Nahum Tate.

Booth's last project was to form a men's club in New York City, The Players, in 1888 to facilitate the social interaction of leading actors and luminaries of other fields, such as Mark Twain and William Tecumseh Sherman, at a personal expense of $200,000. Booth reserved an apartment for himself on the top floor, overlooking Gramercy Park, and continued to tour periodically. His final stage appearance occurred in 1891 at the Brooklyn Academy of Music, where he performed as Hamlet. A huge crowd gathered after the performance to witness his departure from the stage door.

Booth remained at The Players, devoting himself to the club's operations, until his death in New York City. During his funeral there, Ford's Theatre, which had been converted into an office building, collapsed, killing more than twenty persons. Booth was buried beside Mary Devlin Booth in Mount Auburn Cemetery in Cambridge, Massachusetts.

In his greatest roles—Hamlet, Richelieu, Othello, Iago, Bertuccio, and Lucius Brutus—Booth displayed imagination, intuitive insight, spontaneous grace, intense emotional fervor, and melancholy refinement. William Winter described "his controlling attribute, the one which imparts individual character, color, and fascination to his acting, [as] the gently thoughtful, retrospective habit of a stately mind, abstracted from passion and toned by mournful dreaminess of temperament." Booth won almost universal adulation for his portrayal of Hamlet. When, in 1870, at the top of his powers, he produced *Hamlet* in repertory at his own theater, newspaper critics commented, "The most admired actor and manager on the American stage achieved the greatest triumph he has yet known." Another only regretted that Shakespeare himself could not have seen *Hamlet* so brilliantly produced.

Despite his enormous successes, Booth often regretted becoming an actor, writing to a friend, "I wish to God . . . I was not an actor; I despise and dread the d——d occupation. . . . I am a monkey, nothing more." He was much more. His acting might best be called transitional, serving as a bridge between the romantic fury of his father and British actor Edmund Kean and the more subdued realism emerging in the late nineteenth century. In the most public of professions, he was the most private of men, self-effacing, modest, and scornful of pretentiousness and theatrical mock heroics. A statue of Edwin Booth as Hamlet, erected by The Players, surveys Gramercy Park near his final residence, attesting to his enduring fame as the Prince of Players.

• The Players houses the most comprehensive collection of Booth documents. The New York Public Library theatre collection at Lincoln Center has considerable material on Booth, as do the Folger Shakespeare Library in Washington, D.C., and the Harvard Theatre Collection. See L. Terry Oggel, *Edwin Booth: A Bio-Bibliography* (1992), for a definitive listing of works on Booth. Also see Daniel J. Watermeier, ed., *Between Actor and Critic: Selected Letters of Edwin Booth and William Winter* (1971). Booth contributed notes on Shakespearean interpretation to the H. H. Furness's Variorum Editions of *Othello* and *The Merchant of Venice*. The major published treatments include Katherine Goodale, *Behind the Scenes with Edwin Booth* (1931); Edwina Booth Grossman, *Edwin Booth: Recollections by His Daughter* (1894); Laurence Hutton, *Edwin Booth* (1893); Richard Lockridge, *Darling of Misfortune: Edwin Booth* (1932); Eleanor Ruggles, *Prince of Players: Edwin Booth* (1953); Charles H. Shattuck, *The Hamlet of Edwin Booth* (1969); and William Winter, *Life and Art of Edwin Booth* (1894). See also Asia Booth Clarke, *The Elder and the Younger Booth* (1882); Lawrence Estavan, *Monographs* of the San Francisco Theatre Research series (1934); Stanley Kimmel, *The Mad Booths of Maryland* (1940; repr. 1969); and Ella V. Mahoney, *Sketches of Tudor Hall and the Booth Family* (1925). The *New York Times* obituary, 7 June 1893, typifies the adulatory response to his death by most newspapers and magazines.

STEPHEN M. ARCHER

BOOTH, James Curtis (28 July 1810–21 Mar. 1888), chemist, was born in Philadelphia, Pennsylvania, the son of George Booth and Ann Bolton. After attending public schools in Philadelphia and the Hartsville (Pa.) Seminary, he studied chemistry at the University of Pennsylvania, receiving an A.B. in 1829. He then spent a year at Rensselaer Polytechnic Institute in Troy, New York, studying chemistry and geology with Amos Eaton, and presented a series of chemical lectures in Flushing, Long Island, 1831–1832. This took him as far in mastering his subject as was possible in the United States at that time. To complete his training, Booth went to Germany in 1833 and stayed three years in Europe. He studied analytical chemistry in Friedrich Wöhler's private laboratory in Kassel (no student labs existed at the time), and with Gustav Magnus in Berlin. From there he proceeded to Vienna, where he attended lectures, and then went on to tour chemical factories on the Continent and England. For Booth, "touring" was not a passive operation; he took detailed notes, with drawings, and was sometimes admitted to trade secrets because of his obvious interest and understanding. This experience laid the foundation for his lifelong conviction that the chemistry laboratory is a smaller version of the chemical industry, and vice versa.

Returing to Philadelphia in early 1836, Booth lost no time in establishing the country's first and longest-lived consulting firm in analytical chemistry (now Booth, Garrett and Blair) and in giving courses in practical chemistry that offered student laboratories as well as instruction in theory. This schooling quickly became the approved way for American chemists to complete their education, and a distinguished group of professors and chemical manufacturers began their careers with Booth.

From 1836 to 1845 Booth also served as professor of chemistry applied to the arts at the Franklin Institute and took part in geological surveys of Pennsylvania in 1836 and of Delaware in 1837–1838. The latter resulted in his *Memoir of the Geological Survey of the State of Delaware, Including the Application of the Geological Observations to Agriculture* (1841), a thorough study, but weakened by Booth's imperfect knowledge of current geology. Nonetheless he was appointed state geologist of Delaware in 1837–1838. After the survey he gradually gave up his interests in the subject and concentrated on chemistry.

From 1842 to 1845 Booth taught chemistry in the Philadelphia Central High School, where he was the first to apply polarimetric methods to the analysis of molasses and sugar. From 1851 to 1855 he was professor of chemistry at the University of Pennsylvania. During these years he developed a process for recovery of cobalt metal in commercial quantities from the ores of Mine La Motte in Missouri, which had been pronounced too poor in the element for practical recovery; the same study produced a method for nickel. Booth and his former student Campbell Morfit produced a report, published by the Smithsonian Institution as a contribution to a book, *On Recent Improvements in the Chemical Arts* (1852). Booth himself published the pamphlet *Practical Value of the Analysis of Soils* (1853), and he and others produced the substantial (more than 1,000-page) *Encyclopaedia of Chemistry, Practical and Theoretical* (1850). He also edited and annotated a translation from the French of Henri Victor Regnault's *Elements of Chemistry* (1853). During the 1840s and 1850s he published articles in various research journals, including, somewhat unexpectedly for a mineral and inorganic chemist, "On the Conversion of Benzoic Acid into Hippuric Acid" and "Constitution of Glycerin and Oily Acids."

In 1849 Booth became melter and refiner at the U.S. Mint in Philadelphia, a position he occupied until a few months before his death. The title makes the job sound modest and undemanding; in fact, it was anything but that. As Booth took over, the mint was experiencing difficulties with bullion from the new California gold fields, which contained a much higher impurity level than the mint's procedures could handle. Revising existing methods failed to solve the problem, and Booth spent many years inventing and refining methods that had never before been required and simply did not exist in 1849. Later crises arose when the federal government decided to go to coinage—grade silver, then copper, for small denominations of coins, and later to a copper-nickel alloy. All of these modifications, combined with changes in specifications and methods that attended the usual government changes of administration, gradually wore down the aging Booth. He resigned his position in August 1887 having brought about a revolution in the production of coinage metals, essentially by scaling up newly discovered laboratory procedures to the level of manufacture. He died in Haverford, Pennsylvania, less than a year later.

Booth had married Margaret M. Cardoza in 1853; they had three children. He was president of the American Chemical Society from 1883 to 1885. His most lasting contribution to chemistry in America is that which is now buried under a century and a half of academic accretion: getting chemistry away from lectures and demonstrations and into the hands of students.

• Accounts of Booth's life and work include Patterson DuBois, *Proceedings of the American Philosophical Society* 25 (1888): 204–11; *Popular Science Monthly* 40 (1892): 116–22; and E. F. Smith, *Journal of Chemical Education* 20 (1943): 315–18, 357 (reprint of pamphlet, 1922). Valuable information is found in Wyndham Miles, "With James Booth in Europe," *Chymia* 11 (1966): 139–49, and Sidney Edelstein, "An Historic Kit [Booth's] for Blowpipe Analysis," *Chymia* 26 (1949): 126–31.

ROBERT M. HAWTHORNE JR.

BOOTH, John Wilkes (10 May 1838–26 Apr. 1865), actor and assassin of President Abraham Lincoln, was born near Bel Air in Harford County, Maryland, the son of Junius Brutus Booth, an actor, and Mary Ann Holmes. His grandfather, Richard Booth, named him after John Wilkes, the British reformer. As a child Booth dabbled in acting, as did some of his brothers and several neighborhood boys, both at the Booth country home, "Tudor Hall," and at their town house in Baltimore. Booth's father actively discouraged his children from entering the theatrical profession, but he toured extensively and died on the road when John was only fourteen.

Booth grew up as the darling of his family, somewhat spoiled and temperamental, receiving only intermittent education. One of his four sisters, Asia, recalled his "fitful gaiety" as a youth, tinged with a "taint of melancholy." He followed his father and two older brothers onto the stage, making his professional debut in Baltimore on 14 August 1855 as Richmond in *Richard III*. The seventeen-year-old thespian failed miserably but returned home to study the actor's craft. He next appeared at the Arch Street Theater in Philadelphia, then the theatrical center of America. The handsome young actor charmed his audiences, in spite of his overacting, faulty elocution, and general lack of discipline. He appeared once with his brother Edwin, then performed for a season at Richmond, Virginia. During these and later engagements Booth used various names, apparently trying to protect the family name until he could add some professional luster to it. At the same time he began to develop a reputation as a womanizer and a considerable southern chauvinist. He went so far as to try to join a military group, but he had promised his mother he would not enlist and would continue his acting career.

When Booth returned to Richmond for another season, he learned of John Brown's impending trial at Charles Town. Booth abandoned his job at the Richmond Theatre to attend Brown's execution, later claiming to have helped capture Brown, writing, "I thought that the Abolitionists were the only traitors in the land and . . . deserved the fate of Brown." Goaded by reports of his brother Edwin's success as an actor, he soon sought to make himself into a star, thereby increasing his income and fame substantially. He began to appear as J. Wilkes Booth, often in roles that his father had made famous.

As the Civil War approached and theatricals in the South decreased, Booth began a northern tour, continuing to denounce President Lincoln and the North. In Baltimore he joined a rebel secret society called the Knights of the Golden Circle, wholly convinced that the North was unjustly oppressing his beloved South. He meanwhile continued to expand his professional and personal reputations. On 26 April 1861 one of Booth's jilted lovers, actress Henrietta Irving, tried to kill him but succeeded only in slashing his arm.

By 1863 Booth billed himself as "the Youngest Tragedian in the World." His passion for the Confederate cause intensified; he began to plot the kidnapping of President Lincoln, possibly with the intention of ransoming all Confederate prisoners held by the North. Toward the end of the war, he began to assemble a small band of conspirators in Washington, D.C. Whether or not Booth had any official mandate from the Confederacy remains unclear.

On 25 November 1864 Booth and his brothers Edwin and Junius, Jr., appeared together on the stage for the first and only time. The occasion was a benefit production of *Julius Caesar* in New York City to raise funds for a memorial statue of Shakespeare for Central Park. Edwin played Brutus; Junius, Jr., impersonated Caesar, and John Wilkes as Antony cried out for vengeance against the assassins. Mary Ann Holmes Booth, the actors' aged mother, proudly attended the performance.

At his greatest popularity as an actor, Booth earned about $20,000 a year. His repertory grew to include *The Lady of Lyons*, *Money*, *The Robbers*, *The Marble Heart*, *The Apostate*, *The Stranger*, and *The Corsican Brothers*, as well as the Shakespearean roles of Richard III, Romeo, Hamlet, Macbeth, Othello, Iago, Shylock, and Petruchio. Admirers and critics described him as one of the most charming of men, admired by most men and adored by almost all women. His dark good looks resembled those of Edgar Allan Poe; a friend said he was as handsome as a young god. His acting was described as passionate, explosive, and uneven, lacking the intellectuality of his father or the quiet dignity of Edwin Booth, depending on charisma rather than craft or artistry. Later critics would denigrate his work, but John Wilkes Booth was definitely an actor with exceptional potential during the Civil War. He appeared on 18 March 1865, for the last time on any stage, as Pescara in *The Apostate*. The performance took place at Ford's Theatre in Washington, D.C.

Booth grew increasingly obsessed with the subjects of slavery and the Confederacy. He recruited two boyhood friends, Michael O'Laughlin and Samuel Arnold, to assist him in kidnapping Lincoln, which they planned for 20 March. Lincoln did not appear as expected; the conspirators panicked and fled. Later Booth added David Herold and George Atzerodt to his band, completing it with Lewis Powell, known also as Lewis Payne. By this time Booth had become acquainted with a young rebel, John Surratt, and his mother, Mary Eugenia Surratt, a rebel sympathizer who operated a boardinghouse in Washington, in which the group would meet from time to time.

The kidnapping plot evaporated when the city of Richmond fell and the war ended. Five days later, on 14 April 1865, Booth learned that President Lincoln planned to attend *Our American Cousin* (starring Laura Keene) at Ford's Theatre. Working quickly, Booth assigned Atzerodt to assassinate Vice President Andrew Johnson and Payne to kill Secretary of State William Seward while Booth himself murdered Lincoln. Atzerodt lost his nerve and made no attempt on Johnson, but Payne, a young giant, wounded Seward severely, as well as several others who tried to defend him.

Booth meanwhile had entered Ford's Theatre at about ten o'clock, moving across the rear of the balcony to the president's box. Waiting for the audience's laughter to cover the report of his derringer, Booth entered the box and fired a single .44-calibre bullet at point-blank range into the back of Lincoln's head. He shouted "Sic semper tyrannis! The South is avenged!" according to some, slashing with a dagger at Major Henry Rathbone, who tried to restrain him. Booth then leaped the twelve feet from the presidential box onto the stage, breaking his left leg. He escaped from the theater to a waiting horse, and, accompanied by Herold, fled Washington. They stopped at the home of Dr. Samuel A. Mudd in Bryantown, Maryland, to have Booth's leg set, then hid in neighboring woods for six days while federal troops vainly searched for them.

By 23 April Booth and Herold had reached the farm of Richard H. Garrett, three miles south of Port Royal, Virginia, and seventy-eight miles from Washington. Garrett hid the fugitives in one of his tobacco barns. In the early morning of 26 April a band of soldiers arrived and surrounded the outbuilding. Herold surrendered immediately; Booth defied the troops, offering to fight them one by one. Instead the troops set fire to the barn, and they saw Booth inside, using a crutch to stand erect. A bullet felled Booth, but whether he shot himself or was mortally wounded by one of the soldiers, Sergeant Boston Corbett, has never been completely resolved. Booth died at about seven o'clock, his last words being, "Tell Mother I died for my country."

The troops returned the body to Washington and a secret burial at the Arsenal Grounds. A confusing, disorganized trial—a travesty of judicial procedure—ensued. Eventually the government hanged Herold, Payne, Atzerodt, and Mrs. Surratt (who may have known nothing of the plot). Mudd, Arnold, and O'Laughlin received life imprisonment.

Edwin Booth petitioned the government to return John Wilkes Booth's body to his family; on 20 February 1869 the body was buried in an unmarked grave in the Booth lot (Dogwood Number Nine) in Green Mount Cemetery in Baltimore, after identification by several friends and acquaintances. Nevertheless rumors abounded that Booth had escaped, and later a mummified body advertised as Booth's appeared on exhibition around the country. A popular fiction held that Booth committed suicide in 1903 in Enid, Oklahoma, where he was known as David E. George.

Scholars and historians who have examined the evidence carefully agree Booth died at Garrett's farm. Many maintain that by murdering Lincoln, who could have overseen Reconstruction with mercy and justice, Booth struck a staggering blow at his own beloved South. Whatever the case, the first presidential assassination in America forever branded the Booth name with infamy.

• Archival materials on Booth include those in the War Department Records, the Kimmel collection in the Merl Kelce Library at the University of Tampa, and the Library of Congress. Other substantial Booth material appears in biographies of his brother Edwin or the Booth family in general, as in Stanley Kimmel, *The Mad Booths of Maryland* (1940; rev. ed., 1969), Eleanor Ruggles, *Prince of Players* (1953), and Gene Smith, *American Gothic* (1992). Booth's sister, Asia Booth Clarke, gave her brother individualized treatment in *The Unlocked Book: A Memoir of John Wilkes Booth* (1938), richly detailed if undeniably subjective. Less trustworthy is Izola Forrester, *The One Mad Act: The Unknown Story of*

John Wilkes Booth and His Family (1937). See also Clarke, *The Elder and the Younger Booth* (1882), Francis Wilson, *John Wilkes Booth: Fact and Fiction of Lincoln's Assassination* (1929), and Philip Van Doren Stern, *The Man Who Killed Lincoln* (1939). William A. Tidwell (with James O. Hall and David W. Gaddy), *Come Retribution* (1988), speculates on the Confederacy's involvement in the assassination. John Lattimer, *Kennedy and Lincoln* (1980), offers detailed examinations of both assassinations. For Booth's theatrical career, see Gordon Samples, *Lust for Fame: The Stage Career of John Wilkes Booth* (1982). Also see Robert Silvester, *United States Theatre: A Bibliography from the Beginning to 1990* (1993), pp. 168–70.

STEPHEN M. ARCHER

BOOTH, Junius Brutus (1 May 1796–30 Nov. 1852), actor, was born in London, England, the son of Richard Booth, a lawyer, and Elizabeth Game, who named him after the Roman patriot Lucius Junius Brutus. Booth sampled several professions—printing, law, the navy—as a young man, but in 1813 he attended a performance of *Othello* at Covent Garden and soon devoted himself to amateur theatricals in the Bloomsbury area. On 13 December 1813 he made his professional debut with the Jonas-Penley Company at Deptford as Campillo in Tobin's *The Honey Moon*.

Booth next toured the Netherlands, still with the undistinguished Jonas-Penley company, opening in Amsterdam 18 May 1814. During this tour, which took advantage of the recent English victory at Waterloo, the company appeared in Brussels, where Booth met and fell in love with Adelaide Delannoy. She returned with him to London, where they married in May 1815. While Booth sought engagements as an actor, their first child, Amelia, was born in October. After an indifferent engagement at Covent Garden, Booth became a regular at the Worthing and Brighton Theatres Royal.

Booth returned to Covent Garden for a starring engagement, opening as Richard III on 12 February 1817 to cheering crowds. His success challenged London's leading star, Edmund Kean, who invited Booth to appear as Iago to his Othello on 20 February 1817 at Drury Lane, although Booth was contractually bound to Covent Garden alone. The older actor dazzled the Drury Lane audience with a virtuoso display of intensity and passion, surpassing his previous brilliance; Booth retreated to Covent Garden and rioting audiences there who felt he had deserted them. After the disturbances abated, Booth began alternating between provincial tours and London engagements. Metropolitan audiences had lost interest in Booth's novelty, and although they had a second child, Richard Junius Booth, in 1819, his affection for Adelaide had faded. Booth met a Covent Garden flower girl, Mary Ann Holmes, and after settling a separate maintenance with Adelaide, left for America in 1821 with his new companion.

Booth and Holmes arrived in Norfolk, Virginia, on 30 June 1821, and Booth made his American debut in Richmond as Richard III a week later. In October he opened in New York to enormous success, both critical and popular, far greater than he had received in England. Mary Ann delivered a son, Junius Brutus Booth, Jr., in December 1821, and Booth began seeking a permanent base of operations. He settled in Harford County, Maryland, near Bel Air, buying land and moving a log house to his new property. His father, Richard Booth, joined the family there the next year. Booth continued touring while Mary Ann and Richard Booth supervised their free black servants (Booth detested slavery) who did the farm work.

Booth began at this point to show signs of alcoholism and latent madness, causing him to threaten his fellow actors. In 1825 Booth took his American family to England while he fulfilled a London engagement. A London newspaper accused him of deserting Adelaide Delannoy and their son. Booth denied the charges and began to tour the provinces, then returned to America. In 1829 in Boston his madness resurfaced; he broke down during a performance, escaped his captors, and walked to Providence, Rhode Island, before his sanity returned. His depression grew worse when three of his children died in 1833, the same year his son Edwin Booth was born. A few years later, in 1836, Booth sailed again for England with his family.

Once more the English public largely ignored Booth, who abandoned any hopes of success in London. Another of his children died while the family was in London. In 1838, after he returned to the United States, he attempted suicide. The same year a son, John Wilkes Booth, was born. Later Booth savagely attacked his friend and fellow-actor Thomas Flynn, who in defending himself broke Booth's nose. Other incidents clouded the career of the "mad tragedian," as a Baltimore newspaper called him, but he frequently achieved brilliance in his more successful roles: Richard III, Sir Giles Overreach in *A New Way to Pay Old Debts*, Sir Edward Mortimer in *The Iron Chest*, King Lear, Hamlet, Iago, Pescara in *The Mountaineers*, Othello, and Shylock. These nine roles, plus the title role in *Bertram*, constituted 75 percent of his performances, which netted him substantial sums of money. Booth's "line of business," as it was then called, was that of leading tragedian, and although his favorite role was the gentle Hamlet, his most successful characterizations were Machiavellan villains such as Iago and Richard III. In such roles he could demonstrate his enormous passion, his penetrating vocal pyrotechnics, and the depths of his characterizations. Critics called his work "an intellectual feast," "vivid and beautiful," and, toward the end of his career, "majestic and magnificent even in its decay."

Booth's son by Adelaide, Richard Junius, came to the United States to join his father in 1843, touring with him for a few years, but learned nothing of Booth's American family until 1846. He immediately notified his mother, who booked passage to confront Booth in America. Booth offered no defense against Adelaide's charges, and they divorced in 1851. That same year Booth and Holmes, with whom he had already had ten children, married.

In 1852 Junius Brutus Booth, Jr., invited his father and brother Edwin to California for San Francisco and Sacramento engagements. Leaving his sons in California, the elder Booth set out alone to return to Maryland and retirement, stopping in New Orleans for a one-week engagement. Booth died aboard the steamboat *J. S. Chenoweth*.

Booth's major contribution to his profession was not the invention of the explosive and passionate romantic acting; Edmund Kean brought that innovation to the London stage in his 1814 debut. But Booth established this new style in the American theater. Over the course of thirty years Booth played every theater of any significance in North America, spreading the influence of his acting style. Despite his drinking problems and his recurrent madness, he thrilled his audiences with a bright, intellectual enjoyment; many considered him the greatest actor alive after Kean's death. His son Edwin, however, would surpass him professionally, and John Wilkes Booth brought a different sort of notoriety to the Booth name.

• Booth's widow destroyed most of his papers after his death, but some of his letters have survived at The Players and the Harvard Theatre Collection. His daughter Asia Booth Clarke published *The Elder and the Younger Booth* (1881) and *Booth Memorials: Passages, Incidents and Anecdotes in the Life of Junius Brutus Booth* (1886). Other substantial treatments of his life include Thomas Gould's *The Tragedian* (1868) and the anonymous *The Actor; or, A Peep behind the Curtain* (1846). Modern treatments include Stephen M. Archer's *Junius Brutus Booth: Theatrical Prometheus* (1992) and Charles Shattuck's "The Romantic Acting of Junius Brutus Booth," *Nineteenth Century Theatre Research* 5 (Spring 1977): 1–26. The elder Booth is variously treated in biographies of John Wilkes and Edwin Booth. Treatments of the Booth family include Stanley Kimmel's *The Mad Booths of Maryland* (1969) and Gene Smith's *American Gothic* (1992). Among the more substantial obituaries for Booth were those in the *Spirit of the Times*, 11 and 18 Dec. 1852, as well as the New Orleans *Daily Picayune*, 3 Dec. 1852.

STEPHEN M. ARCHER

BOOTH, Marian Agnes (4 Oct. 1843–2 Jan. 1910), actress, was born Marian Agnes Land Rookes, in Sydney, Australia, the daughter of Land Rookes, a British army officer, and Sarah (Smeathman?). She made her first stage appearance at the age of fourteen as a dancer in the role of Columbine at Sydney's Victoria Theatre. Reportedly accompanied by her mother and sister, she immigrated to the United States and on 9 February 1858 appeared under the name of Agnes Land as a dancer with Mrs. John Wood's company in San Francisco. After a brief stint in Adah Isaacs Menken's company, she acted in the stock company at Maguire's Opera House in San Francisco, gaining some reputation for her performance as Hermione in *The Winter's Tale* in 1860. In 1861 she married Harry Perry, a popular young actor in Maguire's company, who died in 1863. In the fall of 1865, billed as Mrs. Agnes Perry, she traveled to New York City to perform in the leading role of Florence Trenchard in Tom Taylor's popular comedy *Our American Cousin* at the Winter Garden Theatre, after which she played supporting roles with Edwin Forrest for a season.

In 1866 Agnes Booth joined the Boston Theatre company, one of the leading stock companies of the period, then under the management of Junius Brutus Booth, Jr., the elder brother of Abraham Lincoln's assassin, John Wilkes Booth, and the notable tragedian, Edwin Booth. In 1867, although she was twenty-five years his junior, she married J. B. Booth, Jr.; they had four children. During their marriage, they also comanaged Masconomo House, a large seaside resort hotel in Manchester, Massachusetts.

Remaining with the Boston Theatre company for eight years, Agnes Booth played opposite many notable stars of the day, including Edwin Booth, John McCullough, Frank Mayo, Lawrence Barrett, and Edward Askew Sothern. In 1874 she toured as a star in her own right and also played special engagements at several New York City theaters, including Booth's, Niblo's, and Union Square. She appeared with particular distinction as Constance in *King John* at Booth's theater in 1874 and at the same theater in 1876 as Myrrah in a scenically spectacular revival of Lord Byron's *Sardanapalus* ("replete with Oriental splendor and suggestiveness," according to contemporary theatrical biographer Lewis C. Strang). In 1877 her performance in Shakespeare's *Antony and Cleopatra* was another great success. From 1878 to 1881, she was the leading lady at Henry E. Abbey's Park Theatre, after which she was the leading lady at A. M. Palmer's new Madison Square Theatre until 1891.

Booth played numerous roles at the Madison Square but earned special distinction as Mrs. Chetwyn in Bronson Howard's *Young Mrs. Winthrop* (1882) and as Mrs. Ralston in Charles Young's *Jim, the Penman* (1886). The noted critic John Ranken Towse called her performance in this latter role "brilliant," commenting in particular on her physical control and expressive face:

> A finer example of the eloquence of facial expression that she exhibited in [the third act] has seldom been shown upon the stage. For several minutes she sat almost motionless, without uttering a word, trusting solely to the play of her features to reveal the course of her thoughts. Any failure of significance would have made the scene tedious, the least exaggeration might have made it ridiculous. She avoided both dangers with the surest instinct, and held the audience in frozen suspense. It was acting of the most subtle, delicate, and intellectual kind.

In 1883 her husband died, and two years later she married John B. Schoeffel, a prominent theater manager. In 1891 she left the stage to travel abroad to Paris and London, returning in 1895 to tour successfully as the Duchess of Milford in *The Sporting Duchess*, by Henry Hamilton, Cecil Raleigh, and Sir Augustus Harris. About this role, Strang wrote:

> The Duchess of Milford dwelt on that vague line betwixt comedy and burlesque; and Mrs. Schoeffel realized a

paradox—she presented a sporting woman who was womanly, a "hail fellow, well met" among men, a frequenter of stables and race-tracks, a female plunger who was not coarse, who never shocked, who was altogether delightful, and who, moreover, was lifelike and not a puppet.

Her final appearance was as Rose in an adaptation of Alphonse Daudet's *L'Arlésienne* (Woman of Arles) in 1897. She then retired from the stage, continuing to manage Masconomo House with her husband until her death in Brookline.

Possessing a singularly rich, distinctive voice, an arresting stage presence, lively features, and a finely honed, if traditional, acting technique, Agnes Booth was an accomplished, exceptionally versatile actress. Indeed, her very versatility and the fact that she mainly acted in stock companies may have prevented her from gaining a reputation equal to the leading actresses of the day. She was widely admired, however. Critics Howard Paul and George Gebbie favorably compared her to the noted British actress Dame Madge Kendal, calling her "the model actress of the American drama." Strang dubbed her "America's leading lady" and quoted the famous French actor Benoît-Constant Coquelin, who called her "the perfect artist."

• Perhaps the best overview of Booth's career is Lewis C. Strang's essay in *Famous American Actors of Today*, ed. Frederic E. McKay and Charles E. L. Wingate (1896), pp. 231–37. See also John B. Clapp and Edwin F. Edgett, *Players of the Present* (3 vols., 1899–1901); Howard Paul and George Gebbie, eds., *The Stage and Its Stars*, vol. 2 (1887), p. 101; Stanley Kimmel, *The Mad Booths of Maryland*, rev. ed. (1969); and John Ranken Towse, *Sixty Years of the Theater: An Old Critic's Memories* (1916), pp. 366–70. Obituaries are in the *New York Times* and the *Boston Transcript*, 3 Jan. 1910.

DANIEL J. WATERMEIER

BOOTH, Mary Louise (19 Apr. 1831–5 Mar. 1889), magazine editor and translator, was born in Millville (later Yaphank), Long Island, New York, the oldest child of William Chatfield Booth, a schoolteacher, and Nancy Monsell. Booth attended local schools at Yaphank and at Williamsburgh, which became part of Brooklyn, where the family moved in 1844 when her father became principal of a public school. Mainly, however, she was self-taught, reading the entire Bible at age five and Racine in the original French at seven. Although her father thought teaching the only suitable career for a woman, and she taught in his school briefly (about 1845–1846), she aspired to a literary career.

Booth moved to Manhattan when she was about eighteen to work as a vest maker by day and to study and write at night. She wrote articles without pay for educational and literary journals and newspapers to gain experience, eventually being hired on a piecework basis by the *New York Times* to cover educational and women's topics. She also began to translate French works at a time when relatively few were engaged in this work. Beginning with *The Marble-Workers' Manual* in 1856, she translated about forty books, chiefly on literary and historical subjects. At the same time she produced her major book, the *History of the City of New York* (1859), the first comprehensive account of the city's founding. Acclaimed by historians, it went through four editions. To earn a regular salary, however, she became secretary to a New York physician in 1860.

Booth also established herself as a reformer. A friend of Susan B. Anthony, she served as a secretary at the women's rights' conventions in Saratoga, New York, in 1855 and New York City in 1860. An antislavery advocate, she translated a variety of pro-Union French works during the Civil War, completing in only one week Gasparin's *The Uprising of a Great People: The United States in 1861* (1862). She had to work rapidly because the New York publisher feared that the war would be over before the book could be sold. Her efforts won praise from Abraham Lincoln and other government leaders.

Because she was widely known for her literary pursuits, Fletcher Harper asked Booth in 1867 to become editor of his new *Harper's Bazar,* a weekly fashion and family magazine that included up-to-the-minute European dress patterns. This was an important feature because other magazines often ran fashion plates redrawn from French publications a year or more after they had appeared. Laboring at her desk daily from nine to four, she combined a shrewd sense of business with Victorian decorum.

Aiming at a conventional, churchgoing audience, Booth provided quality fiction by such writers as Wilkie Collins, Harriet Prescott Spofford, and Mary E. Wilkins Freeman and illustrations by Winslow Homer. She had no intention of advocating woman suffrage, despite her personal views. Writing in 1884 to Thomas Wentworth Higginson, author of the *Bazar*'s popular "Women and Men" column, she stated that "It has always been thought inexpedient to advocate woman suffrage therein, either explicitly or implicitly. It has been a cardinal principle with the *Bazar,* as a home journal, conservedly to abstain from the discussion of vexed questions of religion, politics, and kindred topics."

Booth was proud of her ability to gauge public sentiment and the publication's financial success. Within ten years it had 80,000 subscribers. She ultimately drew a salary of $4,000 annually, which made her one of the highest paid editors of her day. Personally reading every line of manuscript and proof and scrutinizing every illustration, she took total command of the publication, causing Fletcher Harper and his brothers, owners of one of the nation's strongest publishing firms, to treat her with great respect.

Although in Venice in 1887 she became engaged to a suitor she earlier had rejected, Booth never married. She shared a Central Park home with a widow, Annie Wright, a childhood friend. Invariably businesslike in her office, at home she wore ornate gowns and enjoyed entertaining literary lights and other notables. She died in New York City of fibroid phthisis and degeneration of the heart.

Her importance lay in the fact that she built up a magazine that continued to endure more than a century after her death (the spelling was changed to *Bazaar* in 1929) by gathering talented contributors and accurately sensing her audience's attitudes. She personified a new type of career woman. On the one hand, she understood middle-class Victorian women, identifying with their dreams and recognizing their inclination to avoid controversial causes. On the other hand, she proved herself quite capable of wielding power in the male world of publishing. Her contribution to women's advancement lay in the example she provided of a woman who worked with men yet nonetheless personified feminine values of gentility and refinement.

• Letters by Booth are in the New York Public Library. Among her important translations was Henri Martin, *A Popular History of France from the First Revolution to the Present Time* (3 vols., 1877–1882). An interview with her appeared in Charles F. Wingate, ed., *Views and Interviews on Journalism* (1875). A chapter on her life was included in Harriet Prescott Spofford, *A Little Book of Friends* (1916). Another major biographical source is Sarah Knowles Bolton, *Successful Women* (1888). An obituary by Marie E. Zakrzewska ran in the *Woman's Journal*, 6 Apr. 1889.

MAURINE H. BEASLEY

BOOTH, Maud Elizabeth Charlesworth Ballington (13 Sept. 1865–26 Aug. 1948), Salvation Army leader, cofounder of the Volunteers of America, and prison reformer, was born in Limpsfield Surrey, England, the daughter of Samuel Beddome Charlesworth and Maria Beddome, Samuel's first cousin. Her father served as the minister of an aristocratic country parish but was reassigned to a church in a poor section of London in 1868. William Booth, the itinerant Wesleyan preacher who had broken from the Methodist church three years earlier to found the Christian Mission (renamed the Salvation Army in 1878), had rented the building across the street from Maud's father's church, and Booth's open-air meetings introduced Maud to the Salvation Army's noisy style of street-corner evangelism.

When Maud was sixteen, her mother took her to a Salvation Army meeting. William Booth's son, Ballington Booth, spoke that day, and Maud became captivated both by the army's message and the orator. Soon after, Maud met Booth's daughter, Catherine, while on vacation with her father and sisters in Paris after her mother's death in 1882. Catherine was serving as captain of the Salvation Army in France and asked Maud to join her. Maud's father gave his reluctant consent, and Maud became Catherine's assistant.

In these early years of the Salvation Army, members used sensational tactics—singing in cafes, selling pamphlets on street corners—to preach their message. In the course of publicizing what was considered by many a fanatical religion, Salvationists routinely encountered hostility and sometimes outright violence. Persecution against the two women intensified when they were reassigned to Switzerland. When Maud was stoned, arrested, and expelled from the country, she became the focus of contemporary debates about religious persecution and free speech in Switzerland.

Returning to England, Maud assumed her first official Salvation Army post in the London Training Home for Women Officers. In spring 1884 she supervised the first group of "slum sisters." Along with several assistants, Maud took a room in a working-class neighborhood, donned "slum" garb, and tried to convert her neighbors through practical help rather than Bible tracts. "Slum work" granted middle-class women license to an urban public life otherwise unsanctioned by turn-of-the-century gender and class codes, and Maud's accounts ring with excitement.

Maud's commitment to the Salvation Army grew, in spite of her father's fervent opposition. When she announced her engagement to Ballington Booth, her father felt she had betrayed her family, her class, and her religion. Because he refused to give his consent, Maud had to wait until she was twenty-one to marry legally. On 16 September 1886, three days after her birthday, Maud and Ballington married, and Maud was disinherited by her father. The couple would have two children.

In April 1887, soon after the birth of their first child, Maud and Ballington Booth were sent by General William Booth to command the Salvation Army in the United States. They arrived in New York to a poorly organized and factionalized Salvation Army and a hostile American public and immediately set out to improve the organization's standing. Maud was pivotal in the effort to make the Salvation Army respectable. Her strategy of holding meetings in the drawing rooms of homes of prominent people proved extraordinarily effective, attracting supporters from among New York's religious, political, and social elite.

As leaders of an increasingly financially secure, organized, and reputable Salvation Army, Maud and Ballington Booth set out to expand the organization's social work. The Salvation Army had been founded on the philosophy of combining religious appeals with practical help. Booth initiated slum work in the United States in 1889, and in 1890 she started a day nursery to care for babies of working women. The Salvation Army also opened shelters for homeless men and embarked on a temperance crusade—efforts that further heightened the Salvation Army's American popularity.

Despite these advances, the U.S. Salvation Army failed to please General Booth, who visited in October 1894. A number of differences between the general and the Ballington Booths combined to precipitate the schism that followed this visit. The general was offended by the Americanization of the Salvation Army, symbolized by the American flags carried by Salvationists and the display of an eagle on the Salvation Army crest. And the Ballington Booths had long been frustrated by being held to rules formulated in London that seemed to them inappropriate to the American army but over which they had little influence.

These differences soon became unbridgeable. When General Booth ordered the Ballington Booths to mortgage American properties to support Salvation Army ventures elsewhere, they refused. On 6 January 1896 they were ordered to leave their command. Although this order was presented to them as part of a general reassignment of army officers, Ballington and Maud perceived it as punishment and refused to accept the reassignment. The resulting schism was covered with lively interest in the American press, which sided uniformly with Ballington and Maud. A larger context of anti-British feeling, exacerbated by a dispute over the Venezuelan border in 1895–1896, strengthened the American defense of the two popular leaders against what was characterized as the British tyranny of General Booth.

The American Salvationists and their influential supporters urged the Booths to secede from the Salvation Army and form an independent American Salvation Army. Ballington and Maud refused and instead founded a new religious reform organization, the Volunteers of America, on 9 March 1896. Ballington was elected president and served until his death, and Maud was elected vice president.

From the outset, Maud and Ballington made an effort to refrain from committing the Volunteers to work that would compete with the Salvation Army. Maud regretted giving up her slum work but soon found the work she considered her calling and for which she would be most remembered in prison reform. Her inspiration came soon after the break with the Salvation Army, on 24 May 1896, when she was invited to speak to prisoners in the chapel at Sing Sing prison. Appalled by miserable prison conditions and moved by the desire professed by many prisoners to change, Booth dedicated herself to improving prison administration and most of all to the religious rehabilitation of prisoners.

To this end, Booth formed the Volunteer Prison League (VPL), composed of prisoners who were willing to commit themselves to "right living." First organized in Sing Sing and spreading quickly to other prisons, the VPL committed members to a set of rules, including praying every morning and night, refraining from foul language, obeying prison rules, and encouraging fellow inmates to change. To support prisoners after their release, she organized "Hope Halls," to which men could come directly from prison and stay until they found work. Booth also organized assistance for the families of prisoners, providing holiday outings, furnishing used clothes, and offering financial help. She became well known for her dedication to prisoners and her belief in their possibilities for redemption. "My point of view is that of the cell," Booth wrote. "All I know of this great sad problem . . . I have learned from those for whom I work" (*After Prison—What?* [1903], p. 7).

A noted prison reformer from the time of the movement's beginning, Maud Booth belonged to the American Prison Association and served on many committees as well as its board of directors. In 1913 Booth served as president of the association's auxiliary Association of Women Members. In 1918 she was the organization's national vice president.

Booth took over as general of the Volunteers of America when Ballington died in 1940. She continued prison work and national lecturing until her death at the home of her daughter in Great Neck, Long Island. She is most remembered for her pioneering work in the Salvation Army and her leading role on behalf of prison reform and prisoner rehabilitation.

• Maud Ballington Booth's publications include *Beneath Two Flags* (1894), *Branded* (1897), *Did the Pardon Come Too Late?* (1897), *Little Mother Stories* (1906), *The Relentless Current* (1912), and three books of stories for children, *Sleepy Time Stories* (1899), *Lights of Child-Land* (1901), and *Twilight Fairy Tales* (1906). Susan F. Welty, *Look Up and Hope! The Motto of the Volunteer Prison League; the Life of Maud Ballington Booth* (1961), offers the only full biography of Maud Ballington Booth. Herbert E. Wisbey, *History of the Volunteers of America* (1954), provides an account of her work in that organization. See also Wisbey, *Soldiers without Swords: A History of the Salvation Army in the United States* (1955).

REGINA G. KUNZEL

BOOTH, Shirley (30 Aug. 1898–16 Oct. 1992), actress, was born Thelma Booth Ford in New York City, the daughter of Albert J. Ford, a businessman, and Virginia Wright. Throughout her career, Booth continually maintained that she was born on 30 August 1907 rather than 30 August 1898, perpetuating this fiction so successfully that it appears in many of her obituaries. After grade school in Brooklyn and Hartford, Connecticut, Booth's first theatrical experience was in the summer stock company of *The Cat and the Canary* in Hartford in 1921. After a winter at home with her parents, she returned to Hartford and rejoined the stock company. She then switched to the branch of the Poli Stock Company located in New Haven, Connecticut, and eventually appeared in more than 600 stock productions through 1935, touring with Poli and other theatrical troupes. It was during this period that Shirley Booth formally adopted her stage name.

By 1925 Booth was also working on Broadway, starting with the production of *Hell's Bells* (1925), in which she appeared with a young Humphrey Bogart, followed by *Laff That Off* (1925), *Buy, Buy Baby* (1926), *High Gear* (1927), *The War Song* (1928), *The Mask and the Face* (1933), and many other plays and revues. In 1935 Booth finally got a major role in the Broadway production of *Three Men on a Horse*, thanks to the intervention of theatrical impresario George Abbott, who had seen Booth in a series of sketches (some written by Dorothy Parker) at the Barbizon-Plaza Hotel, where Booth worked in exchange for food and lodging. The enormous success of *Three Men on a Horse* lifted Booth out of the ranks of day players and extras and established her firmly as an up-and-coming performer.

When *Three Men on a Horse* finally closed after a two-year run, Booth appeared in rapid succession in the theatrical productions of *Excursion* (1937), *Too Many Heroes* (1937), *The Philadelphia Story* (1939),

My Sister Eileen (1940), *Tomorrow the World* (1943–1944), *Hollywood Pinafore* (1945), *Land's End* (1946), *The Men We Marry* (1948), *Goodbye, My Fancy* (1948), *Love Me Long* (1949), *Come Back, Little Sheba* (1950, for which Booth won both the Tony Award for Best Actress and the New York Drama Critics Circle Award), *A Tree Grows in Brooklyn* (1951), *The Time of the Cuckoo* (1952), and *Desk Set* (1955). At the same time, she worked in radio on the long-running comedy series "Duffy's Tavern," in which she appeared opposite Ed Gardner, whom she had married in 1929 (the couple divorced in 1942). In 1943 she married William H. Baker, Jr., who died in 1951.

In 1952 Booth finally made her debut in motion pictures, starring in the filmed version of her Broadway success *Come Back, Little Sheba*, in which she played a dowdy, yet endlessly optimistic housewife married to a self-destructive alcoholic (played in the film by Burt Lancaster). *Come Back, Little Sheba*, photographed in black and white, was an enormous commercial and critical success, winning Booth the Academy Award as Best Actress, the New York Film Critics Award, and the Cannes Film Festival acting award (all in 1952). Booth made only a few other motion pictures after this auspicious and long-delayed debut, and none of them achieved the distinction of her first film. Her last films were *Main Street to Broadway* (1953), *About Mrs. Leslie* (1954), *The Matchmaker* (1958; this film served as the basis of the musical *Hello, Dolly!*), and *Hot Spell* (1958).

In 1961 Booth accepted the role in "Hazel," a television series chronicling the continuing misadventures of the meddling housekeeper originally created by Ted Key in a series of popular cartoons for the *Saturday Evening Post*. The show lasted until 1966 and gave Booth a comfortable income from residuals. In 1973 she appeared in the short-lived television series "A Touch of Grace." Retiring after the series folded, Booth lived her final years in relative seclusion and died in North Chatham, Massachusetts.

Much of Booth's work is lost to us now, having been created expressly for that most transient of all media, the theatrical stage. The pathos that Booth brought to her characterization of Lola Delaney in *Come Back, Little Sheba* (on stage and screen) is balanced by her superb comedy work as Mabel, a gangster's girlfriend, in the stage version of *Three Men on a Horse*. And although "Hazel" was ground out in predictable television sitcom fashion, Booth's slapstick comedy created a believable character, all energy and motion.

Shirley Booth was one of the most prolific actresses of the twentieth century. She appeared in starring roles in the theater, in motion pictures, on radio, and on television. Whether she played tragedy or comedy, she always made the audience believe in the reality of her characters, which is, finally, a theatrical artist's most important test.

• The most accurate and complete information on Shirley Booth's life and career is Louise Mooney, ed., *Annual Obituary 1992* (1993). See also Thomas G. Aylesworth and John S. Bowman, eds., *The World Almanac Who's Who of Film* (1987), Judith Graham, ed., *Current Biography Yearbook* (1993), and Barry Monush, ed., *65th International Motion Picture Encyclopedia* (1994).

WHEELER WINSTON DIXON

BOOTH-TUCKER, Emma Moss (8 Jan. 1860–28 Oct. 1903), Salvation Army leader and social reformer, was born in Gateshead, England, the daughter of William Booth and Catherine Mumford, founders of the Salvation Army. A few days before her birth, her mother had written a bold and controversial pamphlet defending the right of women to preach the gospel. *Female Ministry* used Scripture to challenge those who condemned women's public speaking, laid the groundwork for an important Salvation Army tenet of equality of leadership between women and men, and offered "a bright omen" of Emma's future success as one of the most popular speakers of her day.

Emma Booth's childhood was intertwined with the early history of the Salvation Army. In 1865, when she was five years old, her father had left the Methodist church to found the Christian Mission, renamed the Salvation Army in 1878 and devoted to redeeming the poor through aggressive evangelicalism and practical help. Along with her seven siblings, Emma's upbringing was rigorously religious, and the Booth children honed their preaching skills on dolls and pillows arranged into a congregation. Emma professed conversion at the age of seven.

Salvation Army leadership was expected of all the Booth children, and Emma plunged in at an early age. She led a children's Bible class from the time she was sixteen. She assumed her first significant post in 1880, when she was placed in charge of the Salvation Army Training College to prepare women for army officership. As the college's head until 1888, Booth distinguished herself as an organizer and administrator and became known as "The Consul."

In 1887 Emma's father asked her to help Frederick St. George de Latour Tucker in selecting fifty officers to develop Salvation Army work in India. Six years earlier, Tucker had given up a career in Indian civil service to serve in the Salvation Army. He had led the evangelical "invasion" of India in 1882 and pioneered Salvation Army missionary work in India along what he termed "native lines," adopting native dress, traveling through India as a religious beggar, and "discarding ordinary European usages." Emma and Frederick worked closely together to select the missionary party and were soon engaged. They were married on 10 April 1888, in spectacular fashion, taking their vows before an audience of 5,000. Booth wore a Salvation Army uniform, and Tucker appeared in a turban, Indian robes, flowing scarf, and bare feet, carrying a begging bowl. Tucker recalled that "there was a tinge of romance, a union of West to East for the salvation of the world's white and colored heathendom" (Frederick Booth-Tucker, *The Consul*, p. 82). As was the practice of men who married into the Booth family, Tucker hyphenated his last name, and the couple became the Booth-Tuckers. In fall of 1888 Frederick and Emma left for India, where they oversaw the expansion of the army's missionary efforts there. Booth-Tucker joined her husband in adopting Indian dress and took the name of Raheeman. The first two of their six children were born in India, and they too were given Indian names.

Booth-Tucker had been working in India for two years when, late in 1890, she was diagnosed with anemia, and her doctors ordered her to return to London. Frederick and Emma returned to the army's international headquarters in London in January 1891 to serve as commissioners for foreign affairs, responsible for overseeing the army's work outside of England. The Booth-Tuckers worked in London for the next six years, until 1896, when they were named co-commanders of the Salvation Army in the United States. They succeeded Emma's brother, Ballington, and his wife Maud in the wake of a controversy known in Salvation Army history as the "great schism." As leaders of the American Salvation Army since 1887, Ballington and Maud Booth had overseen its growth in organization and reputation. But they fell out of favor with General William Booth, who replaced them with Emma and Frederick.

The Ballington Booths had expanded the scope of the American Salvation Army's social welfare efforts, and the Booth-Tuckers devoted themselves to building on that foundation. Soon after their arrival, they initiated an extensive reform program in New York City, opening rescue homes for "fallen women," inexpensive "workingmen's hotels," and orphanages. Emma Booth-Tucker's most important project was the Cellar, Garret, and Gutter Brigade, a group of women who donned working-class attire and engaged in community service while living among the poor. The most ambitious undertaking of the Booth-Tuckers' American command was the establishment of Salvation Army "farm colonies." Under the slogan, "Place the landless man on the manless land," the farm colonies endeavored to alleviate urban poverty by removing the unemployed urban poor from the allegedly corrupting influence of the city and relocating them on rural farms in California, Colorado, and Ohio. The farm colonies received much attention at the time, but problems in farming and irrigation led to the defection of many of the "colonists."

Both of the Booth-Tuckers traveled widely and became well known public speakers of their day. They made innovative use of new popular cultural forms and media, including film and stereopticon, in their lecture tours. Emma Booth-Tucker's most popular lecture, "Love and Sorrow," filled some of the largest opera houses in the country and played in more than fifty cities. In it, she interspersed "living tableaux" such as "The Madonna of the Slums" and "The Drunken Rag-Picker" with music and song and photographs displayed by stereopticon.

At the height of Booth-Tucker's popularity, she was returning from a tour of the Colorado farm colony and on her way to meet her husband in Chicago when she was killed in a train accident at Dean Lake, Missouri. She was forty-three. A memorial service was held for her at Carnegie Hall in New York City to which 15,000 came to mourn and pay tribute.

Although Frederick Booth-Tucker wrote that the contemporary women's movement "did not so much as exist" for his wife, Emma herself wrote, "I have felt from a very little child a great love for my own sex," and she expressed her dedication "to stand beside and help free them from the fetters of their unfavorable surroundings and of their natural timidity, and . . . inspire them to do something with their time and their talents, so that the world might be better for their existence in it" (Frederick Booth-Tucker, *The Consul*, p. 130; quoted in Williams, p. 131). Emma Booth-Tucker is best remembered for her pioneering work in the early Salvation Army and as an innovative public speaker.

• The fullest biographical sources on Emma Booth-Tucker are the biographies that her husband, Frederick Booth-Tucker, wrote for her and her mother, *The Consul: A Sketch of Emma Booth-Tucker* (1903) and *The Life of Catherine Booth: The Mother of the Salvation Army* (2 vols., 1892). See also Margaret Troutt, *The General Was a Lady: The Story of Evangeline Booth* (1980), and Herbert A. Wisbey, *Soldiers without Swords: A History of the Salvation Army in the United States* (1955). Emma Booth-Tucker worked closely with her husband; two biographies of Frederick Booth-Tucker—Harry Williams, *Booth-Tucker: William Booth's First Gentleman* (1980), and Frederick Arthur MacKenzie, *Booth-Tucker: Sadhu and Saint* (1930)—contain useful information about Emma Booth-Tucker as well.

REGINA G. KUNZEL

BOOTT, Kirk (20 Oct. 1790–11 Apr. 1837), a founder of the industrial city of Lowell, Massachusetts, was born in Boston, the son of Kirk "Church" Boott, an importer and merchant who immigrated from Derbyshire, England, and Mary Love. The Bootts lived comfortably in a Boston mansion so elegant that it became a local landmark. Unruly as a young man, Kirk attended several schools in England and returned to the United States in 1806 to attend Harvard, from which he did not graduate. After briefly serving as a bookkeeper for his father's business, Kirk Boott and Sons, Boott returned to England in 1811 to assume a commission as a lieutenant in the British army and served under the Duke of Wellington in Spain during the Peninsular War. In 1813 his regiment was ordered to New Orleans during the War of 1812, but Boott refused to fight against his homeland. He is believed to have enrolled instead at the Royal Military Academy at Woolwich, where he was trained in engineering and surveying; he remained in the British army until 1817. Boott married Anne Haden of Derby in 1818; the couple had six children.

After his father's death in 1817, Boott returned to Boston to run the family business with his brothers. The firm, which dealt mostly in imported British goods, was negatively affected by the War of 1812 and its economic aftermath and was discontinued in 1822.

In the summer of 1821 Boott met Patrick Tracy Jackson, a member of the Boston Associates, an elite group of capitalists who had begun operating a water-powered textile mill on the Charles River in Waltham, Massachusetts. Jackson was the brother-in-law of Francis Cabot Lowell, who established the textile industry in New England when he organized the Waltham mill in 1815. The Boston Associates, looking for an additional site on which to operate water-powered mills, had chosen East Chelmsford, a rural community thirty-five miles northwest of Boston. East Chelmsford was ideally situated along a series of waterfalls on the Merrimack River, with a total drop of about thirty feet; it was accessible to Boston by the Middlesex Canal.

Jackson and his associates named Boott the agent of the newly organized Merrimack Manufacturing Company in the winter of 1821–1822. Before mill operations began, the Merrimack Company bought all the stock of the Pawtucket Canal Company, which built a canal in 1793 to navigate around the falls. The canal gave the Merrimack Company effective control of the water power of the Merrimack River. The Boston Associates also purchased more than 400 acres of the surrounding farmland. Boott and his family moved to the area in the spring of 1822, and a mansion, built for him by the Merrimack Company, was completed the following year. After dam and canal reconstruction and erection of a mill building, textile manufacturing began in September 1823. East Chelmsford became the Town of Lowell in 1826, in honor of Francis Cabot Lowell, despite the desire of Boott to name the town Derby, after his father's home.

The Boston Associates occupied a series of interlocking directorates among what would eventually be nine mill corporations. Boott held the titles of treasurer, clerk, and director of both the Merrimack Company and the Locks and Canals Company, which was reorganized as a separate entity in 1825. Holding the powerful position of agent of both companies, Boott had broad authority to buy and sell real estate, oversee construction of dams and canals, and design mills and company-owned housing for workers, among many other improvements. His financial interest in other firms, including several mills, a railroad, and a bank, allowed him to direct much of the growth of Lowell for more than a decade. Boott served as moderator of the first town meeting in 1826 and was elected four times to the Massachusetts legislature during the 1830s.

Although much admired by the men who employed him, Boott was not well liked by many of the workers in Lowell, who saw him as haughty and aristocratic. In an action praised by some as providing much-needed moral guidance and criticized by many others as excessively paternalistic, Boott constructed an Episcopalian church, St. Anne's, in 1825, and he imposed a mandatory deduction from mill workers' pay to support it. The outcry that followed was so intense that the payroll deduction was discontinued. Boott also generated local rancor for his opposition to the construction of public schools in Lowell in 1832. He argued that the mills were simply an industrial experiment and if they failed, the schools, relying on the mills as the primary source of the town's tax revenue, would fall into decay. Many of the townspeople countered that the Boston-based investors whom Boott represented were simply exploiting the people of Lowell without providing for their betterment. The leader of the school construction initiative was Theodore Edson, the rector of St. Anne's; after the town voted to go forward with the new schools, Boott notified Edson of his withdrawal from the congregation.

At the time of the founding of Lowell, industrialization was a relatively new phenomenon in the United States; many of the first mill workers in Lowell came from rural New England farms. The resulting culture clash produced a series of political and philosophical battles in which Boott, the highest ranking local representative of the mill interests, was inextricably involved. As the nineteenth-century historian Charles Cowley put it, Boott "became, by the general consent of all, *the man* of the place, so that for fifteen years the history of Lowell was little more than the biography of Kirk Boott" (*History of Lowell*, 2d ed. [1868], p. 45).

Boott suffered an apparent aneurysm and fell dead from his carriage on a downtown Lowell street at midday.

• Letters by Boott are at the Massachusetts Historical Society, Boston. Lowell, one of the nation's first industrial cities, has been the subject of considerable scholarship. Especially useful for the study of Boott is Brad Parker's *Kirk Boott, Master Spirit of Early Lowell* (1985), which provides details on Boott's family and his early years. Additional information on Boott can be found at the University of Massachusetts at Lowell's Center for Lowell History. Hannah Josephson, *The Golden Threads: New England's Mill Girls and Magnates* (1949), examines the relationship between the mill owners who developed Lowell and the workers who lived there.

PEYTON PAXSON

BORAH, William Edgar (29 June 1865–19 Jan. 1940), U.S. senator, was born in Jasper Township, Illinois, the son of William Nathan Borah and Eliza West, farmers. Although enamored of the written and spoken word at an early age, Borah was an indifferent student and never finished high school. He refused to agree to his father's wish that he prepare for the ministry and for a brief period worked in an itinerant acting group. At the invitation of an older sister, whose husband was an attorney, Borah moved to Kansas and enrolled at the University of Kansas in the fall of 1885, but lack of financial resources and poor health forced him to drop out in the spring of 1887.

Instead, he read law and passed the bar examination that same year. Borah practiced law with his brother-in-law for three years, after which he headed west. He got no farther than Boise, Idaho, where he ran out of money, according to his own account.

Borah found his element in the boisterous atmosphere of this frontier community and soon gained recognition as a flamboyant criminal lawyer. In 1892 he was named chairman of the Republican State Central

Committee. He served for a time as secretary to Governor William J. O'Connell and in 1895 married the governor's daughter, Mary. The marriage produced no children.

Borah's visibility soared when the Populist crusade and the Free Silver issue shattered party lines in the mid-1890s. He was a superb orator, especially adept at playing upon popular emotion against the "interests." He joined the Silver Republicans in deserting the party in 1896, supporting Democratic presidential candidate William Jennings Bryan and mounting his own unsuccessful campaign for election to the U.S. House of Representatives. In 1902 Borah returned to the Republican party and ran for the U.S. Senate. Clearly the most popular candidate, he was blocked by the party regulars, however, who remembered his defection and disliked his identification with the rising tide of progressivism.

In 1906 Borah served as prosecuting attorney in a sensational murder trial involving the alleged attempt of William "Big Bill" Haywood and other radical labor leaders to contract for the killing of the ex-governor of Idaho, Frank Steunenberg. With Clarence Darrow arguing for the defense, the case made national news. Before the end of that trial, Borah himself was indicted for fraudulent timber deals. He was acquitted, but as one of his biographers observed, for a time doubt existed whether he would go to the Senate or to jail. Nevertheless, in early 1907 the state legislature elected him to the U.S. Senate, where he served without interruption until his death.

During his early years in the Senate, Borah established a reputation for idiosyncratic voting that confounded his critics and admirers alike for the rest of his career. Although counting himself a progressive, he opposed as much progressive legislation as he supported, frequently finding fault with the remedies offered to cure the ills he so eloquently denounced. Borah often voted against measures designed to curb the "interests," for example, on the ground that they would increase the power of the federal government. Although he was very skilled at speaking out, his unwillingness to do more than protest eventually earned him a reputation for futility.

Borah often professed his devotion to the U.S. Constitution but interpreted it to suit his prejudices. A stout defender of civil liberties, even during the emotional atmosphere of World War I and the ensuing Red Scare, he showed less concern about civil rights, preferring to leave to the states matters such as southern blacks' right to vote and woman suffrage. At the same time he indignantly denied that the states had any right to interpret the Prohibition amendment, which he supported.

Despite his erratic behavior, Borah emerged after World War I as one of the nation's most prominent progressives. His oratorical talents, his willingness to speak out on controversial issues, and his indifference to party loyalty earned him a national following. Borah was aided in this regard by excellent relations with the press, which he ardently courted. But his inability over the years to develop a coherent program or to back up his rhetoric with effective action disillusioned many of his early supporters. In 1921 the *Nation* referred to him as "the most effective and virile leader in the Senate"; by 1928, after he had supported Herbert Hoover, that same journal branded him "the sorriest figure in this campaign," one who could "no longer be carried on the roster of independents and Progressives."

The Idahoan's influence waned after Franklin D. Roosevelt became president in March 1933, although he still held important committee assignments. The gravity of the Great Depression led Borah to accept reluctantly the need for more government intervention in controlling the economy. He generally supported those New Deal measures providing work, relief, and aid to farmers and opposed those benefiting the financial and industrial interests. In 1936, at age seventy-two, he made a futile bid for the presidency. He scored well in a few western primaries but had little strength at the Republican convention. In 1937 he used his position on the Senate Judiciary Committee to help defeat Roosevelt's attempt to "pack" the Supreme Court.

Borah was best known for his impact on American foreign policy. He was a militant nationalist during his first two terms. He supported Woodrow Wilson's interventions in Mexico in 1914 and 1916 and the president's request for a declaration of war against Germany in 1917. Borah made clear that he advocated U.S. involvement in the war solely in behalf of national interests and not in pursuit of an idealistic "crusade." Later he opposed U.S. participation in a world organization as one of the leaders of the "irreconcilables"—senators who rejected *any* version of a League of Nations. These sixteen men figured more importantly in preventing American entry into the League than their numbers warranted, owing to Wilson's refusal to compromise with the moderates.

Borah's influence increased greatly after he became chairman of the Senate Committee on Foreign Relations in December, 1924. One quip had it that Secretary of State Frank B. Kellogg made foreign policy by ringing Borah's doorbell. As in domestic matters, the senator was better at fighting the proposals of others than at devising constructive alternatives. For example, the original impetus for the Washington Conference of 1921–1922 came from a Senate Resolution Borah himself introduced in December 1920. By the time the conference met, however, he had convinced himself that President Warren G. Harding and Secretary of State Charles Evans Hughes were conspiring to lead the United States into the League of Nations via "the back door" and therefore voted against some of the conference's most important treaties. Almost as suspicious of U.S. presidents as he was of foreign nations, Borah perceived threats everywhere.

Borah was identified throughout these years with what was known as the Outlawry of War movement, which culminated in the Kellogg-Briand Peace Pact in 1928. However, the evidence suggests that he used the movement primarily as a tactical device; his enthusiasm for the program waxed when such issues as U.S. entry into the World Court were being debated and waned when that danger passed. He was far more consistent in his opposition to interventionist policies in Latin America and the Far East and in his campaign to extend diplomatic recognition to the Soviet Union.

The senator welcomed President Roosevelt's "Good Neighbor" policy toward Latin American and his decision to recognize the Soviets. As the 1930s wore on, however, he became convinced that Roosevelt was leading the United States into a working alliance with Great Britain and France. No admirer of Adolf Hitler, Borah nonetheless argued that the German dictator was trying to redress the grievances of the Versailles peace treaty. To avoid U.S. entanglement in case of war, Borah supported mandatory neutrality legislation rather than granting the president the authority to discriminate between aggressor and victim in supplying aid. In the summer of 1939 he helped block Roosevelt's attempt to amend the neutrality laws to permit selling arms on a "cash and carry" basis. However, after Germany's invasion of Poland, in September, the revision passed despite Borah's opposition.

Borah died in Washington D.C.

• Borah's papers, more than 700 boxes, are in the Library of Congress. The Raymond Robins Papers in the State Historical Society of Wisconsin and the Salmon O. Levinson Papers at the University of Chicago Library contain valuable correspondence both with and regarding Borah. Borah's speeches are collected in Horace Green, ed., *American Problems: A Selection of Speeches and Prophecies by William E. Borah* (1924), and Borah, *Bedrock: Views on National Problems* (1936). Biographies include Claudius O. Johnson, *Borah of Idaho* (1936), and Marian C. McKenna, *Borah* (1961). Leroy Ashby, *The Spearless Leader: Senator Borah and the Progressive Movement in the 1920s* (1972); Robert James Maddox, *William E. Borah and American Foreign Policy* (1969); and John Chalmers Vinson, *William E. Borah and the Outlawry of War* (1957), study particular aspects of Borah's career. An obituary is in the *New York Times*, 20 Jan. 1940.

ROBERT JAMES MADDOX

BORCHARD, Edwin Montefiore (17 Oct. 1884–22 July 1951), professor of international law, was born in New York City, the son of Michaelis Borchard and Malwina Schachne. His father was a prosperous Jewish merchant, and Borchard enjoyed the benefits of a highly cultured upbringing. He attended City College of New York from 1898 to 1902, after which he earned an LL.B., cum laude, from New York Law School (1905), a B.A. from Columbia College (1908), and a Ph.D. from Columbia University (1913). Borchard married Corinne E. Brackett in 1915; the couple had two daughters.

Even before completing his Ph.D., Borchard embarked on a distinguished career in international law. In 1910 he advised the American delegation during the North Atlantic Coast Fisheries Arbitration at The Hague, Netherlands. He served as law librarian of Congress from 1911 to 1913 and from 1914 to 1916. In between, he was assistant solicitor for the Department of State. He worked as an attorney for the National City Bank of New York from 1916 to 1917.

Borchard became professor of law at Yale University Law School in 1917 and ten years later was appointed Yale's Justus H. Hotchkiss Professor of Law, a position he held until he retired in 1950. He continued to serve, however, in a variety of government positions. He was chief counsel for Peru in the Tacna-Arica dispute from 1923 to 1925. President Calvin Coolidge appointed him to the Central American Arbitration Tribunal in 1925. Borchard was technical adviser to the American delegation at The Hague Codification Conference in 1930 and served on the Pan American Committee of Experts for the Codification of International Law in 1938. He also advised various government departments and agencies.

Among his academic honors, in 1925 Borchard became the first American professor to lecture at the University of Berlin after World War I. He also lectured at the International Academy of Law at the Carnegie Peace Palace at The Hague. He served on the board of editors of the *American Journal of International Law*, a publication to which he frequently contributed, from 1924 until his death.

In addition to his scholarship, Borchard was an activist who in several of his writings influenced American civil justice. *Declaratory Judgments* (1934) argues that courts should be permitted to issue declaratory judgments, which establish the rights of parties or express the opinion of the court on questions of law without ordering anything to be done or granting any remedy. The declaration of preexisting rights of litigants would, Borchard argued, remove legal uncertainty before the occurrence of an actual loss or injury. He lobbied strenuously and successfully for passage in 1934 of the Declaratory Judgments Act. *Convicting the Innocent* (1932) consists of case histories of innocent men found guilty of major crimes. In it, Borchard called for restitution for those wrongly convicted and for appellate review of the facts as well as the law in cases of felony or at least in capital cases. The book's publication contributed to the passage of a federal law granting relief to individuals wrongly convicted in U.S. courts. In recognition of Borchard's role, Franklin D. Roosevelt presented him with the pen the president had used to sign the legislation.

A recognized and influential authority on diplomatic protection for alien citizens and property, Borchard advocated the compulsory submission of foreign claims to international tribunals. He addressed these issues in *The Diplomatic Protection of Citizens Abroad* (1915), which still remained the standard work on the subject at the time of Borchard's death, and in a two-volume work written with William H. Wynne, *State Insolvency and Foreign Bondholders* (1951).

Borchard was best known for his advocacy of traditional neutrality, which he defined as a compromise between the claims of a belligerent to stop all trade with its enemy and the claims of a neutral to trade freely. In return for permission to trade in nonmilitary goods, the neutral nation would agree to permit the belligerent to capture, if it could, military goods destined for its enemy.

During the interwar years, Borchard was an active noninterventionist and a harsh critic of the Roosevelt administration. Borchard had criticized President Woodrow Wilson and his secretary of state Robert Lansing for failing to remain neutral and thereby leading America into World War I. He expressed these views in *Neutrality for the United States* (1937), written with William Potter Lage. Borchard opposed discriminatory arms embargoes and cooperation against aggression as flagrant breaches of neutrality. Neutrals, he believed, should trade openly and without preference. He supported the America First Committee but rejected the abdication of neutral rights proposed by the so-called "new neutrality." For Borchard, requiring belligerent nations to pay cash and carry goods on their own ships constituted a surrender of historically established neutral rights. Moreover, Borchard worried that discriminatory embargoes and presidential discretion would not only fail to prevent war but would make American involvement more likely. In addition, he argued, prohibiting all trade with belligerents would have disastrous effects on the American economy.

Throughout the 1930s Borchard corresponded with a number of influential noninterventionists in Congress. When Roosevelt ordered American ships to shoot Nazi submarines on sight after the *Greer* incident, Borchard joined fifty-seven other prominent noninterventionists in signing a statement condemning Roosevelt's policies. Borchard saw American entry into the Pacific war as an imperial venture, and he continued to oppose American foreign policy during World War II and the Cold War. For example, he regarded the Yalta accords and the Truman Doctrine as wrongheaded commitments to unlimited intervention.

A demanding teacher, Borchard was accessible to his students and willing to use his extensive contacts in law and government to place them. A rigorous, if not rigid, scholar, he was, nonetheless, approachable and sociable. He acted on his beliefs by serving on the national committee of the American Civil Liberties Union and by donating generously to antifascist refugees. His death, in Hamden, Connecticut, came after a lingering and painful illness. Borchard remains best known for his unwavering adherence to a legalistic and perhaps anachronistic notion of neutrality.

• Borchard's papers are at the Yale University Library. Works by Borchard not cited above include *Guide to Law and Legal Literature of Germany* (1911); *Bibliography of International Law and Continental Law* (1913); *Commercial Laws of England, Scotland, Germany, and France* (1915), with A. J. Wolfe; *Guide to the Law and Legal Literature of Argentina, Brazil and Chile* (1917); *Latin American Commercial Law* (1920), with T. Esquivel Obregón; and *American Foreign Policy* (1946). He translated into English and wrote an introduction to Pasquale Fiore, *International Law Codified* (1917; trans. 1918). Along with Joseph F. Chamberlain and Stephen Duggan, Borchard edited the papers of a friend and teacher, *The Collected Papers of John Bassett Moore* (7 vols., 1944).

For the most detailed account of Borchard's life and work, see Richard H. Kendall, "Edwin M. Borchard and the Defense of Traditional American Neutrality, 1935–41" (Ph.D. diss., Yale Univ., 1964). A more sophisticated analysis of Borchard's thought is Justus D. Doenecke, "Edwin M. Borchard, John Bassett Moore, and Opposition to American Intervention in World War II," *Journal of Libertarian Studies* 6, no. 1 (Winter 1982): 1–34. Information on Borchard can also be found in Wayne S. Cole, *America First: The Battle against Intervention* (1953) and *Roosevelt and the Isolationists* (1983); Robert A. Divine, *The Illusion of Neutrality* (1962); William O. Douglas, *Go East, Young Man* (1974); Ronald Radosh, *Prophets on the Right* (1975); and Doenecke, *The Literature of Isolationism* (1972). Lengthy obituaries are in the *New York Times*, 23 July 1951; *Yale Law Journal* 60 (1951): 1071; and *American Journal of International Law* 45 (1951): 708.

MICHAEL S. MAYER

BORCHARDT, Selma Munter (1 Dec. 1895–30 Jan. 1968), educator and labor leader, was born in Washington, D.C., the daughter of Newman Borchardt, a soldier and government official, and Sara Munter. She completed a B.S. in education at Syracuse University in 1919 and received an A.B. from the same university in 1922. In 1933 she graduated from Washington College of Law (later known as American University College of Law), and in 1934 she was admitted to the Washington, D.C., Bar Association. In 1944 Borchardt had the honor of being admitted to the Supreme Court bar. In 1937 she received an M.A. in sociology from Catholic University and went on to complete all the requirements for a Ph.D. in sociology except the dissertation.

Borchardt began her career in education as the director of teacher training for Montgomery County, Maryland, in 1920. The following year she served as the supervisor of the county's rural schools. In 1922 she began teaching in the Washington, D.C., public schools, a job she held until she retired as chair of the English department at Washington's Eastern High School in 1960. Borchardt also served as an instructor at the Washington College of Law from 1934 to 1947.

Borchardt's most significant contribution to education was her activism in the American Federation of Teachers (AFT). Her legal expertise made her an invaluable participant in the labor movement. In 1923 she joined Local 8 of the AFT and served as legislative representative and vice president of the AFT both from 1924 to 1935 and from 1942 to 1962. As legislative representative Borchardt lobbied for federal aid to teachers, health care for school-aged children, funding for adult literacy programs, and support for school construction. During this period Borchardt also published numerous articles and reports on education reform in the AFT publication *American Teacher*.

Borchardt also served as secretary of the Education Committee of the American Federation of Labor (AFL) from 1929 to 1955. She authored several studies for the AFL during this period: "Who Selects Our Textbooks" in 1926, "The Relation of School Attendance Laws and Child Labor Laws" in 1930, and "Labor's Program for the Prevention of Juvenile and

Youth Delinquency" in 1943. From 1927 to 1958, as the AFT's representative to the Women's Joint Congressional Committee, Borchardt worked on developing and passing legislation aiding schools. While a representative she also served as chair for the Subcommittees on Federal Aid to Education and Child Labor Standards.

In 1935, in her capacity as the legislative representative of the AFT, Borchardt was appointed to a committee empowered to resolve a conflict over control of the New York AFT Local 5. A younger, more radical leadership that was affiliated with the Congress of Industrial Organizations (CIO) had emerged during the depression to take control of the local, marginalizing the older trade union activists who were affiliated with the more conservative AFL. Although the AFT committee issued a majority ruling suggesting that the factions be dissolved and a temporary union secretary be appointed, Borchardt dissented, arguing for the revocation of Local 5 and the chartering of a new local under the stewardship of the more conservative leaders. This dissent marked Borchardt's emergence as a prominent anti-Communist leader in the AFT.

In 1936 Borchardt was ousted from her position as legislative representative by an emerging pro-CIO faction in the AFT. In the years following Borchardt was immersed in the politics of the union, siding with the pro-AFL faction that sought to oust Communist sympathizers. By 1940 newspaper reports and an investigation of the House Un-American Activities Committee (HUAC) raised public concern about communism in the AFT. By 1942 the pro-AFL conservatives were firmly in control of the union, and Borchardt was reinstated to her positions as vice president and legislative representative.

Borchardt became involved in yet another controversy over alleged Communist infiltration into the AFT in 1947 when she served on a committee investigating a Los Angeles Local 430 affiliation with the Communist-dominated United Public Workers of the CIO. Borchardt and her fellow committee members formally chastised and revoked the charter of the local. Similar action was taken by the committee with locals in San Francisco and Seattle. During this period a national Cold War consensus was emerging that allowed the AFT leadership, including Borchardt, to forcefully purge its locals of any Communist influence. For example, in 1953, when increasing numbers of AFT members were called before the HUAC, Borchardt opposed the use of the Fifth Amendment by members of the AFT, urging teachers to testify in full.

Borchardt was active in several other organizations during her career. In 1927 she was appointed director of the World Federation of Education Associations, established in 1921 "to promote peace and good will among educators of all nations." In 1946 the WFEA disbanded, and Borchardt served on a committee to establish its successor, the Institute of World Studies, a nonprofit organization that sponsored educational institutions in England, France, Switzerland, and Holland. Borchardt was president of the Washington Women's Trade Union League from 1925 to 1927, and she served as a consultant on education for the American Association of University Women from 1931 to 1960.

Government positions held by Borchardt included service on the National Advisory Board of the National Youth Administration (1935 to 1944), on the U.S. Office of Education Wartime Commission (1941), and on a committee to supervise the High School Victory Corps (1941 to 1943). From 1946 to 1952 Borchardt served on the U.S. National Committee on United Nations Educational, Scientific, and Cultural Organization (UNESCO). Borchardt also served as a delegate to the White House Conferences on Children and Youth in 1930, 1940, and 1950 and as a delegate to the White House Conference on Education in 1955.

In 1960 Borchardt retired from the Washington, D.C., public school system and soon afterward resigned her AFT posts as legislative representative and vice president. She spent her remaining years in Washington, D.C., where she died in a nursing home.

Borchardt's active and varied career places her as one of the outstanding education advocates of the twentieth century. Her many appointments to government positions and private organizations serve as a testament to her peers' recognition of her intelligence and acumen. Although her early record of activism and leadership in the AFT was marred by her involvement in the anti-Communist purges of the McCarthy years, Borchardt's willingness to become immersed in the turbulent politics of organized labor also serves as evidence of her continued commitment to improving American education.

• A collection of Borchardt's papers (1911–1967) can be found in the Archives of Labor History and Urban Affairs, Walter P. Reuther Library, Wayne State University. This collection includes correspondence, drafts of articles and fiction, reports minutes, speeches, press releases, and notes. Borchardt wrote articles and reports on her activities as congressional representative to Washington, D.C., in the AFT publication *American Teacher*. Examples of these writings include "Eradicate Illiteracy! Don't Conceal It," *American Teacher* 15 (Oct. 1930): 14–16; "Report of AFT's Washington Representative," *American Teacher* 31 (Oct. 1946): 27–32, 31 and (Apr. 1947): 5–9; and "S717, the AFT-AFL Federal Aid Bill, and Other Federal Legislation," *American Teacher* 29 (Apr. 1945): 4–6. A transcript of Borchardt's U.S. Senate testimony in favor of a bill providing federal aid to private as well as public schools, "Should the Public School System Be Subsidized by Federal Funds?" was published in *Congressional Digest* 25 (Feb. 1946): 56ff. Borchardt also published a column concerning women's working conditions in the Washington *Herald* while she was president of the Washington Women's Trade Union League from 1925 to 1927. Discussions of the impact of Borchardt's career on the AFT may be found in Philip Taft, *United They Teach: The Story of the United Federation of Teachers* (1974); William Edward Eaton, *The American Federation of Teachers, 1916–1961: A History of the Movement* (1975); and Marjorie Murphy, *Blackboard Unions: The AFT and the NEA, 1900–1980* (1990).

VICTORIA W. WOLCOTT

BORDE, Percival (31 Dec. 1922–31 Aug. 1979), Afro-Caribbean dancer and choreographer, was born Percival Sebastian Borde in Port of Spain, Trinidad, the son of George Paul Borde, a veterinarian, and Augustine Francis Lambie. Borde grew up in Trinidad, where he finished secondary schooling at the Queens Royal College and took an appointment with the Trinidad Railway Company. Around 1942 he began formal research on Afro-Caribbean dance and performed with the Little Carib Dance Theatre. In 1949 he married Joyce Guppy, with whom he had one child. The year of their divorce is unknown.

Borde took easily to dancing and the study of dance as a function of Caribbean culture. In the early 1950s he acted as director of the Little Carib Theatre in Trinidad. In 1953 he met the noted American anthropologist and dancer Pearl Primus, who was conducting field research in Caribbean folklore. Primus convinced Borde to immigrate to the United States as a dancer and teacher of West Indian dance at her New York City school. Borde developed courses in traditional Caribbean dance forms for the Pearl Primus School and began performing with the Pearl Primus Dance Company. Shortly thereafter, he and Primus were married (date unknown). The couple had one child.

Performing success with Primus's modern dance company brought Borde appearances on television and the popular stage. He appeared on Broadway as the African Chief in Joyce Cary's 1956 play *Mr. Johnson*. In 1956 and 1957 he toured with the Primus dance company throughout Europe. Borde brought his own self-named dance troupe to the St. Marks Playhouse in New York City on 23 September 1958. He performed his own works and dances created for him by Primus, who acted as the artistic director of the company. John Martin, dance critic for the *New York Times* and a longtime supporter of Primus's dance anthropology, called the concert an "unusually well unified and atmospheric presentation, unpretentious in manner but with a wealth of knowledge behind it." Raves also came from the African-American press, and Borde's arrival as a leading male figure in Afro-dance was confirmed. In 1959 the separate Borde and Primus companies combined to form the Pearl Primus and Percival Borde Dance Company.

Borde's performances always included ethnographic dance characterizations of several Afro-American archetypes. For instance, his four-part 1958 program titled "Earth Magician" included portrayals of an Aztec warrior, a giant Watusi, a Yoruba chief, and a Shango priest. Borde performed sections of this program throughout his career, honing the authenticity of his dance movements through research and study. His performance style was consistently described as dynamic yet elegant, his strong physicality offset by his striking good looks. Martin described him as "light and easy of movement, with strength, admirable control and authority."

In 1959 Borde and Primus toured Africa and performed in Ethiopia, Ghana, Mali, Kenya, Nigeria, and Liberia, which held special import for the couple. It was in Liberia that Borde was named Jangbanolima, or "a man who lives to dance," by Chief Sondifu Sonni during an official adoption ritual. Also in 1959 Borde and Primus became the directors of the Performing Arts Center of Monrovia, Liberia. They remained in Liberia until November 1961. During this time Borde wrote articles for the *Liberian Age* and was active in the Liberian Chamber of Commerce. He was awarded the Gold Medal of Liberia for his work in the dance of the African diaspora.

After returning to the United States, Borde produced *Talking Drums of Africa*, an education-in-the-schools program sponsored by the New York State Department of Education. He was active in the Congress on Research in Dance, a dance scholars' organization, and served on its board of directors. He also continued to work in the theater, serving as the resident choreographer for the Negro Ensemble Company's 1969 season.

Borde completed a bachelor's degree (1975) and coursework toward a master's degree at the School of the Arts of New York University. He taught movement courses there, at the Columbia University Teachers College, and at the State University of New York at Binghamton, where he was an associate professor of theater arts and black studies. Borde's highly popular courses offered participatory, dance-based studies of Afro-Caribbean culture, which emphasized the connections between dance, ritual, and everyday life. He often reminded his students, "Just as one should prepare oneself to enter a temple, one should prepare to dance" (*Wichita Eagle*, 20 Aug. 1969).

Borde died of a heart attack backstage at the Perry Street Theater in New York City immediately after performing "Impinyuza," the strutting Watusi solo he had danced for more than two decades.

Borde's masculine stage presence and dynamic performance style helped to widen interest in concert Afro-American dance forms. His work continued the efforts of dancer-choreographers Primus and Katherine Dunham in the insertion of ceremonial, anthropologically researched dance on the concert stage. After his death, Primus characterized him as "the outstanding exponent of African influences on Caribbean culture."

• Slight documentation of Borde's significant dance career exists. The Dance Collection of the New York Library for the Performing Arts at Lincoln Center holds a file of newspaper reviews of his performances. The New York Public Library's Schomburg Center for Research in Black Culture holds listings of materials from the black press. Reviews are also in the *New York Times*, 29 Sept. 1958 and 5 Oct. 1958; *Dance Magazine*, Dec. 1958, Aug. 1964, and Oct. 1964; and *Dance Observer*, June 1956, Dec. 1958, and Oct. 1959. An obituary is in the *New York Times*, 5 Sept. 1979.

THOMAS F. DEFRANTZ

BORDEN, Gail (9 Nov. 1801–11 Jan. 1874), surveyor and inventor, was born in Norwich, New York, the son of Gail Borden, a pioneer and landowner, and

Philadelphia Wheeler. The Bordens moved at least twice in the early 1800s, first to Kennedy's Ferry, Kentucky, which became Covington soon after their arrival, and then to New London, Indiana, in 1816, where Borden learned surveying. Borden attended school in Indiana during 1816 and 1817.

In 1822 Borden and his brother Thomas set out for New Orleans together but ended up in Amite County, Mississippi. There Borden surveyed land as the county surveyor. He also taught school in Bates and Zion Hill, where he was legendary for running, not walking, to school most days, sometimes even carrying a student along the way. Borden met Penelope Mercer in Amite County and married her in 1828; they had five children.

Following his father and his brother Thomas, Borden moved to Texas in 1829, where he farmed, raised livestock, and surveyed. He quickly became involved in Texas politics, representing San Felipe in the Lavaca district. The Texas political convention of 1833 was held in San Felipe, and Borden appeared as a delegate. He contributed to the premature drafts of a Texas constitution, written before the Texas separation petition was accepted by the Mexican government. He was then called on to perform administrative duties, along with Samuel M. Williams, when Stephen F. Austin was away during much of 1833 and 1834 negotiating terms for a possible union with Mexico. Borden's surveying experience qualified him to help compile the first topographic map of Texas, which was completed in 1835.

With his brother Thomas and Joseph Baker, Borden started the first newspaper in Texas that lasted any length of time—over forty years—the *Telegraph and Texas Register*. Its first weekly issue was published on 10 October 1835. It was published originally in San Felipe, then moved first to Harrisburg (now Houston) and then to Columbia, Texas. After constant financial woes, Borden sold his portion of the paper in 1837 to Jacob W. Cruger.

That same year, Borden was chosen to be the first customs collector for Texas, at Galveston Island. He was ousted from the position in 1838, after Mirabeau Buonaparte Lamar was elected president of Texas and retaliated against Borden and ten other men who had refused to support him for president.

Borden was hired to be an agent for the Galveston City Company in May 1839. The company was responsible for city planning and nearly all real estate sales for the city. He held the position for twelve years, even while accepting another stint as customs collector from December 1841 to the spring of 1843. He left the customs post on very bad terms but busied himself with his Galveston City Company position and his new interest in inventing.

Borden's wife, Penelope, died on 5 September 1844 of yellow fever. In 1845 Borden married Mrs. A. (Augustine?) F. Stearns.

Borden is credited with attempting to create an amphibious vehicle that he called the terraqueous machine in 1848, which he did not pursue past its prototype. He began experimenting in 1849 with a condensed-beef-broth-and-flour concoction that he called a meat biscuit. It was a pemmicanlike food that could be taken into the field or on long trips without spoiling. Even though the meat biscuit was endorsed by the U.S. Army in 1850 and awarded a gold medal at the Great Council Exhibition in London, England, in 1851, it was not profitable. Since Texas had been admitted to the Union a few years earlier, Borden felt free to move to the U.S. financial capital, New York City, in 1851 to market the meat biscuit more advantageously.

While he was promoting his meat biscuit, Borden began to experiment with condensing a number of products, including milk, coffee, tea, and cider. In what proved later to be his most successful venture, he created a commercially viable method for producing condensed milk that was consistently pure and long-lasting. His condensed milk was sweetened with sugar. Later, other manufacturers succeeded in drying milk and evaporating milk without sugar. The meat biscuit, however, commanded most of Borden's attention until 1855, when he all but abandoned it because of continued flagging sales. Then, in 1856, Borden was issued a patent for condensing milk in a vacuum over low heat.

Though Borden had a patent in hand, he did not have the funds to produce and market the product. He found partners, James Bridge of Maine and Thomas Green of Virginia, who helped him build a condensery at Wolcottville, Connecticut, in 1856. A second factory was built the next year in Burrville, Connecticut, with the financial backing of Bridge, Green, and Reuel Williams of Maine. The milk was selling enough to sustain the factories, but not enough to turn a profit.

Borden insisted on particular sanitation methods in the dairies that supplied milk to him, thereby helping to institute cleanliness standards that have persisted to this day. He used a vacuum pan in which to condense the milk, further ensuring purity. Because this was before Pasteur's discoveries and Borden was not a scientist, he did not know exactly why preventing the milk from coming in contact with the air contributed to its purity and longevity.

Jeremiah Milbank, a New York financier, met Borden in 1858. They quickly became partners, founding the New York Condensed Milk Company, and sales increased markedly.

It is not known when or where his second wife died, but Borden married Emeline Eunice Eno Church in 1860.

Borden closed the plant at Burrville and opened another at Wassaic, New York, in 1861 without Milbank's financial backing. Later he opened plants at Brewster's Station, New York, and Elgin, Illinois. The U.S. Civil War offered a large market for the condensed milk. After the war, overexpansion threatened to overwhelm operations, but Milbank and Borden were able to contain the problem and keep the factories running.

In the early 1870s Borden spent summers in White Plains, New York, where he still presided over what was by then the Borden Condensed Milk Company. He died while wintering in Borden, Texas, which was founded in honor of the Borden family.

• More can be found about Gail Borden in Joe B. Frantz, *Gail Borden: Dairyman to a Nation*, as well as S. L. Goodale, *A Brief Sketch of Gail Borden and His Relation to Some Forms of Condensed Food*, and, from *The Borden Eagle* (1922–1923), "The History of the Borden Company: Who Was Gail Borden?" See also Borden's U.S. patent, no. 15,553 (1856), for his method of condensing milk.

SUE ANN LEWANDOWSKI

BORDEN, Lizzie Andrew (19 July 1860–1 June 1927), the accused murderer of her father and stepmother in a celebrated trial, was born in Fall River, Massachusetts, the daughter of Andrew Jackson Borden, who started as a fish peddler and undertaker and ended as an investor worth a half-million dollars, and Sarah Anthony Morse. When Borden was two, her mother died. Her twelve-year-old sister, Emma, became her surrogate mother, even though two years later her father married thirty-seven-year-old Abby Durfee Gray. Borden developed into a pretty young woman with carefully kept red hair and large gray eyes who wore stylish clothes. Often pitted against their miserly father and 200-pound stepmother, Borden and her sister found their home a battleground. But the customs of the time kept the daughters from leaving the small, drab house, located in an area losing its residential character. After graduating from high school, Borden escaped her unhappy home by engaging in activities at the Central Congregational Church. At age thirty she toured Europe with a group of young Fall River women. On her return she taught a Sunday school class of immigrant children, became secretary-treasurer of the Christian Endeavor, and joined the Woman's Christian Temperance Union.

On 4 August 1892, at approximately 9:30 A.M., Abby Borden was struck nineteen times by a sharp instrument, most likely a hatchet, while she was tidying the second-floor guest room. (Abby Borden's time of death was determined both by forensic evidence and by when she was last seen.) About an hour and a half later, Andrew Borden, who, after a short tour of business, had returned home and was napping in the living room, was hit ten times by the same instrument. Lizzie Borden was home that morning, as was Bridget Sullivan, the family servant, who for much of the time was outside washing the first-story windows. Borden's visiting uncle, who had slept in the guest room the night before, returned to the house after the murders. Borden's presence in the house made her a suspect, as did her varied responses to the oft-repeated query, "Where were *you* when it happened?"

After an inquest, during which she was deprived of her counsel and made numerous inconsistent statements, Borden was arrested. The district attorneys prosecuting the case were Hosea M. Knowlton, a formidable cross-examiner with a bulldog manner who insisted that women "make up for lack of strength in cunning; their hates are more undying, more unyielding, and their passions stronger," and William H. Moody, who would later become a U.S. congressman, serve in two cabinet positions, and be an associate justice of the Supreme Court. But they were no match for the defense, which was headed by George D. Robinson, a three-term Massachusetts governor and one of the state's ablest trial lawyers. Patting her arm while assuring her, "It's all right, little girl," Robinson immediately put Borden at ease. She liked everything about him but his $25,000 fee.

Surpassing the simultaneous Chicago World's Fair in newspaper coverage, Borden's trial was the sensation of the year 1893. (The start of the trial had been delayed because the authorities, knowing they did not have an airtight case, had proceeded reluctantly.) Most newspapers thought Borden innocent, as did feminists Mary A. Livermore and Lucy Stone. The 5 to 20 June trial was held in New Bedford, rather than in Fall River, a textile town deeply divided between immigrant millworkers, who thought that Borden was guilty, and those like herself, who came from old, prominent families and rallied in her defense. During the trial, self-possession never deserted Borden. Wearing a stylish black mohair dress with leg-of-mutton sleeves, she entered the courtroom each day on the arm of one of the ministers of her church. Occasionally, when testimony brought tears to her eyes, she covered her face with her fan; twice she fainted in the stifling, hot courtroom; and she waited demurely in the hall when her father's skull was exhibited. Borden half smiled when her eyes met those of Bridget Sullivan, who was testifying about the ever-present mutton, which had appeared at four consecutive Borden meals during her parents' last twenty-four hours.

Robinson managed to get damaging inquest testimony excluded from the trial, as well as testimony that the day before the murders Borden had tried to buy prussic acid, a deadly poison. The chemical tests made by Professor Edward S. Wood of Harvard revealed no prussic acid in the stomachs of the victims, no blood on two axes and two hatchets from the Borden home, and no blood on Lizzie Borden's garments excepting one pinhead-sized spot on an underskirt. One of the hatchets, which fitted the wounds of the murdered Bordens, had been broken from its handle and dusted with ashes. Also it was uncertain whether the garments tested for blood were the garments Borden was wearing the morning of the murders. Descriptions of her dress varied, and just before her trial a second grand jury was called to hear new testimony that she had burned a dress in the kitchen stove. Robinson deftly handled this circumstantial evidence, as well as testimony of bitter feuding in the Borden household.

In making his charge to the jury, Judge Justin Dewey hinted that a finding of not guilty was the only valid option. (Dewey, the father of three daughters, owed his appointment to superior court to Robinson, the former governor.) Evidently, the jury was ready to comply, but it waited more than an hour before giving its verdict. Although applause thundered in the New Bedford courtroom, Fall River people were less satisfied. Few of them wanted Borden executed, but many of them, particularly those of the working class, were not prepared for her complete exoneration. Even in her own church Borden was shunned when she triumphantly returned.

While the real Lizzie Borden moved to a better neighborhood, called herself Lizbeth, befriended the actress Nance O'Neill, and became estranged from her sister, the Lizzie Borden who emerged from the literature of her trial became part of American folklore. Her story was repeated in novels, movies, and plays. Suddenly children had a new rhyme to use in counting-out games:

Lizzie Borden took an ax
And gave her mother forty whacks;
When she saw what she had done
She gave her father forty-one!

When they died ten days apart, Lizzie and Emma Borden were buried with their parents and stepmother. Their wills were generous to institutions and people in Fall River, where Lizzie Borden died. In her will, she also remembered the animals. "Their need is great and there are so few who care for them," she explained, after leaving $30,000 to the Fall River Animal Rescue League (Williams et al., p. 259).

• Material on Lizzie Borden and her trial has been conveniently brought together by Joyce G. Williams, J. Eric Smithburn, and M. Jeanne Peterson, eds., *Lizzie Borden: A Case Book of Family and Crime in the 1890s* (1980). The Fall River Historical Society has a file on the murders and related materials. Books and articles on Lizzie Borden have appeared steadily, beginning with articles in *Woman's Journal*, 20 Aug., 17 Sept. 1892, and 27 May, 24 June 1893; Edwin Henry Porter, *The Fall River Tragedy* (1893); and John H. Wigmore, "The Borden Case," *American Law Review* 27 (1893):819–45. Her story is also a favorite with mystery writers and a constant in collections of famous murders and trials. Among the best of these are those by Edmund Pearson, especially his *The Trial of Lizzie Andrew Borden* (1937). The murders have been charged to her sister, Emma, in Frank Spiering, *Lizzie* (1984), and to the family maid, Bridget Sullivan, in Edward Radin, *Lizzie Borden: The Untold Story* (1961). Victoria Lincoln, *A Private Disgrace: Lizzie Borden by Daylight* (1967), suggests that Borden committed the first murder while in an epileptic fit. Imaginative treatment of the Borden story is in Edward H. Bierstadt, *Satan Was a Man: A Novel of Murder* (1935); two plays: John Colton and Carlton Miles, *Nine Pine Street* (1934), and Lillian De La Torre, *Goodbye, Miss Lizzie Borden: A Sinister Play in One Act* (1948); and the ballet and book of the same name, Agnes de Mille, *Lizzie Borden: A Dance of Death* (1968). Among numerous obituaries are those in the *New York Times*, 3 June 1927, and the Fall River *Daily Globe*, 2 June 1927.

OLIVE HOOGENBOOM

BORDLEY, John Beale (11 Feb. 1727–26 Jan. 1804), agricultural theorist and lawyer, was born in Annapolis, Maryland, the son of Thomas Bordley, a lawyer, and Ariana Vanderheyden Frisby. At the age of twenty-one, Bordley inherited land from his father. In 1751, after his marriage in that year to Margaret Chew, this property was combined with the private fortune of his wife, and he devoted considerable effort to tending his estate near Joppa close to Baltimore. The couple had four children. Bordley also studied law in the office of his brother Stephen, and in 1753 he was appointed prothonotary (chief clerk) of Baltimore County; he simultaneously established a law practice that encompassed Cecil County, Harford County, and Baltimore County. In 1765 Bordley resigned his clerkship in protest of the Stamp Act and moved his law practice to Baltimore, where he soon attracted such renown that in 1766 he was appointed judge of the Provincial Court of Maryland and in 1768 a member of the commission to determine the line between Maryland and Delaware.

As the tension between Britain and the colonies increased in the 1770s, Bordley, despite his strong opposition to British demands, resisted an active participation in the revolution and turned his attention increasingly to agriculture. In 1770 Bordley purchased an estate of 1,600 acres on an island in the Wye River leading to the eastern shore of Chesapeake Bay; here he established a model farm where he grew a variety of grains and fruits and bred cattle and sheep. Bordley became a supporter of the revolutionary movement—in 1774 the Provincial Convention of Maryland appointed him to the Committee of Public Safety—but he believed that he could best serve the cause by demonstrating that the new nation could win its independence by establishing an efficient agriculture and indigenous manufactories. Accordingly he spent most of the revolutionary period experimenting on crop rotation, cattle breeding, and textile production, occasionally demonstrating his prowess in farming by sending boatloads of flour, vegetables, and beef to the local militia.

After his first wife's death in 1773, in 1776 Bordley married Sarah Mifflin and thus became connected to one of Philadelphia's most prominent families. The couple had one child. Accordingly, after the war Bordley spent increasing amounts of time in Philadelphia, and in 1783 he was elected to the American Philosophical Society, then the country's leading scientific organization. The following year he published *A Summary View of the Courses of Crops in the Husbandry of England and Maryland*, and in 1785 he was active in establishing the Philadelphia Society for Promoting Agriculture (PSPA) with the support of local landowners, merchants, and prominent political figures. Bordley wanted the society to encourage progressive agriculture; the PSPA offered awards for crop rotation, livestock breeding, trench plowing, and sowing wheat, encouraged the establishment of similar groups throughout the United States, and petitioned the Pennsylvania legislature to establish a state agricultural society, to endow a chair in the theory of agriculture at the University of Pennsylvania, and to establish a model farm. Bordley served as vice president of the PSPA from 1785 until 1791; since he continued, however, to live at Wye throughout this period, he was not a central figure in the society's affairs. Bordley was intermittently a member of the society's committee of correspondence, sending accounts of his experiments at Wye to the *Columbian Magazine* and the *Pennsylvania Gazette*; most notably, he constructed a horse-drawn drill for sowing wheat. Bordley's experiments and the society's efforts were both nugatory in their influence on American agriculture; those farmers who paid any attention to the society were reluctant to import expensive livestock breeds from England and unwilling to risk experiments in the use of gypsum and crop rotation when land, even in Pennsylvania, was still plentiful and inexpensive.

In 1791 Bordley moved to Philadelphia, but the society had already become temporarily moribund. Bordley spent his remaining years in writing up his agricultural experiments; in 1797 he published *Sketches on Rotations of Crops*, and in 1799 *Essays and Notes on Husbandry and Rural Affairs* appeared; he was also an active member of the Episcopal church in Philadelphia. After a long illness, Bordley died at his country house opposite Fairmount on the west side of the Schuylkill.

• Bordley's letters are in the Bordley Family Papers at the Maryland Historical Society, and account books relating to Bordley's farm are in the Estate Administration Accounts at the Historical Society of Pennsylvania. The manuscript minutes and correspondence of the Philadelphia Society for Promoting Agriculture are in the Van Pelt Library, University of Pennsylvania, and contain additional information on his agricultural experiments and correspondence. A brief sketch of Bordley's farm on Wye Island is in Robert Wilson, "Wye Island," *Lippincott's Magazine* 19 (1877): 466–74, and a hagiography is provided by his daughter Elizabeth Bordley Gibson, *Biographical Sketches of the Bordley Family of Maryland* (1865). See also Olive Moore Gambrill, "John Beale Bordley and the Early Years of the Philadelphia Agricultural Society," *Pennsylvania Magazine of History and Biography* 66 (1942): 410–39, and Simon Baatz, *"Venerate the Plough": A History of the Philadelphia Society for Promoting Agriculture, 1785–1985* (1985), for Bordley's activities as a member of the society.

SIMON BAATZ

BORDONI, Irene (16 Jan. 1895–19 Mar. 1953), actress and singer, was born in Ajaccio, Corsica, France, the daughter of Sauver Bordoni, a tailor; her mother's name is not known. She was reputed to be the great grandniece of Jean-François Millet, the French painter. Her family moved to Paris, and she left school at the age of ten to work in her father's shop.

In 1907 Bordoni joined the chorus at the Théâtre de Variétés. During the next few years she sang and danced in a number of revues without attracting any particular attention. She came to the United States in 1912 to play a small part in *The First Affair* on Broadway and a more substantial one in *Broadway to Paris*. For the next two years she toured in vaudeville. In 1914 she returned to Europe to appear in *L'Impresario* in London. She married Edgard Beeckman, a Belgian actor and manager, in 1915; they had one daughter.

Bordoni returned to the United States in 1915 to appear in *Miss Information* on Broadway. Her breakthrough to stardom came in 1917 in a featured role in *Hitchy-Koo*, produced by Raymond Hitchcock and E. Raymond Hitchcock and E. Raymond Goetz. She triumphed in the 1918 production as well. Having divorced Beeckman in 1917, she married Goetz the following year.

By the early 1920s Bordoni had become an international sensation, starring in revues and musicals on both sides of the Atlantic, many of which were produced by her husband. Her standard role was that of a worldly young French woman in American adaptations of risqué French farces with the occasional song, written by Goetz and various coauthors, for her to sing. In 1920 she starred in *As You Were*, introducing the song, "If You Could Care for Me." In *The French Doll* (1922) she played a saucy French girl whose family sought to marry her to a millionaire. Critics praised her for sparkling performances in *Little Miss Bluebeard* (1923), which she took to London in 1925, and *Naughty Cinderella* (1925–1926). She also headlined vaudeville shows at the Palace in New York City.

Although Bordoni achieved stardom, she did so without great talent. She could sing in English, French, and Spanish, but her voice was neither professionally trained nor particularly memorable. Nor was she a good dancer. Yet she was vivacious, charming, and pretty, always dressed in chic and extravagant style. She performed her signature risqué songs with a charming accent and much flirtatious eye rolling. She reminded many admirers of the near-contemporary popular vaudevillian Anna Held. Above all, she gained fame because she epitomized the Anglo-American stereotype of the French coquette. As a *New York Times* critic observed in the 1920s, "She is everything Americans expect a French girl to be in the theatre and then some."

In 1926 Bordoni tried to escape typecasting by taking the title role in Sacha Guitry's *Mozart*, produced in English by her husband. Neither critics nor audiences could accept *their* Bordoni as the young male composer, and the musical play failed. In 1928 she again triumphed in her usual role as a French coquette in *Paris*, produced by her husband, who assisted Cole Porter in composing the songs. In *Paris* she introduced "Let's Do It," which became part of the Porter canon. In 1929, at Bordoni's request, an Illinois court annulled her marriage to Goetz on the grounds that Illinois law prohibited him from marrying her so soon after his earlier divorce.

Bordoni was eager to repeat her theatrical success in films. In the late 1920s Hollywood studios were equally eager to recruit the latest Broadway sensation for the musical films made possible by the introduction of sound. Bordoni arrived in California in 1929 in the style expected of a Broadway star, accompanied by an entourage of managers, secretaries, servants, lapdogs, and twelve trunks of clothes. To gushing writers of fan magazines, she confessed that she owned 150 pairs of shoes. She appeared in *Show of Shows* (Warner Bros.,

1929), a huge filmed vaudeville show, and with more success in *Paris* (First National, 1929), where she recreated her stage role. However, the rush to use sound had led to a glut of revues and musical plays. By 1930 studio bosses had reacted to audience indifference by deleting musical numbers from completed films and canceling new productions. Moreover, the onset of the Great Depression reduced audiences and made musicals too expensive to produce. The musical films of the early depression years would feature dancing, not Bordoni's strong point.

The economic downturn afflicted Broadway as well as Hollywood, making lavish musicals and revues with high-priced talent uneconomical. Theatrical vehicles for Bordoni's distinctive talent and stock portrayal became increasingly hard to find and less popular with audiences. No longer a star and no longer typecast, she developed into a fine character actress in roles requiring comic talent and a larger than life presence. During the 1930s she toured the United States and Great Britain in road company productions of musicals, light comedies, and such standards as *Blithe Spirit*.

Bordoni did not appear on Broadway again until 1938, when she had a starring role in *Great Lady*, which closed after twenty performances. In 1940 she won critical acclaim for a character part in *Louisiana Purchase*, with music and lyrics by Irving Berlin, which ran for more than a year on Broadway. She repeated this role twice, in the 1941 film starring Bob Hope and in a 1947 revival in California.

In the late 1940s and early 1950s Bordoni continued to play character parts in repertory company and summer stock productions. A final triumph came with the role of Bloody Mary in a 1951 Chicago production of *South Pacific* that toured until September 1952. She died in New York City.

• Gerald Bordman, *American Musical Theatre: A Chronicle* (1992), and Miles Kreuger, comp., *The Movie Musical from Vitaphone to 42nd Street* (1977), contain information on Bordoni's career. Reviews of her performances can be found in *New York Times Theatre Reviews*. Long obituaries are in the *New York Times*, 20 Mar. 1953, and *Variety*, 25 Mar. 1953.

G. F. GOODWIN

BOREMAN, Arthur Ingram (24 July 1823–19 Apr. 1896), lawyer and politician, was born in Waynesburg, Pennsylvania, the son of Kenner Seaton Boreman, a merchant, and Sarah Ingram. Kenner Boreman's father, John Boreman, was a Philadelphia merchant who served as assistant paymaster to the revolutionary army. Kenner Boreman moved his family to Middlebourne, Tyler County, Virginia, when Arthur was four. There Arthur attended a tuition-supported common school. In 1840 the family moved to Elizabethtown, Marshall County, where Arthur Boreman clerked in his father's store. At age twenty he returned to Middlebourne to read law with his brother and brother-in-law, and in 1845 he began practicing law in Parkersburg, Wood County.

From 1855 to 1861 Boreman represented Wood County in the Virginia House of Delegates as a Whig, opposing the dominant Democratic party, which he believed chiefly represented the planter and slaveowning interests of eastern Virginia. During the secession crisis, he joined the Unconditional Unionists in opposing secession, which he feared would mean the end of the best government in the world and a future of "impenetrable gloom."

Because of his outspoken Unionist stand, Boreman was chosen to preside over the Second Wheeling Convention (11–25 June and 6–21 Aug. 1861), which first organized a Restored Government of Virginia and then moved toward creation of a separate state. After the Second Wheeling Convention and while the movement for a separate state proceeded, Boreman served as a circuit judge of Reorganized Virginia, which, led by Governor Francis Pierpont, administered the Unionist counties of western Virginia from Wheeling.

On 24 October 1861 voters in forty-one western counties approved the idea of a separate state and elected members to a constitutional convention. On 13 May 1862 the General Assembly of the Reorganized Government of Virginia gave its consent to the formation of West Virginia, and after much debate Congress passed a statehood bill that required the new state to adopt a plan for the gradual emancipation of slaves. President Abraham Lincoln, distressed at the thought of disrupting the Old Dominion, delayed signing the statehood bill until the last possible moment, but he concluded that as a practical matter the government could not survive if it gave secessionists and loyal Unionists equal consideration.

The candidate of the Constitutional Union party, Boreman was elected the first governor of the new state in the elections on 28 May 1863. West Virginia officially became the thirty-fifth state of the Union on 20 June, when Boreman was inaugurated in ceremonies held at Wheeling, the capital. The new government continued to cooperate with the Pierpont government, which now moved to Alexandria and sought to expand the small Unionist remnant in Virginia while awaiting a move to Richmond. In 1864 Boreman married Laurane Tanner Bullock, a widow with four children. The Boremans had two more children.

Boreman presided over West Virginia's government during extremely difficult times, as the population was much divided over the Civil War and its aftermath. Many West Virginians sympathetic to the Confederacy fought as irregulars or bushwhackers, and some took advantage of the weakness of the new state to engage in robbery and murder. Boreman constantly urged Union military authorities to provide greater security against the irregular forces in West Virginia.

Upon the assassination of President Lincoln, Boreman feared for the survival of the new state. He hurried to Washington and met with the new president, Andrew Johnson, who assured Boreman that he would continue to support the new state and that he would recognize the Restored Government of Virginia as the official government of Virginia after the war. Such assurances encouraged Boreman and the Unconditional Unionists to join the Republican party.

The bitterness of the war spilled over into the postwar period, and West Virginia experienced a Reconstruction era similar to that of the former Confederate states, although racial tensions were less severe. In February 1865, on Boreman's recommendation, the legislature enacted a severe voters' test oath and other measures effectively proscribing teachers, attorneys, and others who did not support West Virginia or the Reorganized Government of Virginia. On 16 January 1866, responding to the outrage of Unionists disturbed by former Confederates eager "to repossess themselves of place and power," Boreman called for a tightening of restrictions, including voter registration boards and a disfranchising amendment to the constitution. Voters passed the measure on 24 May 1866, disqualifying 15,000 to 25,000 former Confederates. Boreman also deplored the depredations of violent criminals who, he charged, continued to operate with the support of disloyal persons. He promised free firearms and ammunition to loyal West Virginians who would "organize themselves into bands for the purpose of hunting down, capturing or killing such outlaws."

Twice reelected as governor, he resigned on 26 February 1869, four days before the expiration of his third term, in order to assure his election to the U.S. Senate by a friendly state senate. During his term as senator, from 1869 to 1875, Boreman served competently but without particular distinction. He chaired the Committees on Political Disabilities and Territories and served on the Manufactures and Claims committees. In West Virginia the Republican coalition of Unconditional Unionists and Conservative Unionists disintegrated as the Conservatives, disgruntled by emancipation and pressures to give freedmen suffrage, joined forces with returning Confederates to put Democrats in control of the state legislature. In 1871 the disfranchising amendment was replaced with one that gave the vote to all males over twenty-one, and a long period of Democratic domination in state politics began, ending any possibility of Boreman's reelection to the Senate.

In 1875 Boreman retired to private life, taking up again his law practice in Parkersburg. In 1888 he was again elected to the position of circuit judge and continued on the bench until his death at his home in Parkersburg.

As one of the founding fathers of West Virginia, Boreman made a substantial contribution to laying the foundations for the new state in the midst of much fratricidal strife. As governor for three terms, he led in building up a new government and new institutions from virtually nothing and reestablishing order where local authority had broken down. Others were more articulate and attracted more attention with speeches and pronouncements, but Boreman was the cohesive force that held the new government together in its perilous early years. Although he and fellow state makers were largely rejected by voters after 1871, they could take satisfaction in having created a new state free of slavery and in having founded most of West Virginia's modern institutions, including a system of free public schools and the state university.

• A small collection of Boreman letters is in the West Virginia Department of Archives and History in Charleston. A few letters from the period during which he was governor and personal and business papers relating primarily to his judgeship and to the law firm of Boreman and Bullock in Parkersburg are in the West Virginia and Regional History Collection, West Virginia University, Morgantown. Isaiah Alfonso Woodward, "Arthur Ingraham Boreman: A Biography," *West Virginia History* 31 (July 1970): 206–69, 32 (Oct. 1970): 10–48, is useful but uncritical, as is a brief essay, John G. Morgan, "Arthur Ingram Boreman, First Governor, 1863–1869," in *West Virginia Governors*, 2d ed. (1980). Brief general accounts of Boreman's role in the making of W.Va. are in Charles Henry Ambler and Festus Paul Summers, *West Virginia: The Mountain State*, 2d ed. (1958), and Otis K. Rice, *West Virginia: A History* (1985). See also Richard Orr Curry, *A House Divided: A Study of Statehood Politics and the Copperhead Movement in West Virginia* (1964), and Richard Lowe, *Republicans and Reconstruction in Virginia, 1856–1870* (1991).

JERRY BRUCE THOMAS

BORGLUM, Gutzon (25 Mar. 1867–6 Mar. 1941), sculptor, was born near Great Bear Lake in Idaho Territory, the son of Jens de la Mothe Borglum, a Mormon-convert carpenter from Denmark, and Christina Mikkelsen (later Cristine Michelson). Jens also had another wife, Christina's sister Ida. Christina was the mother both of the sculptor, christened John Gutzon de la Mothe Borglum, and of a second son. Ida also had a son by Jens. After Christina withdrew from the troublesome plural marriage, Jens took Ida and their son to St. Louis, became a physician, and changed his name to James Miller Borglum, practicing medicine in Fremont, Nebraska. Eventually he and Ida had a total of seven children. Gutzon attended school in Kansas City, Missouri, in 1882, worked in a machine shop in Omaha, became an apprentice lithographer in Los Angeles in 1883, and studied painting. In 1888 he completed a portrait of John C. Frémont so fine that the explorer's influential wife, Jesse Benton Frémont, was permanently impressed. Borglum took art lessons in Los Angeles from Elizabeth ("Lisa") Jaynes Putnam, who was eighteen years his senior and whom he married in 1889; the couple had no children. It is noteworthy that Borglum did much to aid his half-brothers Auguste, a musician, and Francis, a physician.

In 1890 Borglum and his wife went to Paris, where he studied painting and sculpture, even working under Auguste Rodin. After a brief visit to Spain, the Borglums resided in Sierra Madre, California, from 1893 to 1896. Borglum went to London in 1896, followed by his wife the next year. In 1901 they returned to Paris, where his brother Solon was already an established sculptor. Gutzon abandoned his wife, followed his brother to New York, became an adept sculptor, and by 1903 exhibited and was elected to the National Sculpture Society, only to resign in 1904 after a squabble over changing what Borglum regarded as the society's archaic rules. That summer he won a gold medal at the Louisiana Purchase International Exposition—commonly known as the St. Louis World's Fair—for one of two submissions, or possibly both. Amid much other work, he won a contract for his *Philip Sheridan*, unveiled in 1908 in Washington, D.C. This bronze equestrian statue shows the gaunt leader about to regroup his men after the Cedar Creek defeat. The energetic, nettlesome sculptor created an enormous bust of a brooding, shadowed Abraham Lincoln, based, Borglum said, on data in his private possession and carved directly into marble. He persuaded President Theodore Roosevelt to order it displayed in the White House in 1908. In 1909 Borglum obtained a "divorce" by contending that Lisa, who had been previously married, had never been legally divorced; he then married his young longtime secretary and companion Mary Montgomery. He and his new wife, an intelligent influence on him, bought an estate near Stamford, Connecticut—partly on borrowed funds, which were never repaid. He worked steadily, campaigned for Roosevelt and his Bull Moose party (1912), involved himself in the Stone Mountain project near Atlanta, Georgia (from 1915), and autonomously investigated the American aircraft industry (1917–1918) with President Woodrow Wilson's reluctant acquiescence.

After the war, Borglum returned to his Georgia project—planned as a quarter-mile granite carving of Confederate soldiers—but managed to finish only a twenty-foot head of Robert E. Lee (1924) before trouble caused the plan to be scuttled. The hot-tempered sculptor destroyed his models, to prevent their later use by others, and was almost arrested for doing so (1925). (His hatted, roughly bearded head of Lee was later blasted out of existence.) Meanwhile, publicity had already brought Borglum to the attention of South Dakotans who were envisioning mountain sculpture of their own—in the Black Hills. In 1924 Borglum chose Mount Rushmore. After much planning, he started work in 1927, was encouraged when Congress authorized funds in 1929, and with a veritable army of hoisted and sling-seated workmen substantially finished George Washington's sixty-foot head, with calm eyes and a grim mouth. Unveiled and dedicated in 1930, it was immediately visible sixty miles away. Controversies swirled about the combative, irascible artist, who had briefly joined the Ku Klux Klan in Georgia, had also made foolish, inconsistent anti-Semitic remarks, and was irresponsible in discussing and handling finances. Nonetheless, the dynamiting, pointing, drilling, and jackhammer carving proceeded on Mount Rushmore—all on a gargantuan scale. Gradually, the other three faces emerged in nearly final form and were dedicated, Thomas Jefferson in 1936, Abraham Lincoln in 1937, and Theodore Roosevelt, whose spectacles are abstractly hinted at, in 1939. Their enormous size is suggested by the fact that if each president were in full figure he would be 465 feet or more in height. Lincoln's nose measures eighteen feet; the pupil of each eye, four feet in diameter.

Before and even during his Mount Rushmore enterprise, Borglum designed and completed innumerable other sculptures. Of special note are the *Seated Lincoln*, with empty space about him poignantly suggesting his essential loneliness, and the panoramic *Wars of America* (both Newark, N.J.); the energetic, swirling, naturalistically detailed *Trail Drivers' Memorial* (San Antonio, Tex.); and the accurately muscled, fiercely vigorous *Mares of Diomedes* (New York City). For years he worked on dozens of statues for the Cathedral of St. John the Divine, in New York City. Individual memorials are almost legion. He created more items for Statuary Hall in the Capitol in Washington, D.C., than any other artist. The fate of his bronze *Woodrow Wilson*—caped, with right arm extended in peace, and placed in Poznan, Poland, in 1921—was ironic: it was destroyed by the German army in 1939 under orders from Adolf Hitler.

Borglum and his second wife had a son, Lincoln, and a daughter. Lincoln, who also became an excellent sculptor, assisted his father at Mount Rushmore and was superintendent of the project during its last six years. The aging sculptor submitted to prostate surgery in Chicago and died a few days later of a pulmonary embolism while still hospitalized.

Borglum, who constantly sought publicity, was a patriotic, contentious orator much in demand, an eager participant in sports (including boxing and fencing), an enthusiastic joiner, a generous neighbor, and a conscientious environmentalist. Many of his publications in journals and newspapers are of considerable interest. His "Art That Is Real and Beautiful" (*World's Work* 28 [June 1914]: 200–17) suggests that American sculptors should create art out of American history and not imitate Greek and Roman works that quite rightly expressed ancient triumphs. His "Moulding a Mountain" (*Forum* 70 [Oct. 1923]: 2019–26) is an illuminating account of his "herculean" work on the Stone Mountain project. Some of his writings, however, are shrill and even unreliable. For example, he called himself an aeronautical engineer, which he was not. More amusingly, he fibbed about the date and place of his birth, and even about which Mormon sister was his mother. His name, however, will be forever linked to that "Shrine of Democracy," the eternal granite faces jutting out of Mount Rushmore with startling clarity.

• Many of Borglum's papers, including diaries and autobiographical bits, are in the Library of Congress. Gerald W. Johnson, *The Undefeated* (1927), is a rather sentimental account of the Stone Mountain fiasco. Robert J. Casey and Mary Borglum, *Give the Man Room* (1952), includes personal information provided by Borglum's daughter. Rex Alan Smith, *The Carving of Mount Rushmore* (1985), details Borglum's most celebrated artistic endeavor. Howard Shaff and Audrey Karl Shaff, *Six Wars at a Time: The Life and Times of Gutzon Borglum, Sculptor of Mount Rushmore* (1985), is a painstakingly thorough biography, generously illustrated and listing his major works. A. Mervyn Davies, *Solon H. Borglum: A Man Who Stands Alone* (1974), touches on the competitive relationship of the two sculptor brothers. An obituary is in the *New York Times*, 7 Mar. 1941.

ROBERT L. GALE

BORGLUM, Solon Hannibal (22 Dec. 1868–31 Jan. 1922), sculptor, was born in Ogden, Utah, the son of James (Jens) de la Mothe Borglum, a woodcarver turned doctor, and Christina Michelson. Solon's parents had immigrated to America from Denmark in the mid-1860s. They settled in Salt Lake City, Utah, and became Mormon converts. Jens, Christina, and her sister Ida were in the same polygamous union, which was then permitted by the Mormon church. Shortly after the birth of their two children, however, Jens and Christina decided to have their marriage dissolved, whereupon Ida came to be regarded as Solon's mother.

Borglum grew up in the Nebraska frontier towns of Fremont and Omaha before moving with his family to St. Louis. Not fond of school, Borglum thrived in the outdoors, often accompanying his father on medical rounds. He enjoyed nature and wildlife, in particular horses, which he supposedly learned to ride before he could walk. These early experiences prepared him to herd and rope cattle as a cowboy in southern California and at his father's newly acquired 6,000-acre ranch in central Nebraska. Initially Borglum was a self-taught artist, sketching horses and landscapes. His older brother Gutzon, also an artist, later renowned for his carvings of presidential portraits on Mount Rushmore in South Dakota, encouraged him to develop his talent, and following this advice, Borglum studied from 1890 to 1893 with the local painter John Laurie Wallace, a former student of Thomas Eakins. In 1893 Borglum left the family ranch and stayed for a brief period with his brother and sister-in-law in Sierra Madre, California, where the brothers shared a studio. He subsequently worked as an itinerant artist in Los Angeles, California, eventually moving in 1895 to Cincinnati, Ohio, where he enrolled at the Art Academy and studied under Louis T. Rebisso. Inspired by the horses used in the U.S. postal service and his experience of dissecting dead animals at a veterinary school, Borglum modeled clay sculptures of horses. A few of them won prizes, earning him enough money to travel to Paris from 1897 to 1899, "to look around."

Borglum arrived in Paris with only a Nebraska oil stove and a blanket from home. He studied under Denys Puech at the Académie Julian, but he resolved never to let his work "lose its stamp of American life" (Davies, p. 48). This determination was evident in his sculptures, which reflected his experiences of growing up and being a part of the American West, observing the cowboys, pioneers, and Native Americans involved in their daily activities. Most scenes Borglum created were about the drama of humans interacting with horses and the forces of nature. The French were fascinated with Borglum and his work, and numerous newspaper articles referred to his early life on the prairie. Borglum studied the sculptures of the old masters at the Louvre and Luxembourg Gardens and the live animals at the Jardins des Plantes and a livery stable on Boulevard Raspail. Impressed by his work, the animal sculptor Emmanuel Frémiet said, "You are lucky, sir. Many young men go to art school and come out polished with nothing to say. You lived, you had something to say, then you began to think about art" (Davies, p. 41). Borglum's bronzes won prizes at the Paris Salon in 1898 and 1899, and his *Stampede of Wild Horses* was placed at the entrance to the United States Pavilion of the Exposition Universelle in Paris (1900). Borglum's sensitive and warm personality earned him friends wherever he went, including the American sculptors who were then working in Paris, Augustus Saint-Gaudens and Frederick MacMonnies.

In 1900 Borglum returned permanently to the United States with his new bride, Emma Vignal, the daughter of a French Protestant clergyman; eventually the couple had three children. That year they summered at the Crow Creek Reservation in South Dakota, where Borglum created some of his finest work. In 1901 he established a studio in New York City, but ultimately he made Rocky Ranch in Silvermine, Connecticut, his permanent residence and atelier in 1906. By this time his reputation in the United States was established, as his busts and small bronzes of pioneer subject matter were becoming immensely popular with turn-of-the-century patrons. Some of his best-known large-scale groups included the eleven works he submitted for the 1901 Pan-American Exposition in Buffalo, New York, and four staff works (plaster and lath) exhibited on the grounds of the Great Louisiana Purchase Exposition in St. Louis (1904). Notable single-figure equestrian portraits included depictions of General John B. Gordon (Atlanta State House, Ga.) and Bucky O'Neill, a Rough Rider (Prescott, Ariz.). Elected to the council of the National Sculpture Society in 1904, Borglum became an associate member of the National Academy of Design seven years later. The American sculptor Paul Manship worked as an assistant in Borglum's studio from 1905 to 1907 and acknowledged the tremendous influence Borglum had on his own development as an artist.

Borglum was one of a number of sculptors who either came from the West or lived there long enough to make frontier life their primary subject matter. By the early 1900s the "Indian threat" was no longer a concern, and it became popular to romanticize the Native Americans, even to sympathize with them without sentimentality or melodrama. Borglum worked in a realist tradition similar to that of his contemporary Frederick Remington, rendering as authentically and accurately as possible every detail, including the straining muscles of horse and rider and the complete gear and accessories found in a typical equestrian group. Whatever his theme, Borglum was praised by artists and critics alike for capturing the spirit and dignity of his figures.

In World War I, Borglum was accepted by the Young Men's Christian Association for overseas canteen duty. These services took him to Paris, where he was assigned to the French army and, among other things, ran a *Foyer du Soldat*. For his duty he was awarded the Croix de Guerre for "great capacity for organization, generosity and qualities of heart" (Davies, p. 207). After the war Borglum became the director of sculpture at the American Expeditionary Forces Art Training Center at Bellevue, in Seine-et-Oise, a Paris suburb.

During the last years of his life Borglum became increasingly involved with teaching. In 1920 he opened a school of sculpture in New York City and prepared *Sound Construction*, his illustrated instruction manual of comparative anatomy for artists. It was published in 1923 after his death in New York resulting from complications following an appendectomy in 1922.

• The Solon H. Borglum Papers and the Solon Borglum Scrapbook are located at the Library of Congress, and a copy is at the Archives of American Art in Washington, D.C. For Borglum's own manual of instruction, containing hundreds of his drawings, see *Sound Construction* (1923). For an extensive biography, see A. Mervyn Davies. *Solon H. Borglum: A Man Who Stands Alone* (1974). Borglum was included in Charles H. Caffin, *American Masters of Sculpture* (1903), and Lorado Taft, *The History of American Sculpture* (1930). Borglum has been discussed in Wayne Craven, *Sculpture in America* (1968), and Richard H. Saunders, *Collecting the West: The C. R. Smith Collection of Western American Art* (1988). For Paul Manship on Borglum, see the Paul Manship Interview at the Archives of American Art. For Gutzon Borglum on his brother, see Howard and Audrey Karl Shaff, *Six Wars at a Time* (1985), and Gutzon Borglum's letter in the *New York Times*, 5 Mar. 1922, reprinted with illustrations in the *American Magazine of Art*, Nov. 1922. Borglum sculpture exhibitions include *Solon H. Borglum* at the National Collection of Fine Arts, Smithsonian Institution, Washington, D.C. (1972), and *The Solon H. Borglum Collection* at the New Britain Museum of American Art, New Britain, Conn. (1982); exhibition publications were produced for both occasions. An obituary is in the *New York Times*, 31 Jan. 1922.

EFRAM BURK

BORING, Edwin Garrigues (23 Oct. 1886–1 July 1968), psychologist, was born in Philadelphia, Pennsylvania, the son of Edwin McCurdy Boring, a pharmacist, and Elizabeth Garrigues. Boring was reared in cramped quarters above the family drugstore and was not allowed to play with other children. He grew up with an intense desire to escape the stifling confines of the Moravian-Quaker household in which he was viewed as a problem child because of his hyperactivity. Although kept out of school until the age of nine and physically awkward, Boring excelled at the Friends Select School and found electrical engineering first an exciting hobby and then a rationale for escaping his father's hope that he would follow him into the pharmacy. Boring entered Cornell in 1904 and earned his M.E. in 1908, but he struggled to earn ordinary grades. He quit his first job with the Bethlehem Steel Company when offered a promotion, fearing that he might remain an engineer for the rest of his life. An elective psychology course at Cornell, taught by the charismatic E. B. Titchener, had exposed Boring to the ideal of pure research. After a year of teaching science at a Moravian school (1909–1910), Boring returned to Cornell, where he found his calling as an experimental psychologist. In 1914 he received the Ph.D. and married Lucy May Day, who in 1912 had also earned a Ph.D. from Cornell. They had four children.

Beginning in 1912, Boring established his credentials as an experimental psychologist in a series of monographs that included studies of the regeneration of a nerve that he severed in his forearm and of the sensitivity of the alimentary canal and stomach, based upon his mastery in swallowing stomach tubes. Despite his mentor Titchener's emphasis on a pure science of psychophysics and contempt for applied and comparative psychology, Boring maintained a wider perspective in studies of light sensitivity in worms and learning among schizophrenics.

When the United States entered World War I in 1917, Boring left Cornell to work with Robert M. Yerkes, the director of the U.S. Army's mental testing program. After the war Boring stayed with Yerkes to help write the massive National Academy of Sciences monograph that described the tests and made sweeping claims for them as a scientific technology. Although Boring maintained theoretical distance from the test-based claims made by Yerkes and his protégés concerning the inferior mental abilities of immigrants and African Americans, he remained a loyal member of the wartime testing fraternity. In public criticism of the reasoning from statistics made by the mental testers, Boring provided one of his disarming witticisms when he proclaimed that, regardless of the methodological flaws of mental testers, no harm need result if everyone kept in mind that "intelligence is what the tests test" (*New Republic*, 6 June 1923, p. 35).

In 1919 Boring accepted a three-year appointment as professor of experimental psychology at Clark University. Although he quickly established a productive research group, after G. Stanley Hall's retirement in 1920 Boring found himself at odds with President Wallace Atwood, who wanted to emphasize undergraduate education and disciplines other than psychology. In 1922, unsure of his future at Clark because of his public association with a group of faculty critical of Atwood's policies, Boring accepted an appointment as associate professor at Harvard, where psychology was still an orientation within the Department of Philosophy.

Boring succeeded in winning a strong institutional position for psychology at Harvard through 84-hour work weeks and ruthless dedication to his vision of psychology as an exact experimental science. Although Boring published little experimental work of his own, he established a laboratory in which work in the psychophysics of perception and sensation thrived; he also won a loyal following as a dedicated teacher and published histories of psychology and textbooks that provided intellectual coherence for an eclectic academic discipline. Boring's services to his profession were recognized in 1928 with his election as president of the American Psychological Association and his promotion to full professor and in 1934 with his appointment as the first chairman of the new Department of Psychology. From 1925 to 1946 Boring served as coeditor of the *American Journal of Psychology*, and from 1956 to 1961 he was the founding editor of *Contemporary Psychology*.

During World War II Boring served his profession as a member of the Survey and Planning Committee of the American Psychological Association, which set the conditions for professional expansion by including applied psychologists and other specialists. Boring also convinced the National Research Council's Emergency Committee in Psychology that the discipline should provide a handbook for soldiers. Drawing upon the expertise of fifty-two academic specialists and two coeditors, Boring molded *Psychology for the Fighting Man* (1943) into a popular introduction to the value of the psychological perspective for the common man; the book sold 380,000 copies. A second book, *Psychology for the Armed Services* (1945), intended as a college text, was less successful but asserted the value of psychology for military leaders.

By 1946 Boring was widely recognized as "Mr. Psychology," a chief spokesperson and power broker within his academic culture. In 1959 the American Psychological Association awarded him its Gold Medal. He was acutely self-conscious of the contrast between his visibility as the spokesman for a scientific discipline and his modest productivity as an experimental scientist. Boring's professional salience rested upon his ability to reconcile competing tendencies within his discipline and to maintain the ideal of the tightly knit research community in the challenging environment of the expansive research university. While he aggressively opposed the appointment or promotion at Harvard of those who represented humanistic or social approaches in psychology, he accepted the creation of the Department of Social Relations in 1945 and rationalized the differences with his colleagues by explaining that they were "sociotropic" and his experimentalists were "biotropic." A willing servant of many organizations devoted to promoting psychology as an academic discipline, Boring led his colleagues by providing them with perspective and rhetoric that legitimated their vocation and helped them to live with their differences. He died in Cambridge, Massachusetts.

• Boring's papers are in the Harvard University Archives, Cambridge, Mass. His books include *A History of Experimental Psychology* (1929; rev. ed., 1950); *The Physical Dimensions of Consciousness* (1933); *Psychology: A Factual Textbook*, ed. with H. S. Langfeld and H. P. Weld (1935; rev. eds., 1939 and 1948); *Sensation and Perception in the History of Experimental Psychology* (1942); *Psychologist at Large* (1961); *History, Psychology, and Science* (1963); and *Source Book in the History of Psychology*, with Richard J. Herrnstein (1965).

Important memoirs and interpretations of his work include S. S. Stevens, "Edwin Garrigues Boring," National Academy of Sciences, *Biographical Memoirs* 43 (1973): 41–76, which includes a bibliography; Julian Jaynes, "Edwin Garrigues Boring," *Journal of the History of the Behavioral Sciences* 5 (1969): 99–112; Frany Samelson, "E. G. Boring and His History of Experimental Psychology," *American Psychologist* 35 (1980): 467–70; Robert M. Young, "Scholarship and the History of the Behavioural Sciences," *History of Science* 5 (1966): 1–51; John M. O'Donnell, "The Crisis of Experimentalism in the 1920s: E. G. Boring and His Uses of History," *American Psychologist* 34 (1979): 289–95; and James H. Capshew, *Psychologists on the March: Science, Practice, and Professional Identity in America, 1929–1969* (1997). An obituary is in the *New York Times*, 2 July 1968.

JAMES W. REED

BORLAND, Solon (8 Aug. 1811–15 Dec. 1864), editor, U.S. senator, and diplomat, was born in Suffolk, Virginia, the son of Thomas Wood Borland, a physician, and Harriet Godwin. His father was politically active, serving as a member of the Virginia House of Delegates from Nansemond County between 1815 and 1820. In 1831 Borland married Huldah Wright, with whom he had two children. Following in the medical footsteps of his father, he attended the University of Pennsylvania Medical School during the academic year of 1833–1834. He then practiced medicine in Suffolk, but upon the death of his wife in 1836 Borland moved to Memphis, Tennessee. There he entered into a medical career with his brother, who was also a physician. In 1839 Borland married Eliza Hart, who died just a few months later. They had no children. By this time he had forsaken pills for politics, becoming the founding editor of the *Western World and Memphis Banner of the Constitution*, a Democratic paper, in January 1839. Four years later, the Arkansas Democratic party hired him to edit their newly created organ, the *Arkansas Banner*, in Little Rock.

Although the *Arkansas Banner* appeared in September 1843, Borland did not arrive in Little Rock until late November. He soon displayed his violent temper, assaulting Whig editor Benjamin J. Borden and, according to one witness, beating his rival's face into jelly. In 1845 Borland married Mary Isabel Milbourne, with whom he had three children.

Borland embraced President James K. Polk's policy of Manifest Destiny and volunteered for military service at the outbreak of the Mexican War. Captured in northern Mexico on 23 January 1847, he was held for months as a prisoner of war before he managed to escape from Mexico City. He participated in the final American attack in September 1847.

When Borland returned to Arkansas, Governor Thomas S. Drew appointed him to fill a vacancy in the U.S. Senate in March 1848. He was elected to a full Senate term the following fall. Although elected as a Democrat, Borland was opposed to the major Conway-Sevier-Johnson families, who dominated the Arkansas Democratic party. In the Senate, he initiated congressional action on a western branch for the federal court (the future position of the famous Arkansas "hanging" judge Isaac C. Parker), swampland reclamation in Arkansas, and back pay for American prisoners of war.

During the compromise crisis of 1850, Borland vociferously defended southern rights, even physically attacking Mississippi senator Henry S. Foote, who had called Borland a "servile" disciple of John C. Calhoun. Borland discovered that Arkansas public opinion did not support his opposition to the compromise. In a speech in Little Rock in July 1850 the Arkansas senator denounced abolitionists and admitted that he liked neither California coming in as a free state nor ending the slave trade in the District of Columbia. However, he concluded his address by expressing veneration for the Union. Borland never returned to Washington to vote on the Compromise of 1850, and this absence appeared as acquiescence to the accord.

Borland maintained his interest in expansionism. He opposed the 1850 Clayton-Bulwer Treaty, because it placed undue limits on U.S. expansion and it violated the Monroe Doctrine by calling for British participation in any future interoceanic canal project in Central America. Such views were apparently welcomed in the Franklin Pierce administration, so Borland was appointed in 1853 as envoy extraordinary and minister plenipotentiary to Central America, assigned to Nicaragua. Since the Arkansas senator had been involved in a series of Washington brawls, some questioned his diplomatic abilities.

Borland resigned his Senate seat in April 1853 and submitted his credentials to the Nicaraguan government on 14 September. As minister he called for the repudiation of the Clayton-Bulwer Treaty and urged his government to militarily support Honduras in its efforts to remove the British from the Honduran Bay Islands. In mid-October Borland declared in Granada that it was "his greatest ambition to see the State of Nicaragua forming a bright star in the flag of the United States." This speech, given before an audience that included the British vice consul to El Salvador, plus Borland's complaints and demands provoked a reprimand from Secretary of State William L. Marcy that in turn prompted Borland's resignation.

While leaving Nicaragua on 16 May 1854, Borland interfered with the arrest of an American citizen in San Juan del Norte (or Greytown). He was almost arrested but claimed diplomatic immunity, and someone smashed a bottle in his face. The enraged diplomat reported the incident to his government. President Pierce sent a naval warship to demand an apology, but the local governing officials had fled. On 13 July 1854 the U.S. Navy bombarded the town and sent marines to burn what remained, an early example of gunboat diplomacy. It is difficult to judge the full impact of the bombardment of San Juan del Norte, but it may have made the Pierce administration more wary of becoming involved in Central America.

Borland journeyed back to Little Rock, where he soon reentered local politics. The Whigs collapsed by the mid-1850s, and he became in 1855 editor of the *Arkansas Gazette*, the main organ of the American party, a new and short-lived opposition party to the Democrats. Through the *Arkansas Gazette* Borland was able to attack the ruling clique of the Democratic party. By 1857 he retired from politics and returned to Memphis to practice medicine. He reappeared in the Arkansas capital to campaign for the Constitutional Union party in the fall of 1860.

After Fort Sumter, Arkansas governor Henry M. Rector appointed Borland commander of the militia and ordered him to seize the Federal arsenal in Fort Smith, even though the state had not yet formally seceded. Borland arrived on 23 April 1861 to find the Federals had already departed with their supplies. The Arkansas secession convention replaced him as head of the militia the next month. That summer he entered the Confederate service and was placed as commander over northeastern Arkansas. In this capacity, on 29 November, Borland ordered martial law, citing as his reason the runaway inflation in his area. Governor Rector rescinded this order the next month, yet Borland denied that Arkansas's chief executive could countermand a Confederate officer. By January 1862 Confederate secretary of war Judah P. Benjamin revoked Borland's order. Borland was out of Confederate service by March, the *Arkansas Gazette* maintaining that, at fifty years old, he was physically unable to continue in the military.

In June 1862 Borland resumed his medical practice in Little Rock. In October that year his third wife died. Borland wrote his will in Arkansas's last Confederate capital, Washington, on 31 December 1863. Some sources say he died in Houston, Texas, but this cannot be confirmed.

• Many accounts of Borland's life and career contain errors, especially regarding the date and place of his birth, his early education, his Civil War career, and the date of his death. A copy of Borland's will and its probation are in the Arkansas History Commission, Little Rock. For his career in Ark. see the small manuscript holdings on him in the Arkansas History Commission. See also the existing copies of the newspapers he edited, the Little Rock *Arkansas Banner* and the Little Rock *Arkansas Gazette*. For an accurate look at his family background see "Notes and Queries: The Borlands and Godwins," *Virginia Magazine of History and Biography* 17 (1909): 97–98. For a secondary account of Borland's antebellum Ark. political career, consult James M. Woods, *Rebellion and Realignment: Arkansas's Road to Secession* (1987). His role as editor within local politics and society is stressed in Margaret Ross, "*Arkansas Gazette*": *The Early Years, 1819–1866* (1969). Borland's career in the Mexican War up until his capture is told in William W. Hughes, *Archibald Yell* (1988). His short career as a diplomat is presented in Woods, "Expansionism as Diplomacy: The Career of Solon Borland in Central America, 1853–1854," *Americas: A Quarterly Review of Inter-American Cultural History* 40 (Jan. 1984): 399–415. His Civil War career is presented by Michael B. Dougan, *Confederate Arkansas: The People and Politics of a Frontier State in Wartime* (1976). Borland's career in Memphis is briefly mentioned in Thomas H. Baker, *The Memphis Commercial Appeal: The History of a Southern Newspaper* (1971).

JAMES M. WOODS

BORTHWICK, John David (1824–21 Dec. 1892), artist and writer, was born in Edinburgh, Scotland, the son of George Augustus Borthwick, a physician, and Janet Kinnear. He attended Edinburgh Academy and also took private art lessons. At age eighteen he received an inheritance, which he chose to use for travel. He first toured Europe and then in 1847 sailed to the New World. He journeyed to eastern Canada, then to New York City where he heard of the gold rush and was, in his words, "seized with the California fever."

In May 1850 he sailed from New York on a small, overcrowded ship bound for Panama. On reaching

Chagres, the sixty passengers learned that they were responsible for making their own way across the isthmus. Breaking into groups, they hired boats to row them up the Chagres River, and in weather that Borthwick described as alternating between "scorching heat" and "drenching rain," they took turns at the oars. At Cruces, the passengers disembarked and walked for two days to reach Panama City. Finding no space available on the departing mail steamer, Borthwick joined the thousands of impatient goldseekers idling about the "gay" but "outrageously filthy" city whose hotels were all "crammed full." During weeks of awaiting passage on a steamer, he met with a serious accident—upon which he declined to elaborate—and was confined to bed. Upon recovery, he resorted to boarding another small sailing vessel, which was "most shamefully ill supplied with provisions." Their voyage was plagued by fierce gales, followed by periods when they were becalmed; to avert starvation, passengers shot and ate porpoises.

In late September the vessel limped into San Francisco, and Borthwick proceeded inland to the goldfields. After mastering the art of prospecting, he was fortunate enough to make a lucky strike on Weber Creek. Several weeks of mining, however, convinced him that his true interest lay not in accumulating gold, but in exploring the "miraculous" international community gathered at the mines. Commencing in California's northern goldfields, he embarked upon a walking tour of the gold camps, making sketches and taking notes as he traveled. In January 1852 the *Illustrated London News* printed an article that Borthwick had submitted, thus making him one of the first artist-correspondents to cover the gold rush for a British newspaper. Later he also contributed to American periodicals, such as *Hutchings' California Magazine*, *Gleason's Pictorial Drawing Room Companion*, and *Harper's Weekly*. The latter gave one of his illustrated articles a two-page spread.

In late 1853 Borthwick followed the gold rush to Australia and from 1854 to 1856 covered Nicaragua's civil war for *Blackwood's Edinburgh Magazine*. While touring Nicaraguan battlefields, he met and recorded his impressions of American adventurer William Walker, who entered the war on the side of the Nicaraguan Democrats and led them to victory over the Legitimists. After the peace, Borthwick returned to Scotland and compiled his New World adventures in an illustrated book entitled *Three Years in California* (1857), which was reprinted without illustrations in the United States as *The Gold Hunters* (1917).

Determined to devote the remainder of his life to pursuing an artist's career, Borthwick moved to London. There he spent the next eight years painting oils of domestic scenes, the English countryside, and his recollections of the California gold rush. Though he held occasional showings at the Royal Society of British Artists, the Royal Academy of Arts, the British Institution, and Dudley's Gallery, he had no recorded sales. Thus his known paintings—*Too Many Cooks*, *The Man at the Wheel*, *Dead Broke*, *In Hertfordshire*, and *The Miner's Grave, California*—are all untraceable. After his final exhibition (1867), he remained in London, living in a rented room of a family home. When he developed throat cancer, his niece came to reside with him, and she took care of him in London until his death. Borthwick died in obscurity and poverty.

Despite his failure to gain fame as a painter, Borthwick's illustrated writings have captured for posterity the panorama of the California gold rush. Among his memorable images of the robust 1850s mining society is the following description of a ball held at Angel's Camp, California:

> It was a strange sight to see a party of long-bearded men, in heavy boots and flannel shirts, going through all the steps and figures of the dance with so much spirit, and often with a great deal of grace, hearty enjoyment depicted on their dried-up sunburned faces, and revolvers and bowie-knives glancing in their belts. . . . Every gentleman who had a patch on a certain part of his inexpressibles should be considered a lady for the time being. These patches were rather fashionable.

Borthwick's vivid drawings of the gold camps—the gambling halls, bull and bear fights, mining enterprises, and now-vanished towns—are unmatched in both workmanship and historical value. Likewise, his book is one of the most complete and entertaining gold rush accounts available. With rare wit, the keen eye of an artist, and historical insight, he narrated such momentous events as the great Sacramento flood, the Hangtown lynchings, the burning of the town of Sonora, skirmishes between Indians and miners, and the execution of a woman in the remote camp of Downieville.

Borthwick surpassed his contemporary journalists in his analysis of the impact of the gold rush upon the world, pointing out, for example, that California's international mining society would have a profound democratizing influence upon the rest of the world. He predicted that the United States would play a major role in future world affairs, and his perceptive probing of the American character remains relevant. Though he deplored the Americans' coarseness, boastfulness, penchant for expansion, and "utter contempt on the natives," he praised their democratic spirit, ingenuity, and skill for self-rule in the wilderness and for colonization. "It is a fixed idea with the American people," he wrote in *Blackwood's Edinburgh Magazine* (Mar. 1856), "that in due course of time they are to have the control of all the North American continent." Though he warned Central Americans that accepting aid from the United States would result in a loss of national autonomy, he emphasized the economic and social benefits of such aid. The theme of an enlightened world community, inspired by America's best traits, runs through Borthwick's writings, and his vision of international brotherhood is evident in his gold rush art.

• The best sources for viewing Borthwick's art are *Harper's Weekly*, 3 Oct. 1857, pp. 632–34; *Gleason's Pictorial Drawing*

Room Companion, 27 Mar. 1852, p. 197; and the *Illustrated London News*, 24 Jan. 1852, pp. 73–74. The Society of California Pioneers in San Francisco owns two Borthwick pencil drawings, which scholars may view by appointment. A biography, R. E. Mather and F. E. Boswell, *John David Borthwick: Artist of the Gold Rush* (1988), includes a collection of ten of the artist's lithographs, and his *Three Years in California* (1857) contains eight lithographs. A lengthy review of Borthwick's book appears in *Blackwood's Edinburgh Magazine*, Apr. 1857, pp. 480–89.

RUTH E. MATHER

BORZAGE, Frank (23 Apr. 1894–19 June 1962), motion-picture director and producer, was born in Salt Lake City, Utah, the son of Lewis Borzage, a mason and cattle rancher, and Maria Ruegg. As a teenager Borzage began acting with traveling theater groups. By 1913 he had arrived in Hollywood; after mostly bit appearances for the Universal and Lubin film companies, he began playing leads and villains for Thomas Ince's company. He began directing films starring himself—fifteen in 1916 alone—some of which he also scripted. Most were two- and three-reelers distributed by the Mutual Film Corporation. The first of these, the western *The Pitch o' Chance* (1915), is one of the few Borzage films of this period even partially extant. In 1917 and 1918 he was directing five-reelers for producer Allan Dwan and the Triangle Film Corporation; his appearances in these films were generally reduced to supporting roles.

In 1920 Borzage began directing films for William Randolph Hearst's Cosmopolitan Productions, distributed by Paramount Pictures. *Humoresque* (1920), scripted by Frances Marion from a story by Fanny Hurst, was an enormous critical and popular success; it was followed over the next three years by six more films for Cosmopolitan, three of them from Hurst stories. In late 1925, after two years directing for First National and Metro-Goldwyn-Mayer, Borzage signed with the Fox Film Corporation, directing six films in 1925–1926. In 1927 Borzage directed *Seventh Heaven*, a smash hit and his greatest success. In the film, which takes place in Paris, a young sewer worker (Charles Farrell) falls in love with an orphaned petty thief (Janet Gaynor). They are separated by World War I, but their sublime love reunites them at the armistice. At the first Academy Awards ceremony, Borzage won as best director, Gaynor as best actress; the adaptation by Benjamin Glazer was also honored. *Seventh Heaven* was Borzage's first film available with a Movietone syncronized musical score.

Borzage followed with another intense, lyrical romance starring Farrell and Gaynor, *Street Angel* (1928), which was also a triumph both critically and at the box office. Two similar romances followed, both with talking sequences, *The River* (1928) and *Lucky Star* (1929). Borzage was now at the peak of his career, one of the highest-paid filmmakers in Hollywood, earning more than $200,000 a year from Fox. He made two early talkies with Will Rogers, but his next big success came with *Bad Girl* (1931), a modest film with James Dunn and Sally Eilers as a couple struggling to preserve their love in the face of depression-era tenement life. The film was a popular hit and earned Borzage another Academy Award as best director. After two more films for Fox in 1932, Borzage directed *A Farewell to Arms* for Paramount, with Gary Cooper and Helen Hayes. He was involved in extensive preparations for *Cavalcade*, but disagreed with the studio over its direction. His fruitful relationship with Fox, the most successful period of his career, was over.

In great demand in Hollywood, Borzage remade as a talkie his own 1924 silent film *Secrets* (1933), now notable as Mary Pickford's final film. For Columbia, he made two films, including *Man's Castle* (1933), another depression romance about a couple (Spencer Tracy and Loretta Young) desperately eking out life in a Hooverville shack. For Universal, Borzage worked on the preparations for *Showboat*, but the only film he completed for the studio was *Little Man, What Now?* (1934), also about a struggling depression couple, this time in Germany. This was the first of four films Borzage made with Margaret Sullavan.

Signing with Warner Bros., Borzage directed six films for that studio over the next three years, including musicals, romances, and dramas, as well as filling in at Paramount for Ernst Lubitsch on *Desire* (1936), with Gary Cooper and Marlene Dietrich. He also directed *History Is Made at Night* (1937) for Walter Wanger and United Artists, with Jean Arthur and Charles Boyer. In 1937 he parted with Warner and signed a five-year contract with Metro-Goldwyn-Mayer, for whom he completed ten films featuring the studio's biggest stars. In *Three Comrades* (1938) he was reunited with Sullavan in a film from a screenplay coauthored by F. Scott Fitzgerald. The film focuses on three war veterans, in Germany between the wars, who transcend tragedy through the help of a young woman.

Borzage's *Strange Cargo* (1940), with Clark Gable and Joan Crawford, depicts a similar spiritual transformation. A criminal and a prostitute flee a tropical island prison and are brought to a new sense of values by a Christlike figure who shares their torment and suffering. *The Mortal Storm* (1940), featuring Sullavan and James Stewart, was the only Hollywood film of this era to directly portray the moral degradation of the coming of Nazism. A family is nearly destroyed as the fascists' anti-intellectual race theories come to dominate a small university town. *The Mortal Storm* was the third of Borzage's films about the spiritual crisis in Germany.

After several years of freelance directing, Borzage signed his last long-term contract, a profit-participation deal, with Republic Pictures. There he directed several low-budget films, including *I've Always Loved You* (1946) and *Moonrise* (1948). Though strikingly filmed and well reviewed, *Moonrise*, his third and last film for Republic, was not a box-office triumph. Borzage ceased directing films for a decade, pursuing business and sporting interests instead. His final films were *China Doll* (1958), for United Artists, and *The*

Big Fisherman (1959), a three-hour biblical epic in widescreen and color.

Frank Borzage was married three times: to Rena Rogers in 1916 (divorced 1940); to Edna Stilwell Skelton in 1945 (divorced 1949); and to Juanita Scott in 1953. He had no children.

Like his contemporary John Ford, Borzage was a filmmaker very much in the tradition of D. W. Griffith. His romantic melodramas are concerned with nothing less than the salvation of his characters. In his films his characters face the extremes of hardship and peril, from war, poverty, and disaster, but the filmmaker's focus is on their spiritual journeys. The peace achieved by these figures at the end of the films comes from the discovery of selfless love that transcends mortal problems. As John Belton has pointed out, Borzage's theme is explicitly summarized in the opening title of *Street Angel*, "human souls made great by love and adversity."

Frank Borzage died in Los Angeles.

• The early examinations of Frank Borzage's films are in French, in Ado Kyrou's *Amour, éroticisme et cinéma* (1957) and in Henri Agel and Michael Henry's entry on him in *Anthologie du cinéma* (1973). Andrew Sarris summarizes Borzage's themes in *The American Cinema* (1968). See also the special issue devoted to Borzage of *Focus!* 9 (Summer 1973), and Robert E. Smith, "The Films of Frank Borzage," pts. 1 and 2, respectively, *Bright Lights* (Spring 1975), pp. 4–13, and (Summer 1975), pp. 15–22. John Belton explores Borzage's works in *The Hollywood Professionals: Howard Hawks, Frank Borzage, Edgar G. Ulmer*, vol. 3 (1974) and *Cinema Stylists* (1983). The only book-length study of Borzage's films in English is Frederick Lamster, *Souls Made Great through Love and Adversity: The Film Work of Frank Borzage* (1981). The only book-length critical biography is in French, Herve Dumont, *Frank Borzage: Sarastro à Hollywood* (1993); a chapter from this work appears in English in a special Borzage issue of *Griffithiana* 46 (Dec. 1992). An obituary is in the *New York Times*, 20 June 1962.

JONATHAN KUNTZ

BOSONE, Reva Beck (2 Apr. 1895–21 July 1983), judge and congresswoman, was born in American Fork, Utah, the daughter of Christian M. Beck, a hotel and livery stable owner, and Zilpha Ann Chipman, manager of the hotel. Descended both from Mayflower ancestors and early Utah Mormon pioneers, she was born into a family that emphasized education for both boys and girls. She graduated from Westminster Junior College in 1917 and from the University of California at Berkeley in 1919. She taught speech, drama, and debate in several Utah high schools for seven years before entering the University of Utah College of Law in 1927. There she met and married, in 1929, fellow student Joseph P. Bosone. She received an LL.B. in 1930, shortly before the birth of her daughter.

In 1931 the Bosones moved to Helper, a coal-mining community in central Utah, where Bosone practiced law with her husband. In this community of diverse European ethnic groups she was elected in 1932 to the Utah State House of Representatives as a Democrat. In her elected position she seemed to fulfill her mother's admonition: "a country is no better than its laws; if you want to do good, go where the laws are made." After the Bosones moved their law practice to Salt Lake City, she was elected to the Utah House in 1934 from her new urban district. Her colleagues elected her as majority party floor leader—the first woman in this position—and chair of the crucial Sifting Committee, which could advance bills to floor action or kill them. She was able to obtain passage of a minimum wage and hour law for women and children and an amendment to the Utah State Constitution to assure its constitutionality in 1933. In 1935 she won a close battle to obtain the legislature's ratification of the proposed Child Labor Amendment to the U.S. Constitution.

In 1936 Bosone's career took a new turn when she was the first woman elected a Salt Lake City judge. She undertook the least-desired assignment for a judge, that of presiding over the police and traffic court—a position that usually made more enemies than friends. She immediately gained local attention with her stiff fines for traffic offenders, which were sometimes twice as high as other judges had been imposing, and she instituted a successful traffic school. Salt Lake City's traffic accident rate dropped, and Bosone built a reputation that enhanced her political career. The public applauded her tough approach; in 1940 and 1944 she was reelected to the bench.

Divorced in 1940, she gained attention in the 1940s for vigorous activities off the bench as well as for her hard-line decisions as a judge. During the late 1940s she was in demand as a witty and stimulating public speaker. She also hosted a weekly KDYL radio program, "Her Honor—the Judge," which provided a platform for her views on crime, prostitution, juvenile delinquency, alcoholism, and other social issues.

In 1948 she became the first Utah woman elected to the U.S. House of Representatives. She became the first woman to gain a seat on the Interior Affairs Committee, where she sponsored and supported various water, power, and conservation projects that were important to the West, including the Upper Colorado River Project, which was crucial to the development of the arid western states. She was also an advocate of Indian rights but did not succeed in passing her bill to study the feasibility of letting Indian tribes manage their own affairs. Although she concentrated her energies on issues like water development, which traditionally built political careers in Utah, she also proposed a program of national health insurance that drew spirited opposition in her conservative home state. In 1950 she won reelection over another prominent Utah woman, Ivy Baker Priest (who later became treasurer of the United States), in Utah's first all-woman race for national office.

In 1952 she was defeated in the congressional race by William A. Dawson, and again in 1954 she failed to regain her old seat. During this time she hosted a four-day-a-week television program in Salt Lake City, which highlighted issues of interest to women. "It's a Woman's World" won the Zenith Television Award for excellence in local programming in 1953. Returning to Washington in 1957, she served as legal counsel to the Subcommittee on Safety and Compensation of the House Committee on Education and Labor until 1960. In 1961 she was named chief judicial officer and chair of the Contract Board of Appeals of the U.S. Post Office Department, a position she held until 1968.

Bosone's interests were broad and deep. As a judge she had promoted efforts to keep young offenders in school and out of further criminal activity and had pushed for improvement of conditions in the city jail. Alcoholic rehabilitation projects, however, were her most visible activities; she promoted the development of an Alcoholics Anonymous program in Utah, organized the first Alcoholism Institute in Utah in 1946, and in 1947 became the first director (a part-time position) of the Utah State Board on Alcoholism. Her efforts to provide effective treatment for alcoholics prompted her election to the Utah Hall of Fame in 1943. Among many other honors, she received the Distinguished Service in Government Award from her alma mater, the University of California at Berkeley, in 1970. After her retirement in 1968, she moved to Vienna, Virginia, to be with her daughter. She later died there.

Though strong and opinionated, Bosone was willing to negotiate and compromise to reach her goals. She worked well with both men and women, fostering productive relationships with her quick wit and charm. She expressed her philosophy of government throughout her career succinctly: "The biggest need in politics and government today is for people of integrity and courage, who will do what they believe is right and not worry about the consequences to themselves. If it is the right course of action, it will be popular later." Bosone became a role model for many women in Utah and the West not only for her many "firsts" as a woman, but for her tenacity in working for causes in which she believed.

• Bosone's papers are in the Special Collections Department, Marriott Library, University of Utah, Salt Lake City. The collection includes autobiographical and biographical material, correspondence, political and governmental papers, speeches, articles, and scrapbooks. Her biography is Beverly B. Clopton, *Her Honor, the Judge: The Story of Reva Beck Bosone* (1980). A good biographical sketch is in *Beehive History* (Utah State Historical Society) 17 (1991): 6. Obituaries are in the 23 July 1983 editions of the *Deseret News* (Salt Lake City) and the *Salt Lake Tribune*.

JEAN BICKMORE WHITE

BOSS, Lewis (26 Oct. 1846–5 Oct. 1912), astronomer, was born in Providence, Rhode Island, the son of Samuel P. Boss and Lucinda Joslin. Boss received a boarding school preparatory education and earned a bachelor's degree from Dartmouth College in 1870. His college studies were classical in nature, but his preference for astronomy was evident from his frequent visits to the college observatory. There he became familiar with astronomical equipment and the mathematical methods used in the reduction of astronomical observations. He also developed surveying skills in his leisure hours at Dartmouth and conducted an extensive survey of the college grounds. In 1870 Boss moved to Washington, D.C., where he was employed in a clerical position in the Census Office and later as examiner of surveys at the Land Office. In 1871 he married Helen M. Hutchinson: they had four children.

While in Washington, Boss pursued his interest in surveying with a borrowed sextant and chronometer. The thoroughness of these observations secured him a position as an assistant astronomer with the U.S. Northern Boundary Commission in 1872. While executing the duties of this position Boss determined the need for the development of a homogeneous system for the declinations and proper motions of standard stars. A comparison of all available catalogs needed to be made. He undertook this task and his completed catalog was published in 1878 as Appendix H to the *Report of the United States Northern Boundary Commission*. The catalog included tables of systematic corrections for almost 100 previously published fundamental catalogs as well as declinations and proper motions of 500 stars. This system was adopted in the *American Ephemeris 1883 to 1899*.

In 1876 Boss accepted the directorship of the Dudley Observatory in Albany, New York, and began a program of cometary observations. He participated in a total solar eclipse expedition to West Las Animas, Colorado, in 1878. In 1881 Boss, using the pseudonym Hipparchus III, won the Warner Award, presented by H. H. Warner, founder of the Warner Observatory, for his essay on the physical nature of comets. In 1882 Boss was placed in charge of one of the eight government observing parties bound for Santiago, Chile, to observe the transit of Venus. The cometary project was superseded when Dudley Observatory joined in the work of the scientific society; the Astronomische Gesellschaft (AG), an international project designed to determine accurate stellar positions for all northern hemisphere stars ninth magnitude and brighter. Boss began observations in the Albany zone (+0°50′ to +5°10′) ten years after observations had been started at other observatories participating in the project, yet the Albany zone was the first to be completed. The results of the almost 20,000 observations of 8,241 stars were presented for publication in 1887 and published in 1890. Following the completion of the AG observations, Boss returned his focus to the investigation of comets, and Dudley Observatory became a center for orbit determinations.

In 1891 Boss began a campaign to move the Dudley Observatory to a more desirable location and accomplished his plan in November 1893. At the new location in the western part of Albany, he began his most ambitious project, a catalog of more than 25,000 northern and southern hemisphere stars in which he would correlate and supplement the observations made by the astronomical community over the previous 150 years. In 1905 Boss was awarded a gold medal by the Royal Astronomical Society in recognition of his work on determining the positions and proper motions of fundamental stars. In 1906 he received the support of the Carnegie Institution, which established a Department of Meridian Astrometry and named him the director. Observations on the list of 25,000 stars began in 1907 in the northern hemisphere and in 1909 in the southern hemisphere. The fruit of this labor, which included even more stars than he originally intended, was published in four important catalogs: *The Preliminary General Catalogue of 6,188 Stars* (1910), *The San Luis Catalogue of 15,333 Stars* (1928), *The Albany Catalogue of 20,811 Stars* (1931), and the *General Catalogue of 33,342 Stars* (1937). The first catalog was published under the direction of Lewis Boss, the second under the direction of both Lewis and his son Benjamin Boss, and the final two under Benjamin Boss. Lewis Boss made observations, reduced data, and was known to supervise even the smallest details of his projects. Boss's 1908 discovery of a star stream in the constellation of Taurus was reported in the *Astronomical Journal*, a publication for which he served as associate editor and, beginning in 1909, as editor.

In addition to receiving several honorary degrees, Boss was awarded the Lalande Prize from the Paris Academie des Sciences (1911). He was elected a member of the National Academy of Sciences (1889), the American Philosophical Society, the Astronomische Gesellschaft, and the American Academy of Arts and Sciences. He was a corresponding member of the British Association for the Advancement of Science, the Prussian Academy, and the St. Petersburg Academy. He was a foreign associate of the Royal Astronomical Society. Boss also served New York state as the superintendent of weights and measures from 1883 to 1906 and used the salary from this position to subsidize his astronomical research at Dudley Observatory. He served as the editor and manager of the daily paper the *Albany Morning Express* from 1885. Boss died in Albany.

• A collection of Boss papers is at the Dudley Observatory Archives, Schenectady, N.Y. Boss's essay "Comets: Their Composition, Purpose and Effect upon the Earth" is published in Warner Observatory, *History and Work of the Warner Observatory* (1883–1886), pp. 25–30. A complete bibliography of Boss's scientific writings and a biography by Benjamin Boss is "Biographical Memoir of Lewis Boss, 1846–1912" in the National Academy of Sciences, *Biographical Memoirs* 9 (1920): 239–60. Additional biographical information can be found in R. H. Tucker, "Lewis Boss," *Publications of the Astronomical Society of the Pacific* 24 (1912): 256–60. The early work of Boss is summarized in "Address Delivered by the President, H. H. Turner, on Presenting the Gold Medal of the Society to Professor Lewis Boss," *Monthly Notices of the Royal Astronomical Society* 65 (1905): 412–25. An obituary is in the *New York Times*, 6 Oct. 1912.

MERRI SUE CARTER

BOSTIC, Earl (25 Apr. 1913–28 Oct. 1965), alto saxophonist, was born in Tulsa, Oklahoma. Details about his parents are unknown. Bostic played clarinet in school and saxophone with the local Boy Scouts. By 1930 or 1931 when he left Tulsa to tour with Terrence Holder's Twelve Clouds of Joy, he was already a saxophone virtuoso. Fellow saxophonist Buddy Tate recalls that Bostic was asked to join the band because of his dexterity and maturity as a soloist. Holder's band members then informally tested his ability to read difficult music: skipping the opportunity to rehearse, Bostic counted off an impossibly fast tempo and played the piece on first sight with such skill that only he and the drummer made it through to the end. "We let him alone after that," Tate said.

Sometime in the early 1930s Bostic spent a year at Creighton University in Omaha, Nebraska, playing by day in an ROTC band and by night with jazz groups. He was briefly a member of Bennie Moten's band early in 1933. Later that year he enrolled at Xavier University in New Orleans to study music theory, harmony, and various instruments; again he played with military bands at school and jazz groups in the city. One year later he left to work mainly with lesser-known bands, although in 1935–1936 he played and arranged for a band led by Charlie Creath and Fate Marable.

After moving to New York at the beginning of 1938, Bostic joined Don Redman's band in April, played briefly with Edgar Hayes's orchestra, and then led his own band at Smalls' Paradise in Harlem from 1939 intermittently into the early 1940s. In this group he occasionally played trumpet, guitar, or baritone sax in addition to his alto sax. During these years he also contributed his best-known composition and arrangement, "Let Me Off Uptown," to Gene Krupa's big band, which recorded it in 1941, and he was a member of Hot Lips Page's group in 1941 and again around 1943. From June 1943 to August 1944 he played and wrote for Lionel Hampton's big band. He left to resume leading a group at Smalls'. In September 1944 he recorded several sides with Page, including "Good for Stompin'" and "Fish for Supper." His solos on these recordings reveal an alto saxophonist with a full-bodied tone, a precise articulation of notes, considerable technique, and an uncertain sense of melodic architecture, with the result that sometimes he relied on stiff, etude-like figurations. Ironically, in light of what was to come, the worst of these was a blues, "You Need Coachin'," which finds Bostic so busy with technique that he sounded out of touch with characteristic blues timbres, melodies, and emotions.

For the remainder of his career Bostic led bands. In the mid- to late 1940s he changed his stylistic orientation by adopting a ferocious, gritty, vocalized tone; playing simple, singable melodies (although many tunes still left room for improvising); using the catchy dance rhythms of contemporary rhythm and blues; and basing the group's sound on a twangy electric guitar and smooth-toned vibraphone (the vibes perhaps inspired by his year with Hampton, but used in a less aggressive style). Early recordings in this vein were done for the Gotham label, including "That's the Groovy Thing" (1946), "8:45 Stomp," and "Temptation" (probably late 1947). After signing with the King label (which reissued these titles) in 1949, the new approach came to fruition with a recording of "Flamingo," which held the top position on the rhythm and blues popularity chart for twenty weeks in 1951. Other hit records included "Sleep" (also 1951), "Moonglow" and "Ain't Misbehavin'" (both 1952), and "Blue Skies" (1954); incidentally, the 1952 sides included a young John Coltrane in the band.

Bostic toured the country, and as testimony to a level of success unusual in rhythm and blues and jazz, for several years he was able to take six-week vacations. In 1956 he suffered a serious heart attack that, apart from recordings, rendered him inactive. He resumed touring in 1959, but he soon became ill again. After years of semiretirement, he began an engagement in October 1965 in Rochester, New York, only to die there two days after suffering another heart attack.

Tate summarized Bostic's career: "Oh man, he could read. . . . He was a virtuoso. . . . He could play . . . way out, progressive, but he made it big, just playing the melody. That's what people wanted to hear." It might be added that, in pursuing this path, Bostic discovered a musicality that had sometimes been lacking in the earlier part of his career. By the mid-1980s Bostic was felt to be a "forgotten" man (Schonfield), but with the reissue in the late 1980s and 1990s of much of his work for the King label, it is possible for new generations of listeners to discover his best music.

• Ruth Cage supplies a brief biography of Bostic in "Rhythm & Blues Notes," *Down Beat*, 29 Dec. 1954. Changes in personnel under Holder and Moten are traced in Albert McCarthy, *Big Band Jazz* (1974). For an excellent overview of his musical style, see Victor Schonfield, "The Forgotten Ones: Earl Bostic," *Jazz Journal International* 37 (Nov. 1984): 10–11. The best chronology of his activities appears in John Chilton, *Who's Who of Jazz: Storyville to Swing Street* (1985). Tate's story, "Earl Bostic Joins the T. Holder Clouds of Joy," is in Nathan W. Pearson, Jr., *Goin' to Kansas City* (1987). An obituary appeared in *Down Beat*, 2 Dec. 1965.

BARRY KERNFELD

BOSTWICK, Arthur Elmore (8 Mar. 1860–13 Feb. 1942), editor and librarian, was born in Litchfield, Connecticut, the son of David Elmore Bostwick, a physician, and Adelaide McKinley. Bostwick took advantage of the cultural assets in his hometown, reading periodicals from a neighbor's private library, studying romance and classical languages, participating in music ensembles, and attending the Episcopal church where his mother was organist. His innate intellectual abilities were thus stimulated, laying the foundation for an active life of the mind. He attended Yale College, won the first Silliman Fellowship in physical science, graduated Phi Beta Kappa, and earned a B.A. in 1881 and a Ph.D. in physics in 1883. Aspiring to a college professorship, he declined an appointment as a Fellow at the Johns Hopkins University in favor of a temporary position at Yale but, when a permanent post was not forthcoming, he moved to Montclair, New Jersey, where he taught high school from 1884 to 1886. In 1885 Bostwick married Lucy Sawyer, with whom he had three children.

Bostwick's career entered a new phase when, through the influence of his cousin, John D. Champlin, he was appointed to a post with *Appleton's Cyclopaedia of American Biography*, thus beginning lifelong commitments to editorial work and professional writing. He collaborated with Champlin on the *Young Folks' Cyclopaedia of Games and Sports* (1890; rev. ed. 1899). He assisted L. S. Metcalf and Walter Hines Page with *Forum*, a monthly review, from 1890 to 1892 and served for two years as associate editor for *A Standard Dictionary of the English Language*, edited by Isaac K. Funk and Adam W. Wagnalls. His lively interest in the physical sciences was apparent in his contributions on physics in *Appleton's Annual Cyclopaedia* (1886–1902) and in his work with *Literary Digest*, which he served as science editor (1891–1933).

In 1895, again through the auspices of his cousin but also of his former employer, William W. Appleton, Bostwick assumed a new position, that of chief librarian of the New York Free Circulating Library. By entering librarianship, he could bring together his broad intellectual interests, his literary talents, and his scientific attention to detail. Acknowledging his status as a novice, he resolved to make his own library education a continuing process. In 1899 he moved to the new Brooklyn Public Library as director and in 1901 became the first chief of the Circulation Department of the New York Public Library following that institution's merger with the New York Free Circulating Library.

He returned to find the library in great flux: the Astor and Lenox libraries were merging with the Tilden Trust and with circulating and reference libraries to create the New York Public Library under the guidance of John Shaw Billings. Bostwick chafed under the redoubtable Billings and differed with him on the purpose of the library. While Billings regarded libraries as reference institutions designed for scholarly use, Bostwick saw them as instruments of popular education. Despite these differences, Bostwick matured as an administrator and directed the vast building program funded by Andrew Carnegie. By 1909 Bostwick was supervising the largest circulating library in the world, loaning 6.5 million volumes annually through forty-one branches. He also presided over the New York Library Club (1897–1899), the New York State Library Association (1901–1903), and the American Library Association (ALA, 1907–1908).

From 1909 to 1938, Bostwick served as librarian of the St. Louis Public Library and as associate librarian until the end of his life. His flexible administrative style and flair for organization facilitated major improvements. He converted the classification scheme from one devised by William T. Harris to a decimal classification system, occupied a new central building in 1912, expanded the system from four to nineteen branches, and tripled circulation to more than 3 million volumes annually. Less admirably, he joined numerous other librarians who, during World War I, removed pro-German materials from library shelves.

Bostwick distinguished himself as a leading citizen of St. Louis, becoming integral to the city's cultural and social life. He served as president of the New England Society (1911), the St. Louis Archaeological Society (1915), the St. Louis Art League (1920), the St. Louis Branch of the League of Nations Non-Partisan Association (1924–1933), the St. Louis Branch of the Foreign Policy Association (1927), and the Missouri Welfare League (1926–1936). He was active in the Artists' Guild, the Contemporary Club, the Round Table, the Society of St. Louis Authors, and Town and Gown.

Because of Bostwick the St. Louis Public Library gained national stature. Through its library school, the library trained numerous individuals for the profession (1917–1932). Bostwick also presided over the ALA Publishing Board (1918–1921), chaired the ALA Library Survey Committee (1922–1929), and presided over the Association of American Library Schools (1932–1933). Through the Chinese Association for the Advancement of Education, he visited China as ALA representative in 1925 and was appointed honorary director of the Library Association of China. In 1929 he presented a paper on public libraries at the International Library Conference in Rome and Venice.

Bostwick published nineteen books and pamphlets and more than two hundred articles in addition to works he edited or coauthored. He edited the *Classics of American Librarianship* (10 vols., 1914–1933) and *Doubleday's Encyclopedia* (11 vols., 1938). He wrote *The American Public Library* (four eds., 1910–1927), a thorough text used by generations of students and practitioners; *Popular Libraries of the World* (1933); and *A Life with Men and Books* (1939), one of the most engaging autobiographies in American librarianship.

Bostwick died in Oak Grove, Missouri. He believed that his principal work in life had been the writing and editing of periodicals and books and making them available in libraries. He wrote for popular as well as scholarly audiences, and he promoted libraries as tools of mass education. Scientific in outlook, intellectually polished, and keenly perceptive, Bostwick brought to librarianship strong administrative abilities and an unwavering faith in the power of the word to educate.

• Materials related to Arthur Bostwick are located in the Special Collections department of the St. Louis Public Library. In addition to works already mentioned, Bostwick's major publications include *The Different West As Seen by a Transplanted Easterner* (1913), *Earmarks of Literature: The Things That Make Good Books Good* (1914), *A Librarian's Open Shelf: Essays on Various Subjects* (1920), and *Library Essays: Papers Related to the Work of Public Libraries* (1920). See also Phyllis Dain, *The New York Public Library: A History of Its Founding and Early Years* (1972); Margery Doud, "Recollections of Arthur E. Bostwick," *Wilson Library Bulletin* 27 (1953): 818–25; Charles H. Compton, *Twenty-Five Crucial Years of the St. Louis Public Library, 1927 to 1952* (1953); Joseph Alfred Boromé, "A Bibliography of Arthur Elmore Bostwick, 1860–1942," *Bulletin of Bibliography* 18 (1944): 62–66; and Anne Carroll Moore, "Arthur Elmore Bostwick, 1860–1942, Citizen of the World," *ALA Bulletin* 36 (1942): 210–11, 220. Obituaries are in the *New York Herald Tribune* and the *New York Times*, both 14 Feb. 1942.

JOHN MARK TUCKER

BOSWELL, Connee (3 Dec. 1907–11 Oct. 1976), jazz singer, was born Constance Foore Boswell in Kansas City, Missouri, the daughter of Alfred Clyde Boswell, a circus and vaudeville performer, and Meldania Foore. Together with her sisters, Martha and Helvetia (or Vet), Connee (spelled "Connie" until 1941) Boswell was exposed to music very early in life, as her parents and a live-in uncle and aunt frequently sang barbershop harmonies at home. When she was three Boswell was stricken with poliomyelitis, and though her legs remained paralyzed for the rest of her life she gradually regained the use of her arms and torso. While still very young Boswell started playing cello, and in 1914, after the family moved to New Orleans, she took music lessons from Martha's piano teacher, Professor Otto Finck, who later also started Vet on violin.

While growing up in a wheelchair Boswell not only practiced cello and taught herself piano, alto saxophone, and trombone, but she also took up horseback riding, swimming, bicycling, carpentry, and oil painting. Once they were proficient enough, the sisters played classical and semiclassical music on local radio programs and at church socials, fairs, the Young Men's Gymnastic Club, and the Orpheum Theater. They were first exposed to authentic spirituals and the blues through the singing of their parents' house servants, and they also listened to the records of Enrico Caruso and blues singers Mamie Smith and Bessie Smith, whose rich tones and heartfelt expression made a deep and lasting impact. During the early 1920s, with Connie playing sax and Vet banjo, the sisters held jam sessions at home to which they invited Martha's boyfriend, cornetist Emmet(t) Hardy, trumpeters Leon and Louis Prima, clarinetist Leon Roppolo, saxophonist Pinky Vidacovich, and drummer Monk Hazel. In March 1925 the group made its first vocal recordings, "Nights When I'm Lonely," a girlish-sounding, vaudeville-inspired novelty, and "I'm Gonna Cry," a blues solo feature for Connie.

Boswell and her sisters left New Orleans in September 1928 to audition in Chicago for work on a vaudeville theater circuit. Once hired, they were booked on a cross-country tour that ended in San Francisco, where they took on a manager, Harold Leedy, who helped them land a radio spot on KFWB in Los Angeles. While still in Hollywood, in July 1930 the now more mature-sounding trio recorded incidental vocal choruses on two titles with Jackie Taylor's Orchestra, but they received no billing on the single side that was issued. The next October they had four featured releases on the OKeh label, including "Heebie Jeebies," a number that Louis Armstrong had made into a hit in 1926 and one that the trio continued to use as an opening theme on their radio shows and theater performances. Already heavily influenced by Armstrong's rhythmic phrasing, hot intonation, and scat-singing, Connie emerged at this point not only as the leader of the best vocal group in popular music but also as the first fully developed white female jazz singer.

In March 1931, now officially listed on labels as the Boswell Sisters, the trio signed a contract with Brunswick Records that resulted in an uninterrupted series of classic performances lasting until shortly before the group's breakup in early 1936. On virtually all of these many recordings, the trio worked with some of the top New York jazz studio musicians of the time, among them trumpeters Bunny Berigan and Manny Klein, trombonist Tommy Dorsey, clarinetist Jimmy Dorsey, violinist Joe Venuti, pianist Artie Schutt, guitarists Eddie Lang, Dick McDonough, and Carl Kress, bassists Joe Tarto and Artie Bernstein, and drummer Stan King. Although liberally dosed with exciting improvised solos and ensembles, what was truly innovative about this series were Connie's vocal arrangements and the facility with which the trio interpreted them. Grounded in the close harmonies they had absorbed as children, the sisters had an intuitive grasp of line crossing, a choral technique involving simultaneous upward and downward movements between the soprano and alto ranges that imparted a wholly original texture to their voicings. Added to that and their New Orleans–rooted feeling for swing were such finely honed devices as abrupt changes in key and tempo, frequent modulations between major and blues-inflected minor modes, displacement of expected rhythmic accents, scat-singing, and hot breaks, rhythmically phrased glottal stops, the "mouth horn"–style also associated with the Mills Brothers, double-timed patter routines, and expertly synchronized phrasing and timing.

Of the nearly ninety titles the trio recorded between 1931 and 1936, a few of the most memorable include "Whadja Do to Me," "When I Take My Sugar to Tea," "Roll On, Mississippi, Roll On," "Shout, Sister, Shout," "It's the Girl," "It's You," "Makin' Faces at the Man in the Moon," "Heebie Jeebies," "River, Stay 'Way from My Door," "Was That the Human Thing to Do?" "Everybody Loves My Baby," "There'll Be Some Changes Made," "Down among the Sheltering Palms," "Forty-second Street," and "If I Had a Million Dollars." In August 1931 Brunswick also signed Connie to a contract for a series of solo recordings that lasted through July 1935, when she went over to Decca. During the earlier part of this period her accompanists included essentially the same musicians who backed up the trio, but later she was matched with Bing Crosby ("Basin Street Blues," "Bob White," "Between 18th and 19th on Chestnut Street," "Rhythm on the River," "Tea for Two," and "Yes Indeed") and the bands of Bob Crosby, Ben Pollack, and Woody Herman.

In addition to their recordings the trio also appeared on the first CBS television broadcast in July 1931, performed at the Paramount and Roxy theaters in New York, had their own sponsored radio shows, and were often featured with Bing Crosby on "The Woodbury Hour" (1933) and with Rudy Vallee on "The Fleischmann Hour." They also appeared in films such as *Big Broadcast of 1932*, *Sleepy Time Down South* (1932), *Boswell Sisters* (1933), *Moulin Rouge* (1934), and *Transatlantic Merry-Go-Round* (1934) and performed at the London Palladium and the Café de Paris in 1933 and 1935. In early 1936, following their recent marriages, the trio agreed to break up. Martha and Vet decided to leave show business and live with their husbands in Peekskill and Toronto, respectively, but Connie, who had married Leedy in 1935, pursued a career as a soloist, with Leedy continuing on as her manager. Unlike many such unions, the Boswell-Leedy alliance remained happily intact until Leedy's death in 1975. They had no children. Many students of the period believe that Boswell produced her best work after the breakup of the trio, a contention supported by such recordings as "Concentratin'," "My Lips Want Kisses," "Washboard Blues" (with the Casa Loma Orchestra), "A New Moon Over My Shoulder," "Whispers in the Dark" (which was nominated for an Academy Award in 1939 for best presentation of a song in a motion picture), the swing versions of "Martha," "Home on the Range," "Gypsy Love Song," and "Ah! Sweet Mystery of Life" (with the Bob Crosby Bob Cats), and "Sand in My Shoes."

As a featured radio artist, Boswell regularly appeared on "Gloom Chasers" (CBS, 1934), "Good News" (NBC, 1938), "Maxwell House Coffee Time" (NBC, 1940), "Kraft Music Hall" (NBC, 1941–1942), and "Stagedoor Canteen" (1943–1945). She was also an occasional guest star on "Camel Caravan" (CBS) and the shows of Arthur Godfrey and Frank Sinatra as well as hosting her own "Connee Boswell Show" on ABC. While reading some fan mail in 1941 she decided to change the spelling of her first name to "Connee." It seems that because she never bothered to dot her *i*'s when signing autographs, many of her admirers believed that the unconventional spelling was her own preference, record labels and print publicity notwithstanding. On film she had guest appearances in *Artists and Models* (1937), *Kiss the Boys Goodbye* (1941), *Syncopation* (1942), *Swing Parade of 1946*, and *Senior Prom* (1958).

During the war, Boswell toured army and navy training camps and hospitals and assisted in fundraising drives, activities for which she received many citations from the government and the armed forces. Although she also volunteered to entertain the military personnel abroad, her request was rejected by the army on the basis of her own disability (she always performed seated in her wheelchair). However, along with Eddie Cantor and other show business celebrities, she helped found the March of Dimes to aid polio-stricken children. On the professional front Boswell continued recording and appeared in several Broadway revues and performed at hotels and supper clubs across the country. As television grew in popularity she appeared on "The Bell Telephone Hour," Ed Sullivan's "Toast of the Town," "The Perry Como Show," and Jack Webb's "Pete Kelly's Blues" (1959).

Boswell continued recording through 1958, her penultimate album being a 1956 retrospective of 1920s tunes performed with a reassembled Original Memphis Five. From 1960 on she concentrated on performing at benefits for the handicapped and making rare television appearances. In the early 1970s Boswell was diagnosed with cancer of the stomach, but after the shock of her husband's death she requested that her chemotherapy be discontinued. She died in New York City.

Boswell left an indelible mark on her contemporaries and many of her successors as well. It might be said that, along with Louis Armstrong and Ethel Waters, she invented jazz singing. Her intuitive gifts for phrasing, note-shaping, enunciation, intonation, and swing proved demonstrable influences not only on such female jazz singers as Mildred Bailey, Lee Wiley, Ella Fitzgerald, and Peggy Lee, but also on male jazz singers Crosby, Sinatra, Mel Torme, Nat King Cole, and their stylistic descendants.

• Collections of Boswell materials are at Rutgers University, Howard University, and the Berklee School of Music. The most thorough biographical source on Connee Boswell and her sisters is J. Lee Anderson, "The Boswell Sisters: Martha, Connie, and Vet," *Mississippi Rag*, July 1992, pp. 2–8. See also Chris Ellis, "Connee Boswell: 3 Dec. 1907–11 Oct. 1976," *Storyville*, June–July 1977, pp. 166–69, and Jan Shapiro, *Filling in the Gaps in the History of Vocal Jazz* (1991). Some information about Boswell's activities in radio can be found in John Dunning, *Tune in Yesterday* (1976). Discographical listings are in Brian Rust, *Jazz Records, 1897–1942* (1982) and *The Complete Entertainment Discography* (1975), and Erik Raben, *Jazz Records, 1942–1980*, vol. 2 (n.d.). An obituary is in the *New York Times*, 12 Oct. 1976.

JACK SOHMER

BOSWELL, Henry (26 Mar. 1884–16 Dec. 1957), physician and tuberculosis sanatorium administrator, was born in Hinton, Alabama, the son of John Boswell and Georgianna Neal. Nothing is known of his parents' occupations. Boswell grew up in Choctaw County, in west central Alabama, attending grade school in Hinton and public high school in nearby Rock Springs. He moved north to Tennessee to seek a medical education at the University of Nashville, from which he received an M.D. in 1908. After graduation, he held a brief internship at the Nashville General Hospital before accepting a position as house surgeon at Providence Hospital in Mobile, Alabama, where he worked until late 1909.

Following his short stint as a hospital surgeon, Boswell moved to Laurel, Mississippi, about fifty miles southwest of his boyhood home, to establish a private medical practice. There he met and in June 1910 married Iola Saunders, an English teacher at the local high school; they would have five children. Only a few months into this young marriage, Boswell developed active tuberculosis. In November 1910 he removed himself to a sanatorium in El Paso, Texas. After what must have been a long year of separation from his new wife, Boswell achieved recovery from the rest and fresh air he found in El Paso. Not all his fellow patients were so lucky, including another physician who had occupied a bed next to Boswell. As Boswell prepared to depart El Paso, another doctor, suffering from an advanced and obviously terminal case of TB, asked Boswell to dedicate himself to combating tuberculosis. Boswell pledged to follow the wish of his dying friend.

In 1916, a few years after Boswell had returned to his home in Mississippi, the state legislature appropriated $25,000 for the construction of a TB sanatorium on 200 acres of donated land just north of Magee, Mississippi. Appointed its superintendent, Boswell moved to the Mississippi State Tuberculosis Sanatorium, still under construction, in 1917. By the time the first patient arrived on 4 February 1918, the initial buildings were complete, but the structures were quite humble, comprising twenty-bed cottages and two other small buildings. The institution was also severely understaffed during this early phase. Boswell, the only physician, was forced to help with tasks such as meal preparation, scrubbing floors, and routine nursing care because his budget allowed only one nurse and one orderly to be on duty at any given time.

During the state legislative campaign of 1919, Boswell made a bold and overtly political move to improve matters at the sanatorium. He carried his vision of a large, modern, government-financed TB sanitorium across the state and seized every opportunity to engage in public debate with candidates who did not support his plan. Boswell's political efforts brought a dramatic pay-off in the next legislative session: the 1920 Mississippi legislature appropriated $1,043,000 to expand and improve the Mississippi State Tuberculosis Sanatorium. At the time, this was the greatest single appropriation for TB treatment ever made by any state in the union. The figure also represented more than forty times the amount Mississippi had set aside three years earlier to establish the institution.

Boswell's success with the 1920 state legislature was his greatest political triumph, but it was not his sole achievement in the government halls of Jackson. Year after year, he continued to lobby for increased funding for the sanatorium. He also worked toward the enactment of laws to improve public health in Mississippi. Boswell's political acumen was matched by great administrative skill. As superintendent of the Mississippi State Tuberculosis Sanatorium for four decades, he oversaw great institutional expansion and won loyalty among staff members and patients. A former member of Boswell's medical staff offered the following tribute: "During . . . years of close contact with Dr. Henry Boswell, I learned to admire, to love, and to respect him for the man he was, for his unexcelled ability as an administrator, and for the ease and simplicity with which he directed the future of the sanitorium, and at the same time acted as father and advisor to the staff and all the patients" (O'Mara, p. 317). Former patients of the Mississippi State Tuberculosis Sanatorium paid the superintendent a high honor by naming their association the Henry Boswell Society.

Boswell was active in several professional associations and held the presidency of the Mississippi State Medical Association, the Mississippi State Hospital Association, the Mississippi State Tuberculosis Association, the National Tuberculosis Association, and the American Trudeau Society. He was also president and honorary lifetime president of the Mississippi State Golf Association in recognition of his avid devotion to that game. A firm believer that everyone should have a hobby, he excelled at his chosen avocation throughout his life, scoring three holes in one after the age of seventy.

Boswell died just north of Magee, Mississippi, at the institution to which he had devoted so much of his abundant energy, having kept the promise that he had made as a recovering TB patient forty-six years earlier.

• Some of Boswell's papers are at the Mississippi Department of Archives and History, Archives and Library Division, Jackson. The chief source on Boswell is a biographical tribute by B. B. O'Mara, "Conqueror of the White Death," *Journal of the Mississippi State Medical Association* 1 (1960): 317–19. An obituary is in *Journal of the American Medical Association* 166 (1 Mar. 1958): 1068.

JON M. HARKNESS

BOSWELL, John Eastburn (20 Mar. 1947–24 Dec. 1994), educator, historian, and author, was born in Boston, Massachusetts, the son of Henry Boswell, Jr., a U.S. Army officer, and Catherine Eastburn. He traveled around the world with his parents before settling with them in Petersburg, Virginia. He attended the College of William and Mary, receiving his A.B. in 1969. He did graduate work at Harvard, earning his M.A. in 1971 and his Ph.D. in 1975. His life thereafter was devoted to teaching, research (often supported by grants, including a Woodrow Wilson fellowship and a Fulbright scholarship), and writing scholarly publications.

Boswell taught at Yale as assistant professor of history (1975–1981), associate professor (1981–1982), and professor (from 1982). He also served as director of graduate studies in history (1984–1986). In 1982 Yale honored Boswell by awarding him its William Clyde deVane Medal for excellence in teaching and scholarship. He was a voracious reader and a tireless student of languages. While in Petersburg he studied Latin and Spanish in public high school and was tutored by a rabbi in Hebrew. At William and Mary he learned French, German, and Greek. At Harvard he studied Aragonese, Catalan, Old Icelandic, and Provençal. He once said that, beginning in 1969, he tried to master a language a year. Adding Armenian, Church Slavonic, Persian, and Syriac, among other languages, he ultimately read or spoke seventeen languages. He chose at one point to study Arabic in French and German texts in order to improve his competence in three languages at once.

Boswell published four historical studies, almost all concerning life earlier than and during the fourteenth century and all both significant and controversial. They are *The Royal Treasure: Muslim Communities under the Crown of Aragon in the Fourteenth Century* (1977), *Christianity, Social Tolerance, and Homosexuality: Gay People in Western Europe from the Beginning of the Christian Era to the Fourteenth Century* (1980), *The Kindness of Strangers: The Abandonment of Children in Western Europe from Late Antiquity to the Renaissance* (1988), and *Same-Sex Unions in Premodern Europe* (1994). He also published many shorter pieces, including "Revolutions, Universals and Sexual Categories" (*Salmagundi* [1982–1983], repr. in *Hidden from History: Reclaiming the Gay and Lesbian Past*, ed. Martin Bauml Duberman et al. [1989]); "Gay History" (*Atlantic Monthly*, Feb. 1989); and "Concepts, Experience and Sexuality" (*Difference: A Journal of Feminist Cultural Studies* [Spring 1990]). In 1987 Boswell listed as works in progress "Marriage, Love, and the Catholic Moral Tradition," "The Three Religions in Spain: The Interaction of Judaism, Christianity, and Islam in Western Europe," and "Conversion to Judaism in the High and Later Middle Ages."

The Royal Treasure concerns the population of the Muslim community under the crown of Aragon between 1355 and 1366, during part of the reign of Peter the Ceremonious. Boswell analyzed the composition and organization of the Muslims; the legal, financial, and military positions not only of individual persons but also of their communities; and the relation of the Muslims to Aragon society as a whole with respect to rights permitted and discrimination suffered. Boswell limited himself to a small time-frame, even though Muslims were a significant minority in Christian Spain from the eleventh century through the sixteenth. In doing so he sought to demonstrate representative contrary social impulses toward segregation and toward acculturation. Some critics found fault with Boswell's quotations and translations from the Arabic.

Christianity, Social Tolerance, and Homosexuality, which won the American Library Association Gay/Lesbian Book Award and the American Book Award for History in 1981, is a monumental work and the one for which Boswell is most likely to be remembered. It had a considerable period of gestation. While Boswell was in graduate school, a friend who was a divinity student asked him to explicate certain New Testament Greek terms traditionally related to homosexuality. Boswell presented his findings at his friend's seminar; another student's refusal to believe that the Scriptures did not condemn homosexuality impelled Boswell to undertake a decade-long study. In the resulting book he discussed the experiences of European homosexuals over fifteen centuries, arguing that virulent intolerance of homosexuals first appeared in the thirteenth century, as did intolerance toward Jews, Muslims, other infidels, and heretics, especially after the Crusades proved unsuccessful. Boswell argued that prejudice against homosexuals was not exclusively a Christian bias, although under secular pressure it was emphasized by Aquinas and by conservative rural clergy. Boswell used an impressive range of classical, scriptural, patristic, Islamic, medieval, and modern sources to counter traditionally accepted notions.

Many scholars believed that Boswell's study was a revisionist work of enormous importance; others, however, rejected his scriptural commentary as well as his suggestion that clerical friendships were homosexual.

In *The Kindness of Strangers* Boswell studied the widespread practice of abandonment of children in Europe from Hellenistic times through the thirteenth century. He blamed the Catholic church not only for urging families to have many children but also for routinely welcoming abandoned ones into churches and monasteries. His sources, which some scholars regarded as flawed and incomplete, included demographic statistics; legal, theological, and literary documents; and records of foundling hospitals.

Same-Sex Unions, on which Boswell worked for twelve years, theorized that pre–fourteenth-century Christian leaders sanctioned male-male unions. Boswell cited more than sixty church documents and said that the church consecrated such unions by prayers and gestures similar to those employed in male-female marriage ceremonies. He found parallel same-sex bonds in Greco-Roman times. Boswell was here implicitly pleading for liberalization of societal attitudes.

Boswell's early death, caused by complications from AIDS, occurred in New Haven, Connecticut, and cut short the career of a talented and daring scholar in the field of homosexual social history. An indication of his influence is the fact that his work was translated into Dutch, French, German, Greek, Italian, Japanese, and Spanish.

• Boswell is treated briefly in Hal May, ed., *Contemporary Authors*, vol. 121 (1987), which lists several reviews of his works, and in Wayne R. Dynes, ed., *Gay & Lesbian Literature: Introduction to Gay Male Literature* (1994). An interview with Boswell is in *Newsweek*, 29 Sept. 1980. Obituaries are in the *New York Times*, 25 Dec. 1994, and the *Washington Post*, 27 Dec. 1994.

ROBERT L. GALE

BOSWORTH, Welles (8 May 1869–3 June 1966), architect, was born William Welles Bosworth in Marietta, Ohio, the son of Daniel Perkins Bosworth, Jr., a merchant, and Clara Van Zandt. After graduating from the Marietta Academy in 1885, Bosworth enrolled at the Massachusetts Institute of Technology that fall. During his student years Bosworth worked part time in the architectural offices of Henry Hobson Richardson and Shepley, Rutan and Coolidge, where he was involved in the preparation of the first presentation drawings for Frederick Law Olmstead's plan of Stanford University. He received a bachelor's degree in architecture in 1889. After graduation, Bosworth continued to work for Shepley, Rutan and Coolidge, then spent a year traveling in Europe with William Rotch Ware, editor of the *American Architect*. In 1894, having established an architectural practice in New York, Bosworth married Elizabeth Lewis Newton, with whom he would have two children.

After only a few years of practicing on his own, Bosworth decided that he needed the type of advanced architectural training that could be obtained only at the École des Beaux-Arts in Paris. He closed his New York office and traveled to Europe, stopping in London to study briefly with the English painter Sir Lawrence Alma-Tadema. Bosworth then enrolled in the École and participated in the Chaussemiche and Redon ateliers before receiving his diploma in the late 1890s. After another tour of Europe, Bosworth returned to the United States and secured a position in New York with Carrére and Hastings. Shortly thereafter John M. Carrére was named supervising architect of the Pan-American Exposition to be held in Buffalo in 1901, and he made Bosworth resident architect of the project. In that capacity he oversaw construction and designed three exposition buildings, an experience that proved to be invaluable to some of his future work.

Bosworth left Carrére and Hastings in 1902 to reestablish his own practice. By then he was known throughout the architectural community as an exceptional draftsman and landscape designer, and other firms hired him for special projects. In 1903, for example, Carrére asked him to work on drawings for the City of Cleveland Group Plan Commission. In 1904 he prepared the final presentation drawings for Cram, Goodhue and Ferguson's winning entry in the competition to redesign the U.S. Military Academy at West Point, New York.

Bosworth's architectural career over the next twenty-five years was prolific and diverse. He flourished at a time when the upper crust of New York society was enamored with the type of eclectic architecture that Bosworth and his French-trained colleagues could provide. Most of his work was in the formal, classical style favored by his teachers at the École. During the early part of the twentieth century, Bosworth established a successful practice designing gardens and estates in the New York area. His designs were praised in architectural journals, such as the *American Architect* (5 July 1922), which described the Walter Farwell estate in Syosset, New York (1920), as "the most perfect country home in America." Bosworth's Beaux-Arts training was most evident in his garden plans, which emphasized axiality and formality in the French manner; they also contained touches of Italian and English landscape architecture that worked together to create designs that were both controlled and emotional.

In 1913 the Massachusetts Institute of Technology commissioned its distinguished alumnus to prepare the plan for the institute's new campus on the Charles River in Cambridge. Bosworth was selected because of his work with the Pan-American Exposition and his reputation as a landscape designer. His design embodied classical simplicity in the creation of a monumental complex grouped around a central court and anchored by a rotunda in the manner of Charles F. McKim's Columbia University Library and Thomas Jefferson's University of Virginia.

Bosworth's practice also included a considerable amount of commercial work in New York City. His most prominent structure in this line was the 27-story building at 195 Broadway designed as the headquarters for the American Telephone and Telegraph Company and the Western Union Telegraph Company. The AT&T Building (1915–1922), as it came to be known, differed from contemporary skyscrapers in its use of classical ornamentation. The ground level utilized the Doric order, followed by eight levels of Ionic orders stacked one over the other, each covering three floors.

The longest-lasting and most important client in Bosworth's career was John D. Rockefeller, Jr., who hired Bosworth in 1907 to design the gardens for "Kykuit," the Rockefeller family estate at Pocantico Hills, New York. Bosworth's garden plan combined closed and open spaces, terraces, statues, architectural elements, and natural features to produce a spectacular enclave on the hills overlooking the Hudson River. In 1910 Rockefeller asked Bosworth to help remodel the main house at Kykuit, which had been completed only a few years before by William Adams Delano and Chester Holmes Aldrich. Bosworth worked on various projects at Kykuit for almost ten years. He also designed Rockefeller's New York City townhouse (1914, demolished), and a mausoleum for the William Rockefeller family in Tarrytown, New York (1920). When Rockefeller, Jr., created the Comité Franco–Americain pour la Restauration des Monuments in 1925 to help rebuild French architectural treasures damaged during World War I, he asked Bosworth to oversee the project. In order to carry out Rockefeller's request, Bosworth retired from his New York practice and moved his permanent residence to France. Appointed general secretary of the comité by French president Raymond Poincaré, Bosworth also became involved in projects to restore Reims Cathedral and the palaces at Versailles and Fontainebleau.

Bosworth received fewer commissions after moving to France because by then, the movement toward modernism had supplanted his style of Beaux-Arts classicism. In 1927 he and his wife were divorced; that same year he married Reneé Oberle Du Souich, with whom he had two more children. Except for a brief period during World War II, the family lived in the "Villa Marietta," Bosworth's estate in Vaucresson, France, where he died. Bosworth's work on the Comité Franco-Americain earned him the French Legion of Honor and the French Cross of the Commander of the Order of Arts and Letters.

• The Rockefeller Archives contain materials pertaining to Bosworth's work at Kykuit and on the Comité Franco-Americain pour la Restauration des Monuments. Correspondence between Bosworth and William Barton Rogers concerning the Massachusetts Institute of Technology buildings and plans is at the MIT Archives; the MIT Museum has some elevational drawings of the buildings. The National Academy of Design has a Bosworth watercolor of the Parthenon. Bosworth wrote two books: *The Gardens of Kijkuit* (1919), describing the Rockefeller estate, and *The Altoviti Aphrodite* (1920), about a statue displayed at Kykuit. His other writings include "Chartres Cathedral," *American Society Legion of Honor Magazine* 22 (Autumn 1951): 201–12; "Domestic Architecture of Early America," *New York Times*, 4 Feb. 1923; "The Garden at Pocantico Hills, Estate of John D. Rockefeller, Esq.," *American Architect*, 4 Jan. 1911; "Mens Sana In Corpore Sano," *Architectural Record* 30 (Aug. 1911): 151–64; and "Reims Cathedral," *American Society Legion of Honor Magazine* 25 (Spring 1954): 9–21. For biographical material see "Welles Bosworth" in *The Brickbuilder* 24 (Apr. 1915): 102; "Master Draftsmen IX: Welles Bosworth," in *Pencil Points* 6 (Jan. 1925): 59–64; Bosworth, "I Knew H. H. Richardson," *Journal of the American Institute of Architects* 16 (Sept. 1951): 115–27; and Quentin S. Jacobs, "Welles Bosworth: Modern Classicist," *Preservation League of New York State Newsletter*, Spring 1989, pp. 4–5. Also see Hugh J. McCauley, "Visions of Kykuit: John D. Rockefeller's House at Pocantico Hills, Tarrytown, New York," *Hudson Valley Regional Review* 10 (Sept. 1993): 32–33, 42; and Jacobs, "William Welles Bosworth: Major Works" (master's thesis, Columbia Univ., 1988). An obituary is in the *New York Times*, 5 June 1966.

DALE ALLEN GYURE

BOTELER, Alexander Robinson (16 May 1815–8 May 1892), congressman and businessman, was born in Shepherdstown, Virginia (now W.Va.), the son of Henry Boteler, a physician, and Priscilla Robinson. His mother died when he was only four, so Boteler was raised by his grandmother in Baltimore. He graduated from Princeton College in 1835 and married Helen Macomb Stockton the next year; they had at least one child. After his father's death in 1836, Boteler moved to the family farm, where he earned recognition for agricultural experimentation, including the development of farm machinery. He also operated a flour and cement mill. He soon became a man of some wealth and was reported as owning an estate worth $41,000 in the 1860 census, including fifteen slaves.

Boteler was an amateur writer and painter of some talent. His sketches of John Brown (1800–1859) and paintings of several Confederate leaders still survive, and his book, *My Ride to the Barbecue*, was published in 1860. However, Boteler is significant primarily for his political activity just before and during the Civil War and for his promotion of industrial and commercial development in West Virginia after the war. An active Whig, he was one of the electors for Winfield Scott in 1852. When the Whig party disintegrated, he became a member of the American party and was elected to the Thirty-sixth U.S. Congress, serving from March 1859 to March 1861. He was a delegate to the national convention of the Constitutional Union party in 1860, supported the candidacy of John Bell, and was a member of the party's Executive Committee.

Like most Virginia Whigs, Boteler was a Unionist in the crisis of 1860–1861. He made the motion in the House of Representatives to appoint the Committee of Thirty-three that was to find some compromise to avoid the crisis, but he preferred not to serve on the committee himself. Only a week before the secession of Virginia, he advertised himself as an "Independent Union Candidate for Congress," but he fully supported the Confederacy after Virginia seceded. After the war he explained, "When finally against my hopes &

efforts my state seceded, I felt compelled to share her fortune, & to share her fate." He added, "I had been taught to love Virginia more than I loved my life."

Boteler joined the staff of General Thomas J. "Stonewall" Jackson as an aide, but the Virginia state convention appointed him to fill a vacancy in the state's delegation to the Provisional Congress of the Confederacy. He was admitted to Congress on 27 November 1861 and was later elected to represent the Tenth District of Virginia in the First Congress, in which he served from February 1862 to February 1864.

Like most of the members from districts that were occupied or threatened by the Union army, Boteler urged the vigorous exercise of authority by the Confederate central government. He favored a rapid and heavy buildup of the army, sequestration of enemy property, conscription, drastic economic measures, and even suspension of the writ of habeas corpus. He acted as Stonewall Jackson's mouthpiece in Congress and served on his personal staff when Congress was not in session. After Jackson was killed, Boteler served on the staffs of General J. E. B. Stuart and Governors William Smith (1797–1887) and John Letcher of Virginia.

Boteler ran for reelection to the Second Confederate Congress but was defeated when the counties composing his western Virginia district were unable to participate in the election. Liable to conscription because of his age, he returned to the army, and in 1881 he claimed to have been on the staff of General J. B. Gordon when the war ended. When required to give an account of his wartime activities, however, Boteler only admitted to accepting a colonel's commission to serve on one of the military courts attached to the Army of Northern Virginia, claiming he was serving in that capacity when he was captured at Appomattox Court House.

After the war Boteler returned to Shepherdstown and turned to business. He contacted English capitalists to encourage investment in the Covington and Ohio Railroad as well as in Virginia agricultural land, water power, and mines. He also tried to encourage European immigration into Virginia, because "the only hope for our *state* . . . consists in filling it up with white men from our tide water and in opening here facilities for immigrants [*sic*] by Europeans." These efforts were intended to "enable us, not only to compete with the Yankees, but also to be really & truly independent of them by being (so far as they are concerned) a self sustaining commonwealth."

In a lifetime of public service, Boteler held a variety of nonpolitical positions, including county school commissioner, the governing board of the Virginia Military Institute, the governing board of the University of Virginia, and the Centennial Commission in 1876. He was appointed to the U.S. Tariff Commission in 1881 and later served as assistant attorney and pardon clerk in the Department of Justice. He was disappointed, however, in his expectation of having some influence over patronage during the Cleveland administration.

Boteler died in Shepherdstown, just a few days short of his seventy-seventh birthday. He was a moderate in an age when moderation was not in fashion and a supporter of losing causes: the Whig party when it died, the Union as it broke up, and at the end of the war he was in Confederate uniform. Nor was his hope for an economically reinvigorated Virginia realized during his lifetime.

• The largest collection of Boteler's papers is in the Duke University Library. The most significant portions of his political career are covered by the *Congressional Globe* for the Thirty-sixth U.S. Congress; the *Journal of the Congress of the Confederate States of America, 1861–1865*, vols. 1, 5–6, 58th Cong., 2d sess., 1904–1905, S. Doc. 234; and the "Proceedings of the . . . Confederate Congress" [title varies], *Southern Historical Society Papers*, vols. 44–50 (1923–1953). Boteler explained his course and career in his postwar amnesty petitions to President Andrew Johnson, which are found in Case Files of Applications from Former Confederates for Presidential Pardons ("Amnesty Papers"), 1865–1867, RG 94, Records of the Adjutant General's Office, 1780–1917, National Archives Microfilm Publication M-1003. The best depictions of Boteler are in the anonymously written "Alexander Robinson Boteler," *Magazine of the Jefferson County Historical Society* 20 (Dec. 1954): 19–27, and in A. D. Kenamond, *Prominent Men of Shepherdstown during Its First 200 Years* (1963). Brief sketches of Boteler's career are also found in Ezra J. Warner and W. Buck Yearns, *Biographical Register of the Confederate Congress* (1975), and Richard N. Current, ed., *Encyclopedia of the Confederacy*, vol. 1 (1993).

RICHARD E. BERINGER

BOTSFORD, George Willis (9 May 1862–13 Dec. 1917), historian, was born in West Union, Iowa, the son of William Hiram Botsford and Margaret Johnson, farmers. In 1870 the Botsford family homesteaded a farm in Otoe County, Nebraska, living in a sod dugout until 1878. Subsequently, the family prospered and George received some twelve months of elementary education at the public school in Palmyra. In 1881 he enrolled in the Latin School, later the Junior Division, of the University of Nebraska, which was designed to assist the matriculation of students who lacked a formal education. After a year of this preliminary study, he entered the university itself. In 1884 Botsford received his B.A. magna cum laude, graduating first in his class.

From 1884 to 1886 Botsford pursued graduate studies at Johns Hopkins University in Baltimore, studying with Basil Lanneau Gildersleeve, the premier American classicist of his day. Without obtaining a degree from Hopkins, he worked from 1886 to 1890 as professor of Greek at Kalamazoo College in Michigan. In 1889 Botsford received his M.A. from Nebraska—apparently *extra muros*, as there is no record of his attending classes at Nebraska after 1884. In 1890 he went to Cornell University, receiving a Ph.D. in classical philology and Sanskrit a year later, with a thesis entitled *The Development of the Athenian Constitution*

(1893). On 30 August 1891 he married Lillie M. Shaw of Kalamazoo. The Botsfords had two children.

From 1891 to 1893 Botsford was an instructor in history at Worcestor Academy in Massachusetts and from 1893 to 1895 professor of Greek at Bethany College in Virginia. In 1895 he became an instructor in Greek and Roman history at Harvard University and Radcliffe, remaining there for six years. In 1902 Botsford was appointed a lecturer in ancient history at Columbia University in New York. This was the first time a professorship of ancient history had been placed in Columbia's history department rather than in that of Greek and Latin language, thus helping to establish ancient history as a field independent of the classics. Botsford became an instructor in 1903 and adjunct professor in 1905.

Botsford's *Roman Assemblies from Their Origin to the End of the Republic* (1909) was a highly influential book, approaching Roman constitutional history from a broad historical, rather than a narrow juristic, perspective. In discussing the conflict of the orders, he argued for a Social Darwinian view, that the rise of an aristocracy, such as the Roman patrician order, was the result of a process of natural selection of the best individuals in a society, against the older idea, set forth by the German classicist Theodor Mommsen, that the patricians and plebs were originally of different "races."

Botsford was appointed full professor of history at Columbia in 1910. At the time he was one of a handful of professors of ancient history in the United States. Botsford felt it important to pass on university-level scholarship to secondary school teachers. In 1914, in *History Teachers Magazine*, he argued that "it is better [for teachers] to take one [college] course in Greek history under a good instructor than ten courses in the methods of teaching the subject."

Botsford continued his work on Greek and Roman constitutional history, but his main achievement was the writing of textbooks and source books for secondary schools and colleges. He used these works not only to set forth generally accepted facts, but as vehicles to present original research. Though politically independent, Botsford was a devoted Progressive, and his textbooks stressed the importance of social and economic history and the relevance of the understanding of history and politics to the training of good citizens. His *Hellenic History* (1922), edited posthumously by his son, Jay Barrett Botsford, was re-edited by C. A. Robinson in 1939 and remained a mainstay of college history courses for decades. In 1969 Donald Kagan re-edited "Botsford and Robinson," and it continues to be used today.

Although powerfully built, Botsford was a shy man so devoted to his work as to be almost a recluse. While he was greatly admired by his colleagues in the history department, he took little part in its activities, except as an editor of, and frequent contributor to, Columbia's *Political Science Quarterly*. On the day of his death, Botsford arrived at Kent Hall, as was customary, around 9:10 A.M. He complained to the elevator operator of feeling unwell and was escorted to his study, where he collapsed and died. The university physician, who arrived only moments after Botsford's death, diagnosed its cause as "acute indigestion . . . complicated by heart troubles." Only fifty-five years old, Botsford was struck down in the midst of an active and distinguished career as a teacher and a scholar. His original research on ancient constitutional history was important and its impact long lasting, but it was as a writer of textbooks and as a supporter of the teaching of ancient history in high schools and colleges that Botsford made his greatest contribution.

• Botsford's personal papers have been lost. He wrote fifteen scholarly articles, primarily on Greek and Roman constitutional history, and articles for the *Encyclopaedia Britannica* and *Encyclopedia Americana*. Books not mentioned in the text are *A History of Greece for High Schools and Academies* (1899); *A History of Rome for High Schools and Academies* (1901); *A History of the Orient and Greece for High Schools and Academies* (1901); *An Ancient History for Beginners* (1902); with Lillie S. Botsford, *The Story of Rome as Greeks and Romans Tell It* (1903); *A History of the Ancient World* (1911); with Lillie Botsford, *A Source-book of Ancient History* (1912); with E. G. Sihler, *A Syllabus of Roman History* (1915); *Hellenic Civilization* (1915); and, with Jay Barrett Botsford, *A Brief History of the World* (1917). An obituary is in the *New York Times*, 14 Dec. 1917.

JONATHAN ROTH

BOTTA, Anne Charlotte (11 Nov. 1815–23 Mar. 1891), educator, writer, and literary hostess, was born Anne Charlotte Lynch in Bennington, Vermont, the daughter of Patrick Lynch, a merchant, and Charlotte Gray. The family moved to Pennsylvania and later to Windham, Connecticut. In 1819 Patrick Lynch died at sea while going to claim land offered by the Cuban government to Irish refugees. His widow took their young children to Hartford, Connecticut. At sixteen Anne enrolled at the Albany Female Seminary in Albany, New York, graduating with honors in 1834 and staying on for some time to teach.

After two years as a governess with the Gardiner family on Shelter Island, New York, she joined her mother in Providence, Rhode Island, in 1838 and started a boarding school for "young ladies" whom she inspired with a lifelong devotion to learning and to herself. After another spell as a governess in Philadelphia, Pennsylvania, where she developed a friendship with Fanny Kemble, she finally moved to New York City, where she took in pupils, taught at the Brooklyn Academy for Young Ladies, and tried her hand at writing. In Albany she had won school prizes for poetry; on Shelter Island she had kept her "Diary of a Recluse," evidence of her desire for self-knowledge, and in Providence she had written for periodicals and edited *The Rhode Island Book*, an anthology of the state's writers, including herself.

In 1849 Anne published a volume of poetry, with illustrations by contemporary artists. Increasingly, however, she was becoming known as the premier literary hostess of New York. In Providence she had begun holding evening receptions for literary people, both residents and visitors of the city, which included Sarah Helen Whitman, Margaret Fuller, Orestes Brownson, and Ralph Waldo Emerson—gatherings that were said to assemble "the best literary society" in the state capital. When she and her mother set up house in New York in 1845, she continued to receive every Saturday evening.

From 1850 to 1853 Anne visited Washington, D.C. She petitioned Congress in 1851 for military pay owed her in behalf of her deceased maternal grandfather from the revolutionary war. She made influential contacts, served as Henry Clay's private secretary, and dedicated a poem to Daniel Webster. In 1853 she traveled to Europe, where she met Thomas Carlyle and studied art in museums, galleries, and studios in France and Italy. She became an accomplished amateur sculptor, setting up a studio at her house on Thirty-seventh Street in New York, where she had moved after her marriage to Vincenzo Botta in 1855. The couple had no children.

From 1855 until her death in 1891, Botta and her husband kept what Emerson called "the house of the expanding doors"—sought out by aspiring authors or people already prominent in literature, the arts, and public life. These evenings could include musical recitals, dances, poetry readings, and tableaux vivants. Here, Poe recited his "Raven" and met Margaret Fuller. Over the years, her guests included Bronson Alcott, George Bancroft, Henry Ward Beecher, William Cullen Bryant, Alice and Phebe Cary, Horace Greeley, Grace Greenwood, Fitz-Greene Halleck, Nathaniel Hawthorne, Washington Irving, Helen Hunt Jackson, Emma Lazarus, Herman Melville, Catharine Sedgwick, Richard Henry Stoddard, Bayard Taylor, Henry Theodore Tuckerman, and Mary Helen Whitman. Distinguished foreigners, such as the Swedish writer Frederika Bremer, the Norwegian violinist Ole Bull, and British writers Henry Makepeace Thackeray and Matthew Arnold, added their luster.

An early friend of Brook Farm, Botta espoused movements for democracy and national liberation and supported women's education and legal rights but did not herself campaign for reforms. Legendary for her charitable disposition and her devotion to duty (her "hobby," according to Poe), she took care of her mother, adopted her dead brother's son, and contented herself with making room for others. This she did, with resounding success as, for almost four decades, her hospitality made its mark on American culture.

During much of this time, Botta's own literary production continued as she published in the popular journals and giftbooks of the day. Her prose sketches are entertaining, her essays on history and literature are thoughtful and well-informed, and her sonnets are quite competent. Poe singled out "The Ideal" and "The Ideal Found," saying, "I really do not know where to point out anything American much superior to them." Despite such early praise, however, her poetic oeuvre remained largely undistinguished. Several poems are addressed to nature, science, or to personified virtues; others are dedicated to important individuals, for example, Halleck, Peter Cooper, Lamartine, and Kossuth, or support causes, as in "Viva Italia!" and "Nightfall in Hungary"; many reflect reverently on the mysteries of life and death in idealistic terms. Botta was aware of her own limitations. "It is dreadful to think how I have wasted all my life," she wrote at age twenty-five, but she realized what her true strength was: to be a collector of literature. She compiled the *Handbook of Universal Literature* (1860), which became a popular college text. At the time of her death, she was engaged with compiling another compendium, *Handbook of Universal History*. She died in New York.

• Much of Botta's work appeared in periodicals or giftbooks. "Leaves from the Diary of a Recluse" appeared in *The Gift* for 1845, but some of her poems were anthologized in such works as Caroline May's *American Female Poets* (1853) and Evert A. and George L. Duyckinck's *Cyclopedia of American Literature* (1854). Besides those works mentioned, she also compiled *The Rhode-Island Book: Selections in Prose and Verse, from the Writings of Rhode-Island Citizens* (1841). The *Memoirs of Anne C. L. Botta, Written by Her Friends. With Selections from her Correspondence and from Her Writings in Prose and Poetry*, ed. Vincenzo Botta (1894), laudatory but not hyperbolic, continues to be the richest source on her life and work. Poe discussed her in "The Literati of New York City" in *Godey's Lady's Book*, Sept. 1846. Descriptions of her salon can be found in Charles Hemstreet, *Literary New York* (1903); Mrs. Roger A. Pryor, *My Day: Reminiscences of a Long Life* (1909); Hervey Allen, *Israfel: The Life and Times of Edgar Allan Poe* (1926); Madeleine B. Stern, "The House of the Expanding Doors: Anne Lynch's Soirees, 1846," *New York History* 23 (Jan. 1942): 42–51; *The Letters of Margaret Fuller, vol. 4, 1845–47*, ed. Robert N. Hudspeth (1987); and Kenneth Silverman, *Edgar A. Poe* (1991).

FRITZ FLEISCHMANN

BOTTOMLEY, William Lawrence (24 Feb. 1883–1 Feb. 1951), architect, was born in New York City, the son of John Bottomley, a lawyer and businessman, and Susan Amelia Steers. His father was a native of Ulster who had come to the United States to represent the interests of his uncle, scientist William Thomson, first baron Kelvin. Bottomley was educated at the Horace Mann School and at Columbia University, graduating in 1906 with a B.S. in architecture. He went to work for the architectural firm of Heins and La Farge in New York, afterward joining the office of the New York State Architect in Albany. In 1907 he was awarded the McKim Fellowship in Architecture at the American Academy in Rome. He spent the summer of 1908 traveling through northern Italy and southern France and on 1 October entered the École des Beaux Arts in Paris, where he continued his studies. Bottomley returned to the United States in 1909 and that year married Harriet Townsend, a writer on architectural subjects; they had three daughters.

Bottomley began his architectural practice in 1911. He designed many types of buildings, including high schools in Southampton and Port Chester, New York; a church; a restaurant; and the Municipal Building in

Plainfield, New Jersey. He specialized, however, in residential structures, both houses and apartment buildings. He had clients throughout the eastern United States, from Maine and New Hampshire to Florida and Texas, but the majority of his commissions came from the New York metropolitan area. Bottomley did not limit himself to a single style, for he felt strongly that each commission presented a set of problems that needed to be solved in a different way. The most important challenge was to avoid banality: "I work toward interesting silhouettes to the roof lines . . . contrasting plain walls with interesting detail at salient points" (Colton, p. 340). Nor did he limit himself to designing buildings, believing that an architect also "should design the lawns, terraces, and roads immediately about the house. . . . A stucco house, for instance . . . usually looks better when seen through what we call tracery planting, perhaps with accents of evergreens. A brick or stone house, on the other hand, is apt to appear much better when there are open views of it . . . and when there are dense masses of tree foliage behind it" (Boyd, p. 98). To Bottomley, the materials with which a building was constructed were more important than its architectural style.

Bottomley's largest design, and his masterpiece, is "River House," a 26-story apartment building on the block between 52d and 53d streets in Manhattan, next to the East River. Built in 1932, it is an excellent example of the Art Deco style. One writer described it as "ris[ing] in a symmetrical mass of wings and pavilions that reduces gradually, in a series of stepbacks with terraces to a huge central tower, to be occupied by cooperative apartments" (Boyd, p. 51). Bottomley included gardens and terraces in his design, and the apartments were roomy and comfortable. River House even had a private dock on the East River where the residents could tie up their yachts, a feature that disappeared when the FDR Drive was built. When it opened in 1932, the least expensive apartments were those with six rooms, priced at $30,000 to $35,000, and the most expensive was the penthouse at $275,000. By setting aside so much space for gardens and by its placement on the East River, Bottomley guaranteed that River House's occupants would always enjoy ample light and air. It remains one of the city's most exclusive apartment buildings.

What may be Bottomley's most lasting achievement are the many buildings he designed in Richmond, Virginia, most of them private residences in the city's West End. His first work in Richmond was a house at 2309 Monument Avenue, commissioned by H. L. Golsan and his wife in 1916. How they came to choose Bottomley is not known, although Mrs. Golsan, a former resident of New York, may have been familiar with his work there. For the Golsans, the architect produced a design indebted to but not imitative of an English Georgian town house, built of brick and featuring three floors. He took special care with its details and even painted the map over the mantel in the library. For Robert Gamble Cabell III and his wife, Bottomley designed a handsome residence with a facade modeled on that of "Mompesson House" in Salisbury, England. The interior, however, was an original Bottomley plan. The lot on which the house was built, later 2601 Monument Avenue, was larger than other lots on the street, and the architect was thus able to design a bigger house. That he was pleased with the result is demonstrated by his inclusion of the Cabell house in his entry in *Who's Who in America*.

Bottomley designed twenty buildings in Richmond, all of which survive. Most are in a neo-Georgian style, which complements much of the architecture found in Virginia, but three structures—the Parrish house, the Stuart Court Apartments, and the shop at 121 East Grace Street—were designed in the American Mediterranean style influenced by both Italian and Spanish architecture. In addition to his Richmond work, Bottomley designed or worked on twenty-seven residences elsewhere in Virginia.

Bottomley edited the two-volume *Great Georgian Houses of America* (1933–1937), an important source on that subject. He also wrote the book *Spanish Details* (1924). A Republican, he served as mayor of Old Brookville, Long Island, from 1928 to 1934. In the latter year he received the Silver Medal of Honor of the Architectural League of New York and the Apartment House Medal of the New York Chapter of the American Institute of Architects (AIA). He had joined the AIA in 1921 and in 1944 was named a fellow of that organization. He also belonged to the Episcopal church.

Bottomley's reputation went into a decline after his death; his style of architecture came to be regarded as too conservative for a more modern age. The quality and scope of his work, however, continue to be appreciated, and his buildings are admired by serious students of architecture. The noted architect Louis Kahn visited "Milbourne," one of Bottomley's Richmond houses, and observed, "Ah, yes, this was a man who loved and understood building; this was truly an architect, this Bottomley" (O'Neal and Weeks, p. xiii).

• The Valentine Museum in Richmond, Va., owns all of Bottomley's surviving papers associated with his work in Virginia. Studies of Bottomley's life and work include John Taylor Boyd, Jr., "The Country House and the Developed Landscape: William Lawrence Bottomley Expresses His Point of View about the Relation of the Country House to Its Environment in an Interview," *Arts and Decoration* 31 (Nov. 1929): 50–54, 98, 100; Arthur Willis Colton, "The Work of William Lawrence Bottomley," *Architectural Record* 50 (Nov. 1921): 338–57 and *Architectural Record* 50 (Dec. 1921): 418–41; Davyd Foard Hood, "William Lawrence Bottomley in Virginia: The 'Neo-Georgian' Houses in Richmond" (M.A. thesis, Univ. of Virginia, 1975); and William B. O'Neal and Christopher Weeks, *The Work of William Lawrence Bottomley in Richmond* (1985).

DAVID MESCHUTT

BOUCHER, Jonathan (12 Mar. 1738–27 Apr. 1804), priest of the Church of England, was born in Blencogo, parish of Bromfield, Cumberland County, England, the son of James Boucher, a yeoman, schoolmaster and manager of an ale house, and Ann Barnes. When he was only sixteen Boucher ran a school for boys at Raughton-head, and in 1755 he went to Workington in Cumberland to study with the Reverend Mr. Ritson. In 1756 Boucher became an usher, or tutor, in St. Bees' School, Cumberland, which was run by the Reverend Dr. John James, with whom Boucher had a friendship of thirty years. In 1759 John Younger, a Whitehaven merchant, acting as an agent for his factor in Virginia, was seeking a young man to go to the colony as a private tutor. On 12 April 1759 Boucher stepped ashore on the banks of the Rappahanock River at Urbanna and then traveled eighty miles upriver to Port Royal to the home of Captain Edward Dixon to be the tutor of Dixon's two sons, Harry and Turner. Boucher did not particularly enjoy Port Royal or his work as a tutor. "My thoughts had long been withdrawn from the Church; nor could my late course of life in any sense have qualified me for it. Yet happily as I trust for the future rectitude of my conduct, a train of unforeseen circumstances now led me back to this my original bias, and at last made me an ecclesiastic" (*Reminiscences*, pp. 29–30).

Boucher had lately struck a friendship with the Reverend Isaac William Gilberne, rector of Hanover Parish, directly across the river from Port Royal. Gilberne was about to resign his parish, and apparently at his suggestion, the vestry of Hanover Parish recommended Boucher to the bishop of London for ordination, with the expectation that he would be assigned to their parish. Because there was no bishop in the colonies, Boucher had to go to England for ordination. On 26 March 1762 Bishop Richard Osbaldeston of London ordained him deacon, and on 31 March 1762 he ordained him priest. Boucher returned to Hanover Parish and served as rector there until December 1764, when he became rector of St. Mary's Parish, Caroline County, where he was a parish clergyman, schoolmaster, and planter. He found schoolteaching "the most irksome and thankless of all employments," but among his pupils was John "Jacky" Parke Custis, the son of Martha Washington and stepson of George Washington. Boucher and Washington became friends and had an extensive correspondence. While rector of St. Mary's Parish Boucher did much work among the slaves, and on 31 March 1766 he baptized 313 adult slaves.

On 10 May 1770 Boucher became rector of St. Anne's Church, Anne Arundel County, Annapolis, Maryland, where he stayed until November 1771, when he became rector of Queen Anne Parish, Prince George's County, Maryland. In 1772 he married the first of his three wives, Eleanor "Nelly" Addison; they had no children. Because Boucher was a Tory and a firm supporter of established authority, he immediately encountered opposition from his parishioners. On his first Sunday he arrived to discover that he had been locked out of the church. While he was rector of St. Anne's Parish, Boucher also served as curate to the Reverend Henry Addison, his wife's brother, at St. John's Parish, Prince George's County, where the people considered "every sermon of mine as hostile to the views and interests of America." "All the answer I gave to these threats was in my sermons, in which I uniformly and resolutely declared that I never could suffer any merely human authority to intimidate me from performing what in my conscience I believed and knew to be my duty to God and His Church. And for more than six months I preached, when I did preach, with a pair of loaded pistols lying on the cushion; having given notice that if any man, or body of men, could possibly be so lost to all sense of decency and propriety as to attempt really to do what had been long threatened, that is, to drag me out of my own pulpit, I should think myself justified before God and man in repelling violence by violence" (*Reminiscences*, p. 113). On 10 September 1775 Boucher and his wife sailed for England.

From 1776 to 1785 Boucher was rector of Paddington Parish, London, and in 1779 he was appointed assistant secretary to the Society for the Propagation of the Gospel. Nelly Boucher died in 1781. In 1787 he married Mary Forman, and they also had no children. In 1789 he married Elizabeth Hodgson James, the widow of John James, Jr.; they had eight children. Boucher's last church was Epsom Parish, Surrey, which he served until his death in Carlisle.

Boucher was a leading Tory and a forceful advocate for bishops in the colonies. He preached "the divine authority of the status quo" and insisted on "obedience for conscience sake," which he considered to be the "cornerstone of all good government." He preached the doctrine of the divine right of kings and believed that "the Church and the King, do, and must, stand or fall together." He taught that rebellion is a sin against God's authority and that "to resist or to rebel against a lawful government is to oppose the ordinance of God." He was a conservative constitutionalist and advocate of the supremacy of law.

• Boucher's major writings are *A View of the Causes and Consequences of the American Revolution; in Thirteen Discourses, Preached in North America between the Years 1763 and 1775: With an Historical Preface* (1797; repr. 1967) and *Reminiscences of an American Loyalist, 1738–1789. Being the Autobiography of the Reverend Jonathan Boucher, Rector of Annapolis in Maryland and Afterwards Vicar of Epsom, Surrey, England* (1797), ed. Jonathan Bouchier (1925; repr. 1967). He also wrote *Glossary of Archaic and Provincial Words . . . Forming a Supplement to the Dictionaries of the English Language, Particularly Those of Dr. Johnson and Dr. Webster* (1833). Much of Boucher's correspondence is in Worthington C. Ford, ed., *Letters of Jonathan Boucher to George Washington and Letters of Washington to Boucher* (1899); "Documentary History: Correspondence between the Right Reverend John Skinner, Jr., and the Reverend Jonathan Boucher, 1786," *Historical Magazine of the Protestant Episcopal Church* 10 (1941): 163–75; and "Letters of Rev. Jonathan Boucher," *Maryland Historical Magazine* 7 (1912): 1–26, 150–65, 286–304, 337–56; 8 (1913): 34–50, 168–86, 235–56, 338–52; 9 (1914): 54–67, 232–41, 327–36; and 10 (1915): 25–37. Major studies of Boucher are by Anne Young Zimmer, *Jonathan Boucher: Loyalist in Exile* (1978) and "Jonathan Boucher: Moderate Loyalist and Public Man" (Ph.D. diss., Wayne State Univ., 1966).

Other helpful studies are Carol R. Berkin, "Jonathan Boucher: The Loyalist as Rebel," *West Georgia College Studies in the Social Sciences* 15 (1976): 65–78; Michael D. Clark, "Jonathan Boucher and the Toleration of Roman Catholics in Maryland," *Maryland Historical Magazine* 71 (1976): 194–204; Philip Evanson, "Jonathan Boucher: The Mind of an American Loyalist," *Maryland Historical Magazine* 58 (1963): 123–36; Ralph Emmett Fall, "The Rev. Jonathan Boucher, Turbulent Tory (1738–1804)," *Historical Magazine of the Protestant Episcopal Church* 36 (1967): 323–58; Richard M. Gummere, "Jonathan Boucher, Toryissimus," *Maryland Historical Magazine* 55 (1960): 138–45; R. W. Marshall, "What Jonathan Boucher Preached," *Virginia Magazine of History and Biography* 46 (1938): 1–12; James E. Pate, "Jonathan Boucher, an American Loyalist," *Maryland Historical Magazine* 15 (1930): 305–19; Allen W. Read, "Boucher's Linguistic Pastoral of Colonial Maryland," *Dialect Notes* 6 (1933): 353–63; Marcella Wycliff Thompson, ed., "Jonathan Boucher (1738–1804)," *Blackwood's Magazine* 231 (1932): 315–34; Robert G. Walker, "Jonathan Boucher: Champion of the Minority," *William and Mary Quarterly*, ser. 3, 2 (1945): 3–14; and Zimmer and Alfred Kelley, "Jonathan Boucher: Constitutional Conservative," *Journal of American History* 58 (1972): 897–922.

DONALD S. ARMENTROUT

BOUCHET, Edward Alexander (15 Sept. 1852–28 Oct. 1918), educator and scientist, was born in New Haven, Connecticut, the son of William Francis Bouchet, a janitor, and Susan Cooley. Part of New Haven's black community that provided much of the city's unskilled and domestic labor, the Bouchets were members of the Temple Street Congregational Church, which was a stopping point for fugitive slaves along the Underground Railroad, and both Edward and his father were active in church affairs. During the 1850s and 1860s New Haven had only three schools that black children could attend. Edward was enrolled in the Artisan Street Colored School, a small (only thirty seats), ungraded school with one teacher, Sarah Wilson, who played a crucial role in nurturing Bouchet's academic abilities and his desire to learn.

In 1868 Bouchet was accepted into Hopkins Grammar School, a private institution that prepared young men for the classical and scientific departments at Yale College. He graduated first in his class at Hopkins and four years later when he graduated from Yale in 1874, he ranked sixth in a class of 124. On the basis of this exceptional performance, Bouchet became the first black in the nation to be nominated to Phi Beta Kappa. In the fall of 1874 he returned to Yale with the encouragement and financial support of Alfred Cope, a Philadelphia philanthropist. In 1876 Bouchet successfully completed his dissertation on the new subject of geometrical optics, becoming the first black person to earn a Ph.D. from an American university as well as the sixth American of any race to earn a Ph.D. in physics.

In 1876 Bouchet moved to Philadelphia to teach at the Institute for Colored Youth (ICY), the city's only high school for black students founded by the Society of Friends because African Americans had historically been denied admittance to Philadelphia's white high schools. Members of the ICY board of managers like Cope, Bouchet's Yale benefactor, believed firmly in the value of a classical education and were convinced that blacks were capable of unlimited educational achievement. In 1874 Cope had provided $40,000 to establish a new science program at ICY, and soon thereafter began recruiting Bouchet to run it.

Although Philadelphia was as segregated as any southern city, it offered a supportive environment for a man of Bouchet's abilities. The city's black population, the largest in the North, had made considerable progress in education during the decades preceding his arrival. As early as 1849 half the city's black population was active in one or more of the many literary societies established by the black community. After the Civil War, the ICY played an important role in training the thousands of black teachers that were needed throughout the country to provide freedmen with the education they sought.

Bouchet joined St. Thomas' Church, the oldest black Episcopal church in the country, served on the vestry and was church secretary for many years. The bishop also appointed Bouchet to be a lay reader, which gave him the opportunity to take a more active part in church services. Bouchet took his scientific interests and abilities beyond the ICY into the broader black community, giving public lectures on various scientific topics. He was also a member of the Franklin Institute, a foundation for the promotion of the mechanic arts, chartered in 1824. Bouchet maintained his ties with Yale through the local chapter of the Yale Alumni Association, attending all meetings and annual dinners.

By the turn of the century, a new set of ICY managers emerged, more receptive to the industrial education philosophy of Booker T. Washington than to academic education for blacks. In their efforts to redirect the school's programs, the all-white board fired all the teachers including Bouchet in 1902 and replaced them with instructors committed to industrial education.

Over the next fourteen years, Bouchet held five or six positions in different parts of the county. Until November 1903, he taught math and physics in St. Louis at Sumner High School, the first high school for blacks west of the Mississippi. He then spent seven months as the business manager for the Provident Hospital in St. Louis (Nov. 1903–May 1904), followed by a term as a United States inspector of customs at the Louisiana Purchase Exposition held in St. Louis (June 1904–Oct. 1906). In October 1906, Bouchet secured a teaching and administrative position at St. Paul's Normal and Industrial School in Lawrenceville, Virginia. In 1908 he became principal of Lincoln High School of Gallipolis, Ohio, where he remained until 1913, when an attack of arteriosclerosis compelled him to resign and return to New Haven. Undocumented information has Bouchet returning to teaching at Bishop College in Marshall, Texas, but illness once again forced him to retire in 1916. He returned to New Haven, where he died in his boyhood home at 94 Bradley Street. He had never married or had children.

Bouchet had the misfortune of being a talented and educated black man who lived in a segregated society that imposed numerous barriers and thus hindered him from conducting scientific research and achieving professional recognition. Segregation produced isolation as Bouchet spent his career in high schools with limited resources and poorly equipped labs. No white college would have considered him for a position on its faculty even with his superior qualifications. Completely excluded from any means of utilizing his education and talent, Bouchet languished in obscurity. The ascendance of industrial education also served to limit his opportunities as his academic training in the natural sciences made him unattractive as a candidate at the increasing number of black institutions that adopted a vocational curriculum.

Bouchet's full impact on black education will never be known; that he had an impact is undeniable. Lillian Mitchell Allen remembered Bouchet from her childhood days in Gallipolis. Perhaps the most highly educated person in the area, he inspired both black and white young people with hitherto unknown goals, she said, noting that her brother, J. Arnot Mitchell, who graduated from Bowdoin College in 1913 and became the first black faculty member at Ohio State University, was influenced by Bouchet.

The absurdity of the claims made by some proponents of vocational education concerning the innate inability of blacks to undertake an academic education could not have been more obvious to Bouchet. From his own accomplishments and those of his students, it never occurred to Bouchet that blacks could not master the fields of classical education or excel in science. In the face of personal setbacks and a changing public mood on black education, Bouchet never altered his educational ideals.

• Bouchet wrote a short autobiographical piece for the Yale publication *Class Record* (1912). Comments about Bouchet when he was at Yale College are included in a short synopsis of his graduation class by George L. Dickerman, *Yale College Class of 1874* (1879). These publications are available in the Yale University Manuscripts and Archives, Sterling Memorial Library. See also Ronald E. Mickens, "Edward A. Bouchet: The First Black Ph.D.," *Black Collegian* 8, no. 4 (Mar./Apr. 1978): 32, and "Edward A. Bouchet, Ph.D.," *Negro History Bulletin* 31 (Dec. 1968): 11. Information on Bouchet's years at the Institute for Colored Youth can be found in Linda M. Perkins, *Fanny Jackson Coppin & The Institute for Colored Youth, 1865–1902* (1987). An obituary is in the *Bulletin of Yale University, Obituary Record of Yale Graduates, 1918–1919*, no. 11 (1919).

H. KENNETH BECHTEL

BOUCICAULT, Dion (27 Dec. 1820–18 Sept. 1890), dramatist, actor, and man of the theater, was born Dionysius Lardner Boursicault in Dublin, Ireland, possibly the illegitimate son of the Reverend Dr. Dionysius Lardner and Anna "Anne" Maria Darley, the wife of Samuel Smith Boursiquot, a wine merchant. After desultory schooling, supported by Lardner, at age fifteen he wrote his first play. He began work as a peripatetic actor in 1838 under the pseudonym of Lee Moreton, alternately adulated and attacked by critics, his strong Irish brogue by turns an asset and a liability. By 1839 his first play for the professional stage, *Lodgings to Let*, had appeared on the stage of the Theatre Royal, Bristol, with "Moreton" himself as Tim Donoghue, "an Irish Emigrant, and a Genius of the first rate" (playbill), but the play later failed in London. In 1840, encouraged by Charles Mathews, manager of Covent Garden Theatre, to write "a good five-act comedy of modern life," Boucicault wrote *London Assurance*, which, opening on 4 March 1841, established his reputation. Relying on his fluent French, Boucicault began adapting French plays for the English stage. The practice may account for his claim, later in life, to have written some 250 plays in all; other estimates put the figure closer to 150. Increasingly aware of the tastes of a popular audience, Boucicault clung for a while to an idealized self-image as a serious writer of comedy, as in the instance of *Old Heads and Young Hearts* (1844).

In 1845 he married Anne Guiot, a French widow some years older than himself. Little is known about their relationship, and by 1848 she had died. Having quickly spent whatever he had inherited from his wife, and still deeply in debt, Boucicault declared bankruptcy late in 1848. In 1850 he joined forces with Charles Kean as house dramatist at the Princess's Theatre. A series of plays by Boucicault produced by Kean included an original work, *Love in a Maze*, and one of his most successful adaptations, *The Corsican Brothers* (1852), based on an Alexandre Dumas story, which mesmerized audiences for half a century. Queen Victoria, who saw it five times the first season, found the duel scene "beautifully grouped and quite touching." To answer the needs of the dramatic action Boucicault invented a special trap door, thereafter called a "Corsican Trap," which allowed an apparition of the hero's murdered brother to glide eerily up out of the floor and along the stage.

During his time at the Princess's, Boucicault fell in love with a young actress, Agnes Robertson, Kean's ward. Kean's discovery of the relationship caused a permanent rift with Boucicault. Having secured an engagement for Robertson in New York, in September 1853 Boucicault set off for the United States, where he and Robertson began a difficult life, plagued by financial anxiety but punctuated by periods of success and great prosperity. They performed a marriage by mutual agreement, avoiding a church wedding so that Robertson could go on being billed under her own name. They had six children.

Penniless once again, Boucicault tried to resuscitate himself while Robertson supported them both with earnings from triumphant successes in Montreal and New York. Rewriting his own plays under new titles, adapting others' work, and even attempting public lectures, Boucicault was continually busy, yet not making money. For two years he and Robertson toured the East and the South, during which time Boucicault took a lease on a New Orleans theater, renaming it the Gaiety, but failed after three months. Adding to both their reputations as actors and to Boucicault's as dramatist, but not achieving the financial stability they craved, they attempted to settle in New York.

There, Boucicault's fortunes changed for the better. He adapted a French play under the title *The Poor of New York*, an extremely successful melodrama marked by a sensation scene, a spectacular fire in which an apartment house collapses and a real fire engine is driven on stage. Although "never a profound or very original thinker," as his biographer Richard Fawkes observes, he had the journalist's knack of catching "the mood and manners of his time with a deftness and wit few of his contemporaries could match." *The Octoroon* (1859), a case in point, was the story of a mulatto girl (Zoe, acted by Robertson) doomed by a white planter's love. By deftly skirting the deeper issues of race relations, it played successfully to audiences north and south. Even greater success came with *The Colleen Bawn; or, The Brides of Garryowen* (1860).

Boucicault then returned to England in triumph, and *The Colleen Bawn* set a record of 231 performances, earning Boucicault and Robertson thousands of pounds. Intending to capitalize on his success, Boucicault once again became a theatrical entrepreneur, taking a two-year lease on Astley's Amphitheatre, across the Thames in Surrey. At the same time he tried building a huge scene dock and a second theater. Again the victim of his own grandiose schemes, he was forced into bankruptcy for the second time in July 1863.

In 1865 Boucicault crafted a new version of the story of Rip Van Winkle for the American actor Joseph Jefferson, who opened with it in London that September in a production lasting 172 nights. In 1868 Boucicault brought out *After Dark*, whose great sensation scene unashamedly derived from a hit of the previous year, Augustin Daly's *Under the Gaslight*. When an American production opened in New York, Daly sued, and the producers were forced to pay him royalties.

By September 1872 Boucicault and Robertson were back in New York. Early in 1873 they became American citizens, but their marriage was breaking down, increasingly strained by Boucicault's habitual philandering. Robertson returned to London alone, leaving him involved in an affair with Katherine Rogers, whom he took with him on a profitable tour of California.

The next year would mark Boucicault's greatest success in the theater. The most appealing of all his Irish plays, *The Shaughraun*, opened at Wallack's Theater in New York on 14 November 1874 to extraordinary acclaim. At its center was Boucicault himself in the title character of Conn the Shaughraun, the vagabond rogue-hero, the most memorable role of his career. A textbook example of the pathetic-comic play he advocated, *The Shaughraun* played to capacity houses over the next few years and is said to have earned Boucicault a half-million dollars in the United States alone.

Although he earned vast sums during his lifetime, Boucicault was more often deep in debt. Extravagant by nature and generous to fellow performers, he was constantly in want of money. In yet another attempt to recoup his derelict fortunes, he formed a company including the young actress Louise Thorndyke, departed for San Francisco in April 1885 for a month's performances of his plays, and then sailed for Australia in June. There, on 9 September, Boucicault married Thorndyke in a registry ceremony and, after a highly profitable tour performing his Irish plays and other reliable pieces, returned with her to New York. Robertson filed for divorce in May 1886, and after the final decree on 15 January 1889 Boucicault and Thorndyke remarried. His insistence that he and Robertson had never been properly married threatened his children with the stigma of illegitimacy and damaged his professional reputation.

Now nearing seventy, Boucicault continued to sleep little and write much, not only plays but articles on drama and an autobiography. But he was reduced to teaching acting for a living and never completed a play commissioned by American producer Daniel Frohman intended for the fiftieth anniversary of *London Assurance*. The failure of his last original play, *A Tale of a Coat*, in September 1890 was decisive. Shortly after the play closed, Boucicault fell ill with pneumonia and died in New York City.

In an intensive and varied career in the theater that stretched over most of his life, Boucicault contributed extensively to the pleasures of audiences and the discomfort of critics on three continents. He improved the safety of spectators by building or refurbishing theaters on new principles of fire-resistant construction and by introducing a chemical means for fireproofing scenery. He added significantly to the quality of the mise-en-scène by insisting on a voice in the staging of his own plays. A martinet in the theater, he rehearsed his actors tirelessly in minute details of stage business that enhanced the creation of character. In addition, he was instrumental in replacing the earlier system of provincial performance, in which a star arrived and with a minimum of rehearsal performed with a resident company, by a system of self-sufficient touring companies in which the play itself was the real star.

Boucicault also worked to better the financial rewards of English and American dramatists. His lobbying was crucial to Congress's amendment of the 1831 Copyright Act in 1856, giving the author of a dramatic composition the exclusive right to print and publish it and to control the rights to performance.

Left behind in old age by new trends exemplified by such dramatists as Henrik Ibsen and August Strindberg, whom he detested, Boucicault embodied the definitive profile of the nineteenth-century popular playwright, yet paradoxically influenced one of the most important modern Irish dramatists, Sean O'Casey. A witty man and a scintillating conversationalist, Boucicault could instill in his characters a vitality wholeheartedly acknowledged by his audiences, who, it is estimated, paid some $25 million over his lifetime to see him perform. A similar vitality still shines in at least three of his plays—*London Assurance*, *The Octoroon*, and *The Shaughraun*.

• Boucicault's papers survive in the possession of his great-grandson Christopher Calthrop and at the University of South Florida. Printed and manuscript plays and other materials are at the University of Kent at Canterbury, the Harvard Theater Collection, the New York Public Library, and the Theatre Museum, London. Boucicault's writings on the drama include a series in the *North American Review*, of which the most important are "The Decline of the Drama" (125 [1877]: 235–45), "The Art of Dramatic Composition" (126 [1878]: 40–52), and "The Debut of a Dramatist" (148 [1889]: 454–63).

The best biography is Richard Fawkes, *Dion Boucicault* (1979), but Townsend Walsh, *The Career of Dion Boucicault* (1915), is still useful. The plays are studied in Robert Hogan, *Dion Boucicault* (1969); the best discussion of the Irish plays is David Krause's introduction to *The Dolmen Boucicault* (1964). No definitive list exists, but checklists may be found in Hogan and Fawkes. Information on Boucicault's Adelphi plays is contained in Alfred L. Nelson and Gilbert B. Cross, gen. eds., *The Adelphi Theatre Calendar, 1806–1900* (2 vols., 1988, 1993). The most extensive published collection is in the Readex Microprint series *English and American Plays of the Nineteenth Century*, ed. Joseph Donohue and James Ellis. Bibliographies of secondary studies can be consulted in Fawkes, in Hogan, and in Walter J. Meserve, *American Drama to 1900: A Guide to Information Sources* (1980). An obituary is in the *New York Times*, 19 Sept. 1890.

JOSEPH DONOHUE

BOUCK, William C. (7 Jan. 1786–19 Apr. 1859), governor of New York State, was born in Fulton, New York, the son of Christian Bouck and Margaret Borst, farmers. Great-grandson of one of the German pioneers who first settled the Schoharie Valley, Bouck's family was able and willing to furnish him with a liberal education, but his devotion to farming diverted him from anything more than elementary schooling. He entered politics as a Jeffersonian Republican, first in 1807 as the town clerk of Fulton, later as county sheriff (1812–1813), state assemblyman (1813–1815 and 1817), and then as state senator (1820–1821). In 1807 he married Catherine Lawyer, with whom he had eleven children.

In 1821 Bouck was appointed to the Erie Canal Commission and was assigned the task of supervising the construction of the difficult western section of the canal from Brockport to Lake Erie. Although his political hostility to DeWitt Clinton initially led him to oppose the Erie project, he soon recognized its importance for the development of western New York and devoted himself to completing it. He traveled, often through wilderness areas, from one construction site to another until 1825, when the canal was finished from the Hudson River to Lake Erie. Subsequently, as canal commissioner, he devoted himself to the completion of tributaries to the Erie system, namely, the Cayuga and Seneca, the Crooked Lake, the Chemung, and the Chenango canals. In the early 1830s he became convinced that the state had to enlarge the Erie Canal in order to preserve its expanding western business from competition. Throughout the decade he directed further construction, becoming a familiar figure as he rode his favorite white horse from one point to another along the canal. In 1851 his biographer could claim that, during his nineteen years as commissioner, Bouck had "faithfully expended and accounted for upward of eight millions of dollars" for canal purposes.

Bouck would have been content to continue to serve on the Canal Commission, but in 1840 he, a Jacksonian Democrat, was removed from his post after the opposing Whig party gained control of the state government. In removing him the Whigs created a popular martyr, and in 1840 Bouck was nominated by his party to run against the Whig governor, William H. Seward. He lost the election by only 5,000 votes. In 1842 he tried again, this time winning by a majority of 22,000 votes to become the state's eleventh governor, as a deepening depression turned the public against the Whigs.

It was, however, a bad time to be governor. Even before Bouck's inauguration in January 1843, the depression had deepened factional conflict within the Democratic party over government policy. One faction, the Radicals (or "Barnburners"), blamed governmental interference for the depression and demanded that the state withdraw from all but the most essential activities. The opposing Conservative ("Hunker") faction was reluctant to change existing state policy. Bouck had been nominated as the compromise candidate of both factions, but as governor he soon antagonized the Radicals. With a conservative temperament, he favored a status quo policy, especially continued support for the state's canal system.

Unfortunately, further spending for the canal system became a major issue. The Radicals, concerned that new borrowing would bankrupt the state, demanded that the government make no further improvements on the canals unless taxes were enacted to pay for them; in addition, they demanded a change in the state constitution to require that major spending proposals be submitted to the people for their approval. Although he was a fiscal conservative who had been elected with the understanding that he would not challenge the Radicals' "stop-and-tax" policy, Bouck urged continued improvement of the canals, arguing in 1844 that the low wages of labor resulting from the depression would keep down the costs.

Because it was widely believed that he could not carry the state for his party in a presidential election year, Bouck was not renominated for governor in 1844, losing 95 to 30 at the Democratic State Convention to the popular Silas Wright, who won the general election. During Bouck's last months as governor, violence erupted in Upstate New York, when farmers who leased their lands from large landed proprietors refused to pay their rents. Anti-Renters tarred and feathered the sheriff of Albany County when he attempted to enforce rent collections, and in September Bouck promised rewards of up to $100 for each conviction of a culpable farmer. Later in the year he ordered three regiments into action to restore order in Columbia County.

In 1846 Bouck was elected a delegate to the state constitutional convention, but his participation was limited by his new responsibilities as federal assistant treasurer in New York City, where he "discharged his duties," said his biographer, "rendered particularly delicate and onerous during the progress of the Mexican War, with great integrity," especially the rapid transfer of government funds from New York to places where it was required by the war. He was removed in 1849 by the new Whig administration of Zachary Taylor and retired to his Schoharie Valley farm, where he died a decade later. Bouck's conservatism as New York's first farmer governor limited him as a force for change, but he did make a notable contribution to the completion and the successful operation of the Erie Canal.

• Bouck's messages as governor are in Charles Z. Lincoln, ed., *Messages from the Governors* (1909). The principal biography of Bouck remains the eleventh chapter of John S. Jenkins, *Lives of the Governors of the State of New York* (1851). Also of use are D. S. Alexander, *A Political History of the State of New York* (1906–1909), Herbert D. Donovan, *The Barnburners* (1925), and Ronald E. Shaw, *Erie Waters West* (1966). An obituary is in the *New York Times*, 21 Apr. 1859.

EDWARD K. SPANN

BOUDIN, Leonard B. (20 July 1912–24 Nov. 1989), attorney, was born in Brooklyn, New York, the son of Joseph Boudin, an attorney, and Clara Hessner. After graduating from the City College of New York (1933) and St. John's Law School (1935), and serving one year as a law clerk at the New York State Mortgage Commission, Boudin began a fifty-year career devoted to the defense of the Constitution and of individuals threatened by the state. In 1937 he married Jean Roisman, a poet, with whom he had two children.

From 1936, when Boudin joined his uncle's law firm, as an associate, to roughly 1947, when he left that firm to begin his partnership with Victor Rabinowitz, Boudin represented labor unions. From 1948 through the mid-1960s, his practice, largely as an appellate attorney, was shaped by the McCarthy era and the Cold War. From the end of the sixties until his death, the investigation of governmental misconduct occupied much of his efforts.

Boudin joined his uncle's firm in 1936, shortly after the passage of the National Labor Relations Act and shortly before its constitutionality was upheld. During the decade that followed, with the exception of one year spent at the War Labor Board, Boudin represented unions as they organized the workforce. His clients, most importantly the United Office and Professional Workers of America (UOPWA), were often political radicals.

Though the UOPWA followed Boudin to his new firm in 1947, the passage of the Taft-Hartley Act and cold war hysteria quickly forced the new practice to change its focus. Unions were purging either their radical members or their radical policies, and both Rabinowitz and Boudin were tainted by their earlier clients. When, in 1950, Boudin was appointed counsel to Judith Coplon, accused of espionage, his firm's labor practice largely disappeared.

The McCarthy era framed the issues that he confronted throughout the 1950s. Boudin represented victims of McCarthyism before congressional committees, state committees, administrative hearings, and in the courts. In 1952 Boudin began his lifelong tenure as general counsel to the Emergency Civil Liberties Committee, one year after its founding. Throughout this period, he never lost sight of either the constitutional issues or the individual lives at stake. His clients almost invariably invoked their Fifth Amendment rights and lost their jobs. Those with other counsel who invoked only their First Amendment rights lost both their jobs and their liberty.

Two of his legal victories during the McCarthy period merit special attention. In 1952 Boudin began to represent individuals who had been denied passports (or passport renewals) by the State Department. Over the next six years, Boudin argued a series of cases that culminated in *Kent v. Dulles*, in which the Supreme Court held that the United States could not deny passports on the basis of political beliefs. In 1965, in another of the nineteen appearances he would make before the U.S. Supreme Court, he argued *Lamont v. Postmaster General*, in which the Court found unconstitutional a statute requiring individuals specifically to request delivery of "radical" political literature.

The movement against the Vietnam War transformed Boudin from an appellate advocate into a trial attorney. He played a central role in three of the major conspiracy trials of the era: he represented Dr. Benjamin Spock against charges of conspiracy to violate the Selective Service laws; he represented Eqbal Ahmad (one of the Harrisburg Seven) against charges of conspiracy to destroy government property and to kidnap Henry Kissinger; and he represented Daniel Ellsberg against charges of conspiracy, theft, and espionage related to the release of the Pentagon Papers. His handling of these cases reflected the same balance of concern for his client and for the Constitution that his tactics during the McCarthy era had exhibited. On the one hand, his briefs and oral arguments invariably framed large constitutional questions. On the other hand, in none of the cases did he "put the war on trial"; he kept his clients out of jail on any ground. An intermediate appellate court reversed Spock's conviction because of insufficient evidence to prove intent; the trial of Ahmad ended in a hung jury; government misconduct (from wiretapping to illegal break-ins) led to a mistrial and the dismissal of the indictment against Ellsberg.

In the seventies Boudin continued to litigate conspiracy cases, this time acting on behalf of plaintiffs. For example, he successfully represented the Socialist Workers party in a civil action grounded on the United States' surveillance of the party through illegal wiretaps, break-ins, and informants.

Boudin's association with Rabinowitz began when both were associates at Boudin's uncle's firm. Their partnership, which extended continuously from 1947 until Boudin's death, endured periods of economic hardship as well as the arrival and departure of many partners and associates. Its breadth and interest extended well beyond the cases sketched above. In the early 1960s, for example, their firm became counsel to the Cuban government, which pleased Boudin as much for the opportunity to confront Che Guevara at the chessboard as for the opportunity to confront major constitutional issues. This was the first of several instances in which the firm represented governments at odds with the United States. For instance, the firm represented the Allende regime in Chile until the death of Allende in 1971. After the fall of the shah, it represented the central bank of Iran after the United States froze Iranian assets in U.S. banks.

Boudin worked long hours throughout his life. He also played chess and read widely. His rumpled, congenial style in the courtroom also typified his private life, which centered on his clients, often illustrious, his legal associates, and his wife's literary friends. Boudin died in New York.

Starting in the seventies, he had taken periodic leaves from his practice to teach at the law schools of Harvard, Yale, Stanford, and the University of California at Berkeley. There Boudin influenced a new generation of attorneys. His significance in the legal and political history of his times can be measured not only by the cases in the law books but also by the numbers of his students, former partners, associates, and co-counsel who took his legal career as exemplary.

• An oral history is available at the Columbia Oral History Project. Briefs and decisions are available in the nineteen cases he argued before the U.S. Supreme Court, most prominently, *Regan v. Wald*, 468 U.S. 222 (1984), *Kleindienst v. Mandel*, 408 U.S. 7453 (1972), *In re Stolar* 401 U.S. 23 (1971), *Bond v. Floyd*, 385 U.S. 116 (1966), *Lamont v. Postmaster General* 381 U.S. 301 (1965), *Zemel v. Rusk*, 381 U.S. 1 (1965), *Braden v. U.S.*, 365 U.S. 431 (1961), *Uphaus v. Wyman*, 360 U.S. 72 (1959), *Kent v. Dulles*, 357 U.S. 116 (1958), and *Ullmann v. U.S.*, 350 U.S. 422 (1956). The major conspiracy trials attracted various chroniclers, e.g., Jessica Mitford, *The Trial of Dr. Spock* (1969); William O'Rourke, *The Harrisburg 7 and the New Catholic Left* (1972); and Peter Schrag, *Test of Loyalty* (1974), on Ellsberg.

LEWIS A. KORNHAUSER

BOUDIN, Louis Boudinoff (15 Feb. 1874–29 May 1952), political theorist and lawyer, was born Louis Boudinoff in the Ukraine, the son of Peter Boudinoff, a merchant, and Frone Feld. Louis Boudinoff emigrated in 1891 to New York, where he adopted a shortened form of his family name as a surname. He began legal studies at New York University, supporting himself with part-time work as a shoemaker, journalist, and tutor. He earned an LL.B. in 1896 and an LL.M. in 1897. He became a naturalized citizen in 1897 and was admitted to the New York bar in 1898. The next year he married Leah Kanefsky; they had two children. Leah died in 1906, and in 1909 Boudin married Anna Pavitt, a dentist.

Boudin's career before 1919 was spent in socialist politics. He conducted several unsuccessful campaigns for judicial offices in New York as the Socialist party candidate and served as a delegate to internationalist socialist congresses. His first book, *The Theoretical System of Karl Marx in the Light of Recent Criticism* (1907), largely a collection of articles written for the *International Socialist Review*, was a defense of Marxist orthodoxy against revisionism. This book had a wide impact and gave Boudin an international reputation as a theoretician, resulting in a favorable citation from Vladimir Lenin in 1914. He was more favorably regarded abroad than in the United States, where his personal disputes and impatience with what he considered to be unorthodox American socialism hampered his political career. His 1916 book, *Socialism and War*, interpreted World War I as the result of capital accumulation and consequent imperialist competition among the industrial states. His final falling out with socialist politics came with the decision of the United States to enter the war and with the Bolshevik Revolution in Russia. Boudin's personal antipathy for Socialist party leader Morris Hillquit led him to dissent from the party's declaration against American intervention in the war, even though he agreed with the party's anti-intervention decision. He rejected Lenin's leadership of the Bolshevik Revolution and did not join the Communist party, withdrawing from political activity after 1919.

While Boudin was on the left wing of the American socialist movement, progressives of all sorts denounced the federal judiciary, which used the power of judicial review to strike down progressive legislation at the national and state levels. Although historians have shown that the Supreme Court's activism in defense of laissez-faire doctrines has been exaggerated, the federal judiciary was a frequent target of progressive protest. In 1911 Boudin published an attack on the federal judiciary in the *Political Science Quarterly* (26 [1911]: 238), titling his article "Government by Judiciary." Boudin argued that the power of judicial review was an illegitimate usurpation by judges and not part of the U.S. Constitution's original design. This brought him into conflict with the leading progressive critic of the Constitution, Charles A. Beard, who argued in many of his works that the power of judicial review was built into the constitutional system by the framers as an intentionally antidemocratic device, because the framers of the Constitution were themselves propertied persons and wrote the document to protect their interests. Boudin undertook further research to buttress his thesis; in 1932 he published his two-volume major work, *Government by Judiciary*.

Boudin's attack on judicial power was very popular and has continued to be of interest and influence. It is in large part a commentary on long excerpts from original documents, primarily analyses of court decisions. Boudin labored to show that reasonable people will derive different interpretations of the Constitution and that the institution of judicial review ends up becoming a doctrine of judicial despotism. He denied that the sort of review exercised by Chief Justice John Marshall in *Marbury v. Madison* was the same kind of judicial power claimed in later decades, because Marshall was simply claiming a sort of self-defense for the judicial branch in its exercise of equal coordinate power. He refuted many of the alleged examples of judicial review that antedated the Constitution, showing that many were fabricated or vastly exaggerated in importance. As judiciary's power grew, in a long-running accretion of power rather than one dramatic usurpation, it reflected the dominant economic interests of the society and used specious constitutional doctrines to protect big business against government regulation.

Boudin's argument was rhetorically forceful but clearly tendentious. He stated at the outset of his work that he made no pretense of disinterestedness, and he denied that there was any such thing as objectivity in the social sciences. The same force that led him to exaggerate the impact of judicial power in defeating progressive goals in the early twentieth century—ignoring the extent to which the people themselves were divided over questions of regulation—led him to overstate the importance of judicial power in the nineteenth century, for example, by attributing the Civil War largely to the *Dred Scott* decision.

Although many of Boudin's arguments have been surpassed by subsequent historical research, the question of judicial power that he raised is a perennial one. In the aftermath of the Warren Court revolution, in which the Supreme Court engaged in a new kind of activism for liberal purposes, conservative critics again took up the question. Both positivists like Robert Bork, who recognize no authority higher than the people and therefore insist that judges defer to majority opinion, and natural law advocates like Harry Jaffa, who declaim against judges who follow their own faulty reasoning rather than right reason, have attacked a modern version of government by judiciary. Boudin would have stood with the positivists, maintaining a faith in popular sovereignty as the will that the judiciary should consult. He regarded constitutional interpretation as properly practical and "instrumentalist," to be used by people to get things done, rather than a dogmatic control on government. In the light of Marxist theory, constitutional interpretation would evolve with the changing class structure and would reflect the economic factors of the society.

Boudin spent the last two decades of his career as a labor lawyer, arguing before the courts whose arrogance he decried in *Government by Judiciary*; ironically, he enjoyed more success at the bar than as a political leader. In the 1935 case of *New York Lumber Trade Association v. Lacey*, Boudin successfully defended New York teamsters against charges that they conspired with longshoremen in violation of the antitrust laws. Labor unions had been liable to prosecution as conspiracies in restraint of trade, notwithstanding the apparent intent of Congress to exempt them in the Clayton Antitrust Act of 1914. Judges who were hostile to the privileges labor unions enjoyed to coerce employers and fellow workers invoked the antitrust laws and issued injunctions against unions, until Congress and many states passed anti-injunction laws and elaborated the statutory protections for unions in the 1930s. Like farmers who were exempted from antitrust laws and allowed to reduce production and fix prices, labor unions were allowed to engage in control of the labor market as government intervened on their side in labor-management disputes.

Carrying further the power won by organized labor under the New Deal, in *U.S. v. Local 807* (1942), Boudin defended the Teamsters Union against prosecution under federal racketeering laws. In this case, teamsters in New York City extorted payments from out-of-state truckers, compelling them by violence and threats to pay the equivalent of the union rate for a day's work to unload shipments, or simply as protection money. A majority of the Supreme Court held that the federal racketeering law was aimed at "professional gangsters, and not interference with traditional labor union activities."

Boudin also advanced the doctrine announced by the Supreme Court in *Thornhill v. Alabama* (1940) stating that picketing was an exercise of free speech, protected under the First Amendment. In *Cafeteria Employees Union v. Angelos* (1943), in which the union picketed an owner-operated cafeteria, making admittedly false and threatening statements to customers while picketing, Boudin convinced the court that the New York courts had issued an overly broad injunction against picketing. By the end of the 1940s, the court had backed away from this broad protection of picketing as free speech and allowed states to regulate the practice. Boudin also defended the fur workers' union against Justice Department prosecution in the 1940s.

Although Boudin had lamented in *Government by Judiciary* that liberals hoped to fill the courts with "good men" rather than take on the structural illegitimacy of judicial power, by the end of his career the change in judicial personnel and doctrine had begun to reverse the respective powers of capital and labor, which he believed to be at the heart of political and constitutional questions. He continued to work and to teach left-wing ideas while staying out of Socialist and Communist party politics. He died in New York City while working on a never-completed treatise on economic developments in the nineteenth and twentieth centuries.

• Some of Boudin's personal papers are in the Columbia University Library. For a background treatment of the issue of judicial review, see Christopher Wolfe, *The Rise of Modern Judicial Review: From Constitutional Interpretation to Judge-Made Law* (1986). An obituary is in the *New York Times*, 31 May 1952.

PAUL MORENO

BOUDINOT, Elias (2 May 1740–24 Oct. 1821), statesman and philanthropist, was born in Philadelphia, Pennsylvania, the son of Elias Boudinot III, a silversmith and postmaster in Philadelphia, and Elizabeth Williams, daughter of a planter in Antigua, West Indies. He was fourth in a line of notable Elias Boudinots, the first a Huguenot refugee who moved from

London to New York about 1687. Over the generations Boudinots became linked through marriage with a number of prominent families, including those of Thomas Bradbury Chandler, William Tennent (1673–1746), Richard Stockton (1730–1781), and Benjamin Rush. Despite the prominence of the Boudinot family, the fourth Elias Boudinot apparently lacked the funds to attend college where he might have prepared for the ministry. Instead he studied law with his brother-in-law, Richard Stockton, receiving his license in 1760. Boudinot established a successful law practice in Elizabethtown, New Jersey, which he linked with mercantile activities and real estate investments so that by his early thirties he had acquired considerable wealth and social prominence.

Conservative by temperament and social station, Boudinot appears not to have engaged in the political protests of the 1760s, but by 1774 he became a member of the Essex County Committee of Correspondence, chairman of its Committee of Safety, and a member of the New Jersey Provincial Congress. A conservative Whig, he quashed the appeal of John Witherspoon at a meeting in New Brunswick that New Jersey proclaim its independence in April 1776. Boudinot contended that such matters should be left to the Continental Congress, which, among other things, had the best information about the possibility of a "happy reconciliation with the Mother Country" (*Journal*, p. 7).

Boudinot served briefly as aide-de-camp to William Livingston in the New Jersey militia in 1776, and in 1777, yielding to the entreaties of George Washington, he agreed to accept the post of commissary-general of prisoners captured by the British. Although he lamented leaving family and church for what he called the "unnatural and disrelishing state of War and slaughter," Boudinot carried out his mission ably, going so far as to pledge his own fortune to relieve the distress of the American prisoners. It was at this time that he came to know and greatly admire Washington.

Boudinot next served as a delegate from New Jersey (1778–1779) in the Continental Congress, where he managed to recover his outlays on behalf of the prisoners. Reelected to Congress, he served from July 1781 until November 1783. Much more active in his second term, he usually aligned with the nationalists from the middle states, especially in support of the claims of land companies to the West and in efforts to strengthen continental authority. Noting in 1781 that "the affairs of America require now the abilities of a Pitt & a Necker to preside over her Councils," Boudinot was elected to the presidency of the Congress on 4 November 1782. But the office, which then rotated annually from one state delegation to another, was so weak that Boudinot functioned largely in a ceremonial capacity. He served for a while as de facto secretary for foreign affairs after the resignation of Robert R. Livingston (1746–1813) in June 1783, signing the provisional peace treaty with Great Britain on 15 April 1783. He also presided over the problematic removal of Congress to Princeton on 24 June 1783 after the revolt of the Pennsylvania Line. His presidency was characterized by political moderation and social grace.

Preoccupied with investments in western lands, Boudinot was not actively involved in the movement to establish the federal Constitution, but, as was true during the revolutionary era, once the new system was under way he was a prominent participant. Elected to the First Congress, which met in New York on 4 March 1789, he became an outspoken Federalist. Boudinot made the first committee report on standing rules and orders of proceedings in the First Congress and moved for the creation of executive departments, the first being a secretary of finance. When Elbridge Gerry advocated a board of commissioners to manage treasury matters, Boudinot spoke in favor of a single head. Believing that government should regard the "well ordering of the whole Civil Society" rather than serving individual interests, Boudinot defended Alexander Hamilton's (1755–1804) proposal to fund the domestic debt at par value.

Boudinot resigned his seat in the Third Congress to take up the directorship of the U.S. Mint in 1795. He held that position until 1805 despite attempts by some Republicans to abolish the institution. That occasionally stormy tenure completed his public service.

Though characterized by Benjamin Rush (his nephew by marriage) as one who had a "canine appetite for wealth," Boudinot had genuine compassion for the underprivileged and gave generously of his time and fortune to philanthropic causes. A determined opponent of slavery, he went to court to defend blacks of doubtful freeman status. He took particular interest in the plight of Native Americans, to whom he left an endowment, and in his later years he engaged in a study of the culture and origins of Native Americans. The result was *A Star in the West* (1816), in which Boudinot argued from Scripture that the American Indians were descended from the Jews of the Diaspora.

Devoutly religious, Boudinot was alarmed by the rising popularity of deism, especially after the election of 1800. He published two works, *The Age of Revelation* (1801) and *The Second Advent* (1815), which aimed to counter the skepticism associated with Thomas Paine's *Age of Reason* and the secularism of the French Revolution. Perhaps more than any other individual he was responsible for the founding of the American Bible Society of which he was the first president (1816). His many bequests reflected his concern for the propagation of religion, including about 5,000 acres of western lands each to the American Bible Society, the American Board of Commissioners for Foreign Missions, and the Presbyterian Seminary. He endowed two scholarships at Princeton College where he had been an active trustee since 1772. A committed philanthropist, he left the timber on 13,000 acres of land for fuel for the poor of Philadelphia. Among other bequests he left $500 to the Foreign Mission School in Cornwall, Connecticut, where the young Cherokee Galagina was educated and took the name Elias Boudinot (c. 1803–1839) before assuming a leadership role in the Cherokee Nation.

Elias Boudinot died in Burlington, New Jersey. Not an innovative statesman like James Madison, Boudinot nonetheless exemplified the civic virtue so highly prized in the new nation.

• The Historical Society of Pennsylvania and the Princeton University Library hold the preponderance of Boudinot manuscripts. His papers have not been published, but his *Journal . . . of Events during the Revolutionary War* (1894; repr. 1968) contains a brief memoir of his military experience, and Jane J. Boudinot, *The Life, Public Services, Addresses and Letters of Elias Boudinot, LL.D.* (1896), contains many excerpts from his correspondence. In addition to the major published works mentioned in the text, there are some additional printed orations and addresses. The Papers of the Continental Congress, the *Annals of Congress*, and the Records of the United States Mint contain relevant materials as do the papers of leading figures of the period. The definitive biography is George Adams Boyd, *Elias Boudinot* (1952). Barbara Louise Clark, *E. B., The Story of Elias Boudinot IV, His Family, His Friends, and His Country* (1977), also contains information on Boudinot.

H. JAMES HENDERSON

BOUDINOT, Elias (1804?–22 June 1839), editor, was born at Oothcaloga in the Cherokee nation, now northwest Georgia, the son of Oo-watie (later known as David Watie), a Cherokee warrior, and Susanna Reese, the daughter of a white trader and a Cherokee woman. Originally named Galagina, which translates in English to "Buck," he attended the Moravian mission school in the Cherokee nation from 1811 to 1818 and the American Board of Commissioners Foreign Mission School in Cornwall, Connecticut, from 1818 to 1822. Buck took the name of the president of the American Bible Society, Elias Boudinot (although the Cherokee youth sometimes spelled it Boudinott), in 1817 en route to Cornwall. Moravian and American Board missionaries noted Boudinot's intellect and piety, and in 1820 he converted to Christianity.

Upon his permanent return home from school in 1825, Boudinot served as clerk of the Cherokee Council (until 1827), but his real interests were religious and intellectual rather than political. In 1826 he toured major American cities on behalf of his people to raise money for a printing press and types in the Cherokee syllabary invented by Sequoyah. The lecture he delivered in Philadelphia, published as *An Address to the Whites* (1826), is a classic expression of enlightenment attitudes toward culture and "civilization." Boudinot believed that Indians "must either become civilized and happy, or sharing the fate of many kindred nations, become extinct." He envisioned the Cherokee nation, with the assistance of white benefactors, "rising from the ashes of her degradation, wearing her purified and beautiful garments, and taking her seat with the nations of the earth."

While he was in the Northeast in 1826, Boudinot married Harriet Ruggles Gold, whom he had met while he was a student at Cornwall. This interracial union provoked an uproar among New Englanders that challenged Boudinot's belief that accomplished Indians could take their seats alongside whites—that is, be treated as equals—and forced the Foreign Mission School to close. Despite charges that she would become a "squaw," Harriet returned to the Cherokee nation with her husband, and they had six children before her death in 1836. In 1837 Boudinot married American Board missionary Delight Sargent, also a white New Englander, with whom he had no children.

Boudinot's tour was professionally as well as personally successful. The council purchased the press and appointed Boudinot editor of the bilingual, biweekly *Cherokee Phoenix*. The prospectus for the paper appeared in October 1827 and the first issue in February 1828. While Boudinot borrowed material on national and world news from other publications, he also printed Cherokee laws and announcements and penned an editorial. The difficulty of setting type in the syllabary meant that the amount of Cherokee text in the *Phoenix* never equaled the English. The American Board subsidized Boudinot's salary, and so he worked with missionary Samuel Austin Worcester on the translation and publication of hymns and the New Testament. He also translated *Poor Sarah* (1833), an inspirational story originally serialized in missionary periodicals.

Although he was not a politician, Boudinot became convinced in 1832 of the futility of Cherokee resistance to removal west of the Mississippi River. Southern states demanded federal action to extinguish Indian title to land within their chartered borders, and President Andrew Jackson sought to oblige them. In 1832 the U.S. Supreme Court decided in favor of the Cherokees in *Worcester v. Georgia*, a case involving the unlawful arrest of Boudinot's collaborator, who refused to take an oath of allegiance to the state of Georgia, but the Court lacked the power to enforce the decision. As white intruders streamed into Cherokee country and threatened, robbed, and assaulted Cherokees with impunity, Boudinot began to believe that only removal would end the Cherokees' suffering. He wanted to open columns of the *Cherokee Phoenix* to a debate of the issue. Principal Chief John Ross refused on the grounds that the *Phoenix* was the official organ of the Cherokee nation and therefore should print only the nation's official position on the issue—steadfast opposition to removal. Consequently, Boudinot resigned as editor in 1832. He served on official delegations to Washington, D.C., in 1834 and 1835, but he focused his energies on trying to convince Ross to negotiate. Despairing of accomplishing that goal, he joined his cousin John Ridge and uncle Major Ridge in promoting a removal treaty.

In December 1835 a small group of Cherokees met at Boudinot's house and signed the Treaty of New Echota in clear violation of the Cherokee law that made unauthorized land cession a capital offense. The vast majority of Cherokees repudiated the treaty and its signers. Boudinot defended his actions in a pamphlet, *Letters and Other Papers Relating to Cherokee Affairs* (1837): "Instead of contending uselessly against superior power, the only course left, was, to yield to circumstances over which they [the Cherokees] had no control." Because Ross prevented discussion of the issue, "the people have been kept ignorant of their true condition." As a result, he argued, "we can see strong reasons to justify the action of a minority of fifty persons—to do what the majority *would do* if they understood their condition—to save a *nation* from political thraldom and moral degradation."

Boudinot and his family moved west in 1837, a year before the U.S. Army rounded up the majority of Cherokees and imprisoned them in hot, crowded, unsanitary stockades to await transportation to the West over the infamous "trail of tears." They settled at Park Hill, near the new Cherokee capital of Tahlequah (present-day Oklahoma), where Boudinot planned to resume his work with Worcester, who had relocated there following his release from the Georgia penitentiary. After the Cherokees had suffered at least 4,000 deaths on their forced migration to the West under the terms of the Treaty of New Echota, an unknown group of men executed Elias Boudinot and the Ridges for their role in removal. Boudinot died at Park Hill. His ignominious death does not detract from his literary legacy, which rested on a profound belief in the Cherokees' ability to adapt to changing circumstances, triumph over adversity, and "rise like the Phoenix."

• Ralph H. Gabriel, *Elias Boudinot, Cherokee, and His America* (1941), is a full-length biography of Boudinot that focuses on the controversy surrounding his marriage to Harriet Gold. Thurman Wilkins, *Cherokee Tragedy: The Story of the Ridge Family and the Decimation of a People* (1970), is a sympathetic, very readable account of Boudinot's extended family. An analysis of Boudinot's public life along with an annotated collection of his published work can be found in *Cherokee Editor: The Writings of Elias Boudinot*, ed. Theda Perdue (1983).

THEDA PERDUE

BOUDINOT, Elias Cornelius (1 Aug. 1835–27 Sept. 1890), Cherokee lawyer and progressive, was born in New Echota, Georgia, the son of Elias Boudinot, tribal leader and editor of the newspaper, the *Cherokee Phoenix*, and Harriet Gold, daughter of a prominent New England family. His mother died a year after his birth.

Elias Cornelius Boudinot was born the same year his father signed the infamous 1835 Cherokee treaty. His father and his great-uncle, Major Ridge, led the faction that agreed to the Cherokees' removal from Georgia, North Carolina, and Alabama to eastern Oklahoma. The elder Boudinot, convinced that the Cherokees' survival depended upon their continued adoption of white institutions and skills, urged the tribe to move westward where they could "civilize" at their own pace. The majority of the tribe rejected the treaty but failed to convince the federal government to renegotiate. Sixteen thousand Cherokees, many forcibly rounded up, were marched westward by the U.S. Army; approximately 4,000 died from hunger and sickness along the way.

When Boudinot was four, tribal members assassinated his father, great-uncle, and another relative for violating the Cherokee law that forbid any member from ceding tribal lands upon penalty of death. His stepmother returned with the Boudinot children to New England, where Elias studied civil engineering in Manchester, Vermont. At age eighteen, Boudinot moved to Fayetteville, Arkansas, apprenticing himself to the lawyer A. M. Wilson. Admitted to the bar at age twenty-one, Boudinot quickly achieved fame for his adversarial and oratorical skills during the trial of his uncle, Stand Watie, who was ultimately acquitted for murder.

Like his father, Boudinot was drawn to newspaper work, taking the editorship first of the Fayetteville *Weekly Arkansian* and then of the Little Rock *True Democrat* in 1860. Boudinot also became involved in Democratic and Confederate politics during this period, becoming chairman of the Democratic State Central Committee in 1860 and secretary of the Secession Convention the following year.

The Civil War again split the Cherokees into two warring factions, with battles fought throughout the tribal nation between Union and Confederate Cherokee forces. Boudinot served briefly with his uncle Stand Watie's Confederate regiment, achieving the rank of lieutenant colonel. In 1863 the southern faction of the Cherokees elected Boudinot as their delegate to the Confederate Congress at Richmond. At the war's end, Boudinot represented the southern Cherokee faction in the negotiation of the Cherokees' 1866 treaty with the United States.

Article 10 of the treaty guaranteed Cherokee immunity from federal agricultural taxes. Boudinot, cognizant of the economic advantage of this provision, constructed a factory to produce tobacco, which was sold throughout Arkansas, Missouri, and the Indian Territory. Federal officials, disputing the treaty's interpretation, seized the factory for nonpayment of taxes. Boudinot took the case to the Supreme Court, where in 1871 the Court ruled in the famous *Cherokee Tobacco* decision that federal legislation that was passed later could abrogate treaty guarantees.

For the next twenty years, Boudinot devoted his life to continuing the progressive and assimilationist philosophies espoused by his father. He lobbied extensively in Washington, D.C., and on the lecture circuit for the division of Cherokee lands in severalty, the opening of Cherokee lands to the railroads, and the dissolution of tribal governments. Boudinot's wit, charm, shrewdness, and opinions found favor with members of the railroad lobby and Washington society. His talents, however, never provided him with a secure income. Following the failure of his tobacco factory, Boudinot, in addition to his lobbying, lecturing, and lawyering, dabbled in ranching, newspaper work, and commercial enterprises. In 1877, he masterminded the first "Boomer" invasion, a flood of white settlers, into the Cherokee's western lands, an action that brought threats to his life from other Cherokees.

Boudinot married Clara Minear in 1885. His marriage kept him closer to his legal practice in Fort Smith, Arkansas, where he continued to involve himself in the affairs of the Cherokee nation. He died in Fort Smith following a sudden illness.

Elias Cornelius Boudinot, three-eighths Cherokee, was a man caught between two cultures. Unable to leave his Cherokee roots behind and assimilate into white society, Boudinot tried to drag the Cherokees into his white world. His Cherokee brethren simultaneously grudgingly respected and reviled him as a self-serving "sellout."

• Letters from Elias C. Boudinot are in the Western History Collections at the University of Oklahoma and in Edward E. Dale and Gaston Litton, *Cherokee Cavaliers: Forty Years of Cherokee History as Told in the Correspondence of the Ridge-Watie-Boudinot Family* (1939). The earliest biographical information about Boudinot appeared in "Colonel Elias C. Boudinot," *National Illustrated Magazine* 1, no. 6 (1884): 169–73. For important biographical studies of Boudinot, see Lois E. Forde, "Elias Cornelius Boudinot" (Ph.D. diss., Columbia Univ., 1951), and Dewey Whitsett Hodges, "Col. E. C. Boudinot and His Influence on Oklahoma History" (Master's thesis, Univ. of Okla., 1929). Discussions of Elias C. Boudinot's political life are in Robert K. Heimann, "The Cherokee Tobacco Case," *Chronicles of Oklahoma* 41, no. 3 (1963): 299–322; Muriel H. Wright, "Notes on Colonel Elias C. Boudinot," *Chronicles of Oklahoma* 41, no. 4 (1964): 382–407; and Thomas Burnell Colbert, "Visionary or Rogue?: The Life and Legacy of Elias Cornelius Boudinot," *Chronicles of Oklahoma* 65, no. 3 (1987): 268–81. John D. Adams, *Elias Cornelius Boudinot: In Memoriam* (1891), commemorates Boudinot.

SHARON O'BRIEN

BOULANGER, Nadia Juliette (16 Sept. 1887–22 Oct. 1979), composer and teacher, was born in Paris, the daughter of Ernest Boulanger and Princess Raissa Mychetsky. Her family was musical: her father and grandfather had taught singing at the Paris Conservatoire; her mother, a singer who had been one of Ernest Boulanger's students, gave Nadia her first music lessons; and her sister, Lili (1893–1918), was regarded during her brief lifetime as a talented composer.

At age ten, Boulanger began formal musical instruction at the Paris Conservatoire, studying harmony with Paul Antonin Vidal, organ with Louis Vierne and Alexandre Guilmant, and composition with Charles-Marie Widor and Gabriel Fauré. She graduated with prizes in both organ and theory. In 1908 she earned second-place honors in the Prix de Rome competition for "La Sirène," a cantata. Her sister was one of her first composition students and the first woman to win the Prix de Rome, in 1913. After Lili's death in 1918, Boulanger gave up her own composing career and devoted her energies entirely to teaching. She had become an assistant teacher in harmony at the Paris Conservatoire in 1909, and she held this position until 1924. From 1920 to 1939 Boulanger taught at the École Normale de Musique in Paris, and she began teaching at the American Conservatory at Fontainebleau in 1921, becoming its director in 1950.

Boulanger visited the United States for the first time in 1924 at the invitation of her American student Aaron Copland. She appeared as organ soloist in Copland's "Symphony for Organ and Orchestra" with the New York Symphony Orchestra under Walter Damrosch on 11 January 1925. She made several more trips to this country and was admired for her performances, her influence as a teacher on many young American composers, and her conducting. Boulanger became the first woman to conduct a regular concert of the Boston Symphony Orchestra in 1938 and the New York Philharmonic Symphony Orchestra on 11 February 1939. During the occupation of France during World War II, she lived in the United States, teaching at Wellesley and Radcliffe Colleges and the Juilliard School. She returned to her faculty position at the Paris Conservatoire in 1946.

Boulanger earned a reputation as an inspiring but strict and demanding pedagogue, both in her formal composition classes and in private lessons. She demanded that her students study and analyze scores of major composers from all periods in order to develop their own individual modern styles. She emphasized the formal and harmonic construction of works by Igor Stravinsky, Maurice Ravel, and Claude Debussy. Although she appreciated modern music, she did not admire the works of Arnold Schoenberg and the Viennese School. As a result of her broad interests and her insistence on discipline, the work of her students is highly individual and eclectic, not tied to the theoretical dictates of any particular school. Among her American students in the 1920s through the 1950s were many who became influential composers and teachers themselves, including Arthur Berger, Marc Blitzstein, Elliott Carter, Copland, David Diamond, Roy Harris, Douglas Moore, Walter Piston, Elie Siegmeister, Louise Talma, and Virgil Thomson. Boulanger was also influential in the rediscovery of early music by Gesualdo and Monteverdi, which she sight-read with her students at her Wednesday afternoon master classes. Her impact on the direction of American composition was so great that Virgil Thomson once quipped that every American town had "a five-and-ten-cent store and a Boulanger student."

After her return to Paris in 1946, Boulanger continued to teach for as long as her health permitted. Her ninetieth birthday was the occasion of numerous tributes from her students all over the world. Boulanger was honored in Europe with a commandership in the Légion d'honneur and nomination as maître de chappelle to the prince of Monaco. In the United States, Boulanger was elected to the American Academy of Arts and Sciences. She died in Paris.

• Boulanger's life and works are treated extensively in Leonie Rosenstiel, *Nadia Boulanger: A Life in Music* (1982). See also Alan Kendall, *The Tender Tyrant, Nadia Boulanger: A Life Devoted to Music* (1977), and Bruno Mosaingeon, *Mademoi-*

selle: Entretiens avec Nadia Boulanger (1980; English translation, 1985). Boulanger is mentioned as an important teacher in the biographical works of numerous American composers. See also Allen Shawm, "Nadia Boulanger's Lessons," *Atlantic*, Mar. 1983, pp. 78–85, and Vivian Perlis, "Nadia Boulanger," in *The New Grove Dictionary of American Music*, ed. Stanley Sadie and H. Wiley Hitchcock, vol. 1 (1986).

BARBARA L. TISCHLER

BOULIGNY, Dominique (23 Aug. 1773–5 Mar. 1833), soldier, planter, and U.S. senator, was born in New Orleans, Louisiana, the son of Francisco Bouligny, the lieutenant governor of Louisiana, a colonel in the Fixed Louisiana Regiment, and the acting governor of Louisiana, and Marie Louise le Sénéchal d'Auberville. He spent his childhood in the comfort that his father's influence and wealth provided. Surrounded by a large extended family and a full complement of house servants, Bouligny developed a strong attachment to his family, an even stronger admiration for the military that commanded his father's devotion, and pride in being a citizen of Spain. Louisiana offered few opportunities for the sons of army officers outside of military service. Sons of officers entered the army at an early age, and as a senior officer in the Fixed Louisiana Regiment, Bouligny's father arranged an appointment for his twelve-year-old son as a cadet in the regimental school in March 1786. His father's influence assured Bouligny's rapid promotion to the first officer rank of sublieutenant at the age of fourteen.

After Spain declared war on revolutionary France in 1793, Bouligny received orders to help prepare the defenses of the colony against its many potential enemies, including the French, the British, and the intrusive Americans. Initially, Bouligny drilled the regiment's artillery corps. He then served on the *La Fina* in the Gulf of Mexico. Upon receiving news of the Genet-Clark expedition against Louisiana, the Floridas, and Canada in 1794, Bouligny received an appointment to the Mississippi River Squadron. He commanded land troops on the galleys sent to New Madrid and on the galley *La Castilla*. In the Illinois Country he took temporary command of the galiot *La Flecha*, served as the second in command at Fort Celeste in New Madrid, and was charged with overseeing the construction of a new fort, San Fernando de las Barrancas, at the present site of Memphis. Bouligny successfully carried out assignments beyond those normally directed by a sublieutenant, and his promotion to the rank of lieutenant was endorsed in Spain on 20 December 1795. Under the command of Lieutenant Colonel Carlos Howard, Bouligny continued to direct efforts to strengthen defenses in Upper Louisiana, and in 1797 he was at Fort Panmure to assist in deterring angry Americans who planned to beseige the fortification. His first experience of battle came when he participated in a naval engagement with a British warship at the mouth of the Mississippi River.

When his father died in 1800, Bouligny became the head of the family; he advanced his position by purchasing an office on the Cabildo, an institution representative of Spanish-style city government, as regidor perpetuo. He was already a substantial landowner. In 1796 he had taken up a land grant, and in 1803 he purchased a half-interest in a prosperous sugar plantation fronting the Mississippi River a few miles from New Orleans. That year he bought a plantation in the Attakapas area, and he received royal permission to marry Anne Arthemise Le Blanc. The wedding took place early in 1803 at St. Louis Cathedral, and the couple moved to Bouligny's newly acquired sugar plantation; they had fifteen children.

Bouligny resigned his commission and retired to attend to his plantation when the colony was transferred to the United States. In 1805 he was elected to the territorial legislature, in which he joined with other Gallics in opposing Governor William Charles Coles Claiborne and the newly arrived Americans. His hostility toward the unfamiliar principles of representative government and common law innovations prompted him to apply to the Viceroy of Mexico, requesting permission to settle in Vera Cruz. Reelection to the legislature and favorable committee appointments convinced him to remain. He served on the Committee on the Judicial System and the Committee on the Organization of the Militia, and he was appointed a major in the Fourth Regiment of the militia.

After Louisiana was admitted to the Union in 1812, Bouligny became a member of the Orleans Parish Police Jury. He served on the Committee for the Defense of New Orleans in 1814, subscribed $10,000 to defend the state from the British, and fought under Andrew Jackson in the battles for New Orleans. In the postwar years, Bouligny reaped large profits from his agricultural holdings—profits that declined to deficits by 1818. Economic depression, combined with his lingering attachment to Spain, prompted Bouligny to make serious efforts to liquidate his property, remove the entire family to Cuba, and to import tools and equipment to Cuba duty free. However, Spanish restrictions on imports forced him to abandon the scheme.

Bouligny's Americanization was completed in 1824 when the state legislature selected him to fill the unexpired senatorial term of Henry Johnson, who had been elected as the governor of the state. In the Senate, Bouligny followed an independent course. Although the concept of party was alien to him, his consistent support of protective tariffs placed him among the National Republicans. Additionally, he pushed the pension claims of Louisiana veterans of the War of 1812.

Bouligny hoped to be reelected, but he had no political gifts. Ideologically and personally, he preferred the order and discipline of centralized authority. He had remained mute in the Senate, ignored his Louisiana colleagues, and simply could not compete in the political climate inaugurated by the Jacksonians. Defeated in his bid for reelection in 1830, Bouligny thought to run for mayor of New Orleans against Denis Prieur. He soon saw the impossibility of victory against the popular Prieur, withdrew his candidacy, and retired to private life.

In 1830 Bouligny gave up the last of his country property in exchange for property on Royal Street in New Orleans, where he contracted to build a large home that was completed in 1832 and where he died.

• The Bouligny-Baldwin Family Papers, 1710–1900, and the d'Auberville-Bouligny Family Papers, 1618–1873, housed in the Historic New Orleans Collection in New Orleans, contain some useful information. Fontaine Martin, *A History of the Bouligny Family and Allied Families* (1990), provides the most complete account of Bouligny's life. Gilbert Din, *Francisco Bouligny: A Bourbon Soldier in Spanish Louisiana* (1993), examines Bouligny's early career. Ronald Morazán, "Letters, Petitions and Decrees of the Cabildo of New Orleans, 1800–1803; Edited and Translated" (Ph.D. diss., Louisiana State Univ., 1972), provides information on Cabildo activities during Bouligny's tenure. Richard Lowett, "Activities of Citizen Genet in Kentucky, 1793–1794," *Filson Club Historical Quarterly* 22 (1948): 752–67, covers the concerns that prompted Spain's defensive posture and gave Bouligny military experience and promotion.

CAROLYN E. DE LATTE

BOUQUET, Henry (1719?–2 Sept. 1765), soldier of fortune, was born in Rolle, Switzerland, the son of Isaac-Barthelemy Bouquet, a hotel proprietor, and Madeleine Rolaz du Rozay. In 1736 he became a cadet in the Swiss Regiment of Constant in the Dutch service. From 1739 to 1748 he served in the army of the king of Sardinia. He obtained a command in the Dutch army's Swiss Guards, serving until 1755, when Jacques Prevost recruited him with other mercenary officers for the Royal American Regiment, a four-battalion British army unit Prevost was raising for service in America. Embarking in May 1756 to spend the rest of his life in the British army in America, Bouquet commanded as lieutenant colonel, in October 1756, the First Battalion, which was sent to Philadelphia. He clashed with Pennsylvania authorities over troop quarters and the need for a smallpox hospital. In June 1757 he took four companies and part of the Seventy-seventh Highland Battalion to Charleston, South Carolina. Again colonial officials did not provide facilities. With other Swiss officers he invested in South Carolina rice growing lands, although the project collapsed in 1761. Bouquet brought five First Battalion companies to Philadelphia in May 1758 to join Brigadier John Forbes's expedition against the French at the Forks of the Ohio, on which he served virtually as second in command.

Bouquet originally underestimated the time required to assemble a preponderant force before Fort Duquesne, and he unwisely condoned Major James Grant's precipitous attack on the fort on 13–14 September. However, he encouraged Forbes to use the Pennsylvania route to the Forks instead of Braddock's Road, tactfully facing down George Washington, who adamantly objected. Bouquet also recognized the value of the discovery of a short cut across Laurel Ridge, and he was responsible for scheduling the army's movement. The French realized they were outnumbered and destroyed Fort Duquesne on 24 November. In the following eighteen months they abandoned all other posts in western Pennsylvania.

From 1759 to April 1765 Bouquet commanded forces in the upper Ohio Valley, at first as the subordinate, successively, to Forbes, Brigadier John Stanwix, and Brigadier Robert Monckton. When Monckton withdrew in October 1761, Bouquet became full commander of the district; in May 1764 he was made commander of the entire Southern Department. Although the French had disappeared south of the Great Lakes by 1761, British regular garrisons remained, and Fort Pitt was constructed. On 30–31 October 1761 Bouquet issued a proclamation against hunting and settling west of the Alleghenies in order to enforce territorial rights granted the Indians at the Treaty of Easton (1758). However, his forces were too few to fully implement that policy.

Bouquet was thrown into despair by a flood at Fort Pitt and by simultaneously learning that his intended bride, Anne Willing of Philadelphia, had married Tench Francis, Jr. Although he watched "Long Meadow," his plantation near Hagerstown, develop, his personal finances were precarious. Army funds had been stolen from him at Fort Pitt, and he was held accountable for funds of the Seventy-seventh Highlanders he had administered in 1756. Disgusted, in May 1763 he obtained leave to sail to England, but at the outbreak of Pontiac's War, General Sir Jeffery Amherst sent him back to the upper Ohio Valley. He commanded an emergency expedition of 438 soldiers (Royal Americans and Highlander light infantry) and a packhorse train carrying flour, to save besieged Fort Pitt. On 24 June, while Bouquet was en route, individuals at Fort Pitt gave smallpox-infected items to unsuspecting Indians. Not knowing this, Amherst in July got Bouquet to agree to do the same thing. Their exchange has been construed as an endorsement of genocide. On 5 August the war party of Shawnees, Delawares, Wyandots, and Mingoes who had besieged Fort Pitt repositioned near Bushy Run and ambushed Bouquet's expedition there. The British took shelter on the adjacent Edge Hill. Although apparently doomed, the next day Bouquet vanquished the attackers by luring them to expose themselves to a flank attack of bayonets and driving them into cross fire. Despite heavy losses the expedition entered Fort Pitt on 10 August. The Indians did not renew the siege, but their raids in Pennsylvania resumed in 1764.

In July 1764 Bouquet began organizing an expedition from Fort Pitt into Indian strongholds in central Ohio, under commander in chief Major General Thomas Gage's orders, intended to coordinate with Colonel John Bradstreet's amphibious force, which moved from Niagara to the Great Lakes. Unavoidable problems, especially desertion, delayed Bouquet, and his 1,500 soldiers did not leave Fort Pitt until 1 October, long after Bradstreet.

Marching west toward Indian villages on the Muskingum River, Bouquet chose good defensive sites for all encampments to avoid repeating General Edward Braddock's mistakes of 1755. By 12 August Bradstreet had completed an unauthorized treaty at Presque Isle with Indians representing themselves as emissaries of the nations of central Ohio. Gage repudiated the treaty on 2 September, with Bouquet's approval. On 28 October a letter from Bradstreet reached Bouquet stating that rather than create a diversion from Sandusky Bay, as ordered, Bradstreet had gone to Detroit. Through October and early November Bouquet negotiated with Delawares, Shawnees, and Ohio Senecas (Mingoes) near Tuscarawas and at the Forks of the Muskingum. In addition to abandoning the war and admitting that they had started it, these nations agreed to surrender all prisoners, yielding hostages from their own leadership as a guarantee, and to send delegates for a formal treaty with Sir William Johnson, the British Indian superintendent. On 28 November the expedition was back at Fort Pitt with the freed prisoners, hostages, and delegates. Without firing a shot, Bouquet's show of force had ended open warfare with the Indians until Dunmore's War.

On 17 April 1765 Bouquet, now naturalized by Parliament, learned that he had been appointed brigadier in command of forces in the Floridas. Meanwhile, he had an affair with Margaret Oswald, Benjamin Chew's sister-in-law. Chew and Bouquet belonged to a consortium investing in the Shepody coast of Nova Scotia. On 2 July Bouquet set sail from Cape May and arrived at Pensacola on 24 August with a flotilla of troop transports. Deadly fever was rampant aboard and ashore. Bouquet, already stricken, was brought ashore, where he died the next day.

Historians of the British army regard Bouquet as an innovator of light infantry tactics because of his operation at Bushy Run and the organization he devised for the Ohio expedition. His tact and capacity to compromise stand in contrast to the traditional view of bungling, heavy-handed British military administration in colonial America.

• The Bouquet papers, the principal source, are at the British Library, London. Other original records are found in the Amherst papers (Public Record Office W.O. 34 Series), Kew; the Gage papers, American Series, at the Clements Library, University of Michigan, Ann Arbor; the James Abercromby Papers at the Huntington Library, San Marino, Calif.; and the John Forbes Papers at the Tracy W. McGregor Library, University of Virginia. Bouquet papers from these and other repositories are printed for the period through November 1761 in *The Papers of Henry Bouquet*, ed. S. K. Stevens et al. (6 vols., 1951–1994). Two of Bouquet's three orderly books for 1764, both preserved at the Clements Library, are printed in *Western Pennsylvania Historical Magazine* 42 (1959), 56 (1973), and 57 (1974), ed. Edward G. Williams, with an essay locating the road to Fort Pitt. *An Historical Account of Bouquet's Expedition against the Ohio Indians in 1764* (1765), attributed to the Reverend William Smith, includes a condensed version of the negotiations with the Ohio Indians. C. G. F. Dumas's sketch of the life of Bouquet, written as a preface to Dumas's French translation of Smith's *Historical Account* (1769), is one of the few sources for Bouquet's early life.

LOUIS M. WADDELL

BOUQUILLON, Thomas Joseph (16 May 1840–5 Nov. 1902), Catholic priest and moral theologian, was born in Warnêton, Belgium. Little is known about Bouquillon's parents other than their occupations as small landowners and farmers. Bouquillon received his early education in the small hamlet of Warnêton and in 1854 was sent to the episcopal college of St. Louis at Menin, Belgium, where until 1860 he learned languages and studied the liberal arts. Immediately thereafter he entered the petit séminaire of Roulers, Belgium, where he studied scholastic philosophy, and in 1862 he studied theology at the major seminary of Bruges, Belgium. In 1863 he matriculated at the Gregorian University in Rome, where he finished his theological studies, was ordained in 1865, and obtained a doctorate in moral theology in 1867.

During his Roman years he witnessed the antimodernist leadership of Pope Pius IX (1846–1878), the Syllabus of Errors (1864), and the scholastic and Thomistic revival in philosophy and theology. Although the scholastic revival had its ecclesiastical confirmation in Pope Leo XIII's (1878–1903) encyclical *Aeterni Patris* (1878), it had been a developing force in the Roman schools since the mid-nineteenth century. The return to Thomas Aquinas's philosophy was thought to be a particularly secure way of preserving Catholic orthodoxy in response to modern post-Kantian philosophies that the revivalists considered subjectivist and relativist. As his later published works reveal, Bouquillon was especially influenced by the Thomistic realistic metaphysic and natural law tradition.

After receiving his Roman doctorate, Bouquillon returned to Belgium, where he spent ten years (1867–1877) teaching moral theology at the major seminary of Bruges. Like his Roman professors he understood moral theology as a science of the Christian means to salvation, not just the science of ethical activity. During his years in Bruges he published the first of three editions of his *Institutiones Theologia Moralis Fundamentalis* (1873; rev. eds. 1890, 1903), a textbook that was widely used in the moral education of clergy in Belgium and in the Catholic University of America during the late nineteenth and early twentieth centuries. In 1876 and 1877 he also helped organize for lay professionals and businessmen at Bruges theological conferences whose primary aim was to help distinguished laity reflect upon modern moral issues.

In 1877 Bouquillon was appointed to a chair in moral theology at the newly established Catholic University of Lille in the Départment du Nord in France. While at Lille he published two more significant studies in special moral theology, *Tractatus de virtutibus Theologicis* (1878) and *Tractatus de Virtute Religionis* (1880), and edited a major work by the sixteenth-century English Catholic theologian Thomas Stapleton, who had taught in Belgium.

In 1885 he joined the Benedictine Abbey in Maredsous, Belgium. It is not clear why he entered the monastery. His biographer, H. Rommel, believed that he had entertained a vocation to the monastic life at the time, but he never became a monk. Instead, he used his time in the monastery to write a history of moral theology for an introduction to a new edition of his manual of fundamental moral theology. He remained in the monastery doing research, editing, and writing until 1889, when the American Bishop John J. Keane, president of the newly established Catholic University of America, invited him to become a founding member of the new university's theology faculty.

From 1889 until his death Bouquillon taught moral theology at the Catholic University, built up the theological library, revised his textbooks on moral theology, and contributed numerous articles to the new *Catholic University Bulletin*, a journal for the dissemination of contemporary Catholic ideas on theology and social-moral issues. He believed he was particularly well suited to American life. As a Belgian Catholic, he had grown up in a nation where the Catholic clergy had supported the political movements to establish a free nation and where Catholics had experienced and valued the benefits of religious freedom. He was also sympathetic to the scientific spirit of the day in the United States. He called upon moral theologians to establish a dialogue between Thomas Aquinas's moral principles and the new developments in the empirical social sciences (especially sociology and economics). His advocacy of the use of the social sciences had a profound effect upon moral theology, especially in fostering the development of a twentieth-century social Catholicism that focused upon issues of social and economic justice in American society. His teachings significantly influenced his students, two of whom, John A. Ryan and William J. Kerby, became intellectual and social leaders within early twentieth-century American Catholicism.

Bouquillon became most widely known in the United States during his involvement in an American Catholic debate on the state's role in education. Archbishop John Ireland of St. Paul, Minnesota, acknowledged in 1890 the need for public education and the state's right and duty to provide for it, a position some leading American Catholics considered heterodox. In 1891 Bouquillon prepared a pamphlet, *Education: To Whom Does It Belong?*, supporting Ireland's argument, and for the next two years the issue became hotly contested within American Catholic circles. Bouquillon's position was argued on the moral grounds that the state had the duty to provide for the "temporal common welfare" and that the diffusion of knowledge was among the most necessary means for that end. The state, therefore, had a duty to provide education where parents and churches were incapable of doing so. The battle over the state's right and obligation to educate would continue within various pockets of American Catholicism for another fifty years before Bouquillon's position gained universal acceptance.

Bouquillon, considered a member of the more liberal wing of the faculty at Catholic University, sided with the Americanizing bishops and priests of the late nineteenth century. He not only supported Archbishop Ireland's views on education but also encouraged the Americanization of the immigrant Catholic church and a sympathetic Catholic dialogue with modern scientific thought and methods. Affable and open to new directions in thought, he won many students to his perspectives. Although he had a strong mind and rigorous habits of study, he was soft spoken and generally in poor physical health. After 1900 his health deteriorated to such an extent that in 1902 he retired from teaching and, hoping to regain his health, returned to Belgium. While in Brussels he died.

• Bouquillon's letters and unpublished papers are located primarily in the archives of the Catholic Seminary in Bruges, Belgium, and the Catholic University of America, Washington, D.C. In addition to the books mentioned above, Bouquillon edited six volumes of *Leonis Papae XIII Allocutiones, Epistolae, Constitutiones aliaque acta praecipua* (1887), the *Catechismus ex decreto Concilii Tridentini ad Parochos* (1890), and other tracts on spiritual and ecclesiastical topics. He also wrote a number of articles on moral issues for *Revue des sciènces ecclésiastiques*, *Nouvelle revue théologique*, *Revue bénédictine*, *American Catholic Quarterly Review*, and the *Catholic University Bulletin*. The only biography is H. Rommel, *Thomas Bouquillon . . . Notice biobibliographique* (1903). Other studies of his life and thought are C. J. Nuesse, "Thomas Joseph Bouquillon (1840–1902), Moral Theologian and Precursor of the Social Sciences in the Catholic University of America," *Catholic Historical Review* 72 (1986): 601–19, and "Before *Rerum Novarum*: A Moral Theologian's View of Catholic Social Movements in 1891," *Social Thought* 17 (1991): 5–17; J. Forget, "Bouquillon, Thomas J.," *Dictionaire de théologie catholique*; and Laurent Janssens, "Maitre Thomas Bouquillon," *Revue bénédictine* 20 (1903): 2–6. An obituary is in the *Catholic University Bulletin* 9 (Jan. 1903): 152–63.

PATRICK W. CAREY

BOURKE-WHITE, Margaret (14 June 1904–27 Aug. 1971), pioneer photojournalist and industrial photographer, was born in New York City, the daughter of Joseph Edward White, an amateur photographer and an engineer and inventor for a printing press manufacturer, and Minnie Bourke, a teacher. Originally using the name Margaret White, she added her mother's maiden name in 1927.

Bourke-White began photographing as a way to finance her college education, first at the University of Michigan and then at Cornell University. As a freshman Bourke-White had taken a course with the noted pictorialist Clarence H. White at Columbia University in New York City. After studying biology and technology at five different universities, including Rutgers, Purdue, and Case Western, she graduated from Cornell in 1927 with a degree in biology.

In 1924 she married Everett "Chappie" Chapman, a graduate student in electrical engineering whom she had met while at the University of Michigan. They then went to Purdue University but separated two years later, having had no children. Following the breakup of her marriage and her college graduation, she moved to her mother's home in Cleveland to work in the Museum of Natural History, obtain a divorce, and freelance and work as a commercial photographer.

From the beginning of her career Bourke-White was intrigued by architecture and industry, subjects with which she had become acquainted through her father. According to her autobiography, as a child she accompanied her father on trips to factories, where he supervised the setting up of rotary presses, and she was so impressed that she believed "a foundry represented the beginning and end of all beauty. Later when I became a photographer . . . this memory was so vivid and so alive that it shaped the whole course of my career" (*Portrait of Myself*, p. 18). She was only seventeen when her father died, but his influence was imprinted on her for a lifetime.

The two years (1927–1929) Bourke-White spent photographing steel mills in Cleveland as a commercial photographer and freelancer included work that interested publisher Henry Luce. After a trip to New York at Luce's invitation, Bourke-White decided to join the staff of the new business magazine Luce was planning to publish. As an associate editor and the first photographer at *Fortune* (1929–1933), she proved how talented she was. Photographs from the first of several trips to the Soviet Union were published in *Fortune*, the *New York Times Magazine*, and her first book, *Eyes on Russia* (1931). From 1932 to 1937 her freelance work was published in *Vanity Fair* as well.

Bourke-White's skill eventually led to her employment as one of the four original photographers at *Life*, along with Alfred Eisenstaedt, Thomas D. McAvoy, and Peter Stackpole. Bourke-White's photograph of Fort Peck Dam in Montana was *Life*'s lead photo essay and first cover in November 1936. The dramatic flare that characterized her professional life also characterized her photographs for *Fortune* and *Life*. She went on to work for *Life* almost without interruption until 1957, remaining on staff while in semiretirement until her resignation in 1969.

Bourke-White's long tenure with Luce's two magazines meant many exciting assignments that took her to the far corners of the world. Over a 26-year period she photographed a wide variety of topics, primarily because she shot the newsworthy characters of the day, including notables such as Joseph Stalin, Winston Churchill, Franklin D. Roosevelt, Haile Selassie, and Pope Pius XI. Ironically, in a magazine known for its candid photo essays, Bourke-White reportedly made her subjects endure "the torture of long hours, new positions, and recommended changes of clothing" (*Life*, 10 Sept. 1971, p. 3). She was accused of perpetuating stereotypes and choosing "drama over unembellished fact" (Goldberg, *Margaret Bourke-White*, p. 191).

Compassion for other human beings was slow in coming to Bourke-White's work. People served as figures to put in a photograph's frame to show scale until she went on a *Fortune* assignment in 1934 to document the plight of dust bowl farmers. A growing sensitivity to her subjects is noticeable from this point forward.

During the depression she collaborated with southern novelist Erskine Caldwell on a project about southern sharecroppers, resulting in 1937 in the widely circulated publication of *You Have Seen Their Faces*. (Some of her images are mistakenly thought to be part of the Farm Security Administration project.) Caldwell and Bourke-White "used only the material that sustained certain images of the South, and set the rest aside" (Snyder, *Prospects*, p. 398). Critics also took issue with the captions they wrote to accompany the photographs because they were the photographer's and writer's own inventions, their ideas of what the subjects had been thinking at the time rather than direct quotes.

Bourke-White and Caldwell got along so well that they were married in 1939, but they divorced three years later; they had no children. They did, however, collaborate on two other books, *North of the Danube* (1939) and *Say, Is This the U.S.A.?* (1941).

In 1942 Bourke-White became the first woman photographer accredited to the U.S. Air Force. During World War II she was the only foreign photographer in Moscow during the German bombardment. Bourke-White photographed Nazi death camps at the end of the war; critics say some of her best shots were those of the half-crazed victims of Buchenwald when General George Patton arrived to release them in 1945.

Among the many important subjects she covered was India (1946–1948) during Mahatma Gandhi's fight for independence. She photographed Gandhi just a few hours before he was assassinated in 1948. Bourke-White also photographed racial and labor unrest in South African diamond and gold mines (1949–1950), and in 1952 she was a United Nations war correspondent in Korea for *Life*, covering the war from the perspective of the Koreans rather than the American troops.

Bourke-White was accused of subversion during the post–World War II "red" witch hunt and was considered by the Federal Bureau of Investigation to be a communist sympathizer and a national security risk. Although she never knew how closely the FBI was watching her activities, the customs bureau repeatedly searched her luggage when she traveled on assignment, and the post office monitored her mail. There appears to have been no harm done to her career by this surveillance, but it does speak to the age in which she worked.

Bourke-White attempted to balance an inner yearning for a happy domestic life and children with her penchant for industrial photography and photojournalism. Ultimately, it was her career that won out: "Work is a religion to me, the only religion you can count on, a trusted lifelong friend who never deserts you," she said. At a time when most of her contemporaries were homemakers, Bourke-White was making history in a profession dominated by men.

Few people know the extent to which Bourke-White shaped her own public image, conducting a "one-woman publicity campaign" and promoting herself whenever possible. In her time she was one of the best-known American women, not just one of the best-known female photographers. By 1934 Bourke-White was listed in *Who's Who*. A year later she was cited as one of the ten most successful career women in New

York City, and the year after that she was named one of the ten outstanding women in America. She was awarded the American Woman of Achievement Citation from the Boston Chamber of Commerce in 1951, the Achievement Award from *U.S. Camera* magazine in 1963, and the Honor Roll Award from the American Society of Magazine Photographers in 1964.

While Bourke-White was in retirement and battling Parkinson's disease, her portrait hung in the 1965 World's Fair Women's Hall of Fame pavilion, along with those of Helen Keller and Eleanor Roosevelt, as one of the ten outstanding living American women. Even advertisers recognized the vast appeal this attractive woman had for the public: she appeared in print and on radio endorsing coffee, wine, and cigarettes (not even her own brand). "If she had an outsize career, she had an outsize personality as well. People had an astonishing range of reactions to her, as if she were some sort of magnetic force that alternately attracted and repelled" (Goldberg, *Margaret Bourke-White*, preface).

Bourke-White died in Stamford, Connecticut, after a nineteen-year battle with Parkinson's disease, which she had aggressively fought with medication, therapy, and surgery. In fact, one of her last projects for *Life* was the June 1959 story in which Alfred Eisenstaedt photographed Bourke-White's experimental brain surgery and the rehabilitation classes that followed. Her struggle also became a motion picture, *Double Exposure* (1989), featuring Farrah Fawcett as Bourke-White, which furthered the appeal of one of photojournalism's most groundbreaking and memorable characters.

• The chief repository of Bourke-White's papers is Syracuse University's George Argents Research Library. Other locations include the Brooklyn Museum, the Cleveland Museum of Art, the International Museum of Photography at the George Eastman House, the Library of Congress, the *Life* Picture Collection, the Museum of Modern Art, and the New Orleans Museum of Art. Her books of her photographs and text include the autobiographical *Portrait of Myself* (1963), *A Report on the American Jesuits*, with Father John LaFarge (1956), *Halfway to Freedom: A Report on the New India* (1949), *Dear Fatherland, Rest Quietly* (1946), *They Called It "Purple Heart Valley"* (1944), *Shooting the Russian War* (1942), *One Thing Leads to Another: The Growth of an Industry*, with Fred C. Kelly (1936), *U.S.S.R. Photographs* (1934), and *Red Medicine*, with Sir Arthur Newsholme and John Adams Kingsbury (1933). The most recent extensive biography is Vicki Goldberg's *Margaret Bourke-White: A Biography* (1986); also helpful is Theodore M. Brown, *Margaret Bourke-White: Photojournalist* (1972), and Sean Callahan, ed., *The Photographs of Margaret Bourke-White* (1972). Bourke-White is a major part of the discussion in William Stott, *Documentary Expression and Thirties America* (1973). See two insightful pieces by Robert E. Snyder, "Margaret Bourke-White and the Communist Witch Hunt," *Journal of American Studies* 19 (Apr. 1985): 1, 5–25, and "Erskine Caldwell and Margaret Bourke-White: You Have Seen Their Faces," in *Prospects: An Annual Journal of American Cultural Studies*, ed. Jack Salzman, vol. 11 (1987), pp. 393–405. Other pieces of interest include Julia Edwards, "The Unsinkable Maggie White," *Women of the World: The Great Foreign Correspondents* (1988); Goldberg, "In Hot Pursuit: The Life and Times of Margaret Bourke-White," *American Photographer* 16 (June 1986): 38–61; Madelon G. Schilpp, "Margaret Bourke-White, Pioneer Photojournalist," *Great Women of the Press* (1983); C. Zoe Smith, "An Alternative View of the 30s: Hine's and Bourke-White's Industrial Photos," *Journalism Quarterly* 60 (Summer 1983): 305–10; and [anon.], "This Daring Camera Girl Scales Skyscrapers for Art," *American Magazine*, Nov. 1930, pp. 66ff. An obituary is on the front page of the *New York Times*, 28 Aug. 1971, and in *Time*, 6 Sept. 1971.

C. ZOE SMITH

BOURNE, Benjamin (9 Dec. 1755–17 Sept. 1808), U.S. congressman and jurist, was born in Bristol, Rhode Island, the son of Shearjashub Bourne and Ruth Bosworth Church. Bourne began a career in law and public service after graduating from Harvard with an A.B. in law in 1775. In January 1776 he became the quartermaster for the Second Regiment of Rhode Island. He left military service in January 1777 and returned to Bristol. In 1778 Bourne married Hope Child Diman, the widow of Captain Benjamin Diman of Bristol; they had four children.

In 1780 Bourne was elected to the House of Deputies, the lower house of the Rhode Island General Assembly. He served as a clerk of that legislative body and on the Council of War. In 1786 or 1787 he moved his law practice to Providence, where he rose to prominence not only as an attorney but also as a merchant. Providence elected him to the House of Deputies from 1787 to 1790.

During Rhode Island's turbulent Confederation period, Bourne remained an influential member of the minority party, which consisted primarily of merchants; the party objected strenuously to the Country party's policy of alleviating the state's debts by large emissions of paper money. The minority party came out strongly in favor of Federalism after the Constitutional Convention of 1787 because it viewed a strong federal government as the only protection against the agrarian-based Country party. Bourne was an active supporter of the Constitution and tried to convince the general assembly to call a ratification convention during the two-and-a-half years that Rhode Island refused to give its consent to the new federal structure.

Events came to a head in January 1790, after the other twelve states had ratified the new Constitution. The federal government began to fear that it would have to resort to economic pressure to compel Rhode Island's acquiescence; some members of the federal government even considered dissolving the state and distributing its territory to Massachusetts and Connecticut. In addition, Rhode Island Federalists threatened to secede and take Providence, Newport, and Bristol with them if the anti-Federalists persisted in their isolationist policies. In this highly charged atmosphere, Bourne added momentum to the ratification movement by proposing on 14 January 1790 that the general assembly call a ratifying convention; the motion passed in the lower house but was defeated in the upper house by one vote. A second proposal for a ratifying convention, made only days after Bourne's proposal, passed both houses, primarily as a result of the anti-Federalists' fear of federal repercussions and the possible dissolution of the state.

In both of Rhode Island's conventions to ratify the Constitution (the first was held in South Kingstown on 1 March 1790 and the second in Newport at the end of May 1790), Bourne played an active role. After the second ratifying convention agreed that the state should join the Union (and proposed twenty-one amendments to the Constitution), Bourne rose to even greater prominence in state politics. He was a member of the committee to greet President George Washington on his conciliatory visit to Providence in August 1790 and at the end of that month was elected to the U.S. House of Representatives as Rhode Island's first representative. He was reelected three times and served in the first four Congresses (1790–1796). Bourne's congressional career was uneventful. He seldom spoke in the House of Representatives, although he occasionally entered into debate to champion the rights of the Union's small states or to oppose direct taxation of the people. He was a member of the Federalist party.

Bourne resigned from the House of Representatives before the Fourth Congress had adjourned. He returned to Rhode Island and served as a judge for the U.S. District Court (1796–1801) and later as a judge for the U.S. Court of Appeals for the eastern circuit (1801–1802). Bourne died in Bristol.

Bourne was a central figure in Rhode Island's tumultuous entrance into the United States, and he was instrumental in pushing through ratification of the Constitution. After ratification, his election as the state's first representative illustrated the conciliatory nature of post-Confederation Rhode Island politics. Differences between Federalists and anti-Federalists in Rhode Island began to lessen and the state enjoyed a period of political harmony during the Federal period. Bourne symbolized this harmony. Although many of his opinions during the Confederation period were unpopular, after the ratification of the Constitution (and the subsequent end of paper money emissions) Bourne received strong majorities in each of his elections to the U.S. House of Representatives.

• The majority of Bourne's letters are at the Rhode Island Historical Society. Bourne wrote a history of his native town, *An Account of the Settlement of the Town of Bristol, in the State of Rhode-Island: And of the Congregational Church therein, with the Succession of Pastors, from Its Origin to the Present Time* (1785). Bourne's role in the history of Rhode Island is mentioned in Irwin H. Polishook, *Rhode Island and the Union, 1774–1795* (1969); Patrick T. Conley, "Rhode Island in Disunion, 1787–1790," *Rhode Island History* 31 no. 4 (Fall 1972); and Conley, "Rhode Island's Paper Money Issue and *Trevett v. Weeden* (1786)," *Rhode Island History* 30 no. 3 (Aug. 1971). Local histories also mention Bourne, including W. H. Munro, *History of Bristol, Rhode Island* (1880), and W. R. Staples, *Annals of the Town of Providence* (1843).

ELIZABETH DUBRULLE

BOURNE, George (13 June 1780–20 Nov. 1845), clergyman and abolitionist, was born in Westbury, England, the son of Samuel Bourne, a cloth manufacturer, and Mary Rogers. Bourne attended Homerton College, located in a London suburb, to prepare for the ministry. He first visited the United States in 1802 and in 1804 emigrated to Baltimore, Maryland. Rather than enter the ministry, Bourne became a journalist and established the *Baltimore Evening Post* in March 1805. He failed to secure backing for his paper and in November sold out to Hezekiah Niles, perhaps the most successful journalist of the early nineteenth century. Despite his failure, Bourne had made important contacts among American publishers and displayed an uncanny ability to survive in his adopted country. His first book, *The Spirit of Public Journals* (1806), likely impressed several influential publishers, such as Niles and Mathew Carey, who commissioned Bourne to write a biography of Napoleon Bonaparte (1806), which he followed in 1807 with a study of the Methodist leader John Wesley.

Bourne's ambition soon embroiled him in Maryland's heated partisan politics and in allegations that he had mishandled funds entrusted to him by the city's Forensic Society. By 1810 Bourne had worn out his welcome in Baltimore and took his family—Bourne had been married just before departing England, but his wife's name is unknown—to the Harrisonburg area in Virginia's Shenandoah Valley. He returned to the ministry and formed a new congregation among recent Scotch-Irish Presbyterian immigrants. In October 1811 Bourne applied to the Lexington Presbytery for recognition of his new church, which was accepted in April 1812.

Presbyterian ordination required acceptance of the Westminster Confession. While studying for his examination by the Lexington Presbytery, Bourne noted a prohibition against "man-stealing" in the church catechism. His studies revealed further biblical censures against "man-stealing," classifying it as a crime worthy of death. Scant evidence exists that prior to his ordination Bourne had ever questioned the institution of slavery; when he edited the *Post* he accepted advertisements for the sale of slaves and had once "hired" a slave worker. But the revelation he experienced from the Presbyterian catechism, coupled with the likely influence of nascent antislavery sentiment in western Virginia, altered the course of Bourne's life and convinced him that any individual "who holds Slaves and who pretends to be a Christian or a Republican, is either an incurable idiot . . . or an obdurant sinner" (Christie and Dumond, p. 105).

Between 1810 and 1815 he began excluding slave owners from his congregation and sought to convert the Presbyterian church to his antislavery views. At the 1815 Philadelphia Presbyterian General Assembly, Bourne shocked delegates by questioning the Christianity of individuals who owned slaves, condemning them as "man-stealers." Heckling and attempts to silence him only incensed Bourne, who became more vehement in his condemnations. He charged ministers who owned slaves at the time of their ordination with violating church rules and Christian doctrine and repudiated the assembly's attempt to restore peace as "deceptive and two-faced." In response to his attacks, the Lexington Presbytery dissolved his congregation and commenced a three-year campaign that resulted in Bourne's expulsion from the church. In 1816 he published *The Book and Slavery Irreconcilable*, the first sustained examination of the relationship between slavery and the Bible in the United States. Bourne categorically condemned slavery as the most immoral form of theft and called for its immediate end. His book proved to be one of the most important works of the early antislavery movement. William Lloyd Garrison, founder of the nineteenth-century American antislavery crusade, declared that, next to the Bible, no other book had exerted more influence on him.

Bourne continued to battle the Presbyterian church but in 1816 wisely left Virginia. Between 1816 and 1829 Bourne filled a succession of pulpits in Germantown, Pennsylvania; Ossining, New York; and Quebec, Canada. In 1829 he moved to New York City, where he would remain; there he was befriended by the wealthy evangelical reformer Arthur Tappan and published the rabidly anti-Catholic newspaper the *Protestant*. Although usually remembered as one of the first radical abolitionists, Bourne was also one of the earliest leaders of the American nativist, or anti-Catholic, crusade.

Bourne's abolitionism and virulent nativism shared the same evangelical Protestant foundation, commitment to freedom and liberty, abhorrence of tyranny, and a prurient obsession with the sexual exploitation of women. To Bourne, the totalitarian control that masters exercised over slaves found an unseemly analogy in the authoritarian structure of the Catholic church. Both institutions, defended by respectable clerics, subjected the individual to the unchecked power of lordly masters, and each left women vulnerable to the grotesque and apparently unquenchable lusts of depraved men: slave owners and priests, especially Jesuits. Bourne became one of the earliest writers to adapt the captivity narrative (usually stories of white women held by Native Americans) and the slave narrative styles to anti-Catholic propaganda. Although his part in the writing and publication of the fanciful but lurid *Awful Disclosures of the Hôtel Dieu Nunnery of Montreal* by Maria Monk (1836) has been documented (Billington, pp. 99–100), Bourne authored his own lurid tale of rape, murder, and incest two years earlier in *Lorette: The History of Louise, Daughter of a Canadian Nun, Exhibiting the Interior of Female Convents* (1834). The plight of the women who suffered under the tyranny of Jesuits in *Lorette* are indistinguishable from the real-life horrors that Bourne outlined in *Slavery Illustrated in its Effects upon Woman and Domestic Society* (1837). To Bourne, the convent and the "slave States are one vast brothel."

Bourne remained committed to abolitionism and nativism for the remainder of his career. He was a founding member of the American Anti-Slavery Society (1833) and a frequent contributor to Garrison's famous paper the *Liberator*. During the 1830s Bourne ministered to several New York congregations and, until his death in New York City, edited the *Christian Intelligencer*. Frequently overlooked, Bourne was a crucial figure in the history of the antislavery movement and was representative of the darker side of nineteenth-century American Protestantism.

• Although Bourne left no major collection of papers, his many published works mark a fascinating phase of American social and intellectual history. Bourne's other major works include *Marriage Indissoluble and Divorce Unscriptural* (1813), *Secreta Monita Societas Jesu. Secret Instructions of the Jesuits* . . . (1831), *Picture of Slavery in the United States of America* (1834), and *A Condensed Anti-Slavery Bible Argument: By a Citizen of Virginia* (1845). A complete list of his publications can be found in John W. Christie and Dwight L. Dumond, eds., *George Bourne and 'The Book and Slavery Irreconcilable'* (1969). No biography of Bourne has been written; the best information on Bourne and his times can be found in the truculent work of Christie and Dumond, *George Bourne*; Ray Allen Billington, *The Protestant Crusade, 1800–1860* (1938); and David Brion Davis, ed., *The Fear of Conspiracy* (1971) and *The Problem of Slavery in the Age of Revolution, 1770–1823* (1975).

DONALD YACOVONE

BOURNE, Jonathan, Jr. (23 Feb. 1855–1 Sept. 1940), U.S. senator, was born in New Bedford, Massachusetts, the son of Jonathan Bourne, a textile manufacturer and owner of whaling ships, and Emily Summers Howland. He attended private schools and studied at Harvard University from 1873 to 1876, but he left academic studies his senior year to tour the world in one of his father's ships. In 1878, after having been shipwrecked off Formosa, Bourne relocated to Portland, Oregon, where he made his home and studied law. Gaining admission to the bar in 1881, he practiced for only a short time before turning to business activities. His interests in mining, farming, real estate, and various commercial enterprises in both western and eastern states soon earned him a fortune. He headed several corporations in Oregon and also the Bourne Mills at Fall River, Massachusetts, a family-run operation.

Bourne's successful business ventures led to a career in politics. A Republican, he held a seat in the Oregon House of Representatives in 1885, 1886, and 1897. Bourne was a member of the Republican National Committee from 1888 to 1892, during the presidential administration of Benjamin Harrison (1833–1901), and attended some of his party's national conventions, in 1888 and 1892 as a delegate. Yet he temporarily abandoned the Republicans in 1896 to support William Jennings Bryan and the cause of free coinage of silver.

Bourne led the successful campaign in Oregon for the popular election of U.S. senators rather than election by the state legislature, an outmoded constitutional device designed by the founding fathers. With a senatorial preference primary, which Oregon adopted in 1904, and a legislature pledged to support the people's choice, Bourne in 1906 won election to the U.S. Senate, earning the apparent distinction of being the first U.S. senator to be chosen by popular vote. He served one term in the upper chamber from 1907 to 1913. As chairman of the Committee on Post Offices and Post Roads he assumed an active role in inaugurating the parcel post system and authored the Parcel Post Act of 1912. He also chaired the Joint Commission on Federal Aid to Good Roads and the Joint Commission on Railway Mail Pay and Second Class Postage.

Often referred to as the "father of the Oregon System" for his espousal of popular government, Bourne joined forces with William S. U'Ren, a proponent of direct democracy and the single tax, to agitate for social, economic, and political change during the early twentieth century. Bourne was at that time one of the leading and most dedicated progressives in the nation. He advocated numerous reforms, including woman suffrage, the regulation and publicity of campaign expenditures, the initiative, recall, and referendum, a direct presidential preference primary, which he hoped would extend throughout the nation, and the restriction of presidential patronage. A printed version of his speech "Popular versus Delegated Government" (1910) sold several million copies.

In 1908 Bourne at first backed President Theodore Roosevelt (1858–1919) for a second elective term, but when the chief executive removed himself from consideration, Bourne endorsed Roosevelt's designated heir, William Howard Taft. Although he deplored the president's tactic of utilizing his position to influence the nomination of a successor, Bourne campaigned for Taft in Oregon, played golf with the nominee, and bombarded Republican leaders with letters describing significant issues such as the conduct of Taft's campaign and the electoral outlook. Calling Taft "the man of destiny," Bourne took satisfaction in Taft's victory for president over the beleaguered Bryan. Ultimately, the friendship that developed between Taft and Bourne during the 1908 campaign evaporated over political differences that enveloped Taft's problem-plagued presidency. Even though he voted for the controversial Payne-Aldrich Tariff of 1909, Bourne blamed Taft for a clumsy handling of the issue. Other matters, such as the Ballinger-Pinchot controversy regarding conservation, convinced Bourne that Taft was insufficiently progressive and undeserving of another term. Overlooking opportunities to resolve differences with Taft, Bourne concentrated on the president's tarnished image as a fallen hero who had been hastily groomed as a replica of Roosevelt. Bourne would have been a better politician had he exercised more pragmatism and less dogmatism about his attachment to progressivism.

In 1911 Bourne assumed the presidency of the National Progressive Republican League. He worked closely with Senator Robert M. La Follette (1855–1925) of Wisconsin, a Progressive Republican whom he initially supported for president. Following La Follette's breakdown and illness, Bourne in 1912 sanctioned Roosevelt's presidential candidacy. When Roosevelt failed to seize the Republican nomination and bolted the national convention to form a third party, Bourne, remaining a Republican, restricted his endorsement only to Roosevelt rather than to the Progressive party. In the meantime, Bourne hailed Woodrow Wilson's triumph as the Democratic presidential nominee as "a great progressive victory" but doubted the governor's ability to "come through with the advocacy of popular government principles which the American people so earnestly desire."

During his senatorial term Bourne neglected to keep in touch with his constituents, visiting Oregon only twice during the six-year period. In April 1912 he lost his bid for renomination to Ben Selling, whom Harry Lane, a Democrat, defeated in November. More dedicated to a belief in popular government than to his party, Bourne had managed to antagonize influential Republicans with his independent conduct. Ironically, he fell victim to his own crusade for removing power from state bosses and entrusting it to the people. He never again sought elective office.

After leaving the Senate Bourne remained in Washington, where he engaged in newspaper work and chaired an anti-Wilson Republican Publicity Association to promote the tenets of liberal Republicanism. Gradually, however, Bourne grew more conservative in his later years. He opposed the League of Nations, condemned what he considered the dangerous radicalism of organized labor, denounced Samuel Gompers, and criticized policies that he felt represented an undue extension of the power of the federal government, such as government ownership of utilities, special privileges for organized labor, and high income taxes. Although he favored Alfred E. Smith for the presidency in 1928 and Franklin D. Roosevelt in 1932, Bourne detested the steady growth of bureaucracy. The New Deal reforms of the 1930s far outstripped Bourne's obsolete views and uncompromising conservatism.

Despite several political successes, Bourne suffered certain setbacks in his personal life. He had three wives but no children. He married his first wife, Lillian Wyatt, in 1893, but they divorced in 1913. His second wife was Carol B. Sperry, whom he married in 1918 but divorced in 1924. In 1925 Bourne married Frances Barker Turner, a 29-year-old daughter of an Episcopal clergyman. Bourne died in Washington, D.C.

• Bourne's papers are in the University of Oregon Library at Eugene. The most thorough work is Albert Pike, Jr., "Jonathan Bourne, Jr., Progressive" (Ph.D. diss., Univ. of Oregon, 1957). Other studies include Leonard Schlup, "Republican Insurgent: Jonathan Bourne and the Politics of Progressivism, 1908–1912," *Oregon Historical Quarterly* 87 (1986): 229–44; and Marian V. Sears, "Jonathan Bourne, Jr., Capital Market and the Portland Stock Exchange . . . 1887," *Oregon Historical Quarterly* 69 (1968): 197–222. An obituary is in the *New York Times*, 3 Sept. 1940.

LEONARD SCHLUP

BOURNE, Randolph Silliman (30 May 1886–22 Dec. 1918), writer and social critic, was born in Bloomfield, New Jersey, the son of Charles Rogers Bourne and Sarah Barrett. From the start, Bourne's life was star-crossed. At birth, his face was severely deformed, and spinal tuberculosis at age four stunted his growth and left him with a misshapened back. His alcoholic father, a failure at various small businesses, left the family when Bourne was a boy. He was raised by his mother and devoted aunt. Bourne turned to books and friends and graduated from high school in 1903 as the valedictorian and senior class president.

Strained family matters kept Bourne from college until 1909 when he entered Columbia University on a scholarship. He received his B.A. in 1912 and M.A. in sociology in 1913, benefiting from friendships with bright students and a brilliant faculty that included Charles Beard, James Harvey Robinson, and John Dewey. Books, talk, liberating ideas—he had become quite critical of the narrowness of Bloomfield—became Bourne's life; he blossomed into an intellectual, a passionate pragmatist, absorbed in a host of cosmopolitan writers from Henri Bergson to Friedrich Nietzsche to William James. Bourne responded with literate essays in the undergraduate magazine and provocative writings on his generation's concerns in the *Atlantic Monthly*. These (including the poignant but uncomplaining essay, "The Handicapped") and others made up his first book, *Youth and Life* (1913), a lyrical work of cultural criticism that endeared him to others in flight from small-town, conservative America. Later, his friend Van Wyck Brooks immortalized Bourne as "the flying wedge of the younger generation."

Following a year in England, France, and Germany on a travelling fellowship from Columbia, Bourne joined the *New Republic*, a new "journal of opinion" edited by Herbert Croly, Walter Lippmann, and others, including Beard and Dewey, whom Bourne had idolized. Bourne became a wide-ranging cultural and literary critic, championing Theodore Dreiser and young moderns and attacking the genteel tradition and traditional education. His series of articles in 1915 on the progressive schools of Gary, Indiana, and subsequent books, *The Gary Schools* (1916) and *Education and Living* (1917), earned for Bourne a permanent place of honor in the history of progressive educational reform.

But Bourne became disillusioned, and his outlook soured in 1917 when his skepticism about America's professed idealism toward involvement in World War I greatly alarmed Croly and Dewey, who saw in the war a chance for international reform. They gently but firmly reduced and restricted Bourne's writings in the *New Republic*. Brooks secured a forum for Bourne with the new avant-garde monthly, the *Seven Arts*. Here Bourne's searing dissent—a bracing compound of pacifism, socialism, romanticism, and estrangement from traditional ideas linking England with freedom—found unfettered expression. In "The War and the Intellectuals" (June 1917) and "Twilight of Idols" (Oct. 1917) Bourne lashed out at the basic assumptions undergirding American involvement in the war. Never had he written so powerfully, or with such anguish over what he considered the treason of the intellectuals, particularly Dewey and the liberals who supported the war effort wholeheartedly and with little concern for the daily violations of freedom of speech in America. Never had Bourne spoken with such penetration as he punctured the illusions of pragmatism's inherent optimism and prophesied postwar disillusionment. In "A War Diary" he wrote in September 1917, "The war—or American promise: one must choose."

Such uncompromising words frightened Mrs. Rankine, the magazine's benefactor, and largely because of Bourne's articles the *Seven Arts* died on its first birthday in late 1917. Bourne was silenced. In 1918 he wrote noncontroversial reviews and literary pieces for the *Dial*, turned inward to write sophisticated autobiographical essays, and started an ambitious work entitled "The State." He was trying, as he said in "A War Diary," to follow his own advice: "one keeps healthy in wartime not by a series of religious and political consolations that something good is coming out of it all, but by a vigorous assertion of values in which war has no part."

Fortunately, he was rich in friends, particularly women—Elsie Clews Parsons, Elizabeth Shepley Sergeant, Florence Kelley, among others—who admired his honesty, sincerity, feminism, and willingness to listen to them. At the end, just before his early, tragic death from the influenza epidemic that swept America and the world in 1918, he was engaged to be married to Esther Cornell, a beautiful actress. He had often despaired of finding love, but he had.

Bourne's reputation went into eclipse in the 1920s. His name resurfaced only occasionally in the next decades until the intellectual unrest occasioned by the Vietnam War brought his writings back into circulation and refurbished his reputation as a trenchant critic of war and the state and as an inspiring proponent of friendship and community and the responsibility of unfettered intellectuals. His growing literary and intellectual renown rests on his early essays on youth, his wartime dissents, and his intensely personal letters.

• Bourne's papers are at Columbia University. His letters are available in *The Letters of Randolph Bourne: A Comprehensive Edition*, ed. Eric J. Sandeen (1981). For two early and important anthologies of Bourne's writings, including previously unpublished material, see Bourne, *History of a Literary Radical*, ed. Van Wyck Brooks (1920), and Bourne, *Untimely Papers*, ed. James Oppenheim (1919). The most complete, critical biography is Bruce Clayton, *Forgotten Prophet: The Life of Randolph Bourne* (1984). An older, but still useful work is John Adam Moreau, *Randolph Bourne: Legend and Reality* (1966). Christopher Lasch, *The New Radicalism in America, 1889–1963: The Intellectual as a Social Type* (1965), includes a provocative assessment of Bourne as an intellectual. On Bourne as a cultural critic and his era, see Edward Abraham, *The Lyrical Left: Randolph Bourne, Alfred Stieglitz, and the*

Origins of Cultural Radicalism in America (1986), and Casey Nelson Blake, *Beloved Community: The Cultural Criticism of Randolph Bourne, Van Wyck Brooks, Waldo Frank, and Lewis Mumford* (1990). Charles Forcey, *The Crossroads of Liberalism: Croly, Weyl, Lippmann, and the Progressive Era, 1900–1925* (1961), had a major role in reviving Bourne's reputation. An obituary is in the *New York Times*, 23 Dec. 1918.

BRUCE CLAYTON

BOURNEUF, Alice Elizabeth (2 Oct. 1912–7 Dec. 1980), economist, was born in Haverhill, Massachusetts, the daughter of Volusien M. Bourneuf, a businessman, and Jessie d'Entremont. Bourneuf belonged to a large, affluent, and devout family. After the death of her father in 1914, the Bourneuf family moved from Haverhill to Brookline, Massachusetts. In the mid-1920s they moved to the Chestnut Hill section of Newton, Massachusetts, and Bourneuf graduated from Newton High School in 1929.

Bourneuf's career as an economist has its roots in her formal education at Radcliffe College. She was elected to Phi Beta Kappa and was awarded the A.B. in 1933, graduating magna cum laude. She entered Radcliffe Graduate School in 1933 under the prevailing arrangement by which Radcliffe women did graduate work at Harvard University. Bourneuf, Paul Samuelson, John Kenneth Galbraith, and Richard Musgrave were an extraordinary group of graduate students at Harvard in the 1930s who would later achieve distinction in economics. From 1935 to 1937 Bourneuf alternated study with employment in economic research at Harvard, and after serving as an instructor at Rosemont College in Pennsylvania from 1937 to 1939 she was awarded the M.A. from Radcliffe in 1939.

In order to do research for a doctoral dissertation, Bourneuf spent the year 1939–1940 in Belgium working under a Belgian-American Foundation fellowship on Belgian terms of trade. This project was abruptly ended by the German invasion in May 1940, and her year's work was left behind when she fled to France. After her safe return to the United States, she did research for Seymour Harris of Harvard University for about two years.

Bourneuf then moved to Washington, D.C., to begin a career in government service that would span more than a decade and would establish her as an authority on international monetary policy. In the Office of Price Administration she worked on import and export prices during a period of price control. In 1942 she moved to the research department of the Federal Reserve Board to develop postwar international monetary plans. As a participant in the Bretton Woods Conference of 1944, she contributed to the establishment of the International Monetary Fund (IMF) and the World Bank, publishing several scholarly articles on these subjects between 1944 and 1946. In 1946 she moved to the research department of the IMF. There she worked on exchange rates and financial problems related to its mission to advance international trade by promoting stability of foreign exchange.

In 1948 Bourneuf moved to Oslo, Norway, to begin five years of service in the Marshall Plan organization, which had been created to promote European economic recovery in the aftermath of World War II. Bourneuf contributed to the reorganization of the Norwegian economy as a skilled analyst of its economic problems and as a negotiator between the governments of Norway and the United States. In 1951 she moved to the plan's Paris office, where she was responsible for research on Scandinavia and the United Kingdom.

In 1953, at the end of the Harry Truman administration, Bourneuf left public service to return to the academic world. Under a Littauer School of Public Administration fellowship at Harvard in 1953–1954, she wrote her doctoral dissertation based on her research in Norway and published in 1958 by Harvard University Press under the title *Norway: The Planned Revival.* Radcliffe College awarded her the Ph.D. in 1955.

Bourneuf served as an assistant professor at Mt. Holyoke College from 1954 to 1956 and as an associate professor from 1956 to 1958. From her position as a visiting associate professor at the University of California at Berkeley, which she held from 1957 to 1959, she was recruited by Boston College. In 1959 she became the first woman in the College of Arts and Sciences at Boston College to hold the rank of tenured full professor.

Equipped with high academic standards and impressive collegial contacts, Bourneuf became a major force in building a strong economics department at Boston College. Through her recruiting efforts, many noteworthy scholars were attracted to its faculty. Boston College credits her not only with having a role in building its economics department but also with providing vision and guidance to the institution itself as it grew from a local college into a major university. Her appointment as professor opened doors for future women scholars at the predominantly male school.

During her tenure at Boston College, Bourneuf published scholarly articles in the *Review of Economic Statistics*, the *Review of Social Economy*, and the *American Economic Review*. She was awarded a Ford Foundation faculty research fellowship to the Massachusetts Institute of Technology for the year 1962–1963, and in 1963 she was elected second vice president of the Catholic Economic Association.

Bourneuf was recognized in her lifetime for her professional contributions both internationally and locally and for her abiding personal integrity. Her colleagues in economics presented her with a Festschrift, a book of essays dedicated to her, which was published in 1976. In that year Boston College established the Bourneuf Award, to be given each year to an outstanding student of economics. In 1979 an administrative office building at Boston College was named Bourneuf House in her honor.

After her retirement from Boston College in 1977, Bourneuf moved to Ogunquit, Maine. She died in

Boston. Boston College established the Alice E. Bourneuf Lecture Series after her death.

Bourneuf was a macroeconomist in the Keynesian tradition and a recognized expert on international monetary policy. She rose to prominence in a field and in institutions that were heavily dominated by men. She was a prominent economist who was valued for her strength, courage, and generosity as well as for her brilliance. These attributes are recognized in the following excerpt from her honorary degree citation at Boston College: "Daughter of Radcliffe whose early mentors were the legendary Schumpeter, Taussig, Harris and Hansen, her own students rise up and call her blessed, for she has ever sought excellence and opened her mouth in wisdom."

• Biographical material may be found in the Radcliffe Archives and in the Boston College Archives. Bourneuf's own account of her wartime experience is "Chestnut Hill Girl Tells Thrilling Story of Fleeing Belgium," *Boston Globe*, 1 June 1940. A biographical tribute to Bourneuf is given in the preface to her Festschrift, David A. Belsley, Edward J. Kane, and Paul A. Samuelson, eds., *Inflation, Trade and Taxes: Essays in Honor of Alice Bourneuf* (1976). See David Warsh, "At All-Male BC, a Woman Built a Department," *Boston Globe*, 16 Dec. 1980, for a discussion of her contributions to Boston College. Among many obituaries are those in the *Boston Globe*, 12 Dec. 1980, the *Chicago Tribune*, 10 Dec. 1980, and the *Biweekly* (a publication of Boston College), 18 Dec. 1980.

SUSAN WILLIAMSON

BOUSFIELD, Midian Othello (22 Aug. 1885–16 Feb. 1948), physician, was born in Tipton, Missouri, the son of Willard Hayman Bousfield, a barber, and Cornelia Catherine Gilbert. From the start Bousfield exemplified what W. E. B. Du Bois meant by the term "talented tenth." Awarded a bachelor's degree from the University of Kansas in 1907, he earned his M.D. two years later from Northwestern University and did an internship at Howard University's Freedmen's Hospital in 1910. Lured back to Kansas City for his initial medical practice (following an unlikely adventure in Brazil where, when medical prospects dimmed, he took up prospecting for gold), he soon felt a need for a larger stage, and in 1914 with his new bride, Maudelle Tanner Brown, he shifted base to Chicago. There he embarked on a career of astounding breadth that took him to leadership positions in the business, health, medical, philanthropic, educational, and military worlds of Chicago and beyond. Later, the couple would have one child.

Bousfield's first success was in the black business sphere. Perhaps perceiving the larger influence of a corporate career, in 1919 he gave up an affiliation with a fledgling black railroad union and helped found the Liberty Life Insurance Company, remaining on as medical director and vice president. A decade later, as president, he guided the company through a merger and a reorganization as the Supreme Liberty Life Insurance Company. For the next four years he led the new firm as both medical director and chairman of its executive committee.

But the worlds of health, medicine, and philanthropy absorbed most of Bousfield's energy, and his primary interests there lay in improving the opportunities—and quality—of black physicians and the health care of black citizens, especially the underserved majority in the South. His great chance to promote those interests came in 1934, when the Chicago-based Julius Rosenwald Fund named him its director of Negro health.

Although the appointment was due mostly to Bousfield's stature as a business leader, the post, itself, was largely one he created by cultivating the Rosenwald medical director, Michael M. Davis, and convincing him of the need and possibilities for Rosenwald involvement in black health issues. Largely at Bousfield's initiative the fund (both before and after 1934) launched projects aimed at improving black hospitals and nurses' training and creating openings for black doctors within southern health agencies (using the lure of Rosenwald money for their initial salaries). By 1942, when the fund ceased operations, the color line in southern public medicine had been substantially breeched and the black profession greatly strengthened.

For Bousfield, 1933–1934 proved a take-off year apart from the Rosenwald post. It also brought him the presidency of the all-black National Medical Association, making him for a time the leading spokesman of black medicine. Moreover, the year provided him an influential, inside forum from which to exert that prestige to good ends through the annual meeting of the American Public Health Association (APHA), where Bousfield became its first black speaker. He did not mince words: it was simply "inconceivable," he said, that anything but racism could account for the fact that health officers could "so complacently review, year after year, the unfavorable vital statistical reports of one-tenth of the population and make no special effort to correct them" (p. 210). Members must shed their racist blinders and start solving blacks' health problems, using black professionals as partners. For the first time, the APHA got the African-American perspective and learned to its surprise that "darkey" dialect stories and racial disdain raised barriers to black community participation in vital health work. Thanks in part to Bousfield a new racial sensitivity among health professionals had begun.

Yet despite such bluntness Bousfield never lost his ties to white leaderships. Whether this was due to his reputation in business or his visibility as an Episcopal layman (surely a mark of acceptability to whites), Bousfield nonetheless continued to enjoy opportunities to serve his people from the upper reaches of the white establishment. In 1939 Democratic boss Edward J. Kelly named Bousfield the first black member on Chicago's board of education, a move black Chicago had been urging for twenty-five years. Then, in 1942 he got a national call: to take charge of the U.S. Army hospital at Fort Huachuca, Arizona. The army's first all-black hospital, it would also be under the direction of the medical corp's first black colonel. Not only did his leadership give black physicians new opportunities, but the quality of their care was so patently good that neighboring whites sought out Fort Huachuca in preference to their own white facility.

One final creative venture remained. In 1946 Bousfield helped organize the Provident Medical Associates, a group of well-heeled (but progressive) Chicago black doctors, whose purpose was to fund the education of aspiring medical specialists and in the process break another racial barrier in American medicine. At his death, in Chicago, and thanks substantially to his efforts, a momentum was building that in little more than a decade and a half would demolish the structure of medical segregation. Ironically, it was Bousfield's separate-but-(truly)-equal strategy that helped bring on integration, for his approach helped ensure the quality the black medical profession needed to convince white physicians that integration was an acceptable next step.

M. O. Bousfield's career is significant for two reasons apart from his own professional contributions. It demonstrated that African Americans—North and South—were making large strides toward equality well before the civil rights movement, even before World War II. It further showed that a conservative approach to social change, that is, stressing gradualism and reliance on the white power structure for help, did bring some results. This was not to say that Bousfield was an Uncle Tom. Although he never joined the National Association for the Advancement of Colored People (NAACP) or flirted with Garveyism, he did associate publicly and early on with black unionism (the Railway Men's International Association), was a key leader in the National Urban League, and could speak bluntly to white professionals when straight talk seemed a surer course than tact and cajolery.

• Although there are no Bousfield papers, much of his professional correspondence can be found in the papers of the Julius Rosenwald Fund at the Fisk University Library (Special Collection) in Nashville and in the Peter Marshall Murray Papers at the Moorland-Springarn Research Collection at Howard University. Bousfield's own writings were few, but references to them are found in Rayford Logan and Michael Winston, eds., *Dictionary of American Negro Biography* (1982), pp. 51–52. Especially important for his view of the impact of racism on health care is his precedent-breaking speech to the APHA, "Reaching the Negro Community," *American Journal of Public Health* 24 (Mar. 1934): 209–15. A biography of Bousfield has yet to be published, but the obituary in the *Journal of the National Medical Association* 40 (May 1948):120, is by his close professional associate Peter Marshall Murray. An obituary is also in the *Chicago Daily News*, 17 Feb. 1948. An appraisal of his role as a professional reformer is found in E. H. Beardsley, *A History of Neglect: Health Care for Blacks and Mill Workers in the Twentieth Century South* (1987).

E. H. Beardsley

BOUTWELL, George Sewall (28 Jan. 1818–27 Feb. 1905), governor, congressman, and senator, was born in Brookline, Massachusetts, the son of Sewall Boutwell and Rebecca Marshall, farmers. Although his family's poverty prevented him from securing a formal education after the age of ten, he was sufficiently well read and self-taught to take over a district school at the age of sixteen. From 1835 he clerked in a country store in Groton, Massachusetts. He eventually became a partner and worked in the business until 1855. He studied law in the office of Bradford Russell of Groton and was admitted to the bar in 1836. He served as the clerk of chancery court for two years, from 1838 to 1840. In 1839 he was elected to the school committee, the first formal step in what would become a lifelong interest in education. A few weeks later he was chosen as the Temperance party's candidate for the Massachusetts House of Representatives, but he was not elected. Meanwhile, Boutwell continued a serious and intensive course of reading in an effort to make up for his lack of a college education.

Boutwell supported Martin Van Buren's unsuccessful 1840 campaign for president against William Henry Harrison. Boutwell became postmaster in 1841, and in that year he also married Sarah Adelia Thayer, with whom he had two children.

In 1842 Boutwell was elected as a Democrat to the state legislature, where he served until 1851. During this time, he became a leader of the Democratic party. Still, over the course of the next ten years he suffered a series of defeats. In 1844, 1846, and 1848 he was defeated for Congress. In 1849 and 1850 he was the Democratic nominee for governor and lost those contests as well. From 1849 to 1850 he served as state bank commissioner, and he was a member of the 1853 state constitutional convention. Finally, in 1851 he was elected governor of Massachusetts by a coalition of the Democratic and Free Soil parties. Because Boutwell lacked a majority, the candidates' names were sent to the Massachusetts legislature for a final decision. In an agreement hammered out between the two parties, the Democrats and Free Soilers split key political offices in the state. The final terms of the agreement gave the Democrats important state legislative positions and Boutwell the governorship. In exchange, Free Soiler Charles Sumner received the Senate seat. During a sometimes vituperative election battle, opponents had dismissed Boutwell as a "country trader," because after twenty years he was still in business in his store. However, a Free Soil journal characterized him as a "genuine specimen of the self-reliant, inquisitive, ambitious, go-ahead and yet cautious Yankee." During his tenure as governor, Boutwell was able to pass most of his projects—the secret ballot, single legislative districts, the Massachusetts Homestead Act, and reorganization of the Harvard College Board of Overseers.

Although he was a Democrat, Boutwell had always been strongly against slavery. After the Kansas-Nebraska Act repealed the Missouri Compromise, he abandoned the Democratic party for good and ably assisted in organizing the fledgling Republican party. He supported John C. Frémont in the 1856 presidential election, and he served as a member of the 1860 Chicago Republican convention that nominated Abraham Lincoln. In February of the following year, during the secession crisis, he was a delegate to the Peace Convention in Washington. In 1862 Lincoln appointed him first as a member of the commission to adjust the claims against the government arising out of the operations of Frémont in Missouri, then as organizer of the new Department of Internal Revenue. Boutwell became its first commissioner until March 1863, when he resigned to take a seat in Congress.

During the early years of the Civil War, Boutwell wrote articles on Republican principles for the *Continental Monthly Magazine* that attracted wide public attention. He also worked tirelessly to increase recruitment, improve armaments, and promote a vigorous prosecution of the war. In 1862 he was elected to the House of Representatives, where he supported emancipation and black suffrage. He was reelected in 1864, but his hopes for a cabinet post were ended by Lincoln's assassination the following year. He continued to work on his long-term goal of black suffrage and was reelected to his seat in the House in 1866 and 1868.

In February 1868 Boutwell advocated the impeachment of President Andrew Johnson, chaired the Committee to Draft the Articles of Impeachment, and served on the board of managers of the trial. He also played an important role in the drafting, reporting, and debating of the Fourteenth and Fifteenth amendments.

In March 1869 Boutwell became secretary of the treasury under Ulysses S. Grant, in spite of his own disinclination for the post. Grant finally submitted the nomination over Boutwell's refusal. Boutwell opposed bills to cut taxes and was relentless in his determination to reduce the national debt, lowering it by some $364 million by the time he left office. In early 1869 the Treasury Department was shaken by the embarrassment of the gold conspiracy, in which James Fisk, Jr., Jay Gould, and other speculators had concocted a scheme to corner the market and thus force up the price of gold. However, Boutwell's willingness to interfere in gold speculation by releasing $4 million of the government's holdings curbed the inflation of gold prices.

In March 1873 Boutwell resigned his cabinet post and reentered Congress as a senator from Massachusetts. In 1877 President Rutherford B. Hayes appointed him to codify and edit the U.S. Statutes, a task he completed in 1878. He served as counsel for the United States before the French and American claims commission in 1880. Throughout the rest of his life, Boutwell was active in the Anti-Imperialist League, opposing President William McKinley's actions in the Philippines. He felt that the country should not expand overseas while the civil rights of millions of American citizens, the freed slaves, were still being denied.

Continuing his lifelong dedication to education, Boutwell served for six years as an overseer of Harvard University and was for five years secretary of the Massachusetts Board of Education. He returned to Washington to resume the practice of law and to continue fighting for Philippine independence. He died in Groton, Massachusetts. According to his biographer, Boutwell "held aloft the nation's ideal in human liberty."

• Boutwell's papers are in the collections of the American Antiquarian Society in Mass. Books written by Boutwell include *Thoughts on Educational Topics and Institutions* (1859), *A Manual of the Direct and Excise Tax System of the United States* (1863), *Decisions on the Tax Law* (1863), *The Tax-Payer's Manual* (1865), *Why I Am a Republican* (1884), and *Reminiscences of Sixty Years in Public Affairs* (1902). Thomas H. Brown, *George Sewall Boutwell: Human Rights Advocate* (1989), is an in-depth study of Boutwell's career as a reformer and politician. An obituary is in the *New York Times*, 28 Feb. 1905.

SILVANA SIDDALI

BOUVET, Marie Marguerite (14 Feb. 1865–27 May 1915), teacher and author of books for young people, was born in New Orleans, Louisiana, the daughter of Jean François Bouvet, a businessman, and Adelphine Bertrand, a teacher. Though born in the United States, Bouvet spent part of her childhood near Lyons, France. Her father had suffered financially during the Civil War and died when Bouvet was five years old. Her mother, a graduate of the Sorbonne in Paris, found a position teaching French literature at the Loquet-Leroy Female Institute in New Orleans. Under these circumstances, Bouvet's mother accepted an offer from her in-laws to have Bouvet live with them temporarily. This seven-year period in her life proved beneficial to Bouvet, who acquired an ear and voice, as well as subject matter, for storytelling through her grandparents' guidance. She also became fond of foreign travel, a penchant that enriched her life and work.

Returning to New Orleans at age twelve, Bouvet attended the institute where her mother taught. Subsequently, she went to Knoxville, Illinois, for schooling at St. Mary's College, from which she graduated in 1885. Returning to New Orleans, she began a lifelong career of teaching French language and literature.

Despite her success as an educator, Bouvet is best known for the many stories addressed to "my young readers." Most of these juvenile novels are set in Europe and revolve around historical events or characters. For example, *Sweet William* (1890), Bouvet's best-known novel for young people, takes place at Mont St. Michel in Normandy and concerns William the Conqueror. *A Child of Tuscany* (1895), set in Florence, Italy, describes how a young boy, reared in poverty by a woman unrelated to him, becomes reunited with his true family, one of wealth and nobility. London is the location of *A Little House in Pimlico* (1897). Bouvet's early years in France and two extensive European excursions after she began teaching helped her capture accurately the physical features and cultural flavor of her various settings.

Bouvet's most intriguing tales for her young readers concern the French Revolution: a Jacobin soldier keeps a pledge to a dying Royalist soldier, despite their political enmity; a village boy provides food and secrecy for his hidden Royalist master and thereby prevents government officials from arresting him; Jacobin soldiers methodically search a château and, just as they are leaving, accidentally discover the hiding place of a Royalist captain. Through such stories Bouvet enlightened and enchanted her readers, but she also relived the pleasures of hearing them herself from her paternal grandparents.

In *Tales of an Old Château* (1899), Bouvet tells her young readers about "incidents which really occurred in France during the period of the great Revolution." Shaped by stories Bouvet had heard as a child, these tales feature acts of heroism and true love. They also reveal the Bouvet family's sympathies with the Royalists during the French Revolution. This book and several others probably owed some of their popularity to their favorable portrayal of European royalty and nobility, a subject that fascinated Victorian Americans.

Bouvet created deft narratives, and readers found her characters realistic, warm, and humorous. Even the villains have redeeming qualities, and, of course, the endings are always happy. Some of her other books included *Little Marjorie's Love Story* (1891), *Prince Tip Top* (1892), *My Lady* (1894), *Pierrette* (1896), *Bernardo and Laurette* (1901), *The Fortunes of Clotilde* (1908), and *The Smile of the Sphinx* (1911). Her only nonfiction work was a book of French quotations, *Fleurs des Poètes et des Prosateurs Français,* published in 1900.

At the time of her death, Marguerite Bouvet was living in Reading, Pennsylvania, where she had moved in 1896. Never married, she made her home with a former college friend. Bouvet dedicated her life to providing intellectual stimulation to her students and enriching, wholesome entertainment to the children of America.

• References to Marguerite Bouvet are few and not recent. See *Men and Women of America* (1910); *Who's Who in America, 1914–1915; Women's Who's Who of America, 1914–1915,* ed. John William Leonard; *American Authors 1600–1900,* ed. Stanley J. Kunitz and Howard Haycraft (1938); and *Dictionary of American Biography,* vol. 2. An obituary is in the *Reading Evening Herald,* 27–28 May 1915, and in the *New York Times,* 3 June 1915.

DOROTHY MCLEOD MACINERNEY

BOUVIER, John (1787–18 Nov. 1851), legal scholar, was born at Condognan, Department of Gard, France, the son of John Bouvier and Marie Benezet. The family came to Philadelphia, Pennsylvania, in 1802 to enter the mercantile business with the Benezet family. While Bouvier was in his teens his father died and he began learning the printing and publishing trade from Benjamin Johnson of Philadelphia. In 1808 he became the proprietor of a small printing business in West Philadelphia. He married Elizabeth Widdifield of Philadelphia in 1810; they had one child, the author Hannah Mary (Bouvier) Peterson. In 1814 he began a weekly newspaper, the *American Telegraph,* in Brownsville, Pennsylvania, and in 1818 he united it with the *Genius of Liberty* in Uniontown.

While publishing these newspapers Bouvier studied law. In 1818 he was admitted to the bar in Uniontown, where he practiced until his admission to the state supreme court in 1822. Bouvier then moved back to Philadelphia, where he practiced law and published legal treatises until his death. A lifelong Democratic-Republican party functionary, he held only two minor public offices: recorder of the city of Philadelphia from 1836 and associate justice of the Philadelphia Court of Criminal Sessions from 1838.

Bouvier's major contribution to law and American society was his legal dictionary derived from American law and legal practice. Frustrated by attempts to use law dictionaries designed for British lawyers, Bouvier reportedly worked daily throughout his career to produce a "Law Dictionary for the profession on this side of the Atlantic." In 1839 the first of fifteen editions of Bouvier's *A Law Dictionary, Adapted to the Constitution and Laws of the United States of America, and of the Several States of the American Union; with References to the Civil and Other Systems of Foreign Law* was published in two volumes and was widely adopted by practitioners. Bouvier continued to collect new and valuable material, which he added to the second and third editions of the dictionary. Upon his death his papers were mined to produce an important fourth revised edition in 1852.

Bouvier next undertook the task of revising and creating the first index of Mathew Bacon's *New Abridgement of the Law,* which appeared in ten volumes from 1842 to 1846. Determined to relieve the American lawyer from "being obliged to study laws which are not his own, and which do not belong to the present age," Bouvier began preparing a comprehensive, systematic digest of American law based on the analytical system of Robert Pothier. Bouvier's *Institutes of American Law* (1851) appeared in four volumes shortly before his death in Philadelphia.

• A summary of Bouvier's personal and professional life can be found in an unsigned review of Bouvier's two law books in the *North American Review,* July 1861, pp. 71–82. See also Henry Simpson, *The Lives of Eminent Philadelphians* (1859), pp. 111–23. There is a small collection of John Bouvier Papers, which includes his personal and professional papers, at the Henry E. Huntington Library in San Marino, Calif.

GERARD W. GAWALT

BOVARD, Oliver Kirby (27 May 1872–3 Nov. 1945), newspaper editor, was born in Jacksonville, Illinois, the son of Charles W. Bovard, a printer, and Hester Bunn. The family moved from Springfield, Illinois, to St. Louis, Missouri, in 1880. Bovard left school at age fourteen, and after several years of clerical jobs, he took a job as a reporter for the *St. Louis Star* in 1896. He became a reporter in 1898 for the *Post-Dispatch,* where his father was a telegraph editor. Two years later Bovard became city editor. In 1908 he was promoted to managing editor. Bovard married Suzanne Thompson of San Antonio, Texas, in 1902; they had no children.

The founder of the *Post-Dispatch*, Joseph Pulitzer, called him to New York City in 1909 to work on the *World*. Bovard had worked with Pulitzer for ten months when Pulitzer gave him a choice: assistant managing editor at the *World* or managing editor at the *Post-Dispatch*. Bovard chose St. Louis because, as he told Pulitzer, he did not want to be a "second fiddle" on the *World*.

In the forty years Bovard worked for the *Post-Dispatch*, he built a national reputation as a commanding editor, vigilant and relentless in publishing news. He considered his charge as editor to focus always on the news and to report the news completely and correctly. As city editor, he dictated the first paragraph of every story he blue-penciled. He set up the paper's bureau in Washington, D.C., and ordered an investigation into the continued imprisonment of conscientious objectors following World War I. When United Press International (UPI) telegraphed news that World War I had ended 7 November 1918, Bovard suspected the information was wrong after his own analysis of news from the front, and, at the risk of being scooped in the highly competitive world of St. Louis journalism, he did not publish UPI's premature newsflash.

Bovard directed the *Post-Dispatch*'s investigation of the naval reserve oil scandal called "Teapot Dome." He waged the news campaign for six years, charging his reporters to keep one question before the public: "Who got the bonds?" The answer came, in part, because the *Post-Dispatch* published the serial numbers of $233,000 of the missing $2.7 million of Liberty Bonds. *Post-Dispatch* reporter Paul Y. Anderson won a Pulitzer Prize for reporting the Teapot Dome Scandal.

Bovard was known for being irascible and inflexible in service to the news and the reader. "Get all the facts," Bovard commanded his staff, "never leave unanswered a question any reasonable reader might ask." One anecdote boasted that Bovard would fire the reporter who failed to record a person's middle initial or who recorded it wrong. According to *Post-Dispatch* reporter Harry Wilensky in the 1973 update of the newspaper's history, Bovard disdained feature articles and opposed women in his newsroom. To Marguerite Martyn, confined to the fashion page, Bovard declared, "Always remember, your work is not important, it is merely interesting."

Paul Anderson, whose paean to Bovard appeared in the *St. Louis Star-Times* (1 Aug. 1938) on the editor's retirement, noted that Bovard's tongue was "pitiless." Anderson told about a writer importuning Bovard for a job at the *Post-Dispatch*: "Mr. Bovard, I've got to live!" the man begged. "Not necessarily," Bovard said.

During the depression, Bovard earned $75,000 a year, reportedly the highest paid managing editor in the nation, but at the same time, some of the highest paid reporters in the country worked for him. He earned a reputation as an editor who could spot talent; woe betide the cub who had none or was careless with the talent he had, but Bovard worked persistently with anyone possessing a spark. Bovard's name was barely known outside newspaper circles, but his reporters—and their prizes—were well known. Bovard refused an invitation to join the St. Louis Country Club, in part because he thought an editorial writer should not mingle with the people he may write about.

On 29 July 1938 he left the *Post-Dispatch* on a matter of principle, writing his resignation "to the staff" in blue pencil. He cited "irreconcilable differences" with the Pulitzers. Bovard never elaborated. Anderson explained that the reasons were political: Joseph Pulitzer II, who had become the newspaper's publisher, was very conservative, backing Alf Landon for president and decrying the New Deal as too liberal, at a time when Bovard, having read Marx and Lenin thoroughly for two decades, labeled Franklin Roosevelt "a phony liberal."

After retirement, Bovard continued his annual safaris to Saskatchewan, Canada. While hunting in 1944, he contracted a pulmonary infection that nearly killed him but returned in 1945. He was reinfected and died in St. Louis of viral pneumonia.

The *Post-Dispatch* had been Bovard's life. He kept no letters or personal papers. He was rarely seen in public or in print. Legends about him were spread by word of reporters. According to his wife, Bovard grumbled when the story of his retirement made the front page of the *Post-Dispatch*: "To think, after all the years I spent teaching those boys what news is, they should waste so much space on this."

• A vertical file on Bovard is available in the collection of the Missouri Historical Society in St. Louis; the file includes the articles on Bovard's retirement and death, also available in the archives of the *St. Louis Post-Dispatch*. For information on his life and career see James W. Markham, *Bovard of the Post-Dispatch* (1954). An obituary is in the *Post-Dispatch*, 4 Nov. 1945.

MARTHA BAKER

BOW, Clara (29 July 1905–27 Sept. 1965), film actress, was born Clara Gordon Bow in Bay Ridge, Brooklyn, New York, the daughter of Robert Bow, a frequently unemployed waiter and handyman, and Sarah Gordon, his mentally ill wife. Bow attended Public School 98 in Sheepshead Bay until the eighth grade, when she left to become a doctor's receptionist. Bow regarded herself as "the worst looking kid on the street," but at age fourteen she won a personality contest, and in 1921 she received a prize from *Fame and Fortune* magazine: a small part in *Beyond the Rainbow*, starring Billie Dove. Bow was cut from the film, but another director saw her photo in a movie magazine and cast her as a spunky stowaway in *Down to the Sea in Ships* (1922). The show business daily *Variety* noted "It is Clara Bow that lingers . . . when the picture has gone."

Signing for $50 per week with producer B. P. Schulberg's Preferred Pictures in 1923, Bow sometimes worked on three films simultaneously. In 1924, the year she was chosen by the Western Association of Motion Picture Advertisers as a WAMPAS Baby Star, or star of the future, Bow appeared as Orchid McGonigle, a reformed gang member, in *Grit*, based on an F. Scott Fitzgerald story. A representative, according to British film historian David Thomson, of "the first generation to be raised on films," she became a symbol of the exuberance and moral emancipation of the Roaring Twenties. Thomson called Bow "the first actress intent on arousing sexual excitement who is not ridiculous."

Bow's reputation and range grew with *The Plastic Age* (1925), produced by Schulberg. As the fierce-kissing Cynthia Day, she was "the hottest jazz baby in films," ruining college student Hugh Carver's athletic ability and concentration, mending her ways in time to save the big game—and regain Hugh. She played Marie Grizzard, a divorce lawyer's secretary, in *Kiss Me Again*, an Ernst Lubitsch comedy that the *New Yorker* called "a champagne picture in a beery world" and voted one of 1925's ten best films.

In 1926 Bow followed Schulberg to Paramount Pictures and to fame. In *Mantrap*, based on a Sinclair Lewis story, she sat in a tent and saucily lured the sleepy object of her affections by reflecting sunlight into his eyes from a crystal. Her come-hither winks complemented the image. By the end of the year fans were sending Bow over 40,000 letters every week.

In 1927 Bow portrayed Betty Lou, the salesgirl heroine in Schulberg's film based on Elinor Glyn's "hard-breathing" novel *It*. Betty Lou was spirited, able to laugh at a too-late marriage proposal and later to save the proposer's fiancée from drowning, an impulsive act that eventually won him back to her. (Vigorous swimming was a feature of several Bow comedies.) Defining "It" as a generalized sex appeal, social historian J. C. Furnas called Bow "an incarnation of girlish gaiety on the loose." Glyn remarked, "Of all the lovely young ladies I've met in Hollywood, Clara Bow has 'It'" (see J. C. Furnas, *Great Times* [1974]). For the rest of her life, Bow was "The *It* Girl." Bow's fellow star Louise Brooks called everything she did "completely original." "Sliding across a desk in *It* was just *her*," she commented. Director Terence Badger claimed that the camera seemed to cause Bow to grow. At 5′3½″ tall, plumpish in contrast to the flattened-breast look of the time, with Cupid's bow lips, a hoydenish red bob, and nervous, speedy movement, Bow became a national rage, America's flapper. Noting her "gum-chewing sex appeal," Schulberg wrote that she "gave off sparks." At the end of 1927 she was making $250,000 a year.

Fitzgerald wrote in *Motion Picture* (July 1927) that thousands of flappers patterned themselves after Bow: "Pretty, impudent, superbly assured, as worldly wise, briefly clad and 'hard-berled' as possible." In describing her "ideal flapper" for *McCall's* (Oct. 1925), Zelda Fitzgerald might have had Bow in mind: "someone who is seen by and in a crowd, but is intimate with no one, fully airing the desire . . . for dramatizing herself. . . . She is an artist in her particular field, the art of being—being young, being an object."

In 1928 *Vanity Fair* called Bow "orchidaceous . . . the hyper-reality and extra-ideality of a million or more film goers . . . the *genus* American girl, refined, washed, manicured, pedicured, permanent-waved and exalted." She drove a red Kissel roadster filled with red chow dogs and once invited a college football team to a midnight practice on her lawn. In the classic flying film *Wings* (1929) Bow progressed from girl-next-door to ambulance driver, with a failed seduction in between. In 1928 she made another Glyn film, *Red Hair* (with a color sequence), and in *The Fleet's In* (1928) Bow played a dime-a-dance girl with a heart of gold. Further successes included *Kid Boots* and *The Saturday Night Kid* (1929), and *Her Wedding Night* (1930). All told, between 1922 and 1930 Bow made fifty-two films.

Bow's personal life was complicated. Never a Hollywood "insider," she nevertheless collected famous, simultaneous suitors. She also supported her father in various failed businesses. Novelist, playwright, and screenwriter Budd Schulberg, B. P.'s son, called her home a nonstop open house, with poker games, friendly cops, and favored bootleggers: there were blackmail threats about love letters and gangsters trying to collect gambling debts. B. P. Schulberg began to call Bow "crisis-a-day Clara."

Bow had long feared that she might inherit her mother's mental instability, and with the onset of talking motion pictures she began to suffer nervous breakdowns. Though Louise Brooks called Bow's voice charming, not "too Brooklyn," the demands of the fixed microphone apparently hindered her freewheeling, improvisational style. Nevertheless, she sang in three 1930 musical films: *Paramount on Parade*, *Love among the Millionaires* (in which nine-year-old Mitzi Green performed an impersonation of Bow), and *True to the Navy*.

The 1931 trial of former friend and secretary Daisy Devoe for the misappropriation of Bow's money, jewelry, and letters was Hollywood's "most sensational since Fatty Arbuckle." When more litigation and notoriety arose from an alienation-of-affections accusation and a book by Devoe focusing on her sex life, Bow suffered another breakdown.

Concluding that Bow now seemed notorious instead of a public favorite, Paramount fired her in 1931. B. P. Schulberg wrote to her "it has never been my good fortune to have anyone as sweet and loyal, as conscientious and as courageous to work for us as yourself." Six months later she married one of her suitors and defenders, cowboy film star Rex Bell (George F. Beldam), in Las Vegas, Nevada, and retired to his ranch in Searchlight. He became the state's lieutenant governor, and they had two children.

Comeback attempts in 1932 (*Call Her Savage*) and 1933 (*Hoopla*) proved unsuccessful. Bow returned briefly to public awareness in 1947, when she was identified as "Miss Hush" on the radio program "Truth or Consequences." After a number of stays in sanitariums, she died of a heart attack in her home in Culver City, California, though acute drug intoxication was listed as a contributory cause. In any frame of her films, Bow is the irresistible center of attention. But a widespread revival of interest in these films has never come. America's first motion picture sex goddess—a girl with bounce—is imprisoned in her short-skirted, Charleston-kicking era.

• Clippings and papers relating to Bow are in the libraries of the Academy of Motion Picture Arts and Sciences, Beverly Hills, and the American Film Institute, Los Angeles, Calif. Joe Morella and Edward Epstein, *The 'It' Girl: The Incredible Story of Clara Bow* (1976), is a useful biography. Scott and Zelda Fitzgerald's assessments of Bow and flappers in general can be found in Matthew Bruccoli et al., eds., *The Romantic Egotists* (1974), and Bruccoli, ed., *Zelda Fitzgerald: The Complete Writings* (1991). Various movie memoirs and autobiographies, such as Budd Schulberg, *Moving Pictures* (1981), Sheilah Graham, *The Garden of Allah* (1970), and Garson Kanin, *Hollywood* (1979), are helpful. The contributions of Adela Rogers St. John (originally in *Photoplay* [1928]), Louise Brooks, and many other Hollywood pioneers can be found in Kevin Brownlow's 1984 television series *Hollywood*, particularly the twelfth program. The best obituary is Jack Smith's in the *Los Angeles Times*, 28 Sept. 1965.

JAMES ROSS MOORE

BOWDEN, John (7 Jan. 1751–31 July 1817), Anglican clergyman and educator, was born in Ireland, where his father, Thomas Bowden, Esq., was serving as an officer of the King's Forty-fourth Regiment of foot soldiers. (Information about his mother is unavailable.) When his father came to America to fight in the French and Indian War, Bowden soon followed. After a period of private preparation, he studied at the College of New Jersey (later Princeton University) for two years, though he did not take a degree. Instead, when his father returned to Ireland after the cessation of hostilities in 1763, he followed him. Bowden returned to America in 1770 and studied divinity at King's College (now Columbia University), graduating in 1772. Two years later he went to England for ordination as a priest of the Church of England.

Returning to America in 1774, the following year he became assistant minister at Trinity Church in New York City, where he associated himself, as did other Trinity clergy, with the Tory cause. Upon the outbreak of the American Revolution, when Trinity Church closed rather than modify its liturgy by excising prayers for the crown, Bowden retired to Norwalk, Connecticut. After the British recaptured New York in 1776, he returned to the city, but a voice ailment prevented him from resuming his labors at Trinity. He did assist at churches on Long Island and in 1784, after the British left New York, became rector of St. Paul's Church in Norwalk. Even this, however, was too much of a strain on his health, and in 1789 he took up residence in St. Croix in the West Indies in the hope that it would aid his health. This change in climate, however, brought no relief. He returned to Stratford, Connecticut, in 1791 and conducted an academy there before being chosen in 1796 to become the first head of the newly established Episcopal Academy in Cheshire, Connecticut. In the same year he declined, on account of health and other reasons, election as bishop of the Episcopal church in Connecticut. In 1802 he became professor of moral philosophy and belles lettres at Columbia College and served in this position until his death. He was married to Mary Jervis and had three sons. He died in Ballston Spa, New York.

Bowden was a careful, if unimaginative, scholar of the history of the early church and employed his learning in a number of religious disputes during the early national period. He was a representative of the high church tradition of the Episcopal church and held that the only valid Christian ministry was one that stemmed from a succession of bishops going back to the apostles. This position was a controversial one, and he often wrote tracts and pamphlets defending his church against other religious communities. *A Letter to Ezra Stiles [on] Church Government* (1788), *A Letter from a Churchman to His Friend in New Haven* (1808), and *A Full Length Portrait of Calvinism* (1809) were defenses of his church's episcopal polity and Arminian theology against criticisms from Connecticut Congregationalists. During the early nineteenth century he became associated with John Henry Hobart, Episcopal bishop of New York, and became involved in an extensive debate with the Presbyterian divine Samuel Miller over the necessity of episcopal ministry for a true church. His two works: *The Apostolic Origin of Episcopacy Asserted* (1808) and *A Series of Letters Addressed to the Rev. Dr. Miller* (1811) were his major literary efforts and later, reprinted as a single volume, became a standard work of Episcopal apologetical theology.

• Bowden's other works include *A Letter to Ezra Stiles [on] Church Government* (1788) and *An Address from John Bowden, A.M., to the Members of the Episcopal Church in Stratford* (1792). No significant collection of Bowden papers has survived, nor is there a full-scale biography. Sketches can be found in the *Christian Journal* (Jan. 1818); W. B. Sprague, *Annals of the American Pulpit*, vol. 5 (1859); and A. Lowndes, ed., *Archives of the General Convention . . . The Correspondence of John Henry Hobart* (1911–1912). The best modern treatment of his thought is found in R. B. Mullin, *Episcopal Vision/American Reality: High Church Theology and Social Thought in Evangelical America* (1986).

ROBERT BRUCE MULLIN

BOWDITCH, Charles Pickering (30 Sept. 1842–1 June 1921), benefactor and archaeologist, was born in Boston, Massachusetts, the son of Jonathan Ingersoll Bowditch, a merchant and trustee, and Lucy Orne Nichols. Bowditch was the grandson of mathematician Nathaniel Bowditch. Bowditch was graduated from Harvard College in 1863. In 1863–1864 he held commissions in the Fifty-fifth Massachusetts Volunteer Infantry and the Fifth Massachusetts Volunteer Cavalry, attaining the rank of captain. Bowditch received an A.M. from Harvard in 1866. That same year he married Cornelia Livingstone Rockwell, the daughter of a judge and former U.S. senator. The Bowditches had five children, one of whom died in infancy.

Bowditch was involved with several business concerns and numerous charities. Among his business interests were the Pepperell Manufacturing Company and the Boston and Providence Railroad Corporation. He was a vice president of American Telephone and Telegraph (1883–1886) and the president of the Massachusetts Hospital Life Insurance Company (1915). He was also a man of wide-ranging intellectual interests, as reflected by his membership in numerous learned societies, his benefactions, and his own writing. In 1887 he published *The Pickering Genealogy*, a history of his maternal grandmother's family. In *An Account of the Trust Administered by the Trustees of the Charity of Edward Hopkins*, published in 1889, Bowditch traced the litigation surrounding Harvard's receipt of the bequest of Edward Hopkins, former governor of the Connecticut Colony, intended to further education in New England. Bowditch also wrote a short work on the authorship of Shakespeare's works. Published in 1910, *The Connection of Francis Bacon with the First Folio of Shakespeare's Plays* displays Bowditch's interest in mathematics and ciphers. Elected to the American Academy of Arts and Sciences in 1892, he served as treasurer (1905–1915) and president (1917–1919). He was a founder of the American Anthropological Association.

But it was in the then nascent field of Mexican and Central American archaeology that Bowditch made his greatest contributions as benefactor and scholar. Visits to Mexico in 1888 and to Honduras in 1890 sparked a fascination with the pre-Columbian Indian civilizations of Mexico and Central America. From the late 1890s until his death, Bowditch fostered the study of the region's ancient history through his association with the Peabody Museum of Archaeology and Ethnology of Harvard University. His substantial gifts to the museum and, starting in 1894, his service as trustee contributed to building the museum's collections, shaping its research focus, enriching its library, and creating a division (now a department) of anthropology. Bowditch established fellowships for students and endowed a chair in the anthropology department, the Bowditch Professor of Central American and Mexican Archaeology and Ethnology.

Research expeditions by the Peabody Museum to Honduras, Guatemala, the Yucatan peninsula, and Belize, funded largely by Bowditch, began in 1891. These pioneering explorations, many of which included some of the earliest excavations in the region, were instrumental in demonstrating the richness of the Indian, and especially Maya, past. Bowditch supported initial research and publication by Edward H. Thompson (Chichen Itza, Mexico), John Owens and George Byron Gordon (Copan, Honduras), Gordon (the Ulua Valley, Honduras), Teobert Maler (the tropical lowlands of Guatemala), Raymond Merwin (Holmul, Guatemala), and Alfred Marston Tozzer (Belize and Guatemala).

It is Tozzer who perhaps represents Bowditch's greatest legacy to the field. Urged on by Professor of Anthropology Frederick Ward Putnam, Bowditch assumed responsibility in 1901 for the costs of Tozzer's graduate training in linguistics and archaeology. Bowditch provided not only financial support to Tozzer but also advice and friendship that continued after Tozzer joined the faculty at Harvard and began building an academic program in Mexican and Central American archaeology and ethnology.

In an effort to disseminate more widely research on pre-Columbian Mexico and Central America by the German scholars Eduard Seler, Ernst Förstemann, Paul Schellhas, Karl Sapper, and Erwin Dieseldorff, Bowditch commissioned the translation of their works into English. Bowditch himself translated several Colonial-period Spanish documents describing native customs or events of the conquest, including Diego de Landa's *Relación de las cosas de Yucatán* as well as accounts by Andrés de Avendaño y Loyola, Juan de Villagutierre Soto-Mayor, Bernardo de Lizana, and Alonzo Cano. Most of the translations remain unpublished, although parts of Avendaño and Cano appeared in Philip Ainsworth Means's *History of the Spanish Conquest of Yucatan and of the Itzas* (1917).

Copies of two native books, the Codex Nuttall and the Codex Laud, were commissioned and published by Bowditch. In a continuing effort to make primary source material available for research, Bowditch either had made, or purchased from William Gates, photographic reproductions of manuscripts and rare books, with special emphasis on linguistic materials.

Bowditch's research focused on the decipherment of the hieroglyphic writing system used by the Maya from the first century A.D. up to the time of the Spanish conquest in the sixteenth century. Bowditch published a series of privately printed pamphlets and several journal articles dealing with the Maya calendar, including "The Lords of the Night and the Tonalamatl of the Codex Borbonicus" (1900) and "Memoranda on the Maya Calendars Used in the Books of Chilam Balam" (1901), both appearing in *American Anthropologist*. Other works include *Was the Beginning Day of the Maya Month Numbered Zero (or Twenty) or One?* (a 1901 pamphlet) and "The Dates and Numbers of Pages 24 and 26 to 50 of the Dresden Codex" (1909, in *Putnam Anniversary Volume*). In 1910 he wrote and published privately *The Numeration, Calendar Systems and Astronomical Knowledge of the Mayas*, a compendium of available information on these topics based on the codices and stone inscriptions. The lengthy discussion of mathematics reflects Bowditch's own considerable abilities in this area. He stands as one of the pioneers who laid the groundwork for the complete decipherment of the script in the last decades of the twentieth century.

Because of his work and his sustained support of archaeological, linguistic, and epigraphic research on the ancient civilizations of Mexico and Central America, Charles Bowditch is remembered as one of the founders of a new field of study in American anthropology. He died in Jamaica Plain, Massachusetts.

• The archives of the Peabody Museum, Harvard University, hold the Charles P. Bowditch Correspondence for 1893–1921. The Edward H. Thompson Papers, also in the archives, contain material relating to Bowditch. The Harvard University Archives contain other relevant material. Bowditch's book collection, the German translations, his privately printed pamphlets, and his photographic copies of manuscripts are now in the Tozzer Library, Harvard University. Some of the German translations were published as *Bulletin 28* of the Bureau of American Ethnology (1904) and in the *Papers of the Peabody Museum*, vol. 4 (no. 1, 1904; no. 2, 1906). Bowditch's patronage of the Peabody Museum and his interest in archaeology are discussed in Curtis Hinsley, "Wanted: One Good Man to Discover Central American History," *Harvard Magazine* 87, no. 2 (1984): 64A–64H. Two privately printed family histories contain some biographical information on Bowditch and his family. They are Harold Bowditch, *The Bowditch Family of Salem, Massachusetts* (1936), and Francis Williams Rockwell, *The Rockwell Family in One Line of Descent* (1924). An entry in William Bentinck-Smith and Elizabeth Stouffer, *Harvard University: History of Named Chairs* (1991), discusses the nature of Bowditch's endowment to the Peabody Museum. An obituary by Alfred Marston Tozzer in *American Anthropologist* n.s., 23 (1921): 353–59 is the most complete. A shorter obituary is in the *New York Times*, 2 June 1921.

JULIA A. HENDON

BOWDITCH, Henry Ingersoll (9 Aug. 1808–14 Jan. 1892), physician, public hygienist, and abolitionist, was born in Salem, Massachusetts, the son of Nathaniel Bowditch, a mathematician and astronomer, and Mary Ingersoll. Raised in a patrician family, Bowditch, who received his early education at the Salem Private Grammar School and Boston Public Latin School, graduated from Harvard College in 1828. He then studied at the Harvard Medical School and supplemented its didactic lectures by serving in 1831–1832 as house officer at the Massachusetts General Hospital.

After receiving an M.D. in 1832, Bowditch, like a growing number of elite young American physicians, traveled to Paris to continue his medical studies. His father's fame as translator into English of the French astronomer and mathematician Pierre-Simon Laplace's *Méchanique céleste* won the young man a welcome reception into Parisian scientific circles. Bowditch spent most of his time studying clinical examination and diagnosis in the wards of the physician Pierre Charles Alexandre Louis at La Pitié. Along with other students of Louis, including fellow Harvard medical alumni James Jackson, Jr., and Oliver Wendell Holmes, he participated in the newly formed Société médicale d'observation, which cultivated reports of observation at the bedside, correlation of symptoms with lesions found at autopsy, and the use of Louis's "numerical method" to bring statistical order to such clinical information. Bowditch wrote to his mother that Louis had "roused in me a higher feeling" for medicine (*Life*, vol. 1, p. 38), and he embraced his French mentor's empiricist crusade against rationalistic systems of medicine. Louis's commitment to exact observation as the sole means of attaining medical truth would become a central theme in Bowditch's work.

In 1834 Bowditch returned to Boston, where he began to practice medicine and energetically proselytized the new Parisian medical gospel. In 1835 he helped to found the short-lived Society for Medical Observation and, in 1846, the more lasting Boston Society for Medical Observation, which was explicitly modeled after Louis's Parisian Society. In 1836 Bowditch published translations of two of Louis's key books, on phthisis and on typhoid fever. He also vigorously defended the use of the numerical method in medical investigation against American critics, as in his ardent polemical exchange in 1840 with the New York medical professor Martyn Paine, who charged that clinical statistics threatened to undermine appreciation of patient individuality and exercise of clinical judgment. Bowditch, like Louis's other American disciples, had taken up the mission of liberating medicine from its bondage to rationalistic systems, constructing, as Louis put it in a letter to Bowditch of 5 February 1840, "a barrier against the spirit of system."

In 1838 Bowditch married Olivia Yardley, an Englishwoman whom he had met in Paris; together they had four children. He became admitting physician at the Massachusetts General Hospital in 1838 and used its wards for private clinical teaching until 1846, when he won the prestigious position of visiting physician he occupied until 1864. Bowditch vigorously advocated the use of the stethoscope, the recently invented hallmark of Parisian clinical medicine, in understanding diseases of the chest. In 1846 he published *The Young Stethoscopist; or the Student's Aid to Auscultation*, a popular textbook that helped establish Bowditch as a leading authority on chest disorders. From 1852 to 1855 he offered classes on stethoscopic examination at the Boylston Medical School, a non-degree-granting supplementary school in Boston.

For at least a decade and a half after his return from Europe, however, Bowditch's efforts to elevate medicine were subordinate to his passionate antislavery activism. Largely convinced by the writings of British abolitionist William Wilberforce, Bowditch opposed slavery even before he left for Europe, and the moving experience of attending Wilberforce's funeral while in England strengthened his belief in the immorality of slavery. Shortly after his return to America, in October 1835, he witnessed a Boston mob trying to tar and feather abolitionist William Lloyd Garrison. Indignant and radicalized, Bowditch pledged in his diary to devote his "whole heart to the abolition of that monster slavery" (Folsom, p. 313). More radical than most antislavery sympathizers of his social class, Bowditch became a devout follower of Garrison. He advocated physical resistance, assisted fugitive slaves, and fought northern laws that would return them to bondage. He ardently fought the extradition of George Latimer, an escaped slave from Virginia who had been arrested in 1842; "it was a grand moral tonic" (*Life*, vol. 1, p.

137), he later recalled of his efforts in the Latimer affair, which contributed to the passage of a bill by the Massachusetts legislature forbidding the detention of runaway slaves in town or state jails. Bowditch remained committed to the antislavery cause through the 1850s, when he was an activist in the Anti–Man-Hunting League. Bowditch, in some measure socially ostracized for his radical abolitionism, reveled in the moral crusade despite his recognition that it would undercut prospects for a lucrative medical practice.

During the 1850s, Bowditch's attention shifted more toward medicine. Although there had been no growth in his private practice from 1836 to 1846, his practice doubled by 1852 and trebled by 1861. Using a procedure suggested by Morrill Wyman of Cambridge, Massachusetts, Bowditch developed in 1850 a method, which he termed thoracis paracentesis, of puncturing the chest with a small hollow needle to remove excessive fluid by aspiration. This method of relieving patients who suffered from pleurisy quickly came into common use and cemented his reputation as an authority on chest diseases. In 1854 Bowditch began a large-scale survey of consumption, then regarded as the leading cause of death. The evidence he collected from Massachusetts physicians, tabulated, and analyzed using Louis's numerical method convinced him that pulmonary tuberculosis was associated with residence on or near damp soil. From this study, which he reported to the Massachusetts Medical Society and published in 1862 as *Consumption in New England; or, Locality One of Its Chief Causes*, Bowditch drew a conclusion that would govern his medical endeavors for the remainder of his career—namely, that the physical environment was a major determinant of disease and should be a leading target of efforts at prevention and cure. The death of his son, who had been left for over a day wounded and unattended on a Civil War battlefield, prompted Bowditch in 1863 to lobby for an efficient ambulance corp, and his writings proved an important stimulus to the reformed ambulance system that was among the few medical contributions to emerge from the war.

In 1859 Bowditch became Jackson Professor of Clinical Medicine at the Harvard Medical School, a post he held until 1867. At a time when American physicians wavered between the polar extremes of confident heroic therapy and restrained therapeutic skepticism, Bowditch was a nationally prominent advocate of what he urged on his students as "the middle course" or "the golden mean" ("Lectures for Winter 1860–1861," Countway Library). He denounced blind allegiance to aggressive drugging but equally opposed therapeutic nihilism, and in the 1860s and 1870s he cautioned physicians against overreacting against earlier excesses by abandoning such therapeutic practices as bloodletting.

In 1869 Bowditch became chairman of the newly created Massachusetts State Board of Health, the first of its kind in the nation. For Bowditch, the new position meant both a decisive turn in his career toward public health and a return to the crusading zeal that before the Civil War he had invested in abolitionism. Public hygiene—what Bowditch from the outset termed "State Medicine"—gave him a new forum for battling social and physical ills inflicted on the most powerless of the nation's people. Convinced by his investigations on consumption that changing the environment was key to preventing disease, Bowditch looked to hygienic improvement of the environment under state auspices as the crucial first step toward improving the condition of the poor and enabling them to lead healthy and moral lives.

The board of health lacked the enforcement powers needed to enact Bowditch's aspirations for "State Medicine," but the investigations and reports carried out under his direction did draw attention to the state's sanitary ills. Determined, moreover, to use his position as chairman as a pulpit for proselytizing the sanitary reform movement, he set forward a new vision for American medicine and public health. In *Preventive Medicine and the Physician of the Future* (1874), he looked forward to the time when physicians' primary role would be educating the public and the state about how to preserve and improve health. In his 1876 address to the International Medical Congress, published as *Public Hygiene in America* (1877), Bowditch asserted that the founding of the Massachusetts State Board of Health had inaugurated a new epoch in American medicine—state preventive medicine—which he urged physicians to embrace as a sacred duty. In the same year, Bowditch was elected president of the American Medical Association. He resigned from the board of health in 1879, protesting against political interference in its reorganization.

Bowditch had largely shed the credal framework of his protestant religious upbringing by his late twenties, but throughout his life he retained a pietistic sense of mission and zealous Christian moralism. He passed none of his adult life without at least one campaign to focus his energies and viewed all of his battles—against rationalistic systems of medicine, against slavery, and against unhygienic environments—as moral crusades. His health and activity gradually declined after a fall on an icy street in 1879. He died in Boston.

A leading figure in transporting Parisian medical ideas and practices to the United States and a prominent participant in the Massachusetts antislavery movement, Bowditch's most lasting contribution was the impulse he imparted to the American public health movement and especially to promoting the role of the state in preventive medicine.

• A rich collection of Bowditch's medical lecture notes, correspondence, and patient records is in Holmes Hall, Francis A. Countway Library of Medicine, Boston. Among his publications that have not already been mentioned are *Brief Memories of Louis and Some of His Contemporaries in the Parisian School of Medicine of Forty Years Ago* (1872); *A Brief Plea for an Ambulance System for the Army of the United States* (1863); *On Paracentesis Thoracis, with an Analysis of Cases* (1852); *Remarks Relative to Dr. Paine's Commentaries upon the Writings of M. Louis* (1840); and *Venesection, Its Abuse Formerly—Its*

Neglect at the Present Day (1872). Vincent Y. Bowditch, *Life and Correspondence of Henry Ingersoll Bowditch* (2 vols., 1902), provides an account of his life and extracts from his correspondence and journals; a substantive obituary by Charles F. Folsom, "Henry Ingersoll Bowditch," *Proceedings of the American Academy of Arts and Sciences*, n.s., 20 (1893): 310–31, contains an extensive but incomplete bibliography of his publications. For Bowditch's board of health work, see Barbara Gutmann Rosenkrantz, *Public Health and the State: Changing Views in Massachusetts, 1842–1936* (1972); for his medical teaching, see Dale Cary Smith, "The Emergence of Organized Clinical Instruction in the Nineteenth-Century American Cities of Boston, New York, and Philadelphia" (Ph.D. diss., Univ. of Minnesota, 1979); and for his relationship to French medicine and therapeutic stance, see John Harley Warner, *The Therapeutic Perspective: Medical Practice, Knowledge, and Identity in America, 1820–1885* (1986).

JOHN HARLEY WARNER

BOWDITCH, Henry Pickering (9 Apr. 1840–13 Mar. 1911), physiologist, was born in Boston, Massachusetts, the son of Jonathan Ingersoll Bowditch, a successful Boston merchant, and Lucy Orne Nichols. Bowditch enjoyed a comfortable, cultured childhood in Boston and later in West Roxbury, where his family moved when he was thirteen. In preparation for college Bowditch attended a school organized by Epes S. Dixwell, graduating in 1857. After graduating from Harvard College in 1861, Bowditch matriculated at the Harvard-affiliated Lawrence Scientific School in Cambridge to study chemistry and natural history in preparation for a possible career in medicine. His studies were interrupted in November 1861 when he joined the First Massachusetts Cavalry as a second lieutenant. His unit engaged in a number of actions, including one at New Hope Church on 27 November 1863 where Bowditch was shot in the arm while leading a charge. Although honorably discharged in February 1864, he soon rejoined the army as a major in the Fifth Massachusetts Cavalry. He resigned his commission in June 1865 and returned to the Lawrence Scientific School, where he resumed studies of comparative anatomy under Jeffries Wyman, receiving the M.A. in 1866. He also completed the medical course at Harvard Medical School, earning an M.D. in 1868 with a thesis on the physiological actions of potassium bromide.

On graduation Bowditch left Boston in August 1868 to continue his scientific and medical training in Europe. These years following graduation were the most formative of his career; he encountered the research and pedagogic models he would emulate during much of that career. In particular, while visiting French and German physiological laboratories where physicians devoted their entire time to medical research rather than to patient care, Bowditch realized that he was drawn more to teaching and research than to clinical practice. Hoping but unable to obtain a position in the laboratory of Charles Edouard Brown-Séquard, he remained in Paris for only nine months. While there he attended the lectures and clinics of Paul Bert, Paul Broca, Jean-Martin Charcot, Jules Gavarret, Pierre Louis, Étienne-Jules Marey, and Edmé-F. A. Vulpian. Eventually he was also able to spend three days a week in the physiological laboratory of Claude Bernard, and another three days a week in the histological laboratory of Louis-Antoine Ranvier. His experiences in Paris led him to conclude that while French physiologists were excellent scientists, they lacked a vision or unified program to guided their diverse researches, especially in relation to clinical medicine.

In May 1869, on the advice of the German physiologist Wilhelm Kühne, Bowditch departed for Germany. After five months studying microscopic anatomy in the Bonn laboratory of Max Schultze and Eduard Rindfleisch, he obtained a position in Carl Ludwig's physiological institute at Leipzig. Internationally renowned as a scientist and teacher, Ludwig headed one of the most stimulating sites for physiological research during this period, drawing students from throughout Europe and the United States. Within two months of his arrival at Ludwig's laboratory in November 1869, Bowditch made a number of important contributions to Ludwig's research. Most notably, he improved Ludwig's kymograph by developing a mechanism, based on the metronome, which registered the relationship between the blood-pressure readings made by the instrument and the time they were made. Under Ludwig's direction, Bowditch also completed exemplary studies of the characteristics of cardiac muscle stimulation and the influence of arterial blood pressure on the heart's nerves. The instruments, methods, techniques, and laboratory activity Bowditch encountered during his stay with Ludwig greatly impressed him, prompting him to write a detailed letter to the *Boston Medical and Surgical Journal* extolling German physiology and its practices. Bowditch also took time from Ludwig's work to spend November 1870 in Munich attending Carl Voit's lectures on nutrition and metabolism. Before returning to Boston, on 9 September 1871 Bowditch married Selma Knauth, a Leipzig banker's daughter, with whom he had seven children.

At the insistence of Harvard president Charles W. Eliot, Bowditch returned to Boston in September 1871 to assume an assistant professorship in physiology at the newly-reformed Harvard Medical School. Bowditch would remain at Harvard his entire professional career; he was appointed full professor of physiology in 1876 and named George Higginson Professor of Physiology in 1903, and he retired as professor emeritus in 1906. He played an important role in the reform of Harvard Medical School during the 1870s and in the building of a new medical campus; in addition, while serving as medical school dean from 1883 to 1893 he oversaw the extension of the medical course to four years and the establishment of new departments, particularly bacteriology.

The physiological laboratory at Harvard was the first for teaching medical students in the United States, and although it was cramped and makeshift, Bowditch outfitted it with first-rate equipment and instruments he personally purchased while in Europe. Following the example of Ludwig, Bowditch's laboratory pursued a wide variety of work beyond physiology, venturing into experimental biology, pharmacology, pathology, psychology, surgery, and bacteriology. Bowditch was also able to attract a dedicated corps of talented students, including G. M. Garland, G. Stanley Hall, William James, Warren P. Lombard, Robert W. Lovett, Charles S. Minot, Isaac Ott, James J. Putnam, William F. Southard, and Joseph W. Warren. In the laboratory Bowditch and his students developed important new physiological instruments and techniques: induction apparatus permitting intensity variation, a plethysmograph for recording volume changes in organs, and devices for aiding artificial respiration and observing the vocal cords.

After returning to Boston Bowditch continued some of the research he began with Ludwig's guidance in Leipzig. Building on his earlier studies of the "Treppe" or steplike increase of heart conduction, Bowditch demonstrated the incapacity of the ventricle's apex to exhibit a spontaneous rhythm once separated from its base. Another line of interest concerned the nervous control of blood vessels; he showed that chloroform had a more profound effect than ether in depressing vasomotor reflexes, and that it was possible alternately to generate vascular constriction and dilation by varying the nature of stimulation. The functioning of the nervous system was of central interest in another classic study, in which Bowditch demonstrated the indefatigability of the nerve trunk. His contributions to psychology included showing the relative accuracy of sensory knowledge of position in space as adduced by sight and by touch. Another facet of his research was anthropometric studies of Boston children, showing that the quality of their housing and nutrition was more important than race in determining the levels of children's growth, and that loss of weight in growing children suggested impending chronic illness.

Bowditch was very active in professional and civic organizations. A founding member of the American Physiological Society in 1887, he served as its president from 1891 to 1895, a crucial period in its history. The American Society of Naturalists and the Congress of American Physicians and Surgeons both elected him to head their organizations; his presidential address before the 1900 meeting of the Congress of American Physicians and Surgeons, titled "The Medical School of the Future," was prescient and catalytic for reforms in medical education. He recognized that antivivisection campaigns posed a significant threat to the progress of medical research and testified and lobbied government agencies and officials against antivivisectionist legislation. Also active in the public affairs of Boston, Bowditch served as a member of the Boston School Committee (1877–1881), president of the Massachusetts Infant Asylum (1886) and Boston Children's Aid Society, and trustee of the Boston Public Library.

Bowditch was elected to membership in the American Academy of Arts and Sciences (1872), the National Academy of Sciences (1887), the American Philosophical Society, the Royal Society of Medicine and Natural Sciences of Brussels, the Academy of Science of Rome, and many other American and foreign academic societies. A consummate scholar and dedicated teacher, he advanced the cause of physiology and medical research in the United States through his exemplary research and by training many of the most important physiologists of the early twentieth century. He died in Boston.

• Bowditch's extant correspondence and papers are in the Francis A. Countway Medical Library at Harvard Medical School. A complete list of his publications is in Cannon (1924); many of these were collected in *The Life and Writings of Henry Pickering Bowditch* (2 vols., 1980). The most important include "Bromide of Potassium," *Boston Medical and Surgical Journal* 78 (1868): 177–84; "Alcohol as a Nutritive Agent," *Boston Medical and Surgical Journal* 86 (1872): 413–14; with C. S. Minot, "The Influence of Anaesthetics on the Vaso-Motor Centers," *Boston Medical and Surgical Journal* 91 (1874): 493–98; "The Growth of Children," *Eighth Annual Report of the Massachusetts State Board of Health* (1877), pp. 275–325; and "The Relation Between Growth and Disease," *Transactions of the American Medicine Association* 32 (1881): 371–77.

The best biographical study is by his student Walter Branford Cannon, "Henry Pickering Bowditch," National Academy of Sciences, *Biographical Memoirs* 17 (1924): 183–96. W. Bruce Fye considers Bowditch's influence and contribution to American physiology in "Why a Physiologist?—The Case of Henry P. Bowditch," *Bulletin of the History of Medicine* 56 (1982): 19–29, and in "Henry P. Bowditch: The Prototypical Full-Time Physiologist and Educational Reformer," in *The Development of American Physiology: Scientific Medicine in the Nineteenth Century* (1987). See also T. E. Cone, "Dr. Henry Pickering Bowditch on the Growth of Children: An Unappreciated Classic Study," *Transactions and Studies of the College of Physicians of Philadelphia* 42 (1974): 67–76; and, Saul Benison et al., "Changing of the Guard," *Harvard Medical Alumni Bulletin* 56 (1982): 34–41.

D. George Joseph

BOWDITCH, Nathaniel (26 Mar. 1773–16 Mar. 1838), astronomer and mathematician, was born in Salem, Massachusetts, the son of Habakkuk Bowditch, a shipmaster and cooper, and Mary Ingersoll. His family moved to Danvers, Massachusetts, while he was still an infant but returned to Salem when Bowditch was seven. Business reverses forced his family into poverty, and Bowditch's formal education ended at age ten, when he entered his father's cooperage shop. In 1785 he became an apprentice clerk in the ship-chandlery shop of Hodges and Ropes in Salem; five years later he moved to the shop of Samuel C. Ward. Between January 1795 and December 1803, Bowditch made five voyages on merchant ships, including four to the East Indies and one to Europe, serving on the last voyage as master and part owner. In March 1798, between voyages, he married Elizabeth Boardman, who died seven months later. He married Mary Ingersoll, a cousin, in 1800; they had eight children.

In 1804 Bowditch became head of the Essex Fire and Marine Insurance Company in Salem. Although his term as president included the embargo years and the War of 1812, the company flourished. He left Salem for Boston in 1823 to become actuary of the Massachusetts Hospital Life Insurance Company, a position he held until his death in that city. Although he had the opportunity to leave the business world for academia a number of times—he rejected offers of professorships from Harvard University, West Point, and the University of Virginia—he remained in commerce because it provided both an income that American higher education could not match and sufficient leisure for his research and writing. In 1818, for example, the University of Virginia, which at the time paid relatively high salaries to its faculty, offered Bowditch $2,000 and a house. Bowditch's income, however, was already over $3,000. Upon joining the Massachusetts Hospital Life Insurance Company five years later, he earned a salary of $5,000.

Bowditch began his self-education during his apprenticeship years. He began the study of algebra in 1787, calculus two years later, and Latin by 1790. He took up the latter two subjects in order to understand Isaac Newton's *Principia*. In June 1791 the resources of the Salem Philosophical Library were made available to him, including various science texts and the *Philosophical Transactions* of the Royal Society of London. Recognizing that many significant mathematical works were in French, he undertook the study of that language in 1792 and perfected his knowledge during his sea voyages. Continuing to learn throughout his life, he mastered German at the age of forty-five in order to stay abreast of the revolution in astronomical thought and practice that was taking place in Germany through the work of H. W. M. Olbers, Carl F. Gauss, Johann F. Encke, and others. In so doing, Bowditch was the first American to become fully cognizant of this revolution.

Bowditch's first major contribution was his revision of John Hamilton Moore's *The Practical Navigator*. Working in collaboration with his brother William, Bowditch corrected the errors in the thirteenth English edition and produced in 1799 the first American edition. A second edition appeared in 1800, and what would have been the third was prepared in 1801. Because Bowditch's alterations were so extensive, however, this third edition was instead published under his own name as *The New American Practical Navigator* (1802). By the time of Bowditch's death, *The New American Practical Navigator* was in its tenth edition. Widely used throughout the nineteenth and twentieth centuries, this handbook gained for Bowditch public recognition and his election to the American Academy of Arts and Sciences in 1799. His election as professor of mathematics and natural philosophy at Harvard in 1806 (which he did not accept) was based on a reputation acquired through this book, which was more of a practical manual than a scientific contribution; a single article on the application of lunar observations for purposes of navigation, published in the *Memoirs of the American Academy of Arts and Sciences* in 1804; and his 1806 publication of a chart of the harbors of Salem, Marblehead, Beverly, and Manchester, Massachusetts.

Over the next two decades, Bowditch published articles on celestial mechanics, mathematics, and terrestrial magnetism. Examples of his topics include the 1807 meteor explosion over Weston, Connecticut (1811); comet orbits (1815, 1818, 1820); variations of the magnetic needle (1815); and the motion of a pendulum suspended from two points (1815). In the last article, published in the *Memoirs of the American Academy of Arts and Sciences*, Bowditch discussed the paths traced out by a particle that oscillates simultaneously in two mutually perpendicular directions. These curves are now know as "Lissajous figures," in honor of the French physicist Jules A. Lissajous, who published an account of them and their application to understanding accoustical phenomenon in 1855.

Bowditch's work appeared primarily in the American journals *Memoirs of the American Academy of Arts and Sciences*, *The Analyst*, the *Mathematical Diary*, and the *North American Review*, but also in British and Continental journals. These publications established his reputation as the leading American celestial mechanician and mathematician, a reputation ratified by his election to the American Philosophical Society (1809), the Edinburgh Royal Society (1818), and the Royal Irish Academy (1819), and his selection as a member of the Board of Overseers for Harvard (1810). Most significant as an indicator of his international reputation was his election as a foreign member of the Royal Society of London in 1818; this honor was not again bestowed upon an American until 1852. Subsequent honors included the presidency from 1829 of the American Academy of Arts and Sciences and fellow from 1825 of the Harvard Corporation, both until his death.

During these same two decades, Bowditch was working on the publication that marked the climax of his career, his translation and annotation of Pierre Simon Laplace's *Traite de mécanique céleste*. Laplace's five-volume summary of the progress of physical astronomy since Newton had been published between 1799 and 1825. Having read the first volume while on his 1802–1803 voyage and the next three by June 1806, Bowditch translated and provided a commentary for these four volumes between 1814 and 1817. His intention, expressed in the preface to volume one, was to make Laplace's compendium "more accessible to persons who have been unable to prepare themselves for this study, by a previous course of reading in those modern publications, which contain the many important discoveries in analysis, made since the time of Newton." In his commentary Bowditch added the missing intermediary steps in Laplace's demonstrations; noted recent improvements and discoveries in mathematics, in essence providing a summary of the progress in the discipline since Laplace's writing; and supplied the sources from which Laplace had drawn, but to whom no credit had been given.

Although the translation was ready for the press by 1818, the first of the four volumes did not appear until

1829. Bowditch rejected suggestions that the volumes be published either through subscription or by the AAAS, preferring to wait until he could finance the entire enterprise, which cost approximately $12,000, from his own resources. That way, he could maintain control over the final product. During the delay, Bowditch continued to update and revise his commentary, although he did not translate Laplace's fifth volume, which appeared in 1825. The second and third volumes appeared in 1832 and 1834, respectively. Volume four, almost finished at his death, was published posthumously in 1839. As printed, the commentary was approximately one-and-a-half times the length of Laplace's original treatise.

It would be difficult to overestimate the value of Bowditch's translation and commentary to American physical astronomy during the first half of the nineteenth century. The work marked the beginning of American participation in the field of celestial mechanics. Not only did it allow the poorly trained professors of mathematics in American colleges to explore the wonders of French celestial mechanics, but it also became an essential part of the education of some of Bowditch's successors in the field. Benjamin Peirce, the next great American in the field, helped revise and correct Bowditch's proofs. William Ferrel, Daniel Kirkwood, and John Nelson Stockwell were essentially autodidacts like Bowditch who learned celestial mechanics from his translation.

Even if Bowditch had never published his translation of the *Mécanique céleste*, he would still rate as one of the leading American scientists during the Jeffersonian age. His strength lay not in original thought but in his ability to ferret out the errors of others, his command of the scientific literature in many languages, and his immense energy. Almost single-handedly, he kept mathematical astronomy alive in the United States during the first decades of the nineteenth century.

• Shortly before his death Bowditch destroyed many of his personal papers. What remained is in the Boston Public Library. Nathan Reingold has published some of his correspondence in *Science in Nineteenth Century America, A Documentary History* (1964). Bowditch's journal of his fourth voyage was edited by T. R. and M. C. McHale, *Early American-Philippine Trade: The Journal of Nathaniel Bowditch in Manila, 1796* (1962). The best study of his life is the *Memoir of Nathaniel Bowditch* (1839), prepared by his son, Henry Ingersoll Bowditch, and published in volume four of *Mécanique céleste*. For Bowditch in the context of American science, see Dirk J. Struik, *Yankee Science in the Making* (1962), and John C. Greene, *American Science in the Age of Jefferson* (1984). Ronald Story, *The Forging of an Aristocracy: Harvard and the Boston Upper Class, 1800–1870* (1980), considers Bowditch as a member of the Boston financial community.

MARC ROTHENBERG

BOWDOIN, James (7 Aug. 1726–6 Nov. 1790), scientist and statesman, was born in Boston, Massachusetts, the son of James Bowdoin, a wealthy Boston merchant of French Huguenot origins and a member of the Massachusetts Council, the upper house of the General Assembly, and his second wife, Hannah Portage. Young James Bowdoin was educated at Boston Latin School and graduated from Harvard College in 1745. At his father's death in 1747 he inherited a fortune valued at over £80,000 sterling. Independently wealthy, he lived luxuriously on his income from bonds, loans, rentals, and real estate holdings in Maine. In 1748 he married Elizabeth Erving, daughter of John Erving, a Boston merchant. The couple had two children.

Following in the tradition of the English country gentleman, Bowdoin pursued a life of public service, scientific study, and estate development. A representative of the eighteenth-century Enlightenment, Bowdoin took a master's degree at Harvard in 1748 and, inspired by his college mentor, John Winthrop (1714–1779), the next year began purchasing electrical apparatus. In 1750 Bowdoin visited Philadelphia, where he began an enduring friendship with Benjamin Franklin (1706–1790). The next year Franklin sent him the manuscript of his *Observations on Electricity*, and the pair began a correspondence that continued for the next forty years. Bowdoin, however, turned from the study of electricity to astronomy. He was especially interested in optics and in 1761 published a brief article, "An Improvement Proposed for Telescopes," in the *London Magazine*. He encouraged Winthrop's successful observation of the transit of Venus in 1761 and backed a similar abortive venture, planned for the Lake Superior region in 1769.

Gradually Bowdoin assembled a remarkably comprehensive working library, which contained over 1,200 volumes by 1775. Although heavily weighted toward scientific and mathematical works, the collection included extensive holdings in philosophy, religion, politics, history, biography, and belles lettres. In 1759 he published a volume of original verses, *A Paraphrase on Part of the Oeconomy of Human Life*, which he fancied exceeded the scope of Robert Dodsley's original work, *The Oeconomy of Human Life* (1751). His book attracted little attention in Boston, but he was undaunted enough to contribute four poems, two in Latin and two in English, to the "Harvard Verses" presented to the young George III in 1762 in an attempt to gain royal patronage for the college.

Bowdoin was also drawn to Massachusetts politics. He served on several town committees before his election to the House of Representatives in 1753. Four years later he was advanced to the Council, where he continued without interruption until 1769. Like his father, Bowdoin at first endorsed the prerogative or court party, which supported the royal governor. A friend of Governor William Shirley, he was even closer to his successor, Thomas Pownall, who shared his scientific interests. But his attachment to royal government soured after the arrival of the next governor, Francis Bernard, whom Bowdoin soon came to detest personally.

Bowdoin's first opposition to British restrictive policies came when, with the rest of the Council, he condemned the Sugar Act of 1764, claiming that although the act was ostensibly intended to regulate trade, it was unconstitutional because it raised a revenue in the colonies. Bowdoin halted his personal imports of British goods in support of the nonimportation agreements of the 1760s to protest the Stamp and Townshend acts. His final break with Bernard came soon after his daughter Elizabeth married John Temple in 1767. Temple, though a customs agent, was an implacable foe of the governor. Peter Oliver, a Massachusetts Tory, later commented in his *Origin and Progress of the American Rebellion* that Temple had acquired "a rich Father-in-Law to support him in resentment." In 1768 Bowdoin engineered a Council appeal to the king opposing the Townshend Acts, as usual, on economic grounds. By this time he effectively controlled that body through a faction that included his father-in-law, John Erving, and his brother-in-law, James Pitts. Bowdoin's opposition to Bernard became so heated that the governor vetoed his Council membership after the May 1769 election.

Banished from the Council, Bowdoin ever more openly embraced the patriot cause. In 1770, fearing a hostile British reaction to the Boston Massacre, the town meeting chose Bowdoin and several others to prepare a report. His introduction and ninety-six depositions taken from eyewitnesses were quickly published in England as *Short Narrative of the Horrid Massacre in Boston* (1770), a propaganda piece that proved highly effective in minimizing the affair in British eyes. Bowdoin was returned to the House in the May 1770 election and immediately elevated to the Council. The new governor, the native-born Thomas Hutchinson, permitted his election to stand, but Bowdoin consistently opposed Hutchinson in the Council through the Boston Tea Party crisis and Parliament's imposition of the Intolerable Acts. These changes in government brought in Thomas Gage (1721–1787) as military governor and instituted a new Mandamus Council composed of Loyalist sympathizers. Thus in 1774 Bowdoin was again excluded from the Council.

Though Bowdoin declined election to the First Continental Congress on the grounds of ill health, his services to the revolutionary cause were substantial. Fleeing Boston a month after the battles of Lexington and Concord, he recuperated from consumption at the summer estate of Tory absentee Peter Oliver at Middleborough while General John Burgoyne occupied his own Beacon Hill mansion. By May 1776 he was well enough to stand for election to Massachusetts's new revolutionary Council, where he served as president. This position made him head of the Massachusetts government. Here he enthusiastically worked for independence from Great Britain. Recurring tuberculosis forced his resignation from the Council in 1777, but he was well enough to preside over the Massachusetts constitutional convention of 1780 and to chair the subcommittee which, guided by John Adams (1735–1826), wrote the new constitution.

During the war years Bowdoin's fortunes declined as his Maine holdings deteriorated and his Elizabeth Isles, off the Massachusetts coast, were repeatedly attacked by British raiders. Seeking new investment opportunities, he concentrated on shipping ventures. Unfortunately, all of Bowdoin's ships were taken by the British, and Emanuel Pliarne, a partner, drowned while crossing the Potomac River. Later efforts at privateering proved equally disastrous. Meanwhile, renewing his interest in science, Bowdoin was an important founder of the American Academy of Arts and Sciences (AAAS) in 1779, served as first president, and contributed four papers to the first volume of the society's *Memoirs*, published in 1785.

During the postwar years, Bowdoin broadened his financial and philanthropic interests and reentered politics. In 1784 he became founding president of the Massachusetts Bank, and in 1786 was elected president of the fledgling Massachusetts Humane Society, which attempted to find means of resuscitating drowning victims. As a conservative, Bowdoin had opposed the spending policies of his old political enemy John Hancock (1737–1793) since 1780, but before 1785 he had never received more than 15 percent of the vote for the governorship. That year, however, the state was facing bankruptcy, and in February Hancock abruptly resigned, leaving his lieutenant governor, Thomas Cushing, to complete his term. This was Bowdoin's best chance for victory; he narrowly defeated Cushing on a platform of fiscal responsibility and morality, rising to power on the "Tea Assembly" issue of corruption in office. He performed satisfactorily enough to win reelection in 1786 as well but was criticized by many for his overzealous handling of Shays's Rebellion. In the face of state bankruptcy, Bowdoin, ignoring legitimate agrarian grievances, had raised a privately financed army that had crushed the farmer rebels of western Massachusetts. Accordingly, he went down to defeat by a revitalized John Hancock in 1787.

After this setback Bowdoin retired permanently from state politics, his last years brightened by his election to the Royal Society in 1788 as a "foreign" member on the basis of his contributions to the AAAS and the publication of its *Memoirs*. That same year he purchased nine shares in the Ohio Company of Associates, then engaged in the settlement of Marietta. In 1789 he made a final investment, this time in the China trade. As governor, Bowdoin had promoted the creation of a stronger central government, stressing the confederation's need to regulate foreign commerce. Thus he heartily endorsed the new Constitution and entertained George Washington at his home on the president's visit to Boston in October 1789. After an illness of several months, James Bowdoin died in Boston of a "putrid fever and dysentery." His funeral was long remembered as one of Boston's largest and grandest.

James Bowdoin was an exceedingly complex individual. Always a conservative, reserved and aristocratic, he disdained mere popularity but was a determined and fervent Massachusetts patriot. Though relatively unknown beyond New England, this statesman and philosopher, if not in the first rank of revolutionary intellectuals, may still be favorably compared with

Thomas Jefferson and especially with his old friend Benjamin Franklin.

• Both Bowdoin's letter book and cash book have been preserved at the Massachusetts Historical Society, which has published many of his letters in *Bowdoin and Temple Papers*, 6th ser., vol. 9, and 7th ser., vol. 6. Additional manuscripts may be found among the Kennebeck Purchase Papers and Waldo, Knox, and Flucker papers, Maine Historical Society. Alden T. Bradford, ed., *Speeches of the Governors of Massachusetts from 1765–1777; and the Answers of the House of Representatives to the Same* (1818), illustrates Bowdoin's legislative contributions. *Acts and Laws of the Commonwealth of Massachusetts*, vol. 4 (1890), contains his gubernatorial messages. Robert C. Winthrop, a collateral descendant, published early accounts of Bowdoin's life in *Washington, Bowdoin and Franklin* (1876) and *The Life and Services of James Bowdoin* (1876). The best short biography is Clifford Shipton, *Sibley's Harvard Graduates* 9 (1960): 514–50. Gordon E. Kershaw, *James Bowdoin II: Patriot and Man of the Enlightenment* (1991), is a full-length biographical study. Bowdoin's role as governor during Shays's Rebellion is explored in Marion Starkey, *A Little Rebellion* (1955); David P. Szatmary, *Shays' Rebellion: The Making of an Agrarian Insurrection* (1980); and in several essays in Robert Gross, ed., *In Debt to Shays* (1993). His Maine real estate empire is examined in Kershaw, *The Kennebeck Proprietors* (1975).

GORDON E. KERSHAW

BOWDOIN, James (22 Sept. 1752–11 Oct. 1811), merchant and diplomat, was born in Boston, Massachusetts, son of James Bowdoin, a merchant and Massachusetts governor, and Elizabeth Erving. After early schooling at Boston Latin School, he attended Harvard College, from which he received his degree in absentia in 1771, having gone to England in 1770 for health reasons. In England he studied at Christ Church, Oxford University, and subsequently traveled on the Continent until his return home in late 1775.

Because of his chronic poor health, Bowdoin did not participate in the military during the Revolution. Not attracted to the law, although he accepted a brief commission as justice of the peace in 1777, he instead took up the mercantile business, in which he successfully exploited the dislocations of war to make his fortune. Later he added to his wealth through investments in public lands which he later sold, especially in the Kennebec region of the district of Maine, then part of Massachusetts, and through the purchase and sale of federal securities. In 1781 he married his cousin Sarah Bowdoin. They had no children.

In 1786 Bowdoin moved to Dorchester, where he commenced his public career that same year when he was elected the town's delegate to the Massachusetts House of Representatives, in which he served five annual terms until 1791. While serving in the house, he accepted election from Dorchester to the Massachusetts convention called in 1788 to ratify the new Constitution of the United States, which he actively supported. In 1794 he was elected to the first of two annual terms in the state senate, the second being 1801–1802. He served a one-year term on the governor's council in 1796–1797. He lost election to Congress in 1796.

During the 1790s, in contrast to many of his class and connections in Massachusetts, Bowdoin gravitated into the Democratic Republican party, whose vigor he helped establish. In 1796 he moved to Boston, and because of the solidification of Federalist dominance in the Bay State, especially in eastern Massachusetts and Boston, by the late 1790s his political future in local politics became clouded. In effect, he had to look elsewhere for preferment.

In 1797 Bowdoin established his broader reputation with *Opinions Respecting the Commercial Intercourse between the United States of America, and the Dominions of Great Britain*, published anonymously, although he soon became known as its author. In this work, he allied himself with those, such as James Madison, who had been calling for retaliation against British restrictions on American trade. After the Democratic Republicans captured the presidency in 1801 with the election of Thomas Jefferson, Bowdoin hoped to succeed Rufus King as minister (or ambassador) to Great Britain. Instead, in 1804 he was named minister to Spain. His four-year tenure in that post was frustrating and unsuccessful. He was instructed to continue the administration's ongoing and complex efforts to acquire West Florida from Spain, whose title to the territory had been confused by the 1803 cession of Louisiana to the United States. He was also directed to try to settle outstanding issues concerning the boundaries of Louisiana and to seek redress for Spanish assaults on American neutral shipping. Concluding that he would not be welcomed in Madrid, Bowdoin instead went to London and then to Paris. There he was frustrated in his efforts to treat with the Spanish by the obstructionism of American minister John Armstrong, by the deviousness of Charles-Maurice de Talleyrand-Périgord's foreign policy, and by the obduracy of the Spanish, who were falling increasingly under the control of Napoléon Bonaparte, then involved in a Europewide war. Consequently, negotiations with the Spanish led nowhere, and in 1808, having never made it to Madrid, Bowdoin resigned his embassy and returned to the United States.

Bowdoin long devoted himself to philanthropy, agricultural improvement, and endeavors in behalf of education. He was an incorporator of the Massachusetts Charitable Fire Society, trustee of the Massachusetts Agricultural Society, member of the Harvard Corporation, and trustee of the Hopkins Charity. In 1810 he helped incorporate the Massachusetts General Hospital. A lifelong student of French, in 1810 he translated Louis Daubenton's *Instruction pour les bergers et pour les proprietaires de troupeaux* (1782) as *Advice to Shepherds and Owners of Flocks, on the Care and Management of Sheep*. In addition to gifts to his alma mater, he made generous benefactions of land and money to the Maine college named originally after his father and provided in his will that much of the remainder of his estate, including his collections of art and scientific instruments, go to the college after his wife's death. Upon his return to the United States, Bowdoin retired to his estate on Naushon Island, one of the Elizabeth Islands in Buzzards Bay, where he continued to raise dairy and agricultural products for market sale and where he died.

Bowdoin's career reveals the snares and opportunities for talented and well-placed men created by the emergence of a many-tiered party system within the complex federal system of American government. Denied advancement at one level because of party affiliation and political conviction, he found advantage at another. His most lasting legacy was no doubt his substantial bequests to the college that bears his family's name.

• The principal collections of Bowdoin's manuscripts are at Bowdoin College and the Massachusetts Historical Society. The standard study of Bowdoin's political party in Mass. is Paul Goodman, *The Democratic-Republicans of Massachusetts: Politics in a Young Republic* (1964). An obituary is in the *Boston Independent Chronicle*, 21 Oct. 1811.

JAMES M. BANNER, JR.

BOWEN, Catherine Drinker (1 Jan. 1897–1 Nov. 1973), biographer and novelist, was born Catherine Shober Drinker in Haverford, Pennsylvania, the daughter of Henry Sturgis Drinker, an attorney, and Aimee Ernesta Beaux, a musician. After her father became president of Lehigh University in 1905, the family moved to Bethlehem, Pennsylvania. In between travels to such places as the Panama and Suez canals, she attended the Moravian Seminary, Bethlehem, Pennsylvania. From 1914 to 1916 she studied at St. Timothy's boarding school in Catonsville, Maryland, where she cultivated a taste for music and started to play the violin. Although accepted at Bryn Mawr College, she studied instead at the Peabody Conservatory of Music in Baltimore, Maryland (1915–1917), where she further cultivated the violin. Subsequently, she studied at the Juilliard School in New York City when it was still known as the Institute of Musical Arts.

In 1919 she married Ezra Bowen, an associate professor in economics at Lehigh University; they had one son and one daughter. After her marriage, Catherine Bowen gave private music lessons and played in amateur string quartets. She moved to Easton, Pennsylvania, when her husband became head of the economics department at Lafayette College. During this time her love of music compelled her to write about the musicians who inspired her. This enlivened written expression led to other forms of writing—"Writing saved me," she later said. Even after *Yachting Magazine* published her first piece in 1920, she kept her writing a secret. She went on to write articles for *Woman's Home Companion*, *Pictorial Review* and *Good Housekeeping*. Bowen later wrote that once she saw her name in print, "nothing mattered but to get on with the work." The year 1924 also saw the appearance of her first two books, *The Story of the Oak Tree*, a children's book, and *The History of Lehigh University*. Still reticent about telling others of her writing talent, she waited to claim writer status until 1951 with two Book-of-the-Month Club selections to her credit. In 1932 she completed her only novel, the semiautobiographical *Rufus Starbuck's Wife*, in which she addressed the perplexing problem of female writers and their drive for independence. The musician heroine pursues feminism in an attempt to free herself from a domineering husband but soon recognizes the dangers of such subversive reasoning and returns to "the straightest, plainest path," to reconcile with her husband. Bowen and her husband divorced in 1936, and in 1939 she married the surgeon Thomas McKean Downs.

Catherine Bowen continued to incorporate her love for music into her writing. *Friends and Fiddlers* (1935) recalls her experiences as a violinist. She chose Tchaikovsky and his wealthy patron as the subjects of her first biographical work, *Beloved Friend: The Story of Tchaikovsky and Nadejda von Meck* (1937), which soon became a Book-of-the-Month Club selection and sold more than 150,000 copies in the United States alone. Her *Free Artist: The Story of Anton and Nicholas Rubenstein* (1939), which explores the Russian musicians who helped popularize Tchaikovsky's music, brought Bowen to the Soviet Union. In biography, she had found her writer's niche.

After an attempted biography on Mendelssohn was terminated by her inability to travel in Europe during World War II, Bowen moved toward American historical figures to seek "the foundations of our constitutional government." Oliver Wendell Holmes became the subject of her first nonmusical biography, *Yankee from Olympus* (1944). *John Adams and the American Revolution* became her next biographical project in 1950; it was another Book-of-the-Month Club selection. This was followed in 1957 by *The Lion and the Throne: The Life and Times of Sir Edward Coke, 1552–1634*, a biography of the seventeenth-century legal scholar. Besides becoming both Book-of-the-Month Club and History Book-of-the-Month Club selections, this volume won the National Book Award for Nonfiction and the nonfiction award of the Athenaeum of Philadelphia in 1957. During this year Bowen also received the Phillips Prize, the American Philosophical Society's award for an essay on jurisprudence. Her other books include *Francis Bacon: The Temper of a Man* (1963) and *Miracle at Philadelphia: The Story of the Constitutional Convention* (1966). Her final book, *The Most Dangerous Man in America: Scenes from the Life of Benjamin Franklin*, was published posthumously in 1974.

Bowen is remembered as an advocate for female writers. In "Discipline and Reward: A Writer's Life," she echoes Virginia Woolf's voice in *A Room of One's Own*. "Women," Bowen noted, "are trained from the cradle, to please." She staunchly believed that "no woman of spirit can focus her entire life on the raising of two children." And when asked why she never wrote a biographical study of a woman, she replied: "a woman's biography—with about eight famous historical exceptions—so often turns out to be the story of a man and the woman who helped his career."

Bowen described the method of biography in three collections of essays: *The Writing of Biography* (1951), *Adventures of a Biographer* (1959), and *Biography: The Craft and Calling* (1969).

The youngest of six children, Bowen shared success with other family members. Her aunt was the popular portrait painter Cecilia Beaux; her brother Philip invented the iron lung; and another brother, Cecil, served as dean of the Harvard School of Public Health. Throughout her life she cultivated her love for music and was a talented violinist. She died in Haverford, Pennsylvania.

• Bowen's papers, which include correspondence, notes, and drafts, are at the Library of Congress. Biographical information about Catherine Bowen can be found in her *Family Portrait* (1970). Bowen's articles "Discipline and Reward: A Writer's Life," *Atlantic Monthly*, Dec. 1957, pp. 87–92, and "We've Never Asked a Woman Before," *Atlantic*, Mar. 1970, pp. 82–86, provide interesting information on her. Bowen's son reflects on his mother's life in *Henry and Other Heroes: An Informal Memoir of High Dreams and Vanished Seasons* (1974). See also the *American Philosophical Society's Yearbook 1974* (1975) for a more complete account of Bowen's life. An obituary is in the *New York Times*, 2 Nov. 1973.

M. CASEY DIANA

BOWEN, Francis (8 Sept. 1811–21 Jan. 1890), author and philosopher, was born in Charlestown, Massachusetts, the son of Dijah Bowen and Elizabeth Flint. He attended Mayhew Grammar School in Boston, worked as a clerk in a Boston publishing office for several years, and enrolled in Phillips Exeter Academy in January 1829. In August 1830 he enrolled at Harvard College. For several winters while in college he taught school at various places, including Hampton Falls, New Hampshire; and Lexington, Northborough, and Concord, Massachusetts.

After graduating with highest honors from Harvard in 1833, Bowen taught mathematics at Phillips Exeter Academy until August 1835. He then returned to Harvard, first as tutor in Greek and then as instructor in mental philosophy and political economy. In August 1839 he resigned from the college for a year of travel and study in Europe. Up to this point his literary work consisted of biographical sketches of Sir William Phipps (1837) and Baron Friedrich von Steuben (1838) in Jared Sparks's *Library of American Biography*.

Upon returning to Cambridge, Massachusetts, Bowen was editor of the *North American Review* (1843–1852) and, for six years, of the *American Almanac and Repository of Useful Knowledge*. He continued his work as a biographer, publishing lives of James Otis (1844) and Benjamin Lincoln (1847). He also produced an edition of Virgil's writings with notes and commentary (1842) and published his *Critical Essays on a Few Subjects Connected with the History and Present Condition of Speculative Philosophy* (1842) and the Lowell Lectures *On the Application of Metaphysical and Ethical Science to the Evidences of Religion* (1849). He married Arabella Stuart in 1848. They had one son and two daughters.

Bowen distinguished himself in political affairs by repudiating tariffs. He also was embroiled in political controversy during the 1851 visit of popular Hungarian patriot Lajos Kossuth, whom Bowen denounced. This unpopular move prevented the confirmation of Bowen's 1850 nomination to the McLean Professorship of History at Harvard College. His political influence continued, however, for he later served on the U.S. Silver Commission (1876).

In 1853 Bowen was appointed Alford Professor of Natural Religion, Moral Philosophy, and Civil Polity at Harvard, an appointment that lasted until his retirement in 1889. The original bequest for this professorial endowment (1783) called for instruction that would

> demonstrate the existence of a Deity, or first cause; . . . prove and illustrate his essential attributes, both natural and moral; . . . evince and explain his providence and government . . . decide and enforce the obligations which man is under to his Maker . . . together with the most important duties of social life . . . and likewise the several duties which respect ourselves . . . [and] state the absolute necessity and vast utility of a Divine Revelation.

Bowen's immediate successor to the Alford Professorship, George Herbert Palmer, was the first to call into question the terms of this bequest. For his part, Bowen seems to have been overt in his effort to inculcate confidence in the Christian view of the world. In his book *A Layman's Study of the English Bible* (1885), he expressed the conviction "that the only hope for the civilization and the happiness of the generations that are to come in this English-speaking world depends on the continued reverent study of the English Bible" (p. 143). Piety, conditioned by standards then thought appropriate to the academic study of religion, marked his writing and teaching. This is manifest even in his 1856 publication *The Principles of Political Economy*: "These designs, as shown in the economical laws of human nature, (i.e. in the principles of Political Economy,) through their general effects upon the well-being of society, manifest the contrivance, wisdom, and beneficence of the Deity, just as clearly as do the marvellous arrangements of the material universe" (1859 ed., p. 27).

Bowen disparaged the theory of evolution in his prompt review of Darwin's *Origin of Species*, in the *North American Review* (90 [1860]: 474–506). Bowen focused on "the immense gap which now separates man from the animals most nearly allied to him,—a gap . . . between reason and instinct, where nearly all psychologists are agreed that the difference is in kind, and not in degree." He regarded Darwin's speculations to involve him in an unwarranted extrapolation from empirical data to conclusions about human mental reality. This constituted an illicit encroachment upon metaphysics, the special preserve of philosophers.

Bowen thought the principal alternative to ethical monotheism to be the despairing nihilism of Schopenhauer and Hartmann, which could not be true inasmuch as it was impracticable. There is, then, an unmistakable pragmatist element in his reasoning. (C. S. Peirce as student and William James both as student and as professor were at Harvard while Bowen was Alford Professor, and Bowen has been identified as an early source of pragmatism in America.) His philosophical perspective oscillated between German idealism (with its doctrine that there is such an intimate connection between consciousness and reality that the mind may be said to construct reality) and Scottish common-sense realism (with its commitment to the existence of a world of mind-independent objects that can be known accurately in common or ordinary acts of cognition).

Other publications produced during Bowen's long tenure at Harvard include *Behr's Translation of Weber's Outlines of Universal History* (1853); *Dugald Stewart's Philosophy of the Human Mind* (1854); *Documents of the Constitution of England and America, from Magna Charta to the Federal Constitution of 1789* (1854); *The Metaphysics of Sir William Hamilton* (1861); *De Tocqueville's Democracy in America* (1862); *A Treatise on Logic* (1864); *American Political Economy* (1870), a revision of his earlier *Principles of Political Economy*; *Modern Philosophy, from Descartes to Schopenhauer and Hartmann* (1877); and *Gleanings from a Literary Life, 1838–1880* (1880). In 1879 he was awarded an LL.D. by Harvard College. Among the oldest of Harvard professors, Bowen died at his Cambridge home.

• Personal papers, including letters related to Bowen's work for the *North American Review*, are preserved in the Harvard University Archives and the Houghton Library at Harvard. Also of some value is the biographical sketch by Waldo Higginson, class secretary, in *Memorials of the Class of 1833 of Harvard College* (1883), prepared for the fiftieth anniversary of their graduation; also included is a list of Bowen's publications through 1880. For details on the Alford Professorship, see William Bentinck-Smith and Elizabeth Stouffer, *Harvard University History of Named Chairs: Sketches of Donors and Donations* (1991). Herbert W. Schneider seeks to understand Bowen's work within its historical and social context in *A History of American Philosophy* (1946). For a summary and appraisal of his *Treatise on Logic*, see Elizabeth Flower and Murray G. Murphey, *A History of Philosophy in America*, vol. 1 (1977). Flower and Murphey credit Bowen for introducing to America "an interest in logic as a formal discipline."

R. DOUGLAS GEIVETT

BOWEN, Henry Chandler (11 Sept. 1813–24 Feb. 1896), editor-publisher and merchant, was born in Woodstock, Connecticut, the son of George Bowen, a store and tavern keeper, and Lydia Wolcott Eaton. He received his formal education at schools in Woodstock and nearby Dudley, Massachusetts, and worked for four years in his father's store. At age twenty he went to New York and became a clerk in the firm of Arthur and Lewis Tappan, dry-goods merchants and leaders of the antislavery movement. Bowen was among the employees who defended the Tappans' store when it was attacked by an antiabolitionist mob in 1834. In 1838 Bowen established his own dry-goods company, Bowen & McNamee, and in 1844 married Lewis Tappan's daughter Lucy Maria Tappan. They had ten children.

Although not an abolitionist, Bowen was unbending in his opposition to the extension of slavery. His firm gained the hostility of other merchants by refusing to sign a declaration upholding the Fugitive Slave Act of 1850. After criticism in the press, Bowen & McNamee published a newspaper notice asserting that as silk merchants "we wish it distinctly understood that our goods, and not our principles, are in the market." When the company went bankrupt in the crash of 1857, he reestablished himself, only to fail again at the start of the Civil War when his southern customers defaulted.

In the fifteen years before the war, Bowen became a leading Congregational layman. He was a founder of the Plymouth Church in Brooklyn and was primarily responsible for persuading the celebrated Henry Ward Beecher to occupy its pulpit starting in 1847. He also organized backing for a weekly newspaper, *The Independent*, designed to promote Congregationalism and to oppose slavery. The paper began publication in December 1848, with Bowen as publisher. When Bowen lost his business in 1861, the unprofitable *Independent* was the only property he still controlled. He brought in the enormously popular Beecher as editor, and the newspaper prospered.

Bowen's relations with Beecher were deeply troubled, however. There is evidence that starting in the mid-1850s Beecher carried on an affair with Bowen's wife, a supposition bolstered by her purported deathbed confession in 1863. Beecher abruptly left the editorship of *The Independent* shortly after her death and was succeeded by a young assistant editor, Theodore Tilton, who had already been doing much of Beecher's editorial work. Tilton was an immediate success as an editor, and Bowen gave him full independence.

After Bowen married Ellen Holt in 1865 (they had one child), he established an uneasy truce with Beecher, which was broken by a complex series of events in 1870. Early in the year, Bowen bought a local Republican newspaper, the *Brooklyn Union*, and began to dabble in partisan politics. He added the editorship of the *Union* to Tilton's tasks, but they soon quarreled over the *Union*'s failure to support party candidates and its grudging coverage of Plymouth Church. Summoned to a meeting with Bowen on 26 December 1870, Tilton blurted out that his wife had confessed to a liaison with Beecher. In short order, Bowen had Tilton write a letter demanding Beecher's resignation from Plymouth Church, Beecher rejected Tilton's accusations, and Bowen, doubting Tilton, fired him as editor of both *The Independent* and the *Union*. There began a strenuous effort, engineered by friends, to keep the matter from becoming public. In April 1872 Tilton, Beecher, and Bowen entered an agreement under which Bowen paid Tilton $7,000 for having broken his employment contracts and withdrew charges he had aired against Beecher.

But the scandal would not die. Late in 1872 the Beecher-Tilton controversy was laid before the public by *Woodhull & Claflin's Weekly*, operated by the sisters Victoria Claflin Woodhull and Tennessee Claflin. Other newspapers recounted Beecher's encounter with Bowen's first wife. Ultimately the case of *Tilton v. Beecher* was tried in New York in 1875, and Beecher was acquitted of adultery. Because he insisted on Beecher's guilt, Bowen was excommunicated in 1876 by Plymouth Church, which was under control of Beecher's supporters.

When he fired Tilton in 1870, Bowen made himself editor of *The Independent*, a post he held until he died. He led the newspaper into policies that still strongly favored human rights but became, in reaction to Beecher's religious liberalism, conservative on church questions. *The Independent* supported the Republican party (except in the 1884 election) and national expansion. Bowen recruited a strong staff, led by William Hayes Ward, husband of Bowen's niece, and the publication gradually became a magazine rather than a newspaper and became less specifically religious in its focus.

Throughout his long career Bowen maintained his ties to his native town. Each Independence Day he arranged to bring important personages, including, on occasion, presidents, to Woodstock. He was a supporter of Woodstock Academy and created Roseland Park, opened in Woodstock on 4 July 1876. Despite his benefactions, he was not known as an open or engaging person. Paxton Hibben, in his biography of Beecher, depicted Bowen as unpleasantly grasping, and even obituary tributes emphasized steadfastness over warmth. Bowen died in Brooklyn.

Bowen hoped that his son John Eliot would succeed him; but John died in 1890, and Ward became editor when Bowen died. Managed by a family trust, *The Independent* enjoyed a renaissance as a reform journal in the first years of the twentieth century under Bowen's grandson, Hamilton Holt. The publication—Bowen's most important legacy—continued, in one form or another, until 1928.

• Bowen family papers are held at the Society for the Preservation of New England Antiquities, Boston, and at the American Antiquarian Society, Worcester, Mass. There is a Bowen scrapbook at the New York Public Library, and the Hamilton Holt Papers, at Rollins College, Winter Park, Fla., also contain material about Bowen. Clarence Winthrop Bowen, *The History of Woodstock, Connecticut* (1926), has plentiful detail about the Bowen family. Bowen's career was treated extensively in the *Independent*'s sixtieth-anniversary issue, 10 Dec. 1908, notably in William Hayes Ward, "Henry C. Bowen," pp. 1364–66; Ward, "Conflicts and Conquests," pp. 1354–58; and Ward, "The Editors," pp. 1359–63. Among the many treatments of the Beecher-Tilton controversy, Paxton Hibben, *Henry Ward Beecher: An American Portrait* (1927), and Altina L. Waller, *Reverend Beecher and Mrs. Tilton* (1982), are the most revealing of Bowen's role. Bowen is discussed in Louis Filler, "Liberalism, Anti-Slavery, and the Founders of the *Independent*," *New England Quarterly* 27 (Sept. 1954): 291–306; Philip S. Foner, *Business & Slavery* (1941); Frank Luther Mott, "The Independent," in *A History of American Magazines, 1850–1865* (1938), pp. 367–79; and Warren F. Kuehl, *Hamilton Holt* (1960). An obituary is in the *New York Times*, 25 Feb. 1896. Ward's funeral address and other tributes were printed in *The Independent*, 5 Mar. 1896. His will was described in detail in the *New York Tribune*, 14 Mar. 1896.

JAMES BOYLAN

BOWEN, Ira Sprague (21 Dec. 1898–6 Feb. 1973), astrophysicist and first director of the combined Mount Wilson and Palomar Observatories, was born in Seneca Falls, New York, the son of James H. Bowen, a Methodist minister, and Philinda Sprague, who became a teacher after her husband's death. Bowen (always known as "Ike" to his friends) attended the high school and three years of the junior college that formed part of the Houghton Wesleyan Methodist Seminary, at which his mother taught. He was an excellent student. His teacher in physics, mathematics, and astronomy, J. S. Luckey, the president of the college, helped him transfer to Oberlin College for his senior year. Bowen received his A.B. at Oberlin in 1919 and entered the University of Chicago as a graduate student in physics. In two years he took all the graduate courses taught by A. A. Michelson and Robert A. Millikan, the first two American Nobel Laureates in physics, while working as Millikan's laboratory assistant. He did all the experimental work for Millikan's systematic program of ultraviolet spectroscopy of the first twenty elements in the periodic table. When Millikan left Chicago in 1921 to move to the California Institute of Technology as chairman of the executive council (essentially president), he took Bowen with him. Ultimately they published more than twenty joint papers, nearly all of them on the analysis of these spectra, most of which Bowen also did under Millikan's supervision. They also worked on cosmic-ray research, obtaining their data from high-altitude sounding balloons. Bowen had begun teaching at Caltech soon after his arrival there and finally took his Ph.D. in 1926 on a completely different topic (evaporation of water from a lake).

Bowen made his great discovery, the identification of many of the brighter emission lines in the spectra of gaseous nebulae, whose origin was then unknown, in 1927. These lines had puzzled astronomers from the earliest days of precision spectroscopy because their wavelengths did not match those measured in any known laboratory sources. Bowen realized that they might be transitions between known energy levels of ions of abundant elements, which had not been detected in laboratory sources and were therefore regarded as "forbidden." He had all the data, the precisely measured energy levels from his ultraviolet spectroscopic work with Millikan. In one night Bowen was able to check his hypothesis and verify it quantitatively. The first lines he identified were those of oxygen, nitrogen, and sulfur ions; over the next decade he identified many more. These new results and his sound physical knowledge enabled him to lay out the essential nature of gaseous nebulae. Bowen's two key papers on the nature, structure, and composition of gaseous nebulae, published in the *Astrophysical Journal* in 1928 and 1935, provided the basis for all the later detailed theoretical investigations of these objects, until their origin and evolution became fields of study in the 1960s.

In 1938 Bowen spent a year at Lick Observatory, where he got his first experience at astronomical spectroscopic observing. With his insights and laboratory skills, Bowen and young Arthur B. Wyse of the Lick staff were able to record and identify many additional, fainter lines, some of them from even rarer ions, in the nebulae. Their results showed that hydrogen was the most abundant element in nebulae, helium next, and oxygen, nitrogen, and carbon after them, as in stars.

As an expert in optics and spectroscopy, Bowen was deeply involved in all stages of the planning and instrumental design for Palomar Observatory's 200-inch telescope, which began at Caltech in 1928. The work on this telescope and the associated 48-inch Schmidt camera (Bowen also made important contributions to its design) stopped before America's entry into World War II, as physicists at Caltech and other research universities shifted their efforts to weapons development. Bowen played an important role in optical design for the U.S. Air Force and in the Caltech rocket project, which produced solid-fuel rockets for ground and air use.

At the end of the war Bowen was appointed director of Mount Wilson Observatory, owned and operated by the Carnegie Institution of Washington, and when the 200-inch Hale and 48-inch Schmidt telescopes (both owned by Caltech) were completed in 1948, he was named director of the jointly operated Mount Wilson and Palomar Observatories. His superb skills with optical systems were crucial to the completion of the 200-inch Hale telescope, and his design of the large, highly efficient coudé spectrograph used in conjunction with it made it possible for the staff members of the observatories to get reliable, quantitative results on faint stars and nebulae. Though his administrative duties were heavy, Bowen nevertheless managed to find time to use the 200-inch telescope and coudé spectrograph himself for additional forbidden-line work, now aimed at using the astronomical results to improve the precision of the energy-level values. Under Bowen, Mount Wilson and Palomar Observatories flourished as a joint research institution. No small part of the credit is due to him. Bowen's deep instrumental knowledge, modest yet forceful personality, emphasis on high-quality results, and insights into what the most important problems for the world's largest telescope were, made him the perfect director for the time and place.

As director, Bowen introduced the guest investigator program under which astronomers from other institutions were permitted to use the Mount Wilson telescopes (and later those at Palomar) to obtain observational data for their own research programs. In effect Mount Wilson and Palomar Observatories operated in this way as a partially national, or even international, observatory. This new program noticeably increased the productivity of American astronomy, greatly stimulated research by first-class scientists at institutions with small telescopes or poor observing climates, and brought new ideas from outside to the Mount Wilson and Palomar staff members.

Bowen retired as director in 1964 but continued working on optical design of large telescopes and of various forms of Schmidt cameras, especially for use in spectrographs. His papers on these subjects are classics, and he was a consultant on practically every large telescope built before his death. Even while he was still director of Mount Wilson and Palomar Observatories, Bowen was extremely supportive of the early design of the Kitt Peak National Observatory in Arizona and the European Southern Observatory in Chile.

Bowen married Mary Jane Howard in 1929; they had no children. He lived a full life until, at the age of seventy-four, he became ill at his home in Altadena, was taken by ambulance to a hospital in Hollywood, and died there that same evening.

Bowen was an unusual combination of outstanding research scientist, instrument-design expert, and scientific-institution director. He, and the astronomers and astrophysicists who worked with him, used his telescopes and spectrographs, or worked under his supervision, greatly increased our knowledge and understanding of the physical universe.

• Bowen's papers as director of Mount Wilson and Palomar Observatories and some from his postretirement period are in the Department of Manuscripts, Henry Huntington Library, San Marino, Calif. Some of his papers from the time before he became director are in the Ira S. Bowen Papers, California Institute of Technology Archives, Pasadena. The best published memorial biography is Horace W. Babcock, "Ira Sprague Bowen 1898–1973," National Academy of Sciences, *Biographical Memoirs* 53 (1982): 83–119; it contains a complete bibliography of Bowen's published scientific papers. Another excellent, but shorter, biographical memoir is Lawrence H. Aller, "Ira Sprague Bowen," *Quarterly Journal of the Royal Astronomical Society* 15 (1974): 193–96. A historical paper that focuses on one high point of his career is Donald E. Osterbrock, "The Appointment of a Physicist as Director of the Astronomical Center of the World," *Journal for the History of Astronomy* 23 (1992): 155–65.

DONALD E. OSTERBROCK

BOWEN, John Wesley Edward (3 Dec. 1855–20 July 1933), Methodist educator and theologian, was born in New Orleans, Louisiana, the son of Edward Bowen and Rose Simon. His father was a carpenter from Maryland who was enslaved when he moved to New Orleans. After purchasing his own freedom, Edward Bowen bought that of his wife and son in 1858 and served in the Union army during the Civil War. After the war young J. W. E. Bowen studied at the Union Normal School in New Orleans and New Orleans University, which was founded by the Methodist Episcopal church for the education of freedmen. Bowen received a bachelor's degree with the university's first graduating class in 1878. Eight years later, New Orleans University awarded him a master's degree. From 1878 to 1882 Bowen taught mathematics and ancient languages at Central Tennessee College in Nashville.

In 1882 Bowen began theological studies at Boston University. While a theological student, he was the pastor of Revere Street Methodist Episcopal Church in Boston. Bowen earned a bachelor of sacred theology degree in 1885, and soon after he became pastor of St. John's Methodist Episcopal Church in Newark, New Jersey. He continued graduate study in theology and married Ariel Serena Hedges of Baltimore, Maryland, in 1886. They became the parents of four children. Bowen was the second African American to earn a Ph.D. in the United States when Boston University conferred the degree on him in 1887. After leaving St. John's in 1888 Bowen went on to serve as pastor of Centennial Methodist Episcopal Church in Baltimore and of Asbury Methodist Episcopal Church in Washington, D.C. At Centennial Church, he conducted a notable revival in which more than 700 people claimed conversion. He also served as professor of church history and systematic theology at Baltimore's Morgan College from 1888 to 1892 and in 1890–1891 as professor of Hebrew at Howard University in Washington, D.C. From 1889 to 1893 Bowen was also a member and examiner for the American Institute of Sacred Literature. In 1892 he published *What Shall the Harvest Be? A National Sermon; or, A Series of Plain Talks to the Colored People of America, on Their Problems*. He represented the Methodist Episcopal church at conferences of world Methodism in Washington, D.C., in 1891 and London in 1901.

In 1892, after leaving his posts at Centennial and Asbury, Bowen became a field secretary for the Freedmen's Aid Society of the Methodist Episcopal church. He left the Freedmen's Aid Society in 1893, however, to become professor of historical theology at Gammon Theological Seminary in Atlanta, Georgia. As the first African-American professor at the school, founded in 1883 by the Methodist Episcopal church for the preparation of African-American clergymen, Bowen was awarded an honorary doctor of divinity degree by Gammon in 1893. As secretary of the seminary's Stewart Missionary Foundation for Africa, he also edited its periodical, the *Stewart Missionary Magazine*.

In October 1895, after praising Booker T. Washington's emphasis on industrial education and the work ethic in Washington's address to Atlanta's Cotton States' Exposition a month earlier, Bowen delivered his own address, "An Appeal to the King," on "Negro Day" at the exposition. In December 1895 Bowen organized an important three-day conference on Africa held in conjunction with the exposition and published its proceedings as *Africa and the American Negro: Addresses and Proceedings of the Congress on Africa . . . in Connection with the Cotton States . . . Exposition, Dec. 13–15, 1895* (1896). Subsequently, however, Bowen distanced himself from Washington by defending liberal arts education for leadership and joined W. E. B. Du Bois in protesting state legislation to segregate railroad transportation and limit funds for black public schools to taxes paid by black people.

In 1896 Bowen was elected a delegate to the quadrennial general conference of the Methodist Episcopal church, a position he retained until 1912. As the most distinguished African-American clergyman in the Methodist Episcopal church, he received many votes for the episcopacy at the general conferences in 1896, 1900, and 1904. As a member of the Board of Control of the Methodist Episcopal church's Epworth League, he organized a national conference in Atlanta on the Christian education of African-American youth. With I. Garland Penn, Bowen also edited and published its proceedings, *The United Negro: . . . Addresses and Proceedings. The Negro Young People's Christian and Educational Congress, Held August 6–11, 1902* (1902).

In January 1904 Bowen and Jesse Max Barber launched the *Voice of the Negro*, a literary journal addressed to a national audience of African Americans. In September 1905 they endorsed the Niagara Movement, which was organized by Du Bois and others to protest African Americans' loss of civil rights; months later, they promoted the organization of the Georgia Equal Rights League, which had similar objectives. At the peak of its circulation in 1906, the *Voice of the Negro* claimed 12,000 to 15,000 subscribers.

After the death of his first wife in 1904, Bowen married Irene L. Smallwood in 1906. They had no children. That same year Bowen became the president of Gammon Theological Seminary. In September, however, his inaugural year was shadowed by a severe race riot in which white rioters brutally attacked black people in Atlanta. Bowen opened the seminary to shelter black refugees from the riot. Three days after the rioting began, he was beaten and arrested by Atlanta's white police. Barber fled the city, taking the *Voice of the Negro* with him to Chicago, where he continued its publication as the *Voice* for a year without Bowen's assistance.

Bowen survived the Atlanta race riot and served as president of Gammon until 1910, when its administration was merged with that of Clark University. He became vice president of the institution and continued as professor of historical theology. A lecturer on the Chautauqua circuit, Bowen was an active member of the American Historical Association, the American Negro Academy, and the National Association for the Advancement of Colored People. The frustration of African-American hopes for leadership in the church eventually led to Bowen's publication of *An Appeal for Negro Bishops, but No Separation* in 1912. When, finally, the Methodist Episcopal church determined to elect its first two African-American bishops in 1920, however, it chose younger men, Robert Elijah Jones and Matthew Wesley Clair. Bowen retired as head of the church history department at Gammon in 1926 but continued to teach until 1932, when he became an emeritus professor. He died in Atlanta. Throughout a distinguished career, Bowen was an eloquent example of an African-American Christian intellectual.

• The J. W. E. Bowen Papers are in the Gammon Theological Seminary Archives at the Atlanta University Center's Woodruff Library. See also *The Booker T. Washington Papers*, ed. Louis R. Harlan et al. (1972–1989) and unpublished documents in the Washington papers at the Library of Congress. On the context of Bowen's career, see Alphonso A. McPheeters, "The Origin and Development of Clark University and Gammon Theological Seminary" (Ed.D. diss., Univ. of Cincinnati, 1944); Prince Albert Taylor, Jr., "A History of Gammon Theological Seminary" (Ph.D. diss., New York Univ., 1948); August Meier, *Negro Thought in America 1880–1915: Racial Ideologies in the Age of Booker T. Washington* (1963); Harlan, "Booker T. Washington and the *Voice of the Negro*, 1904–1907," *Journal of Southern History* 45 (Feb. 1979): 45–62; Alfred A. Moss, Jr., *The American Negro Academy: Voice of the Talented Tenth* (1981); and Ralph E. Luker, *The Social Gospel in Black and White: American Racial Reform, 1885–1912* (1991). For obituaries, see the *Atlanta Constitution*, 21 July 1933, and J. R. Van Pelt, "John Wesley Edward Bowen," *Journal of Negro History* 14 (Apr. 1934): 217–21.

RALPH E. LUKER

BOWEN, Louise deKoven (26 Feb. 1859–9 Nov. 1953), philanthropist, social reformer, and suffragist, was born in Chicago, Illinois, the daughter of John deKoven, a successful banker, and Helen Hadduck. Louise grew up with all the pleasures and privileges of wealth and power. She graduated from the prestigious Dearborn Seminary at the age of sixteen and soon thereafter began teaching Sunday school and dabbling in charity work. She established the Huron Street Club, one of the first boys' clubhouses in Chicago; helped to create a kitchen garden association for girls; and regularly visited the hundred families of the boys in her church class, offering help when needed. In 1886 she married Joseph Tilton Bowen, a Chicago businessman. She gave up her Sunday school class and other church-related social work so that she would have time to care for their four children. Unwilling, however, to give up all philanthropic activities when her children were very young, Bowen joined the board of managers of the Maurice Porter Memorial Hospital. She later held board positions with other hospitals and helped establish the Visiting Nurse Association of Chicago.

In 1893 Jane Addams, founder of Hull-House, asked Bowen to join and help to lead the settlement's Woman's Club, a public affairs organization consisting of women in the neighborhood. Bowen accepted the invitation, after first taking a class in parliamentary procedure, and for the next sixty years she was deeply involved in the settlement and its activities. She also became a close friend of and adviser to Jane Addams. Bowen ended up serving as an officer of the Woman's Club for seventeen years. Under her leadership, the club was so successful that it quickly outgrew the room in which it had started, so in 1904 Bowen built a hall for the Woman's Club that was named "Bowen Hall." In her 1926 memoir, *Growing Up with a City*, she wrote that "I have always felt that any experience I acquired in speaking was entirely due to practice in this club." The activities there, Bowen said, gave her a "liberal education" and "wide insight into matters of the day." Although the Woman's Club didn't make Bowen into a civic leader, her experiences there did enhance those skills and that concern for others that made her an effective social reformer.

In 1903 Bowen became a Hull-House trustee, and soon thereafter she became treasurer of the Hull-House Association. Bowen was a financial mainstay of the settlement, donating funds herself to the organization in times of crisis if she could not raise them from others. She built a five-story Boy's Club for the settlement and donated seventy-two acres of land in Waukegan, Illinois, as a country club retreat for children and residents of Hull-House. According to one historian, Bowen gave almost $1 million to the association. When Addams died in 1935, Bowen became president of the Hull-House Association. Although she was sometimes a controversial leader, often disagreeing with the head residents of the settlement and causing some women to leave the organization, Bowen was a strong president who ensured the survival of the settlement during this critical period.

Some of Bowen's social service activities grew out of her affiliation with Hull-House. The most significant of these was her participation in the child-saving movement, a Progressive-era crusade to protect children from the physical and moral dangers of an industrial and urban society. In 1899 Bowen was one of a group of club women who prodded Cook County to establish the first juvenile court in the United States. That group then organized themselves as the Juvenile Court Committee with Hull-House member Julia Lathrop as its president. A year later Bowen succeeded Lathrop as the group's top officer, and during Bowen's seven-year tenure the Court Committee procured the salaries of probation officers, administered the civil service exam used to select probation officers, investigated complaints of neglect, sat in juvenile court to advise judges, and established a juvenile detention home.

In 1907, after being relieved of financial responsibility for the detention home and the salaries of probation officers, the Court Committee reorganized itself as the Juvenile Protective Association. Bowen was the association's first president, a position she held for over thirty-five years. The association continued to investigate complaints and lobby for new courts and measures to clamp down on prostitution, to improve working conditions of women, and to clean up dance halls and other places where children gathered. Bowen wrote several pamphlets about the work of the association including *The Welfare of Children*, *The Department Store Girl*, and *The Straight Girl on the Crooked Path*. She also conducted the first study of the living conditions of African Americans in Chicago that was published as *The Colored People of Chicago* (1913), and she wrote about her experiences with the Juvenile Protective Association in *Safeguards for City Youth at Work and at Play* (1914).

During her life Bowen was actively involved in many other social and civic reform efforts, holding over thirty official leadership positions. Those positions included founding member and president of the Woman's City Club in Chicago, vice president of the United Charities of Chicago, member of the Executive Committee of the Committee of Fifteen, auditor of the National American Woman Suffrage Association, vice president of the Illinois Suffrage Association, chairman of the Illinois division of the Woman's Committee of the National Council of Defense, president of the Women's Roosevelt Republican Club, and Republican party national committeewoman from Illinois. She was also the only governmental delegate from the United States to the 1923 Pan-American Conference of Women, and after World War I she became the Woman Fair Price Commissioner for Illinois. Bowen campaigned for the Progressive party in 1912, she raised money to provide food to the children of striking garment workers, she marched and lectured for woman's suffrage, and she used her power as a stockholder to pressure companies to improve their working conditions. Bowen received numerous awards and honors for her activities including, in 1941, the first Gold Medal for Distinguished Service ever awarded to a woman by the Rotary Club of Chicago. In 1944, at the age of eighty-eight, she cut back most of her official duties but remained honorary president of Hull-House, the Juvenile Protective Association, and the Women's City Club. Bowen died in Chicago.

Bowen was one of a generation of powerful women that had a lasting impact on the nation. Her friends included U.S. presidents, chief executive officers of large companies, and renowned physicians and scientists, as well as social reformers. She was a vital link among various civic and social organizations in Chicago, an effective leader of many of those organizations, and the key benefactor of Hull-House. And, she was at the center of the child-saving movement, an effort that laid the groundwork for contemporary programs of delinquency control.

• The Louise deKoven Bowen Papers are kept at the Chicago Historical Society. Some of her correspondence and clippings having to do with her Hull-House activities are in the Jane Addams Memorial Collection at the University of Illinois, Chicago. The Jane Addams Collection also contains the papers of the Hull-House Associates and the Juvenile Protective Association. Bowen wrote three autobiographical books: *Growing Up with a City* (1926), *Baymeath* (1944), and *Open Window: Stories of People and Places* (1946). Copies of some of her correspondence, speeches, and the many pamphlets she wrote based on her research and experiences at the Juvenile Protective Association can be found in *Speeches, Addresses and Letters of Louise deKoven Bowen: Reflecting Social Movements in Chicago*, ed. Mary E. Humphrey (1937). Elisabeth Lasch-Quinn, *Black Neighbors: Race and the Limits of Reform in the American Settlement House Movement, 1890–1945* (1993), has a chapter analyzing the views on African Americans of Bowen and three others connected to the settlement movement in the early twentieth century. Anthony Platt includes a critical analysis of Bowen and other upper-class reformers in his work on the child-saving movement, *The Child Savers: The Invention of Delinquency* (1969). Also see Helen J. Ferris, *Five Girls Who Dared: The Girlhood Stories of Five Courageous Girls As Told by Themselves* (1940), on Bowen's childhood; Michael David Levin, "Louise deKoven Bowen: A Case History of the American Response to Jazz" (Ph.D. diss., Univ. of Illinois, 1985); and Allen F. Davis and Mary Lynn McCree, eds., *Eighty Years at Hull House* (1969). Obituaries are in the *New York Times* and the *Chicago Tribune*, both 10 Nov. 1953.

CYNTHIA R. POE

BOWEN, Norman Levi (21 June 1887–11 Sept. 1956), petrologist and educator, was born in Kingston, Ontario, Canada, the youngest son of William Alfred Bowen, an immigrant from London (Chigwell), England, and Eliza McCormick of Kingston. At the time of Bowen's birth, his father was a guard at the Kingston Penitentiary, later became sexton of St. George's Cathedral, and then was proprietor of a bakery. His older and only surviving brother, Charles Lewis Bowen (1879–1951), retained the bakery business.

Bowen entered the Faculty of Arts, Queen's University, in 1903 and took an honors course in chemistry and mineralogy, graduating in 1907 with an M.A. degree and university medals in both subjects. He continued in mineralogy and geology, completing the B.S. degree in 1909 in the School of Mining, where he studied primarily under Reginald W. Brock, later the director of the Geological Survey of Canada. Two papers were produced from three summers' field work with the Ontario Department of Mines (1907–1909). One paper was awarded a first prize by the Canadian Mining Institute and its President's gold medal.

After winning an 1851 Exhibition Scholarship, Bowen looked abroad for graduate studies, as was then the custom. Because of his interest in the physicochemical relations of rocks, he was attracted to Norway where Johan H. L. Vogt and Waldemar C. Brøgger were doing research, respectively, in the laboratory and the field. Discouraged by them for several reasons, including the language barrier, Bowen then looked to a fellow Canadian, Reginald A. Daly, an imaginative and inspiring teacher at the Massachusetts Institute of Technology (MIT). He registered there in the fall of 1909. Imbued with the principles of physical chemistry related to mineralogical and petrological problems, probably by Charles H. Warren, then associate professor of mineralogy, he applied at the suggestion of his departmental chairman, Thomas A. Jaggar, to carry out research at the Geophysical Laboratory, which had been established in 1905 in Washington, D.C. After Bowen visited the Laboratory, the director Arthur L. Day accepted him with the understanding that he could use the proposed investigation of the thermal relations of mixtures of the minerals nepheline and anorthite for partial fulfillment of the requirements for a Ph.D. degree. In this way, Bowen became, in 1910, the first predoctoral fellow of the Geophysical Laboratory.

Bowen could not have arrived at the Geophysical Laboratory at a better time. The method for investigating silicate systems at high temperatures by very rapid cooling (quenching) had just been developed by Ernest S. Shepherd, George A. Rankin, and Frederick E. Wright; the calibration of the platinum thermocouple element for measuring temperature had just been completed by Leason H. Adams; and the technique for maintaining constant temperatures up to the melting point of platinum was in hand. When Bowen produced the diagram for the thermal relations of the minerals nepheline and anorthite (1911), it was clear that he had found the first example in silicates of limited crystalline homogeneity (solid solution) combined with crystallization in more than one form (polymorphism), a possible relationship deduced previously by Bakhuis Roozeboom of the University of Amsterdam, an expert on heterogeneous phase equilibria, on theoretical grounds. The experiments were completed in time to take advantage of the summer field season, and Bowen served as assistant to R. A. Daly, surveying along the main line of the Canadian Pacific Railway in British Columbia. At the end of the field season, on 3 October 1911, Bowen married Mary Lamont of Charlottetown, Prince Edward Island, Canada, just after she received her doctorate of medicine at the College of Physicians and Surgeons in Boston. They would have one child. On 4 June 1912 Bowen was graduated from MIT. He reported as staff member to the Geophysical Laboratory on 1 September 1912 after another field season, this time in charge of his own field party in British Columbia.

Within the short span of three years Bowen published on the plagioclase feldspars, MgO-SiO_2 (with Olaf Anderson), diopside-forsterite-silica, and diopside-albite-anorthite, the results of which were summarized in his article, "The Later Stages of the Evolution of the Igneous Rocks" (*Journal of Geology* 23, supp. [1915]: 1–89). Thus, by his twenty-eighth birthday he had formulated the major concepts leading to the following conclusions: (1) that basalt was the parental magma for many rock types; (2) that most, if not all, igneous rocks were derived therefrom by a crystallization process, primarily by separation of the residual liquid from already formed crystals (differentiation); (3) that assimilation, the process whereby the magma absorbs by solution the host rocks, was unimportant; (4) that the Soret effect, involving the variation of solute in a solution with temperature, was negligible; (5) that immiscibility, the limited solubility of one magma in another, was not supported by the existing field and experimental evidence; and (6) that volatiles were necessary for the generation of alkalic rocks. He explained the process for deriving monomineralic rocks and the order of crystallization of the important rock-forming minerals, and he interpreted the chilled border facies of igneous bodies. Bowen's proposals, refuting the current popular models requiring each rock type to form from a magma crystallizing minerals in definite proportions (a eutectic), were not immediately received with enthusiasm by his peers. But by 1917, when he applied the process of crystal accumulation under the influence of gravity as an origin for the monomineralic anorthosites of the Adirondacks and Quebec, his ideas won the attention of geologists around the world.

During World War I, research at the Geophysical Laboratory was entirely devoted to the vital problem of developing optical glass, previously imported from Germany. To facilitate the application of physicochemical principles to the systematic manufacture of glass, previously a secretive cookbook endeavor, staff members were posted at the principal optical companies. In this capacity Bowen served at the Bausch and Lomb Optical Company in Rochester, New York, and at the Pittsburgh Plate Glass Company in Charleroi, Pennsylvania.

Following World War I, Bowen returned to Queen's University, Kingston, Ontario, where he taught from January 1919 to May 1920, but he found experimental work more to his liking than teaching and returned to the Geophysical Laboratory. In the next six years his work yielded an incredible sequence of landmark papers. An experimental study in 1921 of diffusion against gravity of a heavy diopside liquid into a lighter plagioclase liquid led to the conclusion that diffusion, the permeation of one substance through another, was not a major factor in the development of the marginal facies of large igneous intrusions. He demonstrated in 1922 the great importance of the reaction principle in petrogenesis, a concept where early formal crystals react with the magma to form new minerals further down the series. This concept is hailed as one of the most significant contributions to petrology. Next he analyzed the principles of assimilation from a physicochemical viewpoint and concluded that assimilation was not essential to the main scheme of igneous differentiation—contrary to the views of his mentor R. A. Daly. This study was followed by the experimental investigation of Al_2O_3-SiO_2 with his ex-student Joseph W. Greig in which the important refractory ceramic compound mullite was discovered. In 1925 Bowen joined with colleagues in studies of portions of the Na_2O-CaO-SiO_2 and K_2O-CaO-SiO_2 systems that bear on the manufacture of common glass (mainly because of their viscosity and low-temperature melting characteristics). This period of his life culminated with the publication in 1928 of *The Evolution of the Igneous Rocks,* based on a series of lectures he gave at Princeton University at the invitation of his friend and former colleague Arthur F. Buddington. This survey and synthesis of the principal petrological problems is often described as the most influential book in petrology ever written.

From 1929 to 1937 Bowen was involved in a program of experimental investigation, primarily with his indefatigable colleague J. Frank Schairer, on silicate systems containing iron oxides. A new method for keeping iron mostly in the ferrous state was achieved by holding the charges in an iron crucible in a nitrogen atmosphere. New results from many systems contributed to the understanding of the crystallization characteristics of the mafic minerals olivine and pyroxene as well as of their relations to the feldspars and feldspathoids. He summarized the implications of these observations at the Harvard tercentenary celebrations, where he received an honorary degree. There he emphasized once more his strongly held view that fractional crystallization yielded residual liquids enriched in alkali-alumina silicates, which he described as petrogeny's residua system. Results of work on that system, $NaAlSiO_4$-$KAlSiO_4$-SiO_2, were first presented in a preliminary way in 1935 and described in full with revisions by J. F. Schairer in 1950. The principles deduced were applied with success to the rocks of the East African volcanic field, which Bowen had studied in the company of Bailey Willis in 1929.

In 1937 Bowen left the Geophysical Laboratory because of uncertainties accompanying the appointment of a new director and because he had an attractive offer from the University of Chicago following the retirement of Albert Johannsen, petrologist, from the department of geology. In addition, the move was prompted by Bowen's conviction that the experimental aspects of petrology should be developed in the universities. For nine years, interrupted by one and one-half years of defense work at the Geophysical Laboratory as coordinator of research under a government contract during World War II, he directed a succession of students as the Charles L. Hutchinson Distinguished Service Professor of Petrology. They worked on selected portions of the Na_2O-CaO-Al_2O_3-SiO_2 system that involved nepheline, gehlenite, wollastonite, anorthite, and albite. His remarkable paper on the "Progressive Metamorphism of Siliceous Limestone and Dolomite" (*Journal of Geology* 48 [1940]: 225–74) opened up a new approach to the interpretation of metamorphic rocks. The idea of a petrogenetic grid was established by expressing quantitatively on a pressure-temperature diagram the boundaries of the various mineral assemblages. During this period, Bowen supervised one M.S. degree and five Ph.D. degrees. Only two of the recipients (Wilfred R. Foster and Julian R. Goldsmith) fulfilled his goal of staffing the universities and perpetuating the experimental approach to petrology. Burdened with the departmental chairmanship (1944–1947) and the constant struggle for funds to build an experimental laboratory, and lured by an exciting new program of research proposed in 1946 for the Geophysical Laboratory, he returned to Washington in 1947.

The investigation of mineral systems in the presence of water was the focus of the last period of Bowen's experimental career. A collaborative study of the MgO-SiO_2-H_2O system with O. Frank Tuttle, who devised a simple hydrothermal quenching apparatus, opened the way to the quantitative calibration of the conditions of formation of metamorphic rocks. Next, they investigated how liquids crystallized in mixtures consisting of $NaAlSi_3O_8$-$KAlSi_3O_8$-SiO_2-H_2O, a close model of granite magmas. They found a thermal trough in which the composition of most natural granites projected. This discovery provided strong support for Bowen's contention that granites were of magmatic origin, whether as residual liquids or as early partial melts. In 1952 Bowen was retired from his position as petrologist at the age of sixty-five. He moved to Clearwater, Florida, only to return again to Washington a year later. Bowen had contributed in large measure to the international renown of the Geophysical Laboratory for its experimental accuracy and focus on the solution of problems pertinent to field geologists.

Bowen was a retiring, quiet, unassuming person with a surprising wit and dry sense of humor. He was not easily provoked into debate, and he usually deferred responding to serious questions overnight or even for days, but ultimately a superbly reasoned reply was offered. For someone who had contributed to the solution of most of the primary petrological questions by entertaining "multiple prejudices," he was adamant in his belief that fractional crystallization was of prime importance in the derivation of magmas. On that issue he laid "no claim to an open mind," and defended his position with rapier strokes of facts and humor. His lectures were classics and were well rehearsed in the early morning hours before presentation. Needless to say, his students held him in awe and were reluctant to approach their world-renowned master. His gentleness and kindly expression did not seem to fit the role expected of a giant in his profession. He clearly preferred the somewhat sheltered life in a research laboratory, free of teaching and administrative duties. Near the end he suffered depression and, complaining of ill health in a final note, took his own life in his home in Washington, D.C. His ashes were scattered on the grounds of the Geophysical Laboratory near his favorite gum tree.

Bowen's applications of the principles of physical chemistry to petrological processes have stood the test of time, and the clarity of his insights into complex geological field problems has been appreciated around the world. Among his honors were the Bigsby Medal (Geological Society of London, 1931), Penrose Medal (Geological Society of America, 1941), Miller Medal (Royal Society of Canada, 1943), Roebling Medal (Mineralogical Society of America, 1950), Wollaston Medal (Geological Society of London, 1950), Hayden Medal (Academy of Sciences of Philadelphia, 1953), and Bakhuis Roozeboom Medal (Royal Netherlands Academy, 1954). Bowen was elected to almost a dozen honorary societies around the world. Shortly after he became a U.S. citizen (1933), he was elected to the National Academy of Sciences (1935). He served as president of the Mineralogical Society of America (1937) and of the Geological Society of America (1946).

• Bowen's letters to the director of the Geophysical Laboratory, collected works, and diplomas are in the archives of the Geophysical Laboratory. Some correspondence during his term as chairman of the Department of Geology, University of Chicago, is held in the archives of that department. His medals were given to the Smithsonian Institution, Washington, D.C. Notes on his early life are given by him in "The Igneous Rocks in the Light of High-temperature Research," *Scientific Monthly* 40 (1935): 487–503, and in an autobiographical sketch in his acceptance speech for the Penrose Medal in the *Proceedings of the Geological Society of America for 1941* (1942), pp. 82–7. A manuscript by an unidentified author (J. W. Greig?) on Bowen's early life at Queen's University, including detailed accounts of his field seasons together with copies of letters from his past students written to A. F. Buddington in 1959–1960, are in the archives of the Geophysical Laboratory. Essentially complete bibliographies are given in the new "Introduction," by J. F. Schairer, of the reprint edition of Bowen's *The Evolution of the Igneous Rocks* (1956), and in his biography by H. P. Eugster, *National Academy of Sciences, Biographical Memoirs* 52 (1980): 35–79. An obituary is in the Washington, D.C., *Evening Star,* 11 Sept. 1956.

H. S. YODER, JR.

BOWEN, Thomas Meade (26 Oct. 1835–30 Dec. 1906), U.S. senator and mining entrepreneur, was born in Burlington, Iowa. His parents' names and occupations are unknown. Bowen was educated at Mount Pleasant Academy (Mount Pleasant, Iowa) and began practicing law in 1853 at the age of eighteen. He was elected to the Iowa House of Representatives as a Democrat in 1856 but served only one term before moving to Kansas, where he joined the Republican party over the issue of free soil. During the Civil War, Bowen organized and commanded the Thirteenth Kansas Infantry and was eventually brevetted a brigadier general in 1863. When the war ended, Bowen was stationed in Arkansas. He settled in Little Rock, where he married Margarette Thurston and established himself as a planter and a prominent lawyer. Whether they had children is not known.

Bowen soon emerged as a key figure in Arkansas's highly factionalized Republican party and its program for Reconstruction. He served as president of a Republican convention in 1867 that claimed that the existing constitution, slightly modified, could serve as an acceptable basis for republican government and advocated the restoration of public credit, support for railroads and internal improvements, and improving the public school system. Bowen subsequently served as president of the constitutional convention of 1868. The convention of 1868 appointed Bowen to the board of commissioners that conducted statewide elections approving the new constitution. Bowen and his fellow commissioners validated the vote despite widespread accusations of fraud on both sides of the issue, and Congress promptly readmitted Arkansas to the Union. Bowen then served four years (1868–1871) as a justice of the Arkansas Supreme Court. He left the court in 1871, when President Ulysses S. Grant appointed him governor of the Idaho Territory. In August of that year, however, Bowen returned to Arkansas and became entangled once more in the raucous politics of Reconstruction.

The years of Republican government in Arkansas were filled with violence and civil disorder. The opponents of Reconstruction were determined to resist Republican governor Powell Clayton, Bowen, and company in any and every way they could. Not confined to the Democrats, the disagreements erupted within the Republican party into a feud between Governor Clayton and Lieutenant Governor James M. Johnson and their followers. Clayton, future governor Elisha Baxter, and Bowen headed the regular faction; Johnson and Joseph Brooks led a "liberal Republican" group that attempted compromise and coalition with moderate Democrats. Patronage, personal animosities, and Clayton's peremptory style influenced that division, but policy differences also affected the split. Regulars supported control of the franchise and railroad bonds, while "liberals" opposed the bonds and favored enfranchising ex-Confederates. Bowen was an important figure in the disputes. He served as counsel for Clayton during the latter's impeachment trial in 1871. The impeachment effort failed when loyal Republican senators refused to attend sessions, thus preventing the calling of a quorum and outlasting the patience of Clayton's opponents. In 1873 Bowen was the regular faction's candidate for the U.S. Senate, but lost when the liberals and Democrats united to support Stephen W. Dorsey.

Bowen's interests in Arkansas were not confined to politics and the law. He served on the Board of Directors of the Little Rock, Pine Bluff, and New Orleans Railroad Company in 1871. He was also president of the Mississippi, Ouachita, and Red River Railroad Company. He had hoped to engage in mining ventures in Idaho, but the lack of lucrative investment opportunities in that state may have contributed to his short stay as governor. Shortly after his failed bid for the Senate, Bowen once more left the turbulent politics of Arkansas to pursue his fortune in the Rockies.

In 1875 Bowen moved west, settling in Del Norte, Colorado. He again took up law and became involved in mining ventures in the San Luis Valley. These endeavors made Bowen a wealthy man and established him as one of the more prominent of the state's numerous mining entrepreneurs. Pursuing public office again, he won the position of judge of Colorado's Fourth Judicial Circuit upon the formation of a state government in 1876. He resigned from the bench in 1880 and was elected to the lower house of the Colorado legislature in 1882. One year later he won one of the most exciting Senate races in Colorado's history.

A number of names emerged in 1883 from the Republican caucus in the state senate as possible candidates. The most prominent was Horace Tabor, another mining entrepreneur, who faced enough opposition to open the door for compromise candidates. Bowen presented himself as a suitable and relatively uncontroversial alternative and was elected after eleven days and ninety-six caucus votes. By making himself acceptable to the two powerful factions in the party, led by Henry M. Teller and Nathaniel P. Hill, Bowen found a middle ground and attempted to ease some of the interparty animosity. Bowen served one term in the Senate and chaired the Committee on Mining. He quickly established himself as a champion of the free coinage of silver, unsuccessfully introducing a bill to that effect in 1887. He also was a vocal advocate of federal irrigation projects in the West and of federal aid for public schools. In 1889 he returned to Colorado to revive his nearly exhausted fortune. The mining business was good to him once more, and he died a wealthy man in Pueblo, Colorado.

Bowen's career was a procession from one public office to another. From Arkansas to Idaho to Colorado, he remained an active figure in Republican politics, eventually being rewarded with a seat in the U.S. Senate. Throughout his career Bowen pursued his financial interests as well, gaining and losing fortunes in the booms and busts of the American West. His support of free silver showed how his personal and political interests were intertwined.

• Bowen left no personal papers or memoirs. Works that provide some insight into his career include William H. Burnside, *The Honorable Powell Clayton* (1991); Hiram T. French, *History of Idaho* (1914); George H. Thompson, *Arkansas and Reconstruction* (1976); and Duane A. Smith, *Horace Tabor: His Life and the Legend* (1973). Bowen's obituary is in the *New York Times*, 1 Jan. 1907.

WILLIAM T. HULL

BOWERS, Bathsheba (c. 1672–1718), spiritual autobiographer and Quaker preacher, was born in Massachusetts, the daughter of Benanuel Bowers and Elizabeth Dunster, English Quakers who had resettled in Boston at the end of the seventeenth century to escape the Anglican faith of her father's father. Because Bowers's adolescent years were disrupted by the ruling Puritans' persecution of Quakers, she and at least two of her eleven siblings were removed to Quaker Philadelphia, were Bowers spent most of her adult life.

After apparently having had a love affair, which evidently failed, at the age of eighteen, Bowers chose not to marry, devoting herself instead to her religion. In *An Alarm Sounded* (1709), her only extant text (which was, notably, published in New York, a safe distance from Bowers's hometown of Philadelphia), she detailed her early struggles against "the Influences of evil" and toward salvation. Even in this text, which in general outline closely follows proscribed patterns for Quaker conversion narratives, Bowers's struggle with the limited roles for women even in the seemingly egalitarian Society of Friends is evident.

While she recognized the Society's belief that "*Obedience is better than Sacrifice*," she insisted in her prefatory remarks on the goodness of ambition when it is directed by and for the propagation of God's work. Under these conditions, she argued, it is rightful for women to publish their religious narratives and to speak publicly; these goals directed the remainder of her life. Rather than settle into what she envisioned as the stasis of marriage and a narrow sense of community service, she separated herself by living alone, never marrying, and creating her own world within the confines of what came to be known as "Bathsheba's Bower," a highly cultivated plot of springs and gardens at the intersection of Little Dock and Second streets in Philadelphia, where the evangelist George Whitefield is said to have preached from the balcony in subsequent years.

For a short period of time she took in her niece, Ann Bolton, whose diaries detail the family history and suggest Bowers's highly unconventional beliefs and lifestyle; most disconcerting to Bolton was Bowers's occasional adherence to the early Quaker practice of nakedness, meant to symbolize the spiritual nakedness of earthly existence.

Though no copies are known to remain of Bowers's writings other than *An Alarm Sounded*, she reportedly was a prolific writer of spiritual texts and letters, the latter most often directed to Philadelphia's noted Quaker preacher Thomas Story. Whether it was her isolated lifestyle, which afforded her the time for reflection and writing, or some other encouragement, Bowers eventually found the courage to pursue her greatest ambition: to be a Quaker preacher.

Late in her life she traveled throughout the Mid-Atlantic states and the South, preaching at public gatherings in order to plant the "little seed whose product outflowrisht all Seeds," a metaphor she had employed in *An Alarm Sounded* to designate the power of her preaching and publishing, even if it caused her to be "the Object of Scorn and Ridicule." Bowers died in South Carolina, having lived an unorthodox life for an early eighteenth-century woman.

• A copy of *An Alarm Sounded* is housed in the Historical Society of Pennsylvania, Philadelphia. Excerpts from Ann Bolton's diaries chronicling the family history are in William John Potts, "Bathsheba Bowers," *Pennsylvania Magazine of History and Biography* 3 (1879): 110–12. See also Lina Mainiero, ed., *American Women Writers* (1979); James A. Levernier and Douglas R. Wilmes, eds., *American Writers Before 1800* (1983); Pattie Cowell, *Women Poets in Pre-Revolutionary America, 1650–1775* (1979); Daniel P. Shea, *Spiritual Autobiography in Early America* (1968); Lucius R. Paige, *History of Cambridge, Massachusetts, 1630–1877* (1877); J. F. Watson, *Annals of Philadelphia* (1905); and Luella M. Wright, *The Literary Life of the Early Friends, 1650–1725* (1932).

SHARON M. HARRIS

BOWERS, Claude Gernade (20 Nov. 1878–21 Jan. 1958), journalist, diplomat, and historian, was born in Westfield, Indiana, the son of Lewis Bowers, a storekeeper, and Juliet Tipton, a milliner and dressmaker. Reared in rural communities in central Indiana, Claude moved to Indianapolis with his divorced mother when he was thirteen. He was a voracious reader and became a confirmed Democrat while at Indianapolis High School. In 1898 Bowers graduated and also won the state oratorical contest but was unable to attend college for lack of funds. Instead he worked for the publishing firm that later became the Bobbs-Merrill Company. In 1900 Bowers became the major editorial writer for the *Sentinel*, Indianapolis's Democratic daily, and he gave the first of hundreds of speeches advocating democracy. His rapid-fire delivery soon earned him the title "Gatling Gun Orator of the Wabash."

Beginning in 1903 Bowers wrote editorials for the *Gazette* and *Star* in Terre Haute, Indiana, advocating progressive reforms. He also served on the Terre Haute Board of Public Works. Bowers ran for Congress in 1904 and 1906 but was defeated by the Republican incumbent. In 1911 he went to Washington,

D.C., as secretary to Senator John W. Kern. During Woodrow Wilson's presidency Kern became the first party whip and shepherded New Freedom legislation through the Senate. Bowers handled many responsibilities, including work with constituents, important office duties, and speeches in Indiana. In 1911 Bowers married Sybil McCaslin of Indianapolis; they had one child. Following Kern's defeat, in 1917 Bowers moved to Fort Wayne, Indiana, where he contributed editorials to the *Journal-Gazette* for six years.

Bowers's national prominence increased following his move to New York City in 1923. He was an editorialist first for the Pulitzer family's *Evening World* and in 1931 for the *Evening Journal*, which distributed his signed columns in other newspapers published by William Randolph Hearst. Bowers wrote speeches for politicians Al Smith, Robert F. Wagner, and Franklin D. Roosevelt. At the 1928 Democratic convention Bowers attacked Presidents Warren G. Harding and Calvin Coolidge in a memorable keynote address, charging that "privilege and pillage are the Gold Dust twins of normalcy." In 1932 Bowers campaigned for Roosevelt.

Bowers's historical works also earned him a national reputation. *The Irish Orators* (1916) was followed in 1918 by a laudatory biography of Senator Kern, and in 1922 he published *The Party Battles of the Jackson Period*, a vigorous defense of the seventh president. Bowers's fame as a historian rests principally on two works: *Jefferson and Hamilton* (1925) and *The Tragic Era: The Revolution after Lincoln* (1929). In the former Bowers recounts his subjects' "Plutarchian struggle" and argues that Jefferson's victory "definitively determined that this [nation] should not only be a republic, but a democratic republic." In *The Tragic Era* Bowers attacks Radical Republicans for their "despotic policies" toward the South following the Civil War. *Jefferson in Power* (1936) and *The Young Jefferson* (1945) complete Bowers's trilogy on his democratic hero. Because Bowers glorified the subjects of his biographies and dismissed the motives of the Radical Republicans following the Civil War, more recent historians have taken issue with his interpretations of Jefferson and Reconstruction. Yet *Jefferson and Hamilton* has gone through twenty-seven printings, and *The Tragic Era* attracted perhaps a larger readership than any other study on Reconstruction. Bowers's other historical works include a biography of Indiana Republican Albert J. Beveridge (1932), the charming *Spanish Adventures of Washington Irving* (1940), and *Pierre Vergniaud* (1950), which praises the French revolutionary orator.

Bowers was also active in international affairs. He was Roosevelt's ambassador to Spain (1933–1939) and then served Presidents Roosevelt and Harry S. Truman as minister to Chile (1939–1953). In Madrid Bowers sought to improve Spanish-American trade. During the Spanish Civil War (1936–1939) he was an outspoken proponent of the Spanish Republic in its unsuccessful fight to defeat General Francisco Franco's rebel forces, aided by Benito Mussolini and Adolph Hitler. Despite his pleas that the United States permit the Spanish Republic to buy arms in America, Washington feared involvement in the conflict and refused. In Santiago Bowers helped convince the reluctant Chilean government to break relations with the Axis in 1943. Bowers also worked to increase Chile's vital wartime exports of copper, and he promoted cultural exchanges and political cooperation during the Cold War.

Back in New York in 1953, Bowers continued his party activities, working with former first lady Eleanor Roosevelt and advising politician Adlai Stevenson. Bowers also wrote two volumes on his ambassadorships to Spain and Chile, *My Mission to Spain: Watching the Rehearsal for World War II* (1954) and *Chile through Embassy Windows: 1939–1953* (1958), and following his death in New York City his almost completed autobiography was published as *My Life: The Memoirs of Claude Bowers* (1962).

Bowers is remembered as an influential Democratic political adviser and orator as well as an editorial defender of liberal democracy. Despite their lively style and popularity during his lifetime, Bowers's many historical works are more recently viewed as too partisan. Many conservative contemporaries in the State Department considered his actions in foreign affairs to be the naive diplomacy of a political appointee. But Bowers's defense of the Spanish Republic during the civil war there and his understanding of the difficulties that Chilean leaders faced in breaking relations with the Axis are increasingly viewed in a more favorable light.

• Bowers's papers, including most of his personal letters, many speeches, and copies of much of his official correspondence, are in the Lilly Library at Indiana University, Bloomington. Reports, telegrams, and letters from his diplomatic years are with the State Department records at the National Archives. For autobiographical material, see Bowers's oral history interview conducted by Louis Starr at the Columbia University Oral History Research Office in New York City, "The Reminiscences of Claude Bowers" (1954), and Holman Hamilton and Gayle Thornbrough, eds., *Indianapolis in the "Gay Nineties": The High School Diaries of Claude G. Bowers* (1964), which also contains an informative introduction written by the editors. For a secondary treatment of Bowers see Sabine Jessner and Peter J. Sehlinger, "Claude G. Bowers: A Partisan Hoosier," *Indiana Magazine of History* 83 (Sept. 1987): 217–43. An obituary is in the *New York Times*, 22 Jan. 1958.

PETER J. SEHLINGER

BOWERS, Elizabeth Crocker (12 Mar. 1830–6 Nov. 1895), actress, was born in Stamford, Connecticut, the daughter of Rev. William A. Crocker, an Episcopal minister; her mother's name is unknown. After her father died when she was five years old, the family was supported by Elizabeth's older brother, John Crocker, an actor in New York City. She made her debut at the Park Theatre, where her brother was a company member, as Amanthis in *Child of Nature* on 3 December 1845. After playing small roles at the Park for the season, she joined the Walnut Street Theatre company in Philadelphia with her brother.

On 4 March 1847 Elizabeth married actor David P. Bowers. For the next ten years the couple worked, primarily in Philadelphia, as members of stock companies. Elizabeth Bowers worked her way up to leading roles and became a local favorite. On 5 June 1857, near the end of a season at the Arch Street Theatre, she took a benefit performance. The next day her husband died of heart failure at the age of thirty-four.

A young widow with three children, Bowers could afford only a brief retirement from the stage. She returned to the Arch in August 1857 and soon ventured into theater management. Assuming the lease to the Walnut Street Theatre, which had been given up by E. A. Marshall, Bowers opened her season on 19 December 1857 with Dion Boucicault's *London Assurance*. Retaining many of the actors and staff from the previous management, Bowers also added her sister and brother-in-law, Mr. and Mrs. F. B. Conway, and local favorites, Mr. and Mrs. John Drew, to her company. The moderately successful first season ran through 15 May 1858. Bowers then took her company to New York City for a three-week engagement at Laura Keene's Theatre, while Keene's company played at the Walnut.

Following her benefit performance on 18 June 1858, Bowers shut the Walnut Street Theatre for the summer and had the auditorium remodeled. During the second season, which began on 21 August 1858, Bowers began to have some difficulty attracting audiences. Bowers's own strength in tragic or darkly melodramatic parts, such as the title roles in *Camille* and *Jane Shore*, led her to produce rather heavy fare. Never adequately supported in the secondary roles, Bowers also had to contend with the loss of the Drews before the start of the second season, followed by the midseason departure of the Conways. Relying primarily on old stock scenery, Bowers provided little in the way of scenic splendor or novelty at the Walnut. Even Bowers herself, the primary attraction, lacked the novelty and drawing power with audiences she would later compel as a visiting star on a limited engagement.

Bowers eventually resigned herself to engaging star performers, but this policy increased her expenses and drove away company members who anticipated decreased opportunities. However, the final blow to her management came when Bowers, who had not closely monitored the day-to-day business arrangements of the theater, demanded an inspection of the books. She apparently angered one of the staff members retained from the previous management, provoking a string of poison pen letters. Bleak financial prospects, on top of the anonymous hate mail, led Bowers to give up the management of the Walnut, bringing her season to an early close on 22 January 1859.

Bowers made another attempt at theater management in Philadelphia, leasing the Academy of Music and presenting short seasons in March and September 1859. When this venture was not a success, Bowers refocused her efforts on her acting career, and it was as a touring star that she made her reputation. Although Bowers married a man named Dr. Brown in 1859, she maintained the stage name Mrs. D. P. Bowers throughout her career.

Bowers toured extensively with her own company playing a repertory that included domestic melodramas and historical pieces, such as *Lady Audley's Secret*, *Mary Stuart*, *Queen Elizabeth*, *Marie Antoinette*, and *East Lynne*. Whether she portrayed a sympathetic heroine in distress or a serious, regal figure, these plays allowed her to perform the passionate, yet refined characters that suited her stately carriage and powerful stage voice. One contemporary critic noted, "She received from nature a voice, which, even in its inarticulate tones, was pathos itself. Her acting, her splendid declamation, her wonderful powers of expression and classic poses gave to her act a higher tint and made popular a piece of little merit beyond its tableaux."

In 1861 she made her first appearance in England, playing Julia in *The Hunchback* at Sadler's Wells. Returning to the United States in 1863, Bowers played an engagement at New York's Winter Garden during late summer, supported by Lawrence Barrett as Robert Audley in *Lady Audley's Secret* and as Sir Thomas Clifford in *The Hunchback*. Bowers brought her company back to the Winter Garden in the fall of 1866. For Bowers's benefit performance on 23 November, the actress played Juliet to the Romeo of her sister, Mrs. F. B. (Sarah Crocker) Conway. The sisters performed *Romeo and Juliet* on several occasions, usually during one of Bowers's frequent starring engagements at Mrs. F. B. Conway's Park Theatre or Brooklyn Theatre.

Touring brought Bowers back to Brooklyn several times, but between 1868 and 1880 she was not seen on the stage in Manhattan. She presumably suffered a slight decline in popularity in this period because her grand acting style began to seem old-fashioned. Nevertheless, she was able to find work, touring in the South and West. Making a critically acclaimed return to the country's theatrical center, she supported Edwin Booth at Booth's Theatre, from 30 March through 24 April 1880. Bowers took the roles of Lady Macbeth, Beatrice in *Much Ado about Nothing*, Queen Margaret in *Richard III*, Emilia in *Othello*, and Portia in *The Merchant of Venice*. Bowers also played the parts of Emilia and Gertrude during Booth's season with Tommaso Salvini at the Academy of Music in New York in 1886.

Bowers's second husband died in 1867, and in 1883 she married James C. McCollum, her touring partner of many years. During the next few years Bowers spent part of her time teaching elocution, but she also played some starring engagements, relying on her favorite old vehicles, such as Lady Audley. Bowers secured her reputation as one of the notable actresses of her age, when late in her life she performed for a new generation of theatergoers. On 3 February 1892 Bowers appeared at Palmer's Theatre as Mme. d'Arcay in *The Broken Seal*. Oscar Wilde's *Lady Windermere's Fan* had its New York premiere at Palmer's on 5 February 1893 with Bowers as the duchess of Berwick. New York theater chronicler George C. D. Odell noted, "Mrs. Bowers came to the younger playgoers as a revelation of what the older school could do in the way of crisp, trenchant diction; nothing like her delivery of Wilde's brilliant lines had for years been heard in New York." On 24 October 1893 Bowers took the role of Mrs. Kirkland in David Belasco's *The Younger Son* at the Empire Theatre. Bowers next appeared at Miner's Fifth Avenue Theatre on 11 December 1893 as Carolina Pontefract in Wilde's *A Woman of No Importance*. Her final stage performances were at Palmer's in 1894. Bowers appeared on 15 October as Mrs. Woodville in A. W. Gattie's *The Transgressor* and on 12 November as Lady Wargrave in Sidney Grundy's *The New Woman*. Bowers died at her daughter's home in Washington, D.C.

• Bowers's career is discussed in T. Allston Brown, *A History of the American Stage* (1870) and *A History of the New York Stage* (1903), and George C. D. Odell, *Annals of the New York Stage* (1927–1941). For details of her managerial career see Jane Kathleen Curry's *Nineteenth-Century American Women Theatre Managers* (1994). For a full listing of plays presented by Bowers at the Walnut Street Theatre, see Kathleen Anne Morgan, "Of Stars and Standards: Actress-Managers in New York and Philadelphia, 1850–1880" (Ph.D. diss., Univ. of Illinois, 1989). Feature articles are in the *Spirit of the Times*, 7 Mar. 1874, and the *New Orleans Daily Picayune*, 8 Apr. 1894. Obituaries are in the *Washington Post* and the *New York Times*, both 7 Nov. 1895, and the *New York Clipper*, 16 Nov. 1895.

J. K. CURRY

BOWERS, Lloyd Wheaton (9 Mar. 1859–9 Sept. 1910), lawyer and solicitor general of the United States, was born in Springfield, Massachusetts, the son of Samuel Dwight Bowers, a jeweler, and Martha Wheaton Dowd. In 1865 his family moved from Springfield to Brooklyn, New York. In 1869 they settled in Elizabeth, New Jersey, where Bowers prepared for college under the Reverend John Young. As the only one of Young's students with an eye set on college, Bowers received Young's focused attention. Bowers considered Young's tutelage an important factor in his later success.

In 1875 Bowers entered Yale College, graduating four years later as the valedictorian with the second-highest rank ever achieved by a Yale student until that time. Upon graduating he accepted Yale's Soldiers' Memorial Fellowship for postgraduate study, but the following spring he resigned the fellowship. That fall he enrolled in the Columbia Law School. Bowers graduated from Columbia in 1882 and was admitted to the New York State bar. He was one of three applicants selected for special commendation by the bar examiners.

Bowers joined the New York City law firm of Chamberlain, Carter and Hornblower in the summer of 1882. He became a managing clerk a year later and a partner in early 1884. His health, however, did not hold, and after a summer of rest and travel with a cousin in the Northwest, Bowers left New York permanently to form a partnership in Winona, Minnesota, with Thomas Wilson, a former chief justice of the Minnesota Supreme Court. Bowers married Louise Bennett Wilson of Winona, in 1887; they had two children.

In June 1893 Bowers left Winona and the private practice of law to become the general counsel of the Chicago & Northwestern Railway Company in Chicago. He represented the railroad in this role with quiet diligence and distinction for sixteen years.

Bowers was a member of the Chicago Bar Association, the Chicago Law Club (of which he was the president in 1900–1901), the Chicago Club, and the Yale Alumni Association of Chicago. His less structured pursuits and interests included the study of literature and old prints. In his later years he also took up the study of calculus and music. In this he said he could "consider [himself] happy, for ordinarily the business man seems to lose whatever other faculties he first had, and most rarely to acquire any new ones" (*A History of the Class of Seventy-Nine—Yale College*, p. 112). Following the death of his first wife in 1897, Bowers in 1906 married Charlotte Josephine Lewis Watson of Detroit, Michigan.

In March 1909 President William Howard Taft appointed Bowers as the solicitor general of the United States, a position for which he had been seriously considered in 1893 by President Grover Cleveland. Later Taft recalled how proud he had been "on securing [Bowers's] services in this administration at great personal sacrifice to himself" (*Washington Post*, 10 Sept. 1910). Bowers's government pay was less than one-fourth of his $30,000-a-year railroad salary.

The high point of Bowers's brief tenure as solicitor general was his argument in the corporation tax cases in March 1910; he argued that the new federal tax on corporations was not a direct tax, but a constitutionally permissible excise tax within Congressional taxing powers. The president opined that the argument "was one of the most able of which that court has any record" (*Washington Post*, 10 Sept. 1910). These cases were reargued after Bowers's death, and Bowers's position prevailed. The corporation tax within the Tariff Act of 1909 was declared constitutional in *Flint v. Stone Tracy Company* (1911).

Bowers's friendship with Taft, which began when both were undergraduates at Yale, had charted his career. Taft's high regard for Bowers's legal abilities enhanced their relationship and improved Bowers's prospects. For example in 1902, when President Theodore Roosevelt asked Taft about Bowers's qualifications to sit on the U.S. Supreme Court, Taft was unqualified in his praise and enthused that Bowers was "one of your kind of men" (Pringle, p. 241). In fact, it was widely reported that Bowers was an almost certain Taft appointee to one of the two places vacant on the Court at the time of Bowers's death. For his part, Bowers had long been known to aspire to the office. There is even a tale, perhaps apocryphal, that while at Yale Taft had inquired of Bowers's "chief ambition in life" in the course of Bowers's initiation into the Skull and Bones senior society; Bowers announced his desire to be an associate justice of the Supreme Court.

Taft supposedly replied: "When I get to be President I'll appoint you" (*New York Times*, 10 Sept. 1910).

Bowers died unexpectedly of complications after contracting an illness at a Boston, Massachusetts, hotel. Only two days before Bowers's death, President Taft visited him at the hotel on his way to the Beverly, Massachusetts, "summer White House."

In his public message of tribute after Bowers's death, Taft indicated that "it was my purpose to have appointed him a justice of the Supreme Court if opportunity offered" (*Washington Post*, 10 Sept. 1910). Later that month Justice Oliver Wendell Holmes, Jr., echoed Taft's sentiment that Bowers's death was the Court's loss: "I know of no one who I so want to see on our Bench as much as I did the late Solicitor General" (Letter from Holmes to Sir Frederick Pollock, 24 Sept. 1910).

• For a biographical treatment see the discussion of Bowers in F. W. Williams, ed., *A History of the Class of Seventy-Nine—Yale College* (1906), and Williams, ed., *The Biographical Record of the Class of '79—Yale College* (1885). His relationships to Taft and Holmes are noted in Ishbel Ross, *An American Family: The Tafts* (1964); Mark De Wolfe Howe, ed., *Holmes-Pollock Letters: The Correspondence of Mr. Justice Holmes and Sir Frederick Pollock, 1874–1932* (2 vols., 1941); and Henry Fowler Pringle, *The Life and Times of William Howard Taft* (1939). Obituaries are in the *Boston Evening Transcript*, the *Chicago Daily Tribune*, the *New York Times*, and the *Washington Post*, all 10 Sept. 1910; and *Obituary Record of Graduates of Yale University Deceased During the Year Ending June 1, 1911*, no. 70 (no. 1 of 6th printed ser.).

ALFRED S. NEELY

BOWES, Major (14 June 1874–13 June 1946), radio producer and talent show host, was born Edward J. Bowes in San Francisco, California, the son of John M. Bowes, a customs agent, and Caroline Amelia Ford. Bowes's father died when he was only six, forcing him to abandon his schooling after he graduated from grammar school. Bowes became a remarkably educated individual nevertheless and entered the real estate business in San Francisco, becoming prosperous if not wealthy. In 1909 he married Margaret Illington, an actress; they had no children. After World War I he gave up his business interests in San Francisco and moved to New York City, where he began operating theaters. This venture brought him into contact with Samuel Rothafel, popularly known as Roxy. The two men ran the Capitol Theatre in New York in the postwar period. In 1923, as radio was beginning to become popular, Roxy started his own show known as the "Capitol Family Theatre," which was broadcast on Sunday mornings and featured amateur talent. Bowes helped with the show and at this time took the name "Major Bowes," although he was not a professional military man. (It was common in radio for performers to assume amusing titles—there were Senators Claghorn and Ford, Judge Hay, and so on—a practice held over from vaudeville.)

After a fight with the American Telephone and Telegraph Company, in 1926 Roxy left the AT&T station in New York (WEAF) and started his own program, "Roxy and His Gang," the first major variety show on radio. In doing so he left Major Bowes in charge of what was then called the "Capitol Family Hour," which was shortly renamed "The Major Bowes Family Hour" and changed again in 1934 to "Major Bowes' Original Amateur Hour." The original format, which featured amateur talent, was a mild success for a number of years, though hardly spectacular in the ratings. But in 1935 it became the object of national notoriety, if not hysteria, when the program began to be broadcast coast-to-coast on the NBC radio network.

Beginning in the summer of 1935 a kind of tidal wave of amateur fever swept the country, and people everywhere wanted to travel to New York to see if they could make it in show business by appearing on the "Amateur Hour." There was a hint in this dark year of the depression that anyone with bus fare and a ukulele might make it big in show business if only they could be introduced by Major Bowes over the airwaves. By 1936 "Major Bowes' Original Amateur Hour" was receiving as many as 10,000 applications a week from aspiring performers. It was the highest-rated program in radio. Winners were selected on the basis of audience response. Between 500 and 700 people were actually auditioned by the show's large staff, but only twenty per week could go on the air. The show caused considerable consternation among officials of New York City, who reported that it acted as a magnet for people from all over the country, drawing 1,500 people to the city in one month alone. Many of these had come to New York hoping to appear on the program, but after failing to get on it they applied to the city for emergency food and shelter.

Bowes himself was now a nationally known figure making $15,000 a week. His program drew country guitar pickers and fiddlers from the South, players of jugs and washboards, pianists, classical singers—sopranos, baritones, tenors—African-American tap dancers, mimes, yodelers, chime ringers, drummers, joke tellers, and down-home comedians. People wheezed and wept, shuffled their feet, sang "Dixie," or recited the Lord's Prayer; some probably had talent, but most were downright awful. Part of the show's appeal seemed to be that many contestants *were* awful. This was, after all, an amateur hour.

Major Bowes, a rotund, heavy-jowled old gentleman, seemed kindly and encouraged all kinds of talent. The performers actually selected to go on the air were personally taken out to dinner by Bowes and paid $10 for their performances whatever the final outcome of their acts. This was not an insignificant sum in the depression, when it was possible to buy a good restaurant dinner for $3.50.

A well-known feature of the "Amateur Hour" was the large gong that Bowes used when a performer was not making it with the audience—an element of sadism in the seemingly kind old Major. The striking of the gong meant that the act was over, and the performer had to shuffle away in disgrace. Security guards were on hand for a few who had to be removed kicking and screaming.

Variously, musical themes for the program were "Stand By" and "There's No Business like Show Business." A catch phrase used regularly by Bowes became one of the outstanding features of the show: "The wheel of fortune goes 'round and 'round, and where she stops, nobody knows."

"Major Bowes' Original Amateur Hour" remained on the air until Bowes's death in New York City, but it was much less popular in its last few years. Originally sponsored by Chase and Sanborn Coffee, the program moved to CBS in 1936 for the Chrysler Corporation. After Bowes's death it was heard on ABC.

It is estimated that some 15,000 people appeared on the program, but very few participants ever made it to stardom. One who did was Frank Sinatra, from Hoboken, New Jersey, who appeared on the program in 1937 as part of a quartet called "The Hoboken Four." Another was Belle Silverman, from Brooklyn, who, as Beverly Sills, became one of the world's great coloratura sopranos.

While the "original" amateur hour died with Major Bowes in 1946, the program was revived two years later by Ted Mack, who had assisted Bowes in the original show. Mack also moved the show to television, where the imaginary "wheel of fortune" was made visual; but never again did the talent-show concept flourish as it did in the middle of the depression, when people actually sold their homes and cashed in their bank accounts to grasp the fleeting and impossible dream of show business success.

• An extensive profile of Bowes is in *Current Biography* (1941). The most detailed accounts of the man and his radio career can be found by consulting show business publications and popular magazines published during the mid-1930s, when Bowes was a national celebrity. See especially *Literary Digest*, Oct. 1935. For an account of "Major Bowes' Original Amateur Hour," see Erik Barnouw, *A History of Broadcasting in the United States* (3 vols., 1966–1970), vol. 2, *The Golden Web, 1933–1953*. See also John Dunning, *Tune in Yesterday: The Ultimate Encyclopedia of Old-Time Radio* (1976). Numerous recordings of the "Amateur Hour" are available. An obituary is in the *New York Times*, 14 June 1946.

GEORGE H. DOUGLAS

BOWIE, Jim (c. 1795–Mar. 1836), popularizer of the bowie knife, speculator, and co-commander of Texan forces at the Alamo, was the son of Rezin Bowie and Elvy Jones; his formal given name was James. Bowie's birthday and his mother's name are the subject of dispute. Some sources claim that he was born in 1795, while others believe the correct year was 1796; some claim that his mother's name was Alvina, perhaps shortened to Elvy, and that the reading of her name as "Jones" from Spanish documents is an erroneous extrapolation from markings that could have been intended as "Jane." Similarly, some sources state that Bowie was born in Burke County, Georgia, while others opt for Elliot Springs, Tennessee. J. Frank Dobie claimed that Bowie was born in Logan County, Kentucky, in 1796. What most biographers agree upon is this: Rezin Bowie married Alvina (Elvy) in Georgia in 1782, lived for a while in Tennessee and then in Kentucky and Missouri, and finally moved to Rapides Parish, Louisiana, in 1802. The greatest likelihood is that Jim Bowie was born in Tennessee.

After moving with his family to the Bayou Boeuf area in Rapides Parish, Bowie grew up in extremely rural conditions. He participated in such family businesses as farming and logging. Early displaying a spirit of adventure, Bowie was associated with Dr. James Long of Natchez, Mississippi, in the latter's filibustering expedition into Texas in 1819 in protest of the Adams-Onís Treaty by which the United States ceded claims to lands west of the Sabine River. Long tried unsuccessfully to establish an American presence in Texas, and eventually was killed in the attempt.

After participating in the early phases of Long's activities in Texas, Bowie and his brother, Rezin P. Bowie, speculated in Texas land and engaged in a scheme to evade the U.S. prohibition of importing slaves by smuggling them through Texas into Louisiana. While involved in such illegal and dangerous activities, Bowie accumulated a reputation as a tough, barroom fighter. Among such activities, accounts of which seem heavily tainted with legend, was the Sandbar Duel that occurred near Natchez. Bowie defended himself in this fight with the unique knife that has borne his name ever since. Like other aspects of his life, the origin of the knife is disputed. Some claim that Bowie designed the knife, which features a guard at the base of the handle to prevent the hand from slipping on to the cutting edge, after doing just that in a fight with a butcher knife. More authoritative sources claim that the knife was designed by Rezin P. Bowie and given to the man who made it famous in various fights. The knife, which is fashioned somewhat like a butcher knife, has a curved blade near the point, a heavier handle and thicker portion above the cutting edge, and a fine balance. Whether as inventor or popularizer or both, Bowie and his knife are linked in both history and legend. It became a favored weapon of many frontiersmen and was also known as an "Arkansas toothpick."

Bowie returned to Texas to live in 1828, as evidenced by his baptism into the Roman Catholic church, a requirement for permanent residence. He spent time searching for a legendary lost mine in the San Saba River area, now known as the Lost Bowie Mine. It probably never existed. Bowie married Ursala Maria de Veramendi, daughter of Vice Governor Juan Martín de Veramendi, in April 1831 and, after a wedding trip to New Orleans, returned to Texas and to speculation in land. With his fortunes increased by marriage, he soon possessed vast holdings, although some charge he did so by persuading Mexicans to apply for land he could not have obtained as an Anglo American and then purchasing it from them.

In the political unrest between states' righters and centralists that developed in Mexican Texas early in the 1830s, Bowie sided with the states' righters. He participated in the battle of Nacogdoches in August 1832, one of the Disturbances of 1832 that began the process of revolution in Texas. Bowie was among those who escorted Colonel José de las Piedras, the defeated Mexican commander at Nacogdoches, to San Antonio to be turned over to the central authorities. He briefly served among Texas Rangers fighting Native Americans but returned to Louisiana in 1833 following the death of his wife and children during a cholera epidemic in Monclova, where they had been sent to escape the disease.

Bowie returned to Texas in 1834 and again engaged in land speculation. When strife between Anglo Americans in Texas, supporting the states' rights movement, and centralists erupted again in 1835, Bowie sided immediately with the Texans. He participated in skirmishes leading up to the siege of San Antonio in November 1835, in an action known as the Grass Fight during the siege, and in the storming of the city, 5–10 December. Because of Bowie's reputation as a fighter, several score of volunteers attached themselves to him and would follow no other leader. Bowie and his men were in San Antonio early in 1836 when Mexican president and general Antonio López de Santa Anna de Lebron came north to drive all Anglo Americans from Texas. Apparently Bowie and the regular army commander, James C. Neill, got along well enough, but when William Barret Travis replaced Neill, the two disputed command. A part of their difficulty probably lay in their age difference; Bowie, in his early forties, did not wish to be subordinate to the 26-year-old Travis.

Bowie and Travis agreed to an election to determine who would command, and Bowie won handily. Quickly they worked out an arrangement for joint command, Travis of the regulars and Bowie of his volunteers. The relationship was strained by Bowie's releasing all the prisoners in San Antonio's jail during a drunken celebration of his election victory and by sending out agents to parley with Mexican leaders without informing Travis when Santa Anna arrived. Eventually, full command fell upon Travis when Bowie, ill with pneumonia and possibly tuberculosis aggravated with dissipation, was confined to bed. He died there at the hands of Mexican soldiers when the Alamo was stormed.

• Primary sources on Jim Bowie may be found in the Texas State Archives and the Eugene C. Baker Texas History Center, University of Texas, both in Austin.

Much of the literature on Bowie is tinged with folklore and legend. See J. Frank Dobie, "James Bowie," in *Heroes of Texas* (1964), and an unpublished master of arts thesis at the University of Texas by Edward Gay Rohrbough, "James Bowie and the Bowie Knife in Fact and Fancy" (1938). An early biography is Evelyn Brogan, *Jas. Bowie: A Hero of the Alamo* (1922); see also Doris Shannon Garst, *James Bowie and His Famous Knife* (1957); Virgil Baugh, *Rendezvous at the Alamo: Highlights in the Lives of Bowie, Crockett, and Travis* (1970); and Jean Flynn, *Jim Bowie: A Texas Legend* (1980). Finally, there is an article on Bowie in Walter P. Webb, *Handbook of Texas* (1952).

ARCHIE P. MCDONALD

BOWIE, Robert (Mar. 1750–8 Jan. 1818), planter and politician, was born near Nottingham, Prince Georges County, Maryland, the son of William Bowie, a planter and politician, and Margaret Sprigg. He was educated by the Reverend John Eversfield near Nottingham and then by the Reverend Thomas Craddock, the first rector of St. Thomas Parish in Garrison Forest, Baltimore County, Maryland. On the eve of the American Revolution, about 1773, tradition has Bowie eloping with Priscilla Mackall, a daughter of the richest man in Calvert County, James John Mackall. Bowie's father gave them a farm near "Mattaponi," the family plantation where Bowie had been born. They had five children who survived to adulthood.

Both Robert Bowie and his older brother Walter Bowie played prominent roles in the events of 1774 that established the patriots' resistance to British parliamentary legislation. Walter was one of the instigators of Maryland's "tea party," the burning of the *Peggy Stewart* in Annapolis in October. Robert was appointed by a meeting of "freeholders and citizens" in Upper Marlborough (now Upper Marlboro) in November to a countywide committee charged with carrying out the resolutions of the First Continental Congress. Robert Bowie then became more and more involved in military defense. In 1775 he became one of a committee for establishing a company of minutemen in Prince Georges County, and early in the following year he was commissioned a lieutenant in a company of militia formed in Nottingham. In June 1776 he was made a captain in the Second Battalion of the Maryland Flying Artillery, which joined General George Washington in the battles of New York, and he remained in that capacity with the Continental army for the duration of the war.

Peacetime introduced a new cycle into Bowie's life. Returning to his plantation in 1781, he spent the first few years rebuilding it and serving in local offices such as tax collector, sheriff, justice of the peace, and vestryman. In 1785 he reentered public life by serving in the Maryland House of Delegates for six consecutive terms. During the 1790s he was not active in politics but served as a major of the militia as well as a justice on the levy court for Prince Georges County.

However, Bowie identified with the Democratic-Republican party that emerged during the 1790s and was part of the "Republican revolution" of 1800 that swept them into office in the states and the federal government. He was elected a member of the Maryland House of Delegates in 1801 and was reelected in 1802 and 1803. This paved his way into Maryland's governorship on the crest of a reform movement in 1803. The incumbent, John Francis Mercer, was a longtime personal friend of President Thomas Jefferson and had learned his law as Jefferson's pupil in 1779–1780.

However, Mercer was a Virginian in Maryland and associated with the anti-Federalist Republicans rather than with those willing to work within the Constitution of 1789. Because Governor Mercer did not sympathize with demands for eliminating aristocratic controls, such as a long residence and high property qualifications for voting, he seemed more and more out-of-date to Maryland Republicans. The differences were intra-party; Bowie was Teddy Roosevelt to Governor Mercer's William McKinley, and Bowie was more radical within the constitutional framework than the governor.

Elected governor by the Maryland General Assembly in 1803, 1804, and 1805, Bowie continued to fulfill his reputation as a radical Democrat. His administrations supported increasing Baltimore city's representation in the House of Delegates to match its fast-growing population; opening the National Road from Baltimore to Cumberland, Maryland; prohibiting immigration of free blacks into the state; and transferring the state's holding of bank stock from Great Britain. After leaving office at the end of 1806, Bowie returned to his home and served as a justice of the peace and a judge on the Prince Georges Levy Court. He also served as a presidential elector for James Madison in 1808. Following the attack of the HMS *Leopard*, a British naval vessel, on an American ship, the USS *Chesapeake*, in the Chesapeake Bay in July 1807, Bowie openly called for a declaration of war on Britain.

Many Maryland Republicans supported the foreign policies of Jefferson and Madison and followed Madison's drift toward war. They were led by Edward Lloyd, who served as governor from 1809 to 1811 and then as state senator representing the Eastern Shore. Lloyd, in turn, was supported by Western Shore Republicans such as Bowie, who was elected governor again in November 1811. This was only the second time in the history of the state that a former governor who had been out of office for several years was reelected, and it had everything to do with Bowie's reputation as a prowar, anti-British radical Democrat.

It also made for a classic tragedy. The news of Congress's declaration of war against Great Britain on 11 June 1812 so elated the governor that he walked bareheaded through the streets in Annapolis to the state house, where he congratulated everyone. He then called the general assembly into special session and directed it to organize and equip the militia. However, opposition to the war was equally vociferous and was led by Alexander Contee Hanson, editor of the *Federal Republican*, a Federalist newspaper published in Baltimore. Hanson's strong editorial on 20 June 1812 roundly condemned the reasons for going to war and charged the Republicans with irresponsibility. Two evenings later a mob attacked Hanson's premises and destroyed the type, the presses, and even the building. Hanson and his supporters were lodged in the city's jail for protection, but the mob broke in and killed and maimed several of them. Public reaction was instant: meetings were held, and Governor Bowie was urged to order an investigation and punish the murderers. He never did and so was accused of protecting them. In that November's elections the Federalists won control of the state government, both the legislature and the governorship, and retained it throughout the War of 1812 by supporting the war effort. Bowie tried to regain office each year from 1813 through 1816, but his response to Baltimore's riot had ruined his reputation. He died at his home in Nottingham.

• Relevant manuscript collections located at the Maryland Historical Society include the Walter W. Bowie Collection (mss. 86; mainly genealogical); the Oden papers (mss. 178; microfilm no. 505); the Oden, West, Bowie collection (mss. 2380); and the Mrs. Sydney Wetherell Collection (G. 5058). Several Bowie items are in the Maryland State Archives, Hall of Records, and are referenced in Edward C. Papenfuse et al., *Inventory of Maryland State Papers*, vol. 1: *The Era of the American Revolution, 1775–1789* (1977). See also Frank F. White, Jr., *The Governors of Maryland, 1777–1970* (1970), and Papenfuse et al., *A Biographical Dictionary of the Maryland Legislature, 1635–1789* (2 vols., 1979).

GARY L. BROWNE

BOWIE, William (6 May 1872–28 Aug. 1940), geodesist, was born at Grassland, near Annapolis Junction, Maryland, the son of Thomas John Bowie, a government official, and Susanna Hall Anderson. After attending local public schools, Bowie received a general education at St. John's College in Annapolis before embarking on engineering studies, first at Trinity College in Hartford, Connecticut, where he received his B.S. in 1893, and then at Lehigh University, where he received his professional engineering certification (C.E.) two years later. Following a family tradition of public and military service, Bowie spent his professional career with the U.S. Coast and Geodetic Survey. He joined the survey in July 1895, working first as a junior officer and later as a chief of survey parties engaged in triangulation work in the United States, Puerto Rico, and the Philippines. In 1899 he married Elizabeth Taylor Wattles of Alexandria, Virginia; they had one child.

After fourteen years of field surveying experience, Bowie was promoted to the position of inspector of geodetic work and chief of the Computing Section (later the Division of Geodesy); he served in this capacity until his retirement in December 1936. As chief of the Division of Geodesy for nearly thirty years, Bowie's overriding concern was the practice of geodesy—the science of determining the size and shape of the earth, and the distances between points on it. His division was deluged with requests for triangulation and leveling data from mining and petroleum companies laying claims, from state and local governments building roads and bridges, and from the survey's own Division of Charts for its continual updating of bathymetric (depth) data in coastal waters. Bowie strove to accommodate these requests by constantly looking for means to improve the productivity of his division. He introduced the portable steel leveling tower, obviating the need for building a wooden edifice at every station, and was the first director to purchase trucks rather than horses for his crews. Motivating these pragmatic innovations was an overriding professional goal: to complete the primary triangulation network for the United States. A triangulation network is a system of accurately located benchmarks at regular intervals, used as a reference for topographical surveys. The position of each benchmark is located by reference to two adjacent benchmarks—hence forming a triangle. The Coast Survey's network was completed when every point was connected to every other point from New York to California—the geodetic equivalent of the Golden Spike. With this, the country could now be accurately mapped. Bowie accomplished this in the mid-1930s when abundant funds became available through the Works Progress Administration. Unlike many scientific administrators, Bowie saw a use for unskilled laborers and put them to work holding rods and chains across the country. As a result of his initiative, the United States was for the first time connected by a complete network of continuous triangulation.

Bowie was also an able scientist who continued the work on isostasy pioneered by his survey mentor and predecessor, John Hayford. Isostasy is the theory, first proposed in the mid-nineteenth century, that the excess mass represented by surface topographic features is compensated by a mass deficit below, and that the earth's crust therefore floats in hydrostatic equilibrium on a denser substrate. In 1909 Hayford had completed a definitive study using the assumption of isostatic compensation to correct triangulation data and produce an improved value for the figure of the earth. The success of Hayford's study seemed to confirm the theory, but Hayford and Bowie realized that an independent test could be found in variations in the acceleration of gravity: if isostasy applied, local topography would make little contribution to gravity. Bowie thus calculated the predicted value of gravity at more than 100 geodetic stations across the United States, using the assumption of isostatic compensation; the results matched measured values to a very high degree of accuracy. In 1914 the great American geologist G. K. Gilbert wrote, "The success of the hypothesis [of isostasy] in reducing [gravity] anomalies . . . show[s] that isostatic adjustment in the Earth's crust is nearly perfect. Starting with geodetic and topographic data . . . Hayford and Bowie have demonstrated isostasy" ("Interpretation of Anomalies of Gravity," *U.S. Geological Survey Professional Paper* 85-C [1914], pp. 29–37).

From 1912 on Bowie published and lectured widely on the demonstration of isostasy and its geological implications; his lifetime publications numbered nearly 400. He became well known in academic scientific circles and was asked to serve on scores of committees. As a member of the U.S. National Academy of Sciences' Committee on Oceanography in the 1920s, he helped to secure the Rockefeller Foundation funds which endowed the Woods Hole Oceanographic Institution. He also served as the first president of the American Geophysical Union (1920–1922) and in 1939 was awarded its first annual William Bowie Medal, for "unselfish cooperation in research." Bowie's efforts were not restricted, however, to academic circles; he strongly believed that if science were supported by the public purse, the public must understand science, so he produced many popular articles and radio addresses.

A founding member of the International Union of Geodesy and Geophysics, Bowie served as its president (1933–1936) and was personally responsible for a number of international geophysical initiatives. In the late 1920s he organized a visit to the United States by a Dutch geodesist, F. A. Vening Meinesz, to cooperate with the U.S. Navy and the Carnegie Institute of Washington on marine gravity surveys. He was also a driving force behind the Worldwide Longitude Operation, an international project begun in 1914 and reestablished in 1924 to use radio wave time signals to detect continental drift. He died in Washington, D.C.

Bowie's interest in continental drift might seem to imply that he was an early advocate of that theory, but he was not. He believed that the complete and local nature of isostatic equilibrium proved that the major features of the Earth had long since achieved their present configuration, and that the crust was too weak to sustain the requisite stresses. Bowie also argued that Wegener's theory was inconsistent with the Pratt model of isostasy on which he and Hayford had based their work, because the tangential forces required to move continents would necessarily disturb the uniformity of the limiting depth of isostatic compensation. Continental drift implied a different version of isostasy—the "roots of mountains" theory proposed by George Biddell Airy—and given the success he and Hayford had achieved, Bowie concluded that the model they used was correct and Wegener's theory was not. Among scientists interested in crustal dynamics, Bowie's arguments against continental drift appeared to strike a fatal blow; in the 1930s tectonic theories were put forth largely within the framework of Pratt isostasy. Ironically, Hayford had not adopted the Pratt model because of a belief in its physical veracity, but rather, as he wrote, because "it happens to be that one of the reasonable assumptions which lends itself most readily to computation." What began as a simplifying assumption became a theoretical constraint and ultimately a belief about reality. Thus Bowie's opposition to drift provides an example of how success in one area of scientific inquiry can constrain and even impede advance in another.

• Bowie's official papers at the Coast and Geodetic Survey are in its records, U.S. National Archives, and at the National Geodetic Survey, now part of the National Oceanic and Atmospheric Agency, Washington, D.C. Correspondence is in the papers of Charles Schuchert at Yale University Libraries; Bailey Willis at the Huntington Library, San Marino, Calif.; and Harry Wood at the California Institute of Technology. His most important work is "The effect of topography and isostatic compensation upon the intensity of gravity," *U.S. Coast and Geodetic Survey Special Publication* 10, *Geodesy*, and his book, *Isostasy* (1927). Important articles include

"Proposed theory, in harmony with isostasy, to account for major changes in the elevation of the Earth's surface," *Gerlands Beiträge zur Geophysik* 15 (1926): 103–15; and "Possible origins of oceans and continents," *Gerlands Beiträge zur Geophysik* 21 (1929): 178–82. For John Hayford's comment on his choice of the Pratt model, see *The Figure of the Earth and Isostasy from Measurements in the United States* (1909).

Biographical materials include J. A. Fleming, National Academy of Sciences, *Biographical Memoirs* 26 (1951): 61–97; N. H. Heck, "Memorial to William Bowie," Proceedings of the Geological Society of America 40 (1941): 163–66; and W. Heiskanen, "William Bowie as an Isostasist and a Man," *Transactions of the American Geophysical Union* 30 (1949): 629–35. For recent scholarship on gravity, isostasy, and continental drift see Naomi Oreskes, "Weighing the Earth from a Submarine: The Gravity Measuring Cruise of the U.S.S. S-21," *History of Geophysics* 5 (1994): 53–68 and idem, "Gravity Surveys in the 'Permanent' Ocean Basins: An Instrumental Chink in a Theoretical Suit of Armor," in *Oceanography: The Pacific and Beyond*, ed. P. F. Rehbock and K. R. Benson, (1998); and Naomi Oreskes, *The Rejection of Continental Drift* (1998).

NAOMI ORESKES

BOWKER, R. R. (4 Sept. 1848–12 Nov. 1933), editor, publisher, and reformer, was born Richard Rogers Bowker in Salem, Massachusetts, the son of Daniel Rogers Bowker, a manufacturer of barrel machinery, and Theresa Maria Savory. Although Bowker's education began in Salem, the majority of it took place in New York City, where his parents moved in 1857 after the failure of a family business. He attended the College of the City of New York, becoming the editor of *The Collegian*, one of the country's first collegiate publications, and the organizer of a student senate, considered to be the first attempt at student government at an American university.

After graduating with a B.A. in 1868, Bowker became the city editor and, after a year, the literary editor of the newly created *New York Evening Mail*. He remained with that newspaper until 1875, at which time he moved on to the literary department of the *New York Tribune*. During this period Bowker also wrote for the book trade publications of Frederick Leypoldt. He became involved with efforts to organize the book trade and attended the first booksellers' convention held in the United States, in Ohio in 1874.

At this time Bowker began to develop an appreciation for libraries that would continue throughout his entire life. In September 1876 he founded, along with Leypoldt and Melvil Dewey, the *Library Journal*. In that year he also helped to found the American Library Association and, with Leypoldt, began publication of the *American Catalogue*, an index of all books published in the United States, which was lauded for its thoroughness and painstaking detail. A reviewer in the *Critic* wrote, "Few but those who have been engaged in similar labors can have any just appreciation of the amount of toil, of skill, of energy, of careful precision, necessary to the successful completion of such an undertaking." Bowker continued as editor of the *American Catalogue* until 1910. He was also a fellow of the American Library Institute and the first president of the New York Library Club.

Bowker's association with Leypoldt led to his purchase of *Publishers Weekly* in 1879. Bowker had been a regular contributor to this journal since its creation by Leypoldt in 1873, and he took editorial control of it upon Leypoldt's death in 1884. In 1880 Bowker set sail for London to start the British edition of *Harper's Magazine*.

Bowker's interests were not confined to the world of publishing; his career took diverse paths. From 1878 to 1879 he served as a member of the executive committee of the New York Prison Association. In 1879 he was a member of the working committee that drafted the postal code. He was also a strong supporter of tax, civil service, and municipal reform and in 1883 helped secure the enactment of the first New York State civil service reform law. He also founded the Society for Political Education in 1880 for the purpose of increasing the public's knowledge of social and political issues. Under its auspices he wrote *Of Work and Wealth: A Summary of Economics* (1883), *A Primer for Political Education* (1886), *Economics for the People* (1886), and *Electoral Reform* (1889). He also served as the editor of *The Economic Fact-Book and Free-Traders' Guide* (1885) and, with George Iles, of *The Reader's Guide in Economic, Social and Political Science* (1891).

Bowker also left a lasting impression on the course of American politics. He was the leader of the independent Republican movement, also known as the "Mugwump" movement, established in 1879. At the Republican national convention the following year, the Mugwumps were instrumental in preventing President Ulysses S. Grant from receiving a nomination for a third term. In the election of 1884 Bowker publicly endorsed Democratic candidate Grover Cleveland, writing many pamphlets and delivering several addresses on his behalf. By 1896 Bowker had aligned himself with the Gold Standard Democrats; during the campaign he wrote a series of anti-silver articles that appeared in the *New York World*.

In addition, Bowker did a great deal of work in the field of copyright law. An early member of the American Copyright League and later its vice president and acting president, he surveyed authors and publishers with a questionnaire on international copyright. In 1886 he wrote *Copyright: Its Law and Its Literature*, an extensive reference book. The *Critic* hailed it as an "excellent compend . . . at last an intelligible statement of the whole subject, freed from all mystification, sophistry, and special pleading." Bowker's second volume in this area, *Copyright: Its History and Its Law*, was published in 1912.

Bowker was a skilled businessman, serving as the first vice president of the Edison Electric Illuminating Company in Brooklyn from 1890 to 1899. A personal friend of Thomas Edison, he traveled to Paris and Sweden in 1895 to study the operation of the De Laval turbine engines and to bring some engines back for the Edison company. In 1901, upon the inception of the De Laval Steam Turbine Company in New York,

Bowker was named its vice president; after 1918 he became vice chairman of the board of directors. From 1902 to 1931 he was also vice president of the De Laval Separator Company. In 1911 Bowker's interests in publishing and industry were merged when his publishing business was incorporated as the R. R. Bowker Company.

After succeeding in establishing *Harper's* in England, Bowker returned home in 1882, saying, "I was afraid I would lose my Americanism if I remained longer in Europe" (*New York Times*, 13 Nov. 1933). There was never any danger in that, however, because Bowker was that rare breed of American who was truly well versed in most aspects of American culture. His vast knowledge is exemplified by the publication in 1900 of his volume of essays, *The Arts of Life*, followed by the subsequent publication of its specialized parts—*Of Business* (1901), *Of Politics* (1901), *Of Education* (1903), and *Of Religion* (1903). In his later years Bowker found time to complete two volumes of verse, *From the Pen of R.R.B.* (1916) and *From Years That Are Past* (1923). He died in Stockbridge, Massachusetts; he was survived by his wife, Alice Mitchell, whom he had married in 1902. He had no children.

• The New York Public Library prepared a scrapbook of Bowker's manuscripts, correspondence, and other papers as a memorial to him and presented it to the Stockbridge, Mass., Library Association. An informative biographical source is Edward McClung Fleming, *R. R. Bowker: Militant Liberal* (1952). An appreciation of Bowker's life is in *Publishers Weekly* 124 (18 Nov. 1933): 1763–68. The *Library Journal* 58 (1 Dec. 1933): 1001–12 and 63 (1 Apr. 1938): 277 contain memorials. An obituary is in the *New York Times*, 13 Nov. 1933.

FRANCESCO L. NEPA

BOWLEGS, Billy. *See* Billy Bowlegs.

BOWLES, Chester Bliss (5 Apr. 1901–25 May 1986), businessman, politician, and diplomat, was born in Springfield, Massachusetts, the son of Charles Allen Bowles, a paper manufacturer, and Nellie Harris. His grandfather, Samuel Bowles (1826–1878), a man Chester frequently identified as his inspiration and role model, transformed the Springfield *Republican* into one of the more influential daily newspapers in mid-nineteenth-century America. The newspaper remained in family hands during Bowles's youth, although with the death of the independent-minded Samuel Bowles in 1878 it lost its crusading, liberal orientation.

Bowles enjoyed the material advantages bestowed by his family's relative affluence and social connections. He attended two exclusive Connecticut prep schools, Choate and Roxbury, before enrolling, as had his father and brother, at Yale University. In later years, Bowles conceded ruefully that athletic and social activities occupied far more of his attention during his four-year sojourn at Yale than did academic pursuits. Following graduation in 1924, he returned to Springfield and worked for a year at the family newspaper. His hopes for returning the *Republican* to the more progressive outlook of his grandfather's era soon faded, however, and the restless and ambitious Bowles moved to New York, where he found employment in the booming advertising business. In 1925 he married Julia Mayo Fisk. They had two children before divorcing in 1933.

After a brief stint as a copywriter for one of Madison Avenue's top agencies, he founded his own firm, Benton & Bowles, in 1929. Together with his partner, fellow Yale alumnus William Benton, Bowles managed to turn the venture into a stunning success. By the mid-1930s, Benton & Bowles ranked as the nation's sixth largest advertising agency and boasted among its clientele such corporate giants as Procter & Gamble, General Foods, and Bristol Myers. Bowles, who devoted most of his attention to the creative side of the business, pioneered the use of consumer surveys as a tool of market research and helped develop and produce many of the popular radio shows of the 1930s that bore his clients' names.

Bowles left the firm that had made him a multimillionaire shortly after the Japanese attack on Pearl Harbor. An ardent New Dealer whose liberal inclinations were strengthened after his marriage to Dorothy Stebbins in 1934 (with whom he had three children), Bowles found himself increasingly drawn to the idea of public service. Early in 1942 he accepted a request by the governor of Connecticut, where he maintained a residence, to become state director of the newly established Office of Price Administration (OPA). His administrative skills and public relations flair brought Bowles to the attention of President Franklin D. Roosevelt, who appointed him head of the national OPA in November 1943. In that difficult post, the former advertising executive proved unusually adept; not only did he manage to contain inflationary pressures but he built strong public and congressional backing for the fiscal controls that the war necessitated. At war's end, Bowles served briefly as director of the new Office of Economic Stabilization for President Harry S. Truman but resigned from that position in 1946, largely because Congress refused to extend the price controls that he considered essential for continued economic stability.

Bowles then returned to Connecticut, where he launched an abortive bid to secure the Democratic gubernatorial nomination. Two years later, in 1948, he did gain his party's nomination and went on to defeat incumbent Republican governor James C. Shannon by a thin margin in the general election. As governor, Bowles pursued an ambitious liberal agenda that emphasized increased spending for housing, education, and medical care. He also spoke forcefully against racial discrimination, becoming the first governor to establish a State Commission on Civil Rights. His record on those issues, coupled with his efforts to streamline state government, catapulted Bowles once again to national prominence. In 1950, however, he suffered a major political setback, losing his bid for a second term to Republican John Davis Lodge, a staunch conservative who unfairly caricatured Bowles as a radical activist.

Long interested in international affairs, Bowles lobbied Truman for a diplomatic assignment in the wake of his disappointing political loss in Connecticut. Truman obliged, offering Bowles his choice of several ambassadorial posts. Bowles chose India and, after a bruising confirmation battle, became the third American ambassador accredited to that newly independent country. Republican critics feared that Bowles would tug too hard at congressional purse strings in his eagerness to see India achieve its ambitious economic goals.

In fact, they were right. Bowles arrived in India in October 1951 and almost immediately began to press the Truman administration and Congress to provide India with as much as $250 million per year in U.S. economic aid. The energetic new ambassador was convinced that India's economic success was crucial not only to the material advancement of India's impoverished masses, but to the triumph of democracy and capitalism throughout Asia. He feared that without sufficient American support India might gravitate toward communism, creating a political and strategic disaster for the United States comparable to that posed by the collapse of the Chinese nationalist regime in 1949. Bowles used his considerable skills as an advocate and publicist in a valiant but ultimately unsuccessful campaign to sell his program to officials in Washington. In the end, he accomplished much as ambassador—developing a warm rapport with Indian Prime Minister Jawaharlal Nehru, imparting a friendlier tone to Indo-American relations, pioneering a personal, "shirt-sleeves" approach to diplomacy, and helping to secure a modest increase in U.S. economic aid—but he never achieved his broader goal. Bowles's urgent pleas for a massive American financial commitment to India largely fell on deaf ears; he seemed unable to grasp the broader forces that pushed India to the margins of American global interests.

Bowles resigned as U.S. ambassador to India early in 1953, following the election of Dwight D. Eisenhower. He subsequently returned to his sprawling home in Essex, Connecticut, where he spent much of the rest of the decade. Bowles emerged during that time as an outspoken critic of the militaristic orientation of Eisenhower's foreign policy and an equally outspoken advocate of warmer ties with the newly emerging nations of the Third World. With characteristic zeal, he offered an alternative vision of the role the United States should play in foreign affairs in a steady stream of books, articles, newspaper columns, letters, and public speeches. The books he authored during this period included *New Dimensions of Peace* (1955) and *Africa's Challenge to America* (1956).

Bowles recognized, however, that he needed a much wider stage in order to influence the direction of Cold War foreign policy. Consequently, in 1956 he joined the unsuccessful presidential campaign of Adlai Stevenson (1900–1965) as a foreign policy adviser. Two years later, he reentered the fractious world of state politics. After suffering a bitter defeat in his bid to gain the Democratic nomination for the Senate, Bowles managed to win a seat in the House of Representatives from his district in eastern Connecticut. His service on the House Foreign Affairs Committee over the next two years allowed him to lend his voice to those on Capitol Hill calling for a more dynamic approach to the challenge of Third World nationalism.

An early supporter of John F. Kennedy's bid for the presidency in 1960, Bowles became a top foreign policy adviser to the Kennedy campaign. He also served as chair of the Democratic party's platform committee. Many observers—including Bowles himself—assumed that Kennedy would make Bowles his secretary of state. Although deeply disappointed when the post went instead to the more moderate Dean Rusk, Bowles agreed to serve as undersecretary of state. The ambitious, self-assured Bowles was never well suited for playing second fiddle. He and Rusk almost immediately developed a strained working relationship; neither their personal styles nor their policy orientations proved compatible. In November 1961 Kennedy fired Bowles, though as a face-saving measure he appointed him to an ill-defined position as special representative for Asian, African, and Latin American affairs. It gave Bowles ample opportunity to gain more firsthand exposure to the problems of the developing nations, but the job carried virtually no policy influence.

Frustrated in his new role, Bowles jumped at the opportunity to serve once again as U.S. ambassador to India, a prospect Kennedy offered him in mid-1963. Bowles remained at the embassy in New Delhi over the next six years, until his retirement from public life in April 1969. Although lengthier than his first tour of duty in India, Bowles's second tour proved considerably less satisfying. Bowles remained a consistent—and often eloquent—advocate of stronger Indo-American ties, but President Lyndon B. Johnson and his senior national security advisers largely lost interest in India after the Indo-Pakistani war of 1965. They tended, moreover, to disparage Bowles as an uncritical advocate of the Indian perspective on world affairs; one quipped that Bowles saw his role more as India's ambassador to the United States than America's ambassador to India.

Following retirement, Bowles returned to his home in Essex, where he spent the remainder of his years. In 1971 he wrote a memoir covering his public career. Soon thereafter, his declining health imposed severe limitations on his activities. Parkinson's disease, from which he had been suffering since the mid-1960s, made the activism, travel, and writing that Bowles so cherished increasingly difficult. He died in Essex.

Bowles left a significant mark on a number of ordinarily distinct areas of American life, including business, politics, and government service. He will likely be remembered best, however, for his role as a formulator—and critic—of Cold War foreign policy. Bowles dissented from the Eurocentric emphasis that dominated American foreign policy during the first two decades of the Cold War era, insisting that the Third

World and not Europe represented the key challenge for the future. His vision was in many respects one rooted in liberal idealism; Bowles genuinely believed that the United States could and should be a catalytic agent in the creation of a more equitable and democratic world order. At the same time, his vision was conditioned by the reflexive anticommunism that shaped the thinking of so many of his contemporaries. The importance of the Third World for Bowles derived not only from his humanitarian impulses, but also from his conviction that the developing nations could play a critical role in the containment of communist expansion. Even though Bowles's ideas never exerted the impact on U.S. policy priorities that he desired, they nonetheless encapsulated a significant alternative to the military-security strategies actually pursued during the Truman, Eisenhower, Kennedy, and Johnson administrations.

• Bowles's voluminous private papers are housed at Yale University's Sterling Memorial Library. Oral history interviews with Bowles can be found at the John F. Kennedy and Lyndon B. Johnson presidential libraries and at the Columbia University Oral History Project. His own account of his career appeared in 1971 as *Promises to Keep: My Years in Public Life, 1941–1969*. Howard B. Schaffer concentrates on Bowles's contribution to U.S. diplomacy in his study, *Chester Bowles: New Dealer in the Cold War* (1993). Robert J. McMahon emphasizes his significance to Indo-American relations in *The Cold War on the Periphery: The United States, India, and Pakistan* (1994). A front-page obituary is in the *New York Times*, 26 May 1986.

ROBERT J. MCMAHON

BOWLES, Eva Del Vakia (24 Jan. 1875–14 June 1943), secretary for colored work for the Young Women's Christian Association, was born in Albany, Athens County, Ohio, the daughter of John Hawkes Bowles and Mary Jane Porter. Unlike most African Americans born during the American Reconstruction period, Bowles grew up in comfortable circumstances. Her grandfather John R. Bowles served as a chaplain for the all-black Fifty-fifth Massachusetts Infantry and later became the first black teacher hired by the Ohio Public School Fund. Her father was the first black postal clerk in Columbus, Ohio.

Eva Bowles was educated in Columbus at a business college and attended summer courses at Ohio State University. After a short teaching career in Kentucky, North Carolina, and Virginia, she was recruited in 1905 to work in New York City as secretary of the Colored YWCA (later affiliated with the New York City YWCA as the 137th Street branch in Harlem). This position made her the "first employed Negro YWCA Secretary in the country." In 1908 she received training in social work at Columbia University School of Philanthropy.

In 1913, after a brief return to Columbus, where she worked as a caseworker, Bowles returned to New York as secretary of the newly formed Subcommittee for Colored Work of the YWCA national board. The position had been created in recognition of the fast-growing interest in association work among urban black women. Among Bowles's responsibilities was the delicate task of helping the organization accommodate its black membership without jeopardizing the support of whites. At a time when race separation was supported throughout the nation, this was no small task.

At the time of Bowles's appointment, the national board had fourteen local colored affiliates. For the most part, these associations were organized by black club women to provide services similar to those offered by white YWCAs—namely, lodging and club activities for young single women who moved into cities to work. Black women, even though their needs were critical, were routinely excluded from white facilities. Furthermore, although local black and white associations were affiliated with the national board, there was often little communication between the local organizations. Bowles's solution was to create a structure whereby there would be only one YWCA in each city. Because the colored associations were usually smaller and less financially stable, they became branches of the larger, white organization.

Although this arrangement made black women accountable to white women, Bowles insisted that the volunteers and staff of the black branches be responsible for day-to-day operations and for fundraising. In addition, she regularly scheduled skills and leadership training opportunities for black volunteers and staff. Bowles believed that integration was inevitable. She felt that this structure would provide a way for the two races to become accustomed to working together and that black women would have the opportunity to prove their administrative and decision-making abilities.

World War I offered a unique opportunity for the YWCA when the national board was granted $4 million by the U.S. War Department Commission on Training Camp Activities to work with women and girls on the home front. The War Work Council of the YWCA set aside $200,000 for colored work, and Bowles was made secretary in charge of expanding services to black women. Under this mandate, the association was able to open recreation centers, industrial work centers, and fifteen hostess houses (facilities that provided entertainment for soldiers and sometimes lodging for their families) near army installations. By the end of the war, black women were being served in forty-five cities, and associations had over 39,000 black members. Most notable was the use of funds left over from the war effort to build a much-needed association facility in Washington, D.C., to accommodate the city's growing black population. Bowles's accomplishments during the war so impressed former president Theodore Roosevelt (1858–1919) that he designated $4,000 of his Nobel Peace Prize to be dispersed according to her directions.

To accomplish this expansion of work during the war, Bowles sought the support of the network of prominent black club women in the National Association of Colored Women. She later used the influence of this group to press the national board for more equitable representation for black women on local and national committees and boards. This move resulted in significant steps toward more biracial cooperation in student and community associations. Furthermore, black women gained their first representative on the national board in 1924.

After the war, Bowles concentrated on the improvement of race relations within the national association. As secretary of the Council on Colored Work, she increased the number of black staff employed by the national board to nine at headquarters and three in the field. Under her leadership, the board led other organizations in negotiations to hold nationally sponsored conventions and meetings only in cities that would guarantee that all members, regardless of race, could be accommodated. She also worked tirelessly as an advocate of the international work of the association, especially in Africa and the Caribbean. She became disillusioned with the YWCA, however, and resigned in 1932, charging that a recent reorganization would "diminish participation of Negroes in the policy making of the Association" by dispersing black staff in a way that she felt diminished their effectiveness in behalf of the specific needs of black women.

Eva Bowles did not confine her interest in race work to the YWCA. She was an active volunteer in such important organizations as the Urban League, the National Interracial Conference, the American Interracial Peace Committee, the National Association for the Advancement of Colored People, the National League of Women Voters, the Commission of Church and Race Relations of the Federal Council of Churches, and her denominational Episcopalian Women's Interracial Council.

After her resignation from the YWCA, Bowles worked briefly as an executive of the National Colored Merchants Association, sponsored by the National Business League. Then, after returning to her native Ohio, she served for a brief time as acting secretary of the West End branch of the YWCA of Cincinnati. During the 1940 presidential campaign, she became the Harlem organizer for the Wendell Willkie Republican organization. She died in Richmond, Virginia.

• Information on the work of Eva Bowles can be found on microfilm in the national board YWCA archives under Colored Work, Interracial Work, and War Work Council. Bowles's work during World War I is detailed in Jane Olcott, comp., *The Work of Colored Women* (1919). Also held by the national board YWCA archives are Juliet O. Bell and Helen Wilkins, "Interracial Practices in Community YWCAs"; "War Work Bulletins," 6 Dec. 1918 and 28 Dec. 1917; Jane Olcott, "The Growth of Our Colored Work," *Association Monthly*, Nov. 1919, pp. 431–32; and "Eva D. Bowles," *Woman's Press*, July 1932. Also see YWCA national board personnel files and association records, 1914–1931. Articles written by Bowles are "Negro Women and the Y.W.C.A. of the United States," *Women's International Quarterly* 9 (Oct. 1919): 20–25; "The Colored Girls in Our Midst," *Association Monthly*, Dec. 1917; and "The YWCA and Racial Understanding," *Woman's Press*, Sept. 1929, pp. 622 and 624. No full-length biography exists, but Bowles's work is chronicled in Gladys Gilkey Calkins, "The Negro in the Young Women's Christian Association" (M.A. thesis, George Washington Univ., 1960). Obituaries are in *Woman's Press*, Sept. 1943, and the *Norfolk Journal and Guide*, 19 June 1943.

ADRIENNE LASH JONES

BOWLES, Jane (22 Feb. 1917–4 May 1973), playwright and fiction writer, was born in New York City, the only child of Clair Stajer and Sidney Auer, owner of a blouse factory who became an insurance agent in the late 1920s. She grew up in affluent circumstances, and the family moved to Woodmere, Long Island, when she was ten. After her father's death in 1930, she returned to Manhattan with her mother to live in a hotel. A year later, while attending Stoneleigh, she fell from a horse and broke her leg. Tuberculosis developed in her knee, and she spent the next two years at a sanatorium in Leysin, Switzerland. In 1935 an operation was performed to permanently stiffen the knee joint.

Jane Auer became part of the Greenwich Village scene and there met Paul Bowles, a young composer and writer who had studied with both Aaron Copland and Virgil Thomson. Although she and Bowles were homosexual, their friendship and respect for each other's talents grew quickly. They married in February 1938 and went on a honeymoon tour of France and Central America. It was a marriage of convenience, affection, and shared intellectual interests, with each partner pursuing his and her own sexual affairs.

By spring of 1939 the Bowleses were renting a farmhouse on Staten Island, where Jane worked on her second novel—she had finished the first in 1936 but had lost the manuscript. Completed near the end of 1941, *Two Serious Ladies* was not published until 1943. Reviews were mostly discouraging, but the novel has since been recognized as a minor masterpiece of female psychology; complex, often ambivalent relationships between strong women are at the thematic center of all of Bowles's creative work. The mordantly comic eccentricities of the female protagonists, as well as a potent erotic undercurrent, in *Two Serious Ladies* reflect its author's interactions with a difficult world and an uncertain self.

From 1943 to 1946 Bowles spent most of her time apart from her husband, living with Helvetia Perkins, either at the latter's Vermont farm or her Manhattan apartment, and working on a brief puppet play called "A Quarreling Pair." In 1947, while Paul Bowles went to Morocco, she stayed at the Connecticut estate of her friend Libby Holman, the renowned torch singer, and tried to write another novel. She soon joined her husband in Tangier, an international free port. Attracted by its low prices, beautiful beaches, sunny climate, ample drugs, Muslim mysticism, and almost complete sexual freedom, they made it their permanent home.

With the publication of his first novel, *The Sheltering Sky*, in 1949, Paul Bowles's career began a steady ascent, which was in marked contrast to his wife's fading ability to concentrate. She had been diagnosed as having an organic heart problem the year before and was subject to bouts of hysteria and depression. In the late 1940s and early 1950s, aside from a few short stories, most of her diminished creative energy was funneled into *In the Summer House*, a character play dealing with two highly neurotic mothers and their peculiar daughters. Morbid, witty, psychologically acute, it lacked sufficient dramatic tension and reach, closing in February 1954 after less than two months on Broadway. A 1964 revival off-Broadway fared worse, lasting only a couple of weeks.

Despite her various ills, which abetted an ever heavier reliance upon drink and drugs, Bowles was a major player in Tangier's busy social life, equally at home among the rich and famous and the various artists, predominantly gay, such as Tennessee Williams, Francis Bacon, and Allen Ginsberg. Truman Capote, who wrote an admiring introduction to *The Collected Works of Jane Bowles* (1966), affectionately described her personality as a "startling blend of playful-puppy candor and feline sophistication."

Her love life proved less happy, however, as she became embroiled in an extended affair with a Moroccan woman named Cherifa, who manipulated her emotionally. Jealousy was another problem as she came to resent the attention her kindly but almost pathologically detached husband lavished on his various Moroccan protégés. Further, when Morocco secured independence in the late 1950s, after several years of riotous unrest, expatriates found themselves under increasingly hostile scrutiny.

Bowles, who had been trying to write another play, suffered a stroke in 1957 that left her with impaired vision and partially paralyzed on the right side. Haunted by fears of insanity, she also could neither read nor write. After a second seizure and suspecting a brain tumor, her husband took her to London for tests, which proved negative. Her continued mental agitation necessitated a return trip, however, during which she underwent seven electroshock treatments, an experience she called "torture."

Though she slowly began to recover some motor skills, Bowles was wracked by spasms of anxiety and paranoia, which did not prevent her from participating in Tangier's social scene. Her mental and physical deterioration, however, was inexorable, and in 1962 she underwent yet another hernia operation, having had two previous ones. Financial worries added to her woes. By 1966, the year her *Collected Works* appeared in the United States to generally respectful reviews, the English edition of *Two Serious Ladies* (1965) had earned a mere $400. The last seven years of her life encompassed a series of hospital and clinic stays, two more sequences of shock treatments, near total loss of speech and sight, and retreat in 1969 to a sanatorium in Malaga, Spain, where she died.

If not major in size or effect, Bowles's contribution to American literature has been permanent. Her unique fictions and single drama pioneered a sounding of feminine depths at odd angles to the culture's traditional absorption in male themes, illuminating as well many subtle interactions between the sexes.

• The bulk of Jane Bowles's letters are at the Humanities Research Center, University of Texas at Austin, and the Virgil Thomson Archive in the Music Library of Yale University. The most accurate source of biographical information is Millicent Dillon, *A Little Original Sin: The Life and Work of Jane Bowles* (1981); Dillon also edited *Out in the World: Selected Letters of Jane Bowles, 1935–1970* (1985). See also Paul Bowles's autobiography, *Without Stopping* (1972), and Michelle Green, *The Dream at the End of the World: Paul Bowles and the Literary Renegades in Tangier* (1991).

EDWARD BUTSCHER

BOWLES, Samuel (8 June 1797–8 Sept. 1851), journalist, was born in Hartford, Connecticut, the son of Samuel Bowles, a grocer. The family would be considered by today's standards to be middle class. At his father's death in 1813, Bowles inherited little of any value other than a watch and a Bible. He received a primary school education while he worked in the family store. Bowles then apprenticed as a printer. That experience played a major role in shaping the future direction of his life. Many years later he recalled,

> During my apprenticeship I was one of some ten or fifteen who formed an association for the improvement of the mind. I was one of the most zealous and steadfast of the club. . . . We met once a week, led discussions and listened to readings. . . . Here I acquired a taste for reading and mental cultivation. Before this my inclination was almost entirely for social pleasure and for evening carousels. . . . My connection with the debating club I consider an important era in my life. . . . It gave a good direction to my habits strengthening my mind to resist temptation, and led me to prefer mental to sensual pleasure.

In 1819 Bowles became a joint proprietor of the *Hartford Times* with John Francis. Francis apparently put the *Times* into deep debt. Bowles suffered from exhaustion and what was likely pneumonia. When the opportunity came to establish a new newspaper some thirty miles up the Connecticut River in Springfield, Massachusetts, he eagerly accepted. With $400 borrowed for type and press machinery, he founded the *Republican* in 1824. Meanwhile, Bowles had married Huldah Deming of Wethersfield, Connecticut, in 1822. Deming was a descendant of Miles Standish. The couple had three children, including a son named Samuel, who became an even more famous editor of the same paper.

In the *Republican*'s early years all the tasks normally associated with newspaper production fell on Bowles's shoulders; he was publisher, editor, reporter, compositor, and pressman. The newspaper concentrated on national and international news. The items were gleaned from other newspapers, sometimes unattributed, a common practice of the time. Its first issue, for example, featured a sketch of Lafayette and an article about building a monument to George Washington. Initially, 250 people subscribed at two dollars a year.

Like most other newspapers of the time, it sold weekly and only by subscription for a set term.

Bowles began to have his voice heard on the larger political and social issues of the day. In the mid-1820s he became secretary to the local chapter of the American Colonization Society. He feared Andrew Jackson as a potential "dictator" and strongly opposed his election in 1828. He praised incumbent president John Quincy Adams as both honest and a major contributor to American prosperity. When Jackson was elected, Bowles editorialized vehemently against the "spoils system" and other administration policies. The administration retaliated by switching its publication of "uncalled-for-letters" at the post office to a rival newspaper, significantly cutting into revenues at the *Republican*.

In the 1830s the paper became an ardent supporter of the Whig party. It enlarged while adding additional political coverage. The *Republican* absorbed several rivals, most importantly the *Hampden Journal*. Despite the financial risks, the paper became a daily in 1844, with son Samuel taking over its editorial operation. The senior Bowles remained in charge of the weekly edition. In 1848 the *Republican* took over the *Springfield Gazette*.

Bowles, weary and weakened from a severe gastrointestinal disorder, died in Springfield.

Bowles was a cautious, methodical, and hard-working man. He was reserved and a man of little wit. He was an honest man and, unlike his son Samuel, had no real enemies. A solid newspaper under Bowles's command, the *Republican* would become one of America's finest under the control of his son.

• Little material exists on Samuel Bowles, the man; he left virtually no personal material of any significance. The best source on the newspaper is Richard Hooker, *The Story of an Independent Newspaper* (1924). A biography of his more famous son contains some additional material on the father; see George Merriam, *The Life and Times of Samuel Bowles* (2 vols., 1885).

STEPHEN G. WEISNER

BOWLES, Samuel (9 Feb. 1826–16 Jan. 1878), newspaper editor, was born in Springfield, Massachusetts, the son of Samuel Bowles, the founder of the *Springfield Republican* in 1824, and Huldah Deming. The boy's formal education was modest. He attended the local schools in Springfield, making satisfactory progress in his studies. He was a diligent student, a trifle slow in absorbing material, but he usually retained most of what he learned. He enjoyed school and had a strong desire for a college education. His headmaster offered encouragement, but Bowles's hopes were dashed by his father, who thought college was unnecessary. College would also have been a financial hardship on the family. Throughout his adult life, in the pages of his newspaper, Bowles rationalized his lack of higher education by denigrating its value in the making of a newspaper editor.

In 1844 Bowles convinced his father that the weekly newspaper should also become a daily. Despite his doubts—mostly financial—his father agreed under the condition that Bowles take over its editorial operation. The first edition of the daily was published on 27 March 1844. Bowles threw himself into his work. The result was a nervous breakdown. He went south to recover. During his recuperation he wrote a long series of letters about the region that were published in his newspaper. By the spring of 1845 he was back in western Massachusetts. The *Republican* gained circulation through the late 1840s and was placed on a firm financial foundation. In September 1848 he married Mary Sanford Dwight Schermerhorn, the grandaughter of James S. Dwight, Springfield's leading merchant of the early nineteenth century. The couple had seven children. The death of his father in 1851 increased Bowles's already excessive workload.

Politically Bowles was a staunch Whig. He was antislavery and called for a "new party of freedom" in the mid-1850s to replace the party torn asunder by its "Cotton" and "Conscience" factions. He became a leader of the new Republican party and supported its presidential nominee John Frémont in 1856. He attended the Republican party convention in Chicago in 1860 that nominated Abraham Lincoln. He was enthusiastic: "Lincoln is a man of the most incorruptible integrity—firm as a rock against duplicity, dishonesty, and all dishonorable conduct, public and private." Throughout the course of the Civil War, Bowles and the *Republican* supported most of Lincoln's policy initiatives.

As the Civil War went on, Bowles could look back with immense satisfaction at the progress of his newspaper. Circulation increases were impressive. The combined totals for the daily and weekly exceeded 18,000 readers, several thousand from outside New England.

Bowles was a combative editor. Thin-skinned, he did not take criticism of himself or his paper lightly. No other newspaper of his era embodied more of its editor's heart and soul than did the Republican. Bowles was a perfectionist who rarely admitted error. Not infrequently Bowles would put in twelve- to sixteen-hour workdays. He once worked nonstop for several straight days. Away from his office he still had his mind on the paper. A friend recalled, "Zeal for his business, zeal, burning zeal for his newspaper which was verily to him bone of his bone and flesh of his flesh, ate him up." Bowles suffered chronic health problems all his life. Aside from the aforementioned nervous breakdown, he was often ailing from sciatica, dyspepsia, headaches (probably migraine), and periodic bowel difficulties.

Bowles loved to travel and did so often. A six-month tour in 1862, it was hoped, would "restore his nervous system." Bowles promised his loyal readers an occasional "gossiping personal letter" but also reminded them that this was a "tour for health," so his writing would be limited lest the trip "cheat its purpose."

A 3,000-mile journey west in 1865 resulted in a long series of letters published in the *Republican*. The letters, compiled and slightly revised, turned into a national bestselling book, *Across the Continent* (1865). Bowles's thoughts on the Indians, Mormons, and Chinese, among other groups, tended to reflect the popular prejudices of the day.

Bowles was deeply troubled by the political atmosphere of post–Civil War America. A scathing editorial about robber baron James Fisk landed the fearless editor in jail for a short spell. Fisk had his Tammany Hall henchmen arrest Bowles on a trumped-up charge while he was visiting New York City and dining at the elegant Fifth Avenue Hotel.

In 1872 Bowles was a leader in the Liberal Republican movement that sought to deny Ulysses S. Grant renomination for president. Bowles believed that the Republican party had to be purified of its corrupt elements. He was one of the four members of the "Quadralateral"—along with three other newspaper editors, Murat Halstead of the *Cincinnati Commercial*, Horace White of the *Chicago Tribune*, and Henry Watterson of the *Louisville Courier-Journal*—that tried and failed to nominate Bowles's choice, Charles Francis Adams. Bowles was warned that his anti-Grant posture would hurt newspaper circulation, but he was undeterred.

Bowles spent much of the winter of 1875 preparing for trial. Earlier, the *Republican* had accused railroad builder Willis Phelps of being the "Boss Tweed of Springfield" as well as a "public robber and corrupter." Phelps responded with a $200,000 libel suit. Judge Endicott in the juryless trial agreed with Bowles on most matters and assessed damages against the *Republican* for a token $100. For the second time Bowles became a hero to most of America's newspaper editors as a champion of a free press.

In the latter part of 1876 Bowles's health deteriorated badly. He may have suffered a minor stroke. In December 1877 he suffered a major stroke. A final stroke killed him. He died in Springfield. Among the many mourners was his friend Emily Dickinson, who idolized the editor.

The *Springfield Republican* was one of America's finest newspapers and perhaps the best published in a large town or small city.

• Most of Bowles's personal papers have been destroyed. Those remaining are at Yale University. Bowles's own writing is instructive. His two travel accounts are *Across the Continent: A Summer's Journey to the Rocky Mountains, the Mormons and the Pacific States* (1865) and *The Switzerland of America: Colorado, Its Parks and Mountains* (1868). The standard account, though hagiographic, is *The Life and Times of Samuel Bowles* (2 vols., 1885), by family friend George S. Merriam. For a modern treatment, see Stephen G. Weisner, *Embattled Editor: The Life of Samuel Bowles* (1986). For a history of the newspaper, see Richard Hooker, *The Story of an Independent Newspaper* (1924).

STEPHEN G. WEISNER

BOWMAN, Isaiah (26 Dec. 1878–6 Jan. 1950), geographer, geologist, and educator, was born at Berlin (now Kitchener), Ontario, Canada, the son of Samuel Cressman Bowman and Emily Shantz, farmers. When he was eight weeks old the family moved to a farm near Brown City, Michigan. After attending country schools, Bowman began teaching. At age twenty-one he enrolled in the Ferris Institute, a college preparatory school in Big Rapids, Michigan, where he was influenced by geographer Harlan H. Barrows. In 1900, after a year of intensive study, he entered the Normal School in Ypsilanti, Michigan, where he studied under Mark Jefferson, a disciple of William Morris Davis, a professor of geology, meteorology, and geography at Harvard University. He also became a naturalized U.S. citizen in 1900. After graduating with a B.Sc. in 1902, following Jefferson's advice, Bowman went to Harvard to study with Davis and there earned a B.S. in 1905. In 1903, while at Harvard, Bowman joined the U.S. Geological Survey as a part-time employee, investigating the geology of surface and ground water. This association continued until 1913, during which time he published *Well Drilling Methods* (1911), which became a widely used, practical manual for water-well drillers.

Inspired by Jefferson and guided by Davis, Bowman decided to continue his geographic studies at Yale University. While working toward his doctorate there, he served as an instructor and headed the Yale South American Geographical Expedition in 1907, which led to lifelong interests in marginal societies and Latin America. On earning his Ph.D. in 1909, he was appointed assistant professor of geography at Yale. In May of that year he married Cora Olive Goldthwaite; they had three children.

Bowman taught at Yale from 1909 to 1915. During those years he continued to be active in field research work, serving with the Yale Peruvian expedition of 1911 and the American Geographical Society expedition to the Andes in 1913 and publishing *South America: A Geography Reader* in 1914. While teaching forestry at Yale, Bowman published *Forest Physiography: Physiography of the United States and Principles of Soils in Relation to Forestry* (1911), defining physiographic subdivisions and presaging the definitive work of University of Cincinnati professor Nevin M. Fenneman on the physiographic subdivisions of the United States.

In 1915 Bowman resigned from Yale to become the director of the American Geographical Society. One of his significant achievements was transforming the society's *Bulletin* (founded as a pedagogical journal in 1853) into a national organ of original research and changing its name to the *Geographical Review*. He assembled a major library and map collection and started a project to prepare a 1:1,000,000 scale map of South America. The 107 sheets of this map (completed in 1945) made up the first comprehensive, detailed map of the continent. As chief officer of "the Inquiry," a program organized by Colonel Edward M. House to gather information preparatory to negotiations at the end of World War I, Bowman devoted the resources of the American Geographical Society to the effort producing three truckloads of files and maps that accompanied the U.S. delegation to Versailles.

Appointed to the post of territorial adviser to the American Commission Negotiating the Peace in 1918–1919, Bowman contributed his expertise in locating post–World War I boundary lines in Eastern Europe. In 1921 he published *The New World: Problems in Political Geography*. This work summarized political and social problems in the postwar world and provided (in revisions through 1928) both historical and regional contexts for government policymakers.

From 1919 to 1935 Bowman served on various committees and councils, including the National Research Council, the board of directors of the Council on Foreign Relations, and the Editorial Advisory Board of Foreign Affairs. In 1933, at President Franklin Delano Roosevelt's request, he served as vice chair of the Science Advisory Committee and as a member of a commission of inquiry into national policy in international economic relations. He also spearheaded American Geographical Society support of Arctic and Antarctic exploration. During this period Bowman published *Desert Trails of Atacama* (1924) and, as the culmination of his study of pioneer communities, *The Pioneer Fringe* (1931), which established a "science of settlement," explicating the process by which organized society spreads into unoccupied lands. In 1934 he wrote a report, *Limits of Land Settlement: A Report on Present-day Possibilities*, for the Council on Foreign Relations.

Bowman left the American Geographical Society in 1935 to become president of Johns Hopkins University. His administration effected the university's recovery from the Great Depression by instigating intensive fundraising, strengthening and expanding the graduate program, and establishing balance between teaching and research. He also instituted a Department of Geography, one of the first in the United States, in 1942–1943. In 1936 Bowman published *A Design for Scholarship*, which outlined his conception of the graduate university as an institution for mobilizing societal resources for the public good. During World War II he encouraged military-oriented research at Johns Hopkins. In 1942 he became de facto director of the "M" project, a secret U.S. government program launched by President Roosevelt to plan resettlement of the displaced persons of World War II. After retiring from the presidency of Johns Hopkins in 1948, he was appointed adviser to the Economic Cooperation Administration, the U.S. governmental agency supporting postwar reconstruction. In this capacity he wrote *Reclamation of New Lands for Agriculture* at the request of the secretary general of the United Nations, Trygve Lie. He died in Baltimore, Maryland.

According to his biographer Geoffrey J. Martin, Bowman was the author of thirteen books and more than 200 articles, excluding a swarm of lesser statements and articles, anonymous writing, and unpublished archival reports. He was an early leader in transforming geography from a science of physiography to one concerned with societal and environmental problems. However, his principal contributions were in developing the American Geographical Society and Johns Hopkins University and in bringing the broad principles of geography to bear in governmental policy.

• Bowman's papers are at Johns Hopkins University, the American Geographical Society, and in family archives held by his son Robert G. Bowman. Geoffrey J. Martin, "Isaiah Bowman 1878–1950," *Geographers Bibliographical Studies* 1 (1979): 9–18, is a concise, well-organized biography that includes a thematic bibliography listing fifty titles; Martin, *The Life and Times of Isaiah Bowman* (1980), is a more detailed account that includes a list of 193 of Bowman's publications. Brief memorials are by Henri Baulig in *Annals of Geography* 60 (1951): 48–50; George F. Carter in *Annals of the Association of American Geographers* 40 (1950): 335–50; and A. G. Ogilvie in *Geographical Review* 114 (1950): 226–30. Two more substantial memorials are John K. Wright and George F. Carter, "Isaiah Bowman 1878–1950," National Academy of Sciences, *Biographical Memoirs* 33 (1959): 39–64, which includes a portrait; and Gladys M. Wrigley, "Isaiah Bowman," *Geographical Review* 41 (1950): 7–65. An obituary is in the *New York Times*, 7 Jan. 1950.

RALPH L. LANGENHEIM, JR.

BOWMAN, Lee (28 Dec. 1914–25 Dec. 1979), actor, was born in Cincinnati, Ohio, the son of Lucien Lee and Elizabeth Pringle Brunson. He attended local schools and worked as a radio singer to finance the study of law at the University of Cincinnati. After joining the university's drama group, he decided to quit law school to become an actor. Bowman went to New York to study at the American Academy of Dramatic Arts. His professional stage debut came in a New Hampshire summer stock production of *The Old Lady Shows Her Medals*.

In 1935 the head of Paramount's talent department noticed Bowman's performance in a summer stock production of *Berkeley Square* in Stockbridge, Massachusetts. The major studios were always looking for new talent, and the tall, dark, and handsome Bowman seemed typecast to become a male movie star of the 1930s. When Paramount offered him the customary six-month contract, which the studio could renew at its option for up to seven years, Bowman took off for Hollywood. His screen debut came in the studio's *Internes Can't Take Money* (1937), the first film based on the Dr. Kildaire stories.

When Paramount didn't renew his contract in late 1937, Bowman signed a contract with RKO for two years. He moved to MGM in 1939 and remained there for four years, although MGM loaned him out to other studios. In 1943 he began a contract with Columbia, whose head, the autocratic Harry Cohn, gave him top billing in several films.

Bowman developed into a versatile film actor who could competently play a variety of dramatic, romantic, and comic parts. Appearing in more than fifty feature films, he was cast opposite some of Hollywood's most glamorous actresses of the 1930s and 1940s, although usually as the second male lead. Always well-groomed and suave, with a pencil-thin mustache, he was attractive enough to make a relationship with a beautiful, desirable woman convincing, but not so appealing that her eventual dismissal of him seemed unlikely.

Bowman made a film career out of not getting the girl. In Paramount's *I Met Him in Paris* (1937), starring Claudette Colbert, Melvyn Douglas, and Robert Young, he played Colbert's handsome but somewhat lifeless fiancé, whom she discards for the more dashing Douglas. RKO's *Love Affair* (1939), starring Irene Dunne and Charles Boyer, had Bowman engaged to Dunne, who leaves him for Boyer. And in Columbia's *Tonight and Every Night* (1945), Rita Hayworth played a British music hall singer who declines to marry Bowman, an RAF pilot, despite her love for him; instead she remains at the music hall, singing to the service personnel gathered there. Bowman's own emotional life was more successful. In 1941 he married Helene Rosson, a writer and radio interviewer. They had two children.

His best roles came in two Columbia films of 1944 and a Universal film of 1947. He costarred with Jean Arthur in *Impatient Years*, the film that helped to make her a star, and he appeared in *Cover Girl* with Rita Hayworth and Gene Kelly. Hayworth, a singer, leaves Bowman, a Broadway producer, at the altar and returns to Kelly, a nightclub owner. In Universal's *Smash-Up: The Story of a Woman*, he costarred with Susan Hayward in her first major screen appearance.

By the late 1940s Bowman's film career was clearly in decline. He appeared in only two films in the 1950s, and his last film appearance came in *Youngblood Hawke* (1964). An attempt to revive his stage career resulted in his Broadway debut in 1954 in *The Magic and the Loss*. The play closed after only twenty-seven performances, but Bowman was praised for his work as the heroine's calculating lover.

Although no more stage roles materialized, Bowman was not washed up as an actor. Even while costarring in feature films, he had played dramatic parts on radio. From the late 1930s to the 1950s he performed frequently on "Cavalcade of America," "Theatre Guild on the Air," and "NBC Radio Theatre." In 1948 he costarred with Lucille Ball in the early episodes of "My Favorite Husband," a CBS radio comedy. He played a stuffy, forgetful husband, and she played a zany housewife, a role she would later perfect in the "I Love Lucy" television series.

Bowman found another outlet for his acting talents in the new medium of television. He made frequent and critically successful appearances on the great television drama series of the 1950s and 1960s, "Studio One," "Robert Montgomery Presents," and "Playhouse 90." In addition, he played the title role in "Ellery Queen" (1951–1952), an early detective series, and he was a regular on two panel shows, "What's Going On?" (1954) and "Masquerade Party" (1958–1960). Looking back at his career, Bowman maintained that his finest performance was in the 1955 production of *The Great Gatsby* on "Robert Montgomery Presents."

After a humiliating experience in which he was cut during the rehearsals for an off-Broadway production of *Private Lives* in 1968, he gave up acting. He supported himself thereafter as a consultant to Bethlehem Steel and other large corporations, coaching their executives on how to speak and behave in public. Like Ronald Reagan, George Murphy, and Robert Montgomery, other film stars whose careers were in decline, he became active in the Republican party. In 1969 the Republican Campaign Committee appointed him as their radio-television consultant with the responsibility of teaching Republican politicians camera techniques and public speaking. In 1972 and 1976 he served as master of ceremonies at the Republican national conventions. Bowman died in Brentwood, California.

• Richard Lamparski, *Whatever Became of . . .* , 5th ser. (1974), contains a brief biography. Bowman's film roles are described in Jay Robert Nash and Stanley Ralph Ross, eds., *The Motion Picture Guide* (1985). Obituaries are in the *New York Times*, 28 Dec. 1979, and *Variety*, 2 Jan. 1980.

G. F. GOODWIN

BOWNE, Borden Parker (14 Jan. 1847–1 Apr. 1910), philosopher, theologian, and educator, was born in Atlantic Highlands (formerly Leonardville), New Jersey, the son of Joseph Bowne and Margaret Parker. His father, a farmer and justice of the peace, served also as a local Methodist preacher. His father was a staunch abolitionist, and his mother, a descendent of Quaker stock, despised sham and vanity. Traits of both parents ran deep in their son.

After graduating from the University of the City of New York in 1871 as valedictorian, Bowne joined the New York East Conference of the Methodist church. He was appointed pastor of the Methodist Episcopal church at Whitestone, Long Island, in 1872. But he served there for less than a year before he undertook advanced theological and philosophical studies in Paris, Halle, and Göttingen (1873–1875). His first book, *The Philosophy of Herbert Spencer* (1874), was published while he was still a student at Halle. Less than a full year after his return from Europe, he accepted a position as assistant editor of the magazine *The Independent* and served also as assistant professor of modern languages at his alma mater. Bowne married Kate Morrison in 1875; the couple had no children.

In 1876 Bowne became chairman of the philosophy department at Boston University. Twelve years later he was appointed dean of the graduate school, where he served until his death. Through the writing of seventeen books and 132 scholarly articles, Bowne developed an independent philosophical system that he called Kantianized Berkelianism, transcendental empiricism, and later personalism, a label that stuck.

It is appropriate to label his early philosophical position objective idealism, because it then represented a fusion of Immanuel Kant's viewpoint (including the categories of understanding) with the idealism of George Berkeley. Bowne's perspective was also a transcendental empiricism because he firmly insisted that human experience was not sense-bound, and he rejected any viewpoint that suggested human freedom was an illusion. Such a viewpoint, he held, would undercut the possibility of knowledge itself.

But personalism is the name most appropriate for his mature perspective. For Bowne, God as the creator-person and human beings as created persons, taken together and in their interrelationships, constitute the real. And it is on account of these persons in relationship that morality and religious living are significant. Religion provided support for ethics even as ethics, in its own fashion, expressed religion. Both religion and morality draw their full meaning from personalism. In this view nature as known by persons is an objectified entity that results in part from the interaction of human finite wills and God's will. The world of nature provided by God is sufficiently ordered both to limit and to provide opportunity for human creative endeavors. God provides the basic rational and moral principles by which humans guide their thought and action in the ultimate given order.

A devoted advocate of theistic idealism, Bowne challenged Thomas Huxley and other natural scientists who, he argued, toyed with metaphysics, relentlessly criticized David Strauss, debated with James McCosh, and defended John Henry Newman's radical change of loyalty. Among his favorite critical targets were naive Darwinianism, easygoing utilitarianism, all forms of materialism, and religious fundamentalism and literalism. He was tried for heresy by the Methodist church on charges brought by the Reverend George A. Cooke, a minister from Brandon, Vermont. He was acquitted, and the acquittal was more an indication of the liberal tilt of Methodism than a confirmation of Bowne's orthodoxy. Bowne's accuser was totally inept at understanding the writings of the man he had labeled a heretic.

One of Bowne's most controversial positions was his rejection of scriptural infallibility. He argued that the conditions of the manuscripts, ancient or more recent, along with the diversity of versions, made inerrancy a fiction. To back his claim he challenged literalists to make historical sense of conflicting reports in Chronicles and Kings.

As an educator Bowne was thoughtful and fair toward his students. But he expected a great deal from them as he did from himself. He was impatient with students who were indifferent or lazy, and he showed no mercy toward the pompous and the satisfied ignorant. About a shallow-minded but verbose student, Bowne quipped: "he should be arrested for intellectual indecent exposure." To a student struggling in a circuitous and long-winded fashion for an answer, Bowne commented: "If you proceed in that way, you will wear out a great deal of philosophical shoe leather." To a critic who had obviously not read the book being criticized, Bowne quipped, "He's bald on the inside of his head."

Bowne's importance and influence have been more pervasive than one might initially suppose. In addition to goading many Christians into reflective changes, he was esteemed by the suffragist movement for a pamphlet he wrote defending their cause.

His more enduring influence in the philosophical realm is evident in his defense of the claim that God is a person. This viewpoint he expounds in *The Philosophy of Theism* (1887). Here his negative arguments seem to be especially cogent. If we deny that God is a personal self-active intelligence, then we are implicitly claiming that an irrational power is doing rational work, an unconscious entity is producing consciousness, nonintelligence is bringing about intelligence, necessity is creating freedom, and the nonpurposive is manifesting itself through purpose. One's credulity is stretched far more by such a mechanistic perspective than by the hypothesis of a self-active person or God. Bowne insisted that only a God who was a conscious person could truly care for creation, and especially express love for human beings. And without the possible interaction between the cosmic person and finite human persons, worship loses all its meaning. And if worship has no meaning then religion is certainly vacuous.

Bowne taught many teachers of theology and philosophy and continues to exert wide influence through the journals *The Personalist*, *Idealistic Studies*, and *The Personalist Forum*, a well-known and respected journal. At Boston University his immediate philosophical heirs were Albert C. Knudson and Edgar S. Brightman, both outstanding teachers and scholars. In the latter half of the twentieth century his views were developed, revised, and renewed by Harold DeWolf, Ralph Tyler Flewelling, and Peter Anthony Bertocci. Bowne is correctly esteemed as the founder of American personalism. He died at his home in Brookline, Massachusetts.

• Papers of Bowne are in the archives of Boston University Library, Boston, Mass. Some of Bowne's letters are considered in Warren Steinkraus, "Bowne's Correspondence," *Idealistic Studies* 2 (May 1972): 182–89. Bowne's most important books include *Metaphysics* (1898), *The Theory of Thought and Knowledge* (1897), *Theism* (1902), and *Personalism* (1908). Works about Bowne include F. J. McConnell, *Borden Parker Bowne* (1929), which contains a virtually complete bibliography. For an account of Bowne's heresy trial, see Harmon L. Smith, "Borden Parker Bowne: Heresy at Boston," in *American Religious Heretics, Formal and Informal Trials*, ed. George H. Shriver (1966). A reflection on Bowne's life is in Francis J. McConnell, "Memorial Address—Borden Parker Bowne," *Zion's Herald* 88 (20 Apr. 1910): 491–94. An obituary is in the *New York Times*, 3 Apr. 1910.

JOHN HOWIE

BOWNE, Eliza Southgate (24 Sept. 1783–19 Feb. 1809), letter writer, was born in Scarboro, Maine (near Portland), the daughter of Robert Southgate, a physician, and Mary King, sister of the eminent Federalist politician Rufus King (1755–1827). Eliza attended finishing schools near Boston in her early teens, completing her formal education at Susanna Rowson's academy. She enjoyed a happy relationship with her parents, with whom she "never felt the least restraint . . . which would induce me to stifle my gaiety" (3 July 1800). But she could write more freely to her cousin Moses Porter, a law student. Challenged by correspondence with an educated young man, she examined conventional beliefs about women. These letters, written regularly between March 1801 and July 1802, when Moses suddenly died, reveal a highly intelligent, though undereducated, seventeen- to eighteen-year-old reacting to assumptions that she found to be disparaging as well as restrictive. Unprepared to rebel outright, she characteristically repeats some conventional view—for example, that inherent differences between women and men entail a differential morality and separate spheres—but then she raises trenchant objections to it and finally retreats by disavowing or making light of what she has said.

For example, after agreeing that women should do no more than passively respond to suitors, because the female mind is naturally pliable, she proceeds to argue vigorously against prudentially restricted love for either sex: "The heart which is regulated by mechanical rules" and convenience is "a mere piece of clockwork which always moves right! How far less valuable than that being who has a soul to govern her actions, and though she may not always be coldly prudent, yet she will sometimes be generous and noble" (Fall 1800). In another letter, after accepting the truism that women excel in sprightliness and lively imagination, men in the more valuable qualities of deep thinking, judgment, and strength of character, Eliza moves on to show how education and experience could create this difference "even though nature had not implanted it." In fact, she cites enough evidence to account for the difference without any predisposition from nature: Men's active pursuits require intellectual and moral exertion, neither of which are called for in women's domestic sphere. "Necessity," she asserts, "is the nurse of all the great qualities of the mind." Although she hastens to affirm the wisdom of separate spheres for men and women, she goes on to plead for the right of women to develop their God-given potential, which they cannot do in a restrictive sphere. Eliza closes, however, with playful self-disparagement, claiming to be too feminine to be at home in the realm of argument: "I hate anything that requires order or connection. . . . when I get a subject I am incapable of reasoning upon, I play with it as with a rattle, for what else should I do with it?" (1 June 1801). Nevertheless, she resented Moses's facetious response and begs him not to trifle with her (July 17).

Moses's plan to withdraw into rural retirement prompted Eliza to reiterate her preference for "the active and generous virtues" over "mere negative goodness," and this led her to contrast the opportunities open to men and women. "In the choice of life one ought to consult their own dispositions and inclinations, their own powers and talents," she generalizes; but then she remembers that this choice is only available to men. She writes that she has "often thought what profession I should choose were I a man," and she imagines herself as an eloquent lawyer, admired in public life. Then she checks herself: "I thank Heaven I was *born* a woman. I have now only patiently to wait till some clever fellow shall take a fancy to me and place me in a situation." She explains, no doubt with a sarcastic edge, "We ladies, you know, possess that 'sweet pliability of temper' that disposes us to enjoy any situation" (May 1802).

Believing that she could not hold her own in a debate with her cousin, Eliza questioned the value of her education, even though she had attended one of the best girls' schools available. On her own initiative she had decided to think for herself, only to find that she was not equipped to do so: "I left school with a head full of something, tumbled in without order or connection. I returned home with a determination to put it in more order; I set about the great work of culling the best part to make a few sentiments out of . . . But I soon lost all patience . . . for the greater part of my ideas I was obliged to throw away without knowing where I got them or what I should do with them; what remained I pieced as ingeniously as I could into a few patchwork opinions." Her words present a touching picture of the difficulties of a very bright girl trying to turn herself into a judicious woman without the benefit of learning or mental discipline (May 1801).

Meanwhile, Eliza was moving into society. During a trip to Saratoga Springs with wealthy friends of the family, she met and fell in love with Walter Bowne, a prosperous businessman from New York City. Her letter to her mother shows how a young woman could manipulate contemporary restrictive manners. Although she submits herself wholly to the will of her parents, she assures them that she is "convinced that my happiness is your warmest wish" and that Mr. Bowne is "better calculated to promote my happiness than any person I have yet seen" (9 Sept. 1802). They were married the following spring and settled in New York City, where they had two children. In a 6 June 1803 letter to her sister, Eliza rejoiced over her unalloyed happiness, but not long afterward she became seriously ill, apparently with tuberculosis. She died a few years later in Charleston, South Carolina.

Had Eliza Bowne been a man, she might have been a brilliant lawyer or a statesman like her uncle. As it was, she was an attractive woman who was beloved in private life. Her letters reveal the mind of an intelligent young woman of the early 1800s who questioned the conventional attitudes that limited her while living gracefully within them.

• Eliza Southgate Bowne's letters were copied by her granddaughter and edited by Clarence Cook as *A Girl's Life Eighty Years Ago: Selections from the Letters of Eliza Southgate Bowne* (1887).

KATHARINE M. ROGERS

BOYCE, James Petigru (11 Jan. 1827–28 Dec. 1888), Baptist seminary founder and theologian, was born in Charleston, South Carolina, the son of Ker Boyce, a wealthy banker and merchant, and Amanda Jane Caroline Johnston. His father was among the richest men in the South. Boyce was educated at Charleston College from 1843 to 1845, Brown University from 1845 to 1847, and Princeton Theological Seminary from 1849 to 1851. He married Elizabeth Llewellyn Ficklen in 1858; they had three daughters.

Boyce's teachers deeply impressed him. Francis Wayland, his mentor at Brown, emphasized the importance of the democratic ideal for Baptist education: the secret of Baptist success was that the churches hired ministers to serve their own membership. A less educated church would naturally secure a minister with less training. The ideal Baptist school for ministers, Wayland believed, would have a place for people of different backgrounds. Boyce may have also learned the recitation method of teaching, a method that he followed throughout his career, from Wayland.

Just as Wayland influenced Boyce's pedagogy, Charles Hodge, his favorite Princeton instructor, shaped his theology. Like Hodge, Boyce was a convinced Old School Calvinist, opposed to revisions by Calvinist theologians trying to make the theology more palatable to Americans. In Hodge's class, Boyce read the *Institutio theologiae elencticae*, by Francis Turretin, a seventeenth-century Reformed Scholastic theologian. Later, he used this work as the basic text in his own Latin theology class. Hodge shaped him in other ways. When Boyce published his own *Abstract of Systematic Theology* (1887), he closely followed Hodge's *Systematic Theology* (1871–1872). Hodge's rigorous doctrine of biblical inspiration affirmed the inerrancy of the original autographs of the Bible. This teaching was particularly important for Boyce's own system. Boyce was also deeply influenced by the belief that theology could be presented systematically and logically. His writings reflected an attempt to demonstrate the interconnectedness of Scripture. Boyce believed that he never fulfilled his promise as a theologian. His greatest regret was that his administrative work did not leave him with time to study as much as he liked.

Boyce eventually became known as the "Father of Southern Baptist Theological Seminary." After serving briefly as the pastor of the First Baptist Church of Charleston, Boyce received a call to teach theology at Furman College, Greenville, South Carolina, in 1855. While there, he became a strong advocate of a seminary that would serve the whole of the new Southern Baptist Convention. He believed that such a central school would enable Southern Baptists to forge their own denominational identity apart from Baptists in the North. Boyce hoped that the school would, like the Presbyterian seminary at Columbia, South Carolina, provide a Christian rationale for the southern way of life.

In 1856 Boyce delivered his inaugural address, "Three Changes in Theological Institutions." In this address, Boyce set forth three ideas. First, any Southern Baptist seminary must be open to people with varying degrees of academic preparation. This meant that the seminary needed to find ways to educate students with only a common school training as well as others with Latin and Greek. Second, Boyce argued that the new school needed to lay the foundation for scholarly excellence. Like many American conservatives, Boyce feared that German rationalism might dominate theological study, and he hoped that a new seminary would educate scholars in a different way, though one as rigorous as that followed on the Continent. Third, Boyce believed that a new school should require every faculty member to subscribe to a confession of faith or abstract of principles that set forth the Baptist tenets.

After several years of traveling and fundraising by Boyce, Southern Baptist Theological Seminary opened in 1859 in Greenville on the principles that Boyce had articulated. Boyce was the chair of the faculty and the first professor of theology. Although Boyce had opposed secession, he joined the Confederate army as a chaplain and served for two years. The war's end found the seminary bankrupt. Further, future prospects were poor. Few southerners had money to keep the school going. Nonetheless, Boyce resolved to hold the institution together. Most of his personal fortune went to finance the school.

After struggling with the poverty of the Greenville location, Boyce decided that the solution to the seminary's problems was to move to Louisville, Kentucky, a border state city that had not suffered from the war but had prospered through its role in banking and manufacturing. Yet, Louisville was sufficiently southern to support a school that was conscious of its southern heritage. Despite the depressions of 1869 and 1873, Boyce made contacts with Baptist business people and secured pledges from them. Southern Baptist Theological Seminary opened in Louisville in 1877. While the school had periodic financial problems, the foundation that Boyce laid was sound. Many families that initially supported the school continued to do so over several generations.

Aside from finances, the most serious problem that Boyce faced at Southern Baptist Theological Seminary was the teaching of Crawford Toy. Toy joined the faculty in 1869 as professor of the Old Testament. As time passed, Toy adopted many newer critical methods that were becoming common in both Europe and the North. As controversy mounted around Toy, Boyce and the trustees agreed that Toy had no place at the school. In 1879 Toy resigned. The controversial professor later taught at Harvard.

Boyce exhausted himself teaching and raising money for the seminary. His strong personality and determination, perhaps inspired by his theological commitments, enabled him to keep his school and denomination alive during a financially constrained period in their histories. He was a skillful administrator and fundraiser. Boyce began his career as an apologist for the religion of the Old South and ended it in the midst of one of the South's most successful industrial cities. He died in Pau, France, where he had retreated to find a cure for his gout and general exhaustion.

• The standard biography of Boyce is by his close friend and colleague John A. Broadus, *Memoir of James Petigru Boyce* (1893). Timothy George, ed., *James Petigru Boyce: Selected Writings* (1989), brings together the most important of Boyce's writings. For further information, see George, "James Petigru Boyce," in *Baptist Theologians*, ed. George and David Dockery (1990), pp. 249–66, which includes an extensive bibliography. An obituary is in the *New York Times*, 29 Dec. 1888.

GLENN MILLER

BOYD, Belle (9 May 1844–11 June 1900), Confederate spy, was born in Martinsburg, Virginia (now West Virginia), the daughter of Reed Boyd, a store owner and manager of a farm, and Mary Rebecca Glenn. Both parents were from prominent Virginia families, and young Belle (christened Isabelle) was educated at Mount Washington Female College in Baltimore. When the Civil War broke out, she returned to her home and began raising funds for the Confederate army.

An early incident revealed Boyd's commitment and courage and ironically brought her praise from Federal officers. After Boyd's father left to join Thomas J. "Stonewall" Jackson's infantry, Union troops invaded Martinsburg on 3 July 1861. The next day, Union soldiers forcibly entered the Boyd home and prepared to hoist the Federal flag and remove the Confederate flags in Belle's room and outside the house. Mary Boyd's protests provoked an officer to address her "in language as offensive as it is possible to conceive," as Belle recalled in her 1865 memoir *Belle Boyd in Camp and Prison*. Infuriated, the seventeen-year-old Belle shot and killed the officer, for which she gained the admiration of the Federal command, who said she had "done perfectly right." Becoming something of a celebrity to Confederates and Unionists alike, Belle became acquainted with many young Union officers posted to protect her home, and she passed on to the Confederates information that the Union officers inadvertently revealed to her, thus becoming an unofficial Confederate spy. Boyd gathered information by flirting with Union officers, listening carefully to what they let drop, and by watching troop movements.

Boyd's success in transmitting information won her growing attention from Confederate operatives, and by the autumn of 1861 she had been appointed a courier for Generals P. G. T. Beauregard and Stonewall Jackson. Then, after working briefly as a nurse, she became engaged in the more adventurous activities of blockade-running and smuggling, in which her knowledge of the Shenandoah Valley and skilled horsemanship proved useful.

The inexperience of both Belle and Federal authorities was telling at first: after she failed to use the correct cipher and was caught sending messages to Confederate officers, she was issued only a reprimand. By early 1862, however, after Rose Greenhow's arrest for espionage in Washington, D.C., led to widespread awareness of the potential danger of women spies, Belle's activities attracted greater attention from Federal authorities, and she was arrested for lacking an official travel pass. After being detained for a week at a Baltimore jail, she returned to Virginia, where she visited an aunt who lived in the Shenandoah Valley town of Front Royal, which was under Union occupation.

It was here that Boyd performed the act that won her lasting fame. In the spring of 1862, General Jackson launched an offensive in the Shenandoah Valley to divert the northern army from its operations against Richmond. In her travels, Boyd had gained information she felt could be of use to the advancing Confederates, especially regarding bridges that the Federals planned to destroy in their retreat from Front Royal. If saved, the bridges would hasten the Confederate advance. As Jackson's troops approached the town, Boyd met them in full view of the Union forces to deliver the information. Jackson's advance succeeded to a great extent. The depot building could not be saved, but fires set to the bridges were doused by the Confederate troops.

After Union forces reoccupied Front Royal in the summer of 1862, Boyd was placed under close surveillance. Arrested on the orders of Secretary of War Edwin M. Stanton, she was confined for a month in Washington, D.C.'s, notorious Old Capitol Prison (where Greenhow had also been held) before being released in a prisoner exchange.

Boyd's daring captured the imagination of both armies, and she became famous throughout the North and South. Northern newspapers accused her of impropriety, *Frank Leslie's Illustrated Newspaper* going so far as to dub her "the Secesh Cleopatra" (23 Aug. 1862) and one of the "feminine desperadoes of the Confederacy" (9 Aug. 1862). The *Philadelphia Inquirer* demurred, claiming that although she "passes far the boundary of her sex's modesty," she "has not yet lost the crowning virtue of woman" (12 July 1862).

After residing briefly in Richmond, Belle returned to her native Martinsburg, which had been recaptured by the Confederates in their drive to Gettysburg. When the town fell after the failed offensive, Boyd was again arrested and sent to the Carroll Prison in Washington, D.C., where she remained, growing dangerously ill with typhoid, until her banishment to the South in December 1863.

After her recovery in early 1864, Boyd undertook what would become her final mission for the Confederacy, carrying dispatches to England. The ship on which she was traveling was captured, and after her mission was discovered, she was once again taken prisoner. This time, Federal authorities banished her to Canada, but she soon made her way to England. There in 1865 she married Samuel Wylde Hardinge, Jr., who had taken command of her captured ship and had himself been imprisoned upon his return to the United States for allowing a Confederate on board to escape. Hardinge died shortly thereafter, leaving Boyd and their young child in a tenuous financial situation that prompted her to write *Belle Boyd in Camp and Prison*. Perhaps the most striking aspect of Boyd's memoir is the pains she took to depict herself in conventional gender terms, despite her remarkable exploits. Amply illustrating the class and race assumptions of the elite Confederates of her time, she portrayed herself as a "southern lady" and depicted slaves as naturally subservient, arguing that they preferred "servitude to freedom," having reached only an "adolescent period of existence" (p. 123).

In the years following the war, Boyd launched an acting career in England and the United States. In 1869 she married John Hammond, a wealthy former British officer; they had four children. They divorced in 1884, after which Boyd resumed her acting career. Two months later she married Nathaniel High, an actor seventeen years her junior. Once again financially pressed, she began making appearances on the lecture circuit, in which she described her war experiences. Significantly, she concluded each engagement by calling for a spiritual reunion of North and South.

In later years Boyd's fame continued to draw crowds, leading several enterprising imposters to claim her identity and forcing Boyd to carry her credentials to speaking engagements. She died after suffering a heart attack while on a speaking engagement in Kilbourn, Wisconsin. Above all, her fame did not rest so much on her successful efforts as a spy—she had been too well known for that—as on being a symbol of the South's insouciant courage.

• The primary source of information on Boyd is her provocative 1865 memoir, the 1968 edition of which includes a very informative introduction by Curtis Carroll Davis, particularly concerning Boyd's later years, that also quotes from Boyd's only extant letters. The definitive biography remains Louis A. Sigaud, *Belle Boyd: Confederate Spy* (1944). Sigaud was allowed access to Boyd's few papers, which were held by her daughter, and his notes are held in Blennerhassett Island Historical Park Museum in Parkersburg, W.Va. See also Mary Elizabeth Massey, *Bonnet Brigades* (1966), for a discussion of Boyd in the context of other women spies in the Civil War. The biography by Ruth Scarborough, *Belle Boyd: Siren of the South* (1983), is a popular account but with careful and useful notes.

LYDE CULLEN SIZER

BOYD, Ernest Augustus (28 June 1887–30 Dec. 1946), literary critic, was born in Dublin, Ireland, the son of James Robert Boyd and Rosa Kempston. He was privately educated by a French tutor. As a young man Boyd established himself in the intellectual circles of Dublin, attending salons and events and writing articles on Irish politics and belles-lettres. In 1910 he became a member of the editorial staff of the *Dublin Irish Times*. After a period of study in Switzerland and Germany, Boyd passed the entrance examinations for the British Consular Service in 1913 and was appointed to the consulate in Baltimore, Maryland, where he met editor and critic H. L. Mencken, a kindred spirit who encouraged and assisted Boyd in his career in the United States.

Boyd was posted to Barcelona in 1916 and to Copenhagen in 1919, but he resigned from the Consular Service that year under suspicion of harboring Sinn Fein sympathies. He moved to New York City in 1920. Boyd plunged into the Greenwich Village literary scene, of which he remained a prominent part for the rest of his life. He worked on the editorial staff of the *New York Evening Post* (1920–1922); was the foreign literature reader for the Alfred A. Knopf publishing firm; a play reader for the Theatre Guild; and literary editor of the *Independent* and, later, the *New Freeman*. Beginning in 1924 Boyd was a freelance contributor to such journals as the *Saturday Review of Literature*, *The Dial*, *Bookman*, *Harper's*, and *American Mercury*. One of the founders of the *American Spectator*, Boyd remained an editor until the magazine folded in 1935, at the height of its popularity (the editors explained that they were "too tired" to bring out another issue).

Boyd continued to write on political topics (particularly those relating to Irish affairs) throughout his career, but he was best known as a translator and literary critic. Before settling in the United States he had authored three books on Irish literature: *Ireland's Literary Renaissance* (1916; rev. ed., 1922), *Contemporary Drama of Ireland* (1917), and *Appreciations and Depreciations* (1917). Among his books on non-Irish literary topics are *Portraits: Real and Imaginary*, which contains sketches of contemporary authors (1924); a biography titled *H. L. Mencken* (1925); and *Literary Blasphemies* (1927). As a critic, Boyd was essentially a reviewer who wrote in the caustic Mencken mode, a leading exemplar of the "bad boy" school. He was an acerbic champion of American realists and other "serious" authors against their "philistine" enemies. The introduction he wrote for the Everyman's Library edition of Sherwood Anderson's *Winesburg, Ohio* (1927) exemplifies both his aggressive style and his desire to create a wider public for serious literature in the United States. His erudition was formidable and his reviews widely read, but his prejudices against such writers as John Milton drew accusations of carelessness, if not actual misrepresentation, from the academic community.

Boyd's greatest contributions to American literary life were his translations and critical efforts to introduce recent European writers to the American reader. A cosmopolitan from an early age, Boyd was eventually fluent in twelve modern languages. His translations include the complete works of Guy de Maupassant (18 vols., 1922–1926, with Storm Jameson) and works by Émile Zola, Anatole France, Jean Cocteau, Henri C'eard, the Goncourts, Barbery d'Aureville, and Gustav Wied. Boyd wrote a full-length biography of de Maupassant (1926), and he was a prolific author of introductions and prefaces for translations. His book *Studies from Ten Literatures* (1925) contains brief appreciations of twenty-nine European writers.

Boyd was active in literary society throughout his adult life, and he became something of a New York institution. He was noted for his abilities as a raconteur and conversationalist and for his striking appearance, including his trademark copper-colored beard. His wife, Paris-born Madeline Reynier, whom he married in 1913, pursued a career as a literary agent and included a thinly-disguised account of their early life together in a forgettable novel, *Life Makes Advances* (1939), written after their divorce. They had no children. Boyd died at his New York home.

• Full-length works by Boyd not mentioned in the text include *The Sacred Egoism of Sinn Fein* (author's name given as "Gnatha'i gan larraidh," 1918); *Secret Springs of Dublin Song* (limited ed., 1918); and *The Worked-out Ward, a Sinn Fein Allegory in One Act* (1918). In addition to the authors mentioned above, Boyd translated works by Louis Verneuil, Heinrich Mann, Mariluise Lange, Simon Gantillon, and Lafcadio Hearn. Boyd edited Honoré de Balzac's *Droll Stories* (1928) and *Standish O'Grady: Selected Essays and Passages* (1918?). Articles by Boyd, not counting reviews, number over one hundred, and many of them were later collected in his books. Articles about Boyd may be found in Stanley J. Kunitz and Howard Haycraft, *Twentieth Century American Authors* (1942); in the 1955 supplement to that work; and in Benjamin DeCasseres, "Portraits en Brochette," *Bookman* (July 1931). Obituaries are in the *New York Times*, 31 Dec. 1946, and the *Times* (London), 1 Jan. 1947.

CHARLES H. BRICHFORD

BOYD, James (2 July 1888–25 Feb. 1944), author, was born in Harrisburg, Pennsylvania, the son of John Yeomans Boyd, an industrialist and lay Presbyterian leader, and Eleanor Herr. A frail child of a wealthy family, Boyd attended Hill School, entered Princeton in 1906, and graduated in 1910. He earned a master's degree in English literature from Trinity College, Cambridge (1910–1912).

After a year's teaching at Harrisburg Academy in Pennsylvania, Boyd retired to a family estate in Southern Pines, North Carolina, to recuperate from a mild case of polio. Still in poor health but eager to participate in World War I, he made several attempts to join the military before being accepted, in 1917, as a lieutenant in the U.S. Army Ambulance Service. Boyd married Katharine Lamont late the same year; they had three children. He served in France until his discharge in 1919 and returned to Southern Pines with plans to become a writer.

During the next two years Boyd's short stories were accepted by *Scribner's*, *Century*, and other respected national magazines. His first novel, *Drums*, was published in 1925. It is an attempt to adjust the conventions of the historical novel to realism by having the fictional initiate display motives, thoughts, and emotions of life-like complexity in encounters with large historical figures and events. This story of a young man in the American Revolution sold more than 50,000 copies and was highly praised by both critics and novelists. Maxwell Perkins—editor at Scribner's for Boyd as well as for F. Scott Fitzgerald and then working to sign Ernest Hemingway—wrote Boyd in 1924, "Old authors . . . seldom surprise us. But the young writers may do anything—at least several of them may, and you are certainly one of those several."

Boyd hoped to build on this early success with a second historical novel, *Marching On*, published in 1927. Similar in many ways to *Drums*, this work is about a poor North Carolina farmer in the Civil War. The novel is a serious attempt at realism, but it contains a sentimental love story that is incongruous with the rest of the plot. Although *Marching On* sold about 80,000 copies, critics gave it a lukewarm reception.

Boyd immediately began writing his third novel, *Long Hunt*, which was published three years later in 1930. Like the first two novels, it is set in North Carolina in the past. But *Long Hunt* treats no famous historical figures or events. It is a realistic, psychological study of an ignorant mountain man caught between conflicting desires for commitment and for independence. Sales were below those of *Marching On*, but the critics were enthusiastic.

As usual, Boyd at once began work on his next novel. Poor health—serious sinus disorders—continued to plague him. He divided the next five years between his writing and sinus operations. In 1935 he completed *Roll River*. The author abandoned both the historical context and the North Carolina setting in this most autobiographical of his longer works. It treats four generations of a wealthy family living in a small Pennsylvania town at the turn of the century. The novel is divided into two parts, each about a central character struggling with and finding moral victory over stultifying and sometimes deadly social convention. Critics praised this novel—which now seems Boyd's best—for its artistic excellence. Sales, however, were slow.

Still fighting illness, Boyd completed his fifth and last novel, *Bitter Creek*, in 1939. Its hero leaves a troubled Illinois childhood for Wyoming, where he finally comes to accept the complexity of life: "Let the specks not grieve too hard about their little lives, so lost in darkness under stars. Nothing that happened to them for good or bad was near as big as it might seem." This attempt to write a naturalistic cowboy story was the author's least successful major effort. Some reviewers, however, thought Boyd advanced the western by showing how it could be a vehicle for serious literary comment, not just a form of light entertainment.

Boyd then devoted most of his energy to organizing and leading the Free Company of Players. The purpose of this group was to produce radio drama explaining and affirming American values on the eve of World War II. Boyd recruited many artists for the Free Company, including Maxwell Anderson, Sherwood Anderson, S. N. Behrman, Stephen Vincent Benét, Louis Bromfield, George M. Cohan, Marc Connelly, Paul Green, George Kaufman, Archibald MacLeish, Elmer Rice, William Saroyan, Robert Sherwood, Orson Welles, and Thornton Wilder. This group created and produced eleven radio plays broadcast to large audiences in 1941. Boyd edited a collection of these plays—including his *One More Free Man*—as *The Free Company Presents* (1941).

His health steadily declining, Boyd abandoned fiction for poetry. The poems, traditional in form and diction, were published in journals such as *Harper's* and the *Atlantic Monthly*. Boyd described his poetic efforts to fellow North Carolina writer Paul Green as "unprofitable, but . . . uniquely satisfying."

When the Free Company broadcasts ended in 1941, Boyd bought and edited a country newspaper, the *Southern Pines Pilot*. The *Pilot* was badly equipped and deeply in debt when Boyd acquired it. By investing time, talent, and money, he made this rural newspaper into a journal respected across North Carolina.

After years of failing health, Boyd died from a stroke in Princeton, New Jersey, while participating in a program to help train British officers. He was admired throughout his life not only for his talent but for his energy, friendliness, and wit.

James Boyd enjoyed critical recognition, the respect of other writers, and popularity with readers during his career. He was selected for the National Institute of Arts and Letters and the Society of American Historians. Despite these and other honors, his reputation waned considerably in the years following his death. Boyd's writings have been neglected in student anthologies of American literature. He has attracted little attention from scholars.

• Manuscripts and galleys for all of Boyd's novels, except *Marching On*, as well as manuscripts for many of his poems, stories, and letters are at Princeton University. Those for other letters, several short stories, and various personal papers are at the University of North Carolina at Chapel Hill. Two posthumous volumes of Boyd's work have been published: *Eighteen Poems* (1944), with a foreword by Paul Green, and *Old Pines and Other Stories* (1952). *Princeton University Library Chronicle* 4 (1945): 77–81, contains a bibliography of Boyd's writings. Another bibliography of works by and about Boyd appears in David E. Whisnant, *James Boyd* (1972), a book-length biographical and critical study of the author. Lewis Leary, *Articles on American Literature, 1900–1950* (1954), lists a few essays on Boyd not cited elsewhere. *Editor to Author: The Letters of Maxwell E. Perkins*, ed. John H. Wheelock (1950), contains several interesting letters to and about Boyd. A reminiscence by Struthers Burt is in the *Princeton University Library Chronicle*, Feb. 1945.

ANDREW T. CROSLAND

BOYD, John Parker (21 Dec. 1764–4 Oct. 1830), army officer and soldier of fortune, was born in Newburyport, Massachusetts, the son of James Boyd and Susanna (maiden name unknown). He developed military interests as a boy, and in 1786 he was appointed ensign in a Massachusetts infantry regiment suppressing Shays's Rebellion. Boyd saw little active service—the Massachusetts militia put down the unrest before the regiment was fully organized—and he left the army in 1787, when the additional force was disbanded.

Undaunted, the young adventurer traveled to India in hopes of plying the soldier's trade. Rejecting a commission in the forces of the British East India Company because of the slowness of promotion, Boyd entered the service of native princes allied with the British—first Nizam Ali, Muslim ruler of a principality in the Deccan of south-central India, and later the Hindu Maratha confederation of north-central India. In the Hindu service, Boyd rose to the command of a brigade and fought in the battle of Kharda in 1795, in which the Marathas defeated his former employer. Later he led an independent partisan corps of 2,000 men.

In 1798 Boyd sold his command for 35,000 rupees and returned to the United States. He settled in Boston and lived on his substantial fortune, engaging in foreign trade and speculating in Maine lands. Boyd was a Democratic Republican, and when Congress expanded the army in 1808, the administration of Thomas Jefferson appointed him colonel of the newly formed Fourth Infantry Regiment. During the summer of 1811 the War Department ordered his command to Indiana Territory for service against the Indian confederation led by Tecumseh and his brother Tenskwatawa, the Shawnee Prophet.

On his arrival at the territorial capital of Vincennes, Boyd was appointed second in command to Governor William Henry Harrison, and his regiment formed the disciplined core of Harrison's largely militia army when it marched up the Wabash River against Prophetstown, the Indian stronghold. On the night of 6 November the army encamped two miles from Prophetstown, as Harrison was under orders to disperse the Indians without force if possible. Urged on by the Prophet, the Indians attacked the camp's perimeter shortly before dawn, and in the confused and bloody fighting that ensued, Boyd displayed courage and energetic leadership. The Indians eventually withdrew, and the troops occupied and destroyed their village. Throughout the West, whites proclaimed the battle of Tippecanoe a glorious victory, and Boyd received the thanks of the territorial legislature. In orders and letters to the administration, however, he disparaged the performance of the militia—and implicitly Governor Harrison—and attributed the victory solely to his regulars, thereby generating an acrimonious political and civil-military controversy.

In August 1812, two months after the declaration of war against Great Britain, the James Madison administration promoted Boyd to brigadier general. He commanded the army's eastern district, embracing the coastline of Massachusetts, New Hampshire, and Maine, during the early stages of the conflict. In the spring of 1813 Boyd was ordered to the Niagara frontier, and he led a brigade in the force of Major General Morgan Lewis that on 27 May captured Fort George, a British bastion just across the Niagara River in Upper Canada. When the American offensive stalled in early June, Boyd was left in command of the large Niagara army with orders to initiate no military action. Through the summer he remained at Fort George, where he engaged in defensive skirmishing against the British and their Indian allies.

During the fall of 1813 Boyd commanded a brigade in the army of Major General James Wilkinson, gathered at Sackets Harbor, New York, as the western part of a two-pronged offensive against Montreal. Wilkinson's force—the largest American field army of the war—entered the St. Lawrence River from Lake Ontario in early November and cautiously pushed downstream. It was followed closely by a British "corps of observation" of about 800 regulars and Canadian militia, under Lieutenant Colonel Joseph W. Morrison. On 10 November as the American force prepared to pass the difficult Long Sault Rapids, Wilkinson ordered Boyd with a detachment of 2,000 men to dispose of the menace to his rear. In the battle of Crysler's Farm the following day, Boyd launched assaults against the outnumbered British, but he failed to dislodge Morrison's forces. Running low on ammunition, he eventually withdrew to the main encampment, leaving the British in possession of the field. This reverse, together with the refusal of Brigadier General Wade Hampton to advance on the Lake Champlain frontier, convinced Wilkinson to abandon the offensive and to go into winter quarters.

Boyd was widely criticized for his generalship at Crysler's Farm. Brigadier General Jacob Jennings Brown, one of the army's rising young leaders, threatened to resign rather than serve with him, and Boyd never again exercised an active command. He spent the first half of 1814 on leave in Boston, attending to his financial interests. During the closing stages of the war, he supervised seacoast defense in New York and New Jersey, and he was discharged in the reduction of the army in June 1815. He returned to Boston and resumed his former business activities; shortly before his death, President Andrew Jackson appointed him to a customs post in Boston. Apparently Boyd never married, but his will mentioned a daughter born in 1797 through a union with Housina, a Muslim woman in India, and a son born in 1814 through a union with Marie Rupell. Boyd died in Boston.

As a military leader, Boyd was personally brave, energetic, and capable of inspiring men; in common with many high-ranking War of 1812 officers, however, he lacked the experience and professional knowledge to direct large forces, and some considered him argumentative and vain.

• No collections of Boyd's personal papers are known to exist. Boyd described his services in India in a letter to Henry Knox, 22 Feb. 1799, in the Henry Knox Papers, Massachusetts Historical Society. After the War of 1812 Boyd published a defense of his military leadership, *Documents and Facts, Relative to Military Events during the Late War* (1816). E. Alexander Powell presents a dramatized and fanciful account of his Indian career in *Gentlemen Rovers* (1913). Boyd's army service may be followed in M. Agnes Burton, ed., "Orderly Book of Col. John P. Boyd and Extracts 1811–1812," *Manuscripts from the Burton Historical Collection*, vol. 1, no. 5 (1917), pp. 145–87; Ernest Cruikshank, ed., *The Documentary History of the Campaign upon the Niagara Frontier* (1896–1908; repr. 1971); National Archives, Records of the Adjutant General's Office, RG 94, Letters Received by the Office of the Adjutant General, 1805–1821; and National Archives, Records of the Office of the Secretary of War, RG 107, Letters Received by the Secretary of War, registered ser., 1801–1870. See also John K. Mahon, *The War of 1812* (1972), and other standard military histories of the War of 1812. Information on his personal life may be gleaned from John P. Sprague, "General John Parker Boyd and Judge Henry Orne, the Original Proprietors of the Town of Orneville, Maine," *Sprague's Journal of Maine History* 1 (July 1913): 43–47.

WILLIAM B. SKELTON

BOYD, Julian Parks (3 Nov. 1903–28 May 1980), documentary editor and historian, was born in Converse, South Carolina, the son of Robert J. Boyd, a railroad telegrapher, and Melona Parks. After graduating with a bachelor of arts degree from Duke University in 1925, he earned a master's degree in political science from that institution in 1926 and then spent 1926–1927 as instructor and principal at Alliance High School in North Carolina; in 1927–1928 he did further graduate work at the University of Pennsylvania. In December 1927 he married Grace Wiggins Welch; the couple had one son.

In 1928 Boyd took up a position as editor of *The Susquehannah Company Papers* for the Wyoming Historical and Geological Society at Wilkes-Barre, Pennsylvania. In 1932 he moved to the New York State Historical Association as its director. In 1934 he joined the Historical Society of Pennsylvania as assistant librarian, becoming its librarian in 1935. From 1940 to 1952 he was head librarian at Princeton University, where he had an important part in the design and construction of the Firestone Library, opened in 1948. Appointed professor of history at Princeton in 1952, he received emeritus status as senior research historian in 1972.

Boyd's career as a documentary editor began with his four volumes of *The Susquehannah Company Papers* (1930–1933). He went on to produce editions of *Indian Treaties Printed by Benjamin Franklin, 1736–1762* (1938), and, significantly, *The Declaration of Independence* (1943), in which he showed how the Declaration evolved through a series of drafts and identified the contributions of individuals other than Jefferson. His other major publication of this period, *Anglo-American Union: Joseph Galloway's Plans to Preserve the British Empire* (1941), was a work of traditional historical narrative and analysis.

At the Historical Society of Pennsylvania, Boyd had come to the attention of Fiske Kimball, director of the Philadelphia Museum of Art and the first serious student of Jefferson's architecture. Kimball, an influential member of the federal Thomas Jefferson Bicentennial Commission, helped to secure Boyd's appointment in March 1943 as its historian; on his recommendation Boyd was named editor of *The Papers of Thomas Jefferson*, the new edition approved by the commission in October 1943 on the basis of a feasibility study Boyd had submitted in September. Scholars had long complained that existing editions of Jefferson's writings were incomplete and frequently unreliable; Boyd had little trouble demonstrating the need for a more comprehensive one that, moreover, would break new ground by including incoming as well as outgoing materials.

The edition Boyd planned was to be more than a work for scholars. The 1943 Jefferson bicentennial popularized the image of Jefferson as the embodiment of the nation's ideals, and the edition's role in the global struggle to win hearts and minds had real importance for its supporters. That link between scholarship and politics continued to be significant for the edition during the early decades of the Cold War. A $200,000 grant from the *New York Times* and $15,000 of federal money allowed the project to begin operations under Boyd's direction in 1944; he remained its editor until his death in 1980.

At first, Boyd's elegantly produced volumes appeared in rapid order and to general acclaim. By 1958 the series had reached its fifteenth volume and Jefferson's final months in France. Thereafter it slowed almost to a halt. Only four volumes appeared during the rest of Boyd's tenure as editor, and together they took in less than two years of Jefferson's life (Nov. 1789–Mar. 1791); a fifth (covering Apr.–Aug. 1791) was nearing completion when Boyd died. Boyd had always stressed the importance of annotation, but after 1958 annotation threatened to overwhelm the edition. He now gave priority to creating exhaustive commentaries that would provide definitive interpretations of Jefferson's life and work. Some of his notes in this spirit went on for scores of pages. They could also exhibit a strong animus against Alexander Hamilton, as in a note in volume 17 that accused Hamilton of "duplicity" in his reports on his contacts with British agent George Beckwith. An expanded version of that note appeared separately as *Number 7: Alexander Hamilton's Secret Attempts to Control American Foreign Policy* (1964).

With intervals between the volumes lengthening, criticism, at first muted, then louder, began to surface, much of it attacking the edition's lack of progress and Boyd's ultimately futile attempt to nail down the meaning of the documents he published. Some took a closer look at his editorial methods and found them wanting; for G. Thomas Tanselle, writing in 1978, it was unfortunate that "an edition in such a strategic position of influence is so unsophisticated in its handling of the actual text" ("The Editing of Historical Documens," *Studies in Bibliography* 31 [1978]: 41). Meanwhile, other documentary editions moved ahead, not least because their editors resisted the temptations that ensnared Boyd. By the 1970s "Boyd" had become an example of how not to do things. His successors at *The Papers of Thomas Jefferson* would restore the forward trajectory lost during Boyd's last decades.

Boyd was president of the American Historical Association in 1964 and president of the American Philosophical Society from 1973 to 1976. His explanation of the principles of documentary editing in the introduction to volume one of *The Papers of Thomas Jefferson* (1950) was highly influential; for years American historian-editors were guided by Boyd's practice. From 1951 to 1964 Boyd served on the National Historical Publications Commission and in that capacity worked to foster the documentary editing movement. The example he set in *The Papers of Thomas Jefferson* helped to inspire the many projects to create modern editions of the papers of American statesmen; as historians' tastes changed, new projects brought women and minorities within scope of the documentary editions that have made the record of the American past more readily available to scholars, students, and other interested readers. Boyd died in Princeton.

• A collection of Boyd's papers is in the Princeton University Library. A list of Boyd's works is *Julian P. Boyd: A Bibliographical Record* (1950). *Current Biography* 37 (1976): 58–61 contains the most comprehensive biography. Merrill D. Peterson, *The Jefferson Image in the American Mind* (1960), places Boyd and his edition in the larger context of Jefferson studies. His role in the development of documentary editing is discussed in Mary-Jo Kline, *A Guide to Documentary Editing* (1987). Boyd's views on editing appear in his introduction to vol. 1 of *The Papers of Thomas Jefferson* (1950). See also Noble E. Cunningham, Jr., "The Legacy of Julian Boyd," *South Atlantic Quarterly* 83 (1984): 340–44. An obituary is in the *New York Times*, 29 May 1980.

HERBERT E. SLOAN

BOYD, Linn (22 Nov. 1800–17 Dec. 1859), congressman from Kentucky, was born in Nashville, Tennessee, the son of Abraham Boyd, a farmer (mother's name unknown). A veteran of the revolutionary war, Linn's father had moved to Tennessee from South Carolina, and in 1803 the family settled in Christian County, Kentucky. There Abraham Boyd was one of the U.S. commissioners who assisted Andrew Jackson in securing the cession of 7 million acres of Chickasaw tribal lands west of the Tennessee River in Kentucky and Tennessee. He later served in the Kentucky legislature. Following in his father's footsteps, Boyd was a farmer, a supporter of Jackson, and a state legislator. He began his public life as a sheriff. In 1827 he represented four counties west of the Tennessee River (the "Jackson Purchase") in the Kentucky House of Representatives. From 1828 to 1830 he represented Calloway County and from 1831 to 1832 Trigg County. Boyd had little formal education and was known to his constituents as a farmer of humble origins. In 1832 he married Alice C. Bennett; they had one son before her death in 1845.

In 1833 Boyd ran as a Democrat for Congress in the First District. He was defeated but tried again in 1835 and was successful. To be a Jacksonian in a state dominated by Henry Clay was difficult, and Boyd failed to secure reelection in 1837. Persistent and always ambitious, he was elected to the Twenty-sixth Congress in 1839 by a mere six hundred votes. Nevertheless he would be returned to Congress for seven more consecutive terms, serving from 1839 to 1855. Several times he faced no opposition.

An infrequent debater, Boyd was a faithful adherent to the Democratic program in and out of Congress, and he represented Kentucky in Democratic national conventions. In 1844 Boyd, anticipating Clay's presidential bid, raised the 1825 corrupt bargain charge in a controversial congressional speech. He was an important player in getting resolutions passed in 1845 for the annexation of Texas, and he also favored the annexation of Oregon. As chairman of the Committee on Military Affairs, Boyd ably defended the Mexican War. James K. Polk also relied on him to support the presidential veto of the Rivers and Harbors Bill of 1846.

Loyal service and a moderate reputation led some to consider Boyd as a candidate for Speaker of the House in 1849. He was devoted to protecting southern rights but "insisted that issues be settled on the basis of national—not sectional—principles" (Hamilton, *Prologue to Conflict*, p. 35). He had spurned, for example, John C. Calhoun's "Southern Address." Another southern moderate, Howell Cobb, secured the Speakership, but Boyd became chair of the Committee on Territories. In that position Boyd came to play a key role in the formulation and passage of the Compromise of 1850. He worked closely with his Senate counterpart, Stephen A. Douglas, in designing a Democratic alternative to Clay's compromise, which would allow the residents of the New Mexico and Utah territories to decide the status of slavery there for themselves. In late August 1850 Boyd presented the "little omnibus" that combined bills for the organization of the New Mexico Territory and the resolution of the Texas boundary and bonds controversies. With considerable parliamentary dexterity, he then guided the little omnibus to a successful conclusion in the House, breaking the last legislative logjam in the Congress. The remainder of the famous compromise passed piecemeal shortly thereafter. In 1850 Boyd married Ann L. Rhey Dixon, who was a relative of Vice President Millard Fillmore. They had one son.

In 1851 and again in 1853 Boyd was elected Speaker of the House. He had a reputation for fairness, although historian Roy F. Nichols assessed him as a "harmless" compromiser who established "a dull routine of presiding ponderously and stupidly over the House" (*The Democratic Machine* [1923], p. 91). During the contentious debate on the Kansas-Nebraska Bill in May 1854 Boyd was not seen as much of a factor. In fact, he resisted Senator Douglas's behind-the-scenes attempts to dictate the Speaker's decision so as to terminate the filibuster against the Kansas-Nebraska Bill. Competition over this and the presidential nomination increased Boyd's resentment toward the "Little Giant." For many years Boyd desired to move beyond the House, but an 1847 attempt to be elected U.S. senator failed. He published a campaign biography in 1852 but was not considered seriously for the Democratic presidential nomination. In 1856 Boyd was his state's favorite son candidate for vice president, but fellow Kentuckian John C. Breckinridge was nominated instead. Boyd hoped to use the governorship in 1859 as a stepping-stone to the U.S. Senate, but he received the nomination for lieutenant governor instead. Four months after his decisive election, Boyd died (cause unknown) at his residence in Paducah.

Boyd was a typical Democratic party stalwart in Congress. His strikingly handsome appearance and unpretentious background endeared him to his constituency. According to Lucius Little, "He had begun life under no other auspices than his indomitable will and tireless energy" (*Ben Hardin: His Times and Contemporaries* [1887], p. 252). Although he never achieved the greatness he craved, Boyd was a critical figure during the formulation of the Compromise of 1850 and a respected nationalistic leader during the years of growing sectionalism.

• Boyd's papers are in the University of Kentucky Libraries and the Filson Club, Louisville, Ky. Substantive information can be found in George Western Thompson, *Biographical Sketch of the Hon. Linn Boyd* (1852); Richard H. Collins and Lewis Collins, *Collins' Historical Sketches of Kentucky, History of Kentucky* (1882); Q. Q. Quigley, "Bench and Bar of Southwestern Kentucky," in *The Lawyers and Lawmakers of Kentucky*, ed. H. Levin (1897); and G. Glenn Clift, *Governors of Kentucky, 1792–1942* (1942). Very useful for Boyd's contribution to the Compromise of 1850 are Holman Hamilton, "Kentucky's Linn Boyd and the Dramatic Days of 1850," *Register of the Kentucky Historical Society* 55 (1957): 185–95; and Hamilton, *Prologue to Conflict: The Crisis and Compromise of 1850* (1964). An obituary is in the *New York Times*, 27 Dec. 1859.

M. PHILIP LUCAS

BOYD, Louise Arner (16 Sept. 1887–14 Sept. 1972), Arctic explorer, photographer, and author, was born in San Rafael, California, the daughter of John Franklin Boyd, Sr., and Louise Cook Arner. Boyd was born to one of the wealthiest families in turn-of-the-century San Francisco. Her maternal grandfather, Ira Cook, had built a fortune in the mid-nineteenth century, and her father ran the family gold-mining business and an investment company. Boyd was educated privately, first by governesses, then at Miss Stewart's School in San Rafael and Miss Murrison's in San Francisco. She did not attend college or university and made her social debut in 1907. Throughout the next decade, during which her father trained her to become the financial manager of the family business, Boyd stayed busy with family concerns and community interests, helping care for her invalid brothers and emerging as a leading patron of music, art, and charitable causes in San Rafael and San Francisco. She also became expert at growing prize camellias.

Events in the 1920s propelled her toward a career as an Arctic explorer. Her father's death in 1920 had been preceded by the deaths of her brothers and her mother. Thus Louise Boyd was the sole survivor, unmarried, and heiress to a fortune at age thirty-two. Thereafter she channeled her grief, her money, and her time into travel. In 1924, after several European tours, she took a pleasure cruise that included Spitsbergen, an archipelago in the Arctic Sea between Norway and East Greenland where she fell in love with the Arctic. "Far north," she wrote, "are lands that hold one spellbound. . . . One enters another world where men are insignificant amid the awesome immensity of mountains, fiords, and glaciers" (Olds, p. 234). Boyd organized, financed, and led seven Arctic expeditions between 1926 and 1941. Each expedition had a specific mission and carried the latest scientific equipment.

On the first two voyages, in 1926 and 1928, Boyd developed her expertise as a photographer and expedition leader that earned her a place in the circles of the American Geographical Society. In 1926 she chartered the Norwegian sealer MS *Hobby*, once the flagship of Roald Amundsen's polar expedition, for a voyage that combined sport with science. Boyd and her six-man team hunted polar bears and studied Arctic flora and fauna in Franz Josef Land, the northernmost point of land in the Eastern Hemisphere. More important, the 1926 voyage launched Boyd's career as a photographer. Thereafter, as official photographer for her expeditions, she was not only patroness but part of the scientific team.

In 1928 Boyd was preparing for another voyage when she learned that Roald Amundsen, "Norway's cherished hero of Arctic and Antarctic exploration," had disappeared in his hydroplane *Latham* on a mission to rescue General Umberto Nobile, whose dirigible *Italia* had crashed while trying to fly to the North Pole (Olds, pp. 239, 240). Boyd immediately changed her plans and committed herself to the search for Amundsen. In the course of the search Boyd and the *Hobby* covered 10,000 miles of Arctic seas between 1 July and 22 September. Although Amundsen was never found, Boyd's rescue mission brought her international publicity as a serious explorer who had scrapped her expedition for a noble cause. That year she received high civilian honors from the nations sponsoring the search: she was the first non-Norwegian woman to receive the Knight Cross of St. Olaf, First Class, and France made her a chevalier of the Legion of Honor. The instant fame also brought her to the attention of Scandinavian Arctic experts and notable American scientists such as Isaiah Bowman of the American Geographical Society.

The four expeditions in the 1930s, in the 125-foot oak-ribbed Norwegian sealer *Veslekari*, added significantly to the knowledge of the fiords and sounds of East Greenland. The 1931 expedition was Boyd's first exploration of the Franz Josef and King Oscar fiord regions of East Greenland, which had been surveyed by Denmark but never studied closely. On this voyage she discovered the true end of Ice Fiord, in the Franz Josef region between De Geer and Jaette glaciers. Previous explorers had misjudged the fiord's terminus. The new area was an important glaciological find, as "one of the three principal sources of icebergs in the entire fiord region." The Danes honored her discovery by christening it "Weisboydlund" (Miss Boyd Land) (Olds, p. 246). On the steamer home from that expedition, Bowman and others from the American Geographical Society convinced Boyd to take a multidisciplinary team of experts on subsequent voyages with the society as official sponsor.

The next voyage, in 1933, mapped the inner reaches of Franz Josef Fiord. Photography became Boyd's top priority, and this expedition yielded the first of her three books, *The Fiord Region of East Greenland* (1935), coauthored with the expedition's scientists. It featured 350 of Boyd's photos and several new maps, including the first echo sound map of the floor of Franz Josef Fiord.

Isaiah Bowman now held Boyd's work in such regard that he named her a delegate to represent the American Geographical Society, the American Academy of Sciences, and the U.S. State Department at the 1934 International Geographical Congress in Warsaw, Poland. The trip resulted in a second book, *Polish Countrysides* (1937), featuring her classic photographs of a vanishing culture.

The 1937 and 1938 Arctic voyages were planned as a unit with a dual agenda, one exploratory, the other scientific. Boyd wanted to go as far north into East Greenland as possible and to continue the study of glacial margins begun in 1933. Unfortunately, the 1937 expedition (4 June–27 Sept.) was trapped by ice in Franz Josef Fiord and had to return by a 100-mile detour through King Oscar Fiord and Sona Sound in order to avoid disaster. Nevertheless, Boyd discovered the western peak of an unknown ocean bank between Bear and Jan Mayen islands, later named Louise A. Boyd Bank.

In 1938, aboard the *Veslekari*, Boyd succeeded in reaching the Isle de France, at 77°48″ north latitude, only about 800 miles from the North Pole—the highest latitude reached by an American expedition and the second highest seagoing latitude in history. For "the notable contribution which her expeditions have made to geography and its related sciences," the American Geographical Society awarded her its Cullum Geographic medal in 1938. She was only the second woman in the society's eighty-six years to receive the medal, joining the ranks of such illustrious recipients as Admiral Robert E. Peary and Captain Robert F. Scott.

By the summer of 1940 Boyd was preparing to publish the results of her 1937–1938 voyages. But Hitler had conquered Denmark, making the Danish island of Greenland strategically important. Consequently, she complied with the War Department's request to forestall publication and turn over all of her records and data on Greenland to them for the duration of the war. In 1941 she financed and led an expedition, sponsored by the U.S. Bureau of Standards, to Canadian Arctic waters to gather data on military uses of long-range radio transmission in the Arctic ionosphere. In 1942 and 1943 she served as a civilian consultant to the Military Intelligence Division of the War Department. After the war she published the accounts of the 1937 and 1938 expeditions in her third book, *The Coast of Northeast Greenland* (1948). Between 1943 and 1955, when not exploring, Boyd lived at "Maple Lawn," her San Rafael estate, and hosted lavish social events. She also worked diligently for the arts and for her favorite charity, the Red Cross.

Her final expedition was by air. On 16 June 1955 she and her American crew made exploration history with a flyover of the North Pole. At age seventy-eight she was the first woman to undertake this endeavor, the first in a nonmilitary plane, and the first by privately financed expedition.

Boyd has been called "the only woman to achieve an outstanding position in Arctic exploration" (Olds, p. 234). However, two obstacles frustrated her bid for recognition as a scientist. First, she was a woman in a field dominated by men, some of whom resented her intrusion into their brotherhood. Second, she was an explorer among scientists. The botanist on her 1937 expedition, Henry J. Oosting, described the dilemma from the scientists' standpoint: "We fear she (Boyd) will develop wanderlust when we hope to concentrate all endeavors on one localized area associated with a single glacier" (Oosting diary, 14 July 1937, p. 46). Because Boyd had no professional credentials, some scientists dismissed her as a wealthy socialite simply indulging a hobby. "Louise had absolutely no scientific training or background," wrote her friend and colleague Walter A. Wood. "I think that Louise tried her hardest to become a member of the scientific fraternity. I'm glad she didn't [succeed]. She was a far better advocate of science in her social environment" (Trussell, p. 12). It was as an explorer, photographer, and friend of science that she joined the inner circles of the American Geographical Society in the 1930s. In 1960 she became the first woman named to its executive council. Twelve years later Boyd died in a San Francisco nursing home, without enough money to satisfy her request that her ashes be scattered over the North Pole. Devoted friends flew her remains as far north as funds permitted, scattering them over the Canadian Arctic.

• The following house manuscript material on Louise Boyd: the American Geographical Society in New York; Henry J. Oosting's diary in the Special Collections Library, Duke University, Durham, N.C.; the Marin County Historical Society in San Rafael, Calif.; the Society of Woman Geographers file at the National Archives in Washington, D.C.; the National Archives' Civilian Personnel Records Office in St. Louis; the University of Colorado, Boulder; and the University of Wisconsin-Milwaukee Library. The scant biographical writings on Boyd include a chapter in Mignon Rittenhouse, *Seven Women Explorers* (1964); Margaret Edith Trussell, "Five Western Woman Pioneer Geographers," in *Yearbook of Pacific Coast Geographers* (1987); a meticulously researched essay in Elizabeth Fagg Olds, *Women of the Four Winds* (1985); and a memorial booklet, *Louise Boyd: Science and Society, Marin County Historical Society Magazine* 14, no. 2 (Fall/Winter 1987–1988).

CHERYL FRADETTE JUNK

BOYD, Richard Henry (15 Mar. 1843–23 Aug. 1922), Baptist clergyman, was born in Noxubee County, Mississippi, the son of Indiana, a slave woman. He was born with the name Dick Gray, having been given the surname of his mother's owner. At the death of his mother's owner, he accompanied members of the Gray family who relocated to Washington County in western Texas, where he lived on a plantation until the outbreak of the Civil War. During the war he served his master in the Confederate camps. Having survived his master, he returned to Texas, where he was given responsibility for managing the Gray plantation. After the war he left the plantation and took on several occupations in Texas, including that of a cattleman. Having had no formal education in his early years, it was not until the mid-1860s that he learned to read and write.

In 1867 he changed his name to Richard Henry Boyd, and two years later he enrolled at Bishop College in Marshall, Texas. Although he did not complete his studies, he was ordained a Baptist minister. In 1868 he married Laura Thomas, who died shortly thereafter. In 1871 he married Harriett "Hattie" Albertine Moore. Boyd had at least three daughters and two sons, but it is not known which children came from which marriage.

During the 1870s and 1880s Boyd became a leader of the black Baptist community in Texas. Forming and guiding churches in towns and cities throughout Texas, he aided in organizing the Texas Negro Baptist Convention (TNBC) and became the convention's education secretary.

Boyd's influential role in American religious history is best understood against the background of racial conflict among the major Baptist denominations of the late 1800s. At the 1892 meeting of the TNBC Boyd opposed a plan that would have allowed the northern and predominantly white American Baptist Home Mission Society (ABHMS) to consolidate schools for black freedmen and that would have given oversight of the publication and dissemination of Baptist school literature to the American Baptist Publication Society (ABPS), which declined to publish the writings of black ministers. Some black Baptists viewed Boyd's opposition as escalating the issue of race. Boyd's vision of a publishing house that served black educational needs eventually led him and his supporters to separate from the TNBC in 1893 and to form the General Missionary Baptist Convention (GMBC) with Boyd serving as superintendent for the new convention's missions program.

Resigning his pastorate of Mount Zion Church in San Antonio, Texas, Boyd worked to create a central repository from which to disseminate Sunday school materials to black churches in the GMBC. He achieved this aim by skillfully negotiating with the Southern Baptist Convention's Sunday School Board for the delivery of materials. Boyd's efforts lessened the dependency of black Baptist Sunday schools on the ABPS's literature and distribution network and would eventually decrease the influence of white northern Baptists in the affairs of southern black Baptists. He was criticized by some black Baptists as having diminished the prospect for cooperation and as having undermined the Fortress Monroe Agreement, a cooperative pact between the Southern Baptist Convention and the ABHMS.

Throughout 1895 Boyd strengthened his position. He prompted a convening of Sunday school teachers and superintendents in Grimes County, Texas, where he convinced church officials to direct their requests for Sunday school materials to his newly established repository. He also received the endorsement of the Palestine Baptist Association of Texas and was able to convince many at a Palestine Sunday school convention of the importance of having a black publishing house.

Boyd's influence grew when he represented the Texas delegation from the GMBC at the predominantly black National Baptist Convention, U.S.A. (NBC, U.S.A.) in St. Louis, Missouri, in 1896. His proposal to establish a publishing board capable of producing materials on a national scale for the black Baptist population was initially rejected by supporters of the ABPS and persons within the TNBC who opposed his efforts. However, the TNBC's Home Mission Board, to which Boyd had been elected corresponding secretary, accepted Boyd's idea to establish a committee in charge of printing Sunday school materials. On Boyd's recommendation, the committee was granted board status by the convention and was named the National Baptist Publishing Board (NBPB). Boyd became the new board's corresponding secretary and treasurer.

In October 1896 Boyd resigned his position as the GMBC's superintendent of missions and proceeded to establish the operations of the NBPB in Nashville, Tennessee. By 1897 the board had begun printing Sunday school materials copyrighted in Boyd's name. In 1898 he obtained a state charter and incorporated the NBPB in Tennessee.

Although Boyd resigned his position as corresponding secretary of the NBC, U.S.A.'s Home Mission Board in 1914, his chartering of the NBPB had begun a long-simmering conflict over the control and legal ownership of the publishing board's operations and copyrights that culminated at a meeting of the National Baptist Convention, U.S.A., in Chicago, Illinois, in 1915. The courts of Tennessee ruled in Boyd's favor, the NBC, U.S.A., having failed to support its legal claims over the publishing board. The conflict, however, led Boyd and his supporters to organize an "unincorporated" faction of the National Baptist Convention in 1915, now known as the National Baptist Convention of America (NBCA). In 1916 the NBCA declared that the NBPB was an independent legal entity and hence was not owned or subject to the control of any convention.

From its inception in 1896 to 1922 Boyd served as secretary and treasurer for the NBPB. During Boyd's tenure, the NBPB held annual congresses of Sunday school leaders and teachers beginning in 1905 and by 1909 had established service training for Baptist teachers.

Boyd also became a successful businessman in Nashville. He founded the National Negro Doll Company in 1911 to manufacture dolls with African-American features; helped to establish and was president (1904–1922) of Nashville's One Cent Savings Bank, a savings and loan bank for African-Americans; aided in organizing and became the president in 1906 of the Globe Publishing Company, which produced the *Globe* newspaper primarily for African-American readership; and served as a national vice president of the Negro National Business League. Boyd died in Nashville.

• Boyd's most important pamphlets and books include *What Baptists Believe and Practice* (1890), *Baptist Sunday School Catechism* (1899), *Boyd's National Baptist Pastor's Guide and Parliamentary Rules* (c. 1900), *Ancient and Modern Sunday School Methods* (1909), *The Separate or "Jim Crow" Car Laws or Legislative Enactments of Fourteen Southern States* (c. 1909), and *A Story of the National Baptist Publishing Board: The Why, How, When, Where and by Whom It Was Established* (1915). An extensive listing of his writings is in Edward C. Starr, ed., *A Baptist Bibliography*, vol. 3 (1953). Bobby L. Lovett assesses Boyd's career and considers his impact on the African-American community in *A Black Man's Dream: The First One Hundred Years* (1993). An excellent historical source on the black Baptists is James Melvin Washington, *Frustrated Fellowship: The Black Baptist Quest for Social Power* (1986). See also C. Eric Lincoln and Lawrence H. Mamiya, *The Black Church in the African-American Experience* (1990). An important source on the NBPB and African-American religious education is James D. Tyms, *The Rise of Religious Education among Negro Baptists* (1979). Valuable perspectives on Boyd, the NBPB, and the NBCA are in Leory Fitts, *A History of Black Baptists* (1985), Owen D. Pelt and Ralph Lee Smith, *The Story of the National Baptists* (1960), and William E. Montgomery, *Under Their Own Vine and Fig Tree: The African-American Church in the South, 1865–1900* (1993). An obituary is in the *Nashville Banner*, 24 Aug. 1922.

ZIPPORAH G. GLASS

BOYD, William (5 June 1898–12 Sept. 1972), film actor and producer, was born in either Cambridge or Hendrysburg, Ohio, the son of Charles W. Boyd, a laborer, and Linda Alberta Wilkins. When Boyd was six the family moved to Tulsa, Oklahoma. His father was killed in a work-related accident before Boyd reached the age of thirteen, and the boy was forced to quit school after the sixth grade to earn money for the family.

Boyd worked his way west in 1918 performing itinerant jobs. Like many photogenic young people of the day, on his arrival in California he tried to break into the fledgling Hollywood film industry. Although he had no dramatic training or experience, his good looks and sturdy physique gained him work earning $30 per week as an extra in pioneer director Cecil B. De Mille's *Why Change Your Wife?* (1920). Boyd signed term contracts, first with Famous Players-Lasky at $25 per week and then with Fox Studios, allowing him to work regularly from 1921 until 1925, several times in De Mille productions. In 1921 Boyd married actress Ruth Miller. They had one child, who died before its first birthday. Boyd and Miller divorced in 1926.

A De Mille favorite by 1926, Boyd was cast as the lead in *The Volga Boatman* (1926), in which he costarred with Elinor Fair, whom he married that year. In 1927 he played a featured part in De Mille's biblical extravaganza *The King of Kings*. That same year Boyd and Fair costarred in two other films. The couple had no children and were divorced in 1929.

During the 1920s Boyd appeared in more than three dozen films. Several biographical accounts describe his personal and social life as fast-paced and hedonistic. In 1930 Boyd's career seemed to falter, with none of his four films a major one. He married actress Dorothy Sebastian that same year, a union that was legally dissolved in 1936; they had no children.

Boyd's fortunes revived briefly in 1932 when he signed a contract with Pathé Studios and appeared in four films. Ironically, it was not Boyd's own fast living but rather the indiscretion of a namesake, stage actor William Boyd, that almost destroyed his career. The stage actor Boyd was arrested in a scandalous gambling and liquor incident, and according to several sources Boyd's photograph was mistakenly published in newspapers. Although a retraction was printed, Boyd's reputation was tarred, and his film roles declined in quantity, quality, and prestige. By the mid-1930s he was effectively washed up.

In 1935 actor James Gleason turned down the opportunity to play the cussing, limping, ne'er-do-well title character in a series of low-budget westerns, and Boyd was chosen in his stead. His one condition for accepting was that the part be thoroughly overhauled. Thus he came to star as the two-fisted, teetotaling hero of the first of sixty-six Hopalong Cassidy feature films—the longest-running western series in Hollywood's first century.

Boyd was paid $5,000 per picture, and the Hopalong series streamed forth at the rate of five or six films a year from 1936 through 1943 (a phenomenal ten pictures were made in 1941, and eight in 1943). Directed by veteran, no-nonsense journeymen, each film cost about $10,000 and required ten shooting days. All of the pictures shared the same basic plot and action ingredients: an illegal act perpetrated by bad guys that upsets the solid citizenry, a saloon brawl, a furious chase on horseback, a gun battle among boulders, a man-to-man fistfight, the unmasking of the real villain, and a warm but sexless thank-you from the heroine. Hoppy (as the main character was also called) rarely killed anyone; rather, he shot the guns from opponent's hands. His distinctive touch was his all-black attire. Astride his white horse, Topper, the silver-haired, midnight-clad Boyd stood out from the era's many low-budget western heroes.

Despite their well-worn plots, the quality of the Hopalong Cassidy pictures placed them above the competition. Each Hoppy film used a deliberately slow buildup that led to a vigorous climax. One group of critics observed, "These climaxes were constructed with long panoramic scenes, and . . . creative tension-building editing." The review went on, "The excitement in these sequences was increased by the sudden and appropriate introduction of background music for the first and only time in the film." The entertainment paper *Variety* noted the pictures' "first-rate photography, excellent locations, and unusually good musical backgrounds." From the start, Hoppy always had a sidekick, either an impetuous youngster or comic grizzled cowpokes like Andy Clyde and George "Gabby" Hayes.

Boyd married Grace Bradley in 1937. They had no children. Inspired by his paragon screen role and his wife's example, he changed his habits.

Most (fifty-four) of the Hopalong Cassidy films were produced for Paramount Pictures by Harry "Pop" Sherman, but in 1943 Boyd took over from him. He signed a distribution deal with United Artists that resulted in twelve more Hoppy features. Boyd also showed remarkable foresight in buying the rights to both studios' entire catalogs of Hopalong Cassidy films. The risky investment soon paid off.

By the late 1940s, with television growing daily in popularity, the Hopalong movies were syndicated individually on profitable terms to urban TV stations, becoming a phenomenon of the small screen. In June 1949 the National Broadcasting Company paid Boyd some $250,000 to produce new Hoppy episodes that were seen in thirty-nine cities. Offshoots of the repeatedly shown older movies and the TV program included a weekly radio show on the Mutual network with an estimated 25 million listeners on 496 stations. A Hoppy daily comic strip, distributed by the *Los Angeles Mirror*, appeared in about fifty newspapers, and 15 million copies of Hoppy comic books were sold in 1949 alone. Novelty products abounded, from black cowboy attire to school lunch boxes, earning Boyd handsome royalties. He made scores of personal appearances nationwide and was President Harry S. Truman's guest of honor at "I Am an American Day" in 1950. Boyd also led the Macy's Thanksgiving Day parade along New York's Broadway and founded Hoppy's Troopers—with ideals that echoed the Boy Scouts'—which enrolled millions of members.

At the peak of the national Hopalong Cassidy craze, Boyd was amassing a multimillion-dollar annual income at a time when millionaires were rare. In turn he gave generously to children's charities. He once remarked, "If it weren't for the kids, I'd be a bum today."

Boyd's final big-screen film role, fittingly, was a cameo in De Mille's *The Greatest Show on Earth* (1952). Boyd retired in 1953 and invested in real estate in Palm Desert, California, where he resided. During his last years he suffered from Parkinson's disease and refused to be interviewed or photographed, wanting Hopalong Cassidy—the good guy in black—to be remembered as he had been. Boyd died in South Laguna Beach, California.

• Useful references to the Hopalong Cassidy films and to Boyd's career in films include the *Saturday Evening Post*, 14 June 1947; Ephraim Katz, *Film Encyclopedia*, 2d ed. (1994); Danny Peary, *Cult Movie Stars* (1991); and George N. Fenin and William K. Everson, *The Western: From Silents to Cinerama* (1962). For information on the Hoppy fad on television and radio, see Gary A. Yoggy, "When Television Wore Six-Guns: Cowboy Heroes on TV," in *Shooting Stars: Heroes and Heroines of Western Films*, ed. Archie P. McDonald (1967); Alex McNeil, *Total Television* (1991); and John Dunning, *Tune in Yesterday: The Ultimate Encyclopedia of Old-Time Ra-*

dio, 1925–1976 (1976). The article on Boyd in *Current Biography 1950* is sanitized and hagiographic but is valuable for biographical details not published elsewhere. An obituary is in the *New York Times*, 14 Sept. 1972.

ROBERT MIRANDON

BOYDEN, Uriah Atherton (17 Feb. 1804–17 Oct. 1879), engineer, was born in Foxborough, Massachusetts, the son of Seth Boyden and Susanna Atherton, prominent local farmers. Boyden came from a mechanically inclined family. His father was not only a farmer but also a blacksmith and inventor of a machine to split leather. His older brothers Seth and Alexander were inventors and manufacturers of note, and five of the six Boyden brothers at some point were involved in manufacturing wrought iron.

Little is known of Boyden's youth, save that he worked on his father's farm and received an ordinary education in the local schools. Some sources suggest that he briefly set up a leather-splitting shop in Cambridge, Massachusetts, probably using his father's invention. In 1825 he moved to Newark, New Jersey, where he worked under his eldest brother Seth in a leather and sheepskin bookbinding business.

Around 1828 Boyden returned to Massachusetts. At the time the standard means of entering the engineering profession was as a surveyor's assistant on a canal or railroad project. Boyden secured such a position, working with James Hayward making the first surveys for the Boston and Providence Railroad. He then secured employment with Laommi Baldwin, a prominent early American engineer who was constructing a dry dock for the Charlestown Navy Yard.

In either 1833 or 1837 (accounts differ), Boyden opened an office in Boston as a consulting engineer. In the mid-1830s he worked on the construction of textile mills in Lowell, Massachusetts, and on the Boston and Lowell Railroad. From 1836 to 1838 he oversaw construction of the Nashua and Lowell Railroad. Then, around 1840, Boyden served as an engineer for the Amoskeag Manufacturing Company in Manchester, New Hampshire, a major water-powered textile industry complex.

With his work for Amoskeag, Boyden turned almost entirely to hydraulic engineering. In the early 1840s Boyden became familiar with water turbines based on the designs of the French engineer Benoit Fourneyron. Boyden sensed the advantages these turbines had over conventional vertical wheels, and in 1844 he introduced an improved Fourneyron machine at the Appleton Mills in Lowell. Boyden's turbine developed an efficiency of 78 percent, considerably higher than the vertical breast wheels previously used. The owners subsequently asked Boyden to install three additional turbines. When completed in 1846, they developed 88 percent efficiency.

Boyden achieved these results by making a large number of detailed improvements to the Fourneyron design. His improvements did not depend heavily on theory. Boyden was ignorant of calculus. He laboriously used arithmetic calculations that were only approximations. Instead, he relied heavily on his mechanical skills, patience, and methodical construction procedures. In designing turbines Boyden employed only the best materials, precision manufactured. He paid close attention to the flow of water into, through, and from the turbine, taking care to eliminate any impediment to flow from friction or impulse. For example, in Boyden's turbines water entered via a special cone-shaped flume that gave it a spiral course and smoothed its entrance into the rapidly rotating wheel. Water exited the wheel via a diffuser that enabled the turbine to gain additional power. In addition, Boyden developed an improved gate to regulate flow of water onto the wheel, a low-friction wheel bearing, and methods of joining parts to eliminate internal projections. Boyden's wheels were expensive, but they delivered high performance and long life.

By the 1850s Boyden's turbines had such a high reputation that large textile mills all over New England began turning from the breast wheel. Among those converted was James B. Francis, chief engineer of the Locks and Canals Company in Lowell. Francis closely observed Boyden's early turbines in Lowell and began working with Boyden to design turbines for other Lowell mills. In 1849 Francis persuaded Lowell's proprietors of locks and canals to purchase from Boyden the rights to his improvements and patents. For some years after, Boyden worked loosely with Francis as Francis oversaw the gradual conversion of Lowell's water-powered mills to turbines.

The most significant result of this collaboration was the development of the mixed-flow, or "Francis," turbine, a design that combined the low cost of the inward-flow turbine design pioneered by Samuel Howd with the high efficiency of the Boyden-modified, outward-flow Fourneyron turbine. Boyden's exact role in the emergence of the Francis turbine is unclear, but he was important, even if only in stimulating Francis's work. The Francis turbine was to become the most widely used water turbine in the world.

In 1850 Boyden moved to Boston. He continued his collaboration with Francis and designed an occasional turbine for a manufacturer. But by now he had sufficient wealth to devote time to personal interests, especially pure science. He experimented widely with equipment of his own design, devoting particular attention to the velocity of sound, the velocity of light, and heat. To determine the velocity of sound, for example, he carried out extensive tests using local water company pipes. In 1874 he deposited $1,000 with the Franklin Institute to be awarded to the first North American to determine the velocity of light. He also studied meteorology, chemistry, and metallurgy. But little came of Boyden's scientific work, for he did not publish. In fact, with only a rare exception, he never published.

Boyden was introverted and secretive. He was a vegetarian in an age when few were. He never drank tea, coffee, or alcohol. He never married. He dressed soberly, in Quaker style, and lived in a Boston hotel in the closing decades of his life, even though he could have afforded better quarters. He never joined professional societies; Francis was his only close professional associate.

Boyden died in Boston, bequeathing an estate of around $250,000 to Harvard University for scientific investigations. Harvard used the funds to establish an astronomical observatory in Peru.

• Boyden's papers are at the National Museum of American History, Smithsonian Institution, Washington, D.C. Some additional materials can be found in the Proprietors of Locks and Canals Papers, Baker Library, Harvard University, Cambridge, Mass. Published biographical material on Boyden is scant. Some details of his parentage, early life, and career can be found in Wallace C. Boyden et al., *Thomas Boyden and His Descendants* (1901), *Foxborough's Official Centennial Record* (1879), and in obituaries (see below). Scholarship relating to Boyden's improvements on the turbine is more widely available and includes James B. Francis, *Lowell Hydraulic Experiments* (1855); Arthur T. Safford and Edward Pierce Hamilton, "The American Mixed-flow Turbine and Its Setting," *Transactions of the American Society of Civil Engineers* 85 (1922): 1237–1356; Louis C. Hunter, *A History of Industrial Power in the United States, 1780–1930*, vol. 1: *Waterpower* (1979); Edwin T. Layton, Jr., "Scientific Technology, 1845–1900: The Hydraulic Turbine and the Origins of American Industrial Research," *Technology and Culture* 20 (1979): 64–89; and Layton, "James B. Francis and the Rise of Scientific Technology," in *Technology in America: A History of Individuals and Ideas*, ed. Carroll W. Pursell, Jr. (1981). Obituaries are in the *Boston Evening Transcript*, 17 Oct. 1879, and the *Boston Morning Journal*, 18 Oct. 1879.

TERRY S. REYNOLDS

BOYÉ, Martin Hans (6 Dec. 1812–5 Mar. 1909), chemist and geologist, was born in Copenhagen, Denmark, the son of Mark Boyé, a chemist and superintendent of the Royal Porcelain Manufactory and of a large pharmaceutical firm. His mother's name is not known. In 1831 Boyé was admitted to the University of Copenhagen, where he passed the philological and philosophical examinations with distinction. In 1832 he entered the Polytechnic School in Copenhagen, where he studied analytical chemistry and physics under Hans Christian Ørsted, William Christoffer Zeise, and Johan Georg Forchhammer; he graduated with honors in 1835.

In 1836 Boyé emigrated to New York "to obtain an open field for research along his chosen line," as a close relative expressed it. In 1837 he moved to Philadelphia, where he attended the lectures of and assisted Robert Hare, professor of chemistry at the University of Pennsylvania School of Medicine. In Philadelphia Boyé became acquainted with the distinguished Rogers family, members of which contributed to scientific research in a number of fields. In 1838, under Henry Darwin Rogers, professor of geology and mineralogy at the University of Pennsylvania, Boyé acted as assistant geologist and chemist in the first geological survey of the state. The two toured the anthracite coal region, and Boyé analyzed magnetic iron ore and prepared a geologic map of the region. In 1839 and 1840 Boyé was associated with Henry's brothers, Robert Empie Rogers and James Blythe Rogers, in further analyzing limestone, coal, iron ores, and other rocks and minerals for the survey. He not only developed his ability as a mineral analyst but also discovered a method of separating quantitatively calcium from magnesium by addition of excess dilute sulfuric acid and 40–41 percent aqueous alcohol, which precipitated the calcium. Together with Henry Darwin Rogers, Boyé discovered a new compound of platinum chloride with nitric oxide—"nitrosoplatinic chloride" (modern, nitrosyl hexachloroplatinate(IV)). The report of this discovery to the American Philosophical Society resulted in Boyé's election to membership in that society in January 1840, making him the youngest member in many years.

In April 1840 Boyé was one of about twenty scientists who met in Philadelphia to organize the American Association of Geologists (later the words "and Naturalists" were added to the name), which in 1848 became the American Association for the Advancement of Science. At the time of his death Boyé was the only surviving member of both the original and successor organizations. He was a fellow of the AAAS for 60 years and a member of the Franklin Institute for 72 years. In the summer of 1840, together with John Innes Clark Hare, Robert Hare's son, who was then a chemist but later became a prominent Pennsylvania jurist, Boyé discovered "perchloric ether" (modern, ethyl perchlorate), the most powerful explosive then known (3⅔ times as powerful as gunpowder). It was manageable only with diluted alcohol, and its instability prevented its widespread application. Konrad Friedrich Beilstein, in his *Handbuch der organischen Chemie* (1881–1883), erroneously ascribed this discovery to Henry Enfield Roscoe. Thus Boyé was an unrecognized pioneer in the field of smokeless powder.

By the summer of 1841 Boyé resumed field work, examining the bituminous coal regions. While he preferred chemistry, he was equally skilled in geology and physics. From 1842 to 1844 he attended the course of medical lectures at the University of Pennsylvania. He received his M.D. degree in 1844 with the thesis, "Structure of the Nervous System," but he never practiced medicine. Because most of the lectures and practical work in the medical school occurred after 4 P.M., during the day he joined James Curtis Booth, possibly the first professional consulting chemist in the United States and later president of the American Chemical Society, to form the firm of Booth & Boyé. Boyé performed the analytical work of the business and analyzed rocks and minerals from Pennsylvania and from the Delaware Geological Survey. He discovered nickel (a metal long used in U.S. coins) in iron pyrites from the Gap Mine in Lancaster County, Pennsylvania. Together with Booth, he wrote a report, "The Conversion of Benzoic into Hippuric Acid" for the centennial of the founding of the American Philosophical Society. Other reports that Boyé made to the society during his long career bear witness to the breadth of his interests: analysis of three varieties of feldspar from Delaware rocks; a white, crystalline mineral (albite) from West

Chester, Pennsylvania; artificially colored tea; fossil infusoria; the aurora borealis; nitric ether; analysis of a concretion from a horse's stomach; brown hematite; calcium acetate; and a tin amalgam.

In 1845 Boyé invented a process for refining the black, viscous oily product extracted from cottonseed into a colorless, bland oil that could be used for cooking, salad dressing, or toilet soap that was superior to the best castile soap. Boyé produced this oil on a large scale in 1847–1848. A sample produced in 1848 was awarded the first premium at the Centennial Exposition (1876) held in Philadelphia's Fairmount Park. In 1845, when Booth retired from the chair of natural philosophy and chemistry at the prestigious Central High School of Philadelphia, an elite, college preparatory school for boys, Boyé succeeded him. An earnest, enthusiastic, and successful teacher, he delivered many public lectures and wrote two books intended primarily for his students—*A Treatise on Pneumatics: Being the Physics of Gases, Including Vapors* (1855) and *Chemistry or the Physics of Atoms* (1857). Many of his students became successful chemists and chemistry teachers. During this period he also wrote many lengthy articles for the first part of Booth's *The Encyclopedia of Chemistry* (1850), one of which, "Analysis," was later published as a separate volume. In collaboration with Foreman Leaming, Boyé translated into English many literary essays and chemical works, including one by Jöns Jacob Berzelius, "The Kidneys and Urine" (1843).

Boyé apparently never married. In February 1859 he resigned his professorship at Central High School "because of ill health." His early geological field work acquainted him intimately with the picturesque eastern region of Pennsylvania, and he selected Coopersburg, about nine miles south of Bethlehem in Lehigh County, as the site of his home in his declining years. He named his home "Keewaydin," the Onondaga Indian name of the northwest wind, taken from Henry Wadsworth Longfellow's *The Song of Hiawatha* (1855). Here he devoted himself to what George Washington called the most noble and useful avocation of man—agriculture. His physical ailments were probably not serious because during his eighties he made long journeys to such distant places as Alaska, Honolulu, where he witnessed the transfer of the Hawaiian Islands to the United States, and Japan. He died in Coopersburg, a full half-century after his retirement. In his will he bequeathed $12,000 to the University of Pennsylvania Hospital. This long-lived and eminent but neglected scientist, inventor, and teacher helped lay the foundations of research in chemistry, geology, and physics in nineteenth-century United States.

• Little information is available about Boyé, especially his early years in Denmark. The few articles available include W. H. Hale, "A Pioneer of Science," *Scientific American* 75, no. 24 (12 Dec. 1896): 430 (with portrait); by an unknown author, "Martin Hans Boyé," *Science* 29 (19 Mar. 1909): 448–49; Edgar Fahs Smith, "Martin Hans Boyè [*sic*], 1812–1909," *Journal of Chemical Education* 21 (Jan. 1944): 7–11 (with portrait); and Harold J. Abrahams, "Martin Hans Boyé," in *American Chemists and Chemical Engineers*, ed. Wyndham D. Miles (1976). Obituaries are in the *Philadelphia Press* and the *New York Times*, both 6 Mar. 1909.

GEORGE B. KAUFFMAN

BOYER, Charles (28 Aug. 1899–26 Aug. 1978), actor, was born in the agrarian town of Figeac in southern France, the son of Maurice Boyer, a merchant, and Augustine Louise Durand. From an early age Boyer was determined to become an actor, having been awed by Max Linder's silent film comedies and mesmerized by plays featuring his idol, French stage actor Lucien Guitry. Boyer's father, at various times a grain merchant, bicycle shop owner, and farming equipment dealer, died in 1909. Soon afterward Boyer took over the abandoned granary and used it to stage amateur plays.

At his mother's insistence, Boyer pursued a college education, first at the College Campollion near Figeac and in 1919 at the Sorbonne in Paris, where he majored in philosophy. He neglected his studies in favor of the theatrical community of Paris, and he dropped out of school in less than a year. He eventually transferred to the Paris Conservatory, where he earned a two-year degree in the early 1920s.

Boyer made his stage debut in Paris in 1920, when the star of *Les Jardins de Murcie* fell ill on the evening before the play's opening. Boyer was hired as a last-minute replacement and was given the task of memorizing the lead role in twelve hours. He won rave reviews and became an overnight sensation in Paris.

Though a stage actor at heart, Boyer was lured by the fame and money offered by motion pictures. He appeared in a handful of silent films, beginning with *L'Homme du Large* in 1920. In the early years of talking pictures, studios often produced foreign language versions concurrently with the corresponding American productions (this practice was eventually abandoned in favor of dubbing). Boyer was first brought to Hollywood by Metro-Goldwyn-Mayer in 1929 to film *Le Proces du Mary Dugan*, the French language version of *The Trial of Mary Dugan*. He was dissatisfied with his early American pictures and was ready to give up on Hollywood entirely when director Walter Wanger offered him the lead in *Private Worlds* (1935), his first American film success.

Boyer's performance in the romance *Algiers* (1938) brought him heightened fame and a reputation as "The Great Lover." It was a label Boyer resisted, and he subsequently turned down countless "lover" roles in favor of character parts. Although *Algiers* was a critical and commercial success and earned him his first Oscar nomination, Boyer later looked back on the film as a hindrance to his career because it had inspired much parody. He became eternally identified with the line "come wiz me to the Casbah" (which he never actually uttered in the film). He later said, "I would say that one line, more than anything else, has hampered my career."

Boyer starred in close to eighty films and was teamed with Hollywood's most famous leading ladies, including Marlene Dietrich, Greta Garbo, Claudette Colbert, Irene Dunne, Rita Hayworth, and Ingrid Bergman. Nominated four times for an Academy Award (*Conquest*, 1937; *Algiers*, 1938; *Gaslight*, 1944; and *Fanny*, 1961), Boyer never won the coveted prize for his acting, but he was awarded a special Oscar in 1942 "for his progressive cultural achievement in establishing the French Research Foundation in Los Angeles." Frustrated by inaccurate depictions of French people in American popular culture, Boyer had founded the organization in 1940. Its primary function from its inception through its dissolution in 1952 was the documentation of France's involvement in World War II.

Boyer returned to the stage intermittently throughout his career, scoring Broadway hits with *Red Gloves* (1950), *Don Juan in Hell* (1951), and *The Marriage-Go-Round* (1958). He also tackled the medium of television, coproducing and starring in "Four Star Playhouse" (1952–1956) and "The Rogues" (1964–1965).

Boyer married British actress Patricia Paterson in 1934. She had been groomed for stardom by Fox Films, but after a handful of forgettable films her career fizzled. Their marriage produced one child, who committed suicide in 1965. The Boyers never recovered from the loss, and they withdrew from their friends and from the Hollywood community. Boyer continued working in films as a means of escaping his gloom.

In the summer of 1977 the Boyers retired to Paradise Valley, Arizona. Pat Boyer passed away on 24 August 1978. Two days later, disconsolate over the loss of his wife, Boyer took an overdose of barbiturates and died in Paradise Valley.

Boyer has been described by his contemporaries as moody and driven, a consummate professional who took his craft very seriously. He was one of the highest-paid and most sought-after actors in Hollywood, but he was plagued by regrets and self-criticism. A major source of contention for Boyer was the label "The Great Lover." He fervently desired to be recognized for his acting skill rather than for his supposed romantic prowess. He told journalist Hollis Alpert in April 1960, "The public has an image of me as lover, playboy, and seducer, while I have an image of myself as a serious actor. I hope we can get together some day."

• Larry Swindell's full-length biography is titled *Charles Boyer: The Reluctant Lover* (1983). Boyer is also profiled in George Tashman, *I Love You, Clark Gable, Etc.: Male Sex Symbols of the Silver Screen* (1976); and in Danny Peary, *Closeups: Intimate Profiles of Movie Stars by Their Co-stars, Directors, Screenwriters and Friends* (1978). Boyer is the subject of innumerable magazine articles, including R. Monsees, "Charles Boyer: Possessed and Projected Much More Than Mere Gallic Charm," *Films in Review*, May 1971, pp. 258–74, which includes a lengthy career analysis with filmography (through 1969). See also Hollis Alpert, "Boyer and Some Thoughts about the Casbah," *Woman's Day*, Apr. 1960, p. 46; Digby Diehl, "Q&A: Charles Boyer," *Los Angeles Times*, 24 Sept. 1972; Amy Porter, "M'sieu Bwayea," *Collier's*, 17 May 1947, pp. 20–21ff.; "The Bedroom Pirate," *Time*, 11 Sept. 1964, p. 66; and "Behind the Scenes: Gentleman Ladykiller," *Newsweek*, 30 Dec. 1957, p. 61. Obituaries are in the *Los Angeles Times*, 27 Aug. 1978; *Variety*, 30 Aug. 1978; and *Newsweek* and *Time*, 4 Sept. 1978.

BRENDA SCOTT ROYCE

BOYESEN, Hjalmar Hjorth (23 Sept. 1848–4 Oct. 1895), author and educator, was born in Fredriksvaern, Norway, the son of Sarolf Boyesen, a mathematics instructor in the naval academy there, and Hanna (or Helga) Tveten Hjorth, the foster daughter of Judge Hjorth of Systrand. In 1854 Sarolf Boyesen, out of favor because he had joined the Swedenborgian church, sent his family to Judge Hjorth and entered the American army, for a period of two years. Hjalmar Boyesen loved the natural setting of Systrand, relished the servants' folktales there, was sad when he was sent away to school, and found consolation in reading and writing. He attended Latin school at Drammen and Gymnasium at Christiania and graduated from the Royal Fredriks University in 1868—adept in several languages. He obtained family permission to go to the United States, which his father had extolled as the land of freedom and opportunity.

Boyesen landed in New York City in 1869, traveled in New England and the South, taught for a year at a Swedenborgian institute in Urbana, Ohio, edited a weekly Norwegian newspaper in Chicago for another year, and made a literary pilgrimage to Boston in 1871. By chance he met author William Dean Howells, who read parts of *Gunnar*, a novel Boyesen was writing. In 1873 Howells serialized it in the *Atlantic Monthly*, of which he was the editor. In preparation for a teaching position at Cornell University, which Howells's connections helped him secure, Boyesen returned to Europe and studied for several months in Leipzig. He taught European languages at Cornell from 1874 until 1880.

During these years Boyesen displayed incredible energy. He filled his spare time by writing tirelessly. *Gunnar* appeared in book form in 1874. His *Goethe and Schiller: Their Lives and Works*, a pioneering study in English, was published in 1879 and became a textbook. In between, he wrote two more novels, *A Norseman's Pilgrimage* (1875) and *Falconberg* (1879); a stream of short stories for the *Atlantic*, the *Galaxy*, and *Scribner's* (many of which were collected in *Tales from Two Hemispheres* [1876]); and more than a dozen poems, essays, and reviews in various journals. Boyesen's bookish English had become almost as natural as that of his numerous literary friends, including George Washington Cable, Edward Eggleston, Richard Watson Gilder, Henry Wadsworth Longfellow, Edmund Clarence Stedman, and Mark Twain, as well as Howells. In 1878 Boyesen married Lillie Keen, the daughter of a wealthy, divorced Philadelphia matriarch. Two years after honeymooning briefly in Europe, Boyesen and his wife, who eventually had three children, moved to New York City and its challenging sophistication. Trying but unable to support his family as a freelance writer, Boyesen became an instructor of German at Columbia College in 1881. He was promoted to full professor of Germanic languages and literature in one year and served in that rank for the rest of his life.

Boyesen combined teaching, scholarly and creative writing, and popular lecturing on the Chautauqua circuit and elsewhere. He sought to bridge the gap between European and American culture. Moving from Scandinavian and American Romanticism to American realism, he simultaneously favored European philosophical idealism and European naturalism. Returning with his family to Norway in 1891 for rest and intellectual stimulation, he sadly concluded that he was at home nowhere. Covering too many topics, he wrote on European literature, mainly German and Scandinavian; lauded the works of Bjørnstjerne Bjørnson, Henrik Ibsen, and Ivan Turgenev; addressed American social, educational, and immigration problems; deplored aspects of women's liberation in his adopted land; reviewed dozens of American books; and mixed most of his concerns into new fiction of his own and even wrote books for children. Such herculean efforts were bound to result in incompletely unified works and professional frustration. To everyone's surprise, he suddenly contracted pneumonia and died two days later in New York City. His total production was eight novels, eight collections of short fiction, eight scholarly and critical books, many poems, and scores of scattered reviews and critical essays.

Boyesen is remembered today only for his literary criticism and his novels. He advanced the cause of German and Scandinavian men of letters, and he urged American playwrights to stop imitating the vapid British theater, follow the lead of German drama and of Ibsen, and help improve American society in the evolving industrial age. He thought that American society would also be stronger if women avoided the professions and confined themselves to marriage, motherhood, and homemaking, and if immigration of persons unable to speak English were restricted. Boyesen's early novels, some of which are romantic and deal with the problems of immigrants, now seem outmoded. His four best novels address significant social issues. In *A Daughter of the Philistines* (1883), the heroine marries a man with moral values instead of a rich man preferred by her socially ambitious parents; she then properly becomes an old-fashioned wife and homemaker. *The Mammon of Unrighteousness* (1891) contrasts two sons of a university president. One son opts for politics, marries an heiress with social clout, and grabs money and power; the other son chooses decency in the workplace, rescues his foster sister from ruin, and marries her for love. The hero of *The Golden Calf* (1892) ignores the precepts of his tutor (a German-born idealist patterned partly after the young Boyesen) and claws his way to financial and political success as a Washington lobbyist but in the process is spiritually damned. In *Social Strugglers* (1893), which bears some resemblance to *A Hazard of New Fortunes* by Howells (1890), a midwestern family—newly rich father, domineering mother, and three daughters—migrate to New York City, where they encounter social problems but also Boyesen's most positive male figure. He is not only decent and bright but also successful in applying Christian reformist policies on both personal and social levels. The struggles implied in the title echo Boyesen's efforts to succeed financially, advance professionally, and improve the social, political, and aesthetic attitudes of his adopted land.

• Most of Boyesen's widely scattered papers are in university libraries at Columbia, Harvard, Princeton, Tulane, and Virginia. The standard biography is Clarence Glasrud, *H. H. Boyesen* (1963). Two critical studies are Robert S. Fredrickson, *Hjalmar Hjorn Boyesen* (1980), and Per Seyersted, *From Norwegian Romantic to American Realist: Studies in the Life of Hjalmar Hjorn Boyesen* (1984); both have extensive bibliographies. In his *Literary Friends and Acquaintance* (1900), William Dean Howells recalls his friendship with Boyesen and comments on his work. Aagot D. Hoidahl, "Norwegian-American Fiction, 1880–1928," *Norwegian-American Historical Association Studies and Records* 5 (1930): 61–83, places Boyesen in the context of Norwegian immigrant authors. George Leroy White, Jr., "H. H. Boyesen: A Note on Immigration," *American Literature* 13 (Jan. 1942): 363–71, explains how Boyesen's works contribute to an understanding of the problems and achievements of Scandinavian immigrants. Arlin Turner, "A Novelist Discovers a Novelist: The Correspondence of H. H. Boyesen and George W. Cable," *Western Humanities Review* 5 (Autumn 1951): 343–73, shows how well Boyesen aided, encouraged, and praised Cable. Marc Ratner, "The Iron Madonna: H. H. Boyesen's American Girl," *Jahrbuch für Amerikastudien* 9 (1964): 166–72, argues that Boyesen was troubled by the role played by American women in the social evolution of their nation and by the effect of racy young American women on the national literary taste. Neil Eckstein compares Boyesen and another Norwegian-American writer in *The Marginal Man As Novelist: The Norwegian-American Writers, H. H. Boyesen and O. E. Rolvaag, as Critics of American Institutions* (1991). An obituary is in the *New York Times*, 5 Oct. 1895.

ROBERT L. GALE

BOYINGTON, Gregory (4 Dec. 1912–11 Jan. 1988), Marine Corps fighter pilot, was born in Coeur d'Alene, Idaho, the son of Guy Boyington and Grace Hallenbeck, apple ranchers. He earned a degree in aeronautical engineering from the University of Washington in 1934, and that year he married Helene Clark. Before divorcing in 1941, they had three children, one of whom became an Air Force fighter pilot in the Vietnam War. After a year with Boeing Aircraft, Boyington entered the Marine Corps as an aviation cadet in 1936.

In 1941 Boyington was a flight instructor at Pensacola, Florida, with the rank of first lieutenant. Widely considered one of the best fighter pilots and one of the worst rule-breakers in the Marine Corps, he resigned his commission that year to join the American Volunteer Group (AVG), the famous "Flying Tigers." In air combat over Burma and China in early 1942 he shot down six Japanese aircraft (three and a half officially confirmed) before the AVG disbanded and its pilots returned to U.S. military service in July 1942. He despised the corruption and administrative arrogance he saw in China but admired the skill and courage of his fellow pilots, two contrasting attitudes he would repeat in every place he served throughout his flying career.

Boyington stubbornly resisted efforts to induct him into the Army Air Corps, preferring and expecting to resume his Marine Corps commission. To his dismay he learned that his marine superiors frowned on all the marine pilots who had "deserted" to join the AVG and on Boyington in particular, whose boisterous, undisciplined reputation and tendency to insubordination made him unpopular with higher authority. Eventually he had to appeal directly to the assistant secretary of the navy to be reinstated as a Marine Corps Reserve major, sacrificing his prewar regular commission, in November 1942.

In January 1943 Boyington went overseas as assistant operations officer of an air base in the New Hebrides, a frustrating desk job that offered few opportunities for action except for occasionally ferrying aircraft to front-line units on Guadalcanal. He managed to obtain reassignment as executive officer and then commanding officer of Marine Fighter Squadron 122 based on Guadalcanal in April 1943 but saw no combat on his first tour of duty. When the squadron was withdrawn to a rear area to reequip with the new F4U Corsair fighter, "a sweet-flying baby," in Boyington's words, he broke his ankle in an alcohol-related sports accident and found himself hospitalized as his squadron returned to action without him.

Boyington spent the summer in various administrative posts that gave him no satisfaction except the opportunity to dismiss every court-martial charge that crossed his desk for review. Fearing his chances for another combat assignment were fading rapidly, he offered to form a new squadron with pilots from the replacement pool, a proposal his sympathetic and shorthanded group commander quickly approved. This became Marine Fighter Squadron 214, the legendary "Black Sheep," in August 1943.

Contrary to popular myth, the squadron was not a gang of brawling misfits; the nickname referred only to their origins as unattached replacements and to Boyington's history of conflict with his superiors. His own nickname, "Pappy," reflected the ten-year age difference between Boyington and his young pilots. Under his tutelage the Black Sheep became one of the most successful fighter squadrons in the South Pacific, and Boyington quickly became one of the leading American aces. With twenty-six official victories, he was tied for the title of leading marine ace when he was shot down in January 1944.

Boyington survived two harrowing years in a Japanese prisoner of war camp by using the combination of toughness and crafty realism that always had seen him through adversity. He emerged not bitter toward his captors but philosophical, convinced cruel and kindly individuals existed in every nation. On his return home in 1945 he was credited with two more victories from his last aerial engagement. With twenty-eight victories, he became the top marine ace of World War II and in fact, the top marine ace ever, for which he received the Medal of Honor and the Navy Cross. He was medically discharged because of his wounds, which "saved the Marine Corps the trouble" of dealing with him, Boyington observed in his frank and revealing 1958 autobiography, *Baa Baa Black Sheep*.

In civilian life Boyington held a variety of jobs, including beer salesman and professional wrestling referee, and continued the struggles with debt and with alcohol that had plagued his entire adult life. In 1946 he married Frances Baker; they had no children. Within ten years Boyington prevailed and found stability through this marriage, working as an air charter pilot and eventually as a salesman for an aircraft sealant manufacturer. In 1959 he and his second wife divorced. In 1960 he married Dee Tatum; they had no children and divorced in 1964. In 1978 he married Josephine Wilson Moseman; they had no children. The exploits of Boyington and his squadron (with some dramatic embellishment) were the subject of a television series, known first as "Baa Baa Black Sheep" and then as "Black Sheep Squadron," in the 1970s. He died in Fresno, California, and was buried in Arlington National Cemetery.

• Boyington wrote a novel, *Tonya* (1960), inspired by his life in China with the Flying Tigers. See also Frank Walton, *Once They Were Eagles: The Men of the Black Sheep Squadron* (1986), by a member of his squadron; Robert Sherrod, *History of Marine Corps Aviation in World War II* (1952); and Peter B. Mersky, *U.S. Marine Corps Aviation: 1912 to the Present* (1983). Obituaries are in *Fortitudine: Bulletin of the Marine Corps Historical Program*, Winter 1987–1988, and the *New York Times*, 12 Jan. 1988.

DAVID MACGREGOR

BOYINGTON, William W. (22 July 1818–16 Oct. 1898), architect, was born in Southwick, Massachusetts, the son of Juba Boyington, a carpenter, and Aurelia Campbell. Boyington received a common-school education; after the family moved to Springfield, Massachusetts, in 1834 he trained as a carpenter and joiner under his father's direction. In 1839 Boyington married Eunice B. Miller; they had nine children.

Boyington's career exemplifies the nineteenth-century professionalization of architectural design in the United States. For over a decade he worked as a journeyman carpenter and builder in Springfield. He often furnished the designs for the buildings he built, and he operated a lumberyard and planing mill to provide necessary materials. In the late 1840s Boyington, who spent his evenings studying pattern books and treatises on "architectural science," sold his interest in the building firm of Decreet, Boyington & Company and changed his professional designation, given in directories, from "carpenter" to "architect." When Boyington moved to the booming city of Chicago, Illinois, in 1853 he assumed a dominant place among the small handful of local architects who designed buildings and oversaw their proper completion, quite apart from the physical labor and contractual relations of construction. In 1870 Boyington became the first president of the Chicago Chapter of the American Institute of Architects.

As Chicago grew from nearly thirty thousand residents in 1850 to over one million in 1890, Boyington became one of the most prominent and successful local architects. His specialization as an architect dovetailed with the rising demand for new types of buildings; he designed railroad stations, department stores, hotels, warehouses, skyscrapers, a board of trade, a water pumping station, and an entrance for a landscaped cemetery. Even his designs for more traditional building types, like residences, fit an increasingly specialized urban landscape that separated buildings according to type and people according to class. Boyington's design for Michigan Terrace (1856), a row of eleven palatial marble-front row houses built on Michigan Avenue, helped give early and monumental form to the rise of class-segregated neighborhoods. Several of the wealthy Michigan Terrace residents had previously lived in the more diverse downtown area. Now, instead of simply building on a single lot, with little control over neighboring development, the Michigan Terrace residents developed an entire block front and thus excluded all other development from their midst. The *Fifth Annual Review* (1857) of Chicago development declared the project "one of the most beautiful blocks of private dwellings which any city in the Union can boast. Its graceful proportions and harmonious style of architecture indicate the good taste and superior ability of the architect" (p. 11).

Boyington, more than any other designer, determined the form of the wealthy residential neighborhood arising south of the downtown area during the 1850s and 1860s. In addition to Michigan Terrace he designed at least twenty other residences in the neighborhood. At the same time he designed an increasingly specialized religious landscape for the leading Protestant congregation. These congregations abandoned their downtown locations where they stood adjacent to residences, civic structures, hotels, stores, offices, and other commercial structures and rebuilt in the elite residential section, with houses and churches their only neighbors. Boyington's fine designs for new churches added to the urgency with which older congregations approached the question of relocation. Boyington designed St. Paul's Church for the First Universalist Society (1856), First Presbyterian Church (1856), Wabash Avenue Methodist Episcopal Church (1857), and the First Baptist Church (1866). These and other Boyington churches in Chicago were built of stone in the Gothic and Romanesque styles; each accommodated between one and two thousand worshippers and had towers and spires reaching 150 to 250 feet high. Boyington later gained commissions for churches in Philadelphia, Indianapolis, Dayton, Ohio, Grand Rapids, Michigan, and Des Moines, Iowa.

Boyington designed similarly prominent commercial structures in downtown Chicago. Crosby's Opera House (1865) on Washington Street cost an estimated $600,000. The Sherman House (1869) and the monumental Grand Pacific Hotel (1871) established Boyington's reputation as a hotel designer. He later designed several other Chicago hotels, along with ones in Montreal, Denver, Milwaukee, and Ottawa, Illinois. The complexity of the programs and plans for Boyington's hotel projects is also evident in his designs for other important commercial projects. The Chicago Board of Trade (1881), built in part on a vacated segment of La Salle Street, enjoyed special prominence. The structure, whose soaring tower closed the impressive La Salle Street vista, housed one of Chicago's major exchange rooms, numerous private offices, and shops. In 1891 Boyington designed the Columbus Memorial Building, one of his most notable commercial designs. Seeking to capitalize on the local enthusiasm for the Columbian Exposition, Boyington designed a sixteen-story office building in the Spanish Renaissance style, with a statue of Columbus over the entrance, richly ornamented ironwork and mosaics in the lobby and halls, and two large murals, the *Landing of Columbus* and *Columbus before Ferdinand and Isabella*.

Boyington also received the major commission for the Columbian Exposition's State of Illinois Building in 1892. The project capped decades of important civic and municipal designs, including Jones Hall (1859), Douglas Hall (1865), and the observatory (1865) all at the first University of Chicago. Other major civic commissions included a high school and armory for Des Moines; an insane asylum for Knoxville, Tennessee; a county jail for Pike County, Illinois; and the Illinois state penitentiary in Joliet.

For many of his civic commissions during the 1850s and 1860s Boyington designed buildings in the castellated Gothic style, using a locally quarried Joliet-Lemont limestone worked in a rough rock-faced manner. The cemetery entrance at Rosehill Cemetery (1864) in Chicago is a good surviving example of this style, but the most notable is the Chicago Water Tower and Pumping Station (1866–1869). The design, with its 154-foot tower, has gained its current prominence primarily because it is one of the few buildings still standing in Chicago that survived the 1871 fire and is thus a focal point of both civic pride and local mythology.

In 1885 historian and biographer Alfred T. Andreas wrote that Boyington "stands in the foremost ranks of the architects of Chicago." Nevertheless, his reputation later languished in obscurity. The Chicago fire destroyed many of Boyington's early buildings, and subsequent urban renewal destroyed even more. In addition to the destruction of Boyington's work, there are important historiographical reasons for his obscurity. Most of Chicago's architectural history has been framed by historians and critics strongly interested in the city's place in a narrative of modern architecture dominated by Chicago architects Louis Sullivan, Frank Lloyd Wright, and Mies van der Rohe. The more eclectic architects like Boyington, regardless of their prominence in their own time, have not fit the narrow conceptions of "Chicago School" architecture and thus have received only scant historical attention. Despite the subsequent critical slight, Boyington worked impressively for over four decades, meeting the new demands for specialized buildings and spaces in the modern metropolis. Boyington died in Highland Park, Illinois.

• The best contemporary biographical sources are *Biographical Sketches of the Leading Men of Chicago, Written by the Best Talent of the Northwest* (1868), pp. 215–22; Alfred T. Andreas, *History of Chicago, from the Earliest Period to the Present Time*, vol. 2 (1885), p. 564; and Peter B. Wight, "Memorial to the Late W. W. Boyington," *Inland Architect and New Record* 32 (Nov. 1898): 32. For discussion and pictures of individual buildings by Boyington, see Daniel Bluestone, *Constructing Chicago* (1991); Alice Sinkevitch, ed., *AIA Guide To Chicago* (1993); and Frank A. Randall, *A History of the Development of Building Construction in Chicago* (1949).

DANIEL BLUESTONE

BOYLE, Hal (21 Feb. 1911–1 Apr. 1974), journalist, was born Harold Vincent Boyle in Kansas City, Missouri, the son of Peter Edward Boyle, a butcher, and Margaret Gavaghan. He was discouraged from his boyhood plan to become a civil engineer by poor grades in mathematics, and in high school he considered a career in teaching, but an interest in writing drew him to journalism. After graduating from high school in 1928, he took a night job as an office boy with the Associated Press in Kansas City, earning $15 for a 58-hour week. He returned to school and attended Kansas City Junior College until 1930 and the University of Missouri in Columbia until 1932, when he received two bachelor's degrees—one in English and one in journalism. His academic work earned him a scholarship from the university, and he stayed on for a year in graduate school studying English.

In 1933 he returned to the Associated Press with a job in Columbia, reporting college and sports news, and after a year and a half was promoted to the post of feature editor in Kansas City. In 1936 he advanced to the agency's much larger St. Louis bureau, where he served as night editor, and in 1937 he went on to its home office in New York City. That same year he married Mary Frances Young, a social worker, who died in 1968. The couple adopted a daughter in 1953. Boyle worked as a reporter in New York for several years and by 1942 had become night city editor.

Boyle's first assignment as a war correspondent came in October 1942, and the next month he accompanied General George S. Patton's Second Corps on their landing, under heavy enemy fire, on the Moroccan coast. It was almost his last assignment, as well; the boat carrying him hit a reef, and he was barely able to swim ashore from an accident that cost some 400 American lives. His dispatches from that campaign across North Africa, written from the standpoint of the foot soldiers whose lot he shared, made him famous. Described by his colleague Saul Pett as "the loving Boswell of the GI," Boyle produced an enormous volume of war reporting during the European conflict, writing as many as twelve spot stories a day. He accompanied the landing of General Mark Clark at Salerno, the First Army's march from Normandy to the Elbe, and the Battle of the Bulge. He once hitchhiked 400 miles to get a story. After the war ended in Europe, he covered the end of the Pacific campaign and went on to write from the battlefront in Korea and Vietnam.

His column "Leaves from a War Correspondent's Notebook," in which he reported the personal experiences of the average soldier, became one of the Associated Press's most popular features and the most widely distributed column in the United States, appearing in more than 500 newspapers, almost one-third of all U.S. dailies, during the 1940s. His columns were frequently read over the radio and dramatized on television. Among his most appreciative readers were the parents of soldiers, who found news of their sons at the front in his accounts of "the bravery, beefs, homesickness, and fears of GI Joe, his craving for a hot meal and bath, a comfortable bed, or a letter" (*Newsweek*, 25 Dec. 1944, p. 80). When the Veterans of Foreign Wars honored Boyle for his coverage of the Korean conflict, General of the Army Omar Bradley, who presented the award, told him, "There are few men who understand the American soldier and how he feels as well as you." Unlike fellow war-correspondent Ernie Pyle, a good friend to whom he was often compared, Boyle produced not only what he called his "day to day stories on soldiers" but battle reports as well. He received the Pulitzer Prize in 1945 for his coverage of World War II. A selection of his columns, *Help, Help! Another Day!*, was published by the Associated Press in 1969.

Known among his colleagues at Associated Press Newsfeatures for his cluttered desk and a filing cabinet so disorganized that one drawer was labeled "God Only Knows," Boyle was convivial with his co-workers, given to horseplay, and always ready for a drink and a conversation. A portly figure who battled endlessly with an expanding waistline, he was described in *Newsweek* (1944) as having "thinning hair, grave blue eyes, a prizefighter's face, and a poet's soul." Boyle loved poetry and collected early editions of Emily Dickinson, a volume of whose work he carried through the war. The title of his book was taken from one of Dickinson's poems, which he ranked after Shakespeare's as the greatest in all literature.

Boyle contracted amyotrophic lateral sclerosis, known as Lou Gehrig's disease, in 1973 and ceased writing the next year. In his last column, dictated by the paralyzed Boyle on 21 February, the reporter noted, "I am somewhat abashed that my wordage output is four times that of William Shakespeare. But I savor the fact that it enables me to have more bylined stories on the major wires of The Associated Press than any other writer in its 126 years." Shortly before his death of a stroke at his home in New York City, a scholarship was established in his name at the journalism school of the University of Missouri.

• For information about Boyle's life and career, see *Newsweek*, 25 Dec. 1944, pp. 79–80, 18 Nov. 1957, p. 76, and 23 Nov. 1959, p. 65; the *New York Times*, 8 May 1945; and *Editor & Publisher*, 30 June 1945, p. 8, 14 Sept. 1968, pp. 13 and 66, and 21 Sept. 1968, pp. 15, 41. Affectionate anecdotal accounts of his personality and working habits are in the *New Yorker*, 15 Apr. 1974, and by Saul Pett, "Unforgettable Hal Boyle," in the *Reader's Digest*, Oct. 1974. Obituaries are in the *New York Times*, 2 and 4 Apr. 1974.

DENNIS WEPMAN

BOYLE, Jeremiah Tilford (22 May 1818–28 July 1871), soldier and railroad entrepreneur, was born in Mercer County, Kentucky, the son of John Boyle, a judge, and Elizabeth Tilford. His father was described as "one of the most conspicuous figures in the public life of Kentucky for more than a third of a century" (Levin, p. 157). Boyle was educated at Centre and Transylvania colleges in his native state and in 1839 graduated from the College of New Jersey (now Princeton University). Admitted to the Kentucky bar in 1841, he practiced law in Harrodsburg and later that year in Danville. In 1842 he married Elizabeth Owsley Anderson; they had twelve children.

A slaveholding Whig, Boyle became a staunch Unionist in conflict with his own economic interests, and in 1860 he supported the presidential candidacy of John Bell. A few months after the outbreak of the Civil War, Boyle and other Kentucky loyalists sought permission to organize forces for local defense. Late in September 1861 Boyle was authorized to raise three infantry regiments, which he led as a brigadier general of volunteers. The brigade was ready for service that autumn, but Boyle's appointment did not come through until early 1862.

In late December 1861 Boyle and his troops reported for service at Louisville, headquarters of the Department of the Ohio. Major General Don Carlos Buell assigned Boyle to command the Eleventh Brigade of the Army of the Ohio, consisting of two Kentucky and two Ohio regiments. The command saw its initial action on the second day at Shiloh, 7 April 1862. Originally Boyle's troops were held in reserve, but near the day's end they advanced and, after hard fighting, seized a strategic position. According to Boyle's immediate superior, Brigadier General Thomas L. Crittenden, throughout the day Boyle displayed "conspicuous gallantry, inspiring his troops with a confidence and courage like his own."

On 27 May Secretary of War Edwin M. Stanton removed Boyle from the field and returned him to Louisville to command forces charged with pacifying western Kentucky. Ostensibly the assignment was made to exploit Boyle's "knowledge of the requirements of the service in [his] State and [his] experience and discretion." In fact, Stanton acted under pressure from the Kentucky congressional delegation, who believed that Boyle's legal acumen would help him set a course acceptable to both Unionists and Confederate sympathizers.

The solons were mistaken. Although Boyle's headquarters were situated in a Unionist enclave, from the first he considered himself an enemy occupation commander. Surrounded by elements he regarded as inimical to peace and order, he felt constrained to rule with a heavy hand. As he informed Stanton in August 1862, "I believe in subjugation—complete subjugation by hard and vigorous dealing with traitors and treason."

The result was an oppressive, dictatorial regime that trampled civil liberties with such impunity as to embarrass the administration of Abraham Lincoln. Boyle arrested so many civilians on the merest suspicion of disloyalty that the War Department forbade the practice without the prior approval of Governor Thomas E. Bramlette. Although Boyle complied with this directive, he continued to distress his civilian and military superiors. He impressed into his defense forces citizens below and above the enlistment age, censored newspapers critical of his rule, and interfered in local elections. He came down especially hard on Confederate irregulars, vowing to eradicate those who "overrun the border and rob banks, sack towns, and pillage the people." With his tacit approval, scores of captives suspected of guerrilla activities were summarily shot or hanged. Boyle even taxed "disloyal men" to finance reparations to Unionists who had suffered at guerrillas' hands. He also displeased the government by criticizing some of its most significant policies, including the recruitment of black units, a practice Boyle considered not only unconstitutional but immoral.

Boyle might have survived these failures and indiscretions had he proven himself an able soldier. On numerous occasions, however, the rumored approach of Confederate forces caused him to despair that "the State . . . will be overrun." During each of the three cavalry raids John Hunt Morgan conducted in Kentucky between July 1862 and January 1863, during the fall 1862 invasion of the state by Braxton Bragg and Edmund Kirby Smith, and again at the outset of Morgan's mid-1863 expedition into Indiana and Ohio, Boyle fell victim to doubt and indecision. He overestimated the numbers opposing him, sent his superiors garbled and inaccurate intelligence of enemy movements and intentions, and pursued slowly if at all.

During Morgan's initial incursion, Boyle's fits of panic alarmed and distressed the government. He importuned numerous superiors and associates for reinforcements, even petitioning the mayors of Ohio River communities for troops and guns. Noting that Boyle and his subordinates seemed constantly "in trouble," an exasperated Lincoln lamented that "they are having a stampede in Kentucky." In August 1862, when Boyle's superiors assigned primary responsibility for the state's defense to Major General William Nelson, Boyle complained that he had been unjustly superseded.

December 1863 spelled the demise of Boyle's regime. On the eleventh the new commander of the Department of the Ohio, Major General John Gray Foster, ordered Boyle to Knoxville, Tennessee, to command the First Division, XXIII Army Corps. Foster ascribed the move to his dissatisfaction with Boyle's support of other commanders in Kentucky.

Doubtless he was also influenced by Washington's loss of faith in Boyle's ability to govern. Boyle vehemently protested his relief, criticizing his superiors' "distrust of me" and their violation of a pledge that his Kentuckians would not serve outside their state. When his grievances went unaddressed, he tendered his resignation, which took effect on 26 January 1864. A few months later he sent Lincoln a letter, in which he attributed his downfall to vengeful disloyalists, declared the war effort a failure, and called for an armistice.

In postwar life, Boyle gave up his legal practice to enter the field of public transportation, in which he amassed a fortune. He helped organize and became president of the Louisville City Railroad Company. In 1866 he headed the Evansville, Henderson, & Nashville Railroad, which he transformed from an unprofitable venture into a thriving enterprise. Until his death in Louisville, he managed these businesses as well as considerable real estate holdings in the western states.

Historians almost universally judge Boyle's administration a failure. They reserve their hardest condemnation for his abuse of civil rights in a region in which habeas corpus was not suspended and martial law was not declared until mid-1864. It is doubtful, however, that any departmental commander could have imposed a fair yet firm rule on the war's most bitterly divided border state. Given the blood-feud nature of the violence infecting western Kentucky, it is not surprising that Boyle resorted to extreme measures to establish and maintain a semblance of peace in his realm.

As for Boyle's inability to meet the several military crises that confronted him, his bailiwick was too extensive, too vulnerable to invasion, and too lightly defended to form the bulwark against Confederate operations that the Lincoln administration apparently considered it to be. Significantly, given Boyle's many shortcomings as both administrator and field leader, among the staunch Unionists of Kentucky he maintained a reputation as a man of good intentions and "irreproachable personal honor," especially in contrast to the even harsher policies of his successors.

• There is no known collection of Boyle's papers. The most comprehensive source on his Civil War service is *The War of the Rebellion: A Compilation of the Official Records of the Union and Confederate Armies* (128 vols., 1880–1901), which contains hundreds of reports, letters, and telegrams he sent to superiors in the field and in Washington. Biographical material is in Z. F. Smith, *History of Kentucky* (1886); H. Levin, ed., *Lawyers and Lawmakers of Kentucky* (1897); and John E. Kleber et al., eds., *The Kentucky Encyclopedia* (1992). Some general accounts of the war in Kentucky highlight his role and offer mostly unfavorable assessments, especially E. Merton Coulter, *The Civil War and Readjustment in Kentucky* (1926); Robert E. McDowell, *City of Conflict: Louisville in the Civil War* (1962); and Lowell H. Harrison, *The Civil War in Kentucky* (1975). Studies of military operations that affected Boyle's administration include Charles K. Messmer, "Louisville and the Confederate Invasion of 1862," *Register of the Kentucky Historical Society* 55 (1959): 299–324; and Allan Keller, *Morgan's Raid* (1961).

EDWARD G. LONGACRE

BOYLE, John (28 Oct. 1774–28 Jan. 1834), congressman and state and federal judge, was born at "Castle Woods," near Tazewell, Botetourt County, Virginia, the son of John Boyle, a farmer, and Jane (maiden name unknown). An 1878 encyclopedia describes Boyle as "descended from a sound but humble stock, he was the carver of his own fortune, and the ennobler of his own name" (*Bio. Enc.*, p. 701). Good friends, good timing, and good luck helped him to advance, especially in his early career. Boyle moved with his family to Kentucky in 1779, settling not far from Boonesborough in Garrard County. Because Kentucky had not yet established public education, he was privately tutored in math, English, Greek, and Latin by the local Presbyterian minister, and in time Boyle developed an interest in the law. He read law under Thomas Davis, a prominent local lawyer in neighboring Mercer County, and he was admitted to practice in 1797 in Lancaster, Kentucky. That same year he married Elizabeth Tilford, with whom he had one child.

His reputation developed, and law practice prospered, no doubt aided by his friendship with Davis, who represented the area in Congress. In 1800, Boyle first entered public service when he was elected to the Kentucky House of Representatives. He followed this political success by being elected in 1802 to the national Congress, succeeding his friend Davis. A Jeffersonian-Republican, he served three terms in Congress (1803–1809). Boyle was active in party politics. He served as a House manager in the successful impeachment of federal district judge John Pickering (1738–1805) in January 1804 and in the unsuccessful attempt to impeach Associate Justice Samuel Chase of the United States Supreme Court in December 1804. Desiring to return to Kentucky and to his law practice, Boyle left Congress in 1809 after turning down President James Madison's (1751–1836) offer to appoint him governor of the Illinois Territory. But his private life did not last long. In 1810 he accepted the appointment as chief judge of Kentucky's highest court, the Court of Appeals. Judge Boyle served in that position until November 1826.

As chief judge, Boyle headed a court that ran afoul of the state legislature on the issue of debt relief. Responding to popular pressures brought about as a result of the Panic of 1819, Kentucky passed a series of debt-relief laws in the early 1820s that absolved some debts and extended others. When litigation challenging these statutes reached the Court of Appeals in the case of *Blair, &c. v. Williams* (1823), for a unanimous court Boyle struck down the relief law as unconstitutional, citing the obligation of contracts clause in both the federal and state constitutions. This decision led the state legislature, dominated by the Relief party, to hold special hearings to which Boyle was called to testify and to defend his decision. Then in 1824 it established a "New Court," packed with pro-debt relief judges, in an attempt to force Boyle and his colleagues on the "Old Court" to resign or reverse the *Blair* decision. For two years, 1824 to 1826, Kentuckians witnessed two competing Courts of Appeals, each holding the other unconstitutional. In 1826, legislative candidates of the antidebt Anti-Relief party won at the polls and thereby secured Boyle's Old Court and its *Blair* decision. The new legislature abolished the New Court. After overcoming that political strife, Boyle resigned from the Court of Appeals and accepted the life-tenured position of a federal district judgeship proffered by John Quincy Adams (1767–1848). He died near Danville, Kentucky.

Boyle is best remembered on the national level for his part in the impeachments of Pickering and Chase and on the state level for his tenure as chief judge of the Court of Appeals. In Boyle's honor, and as a testament to his service to his state, Kentuckians named a new county for him in 1842.

• No private or family papers of John Boyle can be located. Boyle's decisions on the Kentucky Court of Appeals from 1810 until 1826 form the largest single body of his judicial work and can be found in the appropriate volumes in the *Kentucky Reports*. Information on Boyle can be gleaned from a variety of nineteenth- and twentieth-century sources. See William B. Allen, *A History of Kentucky* (1872); *The Biographical Encyclopedia of Kentucky of the Dead and Living Men of the Nineteenth Century* (1878); H. Levin, *The Lawyers and Lawmakers of Kentucky* (1897); Richard H. Collins, *History of Kentucky* (1924); Thomas D. Clark, *A History of Kentucky* (1937); *Judges of the United States*, 2d ed. (1983); and John E. Kleber, ed., *The Kentucky Encyclopedia* (1992).

THOMAS C. MACKEY

BOYLE, John J. (12 Jan. 1851–10 Feb. 1917), sculptor, was born in New York City, the son of Samuel Boyle, a stonecutter, and Catherine McAuley. Boyle's family relocated to Philadelphia before his first birthday, and his father died five years later. As a boy Boyle attended public schools and worked as an apprentice stonecutter and stonecarver. In 1872 he enrolled in the Pennsylvania Academy of the Fine Arts, where he studied with Thomas Eakins while continuing to work as a stonecarver. In 1877 Boyle sailed for Paris and enrolled in the École des Beaux-Arts, where he was awarded a medal within two years. While still a student Boyle executed a series of relief panels and caryatids for a London leather exchange building, and he exhibited a bronze at the 1879 Paris Salon.

Boyle returned to the United States in 1880, when he received a commission from Chicago timber baron Martin Ryerson for a memorial to the Ottawa tribe, which had been forcibly resettled to midwestern reservations. Ryerson insisted that Boyle avoid the stereotypical presentation of Native Americans as inhuman savages. Boyle traveled to the Dakota territory and spent two months studying Native Americans (probably Sioux) in their own milieu. After completing his research Boyle returned to Philadelphia to work on the commission. He married Elizabeth Carroll in 1882. The finished work for Ryerson, titled *The Alarm*, was installed in Chicago's Lincoln Park in 1884. It includes a standing male figure, flanked on his right by a seated woman holding a young child strapped to a cradle, and on his left by his quiver and dog. The figures are relaxed yet alert, and they are solidly rendered with a degree of roughness that adds to the composition's strength.

Boyle exhibited *The Alarm* in Philadelphia before sending it to Chicago, and as a result he received a commission for a similar group from the Fairmount Park Art Association. The completed bronze, *Stone Age in America*, was installed in 1888. In this piece a female figure holds an infant while an older child crouches at her side. The woman holds a hatchet, with which she has dispatched a bear cub that lies at her feet. She stands in contrapposto, with a weight and solidity that is enhanced by her roughly rendered drapery. A plaster version of this work was the only piece by an American exhibited at the Paris Salon of 1886, at which it was awarded an honorable mention. Lorado Taft, a contemporary historian of sculpture, preferred Boyle's depictions of Native Americans to the "class of exquisitely finished and exquisitely foolish Indians of the jewelry stores, with which not a few public works have a close relationship" (p. 407). Boyle's original design showed the woman defending her children against an eagle splayed on its back with wings spread and claws tearing the air. The association objected to this depiction of the nation's symbol, so Boyle grudgingly substituted the inoffensive, but not particularly threatening, young bear.

Sometime during the 1880s the Boyles took an extended trip to Europe, including eight months of study and travel in Italy and tours of Switzerland and Germany. By the early 1890s Boyle was back in the United States, coordinating the decoration of the Transportation Building for the World's Columbian Exposition. Boyle supervised a team of sculptors who executed his designs for five bas-relief panels, eight figural groups, and sixteen single figures. Boyle also exhibited a bronze at the exposition: *Tired Out*, a figural group of a mother with two children, won a medal. In 1893 the artist returned to Philadelphia, where he worked on numerous commissions, including full-length bronzes of Francis Bacon and Plato for the Library of Congress and several busts for local institutions.

Around the turn of the century Boyle worked on a statue of Benjamin Franklin, which was presented to the city of Philadelphia in 1900 by J. C. Strawbridge, one of the city's wealthiest merchants. Franklin is shown seated, with one leg tucked slightly under and the other extended such that the toe of his shoe reaches beyond the edge of the pedestal. The statesman leans forward slightly, rather than sinking back into the chair. His head is turned to the left, and his gaze is directed up and away as if he is observing some interesting activity or phenomenon. Viewed from the side, the slight turn of his shoulders emphasizes Franklin's engagement with his surroundings. Boyle successfully balanced a suitable level of dignity and monumentality with elements that lend the work a liveliness and informality appropriate to the subject. The sculpture received accolades when it was exhibited at the 1904 World's Fair in St. Louis, and in 1905 a reproduction was installed in Paris in honor of the Franklin bicentenary.

In the meantime Boyle had designed two large groups, *The Savage Age in the East* and *The Savage Age in the West*, for the Pan-American Exposition of 1901; like his designs for the 1893 exposition, these were never executed in stone or bronze and do not survive. In 1902 the Boyles moved to New York City, where Boyle participated in many professional organizations, and served on the Art Commission from 1906 to 1907. In 1908, after a controversial competition open to sculptors of Irish descent, Boyle was awarded a $50,000 commission from the federal government for a statue of Irish-American revolutionary war hero Commodore John Barry. Boyle executed a formal eight-foot tall statue of Barry clad in yards of drapery holding his orders and sword in his right hand. A figure of Victory decorates the front of the enormous stone pedestal. The statue was unveiled on 16 May 1914 during a gala ceremony, which included an address by President Woodrow Wilson. Boyle became ill and died in New York City within a few years of completing this work.

Boyle contributed to the development of American monumental sculpture and architectural decoration by applying his traditional European training to uniquely American subjects. A contemporary critic, referring in particular to Boyle's depictions of Native Americans, wrote that "the impulse which his example gave has greatly enriched American sculptural art and turned the efforts of American artists to the rich art field to be found in our own history."

• Early assessments of John J. Boyle include brief discussions in Charles H. Caffin, *American Masters of Sculpture* (1903), and Lorado Taft, *The History of American Sculpture* (1903). See also Edward J. Wheeler, ed., "A Sculptor of American Primitive Life," *Current Literature* 39, no. 5 (Nov. 1905): 507–8, frontispiece. More modern discussions are included in Wayne Craven, *Sculpture in America* (1968), and Donald Martin Reynolds, *Masters of American Sculpture* (1993). See also James M. Goode, *The Outdoor Sculpture of Washington, D.C.* (1974), regarding the statue of Commodore Barry, and Ira J. Bach and Mary Lackritz Gray, *A Guide to Chicago's Public Sculpture* (1983), for an essay about *The Alarm*. Substantive obituaries are in the *Philadelphia Public Ledger*, *Philadelphia Inquirer*, and *New York Tribune*, all 11 Feb. 1917.

MARJORIE A. WALTER

BOYLE, Kay (19 Feb. 1902–27 Dec. 1992), writer, educator, and political activist, was born in St. Paul, Minnesota, the daughter of Howard Peterson Boyle, a lawyer, and Katherine Evans, a literary and social activist. Her grandfather had founded the West Publishing Company, and the financial security afforded by this background allowed the Boyle family to travel extensively. Boyle's education was sporadic, culminating in two years of architecture classes at the Ohio Mechanics' Institute (1917–1919). In 1922 Boyle joined her sister Joan in New York City, where she began to work for Lola Ridge, New York editor of *Broom*. This brief period in New York marked Boyle's entry into the world of the "little" magazines, the avant-garde literary movement that she helped develop and define over the next decade. Boyle married Richard Brault in 1922. They had no children and were divorced in 1932.

After moving to France in 1923 with Brault, Boyle began to work with Ernest Walsh on his magazine *This Quarter*. In 1927, after Walsh's death, she gave birth to a daughter fathered by Walsh; in this same year, she contributed both a review of William Carlos Williams's *In the American Grain* and the short story "Theme" to the first issue of Eugene Jolas's *transition*. Over the next two years Boyle published consistently in *transition*, a magazine that offered itself as the playground for revolutionary literary endeavors, as the forum for the self-proclaimed "Revolution of the Word."

In 1932 Boyle married Laurence Vail, with whom she had been living since 1929. The couple had three children. After moving to Austria in 1933, Boyle solicited contributions for a new experiment in publishing, *Short Stories 1934*. Intended to be a collection of page-length stories by different authors that would encapsulate the year, this work was published as *365 Days* (1936), with contributions by Boyle, Vail, William Saroyan (who gave her 365 stories), Langston Hughes, and Henry Miller. In 1934 Boyle was awarded her first Guggenheim Fellowship, and she also won her first O. Henry Memorial Award for the short story "The White Horses of Vienna." This story is exemplary of much of Boyle's writing, for it articulates an urgent need for art to engage with political and social issues. In this story, set in Austria in the early 1930s, the Viennese Dr. Heine travels into the mountains to assist an older doctor whose knee has been sprained during covert socialist maneuvers, and who can no longer attend to his patients. While the young Dr. Heine argues that art, science, and everyday life are fundamentally more important than politics, the older doctor seems to believe that as long as human dignity is threatened, art is meaningful only in the service of freedom.

This same basic theme is played out, with numerous variants and immense subtlety, in the majority of Boyle's short stories, including such acclaimed pieces as "Defeat" (1941), which won Boyle her second O. Henry Memorial Award, and the often-anthologized *New Yorker* masterpiece "Winter Night" (1946). Boyle's novels, fairly popular in their time, have been largely neglected in comparison with her other works. When the eminent literary critic Edmund Wilson reviewed Boyle's novel *Avalanche* (1944), he summed up the position of many critics on her novels with "I cannot see how a writer with a really sound sense of style could have produced this book even as a potboiler."

Boyle and Vail were divorced in 1943, and that same year she married Baron Joseph von Franckenstein. They had two children. In 1953 Boyle's writing career was nearly devastated when Franckenstein was dismissed from his post in the Public Affairs Division of the U.S. State Department. Although he had been cleared at a loyalty-security hearing, at which Franckenstein was charged with being married to the potentially subversive Boyle, Roy Cohn decided to fire Franckenstein as representing "surplus" labor. Boyle lost her post as foreign correspondent to the *New Yorker*, which she had held since 1947, and was virtually blacklisted by the major magazines to which she had once contributed so abundantly. After a nine-year legal battle against his dismissal, during which Boyle and her family lived in Rowayton, Connecticut, Franckenstein was reinstated by the State Department and appointed cultural attaché to the U.S. embassy in Tehran (1962); he died of lung cancer within a year of assuming his new post.

With a large family to support, Boyle immediately accepted a creative writing position on the faculty of San Francisco State College (1963; now San Francisco State University). She remained on the faculty until 1979. During this time she was also heavily involved in political activism. She traveled to Cambodia in 1966 as part of the "Americans Want to Know" fact-seeking mission; also in 1966 she held daily vigils in front of the San Francisco California Funeral Service, where bodies returning from Vietnam were being processed. In 1967 she was arrested twice and jailed for thirty-one days for participating in sit-ins at the Oakland Induction Center. Until her death in Mill Valley, California, Boyle was involved in a number of activist organizations, particularly Amnesty International. As a political activist and educator, Boyle's legacy of personal commitment and tireless dedication has survived her death. As a literary figure, Boyle remains an important (although often underrated) component of American literary modernism, both for her early experimental work with the émigré avant-garde and for her later pieces in major magazines such as the *New Yorker*.

• Most of Kay Boyle's papers and manuscripts are at the Morris Library, Southern Illinois University, Carbondale. The most comprehensive study of Boyle's life and work is Sandra Whipple Spanier, *Kay Boyle, Artist and Activist* (1986). Less specifically about Boyle, but an excellent introduction to the émigré writing community of the period, is Shari Benstock, *Women of the Left Bank* (1986). For Boyle's firsthand account of the *transition* era, see her additions to the revised edition of Robert McAlmon, *Being Geniuses Together, 1920–1930* (1968). Boyle considered *Monday Night* (1938) to be her best novel, although *Plagued by the Nightingale* (1931) was equally acclaimed; many of her short stories can be found in *Fifty Stories* (1980); her *Collected Poems* appeared in 1962. An obituary is in the *New York Times*, 29 Dec. 1992.

CHRIS ANDRE

BOYLE, Michael J. (11 June 1879–17 May 1958), labor leader, was born in Woodland, Minnesota, the son of Michael Boyle and Ann Kelly, farmers. In 1895 Boyle left school and started working as a utility company lineman in St. Paul. After holding similar jobs in Ohio and Michigan, Boyle moved to Chicago, where he became a wireman with the Chicago Tunnel Company. In 1902 he married Minnie Alice Oberlin; they had three children. Boyle had joined the International Brotherhood of Electrical Workers (IBEW) when he took his first job, and in 1904 he transferred his membership to the union's Local 134, which had jurisdiction over "inside" electrical work in Chicago. In 1908 he became business agent for the local.

Boyle assumed his position at a time when Chicago's building trades unions were reviving after a humiliating defeat in 1900; meanwhile the employers' solidarity had begun to wane. In this climate it became possible for unions like Boyle's to demand payoffs from individual contractors in exchange for labor peace. During these years Boyle acquired the nickname "Umbrella Mike." Reputedly, instead of taking direct bribes he encouraged people to drop contributions into his folded umbrella as it hung from the bar at his informal headquarters in Johnson's Saloon. In 1909 Boyle and a colleague were convicted of extortion but received only light fines. Then, in 1911, Boyle and several others were convicted of conspiring to restrict trade when Local 134 used its power to prevent the use of nonunion-made electrical appliances.

In 1914 Boyle joined the IBEW executive board. That same year he faced legal trouble again when he was charged with violating the Sherman Antitrust Act. This time his fellow defendants included not only three union officers but also five members of the Chicago Switchboard Manufacturers' Association (CSMA). Witnesses testified that the contractors had granted Local 134 the closed shop in exchange for the union's refusal to work on any job involving switchboards that were not produced by the CSMA. It was reported that Boyle had particularly benefited from this arrangement because he had a financial interest in one of the CSMA member firms. (He had other business interests as well, including a valve company and a real estate firm.) Several witnesses reported bribing Boyle; one businessman, for instance, testified that he had paid Boyle a $20,000 "insurance premium" to prevent strikes while his company was erecting a building. Asked to explain how he had accumulated a fortune of $350,000 on his $50 per week union salary, Boyle explained: "It was with great thrift."

On his conviction, Boyle was sentenced to serve a year in prison and to pay a $5,000 fine. However, his sentence was commuted in 1920 after he had served only four months, thanks to the intervention of American Federation of Labor president Samuel Gompers, Attorney General A. Mitchell Palmer and President Woodrow Wilson. That summer Boyle demonstrated his undiminished power by tying up public transportation in Chicago for several days with a strike and then calling out the elevator operators in City Hall. The *Chicago Tribune* explained the situation succinctly, "Umbrella Mike is out of jail." Threatened with arrest, Boyle called off the strike, but in 1921 he led another walkout that stopped public transportation again and threw the entire city into darkness. This time the strike ended when a number of participants were indicted for murder. Local 134 also acquired a reputation for violence within its ranks; in 1924 two men were killed and four were hurt in a union election fight.

In 1921 a state commission appointed to investigate the high cost of construction in Chicago confirmed that the patterns of corruption and collusion described in Boyle's 1914 trial were continuing. According to witnesses, construction sites were besieged by union representatives demanding bribes to prevent strikes; Boyle was cited as one of the major offenders. Moreover, testimony made clear that employers played their own role in the process, quietly paying the unions and passing the additional cost on to their customers.

Boyle's regime was sustained not only by the loyalty of his followers and the cooperation of employers but also by a network of influential political friends. In 1922 Boyle was accused of bribing the jury that acquitted his close associate, Illinois governor Len Small, of fraud charges. Boyle went into hiding for six weeks, resurfaced, refused to testify before the grand jury, and was sentenced to six months in jail. After jumping bail, he was arrested in Wisconsin and brought back to Chicago but was pardoned by Small after serving only fifty days.

In 1930 Boyle became an IBEW vice president for the Sixth District, which covered the upper Midwest. Over the next decade he launched an aggressive organizing campaign throughout his district; called periodic strikes, some of which involved violence between union factions; and worked assiduously to prevent any inroads into his domain by the new Congress of Industrial Organization. In 1936, four years after the death of his first wife, Boyle married Helen Kane; they had no children together.

Boyle faced antitrust charges again in 1940, when he and sixteen local union leaders and businessmen were charged with combining forces to keep out of Chicago any electrical fixtures not manufactured there; three years later the charges were dropped. Meanwhile, as head of a district that accounted for one-quarter of the IBEW's total membership, Boyle had become increasingly influential within the union. He showed the extent of his power in 1946–1947 when he spearheaded the ousting of both the IBEW president and secretary during a struggle over loyalty and rivalry within the union. In his later years Boyle retired to Miami, Florida, where he died, but he retained his union offices until his death.

Despite his many misdeeds, Boyle sustained the power of the IBEW for a half century under extraordinarily difficult conditions. He developed an unemployment insurance program that helped many union members survive the depression. Admiring his drive, negotiating skill, and administrative talent, most members were willing to overlook his sins. "Remember," said one, "the Umbrella has meant higher wages and better working conditions for thousands." Yet there was a darker side. Corruption and violence shadowed his career and brought discredit to labor; but it would not have continued without the acquiescence and cooperation of employers, top labor leaders, political officials, and rank-and-file members. Boyle's story represents a troubling chapter in not only the history of the labor movement but also of the society within which he lived.

• Since Boyle left no personal papers, the best picture of his career is found in the records at IBEW headquarters in Washington, D.C., and in the *Electrical Workers' Journal.* See also Grace Palladino, *Dreams of Dignity, Workers of Vision: A History of the IBEW* (1991), Barbara Warne Newell, *Chicago and the Labor Movement: Metropolitan Unionism in the 1930s* (1961), and Royal E. Montgomery, *Industrial Relations in the Chicago Building Trades* (1927). Boyle's misdeeds are discussed in Harold Seidman, *Labor Czars: A History of Labor Racketeering* (1938), and William Z. Foster, *Misleaders of Labor* (1927). Obituaries are in the *New York Times,* 19 May 1958, and the *Electrical Workers' Journal* (May–June 1958): 20.

SANDRA OPDYCKE

BOYLE, Thomas (29 June 1776?–12 Oct. 1825), shipmaster and privateer, was born reputedly at Marblehead, Massachusetts, although little else is known of his early years. His first recorded appearance was on 15 October 1792, when he registered at the Baltimore Customs House as master of the schooner *Hester.* In 1794 Boyle married Mary Gross of Baltimore; they had five children. In 1804 he purchased his own vessel, the *Traveller,* and conducted many voyages to the West Indies and South America. Boyle quickly established himself as a successful shipmaster, but in 1806 he abandoned seafaring to open a tannery shop. He also served on the Mechanic Bank of Baltimore board of directors and, on 8 April 1808, received appointment as captain in the city's Fifty-first Militia Regiment. When renewed hostilities with England commenced in June 1812, Boyle forsook commercial pursuits and returned to sea as a privateer.

On 11 July 1812 Boyle departed Baltimore commanding the fourteen-gun schooner *Comet.* In quick order he subdued the ships *Henry, Hopewell,* and *John* as well as the brig *Industry* for a total prize value of half a million dollars. Boyle returned home in November 1812, having cruised eighty-three days without the loss of a man. Pausing only to refit and resupply, the *Comet* slipped back into Chesapeake bay on 23 December 1812.

Boyle conducted his second cruise in the West Indian and South American waters that he knew so well. On 14 January 1813 he rashly attacked a convoy of three armed British transports escorted by a Portuguese warship near Pernambuco, Brazil. The *Comet,* firing accurately, disabled the escort and captured the three vessels. Two weeks later Boyle took the *Adelphi,* and on 6 February he seized the ship *Alexis* before enduring a six-hour chase by the frigate HMS *Surprise.* Following repairs at St. Bartholomew's, Boyle eluded additional British warships near St. Croix and reached Baltimore on 20 March 1813. Subsequent cruises in the *Comet* yielded additional prizes but also an unsuccessful nine-hour battle with the high-sided transport

Hibernia. By the time the *Comet* was sold in December 1814, Boyle had taken twenty-seven prizes.

In the summer of 1814 Boyle transferred to a new ship, the sixteen-gun schooner *Chasseur*, which was based in New York. On 29 July he embarked on his most audacious cruise yet, directly into the chops of the English channel. Boyle rapidly subdued the brigs *Eclipse*, *Antelope*, and *Commerce* and the ship *James* without loss. On 30 August he mockingly proclaimed England, Scotland, and Ireland under blockade and had the document sent aboard a cartel vessel to be posted at Lloyd's of London. This bravado induced the Admiralty to dispatch five Royal Navy brigs with specific instructions to capture the *Chasseur*, but Boyle easily outsailed his pursuers. He reached New York on 29 October 1814, having secured eighteen prizes in ninety days.

Boyle departed New York for the last time on 23 December 1814 and sailed directly for Barbados. Arriving there on 5 January 1815, he traded shots with a sloop-of-war, burned a schooner within sight of an admiral's ship, and easily outran a pursuing frigate. Within days Boyle captured two heavily laden cargo ships, *Coruna* and *Adventure*, before proceeding to the Cuban coast. On 15 February he approached an innocent-looking schooner that turned out to be a warship, HMS *St. Lawrence*. A desperate fight ensued at close quarters, but Boyle's superior gunnery wrecked his opponent, and the warship capitulated. *Chasseur* is the only privateer of the War of 1812 to subdue a vessel of the Royal Navy. Word of peace arrived soon after, and Boyle returned to Baltimore in triumph. In two years he had amassed a phenomenal record, having secured eighty prizes valued at more than a million dollars. For its exploits, *Chasseur* became popularly known as the Pride of Baltimore.

After the war Boyle resumed commercial activities and plied the trade routes to the West Indies and South America. On 11 January 1817 he was elected board member of the Vigilant Fire Company of Baltimore. The wars of national liberations were then commencing in Latin America and afforded lucrative prospects to many former privateers and their vessels. Fragmentary evidence suggests that between 1816 and 1818 Boyle covertly ran supplies for the Mexican adventurer Francisco Xavier Mina and the Argentine renegade Luis Aury. When both expeditions failed he returned to the coastal trade and acquired the brig *Panopea* in June 1825. Boyle had apparently lost none of his prowess when, in July 1824, he beat off a pirate attack in the Gulf of Mexico. A major loss occurred on 25 December 1825, however, when *Panopea* ran aground at Turks Island, Jamaica, and was scuttled. In the following spring at Baltimore, Boyle purchased a new vessel, the *Chasseur*, and on 16 August 1825 sailed from New York for Alvarado, Mexico. He died on the return leg of the voyage.

Boyle was a legendary privateer of the War of 1812. Quiet and unassuming by nature, he nonetheless exemplified American naval prowess by sailing under the bows of a powerful enemy and defying all attempts at capture. The accomplishments of his ships the *Comet* and *Chasseur* equaled or exceeded those of contemporaries like *America* and *Grand Turk* of Salem and insured Baltimore's reputation as the nation's privateering center.

• Logs and letters of Boyle are in the Maryland Historical Society. Printed accounts are "Log of the *Chasseur*," *Maryland Historical Magazine* 1 (1906): 168–80, 218–40, and "The *Comet* Harasses the British," *Maryland Historical Magazine* 53 (1958): 295–315. An informative biography is Fred W. Hopkins, *Tom Boyle, Master Privateer* (1976). Old but still informative is William A. Fairburn, *Merchant Sail*, vol. 2 (8 vols, 1945–1955). For greater historical context consult Jerome Garitee, *The Republic's Private Navy* (1977); Thomas V. Huntsberry, *Maryland Privateers: War of 1812* (1983); and Thomas C. Gilmer, *Pride of Baltimore* (1992).

JOHN C. FREDRIKSEN

BOYLE, Tony. *See* Boyle, William Anthony.

BOYLE, William Anthony (1 Dec. 1904–31 May 1985), labor union leader, was born in Bald Butte, Montana, the son of James P. Boyle, a coal miner, and Catherine Mallin. He attended public schools in Idaho and Montana and graduated from high school. Like his father, who came from a family of Irish immigrant coal miners in England and who emigrated to the United States, William A., better known as "Tony" Boyle, became a coal miner. Like most miners in the state of Montana, he joined the United Mine Workers of America (UMWA), the union that by the middle of the 1930s represented nearly all the nation's coal miners. On 3 June, 1928 Boyle married Ethel V. Williams; they had one child.

Boyle rose rapidly in the ranks of his union, by 1940 achieving the presidency of UMWA District 27, which represented all the coal miners in Montana. He served in that capacity until 1948. For a short time before the UMWA withdrew from the Congress of Industrial Organizations (CIO) in 1941, Boyle also served as the CIO regional director for western mountain states as well as a regional director of District 50, UMWA, a catchall unit for noncoal miners. In his capacity as a UMWA district president, Boyle represented the union on several World War II government-industry committees in Washington, where he caught the attention of UMWA president John L. Lewis. In 1948 Lewis appointed Boyle as his special assistant, a position Boyle held until 1960.

Boyle served Lewis and worked out of the Union's national headquarters in Washington during a period in which the UMWA first flourished and then suffered a series of debilitating setbacks. Between 1946 and 1952, under Lewis's leadership, the UMWA won for its members exceptionally high daily wage rates, a generous retirement plan, and company-paid health and welfare benefits, including union-operated hospitals and clinics in southern Appalachia, a region previously lacking modern health services and facilities. The UMWA also dealt cooperatively with the major coal companies and associations, rendering mass strikes a relic of the past.

By the middle of the 1950s, however, competition from cheaper, cleaner energy sources (primarily natural gas and oil) as well as technological improvements reduced the demand for coal miners. Smaller coal operators could not afford to pay union retirement and health benefits, and unemployed miners took work wherever they could find it. As nonunion mining spread, especially in Kentucky and Tennessee, Lewis assigned Boyle to fight the nonunion operators. Throughout the 1950s, working with UMWA officers in the two states and with hired thugs, Boyle used intimidation, outright violence, and even dynamite to put nonunion mines and miners out of work.

Lewis apparently appreciated Boyle's services to the union, for when the UMWA president retired in 1960, he appointed Boyle vice president, making him the logical successor to the new, elderly, and ailing UMWA president, Thomas Kennedy. Suffering from cancer, Kennedy died in 1963, and the union presidency passed on an interim basis to Boyle. As president, Boyle behaved in the manner that he had learned from Lewis. He ran the union as a private fiefdom, appointed his brothers and his daughter to well-paid positions in the union, and used other appointed officials and the UMWA journal to promote his own candidacy for union president. In 1964, despite a challenge from an obscure competitor, Boyle was easily elected president of the UMWA.

Like Lewis, Boyle promoted cooperation with the mine operators, personally serving as a member of the board of directors and a vice president of the National Coal Policy Conference, a joint agency of the largest operators and the union. He opposed strikes and preferred to bargain amicably with the mine operators.

During Boyle's administration, alternative fuels continued to reduce demand for coal, nonunion mines increased, and the number of employed union miners shrank drastically. By 1970, at most 164,000 workers mined coal; 40 percent of the coal they loaded was nonunion; and under 100,000 working miners (as distinct from retired union members) belonged to the UMWA. Although Boyle ran the union autocratically, as Lewis had done for years, he never became a true leader or hero to the rank and file. When a mine disaster in West Virginia in 1968 claimed seventy-eight lives, Boyle dispassionately alluded to it as a natural feature of coal mining and expressed sympathy for the company as a good employer. His lack of empathy for the deceased miners and their families fueled resentment and protest among union members. That, as well as the continued decline of the union, prompted Joseph Yablonski, another former Lewis lieutenant, to challenge Boyle for the presidency in 1969.

Yablonski's candidacy led directly to the undoing of Boyle. Not content to use his control of the union's staff, journal, and treasury to insure reelection, Boyle resorted to violence. On New Year's Eve 1970, thugs hired by Boyle murdered Yablonski, his wife, and daughter. Reelected to the union presidency by a margin of two to one, Boyle found himself beset by foes everywhere. Yablonski's surviving son, an attorney, organized a movement to tie Boyle to the murders and remove him from the presidency; rank-and-file miners linked their cause to that of Yablonski's son through Miners' for Democracy (MFD), an insurgent protest movement; and state and federal officials brought formal charges against Boyle. The U.S. department of Labor invalidated the 1969 election, requiring the UMWA to hold another election for president in 1972 in which the MFD candidate, Arnold Miller, defeated Boyle.

In September 1973 Pennsylvania indicted Boyle for conspiracy to murder the Yablonskis, prompting Boyle to attempt suicide. Even before Pennsylvania tried him on the murder charges, the federal government in December 1973 indicted Boyle for using union funds for illegal political contributions, a charge on which he was convicted and sentenced to serve twenty-eight months at a medical center for federal prisoners in Missouri. While Boyle served his federal sentence, Pennsylvania tried him for murder, a charge on which he was also convicted in April 1974 and sentenced to three consecutive life terms.

Boyle entered the Pennsylvania state prison at Dallas as soon as his federal sentence ended in April 1976. From 1980 until his death, he grew so ill that he moved back and forth between a nursing home and a hospital. He died at Wilkes-Barre (Pa.) General Hospital.

• No separate collection of Boyle papers exists. The UMWA's papers are located in a warehouse in Alexandria, Va. The following books provide the most complete information on Boyle's career in the UMWA: Paul F. Clark, *The Miners' Fight for Democracy* (1981); Melvyn Dubofsky and Warren Van Tine, *John L. Lewis: A Biography* (1977); Joseph E. Finley, *The Corrupt Kingdom: The Rise and Fall of the United Mine Workers* (1972); and Britt Hume, *Death and the Mines: Rebellion and Murder in the United Mine Workers* (1971). An obituary is in the *New York Times*, 1 June 1985.

MELVYN DUBOFSKY

BOYLSTON, Zabdiel (9 Mar. 1680–1 Mar. 1766), surgeon and first physician to perform smallpox inoculation in America, was born in Muddy River (now Brookline) near Boston, Massachusetts, the son of Thomas Boylston, a physician and farmer, and Mary Gardner. He began studying medicine with his father, who died when Zabdiel was fifteen, after which he continued with John Cutler, a leading physician and surgeon in Boston. The fact that he never obtained a college education haunted him throughout his life but may have contributed to his strong drive to succeed.

In the early 1700s Boylston opened an apothecary shop in Dock Square, where he carried on a lucrative medical and surgical practice and took on apprentices. Driven to make money, he developed various medicines and medical equipment and advertised them in local newspapers, in addition to elixirs, sugar, and spices. Advertisements in 1710 and 1720 described a lithotomy and a mastectomy, which Boylston had carried out in the presence of local physicians, surgeons, and clergy. In 1706 he married Jerusha Minot of Boston; they had eight children.

At the end of April 1721, the dreaded epidemic disease, smallpox, was spread to Boston by a traveler from the West Indies. By 27 May there were eight cases of smallpox in Boston, although authorities had tried to contain it with sanitation and isolation. The Reverend Cotton Mather, who was interested in scientific and medical matters and was a fellow of the Royal Society of London, had learned of a folk remedy called "inoculation" from an African and from articles about inoculations in Constantinople in the society's *Philosophical Transactions*. Smallpox inoculation involved insertion of pus from a patient suffering from a mild case of smallpox into the arm or thigh of a healthy person, thereby deliberately infecting the recipient, who then usually had a mild case of the disease followed by permanent immunity. On 6 June Mather circulated "An Address to the Physicians of Boston" containing details of the new medical procedure and urging them to try it. After there was no response to this or a second letter sent out several weeks later, he wrote directly to Boylston, enclosing a summary of the articles in the *Philosophical Transactions*. Two days later, on 26 June, Boylston successfully inoculated his six-year-old son, his slave Jack, and Jack's two-and-a-half-year-old son.

The public outcry was enormous, especially since it was considered sinful to make people ill deliberately. Physicians, led by Edinburgh graduate William Douglass, were opposed because of professional conservatism and the belief that inoculation would spread the disease even further. Some questioned Boylston's competence, citing his lack of university training. Many believed that there were geographical differences in disease, owing to different climates, and that the fact that a new practice worked in southern regions, such as Africa and Constantinople, did not mean that it would work in the North.

Although both Mather and Boylston were publicly ridiculed and threatened, they fought back in the press, and Boylston continued to inoculate. Mather and Boylston distributed a twenty-two–page tract describing the Constantinople inoculations and responding to religious scruples about the procedure entitled *Some Account of What Is Said of Inoculating or Transplanting the Small Pox*. Six of Boston's sixteen ministers publicly endorsed inoculation. Meanwhile, the city of 12,000 inhabitants was ravaged by the disease, which continued into the winter. When the epidemic ended in the spring of 1722, 5,889 people had contracted smallpox, of whom 844 had died. Boylston had inoculated 246, only six of whom had died, probably from other causes. Two other physicians in neighboring towns had performed 36 inoculations.

Simultaneously, unknown to the Bostonians, the new practice had also been introduced into England, and experimentation had occurred under royal sponsorship at the suggestion of Sir Hans Sloane, a royal physician. In September 1721 Mather had sent information about the Boston inoculations to London to be published, and several supportive tracts written by Boston clergymen were reprinted in London.

Since many more people had been inoculated in Boston than in England, knowledge of Boylston's work was crucial to supporters of the new immunological procedure, and English doctors eagerly invited Boylston to London. He arrived in 1725 and remained nearly two years. He was immediately adopted by the inoculationists and was urged to write a detailed account of his experience in Boston. His *Historical Account of the Small-Pox Inoculated in New England, Upon All Sorts of Persons, Whites, Blacks, and of All Ages and Constitutions* was published in the spring of 1726. Based on detailed case histories, the book gave precise clinical and statistical information to demonstrate the validity of the new procedure. On 7 July 1726 Boylston became the first American-born physician to be elected a fellow of the Royal Society of London, the highest scientific honor of the time.

Although Boylston was invited to speak to the Royal College of Physicians as well as to the Royal Society, he did not perform inoculations or practice medicine while in London. After returning home he sent a five-and-a-half-pound stone taken from a horse's stomach to the society for its "Collection of Valuable Rarities." Later he claimed to have unsuccessfully tried to accustom rattlesnakes to confinement so that they could be shipped to London for experimentation.

In Boston Boylston resumed his busy and lucrative practice. He led the inoculation efforts when a new smallpox epidemic struck the city in 1730. In 1740 his health declined, and he sold his Boston shop and moved to his father's farm in Brookline, where he became a selectman, bred horses, and carried on scientific experiments on plants and animals. His stately three-story, fifteen-room mansion still stands in Brookline.

Without Boylston's pioneering inoculation efforts, Edward Jenner's introduction of vaccination against smallpox through cowpox inoculation at the end of the eighteenth century, which refined the procedure by substituting a harmless substance to be inoculated, could not have taken place.

• The most detailed and thoroughly researched study on Boylston is Gerald Marvin Mager, "Zabdiel Boylston: Medical Pioneer of Colonial Boston" (Ph.D. diss., Univ. of Illinois, Urbana-Champaign, 1975). Mager's research at the Boston Public Library, the Massachusetts Historical Society, Harvard University, the British Museum, and the Royal Society, as well as his study of local newspapers and the records of Suffolk County, revealed much about Boylston that was previously unknown. Other publications that contain pertinent information include Reginald H. Fitz, "Zabdiel Boylston, Inoculator, and the Epidemic of Smallpox in Boston in 1721," *Johns Hopkins Hospital Bulletin* 22 (1911): 314–27; John B. Blake, "The Inoculation Controversy in Boston, 1721–1722," *New England Quarterly* 25 (1952): 489–506; G. L. Kittredge, "Lost Works of Cotton Mather," *Proceedings of the Massachusetts Historical Society*, Feb. 1912, pp. 418–79; Otho T. Beall, Jr., and Richard H. Shryock, *Cotton Mather, First Significant Figure in American Medicine* (1954); Raymond P. Stearns, *Science in the British Colonies of America* (1970); and Genevieve Miller, *The Adoption of Inoculation for Smallpox in England and France* (1957).

GENEVIEVE MILLER

BOZEMAN, John M. (7 Jan. 1835–18 Apr. 1867), Montana trailblazer, was born in what is now Pickens County, Georgia, the son of William Bozeman and Delila Sims. His middle name apparently was Merin, but this cannot be determined with certainty. Little is known about John Bozeman's early life. In 1849 his father left the family to seek gold in California but died en route. In 1856 Bozeman married Lucinda Cathrine Ingram; the couple had three children, all daughters. In 1860 Bozeman followed his father's example, leaving his wife and children to join the Colorado gold rush. He arrived in Colorado too late to get a good claim. After less than two years there he joined Thomas Stuart and several others who had been encouraged to head north by glowing reports from Stuart's brothers Granville and James. The party arrived in the Deer Lodge Valley in what is now western Montana on 24 June 1862. Bozeman spent a brief period in Bannack a hundred miles to the south before moving to the Gallatin Valley in February 1863. He quickly recognized the agricultural and commercial potential of the location and filed claim number 60 on 160 acres of Gallatin riverfront property.

As the Montana gold rush began, the two available routes to the goldfields were the slow and expensive route by way of the Missouri River and Fort Benton or north from the Oregon Trail through Fort Hall in what is now southeastern Idaho. Bozeman saw the need for a direct route with adequate grass for large wagon trains and cattle herds. He met John M. Jacobs, an experienced wagon guide who agreed that a route should be possible east of the Big Horn Mountains. The advantages of the eastern route were seen as relatively level terrain, wide-open spaces that would support large herds, and several rivers that would provide adequate water. Bozeman seemingly discounted the main disadvantage of the eastern route—that it crossed prime Sioux hunting grounds.

In mid-March 1863 Bozeman, Jacobs, and Jacobs's young half-Flathead daughter Emma left Bannack to scout out the route. They timed their departure early enough to be able to meet potential emigrant customers at Fort Laramie. Unfortunately, after crossing the Big Horn River they were robbed of their horses and supplies by a band of Indians. Riding the three inferior horses that the Indians provided them in exchange and carrying a gun with five shots of ammunition, the small party was able to make it over 150 miles south to a settlement on the North Platte River at Deer Creek. There they recruited forty-six wagons, eighty-nine men, and a few women and children to take their new route north. They were also accompanied by a guide named Rafael Gallegos. Near present-day Buffalo, Wyoming, the wagon train was met by 150 Sioux and Cheyenne who convinced most of the party to turn back. Bozeman, Jacobs, and eight other men, however, insisted on continuing on the original route. With one packhorse, no wagons, and scant supplies they headed north, traveling at night. Despite losing their packhorse and supplies in a fall, they made it back to the Gallatin Valley.

Bozeman was not discouraged by this inauspicious start to his trail. In December 1863 he headed back to Omaha to recruit another emigrant train for the spring. He also organized the Missouri and Rocky Mountain Wagon Road and Telegraph Company to build tollgates and ferries on the trail. Bozeman's 1864 wagon train was a success, and the establishment of Fort Reno, Fort Phil Kearney, and Fort C. F. Smith along his route in 1866 quickly made it the most popular route to Montana. However, this very success later led to "Red Cloud's War" in 1866–1867, during which Sioux attacked the trail and besieged the forts along it.

After 1864 Bozeman did not personally lead any more wagon trains but instead became more involved with the development of the Gallatin Valley. He helped found the new town of Bozeman, farmed on his 160-acre homestead, carried the mail, helped establish a flour mill and hotel in Bozeman, and promoted the Gallatin Valley in interviews with the *Montana Post.* In November 1864 Bozeman placed advertisements in the paper attempting to raise a military unit to drive out the "marauding Indians." However, the unit never materialized.

In 1866 Bozeman formed a partnership with W. J. Davies to build and sell flatboats to travelers heading back east for the winter. He also planned to construct a ferry or bridge across the Yellowstone River at Boulder River and hoped to make a contract to sell flour to the army at Fort C. F. Smith. In order to further these ends, he left Bozeman on 17 April 1867 with Tom Cover. The following day while stopped for lunch they were attacked by a party of five Indians, possibly Blackfeet. Bozeman was killed, and Cover was wounded. Largely as a result of this incident, acting governor Thomas Francis Meagher authorized the raising of a militia, and the U.S. Army established Fort Ellis at Bozeman. Over the years there have been allegations that Thomas Cover actually murdered Bozeman and invented the story of an Indian attack. However, most historians accept Cover's version of the incident.

John Bozeman's legacy is difficult to evaluate. His vision of the strategic importance of the Gallatin Valley to the development of the territory was prophetic. He died, however, before any of his dreams could be realized. His greatest claim to fame, the Bozeman Trail, had to be abandoned in 1867 as a result of continued Indian opposition. The arrival of the Union Pacific Railroad in Corinne, Utah, the following year provided an easy, safe route to Montana and sealed the fate of the trail as an emigrant route. In the 1880s the route was revived in some of the great cattle drives from Texas.

• There were numerous contemporary newspaper articles on John Bozeman's death. An attempt at a biography is Merrill Burlingame, *John M. Bozeman, Montana Trailmaker*, originally published as an article in *Mississippi Valley Historical Review* 26 (Mar. 1941): 541–68 and revised in 1983 as a pamphlet. It treats certain aspects of his life in Montana in considerable detail but, because of a lack of sources, includes essentially nothing on his life before he came to Montana. The two most complete books on the Bozeman Trail are Grace Raymond Hebard and E. A. Brinistool, *The Bozeman Trail: Historical Accounts of the Blazing of the Overland Routes into the Northwest and the Fights with Red Cloud's Warriors* (1922; repr. 1960), and Dorothy M. Johnson, *The Bloody Bozeman: The Perilous Trail to Montana's Gold* (1971). An interesting, more recent article is Susan Badger Doyle, "Indian Perspectives of the Bozeman Trail," *Montana, Magazine of Western History*, Winter 1990, pp. 56–67.

ELLIE ARGUIMBAU

BRACE, Charles Loring (19 June 1826–11 Aug. 1890), philanthropist and social reformer, was born in Litchfield, Connecticut, the son of John Brace, the principal of the Female Seminary in Hartford, and Lucy Porter. Brace's mother died when he was fourteen. Entering Yale College in 1842, Brace showed an early interest in moral issues, theology, and the ministry. Upon graduating from Yale in 1846, he taught school for a year at Ellington and Winchendon in Connecticut. After returning to Yale Divinity School in 1847, he continued his studies at Union Theological Seminary in New York City, where he was ordained a Congregationalist minister in 1849. In New York City Brace's attention was drawn to the plight of the immigrant poor, particularly Irish street children and the Italians of the notorious Five Points district. From Blackwell's Island, a receiving station in the East River for New York City's poor and diseased where Brace did charitable work in 1849–1850, he wrote to his father in 1849, "I never had my whole nature so stirred up within me, as to what met my eyes in those hospital wards" ([Brace], p. 76).

In 1850 Brace visited Ireland, England, Germany, France, and the interior of Hungary. In Hungary, little visited at that time by tourists, he was arrested and imprisoned, suspected of being an agent of Hungarian revolutionaries and a supporter of Louis Kossuth, the Hungarian patriot. After a month's confinement, Brace was released through the intervention of the American consul. While abroad, he studied the management of schools, visited prisons, and observed charity centers and their methods, all sharpening his interest in social reform.

Brace returned to New York City in 1852 and intensified his efforts on behalf of the poor. In 1853 he was asked to head a "mission to the children" by a committee of prominent New York City citizens (including Abram Hewitt and Cyrus W. Field), all working separately to aid the poor in different areas of the city. Brace accepted and became the secretary of the newly formed Children's Aid Society. In a circular announcing the society's aims, Brace wrote:

> This society has taken its origin in the deeply settled feeling of our citizens, that something must be done to meet the increasing crime and poverty among the destitute children of New York. Its objectives are to help this class, by opening Sunday meetings and industrial schools, and gradually, as a means shall be furnished, by forming lodging houses and reading-rooms for children, and by employing paid agents, whose sole business shall be to care for them.

Brace remained the society's secretary for nearly forty years, helping guide its activities and preparing its annual reports, which were a chronicle of its achievements.

Brace was the architect of the society's "emigration" policy of placing poor children, mostly orphaned or abandoned, in the homes of families willing to care for them. "The best of all Asylums for the outcast child," Brace asserted, "is the *farmer's home*." In his time, he was the country's foremost advocate of home placement for destitute children as opposed to institutionalization, a step in a process Brace called "moral disinfection." In *The Best Method of Disposing of Our Pauper and Vagrant Children* (1859), Brace claimed that "by sending them out [to foster homes in western states], we are supplying the greatest and sorest need in American families, a permanent labor force educated in the habits of the house."

For over twenty years the Children's Aid Society relocated thousands of children to rural communities in New York, adjacent states, and the West. Brace maintained that some 75,000 children from the streets of New York City were placed in homes in the far West. The emigration policy continued, with some modifications, to the end of the nineteenth century. After a revival by the society in the Great Depression of the 1930s, the policy was discontinued because of societal changes. The Children's Aid Society also maintained homes for boys that developed from the Newsboy's Lodging House founded by Brace in 1854. Under Brace's direction, the society helped some 300,000 children in its free reading-rooms and in its ministrations to sick children throughout the city, making it a major force in the amelioration of nineteenth-century urban poverty. Historian Herbert Baxter Adams, writing in 1892, estimated that the number of children aided by Brace, within or outside the Children's Aid Society, was in excess of half a million.

On a second trip to Ireland in 1854, Brace married Letitia Neill of Belfast; they had six children, two of whom died at an early age. In 1856 he attended the international convention of children's charities in London and traveled to Europe in 1865 to investigate the sanitary methods of major cities. In 1872 he was a delegate to the international prison congress that met in London. His widening circle of colleagues and friends established Brace's national and international reputation.

A prolific writer, Brace's major works include *The Dangerous Classes of New York and Twenty Years' Work among Them* (1872) and *Gesta Christi; or, A History of Humane Progress Under Christianity* (1882), which went through four editions. Other works include *The Races of the Old World: A Manual of Ethnology* (1863); popular travel books such as *Home Life in Germany*

(1853); a mystical treatise, *The Unknown God; or, Inspiration among Pre-Christian Races* (1890); and a multitude of tracts.

Brace largely articulated in his works the concept of self-help and opposed all charitable efforts that, in his view, led to pauperization. *The Dangerous Classes*, the only work by Brace remembered today, is a comprehensive sourcebook for the study of nineteenth-century urban poverty and a blueprint (on Brace's terms of religion and regeneration through hope) for its reform. Brace presents a somber picture of urban pathology (for example, crime, family disintegration, alcoholism and vagrancy, prostitution, street gangs, child labor abuse, illegitimacy, and juvenile crime) and interpolates among these grim pictures the remedies and constructs of reform. It is these constructs of reform that intrude into current contexts. One could hardly argue that Brace understood the dynamics of class struggle or that in advocating that the poor become useful "producers" he sought the transformation of a *lumpen proletariat* into working-class coalitions of the poor who would work to confront economic issues—jobs, schools, housing. Yet it is in this direction that Brace's efforts led. He died in Switzerland.

• Some of Brace's papers and memorabilia are in the archives of the Children's Aid Society and in the New York Public Library. The chief source on the life of Brace is [Emma Brace], *The Life of Charles Loring Brace, Chiefly Told in His Own Letters* (1894). Two works that place Brace in the context of nineteenth-century poverty and its reform, both by Robert H. Bremner, are *From the Depths: The Discovery of Poverty in the United States* (1956) and *The Public Good: Philanthropy and Welfare in the Civil War Era* (1980). On the Children's Aid Society, see *The Children's Aid Society of New York: Its History, Plans, and Results* (1893) and *The Children's Aid Society, the Crusade for Children: A Review of Child Life in New York during Seventy-Five Years, 1853–1928* (1928). See also Francesco Cordasco, "Charles Loring Brace and the Dangerous Classes: Historical Analogues of the Urban Black Poor," *Journal of Human Relations* 20 (1972): 379–86.

FRANCESCO CORDASCO

BRACE, Charles Loring (2 June 1855–24 May 1938), social reformer and philanthropist, was born in Dobbs Ferry, New York, the son of Charles Loring Brace and Letitia Neill. His father had founded the Children's Aid Society (CAS) of New York, which the younger Brace would eventually manage and expand. Brace's early years were happy ones, as his son Gerald later recounted in *Days that Were* (1976). Brace was educated at Phillips Academy in Andover, Massachusetts, and at the Sheffield Scientific School of Yale, where he received his Ph.B. in 1876. Upon graduating, Brace traveled abroad.

Brace did not immediately follow in his father's steps. Beginning in 1880 he spent three years in Hudson, Wisconsin, working on the Chicago, St. Paul, Minneapolis and Omaha Railway as a construction engineer. He moved next to the Minnesota and St. Louis Railroad in 1883, apparently building bridges.

Sometime in 1889 or 1890 Brace volunteered or was called by his father to return to New York to become the senior Brace's assistant at the Children's Aid Society; however, Emma Brace, his sister, recalled that Brace volunteered to come to his father's aid. Either way, Brace was in position to take over for his father when the senior Brace died in August 1890. Until this time Brace had little interest in a philanthropic career; nevertheless, he would spend the next thirty-seven years as executive secretary of the CAS. His son Gerald Warner Brace would later compare the first two executive secretaries of the CAS. "My own father . . . was a good and capable executive but was not driven by the need to do miracles," unlike the senior Brace. Nevertheless, it would be a mistake to say that Brace merely continued the organization created by his father. The son in many ways surpassed the father's plans in both scale and scope.

As the *New York Times* wrote on 14 January 1935, Brace took the society from a small organization to "one of the largest and most influential in the city." He continued the programs established by the CAS under his father, most notably the placing-out system, which put children from the streets of New York City in homes throughout the nation; particularly in the West, and the summer camps, lodging homes, and industrial schools. However, under the younger Brace, the Children's Aid Society gradually began to place more emphasis on the children left in the city rather than those sent west on the orphan trains. Furthermore, in these years the CAS began to tackle other issues, such as the health, recreation, happiness, and citizenship of the children of New York City. Health centers, sanatoriums, fresh air homes, playgrounds, club centers, a medical bureau, and a boarding-homes department were established to address these concerns.

Like his father, Brace was greatly concerned about juvenile crime. His father had combated this problem by removing street children from the city and sending them on the orphan trains to the rural West. He believed that crime and poverty would be diminished if the population of street children was dispersed among the nation's farm families. The younger Brace took a different approach. Under him the CAS argued that most crimes occurred after school hours; therefore, Brace concluded, in order to decrease crime, activities must be created to fill the spare time of children after school. Furthermore, Brace claimed that most crimes were committed by boys seeking excitement and adventure, not to feed themselves or their families. Despite the attention that other social reformers at the time drew to the squalid quality of life in the tenements, clubs and playgrounds were the chief means that Brace employed to combat juvenile crime. According to Brace, these social institutions offered an additional benefit. At a time when militant labor protests had engendered fear of foreign ideas and influences among the elite and respectable elements of society, playgrounds and clubs offered the best means to Americanize the children of immigrants.

During these years the CAS became one of the most influential organizations in the field of child health in

New York City. The CAS inaugurated a medical bureau, a clearinghouse to which hundreds of organizations and hospitals came. Other programs he added included medical exams, meals for school children, and health centers. The CAS established a fresh air school for anemic children, where classes and naptimes were held outside as often as possible. Doctors were sent into tenements to bring weak children to these classes. Under Brace the CAS brought handicapped children out of their homes, many for the first time; even transportation was provided.

Brace married Louise Warner in January 1885. She had been living with the Braces for the years since the death of her stepmother. However, when Brace briefly returned East to marry her, his wife was disowned by her father, who claimed that Brace was a fortune hunter. Brace and his wife, who had five children, were close, but in the words of their youngest son, the family kept "their emotions and desires under control" (*Days*, p. 50).

Brace retired from the CAS on 1 January 1928. Two years later his younger brother Robert also retired from the CAS. This marked the end of the Brace family's role in the organization and in social work in general. Brace died in Santa Barbara, California.

The CAS is still an important part of the social welfare scene, due in no small measure to the work of Brace, a man whose dedication led the *New York Times* to note, "He has seen that the case of every child has been treated as an individual problem—as every bridge is to an engineer."

• For information on the Children's Aid Society under Brace, several letters to the editor in the *New York Times* written by him will be helpful; see especially 29 June 1923, 18 Oct. 1923, 14 Dec. 1925, 21 May 1926, and 22 June 1926. Gerald Warner Brace, *Days that Were* (1976), offers the best examination of Brace's personal life. One of the few secondary sources dealing with Brace or the Children's Aid Society during his years as executive secretary is the anonymously written *New York Street Kids* (1978). See also Marilyn Holt, *The Orphan Trains: Placing Out in America* (1992), for information about this program. Emma Brace, ed., *Life of Charles Loring Brace* (1894), while concerned with the senior Brace, offers some insights into the transition of his son from engineer to philanthropist. An obituary is in the *New York Times*, 26 May 1938.

ROBIN E. WALLS

BRACE, DeWitt Bristol (5 Jan. 1859–2 Oct. 1905), physicist, was born in Wilson, New York, the son of Lusk Brace, a farmer and grain mill operator, and Emily Bristol. In the early 1860s, the Braces moved to Lockport, New York, where DeWitt attended the local common and high schools. In 1877 he entered Boston University, receiving a bachelor of arts degree (1881). In 1881 he began graduate study in physics at the Johns Hopkins University, where he worked with Henry Augustus Rowland, one of America's foremost physicists. After receiving a master's degree in physics (1883) from Hopkins, Brace spent the next two years studying at the University of Berlin with Hermann von Helmholtz and Gustav Robert Kirchhoff, two of Europe's leading physicists. He received his Ph.D. in physics from Berlin in 1885 with a dissertation on the magnetic rotation of the plane of polarization (i.e., the Faraday effect) and refraction. This study in optics defined his future career as a research physicist.

In early 1886 Brace obtained his first professional appointment, as acting assistant professor of physics for one semester at the University of Michigan. Although unemployed the following academic year, in June 1887 he was appointed to a one-year instructorship in physics and chemistry at the University of Nebraska in Lincoln. Toward the end of that academic year he was appointed professor of physics and charged with developing a new department of physics (and electrical engineering) at Nebraska. Although he later had offers from Purdue, Texas, and Princeton, Brace stayed at Nebraska for the remainder of his career.

That career assumed two essentially distinct phases: in the first phase (1887–1896), Brace devoted himself to teaching and building the Department of Physics; in the second (1896–1905), he increasingly devoted himself to research. These phases and the development of the department reflect in part the changing nature of American physics in the late nineteenth century.

By the start of his second semester at Nebraska, Brace had established a proper physical laboratory, increased instruction in electricity, and offered a new course in electrical engineering. The following year he opened a more advanced laboratory and further expanded instruction in electricity. To do all this, the new department expanded from a one-room to a nine-room operation. In time, he more than doubled the number of physics courses available to students. To handle the increased teaching load, he gained an additional teaching staff of four, as well as two assistants. At the same time, Brace taught physics courses and helped obtain a new building for the fledgling Department of Electrical Engineering. In 1891 the latter became largely independent of physics and received its own professorship; in 1895 physics and electrical engineering were formally separated. By the second half of the 1890s, the physics department was offering a full line of undergraduate and graduate courses, in theoretical as well as experimental physics, at both the doctoral and master's level. The university's first Ph.D. degree, conferred in 1896, went to a Brace student.

Brace was an enthusiastic and successful teacher. It was said of him that "few men are more interested in the welfare of his pupils than he was" (*Daily Nebraskan*, 3 Oct. 1905). Growth in student enrollment in Brace's and the department's courses came accordingly: in 1895, for example, the department enrolled over 400 students in its classes. Yet Brace had to plead constantly with the university's board of regents to provide him with the financial resources to meet his expanded teaching obligations. In 1895 he began calling for funds to build an entirely new building devoted solely to physics. Not until the summer of 1904, however, did construction begin on the new three-story physics building, which opened in January 1906.

The second phase of Brace's career, that of research physicist, began in 1896, when the university first became a research institution and Brace's department had itself matured sufficiently so that he could consider doing research as well as teaching. Brace not only conducted his own research—publishing twenty-one papers in his career—but also inspired his small staff and still smaller number of advanced students to join him in research. Between 1896 and 1905, Brace's associates produced some fifteen publications. Such productivity placed Nebraska among the nation's leading physics departments at the turn of the century.

Brace devoted himself principally to studying the effect of certain electromagnetic processes on the velocity of light propagation in a transparent medium. In so doing, he made the highly skilled creation, adaptation, and use of optical instrumentation the hallmarks of his research. Above all, he pursued the foundational issue of the motion of matter relative to the so-called ether (the "ether drift"), an issue that called for highly precise instrumentation and great observational and experimental skills, leading to some of the most precise measurements of his day.

Among Brace's publications, pride of place must go to three substantive studies published in the *Philosophical Magazine*, the most important British journal of physics. In 1897 he showed that no optical effect of the magnetic field in a dielectric normal to the lines of force could be detected. In so doing, he cleverly managed to eliminate the Faraday effect. Then in 1901 he managed to resolve light into its circular components in the Faraday effect. The third outstanding study (1904) improved greatly upon the methods and results of Lord Rayleigh, one of the foremost physicists of the day: Brace showed definitively that no double refraction in matter moving through the ether could be detected. Brace's highly sensitive measurement suggested, as the Dutch theoretical physicist H. A. Lorentz soon pointed out, that there may be no ether drift. And, indeed, in 1905 Albert Einstein published his special theory of relativity, wherein he noted that experimental results to detect ether drift had all failed to detect any such motion.

Along with his substantive research, Brace also invented three important precision instruments: a new spectrophotometer that measured light transmission as a function of wavelength and that permitted comparative analysis of color or wavelength (1899); a sensitive-strip spectropolariscope for determining the angle of the plane of polarization of light (1903); and a half-shade elliptical polarizer and compensator (1904) for studying polarized light.

Brace's colleagues found him "unassuming, simple in his tastes, calm and dignified, yet resourceful and energetic" (*Nebraska State Journal*, 4 Oct. 1905). He remained a bachelor until 1901, when, at the age of forty-two, he married Elizabeth Russell Wing; they had three children. In September 1905 Brace, who was in Lincoln at the time, required emergency surgery on his mouth to remove an infected carbuncle. His doctors' efforts proved unsuccessful: the infection soon led to septicemia and to Brace's death in October.

By 1900, Brace had become one of the leading physicists in the United States. He was a charter and council member, and a vice president, of the new American Physical Society (founded 1899); he also was elected vice president of the American Association for the Advancement of Science (for 1901–1902). The public highpoint of his scientific career came in 1904, when he was asked to be one of only six American physicists to speak at the International Congress of Arts and Science held in St. Louis, a congress attended by many of the leading scientists, humanists, and educators in the United States and Europe. As the *Daily Nebraskan* pridefully noted the day after Brace's untimely death at age forty-six: "physicists place him among the first in his line in this country." The University of Nebraska honored him by naming the new physics building the Brace Laboratory of Physics. It was a fitting testament to his entrepreneurial and scientific accomplishments, to one who not only brought the scientific culture of the Atlantic coast and Central Europe to the Great Plains, but to one who, in turn, helped replenish that culture through his own contributions.

• The largest collections of Brace's correspondence, manuscript materials, and other miscellaneous primary source items are at the University of Nebraska–Lincoln Archives. Most of Brace's published writings are listed in *J. C. Poggendorff's Biographisch-literarisches Handwörterbuch*, vol. 4: *1883–1904* (1904), p. 171, and vol. 5: *1904–1922* (1926), p. 157; and in the *Royal Society Catalogue of Scientific Papers*, fourth series (1884–1900), 13:757.

The best scholarly studies on Brace are M. Eugene Rudd, "D. B. Brace's Measurement of Double Refraction Due to Ether Drift," in *The History and Preservation of Chemical Instrumentation*, ed. J. T. Stock and M. V. Orna (1986), pp. 41–50; and Rudd, *Science on the Great Plains: The History of Physics and Astronomy at the University of Nebraska–Lincoln*, University of Nebraska Studies, n.s., no. 71 (1992), pp. 1–51. David Cahan and M. Eugene Rudd, "At the Frontier of Science: DeWitt Bristol Brace. The Life of an American Physicist, 1859–1905" (in preparation) presents a full-length scholarly biography of Brace's life and career. See also Edward L. Nichols, "The Scientific Work of DeWitt Bristol Brace," *Physical Review* 24 (1907): 515–21.

DAVID CAHAN

BRACKENRIDGE, Hugh Henry (1748–25 June 1816), author and judge, was born Hugh Montgomery Breckenridge near Campbeltown, Scotland, the son of William Breckenridge, an impoverished farmer. His mother's name is unknown, but apparently she was a person of great intellect. Seeking to escape poverty, the family moved to Pennsylvania when Hugh was five, later settling in rural York County. Eventually Hugh changed his middle name to Henry, and he altered the spelling of his last name "because I found the bulk of the same stock spelt it so."

Although the backcountry offered few opportunities for learning, a local clergyman provided Brackenridge an introduction to classical studies. When he was fifteen he was hired as a teacher at a free school at Gunpowder Falls, Maryland, where he stayed for three years. In 1768 he entered the College of New Jersey (now Princeton University) and aligned himself with Philip Freneau and James Madison in a Whig literary club. Brackenridge was a devoted American patriot. In *The Rising Glory of America*, a poem written with Freneau as the commencement address in 1771, he lauded "the morning of the world." By 1774 he had received a master's degree in divinity and again provided a commencement poem. During the Revolution he served as a chaplain in General George Washington's army and wrote two plays, *The Battle of Bunkers-Hill* (1776) and *The Death of General Montgomery* (1777), as well as *Six Political Discourses Founded on the Scriptures* (1778). These works did not, however, make him a well-known author.

Brackenridge was a restless man. He never really embraced all of the doctrines of his church, the Presbyterian, and he resigned a year after he was licensed to preach by the Philadelphia Presbytery. He was never ordained. He turned in 1778 to the study of the law under Samuel Chase of Annapolis, Maryland. A year later he was back in Philadelphia, where he cofounded the *United States Magazine*. Brackenridge wrote most of the articles for the magazine, but it folded in December 1779. The next year he was admitted to the Philadelphia bar, and in 1781 he opened a law office in Pittsburgh, where he quickly became one of the most prominent members of the local bar. Five years later he helped found the *Pittsburgh Gazette*, to which he contributed political and literary essays the rest of his life.

In 1785 Brackenridge married an obscure woman surnamed Montgomery; a year later, his son, Henry Marie, was born. The exact date of his wife's death is unclear (it was either 1787 or 1788), but in 1790 he married Sabina (or Sofia) Wolfe, with whom he had three children. The family lived in Pittsburgh until 1801 and then in Carlisle, where they remained until Brackenridge's death there.

Brackenridge's political philosophy and his allegiances were almost as unsettled as the man himself. One source (*Princetonians, 1769–1775*) describes his basic philosophy as "democratic elitism" (p. 143), an apt characterization, although some of his shifts seem matters of personal antipathy or expediency more than matters of ideology. He supported the claims of poorer western settlers against the claims of absentee landlords and was elected to the state legislature in 1786 with the support of radicals who clamored for debt relief. But at the same time he initially embraced Federalism as did his legal mentor, Chase, an uncompromising Federalist and Supreme Court justice. Brackenridge supported the Constitution of 1787 and voted Federalist in the first federal elections. But Federalism was not popular in western Pennsylvania. By 1790 he had antagonized a powerful party leader, General John Neville, and shortly afterward shifted to the Republican camp. Brackenridge then founded the *Tree of Liberty* as a rival paper to the *Gazette* when the latter became a Federalist paper.

Brackenridge's fascination with the west never waned. His view of the Native Americans who lived there was paradoxical. At age seven he had survived the Indian attacks on the English settlers after General Edward Braddock's defeat in 1755, and he despised Native Americans. In the *Freeman's Journal* (May 1783) he even proposed that they be driven to the North, where the cold climate could destroy them, and he consistently held that the seizure of Indian land was moral and lawful, a view representative of white settlers of western Pennsylvania. Incongruously, he exhibited a capacity for benevolence. For example, in the year of his first marriage Brackenridge defended an Indian tried for killing two whites and described the case in *The Trial of Mamachtaga* (1785). Although he had little understanding of Indian cultures, he crafted a realistic and even sympathetic portrait of Mamachtaga.

Brackenridge was representative of western Pennsylvania in another way. He opposed the excise tax on whiskey that triggered the notorious Whiskey Rebellion in the region (1793–1794). Well before the riots he had defended some of the participants when they were prosecuted by the collector of excise. After the uprising he tried to mediate by both opposing the tax and supporting the federal government. He failed, however, as he explained in *Incidents of the Insurrection in the Western Parts of Pennsylvania in the Year 1794*.

Brackenridge's "democracy" remained a peculiar kind. His political views included elements of the classical republicanism embraced by Federalists. In his widely read novel, *Modern Chivalry* (a work he began in 1792 and kept expanding and then revising downward until 1815), he argued that men of merit ought to govern the American republic even as he described himself as a "democrat." Moreover, he revealed his disdain for majoritarianism when he described his brand of "democracy": "I am a democrat," he wrote, "if having no cousin, and no funds, and only to rely on my personal services, can make me one." Brackenridge was a democrat in a stylistic sense: he tried to make his work accessible to ordinary men, offering "good sense expressed in clear language." *Modern Chivalry* was an important early example both of American satire and western literature.

Brackenridge's fortunes rose considerably when Governor Thomas McKean appointed him a justice of the Pennsylvania Supreme Court in late 1799, where he remained until his death. Two events particularly marked his judgeship. The first was his response to efforts to impeach the judges of the court, a major crisis in Pennsylvania politics that paralleled the efforts of Republicans to impeach Federalist federal judges and members of the U.S. Supreme Court, the most prominent being Justice Chase, Brackenridge's law teacher. Though a Republican, Brackenridge, firmly believing in judicial independence, asked to be included in the impeachment trial notwithstanding that he had not sat on the case that gave rise to the impeachment attempt.

His request was met with a legislative motion for his removal, which Governor McKean rejected.

The second notable event was the publication of Brackenridge's important *Law Miscellanies* in 1814. A potpourri of essays on Sir William Blackstone's *Commentaries on the Laws of England*, the law of Pennsylvania, federal statutes, and judgments of the Supreme Court of the United States, this rambling production contained many striking insights. The work was an important contribution to an ongoing debate about the place of English common law in American jurisprudence. Brackenridge admired the common law but only when it was useful to republican society. He urged judicial activism in reforming the law but knew that bold judges were rare and that improvement in the law "*must come from the legislature*." Brackenridge had no trouble condemning the U.S. Supreme Court's decision in *Marbury v. Madison* (1803) striking down an act of Congress as wrongly decided. The Court, he said, should have forced the executive branch to act.

Brackenridge was never a man who could be fitted neatly into any category. One summary of his life described him as a "poet, novelist, satirist, polemicist, Presbyterian clergyman, teacher, lawyer, jurist, publisher, editor, and public official" (*Princetonians, 1769–1775*, p. 138). He was an important, if not always a central, figure in several of these roles. He was a frequent contributor (in numerous forums) to the boisterous debates concerning things such as the relationships among the various social elements of the new American communities (including those on the margins such as Native Americans), relationships among the federal and state governments, the nature of democracy, and the proper content of a truly American jurisprudence. He was a democrat who distrusted much about the bumptious democracy around him. But he was also a republican in the sense that he believed that men of merit should rule. Though devoted to an independent judiciary, he conceded lawmaking power to legislators elected by people who represented the poorer people in society as well as the rich and well born.

• Some Brackenridge manuscripts are at the University of Pittsburgh library, but most of his papers were lost by his son Henry Marie. See the valuable study by Daniel Marder, *Hugh Henry Brackenridge* (1967), and the excellent sketch in Richard Harrison, *Princetonians, 1769–1775: A Biographical Dictionary* (1980). See also Claude Newlin, *The Life and Writings of Hugh Henry Brackenridge* (1932). Useful information can be found in Thomas P. Slaughter, *The Whiskey Rebellion: Frontier Epilogue to the American Revolution* (1986), and Steven R. Boyd, ed., *The Whiskey Rebellion: Past and Present Perspectives* (1985), which includes a portion of *Incidents of the Insurrection*. The best avenue into Brackenridge's life remains his publications, especially his two most important works, *Modern Chivalry* and *Law Miscellanies* (repr. 1972), which are readily available. See also *A Hugh Henry Brackenridge Reader, 1770–1815*, ed. Daniel Marder (1970).

THOMAS D. MORRIS

BRACKETT, Anna Callender (21 May 1836–18 Mar. 1911), educator, was born in Boston, Massachusetts, the daughter of Samuel Eaton Brackett, a dry goods merchant, and Caroline S. Callender. Brackett attended public and private schools in the Boston area, including Abbott's Academy, before enrolling in the State Normal School in Framingham. Graduating at age twenty, she taught briefly in the East Brookfield schools before returning to Framingham as assistant principal. In 1860 she moved to Charleston, South Carolina, to become vice principal of Girls' High and Normal School, remaining there for nearly two years, until the onset of the Civil War forced her and all other northerners to leave. Following a year of teaching at the Cambridge, Massachusetts, high school, she was called, at the age of twenty-five, to the principalship of the St. Louis Normal School in Missouri.

Brackett's salary of $2,000 was extraordinarily high for the era, but Superintendent William T. Harris (later U.S. commissioner of education from 1889 to 1906) intended that both male and female principals assume a degree of responsibility unusual in a city school system. Brackett's nine years at the normal school allowed her to exercise her conviction that teachers, too, must meet a much higher intellectual standard than had become traditional for many western communities. While in St. Louis she adopted many of the pedagogical ideas of the "St. Louis movement" led by Harris and Henry Brokmeyer. Harris followed German philosopher-educators in advocating the abandonment of rote memorization and a new attentiveness to the curiosity and thought processes peculiar to successive stages of childhood. Brackett increasingly found support for her own assumptions in Hegel's philosophy, with its emphasis on the primacy of innate ideas. Deeply imbued in New Testament visions of human possibility, she seems to have developed her own synthesis of Christian and Hegelian concepts of moral perfection during her St. Louis years.

Brackett's sudden resignation from the St. Louis Normal School in April 1872 was probably the result of pressure from school board members who were unwilling to pay for the preparation that she felt teachers needed. She moved to New York City with her assistant, Ida M. Eliot, and in 1872 opened her own private school for girls. The school soon had more than 200 pupils from prominent New York families. Brackett remained its principal through the next twenty-three years.

In evenings and during vacations, Brackett began her second career as a writer during this time. Her writing had the authority and directness of a busy practitioner and appeared in magazines such as *Harper's Monthly*, *Century*, and the *Independent*, as well as in book form. Gifted in languages and well read in the works of Friedrich Froebel and other German educators, she translated *The Philosophy of Education* by Karl Rosenkranz for serialization from 1872 to 1874 in the *Journal of Speculative Philosophy*, a publication of the St. Louis movement (issued in book form in 1886 and edited by W. T. Harris). She directly reproduced several of Rosenkranz's ideas in her introductory essay for *The Education of Girls* (1874). Editing other contributions to this book, she refuted most of the evidence by which the popular physician and writer Edward C. Clarke sought scientifically to prove that girls and women were unfit for extended academic study.

In *The Education of Girls*, Brackett was ready to agree with Clarke that "brainwork" occasioned a "tremendous and unusual strain on the whole nervous system" of young women but insisted that any ill effects could be deflected by nutritious diet, moderate outdoor exercise, looser-fitting clothes, and above all, the quiet orderliness that, she argued, becomes habitual in girls and women who have been gradually led to substitute their natural reason for their natural willfulness. She ridiculed Clarke's prescription for a week of menstrual rest; according to Brackett, a young woman need interrupt her study for no more than six to (rarely) thirty-six hours, after which she could catch up with her male or female classmates. Furthermore, she believed that, throughout girlhood and adolescence, the body, mind, and will should be educated together, with the mother lovingly explaining to her pubescent daughter "the mysterious process of reproduction" to counter the fantasies and obsessions that can indeed divert blood from the brain to the "newly aroused reproductive organs."

This holistic view of education was new to most Americans of the 1870s. Brackett believed that the American girl particularly required it because, while having far more energy than her European counterparts, she lived in an overstimulating and overindulgent social environment, her nervous system "stung into undue activity by the extremes of our climate" and constantly stressed by an urbanizing society's shifting expectations of women. Rules were necessary to help her focus her attention and direct her will, but excessive authority in teachers would only obstruct her unique, developing conscience. Schools should "train character," not cleverness, she insisted. A teacher's sensitive judgment and concern should take the place of grades and marks. Rote memorization and five-hour examinations would discourage love of learning, of logic, and of artistic beauty. In an age that had discovered adolescence and found its sexual energies alarming, Brackett noticed instead the quickening of both "mental development" and imagination. The young woman, properly educated, she claimed, is "a responsible being . . . a reflection of the Creator in his self-determining intelligence."

Women's roles were changing fast in the late Victorian era. In Brackett's New York school, training in needlework and the "hodgepodge of bits of information" that were supposed to fit girls for modern life gave way to intensive study of languages (including Latin for younger girls as well as those bound for college), literary classics, history, and mathematics. Science's role was to engender "a feeling of reverence and wonder for the Creator." Traditional intellectual disciplines developed the judgment and the broad humanity that, she felt, were needed equally by mothers and college-educated professional women.

Increasingly, Brackett thought about what it meant to "manage a great school" and to help its teachers "create, from [what the philosopher Josiah Royce called] 'the chaos of unreason' a world" unified by an "underlying controlling principle." In 1893 she recorded her thoughts and her experienced prescriptions in *Woman and the Higher Education*. She railed against "educational cant," drawing instead on William James's thought to underline her own and her teachers' observations concerning children's developing capabilities. She believed with Kant in "the constructive power of the mind." A teacher's chief challenge and joy is to make students think by building on and recombining what they already know. Though teachers "of original character . . . need no diploma from any school of pedagogy," they must become skilled diagnosticians, observing and listening to students as often as lecturing to them, deciding the order of subjects by each pupil's "mental readiness." Many of Brackett's pupils had accomplished so much by the time they graduated that they entered Vassar and similar colleges with advanced standing. The debt to Brackett's school that is owed by several New York girls' schools founded in the late 1880s and the 1890s is suggested by striking similarities in curriculum, pedagogy, and rationale, as described in catalogs and other documents.

Brackett retired from her principalship in 1895 but continued for some time to teach adult classes in literature, art, philosophy, history, and Bible studies. She had adopted a child, and helped others in need throughout her adult life. She died in Summit, New Jersey. Her former students raised money for a graduate fellowship in her memory to be administered by the American Association of University Women.

A lifelong teacher who founded her own successful school for girls, Brackett was conservative in her adherence to classical academic standards but innovative in her teaching methods and her philosophical justifications for them. Her numerous educational writings, which were grounded in Platonic and Hegelian principles, were conveyed in a style rich in lively exhortation and pungent examples and were widely read during her lifetime.

• None of Brackett's private papers are readily available. Her works *The Technique of Rest* (1892) and *Woman and the Higher Education* (1893) include her most cogent essays. Edith Kendall, *Anna C. Brackett: In Memorium* (1915), has some helpful information, but it is far from being a complete biography.

SUSAN M. LLOYD

BRACKETT, Charles William (26 Nov. 1892–9 Mar. 1969), writer and motion-picture producer, was born in Saratoga Springs, New York, the son of Edgar Truman Brackett, a lawyer and state legislator, and Mary Emma Corliss. For a time, he seemed destined to follow in his father's footsteps as a prominent lawyer in Saratoga Springs. Brackett did, indeed, pursue such a career in his college studies, first taking a B.A. from Williams College in 1915 and then receiving an LL.B. from Harvard Law School in 1920. While at Harvard, Brackett interrupted his studies in 1917 to serve in World War I, positioned in St. Nazaire, France, as a second lieutenant in the American Expeditionary Forces and serving as vice-consul and assistant liaison officer to the French general. His efforts were acknowledged with the awarding of the Medaille d'Honneur en Argent.

After his war service Brackett finished his schooling at Harvard and then began practicing law with his father's firm. He married Elizabeth Barrows Fletcher, daughter of another prominent area family, in 1919 and worked in Saratoga Springs for six years. The first stirrings of movement toward another career began taking place in these early years of marriage and work. He used some of his wartime adventures as subject matter for a short story, "War," which was purchased by a national magazine soon after his return from service. He also completed a novel, *The Counsel of the Ungodly*, which was serialized by the *Saturday Evening Post* in 1920. Through the early 1920s he continued to work as a lawyer, but the pace and success of his writing increased, and he became a featured contributor to several magazines, including the *Post* and *Vanity Fair*. The publication of his next novel, *Weekend* (1925), attracted attention that led to his appointment in 1926 as drama critic for the *New Yorker*, and although he had no theatrical experience his work as critic was generally well received. Brackett continued to write novels as well, including *That Last Infirmity* (1926), *American Colony* (1929), and *Entirely Surrounded* (1934), all dealing somewhat comically and satirically with upper-class life. He stayed with the *New Yorker* until 1929, when he resigned to devote more time to his novels and other writing.

Although both his success as a writer and his family's wealth (as well as his wife's) meant that Brackett could live the life of a country gentleman lawyer and writer if he wished, he pushed on to other challenges and to his most notable achievements in the 1930s and 1940s. He had worked briefly as a motion-picture writer for Paramount in 1932, and after returning east he was soon recalled to California and the beginning of an association with the studio that would last until 1950. Within that association he was teamed with writer-director Billy Wilder, and the pair developed a series of successful films and a reputation as the preeminent writing team in Hollywood. The somewhat reserved and aristocratic Brackett and the aggressive, rebellious Wilder made an odd team, but they worked together on an impressive number of important and well-received films, sometimes producing (Brackett) and directing (Wilder) in addition to writing. Among their thirteen films together, major works include *Ninotchka*, a comedy starring Greta Garbo (1939); *Arise, My Love*, a romantic drama with Claudette Colbert and Ray Milland (1940); *Hold Back the Dawn*, a melodrama starring Charles Boyer and Olivia de Havilland (1941); *Ball of Fire*, a classic screwball comedy with Gary Cooper and Barbara Stanwyck (1942); *The Lost Weekend*, the Oscar-winning Best Picture featuring Ray Milland's struggles as an alcoholic (1945); and their final collaboration *Sunset Boulevard*, starring Gloria Swanson as an aging and deluded Hollywood has-been (1950). Brackett and Wilder won Oscars for their screenplays with the last two films on this list, and they enjoyed increasing levels of creative autonomy and industry respect that came with critical and box-office success.

Changes were afoot in both Brackett's private and professional life in the late 1940s and early 1950s, however. His 29-year marriage to Elizabeth ended with her death in 1948; the couple had two daughters and were well known in Hollywood as skillful party hosts with busy social lives. In 1953 he married his first wife's sister, Lillian Fletcher. Brackett's long association with Paramount and with Billy Wilder ended during this period as well, when in 1950 he signed a seven-year contract with Twentieth Century Fox, reportedly because of some disagreement with Paramount's new management over creative freedom and budget constraints. This move to Fox ended the landmark series of Brackett-Wilder collaborations.

His work at Fox through the 1950s never reached the previous heights, but he did share a third Best Screenplay Academy Award for *Titanic* in 1953, and he also produced *The King and I* (1956), *Journey to the Center of the Earth* (1959), and *State Fair* (1961), among other films, before retiring in 1962. Well respected throughout the Hollywood community, Brackett served as president of the Screenwriters' Guild (1938–1939) and the Academy of Motion Picture Arts and Sciences (1949–1955). He received a fourth Oscar in 1957, a special award for his years of service to the academy and the industry. He died in Bel Air, California.

Charles Brackett exhibited skill and talent as a lawyer, novelist, critic, and movie producer, but he will be most remembered for his writing and producing-directing partnership with Billy Wilder. These two men from very different backgrounds and with very different temperaments reached what was at the time an unprecedented level of prominence as a creative team and, most significantly, left behind a series of powerful and entertaining motion picture classics.

• Brackett's early novels (often serialized) and short stories can be found in magazines of the 1920s and 1930s—primarily the *Saturday Evening Post*—and examples of his drama criticism are in many issues of the *New Yorker* from 1926 to 1929. Biographical information and personality sketches on Brackett are most common in biographies of Billy Wilder and histories of the Hollywood studio system; among the most revealing in their treatment of Brackett are Axel Madsen, *Billy Wilder* (1969); Maurice Zolotow, *Billy Wilder in Hollywood* (1977); Bernard Dick, *Billy Wilder* (1980); Tom Wood, *The Bright Side of Billy Wilder, Primarily* (1970); Ian Hamilton, *Writers in Hollywood 1915–1951* (1990); and Pat McGilligan, ed., *Backstory Two: Interviews with Screenwriters of the 1940s and 1950s* (1991), which features a Joel Greenberg interview with longtime Brackett colleague Walter Reisch. An obituary is in the *New York Times*, 10 Mar. 1969. And, of course for examples of Brackett's writing skill at its peak, there are the films.

ROBERT P. HOLTZCLAW

BRACKETT, Edward Augustus (1 Oct. 1818–15 Mar. 1908), sculptor and writer, was born in Vassalborough, Maine, the son of the Quaker Reuben Brackett, a farmer, clockmaker, and oil cloth manufacturer, and Eliza Starkey. He resisted his parents' attempts to send him to school and passed through a series of six apprenticeships. His parents moved from Boston, Massachusetts, to Cincinnati, Ohio, in early 1837, and he was employed there making patterns for paper strainers. In Cincinnati Brackett became familiar with the portrait sculpture of Shobal Clevenger and a bust of General Andrew Jackson by Joel Hart. By February 1839 he was living with the Frankenstein family and sharing a studio with Godfrey Frankenstein, a landscape painter, and John Whetstone, a sculptor and the son of a wealthy Cincinnati pioneer family.

Brackett's friendship with the socially prominent Whetstone and the artistic Frankenstein family undoubtedly helped him gain the public attention he received that year. His first sculpture was a bust of his sister, and by May 1839 he had modeled four portraits and received his second approving notice in the Cincinnati newspapers. In August 1839 Brackett exhibited in the studio a statue, *Nydia the Blind Girl*, based on a character in Bulwer Lytton's *Last Days of Pompeii*. The local press heralded this as the first full-figure sculpture created in the western states. In October 1838, when the Cincinnati Academy held its first exhibition of painting and sculpture, Brackett exhibited two busts. Other sculptors exhibited that year were Hiram Powers, Shobal Clevenger, John C. King, Joel T. Hart, Miner Kellogg, and John Whetstone. Through the autumn of 1839 praise for *Nydia* was printed repeatedly in the local newspapers. In November a public meeting, reported in the press, was held for the purpose of starting a subscription to buy the sculpture and place it on view at a public institution. A committee of prominent citizens including John Whetstone was established to carry the plan forward. Finally, a newspaper account placed the work in the perspective of a youthful first attempt, pointing out that Powers and Clevenger had both made first attempts at full-figure sculpture and had had the good sense to destroy them. The purchase was never made.

Although Cincinnati nurtured many artists during this period, including Hiram Powers, Shobal Clevenger, John Frankenstein, Henry K. Brown, Nathan F. Baker, Thomas D. Jones, and Carolyn Wilson, it never offered sufficient work to support the artists. Cincinnati was a young city, offering little opportunity to see paintings or sculpture and no professional training for the artists, and with the exception of Whetstone and Wilson, all of these artists left Cincinnati. By the summer of 1840 Brackett was working in New York on a bust of William Henry Harrison, of which he sold a number of plaster copies. Brackett supported himself as Powers and Clevenger had done before him by canvassing the eastern cities for portrait work. By May 1842, however, he had exhibited in New York a sculpture group, the *Binding of Satan*, which consisted of the figure of Satan and an angel. The piece was well received and commented on in the New York press. By September Brackett had moved to Boston and was continuing his portrait work while still exhibiting his *Binding of Satan*. Though critical judgments of his portraiture were full of praise, the *Satan*, though well received, was still considered to be the work of a man who was lacking in academic training.

In 1842 Brackett married Amanda Folger of Cincinnati; they had four children. They settled permanently in Woburn, Massachusetts, after their marriage. One of Brackett's best-known works in this period was a bust of Washington Allston (1844); throughout his career as a sculptor, commissions for portrait busts remained his financial support. In 1844 he published a set of lithographs of sculpture and poetry, and in 1845 he published another book of poems, *Twilight Hours or Leisure Moments of an Artist*. Brackett's main goal in these years was to establish himself as a serious artist by creating full-size figurative work. After the *Binding of Satan*, he produced a plaster *Little Nell* based on the character created by Charles Dickens, and by 1850 he was working on *Shipwrecked Mother and Child*, the main work for which he is known. The plaster was translated into marble, and it is the only figurative work of Brackett's known to have survived (now in the Worcester Art Museum). The work was widely reported on, and it received much critical acclaim.

During the Civil War Brackett served one year in the Massachusetts Cavalry. However, by the 1860s he found himself unable to support himself as a sculptor. In 1869 he accepted an appointment as a commissioner on land fisheries, having in the 1860s become increasingly interested in the habits of fish and artificial propagation. Brackett's brother, Walter Brackett, who had worked closely with him particularly on the carving of *Shipwrecked Mother and Child*, was known in this period as a painter of salmon, trout, and other species of game fish. Brackett abandoned sculpture after 1873 and concentrated on the science of pisciculture.

After his first wife's death Brackett married Elizabeth F. Belville of Cincinnati in 1872; they had one child. Brackett continued as a fish commissioner until 1905, inventing hatching trays and fish ways for dams. He published three books in the last eight years of his life, two on the subject of the material world and the search for a spiritual essence, and one book of poems, *My House, Chips the Builder Threw Away* (1904).

Brackett's success as a sculptor was hampered by his lack of academic training, and he stood in the shadow of men such as Hiram Powers and Thomas Ball, who left the United States for the training Italy offered. Boston, where Brackett was most well known, was a city that by 1850 saw more and more competition among sculptors. Even with fellow sculptor Horatio Greenough's praise for *Shipwrecked Mother and Child*, sufficient enthusiasm could not be raised to buy it for the Boston Athenaeum. After the Civil War Brackett was confronted by a renewed competition from young and well-trained artists and a differing set of esthetic values against which he was ultimately unable to compete.

• Hannah F. Lee, *Familiar Sketches of Sculpture and Sculptors* (1854), is the best early source. Joy S. Kasson, *Marble Queens and Captives* (1990), is the most complete modern assessment. Wayne Craven, *Sculpture in America* (1984), contains a broad list of Brackett's works in sculpture.

THEODORE A. GANTZ

BRACKETT, Joshua (5 May 1733–17 July 1802), physician, was born in Greenland, New Hampshire, the son of Captain John Brackett, a lawyer, and Elizabeth Pickering. Because his parents wanted him to enter the ministry, Brackett was educated by the Reverend Henry Rust in Stratham before he entered Harvard College. Despite his repeated infractions of the school's Sunday rules, he graduated in 1752 and earned an M.A. in 1755. Brackett seems to have been unenthusiastic about his religious calling, but he only pleaded poor health when he ceased to be a minister, probably in 1757. He soon began to study medicine with his physician, Dr. Clement Jackson of Portsmouth, New Hampshire, where he opened his own practice in 1759. Two years later he married Hannah Whipple; they had no children.

Known for the gentleness of his remedies (he did not prescribe emetics, cathartics, or bleeding as often as many contemporary doctors did), Brackett performed no major surgery, but he had an enviable reputation for his obstetrical skills. He attended more births and was asked to deliver more twins than were other Portsmouth physicians. He also inoculated for smallpox when Portsmouth was threatened with an epidemic. Like many eighteenth-century physicians, he sold medicines and household items at his shop to help make ends meet. Active in town affairs, he pushed for legislation that would improve its streets and became an Overseer of the Poor, managing the town's various relief efforts. In the years leading up to the Revolution the ruling clique of New Hampshire did not regard Brackett as a patriot who threatened their hold on the province, and thus he was awarded lucrative land grants. In 1775, however, he became a member of the local Committee of Safety and was elected to the Provincial Congress. In 1761, and again in 1776, he was appointed a judge of the New Hampshire Admiralty Court, on which he served until 1784.

His other wartime efforts, both political and medical, widened his reputation even beyond his own state. In 1783 he was one of the first four men who were awarded honorary fellowship in the newly formed Massachusetts Medical Society. Brackett was a founding member of the New Hampshire Medical Society in 1791 and became its first vice president and then its president from 1793 to 1799, when he resigned because of poor health. He founded its library through a gift of 143 medical books. Harvard awarded him an honorary M.D. in 1792. He bequeathed $1,500 to his alma mater for the establishment of a chair of natural history and botany. Because of her own interest in the same subjects, his widow added to the endowment of the Massachusetts Professorship of Natural History.

Sensing that he had a serious heart disease—perhaps angina pectoris—Brackett traveled to take the famous waters at Saratoga Springs, New York, in late June 1802. Because he rapidly worsened, he returned to Portsmouth, where he died about a week later. Although his funeral eulogies were conventional in their praise, he does seem to have been distinguished among his colleagues for his readiness to treat the poor without charge.

• Little has been written about Brackett. Sources include James Thacher, *American Medical Biography*, vol. 1 (1828), pp. 192–95, and Clifford K. Shipton, *Sibley's Harvard Graduates*, vol. 13 (1965), pp. 197–201.

J. WORTH ESTES

BRADBURN, Juan Davis (1787–20 Apr. 1842), military adventurer and officer of the Republic of Mexico, was born John Davis Bradburn in Virginia. Bradburn was known as Juan from 1817 until his death. Details about his early life are few, and his only child became a priest, leaving no direct descendants.

Bradburn lived in Christian County, Kentucky, between 1800 and 1810 and was briefly a merchant at nearby Springfield, Tennessee. He joined the Gutiérrez-Magee expedition in 1812 that left Natchitoches, Louisiana, to capture Nacogdoches, La Bahía, and San Antonio in support of the Mexican republicans fighting against Spain. The Spanish army defeated the invaders at the battle of Medina, southwest of San Antonio, in August 1813, and survivors fled to Louisiana. Many of the veterans, including Bradburn, served in the Louisiana militia in 1814–1815, joining Andrew Jackson at New Orleans to defeat the British. His unit elected Bradburn third lieutenant, and his military record shows he was discharged on 11 March 1815.

Bradburn remained in New Orleans and joined a second filibuster under the leadership of Henry Perry. The volunteers camped on Galveston Bay in Texas in 1816 and later joined the international force, led by the idealistic Spanish leader Xavier Mina, that arrived at Galveston Island from Baltimore. The combined group sailed to the Santander River, midway between the Rio Grande and Tampico, in 1817 and captured Soto la Marina from the Spanish royalists. Lieutenant Colonel Bradburn succeeded to command of the Anglo-American volunteers during a brutal Spanish attack that forced the survivors to flee. Bradburn retreated to the mountainous interior where he organized a guerrilla powder factory but eventually had to escape to Acapulco, where Vicente Guerrero, republican guerrilla and later president of the Republic of Mexico, was fighting. Bradburn served as Guerrero's aide and became the intermediary between the republican insurgents and General Agustín Iturbide, the Mexican-born royalist officer who subverted his command to join the republicans and defeat the Spanish in 1821.

Iturbide became emperor of Mexico in 1822 and arranged a marriage for Bradburn to María Josefa Hurdado. She belonged to a titled Mexican family, and when the empire collapsed in 1823 and a republic was formed, Bradburn and his wife pragmatically supported the new administration. Anglo Americans in Mexico City who were seeking land grants in Texas between 1822 and 1824 sought Bradburn's influence with the changing leadership. In 1828, still holding his rank in the Mexican army, Bradburn moved to the Rio Grande, where he acquired a ranch on the north side and tried unsuccessfully to organize a steamboat company.

In 1830 the commandant general of northeastern Mexico sent Bradburn to open a new garrison on Galveston Bay and establish a town to be named Anahuac. This step was in accordance with a plan to "Mexicanize" Texas and enforce a new law limiting Anglo-American immigration. It also coincided with the end of the six-year exemption from national tariff duties on goods imported from the United States that had been granted to Stephen F. Austin's colonists, and the garrison was to aid the newly assigned customs collectors.

Many of the Anglo settlers knew Bradburn from earlier times and assumed that he would see issues from their point of view. He, however, was a career officer and enforced national laws despite the fact that these laws often seemed arbitrary and unconstitutional to his former countrymen, who forgot that they were living in Mexico. They did not understand that as military commander of the area, Bradburn's orders could supersede state laws. When runaway slaves from Louisiana sought asylum at Anahuac because Mexico did not permit slavery, except by immigrant Anglo cotton farmers in Texas, a special privilege that had been revoked in 1830, Bradburn refused to relinquish the blacks to an agent of the owner. When a state-appointed land commissioner finally arrived in the area in 1831 to issue titles to longtime Anglo settlers, Bradburn arrested the land commissioner on grounds he was violating the 1830 national ban on immigration. These issues and the enforcement of the tariff laws (the Anglos believed the exemption had been granted in perpetuity), caused friction between Bradburn and local residents.

The issue came to a head in May 1832 when Bradburn arrested lawyer William B. Travis for committing sedition on the military post at Anahuac, an act punishable by death after a trial before the commandant general at Matamoros. Rescue efforts by Anglo Texans resulted in more arrests and led in June 1832 to an attack against Bradburn by an armed force of Anglos from the Brazos River communities. Although the Anglo Texans captured Bradburn's nineteen cavalrymen, their lack of a cannon prevented them from capturing the fort. A ranking colonel from Nacogdoches who had been called to Anahuac by Bradburn arrived, but convinced that the Texans in camp awaiting the arrival of cannon from the Brazos outnumbered his force, he agreed to Anglo demands, including the removal of Bradburn from command. The colonel returned to Nacogdoches while Bradburn considered ways to reach Matamoros to put his case before the commandant general.

The battle of Anahuac coincided with a victory on the Rio Grande by the federalist faction army that had been at war with the centralist administration's forces (to which Bradburn was loyal) for two years. On receipt of the news of the victory, a federalist officer imprisoned at Anahuac staged a mutiny that endangered Bradburn's life, and he fled to New Orleans with the aid of local ranchers loyal to him.

By the time he reached Matamoros, the two factions had reached a settlement that resulted in the election of federalist general Antonio Lopez de Santa Anna as president. Bradburn retired from active duty to cultivate his farm near Matamoros with the aid of his wife and son and to raise cattle on his ranch on the opposite shore. When the Texans declared their independence from Mexico in March 1836, Bradburn was called back to service. He refused to accompany the army into the Anglo-Texan settlements but reluctantly agreed to serve at a small port on Copano Bay southeast of San Antonio where supplies were landed for the Mexican army. After the Texan victory over Santa Anna on 21 April 1836, Bradburn was stranded at Copano when the Mexican army retreated toward Matamoros. Alone and afoot, Bradburn made his way south along Padre Island to reach home. He was again called to service to attack San Antonio in March 1842, but he refused. A month later he died at his ranch in present-day Hidalgo County, Texas.

Maligned as an autocratic despot by chauvinistic nineteenth-century Texas historians, Bradburn emerges from a fuller reading of his life as an adventurer who faithfully served his adopted country of Mexico from 1817 until his death.

• The *Diccionario de insurgentes* compiled by José María Miquel i Vergés in 1969 using Mexican military records gives Bradburn's birthdate and birthplace. Bradburn's file in the hard-to-access military archives in Mexico City would doubtless reveal more details about his military career. In Mexican sources, Bradburn's name is usually indexed under Davis on the erroneous presumption that it was the name of his father, as is Mexican custom. The revisionist monograph by Margaret Swett Henson, *Juan Davis Bradburn: A Reappraisal of the Mexican Commander of Anahuac* (1982), offers a detailed bibliography of Mexican and U.S. source material.

MARGARET SWETT HENSON

BRADBURY, Theophilus (13 Nov. 1739–6 Sept. 1803), lawyer, jurist, and congressman, was born in Newbury (now Newburyport), Massachusetts, the son of Theophilus Bradbury, a wealthy sea captain, and Ann Woodman. Graduated from Harvard College in 1757, he moved to Falmouth (now in Maine but a part of Massachusetts until 1820), where he briefly taught school. When courts were organized in Cumberland and Lincoln counties in 1761, Bradbury was the first man admitted to the bar. Bradbury's knowledge of the law and effective, dignified courtroom manner led to his appointment as collector of the excise on liquor, tea, coffee, and china in Maine for the province. In 1762 he married Sarah Jones; they had seven children.

Bradbury inclined toward the Loyalists as the Revolution approached. In 1768 he was appointed a justice of the peace, and in February 1774 he protested the Falmouth Town Meeting's criticism of the East India Company and Governor Thomas Hutchinson following the Boston Tea Party. But as one of Maine's two lawyers, who had grown "rich very fast" as John Adams noted, Bradbury realized he had to sail with the popular wind and apologized for his February protest. He became a Massachusetts state attorney in 1777 but resigned and moved to Newburyport in 1779 after the British destroyed Falmouth. Bradbury's mansion, however, still survives.

In Newburyport, the wealthy, well-known lawyer immediately took a prominent role in town affairs. He served on the town committee to consider the 1780 state constitution, on the school committee, and joined the board of trustees of the Dummer Academy in 1786. He served in the Massachusetts Senate from 1791 to 1795 and became an overseer of Harvard College.

In 1795 Bradbury was elected to Congress as a Federalist. He enjoyed the theater and elegant soirees at the homes of Philadelphia's elite, but his service was undistinguished. He returned to Massachusetts after one term to take a seat on the state supreme court in 1797. Shortly before assuming that post, he represented his town of Newburyport in a suit against the proprietors of the town's common land, who alleged that in 1771 the town had taken this land away from them to use as a shipyard without compensation. Bradbury was successful, and the landmark decision gave Massachusetts towns the right to dispose of common lands without the proprietors' consent.

Bradbury served on the supreme court for five years until a paralytic stroke laid him low in February 1802. Incapacitated, he offered to resign if he would receive a pension; the Federalists were outraged that the Jeffersonian governor refused. In July 1803 the legislature removed the helpless Bradbury from his post; he died in Newburyport two months later. Bradbury is best remembered as a career lawyer who relocated, adapted his politics, and changed jobs in the new nation to achieve personal success.

• The only prior sketch of Bradbury that is extant appears in Clifford K. Shipton, *Sibley's Harvard Graduates*, vol. 14 (1968), pp. 143–46. See also William Willis, *History of the Law, the Courts, and the Lawyers of Maine* (1863).

WILLIAM PENCAK

BRADBURY, William Batchelder (6 Oct. 1816–7 Jan. 1868), music teacher, composer, and publisher, was born in York County, Maine, the son of David Bradbury and Sophia Chase. When Bradbury was fourteen years old the family moved to Boston, where William began the study of harmony and decided to become a professional musician. He attended the Boston Academy of Music, sang in Lowell Mason's church choir, and studied organ. In 1836 Bradbury relocated to Maine, where he began teaching private music lessons and singing schools. He married Adra Esther Fessendon in August 1838; they had four daughters and one son.

After four years of financially strenuous musical itineracy, the Bradburys moved to Brooklyn, New York, where William became music director at the First Baptist Church and later at the Baptist Tabernacle. There he introduced singing classes for children that developed into highly successful annual music festivals and resulted in the introduction of music instruction in the city's public schools. In response to the need for suitable material for his classes, Bradbury began composing his own music. In 1841 he published *The Young Choir*, later to be revised by Thomas Hastings, a pioneer in church choral singing and psalmody, with whom Bradbury collaborated on four additional collections.

In July 1847 the Bradbury family set sail for Europe with the intention of furthering William's musical studies. At Leipzig Bradbury pursued work in piano, harmony, and composition; he also met Franz Liszt, heard Robert and Clara Schumann, and resided three doors from Felix Mendelssohn. During his two years abroad, his correspondence concerning matters personal and musical was published in the *New York Observer* and the *New York Evangelist*, enhancing his recognition at home.

Upon his return from Europe, Bradbury continued to conduct musical conventions, compose, and edit books. His first book was *The Mendelssohn Collection* (1849), which reflected a continued move away from the musical aesthetics and practices of the American colonial singing school tradition of William Billings toward a more European-based musical approach. In 1854 Bradbury joined Mason, Hastings, and George F. Root in their Normal Musical Institute, the earliest systematic training for music teachers. With his brother E. G. Bradbury, William also formed a partnership to manufacture pianos that soon received widespread recognition for its excellence.

Bradbury's most lasting musical contribution resulted from his work with Sunday School hymnody. At a time when there was little difference in the style of religious music provided for children and adults, Bradbury began composing music that was pleasing, lively, and more attractive to children. Although his first collection in this genre, *Sabbath School Melodies*, was issued in 1850, it was not until after the success of *Oriola* in 1859 that the composer formed the William B. Bradbury Company in 1861 to publish his own music. Its first publication was *The Golden Chain*, which met with such success that a whole "Golden" series soon followed. Unlike the traditional, large, rectangular singing school books containing religious music, Bradbury's Sunday School song collections were a pocketsize five-by-six inches and sold for a quarter. Most significantly, his collections contained not only a more rhythmically animated type of song but also included a more modern musical feature—a chorus or refrain that its proponents boasted would insure the sentiment of a religious text like "a nail in a sure place."

In 1864 Bradbury met the blind poet Fanny Crosby and encouraged her to take up hymnwriting. Soon afterwards, Crosby began writing for Bradbury's company, becoming Sunday School hymnody's most important poet. Combining a keen business sense with the ability to write pleasing melodies for the growing Sunday School movement, Bradbury sold over three million books in less than a decade. By 1867 Bradbury's failing health caused him to sell his interests in both the piano business and his publishing company. The piano company was eventually absorbed by Knabe Piano, and the music publishing business was purchased by Biglow and Main, which billed itself as "Successors to William Bradbury."

Although Bradbury composed several cantatas, thirty anthems, and scores of other sacred and secular works (as well as dozens of collections), it is the Sunday School melodies that have proved his most lasting contribution. Intended primarily for children, many of these tunes and their texts have become standards of Protestant hymnody. Of Bradbury's nearly one thousand hymntunes, the most popular include "Bradbury" ("Savior, like a shepherd lead us"); "He Leadeth Me"; "Jesus Loves Me"; "Olive's Brow"; "Sweet Hour" (of prayer); "The Solid Rock"; and "Woodworth" ("Just as I am").

During his lifetime Bradbury stood squarely at the dawn of a new age of music in the United States, an age that he helped to usher in and to guide. It involved the concept of widespread and systematic music instruction for public school students and their specialist music teachers. It also included a new paradigm of church music based on European aesthetic models combined with the beginnings of the modern music publishing industry. Bradbury was clearly the first important moving force in developing music for the Sunday School movement. He died of respiratory complication at his Monclair, New Jersey, home. His songs continue to be sung around the world.

• A study of Bradbury is Alan B. Wingard, "The Life and Works of William Batchelder Bradbury (1816–1868)," (D.M.A. diss., Southern Baptist Theological Seminary [Louisville, Ky.], 1973). Additional works on church music provide various perspectives on his life. These include Leonard Ellinwood, *The History of American Church Music* (1953); J. H. Hall, *Biography of Gospel Song and Hymn Writers* (1914); Donald P. Hustad, ed., *Dictionary-Handbook to Hymns for the Living Church* (1978), with an introduction tracing the history of Sunday School music; Frank J. Metcalf, *American Writers and Compilers of Sacred Music* (1925); and Bernard Ruffin, *Fanny Crosby* (1976), with a good account of Bradbury's relation to Crosby. Most hymnal companions contain a brief biographical sketch in addition to information about his hymntunes. The most accessible overviews of Bradbury's career, which also contain a fuller list of his publications, are found in both *The New Grove Dictionary of Music and Musicians* (1980) and *The New Grove Dictionary of American Music* (1986). An obituary is in *New York Musical Gazette* 2 (1867–1868): 25.

MEL R. WILHOIT

BRADDOCK, Edward (Jan. 1695–13 July 1755), British officer, was born in London, England, the son of Edward Braddock, an officer in the Coldstream Guards, and Mary (maiden name unknown). He was baptized on 5 February 1695. His father purchased an ensigncy in the Coldstreams for him in 1710, and he advanced through the regiment, becoming a lieutenant in 1716; a captain lieutenant in 1734; a second major in 1743; and first major and then lieutenant colonel in 1745. Although the regiment served on the Continent during the War of the Austrian Succession (1742–1748), it is not known whether Braddock took part in any engagement, but he did perform administrative duties. He left the Coldstreams when appointed colonel of the Fourteenth Foot (Feb. 1753) and spent most of 1753–1754 with his regiment at Gibraltar, serving as governor. In April 1754 he was promoted to major general.

In September 1754, apparently on the recommendation of the duke of Cumberland, Braddock was appointed commander in chief in North America. The reasoning behind this appointment is obscure, but officers who enjoyed greater status or influence seem not to have coveted it. Cumberland may have been impressed by Braddock's record as an administrator at Gibraltar, and the American command involved a heavy administrative burden. Indeed, Braddock was given broad powers to direct both military and civilian affairs in the colonies, and generally to put them on a war footing. However, his primary assignment was military: to take the newly built French stronghold at the forks of the Ohio, Fort Duquesne, and then to sweep the French from the Ohio Valley and pursue them back into Canada. The government set forth this strategy in secret orders to him but provided only two regiments, both undermanned and of poor quality, to carry them out. It further appears that the government grossly underestimated the administrative, political, and military obstacles that Braddock could be expected to encounter.

Braddock arrived at Hampton, Virginia, on 20 February 1755. During the next two months, he and governors of the region coordinated strategy for the ensuing campaign. They also discussed Indian affairs and, least successfully, the question of how to finance the upcoming offensive. In late April Braddock rejoined his army at Wills Creek. His hopes for a prompt departure were stymied by supply problems, which were not relieved until early June, when Benjamin Franklin (technically, acting in the capacity of deputy postmaster general of Pennsylvania), making use of funds provided by Braddock and by the Pennsylvania Assembly, as well as £200 of his own, brought in supplies and wagons. To this point, Braddock had been frustrated by the unwillingness of the Americans to provide for his army, and when, in a subsequent letter to Franklin, he praised the Pennsylvanians, who "had promised nothing and performed everything," he also criticized Maryland and Virginia, for having "promised everything and performed nothing." Braddock was likewise concerned about the quality of his troops, for the regiments had been filled out with draftees and with "Virginians, very indifferent Men, this Country affording no better," as he wrote the adjutant general on 8 June. Nevertheless, the march from Wills Creek began on 10 June, with Braddock apparently confident. He was in any case fearful that if the army were too long delayed, Fort Duquesne would be reinforced—as indeed it was, shortly before his arrival—and this concern also prompted his decision, on 16 June, to divide his army, leaving behind, to advance as best they could, about one-third of the men and most of the wagons. Braddock's force now moved more quickly, and by 9 July was nearing Fort Duquesne, with plans to invest it the following day. Shortly after a second fording of the Monongahela brought the army to within ten miles of the fort, however, it confronted a French and Indian force—about two-thirds the latter—that was roughly half its size. Although the enemy force had planned to attack at the river and was initially confused, it reacted more quickly than did Braddock's army, taking high ground near the line of march and firing on the flanks of the British vanguard from both sides. Braddock, who was with the main body at the start of action, sent a detachment forward, but the vanguard fell back on it, and most of the army lost cohesion. During the two hours or more that followed, Braddock attempted to restore order and rally his men, but, as a result of the confusion and perhaps panic of the troops, he failed. In the heat of the action he was finally wounded, perhaps by the deliberate act of one of his own men. He was removed from the field as his army retreated, and four days later, after resigning his command, he died at the Great Meadows, where the retreating army had encamped. The following morning he was buried under the road that bears his name, and wagons were driven over the grave to obscure it and so preserve it from desecration (remains purportedly his were unearthed in 1812). Before leaving England in late 1754 Braddock, who never married, had prepared a will, leaving his entire estate to a friend, and perhaps mistress, Mary Yorke, and to an army agent, John Calcraft.

Both in England and America Braddock left behind some admirers, most notably George Washington, who served as an aide-de-camp on his expedition. In the wake of his defeat and death, his supporters tried to defend his performance on the battlefield. Nevertheless, the general attitude toward him, somewhat hostile even before the expedition came to its disastrous end, became more harsh as news of the defeat spread, and has tended to remain negative ever since. The bases for this assessment are two. First, he has been seen as a martinet. According to a contemporary historian, John Entick, "His soldiers could not relish his severity in matters of discipline." Undoubtedly, to Americans who observed, perhaps joined, his army, it appeared that the disciplinary system that obtained was harsh, for they were used to the lax discipline of militia. It does not, however, appear that he was more demanding or quicker to punish than were most British commanding officers of the time. A more common and persistent charge against Braddock is that he failed dismally as a general on the day of his climactic battle. Although his courage has never been questioned, contemporaries and historians alike have accused him of poor, even foolish, leadership. His persistent efforts to organize his troops for a counterattack that followed European rules, while at the same time discouraging Americans from seeking shelter behind trees and fighting "Indian-style," have served to reduce him to a metaphor for the British inability to comprehend the realities of American warfare and, by extension, of America itself. It is improbable, however, that the British troops, who were trained to execute standard tactics, would have succeeded if called upon to fight in a different style, and most of the Americans serving under Braddock had little experience in wilderness warfare. Furthermore, the numerous eyewitness accounts of the battle, even those by hostile reporters, suggest that once the army telescoped and confusion spread, Braddock's chances of rallying the troops to victory, regardless of what tactics he relied on, were slim. The evidence suggests that if any British officer can fairly be accused of having demonstrated incompetence it is not Braddock, but rather Thomas Gage, who commanded the advance party on the day of battle, and whose blunders permitted the enemy to seize the initiative. Perhaps the fairest criticism of Braddock is not that he failed to win the battle of 9 July, but that he failed to promptly recognize it as a lost cause and withdraw his army to regroup.

The negative reputation of Braddock is understandable, however. He was known to contemporaries, and is known to historians, primarily for one enterprise, and that ended in disaster.

• Although Braddock has been the subject of a number of articles and encyclopedia entries, there is only one book-length biography, Lee McCardell, *Ill-Starred General: Braddock of the Coldstream Guards* (1958). Winthrop Sargent includes valuable material on his career, as well as providing a fine narrative of the Braddock expedition and the battle, in *The History of an Expedition against Fort Du Quesne in 1755* (1855). An analysis of the documentary evidence relative to the battle is provided in Paul E. Kopperman, *Braddock at the Monongahela* (1977), and most eyewitness accounts of the battle are appended in full. See Kopperman also for a fuller bibliography.

PAUL E. KOPPERMAN

BRADEN, Carl James (1914–18 Feb. 1975), journalist and social justice activist, was born in New Albany, Indiana, the son of James Braden, a railroadman and auto worker, and Elizabeth Braden. He attended Catholic schools in Louisville and was for two years a proseminary student at Mount Saint Francis College in Indiana. In 1930, at the age of sixteen, he left Mount Saint Francis for a job as a reporter for the *Louisville Herald-Post*. In 1937 he moved to Cincinnati,

Ohio, where he worked for the *Cincinnati Enquirer*, first as a labor reporter and later as the editor of the Kentucky edition of the paper. In 1945 he returned to Kentucky to become the labor editor for the *Louisville Times*. He also wrote for other news services including the *Harlan Daily Enterprise*, the *Knoxville Journal*, the *New York Daily News*, the *Chicago Tribune*, the *St. Louis Globe-Democrat*, *Newsweek*, and the Federated Press.

In 1948 Braden married Anne Gamrell McCarty, the education editor at the *Louisville Times*, and thus began a political as well as a personal partnership. Carl and Anne Braden had three children. In the late 1940s they became active in a number of civil rights organizations and campaigns in Louisville including the National Association for the Advancement of Colored People, the Urban League, the 1948 Progressive party campaign, the Militant Church Movement, and efforts to desegregate private hospitals, nurse training programs, parks, and schools. Braden left the *Louisville Times* in 1948 to work for a group of CIO unions. In 1950 he took a job as a copy editor for the *Louisville Courier-Journal*.

In May 1954 the Bradens bought a house in what was then an all-white neighborhood and transferred title to Andrew Wade IV, a black Korean War veteran. When the Wades moved into their new home, they immediately faced intense harassment including cross burnings, random gunfire, and broken windows. On 27 June just after midnight, a bomb destroyed half the home. After several weeks passed without an arrest, the commonwealth attorney for Louisville used a grand jury investigation to attack Wade's white friends. He theorized that the bombing was an "inside job" and charged Braden, his wife, and five others with criminal syndicalism and sedition under a heretofore never-used 1920 Kentucky statute. The prosecutor argued that the Bradens had bought the house in a Communist plot to stir up racial strife and thereby bring about a political revolution that would result in the overthrow of the governments of Kentucky and the United States. In essence, they were accused of intentionally provoking all of the attacks upon the Wade home by selling a house in a white neighborhood to a black family.

Braden was the only person ever brought to trial in connection with the bombing of the Wade home. Although there was no evidence presented at the trial connecting him to the bombing, Braden was convicted of sedition because of the prosecution's allegations that he was affiliated with the Communist Party. The judge sentenced Braden to fifteen years in prison and a $5,000 fine. The conviction was widely condemned as a misuse of state power to punish and suppress civil rights advocates. Nathan Cohen, associate dean of the New York School of Social Work, Columbia University, said that "it was evident that democracy had taken a holiday" during this trial. Braden served eight months of his sentence before he was able to raise the $40,000 appeal bond, which was, as of then, the highest ever set in the state. In 1956 the Kentucky Court of Appeals overturned his conviction, and all charges against him and the other defendants were dropped.

In 1957, blacklisted from employment by local newspapers, Braden became a field organizer for the Southern Conference Educational Fund (SCEF), an interracial organization working to improve economic conditions and end segregation in the South. At the same time, he became coeditor of the *Southern Patriot*, a publication of the SCEF. In 1958 the House Un-American Activities Committee (HUAC) summoned Braden and his wife to appear at a hearing in Atlanta because of letters and petitions they purportedly circulated opposing state antisedition laws and HUAC's hearings. When asked about his political activities and beliefs, Braden refused to testify and said instead that "my beliefs and my associations are none of the business of this committee." HUAC charged him with contempt of Congress, and he was sentenced to one year in prison. By a 5–4 vote, the U.S. Supreme Court upheld his conviction.

Braden entered prison in May 1961. Meanwhile, HUAC had indefinitely postponed the questioning or prosecution of Anne Braden. While Braden was in prison, his wife worked closely with anti-HUAC organizations, wrote a pamphlet attacking HUAC called *HUAC: Bulwark of Segregation*, and traveled widely to rally support for clemency for Braden and other victims of HUAC. Braden left prison in February 1962 after serving nine months of his sentence. Although he lost his case before the Supreme Court, his stand and his wife's subsequent organizing efforts were important pieces of a campaign that ultimately demonstrated to the country and to the Court how federal and state authority was being used to intimidate black civil rights activists and their white supporters.

In 1966 Braden and his wife became the executive directors of SCEF. A year later, they and SCEF came under attack in the Kentucky gubernatorial campaign and were again charged with sedition for their involvement in organizing poor Appalachian whites. That case ended when the state sedition law was held unconstitutional. In 1972 Braden resigned from SCEF because of what he thought to be Red-baiting inside the organization. He then became the director of the Training Institute for Propaganda and Organizing, helped found the National Alliance against Racist and Political Repression, and began the campaign to free the Wilmington Ten, a group of civil rights activists convicted of firebombing a grocery store during protests in Wilmington, North Carolina, in 1971. Their convictions, like the sedition accusations against Braden, symbolized for many the brutal suppression of civil rights activity in the South.

Braden died in Louisville, Kentucky. He devoted his life to ending racial discrimination and to improving the living conditions of poor and working people in the South. Although state and federal authorities continually attacked him as a subversive for this work and attempted to isolate him from the civil rights movement, Braden's stand for the freedom of belief and association earned him the respect of social justice and civil rights activists, helped undermine the authority of HUAC, and helped make First Amendment freedoms more secure for all.

• The Carl and Anne Braden Papers are located in the Archives of the Wisconsin State Historical Society. The collection includes pleadings, correspondence, and notes having to do with the Wade affair; papers from the Southern Conference Educational Fund (1948–1972); and papers from the National Committee to Abolish HUAC. Access to the collection is restricted. There is an account of the Wade affair in Anne Braden's book about segregation, *The Wall Between* (1955). An excellent entry on the Bradens is in the *Encyclopedia of the American Left*, ed. Mari Jo Buhle, Paul Buhle, and Dan Georgakas (1990). Obituaries are in the *New York Times*, 25 Feb. 1975, and the *Washington Post*, 20 Feb. 1975.

CYNTHIA R. POE

BRADFORD, Amory Howe (14 Apr. 1846–18 Feb. 1911), Congregational pastor, was born in Granby, New York, the son of the Reverend Benjamin Franklin Bradford and Mary A. Howe. An eighth-generation descendant of Governor William Bradford of the Plymouth Colony, Bradford prepared for college at Penn Yan, New York, studied for a year at Genesee College, and graduated from Hamilton College in 1867. Three years later, in 1870, he graduated from Andover Theological Seminary and married Julia S. Stevens of Little Falls, New York. They had no children. Also in 1870 Amory Bradford was ordained a Congregational minister and became the pastor of First Congregational Church of Montclair, New Jersey.

Bradford spent a year of postgraduate study at England's Oxford University and was awarded a doctor of divinity degree by Hamilton College in 1884. His early books, *Spirit and Life* (1888), *Old Wine, New Bottles* (1892), *Christ and the Church* (1895), *Heredity and Christian Problems* (1895), *The Growing Revelation* (1897), *The Age of Faith* (1900), *The Return to Christ* (1900), and *Spiritual Lessons from the Brownings* (1900), were elaborations of his articles, sermons, and speeches on Christian philosophy. In 1892 he became president of the American Institute for Christian Philosophy, under the auspices of which *Christian Thought* (11 vols., 1883–1894), coedited by Bradford, Charles Force Deems, and John Bancroft Devins, was published. In 1892 and 1893 he delivered the Southworth Lectures at Andover Theological Seminary. Bradford articulated what was called a progressive orthodoxy. Common among graduates and faculty members of Andover Seminary, it aimed to give a modern voice to all that was of value in traditional Christian thought in light of historical criticism and scientific research. The effect, he argued, was to put "Old Wine" in "New Bottles."

Bradford was also actively interested in the social issues of his day. From 1892 to 1899 he was an associate editor of the *Outlook*. In 1895 the American Board of Commissioners for Foreign Missions sent Bradford to Japan as part of a delegation to inspect missions there. He founded the Whittier House Social Settlement in Jersey City, New Jersey, where his sister, Cornelia Bradford, was head worker. From 1901 to 1903 Bradford served as moderator of the National Council of Congregational Churches. In 1904 he exchanged places with Washington Gladden to become president of the American Missionary Association. African-American Congregational pastor Henry Hugh Proctor held that Bradford was "one of the greatest, wisest, and most courageous friends my people ever had." In *My Brother* (1910), one of the Social Gospel's more important critiques of racism, Bradford developed the racial implications of the doctrines of the fatherhood of God and the brotherhood of man. "We believe in the brotherhood of man, because we believe in the Fatherhood of God," Bradford said. His critique was based on theological personalism, which held that all humanity participates in the divinity of God. "All men, as men, are sacred," he wrote. "Because all human beings have the same parentage, all have by nature the same rights, and should have equal opportunities."

During Bradford's ministry at Montclair's First Congregational Church, it became one of the denomination's leading congregations, the largest outside New England. Bradford retired from its pulpit in January 1911, just six weeks before his death in Montclair.

• There is no known collection of Bradford papers, but there is Bradford correspondence in the American Missionary Association Papers at the Amistad Research Center at Tulane University and in the Washington Gladden Papers at the Ohio State Historical Society. In addition to the standard biographical sources, see the *American Missionary*, May 1911; *Congregationalist*, 4 Mar. 1911; *Newark Sun*, 20 Feb. 1911; *New York Sun*, 19 Feb. 1911; and *Outlook*, 4 Mar. 1911. On the theological and social significance of Bradford's thought see William R. Hutchison, *The Modernist Impulse in American Protestantism* (1976), and Ralph E. Luker, *The Social Gospel in Black and White* (1991).

RALPH E. LUKER

BRADFORD, Andrew (1686?–24 Nov. 1742), printer and journalist, was born in Philadelphia, Pennsylvania, the son of William Bradford, a printer and journalist, and Elizabeth Sowle, whose father, Andrew Sowle, was a printer in London. After being arrested and released for printing a pamphlet by Quaker apostate George Keith, William Bradford moved his family to New York and opened a print shop. Here, Andrew Bradford was trained as a printer. Little is known about his childhood or formal education, but Bradford was probably not the "illiterate" printer Benjamin Franklin was to call him in the disparaging remarks in his *Autobiography* on the state of printing in Philadelphia upon his arrival in the city.

Bradford was listed as a freeman and a printer of New York in 1709, the same year he declined Rhode Island's offer to become the colony's printer. In 1710–1711 father and son were in partnership and published three books together; they maintained close business ties throughout their careers. In 1713 Andrew Bradford returned to Philadelphia and was hired to publish

"The Acts and Laws of the Province of Pennsylvania, October 14th, 1712 to March 27th, 1713," the first printed collection of the colony's laws, and thus became the unofficial provincial printer. He was the only printer in Philadelphia until 1723 and published the acts of the assembly, Indian treaties, and Governor William Keith's letters and proclamations. Almanacs by Jacob Taylor, Titan Leed, and John Jerman bore Bradford's imprint, as did various books and pamphlets on social, political, and religious matters.

Bradford's the *American Weekly Mercury*, the first newspaper in Philadelphia, commenced publication on 22 December 1719 and remained in publication for twenty-six years. The venture was initially a partnership with John Copson, a local bookseller at the time. They were assisted by William Bradford, who remained in New York, but took in advertisements for the *Mercury* until he started his own paper, the *New York Gazette*, late in 1725. The *American Mercury* had a wide circulation, and Bradford enjoyed the advantages of being colonial postmaster from 1728 to 1737, which allowed him to accumulate news and to send his own mail at no cost—both of which greatly increased the *American Mercury*'s circulation.

Until 1728 the *American Mercury* did not have any local competition, but upon hearing that Benjamin Franklin was planning to bring out a newspaper, another Philadelphia printer and one of Franklin's former employers, Samuel Keimer, began publishing the *Universal Instructor in All Arts and Sciences; and the Pennsylvania Gazette*. Franklin, joined later by Joseph Breintnall, sent thirty-two letters modeled on Sir Richard Steele and Joseph Addison's London essay periodical, the *Spectator*, to Bradford for publication in his newspaper. These essays, together called *The Busy-Body*, included remarks designed to attack Keimer and drive him out of the newspaper business; they were a success. Franklin took possession of the *Pennsylvania Gazette* in 1729 and became Bradford's chief competition.

Early in his newspaper's existence, Bradford used it to criticize local government. After a pamphlet critical of the provincial government's financial condition was published, perhaps by Bradford, the *American Mercury* included a remark also critical of the province's "sinking credit." Brought before the council, Bradford denied printing the pamphlet and claimed that the newspaper remarks were inserted by a journeyman. Admonished against printing remarks on the colonial governments, Bradford was released, but in 1723 he published an account of James Franklin's censure and imprisonment in New England for publishing "scandalous libels" against the colonial government there. The account included remarks supportive of Franklin and generally of freedom of the press. In 1727 and 1728 Bradford again printed several pamphlets on political topics but was not censured. In 1729, however, Bradford was called before the council again. The governor and council found Busy-Body essay number twenty-seven, in which Breintnall presents an argument for rotation of public office, to be offensive, appearing, as it did, just before an election. Bradford was jailed but returned to the press shortly, where he continued to publish the *Busy-Body* essays in the *American Mercury*. Bradford's quiet resistance of the council's wishes has been seen as an early principled conflict between the press and government in the colonies.

Bradford also published the first magazine in America. The *American Magazine*, edited by John Webbe, was modeled on Edward Cave's *Gentleman's Magazine*, initiated in London some years earlier. Webbe approached Franklin about the venture, but objecting to Franklin's terms, brought the plan to Bradford. In an advertisement in the *American Mercury* announcing the venture, the editor sets out numerous objectives: to carry the news and laws of colonial governments, to carry news of communities without a press, and to promote liberty and freedom of the press and speech, without engaging in licentious abuses. Franklin, in the meantime, decided to bring out his own *General Magazine*, and he and Webbe waged an editorial battle in the *Gazette* and the *American Mercury*. When the magazines were issued, weeks later, Bradford and Webbe had beaten Franklin into print by three days. Both magazines failed, however, in just a few months.

Bradford was married to Dorcas Boels of Freehold, New Jersey, and after her death in 1739, to Cornelia Smith in 1740. His only child, by Dorcas, died in infancy or childhood. Sometimes mentioned as a foster son, William Bradford III was Bradford's nephew and was apprenticed to him in the 1730s.

After Bradford's death in Philadelphia, Cornelia Bradford continued to publish the *American Mercury* until 1746. Bradford's reputation rests primarily upon his publication of the first newspaper in the middle colonies and the first magazine in America, as well as upon his consistent if undramatic resistance to the provincial government's desire to control the press.

• The papers and manuscripts of Andrew Bradford are collected at the Historical Society of Pennsylvania. The *American Weekly Mercury* has been reprinted in facsimile by the Colonial Society of Pennsylvania and is available on microfilm (1970). The *American Magazine* was reprinted in 1937 and also is available on microfilm. The most comprehensive study of Bradford's life and work is Anna Janney DeArmond, *Andrew Bradford: Colonial Journalist* (1949). See also Horatio Gates Jones, *Andrew Bradford, Founder of the Newspaper Press in the Middle States of America* (1869; repr. 1970). On Bradford's place in the history of printing in early America, see Isaiah Thomas, *History of Printing in Early America* (1810; repr. 1970); Elizabeth Christine Cook, *Literary Influences in Colonial Newspapers* (1912; reissued 1966); and Sidney Kobre, *The Development of the Colonial Newspaper* (1944; repr. 1960).

RAYMOND A. CRAIG

BRADFORD, Augustus Williamson (9 Jan. 1806–1 Mar. 1881), governor of Maryland, was born in Bel Air, Harford County, Maryland, the son of Samuel Bradford and Jane Bond. Educated in Bel Air at the Reverend Reuben Davis's well-known academy, Bradford continued his studies at St. Mary's College in Baltimore where he graduated in 1824. Returning to Bel

Air, he apprenticed with Otho Scott, one of the state's most famous lawyers. He was admitted to the bar in 1827.

In his early career Bradford practiced in Bel Air, where he was also a surveyor. Like many ambitious young men, he soon moved to Baltimore. In 1835 he married Elizabeth Kell. The couple became the parents of twelve children.

Attracted to politics by the dynamic Kentucky legislator Henry Clay and his new Whig party, which supported internal improvements, Bradford served as a presidential elector for Clay in 1844. He was appointed clerk of the Baltimore County Court in 1845, a post he retained until 1851. When the Whig party disappeared in the 1850s, Bradford retired from politics, but his legal reputation gained him an appointment by Governor Thomas H. Hicks as a member of the Maryland delegation to the 1861 Washington Peace Conference. Although this conference of notables failed to prevent war, Bradford gave a stirring Unionist speech to its members. Unencumbered by political attachments, he now represented the patriot restored to public affairs in a crisis—an appealing image to Marylanders, who remembered George Washington as such a figure. In the summer of 1861 Bradford received the gubernatorial nomination of Maryland's Unionist party over a number of candidates whose ties to party organization were more substantial.

Bradford's opponent in Maryland's gubernatorial election of 1861 was Benjamin Chew Howard of the States' Rights party. Clearly the choice of most Marylanders, Bradford won the election with two-thirds of the vote, which included Maryland's soldiers who were given furloughs to return home and vote. Many Democrats boycotted the election; their failure to vote—rather than any interference by the few detachments of soldiers directed to protect Union voters from intimidation and to arrest anyone who had just returned from Virginia—accounted for Bradford's strong showing.

Bradford took office in January 1862 and served until January 1866. Throughout the war he supported the Lincoln government, but at the same time he sought to prevent its encroachment into Maryland's domestic affairs. Three times, when the Confederates invaded Maryland, he called for volunteers. Without waiting for legislative approval, he organized these often elderly male citizens into a home guard ready to defend the state from the Confederates. When Major General Robert Schenck authorized Union officers to support election judges who required an oath of allegiance from suspected Confederates, Bradford assured President Abraham Lincoln that such intrusion by the military was unnecessary. Convinced of the state's loyalty, he walked a narrow path between Unionism and support of the federal government and what he considered to be the rights of Marylanders. Meanwhile he encouraged the passage of a state "Treason Bill," making it illegal to support the Confederacy.

A slaveholder, Bradford came to oppose slavery on both moral and economic grounds, believing that any loss of property was a cost of war—"the direct and anticipated fruits of this atrocious rebellion." By 1864 he encouraged the calling of a state constitutional convention to emancipate slaves, many of whom had already been freed by enrolling in the Union army. The resulting constitution, which was ratified in October 1864, emancipated Maryland's slaves, reapportioned the legislature by basing representation on white not total population, and disenfranchised citizens who had fought for or aided the Confederacy. Some Marylanders opposed these changes, and in order to obtain the broadest vote on the constitution, the governor appointed agents to visit military camps and take the vote of Maryland's soldiers who were temporarily out of the state in military service.

In 1864, during the Confederate general Jubal Early's raid into Maryland, marauding Confederates burned Bradford's home four miles north of Baltimore. He accepted his personal loss as "the special providence of God to tear loose from us a black idol." When the war ended nine months later, Bradford traveled throughout the state, praising Union veterans and offering hope for the future in a restored Union.

In 1867 Bradford was appointed surveyor of the Port of Baltimore by President Andrew Johnson, but later he declined another patronage position in the city's customhouse. Instead, as he had in the 1850s, he returned to his law practice, although he was a presidential elector for Horace Greeley on the Democratic ticket in 1872. Bradford died in Baltimore.

• Bradford's private papers were destroyed when the Confederates burned his home. Some of his official correspondence is found in the Robert Todd Lincoln Collection of Abraham Lincoln Papers, Library of Congress. See also Roy Glashan, *American Governors and Gubernatorial Elections, 1775–1975* (1975), and Jean Baker, *The Politics of Continuity: Maryland Political Parties from 1858 to 1870* (1973).

JEAN H. BAKER

BRADFORD, Cornelia Foster (4 Dec. 1847–15 Jan. 1935), social reformer, was born in Granby, New York, the daughter of Benjamin Franklin Bradford, a Methodist minister, and Mary Amory Howe, a reform activist. Her parents were active in the women's rights, abolitionist, and temperance causes and provided both Cornelia and her sister with college educations in an era when many girls were taught at home. Cornelia Bradford graduated in 1869 from Houghton Seminary in Clinton, New York, and then attended Olivet College in Michigan. Although little is known of her life during these early years, by her mid-twenties she was living with her sister and father in Chester, New Jersey, where she taught Sunday school.

At about the age of forty-five, Bradford became interested in social settlement work. In 1892 she visited the pioneering social settlement, Toynbee Hall, in London and lived briefly at Mansfield House, a settlement in East London. In 1893 she visited Jane Addams's Hull-House in Chicago, beginning a lifelong friendship with Addams. Bradford then moved to Jersey City, New Jersey, where her brother and father now lived. There she worked at the People's Palace, a cultural center, organizing local residents into sports and club activities. In May 1894, with the financial help of her brother, Amory Howe Bradford, a minister, she established the state's first social settlement, Whittier House, which she named for the Quaker poet, John Greenleaf Whittier.

Whittier House, like most social settlements, had as its purpose the promotion of fellowship and mutual helpfulness between people of different "occupations and opportunities," the establishment of a residence for those engaged in the work of the settlement, and the formation of a place for cooperation with churches and other agencies organized "for the improvement of social conditions." It was situated in a slum populated predominantly by Russian, Italian, and Polish immigrants who labored on the docks and in Jersey City's sugar, soap, and tobacco factories. Like Jane Addams and Ellen Gates Starr at Chicago's Hull-House, Bradford succeeded in gaining the financial support of Jersey City's elites to create a social center that she hoped would spread middle-class values and aspirations through offering classes in art, literature, and culture. Whittier House also sponsored programs providing more practical assistance, including the first free kindergarten in the city, the first district nursing program, health clinics, and the first public playground. A branch of the public library was housed at the settlement, as were a savings bank, a legal aid department, and classes in sewing, dressmaking, millinery, and athletics.

Bradford, like other settlement house workers, was also involved in many other progressive social reform movements. Under Bradford's direction, Whittier House residents conducted a number of influential social surveys on housing conditions, the status of women in the trades, and immigration. In 1898 the New Jersey Consumers' League was founded at Whittier House to focus on the working conditions of women and children. Similarly, the Tenement House Protective League, established in 1903, grew out of a housing investigation by Whittier resident Mary Sayles and contributed to the passage of a state tenement housing code. Bradford also organized the New Jersey Association of Neighborhood Workers in 1903, serving as president and chair of its Legislation Committee, which lobbied the state legislature on behalf of progressive reforms, such as limits on child labor and safeguards against the adulteration of foods. In 1911 she was appointed to the Jersey City Board of Education and was later named to the State Board of Children's Guardians and the State Board of Charities, Aids, and Corrections. Bradford became president of the New Jersey Conference for Social Welfare in 1920.

Bradford was also involved in the woman suffrage and peace movements. She considered herself an ardent feminist and worked on behalf of the suffrage movement, particularly for the Congressional Union, forerunner of the National Woman's Party. She also joined the Women's International League for Peace and Freedom. During World War I, however, her attitudes changed. She turned Whittier House into a home for homeless soldiers and, like many reformers with ambivalent attitudes toward immigrants during the war, became active in Americanization and nativist movements.

At Whittier House Cornelia Bradford successfully replicated the settlement house model in New Jersey and left her mark on myriad social welfare and legislative programs in the state. The fortunes of Whittier House—like settlement houses generally—waned during the 1920s, as many of the settlement's programs, especially those involving child welfare, legal aid, and public health, were taken over by city and state government. In 1925 Bradford retired and lived with her brother in Montclair, New Jersey, until her death.

• Primary source material on Bradford is available in the Whittier House Papers, New Jersey Historical Society, Newark. The Whittier House Annual Reports are held at the Social Welfare History Archives, University of Minnesota, and at the Jersey City Public Library. Correspondence between Bradford and Jane Addams is available in the Jane Addams Papers, University of Illinois at Chicago. Bradford's publications, besides her annual reports, include "For Jersey City's Social Uplift: Life at Whittier House," *Commons* 10 (Feb. 1905): 101–6, and "The Settlement Movement in New Jersey," *New Jersey Review of Charities and Corrections* 11 (Apr. 1912): 23–28. Biographical accounts include Roy Lubove's in *Notable American Women*, vol. 1 (1971), and Claudia Clark's in the *Biographical Dictionary of Social Welfare in America*, ed. Walter Trattner (1986). See also Robert Woods and Albert Kennedy, "Whittier House" in *Handbook of Settlements*, ed. Robert Archey Woods (1911), and "Anniversary of Whittier House," *Outlook*, 21 May 1898, p. 188.

LYNN Y. WEINER

BRADFORD, Ebenezer (1746?–3 Jan. 1801), pastor, was probably born in Canterbury, Connecticut. Nothing is known about his familial background. Bradford attended the College of New Jersey (now Princeton University), where he received a B.A. in 1773 and an M.A. in 1786. He married Elizabeth Green, daughter of pastor Jacob Green, in 1776; the couple had nine children. In 1775 Bradford was appointed pastor of the Church of South Hanover in New Jersey. Later he worked as a preacher at the First Church in Danbury, Connecticut. Together with his father-in-law and several other ministers, Bradford left the Presbyterian Church in 1780 over a conflict concerning centralized authority and founded the Associated Presbytery of Morris County. He preached at several other churches before taking up a position at the Congregational Church in Rowley, Massachusetts, a town in Essex County where he spent the rest of his life. During his tenure there, Bradford took part in ecclesiastical and political debates of his day, publishing sermons as well as other prose.

Six of Bradford's nine published sermons, which were delivered between 1785 and 1795, were given at the ordinations of fellow pastors. They were all structured in the same manner, taking their subject from a New Testament quotation, working out its meaning and implications in enumerative style, and closing with direct addresses to the new pastor and the congregation. Bradford's most unusual sermon, *The Nature and Manner of Giving Thanks to God, Illustrated*, was delivered on 19 February 1795, a national day of thanksgiving. In this and his later sermons, Bradford became more political, taking up the official proclamation of thanksgiving but adding several points concerning the freedom of the press, democratic associations, and Republican France. With these prayers Bradford intervened in the Federalist debate as an antifederalist, while nevertheless remaining an admirer of Washington, to whom he had dedicated his earlier *Mr. Thomas Paine's Trial* (1795), an attack on Deism. Although Bradford referred to Washington in the text "Our good and beloved President" again and again, he also points out that he is "*but a man!* subject to like imperfections with his fellow-men." Bradford defended the French as long as they "feel themselves under the controul of Law and Reason." He also lamented "the baneful influence of British politics, spoliation and injustice." His positions were unusual for a Congregational pastor, and they earned him the nickname "Vandal of Rowley." Another Massachusetts pastor, David Trappan, countered *Nature* with a sermon attacking Bradford's opinions, to which Bradford in turn responded two months later with an *Appendix in Answer to Dr. Tappan's Remarks on his Thanksgiving Sermon*. Even though a contemporary newspaper speculated that "the laurels of a Bradford shall bloom with increasing glory" (*Boston Independent Chronicle* 2 Mar. 1795), this debate caused Bradford to become an outsider in Essex County, and his publications ceased after 1795.

All four of Bradford's prose publications are a mixture of the political, religious, philosophical, and moral writing that was characteristic of the period. *A Dialogue between Philagathus, a Young Divine, and Pamela, his Sister, a Young Convert* (1795) takes up themes from earlier sermons such as the depravity of human nature. In this dialogue Philagathus explains the mysterious workings of the Holy Ghost, what he refers to as the "*Common*, *Miraculous*, and *Gracious* . . . operations of the spirit," in an enumerative style with examples from both the Old and New Testaments. Bradford is also considered the author of *The Art of Courting* (1795). This work, described as a sentimental novel by most critics, is actually a compilation of an introductory prose chapter and seven series of letters interspersed with editorial comments narrating variations of courtship. Instead of being a sentimental novel, it attacks the "novels and plays" read by young ladies in an attempt to counter sentimental fashion with educational didacticism and clumsy humor. *The Art of Courting*, which claims to be a collection of real letters, is supposed to "*impress the minds of young people with a lively sense of the love and favour of heaven in granting to the human race*, the Institution of Marriage." All courtships move from mutual friendship, through protestations of love from both the man and the woman, to engagement. The final and climactic set of letters relates the conversion of Damon from Deism, a conversion made possible through the power of his love to Harriot. A contemporary review in the *Massachusetts Magazine* (Feb. 1796) condemned the work for its "scenes of courtship that are detailed without spirit till the vapid narration ends in marriage" and refused to quote from it lest "the Editor of the Magazine will be unwilling to retail such low wares."

Although Bradford was certainly not remarkable for his prose writings, which are typical examples of early American educational fiction, he is memorable for his participation in the Federalist debate and his ability to blur the boundaries between didactic sermons and religious fiction. He died in Rowley.

• All of the works discussed in the text, as well as other writings by Bradford such as his sermon *The Depravity of Human Nature* (1791) and the prose piece *Strictures on the Remarks of Dr. Samuel Langdon* (1794), are available in the Early American Imprints microfiche series. The longest biographical notice is James A. Levernier and Douglas R. Wilmes, eds., *American Writers Before 1800: A Biographical and Critical Dictionary* (1983). There is a short secondary bibliography in Patricia L. Parker, *Early American Fiction* (1984). A brief discussion of Bradford's role as a pastor in the Federalist debate can be found in W. DeLoss Love, *The Fast and Thanksgiving Days of New England* (1895). Lillie D. Loshe, *The Early American Novel 1789–1830* (1907); Herbert Ross Brown, *The Sentimental Novel in America 1789–1860* (1940); and Henri Petter, *The Early American Novel* (1971), all comment on *The Art of Courting*.

NORBERT SCHÜRER

BRADFORD, Edward Hickling (9 June 1848–7 May 1926), orthopedic surgeon, was born in Boston, Massachusetts, the son of Charles F. Bradford, a merchant, and Eliza E. Hickling. After attending preparatory schools, Bradford earned degrees from Harvard College in 1869 and from Harvard Medical School in 1873. Following an internship at the Massachusetts General Hospital, he spent two years in Europe, visiting various medical centers and attending lectures and clinics. Having developed a special interest in orthopedic surgery, he worked for some months in England with Owen Thomas of Liverpool, a pioneer in joint surgery. After his return to America, Bradford studied under another outstanding orthopedic surgeon, Charles Fayette Taylor, in New York before returning to Boston and establishing his practice.

For a long period Bradford worked with Buckminster Brown at the House of the Good Samaritan, the first institution in Boston where bone and joint diseases of children were regarded as a special branch of surgery, later succeeding Brown as surgeon in charge. He also practiced, from early in his career, at the Boston Dispensary (1876), the Children's Hospital (1878–1909), and the Boston City Hospital (1880–1894), gaining much valuable experience. Although he came to devote more and more of his time and energy to orthopedic surgery, he nonetheless maintained a continued interest in general surgery. His work at the Children's Hospital eventually absorbed all his attention, and he became surgeon in chief there. His long connection with the Children's Hospital was concurrent with the gradual foundation and growing worldwide reputation of the Boston school of orthopedic surgery.

Bradford largely thought out and made better known the correct pathology of congenital dislocation of the hip, later instituting effective methods of treatment. For the treatment of Pott's disease (osteitis or caries of the vertebrae) he invented a simple and useful frame that bears his name; he also developed other orthopedic apparatus, including the Bradford induction hip-splint for the treatment of caries of the hip joint.

In 1880 Bradford became clinical instructor of orthopedic surgery at the Harvard Medical School, gradually rising in rank until in 1903 he was appointed professor of orthopedic surgery, a post he held until 1912, when he became emeritus. In 1912 he was made dean of the Harvard Medical School, serving until 1918 on a half-time basis. Bradford was a superb clinician and clinical investigator, but he had little appreciation for the preclinical sciences and academic research. Furthermore, his deanship followed closely the publication of the so-called "Flexner Report" (1910) on the state of medical education, with recommendations for its reform. As a result Bradford was embroiled throughout much of his deanship in controversies and arguments dealing with admission standards, the increasing role of research in medicine, and full-time teaching at Harvard.

After the medical faculty had approved in early 1913 the minimum standards of admission adopted by the Council of Medical Education, which required the bachelor's degree, Bradford publicly came out in favor of a policy of admitting students after they had completed only two years of college. Not only did he become involved in debates over the amount of research at the school and the direction the university administration was advocating; he also opposed efforts by the Rockefeller General Education Board in promoting the full-time system, under which clinical professors had the same status as professors of laboratory (preclinical) subjects. Early in 1915 former president Eliot and others began to maneuver to make Walter Bradford Cannon dean in Bradford's place, in an effort to establish their plan for a full-time system at Harvard and thereby obtain funds from the General Education Board. However, after Cannon expressed his unwillingness to discontinue his teaching and research, Bradford remained in the deanship until he stepped down in 1918. In 1919 he was elected an overseer of Harvard College.

Bradford was author of many pioneering articles on bone diseases and orthopedic procedures but was best known for writing, with Robert W. Lovett, his associate at the Children's Hospital, one of the earliest and best-known texts in the orthopedic field, *A Textbook of Orthopedic Surgery* (1890). This was for many years the standard authority, going through five editions by 1915.

All of Bradford's later activities were carried on in spite of increasing impairment of vision; he had lost an eye and was permanently disfigured as the result of a bicycle accident in middle life. Toward the end of his life he took up the study of Braille to keep in touch with the outside world and derived much enjoyment from it. Bradford married Edith Fiske in 1900; of their four children, one of his sons became an orthopedic surgeon also, and another a governor of Massachusetts. He died suddenly in Boston, of a cerebral hemorrhage. He was described in an obituary in the *British Medical Journal* as "a notable figure from the dwindling group of pioneers in orthopedic surgery."

• George H. Monks, a Boston surgeon and colleague, compiled the most extensive biographical memoir on Bradford, "Edward Hickling Bradford," *Surgery, Gynecology and Obstetrics* 45, no. 1 (Oct. 1927): 564–66. For information on Bradford's term as dean of the Harvard Medical School see Saul Benison et al., *Walter B. Cannon: The Life and Times of a Young Scientist* (1987). An obituary is in the *Boston Medical and Surgical Journal* 194, no. 21 (May 1926): 1005–6.

RICHARD J. WOLFE

BRADFORD, Gamaliel (9 Oct. 1863–11 Apr. 1932), writer, was born in Boston, Massachusetts, the son of Gamaliel Bradford V, a banker, businessman, writer, and reformer, and Clara Crowninshield Kinsman. Gamaliel's mother died of tuberculosis when he was three, leaving him and his brother, who died at age nine, in the care of their aunt Sarah Hickling Bradford. In 1882 Bradford was enrolled at Harvard College but was compelled to withdraw because of ill health; thereafter, he devoted his life to writing. Bradford married Helen Hubbard Ford in 1886; they had two children.

Widely read in several languages and consumed by an almost Elizabethan passion for fame, Bradford attempted virtually every type of creative writing known in his time. *Lee the American* (1912) was his first work to attract wide attention. This book, like nearly twenty subsequent volumes in kind, typified a genre he called "psychography," a form of biographical writing that is organized topically rather than chronologically, with its emphasis not on the events of the subject's life but upon a description and analysis of the subject's character and personality. These studies, which exhibit some similarity to the works of Sainte-Beuve, made Bradford one of the notable figures in the extraordinary revival of interest in biography that reached its height in the 1920s.

Though Bradford published book-length studies of Samuel Pepys, Charles Darwin, and D. L. Moody after the publication of *Lee*, his more characteristic form was the short psychograph, first published in such magazines as the *Atlantic Monthly* and *Harper's* and then collected, seven or eight psychographs to a volume. At the height of his career, he appealed to a wide variety of readers (if he was allergic to Freud, he was also cold to the Victorians), and one of his most ardent admirers was H. L. Mencken, who was then, like Bradford himself, at the height of his vogue and influence. As Bradford wrote in the preface of *Damaged Souls* (1923), he believed that "if the human heart was not worth loving, my work would not be worth doing," and his ability to portray sympathetically yet with a keen critical eye a wide variety of human beings, some of whom seemed almost wholly antipathetic to both his temperament and his principles, amounted at times almost to genius.

Lee the American, Confederate Portraits (1914), and *Union Portraits* (1916) comprised a Civil War trilogy, while *Portraits of Women* (1916), *Portraits of American Women* (1919), *Wives* (1925), and *Daughters of Eve* (1930) formed a distaff tetralogy. *A Naturalist of Souls* (1917; rev. ed., 1926) traces Bradford's early work, revealing how his interest gradually shifted from the study of a writer's work to the study of the subject's character. *Darwin* (1926), *D. L. Moody, A Worker in Souls* (1927), and *Life and I, an Autobiography of Humanity* (1928)—the last is not psychography in the strictest sense—involve the problems of faith and doubt, issues that enthralled and tormented Bradford throughout his mature life. *American Portraits, 1875–1900* (1922), which included studies of Mark Twain, Henry James (1843–1916), and Henry Adams (1838–1918), was designed as the first of a series intended to cover the whole range of American history. This plan was aborted, however, by the unexpected success of *Damaged Souls*, whose portraits of Benedict Arnold, Thomas Paine, Aaron Burr (1756–1836), John Randolph (1773–1833), John Brown (1800–1859), P. T. Barnum, and Benjamin F. Butler (1818–1893) prompted editors and publishers to overwhelm Bradford with suggestions that he write about subjects who were calculated to have a wider appeal than those he had hitherto studied. In *The Quick and the Dead* (1931), Bradford dared for the first time to apply the psychographic method to a group of celebrities over half of whom were still living. Mussolini admired the highly critical portrait of himself, but Coolidge family members were reportedly not pleased by Bradford's "The Genius of the Average: Calvin Coolidge." Bradford had already tested his psychographic method in *Bare Souls* (1924), in which he made use of the rich and abundant material furnished by some of the world's great letter writers. In *Wives*, contrarily, he was faced with the challenge of describing seven women of whom little was known, except through what had been written about their famous and infamous husbands.

Bradford's whole life was a struggle against ill health. For years he was prostrated from time to time by paralyzing attacks of vertigo, and during his years of fame he was rarely able to write for more than two hours a day. He disciplined his resources with amazing care, planning his work in detail before beginning to write, and always sending his first draft to the printer. Temperamentally intensely religious, Bradford never achieved a settled, satisfying faith, primarily because though he could not accept Christian fundamentalism, he was unable to find any modernist modification thereof satisfactory. A kindly man, he had an immense correspondence and a multitude of friends, including established writers like Robert Frost, neophytes whose early activities he advised, and a multitude of persons in other lines of activity. Only one of his plays, *Unmade in Heaven* (1917), and three of his novels—*The Private Tutor* (1904), *Between Two Masters* (1906), and *Matthew Porter* (1908)—achieved book publication, but a number of others survive in manuscript, as do innumerable poems, journals, and letter books. His poems published in *A Pageant of Life* (1904) and in *Shadow Verses* and *A Prophet of Joy* (both 1920) were supplemented by many other poems published in contemporary magazines. His book reviews and editorials in the Boston *Herald* remain uncollected. Bradford died in Wellesley Hills, Massachusetts.

• Bradford's manuscripts, including unpublished works, journals, and correspondence, are in the Houghton Library, Harvard University. His autobiography was once among his papers, but Mrs. Bradford, who thought it did not do him justice, withdrew it, and its condition and whereabouts are unknown. Bradford's *Journal* (1933) and *Letters* (1934), both edited by Van Wyck Brooks, are important sources. All of Bradford's collections of psychographs have been noted in the foregoing discussion except *The Soul of Samuel Pepys* (1924), *As God Made Them* (1929), *Saints and Sinners* (1932), and *Biography and the Human Heart* (1933). Mabel A. Bessey, ed., *Portraits and Personalities* (1933), contains brief psychographs intended by Bradford for high school use, together with reprints of some of his other pieces chosen by the editor. Harold Ogden White, ed., *Elizabethan Women* (1936), contains early literary criticism by Bradford; Bradford's *Types of American Character* (1895) is interesting for the contrast afforded with his later concentration upon individuals. The only book-length study is Edward Wagenknecht, *Gamaliel Bradford* (1982), in Twayne's United States Authors series, whose bibliography lists all earlier significant commentary.

EDWARD WAGENKNECHT

BRADFORD, John (6 June 1749–20 Mar. 1830), first printer in Kentucky, was born in Prince William (later Fauquier) County, Virginia, the son of Daniel Bradford, a surveyor for Fauquier County, and Alice Morgan. He was one of eleven children in a family that probably also farmed. Bradford's father taught him the craft of surveying. In 1771 John Bradford married Eliza James; they had five sons and four daughters.

Bradford saw military service during the revolutionary war. He first made his way to Kentucky in the fall of 1779, when he was hired to survey land around Harrodsburg and Lexington. He returned to Fauquier County, where he was commissioned as an ensign in the county militia on 23 July 1781, and then he traveled back to Kentucky, where he served as deputy surveyor of Fayette County under Colonel Thomas Marshall. During the course of his work, he acquired a claim to 6,000 acres of land in present-day Fayette and Scott counties on the North Elkhorn and Cane Run creeks. Like most Kentucky land claims of that era, however, Bradford's were disputed. Throughout his life he was involved heavily in both real estate trading and litigation.

Bradford fought in various Indian skirmishes, took part in the raid on Shawnee Town at Chillicothe, and acted as deputy surveyor of Kentucky County, Virginia, under George May. In 1784 he returned to Virginia to bring his wife and children back with him to settle in Fayette County on Cane Run in 1785.

Later in 1785 the third or fourth of ten territorial conventions gathered in Danville to deliberate on the propriety of separating from Virginia and sought the services of a printer to publicize its proceedings and unite the citizens of the region in the resolve for statehood. Finding no printer willing to migrate, they employed Bradford—who stepped forward to offer his services even though he had no prior knowledge of the printing trade—to learn the craft. At that time he and his family moved again, this time to Lexington. Bradford and his brother Fielding undertook the trade with the understanding that their business would receive government patronage in the future. The first issue of the *Kentucke* (later *Kentucky*) *Gazette*, the only newspaper within 500 miles of Lexington, was published in a single-fold sheet of four pages on 11 August 1787. Bradford received a plot of land in Lexington in exchange for agreeing to locate the press there.

From this small beginning Bradford generated a printing business founded on the twin pillars of government subsidy and commercial support. He was appointed printer to the Commonwealth upon Kentucky's entrance to the Union in 1792 and continued in that capacity until 1795, assuming the post again in 1797 and 1798. When Bradford lost the contract for public printing to Colonel William Hunter in 1798, he and his son James established a Frankfort version of the *Gazette*, called the *Guardian of Freedom*, in order to compete with Hunter's *Palladium*. In 1797 and 1802 Bradford served in the state legislature representing Fayette County, and by 1801 his tax assessment placed him among the richest third of Lexingtonians. Increasingly a prominent public figure, Bradford served at different times in his career as a founder and trustee of the Lexington Library, as chairman of the board first of Transylvania Seminary and subsequently of Transylvania University, and as high sheriff of Fayette County. Although he had relinquished ownership of the *Gazette* to his son Daniel in 1802 in order to take charge of the *Kentucky Herald*, Bradford assumed control of a merged *Herald* and *Gazette* in 1805. He sold the paper to Thomas Smith in 1809, but it passed back into his family in 1814, when his son Fielding Bradford, Jr. (nephew of the first Fielding), repurchased it. John Bradford served as its editor for yet another stint beginning in 1825.

Although Bradford was a Democratic-Republican and clearly involved in politics, the documentary record yields what are probably only the barest hints of his activity. In 1793 he had been instrumental in the formation of the Kentucky Democratic Society, modeled on the radical Jacobin Philadelphia Democratic Society. The immediate impetus for the formation of this group was Spain's closure of the Mississippi River to western settlers. Bradford was part of a group of prominent Kentucky gentlemen who issued handbills and propaganda and sent remonstrances to the president and to Congress urging that any measure necessary be taken to open the river to the free operation of commerce. The clubs spread across the state and played a role in the self-conscious formation of a regional consciousness during the era.

In August 1826 Bradford took on the role of memorializer of the early history of Kentucky with his publication of his "Notes on Kentucky" in the *Kentucky Gazette*. In the sixty-two papers published in this series before its cessation in January 1829, Bradford recounted the experiences of early settlers whom he had known and made himself a lasting place as historian of the state. Bradford died at his home in Lexington having played a major role in establishing a sense of regional identity through his printing, publishing, and political work.

• The John Bradford Papers are located in the University of Kentucky Special Collections and Archives, with a good number of materials relating to Bradford in the Samuel Mackay Wilson Collection. Other important sources include Willard Rouse Jillson, *The First Printing in Kentucky* (1936); William H. Perrin, *The Pioneer Press of Kentucky* (1888); Samuel M. Wilson, "John Bradford: Kentucky's First Printer," *Filson Club History Quarterly* 11 (1937): 145–51, 260–69; W. H. Venable, *Beginnings of Literary Culture in the Ohio Valley: Historical and Biographical Sketches* (1891); Garrett Glenn Clift, "John Bradford, 'the Caxton of Kentucky,': A Bibliography," *American Notes and Queries* 8 (1948): 35–41; and J. Winston Coleman, *John Bradford, Esq.: Pioneer Kentucky Printer and Historian* (1950). E. Merton Coulter, "The Efforts of the Democratic Societies of the West to Open the Navigation of the Mississippi," *Mississippi Valley Historical Review* 11 (1924): 376–89, provides information on Bradford's role in the formation of the Kentucky Democratic Society. Bradford's "Notes on Kentucky" have been republished as *The Voice of the Frontier: John Bradford's Notes on Kentucky*, ed. Thomas D. Clark (1993).

MARY KUPIEC CAYTON

BRADFORD, Perry (14 Feb. 1895–20 Apr. 1970), blues and vaudeville songwriter, publisher, and musical director, was born John Henry Perry Bradford in Montgomery, Alabama, the son of Adam Bradford, a bricklayer and tile setter, and Bella (maiden name unknown), a cook. Standard reference books give his year of birth as 1893, but Bradford's autobiography gives 1895. Early in his youth Bradford learned to play piano by ear. In 1901 the family moved to Atlanta, where his mother cooked meals for prisoners in the adjacent Fulton Street jail. There he was exposed to the inmates' blues and folk singing. He attended Molly Pope School through the sixth grade and claimed to have attended Atlanta University for three years (there being no local high school). This is chronologically inconsistent, however, with his claim to have joined Allen's New Orleans Minstrels in the fall of 1907, traveling to New Orleans for Mardi Gras performances in February 1908 and then moving on to Oklahoma.

After working as a pianist in Chicago, Bradford toured widely from about 1909 to 1918 with Jeanette Taylor in a song-and-dance act billed as Bradford and Jeanette. His nickname "Mule" came from his being featured in a piano and vocal vaudeville song, "Whoa, Mule," although jazz dance historians Marshall and

Jean Stearns point out that the name also fit Bradford's personality. Bradford learned countless dances from local performers as he toured. When appropriate he memorialized the best dances in lyrics to songs such as "The Bullfrog Hop" (c. 1909) and "Rules and Regulations" (printed in 1911). A shrewd entrepreneur, he initially published his songs as sheet music to be sold after performances. This informal method of distribution was due in part to the racist structure of the publishing industry, which put roadblocks in the paths of aspiring African-American songwriters. (Compare the experiences of lyricist and composer Andy Razaf.) Bradford's financial situation improved slightly with the commercial publication of "Scratchin' the Gravel" (1917) and "The Original Black Bottom Dance" (1919). During these final years of the decade he produced and performed in the musical revues *Sergeant Ham of the 13th District* (1917 and 1919); *Made in Harlem* (at the Lincoln Theater in New York, 1918), for which he wrote "Harlem Blues"; and *Darktown after Dark* (1919). Around 1918 Bradford married his first wife, Marion Dickerson, who took Taylor's place in the revues; details of his subsequent marriage or marriages are unknown.

In 1920 Bradford initiated a revolution in popular music. After several companies had turned him down, Bradford convinced Fred Hager of OKeh records to take a chance in spite of racist warnings "not to have any truck with colored girls in the recording field" (Bradford, p. 118). In February African-American singer Mamie Smith recorded for OKeh Bradford's songs "That Thing Called Love" and "You Can't Keep a Good Man Down," accompanied by a white band; these were not immediately released, owing to an industry-wide patent dispute that was still a half-year from settlement. In August, with a hastily put together African-American band, her Jazz Hounds, Smith recorded "It's Right Here for You" and "Crazy Blues." The latter title became a huge hit, selling perhaps more than a million copies. It initiated the 1920s craze for female blues singers and more broadly opened up the field of recording to African Americans not only in general markets but also in a newly created market: race records.

In 1921 Bradford organized tours for Smith, directed further recording sessions, and established his own publishing company. He quickly made five-figure sums in royalties, and when a Columbia Records lawyer, unaware of the instantaneous success of "Crazy Blues," offered to make the song a big hit if Bradford would waive his rights to royalties, he made the classic reply, "The only thing Perry Bradford waives is the American flag" (Bradford, p. 155). Also in 1921 singer Ethel Waters featured his song "Messin' Around" on the Theater Owners' Booking Association circuit, and Bradford himself performed in the show *Put and Take*. But all did not go smoothly in this year. Bradford reached an out-of-court settlement for having previously sold "Crazy Blues" (a retitled version of "Harlem Blues") to other publishers under the alternative titles "The Broken Hearted Blues" and "Wicked Blues." Also, a series of financial and touring disputes with Smith's husband and her boyfriend led Bradford to switch from OKeh to Columbia to promote singer Edith Wilson, who recorded his "Evil Blues" in 1922. In this year he was sued for publishing a song owned by another publisher, convicted of this charge and also of having witnesses commit perjury while testifying on his behalf, and sentenced to four months in prison.

Among his achievements in the 1920s Bradford claimed to have taught the Black Bottom dance to Ethel Ridley, who introduced it in Irvin C. Miller's show *Dinah* (1923). From this point on his star descended quickly. He assembled great musicians such as Louis Armstrong, James P. Johnson, and Buster Bailey, for undistinguished recordings made from 1923 to 1927 under the name of Perry Bradford's Jazz Phools and in 1927 introduced his song "All I Had Is Gone." He wrote lyrics to the musical revue *Messin' Around* (1929). He seems to have made no further impact, however, apart from a hit song recorded by Louis Jordan's new band in 1939, "Keep a Knockin' (But You Can't Come In)." Singer and songwriter Noble Sissle asserts: "The industry, especially some of the publishers, finally had Perry's terrific catalog of 1,400 songs blackballed from being recorded because he would not sell out to them. They practically broke him. His only brother Negro publisher, Clarence Williams, offered him the same fate. He had to sell out to a white publisher" (Bradford, p. 10). Bradford lived on relief and worked in New York as a mailman at Queens General Hospital, where he died after having spent his last years in ill health and confined to a nursing home.

As a musician Bradford was no match for pianist and composer Jelly Roll Morton, but they resembled one another in crucial ways. Both were aggressive, perceptive self-promoters who backed up brash claims with documented achievements. Touring the country during the developmental years of blues and jazz, they absorbed and disseminated what they heard, thus helping to create an international music from scattered rural and urban folk ways. Both were inflexibly hardheaded and after a period of great success (Bradford's financial and sociocultural, Morton's artistic) found themselves left behind as they stuck doggedly to musical styles that had fallen out of fashion.

Bradford's autobiography is a sustained outburst against his having been left out of early histories of blues and jazz and also against what was in his (probably incorrect) opinion an overestimation of the significance of New Orleans jazzmen in comparison to African-American jazz musicians in other locales. Although he distorts history as much as he repairs it, his essential arguments have been taken into account in most subsequent studies, and the great significance of his personal contribution to the music's flowering is now widely acknowledged.

• Bradford's autobiography is *Born with the Blues; Perry Bradford's Own Story: The True Story of the Pioneering Blues Singers and Musicians in the Early Days of Jazz* (1965). Dan Burley discusses Bradford in the context of Mamie Smith's career in "'Crazy Blues' and the Woman Who Sold 'Em," *Amsterdam News*, 17 Feb. 1940, which is continued as "The 'Crazy Blues,'" 24 Feb. 1940, 2 Mar. 1940, and 9 Mar. 1940. The most informative surveys are Samuel B. Charters and Leonard Kunstadt, *Jazz: A History of the New York Scene* (1962; repr. 1981), pp. 83–92; and Marshall Stearns and Jean Stearns, *Jazz Dance: The Story of American Vernacular Dance* (1968), pp. 103–14. See also Ronald Clifford Foreman, Jr., "Jazz and Race Records, 1920–1932: Their Origins and Their Significance for the Record Industry and Society" (Ph.D. diss., Univ. of Illinois, 1968); Henry T. Sampson, *Blacks in Blackface: A Source Book on Early Black Musical Shows* (1980); and Garvin Bushell and Mark Tucker, *Jazz from the Beginning* (1988). An obituary is in *Down Beat*, 11 June 1970, pp. 11–12.

BARRY KERNFELD

BRADFORD, Roark Whitney Wickliffe (21 Aug. 1886–13 Nov. 1948), fiction writer and journalist, was born on his family's cotton plantation in Lauderdale County, Tennessee, near the Mississippi River, the son of Richard Clarence Bradford, an affluent lawyer and planter, and Patricia Adelaide Tillman. Growing up on the plantation, Bradford played with the children of the nearly twenty black families that worked there. He frequently visited the black quarters and the local black church, all the while absorbing the stories and songs of the black plantation culture. This landscape proved to be the major influence on Bradford's subsequent literary career, providing the basis for the settings and characters of much of the fiction that won him acclaim in the 1920s and 1930s.

Bradford's formal education took place in the local one-room school and in the public schools at Halls, Tennessee. After the U.S. entry into World War I, he served in the Canal Zone as a first lieutenant in the U.S. Army Artillery Reserve. Later, he taught military science and tactics at Mississippi Agricultural and Mechanical College. Bradford was discharged from the army in 1920. He had previously married Lydia Sehorn of Columbia, Mississippi. She died several years later, and he soon married Mary Rose Sciarra Himler of Indianapolis, Indiana; they had one son.

Bradford worked as a newspaper reporter from 1920 to 1926. In Georgia, he was employed first by the *Atlanta Georgian*, then by the *Macon Telegraph*. After moving to Louisiana, he worked for the *Lafayette Daily Advertiser* until 1924, when he became night city editor for the *New Orleans Times-Picayune*. Two years later, Bradford resigned in order to become a freelance writer.

Bradford's writing focused on the stories of poor blacks who labored on the lower South's plantations. Much of his fiction would draw upon the blacks he had known as a boy as well as the storytellers he encountered in Louisiana. He soon developed his own humorous style of storytelling along with a unique representation of black dialect. One of his first stories of black life, "Child of God," appeared in the April 1927 issue of *Harper's* and won that year's O. Henry Memorial Prize. It would be followed over the next twenty years by similar stories that appeared in the pages of such magazines as the *Saturday Evening Post*, *Collier's*, *Harper's*, *Forum*, and the *Dial*.

Bradford's first book of stories, *Ol' Man Adam an' His Chillun*, was published in 1928. The stories in this volume are distorted versions of biblical tales told by a backwoods black preacher. The tone of these stories, and of all those that followed, is patronizing yet sympathetic. Another collection of similar stories, *Ol' King David an' the Philistine Boys* (1930), soon followed. In 1930, dramatist Marc Connelly adapted *Ol' Man Adam*, a highly successful play entitled *Green Pastures*, for which Bradford and Connelly were awarded a Pulitzer Prize. Bradford's popularity as a writer grew rapidly in subsequent years. His work sold well throughout his writing career.

Two of Bradford's novels, *This Side of Jordan* (1929) and *Kingdom Coming* (1933), attempt to treat black life seriously, but most of his prolific fictional production dealing with blacks—as in his first two collections of stories—is a mostly comical rendering of black culture. Bradford's only play, *How Come Christmas* (1930), many of his uncollected stories, and an additional collection of stories, *Let the Band Play Dixie* (1934), reflect this theme. Narrated in standard English, Bradford's *John Henry* (1931) is a collection of basically folkloric tales about the legendary black folk hero. His 1937 novel, *The Three-Headed Angel*, deals with the first white settlers in Tennessee's Cumberland Mountains.

Bradford served in the U.S. Navy from 1942 to 1946. He then became a visiting lecturer in the English department at Tulane University, a position he retained until his death at his New Orleans home.

Undoubtedly, the primary reason for Bradford's popularity was his sentimental and comic interpretation of southern blacks, a portrayal now recognized as stereotypical but accepted by most readers during Bradford's day as realistic. By the time of his death, the world pictured in Bradford's writing no longer existed and a nascent civil rights movement denounced stereotypical images of blacks. Though Bradford's fiction received contemporary critical acclaim and wide readership, it reveals more about white perceptions of blacks rather than providing literary insights into reality.

• Biographical information on Bradford's life and critical interpretations of his work can be found in Grace Leake, "Old Man Fortune and the Bradford Boy," *Holland's* 49 (Nov. 1930): 18, 34; Kenneth Thomas Knoblock, "Uncle Roark," *New Orleanian*, 15 Jan. 1931, pp. 19–20, 38–39; Rupert Norval, Jr., "Roark Bradford: An Analysis of His Works and Technique" (master's thesis, Univ. of Texas, 1941); David L. Cohn, "Strictly Personal: Roark Bradford's Revenge," *Saturday Review* 24 June 1944, pp. 13–14; Cohn, "Straight to Heaven," *Saturday Review*, 4 Dec. 1948, pp. 20–21; and Ruth Louise Durrett, "Roark Bradford's Portrayal of the Negro" (master's thesis, Louisiana State Univ., 1950). Obituaries appear in the *New Orleans Times-Picayune*, 15 Nov. 1948; the *New York Times*, 14 Nov. 1948; and the *Saturday Review*, 27 Nov. 1948.

L. MOODY SIMMS, JR.

BRADFORD, William (1590–9 May 1657), a founder and long-time governor of Plymouth colony, was born of yeoman stock in Austerfield, Yorkshire, the son of William Bradford and Alice Hanson. The parish register records his date of baptism as 19 March 1590. His father died in 1591; his mother remarried in 1593. According to Cotton Mather, whose *Magnalia Christi Americana* supplies details of Bradford's early life, the boy received a "Comfortable *Inheritance*" and was raised as a farmer by his grandfathers and uncles. An early interest in religion brought him to the notice of the Reverend Richard Clyfton, nonconformist rector at Babworth, Nottinghamshire, ten miles distant, and Clyfton's preaching led the young man to join the dissenters who met at the home of William Brewster (1567–1644) in Scrooby, near Babworth. Twenty-three years his senior, the experienced, learned, and devout Brewster became his surrogate father. The Scrooby group formed itself into a separatist church in 1606.

In the spring of 1609 Bradford and some 125 of his coreligionists made their way to Holland to escape local hostility and official repression. Mather records that Bradford was arrested with others en route and briefly jailed in Boston, Lincolnshire, and that he was detained again for a short time on his arrival in Amsterdam. From that city the separatists soon moved to Leiden, where they took up artisanal occupations and, led by the Reverend John Robinson, formed a congregation that Bradford called "as near the primative patterne" of the early apostolic churches "as any other church of these later times." Bradford became a citizen of Leiden and made a living as a weaver. In 1611 he converted inherited properties in England into cash, with which, it appears, he bought a house on the Achtergracht (sold 1619). In 1613 he married Dorothy May, daughter of a member of the English Church in Amsterdam. They had one child, John, who followed his parents to Plymouth.

In 1620, after securing financial support from a group of English investors—the merchant adventurers of Bradford's chronicle—through hard negotiations in which Bradford took part, forty-one Leiden separatists (seventeen men, ten women, and fourteen children) sailed in the *Mayflower* with sixty-one other passengers, including servants and so-called strangers recruited by the merchant adventurers, to a farther refuge in what Bradford terms "those vast and unpeopled countries of America." Relating their motives for moving, he stresses the "great difficulties" and their "answerable courages."

Of Plimmoth Plantation, Bradford's account of the Plymouth colony's early years, was composed over the course of some two decades. Bradford wrote Book 1 about ten years after the landing. By 1650 he had completed the much longer Book 2, carrying the record to 1646 in the form of annals. For sources, he had notes and letters (which he quoted at length), amplified by his own and others' memories. In 1651 he added a list of *Mayflower* passengers. His manuscript was used by colonial historians such as Mather, Nathaniel Morton, William Hubbard, Thomas Prince, and Thomas Hutchinson. Book 1 remained in manuscript until 1841; the full text was printed in 1856 as *History of Plymouth Plantation*.

The designation "Pilgrims" derives from Bradford's poignant memory (echoing Hebrews 11:13–16) of leaving Leiden, "that goodly and pleasante citie, which had been their resting place near 12 years; but they knew they were pilgrimes, and looked not much on those things, but lift up their eyes to the heavens, their dearest cuntrie, and quieted their spirits." The passage, typical of Bradford's best prose, expresses his sense of the dependence of human actions and affairs on divine providence. This faith inspires much of his account of the Pilgrims' adventure as summed up in one of his late verses:

> In wilderness he did me guide,
> And in strange lands for me provide.
> In fears and wants, through weal and woe,
> A Pilgrim passed I to and fro.

The *Mayflower* dropped anchor in Cape Cod harbor (Provincetown) on 11 November 1620, and Bradford began to learn firsthand about the "wilderness" on exploring expeditions that month and the next. The first expedition, finding a cache of corn unguarded by its Nauset Indian owners, rifled it for seed—"a spetiall providence of God," in Bradford's words, without which the English "might have starved." Another took stores of corn and beans, "purposing to give [the Indians] full satisfaction when they should meet, . . . as about some 6 months afterward they did." A third party beat off a Nauset attack and, after a cold, wet sail in the ship's shallop, found, on 11 December, a place with brooks and cornfields fit for settlement. While Bradford was off exploring, his wife drowned in Cape Cod harbor, either by accident or by suicide. The whole company, who had been living on board the *Mayflower* all the while, landed at Plymouth on 16 December.

From 1620 onward Bradford's life was meshed with Plymouth's history. The colony was Bradford writ large in a double sense. First, he was at most times its chief magistrate and at all times its chief man. He served as governor every year but five from 1621 to 1656 by virtue of thirty-one annual elections; in the other five years—1633, 1634, 1636, 1638, and 1644—he was elected one of the governor's assistants. Second, Bradford fused his story with that of the community he both presents and represents. He appears in his text in his public capacity only—as "the Gov[erno]r"—never as a private person. We know from other sources that in 1623 he married Alice Carpenter Southworth, a widow with two small boys who bore him three children, none of whom he mentions. Even as a public man Bradford was modest and reticent; though his authority was great, he does not thrust himself forward in his pages.

Bradford begins Book 2 with the Mayflower Compact, which he signed second of forty-one on 11 November 1620. Prompted by the restiveness of the strangers, the compact formed the signers into a self-selected "civill body politick." This act, in which the disciplinary motive was uppermost, served as the moral foundation of Pilgrim rule. The signers chose a governor, John Carver, who then, with the rest of the "better part," quelled further dissent for the time being by applications, Bradford writes, of wisdom, patience, and justice.

At first, the authority of the governor—as executive, chief judge, and treasurer—was highly personal and discretionary. He had charge of the plantation's business, land distribution, commerce and agriculture, and defense. Bradford's administration was marked by vigor, prudence, humor, plain speaking, and self-denial. He could temporize like a diplomat; he could also act with force and dispatch. Identifying his interests with the Pilgrim purpose, he did not aim at purely personal gain. When the Warwick patent of 1630 made him sole proprietor of Plymouth, he shared his right to the land with the "Old Comers" and confirmed the freemen's electoral and legislative powers. In 1636 he helped draft laws defining the relative duties of magistrates and of the freemen's general court. This code gave his authority a constitutional basis without significantly limiting it. In 1639, under pressure from the freemen, Bradford and the Old Comers yielded the patent to the whole body of freemen, while reserving tracts of land for themselves.

As magistrate, Bradford had primary responsibility for keeping order, dealing with English creditors, directing economic development, conducting relations with the Indians, coping with discordant neighbors, and treating with the other English governments in New England and with the Dutch at New Netherland. All this he did in consultation with such "trusty friends" as Brewster, Edward Winslow (1595–1655), and, for a time, Isaac Allerton.

Communal order was threatened by the presence of people who did not share the Pilgrim esprit de corps. These contingents included the *Mayflower* strangers, the "lusty yong men" deposited by the *Fortune* in 1621 whose Christmas revels that year Bradford peremptorily squelched, and a group that came in 1623 on "their perticuler" and "nurish[ed] a faction" when the colony's poverty and restrictions on private enterprise (e.g., in the Indian trade) frustrated their desire for quick gain. Bradford and his advisers defused challenges from the so-called Particulars and others mainly through skillful accommodations of private and public interest. The most important of these concessions, in 1627, brought all responsible heads of household and single men into a partnership involving a parceling out of land and cattle and a sharing of profits and losses from the colony's trade. Thereafter, Bradford records occasional grumbling but no significant contests over property.

Civil peace was also disrupted by disaffected individuals who sent ill reports to influential sponsors in England. The Particulars had reasons to complain, since they were caught between the promises of the merchants who had sent them and the constraining policies of the colony. Reporting quietly and critically to those same merchants in 1624 were the Reverend John Lyford, a crypto-Anglican, and his accomplice, John Oldham, one of the Particulars. "Knowing how things stood in England and what hurt" such "malicious slander" might do, Bradford acted decisively. As chief magistrate he intercepted Lyford's and Oldham's letters and convened a court to try (and convict) the two men for conspiracy, civil disturbance, and sedition. As chronicler, he carefully corrected their calumnies and made a robust defense of Pilgrim conduct. The incident exposed deep rifts among the merchant adventurers, most of whom now pulled out. The gain was greater than the loss, for the seceders had been stingy toward Plymouth, and their withdrawal relieved the colony of some of the hazards of entanglement in factional contests at home.

For the colony, divisions among the merchants complicated a relationship that was troubled from the start. Bradford quotes at length from correspondence in which both the company and the colony explain, complain, and extenuate in its own cause. Difficulties were only partly composed by an agreement of 1627 whereby eight planters, including Bradford, assumed the colony's debt in exchange for proprietorial rights and powers. It was to help meet this obligation that household heads and others were brought into partnership in 1627; later that year the enlarged body gave a monopoly on the colony's trade to Bradford, Allerton, and Miles Standish. These "Undertakers" took in other members of Plymouth's governing circle plus four of the remaining merchant adventurers. While the Undertakers bent to their formidable task, relations with creditors continued to be roiled, and the colony's economic capabilities undercut, by the entrepreneurial freewheeling of Allerton who, as Plymouth's agent in England, used his public trust for private ends. Until 1630, when Allerton was dismissed, his tangled, obscure dealings baffled Bradford and tested his charity. Five years later the Undertakers were still trying to sort out the agent's accounts and repair the damage.

Concern for Plymouth's economic plight and progress fills many lines of Bradford's history, beginning with his memorable account of the settlers' struggles to stay alive during the first few years. Over half their number had died by the summer of 1621. Hardship continued to pinch until 1625, when, for the first time, Bradford noted that Plymouth had "corn sufficient, and some to spare." He credited this success partly to the privatization of land in 1623 by which every family secured a parcel of its own. Bradford initially resisted this abandonment of communal economy but wrote approvingly that, when tried, "it made all hands very industrious." Survival thus assured, the leadership promoted the trade in furs with the Indians on which the colony's development depended. In addition to local exchange, posts were set up on the Maine coast in the 1620s. Bradford himself, with Winslow, sailed on a trading voyage to Monhegan Island in 1626. By that year, despite setbacks, the trade had become strong enough to warrant the buy-out of the merchants and the launching of the Undertaking. Most important, the Puritan migration of the 1630s to Massachusetts Bay provided a lively market for Plymouth's cattle and crops. By 1633 Bradford could record the shipment of a "great quantity of beaver besides pa[y]ing all their charges and debts at home, which good returne did much incourage their friends in England." Though the "long and tedious bussines" of settling with creditors dragged on until 1650, the plantation's viability had now been placed beyond doubt.

Good relations with the Indians were essential to the fur trade. Peaceful contacts were maintained with the neighboring Wampanoags, who had been "abundantly wasted in the late great mortalitie." It was from the Wampanoag chief, Massasoit, in 1623 that the Pilgrims had forewarning of an Indian attack on Thomas Weston's settlement at Wessagusset on Massachusetts Bay, which they easily suppressed through the superiority of guns to bows and arrows. Though force—actual or show—was always an option, and the plantation kept up its guard, Bradford did not pursue aggressive policies but practiced the diplomacy of commerce. While maintaining a tough stance, he displayed exceptional sensitivity to the humanity of Indians. He movingly describes the frightful impact of European disease on Indian bodies (though he was oblivious to its destruction of their culture); observes (in a letter of 1623) that the Indians, though culpable in the Wessagusset incident, had been provoked by Weston's rowdy young men; records approvingly that Plymouth settlers on the Connecticut River bought their land from its "right owners"; and rebuffs the "rude and ignorante sorte" who grumbled about the hanging of three Englishmen for murdering an Indian (in 1638, the first execution for such cause in New England). Exchange rather than conquest is Bradford's theme: Squanto ("a spetiall instrument sent of God for their good beyond their expectation") showed the settlers how to grow Indian corn; English hoes in turn increased the Indians' own yield. Although from first to last Bradford viewed the Indians as "brutish and savage," he could write that "through grace we have lost no blood, / But rather by them often have found good."

Weston's was one of two English intrusions into nearby territory that roused Bradford's concern by irresponsible dealings with the Indians. The other was the outpost at Mount Wollaston (Merrymount) where Thomas Morton, "the lord of misrule," and his company not only drank and frolicked with Indians, but sold them guns and taught them to shoot. In 1628, on Bradford's orders, Plymouth soldiers under Standish drove out Morton and his men. The Dutch at New Netherland proved better neighbors, despite a sharp contest in 1633 over land and trade on the Connecticut River. With the founding of the Massachusetts Bay Colony in 1630 and the great flow of migration from England to that place during the following decade, the center of power in New England shifted from Plymouth to Boston. Despite religious differences and Massachusetts's occasional arrogance, the colonies consulted on a variety of projects, notably preparations for the campaign against the Pequot Indians and the formation of the Confederation of New England. Bradford vigorously maintained the interests of Plymouth in disputes over land claims and the location of the colonies' common boundary.

As the colony grew, the annual entries in *Of Plimmoth Plantation* got shorter, the last few being barely one-third the length of those that open Book 2. The closing chapters dwell on signs of loss. Bradford noted the deaths of founders such as Brewster and decried the decay of communal spirit when Winslow, Standish, John Alden (1599–1687), and numbers of others moved to satellite villages. An outbreak of "sundrie notorious sins" in Plymouth in 1642 led him to question whether "in 20 years time . . . the greater part be not grown the worser."

The verses of his later years harp on such themes. The longest of these contrasts austere and arduous beginnings with subsequent decline of godliness and goodness brought about by material gain and the intrusion of "loose and profane" persons. It also deplores the selling of English guns to Indians. Bradford warns that God's interest in New England is in doubt; he urges the younger generation to repent and reform in order to avert divine displeasure.

Such poems, devoid of literary art, exemplify the mingled admonitions and incentives of the genre of the jeremiad then being developed in New England. As in *Of Plimmoth Plantation*, Bradford's great theme is God's providence; his paradigm is the experience of biblical Israel. Scholars differ over the degree of his discouragement toward the close of his life, some emphasizing his doubts and fears, others taking his lamentations themselves as evidence of an abiding faith in God's constancy.

Bradford was a moderate separatist and a strong believer in "independent" or congregational church government, which he defended in dialogues between "Ancient-men" and "Yonge-men borne in New-England"; two of the original three dialogues survive. He had an active concern for the Plymouth church, though his efforts to secure and support a worthy minister were sometimes frustrated. He attended the synod of 1647 at Cambridge as delegate from Plymouth. In his old age he studied Hebrew to better understand the word of God in God's own "holy tongue." His biblical learning and inspiration are apparent throughout his writings.

Bradford lived by farming and trading. At his death he owned a house, orchard, and lands valued at £45—equivalent to the "comfortable inheritance" he had given up in England—as well as a large library. He had sold one of his farms in 1648 to help discharge the plantation's debt. He died at Plymouth.

As Plymouth Colony's long-enduring governor, William Bradford had central responsibility for setting the community's course and directing its affairs. The difficulties were numerous and great, and the burden of authority required answerable character and competence. Bradford's chronicle, *Of Plimmoth Plantation*, is his monument. Not only an invaluable record of early English settlement on the North American continent, it is commonly acknowledged the foremost work of history produced in the English colonies in the seventeenth century.

• The best biography is Bradford Smith, *Bradford of Plymouth* (1951). Perry D. Westbrook, *William Bradford* (1978), discusses Bradford's writings and interpretations of his thought and art. The standard edition of Bradford's chief work is *History of Plymouth Plantation, 1620–1647* (2 vols., 1912). A convenient modernized edition is Samuel Eliot Morison, ed., *Of Plymouth Plantation, 1620–1647* (1952); the preface traces the history of the work in manuscript and print.

MICHAEL MCGIFFERT

BRADFORD, William (20 May 1663–23 May 1752), first printer in Pennsylvania and New York, was born in Leicestershire, England, the son of William Bradford and Anne (maiden name unknown). Apprenticed to the London Quaker printer Andrew Sowle, Bradford became a Quaker and married his master's daughter Elizabeth. Only weeks after their marriage in April 1685, the couple sailed for Pennsylvania with a letter from George Fox recommending Bradford as printer for the Society of Friends and the province. Some sources also say Bradford came with the specific endorsement of William Penn.

Bradford probably set up his print shop initially in Oxford township near Philadelphia. His first production, appearing in the fall of 1685, was *Kalendarium Pennsilvaniense,* an almanac for 1686 prepared by Samuel Atkins, a Philadelphia bookseller. A reference to "Lord Penn" in the almanac's text offended Quaker sensibilities, and the printer was ordered to print nothing more without prior license from the colony's council. Though the order was consistent with contemporary English practice and thus not extraordinary, it did set the tone for Bradford's relationship with both the proprietary government and the Society of Friends for the next eight years. He was subjected several times again to governmental censure, but the climactic episode came in 1692. Though Bradford printed for the Philadelphia Yearly Meeting of Friends, he also proved a willing printer of the tracts of George Keith, leader of a schismatic Quaker faction. In 1692 alone he printed thirteen of Keith's writings, including *An Appeal from the Twenty-Eight Judges to the Spirit of Truth,* which the secular authorities construed as seditious. Bradford was arrested and his equipment seized. He was imprisoned for four months pending his inconclusive trial in December 1692. Soon after his release, Bradford accepted the invitation of Benjamin Fletcher, who had just become governor of Pennsylvania as well as New York, to become official printer to the province of New York.

Soon after moving his family to New York City in May or June of 1693, Bradford abandoned the Society of Friends for the Church of England and by 1703 had become a vestryman of Trinity Church. As government printer, not only to New York, but also, beginning in 1703, to New Jersey, Bradford was a prolific printer of public documents including the first records of legislative proceedings to be printed in America, several collections of laws, and the first New York paper currency. He also printed the first American edition of the Book of Common Prayer, but it failed to sell enough copies to pay back the wardens of Trinity Church, who had underwritten it.

In 1725 Bradford founded the *New-York Gazette,* the fifth newspaper in America and the second outside of Boston. Against his inclination to be dignified and uncontroversial, his paper was drawn into political warfare when his former apprentice John Peter Zenger founded the rival *New-York Weekly Journal* late in 1733. The *Journal* was designed specifically as a vehicle for the outspoken political faction opposing Governor William Cosby. Bradford had no choice but to lend his *Gazette* to the recriminations of the other side. It is for that vehement but relatively brief exchange, climaxed by Zenger's celebrated acquittal on charges of seditious libel in 1735, that the *Gazette* is best remembered.

William and Elizabeth Bradford had three children. Andrew, the older of their two sons, established a press in Philadelphia in 1712 and founded the *American Weekly Mercury,* the first newspaper in the Middle Colonies, in 1719. After Elizabeth's death in 1731, Bradford married Cornelia Smith, a New York widow. In 1744 Bradford turned over his business to Henry DeForeest, a former apprentice and partner. He died at the New York home of his son William.

• Bradford's career as a printer, including a partial transcript of his trial in 1692, is readily followed in Isaiah Thomas, *History of Printing in America,* ed. Marcus A. McCorison (1970). A useful supplement is Douglas C. McMurtrie, *Pioneer Printing in New York* (1933). There is a manuscript account of his life, giving what are now presumed to be the wrong dates of his birth and arrival in America but otherwise enlightening, by his son, William Bradford II, to be found in the Society Collection of the Historical Society of Pennsylvania. The early pages of Anna Janney DeArmand, *Andrew Bradford, Colonial Journalist* (1949), summarize the elder Bradford's career in Pennsylvania, and Michael G. Kammen, *Colonial New York—A History* (1975), discusses Bradford's contributions to the changing culture of New York in the early eighteenth century. The role of the *New-York Gazette* in the factional controversy that ended in the famous trial of John Peter Zenger is discussed and illustrated with relevant excerpts in Stephen Botein, *'Mr. Zenger's Malice and Falshood'; Six Issues of the New-York Weekly Journal, 1733–1734* (1985).

CHARLES E. CLARK

BRADFORD, William (19 Jan. 1722–25 Sept. 1791), author and printer, was born in New York City, the son of William Bradford and Sytje Santvoort. He was the grandson of the printer William Bradford (1663–1752) of New York and Philadelphia. In 1739 young Bradford went into partnership in Philadelphia with his uncle Andrew Bradford, who had established Pennsylvania's first newspaper in 1719. After the termination of their partnership, he went to England, where he received additional training and secured printing materials through another relative, the London printer Tace Sowle Raylton.

In July 1742 Bradford opened his own printing office and bookstore in Philadelphia at "The Sign of the Bible." That December, a few days after his uncle's death, he established the *Weekly Advertiser, or Pennsylvania Journal*. Except for two interruptions, the paper continued to be printed by William or his son Thomas Bradford until 1814. The paper achieved much public notice for its protest against the Stamp Act on 31 October 1765. The front page was designed as a tombstone, with a skull and crossbones on the spot set aside for the tax stamp. The *Journal* became the leading vehicle for patriotic opposition to the Stamp Act. According to one story, after William Goddard had printed articles in his newspaper defending actions of Benjamin Franklin (1706–1790) that many Philadelphians perceived to have been in support of the Stamp Act, Bradford and some other patriots threw Goddard bodily out of a coffee house.

Bradford was a rival to Franklin as soon as he began the *Journal*, a better-printed paper than Franklin's *Pennsylvania Gazette*. Bradford also printed books and pamphlets on literature, politics, and religion. He published two magazines: the *American Magazine and Monthly Chronicle*, edited by William Smith (1727–1803) (Oct. 1757 through Oct. 1758), and the *American Magazine, or General Repository*, edited by Lewis Nichola (Jan. to Sept. 1769). In addition to his publishing activities, Bradford formed the Philadelphia Insurance Company in 1762 with John Kidd.

It is for his opposition to the Stamp Act and his role as the "patriot-printer of 1776," however, that Bradford is most remembered. He signed the Non-Importation Resolutions of 1765, he supported a proposed continental congress, and his paper carried the serpent and "Unite or Die" slogan from July 1774 until October 1775. The London Coffee-House, which Bradford owned and frequented, became the Revolution's unofficial Philadelphia headquarters. A leading Son of Liberty, he printed the most extreme material opposing the Crown; he was the first to publish Thomas Paine's *Crisis* essays. Much of the propaganda published in support of the American cause was anonymous, and so it cannot be known how much of what Bradford printed he also wrote, though editors in other colonies introduced articles reprinted from the *Journal* as "the work of William Bradford, printer."

In addition to serving as printer for Congress and although beyond the normal age for military service (he had served in the army in 1747–1748 and in 1756), Bradford organized a militia company, fought at Trenton, and was promoted to a colonelcy after the battle of Princeton, in which he was severely wounded. He then served as chairman of the Pennsylvania Navy Board. After the British retreated from Philadelphia in 1778, Bradford retired from active service, his health and finances ruined by the war.

He had six children by his wife, Rachel Budd, whom he had married in 1742. His sons Thomas and William Bradford (1755–1795) continued in some way the work of their father, both serving as soldiers in the Revolution, Thomas as a printer and William as George Washington's second attorney general.

Shortly after his death in Philadelphia, the *Pennsylvania Mercury* published an "anecdote of the late William Bradford." When in 1773 Philadelphians were about to pay a tax on tea, Bradford, according to the story, was told that "the citizens of Philadelphia were tired out with town and committee meetings, and that it would be impossible to collect a sufficient number of them together, to make an opposition to the tea, respectable and formidable." Bradford replied, "Leave that business to me—I'll collect a town meeting for you—Prepare some resolves;—and,—they shall be executed."

• The Historical Society of Pennsylvania holds a collection of Bradford papers. The one limited edition biography of Bradford is John Wallace, *An Old Philadelphian* (1884). See also C. R. Hildeburn, *A Century of Printing: The Issues of the Press in Pennsylvania* (1885); Frederick D. Stone, "How the Landing of Tea Was Opposed in Philadelphia by Colonel William Bradford and Others in 1773," *Pennsylvania Magazine of History and Biography* 15 (1891): 385–93; Edmund S. Morgan and Helen M. Morgan, *The Stamp Act Crisis* (1953); Arthur M. Schlesinger, *Prelude to Independence* (1957); Richard Alan Ryerson, *The Revolution Is Now Begun* (1978); and Edwin Wolf II, *The Book Culture of a Colonial American City* (1988).

DENNIS BARONE

BRADFORD, William (30 Apr. 1823–25 Apr. 1892), marine painter, was born in Fairhaven, Massachusetts, the son of Melvin Bradford, a storekeeper, and Hannah Kempton. Raised in Fairhaven, in the Quaker faith, his formal education was, in his own words, "quite meagre" (quoted in Ellis, p. 98). Although he was attracted to art from a young age, he was brought up to participate in the family business.

In 1847 he married Mary Breed, a Quaker from an old New England family, with whom he had two daughters, the elder dying at an early age. For eight years after his marriage he devoted himself, halfheartedly, to mercantile pursuits. Working first as a store clerk, he opened his own wholesale clothing business in 1852. Within two years he was bankrupt, having spent, he confessed, "too much time in painting to succeed" (quoted in Ellis, p. 99). With the failure of his business, he turned his attention full time to painting, specializing at first in meticulously drawn ship portraits and coastal scenes, works that celebrated the commercial vitality of maritime New England and the summer pleasures of the regatta set. He found a steady market for such images, selling his first picture in about 1854.

As an artist, Bradford seems to have been largely self-taught, though he must have learned much from the Dutch-born marine painter Albert Van Beest, with whom he shared a waterside studio in Fairhaven for two or three years in the mid-1850s. The two artists collaborated on a number of works, such as *New York Yacht Club Regatta* (1856; New Bedford Whaling Museum), with Bradford painting the ships and Van Beest the sky and water. Other influences on Bradford's style included the tightly painted works of the New England marine painters Fitz Hugh Lane and Robert Salmon as well as the landscapes of his friend Albert Bierstadt.

In the later 1850s Bradford moved to Boston, where he struggled to establish his reputation. In 1860 he began exhibiting his paintings at the National Academy of Design in New York and by 1861 had taken a studio in that city's famous Tenth Street Studio Building, where many other prominent American artists worked. He maintained a residence in New York until the end of his life, though he also kept a home in Fairhaven.

The year 1861 also brought a change in the direction of Bradford's career. That summer, inspired by the exploits of Arctic explorers such as Sir John Franklin and Elisha Kent Kane and, most likely, by the phenomenal success of Frederic Church's painting *The Icebergs* (1861), which had been unveiled to the New York public that spring, Bradford charted a ship to chase icebergs off the coast of Labrador. This was the first of the artist's six or seven arctic voyages, and from that time on he made arctic scenes his specialty. He painted silver icebergs riding on glassy water, ice flows lit by lurid sunset skies, and sailing ships breaking their way through frozen seas under the eyes of inquisitive polar bears. His Arctic is a stunningly beautiful yet treacherous place, where the human presence is always marginal and often threatened. Bradford's arctic paintings include *Ice Dwellers Watching the Invaders* (c. 1870; New Bedford Whaling Museum, New Bedford, Mass.), *Arctic Scene* (1870; Indiana University Art Museum, Bloomington), *Arctic Scene* (1876; University of La Verne, La Verne, Calif.), and *Caught in the Ice Flows* (Addison Gallery of American Art, Andover, Mass.).

On Bradford's last arctic voyage, in the summer and fall of 1869, he was accompanied by the polar explorer Isaac Hayes and two Boston photographers, John Dunmore and George Critcherson, who shot for Bradford nearly four hundred images. That voyage was commemorated in Bradford's lavishly illustrated book *The Arctic Regions*, published in London (where he lived from 1872 to 1874) in 1873. The photographs, sketches, and memories from this and the earlier polar expeditions became the bases of Bradford's work for the rest of his career. He also drew on these sources for his many illustrated lectures on the Arctic, which he delivered to appreciative audiences in both the United States and England.

In the later 1870s Bradford divided his time between San Francisco and New York. He took advantage of his California stays to paint sites such as Yosemite Valley and Mount Shasta, but even during his California sojourns polar scenes remained the staple of his art. On 5 August 1876 the *San Francisco Daily Evening Examiner* described Bradford as an artist who "has taken possession of the Arctic region. The country all up around the North Pole belongs to him by right of artistic possession." His arctic images met with lavish critical acclaim and attracted eager buyers; each selling for as much as $12,000, they were purchased by members of the European nobility, including Queen Victoria (who acquired *The Panther off the Coast of Greenland under the Midnight Sun;* still in the Royal Collection), the duke of Argyle, and Baron Rothschild, as well as by American business magnates, such as Collis P. Huntington, W. H. Havemeyer, and Legrand Lockwood.

Bradford died in New York City, still active as a painter and lecturer. The American art-buying public had by then embraced impressionism, but Bradford's pictures, with their exotic subjects, luminous light effects, and precise detail, were still accorded some esteem. The art critic for the *New York Daily Tribune*, writing on 27 November 1892, lamented that Bradford was "born and fixed in his ways before contact with European schools had widened our views on technique—he was never able to eliminate hardness from his execution . . . [or] to vitalize his canvasses with atmosphere." Yet, this critic conceded, "he could still convey an impression of truth."

Bradford's reputation slipped further in the early decades of the twentieth century. But in the late 1960s and 1970s, with the approaching bicentennial turning attention to the nation's past, and the growing environmental movement sparking a renewed interest in landscape painting, Bradford's reputation was revived. By then, the very qualities that turn-of-the-century critics had dismissed as old fashioned (his meticulous attention to detail, the brilliant clarity of his light effects, and his fascination with marine and polar subjects) were coming to be valued as expressions of reverence for the natural world and as outgrowths of the exploratory zeal of his era.

• The New Bedford Whaling Museum, New Bedford, Mass., holds a significant collection of Bradford's works and papers. The papers, as well as other items relating to Bradford's life and work, are available on microfilm through the Archives of American Art, Smithsonian Institution. Henry T. Tuckerman, *Book of the Artists* (1870), and Leonard B. Ellis, *History of New Bedford* (1892), contain short biographies, as does the Metropolitan Museum of Art's *Catalogue of American Paintings*, vol. 2 (1985). John Wilmerding, *William Bradford* (exhibition catalog, 1969), offers an overview of the artist's life and career and a useful bibliography, whereas Wilmerding's *American Marine Painting*, 2d ed. (1987) and Roger B. Stein's *Seascape and the American Imagination* (1975) place Bradford's work in the context of American marine painting. *American Light*, ed. Wilmerding (1980), relates Bradford's work to the Luminist movement, a mid-nineteenth-century aesthetic concerned with luminous light effects. On Bradford's use of photography, see Frank Horch, "Photographs and Paintings by William Bradford," *American Art Journal* (Nov. 1973): 61–70, and Sandra S. Phillips, "The Arctic Voyage of William Bradford," *Aperture* 90 (1983): 16–27. An obituary is in the *New York Times*, 26 Apr. 1892.

REBECCA BEDELL

BRADLEY, Aaron Alpeora (1815?–Oct. 1882), Reconstruction politician, was born in Edgefield District, South Carolina, the son of unknown slaves on the plantation of Francis Pickens, a prominent politician. Little is known of Bradley's youth and early manhood other than that he was a shoemaker for a time in Augusta, Georgia, and that he escaped slavery and made his way to the North, apparently during the 1830s. He lived for a time in New York and in Boston. In the latter city he not only met abolitionists but also studied the law and eventually became a practicing attorney.

The Civil War opened new horizons. Bradley returned south late in 1865 and settled in Savannah, Georgia, intending, it seems, to open a law practice and a school. Drawn inexorably to the public arena, he began to champion the cause of freedpeople who were resisting President Andrew Johnson's policy of restoring plantation land to its antebellum owners. His advocacy took the form of leading mass public demonstrations as well as petitioning authorities in Washington. Military officials in Georgia deemed his spirited criticism of government policies seditious, convicted him of the charge before a military tribunal, and permitted him to leave the state in lieu of a year's imprisonment. When he returned to Savannah from Boston late in 1866, he resumed his role as champion of the freedpeople with the same militancy he had earlier displayed. He immediately took up the cause of rice-plantation laborers, who were locked in a dispute with the antebellum plantation owners and the Freedmen's Bureau over rights to the land; both sides resorted to threats of using armed force to gain their objectives.

Despite his ambivalent relationship with military authorities, Bradley had no doubt that federal power—military as well as executive, legislative, and judicial—was essential to revolutionize the South. Accordingly, he appealed to federal officials both broadly to protect freedpeople in what he termed the "free enjoyment of Equal Rights and Immunities" and narrowly to redress an assortment of pressing grievances. One representative campaign aimed to remove from office the mayor of Savannah, a former Confederate colonel who treated former slaves with undisguised contempt. Although often unpolished and by turns brazen and elliptical, Bradley's numerous petitions articulated the political aspirations of his constituents in the language of constitutional rights.

For Bradley and like-minded political activists throughout the South, the Reconstruction acts of March 1867 marked a milestone in the struggle to revolutionize the political system. The acts granted the suffrage to black men and required elections of delegates to write new constitutions for the former Confederate states. Bradley placed his name forward as a candidate, won the hearty support of the voters in his majority-black district, and assumed his seat in the constitutional convention that met in Atlanta from December 1867 to February 1868. By downplaying his constituents' demands to press for a redistribution of plantation land and by supporting the package of debtor relief and homestead exemption measures tailored to the needs of white yeoman farmers, Bradley aligned himself behind the state's Republican leadership. He seemed to defer to the Republican strategy of appealing to potential white voters (although he never said so directly); at the same time, his black constituency grew broader—including urban laborers with less interest in land grants than plantation laborers had evinced—and he surely began to see more realistically how slim the prospects of legislating land reform at the state level were. Despite his loyalty, Republicans raised neither hand nor voice in his defense when Democratic delegates maneuvered to expel him from the convention on grounds of a past criminal conviction on a morals charge in New York City in 1851. Unfazed, his constituents promptly elected him to the state senate, only to see him, together with every other black senator, driven from that body as well. He ran unsuccessfully for Congress in 1868 and 1870 but reclaimed his state senate seat in January of the latter year, when federal authorities initiated Georgia's third postwar Reconstruction.

For the next two years, Bradley labored on behalf of his working-class constituents, introducing various bills to lower taxes, shorten the workday for urban workers, and guarantee civil and political rights. Increasingly convinced that state officials cared more about preserving the trappings of office than about satisfying the freedpeople's needs, Bradley castigated Republican governor Rufus B. Bullock and party regulars in Savannah, who were backpedaling before a Democratic onslaught. At the same time, Bradley petitioned Washington officials to grant him a sinecure. Appointed a special customs inspector in 1872, he soon politicked his way out of favor and out of his position.

When Georgia Democrats assumed full control over the state government in 1872, Bradley grew increasingly disenchanted. In his search to realize Reconstruction ideals, he advocated a strategy of migration, to Florida in the mid-1870s and to Kansas at the end of the decade. Frustrated by his inability to garner support for the Kansas exodus among black Georgians, he headed west on his own in 1882, making it to St. Louis, where he died without any known descendants. Whether he ever married is not known.

Assessing Bradley's role in Reconstruction requires an appreciation of his role as a leader in a mass movement for radical social change. He consistently identified his political agenda with that of ordinary former slaves, especially the field laborers on coastal rice plantations and the semiskilled and unskilled workers in Savannah. Their numbers buoyed his strength and their militancy his arrogance. Their collective demand that constitutional rights be extended to all citizens regardless of color or former condition of servitude was frustrated at the time, but it resurfaced with unstoppable force in the twentieth-century civil rights movement.

• Like most of his contemporaries, Bradley lived and died with little concern for the judgment of history. He marked his trail haphazardly when he did so at all; as a result, biographers have had to reconstruct his life from scattered and often biased sources. Newspapers in Savannah and throughout Georgia tended to cover Bradley's public career closely, especially between 1865 and 1872. The official records of the 1868 constitutional convention and the legislative sessions in which he served also record his actions. The National Archives contains the largest single body of material from his pen, although it is scattered among the records of various government agencies, most notably the Freedmen's Bureau. Such general accounts of Reconstruction as Eric Foner, *Reconstruction: America's Unfinished Revolution, 1863–1877* (1988), treat aspects of Bradley's career, as do the standard accounts of Reconstruction in Georgia, C. Mildred Thompson, *Reconstruction in Georgia: Economic, Political, Social* (1915); Alan Conway, *The Reconstruction of Georgia* (1966); Elizabeth Studley Nathans, *Losing the Peace: Georgia Republicans and Reconstruction, 1865–1871* (1968); and Edmund L. Drago, *Black Politicians and Reconstruction in Georgia* (1982). E. Merton Coulter's hostility toward Bradley in *Negro Legislators in Georgia during the Reconstruction Period* (1968) inspired Joseph P. Reidy, "Aaron A. Bradley: Voice of Black Labor in the Georgia Lowcountry," in *Southern Black Leaders of the Reconstruction Era*, ed. Howard N. Rabinowitz (1982). A critical obituary is in the *Savannah Morning News*, 25 Oct. 1882.

JOSEPH P. REIDY

BRADLEY, Abraham, Jr. (21 Feb. 1767–May 1838), public administrator and topographer, was born in Litchfield, Connecticut, the son of Abraham Bradley, a public officer, and Hannah Baldwin. Bradley grew up in Litchfield, graduated from Tapping Reeve's well-known law school, and was admitted to the bar in 1791. For a brief period he practiced law in Luzerne County, Pennsylvania, where he also served as a judge. During this time he met and married Hannah Smith, with whom he had eight children. Though Bradley possessed an excellent knowledge of the law, he did not find legal work congenial because it called for a good deal of public speaking, a skill that he never acquired.

When Bradley was living in Luzerne County, he came to the attention of Timothy Pickering, an influential public figure with close ties to President George Washington. When Washington appointed Pickering postmaster general in 1791, Pickering persuaded Bradley to come with him to Philadelphia to work in the general post office as a clerk. Though Bradley was diffident and shy, he possessed the necessary qualifications for the office: excellent penmanship, a solid knowledge of the law, and an enormous capacity for hard work. He was an "unassuming man," wrote a friend at about this time, "modest and retiring almost to diffidence, yet a lawyer of competent learning, with a clear and discriminating mind, and an industry that knew no relaxation when there was a duty to be performed" (Bradley, pp. 130–31). By 1800 Bradley had risen to the assistant postmaster generalship and had overseen the relocation of the general post office to Washington. Shortly thereafter he recruited his brother, Phineas, to join him in the office. Here the Bradley brothers worked together for almost thirty years, presiding over the expansion of what was then the largest branch of the federal government.

Bradley's best known accomplishment was his authorship of a notable map of the United States, the first edition of which appeared in 1796, and the second in 1804, following the acquisition of the Louisiana territory. Bradley's maps were hung in many of the republic's post offices and were reprinted in Jedidiah Morse's *American Universal Geography*. Historians have agreed that the 1796 edition provides the best source of information about the geographical extent of the United States in the decade following the adoption of the federal Constitution. To a greater degree than almost any other single document published during this period, Bradley's maps helped to impress ordinary Americans with the size of the country and to transform the ill-defined frontier into a sharply etched border.

Bradley also coordinated the movement of the mail and took great pride in his almost encyclopedic knowledge of every single postal route in the country. Since most stagecoach firms relied on mail contracts to cover their costs, Bradley was thus largely responsible for the scheduling of passenger service throughout the United States. Though Bradley supported the subsidization of the stagecoach industry, he remained troubled by the potential for abuse. This was particularly true during the administration of Andrew Jackson; Bradley publicly denounced the Jacksonians for their "stage mania," by which he meant their lavish policy of subsidizing the industry with little regard to cost (John, p. 243).

To help keep expenses under control, Bradley personally supervised the payment of mail contractors, a challenging task. Because the United States lacked a single currency during this period, it was difficult to pay agents who lived at a great distance from Washington. To help overcome this problem, Bradley assumed the presidency of the Union Bank of Georgetown at some point prior to 1820. This made it possible for Bradley's signature to appear on the bank notes that the general post office disbursed. The fact that Bradley's signature was well known facilitated the transmission of postal revenue from the general post office to the contractors in the field.

Bradley's postal career came to an end in 1829, a casualty of the far-reaching changes in American public life set in motion with the election of Andrew Jackson. Determined to gain control of postal patronage, the Jacksonians recognized Bradley as an obstacle in their path. Though Bradley disdained partisan politics and never engaged in electioneering, he was known to have supported Jackson's opponent, John Quincy Adams, in the election of 1828—just as he had supported Adams's father, John, in the election of 1800. More importantly, he could be expected to oppose any changes in contracting or staffing arrangements that were politically inspired. The catalyst for his dismissal—and for that of his brother, Phineas—was the publication of a private letter Bradley wrote in which he defended a Kentucky postmaster against a trumped-up charge. When this letter became public, Postmaster General William Barry felt he had no choice but to dismiss Bradley for insubordination. When Phineas protested, Barry dismissed him, too.

Outraged by his dismissal, Bradley wrote a series of stinging public letters during the next few years to justify his official conduct, expose the Jacksonians' administrative shortcomings, and ridicule Barry's ignorance of geography and postal procedure. Bradley's influential critique did much to damage the Jacksonians' political standing. Even more damning was the widespread perception that Bradley himself had been unfairly dismissed. Much was made of the Jacksonians' determination to destroy his reputation and to prevent him from testifying before Congress on his own behalf. His plight, for example, was among the grievances that National Republican leaders cited in a party platform that they issued in the months preceding the election of 1832.

Following his dismissal Bradley remained in Washington, where he died. Though he never again held public office, between 1836 and 1838 he did serve a term as secretary of the Franklin Insurance Company. Few individuals better exemplified the energy, dedication, and integrity that were a hallmark of American public administration in the generation between the adoption of the federal Constitution and the victory of the Jacksonians in the election of 1828. "The merits and blessings" of that "great establishment," the postal system, wrote one eulogist, were due more to Bradley's exertions, and to those of his brother, Phineas, than to "any other persons who have yet lived" (Bradley, p. 135).

• Bradley's official correspondence is in the records of the general post office at the National Archives. There is no collection of personal papers. Bradley's public career is discussed in Richard R. John, *Spreading the News: The American Postal System from Franklin to Morse* (1995), and Charles S. Bradley, "The Bradley Family and the Times in Which They Lived," *Records of the Columbia Historical Society* 6 (1902): 123–42. His maps are discussed in Walter W. Ristow, *American Maps and Mapmakers* (1985), and Richard H. Kohn, *Eagle and Sword* (1975). For obituary notices, see *National Intelligencer*, 10 May 1838 and 31 July 1845.

RICHARD R. JOHN

BRADLEY, Amy Morris (12 Sept. 1823–15 Jan. 1904), educator, Civil War nurse, and school founder, was born in East Vassalboro, Kennebec County, Maine, the daughter of Abiud Bradley, a shoemaker, and Jane Baxter. As a child Bradley suffered from bronchial problems, a vulnerability that plagued her throughout her life. When she was six, her mother died. Her seven older siblings and elderly father cared for her until she was thirteen; her father then moved away, and her married brothers and sisters took turns boarding her in their homes. From this experience she developed self-reliance and disinclination to marriage.

Although Bradley received thorough training in traditional, gender-specific skills such as dressmaking and cooking, she was always driven to get an education. Like many intellectually inclined women of the mid-nineteenth century, she was constrained by the limited opportunities for higher education available to young women and by limited financial resources. Instead, she took advantage of informal learning opportunities such as the lyceum movement, museums, libraries, and travel.

When Bradley was fifteen years old, she began teaching at a small dame school; she was then hired to teach in the Vassalboro public schools. For several years she divided her time between teaching in country schools and attending school. She used her teaching income to enroll in B. H. Shaw's high school and then spent the fall term of 1842 at Vassalboro Academy, a private girls' school, the culmination of her formal education.

In 1844 Bradley's expanding competence and confidence took her to Gardiner, Maine, where she was appointed principal of a grammar school. Her success in bringing discipline to the school pleased the committee of overseers. This accomplishment, along with her salary of three dollars per week, provided her with personal and financial independence. She remained at the Gardiner school for three years. She visited family and friends throughout New York and New England during school vacations, while also earning money as a dressmaker. This satisfying period ended when adverse financial circumstances closed the school.

Bradley quickly obtained another teaching position in the fall of 1847 as an assistant at the Winthrop School in Boston. In the city she attended lectures, the opera, theaters, and museums; she also joined the Unitarian church, reinforcing her belief in individual freedom and social justice.

In 1850 the Winthrop School closed, and Bradley became an assistant at the Putnam Grammar School in East Cambridge. Illness forced her to resign within a few months, however, and she went to visit relatives in Charleston, South Carolina. She arrived in November 1850 and was immediately surrounded by a combination of southern hospitality and anti-northern sentiment. Exposed to slavery firsthand, she developed a lasting hatred for it. She believed that abolition should take place not through immediate political action but "by a gradual enlightening of the minds of the slave owners"; she thought that emancipation would be "a thing pleasing in the eyes of God" and that people "are happier doing their own work with their own hands" (Cashman, p. 50).

Bradley disliked other features of Charleston life. She believed its schools were backward and resented the pervasive anti-northern sentiment. After the unexpected death of her hostess in May 1851, she returned to Boston.

For two years Bradley kept house for her father and brother, but by 1853 she was again eager to teach. In November 1853 she sailed for Costa Rica to work as a governess, but she and her new employer held conflicting views and parted company. She moved to San José and supported herself as a dressmaker while learning Spanish. She then began tutoring and eventually opened Costa Rica's first English school, with texts she translated herself. Her school enjoyed such a fine reputation that the governor of San José enrolled his children.

Bradley stayed in Costa Rica until March 1857, when her father's ill health, coupled with an unstable political situation in Nicaragua, brought her back to Maine. While caring for her father, in her spare time she organized a temperance league and established a temperance newsletter.

After her father's death in 1858, Bradley moved back to Boston. Her knowledge of Spanish secured her a position as translator for the New England Glass Company in nearby East Cambridge. Ever in search of self-improvement, she took bookkeeping courses at the Mercantile Academy.

After the Union army's defeat at Bull Run in 1861, Bradley volunteered as a nurse to the Third and Fifth Maine regiments. In Virginia, Union general Henry W. Slocum observed that soldiers in Bradley's hospitals were "so much more comfortable than those of other Regiments in the Brigade." He appointed her matron of his brigade hospital, where she worked tirelessly to obtain medical and housekeeping supplies for the soldiers in her care. When the hospital was closed, she volunteered for the U.S. Sanitary Commission (USSC). For eleven weeks she served as a nurse for the USSC Hospital Transport System, on board ships carrying wounded soldiers to military hospitals in New York, Philadelphia, Washington, and Baltimore.

Her dedication to the soldiers and the quality of her work earned Bradley the charge of the USSC Convalescent Home in Washington, D.C., in September 1862. She set up a library, encouraged local citizens to visit "her boys," and wrote letters home for them. As an official commission relief worker, she also visited other camps and hospitals.

Bradley remained in this job until the hospital closed in September 1865. Through these grueling but rewarding years she worked single-mindedly for her soldiers. She personally guided soldiers through the bureaucratic maze of Washington to get them back pay, discharge orders, and amendments or corrections to their military records. She also published in 1864 a camp newspaper, the *Soldier's Journal*, to provide soldiers with information on how to work with government agencies, from securing pensions to obtaining prostheses. Proceeds from this paper were donated to a fund for orphaned children of Union soldiers. By the end of that year Bradley's subscribers included President Abraham Lincoln and General Ulysses S. Grant.

Bradley contacted the American Unitarian Association soon after the war, hoping to continue her volunteer work. In 1866 the association appointed her special agent of the Soldiers Memorial Society for missionary work in Wilmington, North Carolina. This society's mission was "uplifting all, white or black, in the States which have been in the field of our victories" (Cashman, p. 159). Although most post–Civil War missionary activities centered on the needs of African Americans, Bradley followed the lead of her predecessor in Wilmington, who had stated that the poor whites "are the most neglected, the blacks have received the chief attention heretofore" (Cashman, p. 161). Her decision to attend to the education of poor whites fulfilled one of the stated missions of the U.S. Freedmen's Bureau, which aided her work and that of the Soldiers Memorial Society, authorizing funds for teachers traveling south and for the construction of schoolhouses. These federal funds supported work among newly freed slaves and southern white refugees.

Bradley arrived in Wilmington on 30 December 1866. Despite an initially chilly reception, the Yankee "schoolmarm" set to work immediately to gain community support and to identify those the Soldiers Memorial Society had targeted for relief. She secured the key to the Dry Pond Union School in the poor white district of Wilmington, opening it with three pupils on 9 January 1867; within a week it had fifty pupils, with many more wanting to attend.

Bradley's concern for her students extended to their families. Every afternoon she made home visits to judge their needs. By March she had organized the Young Ladies Union Benevolent Society.

Bradley's school soon had a waiting list and two new teachers. She knew the success of her mission would depend on local support, which she slowly gained. By the next fall Wilmington citizens had subscribed to a school addition fund; a new room was added to Union School, and Bradley and her two teachers welcomed 188 students. By early 1869 she had enough support from Wilmington's citizens, northern friends, the Peabody Education Fund, and the U.S. Freedmen's Bureau to open two more schools. Bradley's three schools comprised a faculty of eight and 435 students. She saw this accomplishment as a model system of free public education for the people of Wilmington. On 6 June 1870 she was appointed New Hanover County school examiner, and in December of that year her schools were officially designated Wilmington's Free Public Schools. Two years later she opened Tileston Normal School to train local teachers. Except for a hiatus between 1873 and 1876, when she rested in Europe from her years of hard work, she remained at Tileston for the next two decades, until it also became part of the public school system.

Illness forced Bradley to resign as head of Tileston Normal School in 1891. She lived out her retirement in a cottage on the grounds of Tileston, where she died. In honor of Bradley's achievements, the graduate of New Hanover High School in Wilmington with the highest academic average receives the Amy Bradley Medal.

Bradley's career in the post–Civil War South is distinct from those of many other missionaries because of her decision to educate poor whites rather than African Americans. No evidence exists, however, that she was prejudiced against the latter. The U.S. Freedmen's Bureau provided in 1867 for the care of both blacks and poor whites, but Bradley was one of the few to attend to whites. Her career in North Carolina provided the opportunity for a single, nineteenth-century woman to express her educational, religious, and philanthropic interests in a manner that was personally fulfilling yet within the circumscribed sphere for women of the period.

• Bradley's diaries, correspondence, and financial books from the 1840s to 1900 are at the Special Collections Library, Duke University, Durham, N.C. Reports of Bradley's work and excerpts from her correspondence appear in the *Bulletin* of the U.S. Sanitary Commission (1860s); *Reports* of the Soldiers Memorial Society (1860s), available at the Andover-Harvard Theological Library, Harvard Divinity School; *Annual Reports* of the superintendent of public instruction of North Carolina (1867–1891); and *Proceedings* of the Peabody Education Fund (1868–1876). The most authoritative biography is Diane Cobb Cashman, *Headstrong: The Biography of Amy Morris Bradley, 1823–1904: A Life of Noblest Usefulness* (1990). An earlier, brief monograph is David Y. Sellers, *Miss Amy Bradley: The Story of a Woman from Maine Who Spent Many Years in the Service of Free Education in Wilmington, North Carolina* (1970.) Bradley is mentioned in Frances Willard, *A Woman of the Century* (1893); and Frank Moore, *Women of the War: Their Heroism and Self Sacrifice* (1866). Context for Bradley's North Carolina mission is provided by Jacqueline Jones, *Soldiers of Light and Love: Northern Teachers and Georgia Blacks* (1980). An obituary is in the *Wilmington Morning Star*, 16 Jan. 1904.

VICTORIA-MARÍA MACDONALD

BRADLEY, Buddy (1908–1972), African-American choreographer and jazz tap dancer, was born Clarence Bradley, in Harrisburg, Pennsylvania. His parents' names and occupations are unknown. His father died when he was quite young and his religious mother brought him up strictly. After seeing the tap dancers Jack Wiggins and Clarence "Dancing" Dotson at a local theater, Bradley learned to do the time step on one foot by the time he was eight. He taught himself the Charleston, strut, drag, shuffle, and a vast assortment of African-American vernacular dances from the deep South.

After his mother died when he was fourteen, Bradley went to live with a brother-in-law in Utica, New York, and worked as a hotel busboy. A few months later he ran away to New York City and lived at a Harlem boardinghouse inhabited by many show people, especially dancers. With a group of other youngsters that included Derby Wilson, who would become a well-known tap dancer, Bradley learned tap dance in a blind alley next to Connie's Inn in Harlem and picked up flash and acrobatic steps as a chorus boy at both the downtown Kentucky Club and Connie's Inn. In 1926 he made his stage debut as a dancer in a Florence Mills revue at the Lincoln Square Theatre.

Around 1928, at the Billy Pierce Dance Studios off Broadway, Bradley found himself tailoring routines for specific dancers—from gangsters' molls to Broadway stars—for $250 a routine. His dance formula was radically new: he simplified rhythms for the feet while sculpting the body into shapes from African-American social dance, blending easy tap dance and jazz dance into routines that rose to a climax and finished gracefully. Well paid but known only in show-business circles, Bradley created dozens of dance routines for white stars of Broadway musicals such as Adele Astaire, Ruby Keeler, and Eleanor Powell, although his name never appeared on any program. It was the custom that as long as the "dance director," who grouped scenes and coached the stars, got his pay there was no need for program credit. Bradley coached Tom Patricola, Ann Pennington, and Francis Williams in the Black Bottom musical numbers in George White's *Scandals* (1926). In 1928, he rechoreographed the entire production of *Greenwich Village Follies*, even though Busby Berkeley's name remained as choreographer on the program. Bradley created routines and sometimes staged complete scenes for Mae West, Gilda Gray, Irene Delroy, Jack Donahue, and Paul Draper in shows such as *Ziegfeld Follies* (1929) and Erroll Carroll's *Vanities* (1924). The "High Yaller" routine from the "Moanin' Low" number in *The Little Show* (1929), which established Clifton Webb as one of the hottest dancers since Earl "Snake Hips" Tucker, was choreographed by Bradley.

Inspired by the music of the day, Bradley ignored the melody and translated the accents of improvising jazz musician soloists into dance patterns that were new to Broadway. Bradley received the first full choreographic credit in his career in 1930 in London with *Evergreen*, a new Rodgers and Hart musical at the Adelphi Theatre. His choreography for C. B. Cochran's 1931 revue catapulted him into English musical theater. In the 1930s alone, Bradley choreographed over thirty musical productions in London, including *Revels in Rhythm* (1931), *Words and Music* (1932), *Mother of Pearl* (1933), *Tulip Time* (1935), Cochran's 1936 revue *Follow the Sun*, and Lew Leslie's *Blackbirds of 1936*. *Evergreen*, which was made into a film in 1934, launched him into the emerging English film industry.

In simplifying dance steps, Bradley used the body to express rather than accompany the music; and although he simplified rhythms, he never sacrificed the distinctive accents of rhythm tap. Bradley collaborated with Frederick Ashton in creating the first English jazz ballet, *High Yellow* (1932), which featured Alicia Markova. He also created a cabaret act for the ballet dancers Vera Zorina and Anton Dolin, and collaborated with Agnes de Mille on *Words and Music* (1934), with Antony Tudor on *Lights Up!* (1940), and with George Balanchine on Cochran's 1930 revue.

Bradley lived in London for thirty-eight years, working in Europe as a teacher, choreographer, and producer of musical revues, films, and television. By 1950, the Buddy Bradley Dance School in London had over 500 students. It remained in operation until 1968 when he returned to New York, where he died. He was survived by his wife Dorothy (maiden name unknown). They had no children.

Bradley was a prime figure in the transplantation of African-American jazz and tap dance onto the American and English musical theater stage. "His dance ideas were well ahead of his time, and knowing performers of the musical comedy stage flocked to him," Bradley's obituary in *Variety* (26 July 1972) stated. "He was personally popular in the profession, together with respect given to his creative choreography."

• Bradley's early career is documented in Marshall and Jean Stearns, *Jazz Dance: The Story of American Vernacular Dance* (1968), and his London career in Constance Valis Hill, "Buddy Bradley: The 'Invisible' Man of Broadway Brings Jazz Tap to London," *Proceedings of Society of Dance History Scholars* (14–15 Feb. 1992). His London career in the fifties is described in "Buddy Bradley: Nimble Ex-Harlemite Runs Most Successful School in England," *Ebony*, July 1950, pp. 61–64.

CONSTANCE VALIS HILL

BRADLEY, Charles Henry (13 Feb. 1860–30 Jan. 1922), asylum superintendent and educator, was born in Johnson, Vermont, the son of Harmon Howe Bradley and Sarah Grout Ferguson (occupations unknown). Educated at the state normal school in his hometown, he left Vermont in 1880 to become an instructor at the State Primary School in Monson, Massachusetts, a school for destitute and dependent children. In 1885 he became assistant superintendent. Bradley was married to Mary Chilton Brewster in 1883; they had one child. In March 1888 he accepted the position of superintendent of the Boston Asylum and Farm School for Indigent Boys, on Thompson's Island in Boston Harbor, where he would spend the rest of his life.

The Farm School, as the institution was then known, was the result of an 1835 merger between two early nineteenth-century child-welfare organizations, the Boston Asylum for Indigent Boys, an orphanage that emphasized schooling, and the Boston Farm School Society, a reformatory that stressed agricultural labor. By 1888 the 157-acre Thompson's Island held a working farm where 100 dependent boys between the ages of ten and sixteen divided their time between schooling, farm work, and recreational activities.

Bradley, the first trained educator to hold the superintendency, believed that the school's purpose was to help "the lad to find himself, to bring out the best that is in him, to fit him for productive and effective citizenship." While the Farm School had always emphasized "learning by doing," under Bradley's leadership the program became more individualized and varied. During his 34-year tenure he incorporated a series of innovations that gave the school, and Bradley himself, a national reputation.

In 1889, six years before William R. George's "junior republic," Bradley introduced Cottage Row at the school, a learning community of wooden playhouses built, "owned," and maintained by the boys. Like George, Bradley believed that good citizenship skills were best learned through participation in a small-scale model of the larger economic and political world. Cottage Row had its own town government, a banking system, a sanitation department, and a judiciary, all run by students. In an era when most asylums emphasized hierarchical discipline, anonymity, and routine, this was highly unusual.

Bradley enlarged the curriculum in 1890 to include manual training through sloyd, a highly disciplined Swedish woodworking program that taught the use of hand tools, the principles of mechanical drawing, and the principles of fine carpentry through detailed projects of increasing complexity. The Farm School was the first American site for sloyd, which Bradley called "the A B C in all manual instruction," but it soon was widely adopted in American elementary schools and other institutional settings. Sloyd was seen as an especially valuable system not only because it was a carefully delineated manual training program but also because it taught pride and esthetic appreciation of fine workmanship.

Over the next several years other trades as well as practical methods of promoting traditional academic skills were introduced at the school. In 1897 Bradley launched a newspaper written and printed by students; in 1900 he opened a student-managed store; and in 1905 students built a weather observatory from which teams tracked instruments, mapped and recorded their measurements, and reported their findings to the local U.S. Weather Bureau.

With the aid of his students Bradley also modernized the island; he introduced electricity and central coal-fired steam heating and built seawalls, dikes, and tree breaks to control erosion on the shoreline. In 1907 the name of the school was officially changed to the Farm and Trades School to more accurately reflect its current agenda. Yet Bradley was determined that Farm School boys should also be academically well prepared. By the time he died, in 1922, in response to child labor laws and other trends toward a longer period of formal schooling, the academic program included a first-year high school curriculum.

Although Bradley was an innovator, he also maintained aspects of the traditional institutional program that he believed were effective: the boys continued to live in a congregate setting, to perform agricultural labor including the growing of much of the island's food supply, and to be apprenticed when they could not be returned to their families upon completion of their education.

Bradley saw himself as an educator, not a reformer or philanthropist, and called his institution "a private school for worthy boys of limited means." He was convinced that his program represented the best of modern education without regard to class; that "the classical and the sloyd have united to give the man an opportunity to learn how he can live best and what he can best do."

As his reputation grew, Bradley consulted at other schools, traveled widely, and was offered positions at larger public and private institutions like the New York State Reformatory in Elmira, New York, and the New York House of Refuge, which he declined. During Bradley's tenure the Farm and Trades School became a model for other institutions and gained stature in the local community as well. Bradley was active in professional organizations, such as the National Conference of Charities and Corrections, as well as national and local clubs, especially patriotic organizations, such as the Vermont Association of Boston, of which he was the first president. He died in Boston and was eulogized by the school's board of managers as a man of "rare skill and judgment" for whom "no task seemed too difficult."

• Many of Charles Henry Bradley's papers, including correspondence, a manuscript history of the Farm and Trades School, speeches, and other writings, are collected in the Thompson's Island Collection, 1814–1975, University of Massachusetts Archives, University of Massachusetts, Boston. A memoir was published in the *New England Historical and Genealogical Register* 77 (1923): lx. An obituary is in the *Boston Transcript*, 30 Jan. 1922.

SUSAN L. PORTER

BRADLEY, Joseph P. (14 Mar. 1813–22 Jan. 1892), U.S. Supreme Court justice, was born in Berne, Albany County, New York, the son of Philo Bradley and Mercy Gardner, farmers. (The middle initial *P* does not stand for a second name; Bradley may have chosen it to honor his father.) The first child of very young parents, Bradley grew up in an intellectually stimulating extended family, forming close associations not only with uncles his own age but also with grandparents and a great-grandfather. His father was an avid reader and a talented surveyor, and his maternal grandfather, a lover of mathematics, delighted in posing problems for his children and grandchildren to solve.

As soon as Bradley could lift a hoe, he joined in the farm work, was soon his father's equal in the fields, and while in his midteens took over his father's teaching in a nearby winter school. In 1831, while threshing buckwheat, Bradley told his sympathetic father that his "life was being wasted" and insisted "I *must* have an education" (Pope, p. 121). After the harvest he moved in with a Dutch Reformed minister, who helped him prepare for college while he taught in the winter school.

In the fall of 1833, aided by a church fund and planning to enter the ministry, Bradley enrolled at Rutgers College. It had fewer than ten faculty members, and most of its eighty students were from wealthy Dutch Reformed families in contrast to Bradley, who wore homespun clothing and lodged on a farm several miles from the school. Bradley excelled intellectually, became the best mathematics student in the college, and at the beginning of his second year was advanced to the junior class. By this time he had formed a bond with fellow students Frederick T. Frelinghuysen (later a senator and secretary of state) and Cortlandt Parker (later president of the American Bar Association). These young men, who remained his lifelong friends, opened numerous doors for him. Like them he belonged to the Philoclean debating society, and when the faculty and board of trustees demanded it rescind some of its resolutions, Bradley defended its autonomy. His position paper impressed both the faculty—who, nevertheless, would not budge—and his friends, who convinced him he should become a lawyer. Midway through his senior year, however, Bradley returned temporarily to teaching when the Frelinghuysen family secured a position for him at a classical academy in Millstone (whose principal he soon became). The Rutgers faculty allowed Bradley to receive his college degree in 1836 without completing his final term.

Later in 1836, on the recommendation of the Parker family, Archer Gifford, the customs collector at Newark, made Bradley his assistant and agreed to tutor him in law. Commencing his studies with the goal of mastering the law so completely that he would be the peer of the chief justice of the U.S. Supreme Court, Bradley began to assemble a law library that would later grow to 10,000 volumes. In 1839 he was admitted to the New Jersey bar and with Frelinghuysen and Parker resurrected the previous generation's *Institutio legalis*, a moot court society, which gave Bradley access to Newark's conservative elite. Times were hard after the panic of 1837, and Bradley supplemented his meager income by becoming the Trenton correspondent of the *Newark Advertiser*, for which he had written while in college. Although from 1840 to 1845 he was the junior partner of John P. Jackson, a prominent Whig and head of the New Jersey Railroad and Transportation Company (whom Bradley met through the Frelinghuysens), his earnings remained modest.

In the fall of 1844 Bradley married Mary Hornblower, daughter of Joseph C. Hornblower, the chief justice of the New Jersey Supreme Court. They had seven children, four of whom reached adulthood. Also in 1844 Theodore Frelinghuysen, his friend's uncle, became Henry Clay's running mate in the presidential election, and despite earlier Democratic leanings, Bradley became active in Whig politics. With his friends he formed Frelinghuysen clubs in Newark and in Essex County. Bradley's ability and industry, abetted by his marriage, improved his practice.

In 1849 Bradley began his association with the Camden and Amboy Railroad Company and the Delaware and Raritan Canal Company, which were called the Joint Companies and together formed one of the strongest economic and political forces in New Jersey. Called "the Monopoly" by their enemies, these companies worked closely with the dominant Democratic party. In 1848 former New Jersey governor William Pennington (who was connected by marriage with Bradley's in-laws) headed a commission to investigate the Joint Companies, which had exclusive transportation rights across the state and monopolized rail transportation between New York and Philadelphia. Chosen by Pennington to become secretary of the commission, Bradley wrote its final report exonerating the Joint Companies of any wrongdoing. Enemies of the railroad called the report a whitewash, and when in

1849 they mounted a second investigation, the Joint Companies hired Bradley as counsel.

A precursor of the modern corporate attorney, Bradley became secretary to the Joint Companies' board of directors and a member of its executive committee. He also was the director of several Camden and Amboy subsidiaries. For another client, the Mutual Benefit Life Insurance Company of Newark, Bradley used his skills in mathematics to work out actuarial tables, and for still other clients he argued six cases before the U.S. Supreme Court. After the collapse of the Whigs in the 1850s, there is no record that Bradley joined the American party, but he extolled its pro-Union principles and nativist prejudices in his many Fourth of July orations. In 1860 Bradley's heart was with the Constitutional Union party of old Whigs and conservative Democrats, but when that movement collapsed in New Jersey he reluctantly joined the Republicans.

After the election of Abraham Lincoln and the secession of the lower South, Bradley, as a social and civic leader of Newark, which sent seven-eighths of its manufactured products to southern states, urged "CONCESSION and peace." It could be achieved, he believed, by adopting the Crittenden Compromise that would extend and perpetuate slavery. With the firing on Fort Sumter, however, he enthusiastically supported the war, and later he "equated Southern rebels with traitors and murderers." When he ran as a Republican for Congress in 1862, he was decisively defeated, because in Newark, even more than in the rest of the country, initial enthusiasm for the war had soured.

By 1868 Bradley was an outstanding lawyer, adept at reducing arguments and principles to their bare essentials, and his friends began pushing him for a seat on the U.S. Supreme Court. Chance helped, but the tenacity and shrewdness of Bradley's friends during a two-year period of changing conditions proved instrumental. The mastermind was George Harding, a prominent lawyer whose brother published the *Philadelphia Inquirer*. Encouraged by his backers (who secured support for him in all three branches of the federal government), Bradley plunged into politics. He worked to counter the perception in New Jersey that his politics were more "Camden & Amboy" than Republican. After meeting Grant and Colfax at a Washington dinner, Bradley headed their New Jersey slate of Republican electors and campaigned for them vigorously.

Despite the long and intense maneuvering of Bradley's friends, his nomination and that of William Strong were perceived as a hasty attempt to reverse the court's decision in *Hepburn v. Griswold* (1870), which invalidated the Legal Tender Acts (1862, 1863) requiring that paper money be accepted for debts and taxes. Almost simultaneously with that decision Grant nominated these men in place of Edwin Stanton (who died two days after his confirmation) and Ebenezer Rockwood Hoar (whose nomination was rejected by the Senate). On 23 March 1870 Bradley took his seat on the Court; he had been confirmed two days earlier by a vote of 46 to 9 (with Democratic senators voting for him). As Grant hoped, Bradley and Strong helped reverse the *Hepburn* decision in the subsequent *Legal Tender Cases* (1871).

Joining the Court shortly after the adoption of the Fourteenth Amendment (1868), which defined citizenship and forbade the restriction by states of any citizen's civil rights, Bradley played a prominent role in its interpretation. His dissent in *Blyew v. United States* (1872) justified the use of congressional power to protect the civil rights of former slaves from state interference. In his dissent in the *Slaughterhouse Cases* (1873) he argued that the Fourteenth Amendment's privileges and immunities clause protects economic enterprise—and inferentially human rights—from unreasonable state interference.

Shortly before his dissent in *Slaughterhouse*, Bradley took an opposite tact in *Bradwell v. Illinois* (1873). In a separately filed concurring opinion in that case, in which Myra Bradwell challenged the state's right to prevent her from practicing law because she was a woman, he claimed that "the law of the Creator" limited women to "the noble and benign offices of wife and mother." It is impossible to reconcile his argument in *Bradwell* with his nine-year-earlier lament to his daughter Carry: "I know that the practices of society offer but little opportunity for a woman to earn her bread alone . . . but the times are gradually improving in that respect and I hope to live to see the day when an industrious woman can earn a livelihood . . . as honorably as an industrious man" (Pope, p. 342).

Two years after his early dissents, Bradley began narrowing his interpretation of the Fourteenth Amendment until his majority opinion in the *Civil Rights Cases* (1883) nullified equal access to public accommodations (guaranteed in the Civil Rights Act of 1875). The Fourteenth Amendment, he insisted, referred only to state actions, and the attempt to bar segregation in public inns was beyond the power of Congress. "When a man has emerged from slavery," Bradley stated, "there must be some stage . . . when he takes the rank of mere citizen and ceases to be the special favorite of the laws" (Friedman, p. 1197). The change in Bradley's thinking may reflect his sojourns in the South, where he performed his circuit duties until 1880, and a perception—shared by a majority of his contemporaries—that Reconstruction had failed. He justified his inconsistency by stating, "My own mind is rather in the condition of seeking the truth, than of dogmatically laying down opinions" (Friedman, p. 1197).

Earlier, in 1877, when Congress formed a commission to decide the disputed presidential election, Bradley (a man of integrity who was not an extreme partisan) became its final member. One hundred eighty-five electoral votes were needed to win the election. Samuel J. Tilden, the Democratic candidate, had 184 votes; Rutherford B. Hayes, the Republican candidate, 165 votes; and twenty votes were contested (those from Fla., La., and S.C. seriously, and one from Oregon on a simple technicality). Bradley was selected in place of Supreme Court Justice David Davis, who had disqualified himself after he was elected to the Senate with Democratic support. The only independent available for the commission, Davis had been selected to break an anticipated tie because the commission's other fourteen members were evenly divided between the two parties. As Davis's replacement Bradley "was expected to sink all political bias and act the judge merely."

A man who throughout his career exhibited a "penchant for order, regularity and ceaseless toil," Bradley spent every waking moment searching out what the law said on the subject. He again took up smoking (a habit he had broken twenty-two years earlier) and saw his family only at mealtime. He and he alone had to decide whether the commission should, as the Democrats proposed, go behind the officially recorded vote of the Republican returning boards. In the three southern states these boards had thrown out numerous votes—fraudulently, the Democrats claimed—because of widespread intimidation of black voters.

Bradley gave no indication at commission meetings how he would vote, but Democrats took heart from the fact that he usually sided with them on procedural matters. Since the same questions were involved in the three southern states, Bradley's vote on the Florida case would determine if Tilden or Hayes would be president. When, pale and trembling, he gave his opinion prior to casting the most momentous vote in American history, Bradley did not reveal until the concluding paragraphs his decision that the commission did not have the power to go behind the official Republican-canvassing-board returns. After his verdict, he was "inundated by a flood of vulgar and threatening communications," and Navy Secretary George Robeson, who was his close friend, arranged for detectives to guard him and his home. "Public life, in this country," Bradley complained to his sister, "is a gauntlet through which one passes subject to be struck at by every villain that chooses to do it" (Fairman, p. 80).

Eight months later Bradley further incensed the Democrats by detailing how he arrived at his momentous decision. "I wrote and re-wrote the arguments and considerations on both sides as they occurred to me," he told a newspaper, "sometimes being inclined to one view and sometimes to the other. But finally, I threw aside these lucubrations, and . . . wrote out the short opinion which I read in the Florida case" (Pope, p. 374).

Working independently from his forceful intellectual equals on the Court (Stephen J. Field, Samuel F. Miller, and John Marshall Harlan), Bradley developed an intimate working relationship with Chief Justice Morrison R. Waite, with whom he served for fourteen years (1874–1888). "I will take the credit and you shall do the work, as usual," wrote Waite in a note to Bradley (acknowledging his need for help in an era when there were no law clerks). In Waite's most important majority opinion, *Munn v. Illinois* (1877), Bradley researched the law and formulated the key phrase upholding state regulation of grain elevators in Chicago. In Waite's translation the phrase read, "When private property is affected with a public interest," it ceases to be exclusively private property.

Despite Bradley's railroad background he was the Court's "staunchest defender of state regulation of railroad rates" and "with few exceptions gave the broadest reading to national rights and federal power." When nearly a decade after *Munn*, the Court retreated from its position, in *Wabash, St. Louis and Pacific Railway Co. v. Illinois* (1886), Bradley in his dissent claimed that in the absence of federal regulation the states had every right to regulate. Nudged by Bradley's dissent, Congress almost immediately created the Interstate Commerce Commission.

"With his powerful intellect and moral assertiveness," Bradley, Leon Friedman states, "surpassed all but a handful of judges who have sat upon the Court" (p. 1200). In keeping with his background and interests, he was the Court's expert on railroad practice, insurance litigation, and patent cases (where he used his knowledge of mathematics and physics). Because his circuit duties were in the South for ten years, he also was experienced in deciding cases relating to private contracts disturbed by the Civil War. Not satisfied to base his opinions merely on precedent or the common law, he preferred using history, logic, and axioms and wanted American law to incorporate useful laws and institutions of all peoples. Few of his peers have surpassed him in "craftsmanship and marshalling of legal principles in reasoned opinions to guide lawyers and through them society" (Friedman, p. 1181). He was still on the Court when he died in Washington, D.C.

• Bradley's papers are at the New Jersey Historical Society, Newark; among them are diaries, writings, extensive correspondence, and a scrapbook in which are sketched the seating arrangements of the 189 Washington dinners Bradley attended. Some of his papers have been published in *Miscellaneous Writings of the Late Hon. Jos. P. Bradley*, edited by his son Charles Bradley, in 1902. See also Joseph P. Bradley, *Family Notes Respecting the Bradley Family of Fairfield* (1894) and *Catalog of the Library of the Late Joseph P. Bradley* (1892). Especially helpful are Dennis H. Pope, "Personality and Judicial Performance: A Psychobiography of Justice Joseph P. Bradley" (Ph.D. diss., Rutgers Univ., 1988); Leon Friedman, "Joseph P. Bradley," *The Justices of the United States Supreme Court 1798–1978: Their Lives and Major Opinions*, ed. Friedman and Fred L. Israel, vol. 2 (1980); and Charles Fairman, "Mr. Justice Bradley," in *Mr. Justice*, ed. Allison Dunham and Philip B. Kurland (1964). An obituary is in the *New York Times*, 23 Jan. 1892.

OLIVE HOOGENBOOM

BRADLEY, Lydia Moss (31 July 1816–16 Jan. 1908), university founder, was born in Vevay, Indiana, the daughter of Zealy Moss, a revolutionary war officer, Baptist preacher, and farmer, and Jenny Glasscock. Like many frontier children she was educated in the kitchen of a neighbor who had access to the *Webster Speller*, the *English Reader*, and the Bible.

Her entrée into the business world came in the early 1830s when she traded her pet horse for a tract of timberland. Clearing the land herself, she sold the logs to a sawmill owned by Tobias Smith Bradley. A few years after the sale, in 1837, Lydia Moss and Tobias Bradley were married.

Tobias Bradley eventually opened a wood yard and sawmill in connection with the river trade along the Ohio River. During this time Lydia and Tobias had two daughters and suffered the first of many personal tragedies with their children's deaths in 1845 and 1847. Seeing greater economic opportunity, the Bradleys decided to move to Peoria, Illinois, in 1847 to join Lydia's brother, William Moss. Tobias became a partner with William Moss in a variety of enterprises, including a distillery business, railroading, milling, a telegraph line, real estate, steamboating, farming, and gold mining. Along with money and land Lydia Bradley had been given by family members at the time of her marriage, these partnerships led to the Bradley fortune.

Tragedy continued to haunt the Bradleys. They had four more children, all of whom died before adulthood. Their last surviving child, a daughter, died in 1864 at the age of fourteen. The final tragedy occurred when Tobias was involved in a buggy accident on 1 May 1867; he died three days later.

With her husband's death and the eventual settlement of the estate, Lydia Bradley found herself with 700 acres of land, a bank, a railroad, and other interests totaling $500,000. She assumed these new responsibilities without experience, but with good judgment, careful management, and the assistance of her business manager W. W. Hammond, she was not only able to preserve the estate but to increase it fourfold, primarily through the development of real estate. Being a major stockholder in the First National Bank and owning the building in which the bank was located, Bradley became a member of the board of directors, the first woman member of a national bank board in the state of Illinois.

In 1869 Bradley married Edward Clark, a successful cotton broker from Memphis, Tennessee. Bradley insisted that a prenuptial agreement be signed to protect her growing assets. Bradley and Clark were divorced in 1873.

Bradley's growing assets enabled her to respond to the needs of the Peoria community. She relieved the Universalist church from a $30,000 mortgage and helped finance the establishment of the Grand Old Opera House. She donated the land on which was built the Saint Francis Medical Center, constructed a home for aged women, and gave the city of Peoria 130 acres of land for parks with the provision that a park board be organized. The Peoria Pleasure Driveway and Park District was organized in 1894, becoming the first park system formed in the state of Illinois under the enabling legislation of 1893.

Bradley's greatest contribution was the founding of Bradley Polytechnic Institute, which started with her personal investigation of polytechnic schools across the country. In 1892 she purchased controlling interest in Parsons Horological Institute from LaPorte, Indiana, and moved the school with its 100 students and faculty to Peoria. The school was first housed in the Peoria Watch Company near the location of the future campus. The horology school was the first tentative step toward achieving her goal, but the school did not provide classical education that she desired to support.

With the assistance of William Rainey Harper, president of the University of Chicago, she transformed the horology school into Bradley Polytechnic Institute. According to the charter of incorporation of Bradley Polytechnic Institute, granted on 13 November 1896, "The chief aim of the Institute shall be to furnish its students with the means of living independent, industrious and useful lives by the aid of a practical knowledge of the useful arts and sciences." This institute, which she formally dedicated "for Tobias and the children," was founded on 8 October 1897. Bradley Polytechnic Institute became a four-year college in 1920 and in 1946 became a university offering graduate programs.

On 2 January 1908 Bradley fell ill, and after a two-week illness she died in Peoria, Illinois. Few women at the turn of the century did as much to rejuvenate and modernize an American city as did Lydia Moss Bradley. She enriched every conceivable dimension of Peoria, Illinois, from medicine to religion, from recreation to the arts, from business to education. Bradley University embodies her dream of providing deserving young men and women with opportunities for useful and productive lives through higher education.

• A. A. Upton, *Forgotten Angel: The Story of Lydia Moss Bradley* (1988), contains details of Bradley's life and work. Her contributions to Bradley University are documented in Bradley Polytechnic Institute, *The First Decade* (1908), and Louis A. R. Yates, *A Proud Heritage: Bradley's History, 1897–1972* (1974). J. Klein, *Peoria* (1985), recognizes her contributions to the city. Obituaries are in the *Peoria Star*, the *Peoria Journal*, and the *Peoria Transcript*, all 16 Jan. 1908.

KATHY A. FULLER

BRADLEY, Milton (8 Nov. 1836–30 May 1911), manufacturer of games and educational materials, was born in Vienna, Maine, the son of Lewis Bradley, a craftsman, and Fannie Lyford. After finishing high school in 1854 in Lowell, Massachusetts, Bradley found work in the office of a mechanical draftsman and patent agent. There he earned enough money to enroll himself in the Lawrence Scientific School at Cambridge, where he studied drafting. Half a year short of completing the two-year course, Bradley moved to Hartford, Connecticut, with his parents. Unsuccessful in securing employment there, he left home in 1856 for Springfield, Massachusetts, where he immediately found work with the Wason Car-Manufacturing Company as a draftsman.

After the doors of Wason Company closed in 1858 owing to economic recession, Bradley went into business by himself as a mechanical draftsman and patent agent. However, he made no money until he rejoined the reopened Wason Company to draw up the plans for a luxurious railroad car ordered by the ruler of Egypt. Later he learned the art and craft of lithography, bought a press, and started another business in 1860. Shortly afterward Samuel Bowles, publisher of the *Springfield Republican*, persuaded him to make and sell lithographs of a photograph of a beardless Abraham Lincoln. Although the prints initially sold well, they became worthless after the future U.S. president grew a beard. In that same year, inspired by his own love of playing games, Bradley created "The Checkered Game of Life" and began his career in manufacturing games.

Bradley successfully sold the first batch of this game personally to store managers in New York City. The philosophy behind his creation of this game was that life was oftentimes like a game and a game like life, both involving chance as well as skill. Bradley did not advocate gambling, although some people of this time did not approve of any type of game. His first success was followed by "Games for the Soldiers" in 1861, a kit of nine popular games for Union troops. In 1864 Milton Bradley Company became successful enough to include J. F. Tapley and Clark W. Bryan as partners. Two years later Bradley invented "The Myrioptican," which was a box that was cranked to unroll lithographed historical scenes across a screen. Another popular item was "The Zoetrope, or Wheel of Life," which was an improvement of the former. It consisted of a revolving drum with vertical slits on the side and a paper strip of figures in various stages of action inserted inside. When spun, it appeared that a figure was in perpetual motion. The year 1866 also saw the patenting of Bradley's rules for the popular game of croquet, which soon became standard. Because Americans were beginning to have more leisure time in the late 1800s, Bradley's games were greeted with enthusiasm. The end of the Civil War and economic recession gave the nation additional reasons to indulge in such diversions.

In 1869 Milton Bradley became involved in the kindergarten movement after meeting Edward Wiebe and hearing a lecture by Elizabeth Peabody. As a result, he published a book by Wiebe titled *Paradise of Childhood* (1869) on the ideas of a German named Friedrich Froebel. It was the first work about kindergarten instruction published in the English language. Because Bradley's own parents instilled in him the pleasure of learning and taught him simple arithmetic with objects that better enforced a lesson than did mere memorization, he could sympathize with such a cause. Although the book did not sell well, Bradley began to manufacture kindergarten materials such as the "gifts" named by Froebel, which were objects that taught children the ideas of fractions and division. In addition, Bradley published two magazines for the purpose of promoting his educational materials. One was called *Kindergarten News* (purchased in 1893), which became *Kindergarten Review*, and the other was *Work and Play* (published earlier). Because Bradley's educational venture was unprofitable, J. F. Tapley and Bryan parted with him in 1878 and his longtime friend and clever businessman George Tapley joined the company.

Bradley's interest in children's education led him to develop a new color wheel for color instruction, which had brighter and purer colors than previous models. His experiments with different hues and pigments mixed together in an ice cream freezer led him to write and publish four works himself about teaching colors to children: *Color in the School Room* (1890), *Color in the Kindergarten* (1893), *Elementary Color* (1895), and *Water Colors in the Schoolroom* (1900).

Bradley's first marriage was to Vilona Eaton of Boston in 1860; they had no children. Two years after she died, he married Ellen "Nellie" Thayer in 1869, a schoolteacher from Winchester, New Hampshire. They had two daughters. A somewhat shy man who did not care for the business aspect of his work, Bradley was more comfortable at his drafting board or experimenting with new ideas for games. He believed in using his artistic talents for practical purposes such as mechanical drafting rather than for producing art for its own sake. It was later, when he started painting with water colors, that he enjoyed art for its aesthetic qualities.

Bradley was a persistent character. His perseverance was especially clear in his decision to continue manufacturing the unprofitable educational materials. "It took about all the faith I could muster, all the belief in the final triumph of kindergarten principles, to pull me through those early years of discouragement, when my business associates and other friends and the annual balance sheets of our bookkeeper were all against me" (quoted in Shea and Mercer). Because he helped spread the concept of kindergarten and persisted in producing educational materials, the aids were eventually bought and used. His advocacy and support helped to make kindergarten more of a reality. Most of all, he is known for the company that he founded and remembered for the games that he created to bring enjoyment into the parlors of American homes in the late 1800s. He died in Springfield.

• For a history of Milton Bradley Company, see James J. Shea, Jr., *The Milton Bradley Story* (1973). A full-length biography is James J. Shea and Charles Mercer, *It's All in the Game* (1960). See also *Milton Bradley, a Successful Man: A Brief Sketch of His Career and the Growth of the Institution Which He Founded, Published by Milton Bradley Company in Commemoration of Their Fiftieth Anniversary* (1910), and Jas. E. Tower, ed., *Springfield Present and Prospective* (1905).

DEBORAH S. ING

BRADLEY, Omar Nelson (12 Feb. 1893–8 Apr. 1981), military commander, was born in Clark, Missouri, the son of John Smith Bradley, a schoolteacher, and Sarah Elizabeth Hubbard, a seamstress. Bradley was one of his father's pupils until age twelve, when his parents settled in Higbee so he could attend public school. From his father, who died of pneumonia when Bradley was fourteen, he gained a love of reading, baseball, and hunting.

Described as "calculative" in his Moberly High School yearbook because of his math abilities, Bradley wanted to be a lawyer, but his family had no money for college when he graduated in 1910. He went to work for the Wabash Railroad repairing steam engine boilers to earn tuition for the University of Missouri. During this period a friend suggested that Bradley consider trying to gain an appointment to the U.S. Military Academy, and he was chosen as an alternate by his congressman. In 1911 the top candidate failed the qualifying examinations, and Bradley received word of his appointment four days before he had to report to West Point.

"The four years I spent at West Point were among the most rewarding of my life," he remembered. "I loved every minute of it" (*A General's Life*, p. 30). Although he felt that athletics (four letters in baseball, two in football) kept him from placing in the top twenty of his 1915 class, he still graduated a respectable forty-fourth out of 164, fifteen places ahead of star halfback Dwight D. Eisenhower. In the yearbook Eisenhower wrote that Bradley's "most promising characteristic is 'getting there,' and if he keeps up the clip he's started, some of us will some day be bragging to our grandchildren that, 'Sure, General Bradley was a classmate of mine.'" In fact, fifty-nine graduates in "the class the stars fell on" would become general officers.

Infantry Second Lieutenant Bradley reported to Fort George Wright outside of Spokane, Washington, in September 1915. The Pancho Villa crisis the following spring caused postponement of Bradley's wedding when he was sent to Arizona in May, but he saw no action. In December 1916 he returned to Missouri to marry his high school sweetheart, Mary Elizabeth Quayle. The couple had one child.

In April 1917 the United States entered World War I, but Bradley again was not involved in the fighting. He spent sixteen months in Arizona processing troops before transferring to Montana, where he guarded copper mines. The National Defense Act of 1916 boosted his rank to first lieutenant, and he received a temporary promotion to major during the war. Nevertheless, Bradley was "absolutely convinced" that he was "professionally ruined" because he had not made it to France.

At the end of 1918 Bradley moved to Rockford, Illinois, then the following year he became a Reserve Officers Training Corps instructor at South Dakota State College. He found that he enjoyed teaching, and spent thirteen of his first twenty-three army years in instructing positions. From 1920 to 1924 he taught math at West Point, followed by a year of study at the Infantry Training School in Fort Benning, Georgia, then a three-year stint in Hawaii. In 1924 Bradley was repromoted to major.

After graduating from Command and General Staff School at Fort Leavenworth, Kansas, Bradley went back to Fort Benning in 1929 as an instructor. There he had his first contact with George C. Marshall, who, as assistant commandant, had assembled an outstanding faculty. Bradley taught tactics under Joseph Stilwell the first year, so impressing Marshall that he was named head of the weapons section in 1930. He attended the Army War College in Washington (1933) before going back to West Point to teach in the Department of Tactics (1934–1938). Promotion to lieutenant colonel finally came in 1936.

In late 1938 Bradley reluctantly accepted an assignment to the General Staff in Washington. Marshall was named chief of staff the following April and immediately requested that Bradley be transferred to his personal staff. Together they watched, "shaking our heads in disbelief," as Germany rolled across Europe during the first months of World War II (*A General's Life*, p. 88). Bradley was offered the position of commandant of cadets at West Point in early 1941, but Marshall countered with a better proposal—that Bradley become commandant of the Infantry School at Fort Benning, a vital officer training assignment with the country on the verge of war. The position meant elevation to brigadier general, with Bradley skipping the rank of colonel and earning the first star awarded to a member of the 1915 class.

At Benning, Bradley inherited a prototype of what he would quickly develop into the first Officer Candidate School. The initial airborne training was also taking place on the base, as was development of the Second Armored Division, with George S. Patton, Jr., then second in command. In maneuvers during the year, Patton offended some by breaking many of the accepted rules for tank warfare, but he dazzled Bradley with his ability and drive. It was the beginning of a stormy but propitious relationship.

In late December 1941 Bradley was elevated to major general and given charge of the Eighty-second Division, but the following June his reputation as an excellent training officer led to an assignment he did not relish, transfer to command of the Twenty-eighth National Guard Division. Through discipline and physical conditioning he turned what he described as "a hodgepodge" into "a tough fighting unit." He would not remain to take the division into combat, however, as in February 1943 he received word that he was being sent to North Africa, where the Allied Operation Torch was not faring well against the Axis forces, particularly the Germans.

Uncertain of the reasons for his assignment, Bradley later speculated that "perhaps Marshall was tactfully seeking a way of reinforcing [Eisenhower] on the battlefield with professional generals skilled in infantry tactics, without actually saying so," for he found that while his West Point classmate had "matured into a charming man with a first-class mind," Eisenhower had "little grasp of sound battlefield tactics." Initially slated to become Eisenhower's "eyes and ears" at the front, probably to be regarded as "an odious spy for Ike," Bradley was pleased when it was decided in early March that Patton would be given II Corps (with Bradley as second in command) for a few weeks until he was to leave to prepare for the invasion of Sicily, at which time Bradley would succeed to the top position.

Bradley soon became aware of the delicate political situation within the Allied command. The British did not trust the Americans, and the Americans believed the British generals were too slow and too cautious. Bradley and Patton were convinced that Eisenhower's decisions consistently favored the British.

After seeing his first action under Patton, whom he thought "a superb field general and leader," Bradley took command of II Corps on 16 April, a week before the final Allied campaign in North Africa was launched. The British entered Tunis on 7 May, the same day that Bradley's II Corps took Bizerte, effectively ending Axis resistence in Tunisia. Within a week Bradley left to join Patton in planning the Sicily invasion, and on 2 June he was promoted to three-star general.

The 10 July landing on Sicily was the first major amphibious operation of the war, with Bradley's II Corps going ashore at Gela and Scoglitti. Bradley had not been pleased with the plan, and his skepticism proved correct as Allied forces soon bogged down in bloody fighting. His relations with Patton cooled as Patton told Eisenhower that Bradley was not aggressive enough, then left II Corps heavily engaged in the central part of the island and took off in disobedience of orders on a glory-seeking dash for Palermo. As the campaign progressed, II Corps spearheaded the Seventh Army's drive for Messina, and Patton took unnecessary risks in an attempt to beat British general Bernard Montgomery to the coastal city. Patton won the race, but the lack of Allied coordination allowed 110,000 Germans and Italians to escape to the Italian mainland.

Bradley, not Patton, received the next major assignment. At Marshall's urging, he was selected to coordinate preparation for Operation Overlord, the long-awaited Allied invasion of France. After flying to Washington for briefings with Franklin D. Roosevelt and Marshall, Bradley established his headquarters outside of London in October 1943. When Eisenhower was chosen in December to head Overlord, Bradley became army group commander. All American ground forces were in his charge. Bradley's idea of a night landing in the manner of the Sicily invasion was overruled, but at his insistence, a second American beach was added, and the role of airborne troops was greatly enlarged. After months of planning and training, Bradley watched from the deck of the heavy cruiser *Augusta* as American forces stormed the Normandy beaches designated Utah and Omaha on the morning of 6 June 1944.

Although slightly off course, the Utah landing went smoothly. Omaha was a different matter, however, as a veteran German division was in the area on training maneuvers. The stiff initial resistance it offered led Bradley to consider withdrawing U.S. forces from Omaha, but naval bombardment and determined infantry thrusts established the beachhead. Bradley was able to move the First Army headquarters ashore on 9 June.

Neither the Americans nor the British made much progress in breaking out of Normandy until late July, when Bradley implemented Operation Cobra. His most highly praised operation of the war, it featured "bold concentration and exploitation" (Weigley, p. 729), taking full advantage of the army's mobility. Bradley's follow-up was decidedly less bold, however, as he proposed a broad encirclement of the German army, with U.S. forces swinging southeastward through Brittany. As the movement began, a German counterattack in early August suddenly presented a better opportunity—the chance to trap the same army in less than two weeks by stanching the gap behind it between Falaise and Argentan. In what Bradley described as a "shattering disappointment," the pocket was not closed. Bradley stopped Patton's overextended drive from the south, and Montgomery inexplicably used inexperienced Canadian forces at the van of his hesitant push from the north.

The failure at Falaise further frayed the already-strained relations between Bradley and Montgomery. The British field marshall insisted that he should be placed in charge of all Allied ground forces, while the American commander had little use for Montgomery's lunge for the Rhine River, Operation Market-Garden, which turned out to be a disaster. Bradley fared little better in his November attempt to reach the Rhine by way of crossing the Roer River.

In mid-December the Germans caught the Allies completely off guard with a massive counteroffensive through the Ardennes, splitting the American forces. Bradley had seriously underestimated the threat that resulted in the Battle of the Bulge, but he reacted quickly, planning the Patton counterattack that was launched on 22 December. He was unable to ward off Montgomery's political assault, however, as the British commander convinced Eisenhower to give him temporary charge of the two American armies caught on the British side of the bulge, leaving Bradley with only Patton's Third Army in his Twelfth Army Group.

The U.S. First Army reverted to Bradley in January 1945, but Montgomery clung to the Ninth and continued to insist on only one drive into the German heartland—his—with Bradley and the Americans relegated to a supporting role. Bradley favored a two-pronged attack but was placed on the "aggressive defensive" by Eisenhower in February. While Montgomery delayed his push for the Rhine, however, Bradley launched Operation Lumberjack in early March, reaching the Rhine in four days. On 7 March elements of the First Army seized a railroad bridge at Remagen, affecting the first Allied crossing of the Rhine. Using this bridgehead as leverage, Bradley gained approval from Eisenhower for a "right hook" through Frankfurt toward Kassel. While Montgomery dallied, the Americans leaped, with a breakout beginning on 25 March. By this action, Bradley earned the right to take the lead in the final offensive. He gained his fourth star in March, and on 4 April the Ninth Army was returned to him, giving him charge of 1.3 million men, the largest ground force ever commanded by a U.S. general.

In the first phase of Bradley's operations, elements of the First and Ninth armies circled the Ruhr industrial region, forcing the surrender of 317,000 German troops on 18 April. By that time the Americans, deployed on a 140-mile line, had already reached the Elbe, while the British and Canadians were slowly securing the northern part of the country. The only question remaining was whether to drive onward to Berlin or to leave it for the Soviets. Montgomery and Patton each wanted the glory, but Bradley cautioned Eisenhower that it would cost 100,000 casualties to reach and clear the German capital. The Russian assault on Berlin opened on 16 April, rendering the point moot. At 5:00 A.M. on 7 May Bradley received a call from Eisenhower notifying him that Germany had surrendered.

The euphoria did not last long. Bradley, who had hoped to be sent to the Japanese theater, was "devastated" when he learned in mid-May that Marshall had suggested he be put in charge of the poorly functioning Veterans Administration (VA). With demobilization, 43 percent of the American male population would be veterans, so Bradley faced a monumental task when he took over the position in August 1945. During his two-plus years on the job he oversaw complete reorganization of the government's largest independent agency, placing it on a better footing to handle the postwar influx.

At the end of November 1947 Bradley resigned the VA position and prepared to succeed Eisenhower as chief of staff of the army, which he did the following February. With drastic reductions in defense spending, Bradley faced the difficult task of maintaining military preparedness while also making substantial cutbacks. Crises in Greece and Berlin also arose during this period. The term as chief of staff was supposed to last four years, but when Eisenhower turned down the newly created position of chairman of the Joint Chiefs of Staff, Harry S. Truman offered the job to Bradley, who took over in August 1949.

Cold War tension increased during late 1949 with the fall of China to the Communists and Soviet development of an atomic bomb. Bradley advocated building the exponentially more powerful hydrogen bomb, even though he believed its value was largely "psychological." While successfully lobbying Truman, he emphasized that the United States would be in "an intolerably inferior military posture" if the Soviets developed an H-bomb and the Americans did not.

As chairman of the Joint Chiefs, Bradley also oversaw consideration and approval of NSC-68, a policy statement that outlined uses of the military in support of the doctrine of containment. Implementation was only weeks away, as the Korean War began in June 1950. Early in the conflict Truman considered sending Bradley to replace Douglas MacArthur, but he decided to keep the fellow Missourian in Washington and in September 1950 promoted Bradley to five-star general.

Bradley thought MacArthur "awesomely brilliant" but also "a megalomaniac" like Patton and Montgomery (*A General's Life*, p. 523). He continually urged MacArthur to take a more cautious approach to military affairs, but with little effect. Like Truman, Bradley was appalled at MacArthur's continual public criticism of presidential policy, although he did not think that MacArthur's actions technically constituted military insubordination. He did, however, fully support Truman's April 1951 decision to replace MacArthur.

Bradley's term as chairman of the Joint Chiefs ended in August 1953, a month after the Korean armistice was signed. Law required that five-star generals remain on the active roster, but for all practical purposes Bradley retired, settling in California and accepting a position as head of the research and development laboratories of Bulova Watch Company. In 1957 he and his wife moved back to Washington to be closer to their grandchildren, and a year later Bradley was elected chairman of the board of Bulova, a position he held until 1973. His wife died in December 1965. Soon thereafter he became enamored with Esther Dora "Kitty" Buhler, a Hollywood screenwriter who was interested in filming Bradley's life story; they married in 1966. Two years later the couple settled in Beverly Hills, where the general enjoyed the contact with Hollywood stars that his wife provided. Instead of proceeding with the Bradley movie, they became senior advisers for the Academy Award–winning film *Patton* and earned handsome royalties from a percentage of the profits.

In 1973 Bradley nearly died from a blood clot in his lungs. Two years later a blood clot in his brain left him confined to a wheelchair, and in 1977 he moved to Fort Bliss in El Paso, Texas, to be closer to army hospital facilities. His wife made sure that he remained active, encouraging work on his second memoir and travel around the country for brief speaking engagements. Bradley died in New York while on one of these trips and was buried at Arlington National Cemetery.

Bradley, called the "GI's general" or "soldier's general," lacked Patton's drive and Eisenhower's polish and has been criticized by some historians for being too cautious. His strengths, however, lay in other areas. "Bradley was conspicuous for his ability to handle people and his ability to see things very simply and clearly," said Marshall (*George C. Marshall Interviews*, p. 542). "His tactical skill in the handling of large forces is remarkable," added Eisenhower at the end of World War II. "His brains, selflessness, and outstanding ability as a battleline commander are unexcelled anywhere in the world today" (*The Papers of Dwight D. Eisenhower*, vol. 4, p. 2648).

• Major collections of Bradley's papers are at the Omar N. Bradley Library in the Special Collections Division of the U.S. Military Academy Library, West Point, N.Y.; at the U.S. Military History Institute, site of the Bradley Foundation and Bradley Museum, Carlisle Barracks, Pa.; and at the National Archives. With considerable collaboration, Bradley published two memoirs, *A Soldier's Story* (1951), ghostwritten by Bradley's wartime aide Chester B. Hansen, which focuses exclusively on World War II activities, and *A General's Life* (1983), completed after Bradley's death by journalist Clay Blair, with whom Bradley worked from 1979 to 1981. The latter book contains a useful bibliography. Charles Whiting, *Bradley* (1971), is a brief biography. An excellent assessment by Marshall's biographer Forrest C. Pogue is in *The War Lords*, ed. Michael Carver (1976). Wartime coverage was extensive, including a *Time* cover story, 1 May 1944, and feature articles in *Newsweek*, 31 Jan. 1944, and *Life*, 5 June 1944. Bradley is prominent in practically every postwar history and memoir of the European theater, most notably Russell F. Weigley, *Eisenhower's Lieutenants: The Campaign of France and Germany, 1944–1945* (1981), and Pogue, *The Supreme Command* (1954). Numerous references to Bradley are in *The Papers of Dwight D. Eisenhower* (1970–); Larry I. Bland, ed., *The Papers of George C. Marshall* (1981–); Pogue and Bland, eds., *George C. Marshall Interviews and Reminiscences for Forrest C. Pogue* (1986); and Martin Blumenson, ed., *The Patton Papers*, vol. 2 (1974). Stephen T. Powers, "The Battle of Normandy: The Lingering Controversy," *Journal of Military History* 56 (July 1992), summarizes the literature on the Falaise gap controversy, since augmented by Blumenson, *The Battle of the Generals* (1993). Richard Rhodes, *Dark Sun: The Making of the Hydrogen Bomb* (1995), chronicles Bradley's part in that drama. An obituary is in the *New York Times*, 9 Apr. 1981.

KENNETH H. WILLIAMS

BRADLEY, Stephen Row (20 Feb. 1754–9 Dec. 1830), jurist and senator, was born in Wallingford (now Cheshire), Connecticut, the son of Moses Bradley and Mary Row. Moses Bradley's occupation is not known, but he may have been a silversmith like his father. He had the means, at any rate, to send his son Stephen to Yale College for an education. After receiving his baccalaureate degree in July 1775, Stephen Bradley became captain of the Cheshire Volunteers, a militia unit that joined the Continental army in January 1776. Enlistment periods were brief, typically for ninety days, and Bradley served intermittently from 1775 through 1779. He was an aide-de-camp to General David Wooster when that officer was killed at Danbury, Connecticut, in April 1777. He served as commissary and quartermaster and had risen in rank to major when he moved from Connecticut to Vermont. In the Vermont militia, he achieved the rank of brigadier general.

Between military enlistments, Bradley continued his education. In September 1778 he received the M.A. degree from Yale, after which he began reading law under a distinguished Litchfield jurist, Judge Tapping Reeve. In search of new challenges and opportunities, he moved in 1779 to a remote area of New England known as the New Hampshire Grants, where settlers were struggling to establish the independent state of Vermont. In May 1779 at Westminster, Bradley was admitted to the Vermont bar and was promptly made clerk of the superior court of that "independent" state, a testament to his solid legal learning.

Bradley's knowledge of the law and the skill with which he practiced it quickly gained him a place of respect and leadership in the frontier community. In October 1779 he was given the special trust of serving as one of Vermont's agents to the Continental Congress for the purpose of advancing the case for statehood. For some time New York, New Hampshire, and Massachusetts were rival claimants to the country Ethan Allen and the Green Mountain Boys had proclaimed to be the free state of Vermont. Congress set the first of February 1780 as the date to adjudicate the rival claims, and Bradley was assigned the job of presenting Vermont's views. He prepared a carefully researched and forcefully written treatise entitled "Vermont's Appeal to the Candid and Impartial World," which the Council of Vermont approved and published in December 1779. He presented Vermont's petition for statehood to Congress, but that body postponed the hearing and finally failed to act on the question. Even so, Bradley's efforts to gain statehood for Vermont endeared him to its citizens, who came to regard him as one of their ablest public servants.

From the time he moved to Vermont in 1779 until his retirement from the U.S. Senate in 1813, Bradley was continuously employed in public service. In 1780 he was appointed state's attorney for Cumberland County. In the same year he represented Westminster in the General Assembly, a position to which he was reelected five times over the next two decades. He was speaker of the lower house of the legislature in 1785. From 1781 to 1791 he was register of probate for Windham County, and in 1788 a judge of the county court. In 1789 he was one of the commissioners who negotiated with New York a settlement of the disputed land claims that prepared the way for Vermont's admission into the Union in 1791. He was also a leader of the state convention of 1791 that ratified the U.S. Constitution.

In 1791 Bradley was elected to the U.S. Senate. On the expiration of his initial four-year term he was defeated in his bid for reelection by Elijah Paine, a popular judge of the state supreme court. Bradley was appointed to Paine's unexpired term in 1801 and was reelected to a full six-year term in 1806, remaining in the Senate until March 1813. An able, hard-working senator whose ready wit and boundless store of amusing anecdotes made him popular with his colleagues, Bradley twice served as president pro tempore of the Senate (1802–1803, 1808). Respected for his solid legal knowledge, he was called on to draft the Twelfth Amendment to the Constitution, approved in 1804, providing for separate electoral ballots for president and vice president.

The leading Democratic-Republican senator from New England during his day, Bradley was not blindly loyal to party leaders Thomas Jefferson and James Madison. He did not support President Jefferson's war with John Marshall and the federal judiciary, especially his impeachment of Associate Justice Samuel Chase, and he opposed his party's foreign policy. He organized the party caucus that nominated Madison for president in 1808, but he did not support Madison's 1810 decision to impose non-intercourse against

Great Britain unless that nation repealed its restrictions against American commerce. He strongly opposed war with England and earnestly counseled Madison against declaring it in 1812. Unable to prevent what he thought was "a needless war," Bradley left public life at the end of his Senate term in March 1813.

Bradley retired to Westminster, where he lived until 1818, when he moved to the neighboring village of Walpole. In his retirement he was active in the affairs of Middlebury College, whose charter he had been instrumental in obtaining in 1800, and which he served as fellow and trustee until 1830. He was married three times. By his first marriage on 16 May 1780 to Merab Atwater, he had one child, William Czar Bradley, who became a prominent Jacksonian Democrat and congressman. Following the death in 1782 of his first wife, Bradley married Thankful Taylor, and, following her death, Belinda Willard (dates and issue unknown). Bradley died at his home in Walpole.

• Bradley's principal collection of papers is among the Bradley Family Papers, 1774–1882 (Dalton Collection) at Duke University in Durham, N.C., which contains 775 items of personal and political correspondence along with legal and financial papers. Additional but less important collections are the Stephen Row Bradley Papers at the Boston Public Library, and a box of Bradley correspondence and papers in the Henry A. Willard II collection, Library of Congress. Short biographical sketches are in Franklin Bowditch Dexter, *Biographical Sketches of Yale College with Annals of the College History*, vol. 3 (1903); Benjamin H. Hall, *History of Eastern Vermont* (1858); and *Records of the Governor and Council of the State of Vermont*, vol. 2 (1874).

CHARLES D. LOWERY

BRADLEY, William Czar (23 Mar. 1782–4 Mar. 1867), politician and attorney, was born in Westminster, Vermont, the son of Stephen Row Bradley, an attorney and U.S. senator, and Merab Atwater, who died soon after his birth. He contracted scarlet fever at age two, and it is likely that the disease resulted in hearing loss, which became pronounced. During his early years Bradley lived with his grandparents in Cheshire, Connecticut, and began school at Charlestown, New Hampshire.

A precocious child, Bradley started writing poetry at age six, and by age twelve he had published a short pamphlet and undertaken the study of Hebrew after reading the Bible completely a number of times. This remarkable scholastic aptitude allowed Bradley to gain admission to his father's alma mater, Yale, at age thirteen, where he took great interest in foreign and ancient languages. He would continue to study languages and create poetry throughout his life. Bradley's tenure at Yale was brief, however, as he was expelled during his freshman year for putting a donkey in the university chapel. He denied committing the prank but confessed to others, and he was sent home. The stories of his displeased father's reaction conflict, as the youth was either condemned to farm labor or turned out of the home completely. Bradley eventually made his way to Amherst, Massachusetts, where he began studying law with Simeon Strong, a judge on the state supreme court. His efforts there and with a Mr. Ashmun in Blandford, Massachusetts, redeemed him in his father's eyes, and he was allowed to return to Westminster and continue his legal education in his father's office. At age nineteen, in 1801, Bradley was made secretary to the commissioner of bankruptcy for the town, and the following year he was admitted to the bar. He also got married in 1802, to the daughter of the lieutenant governor, Sara Richards, with whom he would have four children.

At age twenty Bradley asked the legislature for an underage exemption to practice before the state supreme court. The members chose not to set such a precedent but named Bradley the state's attorney for Windham County, a position that allowed him the same access to the high court that he had requested. He remained in that post until 1811, and in 1806 he began a political career with election to a two-year term in the legislature. In 1812 he was appointed to the Governor's Council, the forerunner of the state senate, and later in the year he was elected as a Democrat to the House, entering Congress at the time his father was retiring from the Senate. Unlike his father and many other Vermonters, however, Bradley was an outspoken supporter of James Madison's war policy. In Washington he became friends with several of the other young war hawks, including Henry Clay, John C. Calhoun, and Daniel Webster.

Impressing a number of influential people during his 1813–1815 House term with his knowledge and wit, Bradley was appointed in 1817 to help survey the boundary in the northeastern part of the country between the United States and Canada. The survey, stipulated by the Treaty of Ghent, was conducted under the auspices of the Treasury Department and took five years to complete. Bradley's position was agent to the commissioner, Cornelius Peter Van Ness, meaning that he supervised much of the field activity. When he met with Secretary of State John Quincy Adams in 1819 to give him a report on the proceedings, Adams was impressed with Bradley's diligence on the project, but found Bradley "so deaf that it is scarcely possible to hold a conversation with him" (Adams, *Memoirs* vol. 4, p. 211). The line, which for the most part was drawn along the forty-fifth parallel, was initially rejected by the British, but twenty years later it was adopted as part of the Webster-Ashburton Treaty. Bradley considered the survey his most important accomplishment.

Upon completion of his boundary work, Vermont returned Bradley to the House in 1823 and again in 1825. During the 1824 presidential election, fellow Vermont congressman Rollin C. Mallary told Adams that Bradley was aligned with William H. Crawford, but Adams recorded that "Mr. Bradley himself most distinctly and explicitly professes otherwise" (Adams, *Memoirs*, vol. 6, p. 232). Bradley did split with Adams, however, becoming an ardent Jacksonian Democrat. He went back to his law practice in 1827 but remained active in politics, although his party was in the minority in his home state. When the 1830 gubernatorial election was thrown into the legislature, Bradley was substituted for Democratic candidate Ezra Meech but did not win. A gifted orator and radical thinker, he was said to enjoy campaigning more than officeholding, especially if cast as an underdog. He ran unsuccessfully for governor in 1834 and 1838.

In 1848 Bradley became a member of the Free Soil party, and he returned to the state legislature, serving from 1850 to 1852. An elector for the Republican presidential ticket in 1856, he participated in the state constitutional convention the following year. Bradley retired from both politics and the bar in 1858 and spent his final years in Westminster, where he died.

An important public voice for his state for more than half a century, Bradley's best-remembered national service was helping establish the northeastern boundary between the United States and Canada.

• Bradley correspondence can be found in Sarah B. K. Willard, *A Tribute of Affection to the Memory of Hon. Wm. C. Bradley* (1869). Examples of his poetry are published in Frederick Frothingham, *In Memoriam: A Tribute to the Memory of William Czar Bradley* (1867), which was also issued as *A Tribute to the Memory of William Czar Bradley* (1867). The Treaty of Ghent commission report that was rejected by the British is found in Fred L. Israel, ed., *Major Peace Treaties of Modern History 1648–1967*, vol. 1 (1967), pp. 697–712. A biographical summary is Frank L. Fish, "William Czar Bradley 1782–1867," in *Proceedings of the Vermont Historical Society for the Years 1826–1828*, pp. 105–24. Several mentions of Bradley can be found in Charles Francis Adams, ed., *Memoirs of John Quincy Adams* (12 vols., 1877). An obituary appeared in the *Rutland Herald*, 7 Mar. 1867.

KENNETH H. WILLIAMS

BRADSHAW, Tiny (23 Sept. 1905–26 Nov. 1958), singer, drummer, and bandleader, was born Myron Carlton Bradshaw in Youngstown, Ohio. His parents' names are unknown. He played the drums from the age of ten and soon after was performing professionally as a drummer and vocalist. Early in his career he served as the drummer of the Jump Johnson Band in Buffalo, New York. He attended Wilberforce University in Wilberforce, Ohio, and majored in psychology. Before forming his own big band in 1934, he sang with Horace Henderson's Collegians and in New York either drummed or sang with Marion Hardy's Alabamians, the Savoy Bearcats, Mills Blue Rhythm Band (1932–1933), and Luis Russell (1933–1934).

Bradshaw's own band enjoyed long engagements in the ballrooms and nightclubs of Harlem (notably the Savoy and the Apollo), Philadelphia, and Chicago and toured throughout the United States and Europe, making its reputation with powerful, blues-based jazz. His band was introduced to the public at the Renaissance Ballroom in New York City in 1934. That same year it landed a recording contract with Decca and earned nationwide recognition. The performances and recordings of this ensemble typically featured the highly energized singing of its leader—a combination of blues belting, scat improvisations, and patter reminiscent of Cab Calloway, whom Bradshaw was known to greatly admire. In 1935 the teenaged Ella Fitzgerald won an amateur contest at the Harlem Opera House earning her a week of performances with the newly popular Bradshaw band; these performances with Bradshaw at the Harlem Opera House resulted in her first mention in the press and her introduction to bandleader Chick Webb, with whom she catapulted to national fame. A high rate of turnover in band membership suggests the continual financial and artistic challenges that Bradshaw faced over a fifteen-year period. Such constant changes in personnel, however, also reveal Bradshaw's uncanny ability to identify talent, especially among alto saxophonists. At one time or another his lineup included Russell Procope, Bill Johnson, George Dorsey, Bobby Plater, Sonny Stitt, and Gigi Gryce. With Bobby Plater and Edward Johnson, he composed the evergreen riff song "Jersey Bounce" (1942), which was popularized initially by Glenn Miller and later by Benny Goodman. During World War II, with the rank of major, Bradshaw led a large military show band that performed for the troops both at home and overseas. In 1945 he made a USO-sponsored tour of Japan and in the same year made his last big band recordings.

After World War II Bradshaw downsized his ensemble and shifted its emphasis to the rhythm and blues idiom, in which he achieved great popularity during the 1950s. Between 1949 and 1958 he was affiliated with the King label as leader, piano soloist, and accompanist. In the "jump" tradition he issued approximately sixty recordings and scored several hits, including "Big Town" with R&B vocalist Roy Brown and "Soft" (1953). Bradshaw's hard-driving instrumental pieces and novelty songs were among the models imitated by early rock and roll singers. Toward the end of his life, Bradshaw settled in Chicago, where he worked regularly until two strokes brought his 35-year entertainment career to a close. He died in Cincinnati, Ohio.

In his assessment of Bradshaw's early work, Gunther Schuller praised the bandleader's own jazz-oriented singing and the consistent quality of the solos of trumpeter Shad Collins and alto saxophonist Procope, as well as the effective integration of improvised solos into arrangements, while faulting the formulaic nature of the arrangements themselves. Putting Bradshaw's big band in the context of its era, Schuller wrote, "Bradshaw and his band were a rhythmically exciting, hard-swinging group, perhaps not exactly ahead of its time in that respect, but certainly undeviatingly committed to a strong propulsive swing as the essence of jazz—at a time when so many bands could not swing at all or reserved it only for special up-tempo instrumental numbers" (pp. 423–24). Summarizing Bradshaw's achievement, Schuller continued: "With jazz and the blues always at his side, he was swinging long *before* swing arrived in full force and long *after* it had disappeared" (p. 425).

• Scholarly assessment of Bradshaw's life and career is scant. His ensemble is discussed briefly in Albert McCarthy, *Big Band Jazz* (1974), and Gunther Schuller, *The Swing Era: The Development of Jazz, 1930–1945* (1978). A list of his recordings is given in Kurt Mohr, *Discography of Tiny Bradshaw* (1961), and Roger D. Kinkle, *The Complete Encyclopedia of Popular Music and Jazz, 1900–1950* (1974).

MICHAEL J. BUDDS

BRADSTREET, Anne (c. 1612–16 Sept. 1672), poet, was born in England, probably in Northampton, the second child and eldest daughter of Dorothy Yorke and Thomas Dudley, steward to Theophilus Clinton, the earl of Lincoln. No state records remain of Bradstreet's birth or marriage, and no one knows the location of her grave. Yet she came from a prominent family and attained individual fame. Her mother's extraction and estate were described by Cotton Mather as "considerable," and her father served as deputy governor and, later, governor of Massachusetts. She did not attend school but was well and widely educated at home. From about age six to age sixteen, she lived at Sempringham in Lincolnshire and had the run of the earl of Lincoln's vast library. Her poems reveal a wide range of specific references to the Geneva Bible, the Greek and Latin classics, and to such later writers as Edmund Spenser, Sir Philip Sidney, Elizabeth I, and Francis Quarles. Her historical poems benefit from a detailed knowledge of Sir Walter Raleigh's *History of the World* (1614), and she acknowledged as an inspiration for her own poetry Joshua Sylvester's translation of *The Divine Weekes and Workes* (1605) of the French Calvinist Guillaume Du Bartas.

During Bradstreet's early years, according to her letter "To My Dear Children," she "began to make conscience of my ways" and to find "much comfort in reading the Scriptures, especially those places I thought most concerned my condition," a focus that characterized her religion throughout her life. There was little eschatology in Bradstreet's writing and no asceticism. Though she prayed that God would "wean" her affections from an immoderate love for the things of this world, her attention remained on them as both facts and metaphors, "for were earthly comforts permanent, who would look for heavenly?" In adolescence, "about 14 or 15, I found my heart more carnal, and sitting loose from God," but "vanity and the follies of youth" were repented of at sixteen, a remarkable year in which she survived smallpox, experienced conversion, and married Simon Bradstreet.

In 1630 Bradstreet and her husband journeyed with the Winthrop party on board the *Arbella* to Salem, "where I found a new world and new manners, at which my heart rose." Whatever the precise cause of her anger, her life in this new world was far from easy. She "fell into a lingering illness, like a consumption," and in convalescence she wrote her earliest extant poem, "Upon a Fit of Sickness, Anno 1632. Aetatis suae, 19." That same year, she became pregnant with Samuel, the first of her eight children. Though this second mode of production was more conventionally approved than the first, Bradstreet linked the two. In the early years of her marriage, she worried that her apparent barrenness might result from God's displeasure. Those fears were eased by pregnancy and promptly replaced by another, the fear of dying in childbirth. At such times, it was prudent to leave behind some record for one's family. And Bradstreet's description of her message to her children might serve just as well for her poetry: "I have not studied in this you read to show my skill, but to declare the truth, not to set forth myself, but the glory of God." Writing poetry was a form of meditation, a way of acknowledging God's metaphoric linking of this world with the next, and one way to make somewhat more durable a world both beautiful and transient, "No sooner blown, but dead and gone, / ev'n as a word that's speaking." For the next thirty-seven years, she continued to write poems, which she sometimes enfigured as children.

The years were filled with public event. Bradstreet was among the founders of Newtowne (later Cambridge) in 1631, lived at Ipswich (1635–1645), and was among the settlers of North Andover, where she lived from 1645 until her death. Her husband held a series of public offices as judge, agent, and commissioner during her life and would later become governor, yet hers were not occasional or public poems.

By 1642 she had completed her "Quaternions" on the four elements, humors, ages, seasons, and monarchies. These erudite poems ranged over science, religion, and history, yet they were dedicated to her father in thanks for his part in the education here displayed, and they were focused on what such knowledge might teach a soul journeying through time on the way to eternity.

In 1650 Bradstreet's poems became public when John Woodbridge, the husband of her sister Mercy, took her poems to London, where they were published by Stephen Bowtell, apparently without her permission. However conventional such disclaimers of authorship might have been in her time, there is no evidence that Bradstreet had a chance to edit the manuscript before publication, and it is not likely that she would have chosen the title, *The Tenth Muse Lately sprung up in America. Or Severall Poems, compiled with great variety of Wit and Learning . . . By a Gentlewoman in those parts.* The book was well received and listed in 1658 in William London's *Catalogue of the Most Vendible Books in England.* In subsequent years, Bradstreet revised these early poems and added eighteen others for a second edition, published in Boston in 1678 as *Several Poems . . . By a Gentlewoman in New England.*

Bradstreet was the first American to publish a book of poetry. Her work was highly valued in her time (hers was the only book of poetry found in Edward Taylor's library at his death), devalued in the nineteenth century, and appreciated anew in the twentieth. It is avowedly Puritan but multivocal, sometimes patriarchal, sometimes feminist. Her "Prologue" humors masculine supremacy ironically, while her poem on Queen Elizabeth is more direct and explicit:

Nay masculines, you have thus taxed us long,
But she, though dead, will vindicate our wrong.
Let such as say our sex is void of reason,
Know 'tis a slander now but once was treason.

Her later poems are more personal in their subject matter, but throughout Bradstreet's work the largest issues and greatest truths find expression in humble details, and those details are in turn examined for what they will reveal of God. For that reason, her speakers are humble but not patient: "But he's a beetle-head that can't descry / A world of wealth within that rubbish lie." Her work enacted the quest to find the wealth within the rubbish. For all her doubts about God's will and human actions, Bradstreet was no rebel. Unlike her younger sister Sarah, she was never accused of "irregular prophecying." Indeed, her contemporaries and such successors as Cotton Mather heaped praises upon the poetry in which their own beliefs were so profoundly questioned.

In Bradstreet's work, such paradoxes argue not hypocrisy but integrity. She was what she appeared to be—a poet, a woman, and a Puritan—and her work continues to suggest how complex such categories can be.

• A small notebook containing poetry and prose not in the first two editions of Bradstreet's work belongs to the Stephens Memorial Library in North Andover, Mass. Part of it is in Bradstreet's own handwriting and part of it in the hand of her son Simon. The Houghton Library at Harvard University owns another manuscript of the same material in the same order, except for a passage dated "May 11, 1661"; it is in the hand of her daughter, Sarah Hubbard. This material was first published in *The Works of Anne Bradstreet, in Prose and Verse*, ed. John Harvard Ellis (1867). The best modern editions are *The Works of Anne Bradstreet*, ed. Jeannine Hensley (1967), and *The Complete Works of Anne Bradstreet*, ed. Joseph R. McElrath, Jr., and Allan P. Robb (1981).

An early account of Bradstreet's life is Cotton Mather's *Magnalia Christi Americana* (1702). A good modern biography is Elizabeth Wade White, *Anne Bradstreet: The Tenth Muse* (1971). See also Ann Stanford, *Anne Bradstreet: The Worldly Puritan* (1975), for an overview of Bradstreet's reading and a suggested chronology of her writings; Robert Daly, *God's Altar: The World and the Flesh in Puritan Poetry* (1978), for the role her poetry played in her life, in "weaning" her affections from the love of this world; Ivy Schweitzer, *The Work of Self-Representation: Lyric Poetry in Colonial New England* (1991), for Bradstreet's challenge to conventional readings of gender; and Rosamond Rosenmeier, *Anne Bradstreet Revisited* (1991), for the best reading of Bradstreet's life and work in light of current knowledge and theory, and for an annotated bibliography.

ROBERT DALY

BRADSTREET, John (21 Dec. 1714–25 Sept. 1774), British army officer, was born in Annapolis Royal, Nova Scotia, the son of Edward Bradstreet, a lieutenant of the British Fortieth Regiment in Nova Scotia, and Agathe de St. Etienne de la Tour. On 12 March 1715 he was baptized Jean-Baptiste Bradstreat. After his father's death in 1718, his mother, who was from an old and wealthy Nova Scotian family, married another English army officer, Hugh Campbell.

Bradstreet purchased an ensign's commission (dated 23 Aug. 1735) and was stationed at the army garrison at Canso, Nova Scotia. Sometime after 1739 he married Mary Aldridge, the widow of a kinsman by the same name (Lieutenant John Bradstreet). They had two children.

At Canso Bradstreet found time to engage in trade and fishing. Throughout his army career he found ways to profit in side endeavors. At the outbreak of King George's War, Bradstreet, by then a lieutenant, was captured at Canso by the French and imprisoned at Louisbourg until paroled at Boston and then exchanged. Supposedly while in Boston he convinced Governor William Shirley to employ Massachusetts troops to attack Louisbourg. As an unofficial lieutenant colonel, he was second in command of a regiment of Massachusetts troops involved in the capture of Louisbourg in 1745. As a reward for his services Bradstreet was promoted to captain in the British army and appointed on 16 September 1746 as governor of St. John's in Newfoundland. Always ambitious, Bradstreet left for England in the fall of 1751 primarily to seek military preferment; he returned to America in March 1755 and joined the British Fifty-first Regiment in New York.

When the French and Indian War began, Shirley, soon to be the British commander in chief in America, placed Bradstreet in charge of transporting supplies from Schenectady to Oswego. Bradstreet commanded 2,000 bateaumen and received the unofficial title of lieutenant colonel, though still a captain in the British army. On 3 July 1756 Bradstreet and his men encountered a small French detachment, eight miles from Oswego, and after "a Sharpe fight . . . in the Indian Way" drove off the enemy. On 8 May 1757 he was appointed captain of the Sixtieth Regiment of Royal Americans (regular British troops raised in America). In December 1757 he was promoted to lieutenant colonel and deputy quartermaster general. Bradstreet is credited, with others, with convincing the Pitt ministry on the battle strategy for the remainder of the war.

After participating in the disastrous British-American defeat before Fort Ticonderoga, Bradstreet led an expedition against Fort Frontenac (now Kingston, Ontario). With 2,737 troops and bateaumen, he forced the French garrison (undermanned with only 110 men) to surrender on 27 August 1758, seizing seventy-six cannon and a large amount of military stores. He missed the opportunity, however, to push on to Fort Niagara (manned by forty French soldiers) and to gain control of Lake Ontario. For the rest of the war, Bradstreet performed his duties in the quartermaster department at Albany. In 1762 he received the rank that he so long coveted, colonel in the British army.

When Pontiac's Rebellion occurred, Bradstreet was again called on for field command. In 1764 he was given charge of one of the two punitive expeditions against the Ohio Indians. While Colonel Henry Bouquet set out from Fort Pitt for the Delaware and Shawnee villages, Bradstreet, with 1,404 troops, moved from Niagara toward Detroit, under orders from General Thomas Gage to strike at the Indians in upper Ohio on the way. At Presque Isle (now Erie, Pennsylvania) he met with ten Indians who presented themselves as emissaries of the Delawares and Shawnees. Bradstreet and these Indians agreed to peace terms, and Bradstreet thereby canceled campaigning in the Ohio country. He notified Bouquet to do the same. Bradstreet reached Detroit on 27 August 1764 and there held a conference with delegates from the Ottawas, Hurons, Chippewas, and Potawatomies on 5–7 September. Again Bradstreet thought he obtained a treaty of peace and submission. However, he soon found that the treaties were repudiated by his superiors and that the non-treaty tribes, the Delawares and Shawnees, remained on the warpath. Thus Bradstreet's "bloodless" conquest of the Indians proved an empty one. General Gage wrote Bradstreet on 15 October 1764, "They have negotiated with you on Lake Erie and cut our throats upon the frontiers." Bradstreet's naiveté in dealing with the Indians greatly tarnished his military reputation. Foremost in Bradstreet's mind was the securing of a peace that would pave the way for establishment of a colony at Detroit, where he would be governor and profit from the lucrative fur trade. Unfortunately for his plans, the British government continued to curtail westward expansion. Undaunted, Bradstreet also sought, unsuccessfully, an Indian superintendency.

Because of Bradstreet's rumored marital infidelity and his long absences from his family, his family departed for England in 1765, never to return; the expense of their support abroad drained his finances.

Bradstreet desired to be a great landed proprietor. He saw such an opportunity when the Treaty of Fort Stanwix (1768) moved the Indian boundary beyond much of western New York. He presented to authorities in New York and in England a claim to 300,000 acres between the Susquehanna and Delaware rivers, a deed he had obtained by purchase from the Oneida Indians. The British board of trade, the secretary of state for America (Lord Hillsborough), and the New York government denied Bradstreet's request. At the time of his death he claimed only 5,000 acres of the original tract. Bradstreet, however, in partnership with others, acquired other landholdings. At the time of his death he owned at least 15,212 acres in addition to an estate worth £15,000 sterling, which included English investments.

Bradstreet was embittered during his last years over failure to receive appointment as governor of either New York or Massachusetts, or as commander of the British middle district in America. Promoted to major general in the British army in 1772, he hoped to succeed General Gage as commander in chief in America. However, his health failed. He died in New York City of a combination of cirrhosis of the liver and dropsy. An obituary in the *New-York Gazetteer* (29 Sept. 1774) noted a funeral with full military honors.

• Bradstreet papers are found in many libraries, most notably the American Antiquarian Society, the National Library of Wales, the Public Archives of Canada, the New York State Library, the Public Archives of Nova Scotia, in the General Thomas Gage Papers at the Clements Library, and the Generals Abercromby and Loudoun papers at the Henry E. Huntington Library, San Marino, Calif. The 300 letters and other manuscripts at the American Antiquarian Society are catalogued in "A Calendar of the Manuscripts of Col. John Bradstreet in the Library of the Society," American Antiquarian Society, *Proceedings*, n.s., 19 (1908): 103–81. Published Bradstreet materials include "Will of Gen. John Bradstreet, 23 Sept. 1774," *New England Genealogical and Historical Register* 16 (1862): 315–16; Charles Whittlesey, ed., "Papers Relating to the Expeditions of Colonel Bradstreet and Colonel Bouquet, in Ohio, A.D. 1764," *Western Reserve and Northern Ohio Historical Society Tracts*, nos. 13, 14 (1873); Franklin B. Hough, ed., *Diary of the Siege of Detroit in the War with Pontiac* (1860); and Louis E. De Forest, ed., *Louisbourg Journals 1745* (1932), which includes "Colonel Bradstreet's Journal." See also "The Claims of Col. John Bradstreet to Lands in America," American Antiquarian Society, *Transactions and Collections* 11 (1909): 101–31. Of useful reference is Stanley Pargellis, ed., *Military Affairs in North America, 1748–1765: Selected Documents from the Cumberland Papers in Windsor Castle* (1936). The only biography is thoroughly researched and interpretive as to Bradstreet's proposals and ideas that relate to the British empire in America: William G. Godfrey, *Pursuit of Profit and Preferment in Colonial North America: John Bradstreet's Quest* (1982).

HARRY M. WARD

BRADSTREET, Simon (Feb. or Mar. 1604–27 Mar. 1697), colonial statesman and governor of Massachusetts, was born in Horbling, Lincolnshire, England, and was baptized on 18 March 1604, the son of Simon Bradstreet, vicar of Horbling, and Margaret (maiden name unknown). In 1617 he entered Emmanuel College, Cambridge (of which his father had been a fellow), and received the degrees of B.A. in 1620 and M.A. in 1624. Between 1621 and 1624 he served as assistant to Thomas Dudley, steward to the earl of Lincoln, and then became steward to the dowager countess of Warwick. These connections led to his first marriage, probably in 1628, to Dudley's eldest daughter, Anne, soon to win renown as the poet Anne Bradstreet, and to association with the company of Puritan gentry planning to immigrate to New England. On 18 March 1630, at a meeting in Southampton, Bradstreet was elected an assistant in the newly chartered Massachusetts Bay Company and assumed duties as its secretary. Two weeks later he sailed for America with his wife and the Dudley family in the fleet led by Governor John Winthrop (1588–1649).

In Massachusetts, where the company transformed itself into a colony, Bradstreet settled in Cambridge and continued his administrative tasks. He served as colony secretary until 1636 and, except during the period of direct royal government between 1686 and 1689, continued to be annually reelected to the magistracy (first as assistant, then in 1678 as deputy governor, and, from 1679, as governor) until his retirement in 1692, the longest recorded service of any colonial New England official. Throughout, he sat on numerous General Court committees. He was especially active in the negotiations that in 1643 created the New England Confederation, an alliance between the colonies of Massachusetts, Plymouth, Connecticut, and New Haven. He served as commissioner or alternate from Massachusetts to the confederation for twenty-four of the next thirty-four years.

In political affairs, Bradstreet consistently positioned himself as a moderate anxious to play down authoritarian tendencies in government and conflicts with the outside world. He sided with the Massachusetts deputies against a majority of his fellow magistrates in a prolonged debate over the degree of discretionary authority to be accorded the magistrates in the day-to-day business of government, and he strove to moderate the punishments inflicted on Robert Child when Child tried to appeal beyond Massachusetts to the English Parliament in 1646 for greater civil liberties and a Presbyterian system of church organization within the colony. Bradstreet joined other Essex County magistrates in 1643 in protesting Winthrop's policy of intervening in a dispute over who was the legitimate ruler of French Acadia (Nova Scotia). In 1661, after the restoration of the English monarchy, he was chosen, with Boston minister John Norton (1606–1663), to travel to London in an effort to allay the Crown's reputed hostility to Puritan Massachusetts. Arriving in England the following spring, the two emissaries quickly secured a royal letter confirming the Massachusetts charter and pardoning past offenses. Upon their return in 1663, however, they found that the letter's other provisions, commanding greater religious toleration and a suffrage no longer restricted to church members, only confirmed suspicions among colonists opposed to the mission that Bradstreet had been too passive in presenting their case for virtual autonomy from the Crown.

These fears did not prevent Bradstreet's election as governor in 1679, as England was again pressing Massachusetts for greater conformity to royal authority. But they produced sharp political divisions during his term of office. Some denounced him by 1684 as so accommodating to visiting royal officials as to be an enemy to his own colony. Others, such as his allies Joseph Dudley and William Stoughton, pressed him to bend still further to London's demands. Once more, Bradstreet steered a middle course. He bowed to the Crown's eventual nullification of the Massachusetts charter but refused to accept office in the royally governed Dominion of New England, imposed in place of charter rule in 1686, on the ground that its authoritarian structure abridged the colonists' liberties. When, on 18 April 1689, the dominion and its governor, Sir Edmund Andros, were overthrown by an armed uprising in Boston, the aged Bradstreet was brought out of retirement to serve as president of a council of safety and then, after June, as governor in a restored charter administration, a post he held despite increasing physical weakness until the arrival of a new royal governor, Sir William Phips, in May 1692. From February 1690 until 1692 his governorship also extended over the neighboring province of New Hampshire.

Bradstreet's long political service won him respect and renown as "the Nestor of New England." Jasper Danckaerts, a Dutch visitor to Boston in 1680, found that the "quiet and grave" governor "dwelt in only a common house, and that not the most costly. . . . He was dressed in black silk, but not sumptuously." Joshua Scottow, in "A Narrative of the Planting of the Massachusets Colony" (1694), hailed Bradstreet as "the only surviving Antiquary of us Nov-Angles, the Prime Secretary and Register of our civil and sacred Records, and the Bifronted Janus who saw the Closure of the Old and the Overture of this New-Albion World." Anne Bradstreet's verse provides a more intimate portrait: "If ever two were one, then surely we," she began the lines addressed "To My Dear and Loving Husband" (1678). Together, they raised four sons and four daughters, "eight birds hatcht in one nest," all of whom married into the colony's most prominent families. From Cambridge, the Bradstreets moved to Ipswich in 1635 and, by 1646, to the frontier settlement of Andover (what is now North Andover). After Anne's death in 1672, Bradstreet lived in Boston. In 1676 he married Anne Downing Gardner, thirty years his junior and a niece of former governor John Winthrop. The marriage was childless, and the couple passed their final years at Salem, where Bradstreet died.

Bradstreet never ranked among the wealthier men of the colony, and he took no lasting interest in mercantile affairs. But with the frequent grants of land given him for his public service he became a leading property developer and absentee proprietor, owning lands that fell within the boundaries of the towns of Hadley, Topsfield, Andover, Salisbury, and Lynn, together with large tracts in Maine. After 1660 he was an active member of the Atherton Company, a powerful group of speculators seeking to develop the Narragansett territories between Rhode Island and Connecticut. His 1689 will disposed of over fifteen hundred acres of land in Massachusetts alone.

Bradstreet's life spanned and exemplified many of the themes of the Puritan colonists' transition from old to New England—from primitive settlement to royal province and from the migration of individual families to the creation of a complex social order. Less ardently religious—to judge by his writings—than many of his fellow leaders, Bradstreet was nonetheless a firm opponent of groups such as the Quakers whom he perceived as threatening New England's domestic peace and purity. In the face of external authority, by contrast, he preferred diplomacy to confrontation. Bradstreet inspired unusual respect and affection among his contemporaries, and his life is powerful testimony to the vitality and cohesion of the political community they created.

• Bradstreet's public service is detailed in Nathaniel Shurtleff, ed., *Records of the Governor and Company of the Massachusetts Bay* (1853–1854) and in the New England Confederation records printed in Shurtleff and David Pulsifer, eds.,

Records of the Colony of New Plymouth in New England, vols. 9 and 10 (1855–1861). His correspondence with the London government is excerpted in *Calendar of State Papers, Colonial Series*, vols. 10–13, and more fully for one period in Robert E. Moody and Richard C. Simmons, eds., *The Glorious Revolution in Massachusetts: Selected Documents, 1689–1692* (1988). Cotton Mather, *Magnalia Christi Americana* (1702), bk. 2, ch. 5, contains a contemporary life of Bradstreet; a portrait is in the Boston Athenaeum. A record of his 1604 baptism, suggesting a birth later than the traditional date of 1603, is in *New England Historical and Genealogical Register*, vol. 48 (1894), p. 169. See also Elizabeth Wade White, *Anne Bradstreet* (1971), for Bradstreet's domestic life; Robert E. Wall, *Massachusetts Bay: The Crucial Decade, 1640–1650* (1972), and Jonathan M. Chu, *Neighbors, Friends, or Madmen* (1985), for his part in local politics; John F. Martin, *Profits in the Wilderness* (1991), for his landholdings; and Thomas Hutchinson, *History of the Colony and Province of Massachusetts-Bay*, ed. L. S. Mayo (1936), and Richard R. Johnson, *Adjustment to Empire: The New England Colonies, 1675–1715* (1981), for the larger political context of his life.

RICHARD R. JOHNSON

BRADWELL, James Bolesworth (16 Apr. 1828–29 Nov. 1907), lawyer and publisher, was born in Loughborough, England, the son of Thomas Bradwell and Elizabeth Guthredge, farmers. He came to the United States with his family in 1829, settling first in Utica, New York. In 1833 they moved to west-central Illinois and later to Chicago, making the last journey by covered wagon in 1834. They remained in Chicago only a short time before moving to a site near Wheeling, where they lived in a log cabin. As an adult, Bradwell enjoyed recounting the hardships of his early days in Illinois, which included attacks by Indians.

Bradwell attended Knox College in Galesburg, Illinois, but did not graduate. After leaving college, he was a journeyman in various trades in Chicago before moving to Tennessee, where he studied law and was admitted to the bar. He married Myra Colby in 1852; they had four children, two of whom died in childhood. Both he and his wife taught school in Memphis for a short time before they returned to Chicago.

Bradwell was admitted to the Illinois bar in 1855. His practice there took him to the heights of the legal profession: he was elected president of the Chicago Bar Association (1885) and the Illinois State Bar Association (1890). Early in his half-century of practicing law in Chicago, he served two terms as a judge for Cook County, being elected in 1861 and reelected in 1865. He declined to stand for a third term, preferring instead to return to practice. His partnership with General John Beveridge lasted until Bradwell's retirement. During his judicial service he was renowned as a learned and sensitive probate judge. One of his decisions, validating a marriage between slaves, illustrated his opposition to slavery. He rejected an argument that all precedents were opposed to his decision, writing, "Were there a thousand of these decisions . . . I would brush them aside as I would a spider's web, and decide this case upon what I consider to be the first principles of law—justice and humanity." He also aided runaway slaves, and during the Civil War he strongly supported the Union against local "copperheads."

Bradwell assisted his wife, Myra C. Bradwell, in the management and editing of the *Chicago Legal News*, the first legal journal in the West, which she founded in 1868. He continued its publication after her death in 1894. He served two terms in the Illinois House of Representatives, being elected in 1873 and 1875. During his service, he successfully sponsored bills making women eligible to all school offices and to serve as notaries public. Before that he had been active in the women's suffrage movement. He chaired the organizational meeting of the American Woman Suffrage Association in Cleveland (1869). In addition, he was instrumental in having women admitted to Northwestern University. He was the reporter for the first twenty volumes of the Illinois appellate court reports (1877–1887). At the time of his death, Bradwell still lived in Chicago and served as editor of the *Chicago Legal News*.

Although overshadowed by his wife's historic role as a woman lawyer, Bradwell's life nevertheless mirrored the history of nineteenth-century America, from his humble immigrant and pioneer beginnings to his success as lawyer and statesman. In addition, he never lost his interest in other activities; he was an innovator in photography (he invented a process for half-tone work) as well as a skillful rifleman (he was reputed to be the best shot in Chicago at one time). Bradwell's professional life was identified with the century's legal reform, from the abolitionist movement and women's rights to the organization of the bar.

• The most complete source of information about Bradwell is his obituary in the *Chicago Legal News* 40 (30 Nov. 1907): 126, and two following issues, 40 (7 Dec. 1907): 134, and 40 (14 Dec. 1907): 142. See also J. M. Palmer, ed., *The Bench and Bar of Illinois*, vol. 2 (1899), pp. 831–32.

WALTER F. PRATT, JR.

BRADWELL, Myra Colby (12 Feb. 1831–14 Feb. 1894), publisher and political activist, was born in Manchester, Vermont, the daughter of Eben Colby and Abigail Willey. She spent her childhood in Vermont and western New York, and when she was twelve, her family moved to Illinois. She attended local schools in Wisconsin and Illinois and became a schoolteacher. In 1852 she married James Bradwell. They moved to Memphis where James headed a private school and Myra became a teacher in the school. After two years, they relocated to Chicago, and James became a member of the bar and eventually an Illinois circuit court judge and state legislator. They had four children, but two died young.

Reflecting the influence of her abolitionist family, Bradwell raised funds during the Civil War for the care of wounded soldiers and the support of their widows and orphans. She also served as a member of the Northwestern Sanitary Commission, a post she utilized to good advantage, as did other women of her time, to improve her organizational skills.

Bradwell refused to accept the narrow social role society allowed women. In October 1868 she established the *Chicago Legal News*, the first weekly law journal published in the Midwest and eventually the most widely read. Through her husband's influence, she obtained a special charter exempting her from the state law that prevented married women from entering into contractual arrangements. She served as both editor and business manager of the *News*, and the paper's success was testimony to her skill as a businesswoman and publisher. Under her direction the Chicago Legal News Company published other periodicals and printed and sold stationery and legal forms to a wide clientele.

Bradwell intended to make her paper one "that every lawyer and business man in the Northwest ought to take." Each week she published the opinions in recent state and federal court cases and other legal information. The *News* took on a muckraking function as Bradwell attacked lawyers and judges for incompetence and moral deficiency, urged railroad regulation, and advocated reforms at Cook County courthouse. Her courage and strength of character were demonstrated by the fact that she continued publication of the newspaper after the offices were destroyed by the Great Chicago Fire in 1871.

Bradwell was deeply committed to changing women's second-class status. Using her column, "Law Relating to Women," to urge legal and political equality, she advocated equality in property rights, service on juries, and law school admissions. Insisting that equality for women was not a partisan issue, she exhorted state officials of both parties to end discrimination against women in employment and allow women greater control over their property. The *News* also provided editorial support to women around the country seeking to obtain law licenses in their own states.

Bradwell assisted in writing the Illinois Married Woman's Property Act of 1861 and the Earnings Act of 1869, bills intended to give married women control over their earnings and property. She used her financial status and legal knowledge to successfully lobby the Illinois legislature in Springfield to secure passage of these bills; Elizabeth Cady Stanton, Mary Livermore, and Catharine Waite joined in the lobbying efforts.

Bradwell wanted to be a lawyer at a time when few women were practicing attorneys. Her ambition was first limited to assisting her lawyer husband with research and writing. She worked in his firm before and after the Civil War, determined to become a lawyer herself. At the time, admission to the bar typically followed reading law in a lawyer's office and demonstrating competence and character. In August 1869 an Illinois Seventh Circuit judge and state's attorney examined Bradwell, pronounced her qualified, and recommended to the state supreme court that she be issued a license, but the court denied her application. In a letter to her in October 1869, the clerk of the court noted the court's assumption that she was married and under a legal disability that prevented her from entering into contracts, as attorneys must necessarily do. Bradwell asked the court to reconsider, arguing that under Illinois law marriage was not grounds for disqualification to practice law because the statutes allowing married women to own property should be interpreted as allowing them to enter into contracts as well.

On 5 February 1870, in *In re Bradwell*, the Illinois high court again denied her claim. The court rejected her argument that married woman have a right to contract, emphasizing that married women were only bound by contracts pertaining to their own property. The court stressed that its major objection to her licensure stemmed from the fact that state law prohibited all women, single or married, from practicing law. In an opinion by Chief Justice Charles B. Lawrence, the court stated it had "no doubt" as to her qualifications, but it was "the sex of the applicant . . . [that was] a sufficient reason for not granting the license." Analyzing the legislative intent of the licensing statute, the court found that when the Illinois legislature granted it the right to license attorneys it never contemplated conferring licenses on women. That "God designed the sexes to occupy different spheres of action, and that it belonged to men to make, apply and execute laws, was regarded as an almost axiomatic truth," ruled the court. Because the court grounded its decision on the basis of her sex, rather than on her marital status, it was able to avoid addressing the question she raised: whether married women could make binding contracts in their own names.

Bradwell attacked the court's decision through her editorials in the *News* and filed a writ of error in the U.S. Supreme Court. She acquired the services of Senator Matthew Hale Carpenter to represent her. In his oral argument on 18 January 1872, Carpenter stated that the right to a livelihood was protected by the privileges and immunities clause of the Fourteenth Amendment and that, by refusing Bradwell admission to the bar, the state violated this constitutional provision.

In a 7 to 1 vote in the spring of 1873, the Supreme Court affirmed the state high court ruling by narrowly interpreting the privileges and immunities clause. The Court held in *Bradwell v. Illinois* that this clause only provides protection against state abridgement of a limited number of rights of national citizenship and that "the right to admission to practice in the courts of a State is not one of them."

Although the Court's majority opinion did not address Bradwell's "womanhood," the concurring opinion by Justice Joseph Bradley denied that women enjoyed the same rights as men to pursue an occupation. He contended that their "natural and proper timidity and delicacy" prevented women from assuming an equal place beside men in the workforce. In addition, he noted that it was "the domestic sphere . . . which properly belongs to the domain and functions of womanhood" and that "the paramount destiny and mission of woman are to fulfil the noble and benign offices of wife and mother." While awaiting the Court's decision, Bradwell was disappointed by Illinois Governor

John Palmer's refusal to appoint her a notary public, despite the recommendation of sixty Chicago lawyers. Palmer attributed his refusal to her status as a married woman, saying that she could not execute the bond as the law required.

With the judiciary refusing to support their aspirations to become attorneys, women around the country organized in individual states to lobby legislatures to permit them to enter the legal profession. While Bradwell's appeal was pending before the U.S. Supreme Court, Alta M. Hulett, also of Illinois, was denied a license to practice law. Hulett, a single woman, drafted a bill with Bradwell's help to prohibit the state from enforcing occupational exclusion, except in the military, on the basis of sex. The bill was passed in March 1872, with help from Bradwell's lobbying, and Hulett became the first woman lawyer in Illinois in June 1873.

Bradwell was prominent in the woman suffrage movement on the national level and in Illinois. In 1869 she organized and spoke at a suffrage convention in Chicago and later served as secretary of the Illinois Woman Suffrage Association. Also in 1869 she and her husband joined with suffragists Lucy Stone and Henry Ward Beecher to form the American Woman Suffrage Association in Cleveland, and she served on its executive committee. That same year Elizabeth Cady Stanton and Susan B. Anthony founded the National Woman Suffrage Movement. Eventually, these two groups merged in 1890 to form the National American Woman Suffrage Association.

In 1876 the governor of Illinois appointed Bradwell the state's woman representative to the Centennial Exposition in Philadelphia and later as a delegate to the Prison Reform Congress in St. Louis. She was active in the successful drive to make Chicago the location of the World's Columbian Exposition in 1893. She was the first woman admitted to the Illinois Press Association and the Illinois Bar Association. She had been an honorary member of the state bar association since 1872 and eventually became a vice president and served in that office for four terms. She participated in the founding of the Chicago Bar Association and was a member of the Women's Club, the Daughters of the American Revolution, Eastern Star, the Grand Army of the Republic, the Women's Press Association, and the National Press League.

While Bradwell made no further efforts to gain a license to practice law in Illinois, the Illinois Supreme Court, acting on its own motion in 1890, approved her original application. Two years after her admission to the bar, on 28 March 1892, she was granted the right to appear before the U.S. Supreme Court.

Myra Bradwell died of cancer in Chicago. Her daughter, Bessie Bradwell Helmer, who graduated from Union College of Law (later Northwestern University) in 1882, published her mother's newspaper until 1925. Myra's husband and son, also a lawyer, continued to manage the printing company.

Myra Bradwell was a tireless worker on behalf of legal reform and women's rights in Illinois and the nation. She believed that women's lives should not be restricted by prevailing social norms. She also believed that her legal colleagues should conduct themselves with honor and integrity. Throughout her life she devoted great energy and devotion to her causes—fighting for an end to slavery and racial discrimination, greater equality and opportunity for women, and reforms related to the legal profession.

• For information on Myra Bradwell and the first women lawyers in America, see Charlotte Adelman, "A History of Women Lawyers in Illinois," *Illinois Bar Journal* (May 1986): 2–6; Meg Gorecki, "Legal Pioneers: Four of Illinois' First Women Lawyers," *Illinois Bar Journal* (October 1990): 510–15; Herman Kogan, *The First Century: The Chicago Bar Association 1874–1974* (1974); Martha Minow, "Forming Underneath Everything That Grows," *Wisconsin Law Review* (July–August 1985): 819–98; Karen Berger Morello, *The Invisible Bar* (1986); Frances Olsen, "From False Paternalism to False Equality: Judicial Assaults on Feminist Community, Illinois 1869–1895," *Michigan Law Review* (June 1986): 1518–41; and Marlene Stein Wortman, ed., *Women in American Law*, vol. 1 (1985). The two cases are reported in *In re Bradwell*, 55 Ill. 535 (1869), and *Bradwell v. Illinois*, 83 U.S. (16 Wall) 130 (1873). For information on woman suffrage generally, see Aileen Kraditor, *The Ideas of the Woman Suffrage Movement 1890–1920* (1965), and Eleanor Flexner, *Century of Struggle* (1959). Obituaries are in the *Chicago Legal News*, 17 and 24 Feb. and 12 May 1894.

SUSAN GLUCK MEZEY

BRADY, Alice (2 Nov. 1892–28 Oct. 1939), actress, was born in New York City, the daughter of William A. Brady, a prototypical producer in the twentieth-century American theater, and Marie Rose René, a Paris-born singer and dancer, who died when Alice was just a child. Her stepmother, Grace George, who began as a leading lady and matured into one of the finest stage comediennes of her time, was Alice's greatest mentor, and her half-brother William, Jr., was well on the road to becoming a successful producer when he died tragically in a fire.

Brady's father tried to shield her from the hurly-burly of Broadway by sending her first to the Convent of Saint Elizabeth in New Jersey and then to the New England Conservatory of Music in Boston. Because she possessed a sweet singing voice, he hoped that she could be trained as an opera singer, which he considered a reputable and honorable profession. However, the young Alice rebelled at the thought of spending a decade in training and launched her own career in 1909 by appearing, unbeknownst to her family, as a walk-on in the Robert Mantell production of *As You Like It* in Deal, New Jersey. She was listed on the program as "Marie Rose," her mother's given name. Although her father still disapproved, he allowed her to play one of the three little maids in his own production of *The Mikado* in 1910 in New York. The following year she appeared on Broadway under the name Marie Rose in *The Balkan Princess*, which failed almost immediately. Resigned to his daughter's career in the theater, William Brady gave her running parts in a series of Gilbert and Sullivan operettas, which he produced at the Lyric and Casino Theaters. In 1912 she scored her first personal success in a straight play as Meg in *Little Women* at the Playhouse. For the next two years, she appeared in a number of less than memorable plays and toured with the Gilbert and Sullivan company led by De Wolf Hopper.

In 1914 she began her movie career with an appearance in *As Ye Sow*, and in the following year she signed with her father's company, the World Film Corporation, and eventually played leading roles in a series of eighteen silent movies, the most successful of which were *The Gilded Cage* and *Bought and Paid For*. She returned to the stage in 1918 to star in Owen Davis's comedy *Forever After*. It ran for two years on Broadway and a year on the road and established her reputation as an actress of exceptional talent. During its run she married James Lyon Crane, an actor who played opposite her in several productions. The marriage produced one child before it broke up in 1922.

From 1923 to 1933 Brady played a succession of roles in mostly undistinguished plays. Nevertheless, she showed herself to be an actress of great versatility and emotional power. Some of the plays were presented under her own management. The high point of her career was the role of Lavinia in Eugene O'Neill's *Mourning Becomes Electra* (1931), one of four plays she did with the Theatre Guild. Richard Lockridge, theater critic of the *New York Sun*, described her performance: "Miss Brady, as the Electra of the play, is the spearhead of the whole—a spearhead utterly hard and tempered, driving with a force which seems to come from itself, icy and utterly final. To say that it is the best performance she has ever given is no faint praise, but it is too faint. It is one of the finest performances any contemporary actress has given in any role."

Of medium height, with black hair and pencil-thin eyebrows, she was also known as one of the best-dressed women in the theater. She prided herself on her other accomplishments: she spoke French, German, and Italian fluently, she was a proficient pianist and a fine singer, and she could also play the zither. She refused to be identified with any one kind of role, preferring a broad range of parts in both the theater and the movies.

In 1933 Brady returned to Hollywood to play in her first talking picture, *When Ladies Meet*, a screen version of Rachel Crothers's successful Broadway comedy. For several years she became typecast in Hollywood in fluttery female parts until she took on two serious roles at the end of her career as a film actress. For her portrayal of Mrs. O'Leary in *In Old Chicago* (1937), she won the award for best supporting actress from the Academy of Motion Picture Arts and Sciences, and in her last role, in John Ford's *Young Mr. Lincoln* (1939) opposite Henry Fonda, she received critical accolades. By then she was ill with cancer and returned east with her father to enter a sanitarium for treatment, where she died.

Alice Brady was, perhaps, one of the last of the actresses who had their roots in the late nineteenth century, the prototype of whom was an all-round performer who could play a variety of parts from light comedy to high tragedy, who could sing and dance, who could stride the vaudeville as well as the legitimate stage, who toured the country in popular roles, and who could take on a managerial role as well. Her transition to motion pictures was effected smoothly, and she became one of the earliest stars of both stage and screen.

• A clipping file on Alice Brady is in the New York Public Library for the Performing Arts. See also William A. Brady's *Showman* (1937). An obituary is in the *New York Herald Tribune*, 30 Oct. 1939.

MARY C. HENDERSON

BRADY, Cyrus Townsend (20 Dec. 1861–24 Jan. 1920), Episcopal clergyman and author, was born in Allegheny, Pennsylvania, the son of Jasper Ewing Brady, Jr., a banker and accountant, and Harriet Cora Townsend. He grew up in Leavenworth, Kansas, and graduated from the U.S. Naval Academy in 1883. Brady married Clarissa Sidney Guthrie in 1884; they had three children. After three years of naval service, he became a railroad worker for the Missouri Pacific and Union Pacific railroads. Under the influence of Bishop Worthington of Nebraska, he abandoned his native Presbyterianism and began to read for the Episcopal ministry in whatever hours he could snatch from his regular employment. He was ordained deacon in 1889 and priest in 1890, working mostly as an itinerant missionary in five western states. Brady estimated that in just three years he logged more than 90,000 miles "preaching or delivering addresses . . . marrying, baptizing, and doing all the other endless work of an itinerant missionary" (*Recollections of a Missionary in the Great West*, p. 78). Through this experience Brady developed a deep admiration for what he saw as the vitality, patience, and courage of the men and women of the developing American West, themes often recurring in his later writing. A year after his wife's death in 1890, Brady married Mary Barrett, and they had three children.

After serving as rector of Episcopal churches in Missouri and Colorado and as archdeacon of Kansas, Brady was called to Philadelphia to become archdeacon of Pennsylvania (1895–1899) and then rector of St. Paul's in Overbrook, Pennsylvania (1899–1902). He served as chaplain for the First Pennsylvania Volunteer Infantry during the Spanish-American War (1898), and this experience, together with his abilities as a raconteur, drew him toward a writing career. His first novel, *For Love of Country* (1898), set during the American Revolution, was followed in 1899 by *For Freedom of the Sea*, set during the War of 1812. Encouraged by the success of this work, Brady moved to Brooklyn and devoted himself full time to writing (1902–1905), publishing thirteen novels and historical works in three years. He resumed his ministerial career as rector of Trinity Church, Toledo, Ohio (1905–1909); St. George's Church, Kansas City, Missouri (1909–1913); and the Church of the Ascension, Mt.

Vernon, New York (1913–1914). His last post was assistant minister of St. Stephen's Church, New York City.

Brady's literary output continued unabated, totaling about sixty-six books and numerous short stories, essays, and some plays, published in rapid succession over twenty years. His work included popular biographies of John Paul Jones (1900), Stephen Decatur (1900), and Andrew Jackson (1906). He inaugurated a militantly patriotic series on American wars, including *American Fights and Fighters* (1900), *Colonial Fights and Fighters* (1901), *Border Fights and Fighters* (1902), *Indian Fights and Fighters* (1904), *The Conquest of the Southwest* (1905), and *North Western Fights and Fighters* (1907). His juvenilia and adventure stories, such as the Bob Dashaway series, novels of the sea, camp, and battlefield, and historical romances and love stories, were among the most popular of his time, selling rapidly and adapted in some instances for the stage and cinema. Some of his novels contain autobiographical material, such as *Under Tops'ls and Tents* (1901), which was based on his years at Annapolis and on naval training vessels, as well as on his war service in 1898, and *The Bishop* (1903), about life on the Great Plains. Others are set in remote places and times, such as *The Quiberon Touch* (1901), set in Brittany, and *The Fetters of Freedom* (1912), set in ancient Rome. Brady's characters often represented a virile, intelligent, two-fisted, stoic but tender-hearted ideal of American manhood and a strong-willed, pure but vulnerable womanhood stereotypical of the light literature of his time.

As a well-known preacher, Brady achieved national prominence by his outspoken opposition to woman suffrage, calling it "an insult to God and to man" and telling the Women's League for Political Education that the "average woman today" wanted not a vote but a husband. Upon the entry of the United States into World War I, he railed against "hyphenated Americans," "lukewarm patriots," and "alien propagandists" in his sermons and public addresses. His racial views were expounded in his novel *A Doctor of Philosophy* (1903), which assumed the inferiority of the "dull, unreceptive, superstitious slave-holden negro, so fondly and fatuously dowered with the highest gift of modern citizenship in a day" and whose white heroine commits suicide when she discovers that she is an octoroon.

Brady's fictional writing was at its best when describing scenes of battle. His output had no permanent literary value but was well suited to the popular reading tastes of his time and found a ready market. He died of pneumonia at his home in Yonkers, New York.

• Brady's personal papers and manuscripts are scattered among many collections. The largest holdings are in the Berg Collection, New York Public Library; New York University Library; and especially Princeton University Library. Some early writings of Brady on politics and Prohibition are contained in the papers of the Trinity Memorial Church of Crete, Nebraska, in the Nebraska State Historical Society, Lincoln. Autobiographical material is in *Recollections of a Missionary in the Great West* (1900), and family data are in William G. Murdock, *Brady Family Reunion and Fragments of Brady History and Biography* (1909), pp. 116–17. Obituaries are in the *New York Times*, 25 and 27 Jan. 1920; and the *New York Tribune*, 25 Jan. 1920.

BENJAMIN R. FOSTER

BRADY, Mathew B. (1823?–15 Jan. 1896), photographer and entrepreneur, was born near Lake George, New York, the son of Andrew Brady and Julia (maiden name unknown), poor, working-class parents of Irish heritage. His first name has often been misspelled *Matthew*; Brady himself did not know what his middle initial stood for. Little is known of his childhood and schooling, and there is some question as to how literate Brady was because others handled his correspondence and financial records. His signature is one of the few examples of his handwriting left behind.

In the late 1830s, young Brady developed an interest in art and painting that would later show up in his retouching and portrait composition work. Painter William Page took Brady to New York City in 1841 to meet and later study with Samuel F. B. Morse. Morse was teaching a class on the daguerreotype photographic process, which had been introduced in France two years earlier. During this time, Brady worked as a jewelry salesman at A. T. Stewart & Co. and then sold daguerreotype cases.

Brady became a professional daguerreotypist in 1844, opening his Daguerrean Miniature Gallery at Broadway and Fulton Street in New York City. Soon he began winning awards for his portraits, and his business was a success thanks to his promotional abilities. Brady's skill at retouching opened the door to the production of many different images from a single sitting, a common practice in the daguerreotype era.

In 1845 Brady began working on what would become a book, *The Gallery of Illustrious Americans*, which included a photograph of former president Andrew Jackson at the Hermitage shortly before he died. Credit for actually producing this historic daguerreotype, however, has been given to two other photographers, including Brady's friend and rival, Edward Anthony. *The Gallery*, published in 1850, was to be the first in a series of Brady's portraits of leading Americans. The series never materialized because the project was a financial flop.

A large staff worked for Brady at the gallery, including various cameramen or "operators," who actually exposed the daguerreotype plates (later wet-collodion negatives). By the 1860s Brady participated in the portrait sessions of just his most famous clients, although anything produced at his gallery was labeled "Photo by Brady." The corporate credit line was not considered an unethical business practice at the time.

Brady married Juliet "Julia" Elizabeth Handy, daughter of Maryland attorney Colonel Samuel Handy. They had no children. His wife's family money may have helped Brady finance the opening of a second gallery in Washington, D.C., in 1858 (an earlier attempt in 1847 had been a failure). Alexander Gardner, who came to the United States around 1855 from Scotland, handled everything at this branch office for

Brady, and he employed another young photographer, Timothy O'Sullivan.

On 27 February 1860 Brady photographed Abraham Lincoln for the first time in New York City before Lincoln's Cooper Union speech. Lincoln later credited the success of his presidential campaign to Brady's photograph and that speech. Brady's association with Lincoln was a fruitful one, especially with regard to Brady's famous coverage of the Civil War.

Under Brady's name appeared an eye-level chronicle of the war in pictures, showing the soldiers and their leaders, the bridges, the battlefields, the military camps, the locations where the sons of the North met the sons of the South. The camera technology of the day did not allow for images of men doing battle, but the aftermath could be captured on film at the era's slow shutter speeds.

Acknowledged throughout history textbooks and popular literature as the photographer of the Civil War, Brady was rather the mastermind and businessman behind this documentation, having actually taken very few of the images for which he is known. According to Alan Trachtenberg ("Brady's Portraits," p. 231), "He was the stage-manager of the first phase of photography in America: neither an innovator nor a great artist, not even for most of his career a practicing photographer, nevertheless he epitomized the entire photographic enterprise in antebellum America." It was not until 1949 that Alexander Gardner, for example, received credit for a portrait of Abraham Lincoln previously known as Brady's. In preparing for the Ansco Centennial Civil War Exhibition, researchers found other work previously credited to Brady that was taken by Gardner and his older brother James, Timothy O'Sullivan, D. B. Woodbury, Guy Fox, and other assistants.

In an attempt to show the public that he had actually been there, Brady inserted himself into various photographs taken at the front lines, thus enhancing his reputation as the Civil War photographer. He reportedly invested more than $100,000 in the documentation of the war.

Some sources say a rivalry between Gardner and Brady developed, and by 1862 Gardner left Brady's gallery, opening one of his own in Washington and luring away some of Brady's best operators, including O'Sullivan. Nevertheless, Gardner and Brady continued a professional relationship, which included Brady's purchase of some Gardner photographs after the battle of Gettysburg.

The departure of some of Brady's best photographers, however, seems to have had an adverse impact on his business. As early as 1864 workmen were filing nonpayment suits against him. The public's reluctance to dwell on the war once it was over also meant financial disaster for Brady, who petitioned Congress in 1869 with an offer to sell his negative collection. Finally, in 1875 Brady was able to raise $25,000 by selling 7,000 glass negatives to the federal government, which allowed much of his collection to be preserved while much of the work of the many anonymous photographers who worked for him has been lost or subsumed under Brady's name.

Brady eventually lost both his New York and his Washington galleries, nearing the end of his life in the employ of other gallery owners. After his wife died in 1887, his last years were spent in ill health, including near blindness. Brady died in the "alms ward" of New York's Presbyterian Hospital from injuries sustained in a street accident. He was buried in Arlington National Cemetery in Virginia.

The legend surrounding Brady as the photographer of the Civil War has lived on in spite of more recent revelations. Although he may not have done much of the actual photographing, Brady had the stature, the political connections, the financial resources, the equipment, and the employees to carry out his grand scheme of documenting the war between the states.

Thanks to his business acumen, Mathew Brady helped create, collect, and preserve a majority of the Civil War images and important political figures of the day. Thousands of his glass plate negatives are in the National Archives in Washington, D.C.

• Brady left behind very little written documentation, although George Alfred Townsend did interview him in "Brady, the Grand Old Man of American Photography: An Interview," *New York World*, 12 Apr. 1891, which was reprinted in *Essays & Images: Illustrated Readings in the History of Photography* (1980). What survived of Brady's glass plate negatives are in the National Archives in Washington, D.C., and 2,000 photographs are stored in the War College. Anthony & Company of New York had a less complete set, which Brady used to settle his bill with them for photographic supplies. William S. Johnson, *Nineteenth-Century Photography: An Annotated Bibliography* (1990), is an important source about Brady and his work as well as a great listing of where photographs credited to Brady were published during his lifetime. Also important for the mythology surrounding Brady's work is James Murphy, "Who Made Mathew Brady's Pictures?" *U.S. Camera Magazine*, Aug. 1961, pp. 50–55, and "Discoveries about Brady," *U.S. Camera Magazine*, Nov. 1949, pp. 22–23. See also Roy Meredith, *Mr. Lincoln's Camera Man, Matthew B. Brady* (1946), *Mr. Lincoln's Contemporaries: An Album of Portraits by Matthew B. Brady* (1951), and *The World of Matthew Brady: Portraits of the Civil War Period* (1971, repr. 1976); James D. Horan, *Matthew Brady: Historian with a Camera* (1955); and Dorothy Meserve Kunhardt and Philip B. Kunhardt, Jr., *Matthew Brady and His World* (1977). Also useful are Alan Trachtenberg, "Albums of War: On Reading Civil War Photographs," *representations*, Winter 1985, no. 5, pp. 1–32, and "Brady's Portraits," *Yale Review* 73, no. 2 (1984): 230–53; Philip B. Kunhardt, Jr., "Images of Which History Was Made Bore the Mathew Brady Label," *Smithsonian*, July 1977, pp. 24–35, and "Hold Still—Don't Move a Muscle: You're on Brady's Camera!" *Smithsonian*, Aug. 1977, pp. 58–67; Jennifer Todd, "The Rigors of Business: Matthew Brady's Photography in Political Perspective," *Afterimage* 7, no. 4 (1979): 8–12; and Josephine Cobb, "Matthew B. Brady's Photographic Gallery in Washington," *Records of the Columbia Historical Society of Washington, D.C.* 53 (1953): 28–69. Obituaries are in the *Washington Post* and *Washington Evening Star*, 18 Jan. 1896.

C. Zoe Smith

BRADY, William Aloysius (19 June 1863–6 Jan. 1950), theatrical producer and boxing promoter, was born in San Francisco, California, the son of Terence A. Brady, a newspaper editor, and Catherine O'Keefe, a singer and entertainer. Brady was spirited away to New York at age four by his father when his parents' marriage failed. With the briefest of public school educations, what he learned was mostly from his Shakespeare-loving father and on the streets of the city's Lower East Side.

When his father was killed in an accident, Brady at age fourteen found himself on his own. Taking pity on him, his father's newspaper colleagues got him a job as a steward at the New York Press Club. Restless and ambitious, he left to take a job on the Union Pacific, hawking candy, peanuts, fruit, and newspapers as the trains traveled westward. According to his own account, he was so successful as a candy butcher that he managed to make $400 per week in commissions. With savings of $2,000, he joined a card game and lost his entire cache. In 1882, finding himself jobless in San Francisco and wanting to become an actor, he attempted to get a job through writer-manager Bartley Campbell, then on the West Coast preparing to produce his play *The White Slave*. Brady was hired as a callboy and filled in whenever an actor became ill or left the company.

Shortly thereafter, the pattern of his life began to be set. He ranged up and down the West Coast, acting, stage-managing, doing odd jobs backstage, in every way imbibing the theatrical life. He recognized that the old stock company system was dying and that a new entrepreneurial approach to play production was developing. He concluded that great financial rewards could accrue to someone who "bought" a play, hired actors, rented a theater and surrounded the event with effective publicity. Each production became a single event without the encumbrances of a permanent company of players, a playhouse, and a repertory of plays necessary for operating in the old stock tradition. Brady realized that risk-taking was part of the process, but being a born gambler, he thrived on possibility and decided to launch his career as a theatrical manager. In that role he became a principal architect of the organizing structure of twentieth-century theatrical production, and he helped define the producer's role.

Brady scored a great success with his New York production of *After Dark* (1889), a melodrama by Dion Boucicault. While it brought Brady a small fortune, it also landed him in court to fight a plagiarism charge leveled at the play and playwright by Augustin Daly. He lost the lawsuit, but through the play he found another vocation. Brady had offered a part to a young San Francisco prizefighter, James J. Corbett, who traveled to New York to take it. Recognizing the pugilistic talent of his protégé, Brady became Corbett's manager and issued a challenge to the reigning heavyweight champion, John L. Sullivan. In the fight on 7 September 1892, Corbett won, and Brady had a world champion to promote. Even after Corbett lost his title in March 1897, Brady became manager of another heavyweight, James J. Jeffries, whom he also propelled to a title.

Brady continued his producing career with enough successes to offset the failures that went with the business. At age twenty-two, he married a Paris-born dancer, Marie Rose René, who bore him two children. Their son died at age five, but their daughter, Alice Brady, became a leading theatrical actress of the 1920s and 1930s. After his wife's death in 1896, Brady in 1899 married actress Grace George, with whom he had another son.

Brady believed that audiences of the 1890s wanted to see youth and beauty and sentiment on the stage and decided that a play titled *Annie Laurie* by Lottie Blair Parker had the makings of a hit. It was a sentimental tale of betrayal and redemption, involving a poor farm girl who is tricked into a false marriage. He changed its name to *Way Down East* and, with Florenz Ziegfeld as co-producer, opened it at the Manhattan Theatre in New York in February 1898. Although the play did not fare well in New York—Ziegfeld withdrew from it after its opening—Brady sent it on the road and reaped many millions from it for more than twenty years. Later, he sold the film rights to D. W. Griffith. In 1911 Brady built the Playhouse Theatre at 137 West 48th Street, and a year later, the Forty-eighth Street Theatre, just down the block, to house his productions.

Brady's greatest talent as a producer was in gauging the public's taste and trying to satisfy it. Frank Vreeland, assessing the producer's career in the *Philadelphia Inquirer* in 1943, noted: "More than any key man now in the theater, Brady has seen Broadway pass through a dozen cycles that make a whole history of the drama in themselves—the rural melodrama, the triangle play, the problem play, the naturalistic comedy, the war play, the jazz-age play, the society comedy, the symbolical drama, the kitchen-sink tragedy, the play of social consciousness, and now the war play again." Among his more than 250 productions, Brady managed to have one or more hit plays in every genre.

During his long career Brady earned and lost several fortunes. He invested heavily in the stock market and lost heavily in the Crash of 1929, but he saw his fortunes rebound with a production of Elmer Rice's *Street Scene*, which had opened early in the same year and went on to win a Pulitzer Prize. Brady had entered the nascent film industry in the early decades of the century, founding the World Film Corporation and serving as president of the National Association of the Motion Picture Industry from 1915 to 1922, but he later withdrew from movies to return to the stage. Acting as their manager-agent, he was responsible for shaping the careers of such stars of the day as Wilton Lackaye, Robert B. Mantell, Helen Hayes, Henry E. Dixey, and Mary Nash as well as those of his wife and his daughter. His last production on Broadway was the unsuccessful *Billy Draws a Horse*, which opened at the Playhouse on 21 December 1939.

Although he maintained his interest in the theater to the end, Brady ceased active participation after the 1930s. He died in New York City.

• The New York Public Library has scrapbooks and miscellaneous data on Brady. His two autobiographical works are *The Fighting Man* (1916) and *Showman* (1937). Also by him: "In the Spotlight for Forty Years," *Pictorial Review*, Sept., Oct., Nov. 1924, Jan. and Mar. 1925. See also Frank Vreeland in "Everybody's Weekly," *Philadelphia Inquirer*, 21 Nov. 1943; obituaries (7 Jan. 1950), *New York Times, New York Herald Tribune*, et al.; a tribute by Ward Morehouse, *New York World-Telegram and Sun*, 10 Jan. 1950; and the clipping files of the New York Performing Arts Library.

MARY C. HENDERSON

BRAGG, Braxton (22 Mar. 1817–27 Sept. 1876), Confederate general, was born in Warrenton, North Carolina, the son of Thomas Bragg, a contractor, and Margaret Crossland. His father earned enough to send his children to the best local schools. Upon Braxton's graduation from Warrenton Male Academy, he was accepted by the U.S. Military Academy at West Point (1833). Steadily distinguishing himself, Bragg rose in rank to cadet captain, completing his studies at West Point among the top ten of his graduating class (1837).

Bragg was appointed a second lieutenant in the Third Artillery and ordered to Florida to participate in the military expulsion of the Seminoles. However, plagued with fever, dyspepsia, and boils as a result of combined stress and sultry temperatures, he spent a great deal of 1838 regaining his health and fighting for a more secure appointment. He became impatient about his role in the military and, unfortunately, established a reputation as a quarrelsome albeit rigid commander. Given to outbursts of temper, Bragg alternated between feeling neglected and persecuted, and he often expressed both attitudes in public. Ironically, his insubordination gained him the sympathy of his superiors and with it an order to join General Zachary Taylor's army in the war with Mexico in 1845.

Bragg met the new opportunity with his customary vigor, taking raw soldiers and drilling them to perfection. His engagements in the defense of Fort Brown, Texas, and the capture of Monterrey, Mexico, resulted in his promotion to captain. At the battle of Buena Vista, without reinforcement from cavalry or infantry, Bragg and his men kept up a steady barrage that forced the Mexicans to withdraw from the field. Bragg was brevetted to lieutenant colonel. Having been a hero and excited by the prospects of speedy promotion, he returned to the United States and found his career stalled.

In 1849 Bragg married Elise Brooks Ellis; they had no children. After his marriage, he was ordered to Fort Leavenworth, Kansas. There he again grew cynical about the military establishment and began to openly criticize the War Department, proposing unsolicited reforms. Bragg's criticisms were well placed, and in this enterprise he excelled as a clear and practical administrator. However, when the new administration did not act on all of his reforms, he became discontented and once again felt neglected. He resigned his commission in 1855 and purchased a sugar plantation at Thibodaux, Louisiana, where he lived until the outbreak of the Civil War.

As states began to secede and prepare for war, Bragg was already at work coordinating Louisiana's military board. He negotiated a surrender of a Federal arsenal at Baton Rouge and shortly thereafter was placed in command, at the rank of major general, of the newly formed Louisiana state army. In March 1861 he was appointed brigadier general in the Confederate army and ordered to Pensacola, Florida, to secure the coastal region and hinder the arrival of Federal reinforcements at Fort Pickens. When Bragg arrived, he found that his troops were mainly composed of volunteers and inexperienced soldiers. In addition, the Confederate high command was yet undecided about its military posture. Hence, Bragg received conflicting orders, and finally, when Fort Sumter fell, his post was ignored altogether.

The year 1862 marked a turning point in Bragg's military career. Sensing that the Confederacy would be invaded from the west, particularly after U. S. Grant's successive victories at Forts Henry and Donelson, Bragg requested permission to take his men to join the forces converging at Corinth, Mississippi. There he served under A. S. Johnston and P. T. G. Beauregard in their effort to divide the invading Union forces. During the battle of Shiloh, Bragg's troops were key in surprising the Union forces and sweeping them back to Pittsburg Landing. However, before he could pursue his enemy, Bragg was ordered to withdraw, and the Union forces were permitted to escape. Although he was viewed as a public hero for his contributions, his reputation for bitter complaint and word of the summary executions he ordered for deserters preceded him. After Johnston was injured and Beauregard's health failed, Bragg was given permanent command of the Western Department. Immediately he was faced with problems of low morale, hindered mobility for his troops, and a rebellious staff. He reorganized the staff and improved the discipline of his troops, marching them at a lively pace from Tupelo to Chattanooga by way of Mobile to display his force to the Union commanders in Mississippi and to threaten their northern supply route. As a result, the Union forces retreated from Alabama and central Tennessee. Bragg overlooked the fact that he neglected to link his forces with those of General Edmund Kirby Smith, causing him to abandon plans for an attack at Munfordville and permitting Don Carlos Buell's forces to reach Louisville.

Bragg entered Kentucky next, hoping to rouse its citizens to join the Confederacy. When propaganda failed, he turned to conscription, which meant he had to establish a Confederate governor. Distracted by these political entanglements and undermined by his fellow officers, he could only surmise what the Union forces were planning, and he sought to protect his troops by ordering Leonidas Polk north to Frankfort. Instead, Polk retreated toward Danville, causing

Bragg to lose control of Frankfort. Bragg then accompanied Smith to join Polk. However, his failure to secure Kentucky as a Confederate state cost him the faith of most of his peers, except for Jefferson Davis. Bragg was returned to command the entire Army of Tennessee but was placed under the command of Joseph E. Johnston. From November 1862 through January 1863, at the battle of Murfreesboro, several of Bragg's decisions were ill informed. He misjudged the terrain and subsequently displayed his troops in an inappropriate tactical array, which was further compounded by his weak, textbook maneuvers. By the conclusion of the battle, Bragg was again forced to withdraw his exhausted army.

Bragg was also forced to withdraw at Tullahoma, Tennessee, where he was outmaneuvered by William S. Rosecrans. At this point he had begun to lose confidence in his abilities to command, but a temporary victory over Rosecrans at Chickamauga briefly postponed his retirement. However, instead of destroying Rosecrans's army when he had the chance, he permitted it to escape to Chattanooga, where he laid in a pointless siege. His failure to capitalize on his gains brought him severe criticisms from all levels of the Confederacy and the press. His already bad situation became worse when he suffered humiliating defeats at the battles of Missionary Ridge and Lookout Mountain, and by 29 November 1863 he asked to be relieved of command. After a brief retirement, Bragg was appointed military adviser to the president to oversee conscription of new soldiers, prison administration, and the defense of Richmond. Once again his vigorous activities stimulated controversy. Eight months later he was called upon to provide defense of Fort Fisher near Wilmington, North Carolina, but at this juncture the Confederacy lacked enough personnel to mount an adequate defense. Fort Fisher fell, and with it fell any remaining confidence in Bragg.

Arrested with his wife, Bragg was immediately paroled and, his plantation having been seized by the Union in 1862, spent his remaining years looking for steady employment. He worked briefly in New Orleans as superintendent of the waterworks and then accepted a job with Davis in an insurance firm. In 1874 he moved to Texas and was chief engineer of the Gulf, Colorado, and Santa Fe Railway Company until his death from a stroke in Galveston, Texas.

Bragg was unfairly criticized both by his contemporaries and subsequent historians until efforts were finally made to distinguish facts from the rumors about him. He was a skillful military planner and administrator, but his inability to control his temper, particularly in matters requiring deft, political sensitivity, only amplified the anger and distrust he caused through his mistakes. In addition, while many of Bragg's decisions resulted in disaster, he often was burdened with incompetent and rebellious subordinates and almost always was faced with having to train inexperienced troops. However, the misunderstanding of Bragg's talents placed him in critical positions in the Confederate army, where, hampered by his inability to accept responsibility for his own shortcomings, he ultimately made significant contributions to the defeat of the Confederacy.

• Bragg's papers are distributed among the following libraries: Chicago Historical Society; Duke University Library; Henry E. Huntington Library, San Marino, Calif.; Library of Congress; Lincoln National Life Foundation Archives, Fort Wayne, Ind.; Rosenberg Library, Galveston, Tex.; Samuel Richey Confederate Collection, Miami University, Oxford, Ohio; University of Texas, Austin, Tex.; William K. Bixby Collection, Missouri Historical Society; and the Western Reserve Historical Society, Manuscript Collection 2000, Cleveland, Ohio. A good biography of Bragg is a joint effort published in two volumes, Grady McWhiney, *Braxton Bragg and Confederate Defeat*, vol. 1 (1969), and Judith Lee Hallock, *Braxton Bragg and Confederate Defeat*, vol. 2 (1991). Another book-length treatment of Bragg's life is D. C. Seitz, *Braxton Bragg: General of the Confederacy* (1924). Articles pertaining to specific moments in Bragg's military career are McWhiney, "Controversy in Kentucky: Braxton Bragg's Campaign of 1862," *Civil War History* 6, no. 1 (1960): 5–42; and Daniel T. Kuehl, " 'Double Shot Your Guns and Give 'Em Hell': Braxton Bragg and the War in Mexico," *Civil War History* 37, no. 1 (1991). For military correspondence, see *The War of the Rebellion: A Compilation of the Official Records of the Union and Confederate Armies* (128 vols., 1880–1901).

TIMOTHY P. TWOHILL

BRAGG, Edward Stuyvesant (20 Feb. 1827–20 June 1912), Civil War general, congressman, and diplomat, was born in Unadilla, Otsego County, New York, the son of Joel Bragg, a rural businessman, and Margaretha Kohl. Bragg received his early education at local schools and went on to study law at Geneva College (now Hobart College) in Geneva, New York. He was admitted to the New York bar in 1848. After briefly practicing in Unadilla, he migrated to Fond du Lac, Wisconsin, at the age of twenty-three. He was admitted to the Wisconsin bar and began a lifetime practice of arguing cases before the Wisconsin Supreme Court. In 1854 he was elected district prosecuting attorney. That same year he married Cornelia Coleman; they had four children.

Bragg was a Stephen Douglas delegate at the 1860 Democratic National Convention in Charleston, South Carolina. Following Douglas's lead, he pronounced himself a Unionist and raised a company of volunteer infantry. He entered the Union army in July 1861 and was assigned as a captain to the Sixth Wisconsin Infantry Regiment. In September Bragg was promoted to major and then to lieutenant colonel in June 1862. He saw little activity for almost a year, serving on garrison duty in Washington, D.C. He remained actively concerned with politics during this time, often engaging in debates with abolitionist and Republican officers. He also gained the confidence of his superiors. General John Gibbon related in his memoirs that he sought out Major Bragg's perceptions of a quarrel between his regimental commander and another officer: "He gave it in a calm straightforward dispassionate way which won my confidence at once." As the war progressed

Bragg also won the respect of his men, who fondly referred to him as the "Little Colonel."

Bragg received his "baptism under fire" in Virginia at the second battle of Manassas (29–30 Aug. 1862). When his commander was wounded, Bragg took charge of the regiment for the first time. He also led his men at Turner's Gap in western Maryland during the battle of South Mountain (14 Sept. 1862), forcing the Confederate forces from the high ground until ammunition was scarce and the barrels of the soldiers' weapons were too hot to load. When advised by his brigade commander to allow a relief unit to take his place, Bragg insisted on staying put throughout the night. A few days later Bragg was wounded at Antietam, causing him to be sent home on convalescent leave.

Shortly after Second Manassas, Bragg had been solicited by his home district to run for Congress. In light of military obligations, he reluctantly stated that he would do so if nominated. News of his nomination reached him while his unit was encamped at Sharpsburg. However, the political fallout of the Union defeat at Second Manassas and the Confederate invasion of Kentucky led to his electoral loss thanks to "Copperheads" (sympathizers of the South) within his own Democratic party.

Bragg returned to the Army of the Potomac in time to participate in the battle of Fredericksburg (13 Dec. 1862). Promoted to colonel, he assumed command of the "Iron Brigade," the unit to which his regiment was attached. He participated in every major battle fought by the Army of the Potomac except Gettysburg, an inglorious kick by a horse having put him out of action a few weeks before. During the Petersburg campaign (15 June 1864–3 Apr. 1865), Bragg was promoted to brigadier general of volunteers. In February 1865 he went with the remnants of his brigade to Baltimore, where they remained until the end of the war.

After Bragg was mustered out of service in October 1865, he returned to Democratic party politics. In 1866 President Andrew Johnson appointed him postmaster of Fond du Lac, and that same year he served as a delegate to the Union National Convention, a convention of Democrats who had supported the cause for union. Bragg was elected to the Wisconsin Senate in 1867. His unsuccessful campaign for the U.S. Senate in 1874 did not keep him from winning in 1877 a seat in the House of Representatives, where he served for four terms. As chair of the Committee on Military Affairs, he sought to curtail funding for the army because of its involvement in helping to break the railway strike of 1877. Bragg also opposed the Blair Bill of 1887, which would have extended military pensions to ninety-day soldiers and to those whose service was minimal. In 1893 his second bid for a U.S. Senate seat was for naught when he was defeated by what may have been a corrupt campaign on the part of his opponent.

Bragg was a Wisconsin delegate to the Democratic National Conventions of 1872, 1884, 1892, and 1896. Noted for his oratory, he gave his most memorable speech at the 1884 convention. Seconding the presidential nomination of the governor of New York, Grover Cleveland, he pointed at the delegation of the notoriously corrupt Tammany machine and shouted that the young men of Wisconsin "love [Cleveland] most for the enemies he has made!" The new president rewarded Bragg by appointing him minister to Mexico. In 1896 Bragg opposed the free silver movement and the presidential nomination of William Jennings Bryan at the turbulent convention in Chicago. He then joined forces with other gold standard supporters and formed the National Democratic party, which in a gesture of protest nominated its own candidate for president. In the end Bragg supported Republican William McKinley's candidacy. After McKinley was assassinated, Theodore Roosevelt appointed Bragg consul general to Cuba in 1902 and consul general to Hong Kong later in the same year. Resigning in May 1906, he returned to Wisconsin; he died in Fond du Lac.

A strict military disciplinarian, Bragg displayed an uncompromising sense of honesty, loyalty, and justice, which earned him the respect of his contemporaries. However, he is not a commonly recognized name in American history despite the significant leadership roles he played throughout his lifetime. By 1900 he was no longer an important political player. The very attributes that were his strengths may have contributed to his decline into political obscurity. He was never a compromiser on what he considered to be vital issues. This fact brought him into conflict with Bryan and his own Democratic party, leading to an alliance with Republican leaders who rewarded him with diplomatic positions that ultimately removed him from the political fray.

• Bragg's papers are at the Wisconsin State Historical Society. Three important sources of information for Bragg's Civil War years include Allan T. Nolan, *The Iron Brigade* (1975); General John Gibbon, *Personal Recollections of the Civil War* (1878); and John Michael Priest, *Before Antietam: The Battle of South Mountain* (1992). Information pertaining to the Democratic National Conventions is in Stanley L. Jones, *The Presidential Election of 1896* (1964). Other useful sources include J. G. Hardgrove, "General Edward S. Bragg's Reminiscences," *Wisconsin Magazine of History* 33 (1950): 281–309; Allan Nevins, *Grover Cleveland: A Study in Courage* (1932); and Robert M. Utley, *Frontier Regulars: The United States Army and the Indian* (1973). Also see Ezra J. Warner, ed., *Generals in Blue: Lives of Union Commanders* (1964). Bragg's obituary is in the *New York Times*, 21 June 1912.

MIKE WILLIAM BEATTIE

BRAGG, George Freeman, Jr. (25 Jan. 1863–12 Mar. 1940), Episcopal clergyman, was born in Warrenton, North Carolina, the son of George Freeman Bragg and Mary (maiden name unknown). He was two years old when the family moved to Petersburg, Virginia, where he studied at the elementary school and at St. Stephen's Parish and Normal School. His family helped found St. Stephen's Church for Negroes in 1867. At age six he was employed as a valet by John Hampden Chamberlayne, editor of the *Petersburg Index*. In 1879 he entered a school founded by Major Giles B. Cooke, a former chaplain on Robert E. Lee's staff, that had become a branch of Virginia Theological Seminary. The next year he was suspended for not being "humble" but was appointed a page in the Virginia legislature by the Readjuster party. After a severe case of typhoid fever and a period of teaching school in 1885 he returned to his theological studies, studying at Cooke's school, now named the Bishop Paine Divinity and Industrial School. He was ordained deacon on 12 January 1887 and priest on 19 December 1888 by Bishop Francis M. Whittle. He married Nellie Hill in 1887; they had four children.

Bragg's parish ministry began in 1887 at St. Luke's Church in Norfolk, Virginia, where within four years he built a new church and rectory, renovated a school, organized the Holy Innocents (which became Grace Church), and founded the Industrial School for Colored Girls. After becoming rector of St. James First African Church in Baltimore, Maryland, in 1891, he opened St. James Mission in Portsmouth, Virginia. St. James Church under his leadership became self-supporting, purchased a rectory, and built a new church. By 1931 there were 500 communicants, and the church made annual charitable contributions of $1,000. At least four young men entered the priesthood under his guidance. In addition, he established the Maryland Home for Friendless Colored Children and was associated with St. Mary's Home for Boys and St. Katharine's Home for Little Girls. For thirty-five years he was general secretary of the Conference of Church Workers among Colored People and a special chaplain to the bishop of the diocese of Maryland.

Beyond his service within his denomination Bragg performed many duties. In 1884 he was honorary commissioner to the New Orleans Exposition. Virginia governor Fitzhugh Lee appointed him a curator to the Hampton Normal and Agriculture Institute in 1887. He also served as chaplain to the second battalion of Virginia Colored Militia. In Maryland he was on the board of managers for the House of Reformation for Colored Boys and a member of the State Inter-Racial Commission. He started the Committee of Twelve, a group of black leaders, including Booker T. Washington and W. E. B. Du Bois, that campaigned against the Poe Amendment designed to disfranchise blacks in Maryland. He led the fight to have Negro teachers assigned to Negro schools in Baltimore. In 1905 he joined the Niagara Movement, which advocated leadership as the first principle in raising the status of one's fellow citizens, and became a supporter of Du Bois, its founder.

Bragg's early association with the *Petersburg Index* had generated a lifelong interest in journalism. At nineteen he had begun publishing the *Virginia Lancet*, a pro-Republican paper involved in Virginia politics. In 1886 he founded a new paper, the *Afro-American Churchman*, published, he said, in the interests of the Colored Episcopal church. Also that year he founded the *Afro-American Ledger*, which he later merged with the *Baltimore Afro-American*. The *Church Advocate* served for many years as the unofficial organ of the Conference of Church Workers among Colored People and was filled with biographical sketches of clergy, histories of local black Episcopal churches, and commentary on the continuing struggles of blacks in the Episcopal church. In later years it served as a parish paper for Bragg's church. The *Maryland Home* was a monthly, published to promote the Maryland Home for Friendless Colored Children. Some of his published works, all of which contain some biographical data on him, are *The Colored Harvest in the Old Virginia Diocese* (1901), *Afro-American Church Work and Workers* (1904), *The Story of Old St. Stephen's, Petersburg, Va.* (1906), *The First Negro Priest on Southern Soil* (1909), *Bond Slave of Christ* (1912), *Men of Maryland* (rev. ed., 1925), *The Pathfinder Absalom Jones* (1929), and *Heroes of the Eastern Shore* (1939). A major work still of prime importance is *History of the Afro-American Group of the Episcopal Church* (1922). Many of these were printed on Bragg's own printing press, under the imprint of the Church Advocate Press.

Race relations would be improved, Bragg believed, by morally sensitive, educated people of both races, and he did not hesitate to denounce racial discrimination within his own denomination. Petitions for his selection to the episcopate were made in 1911 and 1917, but he was not elected. He died in Baltimore.

• Bragg's papers are in the Schomburg Center for Research in Black Culture, New York City; the Moorland-Spingarn Research Center, Howard University, Washington, D.C.; and Virginia State University, Petersburg. The Chadwyck-Healey Microfiche Collection, Randall K. Burkett et al., eds., *Black Biography, 1790–1950: A Cumulative Index* (3 vols., 1991), contains reproductions of valuable Bragg materials. George M. Brydon, *The Episcopal Church among the Negroes of Virginia* (1937), is useful. The *Journal of Negro History* 25 (July 1940): 399–400, gives essentials of Bragg's life. See also Mildred L. McGlotten, "Rev. George Freeman Bragg: A Negro Pioneer in Social Welfare" (M.A. thesis, Howard Univ., 1948), and Henry L. Suggs, ed., *The Black Press in the South* (1983), pp. 380–92.

FREDERICK V. MILLS, SR.

BRAGG, Thomas (9 Nov. 1810–21 Jan. 1872), governor and U.S. senator, was born in Warrenton, North Carolina, the son of Thomas Bragg, a carpenter and contractor, and Margaret Crossland. His brother, Braxton Bragg, would become a famous Confederate general. After attending Alden Partridge's military school in Middletown, Connecticut, he studied law under North Carolina Supreme Court Justice John Hall (1767–1833). He moved to Jackson, the seat of Northampton County, in 1833 and soon thereafter was elected county solicitor. He married Isabella M. Cuthbert in 1837; they had eight children.

In 1842 Bragg won election as a Democrat to the House of Commons, where he served as chair of the Judiciary Committee. As a presidential elector in 1844, 1848, and 1852, he canvassed his eastern plantation district and established a reputation as an effective debater. In 1854 he received the Democratic nomination for governor. The campaign centered on the issue of internal improvements. Alfred Dockery, the Whig candidate, came out strongly in favor of a westward extension of the North Carolina Railroad. Bragg's position was more equivocal, reflecting the sectional ambivalence within his own party. While most eastern Democrats opposed publicly financed internal improvements, western Democrats were clamoring for railroad connections to seaport market towns. Bragg pronounced himself a "friend of improvement," provided that it could be carried out within "the means and resources of the State." He won the election by slightly more than 2,000 votes.

In his inaugural address Bragg called for "the prosecution of a liberal system of improvement" and explicitly endorsed a western railroad. The general assembly subsequently approved a state subscription of $4 million in the Western North Carolina Railroad, as well as numerous other transportation improvements. To finance this ambitious program of state development, the legislature doubled both the poll tax and the property tax. Despite grumbling by eastern Democrats about the tax increases, Bragg easily won renomination in 1856. As a result of the popularity of the western railroad, he carried most of the counties in the traditionally Whig mountain region and decisively defeated John A. Gilmer, the American party candidate. In October Bragg met in Raleigh with governors Henry Alexander Wise of Virginia and James H. Adams of South Carolina to discuss the possibility of Republican John C. Frémont's election to the presidency. Bragg acted as a restraining influence on his more impetuous colleagues, who advocated resistance in the event of a Republican victory. The meeting adjourned without issuing a formal statement.

Bragg was a conscientious and hard-working governor, often remaining in his office until late in the evening. His friends admired his "quiet and dignified demeanor" (Cowper, p. 22), which others less favorably inclined construed as sternness and aloofness. Though a man of considerable personal integrity, he pursued his political ambitions with a zeal that sometimes strained the bounds of propriety. In November 1858 he was elected U.S. senator with the help of Thomas L. Clingman, whom he had appointed to a vacant Senate seat just a few months earlier. Bragg's ouster of David S. Reid, the Democratic incumbent, created a rift within the party that was never completely healed.

In the Senate Bragg served on the Committee on Claims and the Committee on Public Lands. Although overshadowed by the flamboyant Clingman, he took an active part in the debates over the Homestead Bill and the Pacific Railroad Bill, both of which he opposed, as well as debates on post office legislation and various appropriation measures. His one set speech (20 Mar. 1860) involved the issue of Florida land claims under the Adams–Onis Treaty of 1819. During the secession crisis Bragg acted as a voice of moderation within the Democratic party. He privately deprecated the "rash and precipitate course of South Carolina," as well as the "impetuous" men in his own state who were attempting to "precipitate disunion." In a speech before the North Carolina General Assembly in January 1861, he announced his opposition to immediate secession, arguing that the South should first exhaust all honorable means to preserve the Union. After the U.S. Congress adjourned in early March without passing any compromise legislation, he finally endorsed secession.

Bragg served as a member of Governor Henry T. Clark's military council but resigned after a few months, reportedly because of differences over coastal defense policy. In August 1861 he was an unsuccessful candidate for the Confederate Senate. In November he succeeded Judah P. Benjamin as Confederate attorney general. He privately complained that his advice was rarely solicited, and he resigned in March 1862 after Jefferson Davis found himself under pressure to appoint a Unionist Whig to the cabinet. After his resignation, Bragg moved to Petersburg, where his family had been residing, and remained there until sometime after 7 November 1862. On 5 February 1863 he attended a meeting of "members of the General Assembly and other citizens" in Raleigh, which passed resolutions endorsing the Davis administration and condemning the Conservative majority in the legislature for creating dissension and obstructing the war. A central committee was created to bring out proadministration candidates for the upcoming congressional elections, and Bragg was named as one of its members. In 1864 he was appointed by the secretary of war to examine the cases of North Carolinians arrested by the military—a position that, as he later acknowledged, brought him "a good deal of obloquy" on the part of those opposed to the suspension of the writ of habeas corpus.

After the Civil War Bragg returned to the practice of law. He was one of the founders of the Conservative party, a coalition of Whigs and Democrats opposed to Republican Reconstruction. At its first state convention on 6 February 1868, he served as chair of the Committee of Resolutions, which drew up a platform declaring unalterable opposition to "political and social equality with the black race." As chair of the state executive committee, he spearheaded the party's successful effort to regain control of the general assembly in 1870. He subsequently was one of the counsel retained by the legislature in the impeachment trial of the Republican governor William W. Holden, who was convicted and removed from office on 22 March 1871.

Despite his partisanship, Bragg was respected by many of his political opponents for his personal honesty and his strong belief in the rule of law. In January 1870 he was appointed by Republican lieutenant governor Tod R. Caldwell to chair a committee investigating corruption in the issuance and disposal of the bonds used to finance North Carolina's railroads. The Republican-controlled legislature denied him sufficient time to conduct a thorough inquiry, and no definitive evidence of corruption was ascertained. Bragg began declining in health soon after the Holden trial.

One of his last public acts was to sign a letter condemning the Ku Klux Klan and calling for its suppression. He died in Raleigh.

Bragg's significance lies primarily in his role in shaping the North Carolina Democratic party, steering it toward a more positive concept of government during the antebellum era and engineering its comeback after the Civil War.

• Bragg's official correspondence as governor, along with some political correspondence, can be found in the Governor's Papers and Governor's Letter Books in the North Carolina Division of Archives and History, Raleigh. A diary kept by Bragg during the periods Jan.–Mar. 1861 and Nov. 1861–Nov. 1862 in the Southern Historical Collection, Univ. of North Carolina at Chapel Hill, contains much valuable material regarding his conduct during the secession crisis and his tenure as Confederate attorney general. Bragg's pardon application (Record Group 94, Records of the Adjutant General's Office, National Archives and Records Administration, Washington, D.C.) is unusually detailed in regard to his actions during the secession crisis and the Civil War. The most comprehensive biographical sketch is Pulaski Cowper, *Sketch of the Life of Gov. Thomas Bragg* (1891). Cowper served as Bragg's private secretary. Also useful are essays by Samuel A. Ashe in *Biographical History of North Carolina*, vol. 6, ed. Ashe et al. (1905–1917); and in the *Raleigh News and Observer*, 30 Dec. 1928 (Clipping Collection, North Carolina Collection, Univ. of North Carolina at Chapel Hill). An obituary is in the *Raleigh Sentinel*, 23 Jan. 1872.

THOMAS E. JEFFREY

BRAHAM, David (1838–11 Apr. 1905), composer, conductor, and violinist, was born near London. His father and brother were musicians, as were two of his sons and four of his nephews. In his teens Braham decided to become a professional harpist but, according to one source, gave up the instrument when a British coach driver informed him that he was welcome aboard but his bulky instrument was not. Shortly thereafter he began studying the violin and became an accomplished performer though he never aspired to a career as a concert soloist. As a youth he played violin in various London music halls.

Braham came to the United States in 1856 and became the bandleader for Pony Moore's Minstrels at the famed Tony Pastor's Opera House in New York City. In the ensuing decade he conducted the pit orchestras in other New York Halls, including Canterbury Hall, Mechanics Hall, and, in 1864, the Theater Comique (at that time called Wood's Theater). His career as a songwriter began almost immediately after his arrival in the United States; he composed show songs to lyrics by several people, including Gregory Hyde and Jennie Kemble.

The year 1872 marked the first of many collaborations between composer Braham and Edward Harrigan, a playwright and lyricist and a partner in the famous Broadway act Harrigan & Hart. One of the Harrigan-Braham sketches from that year, *The Mulligan Guard*, was an immediate triumph in New York. This success led to a series of expanded *Mulligan Guard* sketches and secured their position as an important songwriting team. The first of the Mulligan sketches centered on the activities of the flamboyant Irish character Dan Mulligan (Harrigan's invention); later sketches included Mulligan's friends, family members, and other ethnic characters—Germans, Italians, and others. All of the characters were drawn from ethnic groups in New York's Lower East Side. At first these were small sketches inserted into revues and extravaganzas, but they became so popular that Braham and Harrigan were encouraged to mount them as full-scale musical theater works. The years 1879 to 1880 saw the production of *Mulligan Guards' Ball*, *The Mulligan Guards' Chowder*, *The Mulligan Guards' Christmas*, *The Mulligan Guards' Surprise*, *The Mulligan Guards' Nominee*, and *The Mulligan Guards' Silver Wedding*. On 16 February 1881 *Mulligan Guards' Nominee* reached its 100th performance at the Theater Comique. Like the other Mulligan pieces this one included original incidental music by Braham and songs such as "Down in Gossip Row," "Hang the Mulligan Banner Up," "The Skids Are Out Tonight" and "A Nightcap, a Nightcap."

The Mulligan series ended in 1885, but Braham and Harrigan continued to write hit songs for several more years. They were particularly adept at writing Irish songs that were popular in the 1890s, "Maggie Murphy's Home," "The Last of the Hogans," "Danny by My Side," "Paddy Duffy's Cart," "Mary Kelly's Beau," and "Patrick's Day Parade." In 1859 Braham had married an Irish immigrant, Annie Hanley. They had eight children, one of whom, also named Annie, married Harrigan.

Braham composed his songs on the violin rather than the piano. According to one source, he would cover the wall with music paper and then walk around the room scratching out a tune on the violin while his son George copied down the melody. Most of Braham's melodies and their accompanying harmonies are disarmingly simple, but they are eminently memorable and in their day were whistled or sung by countless New Yorkers, both theatergoers and tenement dwellers.

William A. Pond published a collection of ninety-five Harrigan-Braham songs in 1883. Most of the songs were about immigrant New Yorkers. The collection sold well in New York, but enjoyed only modest success in other parts of the country. Braham died in New York City.

• For more information on Braham's life and career, see Ely Jacques Kahn, *The Merry Partners* (1955); Charles Hamm, *Yesterdays: Popular Song in America* (1979); and Deane Root, *American Popular Stage Music, 1860–1880* (1981).

RONALD BYRNSIDE

BRAINERD, David (20 Apr. 1718–9 Oct. 1747), Puritan missionary to the Indians, was born in Haddam, Connecticut, the son of Hezekiah Brainerd, a prosperous and prominent social and political figure, and Dorothy Hobart Mason, the daughter of a Congregationalist minister and the widow of Daniel Mason. To a large degree, the life of Brainerd as it is generally known was invented by Brainerd in the last months before his death in collaboration with Jonathan Edwards (1703–1758). Edwards at the time needed a vivid example of "true religion" as distinguished from "enthusiasm." To accomplish this end, Brainerd and Edwards "corrected" a daily diary kept by Brainerd since October 1740 by adding and destroying material to suit their purpose. In the version according to Edwards, Brainerd was a predestined saint who felt the stirrings of grace at an early age, culminating in a genuine religious "conversion" on 12 July 1739. Called to the ministry, Brainerd entered Yale College in September 1739, at about the time of the Great Awakening. There young Brainerd suffered a temporary "tinge" of "imprudent zeal" and indulged in behavior "really contrary to the habitual temper of his mind." He was unfairly expelled in January or February 1742, after which he accepted a call to serve as a missionary to the Indians living in the area of present-day Brainard, New York. Over the next four years he worked among Indians on the frontiers of New York, Pennsylvania, and New Jersey, during which time, in June 1744, he was ordained as a Presbyterian minister by the Synod of New York. God blessed his mission with a series of revivals, but his always fragile health broke beneath the strain. In 1747 he went to the Northampton, Massachusetts, home of his colleague and patron, Jonathan Edwards, where he died an exemplary Christian death.

This version of Brainerd's life has inspired generations of Christian believers, including John Wesley, but historians must question its accuracy. What Brainerd construed as his early acceptance of the need to be seriously concerned with religion may have been instead an understandable reaction to the tragedies of his childhood, during which time he lost both of his parents and contracted tuberculosis, the wasting effects of which would eventually kill him. His "conversion" experience, first described eight years after the event, conformed to a pattern that had become stereotypical within the Puritan culture into which Brainerd was born. His choice of a clerical career was undoubtedly influenced by the fact that an older brother and his maternal grandfathers for three generations had entered the Congregational ministry. But for his expulsion from Yale, Brainerd would have lived a short, fulfilling, but obscure life.

Brainerd's offenses at Yale, serious in themselves, stirred a wave of student protest that wracked the school. Brainerd asserted that one of his tutors had no more grace than a chair and that the rector of the college should expect to be struck dead by God at any moment. Brainerd also attended what were considered irregular religious services and refused to apologize for his behavior. After being expelled, Brainerd still believed he could become an ordained Congregational minister and acquired a license to preach. He soon discovered that finding a pulpit without a college degree was difficult, and he offered to make the apology Yale demanded, but that offer was rejected. When Brainerd became a missionary in November 1742, he had no better prospect of employment.

It is impossible to evaluate Brainerd's success as a missionary. His claim that large numbers of Indians were "revived" has always been disputed, and Brainerd apparently expressed the opinion on his deathbed that he had been a failure. Without considering here the legitimacy of the missionary endeavor itself, Brainerd was ill suited for the work. He had never intended to be a missionary, never learned an Indian language, and was often absent from his post. Worst of all, he regarded Indians with utter contempt, describing their religious beliefs, their rituals, their music, their dance, and their language as "savage," "devilish," and "defective." Indians were "unspeakably indolent" and "destitute of natural affection." Their chief character traits were "savage roughness and brutish stupidity." "Not one in a thousand of them," according to Brainerd, "has the spirit of a man."

Brainerd is a more troublesome figure than the saint depicted by Jonathan Edwards. Though he may still be revered as a man who spent his strength bringing souls to Christ, he unknowingly carried an insidious disease that made him dangerous even to those he loved. He probably infected Jerusha Edwards, the daughter of Jonathan Edwards, who nursed Brainerd in his final illness and to whom he may have been engaged. So, too, the Indians among whom Brainerd worked soon suffered outbreaks of tuberculosis. Brainerd preached the Word of Life, but he spoke with a poisoned breath.

• Brainerd first attracted public attention in 1746 when he published two reports on his missionary activities for his employer, The Society in Scotland for the Propagation of Christian Knowledge. These reports, entitled *Mirabilia Dei inter Indicos* and *Divine Grace Displayed*, were in the form of extracts from his diary, and thus constitute his first autobiographical accounts. After Brainerd's death, Jonathan Edwards published *An Account of the Life of the Late Reverend Mr. David Brainerd* (1749), which includes Brainerd's sketch of his childhood and conversion, written by Brainerd as he lay dying; it also contains the sermon preached at Brainerd's ordination and selections from Brainerd's correspondence. For the most part, Edwards's *Account* is an incomplete and unreliable transcription of Brainerd's daily diary, which itself had been significantly altered before Brainerd's death. Edwards's transcription is incomplete because he did not include the extracts already in print and because he often summarized in his own words a number of diary entries, in one case condensing a month into a short paragraph. His transcription is also unreliable because he deleted passages that made Brainerd appear less than saintly or too imaginative. Despite its defects, Edwards's *Account* was long the basic source and has been reprinted frequently. It is probably Edwards's most popular work. For a definitive edition, see Norman Pettit, ed., *The Works of Jonathan Edwards*, vol. 7: *The Life of David Brainerd* (1985). Pettit inserts in correct chronological order the diary extracts that Edwards omitted and demonstrates the extent to which Edwards deviated from the manuscript diary. David Wynbeek, *David Brainerd, Beloved Yankee* (1961), is a good, reverent biography.

JAMES P. WALSH

BRAINERD, John (28 Feb. 1720–18 Mar. 1781), missionary, was born in Haddam, Connecticut, the son of Hezekiah Brainerd and Dorothy Hobart Mason. His father, who was prominent and influential in Connecticut colonial politics, served both in the assembly and in the council. He died when John was seven years old. Brainerd's mother was the daughter of the Reverend Jeremiah Hobart, pastor of the church in Haddam. She died when Brainerd was twelve, leaving him an orphan to be raised by his older siblings. Little is known about John's childhood. He graduated from Yale in 1746 and was licensed to preach by the New York Presbytery on 11 April 1747.

Brainerd quickly became involved in missionary work among the Native Americans. Also in April 1747, the correspondents of the Society for the Propagation of Christian Knowledge (SPCK) in Scotland appointed him as a missionary to the Indians. He went to the Delaware Indian community of Bethel, near Cranberry, New Jersey, to take over the work of his brother, David Brainerd, who had been forced to retire because of illness. Upon David's death in October 1747, Brainerd became the permanent spiritual leader of the settlement. He was ordained in February 1748. In 1752 Brainerd married Experience Lyon.

Brainerd was not as successful in the mission as his brother had been. He faced opposition from local Quakers and had to deal with a dispute concerning who owned the land on which the community was situated. Eventually, the land was taken away. The French and Indian War broke out on the frontier, and many Native Americans in the settlement joined the army to participate in the fighting between the French and the English on the Canadian frontier. Also, a disease, not clearly identified, killed many of the converts and thus weakened the impact of the settlement. Brainerd moved the community twice, and spent nearly £400 of his own money for expenses, in an attempt to resuscitate it, but to no avail. The settlement failed, and the correspondents fired Brainerd on 7 May 1755 for failure to carry out his assignment.

Brainerd had become a trustee of the College of New Jersey in 1754. This position, as well as his being a "New Light" Presbyterian, probably helped him secure his next appointment. Following his dismissal as an Indian missionary, he quickly became the pastor of the First Presbyterian Church of Newark, New Jersey, which had previously been led by Aaron Burr, the president of the College of New Jersey. This church, as one of the most prestigious pulpits in the colonies and a leading "New Light" congregation, could have meant prosperity for Brainerd, but success continued to be elusive. Burr, a very popular pastor, had resigned only because he could not continue to be pastor of the church and president of the college. Burr continued to live in the parsonage, and his presence made Brainerd's job as the new preacher almost impossible. Brainerd led the Newark congregation for over a year without receiving a formal call to become their pastor. Believing that the call would never come, Brainerd returned to his missionary work.

The correspondents of the SPCK still hoped to establish some type of missionary work among the Delaware Indians and they once more turned to Brainerd to carry out their mission. Plans were developed to buy land near New Brunswick, New Jersey, and in June 1756 Brainerd was put in charge of this new effort. Once more Brainerd's attempt failed, and he returned to the church in Newark in September 1757.

Brainerd's first wife died in 1757. He later married Experience Price, although the date of his second marriage is unknown. Brainerd had no children. In January 1758, in his role as a trustee of the College of New Jersey, he journeyed to Stockbridge, Massachusetts, with the Reverend Caleb Smith to secure approval from that church for the appointment of their pastor, Jonathan Edwards, to be the next president of the college. Beyond this official purpose, Brainerd, a friend of Edwards through his brother David, hoped to use his personal influence to convince Edwards to leave the pastorate in order to take on the new challenge of leading the college. In this effort he succeeded, although Edwards died shortly after his installation.

A third attempt to establish a mission among the Delaware Indians began in May 1758. The government had acquired land for the settlement in Burlington County, New Jersey. The village established there became known as Brotherton, New Jersey. Brainerd remained in this community for several years, supervising not only the church in Brotherton but also congregations in several other Indian and white settlements. During the summer of 1758 Brainerd served as a chaplain for the expedition to Crown Point, his only recorded military service.

Over the next ten years Brainerd filled many pulpits throughout New Jersey. Slowly but surely, the emphasis of his work shifted from its earlier emphasis on Native Americans to an ever growing work among the white communities in the area. In 1768 Brainerd moved to Bridgetown (now Mount Holly), New Jersey, where he built a church and developed a growing congregation. This work was disrupted by the American Revolution. Although Brainerd did not serve in the military at this time, he did support the Revolution. In 1776 he preached at least one sermon urging people to enlist in the army and fight for their country. In 1777 he moved to Deerfield, New Jersey, where he served as pastor for the local Presbyterian church until his death there.

Brainerd's missionary efforts among the Native Americans have been overshadowed by the successes of his brother David, probably for good reason. He struggled diligently to continue the work of his brother but met with little success. Brainerd's strengths lay in being a pastor, not a missionary. He discovered this fact late in life and changed the focus of his work in a more successful direction.

• The primary sources for Brainerd's life are his personal journals. The journal for 15 Oct. 1749–21 Nov. 1759, has been published in Thomas Brainerd, *The Life of John Brainerd* (1865). The journal for 1761–1762 is in the library of

Princeton University. Also useful are W. B. Sprague, *Annals of the American Pulpit*, Vol. 3 (1858), and Lucy A. Brainerd, *The Genealogy of the Brainerd-Brainard Family in America, 1649–1908* (1908).

CAROL SUE HUMPHREY

BRAITHWAITE, William Stanley Beaumont (6 Dec. 1878–8 June 1962), poet, critic, and anthologist, was born in Boston, Massachusetts, the son of William Smith Braithwaite and Emma DeWolfe. Of his two preoccupations—American poetry and the status of the American Negro—the second clearly had its origins in an unusual cultural heritage. The Braithwaite family, of mixed black and white descent, was wealthy and held prominent positions in British Guiana. Braithwaite's father studied medicine in London but quit because of apparent mental strain and moved to Boston, where he married DeWolfe, whose family had been in slavery. His father remained aloof from neighbors, educating his children at home. Braithwaite's autobiography mentions no employment held by his father, whose death, when his son was eight years old, left the family destitute.

Braithwaite's mother was forced into menial employment, and, at the age of twelve, so was Braithwaite. After showing interest in reading he was given a job as a typesetter where exposure to the poetry of Keats fixed the course of his life: "Keats had created in me an aspiration that became the most passionate urgency in my life, and Wordsworth and Burns nourished it into an ambition that developed into a fanatical determination" ("The House Under Arcturus," in Butcher, p. 174). Braithwaite read widely and completed a volume of poetry before he was twenty-one, but a series of disappointments while searching for work with literary possibilities made him aware of his position as an American Negro. He became determined to prove that a black poet could be successful despite the fact that he was black—without being forced into a special category as a Negro writer. With this resolve he developed a Keatsian theory of poetry: "It is not the feeling of contemplative anxiety aroused by the philosophic or moral imagination that gives to poetry its highest value, but the agitated wonder awakened in the spirit of the reader by the sudden evocation of magic" ("Imagism: Another View," in Butcher, p. 29–30). Braithwaite's attempted evocations of sheer beauty show virtually no awareness of his racial heritage or of the social problems confronting black Americans, and as a result he has often been criticized or dismissed by those concerned with black literature. It should be remembered, however, that Braithwaite frequently championed black writers, offered his guidance to the Harlem Renaissance, and analyzed the position of black writers in essays such as "The Negro in American Literature."

In this essay he traces the treatment of Negroes in American literature by both black and white writers from *Uncle Tom's Cabin* through the mid-1920s. He does not praise authors whose works show no signs of race, but those whose work transcends the racial. Of James Weldon Johnson he says: "Mr. Johnson's work is based upon a broader contemplation of life, life that is not wholly confined within any racial experience, but through the racial he made articulate that universality of the emotions felt by all mankind" (Butcher, p. 77). Of Jean Toomer's *Cane* he writes: "So objective is it, that we feel that it is a mere accident that birth or association has thrown him into contact with the life he has written about. He would write just as well . . . about the peasants of Russia, or the peasants of Ireland" (Butcher, p. 83). Although Braithwaite's poetry is not a reflection of his black heritage, he admired writers whose work went beyond their black heritage to universal human experience.

In 1903, with his career still before him, he married Emma Kelly, with whom he was to have seven children. A few months after his marriage he dedicated himself full time to literature. His first volume, *Lyrics of Life and Love* (1904), was published by subscription. In 1906 he began writing reviews and criticism for the staid but influential *Boston Evening Transcript*. The collections of the year's best poetry that he published there developed into an annual anthology of magazine verse that appeared from 1913 until 1929.

Braithwaite was an important guiding force during the emergence of modern poetry in the United States. He recognized the genius of Edwin Arlington Robinson before the turn of the century and became a close friend. Among the others whose careers he advanced was Robert Frost, whom he first praised in 1915. He was receptive to imagism, although he did not share American poet and editor Harriet Monroe's enthusiasm for Ezra Pound.

In spite of his influence, Braithwaite was hampered by financial difficulties. He published his yearbooks at his own expense, and he was unable to publish a projected anthology of Negro poetry. His *Poetry Journal*, begun only months after Monroe's *Poetry*, failed after a few issues. It was not until 1935 when he accepted a professorship at Atlanta University that he enjoyed financial security. He taught ten years before retiring to Harlem, where he produced his *Selected Poems* (1948) and his *The Bewitched Parsonage: The Story of the Brontës* (1950). He died at his home in New York City.

It is doubtful that Braithwaite will be remembered as a poet. His *Selected Poems* is a very slim volume, and the poetry is fragile and overly delicate. Between this volume and his first appeared only one other, *The House of Falling Leaves* (1908). His work rarely appears in anthologies. Philip Butcher, editor of the *William Stanley Braithwaite Reader*, predicts: "William Stanley Braithwaite's stature is sure to grow as scholars give attention to the records of his life and work" (Butcher, p. 7). If he is remembered, it will be as an important critical voice of the early twentieth century.

• Forty libraries have papers relating to Braithwaite. The major collections are at Harvard University and Syracuse University. Braithwaite's first annual anthology appeared as *Anthology of Magazine Verse for 1913*. The next was *Anthology of Magazine Verse for 1914 and Year Book of American Poetry*.

This format was followed through 1929. Other anthologies include *The Book of Elizabethan Verse* (1906), *The Book of Georgian Verse* (1909), and *The Book of Restoration Verse* (1910). Philip Butcher's *William Stanley Braithwaite Reader* (1972) is an excellent compendium of critical work, autobiography, and letters. The entire text of the incomplete autobiography "The House Under Arcturus," condensed in Butcher, is serialized in *Phylon* 2 (1941): 9–26, 121–36, 250–59; 3 (1942): 31–44, 183–94. Books that discuss Braithwaite include Richard Bardolph, *The Negro Vanguard* (1961); J. Saunders Redding, *To Make a Poet Black* (1939); William H. Robinson, *Black New England Letters* (1977); and Jean Wagner, *Black Poets of the United States*, trans. Kenneth Douglas (1973). An obituary is in the *New York Times*, 9 June 1962.

DALTON GROSS
MARYJEAN GROSS

BRAMELD, Theodore Burghard Hurt (20 Jan. 1904–18 Oct. 1987), professor of philosophy and philosophy of education, was born in Neillsville, Wisconsin, the son of Theodore E. Brameld, a real estate agent, and Minnie Dangers, a crafts teacher. Brameld was graduated in 1922 from Neillsville High School and attended Ripon College, from which he was graduated in 1926. He then held an administrative position at the college and in 1928 enrolled at the University of Chicago to study philosophy. He received a Ph.D. in 1931, having studied the works of Dewey, Marx, Engels, and Lenin under T. V. Smith, who had just received the first English edition of Lenin's works. Brameld's dissertation, "The Role of Acquiescence in Leninism," was later published as *Philosophic Approach to Communism* (1933).

Brameld served as an instructor of philosophy at Long Island University from 1931 to 1935 and as an assistant and then associate professor of philosophy at Adelphi College from 1935 to 1939. In 1939 Brameld accepted a position at the University of Minnesota in educational philosophy. During this time he published *Design for America* (1945), an account of his 1944 involvement in redesigning a high school curriculum at Floodwood, Minnesota, that adopted a utopian perspective on world affairs and a thoughtful, democratic-socialistic ideology. A community organization in Minneapolis branded the program and Brameld as communistic, and the resulting community reaction led to Brameld's decision to leave Minnesota in 1947. During these years (as well as those of the early 1950s), Brameld defined and developed his conception of "Reconstructionism" and sought to define the relationship between education and social change. In addition, Brameld became quite active with the Progressive Education Association (renamed the American Education Fellowship in 1944) as he sought to bring a more international perspective to the organization. He married Ona J. K. Swanson in 1949; they had three children. Their marriage ended in divorce in 1971.

Brameld served as a professor in educational philosophy at New York University from 1947 to 1958 and, during this period, prepared numerous articles and three widely assigned textbooks: *Ends and Means in Education* (1950), *Patterns of Educational Philosophy* (1950), and *Toward a Reconstructed Philosophy of Education* (1956). In the early 1950s Brameld began to develop a rationale for the inclusion of anthropology as a component of the foundations of education (along with philosophy, history, and sociology) and coined the term "anthropotherapy" as a method of drawing on the scientific perspective of the anthropologist and the normative, cultural perspective of the psychotherapist. Brameld's participation with New Dealer Rex Tugwell in a study of education and general culture in Puerto Rico resulted in his *Philosophies of Education in Cultural Perspective* (1955) and *The Remaking of a Culture* (1959). In 1958 Brameld accepted a professorship at Boston University, where he stayed until his retirement in 1969. At Boston University, Brameld focused on international education and the educator as world citizen. He continued to write prolifically and produced *Education for the Emerging Age* (1961), *Education as Power* (1965), *The Use of Explosive Ideas in Education* (1965), *Japan: Culture, Education, and Change in Two Communities* (1968), and *The Teacher as World Citizen* (1976). During the 1970s a group of Brameld's students formed the Society for Educational Reconstructionism, an organization that published a quarterly journal, *The Cutting Edge*, and held annual lectureships in New York City and periodic conferences at Brameld's summer home in New Hampshire.

Known as a Social Reconstructionist, Brameld is typically included with George S. Counts, Harold Rugg, and John Childs in a group of educators who represented the more radical contingent of the Progressive education movement and who were greatly influenced by the Great Depression. While Progressive education was seen to constitute the *means* for social change and the bettering of society, Social Reconstructionists proposed the actual *ends*, namely, a "genuinely democratic" social order with a planned economy. In determining the role of the school in the social order, the Social Reconstructionists believed that teachers and schools must be actively involved in formulating purpose and shaping the values of its students. While Progressives cried "indoctrination" at this approach and believed that educators should never impose values on students, the Social Reconstructionists viewed America's crisis as being so serious that educators could not stand by and watch the destruction of society.

Brameld saw himself as extending the work of the 1930s Social Reconstructionists into the 1960s. To distinguish his work from that of his predecessors, he coined the term "Reconstructionism" for his perspective that stressed the world situation over domestic issues and saw reconstruction as involving the entire world. Continuing to combat the accusations of indoctrination, Brameld attempted to diffuse criticisms by establishing in 1950 the doctrine of Defensible Partiality: "What we learn is defensible simply in as far as the ends we support and the means we utilize are able to stand up against exposure to open, unrestricted criticism and comparison. What we learn is partial in so far as these ends and means still remain definite and positive to their majority advocates after the defense occurs" (*Ends and Means in Education*, p. 92). In spite of these efforts, Brameld and other adherents of Reconstructionism continued to be accused of indoctrination.

While Reconstructionism achieved recognition from the 1930s to the 1950s, its prominence increased dramatically from the 1950s to the 1980s because of its inclusion in most general textbooks about the field of education. Reconstructionism and Brameld's writings were typically placed in juxtaposition with other philosophies of education, such as Perennialism, Essentialism, and Progressivism, serving as a counterpoint for generations of education students. Brameld's career represents an individual who, while versed in the tenets of Progressivism and educational democracy, sought to address educational issues—social, economic, cultural—of the mid-twentieth century.

During his travels to Japan in the late 1960s, Brameld met Midori Matsuyama, who in 1973 became his second wife. The couple had no children. Brameld retired to Durham, North Carolina, home of his youngest daughter, where he died.

• No archival papers or memoirs of Theodore Brameld exist; a collection of Society for Educational Reconstruction documents are on file at the Museum of Education, University of South Carolina. Critical reviews of Brameld's work include George F. Kneller, *Modern Philosophies* (1962). See also R. H. Thompson, "The Educational Theory of Reconstructionism as Viewed by George S. Counts and Theodore Brameld" (Ph.D. diss., Univ. of Texas at Austin, 1985); D. R. Barnes, "The Origins and Development of Theodore Brameld's Philosophy of Education" (Ph.D. diss., Rutgers Univ., 1971); and J. W. Comer, "Aspects of the Educational Philosophy of Reconstructionism as Set Forth by Theodore Brameld" (Ph.D. diss., Ohio State Univ., 1953). An obituary is in the *New York Times*, 21 Oct. 1987.

CRAIG KRIDEL

BRAMLETTE, Thomas Elliott (3 Jan. 1817–12 Jan. 1875), governor of Kentucky, was born in Cumberland County (now Clinton County), Kentucky, the son of Colonel Ambrose S. Bramlette, a state legislator, and Sarah (maiden name unknown). He received a common school education and began the study of law. In 1837 he was admitted to the bar and began his legal practice in Clinton County. In September of that same year Bramlette married Sallie Travis. The couple had two children. His first wife died in 1872, and he married Mary Graham Adams, a widow, two years later.

In 1841 Bramlette was elected to the Kentucky state legislature for one term. He was appointed Commonwealth attorney in 1848 by Governor John J. Crittenden. In 1850 he resigned the position and established his law practice in Columbia, Kentucky. In 1856 he was elected judge of the Sixth Judicial District.

Bramlette supported the Union cause in 1861. He received the commission of colonel in the Union army and helped raise the Third Kentucky Volunteer Infantry. In 1862 President Abraham Lincoln appointed him to the post of U.S. district attorney for Kentucky. Bramlette received the commission of major general in 1863. That same year he was nominated as the gubernatorial candidate of the Union Democrats of Kentucky. He easily defeated his opponent, Democrat Charles A. Wickliffe, by a wide margin.

Bramlette's devotion to the Union was apparent in his actions as governor of Kentucky. Although the state was badly divided by the Civil War, Bramlette remained adamant in his belief that the Union must be preserved. In January 1864 he issued a proclamation stating that Confederate sympathizers would be punished if guerrilla warfare persisted in the Commonwealth. Fines of up to $1,000 would be exacted from anyone aiding those engaged in guerrilla activities. He also declared that, if a loyal Kentuckian were captured by pro-Confederate forces, five Confederate sympathizers would be seized and held as hostages for the safe return of the loyal Kentuckian.

The devotion of Governor Bramlette to the Union cause was severely tested after General Jeremiah T. Boyle ordered the enlistment of former Kentucky slaves into the Union army. Bramlette appealed to the Lincoln government to pledge that blacks would not be recruited in Kentucky. However, General Boyle's successor, General Stephen G. Burbridge, ordered able-bodied blacks in Kentucky to enlist in the Union army.

In 1864 Bramlette resisted a move by the Kentucky legislature to nominate him on the Democratic ticket for a seat in Congress. Nevertheless, at the Democratic National Convention, the Kentucky delegation nominated Bramlette for the vice presidency. However, he asked that his name be withdrawn from consideration.

Bramlette's relationship with the Lincoln government began to be strained. On 5 July 1864 Lincoln suspended the writ of habeas corpus in Kentucky. Furthermore, General Burbridge interfered with the electoral process in the state by placing Union troops at the polls. Bramlette vigorously protested this intrusion in the internal affairs of the Commonwealth. Strained as his relations with the Lincoln government were, Bramlette, upon Lincoln's death in 1865, proclaimed a day of fasting, humiliation, and prayer to mark the death of the president of the United States.

Bramlette asked President Andrew Johnson to restore the writ of habeas corpus and to withdraw black troops from Kentucky. Despite his opposition to the use of black troops within the state, Bramlette supported the passage of the Thirteenth Amendment. However, he was strongly opposed to the Fourteenth and Fifteenth amendments on the grounds that they would interfere with the balance of power between the states and the federal government. In December 1865 Bramlette announced he would grant pardons to all persons indicted for treasonable activities in Kentucky against the United States. In January 1866 the Kentucky legislature approved this action.

Among the dramatic achievements of Bramlette's administration were improvements to the schools of the Commonwealth and support for mental institutions. He also established an agricultural and mechanical college at Lexington, which became the forerunner of the University of Kentucky. Also among his achievements were the reduction of the state's debt and his proposals for reforms in the Kentucky penal system.

When Bramlette retired from the governor's office in 1867, he established his legal practice in Louisville. He also patronized several charitable concerns in the Louisville area and was a staunch supporter of the Louisville Public Library. He died in Louisville after a brief illness.

• The official papers of Bramlette as governor are located in the Kentucky State Archives and in the Kentucky Historical Society. For a brief biographical sketch of Bramlette, see "Governor Thomas E. Bramlette," *Register of the Kentucky Historical Society* 5 (Jan. 1907): 27–28. Information on Bramlette's term as governor of Kentucky is noted in E. Merton Coulter, *The Civil War and Readjustment in Kentucky* (1926). An excellent article on Bramlette is found in Lowell H. Harrison, ed., *Kentucky's Governors 1792–1985* (1985). A substantial obituary is in the Louisville *Courier-Journal*, 15 Jan. 1875.

RON D. BRYANT

BRANCH, Anna Hempstead (18 Mar. 1875–8 Sept. 1937), poet and reformer, was born in New London, Connecticut, the daughter of John Locke Branch, a lawyer, and Mary Lydia Bolles, an author. Anna Hempstead Branch was born and died in "Hempstead House"; she was the last of ten generations of descendents to live there. Her family was close and supportive. The death of her one sibling Johnny when Anna was thirteen may have intensified an already developing mysticism. Because her father's law practice was in New York, she spent her school years there and in Brooklyn, studying at Froebel and Adelphi Academies before attending Smith College. At Smith, Branch made lifetime friends among professors and classmates, edited the college's literary magazine, and served as Ivy Orator. In 1898 a year after her graduation, *Century Magazine* selected her poem "The Road 'Twixt Heaven and Hell" as the year's best verse by a college graduate. In 1900 she received a degree in dramaturgy from the American Academy of Dramatic Arts in New York.

Nearly as compelling to Anna Branch as literature was her desire for social reform. Shortly after college she wrote to a former Smith professor about her visit to mills in New Hampshire and her desire to work there. She described the long lines of "intensely interesting" people before concluding: "But I suppose my living and working among them is only a plan, for there are so many other things I *must* do." The wording "*must* do" suggests the sense of mission that would always distinguish Branch.

Branch's accomplishments from 1900 to 1910 attest to her dedication to both poetry and social service. Three of the four volumes published during her lifetime appeared in this decade: *Heart of the Road and Other Poems* (1901), *The Shoes That Danced and Other Poems* (1905), and *Rose of the Wind and Other Poems* (1910). Branch was director of the New London Playgrounds Association from 1900 to 1910. Also during this time she began her lifelong volunteer work at Christodora House, a settlement house in Manhattan's Lower East Side. After her father died in 1909, Branch resided at Christodora House in the winters and Hempstead House in the summers. Her mother lived with her in these two locations much of the time until her own death in 1922. Branch never married.

In spite of Branch's high seriousness, she took enormous pleasure in life. While a number of her poems are akin to religious devotional poetry of the seventeenth century, many more, especially in her first volume, are pure entertainment within an unabashedly created fairyland. In musicality, atmosphere, and dramatic episode, they are reminiscent of old ballads. The title selections of the second and third volumes are short poetic dramas, also a favorite genre for Branch. "Rose of the Wind" was produced at the Empire Theatre in New York in 1908.

Branch reached her greatest popularity as a poet before World War I. Probably her most widely admired poem, published in *The Rose*, was "The Monk in the Kitchen," a poem that extols simplicity and clarity as the narrator looks for metaphysical significance in chores and "stolid, homely, visible things." It begins, "Order is a lovely thing; / On disarray it lays its wing, / Teaching simplicity to sing." Many of her most popular poems from this period employ language that to subsequent generations of readers sounds stilted. Yet a number of these that today seem affected still warrant attention; among these are "Ere the Golden Bowl Is Broken" and the epic "Nimrod," which Alfred Kreymborg proclaimed "the greatest single narrative in the whole length of American poetry."

In 1918 Branch served as a vice president of the National League for Women's Service and chaired the education and festival committees in the War Camp Community Service. Many of her remarkable social projects stemmed from her conviction that poetry not only improves lives but also affirms our common humanity. Branch started an International Poetry Society, which from about 1917 to 1920 gathered regularly at Christodora House. She also founded and directed the Poets' Guild of Christodora House, which thrived for years because of her assiduous attention and ability to enlist the participation of an impressive array of fellow poets. Among those involved were Edwin Markham, Josephine Preston Peabody, Percy MacKaye, William Rose Benét, Margaret Widdemer, Ridgely Torrence, Sara Teasdale, Robert Frost, and Edwin Arlington Robinson. The Poets' Guild gave readings and conducted classes for boys and girls. It also created the "Unbound Anthology," individually published poems selected and sponsored by individuals or organizations. With nicely printed poems selling for five cents each, people could get poetry cheaply and profits could go back into the settlement house work. Perhaps most impressive was the Consuls' Series of the Unbound Anthology; this series had a poem gleaned from each of the sixty-three countries with consulates in New York City. Among Branch's own short poetic dramas printed first in this looseleaf form was "The Bubble-Blowers."

As active as Branch was in bringing poetry into people's lives during the 1910s and 1920s, nineteen years elapsed before she published a fourth book of poetry. By 1929, when Branch would have seemed old-fashioned, *Sonnets from a Lock Box and Other Poems* appeared. The poems in this collection are of more interest to later generations of readers; the view expressed in Clarence Britten's 1929 review for the *New Republic* seems typical of critics' responses at that time: "Her place in our poetry is secure, if slight. In this volume, however, there is nothing to extend that place" (vol. 129, p. 357).

Loyalty from old friends and admirers persisted. In 1934 she received an honorary degree from Smith College. After her death in New London, Ridgely Torrence edited her previously unpublished poems for the posthumous volume *Last Poems of Anna Hempstead Branch* (1944). Torrence's introduction speaks of Branch's thorough sense of the world's pain and darkness and then adds, "But only in such a world could saints appear. . . . For she too was a saint." Such praise seems excessive to later generations; still, many who knew her agreed.

Rather than for the critical merits of her poetry, Branch may be remembered more for her unceasing efforts to bring poetry into the public domain and for her ability to inspire and mobilize others in the name of poetry.

• Smith College holds the bulk of Branch's extensive papers. Useful secondary sources include *Twentieth Century Authors: A Biographical Dictionary of Modern Literature* (1942) for information about her family, *American Women Writers: A Critical Reference Guide* (1979) for insightful commentary on her poetry, and *Notable American Women, 1607–1950* (1980) for the nature of her mysticism. Joshua K. Bolles's portrait of Branch and her mother based on a childhood memory of visiting these relatives (in *Father Was an Editor* [1940]) offers an interesting context, as does Margaret Widdemer's chapter in *Golden Friends I Had* (1964). An obituary is in the *New York Times*, 9 Sept. 1937.

MARY HUGHES BROOKHART

BRANCH, John, Jr. (4 Nov. 1782–4 Jan. 1863), governor of North Carolina and Florida Territory, U.S. senator, and secretary of the navy, was born in the borough of Halifax, North Carolina, the son of prominent and wealthy parents, John Branch, Sr., and Rebecca Bradford. The senior Branch was a large landowner and revolutionary patriot who, as high sheriff, gained a reputation for identifying Tories. He represented Halifax County in four sessions of the House of Commons in the 1780s. The well-born Bradford was a daughter of Colonel John Bradford (d. 1787). Young Branch assumed the patrician inclinations of his parents. After receiving an A.B. from the University of North Carolina in 1801, he read law under the supervision of Judge John Haywood. He never practiced, however, preferring instead the life of planter and officeholder. In 1803 he married Elizabeth Foort; they had nine children.

In 1811 Branch was elected as a Democratic Republican to represent Halifax County in the North Carolina Senate, a post he held in the 1813, 1814, 1815, 1816, and 1817 assemblies. He was Speaker in the last two; however, he resigned the Speakership upon his election as governor. From December 1817 to December 1820 he proved a popular chief executive and retired only after completing three terms, the constitutional limit. Governor Branch deemed education essential to enlightenment and republican government. Moreover, he hailed it as a means of reducing crime. He believed money was better spent on statewide common schools than on penitentiaries. Schools would "inculcate such principles in the rising generation, as would supersede the necessity of Houses of Corrections" (*Raleigh Register*, 20 Nov. 1818). Branch also manifested reform tendencies in seeking to regulate the medical profession and in advocating an end to imprisonment for debt. Of the latter reform, he held that imprisonment for debt "seems a remnant of that Gothic policy which prevailed during the ruder ages of society; a policy as barbarous as it is useless" (*Raleigh Register*, 19 Nov. 1819).

Having embraced Jeffersonian precepts, Branch warned against commerce and towns thusly: "North Carolina must long continue to be an agricultural rather than a commercial state; all attempts to make it otherwise, to promote the interest of towns and not that of the country . . . are giving a constrained impulse to the industry of the people contrary to their nature and contrary to the interests of a vast majority of the population" (*Raleigh Register*, 20 Nov. 1820). His agrarian biases also led him to distrust banks and to oppose protective tariffs. After again representing Halifax County in the state senate as a Democratic Republican in 1822, Branch broke with the Old Republicans by abandoning the caucus candidate, William H. Crawford, to support Andrew Jackson in 1824. He became a staunch Jacksonian.

From 1 December 1823 until his resignation on 10 March 1829, Branch represented his state in the U.S. Senate. He gloried in public office, and he and his wife were active in Washington society. Both were genial and gregarious; they gave lavish dinner parties and moved in the best social circles. Branch aspired to higher office and used flattery to advance his career. He wrote fawning letters to Jackson and named a son born on the anniversary of the battle of New Orleans Andrew Jackson Branch. Accepting Jacksonian principles with enthusiasm, Branch supported "Old Hickory's" extended presidential campaign and opposed John Quincy Adams's presidential policies.

Although Branch's Senate tenure was unremarkable, his loyalty led President Jackson to appoint him secretary of the navy in 1829. He became the first North Carolinian to hold a cabinet post. He proved to be a competent naval administrator, but his ambition remained unsated. He expected Jackson's friendship to be the vehicle for further advancement.

In time, however, the Eaton affair soured his relations with the president and led to his dismissal from the cabinet. The Branches joined in attempts to drive Margaret O'Neale Timberlake Eaton, the wife of the secretary of war, from proper Washington society because of her unsavory reputation. Believing that Eaton was a victim of social ostracism similar to that of his beloved Rachel Jackson, the gallant Old Hickory declared Eaton as chaste as the driven snow, a view not widely in vogue. Eventually Martin Van Buren, secretary of state and a bachelor, gained ascendancy with Jackson by befriending the Eatons. Branch, along with other cabinet members, was asked to resign, thus facilitating a reorganization of the cabinet.

The piqued Branch, heretofore a Unionist with states' rights sentiments, aligned himself with John C. Calhoun in the nullification fray. He declined Jackson's offers of a foreign appointment and the governorship of Florida, a post he later accepted from John Tyler. While Branch sometimes spoke fondly of Jackson, he never forgave the wily Van Buren for his "malign influence" and subsequently devoted his efforts to thwarting the New Yorker's political aspirations. The way was prepared for a disgruntled Branch to join the anti-Jackson forces, from which the Whig party developed, though he eventually returned to the Democratic fold.

In seeking popular vindication, Branch ran for Congress in his North Carolina district in 1831. Other candidates withdrew, and he was elected unanimously to the Twenty-second Congress. Again his tenure was undistinguished, and in 1833 he returned to his North Carolina plantations. In 1834 he represented Halifax County in the North Carolina Senate as an anti-Jackson delegate. His defection contributed to the establishment of the Whig party in the state. His last notable service to the state was as the Halifax County representative in the constitutional convention of 1835. Therein he supported proposals to allow free blacks to retain the franchise and to remove all religious restrictions on office holding.

Having acquired several properties in Leon County, Florida, Branch moved to "Live Oaks," a plantation on Lake Jackson, but he retained his North Carolina residence as well. In 1838 he returned to North Carolina long enough to run unsuccessfully as a Democrat against Whig governor Edward B. Dudley. His flirtation with whiggery had been brief, as his admiration for Jackson continued despite their breach. In 1844 President Tyler appointed Branch territorial governor of Florida, a post he held until 24 June 1845. As governor he promoted internal improvements, education, a more efficient militia, and an end to the territorial paper money system. He also sought U.S. indemnification for losses Floridians had suffered in the Seminole Wars. But Branch's greatest contribution was to the statehood movement; he was able to placate disgruntled Floridians and garner support for statehood among his friends in Washington. Upon the admission of Florida to the Union, he opened his Live Oaks home to all who wished to celebrate the event. Because of his wife's health, he declined to represent Florida in the U.S. Senate. After her death in 1851, he returned to North Carolina to manage his extensive holdings there, to enjoy the society of his native state, and to marry Mary Eliza Jordan Bond in 1853. He took no active part in the Civil War but was greatly grieved when Confederate brigadier general Lawrence O'Bryan Branch, his nephew and ward, was killed while commanding a brigade at Antietam. Branch died in Enfield, Halifax County, North Carolina.

Branch possessed fine abilities, and his early years were characterized by noblesse oblige as he saw public service as a duty. After his break with Jackson, he became bitter and less useful. Although aristocratic in demeanor and outlook, he sometimes took positions at odds with his peers. His career rose and declined, but his political ambition waned only after it became apparent that a broadened electorate would no longer choose him for high office.

• Branch manuscripts are in the Southern Historical Collection, University of North Carolina at Chapel Hill, and his governor's letter books are in the North Carolina State Archives, Raleigh. See also the William H. Branch Papers in the Southern Historical Collection and the Andrew Jackson Papers, Library of Congress. The *Raleigh* (N.C.) *Register* contains Governor Branch's addresses to the general assembly and frequent references about important events in his political life. The best secondary treatment is William S. Hoffmann, *Andrew Jackson and North Carolina Politics* (1958). Also see Hoffmann, "John Branch and the Origins of the Whig Party in North Carolina," *North Carolina Historical Review* 35 (1958): 299–315, and Barbara Lou Rich Long, "John Branch, Florida's Last Territorial Governor," *Apalachee* 7 (1968–1970): 120–29. An obituary is in the *Raleigh Register*, 14 Jan. 1863.

MAX R. WILLIAMS

BRANCH, Mary Elizabeth (20 May 1881–6 July 1944), educator, was born in Farmville, Virginia, the daughter of Tazewell Branch, a former slave who served in the Virginia legislature and worked as a shoemaker and tax collector, and Harriett Lacey, a domestic worker. Although she learned to read at home, Branch's quest for formal education began when she was thirteen. Because her mother did laundry for students and teachers at State College in Farmville, Branch often made trips to the school to pick up or deliver clothes; in time, she herself became a maid in the college library. Exposed for the first time to a wide variety of books and knowledge, she determined to obtain her own education. Within a few years she had earned a high school diploma from the normal school of Virginia State College, a land grant college for black students in Petersburg, where she also took teacher education classes.

Eager to share her knowledge, Branch accepted a position as an English teacher at an elementary school in Blackstone, Virginia, soon after completing her secondary education. After a few years she returned to Virginia State, where she taught English for twenty years and also served as housing director for both men's and women's dormitories. While at Virginia State, Branch spent her summers continuing her own education. She studied at the University of Pennsylvania and Columbia University, as well as at the University of Chicago, where she earned a bachelor's degree in philosophy in 1922 and a master's degree in English in 1925. She also began, but did not complete, a doctorate in education. It was unusual for an African American to attend these institutions, and her education gave her distinctive qualifications.

In the late 1920s Branch moved to Kansas City, Kansas, to teach social studies at Sumner Junior College. After one year she moved to St. Louis to serve as dean of girls at Vashon High School, then the largest school in the United States for black girls. Working at Vashon, in a poor urban neighborhood, was challenging, but it paid well and provided Branch with a prominent position within black education circles. By 1930 the American Missionary Association (AMA) had noted her work and invited her to become president of its Tillotson College in Austin, Texas. Branch initially declined two offers from the association, but she accepted after the third request. Noting that many white teachers had gone to the South after the Civil War to help newly freed slaves, Branch determined that accepting the presidency of Tillotson could be no more difficult than that. In taking her new position in 1930, she became the first black woman to serve as a college president in Texas.

The task ahead of her was a formidable one. Chartered by the AMA in 1877 and opened in 1881, Tillotson College was in a state of decline when she was hired to lead it. Originally established as one of several AMA schools for former slaves throughout the South, the school had prospered for many years as it provided industrial and traditional education at the elementary and secondary levels and then achieved collegiate status in 1909. By 1930, however, black migration out of Texas and poor administrative leadership had deeply hurt the school. It was reduced to a junior college in 1925, and in 1926 it converted to a women's college; its enrollment at that time dropped below 150 students.

Branch arrived at Tillotson on 1 July 1930 and found a few run-down buildings on a physically unkempt campus. She appreciated the challenge that awaited her and took advantage of the AMA's promise to let her run the school with minimal interference. Branch quickly established a five-year plan for Tillotson, with immediate goals to improve the physical plant and increase enrollment. Radical and activist in her approach, Branch directed her attention to every aspect of the campus. She was responsible for vastly expanding the library's holdings (often shopping at used bookstores to acquire volumes), renovating several old buildings, and adding numerous others. She solicited donations and initiated a long-term fundraising program for the physical plant. The campus was landscaped, the high school program was dropped, the faculty was doubled, and the minimum requirement for faculty was raised to a master's degree. To attract more students, she sent teachers throughout the Southwest, added scholarships, and invited high school girls to special events on the campus. In 1935 she returned Tillotson to its coeducational status. By this time enrollment had increased to more than 200 students and would top 500 students by the time of her death.

Branch understood the importance of outside recognition for her college. She secured its senior college ranking by the Texas Board of Education in 1931, gained its membership in the American Association of Colleges in 1936, and garnered an "A" rating for it from the Southern Association of Colleges and Secondary Schools in 1943. Branch was an early supporter of the United Negro Fund and made Tillotson one of its first affiliates.

At the same time that she rejuvenated Tillotson and ensured its survival, Branch took a prominent role in the Austin community. She served in 1943 as president of the Austin chapter of the National Association for the Advancement of Colored People, was a member of the state's Commission on Interracial Cooperation, and served on the state's Negro Advisory Board for the National Youth Administration from 1935. In this capacity she worked closely with Lyndon Johnson, then the state's Youth Administration director, and established two freshmen college centers under the auspices of Tillotson to encourage unemployed black youth to further their education. Such efforts, she wrote Johnson, "bolstered up the self-respect of those young folks" (Winegarten, p. 183). She participated in a local book club and women's club and was a regular walker on Tillotson's 23-acre campus.

Branch's efforts garnered nationwide attention. For her work at Tillotson, Virginia State College gave her an honorary doctorate of pedagogy and Howard University presented her with an honorary doctor of laws degree. Never one to be satisfied with past accomplishments, Branch continued to push for needed improvements at Tillotson. She initiated shared faculty and speakers programs with Samuel Huston College, a black Methodist Episcopal college also located in Austin. These arrangements ultimately led to the merger of the two schools into Huston-Tillotson College in 1952. Branch had died in Camden, New Jersey, eight years earlier.

Mary Elizabeth Branch gave singular attention to Tillotson College and moved the college from almost-certain failure to exemplary success. Described by those who knew her as frank and at times even brusque, she was also recognized as one who loved her institution and loved those who shared its life with her. Her interest in the welfare of her students was extensive and included her adoption of one female pupil as her own daughter. She never married. One of only a few black women college presidents in the United States in the 1930s and 1940s, Branch was an inspiring leader for her students, a talented and successful college administrator, and a visionary for the direction of black education in the South.

• Branch's papers are in the archives of the Downs-Jones Library at Huston-Tillotson College in Austin. A thorough assessment of her life is Olive D. Brown and Michael R. Heintze, "Mary Branch: Private College Educator," in *Black Leaders: Texans for Their Times*, ed. Alwyn Barr and Robert A. Calvert (1981). Helpful for placing Branch in the context of the role of black women in higher education in Texas is Ruthe Winegarten, *Black Texas Women: 150 Years of Trial and Triumph* (1995). Other instructive sources on Branch's life are "Making Bricks without Straw" in Mary Jenness, *Twelve Negro Americans* (1936), and Reavis L. Mitchell, Jr., "Mary E. Branch," in *Notable Black American Women*, ed. Jessie Carney Smith (1992).

DEBBIE MAULDIN COTTRELL

BRANCHE, George Clayton (10 Jan. 1896–10 Sept. 1956), physician, was born in Louisburg, North Carolina, the son of Reverend Joel Branche and Hanna Shaw. He attended the Mary Potter Academy in Oxford, North Carolina. The Branche home was located near this Presbyterian school, and George Branche enjoyed playing on the campus where he acquired his early education.

After his high school graduation in 1913, Branche enrolled at Lincoln University in Pennsylvania, where he participated as an athlete. He graduated in 1917 and served in World War I as a master sergeant. After the Armistice, he focused on medicine as a career. Branche graduated from the Boston University Medical School in 1923, and he was an intern at the Boston Psychopathic Hospital.

While Branche was in medical school, federal officials sought a site to establish a hospital for black veterans. African-American World War I veterans suffered from treatment at inferior hospitals or were neglected. Health care for many black Americans was poor, and few black physicians were available to serve the vast population. Government leaders sought a southern town to build a black veteran's hospital, but only black citizens from Tuskegee, Alabama, expressed an interest in the project.

The Tuskegee Veterans Administration (VA) Hospital was approved in 1921 and initially had a white staff. Area residents opposed black physicians securing control of the facility and threatened violence if such measures were implemented. Black medical professionals were disappointed that promises made by government officials to place black physicians in leadership positions at the hospital were not kept. The summer of 1923 erupted into cross burnings and protests after it was announced that six black physicians, including Branche, would soon arrive. General Frank T. Hines, director of the Veterans Bureau, and leaders of the National Medical Association had selected promising physicians to replace the white physicians at the hospital.

Branche moved to Tuskegee in November 1923 as a junior medical officer at the hospital. He served on rotations and treated patients in general medicine, neuropsychiatry, and tuberculosis wards. By 1927 he was accepted for postgraduate study in neuropsychiatry in New York City, returning as chief of Neuropsychiatric Service at the Tuskegee veterans' hospital.

Perhaps Branche's most significant work involved the development of new treatments for neurosyphilis occurring in blacks. He had experimented unsatisfactorily with the tertian strain of malaria to treat neurosyphilis since 1928. In November 1932 he inoculated seven patients with the quartan strain of malaria as a possible treatment for neurosyphilis. Branche considered the results favorable. At the 1934 American Psychiatric Association meeting he first discussed his work. Inoculating thirty-six patients with the quartan strain, he had experienced a 91 percent success rate as compared to a 14 percent rate with the tertian strain injected into twenty-two patients. Psychiatric professionals considered his quartan treatment as some of the most outstanding research performed at Tuskegee.

Branche read his paper "Therapeutic Quartan Malaria in the Treatment of Neurosyphilis among Negroes" at the 1939 American Psychiatric Association meeting in Chicago. During panel discussion, his peers agreed that his work was a "real contribution." Dr. Walter L. Bruetsch of Indianapolis, Indiana, remarked that "The work of Dr. Branche and his associates in Tuskegee represents an admirable contribution and has an important practical application. It also comes at the right moment" because most hospitals at that time were dealing with treatment of malaria. "I believe it is one of the best contributions which have been made in recent years in the treatment of neurosyphilis," Bruetsch concluded (*Journal of the National Medical Association* [1941]: 84–85).

Physicians traveled to Tuskegee to learn Branche's method, and the treatment was quickly adopted. Branche explained that treatment with the tertian type of malaria had failed in blacks because he believed they had acquired an immunity because of the "entrenched endemic nature of tertian malaria in the South." Dr. Toussaint Tourgee Tildon, manager of the Tuskegee VA Hospital praised that "Dr. Branche's greatest single attainment was the contribution he made when he gave to the medical profession and to the world an improved method of treating neurosyphilis by means of quartan malaria" (*Journal of the National Medical Association* [1958]: 140).

World War II interrupted Branche's work. Serving as assistant clinical director since 1941, he embarked on a tour of duty as a lieutenant colonel in the U.S. Army Medical Corps in February 1944. When he was discharged in May 1946, Branche returned to Tuskegee as director of Professional Services at the veteran's hospital.

Branche was a fellow of the American Psychiatric Association and a diplomate of the American Board of Psychiatry and Neurology. He was a member of the American Board of Neuropsychiatry, National Medical Association, American Association for the Advancement of Science, and Association of Military Surgeons of the United States. Branche earned many honors, including the 1944 E. S. Jones Award for research in medical science from the John A. Andrews Clinical Society at Tuskegee Institute. He was named "Omega Man of the Year" in 1954 by Iota Omega Chapter of Omega Psi Phi fraternity.

Branche had married Lillian V. Davidson in 1924; they had two sons, who both became doctors, and a daughter. Branche was active in civic organizations and helped to establish the Presbyterian church at Tuskegee and athletic teams, including baseball, basketball, and tennis, at Tuskegee Institute. After a year's illness, Branche died at the Tuskegee VA Hospital, where he had devoted thirty-three years on staff. He was buried at Arlington National Cemetery.

• Branche's publications include "Syphilis of Brain and Cord," *Journal of the National Medical Association* 21 (1929): 52–57; "Tryparsamide Therapy of Neurosyphilis in Negroes," *U.S. Veterans Bureau Medical Bulletin* 7 (1931): 476–80; and, with Prince P. Barker and Toussaint T. Tildon, "Facts of Interest in Connection with the Veterans Administration Faculty," *Journal of the National Medical Association* 33 (1941): 81–82. For more information on Branche's life and career, see Barker, "Psychiatry at the Tuskegee VA Hospital in Retrospect," *Journal of the National Medical Association* 54 (Mar. 1962): 152–53; Pete Daniel, "Black Power in the 1920s: The Case of Tuskegee Veterans Hospital," *Journal of Southern History* 36 (1970): 368–88; Herbert M. Morais, *The History of the Afro-American in Medicine* (1976); Asa G. Yancey, Sr., "Tuskegee Veterans Administration Medical Center: Genesis and Opportunities It Provided in Surgery," in *A Century of Black Surgeons: The U.S.A. Experience*, ed. Claude H. Organ and Margaret M. Kosiba (1987), pp. 335–75, and Vanessa Northington Gamble, *Making a Place for Ourselves: The Black Hospital Movement, 1920–1945* (1995). An obituary is in the *Journal of the National Medical Association* 50 (1950).

ELIZABETH D. SCHAFER

BRAND, Max. *See* Faust, Frederick Schiller.

BRAND, Virgil Michael (16 Jan. 1862–20 June 1926), brewer and numismatist, was born in Blue Island, Illinois, the son of Michael Brand, a cooper and brewer, and Philippine Darmstädter, the daughter of a flour merchant. Michael Brand was born in Odernheim near Alzey in the Grand Duchy of Hesse-Darmstadt (not to be confused with the larger village of the same name in the Palatinate) and is said to have left Germany because he was involved in the Revolution of 1848. This is certainly possible, but many German immigrants who left for economic reasons later claimed they had left for political reasons, because it was more glamorous. Philippine Darmstädter was born in Framersheim, the next village over from Odernheim. Michael Brand established a brewery in Chicago under his own name, and it became one of the most prosperous breweries in the city. The firm was one of the very first to adopt Carl von Linde's refrigeration machine, which meant that the company had an incalculable advantage over its competitors: in the summer, its beer was cold. Michael Brand became extremely wealthy, and in 1890, after a series of mergers, he sold out to English investors, who formed the United States Brewing Company. Michael Brand also established orchards at Brandsville in the Missouri Ozarks, where he sought to encourage viticulture. He owned an extensive library, and he must have had a great love for the classics, for he named his three sons Virgil, Horace, and Armin.

In addition to a substantial estate, Virgil Brand inherited two important assets from his father: a love of learning, including the classics, and the technique of brewing cold beer. The latter would finance the former. After attending Bryant and Stratton College, a business college in Chicago, he became secretary and treasurer of his father's brewery. He received much in cash and bonds when the company was sold to English investors and served as president of the new firm for a few years, but he soon resigned. In 1899 Brand established his own brewery, the Brand Brewing Company of Chicago, with capital of $300,000, of which he personally subscribed $170,000.

Brand began to collect coins around 1879. From 1 June 1889 he began to enter these purchases in ledgers. By the time of his death he is estimated to have spent $2,057,548.37 to acquire 361,818 coins. Brand's collection was not the largest in the world—coins are extremely abundant artifacts, and it is easy to accumulate a large number of common coins—but it included many rare coins and not single specimens but multiple examples. He had two of the most glamorous rarities of U.S. coins, the 1804 dollar and the Brasher doubloon. Other coins, of which most collectors cannot afford even one, he owned in duplicate, such as two Constantine roubles, two aurei of Diadumenian, and four New Yorke in America tokens (of which between twelve and twenty exist). The 361,818 figure, however, does not necessarily represent the number of coins in his possession at the time of Brand's death. He sold duplicate coins and from 1907 to 1915 operated his own coin dealership, the Chicago Coin Company, in partnership with Theophile E. Leon, who served as Brand's agent, traveling across the country, seeking out rarities.

Brand was a member of many numismatic organizations, including the Chicago Numismatic Society (of which he served as president), the New York Numismatic Club, the American Numismatic Society, and the American Numismatic Association (ANA). In 1909 he resigned from the ANA because of his dislike of the activities of the promoter Farran Zerbe, who was then president. The Chicago Numismatic Society dissolved around 1915.

Brand never married, but from 1908 until his death he had a relationship with Elsie Egelhoff, an artist and a music teacher, who was born about 1885. Brand gave her $50,000 worth of bonds plus a trust fund before his death; his brothers paid her an allowance after his death but stopped it when she married in 1929.

The First World War destroyed Brand's world. His brother Horace purchased in 1912 a German language newspaper, the Illinois *Staats-Zeitung*, which led a campaign for neutrality and against Woodrow Wilson. The hyperpatriotism that followed the declaration of war exposed German Americans to great prejudice. Furthermore, the manufacture of beer was halted during the war; after the war, Prohibition became the law. The brewery made near beer for a few years, but eventually it had to shut down (year unknown).

Anti-German feeling, the closure of the brewery, the end of his activity in numismatic organizations, and a skin disease (boils) from which he had suffered for many years combined to make Brand a recluse. Although he continued to buy coins, he took on some attributes of the true hoarder-recluse: newspapers and rubber bands piled up in his house. He died in Chicago—the death certificate cited acute myocarditis and endocarditis (heart disease) as the proximate cause, with furunculosis (boils) as the secondary cause. No will was found. The estate, which largely consisted of the coins, went to his brothers.

• The chief unpublished records of Brand are his ledgers, now known as the Brand Numismatic Archives, which are in the library of the American Numismatic Society, New York City; some correspondence, mostly from Armin and Horace Brand discussing the estate, also is included. An article by Virgil Brand is "The Objects of Coin Collecting," *Numismatist* 18 (May 1905): 145–47. The one biography is Quentin David Bowers, *Virgil Brand: The Man and His Era: Profile of a Numismatist* (1983). The biography contains errors—Bowers assumes that Brand began collecting in 1889—and the bulk of it is a regurgitation of articles from the *Numismatist*. Bowers, *American Numismatic Association Centennial History* (1991), also largely reprints from the *Numismatist*, contains a reasonable explanation for Brand's resignation from the ANA. The following articles contain useful information about Virgil Brand, "Chicago Numismatists and Their Society," *Numismatist* 19 (Mar. 1906): 80–81; and "Coins as Textbooks: The Chicago Record-Herald Interviews Virgil M. Brand," *Numismatist* 23 (Aug.–Sept. 1910): 213. See also the *Numismatist* 15 (Apr. 1902): 107, for a correction sent in by Brand. Alden Scott Boyer, later president of the ANA, lived in Chicago, knew Brand well, and wrote a regular column for the *Numismatist*. See his columns in the *Numismatist* 35 (May 1922): 241; 46 (Feb. 1933): 104–5; and 46 (Mar. 1933): 195–96. John W. Adams, "The Hall-Brand Saga," *Numismatist* 96 (Jan. 1983): 30–32, is unreliable, because it relied on William Sheldon, a notorious fabulist. On the Chicago Numismatic Society see Carl F. Wolf and Jennie Sochon, "History of Chicago Coin Club," in *Perspectives in Numismatics: Studies Presented to the Chicago Coin Club*, ed. Saul B. Needleman (1986).

JOHN M. KLEEBERG

BRANDEGEE, Frank Bosworth (8 July 1864–14 Oct. 1924), lawyer and politician, was born in New London, Connecticut, the son of Augustus Brandegee, a lawyer, and Nancy Christian Bosworth. Brandegee grew up in an aristocratic family and followed closely in the footsteps of his father. Both men graduated Yale University, practiced law, and entered first state and later national politics as members of the Republican party. Brandegee received a B.A. from Yale in 1885, traveled a year in Europe, and was admitted to the Connecticut bar in 1888. At that time he joined the firm of Brandegee, Noyes & Brandegee. From 1889 to 1902, with the exception of two years, he served as corporation counsel of New London and also as U.S. attorney for his district for a time. Elected to the Connecticut House of Representatives in 1888, he was elected again in 1898 and became Speaker of the house in 1899. During this same period, he served as a delegate to the Republican National Conventions of 1888, 1892, 1900, and 1904.

In 1902 Brandegee embarked upon a national political career. Elected to Congress as a representative from the Third Connecticut District, he remained in the House from 1902 to 1905. He resigned in the latter year to accept his nomination by the Republican-controlled Connecticut legislature to fill the unexpired term of Orville H. Platt in the Senate. Brandegee was elected by popular vote to serve three additional terms as senator, a position he held until his death.

During his years in the Senate, Brandegee made few speeches and very rarely delivered public addresses. His biggest impact on the political process came from his committee work and his behind-the-scenes negotiations. He served as a member of the Committees on Interoceanic Canals, the Library, and Patents as well as chair of the Committee on Forest Reservations and Protection of Game and of the Senate Judiciary Committee. In addition, he was a leading Republican member of the Foreign Relations Committee and became a close personal and political friend of Henry Cabot Lodge (1850–1924).

While a *New York Times* editorial considered Brandegee to be "one of the Senatorial group having most to say in the conduct of Senate affairs" (15 Oct. 1924), some of his colleagues believed the impact of Brandegee to be "largely negative, if not reactionary" (*Dictionary of American Biography*, vol. 1 [1957], p. 598), especially in the area of Progressive reforms. He voted against the Clayton Antitrust Act, the Federal Trade Commission, the Federal Reserve System, the direct election of senators, the extension of the parcel post, federal regulation of child labor, and the income tax. He opposed Prohibition and, despite the passage of the Eighteenth Amendment, kept a supply of whiskey in his office. His vehement statements against woman suffrage earned him the condemnation of the National American Suffrage Association and the National Woman's party. Ironically, he reversed his position in 1920, fearing a female backlash at the polls in the approaching election.

Brandegee is perhaps best remembered for his actions during the war era, particularly in the fight over the Treaty of Versailles. Concerned with executive usurpation of congressional authority, he resisted any increase in presidential power during the war period. He opposed any violation of constitutional guarantees, such as the attempt by the Wilson administration to censor the press. He also rejected any attempt by Assistant Attorney General Charles Warren to bring civilians accused of interference with World War I before military rather than civilian courts. A staunch Irreconcilable, he drafted the famous Round Robin, which stated that "the constitution of the league of nations in the form now proposed to the peace conference should not be accepted by the United States." With his Washington home as the designated meeting place for senators opposed to the league, his colleagues considered him the "brains of the treaty fight." In his own words, Brandegee informed the Senate that he "would not vote for a league of nations based upon the principle that this league of nations is based upon with all the reservations that the wit of man could devise." As Senator George McLean (R.-Conn.) concluded, "No member of this body contributed more than he to the forces which prevented the ratification of the Treaty of Versailles." Despite his fierce support of American isolationism, however, he called upon the Paris Peace Conference to take up the cause of the Irish.

Brandegee's isolationist stance continued throughout his remaining years in the Senate. During the Washington Conference of 1921, he forced the inclusion of the Brandegee Reservation into the Four Power Treaty: the United States would offer "no commitment to armed force, no alliance, no obligation to join in any defense." This amendment basically reasserted his objection to Article Ten of the League of Nations covenant. He also opposed U.S. membership in the World Court because he believed this association could involve the country in the League of Nations through "the back door." His last major stand in the Senate was his strong support of the highly protectionist Fordney-McCumber Tariff of 1922.

To summarize his general political philosophy, Brandegee was an isolationist who believed Congress was wandering far astray of the original principles of the Constitution. He was particularly concerned with what he considered the growing federal infringement on states' rights and the increasing tendency toward centralization.

As for his personal life, Brandegee remained a confirmed bachelor who often operated at the center of Alice Roosevelt Longworth's social circle. A patron of the arts, he preserved a valuable private collection of paintings and antiques in his Washington home. Throughout his life, he maintained a home in New London but spent much of his time in Washington. Health problems associated with an obscure disease following an attack of influenza in the early 1920s as well as adverse real estate investments led Brandegee to end his own life. While historians have focused on Brandegee's role in the fight over the League of Nations, he also helped define the politics of the conservative wing of the Republican party during the Progressive Era.

• The Connecticut Historical Society in Hartford has a small collection of Brandegee's papers, while the Horace B. Clark Collection at the Connecticut State Library, also in Hartford, contains much of his campaign material. For correspondence between Brandegee and other prominent officials during his years in the Senate, see Warren Harding Papers, Ohio Historical Society; Henry Cabot Lodge Papers, Massachusetts Historical Society; and William Borah Papers and Albert J. Beveridge Papers, both at the Library of Congress. The *Genealogical and Biographical Record of New London County, CT . . .* (1905) and N. G. Osborn, *Men of Mark in Connecticut* (1905), provide biographical data on Brandegee. Also useful is Kathleen Lawler, "Reminiscences and Appreciation of Senator Frank B. Brandegee" (1924), an unpublished manuscript in the Orvill Platt Collection at the Connecticut State Library. More information on Brandegee's stand on woman suffrage can be found in the Connecticut Woman's Suffrage Association Papers at the Connecticut State Library. For an analysis of Brandegee and his election campaign of 1920, see Herbert Janick, "Senator Frank B. Brandegee and the Election of 1920," *Historian* 35 (1973): 434–51. Obituaries are in the *New York Times* and the *Hartford Courant*, 15 Oct. 1924, and in the *Congressional Record* (both Senate and House), 68th Cong., 2d sess., 1925.

The most complete study of Brandegee's opposition to the league is Ralph Stone, *The Irreconcilables and the League of Nations* (1970). Other informative works on this topic include Henry Cabot Lodge, *The Senate and the League of Nations* (1925); John Garraty, *Henry Cabot Lodge: A Biography* (1965); and Lloyd E. Ambrosius, *Woodrow Wilson and the American Diplomatic Tradition: The Treaty Fight in Perspective* (1987). The *Proceedings of the Committee on Foreign Relations*, with an introduction by Richard D. Challener (1979), is also worthwhile.

SIMONE M. CARON

BRANDEGEE, Mary Katharine Layne Curran (28 Oct. 1844–3 Apr. 1920), botanist, was born in the wilds of western Tennessee, the daughter of Marshall Bolling Layne, a schoolteacher, and Mary Morris, a weaver. Mary Katharine Layne, known as "Kate," lived as a child in Tennessee, Missouri, Utah, Nevada, and in California at the time of the gold rush. In her own words, "My father, an impractical genius, afflicted with *Wanderlust*, moved continually till stopped by the western ocean, which we reached before my ninth year . . . I passed my childhood in the foothills of El Dorado County in much isolation." They settled in 1853 on a farm in Folsom, California. Kate Layne left home early, taught school, and at age twenty-two married Hugh Curran, an alcoholic local constable, who died in 1874. She had no children. Kate Curran, then thirty, moved to San Francisco and entered medical school; she took her M.D. from the University of California medical school in 1878, just ten years after the university was officially founded. She found herself as a young woman doctor not "overrun with patients." She had become interested in botany, had studied materia medica with Dr. Hans Behr of the College of Pharmacy of the University of California, and was already a member of the California Academy of Sciences. The academy was unusual among contemporary scientific organizations, in the United States and abroad, in welcoming women members. She helped J. W. Harkness, longtime president of the academy, by making microscopic preparations of the California fungi he studied. In her words, "I began to make myself useful especially about the herbarium, which was in a shocking condition. I began to collect plants in 1882, and the next year was offered the curatorship." She accepted, gave up her small practice, and "devoted the succeeding ten very active years to the service of the Academy."

The California Academy was at that time the leading scientific organization in the western United States. The curatorship was a paid position, probably the best held by an American woman botanist at that time. It was the era of botanical exploration and of the discovery of many species new to science in California. Kate Curran made many botanical trips, benefiting from the new transcontinental railroads. "I enjoyed a general pass on the roads, which allowed me to ride on anything from Pullman to engine . . . [which] was of the greatest value in allowing me, without too great expense, to utilize the time of the short desert seasons." She helped to establish a series of *Bulletins* of the California Academy and published her findings there and elsewhere.

In 1889 Kate Curran married Townshend Stith "T. S." Brandegee, also an established botanist. He was by training a civil engineer and had led surveys for several of the western railways, continually making plant collections and sending new species to eastern authorities for identification. He also had collected logs of forest trees for the American Museum of Natural History and had moved to California in the course of that work. A family legacy enabled him to settle in California and devote himself entirely to botany. He joined the California Academy, where he met the "scientific men of the day . . . Dr. H. W. Harkness, Dr. Albert Kellogg, Professor Edward Lee Greene . . . and Dr. Mary Katharine Curran," whom he called the "leading spirit in the affairs of that institution." Kate Curran Brandegee and her husband are said to have spent their honeymoon walking from San Diego to San Francisco, collecting plants along the way.

The Brandegees and Harkness founded the academy journal, *Zoe*, in 1890 to provide, she wrote, "freer scope for discussion and criticism" than was possible in the *Bulletins*. T. S. Brandegee and she both edited it. *Zoe* was called by contemporary botanist Marcus Jones "the only high class magazine on the Pacific Coast." Kate Brandegee wrote articles and reviews, praising and sometimes severely criticizing the work of other botanists, including Edward Lee Greene and Nathaniel Britton. She also started the first West Coast botanical club, the Excursion Club.

In 1893 the Brandegees, together with entomologist Gustave Eisen, made an expedition to Baja California for the academy. The *San Francisco Chronicle* published a popular account of this extended trip under the headline "Off on an Odd Expedition: Two Men and a Woman Chasing after Snakes and Bugs." The Brandegees were, in fact, chasing after new plants. The newspaper writer, aware of the anomaly of a woman scientist, observed that "Mrs. Brandegee on this trip rode astride of her mule man-fashion in the pantalooned suit that she took with her for the purpose." Kate Brandegee returned to San Francisco by boat, was shipwrecked at San Pedro and rescued in a life boat. She managed to save their precious specimens.

In 1894 the Brandegees moved to San Diego, where they built their own herbarium library and botanical garden. Kate Brandegee relinquished the curatorship of the California Academy herbarium to her protégée, Alice Eastwood, another very competent botanist, famed for saving the valuable type specimens during the great San Francisco fire. In San Diego Kate and T. S. Brandegee continued their botanical expeditions, his mostly in Mexico, hers largely in California. She often made expeditions on her own. She wrote her husband, "I am in the oak belt . . . tomorrow I leave on the stage for the Giant [Sequoia] Forest where . . . I will be for nearly a week. Then I try to get higher—with a packer guide and finally fetch up across country to Mineral King. It may be 3 or four weeks before I reach there. Of course you know I am trying by study of their [oak trees] variation to get the bounds of the species." This was the period when California botanists were declaring their independence from the eastern botanical establishment, naming their own new species instead of sending them to Harvard. It was therefore necessary to visit the eastern herbaria and compare the new specimens with those already named. Kate Brandegee was one of the few who did this. She also borrowed specimens by mail from European herbaria.

Brandegee was not a general plant explorer but a botanical problem solver interested in particular genera of California plants. She was always interested in variation, as with the oaks, and made a practice of collecting series of specimens to show the natural variation present. She corresponded with Sereno Watson at Harvard on this subject, sometimes sending him series of specimens, a hundred specimens of *Ceanothus* (California lilac) for example. Botanists at the time were inclined to be either "lumpers" or "splitters" in terms of naming new species. Brandegee could be designated a lumper who espoused broad species concepts; she accepted evolution and viewed the variation she found as part of an evolutionary process. Edward Lee Greene, another leading California botanist, was a creationist and a splitter; to him, every small variant constituted a new species. As stated by Dupree and Gade, Kate Curran Brandegee was "more in tune with [Asa] Gray's evolutionary ideas than with Greene's vituperative anti-Darwinian stand and finely split species." By 1890 California botanists were no longer taking advice from eastern botanists in naming their species; Kate Curran, in her letters and by her specimens, appears to have been instructing Watson in evolutionary plant taxonomy.

In a 1914 paper, Brandegee pointed out the great variation within one species, *Oenothera ovata*, an evening primrose. She discussed self- versus cross-pollination and how cross-fertilization can be brought about, subjects much discussed by Darwin. She had attended Hugo DeVries's lectures when he visited Berkeley and made extensive notes, some critical. She noted:

> The Mutation theory of DeVries aroused much interest. It was given with such a wealth of detail . . . and in the hands of others, carrying on his experiments appeared

to be corroborated [so] that for a time there was danger of its general acceptance, in spite of its inherent improbability. Reduced to its elements, it claims that variability is of [only] two kinds, fluctuating variability, produced by environment, and mutation, which is suddenly produced from inherent tendency, and reproduces itself constantly.

She herself was studying other types of variation. She referred in her 1914 paper to DeVries's work on the better-known *Oenothera biennis-lamarkiana* group. Variation in *Oenothera* is often due to chromosomal translocation, something that was not known at that time. It is clear, however, that the questions she asked and the kind of evidence she looked for indicate an evolutionary mindset, one that obviously ran counter to the more prevalent mindset of finding new species—no matter how narrow the species concept—to be named after the discoverer in the "great naming game" still going on in California.

In 1906 the Brandegees left San Diego and moved back to Berkeley, donating both their extensive herbarium—more than 75,000 specimens, including valuable type specimens—and their botanical library to the University of California. T. S. Brandegee was named honorary curator. According to Setchell, "Daily for the rest of their lives, Mr. and Mrs. Brandegee were to be found at work in the Herbarium of the University and with the exception of an occasional botanical trip to the mountains or the desert, this continued to the end of their lives." Together they explored the Santa Lucia Mountains, where Kate Brandegee broke her leg and had to be carried out over rough terrain. During this last period of her life, in spite of failing health, Brandegee also traveled to Harvard twice, in 1913 and in 1917. She wrote her husband that the people were kind but that there was no hotel in Cambridge; that she had to take the underground from Boston; and that she missed their San Francisco French restaurant. She died in Berkeley and is buried there. Her husband died in 1925.

Marcus Jones, another California botanist interested in evolution, met Brandegee only after she returned to Berkeley, when she was over sixty. He was impressed by what he called the "masculine" quality of her mind, her "keenness of observation and . . . mental grasp she had on any subject she tackled." He called her "a genuine genius for research" but noted her "excessive caution, which led her to put off publication too long." He had hoped she would use her extensive knowledge to write a flora of California. According to Setchell also, some of her many botanical projects were not completed.

Kate Curran Brandegee never wrote a flora of California, though she did publish a flora of Yosemite. Those who have since written California floras describing the state's more than six thousand plants are in her debt. She is listed under "Curran (later Brandegee)" among the authors of species names in Munz's flora of California. Brandegee's research contribution, however, was a different one: she focused on what has since become known as the systematics of particular groups of plants, including the Lobeliaceae, Portulaceae, Cactaceae, *Lupinus*, *Ceonothus*, and *Oenothera*, attempting to solve problems in a very diverse California flora containing very many newly discovered taxa. Her methods of studying variation within these groups were used by later California evolutionary botanists, although they added experimental methods of analyzing variation. Jones mentions her "series of futile experiments to solve the riddle of sex," but that is all we know of them. After she became curator at the California Academy of Sciences in 1883, her influence was especially important in providing California botanists (and other scientists) with journals in which to publish their scientific work, particularly the academy *Bulletins*, which she edited. Later, in *Zoe*, which she was also instrumental in founding, she provided reviews and critical editorial comment on many of the botanical issues of the day, including the "American" system of nomenclature, which she and other California botanists strongly opposed. As Dupree and Gade noted, although Brandegee published little after her return to Berkeley, "her contributions to the herbarium carry . . . a record of her research from which later generations can profit." Indeed, her critical work on several families and genera of the California flora paved the way for monographers who came after her.

• Papers, including an unpublished autobiographical sketch, "Remembrances by Mrs. Brandegee," and many letters, among them those quoted here, and the DeVries lecture notes are in the University Herbarium, University of California, Berkeley. Other papers, including letters, photos, and the 1893 *San Francisco Chronicle* article, are in the California Academy of Sciences Archives. Letters to Asa Gray and Sereno Watson are in the Gray Herbarium library, Harvard University. Her publications from 1884 to 1888 were issued under the name Mary K. Curran; subsequent publications, under Katharine Brandegee or Katharine Layne Brandegee. "The Flora of Yellowstone" was published in *Zoe* 2 (1891): 155–67. The *Oenothera* paper discussed is "Variation in *Oenothera ovata*," *University of California Publications in Botany* 6 (1914): 41–50. Brandegee's reviews in *Zoe*, vols. 1–5, are of considerable interest.

Biographical material and evaluation of her botanical work can be found in William A. Setchell, "Townshend Stith Brandegee and Mary Katharine (Layne) (Curran) Brandegee," *University of California Publications in Botany* 13 (1926): 156–78; a bibliography of her papers and reviews appears here also. Further opinions of a contemporary can be found in two papers by Marcus E. Jones, "Mrs. T. S. Brandegee," *Contributions to Western Botany* 18 (1933): 12–18, and "Katherine [*sic*] Brandegee," *Desert* 4 (1932): 65–70. More recent evaluations include A. Hunter Dupree and Marian L. Gade, "Brandegee, Katharine Curran," in *Notable American Women* (1971), and Nancy Slack, "Botanical and Ecological Couples, a Continuum of Relationships," in *Creative Couples in the Sciences*, ed. H. M. Pycior et al. (1996). For discussion of California's botanical explorers, including Katharine Curran Brandegee, see Slack, "The Botanical Exploration of California from Menzies to Muir (1886–1900)," in *John Muir:*

Life and Works, ed. Sally Miller (1993). See also Marcia M. Bonta's chapter on Kate Brandegee in *Women in the Field: America's Pioneering Women Naturalists* (1991).

NANCY G. SLACK

BRANDEGEE, Townshend Stith (16 Feb. 1843–7 Apr. 1925), botanist, was born in Berlin, Connecticut, the son of Elishama Brandegee, a physician, and Florence Stith. Townshend Brandegee (usually referred to as T. S.) grew up in central Connecticut, where his father was a country doctor and owner of a small farm. Both his father and uncle collected plants and interested him in natural history, especially ferns and birds. He enlisted at age nineteen in the First Regiment of the Connecticut Artillery during the Civil War and wrote in an unpublished autobiographical note that "Gen. Grant and I took Richmond." After the war he attended Yale's Sheffield Scientific School; he received a Ph.B. in 1870 in civil engineering, but he had also studied botany with Daniel Cady Eaton. He subsequently worked as a civil engineer and surveyor in Canon City, Colorado, from 1871 to 1879, but his interest in botany persisted. He collected Colorado ferns and other plants for John H. Redfield, who sent unknown plants to Asa Gray at Harvard.

In 1875 Gray recommended Brandegee as assistant topographer and botanical collector for Ferdinand V. Hayden's exploring expedition in southwestern Colorado and adjacent Utah. Brandegee wrote, "In locating railroad lines and making preliminary surveys I came upon many rare plants." Other railroad surveys and plant collections followed in Arkansas and New Mexico. Brandegee was later in charge of construction for the Denver and South Park Railway in the Sawatch Mountains. "The division extended from 7,000 to 11,000 ft. altitude, which gave me a fine opportunity to collect the Alpine flora, especially on Sunday." There he also collected logs of many tree species for Charles Sprague Sargents "Report on the Forests of North America."

Following his railway work in the west, Brandegee was hired to make a forest map of the Adirondacks in New York State. He then joined the Northern Transcontinental Survey as a forest surveyor and botanical collector, spending two years in the Yakima region and the Cascade Mountains of Washington. In 1886 and 1887 he was sent, again for Sargent, to collect "rare or troublesome tree trunks" from Montana to California for the Jesup Collection at the American Museum of Natural History. They were to be as large as possible, and some were difficult and expensive to transport.

Brandegee was then sent to Santa Cruz Island, California, to collect logs for Sargent, and in 1888 he began a study of the islands off the coast of California and Baja California. He settled in California, devoting himself entirely to botany. Beginning in 1889 he made many expeditions by mule and boat in Baja California and other regions of Mexico, one of the earliest plant explorers and collectors in these regions.

In San Francisco Brandegee became a member of the California Academy of Sciences, the leading West Coast scientific institution of the time. There he met Albert Kellogg, George Davidson, H. W. Harkness, Edward Lee Greene, and Mary Katharine Layne Curran, who was curator of plants for the academy. He married Curran in 1889 in San Diego, and they made a botanical honeymoon trip on foot all the way to San Francisco.

Brandegee continued his botanical explorations and provided financial support from his private income for the academy's journal, *Zoe*, which his wife edited. In 1894 the Brandegees moved to San Diego, where they had their own herbarium and botanical garden. C. A. Purpus sent Brandegee his Mexican collections; Brandegee worked with these and published *Plantae Mexicanae Purpusianae*, containing descriptions of new species found by Purpus as far south as Chiapas.

In 1906 the Brandegees donated their herbarium collections and botanical library to the University of California and moved to Berkeley, where they lived the rest of their lives. They had no children. Brandegee was named honorary curator of the University Herbarium at Berkeley and continued to collect, especially in the Mohave Desert and the state of Puebla, Mexico.

Most of Brandegee's botanical work consisted of exploration for new species. His railway employment enabled him to explore territory unknown botanically. The surveys establishing transcontinental railway routes thus also expanded western American natural history. After he left engineering, log collection, and paid employment, funds from a family legacy allowed him to pursue his interest in the island floras of California and Baja California, on which he became an expert. In California, under the influence of the academy and his wife, Brandegee developed from a botanical explorer to a critical evaluator of his own and others' collections, publishing the results.

Floristics rather than systematic botany was Brandegee's main interest, but that was true of most California botanists during the period of intense botanical discovery. The Brandegee Library and Brandegee Herbarium, the latter containing Brandegee's type specimens, were invaluable contributions to the University of California.

Brandegee read four foreign languages, spoke Spanish on his Mexican expeditions, and wrote his own Latin descriptions of new species. He was a fellow of the American Association for the Advancement of Science and a corresponding member of the Philadelphia Academy of Natural Sciences. He also served on the San Diego Board of Education. Many botanical species and one genus, *Brandegea*, were named for him.

Although Brandegee in his youth was active and outgoing, and often in charge of other workers, in his later California years he was considered quiet and retiring. He suffered from physical disabilities, including deafness and partial paralysis, but he continued his travels into old age and his botanical work until his death in Berkeley.

• Brandegee's papers are in the University Herbarium, University of California, Berkeley; these include two unpublished autobiographical accounts from 1916 and 1921 and many letters. Brandegee published on the plants of California islands and Mexico from 1889 to 1924; his most important publications are the twelve parts of *Plantae Mexicanae Purpusianae*, *University of California Publications in Botany* 3, 4, 6, 7, 10 (1909–1924). The best biographical account is William A. Setchell, "Townshend Stith Brandegee and Mary Katharine (Layne) (Curran) Brandegee," *University of California Publications in Botany* 13 (1926): 156–58, which includes a bibliography of Brandegee's publications. See also Marcus E. Jones, "The Brandegees," *Contributions to Western Botany* 15 (1929): 15–18; and Nancy G. Slack, "Botanical and Ecological Couples," in *Creative Couples in the Sciences* ed. H. M. Pycior et al. (1996), pp. 235–53, as well as her "The Botanical Exploration of California from Menzies to Muir" in *John Muir: Life and Work*, ed. Sally Miller (1993), pp. 193–242.

NANCY G. SLACK

BRANDEIS, Louis Dembitz (13 Nov. 1856–5 Oct. 1941), "people's attorney" and U.S. Supreme Court justice, was born in Louisville, Kentucky, the son of Adolph Brandeis, a successful businessman, and Frederika Dembitz. His parents, non-practicing Jews, had quietly supported the unsuccessful Austrian uprising of 1848 and had immigrated to the United States with their families in the wake of the repression and anti-Semitism that followed. Born as Louis David, Louis changed his middle name as a teenager in honor of his uncle, abolitionist lawyer Lewis Dembitz.

Anticipating the post–Civil War recession, Adolph Brandeis dissolved his business in 1872 and left with his family for a tour of Western Europe. After a year of travel, Louis went to Dresden, where he persuaded the rector of the Annen-Realschule to admit him without the requisite proof of birth, vaccination certificate, and admission examination. There Brandeis vindicated the rector's trust by performing brilliantly. In 1875 he returned to the United States with his family and enrolled in the Harvard Law School.

Brandeis earned his law degree in the usual two years, receiving the highest grades ever achieved at the school and being chosen as valedictorian by the students and faculty. However, Brandeis was twenty years old, and President Charles Eliot at first declined to waive the rule requiring graduates to be twenty-one. Although Eliot and the trustees reversed the decision the morning of commencement so that Brandeis could receive his degree, someone else had already been chosen to give the oration. Brandeis remained at Harvard for a year's graduate work, paying his way by tutoring fellow students and proctoring examinations.

Brandeis was impressed by the case method that had been introduced to Harvard Law School by Dean Christopher Columbus Langdell. Earlier students had been offered only lectures about legal principles. Langdell believed that legal doctrines developed "by slow degrees . . . through a series of cases" and that the best way for the "true lawyer" to learn how to apply them was through reading and discussing the cases. Langdell's approach to the law as a changing entity became the basis of Brandeis's jurisprudence.

Brandeis began his career with a St. Louis firm but missed the intellectual excitement of Cambridge and what he called his "wonderful years" at Harvard. His socialite classmate Samuel Warren invited him to return to Boston to establish their own law firm. The plan became economically feasible when members of the Harvard faculty persuaded Chief Justice Horace Gray of the Massachusetts Supreme Judicial Court to hire Brandeis as his clerk, assuring the young lawyer of an income.

Warren & Brandeis, founded in 1879, rapidly gained a clientele of small and moderate-sized businesses, on whose behalf Brandeis was soon litigating in Massachusetts and other New England states. Members of the local Jewish mercantile class brought him their business. Other clients were referred to him by Harvard faculty members, and Brandeis returned the favor by hiring recent Harvard Law School graduates as the practice expanded, by helping to create the Harvard Law School Alumni Association and the *Harvard Law Review*, and by teaching a course on evidence when James Bradley Thayer went on leave.

Brandeis's course was so successful that Oliver Wendell Holmes (1841–1935) asked one student for his notes, and Harvard offered Brandeis an assistant professorship. However, the twenty-five-year-old attorney turned down the offer because he was afraid that his somewhat uncertain health would preclude his combining teaching with the practice of law and he was loath to relinquish the excitement of litigation. He nonetheless twice taught a course in business law at the Massachusetts Institute of Technology and also found time for writing. In response to overzealous attempts by the press to cover Warren's wedding engagement, Brandeis and Warren wrote an article on "The Right to Privacy," asserting a legally protected "right to be left alone," which was published in the 1890 *Harvard Law Review*. It became the basis for the constitutional right to privacy that was later proclaimed by the U.S. Supreme Court and, as Dean Roscoe Pound commented, "did nothing less than add a chapter to our law."

From the earliest days of his practice, Brandeis began redefining the attorney's role. He considered a major part of an attorney's duty to be the accumulation of facts about a client's business as well as his or her immediate legal concerns, believing that the latter could not be understood without adequate knowledge of the former. The result was that often his clients called him in as a general adviser as well as an attorney. By the time he mediated his first labor strike for a client in 1902, he had begun to rethink the relationship between capital and labor that he had taken for granted both as the son of a small businessman and as the student who had been taught that law developed in tandem with social change. The Homestead Strike of 1892, when the Carnegie Steel Company hired Pinkertons "to shoot at organized labor for resisting an arbitrary cut in wages," as Brandeis described it, made him realize that the power of capital was protected by law but unbalanced by any similar power of labor. He became convinced that arbitrary power inevitably would be abused because "neither our intelligence nor our characters can long stand the strain of unrestricted power." His conversations with labor leaders persuaded him that most labor conflicts could be settled if representatives of business and labor sat down together. He had been delighted at his acceptance by the world of the Boston Brahmins, but he now rejected one of its major axioms by arguing in favor of the legalization of unions and against the uncertain employment that businesses offered in the absence of unions. Boston society responded by turning its back on Brandeis and his second cousin Alice Goldmark, whom he had married in 1891. The couple, immersed in their two young daughters and his burgeoning career, barely noticed.

Brandeis's perception of law as legitimate only to the extent that it reflected societal needs affected his view of the attorney's role. Rejecting the growing tendency of the bar to serve only one side in business-labor disputes, he spoke out against lawyers who "allowed themselves to become adjuncts of great corporations and neglected the obligation to use their powers for the protection of the people." He began working for public causes, initially making himself available for public lectures and then following both his clients' concerns and his own interests into the fields of free trade, public transportation, and utility rates. His dealings with Boston's transportation and utility companies convinced him that monopoly was bad for the public, while his growing familiarity with local and state legislatures demonstrated that big business could corrupt public bodies. Adopting a policy of representing the public for no fee so as to retain his freedom to urge whatever policies he considered fair, he began to spend so much time on public matters that he became known to the public as the "people's attorney" and felt constrained to reimburse his firm for the hours he worked on public causes. His activities inspired a generation of younger lawyers, particularly at Harvard, and helped create the *pro bono publico* (for the public good) bar that became a major force in American legal life during the twentieth century.

Responding in 1905 to the concerns of a potential client, Brandeis became immersed in the practices of the life insurance industry and found the major companies corrupt and wasteful. He considered his life's greatest achievement to be his subsequent creation of the system of savings bank life insurance to provide policies for industrial laborers. When he was asked to mediate the 1910 New York garment workers' strike, he also fashioned an innovative "protocol" that established minimum wages and maximum hours, avoided both the open and the closed shop, and gave labor a voice in disputes. His courtroom creativity was displayed most notably in 1908, when the National Consumers' League asked him to defend Oregon's maximum hours law for women before the U.S. Supreme Court. This period was the heyday of the "liberty of contract" doctrine, which the Court insisted was embodied in the Fourteenth Amendment and interpreted to preclude protective legislation with no direct relationship to workers' health. Determined to demonstrate the constitutionality of the Oregon law, Brandeis presented the Court with only two pages of traditional appeals to legal doctrine and nearly a hundred pages summarizing statistical data from around the world showing that extremely long hours were detrimental to women's health. The Court cited what became known as the "Brandeis brief" in its opinion upholding the law (*Muller v. Oregon*, 1908). The fact-laden brief, consistent with Brandeis's belief that law must follow societal realities, revolutionized constitutional adjudication and was later utilized not only in defense of economic legislation, but in such landmark civil liberties cases as *Brown v. Board of Education* (1954).

As Brandeis worked in the sphere of employee-employer relations and public interest causes that were brought to his attention, he gradually developed a coherent approach to law and politics. A belief in the individual human being, limited in capacity but highly educable and capable of self-government, was central to his thinking. He viewed democracy as the one political system that could decentralize power sufficiently to avoid the pitfalls of corruption that inevitably accompanied unchecked power. Individuals could develop their full potential only through participation in the democratic process, which in turn was dependent upon the informed attention of citizens. Institutions that were created by citizens, such as legislatures, had to be free to experiment with ideas and laws as industrial and technological progress brought both new possibilities and unforeseen problems. Brandeis believed there was an organic relationship between law and society and that it was wrong for judges in a democratic system to attempt to impose their own ideas or outmoded legal concepts to prevent experimentation by citizens and their representatives.

In order for citizens to be informed, Brandeis reasoned, they required access to all available ideas. Thus both state and federal governments had an obligation not to interfere with the free flow of ideas, and states should be encouraged to provide young citizens with an adequate education. In order for citizens to participate fully in government, they required leisure. Overly long work hours were unacceptable both for humane reasons and because they interfered with the democratic process. Brandeis preferred social reform that was undertaken as a result of private decisions rather than as a matter of legal fiat because of his conviction that concentration of power was to be avoided in government as well as in business. However, since he recognized that unions were not sufficiently strong to guarantee shorter working days and decent working conditions, Brandeis supported state legislation setting maximum hours, prohibiting child labor, and establishing unemployment insurance and old-age pensions.

Brandeis saw a correlation between political democracy and what he called "economic liberty." He was Jeffersonian in his belief that a worker who was economically dependent could not be politically free. Beginning with a definition of economic liberty that centered on unionization as a balance to the power of employers, he gradually expanded the meaning to include distribution of excess profits to workers, ultimately redefining the concept as worker participation, whereby workers, by owning and managing businesses, both negate the distinction between capital and labor and prepare themselves for assuming their responsibilities in the political sphere.

Brandeis viewed truth as evolving and depended upon experimentation to demonstrate which institutions would serve humanity best. He therefore supported federalism, lauding both its many possibilities for experimentation and the fact that it saved the American political system from a corrupting overconcentration of power by dividing governmental responsibilities among a multiplicity of entities. Similarly, he deplored overly large businesses. He considered a business "overly large" if its operations were so complex that they could not be understood by the human being supposedly in charge, for such a business could not be run rationally. His disapproval of monopoly, giantism, and the use of corporate wealth to corrupt public bodies converged during his long battle against J. P. Morgan's New Haven Railroad (1905–1913), which eventually was forced to divest itself of most of its holdings.

Many of Brandeis's ideas were shared by his friend, Wisconsin senator Robert La Follette. When La Follette dropped his bid for the presidency after a short campaign in 1912, Brandeis turned his support to Woodrow Wilson, also an enemy of the trusts. Wilson became such a wholehearted student of Brandeis's ideas that his chief biographer, A. S. Link, credits Brandeis with responsibility for Wilson's "New Freedom" and emphasis on elimination of trusts, creation of the Federal Reserve System and the Federal Trade Commission, outlawing of interlocking directorates, increasing the power of the Interstate Commerce Commission, and strengthening the Sherman Antitrust Act.

In August 1914, American Zionists called an emergency conference to consider how to help Palestinian Jews who had been cut off from their usual sources of financial assistance by the outbreak of World War I. Brandeis was invited and was offered what was meant to be only a token leadership position, as Jewishness had never been a major element of his identity, and he had never been involved in the organized Jewish community. He participated in the conference, however, drawn by his conviction that, if properly managed, the Jewish Palestinian community could replicate the democracy that had existed in Periclean Athens. He therefore became the leader of the American Zionist movement and remained intensely involved throughout his life. He frequently compared the socialist Zionists in Palestine to the Pilgrims and helped them fashion a program that reflected his concept of the perfect state: small and agrarian, holding and working all land in common, recognizing the equal rights of all inhabitants, and providing members with an adequate educational system. He had developed most of his ideas on land management while the attorney for *Collier's Weekly* during the Pinchot-Ballinger Alaskan land sales investigation of 1910. The organizations he created as a Zionist leader, such as the American Jewish Congress, the Palestine Endowment Fund, and the Palestine Cooperative Company, incorporated ideas about democratic decision making and institutional accountability that had evolved from his participation in American public life. Brandeis enunciated an idiosyncratic and Americanized form of Zionism that emphasized liberty, equality, democratic governance, fiscal responsibility, and the right of all peoples to national self-determination.

Woodrow Wilson nominated Brandeis to the Supreme Court in 1916—the first time a Jew had been nominated. Although there were traces of anti-Semitism in the battle over confirmation, the bitterness of the fight was much more a reflection of the business community's fear of a reformist, trust-busting "people's attorney" on the Court. However, Brandeis was confirmed and took the judicial oath on 5 June 1916.

He quickly reaffirmed his belief in sociological jurisprudence or law that was based on social needs. When attorneys arguing before the Court failed to demonstrate the constitutionally crucial rational relationship between state statutes and the societal problems they were designed to solve, Brandeis sent his law clerks to gather the sociological and statistical data that were required because the reasonableness of laws "can ordinarily be determined only by a consideration of the contemporary conditions, social, industrial and political, of the community to be affected thereby" (*Truax v. Corrigan*, 1921). For example, when the Court was asked to determine the constitutionality of a consumer protection law that set weight standards for commercially sold loaves of bread, Brandeis presented the Court with fifteen pages of information about the baking industry, most of it in lengthy footnotes (*Burns Baking Co. v. Bryan*, 1924). He viewed judicial opinions as educational essays, written to provide the electorate with the explanation of its officials' decisions to which it was entitled. He was the first Supreme Court justice to cite law reviews (*Adams v. Tanner*, 1917) and developed a symbiotic relationship with them, privately suggesting current topics for articles and then referring to the resultant articles in his opinions.

At the same time, Brandeis insisted on judicial restraint and a limited role for the Court. In a major opinion (*Ashwander v. TVA*, 1936), he spelled out many of the rules that continue to be used in deciding whether it is appropriate for the Court to deal with constitutional issues. He repeatedly emphasized the importance of state independence. His seminal opinion for the Court in *Erie Railroad v. Tompkins* (1938) held that in matters of state law federal courts had to be bound by the decisions issued by each state's highest court. He was wary of federal power, dissenting in *Myers v. United States* (1927) when the Court permitted a president unilaterally to fire a civil servant even though a statute required Senate advice and consent before such a removal and joining the Court whenever, as in *A. L. A. Schechter Poultry Corp. v. United States* (1935), it struck down what he felt was a level of governmental assumption of power not contemplated by the Constitution or inconsistent with democracy.

Brandeis's judicial opinions reflected his insistence that concentrations of power were dangerous, that unions were essential as a balance to corporate power, and that it was wrong for the Supreme Court to negate state experimentation merely because the justices disliked the nature of the experiment. For example, he dissented in *Hitchman Coal and Coke Co. v. Mitchell* (1917), lambasting the Court for upholding "yellow-dog contracts" through which companies forced their employees to agree not to join unions; in *Quaker City Cab Co. v. Pennsylvania* (1928), when the Court overturned a state statute taxing corporations more heavily than individually owned businesses and partnerships; and in *Liggett Co. v. Lee* (1933), when the Court struck down a state law imposing heavier license fees on chain stores than on independent shops.

Brandeis took a fully formed creed to the Court, expressing it in the many opinions he wrote before he retired in 1939. He was, as one colleague noted, an "implacable democrat"; another commented that to Brandeis, "democracy is not a political program. It is a religion." He believed, as he wrote in a 1922 letter, that in a democracy the "development of the individual is . . . both a necessary means and the end sought. For our objective is the making of men and women who shall be free—self-respecting members of a democracy." This creed was particularly apparent in the opinions he wrote concerning free speech and privacy.

Brandeis initially supported Justice Holmes's "clear and present danger" test as a way of determining when the government had the right to penalize speech. Holmes declared that the test should vary in peace and wartime but left open the question of what speech could be punished, saying only that the words had to "create a clear and present danger that they will bring about the substantive evils that Congress has a right to prevent" (*Schenck v. United States*, 1919). In *Schaefer v. United States* (1920), Brandeis rejected differing the criteria for peace and wartime. When a state convicted a speaker under a statute that criminalized the advocacy of pacifism, Brandeis disagreed with Holmes's support of the statute, arguing that the statute violated the right of privacy as well as that of speech (*Gilbert v. Minnesota*, 1920). Finally, in *Whitney v. California* (1927), Brandeis redefined "clear and present danger" as "serious" and "imminent" danger, meaning that there was no time for additional speech to counter the views of a speaker whose utterance raised "the probability of serious injury to the State" and not merely of "some violence or . . . destruction of property." By refusing to endorse governmental power to inhibit or punish speech that was not an imminent danger to the state itself, Brandeis strictly and deliberately minimized the instances in which government action against speech could be held constitutional. His reason for pursuing such a course was his belief in the absolute necessity for the free flow of ideas if democracy was to be possible and that an informed electorate eventually would choose the correct policies.

Brandeis's best-known defense of privacy against governmental intrusion was written in *Olmstead v. United States* (1928), in which he argued that tapping telephone lines was a violation of the Fourth Amendment. "The makers of our Constitution," he wrote in dissent, "undertook . . . to protect Americans in their beliefs, their thoughts, their emotions, and their sensations. They conferred, as against the Government, the right to be let alone—the most comprehensive of rights and the right most valued by civilized men." He noted the crucial connection between speech and privacy, insisting that the protection given by the Constitution to "beliefs, thoughts, emotions, and sensations" had to extend to the expression of them. Brandeis's formulation of the concept of privacy has been cited by subsequent justices in striking down government use of warrantless wiretaps (*Katz v. United States*, 1967) and in upholding constitutional privacy rights to contraception (*Griswold v. Connecticut*, 1965), abortion (*Roe v. Wade*, 1973), and the right to die (*Cruzan v. Director, Missouri Dept. of Health*, 1990). It has also been utilized in the writing of privacy provisions in a number of state constitutions.

Brandeis's extrajudicial activities, including his involvement in Zionism, lasted throughout his judgeship. He had strong ties with the New Dealers who were writing and enforcing many of the social welfare policies he considered crucial for creating a post-Depression economy. While he saw little of President Franklin Roosevelt, he was in frequent contact with other government officials and apparently had as little compunction about telling them what should be included in their laws as he did about striking those laws down when he believed they exceeded the constitutional mandate. He also began and oversaw a program designed to create departmental libraries at the University of Louisville and to upgrade its law school. He continued his involvement with the Harvard Law School, drawing his law clerks from the school, urging many of them to teach there, sending ideas for the law review to Felix Frankfurter, and making personnel and funding suggestions to Dean Roscoe Pound. He also maintained his connection to savings bank life insurance, arranging in 1932 for publication of an inexpensive edition of his articles about his 1914 work, *Other People's Money*, so that the royalties could be used by the Savings Bank Insurance League.

Age and ill health led to his retirement from the Supreme Court in 1939. He died in Washington shortly before what would have been his eighty-fifth birthday. Brandeis left behind a tradition of lawyers contributing their efforts to public service, a jurisprudence based on interpreting the Constitution in light of societal facts, an insistence on privacy and free speech that quickly became the law of the land, an emphasis on individual dignity, and his certainty that, given the efforts of active democrats, liberty would indeed prevail.

• The largest collection of Brandeis letters is at the University of Louisville. Other major collections are in the Library of Congress (Frankfurter papers) and the Harvard Law School Library (Brandeis papers and Frankfurter papers). The Harvard collection also includes many of Brandeis's draft judicial opinions and working folders for Supreme Court cases; see Alexander M. Bickel, ed., *The Unpublished Opinions of Mr. Justice Brandeis* (1957), and Alfred Lief, ed., *The Social and Economic Views of Mr. Justice Brandeis* (1930). Most of the important letters from Brandeis have been published in Melvin I. Urofsky and David W. Levy, eds., *Letters of Louis D. Brandeis* (1971–1978) and *"Half-Brother Half-Son"* (1991). Many of Brandeis's speeches and articles can be found in *Business—A Profession*, ed. Ernest Poole (1914); *Other People's Money and How the Bankers Use It* (1914); *The Curse of Bigness*, ed. Osmond K. Fraenkel (1934); and *Brandeis on Zionism*, ed. Solomon Goldman (1942). Bibliographies of works by and about Brandeis are Roy M. Mersky, *Louis Dembitz Brandeis, 1856–1941: A Bibliography* (1958; repr. 1987), which covers publications through 1957, and Gene Teitelbaum, *Justice Louis D. Brandeis: A Bibliography of Writings and Other Materials on the Justice* (1988), which includes later works.

Among the best of the numerous volumes about Brandeis are Alpheus T. Mason, *Brandeis: A Free Man's Life* (1946); Philippa Strum, *Louis D. Brandeis: Justice for the People* (1984; repr. 1988); and Melvin I. Urofsky, *A Mind of One Piece: Brandeis and American Reform* (1981). Among the works on particular aspects of his life and career are Vincent Blasi, "The First Amendment and the Ideal of Civil Courage," *William and Mary Law Review* 29 (Summer 1988): 653–97; Bernard Flexner, *Mr. Justice Brandeis and the University of Louisville* (1938); Felix Frankfurter, ed., *Mr. Justice Brandeis* (1932); Allon Gal, *Brandeis of Boston* (1980); Alpheus T. Mason, *Bureaucracy Convicts Itself* (1941); Alpheus T. Mason and Henry Lee Staples, *The Fall of a Railroad Empire: Brandeis and the New Haven Merger Battle* (1947); and Alden L. Todd, *Justice on Trial* (1964).

PHILIPPA STRUM

BRANDON, Gerard Chittocque (15 Sept. 1788–28 Mar. 1850), governor of Mississippi, was born on "Selma" plantation near Natchez (then under Spanish control), Mississippi, the son of Gerard Brandon and Dorothy Nugent, planters. He attended Princeton, graduated from William and Mary, began practicing law in the Mississippi Territory in 1810, and was a captain in Ferdinand L. Claiborne's regiment of Mississippi militia during the War of 1812. He married Margaret Chambers in Kentucky in January 1816. The couple had two children before her death in 1820.

Brandon represented Wilkinson County in the territorial legislature in 1815 and in the Mississippi Constitutional Convention in 1817, opposing the division of the territory into two states in both bodies. He served in the state house of representatives in 1821 and in 1822–1823, being chairman of the Committee on Claims during the fourth general assembly and speaker during the sixth. In August 1823 he was elected lieutenant governor, defeating two rivals with 64 percent of the vote. When Governor Walter Leake died on 17 November 1825, Brandon filled out his term until 7 January 1826. The previous August, Brandon had been reelected lieutenant governor by the slim margin of 30 votes out of 9,022 cast. He served until 25 July 1826, when Governor David Holmes resigned. Brandon then again became governor and continued in office until 9 January 1832, defeating four rivals with 52 percent of the vote in 1827 and crushing George Winchester 7,006 votes to 3,764 in 1829.

Always a cautious politician and governor, Brandon was not among the early Mississippi supporters of Andrew Jackson. Brandon was most closely associated with the entrenched and conservative Natchez District political elite in the state, then under assault from the more democratic eastern and northern counties. His gubernatorial style reflected his caution. He was a conscientious administrator but influenced policy primarily through his restrained annual messages to the legislature. Brandon's recommendations on Indian affairs well illustrate his approach. In January 1826 he warned lawmakers that Indian ownership of nearly one-half of the state hindered its development and that the longer the Indians remained, the more difficult it would be to obtain their land; but he failed to suggest what the general assembly could do to hasten their departure. After the well-publicized failure of negotiations with the Choctaws and Chickasaws in late 1826, Brandon again refused to propose any specific action in January 1827. At the next session Brandon ignored Indian affairs except for the brief comment that the prospects of the United States extinguishing Indian title within the state were "flattering." In January 1829 the governor proclaimed that Mississippians would no longer tolerate "an independent [Indian] sovereignty, within our limits, in defiance of the authority of the state." But all he recommended was again petitioning Congress and further patience because the incoming Jackson administration would be better able to convince the Indians to sell their lands in the state. With the approval of President Jackson, Brandon in January 1830 suggested how the general assembly could extend state jurisdiction over Indian territory within Mississippi if it decided to act. Brandon never intended to exercise state jurisdiction over the Indians; rather, the legislation was merely a tool for the Jackson administration to use to convince the Indians to leave the state. The legislature extended state jurisdiction as requested, but, once removal treaties were signed, the governor assured the president that state jurisdiction would be suspended while the Indians were preparing to leave Mississippi. In November 1830 he asked the legislature to suspend jurisdiction, but it failed to act.

Brandon favored a systematic program of internal improvements and in 1829 recommended that the legislature establish a board to undertake such projects. The board was established, but when it was unable to borrow the money needed to execute its plans, Brandon suggested that private corporations be chartered to construct projects that investors thought feasible with the occasional aid that the state could afford. In 1828 and January 1830 the governor opposed the establishment of a branch of the Bank of the United States in Mississippi but, after political sentiment changed, signed a resolution in November 1830 requesting the establishment of a branch in the state. He condemned both the Tariff of 1828 and nullification. Mississippi, Brandon believed, should protest the unjust tariff with a remonstrance "in the strongest terms" to those states supporting it and ask its congressmen to work for repeal of all protective duties. He favored reforming and strengthening the state militia, achieved in legislation passed in 1830. In 1827, 1829, and 1831 Brandon recommended establishing a state penitentiary. His eloquent plea in his final message to "graduate the punishment of crime according to the magnitude of the offence," as most other states were then doing, finally produced results in 1836. In 1828 the governor called slavery "an evil at best" and proposed ending the importation of slaves into the state for sale; he held the office of first vice president of the Mississippi Colonization Society when it was organized in June 1831.

Brandon represented Wilkinson County in the state constitutional convention, which met in September 1832. The ex-governor was barely elected to the convention and received only seven of forty-seven votes for president of that body. He was, however, elected chairman of the committee on the legislative department. On 4 October, as the convention was debating the judiciary, he abruptly resigned his seat. He favored popular election of circuit court judges but opposed it for supreme court justices, which the convention had just approved.

Brandon retired to his plantation, "Columbian Springs," located near Ford Adams in Wilkinson County. Brandon had eight more children with his second wife, Elizabeth "Betsy" Stanton of Natchez, whom he had married in 1824. In the 1830s he owned about eighty slaves and served as the administrator of several estates. In 1838 he was president of the Wilkinson County board of police. He died at his plantation.

• Brandon's annual messages are in the journals of the Mississippi House of Representatives and Senate for 1826–1831. His incoming and some of his outgoing gubernatorial correspondence is in Governors' Correspondence, RG 27, at the Mississippi Department of Archives and History. Other correspondence is in the J. F. H. Claiborne Collection and the Jefferson College Collection at the same repository. Secondary accounts on Brandon and his administrations are in Dunbar Rowland, ed., *Encyclopedia of Mississippi History*, vol. 1 (1907), pp. 287–93, and Claude E. Fike, "The Gubernatorial Administrations of Governor Gerard Chittocque Brandon, 1825–1832," *Journal of Mississippi History* 25 (Aug. 1973): 247–65.

CHARLES H. SCHOENLEBER

BRANDRETH, Benjamin (9 Jan. 1807–19 Feb. 1880), proprietary medicine manufacturer and eclectic physician, was born in Leeds, England, where his father was a merchant. In the mid-eighteenth century, his physician grandfather, William Brandreth of Liverpool, had concocted and sold a Vegetable Universal Pill. Inheriting the formula, Brandreth marketed the pill in 1828. In 1829 he married Harriet Matilda Smallpage; they had five children. In 1835, sensing a larger pill market in the United States, the family migrated to New York City, where his wife died the following year.

Upon his arrival, Brandreth began marketing his Vegetable Universal Pills, and, after a slow beginning, sales expanded rapidly. Brandreth briefly attended New York Eclectic Medical College, the first eclectic college in the United States, which purportedly trained physicians to choose the best practices from different medical theories with an emphasis on the botanical tradition. In 1838, he moved his home and manufacturing operations upriver to Sing Sing (now Ossining). He married Virginia Graham in 1840; they had twelve children, several of whom joined their father's business.

Brandreth's pills became one of the best-selling proprietaries in the United States as well as overseas, especially in South America. The formula contained sarsaparilla and three powerful vegetable cathartics—aloe, colocynth, and gamboge—as well as cinnamon and peppermint for flavor. Americans at this time generally ate a stodgy diet, and constipation was a widespread problem. Brandreth shrewdly asserted that constipation was the source of all ills and acclaimed purgation, by keeping the blood pure, as the universal cure. He condemned the bleeding and mineral medications used in the prevailing therapy of orthodox physicians. Brandreth propagated his doctrines through lavish advertising in the new urban penny press, county weeklies in the expanding West, and popular national weekly magazines. He also distributed a book entitled *The Doctrine of Purgation: Curiosities from Ancient and Modern Literature, from Hippocrates and Other Medical Writers, Covering a Period of over Two Thousand Years, Proving Purgation Is the Cornerstone of All Curatives* (1867). Besides the Father of Medicine, Brandreth sought to make Benjamin Franklin (1706–1790) and the marquis de Condorcet seem to espouse his pills. During the Civil War, he cited soldier testimonials. He appealed to patriotism in his advertisements by including the images of American flags and eagles, and he invoked religion by citing Scripture: "The life of the flesh is in the blood" (Leviticus 17:11). He attracted public attention by creating controversy, accusing druggists of counterfeiting his pills, and battling noisily about the advertising policies of editor James Gordon Bennett (1795–1872) of the *New York Herald* in 1837. In 1848 Brandreth purchased Allcock's Porous Plasters, intended to relieve muscular aches and pains. A congressional committee in 1849 reported that Brandreth was the nation's largest proprietary advertiser, spending $100,000 a year on advertisements. Between 1862 and 1883, Brandreth's average annual gross income surpassed $600,000.

Critics accused Brandreth of quackery. Dan King opined in *Quackery Unmasked* (1858) that Brandreth had brought his pills across the ocean seeing "that the people of the United States, like young birds in their nest, were holding their mouths open for something new."

Brandreth was esteemed in Sing Sing for his lack of ostentation, despite his great wealth. He served as president of the village, was twice elected to the state senate (1850 and 1858), and once ran unsuccessfully for Congress (1857). He was at work in his factory when he suffered the stroke that caused his death. The business continued in family hands, and the pills sold well into the twentieth century.

• Accounts of Brandreth's career appear in J. Thomas Scharf, *History of Westchester County* (1886); James Harvey Young, *The Toadstool Millionaires* (1961); and Henry W. Holcombe, *Patent Medicine Tax Stamps* (1979). See also *Patent Medicines*, House Report 52, 30th Cong., 2d sess., 1849; *Standard Remedies* 15 (Apr. 1928): 64; and "Advertisements of Medicinal Preparations and Devices, 1933–7," Food and Drug Administration Records, RG 88, National Archives. Obituaries appeared in the *Democratic Register* (Sing Sing), 25 Feb. 1880; *New York Tribune*, 20 Feb. 1880; and *New York Times*, 20 and 23 Feb. 1880.

JAMES HARVEY YOUNG

BRANIFF, Thomas Elmer (6 Dec. 1883–10 Jan. 1954), airline executive, was born in Salina, Kansas, the son of John A. Braniff, a businessman, and Mary Catherine Baker. The family moved to Kansas City, Missouri, where Tom and his younger brother, Paul, enrolled in public school. The Braniffs left for the Southwest around the turn of the century, when the Oklahoma Territory opened up under the Homestead Act. Braniff's father started an insurance business, with rural homesteaders as his clients. As a teenager, Tom hit the road for his father, driving a buckboard through the dusty trails of western Oklahoma's "Indian Country."

Young Braniff did well as an insurance salesman. By 1902, in partnership with a friend, he opened his own insurance business in Oklahoma City. He was married in 1912 to Bess Thurman, daughter of a Missouri judge. The Braniffs had two children. When his partner decided to retire in 1919, Braniff bought him out. The T. E. Braniff Company expanded rapidly, fielding dozens of agents and riding the crest of the southwest region's oil boom.

Tom first developed an interest in aviation during the 1920s. After he bought a share in a single-engine Stinson in 1928, his brother, Paul—who had been a pilot in World War I—convinced him to fly it on a 116-mile passenger run between Oklahoma City and Tulsa, two towns joined only by a weather-beaten road and indifferent train service. With backing from two oil companies, Paul R. Braniff, Inc., was organized by the two brothers, with Paul as chief pilot. The operation grew at a surprising speed, acquiring three more six-place Stinsons and carrying a remarkable 3,000 passengers during the first year. By early 1929, the route expanded to include Dallas and Ft. Worth. In 1929 the Braniffs sold out to a larger conglomerate, Universal Aviation Corporation, which eventually became the Aviation Corporation and ended up as American Airlines.

Still fascinated by the airline business, the Braniffs soon launched a new company named Braniff Airways late in 1930, on a route that included Tulsa, Oklahoma City, and Wichita Falls, Oklahoma.

Braniff Airways courted its passengers with appealing schedules and fast airplanes. The new equipment constituted a pair of single-engine Lockheed Vegas with room for six passengers. Not as big as the trimotored Fords of competitors, the Vegas had a reputation for speed that appealed to wildcatters and petroleum executives in a hurry to close a deal or scout new territory.

During the 1930s, Braniff shrewdly built an airline system that ran north and south through a section of the nation that had few paved roads and lacked convenient passenger train connections. Braniff Airways pushed north to St. Louis and Chicago in the mid-thirties and then added southern routes to Houston and other Texas cities, eventually reaching Brownsville, on the Mexican border. Ford trimotors bolstered these early expanded services. Soon, Braniff Airways proudly promoted itself as the "Great Lakes to the Gulf" airline and shed its outdated Fords and Lockheeds. By 1941 Braniff, president of the line, could boast of a modern fleet that included new transports like the Douglas DC-3.

When World War II broke out, Braniff Airways joined other carriers in assigning half its planes to the government. The war brought significant changes for the carrier. Under contract to the Air Transport Command, Braniff Airways not only flew domestic routes but also got its first international exposure. The company's Cargo Air Contract Division operated a route through Central America to Panama. As a result, the company picked up invaluable experience for future operations beyond U.S. boundaries.

At the end of the war, Tom Braniff used cash reserves to buy several war-surplus C-54 four-engine cargo planes, refurbished them as airliners, and introduced them as DC-4 transports on the Dallas–Kansas City–Chicago run in the spring of 1946. Realizing that he would need even more modern planes to keep up with competitors, he introduced pressurized DC-6 service on the same route by the end of the year. Although expansion of domestic routes through the mid-1950s was modest, Braniff paid careful attention to equipment in an increasingly competitive environment. For new service to smaller midwestern cities, Braniff purchased twin-engine pressurized planes like the Convair 340, a modern postwar design. But Braniff's boldest move involved pioneering services into Latin America, where he dueled with powerful Pan American Airways. (Pan Am, because of its government mail contracts, had enjoyed a virtual monopoly on international routes.)

After Civil Aeronautics Board decisions in 1946 opened the door to South America for other airlines, Braniff Airways won authority to fly to Rio de Janeiro and Buenos Aires and to serve several South American countries en route, including Peru and Bolivia. Service got underway in 1948–1949, preparing the way for a major leap across the 20,000-foot Andes to Rio de Janeiro and Buenos Aires, where the first Braniff Airways DC-6 arrived in 1950. Other South American cities appeared on Braniff's route maps, underscoring the company's 1948 name change to Braniff International Airways.

Braniff ran his growing company as a paternalistic enterprise. When he spoke of the "Braniff family," he was not mouthing a slogan but expressing a genuine personal outlook. His was the only major airline to retain its founder's name, an indication of the strong link between the man and the company. A strong Catholic, he was active in both church and civic activities. His humanitarian and international interests gave him a global world view. As an officer of the National Council of Christians and Jews, he was deeply concerned about sectarianism, an issue that made him part of a small group associated with Charles Evans Hughes and led to the founding of the World Council of Christians and Jews in 1947. The goal of religious tolerance took him to Europe in 1950 to help inaugurate the World Brotherhood Organization.

Braniff died in a crash in Louisiana while flying as a passenger in a private airplane. More than many of his contemporaries in the airline industry, he devoted time and energy to civic causes and to the ideal of improved human relations around the world. The glitzy expansion and sudden collapse of Braniff International in the 1980s obscured the sound airline business originally built by Braniff and the significance of the successful postwar network he developed throughout Latin America.

• A collection of Braniff's corporate papers and correspondence is in the Aviation Collection of the University of Texas, Dallas. The most convenient summary of Braniff's life is Charles E. Beard, "Thomas E. Braniff: Southwest Pioneer" (1955), a pamphlet prepared for the Newcomen Society in North America. The early years of airline development are surveyed in Henry Ladd Smith, *Airways* (1942), with good coverage of Braniff's role. R. E. G. Davies, *Airlines of the United States since 1914* (1982), includes many references to the spread of Braniff Airways routes and the role of Tom Braniff. There is an informative profile in *Current Biography* (1952).

ROGER E. BILSTEIN

BRANN, William Cowper (4 Jan. 1855–2 Apr. 1898), journalist and writer, was born in Coles County, Illinois, the son of Noble J. Brann, a Presbyterian minister. When his mother (name unknown) died two years later, his father placed him with a family named Hawkins. At the age of thirteen he left his foster family and also ended his formal education at third grade. Over the next eight years Brann held numerous odd jobs, including railroad work, pitching for a semiprofessional baseball team, and managing a forty-person opera company.

In 1877 in Rochelle, Illinois, Brann married Carrie Belle Martin; they had three children, one of whom, a daughter named Inez, committed suicide at age thirteen. Brann began his career as a journalist and writer in 1883 with the *St. Louis Globe-Democrat* and later with newspapers in Galveston, Houston, Austin, and San Antonio, Texas. In 1891, after an unsuccessful start publishing a weekly, the *Austin Iconoclast*, early in 1894 Brann sold the venture to William Sidney Porter, later famed as the short-story writer O. Henry. Later that same year, Brann arrived in Waco, Texas, repurchased from Porter the rights to the name, and for the four remaining tumultuous years of his life, published the *Iconoclast*.

Brann took on all subjects in his journal and in particular wrote a great deal about politics and economics. His brazenly critical style was suggestive of some of the later writings of H. L. Mencken, and some of his economic commentaries foreshadowed those of the great muckrakers who came after him. His views were similar to those of other populist writers and politicians: he was critical of Presidents Grover Cleveland and William McKinley, and he was a partial supporter of William Jennings Bryan. Unmoved by decorum, Brann once compared President Cleveland to a hog:

> Stubborn, without courage, persevering without judgment and greedy without gratitude, these unpleasant characteristics Cleveland and the hog have in common. There are other points of resemblance, but I have no desire to be hard on the hog.

Brann's political and economic views could be characterized as liberal to radical but with two glaring exceptions: like some other southern populists he was racist toward blacks and sexist in that he did not support woman suffrage. Nonetheless, the *Iconoclast* reached a circulation of more than 90,000 throughout the United States and had a small readership in Europe.

Of all the subjects that Brann wrote about, the one he addressed most frequently was religious freedom and what he perceived as interferences with or threats to First Amendment guarantees, especially as posed by religious particularism. He took pains to make it clear that he was not against religion per se but that he believed in a commonality of beliefs and thus could not abide the tendency of particularists to impose their religious views on others:

> The Sacred Books of all the centuries are essentially the same—the half articulate voice of the world crying for light, the frantic efforts of man to learn whence he came and whither he goes, to lift the veil that shrouds the two eternities—to see and know! I gather them together—the old testament and the new, the Koran and the sacred Vedas, the northern Sagas and the southern mythologies; I search them through, not to scoff, but to gather with reverent soul, every gleam of light that since the birth of Time has been vouchsafed to man. . . . I go forth beneath the eternal stars—each silently pouring its stream of sidereal fire into the great realm of Darkness—and they seem like the eyes of pitying angels, watching man work out, little by little, through the long ages, the mystery of his life.

Baylor University, the largest and best-known college run by the Southern Baptist denomination, was established in Independence, Texas, in 1845, but moved to Waco in 1886. At the time of Brann's arrival there, Waco was the scene of a surge of activity instigated by the American Protective Association (APA), an organization founded to "protect" Americans from the alleged evils of Roman Catholicism. One large APA rally, held very shortly after Brann's arrival, featured an alleged former priest, Joseph Slattery, and his "ex-nun" wife. In his April 1895 issue of the *Iconoclast*, Brann accused Slattery of slander against the Roman Catholic church. In a newspaper article, he also offered to pay Slattery $500 if Slattery could prove that Brann had made a statement that Brann denied making. At a public appearance before a capacity crowd at the Opera House, Slattery called Brann "a pipsqueak scrivener who has soiled [his] city with a calumnious rag called the 'Iconoclast,' a fetid tangle of lies and half-truths." The audience shouted, "Bravo," and shook the Opera House with stamping on the floor. Brann stood up and replied that the *Iconoclast*'s mission was to expose frauds and fakes, and he left the hall shouting, "You lie and you know it!" The audience's hostile response to Brann was the beginning of an ongoing battle, the theme of which, constantly increasing in degree of acrimony, was Brann versus Baptists and, by extension, Brann versus Baylor. Brann added his own coals to the fire, frequently saying of Baptists that he did not believe they had "been held under water long enough." To Baylor, at a time when it was considering relocation, Brann offered "one thousand dollars any time to move to Dallas, and double that amount to go to Honolulu or hell." T. DeWitt Talmadge, well-known Baptist writer whose writings were widely syndicated, regularly struck back and dubbed Brann "the Apostle of the Devil."

In 1892 Baptist missionaries in Brazil sent Antonia Teixeira, a young girl who had been converted from Catholicism, to Baylor to be educated. Because she was about thirteen at the time and thus too young to enter Baylor, she lived with the family of Baylor's president, the Reverend Rufus Burleson. In November 1894 she became pregnant. She claimed she had been assaulted by the brother of Burleson's son-in-law. The baby, born premature in June 1895, died early in 1896. Brann regularly chided Baylor, Baptists, and Dr. Burleson and taunted them about their handling of the legal aspects of the affair. He even alleged that the girl's ultimate retraction of the charge of rape was paid for by funds enabling her to leave Texas.

Not surprisingly, Brann's constant barbs made him many enemies, and he in turn received constant threats. On 2 October 1897 a group of male students abducted Brann, dragged him across campus to a tree, and had a rope affixed to his neck, about to lynch him, when two professors came out and ordered them to release him. Only four days later an angry citizen accosted Brann in downtown Waco, severely injuring him by raining down blows with a cane. Then, on 1 April 1898, the day before Brann was to leave for an extended lecture tour, Tom Davis, the father of a female student at Baylor, lay in wait for him in the downtown business section—according to one theory, he believed Brann had slandered his daughter. Davis ambushed Brann, shooting him in the back, whereupon Brann wheeled around, drew his pistol, and fired at Davis. Several more shots were exchanged, and both Davis and Brann died the next day. Their funerals were two of the biggest in Waco's history. The obelisk at Brann's grave bears only his initials and the word "Truth." Legend has it that the sizable chip in his bas-relief profile on the tombstone was the result of a final shot that some lingering enemy could not resist taking at "the Apostle of the Devil."

• Brann's works are in William C. Brann, *The Complete Works of Brann the Iconoclast* (12 vols., 1919), and Roger N. Conger, ed., *The Best of Brann* (1967). The best work about Brann's life and career is Charles Carver, *Brann and The Iconoclast* (1957). See also E. Haldeman-Julius, *Brann, Who Cracked Dull Heads* (1924); William L. Rivers, "William Cowper Brann and His 'Iconoclast,'" *Journalism Quarterly* 35 (Fall 1958): 433–38; Donna Dickerson, "William Cowper Brann: Nineteenth Century Press Critic," *Journalism History* 5 (Summer 1978): 42–45; Holly Zumwalt, "The Life, Work and Influence of William Cowper Brann" (senior honors essay, Baylor Univ., 1990); and Rufus Jefferson Banks, "Brann vs. Baylor" (M.A. thesis, Baylor Univ., 1956).

PAUL T. ARMITSTEAD

BRANNAN, John Milton (1 July 1819–16 Dec. 1892), soldier, was born in Washington, D.C., the son of John Brannan and Sarah Salome Myer. While Brannan's middle name has been historically recognized as Milton, it actually was Myer, his mother's maiden name. Brannan apparently did not use the appellation "Milton" on official documents, and it may not have been attributed to him until his death. His family operated a boardinghouse that catered to congressional members in Washington. His father compiled a documentary history of the War of 1812 and passed his interest in military affairs on to his son. As a youth, Brannan familiarized himself with martial matters while he worked as a page for the U.S. House of Representatives. As a reward for five years of faithful service, over a hundred representatives, led by Indiana's Ratliff Boon, successfully petitioned for Brannan's admission into West Point in 1837. Four years later he graduated twenty-third in a class of fifty-two cadets. He excelled in infantry tactics but struggled somewhat with artillery training. Nevertheless, he received his first commission as a brevet second lieutenant of artillery.

The young officer's first assignment was garrison duty at Plattsburgh, New York. Prior to the signing of the Webster-Ashburton Treaty (1842), Brannan partook in field exercises to suppress border conflicts between Americans and Canadians over the disputed boundary between Maine and New Brunswick. He first participated in active combat five years later following the outbreak of the Mexican War. Promoted to first lieutenant, he served as regimental adjutant for the First Artillery (1847). The army awarded Brannan a captain's brevet for courageous performance at the battles of Contreras and Churubusco. His daring and recklessness under enemy fire earned him severe wounds during the U.S. Army's successful assault on Mexico City, 13 September 1847.

Brannan recovered and returned to active duty. Over the next few years he served at garrisons in New York, Louisiana, and Florida. Around 1850 he married Eliza Crane; they had one child. On 4 November 1854 he earned a promotion to captain while at Fort Monroe, Virginia. Two years later he took part in military action against Seminoles living in the Everglades. He remained in Florida until 1858, when he suffered a personal tragedy and returned home to Washington. His wife had suddenly disappeared. After an exhaustive search that included posting notices along roads and dredging lakes, Brannan despaired of ever finding his wife. Nearly two years later, however, he discovered that she had left him and their young daughter to live with another man in Europe. Following the public scandal Brannan secured a divorce in 1863.

The outbreak of the Civil War in April 1861 required Brannan either to join the southern rebellion or remain loyal to his country. He had grown up in a Southern city, his family had owned a slave, and he had spent much of his career in the South. Yet he had been exposed to nationalist influences while a boy working for Congress, while a young man studying at West Point, and while a professional soldier in the U.S. Army. Furthermore, his hometown was the nation's capital, which remained in Union hands. Leaving Key West, where he had spent three years, Brannan returned to Washington and accepted an appointment as a brigadier general of U.S. volunteers in September 1861. His first assignment involved maintaining the defenses of his native city that November.

Brannan's experience in Florida led the army to name him commander of the Department of Key West, where he served from January to March 1862. After a transfer to the Department of the South, he was involved in several minor military operations. Laudable performances in the St. Johns River expedition in Florida (25 Sept. 1862) and at the battle of Pocotaligo, South Carolina (24 Oct. 1862), earned him a divisional command in the Army of the Cumberland.

Brannan's most notable action of the war occurred at the battle of Chickamauga (19–20 Sept. 1863), where his Third Division in General George Thomas's XIV Corps saw heavy action. A Confederate attack on the second day nearly routed the army. Brannan's division, despite absorbing considerable punishment, was one of those under Thomas that held fast and covered the army's panicked retreat to Chattanooga, Tennessee. Brannan displayed his normal aplomb during the battle, exposing himself to danger and exhorting his men to fight on. His courage helped establish his corps commander's reputation as the "Rock of Chickamauga." For his actions the regular army brevetted Brannan a full colonel. He supervised the placement of artillery for both the Army of the Cumberland and the Army of the Tennessee during the successful Chattanooga campaign. Subsequently serving as chief of artillery for the Army of the Cumberland, he accompanied General William T. Sherman's invasion of Georgia through the capture of Atlanta.

After the war Brannan served successively as the commander of the District of Savannah and the Department of Georgia and received brevets as major general in both the volunteers and the regular army. Mustered out of the volunteers on 31 May 1866, he remained in the regular army with the rank of major.

Thereafter Brannan was placed in charge of various posts. In 1870 he married Evelyn West Way, a native of Georgia; they had no children. For ten days, in May and June 1870, he commanded troops at Ogdensburg, New York. His orders were to prevent incursions into Canada by the Fenians, an Irish-American terrorist organization out to harm British interests. Brannan also saw duty in the South during Reconstruction. He commanded troops in Edgefield, South Carolina, and Tallahassee, Florida, during the drawn-out presidential election of 1876. The contested electoral votes of those two states and Louisiana were ultimately awarded to Republican Rutherford B. Hayes as part of a deal between congressional Republicans and southern Democrats. The agreement made Hayes president in exchange for an end to Reconstruction.

Following his service in the South, Brannan was promoted to lieutenant colonel and reunited with the First Artillery (1877). That summer his command protected private and public property during strikes and riots by railroad workers in Philadelphia. Around this time, Brannan began suffering from neuralgia, which plagued him for the rest of his life. He was promoted to full colonel on 15 March 1881, and less than three months later he took extended sick leave until 19 April 1882, when he retired. His second wife also left him, although they did not divorce. She returned to Georgia, while Brannan resided in New York City, where he died.

Like the mass of Victorian Americans, Brannan believed that true manhood required demonstrations of courage. Brevetted three times for gallantry, he acted on that belief more than most. In order to satisfy one Victorian ideal, however, he sacrificed another. His private life suffered at the expense of his professional career and caused him a great deal of embarrassment. In an era when patriarchal authority was thought to lead to familial commitment and stability, Brannan had miserably failed twice, a fact family, friends, and chroniclers deliberately obscured following his death.

• Very few of Brannan's papers exist. Useful information is in Brannan's military, pension, and U.S. Military Academy files at the National Archives, Washington, D.C. A straightforward recounting of Brannan's military record is in George W. Cullum, *Biographical Register of the Officers and Graduates of the U.S. Military Academy . . .*, vol. 2 (1891). John Brannan, comp., *Official Letters of the Military and Naval Officers of the United States during War with Great Britain in the Years 1812, 13, 14, and 15* (1823), compiled by his father, is of interest. The best biographical sketch is in Ezra J. Warner, *Generals in Blue: Lives of the Union Commanders* (1964). A celebratory yet useful sketch is in *Twenty-fourth Annual Reunion of the Association of the Graduates of the United States Military*

Academy (1893). A good rendering of the environment in which Brannan grew up, containing the attitudes of elites toward the operators of Washington's boardinghouses, including his family, is in Cynthia D. Earman, "Boardinghouses, Parties, and Creation of a Political Society" (M.A. thesis, Louisiana State Univ., 1992). On the importance of courage in Victorian America see Gerald F. Linderman, *Embattled Courage: The Experience of Combat in the American Civil War* (1987).

DAN R. FROST

BRANNAN, Samuel (2 Mar. 1819–2 May 1889), California pioneer, was born in Saco, Maine, the son of Thomas Brannan, an unskilled laborer, and Sara Knox Emery. At age fourteen, when his sister married a Mormon missionary, Sam shared their honeymoon trip to Kirtland, Ohio, the first Mormon settlement developed by Joseph Smith (1805–1844). Soon a bona fide Latter-day Saint, he helped construct the first Mormon temple and became adept at printing. He met and married Harriet Hatch, daughter of a Mormon farmer, who bore him a son, but she was soon forgotten when Sam was named East Coast publisher of Mormon literature. Such work took little time, giving him ample opportunity for commercial contracts at his New York print shop that made him, at age twenty-five, quite wealthy. He was lucky enough to find a good boardinghouse managed by a Mormon widow, whose daughter, Anna Lisa Corwin, he promptly married. She soon provided him with the first of their eventual brood of five.

After Joseph Smith's murder by an Illinois mob in 1844, the Mormon leaders deemed it best for all the faithful to leave the United States. Most of them headed westward, led by Brigham Young, but those on the East Coast were ordered to go by sea, with Brannan in charge. Using his own money, he bought an old schooner, the *Brooklyn*, loaded its hull with his printing press, a sawmill, a flour mill, and tools of every sort, and hired a captain and crew for what proved to be a five-month voyage around Cape Horn to California. Once well at sea, he assembled the adult passengers and announced the existence of "Samuel Brannan and Company," binding all the Mormons aboard to total obedience. After stops at South American ports for fresh food and water and an extended stay in Honolulu, the voyage ended in late July 1846 at Yerba Buena on San Francisco Bay. There, to Brannan's disgust, an American flag was evidence that California had been claimed by the United States.

Within a few weeks the *Brooklyn* was unloaded, the sawmill and flour mill were both operating, and what had been a sleepy Mexican village was rapidly becoming the first West Coast Anglo-American city, soon renamed San Francisco, with Mormons working under Brannan's direction and on payday, returning a tenth of their wages in lieu of Mormon tithes. His commercial empire steadily expanded, within a year reaching all parts of the Bay area and up the Sacramento River to Sutter's Fort, where he established a retail store outside its walls. He set apart a choice tract of land to serve as a Mormon homeland and, to report it to Brigham Young, in the late spring of 1847 set out on horseback with two companions to Fort Hall in Wyoming, where the overland Mormon party was resting. But Young spurned California, having made his mind up to settle in Utah. Angry and defeated, Brannan never again helped the Mormon cause, and although he never formally severed his ties he is viewed as a prominent apostate.

Early in 1848, when men building a sawmill several miles east of Sutter's Fort found traces of gold in the millrace, Brannan bought up all the nearby land, stocked his store at the fort with everything a gold-seeker might need, gained a monopoly on steamboat landings at Sacramento, and then hurried to San Francisco where, on conspicuous street corners, he brandished a phial of gold dust while shouting, "Gold! Gold on the American River!" He also telegraphed the news to the nation's major newspapers. The result, as he had anticipated, was the human stampede known as the gold rush of '49. It also ushered in Brannan's dominant period as California's first millionaire, able to lavish money on causes both worthy and selfish: donations of land for parks, churches, and cemeteries, and of money for San Francisco's first public library and his private fire brigade and cadet corps. He organized a campaign to eliminate the city's criminal gangs but proved so shrill in demanding immediate punishment that he was forced to resign. He loved to ride about in his fine carriage, often with one or another of the city's fancy women. It so infuriated Anna Lisa that she was willing to escape him by moving to Switzerland, as he suggested, for the better education of their daughters.

Brannan also liked Europe, going often to savor the good life it offered but also to benefit California by buying fine horses, choice vegetable seeds, and grape cuttings of prime importance to the wine industry of the Napa Valley. At the head of that valley he created a hot spring resort on a 2,200-acre site he named "Calistoga," joining elements of the state name and Saratoga. It had a 90,000-gallon reservoir, a skating rink, a mile racetrack, a main hotel and a number of one-family cottages, and a bathhouse with steam, sulfur, and mud. He basked in his role of welcoming host, but there were never enough paying guests, and in 1875 he lost control through mortgage foreclosures.

Being forced to mortgage property was the result of back-to-back lawsuits in 1870. Anna Lisa returned, sued for divorce, and was awarded half of Brannan's property. Brannan then sued the "Big Four" of Central Pacific Railroad fame—Collis Huntington, Charles Crocker, Mark Hopkins, and Leland Stanford—for income due him on stock they had sold him. He not only lost but was forced to pay the trial costs of roughly $100,000. Thereafter, nothing succeeded. He mounted one final grandiose scheme, to colonize a large tract in Mexico, but in spite of an expensive opening campaign in New York there were no subscribers. During his final seven years he sank steadily closer to utter poverty, cared for by an illiterate woman and depending on cash sent irregularly by a nephew, son of the sister whose honeymoon trip he had shared. After his death in Escondido, California, there was no money for a headstone, but one was provided some years later by a man who had never met him.

• Extensive collections of Brannan memorabilia can be found in the California State Library in Sacramento, the Bancroft Library at the University of California, Berkeley, the New York Public Library, and, in San Francisco, both the public library and in holdings of private organizations of which he was a member. Books about Brannan include J. A. B. Scherer, *The First Forty-Niner* (1925), and at least two novels, Reva Scott, *Samuel Brannan and the Golden Fleece* (1944), and Louis J. Stellman, *Sam Brannan: Builder of San Francisco* (1953). See also *Sutter County Historical Society* 13 (Jan. 1974), which is devoted entirely to Brannan and is of particular value for its annotations, Appendix, references, and "gleanings" from local periodicals that together fill the final five pages. For Brannan's contributions to Mormon development, officials of the Church of Jesus Christ of Latter-day Saints in Salt Lake City are consistently generous in responding to queries.

WILLIAM PEIRCE RANDEL

BRANNER, John Casper (4 July 1850–1 Mar. 1922), geologist and university president, was born in New Market, Tennessee, the son of Michael T. Branner, a third-generation Tennessee landowner, and Elsie Baker. Branner attended local schools, read the few books he could find, and developed an active curiosity about the plants, animals, and rocks of his neighborhood. In 1870, after spending two years at nearby Maryville College, he entered Cornell University, where he studied with geology professor Charles F. Hartt, who had made several scientific expeditions to Brazil. Hartt took Branner to Brazil with him in 1874, and the following year, when the Brazilian government appointed Hartt head of a commission to direct the first geological survey of the country, he appointed Branner his assistant. This was the beginning of Branner's lifelong interest in the geology of Brazil, about which little was then known.

When the commission was discontinued in 1877, Branner went to work for a gold mining company in the Brazilian state of Minas Gerais, and in 1880, at the request of inventor Thomas A. Edison, he collected and tested various South American plant fibers for possible use in the incandescent light bulb, which Edison had patented that year. From 1881 to 1883 Branner investigated Brazilian cotton cultivation for the U.S. Department of Agriculture, issuing reports in 1884 and 1885 on the cotton caterpillar and boll worm. He returned to Brazil frequently in later years, often working with Orville A. Derby of the Brazilian geological survey, to investigate black diamonds, evidence of glaciation, the coastline near the mouth of the Amazon, and the geology of other parts of the country. His work on Brazil culminated with the publication in English and Portuguese of a geological map of the country, accompanied by explanatory text (*Bulletin of the Geological Society of America* 30 [1919]: 189–338).

In 1883, the year after receiving a B.S. from Cornell, Branner married Susan D. Kennedy of Oneida, New York, with whom he had three children. Perhaps out of a wish to settle down after being abroad so often, in 1884 he joined the Pennsylvania Geological Survey under J. Peter Lesley, for which he investigated glacial phenomena of the northern part of the state and prepared a topographical map of the anthracite coal fields of the Lackawanna Valley. In 1885 David Starr Jordan, the new president of Indiana University, who wanted to encourage science teaching and research, invited Branner to become professor of geology. Branner received a Ph.D. from Indiana that same year and, as a teacher, soon attracted an enthusiastic group of students.

In 1887 Branner accepted a position as state geologist of Arkansas. Although at first attacked by mining interests because he showed that supposedly valuable gold mines were worthless, he brought together a dedicated staff who mapped in detail 4,500 square miles of the state and discovered the extent of vast bauxite deposits, which made Arkansas the leading producer of this important source of aluminum. Between 1887 and 1893, when the survey ended, Branner published fourteen volumes of reports on iron, coal, manganese, novaculites, marble, and other valuable economic resources. The report also included scientific studies of igneous rocks, stratigraphy, and paleontology. R. A. F. Penrose, Jr., who worked with Branner on the Arkansas survey, called Branner's vigorous and productive direction "doubtless the greatest accomplishment of his life" (Penrose, p. 18).

In 1892 Branner returned to academic life. At the invitation of his friend David Starr Jordan, now president of the newly established Stanford University, he became head of Stanford's geology department. Branner also served as Stanford's vice president from 1899 until 1913 and as its president from 1913 until his retirement in 1916. While at Stanford, he undertook three scientific expeditions to Brazil, in 1899, 1907, and 1911. A prolific author of more than 300 publications on Brazil and other subjects, he also contributed the article on "South America" to the eleventh edition of the *Encyclopedia Britannica*, wrote book reviews, compiled bibliographies, and translated works into and from Portuguese.

In 1906, immediately after the San Francisco earthquake of 18 April, Branner was appointed by the governor of California to an eight-member State Earthquake Investigation Commission, chaired by Andrew Lawson of the University of California. Like most geologists, Branner had a longstanding interest in seismology, but his active involvement was stimulated by the magnitude of the 1906 earthquake and the destruction it caused. For the state commission he investigated a section of the San Andreas fault, observing horizontal and vertical displacements, destruction of property, and changes in geological formations resulting from the earthquake. Branner played an important role in the growth of the Seismological Society of America, which was organized in late 1906 but languished until he became president (1910–1914). He was also a director of the society from 1909 until his death and was instrumental in founding its bulletin in

1911, supporting it with his own money and with manuscripts for the early issues. In 1915 he went to Panama as a member of a National Academy of Sciences committee appointed to recommend a means of controlling landslides that were interfering with the operation of the Panama Canal.

Branner did not often take up matters of theory; most often his work as a geologist was descriptive, based on exploration and reconnaissance. Though well aware of the importance of geology to economic development, as the success of his survey of the natural resources of Arkansas demonstrates, he pursued broad scientific interests, which included entomology and botany as well as the earth sciences. He is perhaps best remembered as an energetic administrator and inspiring teacher, who said late in life that he was more honored to see his students "doing good and honest work in every quarter of the globe" than he was to receive the many honorary degrees and awards that were bestowed upon him (Penrose, p. 22). He died at his home at Stanford University.

• Branner's papers relating to his scientific career and his presidency of Stanford are in the Stanford University Archives. Among Branner's most important papers are "The Supposed Glaciation of Brazil," *Journal of Geology* 1 (1893): 753–72; "Decomposition of Rocks in Brazil," *Bulletin of the Geological Society of America* 7 (1896): 255–314; and his presidential address to the society, "Stone Reefs on the Northeast Coast of Brazil," *Bulletin of the Geological Society of America* 16 (1905): 1–12. He described his work in Arkansas in "The Geological Surveys of Arkansas," *Journal of Geology* 2 (1894): 826–36. Among his contributions to seismology are "Earth Movement on the San Andreas Fault, April 18, 1906, from Crystal Spring Lake to Congress Springs," in *Report of the State Earthquake Investigation Commission*, vol. 1 (1908, repr. 1969), pp. 104–11, and "Suggested Organization for Seismological Work on the Pacific Coast," *Bulletin of the Seismological Society of America* 1 (1911): 5–8. Biographical articles are by R. A. F. Penrose, Jr., *Bulletin of the Geological Society of America* 36 (1925): 15–44, with full bibliography, and Sidney D. Townley, *Bulletin of the Seismological Society of America* 12 (1922): 1–11. On Branner's years in Brazil see Frank Robert Jackle, "John Casper Branner and Brazil" (Ph.D. diss., Stanford University, 1966).

MARGARET D. CHAMPLIN

BRANT, Joseph (1743–24 Nov. 1807), Mohawk chief and captain in the British Indian Department, also known as Thayendanegea, was born while his family was in the Ohio country, the son of Peter Tehowaghwengaraghkwin and Margaret. His father died shortly after Brant's birth, and he may have had several stepfathers, one of them the influential Brant Canagaraduncka, from whom Joseph Brant took his name. His mother's family appears to have been prominent in the Mohawk town of Canajoharie. Brant is reputed to have gone to war as part of the Mohawk contingent allied to the British in the French and Indian War. His sister Mary "Molly" Brant formed a relationship with Sir William Johnson, the superintendent of the Northern Department in the British Indian service, which lasted until Sir William's death in 1774. Mary Brant had at least eight children (the first in 1759) with Sir William in the years they resided on Johnson's estate in the Mohawk Valley. Perhaps because of his relationship to Mary Brant, Sir William enrolled young Joseph Brant in Moor's Indian Charity School run by the Reverend Eleazor Wheelock in Lebanon, Connecticut, in the summer of 1761. Brant, who had had an English vocabulary of only a few words, expanded his English skills while teaching potential missionaries to the Iroquois the intricacies of his own language. He stayed at the school only two years.

After his return to the Mohawk Valley, Brant formed a close relationship with the Anglican missionary to the Mohawk, John Stuart. The two worked together to translate the Gospel of St. Mark, the Church of England catechism, and other religious tracts into Mohawk. Brant also served as an interpreter at councils for the British Indian Department and was appointed an officer in that department in 1775. He was by that time recognized as a chief among the Mohawks.

After the death of Sir William Johnson, the position of superintendent of Indian affairs for the Northern Department passed to his nephew Guy Johnson. With the outbreak of the American Revolution, increasing hostility and violence between rebels and Loyalists in the Mohawk Valley led Guy Johnson and others in the Indian Department to flee to Canada. Joseph Brant went with him. From Quebec City they sailed for London on 11 November 1775.

Brant's trip to London was not especially motivated by the escalating conflict in North America. He was more concerned about the loss of Mohawk lands in the past. The Mohawk towns of Fort Hunter and Canajoharie were surrounded by non-Indian settlements, and the boundary between lands open to non-Indian settlement and lands reserved for Indian use established at the 1768 Treaty of Fort Stanwix was to the west of Mohawk territory. Brant received only minor support for settlement of his land grievances, the government promising to examine them in the future, but he was a sensation in London society. On the commission of the earl of Warwick, George Romney painted his portrait. James Boswell sought him for an interview for the *London Magazine*. He was initiated into the Freemasons and was presented at court. In early June 1776 most of the party boarded ship to return to North America. On the return trip Brant had the opportunity to use his new firearms, acquired in London, to help fend off the attack of an American privateer. They arrived in America in time for Brant to participate in William Howe's capture and occupation of New York City.

British policy had shifted from one dedicated to keeping Indians neutral in the conflict to one in which native allies were to play an active role on the side of the Crown. In November 1776 Brant and a companion set out in disguise to journey from New York City to the Iroquois country. There Brant began agitation to bring the Iroquois (except the Oneida, who were already fighting as allies of the rebels) into action as combatants against the rebels. British restraints, however, prevented him from carrying out an expedition into the Mohawk Valley (where many Mohawks, including his sister Mary, were threatened by the rebel portion of the population). Brant finally led his Mohawk and Loyalist followers (a large number of non-Indians fought in the war under Brant's command) into battle in midsummer 1777. A large contingent of Iroquois accompanied the troops of Lieutenant Colonel Barry St. Leger to besiege Fort Stanwix (or Fort Schuyler as it had been renamed—now Rome, N.Y.). Mary Brant sent word to her brother that the rebel militia from the Mohawk Valley was moving, intent on raising the siege. A force, largely Iroquois, was sent to intercept the advancing army. Brant has been credited with selecting the battlefield at Oriskany. The rebel army was ambushed as it traversed a narrow ravine. Given the number of troops engaged, probably more casualties were inflicted on the rebel forces than in any other battle of the American Revolution.

Brant commanded approximately 300 Indians and 100 Loyalists with distinction for most of the war, often serving with other Iroquois, Loyalists, and British regulars. In 1778 he participated in attacks on Cobleskill, German Flats, and Cherry Valley. In 1779 a major American invasion of the Cayuga and Seneca country was mounted under the command of General John Sullivan. Brant, who had been wounded earlier in the summer, was with the outnumbered force that unsuccessfully attempted to block Sullivan's army at Newtown (now Elmira, N.Y.) on 29 August 1779. Seneca and Cayuga villages east of the Genesee were destroyed, and a major portion of the Iroquois population settled around Fort Niagara as refugees. The following summer Brant was back in the field, however, and his forces destroyed the pro-American Oneida village of Kanowalohale and the towns of Canajoharie and Norman's Kill. In the fall he was part of a major expedition commanded by Sir John Johnson (Sir William's son and heir) that destroyed settlements in the Mohawk and Schoharie valleys and inflicted heavy casualties on local garrisons. In April 1781 Brant left Niagara for Detroit and the Ohio country, in preparation for an anticipated attack on Detroit by the Americans under George Rogers Clark. On 26 August Brant annihilated the rear portion of Clark's forces, under the command of Colonel Archibald Lochry on the Ohio River and frustrated the American campaign. Although the Indians and the British on the northern frontier had enjoyed considerable success, the fortunes of the Crown were less positive in other theaters. As peace negotiations continued, the British Indian Department, in which Brant now held the rank of captain, reined in the activities of the Crown's indigenous allies.

Peace was concluded in 1783, but the Treaty of Paris ignored the Indian allies of the British. The boundary line between British North America and the new American republic ran through the Great Lakes, leaving a large portion of Indians who fought as British allies south of British jurisdiction. The Indian department, now led by Sir John Johnson, and the governor of Canada, Frederick Haldimand, claimed that the Treaty of Paris did not compromise Indian title to land or the boundary between Indian and white settlement established in the Treaty of Fort Stanwix of 1768. Mohawks, like their Loyalist neighbors, had lost their homes to the Americans. Haldimand, urged by Brant, sought lands for them north of the Great Lakes and purchased a large tract for the Mohawk and others of the Six Nations on the Grand River, which flows into Lake Erie near Niagara from the Mississauga. Brant led his Mohawks, a large number of Cayugas and Onondagas, and a few members of the other Six Nations and their allies (including more than 200 Delaware) to the Grand River. The Six Nations Reserve, near Brantford, Ontario, remains from the original grant in the hands of descendants of the nearly 2,000 Indians who followed Brant there in 1785.

For the next decade Brant pursued three ends. One was to enhance his personal political and financial situation. The second was to manage affairs on the Grand River for the benefit of those who had settled there. The third was to foster unity among all western Indians to better resist American expansion beyond the 1768 Fort Stanwix Treaty line. These goals took Brant back to London in the autumn of 1785. He was anxious to convert his commission in the Indian department during the American Revolution into a pension at half pay. He sought aid for publication of Anglican texts in Mohawk and for Mohawk compensation claims for war losses. He enjoyed success in achieving these ends. He also wanted to learn if Britain would support resistance to the advancing American frontier. In this last request he received lip-service support from the British government. Both before and after this trip to London, Brant was active in councils with western Indians urging united resistance to the Americans. In 1783 at Detroit and Lower Sandusky he pressed issues of unity. The Ohio Indians were determined to defend their homes by war if necessary, but Brant was unable to maintain unity, to urge sensible compromises, or to deliver Iroquois warriors to support the confederacy he hoped would oppose American expansion. After the Ohio resistance to American expansion collapsed with the defeat at Fallen Timbers in 1794, Brant experienced a personal tragedy. In 1795 his son Isaac Brant attacked him with a knife, and Brant in self-defense mortally wounded his son, who is believed to have been inebriated.

The original grant awarded the Six Nations was extensive, stretching six miles from each side of the river for almost its entire length. Brant, who had grown up in the Mohawk Valley amid non-Indian settlements, saw benefits in selling surplus lands to white Loyalists and other migrants to Canada. This led to conflict with the British authorities who argued that the Six Nations could not sell these lands to anyone but the Crown. Brant's policy was also unpopular among a portion of the Indians on the Grand River. By 1798 some 350,000 acres (of an original grant of 570,000 acres) had been conveyed to non-Indians. There were unestablished accusations that Brant benefited personally from these transactions. His local support was strong enough, however, that he was able to resist attempts by opponents to remove him from power. Brant lived apart from his Six Nations followers on the Grand River. In 1795 he purchased from the Mississaugas land on Lake Ontario in what is now Burlington, Ontario. There he built a large house said to be staffed by twenty servants, and he established a reputation as a gracious and generous host. It was also there that he died.

Brant married three times. His first wife, whom he had married in 1765, was an Oneida woman known in English as Margaret. She was the mother of Isaac and Christiana but died in 1771. Brant was briefly wed to Margaret's half sister Susanna, but she also left him a widower. In 1779 he married Catherine Adonwentishon, said to be the Mohawk daughter of George Croghan, the famous trader and Indian agent. More important was Catherine's position in a prominent lineage of the Mohawk Turtle Clan. Brant and Catherine were married at Fort Niagara, and they had seven children, of whom his youngest son, John Brant, was the most active in political affairs.

In his lifetime, and in the years since, Joseph Brant attracted lavish praise from his supporters and vehement condemnation from his enemies. The "Monster Brant" of the propaganda of the Revolution and postrevolutionary periods is clearly not supported by careful examination of primary documents relating to his activities during the conflict. However, the ease with which Brant moved in elite circles of British and North American society meant he was credited with far more influence than he probably actually had. With respect to his actions after the Revolution it is difficult to determine if he was acting in favor of a nearly continental pan-Indian view, a pro-British view, a position reflecting the needs of the Six Nations people on the Grand River, or simply looking after his own self-interest. At one time or another he seems to have served each of these ends.

• Brant's papers are widely scattered. Archival collections containing his writings or documents relating to his activities include Colonial Office Papers (especially CO42) in the Public Record Office, London; the Haldimand papers, British Library, London; the Joseph Brant Papers, Draper Manuscripts, State Historical Society of Wisconsin, Madison; and the Claus Family Papers, Public Archives of Canada, Ottawa. Brant has frequently been the subject of biographical treatment. Most important are Isabel Thompson Kelsay, *Joseph Brant 1743–1807: Man of Two Worlds* (1984), and William L. Stone, *The Life of Joseph Brant-Thayendanegea* (1838). The latter prints a significant quantity of primary sources. Also important is Marc J. Smith, "Joseph Brant: Mohawk Statesman" (Ph.D. diss., Univ. of Wisconsin, 1946). Documents relative to Brant's role in Canada after the Revolution are published in Charles M. Johnston, ed., *The Valley of the Six Nations: A Collection of Documents on the Indian Lands of the Grand River* (1964).

THOMAS S. ABLER

BRANT, Molly (c. 1736–16 Apr. 1796), Mohawk, Loyalist, and Anglican, also known as Mary Brant or Konwatsi tsiaienni, was born either at the Mohawk "castle" of Canajoharie in upper New York or in the Ohio Valley, the daughter of Peter and Margaret, both Mohawks of the Six Nations Confederacy of Iroquois. She was the sister of Joseph Brant (Thayendanegea), a staunch Loyalist and renowned war chief and statesman among his people. In 1753 Molly's widowed mother married Brant Canagaraduncka, an influential and wealthy Mohawk sachem, in a Christian ceremony. Molly spent her childhood at Canajoharie in the Mohawk Valley, where the Brants were acknowledged, according to Eleazar Wheelock, a missionary schoolteacher, as "a Family of Distinction" among the Mohawk. Molly received only a rudimentary formal education, but there is evidence that she could write in a proper English style. Although the Brant family was well known and predominant in Mohawk circles, there is no substantive evidence to suggest that Molly was ever a clan matron or mother within the Iroquois matrilineal society.

With the outbreak of the French and Indian War (1756–1763), Molly Brant came increasingly in contact with British and colonial officers, and white people generally, owing to the uneasy military alliance forged between the British and the Mohawk against the French. At a militia rally in the Mohawk Valley in 1759, Brant encountered Sir William Johnson, twenty-one years her senior and the northern superintendent of Indian affairs. Johnson, or Warraghiyagey, meaning "he who does much business," was one of the most successful businessmen and entrepreneurs in colonial New York. His relationships with the Mohawk over several years, which included an acquired knowledge of Six Nations culture and ceremonies, earned him the respect of the Iroquois people. In particular, Johnson's successful courting of the Mohawk and others of the Six Nations Confederacy appeared to focus on his frequent and intimate connections with agreeable, and mostly Mohawk, women. These liaisons produced several children who remained at the villages of their mothers. These families, of whom the mothers tended to be prominent within the clan circles and who wielded power and influence in the decisions of the confederacy councils, strengthened Johnson's ties with the Six Nations and secured a more solid British-Iroquois alliance.

From that meeting in 1759, however, Johnson and Brant were inextricably linked until his death fifteen years later. Brant became the "prudent and faithful Housekeeper" for the powerful Sir William, and together they produced eight children. Johnson treated his Mohawk family with respect and courtesy in accordance with the status of the Brant clan within the Iroquois Confederacy. In his will, he provided them with the financial security that would allow Brant and the children to retain a most comfortable upper-class colonial lifestyle. During their fifteen-year relationship, Brant was of inestimable value to Johnson in facilitating the often difficult and sensitive councils and negotiations between her husband, the senior Crown official for Indian affairs, and the confederacy sachems. In fact, it was observed by one of Johnson's subordinates that "one word from her [was] more taken Notice of by the Five Nations than a thousand from any white man without exception" (NAC, MG24, series B, B114:63, D. Claus to Gov. Haldimand of Québec).

With the death of Johnson in July 1774, Brant and the children were forced to leave the spacious Johnson Hall, which Johnson's white son inherited. Brant remained in the Mohawk Valley and reestablished at Canajoharie, where the family was treated with respect owing to their connection with Johnson and because Brant was acknowledged as a woman of quality and influence in her own right. At this Mohawk village, she enjoyed a comfortable existence, residing in a well-furnished house. She continued to dress in the Mohawk fashion but in the finest cloth. With the help of a generous will, Brant opened a trading store in the area among the Iroquois and conducted a brisk business, predominantly in the sale of rum.

The outbreak of the rebellion in colonial America in the spring of 1775 factionalized the American colonies and produced an internecine rivalry that was as violent in the Mohawk Valley as anywhere, with loyal Americans (king's men) opposed to the American colonial rebels who supported the new Continental Congress. From the beginning of the conflict Molly Brant and the Mohawk stood in support of the king. As an increasing number of Loyalists were driven from the valley, Brant provided these refugees with provisions and other necessaries in order to assist their flight through the forest to the relative safety of Canada. Brant, however, refused to budge from her home at Canajoharie. For the next two years Brant, the Mohawk, and a number of white Loyalists, in spite of harassment, intimidation, and suffering imposed on them by rebel "Committees of Safety," stubbornly persevered and remained on their lands and farms.

In August 1777 Crown forces from Montreal, consisting of British regulars, Loyalists, and various elements drawn from the Six Nations Confederacy, invaded the Mohawk Valley in order to regain the king's control in the region. This force focused its efforts on besieging the rebel stronghold of Fort Stanwix (Rome, N.Y.). During this operation, Brant discovered that a large force of 800 rebels was advancing to the relief of the fort. She immediately dispatched Mohawk runners to warn the British commander of this imminent danger. The result of Brant's decisive action was that at Oriskany, six miles east of Fort Stanwix, the rebel advance was "surprised, briskly attacked, and after a little resistance repulsed and defeated, leaving upwards of 500 killed on the spot" (HLRO, main papers [Burgoyne Campaign], J. Butler to Sir Guy Johnson, 15 Aug. 1777). Two weeks after the battle of Oriskany the British lifted the siege and returned to Canada.

In the Mohawk Valley, Oriskany became a watershed in the conflict, as both sides began increasingly to engage in a brutal partisan struggle. For the Six Nations Iroquois, the battle of August 1777 tore the confederacy apart, with some nations supporting the king while others (notably the Oneida and Tuscarora) committing to the Congress. A rebel invasion force under General John Sullivan that included some Indian supporters ravaged Iroquoia in 1779 and further divided the old confederacy. For the duration of the war, Brant continued to support the interests of the king, and her influence among the Mohawk and others of the Six Nations was paramount to the British war effort. After Oriskany she was forced to leave the Mohawk Valley and subsequently found refuge at the British and Loyalist stronghold of Fort Niagara. At the time of the Sullivan expedition, Brant accepted an offer to settle in Montreal, where her children could be better maintained and receive a good education. The children remained in Montreal until the end of the war. During these years, according to the declared accounts for public expenses for the Indian Department, they were treated generously by the British, as boarding and schooling was provided as well as food and accommodation.

Brant, however, wished to continue her efforts among the Iroquois people in support of the king. Accordingly, in the autumn of 1779 she began a trek back to Niagara but got no further than the British base at Carleton Island, situated on the southeast side of Lake Ontario, where there was a large Iroquois settlement and where Molly could wield her political influence in encouraging the chiefs and warriors to remain loyal to the king. She continued these duties until the end of the war. In 1783 Brant moved across the lake to British Canada and the new Loyalist settlement of Cataraqui (Kingston, Ontario). Here she was provided with the King's Bounty, which included a fine house and a pension of £100 annually for her war service on behalf of the Crown. She apparently lived her last years fairly quietly as a respected member of the community, remaining fiercely loyal to the memory of Sir William Johnson and to the king. Molly Brant died in Kingston, a staunch Loyalist to the end and a devout adherent of the Church of England. She regularly attended service at St. George's, where she "sat in an honourable place among the English." Her grave is located in the lower burial ground of St. George's (now the site of St. Paul's Anglican Church).

• Among the primary material useful to the study of Molly Brant, the National Archives of Canada (NAC), Ottawa, houses RG 10, Records Relating to Indian Affairs, and MG 21, Series B (Haldimand Collection). In the United Kingdom the House of Lords Record Office (HLRO) in London contains an abundance of material on the 1777 campaign of Oriskany. Among the published material relating to Brant, Barbara Graymont, *The Iroquois in the American Revolution* (1972), and Isabel Kelsay, *Joseph Brant, 1743–1807: Man of Two Worlds* (1984), provide details on the life and times of this remarkable Mohawk woman. As well, Robert S. Allen, *His Majesty's Indian Allies: British Indian Policy in the Defense of Canada, 1774–1815* (1992), esp. chaps. 2 and 3, provides information relating to Brant and the British connection and includes an appendix on Indian Department expenses for Brant, her family, and the Six Nations in Canada during the war. Richard Preston, ed., *Kingston before the War of 1812: A Collection of Documents* (1959), is a valuable source, combining narrative details and official documents pertaining to Brant and her importance to the Crown. There are numerous articles focusing on Brant, of which the following can be read with particular profit: Gretchen Green, "Molly Brant, Catherine Brant, and Their Daughters: A Study in Colonial Acculturation," *Ontario History* 81 (1989): 236–50; H. P. Gundy, "Molly Brant—Loyalist," *Ontario History* 45 (1953): 97–108; and Jean Johnston, "Ancestry and Descendants of Molly Brant," *Ontario History* 63 (1971): 86–92.

ROBERT S. ALLEN

BRASHEAR, John Alfred (24 Nov. 1840–8 Apr. 1920), telescope maker, was born in Brownsville, Pennsylvania, the son of Basil Brown Brashear, a saddler, and Julia Smith, a schoolteacher. He attended the common schools of Brownsville. In 1855 he took a brief course in bookkeeping from Duff's Mercantile College in Pittsburgh. The following year he became an apprentice mechanic at the engine works of John Snowden and Sons in Brownsville. After completing his apprenticeship, he went to work as a mechanic in Louisville, Kentucky. From 1861 to 1881 he worked as a millwright in iron mills in Pittsburgh. He married Phoebe Stewart in 1862.

Brashear had been interested in astronomy from childhood. According to his autobiography, he had been taught the constellations by his grandfather when he was eight, and had his first look through a telescope at age nine. After years of naked-eye observations, in 1872 he built his first telescope, a five-inch refractor. Four years later he met Samuel Pierpont Langley, director of the Allegheny Observatory. From Langley Brashear learned that making reflectors, which utilized mirrors rather than the lenses of refractors, was a simpler way to construct a telescope. In 1877 Brashear began constructing a twelve-inch reflector. While working on this telescope he developed a method of silvering the telescope mirror, which became the standard for both large and small telescopes. During this period he also began contributing articles on astronomy to local newspapers.

In 1880 Brashear, who had been doing odd jobs for Langley, began manufacturing, part time, the optics for amateurs desiring to make their own telescopes. With the financial backing of William Thaw, the foremost philanthropist of the Allegheny Observatory, Brashear went into business full time in 1881. He continued to head the John A. Brashear Company until his death.

Brashear had chosen a propitious time to switch professions. American astronomy was entering a period of expansion on both the professional and amateur levels. The number of major observatories doubled during the last two decades of the nineteenth century, while the new discipline of astrophysics demanded new and different forms of auxiliary apparatus. Brashear and his staff were experts in grinding glass to the tolerances needed for astrophysical research. Complementing his technical proficiency were his low prices, a result both of his indifference to profit and the subsidies provided by Thaw.

The John A. Brashear Company manufactured lenses, primary mirrors, spectroscopes, and other optical parts for many observatories in the United States, including Allegheny, Lick, and Yerkes, and for the observatories at the Universities of Michigan and Pennsylvania and Swarthmore College. The pinnacle of Brashear's labor was the production of the 72-inch primary mirror for the Dominion Observatory in Canada. The contract was awarded in 1913 and the telescope completed in 1918. Beginning in 1883 the company was responsible for grounding and polishing the plates for large Rowland Gratings, as well as taking care of distribution. These gratings were essential for diffraction spectra studies in the late nineteenth and early twentieth centuries. Some of the apparatus for Langley's early experiments in manned flight also were produced by Brashear.

Brashear was also extremely active in educational activities in Pittsburgh. From 1896 until his death, he was a member of the board of trustees of Western University of Pennsylvania (which became the University of Pittsburgh), from which he received an honorary doctorate of science in 1893. From 1901 through 1904 Brashear served as the acting chancellor of Western University. He was also a member of the board of trustees of the Carnegie Institute from 1896 until his death and served on the committee that planned the Carnegie Institute of Technology. In 1909 he was named chair of the Educational Fund Commission (subsequently known as the Henry C. Frick Educational Commission), charged with upgrading public education in Pittsburgh by improving the skills of individual teachers, who received scholarships from the commission to attend summer school.

From all indications, "Uncle John," as he was known, was a man of immense personal charm and kindness. He was a very successful participant in the highly personal patronage system that dominated American science between the Civil War and World War I. Part of his success may have lain in his hero-worship of scientists and successful industrialists. There is not a hint in his autobiography that he thought either a patron of science or a scientist could be self-serving or egotistic.

Although Brashear did no significant scientific research of his own, he was one of the more important contributors in the evolution of American observational astronomy to international prominence, if not domination. His life is an example of the essential role of the technologist in the advance of science. His contemporaries recognized this. He received one of the fifty stars given to astronomers in the first edition of *American Men of Science* (1906), indicating that he was among the leading scientists in the United States. He retained his star for the remainder of his life. In 1918 he was selected as a member of the National Research Council. Six years after his death in Pittsburgh, J. W. Fecker bought the John A. Brashear Company.

• Some Brashear papers are at the University of Pittsburgh. Fundamental to understanding Brashear is his autobiography, *A Man Who Loved the Stars: The Autobiography of John A. Brashear* (1924; repr. 1988). Among contemporary obituaries, the best is Frank Schlesinger, "John Alfred Brashear, 1840–1920," *Popular Astronomy* 28 (1926): 373–79.

MARC ROTHENBERG

BRASLAU, Sophie (16 Aug. 1892–22 Dec. 1935), contralto singer, was born in New York City, the only child of Abel Braslau, a physician, and Alexandra Goodelman. Émigrés from the Ukraine in the 1880s, they possessed a lively interest in the arts and availed themselves of the cultural events in their adopted city. In time the home that they established on West Eighty-sixth Street, part of which was set aside for Dr. Braslau's medical practice, attracted the intelligentsia of the day and provided the ideal atmosphere for Sophie, whose many talents, especially in music, asserted themselves in early childhood.

At age six Sophie began piano lessons under a local teacher and continued to make steady progress with the instrument into her teens. While at Wadleigh High School, where her pianism was admired, her unusually rich contralto voice also drew the attention of the music staff, who urged that vocal lessons should not be delayed. In time the Braslaus enrolled Sophie in the newly opened Institute of Musical Arts (later the Juilliard School of Music), where she worked primarily with Arthur Hochmann, her first piano tutor of importance, but some time later she withdrew from the school because of illness. Upon recovery she studied privately with the prestigious Alexander Lambert to become a concert pianist, but her plans were changed in 1910 when composer-teacher Arturo Buzzi-Peccia heard her sing. Astounded by the beauty and power of her voice, he told her parents, "Ah, here you have a contralto of operatic calibre without knowing it!" and eventually persuaded them that Sophie forsake the piano to study voice under his tutelage. This was not an easy task for her and there were many misgivings, but after hearing Alma Gluck sing a recital, her doubts disappeared. "In Alma Gluck's art were all of the things to which I had aspired," she said.

Braslau's three years of intensive vocal study had brought a remarkable polish to her singing and Buzzi-Peccia decided to present her in a private recital to which he invited prominent musicians, most notably Arturo Toscanini, who urged her to audition for the Metropolitan Opera. Encouraged by her teacher as well, she sang for Impresario Giulio Gatti-Casazza and his staff in April 1913, and the result was a three-year contract at twenty dollars a week. She was asked to prepare seven comprimario roles for the coming season.

For a young and inexperienced singer, Braslau found the ensuing months both hectic and fulfilling. Besides her operatic assignment, she made a successful test recording for the Victor Talking Machine Company and signed a contract to make Red Seal recordings. That summer she auditioned for the Wolfsohn Bureau and only a few days after joining the agency, was summoned to substitute for Louise Homer at the Richmond, Virginia, Festival. There in her first professional engagement she scored a triumph. Eager for continued vocal refinement, she began studies with song composer Gabriele Sibella, whom she would later credit for the complete development of her voice so that it encompassed three octaves, from A below the F of the bass clef to the high C. Her other teachers included Marcella Sembrich, Mario Marafioti, and Herbert Witherspoon.

Braslau made her debut at the Metropolitan Opera House as the offstage Voice in Wagner's *Parsifal* in November 1913 but actually appeared on the stage the next evening singing Feodor in Mussorgsky's *Boris Godunov*. Her other roles, such as the Sandman in Humperdinck's *Hansel and Gretel*, the Shepherd in Puccini's *Tosca*, and an orphan in Strauss's *Der Rosenkavalier* offered little to challenge her, a situation that would prevail throughout her succeeding six seasons with the company. With the exception of Marina (*Boris Godunov*) and her acclaimed creation of the title role in Charles Wakefield Cadman's *Shanewis*, she sang comprimario parts, even after her enormous success as Azucena in Verdi's *Il Trovatore*, Amneris in Verdi's *Aïda*, Suzuki in Puccuni's *Madama Butterfly*, and Carmen at the 1918 Ravinia Summer Opera Festival. The critics often lamented her secondary status at the Metropolitan, but her career there was nevertheless a very active one. In all, she sang a total of 242 performances, twenty-five roles in twenty-two operas. She also participated in twenty-five Sunday concerts, four galas, and two concert presentations: Gounod's *Mors et Vita* and Verdi's *Requiem*.

It was on the concert stage that Braslau achieved her greatest fame. Though she had sung some concerts, mostly at festivals, it wasn't until she gave the first of her annual New York recitals in 1916 that she received the unanimous endorsement of the critics. Richard Aldrich in the *New York Times* noted that "she was a recital artist of personality and with serious aims." Fluent in seven languages and facile with various styles of music, she soon developed a repertoire of far-reaching dimensions and skill at programming. In her 21-year career she sang with most of the major symphonic orchestras in the United States, at music festivals, with oratorio societies, and at both solo and joint recitals. Her successes were not limited to the American scene exclusively for she won great favor in Europe, and her tours of England in 1920, Germany in 1925, and the Scandinavian countries in 1931 were unique triumphs.

Braslau's popularity was eminently enhanced by her phonograph recordings. She remained a Victor artist through 1924, having as many as thirty-three titles in the catalog at one time. On the other hand, her Columbia recordings (1927–1929) reveal her voice at its most opulent and in less hackneyed selections. Unfortunately, all of the Braslau recordings have long been unavailable. Radio brought Braslau an even greater audience when she debuted in October 1926. The following year she appeared in a series of weekly concerts and afterward made frequent guest appearances.

During the 1930s Braslau, at the peak of her vocal powers, was in great demand. However, after her highly praised rendition of de Falla's *El Amor Brujo* at the Lewisohn Stadium concert on 18 July 1934, her career came to an abrupt halt when the lingering illness that had plagued her for many months was diagnosed as terminal lung cancer. Early in 1935 she did manage to sing on the radio, but that June she became bedridden and within months died in her New York City apartment. She had never married.

Braslau's funeral was not religious but was instead a celebration of music at which her friends Sergei Rachmaninoff and Jascha Heifetz performed. In his eulogy, critic Olin Downes spoke of "her greatness of heart and depth of affection."

• In 1936 Braslau's mother sold her daughter's priceless collection of music, including original manuscripts, to the Brooklyn Public Library. Two years later she donated Braslau's private papers, programs, and scrapbooks to the music division of the New York Public Library for the Performing Arts, Lincoln Center. James Francis Cooke, *Great Men and Famous Musicians on the Art of Music* (1925), contains an article written by Sophie Braslau titled "The Appeal of the Contralto." The Jan.–Mar. 1996 issue of the *Record Collector* contains a comprehensive article by Edward Hagelin Pearson, which addresses her life and career and also includes a detailed discography. Frederick H. Martens, *The Art of the Prima Donna and Concert Singer* (1923), devotes a chapter to Braslau's discussion of her musical education and singing techniques. Harriet Brower, *Vocal Mastery* (1920), in the chapter "Sophie Braslau Making a Career in America" reveals Braslau's rise to fame as told mostly in her own words.

EDWARD HAGELIN PEARSON

BRATTLE, Thomas (20 June 1658–18 May 1713), astronomer and architect, was born in Boston, Massachusetts, the son of Thomas Brattle, a merchant, and Elizabeth Tyng. The oldest son in one of Boston's wealthiest families, Thomas early devoted himself to mathematics and science. Harvard College, where he earned an A.B. in 1676, was in disarray because of war and bad leadership during his undergraduate years, so Brattle pursued higher education largely on his own. He wrote to Britain's royal astronomer, John Flamsteed, in 1703 and 1705 that no one was able to teach him much mathematics at Harvard, and he had relied on whatever books were available. Young Brattle also worked with and learned from scientifically inclined locals, such as the printer-mathematician John Foster and Dr. William Avery.

With Foster, Brattle made his greatest contribution to astronomy, which earned him a favorable mention in Isaac Newton's *Principia* (1687). Together observing the course of two comets in November and December 1680, Foster and Brattle judged that the two sightings were actually one comet that had changed direction in the vicinity of the Sun. Brattle, who throughout his life hoped "to be acceptable to . . . ye Learned World," sent his precise observations anonymously to be read at the Royal Society of London, where Edmund Halley gathered them with other observations to pass on to Newton. Brattle's data and judgment supported the royal astronomer's data at a crucial point in Newton's development of a theory of universal gravitation.

From 1682 to 1689 Brattle lived in London, where he became a disciple of the aged Robert Boyle, the father of modern chemistry and focal point of London's scientific community, and Royal Astronomer Flamsteed. Brattle seems to have modeled his subsequent life on Boyle. Neither man married, and both men opened their house and laboratories to visitors and young students. Boyle was "very musically given." Brattle returned from England with New England's first chamber organ, probably wrote a treatise on singing with notes, and was music leader at the Brattle Street Church. Boyle was very religious and wrote about being a "Christian Virtuoso." Brattle was also devout and was praised in 1717 as a "Christian philosopher" by his minister, Benjamin Coleman. Finally, just as Boyle endowed educational institutions at the end of his life, Brattle's will endowed a fellowship at Harvard to subsidize a scholar who would teach mathematics and communicate astronomical observations "to the learned abroad, as in some measure I have done."

Brattle's mother and father died while he was in England, and when Brattle returned to Boston, he lived off the rents of inherited property and took on many civic duties. During the Salem witch trials of 1692 Brattle joined with men such as Increase Mather who were trying to show the bad logic being used by the judges. Brattle wrote and circulated an essay that the scholar Perry Miller described as "a milestone in American literature if only for its free-and-easy, its highly literate and satirical tone; in New England it is the first treatment of disaster that steps outside the scheme of the jeremiad" (*The New England Mind: From Colony to Province* [1953], p. 196).

In the late 1690s and early 1700s Brattle became embroiled in a complex religious and political controversy involving the need for a new church in Boston and the control of Harvard College, where Brattle served as a part-time treasurer. In both situations Increase Mather and Cotton Mather led a faction that was losing political and religious power. Brattle and his younger brother William Brattle, minister in Cambridge and former college tutor, were key members of a group that gained power at the college and established what was called the Brattle Street Church. The Brattle brothers were working to adapt Puritan innovations in church membership practices, liturgy, and sectarian orientation that were developed in near isolation during the middle of the seventeenth century to the much more integrated English empire after the Glorious Revolution.

Thomas Brattle's most influential contribution to this controversy and subsequent history of American education and Christianity was architectural. Like most gentlemen mathematicians of the era, he was also an architect and engineer and was consulted regarding building fortifications and bridges. Much circumstantial evidence indicates that Brattle fully designed Stoughton Hall at Harvard College (1698) and his own Brattle Street Meeting House (1699). Stoughton Hall was the first college building in America in what is called the Georgian style, which included a symmetrical facade and classical treatment of dormers and doors and which became iconographic of American higher education. The Brattle Street Meeting House was the first in New England to have a simple tower and steeple derived from Christopher Wren's London city churches, a style that became iconographic of American Protestantism. Both buildings embrace modern styles popular in the greater British empire; however, both were put to specific Puritan use—especially the meeting house, which retained the traditional floor plan of a Puritan meeting house.

Brattle might also be considered an unofficial professor of mathematics and astronomy at Harvard College. No one at Harvard had any expertise in those subjects, and students such as Henry Newman, who later became secretary of the Society for the Propagation of Christian Knowledge in London, and Thomas Robie, who later became a tutor at Harvard, told of doing experiments with Brattle. Brattle's mathematical abilities were not so up-to-date as to teach students the new calculus. However, he was the first New England scientist to explicitly endorse one of the most crucial strategies of the scientific revolution: that the scientist must search for the simplest and most comprehensive terms, usually mathematical, to describe natural phenomena. To this end, Brattle and Robie tried to find mathematical patterns in the smallpox epidemics of 1711 in the way Halley found one for the comet of 1682.

When Brattle died in Boston, Newton, as president of the Royal Society, authorized a plan to procure Brattle's papers "relating to Astronomy, Musick, and other parts of ye Mathematicks." Brattle had succeeded in being acceptable to the learned world. However, his greatest importance was as a provincial New Englander importing scientific and architectural ideas he learned in London in the 1680s to Boston at the turn of the century.

• No record confirms that the Royal Society received any of Brattle's manuscripts. Brattle's papers have disappeared, probably burned in the Harvard Library fire of 1764. The Royal Greenwich Observatory owns several long letters to John Flamsteed. Brattle's almanac, written to earn an M.A. from Harvard, was published as *Almanack of Celestial Motions* (1678). J. Hodgson published "An Account of Some Eclipses of the Sun and Moon, Observed by Mr. Tho. Brattle . . . ," *Philosophical Transactions of the Royal Society* 24 (1704–1705): 1630–38, and "Observatio Eclipsis Lunaris peracta . . . ," *Philosophical Transactions of the Royal Society* 25 (1706–1707): 2471–72. George Lincoln Burr, ed., *Narratives of the Witchcraft Cases, 1648–1706* (1914), includes the "Letter of Thomas Brattle." His will is printed in Edward-Doubleday Harris, *An Account of the Descendants of Capt. Thomas Brattle* (1867). Brattle is discussed in most studies of early American science and Puritanism, the most recent of which are by Rick Kennedy, "Thy Patriarchs' Desire: Thomas and William Brattle in Puritan Massachusetts" (Ph.D. diss., Univ. of California, Santa Barbara, 1987); "Thomas Brattle: Mathematician-Architect in the Transition of the New England Mind, 1690–1700," *Winterthur Portfolio* 24 (1989): 231–45; and "Thomas Brattle and the Scientific Provincialism of New England, 1680–1713," *New England Quarterly* 63 (1990): 584–600.

RICK KENNEDY

BRATTLE, William (22 Nov. 1662–15 Feb. 1717), teacher and minister, was born in Boston, Massachusetts, the son of Thomas Brattle, a merchant, and Elizabeth Tyng. Up to the time William was seven years old, his father was a principal participant in the controversial founding of Third (South) Church of Boston, a church advocating ecclesiastic reforms suited to the fast-growing colony. Extending the example of his father, William devoted his later life to reforming Puritan churches and education to best adapt the formerly isolated colony into the more integrated British empire of the late seventeenth and early eighteenth centuries.

At Harvard College, where he earned an A.B. in 1680, Brattle met his closest associate, John Leverett. The two men devoted the rest of their lives to the college, church, and community. For his M.A. thesis, Brattle published *An Ephemeris of Celestial Motions* (1682), in which he advocated adopting the Gregorian calendar reforms and searching "everything to the bottom." In 1685 President Increase Mather invited Brattle and Leverett to become the two tutors at the college. Because Mather was mostly an absentee president and the college had no professors, Brattle and Leverett were the faculty and on-site administration of the college from 1685 to 1696. The two remained leaders, sometimes unofficially, of the college until their deaths. In 1686, under the influence of the newly immigrated minister Charles Morton, Brattle and Leverett upgraded the content of the curriculum, greatly enhancing the intellectual sophistication of the provincial college. Aside from encouraging a broad range of reading and "searching things to the bottom," Brattle also modified several European textbooks for students' use. The two most influential textbooks were based on the Jansenist Antoine Arnauld's *Port-Royal Logic* (1662), which merged Augustinian with Cartesian epistemology and method. Brattle's logical works and courses were designed to strengthen the Puritan assurance of students while abandoning the outdated Ramist logic of the forefathers. Brattle's textbooks were used long into the eighteenth century and were widely dispersed in the form of student notebooks.

More influential than Brattle's textbooks was the example he gave to his students of an orthodox Puritan, committed to the ideals of the founders of New England but open to the beginnings of the Enlightenment and desirous of ecclesiastical reforms that would help Puritans remain powerful in an increasingly cosmopolitan colony, where Britain was imposing religious toleration. A generation of young ministers, including Benjamin Colman and John Barnard, and important laymen, including Massachusetts chief justice Paul Dudley, were educated by Brattle and Leverett, and a surprising number of accounts survive testifying that Brattle was universally loved, respected, and sought after for advice.

Brattle left the role of tutor to become minister of the Cambridge church in 1696. In 1697 he married Elizabeth Hayman. They had one son who survived to adulthood, General William Brattle, for whom Brattle Street in Cambridge and Brattleborough, Vermont, are named. Increase Mather, Brattle's lifelong patron, recommended him to the Cambridge pulpit, which permitted him to retain intimate contact with the students and faculty as unofficial chaplain and professor of divinity. In his ordination ceremony Brattle insisted that no layperson participate in the laying on of hands. This innovation along with another diminishing the role of the congregation in deciding who should be given full membership in the church enhanced the power of the minister over the laity. Many of the young ministers trained by Brattle made similar innovations. The laity of the churches tended to be more conservative and rigid, fearful of the extensive changes in society being forced by new imperial policies and rapid immigration. Brattle and the young clergy believed that ministers needed more power to embrace new members and set aside old antagonisms to other Protestant groups if Congregationalism were to continue to be a vital part of New England. Tensions reached their height in 1699 and 1700, when Brattle and his former students became embroiled in a complex power struggle over the leadership of the college and the founding of a new church in Boston, the Brattle Street Church.

Many young clergy, former students of Brattle, supported removing Increase Mather from the presidency of Harvard. Cotton Mather and Increase Mather fought hard against what Cotton described in his diary as "a company of head-strong men . . . full of malignity to the holy ways of our churches." Increase Mather eventually had to leave the presidency, and Leverett replaced him in 1707. From 1697 to 1707 Brattle was the on-site, de facto leader of the college. Increase Mather recommended that Brattle's role be formalized as vice president, but Brattle turned down the title in 1714. He also later turned down an offer to become a fellow of the Royal Society of London. Unlike the Mathers, who sought titles and recognition in London, Brattle focused on the duties and rank of being a shepherd to his congregation and students.

Brattle, a peace-loving man, tried to avoid being drawn into the controversy surrounding the Brattle Street Church. One of his students, Benjamin Colman, the church's first minister, wrote a reform *Manifesto* (1699) that extended ideas and attitudes long taught by Brattle. The powerful Brattle family was also involved. In the end, the new church became one of the leading churches of New England and the most visible extension of Brattle's ecclesiastical influence. On Brattle's death, Colman insisted on preaching a sermon honoring his mentor even though Brattle had requested no funeral sermon.

The struggles over the college and church died down after a few years as the young clergy who were trained by Brattle continued to fill more pulpits in New England. Brattle was above all a peacemaker, even maintaining the affection and respect of Increase Mather. Brattle similarly helped his former student Joseph Green, the new minister in Salem after the 1692 witch trials crisis, successfully bring peace to that community.

Brattle's first wife died on 28 July 1715. Sometime in late 1716, a few months before his death, Brattle married Green's widow, Elizabeth Garrish Green. Long after Brattle's death in Cambridge, one of his students, John Barnard, in praising the liberality of his education, described Brattle as "cherished by candidates for the ministry, exceeding prudent, to whom all addressed themselves for advice" (Sibley, p. 204). Such was Brattle's importance. Students long studied his textbooks, and those who knew him honored his teaching and counsel. Harvard tutor Henry Flynt, a former student of Brattle and future teacher of John Adams, wrote in his diary at Brattle's death of losing a father figure, someone with whom he could "unbosom" himself, a "comfort and relief." Brattle was a key figure intellectually and emotionally as New Englanders made the transition from colony to province.

• Brattle's manuscript sermons are in the Houghton Library at Harvard University. Other manuscripts by Brattle, reminiscences by students, and student notebooks including his textbooks are scattered primarily among the Harvard University Archives, the Massachusetts Historical Society, and the American Antiquarian Society, which owns a student notebook by Joseph Sewall that transcribes Brattle's textbook derived from Henry More, *Enchiridium Metaphysicum* (1688). Brattle's will is published in Edward-Doubleday Harris, *An Account of Some of the Descendants of Capt. Thomas Brattle* (1867). See Benjamin Colman, *A Sermon . . . after the Funerals of . . . Mr. William Brattle . . . and . . . Mr. Ebenezer Pemberton* (1717). Increase Mather remembered Brattle in the preface to Joseph Sewall, *Precious Treasure in Earthen Vessels* (1717). John L. Sibley, *Biographical Sketches of Harvard Graduates*, vol. 3 (1873), and Samuel Eliot Morison, *Harvard College in the Seventeenth Century* (1936), give citations of the many disparate sources of information on Brattle. Recent works dealing specifically with Brattle are Rick Kennedy, "Thy Patriarchs' Desire: Thomas and William Brattle in Puritan Massachusetts" (Ph.D. diss., Univ. of California, Santa Barbara, 1987), and Kennedy, ed., *Aristotelian and Cartesian Logic at Harvard: Morton's "Logick System" and Brattle's "Compendium of Logick"* (1995).

RICK KENNEDY

BRAUD, Wellman (25 Jan. 1891–29 Oct. 1966), jazz bassist, was born Wellman Breaux in St. James Parish, Louisiana. Nothing is known of his parents except that they were of Creole heritage, and it is not known when he anglicized his name. Braud began playing violin at age seven and later took up guitar. His earliest work was with string trios playing on the streets of

New Orleans. During the 1910s he worked regularly at Tom Anderson's cabaret, probably playing guitar in a group with violinist Armand J. Piron while also playing drums and trombone in various ad hoc brass bands. In 1917 Braud moved to Chicago, where he began playing bass and toured with John Wickliffe's band, later joining the Original Creole Band (or Orchestra) at the Pekin Café as a replacement for Ed Garland. At the time Braud joined the band, the other members included cornetist "Sugar" Johnny Smith, clarinetist Lawrence Duhé, trombonist Roy Palmer, guitarist Louis Keppard, and drummer Tubby Hall. In 1918 clarinetist Sidney Bechet was added to the group, which during Braud's stay also worked at the Dreamland and De Luxe cafés. From 1920 to 1922 Braud was with Charlie Elgar's orchestra, most likely at the Dreamland, and from March to May 1923 he doubled on trombone and bass with Will Vodery's orchestra in the *Plantation Revue* in London. Later that year he moved to New York, where he worked with vaudevillean clarinetist and bandleader Wilbur Sweatman. In early 1925 Braud and Bechet joined the ten-piece orchestra of the *Seven-Eleven* revue, with which they played vaudeville and burlesque houses in Newark, Baltimore, Washington, D.C., Boston, and Providence, before opening at New York's Columbia Theater. After leaving *Seven-Eleven*, Braud joined the *Lucky Sambo* revue and remained through early 1927.

In mid-1927 Braud joined Duke Ellington's Kentucky Club orchestra and made his first recordings with the band in October. Among the many titles he recorded with Ellington over the next few years, those most revealing of his prominently featured capabilities are "Washington Wobble" (1927), his debut solo performance, which may be the first example of the four-beats-to-the-bar "walking bass" style on record; "Diga Diga Doo," "Move Over," "Hot and Bothered," and "Bandanna Babies" (1928); "Flaming Youth," "Saturday Night Function," "High Life," "Hot Feet," "Stevedore Stomp," "Saratoga Swing," "Freeze and Melt," "Cotton Club Stomp," "Ring Dem Bells," and "Old Man Blues" (1930). Although Braud's technically advanced style of alternately picking and slapping the strings of his bass provided an undeniably powerful lift to the sound of Ellington's late 1920s "jungle-style" band, particularly on fast stomp tempos, by the early 1930s the composer-leader wanted to cultivate a smoother, more sophisticated sound and rhythm. Braud's inability to read music proved no impediment for he could play any of Ellington's arrangements by ear. But his seemingly dated, New Orleans–styled rhythmic conception was no longer what Ellington wanted. Not wishing to fire the mild-mannered older man, he devised a scheme by which Braud would leave the band of his own will, his pride intact. Toward that end, in November 1934 Ellington added the younger, more modern-thinking bassist Billy Taylor to the fold, and the following March Braud quit, probably never realizing how he had been eased out. Ellington, though, must have seen the potential in having two bassists in the band, because in May 1935 he hired the equally young Hayes Alvis as an adjunct to Taylor.

In mid-1935 Braud worked briefly at the Vodvil Club in Harlem in a band he had formed with New Orleans clarinetist Jimmie Noone, and when that ended he spent some time working with drummer Kaiser Marshall at a club in New Jersey. Later in the year he joined the novelty vocal and instrumental group the Spirits of Rhythm as both bassist and manager, but he also worked sporadically with his own trios through 1937. In March 1938 he recorded with trumpeter Hot Lips Page and may have played engagements with his band as well. Either during or after his stay with pianist Edgar Hayes's orchestra in 1939, Braud participated in two important recording dates with Jelly Roll Morton's New Orleans Jazzmen in September. On these sessions he was reunited with old hometown friends such as clarinetist Albert Nicholas, drummer Zutty Singleton, and, most significantly, Sidney Bechet, the most formidable soprano saxophonist alive. In January 1940 Braud recorded three more dates with Morton, once again with Nicholas and Singleton but now with New Orleans trumpeter Henry "Red" Allen as well. The next few months were even more fruitful. In March and April 1940 he recorded with the Bechet-Spanier Big Four, one of the most perfectly realized jazz recording groups of all time, and in May he participated in the reunion of Bechet and Louis Armstrong for Decca's *New Orleans Jazz* album. As a more or less regular member of Bechet's working bands, Braud was present on three of Bechet's dates for Victor between June 1940 and September 1941, while also playing engagements with his quartet at Nick's in Greenwich Village, the Log Cabin in Fonda, New York, and Bill "Bojangles" Robinson's Mimo Club in Harlem.

In 1943 and 1944 Braud worked in the swing bands of saxophonists Al Sears and Garvin Bushell, but in the latter year he also began operating a poolroom and a meat-marketing business in New York, playing music only on weekends. In January 1947 Braud and Bechet appeared at a Town Hall concert produced by clarinetist Mezz Mezzrow to promote his autobiography, *Really the Blues*, and in September Braud replaced bassist Pops Foster on a recording date with the Mezzrow-Bechet Quintet on the clarinetist and author's King Jazz label. Braud was also New Orleans trumpeter Bunk Johnson's choice for three recording dates in December that ultimately appeared on a Columbia album called *The Last Testament*. In early 1956 he joined the equally venerable New Orleans trombonist Kid Ory's band in California and toured Europe with them later in the year. In 1958 Braud settled in Los Angeles, where he worked in clarinetist Joe Darensbourg's band in 1960. After recovering from a mild heart attack in the summer of 1961, Braud sat in with the Ellington band in the fall and later worked with traditional jazz singer Barbara Dane. Braud worked only infrequently after that, including a tour in Oregon in the fall of 1966. He died in Los Angeles.

• There is some oral history material on Braud at Tulane University. References to Braud's activities in both pre- and post-Ellington years are in John Chilton, *Sidney Bechet: The Wizard of Jazz* (1987), and *The Autobiography of Pops Foster: New Orleans Jazzman*, as told to Tom Stoddard (1971). However, Mark Tucker, *Ellington: The Early Years* (1991); Gunther Schuller, *Early Jazz* (1968) and *The Swing Era* (1989); and John Edward Hasse, *Beyond Category: The Life and Genius of Duke Ellington* (1993), provide the best analyses of the role he played in the Ellington orchestra. See also Barney Bigard, *With Louis and the Duke*, ed. Barry Martyn (1986); Rex Stewart, *Jazz Masters of the 30's* (1972); and *The Duke Ellington Reader*, ed. Tucker (1993). Complete discographical information is in Brian Rust, *Jazz Records, 1897–1942* (1982); and Walter Bruyninckx, *Traditional Jazz Discography, 1897–1988* (5 vols., 1989), and *Swing Discography, 1920–1988* (13 vols., 1989).

JACK SOHMER

BRAUER, Richard Dagobert (10 Feb. 1901–17 Apr. 1977), mathematician, was born in Berlin-Charlottenburg, Germany, the son of Max Brauer, a wealthy businessman in the wholesale leather trade, and Lilly Caroline (maiden name unknown). He entered the Technische Hochschule in Berlin-Charlottenburg in 1919 and received a Ph.D. in mathematics from the University of Berlin in 1925 as a student of the noted mathematician Issai Schur. He then moved to Königsberg as an assistant to K. Knopp. He became a privatdozent in 1927 and remained in Königsberg until 1933, when he was dismissed by the Nazis. He spent one year teaching at the University of Kentucky, another at the Institute for Advanced Study at Princeton, New Jersey, and in 1935 he moved to the University of Toronto. In 1948 he moved to the University of Michigan and then, in 1952, to Harvard University, where he remained until his retirement in 1971. Brauer was elected to the Royal Society of Canada in 1945, received the Cole Prize of the American Mathematical Society in 1949, was elected to the National Academy of Sciences in 1955, and received the National Medal for Scientific Merit in 1971. In 1925 he married Ilse Karger; they had two sons, who also became mathematicians.

Brauer's thesis at the University of Berlin dealt with the representation theory of Lie groups, in particular the characters of orthogonal groups; he introduced algebraic methods to the work of Schur and settled an open problem. He followed this line in a number of papers, developing algebraic methods in an area where the pioneering work of Hermann Weyl rested on analytic methods. One of the discoveries Brauer made in this research was the Brauer algebra.

Brauer's years in Königsberg were primarily devoted to the theory of algebras, in particular simple algebras and division algebras. He discovered, in joint work with Emmy Noether, the connection between Schur indices, from the representation theory of finite groups, and division algebras. He then introduced the Brauer factor sets into the theory of division algebras and discovered the Brauer group, a central idea in this area and one that has been influential in many areas of mathematics. Finally, again in joint work with Noether, as well as H. Hasse, Brauer reached a truly outstanding result, the classification of finite-dimensional division algebras over number fields and, in particular, the proof of the longstanding conjecture that all such algebras were cyclic. This result capped decades of research by outstanding mathematicians.

Brauer turned in the mid-1930s to an arithmetic study of the representation theory of finite groups, a topic that he would follow all his life, producing an extraordinary number of outstanding achievements that fit together into a grand theory. Any one of the high points would have been sufficient to establish for him an international reputation. His methods relied on modular representations and the idea, introduced by Brauer, of a block, which, in this area, are analogues of the ideas of congruences and ideals in number theory. In addition to the establishment of the basic ideas, Brauer's formidable accomplishments in this period include the "primes to the first power theory," the three Main Theorems of block theory, and crucial results on Cartan matrices, number of characters in blocks, and applications to the structure theory of groups.

Some of the special and detailed methods that Brauer developed in this area were to pay off in a tremendous way, with a series of papers (beginning in 1947) on Artin L-series and other applications to number theory. In a true breakthrough on old problems, Brauer proved that the Artin L-series were meromorphic functions. The main tool was the celebrated Brauer Induction Theorem, which is important in many areas of mathematics beyond group theory and number theory and has also been the inspiration for a number of important generalizations.

In the 1950s Brauer began yet another great program, this time the study groups of even order based on elementary properties of involutions. Some of the most famous results were the Brauer-Fowler theorem, the Brauer-Suzuki-Wall theorem, and the Brauer-Suzuki theorem, all in that decade. Brauer was able to use the deepest results of the entire theory of blocks. When Walter Feit and John Thompson proved the solvability of groups of odd order in 1961, it became clear that Brauer's ideas were key to the problem of classifying the finite simple groups, a project that then involved many dozens of mathematicians, including Brauer, for two decades. Brauer continued to develop and exploit all these ideas and was a leading figure in research until his death in Boston.

Brauer had many outstanding graduate students over the years. He was always known to be very accessible. He was a careful teacher, always ready to supply details, always assigning interesting problems of greatly varying difficulty. He never used a textbook and would always produce a set of notes for any course at any level. He felt mathematics was alive and each generation should rewrite it.

Brauer's results and influence permeate modern mathematics, and he is one of the most important algebraists of the twentieth century. Achieving great breadth while at the same time having almost all of his work tied in some way to the representation theory of finite groups, he was a colossus with a focus.

• Brauer's personal papers are in the archives at Harvard University. His collected works are the three-volume *Richard Brauer: Collected Papers*, ed. Paul Fong and Warren J. Wong (1980). Two extensive obituaries that include personal memories are by Walter Feit, in *Bulletin of the American Mathematical Society*, n.s., 1 (1979): 1–20, and by J. A. Green, in *Bulletin of the London Mathematical Society* 10 (1978): 317–42.

JONATHAN L. ALPERIN

BRAUN, Wernher von. *See* Von Braun, Wernher Magnus Maxmillian.

BRAUTIGAN, Richard (30 Jan. 1935–Sept. 1984), writer, was born in Tacoma, Washington, the son of Bernard F. Brautigan, a laborer, and Lula May Keho. Richard Brautigan's parents were divorced before he was born, and he never knew his father. Reared by his mother and a series of stepfathers, he had a traumatic childhood. He was deplorably treated and abandoned three times, on one occasion coming home from school to find his mother had disappeared, taking his sister with her. Neighbors discovered her whereabouts and gave him the money to follow her. When he was a young man, he was briefly confined to a mental hospital.

In 1954 Brautigan moved to San Francisco, where he began his career as a writer and formed close friendships with such writers as Lawrence Ferlinghetti, Michael McClure, Philip Whalen, Keith Abbott, Ron Loewinsohn, and, crucially, Jack Spicer. Brautigan initially wrote poems in order "to learn how to write a sentence." Once he had mastered the sentence, he felt, he could turn to fiction. The characteristically spare, wiry sentences that he wrote resemble Ernest Hemingway's in syntactical and lexical simplicity, but they also possess a whimsical, buoyant quality that is Brautigan's own. "I guess you are kind of curious as to who I am," he wrote, for example, in *In Watermelon Sugar* (1968), "but I am one of those who do not have a regular name." His metaphors could be equally whimsical and startling. In "The Weather in San Francisco," he described the interior of a purse as resembling "a small autumn field" with the keys "near the fallen branches of an old apple tree."

Brautigan wrote and published a series of poetry chapbooks, or pamphlets, in the late 1950s. Internal evidence suggests that *Trout Fishing in America*, the book for which he is best known, was written in 1960, but it was not published until 1967. Spicer helped Brautigan to edit *Trout Fishing*. The book was constructed in the form of a "serial poem," Spicer's term for the kind of long work of interrelated shorter pieces that he himself wrote. Although the book pursues various narrative lines, it is less a conventional novel than a collage of loosely related, gently humorous sketches and stories that evoke a deep pathos for lost American innocence. Perhaps its best-known chapter is "The Cleveland Wrecking Yard," in which bits and pieces of landscape have been divided up, and some of them stacked like scrap, for customers to buy and take home.

The second novel Brautigan wrote, but the first to be published, was *A Confederate General from Big Sur* (1964). Like *Trout Fishing in America*, it is a comic work dealing with lost ideals and innocence. Its central figure, Lee Mellon, considers himself a Confederate general, although the Civil War is a hundred years in the past. The book was not popular when first published, but it was reissued after the success of *Trout Fishing in America* and remains one of Brautigan's more respected works.

A profound pathos characterizes the third novel Brautigan wrote, *In Watermelon Sugar*, set in a commune named iDEATH. The commune is an enclosed world of tenuous personal relations, a world lacking all passion—a world in which the ego loses much of its definition and individuality. The fourth novel, *The Abortion*, was the last written before Brautigan's sudden celebrity. The book was finished in 1966 and published in 1971. Dealing mainly with a library where authors bring copies of their books that nobody borrows or reads, it is the least developed of the early novels. Characterization, never one of Brautigan's strong points, is especially thin. Nonetheless, there are fine comic passages.

Trout Fishing in America was published by a small San Francisco press, Four Seasons Foundation, in 1967. The book was not widely publicized, but it soon attracted a sizable following and was reissued by Dell Publishing in 1969 and soon became one of the most widely read works in the counterculture. Brautigan was for hippies what Jack Kerouac had been for the Beat Generation and F. Scott Fitzgerald had been for the Jazz Age. *Trout Fishing in America* remained the most popular of his works, but all of his books published or reissued in the late 1960s and early 1970s sold well. Their flip, lighthearted tone provided diversion for a country torn by an unpopular war in southeast Asia and the exposures of Watergate.

Brautigan's later novels include *The Hawkline Monster* (1974), *Willard and His Bowling Trophies* (1975), *Sombrero Fallout* (1976), *Dreaming of Babylon* (1977), and *The Tokyo-Montana Express* (1980). Although all of these books are marked by a clear, felicitous prose, none are as stylistically adventurous as his earlier fiction. Some of the later books parodied such popular genres as the western, the mystery story, and the gothic, but the results were rarely as imaginatively complex or as amusing as his readers had come to expect.

Brautigan's early stories were published in *Revenge of the Lawn* (1971). His poetry appeared in *The Pill Versus the Springhill Mine Disaster* (1968), which contains early poems, *Rommel Drives on Deep into Egypt* (1970), *Loading Mercury with a Pitchfork* (1976), and *June 30th, June 30th* (1978). Some of these stories and poems equal the four early novels in stylistic brilliance, but there is also much that is bland and unsatisfying. Parts of Brautigan's last book, *So the Wind*

Won't Blow It All Away (1982), were poorly written. The book received some negative reviews, and at the time of his death it had sold only 15,000 copies—a small number in view of his once considerable following.

Much of Brautigan's audience disappeared with the passing of the counterculture. Meanwhile, both of his marriages ended in divorce. (His marriage in 1957 to Virginia Adler ended in 1970. His 1977 marriage to Akiko Nishizawa ended in 1980. He had one child.) He was increasingly depressed and solitary. By 1984 he was living alone in fairly isolated circumstances in Bolinas, California. That October his body was discovered in his house. He had killed himself with a shotgun four or five weeks earlier.

Brautigan's achievement lies in his exquisitely crafted sentences and metaphors and the comic sensibility that runs through them. That comic sensibility was essentially compensation for a darker nature: all of his better-known works concern loss—the loss of friends, affection, and ideals.

• A collection of Brautigan's manuscripts is housed in the Bancroft Library at the University of California in Berkeley, Calif. Keith Abbott, *Downstream from Trout Fishing in America: A Memoir of Richard Brautigan* (1989), is an excellent biographical study with insightful critical commentary. For primary and annotated secondary bibliographies as well as a general assessment of the work, see Edward Halsey Foster, *Richard Brautigan* (1983). Other general assessments include Terence Malley, *Richard Brautigan* (1972); Marc Chenetier, *Richard Brautigan* (1983); Claudia Grossmann, *Richard Brautigan Pounding at the Gates of American Literature* (1986); and Jay Boyer, *Richard Brautigan* (1987).

EDWARD HALSEY FOSTER

BRAWLEY, Benjamin Griffith (22 Apr. 1882–1 Feb. 1939), educator and author, was born in Columbia, South Carolina, the son of Margaret Saphronia Dickerson and Edward McKnight Brawley, a prosperous Baptist minister and president of a small Alabama college. Brawley was an exceptionally bright boy, and the family's frequent moves never stifled his learning. Up until the third grade he was tutored at home by his mother, but he also attended schools in Nashville, Tennessee, and Petersburg, Virginia. During summers when he was not studying the classics, Latin, and Greek at home he earned money by doing odd jobs: working on a tobacco farm in Connecticut or in a printing office. One summer he drove a buggy for a white doctor—and studied Greek while the doctor was out. At age twelve he was sent to Virginia to be tutored in Greek and also studied the language with his father.

By age thirteen Brawley had excelled so much in his studies that he was sent to the preparatory program at Atlanta Baptist College (later Morehouse College). He was surprised and disappointed on his arrival to note that most of the older students there knew nothing of classic literature, much less Greek or Latin. His classmates were equally surprised to find such a young man in their midst, but they soon discovered just how valuable an asset he was. Aware of his intellectual and grammatical prowess, they brought their compositions to him before passing them on to their instructors. Brawley excelled outside the classroom as well. He played football, managed the baseball team, and cofounded the school newspaper, the *Athenaeum* (later the *Maroon Tiger*), for which he wrote numerous articles and poems. Brawley is also said to have initiated the first debate among African-American colleges when his Morehouse team challenged another group from Talladega College.

In 1901 Brawley graduated with honors from Atlanta Baptist College and immediately took a teaching position (a five-month term at $35 a month) in a one-room school in Georgetown, Florida, but then in 1902 took a teaching job at his alma mater, where he stayed until 1910. During his years at Atlanta Baptist College he also earned his B.A. (1906) from the University of Chicago and his M.A. (1908) from Harvard by taking mostly summer courses. Then he accepted a professorship at Howard University and while teaching there met Hilda Damaris Prowd, who became his wife in 1912. They had no children. After only two years at Howard, he returned to Atlanta Baptist, where, in addition to teaching, he became the college's first dean and where his teaching techniques became legendary.

Brawley considered teaching to be a divine profession that should be used to bring students "into the knowledge of truth," the success of which depended as much upon the efforts of the teacher as that of the student. He expected of his students the same high academic and moral standards that he had learned as a child, and he stressed that teaching should take into account the whole student—his or her physical, emotional, economic, and moral background. Brawley would commonly make students memorize long passages from classic literature, and he returned any compositions with even the slightest degree of sloppiness or imprecision, marking them with terse comments like "Too carelessly written to be carefully read" (*Phylon* 10 [1949]). A traditionalist first, last, and always, Brawley was also dissatisfied with the state of education in the country, which emphasized materialism and innovation rather than rote learning.

Although Brawley still earned his primary living as a teacher, he also seriously began to turn toward another profession. He had written articles for his school paper and other publications for several years, but from 1921 on he produced at least ten books and about 100 newspaper and magazine articles, book reviews, editorials, and other efforts. Whether he was writing about African-American life and culture, as in *A Social History of the American Negro* (1921), or more literary topics, as in *A New Survey of English Literature* (1925), Brawley stressed two major themes: first, that literature must rest on a sound artistic and moral basis and, second, that it should present not just the struggles of individuals and races but "a mirror of our hopes and dreams" (*The Negro Genius* [1937], p. 196). He was particularly saddened that most novels and short stories about African Americans that came out of Harlem and other places in the 1920s depicted characters as comic or appealed to their lower natures. "We are simply asking," he wrote in *The Negro Genius*, "that those writers of fiction who deal with the Negro shall be thoroughly honest with themselves" (p. 206). Only by strict adherence to these high ideals, Brawley believed, could the lot of his own race be improved and could race relations be dealt with honestly.

In 1920, after many years at Morehouse, Brawley went to the African Republic of Liberia to conduct an educational survey. Shortly after his return in early 1921, he followed in his father's footsteps and became an ordained Baptist minister at the Messiah Congregation in Brockton, Massachusetts. After only a year, however, he found the congregation's type of Christianity not to his liking and resigned. Brawley returned to teaching, first at Shaw University in North Carolina, where his father, now in failing health, taught theology, and in 1931 at Howard, where he stayed until the end of his life. He died at his Washington, D.C., home from complications following a stroke.

Brawley's impeccable academic credentials and high standards earned him the respect of almost all his students, although that respect was shown in unusual ways. One story goes that a student came to class carrying under his arm a bundle wrapped in newspaper, which everyone assumed was laundry. Instead the student had carefully wrapped his essay in the bundle to be sure that it met Brawley's exacting standards. Brawley's techniques, plus his difficulty in abiding by any standards other than his own, earned him his share of criticism but far more often than not they achieved desirable results.

• The Brawley papers can be found at the Moorland-Spingarn Research Center at Howard University. Scholars interested in a complete bibliography of Brawley's published works should consult the *North Carolina Historical Review* 34 (Apr. 1957): 165–75. Among Brawley's works considered standards are *A New Survey of English Literature* (1925), *The Negro Genius*, and *Paul Laurence Dunbar: Poet of His People* (1936). The best biographical sketches of Brawley are by John W. Parker in *Phylon* 10 (1949): 15–24 and 16 (1955): 183–94. Charlotte S. Price, *Richard LeGallienne as Collected by Benjamin Brawley* (1973), also contains a biographical sketch that is based largely on Parker's work. Obituaries are in the *New York Times*, 7 Feb. 1939, and *The Crisis* 46 (1939).

ROGER A. SCHUPPERT

BRAWLEY, Edward McKnight (18 Mar. 1851–13 Jan. 1923), Baptist minister, educator, and editor, was born in Charleston, South Carolina, the son of free African-American parents, Ann L. (maiden name unknown) and James M. Brawley. Brawley's parents took a keen interest in the education and professional development of their son, providing him private schooling in Charleston, sending him at the age of ten to Philadelphia to attend grammar school and the Institute for Colored Youth, and having him apprenticed to a shoemaker in Charleston from 1866 to 1869. He enrolled as the first theological student at Howard University for a few months in 1870; he transferred to Bucknell University in Pennsylvania in January 1871. The first African-American student at Bucknell, Brawley completed his education with the encouragement and financial support of a white couple named Griffith and his own work teaching vocal music and preaching during school vacations. The white Baptist church in Lewisburg, Pennsylvania, with which he had affiliated, ordained him to the ministry the day after his graduation, 1 July 1875; he was examined by a board composed largely of professors and other learned individuals. In 1878 he received the A.M. from Bucknell and, in 1885, an honorary doctor of divinity degree from the State University in Louisville, Kentucky.

Brawley's first marriage in 1877 lasted only a year; his wife, Mary W. Warrick, and their baby both died. His second marriage, to Margaret Dickerson in 1879, produced four children; one of them, Benjamin Brawley, became a renowned historian and author.

Immediately after Brawley left Bucknell, the predominantly white, northern-based American Baptist Publication Society (ABPS) appointed him as a Sunday school missionary, or agent, for his home state of South Carolina. There he found little organized black Baptist denominational work. He set about establishing new Baptist associations and reorganizing existing ones, as well as encouraging the founding of Sunday school conventions at the state Baptist regional or associational levels. After two years the first statewide Sunday school convention among African-American Baptists was held, with Brawley Serving as corresponding secretary and financial agent. Brawley also aided in efforts among black Baptists to organize for African missions, with South Carolina sending its first missionary, Harrison N. Bouey, to Africa in the late 1870s. Not only did Brawley strengthen denominational structures in the state; he also raised considerable funds for the support of Benedict College in South Carolina.

Eight years of strenuous work in South Carolina took their toll on Brawley's health. Following his doctor's advice, despite the ABPS's strong desire that he continue his duties, in 1883 Brawley traveled to Alabama to assume the presidency of Alabama Baptist Normal and Theological School (later Selma University), a position he had declined several times previously. Once again Brawley's service was successful. He upgraded the school's standards and collegiate rank, graduating the first class in May 1884. Fiercely committed to education to the point of personal sacrifice, Brawley, like many other early educators, both black and white, gave as much as half of his income to needy students.

With his wife's health declining, after only two years Brawley returned to South Carolina to preside over a school he had helped to establish, Morris College. In 1912 he assumed the pastorship of White Rock Baptist Church in Durham, North Carolina. Around 1920 he became professor of biblical history and evangelism at Baptist-supported Shaw University in Raleigh, North Carolina, serving until his death.

Brawley was highly valued as a speaker and lecturer. In addition, he was an accomplished writer and editor. At different points in his career he edited the

Baptist Pioneer in South Carolina, the weekly *Baptist Tribune*, and the monthly *Evangel.* Always concerned about raising the educational standards of both ministers and the laity, he wrote *Sin and Salvation*, which focused on evangelism, and his most significant work, *The Negro Baptist Pulpit: A Collection of Sermons and Papers* (1890; repr. 1971). Of the twenty-eight sermons and addresses in the latter work, Brawley authored four. Throughout his career he also published other sermons, speeches, and addresses.

In addition to his church, educational, and publishing work, Brawley left the theological and philosophical legacy of one committed to uplifting the African-American race by moral and spiritual education that spoke to heart and mind. Furthermore, Brawley passionately supported cooperation with sympathetic whites as a means to advance the race, believing that all racial sentiments should be subject to the greater principle of erecting American Christianity. That position often placed him at odds with African-American leaders who were increasingly restless with the racial parochialism and paternalism of their white benefactors. Whereas some African-American Christians, including Brawley, emphasized the necessity of continued white financial assistance, the more independent complained of the stifling effect of these whites on the development of racial responsibility and self-respect. Nonetheless, Brawley's contributions to denominational organization, church leadership, education, and publishing left an impressive mark on American religious history.

• Brawley's introduction and sermons in his *The Negro Baptist Pulpit* offer a good examination of his theology and devotion to education, religion, and race. The impact of Brawley is captured by two contemporary works: William J. Simmons, *Men of Mark: Eminent, Progressive and Rising* (1887; repr. 1968); and Albert W. Pegues, *Our Baptist Ministers and Schools* (1892). Recent works on Baptist history with brief mentions of Brawley include James M. Washington, *Frustrated Fellowship: The Black Baptist Quest for Social Power* (1986), and Leroy Fitts, *A History of Black Baptists* (1985). Sandy D. Martin, *Black Baptists and African Missions* (1989), notes Brawley's involvement with the African missions movement in South Carolina. Recent biographical sketches are in the *Encyclopedia of African-American Culture and History* (1996).

SANDY DWAYNE MARTIN

BRAWLEY, William Hiram (13 May 1841–15 Nov. 1916), South Carolina politician and federal judge, was born in Chester, South Carolina, the son of Hiram Brawley, a planter, and Harriet Foote. He graduated from the South Carolina College in 1860. When South Carolina seceded, he volunteered for military service as a private in the Sixth South Carolina Volunteers. His unit saw action in the reduction of Fort Sumter and was then transferred to the Virginia front. As a result of wounds he received in the battle of Seven Pines (May 1862), his left arm had to be amputated. Discharged from military duty, he went back home to manage his father's plantation. In 1864, still in poor health, he ran the Union naval blockade and spent the remainder of the war in England and France studying law and literature.

Returning to Chester in November 1865, Brawley read law with an uncle and was admitted to the bar in 1866. In 1868 he married Marion Emma Porter of Charleston. In the same year he was elected solicitor of the sixth circuit; reelected in 1872, he resigned in 1874 and moved to Charleston to practice law with his father-in-law. There he established a lucrative corporate law practice. He became the leading railroad lawyer in South Carolina, serving as a director of the South Carolina Railroad and the Charleston and Savannah Railroad. As general counsel for the latter railroad, he possessed the authority to distribute free railroad passes and to appoint the railroad's attorneys in small low-country towns. As a result, Brawley gained considerable influence in political and legal circles. When the Southern Railway leased the South Carolina Railroad in 1890, he became its general counsel.

By 1882 Brawley had become one of the leading members of the South Carolina bar, and he was elected to the South Carolina House of Representatives in that year. Between 1882 and 1890 Charleston attorneys dominated the county's legislative delegation and the general assembly. For most of this period, Brawley preferred to work behind the scenes, but at the end of the decade he chaired the House Judiciary Committee. The issues he tackled reflected both his interests and his background. An alumnus of the University of South Carolina, he led the fight to reject the legacy of Thomas G. Clemson to create a state agricultural college, seeing it as a threat to his alma mater. The leading railroad lawyer in the state, he also opposed giving the state railway commission the authority to set rates without giving the railroads the right to appeal, loath, as he was, to let popular discontent with the railroads lead to meaningful state regulation. During Benjamin Ryan Tillman's gubernatorial campaign of 1890, Tillman constantly damned the "Charleston Ring" of lawyers, which he believed ran the state. Although Brawley did not succeed in defeating Tillman, he did win election from the First District of South Carolina to the Fifty-second (1891–1893) and Fifty-third (1893–1895) Congresses of the United States.

During his two terms in Washington, Brawley was one of the few southern Democrats who supported President Grover Cleveland's hard-money policies. He spoke against the free coinage of silver and became the only southerner to vote against the Bland Silver Bill. He also favored repeal of the Sherman Silver Purchase Act. When the federal district judgeship for South Carolina became vacant in 1894, Cleveland appointed Brawley to the position. While there is little question that his support of the president's policies figured into his appointment, so too, in all probability, did his railroad connections. Judge Brawley remained on the bench until he retired on 14 June 1911. After the death of his first wife, with whom he had three children, Brawley in 1907 married Mildred Frost of Charleston; they did not have children. Nine years later, he died in the city he had made his home for over thirty years.

Contemporaries considered Brawley one of the best public speakers in South Carolina. His 1905 address on the dedication of the Confederate monument in Chester drew nationwide attention. In it he took the line that through misunderstandings the nation had blundered into the tragedy of civil war. Those who fell in the conflict, whether they wore blue or gray, all "died for their country" (*Charleston News and Courier*). *Harper's Weekly* agreed completely with Brawley's remarks, described the speech as "an oration admirable in thought, word, and spirit," and commended it to its readers.

William Hiram Brawley—leader of the state bar, railroad counsel, legislator, congressman, and federal judge—was one of the most powerful men in late nineteenth-century South Carolina. Yet, only a few years after his death, he had been forgotten. Even David Duncan Wallace's detailed, four-volume *History of South Carolina* (1934) has only one minor reference to him. Brawley generally operated behind the scenes, and his reputation has been eclipsed by the more visible and vocal political figures of the day.

• There are two small Brawley manuscript collections: the William H. Brawley Papers in the South Caroliniana Library (Columbia) and the Brawley miscellaneous papers in the William H. Perkins Library at Duke University. An interesting collection of correspondence (1886) between Brawley and Tillman is in the Joseph W. Barnwell Papers in the South Carolina Historical Society (Charleston). The complete text of Brawley's 10 May 1905 oration can be found in the *Charleston News and Courier*, 11 May 1905, p. 5, and the national reaction to it in *Harper's Weekly*, 27 May 1905, p. 747. Sketches of Brawley can be found in *Cyclopedia of Eminent and Representative Men of the Carolinas, Volume I: South Carolina* (1892; repr. 1972); U. R. Brooks, *South Carolina Bench and Bar* (1908); and J. C. Hemphill, *Men of Mark in South Carolina* (1906). See also his obituary and related stories in the *Charleston News and Courier*, 15 Nov. 1916, p. 10; 16 Nov. 1916, pp. 4, 10; 17 Nov. 1916, p. 10. William J. Cooper, Jr., *The Conservative Regime: South Carolina, 1877–1890* (1968), mentions Brawley briefly in discussing the Conservative opposition to Tillman. The best and most recent assessment of Brawley and his role in post–Civil War South Carolina society is in George C. Rogers, Jr., *Generations of Lawyers: A History of The South Carolina Bar* (1992).

WALTER B. EDGAR

BRAXTON, Carter (10 Sept. 1736–10 Oct. 1797), signer of the Declaration of Independence and legislative leader, was born at his family's estate, "Newington," in King and Queen County, Virginia, the son of George Braxton, Jr., a planter and merchant, and Mary Carter, daughter of Robert "King" Carter, a wealthy landowner in the Northern Neck.

Following his father and older brother George, Braxton attended the College of William and Mary (1754–1756). When Braxton was nineteen he married Judith Robinson, of a politically powerful Middlesex County family. Judith died in childbirth in 1757. In 1761 Braxton married Elizabeth Corbin, daughter of a Crown official who remained a Loyalist during the American Revolution. He fathered eighteen children, ten of whom survived to maturity.

As a burgess for King William County, where he lived at "Elsing Green" and later at "Chericoke," Braxton served in sixteen of the nineteen house sessions between 1761 and 1775. He served also as a visitor of the college, justice of the peace, sheriff, vestryman, and trustee of Indian tribal interests while also managing his father's widespread lands and mercantile activities. He served frequently as chairman of the house committee on religion. With the majority leaders, Braxton opposed Patrick Henry's extreme resolutions on the Stamp Act in 1765, asserting legislative autonomy from Parliament. However, Braxton joined his fellow burgesses in "associations" to restrict British imports and later to assemble, over the protests of the royal governor, the earl of Dunmore, in "conventions" that became an extralegal lower house. After the governor's flight, Braxton was named to the Committee of Safety, which wielded interim executive authority.

In May 1775 Braxton was acclaimed by many Virginians for earlier that month having confronted Patrick Henry at the head of 150 or more "independent" militia from an upland county and stopped his march on Williamsburg, begun by Henry in reprisal for the governor's removal of gunpowder from the public magazine. British naval vessels were threatening a punitive bombardment of Yorktown, and Braxton was credited with preventing civilian bloodshed.

On 15 December 1775 the revolutionary convention added Braxton to its six-man delegation in the Continental Congress. He took his seat on 23 February 1776 and served until August, having supported Richard Henry Lee's resolution for independence and having signed Jefferson's Declaration. He now learned that he was to be cut from the delegation on the pretext of economy. It was rumored in this connection that Braxton's wife, Elizabeth, had uttered Loyalist sentiments. Fearing the lack of unity and democratic tendencies among some of the colonies, Braxton appears to have been faulted for his forlorn hope that Parliament would offer conciliatory overtures to the colonies on generous terms.

While Braxton was still in Philadelphia, Virginia's erstwhile burgesses were proceeding to form an independent government. Because he could not attend their critical deliberations in Williamsburg, Braxton, like Jefferson and Lee, submitted a suggested plan of government. Braxton's pamphlet, suggesting a life-tenure senate and governor, was given little consideration in Williamsburg. George Mason was chiefly responsible for the draft constitution that was adopted.

A few weeks after he returned to Virginia with Harrison, Braxton's home, Chericoke, burned to the ground with all his personal property but with no loss of life. The family moved to the village at West Point (then called Delaware Town) where Braxton established his shipping headquarters. As the British blockade tightened, many of his cargoes moved overland.

He sent large quantities of salt and other provisions to Washington's ill-supplied army.

Braxton's wartime losses were heavy. Tory privateers seized one vessel bound for Nantes with tobacco worth £40,000, according to the *London Chronicle* of 12 August 1779. Braxton's greatest loss resulted from his joint venture with Robert Morris and other shareowners in fitting out the twenty-gun privateer *Phoenix*. Their Boston captain, Joseph Cunningham, misinterpreted his instructions and seized a neutral Portuguese vessel off the Grand Banks in August 1777. The civil suits by the Portuguese captain and the ship's owners were not settled by Braxton and his friends until 1781, and ancillary suits continued as late as 1784.

Braxton, meanwhile, resumed his political career. He was elected to eight terms in the new House of Delegates and was active in fourteen of the twenty-five sessions between 1776 and 1785. He assisted in passing Jefferson's Statute for Religious Freedom, enacted in 1786, as well as certain bills sponsored by Patrick Henry, the new governor, his onetime adversary. Henry supported Braxton's wishes to retire from the house and serve on the new Council of State, an eight-member body whose approval was required on major decisions of the chief executive. In 1785 Braxton moved his family from West Point to the new capital, Richmond, in order to attend the Council of State. Minutes of the council indicate that he suffered a stroke in this period. He withdrew from public affairs other than the council, though he served as a delegate to the conventions that established the Virginia diocese of the Protestant Episcopal church in the United States. Without taking a public role, he supported the federal Constitution in 1787.

Braxton died in straitened financial circumstances at his rented home in Richmond. He had served during the close of his life as an adviser to six of the state's governors, and his role on a simulacrum of the old colonial council must have pleased him. Despite criticism of his views on independence, Braxton was a patriot who desired to assure stability for the political structure of the new state and nation. Benjamin Rush of Philadelphia had found him to be "a decent, agreeable and sensible speaker, and in private life an accomplished gentleman," though "less detached than he should be from his British prejudices" (Corner, p. 152).

• No substantial body of personal papers survives, but small groups are in the New York Public Library, the Henry Huntington Library (San Marino, Calif.), the University of Virginia Library, and the Virginia State Library. Business papers are available in the Rhode Island Historical Society and the Historical Society of Pennsylvania. The Virginia Historical Society's Lee papers and transcripts preserve some of Braxton's correspondence with his uncle Landon Carter on the issue of independence. A rare copy of Braxton's *Address to the Convention . . . by a Native of the Colony* (1776) is preserved in the New York Public Library. At least one Braxton letter is preserved in nineteen or more depositories that have autograph collections of the signers.

Braxton's political career is documented in the published and indexed serial journals of the Virginia Council and House of Burgesses; in leaflets, broadsides, and other documents on the revolutionary conventions; and in printed (serially and individually) journals of the state House of Delegates and Senate and journals of the Council of State, all available at the Virginia State Library and other major libraries. His tenure in the Continental Congress is recorded in the published journals and letters of members, 1776. The affair of the *Phoenix* is told in detail in the *Papers of the Continental Congress, Claims for Captured Vessels* (1777–1784), preserved on microfilm, reel 58, National Archives. The circumstances of Braxton's death are recounted in Elizabeth and Corbin Braxton's letters in the Virginia Historical Society. The Rush quotation is from George W. Corner, ed., *The Autobiography of Benjamin Rush* (1948). A modern biography is Alonzo Thomas Dill, *Carter Braxton, Virginia Signer: A Conservative in Revolt* (1983).

ALONZO THOMAS DILL

BRAY, Thomas (1656–15 Feb. 1730), Anglican activist for the American colonies, was born at Marton in Shropshire, England. Information about his parents and his childhood experiences is unavailable. After early education at Oswestry School, Bray attended Oxford University, earning a bachelor of arts degree at All Souls College in 1678 and a master of arts at Hart Hall in 1693. After being ordained as a priest in the Church of England he served for several years as a curate in Bridgnorth and then as chaplain to the family of Sir Thomas Price at Park Hill in Warwickshire.

In 1690 Bray became rector of the church in Sheldon and there made a name for himself as an effective instructor from the pulpit. His catechetical lectures were quite well received, filling four volumes when published. In them he tried to answer questions on "the whole doctrine of the covenant of grace," as a practical means to doctrinal instruction on all things necessary to salvation. He meant such publications to be particularly useful on shipboard and in colonies, where regular sermons were infrequent because of a lack of clergy. He also arranged in his *Bibliotheca Parochialis* (1697) various books under appropriate theological headings in order to provide trustworthy guidelines for religious teaching.

Activity of this sort drew Bray to the attention of Henry Compton, bishop of London. In 1696 Compton appointed Bray as his commissary with a view to augmenting English missionary efforts in the New World. Though favored with royal support, Anglican churches were few and weak in the early colonial period. During his first years as commissary Bray recruited personnel for colonial parishes, and he soon learned that only the poorer clergy could be persuaded to leave their native land. Their penury prevented them from collecting a modicum of books for an adequate parson's library, and this lack decidedly weakened ministerial efforts. So Bray decided to provide libraries for Anglican clergy in the colonies, thus enabling educational leadership in subsequent generations. By 1699 he had succeeded in establishing the Society for Promoting Christian Knowledge (SPCK), a group which created approximately fifty libraries in colonial plantations from New York to the Carolinas and Bermuda.

In March of 1700 Bray visited the royal colony of Maryland, where the Anglican minority wished to establish a parish system as well as a tax base for its financial support. Traveling at his own expense Bray conducted a tour of inspection, disciplined clergymen in the bishop's name, and laid plans for increasing the number of local churches. His overriding concern was to have Anglican worship established by royal authority as the colony's one religious standard, and he was more instrumental than any other individual in making the English State Church the dominant one. While there he also funneled SPCK contributions to Maryland clergy, placing half of all clerical libraries in that colony alone.

By the summer of 1701 it was clear that Bray could benefit American pastoral work more effectively by returning to England and soliciting royal support there. That year he also helped found another institution to aid missionary endeavors in English territories: the Society for the Propagation of the Gospel in Foreign Parts (SPG). Bray drew up the abstract of its charter and on behalf of that enabling agency delivered scores of reports on the needy state of religion in North America. He issued proposals for recruiting volunteers, presented memorials for raising funds, and campaigned continuously to increase SPG activities. For almost a century thereafter the missionary organization of Bray's devising provided vital funds and manpower to sustain the Church of England on American shores.

In 1706 Bray resigned his post as episcopal assistant and became rector of a church named Saint Botolph, Without, in the Aldgate section of London. He never flagged in his concern for the cause of missionary outreach, however, and he continued to emphasize the importance of libraries at home and abroad. He also espoused philanthropic endeavors such as hospitals, orphanages, charity schools, and prison reform. There is some evidence that Bray influenced James Oglethorpe in his plans for settling debtors in the colony of Georgia. Toward the end of his life he formed still a third corporation notable for its effects on American life. "Dr. Bray's Associates" made significant advances in educating and converting African Americans and local Indian populations. Before his death in London, the associates also succeeded in creating another eighty clerical libraries in England and Wales. The institutional forms set in place by this persistent architect strongly influenced education and social development on both sides of the Atlantic for the bulk of the eighteenth century.

• Bray's writings include his *Catechetical Lectures* (1696) and *Bibliotheca Parochialis* (1697). More pertinent to the colonies are his *A General View of English Colonies in America with Respect to Religion* (1698) and *A Memorial Representing the Present State of Religion on the Continent of North America* (1700). Two studies of the commissary are Bernard C. Steiner, ed., *Thomas Bray: His Life and Selected Works* (1901; repr. 1972), and Henry P. Thompson, *Thomas Bray* (1954).

HENRY WARNER BOWDEN

BRAYTON, Charles Ray (16 Aug. 1840–23 Sept. 1910), soldier and politician, was born in the village of Apponaug in the town of Warwick, Rhode Island, the son of William Daniel Brayton, a Republican congressman (1857–1861), and Anna Ward Clarke. He traced his Rhode Island roots back to 1643 and the founding of Warwick. He first attended nearby East Greenwich Academy, then studied at the Fruit Hill Classical Academy in North Providence, and finally entered Brown University in 1859. He was scheduled to graduate in the class of 1863 but left college in 1861 to organize a Warwick company for the Third Rhode Island Volunteers, a heavy artillery unit. As an artillery officer Brayton served in such sieges and battles as those at Fort Pulaski, Fort Sumter, Fort Wagner, Drury's Bluff, Laurel Hill, Fort Burnham, and Petersburg. In March 1864 he was appointed chief of artillery for the Department of the South, a post he held until his discharge in 1865, when he was allowed to retire with the rank of brigadier general of volunteers. In March 1865 he married Antoinette Percival Belden, daughter of Brayton's headmaster at Fruit Hill Classical Academy; the couple had one child.

Shortly after the Civil War, Brayton became the chief political lieutenant of U.S. Senator Henry Bowen Anthony, the principal organizer of Rhode Island's Republican party. Between 1870 and his death, Brayton manipulated the politics of Rhode Island as the prototypical boss of a highly successful political machine. Anthony secured for his protégé such politically sensitive positions as U.S. pension agent for Rhode Island (1870–1874) and U.S. postmaster for Providence (1874–1880). In 1876 Brayton began his long tenure as chairman of the Republican state party, whose members he addressed as "fellow machinists."

The controversial Brayton resigned from the post office under fire in 1880 for allegedly using the mails to distribute fixed ballots and for converting postal funds to party purposes. When he was stoutly defended by most of the state's elected Republicans and allowed to maintain his party position, the situation gave credence to the lament of a contemporary reformer who had observed that "if a man is an expert in all the deviltry known to politics, in Rhode Island he is made chairman of the Republican State Committee instead of being sent to jail."

For the next three decades Brayton survived repeated political scandals, incurring some dents but no disabling damage to his political machine. After Senator Anthony's death in 1884, Brayton directed his considerable talents toward ensuring the longevity, and hence the seniority, of U.S. Senator Nelson W. Aldrich. Both men weathered a 1905 exposé of their political methodology in an article in *McClure's Magazine* by Lincoln Steffens entitled "Rhode Island: A State for Sale."

Several factors contributed to Brayton's success. Contemporaries described him as a strong leader and stern disciplinarian. He was able to control the general assembly through old-stock rural legislators from the country towns because each of the state's municipalities, regardless of size, had one vote in the senate. Cynically remarking that "an honest voter is one that stays bought," Brayton used the contributions of Providence businessmen to buy up the vote in these small towns. This practice prompted Steffens to allege that "the political system in Rhode Island . . . is grounded on the lowest layer of corruption that I have found thus far—the bribery of voters with cash at the polls."

When growing Democratic strength rendered the office of governor politically insecure, "the Boss" sponsored a law—the so-called Brayton Act of 1901—that placed the appointive and budgetary powers of the state in the hands of the rotten-borough Republican senate. Though not a member of the legislature, Brayton maintained an office in the new state house. In a cause célèbre, the general was ousted from this command post in 1907 by James H. Higgins, the first Irish Catholic Democrat to win Rhode Island's governorship. A gradual loss of sight culminating in total blindness by 1903 diminished Brayton's effectiveness, but only his sudden death seven years later broke his grip on the reins of power. Brayton's forty-year ascendancy, unparalleled in Rhode Island history, ranks him as the most successful and enduring machine politician in a state long renowned for organizational politics.

• For further information on Brayton and his political machine, see Lincoln Steffens, "Rhode Island: A State for Sale," *McClure's Magazine*, Feb. 1905, pp. 337–53; Mary C. Nelson, "The Influence of Immigration on Rhode Island Politics, 1865–1910" (Ph.D. diss., Radcliffe College, 1955); Mary Nelson Tanner, "The Middle Years of the Anthony-Brayton Alliance; or Politics in Post-Office, 1874–1880," *Rhode Island History* 22 (July 1963): 65–76; John D. Buenker, "Urban Liberalism in Rhode Island, 1909–1919," *Rhode Island History* 30 (Spring 1971): 35–50; and Carl Gersuny, "Uphill Battle: Lucius F. C. Garvin's Crusade for Political Reform," *Rhode Island History* 39 (May 1980): 57–75. An obituary by Sidney S. Rider, "De Mortuis Nil Nisi Bonum: Charles R. Brayton, Dead 23 September, 1910," is in *Book Notes*, 29 Apr. 1911, pp. 65–68.

PATRICK T. CONLEY

BREARLY, David (11 June 1745–16 Aug. 1790), jurist and revolutionary war officer, was born at "Spring Grove" farm, near Maidensead (now Lawrenceville), New Jersey, the son of David Brearly and Mary Clark, farmers. The family name was sometimes spelled "Brearley." His early education is unknown, and he may have briefly attended the College of New Jersey (now Princeton University). He studied law and became an attorney at Allentown, New Jersey, where he made his residence. Brearly participated in the revolutionary movement and became associated with men involved in protest against Great Britain before the war who were later dubbed the "early Whigs" and who would dominate East New Jersey politics. In his law practice, he specialized in estate matters; he was appointed Monmouth County surrogate in 1768 and 1771. About 1767 Brearly married Elizabeth Mullen; they had four children before she died in 1777.

Brearly's military career began on 28 October 1775 as captain of the Second Regiment of the Monmouth County militia. He rose to lieutenant colonel and then to colonel on 11 August 1776 in Nathaniel Heard's militia brigade. While he served in the Continental army, he was replaced in the militia by Samuel Forman. On 28 November 1776 Brearly was named lieutenant colonel of the Fourth New Jersey Regiment in General William Maxwell's New Jersey brigade of Continental troops. During the frequent absences of Colonel Ephraim Martin, Brearly was acting commander of the Fourth Regiment. On 1 January 1777 he was transferred, at the rank of lieutenant colonel, to the First New Jersey Regiment. He served with the New Jersey brigade at the battles of Brandywine, Germantown, and Monmouth and, during most of 1777 to early 1779, in the defense of northeastern New Jersey against British raiding parties. In February 1778 he and Colonel Israel Shreve, on behalf of all the New Jersey Continental troops, petitioned the New Jersey governor and legislature to remedy clothing shortages and depreciation in wages.

Upon the resignation of Robert Morris as chief justice of the New Jersey Supreme Court, Brearly, on 10 June 1779, was elected chief justice by a joint session of the houses of the legislature. At the time of his appointment, he was serving in General John Sullivan's expedition against the Iroquois Indians in New York. Brearly resigned from the army on 4 August 1779, and he sold his house in Allentown and moved to Trenton. In 1783 he married Elizabeth "Betsy" Higbee; they had three children.

In October 1780 Brearly was nominated for governor. The legislature, however, reelected William Livingston with twenty-eight votes to six for Brearly and two for Philemon Dickinson. Brearly held the vice presidency of the state chapter of the Society of the Cincinnati from 1783 until his death, and on 18 December 1786 he was selected as the first grand master of the Masonic Order in New Jersey. He was one of the compilers of the Episcopal prayer book in 1785 and the following year represented St. Michael's Church at the diocesan convention in Philadelphia.

During Brearly's tenure as chief justice the New Jersey Supreme Court established the principle of judicial review, a notable decision, sometimes called the New Jersey Precedent, that had influence on the federal judicial philosophy. The New Jersey case arose out of a suit over the confiscation of goods carried from behind enemy lines. By a New Jersey law of 1778, a trial before a justice of the peace and a six-man jury determined the outcome. A verdict in a Monmouth County court found for the defendant, Elisha Walton, a militia officer, who had appropriated the property of John Holmes and Solomon Ketcham. On a writ of certiorari, the New Jersey Supreme Court heard the case,

Holmes v. Walton. In its decision of 7 September 1780, Brearly's court found that the New Jersey law had contravened the state constitution, which had provided for the use of twelve-man juries. In declaring organic law superior to statute law, the court clearly refused to recognize "necessity" or extraconstitutional war power. The New Jersey legislature gave its approval of the decision.

The Congress of the Confederation appointed Brearly one of seven commissioners to settle a longtime jurisdictional dispute between Pennsylvania and Connecticut over the Wyoming Valley in Pennsylvania. Meeting at Trenton, New Jersey, from 12 November to 30 December 1782, the commissioners found in favor of Pennsylvania, chiefly because Connecticut could not produce its 1662 charter or a deed of purchase from the American Indians (both documents were in England).

Brearly, though mostly silent during the debates, left his mark as a delegate to the federal Constitutional Convention in 1787 as one of the sponsors of the New Jersey Plan (small state plan). He accepted the eventual compromises and fully supported the Constitution in its final form. He initially, however, opposed unequal representation of the states in Congress and favored election of the president by each state having one vote. Brearly argued that proportionate representation from the states in Congress would permit several large states to "carry everything before them." He declared that the only remedy concerning fair representation was "that a map of the United States be spread out, that all the existing boundaries be erased, and that a new partition of the whole be made into 13 equal parts." Brearly proposed that the House of Representatives be limited to sixty-five members, which was approved.

At the Constitutional Convention Brearly served on the Committee on Apportionment (congressional representation) and chaired the eleven-man Committee on Unfinished Parts, which decided on the presidential term of office, an electoral college, and the mode of executive appointments. He kept an "imperfect" journal of the proceedings of the convention. William Pierce, a delegate from Georgia, characterized Brearly as "a man of good, rather than brilliant parts"; he "is very much in the esteem of the people. As an orator he has little to boast of, but as a Man he has every virtue to recommend him."

Brearly presided over the New Jersey convention for the ratification of the Constitution, which met in Trenton from 11 December to 18 December 1787. According to a newspaper report, Brearly, "with a perspicuity of argument and persuasive eloquence, which carried conviction with it, bore down all opposition." The Constitution won unanimous approval.

No reports of decisions of the New Jersey Supreme Court while Brearly presided were published. He was considered a hard money man who thought excessive emission of paper money impaired the obligation of contract. On 7 January 1789 Brearly was named a presidential elector by the New Jersey Assembly. In November 1789 he resigned as chief justice for New Jersey to accept a federal district judgeship.

Through inheritance, Brearly was a large landholder in the Lawrenceville vicinity of New Jersey, and he owned public securities, which appreciated in value under the new Constitution. Brearly died at Trenton. A tribute at the time of his death stated that he was "a judicious and conscientious judge, of great capacity and approved integrity." During his brief life, Brearly, as a soldier, a chief justice of New Jersey, and a framer and defender of the new Constitution, made a distinctive contribution to the establishment of the American Republic.

• Brearly's papers are in several collections of the New Jersey Historical Society and in the William Livingston Papers at the Massachusetts Historical Society and the New York Public Library. Published materials by Brearly are in the *Papers of William Livingston*, ed. Carl E. Prince et al. (5 vols., 1979–1988), and the *New Jersey Archives*, 1st ser., vol. 18 (1893) and vol. 29 (1917), and 2d ser., vols. 1–3 (1901, 1903, 1906) and vol. 5 (1917). Max Farrand, ed., *The Records of the Federal Convention of 1787* (4 vols., 1937), depicts Brearly's role at the convention and incorporates his journal. For family history and a short sketch, see William H. Brearley, *Genealogical Chart of the American Branch of the Brearley Family* (1886). For the adjudication of the Pa.-Conn. land controversy, see Henry M. Hoyt, *Brief of a Title in the Seventeen Townships in the County of Luzerne: A Syllabus of the Controversy between Connecticut and Pennsylvania* (1879). A discussion of the New Jersey Precedent is Austin Scott, "*Holmes vs. Walton*: The New Jersey Precedent: A Chapter in the History of Judicial Power and Unconstitutional Legislation," *American Historical Review* 5 (1898–1899): 456–69. See also Clinton Rossiter, *1787: The Grand Convention* (1966). For the N.J. context and political situation see Ruth Bogin, *Abraham Clark and the Quest for Equality in the Revolutionary Era, 1744–1794* (1982); Richard P. McCormick, *Experiment in Independence: New Jersey in the Critical Period, 1781–1789* (1950); and Gertrude S. Wood, *William Paterson of New Jersey* (1933). For Brearly as a Mason, see David McGregor, *History of Freemasonry in New Jersey* (1937), and as a prominent Episcopal layman, see Hamilton Schuyler, *A History of St. Michael's Church, Trenton* (1926). An obituary is in the *New-Jersey Journal and Political Intelligencer*, 25 Aug. 1790.

HARRY M. WARD

BREASTED, James Henry (27 Aug. 1865–2 Dec. 1935), historian and Egyptologist, was born in Rockford, Illinois, the son of Charles Breasted and Harriet Newell Garrison, owners of a small hardware business. Breasted grew up in a family of limited means. Although he entered North Central College (then Northwestern College) at Naperville, Illinois, at the age of fifteen, he did not obtain his B.A. until 1888, as he interrupted his studies in 1882 to attend Chicago College of Pharmacy and to serve an apprenticeship in a pharmacy. Meanwhile he worked as a clerk in local drugstores to finance his studies. In 1886 he graduated as a pharmacist, but at the insistence of an aunt and with her financial support he entered Chicago Theological Seminary in 1887. His doubts about the inerrancy of the biblical text dissuaded him from a career in the ministry, and in 1890 he enrolled in Yale University to pursue graduate studies in Hebrew with William Rainey Harper, who had developed a new method for the study of that language.

When Harper became the first president of the University of Chicago in 1890, he conceived the idea of a biblical studies department that would be protected from fundamentalist pressures by being integrated in the university itself rather than in a divinity school. As such a department required someone to cover Egyptology—a field of study not taught in the United States at that time—he sent Breasted to Berlin in 1891 to study with the Egyptologist Adolf Erman. There Breasted acquired a scientific knowledge of the Egyptian language, and in 1894 he completed a doctoral dissertation on some of Pharaoh Akhnaten's hymns to the sun god. He considered the pharaoh to be a monotheist and of crucial importance to the later development of that religious belief. In 1894 he married Frances Hart and went on a honeymoon to Egypt; the couple had three children. After Frances died in 1934, Breasted married her sister Imogen Hart in June 1935.

In 1898, after two years as an instructor, Breasted was appointed assistant professor at the University of Chicago, becoming full professor in 1905. A small salary and a lack of students forced Breasted to give lectures on Egyptian culture and history throughout the United States. This not only provided him with additional income but also trained him to discuss his field of scholarship in terms accessible to the general public.

In 1897 the Royal Prussian Academy of Sciences in Berlin started a project to produce a complete dictionary of the ancient Egyptian language based on new editions of the texts. Breasted was invited to collate and make new copies of texts in European museums during the years 1899–1901. This enterprise gave rise to his idea to copy all extant ancient Egyptian inscriptions in the Nile Valley itself, and he obtained funding from the University of Chicago to travel to Nubia and the Sudan during the academic years 1905–1907. But after the death of President Harper in 1906, this support was discontinued and the project abandoned.

Meanwhile he published two major works. *Ancient Records of Egypt* (1906–1907), was a five-volume translation of all historical inscriptions until the first Persian conquest of Egypt in 525 B.C. These translations formed the basis for *A History of Egypt* (1905), a chronological survey from prehistory to the same Persian conquest. The latter work was so popular that it was reprinted until long after the author's death, although outdated. His enthusiasm and his ability to communicate with the general public explain this popularity. These works established Breasted as an internationally recognized scholar and America's leading Egyptologist.

He began teaching ancient history courses at the University of Chicago and, after several refusals, agreed to write a high school textbook on ancient history. In 1914 he treated the period from prehistory to the fall of the Roman Empire in *Outlines of European History*, written with James Harvey Robinson. In 1916 he published a textbook, *Ancient Times: A History of the Early World*, which was also extremely popular and raised the public's interest in preclassical civilizations. In 1912 he lectured on Egyptian religion at Union Theological Seminary in New York. When these lectures were published as *Development of Religion and Thought in Ancient Egypt* (1912), it became clear that he had revolutionized the study of this field by stressing evolution and change during the long history of Egypt. In 1919 he was invited to give a series of lectures before the National Academy of Sciences. Soon afterward he was elected to the academy, the first archaeologist to receive the honor. The lectures were published as "The Origins of Civilization" in the *Scientific Monthly* (Oct. 1919–Mar. 1920).

Breasted's popularity was crucial for the success of what became his most important legacy to the field of ancient Near Eastern studies: the establishment of the Oriental Institute of the University of Chicago. He dreamed of creating a research center that would study "the rise of man from Stone Age savagery through successive stages of advance, the emergence of civilization, the history of the earliest great civilized states, and the transmission to Europe of the fundamentals of civilization which we have since inherited" (*American Journal of Semitic Languages* 35 [1919]: 202). His request to John D. Rockefeller, Jr., for $10,000 a year for five years was granted, and in 1919 the institute was created. He directed it until his death. With funds raised from the Rockefeller Foundation, the International Education Board, the General Education Board, and individual donors, the institute sent numerous expeditions to Egypt, Palestine, Syria, Turkey, Iraq, and Iran and published several series of scholarly publications. The institute's activities were not limited to Egypt but covered the entire Near East from prehistory to the advent of Islam. In Egypt efforts were concentrated on the copying of inscriptions, while in other areas more attention was paid to archaeological excavations. Although Breasted's ideal of a large institution where specialists in various disciplines of ancient Near Eastern studies would closely collaborate was never realized, the Oriental Institute remains the world's leading research institution in many of these disciplines. Despite the burdens of his administrative duties, Breasted continued to travel extensively and to publish until he died in New York.

Breasted's written work is infused with his belief that human history shows a progression driven by a positive force continuously improving the morality of humankind. In his last major work, *The Dawn of Conscience* (1934), he depicts humanity as evolving from an "*un*moral savage" to a moral being with a conscience; he accuses the younger generation, however, of "throwing inherited morals into the discard." But he remained an optimist and reacted against the pessimism of the German thinker Oswald Spengler, whom he charged with inappropriate use of ancient Egyptian material. In his opinion Egypt took a primary place in the progression of humankind in many aspects of religion, culture, art, and morality, and he often ignored the contributions made by the surrounding ancient civilizations. These ideas have not always been kindly received by critics and are now of little importance. His major legacy remains his insistence on separating ancient Near Eastern studies from religious prejudices in the United States and his ability to integrate the study of the ancient Near East into that of the ancient world.

• The most detailed biography is by his son Charles Breasted, *Pioneer to the Past* (1943). More useful are two pieces by John A. Wilson: *Biographical Memoir of James Henry Breasted*, in the National Academy of Sciences's *Biographical Memoirs*, vol. 18 (1937), 5th memoir, which contains a complete bibliography of Breasted's publications; and "James Henry Breasted—The Idea of an Oriental Institute," in *Near Eastern Archaeology in the Twentieth Century*, ed. James E. Sanders (1970). A detailed obituary is W. F. Albright, "James Henry Breasted, Humanist," *American Scholar* 5 (Summer 1936): 287–99.

MARC VAN DE MIEROOP

BREAUX, Joseph Arsenne (18 Feb. 1838–23 July 1926), jurist and educator, was born at Bayou Goula in Iberville Parish, Louisiana, the son of John B. Breaux and Margaret Walsh, planters. After completing his undergraduate work at Georgetown College in Kentucky, Breaux studied law at the University of Louisiana (now Tulane) and graduated in 1859. Admitted to the Louisiana bar in 1860, he opened his law office in New Iberia. In 1861 Breaux married Eugenia Mille; they had no children.

Breaux's energetic law practice was soon interrupted by the Civil War, in which he served the Confederacy and distinguished himself by being promoted to the rank of cavalry lieutenant. After the war he returned to the practice of law first in Lafayette and then in New Iberia in 1866. Reconstruction conflicts between northern carpetbaggers and southern aristocrats were mitigated in southern Louisiana by its unique culture. A compromiser more than anything, Breaux was primarily interested in expediting local and state economic, social, and educational progress. Thus, to a large extent his politics and alliances were those of efficiency and efficacy; his talent was the ability to draw upon his cultural background, his established business and community ties, and his service in the Confederate army. Exerting a positive force on the restoration of the area during Reconstruction, he soon gained prestige as one of the leading members of the Louisiana bar. In the late 1860s he devoted himself to advancing the standards of public education in the state and exhibited a degree of business acumen by becoming involved in both the business and educational affairs of his community, first as president of the First National Bank of New Iberia and, more significantly, by being elected president of the Iberia Parish School Board. His success in improving the service of the local schools and in mitigating the cultural conflict between area English and Creole groups attracted statewide attention. His only setback came in the 1870s when he failed to win a seat in the U.S. Congress in a disputed election that was mired in allegations of ballot tampering, for which no conclusive evidence exists. Breaux's reputation was sufficiently respected, however, to ensure his election to the office of state superintendent of public instruction in 1888.

In that position Breaux carefully surveyed the disordered condition of public education in Louisiana. Although the state constitution of 1879 directed the legislature to provide public schooling for all children aged six to eighteen, there was no provision for tax support at the local level. To provide the necessary funding, Breaux drafted the General Public School Act of 1888, which, primarily because of his influence, passed overwhelmingly in both houses of the legislature. The law required local governments to levy property taxes for the support of local public schools. In 1889 Breaux published a compilation of the school laws of Louisiana, together with court decisions that related to those laws, which continued for some time as the standard text on the subject.

Governor Francis Tillou Nicholls appointed Breaux an associate justice of the Louisiana State Supreme Court in April 1890, and he was elevated to chief justice in April 1904. Characterized by Paul E. Mortimer, clerk of the state supreme court for eighteen years, as one of the gentlest and most considerate men ever known on the court, Breaux established a reputation for rendering even-handed justice. In 1901 Breaux assembled and published his *Digest of Decisions of the Supreme Court of Louisiana*, a work that was instantly invaluable to the attorneys of the state.

After his retirement from the court in 1914, Breaux immersed himself in charitable and service work. Especially concerned about victims of tuberculosis, he donated $13,000 for the erection of a building at Charity Hospital, New Orleans, and funded the establishment of five pavilions for the care of these patients. Shortly after retiring, Breaux was appointed chairman of the board of the Louisiana State Museum and later became president of the Louisiana Historical Society. During this period he also served as a member of the board of directors of a number of business, civic, and educational organizations and institutions, including Tulane University, and held a position on the faculty of the Loyola University Law School. Breaux was survived by no immediate family members upon his death in New Orleans. Because of his association with both Tulane and Loyola and his lifelong interest in law and education, Breaux left the bulk of his estate for the benefit of law students at the two schools.

• The *Papers in the Case Breaux vs. Darrall: 3rd Congressional District of Louisiana* (1875) are in the library of the University of Southwestern Louisiana, Lafayette. Biographical information can be found in John Kendall, *History of New Orleans*, vol. 2 (1922). An obituary is in the New Orleans *Times-Picayune*, 24 July 1926.

CLARK ROBENSTINE

BRECHT, Bertolt (10 Feb. 1898–14 Aug. 1956), author, theatrical director, and dramatic theorist, was born Eugen Berthold Friedrich Brecht in Augsburg, Germany, the son of Berthold Friedrich Brecht, a manager of a paper mill, and Sofie Brezing. In 1917 Brecht left the comfort of his respectable provincial family in the Bavarian town of Augsburg, some forty miles northwest of Munich, to enter medical studies at Munich University. After serving as a medical orderly in the Venereal Diseases Ward of the Augsburg Military Hospital during 1918, Brecht briefly resumed his medical studies. His growing interest in theater, however, caused him to leave Munich University in 1921 without receiving a degree.

Brecht, who changed his first name to the less traditional Bertolt (often shortened to "Bert") in 1921, is generally considered to be one of the most important playwrights of the twentieth century, and his status as the century's most influential dramatic theorist is virtually impeccable. Departing from the defamiliarization techniques of the Russian formalists, Brecht created the form of theater known as "epic" theater, alternately named "non-Aristotelian," "dialectical," or "historical" theater. He developed dramatic applications of the defamiliarization process, referred to in his writing as the "estrangement effect" (*Verfremdungseffekt*), whereby everyday objects and activities could be made to appear strange and unfamiliar.

Brecht's dramatic works were designed to defamiliarize social realities to the point where the audience could analyze them critically, as though from a distance; in effect, Brecht wanted to make the present appear historical. He asserted the need to liberate all people, and especially the industrial working classes, from the illusion that the present moment is immutable, the product of an inscrutable form of fate either divine or macroeconomic. Brecht's early interest in America relates to this particular problem; for him as for many intellectuals during the New Sobriety (*Neue Sachlichkeit*) of the German 1920s, America represented the best and worst of modernization, with industrialization and urbanization raised to new levels of excess.

Many of Brecht's early works are thus set in the financial capitals of the United States and deal with both the vertiginous heights of finance capital and the sordid poverty of the workers: the partially completed *Dan Drew* (1925), in New York; *In the Jungle of Cities* (1927), in Chicago; the aborted *Wheat* (1927), in Chicago; the opera *The Rise and Fall of the City of Mahagonny* (1928), in Florida; and *Saint Joan of the Stockyards* (1929–1930; published, 1932), in Chicago. In *Dan Drew* (1925) Brecht had written that in order to understand the workings of the stock exchange, "one would have to have a giant head." America offered Brecht both the opportunity to imagine the workings of these complex operations for himself and the dramatic space within which others might learn how to develop their very own "giant heads."

While in exile from Germany, waiting in Helsinki for a U.S. visa, Brecht wrote a play concerning Adolf Hitler's rise to power, designed especially for the American stage. *The Resistible Rise of Arturo Ui* (1941) combines Brecht's interest in gangster films with the problem of institutionalized violence; in this fictionalized Chicago, as in Hitler's Germany, the general population accepts coercion and reduced rights in order that their domestic lives might remain generally intact. Brecht reached Hollywood in 1941, traveling on the Trans-Siberian railroad with his wife, Helene Weigel (whom he had married in 1929), and their two children.

In Hollywood Brecht felt estranged not only from native Americans but from his fellow exiles as well: "The worst of it is that everybody here is trying to convert himself and everybody else into a hundred per cent American in record time, it makes me feel rather seasick." In his poems from this period Brecht described Hollywood as a leech-filled swamp, a version of Hell, and a market for lies; in order to earn money, however, Brecht quickly adapted himself to working in the film industry, and with fellow German Fritz Lang he wrote the story for the film *Hangmen Also Die* (1943). Although this was the only film project with which Brecht involved himself, it was enough to earn him a subpoena from the House Un-American Activities Committee for their hearings on Communist infiltration of the motion-picture industry. During his appearance before the committee on 30 October 1947 Brecht chainsmoked cigars and spoke only through his interpreter; his carefully rehearsed performance was sufficiently European and congenial for committee chairman J. Parnell Thomas to thank him for being a "good example" to future witnesses. The next day Brecht flew to Zurich, never to return to the United States.

While in Switzerland Brecht composed his "Short Organon for the Theater" (1948), the definitive theoretical exposition of his "epic" theater. After returning to East Berlin (1949), Brecht and his wife founded the Berliner Ensemble, a theater devoted to performing plays written or directed by Brecht. It was the Berliner Ensemble that first brought Brecht truly international fame, with the appearance of their production of his play *Mother Courage and Her Children* (1939; published, 1949) at the Paris International Theater Festival (1954). Since his death of coronary thrombosis in East Berlin, Brecht's influence on world theater has been consistently strong. His techniques and theories have been particularly important in Europe and England, with works by figures such as Jean-Luc Godard, John Arden, and Harold Pinter clearly bearing the marks of Brecht's influence. In the United States Brecht has been less appreciated, but elements of his dramatic theory can be seen in works by dramatists such as Thornton Wilder and David Mamet, as well as in the work of film director David Lynch. Brecht's influence on the whole of twentieth-century dramatic theory, and the importance of his production as a playwright, poet, and short-story author, will ensure that Bertolt Brecht will long remain a viable force in the literary and theatrical fields.

• Brecht's papers are in the Bertolt-Brecht-Archiv, Berlin. In addition to his *Collected Short Stories* (1983), a number of Brecht's important plays not mentioned above include *Baal*

(1922), *A Man's a Man* (1925), *The Threepenny Opera* (1929), *The Measures Taken* (1931), *The Life of Galileo* (1938), *The Good Person of Setzuan* (1938–1941), and *The Caucasian Chalk Circle* (1944–1945). Brecht's *Letters 1913–1956*, ed. John Willett (1990), includes much of his correspondence during his stays in the United States. Important resources for Brecht's relationship to the United States include Patty Lee Parmalee, *Brecht's America* (1981), on Brecht's early writings concerned with America; and James K. Lyon, *Bertolt Brecht in America* (1980), on Brecht's time spent in the United States. The standard reference work for Brecht's theoretical writings is Willett, *Brecht on Theatre* (1964).

CHRIS ANDRE

BRECK, James Lloyd (27 June 1818–30 Mar. 1876), Episcopal missionary, was born in Philadelphia County, Pennsylvania, the son of George Breck and Catharine D. Israell. Senator James Lloyd of Massachusetts, who was married to Breck's paternal aunt, financed his education at the Flushing (N.Y.) Institute and at the University of Pennsylvania. After graduation in 1838, Breck prepared for the ordained ministry of the Episcopal church at the General Theological Seminary in New York City. A sermon on the need for frontier clergy preached there by Bishop Jackson Kemper in May 1840 led Breck to plan a new method of frontier evangelism, which he called the associate mission. The plan was based on the simple premise that a group of clergy could accomplish more than a number of isolated individuals. Drawing on his experience at Flushing, the Oxford Movement's revival of monasticism, and the week-long revivals known as associations conducted by evangelical Episcopal clergy, Breck envisioned a group who would live in a celibate community, establish mission congregations, and operate residential schools.

Between 1841 and 1876, Breck established six such missions. When he and two seminary classmates answered a call for frontier clergy by settling in Nashotah Lakes, Wisconsin, in 1842, they established an academy (later relocated and renamed Racine College), a theological school (Nashotah House), and several congregations. Breck had initially thought of this first mission as self-supporting, but he had to turn for financial support to church and family connections—notably to his brothers-in-law John Aspinwall and William Henry Aspinwall, important backers of educational and missionary projects of both high church and evangelical Episcopalians. This was a pattern that Breck would repeat in later missions. Although the theological seminary at Nashotah survived, it became evident in time that Breck and his fellow faculty members no longer shared the same vision for the school. William Adams, for example, abandoned the idea of a celibate life and married the bishop's daughter. In 1850 Breck decided, therefore, to move on. With the help of others, he established a new mission in St. Paul, Minnesota.

In 1852, a request from Enmegahbowh, the first Native-American Episcopal deacon, led to a new chapter in Breck's ministry. For the next five years Breck would devote his energies to ministry to Native Americans, founding St. Columba's Mission for the Ojibwa at Gull Lake, Minnesota, in 1852 and a second associate mission to the Ojibwa in the same state at Leech Lake in 1856. The Native-American schools and congregations that Breck's missions established were initially successful, though the influx of settlers from the East would inevitably lead to conflict and the forced movement of much of the Native-American population farther west. It may, however, have been family circumstances rather than conflicts between settlers and Native Americans that led Breck to abandon this stage of his work. In 1855 he revised his earlier opinion about the need for celibacy at his missions and married Jane Maria Mills, one of several female workers at St. Columba's Mission; they had two sons.

Withdrawal of U.S. troops from Minnesota in the late 1850s made life among the Native Americans more precarious. In 1857 the Brecks moved to Faribault, Minnesota, and began yet another associate mission. The mission became the site of a boys' school, a girls' school, a theological seminary (Seabury Divinity School, which later merged with Western Divinity School in Chicago), and a diocesan cathedral. Jane Breck died there in 1862, and two years later Breck married Sarah Styles. In 1867 the Brecks and three other clergy established Breck's final associate mission, the Pacific Coast Mission in Benicia, California. At the time of Breck's death, the mission included a college, boy's and girl's preparatory schools, a divinity school, and five congregations. The congregations continued after Breck's death, but the educational institutions did not survive.

Breck was a devout man who took seriously what he understood to be God's call in his life: the bringing of the Episcopal church to the western frontier. He believed that ordained clergy had a central role to play in frontier evangelism and grasped the importance of both cooperative efforts and educational institutions that would prepare westerners for ordination. His devotion and the record of his achievements were unequalled in his denomination.

• James Lloyd Breck's papers are located at Nashotah House. Breck's brother Charles wrote a *Life of the Reverend James Lloyd Breck* (1882), which contained selections of his correspondence. Theodore Holcombe, who as a theological student participated in the St. Paul Mission, produced the biography *An Apostle of the Wilderness: James Lloyd Breck and His Missions and His Schools* (1903). Edward Clowes Chorley, *Men and Movements in the American Episcopal Church* (1946), includes a description of Breck's work, as does William P. Haugaard, "Missionary Vision in America," *Historical Magazine of the Protestant Episcopal Church* 54 (Sept. 1985): 241–51.

ROBERT W. PRICHARD

BRECKINRIDGE, Clifton Rodes (22 Nov. 1846–3 Dec. 1932), politician and diplomat, was born in Lexington, Kentucky, the son of John Cabel Breckinridge, a politician and soldier, and Mary Cyrene Burch. Conscious from an early age that he was heir to a great family political dynasty—the Breckinridges of Kentucky—Clifton Breckinridge struggled to live up to that heritage throughout his life.

While still a youngster, Breckinridge followed his father to war, serving first as a Confederate army private and later as a naval midshipman. At the war's end, he helped his father, then Confederate secretary of war, on the first leg of a dramatic escape to Europe. He worked for two years in a Cincinnati store before his father's friend, British banker and diplomat Lord Ashburton, provided funds in 1867 for him to attend Washington College in Lexington, Virginia, where General Robert E. Lee had become president. He remained in school for three years, developing from Lee's encouragement and from his father's example a resolve to serve in public life.

During the early 1870s Breckinridge tried to make his fortune as a commission merchant and cotton planter in Pine Bluff, Arkansas, where an older brother had a plantation. Wealth came less from business than from his marriage to Katherine Breckinridge Carson in 1876. She was from a prominent, well-to-do Mississippi family, and their marriage was a social event of some note, with the son of Jefferson Davis, president of the Confederacy, serving as Breckinridge's best man. The couple had four children.

Breckinridge began a political career soon afterward, for Redeemer Democrats had overturned Reconstruction in Arkansas. He won local office in Pine Bluff, and then, aided by his late father's fame, he became the state's congressman at large in 1882. Two years later he was elected from the Second Congressional District, which he represented for a decade.

Sponsored by the Speaker, John Carlisle of Kentucky, a family friend, Breckinridge entered the small circle of Democrats who ran the House of Representatives in the 1880s. As a Ways and Means Committee member, his influence steadily increased. Breckinridge faced a serious setback when a Republican-controlled House voted to unseat him. This difficulty resulted from a disputed election in 1888, following which an unknown assassin murdered his Republican opponent. After lengthy investigation of fraudulent voting in Arkansas, the House by a straight party vote in September 1890 declared the dead candidate the election winner. Breckinridge, absolved of personal responsibility for this scandal but tainted anyway, was nonetheless reelected to Congress two months later. He gained national prominence during President Grover Cleveland's second term in the early 1890s, when Breckinridge played important roles in repealing the Sherman Silver Purchase Act and in writing the Wilson-Gorman Tariff Act.

Breckinridge was unable to survive Democratic party splits and populist challenges after the depression of 1893. He loyally supported Cleveland's staunch defense of the gold standard, in which he strongly believed, despite the sentiments of Arkansas farmers, who wanted free coinage of silver. As a result, he failed to receive the Democratic nomination for reelection in 1894. Rewarding political loyalty, Cleveland quickly named him minister to Russia in July.

In official despatches and private letters to the several secretaries of state under whom he served, Breckinridge provided discerning reports of the changing character of Russian-American relations. The century-old friendship between the two nations, he argued, was drawing to a close. Their isolation from each other and their mutual enmity toward Great Britain, which had formed the basis of this friendship, was ending. America's rapprochement with Britain after 1895 and Russia's insistent expansion in the Far East were creating new power alignments. These would threaten potential American commercial interests in Asia, he predicted. He believed that conflict over human rights issues, arising from immigration disputes and Russian mistreatment of Jews, exposed a chasm in values between Russia and the United States that was unbridgeable.

The diplomatic disputes that Breckinridge handled were, on the whole, more routine than the larger picture he described. No major crises in Russian-American relations occurred during this era, so his calls for a stronger policy against Russia, although passed along by the State Department to Presidents Cleveland and William McKinley, had little effect. American leaders remained committed to isolationism toward Europe.

Breckinridge served less successfully in carrying out a diplomat's social obligations. The cost of entertaining in grand style in St. Petersburg was beyond his means. He had to move the American legation's rented quarters to a less expensive location. His family's devout Presbyterianism would not permit Sunday evening dinners, a favorite time for entertaining among Russian aristocracy. Breckinridge pleased the Russian court by acceding to their request that, at the ceremonies marking the coronation of Emperor Nicholas II, he forsake the standard American diplomatic dress of a plain black suit and instead wear knee breeches and silk stockings. The State Department approved this change by reinterpreting an 1867 statute that seemed to forbid it. The Hearst press and cartoonists in newspapers across the United States created an uproar that greatly embarrassed Breckinridge over his supposed abandonment of good "republican" clothes.

After leaving Russia in 1898, Breckinridge accepted President McKinley's appointment in 1900 to the Dawes Commission to the Five Civilized Tribes. Working in Indian Territory to distribute individual allotments of land to Cherokees, Breckinridge and other commissioners were accused in 1903 of setting up trust companies to acquire Indians' land, exploiting Native Americans and benefiting financially from office. Exhaustive investigation eventually cleared Breckinridge of illegal actions, but he found it difficult to bear this blow to his reputation. President Theodore Roosevelt refused his offer to resign, writing that investigators "inform me privately that though they think your actions did not show good judgment in this matter, they are convinced of your absolute probity."

After his work in Indian Territory ended in 1905, Breckinridge largely left public life. He set up the Arkansas Valley Trust Company in Fort Smith, Arkansas, serving as its president from 1906 to 1914. His last involvement in politics occurred in 1917–1918, when he was elected as a convention delegate to write a new Arkansas Constitution, a document voters later rejected. After his wife died in 1921, Breckinridge moved frequently, spending time around the country with his children and grandchildren. He died while living at Windover in eastern Kentucky with his daughter Mary Breckinridge, who was establishing the famed Frontier Nursing Service there.

Breckinridge always lived in the shadow of more famous ancestors. He continued for another generation the Breckinridge tradition of public service but left a mixed legacy. Like many post–Civil War political figures, his reputation suffered scandal without any evidence of personal misdeeds. As a diplomat, Breckinridge served ably in Russia but had little impact on the course of America's foreign relations. As a congressional leader, he made a difference in national affairs. More often in his public life he was on the edge of power, not at its center. In a career spanning more than thirty years, Breckinridge, however, stands out among late nineteenth-century American leaders of lesser rank.

• Breckinridge's letters are scattered throughout the Breckinridge Family Papers at the Library of Congress and at the University of Kentucky as well as in papers of many political figures of his era, including all presidents and several cabinet members from Cleveland to Theodore Roosevelt. Other Breckinridge papers are privately held by his grandchildren. Breckinridge's domestic political career is analyzed in James Duane Bolin, "Clifton Rodes Breckinridge: 'The Little Arkansas Giant'," *Arkansas Historical Quarterly* 53 (Winter 1994): 407–27. His diplomatic service is covered in James F. Willis, "An Arkansan in St. Petersburg: Clifton Rodes Breckinridge, Minister to Russia, 1894–1897," *Arkansas Historical Quarterly* 38 (Spring 1979): 3–31. An authoritative account of his family's place in American history is in James C. Klotter, *The Breckinridges of Kentucky, 1760–1981* (1986). An obituary is in *Arkansas Gazette*, 4 Dec. 1932.

JAMES F. WILLIS

BRECKINRIDGE, Desha (5 Aug. 1867–18 Feb. 1935), newspaper publisher and editor, was born in Lexington, Kentucky, the son of William Campbell Preston Breckinridge, a politician and journalist, and Issa Desha. The Breckinridges were a distinguished Kentucky family; Breckinridge's father was an attorney who had been a Confederate colonel and a U.S. congressman, and his grandfather, Robert J. Breckinridge, was a theologian and antislavery advocate also known as the founder of public education in Kentucky. He was also a great-grandson of John Breckinridge, a U.S. senator and attorney general in Thomas Jefferson's administration. A cousin, John Cabell Breckinridge, was U.S. vice president from 1857 to 1861 and lost to Abraham Lincoln in the 1860 presidential race.

As a youth, Breckinridge was tutored in Lexington by author James Lane Allen. He attended the Lawrenceville Preparatory School in New Jersey and then Princeton University for three years; he did not graduate. After law studies, he was admitted to the Kentucky bar in 1893 and joined his father's Lexington law firm, Breckinridge & Shelby. The young man's reputation was firmly established in Lexington when he helped defend his father in a widely publicized breach-of-promise suit brought by Madeline Pollard, a young woman who claimed that after a long-standing adulterous relationship the elder Breckinridge had promised to marry her after the death of his wife Issa. His father lost the suit, and Breckinridge supported him, nevertheless, in an unsuccessful 1894 Democratic primary for reelection to Congress.

Breckinridge found his calling in life partly as a result of his father's editorial endorsement of Republican presidential candidate William McKinley over Democrat William Jennings Bryan in 1896. His father had written the widely quoted article for Lexington's Democratic *Morning Herald*. When its editor and publisher, Samuel G. Boyle, fell into financial difficulties the next year, Breckinridge leased the newspaper and bought it in 1898. During the Spanish-American War he served as a lieutenant on the staff of an uncle, General Joseph C. Breckinridge. His father continued to write editorials for the *Herald* until his death in 1904; the name was changed to the *Lexington Herald* in that year.

In more than three decades as its publisher and editor, Breckinridge continued the *Herald*'s strong Democratic support even though he sometimes disagreed with state and national party leadership. In the framework of the Progressive Era, he gave broad support to individuals and measures that coincided with his perspectives and conscience. Occasionally he lost advertising revenue and subscriptions because of his editorial stands. Recognized as a strong voice for Kentucky and Kentuckians, the *Herald* had the second-largest circulation in the state and was the dominant newspaper for the Bluegrass region of central Kentucky.

Breckinridge and the *Herald* advocated improved roads for Kentuckians, fought for increased funding for education, campaigned for reform of state prisons, supported a state tuberculosis commission and sanitaria, and criticized the state's "outdated" constitution of 1891. He also denounced the violence and political fights that marred Kentucky's national reputation. Breckinridge supported the formation of a cooperative for Kentucky's burley tobacco growers and spoke out for lowering a federal tax on tobacco. In addition, he joined the successful conservation efforts to keep Kentucky's scenic Cumberland Falls from becoming the location of a hydroelectric dam.

For many years Breckinridge maintained a stable of thoroughbred horses and championed breeding and racing in the state. In 1906 he backed the formation of a state racing commission and marshaled support in 1924 to defeat a state law that would have banned pari-mutuel betting.

Breckinridge frequently participated in national Democratic conventions. He backed Woodrow Wilson after he was nominated for president in 1912 but criticized his slowness in entering the United States into World War I. He supported Alfred E. Smith's presidential candidacy in 1928 and denounced the interjection of religion into the campaign because of Smith's Catholicism. Although not a backer of Franklin D. Roosevelt at first in 1932, he came to support him and the New Deal in the last years of his editorship.

Breckinridge, the editor, did not forget his dependence and involvement with his readers and their concerns. In a 1931 editorial he wrote that the *Herald* pledged "so far as humanly possible, to represent the high spirit of its owners. There may be errors of judgment and sins of commission and omission, but it will endeavor to the limit of its ability to voice the spirit, the faith, the courage, the hope of its people." Breckinridge never sought or held public office, although he was promised political and financial support if he decided to run for Kentucky governor.

Breckinridge's marriage to Madeline McDowell in 1898 cemented a union with another prominent Kentucky family. She was a great-granddaughter of Henry Clay, who was a U.S. senator, a Speaker of the U.S. House of Representatives, and a three-time presidential candidate. Recognized later as a woman suffragist and Progressive reformer, "Madge" Breckinridge brought to the marriage her considerable talents as an organizer and orator. In the early years of their marriage she wrote for the woman's page of the *Herald* and prepared book reviews. Later she used its columns to generate support of the woman's right to vote, which her husband came to espouse in editorials. The couple had no children. Madge Breckinridge died in 1920. In 1929 Breckinridge married Mary Frazer LeBus, the widow of Clarence LeBus, a prominent Kentucky tobacco grower. Breckinridge died at their country home, "Hinata," near Lexington.

• Principal locations of Breckinridge's papers and letters include the Breckinridge Family, Henry Breckinridge, and Breckinridge Long papers at the Library of Congress and the Desha Breckinridge and Chalkley Family scrapbooks at the University of Kentucky Library. A chapter on Breckinridge is in James Klotter, *The Breckinridges of Kentucky: 1760–1981* (1986). Sophonisba P. Breckinridge, *Madeline McDowell Breckinridge: A Leader in the New South* (1921), is a biography of Breckinridge's first wife written by his sister. See also Melba Dean Porter, "Madeline McDowell Breckinridge: Her Role in the Kentucky Woman Suffrage Movement, 1908–1920," *Register of the Kentucky Historical Society* 72 (Oct. 1974): 342–63, and Melba Porter Hay, "Madeline McDowell Breckinridge: Kentucky Suffragist and Progressive Reformer" (Ph.D. diss., Univ. of Kentucky, 1980). The 19 Feb. 1935 issue of the *Lexington Herald* contains an extensive obituary, excerpts from Breckinridge's editorials, a reprint of his 1931 statement of the newspaper's policies, and an editorial tribute from his successor, Thomas R. Underwood. An obituary also is in the *New York Times* on the same date.

CORBAN GOBLE

BRECKINRIDGE, James (7 Mar. 1763–13 May 1833), lawyer and Federalist politician, was born in Augusta County, Virginia (the part of which became Botetourt County in 1770), the son of Robert Breckenridge, a politically active frontier planter, and Lettice Preston, a member of one of the leading families in western Virginia. He and his brothers differed from their father in spelling their surname with an *i*. Young Breckinridge's schooling was erratic because of the disruptions of the American Revolution. In the winter of 1781 he joined the corps of western riflemen that his uncle Colonel William Preston raised, marching to North Carolina to reinforce General Nathanael Greene's army. Breckinridge qualified as deputy clerk of Botetourt County in June 1782 and had become a surveyor by 1784, when he went to Kentucky to survey land for himself and others. Breckinridge returned to Botetourt County in July 1786 determined to settle in Kentucky, but at the urging of his older brother and mentor, John Breckinridge, he entered the College of William and Mary that November. During the next two years Breckinridge studied natural and moral philosophy and read law under George Wythe. Breckinridge's emerging political views were shaped by the debates of the Virginia Ratifying Convention that he observed at Richmond in June 1788. "Y[ou]r Brother Ja[me]s," a convention member wrote John Breckinridge, "has been here from College . . . and he is a flaming federalist." To James Breckinridge's mind, Patrick Henry's attacks on the Constitution were eloquent and all too effective efforts to "lead the ignorant people astray," while James Madison's defense evidenced "plain, ingenious, & elegant reasoning" (Dicken-Garcia, p. 125).

Ill health and lack of money obliged Breckinridge to abandon his studies in December 1788 and return to Botetourt County, where he was admitted to the bar in February 1789. In Richmond in 1791, Breckinridge married Anne Selden, a Tidewater aristocrat who apparently persuaded him to relinquish his Kentucky plans. The couple settled in Botetourt County, living first at "Cloverdale," the 400-acre estate on Tinker Creek that Breckinridge had inherited from his father. In 1794 Breckinridge sold Cloverdale, and during the next nine years, he bought 1,400 acres of land on Catawba Creek near the town of Fincastle. On that land in 1802, he built "Grove Hill," a large federal-style mansion, to house his and Anne's growing family, which eventually numbered ten children. Forty-nine slaves tended the plantation's crops and operated its gristmill, sawmill, tannery, brickyard, and tool-making shops. Breckinridge also established a lucrative law practice, but the drudgery of routine legal work did not satisfy his ambition to attain some "degree of eminence whither at the bar or in the public councils of my country" (Dicken-Garcia, p. 154).

Aided by his influential relatives, Breckinridge was elected in 1789 to the Virginia House of Delegates, the first of his thirteen terms in that body covering the years 1789–1790, 1796–1802, 1806–1808, 1819–1821, and 1823–1824. In 1791 he was named federal revenue inspector for southwestern Virginia, and in the mid-1790s he served as commonwealth attorney of Botetourt County. Breckinridge's political career culminated in April 1809 with his election to the U.S. House of Representatives from Virginia's Fifth Congressional District, and he served four consecutive terms in Congress, the last ending in March 1817.

A steadfast Federalist, Breckinridge was fated to be allied with a minority party in Virginia as a state legislator and in the nation as a congressman, circumstances that thwarted whatever ambitions he had for higher office. He ran as a Federalist candidate for the U.S. Senate in 1796 and for governor three years later, only to be defeated on both occasions by Jeffersonian Republicans whose party dominated the general assembly, where those elections occurred. In the House of Delegates, Breckinridge regularly supported Federalist positions on controversial national issues, casting votes against a 1790 resolution that denounced federal assumption of state war debts, against the Virginia Resolutions of 1798, which denied the constitutionality of the Alien and Sedition Acts, and against an 1808 resolution that endorsed President Thomas Jefferson's embargo. During his four congressional terms, which coincided with Madison's two terms as president, Breckinridge joined his Federalist colleagues in opposing the declaration of war on England in 1812. A nationalist who doubted the wisdom of fighting a great and potentially friendly power, Breckinridge refused to support trade sanctions or a large national army capable of invading Canada, but he consistently voted for defensive measures such as fortifying harbors, maintaining the navy, and strengthening state militia.

Breckinridge was prepared to defend the nation personally once hostilities began. Having been commissioned as an ensign in the Botetourt County militia in 1787, he advanced to captain in 1790 and lieutenant colonel in 1795, and in 1814 Virginia's governor appointed him brigadier general of the Third Brigade of state militia. Breckinridge's brigade was assigned to the defense of Richmond from early September to mid-October 1814, when it marched north to reinforce troops guarding Baltimore. The brigade engaged in no combat before it was discharged in mid-December.

During the later years of his public life, Breckinridge addressed his constituents' growing demands for transportation, electoral reform, and education. He served on a commission that in 1812 marked a road through the Alleghenies to link the navigable waters of the James and Kanawha rivers, and he subsequently supported various internal improvements in the House of Delegates. In 1816 Breckinridge presided over a convention at Staunton that petitioned unsuccessfully to have the state constitution changed to give western counties fair representation in the general assembly. In 1818 Breckinridge was one of the commissioners who adopted plans for the University of Virginia, and he served on its board of visitors until his death at Grove Hill.

Taciturn and stiffly dignified in demeanor, not unlike his Federalist hero George Washington, Breckinridge rarely spoke in public debates, but he closely studied the political issues of his time and took stands that usually commanded the respect if not the assent of a majority of his contemporaries. His careful distinction between offensive and defensive military measures during the War of 1812 offered a "moderate, responsible" alternative to Madison's war policy and the obstructionism of antiwar New England Federalists, and his championing of the domestic concerns of his western small-farmer constituents demonstrates, as historian Norman Risjord has argued, "that neither party in Virginia had a monopoly on progressive reform, democracy, or virtue" (Risjord, p. 517).

• Most of Breckinridge's surviving papers are in the James Breckinridge Papers and the papers of the Breckinridge and Gilmer families (microfilm) at the University of Virginia Library in Charlottesville, the Breckinridge Family Papers at the Library of Congress, and the Breckinridge Family Papers at the Virginia Historical Society in Richmond. Some correspondence about the University of Virginia is in the Thomas Jefferson Papers at the Library of Congress. The only biography is Katherine Kennedy McNulty, "James Breckinridge" (M.A. thesis, Virginia Polytechnic Institute and State Univ., 1970). Roy Albert Lamb, Jr., focuses on politics in "James Breckinridge: Federalist Politician in Jeffersonian Virginia" (M.A. thesis, Univ. of Virginia, 1986). For his youth, see Lowell H. Harrison, *John Breckinridge: Jeffersonian Republican* (1969), and Hazel Dicken-Garcia, *To Western Woods: The Breckinridge Family Moves to Kentucky in 1793* (1991); for local offices, see Robert Douthat Stoner, *A Seed-Bed of the Republic* (1962); and for Grove Hill, see Frances J. Niederer, *The Town of Fincastle* (1983). The most useful political studies are Norman K. Risjord, "The Virginia Federalists," *Journal of Southern History* 33 (1967): 486–517; and Donald Robert Hickey, "The Federalists and the War of 1812" (Ph.D. diss., Univ. of Illinois, 1972). For his brigade, see Stuart Lee Butler, *A Guide to Virginia Militia Units in the War of 1812* (1988); and for the University of Virginia, see Dumas Malone, *The Sage of Monticello* (1981). An obituary is in the *Richmond Enquirer*, 24 May 1833.

PHILANDER D. CHASE

BRECKINRIDGE, John (2 Dec. 1760–14 Dec. 1806), lawyer, planter, and statesman, was born on a farm near Staunton, Virginia, the son of Robert Breckinridge, a farmer and member of the local gentry, and Lettice Preston. While John was still a boy the family moved to the frontier part of Augusta County that became Botetourt County. Determined to acquire an education, John entered William and Mary College in late 1780 or early 1781. His attendance was irregular, but when he left the school in 1784 he had studied for some two years, much of it under the guidance of George Wythe. In 1785 Breckinridge added his shingle to the crowded Virginia bar. If he participated in the American Revolution, it was with the local militia and for brief periods. Breckinridge was elected to the state house of delegates in 1780. Under age, he was not seated until 1781 when his constituents elected him for the third time. He became an accomplished parliamentarian who usually supported James Madison's positions on such controversial issues as freedom of religion and the need for a stable national government.

In 1785 Breckinridge married Mary Hopkins "Polly" Cabell. They had nine children, seven of whom lived beyond infancy. When his farming in Albemarle County and his legal practice did not provide the security Breckinridge sought, his attention turned toward Kentucky, where several family members had already moved. After a personal inspection trip west Breckinridge purchased some 1,600 acres of prime land a few miles from Lexington. Tenants started making improvements and most of his slaves were sent out in advance to ease the journey; he moved his family to the new state in the spring of 1793. Because of the impending move, he refused to be seated after his election to the U.S. House of Representatives.

Breckinridge soon challenged another former Virginian, George Nicholas, for the leadership of the Kentucky bar. He refused to raise tobacco at "Cabell's Dale" for fear it would ruin the good land; instead, he concentrated on the development of a horse farm. Breckinridge also invested in salt springs and the Bourbon Iron Works Company. A cautious speculator in land, his holdings were usually in excess of 20,000 acres. Breckinridge apparently never sold a slave, and by 1806 his fifty-seven slaves made him a large owner by Kentucky standards. Extensive hiring out kept him from becoming slave poor.

As political parties developed Breckinridge became a leading Jeffersonian Republican. After the organization of the Lexington Democratic Society in August 1793 he pressed the West's demand for unimpeded navigation of the Mississippi to the Gulf of Mexico with a violence that alarmed some of his friends. In December 1793 he accepted Governor Isaac Shelby's appointment as attorney general, a position that interfered little with his private practice; he served until 1797. Breckinridge was defeated for the U.S. Senate in 1794 when Humphrey Marshall benefited from a temporary surge of Federalist sentiment.

As a member of the Kentucky House of Representatives from 1797 to 1801 and its Speaker during the last two years, Breckinridge became well known as the supposed author of the Kentucky Resolutions of 1798, which asserted a state's right to pass on the constitutionality of federal actions. The resolutions were secretly drafted by Thomas Jefferson to protest the Alien and Sedition Acts; Breckinridge and his associates modified them slightly and pushed them through the legislature. Because of some adverse state reaction, a long summary resolution, which Breckinridge probably wrote, was passed in 1799. While the states' rights theory was at the heart of the 1798 resolutions, the term "nullification" was not expressed until the following year. Breckinridge worked to reform Kentucky's barbarous penal code in 1798, and he was a leader in an unsuccessful effort to prevent the calling of a second state constitutional convention which he feared might change the land laws and might include constitutional provisions for the emancipation of slaves. Breckinridge and the conservative element dominated the convention, and they were not displeased with the 1799 constitution. Breckinridge also served on the board of trustees for Transylvania University, worked for a subscription library, and sought a passable wagon road to Virginia to be financed by public subscriptions.

Elected a U.S. senator in the Jeffersonian groundswell of 1800, Breckinridge became one of the administration's floor leaders. In an era when presidents did not openly present legislation, Breckinridge introduced and pushed administration measures (such as the repeal of the Judiciary Act of 1801, the reorganization of the federal court system, and the admission of Ohio into the Union), coordinated the efforts of his associates, and countered the moves of the experienced Federalist leaders. During the summer of 1803 Jefferson informed him that the Louisiana Purchase had finally solved the Mississippi River issue. Although he believed in states' rights, Breckinridge was a westerner who wanted no doubt cast on the transaction. Thus he ignored Jefferson's suggestion that a constitutional amendment should make the purchase legal. In the unsuccessful 1805 attempt to remove Supreme Court justice Samuel Chase through the impeachment process, Breckinridge voted guilty on seven of eight charges. Had the attempt succeeded, judges might have been removed for partisan reasons in addition to the constitutional grounds for impeachment, imperiling the independence of the federal judiciary.

In August 1805 Jefferson offered Breckinridge the position of attorney general. He would bring his knowledge of the West's desires, the president wrote, "for which we are often at a loss and sometimes fail in our desire to promote them." Breckinridge, after some hesitancy, accepted the post, which was held in such low esteem that no office or clerical help was provided. Although he made no significant contribution to the office of the attorney general, as the first cabinet member from the West he was able to present the views of that section to the administration. He continued to provide important liaison between Congress and the executive branch, but the Republican majority in the Senate worked less smoothly without Breckinridge's leadership.

His illness during the summer of 1806 was reported as typhus fever or a stomach ailment; it may well have been tuberculosis. He died at Cabell's Dale and was buried there. Years later Albert Gallatin recalled that during the early days of the nineteenth century when he looked for replacements for Jefferson, Madison, and himself he found just two: John Randolph of Roanoke, who was disqualified by his eccentricities, and John Breckinridge of Kentucky.

A member of Jefferson's natural aristocracy, in which position was to depend on merit and not birth, Breckinridge had an important role in the early economic development of Kentucky and in the formation of its second constitution. The resolutions of 1798 and 1799 with which he was associated were among the first overt statements claiming the power of a state to block actions by the federal government it regarded as unconstitutional. As a U.S. senator, Breckinridge helped secure passage of controversial Republican legislation during the Seventh Congress. Before his untimely death, Breckinridge had established himself as one of the important secondary leaders in the Republican party.

• Most of Breckinridge's papers are in the extensive Breckinridge Family Papers, Library of Congress. The most complete biography is Lowell H. Harrison, *John Breckinridge, Jeffersonian Republican* (1969). His role in the establishment of a Kentucky dynasty is well described in James C. Klotter, *The Breckinridges of Kentucky* (1986). His contribution is overemphasized in Ethelbert Dudley Warfield, *The Kentucky Resolutions of 1798* (1887); this should be balanced with Adrienne Koch and Harry Ammon, "The Virginia and Kentucky Resolutions: An Episode in Jefferson's and Madison's Defense of Civil Liberties," *William and Mary Quarterly*, 3d ser., 5 (Apr. 1948) 145–76. Breckinridge's legislative career can be traced in *Journals of the Kentucky House of Representatives* (1797–1801) and *Debates and Proceedings in the Congress of the United States* (1801–1806).

LOWELL H. HARRISON

BRECKINRIDGE, John (4 July 1797–4 Aug. 1841), Presbyterian clergyman and editor, was born at "Cabell's Dale," near Lexington, Kentucky, the son of John Breckinridge, the U.S. attorney general under President Thomas Jefferson, and Mary Hopkins Cabell. He entered the College of New Jersey (now Princeton University) in 1815 and graduated with distinction in 1819.

While at Princeton, Breckinridge came under the influence of the college president, Ashbel Green, and experienced a religious conversion. Joining the Presbyterian church, he entered Princeton Theological Seminary in 1819 to prepare for the ministry. In 1822 he was licensed to preach by the Presbytery of New Brunswick, and shortly thereafter he was elected chaplain of the U.S. House of Representatives for the 1822–1823 session. He was pastor of the Second Presbyterian Church of Lexington, Kentucky, from 1823 to 1826, during which time he edited the *Western Luminary*, one of the earliest religious journals in the West.

From 1826 to 1831 Breckinridge was associated with the Second Presbyterian Church of Baltimore, first as adjunct pastor, then as pastor. In 1831 the general assembly of the Presbyterian church elected him secretary and general agent of its Board of Education. Five years later he went to Princeton Theological Seminary as professor of practical theology, a position he held for two years until he became in 1836 the secretary and general agent of the Presbyterian church's Board of Foreign Missions. This appointment he kept until 1840, when he resigned because of poor health. At the time of his death, at Cabell's Dale, he was the pastor elect of the First Presbyterian Church in New Orleans and the president elect of Oglethorpe University in Georgia. He was married first in 1823 to Margaret Miller, the daughter of Samuel Miller of Princeton Theological Seminary. They had two daughters and a son. In 1840, two years after the death of his first wife, Breckinridge married Mary Ann Babcock of Stonington, Connecticut. They had one daughter.

Breckinridge was a leading representative of the "Old School" party in the Presbyterian church, which, so closely associated with Princeton Theological Seminary, was marked by a commitment to Protestant Scholasticism, Scottish Common Sense Realism, and a conservative political and social perspective.

Breckinridge was best known beyond Presbyterian circles for a series of heated debates with John Hughes, later archbishop of New York. The first debates, conducted in religious periodicals, were published as *Controversy between Rev. Messrs. Hughes and Breckinridge, on the Subject, etc.* (1834?). Breckinridge claimed Protestantism to be "the religion of Christ," while Hughes claimed that honor for Roman Catholicism. In the second set of debates, they disputed political questions, asking first if Catholicism and then if Presbyterianism is "in Any or in All its Principles of Doctrines Inimical to Civil or Religious Liberty?" These debates were published in 1836 as *A Discussion of the Question, Is the Roman Catholic Religion, etc.*

• The Breckinridge Family Papers in the Manuscript Division, Library of Congress, contain more than 500 bound volumes of material arranged in chronological order from 1752 to 1904. Other published works by Breckinridge include *Ministerial Responsibility* (1828); *Spruce Street Lectures on Missions* (1833); and *An Address Delivered July 15, 1835, before the Eucleian and Philomathian Societies of the University of the City of New York* (1836). See also W. B. Sprague, *Annals of the American Pulpit*, vol. 4 (1858). Helpful material on Breckinridge can be found in Edgar Caldwell Mayse, "Robert Jefferson Breckinridge: American Presbyterian Controversialist" (Th.D. diss., Union Theological Seminary, 1974). An extended obituary is in the *Baltimore Literary and Religious Magazine* 7 (Oct. 1841): 475–80.

T. ERSKINE CLARKE

BRECKINRIDGE, John Cabell (21 Jan. 1821–17 May 1875), vice president of the United States and Confederate general, was born in Lexington, Kentucky, the son of Joseph Cabell Breckinridge and Mary Clay Smith. Breckinridge was an only son born into a devoutly Presbyterian family that was distinguished by its leading role in the early history of the Jeffersonian Republican party in Kentucky. His grandfather was a U.S. senator, and his father was a lawyer and Kentucky state representative whose death in 1823 left the young Breckinridge to be raised by his mother and a grandmother at a family estate near Lexington. Breckinridge graduated from Centre College, Kentucky, in 1839, read law at the College of New Jersey in Princeton, and returned home to finish his legal studies at Transylvania University. He received his law degree in 1841 and moved to Burlington, Iowa, to start his law practice. Two years later he was permanently back in Kentucky, where he married Mary Cyrene Burch in 1843; they had six children.

A prospering lawyer in Lexington at the outbreak of the Mexican War, Breckinridge served as a major in the Third Regiment of Kentucky Volunteers. Soon after the war he entered politics as a states' rights Democrat. Aided by his family name and war service, he rose rapidly through party ranks. He was a representative from Fayette County in the Kentucky House from 1849 to 1851 and was elected in 1851 to the U.S. House of Representatives, where he served until 1855. A friend and confidant of both President Franklin Pierce and the Illinois senator Stephen Douglas, Breckinridge was one of the congressional intermediaries who convinced Pierce to accept southern demands that Douglas's bill for organizing the Kansas and Nebraska territories include the statement that the Missouri Compromise restriction on slavery was "inoperative and void." Breckinridge also played a key role in securing approval of Douglas's bill in the House. Until this point he had been viewed as a moderate from the Border South on the slavery issue. Hereafter, although Breckinridge still tried to be a sectional mediator, he was associated with the extreme demands of the Lower South. When the Kansas-Nebraska Act passed in 1854, it triggered a storm of protest in the North that spawned the Republican party. Although he sponsored little in the way of major legislation, Breckinridge was a popular congressman whose charm and affability won him many friends. This popularity, combined with his representation of a key border state that traditionally had voted for the Whigs in presidential elections, gained him the Democratic nomination for vice president in 1856. The Buchanan-Breckinridge ticket carried Kentucky and the election. Breckinridge's service as vice president, however, was even less distinguished than his congressional record. He was virtually ignored by Buchanan and shut out of the administration's policy decisions. It was with some relief that Breckinridge looked forward to entering the U.S. Senate, having been elected in 1859 by the Kentucky legislature to fill the seat to be vacated by John J. Crittenden in 1861.

Much to his surprise, Breckinridge found himself a presidential candidate in 1860. When the Democratic National Convention at Charleston broke up over the issue of federal protection for slavery in the territories, Breckinridge was subsequently nominated for the presidency by a convention of the party's southern wing. Douglas had earlier been nominated by the northern Democrats, and Breckinridge feared that a divided Democratic party would ensure Lincoln's election. He was willing to decline the nomination if Douglas would do the same. Douglas refused, and, citing the "path of duty," Breckinridge went ahead with the race. His running mate was Joseph Lane of Oregon. Breckinridge, himself a slaveowner, had never been part of the radical, secessionist wing of the southern Democrats, but he believed in the right of secession and strongly held that the South was constitutionally entitled to protection for slavery in the territories. Although he insisted he was not a disunionist, he was branded as such by his opponents. He swept the Lower South in the election but finished a distant second to Abraham Lincoln in the electoral college.

As vice president in the dying days of the Buchanan administration and as a senator in the spring and summer of 1861, Breckinridge worked unsuccessfully for a sectional compromise. Bitterly opposed to the war policies of the Lincoln administration, yet still unwilling to go over to the Confederacy, he faced the most agonizing decision of his career. In the absence of any concessions from the North, he was inclined to support the Confederacy, and only reluctantly did he support Kentucky's attempt at neutrality. Kentucky's uneasy neutrality ended in September, when the state legislature declared for the Union. Acting on the recommendation of Kentucky Unionists, federal military authorities then moved to arrest Breckinridge for alleged disloyalty. He now committed himself to the Confederacy and fled east to Virginia, where in November 1861 he accepted a commission as a brigadier general in the Confederate army. On 2 December 1861 the U.S. Senate formally expelled Breckinridge on grounds of treason.

Breckinridge compiled an impressive military record. He fought under Albert Sidney Johnston at Bowling Green and Shiloh in early 1862. Promoted to major general in June 1862, he led an unsuccessful assault at Baton Rouge in August 1862 and then distinguished himself at Stones River in January 1863. Under Joseph E. Johnston during the Vicksburg campaign and Braxton Bragg at Chickamauga and Missionary Ridge in 1863, he continued to be involved in the heaviest fighting of the war in the western theater. In 1864 he was given command of the Department of Southwestern Virginia and took part in Jubal Early's raid on Washington. Breckinridge's greatest contribution to the Confederacy may have been his brief stint as Jefferson Davis's last secretary of war. Appointed to office in February 1865, he worked to ensure that the now inevitable Confederate defeat would be marked by honor and dignity. He opposed efforts to continue the war with guerrilla bands, struggled to preserve the official records of the Confederate government from wanton destruction, and counseled Joseph Johnston in his armistice negotiations with General William T. Sherman in North Carolina.

Fearing for his personal safety, Breckinridge fled to Cuba at war's end. He then moved to England and finally Canada, where he rejoined his family and lived as an exile until he returned to Kentucky in 1869. A voice of moderation and reason during his exile, Breckinridge became for many a symbol of the willingness of former Confederates to accept their defeat and work for a reconstructed nation. The indictments against him for treason were finally dropped in a general pardon issued by President Andrew Johnson on 25 December 1868. Upon returning home in early 1869, Breckinridge renounced any intention of returning to politics. He did speak out against the Ku Klux Klan and in favor of sectional reconciliation. He served as president and then vice president of the Elizabethtown, Lexington, & Big Sandy Railroad from 1869 to 1874 before his death in Lexington.

• The largest collection of Breckinridge's private papers is in the Breckinridge family papers in the Library of Congress. Other holdings are at the Chicago Historical Society, Duke

University, the New-York Historical Society, the Historical Society of Pennsylvania, the Western Reserve Historical Society in Cleveland, and the Filson Club in Louisville. William C. Davis, *Breckinridge: Statesman, Soldier, Symbol* (1974), is a thorough, solid biography. Briefer accounts of his career can be found in *The Biographical Encyclopaedia of Kentucky of the Dead and Living Men of the Nineteenth Century* (1878), and William E. Connelly and E. Merton Coulter, *History of Kentucky*, vol. 3 (1924).

WILLIAM L. BARNEY

BRECKINRIDGE, Madeline McDowell (20 May 1872–25 Nov. 1920), woman suffragist and Progressive reformer, was born at Woodlake in Franklin County, Kentucky, the daughter of Henry Clay McDowell, a lawyer and businessman, and Anne Clay. Members from both sides of her family had been prominent since Kentucky's earliest years. In 1882 her family moved to Ashland, the estate of her great-grandfather Henry Clay, near Lexington. Thereafter, she attended school in Lexington except for the year 1889–1890, which she spent at Miss Porter's School in Farmington, Connecticut. Upon returning home, she took classes at the State College (now the University of Kentucky) but never earned a degree. In late 1890 she sustained an injury to her foot that resulted in tuberculosis of the bone. She subsequently had to have a portion of her leg amputated and periodically underwent treatment at tuberculosis sanatoriums.

Her father's favorite child, she was imbued by him with a sense of noblesse oblige and a desire to match the contributions made by her noteworthy ancestors. In the 1890s she joined the Fortnightly Club and led its members in the study of German literature and philosophy. She also began to write book reviews for the *Lexington Herald* and on 17 November 1898 married the newspaper's editor, Desha Breckinridge, who was also from one of Kentucky's leading political families. These connections by blood and marriage provided a base of support and prestige that greatly benefited her later reform efforts. Moreover, her husband's newspaper gave extensive, invaluable publicity to her activities.

Breckinridge launched her career as a reformer in 1899–1900, when she led the Gleaners of Christ Church Episcopal in establishing a social settlement in Proctor in the mountains of eastern Kentucky. In 1900 she became one of the founders of the Lexington Civic League, organized to promote civic improvements, and the Associated Charities, which was to coordinate and distribute charity by the "scientific," or casework, method. She not only drafted the bylaws of these two groups but also served for many years as their major leader. Many of her ideas for reform seem to have been inspired by her sister-in-law, Sophonisba P. Breckinridge, a University of Chicago professor and the preeminent figure in the professionalization of social work.

Irishtown, the poorest white section of Lexington, became the focus of some of the Civic League's earliest activities. In 1901 the league opened a summer playground there; a kindergarten and then a four-grade elementary school soon followed. Working through the Civic League and the Kentucky Federation of Women's Clubs, Breckinridge promoted such reforms as manual training in the schools and compulsory school attendance and child labor laws. In 1903 she brought Hull-House reformer Jane Addams to Lexington to speak on these issues, and in 1907 the school board finally appropriated money to begin manual training in carpentry and domestic science. While spending the winter of 1903–1904 in Denver, Colorado, Breckinridge investigated the juvenile court system developed there by Judge Benjamin B. Lindsey. After returning home, she brought Lindsey to Lexington to speak. As a result of this campaign, in 1906 state laws were enacted establishing a juvenile court system and restricting child labor.

One of Breckinridge's greatest achievements was the development of a "model" school for Irishtown, which was also designed to serve as a social center for the neighborhood. As president of the Civic League, she raised $35,000 to supplement a $10,000 appropriation from the city to build the school. The Abraham Lincoln School included a laundry, showers, a swimming pool, a gymnasium, and an assembly hall open to residents of the community. The project was initiated in 1908, the cornerstone was laid on 6 December 1911, and the school opened in 1912.

Perhaps spurred by her own and her family's seeming predisposition for the disease, Breckinridge became an avid worker in the fight against tuberculosis. In 1905 the Civic League and Associated Charities opened a free dispensary in Lexington. In 1909 she became a founding member of the Kentucky Association for the Prevention and Relief of Tuberculosis, and from 1912 to 1916 she served on the state tuberculosis commission, advocating a state sanatorium. In 1916 she helped raise $50,000 for building the Blue Grass Sanatorium in Lexington.

Breckinridge became increasingly frustrated by the indifference of politicians to her pleas for reforms in health, education, and welfare. She concluded that only by having the vote could women obtain the power necessary to achieve progressive reforms. This caused her to devote an increasing amount of time to the cause of woman suffrage. In 1908 and 1912, while serving as chair of the Legislative Committee of the Kentucky Federation of Women's Clubs, she lobbied the Kentucky General Assembly for a bill granting women the right to vote in school elections. After winning school suffrage in 1912, she turned her efforts toward full suffrage. From 1912 to 1915 she served as president of the Kentucky Equal Rights Association, and from 1913 to 1915 as a vice president of the National American Woman Suffrage Association. A gifted speaker, she campaigned in several states for the cause. In 1919 she was again elected president of the Kentucky Equal Rights Association. After Congress passed the Nineteenth Amendment that same year, she led the fight to secure Kentucky's ratification of the amendment. This was accomplished on the first day of the legislative session, 6 January 1920.

In the summer of 1920 Breckinridge attended the International Women's Suffrage Alliance in Geneva, Switzerland. When she returned home, she embarked in October on a rigorous speaking tour on behalf of the Democratic presidential ticket and the League of Nations. Back home, she made plans for a meeting to convert the Kentucky Equal Rights Association into a League of Women Voters, but before the scheduled meeting she suffered a stroke and died two days later. Kentucky had lost its leading progressive reformer and women's rights advocate.

• A sizable collection of Madeline McDowell Breckinridge's papers is located amid the huge collection of Breckinridge Family Papers in the Library of Congress. A small group is in the Special Collections Department, Margaret I. King Library, University of Kentucky, Lexington. The most thorough printed source is Sophonisba P. Breckinridge, *Madeline McDowell Breckinridge, a Leader in the New South* (1921). For her suffrage work, see Melba Dean Porter, "Madeline McDowell Breckinridge: Her Role in the Woman Suffrage Movement, 1908–1920," *Register of the Kentucky Historical Society* 72 (1974): 342–63. See also Melba Porter Hay, "Madeline McDowell Breckinridge: Kentucky Suffragist and Progressive Reformer" (Ph.D. diss., Univ. of Kentucky, 1980); and Marjorie Spruill Wheeler, "New Women of the New South: The Leaders of the Woman Suffrage Movement in the Southern States" (Ph.D. diss., Univ. of Virginia, 1990).

MELBA PORTER HAY

BRECKINRIDGE, Mary (17 Feb. 1881–16 May 1965), advocate of nurse-midwifery, was born in Memphis, Tennessee, the daughter of Clifton Rodes Breckinridge, a congressman and ambassador to Russia, and Katherine Carson. Educated at Rosemont-Dezaley in Lausanne, Switzerland, and the Low and Heywood School in Stamford, Connecticut, Breckinridge married Henry Ruffner Morrison in 1904. After her husband's death less than two years later, she attended St. Luke's Hospital School of Nursing in New York City from 1907 to 1910 and graduated as a registered nurse. Her second marriage in 1912, to Richard Ryan Thompson, ended in divorce in 1920, and Breckinridge resumed her maiden name. With her second husband, she had two children; one died at the age of four, and the other died shortly after birth. According to Breckinridge, the deaths of her children prompted her lifelong commitment to improving the health and welfare of mothers and babies.

Breckinridge worked for three months in 1918 as a researcher and spokeswoman for the Children's Bureau, an agency of the Department of Commerce and Labor that investigated a wide range of child welfare issues, including infant mortality, juvenile courts, and child labor. Then she volunteered in a massive relief program for areas of France devastated by World War I. As the director of Child Hygiene and District Nursing for the American Committee for Devastated France from 1919 to 1921, she coordinated food and medical relief for approximately seventy villages and organized a visiting nursing service that provided general and maternity nursing to the local people. Her experiences in France with both French midwives and British nurse-midwives prompted her to write in her autobiography; "After I had met British nurse-midwives, first in France and then on my visits to London, it grew upon me that nurse-midwifery was the logical response to the needs of the young child in rural America" (p. 111).

Upon her return to the United States, Breckinridge took refresher courses in public health nursing at Teachers' College, Columbia University, from 1922 to 1923 and then rode through the eastern Kentucky mountains in the summer of 1923 to survey the local midwives. She found that these midwives provided inadequate care to their rural patients; they had no formal training and did not offer prenatal or postnatal care. By this time Breckinridge had decided that she wanted to set up a demonstration site in nurse-midwifery in eastern Kentucky. She chose this region because of her family connections in the area, her belief that rural mothers and children were in greater danger than urban ones, and her conviction that success in a region so remote and poor would prove that nurse-midwifery could succeed anywhere.

After completing the midwifery survey in Kentucky, Breckinridge wanted to learn more about the British system of nurse-midwifery before she established her program in the United States. She attended the British Hospital for Mothers and Babies in the Woolwich section of London from 1923 to 1924 to become a certified midwife. She then spent several months in Scotland studying the Highlands and Islands Medical and Nursing Service, an organization staffed by nurse-midwives that provided skilled health care to a poor rural population. Returning to England, she enrolled in postgraduate courses in midwifery at the Post Certificate School of the York Road General Lying-In Hospital in London in 1924.

Before Breckinridge left for England in 1923, she had applied to the American Child Health Association to establish a five-year demonstration project in maternal and child health in eastern Kentucky, staffed by public health nurses with midwifery training, but she withdrew her proposal in the face of opposition from the head of Kentucky's Bureau of Maternal and Child Health. Instead, in 1925 she used her wide network of influential family members and friends to establish a private philanthropic organization, the Kentucky Committee for Mothers and Babies (renamed the Frontier Nursing Service in 1928). Breckinridge set up city committees, staffed by wealthy women and men around the country, to solicit funds for her new organization. The money they raised formed the basis of the Frontier Nursing Service (FNS) budget.

Breckinridge designed FNS to serve mothers and families in districts surrounding a central hospital in Hyden, Kentucky. Since nurse-midwives did not exist in the United States, her service employed mostly British public-health nurses, who also were trained as midwives. First by horseback and later by jeep, FNS nurse-midwives traveled through the mountains to offer prenatal, labor and delivery, and postnatal services for women, as well as public health programs for men, women, and children. Although FNS hired a medical director in the early 1930s, the nurse-midwives handled nearly all deliveries at patients' homes without medical assistance. The long distances through difficult terrain meant that physicians were often unavailable, even in emergencies. By 1930 FNS covered more than 700 square miles of territory in three eastern Kentucky counties.

When World War II began, FNS's British nurse-midwives returned home to help with the war effort, forcing FNS to develop an educational program in order to maintain its staff. Under Breckinridge's leadership, the Frontier Graduate School of Midwifery began in 1939, offering midwifery training to registered nurses. From its early years, Breckinridge coped with skepticism from many physicians and nurses about this new type of profession. She worked steadfastly to develop support for her demonstration project, trying to convince her opposition that nurse-midwifery could solve the problem of the United States' alarmingly high maternal and infant mortality rates. She found backing from a number of prominent health-care experts, including George Kosmak, editor of the *American Journal of Obstetrics and Gynecology*, and Louis Dublin, a statistician and maternal welfare expert whose statistics on FNS deliveries showed its very low rates of death in childbirth. Breckinridge also made sure that FNS received publicity in popular magazines such as the *Survey*, the *Nation*, *Harper's*, and *Good Housekeeping*.

Although Breckinridge was unable to find the funding to establish another demonstration project in nurse-midwifery, FNS was in many ways a great success. As its director from 1925 until her retirement in 1959 and the recipient of many honors, Breckinridge proved that a nurse-midwifery service could offer excellent health care at a reasonable cost to a medically underserved population. After she died at her home in Wendover, Kentucky, obituary headlines hailed Breckinridge as the "Angel of Frontier" and "Kentucky's Samaritan."

• For documents on the American Committee for Devastated France and Frontier Nursing Service, as well as some of Breckinridge's personal correspondence, see the Frontier Nursing Service Collection, Department of Special Collections and Archives, University of Kentucky Libraries, Lexington. Breckinridge's autobiography is *Wide Neighborhoods: A Story of the Frontier Nursing Service* (1952). Recent assessments include Nancy Schrom Dye, "Mary Breckinridge, the Frontier Nursing Service and the Introduction of Nurse-Midwifery in the United States," *Bulletin of the History of Medicine* 57 (1983): 485–507; Anne G. Campbell, "Mary Breckinridge and the American Committee for Devastated France: The Foundations of the Frontier Nursing Service," *Register of the Kentucky Historical Society* 82 (Summer 1984): 257–76; Carol Crowe-Carraco, "Mary Breckinridge and the Frontier Nursing Service," *Register of the Kentucky Historical Society* 76 (July 1978): 179–91; and Nancy Dammann, *A Social History of the Frontier Nursing Service* (1982). Obituaries are in the *New York Times* and the *Louisville Courier-Journal*, both 17 May 1965.

LAURA ETTINGER

BRECKINRIDGE, Robert Jefferson (8 Mar. 1800–27 Nov. 1871), theologian and educator, was born at Cabell's Dale (near Lexington) in Fayette County, Kentucky, the son of John Breckinridge, a lawyer and politician, and Mary Hopkins Cabell. Raised in one of the most prominent families in Kentucky, he attended Jefferson College between 1816 and 1818, spent a few months at Yale College in 1818, and finally graduated from Union College in 1819. After completing his schooling, he returned home to study law. Breckinridge married his cousin Ann Sophonisba Preston in 1823; they had four children. He opened his practice in 1824 and a year later was elected to represent Fayette County in the state legislature; he held that position until 1828.

The death of two of his children and a severe illness caused Breckinridge to undergo a religious conversion in the winter of 1828–1829, which eventually led him to abandon his law career and follow his older brother John into the Presbyterian ministry. Following a brief course of study at Princeton Seminary, he was called as pastor of the Second Presbyterian Church in Baltimore, Maryland, and ordained in 1832.

In Baltimore, Breckinridge edited the *Baltimore Literary and Religious Magazine* and its successor, the *Spirit of the XIX. Century*, between 1835 and 1843, and he was known as a militant opponent of intemperance, Sunday mail delivery, and Roman Catholicism. He also entered into the national debate over slavery and, while he condemned abolitionists and proslavery advocates alike, he argued for the gradual emancipation of slaves. Moreover, during the controversy between the Old School and New School factions within the Presbyterian church, Breckinridge helped initiate the "Act and Testimony" of 1834, the statement of the Old School party that outlined the New School's theological "errors," including the looseness with which it interpreted the Westminster Confession, and that was a major factor in the eventual division of the denomination in 1837. When the New School Presbyterians formed a new church body in 1838, he remained loyal to the Old School church.

Breckinridge resigned from his Baltimore pastorate in 1845 and became president of Jefferson College, but he held that position for only two years. His first wife having died in 1844, in 1847 he married Virginia Hart Shelby. They had no children. During that same year he accepted a call to be the pastor of the First Presbyterian Church in Lexington and was also appointed superintendent of public education for Kentucky. Under his guidance, public school attendance in the state grew tenfold, increasing from about 20,000 to more than 200,000 students in just six years. During that same period he helped found Danville Theological Seminary as a bastion of Old School Presbyterianism, and in 1853 he left Lexington to become the principal professor at the seminary. At the outset of the Civil War in 1861, when opposing sectional loyalties tore apart Kentucky, the Old School Presbyterian church, and the Breckinridge family, he was outspoken in his support of the Union and soon became one of Abraham Lincoln's chief advisers in his state. In 1864 he was chosen to be a delegate and temporary chair of the Republican National Convention. His son William and his nephew John C. Breckinridge, on the other hand, served prominently in the Confederate army. His wife died in 1859, and in 1868 Robert Breckinridge married Margaret White.

Besides teaching at Danville Seminary, he served as editor of the *Danville Quarterly Review* between 1861 and 1864 and composed a two-volume systematic theology, *The Knowledge of God Objectively Considered* (1858) and *The Knowledge of God Subjectively Considered* (1859). Convinced of the complete rationality of the Christian faith, he sought to demonstrate how every aspect of existence, including evil and human suffering, could be fit within the theological system he devised. Although he was severely criticized by Robert Lewis Dabney, a rival theologian at Union Theological Seminary in Virginia, Breckinridge's ideas were generally well received within the Old School denomination. Poor health eventually forced his retirement in 1869, but he remained in Danville until his death.

While Breckinridge was neither an original nor a profound thinker, his varied career in the fields of religion, education, and politics made him an important figure in Kentucky public life in the mid-nineteenth century. Within church circles, he was known as an acerbic controversialist, and his attacks on Roman Catholics placed him at the forefront of Protestant nativists in antebellum America. Despite siding with the Union in 1861, Breckinridge and his conservative theological views had their greatest influence on the development of the Presbyterian church in the South after the Civil War.

• There is no nineteenth-century biography of Breckinridge. The principal modern source for information about his life is Edgar C. Mayse's doctoral dissertation, "Robert Jefferson Breckinridge: American Presbyterian Controversialist" (Union Theological Seminary, 1974). Will D. Gilliam, Jr., "Robert Jefferson Breckinridge, 1800–1871," *Register of the Kentucky Historical Society* 72 (July–Oct. 1974): 3–4, is also useful. E. Brooks Holifield, *The Gentlemen Theologians: American Theology in Southern Culture, 1795–1860* (1978), contains a brief scholarly analysis of Breckinridge's theological work.

GARDINER H. SHATTUCK, JR.

BRECKINRIDGE, Sophonisba Preston (1 Apr. 1866–30 July 1948), social scientist and reformer, was born in Lexington, Kentucky, the daughter of William C. P. Breckinridge, a lawyer and U.S. congressman, and Issa Desha. Her father vigorously supported the rights of women and African Americans to secure higher educations. A rich legacy of political achievement and the prominent social standing of the Breckinridge family afforded Sophonisba many advantages in her early life. "Nisba," as she was affectionately known, excelled in school and as an adolescent began taking courses at the Agricultural and Mechanical College in Lexington. In 1884 she enrolled at Wellesley College where she studied Latin and mathematics, graduating with an S.B. in 1888.

The years immediately following college were ones of much emotional conflict. Breckinridge had dreamed of attending law school, but mindful of family responsibilities she accepted a position teaching mathematics at Washington High School in the District of Columbia, where the Breckinridges resided during the congressional term. Illness, followed by a recuperative trip abroad lasting many months, brought an end to her teaching in 1890. She returned home to Lexington in 1892 when her mother died unexpectedly. Breckinridge then read law in her father's office and in 1892 passed the bar examination, becoming the first woman to be admitted to the Kentucky bar.

Opportunities for legal practice proved to be few, however, and an 1894 trip to Chicago pointed to attractive opportunities at the new University of Chicago. At that time her father was embroiled in a sexual scandal that ended his political career. Eager to leave Lexington, Breckinridge began graduate studies in political science at the University of Chicago in 1895. She earned an M.A. in political science in 1897 and a Ph.D., magna cum laude, in 1901. Her dissertation, an important and innovative study of legal tender doctrine in England and the United States, was published by the University of Chicago Press in 1903. After earning her Ph.D., Breckinridge enrolled in the University of Chicago Law School. She graduated with the Law School's first class of students in 1904, thereby becoming the first woman to earn a doctor of jurisprudence from the university and the first to gain admission to Coif, an honorary legal society that recognized academic excellence.

Many years of professional struggle followed as Breckinridge sought a permanent place at the University of Chicago. She held several administrative and teaching appointments at Chicago over the years. Yet in spite of distinguished service, she rose very slowly through the academic ranks from her initial appointment in 1904 as instructor in the Department of Household Administration to her appointment in 1929 as Samuel Deutsch Professor of Public Welfare Administration. Initially one of only a handful of women on the faculty of a major research university, she won her full professorship in a professional school she had helped to found, the University of Chicago's School of Social Service Administration. Breckinridge retired as professor emeritus in 1942. Her career and research interests had gravitated from political science to social welfare and social policy, the latter two having become areas of opportunity for women social scientists in the early twentieth century.

Throughout her career, Breckinridge blended an avid intellectual interest in social problems and public policy with active engagement in reform. She was particularly drawn to the problems of immigrants, African Americans, children, and impoverished women in American cities. She taught and conducted research at the University of Chicago on these subjects, including some of the first courses in what would now be called "women's studies" ever offered in the United States. She spent her free time immersing herself in Chicago's vibrant reform community. By 1908 she had already become a prominent figure in Chicago reform circles and a dedicated member of many reform organizations.

Breckinridge's foray into Chicago reform politics owed much to her association with settlement leaders Jane Addams, Mary McDowell, and Margaret Dreier Robins, head of the Women's Trade Union League (WTUL). An active member of the Chicago chapter of the WTUL, Breckinridge served as a factory inspector in 1905. She lobbied hard and successfully in 1906 to enlist congressional support for a federal research project investigating the conditions endured by women and child laborers in the United States. In 1907 and 1908 Breckinridge helped launch the Immigrants' Protective League, an organization that sought to assist the foreign born in acquiring employment, housing, and education. That same year she began to teach part-time at Graham Taylor's School of Civics and Philanthropy, an independent social work training center with strong ties to the settlement house community.

A frequent visitor to Jane Addams's social settlement, she emerged as one of the most revered and influential figures in the extraordinary community of men and women at Hull House. A close friend of Addams, Breckinridge influenced some of the social survey and research endeavors of Hull House. For fourteen years "Miss Breckinridge," as she was known, took up residence at Hull House during her yearly vacation quarter from the University of Chicago.

Breckinridge's unwavering commitment to improved race relations were an especially notable feature of her academic research and of her reform activities. A founding member of the Chicago chapter of the National Association for the Advancement of Colored People (1911) and the Chicago Urban League (1915), Breckinridge devoted herself to the Association of Colored Women and the black Wendell Phillips Settlement. She served on a fact-finding commission appointed after a brutal Chicago race riot in 1919. Author of the penetrating "The Color Line in the Housing Problem" (*The Survey*, 1913), Breckinridge blamed racial prejudice for the growing residential segregation of African Americans in Chicago. Acutely aware of similar "race prejudice" within the university, she attempted (unsuccessfully) to integrate the women's dormitories at the University of Chicago in 1907. She met with greater success in securing financial aid for black women students at the School of Civics and Philanthropy.

Her colleague, dear friend, and close collaborator Edith Abbott joined Breckinridge in these endeavors for nearly fifty years. The two women met in 1902 when Abbott took Breckinridge's course, "The Legal and Economic Position of Women," at the University of Chicago. They became virtually inseparable from 1908 when Abbott, a brilliant economist, joined Breckinridge at the School of Civics. Together they helped persuade the University of Chicago to absorb the School of Civics in 1920. The School of Social Service Administration then became the first professional school of social work affiliated with a major research university. Though they lived apart for most of their lives, their rich emotional and intellectual ties sustained both women, neither of whom chose to marry. Breckinridge and Abbott undertook several collaborative research projects that led to a series of pathbreaking articles published in the *American Journal of Sociology* between 1910 and 1911 on Chicago's housing problems, *The Delinquent Child and the Home* (1912), and *Truancy and Non-Attendance in the Chicago Public Schools* (1917). In 1927 they founded the *Social Service Review*, which instantly became a leading journal in the field of social work.

Though Chicago remained an intellectual focus and her professional center for Breckinridge's entire career, she gained a national reputation for her social science and social policy expertise. A familiar figure to several generations of congressmen, diplomats, and presidents, Breckinridge participated in several White House conferences on children, advised the U.S. Children's Bureau, attended international congresses at the request of more than one secretary of state, and served as the U.S. representative to the first Pan-American Conference in 1933 at President Franklin D. Roosevelt's invitation. A lifelong Democrat, she abandoned the party to support Theodore Roosevelt and the Progressive party in 1912 in the hope that causes she favored such as social insurance, workmen's compensation, occupational safety and health standards, woman suffrage, and trade unionism would be advanced. A year later she ran for alderman in Chicago on the Progressive ticket at Addams's request but suffered defeat at the polls.

An ardent feminist, Breckinridge served as vice president of the National American Woman Suffrage Association in 1911. She campaigned for women's voting rights by stressing the connection between women's political standing and their economic status. Although not a pacifist, she helped form the Woman's Peace party in 1915, serving as treasurer. That same year she sailed to The Hague with a delegation of women from Hull House to attend the International Congress of Women and later joined the Women's International League for Peace and Freedom. Her experiences as a professional woman in twentieth-century America as well as her brilliant intellectual skills informed her 1933 study, *Women in the Twentieth Century*.

Thin and frail looking to some observers, Breckinridge was a woman of much personal charm who always retained the lilt of her Kentucky accent. Her impeccable manners and gracious style gave hints of aristocratic origins, but friends, students, and colleagues were equally struck by Breckinridge's warmth and democratic demeanor. Her indomitable spirit, fiercely liberal politics, and firm intellectual commitments remained apparent through a long life that ended peacefully in Chicago.

• The Sophonisba P. Breckinridge Papers are located in the Breckinridge Family Papers at the Library of Congress. The University of Chicago holds additional Breckinridge papers, including a fragmented but very useful autobiography in manuscript form. Among the many archival sources of further correspondence are the Graham Taylor Papers at the Newberry Library in Chicago and the Julius Rosenwald Papers at the University of Chicago. Among Breckinridge's many books and articles see especially *New Homes for the Old* (1921), *Madeline McDowell Breckinridge* (1921), a memoir of her sister-in-law, *Public Welfare Administration in the United States* (1927), *Marriage and the Civic Rights of Women* (1931), and *Illinois Poor Law and Its Administration* (1939). For revealing biographical sketches see James C. Klotter, *The Breckinridges of Kentucky* (1986), and a series of reminiscences in the *Social Service Review* 22 (Dec. 1948–Mar. 1949): 417–50.

ELLEN F. FITZPATRICK

BRECKINRIDGE, W. C. P. (28 Aug. 1837–19 Nov. 1904), political leader, was born William Campbell Preston Breckinridge in Baltimore, Maryland, the son of Robert Jefferson Breckinridge, a minister, and Ann Sophonisba Preston, who died when Breckinridge was seven years old. As the grandson of senator and U.S. attorney general John Breckinridge (1760–1806) and the first cousin of vice president and presidential candidate John Cabell Breckinridge, W. C. P. Breckinridge grew up as a member of one of the most prominent families of Kentucky. His father returned to the Bluegrass State in 1847 and became a prominent antislavery leader, state superintendent of public instruction, and college professor. Known to family and friends as "Willie," Breckinridge graduated from Centre College in Danville, Kentucky, in 1855. He began to practice law in 1857 but then attended the Danville Seminary, where his father taught. His departure in less than a year displeased his Presbyterian father, but the two remained close, despite later differences regarding the Civil War.

Breckinridge married Lucretia Clay, granddaughter of Henry Clay, on 17 March 1859; her death in childbirth a little over a year later was followed in two months by the death of the child. Marriage to Issa Desha, granddaughter of a Kentucky governor, came on 17 March 1861; they had seven children.

Starting an antebellum law practice, Breckinridge soon abandoned that for service in the Civil War. Spurning his Unionist father and joining the Confederacy in 1862, he rose to become colonel of the Ninth Kentucky Cavalry and fought with raider John Hunt Morgan in several of his campaigns. Near the end of the conflict, Breckinridge escorted Jefferson Davis in his flight south, then surrendered. The colonel returned to Lexington, where he edited the *Observer and Reporter* newspaper from 1866 to 1868 and rebuilt his legal career.

Very quickly Breckinridge became a leader in the state. Known as the "silver-tongued orator" for the abilities that won him national acclaim, he spoke widely and called out for a New South and a New Kentucky. Breckinridge led the more liberal faction of the Democratic party in his state in advocating an end to sectional bitterness. Though never a racial egalitarian, throughout his career Breckinridge took stands that won praise from the black community. They also cost him political victory. In an 1868 race for commonwealth attorney, he supported the controversial issue of admitting black testimony in the courts. When opponents accused him of favoring blacks, Breckinridge replied that on this issue he did: "Your prejudices blind your judgment. . . . In the after days, when the passions of this hour have cooled, when reason shall assert her sway, when the nobler feelings of your nature shall rule your hearts and judgment—in that hour you will approve though now you condemn me" (*Century Magazine* 31 [1886]: 478). Facing certain defeat, he withdrew from the canvass.

Political success did come his way in time; in 1884 he won a seat in Congress and held it for a decade. Balancing both the central Bluegrass agrarian and the Lexington business interests of his district, he became a spokesman for free trade and, in general, for the Democracy. John S. Sherman, who served in both houses of Congress, termed Breckinridge the greatest natural orator he had encountered, and a contemporary historian, E. Polk Johnson, called the colonel "the most eloquent of Kentuckians past or present" (Klotter, p. 153). Then, at the height of his career, the Pollard affair brought about his defeat by a very narrow margin.

After his spouse's death in 1892, Breckinridge married Louise Wing on 29 April 1893. However, that third union caused Madeline Pollard to sue for breach of contract, charging that he had promised to marry her instead. The trial that followed in 1894 produced sensational national headlines. It was revealed that Pollard had been Breckinridge's mistress for several years after they had met, when she was seventeen years old and he forty-seven. Breckinridge admitted the affair but denied the marriage offer. The jury disagreed and found for Pollard. The scandal ended Breckinridge's career.

Out of political office, Breckinridge became the chief editorial writer for the *Lexington Morning Herald*, a paper owned by his son Desha Breckinridge. Through its pages and through his continuing lectures, he began a fight against free silver, William Jennings Bryan, and, in Kentucky, gubernatorial candidate William Goebel. Breckinridge united for a time with the Gold Democrats, then as a fusion candidate with the Republicans. He served as an attorney for the GOP during the bitterly contested election of 1899, which ended with Goebel's assassination the next January. After that he gradually returned to the Democracy, and the *Lexington Morning Herald* focused on the improvement of public education, opposed black disfranchisement and racial violence, and favored other reforms. Influenced by his daughter Sophonisba Breckinridge, who was a leader nationally in women's rights and other Progressive Era issues, and by his son, Breckinridge became, in a sense, a progressive

Bourbon. Breckinridge died in Lexington, and his funeral, according to contemporary accounts, was the largest in the city since Henry Clay's.

• The chief collection of Breckinridge materials is in the Breckinridge Family Papers, Library of Congress. Other materials include the Craig Shelby Papers and the Breckinridge Family Papers, both in Special Collections, University of Kentucky Library. Many of the public speeches of Breckinridge were printed, and a convenient compilation of them is at the University of Kentucky. The *Congressional Record* should be examined for his years in the House, and the *Lexington Observer and Reporter* (1866–1868) and the *Lexington Morning Herald* (1897–1904) offer his editorial thoughts on a wide variety of subjects, including his own life. The fullest presentation of Breckinridge's life appears in James C. Klotter, *The Breckinridges of Kentucky, 1760–1981* (1986); an earlier work of use is Mary E. Graves, "Contemporary Scenes as Found in the Writings of W. C. P. Breckinridge" (master's thesis, Catholic Univ., 1960). Several books appeared on the Pollard affair: *The Celebrated Trial* (1894); Fayette Lexington (pseud.), *The Celebrated Case of Col. W. C. P. Breckinridge and Madeline Pollard* (1894); and Agnes Parker, *The Real Madeline Pollard* (1894). The University of Kentucky Library has the "Scrapbook concerning the Death of W. C. P. Breckinridge, 1904," which includes obituaries from the *Lexington Morning Herald*, 20, 21 Nov. 1904, and the *Lexington Leader*, 20 Nov. 1904.

JAMES C. KLOTTER

BREECH, Ernest Robert (24 Feb. 1897–3 July 1978), automobile and aviation executive, was born in Lebanon, Missouri, the son of Joseph F. E. Breech, a blacksmith, and Martha Atchley. Ernest gained early experience with mechanics by working with his older brother Earl in his father's blacksmith shop, which specialized in making carriages. In high school he was a stellar football, basketball, and baseball athlete and was offered a try-out with the St. Louis Browns professional baseball team. But he had his sights set on studying law and distinguished himself as a speaker, winning a medal for oratory while in high school. After graduating in 1914, Breech had to defer college because of inadequate family financing. To earn money he worked as a salesman and mechanic in an automobile agency that his father had acquired, thus gaining his first exposure to the automobile industry. He won a scholarship to Drury College in Springfield, Missouri, which he entered in 1915. Despite a strong academic record, Breech left college after his sophomore year in 1917 and moved to Chicago, where his brother Earl had found work for him in the accounting department of Fairbanks, Morse & Company, manufacturers of scales and weighing equipment. He later supplemented the income from this job by working evenings and weekends at O'Connor and Goldberg's State Street Store, the leading ladies' shoe store in Chicago. Also in 1917 Breech married his childhood sweetheart, Thelma Rowden, in Chicago; the couple had two sons.

In 1918 Breech began studying accounting at the Walton School of Commerce in Chicago. In 1921 he received a gold medal for earning the highest grade on the Illinois exam for certified public accountants. He later taught a lecture course at the Wharton School.

After working as a partner in a private Chicago accounting firm, in 1923 Breech became controller of the Yellow Cab Manufacturing Company. In 1925 the Yellow Cab Manufacturing Company merged with General Motors' Truck and Cab Division, and Breech and his family moved to Pontiac, Michigan, where he continued as controller of the consolidated concern, a GM division. In 1929 Breech became a general assistant treasurer at GM's financial headquarters in Manhattan, moving his family to Larchmont, New York. The following year he was named a director and GM's representative on the board of the new Transcontinental and Western Air, Incorporated (TWA), and he played a key role in getting the fledgling company organized and operating efficiently. In 1933 Breech helped to direct the merger of the General Aviation Corporation and North American Aviation (NAA) and became president and chair of the board of NAA. In 1936 he became a group executive at GM; two years later he moved back to Detroit and in 1939 became a vice president for GM's Household Appliances Division and the aviation affiliates. In assuming this new position Breech resigned as president of NAA but remained as chair of the board. That year Breech created a new Aeroproducts Division of GM, which had a factory in Dayton, Ohio, and made constant-speed airplane propellers.

In December 1937 Breech was elected to the board of directors of Bendix, a subsidiary of GM and a major manufacturer of aviation and automobile parts. He began an aggressive cost-cutting operation, firing thousands of people from Bendix payrolls and infusing management with top-flight administrators. By 1939 the company was back in the black. In 1942 Breech resigned as a GM vice president to become president of Bendix Aviation. Under Breech's leadership, Bendix made spectacular gains in output, tripling its production within one year to reach almost $1 billion in annual operations. During World War II Breech served as chair of the Central Aircraft Council for War Production, which coordinated the efforts of aircraft-manufacturing companies to make products for military use.

In 1946, while trying to sell Bendix parts to the Ford Motor Company (FMC), Breech met Henry Ford II. At the time, FMC was experiencing crippling financial difficulties, and Ford asked Breech to join the company, offering him carte blanche to reorganize and decentralize the chaotic FMC empire. Breech became an executive vice president and a company director of FMC in 1946.

Breech's task seemed insurmountable. FMC was an ossified one-man empire left largely without direction since the retirement of Henry Ford I. Its engineering organization was substandard, and with obsolete plants and effete products, FMC was hemorrhaging an estimated $100 million a year. Breech began his Homeric task by luring several former GM associates to FMC, including future U.S. defense secretary Robert S. McNamara. Working closely with Henry Ford II, Breech focused on decentralization. He broke the company into sixteen divisions and put many of his former GM associates in charge of the new divisions, explaining, "We expect each of our division managers to run his business as though he were president and had his own money invested in it." He also set about to reinvest FMC profits, modernizing its operations and cutting costs while increasing production. He instituted what he called a "betterment program," which included the construction of thirteen manufacturing plants in the United States, sixteen parts depots, and four engineering buildings. Breech hired thousands of new engineers and invested millions of dollars in research and development. These sweeping changes put FMC back into a competitive position in the American automobile industry.

FMC rewarded Breech for his services by naming him the first chair of the company's board in 1955, a position he held until 1960, when he resigned to allow younger men to assume "the heavy demands of day-to-day operational responsibilities both in their best interest and for the long-term good of the company." Henry Ford II succeeded Breech as chair. Despite his resignation, Breech continued for two years to serve on the product planning committee and as chair of a newly created finance committee, advising the company on financial policies. In 1967 he ended his career at FMC, retiring from the company's board of directors at age seventy.

The major blemish during Breech's tenure was the introduction of the Edsel Division, whose cars debuted in the 1958 model year. Breech maintained that he opposed the project because he felt it would be a costly gamble of Ford's resources on a car not sufficiently market tested. Ultimately, Breech said, he acceded because other Ford executives appeared enthusiastic about the development of the Edsel. (It was Breech who personally endorsed the name "Edsel" for the new division, named after the only son of company patriarch Henry Ford and the father of President Henry Ford II.) The Edsel Division proved short-lived. Targeted at the medium-price market, the division's cars went into production just when that market was undergoing a contraction. Moreover, Edsel cars became notorious for poor workmanship and unreliability and additionally disappointed consumers by failing to distinguish themselves from Ford and Mercury models. By 1959 the Edsel Division had ceased production altogether, earning distinction as one of the American automobile industry's most costly and infamous failures.

After resigning as Ford's chair in 1960, Breech served as a director for a number of companies, including the Rexall Drug & Chemical Company, the One William Street Funds, and the Lehman Corporation. His most important association was with Trans-World Airlines (TWA). In 1960 Breech was named one of three voting trustees of TWA, and the following year he was elected chair of the board, spearheading a program to create a new image for TWA, which was struggling to stay solvent. By 1964 TWA was the second most profitable airline in the United States. In 1969 Breech finally retired, becoming honorary chair and director emeritus of TWA.

In 1960 Breech, who had become a trustee of Drury College, donated a $450,000 classroom building to the college to house its school of business. Both the building and the business school were named after him.

During retirement, Breech lived with his wife in Bloomfield Township, Michigan, where he owned a farm that he enjoyed working. He also owned a winter home in Phoenix and a summer residence in northern Michigan. Breech died in Royal Oak, Michigan.

• The National Automotive History Collection at the Detroit Public Library maintains a file on Breech. A biography is John Mel Hickerson, *Ernie Breech: The Story of His Remarkable Career at General Motors, Ford, and TWA* (1968). An authoritative account is Allan Nevins and Frank Ernest Hill, *Ford: Decline and Rebirth, 1933–1962* (1963). Also useful is Mira Wilkins and Hill, *American Business Abroad: Ford on Six Continents* (1964). An unsigned interview with Breech, "Reviving the Giants," appears in *Nation's Business*, Oct. 1966, pp. 48–49. Profiles are R. Coughlan, "Co-Captains in Ford's Battle for Supremacy," *Life*, 28 Feb. 1955, pp. 84–86; G. Koether, "How Henry Ford II Saved the Empire," *Look*, 30 June 1953, pp. 48–52; and several unsigned articles, "Mr. Chairman Breech," *Newsweek*, 7 Feb. 1955, p. 58; "Pilot behind TWA's Success," *Business Week*, 23 Apr. 1966, pp. 102–4; and "Why Ernest Breech Gave Drury a New School," *Business Week*, 7 May 1960, pp. 26–28. Obituaries are in the *Detroit News*, 4 July 1978, and the *New York Times*, 5 July 1978.

YANEK MIECZKOWSKI

BREEN, Joseph Ignatius (14 Oct. 1890–7 Dec. 1965), Motion Picture Code administrator, was born in Philadelphia, Pennsylvania, the son of Joseph Breen, an Irish immigrant, and a mother unnamed in biographical sources. His father inspired in him a drive to succeed but also taught him the importance of his Catholic faith. Breen attended parochial schools in Philadelphia and completed his education at St. Joseph's College in that city. He married Mary Derin, a childhood sweetheart, and they had six children who survived infancy.

Breen was a newspaper reporter in Philadelphia for several years and then engaged in public relations work. He also served in the U.S. Consular Service for four years, with posts in Jamaica and Canada, and worked two years in the bureau of immigration of the National Catholic Welfare Conference. In 1926 Breen was publicity director for the International Eucharistic Conference held in Chicago. He made many prominent friends along the way, especially in the ranks of Catholic churchmen and laymen, and was known as a bluff, hearty, outgoing man who could handle any situation capably—and be as tough as the situation might demand.

Among Breen's friends was Will Hays, since 1922 the head of Hollywood's Motion Picture Producers and Distributors Association (MPPDA); a large part of Hays's job was to polish the public image of the movie industry in the wake of a series of headline scandals in 1922. The coming of sound to motion pictures increased public outcry against what many considered sordid and salacious material in films. To ward off censors from outside the industry, in 1930 studio chiefs agreed to voluntary review of their productions for undesirable material by the MPPDA. Father Daniel Lord, a Jesuit priest, and Catholic layman Martin Quigley drew up a Production Code for the MPPDA to spell out what must not be shown in films. In 1931 Hays appointed Breen head of the organization's Production Code Administration—generally known as the "Hays Office" or "Breen office" and viewed as a censoring body. More exactly, the Code was largely a reflection of strictures set up by the censorship boards of seven states of the United States (Fla., Kans., Md., N.Y., Ohio, Pa., and Va.) and the censorship board of Great Britain.

For several years producers were lax in following the Code. But in 1934 increased pressure was brought to bear by religious leaders alarmed at the glorified violence and lawbreaking some producers put on screen in gangster films such as *Little Caesar* (1931) and *Public Enemy* (1931) and at the crude sexual suggestiveness of films like Mae West's *She Done Him Wrong* (1933). The Code was rewritten and enlarged, and a "resolution for uniform interpretation" was adopted by the MPPDA in June 1934. As head of the Production Code Administration, Breen from then on was effectively the arbiter of all screen material, deciding what might be shown and what might not. He became the movie industry's "czar, emperor and dictator in one" whose powers came from the studio heads themselves (*Variety*, 1 Jan. 1935).

The staff Breen headed was made up of seven men from diverse backgrounds, including four professors, two former office managers, and a former theater owner; a 1946 article for *Coronet* speculated that "even in Hollywood no one outside the Breen office could identify them all" (p. 78). Their job was to review all materials that the studios proposed for filming and presentation to the public and interdict anything contrary to the Code. They met daily with Breen to report. Their chief areas of concern were depictions of sex, crime, and brutality; use of vulgar expressions; and demeaning remarks about religions and socioethnic groups. As far as possible, the Code office reviewed story properties and film scripts before expensive studio production began. Often they became uncredited collaborators with studio script writers, suggesting inoffensive ways of saying and showing questionable points. The staff also viewed all completed films and could demand retakes of scenes that went out of Code bounds visually or in line delivery. Only in exceptional circumstances could the Code be bypassed, as when Rhett Butler in the movie *Gone with the Wind* used profanity ("Frankly, my dear, I don't give a damn"), and it was allowed on the screen as part of a famous speech from the novel.

Breen's own job was to act as liaison with the studios and to persuade studio personnel to go along with his office's decrees. Most executives found that if they tried to get along with him, he tried to get along with them. When necessary, however, he would confront and face down recalcitrant producers. His ultimate weapon against the uncooperative was the threat to withhold the Code office seal of approval from a maverick film, which would mean it could not be shown in the 90 percent of the nation's movie theaters controlled by the studios. Almost as potent a weapon was Breen's personality: he could be as loud and profane and obstinate as any studio executive. One description said he had "a vocabulary as colorful as a whirlwind in a paintshop" (*Coronet*, May 1946). But he also had an unerring sense of what approach would work best with a particular individual. Another article put it thus: "Breen knew when to josh and when to genuflect . . . when to glad-hand and when to back-stab" (*American Film*, Dec. 1989).

Pleading exhaustion, Breen left his Code job in 1941 to become general manager in charge of production at the RKO studio but returned to it in 1942. In the years after World War II the power of the Code office, and Breen, began to wane because of changing public morality, the rise of television as the new "family" entertainment, the influx of mature European films, and the studios' divesting themselves of their theater chains by government order. Breen himself dated his office's decline from the successful exhibition of an Italian postwar film, *The Bicycle Thief* (1948), without the Code seal of approval. Other such floutings of the Code followed. He resigned from the Code Administration in 1954, after two years of declining health, and went into retirement. He died in Los Angeles after a long illness.

Though the tenets of the Code may seem petty and constricting to some in the present day, they reflected the mores of millions in the movie going audiences in the 1930s and 1940s. Studio personnel at the time agreed to abide by them, however reluctantly, because Hollywood filmmaking was then a major industry whose profits had to be protected. Breen, doing his job, saw to it that studio product followed the Code. A hard-nosed, profane former newspaperman with a street-fighter's grasp of tactics, he nevertheless successfully defended the purity of a nation's films. He stands today as a colorful figure from an earlier era of Hollywood history.

• Materials on the career of Breen are in the Billy Rose Theatre Collection at the New York Public Library for the Performing Arts, Lincoln Center. Details of his Code office work are in "Censorship at the Source," *Variety*, 1 Jan. 1935; Cameron Shipp, "He Keeps the Movies Clean," *Coronet*, May 1946; Leonard J. Leff and Jerold L. Simmons, "No Trollops, No Tomcats," *American Film*, Dec. 1989; and Leff and Simmons, *The Dame in the Kimono: Hollywood, Censorship, and the Production Code from the 1920s to the 1960s* (1990). Gerald Gardner, *The Censorship Papers: Movie Censorship Letters from the Hays Office, 1934 to 1968* (1987), covers Breen's activities and provides many excerpts from the censor's correspondence concerning specific films. Richard S. Randall, *Censorship of the Movies: The Social and Political Control of a Mass Medium* (1968), raises important issues involved in film censorship in the United States. Obituaries are in the *New York Times* and the *New York Herald Tribune*, both 8 Dec. 1965.

WILLIAM STEPHENSON

BREEN, Patrick (baptized 11 June 1795–21 Dec. 1868), diarist of the Donner Party, was born in Barnahasken Townland, County Carlow, Ireland, the son of Edward "Ned" Breen and Mary Wilson, farmers. Breen spent his youth in Ireland on the family farm, which was left to Breen, his brothers, and mother when his father died in 1816. Breen was reared to be a strict and devoted Catholic, attending chapel from the time he was a baby. His religious convictions helped him tremendously in later life.

Breen immigrated to Canada in 1828 for reasons that are largely unknown. He was joined in Canada by other family members and was married in 1830 or 1831 to Margaret Bulger, eleven years Breen's junior. Seven children were born to Breen and his wife by the time they moved to the United States in 1834. The Breens settled for around twelve years in Keokuk, Iowa Territory, before deciding to join the thousands of emigrants traveling to California.

The family began their journey on 5 April 1846 with three wagons; they had been joined by their friend Patrick Dolan. From Keokuk the family traveled to Independence, Missouri, and then to Fort Laramie in Wyoming, which they reached in the first week of July. At the Little Sandy River the emigrant parties had to decide whether to take the left turn, which led to the new Hastings cut-off, or the right turn, which led to the longer, better established route.

Breen and his family joined the emigrant group that became known as the Donner Party by choosing to follow the Hastings route. This route led the Breens and company to what was then called Truckee Lake (now known as Donner Lake), which they reached in late October. Truckee Lake was high in the Sierra Mountains, which were covered in snow, sometimes more than twenty feet deep. The Breens settled into a cabin built by previous travelers at Truckee Lake around 4 November after they attempted to cross the mountain range and were turned back by severe snowstorms. After selling some of his oxen to the Reeds, another emigrant family in the party, Breen immediately slaughtered the rest of his herd and dried the meat to be stored for the winter to come.

During this time of near death by starvation and cold, Breen tried to provide for his family by storing what little food they had and by praying every night for their rescue and survival. Because of their strong religious faith, Breen and his wife kept hope alive in their family, which may have been a major factor in the survival of all nine of the family members who were trapped in the snow for many months. The conditions were horrible, with freezing temperatures, minimal shelter, and virtually no food.

Breen also began keeping a diary at this time, for which he became renowned. The diary, composed of eight sheets of paper that he folded to make thirty-two pages, includes entries dated from 20 November to 1 March. The entries detail the weather and the deaths of company members, as well as any transfers of property that occurred at the time the party was trapped in the mountains. The entries also give the dates of the arrivals of the three separate rescue parties. There are many lines thanking God for their health, and short prayer-like sentences to God asking for mercy and survival. Only once does Breen speak in plain terms of his own suffering, when he mentions the pain he was in as a result of a kidney stone. Although he was suffering, he helped other members of the party by burying the dead and sharing and trading food and oxen hides. He also invited other party members and their children into his home when they could not care for themselves.

The diary notes the lack of meat and the principal food the family survived on, which was a glue-like substance made from boiling the hairless hides of the oxen for many hours. Many could not stomach this food, but Breen notes that his family ate it with a "tolerable good appetite." There is no mention of the cannibalism that the Donner Party is known for, but it has been determined that the Breen family did in fact survive in part off the bodies of the deceased. This occurred after Breen chose not to attempt escape with the second relief party, because his family was too weak. The family left the mountains with the third party days later.

Upon their arrival at Sutter's Fort in California, Breen gave his diary to the sheriff in case it could be of any use to determine the dates of deaths of the party members and the property transfers that occurred in the mountains. Breen never knew in his lifetime how valuable the diary was or what an important resource it would become in determining what actually happened during those months of entrapment and starvation. Although there are differing versions of what happened to the Donner Party and what Breen was like, the precise and thorough work of Joseph A. King, Breen's biographer, has made it possible to verify many of the events mentioned in Breen's diary and to better understand the man himself. The diary has been found to be factual in almost every instance in which it can be checked.

The Breens eventually settled in San Juan Bautista in February 1848, although they had very little money or property. By 1849, after one son had found some gold, Breen bought land, cattle, horses, and sheep. An eighth child was born to the Breens at this time. Breen worked his land and contributed to the growth and prosperity of the small community of San Juan Bautista. He died at his home in San Juan.

• The largest collection of Breen papers and documents is kept in the Bancroft Library in Berkeley, Calif. Along with newspaper clippings and other important resources, the original copy of Breen's diary is also at the Bancroft. For a modern, well-documented biography of Breen, see Joseph A. King, *Winter of Entrapment: A New Look at the Donner Party* (1992), which focuses on Breen's role in the Donner Party, is thoroughly researched, and contains many citations of important sources and the location of the important Breen documents. Also see George R. Stewart, *Ordeal by Hunger* (1936; rev. ed., 1986), and Frederick J. Teggart, ed., "Diary of Patrick Breen: One of the Donner Party," *Publications of the Academy of Pacific Coast History* 1, no. 6 (July 1910). C. F. McGlashan, *History of the Donner Party: A Tragedy of the Sierras* (1880; repr. 1946), and John Breen, "Pioneer Memoirs" (1877), a handwritten 81-page manuscript on file at the Bancroft Library (file C–D51), also contain information about Patrick Breen's life.

CYNTHIA MARIE CENDAGORTA

BREESE, Edmund (18 June 1871–6 Apr. 1936), actor, was born in Brooklyn, New York, the son of Renshaw Breese and Josephine Busby. He left both public school and home at the age of fifteen to roam the West, working as a farmhand and feed salesman for nine years. Despite his various vocations, Breese nursed acting ambitions and in 1895 obtained a job with an acting company in Eureka Springs, Arkansas, by lying about his stage experience. His first public appearance was at the Opera House there, playing a role in *My Awful Dad*. Other brief engagements with local midwestern companies followed, often with little to no pay.

Through the manager of one such company, Breese was hired for the company of Madame Rhea, at first playing heavies and later leads in standard plays. Next he joined the company of James O'Neill, playing Albert in *The Count of Monte Cristo* for his first appearance in New York in 1898. After four years with O'Neill, Breece spent two seasons with stock companies in Boston and Worcester, Massachusetts. In the 1903–1904 season, after touring with Otis Skinner and Ada Rehan in small Shakespearean roles, he returned to the O'Neill company. Following summer stock in Worcester and Hartford, Connecticut, Breece toured with Robert Edeson, making a successful appearance on Broadway supporting Edeson in *Strongheart* (1905). Breese took two roles in that particular drama, playing a football coach and an American Indian, for which he gained considerable notice.

Later in 1905 Breese was cast as the male lead in what proved to be the greatest hit of the decade, *The Lion and the Mouse*. He played John Burkett Ryder, a multimillionaire who is confronted by the daughter of a man he has ruined. Opinion on Breese's performance was divided. *Broadway Magazine* (Jan. 1906) said "Edmund Breese, as . . . Ryder shows again what a student of character he is. . . . We have not had such a real millionaire on the stage for years. It is as sharply-cut as was his 'coach' in 'Strongheart' last season." The *New York Times* reviewer was more reserved, writing that although "Mr. Breese is at times duly impressive, he lacks a certain sympathy with the role," playing only its harsher side. A wide range of leading men performed the part of Ryder successfully in the play's numerous touring companies. Though comparisons were inevitable, Breese received the prestige of originating the role on Broadway and opening in it in London. He played Ryder in the two theatrical capitals until 1908.

In 1909 Breese appeared in another successful play, *The Third Degree*. Again the play was more lauded than his performance, with the *New York Times* reviewer offering him only faint praise: "Mr. Breese gives an effective performance as the lawyer, though his acting is generally conventional and superficial" (2 Feb. 1909). Nor did the next fifteen years bring Breece stardom, although his portrayal of brutal Bill Sykes in the revival of *Oliver Twist* (1912) was admired.

Breece also tried his hand at writing plays during this period, coauthoring *The Love Leash* (1912) and *A Man's Home* (1917) with Anna S. Richardson. Breese likewise began working in motion pictures, first appearing in 1914 in the film version of a drama about criminals he had previously done on stage, *The Master Mind*. Thereafter, he appeared in films regularly until reviving his stage career, appearing in the audience-pleasing *Why Marry?* (1918) and *Welcome, Stranger* (1920), as well as many other long-forgotten plays. Breece maintained his star status when he played the vaudeville circuit and appeared in touring companies of Broadway hits. His last stage success was in *So This Is London* (1922), both in New York and on tour until 1924. After a Broadway appearance in *Chivalry* (1925), Breese worked only in Hollywood studios for ten years, although his parts were small enough that he was rarely mentioned in movie reviews.

A return to Broadway acting came in 1935, when Breese originated the role of District Attorney Flint in *The Night of January 16*. A few nights before its close in New York, he became ill. Ptomaine poisoning was suspected at first, but the cause proved to be peritonitis. Breece died a few days later in New York City. According to the *New York Herald Tribune* obituary (7 Apr. 1936), "Mr. Breese . . . had told his wife that he liked the part so much he hoped to die playing in it."

Breese was tall, dark, and athletic in appearance. Early photographs show him with curly hair. He was married twice, first to Genevieve Landry in August 1899 and later to Harriet Beach, although the precise date of this second union is unknown. His rating by critics over his career puts him among the "competent" of the second rank: the gist of his notices is that he could be relied on to perform a conventional role in conventional fashion. If Breese has a place in theatrical history, it is because he originated the role of John Burkett Ryder in *The Lion and the Mouse*. Otherwise, his career is notable for following so completely the usual pattern for actors of his generation: early struggles to gain a foothold, beginning stock company appearances far from Broadway, small parts on tour, roles of increasing importance on Broadway—but not always leading roles—accompanied by vaudeville stints and attempts at writing, and eventually a downward slope in motion pictures from leads to character parts.

• Materials on the life and career of Edmund Breese are in the Billy Rose Theatre Collection at the New York Public Library for the Performing Arts, Lincoln Center. For details of his early life, including his hand-to-mouth years, see his article "My Beginnings," *Theatre Magazine*, May 1907, which also includes portraits. Breese's stage roles are listed in *Who Was Who in the Theatre 1912–1976*, along with titles of various films in which he appeared. Obituaries are in the *New York Times* and the *New York Herald Tribune*, both 7 Apr. 1936.

WILLIAM STEPHENSON

BREESE, Sidney (15 July 1800–27 June 1878), politician and jurist, was born in Whitesboro, New York, the son of Arthur Breese, a lawyer, and Catherine Livingston. After graduating from Union College in Schenectady in 1818, he moved west to Kaskaskia, the backwoods capital of the newly admitted state of Illinois. There he became the assistant of Elias Kent Kane, the secretary of state and an old family friend. Breese read law under Kane's direction and was admitted to the bar in 1820. When the government moved to Vandalia in December 1820, Breese transported the state archives to the new capital in a small wagon and supervised the opening of a new office for the secretary of state before returning to his law practice in Kaskaskia. The 82-mile journey through uncleared wilderness took a week to complete. In 1823 he married Eliza Morrison; they had fourteen children.

Through Kane's influence Breese obtained several useful political appointments in the 1820s. He served as postmaster of Kaskaskia in 1821, as state prosecuting attorney for the third judicial circuit from 1822 to 1826, and as U.S. district attorney for Illinois from 1827 to 1829. When President Andrew Jackson removed him for partisan reasons, Breese joined the anti-Jackson faction in Illinois politics and briefly edited a scurrilous anti-administration paper, the *Western Democrat*, under the pseudonym of "R. K. Fleming." But his sympathy for state rights soon drove him into Jackson's Democratic party, and in 1831 he ran unsuccessfully for Congress on a platform that called for placing all public lands under state control. His popularity increased as a result of his service in the Black Hawk War of 1832, in which he rose to the rank of lieutenant colonel in a company of volunteer militia.

Elected circuit judge of the second district in 1835, Breese soon became noted for his lucid and forceful opinions. He had earlier achieved a statewide reputation as a legal scholar with the publication of *Breese's Reports* (1831). This volume made available to lawyers and judges for the first time an authoritative record of the most important decisions handed down by the Illinois Supreme Court during the first eleven years of its existence (1819–1830). Breese was elected in 1841 to the newly expanded supreme court, which the Democratic legislature had increased from four judges to nine. His most noteworthy early opinion, *Stuart v. The People* (1841), upheld the right of a newspaper editor to criticize the conduct of a judge and jury without subjecting himself to summary punishment for contempt of court. In a democratic society, Breese argued, a judge should ignore press criticism unless it was libelous, in which case he should seek vindication through a jury trial.

In December 1842 Breese won election to the U.S. Senate and promptly resigned from the bench. During his single term from 1843 to 1849, he loyally supported most major Democratic policies: a low tariff, a tough stance against England in the longstanding dispute over the Oregon boundary, the annexation of Texas, and the Mexican War. Although in principle he opposed federal grants of public lands to aid internal improvements within the states, he made an exception for railroad and canal projects, especially those that promised to benefit the state of Illinois. Thus, as chairman of the Committee on Public Lands in the Twenty-ninth and Thirtieth Congresses, he urged the passage of bills to aid the construction of two railroads: a transcontinental line from Lake Michigan to the Pacific and another line through central Illinois that eventually would extend southward to the Gulf of Mexico. A poor negotiator, he failed to gain support for either of these measures and suffered the added humiliation of seeing his hated rival, Senator Stephen A. Douglas, push through his own bill in 1850, which made the Illinois Central the first land-grant railroad in American history.

Denied renomination by his party, Breese returned to Illinois and plunged again into local politics. He served a term in the Illinois House of Representatives (1851–1852) and was elected Speaker in his first year. Although his continued efforts to recapture his Senate seat proved unavailing, he achieved lasting fame after he was again elected to the Illinois Supreme Court in 1857. This time he remained on the bench until his death and was chief justice (a rotating post) from 1867 to 1870, in 1873, and in 1874. A war Democrat during the Civil War and a judicial activist, he helped to establish the legal foundations of a modern industrial society.

Breese's creativity was especially evident in the field of tort (personal injury) law. Since the 1840s, American courts had protected developing industries from potentially ruinous liability by holding that workers could not recover damages for workplace accidents unless an employer's personal negligence had caused their injury. Recognizing the harsh consequences of this probusiness policy, Breese devised several important exceptions to the doctrine of nonliability. In *Chicago & Northwestern Railroad Company v. Swett* (1867), he ruled that an employer has a legal duty to provide a safe working environment and safe tools for his employees; in *Illinois Central Railroad Company v. Jewell* (1867), he held that an employer might be liable for retaining an obviously incompetent employee whose carelessness harms a fellow worker. Accident victims, Breese reasoned, should not have to shoulder burdensome medical expenses for injuries that they could not possibly have prevented. His views influenced other state courts and struck a more equitable balance between the interests of management and labor.

Just as he favored the claims of disadvantaged workers in tort law, Breese also supported early legislative efforts to regulate the economy in the public interest.

His most famous case was *Munn v. The People* (1874), in which he upheld the constitutionality of an Illinois law that established maximum rates for the storage of grain in Chicago's warehouses and elevators. The state might legislate on any subject that affected the general welfare, he argued, and its policy choices were not subject to judicial review. On appeal, the U.S. Supreme Court affirmed Breese's opinion in *Munn v. Illinois* (1876), a landmark decision that ushered in a new age of economic regulation, on both the state and national levels.

Breese, whom contemporaries regarded as one of the ablest jurists of his time, died in Pinckneyville, Illinois. Through his long service on an important court during a period of accelerated social and technological change, he contributed significantly to the creation of a distinctively modern American law that responded to the needs of an evolving democratic society.

• Major manuscript collections that include letters from Breese are the John Dean Caton Papers at the Library of Congress, the Ninian Edwards Papers at the Chicago Historical Society, and the Stephen Arnold Douglas Papers at the University of Illinois, Urbana. Breese's extralegal scholarly interests led him to write *The Early History of Illinois . . . until 1763*, which Thomas Hoyne edited for publication in 1884; the book also contains a valuable memoir of Breese by his friend Melville W. Fuller, who later became U.S. chief justice. John W. McNulty provides an able assessment of Breese's formative years in "Sidney Breese: His Early Career in Law and Politics in Illinois," *Journal of the Illinois State Historical Society* 61 (1968): 164–81. McNulty's larger work, "Chief Justice Sidney Breese and the Illinois Supreme Court: A Study of Law and Politics in the Old West" (Ph.D. diss., Harvard Univ., 1962), demonstrates the importance of Breese's jurisprudence for the emerging industrial order. An early study that offers useful insights into Breese's character and accomplishments is Stephen Strong Gregory, "Sidney Breese," in *Great American Lawyers*, vol. 4, ed. William Draper Lewis (1908), pp. 453–95.

MAXWELL BLOOMFIELD

BREESKIN, Adelyn Dohme (19 July 1896–24 July 1986), museum administrator and art historian, was born in Baltimore, Maryland, the daughter of Alfred Dohme, an industrial chemist and founder of the Sharpe and Dohme drug company, and Emmie Blumner. While a student at the Bryn Mawr preparatory school in Baltimore, she planned a career as an artist. Briefly attending first Bryn Mawr College and then Radcliffe College, she graduated from Boston's School of Fine Arts, Crafts, and Decorative Design in 1918. By this time she had become interested in museums.

In 1918, Adelyn moved to New York where she took a job as an assistant in the print department of the Metropolitan Museum of Art. Two years later, in 1920, she married Elias Breeskin, a concert violinist; they had three daughters. They divorced ten years later, over Breeskin's determination to pursue her museum career. Returning to Baltimore with her children, she became the print curator at the Baltimore Museum of Art. Eight years later she was named general curator of the museum. Upon the resignation of the museum's director in 1942, she was named acting director. She later stated that she was given the job only because "all the men had gone away to war." The museum's trustees extended her probationary period until 1947, when they officially named her director.

Among Breeskin's major accomplishments at the Baltimore Museum of Art were the construction of three new additions to John Russell Pope's original building and the acquisition of the Etta and Claribel Cone Collection of modernist works in 1949, including Picasso's *Leo Stein* (1906), Matisse's *Blue Nude* (1907), and Cézanne's *Mont St. Victoire* (c. 1898–1900). Alfred Barr, director of the Museum of Modern Art, expressing a common opinion at the time, called the collection "far too good for Baltimore." Breeskin was undeterred, however, and successfully pursued the Baltimore sisters' collection. Among the other collections acquired by the museum under her direction were the Saidie May collection of late nineteenth- and early twentieth-century art, the Gallagher collection of American painting, and the Woodward collection of sporting pictures. While director, she continued as curator of prints and oversaw the growth of the print collection from less than fifty items when she arrived, to over 80,000 at her retirement in 1962.

A life-long advocate of modern art, Breeskin served as the commissioner for the American contingent of the Thirtieth Venice Biennale in 1960. The artists she selected to represent the United States that year were Hans Hoffmann, Franz Kline, Philip Guston, and Theodore Roszak.

Upon her retirement from the Baltimore Museum of Art in 1962, Breeskin became director of the newly created Washington Gallery of Modern Art. She had hoped the gallery would be a forum for modern art in Washington, D.C., but her own ideas and those of the gallery's board did not always mesh and she resigned after only two years.

Breeskin then became a special consultant in twentieth-century art for the Smithsonian Institution's National Collection of Fine Arts (NCFA). She remained with the NCFA (later renamed the National Museum of American Art), serving as acting curator of contemporary painting and sculpture from 1968 to 1974. At the time of her death, she was senior curatorial adviser.

Among the exhibitions that Breeskin curated in Baltimore as well as Washington were "Abstract Expressionism" (1954), "Baltimore Furniture" (1947), "Age of Elegance" (1959), and (at the Smithsonian) "American Impressionists" (1982), "William H. Johnson" (1971–1972), "Romaine Brooks: Thief of Souls" (1971), "Roots of Abstract Art in America" (1965). Breeskin was also the author of many scholarly works. Her chief contribution to the field of American art was her work on the impressionist painter Mary Cassatt. Her interest in Cassatt, formed during her first days at the Metropolitan Museum of Art in 1918–1920, culminated in the two standard monographs on the artist, *Mary Cassatt: A Catalogue Raisonné of the Graphic*

Work (1948; rev. ed., 1979) and *Mary Cassatt: A Catalogue Raisonné of the Oils, Pastels, Watercolors, and Drawings* (1970; rev. ed., 1980).

Another hallmark of Breeskin's career was her dedication to promoting museums as places of learning. "Education," she said in 1964, "is the single most important advancement American museums have made. We look on them as places of learning" (Gilbert, p. 28). In 1964 Breeskin toured Asia under the joint auspices of the Smithsonian Institution and the U.S. State Department, meeting with artists and museum officials to share ideas on the role of art and museums in their countries.

Affectionately known as "Mrs. B.," Breeskin elicited devotion and respect from all levels of the art world. Her straight-backed carriage and, in later years, perfectly done silver hair, made her a striking figure in the halls of museums and art galleries. On the occasion of her ninetieth birthday, a large celebration was held at the National Museum of American Art with many artists and past co-workers attending. A short while later, while on a trip to Italy, she died near Lake Garda in northern Italy.

• Breeskin's papers as well as transcripts of interviews she gave are in the Archives of American Art, Smithsonian Institution. Avis Berman's two-part interview appeared as "Adelyn Breeskin: 50 Years of Excellence," *Feminist Art Journal* (Summer 1977): 9–14, and "Adelyn Breeskin: A Perseverance of Vision," *Baltimore Sun*, 30 Oct. 1977. See also Rose B. Gilbert, "Professional Profile: Adelyn Breeskin," *Museum News*, Nov. 1964, pp. 27–30; and Elisabeth Stevens, "Baltimore-born Adelyn Breeskin Is a Living Exhibit of Devotion to Museums," *Baltimore Sun*, 18 May 1986. Obituaries are in the *Baltimore Evening Sun*, the *Washington Post*, and the *New York Times*, all 25 July 1986.

MARTIN R. KALFATOVIC

BREIT, Gregory (14 July 1899–13 Sept. 1981), nuclear physicist, was born in Nikolaev, Russia, the son of Alfred Breit and Alexandra Smirnova. The family emigrated to the United States in 1915. Breit matriculated at Johns Hopkins University in Baltimore, and by 1921 he had earned A.B., M.A., and Ph.D. degrees in electrical engineering. In 1923, after a two-year National Research Council fellowship in physics that resulted in the publication of his first papers on quantum theory, he accepted a position at the University of Minnesota teaching quantum physics. He left the following year to experiment with terrestrial magnetism at the Carnegie Institute in Washington, D.C., on the premise that the earth's magnetism was in some way related to the theory of relativity. In 1925, while at the institute, he and Merle Antony Tuve, a doctoral candidate at Johns Hopkins, succeeded in bouncing very short radio-wave pulses off the upper atmosphere in such a way as to establish the existence of the ionosphere as well as determine its height and density. This experiment initiated the scientific investigation of the ionosphere and also served as a major advance toward the development of modern radar. Between 1925 and 1929, Breit and Tuve tried to develop a particle accelerator, or "atom-smasher," which Tuve succeeded in building several years later. During this period, in 1927, Breit married Marjorie MacDill. Although the couple had no children, he adopted Ralph Wyckoff, her son from a previous marriage.

In 1929 Breit became a research associate at the Carnegie Institute as well as professor of physics at New York University. Between 1929 and 1932, he analyzed what is now known as the Breit interaction, the way two electrons affect one another's velocity and spin. In 1931 he and Isidor Isaac Rabi, a physics professor at Columbia University, developed the Breit-Rabi equation as a means of measuring nuclear magnetic moments, or the spin of the protons in an atom's core. In 1934 he moved to the University of Wisconsin and, in collaboration with Eugene Wigner, a physicist at Princeton University, concluded that some force other than electromagnetism governed the interaction of protons and neutrons in a nucleus. Their finding led eventually to the discovery of the strong nuclear force, one of the four basic forces in nature. In 1936 the two collaborators postulated the Breit-Wigner theory, which explained in terms of the resonance, or energy level, of the neutron why some nuclei absorb stray neutrons while others do not. Their theory contributed significantly to the discovery of nuclear fission in 1938.

Breit soon realized that fission could be used to develop nuclear weapons, and in 1940, as a member of the National Research Council, he urged nuclear physicists to refrain from publishing their findings until after the end of World War II. Choosing to devote his attention during the war to the development of conventional weapons, he took a leave of absence from Wisconsin to work at the Naval Ordnance laboratory in Washington. While there, he invented a magnetic extrapolator that could in one day demagnetize a ship's hull, thereby safeguarding it from magnetic mines, whereas the old method had taken a month. But because he was one of a very few physicists with both the requisite knowledge and an American citizenship, in 1942 he was recruited by Arthur H. Compton, head of the Manhattan Project, to be coordinator of rapid rupture of the Fast Neutrons Project; in essence, to plan and coordinate the design of an atomic bomb. He resigned after a few months for several reasons: pessimism about the success of the project, which he felt was progressing too slowly; his own lack of confidence in his abilities as an administrator; concern about security breaches; and a sense that scientists were concentrating too much on developing the A-bomb and neglecting the development of conventional weapons. After his replacement by J. Robert Oppenheimer, Breit worked with the U.S. Army to perfect a proximity fuse, a device that detonates a projectile when it senses, usually by means of radio signals, that the target is nearby. He finished out the war as head physicist at the army's Ballistic Research Laboratory at the Aberdeen Proving Grounds, Maryland.

In 1947 Breit left Wisconsin to accept a professorship at Yale University. In 1950 he was asked to calculate whether the detonation of a hydrogen bomb could set off a chain reaction of explosions involving hydrogen atoms in the oceans and atmosphere. Breit's conclusion that such an eventuality was only remotely possible paved the way for the first hydrogen-bomb test in 1952. That same year, Breit collaborated with R. L. Gluckstern and McAllister H. Hull, Jr., to initiate the study of heavy-ion physics in an effort to facilitate production of the synthetic transuranium elements. After retiring from Yale in 1968, he became Distinguished Service Professor at the State University of New York in Buffalo, a position he held until 1973. In 1973 the Breits moved to Salem, Oregon, where their son lived, and they remained there until Breit's death.

In addition to his work as teacher and researcher, Breit served as associate editor of *Physical Review* (1927–1929, 1939–1941, 1954–1956, 1961–1963), *Proceedings of the National Academy of Sciences* (1958–1960), and *Il Nuovo Cimento* (1964–1970). He became a member of the National Academy of Sciences in 1939, a fellow of the Institute of Radio Engineers in 1945, a fellow in the American Academy of Arts and Sciences in 1951, and the first Donner Professor of Physics at Yale in 1958. He was awarded the Benjamin Franklin Medal for outstanding scientific achievement in 1964 and the National Medal of Science in 1968. Perhaps the greatest testimony to his contributions to the advancement of science and the education of young physicists also came in 1968, when 250 of his students, colleagues, and friends participated in a physics symposium at Yale in his honor.

Breit's 52-year career spanned one of the most exciting and productive periods in the history of physics. During that period the 300-plus papers that he published, most of them related to nuclear structure and particle dynamics, established him as a pioneer in the study of nuclear physics and a fecund source of ideas for his students and colleagues alike.

• Breit's papers are located in the Manuscripts and Archives Division at the Yale University Library. A good exposition of Breit's concepts, as well as some biographical data and a bibliography of his work before his first retirement, can be found in D. Allan Bromley and Vernon W. Hughes, eds., *Facets of Physics* (1970), which also contains the papers presented at the symposium in his honor in 1968. McAllister H. Hull, Jr., "Gregory Breit," *Physics Today* (Oct. 1983), pp. 102–4, presents a eulogy of Breit from one of his former students and collaborators. His obituary is in the *New York Times*, 22 Sept. 1981.

CHARLES W. CAREY, JR.

BREITMAN, Hans. *See* Leland, Charles Godfrey.

BREMER, Edith Terry (9 Oct. 1885–12 Sept. 1964), social worker and reformer, was born in Hamilton, New York, the daughter of Benjamin Stiles Terry, a history professor at Colgate University and a Baptist minister, and Mary Baldwin, the daughter of a Baptist minister. The family moved west in 1892 when Benjamin Terry became a professor at the University of Chicago. Edith spent most of her youth in Chicago and received her A.B. from the University of Chicago in 1907. The following year, she furthered her education by attending the Chicago School of Civics and Philanthropy.

While a student in Chicago, Edith did research on women in industry for the Chicago Women's Trade Union League. In the same year, she also worked as a field supervisor for the Chicago Juvenile Court under the direction of Julia Lathrop. While a resident at the University of Chicago Settlement, Edith became a special agent for the United States Immigration Commission, work she continued when she moved to the Union Settlement in New York City.

She moved to New York City in 1910 to begin a new position as a national field secretary for the National Board of the Young Women's Christian Association (YWCA), focusing on work with immigrant women and girls. That same year she established the first International Institute in New York City as an experimental way of integrating immigrants into American society. Although not everyone in the YWCA shared Edith's expansive approach to immigrant issues, she quickly gained the support of national and local YWCA leadership, and with the first International Institute began a movement that was to shape work on behalf of immigrants for almost half a century. In organizing the International Institutes, she gathered some of the most talented women in the country for her staff. Influenced by her past experiences in settlement work and convinced that existing social service agencies did not meet the needs of immigrant women and girls, she organized the International Institutes to provide basic education, employment skills, English language instruction, and social opportunities for recently arrived, as well as second-generation immigrants. The staff of the institutes comprised mainly immigrants trained as social workers. They extended the work of the institutes into the areas of housing, employment, and counseling services for immigrants.

Two years after arriving in New York, Edith married Harry M. Bremer, a resident social worker at Greenwich House Settlement; they had no children. The couple shared a deep commitment to social causes. Harry Bremer later served as a special agent with the National Child Labor Committee.

Edith Bremer rejected the popular "Americanization movement," and with it the idea that all new Americans should leave behind the culture of their birth and enter the cultural "melting pot." She asserted that immigrants should be first regarded as individuals with a unique cultural identity that should be valued by themselves and others. She rejected the "arrogant assumption that everything American was intrinsically superior to anything foreign." On the contrary, Bremer encouraged cultural pluralism and worked to foster respect for immigrant cultures. Under Bremer's leadership the number of International Institutes expanded rapidly. The second center was organized in Trenton, New Jersey, in 1912; the third in Lawrence, Massachusetts, in 1913; and the fourth in Los Angeles, California, in 1914. By 1918 a total of twenty-one International Institutes were organized across the country.

World War I brought further expansion to the International Institute movement, along with a great need to rapidly integrate new immigrants into society. By the end of the war, sixty-two International Institutes were founded, assisted in part through funding provided by the YWCA's War Work Council. Bremer's staff swelled during the war from between twenty and thirty workers to 168. During these same years, she was also director of the War Work Council and was responsible for training two reconstruction units of foreign-born women as nurses aides and social workers. One of these units was the Polish Gray Samaritans and the other was a Czech-Slovak unit. For her efforts, Bremer was awarded the Order of the White Lion by the president of Czechoslovakia in 1927.

A collaborative leader, Bremer believed the Institutional Institutes should be "possessed by the people they served" and she made immigrants equal partners in providing the services and in setting the policies of the organization. In 1928 a National Network was established to assign caseworkers to welcome new immigrants in New York and San Francisco. By the 1930s many International Institutes withdrew from the YWCA in order to expand their work by becoming independent centers for women and men of all religious backgrounds.

In 1933 Bremer founded the National Institute of Immigrant Welfare, later to become the American Federation of International Institutes, as a new agency combining the work of the newly independent International Institutes with efforts aimed at the reform of immigration laws and the promotion of cultural pluralism. Over fifty cities began to organize ethnic festivals under the International Institute auspices, and an Ethnic Heritage Study was undertaken to encourage the study of ethnic heritage by children, as well as to preserve the native languages of immigrants.

During the 1940s, as executive of the American Federation of International Institutes, Bremer was engaged in efforts to preserve the rights of immigrants from Japan, Germany, and Italy living in the United States during World War II and to oppose the internment of Japanese Americans in prison camps. During the years 1946–1951, the organization under Bremer's leadership resettled thousands of refugees from central and eastern Europe.

Though officially retired in 1954, Bremer served from 1955–1958 as acting deputy of the International Institute of New York—the center she founded in 1910. After a lifetime devoted to the welfare of immigrant people and immigration reform, Bremer died in Port Washington, New York.

• Sources on Bremer's work in the International Institutes movement are in the Archives of the National Board, YWCA, in New York City. The records of the National Board of the YWCA in the Sophia Smith Collection, Smith College, contain Bremer's reports and correspondence, c. 1916–1934. Additional records are located at the Immigration History Research Center, University of Minnesota. See also Nicholas V. Montalto, comp., *The International Institute Movement: A Guide to Records of Immigrant Service Agencies in the United States* (1978). Information on the Terry family is in the Colgate University archives. Bremer's ideas regarding work with immigrants can be found in her book *International Institutes in Foreign Community Work* (1923). Bremer published dozens of articles in the YWCA magazine, *Association Monthly* (renamed *Woman's Press* in 1922), 1913–1934. Other important articles by Bremer include, "Foreign Community and Immigration Work of the National YWCA," *Immigrants in America Review* (1916); "Our International Institutes and the War," National Conference of Social Work, *Proceedings* (1918); and "Development of Private Social Work with the Foreign Born," American Academy of Political and Social Science, *Annals* 262 (1949): 139–47. Helpful secondary sources are Mary S. Sims, *The Natural History of a Social Institution: The Young Women's Christian Association* (1936), and Raymond A. Mohl, "The American Federation of International Institutes," in Peter Romanofsky, ed., *Greenwood Encyclopedia of American Institutions*, vol. 1 (1978). An obituary is in the *Port Washington News*, 14 Sept. 1964.

SHERYL A. KUJAWA

BREMER, Fredrika (17 Aug. 1801–31 Dec. 1865), novelist, travel writer, and poet, was born near Abo, Finland, the daughter of a wealthy merchant and his wife. The family moved to Stockholm, Sweden, in 1804 as Russia prepared to annex Finland, then a year later to a country estate near Arsta, Sweden. Bremer's early life was unhappy; she was isolated and held under her parents' strict control, her days consumed by a demanding academic regimen of history, philosophy, literature, music, art, and languages. She escaped the pressure by consuming romance novels by the British author Fanny Burney. Her health deteriorated, and in 1821 the family took her to the south of France to convalesce.

As a young adult Bremer involved herself in philanthropic work. Her parents opposed her wish to become a nurse, claiming it was below her status, but she tended an invalid sister on the Arsta estate while the rest of the family wintered in Stockholm. Stories, sketches, and poems she wrote during these winters were anonymously published (1828) and welcomed by critics and readers. After her father died in 1830, Bremer governed her own life, choosing to remain unmarried. Between 1831 and 1844 she produced seven highly successful novels, all of which British novelist Mary Howitt translated in 1842–1844: *The H—— Family*, *The President's Daughters: A Narrative of a Governess*, *The Neighbours: A Story of Every-Day Life*, *The Home; or, Family Cares and Family Joys*, *Strife and Peace; or, Scenes in Norway*, and *A Diary*. Howitt translated Bremer's eighth novel, *Brothers and Sisters: A Tale of Domestic Life* (1848), the year it was published in Sweden. The Swedish Academy awarded Bremer a gold medal in recognition of her contribution to national letters after her second book, but her popularity was even greater in the United States and Great Britain. Walt Whitman and John Greenleaf Whittier were among her enthusiastic reviewers.

Convinced of the need for political and social reform in Sweden, Bremer left for a tour of the United States in 1849 to study the influence of democracy on domestic life, women's status, and individual self-fulfillment. Over the next two years she traveled in most of the thirty-one states and Cuba. She visited U.S. prisons, schools, and factories, witnessed slave auctions, attended sessions of Congress, met with women's rights activists, and was befriended by the literati of New York and Boston. On her return to Sweden she published her letters to her sister as *The Homes of the New World: Impressions of America* (1853), which included detailed observations on politics, society, and the famous people she met. A controversy ensued in the English-language press over the accuracy of her report on American life and the propriety of her anecdotes about such notables as Washington Irving, William Cullen Bryant, Ralph Waldo Emerson, and James Russell Lowell. Her defenders, such as an anonymous reviewer in *Putnam's Monthly*, noted that all was written in a spirit of kindness and candor that could not be faulted.

Inspired by American feminists, Bremer campaigned for women's rights in Sweden and organized women's societies for visiting prisons and caring for children orphaned in a cholera epidemic—efforts for which she has been remembered as the first Swedish feminist. She promoted volunteerism with the belief that charitable work was a means by which women could earn recognition and thus improve their status. Infused with feminism, her last two novels, *Hertha* (1856) and *Father and Daughter: A Portraiture from the Life* (1859), led to the founding of a women's rights journal and change in the legal status of unmarried women, but critics condemned her for making art subservient to social message.

Hurt by the negative response to *Hertha*, Bremer left Sweden in 1856 for five years' travel. Her journals of this time were published in English in three volumes: *Two Years in Switzerland and Italy* (1861); *Travels in the Holy Land* (1862); and *Greece and the Greeks: The Narrative of a Winter Residence and Summer Travel in Greece and Its Islands* (1863). She died in Arsta. Her sister later prepared a collection of miscellaneous writings, published in English as *Life, Letters, and Posthumous Works of Fredrika Bremer* (1868).

Bremer's fiction was neglected during the decades of the twentieth century when modernist literary tastes drove the sentimental mode into critical disfavor, but international efforts to recuperate women's writing and recover women's history beginning in the 1970s set the stage for revived interest in her. Her novels have been compared to those of great Victorian novelists such as Charlotte Brontë, Elizabeth Gaskell, and George Eliot, and her travel writing provides insights into the life of an exceptionally independent woman. Her letters about the United States are of enduring interest. Though Bremer's upper-class status limited her view of everyday life, her writings claim a place among those of other international travelers such as Alexis de Tocqueville and Harriet Martineau, who produced sympathetically critical records of nineteenth-century American manners and institutions.

• *Life, Letters, and Posthumous Works of Fredrika Bremer* includes a detailed biographical sketch written by Charlotte Bremer. Lawrence Thompson summarizes Bremer's views on American writing in "Frederika Bremer as a Critic of American Literature," *Edda* 41, no. 28 (1941): 166–76. Signe Alice Rooth reconstructs Bremer's travels in the United States, drawing on newspapers as well as journals and diaries of those she visited, in *Seeress of the Northland: Fredrika Bremer's American Journey, 1849–1851* (1955). Lewis Perry, in a chapter of *Boats against the Current: American Culture between Revolution and Modernity, 1820–1860* (1993), draws comparisons between Bremer's and Tocqueville's observations of American culture.

JANET GRAY

BRENNAN, Walter Andrew (25 July 1894–21 Sept. 1974), actor, was born in Lynn, Massachusetts, the son of William John Brennan, an armature winder for the General Electric Company, and Margaret Elizabeth Flanagan. The elder Brennan also was an inventor who, according to his son, "didn't know how to make money." As a result, Walter Brennan worked at odd jobs from the age of eleven, including driving a horse-drawn express wagon. He attended public schools in Lynn and nearby Swampscott, where the family relocated. After his junior year at Swampscott High School, he enrolled at Rindge Technical School in Cambridge, Massachusetts, where he acted in school plays, played tackle on the football team, and graduated in 1915. Brennan was then employed as a ditch digger on a road gang, an actor in a small repertory company, and a bank messenger in Boston. When the United States entered World War I in 1917, he enlisted in the army and served with Battery C of the 101st Field Artillery, Twenty-first ("Yankee") Division of the American Expeditionary Force in France. During his nineteen months of service, Brennan's unit saw action at St. Mihiel and Verdun, and he got a chance to act again in camp shows behind the lines. After being discharged in 1919, Brennan resumed his job at a Boston bank and later worked for a financial reporting service. He married Ruth Caroline Wells of Lynn in 1920; they had three children.

Finding his work low paying and unfulfilling, Brennan left Massachusetts for what he hoped would be greater opportunities in California. He settled in Los Angeles in 1921 and found employment as a salesman in the booming real estate business there. During the land rush of the early 1920s, when prospective home buyers came to southern California by the busload, Brennan was among those who made a small fortune. He invested his own money in real estate and lost it all when the housing market collapsed in 1923. Brennan subsequently sold stapling machines and insurance door to door and became an extra and stuntman in Hollywood.

Though Brennan never expected to forge a career in the still-young motion picture industry, he was drawn to it because of his previous stage experience. Beginning in 1923 he worked regularly, sometimes on as many as three pictures at a time under different names ("Philip Space" was a favorite alias). By the late 1920s Brennan got some acting credits, mostly in forgotten westerns such as *The Ridin' Rowdy* (1927), *Tearin' into Trouble* (1927), *The Ballyhoo Buster* (1928), *The Lariat Kid* (1929), and *Smilin' Guns* (1929). At some point during Brennan's early film experience a fortuitous accident resulted in the loss of his teeth and gave him a new, highly marketable film persona. Without teeth (or with false teeth) and with prematurely gray, thinning hair, a slender build, and the ability to bend his six-foot frame to look shorter and affect a weary look, he became a serious candidate for old men's roles.

After performing ably but anonymously in several pictures, including *The King of Jazz* (1930), with Paul Whiteman and Bing Crosby; *Baby Face* (1933), with Barbara Stanwyck; and *The Man on the Flying Trapeze* (1935), with W. C. Fields, Brennan landed what would become his breakthrough role in *Barbary Coast* (1935), a boisterous tale set in late nineteenth-century San Francisco directed by Howard Hawks and starring Edward G. Robinson and Miriam Hopkins. His portrayal of Old Atrocity, a character both comic and sinister, won favorable reviews from the critics and led to a ten-year contract with producer Samuel Goldwyn.

In 1936 Hawks cast Brennan as Swan Bostrom, a gentle Swedish-American who befriends a midwestern lumber king (Edward Arnold) and marries a dance hall queen (Frances Farmer) in the film adaptation of Edna Ferber's *Come and Get It*. Despite a dubious Scandinavian accent and the fact that he bore little resemblance to the hulking lumber-camp foreman depicted in the script, Brennan gave another notable performance and won the first award ever given by the Academy of Motion Picture Arts and Sciences to a supporting actor. Two years later he won a second Academy Award for his work as Peter Goodwin, the combative head of a family of horse breeders in *Kentucky*, directed by David Butler. In 1940 Brennan won his third supporting actor Oscar in five years for portraying Judge Roy Bean, the legendary turn-of-the-century Texan who proclaimed himself the "law west of the Pecos," in William Wyler's *The Westerner*. "His clean-cut characterization of the leather-skinned but sentimental judge is one of the finest exhibits of acting seen on the screen in some time," wrote Bosley Crowther in the *New York Times*. The performance upstaged that of Gary Cooper, *The Westerner*'s lead actor and one of the biggest stars of the day.

In the early 1940s Brennan made three more popular movies with Cooper, who had been a friend since their early days as fellow extras on the Universal lot. In Howard Hawks's *Sergeant York* (1941) Brennan, as pastor and confidant to Cooper's York, won his fourth and last Academy Award nomination. He also was the colonel, Cooper's hobo pal, in Frank Capra's *Meet John Doe* (1941) and the sportswriter who discovers Lou Gehrig (Cooper) and helps bring him to the major leagues in Sam Wood's *The Pride of the Yankees* (1942). Brennan, who his friend Hawks believed, "had an amazing quality, to be able to play anything and do it right" had become the best known and most in-demand character actor in Hollywood.

Brennan continued to turn in solid performances in a variety of secondary roles: as a fugitive in Jean Renoir's southern drama *Swamp Water* (1941); as a bearded professor in Fritz Lang's anti-Nazi thriller *Hangmen Also Die* (1943); and, especially, as Eddie, the inebriated crony of fishing boat captain Harry Morgan (Humphrey Bogart) in Hawks's comedy-adventure *To Have and Have Not* (1944). The New Englander was most at home, however, in the western genre. Sometimes lovable, sometimes scheming, always crude and cantankerous, Brennan's western codgers of the 1940s and 1950s were by far his most memorable characterizations. As Old Man Clanton, bête noire of Henry Fonda's Wyatt Earp in *My Darling Clementine* (1946), directed by John Ford, he was the masterful personification of evil. In Hawks's *Red River* (1948), Brennan played the more sympathetic Groot, cook and alter ego of hard-driving cattleman Tom Dunson (John Wayne). The consummate codger, however, was the crotchety Stumpy, deputy to Wayne's Sheriff John T. Chance in *Rio Bravo* (1959), Brennan's final film with Hawks.

In the 1950s television writers Irving and Norman Pincus pursued Brennan to star in their weekly situation comedy about a family of West Virginia mountaineers that moves to northern California. Brennan, who preferred movies to the relatively new medium, resisted for two years before agreeing to play Grandpa Amos, the well-meaning but meddlesome patriarch of *The Real McCoys*, which debuted on ABC on 3 October 1957. Adding a high-pitched southern twang and a pronounced limp to his patented codger repertoire, he created one of the best-loved and most-imitated characters on TV. The show, which featured Richard Crenna and Kathleen Nolan, lasted for six years and inspired a succession of rustic comedies, including *The Andy Griffith Show*, *The Beverly Hillbillies*, *Mayberry RFD*, *Petticoat Junction*, and *Green Acres*.

Because he came to enjoy its conventional five-day work week, Brennan remained in television long after *The Real McCoys*. However, *The Tycoon* (1964–1965), in which he played an Amos McCoy–like corporate chairman, and *The Guns of Will Sonnett* (1967–1969), which revived the western codger, did not come close to replicating his first great TV success. In his last short-lived series, *To Rome with Love* (1970–1971), Brennan took a supporting role as a retired Iowa farmer living with his widower son-in-law and three granddaughters in Italy. He also continued to act in movies throughout the 1960s. Among the films of his later career were *Those Calloways* (1965), a Walt Disney picture that allowed Brennan to play an old New Englander, and *Support Your Local Sheriff* (1969), a western comedy that cast him as Pa Danby, a comically ineffectual version of his brilliant Clanton character. For television he did *The Over-the-Hill Gang* (1969), a comedy-western, and its sequel, *The Over-the-Hill Gang Rides Again* (1970), with an ensemble cast that included Fred Astaire, Pat O'Brien, Edgar Buchanan, and Chill Wills.

Off the set, Brennan generally eschewed the ostentatious Hollywood lifestyle. Despite considerable wealth, including cattle ranches in California's San Fernando Valley and Oregon, he drove a Ford station wagon to the television studio and took along a homemade sandwich for lunch. A traditional Roman Catholic and devoted family man, Brennan deplored the introduction of risqué material to television in the late 1960s and early 1970s. In politics, he was a conservative Republican who actively supported the unsuccessful presidential candidacies of Richard Nixon (1960), Barry Goldwater (1964), and Ronald Reagan (1968). Brennan died in Oxnard, California.

• There is a clipping file on Walter Brennan at the Margaret Herrick Library of the Academy of Motion Picture Arts and Sciences in Los Angeles. An interview with Brennan, conducted by Charles Higham in 1971, is in the Columbia Oral History Collection. Brief biographical sketches and filmographies can be found in James Robert Parish et al., *Hollywood Character Actors* (1978); James Vinson, ed., *Actors and Actresses* (1986); Ephraim Katz, *The Film Encyclopedia*, 2d ed. (1994); Leonard Maltin, ed., *Leonard Maltin's Movie Encyclopedia* (1994); and David Thomson, *A Biographical Dictionary of Film*, 3d ed. (1995). For Brennan's work with director Howard Hawks, see Joseph M. McBride, ed., *Focus on Howard Hawks* (1972), and McBride, ed., *Hawks on Hawks* (1982). His television career is discussed in "Old Pro," *Newsweek*, 3 Feb. 1958, p. 65, and chronicled in Tim Brooks and Earle Marsh, *The Complete Directory to Prime Time Network TV Shows, 1946–Present*, 5th ed. (1992); Alex McNeil, *Total Television: A Comprehensive Guide to Programming from 1948 to the Present*, 3d ed. (1991); and Vincent Terrace, *Television Character and Story Facts: Over 110,000 Details from 1,008 Shows, 1945–1992* (1993). Obituaries are in the *Boston Globe* and the *New York Times*, both 22 Sept. 1974, and *Variety*, 25 Sept. 1974.

RICHARD H. GENTILE

BRENNER, Victor David (12 June 1871–5 Apr. 1924), medalist and sculptor, was born Victor David Barnauskas in Siauliai, Lithuania, the son of George Barnauskas, an artisan, and Sarah Margolis. Brenner's father practiced the trade of metalworking and also carved gravestones, chiseled in soapstone, cut out silhouettes, and engraved rings and brooches. At thirteen Brenner was apprenticed to his father; in addition to learning various crafts, he received instruction in history, languages, and the Talmud. After three years, he became an itinerant journeyman and augmented his repertoire with line engraving.

Whether it was to escape Russian police, who apparently falsely accused him of counterfeiting, or simply to find freedom and opportunity, Brenner departed for New York City in 1890 equipped with little more than his ability and ambition. Upon his arrival he secured employment cutting dies and took advantage of free night classes at Cooper Union. He continued his studies at the Art Students League and in 1896 enrolled at the National Academy of Design. He prospered enough to send for his brother and later for his parents and the remainder of his family. By 1894 he had established himself as a die-cutter for silver and jewelry, and it was not long before he began to obtain an occasional commission. A tiny relief of the composer Ludwig van Beethoven, dating from about 1895, which served as a pendant to a badge for a singing society, prompted Sigmund Oettinger of the City College of New York, a collector of coins, to bring Brenner to the attention of the American Numismatic Society, which immediately ordered from him a few medals and, together with support from his patrons Samuel P. Avery, James Loeb, and George A. Lucas, helped him gain recognition as a medalist.

Brenner went to Paris in 1898 to supplement his formal training. He acquired a thorough education in modeling from Denys Puech and Raoul Charles Verlet at the Académie Julian. He furthered his understanding of the medalic arts with lessons from Alexandre Charpentier and Oscar Roty, to whom he briefly became an assistant. Wanting to exhibit what he had produced during his stay in Paris, Brenner entered several pieces in the Salon of 1900 sponsored by the Société des artistes français, and they were awarded an honorable mention. At the Paris Exposition of 1900 he won a bronze medal for his three submissions. Before returning to the United States in 1901, Brenner traveled in Germany and Italy and branched out from solely creating medals and objects in low relief to modeling in three dimensions, with a bust and works of a decorative nature.

In New York again, Brenner taught a newly organized class in coin and medal design at the National Academy of Design and kept financially afloat for the next three years by cutting dies and making medals and badges. His goal was to be back in Paris, and his year there in 1905 benefited him greatly, with his three-quarter length plaquette of the painter James McNeill Whistler (American Numismatic Society) being a particularly fine example of a sophisticated composition, with its sensuous and fluid modeling and penetrating characterization of the sitter.

By the autumn of 1906, Brenner was in New York once more, intent on becoming known exclusively as a medalist and sculptor. Ironically, in spite of this resolve, he was soon to achieve the fame he so keenly desired, but from a coin. In 1908 Brenner designed the *Panama Canal Service Medal* (American Numismatic Society). During a sitting with President Theodore Roosevelt, whose portrait is on the obverse, Brenner showed him a model for a bronze plaque to mark the centennial of Abraham Lincoln's birth. Roosevelt admired the portrait and suggested to Secretary of the Treasury Franklin MacVeagh that it be used on a coin. The Lincoln penny, the first U.S. coin to bear an image of a president and the first regular issue to feature a likeness of a celebrated American, was placed in circulation in August 1909. The coin itself was widely praised, although the large display of Brenner's three initials met with considerable disapproval. MacVeagh's decision to have the initials removed came just one week following the appearance of the series, after more than twenty million coins had been struck.

The Lincoln penny was clearly the defining moment of Brenner's career; yet even before that commission he had attained a sizable reputation as a medalist. By 1903 his work had been acquired by the Paris Mint, the Munich Glyptotek, the Vienna Numismatic Society, and the Metropolitan Museum of Art, and it has since been collected by many other institutions, among them, the Musée d'Orsay, Paris, the Museum of Fine Arts, Boston, and the Museum of American History in the Smithsonian Institution, Washington, D.C. His expertise in his field led Brenner to write *The Art of the Medal*, published in 1910. In 1913 his personal life was enriched by his marriage to Ann Reed, a social worker. Over the next decade Brenner gratified hundreds of requests from clubs, universities, organizations, and societies to execute tablets, commemorative medallions, and prize medals, some with portraits, some with allegorical figures. The diversity of subjects include the *Ralph Waldo Emerson Plaquette* (1911), the *International Congress on Hygiene and Demography Plaquette* (1912), and the *Warner and Swasey Co. Lick Telescope Medal* (1920; examples of each are in the American Numismatic Society).

His talent and efforts notwithstanding, only a small portion of Brenner's output consisted of sculpture, principally in the form of portrait busts, such as *Simon Sterne* (before 1904; New York Public Library), *Charles Eliot Norton* (1906; Fogg Art Museum, Harvard University), *Samuel P. Avery* (1912; Brooklyn Museum), and *George Walter Vincent Smith* and *Belle Townsley Smith* (both 1913 and both at the George Walter Vincent Smith Museum, Springfield, Mass.). Brenner's over-life-size bronze group, *A Song to Nature*, surmounts the Mary E. Schenley Memorial Fountain, dedicated in 1918 in Pittsburgh. He died in New York City.

Much of Brenner's oeuvre, like that of most medalists of his day, was overly detailed because of the vast amount of descriptive and pictorial information required in such a small space. Technically, however, few individuals at the turn of the century were as capable of designing, engraving, and cutting of medals, not the least because of Brenner's industry and determination. Owing to his mastery of the genre, Brenner elevated the perception of medal-making in America from a trade to an art.

• The American Numismatic Society in New York City is the major repository of information about Brenner and of works by him. Glenn B. Smedley has compiled the most comprehensive listing of Brenner's oeuvre in the following issues of *The Numismatist*: "What Do You Know about Victor David Brenner's Works?" 94 (Feb. 1981): 333–42; "The Works of Victor David Brenner" 96 (July 1983): 1361–92 and (Aug. 1983): 1598–1606; "The Works of Victor David Brenner: A Supplement" 97 (Dec. 1984): 2513–16; and "The Works of Victor David Brenner: Supplement II" 100 (Apr. 1987): 774–77. See also Paul U. Kellogg, "Two New Worlds and a Sculptor's Clay," *Survey* 35 (Oct. 1915): 19–22; Kathryn Greenthal et al., *American Figurative Sculpture in the Museum of Fine Arts, Boston* (1986), pp. 329–35; and Elvira Clain-Stefanelli, "V. D. Brenner," *Medallic Sculpture*, Spring 1985, pp. 3–8. An obituary is in the *New York Times*, 6 Apr. 1924.

KATHRYN GREENTHAL

BRENON, Herbert (13 Jan. 1880–21 June 1958), film director, was born in Dublin, Ireland, the son of Edward St. John Brenon, a writer and journalist, and Frances Harris, a writer. Brenon was educated at St. Paul's School and King's College in London, England, where his family lived and where his father was a drama critic. Always volatile in temperament, Brenon broke away from his family at age sixteen and immigrated to the United States. From work as an office boy for a vaudeville agent and as a call boy at Daly's Theatre, he became an actor and assistant stage manager with Walker Whiteside's touring repertory company. In 1904, while acting with a stock company in Minneapolis, Minnesota, he married a local woman, Helen Oberg.

With the birth of a son in 1906, Brenon desired a more settled way of life and took control of the Auditorium Stock Company in Johnstown, Pennsylvania. He began showing motion pictures as part of the theater's bill of offerings. Competition from the burgeoning nickelodeons in the city led to financial straits at the Auditorium, and in 1909 Brenon went back into vaudeville with a comedy sketch, "The Intruders," written by his mother. *Variety*'s reviewer called Brenon "excellent . . . a very good light comedian" (13 Feb. 1909).

As the movies rapidly increased in importance, Brenon sought employment in that field and was hired as a scenario writer at the Independent Motion Pictures studio of Carl Laemmle in New York. In 1912 he had a chance to direct a film himself, a story of love and sacrifice called *All for Her*. It gave, in film historian George Geltzer's words, "abundant opportunity for those delicate sentimental touches which later came to be called 'the Brenon style'" (p. 117). The next year Laemmle sent him with a film troupe to Europe, where he rapidly made a number of films in England, France, and Germany, not only writing the scenarios and directing but also acting and doing stunt work as well. Two special successes were Brenon's four-reel film version of *Ivanhoe* (1913), using Chepstow Castle as a location and British soldiers as extras, and a spy melodrama, *Across the Atlantic* (1914).

Sentiment, heroic romance, melodrama, and exotic locations remained major elements in Brenon's films in years to come. He entered the realm of film fantasy, another recurrent element, with his next important film, *Neptune's Daughter* (1914), shot in Bermuda. The title role was played by Australian swimming star Annette Kellerman, and Brenon cast himself as the principal villain. Underwater scenes gave a magical, poetic air to the film, but during filming Brenon was seriously injured when a glass water tank burst while he and Kellerman were in it. The film was a great success for Brenon and Laemmle, achieving the longest New York run until *Birth of a Nation*.

Brenon was then considered one of the three leading film directors of the day, along with D. W. Griffith and Cecil B. DeMille. After a disappointing venture in producing his own film, *The Heart of Maryland* (1915), he went to the William Fox studio as a director. His work with Fox star Theda Bara, eliciting her best performances, won him special repute as a "woman's" director. He had an exalted idea of the film director's role: "The director must be . . . a dramatist, an author, a leader of men. . . . He must be a painter [also] . . . because a photoplay is never action alone; it is always, in part, a picture" (Craig, p. 115).

This conception of the artist-director brought him into a giant clash with Fox. He went on location to Jamaica with a large cast and crew in 1915 to film another spectacular underwater fantasy, *A Daughter of the Gods*. Believing he had a free hand, he spent huge amounts of money and time building sets and filming scenes. Fox paid for Brenon's extravagance because the cast and crew refused to finish the film with another director who had been sent to take over, but he used his legal right to re-edit and release the film without Brenon's name as director. Though Brenon sued, he gained no redress.

While *A Daughter of the Gods* was playing to large audiences nationwide, Brenon began several years of hard luck. He formed another production company, and his first film, *War Brides* (1916), opened to enthusiastic reviews and launched Alla Nazimova as a movie star. Its pacifist theme, however, did not suit the temper of audiences at a time when the United States was about to enter World War I. Illness plagued Brenon in the shooting of other films, and his employment of family members was not altogether a wise business decision. Financial problems held up the release of a later melodrama taken from the headlines, *The Fall of the Romanoffs*, until 1918, when its topicality was gone. Shutting down his studio that year, Brenon went to England to make a wartime propaganda film; the results of months of work were lost in a fire, however, and before the reshooting could be completed, the war's end made the film obsolete.

Brenon returned to the United States to become a citizen at the end of 1918 but then went back to Europe, where he could be free of Hollywood's "assembly line" studio system that had grown entrenched during the war years. He directed films in England and Italy and in 1920 was reported abducted by brigands on the side of Mount Etna while filming in Sicily. He was ambivalent about remaining apart from American filmmaking when it was undoubtedly the world leader. A letter from abroad, published in the *New York Times* (7 Mar. 1920) declared that he was "divided between [America's] undoubted mechanical and business supremacy, on the one hand, and the artistic instinct and achievement of the European . . . on the other."

Brenon returned to Hollywood in 1921 in a reluctant surrender to the studio system and its denial of creative freedom and power to directors. A successful series of films starring Norma Talmadge reestablished him as a "woman's" director, and he went on to further work with Pola Negri, Clara Bow, and other female stars. The two films for which he is best remembered, nonetheless, were not of this sort. His film version of *Peter Pan* (1924) was "a brilliant and entrancing production of this fantasy. . . . It is not a movie but a pictorial masterpiece" (*New York Times*, 29 Dec. 1924). His heroic romance *Beau Geste* was one of the smash hits of 1926. It required three months of location work in the Arizona desert, "one of the most elaborate location pictures in movie history," according to Geltzer, but "the results more than justified the effort and money" (p. 122).

Though Brenon had talked the studio into *Beau Geste*, he was unable to win approval of filming another novel, *Sorrell and Son*, in 1927. Believing deeply in this story of a father's sacrifices, Brenon left Famous Players–Lasky to make the film on his own. He declared in a *Theatre* article his desire to bring "truth and beauty to the screen without the aid of the old pap and hokum." His independent production was acclaimed; though some "movieisms" were noted, the *New York Times* said the picture "creates a far deeper impression than the usual film" (14 Nov. 1927).

The arrival of talking pictures in 1927 was deeply distressful to Brenon. In a 1928 article he called talking pictures "this blight of sound and fury," antithetical to "the art of the motion picture . . . the sweep of its canvas, its scenic beauty, its suggestive images, the finesse of its action or interpretative movement, all its significant photographic detail" (*New York Times*, 21 Oct. 1928). Unwilling or unable to adapt fully to sound, his career declined over the next few years. In 1935 he accepted an offer to make movies in England, by now a motion picture backwater. He remained there until the early days of World War II; his last film was *Flying Squad* (1940). Then he returned to Hollywood and a long retirement made comfortable by Los Angeles real estate holdings from the 1920s. He died in Los Angeles.

• Materials on the life and career of Brenon are in the Billy Rose Theatre Collection at the New York Public Library for the Performing Arts, Lincoln Center. Articles by Brenon are "Brenon Abroad," *New York Times*, 7 Mar. 1920; "Breaking Away from Bromidic Formulas," *Theatre*, Aug. 1927; and "Opposition to Sound Film," *New York Times*, 21 Oct. 1928. Contemporary views of Brenon include Johnstone Craig, "The Face That Drives," *Photoplay*, Nov. 1915; Randolph Bartlett, "Brenon—The Man," *Photoplay*, Mar. 1918; and Randolph Bartlett, "Seventy-two Reels of Bad Luck," *Photoplay*, Dec. 1918. Biographical sketches are George Geltzer, "Herbert Brenon," *Films in Review*, Mar. 1955; "Herbert Brenon," in *World Film Directors*, vol. 1: *1890–1945*, ed. John Wakeman (1987). An obituary is in the *New York Times*, 23 June 1958.

WILLIAM STEPHENSON

BRENT, Charles Henry (9 Apr. 1862–27 Mar. 1929), bishop and Christian ecumenist, was born in Newcastle, Ontario, Canada, the son of Rev. Henry Brent, rector of the local Anglican parish, and Frances

Sophia Cummings. His mother filled the rectory with music and many books and was a close companion of her ten children. Although Brent's father was nearly twenty years older than his wife, he, too, shared fully in the children's affections and interests.

After attending the limited Newcastle public school, Brent entered Trinity College School and then the University of Toronto. After graduating, he taught school for two years while reading for Holy Orders. He was ordained to the priesthood in 1887 by Bishop Arthur Sweatman of Toronto, but because there was no opening for him in that diocese, Brent moved to Buffalo, New York, where, in quick succession, he was identified with the Episcopal parishes of St. John's, St. Paul's, and St. Andrew's. A dispute with Arthur Cleveland Coxe, the bishop of Western New York, over Brent's use of altar candles led to Brent's entering the Community of St. John the Evangelist (the "Cowley Fathers") in Boston whose superior at the time, Father Arthur C. A. Hall, was a friend of Brent.

Brent's association with the Cowley Fathers ended abruptly when the order's motherhouse in England summoned Father Hall to explain why he had agreed to the election of low church Phillips Brooks as bishop of Massachusetts. Brent accompanied Hall to England to protest what he considered the order's unjust treatment of his friend. He returned to Boston, but not to the Community of St. John, because, having seen Hall's difficulty, he doubted he could ever accept the monastic vow of obedience. Instead, with Rev. Henry M. Torbert, a former Cowley monk, Brent entered into the work of St. Stephen's Mission, a slum church in Boston's South End.

Brent's work at St. Stephen's, and his writings during his ten years there, became widely known in the Episcopal church. Just as he was about to be appointed to a professorship at the General Theological Seminary in New York City in 1901, he was elected bishop of the Philippine Islands by the General Convention then meeting in San Francisco. He was consecrated in Boston's Emmanuel Church and then sailed to the Philippines in the company of Governor William H. Taft by way of Rome, where Taft attempted to negotiate with the Vatican about the American appropriation of church property on the islands.

Brent's years as bishop of the Philippines (1901–1917) were characterized by his eager cooperation with all other religions, including non-Christian, and his friendship with a broad range of authorities there. He founded the Cathedral of Saints Mary and John as well as hospitals and schools. Always adept at tennis, rugby, hockey, polo, and, later, golf, Brent set up tennis courts, bowling alleys, and swimming pools on the cathedral grounds and encouraged their use. He considered the American army and navy personnel a special responsibility but at the same time was sensitive to and outspoken about the exploitation of native Filipinos. His sincere enthusiasm and magnetic leadership drew men and women to assist him in the Philippines. Brent also built a reputation as a scholar, and this led to the Paddock Lectures (1904) at the General Theological Seminary and the Noble Lectures (1907) at Harvard. He was twice elected bishop of Washington, D.C., and once to the Diocese of New Jersey. He declined these calls despite physicians' advice that the hot climate of the Philippines was damaging his heart.

Perhaps Brent's most conspicuous effort in the Philippines was his work to abolish the opium trade. He urged President Theodore Roosevelt (1858–1919) to call an international conference on opium. Three such conferences eventually convened, in Shanghai (1909), The Hague (1911), and Geneva (1924). Brent was disappointed that these conferences appeared to have sparse results, and he put much of the blame on the British Empire's protection of the opium trade in India.

Brent had long favored American intervention in World War I, and in 1917 he visited the military facilities and his friend General Leonard Wood at Plattsburg, New York. While in upper New York State, Brent was asked by Canadian authorities to visit their troops in Europe, which he proceeded to do. He returned to the Philippines in July 1917. Soon after, he was elected bishop of Western New York and, at about the same time, was asked to return to Europe as a representative of the War Council of the Young Men's Christian Association. Brent's friend, General John J. Pershing had been critical of the War Council, and it was hoped that the bishop could neutralize the general's antagonism. Very soon, Pershing invited Bishop Brent to be senior headquarters chaplain of the American Expeditionary Force. Brent reorganized the American chaplains to serve without insignia or rank (an innovation that was discontinued after the armistice).

Brent assumed duties as bishop of Western New York in 1919, and almost immediately the diocese was invigorated by his ability to inspire co-workers. Such foibles as his fast driving, or his frequent errors in overestimating other peoples' capabilities, endeared him to his new diocese, although it must be added that the bishop's frequent and long absences made some of his colleagues restive. For, by 1920, Brent was entering the final phase of his career: the advancement of cooperation and unity between Christian churches throughout the world.

Brent sought to explore areas of preexisting theological agreement and possible united action. A milestone had been the 1910 World Missionary Conference held in Edinburgh. An important forerunner of the ecumenical movement, it was attended by representatives of all mainstream Protestant church bodies. Brent had been present, and he subsequently thought that authentic unity, rather than limited cooperation between churches, was possible within a century. He urged that a world conference be held to establish bases of agreement. Brent described his views in *The Mount of Vision* (1918). A preliminary world conference meeting was held in Geneva in 1920; forty nations and seventy churches were represented. Finally, after several more preliminary meetings, Brent presided at the great World Conference on Faith and Order held in Lausanne, Switzerland, in 1927. Brent was delighted because the ideal of Christian unity widened at the 1927 conference. Obstacles seemed to be less formidable, and there was a definite sharing of agreement as well as the expected declarations of disagreement. The Lausanne Conference was a major step toward Christian congeniality, and Brent anticipated further steps toward union in the months after Lausanne. It was his persistent follow-up committee work after the 1927 conference that hastened his death.

The Lausanne conference was the culmination of Brent's career. He returned to the Diocese of Western New York, but progressing heart disease prevented his full participation in diocesan affairs. Brent never married, and in his later years two of his sisters kept house for him. In November 1928 he sailed for England, having been appointed to attend the enthronement of the archbishop of Canterbury in December. He had planned to spend the winter in ongoing ecumenical discussions on the Continent, but for most of that time he remained convalescent in the home of the American ambassador to the Court of St. James. He died in Lausanne and is buried there.

• Limited primary material on Bishop Brent may be found in the archives of the Episcopal church (Austin, Tex.), the Diocese of Western New York (Buffalo), and in the Randall papers, Maryland Diocesan Archives. Brent published at least nineteen books, which are collections of his lectures and sermons as well as books of prayers and devotions. The most popular, in addition to *The Mount of Vision*, are *With God in the World* (1899), *Adventure for God* (1905), and *The Mind of Jesus Christ* (1908). Also see reprints of two of Brent's sermons, "The Way to Peace," Episcopal Church *Historical Magazine* 27 (Dec. 1958): 332–39, and "Creation, Old and New," a sermon introducing the ecumenical movement, *Historical Magazine* 19 (June 1950): 139–44. The first biography of Brent is Eleanor Slater, *Charles Henry Brent* (1932). The biography of Brent that is considered "official" is by Alexander C. Zabriskie, *Bishop Brent* (1948). Frederick Ward Kates, ed., *Things That Matter: The Best of the Writings of Bishop Brent* (1949), is a succinct but excellent biography by a friend; among its contents are an article that Brent had prepared for his diocesan magazine, *Our Diocesan Fellowship*, which was published posthumously, quotations from Brent's sermons and diaries, and other excerpts from his writings. Also see by Kates (as editor) "My Little Book of Praise," *Historical Magazine* 27 (June 1958): 89–111; "The Inner Life of a Modern Day Saint," *Historical Magazine* 26 (June 1957): 123–53; "'Walking with God': A Devotional Miscellany from the Unpublished Papers of Bishop Charles Henry Brent," *Historical Magazine* 25 (Dec. 1956): 317–52; and "An Appreciation of Charles Henry Brent," *Historical Magazine* 28 (Sept. 1959): 267–72.

JAMES ELLIOTT LINDSLEY

BRENT, Linda. *See* Jacobs, Harriet.

BRENT, Margaret (1601–1670?), landowner and colonial leader, was born in England, the daughter of Richard Brent, lord of Admington and Lark Stoke in the county of Gloucester, England, and Elizabeth Reed.

When Margaret Brent was about thirty-seven years old, she traveled to the New World with her sister Mary, brothers Giles and Fulke, and their servants. They landed at St. Mary's (later St. Marys) Maryland, in November 1638. Although the two sisters traveled with their brothers, they did not depend on them for their economic survival. They arrived with servants as well as the means to procure large land grants from the proprietor, Lord Baltimore (Cecilius Calvert). Claiming 2,000 acres and their manorial rights, Margaret and Mary established themselves in a feudal landed system much the same as their neighbors had. Thus the Brents quickly acquired political favor as well as land. Margaret obtained a land patent in 1639 for 70.5 acres in St. Mary's, calling the tract "Sisters Freehold." In doing so, she became the first woman in Maryland to obtain title to land in her own right.

Within a few years of her arrival, Margaret Brent had also received 1,000 acres from her brother Giles as payment of a debt. Located on Kent Island, this tract contained a mill, a house, and numerous livestock. As a further symbol of her success, Brent lent money to others, an action that often brought her to the colony's court, in order to collect debts. In the period from 1642 to 1650 Brent appeared in court records no fewer than 134 times, usually as the plaintiff, and in most cases the decision reached was in her favor.

The Brent family, specifically Margaret and her brother Giles, found themselves in influential positions within the colonial government and political realm. One of the assumed reasons for the Brent influence is the possible marriage of Margaret's sister Anne to Governor Leonard Calvert, a brother of Lord Baltimore. Brent, along with Governor Calvert, shared guardianship of Mary Kittamaquund, the daughter of the chief of the Piscataway Indians, who had been sent to be educated among whites. Brent also assisted in the governor's attempt to regain control of Maryland's government after a two-year absence. The governor left Maryland in 1643, spending the year in England. Upon his return in 1644 he discovered the colony on the verge of an insurrection led by William Claiborne and Richard Ingle, who had gained control of some regions. Residents protested the control that the Catholic government had over a predominantly Protestant colony. Fleeing to Virginia, the governor did not return to Maryland until August 1646, at which time he regained control of the government with the aid of recruited soldiers, whom Brent may have helped to assemble.

When Governor Calvert suddenly died in May 1647, Brent was named executor of his estate, and Thomas Greene became governor of Maryland. As executor, Brent had the power to "take all and pay all," a circumstance that she believed was her right. She also was appointed attorney for the proprietor, so that rents could be collected and finances administered. She proved a wise choice as executor of Calvert's estate. She handled problems concerning the payment of soldiers who put down the insurrection as well as a shortage of food supplies. By importing corn from Virginia and paying the soldiers from the sale of cattle from Lord Baltimore's estate (Governor Calvert's estate having been insufficient to cover costs), Brent kept peace within the colony. She did not, however, keep peace with Lord Baltimore, who protested the sale of his brother's property to meet the financial requirements of the colony. When Brent negotiated with Lord Baltimore, both the Maryland assembly and the new governor, Greene, backed her positions. And while Brent dealt with financial and administrative problems, Greene reestablished governmental control over the colony.

While Brent was the executor of Calvert's estate, she also held his power of attorney, and during that time she challenged the governing body in a way that makes her distinctive in Maryland history. On 21 January 1648 she asked to be given two votes in the colonial assembly, one as a freeholder, the other as the proprietor's attorney. Despite her service to and leadership in the colony, she was denied on the basis of her sex any right to vote in the Maryland assembly.

The success of a Protestant Parliament in England also affected the influence and success that the Brents had in Maryland. With the Protestants in power in England, Lord Baltimore felt that his Catholic charter might be in danger, and therefore he attempted to disassociate himself from any Catholic colonial influence, specifically that of Thomas Greene and the Brents. Greene was replaced as governor by William Stone, a Protestant. The Brents, suspected of gaining too much influence and property through Governor Calvert's death and Mary Kittamaquund (Giles Brent had married her), were also in effect removed from the scene.

Because of Margaret's inability to acquire the vote in the colonial legislature and her family's disapproval by Lord Baltimore, the Brents left Maryland. Giles went to Virginia in 1650, Margaret and Mary following shortly thereafter. They acquired lands in Westmoreland County in the Northern Neck of Virginia, brought large groups of settlers to the region, and assisted greatly in the development of that portion of Virginia. On her Virginia plantation, which she named "Peace," Brent lived her remaining days uneventfully; at least it appears as such from her absence from the public record. Brent, who never married, died in Westmoreland County. While the exact date of her death, like that of her birth, is unknown, her will was admitted to probate on 19 May 1671.

In the words of historian Julia C. Spruill, Brent "was one of the most prominent personages in [Maryland], whose business and public activities filled many pages of court records and suggest a career which the most ambitious of modern feminists might envy."

• Information on Brent and her family is located at the Archives of Maryland, vols. 1, 4, and 10, and in the Provincial Court Deeds in the Hall of Records, Annapolis. Sources specifically devoted to Brent include Julia Cherry Spruill, "Mistress Margaret Brent, Spinster," *Maryland Historical Magazine*, Dec. 1934, pp. 259–68; Spruill, *Women's Life and Work in the Southern Colonies* (1938); and Mary E. W. Ramey, *Chronicles of Mistress Margaret Brent* (1915). W. B. Chilton addresses the Brent family genealogy in several issues of the *Virginia Magazine of History and Biography*, mainly in the years from 1905 to 1912, especially Apr. 1905 and Jan., Apr., and July 1908. See also James Walter Thomas, *Chronicles of Colonial Maryland* (1913); Matthew Page Andrews, *The Founding of Maryland* (1933); John L. Bozman, *History of Maryland* (1837); Clayton Colman Hall, ed., *Narratives of Early Maryland, 1633–1684* (1910); and Edwin Warfield Beitzell, *The Jesuit Missions of St. Mary's County, Maryland* (1959).

STEPHANIE A. CARPENTER

BRENTANO, Lorenz (4 Nov. 1813–17 Sept. 1891), German political leader, journalist, and congressman, was born in Mannheim, in the German state of Baden, the son of Peter Paul Bartholomaeus Brentano, a wholesale merchant, and Helene Haeger. He studied law at universities in Heidelberg, Freiburg, and Giessen and afterward practiced in Rastatt and Bruchsal before returning to Mannheim. In 1837 Brentano married Caroline Lentz; the fate of this union is unclear, but Brentano married a second time in later life. Elected to Baden's chamber of deputies in 1845, Brentano fell in with a liberal faction clustered around Friedrich Hecker and Adam Itzstein. He did not participate in the abortive republican insurrections in Baden in 1848, but he subsequently served as counsel for several of the arrested ringleaders, including Gustav Struve, probably saving their lives by securing a civil proceeding rather than a military trial. Brentano also became involved in the broader movement for German unification and constitutional government and was elected to the Frankfurt assembly.

With prominent Baden insurrectionaries in jail or exiled, the more cautious Brentano played a larger role in the final swell of Germany's revolutionary tide of 1848–1849. As local democratic clubs multiplied in Baden, Brentano took the lead in 1849 in welding them into a larger movement. By May he headed a state committee appointed to act on behalf of the clubs. The committee quickly drew up resolutions calling for fundamental political reform, including acceptance of the German constitution crafted by the Frankfurt assembly, the election of a constituent assembly for Baden, and guarantee of trial by jury, but it also embraced such measures as a progressive income tax and pensions for the disabled. After the grand duke fled Baden in mid-May, the state committee became a provisional government. Formally the minister of the interior, Brentano also sat on a four-man executive body charged with executing the committee's decrees. At the beginning of June the larger state committee yielded its authority to a five-man governing body, of which Brentano was a prominent member. Some two weeks later Baden's new constituent assembly placed even greater responsibilities in his hands, naming Brentano to a triumvirate granted nearly dictatorial powers.

Yet the lifespan of the government Brentano led would be counted in weeks. As with many revolutionary movements, bitter divisions quickly emerged between those wishing to proceed at a deliberate pace and those wishing to make the most of the existing momentum. Belonging to the former group, Brentano was anxious that the revolution not degenerate into chaos and, as far as possible, avoid disrupting business and industry. A series of menacing moves on the part of armed groups loyal to the varying factions ended with the brief jailing of several of the more militant "red republicans." Divided internally, the Baden regime was also beset by the superior military force of a Prussian army determined to stamp out revolution in Germany. With the fall of Baden's capital at the end of June, Brentano concluded defeat was inevitable. Several days later, when the constituent assembly abjured negotiation and declared, over his objections, that the fight would continue, he understood himself to have been repudiated and left for Switzerland. The assembly charged that his departure amounted to "cowardly treason" (Dahlinger, p. 258). The old regime, restored after the final surrender of rebel forces in July, likewise condemned Brentano, sentencing him in absentia to life in prison.

The following year Brentano, like many other German revolutionaries, immigrated to the United States. He settled in Pottsville, Pennsylvania, where he briefly edited a German-language antislavery weekly, *Der Leuchtturm* (The Lighthouse). In 1851 he moved to a farm outside Kalamazoo, Michigan. The date of his marriage to Caroline Aberle is not known, but in 1854 they had a son; the couple eventually had three children. Brentano evidently lost touch with his former associates, and some even assumed that he had died. But he was not entirely quiescent. In 1856 he published a statement in a Kalamazoo newspaper urging Germans to back the Republican party. Three years later his rustication ended, and he began to practice law in Chicago. He quickly hired on with the *Illinois Staats-Zeitung*, a German-language daily firmly committed to the Union and the Republican party. In 1862 Brentano bought an interest in the paper and edited it until 1867, when A. C. Hesing assumed sole ownership. The *Staats-Zeitung* was the single most prominent voice for the German community in Chicago, at least until the emergence of independent working-class organs late in the 1860s. Its circulation in 1870 has been estimated at 12,000.

In 1862 Brentano was elected to the Illinois state legislature. The same year he was prominent among the German Americans pressing preferment for Union general Franz Sigel, who had been a military leader in Brentano's Baden government. Early on Brentano's newspaper chided Abraham Lincoln for timidity with respect to the war and emancipation and advertised John C. Frémont as a possible successor. But by 1863 Brentano had distanced himself from the Frémont enthusiasm, and the following year the *Staats-Zeitung* endorsed Lincoln's reelection. For the next two decades Brentano was fairly regular in his Republicanism. A federal appointment allowed him to return to Germany to serve as U.S. consul at Dresden from 1872 to 1876. In the latter year he campaigned for Rutherford B. Hayes and was himself elected to the U.S. House of Representatives. Brentano served a single term in Congress. He opposed the Reagan Bill for federal regulation of railroads, declaring that Chicago business interests would be harmed by its restrictions on rates that discriminated in favor of long-distance shipping. Upon leaving Congress, Brentano occupied himself with a comparative study of American and European jurisprudence. He had seemed to lag behind many of his fellow émigrés in becoming disillusioned with the Republican party, but by 1884 Brentano was a Mugwump. Crippled by a stroke, he died in Chicago. Though Brentano never became as well known in the United States as some other "forty-eighters," such as Sigel or Carl Schurz, his career nevertheless stands as a testament to the continuing contributions exiles and expatriates have made to the nation's political and intellectual life.

• English-language sources on Brentano's life are relatively scarce, but see *In Memoriam: Lorenz Brentano* (1891). His role in the developments in Baden is discussed in Charles W. Dahlinger, *The German Revolution of 1849* (1903). For details about the *Illinois Staats-Zeitung*, see Karl Arndt and May Olson, *German-American Newspapers and Periodicals 1732–1955: History and Bibliography* (1961). Brentano is briefly mentioned in Carl Wittke, *Refugees of Revolution: The German Forty-Eighters in America* (1952), and Adolf E. Zucker, ed., *The Forty-Eighters: Political Refugees of the German Revolution of 1848* (1950).

PATRICK G. WILLIAMS

BRERETON, Lewis Hyde (21 June 1890–19 July 1967), U.S. Army officer, was born in Pittsburgh, Pennsylvania, the son of William Denny Brereton, a mining engineer, and Helen Hyde. Brereton grew up in Annapolis, Maryland, and attended St. John's College, Annapolis, for two years. Desiring a military career, Brereton took the competitive examinations for both West Point and Annapolis in 1907. Though preferring the army (a stance reinforced by uncontrollable seasickness), his exam results dictated that he "take what was left"—the U.S. Naval Academy. Graduating in June 1911, Brereton took advantage of a rule permitting interservice transfers to exchange his ensign's commission for a second lieutenancy in the Coast Artillery.

Brereton was among the first to grasp the potential of flying as a career specialty. He entered the Signal Corps aviation section in 1912 and passed flight qualifications the next year. After tours in the Philippines and Washington, Brereton went to France as one of eight officers in the first contingent of American Expeditionary Force (AEF) aviators. He assumed command of the Twelfth Aero Squadron in March 1918, saw extensive combat, was credited with four German aircraft destroyed, earned the Distinguished Service Cross (DSC), and was himself shot down over St.-Mihiel. Brereton then served as chief aviation officer, I Corps, and as G-3 of the AEF Air Service. Following service in the Army of Occupation and a three-year tour as air attaché in Paris, Brereton returned home in 1922 a much-decorated major in a peacetime military establishment that envisioned only a limited role for America's fledgling air force.

Closely associated with William "Billy" Mitchell (1879–1936), with whom he is jointly credited as having devised dive-bombing, Brereton served as a defense counsel in Mitchell's 1926 court-martial. Zealous advocacy of air power combined with two divorces (Brereton was married to Helen Willis from 1913 to 1929 and Icy V. Larkin from 1931 to 1945) and a penchant for late-night carousing to retard his career. Not promoted to lieutenant colonel until 1935, Brereton thereafter made rapid strides, receiving promotion to brigadier general in 1939 and to major general and command of the Third Air Force in July 1941.

Assigned to command the Far Eastern Air Force in November 1941, the wartime odyssey of this ambitious, high-profile general began disastrously. Despite having several hours warning of an impending Japanese attack, Brereton apparently did not take seriously the threat to his B-17s. Nearly half of the U.S. air force in the Philippines, massed without camouflage and lacking protective revetments, was destroyed on the ground in the 8 December attack on Clark Field. He was, of course, not alone in taking lightly the danger of Japanese attack.

After a short stay as air commander of the Australian-British-Dutch-American Command, during which he earned a second DSC for leading a raid on Japanese bases in the Andaman Islands, Brereton was ordered to India and given the Tenth Air Force. Reporting to General Joseph W. Stilwell, Brereton clashed with his boss over targeting priorities for this ragtag force. In June 1942 he moved to Cairo to organize the Ninth Air Force. After the death of General Frank M. Andrews, Brereton was designated commander of the Middle East Air Force, charged with supporting British operations in North Africa and the Anglo-American invasions of Sicily and Italy. Impatient to use air power in an independent role, Brereton pushed through his plan for a long-range, low-level attack by B-24s against the refinery complex at Ploieşti, Romania—a controversial operation in August 1943 that produced high losses and only modest damage.

A month later Brereton moved yet again, becoming chief of the Ninth Tactical Air Force in Britain. Promoted to major general in April 1944 and always pushing for a free hand, he quarreled over tactical air employment doctrine with his nominal superior, General Carl A. Spaatz. A dispute about air-ground coordination with U.S. ground force commander General Omar N. Bradley turned ugly after Brereton's heavy bombers, diverted to aid the Allied breakout from Normandy in late July (Operation COBRA), dropped short of the assigned bomb line and killed 111 U.S. soldiers.

The last chapter in the Brereton saga involved his role as commander of the First Allied Airborne Army. Although planning for MARKET GARDEN, the Allied airborne/armored attack into Holland in September 1944, was far advanced when he took command, Brereton's performance in this flawed operation was uninspired. Subsequent disputes with Allied commanders over the use of airborne forces and his manifest hesitation—belying reputed aggressiveness—about undertaking a major airborne assault in early 1945 further tarnished Brereton's reputation. A sharp tongue and a propensity to insubordination continued to cause him difficulties in the immediate postwar period. Possibly affected by publication of a self-congratulatory memoir, *The Brereton Diaries: The War in the Air in the Pacific, Middle East, and Europe, 3 October 1941–8 May 1945* (1946), Brereton's career stalled, and he retired in 1948. He died in Washington, D.C.

Brereton was a pioneering aviator who rose to high command during World War II. His wartime career exemplified the global dimensions of American operations and also, some have argued, the weaknesses of a system that selected military leaders largely on the basis of early professional and personal connections. Historian Roger Beaumont has observed of Brereton that "the pattern of bad luck and/or misjudgment that dogged his career during World War II . . . offers a rich possibility for speculation and research." Brereton does appear to have been given difficult assignments and at the worst possible times, but personal traits also played a considerable part.

• Documentation of Brereton's career is scattered widely, and no substantial biographical treatment has been published to date. See Flint O. DuPre, "Lewis Hyde Brereton," in *U.S. Air Force Biographical Dictionary* (1965). To place Brereton's claims in historical context, Wesley F. Craven and James L. Cate, *The Army Air Forces in World War II* (7 vols., 1948–1958), Henry H. Arnold, *Global Mission* (1949), Lee Kennett, *A History of Strategic Bombing* (1982), and Robert F. Futrell, *Ideas, Concepts, Doctrine: A Study of Basic Thinking in the United States Air Force* (1974), are helpful. For the British perspective, see John F. Terraine, *The Right of the Line: The Royal Air Force in the European War, 1939–45* (1985). Brief critical assessments of Brereton's role in spring and summer 1944 are in Russell Weigley, *Eisenhower's Lieutenants: The Campaigns of France and Germany, 1944–45* (1981); Carlo D'Este, *Decision in Normandy* (1983); and Max Hastings, *Overlord: D-Day, June 6, 1944* (1984). An outstanding collection of essays on employment of tactical air power is Benjamin F. Cooling, ed., *Case Studies in the Development of Close Air Support* (1990).

THEODORE A. WILSON

BRESCI, Gaetano (11 Nov. 1869–22 May 1901), silk weaver and regicide, was born in Coiano, Italy, the son of Gaspero Bresci, a peasant/artisan, and Maddalena Godi. At age eleven Bresci was apprenticed to learn the art of silk weaving; he later attended a Sunday school to acquire a specialized trade. While still a youth, Gaetano participated in an anarchist group. First arrested for disturbing the peace in 1892, he was subsequently confined to the penal island of Lampedusa for more than a year for his role in organizing a strike. Now identified as a "dangerous anarchist," Bresci had difficulty securing employment.

Embittered by political as well as economic conditions in Italy, Bresci immigrated to the United States in December 1897. He quickly found employment among his townsmen from Prato in the silk industry of Paterson, New Jersey, and he joined the anarchist movement in that city. He became a dedicated supporter of the group *Diritto all'esistenza* and its organ, *La Questione Sociale*.

Meanwhile, Bresci gained a reputation as a conscientious and valued employee. He earned good wages and indulged his taste for elegant clothes. A handsome ladies' man, he formed a continuing relationship with Sofie Knieland, an Irish-American fellow worker, with whom he had two daughters. Reputed to be a personable, gregarious individual, he learned English, associated with Americans, and developed bourgeois tastes. In a letter to his brother, he wrote, "Here all is different from Italy. Here we are free to express our own opinions. The police respect us, we can write in our newspapers what we please, and the citizens of every social class have the same political rights" (Petacco, p. 29).

Although Bresci hardly fit the profile of the anarchist terrorist, while still in Italy he had conceived of the killing of King Umberto I, and his years in the United States only hardened his resolve. A friend of Errico Malatesta, the leader of the organizational anarchists, Bresci also came under the influence of the individualist Giuseppe Ciancabilla, who advocated the propaganda of the deed. Deeply affected by the brutal suppression of popular uprisings in Italy, Bresci was enraged by the slaughter of scores of people during bread riots in Milan in 1898—and particularly by the king's awarding a medal for this action to General Fiorenzo Bava Beccaris.

On 17 May 1900 Bresci sailed for Europe, ostensibly to visit the Paris Exposition and his family in Prato. During this trip, he enjoyed several dalliances with young women. Following a leisurely tour, on the evening of 29 July, in the city of Monza, Bresci shot Umberto I three times in his royal carriage, killing him on the spot. He was instantly apprehended and confessed to the deed, freely admitting his motives. In addition to his hatred of the king as the author of bloody repressions, Bresci held him personally responsible for his own hard life, which had forced him to emigrate. Referring to the contempt in which Italians were held in the United States, he said, "In America we are even called pigs" (Petacco, p. 123).

The Italian authorities and newspapers seized upon the notion of a conspiracy; hundreds of persons alleged to have been Bresci's accomplices were imprisoned. Speculation regarding elaborate plots focused on the city of Paterson, reputed to be a "nursery of anarchy." With the cooperation of the New York City police department, the governor of New Jersey, and the Department of State, intensive investigations were conducted in the United States. Bresci constantly asserted that he acted alone, and despite elaborate theories, no substantive evidence of a conspiracy was ever produced. In a trial lasting one day (29 Aug. 1900) Bresci was judged guilty and condemned to life imprisonment (Italy had abolished the death penalty). Less than a year later he was "found" hung in his cell. Although officially declared a suicide, many, particularly among the Left, believed that he had in fact been executed. Arrigo Petacco, Bresci's biographer, concludes that he died under "mysterious circumstances" (p. 147).

Bresci's deed was one of a series of assassinations of heads of state committed by Italian anarchists in the 1890s: the French president Carnot, who was killed by Sante Caserio; the Spanish prime minister Canovas, who was killed by Michele Angiolillo; and the empress of Austria Elizabeth, who was killed by Luigi Lucchéni. In Italy, the assassination marked the culmination of a decade of fierce class conflict. While its immediate effect was to unleash a torrent of vituperation and punitive measures against socialists and anarchists alike, the Italian state henceforth embarked on a more moderate course, permitting more freedom of action to workers' parties and organizations. The historian Gaetano Salvemini believed that the great majority of Italians were favorable to Bresci because they viewed Umberto I as a tyrant.

The killing of the king of Italy by an anarchist from Paterson created a sensation in the United States. Newspapers such as the *New York Herald* featured banner headlines and devoted many columns to lurid—and spurious—accounts of sinister plots. Government agencies carried on investigations of the Paterson anarchists. News of the assassination, however, plunged the "Little Italies" into mourning, with memorial services and messages of condolences sponsored by the *prominenti*. Even socialists, both in the United States and Italy, expressed repugnance at the taking of a human life. Although Malatesta and his followers interpreted Bresci's deed as a response to an oppressive political system, they rejected such individual acts as contrary to their concept of anarchy. Only the antiorganizational anarchists openly rejoiced. The anarchists of Yohoghany, Pennsylvania, sent a telegram to the prime minister of Italy exulting upon the death of the king, "massacrer of the people. Hurrah for Comrade Bresci!"

For followers of Ciancabilla and Luigi Galleani, Bresci had entered the pantheon of tyrannicides. In November 1900 the anarchists of Paterson published *Umberto e Bresci* in 50,000 copies, the first of a number of such publications extolling the deed. Groups were formed bearing his name, and 29 July became a holiday on the anarchist calendar to be celebrated with picnics and memorial events. More importantly, Bresci's example served as an inspiration for the terrorist acts of the Galleanisti in the United States during the World War I era.

Although he was in the United States less than three years, Bresci left a lasting impression, not only on the Italian anarchist movement but also on American attitudes toward foreigners. Although his name was soon forgotten, the impression that immigrants were prone to violence and radicalism remained. When President William McKinley was killed by Leon Czgolosz (a second-generation Polish-American who was inspired by Bresci's deed) in 1901, this prejudice was reinforced.

In the "Red Scare" that followed, the Italian anarchists of Paterson were once again a focus of investigations. Bresci's killing of Umberto I was a contributing factor in the enactment by the Congress of the Anarchist Act of 1903, which denied entry to the United States to persons who, among other things, advocated the assassination of public officials.

• Documents relating to Bresci are curiously missing from the public archives in Italy where one would expect to find them. The exception is the record of Bresci's trial, including investigative reports, which is in the Italian State Archives in Milan. Many of these documents, and additional materials, can also be found in Department of Justice, RG 60, National Archives, Washington, D.C.

A brief biography is by Maria Grazia Rosada in *Il movimento operaio italiano: Dizionario biografico, 1853–1943*, ed. Franco Andreucci and Tommaso Detti (1975). For a detailed, if journalistic, account, see Arrigo Petacco, *L'anarchico che venne dall'America* (1969). Giuseppe Galzerano, *Gaetano Bresci* (1988), leans heavily on Petacco but adds some details. Both Petacco and Galzerano include appendices of contemporary documents. On the connection between Bresci and the Paterson anarchists, Luigi Vittorio Ferraris, "L'assassinio di Umberto I e gli anarchici di Paterson," *Rassegna storica del Risorgimento* 55 (1968): 47–64, is useful. United States governmental and press reaction and the role of American agencies in the investigations are reported (but uncritically) in Lowell L. Blaisdell, "The Assassination of Humbert I," *Prologue* 27 (Fall 1995): 241–47. For the impact of Bresci's deed on the Italian anarchist movement in the United States, Paul Avrich, *Sacco and Vanzetti: The Anarchist Background* (1991), is most valuable.

RUDOLPH J. VECOLI

BRESEE, Phineas Franklin (31 Dec. 1838–13 Nov. 1915), Methodist Episcopal minister and official, was born in Franklin, Delaware County, New York, the son of Phineas Philips Bresee and Susan Brown Bresee, farmers. His father also ran a sawmill on his Franklin property until 1851, when the family moved to a larger farm in Davenport.

Bresee maintained a lifelong love of learning, although his sporadic formal education ended in 1855 at the classically oriented Delaware Literary Institute in Franklin. He and his family were devout Methodists in an area served by several early American Methodist noteworthies, including Nathan Bangs, Heman Bangs, and John Bangs. In 1856, in the Methodist Episcopal church in West Davenport, Bresee, led by his pastor James W. Smith, professed a religious conversion and confirmation of a childhood call to preach. In the spring of 1857, in a schoolhouse on the Davenport circuit, Bresee, now licensed as an "exhorter," preached his first sermon.

By June 1857 Bresee had moved with his family to southwestern Iowa County, Iowa. He quickly united with the Methodist "class" at Millersburg, and Presiding Elder William Simpson soon had him holding services. By September the Iowa Annual Conference had admitted Bresee as an itinerant preacher. In 1858 Bishop Thomas Morris appointed Bresee to the Pella Circuit. In 1859 Bresee was ordained a deacon and admitted to full conference membership. He was ordained an elder in 1861.

Bresee married Maria Hebberd in 1860, after counting her by mail; they had seven children. Bresee continued to serve as a Methodist Episcopal pastor and sometime presiding elder in Iowa from 1857 to 1882. At age thirty-two he was elected to the 1872 General Conference of the Methodist Episcopal church. In this capacity he helped significantly in the election of the socially radical integrationist Gilbert Haven to the episcopacy. He also led in the establishment and development of Methodist higher education, including the founding of Simpson Centenary College (now Simpson College) in Indianola.

Bresee left Iowa in 1883 and was very quickly appointed the pastor of the prestigious Fort Street Church (later named First Church) in Los Angeles, California. From 1883 to 1891 he served the congregations of Fort Street, Pasadena First, and Asbury (Los Angeles). In 1891 Bishop Willard Mallalieu appointed a reluctant Bresee as a presiding elder of the Los Angeles District. Bresee spent the year evangelizing and pushing his pastors to evangelize. He also attended several camp meetings sponsored by the National Campmeeting Association for the Promotion of Holiness (NCAPH) (now usually called the National Holiness Association, or NHA) and led the Southern California Annual Conference delegation to the 1892 General Conference.

At this time Bresee and others began to see that Methodism would have to deal with the Holiness Movement and its ethos. Bresee himself had experienced what was known as "entire sanctification" in his term in Chariton (1866–1868); he now increasingly and clearly identified with the principal organization of the Holiness Movement, the NHA.

Opposition to the ecclesiologically and behaviorally radical fringes of the Holiness Movement soon developed into opposition to the movement as a whole, even to that form of it found among Methodist loyalists. By 1891 Bresee had run into this opposition—even among some of the bishops—in his work as a presiding elder.

After the 1892 General Conference, Bresee served two other congregations. In 1894 he requested release from regular appointment in order to work with the independent Peniel Mission. The conference refused his request because it did not wish to set a precedent. But after Bresee decided to go to the mission, forfeiting his status as a Methodist Epicopal preacher, the conference still reelected him to several of its most prestigious posts—including, in 1894, membership in the board of the liberal arts college of the University of Southern California.

The Peniel Mission was established to serve the poor of the city and to serve as a center for the holiness forces in the West. Bresee was to preach on Sunday mornings and to edit the *Peniel Herald*, the mission's paper. But the mission unexpectedly and without explanation terminated the services of both Bresee and Joseph Pomeroy Widney in the late summer of 1894. The terminations likely arose out of differences between the Wesleyan perspective held by Bresee and Widney and the Calvinism of other leaders.

By October 1895 Bresee and Widney had founded the First Church of the Nazarene in downtown Los Angeles. The congregation, many of them members of Methodist congregations that Bresee had served and a surprising number of them socially prominent, elected Bresee and Widney as pastors and general superintendents. The congregation had two aims: ministry to the city's poor and service as a center for Holiness Movement forces in the West. The new body's polity, doctrinal statements, orders and styles of worship, and behavioral expectations were essentially Methodist. Only in certain limitations on clerical authority and in an expansion of lay representation and local control did the Nazarenes decisively depart from episcopal Methodism.

Early in 1897 Bresee, still the pastor in Los Angeles, organized a group in Berkeley into a Nazarene congregation. This was the first of many such organizations in quick succession. By 1905 the Church of the Nazarene was clearly a denomination. Widney's return to the Methodist Episcopal church in 1898 left Bresee to stand alone as the pastor of the Los Angeles congregation and as the general superintendent of the fledgling denomination.

Between 1907 and 1915, Bresee, recognized as a centrist within the Holiness Movement, galvanized a number of leaders and groups within the Holiness Movement (Methodistic and non-Methodist) into a united denomination, the Pentecostal Church of the Nazarene. (In 1919 the adjective "Pentecostal" was dropped to avoid identification as a church that advocated "speaking in tongues.")

Bresee's experience led him to believe that, in spite of importunings, establishing even a modest school lay beyond the fiscal and personnel resources of the Nazarenes. Nonetheless, in 1902 he reluctantly guided the opening of Pacific Bible College and served as its president until 1911. The school passed through many "dangers, toils, and snares," as well as changes of name and location. But in 1910 land was purchased in Pasadena for the establishment of what was by then called Nazarene University. It took two decades before Bresee's dream of a stable postsecondary college of liberal arts under Nazarene auspices was a reality.

Sprightly style, ecumenical interests, and "newsiness" concerning the Church of the Nazarene quickly made Bresee's weekly *Nazarene Messenger* (originally called the *Nazarene*, established in 1896, and regularly published as a monthly beginning in 1898) something of a vade mecum among the Methodistic element in the Holiness Movement. Its nonsectarian spirit was muted somewhat but remained through its merger in 1912 with several other Nazarene papers to form the *Herald of Holiness*.

The 1915 General Assembly of the Pentecostal Church of the Nazarene, held in Kansas City, reelected Bresee to the general superintendency with 210 of the 220 ballots cast, though it was clear that he would not live out his four-year term. He died in Los Angeles.

• Bresee left behind only bits and pieces of autobiographical material in his sermons and speeches. Most of his papers are in the archives of the First Church of the Nazarene in Los Angeles, Calif.; copies are in the archives of the Church of the Nazarene in Kansas City, Mo. Two series of his sermons were published posthumously: *Sermons from Matthew's Gospel* (n.d.) and *Sermons on Isaiah* (1926). Also posthumously published was his *Emmanuel* (1927), a sermonic essay. Some of his editorials and articles are in the *Nazarene Messenger* (1900–1911; from 1896 to 1900 titled the *Nazarene*), including "Social Work and Evangelism," Oct. 1898, "Broadness," 6 Dec. 1900, and "Church Union," 14 Feb. 1907, and in the *Herald of Holiness*. It is quite probable that much of E. A. Girvin, *Phineas F. Bresee: A Prince in Israel* (1916), is from Bresee himself. Also see Donald P. Brickley, *Man of the Morning: The Life and Work of Phineas F. Bresee* (1960), which corrects Girvin on certain points and shows Bresee's connections with both Methodism and the Holiness Movement. Carl O. Bangs, *Phineas Bresee: His Life in Methodism, the Holiness Movement, and the Church of the Nazarene* (1995), puts Bresee in a much broader context and presents the results of archival and other investigations into the wide range of Bresee's ecclesiastical and social connections. Studies of specialized aspects of Bresee's life and work are Timothy L. Smith, ed., *The Certainties of Faith: Ten Sermons by the Founder of the Church of the Nazarene* (1958), and Smith, *Called unto Holiness: The Story of the Nazarenes* (1962). Far more personal is Harrison D. Brown, *Personal Memories of the Early Ministry of Dr. Phineas F. Bresee: Character Study* (1930).

PAUL MERRITT BASSETT

BRESNAHAN, Roger Philip (11 June 1879–4 Dec. 1944), baseball player, coach, and manager, was born in Toledo, Ohio, the son of Michael Bresnahan and Mary O'Donahue, immigrants from Tralee, County Kerry, Ireland. As a youth, Bresnahan played baseball on amateur teams in Toledo, and at age sixteen he earned money playing on a club in Manistee, Michigan. In 1896, while with Lima in the Ohio State League, he impressed scouts with his strong arm, quickness of foot, and all-around ability. The next year he made his major league debut as a pitcher for the Washington Senators of the National League and hurled a shutout in his first game (28 Aug. 1897), finishing the season with a 4–0 mark. The following spring he got into a salary dispute with the Senators and refused to sign. As a result, he played in only a handful of minor league games in 1898 and 1899, and in 1900 he appeared in just one major league contest, as a member of the Chicago club in the National League.

In 1901 Bresnahan, who batted and threw right-handed, joined the Baltimore Orioles, managed by John McGraw, in the fledgling American League. Although he began the season as a pitcher, he became one of the team's catchers after veteran backstop Wilbert Robinson was injured. In mid-1902 McGraw, involved in numerous disputes with American League president Ban Johnson, jumped to the National League New York Giants and persuaded some of Baltimore's better players, including Bresnahan, to join him. In his first two and a half seasons with the Giants, Bresnahan played various positions, but he spent most of his time as the team's center fielder. In 1903 he reached a career-high 142 hits, with 34 stolen bases and a .350 batting average in 113 games. The next season he helped the Giants win their first National League pennant in fifteen years.

During the 1905 season the 5′9″ Bresnahan gradually took over the Giants' catching duties; his speed enabled him to become the first major league catcher to bat regularly in the leadoff position. The highlight of his playing career occurred during the 1905 World Series when he caught all four of his team's shutout victories—three pitched by Christy Mathewson, the other by Joe McGinnity—as the Giants defeated the Philadelphia Athletics.

In 1907 Bresnahan received national attention for the innovations he brought to the game. One day, after having watched the wicket keeper in a cricket match, he took his position behind the plate wearing a primitive set of shin guards, along with the traditional small mask and chest pad. The new protective gear was quickly adopted by other catchers. In June, while batting in a game against Cincinnati, he was struck in the head by a pitch and sidelined for nearly a month. When he returned to the Giants' lineup, he came to the plate wearing a pneumatic head protector, thus becoming the first well-known player to use such a device in a regular season game. Within the next year he likewise started to use a padded face mask, which also soon became standard equipment.

Bresnahan had his best season behind the plate in 1908 when he caught in 139 games and led all National League catchers in putouts. In December St. Louis Cardinals' owner Stanley Robison, desperately seeking a new manager, and McGraw engineered a well-publicized three-way trade with Cincinnati that sent Bresnahan to the Cardinals as player-manager. The move was greeted with much enthusiasm in St. Louis and fulfilled Bresnahan's long-held ambition to manage a major league club.

In his first two seasons at St. Louis, the team under Bresnahan improved only slightly, but in 1911 he was able to keep the club in the pennant race for most of the season. As a result, the team's new owner, Robison's niece Helene Hathaway Britton, rewarded Bresnahan with a new five-year-contract as player-manager at $10,000 per year, plus 10 percent of the club's annual profits. But early in the 1912 season the relationship between owner and manager soured, and, after the Cardinals closed the season in sixth place, he was fired and released. When several clubs claimed him, a league meeting upheld the sale of his contract to the Chicago Cubs, which gave him a $25,000 signing bonus. Soon after, Bresnahan settled out of court on his percentage contract with the Cardinals for $20,000. The $55,000 he received for the 1913 season made him one of baseball's highest-paid players.

With Chicago, Bresnahan shared catching duties in 1913–1914, and in 1915 he was hired as manager. After he piloted the team to a mediocre fourth-place finish, new Cubs' owner Charles Weeghman replaced him as manager with Joe Tinker, who had piloted Weeghman's Chicago entry in the short-lived Federal League. Following his dismissal, Bresnahan returned to his home town, and for $40,000 he bought control of the Toledo Mud Hens of the American Association. He served as playing manager for three seasons and continued as principal owner until 1923, when disgruntled shareholders, tired of the team's lackluster performance, persuaded him to sell his majority interest. In 1924 he married Gertrude Norenberg; they adopted one child.

In 1925 McGraw brought Bresnahan back to the Giants to coach the team's pitchers, including the young southpaw Carl Hubbell. After four seasons with New York, Bresnahan was released for reasons never fully disclosed. He lost most of his personal fortune, estimated at $250,000, during the 1929 stock market crash; eventually he took a job as an attendant at a Toledo warehouse. He returned to the major leagues during the 1930 and 1931 seasons as pitching coach for the Detroit Tigers, but he suffered further financial setbacks, including the loss of his home, during the depression.

In his later years Bresnahan worked in Toledo as a sales representative for the Buckeye Brewing Company. In November 1944 he ran unsuccessfully for Lucas County commissioner on the Democratic ticket. He died in Toledo.

Throughout his baseball career Bresnahan was known for his fiery nature and fierce competitiveness, which won him the respect of teammates and local sportswriters but led him into well-chronicled scuffles with umpires and opposing teams' players and fans. Off the diamond, the "Duke of Tralee," as he was nicknamed, had a fondness for fashionable attire and enjoyed a high-spirited social life. During much of his playing career, he spent the winter months working as a private detective. Although Bresnahan was not the greatest catcher of his era, the innovations he brought to the game and the esteem shown him by some of baseball's most respected figures helped raise his stature in the years following his retirement. A month after his death he was elected to the Baseball Hall of Fame in Cooperstown, New York.

• For information on Bresnahan's role on the great New York Giants' teams of 1903–1908, see John McGraw's autobiography, *My Thirty Years in Baseball* (1923). An early sketch, written by sportswriter Frank Lieb, appeared in *Baseball Magazine*, Oct. 1911, pp. 15–21. Other short pieces on Bresnahan have followed, including Robert M. Smith, *Heroes of Baseball* (1952); Lee Allen and Thomas Meany, *Kings of the Diamond: The Immortals in Baseball's Hall of Fame* (1965); Al Hirschberg, *Baseball's Greatest Catchers* (1967); Milton J. Shapiro, *Heroes behind the Mask* (1968); and Bill James, *The Bill James Historical Baseball Abstract* (1985). The Baseball Hall of Fame's file on Bresnahan contains a wealth of anecdotal information. Obituaries are in the *New York Times*, 5 Dec. 1944, and the *Sporting News*, 7 Dec. 1944.

RAYMOND D. KUSH

BRESSANI, Francesco Giuseppe (6 May 1612–9 Sept. 1672), priest, Jesuit missionary, and astronomer, was born in Rome, Italy. His parents' names are unknown, and very little is known about his early life. Bressani entered the Society of Jesus as a novice on 15 August 1626. Over the next few years he requested repeatedly to be sent to Canada as a missionary. After studying in Rome and later in Claremont, France, he became an accomplished teacher of philosophy, literature, mathematics, and astronomy. In 1642 Bressani got his wish and was sent to Quebec, the seat of the Jesuit mission in New France. Finally, on 27 April 1644, having become sufficiently fluent in Huron to undertake missionary duties, he set off for Sainte-Marie in the Huron country, near the present Midland, Ontario, accompanied by six Christian Hurons and a French boy. Three days later, just east of the mouth of the Richelieu River, the group was captured by twenty-seven Mohawk warriors. Thus began Father Bressani's ordeal.

The war party returned home up the Richelieu River–Lake Champlain route, and on 15 May reached a Mohawk fishing village of 400 people on the upper Hudson River near its junction with the Sacandaga. Here Bressani underwent preliminary torture until his tormentors learned from a Huron captive that he was "an important personage and a captain of the French." He was now told that he would eventually die by fire. The following day, 26 May, Bressani was taken to the Mohawk country, reaching their first village, probably Ossernenon near the present Fultonville in New York State, four days later. At this village and the second one, probably Kanagaro, located a few miles upstream from Ossernenon, his tortures were intensified. In order to keep his sanity, Bressani prayed, observed phases of the moon, and tried to keep track of time. Several times he asked to be spared from death by fire and executed in some other manner. Once, briefly, he contemplated suicide by drowning. On 19 June, thoroughly degraded and physically broken, he was told he would now be burned to death. Instead, however, just as had happened to Father Jogues in 1642, Bressani was ransomed by an old Mohawk woman for "a few beads" as a replacement for her grandfather who had died at Huron hands many years earlier. Totally unfit for work and so horrible in appearance that the Mohawk woman's daughters were afraid to look at him, she permitted the Dutch to ransom him for fifteen or twenty doppias (in value about 150 to 200 French livres or about thirty to forty pounds of beaver pelts).

On 19 August 1644 Bressani left the Mohawk for New Amsterdam, where he was treated by a doctor while staying with the Reverend Johannes Megapolensis. He wrote Megapolensis later and thanked him for his kindnesses. Ever the missionary, he also asked him to consider becoming a Catholic. Finally well enough, Bressani was sent to France and reached La Rochelle on November 15. From there he went to Rome for an audience with Pope Innocent X, who gave Bressani a dispensation to conduct mass without the use of the fingers on his right hand, which had been partially removed by Mohawk torture.

By July 1645 he was back in Canada, and at the Huron mission by the early autumn. He had finally achieved his lifelong goal, to serve as a missionary. According to his colleagues, the ordeal he had suffered had made him a better preacher. He often displayed his mutilated body, especially his hands, to give the Huron a "better conception . . . of the truths of our faith": that, as a Christian, he would endure torture for his faith and still not be afraid of encountering more by returning to Canada.

On 30 January 1646 at Sainte-Marie, 25 May 1649 at Trois-Rivières, and 18 November 1649 at Quebec, Bressani used his scientific knowledge and skill to time lunar eclipses. His results were to be compared with observations made in Europe in order to calculate longitudinal distances. Considering the poor quality of the instruments at his disposal and the difficulties he must have had with his hands, his observations were phenomenally accurate. In fact, they were not equaled for the next hundred years. His calculation for the difference in time between Quebec and Sainte-Marie was exact at thirty-five minutes (8°45′ longitude), while his timing of the eclipse on 18 November at Quebec, which was also timed by Fathers Riccioli and Grimaldi at Bologna, Italy, had an error of only five minutes and thirty seconds (1°22′30″ longitude). As late as 1755, the British cartographer and geographer Thomas Jefferys still cited Bressani as the authority for the coordinates of Quebec at latitude 46°55′ and longitude 52°13′ west of Ferro. These figures carry errors of only 7′ and 29′, respectively.

In 1649, while Bressani was at Quebec, the Huron country faced its final onslaught from the Iroquois League. In June the following year, Bressani, accompanied by about thirty-five Frenchmen and an equal number of Huron warriors, set off with supplies for their beleaguered colleagues. Halfway to Huronia, the group was ambushed by ten Iroquois warriors, and Bressani received three arrow wounds to the head. Shortly after this encounter, they met the survivors of the Huron disaster and all returned to Quebec.

With the Huron mission destroyed, some of the Jesuits, including Bressani, embarked 2 November 1650 for France on the *Chasseur*. Eventually he returned to Italy, where he published *Breve Relatione d'alcune missioni de'PP. della Compagnia di Giesù nella Nuova Francia* (1653), his account of the Huron mission and its martyrs. The book was to be illustrated with a map, which was not ready at press time. The only map fitting the book's description of it is the *Novae Franciae Accurata Delineatio*, engraved by the Italian master Giovanni Federico Pesca in 1657. With its accurate vignettes of native life and the earliest depiction of the martyrdom of Fathers Brébeuf and Lalemant, it is the most beautiful map of seventeenth-century New France.

Bressani spent the remainder of his life in Italy as a priest. By repute he was an effective preacher, continuing the practice of showing his mutilated hands to disbelievers as evidence for the strength of faith against adversity. He died in Florence.

• Most of what is known about Bressani has to be deduced from his letters that he reprinted in his history of the Jesuit missions to New France, *Breve Relatione*. This book was republished by Reuben Gold Thwaites (ed.) as *The Jesuit Relations and Allied Documents* (1896–1901), a work that contains other references to Bressani. An original letter written by Bressani from Iroquois captivity in July 1644, containing a sketch of his mutilated hands, has been published in facsimile by Stelio Cro, "The Original Letter of Father Bressani Written from Fort Orange in 1644," *Canadian Journal of Italian Studies* 4, no. 1–2 (1980–1981): 26–67. Bressani's audience with the Pope is related in Jeanne-Françoise Juchereau and Marie-Andrée Duplessis, *Les Annales de l'Hôtel-Dieu de Québec, 1636–1716* (1939). References to Bressani's skills as an astronomer are in Peter Broughton, "Astronomy in Seventeenth-Century Canada," *Journal of the Royal Astronomical Society* 75, no. 4 (1981): 175–208.

CONRAD HEIDENREICH

BRETT, George Platt (8 Dec. 1858–19 Sept. 1936), publisher, was born in London, England, the son of George Edward Brett, a book salesman, and Elizabeth Platt. In 1869 his father moved with his family to New York City, accompanied by a cargo including the stock necessary to establish an agency for Macmillan & Co., Ltd., of London. He set up shop in a private home on Bleecker Street in Greenwich Village. Brett, who had attended school in London, continued his education in New York schools until he was sixteen. After that he went to work as an assistant in his father's firm and soon became a city salesman.

Brett contracted tuberculosis and sought better health in California, where he worked as a cowboy on a ranch and bought a chicken farm in Santa Cruz. He married Florence Lucy Stikeman in Santa Cruz in 1880; they had one child. His wife died in 1885, and he returned to New York that year when they learned that his father was seriously ill. Although he lacked much experience, Brett combined a strong willpower and a passionate concern for details and became successful almost at once. He also found time to attend night classes at the College of the City of New York. On his father's death in 1890, Brett formally took over the management of the agency, at which time its business amounted to $50,000 annually. In 1891 he married Marie Louise Tostavin and moved to a farm in Darien, Connecticut; they had three children. At about this same time, the owners of the Macmillan firm in London made its American branch an independent partnership composed of British members, with Brett as its resident partner. His New York branch had semiautonomous specialty departments. On the death in 1896 of the last original English founder of Macmillan in London, Brett was named president of the Macmillan Company of New York. He continued to surround himself with able associates but guided all operations personally until his was the most profitable of all American publishing houses. During the 1890s he took business trips to England almost every year.

Brett was responsible for introducing a new method of wholesale distribution of Macmillan books nationwide, with fully equipped and well-stocked branch offices in Atlanta, Boston, Chicago, Dallas, and San Francisco. He was also one of the first American publishers to establish agencies in Shanghai, China; Japan; and the Philippine Islands. He published the following authors and in addition was a personal friend of many of them: James Lane Allen, Gertrude Atherton, James Bryce, Winston Churchill (the American), Francis Marion Crawford, Zona Gale, Lewis E. Gates, Vachel Lindsay, Jack London, John Masefield, Edgar Lee Masters, Ernest Poole, Jacob Riis, Theodore Roosevelt, May Sinclair, Ida M. Tarbell, Sara Teasdale, H. G. Wells, and Owen Wister. Brett had a reputation for keeping his own counsel, sound business sense, admirable literary taste, amiability, and attention to office details. He reportedly received the manuscript of London's *The Call of the Wild* late one afternoon in 1903, took it home and read it overnight, and telegraphed the author its acceptance first thing in the morning.

Brett hailed 1914 as the year initiating a new age of poetry and noted that for the first time since the popularity of Alfred, Lord Tennyson in England and America, poets were becoming bestsellers. Harriet Monroe had founded *Poetry: A Magazine of Verse* two years before, was publishing poems by Robert Frost, Vachel Lindsay, Edgar Lee Masters, and Carl Sandburg, among others, and was starting what became known as the "poetic renaissance." Macmillan was the first book firm to establish a separate department to issue children's books, and from 1920 on, it achieved its greatest financial gains, in large part because Brett began to publish profit-making textbooks for high schools and colleges. In 1923 the firm moved in to its own $800,000, eight-story office building at Fifth Avenue and Twelfth Street, with offices, a book store, a library, and several upper floors reserved for storage. His book list ultimately contained 14,000 titles, to which he added approximately 600 new ones annually. He helped establish an association of American publishers, sought to abolish duty on imported books and to lower postage on books, and lobbied for better international copyright laws.

Brett retired as president of the company in 1931, by which time annual sales amounted to $8 million. He turned over the reins to his son, George P. Brett, Jr., but remained active as chairman of the board. In 1935 one of Brett's manuscript scouts read Margaret Mitchell's nearly completed manuscript of *Gone with the Wind* and snapped it up. When published in 1936, this novel became an instant success, selling 50,000 in one day and a million within six months. Ironically, back in 1925 Brett predicted that the era of the bestseller was over, partly because movies were drawing millions away from reading.

Always a versatile and public-spirited man, Brett combined his hobby of tree-growing with membership in recreational and civic organizations. In his pinetum at Greenfield Hill, Darien, he developed more than

300 varieties of evergreens, and he also grew many varieties of palm trees at his winter home in Cocoanut Grove, Florida. He wrote several articles on tree culture and in addition a few rather amateurish pieces on public affairs and sociology. He was a member of several golf and country clubs in Connecticut and the New York Chamber of Commerce, president of the Greenfield Land Development Company, and a director of the Fairfield Beach Company and of the Fairfield Trust Company. He died in Fairfield, Connecticut, at which time his company employed approximately 650 people.

The American Macmillan publishing house began to be outdistanced by aggressive competitors soon after World War II. It broke completely from its British parent Macmillan & Co., Ltd., in 1952, grew ripe for a takeover, and in 1960 became a subsidiary wholly owned—at a cost of more than $7 million—by the Crowell-Collier Publishing Company. Brett's son was replaced that same year as chairman of the old firm. In the early 1980s what was by then Macmillan, Inc., was divided into the Macmillan Publishing Company, Inc., Collier Macmillan International, and the Macmillan Educational Corporation.

• Correspondence relating to Brett is in the Macmillan Papers, British Library, London, and in the New York Public Library; the Appleton-Century Company records, Lilly Library, Indiana University, Bloomington; the Houghton Mifflin Company papers, Houghton Library, Harvard University; and the McCrady Family Papers, South Caroliniana Library, University of South Carolina, Columbia. Much material, often only incidental, on Brett is contained in Charles L. Graves, *Life and Letters of Alexander Macmillan* (1910); Charles Morgan, *The House of Macmillan (1843–1943)* (1944); *Letters to Macmillan*, ed. Simon Nowell-Smith (1967); William A. Targ, *Indecent Pleasures: The Life and Colorful Times of William Targ* (1975); John Tebbel, *Between Covers: The Rise and Transformation of Book Publishing in America* (1987); and *The Correspondence of Henry James and the House of Macmillan, 1877–1914: "All the Links in the Chain,"* ed. Rayburn S. Moore (1993). An obituary is in the *New York Times*, 20 Sept. 1936.

ROBERT L. GALE

BRETT, George Platt, Jr. (9 Dec. 1893–11 Feb. 1984), publisher, was born in Darien, Connecticut, the son of George Platt Brett, Sr., manager of the New York City branch of Mcmillan & Co. of London, and Marie Louise Tostevin. Although the family home was not far from New York, Brett was ten years old before he ever saw the city, which he immediately disliked. He attended the private Salisbury School in Connecticut and then the Collegiate School in New York. In the autumn of 1913 he began to work as a stock clerk in his father's company. His first job was to remove nails from packing cases filled with books sent from London by the Macmillan firm there. For a few months in 1916 he tried being a salesman for Doubleday, Page and Company, a rival publishing house, but soon thereafter became a tradebook salesman for the Macmillan firm.

Also in 1916 Brett, who was a member of the New York National Guard, saw duty on the Mexican border. He attended officers' training school in Plattsburg, New York, and was commissioned second lieutenant in the U.S. Army in August 1917. That same month he married Isabel Stevenson Yeomans; they had two children. He served in France with the Seventy-seventh Division, was promoted to first lieutenant in January 1918 and to captain that May. He returned home in May 1919.

Brett resumed his employment with the Macmillan Company, worked in 1919–1920 in its Chicago branch, and then returned to New York. His rise in the ranks at the headquarters of the firm was steady. From 1920 to 1928 while he was sales manager of the New York office and a director of the company, he opened branch offices of the trade department in Atlanta, Boston, Chicago, Dallas, and San Francisco. In 1928 he became general manager of the company and held this position until 1934. He was responsible for arrangements enabling Macmillan of New York, Macmillan of London, and Macmillan of Canada to distribute and sell each other's books. The firm also became the U.S. agent to distribute titles published by the Cambridge University Press and the Society for the Promotion of Christian Knowledge. At about this time he humorously defined the company as a "department store of publishing." It had several divisions: the trade department published biographies, fiction, poetry, and books of general appeal; its textbook department, books for all levels of public schools, parochial schools, and colleges and universities; and its smaller departments, children's books, and books pertaining to medicine and health.

In 1929 Brett, who had remained in the Army Reserve Corps, was promoted to major. His father resigned as president of the company in 1931 to serve as chairman of the board until his death five years later. In 1931 Brett was elected company president. Only then was he able to emerge completely from his powerful father's shadow and demonstrate his own qualities as an able leader in business. Doing so required him to counter the personality of Harold Strong Latham, who from 1921 had been the vocal editor in chief of the company. It was Brett's habit to run the firm part of the time from his Manhattan home on West Twelfth Street, which was connected to his office by a 125-foot passageway.

In 1935 Latham was on a cross-country hunt for manuscripts when in Atlanta, Georgia, he was shown the unfinished manuscript of Margaret Mitchell's *Gone with the Wind*. Although Brett at first doubted that such a long first novel could make any money, the company secured the rights to it and published it in 1936. It became one of the bestsellers of all time, with perhaps 20 million copies in print, including translations in more than twelve languages.

In 1941 Brett was commissioned lieutenant colonel in the New York National Guard. In 1942 his firm scored a first in the history of American publishing by producing eighteen books in twenty-eight days for a

Civil Aeronautics Authority project titled the *Air Education Series*. During World War II Brett served the War Production Board by advising it on matters of pulp and paper production, allocation of paper, printing, and publishing. In 1943 he resigned his National Guard commission to accept an invitation from the Department of State to go with heads of four other publishing houses to several South American countries. Their purpose was to determine the feasibility of selling U.S. books there. In 1945 Brett found himself embroiled in a fight over censorship of Kathleen Winsor's novel *Forever Amber*, published by Macmillan. The first case under a new Massachusetts law taking action against an allegedly obscene book, rather than its author, targeted *Forever Amber*. Brett assured the vociferous Boston authorities that he would not try to sell his spicy novel there. Since he already had a quarter of a million back orders for it, his profits were secure.

In 1948 Brett was a member of a five-man panel to visit Germany for the purpose of introducing textbooks in schools in the American zone. In 1958 he left his position as president of the Macmillan Company to assume the position of chairman of the board. After two years he resigned. He died in Southport, Connecticut.

Brett achieved continued success for Macmillan of New York by expanding internationally, continuing to departmentalize, delegating authority and responsibility over choice of titles, including uncontroversial textbooks on its enormous list, and resisting would-be mergers for a longer period than several of his rivals.

• Commercial papers relating to the Brett family are in the Macmillan papers at the British Library in London and in the New York Public Library. Information concerning George Platt Brett, Jr., is in John Tebbel, *Between Covers: The Rise and Transformation of Book Publishing in America* (1987). A brief death notice is the *New York Times*, 16 Feb. 1984.

ROBERT L. GALE

BRETT, William Howard (1 July 1846–24 Aug. 1918), librarian, was born in Braceville, Ohio, the son of Morgan Lewis Brett, an engineer, and Jane Brokaw. At the time of his birth Brett's parents were members of the Trumbull Phalanx, a Fourierist utopian experiment in eastern Ohio. Shortly after his birth Brett's family moved to a modest home in Warren, Ohio, near the Mahoning River. Brett took an early interest in books, learning to read before he started attending the Warren public schools. An early influence on his life was William Porter, owner of W. N. Porter and Sons, a small bookshop near Brett's home. It was here that Brett spent many hours becoming acquainted with the world of books and where he got his first job as soon as he was old enough to be of service. At the age of fourteen Brett was appointed librarian at Warren High School's small library, a position he held until he left school to earn a living in 1862.

During the Civil War Brett made several unsuccessful attempts to enlist in the Union army, finally succeeding in 1864 by joining the 196th Ohio Volunteer Infantry as a musician. In 1868 Brett enrolled for a year at the University of Michigan and later spent another year at Western Reserve College in Hudson, Ohio. In need of money, Brett moved to Cleveland, Ohio, in 1874. He spent the next ten years as a salesman for the Cobb and Andrews Book Store, achieving the reputation of being the best-informed bookman in the city. It was during this period, in 1879, that Brett married Alice L. Allen. They had four sons and a daughter.

Since its founding in 1869 the Cleveland Public Library had suffered from poor organization and management, and by 1884 it had deteriorated into one of the worst metropolitan libraries in the country. That year the trustees of the Public Library Board, none of whom had any idea of the qualifications needed for a librarian, searched for a new librarian who could turn the library around. The trustees offered Brett the job based primarily on his reputation as a knowledgeable bookman. For family reasons Brett was hesitant at first about taking a position of lesser prestige and money, but he finally accepted from a sense of public duty.

From the beginning, Brett's approach was that the role of a library was not to make people wise, but to make them want to be wise. He investigated management practices at other municipal libraries and adopted those practices that were useful for achieving his own goals. In 1885 Brett began a reclassification of the library's collection using principles from Melvil Dewey's first outline of his decimal classification system. He next undertook the tasks of shelf-listing and recataloging the collection, which led to the library's publishing an easily comprehensible one-volume dictionary catalog of the English books in the collection in 1889.

Brett's most significant and most controversial innovation came about when Cleveland Public became the first metropolitan library to institute the open-shelf policy, which allowed borrowers access to the book stacks. Brett was convinced from his experience in the book trade that it was important for borrowers to have direct contact with the books. Up to that time libraries traditionally had housed their collections behind counters with staff members retrieving books for the patrons. Since the open-shelf policy had been tried only in a few small libraries, many librarians and critics believed that in a large library open stacks would cause pandemonium and would result in the widespread loss of books. Brett, however, felt that borrowers must not only be trusted but that they should be challenged to prove their integrity.

In 1890 Brett went against the accepted library practice of physically separating only the reference and circulating collections. He began implementing a flexible organizational structure based on divisional lines by arranging the collection in alcoves by subjects. This gave individual staff members responsibility for the same class of books and allowed them to develop an expertise that better enabled them to answer related reference questions and to select books. As an aid to researchers Brett started publishing in 1896 his *Cumu-*

lative Index to the Selected List of Periodicals, which eventually became *The Reader's Guide to Periodical Literature*.

Brett continually sought new ways to utilize the educational functions of the library and to make its facilities equally accessible to all who were entitled to use it. By the late 1880s Brett recognized that the main library was inconveniently located for many in the city and that the library needed to reach out to the people. In 1890 the library opened its first station and in 1892 its first branch. As a way of providing youngsters a supply of wholesome reading materials, Brett set up the first separate area for children in 1898 and opened a children's department in 1903. By 1918 the library was circulating almost 3.5 million books through more than 700 distribution points, including branches and stations in schools and factories.

Brett also became involved in the development of the profession of librarian. To ensure the efficiency of the library's staff Brett commenced the first of a series of professional training lectures. By 1903 he had developed plans for a new library school, which was established at Western Reserve University in Cleveland, and he served as the library school's first dean until his death.

During his 34-year career Brett developed the Cleveland Public Library from a small, badly organized institution into a great citywide system with an international reputation. A leading innovator in the field, Brett's initiation and adoption of such concepts as open stacks, children's libraries, branch libraries, and extension work helped change the popular impression of libraries as restrictive institutions, lacking in warmth and hospitality, to an image of open and generous ones, accessible to all. Brett died in Cleveland after being struck down on the street by an automobile.

• Most of what has been published about Brett appears to depend on accounts of Brett's life written by Linda Eastman, Brett's successor at the Cleveland Public Library. Eastman's article, "William Howard Brett, 1846–1918" in the Cleveland Public Library's magazine, *The Open Shelf* (Sept.–Oct. 1918), is reproduced in "William Howard Brett: In Memoriam," *Library Journal* (Nov. 1918), which is a compilation of tributes written shortly after his death by people who worked with him. Much of Eastman's article appears in an expanded form in her short book, *Portrait of a Librarian: William Howard Brett* (1940). It is an informative account of Brett's life, but Eastman is too general and too brief. Another brief biography appears in *A History of Cleveland and Its Environs, the Heart of New Connecticut* (1918). Clarence C. Cramer's history of the Cleveland Public Library, *Open Shelves and Open Minds* (1972), relies on Eastman for much of the information on Brett, but Cramer does a fine job of putting Brett's accomplishments in perspective and describing why they are significant. Obituaries are in the *Cleveland Plain Dealer*, 25 Aug. 1918, and the *Cleveland Press*, 26 Aug. 1918.

WILLIAM BECKER

BREUER, Marcel Lajos (22 May 1902–1 July 1981), architect, was born in Pécs, Hungary, the son of Jacob Breuer, a dental technician, and Franciska Kan. His formal education began in the arts at the age of eighteen when he received a scholarship to the Fine Arts Academy in Vienna, Austria. However, it only took a short time before he became tired of the traditional teaching methods and took a job in an architect's office. After hearing about a new design school, the Bauhaus, which had begun in 1919, he traveled to Weimar, Germany, and entered the school in 1920, concentrating on furniture design. He graduated in 1924 and returned soon after in 1925, to the school, now in Dessau, when Walter Adolph Gropius requested his services as the master of the furniture workshop.

On his arrival at Dessau, Breuer bought a bicycle and became intrigued with the idea of using light, hollow metal tubes for furniture similar to those used for bicycles. He soon purchased seamless steel tubes, aluminum being too expensive, and set to work transforming the material into models of which produced his famous tubular steel furniture, the Wassily chair being the most well known. The name was derived from Wassily Kandinsky, who assured a skeptical Breuer of its success. Although Breuer continued to be somewhat doubtful of the design, he used it as the centerpiece in an exhibition of his work held in the Dessau Kunstalle January 1926. Later that year he married Martha Erps. He remained at the Bauhaus until 1928, when conflicts within the school left him dissatisfied. He felt that the separation between the departments was too severe and was a hindrance. In the end, the cooperative nature of the school became too much for Breuer, and he resigned in April 1927.

In 1928 Breuer set up an architectural practice in Berlin, where he had little success. He designed a number of large-scale projects but none that were actually built. The only designs that came to fruition were for furniture; however, he was able to live on royalties from his tubular steel furniture. In 1929 work began to pick up and he designed a number of interiors that included his own furniture designs. He built the Harnismacher house, his first built structure. The house, designed in the International style, was heavily influenced by Le Corbusier.

Breuer, a Jew, left Nazi Germany in November 1931, and for a number of years traveled around without having a permanent home. He was invited by Sigfried Giedion to visit Zurich, Switzerland, where he received several important commissions. He redesigned Warnbedarf stores in Zurich and Basel, along with a line of furniture for the same store and codesigned, with Alfred and Emil Roth, the Doldertal flats in Zurich. Between 1932 and 1934, he worked on a line of aluminum furniture, a similar version of his tubular steel line but much less expensive.

Gropius, having moved to England in 1934, persuaded Breuer to follow. He began corresponding with F. S. R. York, a British architect, and their decision to form a partnership facilitated Breuer's admission into England. Although Breuer was well versed in the new International style that Gropius and his contemporaries were introducing to England, he modified this style by using traditional materials such as Cotswold stone and birch plywood, which gave his modern designs a more traditional aesthetic.

In October 1935 Breuer made England his permanent residence, and with Gropius's suggestion he began to design a new line of plywood furniture based on his aluminum designs. Through Jack Pritchard, who developed the Isoken Company in 1931 with the purpose of promoting modern design, he was able to make his furniture designs a reality. Breuer was dedicated to using natural materials to ensure a comfortable, practical piece of furniture. The most influential was the Isoken long chair made of laminated wood with an upholstered cushion and was directly taken from one of his aluminum designs.

In the fall of 1937 Breuer moved to the United States, where Gropius had not only obtained for him a teaching position at Harvard University but also offered Breuer a partnership position in his architectural firm. At Harvard, Gropius and Breuer were responsible for teaching some of the leaders of the next generation of architects, including I. M. Pei, Philip Johnson, Paul Rudolph, Edward Barnes, and Elliot Noyes. In their architecture practice, Gropius and Breuer mainly designed residences with simple geometric plans, using traditional materials of stone and plywood. Their desire was to transform the International style to fit the New England landscape; as a result, they used stone and timber in their buildings. Although they designed mainly houses for prominent New England families, there were two exceptions, the Wheaton (Mass.) College Art Center (1938) and Wartime Housing in Pittsburgh, Pennsylvania (1943). Throughout this period, Breuer also continued to design furniture. The Franck House (1939) marked the last collaboration between Gropius and Breuer. Together they designed the exterior structure, but Breuer was responsible for the interior, including the furniture and fixture designs. The four-story house, built in rich, natural materials and faced with brick and local fieldstone, was pure, geometric International style.

Breuer married Constance Crocker Leighton in 1940; they had two children. A year later, in 1941, he established his own practice in Cambridge, Massachusetts. In 1946 he relocated the firm to New York City, resigning from Harvard and moving his residence, first to Wellfleet on Cape Cod, then to New Canaan, Connecticut. He designed the Geller House (1945), which was followed by construction of his own residence (1947).

With his growing success, bigger commissions began to come Breuer's way, some of which included the UNESCO Headquarters, Paris (1958); the Institute for Advanced Study, Princeton, New Jersey (1954–1957); the United States embassy, The Hague, Netherlands (1958); and the Whitney Museum in New York City (1966). In many of his later buildings Breuer developed a double Y-shaped plan, an efficient form for an office building. He continued to be active until his retirement in 1976. Although large commissions marked his later career, his best work can be found in his earlier furniture designs and interior work. Breuer died in New York City.

• Breuer's papers and correspondence are in the Marcel Breuer Collection in the George Arents Research Library for Special Collections, Syracuse University. See Marcel Breuer, *Sun and Shadow: The Philosophy of an Architect* (1955), for his own philosophy. Essays and articles by him include "Genesis of Design," in *The Man-made Object*, ed. Gyorgy Kepes (1966), pp. 120–25, "Les buts de l'architecture," *Architecture formes et fonctions* (1962–1963): 6–29; "Project for a Worker's House," *California Arts and Architecture*, Dec. 1943, pp. 24–25; "8 Architects on Exhibition," *Trend in Design of Everyday Things* 1 (Summer 1936): 108–13; and "A House in Bristol," *Design for Today* 3 (Dec. 1935): 459–63. Guido Carlo Argan, *Marcel Breuer disegno industriale e architectura* (1957), is an important early source. Peter Blake wrote *Marcel Breuer, Architect and Designer* (1949), the Museum of Modern Art exhibition catalog. Henry Russel-Hitchcock examined Breuer's early work in *Marcel Breuer and the American Tradition in Architecture* (1938). Cranston Jones spans a forty-year period of Breuer's work in *Marcel Breuer: Buildings and Projects, 1921–1961* (1962), while Tician Papachristou treats later work in *Marcel Breuer: New Buildings and Projects* (1970). See also the catalog for an exhibition at the Museum of Modern Art, Christopher Wilk, *Marcel Breuer: Furniture and Interiors* (1981).

JENNIFER NOELLE THOMPSON

BREWER, David Josiah (20 June 1837–28 Mar. 1910), associate justice of the U.S. Supreme Court, was born in Smyrna, Asia Minor, the son of Josiah Brewer, a Congregational missionary, and Emilia Field, the sister of U.S. Supreme Court justice Stephen J. Field, legal reformer David Dudley Field, and capitalist Cyrus W. Field. In 1838, after eight years in Smyrna, financial problems dictated the Brewers' return to their native New England, where Reverend Brewer held a variety of pastorates throughout Massachusetts and Connecticut. An outspoken opponent of slavery and proponent of peace, the elder Brewer sent his son to Wesleyan College in nearby Middletown, where he attended for two years before completing his studies in 1856 at Yale. After reading law under David Dudley Field and graduating from the Albany Law School in 1858, young Brewer gained admission to the New York bar, but like his other famous uncle, Stephen J. Field, Brewer went west to seek his fortune. After a brief residence in Kansas City and an unsuccessful search for gold at Pike's Peak, in late 1859 he settled in Leavenworth in Kansas Territory, where he lived for the next thirty years. In 1861 he married Louise R. Landon, with whom he had three children.

Brewer soon emerged as a leading member of the state's legal community. By 1861 his reputation as a railroad and business lawyer led to his appointment as commissioner of the federal circuit for the district court of Kansas, a position that exempted him from service in the Union army during the Civil War. Free to pursue his career, Brewer desired a political rather than a judicial office, but his attempt in 1862 to win the county Republican convention's nomination to the Kansas legislature was unsuccessful. Upon defeat he reluctantly accepted an appointment as judge of the county probate and criminal courts, and after a successful term, in 1864 voters elected him judge of the First Judicial District of Kansas. He later served as city attorney of Leavenworth (1869–1870) and as a member of the Supreme Court of Kansas (1870–1884), before President Chester Arthur appointed him to the Eight Federal Judicial Circuit Court. In 1890, after the death of Justice Stanley Matthews, President Benjamin Harrison appointed Brewer to the U.S. Supreme Court, where he served for two decades. At the time of his appointment, his uncle Stephen J. Field was still an active Supreme Court justice.

Brewer's opinions, like those of the Court as a whole around the turn of the century, generally protected business interests and expanded the role of the judiciary. He wrote the majority opinion, for example, in *Reagan v. Farmers' Loan and Trust Company* (1894), where the Court invalidated rates set by the Texas Railroad Commission as violative of the property rights of railroad investors, and in *In re Debs* (1895) he upheld a broad injunction issued by a lower federal court that had crushed a national railway strike. Moreover, Brewer silently joined a number of the Court's most conservative rulings of the period, including those invalidating a federal income tax (*Pollack v. Farmers' Loan and Trust* [1895]), sustaining the legality of the sugar monopoly (*U.S. v. E. C. Knight Co.* [1895]), and striking down a state statute setting maximum hours for bakers (*Lochner v. New York* [1905]). Still, Brewer wrote a few notable opinions that upheld Progressive Era economic regulation. His brief concurrence in *Northern Securities v. United States* (1903), where the Court ordered the dissolution of the Northern Securities Company in accordance with the Sherman Antitrust Act, outlined a distinction between "reasonable" and "unreasonable" restraints of trade that the Court later adopted as its guide in deciding antitrust cases. In *Muller v. Oregon* (1905), moreover, Brewer wrote perhaps his most famous opinion, which upheld an Oregon statute that set a maximum number of hours for women employed in laundries. In short, he was more a moderate conservative on matters of economic regulation than an overt defender of corporate interests.

Brewer produced a mixed record on civil rights issues. He consistently defended the rights of Asian immigrants, almost always in dissent. In *Fong Yue Ting v. United States* (1893), for example, Brewer attacked a congressional act requiring deportation of Chinese who failed to obtain certificates of residence as a violation of the Bill of Rights, which he applied to aliens as well as citizens. Moreover, in *United States v. Sing Tuck* (1904) Brewer argued that the administrative procedures required for deportation of illegal immigrants unconstitutionally denied them access to the federal courts, and in *United States v. Ju Toy* (1905) he similarly asserted that Chinese residents ought to have the right to have their citizenship claims tried in federal courtrooms. Brewer's record on the rights of African Americans was less impressive. Although he broadly interpreted the Thirteenth Amendment and upheld a federal antipeonage statute in *Clyatt v. United States* (1905), he denied relief to the African Americans in that case because of the technical insufficiency of the indictment. Hopes that Brewer might endorse an expansive reading of the Reconstruction amendments were put to rest the following year in *Hodges v. United States*, when the justice denied the federal government power to prosecute a gang of Arkansas whites who had forced a group of blacks to leave their jobs. Furthermore, in one of the most significant segregation cases of the era (he did not participate in *Plessy v. Ferguson* [1896] because of his daughter's untimely death), Brewer upheld a state statute forbidding integrated instruction in private schools and colleges in *Berea College v. Kentucky* (1906). Like his judicial colleagues with antislavery backgrounds, Brewer placed a higher value on the states' power to decide such matters than he did on the constitutional rights of African Americans.

Brewer took an active role in social reform and political affairs both before and during his Supreme Court career. A devout Congregationalist, he served as Sunday school superintendent of his church in Leavenworth and pursued a variety of local civic causes. Most notably, as superintendent of Leavenworth's school system, he modernized the curriculum, upgraded the city's two black schools, and advocated female education. An accomplished orator, during his years on the Court Brewer frequently spoke out on the political issues of the day, and he edited and published two ten-volume sets, *The World's Best Orations* (1899) and *The World's Best Essays* (1900). International peace and disarmament were the subjects of many of his own speeches and writings. In 1895 Brewer served as president of a commission created by Congress to investigate the boundary disputed by Venezuela and British Guyana (and later on the arbitral tribunal that ended the controversy), and he only grudgingly supported the Spanish-American War. After the war, Brewer consistently criticized the American imperial expansion that resulted from the conflict and championed international tribunals to resolve disputes. Consistent with his reform activities, he also advocated woman suffrage and served for five years as president of the Associated Charities of Washington. After the death of his first wife in 1898, he married Emma Minor Mott in 1901; the couple had no children.

Brewer's life reflected the paradox and change of the late nineteenth and early twentieth centuries. His deep religious convictions and belief in the sacredness of property rights rooted him firmly in the nineteenth century, yet his progressive reform activities and internationalist stance foreshadowed the future. In short, Brewer was an idealist and an activist, both on and off the bench. He died in Washington, D.C.

• Brewer's papers are in the Yale University Library, New Haven, Conn., and his U.S. Supreme Court opinions can be found in the *United States Reports*, vols. 123–218 (1890–1910). In addition, his circuit court and state court opinions are in the *Federal Reporter*, vols. 21–64 (1884–1894); the *Pacific Reporter*, vols. 1–3 (1883–1884); and *Kansas Reports*, 2d. ed., vols. 1–29 (1861–1883) and vol. 83 (1911). A few representative speeches, reflecting the themes of peace and disarmament, can be found in Edward Everett Hale and David J. Brewer, *Mohonk Addresses* (1910). A biography of Brewer is Michael J. Brodhead, *David J. Brewer: The Life of a Supreme Court Justice, 1837–1910* (1994), which provides a sound and well researched account of the justice's life and major opinions. Useful articles dealing with Brewer's judicial record include Joseph Gordon Hylton, "David Josiah Brewer: A Conservative Justice Reconsidered," *Journal of Supreme Court History* (1994): 45–64; Hylton, "The Judge Who Abstained in *Plessy v. Ferguson*: Justice David Brewer and the Problem of Race," *Mississippi Law Journal* 61 (1991): 315–64; and Robert E. Gamer, "Justice Brewer and Substantive Due Process: A Conservative Court Revisited," *Vanderbilt Law Review* 18 (1964–1965): 615–41. See also Lynford A. Lardner, "The Constitutional Doctrines of Justice David Josiah Brewer" (Ph.D. diss., Princeton Univ., 1938), and, for a brief and insightful sketch of Brewer's Supreme Court opinions, Kermit L. Hall's entry on Brewer in *The Supreme Court Justices: A Biographical Dictionary*, ed. Melvin I. Urofsky (1994). An obituary is in the *New York Times*, 29 Mar. 1910.

TIMOTHY S. HUEBNER

BREWER, Thomas Mayo (21 Nov. 1814–23 Jan. 1880), ornithologist and journalist, was born in Boston, Massachusetts, the son of James Brewer, a colonial in the revolutionary war (mother's name unknown). He graduated from Harvard College in 1835 and from Harvard Medical School three years later. After a few years of practice in Boston's North End, Brewer virtually abandoned medicine in favor of journalism and natural history.

A strong Whig, he served the party's cause during most of the 1840s and the 1850s as an editor of the Boston *Atlas* and as the paper's Washington correspondent. In 1844 he was elected to the Boston school board, and he later served a second term, shortly before his death. In 1857 he turned to publishing, becoming a partner in the firm of Swan & Tileston. Later he headed the house of Brewer & Tileston. He retired from business in 1875.

Brewer is chiefly remembered for his contributions to ornithology. As a young man he became acquainted with two of the most able ornithologists of the time, John James Audubon and Thomas Nuttall. His earliest scientific papers appeared in the publications of the Boston Society of Natural History, the first significant one being a supplement to Ebenezer Emmons's 1833 list of Massachusetts birds. In 1840, with Audubon's assistance, he brought out an inexpensive edition of Alexander Wilson's *American Ornithology*, giving this classic work a much wider readership than it had hitherto enjoyed. To it he added new information and a "Synopsis of American Birds."

The most important publication of which he was the sole author is part 1 of *North American Oölogy*, published in 1857 by the Smithsonian Institution. In addition to the data on eggs, it contained information on the life histories of the birds treated, plus a great deal of synonymy, and was the standard work on the subject for most of the remainder of the nineteenth century. Because of the high cost of the illustrations, no other parts appeared. Nevertheless, it is well regarded as the first major American work on birds' eggs.

With Spencer Fullerton Baird and Robert Ridgway (1850–1929) he published the three-volume *History of North American Birds* (1874), for which he provided the life-history material, an estimated two-thirds of the text. *The Water Birds of North America*, a two-volume continuation by the same authors—and also nominally the second part of James Graham Cooper's *Ornithology*, vol. 1: *Land Birds*—appeared (in Brewer's case posthumously) in 1884. These two monumental works were standard references for many years. They also provided Brewer the opportunity to insert data intended for the other parts of the aborted *North American Oölogy* series. Most of his later articles, notes, and reviews were published in the *American Naturalist* and the *Bulletin of the Nuttall Ornithological Club*.

In his last years he became embroiled in a dispute with Elliott Coues, ornithologist, and others over the introduction of the English sparrow into the United States, which he had championed and which Coues opposed. Whereas Brewer argued that the sparrow would be a useful addition to the nation's avifauna because it ate insect pests, Coues and others warned (rightfully so in the view of many) that the bird itself would become a pest. Their published exchanges became increasingly acrimonious and personal. Although Brewer was impatient with some of the younger generation of ornithologists, such as Coues and his contemporaries, believing that they should base their work on established, published authorities rather than spend time in the field trying to discover new facts, to others he was a loyal and sympathetic friend.

In 1849 Brewer married Sally R. Coffin, with whom he had two children. Brewer died in Boston. His will provided for the donation of his extensive collection of eggs to Harvard's Museum of Comparative Zoology.

• Some of Brewer's correspondence is located in the George N. Lawrence Papers, American Philosophical Society Library, Philadelphia, and the John E. Thayer Collection of Audubon Papers in the Houghton Library, Harvard University. A helpful source of biographical information is an obituary notice, "Thomas Mayo Brewer," *Bulletin of the Nuttall Ornithological Society* 5, no. 2 (1880): 102–4. See also Robert M. Mengel, comp., *A Catalogue of the Ellis Collection of Ornithological Books in the University of Kansas Libraries*, vol. 1, A–B (1972), pp. 66–8, 205–6.

MICHAEL J. BRODHEAD

BREWER, William Henry (14 Sept. 1828–2 Nov. 1910), explorer-scientist and agriculturist, was born in Poughkeepsie, New York, the son of Henry Brewer and Rebecca DuBois, farmers. Brewer grew up on a farm in Enfield, New York. From 1848 to 1850 he studied scientific agriculture at the School of Applied Chemistry at Yale under Benjamin Silliman and John Pitkin Norton. He then taught at Ithaca Academy and at the Agricultural Institute at Lancaster, New York, while studying for Yale examinations. He received the

Bachelor of Philosophy in 1852, in the first class to graduate from what later became the Sheffield Scientific School. Brewer taught high school from 1852 to 1855 in Ovid, New York, where his duties included agricultural chemistry. In 1855 he traveled to Germany to study chemistry with Robert Wilhelm Bunsen in Heidelberg and with Justus von Liebig in Munich. He made a 600-mile botanical trip across Switzerland in 1856. He also visited agricultural schools and scientific farms in Germany, France, and England.

On his return from Europe Brewer accepted a professorship of natural sciences at Washington College (later Washington and Jefferson College) in Pennsylvania. He married Angelina Jameson in 1858, but in 1860 his wife and infant son both died.

That same year Brewer was recruited by Josiah Dwight Whitney, the California state geologist and director of the proposed California Geological Survey. Brewer, appointed principal assistant, in charge of the botanical department, arrived in San Francisco in November 1860. During the survey he collected 2,000 plants, studied California forests, and measured the giant sequoias. Brewer's botanical collections, titled *Botany*, were published much later, the first volume with the help of Asa Gray and Sereno Watson at Harvard (1876); the second volume was authored by Watson alone (1880). Brewer also made geologic collections and discussed volcanic geology, glaciers, minerals, and fossils in his journal and reports to Josiah Whitney.

Brewer is, however, best known as an explorer, especially of the Sierra Nevada and California coast ranges, and as the leader of field parties for the Geological Survey. The survey was set up by an act of the California Legislature in 1860 to furnish "proper maps and diagrams [of the state] . . . with a full and scientific description of its rocks, fossils, soils, minerals, and of its botanical and zoological productions, together with specimens of the same" (Farquhar, p. x), though its major purpose, in the eyes of the legislature, was to discover gold and other minerals of immediate economic value. It did not fulfill this purpose, but much of scientific value was discovered, in large part owing to Brewer's work. In Francis Farquhar's words, he was a man "of the strongest fiber, of unflagging energy, the soundest judgment, the utmost tact, and of unequivocal honesty and loyalty" (p. x).

Brewer was a very meticulous man, perhaps an unusual trait for an inveterate explorer. In addition to his field notebooks full of observations, measurements, and statistics, he wrote a personal journal in the form of letters to his brother, Edgar, and family. Those of this period, 1860–1864, were collected and published as a book, *Up and Down California*. The letters were often written after a long day in the field, by candlelight or firelight, sometimes with frozen fingers. While climbing unknown, unnamed peaks in the high Sierras they camped at very high elevations. For example,

> Saturday, July 2, we were up at dawn, and [Charles] Hoffman [the topographer] and I climbed this cone which I had believed to be the highest of this part of the Sierra. We had a rough time, made two unsuccessful attempts to reach the summit, climbing terribly steep rocks, and at last, after eight hours of very hard climbing, reached the top [of Mt. Brewer, later named for him]. The view was yet wilder than we have ever seen before. . . . Such a landscape! A hundred peaks in sight over thirteen thousand feet—many very sharp—deep canyons, cliffs in every direction almost rivaling Yosemite, sharp ridges almost inaccessible to man, on which human foot has never trod—all combined to produce a view the sublimity of which is rarely equaled, one which few are privileged to behold. (Farquhar, pp. 524–25)

A letter by Brewer describing the first ascent of Mount Shasta lured Clarence King, a recent graduate of the Sheffield Scientific School, to come west in 1863 and join the Geological Survey as an unpaid assistant. King, later the Fortieth Parallel Survey director, scaled many peaks and wrote *Mountaineering in the Sierra Nevada* (1872), which romanticized mountaineering in California and brought the Sierras and the Survey to the rapt attention of eastern readers. Brewer's own account was not published until 1930.

Brewer worked on the survey in California for four years; during the fourth he was offered the chair of agriculture at Yale's Sheffield Scientific School. In the first three years of the survey he had traveled 13,507 miles, including more than 6,000 on horseback and nearly 3,000 on foot. During the winters he lived in San Francisco, where he was an early member and officer of the California Academy of Sciences. The legislature provided no funds for working up the results of the survey, one cause of the long delay in publishing his botanical findings. He accepted the Yale appointment and moved to New Haven, Connecticut, in 1865. He remained in this position until his 1903 retirement.

In 1868 Brewer married Georgiana Robinson; they had four children. His days of major exploration were over, although he did make three shorter expeditions: to the Rocky Mountains of Colorado in 1869, to Greenland in 1894, and to the Bering Sea in 1899 with the Harriman Alaska Expedition.

Brewer was active in promoting scientific agriculture throughout Connecticut, helping to found the Connecticut Agriculture Experiment Station, the first in the United States. He was interested in microbiology and its bearing on sanitation, water quality, and other areas, as early as the 1870s, and he was a founder of the Connecticut State Board of Health, of which he was president for sixteen years. He wrote many papers and reports and addressed farmers on aspects of scientific agriculture as diverse as soils, seed viability, cereal production, stream pollution, and horse-breeding.

In 1896 the National Academy, authorized by Congress, appointed a Forestry Commission, including Brewer, to recommend national forest policy. John Muir conducted the commission on a tour of forests in California, Oregon, and Arizona. Brewer was also an honorary officer of the Sierra Club and supported forest conservation, particularly promoting the giant sequoia national preserves.

Brewer was elected to the National Academy of Sciences in 1880. In 1902 he chaired a National Academy of Science committee, requested by President Theodore Roosevelt, to promote scientific exploration of the Philippine Islands. In addition to these distinctions, several species were named for him, including a California spruce tree, *Picea breweriana*. He died in New Haven.

Brewer was an outstanding scientific explorer of California on the survey that served as a model for much future exploration. In his Connecticut years, he promoted teaching, research, and institutions that fostered scientific agriculture and public health.

• Brewer's papers relating to the California Geological Survey, including field notebooks and much correspondence, are in the Bancroft Library, University of California, Berkeley. Later papers and the original manuscript of his journal are in the University Archives, Yale University Library. *Up and Down California in 1860–1864: The Journal of William H. Brewer*, ed. Francis P. Farquhar (1930; repr. 1966) is an excellent source. Brewer's botanical and other work on the survey is discussed in Nancy G. Slack, "The Botanical Exploration of California from Menzies to Muir," in *John Muir: Life and Work*, ed. Sally Miller (1993), pp. 193–242. Russell H. Chittenden, "William Henry Brewer," National Academy of Sciences, *Biographical Memoirs* 12 (1928): 289–323, is helpful for his Connecticut years and contains a bibliography of his publications from 1851 to 1904.

NANCY G. SLACK

BREWSTER, Anne Hampton (29 Oct. 1818–1 Apr. 1892), fiction writer and foreign correspondent, was born in Philadelphia, Pennsylvania, the daughter of Francis Enoch Brewster, an attorney, and Maria Hampton. She and her family were middle-class Anglo-American Protestants. Her older brother, Benjamin Harris Brewster, became attorney general of the United States from 1881 to 1885. She was primarily educated by her mother, receiving little formal education.

Despite several suitors, Brewster never married. In 1845 she wrote in her journal, "I am not dependent. I have mind enough & strength to take care of myself. . . . I will never marry for mere convenience." Brewster's attitude toward marriage may have been influenced by her father's abandonment of the family in 1834, when he began living with his mistress, Isabella Anderson, and two illegitimate sons. Anne Brewster and her mother became financially dependent on Benjamin.

Brewster's interest in writing began with poetry, which she wrote freely until 1837, when Benjamin discouraged her. She resumed writing poetry in 1843 with the encouragement of Charlotte Cushman, who managed Philadelphia's Walnut Street Theatre. Brewster regained her confidence as a writer in this supportive relationship and began incorporating verses into short fiction she started publishing in 1845 under the pseudonym "Enna Duval." During her lifetime, she published fifty-two short stories that, like most nineteenth-century American woman's fiction, maintain that marriage for financial security is worse than remaining unmarried. Brewster abhorred economic dependency and believed that all women could develop the Victorian qualities of hard work, morality, and social responsibility in order to find happiness.

In 1848 Brewster converted to Catholicism. In her journal of that year Brewster maintains that "stern, strict duty" is necessary for one's own well-being. Catholicism had a prescribed role for Brewster, which she defines in her first book *Spirit Sculpture* (1849), a moderately successful novella concerning religious conversion: " . . . our [women's] duty lies in a silent performance of the virtues of self-denial, self-control, and the willing performance of the most disagreeable home duties, that we may thereby show the influence of the blessed faith we profess" (p. 94)." A review in *Brownson's Quarterly Review* stated that the novella showed "fine taste, very considerable powers, and much facility on the part of the author." But a harsh critic in Baltimore called the book "heresy" and described Brewster as "a young convert with some presumption." That same year, Brewster's first published poem, "New Year Meditation," appeared in *Graham's Magazine*, where she secured a position as an editor in March 1850. This appointment lasted until May 1851, resulting in numerous published pieces and a $500 yearly salary.

When Maria and Francis Brewster died in 1853 and 1854, respectively, the entire estate was split among Francis's three sons. Benjamin planned to support his sister indefinitely, but she sued him for a portion of the estate in 1856, maintaining that he was a tyrannical alcoholic. The court case and Benjamin's recent marriage, of which Brewster disapproved, prompted her to spend fifteen months in Vevey, Switzerland, and Naples, Italy, beginning in May 1857. On her return to America, she settled in Bridgeton, New Jersey, supporting herself by writing and teaching music and French. Brewster did not win the case but gained control of her rental property and would receive interest on the investments of the family estate that Benjamin controlled. She disapproved of this arrangement, became permanently estranged from Benjamin, yet depended on this variable income for the rest of her life.

Brewster abandoned her pseudonym in 1860 and published her second novel, *Compensation; or, Always a Future* (1860), which was successful enough to warrant a second edition in 1870. The story, set in Switzerland, is similar to her short fiction, with the addition of discourse on art, music, nature, literature, philosophy, and religion, drawn heavily from the personal journals Brewster had kept during her trip to Europe. Her third and last novel, *Saint Martin's Summer* (1866), is a narrated travel journal from Switzerland to Naples and explores the superiority of spiritual to physical love. The novel was both praised and criticized for its extensive descriptions.

Brewster's decision to move to Rome in 1868 was fueled not only by a desire to distance herself further from Benjamin, but by the tradition of Italian travel common among American writers and artists in the nineteenth century. With unreliable income from her inheritance, Brewster needed a more profitable vocation than fiction writing and accepted her first newspaper engagements in 1869 with the *Philadelphia Evening Bulletin* and the *Newark Courier*. During her first ten years in Rome, Brewster worked relentlessly to establish herself in her profession, becoming one of the earliest female foreign correspondents to the United States. Brewster reported on such significant events as the excavations of the imperial palace on the Palatine and Pius IX's announcement of the doctrines of papal infallibility. She was forbidden to enter the Vatican for three years because of her liberal account of Victor Emmanuel's troops entering Rome in 1870. In her report to the *Newark Courier*, Brewster described the pontifical police as "severe." She stated that the Romans saw the Italian troops as liberators and welcomed them enthusiastically with cries of "I nostri fratelli" (our brothers). Throughout her nineteen years in journalism she wrote for at least twelve American newspapers, including the *Boston Daily Advertiser*, the *New York World*, the *Chicago Daily News*, and the *Cincinnati Commercial*. She not only reported on the political, religious, and scientific events in Rome but the cultural ones as well, giving publicity to the artistic, literary, and musical accomplishments of her friends and acquaintances. Her interest in culture resulted in the publication of several articles in *Lippincott's Magazine* and *Blackwood's Edinburgh Magazine*. She was a member of Arcadia, the poetical academy in Rome, and held a weekly salon where she entertained writers, sculptors, painters, and musicians, including Sarah Jane Lippincott, William Wetmore Story, Emma Stebbins, and Franz Liszt. She had a platonic relationship with Philadelphia sculptor Albert E. Harnisch and shared a residence with him from 1871 to 1885.

During the 1880s, income from Brewster's inheritance dropped considerably, and her journalism career declined as newspapers required more concise news items. In 1889 she moved to Siena, Italy, in order to meet her expenses without additional income from writing. Still, she wrote her last article, "Siena's Medieval Festival," while living there and published it in the *Cosmopolitan* in 1890. She died in Siena, leaving several writing projects unfinished, including a revised collection of her newspaper correspondence from Rome between 1868 and 1878. Brewster believed her newspaper work was "elevating and beneficial—it confers a double benefit on myself and others." This accounts for the unique combination of gentility, self-revelation, and scholarship that endeared Brewster to her audience and made her one of the most popular foreign correspondents of the time.

• The Anne Hampton Brewster Manuscript Collection belongs to the Library Company of Philadelphia. It contains personal incoming correspondence, journals, commonplace books, copybooks, miscellaneous article drafts, clippings of Brewster's newspaper correspondence, reviews of her novels, and obituaries of friends and family. The Lloyd P. Smith Papers, also at the Library Company, contain outgoing correspondence. See also Estelle Fisher, *A Gentle Journalist Abroad: The Papers of Anne Hampton Brewster in the Library Company of Philadelphia* (1947); Nathalia Wright, *American Novelists in Italy: The Discoverers—Allston to James* (1965); and Denise M. Larrabee, *Anne Hampton Brewster: Nineteenth-Century Author and "Social Outlaw"* (1992).

DENISE M. LARRABEE

BREWSTER, Benjamin Harris (13 Oct. 1816–4 Apr. 1888), attorney general of the United States, was born in Salem, New Jersey, the son of Francis Enoch Brewster, a lawyer, and Maria Hampton. When Brewster was a year old, the family moved to Philadelphia. Shortly after his fifth birthday Brewster was severely burned, and his badly scarred face affected his personality. Its most obvious manifestation was his adopting—to partially cover his scars—the dress of an 1830s fop with a ruffled shirt, high collar, and white silk hat. His deformity repelled his father, whose reputation caused Brewster more hardship. Considered by proper Philadelphians to be "a blackguard in every sense, degraded & stained by every vice" (Wainwright, p. 155), his father abandoned his family, lived with his mistress, Isabella Anderson, had two sons by her (one of whom, Frederick Carroll Brewster, became a lawyer and jurist), and tried to disinherit Brewster and his sister. After Benjamin Brewster successfully contested the will in 1855, the estate was divided evenly among the legitimate and illegitimate children.

After graduating from the College of New Jersey (Princeton University) in 1834, Brewster returned to Philadelphia and, despite his father's opposition, read law in the office of Eli Kirk Price, a law reformer with broad social concerns. On 6 January 1838 Brewster was admitted to the Philadelphia bar and borrowed $50 to begin his practice. Added to the anxieties of a beginning lawyer were the dependence on him of his mother and sister and the predictions of his father that his scarred face would invite failure and make it conspicuous. It took nearly three months for Brewster's first client to appear, but—befitting a diligent, eloquent attorney with a prodigious memory—his practice grew steadily.

Harboring political ambitions, Brewster, who was a Democrat, became a friend of Simon Cameron as early as 1838 and by 1843 supported James Buchanan for president. Heading the Pennsylvania delegation at the 1844 Democratic Convention, Brewster, who was pledged to support Martin Van Buren, hoped to throw the nomination to Buchanan by helping pass the requirement that the successful nominee must have a two-thirds majority. The change helped nominate James K. Polk, for whom Brewster campaigned vigorously. When Polk triumphed, Brewster demanded a prestigious and lucrative federal office but settled in 1846 for a place on the commission adjudicating claims growing out of the Cherokee's removal to the Indian Territory. During the two years he served on the commission Brewster wrote 90 percent of its decisions.

Disappointed by his meager reward, Brewster concentrated on his law practice and soon was able to travel widely in Europe. Reluctant to expose himself "to the brutal sneers and affected sighs of the 'tender sex' " (Savidge, p. 221), Brewster held himself aloof from women until he settled the estate of a Dr. Shulte of Paris. He was attracted to Shulte's widow, Elizabeth von Myerbach de Reinfeldts, whom he married in 1857. They had no children.

Brewster's political ambitions revived in the mid-1850s, when he flirted briefly with the nativist American party but was not attracted by the emerging Republican party, because he believed that slavery was "a social, commercial, and political necessity" (Savidge, p. 86). Brewster supported his old hero Buchanan for the presidency in 1856 and, as late as April 1858 in the Dangerfield case, demanded that the Fugitive Slave Law be upheld.

Although Buchanan frustrated his desire for a district attorneyship, Brewster remained a Democrat. He supported Stephen A. Douglas for president in 1860 and in January 1861 wished to conciliate the seceding southern states in hopes of wooing them back into the Union. With the Confederate attack on Fort Sumter, however, Brewster concluded that slavery caused "foul treason" (Savidge, p. 94), strongly supported the war, joined the Union League, and brought to it, as his guest, the former slave and abolitionist Frederick Douglass. Joining the Republican party, Brewster was closely allied with Simon Cameron, whose support, he hoped, would help elect him to the U.S. Senate. When Cameron decided in 1867 to return to that body himself, he consoled Brewster by engineering his appointment as attorney general of Pennsylvania. In October 1869, however, Governor John W. Geary, to gratify Philadelphia corrruptionists, who had manipulated returns to reelect him, and whom Brewster planned to prosecute, humiliated Brewster by replacing him with his bastard half-brother Frederick Carroll Brewster, who had close ties to the Philadelphia machine.

When Cameron failed in his attempt to get President Ulysses S. Grant to give Brewster Attorney General Ebenezer Rockwood Hoar's place, Brewster again retreated from politics. Rebounding from his wife's death in 1868, he married Mary Walker in the summer of 1870. The daughter of Robert J. Walker, Polk's secretary of the treasury, she brought a daughter to the union, and together they had a son. Throughout the 1870s Brewster devoted himself to his new family, to his large law practice, to literature, and to orations.

In 1879 he campaigned in New York at the behest of Republican state chairman Chester A. Arthur and a year later was a delegate to the Republican National Convention, where he was one of the 306 diehard Stalwart supporters of Grant. In 1881 Brewster was again an unsuccessful candidate for the Senate. The investigation of the Star Route frauds in the postal service finally gave him his great opportunity. In the late 1870s Second Assistant Postmaster General Thomas J. Brady had expedited service on remote, sparsely used routes (designated on post office registers by three asterisks) by letting contracts to insiders at enormously inflated costs. Among these insiders were friends and relations of former Senator Stephen W. Dorsey, who as secretary of the Republican National Committee in 1880 had managed successfully the James A. Garfield presidential campaign in the doubtful state of Indiana with ill-gotten Star Route money. With President Garfield's approval, his postmaster general, Thomas L. James, and his attorney general, Wayne MacVeagh, investigated. After Garfield was shot but prior to his death, MacVeagh asked Brewster, whom he knew was Vice President Chester A. Arthur's friend, to serve as a special counsel to prosecute the perpetrators of the Star Route frauds. Too much of a reformer to serve under a spoilsman, MacVeagh resigned as attorney general when Arthur became president, and in December 1881 Arthur appointed Brewster to that post.

As attorney general, Brewster pushed the prosecution of Dorsey, Brady, and their associates and at their trial in the summer of 1882 personally summed up the case for the government. The jury, which had been tampered with, illogically found two minor participants in the frauds guilty but divided on Dorsey and Brady; the judge set aside the verdicts and ordered a new trial in December. The second trial lasted six months, and the new jury, also having been corrupted, acquitted all the accused. The Arthur administration then launched twenty-four civil suits to recover monies lost by fraud, but these proved unproductive and were abandoned. Brewster boasted that the "wholesome terror of these trials" eliminated postal frauds and saved the government $2 million annually, but the failure to obtain convictions tarnished his and Arthur's reputations.

Following Brewster's advice, Arthur refused a stay of execution that would allow for an inquiry into the sanity of Garfield's assassin, Charles Guiteau. Arthur also followed Brewster's view that legislative and executive power to tamper with judicial decisions is limited, when he pardoned General Fitz John Porter (who had been convicted of disobeying orders at the second battle of Bull Run) but vetoed a bill restoring Porter to the army, because neither Congress nor the president could overturn the decision of a legal court-martial. During the 1882 campaign Brewster pleased spoilsmen and outraged civil-service reformers by deciding that the 1876 law prohibiting federal employees from collecting political assessments from civil servants did not apply to congressmen. With Arthur's support Brewster pleased reformers and outraged spoilsmen by indicting corrupt federal marshals, particularly in the South and West, who were falsifying their accounts and making arrests on trumped up charges to collect more fees. Arthur also followed Brewster's advice when he opposed the construction of a cantilever railroad bridge across the Niagara River, even though it was desired by William H. Vanderbilt and backed by Congressman Richard Crowley, whose friendship Arthur lost. In the cabinet, Secretary of the Interior

Henry M. Teller later said, Brewster's grasp of international law, political economy, and the science of government revealed that "he was not only a great lawyer, but a great statesman" (Savidge, p. 260).

"Brewster with his famous ruffles," his brilliant conversation, and his prodigious store of literary allusions also contributed to the social success of the Arthur administration. With the end of that administration in 1885, Brewster and his family toured England and the Continent. Following their return to Philadelphia, his wife's health deteriorated, and after her death in 1886 he traveled to Norway for his last trip abroad. As his health declined, Brewster, who died in Philadelphia, arranged for the University of Pennsylvania to acquire his outstanding law library.

• Brewster's papers have not been located, but many of his letters are in the collections of his associates. Because it includes many primary documents, the best source on Brewster is the worshipful Eugene Coleman Savidge, *Life of Benjamin Harris Brewster with Discourses and Addresses* (1891). On Brewster family matters, see Garrick Mallery and Furman Sheppard, *A Brief Statement of . . . Brewster vs. Brewster* (1855). Helpful biographies of Brewster's political associates are Philip Shriver Klein, *President James Buchanan: A Biography* (1962); Erwin Stanley Bradley, *Simon Cameron, Lincoln's Secretary of War: A Political Biography* (1966); and Thomas C. Reeves, *Gentleman Boss: The Life of Chester Alan Arthur* (1975). Also see J. Thomas Scharf and Thompson Westcott, *History of Philadelphia, 1609–1884* (3 vols., 1884); *A Philadelphia Perspective: The Diary of Sidney George Fisher, Covering the Years 1834–1871*, ed. Nicholas Wainwright (1967); Maxwell Whiteman, *Gentlemen in Crisis: The First Century of the Union League of Philadelphia, 1862–1962* (1975); Erwin Stanley Bradley, *The Triumph of Militant Republicanism: A Study of Pennsylvania and Presidential Politics, 1860–1872* (1964); and Frank B. Evans, *Pennsylvania Politics, 1872–1877: A Study in Political Leadership* (1966). An obituary is in the *New York Times*, 5 Apr. 1888.

ARI HOOGENBOOM

BREWSTER, Kingman, Jr. (17 June 1919–8 Nov. 1988), university president and diplomat, was born in Longmeadow, Massachusetts, the son of Kingman Brewster, Sr., a lawyer, and Florence Besse. He was descended on his father's side from Elder William Brewster of the Massachusetts Bay Colony. Brewster's parents divorced when he was six. His mother subsequently married Harvard University music professor Edward Ballentine, and the new family settled in Cambridge, Massachusetts. Brewster attended Belmont Hill School outside Boston (1930–1936), where he took an interest in journalism and debating and also took time to work on the reelection campaign of isolationist Republican senator George William Norris. The Ballentine household in which Brewster grew up was frequented by such notable figures as jurist Felix Frankfurter and pianist Rudolf Serkin. Family summers were spent on Martha's Vineyard, where Brewster developed a lifelong affection for sailing. Skipping his final year of school (a move facilitated by the employment of tutors), Brewster traveled to Europe, where he joined his stepfather on sabbatical and witnessed firsthand the buildup of political tensions that led to World War II.

Entering Yale in 1937, Brewster took the freshman debating prize and joined several campus organizations, although he declined membership in the prestigious Skull and Bones Society. His senior year was filled with activity; he served as chair of the *Yale Daily News* and became embroiled in the controversy over American isolationism. Brewster founded a chapter of the America First organization at Yale and invited Charles Lindbergh to speak at Yale on the subject. He wound up defending a school newspaper editorial before a congressional committee in 1940, and he coauthored (with the editor of the *Harvard Crimson*) an article in the *Atlantic Monthly*, "We Stand Here," in September of the same year.

Brewster graduated in 1941 with an A.B. cum laude in humanities, in the process winning the Andrew D. White Prize for a senior thesis on European history. He was also voted by his classmates as the student who had done the most for Yale. Moving to Washington, D.C., he worked under Carl Spaeth as special assistant coordinator for economics in the Office of Inter-American Affairs, then headed by Nelson A. Rockefeller.

Upon the entrance of the United States into World War II, Brewster joined the Naval Reserve and served as an aviator on antisubmarine patrols in the Atlantic theater, eventually rising to the rank of lieutenant. In 1942 he married Mary Louise Phillips, a Vassar alumna whom he had met while at Yale. They had five children.

Discharged from the navy in 1945, Brewster, although uninterested in a legal career, enrolled at the Harvard University Law School. As he later explained to an interviewer for the *New Yorker*, "I wanted to save the world, and I knew that if you go into politics and public affairs, you always have to deal with lawyers . . . so, in self-defense, you become a lawyer, too" (11 Jan. 1964). While at Harvard he served as note editor on the *Harvard Law Review* and graduated with an LL.B. magna cum laude in 1948. Brewster took his law degree to Paris, where he worked with Milton Katz, a former Harvard law professor, in the Economic Cooperation Administration, which was managing the reconstruction of Europe through the Marshall Plan.

Brewster returned to the United States in 1949 and served for a year as a research associate in the Department of Economics and Social Science at the Massachusetts Institute of Technology. He then joined the faculty of the Harvard Law School in 1950, serving first as assistant professor of law, then, beginning in 1953, as full professor. During this period he wrote *Antitrust and American Business Abroad* (1958) and coauthored with Katz *The Law of International Transactions and Relations: Cases and Materials* (1960). He also undertook consulting work for agencies such as the U.S. State Department, the International Cooperation Administration, the Mutual Security Administration, and the President's Materials Policy Commission.

A long friendship with Yale president A. Whitney Griswold resulted in a job offer—that of university provost—in 1960. Brewster accepted and served as an effective assistant to Griswold, who died in April 1963 after suffering at length from terminal cancer. Brewster then served as acting president until his nomination for the post of president was unanimously approved in October 1963.

The first lawyer and the first individual in the twentieth century without a Ph.D. to hold the position, Brewster was installed as president on 11 April 1964 and soon left his mark on the campus. Greatly concerned with the recruitment and promotion of faculty, Brewster added figures such as writer John Hersey and Charles Henry Taylor, Jr., who succeeded Brewster as provost, to the campus. Minority enrollment increased even as the traditional preference given to sons of alumni declined. Brewster also presided over the advent of coeducation, which was completed in 1969.

While some of these actions did not sit well with the more conservative alumni of Yale, Brewster's activities during the campus upheavals of the 1960s left them even more perplexed. He spoke out strongly on behalf of civil rights and in opposition to the Vietnam War. He helped defend the controversial university chaplain, William Sloane Coffin, Jr., a leader in antidraft counseling, as well as history professor Staughton Craig Lynd, who traveled to Hanoi. His most controversial statement, however, came during the New Haven trial of eight members of the Black Panther party. On 24 April 1970 Brewster declared, "I am appalled and ashamed that things should come to such a pass that I am sceptical of the ability of Black revolutionaries to achieve a fair trial anywhere in the United States." The fallout from Brewster's actions and statements was such that U.S. vice president Spiro T. Agnew urged his removal as president in favor of someone "more mature and responsible." Throughout the period Brewster remained popular with the students, one of whom, Garry Trudeau, created the character "President King" for his comic strip "Doonesbury." Upon the occasion of Brewster's final Yale commencement in 1977, the students were moved to chant "Long Live the King!"

Facing declining alumni donations and a looming budget deficit, Brewster, who had already made up his mind to resign no later than mid-1978, accepted the post of ambassador to Great Britain from President Jimmy Carter on 7 April 1977. While at the Court of St. James, Brewster maintained a low profile yet earned high marks from the English for his careful concern with relaying accurate information to Washington on issues such as Rhodesia, the neutron bomb, and the European monetary system.

With his tenure as ambassador ended by the election of Ronald Reagan, Brewster became the resident London partner of the law firm of Winthrop, Stimson, Putnam and Roberts of New York City. He later (1986) became a master at University College at Oxford University, where he served until his death in Oxford.

The scion of an old New England family, Brewster guided his alma mater through one of the greatest periods of disestablishmentarianism in American history. Although frequently controversial and not universally loved, his administration presided over deep and permanent changes at Yale University. His legacy also included a solid if unspectacular stint at the Court of St. James and an all too short excursion in English higher education.

• Brewster's papers are at the Yale University Archives in New Haven, Conn. His life and career can be traced through numerous publications, most notably the *New York Times*, 13 Oct. 1963, 12 Feb. 1967, and 17 Mar. 1977; "The Y of It All," *Time*, 18 Oct. 1963, p. 51; "Anxiety behind the Facade," *Time*, 23 June 1967, pp. 78–85; "Student to President," *Newsweek*, 21 Oct. 1963, p. 103; "The Once and Future 'King,'" *Newsweek*, 18 Apr. 1977, p. 63; "President Brewster," *New Yorker*, 11 Jan. 1964, pp. 22–24; and John Bainbridge, "Our Far-flung Correspondents: Excellency," *New Yorker*, 12 Dec. 1977, pp. 141–52. His obituary is in the *New York Times*, 9 Nov. 1988.

EDWARD L. LACH, JR.

BREWSTER, William (1567–10 Apr. 1644), a leader of the Pilgrims and of the Plymouth Colony, was born in England, the son of William Brewster and Prudence (maiden name unknown). His specific place of birth has not been determined. The first mention of a William Brewster is in the Scrooby parish records for 1571. At about that time his parents had moved to the Nottinghamshire village, where in 1575 William's father became bailiff and receiver of Scrooby Manor, a property held by the archbishop of York. Archbishop Edmund Grindal appointed the elder Brewster to the posts, and Archbishop Edwin Sandys continued him in office. In 1588 the elder Brewster also assumed the position of postmaster when the town was made a postal stop on the London to York road and, as required, operated a tavern for use of the post riders and other travelers. These positions made him one of the more affluent members of the small community and gave him the opportunity to provide a quality education for his son.

Brewster entered Peterhouse College in Cambridge as a pensioner on 3 December 1580, but he did not stay to receive a degree. Though there is no record of his activities at the university, it is likely that his religious views were refined if not shaped there. At that time Cambridge was in an uproar over the dispute between the Lady Margaret Professor of Divinity Thomas Cartwright, who advocated reforms in the church, and the future bishop John Whitgift, who defended the establishment and used his position as master of Trinity College to have Cartwright deprived of his position and forced from Cambridge. Brewster would also have met John Penry, who entered Peterhouse on the same day as did Brewster and who would be drawn and quartered in 1593 for his Separatist religious activities and criticisms of the established church. In 1583

Brewster entered the service of Sir William Davison, who was a member of the Elizabethan diplomatic service, and he accompanied Davison on missions to the Netherlands in 1584 and 1585. He returned to the simpler life of Scrooby to serve as his father's deputy after Davison was disgraced and the elder Brewster became ill in 1589. The following year his father died, and Brewster assumed the posts both of bailiff and postmaster. If his religious views were evident at this time, they must not have come to the attention of Archbishop Sandys, from whom he received his appointment. By 1593 he had married Mary Wentworth. The couple would have six children.

Brewster was attracted to the views of the reforming clergy in the church, and in 1598 he was presented to the church authorities for repeating sermons to a conventicle of believers. Brewster does not seem to have been deterred and continued to use his influence to protect Puritan preachers. He was sympathetic and helpful to clergymen, such as Richard Clifton, who were deprived on account of the more rigid enforcement of church canons. He was one of those who organized a gathered congregation, which separated from the Church of England in 1606 and chose John Robinson as their pastor in 1607. The authorities pursued Separatists more energetically than they did nonseparating Puritans, and after Brewster and others were cited as Dissenters in December 1607, the Scrooby congregation left England and resettled in the Netherlands. They first located in Amsterdam. Disputes in that city's English Separatist community, which were precipitated by the Reverend John Smith, led the Robinson group to relocate in Leiden.

Robinson was irenic in temper and was not rigid in rejecting contact with nonseparating Puritans, an attitude that Brewster, who served as the congregation's ruling elder, readily endorsed. Brewster tutored students at the University of Leiden in English. He also labored as a printer of religious books by such authors as William Ames, Cartwright, and Robinson that were designed to be smuggled into England. One of the volumes Brewster printed expressed militant Presbyterian views and irritated King James to the point that an official complaint was lodged with the Dutch authorities. Brewster then closed the press and went into hiding. Undoubtedly he was concerned about the effect that any such attention might have on the congregation's plans to emigrate once again.

Worries about how the English community would be affected by the renewal of Dutch-Spanish conflict, which seemed imminent in the late 1610s, combined with concerns about the upbringing of their children and other factors had led the Robinson church to consider moving to the English colonies of the New World. Brewster had traveled to England in 1617, where he met with representatives of the Virginia Company (perhaps including Sir Edwin Sandys, the son of his former employer) and with Crown officials to negotiate details of the move. In the same year he joined with Robinson in drafting seven articles of faith to reassure the Virginia authorities. In keeping with Robinson's semiseparatism, the articles stated the congregation's recognition of the Church of England as a true church and accepted that Anglican institutions could convey saving grace.

In 1620 Brewster journeyed on the *Mayflower* to New England, where he and his fellow colonists established the Plymouth Colony. Because of his experience of Separatist church covenants and of drafting government papers, he is presumed to have had a large role in the drawing-up of the Mayflower Compact. Most of the members of the Leiden church remained behind with plans to migrate at a later date, and Robinson stayed with them. Deacon Brewster, therefore, was the only church officer in Plymouth from the arrival of the Pilgrims until 1629 and for much of the time after that. He conducted prayer services, led scripture readings, and preached twice on each Sunday but never administered the sacraments. Though Separatists reserved the administration of the sacraments to ordained ministers, Robinson had been asked if an exception could be made for Brewster. Robinson had indicated that it would not be proper, and Brewster concurred. In 1633 Brewster argued successfully against those who wished to retain Roger Williams as the congregation's teacher. Brewster feared that Williams would pursue the same course of rigid separatism espoused by Smith that had led to contention in Amsterdam. Indeed, following Williams's settlement in Salem, Massachusetts, his extreme insistence on religious purity did lead to schism and his eventual banishment from the Bay.

As one of the community's leaders and one of its more prosperous citizens, Brewster became one of the undertakers, who in 1627 assumed responsibility for the colony's debt to its English backers. Though he was often consulted by Governor William Bradford (1590–1657), he never sought or held political office. He died in Duxbury, Massachusetts, leaving a modest estate and a library of three hundred volumes.

Brewster was, next to Bradford, the most significant figure in the Plymouth Colony. Well educated and experienced in government, his advice to Bradford was invaluable. He alone held the Pilgrim church together during the early years of settlement, maintaining both its orthodoxy and its willingness to interact with nonseparating Puritans.

• Biographical information on Brewster is in Dorothy Brewster, *William Brewster of the Mayflower* (1970); Mary B. Sherwood, *Pilgrim: A Biography of William Brewster* (1982); and Richard Greaves and Robert Zaller, eds., *Biographical Dictionary of British Radicals in the Seventeenth Century* (1982). See also George Willison, *Saints and Strangers* (1945), and George Langdon, *Pilgrim Colony* (1966). William Bradford's history, *Of Plymouth Plantation, 1620–1647* (1856), has an extended appreciation of Brewster by his contemporary and friend.

FRANCIS J. BREMER

BREWSTER, William (5 July 1851–11 July 1919), ornithologist, was born in Wakefield, Massachusetts, the youngest of four children of John Brewster, a prominent Boston banker and philanthropist, and Rebecca Parker Noyes. Brewster was educated in the public schools of Cambridge. During his youth he became interested in natural history, particularly the study of birds. At the age of ten he fell under the influence of Daniel C. French, a neighbor who was a skilled taxidermist and enthusiastic outdoorsman. Young Brewster quickly mastered the techniques of bird preservation, and by the time he was fourteen, he had acquired an impressive number of mounted birds, which he expanded over the ensuing years into one of the largest ornithological collections in the United States. His father encouraged this activity by procuring Thomas Nuttall's *A Manual of the Ornithology of the United States and Canada* (1832, 1834) and the octavo edition of Audubon's *Birds of America* (1840–1844). Brewster graduated from Cambridge High School in 1869 with hopes of entering Harvard, but his poor health and eyesight caused him to abandon this plan. Instead, at age nineteen, he accepted a position at his father's banking office, but within a year he left his business career for ornithology, a decision supported by his father.

Brewster's major research interest was in local avifauna, particularly in the New England area, where he kept detailed records at Cambridge, Concord, and other localities, such as Lake Umbagog, Maine. He also traveled extensively in the United States, conducting important field studies, usually in the company of other zoologists. These excursions often provided the basis for valuable publications by Brewster and his associates. Among his more notable trips were that to Illinois in 1878 with Robert Ridgway; to West Virginia in 1874 with Ruthven Deane; to the St. Lawrence Valley in 1881 with Alpheus Hyatt; to Colorado in 1882 with Joel A. Allen; and, with Frank M. Chapman, to Florida in 1890 and Trinidad in 1893. He also visited Europe and Britain in 1891, 1909, and 1911. Brewster's South Carolina fieldwork during 1883 and his exploration of the Blue Ridge Mountains of North Carolina in 1885 caused a surge of activity in those locales by other naturalists. He encouraged young amateur ornithologists, establishing a network of correspondents who provided him with data and specimens and published their own local studies.

With his reputation growing, Brewster was placed in charge of the bird and mammal collections at the Boston Society of Natural History from 1879 to 1887. In 1885 he was appointed to a similar position at Harvard University's Museum of Comparative Zoology, and when the bird and mammal divisions there were separated in 1900, Brewster remained as the director of the ornithology collections until the year of his death. Although this appointment provided the basis for his profound knowledge of avian taxonomy, on which he published extensively, his most valuable writings involved the behavior and natural history of living birds; examples include his studies of the elusive Bachman's warbler and Swainson's warbler. Brewster was also a competent amateur botanist, and his garden at Cambridge contained many plants gleaned from his travels in New England.

Perhaps Brewster's most lasting contributions to American science were the key roles he played in establishing the Nuttall Ornithological Club and the American Ornithologists' Union. In 1871 Brewster and a small group of his friends, including Henry W. Henshaw, a classmate at Cambridge High School, began meeting each week at Brewster's home to read Audubon's *Birds of America* and to discuss their own field studies. By November 1873 the group had grown in size and decided to organize as the Nuttall Ornithological Club, named in honor of ornithologist and botanist Thomas Nuttall. Brewster served as first president of the club and was instrumental in establishing the *Bulletin of the Nuttall Ornithological Club*, the first journal in the United States devoted entirely to ornithology. Over the next decade the need for a national society became increasingly apparent, and in September 1883 William Brewster, Elliott Coues, and Joel A. Allen sponsored the founding meeting of the American Ornithologists' Union, held at the American Museum of Natural History in New York. This subsequently grew into the leading organization for scientific ornithology in the United States. Brewster served as president of the union from 1895 to 1898 and was a member of its Committee on Bird Protection.

Brewster was a prolific writer of both technical and popular works. He produced more than 300 scientific papers, mostly during the period 1876 to 1900, when his studies appeared in the *Bulletin of the Nuttall Ornithological Club*, the *Auk*, the *Annals of the New York Lyceum of Natural History*, the *Proceedings of the Boston Society of Natural History*, and the *Bulletin of the Museum of Comparative Zoology*. Among his most important monographs were the classic *Descriptions of the First Plumage in Various North American Birds* (1878–1879), *Bird Migration* (1886), and *The Birds of the Cambridge Region of Massachusetts* (1906). Other valuable books included *Birds of the Cape Region of Lower California* (1902), *Land Birds and Game Birds of New England* (1894), and three works published posthumously, *Birds of the Lake Umbagog Region, Maine* (1924–1925), *October Farm* (1936), and *Concord River* (1937).

An avid conservationist, Brewster was one of the organizers of the first Audubon Society and served as a director of the National Association of Audubon Societies, which later became the National Audubon Society. He was also president of the Massachusetts Audubon Society and a director of the Massachusetts State Fish and Game Commission, working as president of the latter organization from 1906 to 1908. He was a leader in 1911 in establishing the American Game Protective and Propagation Association; he was a member of its advisory committee until his death. He was also a fellow of the American Academy of Arts and Sciences and of the American Association for the Advancement of Science.

Held in high esteem by his peers though modest and retiring, Brewster never sought publicity and was described as totally unselfish in his personal and professional dealings. He was respected for his skills as a scientist, writer, and mentor, as well as for his personal integrity. He received honorary A.M. degrees from Amherst College in 1880 and from Harvard in 1889. He married Caroline F. Kettell of Boston in 1878. He died in Cambridge, Massachusetts. In 1919 the American Ornithologists' Union established the William Brewster Medal, to be awarded to the authors of the most valuable contributions relating to the birds of the Western Hemisphere.

• Most of Brewster's huge collection of bird skins and eggs was donated to the Museum of Comparative Zoology, Cambridge. His manuscripts and correspondence are held mainly at the Museum of Comparative Zoology and also in various collections at the American Museum of Natural History and at the Smithsonian Institution. The two major sketches of Brewster are Frank M. Chapman, "William Brewster, 1851–1919," *Bird-Lore* 21 (1919): 277–86, and Henry W. Henshaw, "In Memoriam: William Brewster," *The Auk* 37 (1920): 1–23. Other sources include Richard H. Dana, "William Brewster," *Harvard Graduates Magazine* (Sept. 1919); an obituary in the *Boston Transcript*, 12 July 1919; and Marcus B. Simpson, Jr., "William Brewster's Exploration of the Southern Appalachians: The Journal of 1885," *North Carolina Historical Review* 57 (1980): 43–77. Material relating to Brewster's role in the American Ornithologists' Union is found in Paul R. Cutright and Michael J. Brodhead, *Elliott Coues: Naturalist and Frontier Historian* (1981), and in a collection of essays in *Fifty Years' Progress of American Ornithology 1883–1933* (1933).

MARCUS B. SIMPSON, JR.

BRICE, Calvin Stewart (17 Sept. 1845–15 Dec. 1898), U.S. senator, railroad builder, and financier, was born in Denmark, Ohio, the son of William Kilpatrick Brice, a Presbyterian minister, and Elizabeth Stewart. He received his earliest education at home and in the public schools of Columbus Grove, Putnam County, where his family moved after his third birthday. When Brice turned thirteen years old, his parents placed him in the preparatory program at Miami University in Oxford, Ohio, where because of his father's limited means he had to work his way through school. He required only one year of preparatory work before being granted admission as a freshman.

After the assault on Fort Sumter in April 1861, Brice volunteered to serve in response to President Abraham Lincoln's call but was denied muster because of his age. He did serve for three months, however, in the 86th Regiment, Ohio Volunteer Infantry, during the summer of 1862. After graduating from Miami in 1863, he returned to Lima, Ohio, to teach in the public school and work in the auditor's office of Allen County. Anxious to return to the war, Brice recruited a company of volunteers in 1864 and, as its captain, led it in service with the 180th Ohio Volunteer Infantry. Before the conflict ended, Brice achieved the rank of lieutenant colonel. Having no desire for an army career, Brice attended law school at the University of Michigan in Ann Arbor and was admitted to the Ohio bar in 1866. He returned to Lima to practice law.

In 1869 Brice married Catherine Olivia Meily; they had six children and maintained a home in Lima throughout their marriage. Although a man of humble means and moderate success as a lawyer, Brice invested in various enterprises, achieving his most memorable success with railroads. He left private practice to take a job in the law department of the Lake Erie and Louisville Railroad, where he learned much about the railroad business. The railroad sent him to Europe in 1871 to secure investments needed to expand the road. This experience prepared him for his future work in planning new railroad lines.

The panic of 1873 slowed the progress of one project, a railroad from Toledo to Ohio's coal fields. Brice, representing a friend who had invested in the scheme, informed other notable investors—such as Allen Thurman, later a U.S. senator, and Charles Foster, later a governor of Ohio—of his plan to save the line. Foster saw in Brice a keen business sense, and with his support Brice used the Lake Erie and Louisville Railroad as the project's nucleus. He secured the loans and investment capital necessary for expanding the road through Lima and on into Indiana and Illinois, and he later became the president of the road, which was then known as the Lake Erie and Western Railroad. Throughout his career Brice was associated with ten other railroads, including the Cleveland, Akron and Columbus Railroad; the Ohio Central Railroad; the Duluth, South Shore and Atlantic Railroad. He also involved himself with other enterprises during the 1880s, such as the National Telegraph Company, the Chase National Bank of New York, and the Lima Car Company. In most of these ventures Brice succeeded by conducting either a reorganization of failing businesses or a sophisticated manipulation of investments, netting millions of dollars in the process.

One of the best examples of Brice's business acumen was his involvement from 1880 to 1882 with the New York, Chicago and St. Louis Railway. Brice shrewdly built this road with support from a New York investment syndicate led by George Seney to parallel William H. Vanderbilt's Lake Shore and Michigan Southern line. Recognizing the competition between Vanderbilt and Jay Gould, Brice and the line's investors hoped to force the Lake Shore line to purchase the new road. Gould feigned interest in the road but did not have the finances to purchase it. To maintain his own Lake Shore line, Vanderbilt bought the competing road, which became known as the "Nickel Plate" because of the profit gained by its builders. On the reputation gained from this success, Brice became instrumental in building railroads across the midwestern and eastern portions of the United States and in Jamaica and China.

Foster, who played such an important role in Brice's business endeavors, may have convinced Brice to enter politics as well—in spite of their partisan differences. In 1876 Brice served as an electoral candidate for Samuel Tilden. He later worked for Grover Cleveland in the 1884 election. In the following presidential campaign Ohio's Democrats elected Brice as a delegate-at-large to the national convention, where he served as a member of the national committee and as the chairman of the Democratic Executive Committee. In 1889, upon the death of William H. Barnum, Brice was chosen as chairman of the Democratic National Committee.

Although Brice had not served in an elective capacity, he garnered enough support among Ohio's Democrats by 1890 to be chosen by the Ohio legislature to replace Democrat Henry B. Payne as a U.S. senator at the end of his term. Payne had gained the seat from Democrat George H. Pendleton under such questionable circumstances that the Senate investigated his selection before granting him a seat. Although some allegations surfaced after Brice's election, he suffered no such ignominy.

Brice was not a great orator, but his senate term was not without merit. He served on the Democratic Steering Committee, the Committee on Appropriations, and as chairman of the Committee on Pacific Railroads. He represented the conservative, business-minded faction of the party known as the Bourbon Democrats. When President Cleveland fostered tariff reform, Brice worked hard to maintain protectionist policies. As elements of the party began to express a growing support for free silver, Brice helped author a party statement on the issue that was evasive and ultimately meaningless. After one term he was replaced by Republican Joseph Foraker. Brice remained involved in party politics until the Democrats adopted free silver in their platform in 1896. He died in New York City after contracting pneumonia.

Brice represented the "Politicos" of the Gilded Age who in the 1930s were accused by writer-historian Matthew Josephson of insider trading and political corruption. From this perspective Brice, like fellow Ohioans Mark Hanna, Payne, and Foster, was a ruthless businessman and unethical politician, a view shared by Brice's political and business opponents. Yet Brice's historical reputation should not be tarnished by these partisan attacks. Brice was actually a typical big businessman-politician of the era, although not the stereotypical "Robber Baron." He and his contemporaries had the daunting task of transforming America into a modern society and weathering all of the resulting growing pains. His life presents a useful picture of the wealthy class of his era in both business and politics.

Brice's career also offers insight into a dying faction within the democratic party that had kept the party divided for decades. Like many Bourbons, his interest in business concerns superseded his regard for political principle. When the Democrats went in a different direction, he did not follow. Gracious eulogies described a man who treated his employees well and gave generously to charitable and societal causes. For example, he was a primary force behind the reopening of his alma mater, Miami University, after it had closed down following the Civil War because of lack of funds. Perhaps he was best characterized by the words of his friend F. T. Adams: "I don't know a man who was loved more by his friends and more cordially hated by his enemies than Mr. Brice was" (*New York Times*, 16 Dec. 1898).

• The Allen County Historical Society of Lima, Ohio, has an extensive selection of sources about Brice. The *Biographical Directory of the United States Congress, 1774–1989* (1989) contains basic biographical material, as does the *Congressional Record*, Fifty-second Congress, 2d session. Although somewhat sketchy, the best overview of Brice's life is Walter Havighurst, "The World of Calvin Brice," in *Men of Old Miami* (1974). Philip D. Jordan, *Ohio Comes of Age, 1873–1900* (1943), vol. 5 of *The History of the State of Ohio*, provides an analytical perspective of Brice's political career, while John A. Rehor, *The Nickel Plate Story* (1965), examines his business dealings related to that particular railroad. An interview with Charles Foster on his close friend and business associate is in Harvey S. Ford, "Foster on Brice—A Forgotten Interview," *Northwest Ohio Quarterly* 22 (1950): 202–08. Obituaries are in the *Lima Times-Democrat*, 16–20 Dec. 1898, and the *New York Times*, the *New York Tribune*, and the *New York Sun*, all 16 Dec. 1898.

THOMAS S. MACH

BRICE, Fanny (29 Oct. 1891–29 May 1951), comedienne and singer, was born Fania Borach in New York City, the daughter of Charles Borach, a bartender, and Rose Stern. The third of four children, all born on New York's Lower East Side, she was raised in a Newark, New Jersey, middle-class home complete with household servants and material comforts. Her parents separated in 1902, and Rose moved the family to St. Marks Place in Brooklyn, New York, where Fanny got the remnants of her formal education at public schools.

Brice made her stage debut on amateur night at Keeney's Theatre in Brooklyn in the spring of 1906, winning first prize with her singing of "When You Know You're Not Forgotten by the Girl You Can't Forget" and other popular songs. She competed in numerous other amateur-night contests in Brooklyn and Manhattan before accepting an engagement in *A Millionaire's Revenge*, a melodrama based on the then-recent murder of architect Stanford White. Forced to withdraw from the cast after two weeks on tour, Brice returned to amateur contests, earning as much as thirty dollars a week, for the remainder of the season.

Hired as a chorus girl for *The Trans-Atlantic Burlesquers* in November 1907, Brice made valuable contacts in the show world. In the chorus of *The Girls from Happyland* the following season, Brice advanced through the ranks to principal performer by May 1909 and was engaged as leading ingenue of *The College Girls*, another burlesque show, in 1909–1910. While with this show, Brice married barbershop owner Frank White; they separated after three days and were divorced in 1913.

Broadway producer Florenz Ziegfeld hired Brice for the *Follies* of 1910, and she scored a huge success by singing "Lovey Joe" by Joe Jordan and Will Marion Cook. Brice appeared in the *Follies* of 1911 but signed with the Shuberts, rival producers, when Ziegfeld did not renew her contract in 1912.

Following appearances in vaudeville and two Shubert shows, *The Whirl of Society* (on tour, 1912) and *The Honeymoon Express* (on Broadway, 1913), Brice sailed for England with her lover, con man Jules W. "Nick" Arnstein, and appeared in three revues in London. Returning to the United States, she played in vaudeville until 1915, when she appeared in the musical revue *Hands Up* and *Nobody Home*, the first of several Princess Theatre musicals by Jerome Kern and Guy Bolton.

Brice toured the Orpheum Circuit in 1916 prior to appearing in the *Ziegfeld Follies* of 1916, where she scored a major success with a burlesque of silent screen actress Theda Bara. Brice was also in the *Ziegfeld Follies* of 1917 before leaving Ziegfeld to appear in *Why Worry?*, a "melodramatic farce" that closed after three weeks on Broadway.

Brice was in Ziegfeld's *Nine O'Clock Revue* and *Midnight Frolic*, two entertainments providing close to six hours of entertainment, on the roof of the New Amsterdam Theatre from 9 December 1918 through 24 May 1919. After she married Nick Arnstein in April 1919, he discovered that his divorce from his first wife had not yet been finalized. Brice and Arnstein therefore had an additional ceremony in June 1919 to make their marriage official. Two months later Brice gave birth to the first of their two children. Brice returned to work in a new edition of the *Midnight Frolic* on 3 October 1919.

Brice appeared in yet another edition of the *Midnight Frolic*, with the *Nine O'Clock Revue*, beginning in March 1920 and was a principal in the 1920 edition of the *Follies*. The *Ziegfeld Follies* of 1921, which leaned heavily on Brice's talents, saw her introduce "Second Hand Rose," the seriocomic lament of the daughter of a Second Avenue secondhand dealer, and "My Man," a song commonly associated with her husband, then a fugitive. Arnstein had been imprisoned before their marriage from 1915 to 1917 on fraud charges and served a second prison term (1924–1925) for his part in the disappearance of $5 million in securities.

In contrast to the rather high, almost facetiously pitched Yiddish dialect in which Brice sang her comic songs, her "legitimate" singing voice was low and vibrant, plaintive and strongly emotional, without the false vibrato that characterized many "torch" singers. She was equally adept with comedy songs and ballads.

Brice performed in vaudeville from 11 May 1922 through 28 March 1923 before joining rehearsals for the *Follies* of 1923, her last stage show for Ziegfeld. She subsequently appeared in the fourth annual *Music Box Revue* and *Fanny*, an unsuccessful attempt to launch her as a star in nonmusical plays by David Belasco. Brice appeared in the *Hollywood Music Box Revue* in 1927 and, following a year in vaudeville, starred in *My Man*, a part-talking feature film produced by Warner Bros. In 1927 she divorced Arnstein on grounds of adultery.

Brice reappeared on Broadway in *Fioretta*, an operetta presented by Earl Carroll in 1929. Returning to Hollywood, she starred in *Be Yourself!* (1930), a sound motion picture similar to *My Man*, with Robert Armstrong as leading man. Brice married popular songwriter Billy Rose in February 1929 and subsequently appeared in *Sweet and Low* (1930) and *Crazy Quilt* (1931), two closely related Broadway revues produced by and partially written by him. The marriage was childless. Brice appeared in the *Ziegfeld Follies* of 1934 and 1936, Broadway revues produced by the Messrs. Shubert following the death of the famed showman.

Brice had introduced the character "Babykins," a mischievous tot, in the show *Sweet and Low*. The child's name was changed to "Baby Snooks" in the 1934 *Follies*, and the character developed the precocious traits that would make her a national favorite for more than fifteen years.

Brice played herself in *The Great Ziegfeld* (1936) and returned to Hollywood to play the maid in *Everybody Sing*, with Judy Garland, the following year.

Although Brice made numerous radio appearances from 1930 to 1936, it was with "Good News," a one-hour NBC program produced by General Foods with the cooperation of Metro-Goldwyn-Mayer beginning in 1937, that she finally established herself in that medium, sublimating her other talents and devoting the remainder of her career to Baby Snooks, the enfant terrible based on the child star Baby Peggy.

Brice divorced Rose in 1938 and never married again, spending her off-air time doing interior decorating and entertaining family and friends. In 1944 she shot two scenes—"Baby Snooks Captures a Burglar" and "The Sweepstakes Ticket"—for *Ziegfeld Follies*, an MGM musical revue released in 1946. (The former scene was cut from U.S. release prints.) Brice died of a cerebral hemorrhage at Cedars of Lebanon Hospital in Los Angeles, two weeks prior to what would have been her final broadcast.

The hit Broadway musical, *Funny Girl* (1964), was based on Brice's life to 1927. A film version was released in 1968, and a sequel, *Funny Lady*, in 1975.

Brice was a satirist, her commentaries dealing mostly with young Jewish women coping with their lives in immigrant America and the pride of nouveau riche but poorly educated Jews with sociocultural pretensions. Her broad style of humor, though most closely linked with stage work, has been seen on television through the work of Jackie Gleason, Carol Burnett, Second City, and others. It must be performed in front of a live audience. Brice is generally considered one of the greatest comediennes of all time, ranking with Bea Lillie, Carol Burnett, and Joan Davis.

• Brice's unpublished memoir, "Don't Pick Your Money Up until You've Finished Singing" (in the New York Public Library Theatre Collection), provides valuable but far from adequate biographical information. The first published biography, *The Fabulous Fanny* (1953) by Norman Katkov, consists of quotes from Fanny's memoirs, interviews with people close to her, and the author's imaginative fleshing out of different scenes and segments. Barbara Wallace Grossman, *Funny Woman* (1991), is a painstaking examination of Miss Brice's stage career. Herbert G. Goldman, *Fanny Brice* (1992), is an attempt at a definitive biography through interviews, memoirs, and contemporary trade sources. (The appendixes list all of Brice's stage appearances, films, radio programs, and recordings. A listing of important newspaper articles and ghosted autobiographical magazine pieces is in the bibliography.) Gene Fowler, *The Great Mouthpiece* (1931), a biography of criminal lawyer William Fallon, provides an interesting look at Nick Arnstein.

HERBERT G. GOLDMAN

BRICKER, John William (6 Sept. 1893–22 Mar. 1986), governor and U.S. senator, was born in Madison County, Ohio, the son of Lemuel Spencer Bricker and Laura King, farmers. Bricker graduated from Ohio State University in 1916, and when a slow heartbeat disqualified him from military service during World War I, he was ordained as a minister so he could serve as an army chaplain. He received his law degree from Ohio State and began practicing law in Columbus, Ohio, in 1920, the same year he married Harriet Day. They had one child.

Bricker became very active in Republican politics and state and local government. He was appointed solicitor of Grandview Heights, Ohio, in 1920 and held that position until 1928. He served concurrently as assistant attorney general of Ohio from 1923 to 1927. After unsuccessfully seeking the Republican nomination for attorney general in 1928, Bricker was appointed to the Ohio Public Utilities Commission, where he served from 1929 to 1932.

Bricker was elected attorney general of Ohio in 1932, despite Democratic victories nationally and in other races in Ohio. Reelected in 1934, he sought the governorship in 1936, charging that incumbent Democratic governor Martin L. Davey's administration was riddled with corruption. Bricker ran well ahead of the rest of the Republican ticket, but popular support for Franklin D. Roosevelt's New Deal carried over to other Democratic candidates and was too much for Bricker to overcome. In 1938, however, Bricker capitalized on growing dissatisfaction with Roosevelt and the Democrats stemming from both the president's attempt to pack the Supreme Court and the recession of 1937–1938 to win the governorship over Democratic candidate Charles Sawyer. Bricker was reelected easily in 1940 and again in 1942.

As governor of Ohio, Bricker earned a reputation for honesty, economy, and efficiency. He took great pride in transforming an inherited budget deficit of $40 million in 1939 into a surplus of more than $70 million by 1945, even though this accomplishment was more the result of the economic growth and prosperity that accompanied U.S. involvement in World War II than the product of any of Bricker's specific actions.

Bricker vehemently opposed the New Deal and the federal government's growing involvement in matters that he believed should remain under state and local jurisdiction. He asserted that unemployment relief, minimum wage laws, and old-age pension systems should be established by the states not the federal government, and he warned against the dangers of an uncurbed federal bureaucracy. He especially criticized the New Deal's close association with organized labor and condemned the union shop and the sit-down strike.

Bricker's success in Ohio and his conservative beliefs made him a strong contender for the Republican nomination for president in 1944, but he had to settle for the vice presidential slot on a ticket headed by Governor Thomas Dewey of New York. During the campaign, Bricker denounced Roosevelt and the Democratic party as a front for organized labor and the Communist party. Dewey and Bricker promised to "win the war quicker," but they were easily defeated by Roosevelt and Harry Truman.

In 1946 Bricker was elected to the U.S. Senate, as Republicans swept to victory in congressional elections all across the nation. As a senator Bricker was more noted for his physical appearance than for any specific legislative accomplishments. Senator Norris Cotton (R.-N.H.) once remarked that the tall, handsome, white-haired Bricker was one of only two legislators "who really looked like senators." Bricker won reelection handily in 1952 and served as chairman of the Senate Committee on Interstate and Foreign Commerce in 1953–1954.

In the Senate Bricker aligned himself with the conservative wing of the Republican party. He tried to cut federal spending, opposed government regulation of business, and fought against any expansion in federal authority over social and economic matters. Bricker consistently voted to reduce or eliminate foreign aid and staunchly defended Senator Joseph McCarthy when the Wisconsin Republican charged that the federal government was riddled with communists.

In 1951 Bricker proposed an amendment to the Constitution, which came to be known as the Bricker Amendment. He sought to prevent the United Nations from interfering in the internal affairs of the United States by requiring that Congress pass implementing legislation before treaties such as the UN Charter, the Genocide Convention, and the UN's draft covenant on human rights would go into effect within the United States. To protect the states from further encroachments by the federal government in such areas as civil rights and labor-management relations, the Bricker Amendment also would have limited Congress, in enacting laws to implement international agreements, to passing only those laws that it could already enact under its enumerated powers. Finally, to prevent future presidents from entering into controversial agreements such as Roosevelt had done at Yalta in 1945, the Bricker Amendment included a provision giving Congress the power to regulate executive agreements.

By 1953 the Bricker Amendment had sixty-four cosponsors in the Senate, including isolationists, conservative Democrats, and nearly all the Republicans, and the measure had been endorsed by the American Bar Association and other organizations. But much to Bricker's surprise and dismay, President Dwight D. Eisenhower opposed the Bricker Amendment even though Republican complaints about the growth of federal and presidential power under Roosevelt and Truman had helped him win the presidency in 1952. Eisenhower feared the amendment would deprive the president of the authority and flexibility needed to conduct the nation's foreign affairs. After a long debate in the Senate in early 1954, the Eisenhower administration persuaded just enough of its supporters in the Senate to join with liberal Democrats to defeat the Bricker Amendment and a series of substitute measures. Bricker kept proposing the amendment until he left the Senate in 1959, but it never again reached the floor for a vote.

Bricker enjoyed strong support in Ohio, but he encountered serious obstacles when he sought reelection to a third term in the Senate in 1958. A referendum on adding a right-to-work provision to the Ohio constitution had been placed on the ballot. The measure would have prohibited union shops, which required workers to join unions to retain their jobs. Organized labor welcomed the opportunity to demonstrate its opposition both to the right-to-work proposal and to Bricker. A recession in 1958 also hurt Republican candidates nationwide, and even though Bricker ran well ahead of the rest of the Republican ticket in Ohio, he was defeated in the election by Democrat Stephen Young. Bricker returned to his law practice in Columbus, where he resided until his death there.

Throughout Bricker's public career, he was often the butt of sharp attacks and criticism. William Allen White reported that Alice Roosevelt had once dismissed Bricker as "an honest [Warren G.] Harding," and John Gunther, in his bestseller *Inside U.S.A.* (1947), asserted that intellectually, Bricker was "like interstellar space—a vast vacuum occasionally crossed by homeless, wandering clichés." A poll of 211 Washington, D.C., reporters conducted by *Pageant* magazine in 1949 unfairly rated Bricker as the "worst senator," and even Senator Robert Taft, Bricker's Republican colleague from Ohio, privately questioned Bricker's intelligence and ability.

Bricker was typical of the midwestern conservative Republicans who rose to national political prominence in the 1940s and 1950s. He opposed the New Deal with its expanded role for the federal government and he rejected America's new role in world affairs. Bricker was the product of an older, simpler time, and he never really adjusted to the changes wrought by the depression and World War II. His legacy is mostly one of failure: he is best remembered as the defeated Republican vice presidential candidate in 1944 and as the sponsor of a constitutional amendment that was rejected by the Senate.

• Bricker's papers are in the Ohio Historical Society. Richard O. Davies, *Defender of the Old Guard: John Bricker and American Politics* (1993), provides the essential biographical information and places Bricker's life and career in perspective. It replaces Karl B. Pauly, *Bricker of Ohio: The Man and His Record* (1944), an uncritical campaign biography. The most complete discussion of the Bricker Amendment is Duane Tananbaum, *The Bricker Amendment Controversy: A Test of Eisenhower's Political Leadership* (1988). For additional views, see Marvin Zahniser, ed., "John W. Bricker Reflects upon the Fight for the Bricker Amendment," *Ohio History* 87 (Summer 1978): 322–33; and Cathal Nolan, "The Last Hurrah of Conservative Isolationism: Eisenhower, Congress, and the Bricker Amendment," *Presidential Studies Quarterly* 22 (1992): 337–49. See also Bricker's obituary in the *New York Times*, 23 Mar. 1986.

DUANE TANANBAUM

BRICKMAN, William Wolfgang (30 June 1913–22 June 1986), scholar of the history of education and of comparative education, was born in New York City, the son of David Shalom Brickman, a cutter in the clothing industry, and Chaya Sarah Shaber. After attending Jewish religious elementary and secondary schools in New York City, Brickman entered the City College of New York, where he earned a B.A. in education in 1934 and an M.S. in education in 1935. He received a Ph.D. in education, with a dissertation on Hermann Lietz, an early twentieth-century German educational reformer, from New York University (NYU) in 1938.

By 1940 Brickman was an instructor in education at NYU. Drafted into the U.S. Army, he then transferred to the air force, where he served as historian, historical editor, and supervisor from 1943 to 1944. He rejoined the army as special agent and special agent in charge, Counterintelligence Corps, Bavaria, West Germany, in 1945. Returning to NYU in 1946, he worked his way up from instructor to full professor. In 1958 he married Sylvia Schnitzer; they had one child, and he adopted her two children from her previous marriage. In 1962 he moved to the University of Pennsylvania, where he served as professor in its Graduate School of Education until he retired in 1981. He died in Philadelphia and was buried in Israel.

A man of prodigious energy, Brickman was author, coauthor, editor, or coeditor of more than twenty books, monographs, and pamphlets. He also served in important editorial positions on numerous academic journals and contributed prolifically to academic journals and reference books.

Brickman's first book, *Guide to Research in Educational History* (1949), was reprinted as *Research in Educational History* (1973). In 1959 he coauthored, with George Z. F. Bereday and Gerald H. Read, one of his best-known books, *The Changing Soviet School* (1960). In addition, he wrote *Educational Systems in the United States* (1964); coedited, with Stewart E. Fraser, *A History of International and Comparative Education: Nineteenth-Century Documents* (1968), and, with Francesco Cordasco, *A Bibliography of American Educational History: An Annotated and Classified Guide* (1975); and wrote *The Jewish Community in America: An Annotated and Classified Bibliographical Guide* (1977), *Educational Historiography: Tradition, Theory, and Technique* (1982), *Educational Roots and Routes in Western Europe* (1985), the posthumously published *Pedagogy, Professionalism, and Policy: History of the Graduate School of Education at the University of Pennsylvania* (1986), and, with John T. Zepper, *Russian and Soviet Education, 1731–1989: A Multilingual Annotated Bibliography* (1992).

Throughout his career Brickman was an ardent proponent of exacting scholarly standards in educational research. Blaming the "dogmatism, superficiality, repetitiousness, and bombast" of most educational literature for the skeptical attitude of many academics toward the field of education, Brickman cautioned, "Many educationists do not yet seem to appreciate the fact that professional respect can only be earned in the open market of scholarship. The more education makes use of the recognized techniques of scholarly inquiry, the better will be its chances of attaining first-class citizenship in the academic community" (*Guide to Research in Educational History*, p iii).

Throughout his career Brickman was extremely active as an editor of educational journals and reference books. His principal editorship was of *School and Society* (later called *Intellect*) from 1953 to 1976. He also served as editor of *Education Abstracts* (1942–1944), as assistant managing editor of *Modern Language Journal* (1942–1946), as editorial board member of *Soviet Society* (1961–1968) and of *Paedagogica Historica* (1961–1986), as editorial adviser, for the field of education, of the *Grolier International Encyclopedia* (1962–1970), as departmental editor of *Encyclopedia Judaica* (1962–1971), as editorial adviser for the *Encyclopedia of Education* (1967–1971), and as contributing editor of *Western European Education* (1979–1986).

Brickman published, throughout his career, on a wide range of topics. According to Elizabeth Swing, the breadth of his research interests astonished his peers. An expert on education in the Soviet Union, he also collected documents on a wide variety of topics, including church/state relations, nineteenth-century international and comparative education, automation and human values, and student activism.

He contributed articles to many important journals, including *Comparative Education Review*, *Journal of Educational Sociology*, and *Western European Education*, as well as numerous entries to various encyclopedias. A remarkable linguist, Brickman reportedly knew some twenty languages and was fluent in Hebrew, classical Greek and Latin, and Yiddish as well as German, Danish, Swedish, Russian, Polish, Hungarian, Portuguese, Romanian, Bulgarian, and several Asiatic and African languages.

Brickman took a fundamentalist approach to teaching, stressing effort, discipline, the logical organization of material, and the setting of long-term goals. An exacting teacher, he demanded as much from his students as from himself. He was known for compiling lengthy reading lists, for giving extremely difficult oral examinations, and for requiring numerous revisions to doctoral dissertations. He also was known, however, for being compassionate and generous.

Brickman's numerous, wide-ranging publications did not achieve a quality commensurate with their quantity. Few of his books were published by distinguished presses, and his publications were cited in the *Social Sciences Citation Index* far less often than could be expected of such an enormous oeuvre. Brickman remains noteworthy nevertheless for the immense number of his publications, his prodigious editing work, and his great abilities as a linguist. His most notable achievement was helping to stimulate in the fifties and sixties, the development of the nascent field of comparative education.

• Most of Brickman's papers are housed in the Hanna collection of the Hoover Institution on War, Revolution, and Peace at Stanford University. The rest of his papers will eventually be sent there. Brickman's other writings include two pamphlets on international education, *Denmark's Educational System and Problems* (1967) and *Educational Reform and Renewal in Contemporary Spain* (1972). His coedited books with Stanley Lehrer include *John Dewey: Master Educator* (1959; rev. ed. 1961), *Religion, Government, and Education* (1961), *Automation, Education, and Human Values* (1966), and *Conflict and Change on the Campus: The Response to Student Hyperactivism* (1970). A good discussion of his life and work is Elizabeth Sherman Swing, "In Memoriam: William W. Brickman, 1913–1986," *Comparative Education Review* 31 (1987): 1–6. A brief account of his career is by Saul Sack, "William W. Brickman Retires," University of Pennsylvania Graduate School of Education *Newsletter* 6 (1981): 1. Franklin Parker wrote a fine, apparently unpublished obituary, "William Wolfgang Brickman, 1913–1986"; it is available at the University of Pennsylvania Archives. Other obituaries are in the *New York Times*, 24 June 1986; the *Philadelphia Inquirer* and the *Philadelphia Daily News*, both 25 June 1986; and the University of Pennsylvania *Almanac* 33 (1986): 7.

DAVID S. WEBSTER

BRICKTOP (14 Aug. 1894–31 Jan. 1984), entertainer and nightclub operator, was born in Alderson, West Virginia, the daughter of Thomas Smith, a barber, and Hattie E. (maiden name unknown), a domestic worker. Christened Ada Beatrice Queen Victoria Louise Virginia, because her parents did not wish to disappoint the various neighbors and friends who offered suggestions for naming her, Bricktop received her nickname because of her red hair when she was in her late twenties from Barron Wilkins, owner of a nightclub called Barron's Exclusive Club in Prohibition Harlem.

Bricktop's father died when she was four, and her mother moved with the children to Chicago to be near relatives. Hattie Smith worked as a domestic in Chicago, and her children attended school. Bricktop showed early musical talent and interest in performing. She made her stage debut as a preschooler, playing the part of Eliza's son Harry in a production of *Uncle Tom's Cabin* at the Haymarket Theatre. As an adolescent, she had the opportunity to perform onstage again when she was hired as part of the chorus for a show at the Pekin Theatre. She quit school at age sixteen to pursue a career as an entertainer, first touring with (Flournoy) Miller and (Aubrey) Lyles, a well-known black comedy team.

After the Miller and Lyles show folded, Bricktop toured with a variety of black vaudeville acts across the northern half of the United States. In the early 1920s she returned to Chicago and worked as a saloon performer at Roy Jones's and the Cafe Champ, owned by heavyweight champion Jack Johnson. In 1922 she went to Harlem, where she worked in Connie's Inn, among other nightclubs, and received her nickname. In 1924 she was invited to work in Paris at Le Grand Duc, a tiny club in Montmartre managed by Eugene Bullard, an African American who had distinguished himself during World War I in the French Foreign Legion and the Lafayette Escadrille.

Never a great song stylist, Bricktop attracted the attention of white Americans in Paris because of her charming personality and her ability to make them feel at home. T. S. Eliot wrote a poem for her. F. Scott Fitzgerald liked to say, "My greatest claim to fame is that I discovered Bricktop before Cole Porter." But it was her discovery by Porter, who later wrote the song "Miss Otis Regrets" for her, that put the imprimatur of acceptance upon her. Under Porter's aegis, Bricktop became a darling of the American celebrity set in Paris. By the fall of 1926, Bricktop had opened the first Bricktop's nightclub in Paris, catering to such American luminaries as Fitzgerald, Elsa Maxwell, Tallulah Bankhead, Ernest Hemingway, and Barbara Hutton, and to international celebrities like the Aga Khan. "Everybody belonged, or else they didn't bother coming to Bricktop's more than once," she wrote in her autobiography.

A succession of Bricktop's nightclubs followed, both in Paris and, in the summertime, at Biarritz, where Bricktop claimed to have cradled the romance of the duke of Windsor and the American divorcée Wallis Simpson. Among the careers she nurtured was that of the British-born black singer Mabel Mercer.

The stock market crash in the United States in October 1929 had no effect, at first, on the "gay" life in Paris. In December 1929 Bricktop married Peter Ducongé, an African-American saxophonist from New Orleans, and the two purchased a country home in Bougival, outside Paris. Childless, each led an independent life, as well as sharing a life together. Some years after their marriage, however, Peter had an affair with a young African-American singer whom Bricktop had taken under her wing in Paris. On learning of her husband's infidelity, Bricktop refused to sleep with him again, although she never divorced him. He died in 1967.

In 1939, as war in Europe and the invasion of France seemed imminent, the duchess of Windsor (the former Wallis Simpson) and Lady Mendl (Elsie de Wolfe) helped Bricktop escape from Paris to New York, where her friend Mabel Mercer had already relocated. Mercer managed to find a niche as a singer in New York cabarets, but Bricktop's special talents as a self-described "saloonkeeper par excellence" went unappreciated. Bankrolled by the tobacco heiress Doris Duke, she relocated to Mexico City, where she successfully ran clubs until the war in Europe was over. In 1943 she converted to Catholicism and remained a devout Catholic for the rest of her life.

Returning to Paris in 1950, she found her old stomping grounds much changed, as was the clientele. After trying and failing to revive the prewar atmosphere, Bricktop removed to Rome, where on the Via Veneto from 1951 to 1965 she recreated the feeling of the old Bricktop's for a new celebrity crowd, primarily American film stars. The romance of Richard Burton and Elizabeth Taylor first made the gossip columns when they were seen together at the Rome Bricktop's during the filming of *Cleopatra*. To Bricktop her career in Rome was secondary to the golden years in Paris, and she never fully accepted the Hollywood film stars as the nouveau royalty.

When Bricktop's older sister Blonzetta became ill in 1965, Bricktop returned to Chicago to nurse her and, after her death, went back to straighten out her affairs. Blonzetta left Bricktop a substantial inheritance. In her early seventies, Bricktop moved to Los Angeles, returned briefly to Europe, and then in 1970 settled in New York City. She made a recording of "So Long, Baby" with Cy Coleman, briefly ran a club owned by Huntington Hartford and then one called Soerabaja, and appeared from time to time at clubs in Chicago, at the Playboy Club in London, and at "21" in New York. Ill health caused her to cease working in 1979.

In August 1983 Bricktop published her autobiography, written with Jim Haskins. Five months later she died in New York City. To the end she was a lady of the dawn who drank only champagne and expected a rose from every male visitor.

• Bricktop's papers are in the collection of the Schomburg Center for Research in Black Culture, New York Public Library, Astor, Lenox, and Tilden foundations. Besides her autobiography, *Bricktop* (1983), only two other books contain considerable information about her life, Kay Boyle and Robert Altman, *Being Geniuses Together, 1920–1930* (1968), and Jim Haskins, *Mabel Mercer: A Life* (1968). A substantial obituary appears in *Rolling Stone*, 29 Mar. 1984.

JIM HASKINS

BRICO, Antonia (26 June 1902–3 Aug. 1989), conductor, was born in Rotterdam, the Netherlands, the daughter of parents who were of Italian and Dutch ancestry. Brico's parents, whose names are unknown, died in 1904, and she moved to the United States with her foster parents in 1906. As a child she showed promise as a pianist but decided at the age of ten that she wanted to be a conductor after hearing a concert conducted by Paul Steindorff, the director of the San Francisco Opera. Brico graduated from the University of California at Berkeley in 1923 with honors and a degree in music.

In 1925 Brico went to New York City to study piano under Sigismund Stojowski. Two years later she moved to Berlin to pursue her passion for conducting. There she met Karl Muck, head of the Hamburg Philharmonic, who accepted Brico as his only student. In 1929 Brico became the first American to graduate from the Master School of Conducting of the Berlin State Academy of Music. Her conducting debut was on 10 January 1930 with the Berlin Philharmonic. At the age of twenty-eight she became the first woman to conduct this internationally renowned orchestra. With the headline "Miss Brico Triumphs as Berlin Conductor," the *New York Times* heralded Antonia Brico's inaugural performance (15 Feb. 1930). Her American debut was on 1 August 1930 with the Los Angeles Philharmonic. She was also the first woman to conduct this major orchestra.

In the early 1930s Brico conducted to great acclaim in many of the major cities of Europe and the United States—Berlin, Hamburg, San Francisco, Warsaw, Lodz, Detroit, Posnan, and Riga. Yet she received no offers for a permanent conducting position. In 1932 Brico returned to the United States because foreigners were no longer welcome in Germany. She arrived in New York City at the height of the depression, when thousands of musicians were out of work. Her New York conducting debut was the following year with the Musicians Symphony Orchestra, an ensemble of unemployed union musicians. One critic said of her performance that "Miss Brico knew what she was doing a good deal better than many a young man who has been tooted and feted and given golden opportunities in this city" (*New York Times*, 11 Jan. 1933). Brico had been engaged for a series of concerts with the Musicians Symphony, but despite glowing reviews, she conducted only two of them. The third concert was cancelled because John Charles Thomas, a soloist, refused to perform under a female conductor. Shortly thereafter, the Works Progress Administration engaged Brico to conduct the WPA Orchestra in three concerts a week in the New York City area.

In 1934 a small group of women musicians approached Brico and asked her to conduct for them. This group became the foundation of the New York Women's Symphony, which had its debut on 18 February 1935. During the late nineteenth and early twentieth centuries many women could perform publicly only by creating or joining orchestras for women. As was the case for other all-female ensembles, Brico's goals for the New York Women's Symphony were to provide opportunities for women musicians and to prove that women could play any position in the orchestra as well as any man. She quickly molded the group into a professional symphony that flourished for several years.

Brico reached the height of her first wave of popular acclaim in 1938. In August she became the first woman to conduct the New York Philharmonic. Thereafter, however, success became evasive. In 1939 she renamed her orchestra the Brico Symphony Orchestra and allowed men to audition. With the addition of male musicians, however, the Brico Symphony Orchestra lost its novelty, and the public and the orchestra's board of directors lost their interest. Support for the orchestra dissipated, and it disbanded after one season. Brico no longer had a regular showcase for her talents.

Brico moved to Denver, Colorado, in the early 1940s. She had hoped to become the conductor for the Denver Symphony, but the symphony's board hired Saul Caston instead. In Denver, Brico taught piano, voice, and conducting. She continued to give lectures and to guest-conduct European orchestras. In 1947 Brico became the permanent conductor of the Denver Businessmen's Symphony, a semiprofessional orchestra started by musicians who had been fired from the Denver Symphony when Caston took over. In 1969 the Denver Businessmen's Symphony was renamed the Brico Symphony in honor of the orchestra's conductor. Brico also directed the Greater Denver Opera Association, the Women's String Orchestra, and the Boulder Philharmonic.

Throughout her career Brico impressed and gained the support of well-known and influential persons in the music world. The sponsors of her New York Women's Symphony included Eleanor Roosevelt, Bruno Walter, and Sigismund Stojowski. During her career Brico had the support of men such as Arthur Judson, Karl Muck, and Arthur Rubinstein. Jean Sibelius was a friend and admirer as was Albert Schweitzer, the famous physician, missionary, and Bach expert. Brico visited Schweitzer in Africa several times. They maintained a lively correspondence, and in 1978 Brico conducted a benefit concert on behalf of the Albert Schweitzer Foundation.

In 1974 Judy Collins, a former piano student of Brico's, and Jill Godmillow produced a documentary about Brico's life titled *Antonia: A Portrait of the Woman.* The film revived Brico's career, bringing several conducting engagements with prestigious symphony orchestras and more honors and tributes. At the age of seventy-two, when asked if she might find the interviews, traveling, and conducting a bit tiring, Brico said, "My goodness, no. I've been waiting forty years for this" (*New York Times*, 19 May 1975). Brico continued to conduct for another ten years, but she never did get a permanent position with a major professional orchestra. In 1985 she resigned her position with the Brico Symphony. Brico died in Denver, Colorado. She never married and had no children.

Antonia Brico was a woman of immense talent and unfulfilled ambition who struggled all her life against sex discrimination in the orchestral world. She vociferously challenged those who said women could not play or conduct; she created opportunities for female musicians to perform; by her words and deeds, she encouraged girls and women to pursue their dreams; and when given the opportunity, Brico moved and delighted audiences with beautiful, brilliantly interpreted music.

• Brico's papers are at the Colorado Historical Society in Denver. Some of her letters are kept by the Music Division of the Library of Congress, in the Olin Downes Collection at the Hargrett Rare Book and Manuscript Library of the University of Georgia, and in the archives of the Albert Schweitzer Institute for the Humanities in Hamden, Conn. The Music Division of the Boston Public Library has a small clippings file on Brico. The Denver Public Library Music Division has the papers and programs for the Brico Symphony Orchestra/ Denver Businessmen's Symphony that she conducted for thirty-eight years. An important source is Patricia Stanley,

"Dr. Antonia Brico and Dr. Albert Schweitzer: A Chronicle of Their Friendship," in *Literary and Musical Notes: A Festschrift for Wm. A. Little*, ed. Geoffrey C. Orth (1995), pp. 185–203. A 1976 interview with Brico is reproduced in Carol Neuls-Bates, *Women in Music: An Anthology of Source Readings from the Middle Ages to the Present* (1982), pp. 253–59. Obituaries are in the *New York Times* and the *Los Angeles Times*, both 5 Aug. 1989, and the *Denver Post*, 4 Aug. 1989.

CYNTHIA R. POE

BRIDGE, Horatio (8 Apr. 1806–20 Mar. 1893), naval officer and author, was born in Augusta, Maine, the son of James Bridge, a judge and financier, and Hannah North. He attended local schools in Augusta before entering Hallowell Academy and then Bowdoin College, from which he graduated in 1825. At Bowdoin, Bridge was a classmate of Nathaniel Hawthorne and Henry Wadsworth Longfellow, and it is his association with Hawthorne at Bowdoin and throughout their lives that has made him important in literature and history.

After leaving Bowdoin, Bridge studied at Northampton law school and was admitted to the bar in 1828. His career as an attorney lasted only until 1838, when it was effectively ended by a disastrous venture in the construction of a dam across the Kennebec River, near his ancestral home. The dam failed, and the river literally washed away the Bridge home and fortune. Part of that fortune had been used to underwrite the cost of printing Hawthorne's first book, *Twice-Told Tales* (1837), an act of friendship that was of paramount importance in advancing Hawthorne's literary career. This was only one of the many important actions Bridge carried out to further Hawthorne's development, which was often threatened by doubts and discouragement.

The two men were in constant touch throughout Hawthorne's life after they met at Bowdoin. Bridge lent a confiding ear to outpourings on topics from gambling to drinking to love. He imparted valuable advice on the other man's writing career; he intervened, indeed schemed, for Hawthorne on a number of occasions in the interest of securing him employment that would also give him time to write. More than once he sent money to help the Hawthornes when they were particularly in need of cash. He was Hawthorne's trusted adviser and, above all, beloved friend. His correspondence with Hawthorne, furthermore, is one of the principal sources for biographical data on Hawthorne's life.

Bridge entered the navy as a purser in February 1838 and saw duty in the Mediterranean before being assigned, in 1843, to the sloop *Saratoga*, which was about to go on a long cruise along the African coast. His journal of that expedition, the composition of which the two men discussed before Bridge departed, was edited by Hawthorne, who knew well the commercial possibilities of a sailing volume in this time that had welcomed *Two Years before the Mast* (1840), by Richard Henry Dana, Jr., and Herman Melville's *Typee* (1846) and *Omoo* (1847). Bridge's book became a commercial success, and the proceeds went to Hawthorne.

Both Bridge and Hawthorne married late, Hawthorne when he was thirty-eight, and Bridge when he was forty. Bridge and his wife, the former Charlotte Marshall, had one child, who died in her fourth year.

Bridge rose to become paymaster general of the U.S. Navy and chief and founder of its Bureau of Provisions and Clothing (later the Bureau of Supplies and Accounts). He served as paymaster general for fifteen years, including the years of the conflict he called "The War of the Rebellion." He retired from the service in 1868, with the rank of commodore, and continued to serve as a civilian until 1873, when he went to live in the country home he called "The Moorings," in Athens, Pennsylvania. The Supply Corps he founded was cited by the Hoover commission a half-century after his death for the quality of its organization.

Both of Bridge's books are associated with Hawthorne. Long after *The Journal of an African Cruiser* (1845), in fact, almost forty years after Hawthorne's death, came *Personal Recollections of Nathaniel Hawthorne* (1893). On the fourth page of that second book, Bridge tells of their first meeting, at Bowdoin, and what it meant to him: "He interested me greatly at once, and a friendship then began which, for the forty-three years of his subsequent life, was never for a moment chilled by indifference nor clouded by doubt. Though our paths in life, like our characters, were widely different, our friendship never wavered till the sad end came."

The importance of Horatio Bridge in Hawthorne's literary career was best stated, and perhaps not exaggerated, by Hawthorne himself, in the preface to his *The Snow Image and Other Twice-Told Tales*, addressed to Horatio Bridge, Ensign, U.S.N. His words were: "If anybody is responsible for my being at this day an author, it is yourself." Bridge died in Athens, Pennsylvania.

• The principal sources for basic information on Bridge's life are the Library of Bowdoin College, Brunswick, Me., and the Maine Historic Preservation Commission, Augusta. His first book, *The Journal of an African Cruiser* (1845), was republished in 1848 and 1853. His second book, *Personal Recollections of Nathaniel Hawthorne* (repr. 1968), though nominally on Hawthorne, provides much information on Bridge himself.

Bridge's name appears over and over in books on Hawthorne's life and correspondence. Letters from him appear throughout *The Centenary Edition of the Works of Nathaniel Hawthorne*, ed. Thomas Woodson et al., vols. 15–18 and 20 (1984). One biography that shows well how important the Bridge materials are to the Hawthorne scholar is Edwin Haviland Miller, *Salem Is My Dwelling Place: A Life of Nathaniel Hawthorne* (1991). Patrick Brancaccio, "The Black Man's Paradise: Hawthorne's Editing of *The Journal of an African Cruiser*," *New England Quarterly* 58 (1980): 23–41, pays close attention to Hawthorne's part in the production of the book on which he and Bridge in a sense collaborated.

ALFRED H. MARKS

BRIDGER, James (17 Mar. 1804–17 July 1881), fur trapper and trader, explorer, and scout, was born in a tavern near Richmond, Virginia, the son of James Bridger, a surveyor and innkeeper, and Chloe Tyler, a barmaid. Bridger and his family moved in about 1812 to a farm near St. Louis, where, on being orphaned five years later, he became a blacksmith's apprentice. In 1822 he responded to an advertisement calling for a hundred able-bodied young men to join a fur-trapping expedition, lasting from one to three years, up to the headwaters of the Missouri River. The organizers of the expedition were William Henry Ashley, then lieutenant governor of Missouri and a brigadier general in its militia, and his business partner Major Andrew Henry. Bridger thus embarked on a lifelong career of trapping, trading, and exploring.

The Ashley-Henry group built a post called Fort Henry (later Fort Union) at the junction of the Yellowstone and Missouri rivers in Montana. In 1823 Hugh Glass, one of the members of the expedition, was horribly mauled by a grizzly bear near what is now Grand River, South Dakota. Bridger and another explorer, John S. Fitzgerald, agreed to stay behind with him until he died. But they abandoned Glass, who survived his injuries, crawled an alleged 300 miles to Fort Kiowa near the Missouri and White rivers, returned up the Yellowstone, and found and forgave Bridger on account of his youth. By this time, Bridger was among the first non-natives to see the geysers and other natural phenomena in the Yellowstone region. It is likely that a little later he was the first non-native to see the Great Salt Lake, perhaps in late fall 1824 or early spring 1825. Its salty taste convinced him that it was an arm of the Pacific Ocean.

In 1830 Bridger, with Thomas "Broken Hand" Fitzpatrick and other explorers, bought out Ashley and Henry and formed the Rocky Mountain Fur Company. Until 1834 they competed with rival concerns, including the Hudson's Bay Company from British Canada and John Jacob Astor's American Fur Company, for the lucrative beaver-pelt trade in the north-central section of the country. In 1838 Bridger and his friend Louis Vasquez built a store on the Green River in southwest Wyoming and expanded it by 1843 into a trading post (later called Fort Bridger) for emigrants on the Oregon and California Trail.

By the 1840s Bridger had walked and was intimately familiar with most of the region bounded by Canada, the Missouri River, and the Colorado–New Mexico border. Evidently he possessed an unusually strong constitution, having been shot with arrows by Blackfoot Indians and having lived with an iron arrowhead in his back for three years. Bridger served as a guide on a variety of missions. In 1849 he led a railroad surveying party under Captain Howard Stansbury to Utah; in 1851 he scouted for a hunting party headed by Sir George Gore, a wealthy Irishman. During 1857–1858 he participated in Colonel Albert Sidney Johnston's campaigns against the Mormons, who in 1853 had driven Bridger from his trading post. He was involved in seeking a direct route from Denver to the Great Salt Lake in 1861 and took part in the expedition to measure distances along the 967-mile Bozeman Trail during 1865–1866. Among later acquaintances were scout Kit Carson; explorer John Charles Frémont; trapper Joe Meek; John Augustus Sutter, the instigator of the California gold rush; and Mormon leader Brigham Young.

In 1835 Bridger married a Flathead Indian whom he named Cora and with whom he had three children. After Cora died in 1846, he married Little Fawn later that year; she was the fourteen-year-old daughter of Washakie, the distinguished Shoshone chief. Called Mary Washakie Bridger, she died in childbirth in 1849. He then married, in 1850, a Shoshone Indian with whom he had two children. Some of Bridger's children were sent to Missouri to be educated.

Bridger spun tall tales about bizarre phenomena, such as petrified forests along the Yellowstone complete with petrified birds. Although illiterate, he could converse in French, Spanish, and a few Native American languages. He enjoyed having literature read to him; in one such instance, he listened to passages from Henry Wadsworth Longfellow's *Song of Hiawatha* until he objected to that poet's ignorance of Indian life. On being informed that William Shakespeare was the world's greatest writer, Bridger traded a team of cattle worth $125 for a book of Shakespeare's plays.

The names given to him by Indians included Casapy (Crow for "Blanket Chief," because of his alleged sexual prowess), Peejatowahooten (Shoshone for "Mysterious Medicine Man," because of his uncanny intelligence), and Big Throat (because of his goiter).

In 1865 Bridger received his discharge at Fort Laramie from service as an army scout and guide during the Powder River campaign against Sioux and Cheyenne Indians blocking the route to the Montana goldfields. Severely pained by his goiter, arthritis, and rheumatism, among other problems with his health, he returned in 1868 to his farm at Westport, Missouri. He requested back rent due him for the government's use of Fort Bridger, but he received nothing. By 1875 Bridger was totally blind. He died in Washington, Jackson County, Missouri. As much a legend as he was a genuine adventurer, Bridger can be counted among the most knowledgeable explorers who opened the West to pioneers from the eastern United States.

• Biographies of Bridger include Grenville M. Dodge, *Biographical Sketch of Jim Bridger: Mountaineer, Trapper and Guide* (1905); J. Cecil Alter, *James Bridger* (1925; rev. ed., 1962); Stanley Vestal (Walter Stanley Campbell), *Jim Bridger: Mountain Man, a Biography* (1946); and Gene Caesar, *King of the Mountain Men: The Life of Jim Bridger* (1961). The following works place Bridger's actions in their historical context: J. Lee Humfreville, *Twenty Years among Our Savage Indians* (1897; later editions titled *Twenty Years among Our Hostile Indians*); Grace Raymond Hebard and E. A. Brininstool, *The Bozeman Trail* (1922); Bernard DeVoto, *The Year of Decision 1846* (1943); William H. Goetzmann, "The Mountain Man as Jacksonian Man," *American Quarterly* 15 (Fall 1963): 402–15; Dale Van Every, *The Final Challenge: The American Frontier 1804–1845* (1964); Fred R. Gowans and Eugene E. Campbell, *Fort Bridger: Island in the Wilderness* (1975); and Ted Morgan, *A Shovel of Stars: The Making of the American West, 1800 to the Present* (1995). Dee Brown, *Wondrous Times on the Frontier* (1991), repeats some of the whoppers told by Bridger.

ROBERT L. GALE

BRIDGER, Jonathan (fl. 1696–1722), colonial official, also recorded as John Bridger, was of obscure origin. He worked early in his career as a shipwright for the Royal Navy at the naval dockyard in Portsmouth, England, and later served as a navy ship's purser on a voyage to the northern American colonies, probably in the early 1690s.

Bridger's 22-year career in New England began with his arrival in Boston in May 1698 as part of a four-member commission appointed by the Navy Board to encourage the production of naval stores (pitch, tar, resin, turpentine, masts, and spars) in the northern colonies and to investigate wasteful woodcutting practices. Of the four commissioners, one died en route to America, while two, already resident in New England, were active exporters of timber. Thus Bridger, without authority, appointed another New England timber merchant to replace the dead commissioner and entered into his duties fully committed to enhancing his career as a government official without regard to local timber interests. Consequently, there was little cooperation among the commissioners. Bridger complained to the Navy Board and to the Board of Trade that he was working alone and that one of his fellow commissioners, Lieutenant Governor William Partridge of New Hampshire, was shipping large quantities of pine masts and boards to Spain, Portugal, and Algiers, although Britain was experiencing a serious timber shortage. The other members complained that, in securing specimens of timber, tar, and pitch for the navy, Bridger ignored the advice of Partridge, whose years in the woods had taught him how to secure these materials at a much better price than Bridger had paid. Partridge's superior, Lord Bellomont, governor of New York, Massachusetts, and New Hampshire, reported that the commission suffered from Bridger's "private management," though he later joined with Bridger in complaining of the trade in ship timber and masts to Spain and Portugal, from which Partridge was profiting.

The Navy Board's dissatisfaction with the quality of the specimens from New England resulted in the disbanding of the commission. Bridger returned to England in 1702. In 1705, largely as a result of Bridger's recommendations to the Board of Trade, Parliament passed a comprehensive naval stores act, combining provisions to encourage the importation of naval stores from America with other provisions aimed at preserving the forests. To carry out the new law, the Board of Trade reinstituted the then defunct office of surveyor general of the woods in America, to which Bridger, whom one historian has called "the solitary and persistent applicant" (Malone, p. 29), was appointed.

The purpose of both the new legislation and the revived office was two-fold: to stimulate the production of pitch, tar, resin, turpentine, hemp, masts, and spars both through instruction and the payment of premiums, and to preserve the forests by prohibiting the felling of pitch pine trees under a certain size if they were growing on ungranted—and therefore royal—land. The act did not mention white pine, New England's great source of ships' masts, because provisions in the Massachusetts charter of 1691 for protecting trees of that species over a certain size were already in effect. Bridger showed a far greater interest in the latter part of his charge, the policing function, than in the first part, the teaching function. Over the next fifteen years, Bridger devoted his main energies to refining British forest policy in America and to its vigorous enforcement. In the process, he made himself one of the most unpopular men in New England.

Bridger concentrated his attention on southern New Hampshire and Southeastern Maine, where cutting, sawing, and exporting lumber through the Piscataqua River ports of Portsmouth and Kittery formed the backbone of the local economy. Convinced that the mast supply was in danger of drying up, he began persistent and annoying investigations of the region's scores of sawmill operators, brought legal actions against government mast contractors who were supplying foreign markets as well as the Royal Navy, and began the practice of marking pine trees of suitable dimensions with the "broad arrow," the sign of royal ownership. He gained the cooperation of Joseph Dudley, then governor of Massachusetts and New Hampshire, in securing passage of a New Hampshire act of 1708 providing for a £100 fine for the unauthorized felling (the felling of a tree without proper consent, usually in the form of a license issued by the Crown to contractors for the navy, and shipping it to parties other than the navy) of a white pine twenty-four inches or more in diameter not on private property. His failure to get a similar act passed in Massachusetts, which then encompassed Maine, resulted in parliamentary passage of the White Pine Act of 1711, which applied provisions similar to those of the New Hampshire law to all of New England, New York, and the Jerseys. Loopholes of various kinds made the law difficult to enforce, so Bridger pressed for still tougher provisions, most of which were incorporated into a parliamentary act of 1722 after Bridger had been replaced in the surveyorship.

In his zeal to police the woods, Bridger made enemies not only of the woodsmen but also of some of the most influential political figures in New England. Accusations against him of bribery and corruption were never pressed to their legal conclusion, but his lack of moderation and realism eventually alienated even those such as Governor Dudley who had once cooperated with him. At one point, Jeremiah Dummer, the agent for New England in London, protested to the Board of Trade that Bridger had even tried to forbid anyone from entering the woods or cutting any trees whether fit for naval use or not.

In 1718, largely as a result of complaints against him, Bridger was replaced in the surveyorship by Andrew Burniston, a London merchant, who appointed Thomas Armstrong, a customs official at Portsmouth, New Hampshire, to serve as his deputy. Armstrong assumed his duties in November 1720, after which Bridger returned to England to argue, unsuccessfully, for the return of his commission. The final plea on record is that received by the Board of Trade in May 1722, in which he argued that Armstrong's incompetence and lack of experience would encourage the further destruction of the forest. He reported that, during his surveyorship, he and his deputies had marked 3,030 trees with the king's broad arrow. At this point, Bridger disappears from the record.

The two principal twentieth-century assessments of Bridger's career in America are strikingly at odds. In 1926 Robert G. Albion portrayed him as a dedicated and principled public servant who suffered the fate of any official "who rigorously enforces an unpopular law which affects the interests of those in influence" (Albion, p. 97). In 1964 Joseph J. Malone called him a "scoundrel, whose dishonesty cost his government vast sums of money and whose egoism and foolishness proved more costly still" (Malone, p. 29). Both historians agree that Bridger was mainly responsible for the development of British forest policy in New England, and both suggest that its enforcement by subsequent surveyors general was one of the earliest and most consistent sources of irritation and resistance to British rule.

Despite Bridger's apparent preoccupation with forest policy, his American career included at least one other accomplishment. Consistent with his dedication to royal interests in New England against local opposition, he apparently played a central role in the organization in 1712 of a Church of England congregation in Newbury, Massachusetts, the second in New England. In a letter to England in 1713, Bridger enclosed a petition to Queen Anne, in which the minister and twenty-nine other signatories commended Bridger's services in protecting the new church against persecution by the dissenting provincial government and in securing its members' exemption from the local ministerial tax.

While Malone's evidence against Bridger persuasively portrays a man who was self-seeking, self-serving, untactful, and prejudiced against New Englanders, and probably occasionally dishonest, it may be that his appellation "scoundrel" is a bit strong. Bridger did possess a number of unattractive qualities, but no man ever labored more diligently and creatively, or with greater long-term effect, in the interests of a limited but important colonial objective of the British Crown.

• Extensive correspondence from and concerning Bridger is in *Calendar of State Papers, Colonial Series* for the years 1696–1722. The letter and enclosed petition regarding Bridger's role in the Church of England at Newbury is in vol. 27, docs. 519 and 519.i, pp. 257–58. The text of Bridger's commission as surveyor general, somewhat abridged, along with other correspondence is printed in *Provincial Papers of New Hampshire*, vol. 3 (1869). Bridger's printed instructions for making tar are contained in a two-page publication under his name entitled *Information and Directions for the Making of Tar, and Choice of Trees for the Same* . . . (1707). A copy is in the New-York Historical Society, and photostats are at the Massachusetts Historical Society and the State Historical Society of Wisconsin. Three monographs on aspects of colonial industry and timber policies comprise the main secondary literature on Bridger: Eleanor L. Lord, *Industrial Experiments in the British Colonies of North America* (1898; repr. 1969); Robert Greenhalgh Albion, *Forests and Sea Power: The Timber Problem of the Royal Navy, 1652–1862* (1926); and Joseph J. Malone, *Pine Trees and Politics: The Naval Stores and Forest Policy in Colonial New England, 1691–1775* (1964). A briefer treatment is in Lawrence Shaw Mayo, "The King's Woods," *Massachusetts Historical Society Proceedings* 54 (1920–1921): 50–61.

CHARLES E. CLARK

BRIDGES, Calvin Blackman (11 Jan. 1889–27 Dec. 1938), geneticist, was born in Schuyler Falls, New York, the only child of Leonard Bridges and Charlotte Amelia Blackman. His mother died when he was only two, and his father when he was three, leaving young Bridges to be raised by his paternal grandmother on a small farm near Plattsburgh, New York. Because he worked at various jobs through his early years, Bridges did not finish high school until 1909, when he was twenty. Nevertheless, he did well enough to win scholarships to both Cornell and Columbia Universities. He entered Columbia and graduated in three years (B.S., 1912). During his second and third years (1910–1912) he began work on the genetics of the fruit fly, *Drosophila melanogaster*, in the laboratory of Thomas Hunt Morgan, work that was to occupy him for the remainder of his life. Bridges's marriage in 1912 to Gertrude F. Ives resulted in four children, three of whom survived him.

Bridges's contributions to the development of Mendelian genetics were multifold: as a particularly astute observer he was credited with spotting more new *Drosophila* mutants than any other investigator in Morgan's lab; clever at designing equipment, he introduced a special type of binocular microscope for observing flies, replacing the older, lower-powered hand lens; and he developed new staining techniques for distinguishing the chromosomes more clearly in microscopic preparations. Most of his research centered on problems in cytogenetics, a rapidly developing field at the time that involved the correlation of genetic studies (carried out by breeding experiments) with alterations in chromosome structure as observed by microscopy. On the theoretical level, he developed far-reaching theories about the mechanism of sex determination and the role of the chromosomes in development. Bridges worked for most of his career in Morgan's laboratory as a research associate of the Carnegie Institution of Washington, and, after the group moved to Pasadena in 1928, as a research associate of the California Institute of Technology.

To understand the significance of Bridges's work it is necessary to describe briefly the genetic basis of sex determination in normal *Drosophila* (a process that applies with some variations to most other multicellular organisms). *Drosophila* and other organisms have in their cell nuclei groups of rod-shaped structures known as chromosomes that consist of linear arrays of genes, each of which specify certain bodily traits (what is known as the organism's phenotype, such as eye color or wing shape). Every species has its own specific number of chromosomes: *Drosophila* has a total of eight, while humans have a total of forty-six. These chromosomes exist in pairs, or homologues, so that *Drosophila* has four pairs and humans twenty-three. The two members of a pair are the same size and shape and have the same linear arrangement of genes, though the corresponding genes on each pair may not determine the trait in the same way—for example, one chromosome could contain the gene for white eye color while its homologue contains the gene for red eye color. When an adult *Drosophila* or other organism forms gametes (egg or sperm), the two homologous members of each chromosome pair normally separate from each other (in a process known as meiosis) and end up in different egg or sperm cells. Thus, gametes contain half the chromosome number found in body cells; the double number is restored when gametes join at fertilization. One pair of chromosomes, called the sex-chromosomes, is responsible for determining the sex of the individual; the remainder of the chromosomes are referred to as autosomes. In *Drosophila*, females have two X-chromosomes that are identical in size and appearance, making up a homologous pair; males have one X and a much smaller, nonhomologous chromosome known as the Y. The X-chromosomes contain genes for many traits other than sex; those other traits determined by genes on the X-chromosome are said to be sex-linked traits, one of the first and most fundamental discoveries made by the Morgan group between 1910 and 1912.

In 1913, while still a graduate student, Bridges was studying several sex-linked traits in *Drosophila*. While in standard sex-linked traits, male offspring tend to resemble their mothers and female offspring their fathers, Bridges found that when he observed a large enough sample of offspring, in about 5 percent of the cases the male offspring resembled their fathers and female offspring resembled their mothers. He realized that it would be possible to explain these results by hypothesizing that in some cases the normal female's two X-chromosomes had failed to separate from each other during meiosis, a process Bridges called "nondisjunction." As a result of nondisjunction, some of the female's eggs would have no X-chromosome, and others would have two. The idea seemed farfetched at the time, but it had the advantage of being testable. Using as the parents a nondisjunction female (symbolized chromosomally XXO, or later, XXY) who had genes for white eyes on both the X-chromosomes and a normal male who had the gene for red eyes on his single X-chromosome, Bridges predicted that, with regard to the characteristics of eye color, sex, and ability to transmit the nondisjunction trait, there should be eight categories of offspring. Although one category (the one containing no X-chromosomes, that is, having only a Y) was missing (the embryos are not viable), the remainder of the categories occurred in the ratios expected by Bridges's theory. This work not only provided additional proof that genes were physically located on chromosomes, a point still much disputed at the time, but it also gave Bridges an insight into the solution to another problem, the relation of chromosomes to sex determination.

Although it had become generally accepted after 1905 that the X and Y chromosomes are involved with sex determination, the actual mechanism was not understood. Using his nondisjunction strains of *Drosophila*, Bridges found that, with the proper matings, he could produce offspring with a varying number of X-chromosomes, from none (nonviable) to four or more. The original hypothesis that the absolute number of either one or two X-chromosomes determines a male and female, respectively, was undermined by Bridges's observation that flies with two, three, or even four X's all turned out to be females, and that flies with either one or sometimes two X's all turned out to be males. Comparing the number of X-chromosomes to the number of autosomes (also using special strains in which nondisjunction had occurred in autosomes) he found that when the number of X chromosomes was equal to the number of autosomes in each pair (for example, 2X / 2A, or 3X / 3A) the flies were females; conversely, the case where the number of X-chromosomes was half the number of autosomes in each pair (for example, 1X / 2A, 2X / 4A) gave rise to males. From these observations Bridges elaborated what became known as the balance theory of sex determination, in which he argued that it was not the number of X-chromosomes, but the ratio of X to autosomes that determined which sex a given fly developed. This work later formed the conceptual framework for understanding not only the chromosomal basis for certain human sex abnormalities, but also for investigating the developmental effects of different dosages of genes (for example, extra chromosomes above the usual two per pair).

With his cytological skills, Bridges also pioneered in correlating abnormalities of chromosome structure with changes in phenotype of offspring. For example, he noted that in some strains the end of one arm of one chromosome (an X, or one of the autosomes) was missing, though its homologue was intact. In the offspring of those flies the genes present on the missing segment would never be expressed, and, conversely, the genes present on the homologous chromosome, even if recessive, would be expressed. For example, if a female inherited from her mother an X-chromosome that lacked the segment containing the eye-color gene, and from her father a normal X-chromosome containing the recessive gene for white eye (which would normally not be expressed in a female if the other X had a gene for the dominant red eye), the female would appear phenotypically white-eyed. By studying chromosomes with missing segments in different regions of the chromosomes, Bridges was able to begin pinpointing where actual genes were localized along the chromosome length. The linear genetic "maps" of the chromosome groups constructed up to this time had been based on breeding data, and thus gave only relative positions of genes. Bridges pioneered the conversion of relative map positions to absolute chromosome positions.

When T. S. Painter (among others) discovered in the early 1930s the extraordinary "giant chromosomes" in the salivary gland cells of *Drosophila* larvae, Bridges undertook a detailed microscopic analysis of the many newly visible details. His detailed drawings of the four chromosome groups of *Drosophila*, with precise positions indicated for numerous genes, remained the standard "picture" of the *Drosophila* chromosomes for decades.

Described as an extremely friendly and generous person, Bridges had a zest for life that brought him into contact with a wide variety of people. He formed a close friendship with a fellow student in the Morgan lab, Hermann J. Muller (who showed that high-energy radiation causes gene mutations), and the novelist Theodore Dreiser, who visited Bridges in Woods Hole, Massachusetts, in the summers of 1928 and 1929. A socialist, Bridges's letters to Muller are gems of political insight. He visited the Soviet Union in 1931–1932 and returned enthusiastic about the Soviet experiment. An advocate of free love, Bridges indulged in periodic liaisons that estranged him from his wife and often embarrassed Morgan and his colleagues. Bridges died at an early age from a deterioration of the heart thought to have been caused by syphilis.

• There is no single collection of Bridges's letters; whatever was extant at the time of his death was destroyed by Thomas Hunt Morgan to avoid embarrassment about Bridges's personal life. A few interesting items are contained in the H. J. Muller Papers, Lily Library, Indiana University, and in the Morgan papers at the library of the California Institute of Technology. Bridges's annual reports to the Carnegie Institution of Washington are printed in that organization's *Annual Reports* (1916–1939). His other scientific publications, mostly technical papers, address such topics as the physical basis of genes linked together on chromosomes (e.g., *Genetics* 1 [1916]: 107–63), the origin of gynandromorphs (e.g., *Carnegie Institution of Washington Publications* 278 [1919]: 1–122), and the balance theory of determination (e.g., *American Naturalist* 56 [1922]: 51–63). The only modestly complete biographical sketch is Morgan's obituary of Bridges in the *Biographical Memoirs of the National Academy of Sciences* 22 (1941): 31–48, which also contains a complete bibliography.

GARLAND E. ALLEN

BRIDGES, Fidelia (19 May 1834–14 May 1923), watercolorist and illustrator, was born in Salem, Massachusetts, the daughter of Henry Gardner Bridges, a ship captain, and Eliza Chadwick. The family was comfortably established, but when Captain Bridges died in China in December 1849 and Mrs. Bridges died just three months later, the family house and furniture had to be sold to pay estate debts. Since Fidelia was not yet sixteen and her brother was a year younger, the older sisters, Eliza and Elizabeth, tried to support the family by starting a school. Fidelia probably helped, as she had been given drawing lessons and was qualified as a teacher of drawing. The school was not a success, and in 1854 the sisters, at the suggestion of Eliza's friend, poet and later sculptor Anne Whitney, moved to Brooklyn, New York. There, a situation was found for Fidelia as a governess in the family of merchant William Augustus Brown.

In Brooklyn, Fidelia Bridges developed a firsthand acquaintance with contemporary art through exhibitions in both Brooklyn and New York. She had already read John Ruskin's influential *Modern Painters* and probably saw the 1857 American Exhibition of British Art, the first American showing of the English Pre-Raphaelite painters whom Ruskin had championed. In the spring of 1860, Anne Whitney invited Bridges to go with her to a series of lectures at the Pennsylvania Academy of Fine Arts to be given by painter William Trost Richards. Partly financed by the Brown family, Bridges began studying at the Pennsylvania Academy in March 1860. She established a warm friendship with Richards and his family and was invited to spend the summer with them in Bethlehem, Pennsylvania, for outdoor landscape study.

Richards became Bridges's mentor and his style the model for Bridges's subsequent work. His meticulous technique, learned from his teacher, landscape painter Paul Weber, had been reinforced by seeing the Pre-Raphaelite paintings in the British Art exhibition. Bridges's close association with Richards continued for several years, and in 1862 she had two paintings, *A Wheat Field* and *View on the Lehigh*, accepted for exhibition at the Pennsylvania Academy. These paintings, as well as subsequent ones shown there, *Ferns* in 1865 and *Violets* and *Study from Nature* in 1866, show the close focus on landscape details that was characteristic of paintings by Richards and the newly formed group of artists known as the American Pre-Raphaelites. Although Bridges never became a member of the short-lived American Pre-Raphaelite group, its tenets had a profound effect on her subsequent work.

Bridges returned to Brooklyn in the fall of 1863 to live with her sister and exhibited for the first time at both the National Academy of Design and the Brooklyn Art Association. Her work began to sell steadily, and she was able to maintain a studio in Brooklyn until 1867, when she accompanied Anne Whitney and several friends to Europe. Bridges painted in Switzerland during the summer and then spent the winter in Rome with Whitney, who had gone there to study sculpture. Bridges returned to Brooklyn in the fall of 1868, again living with her sister, spending her days in a rented studio on Broadway in Manhattan. The European trip seems to have had little effect on her style and furnished the subject for only one exhibited landscape. Instead she sought American locales and in 1871 began spending summers in Stratford, Connecticut. Her studies from nature done there, while complete in themselves, served as the basis for more elaborate compositions painted during the winter months, in watercolor as well as oil.

Bridges's paintings of the 1870s evidence the continuing importance of Pre-Raphaelite subject matter as well as technique—intensity of focus on foreground plants or birds meticulously rendered against a flattened background, a high key palette, and tight brushwork. The sparkling watercolor studies in particular exemplify the Ruskinian aim of conveying the actual presence of growing things in the open air, suffused with sunlight. Bridges's popular success at this time was paralleled by her professional standing—she was elected an associate of the National Academy in 1873 and a member of the American Society of Painters in Water Color in 1875. She began to sell paintings to Prang Publishing Company and to contribute illustrations to *Scribner's* and other periodicals and collaborated on several books with bird themes. In 1881 she was selected as one of Prang's permanent designers, a position she held until 1899 and that gave her for the first time a measure of financial security.

During the 1880s Bridges's style underwent a gradual shift from close views of meadow or forest to more expansive landscapes, or decorative arrangements of birds and plants that evidenced her interest in Japanese scroll painting. Although her technique is free and broad in later oils such as *Pastures near the Sea* of 1885 and *Corn Stacks*, shown at the National Academy in 1892, plants remain botanically specific. She maintained a studio in Manhattan and continued to live with her sister in Brooklyn until Elizabeth's death in 1882.

In 1890 Bridges decided to settle permanently in Canaan, Connecticut, where she rented a house with an extensive garden beside the Blackberry River. Her life remained an active and social one, enlivened by her many friendships, which included the children of the Browns, the Richardses, and the son of another close painter friend, Oliver Lay. She occasionally visited England, where her brother had settled, and more frequently traveled to New York, where she exhibited with the Water Color Society until 1912. Although she continued to paint each day, her exuberant flower garden became her consuming passion in later life. She died in Canaan.

As a woman, and particularly as a well-brought-up young lady of good family, Bridges was barred at the outset of her career from full participation in the New York art world and was unable to join a group such as the American Pre-Raphaelites, her logical peers. Her adherence to Ruskinian subject matter and execution and her preference for watercolor further removed her from the mainstream. Without her virtual adoption by the Brown and Richards families, her initial professional study and subsequent career would have been unlikely. Her determination to succeed as a professional and her steadfast commitment to her personal vision in the face of changing tastes resulted in a fresh and appealing oeuvre of small paintings and watercolor studies of the natural world seen clearly and at close hand. A knowledge of Bridges's work, together with that of other dedicated and talented artists of the time who have long been considered "minor," can tell us as much about the role of the artist and vagaries of taste in nineteenth-century America as the careers of those much better known.

• Letters from Bridges to Anne and Sarah Whitney, and Anne Whitney's correspondence are in the archives of Wellesley College; letters from Fidelia, Eliza, and Elizabeth Bridges to their friend Rebekah Northey are at the Essex Institute Library, Salem, Mass.; and correspondence with the Brown and Lay families is owned by George C. Lay. Bridges's life and work was the subject of an exhibition at the New Britain Museum of American Art, Nov. 1981, with a catalog essay by May Brawley Hill, *Fidelia Bridges: American Pre-Raphaelite*. A study of Bridges's life by Frederick A. Sharf appeared in the *Essex Institute Historical Collections* 104, no. 3 (1968): 217–38. See also "Our Artists and Their Works: Fidelia Bridges," *Brooklyn Monthly* 2, no. 3 (1878): 70–71; Alice Sawtelle Randall, "Miss Fidelia Bridges in Her Studio at Canaan," *Connecticut Magazine*, Feb.–Mar. 1902, pp. 583–88; Samuel Benjamin, *Art in America* (1880), pp. 129 and 131 and Walter Shaw Sparrow, *Women Painters of the World* (1905), p. 76. An obituary is in the *American Art News*, 5 Apr. 1924, p. 6.

MAY BRAWLEY HILL

BRIDGES, Harry Renton (28 July 1901–30 Mar. 1990), labor leader, was born Alfred Renton Bridges in Kensington, Australia, a suburb of Melbourne, the son of Alfred Bridges, a real estate agent and promoter, and Julia Dorgan, a sometime shopkeeper whose parents were Irish. He began while a teenager to call himself Harry, after an uncle who advocated trade unionism and the socialism of the Australian Labor party. Upon completing the tenth grade, Bridges began a college preparatory program but dropped out and soon went to sea.

In 1920 Bridges arrived in San Francisco, joined the Sailors' Union of the Pacific (SUP), and began to sail in the American coastal trade. He participated in a nationwide seamen's strike in 1921 and briefly joined the radical Industrial Workers of the World (IWW). In 1922 he began to work on the San Francisco docks and to live with Agnes Brown, with whom he had a daughter; they were married in 1934.

Dock work was harsh and dangerous, and longshoremen were hired through the daily shape-up, when thousands gathered on the waterfront, and gang bosses (foremen) picked those who would work that day; hiring through the shape-up meant that longshoremen had no job security and were subject to many abuses. In 1933 the International Longshoremen's Association (ILA) chartered Local 38-79 in San Francisco. Bridges emerged as a leader among some two dozen longshoremen—including some Communist party (CP) members—who met at Albion Hall, a room off Albion Street. They used the *Waterfront Worker*, a mimeographed newsletter, to advocate militant action and oppose racial, ethnic, religious, or political discrimination.

In 1934 the ILA's Pacific Coast District (locals in California, Oregon, and Washington) sought a coastwise contract with a union hiring hall. When waterfront employers refused, a coastwise longshore strike began, and seafaring unions promptly struck with issues of their own. Elected chairman of his local's strike committee, Bridges quickly became a prominent figure. He refused a bribe from employers and was conspicuous among those who opposed Joseph Ryan, the ILA's international president, who came from New York to seek a settlement. After a July fifth confrontation in which San Francisco police killed two men, a striker and a strike supporter, and injured hundreds, the governor dispatched the National Guard to the San Francisco waterfront, and strikers stepped up agitation for a general strike. The San Francisco Labor Council reluctantly agreed. The general strike began on 16 July and lasted four days; at its height, it shut down most economic activity in San Francisco and surrounding communities and may have involved as many as 100,000 workers. All sides to the maritime strikes agreed to arbitration, and the longshoremen secured nearly all their demands.

The strike propelled Bridges to the presidency first of Local 38-79 and then of the Pacific Coast District. Other Albion Hall members also moved into leadership positions; within the local, they prohibited racially segregated work gangs and promoted democratic reforms. Bridges also played a major role in the Maritime Federation of the Pacific (MFP), an effort to unite West Coast maritime unions. In 1937 he led the Pacific Coast District into the Congress of Industrial Organizations (CIO) as the International Longshoremen's and Warehousemen's Union (ILWU) and became its first president. John L. Lewis, CIO president, appointed Bridges as CIO western regional director. In California, Oregon, Washington, British Columbia, Alaska, and Hawaii, the ILWU forged a strong union among longshoremen and achieved some organizing successes with warehouse workers. The MFP foundered, however, when the SUP remained in the American Federation of Labor (AFL) and opposed Bridges's leadership among maritime unions. Found in contempt for publicly criticizing a court order involving ILA loyalists in Los Angeles, Bridges appealed; in *Bridges v. California* (1941) the Supreme Court ruled in his favor, thereby extending First Amendment protections. Bridges's growing fame as a militant, left-wing labor leader put him on the cover of *Time* magazine in 1937. Fame had its price: he developed severe stomach ulcers and was divorced.

When Bridges emerged as a strike leader in 1934, some business leaders and public officials began to demand that he be deported. Rumors circulated that he was a CP member, grounds for deportation; he openly supported the CP but always insisted that he never joined. (In 1992, however, evidence from recently opened files of the Communist International indicated that Bridges was elected to the CP's national Central Committee in 1936.) In 1939, bowing to political pressure, Secretary of Labor Frances Perkins ordered the Immigration and Naturalization Service (INS) to determine if Bridges was subject to deportation. The hearing officer ruled that he was not, whereupon the House of Representatives, in June 1940, passed a bill specifically ordering his deportation. Constitutionally questionable, the measure died in the Senate. Congress had recently approved President Franklin D. Roosevelt's proposal to move INS from the Labor Department to the Justice Department and now established new criteria for deportation. In August 1940 Attorney General Robert H. Jackson ordered the FBI to investigate Bridges; by 1956, Bridges's file had grown to nearly 38,000 pages. In a second INS hearing, in 1941, the hearing officer found against Bridges. On appeal, the Supreme Court reversed that decision (*Bridges v. Wixon* [1945]), and that year Bridges completed his naturalization.

With the onset of the Cold War, left-wing unions came under pressure from CIO leadership to espouse anti-Communist views. In 1948, however, Bridges and the ILWU opposed CIO leaders by criticizing the Marshall Plan and supporting the presidential candidacy of Henry A. Wallace; the CIO subsequently expelled the ILWU on the grounds that it was Communist led. Expulsion from the CIO ended ILWU efforts—never very successful—to organize longshoremen and warehouse workers in eastern states. In Hawaii, however, after World War II, the ILWU became the largest union and a powerful political force, representing a racially diverse work force in the longshore, warehouse, sugar, pineapple, transportation, and hotel industries.

In 1949 Federal authorities brought Bridges to trial, charging him and his two witnesses with lying at his naturalization when he swore he never belonged to the Communist party; in 1950 they were convicted of criminal conspiracy. During the appeal, Bridges's bail was briefly revoked, and he went to jail when he criticized American actions in the Korean War. In *Bridges v. U.S.* (1953), the Supreme Court overturned the conspiracy conviction on procedural grounds. In 1955 federal attorneys initiated a denaturalization proceeding, but the trial judge dismissed the charges.

In 1946 Bridges married Nancy Feinstein Berdecio, a dancer who performed under the name Nancy Fenton. They had two children; partly due to pressures from his work and trial, they were divorced in 1953. In 1958 Bridges and Noriko Sawada, a legal secretary, planned a quiet marriage in Reno, Nevada. Once there, they discovered that Nevada law prohibited them from marrying because Sawada was of Japanese parentage; they secured a court order permitting their marriage on grounds that the statute was unconstitutional. They had one child.

With Bridges as its president, the ILWU institutionalized extensive rank-and-file participation in many key decisions; in the longshore caucus, for example, local delegates met regularly to decide contract issues. Major decisions were usually made through membership referendum. Throughout his career, Bridges always insisted that 15 percent of ILWU members be able to petition for recall of any officer, himself included, and that his salary be no higher than a longshoreman's wages.

As president, Bridges always led the ILWU committee in longshore bargaining. In 1948 representatives of waterfront employers refused to negotiate with him because of his political views; after a bitter, three-month strike, however, the companies hired new negotiators and initiated a "New Look" in labor relations. Thereafter, Bridges and the ILWU built a stable—sometimes even comfortable—relationship with the Pacific Maritime Association (PMA), representative of waterfront and shipping companies. In the late 1950s, recognizing that technology could transform longshoring, Bridges argued that the ILWU should not fight change but instead try to benefit from it. After extensive discussion in the union newspaper and union meetings, and with endorsement by the membership, Bridges led negotiations through which the ILWU accepted full mechanization in return for generous retirement arrangements and a guarantee of full pay for those who did not retire, even if there was no work.

The ILWU-PMA Modernization and Mechanization Agreement (M&M) of 1960 led Secretary of Labor James P. Mitchell to judge that "next only to John L. Lewis, Bridges has done the best job in American labor of coming to grip with the problems of automation." Arguments that Bridges settled too cheaply were largely from hindsight. Some ILWU members, however, criticized the M&M for undermining the hiring hall by permitting employers to choose "steady men" for certain jobs; the steady-man issue, especially, fueled a four-month strike in 1971–1972.

Despite his lifelong, outspoken admiration for the Soviet Union, Bridges after 1960 was often praised for his contributions to the maritime industry and was even lauded as a "labor statesman." He disavowed such honorifics, claiming that he had not changed his views. Joseph Alioto, mayor of San Francisco, appointed Bridges in 1968 to the Citizens Charter Revision Committee and in 1970 to the San Francisco Port Commission. Bridges retired as ILWU president in 1977. He died in San Francisco.

By the 1950s, Bridges had become a living legend: the militant, democratic leftist who repeatedly triumphed over federal persecution. His defense committees attracted widespread support from the Left, liberals, and even business leaders who saw Bridges as the victim of governmental harassment. Many ILWU members did not share Bridges's left-wing politics or his admiration for the Soviet Union, but most nonetheless pledged him their respect, loyalty, and affection. In 1992 a group of ILWU pensioners in the Pacific Northwest demonstrated this by collecting $1 million—mostly in small amounts from pensioners—to endow a Harry Bridges Chair in Labor Studies at the University of Washington.

• The most important collections of papers are those maintained by the ILWU at its headquarters in San Francisco and those of Bridges's attorneys, Richard Gladstein (Harry Bridges Legal Collection, Southern California Library for Social Studies and Research, Los Angeles) and Norman Leonard (Norman Leonard Collection, Labor Archives and Research Center, San Francisco State University). Other important sources include the *Voice of the Federation*, a newspaper published by the MFP in San Francisco, and *The Dispatcher*, the ILWU's newspaper since 1942; "On the Beam," Bridges's column in *The Dispatcher*, presented his views on union and public issues.

The only published biography is Charles P. Larrowe, *Harry Bridges: The Rise and Fall of Radical Labor in the United States* (1972). Stanley I. Kutler summarizes the deportation proceedings in "'If at first . . .': The Trials of Harry Bridges," in his *The American Inquisition: Justice and Injustice in the Cold War* (1982). Estolv E. Ward, *Harry Bridges on Trial* (1940), provides a popular treatment of the 1939 hearing and Bridges's career up to that time. Evidence that Bridges was a member of the CP Central Committee in 1936 is presented by Harvey Klehr and John Haynes in "The Comintern's Open Secrets," *American Spectator*, Dec. 1992, pp. 34–35.

ROBERT W. CHERNY

BRIDGES, Robert (5 Mar. 1806–20 Feb. 1882), chemist and botanist, was born in Philadelphia, Pennsylvania, the son of Culpeper Bridges, a merchant, and Sarah Cliffton. He was a student at the University Grammar School in Philadelphia and graduated from Dickinson College in 1824. He then studied medicine in the private medical school of Thomas D. Hewson in Philadelphia. There he became assistant to Franklin Bache, who taught chemistry, a relationship that continued when Bache went on to teach chemistry at the Philadelphia College of Pharmacy and the Jefferson Medical College. Bridges obtained his M.D. from the University of Pennsylvania in 1828.

Bridges was vaccine physician of the southwestern district of Philadelphia from 1830 to 1840, and he kept a careful record of 2,099 vaccinations that came under his observation during those years. In 1832 he was appointed attending physician for the district and had responsibility for the cholera patients at the Eastern Penitentiary. His main interests, however, were not in medicine but in botany and chemistry.

Bridges was elected to the Academy of Natural Sciences of Philadelphia in 1835 and became a member of its botanical committee the next year. He served as chairman of that committee from 1846 to 1857 and was directly involved in indexing three of the main herbaria of the academy. He served the academy as librarian, recording secretary, corresponding secretary, auditor, council member, vice president and, finally, in 1864, president. He devoted many years and served on a variety of committees, for example the publications committee and the committee on herpetology and ichthyology.

Bridges was elected to the Franklin Institute in 1836, elected a fellow of the College of Physicians of Philadelphia in 1842, and elected a member of the American Philosophical Society in 1844. He served as librarian of the College of Physicians from 1867 to

1879 and served the American Philosophical Society as a member of its council from 1855 to 1863 and from 1877 to 1882, as chairman of its publications committee (for six years), and on other committees. He became a member of the Philadelphia College of Pharmacy in 1838, was appointed to the board of trustees in 1839, and was chairman of the board from 1857 until the time of his death.

Bridges's teaching career began at the Philadelphia College of Pharmacy where he became professor of general and pharmaceutical chemistry in 1842. He continued as assistant to Bache at Jefferson. He taught chemistry also at the Association for Medical Instruction from 1842 to 1860 and at the Franklin Medical College from 1846 to 1848. In 1846 his title at the Philadelphia College of Pharmacy became professor of chemistry and he remained in that post until his retirement in 1879. Bridges also assisted George Bacon Wood in teaching the course in materia medica at the University of Pennsylvania from 1835 to 1850.

Although not a research chemist, Bridges discovered a method of obtaining virtually pure oxygen for experimental use and published some articles in the field. Described as "an efficient teacher," his main contribution to chemistry, however, was the editing of two British texts in chemistry. At least five issues of Thomas Graham's *Elements of Chemistry* (1843–1866) and at least twenty-five issues of George Fownes's *A Manual of Elementary Chemistry* and its variant titles (1845–1878) that were published in Philadelphia bear his name as editor. The last was a very popular text, especially in medical and pharmaceutical colleges.

Bridges served on the College of Pharmacy committee on the revision of the *United States Pharmacopoeia* of 1850, assisted the College of Physicians committee on the 1870 revision, and served on that college's committee on the 1880 revision. After the death of Franklin Bache in 1864, Bridges assisted George B. Wood in bringing out the next three editions (1865, 1870, 1877) of the *United States Dispensatory*. He served as assistant to the editor of the *American Journal of Pharmacy* from 1839 to 1847 and contributed numerous articles to that journal as well as to the *Proceedings of the Academy of Natural Sciences of Philadelphia*. From 1847 to 1877 he contributed many bibliographic notices and reviews, primarily of works in chemistry, to the *American Journal of the Medical Sciences*.

Bridges died in Philadelphia. He had never married. Described as shy and modest and lacking an aggressive spirit, the esteem in which he was held was evident when the College of Pharmacy "asked, as a privilege . . . to be permitted to defray the expenses of his funeral and to pay to his heirs an extra quarter's salary of the emeritus professor" (Ruschenberger, "Obituary," p. 447).

• Robert Bridges left no personal papers other than a few letters preserved in the papers of their recipients in Philadelphia repositories. The chief biographical sources are W. S. W. Ruschenberger, "Obituary Notice of Robert Bridges," *Proceedings of the American Philosophical Society* 21 (1883–1884): 427–47, and Ruschenberger's "A Sketch of the Life of Robert Bridges, M.D.," *American Journal of Pharmacy* 56 (1884): 241–51. Short biographical sketches of Bridges are in J. W. England, *The First Century of the Philadelphia College of Pharmacy* (1922), pp. 401–2, and in J. W. Harshberger, *The Botanists of Philadelphia* (1899), pp. 195–96.

DAVID L. COWEN

BRIDGES, Styles (9 Sept. 1898–26 Nov. 1961), governor of New Hampshire and U.S. senator, was born Henry Styles Bridges in West Pembroke, Maine, the son of Earl Leopold Bridges, a tenant farmer, and Alina Roxana Fisher. After his father's early death, Bridges bore heavy responsibilities on the farm, even while attending school. Upon graduation with a degree in agriculture from the University of Maine in 1918, he worked as an agricultural agent until 1922, when he became executive secretary of the New Hampshire Farm Bureau Federation. Later in the 1920s, while serving as secretary of a New Hampshire investment company, he became a protégé of former governor Robert P. Bass, a political ally of the current governor at that time, Charles Tobey.

Bridges was married briefly during his youth to Ella Mae Johnston; they had one child. The marriage ended in divorce. (During his later political career, Bridges kept information about this marriage secret. After his death, Johnston was not even mentioned in his obituaries, and she was not acknowledged as the mother of his first child.) In 1928 he married Sally Clement; they had two children. Sally Bridges died in 1938.

In 1930, Bridges was appointed to the New Hampshire Public Service Commission. Four years later, with the backing of Bass and Tobey, he defeated Senator George Moses for the Republican gubernatorial nomination. Easily elected, he became at age thirty-six the youngest governor in the nation. He was a good one-term governor, balancing the budget while sponsoring state unemployment compensation and old-age benefits. In 1936 he chose to run for the Senate, and despite the Roosevelt landslide, he won, one of the few Republican freshmen elected that year. Settling comfortably into the life of the powerful in Washington, D.C., in 1944, after six years as an eligible widower, he married his third wife, Doloris Thauwald.

In the Senate, Bridges sided with the "Old Guard" Republicans, opposing Roosevelt's proposals to enlarge the Supreme Court and reorganize the executive branch, voting against virtually all New Deal measures, and leading efforts to launch a congressional investigation of the Tennessee Valley Authority. In the late 1930s, he even ceased to use his given name, Henry, in order to avoid any possibility of his being confused with leftist labor union leader Harry Bridges. He was unusual among conservative Republicans of the time, however, in supporting Roosevelt's internationalist policies prior to American involvement in World War II.

Although not an outstanding public speaker, Bridges was plainspoken, direct, and effective in face-to-face dealings and showed political savvy. He quickly emerged as a party leader in the Senate, becoming chairman of the Appropriations Committee when the Republicans captured control of Congress in 1946. He served as Appropriations chairman in 1947–1948 and 1953–1954, as Senate minority leader in 1952, and as president pro tem of the Senate in 1953–1954. As ranking Republican member of the Senate, he was consulted frequently by President Dwight Eisenhower, although they did not always agree.

In addition to his involvement in budgetary matters (he ardently advocated a balanced budget) through his committee participation, Bridges was very outspoken on foreign policy and national security issues. In the early 1950s, like other conservatives such as Robert A. Taft and Joseph McCarthy, he sharply attacked Democratic administration foreign policies, especially the earlier Yalta agreements and the failure to give the Nationalist Chinese adequate support to stave off defeat by the Communists in 1949. During Eisenhower's presidency, Bridges regularly criticized foreign aid spending and grew even more rigidly hostile to the Soviet Union. As late as 1960, he was still warning Eisenhower against replicating the "sellout" that had occurred at Yalta.

Bridges died in Concord, New Hampshire, of complications from a heart attack. At the time, he was in his fifth Senate term and an acknowledged leader of the GOP's conservative wing. Although no major piece of legislation ever bore his name, he was widely recognized as a power in the Senate during an era of legislative giants.

• Bridges's papers are available to scholars at New England College in Henniker, New Hampshire. There is no published biography of Bridges. The most useful study of "Old Guard" Republicans during most of the period he served in Congress is David Reinhard, *The Republican Right since 1945* (1983).

GARY W. REICHARD

BRIDGMAN, Elijah Coleman (22 Apr. 1801–2 Nov. 1861), pioneer missionary of the American Board of Commissioners for Foreign Missions, was born in Belchertown, Massachusetts, the son of Theodore Bridgman and Lucretia Warner. He joined a church at the age of ten, an unusual move at that time. Bridgman graduated from Amherst College in 1826 and Andover Theological Seminary in 1829.

Robert Morrison, the first missionary to China, requested that the Prudential Committee in Boston send him a colleague, and Bridgman was the first candidate accepted for service in China. He was ordained on 6 October 1829 and sailed for China eight days later, arriving in Canton on 19 February 1830. He began studying the Chinese language almost immediately, reporting in June that he was then studying the *Four Books*. In 1832 he founded and became the editor of the *Chinese Repository*, the English-language missionary newspaper published in Canton. He was one of the originators of the Morrison Education Society, which in 1835 established the Morrison School in Macao under the charge of the Reverend Samuel R. Brown. The school, which moved to Hong Kong in 1842, used English to teach young Chinese men Western literature and science. Bridgman was also a founder of the Medical Missionary Society of China. When the Opium War (1839–1840) broke out in Canton, Bridgman declined a request from Chinese authorities to receive a letter for the queen of England. In August 1839, along with the other missionaries, he moved to Macao to avoid the hostilities. While there he published *The Chinese Chrestomathy in the Canton Dialect* (1841), using the press of Samuel Wells Williams.

Bridgman moved to Hong Kong in July 1842, following the Treaty of Nanking, which ceded that island to Britain as a colony. Among the provisions of the Nanking treaty was the opening of five ports in China to Westerners, which missionaries viewed as favorable to their work. On 28 June 1845 Bridgman and Dr. Peter Parker, who had arrived in China in 1836, were appointed as Chinese secretaries to Caleb Cushing, who had been sent to China to negotiate the American treaty of 1844. That treaty, which ended U.S. participation in the Opium War, included a toleration of Christianity clause and was expected to open the way for the Christianization of the country.

In 1845 Bridgman married Eliza Jane Gillette, who had just arrived in China under the auspices of the American Episcopal mission. They had no children of their own but adopted several, including two Chinese girls from Hong Kong who accompanied the Bridgmans when they moved to Shanghai in June 1847. The girls were the first students in Eliza Bridgman's school, believed to have been the first mission school for girls in China.

The family moved to Shanghai so Bridgman could become the Canton representative to the union committee of delegates, which was working on the translation of the Bible into Chinese. Arguments over the correct way to render the word *God* into Chinese characters split the committee and eventually resulted in the publication of two separate versions of the Bible. The translation produced primarily by Bridgman and his colleague M. Simpson Culbertson aimed at an exact translation that was easily comprehended by those without a literary education. It was thought not scholarly enough, however, to appeal to the Chinese intelligentsia. The Old Testament was published in 1862, and Bridgman and the others subsequently published a New Testament to accompany it.

After more than twenty years in China, Bridgman in 1852 took his first furlough, which was aimed at recovering his health. He spent less than four months in the United States. Travel to and from China was arduous and lengthy, and the missionary was dependent upon free passage offered by shipping merchants sympathetic to Christian work in China. When Bridgman embarked for his return to China, he sailed from New York via Cape Horn for San Francisco, where he arrived after a voyage of four months, and then embarked for the transpacific journey.

In 1854 the Bridgmans moved their mission to Shanghai, which was becoming the center of all missionary activity in China. In Shanghai Bridgman was a member of the Society for the Diffusion of Useful Knowledge to China. He was president of the Shanghai Literary and Scientific Society and the North China Branch of the Royal Asiatic Society, whose journal he edited. He died in Shanghai. After Bridgman's death, his wife relocated to Peking (Beijing), and the mission in Shanghai ceased to exist.

• Bridgman's papers are at Harvard University's Houghton Library in the Manuscripts Collection. Kathleen L. Lodwick, comp., *The Chinese Recorder Index: A Guide to Christian Missions in Asia, 1867–1941* (1986), includes references to Bridgman. See also Eliza J. G. Bridgman, *Life and Labors of Elijah Coleman Bridgman* (1864); Donald McGillivray, *A Century of Protestant Missions in China (1807–1907)* (1907); William E. Strong, *The Story of the American Board* (1910); and Kenneth Latourette, *A History of Christian Missions in China* (1929).

KATHLEEN L. LODWICK

BRIDGMAN, Eliza Jane Gillette (6 May 1805–10 Nov. 1871), pioneer missionary to China, was born in Derby, New Haven County, Connecticut, the daughter of Caufield Gillette, a merchant and justice of the peace. (Bridgman's mother's given name is unknown, but she was the daughter of Sheldon Clarke of Derby.) Eliza Jane was the youngest of nine children, and the family, descendants of French Huguenots, attended the Episcopal church. After her father's death in 1815, her mother, she recalled, "scrimped to educate me." Eliza Jane was converted, along with other girls at the school she was attending, at a religious revival in August 1820 and joined the Episcopal church in 1821. At the age of thirteen she had read Claudius Buchanan's *Christian Researches in India* (1811), and she later remarked that "the impression of that book never left me. To be a *missionary* to the heathen seemed to me to be the highest honor that can be conferred upon a Christian." In the summer of 1822 she attended a farewell meeting for two missionaries of the American Board of Commissioners for Foreign Missions (ABCFM) who were departing for the Sandwich Islands (Hawaii).

In 1823 she moved with her mother to New York to be near her three brothers. There she joined an Episcopal church, but she "loved all denominations who believe in Jesus Christ." In New York, "after many disappointments," she found a job as an assistant teacher at a seminary, and Bethune McCartee, who also became a missionary to China, was among her students. In 1827 she began her own school, which "prospered and made me happy and independent." She wanted to be a missionary but could not leave her feeble mother. After her mother's death, one of her brothers married, and with his family she moved in 1837 to a house large enough to accommodate her school, which then had 100 pupils.

With her brother's death in late 1837, she wrote, "I was now no longer young, but still of the same mind that I had always been to go when the way should open as a missionary to the heathen." She was accepted by the Episcopal church in 1843 and sailed with Bishop and Mrs. William Boone, and a large company, in December 1844. Bound for Shanghai on the *Horatio*, she studied Chinese on the voyage. Arriving in Hong Kong on 24 April 1844, she met the missionaries resident there including the Reverend Elijah Bridgman of the ABCFM, who had been in China for fifteen years. The group journeyed to Canton (Kuangchou), where the Reverend Bridgman wanted to work; during the trip he proposed to Eliza Jane Gillette. As Bishop Boone had two other single women to assist him in his work, he agreed to release Gillette, and the reverend paid the Episcopal Board of Missions $600 to cover the cost of her outfit and passage. They were married by the colonial chaplain in Hong Kong on 28 June 1845 and went to Canton several days later.

In Canton Eliza Jane Bridgman opened a school that had two girls among its students. The ABCFM mission in Canton closed in 1847 when the Bridgmans moved to Shanghai, where the Reverend Bridgman was to work on the committee translating the Bible into Chinese. The two girl students accompanied the Bridgmans to Shanghai, and Eliza Jane Bridgman opened a boarding school for girls, thought to be the first in Shanghai and certainly one of the first in China. Eventually, she had three schools for girls and also taught older women in her home.

The Bridgmans left China on furlough, the Reverend Bridgman's first, in February 1852, visiting the island of St. Helena on the voyage home. During the four months they spent in the United States, Eliza Jane Bridgman wrote *Daughters of China*. They embarked on the *Wild Pigeon* in October 1852, rounded Cape Horn, stayed briefly in San Francisco, sailed again in February 1853, and arrived in Shanghai in May, where the Taiping Rebellion was threatening the city. During this time in China she "adopted" four motherless children, one Japanese and three English, who, when the family moved to Peking (Beijing), were joined by a fifth, nationality unknown. She also ran a school where she taught Scriptures, geography, arithmetic, and music.

When the Reverend Bridgman died in 1861, his widow went to Japan for a month and then returned to Peking for most of 1862. That year she visited Hankow, where she reported she met a French priest who had been thirteen years in Szechwan (Sichuan) without seeing another foreigner. In late 1862 she embarked for the United States via England, where she spent several months speaking to church groups about mission work; she was in London in March 1862 at the time of the wedding of the Prince of Wales to Princess Alexandra of Denmark. Back in New York, she participated in "a seance or pentecostal experience" with friends and relatives in August 1863. In New York she edited *The Life and Labors of Elijah Coleman Bridgman.* Offered free passage aboard an Olyphant Company ship, she accepted but then was seriously injured when a runaway horse overturned a sleigh in which she was riding.

Recovered sufficiently to depart, Bridgman took ship and returned to China in 1864 via Capetown, arriving in Hong Kong on her fifty-ninth birthday. She proceeded on to Shanghai and then to Peking, where the mission had relocated. In Peking in 1864 she wrote her autobiography of more than ninety manuscript pages (now at Harvard University's Houghton Library). She again founded a girls' school, using her own money because the American Civil War had put the ABCFM in financial difficulties. During her years in Peking she donated more than $10,000 to the work of the mission in which she was engaged. She died in Peking.

• Eliza Jane Gillette Bridgman's papers, along with those of her husband, Elijah Bridgman, are located in the archives of the American Board of Commissioners of Foreign Missions at the Houghton Library, Harvard University. There are numerous references to her in the *Chinese Recorder* (the periodical concerned with Protestant missions in China), where her obituary appeared in 1871.

KATHLEEN L. LODWICK

BRIDGMAN, Frederick Arthur (10 Nov. 1847–13 Jan. 1928), figure painter, was born in Tuskegee, Alabama, the son of Frederick Bridgman, a physician, and Lovina (or Lovinia) Jennings, a music teacher. When Bridgman was three his father died, leaving his mother to support the family by teaching music in seminaries in Alabama and Tennessee. In 1860, just before the outbreak of the Civil War, Frederick's mother took him back to her family's home in Massachusetts. Wanting to pursue a career as an artist, Bridgman moved to Brooklyn, New York, and was apprenticed in 1863 to the American Bank Note Company of New York, progressing quickly to the level of vignette draftsman. During this period he also attended night classes sponsored by the Brooklyn Art Association and antique life classes at the National Academy of Design in New York. In 1865 he began showing religious paintings at the exhibitions of the Brooklyn Art Association. In May 1866 Bridgman left New York to study in Paris. Thereafter he only sporadically visited the United States, usually to attend specific exhibitions. However, he remained a regular contributor to the major annual exhibitions in the United States for the rest of his life.

In Paris, Bridgman studied briefly at the Académie Suisse, but he had traveled to France to study with Jean-Léon Gérôme, one of the leading academic French painters specializing in Orientalist themes. In February 1867 Bridgman entered the Écoles des Beaux-Arts, at which Gérôme taught. He remained under Gérôme's tutelage for two years, learning the rudiments of academic art—figure drawing and composition. Bridgman's first paintings from France, meticulously detailed scenes illuminated with studio lighting and painted with a tight, linear brushwork and a smooth surface, reveal Gérôme's influence.

Bridgman spent his first summer in France in Pont-Aven, a fishing village in Brittany, and he returned there regularly over the following four years. He soon became one of the major figures of the first generation of Americans to congregate in what became a well-known artist colony. He spent the majority of his time there painting the local inhabitants in their folk dress, almost always presenting them in dark, realistic interiors. It was with these genre scenes that Bridgman established his presence and received his first critical recognition at the Paris Salon. Only when he visited the sun-filled mountain region of the Pyrenees during the summer and autumn of 1872 and 1873 did his repertoire expand to include landscapes. French rural imagery occasionally reappeared thereafter in Bridgman's art, experiencing a slight resurgence in the 1890s and a flowering during his last decades, but never again did it play the crucial role it had during his earlier years.

Bridgman's association with Gérôme was the turning point in his career for he, like his teacher, became a proponent of academic art and a specialist in Orientalist subject matter, particularly a portrayal of the East as a rarified exotic land of sensual pleasures. From the late autumn of 1872 to the spring of 1873 Bridgman traveled to the Maghrib (Morocco, Algeria, and Tunisia), visiting the major tourist spots of the time, including Tangier, Oran, Algiers, Constantine, and Tunis. Bridgman was one of the earliest American artists to travel to Morocco and possibly the first to explore Algeria. Algiers remained Bridgman's favorite Eastern city because of its picturesque quality and rich colors. The winter of 1873–1874 Bridgman and his friend and fellow painter Charles Sprague Pearce went to Egypt, visiting Cairo and traveling down the Nile as far as Abu Simbel in Nubia. Bridgman was most captivated by the people, but during his two North African excursions he also developed a strong interest in naturalist landscape painting.

The second half of the 1870s witnessed Bridgman's emergence as an Orientalist and the subsequent rise in his reputation as he quickly achieved international status. Returning to Paris from North Africa with more than 300 sketches, he began work on a series of Eastern figure and landscape paintings. In 1875 he exhibited his first Orientalist paintings of contemporary North Africa at the Paris Salon. The following year he returned to the United States to visit the Centennial Exposition in Philadelphia, at which five of his paintings were on view, all lent from private collections. On his return to Paris Bridgman began *Funeral of a Mummy* (1876–1877, J. B. Speed Art Museum, Louisville, Ky.), the painting that in 1877 became his first major Salon success. A large-scale and elaborate archeological reconstruction, the scene was praised by French and American critics for its historical accuracy and its delicate treatment of atmosphere and color. *Diversions of an Assyrian King* (1877–1878) and *Procession of the Apis Bull* (c. 1878–1879) followed in successive Paris Salons, but Bridgman did not create another major history painting for over a decade.

During the late 1870s Bridgman's large, theatrical archeological scenes overshadowed his smaller, contemporary views of Eastern life. His earliest images of present-day North Africa reflect Gérôme's influence in painting style and interpretation, but during the 1880s Bridgman's Orientalism changed in response to two more trips he made to North Africa and to contemporary developments in art. In 1879 he visited Algeria and eastern Tunisia, traveling for the first time to the remote southern area. He was one of the few American artists in the nineteenth century to explore the Saharan region, an area that had been far less affected by French colonization than had the northern coastal region. The oasis towns of El-Kantara and Biskra offered Bridgman glimpses of a disappearing native culture, and back in Paris at the 1880 Salon he exhibited paintings about the domestic existence of the nomads and rural poor. These and other images of the Egyptian *fellaheen* (peasant), painted with sketchier brushwork—less tight drawing and less exacting in details—than his earlier works, mark the first break with Gérôme's urban images of the East as Bridgman responded to the Orientalism of the French painter and writer Gustave Guillaumet.

During the winter of 1885–1886 Bridgman visited Algeria again. He stayed primarily in Algiers and its suburbs, frequenting the city's bazaars, gardens, shops, and cemeteries more than on previous trips. His scenes of Arab life were increasingly set outdoors, on terraces, balconies, and streets, reflecting his new desire to set his narratives in fresh, natural light rather than in the artificiality of the studio. As a result his paintings became brighter in color and looser in paint handling. A fascination for light effects at different times of day, especially twilight, arose during the late 1880s, and such effects characterize much of Bridgman's work from the following decade. Bridgman wrote of his North African experiences in a two-part article published in 1888 in *Harper's New Monthly Magazine*; an expanded version was published in 1890 as the book *Winters in Algeria*.

During the late 1870s and 1880s Bridgman was accorded numerous solo exhibitions, which were always well received. His first large showing, almost a one-man display, was in December 1877, when twenty-four of his paintings were shown in Brooklyn. At the 1878 Paris Exposition universelle, Bridgman received the Legion of Honor for his two exhibits, *Funeral of a Mummy* and *Allah, Allah, Achbar*, a contemporary Eastern scene. In 1881 the American Art Gallery in New York accorded Bridgman his first one-man exhibition. Six years later the Fine Art Society in London gave him a comparable show, and two years after that the Cercle Artistique et Litteraire sponsored his first one-man display in Paris. In the 1881 American showing Bridgman was commended for including both his finished paintings and his studies, a practice quite rare in the United States at that time. Bridgman visited New York for his solo exhibition and was honored by several receptions organized by friends and colleagues. He participated in the 1889 Paris Exposition universelle and continued to be well represented in other major international fairs for the next fifteen years.

Bridgman had married Florence Mott Baker, the daughter of a wealthy Boston chocolate maker, in 1877. By the 1880s he and his wife and their three children had settled in a grand house on the boulevard Malesherbes in the fashionable section of Paris. The couple entertained some of the wealthiest Americans, French, and English of the day. Bridgman's studio occupied a second smaller building, consisting of separate rooms in different period decor. He was an accomplished violinist, and his salon was frequented by musicians as well as artists. In the 1890s he began to compose, and during the twentieth century several of his compositions were performed in Vichy, Nice, and Monte Carlo.

The foremost Orientalist specialist from the United States, Bridgman was praised as the American Gérôme, and his success was based largely on his academic painting style. But by the end of the nineteenth century tastes had begun to change. Bridgman realized this, for in 1898 he published *L'Anarchie dans l'art* to counteract the spreading influence of impressionism, and in 1901 he wrote the poem "L'Idole et l'idéal." Although Bridgman was elected an officer of the Legion of Honor in 1907, he had outlived the popularity of his Eastern imagery. He continued to paint exotic scenes of North Africa until his death, but the late images were merely repetitions of his earlier work. Shortly before World War I Bridgman, his second wife, Marthe Jaeger, whom he had married in 1904 after the death of his first wife in 1901, and their son retired to Lyons-la-Forêt. There he returned to painting rural France, depicting the rolling countryside and farms of Normandy in nostalgic, pastoral terms. With the diminished interest in his art, Bridgman spent his last years struggling to support his second family. He died in Rouen.

• The best early articles on Bridgman are Earl Shinn (writing as Edward Strahan), "Frederick A. Bridgman," *Harper's New Monthly Magazine*, Oct. 1881, pp. 694–705; Antony Valabrègue, "F. Arthur Bridgman," *Galerie contemporaine des illustrations françaises* 8 (1882?), a series of three articles; and Lillian K. Byrn, "Frederick A. Bridgman," *Taylor-Trotwood Magazine*, Feb. 1907, pp. 489–92. A complete biography and posthumous study of his entire career is Ilene Susan Fort, "Frederick Arthur Bridgman and the American Fascination with the Exotic Near East" (Ph.D. diss., Graduate Center, City Univ. of New York, 1990). A catalog entitled *The Drawings of F. A. Bridgman* (1983), with an introduction by Fort, includes a published chronology of Bridgman. See also H. Barbara Weinberg, *The American Pupils of Jean-Léon Gérôme* (1984); Weinberg, *The Lure of Paris: Nineteenth-Century American Painters and Their French Teachers* (1991); the exhibition catalog by David Sellin entitled *Americans in Brittany and Normandy, 1860–1910* (1982); and Gerald M. Ackerman, *American Orientalists* (1994). An obituary is in the *New York Times*, 17 Jan. 1928.

ILENE SUSAN FORT

BRIDGMAN, Herbert Lawrence (30 May 1844–24 Sept. 1924), newspaper executive and explorer, was born in Amherst, Massachusetts, the son of Richard Baxter Bridgman and Mary Nutting. Educated at local schools and at Amherst College, from which he graduated in 1866, Bridgman received a master's degree in English from Amherst three years later.

Bridgman began his career in journalism as an undergraduate, serving as an apprentice at several area newspapers. In 1866 he joined the staff of the *Springfield (Mass.) Republican*, eventually becoming city editor. He subsequently worked for the Associated Press and for the periodical *Frank Leslie's*, as well as the *New York Tribune*, before becoming in 1887 business manager and part owner of the *Brooklyn Standard Union*, a position he held until his death. In 1886 Bridgman participated in preliminary meetings that led to the founding a year later of the American Newspaper Publishers Association (ANPA); he served as vice president of the ANPA in 1911 and as president from 1914 to 1916. Bridgman married Melia Newhall in 1868; after his wife's death in 1884, he married three years later Helen Bartlett, a New York writer. Neither marriage produced children.

Already distinguished as a journalist and publisher, Bridgman became even more well known in the 1890s in the field of exploration. The catalyst for his new interest was his friendship with Arctic explorer Robert E. Peary, whom Bridgman met in 1892. Bridgman became an enthusiastic supporter of Peary and helped raise funds for the explorer's 1893 journey to Greenland. A year later Bridgman led a relief mission to the Arctic with supplies for Peary's expedition; during this mission Bridgman was also instrumental in bringing back to the United States Peary's wife and the Pearys' infant daughter, who had been born in Arctic Greenland.

Bridgman's association with the noted explorer continued for more than a decade, and the grateful Peary named a cape in northeast Greenland after his friend and benefactor. In 1899, after Bridgman had led a relief mission to another Peary expedition in the Arctic, the newspaper executive founded the Peary Arctic Club; its purpose was to underwrite future explorations by Peary, who was now intent on reaching the North Pole.

While continuing to support and encourage Peary—in 1901 he led a third relief mission to the explorer in the Arctic—Bridgman became interested in African exploration. In 1904 he traveled to the Congo and the headwaters of the Nile and a year later published a book about his journey, *The Sudan: Africa from Sea to Center*. An active member of the U.S. National Geographic Society, the Explorers Club, and the Arctic Club, as well as his own Peary Arctic Club, Bridgman represented all four organizations at the International Congress for the Study of the Polar Regions, held in Brussels in 1906; he was also the U.S. delegate to the International Polar Commission that met in Brussels two years later.

Bridgman's continuing support of Peary was rewarded when on 6 September 1909 the explorer sent him a telegram from Labrador, claiming that he had finally reached the North Pole the preceding April. Several days earlier, American physician Frederick Cook had announced publicly his discovery of the North Pole in 1908, but Bridgman acted quickly to refute Cook's claim, and he used his newspaper as a podium to champion Peary; he also published articles in Peary's defense in popular magazines. Largely through Bridgman's efforts, Peary was hailed for several decades as the rightful claimant while Cook was discredited.

Bridgman's interest in travel and exploration continued until his death. In 1913 he served again as the U.S. delegate to the International Polar Commission, which met in Rome, and then traveled extensively through the Balkans. A strong supporter of public education, Bridgman became head of the geography department at the Brooklyn Institute of Arts and Sciences in 1915 and two years later was named a regent of the State University of New York. He was also a recipient of honors from the Belgian and Bulgarian governments.

Bridgman undertook his penultimate voyage in 1923, when he traveled by steamer through the Panama Canal to Hawaii. In the summer of 1924, in his eighty-first year, Bridgman sailed to Europe aboard a naval training ship, the *Newport*. Ostensibly on vacation, Bridgman remained a reporter to the end, sending back a dozen articles for publication in his newspaper that recorded his impressions of visits to England, Belgium, Spain, and Madeira. En route home, Bridgman died suddenly at sea of a cerebral hemorrhage. His body was returned to the United States and he was buried in Brooklyn. A posthumous editorial tribute in the *New York Times* praised him for his "rare devotion to public service" and for helping "to keep the spirit of adventure alive in a workaday world" (27 Sept. 1924).

• A memoir by Bridgman's second wife, Helen Bartlett, *Within My Horizon* (1920), describes their life together. Other biographical information on Bridgman appears in the *Amherst College Biographical Record* (1927); and in *His Last Voyage: Herbert Lawrence Bridgman, 1844–1924* (1924), a privately printed pamphlet. An obituary and an editorial tribute are in the *New York Times*, 27 Sept. 1924; see also related articles in the *New York Times*, 30 Sept. and 1 Oct. 1924.

ANN T. KEENE

BRIDGMAN, Laura Dewey (21 Dec. 1829–24 May 1889), first deaf-blind person to receive a formal academic education, was born near Etna, New Hampshire, the daughter of Daniel Bridgman and Harmony Downer. Her father, a substantial farmer and pillar of the Baptist church, served two sessions in the New Hampshire legislature. At age two, Laura and her two older sisters suffered an attack of scarlet fever. Her sisters died, and it was two years before Laura was able to sit up all day and three years until she regained her full strength. The illness left her without any sight or hearing and little sense of smell and taste. The speech she acquired before her illness was forgotten.

During the next few years, Laura Bridgman learned to sew, knit, braid, and do minor work around the house. She also learned some signs to communicate her basic needs: extending the hand a certain way meant "bread"; raising it to the lips as if tipping a cup, "drink." The one person with time and patience for her was Asa Tenney, an eccentric old bachelor with a speech impediment. "Uncle" Asa was Bridgman's companion, playmate, and friend. They developed no formal communication scheme, yet from him she learned about trees and flowers and the difference between earth and water.

In 1837 James Barrett, a student at Dartmouth College, went to work at the Bridgmans' farm. He talked about Laura Bridgman to Reuben Mussey, head of the medical department of Dartmouth, who later wrote an article about her in *Barnard's Magazine*. This article brought her to the attention of Samuel Gridley Howe, the first director of the Perkins Institution for the Blind in South Boston (now the Perkins School for the Blind in Watertown, Mass.). After Howe visited the Bridgmans in 1837, Laura Bridgman was enrolled at Perkins in October of that year.

Howe started Bridgman's education by cutting out the names of common objects and pasting them onto the objects. The letters he used were in the embossed or Boston Line Type then used by the blind, as the Braille system was not yet commonly known. Once the association had been made with the object, he then formed the name from the individual letters. After a long time Bridgman learned the letters. Howe's efforts were first recorded in the *Annual Reports of the Perkins Institution* starting in 1839. He did achieve success, and once Bridgman learned the alphabet and built up her vocabulary, Howe then taught her the manual alphabet or finger spelling that had been developed for the deaf by Abbé de l'Epée. After this, Howe assigned others, Miss Drew and Mary Swift, to help teach her. He dictated what she was to study. Her curriculum included spelling, reading, writing, arithmetic, and geography, the latter improved by the large globe that Howe had built in 1837 (it was the first globe for the blind made in America). Lessons lasted no longer than an hour and were interspersed with recreation. By 1841 Howe and Drew had taught Bridgman to write, guided by a grooved board, the square-hand script favored by Howe. By this means Bridgman was able to keep a journal, filling each page with neat pencil writing.

A major event in Bridgman's life and that of the education of the deaf-blind came in 1842 when Charles Dickens visited Perkins on 29 January. Although Howe was not at the school, Dickens and Charles Sumner were given a tour of the whole establishment. Bridgman made such an impression on Dickens that he wrote extensively about her. This, along with large tracts taken from Howe's reports, he included in his journal that was later published in *American Notes*. It was this work that first brought Bridgman and Howe worldwide attention, and many people came to see her at Perkins Institution for the Blind. Although other deaf-blind persons were educated before Bridgman (such as Victorine Morreseau in France), their educations were not conducted in a formal academic environment. Howe's work with the deaf-blind did not stop with Bridgman. He enrolled others, such as Oliver Caswell (whom Bridgman helped to teach) and Julia Brace. Brace was an older woman when she came to Perkins from the Hartford School for the Deaf in 1842. She stayed only a few months, as little was accomplished in her education.

In 1852 Bridgman returned to live with her family in Hanover, as she had learned as much as it was thought possible. But after the busy and interesting life she had led at Perkins, life back on the farm was tedious and boring. She lost her appetite, and her health soon declined to such an extent that it was thought she might die. She returned to Perkins, recovered to full health, and decided to remain there. Being an excellent seamstress, she sometimes taught sewing to the Perkins girls. She was a very strict teacher. In addition to teaching she also made beds and cleaned. She remained active by making most of her own clothes, knitting, crocheting, and fashioning lace, which she sold. She loved to read, especially the Bible. Bridgman also became busy with correspondence to her family, friends, and many of the celebrities and politicians who came to see her. Among her closest friends was Morrison Heady in Kentucky, who also was deaf-blind. She kept a journal and wrote poetry, simple, devoted verse filled with images of darkness and light. She spent the summers with her family in New Hampshire, returning to Perkins in the fall.

On 9 January 1876 Howe died. In his will he remembered his most famous pupil by making provision for Bridgman so that so she could remain at Perkins for the rest of her life. The second director of Perkins, Michael Anagnos, Howe's son-in-law, saw to it that Bridgman was taken care of. Some of the older Perkins girls were assigned in turn to share Bridgman's room; one of these young women was Anne M. Sullivan, who was partially sighted and became famous, after she graduated in 1886, as Helen Keller's teacher. Bridgman died of pneumonia at Perkins.

In the last years of her life Bridgman was remembered little, except by those who taught the deaf-blind and by a few of a new breed of experimental psychologists who, returning from Europe, were interested in learning about how she was able to learn and function. Her legacy and that of Howe and her other teachers is that they proved that it was possible for a deaf-blind person to be formally educated. The success of her education helped lead to the education of other deaf-blind persons. Although she did not lead a completely independent life outside of Perkins, she was able to gain a good deal of self-sufficiency as well as employment as a teacher. The records kept by Howe and by Bridgman's teachers are invaluable to modern researchers investigating the education of the disabled, as they are the first detailed records of the education of a deaf-blind person. They are also some of the first to detail the education of the disabled in the United States. Since the very start of her education in 1837, Bridgman has been of interest to those studying the behavior of the brain and how sensory loss is compensated by the brain. Until detailed studies of Bridgman were made, it was thought by many that persons who lost both their sight and their hearing could not be educated. The education of Helen Keller by Anne Sullivan was made possible because of Howe's work with Laura Bridgman.

• The largest collection of materials about Laura Bridgman is in the archives of the Perkins School for the Blind, Watertown, Mass. Included in this collection are school records, journals, letters by her and about her, pictures, photographs, and items that she used and made. Charles Dickens's famous account of Bridgman's education appears in *American Notes and Pictures from Italy* (1868). Mary Swift Lamson, who worked with Bridgman, authored *Life and Education of Laura Dewey Bridgman, the Deaf, Dumb, and Blind Girl* (1879); also useful is a book by Howe's daughters, Maud Howe and Florence Howe Hall, *Laura Bridgman: Dr. Howe's Famous Pupil and What He Taught Her* (1903). The results of a postmortem on Bridgman are reported in Henry H. Donaldson, "Anatomical Observations on the Brain and Several Sense-Organs of the Blind Deaf-Mute, Laura Dewey Bridgman," *American Journal of Psychology* 3 (1890): 293–344. More recent works on Bridgman's education include P. Bradley Nutting, "The Education of Laura Bridgman," *Yankee Magazine*, Oct. 1987, pp. 138–41, 198–201, and Ernest Freeberg, "'More Important Than a Rabble of Common Kings': Dr. Howe's Education of Laura Bridgman," *History of Education Quarterly* 34 (1994): 305–27. On the education of deaf-mutes more generally, see Gabriel Farrell, *Children of the Silent Night: The Story of the Education of Deaf-Blind Children Here and Abroad* (1956), and Elisabeth Gitter, "Deaf Mutes and Heroines in the Victorian Era," *Victorian Literature and Culture* 20 (1993): 179–95.

KENNETH STUCKEY

BRIDGMAN, Percy Williams (21 Apr. 1882–20 Aug. 1961), physicist and philosopher of science, was born in Cambridge, Massachusetts, the son of Raymond Landon Bridgman, an author and journalist, and Mary Ann Maria Williams. As a boy, Bridgman was shy but independent and competitive. He participated in track and field sports, played chess, and studied the piano. Although his family was deeply religious (Congregational), the young Bridgman, to the great disappointment of his father, rejected religion as being factually unverifiable. Raymond Bridgman later came to accept his son's commitment to honesty and intellectual integrity as a moral equivalent to religion. A good student, Percy Bridgman attended the public schools of Newton, Massachusetts, and upon graduation in 1900 entered Harvard College, earning an A.B. summa cum laude in 1904. He remained at Harvard to study physics, receiving an A.M. in 1905 and a Ph.D. in 1908, and was subsequently appointed research fellow in the Department of Physics. He became instructor in 1910. In 1912 he married Olive Ware, of Hartford, Connecticut, daughter of Edmund Asa Ware, founder and first president of Atlanta University. The couple had two children. Bridgman was made assistant professor in 1913, full professor in 1919, Hollis Professor of Mathematics and Natural Philosophy in 1926, Higgins University Professor in 1950, and professor emeritus in 1954.

Except for a short time during World War I when they lived in New London, Connecticut, the Bridgmans resided in Cambridge, Massachusetts. They spent their summers in Randolph, New Hampshire, where Bridgman had refashioned a barn into a vacation home. He also built for himself a small study, some distance from the main house, to which he retreated each day to write his scientific papers and philosophical essays. It is an indication of the fondness that Bridgman felt for his Randolph home that he chose to live out his last days there. Throughout his life Bridgman showed the same vigor and proud independence that he had as a child, whether as a working physicist, philosopher of science, or concerned citizen and social critic. He was highly disciplined in his work, painfully honest and literal-minded in his philosophical thinking, and politically and socially, a libertarian. He was also a dedicated family man, considerate of his wife, demanding of his children.

Bridgman is the undisputed founder of high pressure physics. Throughout his scientific career, his work dominated the field. His output was prodigious; he wrote more than 250 papers and thirteen books. He was much admired by his colleagues for his intuitive understanding of physical processes, the simplicity, economy, and originality of his apparatus, and his shop skills, as well as for his perseverance and drive.

At the foundation of Bridgman's experimental program (measuring the physical properties of matter under high pressure) was his invention of a seal that becomes tighter as pressure increases, the enabling principle of which was first discovered when he was a graduate student. Until then, leakage had limited the maximum achievable pressures to about 3,000 atmospheres, reached by the nineteenth-century French investigator Emile-Hilaire Amagat. With the self-tightening seal, there was no upper limit to the pressure except that imposed by the strength of the apparatus (the containing vessel, the connecting tubes, and pressure-transmitting piston).

The physical characteristic that made the self-tightening seal possible Bridgman called "the principle of unsupported area." The name reflects the design of the seal, which, in turn, depends on the physical fact that a given force produces a greater pressure if the area upon which it acts is decreased. Leakage is prevented by designing a joint (or piston) so that the area of the sealing washer or packing that comes in contact with the compressive force is smaller than the area of the surface interfacing the medium transmitting that force. (A simple example is a drain stopper that depends on the weight of the water pressing on its entire surface to seal the outer edge. The part of the stopper that covers the hole and that is thus not in contact with the circumference of the drain is the "unsupported area.") This principle ensures that the sealing medium is always subjected to a higher pressure than the material being compressed. Bridgman claimed that his discovery of this arrangement "had a strong element of accident," meaning that at the time he was not specifically looking for it.

There were three problems Bridgman had to deal with before he could take full advantage of his discovery: installing an efficient compressor, finding a steel strong enough to support the newly accessible pressures, and designing gauges to measure these pressures. The solution to the first was to replace the original inefficient screw compressor with a hydraulic ram (press). The second problem was solved indirectly by contemporary advances in industrial metallurgy that enabled the production of high strength steels not previously available. The solution to the third problem required the full scope of Bridgman's skills as a mechanic. In a 1909 paper Bridgman described how he constructed, by hand, drilling solid steel rod, a primary free-piston gauge capable of measuring pressures up to about 6,800 atmospheres. This was then used as a standard to calibrate a secondary gauge based on the variation of electrical resistance of mercury with pressure. By 1911 an improved primary gauge permitted measurement of pressures up to 13,000 atmospheres, and a new secondary gauge based on the pressure variation of electrical resistance of the alloy manganin permitted, by extrapolation, measurements up to 20,000 atmospheres.

Between 1911 and 1916 Bridgman used these tools to measure the thermodynamic properties of water and other liquids and study polymorphic transitions (phase changes) of solids under pressure, plotting new melting curves. He discovered five forms of water-ice and showed that there is no critical point (point at which the two phases are indistinguishable) for the solid-liquid transition. For about the next twenty years, he turned much of his attention to the measurement of the thermoelectric properties of metals under pressure and, based on his early measurements, formulated a theory of metallic conduction that earned him an invitation to the 1924 Solvay Conference in Brussels, Belgium. This was a rare honor for an American since, as a community, American physicists had not yet achieved stature as theoreticians. However, Bridgman's theory was quickly made obsolete by the appearance of wave mechanics in 1925. During this time he also made measurements of the compressibility of solids, the viscosity of liquids, and the thermoelectric properties of single metal crystals. In 1931 he published a textbook, *The Physics of High Pressure*.

From the mid-1930s on, using new methods to support the pressure vessel, by constructing the pressure-transmitting piston from carboloy (tungsten carbide cemented with cobalt), a material recently developed by General Electric, and by miniaturizing his apparatus, Bridgman extended his measurements to 30,000, then to 50,000 atmospheres. With further modifications he reached 100,000 atmospheres. In 1941 he reported having achieved a pressure of 400,000 atmospheres. The results of his measurements were of significance to investigators in fields ranging from solid state physics to geophysics and cosmology.

During World War I Bridgman worked on submarine detection devices for the U.S. Navy. In World War II he studied the plastic flow in steel, a problem related to the penetration of armor plate by projectiles. For the Manhattan Project he measured the compressibility of uranium and plutonium. However, Bridgman's expression of patriotism went beyond practical contributions to matters of principle. In 1939 Bridgman issued a manifesto in which he declared that he would no longer share his work with citizens of any totalitarian state because these persons were no longer free individuals.

In 1946, after having been twice before nominated for the honor, first in 1917 and again in 1933, Bridgman received the Nobel Prize for his "outstanding pioneer work in the field of high-pressure physics." In addition, during his lifetime, Bridgman was awarded many other prizes and honors, including the Rumford Medal of the American Academy of Arts and Sciences (1917), the Cresson Medal of the Franklin Institute (1932), the Roozeboom Medal of the Royal Academy of Sciences of Amsterdam (1933), the Comstock Prize of the National Academy of Sciences (1933), the Research Corporation of America Award (1937), and the Bingham Medal of the Society of Rheology (1951). He was elected to the American Philosophical Society in 1916. Bridgman was a member of the American Academy of Arts and Sciences (1912), the National Academy of Sciences (1918), the Washington Academy of Sciences, and the American Association for the Advancement of Science (member, 1918; fellow, 1921) and was president of the American Physical Society (1942). He was a foreign member of the Royal Society, an honorary fellow of the Physical Society of London, a corresponding member of the Academia Nacional de Ciencias in Mexico, and a foreign member of the Indian Academy of Science.

As a philosopher of science, Bridgman is best known and most influential as the author of the operational method, later called *operationism* or *operationalism*, which he articulated in *The Logic of Modern Physics* (1927). He stated its central tenet as follows: "In general we mean by any concept nothing more than a set of operations; *the concept is synonymous with the corresponding set of operations*." An "operation," according to Bridgman, was the physical act of measurement. By means of this precept Bridgman meant to convey his belief that the only entities we can meaningfully talk about in science are those we can measure.

Operationism is often represented as a variant of pragmatism or logical positivism. It is also the name given to a methodological precept advanced by the behavioral psychologists, which is an adaptation of Bridgman's operational method. While a family resemblance exists among these doctrines, in fact, Bridgman intended his operational method to be an instrument for cleansing physics of "meaningless" metaphysical concepts, such as Newton's absolute time and space. Thus, for Bridgman, any concept that did not correspond to an actual physical operation was to be discarded as meaningless. However, Bridgman later extended his operational standard to include what he called "paper and pencil" operations—formal logical or mathematical procedures—and in so doing made the interpretation of his operational method more difficult.

In advancing his operational method, Bridgman claimed that he was following the example that Albert Einstein set forth in his 1905 paper on special relativity, the work in which Einstein showed that the only knowledge we can have of time and space is gained by means of actual physical clocks and measuring sticks. However, it can be argued that Bridgman overemphasized the "operational" aspect of Einstein's methodological rationale and that Bridgman's operational method is, in fact, more directly related to dimensional analysis, a subject on which Bridgman had published a book in 1922. (Dimensional analysis is a shortcut method for constructing the mathematical form of an equation expressing a physical relationship.) In any case, because it included no rules for recognizing a "good" operation, that is, a way of distinguishing a theoretically relevant operation/measurement from one that was not, and also overlooked the need for defining classes of equivalent operations (so that operations would not be multiplied ad infinitum), the operational method failed, even on its own terms, to establish unique and rigorous criteria for judging scientific meaning. Nonetheless, Bridgman's operational ideal has served time and again to caution scientists against overreaching their methodological capabilities.

Less widely known, but increasingly prominent in his later thinking, are Bridgman's views on scientific method and the nature of scientific knowledge. In *The Nature of Physical Theory* (1936) he stunned his readers with the announcement that there is no scientific knowledge except in the privacy of the individual mind. It seemed to him evident that by its very nature, knowledge, including scientific knowledge, can exist only in the understanding consciousness of an individual. Thus Bridgman repudiated the idea that science is authoritative because it is public or shared knowledge. By the early 1940s he had also rejected the notion that there is a unique scientific method, asserting that it is merely an instance of "the method of intelligence."

In 1938 Bridgman published *The Intelligent Individual and Society*. He considered the work his favorite and regretted that it had not received much attention. In it he attempted to apply the operational method to demystify social institutions. The outcome was his "discovery" that social truths have no absolute basis. They are but sublimations of human will, enforced by superior physical power. There is no higher meaning outside the individual. In the final analysis, he concluded, the truth from which there is no escape is that the individual is isolated in his own consciousness. He stands alone in an indifferent universe.

As a physicist, Bridgman was regarded with the highest respect, and his operational method was very influential in both the physical and social sciences. However, his views on the nature of scientific knowledge and method were outside of the mainstream, and his social philosophy had similarly little impact. He is best remembered as a brilliant experimental physicist.

Bridgman, suffering from incurable bone cancer, took his own life at his vacation home in Randolph.

• The greater part of Bridgman's papers are in the Harvard University Archives. Some material is at the Center for History and Philosophy of Science, American Institute of Physics, New York City. Experimental apparatus is held in the Smithsonian Institute and Harvard's Collection of Historical Scientific Instruments. Many letters, as well as a family chronicle written by Bridgman and his wife, and some apparatus remain in the possession of his family. Most of Bridgman's scientific papers have been reprinted in his *Collected Experimental Papers* (7 vols., 1964), and a good many of his nonscientific essays have been published in the 2d ed. of *Reflections of a Physicist* (1955). Books by Bridgman not mentioned above include *Dimensional Analysis* (1922; rev. ed., 1931), *The Thermodynamics of Electrical Phenomena and a Condensed Collection of Thermodynamic Formulas* (1925), *The Nature of Thermodynamics* (1941), *The Nature of Some of Our Physical Concepts* (1952), *Studies in Large Plastic Flow and Fracture, with Special Emphasis on the Effects of Hydrostatic Pressure* (1952), *The Way Things Are* (1959), and *A Sophisticate's Primer of Relativity* (1962; rev. ed., 1983).

A biography of Bridgman is Maila L. Walter, *Science and Cultural Crisis; An Intellectual Biography of Percy Williams Bridgman (1882–1961)* (1990). Other biographical material is in Francis Birch et al., "An Ingenious Invention, Percy Williams Bridgman," *The Lives of Harvard Scholars* (1968); Edwin C. Kemble and Birch, "Percy Williams Bridgman, 1882–1961," National Academy of Sciences, *Biographical Memoirs* 41 (1970): 23–67; D. M. Newitt, "Percy Williams Bridgman," *Biographical Memoirs of the Royal Society* 8 (1962); John H. Van Vleck, "Percy Williams Bridgman," *Year Book of the American Philosophical Society, 1962* (1963); and in the essays presented at the memorial meeting at Harvard University on 24 Oct. 1961.

MAILA L. WALTER

BRIERTON, John (1572–c. 1619), explorer and historian, whose name was sometimes spelled Brereton, was born in Norwich, Norfolk, England, the son of Cuthbert Brierton, a dealer in textile fabrics, and Joan Howse. He was educated at Gonville and Caius College, Cambridge University, from which he earned a B.A. in 1592–1593 and an M.A. in 1596. In 1598 he became an Anglican deacon and entered the priesthood later the same year. His first curacy was in Lawshall, Suffolk. While there he met a family named Bacon, members of which were cousins of Bartholomew Gosnold, the English navigator who lived in nearby Otley. Through the Bacons, Brierton met Gosnold.

Early in the seventeenth century there was a revival of interest in establishing colonies in the New World for commercial purposes. Sir Humphrey Gilbert, the English navigator, soldier, and half-brother of Sir Walter Raleigh, had failed in 1579 but succeeded four years later, at St. John's, Newfoundland, to establish the first British colony in North America. Sir Humphrey called the region to the south Norumbega, which later was called North Virginia and finally became New England.

On 26 March 1602 Gosnold sailed from Falmouth as commander of a small bark, the *Concord* of Dartmouth. Accompanying him were Captain Bartholomew Gilbert (Sir Humphrey's son), Gabriel Archer, Brierton, twenty other gentlemen, and eight sailors (whom Brierton later described as "none of the best"). The leaders planned to establish an outpost, leave a holding party, return to England, and come back with more men and supplies. Instead of going north via Newfoundland or south via the Canary Islands, they set a more direct western course, landed briefly at St. Marie in the Azores, and made landfall on 14 May 1602 near what is now Portland, Maine. Coasting southward, they saw a "mightie headland," which Gosnold named Cape Cod because of the area's abundant supply of codfish. Brierton, Gosnold, and three others spent an afternoon in the hills past "a white sandie and very bolde shore," thus becoming the first white men to set foot on New England soil. They stopped at what they called "Marthaes vineyard" (no doubt No Man's Land, just south of present-day Martha's Vineyard) and camped on an island they named "Elizabeths Ile" (now Cuttyhunk Island), northwest of Martha's Vineyard. For nineteen days they scouted the region, traded with the friendly natives, and built a makeshift fort. Supplies were limited, and too few men volunteered to remain. So, loaded with cedar logs, furs, skins, and 2,200 pounds of sassafras roots, they set sail on 18 June and landed at Exmouth, Devon, on 23 July 1602.

Temporary trouble ensued. When Raleigh, undoubtedly unaware of the expedition, met Bartholomew Gilbert in Weymouth and learned about the voyage, he had mixed feelings. He had a Crown patent authorizing him to confiscate all vessels and their contents trading in the New World without his permission. He was afraid that the new load of sassafras would lower profits from the sale of his South Virginia sassafras, which was popularly considered in England at the time as a cure for syphilis, the plague, and other ills. In a letter to Robert Cecil, the earl of Salisbury and secretary of state in Queen Elizabeth's court, Raleigh complained of this infringement but added that because Gilbert was cooperative he would be reimbursed. Later, Raleigh even took Gilbert into partnership.

Meanwhile, Brierton decided to write an account of the voyage. Encouragement may have come from Gosnold or possibly from Richard Hakluyt, the English geographer and a member of the Virginia Company of London. The result was *A Briefe and True Relation of the Discouerie of the North Part of Virginia; Being a Most Pleasant, Fruitfull and Commodious Soile: Made This Present Yeere 1602, by Captaine Bartholomew Gosnold, Captaine Bartholowmew Gilbert, and Diuers Other Gentlemen Their Associats, by the Permission of the Honourable Knight, Sir Walter Ralegh, &c.* (1602). The 48-page book proved so popular that it was reprinted in 1602, with material written earlier and separately by Hakluyt and by Edward Hayes, a Liverpool adventurer and the historian of Sir Humphrey Gilbert's 1583 exploration. This edition was reprinted in 1603.

Brierton's *Briefe and True Relation* is a straightforward, informative narrative. It depicts "North Virginia" as a land of "finest soile," broad rivers, and good harbors, with an abundance of animals and fish, "all sorts of fowles," fruits, nuts, "Tabacco," and various trees. The natives, "exceeding courteous, gentle of disposition, and well conditioned," and even "very wittie," traded cedar, furs, skins, and sassafras for what Brierton simply calls "certaine trifles which they wondered at, and highly esteemed." The "Climat" had such "holsomnesse" that the Englishmen grew "fatter and in better health than when we went out of England." Brierton was too tactful even to hint at what Hakluyt boldly stated to be the "ends" of such expeditions, namely, to spread Christianity, to trade, and to conquer.

The fortunes of Raleigh, praised on Brierton's title page, declined after 1602. That year Raleigh licensed Hakluyt for an expedition that began in April 1603, and Gilbert for another, beginning in May 1603 and ending in Gilbert's death a month later. Queen Elizabeth, as anti-Spanish as Raleigh was, died in March 1603, and Raleigh was imprisoned in July on a charge of treason against her pro-Spanish successor, James I. All this while and a little later, Brierton's book enjoyed a considerable influence. Partly because it propagandized effectively for commerce in North Virginia, still other expeditions were financed, including one commanded by Martin Pring in 1603 and another by George Weymouth in 1605. A far-reaching consequence of these only partial successes was the conclusion that single and even groups of wealthy individuals could not finance such efforts; consequently, when various European rulers continued to offer expeditions moral support but no money, joint stock companies were formed to colonize New England and the seaboard to the south.

Little information is available concerning Brierton's last years. It is known that in 1604 he was in Lawshall and that in 1619 he was rector of Brightwell, in a Suffolk parish near the home of his old friend Gosnold in Grundisburgh. The place of his death is not known.

• A. W. Pollard and G. R. Redgrave, *A Short-title Catalogue of Books Printed in England, Scotland and Ireland and of English Books Printed Abroad 1475–1640* (1926), describes editions of Brierton's book in detail. Henry S. Burrage, ed., *Early English and French Voyages Chiefly from Hakluyt 1534–1608* (1906; repr. 1967), includes Brierton's account. A facsimile reprint is John Brereton, *Discoverie of the North Part of Virginia* (1966). Warner F. Gookin and Philip L. Barbour, *Bartholomew Gosnold, Discoverer and Planter* (1963), discusses the 1602 expedition. Background to English colonization in New England is provided in Oliver Perry Chitwood, *A History of Colonial America* (1931); David Beers Quinn, *England and the Discovery of America, 1481–1620, from the Bristol Voyages of the Fifteenth Century to the Pilgrim Settlement at Plymouth: The Exploration, Exploitation, and Trial-and-Error Colonization of North America by the English* (1974); Kenneth R. Andrews, *Trade, Plunder, and Settlement: Maritime Enterprise and the Genesis of the British Empire, 1480–1630* (1984); and Jerome R. Reich, *Colonial America* (1984).

ROBERT L. GALE

BRIGGS, Charles Augustus (15 Jan. 1841–8 June 1913), clergyman and theological scholar, was born in New York City, the son of Sarah Mead Berrian and Alanson Briggs, the owner of the largest barrel-making company in the United States. He studied at the University of Virginia, where he had a personal conversion experience on 30 November 1858 in the midst of the urban revival of that year. He joined the First Presbyterian Church of Charlottesville and subsequently announced to his family that he would enter the ministry instead of the family business. After spending three months with New York's Seventh Regiment at Camp Cameron near Washington, D.C., he entered Union Theological Seminary in New York in October 1861. There Edward Robinson (1794–1863) taught him biblical research and Henry Boynton Smith showed him how to use historical-critical scholarship in the service of a traditional Reformed faith.

Briggs interrupted his theological studies for three years (1863–1866) to manage the family business for his ailing father. In 1865 he was married to Julia Valentine Dobbs, with whom he later had one child. Licensed to preach on 18 April 1866 by the First (Old School) Presbytery of New York, in June 1866 he and his wife went to Berlin, where he studied under Isaac August Dorner, an advocate of historical-critical scholarship as a tool of the evangelical faith. Prompted by his father's poor health, he returned to the United States in June 1869 and accepted a call as the first pastor of the First Presbyterian Church of Roselle, New Jersey.

While successful in his pastoral role, he began in 1870 to publish articles in the *American Presbyterian Review*. His translation and critical introduction to Karl Moll's *Commentary on the Psalms* (1872) led to his appointment to the Union Seminary faculty in 1874. Committed to the union of the Old and New School wings of the Presbyterian church, he proposed to Charles W. Hodge of Princeton Seminary that the two of them establish a theological journal, managed jointly by Union and Princeton, representing the two sides. Hodge agreed, and the *Presbyterian Review* began publication in 1880. Briggs's first contribution, "The Documentary History of the Westminster Assembly," applied critical historical principles to the Westminster Confession, a document produced by the Westminster Assembly in 1647 and considered the classical doctrinal statement of English-speaking Presbyterians. Briggs argued in his article that excessive claims for the confession's authority went beyond what the authors themselves claimed.

Rather than uniting the two wings of the church, the *Presbyterian Review* revealed the deep differences between them, particularly regarding historical criticism. During the heresy trial of William Robertson Smith before the General Assembly of the Scottish Free Church, Briggs wrote a historical account of the proceedings for the *Review*, casting doubt on the rights of church courts to judge the new critical theories espoused by Smith. When Briggs refused to delete these judgments from the article, the editorial board published a series of essays from both sides. The Princeton theologians argued that the original autographs of the Bible were verbally inerrant. Dismissing those views as new and idolatrous theories, Briggs defended biblical criticism as part of the heritage of the Reformation and a superior means of discerning the ways of God in history.

The differences might not have led to accusations of heresy had Briggs not become so active in Presbyterian debates over proposals to revise the Westminster Confession. In 1889 he published *Whither? A Theological Question for the Times*, a vigorous argument for revision, fanning the fury of conservatives. However, it was his inaugural address in the new Edward Robinson Chair at Union on 20 January 1891 that occasioned charges of heresy. The address, published as *The Authority of Holy Scripture* (2d ed., 1891), called for criticism in the service of faith and attacked the traditionalists, but it contained little that Briggs had not already written. He criticized six "barriers" between the Bible and its usefulness in the church, including verbal inspiration (i.e., the view that the words of the Scripture were spoken directly by God to the writers), inerrancy, and traditional views about authorship, pointing out that Moses did not write the Pentateuch and that Isaiah wrote no more than thirty-nine of the sixty-six chapters of the Book of Isaiah.

A group in Briggs's New York presbytery brought charges against him. On 11 May 1891 a committee recommended proceedings against him on the grounds that he held positions contrary to the Westminster Confession. In a public hearing before the presbytery in November, Briggs reaffirmed the Scriptures as the only infallible rule of faith and practice and the Westminster Confession as containing doctrine taught in Holy Scripture. He dismissed the charges as invalid because they failed to specify what doctrines he had violated. The presbytery agreed and dismissed the charges, but the prosecution appealed to the General Assembly of the Presbyterian Church in the United States, which remanded the case to the New York presbytery with instructions to reconsider the charges, now modified to include violation of the general assembly's statement that the Scriptures were infallible. Briggs accused the general assembly of unconstitutional action and appealed to the facts of history in support of his positions, and the presbytery found him innocent of all charges. Again the prosecution appealed to the general assembly, which conducted a seven-day trial in Washington, D.C., in May 1893 that upheld the appeal, 405 to 145, and suspended him from the ministry. Briggs left the Presbyterian church and on 14 May 1899 was ordained into the Episcopal church. Controversy over his appointment to the Robinson Chair led Union Seminary on 13 October 1892 to terminate its connection with the Presbyterian church.

Briggs became the center of controversy not because he was radical but because he stood in the middle, believing it was possible to combine critical biblical scholarship with an orthodox Presbyterian faith. In the end he was alienated from both. In his last decades at Union, he contemplated charging his colleague Arthur McGiffert with going beyond the bounds of sound doctrine because he questioned the historicity of Jesus' physical resurrection, considered the virgin birth of Jesus a myth, and challenged the traditional authorship of the Gospels of Matthew, Mark, and Luke. In 1904 Briggs moved from the Robinson Chair to a new one in "theological encyclopedia and symbolics," reflecting his broad theological and ecumenical concerns.

Briggs's personality created enemies within the church. He was stubborn and self-confident to the point that some considered him truculent and arrogant. In his first article for the *Presbyterian Review*, he asserted that he was the "first authority on the Westminster Standards in our country" (1 [1880]: 128). One historian has written of his "bellicose personality, which made him democratically adept at alienating people of widely disparate beliefs" (Massa, p. 162). He was also beloved and admired by a large number of friends around the world. He died at home in the Union Seminary apartments.

Briggs was one of the most accomplished biblical scholars and historians of his day. Virtually all English-speaking students of biblical Hebrew know his name, for he was one of the editors of the standard lexicon of biblical Hebrew, Brown, Driver, and Briggs's *Hebrew Lexicon* (1891–1906). He was coeditor of the International Critical Commentary and contributed the two volumes on the Psalms. He established the International Theological Library, which published important works in a variety of fields, including Old and New Testament studies, the history of religion, and Christian doctrine. He was a founding member of the Society of Biblical Literature in 1880 and its fourth president in 1889–1891. He and Frederic Gardiner began the *Journal of Biblical Literature* in the next year. Typical of his contributions to biblical criticism was *A General Introduction to the Study of Holy Scripture* (1899). He also made numerous significant contributions to biblical theology and the history of Christian thought, including *The Bible, the Church, and the Reason* (1892), *Messianic Prophecy* (1886), *American Presbyterianism: Its Origin and Early History* (1885), and *A History of the Study of Theology* (2 vols., 1916).

• Archives and documents from Briggs's trials are in the library of Union Theological Seminary. Charles R. Gillett published an extensive bibliography of Briggs's publications in *Essays in Modern Theology and Related Subjects*, ed. C. H. Toy (1911). Biographical information is in H. P. Smith, "Chas. Augustus Briggs," *American Journal of Theology* 17 (Oct. 1913): 497–508. An excellent recent study of the controversy, including a bibliography of both primary and secondary sources, is M. S. Massa, *Charles Augustus Briggs and the Crisis of Historical Criticism* (1990). See also J. Brown, *The Rise of Biblical Criticism in America, 1800–1870: The New England Scholars* (1969); Carl E. Hatch, *The Charles A. Briggs Heresy Trial: Prologue to Twentieth-Century Liberal Protestantism* (1969); Mark A. Noll, *Between Faith and Criticism: Evangelicals, Scholarship, and the Bible in America* (1986). Major documents from the trials are *Response to the Charges and Specifications Submitted to the Presbytery of New York* (1891), *The Case against Professor Briggs* (1892), *The Defence of Professor Briggs before the Presbytery of New York, December 13, 14, 15, 19, and 22, 1892* (1893), *The Question of the Original Party in the Case of Dr. Briggs* (1892), *The Presbyterian Church in the United States of America against the Rev. Charles A. Briggs, D.D.* (1892), and *Proceedings of the General Assembly of 1893 against Charles Augustus Briggs, 105th Annual Meeting* (1893). His obituary is in the *New York Times*, 9 June 1913.

GENE M. TUCKER

BRIGGS, Clare A. (5 Aug. 1875–3 Jan. 1930), cartoonist, was born in Reedsburg, Wisconsin, the son of William Pardee Briggs, who sold farm machinery, and Nancy Ellen Stewart. His family later moved on to Dixon, Illinois, and finally to Lincoln, Nebraska, where he studied drawing at the normal school. He had shown some talent for drawing as a boy and some of his sketches were printed in the *Western Penman* (1895). He attended the University of Nebraska for two years, but dropped out because he wanted to draw. In 1896, after leaving college, he began his newspaper career as a sketch artist for the *St. Louis Globe Democrat*. The new half-tone process of photographic reproduction was perfected in 1897 and quickly reduced the demand for sketch artists, so Briggs turned to drawing cartoons. In 1898 he was hired by the *St. Louis Chronicle* as a political cartoonist, but because his work was limited to drawing war-related cartoons, he lost his job when the Spanish-American War ended in 1899. Later that year, he moved to New York City and attended the Pratt Institute studying art, and supporting himself with odd jobs while submitting cartoons to the *New York World* and *New York Journal*.

In 1900 Briggs returned briefly to Lincoln, Nebraska, to marry Ruth Owen; they had three children. In the same year William Randolph Hearst, recognizing his talent, hired Briggs and sent him to Chicago as a cartoonist for the Hearst dailies, the *Chicago American* and *Chicago Examiner*. His development as a famous cartoonist began with a comic strip called "A. Piker, Clerk," which ran in both the *Chicago American* and *Chicago Examiner*. It had a racetrack background at a time when horse racing was very popular and was printed on weekdays in the sports section. Some think that "A. Piker, Clerk" may have been the first daily comic strip. Unfortunately, it was capriciously canceled by Hearst just as it gained a following.

Briggs's pen made him a local celebrity in Chicago. He was eventually hired in 1907 by the *Chicago Tribune*, where he developed "Oh Skinnay, In the Days of Real Sport" loosely based on his own boyhood adventures. This was the first of Briggs' panels to become a real success. It followed the adventures of a boy growing up in a small town and was used as the basis for a motion picture in 1919. Briggs used commonplace topics such as tracking mud, setting off fireworks, being seen with a girl, and having to dress up to recall the "good old days."

Briggs developed several other popular series: "When a Feller Needs a Friend"; "Ain't it a Grand and Glorious Feelin'"; "Somebody's Always Taking the Joy out of Life"; and "How to Start the Day Wrong," in the years he worked in Chicago. He excelled in the nostalgic recreation of boyhood in the recent past, which had great appeal in an increasingly fast-paced world, delighting his readers with stories about the highs and lows of childhood. His strips were well drawn and both adults and children enjoyed their gentle humor.

In 1914 Briggs was signed by the *New York Tribune* Syndicate and remained with it until his death, working at the flagship paper, the *New York Herald-Tribune*. He broadened his scope. Without discarding his original topics, he developed strips that depicted the problems and triumphs of the urban lower-middle class male and female at home and at work. He worked in a realistic but incisively humorous style that is still fresh and enjoyable. In 1919 he began his most famous strip "Mr. and Mrs." It featured the true-to-life marital warfare conducted by Vi and Joe Green. It did not have an ongoing plot; each strip focused on some foible of married life. This strip was made into a radio serial in 1929 and was the only one of his creations to be continued after his death.

Briggs credited his colleague John McCutcheon with having the most influence on his work as a cartoonist. McCutcheon, five years Briggs's senior, was the first to draw small-town boys in a motto series. However, Briggs went on to develop a different and distinctive style of his own. Although Briggs's draftsmanship was excellent, it was always subordinate to his ideas. He had a highly developed sense of the ridiculous and an innate ability to write captions that exactly matched his panels. In addition, his drawings of small town and city life are so accurate that they provide a historical record of their era.

Briggs also displayed a social conscience that was rare in the comic pages at this time. Some of his "city kids'" cartoons point out the callous unconcern of the wealthy toward the needy. Every summer Briggs devoted one of his cartoons to the cause of the Fresh Air Fund. In 1929, "When a Feller Needs a Friend" featured a group of tenement house children on a roof top, surrounded by tall buildings. Its caption read "Fresh Air."

In "Real Folks at Home" Briggs drew attention to the importance of ordinary people, including street cleaners, cabdrivers, traffic cops, and hod carriers by basing a strip on their homelife. Disdaining didacticism, he celebrated Instead the commonplace events of life. His drawings were published as a series of compilations of his newspaper work and were very popular because they dealt with the idiosyncrasies and weaknesses of humanity. His panels also provide an excellent source of information about everyday life during his generation.

By 1920 Briggs was listed as one of the country's highest paid cartoonists in the *Literary Digest*. He, his wife and their three children enjoyed a comfortable life in New Rochelle, New York. But his financial success and personal acclaim were cut short by illness. Briggs suffered from lung congestion coupled with a nervous disorder that caused the degeneration of his optic nerve which made drawing difficult in his last years. He died in New York City.

• Biographical information concerning Briggs can be found in his books: *Oh Skinnay, In the Days of Real Sport* (1913), *When a Feller Needs a Friend* (1914), *How to Draw Cartoons* (1926), and *Selected Drawings of Clare Briggs, Memorial Edition* (1930). Obituaries are in the *New York Herald Tribune* and the *New York Times*, both 4 Jan. 1930.

ELSA A. NYSTROM

BRIGGS, Ellis Ormsbee (1 Dec. 1899–21 Feb. 1976), diplomat, was born in Watertown, Massachusetts, the son of James Briggs and Lucy Hill. The family moved to the Riverdale section of the Bronx, New York, where his father worked as an insurance broker. Briggs attended Dartmouth College, graduating in 1921. For two years afterward he taught English and geography at Robert College in Constantinople, Turkey. From 1923 to 1925 he worked as a freelance writer before passing the foreign service examination. He received his first assignment in 1926 as vice consul in the U.S. embassy in Lima, Peru.

For the next thirty-seven years Briggs served in the U.S. Department of State. His career had two distinct stages. From 1926 to 1947 he rose through the professional ranks, with service in various posts in Latin America, Asia, and Washington, D.C. He also participated in special missions to Liberia, London, and Geneva. In 1944 he became ambassador to the Dominican Republic. He served in that position until 1945, when the State Department transferred him to the position of minister-counselor to the U.S. embassy in Chungking, China, assisting Ambassador Patrick Hurley. After a brief stint in China Briggs returned to Washington to work as director of the Office of American Republic Affairs. From that position he helped to clarify U.S. policy on multilateral interventions and opposition to authoritarian regimes in Latin America.

In the second stage of his diplomatic career Briggs served as the chief U.S. representative in several nations. He received a post as ambassador to Uruguay (1947–1949), and later he was sent to Czechoslovakia following the 1948 Communist takeover and purge. He accepted and implemented the hard-line position adopted by U.S. officials to contain the perceived spread of communism in Central Europe and elsewhere. He also won notoriety among State Department officials for his attempts to cut the embassy staff, arguing that the bureaucracy had become overburdened by the presence of the representatives of too many U.S. government agencies other than the State Department. Czech officials aided the process when they demanded the recall of two-thirds of the U.S. staff in 1950. Another crisis developed in 1951 during Briggs's tenure when Czech officials arrested an American correspondent, William Oatis, on charges of spying and sentenced him to ten years in prison. After intense negotiations Briggs secured a pardon for Oatis in 1952, the same year he left for a new assignment.

Briggs's next challenge eclipsed the problems he had faced in Czechoslovakia. In 1952 he arrived in South Korea to replace Ambassador John J. Muccio. For three years he worked with U.S. military officials and other diplomats to craft an acceptable armistice with North Korean and Chinese officials. For his tireless service President Dwight D. Eisenhower awarded him the nation's highest civilian honor, the Presidential Medal of Freedom. After leaving Korea, Briggs returned as ambassador to his first station in Peru (1955–1956) and then went to Brazil (1956–1959); the posts were uneventful compared to his previous two stations. During this period Briggs found time to publish a book on his avocation, bird-hunting—*Shots Heard round the World: An Ambassador's Hunting Adventures on Four Continents* (1957). In 1959 the Dwight Eisenhower administration appointed him U.S. ambassador to Greece. The following year Briggs received the highest rank in the Foreign Service, career ambassador. In 1961 President John F. Kennedy nominated him as ambassador to Spain, but an illness forced his resignation from the Foreign Service and he never took the position.

For the remainder of his life Briggs devoted himself to writing and lecturing about diplomacy and the foreign service from his summer home in Hanover, New Hampshire, and his winter home in Gainesville, Florida. He contributed to the *New York Times Magazine*, *Saturday Evening Post*, *Esquire*, *Reader's Digest*, and several other periodicals. He also published two more books, *Farewell to Foggy Bottom: The Recollections of a Career Diplomat* (1964) and *Anatomy of Diplomacy: The Origins and Execution of American Foreign Policy* (1968). Briggs testified before Congress on several occasions regarding foreign policy issues, including foreign-service reform. He served as chairman of the Dartmouth Alumni College and worked with the Dartmouth *Bulletin*. He died in Gainesville. He was survived by his wife, Lucy Barnard, whom he had married in 1928, and two children who had followed him into the foreign service.

Ambassador Briggs represented a new type of diplomat that emerged during the twentieth century. He was a product of the Rogers Act, which professionalized the Foreign Service in 1924. After that time political appointments ceased to dominate the foreign service, leading to more consistent and professional representation. More importantly, Briggs served in some of the most difficult positions during U.S. foreign relations of the postwar era, especially during the early Cold War. As an ambassador behind the Iron Curtain in Korea during the latter stages of the conflict, and during potentially volatile periods in Latin America, Briggs participated in formulating policy as the United States emerged as the dominant world power in competition with the Soviet Union. People like Briggs effectively set the course of containment that the United States followed through the end of the Cold War.

• An oral history interview with Briggs is at the Dwight D. Eisenhower Presidential Library in Abilene, Kans. Obituaries are in the *New York Times*, 23 Feb. 1976, and the Department of State *Newsletter*, Mar. 1976. Other information can be found in the State Department edited series, *Foreign Relations of the United States*, and contemporary issues of the State Department *Bulletin*.

KYLE LONGLEY

BRIGGS, Emily Pomona Edson (14 Sept. 1830–3 July 1910), journalist who wrote under the pseudonym "Olivia," was born in Burton, Ohio, the daughter of Robert Edson, a blacksmith, and Mary Umberfield (or Umberville). In 1840 the family moved to an Illinois farm, and fourteen years later they moved again, to Chicago, Illinois, where Emily's father succeeded in real estate ventures. Emily attended local schools and had a short career as a schoolteacher in Ohio before she married John R. Briggs, Jr., a former Wisconsin legislator, in 1854; they had two children, one of whom survived to adulthood.

In August 1854 Briggs's husband became part owner of the *Daily Whig* in Keokuk, Iowa, so they traveled westward. The newspaper was renamed the *Gate City* the following year, but it foundered and ultimately failed. John Briggs, who had become friendly with Abraham Lincoln when he reported on the future president's debates with Stephen Douglas, joined the newly created Republican party. Those associations helped him in 1861 to secure a position in Washington, D.C., as the financial clerk in the House of Representatives. Emily Briggs reminisced years later in an interview in the *Washington Post* (10 July 1904) that her husband was able to provide inside information to Lincoln about activities in the Border states and that the couple often visited the White House.

As a clerk, John Briggs reported to Colonel John W. Forney, who also was the owner of the *Philadelphia Press* and the *Washington Chronicle*. Emily Briggs, angered by criticism of women clerks in the newspapers, wrote an unsigned letter to Forney's Washington paper defending the work of women. Briggs told her interviewer that "something in its style" caught the attention of Forney, who tracked down the letter's author and asked to meet her. "I was scared to death," she remembered, "Of course, I thought that he was going to blame me for that article. 'I can't go, John. I can't meet him.' My husband explained that I would have to, that it wouldn't be wise to refuse such a request and I went in fear and trembling" (*Washington Post*, 10 July 1904).

From this encounter came Briggs's first foray into journalism. Forney asked her to work for the Philadelphia newspaper, and she began by writing book reviews. She eventually wrote up to six columns a week, most of them about society news from Washington. Because social taboos discouraged the printing of a woman's name in the newspaper except when she married or died, an editor in Philadelphia chose the pen name "Olivia" to sign to Briggs's work. The "Olivia" byline quickly became a popular item in the Philadelphia paper at a time when few women were being published—although editors were becoming more aware that women writers could encourage women readers, who, in turn, could bring in advertising. Briggs stayed with the Philadelphia newspaper despite an offer from a New York paper, partly because she was earning $3,500 annually for her efforts.

Unlike scores of women journalists who were forced to earn a living when their marriage failed or their source of family support disappeared, Briggs worked free of most domestic obligations. In fact, the Briggs family lived in a hotel so that she was unburdened by of household chores. She said that she completed her news-gathering by day and finished her writing by 8 P.M., when a messenger on horseback would claim the column and rush it to the train station so that it could arrive in Philadelphia for printing in the next day's editions.

One of only four women to break down the gender barrier at the Congressional Press Gallery, Briggs opened doors throughout the city for her readers. She described a visit to the House of Representatives as being "hermetically sealed up in a huge can" (31 Jan. 1866). An essay on a night session of the U.S. Senate described for readers how the Capitol dome was lit "like the great flaming carbuncle on the mountain's brow" and how the chamber itself "seemed touched with the fairy hand of enchantment at night" (20 Mar. 1869).

But while Briggs wooed her readers with prose laden with metaphor and description and primarily gained a reputation as a social commentator, she addressed timely subjects. She deplored the treatment of blacks in the wake of the Civil War. "Slavery is dead, it is true, but the black man is not a citizen," she wrote. However, she stated, "This is not a political view of the subject, only a feeble woman's, who can do not for the freedman but utter shriek after shriek for him" (9 Mar. 1866). And in an essay on woman suffrage, rather than focus on the highly charged issue itself, she lamented that no woman's voice was strong enough to project throughout a lecture hall. Briggs then described how the heavy black silk trimmed in scarlet complimented the main speaker that evening. The essay (18 Jan. 1870), describing the fashions worn by women's rights luminaries Elizabeth Cady Stanton, Susan B. Anthony, Pauline Davis, and others, sidestepped the actual issue of suffrage. Despite her personal ambivalence toward suffrage, Briggs dedicated five consecutive columns to coverage of the most minute detail of the National Woman Suffrage Convention in 1870 and gave even more space to the annual meeting the following year.

After Briggs's husband died in 1872, she continued her commentary on Washington's social life, deliberately embracing a writing style dependent on description and devoid of serious political overtones. With important social connections herself and a reputation among the town's Republicans, she enjoyed great success throughout Ulysses S. Grant's presidency. After Rutherford B. Hayes's election, the White House doors closed to her for reasons that remain unclear. Her status as a regular correspondent for the *Philadelphia Press* ceased, although she did send letters to other newspapers. She served as first president of the Women's National Press Association, which was founded in 1882. Also that year she stopped her regular journalistic work.

Briggs's columns had provided readers in Philadelphia and other cities where her work was reprinted with a glimpse of the social and political life of the nation's capital from 1866 to 1882. In 1882 she retired to "the Maples," a mansion on Capitol Hill, and held court as a popular hostess. She selected her favorite columns for inclusion in the collection *The Olivia Letters* (1906). After she died in Washington, D.C., she was remembered as one of the first women to be a regular contributor to a newspaper and also to open the doors to women journalists in the nation's capital.

• A series of letters by Briggs is in the Vinnie Ream Hoxie Papers at the Library of Congress, but the letters were written after her career in journalism had ended. The most complete treatment of Briggs's life is in Maurine Hoffman Beasley, "Pens and Petticoats: The Story of the First Washington Women Correspondents" (Ph.D. diss., George Washington Univ., 1974), which includes an interview with Briggs's granddaughter and a feature interview with Briggs from the *Washington Post*, 10 July 1904. See also Lina Mainiero, ed., *American Women Writers from Colonial Times to the Present*, vol. 1 (1979). Obituaries are in the *Washington Evening Star*, 4 July 1910, and the *Washington Post*, 5 July 1910.

AGNES HOOPER GOTTLIEB

BRIGGS, George Nixon (12 Apr. 1796–12 Sept. 1861), lawyer, congressman, and governor, was born in Adams, Massachusetts, the son of blacksmith Allen Briggs, a veteran of the revolutionary war, and Nancy Brown. As with many settlers in the Berkshire area of Massachusetts, the Briggses had moved north from Rhode Island and were earnest Baptists (although Nancy Briggs had come from a Huguenot family). At age thirteen Briggs, one of twelve siblings, was apprenticed to Quaker John Allen, a hatter in White Creek, New York. He returned home in 1811 to help his father and attended grammar school for about a year. In 1813 he studied law with Ambrose Kasson (also spelled Kapen) of Adams, Massachusetts; the following year he moved to the office of Luther Washburn in Lanesboro. During his apprenticeship in White Creek, Briggs, then a Quaker, had experienced a conversion at a revival and thereby became a Baptist. While studying law in Lanesboro and helping to found a Baptist church there, he met Harriet Hall, whom he married in May 1818; they would have at least two children.

After being admitted to the bar of Berkshire County, Massachusetts, in October 1818, Briggs practiced law in the towns of Adams, Lanesboro, and Pittsfield. In 1824 he served as the Lanesboro town clerk; from 1824 until 1831 he was registrar of deeds of Berkshire

County; and during 1826 he was chairman of the county commissioners of highways. Although he gained respect and prominence—especially after his 1827 defense of a Stockbridge Indian whom he believed was unjustly accused of murder—his law practice did not make Briggs wealthy. This circumstance delayed his political career, for when his name was submitted for consideration as a representative in the state legislature, it was not accepted because he was not a property owner.

In the election of November 1830 the Eleventh Congressional District chose Briggs as its representative to the U.S. Congress (which did not require property ownership), and he served there from 1831 to 1843. Although he was once a Democrat, Briggs entered the Twenty-second Congress as an Anti-Jacksonian and a supporter of Henry Clay. He was returned to the Twenty-third Congress as an Anti-Jacksonian and to the Twenty-fourth through the Twenty-seventh Congresses as a Whig. Briggs was a member of the Committee on Public Expenditures, which he chaired in the Twenty-sixth Congress, and the Committee on Post Offices and Roads, which he chaired in the Twenty-seventh Congress.

A strong supporter of protective tariffs, Briggs accurately represented the economic interests of his constituents when, on 14 January 1833 he spoke in opposition to a bill designed to reduce duties on imports. On the most divisive issue of his tenure, Briggs was totally opposed to the extension of slavery. In June 1836 the House considered a bill admitting Arkansas to the Union. Because the constitution for the proposed new state forbade the abolition of slavery without the consent of slave owners, Briggs gave a forceful speech supporting the amendment proposed by John Quincy Adams that denied congressional sanction of the offensive article.

As much as Briggs worried about issues that were dividing the country, he addressed them in a temperate manner. He was not an orator in the House of Representatives; his style was modest, and his appeal was to reason. Briggs's frequent letters to family and friends reveal his concern for his country, his compassion, and his humor. To Harriet, he wrote of his hope that a Supreme Court decision on Cherokee lands would restore just treatment to that "much injured race." For his nephew, he described Vice President John C. Calhoun as "nearly six feet high, a little round shouldered, and stoops; . . . he appears as if he were made of nail-rods" (quoted in Richards, p. 104).

Briggs declined renomination for the Twenty-eighth Congress, and in 1843, after twelve years in Washington, he moved back to the Berkshires. That same year the Whigs of Massachusetts nominated him for governor; it was a wise choice for several reasons: Briggs supported temperance, he was a conservative regarding the slavery problem and thus acceptable to the cotton manufacturers, and he was from western Massachusetts where he might capture some rural Democratic votes.

Briggs served as governor from 3 January 1844 until 11 January 1851. His seven one-year terms occurred during a decade of increasingly bitter controversy over national issues and the strengthening of abolitionism as a political factor in Massachusetts politics. This precipitated the breakup of the state Whig and Democratic parties and the inclusion on Massachusetts ballots of Native-American (anti-immigrant), Liberty (abolition), and later, Free Soil candidates. Consequently, four of Briggs's seven elections had to be decided by the state senate; his popular vote in each case was only a plurality, and state law required an absolute majority.

Although Briggs condemned the Mexican War (1846–1848) as unjust and designed to extend slavery, he explained in his address to the state legislature on 12 January 1847 that loyalty to the Union compelled him to supply the Massachusetts troops requested by the federal government. For this, abolitionist preacher Wendell Phillips denounced him as a traitor to his principles.

Despite his lack of formal schooling Governor Briggs was a particularly strong advocate for the schools and colleges. He cooperated with educator Horace Mann's efforts to improve schools and teacher training, and he constantly urged the legislature to increase its support for education. He also attended teacher institutes and spoke out in favor of better educational opportunities at all levels.

Briggs attracted nationwide attention and withstood extreme social pressure because of an extraordinary criminal case that took place while he was governor. In 1849 Harvard professor John Webster was sentenced to death for the murder of Dr. George Parkman. Although his guilt was indisputable, the state attorney general appealed for executive clemency because Webster was a distinguished professional man. In spite of public sentiment, attempted bribes, and even threats to his person, the governor refused to either commute the sentence or pardon Webster.

When his gubernatorial duties permitted, Briggs worked on his beloved farm on the sunny slope of a Berkshire hill and carried on his religious and philanthropic work. At various times between 1846 and his death, he was president of the American Baptist Missionary Union, the American Temperance Union, and the American Baptist Missionary Union, the American Temperance Union, and the American Tract Society. For sixteen years he was a trustee of Williams College (Williamstown, Mass.). On retirement, in 1851, he became even more active in those endeavors and practiced law, with his youngest son as his partner. In 1853 he was a member of the Massachusetts Constitutional Convention and was appointed judge of the Court of Common Pleas. His public service concluded in 1858 when that court was abolished, but he remained concerned about public affairs. Briggs was a founder of the state Republican party and a strong supporter of Abraham Lincoln and the preservation of the Union. In 1861 he was appointed a commissioner to adjust a claims dispute between the United States and New Granada (now part of Colombia), but before he could serve, he was mortally wounded by a gunshot wound that was accidentally self-inflicted. He died at home and is buried in Pittsfield Cemetery.

Sometimes criticized for his religious and temperance activities, Briggs met such criticism by asking how he might better spend his time. Unlike influential thinker Ralph Waldo Emerson, who saw slavery as a simple wrong and therefore could justify the lawlessness of extreme abolitionists, Briggs had a profound respect for the orderliness of government and for the complexities of preserving the Union. His beliefs were strong, his pragmatic policies clearly stated; no matter what the issue or the intensity of his belief, his politics did not descend to the personal level.

• Briggs's remarks in the U.S. House of Representatives are reported in the *Congressional Globe* for the years 1831–1843. *Massachusetts Acts and Resolves* for the years 1844–1850 include Briggs's seven inaugural addresses as governor. *Great in Goodness: A Memoir of George N. Briggs, Governor of the Commonwealth of Massachusetts, from 1844–1851* (1866), by the Reverend William C. Richards, is an encomium, but it contains important biographical details and many of his letters, which provide valuable insights into his private as well as his public life. A century later Briggs was the subject of an admiring biographical sketch that focused on the Parkman murder case in Theodore A. Stevens, *Anecdotes about 101 Distinguished Americans* (1964). A contemporary sketch is included in *Williams Biographical Annals* (1871). For Briggs's role in the Massachusetts political scene of the pre–Civil War decades see Albert B. Hart, ed., *Commonwealth History of Massachusetts*, vol. 4 (1930), and Arthur B. Darling, *Political Changes in Massachusetts 1824–1848: A Study of Liberal Movements in Politics* (1925), which contains a lengthy bibliography. For a more recent assessment see Thomas H. O'Connor, *Lords of the Loom: The Cotton Whigs and the Coming of the Civil War* (1968). An obituary is in the *New York Times*, 14 Sept. 1861.

SYLVIA B. LARSON

BRIGGS, LeBaron Russell (11 Dec. 1855–24 Apr. 1934), educator, was born in Salem, Massachusetts, the son of George Ware Briggs, a minister, and his second wife, Lycia Jane Russell. In 1867 George Briggs accepted a position at Cambridge as minister of the Third Congregational Society, in large part so that his sons might eventually attend his alma mater, Harvard College. In 1871, after attending Cambridge High School, LeBaron matriculated at Harvard College and graduated four years later, fourth in his class. As an undergraduate, he was most impressed by two professors, George Lane and G. H. Palmer, who taught him Latin and Greek, respectively. The next year, Briggs and his close friend Denman Ross spent several months at the University of Leipzig in graduate study. On returning to the United States, Briggs contemplated obtaining a Ph.D. in Greek while doing private tutoring and teaching in and around Cambridge. In the fall of 1878 he received a call from Harvard president Charles Eliot, offering him a one-year position as a tutor in Greek. Briggs accepted and at the end of the year found his appointment extended for two more years.

In the meantime, Briggs discovered that the field of English was emerging as an area of study. He decided to pursue his graduate coursework in English instead of Greek and began work toward an M.A. in 1881. His mother, a major figure in his young life, passed away in November 1881. After completing his degree in 1882, Briggs, still in mourning, left to study at Oxford. None of the courses in English offered at Oxford suited Briggs. Instead he and his now elderly father spent the better part of the year traveling across the Continent and becoming better acquainted. By the end of the trip, having resolved his bereavement and gained a parent, Briggs returned to Cambridge refreshed and invigorated. In 1883 he married Mary deQuedville, whom he had met in 1879 when he offered his course in Latin to the Society for the Collegiate Instruction of Women (later the Harvard Annex and now Radcliffe College). The Briggses had three children.

On his return to Harvard in 1883, Briggs was assigned to Professor Adams Sherman Hill, a member of the faculty since 1872, as a lecturer in English. President Eliot, who shared with Hill a strong belief in the discipline of good writing and command of the language, had asked Hill to instruct all Harvard men in English, but Hill's age and poor health would not permit him to undertake such a task alone. In anticipation of rapidly increasing enrollments, Eliot assigned Briggs and two of his colleagues to assist Hill. Although English composition was required in the sophomore year, Hill and Briggs soon decided that the requirement was more appropriate for the freshman year of study. When the course was moved, Briggs discovered that most freshmen students were in dire need of instructions for life, not just academics. Accordingly, he began to offer advice, support, and fatherly assistance to many of the new students who attended his classes. In short order he became legendary among the young men as a confidante and mentor.

Briggs and Hill developed a pattern of English instruction that became widely known as "freshman composition." They emphasized the value of daily themes and journals. Their new pedagogy was celebrated widely and set a standard for college English courses. In addition to freshman composition, Briggs taught an advanced writing course that was very popular. Over the course of forty-six years, Briggs taught many aspiring writers in "English 5," among them novelist John Dos Passos, poet E. E. Cummings, and humorist Robert Benchley.

Impressed by Briggs's natural charm with students, Eliot appointed him in 1891 to be dean of the college, the first dean of student affairs in American higher education. Relatively young and more youthful in appearance than his thirty-five years, Briggs was an immediate success. He continued to teach but also provided a strong, student-oriented voice to the administrative circle of Harvard College. The demands of serving students at all hours, often seven days a week, in addition to his teaching, were unrelenting. Briggs's popularity was exhausting him. To provide some relief, Eliot reassigned Briggs to the deanship of the faculty of arts and sciences in 1902. Yet in 1903, in addition to his other duties, Briggs took on the "part-time" job of president of Radcliffe College, a position he held for the next twenty years. He also held the Boylston Chair in Rhetoric and Oratory in recognition of his faculty service.

In his roles as dean, president, and teacher, Briggs exhibited a passion for his work and a dedication to students and the betterment of the institution that earned him immeasurable respect as well as the loyalty and adoration of those who knew him. As a measure of his importance to the men of Harvard, at Briggs's last commencement in 1925, President A. Lawrence Lowell announced that an endowment fund of $63,490 had been established by alumni "out of the depth of their respect, loyalty, gratitude, and affection for Dean Briggs." Two years earlier, at the end of his Radcliffe career, a new residence hall had been named for him in honor of his service to the women of Radcliffe. He died in Milwaukee, Wisconsin, while visiting his daughter.

Briggs spent the majority of his adult life in the service of his alma mater, Harvard College. His self-effacing, warm, and open manner personified the best of the Harvard experience for thousands of graduates in the late nineteenth and early twentieth centuries. While serving under Presidents Eliot and Lowell, he set patterns for student affairs, institutional governance, and leadership in college administration that extended well beyond Harvard and continued to influence higher education long after his career was over.

• Briggs's writings include *School, College, and Character* (1901) and *To College Teachers of Composition* (1928). His actions and activities are chronicled in annual reports of Harvard College and Radcliffe as well as in the archival collections of Harvard. The most complete account of his life is Rollo W. Brown, *Dean Briggs* (1926).

ROBERT SCHWARTZ

BRIGGS, Lyman James (7 May 1874–25 Mar. 1963), physicist, was born in Assyria, Michigan, the son of Chauncey Lewis Briggs and Susanna Isabella McKelvey, farmers. At age fifteen Briggs entered the agricultural program of Michigan Agricultural College (later Michigan State University). There he met Katherine Elizabeth Cook, a classmate and the daughter of a professor of zoology and entomology at the college. He graduated first and she second in the class of 1893, and they were married in 1896. They had two children, though the son died in infancy.

Briggs obtained a master's degree in physics from the University of Michigan in 1895. He then entered the doctoral program at Johns Hopkins University and, under renowned experimental physicist Henry A. Rowland, took part in the first studies at that institution of the newly discovered X-rays. In 1896, while a graduate student, Briggs secured an appointment to the Bureau of Soils in the U.S. Department of Agriculture. He received his Ph.D. in physics from Johns Hopkins in 1901.

Between 1897 and 1917 Briggs published extensively on the physical properties of soils. He introduced a number of powerful experimental methods and fundamental concepts into the science of soil mechanics. One such innovation was a procedure for classifying soils according to their ability to retain moisture after centrifuging, which became the standard methodology in the field. He and frequent co-investigator H. L. Shantz introduced the "wilting coefficient," a measurement indicating the lower limit of soil water usable for plant growth. These and many other of his investigations were central to a scientific understanding and evaluation of the nature of soils and were important in developing and maintaining arable land, particularly in the plains states. Beginning in 1906 Briggs organized and then directed the Biophysical Laboratory in what was later the Bureau of Plant Industry of the Department of Agriculture.

Briggs's research at the agriculture department was interrupted with the United States's entry into World War I in 1917, when he was assigned to work at the National Bureau of Standards (NBS, in 1988 renamed the National Institute for Standards and Technology). NBS had been established in 1901 to determine and maintain standards of measurement. It had grown and developed dramatically under the leadership of its first director, Samuel W. Stratton. Even before the war NBS became the largest institution of its kind in the world and the only U.S. laboratory with research responsibilities touching virtually all the physical and engineering sciences. Throughout mobilization NBS conducted war-related research in areas as diverse as radio communications, photography and optical instrumentation, synthetic substitutes for critical materials, and the testing and specification of supplies. During this period Briggs helped develop navigational instruments for the navy and directed the installation and early investigations of the first wind tunnel at NBS. One result of his work was the earth inductor compass, a navigational instrument that solved some of the difficulties in direction-finding for aircraft by using the electrical effect of motion in a magnetic field, for which he and collaborator Paul R. Heyl received the American Philosophical Society's Magellan Medal in 1922. In 1927 Charles A. Lindbergh (1902–1974) used the compass in his historic transatlantic flight.

Briggs received a permanent appointment to NBS in 1920 as chief of the Division of Mechanics and Sound, and in 1926 was promoted to assistant director for research and testing. In 1919 he brought a promising young scientist, Hugh L. Dryden, to the bureau. Dryden, who earned his doctorate from Johns Hopkins the following year at age nineteen, was appointed head of the NBS aeronautics section by age twenty and later became a deputy administrator of NASA. Briggs and Dryden conducted important wind tunnel research on airfoils into the supersonic range.

When the second NBS director, George K. Burgess, died in 1932, Briggs became acting director. He was confirmed permanent director in 1933 after Franklin D. Roosevelt assumed the presidency. The next six years were extraordinarily difficult for the bureau. The country was well into the depression, and the new administration slashed the bureau's funds by half. Briggs was forced to lay off one-third of the bureau's staff, reducing their number to less than 700, the lowest level in seventeen years. The remaining staff were kept engaged largely through imaginative use of alternative funding and many part-time appointments. Briggs kept the NBS operational until the mobilization for World War II again brought robust growth to the laboratory. By the end of the war the staff numbered well above 2,000, and that number would double during the Korean War.

In 1939 President Roosevelt appointed Briggs chairman of the original Uranium Committee, which was created in response to the warning of physicists Albert Einstein, Eugene Wigner, and Leo Szilard that the fissioning of uranium might make possible a superweapon that could determine the outcome of the war. During the war Briggs served as an administrator for the Manhattan Project, which involved about sixty Bureau of Standards scientists. The single most intensive war-related project at NBS, however, was not the atomic bomb but the radio proximity fuze, or VT fuze. The VT fuze detonated a piece of ordnance, such as a bomb, rocket, or shell, in the vicinity of its target rather than on contact, vastly multiplying its effectiveness. This innovation was considered so strategically significant that it barely saw combat until near the end of the war, because many feared that a fuze that failed to detonate would fall into the hands of the enemy, providing a prototype. The fuze project and several other NBS efforts, such as the guided missile program, led directly to the many large and vigorous programs in advanced electronics at NBS after the war.

Briggs retired from the NBS directorship in November 1945. He was succeeded by the noted nuclear physicist Edward U. Condon. After forty-nine years of service in the federal government, Briggs was designated emeritus director of NBS and given laboratory space to conduct his own laboratory work. He continued research and publication on negative pressure in fluids, an abiding interest, nearly until his death.

Several characteristic threads run the length of Lyman Briggs's distinguished career. In the words of friend and later NBS director Allen Astin, Briggs "was not a powerful administrator, yet his wisdom and skill coupled with a gentle firmness inspired the staff and won high respect from the other officials in the government with whom he had to work." It was patience and constancy rather than boldness of new initiatives that preserved what was the nation's most important national physical laboratory during the depression. Had he been given the choice, Briggs might have chosen to return to the laboratory, where he felt truly at home. In his research Briggs showed imagination as a practical problem solver rather than as a theorist, and his great talent was in the design and application of experimental equipment and instrumentation.

Briggs was for many years intimately associated with the National Geographic Society and was chairman of its Research Committee beginning in 1934. He helped design the instrument packages for the stratospheric balloon launches of 1934 and 1935 (Explorers I and II) and led the society's solar eclipse expedition in 1947. He was president of the American Physical Society in 1938 and was a member of many other learned societies, including the National Academy of Sciences and the American Association for the Advancement of Science. Among other awards he received six honorary doctorates and, for his contributions during World War II, the Medal of Merit, awarded in 1948.

Briggs died at his home in Washington, D.C.

• Briggs published over 100 articles in professional journals, including *Physical Review*, *Journal of Physical Chemistry*, and journals of the U.S. Department of Agriculture and the National Bureau of Standards. A selective partial listing of these publications is included in "Lyman J. Briggs: Recognition of His Eightieth Birthday," *Scientific Monthly* 78 (May 1954): 269–74. The issue includes seven articles that together provide the single best source on his scientific and administrative career. The Briggs papers are held in the National Archives, Washington, D.C. Biographical essays have appeared in the *American Philosophical Society Yearbook* (1963) and *Bulletin–Cosmos Club* (Mar. 1974) among others. An overview of the activities of the NBS, from its organization to the mid-1960s, can be found in Rexmond C. Cochrane, *Measures for Progress: A History of the National Bureau of Standards* (1966). An analysis of the NBS during its first two decades, including some discussion of the Briggs administration, may be found in Nelson R. Kellogg, "Gauging the Nation: Samuel Wesley Stratton and the Invention of the National Bureau of Standards" (Ph.D. diss., Johns Hopkins Univ., 1991).

For useful material on the personal life of Briggs and his relationship with his daughter Isabel, who developed the Myers-Briggs Type Indicator (a method of determining personality profile), see Frances Wright Saunders, *Katherine and Isabel: Mother's Light, Daughter's Journey* (1991).

NELSON R. KELLOGG

BRIGGS, Robert William (10 Dec. 1911–4 Mar. 1983), developmental biologist, was born in Watertown, Massachusetts. His parents' names are not known. His mother died while he was very young, and he was reared by an uncle and aunt in Epping, New Hampshire.

Briggs attended Boston College, graduating in 1934 with a B.S. degree in biology. He then went to Harvard University, where he worked with Leigh Hoadley, receiving his Ph.D. degree in 1938. He was a postdoctoral fellow at McGill University until he joined the research staff at the Lankenau Hospital Research Institute (Institute for Cancer Research) in Philadelphia in 1942, where he eventually became head of the embryology department. He married Janet Bloch in 1940; they had two sons and a daughter.

Briggs's early research was on renal adenocarcinoma (kidney cancer) in frogs, and he was one of the first to use carcinogens to induce neoplasms in frog larvae. He developed a technique to produce triploidy in frogs and studied the effect of ploidy (abnormal numbers of chromosomes) on amphibian embryos. He studied a group of abnormalities occurring during the development of haploid embryos (with half the normal chromosome complement) and demonstrated that the effects of haploidy could be decreased, but not eliminated, by removing some of the egg's cytoplasm. This work showed the importance of the nucleocytoplasmic ratio.

Briggs encouraged students to read the older literature, and he did so himself. For example, about 1938, Hans Spemann, professor emeritus of zoology at the University of Freiburg, delivered the Silliman Lectures at Yale University. These lectures mentioned Spemann's work on early embryonic development and induction. One research question at that time (and much later) was whether the amphibian egg nucleus is forever altered in the course of early development. Spemann suggested that the question might be answered by introducing an isolated nucleus into an enucleated egg. Furthermore, he suggested that older, more differentiated nuclei could be tested in this way to see whether these nuclei could support the normal development of an amphibian. At that time, a method for accomplishing this transfer was unknown. Briggs read the Silliman Lectures, which were published by the Yale University Press. He and Thomas King used a micromanipulator to remove the nucleus from an embryonic cell and transferred that nucleus into enucleated amphibian eggs. This technique became the foundation of many years of research by Briggs and others investigating whether irreversible changes occur in the genome as development and differentiation of an embryo progresses.

Briggs joined the faculty of the zoology department at Indiana University in 1956. While at Indiana, Briggs brought Rufus Humphrey, who had retired from the University of Buffalo (now the State University of New York at Buffalo) Medical School. Humphrey had assembled a colony of salamanders and was searching for developmental mutants. He discovered and described many mutant genes in these animals. Briggs and his graduate students studied several of these mutants and through the years established Indiana University as an outstanding institution for developmental genetics.

There was much more to Bob Briggs than science. He appreciated chamber music and would frequently make the rounds of the laboratories in the evening to invite the graduate students to concerts of baroque music in the College of Music. He established a tradition of taking visiting scientists along with the graduate students for beverages and bowling. He instilled in his graduate students not only a love for science, especially developmental genetics, but a love for music and camaraderie as well. He became interested in motorcycles and purchased several until he found the make he liked best. Some of his graduate students and one or two other faculty members would climb aboard their motorcycles for an afternoon of riding in southern Indiana.

Briggs received many awards, including the Charles-Leopold Mayer Prize of the Academy of Sciences, Institute of France, which was awarded to Briggs and Thomas King in 1973. He was elected to the American Academy of Arts and Sciences in 1960 and to the National Academy of Sciences in 1962. In 1963 he was appointed a research professor of zoology at Indiana University.

Briggs's lecturing style was one of nervous energy that some thought distracting, but those who listened carefully discovered a profound knowledge of the literature and critical analyses of papers presented in an exciting way. To the graduate students, he was truly remarkable. With all the accolades, he remained approachable and humble. His research was highly professional, and his writing exhibited the highest ethical standards; he inspired all who had the privilege of working with him.

• Important publications by Briggs include "Tumour Induction in *Rana pipiens* Tadpoles," *Nature* 146 (1940): 29; "Transplantation of Kidney Carcinoma from Adult Frogs to Tadpoles," *Cancer Research* 2 (1942): 309–23; "The Influence of Egg Volume on the Development of Haploid and Diploid Embryos of the Frog, *Rana pipiens*," *Journal of Experimental Zoology* 111 (1949): 255–94; with T. J. King, "Transplantation of Living Nuclei from Blastula Cells into Enucleated Frogs' Eggs," *Proceedings of the National Academy of Sciences* 38 (1952): 455–63; with J. T. Justus, "Partial Characterization of the Component from Normal Eggs Which Corrects the Maternal Effect of Gene *o* in the Mexican Axolotl (*Ambystoma mexicanum*)," *Journal of Experimental Zoology* 167 (1968): 105–15; and "Developmental genetics of the Axolotl," in *Genetic Mechanisms of Development*, ed. F. H. Ruddle (1973), pp. 169–99.

JERRY T. JUSTUS

BRIGGS, Walter Owen (27 Feb. 1877–17 Jan. 1952), manufacturer and baseball executive, was born in Ypsilanti, Michigan, the son of Rodney Davis Briggs, an engineer with the Michigan Central Railroad, and Ada Warner. When Walter was an infant the family moved to a western suburb of Detroit where the Tigers played Sunday baseball, which was forbidden in the city at that time. There he attended John Newberry Public School and played first base and catcher for the baseball team. Leaving school at age 14, Briggs worked in the car shops of the Michigan Central, earning $20 per month.

After a brief stint as a foreman with the C. H. Little cement company, in 1904 he became vice president and general manager of the Everitt Manufacturing Company. This Highland Park, Michigan, business, which painted and trimmed automobile bodies, was owned by boyhood friend Barney Everitt. In 1906 Briggs was elected president. By 1909 Everitt had sold the company to Briggs, the business becoming the Briggs Manufacturing Company. Until 1919 most automobiles were open to the weather; but Briggs's research and production pioneered the "closed body" car, and his enterprise became one of the main sources of auto bodies for the industry. Soon Briggs became the authority on forecasting styles and designs, expanding to nine plants including one in England (1930); his company became the world's largest independent producer of auto bodies, supplying Ford and Chrysler. During World War II the enterprise made a significant contribution to Allied success, providing vehicles and aircraft fuselages. Under Briggs's imaginative leadership his business empire continually grew. He founded an investment company (1922) and acquired such companies as plumbing hardware (1944 and 1946), potteries (1947), and a steel mill (1949). In 1952 Briggs Manufacturing Company and its subsidiaries had sales of $400 million and employed 35,500 people. Along the way the astute businessman became a respected civic and community leader.

On 22 November 1904 Briggs had married Jane Elizabeth Cameron. Their marriage of over 47 years produced one son and four daughters. The growing fortune made in automotive manufacturing allowed Briggs to purchase a 236-foot yacht in 1929, the *Cambriona*, which he kept until 1948. He also maintained the finest steeplechase stable in the nation; in September 1930 his horses won the historic Meadowbrook Cup and the Bloomfield Cup race. The stable also included show horses and hunters. His wealth supported other interests, including the Detroit Symphony Orchestra, the Detroit Zoo, a school, a chapel, and athletic facilities for Eastern Michigan University in Ypsilanti. Although offered many political offices as a staunch Republican, he declined. The physically impressive Briggs was a prudently generous man, an amateur horticulturist, a trustee of hospitals, a leader in many organizations, and president of the Detroit Athletic Club. Because of his own personal difficulty trying to find housing when newly married with a family, Briggs built the Covington Drive Apartments in Detroit where no one could be a tenant without a baby.

But it was through his love of baseball that Briggs became a "symbol of the city of Detroit." Reportedly he had trouble obtaining tickets to the 1907 World Series, owing to the fact that old Bennett Park seated only 5,000 fans for the Ty Cobb–led Tigers. That frustration led Briggs, a die-hard Tigers fan, to purchase a one-quarter interest in the Detroit club in 1920. When partner John Kelsey died in 1927, Briggs bought his 25 percent of the club's holdings; with the death of close friend and partner Frank Navin in 1935, he purchased the remaining 50 percent and became sole owner. Briggs, whom Detroit residents respectfully referred to as "Mr. Briggs," was unfailingly honest and held high expectations of people. According to sportswriter H. G. Salsinger, Briggs intended to give Detroit the best ballpark in the major leagues and the best baseball team in the country. Operating the club without salary, he invested all profits into improving the team and the ballpark. More than one million dollars was spent in remodeling the stadium to seat 56,000, second only to Yankee Stadium.

Briggs Stadium, renamed from Navin Field in 1938, became one of the nation's finest and best maintained of the 1930s and 1940s. Briggs's money brought several star players to the Tigers, including Al Simmons and catcher Mickey Cochrane from Connie Mack's Philadelphia Athletics during the Great Depression. In 1936 the competitive Briggs expanded the scouting staff to 12, three more than the rival New York Yankees. He delighted in offering new suits of clothes from the best tailors to all team members if they won a crucial series. Sometimes his enthusiastic support was excessive. In January 1940 Commissioner Kenesaw Mountain Landis fined the club for illegally manipulating minor league player contracts and transfers and declared free agency for 91 Detroit players. Tigers general manager Jack Zeller claimed that Briggs had no knowledge of technical violations, but Briggs took the fine and penalty without a whimper. He simply hired quality managers (such as Steve O'Neil and Robert Rolfe) and players (such as Leon "Goose" Goslin, Fred Hutchinson, George Kell, Jerry Priddy, and Dick Wakefield) with top salaries. In 1939 the canny Briggs landed the boisterous Norman "Bobo" Newsom from the St. Louis Browns for the then bloated salary of $20,000; the veteran pitcher promptly won 21 games in leading the 1940 Tigers into the World Series.

In 1941 the *Sporting News* named Briggs baseball's executive of the year. Under his benevolent ownership the Tigers won four American League pennants (1934, 1935, 1940, and 1945) and World Series championships in 1935 and 1945. Baseball traditionalist Briggs succumbed to the pressure for night baseball when Detroit became the last American League team to schedule a home game under the lights on 15 June 1948; characteristically, Briggs had the most expensive arc lights ever made installed to illuminate the park.

In 1940 polio left Briggs paralyzed, his once powerful frame restricted to a wheelchair. For the last 10 years of his life the ailing owner rooted on the Tigers from his chair wheeled into a box down the foul lines. The perennial fan, Briggs was a hard loser, as Malcolm Bingay deemed him in the *Saturday Evening Post*, "The Fan Who Bought the Ball Park." One of the richest men in the United States, he never forgot his trouble in getting tickets to see the Tigers; as a result, every year at least 100,000 youngsters saw the games free as his guests.

Briggs died from a kidney infection at his winter home in Miami Beach, Florida. His funeral attested to his stature in the sports world and his eminence in Detroit. In attendance, on a chilly January day in Detroit, were president Will Harridge of the American League, players and managers from all of baseball's family, and many golf and pro football figures. Detroit mayor Albert E. Cobo ordered city flags at half mast, in part because of Briggs's service to the Zoological Commission since 1924. A reporter noted, "His passion was baseball. Without thought of costs he poured forth his money to create winning clubs, to give our baseball-loving community not only recreation but inspiration." Upon his death, son Walter "Spike" Briggs, Jr., assumed the presidency of the Tigers for a turbulent four years. In 1956 Spike sold the team to an 11-man syndicate, and Briggs Stadium became Tiger Stadium.

• The State Library of Michigan in Lansing has a file of Briggs clippings from Detroit newspapers. References with background on Briggs include William M. Anderson, *The Detroit Tigers: A Pictorial Celebration* (1991), pp. 66–121; Frederick G. Leib, *The Detroit Tigers* (1946); and Erik J. Pedersen, "The Briggs Athletic Complex," in *A History of Physical Education at Eastern Michigan University, 1852–1996* (1996), pp. 13–18. Obituaries include the *New York Times*, 18 Jan. 1952; the *Sporting News*, 23 Jan. 1952; H. G. Salsinger's columns in the *Detroit News*, 18 Jan. and 21 Jan. 1952; Walter Spoelstra, "Four from World Championship Team among Briggs' Mourners," *Detroit News*, 18 Jan. 1952; E. A. Batchelor, "He Left a Stamp on Detroit Sports . . . ," *Detroit Times*, 18 Jan. 1952; George W. Stark, "Tiger Owner Passes at Home in Florida . . . ," *Detroit News*, 17 Jan. 1952; and three articles from the *Detroit Free Press*, 18 Jan. 1952: Lyall Smith, "W.O. Briggs, Mogul of Industry, Just a Fan of Baseball"; Leo Donovan, "Industrialist, Sportsman, 74, Dies," p. 1; and an editorial "Tribute to Briggs," p. 6. E. A. Batchelor, "Detroit Almost Had Two Teams," *Detroit Saturday Times*, 19 Jan. 1952, recounts how close Briggs came to moving the St. Louis Cardinals to Detroit. See also "Lost Leaders," *Newsweek*, 28 Jan. 1952, pp. 50–51; and "Died: Walter O. Briggs," *Time*, 28 Jan. 1952, p. 94. Useful articles include "Briggs Mixture," *Time*, 21 Dec. 1936, pp. 50–51; Malcolm Bingay, "The Fan Who Bought the Ball Park," *Saturday Evening Post*, 6 Mar. 1943, pp. 18, 83–84; and H. G. Salsinger, The Umpire column, "W. O. Briggs Liberal Arts Building," *Detroit News*, 10 Aug. 1957.

HAROLD L. RAY

BRIGHAM, Amariah (26 Dec. 1798–8 Sept. 1849), physician and asylum superintendent, was born in New Marlboro, Massachusetts, the son of John Brigham and Phoebe Clark, farmers. Orphaned at the age of eleven, Brigham spent ten months with his uncle, a doctor in upstate New York, before his uncle, too, died. Undaunted, Brigham found work as a clerk in a bookstore and later as a teacher in the local schools of Albany. He prepared himself for the medical profession by studying with doctors in his hometown and in Canaan, Connecticut, and by attending one term of lectures in New York City.

At the age of twenty-one Brigham opened his first medical practice in Enfield, Massachusetts, moving on within two years to the nearby town of Greenfield. Finding little success in a profession that was highly competitive and far from lucrative for most of the nineteenth century, Brigham sojourned to Europe for a year, mingling leisurely travel with serious study of mental illness with eminent Scottish, English, and French alienists (the nineteenth-century term for psychiatrists). On his return to the United States in 1831, Brigham again opened a medical practice, this time in Hartford, Connecticut.

Brigham's peripatetic youth exposed him to the revivalist and reformist atmosphere of early nineteenth-century New England, and as an adult his inquiring mind and persuasive pen were seldom at rest. In the 1830s alone he published a study of the cholera epidemic (1832) and two treatises on the interrelationship of social conditions and health, *Influence of Mental Cultivation on Health* (1832) and *Observations on the Influence of Religion on the Health and Physical Welfare of Mankind* (1835). For a year and a half he served as a medical lecturer at the New York College of Physicians and Surgeons. In 1840 the publication of his book *An Inquiry concerning the Diseases and Functions of the Brain, the Spinal Cord and the Nerves*, together with his expressed opposition to religious enthusiasm, won him an appointment as superintendent of the Retreat for the Insane at Hartford. While some of the directors had been leery of his democratic leanings, others had been impressed with his admonition to churches about their eagerness to open their doors for "what are called Monthly Concerts for prayer meetings to hear accounts of, or to aid, the Bible, Tract, Missionary, Education, Seaman, Colonization, Abolition, and other charitable and religious societies." Believing that social conditions precipitated mental illness, the directors agreed with Brigham's objections to camp revival meetings when he warned that "in nothing should we be more careful . . . than in powerfully exciting the minds of the young, and particularly of females" (*Observations*, pp. 143–44).

At the Retreat for the Insane, Brigham practiced a plan of moral treatment. He, and an increasing number of his colleagues, believed that institutionalization, individual attention, a family-like atmosphere set in a carefully designed asylum, and programs of recreational, religious, occupational, and educational therapy would cure mental illness in most cases. Institutionalization was crucial in order to undo the effects of a volatile and uncertain society on the individual. As the number of asylums grew, popular belief in institutionalization and moral therapy deepened and a number of states built publicly funded asylums. Brigham moved to the New York State Lunatic Asylum (later known as the Utica State Hospital) in 1842—a larger opportunity for him to fulfill his personal ambitions and to advance his professional agenda.

Having struggled intellectually with the interplay of society and mental illness and practiced moral therapy in two different types of asylums, Brigham looked to professionalization as a means to promote the proper care of the insane. In 1844 he founded the *American Journal of Insanity* (later the *American Journal of Psychiatry*) as a sounding board for his ideas and those of his colleagues and, in the same year, became one of the thirteen founding members of the Association of Medical Superintendents of American Institutions for the Insane (later, the American Psychiatric Association).

Brigham's insistence on a wide dissemination of the journal, his open editorial policy, and his personal financial sacrifice in keeping the journal afloat contributed significantly to the spread of ideas about the asylum and moral treatment as the humane way to deal with mental illness. Without the journal the influence of the fledgling professional organization would have been severely limited; with it the Association of Medical Superintendents of American Institutions for the Insane outshone the American Medical Association (founded in 1847) for the next half-century.

Brigham and his fellow superintendents of asylums for the insane brought the confluence of humanistic, scientific, and practical approaches to mental illness and to the care of their patients. The promoted the medicalization of mental illness and rescuing the mentally ill from jails, poor farms, and sheds of incarceration. The asylum superintendents' insistence on the necessity of institutionalization, the implementation of an active plan of treatment, and the acceptance of public responsibility for the care of dependent people altered profoundly the attitudes of American society toward the mentally ill.

In 1833, at the age of thirty-five, Brigham had married Susan Root of Greenfield; they had five children. Brigham's health failed in 1848, and the next year, after a journey to the South, he died at Utica, New York.

• A collection of the European journals of Amariah Brigham is at the Butler Hospital in Providence, R.I., and numerous letters are in the Pliny Earle Papers at the American Antiquarian Society, Worcester, Mass., and in the Thomas Kirkbride Papers at the Pennsylvania Hospital Medical Archives in Philadelphia. The best biographical sketch (with a complete bibliography of Brigham's writings) is Eric T. Carlson, "Amariah Brigham: I. Life and Works," *American Journal of Psychiatry* (Apr. 1956): 831–36, and "Amariah Brigham: II. Psychiatric Thought and Practice," *American Journal of Psychiatry* (Apr. 1957): 911–16. Ellen Dwyer, *Homes for the Mad: Life Inside Two Nineteenth-Century Asylums* (1987), is helpful for Brigham's years at Utica. An obituary is in the *American Journal of Insanity* 14 (1857).

CONSTANCE M. MCGOVERN

BRIGHAM, Carl Campbell (4 May 1890–24 Jan. 1943), educational psychologist, was born in Marlboro, Massachusetts, the son of Charles Francis Brigham and Ida Campbell, occupations unknown. Brigham did not become a serious student until his junior year at Princeton University, when he became deeply interested in experimental psychology. After completing two years of psychology course work in one, he spent much of his senior year performing experiments in Professor Howard C. Warren's laboratory. By the time of his graduation, Brigham was considered the "most highly educated and learned member" of the class of 1912 (Carmichael, p. 444).

Supported by prestigious fellowships, Brigham continued his education at Princeton, earning his M.A. in 1913 and, after defending his dissertation concerning the Binet IQ tests, a Ph.D. in May 1916. After a close examination of Binet's tests, the first widely used intelligence test, Brigham had found that some scores were reflective of school training rather than innate intelligence, whereas others were influenced by the behavior of the test administrator.

In September 1916 Brigham was appointed instructor in psychology at Princeton. The following year Princeton published his dissertation, along with a report of his undergraduate research, in his first book, *Two Studies in Mental Tests*. He left Princeton in March 1917 to work as a psychologist in the veterans reeducation division of the Canadian Military Hospitals Commission. Soon after his arrival, Brigham was visited by Harvard psychologist Robert M. Yerkes, president of the American Psychological Association (APA). As a result of their discussions concerning the future role of American psychologists in the war effort, Yerkes became Brigham's mentor. Their relationship had significant ramifications for both the field of psychology and Brigham's career.

A few weeks later, the United States declared war and Yerkes, crediting Brigham for his advice, organized the first application of standardized intelligence tests on a mass scale to select recruits for officer training and to help identify incompetent men for discharge. Brigham returned to the United States and played an active role in early experimental test administrations at Fort Dix (N.J.) and later on Yerkes's staff in Washington, D.C. By the end of the war, about two million tests had been administered. To a significant extent, this military testing program led to the popularization and spread of other standardized, short-answer (including multiple-choice) tests for educational purposes in the 1920s and 1930s. For example, one spinoff, the National Intelligence Test, was given to millions of schoolchildren in the 1920s. Brigham, hoping to see active service, transferred to the Tank Corps in April 1918 but was relegated to a desk job. After the armistice he served as chairman of the case board in, and assistant to the chief of, the Rehabilitation Division of the Federal Board for Vocational Education.

In 1920 Brigham returned to Princeton University, where he remained until his death. He held appointments as assistant professor (until 1924), associate professor (1924–1928), and professor (1928–1943). In 1923 he married Elizabeth Duffield, with whom he would have one child.

Like other army psychologists returning to academe, Brigham began experimenting with the use of "alpha"-type tests for college admission and guidance purposes, and this interest led him to become the secretary of Princeton's committee on admissions for many years. In a related effort, Brigham also reanalyzed the results of the army examinations to determine whether immigrant groups varied in intelligence. This research resulted in his first major book, *A Study of American Intelligence* (1923).

In this polemical work, written under the guidance of Yerkes and with the financial support of wealthy white philanthropist Charles Winthrop Gould, who advocated racial purity, Brigham claimed that World War I test results proved that the intellectual level of the U.S. population was declining, primarily as a result of both miscegenation between white and black Americans and by immigration from southern Europe. To help deal with this problem, Brigham advocated a restrictive immigration policy. Soon after the book's publication, he addressed the National Republican Club on this topic, and related legislation was passed in 1924. It is unlikely that the efforts of Brigham, Yerkes, and other like-minded colleagues directly affected the result, but Brigham clearly contributed to the intellectual climate of the 1920s, which supported immigration quotas based on race and ethnicity.

Brigham's views began to shift a few years later. In 1926 he characterized geographically based immigration quotas as "stupid" but suggested that the tests could be used to evaluate individual applicants ("Validity of Tests in Examinations of Immigrants," *Industrial Psychology* 1 [June 1926]: 417). In 1928 he publicly withdrew support for his 1923 claims at a meeting of eugenics advocates, and in 1930, while serving as secretary of the APA, he published a formal retraction, characterizing his only significant book as "pretentious" and "without foundation" ("Intelligence Tests of Immigrant Groups," *Psychological Review* 2 [1937]: 165).

The changes in Brigham's views on the usefulness of the concept of intelligence were dramatic. Whereas in the early 1920s Brigham had assumed that intelligence was a largely inherited characteristic that could be measured with a test, he gradually came to believe, as stated in an unpublished 1934 manuscript in the Educational Testing Service archives, that "native intelligence" was "one of the most glorious fallacies in the history of science," merely a concept invented by psychologists to explain test scores, which "very definitely are a composite including schooling, family background, familiarity with English, and everything else, relevant and irrelevant. The 'native intelligence' hypothesis is dead." In just a few years Brigham had shifted from the use of intelligence test data as propaganda to buttress eugenics arguments to a much more cautious, research-oriented approach that encouraged the application of the new testing methodology to serve the more utilitarian, academic purposes of college admission and guidance. This shift is reflected in the name he chose for his next major project, the Scholastic Aptitude Test (SAT), replacing the working title, "psychological examination."

By 1923 over thirty adaptations of alpha were in use in higher education, with that of Columbia University's Edward Lee Thorndike the most popular. Brigham's own version, initially used at Princeton for guidance and experimental purposes in 1923, was made an admission requirement for borderline candidates in 1925. In that year the College Entrance Examination Board appointed Brigham to chair a committee charged with the development of a "psychological examination" that could serve as an indicator of college potential for those not prepared to take its written examinations. The written exams (College Boards), which had been introduced in 1901 to reduce duplication of effort among selective institutions, were based for the most part on a prescribed curriculum offered by private secondary schools and took five days to administer. While useful, they did not meet the needs of colleges to evaluate the credentials of public school applicants.

The College Board leaders were aware that alpha-type tests could be administered more quickly and scored more objectively than written or oral examinations. Another advantage of the new type of tests, Brigham contended, was that the prevailing system for selective college admission favored wealthy students with a "high pecuniary endowment," which enabled them to attend a high-quality preparatory school or pay for costly tutoring to ready them for the achievement tests of the College Board. In theory, students could not prepare for the new test, so it gave college applicants from various backgrounds an opportunity to demonstrate their ability. In fact, Brigham asserted that the alpha-type tests were "one of the most important instruments that science has yet found for alleviating the conditions of the depressed classes" ("Validity of Tests in Examinations of Immigrants," *Industrial Psychology* 1 [June 1926]: 416).

The first administration of the new SAT was held in June 1926, although the written tests continued to be offered until World War II, when they were superseded by a test battery consisting of the SAT and multiple-choice achievement tests. As associate secretary (1930–1935) and research secretary (1935–1942) of the College Board, Brigham worked diligently to improve the reliability of scoring the board's written examinations as well as to improve the SAT and extend its application to guidance and placement. During the SAT's first decade, Brigham substantially revised the examination and introduced several important methodological changes and innovations, which have continued in both the SAT and other standardized tests administered by Educational Testing Service (ETS). (ETS has been conducting testing programs for the College Board since it began operations on 1 Jan. 1948.)

Perhaps the most significant innovation was the introduction of two SAT scores for each test. Brigham and his statistician, Cecil Brolyer, who previously had worked on mental tests for both Lewis M. Terman and Thorndike, determined that the verbal and mathematical subtests were measuring different abilities and that two scores (V and M), rather than one, should be reported. This implied that academic aptitude (and perhaps intelligence to the extent that it influenced success on such tests) was not a unitary construct as was the abstract concept of IQ. Other innovations, to which Brolyer also made significant contributions, included the 200 to 800 SAT score scale, later adopted for use in the Graduate Record Examinations and other major testing programs; the practice of including experimental, unscored sections in actual test forms to evaluate new test questions; and unprecedentedly rigorous statistical analyses of both how individual test questions functioned and how well test results predicted freshman college grades. Brigham published a thorough account of his early years of research on the SAT in his informative if somewhat arcane work, *A Study of Error* (1932), his second major book. While such contributions helped professionalize educational measurement, Brigham's consistently cautious claims concerning the accuracy of college admissions tests for predicting academic success were probably even more influential on his peers and successors.

Brigham's concern for continued research to improve testing led to the last major controversy of his career. In 1937 Harvard University president James

B. Conant proposed that the several nonprofit testing agencies be merged, including both the College Board and the Cooperative Test Service. The latter, under the leadership of Ben D. Wood, had developed and marketed hundreds of standardized educational tests since 1930. Brigham expressed his opposition to this suggestion in "The Place of Research in a Testing Organization" (*School and Society*, 11 Dec. 1937, pp. 756–59). He was convinced that a larger organization would be more concerned about selling tests than conducting research to develop better ones, and the weight of his opposition effectively terminated the discussion until more than two years after his death, when merger negotiations began that led to the formation of ETS in December 1947. Not forgetting Brigham's earlier concerns, the authors of the ETS charter emphasized research as one of its missions.

After a heart attack in 1937, Brigham's health declined and John M. Stalnaker gradually assumed his responsibilities at the College Board. Among Brigham's last accomplishments were the introduction of the SAT for the Blind, which featured the first use by the College Board of phonograph records, and test development for the Foreign Service Examinations of the Department of State, both activities that have continued at ETS.

At his death in Princeton, Brigham was remembered by his close colleagues and friends as a dedicated, dignified professional who possessed a keen intellect and a fine sense of humor. Those with whom he clashed could find him intolerant and scornful of their viewpoints, but he was widely respected by both his friends and his enemies. Although his most notable accomplishment was the creation of the SAT, he has more often been remembered for the marked change in his views regarding the usefulness of standardized tests in drawing conclusions about the intelligence of racial and ethnic groups.

• Brigham's extant files are scanty, but many primary sources, including oral histories with associates, are in the ETS Archives at the Carl Campbell Brigham Library in Princeton, N.J. Brigham correspondence can be found in the papers of Yerkes (Yale), Edwin G. Boring (Harvard), Charles B. Davenport (American Philosophical Society, Philadelphia), Lewis M. Terman (Stanford), and Ben D. Wood (ETS). Matthew T. Downey, *Carl Campbell Brigham: Scientist and Educator* (1961), the only biography, includes a nearly complete bibliography. Other writings that focus on Brigham are Thomas F. Donlon, "Brigham's Book," *College Board Review* 113 (Fall 1979): 24–30, concerning *A Study of Error*; Warren G. Findley, "Carl C. Brigham Revisited," *College Board Review* 119 (Spring 1981): 6–9, 26; and Gary D. Saretzky, "Carl Campbell Brigham, the Native Intelligence Hypothesis, and the Scholastic Aptitude Test," ETS RM-82-04 (1982).

Important sources for Brigham's early SAT work include the College Board's annual reports and its *The Work of the College Entrance Examination Board* (1926); Claude M. Fuess, *The College Board: Its First Fifty Years* (1950); Michael S. Schudson, "Organizing the 'Meritocracy': A History of the College Entrance Examination Board," *Harvard Educational Review* 42 (Feb. 1972): 34–69; and David R. Hubin, "The Scholastic Aptitude Test: Its Development and Introduction" (Ph.D. diss., Univ. of Oregon, 1988). A key early source regarding Brigham and the controversy over the measurement of intelligence is Robert M. Yerkes, *Psychological Examining in the United States Army* (1921). Paul L. Houts, ed., *The Myth of Measurability* (1977), includes a memorable attack on Brigham by Leon Kamin. Franz Samelson, "World War I Intelligence Testing and the Development of Psychology," *Journal of the History of the Behavioral Sciences* 13 (1977): 274–82, provides the context for Brigham's evolving views. Steven Jay Gould, *The Mismeasure of Man* (1981), praises Brigham's recantation; it prompted a new attack on him by Elaine Mensh and Harry Mensh in *The IQ Mythology: Class, Race, Gender, and Inequality* (1991). Mark Snyderman and R. J. Herrnstein, "Intelligence Tests and the Immigration Act of 1924," *American Psychologist* (Sept. 1983): 986–95, minimizes Brigham's direct influence on the legislation. An obituary with photo is in the *New York Times*, 25 Jan. 1943. A memorial by Leonard Carmichael is in *Psychological Review* 50 (Sept. 1943): 444.

GARY D. SARETZKY

BRIGHAM, Mary Ann (6 Dec. 1829–29 June 1889), educator, was born in Westboro, Massachusetts, the daughter of Dexter Brigham, a teacher, and Mary Ann Gould. After attending Mount Holyoke Seminary, Brigham began her distinguished career as a teacher and administrator. Between 1855 and 1858 she worked as an instructor at Mount Holyoke. She assumed her first administrative post in 1859, serving for five years as principal of Ingham University in Leroy, New York. In 1863 Brigham became associate principal of Brooklyn Heights Seminary in Brooklyn, New York, a position she was to hold for twenty-five years. As one of the elite group of women who had attended seminaries and colleges, Brigham participated actively in the Mount Holyoke alumnae organization in the metropolitan New York area.

An accomplished and well-respected administrator, Brigham received numerous opportunities for employment at the collegiate level, including offers of a professorship at Wellesley College and the presidencies of both Wellesley and Smith College. She also retained the loyalty and respect of both Mount Holyoke and Brooklyn Heights alumnae. When she accepted the presidency of Mount Holyoke in 1889, she had the enthusiastic support of alumnae in the New York City area; likewise, graduates of Brooklyn Heights Seminary and other Brooklyn residents petitioned her to remain at Brooklyn Heights.

As her primary goal, Brigham hoped to secure for Mount Holyoke collegiate status, comparable to that of women's institutions such as Vassar College and Smith. Unfortunately, she did not live to achieve this goal. A couple of months prior to assuming the presidency at Mount Holyoke, Brigham died in a railway accident in South Norwalk, Connecticut. In its account of her death, the *Morning Journal and Courier* of New Haven, Connecticut, observed on 1 July 1889 that Brigham had "risen to the foremost rank among Christian women of the land." Mount Holyoke College honored Brigham by naming one of its dormitories in her memory.

• There are several sources from which one can construct the chronology of her life and career. For an account of Brigham's family, one of the earliest to settle in Massachusetts, see W. I. T. Brigham, *History of the Brigham Family* (1907). For a description of the fatal railway accident, see the *New Haven Morning Journal and Courier*, 1 July 1889, and the *New York Tribune*, 30 June 1889; the latter includes a detailed description of Brigham's career.

CAROLYN TERRY BASHAW

BRIGHT, Jesse David (18 Dec. 1812–20 May 1875), U.S. senator, was born in Norwich, Chenango County, New York, the son of David G. Bright, who held a succession of minor government posts, and Rachel Graham. Originally from Virginia, the family in 1819 relocated briefly to Shelbyville, Kentucky, before settling in Madison, Indiana, by 1820. A robust if combative young man, Jesse received a limited public school education before entering the legal profession and politics. He was admitted to the Indiana bar in September 1833.

In 1835 Bright married Mary E. Turpin; they had seven children. At two hundred pounds, Bright walked with a swagger and presented a formidable appearance. While brusque, ambitious, and stubborn, he was also admired by some for his direct manner and strong loyalty to friends and party. Despite his educational deficiencies, he proved to be a shrewd political operator and a successful businessman.

Bright built a successful practice and was quite popular with his clients, but his brother Michael Bright was the more accomplished lawyer and helped shape his political career as well. From August 1834 through March 1839 Jesse Bright served as a probate judge, elected as a Democrat in a Whig county. Through fortunate political connections, he gained appointment in 1840 as a U.S. marshal. In 1841 he took advantage of a Whig split to win election to the state senate from Jefferson County with 43 percent of the vote. In 1843 he joined the Democratic ticket as the party's candidate for lieutenant governor with James Whitcomb running for governor. Both easily won election, and Bright earned 51 percent of the vote.

Always strongly partisan, Bright as president of the state senate in 1845 was in an ideal position to influence the selection of a new U.S. senator. Using his tie-breaking vote to prevent the evenly divided senate from going into session with the Whig house, he was able to delay selection of a senator until the subsequent session. Not surprisingly, the newly elected Democratic house promptly rewarded Bright with the coveted U.S. Senate seat.

Bright took his seat in the Senate on 27 December 1845 and served until expelled in early 1862. Thanks to his confrontational political style, his tenure in the Senate seemingly never went uncontested. In 1851 Robert Dale Owen challenged Bright for his seat but quickly withdrew when Bright went to extraordinary lengths to return to the state capital before the balloting took place. His 1857 reelection was again contested, in this case by Republicans bitter about the way he and his Democratic colleague had been selected. The Republican state senate refused to meet in joint session with the Democratic house, hoping to prevent the combined Democratic majority from prevailing. After prolonged debate the U.S. Senate eventually seated both Democrats in 1858. While building a powerful political machine in Indiana, Bright constantly fought for control of the state party with Governor Joseph A. Wright. Bright's financial resources helped bolster his power, but his machine tactics eventually antagonized many Indiana Democrats.

Bright was rarely impressive in debate on the Senate floor, but his influence was felt in committee work and in private negotiations. He served on a number of committees, eventually as the ranking member on the important Finance and Territories committees. He took characteristic Democratic stands on most issues, supporting the Mexican War and compromise on the Oregon boundary, while he broke with many northern Democrats to join southerners in opposing the Wilmot Proviso, which sought to prohibit slavery in the territories acquired from Mexico. After proposing extending the Missouri Compromise line across the new western territories, he supported Henry Clay's compromise efforts in 1850 but abstained on the Fugitive Slave Bill. In 1854 he endorsed the controversial Kansas-Nebraska Bill, which opened those territories to the possibility of slavery under the doctrine of popular sovereignty. Serving as president pro tempore of the Senate from 1853 to 1857, he further antagonized antislavery elements when he refused to place Charles Sumner or Salmon P. Chase on any committees. A bitter enemy of what he considered "fanatical abolitionists," Bright maintained that the Free Soil senators, who would eventually become leading Republicans, were not members of "any healthy political organization." He evidently declined opportunities for appointment to the cabinet of President James Buchanan.

Bright's hostility toward Illinois senator Stephen A. Douglas, who had voted against seating fellow Democrat Bright in the Senate in the debate of 1857–1858, led him to support the proslavery Lecompton constitution for Kansas and to oppose Douglas for the Democratic presidential nomination in 1860. Hoping to punish Douglas while regaining control of the Indiana Democratic party, he was one of the few northern politicians to support the 1860 candidacy of John C. Breckinridge, a Kentuckian who favored federal protection of slavery in the territories. Although many in Indiana shared southern roots and an aversion to antislavery politics, Bright's Kentucky ties were strengthened by his slaveholding interests (he owned some twenty slaves in Kentucky) and his corresponding southern political alliances. Added to these economic and political considerations, Bright's contrary and contentious political personality no doubt contributed to such southern leanings. Thus, as civil war threatened, Bright's position soon proved out of step with majority opinion in Indiana and the rest of the Union.

While Bright did not accept secession, he also did not favor coercion of the departing southern states. With many of his former political associates now in the Confederacy, his dilemma was partly understandable. Others, however, took his position to be proslavery and perhaps disloyal. Indiana legislators, including fellow Democrats, sought to declare his seat vacant because of his residence in Kentucky and his evident unwillingness to support Unionist objectives. But a controversial letter of introduction that he wrote to Jefferson Davis on 1 March 1861 brought about his expulsion from the Senate. Besides introducing a dealer in firearms to Davis, Bright addressed the southern leader as "His Excellency," the "President of the Confederation of States." Although written before the outbreak of hostilities, this letter provided ammunition to Republicans and his Democratic rivals who wished to make an example of Bright.

On 16 December 1861 Minnesota's Morton S. Wilkinson proposed a resolution for Bright's expulsion. On examining the evidence, the Senate Judiciary Committee reported on 13 January 1862 that it did not support expulsion. After listening to some six weeks of severe criticism from many of his Senate colleagues, Bright defiantly responded in front of packed galleries on 5 February 1862 before dramatically leaving the floor of the Senate. The subsequent vote of 32–14 sealed Bright's rejection. Indiana governor Oliver P. Morton thereupon named Bright's old rival Wright to take his seat in the Senate.

Following his expulsion Bright mounted an unsuccessful effort in 1863 to return to the Senate. In 1864 he returned to Kentucky, where two years later he was sent to the state legislature to represent Carroll and Trimble counties until 1871. He moved to Baltimore, Maryland, in 1874 to oversee his lucrative investments in West Virginia coal mines. He died in Baltimore.

• Bright's personal correspondence is available primarily in the collections of his contemporaries, especially "Some Letters of Jesse D. Bright to William H. English (1842–1863)," *Indiana Magazine of History* 30 (1934): 370–92. Bright's career is detailed in William Wesley Woollen, *Biographical and Historical Sketches of Early Indiana* (1883); Charles B. Murphy, "The Political Career of Jesse D. Bright," *Indiana Historical Society Publications* 10 (1931): 101–145; and Wayne J. Van Der Weele, "'With My Face toward My Accusers': The Expulsion of Jesse David Bright from the United States Senate," in *Their Infinite Variety: Essays on Indiana Politicians* (1981). A characteristic episode is discussed in William S. Garber, "Jesse D. Bright and Michael C. Garber," *Indiana Magazine of History* 28 (1932): 31–39. Election data is provided by Dorothy Riker and Gayle Thornbrough, comps., *Indiana Election Returns, 1816–1851* (1960). Bright's role in national politics is discussed in Roy Franklin Nichols, *The Disruption of American Democracy* (1948). For Ind. politics, see Kenneth M. Stampp, *Indiana Politics during the Civil War* (1949), and Emma Lou Thornbrough, *Indiana in the Civil War Era, 1850–1880* (1965).

VERNON L. VOLPE

BRIGHT EYES (1854–26 May 1903), Indian rights advocate and author also known as Inshtatheamba or Susette La Flesche, was born on the Omaha Reservation near Bellevue, Nebraska, just south of present-day Omaha, the daughter of Joseph La Flesche, also known as Inshtamaza or Iron Eye, a chief of the Omaha, and his wife Mary Gale, a mixed-blood Omaha and Iowa whose Indian name was The One Woman. Susette's paternal grandparents were a Frenchman, also named Joseph, who was a trader and trapper for the Hudson's Bay Company in Canada, and either an Omaha or Ponca woman named Watunna. Because her husband often was away trading or trapping, Watunna left him and married a member of the Omaha tribe. For a while the younger Joseph La Flesche was raised by two aunts who spent part of their time among the Sioux. Later, when his father returned, the younger La Flesche joined him when he once again left on his trading expeditions.

Susette La Flesche's mother was the daughter of Nicomi or Voice of the Waters, a mixed-blood Omaha and Iowa, and John Gale, a surgeon assigned to Fort Atkinson on the Missouri River in present-day Nebraska. After Gale was transferred, Nicomi married Peter Sarpy, an official of the American Fur Company and the employer of the younger Joseph La Flesche. Mary Gale was educated in St. Louis, Missouri, from a fund her father had left with Sarpy. In 1843 she returned to Nebraska and married Joseph La Flesche. Later he took a second wife, Tainne. Eventually, in addition to Susette, Joseph La Flesche had three other daughters with Mary Gale, and a son and two daughters with Tainne.

As a leader of the Omaha, Joseph La Flesche recognized that for the tribe to survive it would have to adapt to the encroaching non-Indian culture that was filling Nebraska with settlers; therefore he enrolled his daughter in the Presbyterian Mission School on the Omaha Reservation. La Flesche was baptized a Catholic on 27 December 1850. In 1859 La Flesche stepped on a nail and, because of the resulting infection, had his leg amputated below the knee; however, the operation was crudely done, and the infection eventually caused his death.

In 1868 Susette La Flesche started school at the agency school in Nebraska. Later she was sent to a private finishing school, Elizabeth Institute, in Elizabeth, New Jersey. In 1875, after fulfilling the requirements to be a teacher, she returned to the Omaha Reservation and taught in the government school.

In 1877 Susette La Flesche witnessed the forced removal of the Ponca tribe from its homeland in South Dakota to a reservation in Indian Territory (present-day Okla.). The suffering of the Ponca, who were closely allied with the Omaha, deeply affected her, and in 1878, along with her father, she visited them on their new reservation among the Quapaw in Indian Territory, where they had temporarily settled pending the assignment of a permanent reservation. After returning to Nebraska, Susette La Flesche became an outspoken opponent of the government's treatment of the Ponca.

Her partner in this was her future husband, Thomas Henry Tibbles. A "crusader," Tibbles had spent time in Bleeding Kansas supporting the efforts of Henry Ward Beecher to bring the territory into the Union as a free state. Once during the fighting in Kansas, Tibbles almost was hanged for his abolitionist beliefs. Later, after studying at Mount Union College in Ohio, he became a Methodist minister and a newspaper reporter, first in Missouri and then Nebraska. It was while serving as a minister in Republican City, Nebraska, that he became involved with the suffering of the Plains Indians. During the drought of 1874 he raised funds to feed the destitute tribes to keep them from starving. Tibbles continued to support the Indians in their efforts to maintain their tribal identity after he became a reporter for the *Omaha Herald*.

In 1879 a group of Ponca led by Standing Bear were arrested in an attempt to return to their ancient homeland. While Standing Bear and his followers were imprisoned at Fort Omaha, Tibbles and a fellow reporter, W. L. Carpenter, took up their cause and implemented a campaign to gain their release. Tibbles's work *The Ponca Chiefs: An Indian Attempt to Appeal from the Tomahawk to the Courts*, published in 1879, helped win support for Standing Bear and his followers. Successful in having the Poncas released, Tibbles and Carpenter then formed what often was called the Indian Ring, a group that advocated fair treatment for Native Americans.

Susette La Flesche quickly became involved in the movement and, apparently at Tibbles's suggestion, took the name Bright Eyes. Along with her brother, Francis La Flesche, and Standing Bear, Bright Eyes undertook a speaking tour of such eastern cities as Boston in an effort to end the government's policy of forced removal of the northern tribes to Indian Territory.

Following the death of Tibbles's first wife, Amelia Owen, he married Bright Eyes on 23 July 1881 in a ceremony performed by the Reverend S. N. D. Martin at the Ponca Reservation Mission. Tibbles's two children by his first marriage were raised by Bright Eyes. The couple had no children of their own. At first Tibbles and Bright Eyes lived in Tibbles's house in Omaha, but in 1882 they moved to a new home on the Omaha Reservation.

Traveling widely with Tibbles, including one visit to Europe, Bright Eyes continued to be a proponent of Indian rights during the latter decades of the nineteenth century. She believed that the effort to assimilate Native Americans into American culture was a mistake and that the greatest error in government Indian policy was to treat the Indians as wards, incapable of caring for themselves. She also advocated American citizenship for Native Americans and continually pressured federal officials for equitable treatment for Indians.

At Tibbles's urging she discovered her talent for writing—a means of communication that allowed them to expand dramatically their audience. In 1881 Bright Eyes published *Ploughed Under, the Story of an Indian Chief*, telling of the struggle of the Native American to adapt in a changing world. Her brother also became active in Native American affairs as an ethnologist and joined with Alice Cunningham Fletcher, a friend of Bright Eyes, to publish *The Omaha Tribe* (Twenty-seventh Annual Report of the Bureau of Ethnology, 1905–1906).

Bright Eyes spent much of her later years on the Omaha Reservation. She also maintained a residence in Lincoln, Nebraska. She died near Bancroft on the Omaha Reservation.

• The La Flesche family papers are in the Nebraska State Historical Society in Lincoln. The best biography of Susette La Flesche is Dorothy Clarke Wilson, *Bright Eyes: The Story of Susette La Flesche, an Omaha Indian* (1957). Additional information may be found in Thomas H. Tibbles, *Buckskin and Blanket Days: Memoirs of a Friend of the Indians Written in 1905* (1957), and "Bright Eyes," *Frank Leslie's Journal*, 3 Jan. 1880.

KENNY A. FRANKS

BRIGHTMAN, Edgar Sheffield (20 Sept. 1884–25 Feb. 1953), philosopher and leading spokesman of personalism, was born in Holbrook, Massachusetts, the son of George Edgar Brightman, a Methodist minister, and Mary Sheffield. Brightman received his B.A. (1906) and M.A. (1908) from Brown University and the bachelor of sacred theology (1910) and Ph.D. (1912) from Boston University. While at Brown he was an assistant in Greek and philosophy. At Boston he studied under Borden Parker Bowne, one of the first philosophers to call himself as a personalist, and as Jacob Sleeper Fellow in 1910–1911 continued his studies at the Universities of Berlin and Marburg, Germany.

Brightman was admitted as a Methodist minister to the New England Southern Conference in 1910. He kept his Methodist affiliation throughout his life and often taught at pastors' schools. In 1912 he married Charlotte Hülsen; they had one child. Charlotte Brightman died in 1915, and in 1918 he married Irma Fall, with whom he had two children.

Brightman began his teaching career at Nebraska Wesleyan University (1912–1915), where he taught psychology, philosophy, and the Bible. From 1915 to 1919 he served as associate and full professor of ethics and religion at Wesleyan University in Middletown, Connecticut. From 1919 until 1925 he served as professor of philosophy at Boston University and from that year until his death served as Borden Parker Bowne Professor of Philosophy at Boston.

Through four decades of teaching and the publication of fourteen books and more than 200 articles, Brightman developed his perspective as an exponent of personalistic idealism. Adopting the essential personalism of his teacher Bowne, Brightman insisted that persons constitute reality and their experiences offer us the only reliable information and clues to other aspects of the universe. In *Person and Reality* (1958) Brightman argues that data found in personal experience ("the shining present") can provide us with metaphysical hypotheses concerning the reality other than us (the "illuminating absent"). Personhood, the "key to reality," is a complex unity of activities, including self-reflectiveness, moral purposes, and religious sensitivity. This personhood, properly understood, provides a reliable basis for rational inferences about the major attributes and power of God.

One of Brightman's contributions to philosophy includes his detailed and careful formulation of twelve ethical principles that taken together, constitute a system. In his *Moral Laws* (1933) Brightman unfolds an interlocking system of moral principles that include logical, axiological, and personalistic ethical directives that fit together coherently. One of these, for example, is "the law of consequences." Embodying in a more inclusive manner the chief insight of John Stuart Mill, the principle succinctly states: "Each person ought to consider and, on the whole, approve of the foreseeable consequences of their actions." Formulated in this way, the principle includes the results of a person's actions, if these are capable of being foreseen, and excludes from the individual's responsibility those results that individual could not anticipate and hence could not prevent. At the same time he intends that "consequences" be interpreted in a more inclusive fashion than Mill would have allowed. Consequences include far more than "happiness." They include the results of one's actions as they affect the character and traits of the doer as well as how the action affects others on whom the deed has impact.

Another of Brightman's contributions is his bold hypothesis about the nature of God, which offers an account of natural evil in the world created by a loving God. In his conception of a God of limited power, Brightman boldly suggests that the limitation is found in the very nature of the deity, not in some outside entity or force. Limitation of God's power is an expression of a nonrational "given" in God's own nature. Natural evils (e.g., tornadoes, earthquakes) are not the result of some other being obstructing the exercise of God's power. Rather, inexplicable outcomes indicate a struggle within God to overcome and completely control this nonrational "given" within God's being. Because of this internal obstacle God cannot prevent and must endure (in some manner even as his creatures do) the calamities and disasters that seem to follow inexorably from physical nature. But Brightman insists that in these tragedies God invariably suffers with human beings. Through this shared suffering and correlative struggle to control recalcitrant aspects, divine and human creativity are lifted to a higher plane. So viewed, God is the "controller" of the "given." And this "given" has a rational aspect (the laws of reason, mathematical relations, and Platonic ideas) and nonrational aspects analogous to qualities of sense objects, disorderly impulses, and rampant desires. God's inability to bring this nonrational aspect under the control of his will is the source of natural evils with their attendant pain and suffering. Brightman seems assured that although God's will may be temporarily thwarted or frustrated, it can never be brought to final defeat.

Brightman's personalism was an influential viewpoint in theology and philosophy during his lifetime. It continues to have its appeal to theologians and philosophers who are dissatisfied with a narrow behaviorist understanding of personhood and who are unwilling to abandon the religious tradition of God conceived as a person.

Brightman died in Newton, Massachusetts.

• Of Brightman's books four are most important for an understanding of his perspective in philosophy of religion. They are *Immortality in Post-Kantian Idealism* (1925), *The Problem of God* (1930), *Is God a Person?* (1932), and *A Philosophy of Religion* (1940). The most significant of his books that deal with ethics are *An Introduction to Philosophy* (rev. ed., 1951), *A Philosophy of Ideals* (1928), and *Moral Laws* (1933). A longer listing of Brightman's books and articles is based on a compilation of his writings by Jannette E. Newhall in Edgar S. Brightman, *Person and Reality: An Introduction to Metaphysics*, ed. Peter Anthony Bertocci et al. (1958), pp. 367–70. A more nearly complete bibliography of Brightman's writings (prepared by Brightman himself) includes more than 700 items and can be found in the Library Archives of Boston University. This list includes philatelic writings (1900–1902), numerous "letters to the editor," some popular and short articles in the religious press, and all of his scholarly writings. Newhall gives a brief account of some aspects of Brightman's life in "Edgar Sheffield Brightman, A Biographical Sketch," *Philosophical Forum* 12 (1954): 9–21. Obituaries are in the *New York Times*, 27 Feb. 1953; *School and Society*, 7 Mar. 1953, p. 159; and *Wilson Library Bulletin*, Apr. 1953.

JOHN HOWIE

BRIGNOLI, Pasquilino (1824–30 Oct. 1884), tenor, was born in Naples, Italy. His father (name unknown) was reportedly a glove manufacturer. His mother's name is also not known. He received a well-grounded musical education in Naples and composed an opera at age fifteen. By 1849 he was in Paris, where his singing at a party attracted the attention of Madame Marietta Alboni, the noted contralto. Dark, handsome, and thin, Brignoli made his Paris operatic debut in Gioacchino Rossini's *Moise en Egypte*. He then decided to study further at the Paris Conservatoire, making a second debut at the Theatres des Italiens as Nemorino in Gaetano Donizetti's *L'elisir d'amore*. He apparently sang at the Paris Opera in 1854. The next year Maurice Strakosch recruited Brignoli for an American company formed by Norwegian violinist Ole Bull. Brignoli made his New York debut on 15 March 1855 in Donizetti's *Lucia di Lammermoor*, although the company had become the property of Bull's creditors by the time Brignoli arrived. Critics were impressed with his silver voice, expressive of sentimental sweetness, and considered him second only to Mario (stage name of Giuseppe, conte de Candia), then the most famous tenor in the world. Except for four trips to Europe, the remainder of Brignoli's career was spent in the United States.

Brignoli arrived in the United States during the time Giuseppe Verdi was composing the highly popular operas of his middle period. Brignoli debuted the tenor leads in the American premieres of *Il trovatore*, *La traviata*, *I vespri siciliani*, and *Un ballo in maschera*, singing the last role on one occasion for an audience that included President Abraham Lincoln. In addition to these Verdi roles, he also sang in the American premieres of Donizetti's *Betly* and the largely unknown American opera *La Spia* by Luigi Arditi, based on the James Fennimore Cooper novel *The Spy*. Also notable was Brignoli's appearance on 25 February 1857, singing Manrico in *Il trovatore* for the opening of the Academy of Music auditorium in Philadelphia. Twenty years later he repeated that role with some members of the original cast. On 24 November 1859 he sang opposite soprano Adelina Patti in her adult operatic debut in *Lucia di Lammermoor*. Patti and Brignoli sang together extensively in the United States during the 1860s, as well as in London and Paris at the end of the decade.

Called the "Adonis of Opera," Brignoli was the first male singer in the United States to become a cult object. During the late 1850s large crowds gathered in New York's Central Park to watch him drive his vermilion-wheeled and silver-ornamented dogcart pulled by two matched horses. Sporting canary kid gloves and deploying a delicate whip, he smiled beneath his long waxed Louis Napoleon mustache at the adoring females who lined the route. In the opera house, women focused their glasses on him; others wrote him passionate love letters. Such enthusiasm declined as Brignoli grew progressively stouter.

The outbreak of the Civil War curtailed opera productions, so in 1862 Brignoli and pianist Louis Moreau Gottschalk turned to concerts, venturing as close to the front line as St. Louis. Later in the decade Brignoli organized his own opera companies and began extensive tours of the hinterland. He performed in Chicago, St. Louis, Cincinnati, Cleveland, Milwaukee, and Washington, D.C., and after the war he traveled to Richmond, Norfolk, Raleigh, Charleston, Savannah, Atlanta, Memphis, Little Rock, Mobile, Galveston, and San Francisco. In addition he visited Montreal, Canada, and Havana, Cuba. The sopranos for these companies included Pauline Colson, Marie Louise Durand, Isabella McCulloch, Euphrosyne Parepa-Rosa, Christine Nilsson, Clara Louise Kellogg, and Emma Abbott. Repertoire was determined based on the company assembled, but Charles-François Gounod's *Faust*, Rossini's *Il barbiere di Siviglia*, and *Lucia di Lammermoor* frequently supplemented the always-present *Il trovatore*. Popular songs and arias from other operas were often inserted into the programs. Chorus and orchestra were minimal, and sets consisted of just a few painted drops.

Also active as a composer, Brignoli wrote "The Sailor's Dream" (1868), an Ave Maria dedicated to Patti; "A Night in Naples" for soprano and tenor; and other songs. His "Crossing of the Danube" is a march dedicated to bandleader Patrick Sarsfield Gilmore, and "Grand Military March" is dedicated to Civil War general Thomas E. Chickering of the famous piano-making family.

Although hailed for the great beauty of his voice, Brignoli was also noted for his peculiarities. Afflicted with severe stage fright, he failed to act on stage. One critic reported that in Vincenzo Bellini's *I puritani* he stood in one spot and thrust out first one then the other arm twenty-three times. In addition, his method of vocal projection was accompanied by a large volume of saliva, leading other singers to avoid him on stage as much as possible. His trademark was the song "Goodbye, Sweetheart, Goodbye," written by the popular songwriter John L. Hatton.

Brignoli's career declined in the 1870s and 1880s. He died in New York just before the twenty-fifth anniversary of Patti's debut, thus frustrating a reported planned reunion. Poet Walt Whitman delivered a eulogy to Brignoli in the poem "The Dead Contralto," included in *Leaves of Grass*.

Brignoli was twice married, first to an English soprano named Kate Duckworth, who sang under the stage name of Madame Morensi. Sometime after her death he married South Carolinian Isabella McCulloch. It is not known if there were any children from either marriage.

Whitman called Brignoli's voice "the perfect singing voice." Equally appreciative was noted critic Henry E. Krehbiel. Critics who expected good acting, however, disliked him. Robert Grant White wrote, "There never was a tenor of any note in New York whose singing was so utterly without character or significance" (*Century Magazine*, June 1882). Park Benjamin recalled how in the aria "Di quella pira" in *Il trovatore* Brignoli would rush to the footlights waving his sword and explode the high note "so that perhaps you might have heard it half way to Harlem" (clipping, 3 Mar. 1921). Brignoli credited his vocal longevity to his refusal to sing higher than a B or to force his voice.

Almost without serious rivals during his life, Brignoli set the standard for singing during the first age of opera in the United States. Not until Enrico Caruso early in the twentieth century did another tenor assume such nationwide fame. Ironically, that his career was so extensively American led after his death to neglect and his disappearance from standard musical reference books. The large portrait of Brignoli that once hung in the Green Room of Philadelphia's Academy of Music disappeared sometime in the twentieth century.

• Modern studies include Michael B. Dougan, "Pasquilino Brignoli: Tenor of the Golden West," in *Opera and the Golden West: The Past, Present, and Future of Opera in the U.S.A.*, ed. John L. DiGaetani and Josef P. Sirefman (1994). Although few Brignoli manuscript materials have been found, nearly every book on opera in the United States in the nineteenth century contains anecdotes about him. Notable examples include Max Maretzek, *Sharps and Flats* (1890); Clara Louise Kellogg, *Memoirs of an American Prima Donna* (1913); Louis M. Gottschalk, "Notes of a Pianist," *Atlantic Monthly*, Apr. 1865, pp. 573–75; and George P. Upton, *Musical Memories* (1908). General accounts include Henry C. Lahee, *Grand Opera in America* (1902); Henry E. Krehbiel, *Chapters of Opera* (1909); John F. Cone, *Adelina Patti: Queen of Hearts* (1993); and, for Brignoli's New York appearances, George C. D. Odell, *Annals of the New York Stage* (1931). Dougan, "Bravo Brignoli! The First Opera Season in Arkansas," *Pulaski County Historical Review* 30 (Winter 1982): 74–80, recounts one trip into the hinterland. A flowery and somewhat erroneous obituary is in the *New York Times*, 31 Oct. 1884.

MICHAEL B. DOUGAN

BRILL, Abraham Arden (12 Oct. 1874–2 Mar. 1948), psychoanalyst and psychiatrist, was born in Kanczuga, Galicia, in the Austro-Hungarian empire, the son of Philip Brill, a noncommissioned commissary officer, and Esther Seitelbach. His parents were pious and provincial Jews with traditional expectations for their son. Brill found these stifling and at fifteen he fled to the United States, arriving destitute and alone in 1889. With fierce ambition and through hard work Brill rose out of the Lower East Side ghetto in New York City where he worked at diverse, petty jobs to fulfill his father's wish that he become both an educated man and a doctor. Although Brill could not afford to complete his course work at the City College of New York, where he had started his studies at night, he managed to educate himself in several languages, in the classics, and in philosophy, accomplishments in which he took pride throughout his life. He finally received a Ph.B. from New York University in 1901 and a medical degree from Columbia University's College of Physicians and Surgeons in 1903. In many ways, however, his real education in his destined métier had not yet begun.

In 1903 Brill took up a post at the New York State Hospital in Central Islip, Long Island, where he came under the tutelage of Adolph Meyer, the Swiss-born psychiatrist who was remaking the profession through a new dynamic approach and the application of rigorous clinical procedures. Since Brill sought further training in techniques to treat the mentally ill and was at a personal crossroads, he found himself paradoxically on a journey back to Europe. At Zurich's Burghölzli Clinic, then under the aegis of Eugen Bleuler and his assistant, Carl Jung, Brill came into the intensely exciting atmosphere created by the discussion and application of the provocative new ideas of Sigmund Freud that were to transform his life. He subsequently traveled to Salzburg to attend the first international psychoanalytic congress and then to Vienna to meet the master himself. Brill now had a firm mission—to transmit his newfound insights into the human psyche to American soil and to plant them firmly within American psychiatry.

On his return to the United States in 1908, Brill began to introduce Freudian ideas in America with passion and purposefulness. Psychoanalysis and the circle of Freudians had given Brill a sense of personal fulfillment and identity that allowed him to do energetically what Freud described as the essence of adulthood—to love and to work. In 1908 he married Dr. Kitty Rose Owen, with whom he had two children. He acted quickly to anchor psychoanalysis in the United States, setting up a personal practice, beginning a series of translations of Freud's writing, and initiating the personal contacts among physicians and laypersons that would eventuate in the founding of important professional societies and create consequential cultural resonances among influential intellectuals. When Freud came, at the invitation of psychologist G. Stanley Hall, for his only visit to the United States in 1909 to speak at Clark University, Brill accompanied him to his lectures. By then, Brill already had opened the practice on Central Park West where he spent the rest of his career.

Brill began his translations of Freud's works in 1909. Eventually he would provide the first English translation of many of the fundamental texts, including *The Interpretation of Dreams* (1913), *The Psychopathology of Everyday Life* (1914), *Three Contributions to the Theory of Sex* (1910), and a collection of Freud's *Basic Writings* (1938), which served as the cornerstone of American knowledge about Freud. Although inelegant and sometimes flawed, these gave the often monolingual Americans critical access to Freud's ideas. They also soon had an introduction by Brill himself, who published *Psychoanalysis: Its Theories and Practical Applications* in 1912. Written quickly and somewhat carelessly, this was the first of his voluminous writings. Brill lectured wherever and whenever he could in medical settings around New York, and he found an eager audience among New York intellectuals who were questioning Victorian sexual inhibitions. New York was central to, but not an exclusive enclave for, psychoanalytic ideas, which had also spread to Washington, Baltimore, Boston, and even westward. As the capital of avant-garde culture and new ideas, however, New York was an ideal locale for Brill's fervent Freudian proselytizing. Blunt in his sexual language, outgoing, and voluble, Brill was soon in demand at the gathering places of such pre–World War I intellectuals as Alfred Kuttner, Walter Lippmann, Max Eastman, Lincoln Steffens, Theodore Dreiser, Floyd Dell, and Mabel Dodge Luhan. Some, like Luhan and Eastman, became his patients. As "a brilliant clinician," Brill quickly developed a thriving practice and a luminous reputation.

In 1911 Brill founded the New York Psychoanalytic Society, a seedbed for American psychoanalytic discussion and practice and a continuing venue for Brill's influence until the 1930s when newer, younger men began to challenge his control. In 1931 he founded the New York Psychoanalytic Institute. By then his rigid adherence to the Freudian ideas he had adopted in Zurich began to backfire as American practitioners, such as Abraham Kardiner, Lawrence Kubie, and Henry Stack Sullivan, pressed forward in new directions. But Brill's influence had already defined the formative stage of American experience, especially the emphasis on medical training as a background for psychoanalytic practice. He upheld this requirement even at the risk of a rift with Freud, who supported the principle of lay analysis. Brill's early experience in America had confirmed that professional status would come from a firm connection with medicine, and he actively sought to situate psychoanalysis in various medical societies, including the American Psychiatric Association and the New York Academy of Medicine. These organizations often elected him chairman of newly formed subdivisions. "I started as a psychiatrist and still am a psychiatrist," he declared in 1944, and he was committed to the view that psychoanalysis had transformed psychiatry into effective practice. Psychoanalysis provided a systematic theory of behavior and a method of practice, and it required a rigorous apprenticeship through a didactic analysis that distinguished its acolytes from the more eclectic, hospital-oriented practitioners of psychiatry. "Without psychoanalysis psychiatry would not have progressed much." As Brill's personal influence grew, he saw psychoanalysis gain in legitimacy and stature. Toward the end of his life, he gave Columbia's prestigious Salmon Lectures (published as *Freud's Contribution to Psychiatry* [1944]) and held visible posts at the New York University College of Medicine and at Columbia University.

Brill spent his life making psychoanalysis legitimate as well as popularly known. He was an indefatigable spokesman for its claims in pedagogy, criminology, and other social sciences and for its value as a tool to illuminate the nature of creativity and art. He was often interviewed in the press as America's "most famous psychoanalyst" as he was in 1932 during the Lindbergh kidnapping, when he assured readers that the child would not be traumatized by his experience. Brill never hesitated to give his opinions because he believed that psychoanalysis was universally relevant, a comprehensive system of human understanding. As a result, his interpretation of psychoanalysis tended toward the reductive and simplistic as he provided little homilies and practical lessons in personal adjustment. Later, critics berated Brill for his idiosyncratic stance and his simplified if enthusiastic renditions of Freud's complex, subtle, and often darkly pessimistic thought.

Yet Brill was an American success story and he supported an optimistic, pragmatic, and multipurpose application of Freudianism. His interpretations suited the times and the place and projected Freud into the center of twentieth-century therapeutics and culture. As Freud's tireless proselytizer, Brill introduced a generation of Americans to Freudian ideas and helped to frame how those ideas were understood and applied in the American context. He died in New York City.

• The Brill papers are at the Library of Congress. A list of Brill's writings (including the translations) is available in the *Psychoanalytic Quarterly* 17 (1948): 164–72. He wrote briefly about himself in "A Psychoanalyst Scans His Past," *Journal of Nervous and Mental Disease* 95 (1942): 537–49; "The Introduction and Development of Freud's Works in the United States," *American Journal of Sociology* 45 (1939): 318–25; and throughout *Freud's Contribution to Psychiatry* (1944). Secondary sources include John Chynoweth Burnham, *Psychoanalysis and American Medicine, 1894–1918: Medicine, Science, and Culture* (1967); Paula S. Fass, "A. A. Brill: Pioneer and Prophet" (M.A. thesis, Columbia Univ., 1968); Nathan Hale, Jr., *Freud and the Americans: The Beginning of Psychoanalysis in the United States, 1876–1917* (1971) and *The Rise and Crisis of Psychoanalysis in the United States: Freud and the Americans, 1917–1985* (1995); Clarence Oberndorf, *A History of Psychoanalysis in America* (1953); May E. Romm, "Abraham Arden Brill, 1874–1948," in *Psychoanalytic Pioneers*, ed. Franz Alexander et al. (1966); and David Shakow and David Rapaport, *The Influence of Freud on American Psychology* (1964). Obituaries are in the *New York Times*, 3 Mar. 1948; *Psychoanalytic Review* 35 (1948): 394–402; *Psychoanalytic Quarterly* 17 (1948): 146–72; and the *International Journal of Psychoanalysis* 29, pt. 1 (1948): 1–3.

PAULA S. FASS

BRIMS (fl. 1670–c. 1730), tribal leader of the Lower Creeks, was born to parents whose names are not recorded. His place of birth is likewise lost to history, although it may have been at Coweta, on the Chattahoochee River (Ala.), one of the four founding towns of the Creek confederation. He had apparently achieved the status of "emperor" or supreme *mico* of the Lower Creeks by 1670, although his first definite recorded appearance was in May 1711. At that time English settlers from the Carolinas were attempting to instigate a war between the neighboring Chickasaw and Choctaw tribes to the west. Brims joined an expedition against the Choctaws in the fall of that year, leading 1,300 men (along with English captain Theophilus Hastings) in a series of attacks on Choctaw settlements. Although Choctaw casualties were light (80 killed and 130 taken prisoner), some 400 dwellings were destroyed during the attacks. In the aftermath of the war, Brims met with Governor Charles Craven at Charles Town (modern Charleston, S.C.) in order "to acknowledge his Loyalty and Obedience to the British Nation."

The Creek confederation during this period was caught among the nations of England, France, and Spain as well as neighboring tribes (such as the Cherokees), all of whose presence in the area offered the potential for conflict. The Creeks, although bound to the English settlers by trade, found themselves increasingly swept up in the ever-shifting political alliances of the period. These alliances underwent a dramatic shift with the outbreak of the Yemassee War in April 1715. A neighboring tribe that was allied with the Creeks, the Yemassee reacted to a long string of abuses by English traders by attacking settlements in present-day South Carolina. Brims was accused by the English of instigating the attack, which included a massacre at the town of Pocotaligo, South Carolina. After a period of initial success (Brims's brother Chigelley, who held the position of head warrior of Coweta, led one attack almost to the gates of Charleston before being thrown back), a hoped-for Creek alliance with the Cherokees evaporated when English diplomatic efforts resulted in the murder of Creek envoys by the Cherokees. With their forces in retreat and plans for a military alliance with the Cherokees dashed, the Lower Creeks faced a difficult future.

Having suffered at the hands of the European powers, the Creeks returned to their former home on the Chattahoochie River in early 1716 (they had moved en masse to a site near present-day Macon, Georgia, on the Ocmulgee River in 1690 in order to more readily profit from trade with the English). Brims at this point developed a policy of neutrality between the Creeks and all three competing powers. In order to put his plans in place, however, relations with the English had to be normalized. Seeking protection against the English until matters cooled down, Brims initiated diplomatic efforts with the Spanish. He sent his son Sepeycoffee to the Spanish outpost of St. Augustine, where he sought the establishment of a Spanish fort at Coweta. After receiving a warm reception in Florida, Sepeycoffee returned to Coweta in August 1717, only to find Brims in serious peace negotiations with the English. As a result of careful diplomacy on the part of Brims, who gave his niece Coosaponakeesa (later known as Mary Musgrove or Mary Bosomworth) to Johnny, a mixed-blood son of English colonel John Musgrove, as a regal pledge, a peace treaty with the English was signed at Charleston, South Carolina, in the fall of 1717. With a tenuous peace in place with the English, a French fort (Toulouse) well established on the nearby junction of the Coosa and Tallapoosa rivers, and the Spanish assured of Creek esteem if not outright loyalty, Brims established a delicate balancing act that he maintained for the rest of his life. Brims's talents did not go unnoticed. One anonymous Carolinian declared that he was "as great a Politician as any Governor in America," while a Frenchman whose name is similarly lost to history stated that "no one has ever been able to make him take sides with one of the three European nations who know him . . . he alleging that he wishes to see everyone, to be neutral, and not to espouse any of the quarrels which the French, English and Spanish have with one another."

The period of relative calm did not proceed unchallenged, however; hostilities toward the Cherokees lingered, and the English made repeated efforts to get the Creeks to declare war against the remainder of the Yemassees, now under the protection of the Spanish in St. Augustine. Brims sent another son, Ouletta, to Charleston for additional peace talks that proved desultory in 1722, and in 1724 the English embargoed trade with the Creeks in an effort to force their hand. Brims remained loyal to his Yemassee allies (although divisions arose among the Creeks on this point) until a band of Yemassees killed Ouletta, who was strongly pro-English in his sentiments. In the late summer of 1724 Sepeycoffee led a war party against the Yemassee at St. Augustine. English pressures for war on the Yemassee and a complete Creek break with the Spanish nearly resulted in both actions, but a peace delegation from St. Augustine arrived in Coweta bearing the three severed heads of Ouletta's murderers. Appeased, Brims later (early 1726) renewed his talks with the Spanish when English-armed Cherokees appeared in Lower Creek country. Failing to gain the support of the Upper Creeks regarding a Spanish alliance, Brims then sent out diplomatic feelers to the English in Charleston. A preliminary meeting between the Creeks and Cherokees took place in Charleston in January 1727, but the delegates returned to Coweta only to find Brims unwilling to make peace with the Cherokees or to break with the Spanish. Brims's position weakened in the summer of 1727 when a rogue band of Creeks combined with several Yemassees in renewed attacks on English settlements. Faced with the threat of a renewed offensive by the Cherokees and a retaliatory embargo of Lower Creek towns by the English, Brims in December 1728 relented and consented to a final breaking of relations with both the Yemassees and the Spanish.

Brims had at least two wives and four sons. He sought to pass on his legacy of neutrality to his underage twin sons, Essabo and Malatchi, before dying sometime between 1730 and 1733 at an undisclosed location. He was succeeded as emperor by his brother Chigelley.

Faced with potential enemies on all sides, Brims led his people through some of the most difficult times that they had faced. Although the Creeks later suffered removal from their homelands (as did all southeastern tribes), their relative strength at the time of Brims's death stands as a testimony to his leadership.

• Primary sources relating to the activities of Brims and the Creeks can be found in the Journals of the Commons House of Assembly, South Carolina State Archives, Columbia, and among the Colonial Office Papers, British Public Record Office, London. The best secondary sources are Verner W. Crane, *The Southern Frontier, 1670–1732* (1928); David H. Corkran, *The Creek Frontier, 1540–1783* (1967); and John R. Swanton, *Early History of the Creek Indians and Their Neighbors*, bulletin no. 73 of the Bureau of Ethnology, Smithsonian Institution (1922).

EDWARD L. LACH, JR.

BRINKERHOFF, Jacob (31 Aug. 1810–19 July 1880), politician and jurist, was born in Niles, New York, the son of Henry I. Brinkerhoff and Rachel Bevier, farmers. Raised in rural New York, where he studied law, Brinkerhoff moved to Ohio in 1836 and began a legal practice in Mansfield. Combining politics with law, he served two terms as county prosecutor before he was elected to Congress as an expansionist Democrat. He served two terms (1843–1847), during which he represented a district of northeastern Ohio characterized by antislavery sentiment. Although a party regular on most issues, he broke with fellow Democrats over the joint resolution annexing Texas in 1845. As an opponent of the extension of slavery, he proposed an amendment prohibiting the institution in half of Texas; without it, he believed, northern whites would refuse to settle there. When the House rejected his proposal, he voted against annexation.

During the Polk administration, Brinkerhoff urged the end of the joint occupation arrangement with Great Britain in the Oregon Country. He claimed American title to the whole region. He voted for the declaration of war against Mexico in 1846 but soon joined the war's critics. His motivation included anger with the president over his patronage policy and a sincere opposition to the extension of slavery into any new territories acquired from Mexico.

Because of his opposition to slavery, Brinkerhoff helped to formulate the Wilmot Proviso, a proposal to ban slavery in any territory acquired from Mexico. (Although he claimed to be its author, and he played a role in the deliberations leading to the proviso's introduction, the evidence suggests that the idea originated with fellow Democrat David Wilmot of Pennsylvania.) Retiring from Congress in 1847, Brinkerhoff followed his antislavery convictions and in the following year joined the Free Soil party, which strongly endorsed the proviso. He believed the Democratic presidential nominee, Lewis Cass, to be a tool of the slave interests and instead supported Martin Van Buren. He also made an unsuccessful attempt to return to Congress. Like many other Free Soilers, his advocacy of the proviso had as much to do with the interests of his white constituents as it did with a concern over the plight of black Americans. He believed slavery would drive free white labor out of the territories and suggested he had "selfishness enough greatly to prefer the welfare of my own race to that of any other and vindictiveness enough to wish to leave and keep upon the shoulders of the South the burden of the curse which they themselves have created and courted" (letter to S. P. Chase, 11 Nov. 1847, Chase Papers, Historical Society of Pennsylvania).

Brinkerhoff followed a logical progression from the Free Soil to the Republican party, with a brief association with the nativist Know Nothing movement in the mid-1850s. His interest in the latter resulted from a concern shared by many Ohioans over the influx of large numbers of German and Irish Catholics into the state. In fact, he opportunistically sought (as an alternative nominee to Salmon P. Chase) the backing of nativists to become governor of Ohio on a fusion ticket in 1855. Nominated instead for a seat on the state supreme court, his election meant the start of a fifteen-year career as a jurist (1856–1871). The case that brought him the greatest attention was his dissent in the trial of those involved in the Oberlin-Wellington fugitive slave rescue of 1858. The court upheld the Fugitive Slave Act of 1850 by a 3 to 2 margin, with Brinkerhoff dissenting. He advanced a states' rights argument denying Congress the authority to legislate on the fugitive issue. Despite the constitutional provision that fugitives must be returned to their owners (Art. IV, Sec. 2), Brinkerhoff, like many other antislavery advocates, contended that slavery was a purely state institution and that it merited no protection by the federal government. After completing his third term on the court, he ended his political career as an active participant in the Liberal Republican movement of 1872.

Like so many leaders of his era, Brinkerhoff combined strong antislavery conviction with political expediency. In changing from Democrat to Free Soiler to Know Nothing to Republican, he revealed both a desire for influence and a genuine opposition to the expansion of slavery. Before his death in Mansfield, he had been married twice, in 1839 to Caroline Campbell, and, after her death, in 1842 to Marion Titus, with whom he had four children.

• There is no collection of Brinkerhoff papers. The most complete accounts of his activities in politics and as a jurist are in two volumes of *The History of the State of Ohio*, ed. Carl Wittke: vol. 3, Francis P. Weisenburger, *The Passing of the Frontier, 1825–1850* (1941), and vol. 4, Eugene H. Roseboom, *The Civil War Era, 1850–1873* (1944). Chaplain Morrison, *Democratic Politics and Sectionalism: The Wilmot Proviso Controversy* (1967), includes coverage of Brinkerhoff's two terms in Congress, while Henry Wilson, *History of the Rise and Fall of the Slave Power in America*, vol. 2 (1874), provides a contemporary account. His speeches in the House of Representatives are found in the *Congressional Globe* (28th and 29th Cong.), and his court opinions are included in *Ohio State Reports*, vols. 5–20 (1910). Stephen E. Maizlish, *The Triumph of Sectionalism: The Transformation of Ohio Politics, 1844–1856* (1983), includes an account of Brinkerhoff's role in both state and national politics before the Civil War.

FREDERICK J. BLUE

BRINTON, Crane (2 Feb. 1898–7 Sept. 1968), historian and educator, was born Clarence Crane Brinton in Winsted, Connecticut, the son of Clarence Hawthorne Brinton, a department-store buyer, and Eva Crane. He was educated at Harvard University, receiving his B.A. summa cum laude in 1919, and a Rhodes Scholarship in 1919 enabled him to study at Oxford University, where he earned a D.Phil. in 1923. His teaching career was spent solely at Harvard, beginning as an instructor in 1923 and rising through the academic ranks to professor in 1942. From 1942 to 1968 he was McLean Professor of Ancient and Modern History. Brinton married Cecilia Washburn Roberts, a psychologist, in 1946; they had no children.

First and foremost, Brinton was an intellectual historian. The task of such specialists, he held, was to bridge abstract ideas with the concrete actions of human beings. This involved being a philosopher in some ways and a social historian in others; the principal question for him was, "How do great issues manifest themselves in the every day lives of real people?" History, he wrote in *Ideas and Men: The Story of Western Thought* (1950), is a most useful guide in the formation of common sense. His own orientation to the intellectual progress of Western civilization arose from the debate between his two Harvard mentors, Harold Laski and Irving Babbitt, who taught him to appreciate both an optimistic rationalism and a healthy respect for the place of prejudice, the conscious, and the unconscious. He remained committed to the rightness of human reason.

The teaching of history in colleges and universities was of great interest to Brinton. He possessed a grand conception of "Western civilization," which became a foundational course. He found that in the West there was a high value placed on the natural sciences, a quality of human dignity, and an underlying belief that the good life was attainable on earth. In his post–World War II classic, *Ideas and Men: The Story of Western Thought*, he virtually created the syllabus for a course on the history of Western civilization, providing both suggested readings and topics for student essays. Fundamental to his approach was the reading of the classics of Western thought, which in itself spawned a generation of anthologies. With John B. Christopher of the University of Rochester and his colleague at Harvard, Robert Lee Wolff, Brinton produced the reliable two-volume *History of Civilization* (1955), used widely in North America as a standard introductory text. His own course at Harvard on the intellectual history of Europe in the eighteenth and nineteenth centuries attracted the largest enrollment for a single course at the university.

Brinton was one of the most respected historians of the mid-twentieth century. His more than twenty published books were used as texts in university courses and by specialists in several fields of intellectual history. His fields of specialization were Western intellectual history and the pattern of revolution. His Oxford doctoral dissertation, "The Political Ideas of the English Romanticists," led to several later publications. In his oft-quoted work on revolution, he studied the character of the English, American, French, and Russian revolutions. He concluded that revolutionaries are optimistic and desire less restraint and that in countries that experience a revolution there are usually bitter class antagonisms, the ruling class typically becomes politically inept, the government machinery becomes ineffective, and the intellectuals gradually desert the old regime. In analyzing the post–World War II situation, Brinton was asked to write an introduction to the British–U.S. diplomatic relationship, based on his residence in Britain from 1942 to 1944 with the Anglo-American Brains Trust. He wrote lucidly of the situation, proposing a major realignment of Western powers suggested by Russian communism. Similarly, in 1967 he wrote a volume for the American Foreign Policy Library on U.S.–French relations, in which he suggested a new pattern in recognition of the post-de-Gaulle era. Ever the ideological historian, he wrote an in-depth study of English political thought in the nineteenth century (republished in several editions) that found that era to be a period of reconstruction, dynamic progress, and a witness to the emergence of popular democracy. He understood his own century in light of the nineteenth.

One of the most honored practitioners of his craft, Brinton received many awards in his over half a century of work as an historian. A fellow of the National Institute of Arts and Letters, the American Philosophical Society, and the American Academy of Arts and Sciences, he was also a chevalier of the Legion d'Honneur and president of the American Historical Association. He died in Cambridge, Massachusetts.

• Brinton's papers are in the Harvard University archives. His works not mentioned above include *Political Ideas of the English Romanticists* (1926), *Jacobins: An Essay in the New History* (1930), *English Political Thought in the Nineteenth Century* (1933), *Decade of Revolution* (1934), *French Revolutionary Legislation on Illegitimacy* (1936), *Lives of Talleyrand* (1936), *Anatomy of a Revolution* (1938), *The United States and Britain* (1945), *From Many, One: The Progress of Political Integration and the Problem of Government* (1948), *Nietsche* (1948), *Shaping of Modern Thought* (1953), *A History of Civilization* (2 vols., 1955), *History of Western Morals* (1959), and *The Americans and the French* (1968). An obituary is in the *New York Times*, 8 Sept. 1968.

WILLIAM H. BRACKNEY

BRINTON, Daniel Garrison (13 May 1837–27 Oct. 1899), ethnologist, was born in Chester County, Pennsylvania, the son of Lewis Brinton and Ann Carey Garrison. Many members of his influential Quaker Philadelphia family had emigrated in 1684 from England. Prepared for college by a private tutor, Brinton took an interest in American Indians by reading Alexander von Humboldt's books of explorations and George McClintock's *Antiquarian Researches*, as well as conducting local searches for Delaware Indian artifacts. In 1858 he received a B.A. from Yale University, where he earned prizes in English composition and served as editor of the college literary magazine.

During his college years, ill health forced Brinton into an extended Florida holiday, resulting in his first book, *Notes on the Floridian Peninsula, Its Literary History, Indian Tribes and Antiquities* (1859). His lifelong preoccupations with assessment of documents, origin of the Indians, and evolutionary theory all appeared in this work.

Brinton was one of the first to argue that the Mississippi Mound Builders were the ancestors of the present-day Indians; he used etymology and philology as evidence for their history, as in his *Notes* and in *The Mound-Builders of the Mississippi Valley* (1866) and *The Probable Nationality of the Mound-Builders* (1881). A strong proponent of the "psychic unity of mankind"—a spontaneous outpouring of universal insights—Brinton linked this argument to his monogenist position of a single origin for the human species. When Brinton found similarities among cultures, therefore, he concluded that no historical explanation was needed. During his career, emphasis on diffusion, or borrowing of culture traits, became the most widely accepted explanation of cultural similarity. Brinton, however, never seriously reconsidered his 1859 position. This theoretical conservatism kept his work from being acknowledged by contemporaries and successors.

From 1858 to 1860 Brinton attended Jefferson Medical School in Philadelphia. He then traveled in Europe for a year, studying at the Universities of Paris and Heidelberg. On the eve of the Civil War, he returned to West Chester, Pennsylvania, to practice medicine. In Europe, Brinton came to lament the absence of clinical training in American medical education. Although he had no such training, he was better educated than most doctors of his generation. Brinton's medical degree and liberal arts education placed him among the elite who spearheaded the professionalization of American medicine.

In 1862 Brinton joined the Union army and was soon commissioned as a surgeon. He saw extensive action before suffering sunstroke at Gettysburg. Transferred to less active duty, he met and married in 1865

Sarah Tillson of Quincy, Illinois; they had two children. Health problems continued through his life.

Brinton practiced medicine until 1874, when he became editor of the weekly *Medical and Surgical Reporter*. His scientific reputation, however, was established primarily in ethnology. Between 1882 and 1890, Brinton published eight volumes, five of which were his own editings of Meso-American texts and another containing his own work on Lenape Delaware, of a *Library of Aboriginal American Literature*. In retrospect, the texts set an important standard for later work; at the time, however, they generated little interest.

Brinton was elected to the American Philosophical Society in 1869 and quickly became its most distinguished ethnologist. He served as secretary from 1888 to 1895 and chaired the publication committee at the time of his death. He was active in various other Philadelphia societies. During most of the 1890s he wrote an anthropology column for *Science*; he was one of only four nineteenth-century anthropologists to serve as president of its sponsoring American Association for the Advancement of Science. He was president of the International Congress of Anthropology in Chicago in 1893.

Brinton's interests were remarkably consistent throughout his long career. *Myths of the New World* (1868) began a focus on religion and psychology that persisted through his posthumous *The Basis of Social Relations* (1902). His books *Races and Peoples* (1890) and *The American Race* (1891) were culled from lecture courses at the Philadelphia Academy of Natural Sciences. He argued for the racial, linguistic, historical, and ethnic identity of the American Indian. In 1886 Brinton became the first university professor of anthropology ("Archaeology and Linguistics") in North America, at the University of Pennsylvania. His position was tied to research in the affiliated University Museum and apparently involved no students. Committed, nonetheless, to the professionalization of anthropology, he tried unsuccessfully to increase the university's commitment to it.

Brinton clashed with the new anthropology developing at Columbia University in association with Franz Boas, the major figure in twentieth-century American anthropology, at the end of the century. Boas, nevertheless, developed the academic base Brinton had failed to establish, emphasized fieldwork rather than armchair scholarship, and used Brinton as a convenient target for his critique of social evolution in anthropology. This resulted in a permanent eclipse of Brinton's reputation in American anthropology.

An amateur ethnologist whose career spanned the transition from gentleman scholarship to professional anthropology, Brinton earned his living as a medical doctor and scholarly editor; his anthropological publications appeared primarily through Philadelphia learned societies whose interests were not specific to his avocational discipline. He died in Media, Pennsylvania.

• Some of Brinton's papers are at the University of Pennsylvania Museum. Secondary sources include Regna Darnell, *Daniel Garrison Brinton: The "Fearless Critic" of Philadelphia*, University of Pennsylvania Museum Monograph 3 (1988). An obituary is in Albert Smyth et al., *Brinton Memorial Meeting: American Philosophical Society* (1900).

REGNA DARNELL

BRINTON, Howard Haines (24 July 1884–9 Apr. 1973), and **Anna Shipley Cox Brinton** (19 Oct. 1887–28 Oct. 1969), Quaker educators, were born in Chester County, Pennsylvania, and Iowa, respectively. Howard was the son of Edward Brinton and Ruthanna Brown, farmers. Anna was the daughter of Charles E. Cox, a businessman and educator, and Lydia Shipley Bean. Howard Brinton attended high school in West Chester and received a B.A. from Haverford College in 1904 with a specialization in science. After spending an extra year studying mysticism with Haverford professor of philosophy Rufus Jones, Brinton received his M.A. in 1909. Between 1905 and 1915 he taught mathematics and science at several Quaker secondary schools. He joined the faculty of Guilford College in North Carolina in 1915 and served as dean and acting president. He later returned to graduate school and received a Ph.D. in philosophy in 1924 from the University of California.

Anna Cox's grandparents, Joel and Hannah Bean, had established the Quaker meeting in 1884 in San Jose, California, in an effort to escape the revival influences of midwestern Guerneyite Friends and to preserve the evangelical doctrines and unprogrammed worship practices characteristic of Philadelphia and London Yearly Meetings. Her parents preserved the Philadelphia connection by sending Cox to Chester County's Westtown School, which was controlled by the Philadelphia Yearly Meeting. There she became enthralled with Latin before graduating in 1905. She received from Stanford a B.A. in 1909, an M.A. in 1913, and a Ph.D. in classical languages and archaeology in 1917. She had been studying at the American Academy in Rome in 1913 and was in Berlin when World War I began. She served as an instructor of archaeology at Mills College in Oakland, California, from 1916 to 1922.

In 1919–1920 Howard Brinton served as secretary and director of publications for the American Friends Service Committee (AFSC), and in 1920–1921 he worked on relief projects in Germany and Upper Silesia, Poland. In 1920 Cox was a member of an AFSC student relief group in Germany, where she met Brinton. She and Brinton were married in 1921. They had four children. In 1922 she became a professor of Latin at Earlham College in Richmond, Indiana; he was a professor of physics and also taught classes in religion and the Bible. They were early examples of husband and wife combining academic careers and child rearing. From 1928 to 1936 Anna was the first professor of archaeology at Mills College; she was also dean of the faculty from 1933 to 1936. Howard dropped science in favor of philosophy and religion and came to Mills as a professor of philosophy. His first book, based on his dissertation, was a study of European mystic Jacob Boehme. Howard and Anna Brinton held a joint fellowship at the Quaker study center in Woodbrooke, England, in 1931.

In 1936 the Brintons moved to Pendle Hill to serve as codirectors. Located in suburban Philadelphia, Pendle Hill provided a setting in which the AFSC could train its workers and in which more evangelical Orthodox and more liberal Hicksite Friends from the two Philadelphia Yearly Meetings and elsewhere might work together. Howard was shy and retiring, Anna more outgoing and practical. Together they shaped Pendle Hill. The Brintons recruited students, raised money, taught classes, and helped to define the mission of Pendle Hill as a school that offered neither grades nor diplomas, but rather combined an academic institution with a religious community and retreat center for the study of Quaker mysticism. The Brintons helped to create the Pendle Hill Pamphlets, a series of tracts that combine scholarship and religious devotion. Anna wrote three, Howard fifteen; together they edited more than one hundred. Most of Howard's books originated as Pendle Hill Pamphlets. Anna published works on fine arts, including two books about illustrated versions of Virgil's *Aeneid*, one on wood engravings of the fifteenth and sixteenth centuries and another on a nineteenth-century pre-Raphaelite version. She also published Pendle Hill Pamphlets on the Quaker art of silhouette cutting, Quakers in Russia, and women's issues.

Howard Brinton's writings define Quakerism as a mystical religion in which an inward sense of the presence of God supersedes outward creeds, liturgy, and sacraments. He disagreed with scholars who saw early Quakers as offshoots of English Puritans, stressing instead the influence of Continental mystics like Boehme. Brinton's historical works argue that, in spite of the many differences among Friends over a period of three centuries, mysticism remained the common denominator of Quakerism. In his writings Brinton relied heavily on the journals and religious diaries of prominent Friends that he considered a most important source of information on religious life.

Brinton used a variety of terms to describe mysticism. He did not believe that it could be precisely defined, calling it a "philosophy" and a "theology" and contrasting positive life-affirming Christian mysticism with negative Platonic and Eastern mysticism, which seeks escape from the world. He described Quaker mysticism as "ethical" and "prophetic," contemplative and active, grounded in a sense of "Inward Light" and resulting in social action. Brinton also insisted that Quaker mysticism, though originating in the Christian tradition, is part of a universal religious impulse. Thus Brinton could cite with approval the studies of psychologist Carl Jung on archetypes and the writings of Buddhists, Hindus, Muslims, and Native Americans. Without repudiating its Western heritage, he saw Quakerism as bridging the differences between Christianity and religions of the East. In content, Howard's writings resemble those of his mentor, Rufus Jones. Both men's books combine Quaker traditions, psychological insights, idealistic philosophy, historical research, and the authors' own religious experiences.

The Brintons supported the work of the AFSC. Anna Brinton served as commissioner in India and China (1946), was a member of the board of directors (1938–1952), and acted as vice chairman (1958–1960 and 1962–1965). After retiring from their directorships at Pendle Hill, the Brintons went to Japan to supervise AFSC work from 1952 to 1955. They then returned to live at Pendle Hill, where both continued to teach and write. Anna served as the representative from the Philadelphia Yearly Meeting to the World Council of Churches from 1962 to 1969. After her death in 1969 Howard was very frail and nearly blind, but he continued to write books and pamphlets. In 1972 he married Yuki Takahashi, his former secretary, who for years had served as housekeeper and companion to the Brintons. Both Anna and Howard died at Pendle Hill.

• The Brinton papers are at the Quaker Collection, Haverford College. Works by Howard Brinton include *The Mystic Will* (1930); *Creative Worship* (1931); *Quaker Education in Theory and Practice* (1940); *Friends for Three Hundred Years* (1952); *Quaker Journals* (1972); *The Religious Philosophy of Quakerism* (1973); and many Pendle Hill Pamphlets. He edited *Children of Light* (1938) and *Byways in Quaker History* (1944). Books by Anna Brinton include *Maphaeus Vegius and His Thirteenth Book of the Aeneid* (1930); *Descensus Averno: Fourteen Woodcuts* (1930); *A Pre-Raphaelite Aeneid* (1934); and *Quaker Profiles* (1964). She was editor for *Then and Now* (1960). For information about the Brintons, see Eleanor Price Mather, *Anna Brinton* (1971); Mather, *Pendle Hill, a Quaker Experiment in Education and Community* (1980); Dan Wilson, "Howard and Anna Brinton," in *Living in the Light*, vol. 1, ed. Leonard Kenworthy (1984).

J. WILLIAM FROST

BRINTON, John Hill (21 May 1832–18 March 1907), surgeon, was born in Philadelphia, Pennsylvania, the son of George Brinton and Mary Margaret Smith, upper-class Quakers. He entered the University of Pennsylvania in 1846 and graduated with a B.A. in 1850. Two years later he received his M.D. from Jefferson Medical College. Following his graduation he spent a year in postgraduate medical studies in Europe; in Paris he studied surgery, and in Vienna he studied with Joseph Hyrtl, the dean of topographic and regional anatomy. In 1853 he was awarded an M.A. degree.

Brinton returned to Philadelphia in April 1853 and began his practice in general medicine. Between 1853 and 1861 he maintained a busy schedule as a physician, teacher, and researcher. His interest in anatomy prompted him to participate in research and to lecture on anatomic dissection, experimentation, and operative and general surgery at the Philadelphia Association for Medical Instruction. In 1854 he edited the American edition of Sir John Erich Erichsen's *The Science and Art of Surgery, Being a Treatise on Surgical Injuries, Diseases and Operations*. In 1859 Brinton was appointed to the staff of St. Joseph's Hospital as surgeon and consultant.

At the outset of the Civil War Brinton enlisted in the Union army. In August 1861 he was commissioned as a brigade surgeon in the United States Volunteers. He was assigned to the staff of Brigadier General Ulysses S. Grant, who appointed him medical director of the military district of Southeast Missouri with the rank of major. Without any military training, Brinton had to depend on his intelligence and ingenuity, his medical education, his practical training as a surgeon, and the assistance provided by the United States Sanitary Commission; all helped him to cope with the turbulent, confusing, unsanitary conditions in the army. Concerned about the lack of experience and knowledge of surgery among his medical associates, Brinton organized the Army Medical and Surgical Society of Cairo (Illinois) as a school to improve their skills.

After the battle of Shiloh, 6–7 April 1862, Brinton was assigned to duty in the office of Surgeon General William A. Hammond in Washington, D.C. In June 1862 Brinton was asked to prepare for publication *The Medical and Surgical History of the War of the Rebellion*, designed to provide accurate statistics on the sick and wounded during the first year of the war. In 1863 he completed the section on gunshot wounds. In August 1862 he was assigned to collect and arrange for exhibition all the morbid (pathological) specimens that had been collected in military hospitals and by individual physicians. Brinton organized the establishment of the Army Medical Museum and was its first curator.

While on duty in Washington Brinton received many varied assignments: to determine more accurately the ratio of wound to death statistics; to collect specimens for the museum; and as an epidemiologist, to investigate hospital gangrene among Union soldiers returning from prison camps in the South. He initiated an effort to establish an Army medical school for graduate medical studies, but Secretary of War Edwin N. Stanton refused to grant authorization. Much later, however, on 13 March 1896, Brinton had the pleasure of giving the valedictory address to the second graduating class of the Army Medical School in Washington, D.C.

As a surgeon assigned to the Army of the Potomac, Brinton participated in many of the major battles of the war. In September 1864 he was transferred to the Department of Missouri, where he served as medical director under General William S. Rosecrans. He was subsequently appointed superintendent of hospitals in Nashville and medical director of the Army of the Cumberland. With the end of the war in sight and family matters to be resolved, on 11 February 1865 he resigned from the army.

Brinton returned to Philadelphia and resumed his medical practice. In 1866 he married Sarah Ward of Genesco, New York; they had six children, but only three survived their parents. In addition to a busy clinical practice and his research activities, Brinton conducted private classes in surgery. In 1866 he was appointed by the faculty of the Jefferson Medical School as lecturer on operative surgery in the newly established Summer Association, a program that provided classes for medical students during the extended summer recess, and in 1867 he was elected as one of the surgeons of the Philadelphia Hospital. On 6 January 1869 Brinton was awarded the prestigious Mütter Museum lectureship of the College of Physicians of Philadelphia. His lectures focused on "Gunshot Injuries, Their Surgery and Pathology." Brinton remained an active participant in the affairs of the museum throughout his life. When the new Jefferson Hospital was being planned, he raised $150,000 through the alumni association, and when it opened in 1877, he was appointed surgeon. He served for five years as president of the hospital medical staff.

In 1882 Brinton was appointed professor of the practice of surgery and clinical surgery at Jefferson Medical College. His lectures were said to be well prepared, informative, and interesting. Brinton was not a prolific medical writer; his main contributions to medical literature were his published lectures, his articles on gunshot wounds, and his valedictory speech to the graduates of the Army Medical School in 1896. *Personal Memoirs of John H. Brinton, Major and Surgeon, U.S.V., 1861–1865* was published in 1914.

Brinton was an active member of many social, civic, cultural, scientific, and professional organizations. He assisted Samuel David Gross in establishing the Jefferson Alumni Association in 1870, the Philadelphia Academy of Surgery in 1879, and the American Surgical Association in 1880. In May 1906, Brinton resigned his position and was appointed professor emeritus at Jefferson Medical College. He died at his home in Philadelphia. His colleagues at Jefferson Medical College and his peers in the Philadelphia medical fraternity viewed his intense ambition, boundless energy, scientific curiosity, teaching ability, and cultural refinement as the source of his professional success.

• Details of Brinton's career are noted in Edward Louis Bauer, *Doctors Made in America* (1963), Burton A. Konkle, *Standard History of the Medical Profession of Philadelphia* (1977), W. S. W. Rauschenberger, *An Account of the Institution and Progress of the College of Physicians of Philadelphia during a Hundred Years from January 1787* (1887), and Frederick B. Wagner, *Thomas Jefferson University: Tradition and Heritage* (1989). See also biographical sketches in *Military Surgeon* 22 (1907): 221–23; and *New Medical Journal* 85 (23 Mar. 1907): 559. An obituary is in the *Philadelphia Press*, 19 Mar. 1907.

SAM ALEWITZ

BRISBANE, Albert (22 Aug. 1809–1 May 1890), utopian socialist, was born in Batavia, New York, the son of James Brisbane, a merchant and landowner, and Mary Stevens. His father, a former agent of the Holland Land Company, amassed a fortune in real estate; his mother was an amateur scholar.

The young Brisbane, carefree and inquisitive, developed a passion for philosophy. In 1828, after two years of being tutored in French and philosophy in New York City, Brisbane sailed to Europe for what turned out to be six years of study and travel. He attended the lectures of the eclectic philosopher Victor Cousin in Paris, then departed for the University of Berlin, where he adopted Hegel's social theories. Gradually, however, his acceptance of Hegel's absolute philosophical idealism was eclipsed by his direct observation of social conditions. Leaving Berlin, he journeyed eastward to Greece and Turkey, then returned via Italy to Paris shortly after the revolution of 1830. In Parisian soirées the reform faith promoted by the disciples of Henri de Saint-Simon confirmed his impression that only a thorough transformation of society, not metaphysics or politics, could eliminate the poverty he had seen. During the winter of 1831–1832, Brisbane brought Saint-Simonianism to the liberal circle in Berlin that centered around Jewish salon hostess Rahel Varnhagen von Ense and included the poet Heinrich Heine. But when a friend sent him a copy of Charles Fourier's *Traité de l'Association Domestique-Agricole* (1822), he found in its elaborate rationale for planned communities (called *phalanxes*) "the means of solving the great problem of human destiny" (R. Brisbane, p. 172). He rushed back to Paris, paid Fourier for six weeks of private lessons, and spent the next two years studying the master's visionary system of psychology and social philosophy with members of the French Fourierist school.

In 1834 Brisbane returned to the United States and plunged into land speculation with the hope of underwriting a model phalanx in America. When the financial collapse of 1837 ruined this scheme, Brisbane turned to propaganda. In 1840 he published *Social Destiny of Man*, which condensed and translated Fourier's theory, and began organizing Fourier clubs in New York, Philadelphia, and Buffalo. His readership mushroomed when he arranged with Horace Greeley of the *New York Tribune* to run a daily column devoted to "Association; or Principles of a True Organization of Society" on its front page. From March 1842 to September 1843 these articles brought Fourierism into thousands of reform-minded households in the antebellum North. Brisbane gathered his articles into a tract, *A Concise Expositon of the Doctrine of Association* (1844), which sold 10,000 copies.

Brisbane's propaganda effectively channeled into Fourierism both the idealism of middle-class reformers and the anxieties of workers displaced by economic depression in the early 1840s. He shrewdly edited Fourier's theory for Americans, stripping its frank hedonism and futuristic fantasies and whittling the remainder to a simple blueprint guaranteeing generous profits for cooperative communities. Persistent and indefatigable, he gave public lectures, drafted model constitutions, and buttonholed writers and politicians. "His utterance was a monologue always," Mary Gove Nichols complained in her memoir *Mary Lyndon* (1855), "and his endurance only measured by the attention he received. If you would listen ten, twenty, thirty hours, it was all the same to him." But those in sympathy with the idea of model communities found him enthralling, "so full of feeling and entire devotion to the cause of God and humanity, that he has won our hearts" (Dwight, p. 91).

Brisbane's energetic promotion of Fourier's theory marked the antebellum era, according to F. O. Matheissen, as the "Age of Fourier" in American social thought (*American Renaissance* [1941], p. viii). In the North, Ralph Waldo Emerson developed his concepts of self-reliance and individualism in opposition to utopian socialism; feminists and free-love advocates adopted Fourier's critique of the "isolated household"; and abolitionists debated Fourierists over the comparative evils of chattel slavery and "wage slavery." Southern proslavery theorists such as George Fitzhugh used Fourierist concepts to criticize northern capitalism.

As a communitarian plan, Fourierism enjoyed a brief but spectacular triumph in 1843 and 1844. Brisbane established the *Phalanx*, which endured six years under various names as the movement's journal; he helped convert Brook Farm, the prestigious Transcendentalist community founded in 1841 at West Roxbury, Massachusetts, by George Ripley, into a phalanx; and he encouraged the formation of twenty miniature Fourierist experiments from New York to Iowa. But Brisbane was unprepared for Americans' sudden rush into poorly organized communal experiments and proved incapable of imposing discipline on the movement. He retreated in 1844 to Paris to study Fourier's manuscripts. By the time he returned the following year, most of the tiny communal experiments had failed. Brisbane urged concentration on a single phalanx: either Brook Farm, which disbanded in 1847, or the North American Phalanx in New Jersey, which survived as the most elaborate American Fourierist experiment until 1855.

In 1847 Brisbane retired from the declining Fourierist movement, but the French Revolution of 1848 revived his hopes. He went to Paris, witnessed the bloody June workers' insurrection, then traveled to Germany and Italy to inspect revolutionary movements there. He brought back from the failed European revolutions a commitment to practical workers' reforms such as producer and consumer cooperatives. Brisbane also convinced exiled French Fourierist leader Victor Considerant to undertake a communal experiment in America. In 1853 the two traveled through the northern states and then down the Great Plains to Texas, where Considerant decided to locate a settlement of French Fourierists to be supplemented by American sympathizers. The result was the ill-fated colony of La Réunion (1855–1859), which Brisbane invested in but did not join.

Throughout the period of Fourierist influence Brisbane never led or joined a communal venture. His wife Redelia, recalling his guileless and impractical nature, noted that "no one could have been less adapted to the great work undertaken" (R. Brisbane, p. 7). Yet Brisbane was shrewd enough not to squander his inheritance on utopian projects, and his unconventional private life blended expediency with sentiment. Although his edition of Fourierism postponed sexual liberation to future generations, he considered himself exempt from bourgeois norms. His first wife, Adèle Le Brun, whom Brisbane had married in 1833, returned to Europe in 1838, although the couple never obtained a divorce. In 1839 Brisbane had an affair with Lodoiska Durand, his New York tutor's married daughter, and later they lived in common-law marriage. In 1860 he married Sarah White; after she died six years later Brisbane again cohabited with Mrs. Durand until he married the young, adoring Redelia Bates. Though he denied endorsing free love, Brisbane went through four marriages of varying legality, pursued other women, and fathered ten children, three of whom were illegitimate. Such activities did not become public until a sensational divorce suit by Mrs. Durand in 1883, but his behavior privately alienated several key Fourierist colleagues.

After the Civil War Brisbane continued to advocate Fourierism. He debated John Humphrey Noyes of the Oneida community on the merits of their respective socialisms. He assisted in organizing Silkville, a Kansas colony founded in 1869 by French expatriate Ernest Valenton de Boissiere, but was denied a guiding role. In published treatises and in manuscripts circulated among friends, he searched for compelling new ways to restate Fourier's theory and churned out proposals for mechanized agricultural colonies. Latching on to newer reform crusades—currency reform, the American Social Science Association, the Knights of Labor—Brisbane sought with limited success to inject Fourierist influence into them.

Much time in Brisbane's later years was taken with promoting several inventions he conceived after the Civil War, including a greenhouse heater, a method of preserving corpses using evaporation, and a system of transport by hollow spheres through pneumatic tubes. (A pilot underground tube of the latter sort for Washington, D.C., was funded by Congress in 1872 but never completed.) He attempted without success to progress beyond Fourierism to a "science of laws" or "method of study" to bequeath to later social theorists. Having returned to the United States after an extended stay in France, he died in Richmond, Virginia.

To the end Brisbane "acknowledge[d] but one Mind on this earth—the great Fourier" (letter to Redelia, 7 Apr. 1875, Univ. of Illinois). Idealistic and ambitious but not a deep or original thinker, he was by temperament a disciple and publicist. By the 1890s most radicals had abandoned the Fourierist idea of model communities in favor of socialist or Populist programs of government ownership. But a half-century earlier Brisbane had succeeded in hitching many Americans' quest for utopia to the meteoric ascent of Fourierism.

• Brisbane's papers, dating mainly from the 1830s and the period from 1866 to his death, are scattered: letters and notebooks are in the Illinois Historical Survey at the University of Illinois, Urbana; travel diaries (1830–1832) and other materials are in the Arents Library at Syracuse University; and numerous letters from the French National Archives are on microfilm at the Western Historical Manuscripts Collection, University of Missouri, Columbia. See also Terry H. Pickett and Françoise de Rocher, *Letters of the American Socialist Albert Brisbane to K. A. Varnhagen von Ense* (1986). Personal papers from the crucial 1840s are scarce, but Brisbane's role in the Fourierist movement can be glimpsed in Marianne Dwight Orvis, *Letters from Brook Farm 1844–1847* (1928). Among his published outlines of Fourierism are *Treatise on the Functions of the Human Passions* (1857) and *General Introduction to Social Science* (1876). Redelia Brisbane, comp., *Albert Brisbane: A Mental Biography* (1893), is actually a disjointed, incomplete autobiography that includes a character sketch by his last wife; many of its errors are corrected in Arthur Bestor, "Albert Brisbane—Propagandist for Socialism in the 1840s," *New York History* 28 (1947): 128–58. The fullest analysis of Brisbane's writings and activities is Carl J. Guarneri, *The Utopian Alternative: Fourierism in Nineteenth-Century America* (1991). See also Richard N. Pettitt, Jr., "Albert Brisbane: Apostle of Fourierism in the United States, 1834–1890" (Ph.D. diss., Miami Univ. [Ohio], 1982), on his inventions and private life.

CARL J. GUARNERI

BRISBANE, Arthur (12 Dec. 1864–25 Dec. 1936), journalist and newspaper editor, was born in Buffalo, New York, the son of Albert Brisbane, a propagator of Fourier socialism, which advocated the establishment of model utopian communities, and his second wife, Sarah White. Extensive family real estate holdings had enabled Albert Brisbane to pursue a polymathic career, and when his wife died in 1866, Albert decided to use their two sons as test cases of his ideas on education. Arthur and his brother Fowell were brought up primarily on the family estate, "Fanwood Farm," in New Jersey, where, as Albert put it, they were encouraged to run free "like wild colts." Reared on a diet of salad, yogurt, and diluted red wine, the boys were forbidden to play with other children, to learn to read, or to cut their blond tresses. These methods failed to improve the health of Fowell, who was mildly retarded from birth. But Arthur, who learned to read in defiance of his father's orders, appeared to thrive.

Albert's third marriage, to Redelia Bates, put an end to this experiment. Arthur, then thirteen, was sent to Europe, where he received a rigorous education in a French boarding school. Returning to the United States shortly before his nineteenth birthday, he decided to forgo college in favor of newspaper work.

Hired by Charles Dana as a reporter for the *New York Sun*, Brisbane was barely literate in English and resorted to writing his stories in French and translating them with the aid of a pocket dictionary. In the long run, however, his lack of familiarity with the culture of his native land proved an asset, infusing his prose with naive enthusiasm. In 1885 Brisbane became the *Sun*'s European correspondent. An avid amateur boxer and sometime sparring partner of Jim Corbett, he covered the John L. Sullivan–Charlie Mitchell title fight in Chantilly, France, as well as the Jack the Ripper murders in London. In 1887 he was summoned back to New York to take over the *Sun*'s evening edition, where he promoted the careers of Richard Harding Davis and Jacob Riis.

Widely regarded as the reform-minded Dana's chosen successor, Brisbane stunned his colleagues in 1890 by resigning to join Joseph Pulitzer's *World*, a paper whose appeal to recent immigrants was considered, in some quarters, tantamount to rabble-rousing. During the following six years Brisbane held various responsible positions in both the editorial and the business offices of the paper. His greatest challenge came in January 1896, when William Randolph Hearst hired away Morrill Goddard, editor of the *World*'s Sunday edition. Goddard and his entire staff decamped without notice, leaving Brisbane to manage the transition in the midst of a circulation war. Brisbane triumphed, demonstrating his mastery of the "crime, underwear and pseudoscience" school of journalism that Goddard had pioneered. When a decapitated corpse was found in the Hudson River, he published an artist's drawing of "The Missing Head of Pearl Bryan." The impending execution of a woman in the electric chair at Sing Sing penitentiary prompted an interview with the executioner, accompanied by an illustration of reporter Kate Swan posing in the death chair. Brisbane was accused of condescending to his working-class readers, but his enthusiasm for lurid crime news as well as for phrenology and certain other bypaths of established science was genuine.

Blind and increasingly reclusive, Pulitzer valued Brisbane's skill as a raconteur and expected him to wait in attendance daily. Gradually it became apparent to Brisbane that Pulitzer's desire to employ him as a glorified private secretary was inhibiting his career, and in early 1897 he, too, defected to the Hearst organization. There, once again, he became his employer's most trusted associate. Under Brisbane's leadership, the Sunday *Journal* increased its circulation eight times over, and he was soon assigned to rescue the paper's evening edition, a perennial money loser.

Hearst was a vigorous advocate of American intervention in Cuba, but when the USS *Maine* sank in Havana harbor in February 1898 the *Journal* found itself in the embarrassing position of being without a senior correspondent on the scene. After a brief hesitation, Brisbane published an inflammatory story by a stringer under the headline WAR! SURE! MAINE DESTROYED BY SPANISH . . . PROVED ABSOLUTELY BY THE DISCOVERY OF THE TORPEDO HOLE! Neither the navy's court of inquiry nor independent divers hired by the *Journal* was able to produce solid evidence of Spanish sabotage, a problem Brisbane disguised by resorting to ever-larger headlines, shorter stories, and the creative use of illustrations and blank space.

After war was declared, Brisbane had editions of the *Journal* delivered by train throughout New York State, an innovation that made the paper a voice of the regional Democratic party and set the stage for Hearst's entry into electoral politics. In the years that followed, Brisbane played a key role in the expansion of the Hearst newspaper empire, a cause close to his heart. A shrewd businessman, Brisbane prided himself on his ability to woo advertisers, win circulation wars, and control costs. He once said, only half in jest, that when he took over the *Evening Journal* he needed only two reporters, one of whom was assigned to rewrite the lead stories of the paper's chief rival, the *World*. Later in his career, he took on difficult assignments, including the launching of the *Chicago American* in 1900 and the editorship of the tabloid *New York Daily Mirror* during the 1930s.

Brisbane was well compensated for his efforts; in 1900 his salary was an unprecedented $50,000, rising to $260,000 in 1936. In addition, he augmented his private fortune through investments in mid-Manhattan real estate. Among other projects, he was the developer of the Ritz Tower, New York's first residential skyscraper. At one time or another, he purchased newspapers in Milwaukee, Wisconsin, New Jersey, and Washington, D.C., which he resold to Hearst at a profit.

Brisbane's desire to write a signed editorial column had been a source of friction in his relationship with Pulitzer. At the *Journal* he wrote many unsigned editorials, including an intemperate attack on William McKinley thought by some to amount to a call for the president's assassination, but he was not given a byline of his own until 1917. For the ensuing two decades, his column "To-Day" appeared on the front page of the larger Hearst papers and was syndicated in 200 daily newspapers and as many as 800 weeklies in the United States and abroad, prompting the Hearst chain's public relations department to claim that he was the most widely read writer in the history of the world. The subject matter of the column ranged from political commentary to homilies on self-improvement through self-education, thrift, and clean living.

As a young man, Brisbane kept a home in Brooklyn and, later, a farm on Long Island, both of which he shared with his brother Fowell, to whom he was devoted. For the most part, however, he was to be found at one or another of his Manhattan clubs. Having followed a health-food diet since infancy and avoided tobacco, he confidently expected to live to be a hundred. According to an unpublished memoir by his friend David Gray, Brisbane had his course planned out: "He would experiment with life for fifty years, then he would marry and give twenty years to educating his children. After seventy he would begin his mature work." Following the second part of this agenda, Brisbane was married in July 1912 to Phoebe Cary, a distant family connection. The union produced six children.

After Brisbane's seventieth birthday, however, his health began to deteriorate. He had grown irritable with the years, and his denunciations of Franklin Roosevelt's New Deal (which he called the "Raw Deal") evoked so many protests that Hearst pressed him to consider retirement. Nevertheless, in 1936 he accompanied "the Chief" on a tour of Italy, where he contracted dysentery. He never completely recovered and died at his home in New York City a few months later.

Well into middle age, Brisbane identified himself as a socialist and often spoke of leaving the Hearst organization to found a small newspaper that would promote his views. Nevertheless, he was most comfortable in the role of the loyal lieutenant. A profile in the December 1925 issue of *Collier's Weekly* summarized his role in the organization: "When a newspaper is to be bought, Brisbane does the buying and starts the paper on its way." As a writer and editorialist, Brisbane devoted himself to popularizing the ideas of others, yet he left his mark on American journalism, developing many of the layouts and story angles that have become staples of the tabloid style.

• Brisbane's papers, including personal correspondence and an extensive series of scrapbooks, are in the George Arents Research Library at the University of Syracuse. See also the Albert Brisbane Collection in the same location. His published works include a biography, *Mary Baker Eddy* (1908), as well as several collections of his columns, distributed largely to subscribers of the Hearst newspapers. Oliver Carlson, *Brisbane: A Candid Biography*, appeared in 1938. Also useful is Samuel Crowther, "A Talk with Arthur Brisbane," *Collier's*, 5 Dec. 1925, and various obituary notices, especially in *Editor & Publisher*, 2 and 9 Jan. 1937. In the absence of a thoroughly researched modern biography, students of Brisbane must rely on works that touch on aspects of his life. These include Redelia Brisbane, *Albert Brisbane: A Mental Biography* (1903); Emile Gaubreau, *My Last Million Readers* (1949); Alan Churchill, *Park Row* (1958); Joyce Milton, *The Yellow Kids* (1989); and, most importantly, W. A. Swanberg, *Citizen Hearst* (1961).

JOYCE MILTON

BRISBIN, James Sanks (23 May 1837–11 Jan. 1892), soldier, was born in Boalsburg, Pennsylvania, the son of Ezra Brisbin, a farmer, and Margaret Packer. He received a good education at the Boalsburg Academy. While still in his teens, he moved to Bellefonte, Pennsylvania, where he read law and wrote for the *Centre Democrat*, of which he later became editor in chief. He achieved notoriety as an antislavery orator and in 1860 was attacked by a mob in Wheeling, Virginia (now West Virginia), for advocating the election of Abraham Lincoln. By his own account the treatment he received so increased his hatred of slavery that he published a letter offering to lead an armed force into Virginia to liberate slaves, causing considerable stir.

At the outbreak of the Civil War, Brisbin closed his printing office and enlisted as a private in the Pennsvalley Volunteers from Boalsburg. He then tried to go to Washington, D.C., in the hope of obtaining a commission. He was recognized at Baltimore as the man who had offered to "invade Virginia," was arrested by Marshall Kane, but escaped on the way to the police station.

Having obtained a commission as a second lieutenant in the regular army, Brisbin reported to Carlisle Barracks, Pennsylvania, with the First Regiment of United States dragoons, afterward the First Cavalry. In July 1861 he marched to Washington with a detachment of recruits and thence to Centreville, Virginia, where he arrived at midday during the first battle of Manassas. First wounded by rebel artillery and small arms fire, he was later sabered by a Union officer whose unit he had attempted to block in its retreat. Promoted to first lieutenant and shortly thereafter captain, and having read of his own death in the newspapers, Brisbin returned to Pennsylvania to convalesce.

Also in 1861 Brisbin married Mary Jane Wagner of Bellefonte. Only fifteen at the time of the marriage, she had seven children, mostly at frontier forts, before her death in 1887. In 1890 Brisbin married Amelia Wilson of Red Wing, Minnesota; they had no children together.

After a stint in Ohio on recruiting duty, Brisbin was assigned in May 1862 to active duty with the Sixth Cavalry. He served in the Peninsular campaign under General George McClellan, and at Malvern Hill. He was with General Alfred Pleasanton in the campaigns along the base of the Blue Ridge. In the battle of Beverly Ford, on 9 June 1863, he was conspicuous for gallantry and for this received the brevet rank of major in the regular army. During Robert E. Lee's invasion of Pennsylvania, Brisbin served as chief of cavalry on the staff of General Darius N. Couch, then commanding the Department of the Susquehanna. He commanded Pennsylvania militia at the battle of Gettysburg. He was twice elected a colonel of cavalry by Pennsylvania troops, but Governor Andrew G. Curtin refused to commission him because he had opposed his nomination as governor of Pennsylvania in 1860. Camp Brisbin, near Harrisburg, was named in his honor.

In the fall of 1863 Captain Brisbin rejoined the Army of the Potomac and in December of that year wrote to Congressman Benjamin Wade of Ohio advocating increased enlistment of blacks. Brisbin was thereafter appointed a colonel of Colored Troops. Eventually assigned to the Fifth Cavalry under General Albert Lee (1864), he accompanied General Nathaniel Banks on his expedition up the Red River and was again wounded at Sabine Cross Roads in April 1864. After Banks's defeat, Brisbin was reassigned to recruiting duty in Kentucky and as chief of staff to General S. G. Burbridge, serving in all the battles of Burbridge's command. He raised nearly 20,000 Colored Troops in Kentucky, including the 107th, 108th, 109th, 14th, 15th, 17th, 18th, 19th, 122d, 123d, 124th, and 125th regiments of Colored Infantry, the 12th and 13th regiments of Heavy Artillery, and the 5th and 6th regiments of Colored Cavalry.

Brisbin's recruiting efforts in Kentucky were so successful as to rouse intense local opposition. In defense of his programs, he asserted that enlistment of blacks would prevent bands of escaped slaves from pillaging the countryside. He advocated their full enfranchisement and stated that his black troops had higher literacy and lower desertion rates than whites of the same region. He went on to urge that women be given the right to vote and that the property of Confederate officers be confiscated. One of his speeches in this vein was published at Louisville in 1864 and was widely reprinted in the national press. In October and December 1864 Brisbin's Colored Troops saw action in the expeditions against the Virginia salt works, and Brisbin was appointed brigadier by brevet, with promotion in May 1865 to brigadier general of volunteers.

According to a letter by General John McNeil, Brisbin was "one of the few officers of the old army who early sought . . . to command negroes in the field and who has full faith in their abilities as soldiers."

Brisbin mustered out of the U.S. Volunteers in 1866 and rejoined the Sixth U.S. Cavalry as a captain, having served in twenty-eight pitched battles throughout the Civil War. In 1868 he was made major of the Second U.S. Cavalry, serving with General Philip H. Sheridan in the Indian wars on the Republican River and northern Kansas from Fort Russell, Wyoming. From 1869 to 1871 he was sent to Wind River Country, in command of two troops of the Second Cavalry. After three years at Omaha Barracks, he was sent in 1875 to Fort Ellis, Montana, and took part in the campaigns against the Sioux. He was present at the conference in which General Alfred H. Terry planned the operations that led to the annihilation of George Custer and his force at Little Big Horn River. According to one widely accepted account, Terry's initial proposal to attach Brisbin and his troops to Custer's was rejected by Custer, so Brisbin remained with the forces under Terry. A detailed description of the campaign and its aftermath that appeared in the *New York Herald*, 8 July 1876, was probably written by Brisbin. Appointed Custer's successor by Terry, he maintained to the end of his life that Custer's debacle was a result of his disobeying orders "in letter as well as spirit." He continued the campaign against the Sioux as commander of Fort Ellis and later Fort Custer and as chief of cavalry of Dakota Territory. In 1879 and 1880 Brisbin was stationed at Fort Assinniboine and Fort Keogh, Montana. In 1884 his Second Cavalry was sent to the Pacific Coast, and Brisbin took command of Boise Barracks, Idaho.

The next year he was promoted to lieutenant colonel of the Ninth U.S. Cavalry, commanding at Fort Niobara, Nebraska, and in 1887 at Fort McKinney, Wyoming. A year later Brisbin was shocked and embittered to be relieved of his command there for debility and general ineptitude. Transferred to Fort Robinson, Nebraska, Brisbin was promoted colonel at the death of the commander of the First Cavalry, commanding at Fort Custer, Montana. Plagued by ill health and partial paralysis, he retired in 1891 after thirty years of service in the U.S. Army.

Brisbin was a prolific author. He produced a pamphlet on the postwar reorganization of the U.S. Army (1865) and contributed numerous letters and articles to the public press, especially concerning affairs in the Northwest. He took considerable interest in military biography and wrote biographies of Ulysses Grant (1868) and James Garfield (1880), the latter reissued under the name of newspaperman William Ralston Balch, leaving Brisbin uncredited. He also published a biography of the Union general Winfield Scott Hancock (1880).

Brisbin edited the memoirs of a raconteur and adventurer named James Belden (1870) and in *The Beef Bonanza* (1881) sought to persuade settlers to undertake large-scale cattle raising in the West. He published a description of Yellowstone in 1882. In a series of articles and a book titled *Trees and Tree-Planting* (1888), Brisbin urged that Congress protect the great forests of Montana, Washington, and Oregon and advocated systematic replanting of what were considered "wild" or "forest" trees. His pleas went largely unheard.

Contemporary description records that Brisbin was a splendid figure of a man, with a commanding presence and tactical sense that suited him for military life. Later sources, fairly or not, portray a crotchety, garrulous officer, loath to mount a horse, viewed with impatience by his superiors though with affection and respect by those he commanded. In Montana his men called him "Grasshopper Jim," perhaps because of his having led a relief effort in 1874–1875 for locust-scourged Nebraska and Kansas, although some attribute the name to his fondness for expatiating on the agricultural potential of Montana. His writing suggests keen powers of observation, narrative skill, and a strong historical sense.

After Brisbin's retirement a bank failure wiped out his savings and left him and his family nearly destitute. He died in a Philadelphia hotel.

• Archival sources include the personnel file of James Brisbin in the National Archives, letters received by the Appointment, Commissions, and Personal Branch, Adjutant General's Office (1871–1894), in which some earlier material is included. This file contains an autobiographical memoir on his Civil War service. His pension file contains a comprehensive statement of his service and family information. A scrapbook in the Rollins Collection, New Jersey Public Library, contains a collection of newspaper articles written by Brisbin. Published sources include a sketch in vol. 4 of the *Cyclopaedia of American Biography*, written during his lifetime, and Ezra J. Warner, *Generals in Blue: Lives of the Union Commanders* (1964), p. 45 (with an early photo). For Brisbin's assessment of Custer, letters are quoted by Cyrus Townsend Brady, *Indian Fighting and Fighters* (1913), pp. 377–78; additional material on this topic is in the Francis R. Hagner Papers, Manuscripts Division, New York Public Library. For his part in the Sioux campaigns, see Edgar L. Stewart, "Major Brisbin's Relief of Fort Pease," *Montana, the Magazine of Western History* 6 (1956): 23–27, and *Custer's Luck* (1955); see also "Fred Munn: Memoirs of a Cavalry Veteran," *Montana, the Magazine of Western History* 16, no. 2 (1966), with a photo of Brisbin on p. 59. For "Grasshopper Jim," see Joseph M. Hanson, *The Conquest of the Missouri: Being the Story of the Life and Exploits of Grant Marsh* (1946), p. 249. An obituary is in the *Bellefonte Democratic Watchman*, 22 Jan. 1892.

BENJAMIN R. FOSTER

BRISCOE, Benjamin (24 May 1867–27 June 1945), automobile manufacturer, was born in Detroit, Michigan, the son of Joseph A. Briscoe, an inventor associated with Michigan's railroad industry, and Sarah Smith. Briscoe attended Detroit public schools and after graduating from the Jones Academy found work as a clerk for the wholesale firm of Black and Owen.

In 1885, at the age of eighteen, Briscoe organized the Briscoe Manufacturing Company (BMC), with a capital of just $472. The company started as manufacturers of sheet metal stampings and grew to produce goods such as garbage cans, oil cans, pails, sprinkler cans, and numerous other items manufactured from sheet metal. The firm eventually employed over 1,000 men and later became a part of the American Can Company. Because the BMC eventually became Michigan's major manufacturer of sheet metal, the firm attracted the attention of Detroit automobile manufacturers who needed sheet metal for their vehicles. Briscoe, who was joined in the company by his brother Frank, developed a successful automobile radiator from sheet metal, and the BMC became one of the largest manufacturers of automobile radiators and sheet metal automobile parts in America.

Although Briscoe's firm fell on tough times during a Detroit financial crisis in 1901, it was reinvigorated by a $100,000 investment from financier J. P. Morgan, which allowed Briscoe to purchase advanced new equipment. When automaker Ransom E. Olds contracted Briscoe to make 4,400 coolers for Olds's famous curved-dash car, Briscoe's company was again financially secure. The 1902 contract for radiators led to additional contracts for such items as fenders, fuel tanks, and tool boxes, and the relationship with Olds created opportunities to supply parts to other automobile manufacturers.

Briscoe's next major business deal came with David Buick, an aspiring automaker who owed Briscoe money for supplies. Buick was designing a new automobile and struck a deal with Briscoe whereby he would buy the incomplete car, advance Buick more money, and supply sheet metal parts to complete the car. The car was finished in 1903 and Briscoe promptly took delivery of it. (This car represented the beginning of the Buick Manufacturing Company.)

Briscoe found himself captivated by the automobile industry, writing, "When a man became infested by the automobile germ, it was as though he had a disease." He resolved to manufacture automobiles, and while he initially considered entering a joint venture with Buick, the company's slow production and inordinate spending dissuaded him. Instead Briscoe turned to Jonathan Maxwell, who had plans to develop a successful automobile engine.

Attracted by Maxwell's mechanical ideas, Brisco advanced Maxwell funds to build a prototype car. In 1903, after the prototype car was successfully tested, the two men pooled their resources and organized the Maxwell-Briscoe Motor Company. In 1904 they leased a plant at Tarrytown, New York, that John Brisban had previously used to manufacture Mobile steam automobiles. Although Briscoe found difficulty in promoting his new venture because potential investors feared that the automobile business had reached its peak as an industry, his company nonetheless grew steadily. Briscoe was able to secure a $100,000 investment from the banking concern of Richard Irvin and Company of New York, as well as financial support from J. P. Morgan and Company.

By 1906 the Maxwell-Briscoe Motor Company expanded to factories at Pawtucket, Rhode Island, New Castle, Indiana, and Auburn, New York. The company's first car was a two-cylinder, two-passenger runabout. As the only company that posed any challenge to eastern Michigan's dominance, the company's production soared from 540 automobiles during its first full year of production to almost 20,000 by 1910, making Maxwell-Briscoe the fifth largest automaker in the country.

In 1907 Briscoe proposed to automobile financier William Durant that they merge their Buick and Maxwell-Briscoe companies, and before the end of the year Briscoe extended the offer to the other two largest automobile companies in the United States, owned by Henry Ford and Ransom E. Olds. But the Big Four companies were unable to agree on a plan for a large-scale consolidation; they were especially divided on Briscoe's plan for a unified management. Briscoe was particularly dissatisfied because he considered that the other participants had undervalued his company, which would have given him a smaller proportion of stock in the proposed new corporation.

When negotiations collapsed, Durant organized the General Motors Company, and in January 1910 Briscoe created a rival company by founding the United States Motor Company (USMC), using Maxwell-Briscoe as the central element and first acquisition. Briscoe's principal financial backer was Wall Street investor Anthony Brady, who was a major stockholder in the Columbia Motor Company of Hartford, Connecticut. Columbia subsequently joined the USMC in March 1910, followed by other acquisitions: the Alden Sampson Company, the Brush Runabout Company, and the Dayton Motor Company of Dayton, Ohio. But the USMC was built on rickety foundations. It held in an uneasy embrace seven marquee names, fifty-two models, and eighteen factories; moreover, the companies that Briscoe had drawn into his new venture were hardly the big-name volume producers that could make the USMC successful. In fact, only Maxwell-Briscoe was a money-making operation. In September 1912, just two years after its formation, the USMC went into receivership, and Briscoe resigned from the company.

Despite the failure of the USMC, Briscoe showed an unflinching determination to remain in the automobile industry. He moved to France and, in the city of Billancourt, established a new concern, Briscoe Freres, which made a light car and a "cyclecar" designed by French engineers. In late 1913 Briscoe returned to the United States and founded the Briscoe Motor Company in Jackson, Michigan, to produce the new Briscoe car. In March 1914 he founded the Argo Motor Company in New York City to produce the French cyclecar.

But World War I impinged on Briscoe's plans to produce automobiles. He converted his company's manufacturing facilities to wartime production, worked in Washington on naval aircraft production, and at the age of fifty he served in Italy and France as a U.S. Navy lieutenant commander. In 1919 he was promoted to commander and awarded the Navy Cross.

At war's end Briscoe turned to new ventures, forsaking automobiles. He helped to develop an improved process for refining crude oil, the rights for which were given to the Barnsdale Oil Company of California. Briscoe later went to Montreal as an executive of the Frontenac Oil Company, which the Texas Oil Company (Texaco) eventually acquired. Briscoe next turned his attention to gold mining in Alma, Colorado, and to ore milling in Idaho Springs, Colorado.

In 1938 Briscoe suffered a paralytic stroke that forced his retirement from business. He moved to Florida and purchased a 3,000-acre plantation in Dunnellon, located in Marion County. There he experimented with tung trees and with Alyce Glover hay and seed.

Briscoe was twice married. His first wife, Lewis Snyder Price of Jackson, Michigan, died in 1938. They had three children. His second wife was Ellen Lustig of Chesley, Ontario. Briscoe died at his home near Dunellon, Florida.

• The National Automotive History Collection of the Detroit Public Library maintains a file on Briscoe. A posthumous tribute to Briscoe by Alfred Reeves can be found in *Automobile Old Timers News*, July 1945, pp. 31–33. A number of books contain information on Briscoe's 1907 attempt to form a merger with the automobile companies of William Durant, Henry Ford, and Ransom E. Olds. These books include Terry Dunham et al., *Buick: A Complete History* (1992); George May, *R. E. Olds: Auto Industry Pioneer* (1977); Glenn Niemeyer, *The Automotive Career of Ransom E. Olds* (1963); and Bernard Weisberger, *The Dream Maker: William C. Durant, Founder of General Motors* (1979). An obituary is in the *New York Times*, 28 June 1945.

YANEK MIECZKOWSKI

BRISSON, Frederick (17 Mar. 1913–8 Oct. 1984), stage and film producer, was born Carl Frederick Brisson, Jr., in Copenhagen, Denmark, the son of Carl Frederick Brisson, a Danish cabaret singing idol, and Cleo (maiden name unknown). At age ten, Brisson was taken to England, where he was educated and where he later began his lengthy career, the foundation of which had been formed when as a youngster he often accompanied his father on tour. After graduation from public school, he traveled as an advanced publicity man for Moss Empire Ltd., the owner of legitimate theaters in England.

Brisson's career behind the footlights began in London, first in a managerial capacity, but he quickly moved into the position of coproducer. His first stage productions in 1930, *Wonder Bar* at the Savoy and *The Merry Widow* at the Hippodrome, when he was only seventeen, marked him as one of London's youngest in the business side of the theater. His father's reputation may have provided him with the original break he needed, but Brisson went on to have a brilliant career. In 1935 he began his first association in North America as the sales representative for the Mitchell Camera Company in New York. Back in London in 1937 he entered film production with the Gaumont-British Studios as the co-producer of two films, *Transatlantic Rhythm* and *Two Hearts in Three-Quarter Time*. In 1938 as an independent producer for United Artists, he convinced the world-famous pianist Ignacy Paderewski to make the film *Moonlight Sonata*. It was Paderewski's only movie appearance.

Brisson came to the United States in the 1920s with his father when the elder Brisson starred in films for Paramount Pictures. While in Hollywood, he joined the Joyce-Selznick Talent Agency. In 1938 he began to settle in there, living with his friend Cary Grant, but for business he made transatlantic trips, which he continued for the rest of his life. At the outbreak of World War II, he enlisted in the U.S. Army Air Corps, from which he was discharged in 1945 as a lieutenant colonel; he was awarded the U.S. Legion of Merit and Denmark's King Christian X Medal.

Back in Hollywood, when the major studios still dominated production, he formed Independent Artists Pictures. This company produced *The Velvet Touch* (1948), which starred Rosalind Russell, who had become his wife in 1941, and later, *Never Wave at a Wac* (1952). Later, he re-created many of his Broadway hits on film.

Brisson's first musical on Broadway, in partnership with Harold Prince and Robert Griffith, was the 1953–1954 season's resounding success, *The Pajama Game*, followed by another huge success in 1955, *Damn Yankees*. Both shows won the Tony award for the best musical and earned immense financial gains for the producers. In his lifetime, Brisson oversaw some twenty-one Broadway shows and turned many of them, like *Damn Yankees*, into successful movies. He also was responsible for the first appearances on Broadway of British playwrights Peter Shaffer (*Five Finger Exercise*, 1959), which won the New York Drama Critics' Circle Award and a similar award in London, and of Harold Pinter (*The Caretaker*, 1961). He attributed his successes to growing up in English theater and then having spent his adult life in the United States, giving him the advantage of knowing something of the taste of both countries. Also, he credited his father for teaching him the meaning of "universality"—what touches emotions and what endures.

In 1969 Brisson produced *Coco*, a Broadway musical based on the life of the famous French couturière, Gabrielle "Coco" Chanel, which starred Katharine Hepburn; although Hepburn was well received, the show was not especially successful. His final Broadway musical, in 1983, was *Dance a Little Closer*, loosely based on Robert E. Sherwood's *Idiot's Delight*.

His 35-year marriage with Russell—they met when he was a house guest of Cary Grant, who later was best man at their wedding—was a Hollywood success story. Her thirteenth film, *Craig's Wife* (1936), had made her a star before their marriage, but together they combined their talents for even greater success. Brisson said that he was fortunate in having an ideal playgoing companion whose reactions to stage situations and characters were acute and immediate; that she was a keen critic whose stage and screen roles had made her intensely aware of the effort behind the creation.

Away from their work, the Brissons were always welcomed whether in California, New York, or Europe, and they were envied for both their professional and marital success. Russell, who died in 1976, suffered for many years with painful and crippling rheumatoid arthritis. In her memory, Brisson established the Rosalind Russell Medical Research Fund at the University of California, Los Angeles.

In 1978, two years after Russell's death, he married Belgian-born Arlette Jannsen, twenty-five years his junior, a public relations executive. At the time of his death, Brisson was engaged in a bitter litigation, having been ousted from the marital apartment after making his wife a party to a substantial fortune.

In the theater Brisson had the producer's knack of knowing what the public wanted and then supplying it. His hits were known for taste and quality—and for the quality of their stars. He belonged to an almost obsolete breed—the gentleman producer. Brisson died in New York City.

• UCLA's Film/Television/Radio Archives and Theatre Arts Library houses the archival collection of Russell and Brisson, which covers fifty years of Broadway and Hollywood history. Brisson's career is documented in the clipping files at the Library for the Performing Arts, Lincoln Center, New York Public Library, and in *Who's Who in the Theatre* (1982–1983). Additional material is found in *Rosalind Russell* by Nicholas Yanni (1975) and *Life Is a Banquet*, as told to Chris Chase, a biography of Rosalind Russell (1977). Obituaries are in the *New York Times*, 11 Oct. 1984, *New York Post*, 10 Oct. 1984, *Variety*, 17 Oct. 1984, and *Time* and *Newsweek*, 30 Oct. 1984.

PATRICIA FOX-SHEINWOLD

BRISTOL, Mark Lambert (17 Apr. 1868–13 May 1939), naval officer and diplomat, was born in Glassboro, New Jersey, the son of Mark Lambert Bristol and Rachel Elizabeth Bush, farmers. He was appointed to the U.S. Naval Academy in 1883 and graduated in 1887. After service aboard the converted bark *Monongahela* (1890), the gunboat *Petrel* (1891–1894) in the Far East, and the gunboat *Alert* (1894), he worked with torpedoes and gunboats in the equipment department of the Norfolk Navy Yard and aboard the schoolship *St. Mary's* in New York (1895–1896). During the Spanish-American War, he served aboard the battleship *Texas*, which fought in the battle of Santiago.

Bristol's next assignments took him aboard the battleships *Massachusetts* and *Kearsage* in 1901, then he served as aide to the commander in chief of the North Atlantic Fleet, Admiral Francis Higginson. He continued his work in ordnance and torpedoes, and he participated in the round-the-world cruise of the Great White Fleet in 1907–1909. In 1908 he married Helen Beverly Moore; they had no children.

As Bristol's career developed, he demonstrated a combination of technical interest in new equipment and a knack for diplomatic resolution of international problems. In 1911 he commanded the monitor *Monterey* and in 1912–1913 the protected cruiser *Albany* in the Far East. During the revolution that overthrew the Manchu dynasty, Bristol showed diplomatic tact in a crises at Swatow by ordering the first U.S. salute to the Chinese republican flag. Promoted to captain in 1913, he was appointed director of naval aeronautics and visited aeronautical engine companies. In 1915 he was appointed a member of the National Advisory Committee on Aeronautics and commander of the new naval air station at Pensacola, Florida.

In 1916–1917 Bristol commanded the aviation station ship cruiser *North Carolina*. He served briefly at the Naval War College, then in 1918 commanded the battleship *Oklahoma* in the North Atlantic and was promoted to rear admiral. Later that year he was commandant of the U.S. naval base in Plymouth, England, and was briefly a member of the Inter-Allied Naval Commission in Belgium that dealt with maritime aspects of the armistice after World War I.

Bristol's diplomatic career began in earnest in 1919 with command of a naval detachment to protect American interests in the eastern Mediterranean and the Near East. During the Turkish nationalist revolution and the Greek-Turkish War, Bristol represented the neutrality of the United States and helped with humanitarian relief for refugees.

Early in his stay in the Near East, Bristol was instrumental in arranging the evacuation of hundreds of Americans from the Crimea during the defeat of the White Russian counterrevolutionaries in 1919–1920. Several hundred wives and children of officers in the army of General Pyotr Nikolayevich Wrangel evacuated from Odessa and Batum (now Batumi) on U.S. ships under Bristol's command.

Bristol played a major role in winning the friendship of Turkey, a former enemy power. In recognition of the diplomatic work he was called upon to perform, he was appointed U.S. high commissioner to Turkey with headquarters in Constantinople. He won the confidence of Mustapha Kemal Atatürk and negotiated an agreement to restore U.S.–Turkish trade and to settle claims against both governments by a joint commission. Bristol was the first diplomat of any Western power to open relations with the Atatürk government in the new capital at Ankara. He assisted in humanitarian relief for both Greek nationals and U.S. citizens after the Turkish defeat and the burning of the city of Smyrna in 1922. U.S. destroyers under Bristol's command helped in the evacuation and in providing food and medical supplies. Bristol, Richard Washburn Child, and Joseph C. Grew were the U.S. representatives at the Lausanne conference in Switzerland that brought an end to the Greek-Turkish War of 1921–1923. Secretary of State Charles Evans Hughes remarked on Bristol's "important services which have been rendered this government." Bristol's work was also recognized by Secretary of State Frank P. Kellogg and President Calvin Coolidge.

For his success in Turkey, Bristol was promoted to commander in chief of the Asiatic Fleet with the rank of admiral. In mid-1927 he attempted to make peace in the civil war between the Kuomintang and Communist forces in China. During his two years representing

American interests in China, he befriended Chiang Kai-shek and C. C. Wu, who later represented republican China in Washington. Bristol's personal reputation for support of modernizing nationalism in Turkey was well-received in China.

Bristol returned to the United States in 1929, assigned to the General Board. He retired in May 1932 and lived in Washington until his death there.

Bristol's career typified the long tradition in the U.S. Navy of diplomatic service and humanitarian work by senior naval officers, who often served as an informal auxiliary to the State Department. Bristol contributed particularly to the changing American attitude toward Turkey by his recognition that the New Turk movement represented a sharp departure from the corruption and decadence of Ottoman rule.

• Bristol's papers and diary are in the Manuscripts Division of the Library of Congress. Bristol was coauthor, with George F. E. Harrison, of *Rules for Army and Navy Maneuvers* (1903). See also William R. Braisted, "Mark Lambert Bristol: Naval Diplomat Extraordinary of the Battleship Age," in *Admirals of the New Steel Navy*, ed. James C. Bradford (1990); and John A. De Novo, *American Interests and Policies in the Middle East, 1900–1939* (1963). An obituary is in the *New York Times*, 14 May 1939.

RODNEY P. CARLISLE

BRISTOW, Benjamin Helm (20 June 1832–22 June 1896), lawyer and statesman, was born at Elkton, Kentucky, the eldest son of Francis Marion Bristow and Emily Edwards Helm. His father was a planter, lawyer, and politician while his mother was a member of one of Kentucky's most distinguished families. Graduating in 1851 from Jefferson College in Canonsburg, Pennsylvania, Bristow studied law in his father's law office and was admitted to the bar in 1854. He married Abigail ("Abbie") Slaughter Briscoe in 1854, and they had two children.

Although Bristow's father owned slaves, he had freed them by the outbreak of the Civil War. As a member of the Thirty-sixth Congress F. M. Bristow worked to prevent the secession of the southern states, but when war erupted in 1861, the family fled to Indiana. Benjamin remained in Kentucky, where he helped raise the Twenty-fifth Kentucky Volunteer Regiment for the Union army. He fought at the battles of Fort Donelson and Shiloh, where he was wounded. Upon recovery he helped to recruit the Eighth Kentucky Cavalry, which assisted in the 1863 capture of Confederate raider John Hunt Morgan. For his services Bristow was offered the brevet of brigadier general, which he refused. Bristow resigned his commission as a colonel in 1863 and was elected to the state senate, where he served on the Committee on Military Affairs and the Committee on Federal Relations. An ardent supporter of President Abraham Lincoln, Bristow bolted the Union party and helped form the Unconditional Union party, which became the nucleus of the Republican party in Kentucky. Bristow also helped establish a Republican newspaper, the *Daily Commercial*, in 1869.

In 1865 Bristow was appointed assistant U.S. attorney and, later, U.S. attorney for the District of Kentucky. Since Kentucky was experiencing a "rule of terror" as a result of the activities of the Regulators and the Ku Klux Klan, Bristow used the writ of *habeas corpus* to transfer to federal courts those cases in which blacks were prevented from testifying in state courts (*United States v. Rhodes*; *United States v. Blyew and Kennard*). His outstanding record commended him to President Ulysses S. Grant, who in 1870 appointed Bristow the first solicitor general of the United States. In this capacity he wrote opinions, advised U.S. attorneys, reviewed cases in the district and circuit courts, and argued the majority of the Reconstruction cases before the U.S. Supreme Court. He continued to use his position to extend the Republican party's influence in Kentucky, supporting John Marshall Harlan for governor in 1871. Because of a conflict with Attorney General Amos Akerman, Bristow resigned as solicitor general in 1872 and became counsel for the Texas & Pacific Railroad and president of the California and Texas Railway Construction Company. When rumors began to circulate in 1874 that he was being considered for the Supreme Court, Bristow resigned his presidency, remaining as legal counsel for the company. Instead President Grant nominated him as attorney general. Grant sought to name Attorney General George H. Williams minister to Spain, but when Williams did not resign, Bristow requested that his own nomination be withdrawn. During these years Bristow was counsel for such companies as the Pullman Palace Car Company and the Louisville & Nashville Railroad.

Plagued with second-term scandals, Grant sought an honest man to fill the tarnished post of secretary of the treasury and in June 1874 nominated Bristow to that position. Because of his vigilant administration as secretary of the treasury, Bristow won the epithet of "Bulldog of the Treasury." Facing a shortage of revenues, Bristow reviewed the collections of the custom houses at New York, Boston, and New Orleans, insisted upon a rigid economy in public spending, and pressed western railroads for repayment of delinquent government loans. A sound economist, Bristow urged Congress to pass the Resumption Act of 1875, which would redeem the wartime greenbacks by 1 January 1879. Bristow also favored American banking houses over foreign financiers in the sale of government bonds. Bristow helped expose numerous scandals, including the notorious Whiskey Ring Scandal. Evidence was brought to Bristow in 1874 that extensive frauds were being perpetrated by distillers at St. Louis. Upon investigation it was discovered that tax was being paid on only one third of the whiskey produced. Tax stamps were being used several times over while 150 proof whiskey was being certified as 135 proof. Further investigation implicated distillers in Evansville, Indiana; Milwaukee; Indianapolis; New Orleans; and Chicago. The president initially supported Bristow, but when it was discovered that two of Grant's closest friends were involved (his private secretary, General Orville Babcock, and General John

McDonald of St. Louis), the president believed that Bristow had betrayed him. Bristow secured indictments against 253 persons, and to his great embarrassment, Grant appeared as a witness at Babcock's trial. As a result, over $1.5 million worth of property was seized, and over $1.5 million in assessments was collected. In addition to a total recovery by the government of $3,365,295, the annual revenues increased by $2 million.

Having lost Grant's confidence, Bristow resigned in 1876 and almost immediately became the presidential nominee of the moderate faction of the Republican party. He was extolled as a man of courage, honesty, and integrity, and Bristow Clubs were formed across the nation. Among his many supporters were James Russell Lowell, Richard H. Dana, and George William Curtis. Bristow's name was placed in nomination at the Republican National Convention in Cincinnati by his friend and former law partner, John Marshall Harlan. His chief opponent was James G. Blaine of Maine. Bristow was urged by his supporters to court Blaine. When Blaine fell ill a few weeks before the convention, Bristow called at the house only to be turned away by Mrs. Blaine. The Blaines blamed Bristow for rumors that were circulating about Mrs. Blaine's early life. This hostility carried over to the convention. When neither Bristow nor Blaine could win the necessary majority, a compromise candidate, Rutherford B. Hayes, was nominated on the seventh ballot. As secretary of the treasury, Bristow had antagonized too many of the party bosses to win the nomination. However, Bristow campaigned for Hayes, urging the nation to lay aside the animosities of the Civil War and to accept the challenge of rebuilding the republic.

Retiring to New York City, Bristow became a successful corporate lawyer, founding the firm of Bristow, Peet, Burnett, & Opdyke. He became counsel for a number of railroad, telephone and telegraph, and industrial corporations, as well as a trustee of Vassar College. His great ambition to sit on the Supreme Court was frustrated by the appointment of John Marshall Harlan to the bench in 1877. Bristow refused an appointment as minister to the Court of St. James and declined to be a presidential candidate in 1880. He continued to be an outspoken advocate of civil service reform and in 1881, with George W. Curtis, formed the Civil Service Reform Association. He was also one of the founders of the American Bar Association and its second president. While involved in many significant legal cases, perhaps the most famous was the 1895 case of *Pollock v. The Farmers' Loan and Trust*. As one of the counsel for the appellants Bristow argued that the Wilson-Gorman Act was unconstitutional since income taxes were direct taxes subject to apportionment among the several states. By a five-to-four decision the Supreme Court upheld his argument.

President Hayes consulted Bristow particularly on money matters and upon Bristow's advice vetoed the Bland-Allison Act, though Congress later overrode the veto. In the presidential election of 1884 Bristow refused to support Blaine and joined the "Mugwumps" in their support of Grover Cleveland. Cleveland sought Bristow's counsel on numerous issues, including money matters and regulation of the nation's railroads. Bristow returned to the Republican fold in 1888, supporting the election of Benjamin Harrison. Suffering from an acute attack of appendicitis, Bristow died in New York.

• The principal collection of Bristow papers, consisting of letter books, correspondence, pamphlets, briefs, speeches, photographs, and scrapbooks, is in the Library of Congress. Two other significant collections are the Gill papers at the University of Kentucky and the Draper papers, which are still in the family's possession. For biographical information, see Ross A. Webb, *Benjamin Helm Bristow: Border State Politician* (1969). Aspects of Bristow's career are discussed in W. D. Gilliam, Jr., "Political Career of Benjamin Helm Bristow" (M.A. thesis, Indiana Univ., 1930), and E. B. Thompson, "Bristow, Symbol of Reform" (Ph.D. diss., Univ. of Wisconsin at Madison, 1940). Obituaries appear in the *New York Times*, 24 June 1896; the *New York Evening World*, 23 June 1896; and the *Nation*, 25 June 1896.

ROSS A. WEBB

BRISTOW, George Frederick (19 Dec. 1825–13 Dec. 1898), violinist and composer, was born in Brooklyn, New York, the son of William Richard Bristow, a musician, and Anna Tapp. His musical training began at an early age with piano and violin lessons from his father, supplemented by instruction from one of the premier violinists of the day, Ole Bull, cello lessons, and studies in counterpoint and orchestration. At the age of thirteen Bristow began his performing career as a violinist with the Olympic Theater Orchestra; when he was eighteen he joined the first violin section of the New York Philharmonic Society Orchestra, where he continued to perform until his retirement in 1879. Bristow played in orchestras that accompanied singers Jenny Lind and Marietta Alboni on their American tours (1850–1851, 1852), and he served as concertmaster (1853–1854) under the baton of the flamboyant French conductor Louis Antoine Jullien, who added American players to an orchestra he had brought from Europe.

Beginning in 1851, Bristow conducted major New York choral groups, including the New York Harmonic Society (1851–1863) and the Mendelssohn Society (1867–1871); during that same period he served as choir director and organist for several churches. His championing of American musicians also began in the 1850s, when he took a leading role in the founding of the American Musical Fund, the American Music Association, and the Metropolitan Music Association, organizations that promoted the works and welfare of American composers. When a spirited controversy over the relative merits of American compositions erupted in 1853 in the pages of *Dwight's Journal of Music*, Bristow joined Americanist William Henry Fry in deploring the lack of opportunities for American composers to present their works. Bristow even resigned temporarily from the Philharmonic to protest its failure to include American music in its public concerts.

For his own compositions, which date from the 1840s to the end of his life, Bristow often drew upon American subject matter but continued to employ the musical language of Europe. His first real success was *Rip Van Winkle*, an opera that premiered in 1855 at Niblo's Garden in New York and ran for thirty successive nights. Ten years later, a second run was thwarted when the New York Academy of Music, where it was to be performed, was destroyed by fire. Among his other works based on American subjects are *Niagara Symphony* (1898); two overtures, *Columbus* (1866) and *Jibbenainosay* (1889); and two choral works, *The Pioneer* (date unknown) and *The Great Republic* (1879). His compositions range from small chamber pieces in classical European style, composed earlier in his career, to large works for chorus and orchestra in the style of Beethoven and Mendelssohn. Many of his works were intended for groups that he conducted or in which he performed. He also composed sacred and secular choral works, solo songs, overtures and symphonic works, keyboard and organ compositions, and pedagogical works. In 1856 Jullien commissioned and performed one of his symphonies, the *Jullien Sinfonia*; F. O. Jones said that it was "of more than ordinary merit." Other works were programmed by the Philharmonic and by the choral societies he conducted. Still, none received the sustained exposure afforded the established European repertory.

Bristow's long career as a music educator began in 1854 as a teacher in the New York public schools. He often called on professional colleagues to appear on programs with his students as a way of encouraging young musicians to aspire to higher performance levels. He taught privately as well and eventually published vocal exercises and other instructional works based on his own pedagogical methods.

Bristow married Harriet Newell Crane in 1853; they were subsequently divorced in 1863. They had no children. In 1864 he married Louise M. Westervelt Holder; they had one child. He died in New York City.

Bristow's contribution to American music rests on the sum of his musical activities rather than on a single facet. His career was typical of professional musicians of his day who, in order to earn a living, seldom confined their activities to one aspect of music making. His roles as performer, conductor, teacher, and composer reflect both the restrictions and the opportunities that existed for musicians in America's major urban center at the time. American musicians had to struggle against the hegemony of European music and performers as exemplified by the lack of venues for works by American composers, the prevalence of European conductors and soloists, and at the outset of Bristow's career, a lack of support organizations devoted to the welfare of American performers. While not a trailblazer in creating a melodic, harmonic, or structural musical vocabulary that was uniquely American, he encouraged its eventual development through his depiction of American subject matter and his ongoing efforts to gain performance opportunities and to attract audiences for American compositions. By all accounts he was an accomplished performer, an effective teacher, and an able conductor, who elicited impressive performance levels from the musicians and students under his direction.

• Most of Bristow's unpublished manuscripts are in the New York Public Library. A general list of Bristow's works can be found in the *New Grove Dictionary of American Music* (1980). For a more comprehensive list and an account of his life and career, see Delmer Dalzell Rogers, "Nineteenth-century Music in New York City as Reflected in the Career of George Frederick Bristow" (Ph.D. diss., Univ. of Michigan, 1967). A biographical sketch appears in F. O. Jones, *A Handbook of American Music and Musicians* (1886; repr. 1971). See also B. F. Kauffman, "The Choral Works of George F. Bristow (1825–1898) and William H. Fry (1815–1864)" (Ph.D. diss., Univ. of Illinois, 1975).

JEAN W. THOMAS

BRISTOW, Joseph Little (22 July 1861–14 July 1944), newspaper publisher and U.S. senator, was born in Wolfe County, Kentucky, the son of William Bristow, a farmer and Methodist circuit rider, and Savannah Little. After his mother's death in 1868, Bristow lived with his grandparents, but in 1873 he was reunited with his father, who had been transferred by the denomination to Fredonia, Wilson County, Kansas. The younger Bristow returned to Kentucky at the age of fourteen to live with his grandfather and uncle. There he met Margaret Hester Hendrix. The couple married in 1879 and soon removed to Elk County, Kansas, where they purchased an eighty-acre farm and set up house in a one-room log cabin.

In 1881, after the birth of the first of five children (two died in infancy), Bristow sold the farm, moved his family to southern Douglas County, and entered Baker University, a small Methodist school located in Baldwin City. Initially, Bristow planned to prepare for the ministry, but he embarked on his life's career in journalism with the *Baldwin Ledger* before completing his B.A. at Baker. Soon after graduation in 1886, he entered politics, winning the office of clerk of the Douglas County District Court. Near the end of his second two-year term, Bristow purchased the *Salina Daily Republican* and moved his family to this central Kansas town, which, according to his son, "he called home for most of the remainder of his life. He also thereafter regarded himself as primarily a newspaperman" (quoted in *Fraud and Politics*, pp. 11–12).

Bristow was identified continuously with Kansas journalism and was involved in several other publishing ventures during the next few decades, including the *Irrigation Farmer*, which he edited at Salina in 1894–1895. Beyond the Kansas borders, however, Bristow gained fame as a public servant and politician. He was chosen secretary of the Republican State Committee in 1894, played a key role in his party's victory that year over the upstart Populists, and was appointed private secretary to Governor E. N. Morrill. Bristow was aligned during this period with a cadre of young Republicans, many of whom were fellow editors—William Allen White, Charles Harger, Edward W. Hoch, and Arthur Capper, among others—who were vociferous in their opposition to the People's party and harbored designs for wresting control of their Grand Old Party from "the old soldiers." Like their counterparts across the country, the Kansas cadre had no interest in a third party and no desire to abandon the party of Lincoln. They did, however, come to see a need for some reform and were, admitted White in his 1946 autobiography, "greedy for power—young buffaloes horning the old bulls out of the old herd" (p. 220). Ironically, when these so-called "Boss Busters" made their move just after the turn of the century, they did so championing many of the reforms—primary elections, direct election of U.S. senators, tariff reform, and railroad regulation—popularized by their old nemesis, the People's party.

Notwithstanding the efforts of Bristow and his Republican colleagues, Kansas voted for the Populist-Democrat fusion ticket in 1896. Nationally William McKinley defeated William Jennings Bryan, however, and Bristow was appointed fourth assistant postmaster general, a position with considerable power over appointments and inspections. Bristow vigorously executed the duties of this office from 1897 to 1905 and was instrumental in uncovering corruption in the department. As an investigator, the fourth assistant reportedly spared no one; according to the *Saturday Evening Post* (12 Sept. 1908), to the chagrin of many members of Congress, when it came to appointments the Kansan "had a queer obsession that induced him to select men for their fitness for the places . . . instead of for their politics." Bristow's commitment to honesty and efficiency in government threatened several prominent Republican lawmakers and ultimately led to his forced resignation.

After spending part of 1905 as special commissioner to the Panama Railroad Company, Bristow returned to Kansas, occupied himself with his Salina newspaper and Kansas politics, and set his sights on the U.S. Senate. Bristow attained that high office in 1909 after defeating the "old guard's " candidate, Senator Chester I. Long, in Kansas's first statewide primary election. In a brief article for the *American Magazine* (Oct. 1909), Kansas humorist Walt Mason warned the nation that his state's junior senator had a deadly serious nature. "His earnestness is almost tragic; and humor is to him a mere theory, unsupported by Facts, and consequently unworthy of consideration." A tireless seeker of truth with "a peculiarly active and healthy conscience" that he consulted frequently, Bristow would let no obstacle stand in his way. "Above all things," Mason continued, "Bristow is distinguished for his zeal and his industry. . . . He will become a nightmare to those whom he opposes in the Senate; they may think that they have him expunged today, but to-morrow he will be in the same old place, the same old Bristow; six feet of protest; one hundred and sixty pounds of defiance" (pp. 556–58).

Senator Bristow entered the Senate a vocal supporter of the Republican president, William Howard Taft. He left a critic of Democrat Woodrow Wilson, whose progressivism was too conservative for the Kansan. In between he was embroiled in the tariff debate and allied himself with Robert M. La Follette (1855–1925) in opposition to much of the Wilson administration's program. With Idaho Senator William E. Borah, Bristow also played a key role in the process that led to the ratification of the Seventeenth Amendment, providing for the direct election of U.S. senators. During this protracted debate the Kansas senator warned the upper house to heed the wishes of the American people: "The people will govern this country and protect themselves from the powers of greed and avarice—in spite of the Constitution if they have to" (*Saturday Evening Post*, 30 Sept. 1911, p. 52).

Bristow's devotion "to the fundamental principles of the [Republican] party" would not allow him to bolt the party with many of his Kansas colleagues in 1912. Although he belatedly supported the Bull Moose candidacy of Theodore Roosevelt, Bristow refused to join the third party; thus, before his term expired in 1915, his former allies were working for their own Progressive candidate for the Senate, Congressman Victor Murdock. Without this group's primary support, Bristow lost the Republican nomination in 1914 to Charles Curtis (1860–1936), the "old guard's" candidate. Bristow served as chairman of the Kansas Public Utilities Commission (1915–1918) and made an unsuccessful bid for the senatorial nomination in 1918. Thereafter he spent most of his remaining years on the Fairfax County, Virginia, estate he first acquired as a residence while serving in the Senate. Kansas, however, remained Bristow's official home for voting purposes, and after he died in Virginia, his body was returned to Salina for burial.

Through nearly four decades of public service at the local, state, and national levels, Bristow built a distinguished record. The "tall, lanky Kansan" was widely known among his contemporaries as a man of convictions and was recognized as the coauthor of the Seventeenth Amendment to the U.S. Constitution. Although he was overshadowed historically by several of his more boisterous colleagues, in many respects Bristow's career typified early twentieth-century progressive Republicanism.

• The papers of Joseph Little Bristow are among the holdings of the Kansas State Historical Society, which also has a large collection of other relevant material, including campaign literature, compiled speeches, clippings, and a near complete run of Bristow's various publications—the *Salina Daily Republican*, the *Irrigation Farmer*, the *Ottawa Herald*, and the *Salina Daily Republican-Journal*. Bristow also wrote *Fraud and Politics at the Turn of the Century: McKinley and His Administration as Seen by His Principal Patronage Dispenser and Investigator*, ed. Joseph Q. Bristow and Frank B. Bristow (1952). A. Bower Sageser, *Joseph L. Bristow: Kansas Progressive* (1968), is a relatively brief but sound biography. Bristow's role in the fight to amend the Constitution is well treated in Larry J. Easterling, "Sen. Joseph L. Bristow and the Seventeenth Amendment," *Kansas Historical Quarterly* 41 (1975): 488–511; his senatorial career is further developed by

William H. Mitchell, "Joseph L. Bristow: Kansas Insurgent in the U.S. Senate, 1909–1915" (master's thesis, Univ. of Kans., 1952); and Bristow's place within the Kansas progressive movement is assessed in Robert S. LaForte's fine study, *Leaders of Reform: Progressive Republicans in Kansas, 1900–1916* (1974). *The Autobiography of William Allen White* (1946) is also invaluable in this regard. See also Clarence H. Matson, "Joseph L. Bristow: The Argus of the Post-Office Department," *Review of Reviews*, Jan. 1904, pp. 45–48. An obituary is in the *New York Times*, 15 July 1944.

VIRGIL W. DEAN

BRITTEN, Emma Hardinge (1823–2 Oct. 1899), Spiritualist, trance lecturer, and author, was born Emma Floyd in London, England, the daughter of a sea captain and Anna Sophia (maiden name unknown). Her father's death during her childhood left the family in poverty, and from an early age Emma supported herself and her mother by teaching music and acting. According to her autobiography, her youthful mediumistic tendencies interrupted a promising musical career and caused her to be "called" into a secret society of London occultists, who used her as a "clairvoyant and magnetic subject." She later wrote that a man she called a "baffled sensualist" manipulated her, preventing her from obtaining work and forcing her into dependence on him. This experience made her a lifelong enemy of the double standard of morality and of economic discrimination against women. She fled to France with a troupe of British performers, then sailed from Paris to New York in 1855 to pursue a career as an actress. When she arrived in the United States, she was using the name Emma Hardinge, although it is unclear how she acquired it.

In New York she was exposed to a popular new religious movement, Spiritualism, in which adherents tried to make contact with the spirits of the dead. She began visiting Spiritualist séances, intending to write an article about the gullibility of Americans. In the process, however, she experienced mediumistic trances that recalled mysterious events during her childhood. The Spiritualist Horace Day provided her with space to hold séances in the Society for the Diffusion of Spiritual Knowledge. Although initially reticent to challenge public strictures against women speaking in public, she soon became an enormously popular "trance lecturer." She also directed the musical program at the weekly Spiritualist meetings in New York's Dodsworth Hall.

Shortly before the Civil War she toured the South, where Spiritualism was especially suspect, both for its criticism of Christianity and for its association with the abolition movement. On her return in 1860, she announced her "Plan for a Self-Sustaining Institution for Homeless and Outcast Women," which she hoped would help fallen women escape prostitution. In 1865 she was employed by the California Union party to lecture every day for a month before Abraham Lincoln's reelection. In addition to her success as a lecturer, she became the historian of Spiritualism. She assembled a wealth of documentary material for her *Modern American Spiritualism* (1870), which still provides the most detailed account of the first twenty years of the new faith. In *Nineteenth-Century Miracles* (1884), she chronicled the movement's spread beyond the United States.

In 1870 she married William Britten, a fervent Spiritualist who joined her in promoting their beliefs. In 1875 she supported the new Theosophical Society, but she soon disassociated herself from its leader, Helena Blavatsky. Her books *Ghost Land* (1876) and *Art Magic* (1876) show the influence of Theosophy. Emma Hardinge Britten and her husband spent 1878 as Spiritualist missionaries in Australia and 1879 in New Zealand, returning to England periodically. She died in Manchester, England.

• Britten left an incomplete autobiography that was edited and published by her sister Margaret Wilkinson as *Autobiography of Emma Hardinge Britten* (1900). Biographical information also appears in E. J. Dingwall's "New Introduction" to the 1970 reprint of *Modern American Spiritualism*. See also *Banner of Light*, 31 July 1858. In addition to those mentioned in the text, Britten's publications include *Six Lectures on Theology and Nature* (1860), *Extemporaneous Addresses* (1866), *The Electric Physician* (1875), *Faiths, Facts and Frauds of Religious History* (1889), and *The English Lyceum Manual* (1889). For her career in England, see Alex Owen, *The Darkened Room* (1990). See also Ann D. Braude, *Radical Spirits: Spiritualism and Women's Rights in Nineteenth-Century America* (1989), and R. Laurence Moore, *In Search of White Crows: Spiritualism, Parapsychology, and American Culture* (1977).

ANN D. BRAUDE

BRITTON, Elizabeth Gertrude Knight (9 Jan. 1858–25 Feb. 1934), botanist, was born in New York City, the daughter of James Knight, a furniture manufacturer and sugar plantation operator, and Sophie Ann Compton. Britton spent most of her childhood at the family sugar plantation near Matanzas, Cuba, where she developed a love of the outdoors with the encouragement of her father, who had an interest in natural history. She was later sent to New York to live with her maternal grandmother so that she could attend school. She graduated from the Normal College (now Hunter College) in New York in 1875. Despite her youth, she was immediately appointed a "critic teacher" at the Normal College's teacher-training institution, the Model School; in 1883 she became a tutor in natural history at the Normal College. Upon her marriage in 1885 to Nathaniel Lord Britton, then an assistant in geology at Columbia University with a growing interest in botany, she resigned her position. In the ensuing years she served as a botanical helpmate while also pursuing work of her own. She accompanied her husband on collecting trips to the West Indies, where her knowledge of Spanish served them well. Each collected in individual areas of interest: she, the bryophytes; he, vascular plants.

In 1879 Britton had joined the Torrey Botanical Club, where she began presenting her research, quickly developing a focus on mosses. Her first bryological paper, on the fruit of *Eustichium norvegicum*, appeared in the *Bulletin of the Torrey Botanical Club* in 1883.

This interest in the mosses and her marriage to Britton led to her becoming the unofficial curator of the small moss collection at Columbia, to which she added considerably by collecting in the field while accompanying her husband and going on a number of expeditions by herself. She also exchanged and purchased specimens for the collection, pulling off a major coup in 1893 by securing (with the help of donors) the herbarium of the Swiss bryologist August Jaeger. Her position in the herbarium brought her into close contact with students who came to consult the specimens, including Abel Joel Grant, whose dissertation work she supervised.

Britton's work with the Torrey Botanical Club provided an outlet for her considerable talents and energy in an era when employment for a married female scientist was difficult to obtain—and for Britton, financially unnecessary. She served as the editor of the club's *Bulletin* (1886–1889), curator of its herbarium (1884–1885), and on a number of committees, including the Committee on the Cryptogamia, which evolved into the Sullivant Moss Chapter, of which she was president from 1916 to 1919. Through the *Bulletin* and other periodicals, especially the *Observer*, she disseminated well-written, scientifically-sound information in a form accessible to amateurs and professionals alike.

With her husband, Britton led the movement in the 1890s for the creation of a botanical garden in New York. The Torrey Botanical Club readily supported the idea, and in 1896 Nathaniel Britton became the first director of the New York Botanical Garden; his wife was a full-time volunteer at the garden, still focusing on moss collections. Their leadership in raising the necessary funds from New York's elite and their shaping of the nascent botanical garden was a team effort typical of their working relationship.

Late in the century Elizabeth Britton's interests shifted to wildflower preservation, a passion that shaped the final thirty-five years of her life. In 1902 she was intrumental in the creation of the Wild Flower Preservation Society of America, which she served intermittently for a number of years as secretary and as treasurer. Through her work with the preservation society and the botanical garden, as well as independently, she played an important role in raising public awareness of the desirability of protecting native species through education, boycotts, and legislation. The most successful of the actions she led was a national boycott of the practice of decorating for Christmas with wild American holly; Britton and her colleagues promoted the use of nursery-grown holly instead.

Britton died at her home in New York. Her chief legacy was the institution-building she had done in many different contexts.

• The largest collection of Britton's papers is at the New York Botanical Garden. She wrote hundreds of articles, described by John Hendley Barnhart, "The Published Work of Elizabeth Knight Britton," *Bulletin of the Torrey Botanical Club* 62 (1935): 1–17. The best biographical sources are Marshall Howe, "Elizabeth Gertrude Britton," *Journal of the New York Botanical Garden* 35 (1934): 97–103; A. J. Grout, "Elizabeth Gertrude (Knight) Britton," *Bryologist* 38 (1935): 1–3; E. D. Merrill, "Biographical Memoir of Nathaniel Lord Britton, 1859–1934," National Academy of Sciences, *Biographical Memoirs* (1938): 147–02; C. Stuart Granger, "Elizabeth G. Britton and the Movement for the Preservation of Native American Wild Flowers," *Journal of the New York Botanical Garden* 41 (1940): 137–42; and Nancy Slack's essay on the Brittons as collaborators in *Uneasy Careers and Intimate Lives*, ed. Pnina Abir-Am and Dorinda Outram (1987). The journal of the New York Botanical Garden, *Brittonia*, which has become one of the preeminent American botanical journals, commemorates the work of Elizabeth Britton and her husband Nathaniel.

LIZ KEENEY

BRITTON, Jack (14 Oct. 1885–27 Mar. 1962), professional boxer, was born William James Breslin near Clinton, New York, the son of Charles Breslin, a day laborer, and Eliza Jane Sweet. He lived in Oneida County, New York, and New Britain, Connecticut, until he was ten years old, when his family moved to Chicago. There he became a newsboy and learned to fight on the streets to protect his territory. By 1900 he was fighting in privately staged boxing events called "smokers," especially in the mail room of the *Chicago Journal* newspaper. He adopted his nickname "Britain," which had been given to him because of his former home city, for use in the ring as "Britton."

Britton turned professional in 1905 but lost his first two fights; in the second fight he suffered the only knockout of his long career. In 1906 he went to Philadelphia and boxed frequently and successfully in the eastern United States as a lightweight until 1909. From the late months of 1909 until 1912 he boxed in the southern and western states. During this time he achieved main event status and gained experience, but not much fame, from fights with notable opponents such as Willie Ritchie, Packy McFarland, Ray Bronson, and Young Erne. His greatest success in these years was to hold McFarland, possibly the best fighter in the world during that period, to a draw in Memphis on 30 January 1911.

Britton's career was transformed in 1912 when Dan Morgan became his manager. The knowledgeable and well-connected Morgan recognized Britton's superior boxing skills and maneuvered him into numerous fights, mostly in eastern cities and often against the best opposition available. As Britton faced more difficult opponents, he consistently raised the level of his own performance. Although no official decision was given in fights held in most of the eastern states during these years, Britton was generally named the unofficial winner of his contests by newspaper reporters, and his reputation rose through "newspaper decisions" over Leach Cross, Matty Baldwin, and many others, and knockouts of Charley White and Tommy O'Keefe. He was unofficially outpointed twice by McFarland in return fights and occasionally by other outstanding fighters. By 1915, however, he was ranked at the top of the welterweight division by most authorities.

At this time no boxer was universally regarded as the welterweight champion. On 1 June 1915 Mike Glover of Boston defeated the most highly regarded claimant, Matt Wells of England. Three weeks later Glover risked his claim against Britton in Boston, and Britton won. However, Britton then lost to Ted "Kid" Lewis of England in Boston on 31 August 1915 and lost again to Lewis on 27 September. In 1916 Britton defeated Lewis unofficially in two rematches, setting the stage for a 20-round world title fight between the two rivals in New Orleans on 24 April 1916. By this time Lewis and Britton were rated clearly above all others in their weight division, and their meeting was widely considered sufficient to establish a true world champion. Lewis tried for a knockout, but Britton outboxed him to win the title.

The rivalry between Britton and Lewis is one of the most famous in boxing history. Between 1915 and 1921 they fought 20 times in 11 cities, usually without an official decision being given. Their well-matched styles pitted Britton's clever boxing against Lewis's impetuous aggressiveness. On 25 June 1917 Lewis regained the title from Britton by a 20-round official decision in Dayton, Ohio. On 17 March 1919 in Canton, Ohio, Britton took the title back by knocking out Lewis in nine rounds after flooring him nine times, the only knockout in the series. On 7 February 1921, in their last fight, Britton defeated Lewis by official decision in 15 rounds in New York City, allowing him to retain the title.

From 1917 to 1921 Britton also had many fights with opponents other than Lewis, almost all without official decision, but he was usually reported to be the winner. Among his opponents were Benny Leonard, Mike O'Dowd, Bryan Downey, and Jock Malone, all of whom were either world champions or claimants at some point during their careers. Other capable and persistent rivals included Soldier Bartfield, Johnny Griffiths, and Johnny Tillman. It is uncertain how many times during these years Britton risked his title in fights against opponents who weighed below the welterweight limit; in these fights no official decision was given, but a knockout would have caused the title to change hands.

Britton was one of the most able defenders in boxing history. Never hesitant to retreat from a determined attack or to hold when in difficulties, he would cleverly sidestep and block punches and would keep his opponents off-balance with feints and left jabs. Economical in his movements, Britton concentrated on making his opponents miss their punches while landing his own counters. When hit hard he was not easily hurt, and he would not become excited or reckless. Although he won few fights by knockout and did not hit especially hard, he could punch effectively.

In 1922 Britton successfully defended his title twice, against Dave Shade on 17 February and against Benny Leonard on 13 June, both in New York City. The Shade fight ended in a draw, and the Leonard fight ended controversially. Leonard was the lightweight champion, younger than Britton, and generally considered to be the best fighter in the world. Britton led on points after 10 rounds, but Leonard then took charge. In the 13th round Britton was knocked down by Leonard and appeared near defeat. However, Leonard then struck him while he was down and was disqualified. It appeared to some onlookers that Leonard chose to lose the fight in this manner, although he denied that the foul blow was intentional.

On 1 November 1922 Britton's long reign as champion ended when Mickey Walker decisively defeated him in a 15-round decision in New York City. Britton continued to box until 1930, winning more than he lost.

One factor that prolonged his career was that Britton had suffered heavy financial losses from investments in Florida real estate when that market crashed in the late 1920s.

Britton married Rene Morton, and they had five children. His son Bobby became a professional fighter under his father's tutelage and had a long career, but he failed to approach championship status. Britton served as a boxing instructor at the Downtown Athletic Club and the Catholic Youth Organization in New York City from 1930 to 1937. He then moved with his family to Miami Beach, Florida, where he and his wife operated a drugstore. Britton died in Miami Beach.

Britton had 342 professional fights in his 24-year career, more than any other champion. He was an inaugural inductee to the International Boxing Hall of Fame in 1990.

• Britton's professional record is in Herbert G. Goldman, ed., *The Ring Record Book and Boxing Encyclopedia* (1986–1987). Several articles on Britton appeared in *The Ring* magazine; see esp. George T. Pardy, "Jack Britton: Ex-Welter King," May 1935, pp. 6–9, 48; Dan Daniel, "Britton vs. Lewis: Series of 20 Bouts Set Record," Nov. 1946, pp. 22–24, 34; Jersey Jones, "Jack Britton," June 1962, pp. 28–29, 46; and Johnny Brannigan, "Jack Britton: The Class of the Welterweights . . . for More Than a Quarter-Century," Dec. 1991, pp. 22–23, 55–56. Ted Lewis told his side of the Britton-Lewis fights in "Punching Through," which was serialized weekly in *Boxing News* (England), 28 July 1948 to 26 Jan. 1949. A biographical article on Britton appeared in the *Pittsburgh Post*, 27 Nov. 1921. John D. McCallum included an article on Britton and Lewis in his *The Encyclopedia of World Boxing Champions since 1882* (1975). Britton's obituary appears in the *New York Times*, 28 Mar. 1962.

LUCKETT V. DAVIS

BRITTON, Nathaniel Lord (15 Jan. 1859–25 June 1934), botanist, was born in Staten Island, New York, the son of Jasper Alexander Hamilton Britton and Harriet Lord Turner. Britton studied at the School of Mines of Columbia College under John Strong Newberry, receiving an E.M. (engineer of mines degree) in 1879. Newberry, a geologist, published on fossil plants and gave lectures on botany, but Britton was a largely self-taught botanist. He joined the Torrey Botanical Club in 1877 and in 1879 published, with his classmate Arthur Hollick, *The Flora of Richmond County, New York*. For the next five years Britton was botanist and assistant geologist on the Geological Survey of New Jersey, publishing *Preliminary Catalogue of the Flora of New Jersey* in 1881. This work earned him a Ph.D. from Columbia College the same year. He became instructor of botany and geology at Columbia in 1887 and in 1891 was appointed professor of botany. He became professor of botany emeritus at age thirty-seven, when he resigned in 1896 to become director of the newly established New York Botanical Garden.

In 1885 Britton married Elizabeth Gertrude Knight, a fellow member of the Torrey Botanical Club, an instructor at Hunter College, and a published author who went on to a distinguished botanical career. The Brittons had no children; they continued their botanical work at the New York Botanical Garden until shortly before their deaths, both in 1934.

One of Nathaniel Britton's most important works, coauthored with financier Addison Brown, was *Illustrated Flora of the Northern United States and Canada and the British Possessions*, published in three volumes from 1896 to 1898, with a second edition in 1913. A revised edition by Henry Gleason, *The New Britton and Brown Illustrated Flora of the Northeastern United States and Adjacent Canada*, appeared in 1952. During the period from 1889 to 1897 Britton was editor of the first American botanical journal, the *Bulletin of the Torrey Botanical Club*. Of his major publications, often coauthored, his geographical floras and treatments of the plant families Cactaceae, Crassulaceae, and Leguminosae remained important sources late into the twentieth century.

Britton's most important contribution to science was the establishment and development of the New York Botanical Garden, of which he was director in chief from 1896 until his retirement in 1929. The original idea for the garden was Elizabeth Britton's, who asked on a visit to the Royal Botanical Gardens at Kew why New York could not have such a botanical garden. A committee of the Torrey Botanical Club was formed to pursue the project, and in 1891 the New York State Legislature chartered the New York Botanical Garden and authorized the Park Commission to set aside 250 acres in the Bronx, provided that $250,000 could be raised by private subscription. Both Brittons were active in fundraising, and Elizabeth Britton (the only woman included in the charter membership of the American Botanical Society) and her committee raised much of the money. The Brittons had only a minor fortune, but they had friends among New York's elite; Cornelius Vanderbilt, Andrew Carnegie, J. Pierpont Morgan, and Nathaniel Britton were the officers of the garden's first board of managers. Columbia University donated its herbarium and botanical library to the garden, which in turn provided Columbia with graduate instruction and laboratory facilities. New York City provided $500,000 for buildings.

Britton was the ever-present administrator, supervising construction, hiring staff, and launching expeditions. He founded several New York Botanical Garden journals as well as the uncompleted *North American Flora*. A later botanical garden journal, *Brittonia*, was founded in his name. During Britton's long tenure as director, the garden became a major research institution as well as an important public showplace, with gardens and greenhouses. It had ample greenhouses and conservatory facilities, one of the great botanical libraries of the world, a reference herbarium with more than 1.7 million specimens, well-equipped laboratories, and a publishing program. Its initial endowment increased to approximately $2.5 million.

Britton initiated New York Botanical Garden expeditions in North America, the West Indies, South America, and the Philippines. Both he and Elizabeth Britton collected plants in Cuba, Jamaica, Puerto Rico, and other Caribbean islands on which they spent many winters. Seventy-four living and fossil plant taxa, including five genera, were named for Nathaniel and fifteen for Elizabeth Britton. In addition, Mount Britton in Luquillo National Park, Puerto Rico, was named for him in honor of his leadership of the scientific survey of that island.

Britton was involved in a sometimes vitriolic controversy over nomenclatural rules. He was a champion of the so-called American (or Rochester) code of botanical nomenclature, defending it against supporters of the International Code. Britton's views were not popular at the time, particularly among western American botanists, and were often criticized in print. Britton, for example, advocated descriptions of new species written in English, whereas the International Code mandated Latin. The American code was rejected by the 1905 International Botanical Congress; nevertheless, Britton continued to use it in his own and in New York Botanical Garden publications. Britton was also criticized as a "splitter" for classifying plants into too narrow genera, many of which have not survived later taxonomic treatments.

Britton received many honors, among them membership in the National Academy of Sciences in 1914 and foreign membership in the Linnean Society of London in 1925. He was president of the Botanical Society of America in 1898 and 1920 and of the New York Academy of Science in 1907. He died in New York City.

• Britton's papers are at the New York Botanical Garden. His important works, in addition to those cited in the text, include *Flora of Bermuda* (1918), *The Bahama Flora*, with Charles F. Millspaugh (1920), *The Cactaceae*, with J. N. Rose (4 vols., 1919–1923), and *Botany of Porto Rico and the Virgin Islands*, with Percy Wilson (2 vols., 1923–1930). Useful biographical sources include M. A. Howe, "Nathaniel Lord Britton," *Journal of the New York Botanical Garden* 35 (1934): 169–80; and Elmer E. Merrill, "Memoir of Nathaniel Lord Britton: 1859–1934," National Academy of Sciences, *Biographical Memoirs* 19 (1938): 137–201, which includes John H. Barnhart's bibliography of Britton's publications from 1877 to 1932. See also Henry A. Gleason, "The Scientific Work of Nathaniel Lord Britton," *Proceedings of the American Philosophical Society* 104 (1960): 205–26. For the founding of the New York Botanical Garden see Douglas Sloan, "Science in New York City, 1867–1907," *Isis* 71 (1980): 37–76. For Nathaniel and Elizabeth Britton and their scientific work, see Nancy G. Slack, "Botanical and Ecological Couples: A Continuum of Relationships," in *Creative Couples in the Sciences*, ed. Helena M. Pycior et al. (1996).

NANCY G. SLACK

BROADDUS, Andrew (4 Nov. 1770–1 Dec. 1848), Baptist minister, was born in Caroline County, Virginia, the son of John Broaddus, a teacher and farmer, and Frances Pryor. Andrew received only a few months of formal schooling, but his studious inclinations convinced his father that he should seek ordination in the Episcopal church. Against his father's admonition, however, he frequented sermons by the Baptist revivalist Theodoric Noel, who baptized him in 1789 as a member of the Upper King and Queen Baptist Church. In 1791 he was ordained as a Baptist minister.

Broaddus settled in Caroline County as the pastor of Burrus's Church and the County Line Church. Eventually he served a large number of Baptist congregations. Being uncomfortable with genteel congregations, he remained in Caroline and Upper King and Queen counties, declining opportunities for pulpits in Boston, Philadelphia, Baltimore, Norfolk, and New York City. What he described as "distressing nervous feelings," and what others saw as "constitutional timidity," probably affected his decisions not to leave rural Virginia. He also declined the offer of an honorary doctor of divinity degree from Columbian College because he considered such honors unseemly for a minister.

Once in the ministry, Broaddus pursued an informal education, learning enough Greek, Latin, and English grammar to teach these subjects in a private school that he founded. In 1832 he became the moderator of the Dover Association and held that position for eight of the subsequent nine years.

His influence extended beyond his home counties, partly because of his abilities as a writer. In his *Age of Reason and Revelation* (1795) he argued against the deism of Thomas Paine. He also wrote for a popular readership in the *Religious Herald*, the newspaper of the Baptist General Association of Virginia. He completed a *Bible History Particularly Adapted to the Use of Schools and Families* (1816), a catechism for children, a manual of Baptist polity, and a polemical treatise against the teachings of Alexander Campbell, principal founder of the Disciples of Christ. His thought embodied both the orthodox rationalism and the evangelical piety that would become normative in popular southern Protestantism.

He gave further expression to evangelical piety by publishing in 1790 *A Collection of Sacred Ballads*, in 1828 *The Dover Selection of Spiritual Songs*, and in 1836 *The Virginia Selection of Psalms, Hymns, and Spiritual Songs*, designing the books not for "the critic's taste" but for "popular use" in worship and social meetings. The hymnals represented the democratizing of religious music in the revivals of the early national period.

He married four times: to Fanny Temple (c. 1793), Lucy Honeyman (after 1804), Jane Honeyman, and Caroline Boulware (1843). Jane Honeyman was the sister of his deceased second wife (his first wife had also died), and the marriage to her scandalized a segment of the community. For this reason, the couple soon separated, and Broaddus endured a brief suspension from the ministry. He remarried after her death. The four marriages produced nine children. Broaddus died in Caroline County, Virginia.

• Some of Broaddus's papers are in the collections of the Baptist Historical Society at the University of Richmond. See also Andrew Broaddus, *The Extra Examined: A Reply to Mr. A. Campbell's M. Harbinger, Extra, on Remission of Sins, Etc.* (1831), and Andrew Broaddus, "A Baptist Minister Visits Kentucky: The Journal of Andrew Broaddus I," *Register of the Kentucky Historical Society* 71 (1973): 393–425. His biography appears in J. B. Jeter, *The Sermons and Other Writings of the Rev. Andrew Broaddus, with a Memoir of His Life* (1852); Andrew Broaddus, Jr., *A History of the Broaddus Family* (1888); James B. Taylor, *Virginia Baptist Ministers* (1859); and William B. Sprague, ed., *Annals of the American Pulpit*, vol. 6 (1860). See Paul A. Richardson, "Andrew Broaddus and Hymnody," *Virginia Baptist Register* 24 (1985): 1198–1209.

E. BROOKS HOLIFIELD

BROADHEAD, James Overton (29 May 1819–7 Aug. 1898), congressman and diplomat, was born in Charlottesville, Virginia, the son of Achilles Broadhead, a farmer and justice of the peace, and Mary Winston Carr. He attained his preparatory education at a subscription school in Red Hills, Virginia, run by his uncle Dr. Frank Carr and then spent a year at the University of Virginia, paying his own expenses by tutoring the children of one of the professors. He then served as tutor in a private home in Baltimore for a short time before emigrating to St. Louis, Missouri, in June 1837. There he secured employment as a tutor in the home of Edward Bates, with whom he also began the study of law. Bates would have a strong influence on Broadhead, and the two would be closely associated politically throughout their careers. Admitted to the bar in 1842, Broadhead established his practice at Bowling Green, Pike County. In 1847 he married Mary S. Dorsey; they had three children.

Broadhead quickly became interested in politics and, following the lead of his mentor Bates, adhered to the Whig party. He was elected a delegate to the state constitutional convention in 1845 and the following year secured election to the state house of representatives, although Pike County was normally Democratic. In 1850 he advanced to the state senate, where he served one term, taking a leadership role in the struggle that unseated the venerable U.S. senator Thomas Hart Benton (1782–1858). In the political turmoil of the 1850s, Broadhead became associated with Frank Blair, Jr. (1821–1825), James S. Rollins, and others in the formation of the Missouri Republican party. He moved to St. Louis in 1859 and established a long-term law partnership with Fidelio C. Sharp. His forte was constitutional law. One of his best known later cases was that of the Church of Jesus Christ of Latter

Day Saints (Mormons) against the United States in 1889, in which he contended that the act of Congress escheating the Mormons' personal property was unconstitutional.

With the outbreak of the Civil War, Broadhead took a firm stand for the Union, playing a prominent role in the February 1861 state convention that decided against secession. When Governor Claiborne F. Jackson sought to move Missouri toward the Confederacy in spite of this, Broadhead joined with Blair and others on the Union Committee of Safety in St. Louis to thwart his plans. They supported General Nathaniel Lyon's move against the state militia encampment at Camp Jackson, which was suspected of prosecessionist activities, and then worked to secure the enlistment of Union volunteers when the governor refused to honor President Abraham Lincoln's call for troops. In the aftermath of this activity, when Lyon's forces drove Governor Jackson into exile, the earlier state convention was reconvened. Broadhead now served as chair of the committee that recommended the ouster of the state officials and the establishment of the provisional government, which would rule Missouri for the remainder of the war.

In November 1861 President Lincoln appointed Broadhead U.S. district attorney for eastern Missouri, in which capacity he continued for approximately one year. When General John M. Schofield became commander of the Department of Missouri, which included Missouri, Kansas, Arkansas, southern Iowa, and the Indian Territory, in June 1863, he selected Broadhead as his provost marshal general with rank of lieutenant colonel. In November 1863 Broadhead stood as the Conservative Republican candidate for the U.S. Senate but lost the election to the Radical Republican candidate, B. Gratz Brown. He served as a member of the Conservative delegation to the 1864 Republican National Convention, which was denied seating in favor of the Radicals.

Broadhead opposed the Radical state constitution of 1865, which provided for immediate emancipation of slaves and disfranchisement of southern sympathizers. Following its adoption, he joined Blair and others in organizing the Conservative Union party in February 1866 to fight Radical rule and support President Andrew Johnson in the fall elections. Although not a candidate for office himself, Broadhead became one of the new party's principal spokesmen on the campaign trail. Following their defeat that year, the Conservatives reorganized as Missouri's Democratic party.

In the canvass for delegates prior to the 1868 Democratic National Convention, Broadhead received a letter from would-be presidential candidate Blair denouncing the national Reconstruction policies and maintaining that a new Democratic president, if elected, should personally work to nullify them. Although Blair secured the nomination for vice president at the convention, the "Broadhead letter" was used by the Republicans with telling effect against the Democratic ticket. When the Missouri Radical party split in 1870 over the franchise issue, Broadhead joined other Democratic leaders in supporting a coalition with the Liberal Republicans, which eventually paved the way for a return of the Democratic party to power in Missouri.

Broadhead served as a member of the 1875 constitutional convention, which replaced the Radical document of ten years earlier with a more conservative one. Following its adoption, he served as a member of the commission framing St. Louis's charter under its provisions. In 1876 he was retained as special counsel by the federal government in the Whiskey Ring cases in St. Louis. Two years later he was elected president of the American Bar Association. Elected to the Forty-eighth Congress as a Democrat in 1882, he served one term. In 1885 President Grover Cleveland appointed him a special commissioner to examine the archives of the French government with regard to spoliation claims of American citizens against the French during the administrations of George Washington and John Adams (1735–1826). His detailed report finally brought action by Congress on an adjustment. President Cleveland in 1893 appointed him minister to Switzerland, where he served two years, after which he resumed his law practice in St. Louis while also teaching international law at Washington University. He died in St. Louis.

Broadhead was a major figure on the Missouri political scene for nearly a half-century. Staunchly conservative, he moved from prewar Whig to wartime Republican to postwar Democrat as political patterns changed. Considered one of the state's foremost lawyers, he earned the respect of colleagues in all political parties.

• Broadhead's papers are in the Missouri Historical Society, St. Louis. A good biographical sketch, which emphasizes his legal career, is Walker LaBrunerie, Jr., "James Overton Broadhead: Lawyer and Public Servant," *Journal of the Missouri Bar* (Jan. 1957): 8–10. The best contemporary sketch is in Howard L. Conard, ed., *Encyclopedia of the History of Missouri*, vol. 1 (1901). Broadhead's career during the Civil War and Reconstruction in Missouri is detailed in William E. Parrish, *Turbulent Partnership: Missouri and the Union, 1861–1865* (1963) and *Missouri under Radical Rule, 1865–1870* (1965).

WILLIAM E. PARRISH

BROADHURST, George Howells (3 June 1866–31 Jan. 1952), playwright and producer, was born in Walsall, England. His parents hoped that he would enter the clergy, especially after the local bishop presented him with an award for his theological knowledge. To avoid a clerical life, he ran away to America, probably in 1886. He settled in Chicago and obtained work as a clerk at the Board of Trade. Subsequently he moved to Milwaukee, where he had been offered the job of managing a theater. Similar assignments followed in Baltimore and in San Francisco. He then spent a while as a journalist, serving briefly as editor of a newspaper in Grand Forks, North Dakota.

It was at this time that he wrote his first play, *The Speculator* (1896), suggested by his experiences at the Chicago Board of Trade, where he had watched the enmity of two traders exacerbated by the romantic leanings of the traders' children. But the play was a failure. Success came when he turned his pen to comedy with *The Wrong Mr. Wright* (1897), *What Happened to Jones* (1897), and *Why Smith Left Home* (1899). For the next several seasons, either alone or with collaborators, he wrote a sizable number of works, many of which were produced in New York and London but none of which was a major success. These plays included comedies, farces, dramas, adaptations of novels, and musicals. Among his efforts from this period were *Nancy Brown* (1903), with co-librettist and co-lyricist Frederic Rankin, *A Fool and His Money* (1903), *The Crown Prince* (1904), *The Duke of Duluth* (1905), and *The American Lord* (1906), with Charles T. Dazey.

Notable success did not come again until Broadhurst fell in line with the then-current vogue for muckraking and produced a hard-hitting melodrama. *The Man of the Hour* (1906), with its tale of a reforming mayor's battle against a corrupt, entrenched political machine, enjoyed a run of 479 performances in New York. *The Mills of the Gods* (1907) and *Wildfire* (1908) were less successful, although neither was without interest. The former centered on a hero who must overcome his inherent cowardice when confronted by a vicious blackmailer. It found some popularity on the road under the title *The Coward. Wildfire* was written in collaboration with George V. Hobart expressly as a vehicle for Lillian Russell, the former queen of the American musical stage, and drew its audiences primarily on the strength of her appeal.

Broadhurst's next major success was *Bought and Paid For* (1911), which told how a lowly telephone operator humbles her arrogant millionaire husband, who sees her only as property. This situation was somewhat reversed in *Today* (1913), which Broadhurst wrote with Abraham S. Schomer and which told of a man who finds his money-mad wife working in a brothel. *Innocent* (1914), based on a Hungarian play and describing how a man is driven to suicide, had a modest run. One last, huge success was *The Law of the Land* (1914), in which Broadhurst returned to the device of melodramatic marriages, in this case recounting an abused wife's murder, seen as justified, of her cruel husband.

World War I proved a turning point in Broadhurst's career. In 1917 the Shuberts built a theater named in his honor, which he jointly managed with them for a time. But this accolade masked the beginnings of a sharp decline in his playwriting and in his producing. When Actors' Equity called its first strike in 1919, among the shows closed was Broadhurst's production of his own play *The Crimson Alibi*. Broadhurst noted that the union had promised to make an exception of his show because of the unusually liberal contract he had given his performers. He later attributed his gradual withdrawal from theatrical activity to his bitterness over the betrayal. However, an equally likely explanation is that the change in playwriting styles and audience tastes brought about by the war made his sort of work less popular. Broadhurst was essentially a competent craftsman writing for a middlebrow audience that was increasingly deserting the theater for films. As he aged, he could no longer keep up with the times.

Broadhurst was married twice. His first wife was Ida Raymond, whom he wed in 1889, left in 1914, and divorced in 1925. He then married Lillian Trimble Bradley, a playwright and director with whom he had first collaborated in 1918. The number of his children, if any, is unknown. In the early 1940s he moved to California and continued to write plays until a year or two before his death, although none reached Broadway after 1924. Broadhurst died in Santa Barbara.

• There is no biography of Broadhurst, and no collections of his personal papers have been located. See Gerald Bordman, *American Theatre: A Chronicle of Comedy and Drama*, vol. 1: *1869–1914* (1994) and vol. 2: *1914–1930* (1995). The *New York Times* printed an obituary on 1 Feb. 1952.

GERALD BORDMAN

BROADUS, John Albert (24 Jan. 1827–16 Mar. 1895), Baptist clergyman and professor, was born in Culpeper County, Virginia, the son of Edmund Broadus, a state legislator, and Nancy Sims. Broadus stood in a long line of preachers, politicians, and revolutionary heroes, which included his father, who served for twenty years in the state legislature of Virginia. After a brief period of teaching, in 1846 he entered the University of Virginia, graduating in 1850 with an M.A. in the humanities and ancient languages (in later years he was offered two different chairs at the university, those in Greek and moral philosophy, which he declined). During college he was converted to Christianity and joined the Baptist denomination. With his vocation as yet undecided, he accepted the pastorate of the Charlottesville Baptist Church but also kept his hand in education by serving as chaplain to the university and teaching classical languages. Thus began his lifelong attempt to synthesize faith and reason, piety and learning. His efforts resulted in the university's becoming an unofficial educational center for Baptists in Virginia at a time when the denomination sponsored few institutions of higher learning. He served both the church and the university between 1851 and 1859.

In 1850 Broadus married Maria Carter Harrison; they had three daughters before her death in 1857. Two years later he married Charlotte Eleanor Sinclair; they had five children.

In 1858 he took a turn in his professional pilgrimage when the Educational Convention of Southern Baptists, sensitive to the educational needs of its ministers, established its "mother seminary" in Greenville, South Carolina. Broadus served on the first faculty of this seminary as professor of New Testament and homiletics. He joined James P. Boyce, Basil Manley, Jr., and William Williams in an effort to give to the Baptists in the South what had been given earlier to Baptists in the North in the founding of Newton Theological Institute in Massachusetts. From the planning stages, Broadus played a commanding role in molding the curriculum of the new school, which he called a "theological university." His decisions about curriculum benefited from correspondence with Philip Schaff at Mercersburg. The seminary opened in 1859 with twenty-six students.

Within three years the Civil War caused the seminary to close temporarily. Broadus confided to his journal that he was no secessionist but that he was a Virginian. During the Civil War he preached in various Confederate army camps, preached part-time in rural Baptist churches, and served during the last year of the war as aide-de-camp to the governor of Virginia. Broadus also began a pattern of practical contributions to his denomination. From 1863 to 1866 he served as corresponding secretary of the Sunday School Board, and in the 1870s he made numerous editorial contributions to the *Religious Herald* as "J.A.B." From 1878 until his death he also served on the International Sunday School Lesson Committee and in 1884 served as the host in Louisville to the International Sunday School Convention. During these decades he wrote dozens of popular tracts and articles for numerous Baptist publications. At the same time he was also involved in a number of scholarly publication ventures such as the *Nicene Library* edited by Philip Schaff.

After the war, the four founding faculty members reopened the seminary under trying economic circumstances. Only seven students enrolled for classes in 1865. One blind student received individualized homiletical lectures by Broadus who later polished them into the standard preaching text that Baptist seminaries used well into the twentieth century—*A Treatise on the Preparation and Delivery of Sermons* (1870). Tired and drained, Broadus took a year abroad in 1870 and returned to the seminary renewed in energy and educational vision.

In 1877 the seminary moved to Louisville, Kentucky, where it experienced immediate success. In its first year in the larger city, the school's enrollment climbed to ninety-six students. In Louisville Broadus continued his writing career. He not only contributed numerous articles to scholarly publications but also published such important volumes as *Lectures on the History of Preaching* (1876), *Commentary on the Gospel of Matthew* (1886), and *Jesus of Nazareth* (1890). He also gained a national reputation as the preeminent homiletician of the last decades of the nineteenth century. He was invited to give lectures at such institutions as Newton Theological Institute and Johns Hopkins University and was the only Southern Baptist in the nineteenth century to be invited to give the Lyman Beecher Lectures on preaching at Yale University (1889). In that same year he became the second president of the Southern Baptist Theological Seminary, a post that he held until his death. During his years as president of the seminary he continued to achieve national prominence and visibility through his numerous speaking engagements and fundraising trips. On a trip to New York City in 1881, he demonstrated his fundraising ability when he collected $40,000 for the seminary—$25,000 alone from the Baptist oil king John D. Rockefeller.

In sermons, lectures, and published works, Broadus was one of the foremost Baptist scholars who dealt with the question of New Testament criticism. He was an evangelical conservative who attempted a synthesis of evangelical faith and the best of nineteenth-century theological scholarship. He blended piety and reverence with erudition and scholarly effort. He was a scholar of international stature as well as a respected Baptist in his own denomination. As a linguist alone, he was competent in Latin, Hellenistic Greek, Hebrew, German, French, Spanish, Italian, Coptic, and modern Greek. In his preaching and teaching he urged intellectual rigor and evangelical warmth. His formal works on preaching still stand as the foundation of evangelical preaching. Revised through the years, his *Treatise* of 1870 was a watershed work blending biblical preaching with common sense as well as sound biblical scholarship. His work continues to instill Christian preachers with evangelical zeal as well as a love of learning.

Because of his wide-ranging contributions, Broadus was probably the greatest intradenominational Baptist ecumenist in the last two decades of his century. Through his writings, speeches, travels, and ecumenical efforts, he brought a semblance of unity between the Baptists of the North and the South. To the last, he pursued a synthesis of faith and reason for young ministers as well as laypersons. He died in Louisville.

• The most important archival materials are in the library of the Southern Baptist Theological Seminary in Louisville, Ky. Broadus's other major works include *Sermons and Addresses* (1877), *A Harmony of the Gospels* (1893), and *Memoir of James Petigru Boyce* (1893). The most complete studies of his life, thought, and contributions are Archibald T. Robertson, *The Life and Letters of John Albert Broadus* (1901), and Thomas R. McKibbens, Jr., *The Forgotten Heritage: A Lineage of Great Baptist Preaching* (1986).

GEORGE H. SHRIVER

BROCKWAY, Zebulon Reed (28 Apr. 1827–21 Oct. 1920), penologist, was born in Lyme, Connecticut, the son of Zebulon Brockway, a merchant and shipyard owner, and Caroline Brockway. After graduating from a local academy Brockway worked as a store clerk, first in Austinburg, Ohio, and then in Guilford, Connecticut. In 1848 he became a clerk at the Connecticut state prison and three years later was chosen as deputy superintendent of the penitentiary in Albany, New York. Appointed superintendent of the Albany almshouse in 1853, he built America's first county hospital designed specifically for the insane. That same year he married Jane Woodhouse; they had two daughters. In 1854 he became the first superintendent of the new Monroe County prison in Rochester, New York. There he began his innovations in penology, treating prisoners with a leniency unusual for the time and stressing education rather than punishment. During this period Brockway was deeply stirred by the local revival movement and began to institute evangelistic programs, including a prison Sunday school. At the same time he won favorable public notice by devising a system of contract labor that made the prison self-supporting.

Brockway wanted to work with younger prisoners, so in 1861 he accepted the superintendency of Detroit's new House of Correction, which was being built for inmates aged sixteen to twenty-one. A court decision soon made it impossible to restrict the institution to the young, but Brockway nevertheless initiated a strong rehabilitative program, including academic courses taught by local college students, vocational training, outside lecturers, calisthenics, a brass band, a prisoners' newspaper, and morning chapel. He also broke new ground in addressing the problems of discharged prisoners, promising jobs in the community to those with good records and opening a separate House of Shelter to sustain discharged women prisoners until they found employment. The House of Shelter developed into an entire women's reformatory—the first in the nation, and the first American prison for adults with a graded system of privileges based on inmates' behavior.

Among Brockway's priorities was "indeterminate sentencing," under which the length of an inmate's sentence would depend on his behavior in prison rather than on his crime. This approach had been tried with apparent success in Europe and had long been a goal of American reformers. Brockway argued that rehabilitation was the right of every convict and the duty of the state; when the job was done, the prisoner should be released. In 1868 he persuaded the Michigan legislature to lengthen the maximum sentence at the House of Corrections to three years so that his rehabilitative programs would have a chance to work, but early release was permitted for prisoners who responded well. Brockway's innovations made the House of Corrections, according to one historian, "the most significant experiment station in the whole world of penology" and brought him national recognition. The following year he helped organize the National (later American) Prison Association and presented one of the most important papers at its initial congress. Titled "The Ideal of a True Prison System for a State," the paper laid out an ambitious reform agenda, including indeterminate sentencing and graded privileges. Though hotly debated, most of his ideas were incorporated in the Association's Declaration of Principles, and they helped shape prison reformers' thinking for years to come.

Despite Brockway's growing standing in national circles, he faced opposition in Detroit. When a broader indeterminate sentencing law was rejected by the state legislature in 1871, he resigned; some sources indicate that he was forced out. He spent the next four years in business. Then in 1876 he won a plum assignment as superintendent of the Elmira Reformatory, which was being built specifically for first offenders between the ages of sixteen and thirty. Over the next quarter century Brockway made Elmira the best-known and most imitated reformatory in the country.

At Elmira, Brockway reestablished, refined, and expanded nearly all the programs he had developed in Detroit. He also instituted the nation's first parole system, requiring prisoners to report to volunteer sponsors in the community for six months after their release. The idea spread rapidly; by 1900 it had been adopted in twenty states. By the time Brockway took over Elmira he had lost faith in evangelism; he now believed that only administrative and coercive power could "socialize the anti-social." This gave new urgency to his belief in indeterminate sentencing, and in 1877 he persuaded the New York legislature to adopt the first comprehensive law of this kind in the United States. The legislature refused his request to hold refractory inmates longer than the state penal code allowed, but it permitted them to be released early if they gave evidence of genuine rehabilitation. Similar laws were soon adopted throughout the country.

By the 1890s prison reformers' hopes were being eroded by serious overcrowding, insufficient funds, and a series of administrative scandals. Elmira was no exception; Brockway found it difficult to maintain his programs in a facility that now held double the original number of inmates. In addition, it had become clear that even under ideal conditions, many prisoners remained unreformed. This led critics to question Brockway's approach, while he himself treated recalcitrant inmates with increasing harshness. In 1894 he was nearly dismissed when claims that he had "paddled" uncooperative prisoners led to an investigation. Accusing his critics of "sentimentalism and mendaciousness," Brockway insisted that "coercive measures" like paddles were sometimes necessary. He gained a reprieve after a second review of his case. His professional standing remained high, as evidenced by his election to the presidency of the National Prison Association in 1897. Nevertheless, a new board of managers at Elmira forced his resignation in 1900 on the grounds of "disability due to old age." Brockway spent the following year lecturing on penology at Cornell University. Elected mayor of Elmira in 1905, he proved, according to an admirer, to be "active, efficient, and incorruptible." But he also made enemies and was defeated when he ran again in 1907. He died in Elmira.

In 1865 Brockway wrote to a colleague, "I feel that there are very gross defects in the prison system of the land, and that as a whole it does not accomplish its design; and that the time has come for reconstruction." If his proposed solutions were not always successful, he galvanized a generation of prison reformers with his bold willingness to apply and build upon the best penological thinking of his time. Many of his innovations became central to the U.S. prison system.

• A significant amount of Brockway's correspondence can be found among the papers of the Monroe County Penitentiary at the University of Rochester Library and the Samuel Barrows Papers at the Houghton Library at Harvard University. Brockway's memoir, *Fifty Years of Prison Service* (1912), gives the fullest discussion of his ideas and experiences. See also Blake McKelvey, *American Prisons: A History of Good Intentions* (1977); Ronald L. Goldfarb and Linda R. Singer, *After Conviction* (1973); Paul W. Keve, *Corrections* (1981); and Frederick Howard Wines, *Punishment and Reformation* (1895). His mayoralty is discussed in Crystal Eastman, "A Non-Partisan Mayor," *Charities and the Commons* 19 (2 Nov. 1907): 953–54. An obituary is in the *New York Times*, 22 Oct. 1920.

SANDRA OPDYCKE

BRODBECK, May (26 July 1917–1 Aug. 1983), philosopher, teacher, and university administrator, was born in Newark, New Jersey, the daughter of Louis Brodbeck and Etta Bragar. In 1941 she took a B.A. in chemistry from New York University. Upon graduating she spent a few years teaching high school chemistry, working in industry, and participating as a physicist in the Manhattan Project.

In 1945 Brodbeck completed an M.A. and in 1947, a Ph.D. in philosophy, both under the guidance of Gustav Bergmann at the University of Iowa. Immediately after graduate school she accepted a position at the University of Minnesota, where she remained for the next twenty-seven years. In 1959 she became a full professor and, in addition to pursuing her scholarship, ventured into university administration. She became chair of the philosophy department in 1967 and maintained that position for three years. In 1972 she became dean of the graduate school at the University of Minnesota.

While at Minnesota, Brodbeck had the opportunity to serve as visiting lecturer at the University of Maryland (1964) and at Cambridge University (1970). In 1971 she combined her academic and administrative skills as director of the Graduate Record Exam Board; she would keep this position until 1977, when she embarked on her last administrative assignment at the National Center for Higher Education and Management Systems, where she served until her retirement in 1983.

In 1952 Brodbeck published her first and only monograph: *Philosophy in America: 1900–1950*. In it she offered a general discussion of William James, C. S. Peirce, A. N. Whitehead, John Dewey, and George Santayana. Her two dozen or so articles appeared in reputable journals, such as *Philosophy of Science: The Official Journal of the Philosophy of Science Association*, which began publication in 1934, and *Journal of Philosophy*, founded in 1903. She was also on the editorial board of *Philosophical Studies* (1950–1974) and *Philosophy of Science* (1959–1981). In 1953 Brodbeck coedited with Herbert Feigl, *Readings in the Philosophy of Science*, to which she contributed the introductory essay, "The Nature and Function of the Philosophy of Science." This anthology was often cited, widely used, and well regarded.

Brodbeck's coauthor, Herbert Feigl, was a member of the Vienna Circle until he emigrated to the United States in 1930 to flee Nazi persecution. In 1953 Feigl established the well-known *Minnesota Studies in Philosophy of Science* series, in which would appear such highly influential papers as Feigl's "The 'Mental' and the 'Physical'," Paul Feyerabend's "Against Method," Wilfrid Sellars's "Empiricism and the Philosophy of Mind," and Hilary Putnam's "The Meaning of 'Meaning'." In this series Brodbeck published in 1962 "Explanation, Prediction, and 'Imperfect' Knowledge," which along with three others of her papers were reprinted in a large anthology edited by Brodbeck, *Readings in the Philosophy of the Social Sciences* (1968). The series also contained Donald Davidson's "Actions, Reasons, and Causes" (published in 1963), another classic paper of which anyone interested in twentieth-century philosophy of mind, philosophy of psychology, or philosophy of social science must become familiar. Brodbeck's paper of the same year "Meaning and Action," in which she critiques Ludwig Wittgenstein's account of mind and its relationship to behavior, has almost been as widely anthologized as Davidson's.

Brodbeck's 789-page anthology, *Readings in the Philosophy of the Social Sciences*, represents the culmination of her studies in social science. There are forty-one essays broken into eight thematic units, and Brodbeck supplies an introduction to each individual section as well as an eleven-page general introduction. She completed work on this volume while she was a National Science Foundation research grantee in 1966–1968. The work was a widely treasured collection for many years.

Brodbeck was a longtime member of the American Philosophical Association (APA) to which she lended her administrative acumen: For the APA's Western Division she was secretary-treasurer from 1955 to 1957, vice president in 1970–1971, and president in 1971–1972. In her presidential address of 1972, "Mind: From Within and from Without," Brodbeck maintained her opposition to the materialist conception of mind popular among many of her colleagues. Feigl, for example, was well-known for his materialist "identity theory" of the mind.

Having established her reputation as a scholar and able administrator, in 1974 her alma mater, the University of Iowa, made her R. J. Garver Professor of Philosophy, vice president for academic affairs, and dean of the faculties. She retired from administrative duties in 1981 and from professorial duties in 1983. Her retirement from administration allowed her to take her last research position, as fellow for the Center for Advanced Studies in the Behavioral Sciences at Stanford University in 1981–1982. She died in Menlo Park, California.

Brodbeck did not view philosophy and social science as aloof disciplines only significant for the specialist. With regard to the social sciences, she explained that "the intriguing facts they uncover about the patterns of individual and group behavior enter into our common consciousness of the social environment and the way we talk about it" (*Readings in the Philosophy of the Social Sciences*, p. v). Examining the connections between science, social science, and philosophy in the introduction to her 1968 anthology,

Brodbeck acknowledged that "the possibility of a social science in principle as perfect as physics remains the unexamined premise of the vast majority of present-day social scientists," and posited that "the philosophy of science seeks to examine certain fundamental ideas and principles which the working scientist himself takes for granted" (p. 1).

• An obituary appears in the *Proceedings and Addresses of the American Philosophical Association* 57, no. 4 (1984).

JOHN M. MIZZONI

BRODE, Robert Bigham (12 June 1900–19 Feb. 1986), physicist, was born in Walla Walla, Washington, the son of Howard Stidham Brode, professor of biology at Whitman College, and Martha Catherine Bigham. After receiving his B.S. from Whitman in 1921 he enrolled at the California Institute of Technology and, in 1924, received the first Ph.D. in physics awarded by that school. After a brief stint as an associate physicist with the U.S. Bureau of Standards, he spent the next two years studying molecular structure as a Rhodes Scholar at Oxford University in England and then as a National Research Board fellow at the University of Göttingen in Germany.

In 1925 Brode demonstrated that the arrangement of a molecule's valence electrons, those electrons that orbit in an atom's outer shell and are shared with other atoms to form molecules, determines to a significant degree the molecule's slow-electron cross-section, the area its nuclei present as a target to a relatively slow-moving electron. The greater the area, the greater the probability that the electron will collide with one of the nuclei and thereby induce a nuclear reaction. The implications of this finding were not fully grasped until 1966, when it became possible to analyze the wave behavior of electrons and other charged subatomic particles by means of computers, and from that time on his work formed the basis of the analysis of low-energy charged-particle scattering.

In 1926 Brode married Bernice Hedley Bidwell, with whom he had two children. That year he became affiliated with Princeton University as a National Research Council fellow. In 1927 he accepted a position as assistant professor of physics at the University of California at Berkeley. He continued to study slow-electron cross-sections by experimenting with the three zinc-group elements and the six alkali metals. The elements in these two groups possess two and one valence electrons, respectively; moreover, they frequently donate their valence electrons to form positive ions. By 1930 he had discovered that an atom's cross-section is also related to its ionization potential, the amount of energy required to strip it of one of its valence electrons; the less energy required to remove an electron, the larger the cross-section. This line of investigation contributed significantly to a better understanding of the relationship between a nucleus and its valence electrons, as well as the many complex factors that determine the outcome of bombarding nuclei with charged subatomic particles.

Brode was promoted to associate professor in 1930 and to full professor in 1932. In 1938 he developed a method for using a cloud chamber, an instrument that coats ions with tiny liquid droplets of ethyl alcohol vapor, to study the ionizing effects of cosmic-ray electrons, which move at velocities approaching the speed of light. His study confirmed the theory that high-energy charged particles transfer some of their energy to atoms in a gaseous state and thereby free valence electrons from their orbits.

Brode contributed to the American military effort during World War II by joining the Office of Scientific Research and Development in 1941. He served as a unit supervisor at the Applied Physics Laboratory at Johns Hopkins University, where he helped to develop the proximity fuse, a radio-controlled detonating device that greatly increased the effectiveness of artillery shells against rapidly moving targets such as aircraft. Because the proximity fuse triggered the explosive when it came within a predetermined range of the target, it permitted the shell to damage the target without scoring a direct hit. From 1943 to 1946 he supervised a group of over sixty researchers at the Los Alamos Atomic Laboratory who were developing a fuse for the atomic bomb. This group devised an arming and detonation system consisting of switches controlled variously by radar, clocks, and barometric pressure, so that the bomb would explode at a specific altitude—thereby maximizing blast damage—without doing so while in flight.

After the war Brode returned to Berkeley, where he took up the study of cosmic-ray mesons, subatomic particles that were thought to hold the atomic nucleus together by interacting with protons and neutrons. He also established the mass of the muon, a subatomic particle found in cosmic rays, whose loss of energy via radiation decay creates ions at approximately 210 times the rate of the electron.

Brode served as vice president of the International Union for Pure and Applied Physics from 1954 to 1960 and the American Association of University Professors from 1960 to 1961. He chaired the Physics Advisory Panel of the National Science Foundation and was its associate director for research from 1958 to 1959. He was vice president of Section B of the American Association for the Advancement of Science and president of its Pacific Division. He also served as a member of the executive committees of the American Physical Society, the American Association of Physics Teachers, and the American Institute of Physics. The Presidential Certificate of Merit was awarded to Brode for his research achievements during World War II. He was elected to membership in the National Academy of Sciences in 1949 and to fellowship in the American Academy of Arts and Sciences in 1960; he received the University of California's Centennial Award in 1968. He retired in 1967 and died in Berkeley.

Brode contributed to the advance of nuclear physics in two ways. His pioneering work with slow-moving electrons and fast-moving mesons contributed significantly to the understanding of the behavior of charged subatomic particles. His role in the development of sophisticated fuses facilitated the successful detonation of the first atomic bomb.

• A biography of Brode, which includes a bibliography, is William B. Fretter and David L. Judd, "Robert Bigham Brode," National Academy of Sciences, *Biographical Memoirs* 61 (1986): 27–37. An obituary is in the *New York Times*, 27 Feb. 1986.

CHARLES W. CAREY, JR.

BRODE, Wallace Reed (12 June 1900–10 Aug. 1974), chemist and physicist, was born in Walla Walla, Washington, one of the triplet sons of Howard Stidham Brode and Martha Catherine Bigham. His father, for more than forty years professor of zoology at Whitman College in Walla Walla, aroused an interest in science in his four sons by making them a hiking class of nature students. All four earned B.S. degrees at Whitman College—Brode in 1921—and all became academic scientists.

After serving in the army during World War I, Brode attended the University of Illinois at Urbana and received his M.S. (1922) and Ph.D. (1925) degrees there. He worked under Roger Adams, one of the country's most prominent organic chemists and a government scientist-diplomat, who exerted an early and lasting influence on Brode by thoroughly grounding him in the politics of science. Brode's doctoral research focused on the determination of the adsorption of optically active dyes on wool. Because the color differences to be measured were small, he used absorption spectroscopy. The three fields in which he was destined to find scientific fame—organic chemistry, especially of dyes; optical activity; and spectroscopy—were joined in this research. During 1924–1925 he was assistant chemist and associate chemist at the U.S. National Bureau of Standards, where he had done his last year of graduate research. He then spent 1926–1928 as a Guggenheim Fellow at European universities, working with Arthur Hantzsch in Leipzig, Germany; with Victor Henri in Zürich, Switzerland; and E. C. C. Baly in Liverpool, England.

Brode spent the next twenty years (1928–1948) at Ohio State University, advancing from assistant professor of organic chemistry (1928) through associate professor (1932) to professor (1939). Soon a leader in dyes, spectroscopy, and applied optics, he became almost as well known for his work in physics as in chemistry. His research and textbooks combined synthetic organic chemistry with optical methods of analysis and control. He carried out numerous studies of rotatory dispersion and optical resolution of asymmetric compounds. He became well known for producing and promoting tinkertoy-like, peg-and-ball molecular models to represent the structures of organic molecules and to visualize steric effects on properties and chemical reactions. These innovative models, which are universally used today, formed the basis for the special exercises in the *Laboratory Manual of Organic Chemistry* (1940), on which he collaborated with Cecil Boord and Roy G. Bossert. His internationally famous pioneering textbook *Chemical Spectroscopy* (1939) was widely used for more than two decades and became the standard reference on the subject, especially during World War II. His spectrophotometric measurements and numerous syntheses of organic dyes elucidated the influence of structure on color and showed how spectrophotometry could be used to predict structure. Brode's work on dyes made him an authority on black-and-white and color photography. His photographic talents and knowledge of spectroscopy led him to become a member of several expeditions to photograph solar eclipses, one of which was the Harvard-MIT Siberian expedition of 1936. During his tenure at Ohio State, in addition to lecturing to beginning and advanced students, he supervised the doctoral research of some forty graduate students, and he instituted lecture and laboratory courses in chemical spectroscopy.

After a first marriage ended in divorce in 1936, in 1941 he married Ione "Sunny" Sundstrom. The couple, who did not have children, shared the hobby of collecting Indian artifacts in the field. An accomplished flutist, Brode was a high-fidelity aficionado who had an extensive collection of tape recordings from both verbal and musical radio broadcasts. He also was an amateur researcher of archery principles.

During World War II, while on leave from Ohio State, Brode held a number of government positions: consultant and project leader for the War Metallurgy Committee (1942–1945) and the National Defense Research Committee (1942–1944); during 1944–1945 a member of the liaison office of the Office of Scientific Research and Development (OSRD) in London and Paris; and a member of the U.S. naval technical mission in Europe and of the Alsos Mission, which collected information on nuclear energy and weapons research from captured enemy scientists. In 1945 he received the Presidential Certificate of Merit for his wartime service.

From 1945 to 1947 Brode was head of the Science Department and deputy to the director at the U.S. Naval Ordnance Test Station at Inyokern, California, the navy's largest rocket laboratory, of whose advisory board he was later (1948–1958) a member. He was also a member of the advisory boards of the army, navy, and air force and of the Atomic Energy Commission from 1946 to 1962. He returned to Ohio State in 1947 but resigned in 1948 to become associate director of the U.S. National Bureau of Standards (NBS) in Washington, D.C., where he remained for a decade, supervising work in the chemical, metallurgical, optical, and mineral product areas. He also directed activities in foreign relations, education, and publishing. As chairman of the NBS editorial committee, he oversaw the publication of periodicals, reports, and handbooks. In addition to his heavy administrative duties, he maintained a basement laboratory, where he worked on steric effects in dyes and on absorption spectra related to dyes and color. In 1958 he received the Exceptional Service Gold Medal of the Department of Commerce (of which NBS is a member agency) and the Society for Applied Spectroscopy's Distinguished Service Medal.

In the aftermath of the 4 October 1957 launching of Sputnik by the USSR, the U.S. Department of State, in January 1958, revived its program of assigning scientific attachés to U.S. embassies overseas. In what constituted the pinnacle of his governmental career, on 13 January 1958 Brode was sworn in as science adviser to Secretary of State John Foster Dulles, filling a position that had been vacant for four years. As the country's "top science diplomat" during 1958–1960 Brode directed and expanded the scientific attaché program and served as consultant to the President's Scientific Advisory Committee (PSAC). From 1960 until his death in Washington, D.C., he was a widely sought scientific consultant.

Brode was a member of the National Research Council (from 1947) and the National Academy of Sciences (elected 1954), co-chairman (1957–1958, 1964–1974) and president (1970–1974) of the People-to-People Committee for Scientists and Engineers, foreign secretary of the American Chemical Society (1965–1967), member of the President's Committee of Scientists and Engineers (1958–1960), member (1960–1974) and president (1972–1974) of the Scientific Manpower Commission, and American delegate to the International Union of Pure and Applied Chemistry (Zürich, 1936, 1955; New York City, 1951; Paris, 1957). He served as president (1960) of the American Chemical Society; director (1951–1960) and president (1961) of the Optical Society of America; governor (1948–1952, 1960–1963) of the American Institute of Physics; governor (1950–1958, 1960–1963) and chairman (1954–1957) of the Science Research Society of America; director and treasurer of Science Service (1958–1972); director (1953–1960), president (1958), and chairman of the board (1959) of the American Association for the Advancement of Science; and national lecturer (1952) and president (1961–1962) of Sigma Xi. The recipient of four honorary doctorates, in 1960 he was awarded the American Chemical Society's Priestley Medal, its highest award, "for his distinguished services to chemistry as a teacher, in research administration, and as a contributor to the development of chemistry in his many activities in professional societies and as a public servant."

• Six cartons (7.5 linear feet) of Brode's papers and manuscripts are in the Bancroft Library of the University of California, Berkeley. Biographical articles include "Chemist to Head AAAS," *Chemical & Engineering News*, 31 Dec. 1956, p. 6380; "Wallace Brode Chosen ACS President-Elect for 1968," *Chemical & Engineering News*, 4 Dec. 1967, p. 21; Roger Adams, "W. R. Brode, President Elect," *Science* 125 (15 Feb. 1957): 279–80; "Dr. Brode Named Science Adviser to Department of State," *U.S. Department of State Bulletin* 38 (3 Feb. 1958): 190–91; Howard Simons, "Scientist of Statecraft: Symbol of New Power," *Saturday Review*, 1 Mar. 1958, pp. 46–47; and Mary E. Warga, "Wallace Reed Brode," *Journal of the Optical Society of America* 64, (Oct. 1974): 1353–54. An obituary is in the *New York Times*, 13 Aug. 1974.

GEORGE B. KAUFFMAN

BRÖDEL, Paul Heinrich Max (18 June 1870–26 Oct. 1941), medical illustrator and anatomist, was born in Leipzig, Germany, the son of Paul Heinrich Louis Brödel, an employee of the Steinweg piano works, and Christiane Henriette Frenzel. As a child, Max Brödel showed talent in both music and the visual arts, and at age fifteen he enrolled in the Königliche Kunstakademie und Kunstgewerkeschule zu Leipzig. Required by the Leipzig art school to learn at least one graphic technique, Brödel always acknowledged the importance of his training in lithography. In 1888, he began working part-time as an illustrator for the renowned physiologist Carl Ludwig. At the time, the Leipzig medical school drew physicians and investigators from around the world for advanced training and research opportunities, and, while working for Ludwig, Brödel met the American anatomist Franklin Paine Mall.

Brödel was drafted into the military soon after graduation in 1890. Upon his discharge in the fall of 1892, he returned to work for Ludwig but was not hopeful of making a good living. Soon he responded positively to an invitation from Mall to join him at the newly founded Johns Hopkins Medical School, but by the time Brödel arrived in Baltimore early in 1894, Mall's workload made it impossible for him to devote much time to the new immigrant.

Fortunately for Brödel, Howard A. Kelly, professor of obstetrics and gynecology at Johns Hopkins, was beginning work on his *Operative Gynecology* and needed an illustrator. Early in their collaboration, Brödel recognized Kelly's ability to create diagrams in which "every clinical phenomenon, every operative procedure flowed in simple, eloquent lines"; and he incorporated Kelly's conceptions into his own illustrations, which were very well received when Kelly's book appeared in 1898. While working for Kelly over the next decade and a half, Brödel took advantage of the opportunity to use Johns Hopkins facilities for his own investigations in anatomy and pathology. He worked on projects for other hospital and medical school personnel and began providing informal instruction in medical illustration to students and faculty, believing that the ability to sketch would provide the doctor or scientist "a better memory of facts, forms and relationships." In 1905 the medical faculty appointed Brödel to a nonpaying position as instructor in art as applied to medicine. He became a U.S. citizen the same year.

Brödel had quickly become comfortable in Baltimore. He developed close relationships with several young members of the Johns Hopkins medical faculty and eventually joined the musical social circle around newspaperman H. L. Mencken. As people at Johns Hopkins came to appreciate the work of a capable artist, Brödel was encouraged to bring other graduates of the Leipzig academy to Baltimore, and Franklin Mall recruited Ruth Marion Huntington, an illustrator pursuing postgraduate studies in anatomy at Smith College, to study with Brödel and become part of the Johns Hopkins medical illustration team. Brödel and Huntington married in 1902; they had four children. Their oldest surviving child, Elizabeth, became a noted medical illustrator in her own right.

Once Brödel's reputation was established, the Mayo Clinic repeatedly tried to recruit him to a better-paying position. Brödel's attachment to Johns Hopkins and the opportunity it provided for teaching were enough to keep him in Baltimore, though, until Kelly ceased being able to pay his salary in 1911. Just as Brödel was about to accept the most recent Minnesota offer, his close friend gynecologist Thomas S. Cullen convinced Baltimore art patron Henry A. Walters to institutionalize Brödel's teaching efforts by supporting a Department of Art as Applied to Medicine at the Johns Hopkins Medical School. Brödel conceived of the department providing instruction to medical students and faculty, a rigorous program for medical illustration students, and special courses for accomplished artists who wanted to learn the principles of medical illustration. In fact, he succeeded mainly in the second point—but he succeeded very well, training nearly two hundred students over the next three decades. Brödel regarded most of his students as mediocre but cherished the few he knew to have superior talents, some of whom founded similar programs at other medical centers or otherwise became important in the field.

While directing the art program at Johns Hopkins, Brödel continued to work as an illustrator for Johns Hopkins doctors and scientists. After retiring from teaching in 1940, he concentrated on his work in anatomy and illustration, especially at the Johns Hopkins Otology Research Laboratory, where he produced his final works, stunning depictions of the anatomy of the ear. He died in Baltimore.

In earlier times, artists who sketched for publication had worked with skilled engravers, lithographers, or etchers who could repair inadequate drawings. Brödel saw how photomechanical reproduction—which appeared to leave no room for the artist in the printing process—both constrained illustrators and offered them new opportunities. He developed techniques for representing human tissue, naturalistically or schematically, that would create illustrations particularly suitable for the newer printing technologies. In his day, virtually no one in the world, and certainly no one in the United States, could compete with him as an innovator or as a producer of illustrations of such clarity and practical value.

Brödel also brought to his work a profound scientific curiosity. He believed that the illustrator must know practical anatomy, and he insisted that to properly depict an operation, the artist must practice the same procedure on a cadaver. He published several scientific articles of his own, including anatomic work on the kidney that led to the development of new surgical techniques. He regarded medical illustration as a field that demanded highly specialized knowledge—in both science and drawing technique—and he regretted that, because it was not lucrative and had a reputation as "hack work," the field was unable to attract the most talented young artists. Above all, Brödel taught that the "planning of the picture and the registration of scientific facts are what gives it its value, not the execution."

• Brödel's personal and professional papers, and virtually all of his original artwork, are held by the Johns Hopkins Department of Art as Applied to Medicine. For his ideas on the significance of medical illustration and how to teach it, see "How May Our Present Methods of Medical Illustration Be Improved?" *Journal of the American Medical Association* 49 (1907): 138–40; "In Memoriam August Horn," *Bulletin of the Johns Hopkins Hospital* 22 (1911): 21–22; "The New Department in the Johns Hopkins University: Art as Applied to Medicine," *Bulletin of the Johns Hopkins Hospital* 22 (1911): 350; "The Origin, Growth and Future of Medical Illustration at the Johns Hopkins Hospital and Medical School," *Bulletin of the Johns Hopkins Hospital* 26 (1915): 185–90; and "Medical Illustration," *Journal of the American Medical Association* 117 (1941): 668–72. A good example of his scientific writing is "A More Rational Method of Passing the Suture in Fixation of the Kidney," *American Medicine* 4 (2 Aug. 1902): 176–78. The authoritative biography of Brödel, co-written by the emerita director of the Johns Hopkins medical art department, is Ranice W. Crosby and John Cody, *Max Brödel: The Man Who Put Art into Medicine* (1991). It includes as an appendix excerpts of previously unpublished drafts of Brödel's planned textbook on medical illustration technique. Another useful source, also by a medical illustrator, is Ida Dox Melloni, "Max Brodel and Visual Communication: The Effect of the Hopkins Intellectual Context in the Genesis of Modern Medical Illustration" (Ph.D. diss., Univ. of Maryland, 1990).

EDWARD T. MORMAN

BRODERICK, David Colbert (4 Feb. 1820–16 Sept. 1859), U.S. senator, was born in Washington, D.C., the son of Thomas Broderick, a stonemason, and Honora Colbert. In 1817 Thomas Broderick moved his family from County Cork, Ireland, to Washington, D.C., where he worked on the Capitol. In 1825 the Brodericks moved to Greenwich Village, New York, where Thomas Broderick died in 1834. At age fourteen, David Broderick began a five-year apprenticeship as a stonemason, while his mother opened a china shop. China importer Townsend R. Harris, later the first envoy to Japan and founder of the City University of New York, revealed the world of books to young Broderick, and journalist George Wilkes broadened his reading.

Broderick worked as a saloon keeper, first at the Subterranean in 1840 and then at the Republican, which provided a political headquarters and a place for the teetotaling barkeeper to read. In 1841 he became foreman of Howard Engine Company No. 34, where his mason's hands proved good in a brawl. A few months in the customhouse in 1843 taught him the value of patronage. He studied human nature, learned political organization, and mastered the intricacies of shifting alliances in the Ninth Ward.

"The class of society to whose toil I was born," Broderick declared, "under our form of government, will control the destinies of this nation." As a delegate selected to revise the New York City charter in 1846, Broderick advocated that a wide variety of offices be filled by election rather than appointment and proposed decentralized, autonomous wards. The Democratic party nominated him for Congress, but class-conscious aristocratic leaders, rather than support an Irish-Catholic workingman, threw the election to the Whigs through the selection of an additional candidate.

Broderick's mother died in 1843 and his brother in 1845, leaving him with no family and long periods of depression. His magnetism and fidelity to promises drew men to him, but his drive to achieve made him humorless, irritable, and subject to vehement outburst. He even felt isolated from workingmen, who were "too prone to neglect their rights and duties as citizens." They could not decipher him. The self-made Broderick once said, "I was tired of the struggles and the jealousies of men of my class, who could not understand why one of their fellows should seek to elevate his condition above the common level."

Blocked politically and having no power base, Broderick left New York City for the unsettled society of California. He arrived in mid-1849 and with Frederick D. Kohler began striking $5 and $10 gold coins, the lightest of any gold rush coinage. Seigniorage made his fortune, real estate investments financed his political battles, and a well-oiled political machine in urban San Francisco gave him power. In January 1850 Broderick entered the California Senate through a special election, and on 14 April 1850 he became the first foreman of Empire Fire Engine Company No. 1. Voters returned him to the legislature that fall. His ability to control men made him a dominating figure for three sessions, and in 1851 his mastery of parliamentary procedure led to his selection as presiding officer.

Broderick's animosity to slavery at once became manifest. He killed proposals to prevent free blacks from coming to California, to amend the constitution to divide California and create a new slave state, and to allow the importation of Chinese coolies. He also fought the foreign miners tax and battled a fugitive slave law. His egalitarianism led to a San Francisco city charter similar to the one he had proposed for New York, support for "squatters" in the tumultuous battles for land, and vigorous opposition to the San Francisco Vigilance committees of 1851 and 1856 that, in 1856 especially, targeted Broderick's political operatives and ballot-box stuffers.

Broderick did not challenge the cardinal principle of white supremacy in the dominant Democratic party but spoke instead for free labor. With implacable hatred, he battled proslavery southerners. His barrier to a senate seat was the aristocratic senator William M. Gwin, who had controlled federal patronage since 1850. After years of intrigue, on 9 January 1857 the state legislature elected Broderick U.S. senator. His earlier political maneuvering had delayed the selection of the second senator, and now Broderick picked his colleague. He spurned the deceitful Milton S. Latham to choose the cunning Gwin. However, incoming president James Buchanan blocked Broderick's patronage choices. A miserably weak man, the president deferred to southerners. His support for the repeal of the Missouri Compromise drove Broderick and Senator Stephen A. Douglas of Illinois into opposition.

When Buchanan attempted to force a proslavery constitution on Kansas Territory, Broderick charged in his maiden Senate speech, on 23 December 1857, that the president personally was attempting "to create civil war in Kansas." On 22 March 1858 he elaborated that now, thanks to Buchanan's actions, "slavery and freedom confronted each other in the territories." Where did Broderick stand? "I represent a State, sir, where labor is honorable." He bluntly denounced the aggressive Slave Power and asserted that Buchanan's support for the "fraud" in Kansas represented "the trembling dotage of an old man."

The next year California's Southern Democrats effectively isolated Broderick, forcing him to break away and create a separate Free Soil party. In contrast, Douglas stayed within the Democratic party. By delaying the rupture for a year, Southern Democrats became the ones who left, while Douglas became the regularly nominated Democratic party candidate for president. "I have been unwavering in my attachment to the Democratic party, and to Democratic principles," Broderick proclaimed, but in 1859 he was vulnerable to charges of bolting and holding black Republican beliefs. On 26 June Broderick read that Supreme Court justice David S. Terry had characterized his party as an unprincipled, "miserable remnant of a faction" that Broderick owned "heart and soul." Worst of all, according to Terry, Broderickites were no longer Democrats; their only guidance came from "the banner of the black Douglass, whose name is Frederick." Being called a "Negro lover," anathema to Democrats and workingmen, coupled with Terry's surprise assault prompted Broderick's volatile temper to explode. He lashed out violently at his supposed friend. Word reached Terry, who valued honor above life, but he let the campaign proceed. Out on the stump, Gwin and Broderick began abusing each other. Broderick was no orator, and his flailing charges brought Southern Democratic scorn. The press anticipated that Broderick would be in a duel following the 7 September election.

Although Broderick's Northern Democrats had attempted fusion with Republicans on some offices, Southern Democrats swept California. As Broderick received devastating election returns, Terry began a hostile correspondence. The two duelists met on 13 September 1859 south of San Francisco by Lake Merced. Broderick fell at the first fire, pierced through a lung, and died in San Francisco three days later. His funeral brought together the largest crowd that had yet assembled in San Francisco. On 18 September Republican Edward D. Baker summed up the somber mood of the mourning Golden State, stating, "His death was a political necessity, poorly veiled beneath the guise of a private quarrel." Baker eloquently asked, "What was his public crime? The answer is in his own words: 'I die because I was opposed to a corrupt administration and the extension of slavery.'" When Senator Gwin left California to return to Washington, he walked under a banner on the steamship landing that declared, "It is the will of the people that the murderers of Broderick do not return again to California."

In death Broderick achieved what he could not do alive. Building on Broderick's strong antislavery image, a political revolution barred southerners from office for a decade. His name became a political symbol for liberty and a rallying cry for laboring men during nineteenth-century elections and a shrine to freedom in twentieth-century textbooks. "He died a Senator in Congress," Baker said, "having written his name in the history of the great struggle for the rights of the people." The martyred Broderick's epitaph reads simply, "Mechanic: Senator." He never married.

• Broderick did not save his letters, but his public record is accessible in the Sacramento *Union* and the *Congressional Globe*; *Speech of Hon. D. C. Broderick of California, against the Admission of Kansas under the Lecompton Constitution, March 22, 1858* (1858); and Winfield J. Davis, *History of Political Conventions in California, 1849–1892* (1893). Valuable for day-to-day details and political intrigue is James O'Meara, *Broderick and Gwin: A Brief History of Early Politics in California* (1881), by a polished journalist who was Senator Gwin's ally. Donald E. Hargis delineates "The Issues in the Broderick-Gwin Debates of 1859," *California Historical Society Quarterly* 32 (Dec. 1953): 313–25. Carroll Douglas Hall presents the best account of *The Terry-Broderick Duel* (1939), while Donald Gill, "The Dueling Doctors of Stockton," *Pacific Historian* 25 (Spring 1981): 52–58, exposes the secret of Broderick's defective pistol. David A. Williams, "The Forgery of the Broderick Will," *California Historical Society Quarterly* 40 (Sept. 1861): 203–14, illustrates how the senator's closest aides divided $300,000 worth of real estate. Baker's oration is in Oscar T. Schuck, *Masterpieces of E. D. Baker* (1899). Donald E. Hargis presents a memorial by the senator's political mentor, "'Straight toward His Heart': George Wilkes' Eulogy of David C. Broderick," *California Historical Society Quarterly* 38 (Sept. 1959): 196–217. A balanced, scholarly work is David A. Williams, *David C. Broderick: A Political Portrait* (1969). Also see Philip J. Ethington, *The Public City: The Political Construction of Urban Life in San Francisco, 1850–1900* (1994).

ROBERT J. CHANDLER

BRODERICK, Helen (11 Aug. 1891–25 Sept. 1959), actress and singer, was born in Philadelphia, Pennsylvania, the daughter of William Broderick, an actor and singer. Her mother's name is unknown. Influenced and encouraged by her father, Broderick began performing when she was fourteen. She began her professional stage career at the age of sixteen in the first of Florenz Ziegfeld's *Follies*, which opened on 8 July 1907 at the Jardin de Paris (located on the roof of the New York Theatre) in New York City. The revue ran seventy performances with a cast that included Grace La Rue, Emma Carus, and Harry Watson, Jr. Broderick's comedic talent was evident in several sketches, including a satire called "The Modern Sandow Girl," which spoofed Sandow the Strongman and Ziegfeld's early career as a showman. The success of the revue led Ziegfeld to take the show to Baltimore and Washington, D.C., and to produce an annual *Follies*.

Broderick spent the next few years playing in the Broadway chorus and in vaudeville, appearing in *The Girl in Question*, which opened in August 1908 at Wallack's Theatre, and as Miss Winston in *Jumping Jupiter*, which opened in March 1911 at the New York Theatre. In 1909 Broderick married Lester Crawford, with whom she performed in vaudeville successfully for the next several years. The year after they were wed the couple had their only child, the actor Broderick Crawford. Male/female comedy teams were popular in vaudeville at the time—Crawford would play the straight man as Broderick developed her trademark "caustic, wisecracking style."

Over the next fifteen years Broderick played on Broadway while continuing her vaudeville career, appearing in *The Kiss Burglar* (1918) at the Cohan Theatre; *Nifties of 1923* at the Fulton Theatre; *The Wild Westcotts* (1923) at the Frazee Theatre; *Puzzles of 1925* at the Fulton Theatre; *Mama Loves Papa* (1926) at the Forrest Theatre; and *Oh! Please!* (1926) at the Fulton Theatre. In 1924 Broderick appeared in her first film, *High Speed*, followed by *The Mystery Club* in 1926.

Beginning in 1929 Broderick's career took an important turn as she appeared in a series of hit Broadway shows and films. On 27 November 1929 she opened as Violet Hildegarde in Cole Porter's *Fifty Million Frenchmen*, a musical spoof of American tourists, at the Lyric Theatre. In the musical Broderick played a bored spinster in Paris who sends risqué French postcards home to her family and friends and buys copies of James Joyce's controversial *Ulysses* to give as gifts to kids. Her performance won rave reviews, and in 1931 she reprised her role for the film version. Also in 1931 she appeared in *The Band Wagon*, which opened at the New Amsterdam Theatre on 3 June. The showstopper of this revue, whose cast included Fred and Adele Astaire, was a comedy sketch in which Broderick's character shops for bathroom appliances. The off-color sketch was almost cut by the producer, Max Gordon, but the director, Hassard Short, talked him out of it, and the sketch became the highlight of the revue. Broderick also performed a satiric revue of torch singers, singing "Where Can He Be?"

In 1932 Broderick appeared in *Earl Carroll's Vanities* with Milton Berle and Will Fyffe. In 1933 she continued her Broadway success in Irving Berlin and Moss Hart's *As Thousands Cheer*, which opened at the Music Box Theatre on 30 September and also starred Marilyn Miller, Clifton Webb, and Ethel Waters. *As Thousands Cheer*, a satiric revue of current events, had Broderick impersonating Mrs. Herbert Hoover and evangelist Aimee Semple McPherson. As the Statue of Liberty she sang, "We'll All Be in Heaven When the Dollar Goes to Hell." The revue was a great success, running more than 300 performances.

Broderick's film career also was successful. She appeared in thirty-eight films between 1924 and 1946. Acting primarily as a comedienne in musical films, she is best known as Ginger Rogers's pal in *Top Hat* (1935) and in *Swing Time* (1936). Released by RKO pictures, *Top Hat* opened to mixed reviews but later became a classic Astaire-Rogers film. According to *Variety*, Broderick's performance was favorable despite the script. "That the material is far from unusual, is particularly evidenced in the case of such an expert comedienne as Helen Broderick," the *Variety* reviewer wrote. "That her material isn't what it should be is unfortunate, but she shows enough here to stick on the Coast because she is one of the stage's top comediennes." *Swing Time* also highlighted Broderick's comedic talents as she teamed with Victor Moore to "bolster the comedy in great style" (*Variety*, 2 Sept. 1936). Her last film was *Because of Him* (1946). She died in Beverly Hills, California.

Broderick remained in the public eye as a vaudeville, stage, and film celebrity for two decades. According to *The Encyclopedia of the Musical Film* her "dead pan, sharp-eyed delivery provided a witty, worldly touch to Hollywood musicals." *Who's Who in Hollywood* called Broderick a "plainspoken, sharply funny femme with a crooked nose, bug eyes, and a worldly soul." Through her work on the stage and screen, Broderick helped raise the quality of musical comedy, often turning two-dimensional characters into comic figures of depth and substance.

• Information on Broderick's stage career can be found in David Ewen, *The New Complete Book of American Musical Theatre* (1970); Gerald Bordman, ed., *The Oxford Companion to the American Theatre* (1984); and *Who Was Who in the Theatre* (1979). Information on her film career can be found in David Ragan, *Who's Who in Hollywood, 1900–1976* (1976); Stanley Green, *The Encyclopedia of the Musical Film* (1981); Evelyn Mack-Truitt, *Who Was Who on Screen* (1983); Mel Schuster, *Motion Picture Performers* (1965; rev. ed., 1971); and Leslie Halliwell, *The Filmgoers Companion* (1970). An obituary is in *Newsweek*, 5 Oct. 1959.

MELISSA VICKERY-BAREFORD

BRODHEAD, Daniel (17 Sept. 1736–15 Nov. 1809), revolutionary war soldier, was born in Albany, New York, the son of Daniel Brodhead II, a merchant, and Hester Wyngart. When Brodhead was young his father moved the family to "Brodhead Manor" on the Pennsylvania frontier in Bucks (now Monroe) County. In his youth he made many trips over the Allegheny Mountains, and by the time he reached manhood he was a capable frontiersman, learned in the ways of the forest and of local Indian tribes.

Brodhead was widely perceived to be an "Indian hater," an attitude that stemmed from a ferocious attack on Brodhead Manor by a French–Indian raiding party on 11 December 1755. In 1773 he moved to Reading and established himself as a prosperous merchant. That year, because of his political connections with Benjamin Franklin, he was appointed deputy surveyor general of Pennsylvania. When Americans took up arms against Britain in 1775, he helped organize the committee of correspondence for Bucks County and was elected to the Pennsylvania Convention. In May 1775 he raised a company of riflemen and joined the Continental army, commanded by General George Washington, at the siege of Boston. When the Pennsylvania State Rifle Regiment was organized under Colonel Samuel Miles on 13 March 1776, Brodhead was appointed lieutenant colonel of the regiment's Second Battalion. With this battalion he marched in the spring of 1776 to New York City.

On 17 August 1776 Brodhead fought in the battle of Long Island, where he acquitted himself well but barely managed to extricate himself before being killed or captured. Of the American officers' confusion during the battle, he wrote disgustedly, "Less generalship never was shown . . . since the Art of War was understood." However, he was pleased with patriot soldiers, declaring that "no troops could behave better." After Miles was captured during the battle, Brodhead was appointed acting commander of the remnants of Miles's Regiment and the Pennsylvania State Battalion of Musketry, which were consolidated into a single provisional battalion. On 25 September 1776 he was administratively transferred to the Third Pennsylvania Battalion but seems never to have joined the unit. During the remainder of the year he fought in a number of skirmishes and battles around New York. On 12 March 1777, while serving under General Benjamin Lincoln at Morristown, New Jersey, he was promoted to colonel and appointed commander of the Eighth Pennsylvania Regiment, to rank from 29 September 1776. His regiment sustained losses at Brunswick, New Jersey, on 12 April 1777 when it was surprised by a British attack on Lincoln's encampment. At the battles of Brandywine, on 11 September; Paoli, on 20 September; Germantown, on 4 October; and Whitemarsh, on 4 December, Brodhead led the Eighth Pennsylvania Regiment as part of General Anthony Wayne's division.

After wintering at Valley Forge, Brodhead was ordered by Washington on 8 March 1778 with his regiment to Fort Pitt, in western Pennsylvania. On 12 July, while on the march westward, he was ordered by his new commander, Brigadier General Lachlan McIntosh, to the west branch of the Susquehanna River to thwart Indian raids there and in the Wyoming Valley. He and his troops reached Fort Pitt on 10 September and in early October accompanied McIntosh on an expedition down the Ohio River to the mouth of Beaver Creek, where Fort McIntosh was erected. Brodhead was appointed commander of the fort and spent a terrible winter there, while McIntosh wintered at Fort Pitt after ineffectual attempts to reach Detroit. Angrily, Brodhead complained to Washington that McIntosh was a poor planner, a poor manager, and a lethargic officer. Brodhead was particularly disgusted with McIntosh's construction of Fort McIntosh, which he referred to as the general's "Hobby Horse." Washington responded on 5 March 1779 by appointing Brodhead commander of the Western Department in Mc-

Intosh's stead. On 11 August 1779, with Washington's approval, Brodhead led an army of 605 men up the Allegheny River to attack Seneca and Delaware Indian villages near the river's headwaters. Successful in neutralizing his Indian foes, he returned to Fort Pitt on 14 September. Later that month, despite his hatred of Indians, he amicably concluded a treaty with the Delawares, who gave him the ceremonial name "Great Moon." For his successes in 1779, Brodhead received a vote of thanks from Congress and Washington's warm congratulations.

On 17 January 1781 Brodhead was transferred from command of the Eighth Pennsylvania Regiment to the Second, when the former regiment ceased to exist. In April 1781 he led an expedition against the Delaware Indians, ostensibly because the Delawares had broken their treaty. In fact, many people thought Brodhead's real reason was to avoid cooperation with George Rogers Clark, who was marching against Detroit. Brodhead assaulted the Delaware town of Conshocton, with no clear result, then returned to Fort Pitt. Because he was a strict military disciplinarian, a land speculator, and an ambitious officer who tended to be jealous of his subordinates, he was unpopular with his troops. Accused by critics of various charges of malfeasance, he was removed from command of the Western Department by Washington on 6 September 1781 and ordered to face a court-martial. Before he departed Fort Pitt in October to join Washington's army in New York, he quarreled with Colonel John Gibson and other officers. On 28 February 1782 he was acquitted with honor by the court-martial of all charges against him. Continuing to retain the goodwill of Washington, he was promoted brevet brigadier general on 30 September 1783.

After he was discharged in 1783 Brodhead returned to his farm, "Milford," which he had purchased during the war, in Pike County, Pennsylvania. Settling down with his wife, Elizabeth Dupui, he held various public offices over the next two decades. He was an ardent supporter of the Constitution of 1787 and a partisan of Alexander Hamilton and the Federalists. In 1790 he was appointed state surveyor by the Pennsylvania General Assembly and held the position until his death. When his wife Elizabeth died, he married Rebecca Mifflin, widow of General Thomas Mifflin. He died at Milford, honored by his neighbors as a competent officer, businessman, and politician.

• Brodhead's papers are in the State Historical Society of Wisconsin, Madison. Published primary materials are in *Colonial Records of Pennsylvania, 1683–1790*, vol. 10 (1853); Samuel Hazard et al., eds., *Pennsylvania Archives*, ser. 1, vol. 5, ser. 2, vols. 1 and 14, ser. 5, vols. 2–3; John C. Fitzpatrick, ed., *The Writings of George Washington from the Original Manuscript Sources, 1745–1799*, vols. 7–24 (1932–1937); William W. Abbot et al., eds., *The Papers of George Washington*, Revolutionary War Series, ed. Philander C. Chase, vols. 5–6 (1993–1994); and Louise Phelps Kellogg, ed., *Frontier Advance on the Upper Ohio, 1778–1779* (1916), and *Frontier Retreat on the Upper Ohio, 1779–1781* (1917). Information on Brodhead's army ranks are in Francis B. Heitman, *Historical Register of Officers of the Continental Army during the War of the Revolution, April 1775 to December 1783* (1914). John B. B. Trussell, Jr., *The Pennsylvania Line: Regimental Organization and Operations, 1776–1783* (1977), discusses his service in the Pennsylvania line. His role in Indian warfare is covered in Obed Edson, "Brodhead's Expedition against the Indians of the Upper Allegheny, 1779," *Magazine of American History* 3 (1879): 649–75; Edgar W. Hassler, *Old Westmoreland: A History of Western Pennsylvania during the Revolution* (1900); C. Hale Sipe, *The Indian Wars of Pennsylvania* (1929); Solon J. Buck, *The Planting of Civilization in Western Pennsylvania* (1939); Albert H. Wright, "Brodhead's Expedition," pt. 2 of *The Sullivan Expedition of 1779: Contemporary Newspaper Comment* (1943); William Y. Brady, "Brodhead's Trail up to the Allegheny, 1779," *Western Pennsylvania Historical Magazine* 37 (1954): 19–31; and John C. Appel, "Colonel Daniel Brodhead and the Lure of Detroit," *Pennsylvania History* 38 (1971): 265–82.

PAUL DAVID NELSON

BRODHEAD, John Romeyn (2 Jan. 1814–6 May 1873), diplomat and historian, was born in Philadelphia, the son of the Reverend Dr. Jacob Brodhead, minister of the First Reformed Dutch Church, and Elizabeth Bleecker. He lived in Philadelphia until 1826, when his father was called to the Broome Street Reformed Dutch Church in New York City. Brodhead thereafter attended Albany Academy and Rutgers College. Graduating with honors from Rutgers in 1831, he studied law in the office of Hugh Maxwell for four years. After being admitted to the New York bar in 1835, he commenced a legal practice as Maxwell's partner, but when his father fell ill two years later, Brodhead abandoned a legal career to care for his father at a summer home in Saugerties, New York, where he developed an interest in early American history.

In 1839 Harmanus Bleecker, a relative and chargé d'affaires to the American legation to the Netherlands, invited Brodhead to serve as an attaché at The Hague. His growing interest in the Dutch colony of New Netherland and its contribution to American history surfaced while he was in Holland. Brodhead resigned his post at the legation after serving for a year; he sought a post, created by the New York State legislature, as an agent authorized to obtain from European archives relevant documents that would complete the state archives. After his appointment by Governor William H. Seward in 1841, Brodhead examined the archives of Holland, France, and England during the next four years. Even with heavy financial constraints, he obtained eighty volumes of manuscript copies of documents. In 1845 he published his report with the hope that it would encourage the state legislature to appropriate funds for the arrangement and translation of these documents. With his knowledge of Dutch and French, he was well qualified for this task. But when the funds were finally appropriated by the Whig-controlled legislature in 1849, Brodhead, a Democrat, was passed over for the position. Edmund B. O'Callaghan and Berthold Fernow subsequently edited the collection, which the state published as *Docu-*

ments relative to the Colonial History of the State of New York (1853–1887).

In 1846 George Bancroft, who had been appointed minister to Great Britain, persuaded Brodhead to serve as secretary to the American legation in London. For the next three years Brodhead supervised the American embassy there.

After Bancroft's recall in 1849, Brodhead retired from the diplomatic service to write his *History of the State of New York*; the plan was for a four-volume work. The first, covering the period 1609–1664, was published in 1853. That same year, President Franklin Pierce appointed Brodhead naval officer of the port of New York. In 1856 he married Eugenia Bloodgood. Brodhead's duties as naval officer delayed publication of the second volume (1664–1691) until 1871. Brodhead never completed the third volume (1691–1789). In addition, he produced during this period several important essays on the early history of New York.

Brodhead was an active member of the New-York Historical Society, serving on its editorial board and executive committee. From 1853 he was a trustee of Rutgers College; he and his father founded its Brodhead Prize in the classics. An active supporter of the Astor Library, he served as a trustee from 1867 until 1871. He died in New York City.

In an era when document copies were made by hand, Brodhead's massive collection of early New York papers was remarkable. Unfortunately, the quality of the transcriptions vary from highly accurate to extremely poor. His *History of the State of New York*, still the standard work on New Netherland, earned Brodhead his reputation as a historian.

• Brodhead's papers are at Rutgers University. His manuscript copies of early New York documents are held by the New York State Library at Albany.

Brodhead's works not cited in the text are *The Final Report of John Romeyn Brodhead, Agent of the State of New York* (1845); *Addresses of John Romeyn Brodhead and Gov. Horatio Seymour, Delivered before the Clinton Hall Association and Mercantile Library Association . . . 8th June, 1854* (1854); *Commemoration of the Conquest of New Netherland, on Its Two Hundredth Anniversary* (1864); *The Government of Sir Edmund Andros over New England, in 1688 and 1689, Read before the New-York Historical Society, on Tuesday Evening, 4th December, 1866* (1867). Brodhead translated Isaack de Rasiers, "New Netherland in 1627," *Collections of the New-York Historical Society*, 2d ser., 2 (1849): 339–54, and Johannes Megapolensis, "A Short Sketch of the Mohawk Indians in New Netherland," *Collections of the New-York Historical Society*, 2d ser., 3 (1857): 137–60. In addition he produced "Memoir on the Early Colonization of New Netherland," *Collections of the New-York Historical Society*, 2d ser., 2 (1849): 355–66, and contributed to *Papers concerning the Boundary between New York and New Jersey* (1866).

An early biographical sketch of Brodhead appeared in *Scribner's Monthly* 13, Nov. 1876–Apr. 1877, 459–63; Adriaan J. Barnouw, "John Romeyn Brodhead, 1814–1873," *de Halve Maen* 39, no. 3 (1964): 11–12; Ronald Howard, "John Romeyn Brodhead," *Dictionary of Literary Biography* 30 (1984). Several of his letters (1840–1842) are printed in Harriet Langdon Pruyn Rice, *Harmanus Bleecker: An Albany Dutchman, 1779–1849* (1924).

DAVID WILLIAM VOORHEES

BRODIE, Bernard Beryl (7 Aug. 1907?–27 Feb. 1989), pharmacologist, was born in Liverpool, England, the son of Samuel Brodie and Esther Ginsberg. Some sources give his birth year as 1909. When Brodie was four, the family moved to Ottawa, Canada, where his father owned a men's furnishings store. Brodie attended public schools, recalling later that he was a poor student and was even expelled for insubordination before completing high school.

In 1925 Brodie joined the Canadian army signal corps for three years. Up until that point, he had been very shy, but a sergeant major urged him to learn to fight to avoid being beaten, and so he learned boxing and became the Canadian army champion in his weight class. He also read library books on the statistics of poker, and during his military service he won about $5,000 at the game. After his discharge he attended McGill University in Montreal with those funds. Although in his freshman year he was suspended from a chemistry course for sleeping, he majored in chemistry, encouraged by W. H. Hatcher, the professor who had suspended him. Hatcher also asked his help on an experiment that required round-the-clock attention, which led to Brodie's first scientific paper, "Polymerization of Acetaldehyde," which they wrote jointly for the *Canadian Journal of Research* (4 [1931]: 574–81). He received the B.S. in 1931.

Brodie then entered New York University on an assistantship and received his Ph.D. in organic chemistry in 1935. His professor recommended that he go into pharmacology instead of laboratory chemistry because, Brodie said, "I was unable to remember simple structures or the Geneva nomenclature and because I was accident-prone" (*Science News*, 11 Nov. 1967). He became a research assistant in 1935 to George B. Wallace, professor of pharmacology at the medical school of New York University. Wallace encouraged Brodie to use his knowledge of chemistry in pharmacology. With Wallace he published on the relationship of administered pharmaceuticals to body fluids. Brodie was appointed instructor in pharmacology at New York University in 1938 and became a U.S. citizen the next year. His brief marriage to Frieda Harris ended in divorce in 1939; they had no children. He advanced to assistant professor in 1943 and from 1947 to 1950 was associate professor of biochemistry.

From 1941 to 1950 Brodie was also a research associate in biochemistry with the Research Service of New York University at Goldwater Memorial Hospital in New York City. This facility began under the auspices of the National Research Council for medical needs of World War II and was directed by James Augustine Shannon, who suggested the significance of determining the levels of drugs in the blood. With Sidney Udenfriend, Brodie looked into problems with the synthetic alkaloid quinacrine for treating malaria. The standard drug for treatment, quinine, was in short supply after Japan's conquest of the Dutch East Indies in March 1942. Quinacrine was proving to be ineffective in the recommended doses. By late 1942 Brodie and Udenfriend had determined that the product broke down readily into inactive components and that a large dose was necessary at first to reach an effective level, followed by smaller daily doses to maintain it. This became the standard practice by military physicians. Brodie and Udenfriend developed other treatments for malaria, which came into use after the end of World War II. During this work they tested colored dyes to trace solutions of alkaloids, and, almost by accident, tried methyl orange, a common laboratory chemical. It worked and led to techniques of determining concentrations of drugs in solution. They published six papers, with coauthors, in a series called "The Estimation of Basic Organic Compounds in Biological Material" in the *Journal of Biological Chemistry* (168 [1947]: 299–344), which summarized much of their work on the body's response to drugs.

Brodie continued studies to define the interaction of drugs with the body in which they are ingested. Using different species of animals, he found that individuals of any one species had widely different responses to the same drug, and this applied as well to humans. He determined that the proper dosage depends upon the concentration of the drug in the blood, not the size or weight of the subject. This was essentially a new concept in medicine, and he was a pioneer in the techniques of measurement. Brodie later considered his work on drug dosage in the blood his most significant contribution to medical practice. It has proven valuable in the development of synthetic medications.

In 1950 Brodie joined the National Heart Institute of the National Institutes of Health, at the urging of his earlier superior James Shannon, who was scientific director of the heart institute and was expanding its research program. Brodie's role was to found its Laboratory of Chemical Pharmacology. Also in 1950 he married Anne Lois Smith; they had no children. He stayed at the institute until 1970. At the same time he was a lecturer at George Washington University and Georgetown University Medical School. His studies on metabolism continued, usually starting with studies on animals and continuing with humans. He found that metabolism can vary greatly from one species to another, so that correlations cannot necessarily be made between certain other animals and humans. An example was the muscle-relaxing phenylbutazone, which proved to be helpful for rheumatoid arthritis in humans but not for other animals in equivalent dosage. Brodie and colleagues found that mammals do not acquire drug-destroying enzyme systems until some time after birth, a finding that made it possible to prescribe drugs more knowledgeably to pregnant women and newborn infants.

In the mid-1950s Brodie set out to determine the roles of drugs in emotional disorders and mental illness. He found that one of the earliest tranquilizers, reserpine, triggered the release of the neurohormone serotonin from the brain, which lowered blood pressure. He also found that the antidepressant iproniazid caused a buildup in the brain of the neurohormone norepinephrine. He continued with researches into the manner in which nerve impulses are transmitted in the central nervous system and concluded that mental illnesses are not associated with biochemical abnormalities or defects. He suggested that their causes might derive from faults in the nerve-transmission system.

Among Brodie's other studies was finding a chemical variation of procaine (procaine-amide) that had a prolonged effect for patients with severe irregularities in heart rhythm. With Julius Axelrod in 1948, he determined the chemical nature of acetanilide, used as an analgesic and fever reducer, so that they could pinpoint the toxic side effects. Their work led to the development of acetaminophen by about 1955 as a substitute for aspirin.

After retiring from the National Heart Institute, from 1971 to 1980 Brodie was a visiting professor of pharmacology at Pennsylvania State University College of Medicine in Hershey, Pennsylvania, and then an adjunct professor until his death. He was a lecturer or visiting professor of pharmacology at several other locations in the 1960s and 1970s and a consultant to medical institutes after 1970.

Brodie's scientific field came to be called chemical or neurochemical pharmacology and was interdisciplinary among pharmacology, biochemistry, physiology, and psychiatry. He was noted for entering various other disciplines and challenging established ideas, which was not always welcomed by researchers in those fields.

Within his working group, when considering a project for study, Brodie often used the phrase "Let's take a flier on it." The phrase helped earn him the nickname "Steve" for the unrelated Steve Brodie who, on a bet, had survived a jump off the Brooklyn Bridge in 1886, from which came the phrase "to pull a Brodie," meaning to take a long shot. He was accustomed to beginning his day's work at about noon and continuing until the early hours of the morning. He had what his biographer Robert Kanigel called a "frighteningly original mind," which impressed and sometimes dismayed his colleagues, who recalled grueling discussions and bleary-eyed night sessions. Lewis Aronow, who worked for him, said, "He was a slave driver" (Kanigel, p. 32). Julius Axelrod, one of the younger researchers who worked with him and later received a Nobel Prize, said that Brodie "made every experiment seem earth-shattering" (Kanigel, p. 59). Brodie's only interest seemed to be accomplishing something in science, and he expected his associates and employees to take as keen an interest.

Brodie published about 400 articles in scientific journals. He was a founder and editor of *Life Sciences* and was a cofounder and U.S. editor of *Medicina et Pharmacologia Experimentalis*. He was elected to the National Academy of Sciences in 1966, he received the Torald Sollmann Award in pharmacology and experimental therapeutics (1963), the Albert Lasker Medical Research Award (1967), the National Medal of Science (1968), and other recognitions.

In retirement Brodie lived in Florida and Arizona for a time, but he later moved to Charlottesville, Virginia, where he died.

• Robert Kanigel's *Apprentice to Genius: The Making of a Scientific Dynasty* (1986) includes considerable biographical information on Brodie. Obituaries are in the *New York Times* and the *Washington Post*, both 2 Mar. 1989.

ELIZABETH NOBLE SHOR

BRODIE, Fawn McKay (15 Sept. 1915–10 Jan. 1981), writer, educator, and editor, was born in Ogden, Utah, the daughter of Thomas Evans Brodie and Fawn Brimhall McKay, both of whom were Mormons. Her father was a chronically indebted farmer, a respected church leader, and later a state senator and public utilities commissioner. She earned her B.A. at the University of Utah in 1934, was an instructor in English at Weber State College (now Weber State University, Ogden, Utah), and obtained her M.A. in English at the University of Chicago in 1936. She married Bernard Brodie in 1936. During the next several years, her husband, who had earned his Ph.D. in 1940 in political science at the University of Chicago, taught at a variety of places, served in the U.S. Navy, and became a writer and a consultant on matters of national defense, weaponry, and foreign affairs. Meanwhile, the Brodies had three children.

Fawn Brodie taught as a senior lecturer in history at the University of California in Los Angeles (1968–1970) and then as a full professor (1970–1977). She took early retirement to devote herself exclusively to writing. The main work of her professional life was five biographies. They are *No Man Knows My History: The Life of Joseph Smith* (1945; rev. and enl. ed. 1971), *Thaddeus Stevens: Scourge of the South* (1959), *The Devil Drives: A Life of Sir Richard Burton* (1967; repr. 1984), *Thomas Jefferson: An Intimate History* (1974), and *Richard Nixon: The Shaping of His Character* (1981). In addition, she and her husband coauthored *From Cross-Bow to H-Bomb* (1962; rev. ed. 1973), a history of weapons and their wartime use. She edited in 1962 Frederick H. Piercy's 1855 *Route from Liverpool to Great Salt Lake Valley* and in 1963 Richard F. Burton's 1861 *The City of the Saints, and Across the Rocky Mountains to California*, and was a contributor to the *New York Times* and the *Encyclopaedia Britannica*. Her husband died in 1978. Three years later, she died in Santa Monica, California, shortly after completing her study of Nixon.

Fawn Brodie grew up hearing accounts of the visions, golden plates, and murder of Joseph Smith, founder of the Church of Jesus Christ of Latter-Day Saints. In her *No Man Knows My History*, she handles sensational material—some of it previously untapped—with sympathy and detached intelligence, and she adopts a point of view rejecting supernaturalism. In a supplement, she speculates on Smith's controversial nature and his evolution from "bucolic scryer" (that is, a crystal-gazing seer) to "religious prophet." Mormon leaders regarded as heretical her comments on the psychological bases of Smith's religious visions, on "the barrenness of his spiritual legacy," and on the "chance event" of his martyrdom. Accordingly, she requested and was granted excommunication from the church.

In her *Thaddeus Stevens*, Brodie concentrates on her controversial subject's private life and complex personality, discusses his parents, the effect of his being clubfooted, rumors that he seduced and murdered a slave girl, his being a surrogate father to two nephews, his friendship with his mulatto housekeeper, and his energizing hates. She deals with his turbulent political career, his relations with Abraham Lincoln, and his battles for African-American suffrage and schooling. Her biography is comprehensively documented, thoughtful, and nicely balanced between the common pitfalls of making Stevens an unscrupulous, tricky demagogue and a wise if rude leader.

The Devil Drives is a thoroughly researched, richly informative, and profound analysis of Sir Richard Burton and his adventures. He was Brodie's most challenging subject, being archaeologist, botanist, ethnologist, explorer, folklorist, geologist, linguist, master of disguises, poet, soldier, translator, traveler, and zoologist. He wrote forty-five books (exploration, travel, poetry) and more than a hundred articles; his translations came to twenty-eight volumes (*The Arabian Nights*, Portuguese poetry, Latin poetry, folklore); and he left many autobiographical items. Brodie mastered this mass and also traveled in search of and otherwise sought out unpublished material. An especially exciting part is her level-headed treatment of Burton's sexual activities, his probably frigid wife, and her burning of his forty-year journal and other juicy items.

Brodie called her well-researched *Thomas Jefferson* "a book about Jefferson and the life of the heart" and not about "his luminous mind and its impact upon society." She explores the links between his public life and intimate inner life. The most compelling sections concern the negative influence of Jefferson's wife, his love affair with the artist Maria Cosway in Paris and Italy, and especially his liaison with his quadroon mistress Sally Hemings, who, Brodie feels, gave him thirty-eight years of "much happiness." Brodie was Jefferson's first biographer to present the known facts in detail and to theorize that his relationship with Hemings was romantic and not strictly sexual. Brodie's conclusions, based on psychoanalytical speculation sometimes shaky but never lurid or demeaning, spurred considerable pro-and-con criticism when her biography first appeared.

Brodie's *Richard Nixon* relentlessly documents his childhood and early maturity, college years, law work, marriage (to a sheltering but silenced woman), and political career up to the assassination of John F. Kennedy, his preeminent rival. Brodie psychoanalyzes Nixon as the product of a sadistic father and a fine but reserved mother and as a personality conditioned by the death of two brothers (particularly that of the older, favored brother). She stresses Nixon's sense of loss, loneliness, mistrust of others, theatrical personality, chronic viciousness, and self-absorption. Her main themes are death as Nixon's "ally," his delight in slaughtering enemies, his inability to love, and his "ineffable dirtiness." Brodie alternately defines Nixon as "responsible decision-maker" and as "shabby, pathetic felon."

Fawn Brodie was a uniquely talented biographer. She will long be esteemed for her treatment of five eminent, controversial men in outstanding book-length studies, all of which are built on an extraordinary base of general and specific knowledge, are richly informative, and are notable for an agreeable, leisurely prose style. In her psychohistories, she advanced well beyond the norms of standard biographical writing by the use of intense psychological probing and occasional autoprojection; the results may be fraught with dangers but are always rewarding.

• Fawn Brodie's papers are in Special Collections, University of Utah Library. Brodie's "Inflation Idyl: A Family Farm in Huntsville," *Utah Historical Quarterly* 40 (1972): 112–21, is a brief autobiographical essay. Newell G. Bringhurst in "Fawn M. Brodie—Her Biographies as Autobiography," *Pacific Historical Review* 59 (May 1990): 203–29, combines detailed biographical data concerning Brodie with an astute comparison of the tensions of her life and personal and intellectual problems confronting the subjects of her five biographies. For an analysis of the evolution of Bernard Brodie's thoughts on nuclear arms—thoughts that undoubtedly contributed to his wife's often gloomy approach to history—see Robert Jervis, *The Meaning of the Nuclear Revolution: Statecraft and the Prospect of Armageddon* (1989). An obituary appears in the *New York Times*, 13 Jan. 1981.

ROBERT L. GALE

BROKMEYER, Henry Conrad (12 Aug. 1828–26 July 1906), philosopher and politician, was born in the vicinity of Minden, Prussia, the son of Frederick William Brockmeyer (Henry used both spellings), a Jewish businessman, and Sophia (maiden name unknown). Brokmeyer spent his youth in Prussia, but at age sixteen, apparently fleeing Prussian militarism, he emigrated to New York City with little money and little knowledge of English. On arrival, Brokmeyer worked his way as far south as Mississippi, where, it is said, he made a small fortune using slave labor in shoemaking.

In 1850 Brokmeyer began two years of schooling at Georgetown College in Kentucky. After two years he moved back east to Brown University, where he learned New England Transcendentalism from the university's president, Francis Wayland (1796–1865). There is no evidence that Brokmeyer actually took a degree. However, despite philosophical disagreements with Wayland, something of Transcendentalism's interest in bringing philosophy closer to lived experience reached him, and in 1854 Brokmeyer moved west to live as a recluse in Warren County, Missouri. About this time, he also lost what remained of his fortune with the collapse of a lending house in which he had invested. Like Henry David Thoreau, Brokmeyer took both books and his philosophical interest to the woods; in particular, he brought with him a growing passion for the study of G. W. F. Hegel.

After this initial hermitage, Brokmeyer returned to civilization in 1857, taking a job as an iron-molder in St. Louis. Some of this part of his life he recorded in *A Mechanic's Diary*, which was published in 1910. While working in St. Louis, Brokmeyer was introduced to William Torrey Harris to whom he introduced the philosophy of Hegel. A second venture into the woods ended in 1858 with an illness that required Harris to bring Brokmeyer to St. Louis in order to recover. Harris and two friends then provided a small pension for Brokmeyer so that he could work on a translation of Hegel's *Larger Logic*, the first draft of which was completed by 1860. During this time, Brokmeyer also wrote and privately published a play entitled *A Foggy Night at Newport*.

Brokmeyer's family life began in 1861 when he married Elizabeth Robertson of St. Louis, with whom he had two children. However, life was interrupted by the Civil War. Brokmeyer helped organize a regiment and became a provisional colonel in the militia. Despite unanimous support from his regiment, he was imprisoned on fabricated charges of disloyalty in St. Louis for a brief period. Fully exonerated, he was elected by an overwhelming majority of the people of Warren County to the state legislature in 1862. Brokmeyer served as a Union Democrat, supporting Abraham Lincoln and later encouraging his reelection. His first marriage ended when Elizabeth Brokmeyer died in 1864. He was remarried in 1867, to Julia Kienlen, with whom he had three children.

Over the course of the next fourteen years, Brokmeyer's public life developed on two fronts: as a philosopher and as a public servant. Together with Harris, Brokmeyer organized the St. Louis Philosophical Society in 1866. The society, which included as members Denton Snider, George Holmes Howison, and Thomas Davidson, provided a midwestern, Hegelian counterpart to the more Platonic transcendentalist movement of New England by which both Harris and Brokmeyer had earlier been influenced. Brokmeyer, who was appointed president of the society, was the admitted philosophical leader, and his optimistic interpretation of Hegel was played out in the dynamic public lives of the society's members. Snider, reflecting on Brokmeyer's leadership, identified both his strength and his weakness: "Particularly I had to be reinforced and underpropped by Brockmeyer's philosophical genius, equal to that of Hegel and more poetical; but he lacked Hegel's industry and organizing power, which Brockmeyer's wild and wayward but very inspiring effervescences spurned" (p. 119). Brokmeyer employed his strength when easterners such as Bronson Alcott and Ralph Waldo Emerson visited, subjecting them to his dialectical abilities. Besides functioning as a philosophical leader, Brokmeyer continued to work on revisions of his Hegel translation and published several essays in Harris's *Journal of Speculative Philosophy.*

Well known from his law practice and from having been on the board of aldermen in St. Louis in 1866, Brokmeyer was elected to the state senate in 1870. He served as a member of Missouri's constitutional convention in 1875 and played a significant role in the drafting of the state constitution. Subsequently he was elected lieutenant governor, running on the Democratic ticket with Governor John S. Phelps. When Governor Phelps became ill, Brokmeyer became acting governor during 1876–1877. Brokmeyer was both charismatic and controversial. Nevertheless, by 1885 he chose to end his career in politics both because he had lost a bid for the U.S. Senate and because he was interested in returning to his intellectual work. To the chagrin of some of his friends and supporters, he then became a lobbyist for the Gould System of Railroads.

The final twenty years of Brokmeyer's life were marked by wandering and a general disappointment in his failure to realize his hopes to make Hegel's work a central feature of American culture. For some time he lived among the Creek Indians in the Oklahoma Territory and apparently impressed them with his abilities in their ways. Besides dwelling off and on among Native Americans, he, on several occasions, attended meetings to give lectures in Milwaukee, St. Louis, and Cincinnati. However, Snider indicates that a great distance had developed between the "frontiersman" Brokmeyer and the intellectuals with whom he had earlier associated. He nevertheless continued to revise his translation of Hegel's *Larger Logic*, but he died in St. Louis with a copy of the manuscript in his attic and the book still unpublished. Despite its accuracy, the text was considered too dry to be worth publishing. As Pochmann maintains, "Its only fault is that it is so literally true to the original of Hegel that the reader who is unfamiliar with the involved Teutonic sentence structure finds the reading extremely wearisome" (p. 21).

Because he published so little, Brokmeyer's philosophical influence was limited to his own time and place. As his contemporaries noted, it was the immediate force of his genius that gave him power. In politics, Brokmeyer's influence was equally localized; as a practicing Hegelian he found himself at the center of the *Geist* of St. Louis in its heyday as the gateway to the frontier. His only lasting mark lies in his contribution to Missouri's constitution. Despite the pathos of his final years, Brokmeyer continues to capture the imagination as an exemplary American frontier intellectual, as a living locus of theory and practice.

• Brokmeyer's papers are in the Missouri Historical Society, St. Louis. Useful accounts of Brokmeyer's life appear in William H. Goetzmann, *The American Hegelians* (1973); Kurt F. Leidecker, *Yankee Teacher* (1946); Henry C. Pochmann, *New England Transcendentalism and St. Louis Hegelianism* (1948); and Denton J. Snider, *The St. Louis Movement in Philosophy, Literature, Education, and Psychology* (1920). An obituary is in the *St. Louis Republic*, 27 July 1906.

DOUGLAS R. ANDERSON

BROMFIELD, Louis (27 Dec. 1896–18 Mar. 1956), novelist, experimental farmer, and newspaper columnist, was born in Mansfield, Ohio, the son of Charles Bromfield, a banker and local Democratic office holder, and Annette Marie Coulter. His father was from an old New England family, and his mother was the daughter of a pioneer family of Richland County, Ohio; both ancestries would influence his later fiction. Bromfield attended Mansfield public schools, spending summers on his mother's family's farm. In 1914–1915 he studied agriculture at Cornell University and then briefly attended Ohio Northern University in Ada, Ohio. He then studied journalism at Columbia University until his enlistment in the U.S. Army Ambulance Service in June 1917. He served with Section 577, attached to the French army, from December 1917 to February 1919. He participated in seven major battles during World War I and was awarded the Croix de Guerre. He was discharged in June 1919 while still in France.

Although Bromfield had earlier planned to become a scientific farmer on his maternal family farm, by 1917 he had decided to become a writer, his mother's ambition for him. In late 1919 he returned to New York City, where he received his degree from Columbia and worked for the New York City News Service (1920–1922) and then for the Associated Press as a reporter and night editor. In 1921 he married Mary Appleton Wood; they would have three daughters. Between 1922 and 1925 he worked at a variety of jobs: foreign editor and critic for *Musical America*; writer of a monthly column of drama, art, and music criticism called "The New Yorker" for the *Bookman*; assistant to Brock Pemberton, a producer; music critic for *Time* magazine; and, briefly, advertising manager for G. P. Putnam's Sons.

Prior to 1923 Bromfield wrote and destroyed three unpublished novels. In 1924, however, *The Green Bay Tree* was published by F. A. Stokes. A success both critically and commercially, it freed Bromfield to write full time. *The Green Bay Tree* is one of Bromfield's best and most deeply felt novels. It reflects Bromfield's Ohio background in "the Town" and on the farm, as well as his love of France, and it reflects the strong Jeffersonian beliefs and the distaste for industrialism and commercialism that his father expressed. Both characteristics were mistakenly interpreted as anticapitalistic by some critics.

Living in Cold Spring Harbor, New York, Bromfield wrote the second of what he called "panel" novels, in which he used similar settings, characters, and values over the same time span. The success of *Possession* (1925) enabled him to take his family to France in 1925 for a vacation that extended to a fourteen-year residency. While in France Bromfield took a fifty-year lease on an old presbytère near Senlis, north of Paris, where he wrote, entertained, and gardened. He introduced several American varieties of vegetables to French gardeners, for which he received much recognition, and he taught gardening techniques to Gertrude Stein. There, too, he wrote *Early Autumn*

(1926), another of his panel novels, for which he was awarded the Pulitzer Prize in 1927.

Bromfield's publishing successes continued with *A Good Woman* (1927), *The Strange Case of Miss Annie Spragg* (1928), *Twenty-four Hours* (1930), and *A Modern Hero* (1932), all of which resulted from his attempts to fuse his Ohio background with his European experiences. In 1933 he published *The Farm*, his most personal and perhaps his best novel, the story of three generations and a hundred years of the history of his Ohio countryside. He returned on occasion to the United States to lecture, to visit, and in 1930 to work briefly for Samuel Goldwyn as a screenwriter. He spent the winter of 1933–1934 in America and began to consider returning to Ohio and buying a farm there. Beginning in 1932 he visited India on four occasions; these travels resulted in two novels: *The Rains Came* (1937), the better of the two, and *Night in Bombay* (1940).

By the early 1930s, as the world moved into depression, and proletarian literature and Marxist critical principles began to dominate American writing, Bromfield continued to emphasize Jeffersonian and agrarian values as well as the destructive nature of industrialism. This led many critics to score his work as overly romantic, and as a result his reputation began a decline from which it never recovered in his lifetime. However, he remained popular with the reading public, and he became increasingly active in public causes. During the Spanish Civil War he was president of the Emergency Committee for American Wounded in Spain, and he was made a chevalier of the Legion of Honor. As war in Europe became imminent Bromfield arranged for his family to return to America in late 1938. He himself returned early the next year.

Settling back in Ohio, Bromfield purchased three exhausted farms in Richland County and began their restoration as a single unit, which he named "Malabar Farm." He continued to travel extensively, to take part in wartime activities, and to publish fiction, including *Wild Is the River* (1941), *Until the Day Break* (1942), *Mrs. Parkington* (1943), and *What Became of Anna Bolton* (1944), the subject of a vicious review by Edmund Wilson. However, his primary interests had become land restoration, experimental agriculture, and nature writing. Beginning with *Pleasant Valley* (1945), a fusion of past and present in the Ohio countryside, he produced a series of fine works, including *Malabar Farm* (1948), *From My Experience* (1955), and *Animals and Other People* (1955), all of which are substantial additions to both agricultural literature and nature writing. For a number of years he also wrote a syndicated newspaper column of experience and opinion called "A Voice from the Country."

When Bromfield died at University Hospital in Columbus, Ohio, his literary reputation was at the low point at which it has remained, and his fine early novels *The Green Bay Tree*, *Possession*, and *Early Autumn* are generally overlooked by literary historians in the late twentieth century. However, these novels, along with *The Farm*, are excellent interpretations of the Midwest in transition. They also constitute an important part of the midwestern literary tradition that, in the hands of Sherwood Anderson, Theodore Dreiser, and others, shaped American writing in the 1920s and 1930s. Moreover, Bromfield's works have remained popular and have been the bases of a number of successful film productions.

At his death Malabar Farm passed into the hands of a foundation sponsored by the Cobey Corporation, a manufacturer of farm implements, that operated it as the Louis Bromfield Ecological Center. It was later owned by the state of Ohio and operated as Malabar Farm State Park, a working farm, campsite, and memorial to Bromfield.

• Bromfield's papers are at the Ohio State University, Mansfield campus. Bromfield outlined his later social and economic views in *A Few Brass Tacks* (1946) and *A New Pattern for a Tired World* (1954). Books about him include Morrison Brown, *Louis Bromfield and His Books* (1957), offering a favorable assessment of his work; Ellen Bromfield Geld, *The Heritage, a Daughter's Memories of Louis Bromfield* (1962), a delightful, accurate memoir; and David D. Anderson, *Louis Bromfield* (1964), a critical biography. Also see Mary Bromfield, "The Writer I Live With," *Atlantic Monthly*, Aug. 1950. For contrasting critical assessments, see Clifton Fadiman, "Louis Bromfield Looks Backward," *Saturday Review of Literature*, 19 Aug. 1933, a favorable review; and Edmund Wilson, "What Became of Louis Bromfield," *New Yorker*, 1 Apr. 1944, a highly unfavorable review. A bibliography of Bromfield's work is by Merle Derrenbacher in *Bulletin of Bibliography* 17 (Sept.–Dec. 1941), and 18 (Jan.–Apr. 1942). Obituaries are in the *New York Times*, 19 Mar. 1956, and *The Times* (London), 20 Mar. 1956.

DAVID D. ANDERSON

BRONK, Detlev Wulf (13 Aug. 1897–17 Nov. 1975), biophysicist, was born in New York City, the son of Mitchell Bronk, a Baptist minister, and Mary Wulf. Bronk's family moved to Bayonne, New Jersey, in 1900, and Bronk received his early education there. From 1912 until 1919 he lived in Troy, New York, graduating from high school in 1915. He then enrolled at Swarthmore College.

When World War I started, Bronk first served as an inspector enforcing the law regulating food prices and then enrolled as a volunteer in the navy flight school, receiving his wings and an ensign's commission in 1918. When the war ended, Bronk returned to college and graduated from Swarthmore in 1920. After a short period working at a brokerage firm, he became an instructor in physics at the University of Pennsylvania and began graduate study. In 1921 he married Helen Alexander Ramsey, with whom he had three children. They moved to Ann Arbor, Michigan, where Bronk continued his graduate studies in physics. In 1922 he received his M.S. from the University of Michigan and began working for a Ph.D., pursuing studies on the infrared spectrum of hydrochloric acid. After declining a job at Pennsylvania, he continued at Michigan under H. M. Randall, who stimulated Bronk's interest in biophysics by pointing out to him this was an undeveloped field with many possibilities.

In 1926 Bronk received a combined Ph.D. in biology and physics. Through the assistance of Winthrop Wright; Frank Aydelotte, president of Swarthmore; and H. C. Bazett, he was given an academic position at Swarthmore and space for research in the physiology department at the University of Pennsylvania.

After a few years at Swarthmore and Pennsylvania, Bronk felt he was not advancing and applied to E. D. Adrian at Cambridge University for a position in his laboratory. Adrian invited him to come to England, work a few months at Cambridge, and then spend some time working on muscle physiology with the Nobel Prize–winning physiologist and biochemist A. V. Hill in London.

In 1928 Adrian had been able to amplify and record signals from individual sensory nerve fibers in the skin and subcutaneous tissue. He had been unable, however, to record the signals from single motor fibers, because during motor activity a large number of fibers fire simultaneously. Bronk solved Adrian's problem by developing a method and electrode that measured a manageable number of neuronal signals. This instrument was later modified to become the electromyograph. Because of Bronk's work in Adrian's laboratory, he spent only two months of his fellowship with Hill.

The work in England was significant for Bronk's career as well as for science. It gave him the background he required to develop instruments for the amplification and measurement of biological signals, work that led to the introduction of instruments for the electronic monitoring of physiological functions of patients.

On his return to the United States in 1929, Bronk was appointed professor of biophysics and dean of men at Swarthmore. Before his departure for England, however, Bazett had told him of the possibility that an institute for medical physics would be established at the University of Pennsylvania. After his return Bronk met with Alfred Stengel, who had originated the idea for this institute. He offered Bronk the directorship of the new Johnson Foundation for Medical Physics, which Bronk accepted in April 1929.

Bronk promptly gathered a group of remarkably talented scientists, specialists in different but closely related fields of biophysics, whom he felt would interact to build a department for advanced biophysical studies. H. Keffer Hartline was Bronk's first faculty recruit, although he did not begin work in the foundation until 1931. Other early recruits were Ragnar Granit of Stockholm and W. A. H. Rushton from Cambridge. Shortly thereafter Bronk added other investigators and then his lifetime collaborators, Martin Larabee, Frank Brink, and Philip Davies. Granit and Hartline later won the Nobel Prize for their work on the biophysics of vision. To make the instruments required for the infant field of biophysics, Bronk persuaded Arnold J. Rawson, a designer and maker of instruments at Swarthmore, and John Hervey, an electronic engineer from Harvard, to join the Johnson Foundation.

The new institute, unique in the early 1930s, under Bronk's leadership enjoyed ample funding and drew many gifted scientists from all over the United States and Europe. As the foundation developed, Bronk demonstrated two remarkable traits: the abilities to recruit talented scientists and to stimulate them. Bronk's policies in the 1930s resulted in important research on vision, radiation effects on cells, smooth muscle mechanics, synaptic transmission, chemical excitation, nerve respiration and metabolism, control of the heart and circulation, and electron microscopy.

Bronk evolved an unusual combination of administration, experimentation, and scientific cooperation. Work in the laboratories did not begin in earnest until after dinner. Loudspeakers announced single nerve fiber recordings, a response of a visual receptor, or even the music of enzyme kinetics; these noises continued until the wee hours of the morning.

Bronk accepted a position as professor of physiology at Cornell University Medical School in 1940. At the same time, he was considering appointments to develop a department of biophysics at M.I.T. and to head the physiology department at the University of Chicago Medical School.

Bronk moved to Cornell in 1940, and his colleagues Hartline, Larrabee, Brink, Davies, Rawson, Hervey, and Glen Milligan all went with him. In March 1941, however, they all returned with Bronk to their old positions in the Johnson Foundation. He was apparently dissatisfied at Cornell because students did not work with the institute scientists and because work on war-related problems was not encouraged.

To solve war-related problems, ample money now became available to support the staff of the Johnson Foundation. Bronk immediately pointed the staff to investigations of military interest. In 1942 he was appointed chair of the Committee on Aviation Research of the Division of Medical Sciences of the National Research Council. Two high-altitude chambers were built at Pennsylvania, and research was carried out on night vision and on the oxygen saturation of hemoglobin during flight that solved many problems peculiar to aviation.

Bronk, despite these practical accomplishments, knew the importance of basic research and its relationship to applied research. To be able to apply his knowledge to basic problems, he again left Pennsylvania, this time to assume the presidency of Johns Hopkins University (1949–1953). He also took on administrative positions in the government, to the extent that he had to give up his direct contact with the laboratory. In the early 1950s he became president of the National Academy of Sciences and head of the National Research Council. In 1953 he was chosen to head the Rockefeller Institute for Medical Research, a position he held until 1968. Applying his ideas about the training of scientists resulted in the Rockefeller Institute being transformed into Rockefeller University. Bronk's goal was to create an ideal community where a few gifted scholars and students would be trained to be extraordinary scientists.

There were two constants in Bronk's life: his home, in Sycamore Mills, near Media, "Hill House Farm," where he entertained his colleagues, and his love of the sea. He became an avid sailor, cruising and racing in the New England waters. He died in New York City.

Even though Bronk was an administrator for many years, his true devotion was to science. Through his insight, respect for his collaborators, and enthusiasm, he was able to convince the government to increase its commitment to scientific research and to make the universities and their laboratories better places for scientists to work.

• The most complete account of Bronk's life is by Frank W. Brink, Jr., in the National Academy of Sciences, *Biographical Memoirs* 50 (1979): 2–87. A brief sketch is Britton Chance, "Detlev W. Bronk (1897–1975)," *Year Book of the American Philosophical Society* (1978): 54–56. His work at the Johnson Foundation features in David Y. Cooper, "The Johnson Foundation for Medical Physics: The First Department of Medical Physics and Biophysics," *Transactions and Studies of the College of Physicians of Philadelphia*, ser. 5, 6, no. 2 (1984): 113–64.

DAVID Y. COOPER

BRONNER, Augusta Fox (22 July 1881–11 Dec. 1966), psychologist and expert in juvenile delinquency, was born in Louisville, Kentucky, the daughter of Gustave Bronner, a wholesale milliner, and Hanna Fox. Both of his parents were of German ancestry. Bronner's maternal grandfather had been the founder of Louisville's Reform Jewish Temple, and the Bronner family was active in the town's Jewish community. Augusta, the middle child of three, was encouraged by her open-minded family to pursue a career instead of confining herself to housework.

After graduating from public high school in Louisville in 1898, Bronner entered the Louisville Normal School, following her childhood ambition of becoming a teacher. Impaired eyesight interrupted her studies after one year, but she returned to school in 1900 and finished the following year. In 1903 she continued her education at Columbia University's Teachers College, receiving a bachelor's degree in 1906 and a master's degree in 1909. During that time she also assisted the distinguished educational psychologist Edward L. Thorndyke by grading papers.

From 1906 to 1911 Bronner taught English in Louisville at her former girls' high school. In 1911 she took up doctoral study, again at Columbia's Teachers College, once more working for Thorndyke. Her dissertation, based on a study of groups of girls with different backgrounds and careers, challenged the then-prevailing belief of a biological cause for delinquency by showing that there was no significant correlation between delinquency and retardation. Her thesis, published in 1914, was not only a pioneer attempt in using mental testing but quickly became an influential standard work.

In 1913 Bronner attended a Harvard summer school course on the motivations of juvenile offenders taught by William Healy, a Chicago neurologist who had pioneered the individual case approach to deviant behavior. Healy, the head of the Chicago Juvenile Psychopathic Institute founded in 1909 by Ethel Sturges Dummer and her Hull-House associates, was impressed by Bronner's rejection of biological notions of inherited mental defects. He hired her later that year as a psychologist at the institute, and there they continued to develop the individual or clinical method of studying juvenile delinquency. Bronner expanded on Healy's argument that each individual was a special case and that a multiplicity of factors induced social behavior and conduct. In addition, she scrutinized group norms by examining the individual social setting to stress separation from the average. Together Bronner and Healy established that heredity was of very little importance in causing social deviance if compared to such influences as mental repressions and conflicts as well as social and family relations.

In 1914, at the height of their efforts, Bronner and Healy's five-year grant, which funded the institute, expired. Cook County (Illinois) took over funding, and the name was changed to the Psychopathic Clinic. For the next three years their work was completely diagnostic, involving twice as many juvenile court cases as before. This situation became frustrating for both Healy and Bronner because it negated their fundamental belief that diagnosis pointed the way to understanding treatment. Because of their frustration, they considered moving to another city. Bronner made connections with Boston philanthropists, who took great interest in Healy's approach to delinquency. Once the financial support was available, they moved to Boston. The city offered a network of social agencies that allowed the treatment they had in mind, and full cooperation from the local government was promised. In 1917 the Judge Baker Foundation (later the Judge Baker Guidance Center), headed by Healy as director and Bronner as assistant director, opened its doors. Conceived as a facility for treating delinquent and difficult juveniles, the new institution served as the model for many child guidance clinics that were soon established in many cities in the United States and abroad.

Bronner and Healy concentrated on spreading what they felt was "scientific knowledge" about the "ever-changing situation of the delinquent." Bronner, continuing to publish on her own, produced studies of long-term significance. For example, using test material from the Chicago clinic, she published "Attitude As It Affects Performance of Tests" (1916), a widely cited article that emphasizes affective factors, including situational factors and the dependence of test scores on probants' attitudes. In addition, *The Psychology of Special Abilities and Disabilities* (1917), which was reprinted several times, was not only the first work on the limitations of language-based mental testing but also the first generally available recognition of psychological disabilities in reading or visualization.

With Healy, Bronner went on to publish joint work on treatment and diagnostic tools that had a lasting influence on clinical psychology and criminology. In *Delinquents and Criminals* (1926) they showed the discrepancy between predictions and eventual outcomes in juvenile court. In contrast, they demonstrated in *Reconstructing Behavior in Youth* (1929) that delinquents who receive some kind of therapy fair better. *A Manual of Individual Mental Tests and Testing* (1927) became a major resource to the mental-testing movement just as it was getting under way.

By the early 1930s, Healy and Bronner shifted from their diagnostic work for the courts to a combination of diagnosis and treatment for their clients. This allowed them to follow up their cases and led to the publication of *Treatment and What Happened Afterwards* (1940). Their development of the "team" concept in guidance work was particularly notable, joining social workers, psychologists, and representatives of other fields with physicians in case planning. Bronner scheduled these case conferences and supervised the psychological work. Additionally, she was responsible for the training of students in residence at the clinic.

Bronner became the center codirector in 1930, but her professional commitments took her outside the clinic as well. From 1929 to 1933 she was an associate director of the Yale Institute on Human Relation, and from 1942 to 1949 she was a lecturer in mental hygiene at Simmons College. She lectured to students at the Boston University School of Education and with Healy in a special course training FBI agents. Among Bronner's many professional commitments were memberships in the American Psychological Association, the Association of Clinical Criminologists, and the American Orthopsychiatric Association, which elected her president in 1932. She also held a fellowship in the American Academy of Arts and Sciences.

After the death of Healy's wife, Bronner married him in 1932. Though a respected psychologist in her own right, she deliberately stayed in his shadow and often did not publish the results of her own research. The overall influence of her work was further reduced by their joint decision to keep the clinic small enough to be personal.

Bronner and Healy retired in 1946 and moved to Clearwater, Florida, in 1950. Three years after the death of her husband, she died at home in Clearwater. Though her work is forever linked to Healy, Bronner made important contributions in the fields of mental testing, delinquency, and mental health. Numerous deviant children and adolescents benefited from her caring counsel during her years at the Judge Baker Guidance Center.

• Bronner destroyed most of her papers when she retired. Some papers have survived in the Judge Baker Guidance Archives in the Francis A. Countway Library of Medicine in Boston. The Ethel Sturgess Dummer Papers in the Radcliffe College Schlesinger Library contain some of her letters. Oral history interviews with Healy and Bronner were conducted by John Burnham in 1960 and 1961; copies of the typescript are available at the Chicago Historical Society, the Judge Baker Guidance Center, and the Houghton Library, Harvard University. An autobiographical account by Bronner and Healy is "The Child Guidance Clinic: Birth and Growth of an Idea," in *Orthopsychiatry, 1923–1948: Retrospect and Prospect*, ed. Lawson G. Lowrey and Victoria Sloane (1948); this work also gives a useful bibliography. An obituary is in the *Boston Globe*, 12 Dec. 1966.

KARL TILMAN WINKLER

BRONOWSKI, Jacob (18 Jan. 1908–22 Aug. 1974), mathematician and historian and philosopher of science, was born in Łódź (in what is now Poland), the son of Abram Bronowski and Celia Flatto, occupations unknown. During his childhood his family moved first to Germany (1912) and then to England (1920). In 1927 he entered the University of Cambridge to study mathematics, receiving his Ph.D. in 1933. He also helped found and edit a literary magazine, *Experiment*, thus beginning his secondary career in literary studies. Over his life he published numerous mathematical papers on a wide range of topics, such as topology, statistics, and mathematical applications to biology. From 1934 to 1942 he was senior lecturer in mathematics at University College, Hull. In 1939 he published his first book, *The Poet's Defence* (rev. 1966), a work on literary criticism that was widely discussed although not necessarily favorably. In 1941 he married Rita Coblentz, a sculptor (professional name Rita Colin). They had four children.

During World War II Bronowski was involved in mathematical studies on the effects of bombing, thus pioneering what has become known as operations research. After the war he went to Japan as scientific deputy to the British Chiefs of Staff Mission; he wrote the British report on the *Effects of the Atomic Bomb at Hiroshima and Nagasaki* (1945). From 1945 to 1963 he worked for the British government in applied science; his work for the National Coal Board (1950–1963) as director of research and director general of process development involved developing smokeless coal, a project that revealed a sensitivity to environmental matters.

Bronowski moved in 1964 to the Salk Institute for Biological Studies at San Diego, California, where he was a Fellow until his death. This move reflected his interest in a new field, what he called "human specificity," namely, the study of what makes humans unique among animal species. His theory of human specificity is succinctly presented in *The Identity of Man* (1965; rev. ed. 1972).

Bronowski's wider fame grew out of his work in the history and philosophy of science. Through lectures, essays, films, and television he was one of the most eloquent popularizers of science of his day. In 1953 he was invited by the Massachusetts Institute of Technology (MIT) to begin a study of science and ethics; he also delivered a series of lectures later collected as *Science and Human Values* (1958), a book widely read for many years. A revised edition was published in 1965 containing the dialogue "The Abacus and the Rose," which was also a radio broadcast. A theme of the book was the argument that certain fundamental values of a free society grew out of science: rationality, the appeal to experience, the communal sharing of ideas and knowledge, independence and originality of thought in the face of authority, and tolerance of dissenting views. The other theme of the book reflected Bronowski's dual career, for he argued—contrary to the popular belief in the dichotomy of science and art—that they in fact are united in the creative act. Thus Bronowski dealt with the so-called "two cultures" issue several years before it was centered around the scientist/novelist C. P. Snow. These themes Bronowski explored through various media, in many ways culminating in the thirteen-part television series "The Ascent of Man"; published in book format in 1973, it became a bestseller. In the book version he put forward his belief in the human value of science and the fundamental unity of science and art; as he often said, he wanted "to create a philosophy for the 20th century which shall be all of one piece." *Ascent* also dovetailed nicely with Bronowski's belief that science can and should be accessible for all intelligent persons, not just specialists. It is fitting that in his last major work he reached his widest audience. Bronowski died of a heart attack while on vacation with his wife in East Hampton, New York.

During his life Bronowski published, coauthored, or edited twelve books and numerous articles. After his death his wife assembled four books from his published and unpublished material. Much of this material is on aspects of the history and philosophy of science and his belief in a common ground between art and science. He was also a published poet (for example, *Spain: Four Poems* [1939]) and a playwright, his radio play "The Face of Violence" winning the Italia Prize as the best European drama for 1950–1951. As noted, he also wrote literary criticism; much of this focused on the work of William Blake, as in his 1944 study, *William Blake: A Man without a Mask* (rev. ed. 1965, published as *William Blake and the Age of Revolution*). His fascination with Blake is prima facie ironic given Blake's hostility to science and his professed antirational, romantic view of nature. But it must be remembered that, in the first place, it was Blake the person who initially attracted Bronowski, that is, Blake the lonely, self-taught rebel who would not submit to authority. In addition, Blake's seemingly hostile view of science was, according to Bronowski, directed against the materialistic view of nature that Blake associated with the science of his day. Bronowski agreed with Blake that this materialistic view stifled the imagination. In the creative act of discovery, the imagination must be given free rein; so, like Blake, Bronowski opposed reductionism, the supposition that humans should ultimately be understood as machines or that the human mind works mechanistically. He became increasingly convinced of the error of this view in his later work on human specificity, postulating that human imagination—for example, the ability to hold images in the mind—is a key source of our uniqueness. Yet at the same time, and unlike Blake, Bronowski had no sympathy for a mystical or vitalistic view of nature; this he associated with an antirational, pre-Enlightenment world in which belief based on authority (not experiment) was paramount. Finally, his focus on the imaginative act of scientific discovery led him away from an inductivist approach to scientific methodology; instead, he asserted that science is an open-ended system, ever revising its image of nature.

The range of topics pursued by Bronowski in his multifaceted life is breathtaking. That he was involved in the pioneering phase of so many fields is remarkable. A friend and colleague who knew him since his Cambridge days spoke of him this way: "I saw and admired his voracious appetite for new knowledge and new insights and his incredible capacity (maintained to the end of his life) to learn" (Eric Roll, *Leonardo* [1985], p. 215).

• Bronowski's papers are on file at the Bronowski Archive, Thomas Fisher Rare Books Library, University of Toronto, Canada. A special issue of *Leonardo* 18, no. 4 (1985) contains eight essays on Bronowski's life and work as well as reprints of seven of his essays; importantly, it contains a comprehensive bibliography (pp. 282–87). The essays collected by Rita Bronowski and Piero E. Ariotti in *A Sense of the Future* (1977) present a broad sample of Bronowski's writings. An obituary is in the *New York Times*, 23 Aug. 1974.

DAVID TOPPER

BROOKE, Abraham (1806–8 Mar. 1867), physician and radical reformer, was born at Sandy Spring, Maryland, the son of Samuel Brooke and Sarah Garrigues, farmers. The Brooke family had been leading Quakers in Maryland for several generations, and Abraham attended Quaker schools at Sandy Spring before entering medical college in Baltimore. In 1829 he married Elizabeth Lukens, a fellow Quaker from Sandy Spring; they had three children. When the Hicksite-Orthodox schism took place among Quakers, the Brookes, like most Maryland Friends, sided with the Hicksite group.

In 1831 Brooke moved his family to Marlborough, a largely Quaker community in Stark County, Ohio. In his first years there Brooke did little to attract notice, practicing his profession and serving as the village postmaster. He first entered reform work in 1836 when a traveling abolitionist lecturer converted him to the cause of the immediate abolition of slavery. In 1837 Brooke, accompanied by his parents and most of his family, moved across the state to the village of Oakland in Clinton County, Ohio.

After becoming an abolitionist, and especially after moving to Oakland, Brooke emerged as the leading figure in the Garrisonian wing of the abolitionist movement in Ohio. Late in the 1830s there emerged a bitter split in the movement for immediate abolition of slavery. More radical abolitionists looked especially to the leadership of William Lloyd Garrison and his journal, the *Liberator*. Garrison and his followers were increasingly prone to question, not just slavery, but other institutions. All abolitionists agreed that the great national denominations had temporized too much on slavery, but by 1837 Garrison was disturbing many abolitionists with the vehemence of his attacks on the churches.

There were also divisions about the roles of women in the movement. Garrison supported the right of women to participate publicly in antislavery activities, and he generally made support for women's rights part of the antislavery movement. Other abolitionists saw this as a distraction from the true business of abolitionists. Finally, Garrison and many of his sympathizers had become committed to nonresistance, the repudiation of all coercive force in human relationships, replacing it instead with the Government of God (government having no human laws but based solely on God's laws). In 1840 the national American Anti-Slavery Society split, with Garrison's opponents leaving to form a separate organization, the American and Foreign Anti-Slavery Society.

By 1842 Brooke had established a national reputation as an articulate and uncompromising Garrisonian. He was a regular contributor to abolitionist journals such as the *Philanthropist* in Cincinnati and the *National Anti-Slavery Standard* in New York City, and his subjects included politics, aiding fugitive slaves, and using products of slave labor. He had become a leader in aiding fugitive slaves and had even been briefly jailed for his involvement in one case. When the Ohio Anti-Slavery Society split into pro- and anti-Garrisonian factions in 1842, Brooke was one of the leaders of the new Garrisonian Ohio American Anti-Slavery Society.

By 1842, moreover, Brooke had become committed—partly through his communitarian interests, partly through contacts with New England abolitionists such as John A. Collins and John O. Wattles, partly through his commitment to nonresistance—to a wider and much more radical vision of reform. This led Brooke in October 1842 to help organize the Society for Universal Inquiry and Reform at a convention held in Oakland. The Universal Reformers envisioned a world based completely on nonresistance, ushering in the Government of God by founding a series of communities based on cooperation and noncoercion. They tried to attract support from Garrisonians by naming a number of abolitionist luminaries in Great Britain and the United States as honorary officers and scheduling the society's first meeting to follow the annual meeting of the American Anti-Slavery Society in New York City in the spring of 1843. That meeting broke up in confusion when Brooke, the president, refused to preside on the ground that such an attempt at organization was an immoral restraint on liberty.

Although eight communities grew out of the agitation for Universal Reform, and the one at Marlborough, Ohio, was partly on Brooke's land, Brooke never joined any, arguing that none was sufficiently committed to the Government of God. By 1844 he had become a notorious eccentric because of his attempts at complete nonresistance. To Brooke money, for example, represented a compromise with greed and a competitive economy, so he refused to buy anything or to receive money for his services, relying on barter or the voluntary gifts or services of neighbors. He refused to send or receive letters through the post office, because he believed that to do so would implicate him with coercive government. He also embraced a strict vegetarianism and refused even to cut his hair or beard.

By 1847 the last of the Universal Reform communities had collapsed, and Brooke had moved away from his more extreme views. Nevertheless he remained a committed reformer. A split had developed among Hicksite Friends in Ohio, with the more conservative majority opposing membership in antislavery societies. Brooke was a leader in the formation of a separatist group, the Congregational Friends, noted for their radical reform commitments.

By 1850 Brooke had also become a spiritualist. He and his wife had both become active supporters of the women's rights movement. In 1853 they moved back to Marlborough. By this time Salem, Ohio, about twenty miles east, had become the center of Garrisonian abolition in Ohio. Brooke became a leading figure in the new Garrisonian group, the Western Anti-Slavery Society, and a regular contributor of essays on slavery, politics, reform, and spiritualism to the *Salem Anti-Slavery Bugle*. In 1855 Brooke, at the request of a black neighbor, went to Tennessee in an unsuccessful attempt to help her daughter escape from slavery. In 1859 he was a leader in the rescue of a young slave girl from a train in Salem. There is no record of Brooke's activities after the collapse of the Western Anti-Slavery Society in 1861. He died in Marlborough.

• No collection of Brooke's papers survived. His published works consist of numerous letters and articles in antislavery journals. Significant material concerning him is in the Antislavery Collection and the Weston Family Papers in the Boston Public Library, the Valentine Nicholson Papers at the Indiana Historical Society, the Wilbur Siebert Collection at the Ohio Historical Society, and the A. J. MacDonald Collection at the Beinecke Library at Yale University. Secondary accounts with extended treatments of Brooke include Douglas Andrew Gamble, "Moral Suasion in the West: Garrisonian Abolition, 1831–1861" (Ph.D. diss., Ohio State Univ., 1973), and Thomas D. Hamm, *God's Government Begun: The Society for Universal Inquiry and Reform, 1842–1846* (1995).

THOMAS D. HAMM

BROOKE, Henry (1 Oct. 1678–6 Feb. 1736), poet and politician, was born at Norton Priory in England, the youngest son of Sir Henry Brook, baronet of Norton. His mother's name is not known. He was probably the Henry Brooke who graduated from Bracenose College, Oxford, in 1693. He went to Pennsylvania in 1702 seeking his fortune. An Episcopalian, Brooke had difficulty securing a place in Quaker-controlled Philadelphia, so he accepted the office of queen's customs collector for Lewes Town, a trading settlement at the mouth of the Delaware River. While serving as collector he saved Newcastle from plunder by a French privateer in 1709, leading local inhabitants in a sortie against the raider.

Traveling frequently upriver to Newcastle and Philadelphia, Brooke became a familiar and welcome figure in coffeehouse society. He served as laureate of a coterie of young gentry that met at Enoch Story's Inn in Philadelphia. This club, chafing at the restriction imposed on public life by the Quaker city corporation, provoked a street war against the town watch, engaging in repeated acts of riot from 1703 through 1704. Brooke was arrested in 1703 for participating in one of these escapades. Late in 1703 Brooke began to regret his group's increasingly libertine and violent behavior. In "A Discourse upon Jesting Attempted in the Way of Horace," addressed to club member Robert Grace, Brooke attempted to reform the manners of his set, injecting politeness and wit into a conversation characterized by nonsense, crudity, and jest.

For Wit, my Friend—but you regard not me,
Regard our Dryden then; True Wit (says He)
Is true propriety of Sence & Words:
How little to a Jest this Rule affords!
Propriety of Sence is where a Tho'ght
Of Nature is a just, & faithful Draught;
Of Words, where w[i]th the tho'ght they so agree,
As fully to convey anothers sense to me.
These are the sum of Wit: and mingle then
If due regard be had to How, and When,
To What, Where, Whome; by these directions steer,
By these, in time you'l speak, in time forbear.

In a series of epigrams "written in company," Brooke demonstrated that raillery and satire could be more effective weapons against Quakerism than curses and fists. His impromptu on William Penn's portrait, "P—painted in armor and a scarf," showed how wit could imbue malediction with sufficient grace to compel admiration. His travesty ballad, "The New Metamorphosis," dressed a humorous tavern yarn about a greenhorn tobacco merchant's commercial failure into an Ovidian mock-myth about the sanctity of contracts. It is one of the comic masterpieces of colonial literature. As Pennsylvania's first belletrist, Brooke provided the model for the generation of poets that emerged during the 1720s.

As a politician, Brooke gradually rose to eminence during the 1710s and 1720s. At that time, the three lower counties of Pennsylvania (present-day Delaware) were governed by a separate legislature. In 1717 Brooke became speaker of this assembly. In 1721 Governor William Keith appointed Brooke to the seat on the Pennsylvania Provincial Council reserved for a resident of the lower counties. In 1726 he was appointed associate justice of the supreme court for Sussex County. After Keith's fall from power in 1727, Governor Patrick Gordon maintained Brooke in office. Lacking a wife and children, Brooke did not share in the almost universal desire to amass land and build an estate. During the latter years of his life, Brooke boarded with Rev. William Becket, the missionary to Sussex County of the Society for the Propagation of the Gospel in America. Perhaps for this reason, the governor and the proprietary party looked on Brooke as a singularly disinterested public official.

While respected as a politician, Brooke was best known as a literary artist. He was the most elegant spokesman of the literary culture of sociability in Pennsylvania. His poetry, written impromptu, designed for oral performance to a familiar audience, and disseminated in manuscript, is the most important corpus of writing surviving from the era before the consolidation of a provincial market for polite letters, a time when the tavern club and the coffeehouse were the dominant institutions of provincial literary culture. Elizabeth Magawley, Philadelphia's foremost woman wit, praised Brooke for being the figure who invited women to participate in the province's literary conversation. He died in Philadelphia. Upon his death he was elegized in the pages of the *American Mercury* as the paragon of New World gentility.

• Brooke's poetry is found in the Peters Collection, Historical Society of Pennsylvania. Details of his career are found in William Becket, "Notices and Letters concerning Incidents at Lewes Town 1727–1744," Manuscript Am .0165, Historical Society of Pennsylvania. His political career is discussed in Charles P. Keith, *The Provincial Councilors of Pennsylvania* (1883). The standard critical assessment is David S. Shields, "Henry Brooke and the Situation of the First British American Belletrists," *Early American Literature* 23 (1988): 1–24.

DAVID S. SHIELDS

BROOKE, J. Clifford (1873?–28 Dec. 1951), actor and director, was born in England; his parents' names are unknown. He began his career as an actor in London with Cyril Maude in *The Second in Command* (Nov. 1900) at the Haymarket Theatre. In the early years of the twentieth century he crossed the Atlantic and began his career in the United States doing walk-ons, then small roles. Eventually, in 1915, he distinguished himself on Broadway and in the touring company playing the title role in *Joe Quinney* (*The Antique Shop*), a clever comedy of British provincial life. His performance was reviewed as a "masterpiece," and one critic in the *Newark News* went on to say, "his presentation was one of the most deftly drawn, humorous, and amusing English characters to whom we've been introduced by a true son of English soil." Brooke remained on Broadway for the next twenty years as an actor and director but rarely again enjoyed a major success. Some of his better-known directorial assignments were *Within the Law* (1912); *Peter Ibbetson* (1917), which starred John and Lionel Barrymore; *Lombardi Ltd.* (1918); and *East Is West* (also 1918). Brooke also staged quite a few Broadway plays, notably *The Man Who Changed His Name* (1932), which featured Fay Bainter, and three productions in 1934, *Caviar*, *Allure*, and *Piper Paid.* In 1930 he acted again in *Mr. Samuel*, which starred Edward G. Robinson, and he directed Jane Cowl in *Art and Mrs. Bottle.* In 1935 he acted in and staged *A Lady Detained.*

All of the above proved to be invaluable training and experience for the school he founded in 1934. S. E. Cochran as manager and Brooke as director opened the Clifford Brooke Academy of Stage Training in the Dramatic Arts in Washington, D.C., "affording essential preparation for a career on the professional stage, for Motion Picture Work, Radio, Directing, or Teaching." A ten-week term, five days a week, cost $100, and courses were taught in Shakespeare, old comedies, and modern plays. The school was under the personal direction of Brooke, who was, as stated in the school's brochure, "considered a keen student of the drama in all of its phases and one of the foremost directors of the professional stage with a wide European background and extended experience." At the same time, based in Washington was an outstanding stock company, the National Players, in which Brooke participated, thus affording his students performing opportunities in its productions. Two of the plays presented were *As You Like It* and *Waterloo*. Brooke taught his students that "a director must bridge the gap between author and actor . . . there's got to be a real reason behind every movement."

His final years were spent as a director and sometimes a performer in films. Often quoted about his style, he said, "Henry Irving was a great tragedian because he had a sense of comedy behind his acting. Charlie Chaplin is a great comedian because behind his acting, he has a sense of tragedy." Brooke used the same method for comedy and tragedy because he believed that there was an intrinsic similarity between the two forms. Also, his directing style was adapted in the style of the actor George Arliss: he would rehearse the whole picture through like a play. And, much to the consternation of MGM executives, he cost the studio $1,000 a minute when he insisted that the company break for afternoon tea. But he was always highly respected in any of his many endeavors. He was also considered a good sport, especially when he volunteered to step in and do a trivial part for an actor who had walked out after objecting to his part being cut.

Brooke was described as a serious and earnest man with a serious and earnest faith in his profession. Photographs reveal an amused glint behind his eyes and around his mouth. There is no record of his marriage, but it was reported that a son survived.

Brooke's life ended suddenly when he was struck by a car in Santa Monica, California.

• Brooke's work is documented in a clipping file at the New York Public Library for the Performing Arts; in Gerald Bordman, *Oxford Companion to American Theatre* (1984); and in Donald Mullin, comp., *Victorian Plays, 1837–1901* (1987). An obituary is in *Variety*, 9 Jan. 1952.

PATRICIA FOX-SHEINWOLD

BROOKE, John Mercer (18 Dec. 1826–14 Dec. 1906), naval officer, scientist, and inventor, was born at Fort Brooke, Tampa Bay, Florida, the son of George Mercer Brooke, a brevet brigadier general in the U.S. Army, and Lucy Thomas. His Brooke forebears had been prominent in affairs of the state of Virginia since the late seventeenth century. Brooke's family moved frequently before he accepted an appointment as acting midshipman at age fourteen. His irregular formal education included a short stint at Aaron's School in Burlington, New Jersey. His scientific education continued in the navy. Brooke served briefly aboard the warship USS *Delaware* in Brazilian waters, under David Glasgow Farragut, then a first lieutenant. Transferred to the sloop of war *Cyane*, he cruised via Cape Horn to the Pacific under Commodore Thomas ap Catesby Jones, returning to Norfolk in 1844. Briefly assigned to the flagship of the Brazil Squadron, USS *Columbia*, Brooke returned to the United States in 1846 to attend the newly established Naval Academy. There he studied navigation, seamanship, gunnery, and the rudiments of hydrography and ordnance, graduating with the first class in 1847.

As a passed midshipman, Brooke spent two years in the Mediterranean, first aboard the new steamer *Princeton*, then the flagship *United States*. From 1849 to 1850 Brooke served with a Coast Survey hydrographic party under Lieutenant Samuel P. Lee. He developed a preference for shore-based scientific duty after his 1849 marriage to his cousin Elizabeth Selden Garnett. From 1851 to 1853 he worked under Mathew Fontaine Maury at the Naval Observatory in the fields of astronomy, meteorology, and hydrography. There he invented a simple but practical deep-sea sounding apparatus with a detachable lead that recovered specimens from the sea floor. Brooke's sounder permitted the first accurate mapping of bottom topography. Maury acknowledged, "Brooke's lead and the microscope . . . are about to teach us to regard the ocean in a new light." The king of Prussia awarded Brooke the gold medal of science from the Academy of Berlin in 1860. Brooke profited little from his invention, receiving $5,000 from the U.S. government just before the Civil War, which he invested in Confederate bonds. Hydrographers continued to acknowledge his contribution in their writings, however.

In recognition of his scientific qualifications, Brooke was attached to the North Pacific and Bering Straits Surveying and Exploring Expedition in 1854, sailing on the *Vincennes* under Commodore Cadwallader Ringgold (succeeded by Commodore John Rodgers). The only officer with purely scientific duties, he made astronomical determinations of the geographical position of ports and took care of the chronometers. He also conducted the first deep-sea soundings in the Pacific, including the deepest ever made in that ocean to date, 2,150 fathoms in the Coral Sea. When the expedition returned in 1856, he went to Washington to prepare charts and records for publication.

Promoted to lieutenant on 15 September 1855, Brooke was ordered in 1858 to survey a route from California to China to complete the work of the North Pacific Expedition. From the schooner *Fenimore Cooper*, he made deep-sea soundings and surveyed Pacific islands and the east coast of Japan along important shipping routes. While Brooke was ashore with the American minister, a cyclone wrecked his ship at Giddo, Japan, forcing him to abandon the survey and wait at Yokohama for passage home. While there, Japanese authorities consulted him as they prepared their first warship to visit the West. Because Japanese mariners had little experience with blue-water sailing, Brooke assisted the captain of the *Karin Maru* with navigation. His crew also instructed their Japanese counterparts. Brooke declined the large purse that Japanese authorities offered him for his service.

Until the outbreak of the Civil War, Brooke worked on the charts and results of his Pacific survey but resigned his commission on 20 April 1861 to join the Virginia state navy and, soon afterward, the Confederate navy. He sided with the Confederacy, in spite of his mother's New England roots, because of his father's ties to Virginia and especially his wife's loyalties. Although commissioned as a lieutenant, he received a promotion to commander for the war's duration on 13 September 1862 as a reward for his initiative and hard work. He devised a plan for reconstructing the USS *Merrimac* into an ironclad using the "submerged ends principle." He was granted patent number 100 by the Confederate government on 29 July 1862 in response to an effort to deny him credit. Working closely with the Tredegar Iron Works, Brooke oversaw the production of the armor and guns for the ship, renamed CSS *Virginia*. Having become the de facto clearinghouse for ordnance plans, he took over as chief of the Bureau of Ordnance and Hydrography from March 1863 until the end of the war. There he invented the most powerful weapon produced by the Confederate government, the "Brooke" gun, a rifled cannon made of cast iron strengthened by shrinking bands of wrought iron around the weakest sections of the barrel. Brooke recognized that a major cause of guns exploding was the practice of ramming the cartridge to the back of the gun. He advocated leaving air space for gas to expand between the charge and the bottom of the bore to lessen the strain on the gun.

Brooke's wife died of consumption in June 1864. Alone except for a young daughter and in need of employment, he renewed contact with northern Coast Survey and naval colleagues after the Civil War and obtained a presidential pardon. In 1865 he took the professorship of physics and astronomy at Virginia Military Institute, assuming that the job would be temporary. He continued inventing and tried to capitalize on prewar inventions such as the sounder and a boat hook. He formed a company with former Confederate associates to supply naval matériel to foreign governments, but teaching responsibilities precluded the travel necessary to promote the business. He grew accustomed to teaching and in 1871 strengthened his ties to the area by marrying Kate Corbin Pendleton, with whom he had two children. He retired in 1899 after thirty-four years of teaching and died in Lexington.

Although not published separately, Brooke's Pacific astronomical and hydrographical work was incorporated into naval charts. As a scientist and inventor, his contributions to ordnance were recognized at the time as important innovations. His deep-sea sounding work, especially the Brooke lead, substantially aided the progress of submarine telegraphy and oceanography.

• Brooke's papers are held by his grandson George M. Brooke, Jr., who wrote *John M. Brooke: Naval Scientist and Educator* (1980), a book-length biography, and edited *John M. Brooke's Pacific Cruise and Japanese Adventure* (1986), based on Brooke's journal of the North Pacific Survey Expedition. Accounts of Brooke's sounder and the early hydrographic and scientific work it permitted can be found in Matthew Fontaine Maury, *Physical Geography of the Sea* (1855), as well as any edition of his *Explanations and Sailing Directions to Accompany the Wind and Current Charts*.

HELEN M. ROZWADOWSKI

BROOKES, James H. (27 Feb. 1830–18 Apr. 1897), Presbyterian clergyman, was born in Pulaski, Tennessee, the son of the Reverend James Hall Brookes, Sr., a clergyman who died when his son was three, and Judith Smith Lacy. Both father and mother had deep ties with the Presbyterian church. In 1851 Brookes matriculated at Miami University in Oxford, Ohio, graduating in 1853. He attended Princeton Theological Seminary during the 1853–1854 term but did not return to complete his studies because of a lack of funds.

Brookes was ordained on 20 April 1854 by the Miami Presbytery in Ohio. Two weeks later he married Susan Oliver, the daughter of an elder in the Presbyterian church in Oxford; they had three daughters. He then moved to Dayton, Ohio, to accept his first charge, the First Presbyterian Church. In 1858 he accepted a call to the Second Presbyterian Church of St. Louis, Missouri, and in 1864 he moved to the Sixteenth and Walnut Street Church, which had been organized by former members of the Second Presbyterian Church. There he remained until his retirement.

Brookes is best known for his extensive ministry as a conference speaker and as an author. He was a founder of the Niagara Bible Conference (1875–1900), over which he presided for more than twenty years. This annual gathering of clergy and laity at Niagara-on-the-Lake, Ontario, became an extremely important source of inspiration for a growing body of theologically conservative preachers, evangelists, teachers, and laypersons from primarily Presbyterian and Baptist churches and schools. Brookes also appeared from time to time at other summer conference centers, such as Northfield, Massachusetts, and Lake Geneva, Wisconsin. He was active in the International Prophetic Conferences in New York in 1878 and in Chicago in 1886. He wrote seventeen books, dozens of sermons and pamphlets, between 250 and 300 tracts, and many articles. From 1875 until his death, he edited the *Truth; or, Testimony for Christ*, an influential monthly Bible study and devotional journal devoted to "the maintenance of the inerrancy of the Bible, to the defense of our Lord's personal and premillennial coming, and to expositions of scripture."

His most important book, *Marantha; or, The Lord Cometh*, went through ten editions between 1874 and 1889. As a dispensational premillennialist, Brookes promoted the doctrine of the secret rapture—the view that Christ might return at any moment to take the Church away before the wrath of the Great Tribulation. He was highly respected and frequently quoted by a growing body of premillennialists in the late nineteenth and early twentieth centuries. His essay, "How I Became a Premillennialist," is one of the most frequently reprinted pieces of premillennialist literature. Among the most notable of his parishioners and disciples were Hamilton R. Gamble, Civil War governor of Missouri, Lyman Stewart, president of Union Oil Company of California, and C. I. Scofield, editor of the influential *Scofield Reference Bible* (1909).

Brookes served his denomination as a commissioner to the General Assembly in 1857, 1880, and 1893 and as stated clerk of the Missouri Synod in 1874. He died in St. Louis, Missouri.

• Copies of Brookes's books, sermons, pamphlets, and tracts are in widely scattered libraries. The most extensive collections are in the Princeton Seminary Library, Princeton, N.J., and the Moody Bible Institute, Chicago, Ill. The Colgate Rochester Divinity School/Crozer Theological Seminary Library in Rochester, N.Y., contains a complete file of the *Truth; or, Testimony for Christ.* David R. Williams, Brookes's son-in-law and a St. Louis newspaperman, wrote *James H. Brookes: A Memoir* (1897).

PAUL C. WILT

BROOKHART, Smith Wildman (2 Feb. 1869–15 Nov. 1944), U.S. senator, was born in Scotland County, Missouri, the son of Abram Colar Brookhart and Cynthia Wildman, farmers. The family moved to Van Buren County, Iowa, where Smith attended the local schools and graduated from the Southern Iowa Normal School in 1889. While teaching school in Keosauqua, Iowa, he read law and passed his bar exam in 1892. Later that year he began practicing law in nearby Washington where he would live for most of his life. On 22 June 1897 he married Jennie Hearn with whom he had seven children.

Brookhart's lifelong interest in politics began in the early 1890s while sipping tea in James B. Weaver's parlor and listening to the former Greenback and future Populist presidential nominee discuss his ideas. Although initially unimpressed with Weaver's rhetoric, Brookhart eventually adopted many of the Populist standard-bearer's positions. In 1894 he was elected county attorney. A lifelong Prohibitionist, he used his office to keep Washington County dry, and he was reelected in 1896 and 1898.

Having served in the Iowa National Guard since 1894, Brookhart joined the Fiftieth Iowa and was stationed in Florida during the Spanish-American War. He became an expert marksman and during World War I taught marksmanship, rising to the rank of lieutenant colonel. The National Rifle Association published his *Rifle Training for War* in 1919.

Iowa politics at the turn of the century was torn by conflict between standpat, old-line conservatives and insurgent progressives. Brookhart strongly favored regulation of railroads, which engaged him in the first of many political disputes with the entrenched Iowa Republican party leadership. He enthusiastically supported Governor Albert B. Cummins for reelection in 1906, but four years later he failed in his own attempt to win nomination for a congressional seat. Undeterred, he exclaimed that he "would rather be right than regular any day," a principle that would serve him both well and ill during his years in politics. In 1911 Brookhart and two of his brothers bought the *Washington County Press,* using its pages to advance progressive ideals over the next decade. He remained active in Iowa politics, chairing the 1912 Republican State Convention and supporting Theodore Roosevelt's (1858–1919) Bull Moose party.

After the First World War, the Iowa farm economy slumped and began its decade-long descent into depression. Convinced that Wall Street bankers and the Federal Reserve Board were the cause of agriculture's economic woes, Brookhart became a vocal champion of the farmers. He broke with Senator Cummins in 1920 when Cummins cosponsored a bill that would return the railroads to private ownership. Unsuccessful as a challenger to Cummins in the 1920 senatorial primary, Brookhart ran again in 1922 when Iowa's junior senator, William S. Kenyon, retired early to take a seat on the U.S. Circuit Court of Appeals. The Republican leadership tried to thwart Brookhart by running several candidates, but he took his case to the people and received 41 percent of the vote and the nomination. He easily won the general election without any support from the party.

In 1924, when Brookhart ran for reelection, the forces against him were mounting. His opponents included the Iowa Republican party, the American Legion, and the Republican Service League (a veterans group with loose ties to the legion). His speeches damaged his own cause. He urged the removal of vice presidential nominee Charles G. Dawes, calling him an "agent of international banking powers," a "plutogogue," and no friend of the farmer. He attacked President Calvin Coolidge as a tool of Wall Street and publicly supported Robert M. La Follette's (1855–1925) Progressive party candidacy. The Iowa Republican party supported his Democratic opponent, Daniel Steck. Brookhart won the election by 755 votes, but Steck demanded a recount. Fourteen months later the Senate Committee on Elections and Privileges declared Steck the winner. Brookhart immediately returned to Iowa where he defeated Senator Cummins in the June 1926 primary. He won his first full term as senator in the general election.

In the Senate, Brookhart allied himself with other progressive Republicans like George W. Norris (1861–1944) of Nebraska, William E. Borah of Idaho, and the senior Robert M. La Follette of Wisconsin. Less politically astute than his progressive colleagues, he alienated the leadership and chaired only one committee: the 1924 Select Committee to Investigate Attorney General Harry Daugherty on charges of defrauding the government. Primarily concerned with obtaining farm relief, he repeatedly introduced bills to enable farmers to manage their own economic affairs through cooperative banks and markets. His efforts came to naught, however, and he eventually joined other farm bloc senators in supporting the McNary-Haugen Bill in 1927. His interest in cooperative solutions to economic problems had been stimulated in 1923 on an approving tour of the new Soviet Union. In those early post–red scare years, his discourses on the merits of the Soviet system served to isolate him further from the prevailing conservative Republican position and from majority opinion in the nation at large.

Brookhart also lobbied on behalf of small businessmen who were competing unsuccessfully with the growing national chain stores. He sought protection for independent small theater owners from buyouts by conglomerates, and he urged that the fledgling radio industry be operated by the government in the public interest. He opposed the tax policies of Coolidge and Treasury Secretary Andrew Mellon and pressed for abolition of the gold standard. A staunch believer in government regulation, he introduced measures for federal control of stock market speculation and public ownership of railroads. He spent his final months in the Senate battling repeal of the Eighteenth Amendment.

Brookhart supported Herbert Hoover's (1874–1964) 1928 presidential bid but soon returned to his status as political gadfly. Despite his noisy profarm rhetoric, he had not successfully sponsored any legislation to help farmers, and he failed to win renomination in the 1932 Iowa senatorial primary. Brookhart supported Franklin D. Roosevelt in 1932 and 1936 and was rewarded with appointment as special adviser for Soviet trade in the Agricultural Adjustment Administration. Retiring from politics in 1936 after failing to win the Iowa Republican nomination for senator, he resumed his law practice in Washington, D.C., until 1943, when he moved to his daughter's home in Prescott, Arizona. He died in Whipple, Arizona.

The political career of Smith Brookhart bridged late nineteenth-century populism and Franklin D. Roosevelt's New Deal. He wedded the Jeffersonian ideal that guaranteed the rights of the yeoman farmer and small businessman to the twentieth-century liberal view that the power of a centralized government should be used to protect individuals from the corrupting influence of big business. Although he was ineffective as a legislator, Brookhart's success at the polls illustrated the attractiveness of the populist critique for many Americans during the economic boom of the New Era 1920s.

• A small collection of Brookhart's papers is in the Department of History and Archives, Des Moines, Iowa. Important correspondence is also held privately by members of Brookhart's family. The best biographical treatment is George William McDaniel, *Smith Wildman Brookhart: Iowa's Renegade Republican* (1995). Also useful is Jerry A. Neprash, *The Brookhart Campaigns in Iowa, 1920–1926* (1932).

EDWARD A. GOEDEKEN

BROOKINGS, Robert Somers (22 Jan. 1850–15 Nov. 1932), philanthropist, was born in Cecil County, Maryland, the son of Richard Brookings, a physician, and Mary Carter. When Robert was three, his father died. His mother subsequently moved the family to Baltimore, where she later married Henry Reynolds, a carpenter. At the age of seventeen, Brookings moved to St. Louis, Missouri, where he joined his older brother Harry to work for Cupples and Marston, a dry goods firm. He became a partner in 1872, and when he retired in 1895, he had accumulated more than $6 million.

Ambivalent about continuing to pursue a business career, Brookings decided to devote the rest of his life to philanthropy. At the suggestion of his former business partner, Samuel Cupples, in 1896 Brookings was appointed president of Washington University, a small university occupying a single building in downtown St. Louis. Brookings devoted himself unsparingly to transforming Washington University into a first-class institution. He supervised construction of a new campus west of the city, completed in 1906, and played a key role in devising a new curriculum and hiring new faculty. A substantial endowment was raised from leading St. Louis businessmen, including Cupples, William K. Bixby, president of the American Car and Foundry Company, Edward Mallinckrodt, founder of National Ammonia Company, lawyer Charles Nagel, and brewer Adolphus Busch. Additional support came from the St. Louis World's Fair committee, which in 1904 agreed to build a library, stadium, and gymnasium for the university in exchange for use of university property during the fair.

After a 1907 report by Abraham Flexner, commissioned by the Carnegie Foundation for the Advancement of Teaching to survey medical education in the United States, rated the medical school at Washington University as mediocre, Brookings turned his attention to improving the school's standing. Working with the trustees of Barnes Hospital and Children's Hospital, Brookings oversaw the construction of a medical center for the school in 1913. David L. Edsall, professor of medicine at the University of Pennsylvania, was appointed dean of the reinvigorated medical school and, with Brookings's support, acquired a first-rate medical faculty. The Carnegie Foundation provided additional funding for the project.

Brookings's association with the Carnegie Foundation opened up new opportunities for philanthropic endeavor. Through the foundation's president, Henry S. Pritchett, a former mathematics professor at Washington University, Brookings became acquainted with Andrew Carnegie. At Carnegie's invitation, he became a founding member of the Carnegie Corporation and a trustee of the Carnegie Peace Foundation in 1910. In 1916 Brookings became a founding trustee for the Institute for Government Research in Washington, D.C., which was heavily funded by the Carnegie Foundation. The institute's purpose was to bring efficiency and economy to government through the establishment of an executive budget system.

World War I brought Brookings the chance to expand his horizons. Four months after the United States declared war, President Woodrow Wilson appointed Brookings to the War Industries Board (WIB), the principal economic coordinating agency of the war. There he joined commissioners Bernard Baruch, a Wall Street financier, and Robert S. Lovett, chairman of the Union Pacific Railroad. In 1917 Wilson expanded the powers of the WIB to fix prices and set priorities in the production and manufacture of war goods, appointing Brookings to head the price-fixing committee and Baruch to head the priorities committee. Although Brookings and Baruch agreed on the need for price-fixing, their personality conflicts reduced their effectiveness on the board.

After the end of the war, Brookings left government service, convinced that social problems must be solved through economic expertise. "Practically all of the problems that have been submerging the world since the signing of the Armistice," he told a friend, "are economic problems, more or less poisoned by political traditions." He proposed to his close friend Henry Pritchett, that the Carnegie Corporation sponsor the establishment of an economic research institute, "free from any political or pecuniary interest." In 1922 the Carnegie Corporation offered a five-year grant of $200,000 to establish the Institute of Economics in Washington, D.C. Brookings then persuaded Washington University to establish a joint graduate program with the Institute of Economics and the Institute for Government Research. The board of trustees of these three institutions were interlocked to allow a complete consolidation of the three in the future.

Brookings selected a young University of Chicago economist, Harold G. Moulton, to head the new economic research institute. Walton Hamilton, an Amherst economics professor, was chosen as the first dean of the Robert S. Brookings Graduate School, in Washington, D.C., which opened its doors in 1924. The school trained a generation of scholars, including Isador Lubin, John U. Nef, Stacy May, Frank Tannebaum, Max Lerner, Carl Swisher, and Mordecai Ezekiel. Fearing that the graduate school had diverged from its original intent by becoming a training ground for professors instead of providing "the direct service I have always had in mind," however, Brookings in 1928 instructed Moulton to consolidate the Institute for Government Research, the Institute for Economics, and the graduate school into a single institution. After a heated controversy, the consolidation took place, and the Brookings Institution was established in Washington, D.C. Under Moulton's direction, in the 1920s the institution conducted major studies on the tariff, international debt, the coal industry, agriculture, and Indian affairs.

Brookings became increasingly reform-minded as he grew older. In 1925 he published his first book, *Industrial Ownership: Its Economic and Social Consequences*. A half-dozen pamphlets and two other books followed, including *Economic Democracy: America's Answer to Socialism and Communism* (1929) and *The Way Forward* (1932). In these works, Brookings called for more and "wiser" government intervention in the economy to provide "intelligent public supervision" of corporations. He favored a federal incorporation law, agricultural cooperatives, federal unemployment insurance, free trade, and a European trading union. After the stock market crash of 1929, Brookings expressed concern about a growing disparity of wealth in the nation. Although he endorsed Herbert Hoover for reelection in 1932, he stressed the need for reform. He urged Moulton to guide the Brookings Institution to the forefront of reform.

In 1927 Brookings married Isabel January, the daughter of a longtime St. Louis friend and a woman over thirty years his junior. In the autumn of 1932, he fell ill. Shortly before his death in Washington, D.C., he declared, "I have done everything I wanted to do."

• Brookings's Washington University papers can be found in the Chancellor Files, Washington University, St. Louis. Some correspondence is in the Brookings Institution files, Washington, D.C. The only complete biography of Brookings is Hermann Hagedorn, *Brookings: A Biography* (1936). Other biographical information can be found in Donald T. Critchlow, *The Brookings Institution, 1916–1952: Expertise and the Public Interest in a Democratic Society* (1985), and James Allen Smith, *The Idea Brokers: Think Tanks and the Rise of the New Policy Elite* (1991) and *Brookings at Seventy-Five* (1991). An obituary is in the *New York Times*, 16 Nov. 1932.

DONALD T. CRITCHLOW

BROOKS, Alfred Hulse (18 July 1871–22 Nov. 1924), geologist, was born in Ann Arbor, Michigan, the son of Thomas Benton Brooks, a mining engineer and geologist, and Hannah Hulse. Educated in schools and by private tutors at the elementary and secondary levels, Brooks began his fieldwork as a junior field assistant for a topographic party of the Geological Survey in southern Vermont in 1888. He then served with another topographic party in Marquette, Michigan, in 1889.

While living in Germany with his family, Brooks studied at the Polytechnik at Stuttgart and Munich in 1890 and 1891. He then returned from Germany in 1891 to take part in fieldwork in northern Michigan. After graduating from Harvard in December 1894 with his B.S., Brooks accepted a position with the Geological Survey in the southern Appalachian region. This period marked the appearance of his first professional piece of writing, "Preliminary Petrographic Notes on Some Metamorphic Rocks from Eastern Alabama" (*Alabama Geological Survey* 5 [1896]: 177–97). Brooks started graduate work at the Sorbonne in 1897 but only spent a few months in Paris. In 1898 he was sent to Alaska with the U.S. Geological Survey, where he spent the major part of the next quarter century.

In his previous posts, Brooks had gained plenty of professional experience, which he put to valuable use in Alaska. In his memorial to Brooks, Philip Smith commented on the long stay in Alaska, writing, "Brooks . . . established a reputation not only in his chosen profession, but as an empire builder, that made him more revered and better known than any other man connected with the development of this great territory."

Brooks's first Alaskan assignment (May 1902) was to aid in the surveying of the White and Tanana rivers. This was followed by many other trips in and around the Yukon, Nome, southeastern Alaska, and the Mount McKinley region, areas where the members of his party were usually the first nonnative peoples on record. According to Brooks's report, the Mount McKinley expedition was the longest cross-country exploration ever attempted in Alaska to that time. In most cases the geologists hoped to survey the areas for use in topographic maps and study the geologic formations and mineral deposits. One interest of the Geological Survey was to investigate the gold fields of Alaska for future exploitation. Rough terrain, horrendous living conditions, swarms of insects, disease, and sheer physical and mental exhaustion made these surveys a monumental undertaking.

From 1902 until he joined the American Expeditionary Force (AEF) in 1917 Brooks supervised all U.S. Geological Survey work in Alaska. Brooks wrote more than 100 articles and reports, cataloging his observations and recommendations on the development of Alaskan natural resources. In 1909 he wrote that, although the discovery of gold had led to a sharp increase in the Alaskan export trade, potential development of copper and iron ore mining, seal rookeries, and salmon, halibut, cod, and herring fisheries could be profitable in the long term if not exploited or hunted to extinction.

In 1912 and 1913 Brooks served as the vice chair for the Alaskan railroad commission. In 1914 he wrote "The Development of Alaska by Government Railroad," analyzing the potential for government involvement in moving large quantities of industrial and agricultural products to market. Government aid in creating a trans-Alaskan railroad would allow large commercial development without creating prohibitive freight rates. Brooks believed that the bitterly cold winters should not hinder the future permanent settlement of "Alaska, our most valuable outlying possession."

In 1916 Brooks, along with many businessmen and industrialists, became interested in the cause of preparedness in case of American involvement in the European war. The Woodrow Wilson administration recognized the need to open channels of communication among government, industry, and labor to better coordinate wartime supply needs. Brooks recommended that the War Department establish a reserve of professionally knowledgeable and militarily trained engineers ready in time of war. Following U.S. entry into World War I in April 1917, Brooks, already a member of the Engineer Officers' Reserve Corps, was commissioned major and sent to France. As chief geologist of the AEF, he handled supply routes, water transport, topographic maps, and fieldwork installations. Following the armistice, Brooks, now a lieutenant colonel, joined the American Commission to Negotiate Peace in Paris, where he helped compile data on the coal- and iron-rich regions of the Saar and Lorraine. He left the service in 1919 with General John Joseph Pershing's grateful acknowledgement of a job well done.

In 1919 Brooks returned to the Geological Survey in Alaska and in 1920 was appointed by the Interior and Commerce departments to advise the government on Alaskan development. As a result, he spent more time in Washington, D.C., and on overseas trips to areas interested in using Alaskan products. Brooks's contributions to the understanding of the Alaskan frontier are hard to measure. He was a pioneer in the exploration and study of Alaskan natural resources and thus provided the foundation for important scientific study. His reports were used by later geologists and explorers of Alaska, and he played a major role in bringing the Alaskan railroad into existence. Brooks's hard work, dedication, and professionalism exemplified his passion for science. He was recognized for his professional accomplishments with the Charles Peter Daly gold medal of the American Geographical Society of New York and the Conrad Malte-Brun gold medal of the Geographical Society of Paris (1913) and later served as president of the Washington Academy of Science (1921). The chain of mountains marking the continuation of the Rocky Mountains into Alaska bears Brooks's name as does a peak in the Seward Peninsula and a river in southwest Alaska.

In 1903 Brooks had married Mabel Baker; they had two children. Brooks suffered a slight stroke in 1922 while in Japan. Shortly thereafter, while working on a lecture on the "future of Alaska," he collapsed in his Washington office and died twelve hours later.

• Brooks's Alaskan field notes are included in the collection at the Alaskan Geology Branch of the U.S. Geological Survey, Menlo Park, Calif. Brooks wrote numerous monographs on Alaskan geology, including *Geography and Geology of Alaska* (1906), *Geologic Features of Alaskan Metalliferous Lodes* (1911), *The Future of Gold Placer Mining in Alaska* (1915), and *The Future of Alaska's Mining* (1920). His history of Alaska's resources and geology was published as *Blazing Alaska's Trails*, ed. B. L. Fryxell (1953). Brooks wrote more than 100 technical and popular journal articles over the course of his career. The most comprehensive study of Alfred Brooks's life and work is included in Philip S. Smith, "Memorial to Alfred Hulse Brooks," *Bulletin of the Geological Society of America* 37 (1926): 15–48, which contains a full bibliography. An obituary is in the *New York Times*, 23 Jan. 1924.

VERONICA JUNE BRUCE

BROOKS, Cleanth (16 Oct. 1906–10 May 1994), teacher, critic, and scholar, was born in Murray, Kentucky, the son of Cleanth Brooks, Sr., an Episcopalian minister, and Bessie Lee Witherspoon. The family soon moved to Tennessee where his father served a number of parishes near Memphis. Despite their peripatetic lifestyle, Cleanth's parents helped their shy, precocious son to find the stability that he needed by encouraging in him a devotion to the great literature of the world. Eventually, Cleanth attended the Mc Tyeire School, where, in addition to the standard academic fare of the era, he learned Greek and Latin and continued the education in classical literature that had begun at age five with his father's present of a collections of tales from the *Iliad*.

When he was still seventeen Brooks entered Vanderbilt University to study law. The year was 1924, and several of the original members of the fugitives, the pro-agrarian, anti-industrial literary movement of the 1920s, were still in residence and teaching. Of these, Professor Donald Davidson became immediately influential in Brooks's intellectual development. During this period the other major Agrarian critic remaining at Vanderbilt, John Crowe Ransom, only indirectly affected Brooks. It was Ransom's protégé Robert Penn Warren, then a senior and a rather glamorous figure to the freshman Brooks, who taught Brooks that literature was not simply a historical artifact, to be studied as one might study a fossil, but an immediate presence in the lives of living human beings who cared about it passionately and who actually wrote and published. Thanks to Warren, Donaldson, Ransom, and to the vitality of the literary studies that their personalities helped to generate at Vanderbilt, Brooks quickly gave up his notion of becoming a lawyer and began the study of literature that would last the rest of his long and productive life.

In 1928 Brooks received his B.A. from Vanderbilt and moved on to graduate work at Tulane University. There he met Edith Amy Blanchard. Though they quickly became engaged, the economic reality of the Great Depression convinced them to postpone marriage until Brooks had secured an academic appointment. Tulane awarded him his M.A. in 1929 and nominated him as the Rhodes Scholar from Louisiana. This allowed him to study for three years at Exeter College, Oxford, where he was reunited with Warren, who was also at Oxford as a Rhodes Scholar. During his stay at Exeter, Brooks read for an honors degree in English under the tutelage of Nevill Coghill. It was under Coghill's watchful eye that Brooks was first exposed to I. A. Richards's *Principles of Literary Criticism* (1924) and *Practical Criticism: A Study of Literary Judgment* (1929). He earned his B.A. with honors from Exeter College in 1931 and an honorary graduate degree in 1932.

At the beginning of the 1932 academic year Charles Pipkin enticed Brooks back to Louisiana to teach literature at Louisiana State University. Pipkin, a former Rhodes Scholar and the dean of the graduate school at LSU, had met Brooks in Paris in 1929 and was impressed with him. Pipkin also soon hired Warren. When Warren arrived in Baton Rouge, he and Brooks continued the personal and professional relationship that had begun years before at Vanderbilt and that would eventually lead to the founding of the *Southern Review* at LSU in 1939.

Brooks's appointment at LSU allowed him to feel secure enough after two years to marry Edith Blanchard. In 1934 they began a life together that would last until her death in 1986. They had no children. In addition to beginning married life, Brooks also began his first major work, *The Relation of the Alabama-Georgia Dialect to the Provincial Dialects of Great Britain*, which was published in 1935. Despite the rather traditional nature of his scholarship during this period, Brooks again found himself at the center of a burgeoning intellectual life that in many respects brought LSU to its first stage of maturity as an institution of national importance. Brooks and his wife found themselves playing host to many of the brightly shining lights of academe and the arts, such as I. A. Richards, Marshall McLuhan, John Crowe Ransom, and Katherine Anne Porter. It was also during these years that Brooks and Warren began with Pipkin's blessing what Ransom called "the organ of the most powerful critical discussion in the language," the *Southern Review*, and began to formulate a solution to the problem of introducing ill-prepared undergraduates to the study of literature. In answer to what they determined to be a pressing need they developed and edited with John Thibaut Purser a textbook for sophomores titled *An Approach to Literature: A Collection of Prose and Verse with Analyses and Discussions* (1936). Two years later they wrote and edited the more important and ambitious *Understanding Poetry: An Anthology for College Students* (1938). Though they realized that the analyses that they provided of the different poems in the text were somewhat controversial (in that they eschewed the traditional historical and biographical approach in favor of a text-oriented criticism), Brooks and Warren were confident that theirs was the appropriate solution to the problem of teaching students to read closely and critically.

This confidence was reemphasized in 1939 when Brooks published *Modern Poetry and the Tradition*, his first collection of critical essays. This book incorporated what he had been busy learning from Richards, T. S. Eliot, and Ransom, and was, in large part, an attempt to reconcile his own formal approach to textual analysis with Richards's more "subjective" method. It was this work that established Brooks as a new and important voice in the critical appreciation and exploration of literature. Its success and the adoption in 1940 of *Understanding Poetry* by Yale University triggered a steady sequence of invitations from around the country to visit and teach: in 1941 he spent the summer teaching at the University of Texas; 1942 found him teaching as a visiting professor at the University of Michigan; in 1945 he took part in the Bread Loaf Writers' Conference; and in 1946 he accepted an invitation from R. S. Crane to teach as a visiting professor at the University of Chicago. Later that year he accepted an invitation from Yale to become a permanent member of its faculty.

At Yale Brooks joined a group of scholar-critics that included many of the best minds of his generation, such as René Wellek, William K. Wimsatt, Maynard

Mack, and Louis Martz. Once again, Brooks found himself contributing to and benefiting from a circle of especially gifted and dedicated colleagues. The next year he published *The Well Wrought Urn: Studies in the Structure of Poetry* (1947) and established himself as both one of the preeminent literary critics of his generation and the exemplary representative, much to his chagrin, of what was being called the "new criticism."

After serving as a visiting professor at Kenyon College during the summer of 1948, Brooks worked with Warren to produce *Modern Rhetoric* (1949). Another product of their collaboration, *Fundamentals of Good Writing: A Handbook of Modern Rhetoric*, followed in 1950. In 1953 Brooks was awarded a Guggenheim Fellowship and began the first of his ten years as a fellow of the Library of Congress. He was appointed Gray Professor of Rhetoric at Yale in 1958 and received another Guggenheim Fellowship in 1960.

Now the leading proponent of new critical methodology, Brooks turned his attention in the early 1960s to another of his fellow southerners and published *William Faulkner: The Yoknapatawpha Country* in 1963. He also collected together a series of lectures presented at a 1955 conference on theology at Trinity College, Hartford, Connecticut, that examined the relationship between modern literature and religion and published them as *The Hidden God: Studies in Hemingway, Faulkner, Yeats, Eliot, and Warren* (1963). The following year he accepted an appointment as cultural attaché at the American Embassy in London. The two years he spent in England provided him with the especially poignant experience of representing the United States at the memorial service in Westminster Abbey for his beloved favorite poet, T. S. Eliot. In 1971 he gathered together with several others those papers delivered while he was cultural attaché and published them as *A Shaping Joy: Studies in the Writer's Craft*. He retired from Yale in 1975 as professor emeritus.

After retirement Brooks produced his second book on Faulkner, *William Faulkner: Toward Yoknapatawpha and Beyond*, in 1978 and his third, *William Faulkner: First Encounters*, in 1983. At what would ordinarily have been the close of an active and extremely successful career, Brooks brought his perceptive intellect, his imagination, and his critical integrity to bear on a seemingly monumental project and established himself as one of the major interpreters of Faulkner's work. He even returned to his first love, the sheer beauty and fascination of language itself, and continued the philological project he had started in the 1930s with the publication in 1985 of *The Language of the American South*. Brooks died of cancer at his home in New Haven, Connecticut. The next year his legacy continued with the posthumous publication of *Community, Religion, and Literature*, a collection of late essays that reveals the tact and modesty characteristic of Brooks and that once again displays the "high, noble, and strenuous view of art and human nature" (Spears, p. 252) that was his hallmark through his life and career.

Though it may be convenient to label Brooks the representative new critic, to do so (whether mistakenly or purposefully) minimizes his contribution to literary study, trivializes his long and accomplished life, and, as he himself writes in *Community, Religion, and Literature*, forces him "to assume responsibility for the collective sins of a vague, undefined group." However, he can (along with Warren) assume the responsibility of having institutionalized "close reading" and the concomitant formal analysis of the literary text as a symbolic structure. Yet, despite the very obvious emphasis in his critical method on the rhetorical structure of the literary text, in all he wrote Brooks drove home the principal lesson he had to teach—that "language itself carries us outside the poem: that the very words can be understood only in the context of an inherited language and that their meaning is circumscribed by external reality" (Wellek, p. 204). Not to understand this about Brooks can lead to great confusion and has done so. His much vaunted and much criticized use of wit, irony, and paradox provides only the concepts so necessary to him for an adequate understanding of the so much more important vital tension that exists between the self-conscious, imaginative use of language and the truth to experience upon which all use of language is dependent and before which even the greatest poetry must ultimately fall short.

• Collections of Brooks's papers exist at the Beinecke Rare Book Room and Manuscript Library, Yale University; the University of Kentucky; the Joint University Libraries at the University of Tennessee; and the Newberry Library, Chicago. In addition to the texts mentioned, Brooks coauthored *Literary Criticism: A Short History* (1957), with William K. Wimsatt. Other major works include the important essay "The Poem as Organism: Modern Critical Procedure," in *English Institute Annual*, ed. Rudolph Kirk (1940); *The Percy Letters*, ed. with David Nicol Smith (6 vols., 1944–1961); "The New Criticism and Scholarship," in *Twentieth Century English*, ed. W. S. Knickerbocker (1946); "Literary Criticism," in *English Institute Essays 1946*, ed. James L. Clifford et al. (1947); "Irony as a Principle of Structure," in *Literary Opinion in America: Essays Illustrating the States, Methods, and Problems of Criticism in the United States in the Twentieth Century*, vol. 3, ed. Morton D. Zabel (1937); "Metaphor and the Function of Criticism," in *Spiritual Problems in Contemporary Literature* (1952); *The Poems of John Milton: The 1645 Edition with Essays in Analysis*, ed. with John Edward Hardy (1952); "Implications of an Organic Theory of Poetry," in *Literature and Belief*, ed. M. H. Abrams (1958). Important selected periodical publications include "A Note on the Limits of 'History' and the Limits of 'Criticism'," *Sewanee Review* 61 (Winter 1953): 129–35; "Metaphor and Paradox and Stereotype," *British Journal of Aesthetics* 5 (Oct. 1965): 685–97; "The New Criticism," *Sewanee Review* 87 (Fall 1979): 592–607; "The Critics Who Made Us: I. A. Richards and Practical Criticism," *Sewanee Review* 89 (Fall 1981): 586–95. For a complete listing of all of Brooks's works through 1990 see John Michael Walsh, *Cleanth Brooks: An Annotated Bibliography*. For critical appreciations and appraisals of Brooks's work see R. S. Crane, "The Critical Monism of Cleanth Brooks," in *Critics and Criticism: Ancient and Modern*, ed. Crane (1952); Gerald Graff, "Cleanth Brooks: New Critical Organicism," in his *Poetic Statement and Critical Dogma*

(1970); and René Wellek, "Cleanth Brooks, Critic of Critics," and Monroe K. Spears, "Cleanth Brooks and the Responsibilities of Criticism," both in *Possibilities of Order: Cleanth Brooks and His Work*, ed. Lewis P. Simpson (1976). Biographical information can be gleaned from Thomas W. Cutrer, *Parnassus on the Mississippi: The Southern Review and the Baton Rouge Literary Community* (1984); Simpson, ed., *The Possibilities of Order: Cleanth Brooks and His Work* (1975); and Kermit Vanderbilt, *American Literature and the Academy: The Roots, Growth, and Maturity of a Profession* (1986). An obituary is in the *New York Times*, 12 May 1994.

WILLIAM W. KIMBREL

BROOKS, Erastus (31 Jan. 1815–25 Nov. 1886), journalist and politician, was born in Portland, Maine, the son of the late James Brooks (c. 1788–1814), a commander of a privateer in the War of 1812 who had gone down with his ship, and Betsey Folsom. The financial problems caused by his father's early death meant that Erastus had to begin work at age eight as a grocery store clerk in Boston. Ever enterprising, he used his pocket money to buy books and attend night school. He soon was placed in a printing office, where he learned to set type. Knowledge of this trade enabled him to earn enough money to attend classes at Brown University, although he did not complete the course of study. Eager to work for himself, he started his own newspaper, the *Yankee*, at Wiscasset, Maine, while still a teenager. About 1834 he moved on to Haverhill, Massachusetts, where he taught school and briefly edited the Haverhill *Gazette*.

Meanwhile Brooks's older brother, James Brooks (1810–1873), had also become interested in newspapers and begun writing on political topics for the Portland *Advertiser*. Erastus joined him. In 1832 James expanded his political reporting by going to Washington to report on Congress in the form of gossipy letters, which were reprinted in the *Advertiser* and other papers. As the presidential election of 1836 approached, James was asked to begin a Whig paper in New York City. Erastus, whose knowledge of printing was invaluable to the enterprise, became a part proprietor (later editor) of the New York *Express*, with which he would be associated for forty-one years, thirty-four as editor. In the meantime, he took his brother's place in Washington in 1835, writing about political events for the *Express*, the *Advertiser*, and various other papers. During William Henry Harrison's presidential campaign in 1840, Brooks edited the Portland *Advertiser*. When he returned to Washington in 1841, he married Margaret Dawes Cranch, with whom he had seven children.

Although New York City was a highly competitive market for newspapers, Erastus and James Brooks hoped to make the *Express* a success. Whig subsidies were helpful but hardly sufficient. Like other editors, the Brookses tried to establish a reputation for being first on the street with breaking news. Once Erastus went to Albany to collect state election returns, taking along type so that he could set the results on the trip home. Later, in 1845, he made an arrangement with Ezra Cornell to use the recently laid telegraph lines to send the governor's inaugural address from Albany to New York City, thus beating the *Herald*'s pony express. During a cholera epidemic, when printers refused to work, Brooks composed and set stories himself so that the paper would not miss an issue.

The brothers also sought popular features. In 1843 Erastus made a walking tour of Europe from Ireland to Moscow, sending back colorful letters to the paper describing his adventures. On his return he had an unanticipated adventure: the packet *Sheffield*, on which he was traveling, went down off Sandy Hook with only a handful of survivors. Also popular, although more mundane, was the *Express*'s daily listing of hotel arrivals, which was important to salesmen. For many years Brooks also helped direct the Associated Press, a pioneering news-gathering organization.

Brooks also used controversy to attract readers. Taking advantage of the powerful nativism gripping the city in the wake of the heavy influx of Irish Catholic immigrants after the Irish potato famine, Brooks in 1852 attacked a measure favored by Archbishop John Hughes (the Taber bill), which would have recognized the right of Catholic bishops in New York to hold title to church property. (Protestant churches vested control in lay congregations.) Decrying the potential for papal influence in the United States, Brooks rode the issue into the state senate in 1853 and 1855. He coauthored legislation that would have severely penalized clerical ownership. He and Archbishop Hughes carried on a running argument in the newspapers over the merits of the bill. The controversy was closely followed in newspapers well beyond New York.

Brooks's notoriety won him the American party's gubernatorial nomination in 1856, an election in which he repeatedly made the false claim that Republican presidential candidate John C. Frémont was a Catholic. Brooks's antics aroused much anger in his opponents. Diarist George Templeton Strong confessed after meeting him socially, "If men are to develop into animal forms, each according to the laws of his individual being, Erastus will be a very ugly, cunning, and vicious rat some of these days" (*The Diary of George Templeton Strong*, abr. ed. [1988], p. 120). Brooks, who had also managed to alienate protemperance and antislavery Know Nothings, finished third in the balloting, receiving 22 percent of the vote.

As the American party waned, Brooks promoted the Constitutional Union party as an alternative to the Republicans, whose agitation of the slavery issue, he believed, would destroy the Union. During the Civil War he became a Democrat and a vigorous critic of emancipation, conscription, and suppression of civil liberties. The *Express*, like many Democratic papers, faced charges of treason and occasional impediments to its distribution. After the war he was elected to a convention to revise the state's constitution (1867–1868). This constitutional reform having failed, he was appointed to a constitutional commission that met in 1872–1873 and proposed amendments to the constitution.

Although Brooks always retained his nose for news, he did not see that a newspaper's financial success could also depend on adopting newer technologies and management techniques, meeting changing popular expectations for more accurate, less partisan reporting, and even owning the building where the paper was produced. (The value of urban real estate was skyrocketing.) The *Express* was past its prime when Brooks sold it in 1877.

In retirement Brooks was elected to represent Richmond County (Staten Island) in the assembly in 1878, 1879, 1881, 1882, and 1883. Well versed in most issues, he served on the Ways and Means and other influential committees. Although not personally wealthy, he was active in charitable work. His causes included public health, the deaf and dumb, American Indian rights, medical care for children, and the prevention of cruelty to animals. He was an active member of Cornell University's board of trustees. Brooks died at his home in West New Brighton, Staten Island. The public services of his later years had done much to erase the hostility generated by his earlier partisan journalism.

• There are no Brooks manuscripts. The unsigned *Biography of the Hon. Erastus Brooks* (1882) is a brief pamphlet. See also Ira K. Morris, *Morris's Memorial History of Staten Island* (1900); Elizabeth Folsom, *Genealogy of the Folsom Family, 1638–1938* (1938); Ray Allen Billington, *The Protestant Crusade, 1800–1860* (1938); and Tyler Anbinder, *Nativism and Slavery: The Northern Know Nothings and the Politics of the 1850s* (1992). Lengthy obituaries are in all the New York papers, 26 Nov. 1886.

PHYLLIS F. FIELD

BROOKS, James (18 Oct. 1906–10 Mar. 1992), abstract expressionist painter, was born James Ealand Brooks in St. Louis, Missouri, the son of William Rodolphus Brooks and Abigail Williamson. He grew up in Denver, Colorado, and Dallas, Texas. After attending Southern Methodist University in Dallas (1923–1925) and the Dallas Art Institute, Brooks went to New York City in 1926 and worked as a letterer to finance his study from 1927 to 1930 at the Art Students League, where his teachers were Kimon Nicolaides and Boardman Robinson.

In the summer of 1931 Brooks shared a studio in a barn in Woodstock, New York, with an abstract expressionist, Bradley Walker Tomlin, whose colorist paintings are frequently compared to those of Brooks. During the 1930s Brooks's connections with the Federal Arts Project (FAP) enabled him to participate—along with Arshile Gorky, Philip Evergood, Karl Knaths, and others—in an exhibition titled New Horizons in American Art, which had been selected by the national director of the FAP, Holger Cahill.

In 1938 Brooks married Mary McDonald. Like so many artists of his generation, Brooks was employed by the Works Progress Administration, under the aegis of which he executed two murals in the New York City area: *The Acquisition of Long Island* (1937–1938) for the Queensborough Public Library, Woodside Branch, and *Flight*, painted on canvas (1938–1942) for the International Overseas Air Terminal at La Guardia Airport. Although these were judged to be among the very best mural paintings produced in the United States during that period, both were subsequently destroyed. A remnant of the latter, however, is extant. At this time Brooks became associated with proud American regionalism rather than the social realism espoused by the leftist intelligentsia. While working on *Flight*, Brooks, who greatly admired Henri Matisse and Pablo Picasso, became increasingly interested in the abstraction of cubism. The direction he might then have taken was deflected by World War II. His service in the U.S. Army sent him to Egypt and the Middle East (1942–1945). After his first marriage had ended, in 1947 he married Charlotte Park.

After the war Brooks took up abstraction in the manner of synthetic cubism (painting with elements of collage) as the abstract expressionist movement was coming into its own. Younger than some of the major adherents to the new "school," including Adolph Gottlieb, Mark Rothko, and his friend Tomlin, Brooks joined the group slightly later but was able to take part in several key early exhibitions. His typical subtlety and refinement brought him closer to the harmonious approach of colorists such as Tomlin than to the aggressive effects of action painters such as Franz Kline and Jackson Pollock. In 1949 Brooks did, however, experiment with poured pigments in the manner that Pollock had adopted. Around this time Brooks also created calligraphic motifs and became an advocate of the surrealist legacy of automatism, then popular with the New York school of abstract expressionists.

On occasion an innovator, Brooks anticipated several significant technical and stylistic developments in American painting, including the staining of unprimed canvas (at first with black and later with color), a method subsequently practiced by Helen Frankenthaler, among others. He created large harmonies of color and assimilated the decorative and tranquil essence later associated with the color field artists, such as Morris Louis and Kenneth Noland. And he added the technique of gestural painting in the vein of Willem de Kooning, so that he could produce a worked and reworked effect of paint seen to have been applied by brush, with the brushstroke manifested by the dried paint, and then reapplied or obscured by a fresh application of a different color. Brooks's palette was both commanding and nuanced, with bright as well as muted tones, and often idiosyncratic. His canvases usually have a predominant color—such as russet, magenta, pink, or forest green—and form and space are projected by variations in the tones of the major hue. Brooks emphasized the outward aspect of his work and maintained that his paintings were "done with as much spontaneity and as little memory as possible." Many of his mature pieces are identified only by a number and the year in which they were executed, a common practice among members of the New York school. But after about 1954 he assigned them enigmatic one-word titles such as *Qualm* or *Boon* or *Hecla*.

In 1951 Brooks was part of the Irascible 18, a famous group of New York moderns, including Ad Reinhardt, who protested against what they considered to be the Metropolitan Museum of Art's neglect of the American avant-garde. Brooks came to temper his avowed reliance on the subconscious in the process of making art, as is indicated by his statement in *The New Decade: Thirty-five American Painters and Sculptors* (1955): "Any conscious involvement . . . is good if it permits the unknown to enter the painting almost unnoticed." Always wary of associations of his work with landscapes, he refused to participate in the Whitney Museum's 1958 group exhibition Nature in Abstraction. By 1960 he had begun to introduce in his paintings jarring elements that counteracted a pervasive and monumental calm.

During the 1940s and 1950s, while residing in New York and The Springs, Long Island, Brooks taught at the Pratt Institute and Columbia University (1946–1948); at Yale University, where he was a visiting critic (1955–1960); and during the 1960s at New College in Sarasota, Florida. He exhibited widely in the United States and Europe, with group shows at the Whitney Museum of American Art in New York (1950 and 1955), the University of Illinois at Champaign-Urbana (1952–1963), the Guggenheim Museum in New York (1954 and 1961), the Galerie de France in Paris (1952), and elsewhere. His one-man exhibitions were at the Peridot Gallery, the Grace Borgenicht Gallery, the Stable Gallery, and the Samuel M. Kootz Gallery in New York City. The major retrospective in his lifetime was held at the Whitney Museum of American Art in 1963. Brooks received awards from the Museum of Modern Art, the Carnegie Institute in Pittsburgh, the Art Institute of Chicago, and the Ford Foundation. He died in Brookhaven, Long Island.

• Brooks's paintings are in the Albright-Knox Art Gallery, Buffalo, N.Y.; the Art Institute of Chicago; the Detroit Institute of Arts; the Wadsworth Atheneum, Hartford; the Guggenheim Museum, the Metropolitan Museum of Art, the Museum of Modern Art, and the Whitney Museum of American Art, all in New York City; and the Tate Gallery in London. *Twelve Americans* (1963) is the catalog for a group exhibition at the Museum of Modern Art that, for the most part, presented young talent; it includes a statement from Brooks, even though he was fifty years old at the time. Sam Hunter, *James Brooks* (1963), documents Brooks's major one-man retrospective at the Whitney. Irving Sandler, "James Brooks and the Abstract Inscape," *Art News*, Feb. 1963, is informative and insightful; also worth consulting are two books by Sandler, *The Triumph of American Painting: A History of Abstract Expressionism* (1970) and *The New York School: The Painters and Sculptors of the Fifties* (1978). See also the catalogs *James Brooks/John Opper: Paintings of the Seventies* (Montclair Art Museum, N.J. [1978]) and *Abstract Expressionism Lives! James Brooks, Willem de Kooning, Robert Motherwell, etc.* (Museum and Nature Center, Stamford, Conn. [1982]). An obituary is in the *New York Times*, 12 Mar. 1992.

JEANNE CHENAULT PORTER

BROOKS, John (4 May 1752–1 Mar. 1825), revolutionary war officer and governor of Massachusetts, was born in Medford, Massachusetts, the son of Caleb Brooks and Ruth Albree, farmers. John Brooks studied medicine with Dr. Simon Tufts of Medford from 1766 to 1773, leaving at age twenty-one to establish his own practice in Reading, Massachusetts. In 1774 he married Lucy Smith; they had three children.

In 1775 Brooks was elected captain of militia in Ebenezer Bridge's regiment, though at first he declined because service would interfere with his attending patients. He fought the British on their retreat from Concord on 19 April 1775 and then joined militia forces at Cambridge. The next month he was made a major. Though helping to throw up entrenchments at Charlestown Heights, he was sent by Colonel William Prescott on 17 June 1775 to obtain reinforcements from General Artemas Ward's command and so missed the battle of Bunker Hill. Brooks stayed with George Washington's army during the siege of Boston.

Brooks served throughout the war and earned a reputation as an enterprising and intelligent soldier. At White Plains on 28 October 1776, his regiment, along with General Alexander McDougall's (1732–1786) brigade, took the brunt of the British attack on Chatterton's Hill. Four days later Brooks was appointed a lieutenant colonel in the Eighth Massachusetts Regiment of the Continental line. Joining the northern army, he accompanied Benedict Arnold's advance against St. Leger's army in western New York and was credited with the ruse (sending the mentally defective Hon Yost Schuyler with false intelligence to the Indians exaggerating the strength of Arnold's troops) that led to the withdrawal of St. Leger's Indians. In 1777 he distinguished himself at the two battles at Saratoga: Freeman's Farm (19 September) and Bemis Heights (7 October). At Bemis Heights he commanded the advance unit that broke through the Hessian lines by capturing Breymann's redoubt. Brooks's regiment joined Washington's army after the battles of Brandywine and Germantown. At Valley Forge on 5 January 1778, he wrote a friend of "our poor brave fellows living in tents, bare-footed, bare-legged, bare-breeched." At Monmouth, Brooks served as adjutant to General Charles Lee's (1731–1782) field division, and at the ensuing court-martial of Lee for insubordination and needless retreat before the enemy, he testified on behalf of Lee versus Washington's aides and generals. Next, he served briefly as a subinspector on Baron von Steuben's staff. In November 1778 Brooks was appointed lieutenant colonel and commandant of the Seventh Massachusetts Regiment, in which capacity he served until the unit's disbandment in June 1783. Brooks defended his commander in chief at the time of the "Newburgh conspiracy" (which centered on the circulation of addresses in camp implying that Washington had neglected the interests of the officers and in effect declaring that the army would desert Congress if pay and pension demands were not met), though he was one of three officers selected to present complaints to Congress.

After the war, Brooks tried trade for a while before beginning a medical practice in Medford. Brooks served two terms as representative in the Massachusetts General Court (1785–1786). In 1786 he served as major general of Middlesex County militia during Shays's Rebellion, though he himself did not march against the insurgents. He was a delegate to the Massachusetts convention that ratified the Constitution. In 1791 he was appointed a federal marshal, and from 1792 to 1796 he served as a brigadier general in the U.S. Army. President John Adams (1735–1826) nominated him for major general in 1800, but the Senate refused to act because the expected war with the French did not materialize.

During the War of 1812, to which he was opposed, Brooks declined the Federalist nomination to Congress, but from 1812 to 1816 he served as adjutant general for Massachusetts (the state's chief military officer). He then served seven terms as governor of Massachusetts (1816–1823) and was the last Federalist governor in the nation. The postwar depression, the dumping of European goods in America, and the advent of the "Era of Good Feelings," with its spirit of "amalgamation" between political parties, aided his success over Democratic-Republican candidates. In annual election campaigns Brooks won decisively in the popular vote over his Democratic-Republican opponents. As Shaw Livermore states: "John Brooks beat back successive Republican challenges with a policy of moderation, smooth and continuous praise of the national administration and constant reminders of his fine Revolutionary War record." In a letter dated 27 February 1818, Daniel Webster commented on Brooks's "disposition to oblige."

One leading issue during Brooks's administration, on which both political parties united, was pressing the federal government for reimbursement of some $800,000 for the state's militia expenses during the War of 1812; ironically, the state had refused to allow federal command of its militia during the war. Congress finally voted to reimburse Massachusetts in 1831. Another issue concerned the revision of the state constitution after the District of Maine separated from Massachusetts and became a state. The convention for revising the constitution met between 15 November 1820 and 9 January 1821; nine of fourteen amendments were adopted, including democratic reforms such as substituting a poll tax for a property tax and the removal of religious tests for officeholding. Economically, the period witnessed a shifting from commerce to industry. Brooks, however, had favored the interests of the former during his political career, reluctant to support a protective tariff on manufactures. He left office in May 1823. After an illness of several weeks, Brooks died at his Medford residence. An obituary refers to Brooks as "the hero of Saratoga" and mentions his "unyielding integrity" and "unaffected manners."

• War correspondence of Brooks is in the George Washington Papers, Library of Congress. The papers of the Continental Congress, National Archives, has regimental documents pertaining to Brooks. There is no substantial biography. The short biographical sketches are John Dixwell's address before the Massachusetts Medical Society, published in Charles Brooks, *History of the Town of Medford, Middlesex County* (1886); Brooks, "Memoir of John Brooks, Governor of Massachusetts," *New England Historical and Genealogical Register* 19 (1865): 193–200; and "Biographical Sketch of Governor Brooks" (a sermon), *Christian Examiner* 2, no. 2 (1825): 103–17. See also Shaw Livermore, *The Twilight of Federalism: The Disintegration of the Federalist Party, 1815–1830* (1962). An obituary is in the *New England Galaxy*, 4 Mar. 1825.

HARRY M. WARD

BROOKS, John Graham (19 July 1846–8 Feb. 1938), reformer and sociologist, was born in Acworth, New Hampshire, the son of Chapin Kidder Brooks, a merchant, and Pamelia Graham. During his youth he worked at the store owned by his father, who also represented the town of Acworth in the state legislature. After graduating from Kimball Union Academy in 1866, Brooks attended the University of Michigan Law School but soon changed his mind about studying law. He left after a year and taught the next year on Cape Cod. In 1868, after a summer in Quebec perfecting his French, he enrolled in Oberlin College, in Oberlin, Ohio. After graduating in 1872 Brooks returned to New England and enrolled in the Harvard Divinity School, where he graduated with a degree in sacred theology in 1875. He was soon ordained and served as a Unitarian minister in Roxbury, Massachusetts. In addition to his pastoral duties, he involved himself in labor reform and organized classes in history and economics for the workingmen of the neighborhood. His liberal sermons attracted listeners from Cambridge and Beacon Hill. He was soon addressing informal groups on social problems. In 1880 he married the widow of another Unitarian minister, Helen Lawrence Appleton Washburn, who shared his reform impulses; they had three children.

Brooks resigned his pulpit in 1882 and began graduate studies in history and economics at the Universities of Berlin, Jena, and Freiburg, spending academic leaves studying labor conditions throughout Europe. After Brooks completed his academic work in 1885, the family lived in London and Oxford for a few months. He was elected to the Reform and Cobden clubs, lectured at the universities, and preached at South Place Chapel in London, among other places. While there he received an invitation to teach at Harvard with an appointment as lecturer on socialism, inaugurating the university's first course on this subject. Returning to the United States in 1885, he held a pulpit in the manufacturing town of Brockton, Massachusetts. He involved himself in social issues with employers and their workers and lectured in Cambridge twice a week. Brooks also began to publish articles in such journals as *Forum*, the *Nation*, and the *Journal of Economics*. He organized classes for factory workers and delivered lectures in Brockton and the Boston area. In 1887 he spoke before the American Social Science Association on the political and economic benefits of labor organizations.

In 1891 Brooks left the ministry in order to concentrate on the analysis of labor-employer relations as an investigator for the U.S. Department of Labor. He and his family left again for Europe, where he had been commissioned to study the system of compulsory insurance in Germany. From this research trip came the 1895 publication of *Compulsory Insurance in Germany*, a workmanlike study based upon traditional sources and a large number of personal interviews and including a comparative study of compulsory insurance in other European countries. He also wrote journal articles on English old-age pensions, Swedish temperance reform, and German coal miners. In 1893 Brooks returned to Cambridge, Massachusetts, and became acquainted with other reformers such as Jane Addams and John Dewey. In an article on an encyclical written by Pope Leo XIII, he defended the view expressed in *Rerum Novarum* that wages "must be enough to support the wage earner in reasonable and frugal comfort" ("Papal Encyclical upon the Labor Question," American Economic Association, *Proceedings* 7 [1895]). He traveled about the country as an investigator of strikes and labor unrest for the federal government and as a lecturer on such topics as unions, cooperatives, consumer groups, and settlement houses. He gave dozens of lectures in New York City for the League for Public Education, and out of "the extraordinary public response" to these lectures the city's Town Hall was formed. In his second book, *The Social Unrest: Studies in Labor and Socialist Movements* (1903), Brooks rejected socialism, in which he had believed for fifteen years in a nondoctrinaire way, and called for greater cooperation between capital and labor. He expressed his belief in immediate public regulation of monopolies, enactment of social security programs, and voluntary trade unionism.

In 1904–1905 Brooks was president of the American Social Science Association, and from 1899 to 1915 he served as the first president of the National Consumers' League. In that period he also was commissioned to study conditions in the Colorado mines. He reported his findings to President Theodore Roosevelt at the White House. In 1908 his answer to foreign critics of the United States was published as *As Others See Us: A Study of Progress in the United States*, in which he emphasized the cooperation between employers and workers and the benefits of immigration. In 1911 he gave a series of lectures at the University of California in Berkeley about the American background of the Industrial Workers of the World (IWW). These lectures appeared in book form as *American Syndicalism* in 1913, and in them Brooks traced the violence of the American-born Wobblies to its origin in the confrontations between the earlier Knights of Labor and their hostile entrepreneurial employers. He praised the IWW for including in its movement the unskilled laborers whom the earlier unions had rebuffed.

Increasingly afflicted with asthma, Brooks retired in 1920 upon the publication of his final book, *Labor's Challenge to the Social Order: Democracy Its Own Critic and Educator*. In it he looked back at his forty-five years as a reformer. He found advances by labor that would have been dismissed as utopian when he began his work, and he asked for more cooperation toward the ideal of enlightened liberalism with a constructive social policy and the acceptance of all unskilled workers within the labor unions. In retirement Brooks kept in touch with old friends in the reform movement, wrote the obituaries of many of them, and served on the advisory board of the Carnegie Foundation Study of Methods of Americanization. During one week of his retirement he demonstrated his continued broad appeal by lecturing to a group of trade unionists and a philosophy class at Harvard College. In 1925 the National Consumers' League held its annual meeting in Boston where a dinner was held in Brooks's honor with such speakers as John R. Commons, Felix Frankfurter, and Florence Kelley. Brooks died in Cambridge.

Brooks was one of the first social scientists to use personal interviews and on-site observations to support his traditional research. Through his lectures and writings he inspired reform-minded men and women to adopt his causes; he even inspired one of them, Robert Woods, to found a settlement house in Boston. He accepted with enthusiasm the need to defend the rights of workers, the poor, women, and children. His crusades were founded upon practical realities arrived at through energetic research and informed discussion and aimed at an optimistic betterment of society that was specifically American and humanitarian. Brooks exemplified, in the period from 1900 to 1920, the leisured, academic group of progressives who were heeded by presidents and congressmen, shop stewards and stockbrokers, social workers and socialites.

• The papers of Brooks and his wife are at the Schlesinger Library on the History of Women at Radcliffe College in Cambridge, Massachusetts. James E. Mooney, *John Graham Brooks: Prophet of Social Justice* (1968), has a listing of over fifty of the published writings of Brooks. Also useful are George W. Coleman et al., *John Graham Brooks, Helen Lawrence Brooks, 1846–1938: A Memorial* (1940), and *The Memoirs of Lawrence Graham Brooks* (1981).

JAMES E. MOONEY

BROOKS, Louise (14 Nov. 1906–8 Aug. 1985), actress and dancer, was born Mary Louise Brooks in Cherryvale, Kansas, the daughter of Leonard Porter Brooks, a lawyer, and Myra Rude. Louise trained as a dancer, beginning her professional career at age fifteen with Ruth St. Denis and Ted Shawn's Denishawn Dancers in New York City. Often rebelling against the directors' strict discipline, Louise was dismissed from the company in 1924. She danced in the chorus of *George White's Scandals* for three months before suddenly departing for London. Her capricious behavior and tendency to make quick, sudden decisions continued upon her return to the United States. For a time she appeared in Florenz Ziegfeld's musical comedy *Louie the 14th*, and despite her erratic behavior and frequent absences, Ziegfeld hired her for specialty dancing in the 1925–1926 edition of the Ziegfeld *Follies*.

Brooks's career as a dancer soon led to her screen debut in *Street of Forgotten Men*, filmed at Famous Players–Lasky studios in Astoria, Long Island, in May 1925. After a succession of roles in flapper movies, she emerged as an actress of considerable potential in Howard Hawks's *A Girl in Every Port* and William Wellman's *Beggars of Life*. With her famous bobbed black hair, spit curls curving across white cheeks, sultry eyes, and penetrating gaze, Brooks created a screen persona of beauty, sensuality, and eros.

In 1928, amidst a salary dispute, Brooks decided to leave Paramount. After her decision, B. P. Schulberg, head of production, informed Brooks that German filmmaker G. W. Pabst was interested in her for his next film. Schulberg cabled Pabst, and, in typical fashion, Brooks promptly sailed for Europe. Pabst had developed a script from Frank Wedekind's works *Der Erdgeist* (*The Earth Spirit*) and *Die Büchse der Pandora* (*Pandora's Box*). An expressionist, Wedekind was fascinated with Freudian theories of sexual repression and with the depraved lives of upper-class German society. In response he created "Lulu," a mythic character of beauty and intelligence whose primitive sexuality created havoc between men and women, often resulting in their destruction, and, eventually, her own.

Silent film provided Pabst the perfect vehicle for *Pandora's Box* as he utilized visual image and Brooks's erotic screen persona to fashion "his" Lulu. "I revered Pabst," Brooks recalled in her collection of essays, *Lulu in Hollywood* (1982), "for his truthful picture of this world of pleasure which let me play Lulu naturally." Although the special rapport of Pabst and Brooks created a Lulu who symbolized an era, resulting in one of cinema's most intriguing and erotic portrayals, the film was initially panned by critics and audience alike, and "for its open treatment of lasciviousness and prostitution . . . it ran afoul of the censors in and out of Germany" (Paris, p. 305).

After Lulu, in 1929 Brooks starred in Pabst's *Das Tagebuch einer Verlorenen* (*The Diary of a Lost Girl*), a film based on Margarethe Boehme's novel. Her last European film was *Prix de Beauté* (*Beauty Prize*), directed by Augusto Genina (Sofar Film, 1930). According to Brooks's recollections in "Pabst and Lulu" (1965), she went against Pabst's advice and his warning that her life was "exactly like Lulu's" and that she would "end the same way," returning to the United States to pursue a contract with Columbia Pictures. The contract never materialized. The popularity of talkies versus silent films was an issue Brooks could no longer ignore. Her films with Pabst had not been received well, and "Europe was thus a double flop: Louise not only failed to gain any sound-film experience there, but she appeared to be faltering even in the obsolete silent medium" (Paris, p. 349). In addition, Brooks was blacklisted by Paramount, who maintained that she owed them another film during her previous contract. She was also outspoken about her attitude toward Hollywood. Biographer Barry Paris reports, "It wasn't making pictures she hated—it was Hollywood" (Paris, p. 359), and her career irreversibly declined.

With the help of friends, Brooks appeared in minor roles in several movies. For a short time she returned to her first training—dance—and performed in a nightclub act before giving the movie industry one last opportunity. She appeared in *Empty Saddles* (1936), *King of Gamblers* (1937), *When You're in Love* (1937), and *Overland Stage Raiders* (1938), her last film, which also featured John Wayne. Finally finished with Hollywood, Brooks operated a dance studio from 1940 to 1943 in Wichita, Kansas, before moving to New York City. There she worked in radio soap operas and as a salesclerk for Saks Fifth Avenue. She quit Saks in 1948, existing solely on the generosity of friends and small loans from family members. In 1953 she was baptized into the Roman Catholic faith.

A quarter of a century after Brooks's films with Pabst, the efforts of James Card of Eastman House in Rochester and Henri Langlois of Cinémathèque Française in Paris revived public interest in her career. In 1955 Langlois featured Brooks in his "Sixty Years of Cinema" exhibition located at the Musée National d'Art Moderne. Through Card's urging, Brooks moved to Rochester in 1956 and began a new career as a writer and film historian. Although Card and Langlois generated new interest in Brooks and her films, Kenneth Tynan's article "The Girl in the Black Helmet—Louise Brooks" for the *New Yorker* created the "Brooks cult" and a horde of adoring fans. She was suddenly rediscovered and heralded as the most engaging and erotic actress of early film.

After her move to Rochester, Brooks wrote a number of articles for various film journals, including *Sight and Sound* and *Image*, among others. She emerged as an interesting writer with exacting, sometimes scathing observations of Hollywood and the film industry. She also compiled a collection of her writings loosely formatted as an autobiography entitled *Lulu in Hollywood* (1982).

Brooks was married twice, first to director Edward Sutherland (1926–1928), and then to Deering Davis for approximately six months in 1933. She was involved in numerous relationships, especially a long-term, stormy one with George Marshall, owner of the Washington Redskins. During the latter years of her life, she isolated herself from friends and family as she struggled with the aging process and the debilitating effects of osteoarthritis and emphysema. She died alone at her home in Rochester, New York.

Although Brooks glided before the movie camera with a dancer's ease, creating perhaps one of the most erotic screen personas in the history of film, her personal life and career often fell victim to her outspoken, quixotic personality. She was intelligent, quick-witted, and well read. At times, her life and that of the character Lulu seemed to merge until it was difficult to discern one from the other. It is not surprising that she never considered herself an actress, only someone who played herself.

Worth examining for writing style and content are Louise Brooks's essays published in various film journals, including: "Mr. Pabst," *Image* 5 (7 Sept. 1956); "Gish and Garbo," *Sight and Sound* (Winter 1958–1959); "ZaSu Pitts," *Objectif* (Aug. 1963); "Filmography—Positive and Negative," *Objectif* (Feb. 1964); "Pabst and Lulu," *Sight and Sound* (Summer 1965); "Marlene," *Positif* no. 75 (May 1966); "Letter to Andrew Sarris," *English Cahiers du Cinema* no. 3 (1966); "Charlie Chaplin Remembered," *Film Culture* no. 40 (Spring 1966): 5–6; "Buster Keaton," in *Double Exposure*, ed. Roddy McDowall (1966); "Humphrey and Bogey," *Sight and Sound* (Winter 1966–1967); "On Location with Billy Wellman," *London Magazine* (May 1968); "The Other Face of W. C. Fields," *Sight and Sound* (Spring 1971); "Actors and the Pabst Spirit," *Focus on film* no. 8 (Feb. 1972): 45–46; "Marion Davies' Niece," *Film Culture* nos. 58–60 (Oct. 1974); "Duke by Divine Right," introduction to Allen Eyles, *John Wayne* (1976); and "Why I Will Never Write My Memoirs," *Focus on Film* no. 15 (Mar. 1978): 31–34.

• Barry Paris's biography *Louise Brooks* (1989) is an important source for those interested in an in-depth view of her life. Roland Jaccard, ed., *Louise Brooks: Portrait of an Anti-Star* (1986), translated by Gideon Y. Schein, provides a unique look at Brooks through essays by the actress, Jaccard, Jean-Michel Palmier, Lotte H. Eisner, and others. Richard Leacock, *Lulu in Berlin* (1974), an interview with Louise Brooks and the only full-length documentary footage of her, is an excellent presentation of her wit, intelligence, and gift for storytelling. The great revival of interest in Louise Brooks can be partially attributed to Kenneth Tynan, "The Girl in the Black Helmet—Louise Brooks," *New Yorker*, 11 June 1979; it was reprinted in Tynan's *Show People* (1979). An obituary is in the *New York Times*, 10 Aug. 1985.

VIRGINIA A. PARRISH

BROOKS, Maria Gowen (c. 1795–11 Nov. 1845), poet, also known as "Maria del Occidente," was born Abigail Gowen in Medford, Massachusetts, the daughter of William Gowen, a goldsmith, and Eleanor Cutter. At her father's encouragement, by age nine Brooks had memorized extensive passages from a number of works, including John Milton's *Comus* and Joseph Addison's *Cato*, and "her conversation excited special wonder by its elegance, variety and wisdom" (Griswold, p. 61).

Following her father's bankruptcy and death in 1809, she came under the care of her widower brother-in-law, John Brooks, a successful Boston merchant with two sons. While she admired rather than loved him, they married in 1810 when she was probably fifteen and he was approaching fifty. Her new life was happy at first; however, shipping losses related to the War of 1812 drastically reduced her husband's wealth, and her family, which now included two newborn sons in addition to her stepchildren, moved to Portland, Maine. Finding little intellectual stimulation in these new surroundings, she wrote poetry to relieve her boredom. When she was nineteen or twenty, she completed an octosyllabic poem in seven cantos, which was never published, and began to compose numerous romantic lyrics. At this time she fell passionately in love with a young Canadian officer. This love interest is fictionalized in Brooks's prose romance, *Idomen: or, the Vale of Yumuri* (1843), in which the officer's name is given as Ethelwald, and it is alluded to in her poetry and correspondence, but little is known of the affair. For unknown reasons, in 1819 she changed her baptismal name legally to Mary Abigail Brooks, and shortly thereafter she began to call herself Maria Gowen Brooks.

In 1820 Brooks collected many of her lyrics in *Judith, Esther, and Other Poems, by a Lover of Fine Arts*. Although it did not receive extensive circulation, its critical reception was enthusiastic enough to convince her that she should continue to write and publish. John Brooks died in 1823, and Maria then moved with her children to Matanzas, Cuba, where her brother William lived on a coffee plantation owned by her maternal uncle. Enamored by the tropical beauty of Cuba, she made it the setting of *Idomen* and wrote in some of her lyrics of this "fair isle." At her request, a small summer house modeled after a Grecian temple was built on the plantation about 1825, and there she composed her poetry. On a visit to relatives in Canada she again met her beloved officer who now proposed marriage. Their engagement soon was mysteriously broken off, however, and Brooks in despair attempted suicide. Returning to Cuba helped alleviate her depression, and when her uncle died soon after, she became owner of the plantation. Relieved of financial worries by this inheritance, she began to work even more diligently on her poetry.

In 1825 she published in Boston the first canto of *Zóphiël; or, the Bride of Seven*. Based loosely on a story recounted in the apocryphal Book of Tobit, the poem is remarkable for its impassioned narration of a fallen angel's love for a mortal woman and for its mellifluous verse. Having nearly finished the remaining five cantos by 1829, Brooks took the manuscript to Hanover, New Hampshire, where her son Horace was studying for admittance to West Point. While in Hanover, she used the Dartmouth Library to write many of the explanatory notes that ultimately were published with *Zóphiël* and that demonstrate the wide range of her reading. Brooks then visited Europe with her brother Hammond and met Washington Irving, who encouraged her to publish her poem; Irving in turn introduced her to General Lafayette, the French hero of the American Revolution, who exerted his influence to ensure her son's entry to West Point.

Traveling to Keswick, England, in 1831, Brooks met the poet Robert Southey, an event she felt later was one of the most important of her life. She greatly admired Southey's works and several years earlier had sent him copies of *Judith, Esther, and Other Poems* and the first part of *Zóphiël*, along with a letter in which she described how she had "been crossed in love."

Southey, who called her epistle "the strangest letter" ever addressed to him (Granniss, p. 6), reluctantly paid the American a visit and was won over by her charm, intelligence, and poetic skill. He subsequently became one of her most vocal supporters, naming her "the most impassioned and most imaginative of all poetesses" (Granniss, p. 24), and offered to find an English publisher for *Zóphiël*. Leaving the manuscript in Southey's hands, she returned to the United States in 1831. The poem appeared in 1833 in both England and the United States under the pen name "Maria del Occidente," a pseudonym Brooks apparently had adopted before her meeting with Southey. The passionate heroine of *Zóphiël*, Egla, shocked some readers; the second stanza of "Egla's Song," from section seven of the sixth canto of the poem, is particularly notable for its depiction of sexual longing:

> Thou to whom I love to hearken,
> Come, ere night around me darken.
> Though thy softness but deceive me,
> Say thou'rt true and I'll believe thee;
> Veil, if ill, thy soul's intent,
> Let me think it innocent!

Brooks published a second American edition in 1834 at her own expense; only about twenty copies were sold, however, and she withdrew the book from the market. In spite of its poor sales, *Zóphiël* won the praise of several influential authors, among them John Quincy Adams (1767–1848), Rufus Wilmot Griswold, and Charles Lamb.

Brooks's last book, *Idomen* (1843), was a prose romance about which she claimed that "the principal incidents are related from the life" (Granniss, p. 31), although it is difficult to tell how far to trust the biographical accuracy of her narration. Certain events, such as Idomen's residence in Portland, Maine, accord with known facts of Brooks's life, while others, like Idomen's death, do not. The tale appeared serially in the Boston *Saturday Evening Gazette* (1838). Unable to secure a commercial publisher for a collected edition of her writings, she finally printed *Idomen* privately. The deaths of a son and a stepson in Cuba during this period necessitated her return to the island in December 1843 to oversee her business affairs. In 1844 she began composing her next epic poem, "Beatriz, the Beloved of Columbus," an unpublished work for which no manuscript has been discovered. She and her remaining stepson died in Matanzas of tropical fever.

Following her death, Henry Wadsworth Longfellow paid her the compliment of quoting from *Zóphiël* in *Kavanagh*, and Thomas Buchanan Read ranked her epic as "one of the most remarkable poems of the day" (*Female Poets of America* [1848], p. 17). Griswold articulated a widespread belief when he called her the most accomplished female poet America had yet produced. Although she has been neglected in the twentieth century, the estimations of these authors should not be carelessly dismissed. Sophisticated, passionate, and skillfully wrought, her work contains some of the most intriguing American poetry written in the first half of the nineteenth century.

• The manuscript of *Zóphiël* and a substantial collection of letters to and from Brooks are in the New York Public Library. Other correspondence and manuscripts are in the Beinecke Library, Yale University, and the Historical Society of Pennsylvania, Philadelphia. Zadel B. Gustafson's biographical introduction to her rare edition of *Zóphiël* (1879) contains information about Brooks provided by her son Horace; this essay is more widely available in *Harper's New Monthly Magazine*, Jan. 1879, pp. 249–61. Ruth Shephard Granniss, *An American Friend of Southey* (1913), is the standard biography. Granniss is usefully supplemented and corrected by Thomas Ollive Mabbott, "Maria del Occidente," in *The American Collector* 2, no. 5 (1926): 415–24. Rufus Wilmot Griswold's appreciative obituary, "The Late Maria Brooks," is in *Graham's Magazine*, Aug. 1848, pp. 61–68.

JEFFREY D. GROVES

BROOKS, Noah (24 Oct. 1830–16 Aug. 1903), journalist and author, was born in Castine, Maine, the son of Barker Brooks, a shipbuilder, and Margaret Perkins, the daughter of a ship captain. He attended schools in Castine until he left for Boston at age eighteen to study painting. His interests, however, soon turned to writing, and Brooks began submitting brief essays and funny stories to weekly periodicals such as the *Carpet Bag*, a small literary journal. Brooks also joined the staff of the *Boston Atlas*, an important Whig daily.

In 1855 Brooks moved to Dixon, Illinois, to start a cabinet-ware business with his friend John G. Brooks. The business failed as did his attempt at farming. In 1856 he married Caroline Augusta Fellows of Salem, Massachusetts, and returned to journalism as a reporter for the *Dixon Telegraph*. While covering the presidential election of 1856, Brooks met Abraham Lincoln, who was campaigning for John C. Frémont. Brooks and Lincoln became friends and remained so through the Lincoln-Douglas debates of 1858. When his financial situation worsened in 1859, Brooks left Dixon and set out on a five-month journey to California, with a brief stop in Kansas where he was active in the free state movement.

After settling in Marysville, California, in 1860, Brooks became co-owner of the *Daily Appeal*, along with Benjamin P. Avery who later served as U.S. minister to China. The *Daily Appeal* was a staunch Republican voice in a stronghold of proslavery Democrats, and it gave strong editorial support to Lincoln in the election of 1860. Brooks also contributed articles to the *Overland Monthly*, an arrangement that began a long-time friendship with its editor, Bret Harte. Brooks's wife died in 1862, apparently in childbirth. (Although there is no record of a child, Brooks later told friends that a son had died with his wife in childbirth.) In November 1862 Brooks sold his share in the *Daily Appeal* and left California for Washington, D.C., to serve as the correspondent of the *Sacramento Union*, the most important newspaper in California between 1851 and 1875.

Brooks, whose pen name was "Castine," gave the *Union*'s readers an insider's view of the Lincoln White

House that was unprecedented in the history of American journalism. He wrote 258 "letters," or major news stories, for the *Union* from December 1862 through 1865. Brooks is remembered for his intimate coverage of Lincoln and his family and is often quoted as an authority on Lincoln, despite the fact that his reporting covered the breadth of life during wartime in the federal capital. Brooks filed news reports about the Civil War from ten states and covered the Republican and Democratic national conventions of 1864. He also went into the field with the Army of the Potomac to report on the fighting firsthand.

Brooks visited the White House as often as two or three times a week. He grew close to the Lincoln family and was one of the few friends Mary Todd Lincoln had in the capital. Brooks also accompanied Lincoln on political trips and visits to various battlefields. The president sought Brooks's advice on California politics, patronage, and congressional issues that affected the state. Lincoln relied on Brooks for personal reports on the national political conventions of 1864 and would have named him to replace John G. Nicolay as his private secretary had Lincoln not been assassinated before he could do so. After the war ended, President Andrew Johnson appointed Brooks customs officer in San Francisco, but he was removed from the position after one and a half years because he refused to comply with Johnson's administration policies.

Brooks joined the staff of the *San Francisco Daily Times* in 1866 but left to become managing editor of the *Alta California*, the state's oldest newspaper, only a year later. While with the paper, Brooks encouraged a young typesetter, Henry George, to pursue writing, going so far as to publish some of George's early work. The *Alta California* was also responsible for publishing Mark Twain's travel letters from Europe, which were later published as *The Innocents Abroad*. During his tenure at the paper, Brooks befriended Twain and also resumed his relationship with Harte, who retained him as an adviser to the *Overland Monthly*.

Whitelaw Reid, editor of the *New York Tribune*, eventually persuaded Brooks to leave California in 1871 and become night editor of the paper. Five years later Brooks left the *Tribune* to become an editorial writer for the *New York Times*, in turn leaving that paper in 1884 when he was appointed editor of the *Newark Daily Advertiser* in New Jersey. However, none of Brooks's journalistic work was as significant as his Washington coverage of the Lincoln administration. He retired from journalism in 1892 but continued to write articles for magazines such as *Scribner's Monthly*, *Century*, and the popular juvenile magazine *St. Nicholas*. Brooks also wrote a number of books, including juvenile fiction. *The Boy Emigrants* (1876) and *The Boy Settlers* (1891) are considered excellent works of their genre. Brooks spent his remaining years at his home in Castine, Maine, which he called "The Ark." Suffering from chronic bronchitis, Brooks went to Pasadena, California, in 1903 to improve his health. He died there.

• The major source on Brooks's Washington career is his own *Washington in Lincoln's Time* (1895). First reprinted as *Washington, D.C., in Lincoln's Time* in 1962, the 1971 edition contains a useful biographical introduction by Herbert Mitgang. Helpful sources covering the history of Washington correspondence in Brooks's time are F. B. Marbut, *News from the Capital: The Story of Washington Reporting* (1971), and Donald A. Ritchie, *Press Gallery: Congress and the Washington Correspondents* (1991). James E. Pollard, *The Presidents and the Press* (1947), discusses the relationship between Brooks and Lincoln. Obituaries are in the *Los Angeles Times*, 17 Aug. 1903, as well as the *New York Times* and the *New York Herald Tribune*, both 18 Aug. 1903.

JOSEPH P. MCKERNS

BROOKS, Nona Lovell (22 Mar. 1861–14 Mar. 1945), cofounder of Divine Science (a New Thought religious movement), was born in Louisville, Kentucky, the daughter of Chauncey Brooks, a merchant and miner, and Lavinia Brigham. Brooks's family was large and prosperous, but her father's business reversal, followed by his death, caused the family's living standards to significantly decline. While Brooks was attending Charleston Female College (1878–1879), her mother and much of the family moved to Pueblo, Colorado. After graduating, Brooks joined them. Although Brooks's mother had hoped the move west would improve her health, she and several other family members, including Brooks who had a throat ailment, suffered from physical ills.

The family's poor financial condition, her failure to secure a satisfactory marriage proposal, and especially her declining health led Brooks and one of her sisters, Alethea Small, to attend a class on mental healing in 1887. Small's husband was a real estate partner of Charles Fillmore, who, together with his wife, Myrtle Fillmore, would found the Unity movement in 1889. The class was led by Katie Bingham, a student of Emma Curtis Hopkins, founder of the New Thought movement. Having been staunch Presbyterians, the sisters were reluctant to accept religious education from a teacher outside their tradition, but they finally decided to attend Bingham's class—apparently because of Brooks's continued ill health. Shortly thereafter, she was healed (1887), and the sisters abandoned Presbyterianism.

The class on mental healing marked the turning point in Brooks's life and began a process that led to the establishment of Divine Science. The sisters became active in the mental healing movement, and Brooks, with some reluctance, became a successful mental healer. Because she lacked confidence, Brooks reportedly hesitated to engage in mental healing, although from the outset she was a proficient healer. Although from 1887 onward she facilitated healings when requested by friends and family, she did not engage in the practice as a vocation until 1896.

Before that time, Brooks lived in Denver with her sister, Fannie James (1887), and in Louisville with her cousin, Lizzie Cecil (1888), and experienced disappointment in several courtships. James had been exposed to New Thought through another Hopkins protégée, Emma McCoy, and had become active in the movement. Brooks briefly pursued a teaching career, studying at the Pueblo Normal School and attending Wellesley College from 1889 to 1890. On her return to Colorado (1890) she taught elementary school in Pueblo and later Denver.

In Denver, Brooks found James leading a group of women in the study of mental healing. In 1893 Alethea was asked to come to Denver to assist James because James's husband would not allow his wife to leave the house in her healing work. The sisters' reunion helped lay the groundwork for the institutional establishment of Divine Science. Each sister played an important role in the group's early years, but the organizational impetus came from Malinda E. Cramer, another of Hopkins's students, who had established a mental healing group in San Francisco. Cramer called her group Divine Science, and after correspondence and a visit with James she approved the Denver ministry's use of the name. After Cramer's death in 1907, Denver became the center of Divine Science.

In 1896 Brooks gave up teaching school and fully committed herself to the ministry. Initially her work was devoted to mental healing, a service for which she was seldom paid. Unlike other mental healers, she apparently was timid about asking for remuneration. She remained steadfast in her commitment, however, and through her efforts and those of her sisters the Denver ministry attracted growing numbers of participants. Reportedly, Brooks excelled as a teacher and later as a preacher; of the three sisters, she appears to have been the most successful at healing.

By 1898 the ministry was incorporated as the Divine Science College, and Brooks was selected minister. At first reluctant to accept the calling, she later relented. She was ordained by Cramer in 1898 and conducted the first Sunday morning service in Divine Science history on 1 January 1899. Although reserved, even timid, Brooks served as minister of the Denver church and as leader of the Divine Science movement for thirty years. She was the first woman minister to perform a wedding in Denver. Although the Denver church prospered during her tenure, and many studied at the Divine Science College, she was not strongly committed to institutional development, and the number of churches affiliated with the movement remained small.

After resigning as leader of the Denver church in 1929, Brooks traveled widely, spending a year in Australia and later accepting many invitations to speak at churches, retreat centers, and the International New Thought Alliance (INTA). She finally settled in Chicago. There, she concluded her ministerial career as leader of a small Divine Science church from 1935 to 1938. In 1938 she returned to Denver to serve as president of the Divine Science College. Brooks never married. She died in Denver.

Although her own movement never extended beyond a few churches, Brooks's influence on the emergence of New Thought was significant. She contributed to the development of INTA, helped popularize New Thought in the Denver area, and directly influenced Ernest Holmes, Emmet Fox, and many less significant leaders of the movement. Much smaller than the two largest New Thought denominations (Unity and Religious Science), Divine Science, with some thirty churches, remains the movement's third largest group. It has always been the most loosely structured of the three. Like other New Thought groups, Divine Science has stressed the primacy of Mind in spiritual healing, the omnipotence and omnibenevolence of Deity/Mind, and the importance of personal freedom in religious pursuits.

• Reliable data on Brooks's life are difficult to find. Dates in several sources conflict, and details are scant. There are considerable biographical gaps, and no explanations are given for critical actions and events. Where information is lacking or obscure, the author's best judgment was used in selecting details and dates. Brooks wrote only a few booklets, *Basic Truths* (1921), *Mysteries* (1923), *The Prayer That Never Fails* (1935), *Short Lessons in Divine Science* (1928), and *Studies in Health* (1953). Her biography, *Powerful Is the Light* (1945), by Hazel Deane, is noncritical and lacks many dates. Brief biographical data can be found in chapters on Divine Science in Charles Braden, *Spirits in Rebellion* (1963); J. Stillson Judah, *The History and Philosophy of the Metaphysical Movements in America* (1967); and Martin A. Larson, *New Thought Religion* (1985).

DELL DECHANT

BROOKS, Peter Chardon (11 Jan. 1767–1 Jan. 1849), merchant, was born in North Yarmouth, Maine, the son of Congregationalist minister Edward Brooks and Abigail Brown. Brooks began his accumulation of wealth in 1789 when he presented himself in Boston for a mercantile apprenticeship. The colonies had only separated from England a dozen years earlier, France was in revolution, Europe was at war with itself, ports were closed, and the absence of an effective government under the Articles of Confederation had left American commerce in chaos, to be preyed upon by all belligerents. The high risks of the period made the writing of maritime insurance a profitable, if risky, endeavor. Brooks, operating from a Boston pub, established himself as agent for the Boston insurers, of whom there were only two or three, earning commissions by matching buyer and seller and taking occasional forays into trade.

For Brooks and other merchants like him, the 1790s were boom times. It was not long before Brooks began assembling insurance consortiums, taking for himself a management profit as well as commissions, enabling him to retire in 1803 at age thirty-six. Though he withdrew from commerce, he remained active as an investor until his death. By 1822 he was among a select handful of Boston's largest taxpayers.

Boston merchants of Brooks's generation had operated according to an informal code, forged amid the commercial turbulence of the 1790s, that sought to protect them from the consequences of exuberance and excessive greed. Raw, uninformed speculation was a specific taboo. Merchants so acculturated were uncomfortable with the speculative financial practices prevalent in the Jacksonian era. They were accustomed to dealing in tangibles, knew how to diversify and manage risk, and were meticulous in documenting their transactions. Investment in remote mill corporations whose stock prices fluctuated for incomprehensible reasons was at odds with Brooks's code concerning investment. Also, it must have been apparent to him and other successful and shrewd merchants that the textile industry's promotional orientation was rigged in favor of insiders and contained the seeds of its own downfall. Latecomers were more likely to be victims than beneficiaries of such frenzied expansion.

Such younger financiers as William Appleton viewed the reclusive Brooks as an independent thinker, not a trend follower and accorded him respect as a proven money maker. Brooks and his family invested modestly in early Lowell and Dover, New Hampshire, textile mills but avoided subsequent ill-conceived and eventually ruinous promotional fiascoes at Holyoke and Lawrence. Such infrequent entries in Brooks's diary as "Chardon gone to Lowell on factory business" suggest that textiles were never of overwhelming importance to him, and he remained aloof from the "cotton mill fever" craze that was to be the ruin of so many others. Short-term stock trading on inside information was a source of profit for many, but Brooks was not among these speculators. His papers suggest that he preferred investing in consortiums, pursuing conservative ventures that he knew and understood.

Brooks had a minor and undistinguished public career, but largely as an observer, for he seldom was vocal or at the center of events. As a merchant in the 1790s he supported the Federalist cause, and between 1815 and 1825 he served several terms as a Federalist in the Massachusetts legislature, long after that party's reason for existence had eroded. He is remembered for opposing the use of lotteries to finance public works, and he supported the construction of bridges and projects abetting commerce but little else. His Medford country estate was made into a model experimental farm. He actively supported causes promoting agriculture, serving as president of the Massachusetts Agricultural Society. Cryptic handwritten notations in the margins of his account books reveal a literal, taciturn, and slightly pompous individual who was taken with his own material success but not entirely secure about its permanence. He made frequent excuses for purchasing an expensive carriage, saying that if his fortunes changed he could always discard it.

Brooks's principal legacy, as with the Appletons and Lawrences, was to provide his descendants with an economic stepping stone to the aristocracy. Money, and the power that went with it, was to take on a greater role in class relations as the economy expanded. While Brooks's ambitions appear to have been fulfilled with wealth, aristocratic status had to await his children. Members of his generation were still too close to the source of their wealth, the rough and tumble of the counting house and quarter deck, and they never quite acquired the polish, aloofness, self-satisfaction, and contempt for the mundane that was to characterize their leisured descendants. Brooks's personality, like that of most first-generation merchants, had been forged amid the white hot fires of the commercial turbulence that followed the Revolution. Success in that world depended on being shrewd, intense, aggressive, and tough, as well as developing a hard outer shell, hardly the genteel cloth from which aristocracy is cut. Brooks died Boston's richest man, with an estate of $3.1 million, a sum that only David Sears, Eben Francis, and a few other merchants could approach.

• The Brooks family manuscripts, including the diaries and account books of Peter Chardon Brooks, are at the Massachusetts Historical Society. Reliable biographical resources are sparse and consist of sanctimonious memoirs by Brooks's sons-in-law. These include C. F. Adams, "A Memoir of Peter Chardon Brooks," *N.E. Historical and Genealogical Register* 8 (Oct. 1854) and 9 (Jan. 1855); and "Peter Chardon Brooks," in Freeman Hunt's *Lives of American Merchants*, vol. 1 (1858), pp. 333–83. Both were written when the textile industry was suffering the consequences of earlier promotional excesses, and they canonize Brooks as the archetypal prudent Boston financier. Background about the Boston financial community and the textile industry, based on extensive personal and corporate manuscript collections, including the Brooks papers, is in Robert V. Spalding, "The Boston Mercantile Community and the Promotion of the Textile Industry in New England, 1811–1860" (Ph.D. diss., Yale Univ., 1963).

ROBERT VARNUM SPALDING

BROOKS, Phillips (13 Dec. 1835–23 Jan. 1893), preacher and Episcopal bishop of Massachusetts, was born in Boston, Massachusetts, the son of William Gray Brooks, a successful businessman, and Mary Ann Phillips. Brooks's parents were of the New England aristocracy and keenly interested in the education of their six sons. Members of Mary Brooks's family had founded Phillips Andover Academy (1778), Phillips Exeter Academy (1781), and the conservative, Congregationalist Andover Theological Seminary (1805). Brooks and his brothers went to the Boston Latin School and to Harvard College, where they excelled. Phillips entered Harvard in 1851 and received his A.B. in 1855. Because he was an accomplished linguist, Brooks was then hired to teach Latin at the Boston Latin School, but he was unable to keep discipline in his class, and he was asked to hand in his resignation. It was a disastrous experience, a failure that left him deeply depressed.

In October 1856 he decided to attend Virginia Theological Seminary. He had been baptized in the elite First Church of Boston, of which his ancestor John Cotton had been the first minister. That same year, 1835, the congregation became Unitarian, and in 1839 a discontented Mary Brooks moved the family to the more Calvinistic and evangelical St. Paul's Episcopal Church. While the Brookses held family prayers, and the boys memorized a new hymn each week, Phillips showed no unusual interest in religion, and only after his first year at seminary did he seek the rite of confirmation. He did not find Virginia Theological Seminary intellectually stimulating, however, and read widely on his own: the church fathers, Goethe, Shelley, Browning, Coleridge's *Aids to Reflection*, and later F. D. Maurice. From his extensive notebooks it is clear that he focused on Christology, emphasized the doctrine of justification by grace through faith, and had a high regard for the Puritan tradition of preaching. By the time he received his B.D. in 1859, he had worked out an unusually mature theology for a twenty-three year old. His letters reveal as well the tensions under which he studied: dislike of southern society, revulsion at slavery, and a sense of impending national catastrophe.

Brooks was ordained on 1 July 1859 and became rector of the Church of the Advent in Philadelphia. In 1862 he moved to Holy Trinity Church in the same city, where he remained until his election in 1869 as rector of Trinity Church, Boston. During the Civil War he was an outspoken supporter of the Union. He believed not only in the abolition of slavery, but in black enfranchisement; he preached regularly to Negro regiments, was an active member of the Freedmen's Relief Association, and was successful in opening the city's streetcars to black passengers. Immediately after the assassination of the president in April 1865, Brooks preached a sermon, "The Character, Life, and Death of Abraham Lincoln." It drew national attention. On 21 July 1865 Brooks was invited to give the invocation at Harvard's Commemoration Day for the college's war dead. His prayer, given without notes, was described as a "fiery stream of thanksgiving and supplication." President Charles W. Eliot judged that "a young prophet had risen up in Israel." Brooks also gained attention as a poet when, sometime shortly after attending a Christmas Eve service in the Holy Land in 1865, he wrote "O Little Town of Bethlehem."

At Trinity Church in the 1870s Brooks reawoke the somnolent aesthetic strain in the New England mind and combined it with moral earnestness. The professional and social leaders of Boston who attended Trinity Church wanted beauty in language, in architecture, and in worship, and they responded both to Brooks's analytical intellect and to his poetic imagination. He appeared to converse with his congregation rather than lecture to them. He preached rapidly, but without emotional display. His voice was high-pitched and easily heard; his language was neither ornamented nor extravagant. He never wore clerical garb other than the traditional preacher's black gown, and he showed no sign of ecclesiastical *hauteur*. In 1873 a new church was designed to provide a stunning architectural setting for Brooks's preaching. It was the work of the great architect Henry Hobson Richardson; interior designer Stanford White, and artist John La Farge, all friends of Brooks's cousin Henry Adams. The building was not completed until 9 February 1877. In 1884 Adams wrote *Esther*, a thinly disguised novel about Brooks and the building of Trinity. Though Romanesque in style, Trinity marked a reaction against the anglo-catholic, Gothic revival; its massive pulpit signaled a self-conscious renewal of Protestant preaching.

In 1877, in his famous "Lectures on Preaching" at Yale University, Brooks defined the sermon as the proclamation of truth through personality. In 1879 he spoke more of substance than of form in the Bohlen Lectures given in Philadelphia, "The Influence of Jesus." These lectures were the culmination of two decades of attention to the literary sense of the New Testament. Reflecting, respectively, the English theologian F. D. Maurice and the American Horace Bushnell, Brooks asked: What is the relation between divinity and humanity in the Incarnation and in the Atonement? Again and again Brooks emphasized that in Christ God and man had met. What then, he continued, were man's capabilities as seen in Jesus Christ? Considerable, was the reply, if individuals grow into the image of Christ. For Brooks the gospels were not so much about Jesus of Nazareth, recognizably himself in his severity, unobsessive love, and natural gentleness, but about the aesthetic and moral potential Jesus promises in the midst of, to quote Brooks's hymn, our "hopes and fears."

Throughout his life Brooks traveled widely in Europe, Asia, and America. He once preached before Queen Victoria (1880) and was offered but turned down numerous college presidencies, professorships, and bishoprics. On 29 April 1891 he accepted election to be bishop of Massachusetts, but his rejection of theories of apostolic succession; his New England "Congregationalism," as his opponents put it (that is, his openness to Protestantism); and his participation in interdenominational services of both preaching and ordination elicited a storm of protest from anglo-catholics. Not until 10 July 1891 were the necessary consents of diocesan standing committees and bishops obtained. In the meantime, both the secular and the religious press throughout the nation kept track of the balloting. Brooks was consecrated bishop on 14 October 1891. Fifteen months later he died, probably of diphtheria. On the day of his funeral, 26 January 1893, businesses closed throughout Boston; thousands gathered in Copley Square and witnessed the long procession to Harvard Yard and then to Mount Auburn Cemetery where he was buried.

Brooks never married, but speculations of two unrequited loves have persisted. As a young man within the Episcopal church his flashes of wit and sarcasm made him enemies; Christians in other denominations, however, responded to his fellow feeling. On Brooks himself the denominational label barely stuck. Theologically he has been called a Christo-centric liberal, that is, a "broad churchman," though he denied it. Toward the end of his life he reasserted the Augustinian Calvinist doctrine of the will, rather than the intellect, as the source of Christian response to the Gospel. William Lawrence declared about Brooks that the "theology of Calvinism ran in his blood."

Against the background of nineteenth-century religious divisions in New England between Unitarians, Edwardsean Calvinists, and Transcendentalists, Brooks sought to restate orthodox trinitarianism. He avoided formal, doctrinal preaching, however, and by means of neoplatonic imagery of light sought to awaken faith in the divine-human person, Jesus Christ. Brooks was a moralist and antimodernist who preached to the hopes and consciences of individuals. As a result, he has been claimed by both conservative evangelicals and by liberal Christians.

• Phillips Brooks's papers, including sermons, notebooks, photographs, and voluminous correspondence, are in the Houghton Library of Harvard University. His most important publications are *Lectures on Preaching* (1877), *The Influence of Jesus* (1879), and *Essays and Addresses: Religious, Literary, and Social* (1892). There are ten volumes of his sermons; the most notable are *Sermons* (1878), *The Candle of the Lord* (1881), and *The Light of the World and Other Sermons* (1890). The famous "Character, Life, and Death of Abraham Lincoln" was published in the *Historical Magazine of the Protestant Episcopal Church* 49 (Mar. 1980), with an introduction by Bayard S. Clark. See also Clark, "My Treasure Hunt for the Unpublished Manuscript Sermons of Phillips Brooks," and a formerly unpublished sermon of Brooks's, "The Witness of His Own Mouth," published together in *Anglican and Episcopal History* 60 (Mar. 1991). A. V. G. Allen, *Life and Letters of Phillips Brooks* (2 vols., 1900), and Raymond W. Albright, *Focus on Infinity: A Life of Phillips Brooks* (1961), are important, if uncritical, sources. Albright's bibliography is helpful. There are two extant portraits of Brooks; one is in the library of Trinity Church, Boston, the other in St. Paul's Cathedral, Boston (the best portrait, by Mrs. Henry Whitman, has been lost; a photograph of it appears in the Allen biography, vol. 2, opposite p. 664).

JOHN F. WOOLVERTON

BROOKS, Preston Smith (6 Aug. 1819–27 Jan. 1857), U.S. congressman, was born in Edgefield, South Carolina, the son of Whitfield Brooks, Sr., a planter, and Mary Parsons Carroll. Brooks was an eldest son born into one of the most influential planter families in antebellum South Carolina. Connected by marriage to the leading families in Edgefield District and upcountry South Carolina, the Brooks line stood proudly among the state's ruling elite. The sons of planters, as befitting their status and wealth, were socialized to live by a code of honor that placed a premium on absolute loyalty to family, kin, and section. Manliness of spirit in defense of honor, the direct antithesis of the presumed submissiveness of the docile slave, was the highest and most esteemed male virtue. This was one of the most important lessons Brooks learned in his private education, first at the Moses Waddel school in Willington and then at the College of South Carolina, the training ground for the state's future leaders.

Brooks was a bright student but something of a headstrong troublemaker during his college days, and in 1839, the year he was to graduate, the trustees expelled him and denied him his diploma. The following year, in an affair that originated in insults directed against his father, Brooks fought a duel with future U.S. senator Louis T. Wigfall. Although wounded in the hip, Brooks survived the duel and in 1841 married Caroline H. Means. After Caroline's death in 1841, he married her cousin, Martha C. Means, in 1843; they had four children.

By the mid-1840s Brooks was settling down to the life of a lawyer-planter. He was admitted to the bar in 1845 and served two years in the South Carolina legislature. With the outbreak of the Mexican War in 1846, however, he eagerly grasped the opportunity to win military glory and honorific fame for himself and his family. He enlisted as a captain in the Palmetto Regiment, a group of volunteers that included many of the sons of Edgefield's most distinguished families.

While on duty in Mexico, Brooks contracted typhoid and was forced to return home in June 1847. Although he rejoined his regiment in September, the bulk of the fighting was over, and he saw no action in any major battle. The fame he desired had eluded him. Especially in light of the fact that his younger brother, Whitfield Brooks, Jr., had died a hero's death in Mexico, Brooks emerged from the war with a sense of inadequacy and personal failure. His honor was further slighted when the Edgefield community ignored him in a ceremony on 4 July 1849, in which swords were presented to Edgefield's gallant sons who had fought in Mexico. Considering himself "unjustly neglected," Brooks reacted by questioning the courage of Milledge Luke Bonham, who had received a sword, and almost fought a duel with Bonham.

In a diary that he kept in the early 1850s, Brooks revealed himself as a loving husband, a caring parent, and a deeply religious individual wracked by doubts over his worthiness as a Christian. For all the tenderness and sensitivity of his private side, however, Brooks the public figure remained committed to the southern code of chivalry, a code that sanctioned the use of violence to avenge a personal insult. That code, and perhaps his desire to win the honor denied him in the Mexican War, drove Brooks to attack Senator Charles Sumner of Massachusetts on 22 May 1856 in the U.S. Senate. The attack was a tremendous boost to the Republicans in the election of 1856, for it gave the party a martyr and was a potent symbol of southern violence against the antislavery movement.

Brooks had been in Congress as a representative from the Fourth South Carolina District since March 1853. He spoke only occasionally and was identified with the moderate faction of South Carolina politicians willing to work with the national Democratic party. Had it not been for his reaction to Sumner's "Crime against Kansas" speech of 20 May 1856, Brooks most likely would have remained a relatively obscure congressman. Sumner's vituperatively antisouthern speech, which included insulting references to Senator Andrew Pickens Butler of South Carolina, violated Brooks's sense of honor. Butler, Brooks's cousin, was absent during the speech, and Brooks sought revenge for his kinsman, his state, and his section. On the afternoon of 22 May, after the Senate had adjourned, Brooks entered the Senate chamber and savagely beat Sumner on the head with ten to thirty blows from a gutta-percha cane.

The caning provoked a storm of reaction throughout the nation. In the North Brooks was denounced as a savage, the bestial product of an inhumane system of slavery. In the South he was hailed as a hero with the courage to defend southern honor. In July, after hearing the report of a special Investigating Committee, a majority in the House voted to expel Brooks. The very sectionalized vote, however, fell short of the necessary two-thirds majority to force expulsion. After declaring to the House in defense of his attack on Sumner that he would have "forfeited my own self-respect, and perhaps the good opinion of my countrymen, if I had failed to resent such an injury," Brooks resigned from Congress and ran for his vacated seat in a special election. He was overwhelmingly reelected.

Shortly after his return to Congress, Brooks died at his boardinghouse in Washington from a severe cold. Funeral services were held in the Capitol, and an immense crowd attended the ceremony. Large groups of well-wishers and glowing tributes followed his hearse on its journey south to Edgefield. Brooks would have been proud of the engraving on the monument erected in his honor in the Edgefield cemetery. It proclaimed him "ever able, manly, just and heroic."

• The Preston Brooks Papers are in the South Caroliniana Library at the University of South Carolina. There is no biography of Brooks, but a fine short treatment can be found in Robert Neil Mathis, "Preston Smith Brooks: The Man and His Image," *South Carolina Historical Magazine* 79 (1978): 296–310. The best source for the caning of Sumner is U.S. Congress. House. *House Report No. 182.* 34th Cong., 1st sess. For the political impact of the caning, see William E. Gienapp, "The Crime against Sumner: The Caning of Charles Sumner and the Rise of the Republican Party," *Civil War History* 25 (1979): 218–45. For the local community and culture that were so central in shaping his character, see Orville Vernon Burton, *In My Father's House Are Many Mansions: Family and Community in Edgefield, South Carolina* (1985).

WILLIAM L. BARNEY

BROOKS, Richard Edwin (28 Oct. 1865–2 May 1919), sculptor, was born in Braintree, Massachusetts, the son of John Brooks, a spinner, and Julia Arnold, both emigrants from the British Isles. Brooks belonged to the class of largely self-trained artists (he had no formal training until the age of about twenty), but early on he displayed an artistic flair and spent most of his formative years modeling and carving. He worked for a time in the workshop of a terra-cotta company and subsequently studied in Boston with Truman H. Bartlett at the Massachusetts Institute of Technology.

Around 1888 Brooks was sufficiently encouraged by his work with Bartlett to open his own business as a commercial sculptor and designer of cemetery monuments. His work was noticed by Massachusetts governor William Eustis Russell who commissioned Brooks to do his portrait. Before embarking on the project, Brooks went to Paris for additional study, first at the Académie Colarossi with Jean Paul Aubé and then with Jean Antoine Injalbert. He completed the Russell bust and had it cast in bronze by 1894 and entered it in the Paris Salon of that year. In the Paris Salon of 1895, Brooks entered his *Chant de la Vague* (The Song of the Wave), a nude female figure. It won an honorable mention, and Brooks began to be noticed. At the Paris Salon of 1899 he received a gold medal, third class. In 1897 he had received a commission to do a statue of Colonel Thomas Cass, commander of an all-Irish regiment, who had died in the American Civil War. This statue won the gold medal, first class, for Brooks at the 1900 Paris Exposition and is now in the Boston Public Garden. These awards were followed in 1901 with a gold medal from the Pan-American Exposition held in Buffalo, New York, for the Cass statue and other pieces.

Brooks remained abroad until 1911, when he returned to the United States to supervise the placement of his statue of John Mifflin Hood, a longtime railroad president and civic leader, in Baltimore, Maryland. This bronze statue, now situated at St. Paul and Saratoga streets, was erected by the city of Baltimore to commemorate the civic services of Hood. Brooks returned to Paris late in 1911, hoping to quickly wrap up his affairs there so that he could move back to the United States. He wound up having to stay for a couple of years. Early in 1914 he opened a studio in Washington, D.C.; later, and until his death, he worked and lived in Boston. In 1915 his work was awarded a silver medal at the Panama-Pacific International Exposition held in San Francisco.

Brooks's work can be found in several major U.S. museums. The Metropolitan Museum of Art in New York City owns *Chant de la Vague* as well as another Brooks bronze, *The Bather*, both of which were acquired in about 1911. Two statues by Brooks that were commissioned by the state of Maryland, one of Charles Carroll of Carrollton, the other of John Hanson, were that state's nominees to National Statuary Hall in the U.S. Capitol, which houses ninety-three such statues. A commission named by the Maryland General Assembly had approached Augustus Saint-Gaudens and Daniel Chester French. Both declined the job, but Saint-Gaudens highly recommended Brooks, and on the basis of his recommendation, Brooks was given the commission in late 1899 or early 1900. He is also represented in Seattle, Washington, by public statues of William H. Seward and one-term governor John Harte McGraw. Brooks also worked on a facade of the Connecticut State Capitol in Hartford and sculpted a bronze tablet for the Corcoran School of Art in Washington, D.C. The tablet, which depicts the school's first principal, E. F. Andrews, was unveiled in 1917.

The last work by Brooks, a plaque of Boston mayor James M. Curley, received favorable reviews. He also completed medallions of fifteen mayors of Boston that still hang in the mayor's office of that city. Brooks is remembered as a fine portrait medalist, having learned the French technique of lightness of touch and subtlety of expression. Also in Boston are the aforementioned bust of Governor Russell as well as a marble bust of Colonel Gardiner Tufts, both in the State House. The Boston Public Library has a bust of General Francis Amasa Walker, who was a library trustee, and a bronze bust of physician Oliver Wendell Holmes (1809–1894).

Brooks belonged to the standard professional societies of his time: the National Sculpture Society, the National Institute of Arts and Letters, and the Society of Washington Artists. He served as chairman of the jury of awards on sculpture at the Louisiana Purchase Exposition held in St. Louis, Missouri, in 1904. Brooks's legacy consists not only of full-size statues but also of busts and medallions. His work is found on both the Atlantic and Pacific coasts, with a concentration in his home city of Boston, where he died.

• The files of the Curator's Office, Architect of the Capitol, Washington, D.C., contain some general biographical information on Brooks. These files are kept in connection with his National Statuary Hall work. See the *Baltimore American*, 12 Jan. 1900, for more information on the selection of Brooks by Maryland's Statuary Hall commission. Also see *Leslie's Weekly Illustrated*, 25 Nov. 1897, p. 341, for information about his work in Boston and on the Cass monument.

PHILIP H. VILES, JR.

BROOKS, Van Wyck (16 Feb. 1886–2 May 1963), literary critic and cultural historian, was born in Plainfield, New Jersey, the son of Charles Edward Brooks, a stockbroker, and Sarah Bailey Ames. From the beginning, Van Wyck Brooks was precocious. He did well in the Plainfield public schools, profited intellectually from a whirlwind year mostly with his mother and brother in England, France, Germany, and Italy (1898), and in due time entered Harvard (1904). While there, he associated with many fellow students, notably Maxwell Perkins, who were also inclined toward literary careers. Brooks privately published some poetry (1905), became an editor of the *Harvard Advocate* (1905), and, although enrolled in the class of 1908, graduated a year early and was a member of Phi Beta Kappa.

Brooks tried briefly but could not manage to initiate a literary career in New York City; so he went for two years to England, wrote for journals, and published *The Wine of the Puritans: A Study of Present-day America* (London, 1908; New York, 1909). Cast in the form of a dialogue between a practical and an idealistic American, this book deplores the fact that the original settlers of New England poured their European culture (old wine) into an explosive new environment (new bottles)—the twofold result being American Transcendentalism (delicate aroma) and commercialism (spoiled wine). Taking to heart his pleas for the emergence of an organic American culture, he returned to New York, where he supported himself by various writing chores (1909–1911).

After moving to Carmel, California, in 1911 he married Eleanor Kenyon Stimson, a Plainfield friend from childhood. The couple had two children. Brooks wrote as much as he could while spending what he felt was too much time and energy teaching composition and survey courses in British and American literature at Stanford (1911–1913). While there, he attended meetings held by local Socialists and was influenced by Stanford faculty Socialists, including Hindu philosopher Har Dayal and economist Max Lippett. (It is thought that in the 1912 presidential election Brooks voted for Socialist party candidate Eugene V. Debs.) Meanwhile, Brooks was working on biographies of H. G. Wells and John Addington Symonds.

The years 1913–1914 found the Brookses back in England and France. Brooks taught at a workers' association and also published *The Malady of the Ideal* (1913), concerning French novelist Étienne de Sénancour, French poet Maurice de Guérin, and Swiss critic Henri Frédéric Amiel. In this work, Brooks theorizes that writers obsessed by universal ideality fail to compromise with reality and hence wither. More significant were three books he completed in England but published after he and his family returned home at the outbreak of World War I. They are *John Addington Symonds: A Biographical Study* (1914), *The World of H. G. Wells* (1915), and *America's Coming-of-Age* (1915). Brooks reasoned that whereas Symonds let the puritanical establishment force him to hate the world, Wells saw science and socialism combining to create a fine new order. In *America's Coming-of-Age*, a manifesto containing astute theoretical insights, Brooks divided America into "Highbrow" (post-Puritan, Transcendental gentility—often meaningless) and "Lowbrow" (opportunistic, materialistic commercialism—often mindless). He praised Walt Whitman for uniquely harmonizing American idealism and materialism, reviled capitalism (even when paternalistic) in favor of socialism, and called for the gradual, not radical, humanizing and liberalizing of American culture. During the years 1918–1924 Brooks published translations of books in French by Henry Malherbe (an appeal to French patriotism) and by Léon Bazalgette (on Henry David Thoreau); Brooks and his wife also translated Georges Berguer's psychological biography of Jesus.

Brooks coedited and published in the *Seven Arts*, a short-lived liberal, pacifist magazine (1916–1917). It called for a conscious effort to unify America culturally, decried political nationalism and materialism, and encouraged experimental literature. Brooks collected his seven essays from it in *Letters and Leadership* (1918), in which he criticizes America's excessive reliance on puritanism, materialism, false optimism, and unimaginative pragmatism, and urges cultural leaders to develop an organically centralized community of the arts. The book gained him national prominence as a critic.

His next two major books stirred violent controversy. They are *The Ordeal of Mark Twain*, published in 1920, during which year he and his family moved to Connecticut, and *The Pilgrimage of Henry James*, published in 1925. Brooks theorized that Twain crippled himself by surrendering to eastern Christian commercialism and profeminist criticism, failed to express what should have been an unbridled personality, and developed a dual nature because of the vestigial remains of his Calvinistic Mississippi Valley childhood. Brooks theorized that James disastrously deracinated himself from his vigorous American heritage by expatriating himself in England, where he failed to sink nourishing roots, and came to stress "vapid" form over popularly meaningful content. Brooks contended that American acquisitiveness caused both Twain and James to miss true greatness. While working on these two controversial studies, Brooks also wrote critical articles and weekly reviews for the *Freeman* (1920–1924), which he also coedited.

Even as he was planning a biography of the idealistic Ralph Waldo Emerson, Brooks grew depressed, harbored thoughts of suicide, suffered nervous breakdowns, and was periodically hospitalized (1926–1931). He became a worry and a burden to his family. While recovering, Brooks was flattened by the suicide of his devoted brother Ames in 1931. In 1932 Brooks published *The Life of Emerson* and *Sketches in Criticism* (containing some of his *Freeman* pieces). More significant, however, was what followed. With great patience and care, Brooks wrote his five-volume masterpiece, *Makers and Finders: A History of the Writer in America, 1800–1915* (1952), the five parts of which are *The Flowering of New England, 1815–1865* (1936; Pulitzer Prize winner in history, 1937), *New England: Indian Summer, 1865–1915* (1940), *The World of Washington Irving* (1944), *The Times of Melville and Whitman* (1947), and *The Confident Years: 1885–1915* (1952). These classics trace the history of mainstream American literature. They have been praised and criticized for being solid, detailed, and knowledgeable but also sentimental, replete with unneeded information, and reductive.

Brooks's last busy decades were marked by an ever-increasing conservatism and a kind of "middlebrow" style—neither "high" nor "low." Brooks assembled old and new critical perceptions in book form: *A Chilmark Miscellany* (1948) and *From a Writer's Notebook* (1955; enl. ed., 1958). He also wrote biographies of John Sloan (1955), Helen Keller (1956), William Dean Howells (1959), and Ernest Francisco Fenollosa (1962). A unique book by Brooks is *The Dream of Arcadia: American Writers and Artists in Italy, 1760–1915* (1958). It dramatizes its author's lifelong dilemma: Brooks intellectually admired Americans who sought cultural inspiration abroad, but at the same time he patriotically—even jingoistically—lamented their prolonged expatriation. Eleanor Brooks died in 1946. Brooks married Gladys Rice Saltonstall Billings in 1947, and they traveled together to the British Isles (1951, 1959) and Italy (1956). Brooks reminisces charmingly in a three-volume autobiography: *Scenes and Portraits: Memories of Childhood and Youth* (1954), *Days of the Phoenix: The Nineteen Twenties I Remember* (1957), and *From the Shadow of the Mountain: My Post-Meridian Years* (1961). He died in Bridgewater, Connecticut.

Van Wyck Brooks was one of the important literary critics of his era. He helped fellow American intellectuals, and less academically trained readers as well, recognize the dangers of rigid puritanism, indifferent expatriation, and capitalistic industrialism, and also appreciate the accomplishments of all of the major and many of the minor figures in America's complex literary past.

• Brooks's papers are located in more than seventy American library collections, but the most important collections are in the Museum of the American Academy of Arts and Letters, New York, and in the Charles Patterson Van Pelt Library, University of Pennsylvania. A lengthy primary and secondary bibliography is in *Van Wyck Brooks: The Early Years, A Selection from His Works, 1908–1925*, ed. with an introduction and notes by Claire Sprague (1968; rev. ed., 1993). Brooks's three autobiographical volumes were reprinted in one volume as *An Autobiography* (1965, foreword by John Hall Wheelock and introduction by Malcolm Cowley). *The Van Wyck Brooks–Lewis Mumford Letters: The Record of a Literary Friendship, 1921–1963* (1970), with an illuminating introduction by the editor, Robert E. Spiller, reveals the separate strengths but mainly the intellectual and emotional symbiosis of two of the leading minds of their epoch. Three excellent evaluative biographies are James R. Vitelli, *Van Wyck Brooks* (1969); James Hoopes, *Van Wyck Brooks: In Search of American Culture* (1977); and Raymond Nelson, *Van Wyck Brooks: A Writer's Life* (1981). William Wasserstrom in *The Legacy of Van Wyck Brooks: A Study of Maladies and Motives* (1971) theorizes on Brooks's love-hate relationship to American culture. Critical essays on Brooks, ranging from laudatory to venomous, are collected in Wasserstrom, ed., *Van Wyck Brooks: The Critic and His Critics* (1979). A lengthy obituary, including a portrait, is in the *New York Times*, 3 May 1963.

ROBERT L. GALE

BROOKS, Walter Henderson (30 Aug. 1851–6 July 1945), clergyman, temperance leader, and poet, was born in Richmond, Virginia, the son of Albert Royal Brooks and Lucy Goode, slaves. Brooks's father was an enterprising slave who owned his own "snack house" and a livery business that brought him into contact with some of Virginia's wealthiest citizens, including his wife's owner, German consul Daniel Von Groning. Albert Brooks purchased his wife's freedom in 1862 for $800. Still a slave, Walter Brooks at age seven was sold to the Turpin & Yarborough tobacco firm. He woefully recalled his time there, writing: "It was all I could do to perform the task assigned to my little hands. What I do remember is that I stood in mortal fear of 'the consequences' of failing to do what was required of me." When the Richmond manufacturer fell victim to wartime economic decline, Brooks was allowed to reside with his mother and began working in hotels, boardinghouses, and restaurants. In his youth he acquired the doctrines that served as the foundation for his life's work. He learned temperance from his pastor, the Reverend Robert Ryland, who taught songs at Christmas to curb the consumption of "egg-nog and the drinking of wine in countless homes," and Brooks's parents instilled "lessons of uprightness and sobriety."

After the Union victory in the Civil War, Brooks worked to make a place for himself in the world. In 1866 he entered the preparatory program at Lincoln

University, a Presbyterian school founded for African Americans in Pennsylvania. He obtained his college degree in 1872 and one year later earned his theological degree. He joined the Ashmun Presbyterian Church in Lincoln in 1868. When he returned to Richmond after graduation, he changed denominations and was baptized into the First African Baptist Church. In 1874 he married the pastor's daughter, Eva Holmes; they had ten children.

Between 1874 and 1876 Brooks worked with the American Baptist Publication Society as a Sunday school missionary in Virginia. He gained national attention for his views on temperance when he addressed the society at its anniversary meeting in Philadelphia in 1875. His speech, entitled "Facts from the Field," sparked controversy when he "drew a picture of the drinking habits of preachers" in an effort to illustrate the critical need for temperance. That same year Brooks became the chaplain of the Anti-Saloon League of the District of Columbia. He retained this position until 1882.

Brooks's greatest legacy came from his work as a Baptist minister. In 1876 he was formally ordained into the ministry and a year later became pastor of the Second African Baptist Church of Richmond. In 1880 he momentarily returned to his missionary work, but by 1882 he had accepted the pastorate of the Nineteenth Street Baptist Church in Washington, D.C. Over the next sixty-three years Brooks established a national reputation. He assisted John W. Cromwell in creating the Virginia Historical and Literary Society and for a time served as vice president in the Bethel Literary and Historical Association in Washington, D.C. Brooks was a trustee of Nannie H. Burroughs's National Training School for Women and Girls and the Virginia Theological Seminary and College in Lynchburg, Virginia. He supported the black women's club movement, and in 1896 his church was the site of the foundational meeting of the National Association of Colored Women.

Brooks played an important role in efforts to build and maintain a national black Baptist convention. He was chairman of the American National Baptist Convention's Bureau of Education, a black organization founded in 1886, and he continuously mediated relationships with national white Baptist conventions. In 1889 the American Baptist Publication Society, in an effort to increase black participation, agreed to accept literary contributions from Brooks and two of his colleagues for its regular publication. The society, however, reneged on its offer when its southern white contingency voiced opposition. The society opted instead to create a special publication for black clergymen, the *Negro Baptist Pulpit*. Though Brooks authored an article for that volume, he and his colleagues were infuriated by this palliative act and predicted it would typify future relations. Further difficulties led eventually to the formation of a black-controlled denominational body, the National Baptist Convention, U.S.A., in 1895.

Brooks's intellectual capabilities and dedication earned him recognition as an exceptional scholar. He wrote a number of essays on the history and development of black Baptist organizations and their relationships with white Baptists. For the *Journal of Negro History* he wrote "The Evolution of the Negro Baptist Church" (Jan. 1922) and "The Priority of the Silver Bluff Church and Its Promoters" (Apr. 1922). For *The Crisis* he wrote "Unification and Division among Colored Baptists" (May 1925). In his work with the Bethel Literary and Historical Association, he offered a "severe but eloquent criticism" of Frederick Douglass's lecture "The Philosophy and History of Reform" that "occasioned a battle royal between him and Mr. Douglass, in which 'Greek met Greek' with vigorous onslaught and heroic defence [*sic*]." Brooks was a member of the American Negro Academy and a lifelong member of the Association for the Study of Negro Life and History, where he worked closely with Carter G. Woodson.

Brooks's first wife died in 1912, and three years later he married Florence H. Swann. Following Florence's death, he married Viola Washington in 1933. Late in his life Brooks established himself as a poet. Two books of his poetry were published, *Original Poems* (1932) and *The Pastor's Voice* (1945). His poems thematically reflect his lifelong concerns for temperance, faith in God, and racial progress.

Brooks, like many black clergy of his time, used the church and his role as pastor for purposes that extended beyond the sacred. He was uncompromising in his struggle to promote education and the use of Christian morals as means to improve the quality of life for black Americans. As racial segregation gained legal precedent and race-related violence reached new heights, Brooks fought for equality and clung to a faith in the American creed that was second only to his faith in God.

• Brooks's granddaughter Evelyn Brooks Higginbotham wrote but did not publish "Walter Henderson Brooks: Some Additional Comments," and she possesses some unpublished writings by Brooks, including an autobiographical piece, "Memories of a Life Time" (1935); some untitled autobiographical notes; and a genealogical "History of the Brooks Family." Brooks's contribution to the publication sponsored by the American Baptist Publication Society, "The Doctrine of God: His Existence and Attributes," is reprinted in *The Negro Baptist Pulpit: A Collection of Sermons and Papers*, ed. Edward M. Brawley (1890; repr. 1971). The most extensive biography of Brooks was written by Carter G. Woodson and published as the introduction to *The Pastor's Voice* (1945). A number of brief biographical sketches can be found by using Randall K. Burkett et al., eds., *Black Biographical Dictionaries, 1790–1950* (1991). The most informative of these sketches are in A. W. Pegues, *Our Baptist Ministers and Schools* (1892); Henry Norval Jeter, *Pastor Henry N. Jeter's Twenty-five Years Experience with the Shiloh Baptist Church and Her History* (1901); D. W. Culp, ed., *Twentieth Century Negro Literature* (1902); and A. B. Caldwell, ed., *History of the American Negro* (1922). For Brooks's interaction with national Baptist groups, the formation of national Baptist conventions, and black relationships with white Baptist organizations, consult Higginbotham, *Righteous Discontent: The Women's Movement in the Black Baptist Church, 1880–1920* (1993), and James Melvin Washington, *Frustrated Fellowship: A Black Baptist Quest for Social Power* (1986). For Brooks's involvement with the intellectual black elite in Washington, see Alfred A. Moss, *The American Negro Academy* (1981). Obituaries are in the *Journal of Negro History* 30 (Oct. 1945) and the Washington, D.C., *Evening Star*, 8 July 1945.

ADAM BIGGS

BROOKS, William Keith (25 Mar. 1848–12 Nov. 1908), zoologist, was born in Cleveland, Ohio, the son of Oliver Allen Brooks, a prosperous importing merchant, and Ellenora Kingsley. Brooks attended public schools in Cleveland. He suffered from a congenital heart defect that limited his athletic activities and may have contributed to his early intellectual development. He was said to have inherited from his mother an artistic skill and a highly studious and idealistic set of values.

As a child, Brooks displayed a precocious interest in reading and in the study of nature. He developed collections, set up a small personal museum in the family barn, used a microscope, learned to stuff and mount birds, and studied classic works of naturalism. Among his childhood friends were the sons of the geologist J. S. Newberry. While in secondary school, Brooks had private tutoring in Greek and developed a lifelong interest in the language. Sometimes working for his father's import business, he invented a calculator for computing interests, discounts, and percentages in British sterling money.

Brooks entered Hobart College in 1866 and transferred in his junior year to Williams College, from which he graduated in 1870, with Phi Beta Kappa honors. At both Hobart and Williams, he furthered his interest in natural science. After completing the bachelor's degree, he taught for two years at DeVeaux College in Niagara Falls, New York, before entering graduate school at Harvard University. There he studied under Louis Agassiz, who had attracted many students to the study of zoology. Brooks spent the summers of 1873 and 1874 at Agassiz's seaside laboratory at Penikese in Buzzard's Bay, Massachusetts, where Agassiz had brought together a group of young scholars. Brooks's work at Penikese converted him to a life of study of marine biology. He completed work for his doctorate in 1874, receiving only the third doctoral degree granted by Harvard, in 1875. He then worked at the private laboratory of Alexander Agassiz in Newport, Rhode Island, making further contacts among the generation of young biologists coming out of the program at Harvard. In 1875 he was instrumental in establishing a laboratory for the study of biology in Cleveland, Ohio.

For the next two years Brooks served as an assistant at the Boston Museum of Natural History. With the founding of Johns Hopkins University in 1876, he applied for a position there and was accepted as one of the first twenty fellows; he also received an associate position in biology at the university. In 1878 he married Amelia Katharine Schultz, and they settled near Baltimore at a large country home, "Brightside," on Lake Roland. They had two children.

In 1883 Brooks was appointed associate professor of morphology, and in 1889, professor of morphology, at Johns Hopkins University. In 1894 he was selected as head of the department of biology, as successor to H. Newell Martin. Brooks had learned much from Martin, who had studied at Cambridge under Thomas Huxley. Brooks worked closely with Martin in modeling the Johns Hopkins graduate program on that of the German type of university. He continued to chair the department until his death. Under his direction, the program at Johns Hopkins led the way in the growth of the biological sciences in the United States in the last decades of the nineteenth century and served as part of the larger reform of graduate education in the United States in that period through regularizing doctoral programs.

A scholar, popularizer, and teacher of zoology, Brooks was well liked and influential as a lecturer. His lectures, which were noted for lively style, clear presentation, and charm of delivery, were widely attended by faculty and students from other departments. His works included a book of lectures, *The Foundations of Zoology* (1899), which went through several editions up to 1915, and a textbook, *Handbook of Invertebrate Zoology*, published in 1882 and republished through 1897.

Brooks's area of specialty was the invertebrate, especially the oyster, and in addition to some seventeen scholarly papers on oysters, he published a popular work on the topic, *The Oyster: A Popular Summary of a Scientific Study* (1891), which was frequently reprinted until 1905. He was a prolific author, publishing more than 100 scientific articles as well as his more widely read texts, handbooks, and popular works. He was also interested in the history of biology, publishing a life of Thomas Huxley, *The Lesson of the Life of Huxley* (1901). He often richly illustrated his own scientific works in pen and ink, and created his own lithographs. His first book, *Development of the American Oyster* (1880), was reprinted in many journals and earned him a medal from the Societe d'Acclimation in France.

Brooks was a descriptive evolutionary morphologist with a liking for studies of the whole organism and their place in the environment. He was a close observer and collector of data and, at the same time, a biologist interested in the larger philosophical implications of life. He saw each species as having a place in the history of the world and as dynamically adapted to the circumstances of its environment. To Brooks, the core issue of life was adaptation, and the significance of a species was exactly how it functioned in its environmental setting. This led him to consider, from a philosophical point of view, the function of each species. As such, Brooks's work was noted for having philosophical and metaphysical overtones, and his *Foundations*, based on a series of lectures, was widely read and well received by critics as a work of literature. In general, his studies were full of rhetorical speculations and thought-provoking asides, some of which struck later generations of marine biologists as premature or ill founded. Yet his literary style and his excellent close work on the embryology and life-cycle of marine invertebrates left a model that others sought to emulate.

Brooks's scientific contributions centered around his work with the conservation and embryology of the oyster, studies of the tunicates, and papers on mulluscan structure and embryology. He published studies of the larval stages of Crustacea and produced a readable and richly illustrated study of the life history of the Hydromedusae. He was the first to follow the life history of a crustacean from a single egg, which he did for the *Lucifer*, a remarkable arthropod. His study of the pelagic tunicate *Salpa*, "The Genus *Salpa*, A Monograph with Fifty-Seven Plates" (1893), was regarded as a classic. In this work he described the development of the *Salpa* buds and demonstrated their relationship to the buds of the sessile tunicates. His works on the embryology of this species and of other marine invertebrates continued to stand out decades later for their clarity and perceptiveness. He studied the life histories of several hydroid coelenterates, giving original and perceptive assessments of their phylogenetic relationships. Thus his work showed not only linkages between a species and its function in the environment, but also its historic situation in evolution, through embryonic relationships and phylogenetic placement. From the species, he would build a picture of a relationship in spacial setting to other organisms in the environment and a picture of a relationship in time to other organisms in the hereditary structure of life itself.

Brooks was deeply involved in what would later be called environmental issues. He advocated the establishment of the Maryland Oyster Commission and was appointed its first chairman in 1882, devoting time to the problems of perpetuating the oyster beds of the Chesapeake. Unfortunately, his warnings about overfishing and preserving the beds went unheeded. He also established in 1878 the Chesapeake Zoological Laboratory in Hampton Roads, Virginia, which he directed for many years. He served at the U.S. Fish Commission Laboratories at Beaufort, North Carolina, and at Woods Hole, Massachusetts. In 1905 and 1906 he worked at the marine laboratory of the Carnegie Institution at Tortugas, Florida. He died at his country home in Maryland.

Colleagues and students remembered Brooks as warmhearted, companionable, and supportive, while at the same time often intense, with a degree of quiet reserve. He had taken great pride in the achievements of his students, many of whom later gained fame for their work, including E. B. Wilson, T. H. Morgan, E. G. Conklin, and R. G. Harrison, who worked in such fields as cytology, embryology, and genetics.

• Brooks left a rich collection of research notes and drawings, preserved in the Milton S. Eisenhower Library at Johns Hopkins University. The research notes cover the genuses Modera, Eucopidea, Lucifer, and the vesiculated medusae, and the drawings were from the illustrations of his morphological studies. Most of the sketches were of the tunicates *Salpa* and the coelenterates *Hydromedusea* and *Physalia*. Among Brooks's monographs published in the *Memoirs of the Biological Laboratory of the Johns Hopkins University* series are "The Life-history of the Hydromedusae: A Discussion of the Origin of the Medusae, and of the Significance of Metagenesis" (1887) and "Lucifer, a Study in Morphology" (1887). Other of his works not already mentioned in the text are *The Law of Heredity: A Study of the Cause of Variation, and the Origin of Living Organisms* (1883); *The Development and Protection of the Oyster in Maryland* (1884); *On the Lucayan Indians* (1889); *The Affinities of the Pelagic Tunicates* (1906); and *Biographical Memoir of Alpheus Hyatt, 1838–1902* (1908). Biographical sources include E. G. Conklin, "Biographical Memoirs of William Keith Brooks, 1848–1908," National Academy of Sciences, *Biographical Memoirs* 7 (1910): 23–88; C. P. Swanson, "A History of Biology at the Johns Hopkins University," *Bios* 22 (1951): 223–62; "William Keith Brooks. A Sketch of His Life by Some of His Former Pupils and Associates," *Journal of Experimental Zoology* 9 (1910): 1–52.

RODNEY P. CARLISLE

BROOKS, William Thomas Harbaugh (28 Jan. 1821–19 July 1870), soldier, was born in New Lisbon, Ohio, the son of DeLoma Brooks. (His mother's name is unknown.) On 18 March 1837 he accepted an appointment to the U.S. Military Academy. Four years later he graduated near the foot of a class that produced twenty future Union and Confederate generals. As a subaltern in the Third U.S. Infantry, "Bully" Brooks served in the Seminole War of 1842–1843 and did garrison duty in the Kansas Territory. During the war with Mexico he saw action at Palo Alto, Resaca de la Palma, Monterrey, Veracruz, Cerro Gordo, Contreras, and Mexico City. For conspicuous service at Monterrey and Contreras he won the brevets of captain and major. In the later stages of the conflict he served on the staff of Brigadier General David E. Twiggs, a profane, hard-driving commander who appears to have exerted a lasting influence on his youthful aide.

Returning to the United States in 1848, Brooks was posted to Texas and the New Mexico Territory, where he wrestled with health problems probably contracted below the Rio Grande. When not on sick leave he fought roving bands of Indians, distinguishing himself in an October 1858 skirmish with the Navajo in New Mexico.

When the Civil War broke out, Brooks's tactical and administrative experience recommended him for a command. On 28 September 1861 he was appointed a brigadier general of volunteers and assigned a brigade of Vermont infantry, later a part of William Farrar "Baldy" Smith's division of the IV Corps, Army of the Potomac. Brooks led his Vermonters throughout Major General George B. McClellan's Peninsula campaign, performing conspicuously at Lee's Mill (16 Apr. 1862) and Savage's Station (29 June), where he was severely wounded. He recovered in time to participate in the Antietam campaign but on 17 September took another wound that kept him out of action for almost a month.

When Brooks returned to the field he was given command of the First Division, VI Corps, which he led at Fredericksburg and Chancellorsville. Only lightly engaged in the former battle, the division was heavily involved in the latter, on 3 May 1863 suffering nearly 1,500 casualties in driving the enemy from a heavily fortified position near Salem Church. In a postaction report his corps commander, Major General John Sedgwick, lauded Brooks's "gallant and spirited" leadership throughout the fight.

After Chancellorsville, Brooks took leave of the army, apparently to recuperate from wounds and fatigue. He was in Pittsburgh, Pennsylvania, early in June when Secretary of War Edwin M. Stanton appointed him commander of the Department of the Monongahela, with the rank of major general. Over the next three weeks Brooks organized, armed, and equipped regular and "emergency" troops to oppose Robert E. Lee's Army of Northern Virginia. Although the invaders of Pennsylvania passed well to the east of Brooks's fiefdom and returned to Virginia after their defeat at Gettysburg in mid-July, Brooks remained in departmental command for another nine months.

By the spring of 1864 Brooks was restive for active duty, but he was not recalled to the Army of the Potomac. A greater blow was the revocation of his appointment as major general in April. The reasons apparently were Brooks's friendship with the deposed General McClellan and his vocal criticism of two of McClellan's successors, Ambrose E. Burnside and Joseph Hooker, both favorites of the Abraham Lincoln administration. Burnside so resented Brooks's opposition that in January 1863 he tried unsuccessfully to have the Ohioan dismissed from the service.

Soon after losing his second star Brooks was rescued from his backwater assignment by Major General Benjamin F. Butler, leader of the Army of the James. Seeking experienced subordinates for his newly formed command, Butler offered Brooks a division in the XVIII Corps under his old superior, Baldy Smith. Brooks served creditably in the Bermuda Hundred campaign, breaking enemy communications and arguing against retreating on 16 May from Drewry's Bluff, where Butler's promising offensive against Richmond fell apart. Late that month Brooks accompanied Smith to Cold Harbor, where on 3 June he led his command in a series of resolute but doomed assaults against Lee's fortifications. Afterward he transferred to the X Corps, another component of the Army of the James, which he led for some time on a provisional basis. Butler, who admired and trusted Brooks, wished to appoint him permanent commander of the corps, but his candidate relinquished the position when he learned that the Senate would not confirm his promotion to major general.

Convinced he could not flourish in the Byzantine world of army politics and borne down by his wounds, Brooks resigned his commission on 14 July 1864, rejecting Butler's plea that "the country . . . can ill afford to spare so good a soldier." After a partially successful attempt to restore his health, the lifelong bachelor took up farming near Huntsville, Alabama, an area occupied by Union forces. His "amiable disposition, simplicity of character, and sound common sense" gained him the respect of both the hill country "tories" and the more numerous secessionists, among whom he resided for the last six years of his life. He died in Huntsville.

Brooks was one of many Civil War commanders whose career was cut short by nonmilitary liabilities. When not hobbled by fragile health, he proved himself a vigorous and decisive field leader who enjoyed the confidence of his troops. One subordinate called him "as modest and devoid of self-seeking as he was conspicuous for skill and personal bravery in action." Another referred to him as "a sturdy . . . splendid fighter." Brooks's positive qualities, however, were somewhat undermined by a temper that could turn him into "a most profane, uncomfortable, irascible man," especially when ordered to withdraw from a fight he believed he could win. At Drewry's Bluff, such a directive left him so angry that, as a staff officer reported, "the air became blue with sulphurous words."

An even greater detriment to Brooks's standing in the army was his impolitic words and deeds. His identity as a "McClellan man" and his association with other partisans of "Little Mac," such as the contentious and egotistical Baldy Smith, ensured Brooks's inability to remain with the Army of the Potomac or to gain promotion in the Army of the James. A conservative Democrat, distrustful of the wartime policies of the Lincoln administration and not hesitant to voice his beliefs, Brooks proved to be more welcome among his Confederate neighbors in Alabama than in the halls of the Republican-dominated War Department.

• Although no body of Brooks's personal papers is known to exist, a small number of his wartime letters are in the Benjamin F. Butler Papers at the Library of Congress and the Ferdinand Dreer and Simon Gratz collections in the Historical Society of Pennsylvania. Brooks's battle reports and dispatches are in several volumes of *The War of the Rebellion: A Compilation of the Official Records of the Union and Confederate Armies* (128 vols., 1880–1901). Works by subordinates who characterized Brooks at some length include George A. Bruce, "General Butler's Bermuda [Hundred] Campaign," *Papers of the Military Historical Society of Massachusetts* 9 (1912): 303–46; Newton Martin Curtis, *From Bull Run to Chancellorsville* (1906); and the Charles A. Currier memoirs at the U.S. Army Military History Institute, Carlisle Barracks, Pa. For a detailed obituary, see *Second Annual Reunion of the Association of the Graduates of the United States Military Academy* (1871).

EDWARD G. LONGACRE

BROOM, Jacob (1752–25 Apr. 1810), civic leader and delegate to the Constitutional Convention in 1787, was born in Wilmington, New Castle County, then part of Pennsylvania, later Delaware, the son of James Broom, a blacksmith who prospered through real estate ventures, and Ester Willis, a Quaker. Broom was educated as a lawyer and as a surveyor at a private school that later became the College of Wilmington. In 1773 he married Rachel Pierce, a widow from nearby Christiana Hundred. She and six of their eight children survived Jacob.

Broom's political career began in 1776 with his election as second burgess of the borough of Wilmington, a town of 2,000. A year later his competence as a surveyor led to a commission by General George Washington to map the roads and significant landmarks of New Castle County. Washington reported to Congress on 30 August 1777 that he had checked the different roads. Washington's notes appear on Broom's 22-by-60-inch map, now at the Pennsylvania Historical Society. In December 1783, as chief burgess of Wilmington, Broom had the honor of welcoming the retired general to the city.

Broom was elected a member of the Delaware Assembly in 1784, a justice of the peace the following year, a member of the Annapolis Convention in 1786, and one of Delaware's five delegates to the Constitutional Convention in Philadelphia in 1787.

Described by Georgia delegate William Pierce as "a plain good Man, with some abilities, but nothing to render him conspicuous . . . silent in public but cheerful and conversable in private," Broom saw many of his wishes outvoted at the Constitutional Convention: the length of the president's term (he thought that presidents should serve until voted out for bad conduct), senators' terms (he thought these should be nine years), and the location of the capital (he had suggested Wilmington). But his views prevailed on 16 July as the convention nearly dissolved over a controversy regarding the composition of the national legislature. The convention had just approved a two-chambered assembly rather than a unicameral assembly in which state representation would be proportional to population. In the second chamber, every state would have the same number of delegates regardless of population. Populous states answered this small-state victory by calling a recess and setting no date for reconvening.

According to *The Records of the Federal Constitution of 1787* (1911), edited by Max Farrand from the notes of James Madison and others, "Mr. Broome thought it his duty to declare his opinion against an adjournment sine die, as had been urged by Mr. Patterson. Such a measure he thought would be fatal. Something must be done by the Convention tho' it should be by a bare majority." Jacob Broom's speech changed enough votes to allow the convention to reconvene the next day.

At home his career as an expediter continued as he became the first treasurer of Wilmington's library in 1788, the president of the Street and Water and Sewer Department, the first postmaster of the city (appointed by President Washington in 1790), a member of the first board of trustees for the College of Wilmington in 1803, chairman of the first board of directors of the Delaware Bank in 1795, and a director of a company to build canals in 1801 and of another for bridges in 1807. He built the first known cotton mill in 1795 but disapproved of a lottery to raise money to rebuild it when it burned.

He died, probably in Philadelphia, a very wealthy man. The inventory of his house near Wilmington lists the contents of a large library and a piano but a modest amount of clothing. He left $500 to the Friends' Female Benevolent Society and the same amount to the "school for instruction of blacks under their direction."

Quiet, unassuming Jacob Broom served his peers and the institutions they chose him to guide well. His abilities made him conspicuous. His advice was taken when the Constitutional Convention delegates might have abandoned their efforts to organize a government.

• Jacob Broom's will, inventory, and two letters are in the state archives in the Hall of Records, Dover, Del. The Pennsylvania Historical Society in Philadelphia has several letters, the 1777 map, and two other maps. The Historical Society of Delaware in Wilmington has copies of these as well as biographical files. No essay, portrait, or silhouette of Jacob Broom is known to exist.

Broom's 1783 address welcoming George Washington to Wilmington and Washington's reply appear in the Reverend William W. Campbell, "The Life and Character of Jacob Broom," in the *Historical and Biographical Papers of the Historical Society of Delaware* (1937). A brief biography is included in Dorothy Horton McGee, *Framers of the Constitution* (1968), and in Betty C. Homan, "The Elusive Jacob Broom—Signer," *Daughters of the American Revolution Magazine* 121, no. 10 (1987): 861, 897. Anna Lincoln mentions Broom's activities in *Wilmington, Delaware, Three Centuries under Four Flags* (1937). His career is recorded in Roger Martin, "Jacob Broom 1752–1810," *Delaware Lawyer Magazine* 6, no. 2 (1987): 45–46.

DOROTHY ROWLETT COLBURN

BROONZY, Big Bill (26 June 1893?–15 Aug. 1958), blues singer and guitarist, was born William Lee Conley Broonzy in Scott, Bolivar County, Mississippi, the son of Frank Broonzy and Nettie (or Mittie) Belcher, former slaves who became sharecroppers. One of at least sixteen children, including a twin sister, he lived in Mississippi until age eight, when his family moved to Arkansas, near Pine Bluff, to try sharecropping. As a youngster he made violins out of cornstalks, learning music from an uncle, Jerry Belcher, and a local musician known as See See Rider. He and a friend began playing homemade instruments to entertain local children, though always out of sight of his parents—stern Baptists who frowned on secular music. The parental disapproval eased, however, when he graduated to a real instrument (supposedly bought for him by a white patron) and began earning money as a musician. When he was twelve, the family moved to Scotts Crossing, Arkansas, where he continued to play, mainly for white dances.

In 1912, however, he joined the Baptist church, briefly putting music aside to try his hand at preaching. In 1914 (some accounts say 1916) he married a fellow church member, seventeen-year-old Guitrue (or Gertrude) Embria, who allowed him to take up music again, he said later, because it paid more than preaching.

In 1918 he was drafted, serving with an army supply company in France. Returning to Arkansas, he grew dissatisfied with life in the South. In early 1920 he left his wife and went to Chicago, where he eventually found work as a Pullman railroad sleeping-car porter. He took guitar lessons from Papa Charlie Jackson, a recording artist who introduced him to Paramount Records executive J. Mayo Williams. After an unproductive session for Paramount in 1926, Broonzy and guitarist John Thomas cut four sides in late 1927 and early 1928, launching Broonzy on one of the most prolific recording careers in blues history.

Through the 1930s and 1940s, he recorded hundreds of sides for a dozen labels, including the most important blues labels of that era: Bluebird, Columbia, OKeh, and Vocalion. He recorded both as a solo artist and in small-combo formats. He became active on Chicago's house-party circuit, then the tavern and club scene as it developed in the late 1930s and 1940s, working with such artists as Memphis Minnie and John Lee "Sonny Boy" Williamson.

As early as 1938, he began making inroads on a new market, participating in John Hammond's *From Spirituals to Swing* programs at Carnegie Hall in New York City—possibly the first appearance of a Mississippi-born blues musician in concert format. He also worked New York's Cafe Society nightclub in 1939 and 1940. In 1941 and 1942 he toured with a Mississippi protégé, vocalist Lil Green, until she started singing with big rhythm-and-blues bands. On tour in Houston, Texas, Broonzy married a "Creole woman," Rosie Syphen, who returned with him to Chicago, where he plunged back into a steady schedule of club work. They had five children.

Although World War II interrupted his recording career, the interruption apparently did not cause a major financial blow. Partly because he recorded under contract to music publisher Lester Melrose, not to any specific labels, Broonzy received little more than session fees as a recording artist. He once claimed that he earned a total of only $2,000 for the hundreds of songs he had recorded. As a result, even during his tenure as the nominal king of Chicago blues, he always worked nonmusical jobs on the side.

Broonzy returned to the recording studio in 1945, working in a new band format as he tried, with diminishing success, to keep pace with the postwar R&B sound. In 1947 folklorist Alan Lomax brought Broonzy to New York, along with Memphis Slim and Sonny Boy Williamson, for a Town Hall concert. The next day, Lomax supervised a recording session at which the three blues artists, identified by pseudonyms (Broonzy's was "Natchez"), played music and talked candidly about life in the South. That session, like the *From Spirituals to Swing* concert, marked another stage in Broonzy's shift from racial/ethnic recording star to interpreter of blues for white audiences.

By the 1950s African-American popular musical tastes had passed Broonzy by, and his recordings were more of a documentary or folk-music nature. In 1950 and 1951 he briefly left the Chicago blues scene and took a job as a janitor at Iowa State University, where he learned to read and write. Returning to music, Broonzy looked more and more to the predominantly white folk-revival audiences for work—for example, touring with Chicago critic Studs Terkel's program *I Come for to Sing*. He also looked to overseas markets and was one of the first artists to bring traditional American blues to British, European, Australian, African, and South American audiences in the 1950s. He appeared in several films and, with his newly acquired literacy, became the first Delta artist to be credited with an autobiography, *Big Bill Blues* (1964), a compilation of anecdotes, tall tales, and recollections originally written as letters to Belgian enthusiast Yannick Bruynoghe.

On tour in England in 1957, Broonzy was forced by health problems to return to Chicago where he was diagnosed with lung cancer. He died in Chicago.

Big Bill Broonzy's performing career spanned five decades, taking him from the Deep South to Chicago and on to Europe, where he became one of the first and most effective ambassadors for American blues. As a recording artist, he recorded over 250 songs—many of them his own—prior to World War II and hundreds more in the postwar era. He also played as a sideman at countless sessions for other artists. As an instrumentalist, he could handle down-home finger picking or single-string electric styles and, even late in his career, could flash techniques that dazzled the guitar-oriented folk-music audience. Although he ended his career singing protest songs and other folk material in coffeehouses and cabarets, Broonzy was the central character in the first generation of Chicago blues musicians and spent most of his adult life performing blues, ragtime, hokum, and pop material for the so-called race market. Because he was one of the first blues artists to work successfully for white audiences, though, Broonzy helped shape the way several generations thought about the blues.

He was elected to the Blues Foundation Hall of Fame in Memphis, Tennessee, in 1980.

• Broonzy's comments on his life and career are in Big Bill Broonzy, "Truth about the Blues" and "Who Got the Money," *Living Blues* no. 55 (Winter 1982–1983): 17–21, and *Big Bill Blues: Big Bill Broonzy's Story As Told to Yannick Bruynoghe* (1964). For additional information see Sheldon Harris, *Blues Who's Who: A Biographical Dictionary of Blues Singers* (1989), and Alan Lomax, *The Land Where Blues Began* (1993). For discographical information, see Robert M. W. Dixon and John Godrich, *Blues and Gospel Records: 1902–1943*, 3d ed. (1982); Mike Leadbitter and Neil Slaven, *Blues Records 1943–1970: A Selective Discography*, vol. 1 (1987); and Paul Oliver, ed., *The Blackwell Guide to Blues Records* (1989).

BILL MCCULLOCH
BARRY LEE PEARSON

BROPHY, John (6 Nov. 1883–19 Feb. 1963), coal miner and union organizer, was born in St. Helens, Lancashire, England, the son of Patrick Brophy, a coal miner, and Mary Dagnall. John spent his early childhood in a predominantly Catholic working-class community where union membership was the norm for most coal miners. He attended parochial school until the age of nine when, in December of 1892, his family immigrated to Philipsburg, Pennsylvania.

The family arrived in the United States at the onset of the panic of 1893, when economic conditions in Pennsylvania's mining towns were unusually harsh. John's father eked out a poor existence as a coal miner, and the family was often forced to move from one mining town to another in search of work. Living conditions were so difficult that six of eight brothers and sisters born during this time died in infancy or early youth. John attended the public schools sporadically and was often unable to afford textbooks but, nonetheless, developed a lifelong appreciation for the value of reading and education.

At age twelve, to supplement the family's income, John entered the coal mines, where he worked alongside his father. In 1899, at age fifteen, he first joined the South Fork local of District 2 of the United Mine Workers of America. His honesty and outspoken leadership of the rank and file led to his election as president of the South Fork local in 1906. The following year he moved to Nanty Glo, Pennsylvania, where he was elected secretary, and then president, of the local miner's union. However, Brophy was blacklisted following a bitter coal strike, while conditions deteriorated in the bituminous coal industry. In 1911 he moved to Bay City, Michigan, where he again found work as a miner, and from 1913 to 1914 he served as president of the United Mine Workers local. He return to Nanty Glo in 1914, and the miners soon elected him as their checkweighman. Brophy's tireless activism soon resulted in his election as president of the UMW's District 2, which encompassed central Pennsylvania, in 1916. Despite his later rise through the ranks of the union movement, he continued to think of himself "as a militant rank and filer." Brophy married Anita Anstead in 1918; they had two children.

Although his education was minimal, Brophy was highly intellectual in his understanding of labor problems. He developed a labor philosophy that favored industrial over craft unionism, aggressive efforts at organizing the unorganized, an independent labor party, union-sponsored workers' education programs and, in government, democratic economic and social planning. Brophy was a leading proponent of nationalizing the coal industry, which he considered "the key to the entire problem of the miners." In 1921 he was appointed chairman of the UMW's Nationalization Research Committee, which proposed legislation for nationalizing the coal industry the following year. Brophy was well versed in socialist theory, but he regarded himself as "basically a trade unionist" adhering to the principles of "Christian humanism." Indeed, in matters of social and economic philosophy, he was most deeply influenced by Leo XIII's papal encyclical *Rerum Novarum*.

Brophy was also a leading figure in the workers' education movement of the 1920s and 1930s. He had educated himself in economic theory, industrial history, and political philosophy, and he came to believe that all workers should possess such knowledge if they were to play a more prominent role in making economic and government policy. To advance this ideal, he was a founding member of the Workers' Education Bureau, and from 1921 to 1931 he served on its executive board. He was also a member of the Labor Cooperating Committee of Brookwood Labor College from 1921 to 1938.

Brophy's progressive agenda quickly brought him into conflict with officials of the American Federation of Labor and the United Mine Workers. Dissatisfaction with the conservative union leadership led him to challenge John L. Lewis for the presidency of the United Mine Workers in 1926. Brophy was defeated in the election and expelled from the UMW. He then worked as a real estate salesman in Pittsburgh from 1927 to 1929 before moving to Indianapolis, where he was a salesman for Columbia Conserve Company from 1929 to 1933.

Despite their previous disagreements, Lewis agreed to make peace with Brophy as union organizing accelerated because of New Deal legislation. In 1933 Brophy was appointed a special representative of the UMW, and the following year he was appointed national director of the Committee for Industrial Organization (CIO). In this position, Brophy played a prominent role in the strikes and union organizing drives that led to the formation of the United Auto Workers, the United Rubber Workers, and the United Steel Workers.

Having laid a substantial foundation for the new Congress of Industrial Organizations, Brophy relinquished his post in 1940 to become the director of industrial union councils for the CIO. He served as a labor representative on the National Resources Committee (1940), the National Defense Mediation Board (1940), the Fair Employment Practices Committee (1941), the War Labor Board (1942–1945), and the Wage Stabilization Board (1951–1953). He was also a CIO representative to numerous international labor organizations and conferences following World War II. During the early years of the Cold War, he assisted local CIO leaders in expelling Communists from the labor movement. In 1956 Brophy became director of community service activities in the new AFL-CIO's Industrial Union Department, where he served until his retirement in 1961.

Brophy died in Falls Church, Virginia. Shortly after his death Walter Reuther, president of the United Auto Workers, observed that "our industrial unions are living testimonials" to Brophy's dedicated work in the labor movement.

• John Brophy Collection at the Catholic University of America includes his personal papers, union publications, minutes of conferences and conventions, newspaper articles, taped interviews, and other documents related to his work in the labor movement. Columbia University has several audiotapes of interviews with Brophy that were conducted as part of the Columbia University Oral History Project in 1955. *A Miner's Life* (1964), is an autobiography that was edited extensively and supplemented by John O. P. Hall.

CLYDE W. BARROW

BROPHY, Truman William (12 Apr. 1848–4 Feb. 1928), oral surgeon, was born in Goodings Grove, Illinois, the son of William Brophy and Amelia Cleveland, farmers. Brophy spent his boyhood on his parents' farm about fifteen miles southwest of Chicago and attended local public schools. From 1863 to 1865 he received more advanced general education at the Elgin Academy (later part of Northwestern University). In 1866 he moved to Chicago, taking an opportunity to apprentice in the office of J. O. Farnsworth, a well-established dentist. In 1870 Brophy took over Farnsworth's prosperous practice.

At age twenty-two Brophy might have been content with his new dental business, but his aspirations were higher. At a time when relatively few dentists honed their skills in an academic setting, he left Chicago, which did not have a dental school, and traveled to Philadelphia for advanced training at the Pennsylvania College of Dental Surgery. He graduated with a D.D.S. in 1872 and embarked on a tour of prominent surgical clinics in Washington, Baltimore, New York, and Boston. During this journey he had an experience that he later called the primary inspiration for a lifetime of work and achievement. In the New York clinic of Louis Sayre, he saw a poor woman present her two-week-old infant, who had protruding premaxillae, a double-cleft lip, and complete cleft of the palate. The surgeon, Brophy recalled, said, "I can move the maxillary bones toward each other. If we had some way by which these bones might be placed in contact . . . we could go far toward correcting the most conspicuous deformity known to mankind. But such an operation has never been performed." Brophy continued, "It was then that I was obsessed with a desire which has been never-failing, but increasing, to devise a way that would enable me to bring about a union of the separated, misplaced bones in such deformities" (quoted in *Dental Cosmos*, pp. 468–69). Brophy returned to Chicago to marry Emma Jean Mason in 1873. They had four children. She died in 1899, and in 1908 he married a woman identified only as Mrs. E. W. Strawbridge.

Back in Chicago Brophy quickly established a reputation as one of the city's leading dental surgeons and built an exceptional practice based on many difficult cases referred to him. After a few years he became convinced that he should augment his dental training with a general medical education, so he enrolled at Chicago's Rush Medical College in 1878. On his receipt of the M.D. in April 1880 he was immediately elected to the Rush faculty as professor of oral surgery, a part-time position he held for twenty-six years. Shortly after this he began to plan the establishment of a dental school in Chicago. In 1883 Brophy's efforts materialized with the opening of the Chicago College of Dental Surgery, which later became part of Loyola University. Brophy served as president and dean of the dental college until 1920, then became dean emeritus but continued to hold the presidency until his death.

During the dozen years of intense activity immediately after Brophy's return to Chicago, he did not forget the scene he had witnessed in Sayre's clinic. He continued to focus most of his investigative energy on the problem of the cleft palate. In 1886 he first employed a novel system of early intervention with an infant patient afflicted with the deformity. He began by forcing together the separated bones of the palate with an elaborate arrangement of lead plates and silver wires; then he stitched together the skin of the cleft lip. Later, when the child was almost old enough to attempt speech, he closed the posterior palate.

Brophy met remarkable success with his first patient and soon added a large number of other success stories. His techniques quickly became the standard approach to ameliorating cleft palate. Brophy was invited to travel around the nation and the world to work his surgical wonders and instruct others in his methods. Before he died, he had operated in every state in the Union and in most of the leading cities of Europe. He also presented his knowledge in two major books, *Oral Surgery* (1915) and *Cleft Lip and Palate* (1923).

Brophy actively participated in a number of national societies, including the American Dental Association and the American Association of Dental Schools; he was a founder of the American College of Surgeons. He was also active in associations at the local and international level, such as the Physicians' Club of Chicago and the International Dental Federation. He died in Chicago.

Brophy left a lasting professional legacy. He played a significant role in elevating the standing of dentistry in the United States; he improved the international reputation of American surgeons; and through his skill as a surgeon and as a teacher he alleviated the suffering of untold numbers who were able to live without the debilitating disfigurement of an unrepaired cleft lip and palate.

• The chief source of biographical information on Brophy is an obituary in *Dental Cosmos* 70 (Apr. 1928): 468–70.

JON M. HARKNESS

BROUGH, John (17 Sept. 1811–29 Aug. 1865), journalist and governor of Ohio, was born in Marietta, Ohio, the son of John Brough, a tavern keeper, and Jane Garnet. Born in the building that housed both the county courthouse and his father's tavern, Brough was orphaned at age eleven. Provided a home by a local editor, he soon became a printer's apprentice. In 1830 he briefly attended Ohio University and the next year organized a Democratic newspaper in Marietta, the *Western Republican*. In 1833 he bought and briefly operated the Lancaster *Ohio Eagle* and with his brother Charles published the *Cincinnati Enquirer* from 1844 to 1848.

Brough combined a journalistic career with an active role in Democratic politics. At age twenty-six he was elected to the Ohio House of Representatives, where he emerged as a leading Jacksonian partisan and chaired the committee on banking and currency. He opposed any expansion of civil rights for Ohio's black community, such as the right of petition, and he viewed abolitionists as dangerous agitators. A strenuous advocate of state regulation of the banking system, Brough was elected state auditor by the legislature in 1839. During the next six years he successfully coped with the state's financial problems and Whig attacks on his economic policies by increasing tax revenue and helping to restore the state's credit. When the Whigs gained control of state government in 1845, he devoted his attention first to journalism and then, from 1848 to 1863, to the management of several railroads that included the Madison and Indianapolis, the Bellefontaine, and the Indianapolis, Pittsburgh and Cleveland. He moved to Indiana, and then eventually to Cleveland.

Brough reentered politics in a dramatic way during the Civil War. Although a Democrat until the outbreak of the war, he supported the war effort and cooperated with the Lincoln administration by making his railroads available to transport troops. In June 1863 he delivered a dramatic speech in support of the military effort, calling his country "the last hope of freemen throughout the world" (quoted in Ervin, p. 110). A week later the Union party nominated him for governor by a narrow margin over incumbent David Tod. The campaign received nationwide attention because his opponent was the recently exiled Peace Democrat Clement Vallandigham. Brough's victory by 100,000 votes (including a 20 to 1 margin in the soldier vote) was the largest in the state's history to that time.

Brough's brief term as governor, which began in January 1864, revealed both strengths and flaws. Though capable and efficient as an administrator and a powerful orator, he bluntly spoke and acted on his convictions without concern for whomever he might offend. His appearance and personal habits did not engender respect: he was corpulent and untidy to an extreme and an inveterate tobacco chewer. His wartime policies were successful, but excessive bureaucracy frustrated him. Under his urging, the legislature approved taxes to aid the needy families of soldiers. He persuaded midwestern governors to support his plan to facilitate a quick end to the war: to supply extra troops for 100-day service who would relieve the regulars from routine tasks and free them for service on the battlefield. In sixteen days, Brough raised close to 36,000 men for this purpose.

Rejecting military convention, he produced discontent with his outspoken insistence on a promotion policy based solely on seniority, ignoring the recommendations of senior officers. This policy caused such opposition among the officers that in 1865 he announced he would not seek renomination. He was honest, energetic, and zealous, but he had made enemies and was not in good health. Earlier he had expressed his indifference "to the political consequence to myself of . . . my public acts" (quoted in Hooper, p. 67). The most forceful and unpopular of Ohio's three war governors, Brough died in Cleveland four months before completing his term; his death was caused by gangrene of the foot and hand. He had married Achsa Pruden in 1832. They had two children before her death in 1838. In 1843 he married Caroline Nelson, with whom he had four children.

• Brough manuscript collections include correspondence in the Cincinnati Historical Society and papers relating to his governorship in the Ohio Historical Society. Several descriptions of Ohio Civil War politics provide significant accounts of his governorship. Most important are Richard H. Abbott, *Ohio's War Governors* (1962); Eugene H. Roseboom, *The Civil War Era, 1850–1873*, vol. 4: *The History of the State of Ohio*, ed. Carl Wittke (1944); and Whitelaw Reid, *Ohio in the War*, vol. 1 (1867). William B. Hesseltine, *Lincoln and the War Governors* (1948), deals with the governor's relationship with the president. Osman C. Hooper, "John Brough," *Ohio Archaeological and Historical Society Publications* 13 (1904): 40–70, includes a brief overview of his entire life. See also Richard C. Knopf, *The Governors of Ohio* (1969), pp. 83–85, and Edgar Ervin, "Birthplace of John Brough," *Ohio Archaeological and Historical Society Publications* 17 (1907): 105–11.

FREDERICK J. BLUE

BROUGHAM, John (9 May 1810–7 June 1880), actor and playwright, was born in Dublin, Ireland, of Irish and French Huguenot parentage. Schooled at Trinity College, University of Dublin, he participated in amateur theatricals during his university years and attended productions by touring companies in Dublin.

In 1830 he made his theatrical debut in *Tom and Jerry* at Tottenham Street Theatre, London, and soon joined Madame Vestris's company at the Olympic Theatre and Covent Garden. He tried writing as well as theater management during these early years but studied the acting of both the troupe's low comedian, John Liston, and the light comedian, Charles Mathew, as well as such touring stars as Tyrone Power. Controversy still surrounds Brougham's contribution to the writing of *London Assurance* (1841), usually credited solely to Dion Boucicault. The role of Dazzle may have been written by Brougham for himself, but Charles Mathews played Dazzle in the London premiere. In 1842 Brougham and his handsome wife, actress Emma Williams, whom he had married in 1838, left England for America.

Mr. and Mrs. Brougham first performed in New York at the Park Theatre on 4 October 1842, Brougham playing O'Callaghan in the farce *His Last Legs* and Emma Brougham playing Lady Teazle. In their first three years in America, the Broughams performed in several New York and Philadelphia theaters and toured such cities as New Orleans and Mobile, Alabama. Brougham continued to write, often including an Irish role for himself. In 1845 Emma Brougham returned to England, and in late 1847 Annette Nelson, actress and theater manager, was introduced as the new Mrs. Brougham. In 1847 Brougham became comanager of the Adelphi Theatre in Boston, where the burlesque *Met-a-mo-ra; or, The Last of the Pollywogs* was first produced on 27 November 1847. One of Brougham's most popular works, it is a genteel spoof of John Augustus Stone's successful Indian melodrama, *Metamora*.

When William Burton opened his Chambers Street Theatre in New York on 10 July 1848, he hired Brougham as stage manager. This soon became the premiere theater in New York, and Burton and Brougham began an extremely productive two-year association. They often played comic roles in such farces as *Mr. and Mrs. Macbeth*, which featured Burton as Lady Macbeth and Brougham as Macbeth. Brougham adapted several novels of Dickens for the stage. *Dombey and Son*, which premiered on 24 July 1848, with Brougham playing two roles, was so popular that it was performed at least once a week for the next two seasons.

After the 1849–1850 season Brougham attempted theater management again, building the Lyceum Theatre, which opened on 23 December 1850. While the audience was reportedly delighted with the performances, serious financial problems developed, and Brougham closed it in March 1852. James W. Wallack reopened the theater in September 1852, hiring Brougham as a member of his company. Brougham remained with Wallack for eight years, a stint interrupted by other short-lived attempts at management of the Bowery and the Broadway Theatres. At Wallack's a number of Brougham's new plays were produced, including his extravaganza, *Po-ca-hon-tas, or The Gentle Savage*, which premiered on Christmas Eve, 1855. This burlesque continued in the repertory for many years, with Brougham playing Pow-ha-tan through 1876. While at Wallack's he occasionally acted at Niblo's Gardens, where he comanaged two successful summer seasons. He also appeared at Burton's New Theatre and elsewhere until 17 July 1860, when he made a farewell appearance at Niblo's Gardens before leaving for England.

In the fall of 1860 Brougham appeared at the Haymarket Theatre, London. While there he wrote *The Duke's Motto*, a drama derived from Paul Feval's *Le Bossu*, for the actor-manager Charles Fechter. Brougham played Carrickfergus, an Irish soldier of fortune, when this play opened at the Lyceum Theatre on 10 January 1863; its run continued for 174 performances. In November 1864 and March 1865 he appeared in Dublin and at the Princess Theatre as The O'Grady in Dion Boucicault's *Arrah-na-Pogue*.

When Brougham returned to America in late 1865, he took short-term starring engagements with New York and Philadelphia companies and made extensive tours of the United States, including one to California. He wrote plays, not only for himself but also to encourage young performers. Among these was *Little Nell and the Marchioness*, first performed on 12 November 1866, an adaptation of Dickens's *The Old Curiosity Shop*, which was written for Lotta Crabtree and performed by her for many years: this play has frequently been acknowledged as a prototype of early musical comedy. His Shakespearian burlesques included *Much Ado about a Merchant of Venice*, first performed on 8 March 1869, in which he appeared as Shylock. His melodrama *The Lottery of Life*, which debuted on 23 September 1867, had extensive runs in several American cities. Although Brougham is usually given credit for writing only burlesques and other comic genres, he wrote well over 100 dramatic pieces of many types. Although he is remembered primarily as a comic actor who appeared in his own plays, throughout his acting career he performed many roles in the standard repertoire as well as in contemporary plays.

Brougham spent almost fifty years as a theater professional in England and America. He continued to act until near the end of his life, in the last few years almost exclusively with companies managed by Augustin Daly or Dion Boucicault. Brougham was a founder and early president of the Lotos Club, a social club for men associated with journalism and the arts, which entertained such distinguished visitors as Charles Dickens and Jacques Offenbach. He was also a founding member and the first secretary of the American Dramatic Fund Association, which was founded in April 1848 and was open to any person in the United States who practiced the art of acting, singing, or dancing as a means of subsistence for at least three years. The purposes of the fund were to provide financial support to members who were incapacitated, their widows, and their children, and to defray funeral expenses for members. Known for his generosity to friends and acquaintances throughout his life, he was in such severe financial straits during his later years that friends gave a testimonial benefit to provide him an annuity.

Brougham's jovial spirit was widely acknowledged but perhaps no more aptly than by Laurence Hutton, who claimed in his *Curiosities of the American Stage* that "if America has ever had an Aristophanes, John Brougham was his name." He died in New York City.

• Brougham's papers are widely scattered; the best source is the Theater Collection at Harvard University. Other primary sources include the New-York Historical Society; the Boston Public Library; the Billy Rose Theater Collection at the New York Public Library for the Performing Arts, Lincoln Center; the theater collection at the Philadelphia Free Library; and the Brander Mathews Collection, Baker Library, Columbia University. The most complete biographical study of Brougham is *Life, Stories and Poems of John Brougham*, ed. William Winter (1881). David S. Hawes, "John Brougham: American Playwright and Man of the Theatre" (Ph.D. diss., Stanford Univ., 1951), focuses on Brougham's early career and on his plays rather than his performances. Pat Ryan wrote several articles on Brougham's plays and provided an extremely complete and well-documented list in "John Brougham: The Gentle Satirist," *Bulletin of the New York Public Library*, Dec. 1959, pp. 619–40.

DANA SUTTON

BROUN, Heywood (7 Dec. 1888–18 Dec. 1939), journalist, was born Matthew Heywood Campbell Broun in Brooklyn, New York, the son of Heywood Cox Broun, an immigrant Scots businessman, and Henrietta Brosé, from a prosperous German-American family. When he was two his family moved to Manhattan, where he grew up in the comfortable circumstances that both of his parents had enjoyed. He graduated in 1906 from the prestigious Horace Mann School. Four years later Broun left Harvard without a degree, short of credits because of distractions that included poker, theater, and the Red Sox. The Harvard *Crimson* had rejected Broun, but the raffish *New York Morning Telegraph* hired him in 1910 as a reporter. Fired in 1912 after asking for a pay raise, Broun was hired by the *New York Tribune*, where he flourished as a reporter, sportswriter, and after 1915 as an able drama critic. After U.S. entry into World War I, Broun went overseas as a correspondent; not properly deferential, sufficiently propagandistic, or admiring of the American Expeditionary Force (AEF) commander, General John Joseph Pershing, Broun was often critical of the military. His war stories were anthologized in 1918 in *The A.E.F.: With General Pershing and the American Forces* and in *Our Army at the Front*.

Resuming his role as *Tribune* drama critic after the war, in 1919 Broun also became literary editor, launching a column, "Books and Things," that soon dealt more with things than books. A pioneer of the signed syndicated column of opinion, Broun moved in 1921 to the prestigious *New York World*, where his column, "It Seems to Me," quickly made him one of the best-known, most-respected, and highly paid American journalists. Discussing domesticity, he declared, "I have no feeling of being a traitor to my sex when I say I believe in at least a rough equality of parenthood." Dealing with controversial issues, such as the unfair trial of anarchists Sacco and Vanzetti, Broun cut to the quick: "What more can the immigrants from Italy expect? It is not every person who has a President of Harvard University throw the switch for him." Many of these columns are anthologized in *Seeing Things at Night* (1921), *Pieces of Hate* (1922), and *Sitting on the World* (1924).

Broun's 1927 biography of antivice crusader Anthony Comstock, written with Margaret Leech, was the first selection of the newly formed Literary Guild. *Christians Only*, a 1931 book written with George Britt, was a controversial, unflinching treatment of anti-Semitism in the United States. Neither critical nor commercial acclaim greeted *The Boy Grows Older* (1922), an autobiographical novel; *The Sun Field* (1923), a fable about a baseball player in politics; or *Gandle Follows His Voice* (1926), a fantasy about a shepherd boy tending sheep menaced by dragons.

A hulk of a man (6′4″ tall and weighing over 275 pounds), Broun was often likened to "an unmade bed" because of his personal sloppiness and sartorial defects. Pugnacious and sentimental, lazy, amiable, talented—he wrote columns quickly, often while sitting out poker hands—capable of great compassion and ingratitude, and overly fond of drink, Broun was a charter member of the Algonquin Round Table in New York City during the 1920s, and as that self-promoting "merry group of writers" became politicized, so did Broun. His passionate campaign in 1927 for Sacco and Vanzetti led the *World* to temporarily suspend his column. Attacks he wrote in *The Nation* on the *World*'s supposed political "timidity" resulted in his discharge a year later. Broun moved to the *New York Telegram* (which in 1931 acquired his former employer and became the *World-Telegram*). Broun never lost his bonhomie but became increasingly political, as evidenced by the 1935 compilation of his writings, *It Seems to Me*. He ran for Congress in 1930 as a Socialist in New York's Seventeenth District, finishing a poor third but garnering enough votes to allow the GOP incumbent to squeak by. He pushed a "Give a Job till June" campaign to help offset the depression's unemployment. With funds he raised, Broun masterminded and appeared in *Shoot the Works*, a 1931 revue designed to employ out-of-work show folk, which collapsed after eighty-nine performances when an exhausted Broun withdrew.

In 1933 Broun spearheaded the establishment of the American Newspaper Guild, the first successful national organization of editorial employees. Although he did not initiate the call to organize, which grew out of the employees' desperate circumstances, more than anyone else Broun was instrumental in the creation of the guild at a December 1933 Washington, D.C., convention. Elected president, he was reelected to the unpaid job until his death. Broun had little to do with the guild's day-to-day operations, but he marched on picket lines, addressed organizational meetings across the country, and helped transform the guild from a professional association into an industrial union. He fought for affiliation with the American Federation of Labor (AFL) as a labor union in 1936, for the inclusion as guild members of noneditorial newspaper workers such as elevator operators, and for the guild's switch in 1937 to the militant Congress of Industrial Organizations (CIO).

The feminist Ruth Hale married Broun in 1917. The couple led an unconventional married life, often occupying separate quarters. The independent and militant Hale—first president of the Lucy Stone League, whose members believed that wives should keep their maiden names—chafed at being called Mrs. Heywood Broun. She was responsible, without accreditation, for some of his best work. Their son Heywood Hale Broun affirmed that both of his parents had what he called "well-advertised affairs." Anxious to reclaim her identity, Hale obtained a Mexican divorce in 1933, but she and Broun remained close. After her death in 1934, Broun declared that "my best friend died." In 1935 Broun married Maria Incoronata Fruscella, a much younger woman and a dancer, known professionally as Connie Madison, who had performed in *Shoot the Works*. The widow of vaudevillian Johnny Dooley, she had a nine-year-old daughter, whom Broun adopted.

Broun's support of the underdog during the 1930s led to his radical political activity, which resulted in a 1938 appearance before the House Un-American Activities Committee and unwarranted charges of his being a "fellow traveler" with Communists. His conversion to Catholicism (he was baptized in 1939) shocked many of his left-wing supporters, who felt betrayed and did not understand that the Episcopal, free-thinking Broun had always had a mystical streak. His guild activity resulted in the *World-Telegram*'s not renewing his contract in 1939; the *New York Post* took him on but at a humiliating cut in pay. Broun wrote only one *Post* column before he died of pneumonia in New York City.

Broun was a good-natured yet complex talent who wrote well, excelling in the topical. He believed in progress and fought for it, and using his column (in the words of one admirer) he was "a cheer leader for the human race." Perhaps the most tangible result of his efforts was the guild, which for decades helped to stabilize the lives of newspaper workers.

• Heywood Hale Broun wrote a fascinating memoir of his family, *Whose Little Boy Are You?* (1983), and edited a collection of his father's writings, *The Collected Edition of Heywood Broun* (1941). Useful biographies are Dale Kramer, *Heywood Broun: A Biographical Portrait* (1949), and Richard O'Connor, *Heywood Broun: A Biography* (1975). A touching if flawed memorial is John L. Lewis et al., *Heywood Broun As He Seemed to Us* (1940). For Broun's guild career see Daniel J. Leab, *A Union of Individuals: The Organization of the American Newspaper Guild* (1970). Touching obituaries are in the *New York Times*, 19 Dec. 1939, and the *Guild Reporter*, 1 Jan. 1940.

DANIEL J. LEAB

BROUTHERS, Dan (8 May 1858–2 Aug. 1932), professional baseball player, was born Dennis Joseph Brouthers in Sylvan Lake, New York, the son of Irish working-class immigrants Michael Brouthers and Mary (maiden name unknown). He was raised in nearby Wappingers Falls, where he attended school until age sixteen. Brouthers was recruited by the semiprofessional Wappingers Falls Actives baseball team, beginning a lifelong career.

In the late 1870s, Brouthers played for several regional semipro teams. A large and powerful man for his era (6′2″, 207 pounds), he soon earned the nickname "Big Dan" and gained the attention of baseball scouts. Signed by the Troy, New York, Trojans of the National League, Brouthers made his major league debut on 23 June 1879. During that season and the next he occasionally pitched, but he found his career position at first base.

From 1881 through 1885 Brouthers played for the upstate Buffalo Bisons, where his batting exploits became legendary. He was said to have originated the phrase "keep your eye on the ball," and he rarely struck out. In 1881, during an era when few home runs were hit, Brouthers led the National League with eight. He also led the league in hits and batting average in 1882 (129; .368) and 1883 (159; .374), becoming the first player to gain those honors in consecutive seasons. In a 19 July 1883 game, he had six hits (four singles, two doubles) in as many at-bats. During those years, Brouthers gained national recognition as the leading member of the team's "Big Four," which included Hardy Richardson, Jack Rowe, and Deacon White.

In 1884 Brouthers married Mary Ellen Croak of Wappingers Falls. Their marriage produced four children. Among his contemporaries, Brouthers's congenial disposition, love of family, and fondness for a good story were well known.

After the 1885 season the contracts of the entire Big Four were sold to the Detroit Wolverines for the then-lavish combined sum of $7,500. In 1886 Brouthers again led the National League in home runs (11), including three in one game and famous home runs at ballparks in Boston and Washington, D.C. The high point of his three-season stay with Detroit, however, came when the 1887 team won the league pennant, then defeated the American Association champion St. Louis Browns in a challenge series, ten games to five. Brouthers's comment: "We slugged 'em to death."

In 1887 Brouthers joined John M. Ward and Ned Hanlon in representing the National Brotherhood of Professional Base Ball Players, as grievances were presented to National League management. The issues focused on a clause that bound each player to only the team that held his contract. When the grievances went unresolved, the stalemate led to the "Brotherhood War" and formation of the Players League in 1890.

Late in 1888, following a fifth-place finish and financial losses, the Detroit team was disbanded. Brouthers's contract was sold to the Boston Braves, for whom he starred as the 1889 National League batting champion with a .373 average. In 1890 his new Boston team won the Players League championship. When the players' revolt dissolved, he was awarded to the Boston Reds of the American Association, which he led with a .350 average as that team won the league title.

Playing in 1892 with the Brooklyn "Trolley-dodgers," he led the National League in hits (197) and runs batted in (124), while capturing his fifth batting championship with a .335 average. After an injury-marred 1893 season, he was traded, with Willie Keeler, to the Baltimore Orioles of the National League.

In 1894 the Orioles, led by player-manager John McGraw, captured their first pennant and the imagination of the baseball world. Their blend of strategy, confidence, and power provided the perfect setting for Brouthers's final great season, in which he batted .347 with 128 runs batted in.

The following year the Orioles repeated as champions. Brouthers began the season with them but, slowed by age and excess weight, saw his contract sold to the Louisville Colonels for $700 on 9 May. He batted well at .344 for the Philadelphia Phillies in 1896, but before season's end the veteran slugger with the closely cropped hair and handlebar mustache was sent to the minor leagues. His only subsequent major league duty came in 1904, when he appeared in two New York Giants games at first base for his old manager, McGraw.

Brouthers played minor league baseball in the Eastern League from 1896 through 1899, largely at Springfield, Massachusetts, but with brief stops at Toronto and Rochester, New York. In 1897 he led the league in batting with a .415 average. After the 1899 season he retired and worked as a tavern owner until his 1904 appearance with the Giants, which stirred the graying left-hander to two final seasons (1904 through 1905) with Poughkeepsie, New York, in the Hudson River League. He then retired for good as an active player at age forty-seven.

Until his death, Brouthers remained active in baseball with the Giants, first as a coach and scout, discovering players such as Larry Doyle, Buck Herzog, and Fred Merkle, and later at the Polo Grounds as a night watchman and stadium/press box attendant. He died in East Orange, New Jersey.

Brouthers was baseball's greatest slugger of the nineteenth century. In 1,673 major league games he had 2,296 hits (league leader three times), 1,523 runs (led the league twice), 460 doubles (led three times), 205 triples (second only to Roger Connor in baseball's early era), 106 home runs (led the league twice), 1,295 runs batted in (more than 100 five times), and a .342 batting average (five titles). Through the twentieth century he remained among the top-ranked all-time hitters for triples, batting average, and on-base percentage (.423). As determined by modern calculations, his slugging average of .520 was by far the best in the nineteenth century. He was elected to the National Baseball Hall of Fame in 1945.

• A concise article with a bibliography by Frederick Ivor-Campbell is in David L. Porter, ed., *Biographical Dictionary of American Sports: Baseball* (1987). A sketch of Brouthers is in Martin Appel and Burt Goldblatt, *Baseball's Best: The Hall of Fame Gallery* (1977). For biographical and statistical details of his career, see John Thorn and Pete Palmer, eds., *Total Baseball* (1989). An obituary is in the *New York Times*, 3 Aug. 1932.

JAMES D. SMITH III

BROUWER, Dirk (1 Sept. 1902–31 Jan. 1966), astronomer, was born in Rotterdam, the Netherlands, the son of Martinus Brouwer, a civil servant, and Louisa van Wamelen. Brouwer attended school in Rotterdam before enrolling at the University of Leiden, where he studied mathematics and astronomy and served as an assistant in theoretical astronomy from 1923 until he received his Ph.D. in 1927. His dissertation on the observations of the satellites of Jupiter, "Diskussie van de Waarnemingen van Satellieten I, II en III van Jupiter," was written under Willem de Sitter, an important figure in European astronomy. He then received an International Education Board fellowship that enabled him to spend the 1927–1928 academic year in postdoctoral study at the University of California at Berkeley and at Yale University. In 1928 Brouwer married Johanna de Graaf; they had one son. Brouwer remained in the United States and spent the rest of his life at Yale: first as an instructor, acting as research assistant for Ernest W. Brown (1928–1933); assistant professor (1933–1939); associate professor (1939–1941); and professor and chairman of the Department of Astronomy and director of the observatory (1941–1966). He also held the positions of Munson Professor of Natural Philosophy and Astronomy (from 1944) and director of the Research Center in Celestial Mechanics (from 1962) until his death.

Brouwer's early work at Yale was devoted to checking the lunar theory of his mentor Brown. In collaboration with him Brouwer showed that the differences between the predicted and observed lunar positions were due not to an error in Brown's theory but rather to incorrectly located reference stars (1930). This led him to study the origin and theory of asteroids (1935). In particular, this included an extension and revision of the Hirayama families of minor asteroids, which appear to have a common origin (1951), and the so-called Kirkwood gaps (1963), which are observable gaps in the asteroid ring. From 1937 to 1946 he devised a method for the direct determination of positions in planetary orbits by stepwise numerical integration. This ultimately led to a method for handling differential corrections of the rectangular coordinates (1944), which was systematically applied in the monograph *Coordinates of the Five Outer Planets: 1653–2060* (1951). Written with Wallace J. Eckert and Gerald M. Clemence, this work marked the first time that high-speed computers were used to solve a major astronomical problem. During World War II, in collaboration with Frederic W. Keator and Drury A. McMillen, Brouwer coauthored the textbook *Spherographical Navigation* (1944), which was based on his lectures for naval officers.

Brouwer's most famous research was his solution of the problem of the motion of an artificial satellite around Earth. This treatment included oblateness effects for Earth (1959); subsequently, with Gen-ichiro Hori (1960, 1961), he incorporated drag effects due to the atmosphere. This complicated investigation was of crucial importance in the early years of the space age. His book *Methods of Celestial Mechanics* (1961), written with G. M. Clemence, served as both a textbook and a research volume. It achieved international success (it was immediately translated into Russian), and it has remained one of the standard books on the subject. From 1950 to 1963 Brouwer was also active in the work of the International Astronomical Union: serving as president of commissions on Asteroids and Comets (six years) and on Celestial Mechanics (six years), as well as a member of a working group on astronomical constants. In 1950 he proposed the term "*ephemeris time*," which is a measure of astronomical time based on the rotation of the planets and the Moon rather than merely Earth's rotation, which has random fluctuations. This term has continued to be in standard use.

From 1941 until his death Brouwer was the leading figure in celestial mechanics in the United States. In that year he was named editor (later senior editor) of the *Astronomical Journal* after its acquisition by the American Astronomical Society, and he served in that capacity to the end of his life. He became a U.S. citizen in 1937, and in 1951 he was elected a member of the National Academy of Sciences. He was a corresponding member of both the Royal Netherlands Academy of Sciences and the Buenos Aires Academy of Science. Brouwer received the Gold Medal of the Royal Astronomical Society in 1955 and shortly before his death was notified that he would receive the Bruce Gold Medal of the Astronomical Society of the Pacific. He also engaged in various advisory/consulting duties for the Office of Naval Research, the Air Force Office of Scientific Research, and the National Aeronautics and Space Administration.

Brouwer was a big, cheerful, naturally ebullient man who seemed to thrive on his staggering responsibilities and workload. A gifted lecturer and an impeccable scholar who welcomed innovation, he had an unfailing interest in his students. His forte was in perfecting "known" methods of analysis and adapting them to changing astronomical situations, rather than seeking bold new theoretical ideas that offered little immediate value. In such practical situations he was considered the world authority, and during his lifetime the group of colleagues around him at Yale constituted the international center of astronomical activity in celestial mechanics. While this group did not long survive him, his influence remains lasting and ongoing. Brouwer died in New Haven, Connecticut.

• There is no known collection of Brouwer's papers. Tributes on the award of his Gold Medals are in *Monthly Notices of the Royal Astronomical Society* 115 (Feb. 1955) and *Publications of the Astronomical Society of the Pacific* 78 (June 1966), both of which contain peer evaluations of his contributions. Brouwer prepared an interesting scientific sketch in *McGraw-Hill Modern Scientists and Engineers* 1 (1980). Obituaries are in National Academy of Sciences, *Biographical Memoirs* 41 (1966): 68–87; the *Quarterly Journal of the Royal Astronomical Society* 8 (Mar. 1966); and the *New York Times*, 1 Feb. 1966.

JOSEPH D. ZUND

BROWARD, Napoleon Bonaparte (19 Apr. 1857–1 Oct. 1910), governor of Florida, was born in Duval County, Florida, the son of Napoleon Bonaparte Broward, a planter, and Mary Parsons. The Broward plantation, which was moderately successful and included an unknown number of slaves, was destroyed during the Civil War, forcing the family to flee Duval County. Broward's father was unable to restore the family's prosperity after the war. Following the deaths of his mother in 1869 and his father in 1870, Broward was raised by aunts and uncles and received no formal higher education.

Broward's subsequent early years were spent working on ships, where he acquired the skills for master and pilot licenses. After several years at sea, he returned to Jacksonville and the St. Johns River area to enter the trade of riverboating. In addition to owning several boats, he operated a lumberyard and developed phosphate mines. In January 1883 he married Georgiana Carolina "Carrie" Kemp, who was also his partner in the riverboat business. Carrie died in childbirth the following year, and the infant died six weeks later. In 1887 Broward married Annie Isabel Douglass, with whom he had nine children.

Broward operated his maritime and other business ventures until 1903 when he ran for governor. He became involved in politics in January 1888, when Governor Edward Perry appointed him to fill a vacancy as sheriff of Duval County. At this time Broward adopted the philosophy for which he would be remembered as governor, a concern for public morality and social and political reforms that reflected the goals of the national Populist and Progressive political movements. While sheriff, he became the leader of a local faction of Democrats known as the "straight-outs," a group determined to attack perceived corruption in railroads and corporations.

Broward's early political years were colorful. After serving the interim appointment as sheriff, he lost the post in the regular election of 1888 but was again appointed to the office in March 1889, when the elected sheriff was disqualified on an electoral technicality. Broward won election as sheriff in 1892 but was removed by Governor Henry Mitchell in 1894 for "excessive zeal in supervising an election . . . [that] was called interference" (Tebeau, p. 328). In 1896, after first refusing to run and then being drafted by his supporters, Broward was reelected sheriff. In addition, he served several years as a member of the Jacksonville City Council.

Most notably during this period prior to the outbreak of the Spanish-American War, Broward was involved directly in a number of covert missions to land supplies and ammunition for Cuban rebels engaged in rebellion against Spain. These actions, then commonly called filibustering, were in violation of a policy of American neutrality declared by President Grover Cleveland. Although Broward was indicted, his filibustering was popular among many Floridians who supported efforts to liberate Cuba. The indictment was eventually dropped owing to a lack of evidence, but Broward and his ship, the *Three Friends*, achieved a level of notoriety that greatly aided him later when he ran for governor.

In 1900 Broward was elected to the state house of representatives. After his term ended in 1901, he was active for a brief period in a maritime towing and wrecking business in southern Florida. By 1903 he decided to run for governor and returned to Jacksonville to organize his campaign. He was appointed to the Florida State Board of Health in 1904. Broward built upon his previous association with the "straight-outs" and his Cuban filibustering fame and entered the 1905 primary election. Running as a populist "man of the people" on a generally Progressive platform that emphasized the regulation of trusts and the prohibition of alcohol, he conducted a well-organized and charismatic campaign and received the support of the outgoing governor. Advancing to a runoff primary election that turned largely on the issues of drainage of the Everglades and control of the railroads, he won by 714 votes out of 45,244. He then easily won the general election by a margin greater than 4 to 1.

As governor, Broward initiated many reforms and programs that were important to the development of Florida in the twentieth century. Skillful in shaping debate and in dealings with the legislature, he achieved passage of Progressive-style laws that banned child labor in factories and mines; regulated the purity and quality of food and drugs; reorganized the state's higher educational system, laying the groundwork for the university system; better organized and supported the public secondary schools; began construction of a canal to drain the Everglades; and modernized the workings of the government and bureaucracy. Broward recommended numerous additional reforms aimed at regulating businesses and increasing the role of the government in social and economic affairs that, while not enacted, shaped the terms of the political debate for the next decade, formally termed the Broward Era.

Constitutionally prohibited from a second term, Broward ran for the U.S. Senate in 1909, losing narrowly in a runoff primary election. In 1910 the state's other Senate seat became available, and he again ran, this time wining the Democratic primary nomination, which was virtually the equivalent of election at the time. However, he died suddenly five months before the general election. Despite Broward's relatively short tenure, scholars regard him as among Florida's most influential and constructive governors. As a politician, he reflected the Progressive and Populist tendencies of the period rather than originating them, but he is remembered as an honest and skillful champion of change who left a profound and positive legacy in the development of Florida. Broward County, Florida, is named after him.

• Broward's public papers are in the Florida State Library in Tallahassee; a collection of private papers is in the P. K. Yonge Library of Florida at the University of Florida, Gainesville. Charlton W. Tebeau offers an interesting and informative chapter on Broward in his authoritative *History of Florida* (1971) and includes an extensive bibliography on Florida's history with many works that touch on Broward. More specific but dated are Samuel Proctor, *Napoleon Bonaparte Broward: Florida's Fighting Democrat* (1950) and "Napoleon B. Broward: The Years to Governorship," *Florida Historical Quarterly* 26, no. 2 (Oct. 1947). David R. Colburn and Richard K. Scher, *Florida's Gubernatorial Politics in the 20th Century* (1980), examines Broward in a scholarly comparative and empirical fashion and includes an informative bibliographic essay on the problematic literature on him as a Florida politician.

MICHAEL HAUSENFLECK

BROWDER, Earl Russell (20 May 1891–27 June 1973), American Communist party (CPUSA) leader, was born in Wichita, Kansas, the son of William Browder, an elementary school teacher, and Martha Hankins. Acute poverty and early politicization marked Browder's childhood. Kansas was the epicenter of Populism—agrarian protest against federal mercantilist economic policies that protected industry but not agriculture. Wichita suffered a separate calamity: real estate speculation had brought sudden collapse and flight of 30 percent of the population. Even greater hardship befell the Browder family directly. When Earl was nine years old, a nervous breakdown disabled his father, forcing the boy to drop out of third grade to help support his parents and five siblings. At night William Browder tutored him in the "three r's," praised Populist heroes, and preached class struggle. Martha Browder imparted passionate anticlericalism, love of literature, and high expectations to all her children. Earl joined the Socialist party in 1906 but never fully overcame his intellectual deprivation. Indeed, he pursued self-improvement projects until his death.

As a young adult Browder became an accountant but considered family and politics more interesting than his livelihood. In 1911 he married his childhood sweetheart, Gladys L. Groves. The following year they moved to Kansas City, Kansas, and Gladys bore a child. There Earl tended books for a Standard Oil trust subsidiary by day and proved a restless radical at night. Between 1912 and 1916 he roamed from organization to organization, trying Socialism, syndicalism, American Federation of Labor (AFL) trade unionism, and cooperativism, but never found a political home. He had escaped grinding poverty, which was no small achievement, but his drifting revealed immaturity. Yet these were not wasted years. During this decisive, formative period Browder developed a keen understanding of American radical politics and nativist tendencies that never completely deserted him.

In 1917 Browder finally found a cause that commanded all his spare time: nonviolent resistance to American participation in World War I. He paid a high price for his subsequent actions. Defiance of the Selective Service sent him to the Platte County (Mo.) jail from December 1917 to November 1918 and to Leavenworth Penitentiary in Kansas from July 1919 until November 1920. While incarcerated, Browder, angry over political repression and brutal prison conditions, became transfixed by the Bolshevik Revolution in Russia. Upon release he deserted his wife and child, moved to New York City, and joined America's infant Communist party. His actions, though cruel, could hardly have been better-timed politically.

The Communist International (Comintern) had recently made its first historic "change of line"—from advocating violent revolution to cooperating with reform elements. A chasm of ill will separated domestic party leaders from most of organized labor, but Browder possessed significant AFL experience. Visiting Soviet observers asked him to join the American delegation to the first Congress of the Red International of Labor Unions (Profintern), which was subordinate to the Comintern and was scheduled to begin functioning in July 1921. The project catapulted Browder into the American party's second stratum of leaders.

Once in Moscow, Browder charmed his Soviet hosts, starting a long, propitious friendship with Profintern head Solomon A. Lozovsky. Subsequent visits developed an even closer tie to Georgi Dimitrov, who led the Comintern from 1934 until 1943.

Browder's first Moscow visit had another significant result. An observer, William Z. Foster, perhaps America's best-known left-wing unionist, decided to join the party. He brought along his Chicago-based Trade Union Educational League (TUEL), the power of which soon rivaled the Communist party's political leadership in New York. Browder became his assistant, editing the TUEL's paper, the *Labor Herald*, and working as liaison between the two factions. His energy and efficiency brought him recognition but not respect. As Foster's "man Friday," he seemed destined to remain a high-level apparatchik for life. By mid-decade he had developed a reputation as the organization's playboy. Indeed Browder's appearance—well-dressed, slender, blue-eyed, ruddy-complected, and sandy-haired—contrasted sharply with that of some of his rougher comrades. Forever after, his intraparty rivals underestimated both his abilities and his ambition.

The year 1926 brought a dramatic turning point in Browder's life. Summoned to assist Foster in Moscow, he broke with his mentor and linked his future to the rising Joseph Stalin. For the next twenty-five years Browder tried to champion Stalinism and domestic reform simultaneously. The angry Foster left him in the Union of Soviet Socialist Republics (USSR) as America's Profintern delegate. Shortly thereafter Browder became intimate with 31-year-old Raissa Luganovskaya, a legal scholar and former Kharkov-area commissar of justice. She quickly became pregnant with the first of their three children. Luganovskaya, known as a climber in high Moscow circles, pestered Lozovsky to give Browder a career break.

Soviet leaders sent Browder to civil war–torn China to help establish the Pan-Pacific Trade Union Secretariat, which he headed in 1927 and 1928. The illegal organization, designed to unionize local workers and subvert right-wing Asian governments, ultimately provided undercover experience for numerous American Communists. There Browder proved his courage and dedication to the Comintern, becoming noted overseas while still little-known domestically.

In 1928 Stalin consolidated his power in the USSR and opened the international struggle's "Third Period," predicting a revolutionary upsurge and capitalism's final demise. Communists everywhere had to prepare for seizing power, attack Social Democrats, and sponsor dual unions. He purged the CPUSA's general secretary, Jay Lovestone, and his followers for arguing that America was not ready for such tactics. This, plus an earlier expulsion of Leon Trotsky's admirers, left a void among the party's top ranks.

In 1929 Browder returned from East Asia and again displayed independence from Foster as the leadership crisis continued. By October the dark horse Browder found himself amid a troika that had replaced the general secretary's position. Behind a facade of public unity, after another reorganization the following year, he battled Foster and William W. Weinstone for complete control. Both pluck and luck allowed Browder to win in 1932. Decisive factors included his surprising skill at infighting, Foster's heart attack, and Weinstone's aversion to hard work. At its April 1934 convention the CPUSA re-created the general secretary's post to celebrate Browder's standing.

Browder accurately anticipated the Comintern's monumental strategy shift of 1935. As German dictator Adolf Hitler's shadow lengthened over Europe, the Comintern abandoned revolutionary rhetoric. Led by anti-Nazi hero Georgi Dimitrov, it sought accord with all anti-fascists (the Popular Front), stressed links to indigenous radical traditions, and urged Western democracies to arrange collective security with the USSR. Luganovskaya, bringing their two children, joined Browder in the United States and began calling herself Raissa Browder. Years later Earl produced both a dubious Moscow decree, dated 1926, divorcing him from Gladys, and a Russian marriage certificate that even his close friend Philip Jaffe eyed suspiciously.

Browder, a man of many contradictions, could never match the charisma of Socialist party leaders Eugene Debs and Norman Thomas. Yet by championing Stalinism and patriotism simultaneously, Browder inspired domestic Communists as did no other general secretary. Claiming links to American revolutionaries and abolitionists, he rapidly became a public figure despite his shy, secretive personality. In a country that still stereotyped Marxists as swarthy, stocky figures advocating revolution in thick Slavic accents, the slender Browder, who still retained his boyish good looks into his forties, made quite a different impression. Using his Great Plains twang—which one conservative commentator conceded was more Kansas than that of Governor Alf Landon—Browder popularized the slogan "Communism Is Twentieth Century Americanism." He spoke on national radio in 1936 and appeared on *Time* magazine's cover in 1938. His depression-era contributions to the movement were not purely cosmetic. Over William Z. Foster's vigorous objections, Browder convinced doubters in Moscow that CPUSA support for President Franklin D. Roosevelt was the specific form the Popular Front should take in the United States.

After Britain and France appeased Hitler at Munich in 1938, the USSR signed a nonaggression treaty with the Nazis a year later. Within days Hitler ignited World War II by invading Poland, which the West had pledged to defend. The Comintern gave the CPUSA no advance warning, leaving Browder a painful choice between domestic radical needs and those of the Soviet Union. Despite direct shortwave orders from Dimitrov to end support for Roosevelt, Browder dragged his feet. He supported the Nazi-Soviet pact but tried to preserve the Democratic Front as well. By refusing to take a principled, independent stand, Browder forfeited a critical portion of his party's following. At the height of the CPUSA's crisis, federal authorities intervened unexpectedly, indicting Browder on a minor, decade-old charge.

Convicted on a passport fraud technicality, Browder spent fourteen months during 1941 and 1942 in Atlanta Penitentiary. The incarceration left psychological scars that never fully healed. Worried about rivals within the CPUSA hierarchy and carrying all the midlife fears of a prisoner approaching age fifty, he faced a situation he had not encountered at Leavenworth a generation earlier. Federal investigators, after giving him the customary prison physical, probed his psyche. For Browder, as for many Americans at the time, psychiatric and psychological examinations were unfamiliar and threatening. He especially feared involuntary commitment to a mental institution. That it was rarely employed against political dissenters did not reduce Browder's fright.

During Browder's incarceration, Hitler's invasion of the USSR and the entry of the United States into World War II changed the political environment in which Browder and the CPUSA operated. Stalinists everywhere began advocating collective security arrangements between the USSR and the Western powers, and the CPUSA espoused the very preparedness efforts it had resisted since late 1939. The U.S. government ceased its persecution of Communists, and on 16 May 1942 President Roosevelt commuted Browder's sentence to further national unity. Liberty rejuvenated Browder, and he swiftly resumed active party leadership.

During 1942 and 1943 Browder received unprecedented acceptance in Washington. Three times he discussed foreign policy with Undersecretary of State Sumner Welles, and the two corresponded frequently. Nothing since 1934 did more to enhance Browder's already abundant self-esteem. Although he had always enjoyed the limelight, for the first time he began to take seriously his cult of personality. He showed every sign of believing party propaganda lauding his brilliance, wisdom, and originality of thought. He believed himself vindicated by history and a recognized figure in national politics. Credulity crept in also, and a severe error in judgment quickly followed.

Josephine Truslow Adams, an unbalanced charlatan with a famous family name and impeccable credentials from the Daughters of the American Revolution, duped Browder into believing she enjoyed access to the president. The inflated Browder sought appropriate acclaim among international Communist circles. His party's wartime isolation from Moscow and the Comintern's 1943 liquidation allowed the illusion that he commanded a truly autonomous Marxist organization.

In November 1943 Roosevelt and British prime minister Winston Churchill met Stalin for the first time at Teheran, Iran. They displayed harmony exceeding the most optimistic expectations, set the date for invading Western Europe, and issued a deliberately vague pledge to work together after the end of the war. Browder, who felt an overwhelming desire to maintain the East-West alliance, insisted the declaration signified "a fundamental and long-term policy" that accepted the Soviet Union "as a permanent member of the family of nations" and that "civilization in our time" required extended postwar unity.

Browder concluded that his role as an independent Communist boss required him to apply the forthcoming East-West détente to domestic politics. Although he possessed neither philosophical aptitude nor economics training, he fancied himself a pioneering Marxist theoretician. He offered what he considered his greatest contribution: the Teheran Thesis.

Because Browder believed unity required prosperity, he envisioned a bold economic program. Mobilization had ballooned America's economy, but military orders comprised nearly half of all government spending. Browder proposed class collaboration to expand foreign sales geometrically and double the domestic adult wage earner's purchasing power. He seemed unaware of Third World objections to economic imperialism, the strength of national liberation movements, or the dread of wealth redistribution at home.

Browder never foresaw the possibility of extended Cold War prosperity. Like many Americans of his generation, he feared peace would presage a return to depression conditions. Beyond doubt, his Teheran program represented wishful thinking run wild. East and West, political leaders ignored it.

Browder's next move made greater sense but shocked his comrades even more profoundly. He announced they would reorganize as a nonpartisan leftist pressure group, the Communist Political Association. He had not consulted Moscow and boasted that the movement was "standing on its own feet for the first time." Browder spent 1944 idolized by his followers, who believed he would lead them to full political legitimacy as an integral, albeit minor part of the New Deal coalition.

Browder's ambition had finally eclipsed his abilities. In early 1945 the Soviet-American alliance crumbled after Hitler's defeat removed the common enemy. The French Communist party's theoretical journal, which generally followed the Russian party's positions, attacked Browder's revisions of Marxism, echoing rival William Z. Foster's intraparty criticisms and praising Foster by name.

Although Browder's followers quickly stampeded, he defiantly refused to humble himself and confess his heresy. Foster blocked face-saving compromises. In July, America's Communists deposed Browder and reconstituted the CPUSA. Expelled in February 1946, he never gained reinstatement and left public life an outcast in 1951. After Raissa died in 1955, he lived alone, but he ultimately spent his final years with his youngest son's family in Princeton, New Jersey, where he died.

Inspired by Foster, the party issued weekly blasts against "Browderism" and remained a force until the 1948 election. Thereafter it succumbed to the Cold War and the 1956 Soviet revelations of Stalin's crimes. The truncated CPUSA was eclipsed by a broader, antihierarchical New Left during the 1960s but enjoyed generous Soviet financial support until the USSR's 1991 implosion.

Some writers have likened Browderism to the liberal "Eurocommunist" parties in Italy, France, and Spain during the 1970s because they, too, sought a democratic route to power. Actually Browderism was an idiosyncratic, mutant form of Stalinism less akin to Eurocommunism than was once believed.

Browder's secretive nature served him well. Both Russian and American government archives reveal that he supervised at least some Soviet espionage in the United States and knew of more. Under Browder, the CPUSA during its heyday dominated politics left of the New Deal. The movement's stress on native roots and local organization meant that its day-to-day operations in union struggles and on behalf of racial minorities and the poor had little to do with the machinations of the leadership. Still, Browder's leadership, through ties to a foreign dictatorship, compromised and betrayed American radicalism's historically democratic nature.

• Browder's papers are at Syracuse University, and his FBI file is available at the Washington, D.C., headquarters. Other government documents are at the National Archives. Browder published more than sixty-five pamphlets. Books that he wrote include *Communism in the United States* (1935), *What Is Communism?* (1936), *The People's Front* (1938), *Fighting for Peace* (1939), *The Second Imperialist War* (1940), *The Way Out* (1941), *Victory and After* (1942), *Teheran: Our Path in War and Peace* (1944), *War or Peace with Russia?* (1947), and *Marx and America* (1958). On Browder's life, see James G. Ryan, *Earl Browder: The Failure of American Communism* (1997). See also Harvey Klehr et al., *The Secret World of American Communism* (1995); Klehr, *The Heyday of American Communism: The Depression Decade* (1984); Maurice Isserman, *Which Side Were You On? The American Communist Party during the Second World War* (1982); Joseph Starobin, *American Communism in Crisis, 1943–1957* (1972); Theodore Draper, *American Communism and Soviet Russia: The Formative Period* (1960); and Draper, *The Roots of American Communism* (1957). An obituary appears in the *New York Times*, 28 June 1973.

JAMES G. RYAN

BROWDER, George Richard (11 Jan. 1827–3 Sept. 1886), Methodist preacher and diarist, was born near Olmstead in southern Logan County, Kentucky, the son of Robert Browder and Helen Walker, farmers. His father had migrated to Kentucky from Virginia in 1820 as a part of the westward surge following the War of 1812. Seven months after Browder's birth, his mother died. In 1828 his father married Sarah L. Gilmer, who, by her godly life and faithful instruction in the catechism, exerted a profound influence on young Browder and prepared the way for his conversion at the nearby Ash Spring camp meeting in 1838. Browder attended neighborhood schools and the Male Academy in Clarksville, Tennessee.

While a student at the academy, Browder decided to become a Methodist preacher, and in 1846 he was licensed to preach by the quarterly conference of Logan Circuit. The Louisville Conference of the Methodist Episcopal Church, South, admitted him on trial the same year. He was ordained a deacon in 1848 and an elder in 1850. During his years of preparation for the ministry, Browder courted Ann Elizabeth "Lizzie" Warfield, daughter of a well-to-do Clarksville merchant and farmer, and they were married in 1850; six of their eight children survived to adulthood.

Disappointment characterized the first twenty years of Browder's preaching career. A series of physical problems, including a persistent sore throat, nausea, boils, and cholera, forced him to withdraw from the full-time ministry. Nevertheless, he preached as often as his health allowed and became a popular speaker for such causes as temperance, education, and the Sunday school movement. He also attended to his 143-acre farm, located near Olmstead, on which he grew corn, wheat, oats, and tobacco. Reflecting the society in which he was reared, Browder became a slave owner, a role that troubled him somewhat. In 1854 as the owner of three slaves, he considered moving his family to a free state—"for the sake of our children"—and when in June 1864 all ten of his slaves ran away he confided in his diary, "I think the loss of my negroes may prove a blessing to my children—active exertion may give them stronger constitutions & they will learn self reliance."

Browder and his family experienced the full impact of the Civil War when the fighting reached south-central Kentucky in the fall of 1861. In his diary he recorded troop movements of both Union and Confederate forces as they met in battle throughout the region; he described the terror elicited by marauding bands, the bitterness caused by the pitting of family against family, and the growing restlessness of the slaves. Fear, horror, and destruction were routine.

Browder's health had improved enough by 1872 that he was able to rejoin the itinerant ranks, and he soon caught the eye of those in leadership positions. In 1876 he was appointed a presiding elder in the Louisville Conference and served the following districts: Bowling Green (1876–1880), Russellville (1880–1884), and Owensboro (1884–1886). As presiding elder he was responsible for the approximately twelve preachers who ministered in each of his districts. In addition to advising the bishop in the appointment of preachers, he also worked closely with each minister in a regular schedule of visitation, as required by the Methodist system.

Browder's work as presiding elder required a great deal of time on the road, much of it spent on horseback. Several times, despite his frail health, he recorded rides of thirty-five or forty miles in one day. He also was absent from home for long periods of time, a hardship that took its toll on both him and his wife and undoubtedly shortened his days as Browder pushed himself beyond his physical capabilities. He died of heart disease at his home near Olmstead.

Browder's significance lies not so much in his career as a Methodist preacher, but in his private recordings as a diarist. He began keeping a journal at the age of nineteen and, with two or three lapses, recorded his thoughts almost daily; he filled twenty-three copybooks, of which fifteen survive. Many of his entries are understandably commonplace, but when the occasion warranted he was capable of considerable descriptive power. The 4 July 1862 observance of Independence Day, for example, inspired the following entry: "Our nation then will celebrate this day with heavy hearts—the waving plumes—the measured step & skillful evolutions of the soldiers & the peal of booming cannon will seem a cruel mockery, to the countless thousands, whose hearts & hearthstones are desolated by the ravages of this unholy war." He also had a humorous eye, as shown in this January 1876 entry recalling the conversion of Wilson Mason, an auctioneer: "Long in the habit of crying 'going' 'going' 'going' 'gone'—he cried out in heavenly hopes—'Glory to God, I'm going to Heaven'—'going' 'going' 'going'–but he did not say '*gone*' he said glory."

Browder's diaries reveal a man who held to evangelical, middle-class, and southern values. As a preacher Browder emphasized the importance of the conversion experience and Christian growth, but he also spoke out against such evils as dancing, alcohol, horse racing, Sabbath breaking, swearing, and moonlight parties. He applauded hard work and thrift and cried out for discipline and responsibility in the family, church, classroom, and society. At the same time he had great compassion for the poor and responded generously to their needs.

Browder's views on the great national issues of his day were representative of most slave-owning Kentuckians. He opposed the breakup of the Union, but when war came his sympathies were with the Confederacy. Nevertheless, as a devout Christian he "cheerfully acquiesced" to God's will, believing at the outset that the outcome of the war would be "a providential settlement of the great slavery question." Browder always expressed considerable compassion toward slaves and freedmen, but he also held to the prevailing belief, especially in the South, that they had a subordinate place. His descriptions of ordinary people living through real events and crises, such as the Civil War, bring nineteenth-century America to life in such diverse areas as the family, religion, agriculture, medical practices, slavery, race relations, education, communication (the telegraph and even the telephone), and transportation.

• Browder's journals are located in the Kentucky Library, Western Kentucky University, Bowling Green. A biographical sketch of Browder is in Richard L. Troutman, ed., *The Heavens Are Weeping: The Diaries of George Richard Browder, 1852–1886* (1987).

RICHARD L. TROUTMAN

BROWERE, John Henri Isaac (18 Nov. 1790–10 Sept. 1834), sculptor, was born John Henry Brower in New York City, the son of Jacob Brower and Ann Catherine Gendon. At some later date he added an "e" to his last name, adopted the French spelling of his middle name, and added the name of Isaac. He attended but did not graduate from Columbia College. He married Eliza Derrick in 1811; their son Albertus del Orient became a painter. Browere studied drawing with the artists Archibald and Alexander Robertson, and from 1812 to 1815 he was a schoolteacher in Tarrytown, New York. In 1815 he moved back to New York City and began painting portraits and miniatures. He also became interested in sculpture around this time and executed his earliest-known work in this medium, a plaster mask of Alexander Hamilton (New York State Historical Association, Cooperstown) derived from a portrait by Archibald Robertson.

At that time Browere developed an interest in life masks, motivated by a desire to secure the most accurate reproduction of a person's features. According to family tradition, his first subjects were his children; but his first known subject was his former teacher, Archibald Robertson, and his second was Judge Pierpont Edwards of Connecticut (both masks are unlocated). He continued to paint portraits, although none of his work in that medium has been located. In 1817 he received a commission to paint John Paulding, one of the captors of Major John André. Paulding could not spare the time to pose, so Browere made a life mask to serve as the model for the portrait. It is not known whether he executed the painting, but the mask (owned by the New York State Historical Association) is the earliest of Browere's life masks known to survive. He subsequently spent two years traveling through Italy, France, and England, studying art and visiting galleries. Then he returned to New York, where he continued to work as a painter and sculptor.

When the marquis de Lafayette made his triumphal tour of the United States in 1824–1825, Browere was one of the artists for whom he consented to pose. The resulting life mask (New York State Historical Association), made in Independence Hall in Philadelphia, received much favorable attention. The success of the Lafayette portrait gave Browere the idea of taking the life masks of other prominent men and women and creating a national portrait gallery that would be cast in bronze and displayed in Washington, D.C. Browere eschewed the use of plaster of Paris, a heavy material that can rest uncomfortably on a subject's face and distort the features. He used a lightweight substance of his own invention, the recipe for which remained a closely guarded secret but probably was similar to present-day *moulage*. He applied it in layers and allowed about twenty minutes for it to set before removing the hardened material. Into this negative mold he poured plaster, resulting in a positive cast. Affixing the mask to an armature, he sculpted the torso in plaster and refined the likeness by carving open eyes and hair. The finished work was a most lifelike and realistic portrayal.

Browere traveled from Virginia to Massachusetts taking the likenesses of Thomas Jefferson, James and Dolley Madison, Henry Clay, David Porter, Alexander Macomb, Charles Carroll of Carrollton, John and John Quincy Adams (all New York State Historical Association), Gilbert Stuart (Redwood Library and Athenaeum, Newport, R.I.), and other prominent Americans. Most of his sitters thought the process was very pleasurable; the only one who felt otherwise was Jefferson, who found the experience so unpleasant that he vowed never to pose for another portrait. (In this instance Browere's material seems to have dried more rapidly than usual, probably because of atmospheric conditions peculiar to Monticello, where the sitting took place.) Jefferson forgave the sculptor, but garbled accounts of his ordeal found their way into the newspapers, causing Browere a great deal of embarrassment.

Browere devoted most of his time, energy, and money to his portrait gallery. He seems to have continued to accept private commissions, but very little is known of such work. His most unusual commission was for a death mask of the Quaker leader Elias Hicks to serve as the model for a formal portrait. As burial had already occurred, Browere surreptitiously exhumed the body in the dead of night, made the mask, and reburied the corpse.

Browere also published art criticism under the pseudonym "Middle-Tint the Second." His sharp criticisms were not appreciated by his fellow artists, who were well aware of Middle-Tint's true identity. Among his enemies were John Trumbull and William Dunlap, and he was never elected either to Trumbull's American Academy of the Fine Arts or to the National Academy of Design, of which Dunlap was vice president. Contemporary and later accounts suggest that Browere was gregarious, opinionated, boastful, and proud of his achievements as an artist.

In 1833 he traveled to Washington to take a life mask of Martin Van Buren (New York State Historical Association), his last known work. After only a few hours illness, he died of cholera the following year at his home in New York City and was buried in the Carmine Street churchyard. On his deathbed he had directed his family to put his portrait gallery in storage for forty years. Several of the life masks were exhibited at the Centennial Exposition in Philadelphia in 1876, but they received little attention and were returned to storage. Several of the masks were sold or otherwise disappeared over the next sixty years. The remaining works remained in the possession of Browere's descendants until 1940, when Stephen C. Clark purchased the seventeen busts and four masks that then composed the collection. He had all of the busts cast in bronze, and in 1960 he bequeathed both the originals and the bronze copies to the New York State Historical Association in Cooperstown.

Because Browere's busts were not modeled entirely by hand but incorporated life masks, most of his fellow artists did not consider them to be works of art. Moreover, most people preferred the dry neoclassicism then prevailing to the lifelike naturalism of Browere's portrayals. His work, however, was the forerunner of the realism that dominated American portrait sculpture later in the nineteenth century, and his portraits are remarkably accurate likenesses of some of the United States' most prominent early leaders.

• A plaster bas-relief of Browere, evidently a self-portrait, was given by his descendants in 1934 to the New-York Historical Society, New York City. In addition to the collection of life masks, the New York State Historical Association in Cooperstown owns a collection of nineteenth- and twentieth-century documents relating to Browere's work, including an unpublished biography written in 1942 by the sculptor's great-great-great-grandson, Everett Lee Millard. A recent account of Browere's life and work is David Meschutt, *A Bold Experiment: John Henri Isaac Browere's Life Masks of Prominent Americans* (1988), which contains a full bibliography. Meschutt discusses Browere's life masks of Thomas Jefferson in "A Perfect Likeness: John H. I. Browere's Life Mask of Thomas Jefferson," *American Art Journal* 21, no. 4 (1989): 4–25.

DAVID MESCHUTT

BROWN, Aaron Venable (15 Aug. 1795–8 Mar. 1859), politician, was born in Brunswick County, Virginia, the son of Aaron Brown, a Methodist minister, and Elizabeth Melton. Born into a slaveowning family, Brown graduated from the University of North Carolina in 1814. After his matriculation his parents moved to Giles County, Tennessee, so upon the completion of his studies Brown studied law in Nashville. In 1817 Brown was admitted to the Tennessee bar and opened a law practice in Nashville; shortly thereafter he moved to Pulaski in Giles County. While practicing law he also invested in cotton planting and established himself as a member of the wealthy planter class. At an unknown date he married Sarah Woodford Burrus; the couple had four children. Sarah Woodford Brown died, apparently in 1844. The next year Brown married the widowed Cynthia Pillow Saunders. This union produced one child.

Brown embarked on his political career in 1821 with his election to the Tennessee state senate. He served four times as state senator and once as a member of the state house of representatives, and he took a particular interest in the reorganization of Tennessee's judicial system and advocated limiting the number of crimes punishable by death. At the same time he emerged as a staunch supporter of Andrew Jackson and as a close personal and political ally of James K. Polk, with whom Brown practiced law from 1822 until 1824. When in the 1830s Tennessee's Jackson party divided into Whigs and Democrats, Brown remained loyal to Jackson's Democracy. In 1839 he won election to Congress, and as a congressman for six years he spoke often for cardinal Democratic policies, such as the independent treasury and opposition to protective tariffs and a national bank. John Quincy Adams in his diary referred to him as one of "the Jackson trumpeters" in Congress who "blew till they brayed like jackasses." Brown also became an early and zealous advocate for the annexation of Texas, and in February 1843 he obtained from Jackson a letter expressing the former president's support for annexation, which proved instrumental in obtaining the 1844 Democratic presidential nomination for his friend Polk.

After Polk's election Brown determined to retire from Congress, probably because he expected an appointment in the new administration. Brown did serve as the president-elect's agent in Washington during the winter of 1845, but Polk never offered him an official position; instead, the Tennessee state Democratic convention nominated him as the party's gubernatorial candidate. Brown accepted the nomination only reluctantly, but he nevertheless defeated the Whig former senator Ephraim H. Foster in a close election. His administration coincided with the beginning of the Mexican War, and Whigs accused Governor Brown of inefficiency and incompetence for delaying the organization of the state's volunteers for service in the war. His candidacy for reelection in 1847 also suffered from the popular backlash in the state to "Jim Polk's War." Despite a declaration of his willingness to support the popular general Zachary Taylor's presidential claims—on the condition that Taylor receive the nomination of the Democratic national convention—Brown lost to the Whig candidate Neill S. Brown (who was no relation).

Although Aaron Brown never again held elected office, he remained active in politics as a leading figure in the Southern rights wing of Tennessee's Democratic party. In 1849 he was a principal manager of the gubernatorial candidacy of William Trousdale, who pledged in his campaign to defend "at all hazards and to the last extremity" the South's right to expand slavery into territory acquired in the Mexican War. Trousdale won his race, but Tennessee's Democrats were forced to modify their call for the defense of southern rights "to the last extremity" when popular support for the Compromise of 1850 left them open to the charge of advocating disunion. Thus, although Brown criticized the compromise for failing to provide justice to the South, his "Tennessee Platform," composed for and presented to the Southern Convention at Nashville in November 1850, declared his willingness to abide by the compromise while threatening commercial nonintercourse with the North should that section attempt to undermine the agreement.

Brown continued in the 1850s to promote the defense of southern rights as a national priority. In 1852 and 1854 he attended the Southern Commercial Conventions at New Orleans and Charleston, and he held a convention office at the latter gathering. Still, he remained active in the national Democratic party, viewing it as the best institution for maintaining southern rights; at the 1852 national party convention he chaired the committee on resolutions and was thought by many to have authored the platform for Franklin Pierce's presidential campaign. Widely regarded as one of the most prominent southern Democrats, in the early 1850s he was contending against rivals in Tennessee for preferment in the national party. His exertions finally paid off when he used his influence to swing Tennessee's delegation at the 1856 Democratic national convention in favor of the presidential nomination of James Buchanan. Brown received only twenty-nine votes for his own vice presidential nomination, but he campaigned energetically for the Democratic ticket and was rewarded with an appointment as Buchanan's postmaster general. This appointment marked the pinnacle of his political career, but his service as a cabinet officer was generally undistinguished. Buchanan's biographer noted only that Brown and his wife "brought with them from Tennessee more wealth than they knew what to do with and determined to show it off to Washington society."

One Tennessee Whig noted in 1859 that a local newspaper had been established for the purpose of promoting Brown's claims for the Democratic presidential nomination in 1860. Although little evidence exists to suggest that Brown intended to seek the nomination, and while his prospects were remote at best, one could understand Brown's desire for the presidency, for he had played an important role in the elevation of three successful party nominees. Any presidential aspirations he may have had could not be pursued because, after two years in the cabinet, Brown contracted pneumonia and died in Washington.

• A small collection of Brown's private papers and a larger one containing papers relating to his service as governor are at the Tennessee State Library and Archives in Nashville, but the best available collection of Brown's letters are those to James K. Polk, published in Herbert Weaver et al., eds., *Correspondence of James K. Polk* (8 vols., 1969–). Brown's most important public papers and addresses are published in *Speeches, Congressional and Political, and Other Writings, of Ex-Governor Aaron V. Brown, of Tennessee* (1854). Charles G. Sellers's two-volume biography, *James K. Polk: Jacksonian, 1795–1843* (1957) and *James K. Polk: Continentalist, 1843–1846* (1966), provides the best account of Brown's congressional career and his relationship with the eleventh president. Philip S. Klein, *President James Buchanan: A Biography* (1962), comments on Brown's service as postmaster general. On Brown's career in politics in Tennessee, see volumes two and four of Robert H. White, ed., *Messages of the Governors of Tennessee* (8 vols., 1952–1972); Jonathan M. Atkins, *Politics, Parties, and the Sectional Conflict in Tennessee, 1832–1861* (1996); and John E. Tricamo, "Tennessee Politics, 1845–1861" (Ph.D. diss., Columbia Univ., 1965). Obituaries are in the *Nashville Republican Banner* and the *Nashville Union and American*, 9 Mar. 1859.

JONATHAN M. ATKINS

BROWN, Abbie Farwell (21 Aug. 1871–5 Mar. 1927), writer, was born in Boston, Massachusetts, the daughter of Benjamin F. Brown, a merchant, and Clara Neal, a writer. The family prided itself on its distinguished New England ancestry, which could be traced back to the *Mayflower* settlers. The weight of this family history, which encompassed ten generations of New Englanders, probably helped keep Brown and her sister Ethel at the family home, 41 West Cedar Street on Beacon Hill; they spent their entire lives there with their mother. Clara Neal Brown had a particularly strong influence on her daughters. She encouraged them to develop their artistic skills and exercise their creativity at home, for example, in *The Catkin*, a family magazine that the girls helped write and illustrate.

Brown's parents provided her with an excellent formal education, which shaped her literary career in many different ways. After she graduated as valedictorian of the Bowdoin School in 1886, she attended Boston Girls' Latin School. Among the close friends she made there was Josephine Preston Peabody, who also became a writer and, along with Caroline Ticknor, one of Brown's closest colleagues. Brown considered her own work as editor of the school's periodical, the *Jabberwock*, to be the start of her literary career. Soon after her graduation in 1891 she began to publish verses—illustrated by her sister Ethel—in the popular children's magazine *St. Nicholas.* The years she spent at Radcliffe College (1891–1892 and 1893–1894) may have inspired another early literary effort, *Quits*, a one-act comedy set in a women's college. Beginning in 1898 Brown wrote regular columns for the *St. Louis Globe-Democrat* under the pseudonym Jean Neal, covering subjects from women's athletics to picnics and flirtations. She became a special foreign correspondent for the newspaper when she went on her first trip abroad in 1899. A series of monthly letters reported the activities of four "Bachelor Girls" traveling through Scotland, the Alps, Paris, and London.

While in England on this trip, Brown visited lovely Chester Cathedral; its enchanting carved choir stalls, depicting episodes in the life of St. Werburge, gave her the idea for her first book. Brown's *The Book of Saints and Friendly Beasts*, a collection of stories for children based on old Christian legends, was published in 1900 by Houghton Mifflin Company. Critics praised the book for its imagination and charming style, as well as for the subtlety of its moral message. Brown followed this success with two more widely acclaimed books for children: *The Lonesomest Doll* (1901) and another adaptation of popular European traditions, *In the Days of Giants: A Book of Norse Tales* (1902).

Though Brown wrote plays, lyrics, and poetry for adults throughout her life, she quickly became known as a talented author for younger readers and concentrated her work in this genre, eventually producing more than thirty books for children. In 1902 the publishing firm Hall and Locke named her editor of their series, the Young Folks' Library, while in her own writing, Brown experimented with subject matter and with the boundaries of juvenile literature. Though Brown usually drew upon elements of myth and legend, she attempted to integrate fantasy with a more modern, realistic story in *The Lucky Stone* (1914). The novel's protagonist is a tenement girl whose belief in fairies inspires a rich young lady to reject a life of uselessness and devote herself to charity instead.

Brown also penned a biography for the juvenile market, *The Boyhood of Edward MacDowell* (1924), and wrote poetry, plays, and lyrics for children. Among her best-remembered efforts in music was "On the Trail," the official song of the Girl Scouts, written with melodist Mabel W. Daniels. Daniels collaborated with Brown on vocal music for adults as well, including "Apple Blossoms" and "In Springtime," a cycle for women's voices. Brown's ear for the types of rhythms and rhymes that children would love made her a popular lyricist; she worked for many years on the Music Hour and the Progressive Music Series for Silver, Burdett and Company. In her last, unfinished effort in this vein, Brown began to compose original verse that would fit Filipino folk melodies and translate Filipino verse to set to original tunes—a sizable project in cross-culturalism.

Brown was less successful when she wrote outside the field of juvenile literature. Her most notable poem for adults was "Peace—With a Sword," first published in the *Boston Transcript* in 1916 and the following year performed in Symphony Hall, Boston, to chorus and orchestral music by Mabel Daniels. Reverend William Harman van Allen called it "the noblest poem of the World War from any American voice." Brown wrote the poem as part of her work as a "Vigilante," a member of a group of 200 writers who "pledged their pens to serve the country during the war" (*Abbie Farwell Brown*, p. 22). She was an active leader of many other writers' organizations as well, including the Boston Authors Club, the Boston Drama League, the Poetry Society of America, and the American Folklore Society. A charter member of the New England Poetry Club, Brown was affectionately regarded and appreciated by her fellow writers. Her energy, productivity, and unflagging hard work animated the group. "I always feel inevitable sadness when anything I have greatly enjoyed doing is at last done, *doing* being the greatest joy in life," Brown wrote, inspiring her peers to keep "doing" as well (quoted in *Abbie Farwell Brown*, p. 3). She wrote the official history of the club in 1923, while a vice president, and was serving as its president at her death. Scholars regard Brown's leadership within the community of New England poets to be of even greater long-term significance than her own efforts as a poet. However, her later poetry, including her last book, *The Silver Stair* (1926), did receive some critical acclaim.

Brown's veiws on juvenile literature, as articulated in her frequent and passionate public lectures, help explain her books' original acclaim and long-lived popularity. She rejected the artificiality and sentimentality that marked an earlier generation of fiction for children. Instead, she insisted, stories and poems should appeal to their readers' preferences and instincts to capture children's attention and imagination by striving toward naturalness. Her recastings of legends, myths, and other popular traditions succeeded precisely because she made them seem real to young readers while preserving the romanticism and ideality of the stories. This careful navigation between style and substance has earned Brown a secure place in the field of children's literature.

• Abbie Farwell Brown's papers, held by the Schlesinger Library at Radcliffe College, include manuscripts of many of her stories and novels, correspondence, travel diaries, and newspaper clippings. The Radcliffe College Archives houses additional materials. The *Boston Post*, 12 Dec. 1902, and the *Boston Herald*, 10 Jan. 1904, published biographical sketches of Brown. Caroline Ticknor wrote a memorial tribute to Brown that appeared in the *Boston Transcript*, 23 Mar. 1927;

she and many other Boston writers contributed to *Abbie Farwell Brown: A Tribute to Her Life and Work*, published by the Boston Authors Club (1929). A more recent biography of Brown is in Edward T. James, ed., *Notable American Women* (1971). See also "Abbie Farwell Brown and Josephine Preston Peabody: The Intimate Letters of Youth," *Poetry Review* (Mar./Apr. 1931), and Cornelia Meigs, *A Critical History of Children's Literature*, rev. ed. (1969). Obituaries are in the *New York Times*, 6 Mar. 1927, and in the *Boston Transcript*, 5 Mar. 1927.

LAURA PRIETO CHESTERTON

BROWN, Albert Gallatin (31 May 1813–12 June 1880), U.S. and Confederate congressman, was born in Chester District, South Carolina, the son of Joseph Brown. (His mother's identity is unknown.) The second son of a struggling, ambitious farmer, Brown moved with his family in 1820 from South Carolina to Copiah County, Mississippi. In this raw frontier setting his father acquired land and slaves. After attending Mississippi College and Jefferson College from 1829 to 1832, Brown wanted to attend Princeton or Yale, but when his father refused to pay the costs, he turned to law and politics. He won his first elective office in 1832 as a colonel of militia. He was admitted to the Mississippi bar in 1833 and had just started his law practice in the now extinct town of Gallatin when he was elected a brigadier general in the militia. Soon after his marriage in 1835 to Elizabeth Frances Taliaferro, he entered the Mississippi legislature as a Democratic representative. He began a remarkable record of holding elective office virtually without interruption for the next thirty years.

Although he had inherited a slave from his father and was to own seventy-eight slaves by 1860, Brown built his political career by championing the interests of Mississippi common whites, poor farmers who owned no slaves or a few at most. As a state representative from 1835 to 1839 and a congressman from 1839 to 1841, he opposed Whig attempts to resurrect a national bank. He depicted the bank as a tool of the monied aristocracy that cheated laborers and farmers out of their hard-earned income through inflated paper currency. It was "an institution," he claimed, "which makes the weak weaker and the potent more powerful, ever filching from the poor man's hand to replenish the rich man's purse." He also emerged as a bitter opponent of northern abolitionism. He won the support of nonslaveholders by appealing to their racial pride. The abolitionists, he insisted, would degrade southern poor whites by stripping them of their privileged social position over the slaves.

Brown's first wife had died five months after their marriage, and in early 1841 Brown married Roberta E. Young, with whom he had two children. Citing a pressing need to rebuild his personal finances, Brown declined to run for reelection to Congress in 1841. However, he did consent to run for the Mississippi Circuit Court, and he easily won election. He resigned his judgeship in 1843 and accepted his party's nomination for governor, handily winning in 1844 and again in 1846. As governor, Brown compiled an outstanding record of state-supported social reform. Under his leadership, the state legislature established a school for the blind and an asylum for the mentally ill and secured funds for a state university and Mississippi's first system of free schools. He returned to Congress in 1848 and served in the House until 1853. From 1854 until the secession of Mississippi he was in the U.S. Senate.

By the beginning of the 1850s, Brown emerged as the head of the radical wing of the Mississippi Democratic party. He strongly opposed the Compromise of 1850, especially California's admission as a free state, and he unsuccessfully tried to commit Mississippi to secession in the state election of 1851. Much of his radicalism resulted from his fear that growing northern majorities were on the verge of completely shutting slavery out of the territories, a policy that he felt would lead to emancipation and a race war in the South. To counter the northern policy of exclusion, he preached a southern version of Manifest Destiny in which slaveholders would carve out a tropical empire in Central America and the Caribbean. Frustrated by the inability of the South to bring Kansas into the Union as a slave state during the presidency of James Buchanan, Brown introduced resolutions in the Senate in February 1859 calling for a federal code of laws to protect slavery in the territories. This issue of a federal slave code played a major role in the disruption of the Democratic party in 1860, which paved the way for Abraham Lincoln's election.

Much more so than Mississippi's other senator and his party rival, Jefferson Davis, Brown was an ardent southern nationalist who urged secession in response to Lincoln's victory. Although he would have preferred that Mississippi leave the Union in a cooperative move with other slave states, he readily supported the decision of the secession convention in January 1861 to secede by separate state action. In the early months of the war, he organized a company that joined the Eighteenth Mississippi Infantry. As its captain, he fought at First Manassas. He also saw service at Lessburg. For most of the war, however, he was in the Confederate Senate. Totally committed to southern independence, by late 1863 he called for a series of extreme nationalist measures that went well beyond what the Davis administration would sanction. He demanded forced restrictions on cotton production, heavy direct taxes, and a conscription policy shorn of exemptions that would sweep virtually all able-bodied white males into Confederate armies. By February 1865 he even favored the arming and freeing of 200,000 slaves in a last-ditch effort to save the Confederacy.

Brown's postwar career was both anticlimactic and disillusioning. He accepted the finality of southern defeat and urged compliance with the northern terms, including those conferring political rights on the freedmen. His finances were ruined, and he viewed the states of the former Confederacy as conquered provinces whose residents had no choice but to submit to the will of the victorious North. Although he believed that black suffrage was "unnecessarily harsh" and "extremely dangerous to the safety and best interest of the whole country," he counseled his fellow whites to accept the inevitability of a political role for the freedmen and to work with blacks to bring them under the leadership of conservative whites. Most white Mississippians scorned his advice, and he never again ran for public office. He died at his estate in Terry, Mississippi.

• Most of Brown's letters have been lost, but some of his correspondence can be found in the J. F. H. Claiborne Collection of the Mississippi Department of Archives and History. A brief biography of his prewar career is included in M. W. Cluskey, ed., *Speeches, Messages, and Other Writings of the Hon. Albert G. Brown* (1859). The standard biography is James Byrne Ranck, *Albert Gallatin Brown: Radical Southern Nationalist* (1937). See also James D. Lynch, *Bench and Bar of Mississippi* (1881), and Dunbar Rowland, *Official and Statistical Register of Mississippi* (1908).

WILLIAM L. BARNEY

BROWN, Alexander (17 Nov. 1764–4 Apr. 1834), founder of an Anglo-American mercantile and financial services firm, was born in Ballymena, Ireland, the son of William Brown and Margaretta Davison. As a young adult he moved to Belfast, where he became involved in the linen trade, reportedly working as an auctioneer on occasion. His brother Stewart left for Baltimore in the mid-1790s, and Alexander followed in 1800. He had married Grace Davison in 1783, and after his arrival in Baltimore he opened a shop that featured linen goods supplied primarily by his in-laws and business associates in Ireland. The mercantile business prospered, and Brown soon widened the scope of his activities. He typified the all-purpose merchant of the early national era (c. 1790–1820), dabbling in various goods and services, including insurance and shipping. When his second son, George, joined the Baltimore firm in 1808, the capital account had risen to $120,000.

Within a few years of the firm's founding, Brown made agency agreements with merchants in other southern ports involved in the transatlantic trade in tobacco and cotton. In 1803 he arranged through an agent in Savannah, Georgia, to purchase raw cotton for direct shipment to the English market. This purchase was one of the earliest in a long series of business transactions that kept the Brown firm deeply involved in the Anglo-American cotton market for decades.

Brown also became a participant in the rapidly maturing foreign exchange market. Most foreign bills of exchange were drawn in British pounds sterling, although some Dutch guilders and French francs linked to tobacco exports were traded as well. Foreign exchange transactions involving overseas shippers can be traced back to the seventeenth century, but markets remained local or regional in scope and were served by few, if any, financial specialists. Brown entered this market by performing essentially brokerage functions that entailed only a limited degree of risk. He bought sterling bills from American exporters with credit balances in England, endorsed them, and within a few days, or weeks at most, resold the bills at modest profit margins to Baltimore importers who owed trade debts overseas.

The character of the firm's business changed dramatically when Brown's eldest son, William, was sent to establish a branch office in Liverpool in 1810. The creation of a network of branch offices in the United States and England was an institutional strategy unduplicated by the firm's leading rivals in the merchant banking field. The solicitation of consignments from cotton shippers in ports along the entire South Atlantic coastline became an important aspect of the partnership's operations. To attract consignments, the firm's southern representatives offered prospective shippers advances covering roughly 75 to 80 percent of the anticipated sales proceeds in Liverpool. The advance took the form of a sterling bill of exchange drawn on the Liverpool office that the American shipper could sell locally to third parties. Later, the New York branch handled an increasing volume of consignments of British finished goods.

The existence of a branch office across the Atlantic gave the firm the chance to shift from the status of foreign exchange broker to full-fledged dealer. No longer dependent on exporters to generate credit balances, Alexander Brown & Sons could create internally a supply of sterling bills drawn in the right amounts to meet the requirements of American importers. The U.S. branches no longer needed to closely match their purchases and sales of foreign exchange, since the Liverpool office had access to financing in the English money market at low interest rates to ride out any temporary imbalances. Gradually, the Brown firm adopted seasonal strategies to enhance profit margins; the partners sold heavily to American importers in the spring and summer months and replenished their overdrawn accounts in fall and winter by purchasing bills of exchange from cotton exporters.

During the 1820s the firm emerged as the second leading foreign exchange dealer in the United States, just behind the Second Bank of the United States, which conducted its operations in cooperation with the House of Baring. Brown's third son, John, opened a branch office in Philadelphia in 1818, and the youngest son, James, did the same in New York in 1825. The partners in this family enterprise occasionally bragged that bills of exchange drawn on their London office periodically commanded the same premium prices as similar bills drawn by the Second Bank on Baring Brothers—something that could not be said about any other competitor in the U.S. market. When the charter of the Second Bank expired in 1836, two years after Alexander's death, the Brown firm assumed the leadership position in the U.S. foreign exchange market and maintained that status until late in the nineteenth century.

In the 1820s the Browns broadened their range of financial services to include the opening of letters of credit for American importers. Customers paid a commission, initially in the range of 2.5 to 5 percent, that allowed them to benefit from the high credit rating that the Brown firm had established in foreign mercantile and financial markets over the years. The Browns, in essence, guaranteed their customers' foreign debts and earned a fee for providing this service. With a letter of credit in hand, the American foreign trader could readily purchase goods overseas in markets where they were personally unknown, and typically at lower prices, since the seller had little fear of any exposure to bad debts. The U.S. branches issued the letter of credit, and the Liverpool office honored the bills of exchange drawn under its terms. This business was potentially highly profitable, since the Browns tied up none of their own capital in letter of credit operations during normal times. The firm was only contingently liable for these debts; the partners had to invest their own monies only when American importers failed to live up to their financial obligations. Unfortunately, letter of credit operations were also extremely risky because sudden downturns in the economy could force many customers to appeal to creditors simultaneously and thereby strain the resources of merchant banking firms to stay afloat. The Browns were one of the major letter of credit issuers in the 1830s, and they required financial assistance from the Bank of England to survive the Panic of 1837. When the economy revived in the 1840s the firm became the leading issuer in the U.S. letter of credit market, a position it held into the early twentieth century.

By the 1830s Alexander Brown could look back upon a long, varied, and enormously successful business career. During his lifetime the firm had generally maintained its involvement in both mercantile activities and financial services. The capital account of Alexander Brown & Sons grew to more than $4.5 million. Soon after Alexander's death in Baltimore, the mercantile activities in the United States were sharply curtailed, although the Liverpool office continued to accept cotton consignments. The partners decided to focus on foreign exchange and letters of credit—two oligopolistic markets where the Brown firm was well positioned. Under the sons' leadership, the enterprise rose to the pinnacle of the Anglo-American merchant banking field.

• Letterbooks of Alexander Brown & Sons are located in the Manuscript Division of the Library of Congress. With some gaps, the letterbooks provide a record of the outgoing correspondence of the Baltimore office from 1800 to 1840. Some materials that pertain to Alexander are located in the Brown Brothers & Co. papers at the New-York Historical Society. None of his personal papers have survived, nor is there any biography. Information on his background and business career is in several histories of the firm that he founded, including John Crosby Brown, *A Hundred Years of Merchant Banking* (1909); Frank R. Kent, *The Story of Alexander Brown & Sons* (1925); John A. Kouwenhoven, *Partners in Banking* (1968); and Edwin J. Perkins, *Financing Anglo-American Trade: The House of Brown, 1800–1880* (1975). An obituary is in the *Baltimore American*, 4 Apr. 1834.

EDWIN J. PERKINS

BROWN, Alexander Ephraim (14 May 1852–26 Apr. 1911), inventor and manufacturer, was born in Cleveland, Ohio, the son of Fayette Brown, a prominent local businessman, and Cornelia Curtis. After receiving his early education in the public schools of Cleveland and graduating from Central High School, he entered the Brooklyn Polytechnic Institute in Brooklyn, New York, in the fall of 1869. Following his graduation with a degree in civil engineering in June 1872, Brown joined the U.S. Geological Survey and spent the next several months exploring and surveying the Yellowstone region of the western United States. While working for the survey, he received an offer of employment from the Massillon Iron Bridge Company in Masillon, Ohio. Returning east, he served that firm for two years as chief engineer. He gained further practical engineering experience from 1875 until 1878 as supervisor of iron mining and engineer of construction in the iron regions near Lake Superior. Brown returned to Cleveland to marry Carrie M., the daughter of General James Barnett, in 1877; the couple eventually had a son and a daughter.

Brown returned to Cleveland for good in 1878. In that year he took a position as a mechanical engineer with the Telegraph Supply Company (later known as Brush Electric Company), a firm that developed and promoted the inventions of its founder, Charles F. Brush. An engineer of both vision and talent, Brown utilized old iron and steels rails (previously useful only as scrap) in the construction of bridge columns. This innovation resulted in substantial monetary savings. Brown spent much of his spare time in mechanical experimentation and research, continually seeking ways to save money and use manpower more efficiently.

Brown's insights and innovations often proved useful, but one incident in particular changed the focus of his career. While observing the unloading of a vessel carrying a load of iron ore, he noted the large numbers of men required to empty the ship. Under the system then in use, long lines of workers pushed heavily loaded wheelbarrows in a never-ending cycle of manual toil. Struck by the inefficiency of this method, Brown remarked to a friend, "All that work ought to be done automatically and all those laborers ought to be otherwise employed" (Avery, p. 533). After about five years of experimentation, Brown in 1879 demonstrated the first "Brown Hoisting Machine" on the shores of Lake Erie in Cleveland. The predecessor of the modern-day bridge crane, the device proved an immediate success because of the efficiency with which the operator could load and unload cargo by manipulating cables attached to the loader. In 1880 Brown obtained the first of many patents on his invention (and its subsequent improvements), and the Brown Hoisting Machinery Company was organized with a view toward the production of the new machines. Brown's father, who had assumed an early leadership in the shipping of iron ore from the Lake Superior region to Cleveland, served as the new company's president until his death in 1910, at which time the younger Brown, who had previously served as vice president and general manager of the firm, assumed the title.

The effects of Brown's invention were immediate and profound. The advent of the Bessemer process of steelmaking created an increase in the demand for the coal and iron ore needed in steel production. Brown's hoists enabled shippers to move their material with far more speed and cost efficiency than ever before. By 1925 it was possible to unload a 12,000-ton ore vessel in as many hours as it formerly took to unload a 500-ton ship.

Recognition followed Brown's achievements in due course. He served as president (1904–1905) of the Cleveland Civil Engineers Club and held memberships in the American Society of Mechanical Engineers, the American Institute of Mining Engineers, and the Engineers Club of New York. Brown died at his home in Cleveland on the day his daughter was to be married. First his brother Harvey Huntington Brown and then his son Alexander C. Brown succeeded him as president of the Brown Hoisting Machinery Company.

Alexander Ephraim Brown was one of a score of mechanically gifted individuals who, through their collective efforts, contributed greatly to the development of American heavy industry.

• The papers of Alexander Ephraim Brown are at the Western Reserve Historical Society archives, Cleveland, Ohio. Little has been written on Brown's life or career; the best sources remain his biographical entry in Elroy McKendree Avery, *A History of Cleveland and Its Environs: The Heart of New Connecticut*, vol. 3 (1918), and his son Alexander C. Brown's article, "Meeting the Demand: A Pictorial History of Ore and Coal Handling on the Great Lakes' Docks," *Trade Winds*, Apr. 1925, pp. 5–9. An obituary is in the *Cleveland Plain Dealer*, 27 Apr. 1911.

EDWARD L. LACH, JR.

BROWN, Alice (5 Dec. 1857–21 June 1948), author, was born in Hampton Falls, New Hampshire, the daughter of Levi Brown and Elizabeth Lucas, farmers. She attended the Robinson Academy in Exeter, New Hampshire, from which she graduated in 1876. Upon graduation, she assumed teaching duties in a country school. In 1880 she accepted a job teaching in Boston. There she also found a staff position at the *Christian Register*, a Unitarian publication, for which she wrote and edited; in 1885 she joined the staff of the *Youth's Companion*. While she worked for both publications, Brown published her first books, *Stratford-by-the-Sea* (1884) and *Fools of Nature* (1887), the latter a study of New England village people.

In Boston, Brown became close friends with the poet Louise Imogen Guiney, a devout Roman Catholic. Through Guiney, Brown (a Unitarian) learned about the traditions and teachings of Catholicism. In 1890 Brown and Guiney toured England for the summer. The next year they founded the Women's Rest Tour Association to enhance women's opportunities for travel. Brown soon began working on *Pilgrim Scrip*, the association's magazine. In 1911 she became association president, remaining in that office until her death. In 1895 she and Guiney took a walking tour of England and Wales, commemorated in her 1896 travel memoir *By Oak and Thorn*.

In 1894, with Guiney and Harriet Prescott Spofford, Brown coauthored *Three Heroines of New England Romance*. The following year, her collection of short stories *Meadow-Grass: Tales of New England Life* appeared. It was well received, and Brown was soon compared to other successful New England writers, including Sarah Orne Jewett, Rose Terry Cooke, and Mary Wilkins Freeman. The stories in *Meadow-Grass* are set in Tiverton, a fictional town modeled on Hampton Falls, that also provided the locale for her 1899 collection, *Tiverton Tales* (1899). Brown's interest in New England's past is also reflected in *Mercy Warren* (1896), an insightful biography of the revolutionary war historian and poet, in which Brown notes the importance of female friendships for women. In the two decades that followed the publication of *Meadow-Grass*, Brown published more than 120 stories in prestigious and popular magazines. A number of these stories are collected in *The County Road* (1906) and *Country Neighbors* (1910).

In 1895 Brown collaborated with Guiney on the biographical study *Robert Louis Stevenson*. The following year she published a collection of verse, *The Road to Castaly*. At the end of the decade, Brown resumed writing novels, publishing two, *King's End* and *Margaret Warrener*, in 1901. Although attracted to the novel as a form for exploring the complexities of human relationships, she seldom achieved the unity and the quality of characterization that are hallmarks of her short fiction. In addition to realist work, Brown also wrote pieces that explored the supernatural and the mystical element in human experience. Her efforts in this vein include *The Day of His Youth* (1897), the collection *High Noon* (1904), and *Kingdom in the Sky* (1932).

From 1907 to 1908 Brown participated in the experiment that produced *The Whole Family: A Novel by Twelve Authors*, which appeared serially in *Harper's Bazar* and then in book form. Other contributors included William Dean Howells, Henry James (1843–1916), and Mary Wilkins Freeman. Critic Alfred Bendixen has argued that "Peggy," the chapter Brown contributed, succeeded in resolving the complexities of the plot that had threatened the unity of the project. A willing collaborator and editor, Brown enjoyed the social side of her literary endeavors as well. In 1913 she joined the Boston Authors Club and served as its president from 1920 through 1922. Her home on Pinckney Street in Boston's Beacon Hill neighborhood frequently served as a location for club activities, and she often entertained summer visitors at her farm in Hill, New Hampshire.

Brown was also drawn to the theater. In 1914 she won the Winthrop Ames Prize ($10,000) for her full-length play *Children of Earth: A Play of New England*, which Ames produced on Broadway in 1915. Receiving mixed reviews, the play had only a short run. Brown fared better with her one-act plays, some based on her short stories, that were often produced by little theater groups. Her most successful was *Joint Owners in Spain* (1914), its enduring popularity evidenced by its production in the Little Theatre Tournament in 1929 and its inclusion in the anthology *Fifty One-Act Plays* in 1934. Brown's additional work in this genre appeared in *One-Act Plays* (1921).

Alice Brown remained active as an author through the 1920s and 1930s, during which she experimented with new genres. She published a biography of Guiney in 1921; a five-act play, *Charles Lamb*, in 1924; and *The Mysteries of Ann*, a detective novel, in 1925. In 1930 she began corresponding with the Reverend Joseph Mary Lelen, a Catholic priest and member of the Glenmary Missioners. Their eighteen-year correspondence led Brown to explore her religious faith, and this line of thought influenced her final work, a play titled *Pilgrim's Progress*, privately printed in 1944. Just prior to her death, she wrote to Father Lelen requesting baptism into the Catholic faith, but the sacrament was delayed. Alice Brown died in Boston.

The best of Alice Brown's prolific output has earned her a place in the circle of significant New England authors of her generation. Many of her novels and plays suffer from weakness in structure and development, but her short stories offer insightful portraits of New England life and character. The stories are finely crafted and often told with a gentle humor that acknowledges the frailties and foibles of human nature.

• Alice Brown's papers can be found in Beinecke Library, Yale University; the Sophia Smith Collection, Smith College; the Boston Public Library; and Dinand Library, College of the Holy Cross. Additional principal works by Brown include *Rose MacLeod* (1908), *The Story of Thyrza* (1909), *John Winterbourne's Family* (1910), *My Love and I* (1912), *Vanishing Points* (1913), *The Prisoner* (1916), *Bromley Neighborhood* (1917), *The Flying Teuton and Other Stories* (1918), *Old Crow* (1922), *Ellen Prior* (1923), *Dear Old Templeton* (1927), and *The Willoughbys* (1935). Two bibliographical articles are Susan Allen Toth, "Alice Brown (1857–1948)," *American Literary Realism* 5, no. 2 (1972): 134–43; and Margaret Ann Baker, "Alice Brown: A Bibliography of Books and Uncollected Prose," *American Literary Realism* 17, no. 1 (1984): 99–115.

There is no book-length biography of Brown, but both biographical and critical information can be found in Dorothea Walker, *Alice Brown* (1974). An early, though not very positive, appraisal of Brown's work appears in Charles Miner Thompson, "Short Stories of Alice Brown," *Atlantic Monthly*, July 1906, pp. 55–65. Assessments of Brown's contributions to New England fiction can be found in two essays by Susan Allen Toth, "A Forgotten View from Beacon Hill: Alice Brown's New England Short Stories," *Colby Library Quarterly* 10 (1973): 1–16, and "'The Rarest and Most Peculiar Grape': Versions of the New England Woman in 19th-Century Local Color Literature," *Kate Chopin Newsletter* 2, no. 2 (1976): 38–45. Also helpful are two essays by Beth Wynne Fisken, "Within the Limits of Alice Brown's 'Dooryards': Introspective Powers in Tiverton Tales," *Legacy* 5, no. 1 (1988): 15–25, and "Alice Brown," *Legacy* 6, no. 2 (1989): 51–57.

MELISSA MCFARLAND PENNELL

BROWN, Benjamin Gratz (28 May 1826–13 Dec. 1885), U.S. senator and governor of Missouri, was born in Lexington, Kentucky, the son of Mason Brown, a lawyer, and Judith Bledsoe. He was educated at Transylvania and Yale Universities, graduating from the latter in 1847. He then earned a degree from Louisville Law School. Upon being admitted to the bar in the fall of 1849, he moved to St. Louis to join his cousins Montgomery Blair and Frank Blair (1821–1875) in their law firm. Brown married Mary Gunn in 1858; they had eight children.

Brown was originally a Henry Clay Whig and a moderate emancipationist; his family, though slaveholders, favored gradual emancipation with colonization of freed slaves. The Browns, angered by the new Kentucky constitution of 1849, which would either expel all slaves subsequently emancipated or send them to prison, allowed several of their slaves to purchase their freedom before the new constitution went into effect. Under the influence of his cousins, Brown became associated with the efforts of Senator Thomas Hart Benton (1782–1858) to resist the proslavery wing of the Missouri Democratic party. He joined with Frank Blair and others in July 1852 to purchase the St. Louis *Morning Signal* as a Benton organ, renaming it the *Missouri Democrat*. He became a frequent contributor to its editorial pages and within two years assumed the post of editor in chief. From the outset the paper assumed a strong Free Soil position and later became the principal organ for Missouri's fledgling Republican party.

Cultivating the strong antislavery German element in St. Louis, Brown was elected to the legislature in 1852 on a pro-Benton ticket. One of his rivals for the German vote was Thomas C. Reynolds, a German-educated United States district attorney and a leader of the proslavery Democrats. Brown attacked Reynolds with venom in his editorials, and Reynolds responded with scorn. The two finally agreed to settle their differences with dueling pistols in August 1856. Brown was struck in the knee; he would limp the rest of his life. Reynolds was not harmed.

Brown continued to serve in the legislature until 1859, persistently assailing, in this slave state, the institution of slavery as the foe of free labor. Certainly no root and branch abolitionist, he advocated at this time gradual emancipation with compensation to owners and voluntary departure by freed blacks through colonization. In the volatile Missouri political climate of the 1850s, this view met with a mixed reaction. The dissolution of the Whig party and the emergence of the Know Nothings left many former Bentonites searching for new party affiliations. Although strongly attracted to the new Republican party, Brown was not yet ready to move openly into its ranks. The death of Benton in 1858 had freed Brown from his personal allegiance to him, but in an effort to hold on to some of Benton's more conservative supporters, Brown decided to run for reelection in 1858 simply as the "Opposition." The absence of a party organization contributed to his defeat as many Bentonites moved back into the regular Democratic party.

Shortly thereafter Brown resigned as editor in chief of the *Missouri Democrat* under pressure from Frank Blair for reasons not altogether certain. Brown spent this brief time away from antislavery politics organizing the Citizens Railway Company to construct St. Louis's first "street railroad." With the formation of the Missouri Republican party in 1860, however, Brown returned to the political wars as a delegate-at-large to the national convention in Chicago. Although he reluctantly supported Missouri's favorite son, Edward Bates, in the early balloting for president, Brown led the Missourians in throwing their votes behind Abraham Lincoln when the trend toward him became clear.

In the aftermath of Fort Sumter, Brown organized a volunteer regiment under President Lincoln's ninety-day enlistments and became its colonel. The outfit saw no military action, and he did not seek to extend his enlistment. When General John C. Frémont, commanding in Missouri, issued his emancipation order as a part of martial law in August 1861, Brown and many of his German supporters rallied to Frémont's support. Although Lincoln countermanded Frémont's order and ultimately removed him, the emancipation issue would not go away.

Brown now resumed editorial responsibility for the *Missouri Democrat* and moved to organize those forces rallying to the cause of immediate emancipation. The legislative election of 1862 centered around that issue, but no clear consensus emerged. Brown's supporters nominated him for the U.S. Senate, but a divided legislature could not agree on either his election or on emancipation. The state convention, which had kept Missouri from secession, reconvened in the summer of 1863 and passed a gradual emancipation ordinance for an end to slavery by 1870.

The more ardent emancipationists, led by Brown and Charles D. Drake, now organized the Radical Union party to press for a quicker resolution of that issue. By the time the legislature reconvened in December 1863, the Radicals had gained sufficient strength to elect Brown to the Senate for a four-year term. There he had great difficulty in supporting Lincoln, considering the president's reconstruction program too lenient. He joined other Senate Radicals in demanding the immediate emancipation of all slaves and instigated a "Freedom Convention" in Louisville in February 1864 to try to unite the border states behind the issue. Brown helped organize a Radical convention in May 1864, which nominated Frémont for the presidency.

The Missouri Radical Union party remained within the Republican fold, however, and carried the state elections that fall. Led by Drake, the Radicals also passed a referendum for a new state convention and elected a strong majority of the delegates. While Brown quickly endorsed the convention's passage of an immediate emancipation ordinance, he was dismayed when it did not back this up with suffrage for the newly freed slaves. He also had serious concerns about its stringent disfranchisement of southern sympathizers. Feeling increasingly out of touch with his own party, Brown took no part in the 1866 election and announced that because of ill health he would not be a candidate for reelection to the Senate.

In the aftermath of the Radical triumph that fall, Brown called a meeting of leading Radicals to consider the party's future. The presented resolutions calling for "Universal Suffrage and Universal Amnesty" that included the enfranchisement of blacks and the removal of restrictions against ex-Confederates. Drake and the more ardent Radicals walked out of the meeting in disgust. Those who remained endorsed Brown's views and thus formed the nucleus of the Liberal Republican movement that would split the Radical party in 1870.

Following his retirement from the Senate in 1867, Brown did not seek elective office for three years. He plunged back into politics in 1870 with a Decoration Day speech reiterating his "Universal Amnesty and Universal Suffrage" theme. He also endorsed woman suffrage, the eight-hour day for labor, and civil service reform. When the Radical State Convention refused to endorse the removal of disfranchisement restrictions, which the legislature had placed on the fall ballot, Brown joined Carl Schurz and other Liberals in bolting the party. Brown became the Liberal Republican gubernatorial candidate on a platform embracing his aforementioned slogan as well as tariff and civil service reform. With the Democrats endorsing the Liberal ticket, Brown was elected governor, and disfranchisement was repealed. The Democrats ran their own legislative candidates, however, and gained a majority in the House of Representatives against the divided Republicans. Brown believed it important to woo the Democrats to support his programs, but in doing so he alienated Schurz and other Liberal Republicans who did not want to acknowledge the Democratic role in their victory.

The success of the Liberal Republicans in Missouri encouraged those opponents of President Ulysses S. Grant within the Republican party to develop a national movement. At the national Liberal Republican convention in 1872, Brown unexpectedly endorsed Horace Greeley for president, in part to avenge himself against Schurz for sabotaging his own chances for the nomination. In return, Brown received the vice presidential nomination to the dismay of many of his former Liberal allies. The platform endorsed most of the Liberals' issues: civil service reform, local self-government, the postwar amendments, the resumption of specie payments, and a single term for president. In a compromise with the Greeleyites, however, it took a neutral stance on the tariff, which caused the Schurz Liberals additional concern.

Following the Liberal defeat, Brown retired from politics to devote himself to his law practice, although he did attend the Democratic National Convention in 1876. He died in St. Louis from overwork and exhaustion.

• There is a small body of Brown's papers in the Missouri Historical Society, St. Louis. The only biography is Norma L. Peterson, *Freedom and Franchise: The Political Career of B. Gratz Brown* (1965). The relationships between the Brown and Blair families are traced in Elbert B. Smith, *Francis Preston Blair* (1980). The origins of the Liberal Republican movement in Missouri are traced in William E. Parrish, *Missouri under Radical Rule, 1865–1870* (1965). The best study of the national movement remains Earl D. Ross, *The Liberal Republican Movement* (1919).

WILLIAM E. PARRISH

BROWN, Charles Brockden (17 Jan. 1771–22 Feb. 1810), novelist, historian, and editor, was born in Philadelphia, Pennsylvania, the son of Elijah Brown, a merchant and land conveyancer, and Mary Armitt. The fifth of six children in a prosperous Quaker family in the nation's most cosmopolitan city and first capital, Brown was shaped in his early years by his Quaker background and the era's tumultuous revolutionary politics. From 1781 to 1786 he received a classics-oriented secondary education under Robert Proud at the Friends' Latin School of Philadelphia and displayed an enthusiasm for literary composition. Although his earliest work is lost, he composed derivative poetry in the "primitive" vein, based on the Psalms and Ossian and planned but never completed verse epics on the exploits of Columbus, Pizarro, and Cortez. The period's political and ideological conflicts touched Brown's family directly when revolutionary authorities exiled his father to Virginia for several months, deeming the father's Quaker position of principled neutrality an aid to the British. While Brown's Quaker background facilitated his early exposure to progressive British dissenting writers such as William Godwin and Mary Wollstonecraft, who would become crucial influences, it left him outside the period's Congregationalist and Presbyterian cultural elite and predisposed him to his lifelong stance of reasoned skepticism of utopian or perfectionist notions for political change. That is, Brown's background and early years helped shape his career-long concern with the violent ideological controversies of the early republic, as well as his characteristic tendency to see both the destructive and productive aspects of the period's far-reaching political upheavals.

From 1787 to 1793 Brown accepted his family's plan to make him a lawyer and worked as an apprentice to Alexander Wilcocks, a prominent Philadelphia jurist. In 1793, however, he rejected this path and left his apprenticeship with the intention of making a living as a writer. In that time and place this was a remarkable and questionable decision. It was risky in practical terms because there was no precedent for earning one's livelihood as a literary artist and in a more complex cultural and class sense because literature was not considered a gentlemanly occupation. In particular, the novel, the genre in which Brown was to make his reputation, was considered a lowbrow and in some senses pernicious and disreputable branch of literature. Thus Brown's decision to become a writer was a bold one. He was not the first significant American novelist, as some older accounts suggest (figures such as Susanna Rowson and Hannah Foster preceded him), but he was the first important American writer to envision an exclusively literary career based on the romantico-modern assumption that literature constituted a separate sphere of culture worthy of pursuit in its own right.

Brown's earliest publications and novelistic projects date from the late 1780s to 1798, a lengthy period of literary and intellectual experimentation. He helped establish one literary group, the Belles Lettres Club, while a law student, and participated in another, the Friendly Club, while in New York in the late 1790s. Along with numerous unfinished narratives, extensive correspondence with fellow law students and club members during this period was an important vehicle for literary development. In these letters, Brown created fictional personas, developed ideas for original narratives, and gave free rein to exaggerated, melodramatic states of elation and depression. Both the correspondence and early works like *The Rhapsodist* (1789), his first published essay series, and *The Henrietta Letters* (c. 1790–1793), an attempt at an epistolary novel, derive from the eighteenth-century tradition of sensibility associated with writers such as Samuel Richardson, Jean-Jacques Rousseau, and Lawrence Sterne. Emphasizing this tradition's focus on private, inner feelings and extreme or estranged emotional states, these writings signal Brown's distance from the neoclassical ideals still dominant during this period. Although by no means as challenging or unorthodox as his later novels, these early writings suggest Brown's growing willingness to violate conventional standards of taste and to produce idiosyncratic narrative forms that tend toward fragmentation and incompletion. Similarly, Brown's intellectual enthusiasm during these years for British radical dissenters, notably the novels and political writings of Godwin and Wollstonecraft, indicates that, in both intellectual and literary terms, his early development occurred in more or less open opposition to the neoclassical principles advocated by the period's cultural conservatives. The final and most important work written during this period is *Alcuin: A Dialogue* (1798), a Wollstonecraft-influenced meditation on women's rights that is the first manifestation of Brown's career-long concern with this subject.

By 1798, living in New York and in the context of his close personal and intellectual associations with Friendly Club members William Dunlap and Elihu Hubbard Smith, Brown was poised to begin his brief but astonishingly productive novelistic career. From 1798 to 1801, in addition to editorial work and numerous significant essays and pieces of short fiction, Brown wrote the six novels for which he is known. In order of their appearance in book form (as distinct from serialization), these novels are *Wieland; or, The Transformation* (1798), *Ormond; or, The Secret Witness* (1799), *Arthur Mervyn or, Memoirs of the year 1793* (2 pts., 1799–1800), *Edgar Huntly; or, Memoirs of a Sleep-Walker* (1799), *Clara Howard: In a Series of Letters*

(1801), and *Jane Talbot: A Novel* (1801). One other novel, *Memoirs of Stephen Calvert*, was also written during this period but remained unfinished, appearing in serial installments from June 1799 to June 1800. While earlier, often hostile commentators begrudged Brown his very productiveness, claiming for example that "his novels all bear the marks of haste, immaturity, and Godwin" (Carl Van Doren, *Dictionary of American Biography*, vol. 2), critics of the post–World War II period have increasingly concurred in finding Brown the most intellectually ambitious and artistically complex of Early American novelists before James Fenimore Cooper.

Brown's novels are remarkable in three principal ways. They are complex and fascinating artworks in their own right, they explore the political and ideological conflicts of the 1790s in an insightful and revealing manner, and, in historical terms, they represent the immense transition from the eighteenth-century world of shared neoclassical cultural standards to the nineteenth-century world of market-based individualism and romantico-modern artistic experimentation. Despite the visible consequences of their rapid composition, the first four books in particular are dramatic, suspenseful tales of crisis and psychological derangement that successfully combine the conventions of British "Jacobin" fiction (the progressive fiction associated with Godwin), and of Gothic, seduction, and picaresque, or adventure, novels with an emphasis on the period's deepest social and political anxieties. These novels are first-person narratives that hold the reader uncomfortably close to spectacular forms of madness and extreme anxiety. *Wieland* gothicizes the period's anxieties about foreign subversives and homegrown conservative extremism as its female narrator is torn between the twin figures of a subversive, lower-class ventriloquist and an upper-class pillar of respectability who lapses into religious hysteria and homicidal rage. *Ormond* employs the model of the seduction novel, contrasting a sophisticated foreign political subversive and a native-born religious zealot who struggle to control a female paragon of youthful American political and cultural virtue. *Arthur Mervyn* and *Edgar Huntly* develop as tales of adventure in which penniless young men set out confidently in the postrevolutionary world only to encounter yellow fever epidemics, Indian warfare, maniacal confidence men, and casualties of revolution that dramatize the period's deep fears about rapid changes in its new, market-based society. The last two novels, *Clara Howard* and *Jane Talbot*, ironically use the genteel conventions of the sentimental and epistolary novel to explore emerging nineteenth-century standards of middle-class gentility and the regimen of psychological and social conformity they require. The almost gleefully exaggerated atmosphere of cultural unrest, psychological turmoil, and baneful paternalism in Brown's novels is aptly summarized by the well-known lament of his hero Edgar Huntly: "Disastrous and humiliating is the state of man! By his own hands, is constructed the mass of misery and error in which his steps are forever involved."

Although they earned him a modest degree of celebrity and critical acclaim in the United States and England (where, for example, he became a favorite of Percy Shelley, son-in-law of Godwin and Wollstonecraft), Brown's novels did not sell, and he emerged from this period as a 31-year-old novelist and editor with a vaguely radical reputation who was still dependent on his family for financial support. Consequently, in an era of conservative cultural norms, he turned to magazine journalism, the only form of literature that could produce an income in this period, and endeavored to adopt a more respectable persona. Likewise, he developed a more conventional personal routine than the hectic and itinerant novelistic years had allowed. He settled down in Philadelphia in 1801 and worked as a merchant in partnership with his brother until 1806 and independently thereafter. In 1804 Brown married Elizabeth Linn, daughter of a Presbyterian minister. The couple had four children.

During this late period, from 1802 to his death, Brown worked primarily as editor and primary contributor for two important magazines, the *Literary Magazine and American Register* (1803–1807) and the *American Register, or General Repository of History, Politics, and Science* (1807–1809). He filled the *Literary Magazine* with miscellaneous essays and a significant amount of short fiction. In the *American Register* he authored a continuing analysis of North Atlantic politics titled "Annals of Europe and America" that earned him recognition as a leading American historical writer of the period. Although this period was long held to represent a decline in Brown's writing, a turn toward hack work on the one hand and conformism or conservatism on the other, criticism since the 1960s has gradually revealed a more complex picture. On closer examination, the journalistic and historical work stands as an impressive accomplishment. It suggests that, although Brown had jettisoned the antagonistic and confrontational elements of his earlier writing, he remained an opponent of conservative theory and an advocate of natural rights, social improvement, education, and the liberal view of commerce as the basis of democratic social order. This period also includes three important pamphlets that argued for territorial expansion and against Thomas Jefferson's administration's restrictions on commerce, a translation of a geographical work by Constantin Volney, and, most surprisingly, given long-standing assumptions that Brown abandoned fiction in these years, the short fiction of the magazines, a now-lost play, and the important book-length novel *The Historical Sketches* (1803–1807). Published posthumously in an 1815 biography, *The Historical Sketches* represent perhaps Brown's most enigmatic narrative experiment, a sprawling novel-length fictional history of a powerful family and its lands in Great Britain, France, and the Mediterranean. The work emphasizes themes concerning political power and corruption, such as the demonization of marginalized individuals and groups, and the ways in which culture is used to create and reinforce political domination. It is related to Brown's orthodox historical writings in its emphasis on the dynamics of power and historical change and to his novels in its creation of a dystopian world of violent psychosocial aberration and historical upheaval.

When Brown died form tuberculosis in Philadelphia, he was an obscure author who had struggled to establish himself in an era that financially and socially discouraged literary careers. Although he was a prolific writer who excelled in a range of genres, from poetry and fiction to essays and historiography, his reputation developed almost exclusively around his six major novels. Mixed evaluations during the nineteenth and early twentieth centuries were consistently colored by debates and assumptions concerning his politics, and the dark, intensely chaotic world of his fiction was simultaneously admired by some nineteenth-century writers, for example Nathaniel Hawthorne, Edgar Allan Poe, and Margaret Fuller, and viewed with hostility by others, such as historian William Prescott. Twentieth-century literary scholars, primarily those working after 1945, have brought the previously unacknowledged breadth of Brown's accomplishment to light and concur in finding him a more fascinating, challenging, and historically significant writer than imagined by most earlier readers. By the end of the twentieth century, Brown was recognized as the most important of Early American novelists, a figure whose reputation is based on the way all of his writings, not only the novels, engaged in artistically complex and intellectually ambitious explorations of some of the major cultural debates and anxieties of American culture at the turn of the nineteenth century.

• A complete collection of Brown's manuscripts, papers, and early editions is located at the Bibliographical and Textual Center of Kent State University. This collection contains copies of all manuscripts and correspondence located at other libraries, with the exception of the early correspondence with Joseph Bringhurst, which is at Bowdoin College. The modern scholarly edition of the novels and *Alcuin* is Sydney J. Krause et al., eds., *The Novels and Related Works of Charles Brockden Brown* (1977–1987). Although neither are complete, modern collections of the short fiction are Harry Warfel, ed., *The Rhapsodist and Other Uncollected Writings* (1943), and Alfred Weber, ed., *Somnambulism and Other Stories* (1987). The best biographies of Brown are William Dunlap, *The Life of Charles Brockden Brown: Together with Selections from the Rarest of His Printed Works, from His Original Letters, and from His Manuscripts before Unpublished* (1815), and David Lee Clark, *Charles Brockden Brown: Pioneer Voice of America* (1952). Major critical studies are Richard Chase, *The American Novel and Its Tradition* (1957); Norman Grabo, *The Coincidental Art of Charles Brockden Brown* (1981); Cathy Davidson, *Revolution and the Word: The Rise of the Novel in America* (1986); and Steven Watts, *The Romance of Real Life: Charles Brockden Brown and the Origins of American Culture* (1994). Watts's study includes an extensive and up-to-date bibliography.

PHILIP BARNARD

BROWN, Charles Reynolds (1 Oct. 1862–28 Nov. 1950), pastor and educator, was born near Bethany, Virginia (later W.Va.), the son of Benjamin F. Brown and Sarah Jane Kinkade, farmers. In 1866 Brown's family moved to a farm in Washington County, Iowa, where he spent his youth. After being schooled at Washington Academy, he graduated from the University of Iowa in 1883. Originally intending a career in law and politics, Brown served as a law clerk, first in a Rock Island, Illinois, firm and then in Davenport, Iowa, while he studied to prepare for law school. He could not, however, escape a sense that God was calling him to the ministry. After working fifteen months for an insurance company in Des Moines, Iowa, to raise money for tuition, he entered the Boston University School of Theology in 1886, grateful for having had three years of practical experience before attending seminary. While studying at this Methodist institution, Brown regularly heard the sermons of one of America's leading preachers, Phillips Brooks, the rector of Trinity Episcopal Church in Boston. During his preparation for the ministry, Brown preached at a small Congregational church in Plympton, Massachusetts, for two summers and spent a semester studying at Harvard Divinity School.

After his graduation from seminary in 1889, Brown became the pastor of Wesley Chapel, a small Methodist congregation in Cincinnati. During his three years there he brought many young people into the church, taught an evening class in stenography to thirty young people, and worked to improve his preaching. Although Brown had been raised as a Methodist and educated in a Methodist seminary, he decided that his style of ministry and his theological views were more in tune with Congregationalism and in 1892 requested to be transferred to this denomination.

That fall Brown accepted a call from the Winthrop Congregational Church in Boston. In 1896 he married Alice Tufts, a student at Radcliffe College; they had no children. Soon after marrying they journeyed to Oakland, California, where Brown became the pastor of the First Congregationalist Church. During a fifteen-year ministry to this downtown congregation, he built its membership to 1,900 and significantly expanded its program and community outreach. For seven of his years in Oakland, he taught a course at Stanford University in either Old Testament or social ethics to about 200 students each year. He served for more than a decade as the president of the board of trustees of Mills College, a women's college on the outskirts of Oakland. As president of the California Home Missionary Society, he visited many struggling congregations in lumber camps and mining towns. An advocate of the social gospel, a movement among American Protestants from the 1880s to the 1920s to reform industrial and urban conditions, Brown investigated and sought to arbitrate strikes, attended many labor meetings, and for six years served as a delegate of Oakland's Ministers' Union to the town's Central Labor Council. For ten years he also regularly attended the Ruskin Club and conferred with its socialist members, who included Jack London, Upton Sinclair, and Edwin Markham. These conversations helped to dampen his initial enthusiasm for socialism.

In 1906 Brown gave the Lyman Beecher Lectures on preaching at Yale, which were published as *The Social Message of the Modern Pulpit*. This analysis of the relation between Christianity and labor helped to make Brown known in religious circles around the country. In 1910 he resigned his pastorate, due in large part to nervous exhaustion, and in 1911 he accepted a position as the dean of the Divinity School at Yale University. Although he was a newcomer to higher education, during his seventeen-year tenure as dean the size of the faculty and the student body increased significantly. While serving as an administrator and as the pastor of Battell Chapel, the campus church at Yale, he also regularly taught courses in preaching and pastoral ministry. While at Yale he frequently spoke at preparatory schools, college chapels, and churches throughout the country. He also supplied the pulpit for several months each at some of the nation's leading churches in Boston and New York, including George A. Gordon's Old South Church and Charles E. Jefferson's Broadway Tabernacle. In 1913 he was elected to a two-year term as the moderator of the National Council of Congregational Churches. After his retirement from Yale in 1928, Brown traveled extensively and preached and lectured around the world.

A prolific author, Brown wrote a column for the *Congregationalist* for seven years and published thirty-nine books, many of which were based on lectures given at many institutions or on chapel talks given at Yale. His books include *The Strange Ways of God* (1910), a study of the book of Job; *Two Parables* (1898), ten sermons on the Good Samaritan and the Prodigal Son; *Why I Believe* (1923); and *Social Rebuilders* (1921), an argument for reforming industrial conditions and applying Christian values to all areas of life. His two bestselling books were *The Main Points* (1899), a discussion in laypersons' terms of ten primary planks of Christian belief, and *These Twelve* (1926), a study of nine of the apostles, Barnabus, Paul, and Jesus as illustrations of various temperament types. More than a million copies of two pamphlets he wrote were distributed to soldiers during World War I, *Who Is Jesus Christ?* and *Do You Win?* an examination of gambling. Several of his books were translated into other languages, primarily for use in the mission field.

Through his many publications, his many lectures and sermons delivered throughout the country, and his prominent position at Yale, Brown helped to shape the theology of mainline Protestant denominations in the direction of his own evangelical liberal beliefs. Like others who held this position, he sought to preserve traditional Christian doctrine and worship, especially the centrality of Jesus Christ as Lord and Savior, while seeking to adjust the faith to modern intellectual currents. A 1924 poll of American Protestant ministers selected him as one of the nation's twenty-five most influential living preachers. At the Yale commencement of 1928, where Brown was awarded an honorary doctorate, William Lyon Phelps, a professor of English, declared that the former dean was widely considered to be "one of the greatest living teachers of the art of preaching. His strong, robust personality, his religious vitality, his command of picturesque language, his wisdom and tact, his hearty love of human beings, have made him a powerful force in the spiritual life of our time" (quoted in *My Own Yesterdays*, p. 158). He died in New Haven.

• Brown's personal papers are at the Yale University Divinity School Library. The best source for understanding Brown's life and work is his autobiography, *My Own Yesterdays* (1931). Several of his books explain his theological views, social commitments, and approach to preaching: *The Modern Man's Religion* (1911), *The Art of Preaching* (1922), *Why I Believe in Religion* (1924), *What Is Your Name?* (1924), and *Have We Outgrown Religion?* (1932). Brown's ecumenical spirit and appreciation for various religious traditions is evident in *The Larger Faith* (1923), in which he analyzes the contributions nine major denominations, including Roman Catholics and Universalists, had made to American society. His contributions to Yale Divinity School are examined in James Glover Johnson, "The Yale Divinity School, 1899–1928" (Ph.D. diss., Yale Univ., 1928). See also the *Yale Divinity News*, "Biographical Sketch," Jan. 1921; "Retirement of Dean Brown," Mar. 1928; "The Dean and the Dean-Elect," Mar. 1928; and "Charles Reynolds Brown," Jan. 1951.

GARY SCOTT SMITH

BROWN, Charlotte Amanda Blake (22 Dec. 1846–19 Apr. 1904), physician, was born in Philadelphia, Pennsylvania, the daughter of Charles Morris Blake, a teacher who directed a private boys' school and at the time of her birth was studying medicine, and Charlotte A. Farrington. In 1849 her father moved to San Francisco, where he edited the *Pacific News*. Two years later the family traveled across the Isthmus of Panama to join him. After establishing another boys' school, Charles Blake answered a call to be a Presbyterian minister to Cornish miners in Chile. En route the family's ship was blown off-course by storms, and they visited Tahiti before reaching their destination. The Blakes lived in Chile for three years, returning to Pennsylvania in 1857. Charlotte Blake lived with relatives in Maine (both of her parents were natives of Brewer) and attended high school in Bangor. After graduating from Elmira College in New York in 1866, she proceeded to Arizona, where her father was serving as an army chaplain. In Arizona she met and in 1867 married Henry Adams Brown, also from Maine.

In 1869 the couple moved, along with her parents, to California, where her older brother, Charles, was a physician (in San Francisco). The Browns settled in Napa, where they had three children. After the birth of her third child, Brown began to study anatomy with the help of a physician friend, and in 1872 she entered the Women's Medical College of Pennsylvania, graduating in 1874. (That same year her father returned to medical school at the University of California, graduating in 1876.) Brown opened a medical practice in

San Francisco, but her initial application for admission to the San Francisco Medical Society (1876) met with opposition from male physicians. Her subsequent membership in the California Medical Society, appointment to an important committee by that group, and performance of the first ovariotomy by a woman physician on the West Coast likely influenced the society's decision to admit her in 1878.

Very concerned about the health and welfare of poor women and children, in 1875 Brown gathered together a group of other women physicians and prominent San Franciscan women who, like her, wanted to establish a free clinic. Their efforts resulted in the Pacific Dispensary for Women and Children, which opened later that same year. The clinic served a dual purpose: as well as providing health care for poor women and children, it enabled women physicians to utilize their medical training, as they were not welcome at most other institutions. Within three years the dispensary had developed into a hospital, and by 1880 the first nurses' training school on the Pacific Coast had been organized. In 1885, when the Hospital for Children and Training School for Nurses (informally known as Children's Hospital) was incorporated, the emphasis of attention and care had become children's health.

Brown's energy, inquiring mind, and breadth of interest were reflected by her active participation within the medical community. A progressive thinker who published at least eighteen articles in medical journals, she proposed the establishment of a tumor registry and even designed a milk sterilizer. In addition to maintaining a surgical practice, she was active in the investigation of adolescent gynecological problems, called for upgrading training for doctors and nurses, and urged her colleagues to take on greater social responsibility. Putting words into practice, she administered gynecological and obstetrical care to Chinese women at San Francisco church missions at a time when many doctors would not attend to Asian patients at all. Concerned as well with preventive health measures, Brown demanded enforcement of city health laws and called for stringent public health standards.

In 1895, having served Children's Hospital virtually for two decades, Brown withdrew from active practice and with her two older children, who also were physicians, founded a small, private hospital. In her later years she also was involved with the California branch of the National Conference of Charities and Corrections, which she had helped establish. She died in San Francisco of paralytic ileus (intestinal paralysis) and was buried at Colma, California. Not simply one of a small group of early women physicians in the San Francisco Bay area, Charlotte Blake Brown was a leading woman surgeon who served as an experienced professional consultant as well as a supportive and willing mentor for younger women medical students and physicians. She was also a significant figure in the provision and investigation of health care for women and children on the West Coast and in the promotion of professional health education.

• Charlotte Brown's papers were destroyed in the 1906 San Francisco earthquake. Her published articles include "A Bureau of Information: The Need of a Post-Graduate School for Nurses," National Conference of Charities and Correction, *Proceedings* (1890), pp. 147–54; "Practical Points in Obstetrics," *Occidental Medical Times* 14 (1900): 12–16; "Report on Obstetrics," California State Medical Society, *Transactions* (1893), pp. 129–39; and "Report on Diseases of Women and Children," California State Medical Society, *Transactions* (1881), pp. 252–60. For examples of her medical case presentations see "A Case of Caesarean Section Necessitated by Ventro-suspension" and "Anti-Partum Diagnosis," *Occidental Medical Times* 16 (1902): 142–43, 290; and "Notes on Surgical Work in the Hospital for Women and Children for the Year Ending Oct. 1, 1888," *Pacific Medical Journal* 32 (Jan. 1889): 1–6. For additional biographical information see Adelaide Brown, "The History of the Development of Women in Medicine in California," *California and Western Medicine* 23 (May 1925): 579–82. For Brown's early work at Children's Hospital see *First Report of the Pacific Dispensary for Women and Children* (1876) and later reports; H. E. Thelander, "Children's Hospital of San Francisco," *Medical Woman's Journal* 41 (July 1934): 184–86; and Lois Brock, "The Hospital for Children and Training School for Nurses, 1875–1949," *Journal of the American Medical Women's Association* 5 (Jan. 1950): 28–31. Additional information is in J. Marion Read and Mary E. Mathes, *History of the San Francisco Medical Society*, vol. 1, *1850–1900* (1958). A brief obituary is in the *San Francisco Call*, 20 Apr. 1904; a death notice is in the *Pacific Medical Journal* 47 (1904): 290.

SANDRA VARNEY MACMAHON

BROWN, Charlotte Emerson (21 Apr. 1838–5 Feb. 1895), first president of the General Federation of Women's Clubs, was born in Andover, Massachusetts, the daughter of Reverend Ralph Emerson, a clergyman and professor, and Eliza Rockwell. Charlotte's father came from a distinguished New England heritage and was related to Ralph Waldo Emerson. As a child, Charlotte exhibited a great aptitude for learning languages and was fluent in French by age twelve. Her interest and skill in languages remained throughout her life. After her graduation from Abbott Academy in Andover, she learned additional languages, including Latin and Greek. Beyond furthering her education in languages and music, she taught Latin, French, and mathematics in Montreal at a seminary for a year, working with Hannah Lyman, who later headed Vassar College. After her teaching experience, Charlotte went abroad for several years. She traveled to Germany, Austria, France, Italy, Greece, Turkey, Egypt, and Syria, studying languages and music in the countries she visited. By the time she returned to the United States, she had become proficient in several more languages.

By 1859 the Emerson family had moved to Rockford, Illinois, and Charlotte joined them there after she returned. She felt that she now needed a business education, and she completed a six-week commercial course in Chicago. After graduation she worked as a private secretary to her brother Ralph, a manufacturer, in addition to teaching modern languages at Rockford Seminary. She also organized two clubs that met at her home—a musical club, called the Euterpe, and a

French club. On 27 July 1880 Charlotte Emerson married Reverend William Bryant Brown, a Congregational minister. Soon after their marriage the couple traveled throughout Europe for a period of two to three years, and Charlotte continued her studies of languages and music during their travels.

The Browns settled in East Orange, New Jersey, after they returned to the United States. Charlotte Brown became involved in the Woman's Board of Missions of the Congregational Church, arranging plans of work for the organization. Her interest in clubs also continued, and by 1888 she had been elected president of the Woman's Club of Orange, serving a two-year term of office. She also organized the Fortnightly Club of East Orange. It was in club work and the women's club movement that Brown found her true mission in life. On behalf of the Woman's Club of Orange, she attended a meeting held in New York City in 1889 of representatives of women's clubs from all over the country. The purpose of the meeting was to discuss uniting the many clubs formed as a means of self-education and development for women throughout the latter nineteenth century into one organization "in order that they may compare methods of work and become mutually helpful" (Wells, p. 26). Jane "Jennie June" Cunningham Croly, the founding mother of the women's club movement, believed that the club movement would attract more supporters than the suffrage movement because it did not threaten abolition of the home. Croly also felt that by exercising their right to organize, clubwomen would be provided a further opportunity for self-improvement, and that clubs would ultimately elevate women's status. In addition to literary and self-improvement interests, some clubs also were investing their energies in public reform and social programs, applying their female influence to the problems of their communities. The clubwomen who convened to found a federation, while homogeneous in background, brought together diverse geographic perspectives and a broad range of concerns in an effort to become mutually supportive.

Chosen at the 1889 meeting to serve on a committee charged with creating the proposed federation of clubs, Brown also served on a smaller advisory board and worked on developing the program for a convention of women's clubs the next year. At the 1890 convention, the General Federation of Women's Clubs was officially formed, and Brown was elected as the organization's first president. After serving a two-year term of office, she was reelected GFWC president in 1892. Brown gave direction and guidance to the fledgling organization, uniting women with diverse interests and goals for a common good. She presided over GFWC biennial conventions in Chicago and Philadelphia. She encouraged membership growth of the federation and traveled extensively to visit existing clubs and recruit new ones. GFWC grew from fifty clubs at its start to over 120 clubs with 20,000 women in twenty-nine states two years later, and the rapid growth continued during her second administration. Brown was also responsible for ensuring that GFWC was incorporated (under the laws of New Jersey) in 1893. Her second term of office concluded in 1894. She was well liked by clubwomen and was known for her businesslike power to focus her energy and enthusiasm to accomplish her goals, her phenomenal memory, and her pleasant personality and ability to inspire others. As a proposed motto for a federation banner, Charlotte Brown wrote, "Our club women must be the synonyms of light, life and love. . . . Such a mission is uplifting, ennobling and inspiring. It is a voice from heaven calling upon every club woman to stand in her appointed place and do her whole duty" (Wells, p. 54).

Brown, who wrote speeches and articles about club work during her GFWC presidency, was asked after her retirement in 1894 to serve as chairman of foreign correspondence and to compile a history of the women's club movement. She had collected material for this book when she died the following year in East Orange, her presidency and workload having adversely affected her health. Ellen M. Henrotin, GFWC president at the time of Brown's death, assessed her contributions by saying, "Beautiful in person, high minded, liberal in spirit, she made no mistake in the organization of the General Federation of Women's Clubs. She brought into it her personality, her individuality that encouraged others to come into it. The whole success of this women's movement was due to the devotion and the unselfishness of Charlotte Emerson Brown" (Wells, p. 52).

• Papers pertaining to Brown's involvement with the women's club movement, especially at the national level, are in the General Federation of Women's Clubs Archives, Washington, D.C., and include biographical information, speeches, clippings, and memorials as well as family papers and photographs. Books containing general biographical information on Brown include Benjamin K. Emerson, *The Ipswich Emersons* (1900); Frances E. Willard and Mary A. Livermore, eds., *A Woman of the Century: Fourteen Hundred-Seventy Biographical Sketches Accompanied by Portraits of Leading American Women in All Walks of Life* (1893; repr. 1967); and Frances E. Willard and Mary A. Livermore, eds., *American Women: Fifteen Hundred Biographies*, vol. 1 (1897). Books with both biographical and more specific information on Brown and the women's club movement include Mary Jean Houde, *Reaching Out: A Story of the General Federation of Women's Clubs* (1989), and Mildred White Wells, *Unity in Diversity: The History of the General Federation of Women's Clubs* (1953). Obituaries are in the *New York Tribune* and the *New York Times*, 6 Feb. 1895.

CYNTHIA N. SWANSON

BROWN, Charlotte Eugenia Hawkins (11 June 1883–11 Jan. 1961), educator, was born Lottie Hawkins in Henderson, North Carolina, the daughter of Edmund H. Hight, a brick mason, and Caroline Frances Hawkins. Accounts vary as to whether her father and mother separated before or after her birth, and it is also unclear as to whether her parents ever married. After her mother married Nelson Willis, Lottie (as she was called until she changed her name to Charlotte Eugenia in high school) relocated with nineteen members of her extended family to Massachusetts in 1888. By joining the widespread migration of African Americans, the family hoped to enjoy greater economic opportunities and a better life. After settling in Cambridge, her stepfather worked odd jobs to support the family while her mother boarded African-American Harvard students, operated a laundry, and baby-sat. Hawkins began her elementary education at the Allston School in Cambridge, where she befriended two of Henry Wadsworth Longfellow's daughters and excelled in her studies. She also attended Baptist Sunday school, where at the age of twelve she organized a kindergarten department.

Hawkins then attended Cambridge English High and Latin School. During her senior year she met and made a favorable impression upon former Wellesley College president Alice Freeman Palmer. Although Hawkins wanted to attend Radcliffe in order to gain the best possible preparation for a teaching career, her mother urged her to enter teaching immediately. As a compromise, Hawkins entered the Salem Normal School (later Salem State College) in 1900. Having spotted Palmer's name in the school catalog, Hawkins wrote to her in search of advice; her inquiry gained her a letter of recommendation and an offer of financial assistance from Palmer.

A second chance encounter at the beginning of Hawkins's second year at Salem determined the course of her life. After meeting a representative of the American Missionary Association on a train between Salem and Cambridge, she decided to accept an offer to return to her native state and operate a school for the association. Leaving Salem before graduating (she later received credit for her work in the South, and was awarded a diploma), she traveled south by train and arrived in McLeansville, North Carolina. After walking four miles to the community of Sedalia, she boarded with a local minister and on 12 October 1901 welcomed fifteen children to the poorly maintained one-room shack that comprised the Bethany Institute.

Although Hawkins was accepted by the community and encouraged by her accomplishments during the five-month school term, her future in Sedalia looked bleak when the association moved to close all its smaller schools at the end of the school year. Undaunted and determined to complete her work in the community, Hawkins rejected an offer from the association to teach elsewhere and returned north with the goal of raising sufficient funds to open her own school.

Upon returning to Cambridge, she approached Palmer for assistance, only to find her benefactress in poor health and bereft of fortune. Palmer did, however, provide her with the names of several possible financial contributors. After soliciting funds from these individuals, Hawkins traveled to the resort community of Gloucester, Massachusetts, where she gave dramatic recitations and musical performances in order to raise money. She returned to Sedalia with less than $400 and, with a donation of fifteen acres of land and an old blacksmith shop, she opened the school on 10 October 1902.

The school, which was named the Palmer Memorial Institute the following summer in honor of her recently deceased mentor, soon became a success story. Inspired by and patterned after Booker T. Washington's institute, Palmer in its early years emphasized basic instruction and manual training. Students were responsible for daily chores and farm work as well as academics. The school filled a dire need in a state in which educational opportunities for African Americans were few (no teacher training institutions existed until the 1930s, and no public schooling existed in the Sedalia area until 1937). Fundraising was a constant concern; fortunately, wealthy northerners such as Charles W. Eliot (who also served as the president of the first board of trustees), Seth Low, and Galen S. Stone were generous in their support. The American Missionary Association added its resources in 1924, and Hawkins's own fundraising efforts resulted in a permanent endowment of $250,000.

In spite of her many commitments, Hawkins did not neglect her own intellectual development. She took summer and regular courses at Simmons College, Temple University, and Harvard University. It was at the latter that she met Edward S. Brown, whom she married in June 1911. Although he initially returned with Hawkins to Sedalia and taught at Palmer, he left after five years to teach at a similar school in South Carolina and the marriage ended in divorce. Charlotte Hawkins Brown, though childless, did raise several nieces and nephews at her on-campus home, the "Canary Cottage."

The Palmer Institute eventually grew to 300 acres in size and shifted its academic emphasis; in its latter years it became a preparatory school with a focus on high school and junior college–level instruction. While her students remained central in her life, she also engaged in professional activities and social activism. She helped found the North Carolina State Federation of Negro Women's Clubs in 1909 and also served as its president (1915–1936). While she was president, the federation purchased and maintained the Efland Home for Wayward Girls in Orange County, North Carolina; it was the only institution of its type for African-American women in the state.

Charlotte Hawkins Brown's interest in interracial harmony led to her work in founding the Commission on Interracial Cooperation in 1919. That same year she published *Mammy: An Appeal to the Heart of the South*, a fictional indictment of the treatment of African Americans during slavery. Fully supportive of civil rights, Brown chafed under the restrictive racial atmosphere of her day and frequently challenged established Jim Crow standards. She refused to ride in segregated elevators and was sometimes ejected from "whites only" Pullman berths. Nonviolent in outlook, she occasionally resorted to lawsuits in order to challenge the discriminatory practices that she encountered during her travels.

Despite her outspoken nature, Brown was a firm believer in the social graces. She constantly sought to inculcate manners as well as education into her students and published *The Correct Thing to Do, to Say, and to Wear* in 1941 as a guidebook in this area.

Brown remained busy throughout her life. She was named in 1940 to the North Carolina Council of Defense—one of the first African Americans so nominated—and also served as a member of the Executive Committee of the Home Nursing Council of the American Red Cross during World War II. Although she retired as president of Palmer in October 1952, she retained the post of director of finance until 1955. She died in Greensboro, North Carolina, after a lingering illness.

Charlotte Hawkins Brown is remembered for her pioneering efforts at Palmer Memorial Institute. Given early advantages of education and upbringing, she returned to her native state in order to provide educational opportunities for her fellow African Americans at a time when those opportunities were not readily available. She succeeded against often overwhelming odds in creating a preparatory school that provided hundreds of students with an opportunity for a better life. Although Palmer Institute closed because of financial problems in 1971, its graduates are Brown's greatest legacy.

• The papers of Charlotte Eugenia Hawkins Brown are held at the Schlesinger Library of Women in America at Radcliffe College, Cambridge, Mass. Additional material on Brown and on Palmer Institute (which is being developed as a historical site by the state of North Carolina) is available in the W. C. Jackson Library at the University of North Carolina at Greensboro, and in the North Carolina Historical Room at the Greensboro Public Library. A recent scholarly treatment of her life and career is Constance Hill Marteena, *The Lengthening Shadow of a Woman: A Biography of Charlotte Hawkins Brown* (1977). An obituary is in the *New York Times*, 12 Jan. 1961.

EDWARD L. LACH, JR.

BROWN, Clarence J. (14 July 1895–23 Aug. 1965), U.S. representative and publisher, was born in West Union, Ohio, the son of Owen Brown, a schoolteacher, and Ellen Barerre McCoppin. Brown was descended from early Ohio settlers, and his paternal grandfather, Jehu Brown, drove the first horse car over the streets of Cincinnati. Brown's birth year is sometimes given incorrectly as 1893, and his middle name is occasionally given incorrectly as "James" rather than just the initial.

In his formative years, Brown sold popcorn and newspapers from a baby carriage and worked as a janitor in a bank. After graduation from high school, he studied law for two years at Washington and Lee University, Lexington, Virginia. He married Ethel McKinney on the day after he turned twenty-one in 1916. They had three children and lived in Blanchester, Ohio. His marriage came a year after his first political appointment—as state statistician and election supervisor in the office of the Ohio secretary of state—and a year before he purchased his first newspaper. As editor he began a career in publishing that was continued by succeeding generations. His newspaper activities earned him membership in Sigma Delta Chi. President of the Brown Publishing Company until his death, his twin loves in life were politics and publishing.

Following three years in his first state post, Brown was elected lieutenant governor of Ohio on the Republican ticket, serving two terms. At twenty-three, he was the youngest lieutenant governor in Ohio to that time. His first term (1919–1921) was under Democratic governor James Cox, who during this time won the Democratic nomination for president of the United States. Because Cox often traveled out of the state, Brown was able to play a very active role in state government. (Cox was handily defeated by the Republican, Warren G. Harding, in the general election.) Brown's second term as lieutenant governor (1921–1923) was under a fellow Republican, Harry L. Davis.

Brown held no public office for the next three years. In 1926 he was elected secretary of state for Ohio, serving in this office for six years. He then suffered the first of two losses in his quest for election to the governorship of Ohio. Both losses (in the Republican primary in 1932 and as the Republican nominee in the general election in 1934) were narrow, but he chose not to run again in 1936. Instead he managed the campaign of Colonel Frank Knox for the GOP presidential nomination. Kansas governor Alfred M. Landon won the nomination and selected Knox as his vice-presidential running mate. Brown thereupon continued in his role as Knox's campaign manager.

In 1938 Brown won election to the U.S. House to represent central Ohio's Seventh Congressional District. He thereafter won reelection until his death, serving thirteen terms and part of a fourteenth. During his long tenure he became, by the late 1950s, the ranking Republican on the House Rules Committee, where he worked with the conservative chairman Howard W. Smith (D.-Va.) to delay liberal legislation. A coalition of Republicans and southern Democrats, of which he was a part, successfully blocked much of the John Kennedy administration's social legislation. Brown's influence declined during Lyndon Johnson's presidency, although the congressman endorsed Johnson's civil rights legislation.

As a member of the House, Brown had a consistently conservative voting record. Even before entering Congress he had publicly opposed Franklin Roosevelt's New Deal legislative programs, and he continued to do so after 1939. He later opposed much of Harry Truman's Fair Deal. As a conservative isolationist, Brown opposed the Roosevelt administration's interventionist foreign policies during 1939–1941. After the Japanese attack on Pearl Harbor in December 1941 plunged the country into war, however, he supported the effort and later called for international collaboration after the war.

In 1947 Brown cosponsored legislation with Senator Henry Cabot Lodge to create the "Hoover Commission," formally known as the Commission on the Organization of the Executive Branch of Government. Brown served on this and a second (1953) commission, both of which took their names from their chairman, ex-president Herbert Hoover. The commissions were to investigate the federal bureaucracy, which had radically expanded under the Roosevelt New Deal, and suggest a more efficient organization of the executive branch. Many of the commissions' recommendations were enacted into law. An ardent anti-Communist during the Cold War years, Brown endorsed legislation curbing Communist activities and criticized the various Democratic administrations' foreign policy decisions. He continued to oppose endeavors to expand the federal government's role in the economy and in alleviating social problems.

A partisan Republican, Brown served as floor manager at Republican National Conventions for presidential nomination candidates Senator Robert A. Taft (1940) and Senator John Bricker (1944), the latter a former Ohio governor. Brown is thought to have attended every Republican National Convention from 1912 through 1964. Within the House itself, he was a passive candidate for House majority leader in 1948, agreeing to serve if chosen.

Brown enjoyed fishing and horseback riding. A large and genial man, he was the 1947 Smelt Eating Champion of the U.S. House. In the year before his death, Brown's mother, wife, and seven-year-old granddaughter had all died. Brown died at the National Naval Medical Center in Bethesda, Maryland. At his death, he was fifteenth in House seniority. His son successfully ran for Brown's congressional seat and was reelected eight times.

• The papers of Representative Brown are in the Ohio Historical Society, Columbus. Items include correspondence, speeches, scrapbooks, pamphlets, and memorabilia from his political career and private life and the business records of the Brown Publishing Company for the period 1922–1952. The collection is inventoried and covers ninety-five feet. The best sources are contemporary biographical magazine articles and reference book entries, especially *New York Times Magazine*, 29 Dec. 1946, p. 11; *U.S. News*, 22 Nov. 1946, pp. 69–71; and *Current Biography Yearbook* (1947). Also see *Political Profiles*, vols. 1–3: Arthur Scherr, *The Truman Years* (1978), Michael L. Levine, *The Eisenhower Years* (1977), and Frank H. Milburn, *The Kennedy Years* (1976). Brown is profiled in each, and the index contains entries for his associates and for information on the two Hoover Commissions. Representative obituaries are in the *Columbus Dispatch*, 23 Aug. 1965, and the *Washington Post* and the *Cleveland Plain Dealer*, both 24 Aug. 1965. Each has an accompanying editorial.

PHILIP H. VILES, JR.

BROWN, Clifford (30 Oct. 1930–26 June 1956), trumpeter, was born in Wilmington, Delaware. Brown's parents' names are not known. Brown's father was a self-taught musician who played the trumpet, violin, and piano for his own amusement. He kept several instruments around the house. Young Clifford eventually picked up the bugle and demonstrated an aptitude for it. When he was twelve, Clifford was taken by his father to study with the renowned Wilmington teacher and bandleader Robert Lowery. Clifford spent three years with Lowery, studying jazz harmony, theory, trumpet, piano, vibraphone, and bass and playing in Lowery's big band.

Brown's father bought Brown a trumpet in 1943, the year he entered high school. He studied the trumpet with his high school band director, Harry Andrews, who had done advanced brass study at the University of Michigan. Brown became an outstanding trumpet player under Andrews's tutelage. He perfected octave jumps, developed a beautiful range, and ornamented melodies with little grace notes. These grace notes became a hallmark of his jazz trumpet style. Brown also began writing arrangements for his high school band. He left a lasting impression on Andrews with his brilliant *Carnival of Venice* graduation solo.

Brown showed a Dizzy Gillespie bebop trumpet influence all the way through high school. He graduated from high school and enrolled at Delaware State College in 1949. The school did not have a music department, so he studied mathematics. The following year he transferred to Maryland State College on a music scholarship. This school had a good fifteen-piece band, which gave Brown playing and arranging experience. While at Maryland State, Brown played a couple of times a month as a member of a Philadelphia house band for jazz concerts. He played with innovators such as trombonist J. J. Johnson, drummer Max Roach, alto saxophonist Ernie Henry, and trumpeters Miles Davis and Fats Navarro.

Navarro encouraged Brown and became his major stylistic influence. Navarro's trumpet roots were in the Cuban trumpet tradition and the American bebop style. He was known for his clear articulation, melodic inventiveness, and ringing, bell-like tone. Brown's melodic inventiveness, clear articulation, and fat, bell-like tone can be traced to Navarro's influence. Gillespie's big band played a date in Wilmington one night in 1949. Benny Harris, one of Gillespie's trumpet players, was late. Brown got the opportunity to replace Harris for forty-five minutes. Gillespie was impressed and encouraged the youngster to pursue a jazz career.

Brown was seriously injured in a 1950 car crash and was hospitalized from June 1950 to May 1951. Gillespie visited him during this period and encouraged him to resume his trumpet career. Brown left the hospital and played successful gigs on the piano until he was able to resume his trumpet playing. One of his trumpet gigs was with alto saxophonist Charlie "Bird" Parker. Brown said about this gig: "Benny Harris was the cause of that one, too. He left Bird shortly after the engagement began so I worked in his place for a week. Bird helped my morale a great deal. One night he took me into a corner and said, 'I don't believe it. I hear what you're saying, but I don't believe it'" (quoted in Hentoff, "Clifford Brown").

Brown toured with Chris Powell's rhythm-and-blues band for a year and a half during 1952 and 1953. He played both trumpet and piano with this group. Brown made his first modern jazz recordings during this period, playing on a Blue Note recording date for alto saxophonist Lou Donaldson. Brown played with composer-pianist Tadd Dameron in Atlantic City, New Jersey, in 1953 and recorded for Prestige Records with Dameron. During the summer of 1953, arranger-trumpeter Quincy Jones was working with the Lionel Hampton Band in Wildwood, New Jersey. Jones begged Hampton to hire three musicians from Tadd Dameron's band, which was nearing the end of its Atlantic City engagement: alto saxophonist Gigi Gryce; tenor saxophonist Benny Golson; and trumpeter Brown. Hampton listened to them and hired all three. Brown stayed with Hampton from July until November 1953. During the band's European tour, Brown recorded several albums with Swedish, French, and American musicians, including Gryce.

Brown freelanced in New York City in 1953 and 1954. He recorded with drummer Art Blakey and pianist Horace Silver in the band that subsequently became the Jazz Messengers. Brown won the 1954 *Down Beat* magazine Critic's Poll as the new star of the year on trumpet. Late in March 1954 Brown joined Max Roach in California to form and co-lead a new quintet. During this time he met and married a University of California music student named LaRue Watson; they had one child.

The Clifford Brown–Max Roach Quintet became one of the most important jazz combos in history. The quintet's 1954–1955 personnel consisted of Brown on trumpet, Harold Land on tenor saxophone, Richard Powell on piano, George Morrow on bass, and Roach on drums. In January 1956 tenor saxophonist Sonny Rollins replaced Land.

The Brown-Roach Quintet established new standards of quality and balance between combo arrangements and improvisations. Roach commented that they desired the quintet "to be interesting musically and emotionally at the same time" (quoted in Hentoff, "Roach & Brown, Inc."). The quintet's 1955 and 1956 Em Arcy recordings are masterpieces of artistry and creativity. Brown's solos are unequaled in their melodic beauty and emphatic clarity. Brown introduced a new trumpet style. Bebop trumpeter Gillespie said that "Brown was gifted. And he established a new style, a way of playing the trumpet that was a little different from what we were doing before" (quoted in West, p. 30). Brown's career was short but long enough to influence virtually every major trumpeter that followed him. Brown, Richard Powell, and Powell's wife died in an auto accident on the Pennsylvania Turnpike.

• For further insight into Brown's life and work, see Nat Hentoff, "Clifford Brown: The New Dizzy," *Down Beat*, 7 Apr. 1954; Hentoff, "Roach & Brown, Inc.: Dealers in Jazz," *Down Beat*, 4 May 1955; Hollie West, "Clifford Brown: Trumpeter's Training," *Down Beat*, July 1980, p. 31; Milton L. Stewart, "Structural Development in the Jazz Improvisational Technique of Clifford Brown" (Ph.D. diss., Univ. of Michigan, 1973); *Jazzforschung* 6, no. 7 (1975): 141–273; and Stewart, "Some Characteristics of Clifford Brown's Improvisational Style," *Jazzforschung* 11 (1979): 135–64.

MILTON STEWART

BROWN, Elmer Ellsworth (28 Aug. 1861–3 Nov. 1934), educator and university president, was born in Kiantone, Chautaugua County, New York, the son of Russell McCrary Brown and Electa Louisa Sherman, farmers. When Brown was very young his family moved to Sublette, Lee County, Illinois. They returned briefly to Kiantone while his father served in the Union army but settled in Sublette in 1864. Brown received his early education in local schools and in his early teens passed the county examination for a teacher's certificate. A teaching position was subsequently denied him because of his youth. In 1878 he finally obtained a position in the field of education, as principal of the public school in Rockport, Illinois. After a year he left Rockport and taught at the high school in Astoria, Illinois, before enrolling in the Illinois State Normal College (now Illinois State University) in Normal, Illinois. After graduating in 1881, he served as superintendent of schools in Belvidere, Illinois, until 1884. Brown's brother Isaac Eddy Brown was secretary of the Illinois Young Men's Christian Association, and in 1884 Brown began serving as his assistant. He remained in that position until 1887, when he enrolled as a freshman at the University of Michigan, earning a bachelor's degree in 1889.

Brown married his cousin Fanny Fosten Eddy in Detroit in 1889; the couple had no children. Brown then spent a year in residence at the University of Halle, Germany. He received his Ph.D. in 1890, having completed a dissertation on the role of relations between church and state in England, Prussia, and the United States as reflected in contemporary teaching practices in public schools.

Brown returned to the United States and served as principal of the high school in Jackson, Michigan, during the academic year of 1890–1891. The following year he returned to the University of Michigan as an assistant professor in education. After a year in that position, the peripatetic Brown moved to the University of California at Berkeley, where he spent the next fourteen years building up that school's department of education. During his tenure there, he wrote numerous articles on education, along with *The Making of Our Middle Schools* (1903).

In July 1906 President Theodore Roosevelt appointed Brown as U.S. commissioner of education, a position then located in the Department of the Interior. During his five years as commissioner, Brown continued to write on the subject of education, and a collection of his writings and addresses was published as *Government by Influence, and Other Addresses* in 1910. He used the office, whose responsibilities were limited to the collection and dissemination of information, to urge all concerned citizens to work for a better educational system. Brown advocated, among other things, merit-based teacher promotions, the establishment of agricultural high schools, the use of apprenticeships in technical collegiate curricula, state aid for local high school maintenance, and a general upgrading of rural schools.

Brown was named as the chancellor of New York University in June 1911, after the retirement of Henry Mitchell MacCracken. NYU had begun its rise to prominence under MacCracken's leadership, and Brown built on the work of his predecessor. Acting chancellor John H. MacCracken (Henry MacCracken's younger brother) had increased the requirements for law school graduation from two to three years of study. Brown continued this trend toward stricter standards within the professional schools. Entrance requirements were gradually raised for the medical school, so that by 1930 only students possessing a bachelor's degree were admitted.

Early in his administration, Brown solicited suggestions from the faculty regarding improvements to the university and also initiated a review of each department by the federal Bureau of Education. The subsequent report indicated that NYU's greatest need (as was the case with so many institutions of higher learning) was funding. While a rapid increase in enrollment (from 4,300 in 1912 to 9,300 in 1917) provided additional funds from tuition, the growth of the university's endowment had not kept pace, and with the advent of World War I the corresponding loss of students caused the university a short-lived budget deficit. A resumption in the growth of the student body, increased alumni support, and aid from the Carnegie Corporation and the General Education Board helped to make up the difference.

Under Brown's leadership, the university grew by leaps and bounds. At the beginning of his administration NYU was divided into two campuses: the University Heights campus, founded in 1894 by the transfer of most university functions from lower Manhattan to the Bronx, and the Collegiate Division at Washington Square. The Collegiate Division, which offered primarily postgraduate training for normal school graduates, was expanded in 1914 to full collegiate status. The Graduate School of Business Administration, founded in 1916, was joined in 1921 by the School of Retailing. The School of Pedagogy became (in 1922) the School of Education, with the authorization to grant graduate degrees for the first time. In 1925 the Dental School opened, and in that same year the Department of Aeronautics was founded within the College of Engineering. The last major addition of the Brown administration was the School of Fine Arts, which opened its doors in 1928. Another welcome addition to the university was the New York University Press, founded in 1916. By the time of Brown's retirement on 30 June 1933, enrollment had reached nearly 40,000. The faculty had grown from 381 at the beginning of his administration to 1,812.

Having received numerous honors during his career, including commander of the Order of the Crown of Italy (1932) and Belgium (1933), Brown enjoyed only a brief period as chancellor emeritus. He died in New York City less than a year and a half after his retirement. The leadership he provided during his long tenure as NYU chancellor was a major influence on the evolution of the school from an academic institution of modest means to today's world-renowned center of learning.

• Brown's papers are held at the New York University Archives. The best source of information on his career at NYU remains Theodore Francis Jones, ed., *New York University, 1832–1932* (1933). An obituary is in the *New York Times*, 4 Nov. 1934.

EDWARD L. LACH, JR.

BROWN, Emma V. (c. 1843–Oct. 1902), educator, was born Emmeline Victoria Brown in Georgetown, District of Columbia, the daughter of John Mifflin Brown, a bishop of the African Methodist Episcopal church, and Emmeline (maiden name unknown), a dressmaker. Emma Brown and her siblings were born and raised into what the racial climate of the period called a "better class of colored." While Brown was still a young girl her father died, and her mother worked to support the family. Brown attended Miss Myrtilla Miner's School for Colored Girls, which opened in 1851 with the goal of training teachers for public schools in the Washington, D.C., area. Brown soon distinguished herself as an outstanding student. When illness forced Miner to take a leave of absence, Brown was recruited to stay on and assist Emily Howland, who had moved from New York as Miner's replacement. In 1858 Brown ran the school during Howland's temporary absence, and by the summer of 1859 Brown was ready and able to open her own small school (twelve students) in Georgetown. At the insistence and encouragement of Miner and Howland, Brown chose to continue her education and enhance her teaching skills at Oberlin College.

Located in Oberlin, Ohio, Oberlin College was the institution of choice for many African-American women. Founded by abolitionists, Oberlin was the first coeducational and interracial college in the country. Accompanied by a friend, Matilda A. Jones, Brown arrived in February 1860 for the spring term and enrolled as a literary degree candidate. Her matriculation at Oberlin was cut short due to long-standing health problems that included a humor in her blood, severe headaches, insomnia, and stress. So determined was Brown to continue her studies that she consented to the drastic treatment of having her head completely shaved in an effort to combat her debilitating headaches. The combination of complaints proved to be too much for Brown, and she was forced to leave Oberlin in June 1861.

On returning to Washington, D.C., Brown's health gradually improved to the point where, in 1862, she was able to start her own modest school. Armed with a new spirit of abolition and reform, Brown became one of a new class of "black schoolmarms" dedicated to educating and improving the lives of newly freed slaves. During the 1860s and 1870s Washington attracted many educators and reformers since it was the first southern city to offer blacks a free, tax-supported school system. On 1 March 1864 the Board of Trustees of Public Schools in Washington opened a black school in Ebenezer Church on Capitol Hill and offered Brown the first teaching position. Brown began with an annual salary of $400 and forty students. By summer enrollment reached 130. Brown continued at the school until 1869 when recurring health problems forced her to abandon teaching and secure less stressful work as a clerk in Washington's Pension Office.

During 1870 Brown lived and worked among the black social elite of Charleston, South Carolina, where she taught school, and Jackson, Mississippi, where she copied the acts of the legislature. Her health renewed, Brown returned to Washington and became the principal of the John F. Cook School on Capitol Hill. Brown received a prestigious appointment in the Washington school district in 1872, when she was named principal of the new Sumner School. The school, named for Senator Charles Sumner, was very modern with ten classrooms, offices, playrooms, and an auditorium. At a starting annual salary of $900, the appointment was the pinnacle of Brown's teaching career.

In 1879 Emma Brown married Henry P. Montgomery, a former slave from Mississippi, former Union army soldier, and principal at the John F. Cook School. They had no children. Since married women were banned from the teaching profession, Brown's career in Washington's school system ended. Her educational interests remained strong, however, and she worked as a corresponding secretary for the Manassas Industrial School in Virginia. Suffering from declining health, Brown died at the age of fifty-eight. Her last known address was Washington, D.C.

Brown was a pioneer and a crusader in the mid to late nineteenth-century movement directed toward educating and improving the lives of freedmen. Whether the subject was astronomy or algebra or botany, Brown taught adults and children to have self-respect and to use education as their chief tool for personal and social betterment.

• The Oberlin College archives, Record Group No. 28, contains useful information on Brown, especially her voluminous correspondence with Miner and Howland. Ellen N. Lawson and Marlene Merrill, "Antebellum Black Coeds at Oberlin College," *Oberlin Alumni Magazine* (Jan.–Feb. 1980): 18–21 (repr. in Darlene Clark Hine, *Black Women in United States History*, vol. 3 [1990]), provide a list of African-American students at Oberlin up to 1865. Perhaps the best and most comprehensive secondary source on Brown is Dorothy Sterling, *We Are Your Sisters: Black Women in the Nineteenth Century* (1984).

THEA GALLO BECKER

BROWN, Ernest William (29 Nov. 1866–22 July 1938), mathematical astronomer, was born in Hull, England, the son of William Brown, a farmer and sometime lumber merchant, and Emma Martin. He was educated at the Hull and East Riding College, and upon winning a scholarship in mathematics in 1884 he entered Christ's College, University of Cambridge. He received his B.A. in 1887 having been ranked sixth in the Mathematical Tripos, and subsequently he became a Fellow of Christ's College from 1889 to 1895. Brown received his M.A. in 1891, after which he came to the United States and to Haverford College in Haverford, Pennsylvania. There he was successively an instructor (1891–1893), professor of applied mathematics (1893–1900), and professor of mathematics (1900–1907). Brown was awarded a Cambridge Sc.D. in 1897 and won the John Couch Adams Prize in 1907 for his essay "Inequalities in the Motion of the Moon Due to the Direct Action of the Planets." In 1907 he accepted a position at Yale University as professor of mathematics. From 1921 to 1931 Brown was the Sterling Professor of Mathematics at Yale, and from 1931 until his retirement in 1932 he was the first Josiah Willard Gibbs Professor of Mathematics there. In 1903 in a poll conducted by *American Men of Science* of the leaders of science in America, he was ranked seventh out of eighty in mathematics. Brown became a U.S. citizen in 1922. Although his interests were primarily in astronomy, he was active in the American Mathematical Society as a joint editor of both the *Transactions of the American Mathematical Society* (1899–1907) and the *Bulletin of the American Mathematical Society* (1910–1913). He gave the fifth Gibbs' Lecture of that society in 1927. He also served as an associate editor of the *Astronomical Journal* (1912–1938).

Brown's research began as a postgraduate student in Cambridge when his advisor, Sir George H. Darwin, suggested that he read the memoirs of the American mathematical astronomer George W. Hill on lunar theory. The perfection and practical implementation of Hill's ideas was to be Brown's lifelong work. Upon coming to the United States, Brown met Hill and Simon Newcomb, who encouraged his studies, and he subsequently produced his first book, *An Introductory Treatise on the Lunar Theory* (1896). This gave a critical examination of the previous theories, and was followed by five large papers, "Theory of the Motion of the Moon, Containing a New Calculation of the Coordinates of the Moon in Terms of the Time" (1897–1908), which contained Brown's new theoretical contributions. This contained equations containing some 2,000 terms, and perhaps five times that number of terms had to be examined to determine the significance of their values to higher order. Brown estimated that so far as the Moon is concerned Newton's law of gravitation was accurate to within 1/250,000 of one percent. Brown then contributed the survey article, "Theorie des Erdmondes," to the prestigious German *Encyklopädie der mathematischen Wissenschaften* (1915).

Having largely completed the theory, the next step was to construct tables containing explicit numerical values, and when Yale offered to subsidize this project, Brown moved from Haverford to New Haven. This project would last twelve years and would result in Brown's three-volume work in collaboration with Henry B. Hedrick, *Tables of the Motion of the Moon* (1919). In this work Brown and Hedrick exhibited values of the coefficients of longitude, latitude, and parallax accurate to within 1/100 of a second of arc. From

1923 until 1960, when computers came into use, these tables were used in computing the lunar ephemeris. While Brown's theory contained no serious errors or omissions, there remained fluctuations of the order of tens of seconds of arc over several centuries in the Moon's secular acceleration that required explanation. After much consideration, Brown suggested in his paper, "The Evidence for Changes in the Rate of Rotation of the Earth and their Geophysical Consequences (1926)," that these fluctuations are due to irregularities in the Earth's rotation. Confirmed by the independent work of Sir Harold Spencer Jones (1932, 1939), these irregularities were accepted as a cause, but not the full explanation, for the fluctuations.

In addition to his purely lunar studies, Brown had a broad interest in celestial mechanics, which included the termination of long period orbits in the restricted three-body problem. In particular, this led him to the so-called Brown Conjecture (1911), which has remained unresolved although the numerical evidence has seemed to confirm it. Finally, Brown's interest in planetary theories was summarized in his final book, *Planetary Theory* (1933), written with Clarence A. Shook.

Brown's contribution to lunar theory became the undisputed basis of late twentieth-century understanding of the subject. His genial personality and interest in the work of others made him one of the most revered mathematical astronomers of his day. While he was not fond of teaching, he created the Yale school of celestial mechanics, which was to flourish as an international center under his colleague and coworker, Dirk J. Brouwer.

Brown was much honored in his lifetime and was elected a fellow of the Royal Society (1898); a corresponding member in astronomy of the French Academy of Sciences (1921); a member of the National Academy of Sciences (1923); and a corresponding member of the Belgian Academy of Sciences, Letters, and Arts (1926). He was also president of the American Mathematical Society (1915–1916), the American Astronomical Society (1928–1931), and the American Society of Variable Star Observers (1934–1936). He was awarded the Gold Medal of the Royal Astronomical Society in 1907, the Pontècoulant Medal of the French Academy of Sciences in 1910, the Royal Medal of the Royal Society in 1914, the Bruce Gold Medal of the Astronomical Society of the Pacific in 1920, and the Watson Medal of the National Academy of Science in 1937.

Brown never married, and for many years in New Haven his sister Mildred Brown handled his domestic affairs and shielded him from everyday cares and disturbances. She predeceased him by several years, and he spent his six years of retirement in failing health, although he did not allow it to interfere with his work. He died in New Haven.

• Most of Brown's publications are heavily mathematical, but two of his more expository articles are noteworthy and of general interest: "The History of Mathematics," *Scientific Monthly* 12 (May 1912), and his Gibbs' Lecture, "Resonance in the Solar System," *Bulletin of the American Mathematical Society* 34 (May/June 1928). Brown's work on lunar theory is generally covered in advanced textbooks on celestial mechanics; an especially good presentation of this work is in Sir Alan Cook, *The Motion of the Moon* (1988). Obituary notices appear in the National Academy of Sciences, *Biographical Memoirs* 21 (1939): 243–73, and the *American Mathematical Society Semi-Centennial Publications* 1 (1938); these contain portraits and a complete list of his publications. Brief obituaries are in *Obituary Notices of Fellows of the Royal Society* 3 (1940), and the *New York Times*, 24 July 1938.

JOSEPH D. ZUND

BROWN, Ethan Allen (4 July 1776–24 Feb. 1852), governor of Ohio, U.S. senator, and diplomat, was born in Darien, Connecticut, the son of Roger Brown, a prominent landholder, and Mary Smith. The youngest of seven children, Brown studied under private tutors who stressed a wide knowledge of languages, most beneficial later in his brief diplomatic career. With the American Revolution playing havoc on his father's finances, Brown's later education was sporadic, but in 1797 he began to study law in Alexander Hamilton's office and gained admission to the New York bar five years later.

With his cousin, Captain John Brown, the new attorney went west in 1804. He purchased a tract in Rising Sun, Indiana, near Cincinnati, established a law office in the queen city, and gained security as director of the Bank of Cincinnati. Quickly immersed in Ohio politics, Brown served as inspector of the Cincinnati land office from 1807 to 1809 and in 1810 received legislative appointment to the state supreme court, where he sat for eight years. In 1818 as the Democratic-Republican caucus nominee, Brown won the governorship in a landslide vote (30,194 to 8,075) over James Dunlap.

Brown's tenure as governor, coinciding with the calamitous panic of 1819, was a period of economic chaos for Ohio. Encouraged by the wartime demand for grain, pork, and distilled spirits, settlers had flooded into the western states and territories after 1815. The deluge lasted until the eve of the panic, bringing runaway land speculation as well as concentrated settlement along the Ohio River and its tributaries. When the crisis hit, nearly 600,000 people clustered in those fertile valleys, depending on flatboat transportation to carry their ample produce downriver to New Orleans. With the panic, state banking collapsed, land and crop prices plummeted, and confidence in frontier prospects ebbed.

The new governor faced mounting popular hostility toward the Second Bank of the United States, which many Ohioans blamed for precipitating the panic and causing their economic distress. Joining in that sentiment, Brown in February 1819 signed a bill authorizing an annual $50,000 tax on federal branch banks in Cincinnati and Chillicothe. The law clashed with the U.S. Supreme Court's ruling the following month in *McCulloch v. Maryland* and resulted in the 1824 case of *Osborn v. Bank of the United States*, which Brown helped to argue, without success, before the high court. In both decisions Chief Justice John Marshall upheld the national bank and disallowed state efforts to tax its branches, arguing that a valid federal law supersedes state law whenever the two are in conflict.

Of greater long-range importance to Ohio and to Brown's political reputation was his avid promotion of a state canal system to connect the Great Lakes and the Ohio River commercially. With the Hudson soon to be linked to the northwest by the Erie Canal, Brown's vision stimulated plans for the Ohio-Erie Canal and made him the Ohio equivalent of his close friend, De Witt Clinton of New York. His inaugural address in December 1818 declared the need for "a cheaper way to market for the surplus produce of a large portion of our fertile country." Brown got the state legislature to set up a seven-member commission to oversee exploratory surveys and loans for canals, sought federal land grants to finance canal building, and lobbied against the "Maxcy proposal" of 1821, which threatened a sharing of western public lands with the eastern states. Ohio voters rewarded him in 1820 with a lopsided reelection victory over Jeremiah Morrow and William Henry Harrison (34,836 to 9,426 to 4,348 votes, respectively).

In 1822 Brown resigned the governorship to accept legislative selection, by a margin of one vote, for the unexpired U.S. Senate seat of the late William A. Trimble. In an era when members speedily rose to positions corresponding to their special expertise, Brown secured the chairmanship of the Senate Committee on Roads and Canals, an ideal post for one so consumed with transportation improvement in Ohio and, now, the nation at large. He regularly voted to extend and repair the Cumberland Road, which he saw as boosting the value of property. He also pushed for resurrection of Albert Gallatin's plan for a canal system uniting the entire inland coast by water, first advanced by the former treasury secretary in 1808. Though he voted for Henry Clay's Tariff Bill of 1824, the Ohio senator backed Clinton's rather than Clay's bid for the presidency until hope faded for the New York governor. Replaced in the Senate by William Henry Harrison in 1825, Brown brought his national prestige and eastern business connections to the Ohio Canal Commission, serving there for five years.

Having supported Andrew Jackson in 1828, Brown's share of the spoils was appointment in 1830 as chargé d'affaires to Brazil, a nation dominated by slaveholding planters; the United States had been the first to recognize formally Brazil's independence from Portugal in 1824. During this time of wars and internal revolts in Latin America, Brown pressed for settlement of American credit claims, demanded equal access to Brazilian commerce, and worked to end Brazil's continuing foreign slave trade.

Returning home in 1834, Brown's last federal position came a year later as commissioner of the General Land Office in Washington. For two years the Ohioan stood as President Jackson's closest adviser on public lands administration. In 1836 he retired to his Indiana farm where, having never married, he planned to live out his bachelor days. Brown returned to politics in 1841 to serve a two-year term in the Indiana House. He collapsed and died while presiding as vice president of the Indiana Democratic convention in Indianapolis.

• The Brown papers are gathered at the Ohio Historical Society, Columbus. On his advocacy of canal building in Ohio, see John S. Still, "Ethan Allen Brown and Ohio's Canal System," *Ohio Historical Quarterly* 66 (Jan. 1957): 22–43, and, more generally, Harry N. Scheiber, *The Ohio Canal Era: A Case Study of Government and the Economy, 1820–1861* (1968). A full-length biography of Brown is John S. Still, "The Life of Ethan Allen Brown, Governor of Ohio" (Ph.D. diss., Ohio State Univ., 1951).

JOHN R. VAN ATTA

BROWN, Francis Donaldson (1 Feb. 1885–2 Oct. 1965), industrialist and business executive, was born in Baltimore, Maryland, the son of John Willcox Brown, a banker, and Ellen Turner MacFarland. (Early on he dropped his first name and thereafter went by "Donaldson.") He graduated from Virginia Polytechnic Institute in 1902 with a degree in electrical engineering; he started graduate work at Cornell, but left to return to Baltimore after his father died. He worked briefly for the Baltimore and Ohio Railroad before becoming the Baltimore sales manager of the Sprague Electric Company. In 1908 he joined the Du Pont Company at the urging of his cousin, Hamilton MacFarland Barksdale, who was then an executive of the explosives firm.

Brown spent the next four years in Du Pont's sales department. In 1912, when Du Pont was reorganized, Barksdale—by then the general manager—made Brown an analyst in his office. Two years later, Brown was assigned to the financial department to appraise the performance of Du Pont's operating departments. In his report, he presented a formula: $R = T \times P$, where R = the rate of return on investments, T = the rate of turnover of invested capital, and P = the percentage of profit on sales. As Brown observed in his autobiography, this simple formula provided "a final and fundamental measure of industrial efficiency in terms of management's primary responsibility." Adopted by Du Pont and subsequently by other leading firms, it soon became the standard tool used by American businesses to assess corporate performance. Brown's report so impressed Du Pont executives that they made him assistant treasurer. In 1918 he succeeded John J. Raskob as treasurer and was appointed to Du Pont's board of directors and executive committee; in 1919 he joined its finance committee.

After 1915 Raskob and another Du Pont executive, Pierre S. du Pont, became involved in the affairs of another large enterprise, General Motors. In 1917 du Pont and Raskob—then chairmen, respectively, of GM's board and its finance committee—persuaded Du Pont to invest $25 million of its surplus earnings in GM common stock. Three years later, with GM near collapse due to heavy indebtedness and poor management, du Pont and Raskob forced a corporate shake-up. They appointed the head of one of the subsidiaries, Alfred P. Sloan, Jr., as GM president; the three men then embarked on an ambitious program to restructure the corporation. To assist in streamlining GM's accounting procedures, in 1921 Raskob recruited Brown, who, after resigning from Du Pont (though retaining his finance committee membership), became GM's vice president in charge of finance; he also joined GM's board and finance committee. Brown had his office in New York, where GM's policy-making groups were located; he continued to reside in Wilmington, Delaware, until 1936, when he purchased an estate in Port Deposit, Maryland.

Brown soon became one of Sloan's leading advisers and a key figure in implementing GM's new decentralized administrative structure. In 1928 he became the finance committee chairman, overseeing GM's accounting, dividend, and capital expansion policies. He introduced several new tools for accounting and planning, the most significant of which was the concept of "standard volume." Seasonal and annual fluctuations in sales made it difficult for automobile plants to operate at a uniform rate throughout the year. The standard volume represented an effort to resolve this problem by establishing a percentage of capacity at which it was considered desirable for a plant to operate, given its capacity and anticipations of future demand. Based on the standard volume percentages for all plants, GM executives more effectively scheduled production, estimated manufacturing costs, prepared sales forecasts, developed pricing policies, and predicted rates of return on their investment.

During the 1930s Brown increasingly focused on some of the broader social and political problems confronting GM and the automotive industry as a whole. In 1933 he chaired the committee that drafted an automobile industry code under the National Industrial Recovery Act; he also acted as chief industry spokesman in negotiations with William Green (1870–1952), president of the American Federation of Labor, over the AFL's claim to represent automobile workers in collective bargaining. When the United Automobile Workers of the Congress of Industrial Organizations waged their famed "sit-down" strikes against several GM plants in 1936 and 1937, Brown, as Sloan's designated adviser on labor relations, directed the company's strategy in dealing with the union. Although GM ultimately was forced to recognize the UAW-CIO, the tough stance Brown adopted during these negotiations came to characterize the company's—and the automobile industry's—subsequent dealings with this union in the 1940s and 1950s.

Soon after the settlement of the sit-down strikes, Sloan became GM chairman and chief executive officer in the wake of another corporate reorganization, while Brown was named vice chairman. During World War II Brown was GM's primary representative in matters relating to governmental relations and defense mobilization. In 1946, contemplating retirement from GM, Sloan urged Brown to succeed him as chairman. Brown agreed in principle with the idea, but he was willing to accept only if certain conditions were met—that he not be required to assume the duties of chief executive officer, and that as chairman, he, and not GM's president, would be the architect of corporate policy. In the meantime, however, GM president Charles E. Wilson prevailed upon Sloan to retain his post as chairman. Declining Wilson's offer to chair a new "Financial Policy Committee," Brown retired from active duty at GM.

Shortly thereafter, Brown became a director of Gulf Oil Corporation. He stayed on the board for ten years, serving on its finance and executive committees. Increasingly, however, his interests centered around two other concerns. He became a leading contributor to politically conservative business organizations such as the Foundation for Economic Education, a successor to the anti–New Deal American Liberty League (which he had also backed heavily). Brown also devoted much attention to the affairs of his personal holding company, Broesco, which he formed in 1946 to provide for his wife, Greta McFarland du Pont Barksdale (the daughter of Hamilton McFarland Barksdale), whom he had married in 1916, and their six children. After retiring in 1956, Brown gave occasional speeches on business, wrote his memoirs, and hunted and fished. He died at his home in Port Deposit.

• Two collections of Brown's personal papers are housed in the Hagley Museum and Library, Wilmington, Delaware. They consist of materials Brown assembled for his memoirs, including correspondence with officials of Du Pont and General Motors and with leading figures in conservative politics; memoranda relating to GM finances, policies, organization, and employee relations; speeches and drafts of his writings on business topics; and files relating to Gulf Oil Corporation and to Broesco Corporation. The papers of several other Du Pont and GM executives, which are also at Hagley, contain correspondence to or from Brown. The major source of information on Brown's life is his memoirs, *Some Reminiscences of an Industrialist* (privately printed, 1957). Other information on his career may be found in Alfred P. Sloan, Jr., *My Years with General Motors* (1964); Alfred D. Chandler, Jr., *Strategy and Structure: Chapters in the History of the American Business Enterprise* (1962), especially chapters 2 and 3; Sidney Fine, *The Automobile under the Blue Eagle* (1963); Sidney Fine, *Sit-Down: The General Motors Strike of 1936–1937* (1969); and Robert F. Burk, *The Corporate State and the Broker State: The Du Ponts and American National Politics, 1925–1940* (1990).

JOHN C. RUMM

BROWN, George Scratchley (17 Aug. 1918–5 Dec. 1978), air force officer, was born in Montclair, New Jersey, the son of Thoburn Kaye Brown, a career army officer, and Frances Katherine Scratchley. After graduating from high school in Leavenworth, Kansas, in 1936, Brown attended the University of Missouri for a year before enrolling in the U.S. Military Academy. He graduated in 1941 and was commissioned a second lieutenant in the infantry. Brown entered flight training in August 1941, and the following March he received his wings and was assigned to the army air forces. In 1942 he married Alice Norvell Calhoun; they had three children.

Brown became a B-24 bomber pilot with the Ninety-third Bombardment Group, and after completing training in August 1942, he went to England with his group. Promoted to first lieutenant in May 1942, captain in October 1942, major in February 1943, and lieutenant colonel in September 1943, he flew numerous combat missions over Europe and served as squadron commander, group operations officer, and executive officer of the Ninety-third Group. While executive officer, he participated in the low-level bombing raid against the oil refineries at Ploieşti, Romania, on 1 August 1943, earning the Distinguished Service Cross for demonstrating steady leadership in assuming control of his formation after the commander's plane was shot down and leading the formation over the target and back to the base in Libya. Brown returned to the United States in 1944 and until 1946 served as assistant operations officer with the Second Bomb Division and, promoted to colonel, in a similar capacity with the Air Training Command.

From 1946 to 1974 Brown rose to the rank of full general while holding a variety of staff and command assignments, in which he demonstrated considerable political savvy, understanding of the complexities of nuclear strategy, and skill in public relations—qualities that eventually led to his appointment as chairman of the Joint Chiefs of Staff (JCS). He was a likable individual who worked well with colleagues, and, while serving as a military assistant in the Office of the Secretary of Defense in the period 1959–1963, he proved particularly adept at handling the longstanding problem of interservice rivalry by helping to reconcile the disagreements that often developed in the JCS. When relations between Secretary of Defense Robert McNamara and the JCS deteriorated in the early 1960s, Brown was an effective buffer between the two. He played a similar role in the years 1966 to 1968, when he was an assistant to General Earle Wheeler, chairman of the JCS.

Between August 1968 and August 1970, Brown commanded the Seventh Air Force in South Vietnam. In that capacity he was responsible for air force operations in Vietnam and was the air deputy for General Creighton Abrams, commander of American forces in Vietnam. The most significant air force operation in Vietnam during these years was the controversial secret bombing of Cambodia in 1969 and 1970. Brown was drawn into the controversy during his Senate confirmation hearings after President Richard M. Nixon named him air force chief of staff in July 1973. Under sharp questioning, Brown denied any direct involvement in the operation, but he justified the falsifying of reports about the raids by air force personnel as "a special security precaution" ordered by higher authority.

From August 1970 to his appointment as chief of staff, Brown headed the Air Force Systems Command, which conducted experiments to determine the best way to exploit America's technological edge over the Soviet Union. This assignment gave him expertise in the highly technical and costly business of developing new weapons and in nuclear strategy. During these years Brown, a frequent speaker and debater on defense issues, was also an able spokesman for military readiness.

As chief of staff, Brown streamlined the operations of the chief's office and granted his subordinates wide leeway in carrying out their responsibilities. He devoted much of his attention to increasing benefits for air force personnel, improving the air force's relations with the other services, and emphasizing cost consciousness in the procurement of new weapons. In the process Brown impressed Secretary of Defense James Schlesinger and President Nixon with his candor, levelheadedness, and ability to deal with Congress. Convinced that Brown possessed the attributes to lead the U.S. military into the post-Vietnam era, to rebuild gutted forces, and to reconstitute America's strategic response to the Soviet threat, Nixon appointed him JCS chairman in May 1974.

Brown's major task was to persuade a fiscally conservative Congress to increase defense spending. At first matters went well, as Brown was articulate, convincing, and realistic in his presentations. Congress, despite the post–Vietnam War bias against the military, seemed receptive to his argument that détente with the Soviet Union must be undergirded by higher defense appropriations. Brown's effectiveness was soon severely tested. In response to a question after a speech at Duke University in October 1974, Brown inexplicably implied that American Jews exercised an unhealthy influence on Congress, saying, Jews "own . . . the banks in this country, the newspapers." Brown's off-the-cuff comment sparked widespread calls for his dismissal, and President Gerald Ford publicly rebuked him. Eventually the uproar cooled when Brown apologized for the remark and denied any anti-Semitism. The incident weakened his standing before Congress, however, and thereafter he played a less prominent role in the budget fights. When not handling budget matters, Brown effected the first major reorganization of the JCS since 1958 and, typical of his leadership style, delegated considerable responsibility to his subordinates in such crises as the Cyprus civil war and the evacuation of American and British civilians from the island, the Cambodian seizure of the American merchant ship *Mayaguez*, the evacuation of American nationals from Lebanon, and the murder of two American soldiers by North Koreans.

Ford reappointed Brown JCS chairman in 1976, and again Brown stirred controversy by publicly criticizing Britain, Iran, and Israel and by describing Congress as meddlesome and irresponsible in its handling of defense and foreign aid. Despite the furor these remarks aroused, President Jimmy Carter kept Brown in his post. In 1977–1978 Brown loyally supported Carter's controversial initiatives to cancel the B-1 bomber and to withdraw American troops from South Korea and his endorsement of the Panama Canal treaties, although he did not always approve of the president's decisions. Brown remained as JCS chairman until prostate cancer forced his retirement in June 1978.

A highly intelligent and affable military professional with an impressive understanding of weapons and strategy, Brown was a capable officer who combined military leadership with managerial ability. He died at Andrews Air Force Base, Maryland.

• Brown's papers are in the Historical Division, Joint Staff to the JCS, at the Pentagon. Edgar F. Puryear, Jr., *George S. Brown, General, U.S. Air Force: Destined for Stars* (1983), is a biography that emphasizes Brown's leadership style. References to Brown's tenure with the JCS are in Mark Perry, *Four Stars* (1989). An obituary is in the *New York Times*, 6 Dec. 1978.

JOHN KENNEDY OHL

BROWN, Gertrude Foster (29 July 1867–1 Mar. 1956), suffragist, concert pianist, and music educator, was born Gertrude Marion Foster in Morrison, Illinois, the daughter of Lydia Ann (or Anna) Drake and William Charles Foster, an agricultural commodities trader and real estate investor. At the early age of five, Gertrude displayed a talent for music by teaching herself to play short piano pieces that she had heard her older brother practicing. When she was twelve years old, she was hired as the organist for the local Presbyterian church, the first organist for that church ever to be paid a salary.

Eager to pursue full-time piano studies, she completed high school at the age of fifteen and persuaded her father to let her go to Boston in 1883 to study at the New England Conservatory of Music. She received a diploma from the conservatory in 1885 and was hired as the head of the department of instrumental music at the Cooper Academy in Dayton, Ohio. The following year she went to Europe to study piano under Xaver Scharwenka at the conservatory in Berlin. For several months in 1888 she studied with De la Borde in Paris, and she then returned to Germany to make her professional debut with the Berlin Philharmonic Orchestra.

In 1889 she moved to Chicago and made her American debut. On the whole, her performances received favorable reviews. The *Chicago Indicator* said that she had "excellent technical ability and a daring bravura style," but the *Chicago Herald* noted that her playing lacked "finish and refinement." She also began teaching at the Chicago Conservatory of Music that year.

In August 1893 she married Arthur Raymond Brown, a newspaper artist, reporter, and humorist with the *Chicago Times*. They had no children. The couple moved to New York City in 1896 when Ray Brown was made art director of the *New York Evening Journal* and the *Morning Journal*. Later, he was head of the art department at *Everybody's* magazine before establishing a private advertising firm. In New York, Gertrude Brown studied piano under Rafael Joseffy for several months and then launched a new decade-long career giving lecture-recitals on Richard Wagner and other great composers to audiences across the nation.

Curious about the suffrage movement, Brown visited the New York suffrage headquarters in 1909. The visit inspired her to organize a suffrage study club that met in her home and was composed of a group of well-known women in the arts and professions. Brown's exposure to the suffrage movement brought about a change that she likened to a religious conversion. "On Account of Sex," an unpublished manuscript about her work in the suffrage movement between 1910 and 1920, she wrote, "my profession, my social life, even my family duties soon took second place, and for the next ten years, until the nineteenth amendment to the Federal Constitution was ratified, . . . I gave work for woman suffrage precedence over everything else in my life." She became a strong public advocate of suffrage, shouting to passers-by from the top of a motorcar at a street corner in Harlem, speaking from the stage in vaudeville theaters in Philadelphia and the Bronx, and marching with fellow suffragists, including her husband, in parades down Fifth Avenue.

During the early years of her suffrage work, Brown met and became friends with Carrie Chapman Catt, head of the New York State Woman Suffrage Party. In 1913, with Catt's persistent prodding, Brown became president of the New York State Woman Suffrage Association. For four years she spearheaded that group's statewide campaign to get a female suffrage referendum passed. When the suffrage referendum of 1915 failed, the New York State Woman Suffrage Party was reorganized, and for two years Brown served as that group's second vice president, organization committee chair, and state congressional chair. In addition to writing extensive campaign literature, she organized and wrote a citizenship correspondence course for New York women on "how to use the vote," educational information that was serialized in the *New York World* and later expanded in Brown's book, *Your Vote and How to Use It* (1918).

After suffrage was achieved for New York women in 1917, Brown became a vice president of the National American Woman Suffrage Association (NAWSA), a position she held until 1920 when the Nineteenth Amendment was ratified. Though suffrage remained a priority concern with Brown during this period, she, like other suffragists, focused on the war effort after the United States entered World War I. When the U.S. government refused to allow a group of female physicians and surgeons to serve overseas, the group went to France under the auspices of the French war department, and NAWSA agreed to help maintain the unit as one of its four wartime programs. Brown accompanied the medical team to France and served throughout most of 1918 as the director general of the Women's Overseas Hospitals, USA.

After the ratification of the Nineteenth Amendment in 1920, some of the suffrage groups disbanded while others reorganized for new purposes. Brown helped establish the National League of Women Voters as the successor to NAWSA. In 1921 she also became the managing director of *Woman Citizen*, formerly the *Woman's Journal*, a magazine that was founded by Lucy Stone in 1870. Although the *Woman Citizen* was popular as a "magazine of information for the new woman voter," the management was unable to maintain its financing after the onset of the Great Depression and the magazine ceased publication in 1931.

When the magazine folded, Brown retired and was able to devote time to music and to travel abroad with her husband. In several articles written during this period, she reflected on the suffrage campaign, its success, and the role of women. She voiced a viewpoint that she consistently had expressed throughout her involvement with suffrage and women's rights, one that she contrasted with women's equality advocates who rejected women's special needs. Brown stressed women's "difference" from men in their basic natures and in their political and civic concerns. She believed that suffrage had allowed women to bring into the public arena special "female" concerns with the human side of government (children, health, the poor) that counterbalanced men's concerns with business and material affairs. She emphasized that women had finally succeeded in gaining the vote because they had learned not to try to be as aggressive as men but to utilize feminine traits such as quiet persuasion, deference, tact, and patience as well as organizational skills and the force of numbers.

In 1941 Brown and her former suffrage friends returned to the public sector to organize the Women's Action Committee for Victory and a Lasting Peace, a group that supported the war effort and U.S. participation in the United Nations. Brown served as chair of the group's campaign committee. In 1944 she was widowed. She unofficially retired from community work in the late 1940s in order to travel and enjoy her musical pursuits, including a chamber music ensemble she organized with a group of friends. She died in Westport, Connecticut.

• Brown's papers are at the Schlesinger Library at Radcliffe College. (Citations in the above text refer to folders in this collection.) The collection contains manuscript versions of her autobiographical writings, "Breaking into the Human Race" and "On Account of Sex: Memories of a New York Suffragist," and a microfilm of "Suffrage and Music: My First Eighty Years." The collection also includes diaries, correspondence, articles about her musical career and suffrage activities, and records of the Woman's Citizen Corporation, the Women's Overseas Hospitals project, and the Women's Action Committee. Brown's "Wangling the Men," *Ladies Home Journal*, Dec. 1933, gives a perspective on her attitude concerning the role of women in politics and government. Her niece, Mildred Adams, wrote a study of the suffrage movement, *The Right to Be People* (1967), which contains biographical information on Brown. Her husband, Ray Brown, anonymously published *How It Feels to Be the Husband of a Suffragette* (1915), a brief book that gives humorous insight into his experience as a suffrage spouse and supporter. An obituary notice appears in the *New York Times*, 3 Mar. 1956, but it contains some incorrect information.

MARILYNN WOOD HILL

BROWN, Gilmor (16 June 1886–10 Jan. 1960), actor, director, and theater manager, was born George Gilmor Brown on a ranch and farm twelve miles outside New Salem, North Dakota, the son of Orville A. Brown and Emma Louise Gilmor. The seeds of Brown's very active and fertile imagination seem to have been rooted in the loneliness and rural isolation of his early childhood. When he was six, however, the family moved to Denver, Colorado, where Brown began formal schooling and finally could socialize. There he became interested in theater. His father, who had wanted to become an actor but was not permitted to by his family, sometimes took him to vaudeville shows. When Brown was about eight, his mother encouraged and assisted him in forming his own theatrical company of neighborhood children dubbed the Tuxedo Stock Company. They performed their own plays, mostly tragedies and melodramas written by Brown. Brown worked with the troupe into his early teenage years. Despite his youth and lack of any theatrical training, his dedication and skill as a director impressed many, including Denver journalists. His efforts also attracted the attention of the pastor of St. Mark's Episcopal Church, who encouraged his interest in drama and invited Brown to participate in a summer camp in the Colorado Rockies. Brown founded a theater at the camp, staging Greek tragedies and classical drama outdoors in a magnificent alpine setting. Brown and others continued to mount such alfresco productions in the years that followed.

A 1901 touring production of *Becky Sharpe* with Minnie Maddern Fiske in the title role confirmed Brown in his determination to make theater his life's endeavor. He commenced a self-directed education: reading, attending all sorts of stage entertainments (including circuses, medicine shows, and vaudeville), and living and breathing all things theatrical. This self-education was supplemented by attendance at a number of generally unimpressive theatrical schools. Mrs. Florence J. (Milward) Adams's school in Chicago proved the exception. The training Brown received there between 1903 and 1905 involved "learning by doing," a principle that would be the foundation in later years of the curriculum at the Pasadena School of the Theatre. After leaving Mrs. Adams's school, Brown began a decade's worth of traveling with touring repertory companies, including that of British actor and producer Ben Greet.

In 1916 Brown landed in Pasadena, California, with his own company, the Comedy Players (later renamed the Savoy Players), and founded the Pasadena Community Playhouse. With the playhouse's opening the following year, Brown's considerable influence on the American theater began. The Pasadena Community Playhouse became southern California's most dynamic theater and one of the pioneers in the community theater (or "little theater") movement, which sought to free American audiences from dependence on Broadway and touring companies by developing local amateur talent. Community theaters, Brown contended, responded to "the desire of the American people for a non-merchandized, personal theatre. . . . They are closer to the people than any professional theatre can be and, therefore, at their best they present a truer and more fundamental reflection of American life and thought" (McCleery and Glick, p. v.).

With Brown as producer/director, the playhouse—employing chiefly amateur actors and a volunteer staff—staged everything from revivals both of Shakespeare's works and of lesser-known classics to fresh material by unheralded playwrights. In its first dozen years it mounted some 300 productions, including more than fifty plays never before staged, most notably Eugene O'Neill's *Lazarus Laughed* in 1928. The community clearly welcomed its efforts. As early as 1925 the playhouse had outgrown its original, rather ramshackle headquarters and moved into its own ornate Spanish-style theater seating over 800. In 1928 Brown, after raising funds door-to-door, founded the Pasadena School of the Theatre (later known as Pasadena Playhouse College of the Theatre). Befitting Brown's own experience, the highly regarded school offered practical rather than academic training. Students at the school's "laboratory" theater regularly staged experimental work by new authors. Both the playhouse and the school nurtured many acting careers, including those of Hollywood stars Dana Andrews, Lee J. Cobb, Tyrone Power, Robert Preston, Victor Mature, Randolph Scott, and Robert Young.

Brown's success both in developing a vital community-based regional theater and in maintaining it through the Great Depression recommended him in 1935 for an important post in the Federal Theatre Project. Serving as western regional director through the end of 1937, he headed what project director Hallie Flanagan declared was one of the Federal Theatre's most vigorous divisions. Though remaining at the helm of the Pasadena Playhouse, Brown also managed at various times to lecture on drama at the University of Southern California and the California Institute of Technology, and he was president of the National Theatre Conference, an association of local nonprofit theater companies.

Brown's health began to fail in 1957. In July 1959 he resigned as president of the Pasadena College of Theatre Arts. He died six months later in Palm Springs, California. Brown never married. Whenever anyone had asked, "When does Gilmor Brown get any time for his personal life?" the response had invariably been, "He has no personal life. His life is the theater."

• There are tapes and transcripts of interviews with Brown and several other principals in the Pasadena Community Playhouse in the collections of the UCLA Oral History Program. Brown's childhood and training, as well as his theater, is discussed in Gail Leo Shoup, Jr., "The Pasadena Community Playhouse: It's Origins and History from 1917 to 1942" (Ph.D. diss., UCLA, 1968). See also Diane Alexander, *Playhouse* (1984); Kenneth MacGowan, *Footlights across America: Towards a National Theater* (1929); and Albert McCleery and Carl Glick, *Curtains Going Up* (1939). Discussions of Brown's work with the Federal Theatre Project may be found in Hallie Flanagan, *Arena: The History of the Federal Theatre* (1940); Jane DeHart Mathews, *The Federal Theatre, 1935–1939: Plays, Relief, and Politics* (1967); George Kazacoff, *Dangerous Theatre: The Federal Theatre Project as a Forum for New Plays* (1989); and Tony Buttitta and Barry Witham, *Uncle Sam Presents: A Memoir of the Federal Theatre, 1935–1939.* An obituary is in the *New York Times*, 12 Jan. 1960. In several sources Brown's first name is spelled Gilmore.

MONICA J. BURDEX

BROWN, Glenn (13 Sept. 1854–22 Apr. 1932), architect, was born in Fauquier County, Virginia, the son of Bedford Brown II, a physician, and Mary E. Simpson. Between 1871 and 1873 Brown attended Washington and Lee University, receiving a traditional education in the classics, and at age nineteen returned to Alexandria to become his father's apprentice in preparation for a career in medicine. Brown soon thereafter discovered an aptitude for design, however, and attended the architecture school at the Massachusetts Institute of Technology in Boston from 1875 to 1876. While in Boston, he found employment with the contracting firm of Norcross Brothers, builders of much of master architect Henry Hobson Richardson's work, and became the shop draftsman and paymaster for Richardson's Cheney building in Hartford, Connecticut. While working in Hartford, Brown married Mary Ella Chapman of Staunton, Virginia, the granddaughter of General William Madison, brother of President James Madison. This marriage, which produced one child, enhanced Brown's identification as a "man of the South" and incidentally promoted an important personal interest in the historic Octagon house, where James and Dolley Madison had lived following the burning of the White House in 1814, and its architect, William Thornton. In 1877 Brown returned to Washington and began a diverse fifty-year career in the nation's capital as an architect, city planning and professional activist, and author.

Brown's work during his 45-year practice ranked with the finest architecture produced by Washington architects in the period. His best-known commissions in the capital include the Romanesque revival National Union Fire Insurance Building on F Street, NW (1890), the Massachusetts Avenue neoclassical revival Beale House (1907), and the Dumbarton Bridge (1913) on Q Street. Brown was also a noted restoration architect who worked on early preservation projects including Christ Church, Alexandria, Virginia (1894); the old Supreme Court chamber in the U.S. Capitol, Washington, D.C. (1901); and Gunston Hall, Fairfax, Virginia (1915).

Brown's contributions to the political influence and organizational development of the American architectural profession were formidable. He was instrumental in the founding of the Washington chapter of the American Institute of Architects (AIA) in 1887 and directed the organization's professional activities for nearly three decades. In 1895 Brown organized the Public Art League, a national fine arts lobby formed to advocate legislation that would establish an expert commission of architects and artists to advise the federal government on its patronage of architecture, art, and sculpture. This national initiative ultimately failed, but it spurred Brown's election as a national AIA officer in 1898.

Brown related in his memoirs that he became AIA secretary with a clear purpose in mind—to use the institute as a lobby to create an architect-dominated fine arts commission in the national capital to revive and protect Pierre Charles L'Enfant's 1791 plan for Washington. Brown orchestrated the important AIA campaigns between 1900 and 1913 that advanced the City Beautiful movement in the capital. He became a trusted fine arts adviser to Presidents Theodore Roosevelt and William H. Taft. During this period Brown engineered AIA sponsorship of the Senate Park Commission (popularly known as the McMillan commission in honor of its legislative sponsor, Senator James McMillan) and directed a lobbying campaign that assured the early implementation of the now famous 1901–1902 McMillan plan for the Mall and the enactment of legislation establishing the U.S. Commission of Fine Arts in 1910.

Brown also initiated the establishment of the institute's headquarters at the Octagon in Washington; created the present AIA archives and library; founded the first journal of the organization; and greatly increased both the membership network and regional representation of the AIA so that by 1913 the organization attained public recognition analogous to the American bar and medical associations.

Brown's emergence as a leader of the architectural profession was built on his national reputation as a scholar and his prolific writing ability. Brown wrote or edited more than eighty articles on subjects ranging from plumbing systems and city planning to architectural history and professional ethics as well as a dozen major books. The centerpiece of Brown's writing career was his two-volume *History of the United States Capitol* (1900–1903). No American work preceding Brown's *History* had provided as extensive an array of architectural drawings, prints, and photographs or narrative documenting the historic design evolution of a national monument and its site. Foreign reception to the book was enthusiastic and led to Brown's election as an honorary member of the British, French, Italian, and Belgian architectural societies. In 1915 Brown contributed a minor classic to the literature of historic preservation by publishing *The Octagon*, a historical monograph that includes an extensive set of measured drawings of the building.

In 1925 Brown retired and during his final years prepared *Memories: A Winning Crusade to Revive George Washington's Vision of a Capital City* (1931), which has become a seminal account of the early twentieth-century planning history of the nation's capital. Brown became gravely ill in 1931 and died in Buxton Hospital in Newport News, Virginia. He was buried at Rock Creek Cemetery, Washington, D.C., next to his wife. The simple shared gravestone was designed by Brown after his wife's death in 1926.

• A collection of Brown's personal papers, drawings, and official correspondence and records as AIA secretary is in the American Institute of Architects Archives, Washington, D.C. A modern treatment of Brown's career is William Bushong, "Glenn Brown, the American Institute of Architects and the Development of the Civic Core of Washington, D.C." (Ph.D. diss., George Washington Univ., 1988). See also Bushong, *A Centennial History of the Washington Chapter of the American Institute of Architects* (1987) and "Glenn Brown and the Preservation of the Octagon as the Headquarters of the American Institute of Architects," *Symposium Proceedings Celebrating the Centennial of the Founding of the AIA Committee on Historic Resources* (1990). Important obituaries include Charles Moore, "Glenn Brown: A Memoir," *Royal Institute of British Architects Journal* 39 (15 Oct. 1932): 858, *American Architect* 141 (June 1932): 44, and the *New York Times*, 23 Apr. 1932.

WILLIAM BUSHONG

BROWN, Hallie Quinn (10 Mar. 1849–16 Sept. 1949), educator, elocutionist, and entertainer, was born in Pittsburgh, Pennsylvania, the daughter of Thomas Arthur Brown, a steward and express agent on riverboats, and Frances Jane Scroggins. Both her parents were former slaves. When Hallie was fourteen years old she moved with her parents and five siblings to Chatham, Ontario, where her father earned his living farming, and the children attended the local school. There Brown's talents as a speaker became evident. Returning to the United States around 1870, the family settled in Wilberforce, Ohio, so that Hallie and her younger brother could attend Wilberforce College, a primarily black African Methodist Episcopal (AME) institution.

In 1873 Brown received her B.S. from Wilberforce. The next year she began her work as a lecturer and reciter for the Lyceum, a traveling educational and entertainment program. She would continue both of these careers, as educator and entertainer, throughout much of her life, often doing them simultaneously. After graduating she moved south to help with the educational needs of southern blacks identified under Reconstruction. She taught at plantation schools and grade schools in Mississippi and South Carolina for several years.

In the early 1880s Brown quit teaching and started to tour with the Lyceum full time. She was an immense success throughout the Midwest. In 1882 she joined a group of singers known as the Wilberforce Concert Company (later the Stewart Concert Company) that toured throughout the nation for four seasons, raising money for Wilberforce College. Throughout her American travels, Brown received accolades for her elocution.

From 1885 to 1887 Brown served as dean of Allen University in Columbia, South Carolina, after which she returned to Ohio to teach public school in Dayton from 1887 to 1891. Her concern for southern blacks continued, and she established a night school for migrants. From 1892 to 1893 she taught under Frederick Douglass at Tuskegee Institute in Alabama before returning to her alma mater, now Wilberforce University, as both a professor of elocution and a trustee.

Brown's lyceum work made her unable to accept the Wilberforce appointment immediately. In 1894 her work as an entertainer and educator took her to Europe, where she remained for five years, spending most of her time in the United Kingdom, although she also visited Germany, Switzerland, and France. During this time, Brown lectured to Europeans on black life in the United States and Negro song and folklore. She was presented twice to Queen Victoria, in 1897 and 1899, and helped to form the first British Chatauqua (another touring educational and entertainment organization) in North Wales in 1895. After returning to the United States she continued her elocutionist career, attending a variety of conferences in the early years of the new century. During all of this time she remained affiliated with Wilberforce, although her teaching requirements were obviously minimal.

In 1906 William S. Scarborough, the president of Wilberforce, reappointed Brown to the position of professor of elocution and also named her as the traveling agent for the institution. Her assignment was to raise money for the construction of a new men's dormitory. In 1910, during a second trip to Europe, she managed to pique the interest of E. J. Emery, a female philanthropist in London. Two years later, Emery donated $16,000, which was used to build a new women's dormitory at Wilberforce. The building was named Keziah Emery Hall in honor of Emery's mother. In 1914 Brown's appointment at the college was reestablished, with the more specific addition of the title of "soliciting agent." From 1915 to 1919 Brown, then in her sixties, taught freshman English at Wilberforce.

Brown never married, and she was very active in the reform movements and politics of her time. In 1893 she attended the World's Columbian Exposition in Chicago, where she approached the Board of Lady Managers that oversaw the exhibits of accomplishment of American women. Brown asked that she be appointed to the board to ensure that the achievements of black women would receive recognition. She was rejected on the ground that she did not represent an organization. Returning home to Ohio, Brown responded, that same year, by forming the Colored Women's League, the forerunner of the National Association of Colored Women.

In 1920 Brown was appointed as the seventh president of the National Association of Colored Women. She held the position for two successive terms until 1924. During her presidency the organization initiated a move to preserve abolitionist Douglass's Anacostia home. It also instituted a fund to be used for higher education of black female students. Brown remained the honorary president of this organization until her death.

During the 1890s Brown also was an active member of the Women's Christian Temperance Union and the British Women's Temperance Association. In 1895 she was a speaker at the World's Women's Christian Temperance Union in London. She was also very involved in the African Methodist Episcopal church. In 1900 she was the first woman to campaign for an office in the AME church's general conference, an endeavor at which she was unsuccessful.

In addition to her active pursuit of rights for women and blacks, Brown was involved in mainstream American politics. In 1920 she campaigned for Warren G. Harding for the presidency, becoming the first woman to speak from his famous front porch during the campaign. She also was involved in the Ohio campaign for Herbert Hoover in 1932.

Brown died at her home in Wilberforce, Ohio.

• Brown wrote seven books and many pamphlets during her life, including *Bits and Odds: A Choice Selection of Recitations* (1880), *First Lessons in Public Speaking* (1920), *The Beautiful: A True Story of Slavery* (1924), *Our Women: Past, Present and Future* (1925), *Tales My Father Told* (1925), *Homespun Heroines and Other Women of Distinction* (1925), and *Pen Pictures of Pioneers of Wilberforce* (1937); she also dramatized *Trouble in Turkeytrot Church* by P. A. Nichols.

During her life, her activism was documented in Elizabeth Lindsay Davis, ed., *Lifting as They Climb* (1933), and a brief biography is in A. Augustus Wright, ed., *Who's Who in the Lyceum* (1906). A more recent article, Ann Jennette S. McFarlin, "Hallie Quinn Brown: Black Woman Elocutionist," *Southern Speech Communication Journal* 46 (Fall 1980): 72–82, discusses her elocution career as well as her life in general. Erlene Stetson, "Black Feminism in Indiana, 1893–1933," *Phylon* 64, no. 4 (1983): 292–98, further discusses Brown's impact on the women's and civil rights movements.

CLAIRE STROM

BROWN, Harrison Scott (26 Sept. 1917–8 Dec. 1986), geochemist and specialist in international relations, was born in Sheridan, Wyoming, the son of Harrison H. Brown, a rancher and cattle broker, and Agnes Scott, a music teacher. After his father's death, when Brown was ten, he moved with his mother to San Francisco, California. A precocious student with a talent for music and the sciences, Brown is credited with building his own chemistry laboratory while attending Galileo High School. He then attended the University of California at Berkeley, earning a B.A. in physics in 1938.

Fascinated by the lectures of the nuclear chemist Robert D. Fowler, Brown continued his studies at the Johns Hopkins University in Baltimore after Fowler transferred there from Berkeley. In 1941 he earned a Ph.D. in chemistry at Johns Hopkins with a thesis, guided by Fowler, on the isotopic composition of cobalt. Shortly thereafter Brown began studying the diffusion properties of uranium hexafluoride, and with Fowler he supplied gaseous uranium products to the nascent atomic bomb program. In 1942 Brown joined the Manhattan Project, assisting efforts to produce plutonium at the wartime Clinton Engineering Works at Oak Ridge, Tennessee.

After the war, Brown became a charter member of the University of Chicago's new Institute for Nuclear Studies. At this facility, home to numerous Manhattan Project veterans, including the Nobel laureate Harold C. Urey, Brown studied atomic abundances as a way to address fundamental problems in geochemistry. In the late 1940s Brown attempted to use geochemical abundances in meteorites to infer the internal structure of the Earth. He also worked to update nuclear abundance curves through new abundance estimates, made possible by wartime advances in atomic accelerators and mass spectrometers; he used these results to produce an extensive bibliography of meteorite analyses. Finally, with the aid of former graduate students, including Claire Patterson, Brown sought to use radioactive abundance measurements to yield reliable methods for determining the ages of ancient rocks and the age of the Earth itself. In 1951 Brown transferred to the California Institute of Technology, where he created an advanced laboratory for geochemical research; at this facility, Patterson made the first modern determination of Earth's age (c. 4.5 billion years) in the mid-1950s. Brown stressed the importance of integrating geochemistry into traditional geological practice and by the 1960s, as lunar and planetary exploration began, encouraged new programs of planetary research at Caltech.

Brown remained active in scientific research at Caltech during the 1960s, although his attention increasingly turned to social issues and science policy. While still at Chicago, Brown published a book highly critical of nuclear proliferation, *Must Destruction Be Our Destiny?* (1946). Brown concluded this essay on a somber note, writing that a planned chapter on the peaceful applications of atomic energy was omitted because these "seemed insignificant when compared to the immediate considerations of life and death that now confront us" (p. 107). In 1954 Brown produced a more substantial study, *The Challenge of Man's Future*, which analyzed trends of population growth together with projections of food resources, energy consumption, and natural resource depletion. While Brown's forecasts were initially attacked as overly pessimistic, his arguments about industrial development and pollution began gaining acceptance from a widening circle of scientists and planners in the 1960s and 1970s.

In the 1960s Brown also became actively engaged in international scientific organizations and programs. Between 1962 and 1974 Brown served as foreign secretary of the National Academy of Sciences, to which he had been elected in 1955. Brown used this office to promote an activist social agenda, including increased support for scientific work in Latin America, Asia, and sub-Sahara Africa. After the Berlin Wall was built in June 1961, Brown was instrumental in securing an arrangement that allowed East German scientists to participate in international scientific meetings in western countries. Beginning in 1957 he chaired a major NAS committee on oceanography that helped to dramatically expand federal support for this discipline. Brown made substantial contributions to the annual Pugwash conferences, which rested on the idea that scientists had responsibility for their inventions. The conferences especially emphasized the devastation that would come from the use of atomic weapons. He also helped found the Austrian-based Institute for Applied Systems Analysis and from 1974 to 1976 served as president of the International Council of Scientific Unions.

By the 1970s Brown's contributions were almost entirely in population and resource studies. Feeling that the social sciences at Caltech were growing too slowly, Brown in 1977 joined the East-West Center in Honolulu, Hawaii, becoming director of its Resources Systems Institute. At the center, Brown focused on the problem of natural resource use in the Asia-Pacific region, especially agriculture, energy, and raw materials. Increasingly convinced that existing economic and political mechanisms would not solve heightened demand for resources, Brown sought to improve the accuracy of growth-rate predictions; unlike most mid-twentieth century analysts, he conducted his discussions of resource issues within a broad social and political context.

Brown received several honorary degrees and numerous professional awards for his geochemical and policy studies. In addition to winning a prize for best paper delivered at the American Association of Arts and Sciences meeting of 1947 and an award from the American Chemical Society (1952), Brown won the Lasker Foundation Award (1958) and the Mellon Institution Award (1971).

Brown had married Adele Scrimger in 1938; they had one son. After their divorce in the late 1940s, Brown married Rudd Owen, who worked with Brown during his years at Caltech on his humanitarian writings and social projects. This marriage also ended in divorce, and late in his career Brown married Theresa Tellez, an anthropologist and his former collaborator in the National Academy of Sciences.

After retiring from the East-West Center in 1983, Brown moved to Albuquerque, New Mexico. For several years he served as editor in chief of the *Bulletin of the Atomic Scientists* and wrote essays on nuclear disarmament. Radiation therapy treatments of his spine following an earlier bout with lung cancer caused progressive paralysis, confining him to a wheelchair. Active until shortly before his death, Brown died in Albuquerque.

Brown's pioneering efforts to incorporate geochemical techniques into traditional geology, and his role in training researchers such as Patterson, were more consequential than his own geochemical studies. His investigations of industrial civilization and natural resources, although overshadowed by later findings of policy analysts and environmental researchers, helped to define these issues and underscore their social importance. His successes in furthering East-West relations in science during the height of the Cold War are increasingly appreciated by historians of this period.

• A limited collection of correspondence dealing with Brown's work at the National Academy of Sciences is in the academy's archives. Brown's other books, primarily on the application of science and technology to significant social issues, include *The Human Future Revisited: The World Predicament and Possible Solutions* (1978) and *China among the Nations of the Pacific* (1982); with Chole Zerwick, he also wrote a work of science fiction, *The Cassiopeia Affair* (1968), which addresses the consequences of Earth receiving a message from an intelligent civilization. The most complete modern assessment is Roger Revelle, "Harrison Brown, 1917–1986," National Academy of Sciences, *Biographical Memoirs* 65 (1994): 41–55. Brown's geochemical studies are discussed in Ronald E. Doel, *Solar System Astronomy in America: Communities, Patronage, and Interdisciplinary Research* (1996), pp. 78–114. On his general scientific career, as well as his contributions to population and natural resource studies, see Kirk R. Smith et al., *Earth and the Human Future: Essays in Honor of Harrison Brown* (1986). An obituary is in the *New York Times*, 9 Dec. 1986.

RONALD E. DOEL

BROWN, Harry Gunnison (7 May 1880–18 Mar. 1975), economist, was born in Troy, New York, the son of Milton Peers Brown, an accountant, and Elizabeth H. Gunnison. Brown suffered from tuberculosis as a youth, which ended a career in factory work and led him to attend Williams College (1900–1904), from which he received a B.A. He next attended Ohio State University (1905–1906) and then enrolled at Yale University, where he was awarded a Ph.D. in economics in 1909. His dissertation, "Some Phases of Railroad Combination," was supervised by Irving Fisher. Brown started his extensive publishing career while a graduate student, writing essays beginning in 1907 for the *Yale Review*.

Brown dedicated the next five decades to the enthusiastic teaching of economics; he wrote eleven books and more than 100 journal articles and, somewhat reluctantly, was involved in academic administration. While teaching at Yale as an instructor (1909–1915) Brown assisted in Fisher's *The Purchasing Power of Money* (1911). Also in 1911 he married Fleda Phillips; they raised three children before her death in 1952. While at Yale, Brown solidified his interest in the teachings of Henry George, and he became the foremost advocate among economists of land value taxation in the tradition of the single tax of George and his precursors. Brown's open and determined advocacy of this economic "heresy" lent an air of notoriety to his career that unfortunately came to overshadow his accomplishments in other areas of economics, especially for succeeding generations of economists.

Before leaving Yale, Brown's first book, *International Trade and Exchange: A Study in the Mechanisms and Advantages of Commerce* (1914), was published by Macmillan Company. In it, and three other books on the subject, he demonstrated his competence and showed himself to be an uncompromising free trader. Brown, who had debated as an undergraduate and coached debate at Ohio State, entered into an exchange in 1913 on the role of capital's productivity in the determination of interest rates. The debate was first with Frank A. Fetter, whose position was that interest rate determination was wholly subjective, but the debate ultimately also involved Fisher. Although he was closer to Fisher's view (that the productivity of capital must play a role, along with time preference) than most of his contemporaries, he never accepted his former mentor's theory that capital's productivity only indirectly influenced interest rates.

Brown was invited by economic theorist Herbert J. Davenport to join the faculty at the University of Missouri in 1915 and taught there until 1950. He served frequently as chair of the economics department and twice as dean of the School of Business and Public Administration (1934–1936, 1942–1946). In 1916 he published *Principles of Commerce*, a text for business students based on economic principles. Brown's *Economic Science and the Common Welfare* (1923) became the nucleus of his later textbook *Basic Principles of Economics* (1942); each had several editions and was characterized by clear and concise exposition.

Also in 1916 Macmillan Company published Brown's *Transportation Rates and Their Regulation*. J. M. Clark, a business cycle theorist, had special praise for his meticulous treatment of freight discrimination. Brown's talent for exploring and explaining complex economic interrelationships became a hallmark of his work. In a 1925 article he entered into a protracted exchange over the merits of reproduction cost versus original cost pricing for railroads or public utilities. He argued for reproduction cost pricing against the current opinion in the discipline. James C. Bonbright, an opponent then, later described Brown's analysis as "a classic in rate regulation" (*Principles of Public Utility Rates* [1961], p. 226). Alfred Kahn has said that his own *Economics of Regulation* (1970) was greatly influenced by this exchange and Brown's writings on competition and regulation (Ryan, p. xiii).

Brown's advocacy of land value taxation was formally introduced in book form in *The Theory of Earned and Unearned Incomes* (1918); this book and *The Taxation of Unearned Incomes* (1921) were superseded by his definitive treatment of the subject, *The Economic Basis of Tax Reform* (1932). In addition to these books Brown wrote more than fifty articles that analyzed or advocated land value taxation, that is, assessing the worth of the land itself, as opposed to the value of the improvements on it. Many of these were published in the *American Journal of Economics and Sociology*, a journal for which he served on the board of editors from its inception in 1941 to his death. During his last years of teaching at various colleges, including Franklin and Marshall, following retirement from Missouri, he and his second wife, librarian Elizabeth Read, whom he married in 1953, actively campaigned for the adoption of land value taxation by the municipalities of Pennsylvania.

The Economics of Taxation (1924) was Brown's most acclaimed publication. When the University of Chicago Press reprinted it in 1979, Arnold Harberger, a public finance theorist at the university, stated: "This is truly a classic. . . . My respect for him is enormous. He belongs in a league with Seligman and Hotelling as the best contributors to the literature of public finance over an entire generation of economists" (Ryan, p. 76). Brown's analysis of the incidence of taxes on general output and on capital were particularly noteworthy. He made early use of the kinked-demand curve concept.

As a student and colleague of Irving Fisher, Brown maintained an interest in macroeconomic questions. He accepted Fisher's version of the quantity theory of money, which states that nominal income is determined solely by movements in the quantity of money. His collaboration with Fisher led Charles Kindleberger to describe their early explanation of business cycles as the "Fisher-Brown" thesis (*Manias, Panics and Crashes* [1978], p. 30). Brown faulted the Federal Reserve Board for helping to cause the Great Depression and for failing to provide an adequate stimulus for recovery. Although a monetarist, Brown qualified his position: "No theory of prices can be accepted as perfect and complete which makes the price level depend on the quantity of money and bank deposits without reference to the general willingness to spend or hesitancy in spending" (Brown, *Basic Principles*, pp. 89–90). In the post–World War II era he became concerned with the growth of the national debt and questioned whether the acceptance of this growth by economists was sufficiently critical.

Brown retired from the University of Missouri in 1950 but continued to teach economics at the New School for Social Research, the Institute for Economic Inquiry, the University of Mississippi, and Franklin and Marshall College. As a colleague pointed out, "Dr. Brown was first and foremost a teacher" (*In Memoriam* [1975]). His colleagues and students praised highly his ability as a speaker, a logician, and a debater. The famous economist Milton Friedman, who never met Brown but did come to know several of his students, wrote that "he clearly was one of the great teachers of economics."

Brown's later publications were in collaboration with the Robert Schalkenbach Foundation, wherein he coedited *Land Value Taxation around the World* (1955) and coauthored with his wife *The Effective Answer to Communism and Why You Don't Get It in College* (1958). He was a member of the American and Midwest Economic associations, serving the latter as president in 1945. He died in Columbia, Missouri.

Although Brown made no signal, original contribution to economic theory, his skill in its application allowed him to make contributions in several areas. His careful studies of tax incidence and regulatory principles bore demonstrable fruit. As a monetarist he belied with flexibility and imagination the usual caricature of pre-Keynesian monetary thought. His advocacy of free trade and land value taxation underscored his lifelong dedication to improving the common welfare.

• *Selected Articles of Harry Gunnison Brown: The Case for Land Value Taxation* (1980), ed. Paul Junk, contains thirty-two of Brown's articles. *Miscellaneous Papers and Articles of Harry Gunnison Brown*, vol. 1, comp. E. Wood, vol. 2, comp. E. R. Brown, is in the Special Collections department of the University of Missouri Library. It contains almost all of Brown's published articles and a few privately printed ones, from 1907 to 1969. Some of Brown's correspondence may be found in the Yale Library and in the Joint Collection, University of Missouri Western Historical Manuscript Collection, Columbia. For a detailed study of Brown's economic thought, see Christopher K. Ryan, *Harry Gunnison Brown: Economist* (1987). For personal views of Brown see Junk, preface to *Selected Articles* above; Will Lissner, "In Memoriam: H. G. Brown, 1880–1975" and "H. G. Brown, Crusader for a Rational Tax System," *American Journal of Economics and Sociology* 34 (1975): 246–48, and 48 (1989): 111–12; and *In Memoriam, Harry Gunnison Brown*, in Special Collections, University of Missouri Library.

CHRISTOPHER K. RYAN

BROWN, Henry Billings (2 Mar. 1836–4 Sept. 1913), associate justice of the U.S. Supreme Court, was born in South Lee, Massachusetts, the son of Billings Brown, a well-to-do merchant and manufacturer, and Mary Tyler. After graduating from Yale College in 1856, he attended Yale and Harvard Law Schools. He moved to Detroit in 1859, where he continued to read law and was admitted to the bar. In 1863 he became assistant U.S. attorney in Detroit. After brief service as a state judge in 1868, Brown returned to private practice and specialized in admiralty law. In 1875 President Ulysses S. Grant appointed Brown to the federal district court, on which he served for fifteen years. President Benjamin Harrison appointed Brown in December 1890 to the Supreme Court, on which he served until his retirement in 1906. Thereafter he lived in Bronxville, New York, which is also where he died.

As a justice Brown wrote more than 450 majority opinions and dissenting or concurring opinions in some fifty other cases. Brown's jurisprudence revealed ambivalence—even contradiction—as he struggled to perform the judicial function. In one dimension, Brown glorified private property and free competition. He considered the right of private property "the first step in the emergence of the civilized man from the condition of the utter savage" ("The Distribution of Property," 1893), and he joined the majority in *Lochner v. New York* (1905), which struck down a state law that limited the hours of bakery workers to a maximum of sixty per week or ten per day. Yet Brown usually construed the state police power broadly and sanctioned legislative modification of laissez-faire principles. In *Holden v. Hardy* (1898), Brown upheld Utah's maximum hours act for miners, rejecting arguments that the state had violated the contract clause and denied property without due process. He looked realistically at the disparity in the bargaining position between employer and employee, recognizing that fear of losing their jobs prompted laborers to perform work that was detrimental to their health. In the decision, concern for public health and inequality of bargaining power justified the state regulation.

Pollock v. Farmers' Loan & Trust Co. (1895) also revealed Brown's willingness to permit legislative regulation of private property. When the Court struck down a congressional tax on incomes, Brown eloquently dissented, protesting that the decision ignored a century of "consistent and undeviating" precedent and represented "a surrender of the taxing power to the moneyed class." Although opponents of the tax had raised the specter of socialism to dissuade Congress from raising funds, Brown construed *Pollock* as "the first step toward the submergence of the liberties of the people in a sordid despotism of wealth." Brown supported the gradual development of federal power as a necessary concomitant to a modern industrial economy. Drawing on his prior experience, Brown wrote many of the Court's admiralty opinions, broadly interpreting federal jurisdiction and the scope of federal maritime law. He also endorsed expansive federal power under the commerce clause, joining, for example, Justice Oliver Wendell Holmes's classic statement of the stream of commerce doctrine in *Swift & Co. v. United States* (1905).

Brown's criminal procedure and civil liberties opinions reflected the general attitude of the era toward criminals, blacks, and women. In *Brown v. Walker* (1896), he held that the Fifth Amendment right against self incrimination was not violated if the state coerced testimony and afforded immunity from criminal prosecution. Social disgrace and ridicule might result from invoking the Fifth Amendment, but a "self-confessed criminal" did not deserve protection from his neighbors' negative judgment. Brown's callousness to civil rights is manifest in *Plessy v. Ferguson* (1896), in which he upheld a Louisiana statute requiring railroads to provide "equal but separate accommodations" for "white" and "colored" patrons. In a remarkably disingenuous opinion, he reasoned that the statute had "no tendency to destroy the legal equality of the two races" and did "not necessarily imply the inferiority of either race to the other." Brown rejected an equal protection challenge to the statute, relying on state cases that were decided before the Fourteenth Amendment was adopted. To Brown, the Louisiana law was a reasonable legislative decision consistent with "the established usages, customs and traditions of the people." In other words, Brown believed that civil rights were adequately protected in the legislative process and did not believe that courts had to protect the civil rights of a minority against overreaching by a majority. *Plessy* mirrored the late nineteenth-century belief in physical and social differences between the races. Contemporary scientific and social science thought considered the Negro and Caucasian races as biologically separate and the Caucasian race as superior. In *Plessy*, Brown constitutionalized the prevailing prejudices of his era.

• Brown's papers are in a special collection housed at the Detroit Public Library. A biographical account is Robert J. Glennon, "Justice Henry Billings Brown: Values in Tension," *University of Colorado Law Review* 44 (1973): 553–604.

ROBERT JEROME GLENNON

BROWN, Henry Kirke (24 Feb. 1814–10 July 1886), sculptor, was born and raised near Leyden, Massachusetts, the son of Elijah Brown and Rhoda Childs, farmers. Toward the end of his education at secondary school his artistic talent asserted itself in the cutting of little silhouette portraits. The next stage of his development came when, using homemade brushes, paints borrowed from a housepainter, and a stretched sheet for a canvas, he painted a portrait of a neighbor. In 1832 he was apprenticed to Chester Harding, a successful Boston portrait painter. Four years later he moved to Cincinnati, then a burgeoning metropolis on the Ohio River with remarkable activity in the arts, and established his studio as a portrait painter. There he met a young sculptor, Shobal Vail Clevenger (1812–1843), and soon afterward modeled his first bust in Clay. Returning in 1839 to Boston and Albany, Brown worked increasingly as a sculptor and found numerous commissions for portrait busts. That same year he married Lydia Udall, daughter of Judge James Udall of Quechee, Vermont. The couple had no children of their own but raised Henry Kirke Bush-Brown, the son of one of Lydia's sisters.

Brown's success as a portrait sculptor enabled him to take the obligatory trip to Italy. He and his wife departed in the summer of 1842, stopping first in London to see the famed Elgin Marbles that had originally decorated the Parthenon in Athens, and then moving on to Florence. Committed to American subject matter, Brown was ambivalent toward the art of classical antiquity and contemporary European styles. This struggle is evident in his major project during these Florentine years; he started work on a standing figure of an American Indian boy but transformed it into a classical Apollino after he moved to Rome in 1844. Also showing the impact of Roman antiquity is a classical head titled *La Grazia* (1845, New-York Historical Society). His marble statue *Ruth* (1845, New-York Historical Society), with its "melancholy sweetness and modesty," appealed to Romantic tastes. But Brown soon rejected the neoclassical ideal as foreign to the values and character of America and, with the zeal of a convert, took up naturalism as the style appropriate for the art of his native land.

Brown returned to the United States in 1846, establishing his studio in Brooklyn. The American Art Union, an art lottery that catered to the expanding artistic interests of the upper middle class, commissioned several small statuettes to be awarded as premiums. To produce them from his own models he built a bronze foundry in his studio, thereby becoming one of the first in America to develop the technology of bronze casting for sculpture. His busts of the painter Thomas Cole (c. 1840, Metropolitan Museum of Art) and the poet William Cullen Bryant (c. 1846, New-York Historical Society) are among the best of their day. It was, in fact, in portraiture rather than ideal pieces that he established his reputation as one of the leading American sculptors of the third quarter of the nineteenth century.

Brown's claim to that position came in 1851 when he unveiled a heroic bronze statue of Governor DeWitt Clinton (Greenwood Cemetery, Brooklyn). Recognition from his fellow artists came that same year with his election to the National Academy of Design in New York, and in 1859–1860 he was one of three artists appointed by President James Buchanan to the National Art Commission. The Clinton statue was followed with an even greater success, the bronze equestrian statue of George Washington, which was unveiled in New York's Union Square in 1856. The *Washington* was cast at the Ames Manufacturing Company in Chicopee, Massachusetts, a foundry that had previously specialized in cannons and other armaments. The image of Washington commanding his troops is one of great dignity, and all who saw it took pride in the technological feat of casting such a large and complex object in an American foundry. The basis of Brown's style was the naturalism to which he was by then totally committed, and he impressed upon his students, such as John Quincy Adams Ward, that it was unnecessary to go abroad to study.

Brown was unsuccessful in obtaining a commission for the Senate pediment sculptures of the U.S. Capitol, and the Civil War ended work on his sculptures for the South Carolina state capitol. However, following the war he received several commissions for works that were installed in the U.S. Capitol or elsewhere in Washington. Statuary Hall, in the Capitol, contains his statues of Nathanael Greene (1870), George Clinton [1739–1812] (1873), Richard Stockton [1730–1781] (1874), and Philip Kearny (1886), while his bronze equestrian image of General Winfield Scott (1871) adorns Scott Circle in Washington, and his statue of General Nathanael Greene (1877) astride his horse is the centerpiece of Greene Square in the same city.

A robust sportsman, Brown was known as an excellent horseman with a splendid knowledge of "horse flesh" that contributed greatly to the success of the animals in his equestrian groups. He was intellectual and philosophical, admired by his students and assistants, among whom was his adopted son. Brown's straightforward naturalism suited the taste of America in the middle of the century, but after 1880 preference shifted toward the richly modeled Parisian style with its lively surfaces; by contrast, Brown's sculptures may seem dry of surface and simplistic in modeling. The critic Adeline Adams was probably too harsh when she wrote that his art often descended into "a commonplace pedestrian interpretation of great themes." He died at his home in Newburgh, New York, where he had maintained a studio since 1857.

• A typescript of Brown's letters, prepared and edited by Henry Kirke Bush-Brown, is in the Library of Congress, and a second copy is owned by the Beinecke Library, Yale University. See Lorado Taft, *History of American Sculpture* (1903), pp. 114–23, for an early assessment of Brown's work. James Lee, *The Equestrian Statue of Washington in Union Square* (1864), and Charles Edwin Fairman, *Art and Artists of the Capitol of the United States of America* (1927), give useful information on portions of his career. For more recent studies see Wayne Craven, *Sculpture in America* (1984), pp. 144–58; Craven, "Henry Kirke Brown in Italy, 1842–46," *American Art Journal* 1 (Spring 1969): 65–77; and Craven, "Henry Kirke Brown: His Search for an American Art in the 1840s," *American Art Journal* 4 (Nov. 1972): 44–58. His obituary appears in *Studio*, n.s. 2, no. 2 (Aug. 1886): 29–32.

WAYNE CRAVEN

BROWN, Jacob Jennings (9 May 1775–24 Feb. 1828), army officer, was born in Bucks County, Pennsylvania, the son of Samuel Brown and Abi White, farmers. Brown was raised a Quaker and graduated from the University of Pennsylvania in 1790. Perhaps because of his family's declining financial circumstances, Brown took up school teaching, first at Crosswicks, New Jersey, and, after a stint as a government surveyor on the Ohio frontier, in New York City. There, he wrote political articles for the press and may have served briefly as a military secretary to Major General Alexander Hamilton (1755–1804) during the early months of the Quasi-war with France. Brown also became involved in land speculation projects in northern New York, and in 1798 he and his family purchased a large tract in what is now Jefferson County, near the eastern shore of Lake Ontario. Moving to the region in 1799, he prospered as a surveyor, land developer, and farmer, and he was the founder and leading figure of the town of Brownville. In 1802 he married Pamelia Williams, with whom he had at least two sons and one daughter.

Although he lacked formal military training and experience, Brown held the rank of brigadier general in the New York militia at the outbreak of the War of 1812. He had resisted Jefferson's embargo and opposed the declaration of war. Nevertheless, he raised a militia force in his region, and during the summer and fall of 1812 he participated in defensive operations along the Lake Ontario and St. Lawrence frontiers. Brown's first major combat test occurred in the spring of 1813 when he took command of a mixed force of militia and regulars left at the American base at Sackets Harbor, on Lake Ontario, during the offensive against Upper Canada. On the morning of 29 May, a British flotilla under General George Prevost landed a force of about 750 troops near the town. The militia broke at the first fire, but the regulars stoutly defended the town's fortifications. Demonstrating the energy and force of will that would henceforth characterize his generalship, Brown managed to rally and inspire enough of the citizen soldiers to threaten Prevost's flank and compel the British to reembark. Brown's performance at Sackets Harbor, coming after a succession of American reverses, won him national recognition and, in July, an appointment as brigadier general in the regular army. During the fall of 1813, he commanded a brigade under Major General James Wilkinson in the abortive offensive down the St. Lawrence against Montreal.

Early in 1814, Brown was promoted to major general and placed in command of the forces on the Lake Ontario frontier. The administration planned a summer offensive through the Niagara peninsula into Upper Canada, intended to capture York (Toronto) and threaten British communications to the west. Under Brown's general supervision, Brigadier General Winfield Scott organized a camp of instruction at Buffalo and molded the forces on the Niagara frontier into the most cohesive and disciplined segment of the generally amorphous wartime army. Early in July, Brown's small field army crossed the Niagara River into Canada and quickly captured Fort Erie. A British force under General Phineas Riall advanced southward, and on 5 July it engaged the Americans near the village of Chippewa. Although the two armies were roughly equal in size, the discipline of the American forces and the energetic leadership of Brown and Scott resulted in a tactical victory that forced the British to withdraw from the battlefield. Brown's hopes of continuing the offensive against York were frustrated when the navy's Lake Ontario squadron, commanded by Captain Isaac Chauncey, failed to support him—resulting in a bitter interservice feud. Brown's army remained in Canada, however, and on 25 July it again clashed with Riall's forces at Lundy's Lane, near Niagara Falls. This battle was one of the hardest fought of the war—about a third of both armies were killed or wounded—and ended in a standoff. Twice wounded, Brown ordered his exhausted army to retire from the field and turned over command to Brigadier General Eleazar W. Ripley. Much to Brown's dismay, Ripley chose not to renew the battle the following day and withdrew to Fort Erie. The British army, reinforced and now led by General Gordon Drummond, followed and began a siege. Brown had been evacuated to Buffalo, but he recovered sufficiently from his wounds to resume command of his beleaguered forces. Ever the aggressive combat leader, he launched a sortie in force on 17 September that caught the British by surprise and broke the siege.

Although a strategic stalemate, Brown's campaign on the Niagara frontier was the army's most impressive performance of the War of 1812, and it made him a national hero. He remained in service after the Peace of Ghent and commanded the army's Northern Division. A citizen soldier rather than a committed professional, he established his headquarters at his home in Brownville, where he mixed agriculture, politics, and military administration. As the result of a major reduction and reorganization of the army in 1821, Brown was left as the only major general in the service, and the Monroe administration ordered him to Washington, D.C., to fill the newly created position of commanding general of the army. Although this office became a fixture of nineteenth-century army administration, its powers and functions were ill defined. Soon after taking the office, Brown suffered a stroke that left him partially paralyzed for a year and too weak permanently to assert his command powers. He served as a military adviser to the administration, but his practical authority was circumscribed by the secretary of war, the commanders of geographical departments, and the chiefs of the army's staff bureaus at the capital. His most important contribution as commanding general was his promotion of advanced "schools of practice" for the artillery and infantry; though eventually discontinued, these schools constituted the army's first experiment with advanced professional training.

As with many officers of his generation, Brown dabbled in politics. He was a strong supporter of Governor DeWitt Clinton of New York, and in 1824 he served as an intermediary in the negotiations through which Secretary of War John C. Calhoun agreed to run for vice president under John Quincy Adams. Brown died at his Washington home.

• Collections of Brown's papers are in the Library of Congress, the Massachusetts Historical Society (Boston), and the William L. Clements Library at the University of Michigan, Ann Arbor. Although not a scholarly work, the most complete biography is C. Gerard Hoard, *Major General Jacob Jennings Brown* (1979). On Brown's wartime career, see Ernest Cruikshank, ed., *The Documentary History of the Campaign upon the Niagara Frontier* (1896–1908; repr. 1971); John K. Mahon, *The War of 1812* (1972); and other histories of the War of 1812. Much material on his postwar career is in Robert L. Meriwether and W. Edwin Hemphill, eds., *The Papers of John C. Calhoun* (1959–1989). See also William B. Skelton, "The Commanding General and the Problem of Command in the United States Army, 1821–1841," *Military Affairs* 34 (1970): 117–22.

WILLIAM B. SKELTON

BROWN, James (11 Sept. 1766–7 Apr. 1835), senator and diplomat, was born near Staunton, Virginia, the son of John Brown, a clergyman, and Margaret Preston. After schooling at the academy at Lexington, Virginia, that became Washington and Lee University, he probably attended William and Mary College; he then studied law under George Wythe. He began practicing law in Kentucky, settling in Lexington in 1789. About 1791 he married Ann (or Nancy) Hart; they had no children.

Brown became a close associate of his older brother John, whose brief flirtation with Spanish proposals that the Kentuckians separate from the United States caused angry controversy in the last years before Kentucky became a state. James Brown was also a close friend of Henry Clay, his wife's brother-in-law, beginning in the 1790s. When Kentucky became a state in 1792, Brown was appointed its first secretary of state, serving until 1796. As a member of the state's Democratic Society in the 1790s, he agitated for free navigation of the Mississippi River and advocated the abolition of slavery in Kentucky. He was professor of law and politics at Transylvania University from 1799 to 1804. In 1803, when it was feared that Spain would oppose the implementation of the Louisiana Purchase, he helped raise forces in Kentucky and Tennessee to protect the U.S. claim.

President Thomas Jefferson appointed Brown secretary of the Territory of Orleans in 1804, and Brown settled in New Orleans later that year. He had become a substantial landowner in Kentucky and soon increased his fortune practicing law in Louisiana; he was helped by his command of all three local languages, French, Spanish, and English. He invested some of his wealth in a profitable sugar plantation north of New Orleans, although he did not reside there much. Jefferson soon replaced him as secretary and appointed him judge of the Superior Court for Orleans Territory (Dec. 1804), but he refused to serve, explaining that he could not afford to give up his practice. He then accepted an appointment as U.S. attorney for the

District of Orleans (1805–1808) and as U.S. land agent for the Eastern District of Orleans Territory (1805–1812). In 1806 he and Louis Moreaù Lislet were appointed by the territorial legislature to prepare a civil code for the territory, which was adopted in 1808. He was one of the original regents of the College of Orleans, which opened in 1812. Disapproving of the domination of the territorial government by local francophones, he implored Washington to bolster the anglophone population by seizing West Florida and combining it with Orleans Territory. For many years before the British invasion of 1814, he warned that New Orleans was too vulnerable to enemy attack by England or France and that it would not be recovered easily if lost.

After serving as a member of the convention that framed the first constitution of Louisiana in 1811–1812, Brown was elected in 1813 to the U.S. Senate, where he served from 5 February 1813 to 3 March 1817. The only notable speech he made there was an 1817 argument against reduction of the standing army. He was defeated for reelection by former Louisiana governor W. C. C. Claiborne, a man he had long despised. Brown then spent a year in France, in part to advise General Lafayette on the lands the latter was to be granted in the United States; in 1824–1825 he facilitated Lafayette's U.S. tour. Claiborne soon died, and Brown was again elected to the Senate, serving from 6 December 1819 until he resigned on 10 December 1823 to accept an appointment by President James Monroe to succeed Albert Gallatin as ambassador to France.

Brown served in Paris from 1824 until 1829. He became known for his princely lifestyle there, described by James Fenimore Cooper. His main task was to press the French government to honor claims by American shippers who suffered losses resulting from seizure of their property during the Napoleonic naval wars. The French refused to settle because the United States had not honored a commitment in Article 8 of the Louisiana Purchase Treaty to give France the status of most favored nation in the ports of Louisiana, an argument to which Brown was not unsympathetic. At first he fretted about the restoration of the Jesuit order and other elements he regarded as anti-republican in France, but sensing the strong surge of "liberal and constitutional principles" there in the last two years before 1830, he predicted correctly that the U.S. spoliation claims would one day be settled by a friendlier government.

While in Paris, Brown noted with anxiety the rising spirit of angry confrontation in American politics in the 1820s, yet his own political passions were marked, and he approved when President John Quincy Adams was defeated for reelection. He probably did not know that Adams, then secretary of state, had been responsible for his own appointment in 1823, when the doubtful majority of Monroe's cabinet had a negative view of Brown as "timid," "indolent," and married to a "showy wife." Adams had defended him as "peculiarly fitted for that mission, or indeed any other—a man of large fortune, respectable talents, handsome person, polished manners, and elegant deportment."

On returning to the United States in 1829, Brown thought civil war between the North and the South was near; he was convinced that it could be prevented only if Andrew Jackson was president for two terms. From 1829 to 1835 he lived in Philadelphia, visiting New Orleans occasionally. He died in Philadelphia. A man who had benefited most from his caution not to offend politicians who could further his career, he had nevertheless played an important role in mobilizing the military defense of New Orleans in the era of the War of 1812, and he had partial credit for the eventual success of American spoliation claims against France.

• Correspondence by Brown is in the Gilpin Family Papers and the Josiah Stoddard Johnson Papers at the Historical Society of Pennsylvania; other documents related to Brown are in the John Mason Brown Papers, Yale University, and the James Brown Papers at the Library of Congress. Some of his letters and other writings were edited by James A. Padgett and published in *Louisiana Historical Quarterly*: "Some Letters of James Brown of Louisiana to Presidents of the United States," 20 (1937): 58–136; and "Letters of James Brown to Henry Clay, 1804–1835," 24 (1941): 921–1177. See also Clarence E. Carter, ed., *The Territorial Papers of the United States*, vol. 9: *The Territory of Orleans, 1803–1812* (1940).

THOMAS N. INGERSOLL

BROWN, Jesse Leroy (13 Oct. 1926–4 Dec. 1950), naval aviator, was born in Hattiesburg, Mississippi, the son of John Brown, a farmer. His mother's name is not known. From the time he was a small boy, Brown was interested in flying: at the sight of an airplane flying above, he turned to a friend and said, "Some day I'm going to fly one of those" (Weems, p. 36). He held fast to his dream. He studied hard at the all-black Eureka High School, and his principal, recognizing that the school did not prepare students well for college, taught Brown and other promising students more advanced subjects. He was also an excellent athlete, participating in basketball and track and playing halfback on Eureka's state championship football team.

These preparations and Brown's determination enabled him to enroll in Ohio State University in 1944. In 1946 he entered the naval reserve program and, while continuing to work on his degree, earned money by unloading boxcars for the Pennsylvania Railroad. He graduated in 1947. At the conclusion of his education, he entered the navy and applied for flight training.

Brown passed the rigorous physical and mental tests required of prospective aviators and was sent to flight school at Pensacola, Florida, in 1948. In so doing, he became the first black aviation trainee in the U.S. Navy. In the midst of this experience and in defiance of navy regulation, Brown married his high school girlfriend, Daisy Pearl Nix. They had one child. His wife provided him support and encouragement while he was in flight school. "There were times when [Jesse] would come home angry and distressed" because of racial discrimination, she said. "We decided that he would just have to stick it out." Brown adapted to the situation and quietly worked to earn the respect of his associates. This strategy worked, and on 21 October 1948 he graduated from basic flight instruction and secured the right to wear the golden wings of a naval aviator. He also received a commission as ensign.

After completing flight training, Brown was assigned to Quonset Point Naval Air Station, Rhode Island, but he and his family continued to suffer from racial discrimination. The situation in his squadron, however, was somewhat better. A fellow aviator, Glenn Ferris, later commented that few in Brown's squadron cared about race: "In aviation everyone is more concerned about an individual's flight ability than the color of his skin."

Even though color blindness was not universal in the navy during peacetime, when the United States entered the Korean conflict in the summer of 1950 the reality of daily combat proved to be something of an equalizer between the races. Brown was assigned to Fighter Squadron Thirty-two in January 1949, and when the conflict began he was sent aboard the *USS Leyte* to the Sea of Japan. He flew his first combat mission on 13 October 1950, a Friday, and flew eighteen more missions through 3 December 1950. By all accounts he performed well and was a valued member of the squadron.

The North Koreans and Chinese began an offensive on 27 November 1950 that sent allied forces reeling. The Chosin Reservoir campaign was one of the most savage of these operations, pitting about 15,000 United Nations troops against an estimated enemy strength of 120,000 men. Brown and three comrades were flying a close air support mission in Corsair aircraft on the afternoon of 4 December 1950 over the Chosin Reservoir when tragedy struck. At an altitude of only 500 feet, Brown's Corsair was hit, and he was forced to make a crash landing behind enemy lines. On impact at the top of a snow covered peak, the aircraft fuselage split open and caught fire. The three pilots of the remaining airplanes saw Brown waving his arms. He was pinned in the cockpit, however, and suffering from broken bones and internal injuries.

While the flight leader called for a rescue helicopter, Lieutenant (j.g.) Thomas Hudner decided to make a crash landing nearby to attempt a rescue, an act of valor for which he received the Medal of Honor. Hudner successfully joined Brown on the ground and tried to free him from the aircraft. He worked for about forty-five minutes to pry the partially conscious Brown from the Corsair but was unsuccessful. Then he tried to put out the fire in the aircraft by shoveling snow into the engine compartment and cockpit. When the rescue helicopter arrived, its crew joined Hudner, but they were unable to free the dying Brown from the aircraft. At sunset they were forced to leave the crash site without recovering Brown's body. A week later, with Brown's crash site still in enemy hands and no chance of retrieving his body, a flight of Corsairs from the *Leyte* performed a bizarre tribute by dropping napalm on the aircraft to cremate Brown's body.

Brown was awarded the Distinguished Flying Cross and the Purple Heart posthumously. He was the first black naval aviator, the first black aviator to die in combat, and the first black U.S. Naval officer to be killed in combat. As a recognition of his service, on 17 February 1973 the navy commissioned the USS *Jesse L. Brown,* Destroyer Escort 1089.

• There is no formal collection of Brown's papers. Material about him can be found at the Naval Historical Center, Washington, D.C. Sketches of his career can be found in "The Last Days of a Navy Pilot," *Ebony,* Apr. 1951, pp. 15–18, 21–22, 24; John E. Weems, "Black Wings of Gold," *Proceedings of the United States Naval Institute* 109 (July 1983): 35–39; Yvonne Price, "Navy Honors Black Hero," *Crisis* 80 (Oct. 1973): 277–78; and Ronald Taylor, "Jesse Brown, Remembered," *Washington Post,* 19 Feb. 1973.

ROGER D. LAUNIUS

BROWN, Joe E. (28 July 1892–6 July 1973), comic actor, was born Joseph Evans Brown in Holgate, Ohio, the son of Mathias Brown, a house painter, and Anna Evans. Lacking formal education beyond the early grades, Brown embarked on a show business career at age nine when his extraordinary athletic talents caught the eye of a neighbor, Billy Ashe. Ashe brought the boy into his family's circus act, the Five Marvelous Ashtons. Touring cities and towns of the Midwest in such traveling shows as the John Robinson Circus and the Floto Circus, Brown grew into his teens developing skills as an acrobat, trapeze artist, and clown. His affinity and aptitude for sports allowed him to supplement his income by playing semiprofessional baseball. In 1915 he married Katherine Frances McGraw. The couple raised four children.

From the circus Brown moved on to stage work in burlesque and vaudeville around 1908, gradually advancing to roles in legitimate Broadway productions, which included such musical comedies as *Listen, Lester* (1919) and *Greenwich Village Follies* (1921). He shifted focus to film work during the twenties, appearing in silent screen comedies including *Song of the West* (1921), *Hit of the Show* (1926), and *Take Me Home* (1928). He achieved even greater success in talking pictures, appearing in more than fifty feature films during the next three decades.

Often dressed in a gaudy, checkered suit, Brown usually played the quintessential rube, a small-town midwestern glad-hander, gullible and good-hearted, who always managed to find his way into trouble. Brown's signature gesture, known to millions, was opening wide his cavernous mouth to cry out for help. The hyperbole of the image was typically augmented by camera close-ups of his lower face. His feature film credits include comic roles in *Hold Everything* (1930), *Alibi Ike* (1935), and *When's Your Birthday?* (1937). He appeared as Flute in the 1935 Warner Bros. production, *A Midsummer Night's Dream,* directed by Max Reinhardt and William Dieterle. One of his final Hollywood parts was in *Some Like It Hot* (1959), in which he played a lascivious, aging millionaire who unwittingly courts a man in woman's clothing (played by Jack Lemmon).

During World War II Brown was active in entertaining American troops, touring with USO shows throughout the Pacific. His efforts were recognized with a certificate of appreciation from the Defense Department in 1945.

The visual nature of Brown's comedy limited his involvement in broadcasting during the radio era, but the advent of television presented fresh opportunities. He appeared regularly as the clown on *The Circus Hour* (NBC, 1951–1953), a dramatic series about a traveling tent show. Each episode contained circus performances, and Brown was able to re-create bits he had developed almost a half-century earlier. He appeared in a dozen or more TV roles until he semiretired in the mid-1960s.

Brown's interest in sports, particularly baseball, endured throughout his life. He appeared on screen as a baseball player in *Elmer the Great* (1933) and *Alibi Ike* and in athletic roles in such comedies as *The Six-Day Bike Rider* (1934) and *Polo Joe* (1936). He also invested financially in baseball franchises, including the minor league Kansas City Blues and the major league Pittsburgh Pirates. A collector of sports memorabilia, Brown maintained that the trophies, uniforms, and other items he kept in a special room in his home was the finest privately owned collection in the world. In 1946 he donated it to the UCLA libraries. The comedian spent the 1953 season as a TV announcer with the New York Yankees.

In his later years Brown occasionally appeared in cameo roles in films, television programs, and stage shows. He died in Los Angeles, only two months after completing a nightclub engagement in Las Vegas.

• An autobiography, *Laughter Is a Wonderful Thing*, written with Ralph Hancock, was published in 1956. For other views, see Joe Franklin, *Joe Franklin's Encyclopedia of Comedians* (1979); Tim Brooks, *The Complete Directory to Prime-time TV Stars* (1988); and David Inman, *The TV Encyclopedia* (1991). An obituary appears in *Current Biography*, Sept. 1973.

DAVID MARC

BROWN, John (19 Oct. 1744–19 Oct. 1780), revolutionary war soldier, was born in Haverhill, Massachusetts, the son of Daniel Brown and Mehitabel Sanford. When he was eight years old his parents moved to Sandisfield, Massachusetts. In 1771 he graduated from Yale College, then the following year studied law with Oliver Arnold, his brother-in-law, in Providence, Rhode Island. Admitted to the New York bar in late 1772, he opened a law office in Caghnawaga (now Johnstown), New York, and that same year was appointed king's attorney. Also in 1772 he moved to Pittsfield, Massachusetts, where (apparently) he met and married Huldah Kilbourne. He quickly gained a reputation for ardent advocacy of American rights in the growing quarrel with Britain and was chosen in June 1774 to serve on the Pittsfield Committee of Correspondence. A month later he helped write nonintercourse proposals that were adopted by a convention at Stockbridge, Massachusetts; in October he was elected to the Provincial Congress. In February 1775 he was sent to Canada by Boston patriots to encourage Canadians to revolt and to establish communications with others who were inclined to do so. Although he pretended to be a horse dealer during his unsuccessful two-month sojourn in the province, Canadian citizens thought it singular that he purchased not one steed.

On his way to Canada, Brown passed Fort Ticonderoga, at the southern end of Lake Champlain, and was struck by the idea that Americans would need to control that bastion should war break out between Britain and the colonies. Hence, on his return to Massachusetts, he encouraged Massachusetts patriots to seize it. Finally, militiamen from the New Hampshire Grants and Connecticut, under Ethan Allen and Benedict Arnold, along with Brown and a few of his Pittsfield neighbors captured Fort Ticonderoga on 10 May 1775. Brown was entrusted with care of British prisoners and also was chosen to deliver the news of the victory to the Continental Congress. On 6 July 1775 he was commissioned a major in Colonel James Easton's Pittsfield militia company. He spent the next two months scouting in Canada for General Philip Schuyler, commanding gunboats on Lake Champlain, and recruiting soldiers. In late September, as an American invasion of Canada was getting under way, he joined forces with Ethan Allen at Longueuil to attack Montreal. Apparently, he did not support Allen adequately during these operations, for the latter was captured, and Brown came in for considerable criticism from Allen's admirers. On the evening of 19 October Brown, with assistance of James Livingston, overcame an enemy garrison at Fort Chambly on the Sorel River and seized six tons of precious gunpowder for the patriots. After St. Johns fell on 3 November, he and Colonel Easton pushed down the Sorel to the St. Lawrence River and captured enemy earthworks dominating the latter stream. On 19 November he and Easton captured a British fleet fleeing down the St. Lawrence River from Montreal by threatening to bombard the enemy vessels from their commanding position.

In December 1775 Brown accompanied the American army under Richard Montgomery down the St. Lawrence to Quebec and took part in the unsuccessful fighting on 31 December to capture the city. In the spring of 1776 he was with the American army in its retreat from Canada. During the seige of Quebec, Brown had fallen out with Benedict Arnold, openly declaring that he did not trust Arnold. The latter had reciprocated by accusing Brown of looting enemy officers' baggage at Fort Chambly and had refused to promote Brown. For more than a year Brown and Arnold hurled charges and countercharges against each other, each trying to outdo the other in personal vindictiveness and spite. Despite Arnold's enmity, Brown was promoted to lieutenant colonel in the Continental army on 1 August and in early 1777 took part in fighting along the shores of Lake George. He resigned from the army in February 1777, refusing any longer to serve under Arnold. He continued to publish handbills against his nemesis, accusing Arnold of levying contributions on Canadians for personal gain.

When General John Burgoyne invaded upstate New York in the summer of 1777, successfully recapturing Fort Ticonderoga in July and threatening Albany a month later, Brown returned to military service. He was elected colonel of a Massachusetts militia regiment and on 18 September surprised a British force in its outworks near Fort Ticonderoga, capturing 293 British soldiers and liberating 100 American prisoners. Thereupon, he joined General Horatio Gates's American army at Bemis Heights, New York, and served with him until Burgoyne surrendered on 17 October. His military labors temporarily in abeyance, Brown returned to Pittsfield and recommenced the practice of law. He was elected to the state legislature in 1778 and was appointed county judge a year later. In the summer of 1780 he was called once more to arms, marching with 300 Massachusetts militiamen into the Mohawk Valley to assist Governor George Clinton in fending off attacks by Sir John Johnson in that vexed region. On 19 October he marched into an ambush of Canadians, Tories, and Indians near Stone Arabia and was killed, along with forty-five of his men. Although of no consolation to Brown, Sir John Johnson seven days later fled the region, and the devastation ceased. Brown is best remembered for the soldierly qualities he manifested during the fight for Canada (1775–1776) and in fending off Burgoyne's invasion a year later. But he is also remembered for his quarrel with Benedict Arnold.

• Brown's letters and other records are printed in various sources, including Peter Force, ed., *American Archives: A Documentary History of the Origin and Progress of the North American Colonies*, ser. 4 and 5 (1837–1850); Albert S. Batchellor, ed., *Miscellaneous Revolutionary Documents of New Hampshire, Including the Association Test, the Pension Rolls, and Other Important Papers* (1910); and John Brown, "Col. John Brown's Expedition against Ticonderoga and Diamond Island, 1777," *New-England Historical and Genealogical Register* 74 (1920): 284–93. For sketches of his life see Garret L. Roof, *Colonel John Brown: His Services in the Revolutionary War, Battle of Stone Arabia: An Address* (1884); Archibald M. Howe, *Colonel John Brown of Pittsfield, Massachusetts, the Brave Accuser of Benedict Arnold: An Address* (1908); and Franklin Bowditch Dexter, *Biographical Sketches of the Graduates of Yale College, with Annals of the College History*, vol. 3 (1903). His attack on Fort Ticonderoga is described in Walter B. Sturtevant, "John Brown's Raid, September, 1777," *Infantry Journal* 36 (1930): 475–78, and "Col. John Brown's Attack of September, 1777, on Fort Ticonderoga," Fort Ticonderoga, N.Y., Museum, *Bulletin* 11 (1964): 207–14. Charles A. Jellison, *Ethan Allen: Frontier Rebel* (1969), describes Brown's relations with Allen, and Willard M. Wallace, *Traitorous Hero: The Life and Fortunes of Benedict Arnold* (1954), and Clare Brandt, *The Man in the Mirror: A Life of Benedict Arnold* (1994), give Arnold's side of the Brown-Arnold quarrel. The best background on the Canadian invasion is still Justin H. Smith's classic, *Our Struggle for the Fourteenth Colony* (2 vols., 1907). For Brown's insurgency activities in Canada, see Alfred Leroy Burt, *The Old Province of Quebec* (1933).

PAUL DAVID NELSON

BROWN, John (27 Jan. 1736–20 Sept. 1803), merchant and congressman, was born in Providence, Rhode Island, the son of James Brown, a merchant and shipowner, and Hope Power. The Brown family was long dominant in the mercantile life of Rhode Island, and during the Revolution Brown and his brothers Moses and Nicholas amassed great wealth from their various enterprises. His education did not go beyond that of the common schools. At age fourteen he wrote in his "Cipher Book," "John Brown the cleverest boy in Providence Town." Upon his father's death in 1739, an uncle, Obadiah Brown, became in loco parentis for Brown and his four brothers. Obadiah Brown took the brothers into his firm, which enhanced its profits by privateering and trading with the enemy during the French and Indian War. By 1760 the company had eighty-four vessels at sea, one of the largest fleets in New England. In 1760 Brown married Sarah Smith; they had six children. Brown was an active member of the First Baptist Church in Providence.

Upon Obadiah Brown's death in 1762, his firm was reorganized as Nicholas Brown & Company, involving the four brothers although Joseph would take only a minor part. Brown withdrew from this firm in 1771, while keeping an interest in the company's spermaceti candle and whale oil industry and the Hope Furnace for manufacturing pig iron in Scituate, Massachusetts.

Allied with Governor Samuel Ward of Newport in his struggles with Stephen Hopkins of Providence for control of Rhode Island's colonial government, Brown was known as a fiery partisan in the political fighting that distinguished eighteenth-century Rhode Island. His support of Joseph Wanton in the imperial debates of the early 1770s placed him in the forefront of the revolutionary movement. Brown led the party that burned the British customs schooner *Gaspee*, which ran aground on 9 June 1772 at Namquit Point, seven miles below Providence. No one would incriminate the culprits, and Brown went free, though he was detained in Boston briefly three years later by General Thomas Gage because of lingering suspicion of his key role in the *Gaspee* affair.

At the start of the revolutionary war Brown was one of a committee named by the second Continental Congress to supervise construction of naval vessels. The work lagged, and Brown was accused of diverting labor and materials for his own privateering vessels. During the war Brown held government contracts to provide munitions, cannon, and supplies for the Continental army. The cannon was manufactured at the Brown brothers iron foundry. The Browns, George Bēnson, and Welcome Arnold operated a rum distillery, but disagreement among the partners eventually led to its closing in 1794.

During and after the Revolution, Providence, which was more militarily secure than Newport, grew rapidly and overtook Newport as the state's chief port. The Browns prospered accordingly. In 1787 Brown established a new firm, Brown & Francis, with his son-in-law, John Francis. Brown & Francis sent out the first ship from Providence for the East Indies and

China. The *General Washington* left Providence 24 December 1787, making ports of call at Madeira, Madras, Pondicherry, and Canton and on its return at St. Helena, St. Ascension, and St. Eustatia islands, arriving at the home port on 5 July 1789. The journey covered 32,758 miles. Cannon shot, anchors, bar iron, tar, ginseng, Madeira wine, brandy, Jamaican spirits, and New England rum were exchanged for tea, silks, china, cotton goods, lacquered ware, gloves, and flannels. The *General Washington* made successive trips to the Orient under the auspices of Brown & Francis. Three other ships were also launched for the same trade: the *Warren*, 1789; the *President Washington*, at 950 tons the largest ship to leave from Providence, 1791; and the *George Washington*, 1794. Brown & Francis owned its docks and built the company's ships.

Brown favored keeping open the African slave trade, even when such a position was very unpopular in New England. He was at odds with his brother, Moses, who had converted to Quakerism and abolitionism. Before the Revolution the Brown family had been involved in sending three slave ships to the African Guinea coast. The *Sally*, under the auspices of Nicholas Brown & Company, went to Africa with 17,274 gallons of rum and various provisions. Of the nearly 200 slaves received, 108 died from disease, mutiny, or suicide. The ninety-two slaves that completed the journey were sold at a low price in Antigua. Brown was also involved with the slave ship *Sultan*, which went to Africa in 1769. Financial failure in the slave trade led Brown to seek profits from privateering during the war and later in far eastern commerce. A Rhode Island law of 1787 prohibited citizens from the slave trade, and in 1794 Congress closed the foreign slave trade to Americans. Not to be deterred, Brown was again involved with a slave ship in 1797. Litigation was brought against him by the Abolition Society; the ship was condemned, and Brown stood trial before the federal court at Newport but was acquitted.

Brown was a selectman in the Providence town meeting and from 1776 to 1783 sat in the Rhode Island General Assembly as a deputy from Providence. He was elected to the Confederation Congress, 1784–1785 but did not attend any sessions. Elected to Congress in 1799, Brown served one term. In the national legislature Brown supported expansion of the navy, which would give added protection to his ships. He staunchly opposed congressional prohibition of Americans from the foreign slave trade. Brown cast one of the five votes against an act for strengthening the 1794 law. He argued that U.S. citizens should benefit from the slave trade as long as those of other nations did, that African slaves had a better life in America, and that the foreign slave trade produced revenue. Moses Brown wrote to Dwight Foster on 30 January 1800 that John "has now a Ship he has been refiting which if he does not Sell I fear he would, again, be tempted to send on a Slave Voyage" (Hedges, *The Browns of Providence Plantations*, p. 84).

A member of the Baptist Society, Brown joined his brothers, Moses and Nicholas, as benefactors of the Baptist-sponsored College of Rhode Island (now Brown University). He used his influence along with Hopkins, a leading politician, to obtain the move of the school from Warren to Providence instead of Newport. Part of the land on which the school was located belonged to the Brown family. Brown laid the cornerstone of the first college building, University Hall, on 27 March 1770 and was treasurer of the college, 1775–1796.

Although Brown was opposed in the 1780s to the conferral on Congress of the authority to levy impost duties, he played a key role in the state's belated ratification of the Constitution. He was a principal holder of public securities, the full value of which would be guaranteed by a new U.S. government under the Constitution.

After failing in 1784 to start a bank, Brown and Francis finally succeeded in establishing the Providence Bank, chartered by the general assembly on 3 October 1791. Brown was elected president of the institution. In addition to his vast mercantile business, Brown had substantial landholdings that included Spring Green Farm (670 acres at Patuxet), a farm in Bristol, and properties at Newport, Warwick, North and South Kingston, and Providence Island. The John Brown house (1787) stands as the home of the Rhode Island Historical Society. Brown died in Providence, Rhode Island.

An obituary noted that Brown had been "one of the foremost to resist the tyrannical attempts of the English ministry to prostrate the liberties of his country." His tombstone read: "The Enterprising and Accomplished Merchant. The Tried Patriot and Legislator. The Universal Philanthropist and Sincere Christian." Of the Brown brothers he was the most adventurous in taking risks. Certainly he benefited from mixing business with patriotism and public and community service.

• John Brown's correspondence and records are in the Brown papers at the John Carter Brown Library of Brown University and the Moses Brown Papers of the Rhode Island Historical Society. James B. Hedges, "The Brown Papers: The Record of a Rhode Island Business Family," *Proceedings of the American Antiquarian Society* 51 (1942): 21–36, analyzes the collection at the John Carter Brown Library (some 350,000 pieces, 1726–1913). John Brown's limited formal education (deficiency in spelling and grammar) is quite evident in Frank H. Brown, ed., "A Colonial Merchant to His Son: From the Unpublished Letters of John Brown to His Son James (1782–83)," *Rhode Island Historical Society Collections* 34 (1941): 47–57. Hedges, *The Browns of Providence Plantations*, vol. 1: *The Colonial Years* (1968), contains a full appraisal of John Brown's business activity. Abby Brown Bulkley, *The Chad Browne Memorial, Consisting of Genealogical Memoirs of a Portion of the Descendants of Chad and Elizabeth Browne, 1638–1888* (1888), has the early genealogy. Brown's connection with the slave trade is related in Elizabeth Donnan, ed., *Documents Illustrative of the History of the Slave Trade to America*, vol. 3 (1932; repr. 1965); James A. Rawley, *The Transatlantic Slave Trade* (1981); and Darold D. Wax,

"The Browns of Providence and the Slave Voyage of the Brig *Sally*, 1764–1765," *American Neptune* 32 (1972): 171–79. For Brown's speech against prohibition of the slave trade, see *The Debates and Proceedings in the Congress of the United States*, 6th Cong., 1851, 686–87. Of interest are Hope F. Kane and W. G. Roelker, "The Founding of the Providence Bank (October 3, 1791)," *Rhode Island Historical Collections* 34 (1941): 113–28, and Harrison S. Taft, "John Brown's Mansion House on the Hill," *Rhode Island Historical Society Collections* 34 (1941): 107–12. An obituary is in the *Providence Gazette*, 24 Sept. 1803.

HARRY M. WARD

BROWN, John (4 Oct. 1750–31 Oct. 1810), court clerk, was born in Williamsburg, Virginia, the son of John Brown and Judith (maiden name unknown). He learned the skills of a court clerk as an apprentice in the office of Benjamin Waller, the secretary of state of the colony and the official clerk of the General Court of Virginia. When his training was finished, Brown was appointed clerk of the court of Mecklenburg County and sworn into office on 10 July 1775. At this period of Virginia history, the county courts were composed of lay justices, and the clerk was responsible for managing the office and records of the court, hearing motions at rule days, and generally guiding the justices through the court procedures. During the American Revolution he served in the Virginia militia.

In 1781 Brown was appointed clerk of the General Court of Virginia, which required him to move to Richmond. He then appointed William Baskervill on 4 June 1781 to act as his deputy in Mecklenburg County. (He resigned in favor of Baskervill in February 1795.) Brown was appointed clerk of the court of appeals, the highest court in Virginia, in 1785. In addition he was clerk of the court of chancery in 1787 and clerk of the district court at Richmond from 1789 to 1797. He resigned the clerkship of the general court in 1797 but remained clerk of the court of appeals until his death. "From the records left in his office, he was a good clerk, and everything [was] kept in good order" (Johnston, *Memorials*, p. 245).

Brown was active in civic and legal matters in a supportive way. In December 1792 he was elected a common councilman for the City of Richmond, but he declined to serve. In 1795 he was appointed by the general assembly to a committee that also included George Wythe, John Marshall, Bushrod Washington, and John Wickham. The duties of this group of eminent lawyers was to collect and superintend the printing of the Virginia acts concerning land. They requested the aid of Thomas Jefferson, who had the best collection of law books in the state, having purchased the libraries of Peyton Randolph and Richard Bland to add to his own books. Jefferson put his library at their disposal but suggested expanding the scope of the work to include all of the statutes of Virginia. This advice was accepted, and the general assembly arranged several years later to have William Waller Hening edit the *Statutes at Large of Virginia* (1809–1823). In 1797 and 1798 Brown was again associated with Marshall; this time he accompanied him to France on the XYZ Affair as his secretary.

Brown married Nancy Geddy in Williamsburg in 1772; they had five children. Brown died in Richmond, Virginia, and was buried in St. John's churchyard. He was characterized in his *Virginia Patriot* obituary as "long well known for his superior talents in the line of his profession, and highly esteemed for his urbanity of manners and general good deportment."

In addition to his support of persons of national importance, he left behind reports of law cases in the Court of Appeals of Virginia for the period 1791 to 1799. These are valuable because of the scarcity of American law reports during the time of the formation of a national law.

• There is a sketch of Brown's life in W. H. Bryson, *The Virginia Law Reporters Before 1880* (1977), pp. 87–89; see also Frederick Johnston, *Memorials of Old Virginia Clerks* (1888). Brown's reports are published in W. H. Bryson, ed., *Miscellaneous Virginia Law Reports* (1992), pp. 25–65. An obituary is in the *Virginia Patriot*, 2 Nov. 1810.

W. HAMILTON BRYSON

BROWN, John (12 Sept. 1757–28 Aug. 1837), lawyer, congressman, and U.S. senator from Kentucky, was born in Staunton, Virginia, the son of John Brown, a prominent Presbyterian minister in the Shenandoah Valley, and Margaret Preston, whose brother William held a number of important government posts in western Virginia. Schooled at his father's Liberty Hall Academy, which later became Washington and Lee University, the younger John Brown continued his education at Princeton, his father's alma mater. Brown's tenure at Princeton was interrupted by the Revolution. When George Washington retreated through New Jersey in November 1776, Brown enlisted as a private in the American army. After his military service he returned to school in 1778, not at Princeton but at William and Mary, where he became one of the earliest members of Phi Beta Kappa. Torn between a career in medicine or law, Brown chose the latter, studying for a year under the tutelage of Thomas Jefferson.

In the summer of 1783 Brown headed west to Kentucky, then a district of Virginia, to claim a land grant bestowed on him for military service, look after the extensive holdings of his recently deceased uncle William Preston, and practice law. After a harrowing journey through the Cumberland Gap and along the Wilderness Road, during which Brown narrowly escaped from a party of Indians, he arrived in Danville, then the seat of the superior court of Kentucky. Because conflicting land claims were endemic and skilled lawyers scarce in frontier Kentucky, Brown's law practice thrived.

Well respected as an attorney and well connected with Virginia's leaders, Brown quickly emerged as one of the principal political figures in Kentucky. In the spring of 1784 he was elected as the representative of Kentucky in the Virginia Senate. Three years later the Virginia legislature appointed Brown to the Continental Congress in New York, making him the first congressman from the Mississippi Valley. In Richmond and New York, Brown pushed Kentucky's case for statehood. He also pressed Congress to negotiate an agreement with Spain to secure navigation rights on the Mississippi River for American shipping.

Rebuffed by the Virginia Assembly, which passed the issue of the separation of Kentucky on to Congress, and frustrated by congressional inaction on statehood and Mississippi navigation, Brown entered into talks with Spain's ambassador, Don Diego de Gardoqui, in June 1788. Just what Gardoqui promised and what Brown agreed to have remained points of controversy. Political opponents later accused Brown of plotting with James Wilkinson and others to declare Kentucky's independence and ally the new nation with Spain in exchange for commercial concessions, land grants, and military protection. Enemies exaggerated Brown's complicity in Wilkinson's conspiracy, but his correspondence reveals that he was not as innocent as he protested. In letters from New York to friends in Kentucky, Brown indicated how desperate he was to attain a separation of Kentucky from Virginia and to secure the free navigation of the Mississippi. While he waffled about the wisdom of a connection with Spain, he certainly did not dismiss the idea. Only after returning to Kentucky did Brown back away from the "Spanish Conspiracy" and then only gradually.

Brown's return to Kentucky was of brief duration, for he shortly won election to the First Congress of the United States. Reelected to a second term, he resigned his post in 1792 after being elected as one of the first senators from the new state of Kentucky. Brown served two terms in the U.S. Senate, including a stint in 1803–1804 as president pro tem. Through his senatorial career, he continued his fight to open the Mississippi permanently and to provide greater protection from Indians for western settlers. Brown also became a devoted member of the party of Thomas Jefferson, his longtime friend.

In 1804 Brown lost his bid for a third term and retired to private life in Frankfort, Kentucky. There, he returned to the private practice of law and served as a director of the Bank of Kentucky. He had married Margaretta Mason in 1799. Together they had five children, though only two sons survived to maturity. Brown and his family resided for more than three decades in an impressive Georgian home, which he named "Liberty Hall." While Liberty Hall was just a few blocks from the Kentucky capitol, Brown steered clear of political office. He continued, however, to advise his many friends in the Kentucky and national governments, including several presidents. Brown died in Frankfort.

Before and after Brown's death, questions about his role in the "Spanish Conspiracy" overshadowed consideration of his other accomplishments. That is unfortunate, for what looked like treason to a later generation was merely one moment in a political career dedicated to strengthening Kentucky.

• Manuscripts include the John Brown Papers at the Kentucky Historical Society; the Orlando Brown Papers at the Filson Club, Louisville, Ky.; and the John Mason Brown Papers at Yale University. In addition to these family collections, the Harry Innes Papers and the Breckinridge Family Papers at the Library of Congress, the Garodqui papers in the Durrett collection at the University of Chicago, and the Preston papers in the Draper collection at the Wisconsin State Historical Society contain numerous letters to and from John Brown. The secondary literature on the "Spanish Conspiracy" is extensive. For opposing views of Brown's participation, see Elizabeth Warren, "Senator John Brown's Role in the Kentucky Spanish Conspiracy," *Filson Club History Quarterly* 36 (1962): 158–76, and Patricia Watlington, "John Brown and the Spanish Conspiracy," *Virginia Magazine of History and Biography* 75 (1967): 52–68. For a broader consideration of Brown's career, see Stuart Sprague, "Senator John Brown of Kentucky, 1757–1837: A Political Biography" (Ph.D. diss., New York Univ., 1972); Elizabeth Warner, "John Brown and His Influence on Kentucky Politics, 1784–1805," *Register of the Kentucky Historical Society* 36 (1938): 61–65; Bayless Hardin, "The Brown Family of Liberty Hall," *Filson Club History Quarterly* 16 (1942): 75–87; and Richard A. Harrison, ed., *Princetonians, 1776–1783: A Biographical Dictionary* (1981), pp. 217–22. See also Thomas Marshall Green, *The Spanish Conspiracy: A Review of Early Spanish Movements in the Southwest, Containing Proofs of the Intrigues of James Wilkinson and John Brown . . .* (1891; repr. 1967), and Watlington, *The Partisan Spirit: Kentucky Politics, 1779–1792* (1972).

STEPHEN ARON

BROWN, John (9 May 1800–2 Dec. 1859), abolitionist, also known as Old Brown of Osawatomie, was born in Torrington, Connecticut, the son of Owen Brown, a tanner and farmer, and Ruth Mills. Brown believed that the American republic was to be God's instrument for the return of Christ to earth and that, as the "embodiment of all that is evil," slavery alone stood in the way. That millennial vision was a legacy of Brown's formative years in Hudson, Ohio, as the first surviving son of pious "Squire" Brown, an early settler, prominent landowner, and zealous reformer. The father of sixteen children by two wives, Owen Brown claimed descent from Peter Browne of the *Mayflower* company, a claim (now believed doubtful) that John Brown exploited in seeking financial contributions for the cause of antislavery among New Englanders who revered the "Pilgrim Fathers."

His father was a lifelong mentor to John Brown and inculcated in him a stern sense of piety and civic duty. John had little formal schooling, but his father exposed him to books, especially the Bible, the conversation of business and church leaders, and antislavery newspapers, which Brown read assiduously. The death of Brown's mother when he was eight and his inability to bond with his stepmother strengthened his father's influence over him. Brown's failure to finish a course of study at an eastern academy intended to prepare him for the ministry disappointed his father, but Brown returned to Hudson to become, by his own account, an "imperious" foreman at his father's tannery. Although remembered for the restlessness of his later years, Brown did not move from Hudson until he was twenty-five and himself a father of three.

Like his father, John Brown reared two families. Prospering as a tanner, in 1820 he married nineteen-year-old Dianthe Lusk, the daughter of his widowed housekeeper. In twelve years of marriage she bore him seven children, five of whom reached adulthood, and supported Brown's struggle against slavery. She died in 1832 after giving birth to a stillborn son.

The following year Brown married Mary Ann Day, the daughter of a blacksmith from New York. At sixteen she was just half his age and wholly uneducated. Mary was a large, strong, shy woman who bore in silence the many hardships Brown's devotion to the cause imposed on her. Only six of her thirteen children survived childhood. Although she shared Brown's evangelical faith and antislavery convictions, Mary quietly opposed her sons' going to Kansas and Harpers Ferry. In the summer of 1864 Mary, her three girls, and her surviving son, Salmon, went by wagon to California, where Mary supported herself as a practical nurse in Red Bluff. She died in San Francisco in 1884.

Brown's long struggle to provide for his growing family and gain respect in the community at first bore fruit. Lured to the new settlement of Richmond in Crawford County, Pennsylvania, in 1825 he opened a successful tannery, won appointment under John Quincy Adams as postmaster, joined the Masons, established a school in his home, and founded a Congregational church. Ten years later, his tannery faltering, Brown entered into partnership in a tanning business in Franklin Mills (now Kent), Ohio. Borrowing from business acquaintances, Brown secured a contract to build a canal from Franklin Mills to Akron, purchased a 700-acre farm for development as an addition to the town, and formed the Franklin Land Company with other locally prominent men. During the hard times that followed the panic of 1837, Brown and his father lost heavily, and Brown was never able to pay off all his accumulated debts, facing legal judgments against him. Finally, in 1842, Brown went through bankruptcy and the court took most of his few possessions.

But in 1844 Brown's fortunes changed. He was raising Saxony sheep in Richfield, Ohio, when a wealthy Akron businessman, Colonel Simon Perkins, rescued him from obscurity by entering a partnership with Brown to market wool. The business grew for a time, and Brown soon gained a reputation among Ohio growers for his crusade to force northeastern buyers to pay higher prices for better grades of wool. In 1847 he even moved his family to Springfield, Massachusetts, where the firm was headquartered. To recoup the firm's mounting losses, Brown in 1849 took 200,000 pounds of wool to Britain, where he hoped to outflank New England buyers. Although the trip proved financially ruinous, Brown seized the opportunity to meet British abolitionists and study military fortifications and guerrilla tactics on the Continent. Soon after, the firm of Perkins and Brown collapsed under an avalanche of lawsuits resulting chiefly from Brown's mismanagement. But Perkins cast no blame on Brown for his losses and in 1854, the civil suits finally disposed of, the two men parted as friends. At age fifty-four Brown possessed only a few head of cattle in Ohio and title to an unpaid 244-acre farm in North Elba in upstate New York.

The origins of Brown's war against slavery are disputed. Brown and his defenders claimed that he nurtured a lifelong dedication to the cause. In a letter written to the thirteen-year-old son of one of his financial supporters in 1857, Brown declared that he had sworn "*Eternal war* with Slavery" at about age twelve after seeing a slave boy beaten with a shovel. Later experiences inspired renewed vows. Long after his death, three of Brown's aging sons, beleaguered by criticisms of the family's past "fanaticism," claimed that as early as perhaps 1836 or 1839 their father had led them in a sacred family oath to "make war on slavery," but no contemporary evidence of this incident survives. Brown's letters during this period betray no plans to attack slavery by force of arms.

Critics have favored a later origin and a less conventional explanation for Brown's antislavery. Allan Nevins argued in *The Emergence of Lincoln* (1950) that a "peculiarly hard, failure-ridden life" drove Brown to take refuge from himself "in fighting the wrongs of others." But this oft-repeated thesis fails to account for Brown's first documented efforts to help "those in bondage," which he undertook in November 1834 as "prospects about business [were] rather brightening." At the time Brown planned to raise a "negro boy or youth" as one of his own sons. He believed that if Christians would only educate young blacks to become self-sufficient, slaveholders would be "constitutionally driven" toward emancipation. Planning to found a school for black children, Brown urged his brother Frederick to move to Richmond with some "firstrate abolitionist families" to create a safe environment for it. Brown then lived in the "confident expectation" that God would soon end slavery.

But events farther from home prodded Brown to adopt a more militant stance. When a mob in Alton, Illinois, killed abolitionist printer Elijah Lovejoy in 1837, Brown followed his father's example in publicly pledging his life to opposing slavery. In 1846, while he was a wool merchant in bustling Springfield, Brown met leading reformers and aided fugitive slaves. Perhaps influenced by black militants like Henry Highland Garnet and David Walker, Brown embraced "forcible means," and in 1847 he confided to Frederick Douglass a sweeping plan to attack slavery in guerrilla raids from Allegheny Mountain hideaways throughout the South and send slaves north on a "Subterranean Pass Way."

Brown's growing sense of stewardship toward African Americans led him in 1848 to publish a satirical essay called "Sambo's Mistakes" in the *Ram's Horn*, an obscure, black-owned New York abolitionist newspaper. In that article he chided blacks for self-indulgence, submissiveness, and failure to support one another in the face of "brutal aggressions." In response to the enforcement of the Fugitive Slave Act, Brown in 1851 recruited Springfield blacks into a secret society he named the League of Gileadites. He urged members to arm themselves to prevent the arrest of suspected fugitives and to "make clean work with your enemies."

With the dissolution of his partnership with Perkins in 1854, Brown determined to devote his remaining years to the "service" of blacks. Now grown to manhood, five of his sons had left drought-plagued Ohio to take up homesteads in the newly opened Kansas Territory. But Brown decided to return to the North Elba farm he had acquired from the reformer Gerrit Smith, hoping to be a "kind of father" to a colony of blacks learning to farm on neighboring properties. Soon after reaching his farm, however, Brown received an appeal from his pioneer sons for weapons to protect themselves from Missouri "Border Ruffians." Brown interpreted the letter as a religious call. "I think could I hope in any other way to answer the end of my being," he wrote to Mary in September 1855 as he hurried with a wagonload of rifles and swords to Kansas, "I would be quite content to be at North Elba." Brown expected to return home in a short time and did not go to Kansas either to "stir the waters" or to free slaves, but simply to help his sons survive against human and natural adversaries.

After the bloodless Wakarusa War in December 1855 during which free-state leaders at Lawrence named him captain of a short-lived militia company, Brown believed for some months that Kansas had been won for freedom. When a proslavery force "sacked" Lawrence the following spring, he determined to act. Brown had long been angered by the failure of the proslavery territorial courts to prosecute the accused killers of five free-state men. He feared an attack from proslavery settlers on Pottawatomie Creek who had burned out a free-state storekeeper and threatened Brown's neighbors. Brown accompanied a militia company led by his son John, Jr., to the relief of Lawrence, but when the unit arrived too late, Brown persuaded a small party to return with him to the Pottawatomie.

On the night of 24 May 1856 Brown descended on the cabins of his victims in what his sons later defended as a "retaliatory blow" against the proslavery party. Dragooning five men from their beds, Brown's party butchered them with short, heavy cavalry broadswords. When the party failed to locate other intended victims, Brown's men "confiscated" horses and disappeared into the night. Although a meeting at Osawatomie near the Brown claims condemned the "massacre," a large proslavery "posse" easily dispersed Brown's men and burned the town on 30 August in retaliation for the killings. Intended to create a "restraining fear" among proslavery men generally, the Pottawatomie killings anticipated the terrorism of a later era.

His role in the killings still unknown in the East, Brown raised money from reformers for the defense of Kansas. For many months he led a guerrilla band in skirmishes with rival guerrillas, and he joined with Captain James Montgomery in a free-state offensive along the Kansas-Missouri border. In December 1858, with peace restored, Brown led a raid into Missouri, where his men seized eleven slaves and several horses and killed a slaveowner in the process. With a price on his head, Brown boldly transported the blacks by wagon and railroad boxcar to freedom in Canada.

Even before peace had settled over Kansas, Brown had revived his plan to attack slavery in the southern states. In May 1858 he organized a secret constitutional convention among blacks in Chatham, Ontario, which adopted Brown's Provisional Constitution for the government of a temporary black state and declared slavery to be "a most barbarous, unprovoked, and unjustifiable war" upon an oppressed people. Supported by contributions from a committee of reformers later dubbed the Secret Six, Brown gathered a force of twenty-one volunteers at a farmhouse on the Antietam Road across the Potomac River from Harpers Ferry.

On Sunday night, 16 October 1859, Brown's men crossed into Virginia and seized the federal arsenal, the armory yard, and other strategic points. Sending parties into the countryside, Brown gathered hostages and slaves from nearby plantations. He arrested employees of the arsenal as they arrived for work Monday morning, but he unaccountably did not thereafter withdraw across the Shenandoah Bridge to the relative safety of Loudoun Heights. That afternoon local militia companies captured both bridges and forced Brown's men to retreat into a small fire engine house in the armory yard. At dawn on Tuesday a storming party of U.S. Marines from Washington commanded by army colonel Robert E. Lee battered in the engine house door, bayoneted two of Brown's volunteers, and captured Brown himself. Ten of Brown's men were killed, including his sons Watson and Oliver and two young in-laws, seven were eventually captured, and five managed to make their way through the mountains to safety in the North. Two slaves, who seem to have sided with Brown, died during or soon after the raid. Brown's men killed three residents of Harpers Ferry, a local slaveowner, and a marine. Brown's saber wounds proving superficial, he promptly determined to wield the "sword of the spirit" on behalf of God's cause. He declared he was ready to "mingle my blood further with the blood of . . . millions in this slave country whose rights are disregarded by wicked, cruel, and unjust enactments."

During his trial Brown spurned efforts by friends and relatives to win him a commutation of sentence on grounds of insanity. The petitioners cited evidence of insanity in his mother's family (though not, as often claimed, in his mother herself). Although the affidavits attesting to Brown's alleged "monomania" benefited from hindsight, it was true that Brown exhibited "agitation" or outrage toward any tolerance of slavery. As Virginia governor Henry Wise insisted, however, Brown had been rational and composed during the raid. But Brown's moods did vary markedly. After Harpers Ferry, he seemed elated and grandiose despite his failure to free any slaves and the deaths of two of his sons. At other times Brown confessed himself profoundly discouraged. Yet his moods were not cyclical or disabling and his bouts of depression were linked to bereavements and disappointments. He was apparently never clinically depressed. His claim that he was an instrument of God to free the slaves seemed to some delusional, but as a prisoner he acknowledged the hubris of that claim. If his judgment was deeply flawed, Brown was neither legally insane nor manifestly psychotic. Facing execution, an unrepentant Brown prophesied that "the crimes of this *guilty, land: will* never be purged *away*; but with Blood." On the scaffold, surrounded by hundreds of Virginia militiamen, Brown met death like a soldier, perfecting his martyrdom.

Though a military fiasco, Brown's raid was for many a jeremiad against a nation that defied God in tolerating human bondage. It sent tremors of horror throughout the South and gave secessionists a persuasive symbol of northern hostility. It hardened positions over slavery everywhere. It helped to discredit Stephen A. Douglas's compromise policy of popular sovereignty and to divide the Democratic party, thus ensuring the election of Abraham Lincoln in 1860. In a longer view, African Americans especially have seen in Brown hope for the eventual redemption of an oppressive America, while critics have condemned his extremism and deplored his divisive impact on the sectional crisis. Both Brown's fanaticism and his passion for freedom make him an enduring icon.

• Brown's letters and papers are scattered in more than a dozen major collections across the United States. The most important are the Boyd B. Stutler Collection at the West Virginia Department of Culture and History in Charles Town; the Henry A. Wise Collection and others at the Library of Congress; the John Brown, Richard J. Hinton, and other collections at the Kansas State Historical Society in Topeka; the Oswald Garrison Villard Collection at Columbia University; the Ferdinand J. Dreer Collection at the Historical Society of Pennsylvania in Philadelphia; the Clarence S. Gee Collection at the Hudson Library and Historical Society in Hudson, Ohio; the John Brown, Jr., Papers at the Ohio Historical Society in Columbus; and the James W. Eldridge and Horatio N. Rust collections at the Henry E. Huntington Library in San Marino, Calif. The Richard O. Boyer Papers at the Massachusetts Historical Society include copies of documents from many of the above, and the Stutler and John Brown, Jr., collections are available on microfilm.

Brown's antislavery career spawned rival biographical legacies. A celebratory abolitionist tradition culminated in Oswald Garrison Villard's still valuable *John Brown, 1800–1859: A Biography Fifty Years After* (1910), which is based in part on interviews with surviving Brown relations and acquaintances. W. E. B. Du Bois's *John Brown* (1909) is an insightful tribute by a distinguished black scholar. Where these authors see heroism, Brown's detractors see criminality or moral failure. The youthful Robert Penn Warren's critical *John Brown: The Making of a Martyr* (1929) relies on secondary sources, but James C. Malin's research for his influential debunking *John Brown and the Legend of Fifty-Six* (1942) is exhaustive. Joseph Chamberlain Furnas's *The Road to Harpers Ferry* (1959) sees growing mental instability in Brown.

In the early 1970s several scholarly biographies bridged the moral issues with varying success. Stephen B. Oates's *To Purge This Land with Blood* (1970) is reliable and even-handed but cautious. Jules Abels's lively *Man on Fire: John Brown and the Cause of Liberty* (1971) is sympathetic but less thoroughly researched. Richard O. Boyer's admiring *The Legend of John Brown* (1973) puts Brown's life before he went to Kansas into the context of his times. Benjamin Quarles's *Allies for Freedom: Blacks and John Brown* (1974) adds valuable information, and Jeffery Rossbach's *Ambivalent Conspirators: John Brown, the Secret Six, and a Theory of Slave Violence* (1982) clarifies why leading reformers like Samuel Gridley Howe and Theodore Parker supported Brown's war against slavery. Paul Finkelman, ed., *His Soul Goes Marching On* (1995), reassesses Brown's impact on the sectional crisis.

ROBERT MCGLONE

BROWN, John (1810?–1876), field hand and author, was born in Southampton County, Virginia, the son of slaves Joe and Nancy. For most of his life as a slave he was called Fed or Benford. At around age ten he and his mother were moved to nearby Northampton County, North Carolina; eighteen months later he was sold alone and sent to Georgia, never again to see any of his kinfolk.

Bought by ambitious, quick-tempered Thomas Stevens, Fed grew to maturity on a farm in central Georgia near the state capital at Milledgeville. Stevens drove his slaves hard, often employing whippings and other brutal punishments. Gradually he accumulated much land and more than twenty slaves, becoming a "planter" by federal census standards. In the 1820s Stevens expanded his family enterprises into DeKalb County, near Cherokee territory in northwestern Georgia, and when these Indians were driven west in the late 1830s, he settled in Cass (now Bartow) County (northwest of modern Atlanta). Fed went with his master, of course, and when Stevens died in 1840 his considerable estate, now including more than forty slaves, was divided among his heirs. Fed became the property of 22-year-old Decature Stevens, an even harsher and more erratic master, who made Fed doggedly determined to escape slavery.

The most influential person in Fed's life, the man who taught him to love freedom, was a slave named John Glasgow. Born a free black in British Guiana, Glasgow became a sailor in the British merchant marine and married an Englishwoman from Liverpool. On a voyage to Savannah he made the mistake of going ashore where Georgia law took effect. As a foreign free black he was interned in the city jail; several weeks later, when his ship sailed without him, he was sold as a slave. Glasgow became the property of Thomas Stevens; free all his life, he could not adjust to slavery, and brutal beatings left him crippled. But he planted the image of freedom in England in the mind of provincial, uneducated young Fed.

Fed finally ran away from Decature Stevens. Caught in Tennessee when his white accomplice betrayed him, he was brought home to face harsh punishment. But in the mid-1840s he ran away again. He had no idea how to reach England, and he finally ended up in a slave pen in New Orleans with the new name Benford. There he was sold to Theodoric J. "Jepsey" James, who owned rich cotton land in Washington County, Mississippi, and ninety-five slave laborers. The environment was primitive and the work exhausting on the James plantation, and after only three months Benford ran for freedom again.

This time he understood that he could reach free country by heading north up the nearby Mississippi River. Traveling by night and hiding by day, Benford reached St. Louis in three months. Then he crossed over into Illinois, got directions from a free black, and headed for Vandalia. A few days later another black man gave him a free pass made out to John Brown, the name he carried for the rest of his life. After spending two weeks in a black community near Terre Haute, Indiana, he walked toward Indianapolis and got help from Quakers involved in the Underground Railroad. They sent him on to Marshall, Michigan, where he worked as a carpenter in the black community for a year. Then Brown moved to Detroit, where he joined Cornish miners and worked as a carpenter for eighteen months until his English friends returned home. Brown planned to follow them, but first he went to Canada and worked for almost six months in a sawmill at the Dawn Institute, a vocational training school for runaway slaves from the United States.

In August 1850 Brown sailed on a ship bound for Liverpool and soon rejoined his miner friends in Redruth, Cornwall. After two months he moved to Bristol and then to Heywood in Lancashire, still working as a carpenter. But he encountered strong white racism, and in the spring of 1851 he went to London, where he lived the remainder of his life. There he contacted the British and Foreign Anti-Slavery Society, whose secretary, Louis Alexis Chamerovzow, was particularly impressed with Brown's plain, direct description of American slavery from the black perspective.

The society carefully checked Brown's story for accuracy and authenticity and then sent him on a speaking tour. British audiences responded well, especially to the sad story of John Glasgow. For a while his speaking fees supplemented his carpentry wages, allowing him to live frugally in a boardinghouse in a working-class area of London. The British and Foreign Anti-Slavery Society's *Anti-Slavery Reporter* ran an account of Glasgow's tragedy on 1 July 1853, and other British journals repeated it. The *Leeds Anti-Slavery Series* covered it in tract eighty-nine, and *Frederick Douglass's Paper* and a few other American journals also repeated the story. In 1854 Brown and his abolitionist friends took a notarized account of Glasgow's life to the British Foreign Office, but inquiries by consuls in Charleston and Savannah led nowhere.

A year later the British and Foreign Anti-Slavery Society published *Slave Life in Georgia: A Narrative of the Life, Sufferings, and Escape of John Brown, A Fugitive Slave, Now in England.* This small, 250-page volume included the Glasgow material but covered Fed–Benford–John Brown's entire life. Brown remained illiterate so Chamerovzow actually wrote the book in standard middle-class English. However, the story is Brown's well enough, the authentic autobiography of a real man and a real slave that has been documented in great detail by modern scholars.

A second limited edition was soon published, and it was also translated into German. Americans were already quite familiar with fugitive slave narratives, so *Slave Life* drew little attention in the United States even though it was one of the few that focused on the Deep South. Its limited royalties augmented Brown's income for a while. Soon he married an Englishwoman and became an "herbalist" (herb doctor) in London, where he died. An ordinary man, Brown told an extraordinary story of black bondage in white America.

• Illiterate, Brown left no manuscripts, but the papers of the British and Foreign Anti-Slavery Society at the Rhodes House Library, Oxford University, include an 1876 letter from his wife announcing his death. The main source for Brown's story is his autobiography. F. N. Boney edited, evaluated, documented, and authenticated this work in *Slave Life in Georgia: A Narrative of the Life, Sufferings, and Escape of John Brown, a Fugitive Slave* (1972; rev. ed. 1991). Boney also has published articles dealing with particular episodes in Brown's life, "Doctor Thomas Hamilton: Two Views of a Gentleman of the Old South," *Phylon: The Atlanta University Review of Race and Culture* 28 (1967): 288–92, "The Blue Lizard: Another View of Nat Turner's Country on the Eve of Rebellion," *Phylon* 31 (1970): 351–58, "Thomas Stevens: Antebellum Georgian," *South Atlantic Quarterly* 72 (1973): 226–42, and "Slaves as Guinea Pigs: Georgia and Alabama Episodes," *Alabama Review: A Quarterly Journal of Alabama History* 37 (1984): 45–51. See also Boney, *Southerners All* (1984; rev. ed. 1990).

F. N. BONEY

BROWN, John Calvin (6 Jan. 1827–17 Aug. 1889), governor of Tennessee, was born in Giles County, Tennessee, the son of Duncan Brown and Margaret Smith, farmers. He attended Jackson College in Columbia, Tennessee, and graduated in 1846, reputedly one of the best-educated men in his region and speaking both Latin and French. He then studied law and, admitted to the bar in 1848, soon became successful as a lawyer, practicing in Giles County and the surrounding area. Though a Whig and the brother of Neill S. Brown, governor of Tennessee from 1847 to 1849, Brown did not become active in politics until the 1860 campaign, when he ran as an elector on the Constitutional Union party ticket of John Bell and Edward Everett. He campaigned aggressively against secession but also against the Republican party. The strain of the election seems to have been too much for his health, for he decided to take a cure popular among the well-to-do at the time, extensive travels through much of North America, Europe, and the Middle East. He returned just before the outbreak of the Civil War.

Despite his opposition to secession, Brown promptly enlisted as a private in a Confederate Tennessee regiment. In short order he rose to captain and then, on 16 May 1861, to colonel of the Third Tennessee. By 28 October he was commanding a brigade with the Confederate forces in central Kentucky. In February 1862 he and his brigade were among the troops sent to reinforce Fort Donelson, Tennessee, a key Confederate stronghold on the Cumberland River. On 16 February the fort surrendered, and Brown and his men were taken prisoner. After being held in Fort Warren in Boston Harbor, he was exchanged on 27 August 1862 and three days later was commissioned a brigadier general. He led another brigade in the Kentucky campaign in the fall of 1862 and on 8 October fought at the battle of Perryville, where he was wounded. He returned to duty that December and was given a brigade. Frequently during 1863 he was called upon to exercise temporary command of the division. He served through the Tullahoma campaign and the battle of Chickamauga (19–20 Sept. 1863). During the siege of Chattanooga that followed, he briefly commanded the division again. At the battle of Missionary Ridge, 25 November 1863, the horse he was riding was killed under him.

In the Atlanta campaign the following year, Brown began in command of a brigade but was soon elevated to division command. In this capacity he served throughout the siege of the city and the subsequent campaigning in northern Georgia. In the fall of 1864 General John B. Hood took the Army of Tennessee north into the state of Tennessee. At Franklin, in a series of reckless assaults, Hood hurled his army at a well-entrenched Union army. Brown was among the remarkably large number of general officers hit in this action, and, seriously wounded, he was unable to rejoin the army until 2 April 1865. By that time it amounted to mere remnants and was operating in North Carolina, attempting to oppose the northward march of Federal troops under General William T. Sherman. On 18 April 1865 the army surrendered at Durham Station, North Carolina.

Brown was paroled early in May at Greensboro, North Carolina, and he returned to Giles County and to the practice of law. In 1869 he ran successfully for a seat in the state legislature. In 1870 he was elected to the convention for creating a new state constitution and then became president of the convention. The recognition he won in this position helped him win election as governor that year and reelection two years later. As a prewar Whig who had nevertheless gone with the Confederacy, he occupied a strong central position in Tennessee politics. He strove to unite both factions of anti-Reconstruction Tennesseans, the former Whigs (known as Conservatives) and the Democrats, even accepting the latter title as the only practical alternative to the Republicans, or "Radicals" as they were called. His political philosophy continued to be consistent with the prewar Whigs' desire for activist government and aggressive reform, and these characterized his administration. He favored state subsidization of railroad construction, the establishment of a state system of tax-supported public schools, the reorganization of the state prison and court systems, and a large-scale reapportionment of election districts.

Brown was a staunch defender of funding the debt Tennessee had incurred both during his own and previous administrations. His position was unpopular and probably contributed to his 1875 defeat by former U.S. president Andrew Johnson in a race for U.S. senator. Returning to private life in Tennessee, Brown again practiced law. Later he was even more successful in the railroad business. He became vice president of the Texas & Pacific Railroad in 1876 and played an important role in railroad building and organization. In 1880 Jay Gould took control of the Texas & Pacific, but Brown kept his position and the next year became general solicitor for all of Gould's railroads west of the Mississippi. In 1888 he became president of the Texas & Pacific. During the last few months of his life, he headed the powerful Tennessee Coal, Iron & Railroad Company. He died in Red Boiling Springs, Tennessee.

During the course of his life, Brown was twice married. His first wife was Ann Pointer; they had no children. After Ann's death, Brown married Elizabeth Childress, with whom he had four children.

• Information on Brown's Civil War career is in William C. Davis, ed., *The Confederate General* (1991); Shelby Foote, *The Civil War: A Narrative* (1958–1974); and Ezra J. Warner, *Generals in Gray: The Lives of the Confederate Commanders* (1959). His postwar political career is dealt with in Roger L. Hart, *Redeemers, Bourbons & Populists: Tennessee, 1870–1896* (1975).

STEVEN E. WOODWORTH

BROWN, John Carter (28 Aug. 1797–10 Jun. 1874), book collector and philanthropist, was born in Providence, Rhode Island, the son of Nicholas Brown, a merchant and philanthropist, and Ann Carter, daughter of John Carter, the second printer of Providence. In 1816 he received an A.B. from Brown University, named for his father, and immediately joined the family mercantile firm, Brown & Ives. Although he was involved in several aspects of the shipping business and became a partner in 1832, he found time to travel extensively in Europe and the United States and to pursue his interests in historical subjects and books. Accustomed from childhood to a growing family library, he and his elder brother, Nicholas, "were predisposed to infection with the epidemic Bibliomania" and belonged to "a small group of American gentlemen of means who found in the London and Continental bookshops a reason for a European holiday" (Winship, pp. 9, 12). He resided in Europe from 1823 to 1826 and bought many books, most of which he shipped back to Brown University as gifts. The university made him a trustee in 1828 and a fellow in 1842. He continued to make donations to the university and to be involved in its affairs throughout his life.

In the beginning Brown's book collecting lacked a focus. "Before he discovered it was Americana he really liked, he was in a fair way to becoming the possessor of an undistinguished 'gentleman's library" (Cannon, p. 65). Like his brother, he bought fine editions of the classics, rare polyglot Bibles, extra-illustrated volumes, and Aldine imprints. Nevertheless, he always had some interest in the history of the Americas and of his own region in particular. In the 1820s he acquired some of the earliest published accounts of the settlement of New England and made note of almost every reference to Rhode Island. He also wrote comments in the margins next to controversial statements about Roger Williams. He purchased White Kennet's *Bibliothecae Americanae Primordia* (1713), the earliest bibliography on the New World, and in the 1830s he acquired Obadiah Rich's new catalogs of books on the Americas. Upon the death of his father in 1841, Brown inherited additional wealth and the opportunity to purchase most of the family library, including the Americana, from his brother for $10,000. Nicholas had inherited the library but wanted to sell it before taking a consular post in Europe. Passing "three anxious days and three sleepless nights," Brown finally agreed to buy the books (Kellen, p. 19).

It is not clear exactly when Brown set himself the task of collecting all materials printed before the nineteenth century relating to the discovery and history of the New World, but between 1845 and 1847 he acquired over 1,500 volumes of Americana from Henry Stevens, a Yankee bookdealer who had just moved to London, England. Stevens had access to the store of Obadiah Rich, which contained a lot of early Americana formerly belonging to the French bibliographer Henri Ternaux-Compans, compiler of the *Bibliothèque Américaine* (1837), a catalog often referred to by Brown. The first of Stevens's now-legendary shipments included Pierre d'Ailly's *Ymago Mundi* (1483), three editions of the Columbus Letter (1493), five editions of the "Cortez letters," Champlain's *Voyages* (1613), and long runs of Jesuit "Relations." No single item cost Brown more than eighty-five dollars.

His acquisition of so many of Ternaux's books "greatly increased his lead in the race that was now beginning in this new and exciting field" (Cannon, p. 67). His main competitor in the quest for Americana was his Newport summer neighbour, James Lenox of New York City. Lenox was a client of Stevens, too, and often complained to him of Brown's receiving preferential treatment. Once, after both collectors had each bid more than enough for a 1493 Basel edition of the Columbus Letter, and Stevens had awarded it to Brown, Lenox insisted on having it and threatened to boycott Stevens. Stevens recalls that Brown, "very kindly, to relieve me of the dilemma, sent the book to Mr [*sic*] Lenox without a word of comment or explanation. . . . Mr Brown was exceedingly vexed with Mr Lenox, and pronounced the demand selfish, and under all the circumstances both illiberal and unbusinesslike. They were both old bachelors, and I suppose found it unpleasant to be crossed" (Stevens, p. 91). Two months later Brown and Lenox met for the first time "and began a friendship that grew steadily through the years" (Adams, p. 4).

Books were not Brown's only concern. In the late 1840s and 1850s he participated in the antislavery Free Soil movement. Some of his Providence ancestors had been abolitionists since before the revolutionary war, and his father's firm had been investing in western land and transportation for years. He was one of the first to join the New England Emigrant Aid Company and became its president around 1854, the year of the Kansas-Nebraska Act. This federal legislation opened the new territory to settlement, but overthrew the Missouri Compromise of 1820 with the idea of popular sovereignty. The company responded by sending more than 2,000 settlers opposed to slavery into Kansas to assure that the territory would vote to become a free state.

On 23 June 1859, at age sixty-one, Brown married a woman he had recently met on a ship returning from Europe, Sophia Augusta Brown (no relation); they had three children. During the Civil War Brown helped found the Rhode Island Hospital. He was a major contributor to the Butler Hospital, too, and served on its board. He also gave to cultural institutions besides Brown University, such as the Providence Athenaeum and the Redwood Library at Newport, Rhode Island.

By the 1860s Brown's collection had doubled in size and "overflowed from the upstairs hallway" (Winship, p. 25). At the request of his wife he constructed a fireproof book room adjoining the house. Scholars were amazed at how generous he was with his books. Sometimes he volunteered to send extremely rare volumes to scholars in Europe. In order to keep track of his growing collection he engaged his friend John Russell Bartlett to compile a catalog. Published from 1865 to 1871 in four volumes, the first edition of *A Catalogue of Books Relating to North and South America* describes over 5,600 selected titles printed between 1493 and 1800. Upon his death in Providence, Brown's library had about 7,500 volumes, but it continued to expand in size and scope under the supervision first of his widow and then of his sons. On 17 May 1904 the library, with a new building and an endowment of $500,000, was donated to Brown University.

Brown's wealth and education, in combination with a timely decision to concentrate on Americana just as the pioneers in the field, Ternaux-Compans and Rich, were selling their stock, enabled him to build a very significant and useful collection. In contrast to Lenox's superb but "patchy" collection, Brown's was limited in scope but comprehensive. His concept of Americana was broad and included all pre-nineteenth-century books relating to the Western Hemisphere, "a subject which literally embraced the globe" (Cannon, p. 65). His library attracted scholars from many countries during his lifetime, and it continues to be an outstanding center for research in American history.

• Brown's papers are in the John Carter Brown Library. Published works on Brown invariably focus on his book collecting and reveal relatively little about his personality and social life. An early source of information on how he acquired parts of his collection and on his rivalry with James Lenox is Henry Stevens, *Recollections of Mr. James Lenox of New York and the Formation of His Library* (1886). Straightforward accounts of the collection's history and treasures, are the "Address" by William Vail Kellen in the John Carter Brown Library, *The Dedication of the Library Building: May the Seventeenth A.D. MDCCCCIIII* (1905), pp. 17–38; George Parker Winship, *The John Carter Brown Library: A History* (1914); and Lawrence C. Wroth, *The John Carter Brown Library in Brown University, Providence, Rhode Island* (1936). For a comparison of Brown with other collectors of Americana, especially Lenox, see Carl L. Cannon, *American Book Collectors and Collecting from Colonial Times to the Present* (1941). Additional anecdotes about Brown's relationship with Lenox and Stevens and about Brown's wife, sons, and other caretakers of the collection are found in Thomas R. Adams, "A Collections Progress," *Gazette of the Grolier Club*," n.s., 8 (Oct. 1968): 2–13. See also the obituaries in the *Providence Daily Journal*, 11 June, 1874 and 24 June, 1874.

ROBERT S. FREEMAN

BROWN, John George (11 Nov. 1831–8 Feb. 1913), artist, was born near Newcastle-on-Tyne, England, the son of John Brown, an attorney's clerk, and Ann Greener. At age fourteen the young "J. G." began a seven-year apprenticeship to a glass cutter in Newcastle-on-Tyne. During his last three years there, he attended evening drawing classes taught by William Bell Scott at the Government School of Design in Newcastle. In 1852 Brown moved to Edinburgh, Scotland, and he worked days at the Holyrood Glass Works and at night studied at the Trustees Academy in Robert Scott Lauder's antique class, drawing from ancient and Renaissance sculpture casts. After spending the summer of 1853 in London, England, he emigrated to the United States, arriving in New York City on his twenty-second birthday. He immediately settled in Brooklyn, New York, and found work at the Brooklyn Flint Glass Company. In 1855 he married his employer's daughter, Mary Owen; they had two children who survived to adulthood.

On marrying Brown left the glass factory to pursue a career as a portrait painter, supported initially by his father-in-law. He enrolled in the life and antique classes at the National Academy of Design in New York City in 1857 and 1858. He became a founding member of the Brooklyn Art Social in 1859 and of the Brooklyn Art Association in 1861. It was probably Samuel P. Avery, a prominent collector-dealer living in Brooklyn, who encouraged Brown to shift from painting portraits to genre subjects about 1859 and facilitated his move to New York's Tenth Street Studio Building in the summer of 1860. Brown resided in Brooklyn until 1863 and then in Fort Lee, New Jersey, until 1869, all the while deepening his involvement with the New York art world. In 1861 he joined the Artists' Fund Society, an organization whose members held exhibitions and sales of their work to contribute to a fund to benefit the widows of members. He was elected a full member of the National Academy of Design in 1863 and a member of the American Watercolor Society in March 1867, two months after its founding. He exhibited steadily at the Brooklyn Art Association and almost without interruption at the National Academy of Design from 1858. A canny businessman, by the 1870s Brown also showed his work locally at Artists' Fund Society and American Watercolor Society annual exhibitions, private clubs like the Century Association, and commercial galleries, as well as in cities as widespread as Buffalo, Chicago, Boston, and Philadelphia.

Brown specialized in depicting children, often presenting them in humorous situations that mimicked adult behavior. His urban scenes of the 1860s featured feisty bullies, cocky smokers, and varied street vendors. More numerous in this decade and the next were his country scenes of middle-class children playing or flirting in idyllic, sun-dappled settings. Combining both English Victorian and American genre traditions, his strong narrative emphasis and descriptive, realist style brought him ready recognition and rising income. Between 1864 and 1866, influenced by the exacting detail and close focus on nature of American pre-Raphaelite painters, Brown produced some of his finest work, including *Watching the Woodpecker* and *Resting in the Woods* (both 1866, private collections). A summer trip to Europe in 1870 had no discernible effect on his art, and about that same time he settled permanently in New York City. His wife having died in 1867, in 1871 he married his eighteen-year-old sister-in-law, Emma Owen; they had five children. During the 1870s he frequently summered in New York's Catskill region, where he sketched country children and also pure landscapes to serve as expanded settings for his genre scenes. Departing from this pattern, he spent the summers of 1877 and 1878 painting rugged fishermen on Canada's Grand Menan (now Grand Manan) Island.

After 1880 Brown made New York's exploding population of street children his principal subject. He replaced his country children with a different country type, old men and women in rustic interiors, but old folks remained clearly secondary. By the end of the 1880s Brown's name was indelibly linked to the image of the street urchin, particularly the boy bootblack, whom he portrayed with brushes and blacking box waiting for customers on the sidewalk. Brown typically characterized his waifs, whether bootblacks, newsboys, flower girls, or crossing sweepers, as independent entrepreneurs freed from society's restrictions and supported by numerous comrades of the streets. Often the children smile engagingly; adults are never present. He represented many nationalities, including "German, Irish, Irish-American, English, or Jewish types" (*Art Amateur* [Nov. 1881]: 113) alone or coexisting harmoniously. They wear tattered clothing but never appear filthy, diseased, or starving, as many actual street children did. Brown derived his idealized vision, which conformed to only some truths of poor children's lives, from the ideas of Charles Loring Brace, the prominent reformer and founder of the Children's Aid Society. His paintings found a literary parallel in the exactly contemporary novels of Horatio Alger, whose newsboys and bootblacks earn success by hard work. Brown often expressed sympathy with his subjects, recalling his own working-man origins and early poverty: "I do not paint poor boys solely because the public likes such pictures and pays me for them, but because I love the boys myself, for I, too, was once a poor lad like them" (*New York Times Magazine*, 27 Aug. 1899).

In the last two decades of his life, as his work grew more formulaic and his critics less favorable, Brown immersed himself in the art establishment. From 1887 to 1904 he served as president of the American Watercolor Society, from 1897 to 1907 as president of the Artists' Fund Society, and from 1899 to 1903 as vice president of the National Academy of Design. Not long before his death in New York City, he ruefully, but correctly, predicted that he would be known for "one idea," the city shoeshine boy (*New York Herald*, 9 Feb. 1913). Though other artists of his time portrayed child street workers, Brown did so most consistently, creating a type widely reproduced in engravings, wood-engravings, and photographs. One of the most popular artists of his time, he almost singlehandedly made working-class, immigrant children acceptable subjects for high art, pointing out the potential of gritty urban themes even while he did not paint them.

• Brown's paintings are widely distributed among many museums, including the Metropolitan Museum of Art, the Brooklyn Museum of Art, the Museum of Fine Arts in Boston, and the Fine Arts Museums in San Francisco. Two of the most valuable nineteenth-century articles are "John G. Brown," *Harper's Weekly*, 12 June 1880, pp. 372–74, and S. G. W. Benjamin, "A Painter of the Streets," *Magazine of Art*, Apr. 1882, pp. 265–70. George Sheldon, *American Painters* (1879), provides Brown's views on art and artists. Two important sales catalogs document his work: *Catalogue of Paintings by J. G. Brown, N.A.*, Ortgies and Co., 26 and 27 Jan. 1892; and *The Finished Pictures and Studies Left by the Late J. G. Brown, N.A.*, American Art Galleries, 9 and 10 Feb. 1914. The fullest treatment of his career is Martha J. Hoppin, *Country Paths and City Sidewalks: The Art of J. G. Brown*, George Walter Vincent Smith Art Museum exhibition catalog, Springfield, Mass. (1989). An obituary is in the *New York Herald*, 9 Feb. 1913.

MARTHA J. HOPPIN

BROWN, John Mason, Jr. (3 July 1900–16 Mar. 1969), critic, author, and lecturer, was born in Louisville, Kentucky, the son of John Mason Brown, a lawyer, and Caroline Carroll Ferguson; they divorced when Brown was two. John and his older sister were brought up by their mother and maternal grandmother. Brown became stagestruck at the age of eight, when he saw the aging Robert B. Mantell play King Lear. Brown's journalistic career began when, at age seventeen, he joined the staff of the *Louisville Courier-Journal*. In 1918 he joined the Williams College Reserve Officers' Training Corp for a summer of training, but World War I ended before he could serve.

In 1919 Brown was accepted at Harvard to study drama with George Pierce Baker, and he participated in Baker's famous 47 Workshop, an extracurricular laboratory theater that staged plays by Baker's playwriting students. Brown acted, wrote plays, and served as director and president of the Drama Club during his last two years at Harvard. Baker encouraged him to pursue a career in dramatic criticism. After receiving his B.A. and graduating cum laude from Harvard in 1923, Brown spent the summer teaching history of the theater and Shakespeare at the University of Montana. He then traveled on the Continent with classmate Donald Oenslager to explore European theater; colleague Brooks Atkinson later described Brown as the only drama critic who had deliberately prepared himself for the job.

In 1924 Brown became associate editor and drama critic for the newly founded *Theatre Arts Monthly*, positions he held until 1928. From 1925 to 1931 he also taught history of drama at Richard Boleslavsky and Maria Ouspenskaya's American Laboratory Theatre in New York. Further travel in Europe and Russia resulted in his publication of *The Modern Theatre in Revolt* (1929), which established his reputation and led to his securing a job as drama critic of the *New York Evening Post* in 1929, where he remained until 1941. In 1931–1932 Baker hired Brown to teach history of dramatic criticism at the Yale University school of drama, which Baker had founded in 1925. Baker and Brown's friendship lasted until Baker's death in 1935.

In 1933 Brown married Catherine Screven Meredith, a young actress he had taught at the Laboratory Theatre. They had two children. Unable to support his family by writing alone, Brown continued teaching during the summers, at Middlebury College and the Bread Loaf Writers' Conference (1935–1936), and at Harvard (1937–1940). In the spring of 1940 he delivered Harvard's Winthrop Ames Memorial Lectures. Brown also augmented his income by touring on the national lecture circuits, where he proved a great success. Helen Hokinson's *New Yorker* cartoon, captioned, "Next week, our intellectual cocktail—John Mason Brown," immortalized his popularity with America's women's clubs. Brown humorously reported his experiences as a platform speaker in *Accustomed As I Am* (1942).

World War II profoundly changed Brown, as it did many servicemen. He turned a minor operation to meet enlistment requirements into a book entitled *Insides Out: Being the Saga of a Drama Critic Who Attended His Own Opening* (1942). Commissioned a Naval Reserve lieutenant, he joined the staff of Rear Admiral Alan G. Kirk in April 1943. Aboard his flagship, which was sailing to invade Sicily, Kirk assigned Brown to broadcast daily reports to the crew. Brown reported enthusiastically across the Atlantic, concluding with twenty consecutive hours of broadcasts during the invasion. These reports were collected in his bestseller *To All Hands: An Amphibious Adventure* (1943), published while on leave with his family. Brown served under Kirk again a year later and broadcast reports during the D-Day Normandy invasion; he recounted his experience in *Many a Watchful Night* (1944). Brown's service earned him the Bronze Star.

Leaving active service in 1944, Brown decided not to resume his daily reviewing of Broadway. With the "real world" still at war, he felt that he needed to "bring the conflict home to those indifferent to it." Brown believed that New York reviewers who had not seen war were judging new plays "by standards utterly divorced from those who have been 'there'." He accepted an assistant editorship at the *Saturday Review of Literature*, writing reviews and a weekly page of commentary. Sent to Germany by editor Norman Cousins, Brown wrote about the Nuremberg Trials, detailing the horrors he had seen in uncut films of the extermination camps.

As a broadcasting celebrity, Brown did a series of "solo literary discussions" titled "Of Men and Books" for CBS Radio (1944–1947), and he appeared frequently on the CBS program "Invitation to Learning" (1944–1964). He was on the BBC London "Transatlantic Quiz" team (1945–1946), moderated ABC-TV's "Critic-at-Large" program (1948–1949), and served as a panelist on CBS-TV's "The Last Word" (1957–1959). He also appeared as a frequent guest on other panel and quiz shows.

Brown was a founding member of the New York Drama Critics Circle, formed in 1935 in response to dissatisfaction with the Pulitzer prizes for drama. The critics felt the prizes were going to plays inferior to others onstage at the time; they wanted to make awards to plays they felt were more worthy. Brown served as president in 1941–1942 and again from 1945 to 1949. He later served for several years as a drama adviser for the Pulitzer awards but resigned in 1963, along with John Gassner, after Columbia University's trustees overruled their recommendation of Edward Albee's *Who's Afraid of Virginia Woolf?* Among other activities, Brown served as an overseer of Harvard College (1949–1955), as a trustee of the Metropolitan Museum of Art (1951–1956), as a board member of Recording for the Blind (beginning in 1951), and as a judge for the Book-of-the Month Club (beginning in 1956).

Brown's 1948 review of Robert E. Sherwood's *Roosevelt and Hopkins* (1948) in the *Saturday Review* signaled a change in his writing and in the course of his career. He saw parallels to his own war experience in Sherwood's evolution from Broadway playwright to political historian. Brown covered the 1952 conventions for the *Saturday Review* and accompanied candidates Dwight D. Eisenhower and Adlai Stevenson on their campaigns. Devoted to serious writing about figures on the national scene, Brown wrote *Through These Men* (1956). He then committed himself to writing a biography of Sherwood, a monumental task involving the study of 30–45,000 documents. The first volume, *The World of Robert E. Sherwood; Mirror to His Times 1896–1939*, appeared in 1965; the second, *The Ordeal of a Playwright; Robert E. Sherwood and the Challenge of War*, was unfinished at Brown's death; old friend Norman Cousins edited it for publication in 1970.

Brown was an important and influential member of a white Anglo-Saxon Protestant, largely Ivy-league establishment prominent in New York's cultural scene from the 1920s through the 1950s. He also reviewed and, for many, epitomized a Broadway theater dominated by George Pierce Baker's "Yale-ies" and earlier Harvard 47 Workshop graduates. Younger critics found Brown's critiques too nice. John Simon, reviewing Brown's *Dramatis Personae* (1963), found him lacking "discrimination" and more an "appreciator" than a critic, but Charles Poore of the *New York Times* regarded him as "the Confederate Aristotle," and Alistair Cooke eulogized him in the *Guardian* as "the blithe and irrepressible gentleman from Kentucky, who managed . . . by some subtle chemistry of character, to applaud the brave, to slap down fools without malice, to combine gaiety with goodness, to blast pretension, and leave no enemies" (Stevens, p. 291). Brown brought a sense of proportion and humor to his work and entertained readers and audiences with his often mischievous wit. Brown's life and career both mirrored and helped to shape his public's awareness of the American experience in the first half of the twentieth century.

• Brown's writings reveal the variety of his interests and include *Daniel Boone: The Opening of the Wilderness* (1952); *Morning Faces: A Book of Children and Parents* (1949); *Beyond the Present* (1948); *The Art of Playgoing* (1936); various theoretical and critical essays; and the imaginative *Letters from Greenroom Ghosts* (1934), which Brown wrote in the personae of great actors of the past advising modern performers. Other books are collections, rearrangements, and revisions of his reviews and columns, and thus offer his running commentary on the culture. They include *Upstage: The American Theatre in Performance* (1930; repr. 1969); *Two On the Aisle: Ten Years of the American Theatre in Performance* (1938; repr. 1969); *Broadway in Review* (1940; repr. 1969); *Seeing Things* (1946); *Seeing More Things* (1948); *Still Seeing Things* (1950); and *As They Appear* (1952). With Montrose J. Moses, Brown edited *The American Theatre As Seen By Its Critics, 1752–1934* (1934; repr. 1967); and as sole editor he published *The Portable Charles Lamb* (1949), and *The Ladies Home Journal Treasury* (1956). George Stevens's affectionate biography *Speak for Yourself, John* (1974), is the most detailed source on Brown's life, much of it in Brown's own words. It provides information on the locations of collections of letters, papers, recordings, and a complete list of Brown's books, though not of his many shorter publications. Obituaries are in the *New York Times*, 17 Mar. 1969; *Time*, 28 Mar. 1969; *Saturday Review*, 29 Mar. 1969; and *Newsweek*, 31 Mar. 1969.

DANIEL S. KREMPEL

BROWN, John Mifflin (8 Sept. 1817–16 Mar. 1893), African Methodist Episcopal (AME) bishop, was born in Cantwell's Bridge, New Castle County, in Delaware. Little is known of his family or early childhood. He lived in Cantwell's Bridge until he was ten. He then moved to Wilmington, Delaware, where he lived for two years with the family of William A. Seals, a Quaker. At Cantwell's Bridge, he attended a predominantly white private school. His older sister encouraged him to move to Philadelphia, Pennsylvania, where he lived with and worked for attorney Henry Chester, who tutored him and provided him with limited religious training. Brown attended St. Thomas Colored Protestant Episcopal Church in Philadelphia.

In January 1836 Brown became a member of Bethel AME Church in Philadelphia and began private studies under Rev. John M. Gloucester to prepare for the ministry. He also studied barbering and worked as a barber in Poughkeepsie, New York, and New York City between 1836 and 1838. In 1838 he studied at Wesleyan Academy in Wilbraham, Massachusetts. In 1841–1842 he studied at Oberlin College in Ohio but did not complete a degree. He moved to Detroit in 1844 and opened the first school for African-American children in that city. After the death of a local AME pastor, Brown was appointed acting minister, serving from 1844 to 1847. His success in the pastorate led to rapid advancement in denominational affairs. He joined the AME Ohio Conference, was ordained a deacon, was assigned to the AME church in Columbus, Ohio, and was appointed principal of Union Seminary, which was the first school to be owned and operated by the AME church.

In 1852 Brown became pastor at Allen Station AME Church in Pittsburgh, Pennsylvania, and joined the Indiana Conference. In February of that year he married Mary Louise Lewis; they had eight children. Bishop Daniel A. Payne commissioned Brown to participate in a mission to New Orleans, Louisiana, where—over a five-year period—Brown took responsibility for building the Morris Brown Chapel. He purchased Trinity Chapel and started congregations in Algiers and Covington, serving as pastor of St. James AME Church. During his mission to New Orleans, he was imprisoned five times for allowing slaves to attend religious services. In April 1857 he requested a transfer and was reassigned to Asbury Chapel in Louisville, Kentucky. In May 1858 he was again transferred to Bethel AME Church in Baltimore, Maryland. He added 700 members to the Baltimore congregation. He also served pastorates at the Ebenezer AME Church and at the Brite Street AME Church in Baltimore.

Brown accompanied Bishops Payne and Wayman on their mission to Virginia and established St. John's AME Church in Norfolk. He was elected corresponding secretary of the Parent Home and Foreign Missionary Society in 1864 and successfully raised over $10,000 to establish AME churches and schools in the southern United States.

In recognition of his exceptional organizational abilities, Brown was elected an AME bishop at the General Conference in Washington, D.C., and was consecrated on 25 May 1868. His first assignment (1868–1872) was to the Seventh Episcopal District (South Carolina, Georgia, Florida, and Alabama). In 1871 he was instrumental in establishing Payne Institute (later Allen University) in South Carolina. He was assigned to the Sixth District (Tennessee, Arkansas, Louisiana, and Texas) from 1872 to 1876 and organized the West Texas, South Arkansas, West Tennessee, Denver (Colorado), Columbia (South Carolina), and North Georgia conferences as well as setting the groundwork for an AME college in Waco, Texas (later to become Paul Quinn College). In 1876–1880 he served the Third Episcopal District (Baltimore, Virginia, North Carolina, and South Carolina). From 1880 to 1884, he served the First District (Philadelphia, New York, New Jersey, and New England), and from 1884 to 1888 he served the Fourth Episcopal District (Missouri, Kansas, Illinois, Iowa, and California). His last assignment (1888–1892) was to the Fourth Episcopal District, which had been restructured to include Indiana, Illinois, Michigan, and Iowa.

In 1878 Brown organized and raised funds for the Liberian Mission Church. He was a supporter of the "Back to Africa" movement and a strong advocate for the ordination of women. He was a delegate to the World Methodist Ecumenical conference held in London, England, in 1881 and again in Washington, D.C., in 1891. He died in Washington, D.C.

Brown's nearly twenty-five years as a bishop had a profound impact on his denomination. Described by Bishop Henry Tanner as "more of an Episcopal than a Methodist by temperament," Brown's keen organizational skills and abilities as a fundraiser did much to foster the dynamic growth of AME churches throughout the United States, Africa, and the Caribbean.

• Major sources on Brown's life include R. R. Wright, Jr., *Bishops of the African Methodist Episcopal Church* (1963); Dorothy E. Hoover, *A Layman Looks with Love at Her Church* (1970); James T. Campbell, *Songs of Zion: The African Methodist Episcopal Church in the United States and South Africa* (1995); Stephen Ward Angell, *Bishop Henry McNeal Turner and African-American Religion in the South* (1992); and Katherine L. Dvorak, *An African-American Exodus: The Segregation of the Southern Churches* (1991).

STEPHEN D. GLAZIER

BROWN, Johnny (1 Sept. 1904–14 Nov. 1974), college football player and film actor, was born John Mack Brown in Dothan, Alabama, the son of John Henry Brown and Hattie McGillary. Brown's father owned a small retail shoe store in Dothan that brought the family only a small income. Johnny had to go to work at an early age selling newspapers. He spent much of his youth fishing, hunting, and playing football and other sports with his five brothers. Brown attended Dothan High School, where he earned letters in track, baseball, and football and was an all-state football player. In 1923 Brown earned a scholarship to play football all four years at the University of Alabama.

At Alabama, Brown earned a national reputation as a halfback and gained the nickname the "Dothan Antelope." He was noted for both his speed and his pass catching ability. With Brown in the backfield, the Crimson Tide became the first southern team to win the Rose Bowl, defeating Washington, 20–19, in 1926. Brown caught two touchdown passes in the game. Named to the 1926 All-America team at halfback, Brown graduated from Alabama the following spring. The next year Alabama was back in the Rose Bowl, this time with Brown as an assistant coach.

George Fawcett, an actor friend of Brown's, encouraged Brown to make a screen test with MGM while he was in California for the 1927 Rose Bowl. The successful test put Brown on a path to Hollywood stardom. Brown made ten films (melodramas and romances) with MGM before starring in the 1930 western *Billy the Kid*, an all-talking picture directed by King Vidor and costarring Wallace Beery. It remains Brown's most memorable film. Not then identified as a cowboy star, however, Brown also made features for MGM, Fox, Pathe, United Artists, RKO, Cosmopolitan, First National, Paramount, and other studios although he was not under contract to them. He was cast with such film greats as Greta Garbo, Mary Pickford, Joan Crawford, Mae West, Jean Harlow, Ralph Bellamy, Clark Gable, and Robert Young.

In 1935 Brown signed with Supreme Pictures to star in a series of eight westerns, including *Branded a Coward* (1935), *Rogue of the Range* (1936), *Everyman's Law* (1936), and *The Crooked Trail* (1936). The financial success of these films made Brown a prized commodity. Leaving Supreme in 1936, he signed with Republic Pictures to make another eight serials. In 1937 Brown teamed with John Wayne in *Born to the West* and Joel McCrea in *Wells Fargo*, both for Paramount Pictures. By this time he had added the *ny* to his first name and was making a half dozen films a year.

By the end of the 1930s Brown had earned a reputation as one of Hollywood's top ten money-making western actors, ranking with Gene Autry and Tim McCoy. Universal signed Brown to make two more serials in 1938 and 1939, but thereafter he made only features. Beginning with the 1939 film *Desperate Trails*, Brown teamed with sidekick Fuzzy Knight for the first of twenty-eight western films they made together. In the final seven they were joined by Tex Ritter. In 1943 Brown began a film association with Raymond Hatton, and until 1946 the two were familiar to moviegoers as, respectively, "Nevada Jack McKenzie" and his sidekick "Sandy Hopkins." Brown and Hatton costarred in forty-five western films until 1949. Although his films continued to make money, Brown was older and heavier, and in 1952 he had his last starring role in Monogram Picture's *Canyon Ambush*. He appeared in three more westerns as a guest star and finished his career in television cameo roles. His last film was Paramount's *Apache Uprising* in 1966.

Tall and athletic, Brown was a fine actor and rider. A testament to his ability as a dramatic actor is the forty other films in which he appeared. His westerns featured gunfighting and brawls and generally had better story lines than the typical "B" westerns. Like all Hollywood cowboys, Brown had a faithful steed, "Rebel." One of only a few film cowboys honored with a star on Hollywood Boulevard, Brown starred in 121 of the 127 westerns he made.

Brown had married his hometown sweetheart, Cornelia Foster, in 1927. They had four children. During Brown's movie career the family lived in a Beverly Hills mansion. Once his career was over and the children had left home, the Browns moved into a luxury apartment in Los Angeles. Brown spent his later life quietly with his wife. He continued to find pleasure in hobbies such as fishing, golf, tennis, and swimming. In 1957 Brown was inducted into the College Football Hall of Fame. In his last years Brown worked as a greeter at the Tail of the Cock restaurant in Hollywood. He died at the Motion Picture Country Home and Hospital in Woodland Hills, California.

• A short profile of Brown is in Ted Holland, *B Western Actors Encyclopedia: Facts, Photos and Filmographies of More Than 250 Familiar Faces* (1989); and Buck Rainey, *Heroes of the Range: Yesteryear's Saturday Matinee Movie Cowboys* (1987). An obituary is in the *New York Times*, 16 Nov. 1974.

BRIAN S. BUTLER

BROWN, John Young (28 June 1835–11 Jan. 1904), governor of Kentucky, was born in Elizabethtown, Kentucky, the son of Thomas Dudley Brown and Elizabeth Young. Brown's father, a trader and court clerk by profession, achieved local prominence as a politician and encouraged his son to pursue a career in politics. Following his graduation from Centre College in 1855, Brown studied law in Elizabethtown where he commenced law practice in 1856. He married Lucie Barbee in 1857. She died a year later, and in 1860 he married Rebecca Hart Dixon, a daughter of former U.S. senator Archibald Dixon. This marriage produced eight children.

Brown served in the U.S. House of Representatives as a Democrat from 1859 to 1861, but the federal occupation of Kentucky resulted in his declining support for the Union war effort. In 1867, he was again elected, but the House denied him a seat because of his alleged disloyalty to the Union as evidenced in a letter published in 1861 in which he advocated killing anyone who volunteered to fight for the North. He returned to the House in 1873 where he served until 1877. During this sojourn he opposed Reconstruction, delivering a major speech against the Civil Rights Act of 1875 in which he argued its unconstitutionality and so castigated Benjamin F. Butler (1818–1893) that he was censured by the House. (The next Congress revoked the censure.) He also unsuccessfully fought protectionism and federal taxation of tobacco and whiskey, and he opposed the merger of competing railroads.

An excellent lawyer, Brown retired from the House to practice law in Henderson, Kentucky, from 1879 to 1891, when he returned to politics by campaigning successfully for the Democratic nomination for governor. Nominated because he received support from western Kentucky agrarians, who supported railroad reform, and the Louisville & Nashville Railroad, which opposed it, in the general election Brown tried to focus on national political issues, including tariff reform and free coinage of silver. Ultimately, pressure from his Republican opponent forced him to endorse the newly proposed state constitution that was regarded as antirailroad in nature. Brown was elected, but not as comfortably as the new constitution, which was ratified by a margin of nearly three to one.

As governor, Brown endeavored to steer a middle course between the reform and antireform wings of his party but was less than successful. While he gained legislative approval of his proposed reforms of tax collection, state printing contracts, foreign corporations, lotteries, and asylums, he failed to secure legislation that could have strengthened the railroad commission, improved railroad safety, reformed prison management, toughened bank regulation, and abolished the newly created state parole board. More serious than his legislative failures were his political ones, which caused two of the most powerful corporations of the state, the Louisville & Nashville Railroad and the Mason & Foard Company, a railroad construction firm, to oppose his administration. He vetoed some of the bills intended to implement the new constitution because they had not received requisite majorities, and he criticized the attorney general and state auditor, causing some of his enemies within the party to seize leadership from him on several important state boards. The auditor's control of valuable patronage enabled him to become a more dominant force than Brown within the Democratic party. Brown's rather clumsy governorship contributed to a growing split within the Democratic party.

Brown's deteriorating political position and the divisions within the Democratic party manifested themselves in the 1895 gubernatorial campaign. Constitutionally unable to succeed himself, Brown unsuccessfully campaigned for Cassius M. Clay, Jr., who lost the Democratic party's nomination to the anti-Brown candidate, P. "Wat" Hardin. In part because Brown refused to endorse him, Hardin lost the general election to the Republican candidate, William O. Bradley, the first of his party to occupy the state house.

By 1896 Brown's political fortunes had not improved, and he lost a bid to return to the U.S. House of Representatives. In 1899, in keeping with his erratic record regarding railroad reform, Brown became reconciled with the Louisville & Nashville Railroad and ran as an Independent Democratic candidate for governor. He finished a poor third behind controversial reform Democrat William Goebel and a Republican. The disorder surrounding the election eventually led to Goebel's murder. Brown defended one of the men charged in the assassination at his first trial. Following his retirement from politics, he practiced law in Louisville and Henderson. He died in Henderson.

• There is no significant collection of Brown's papers. For an updated biographical sketch see Robert M. Ireland, "John Young Brown," in *Kentucky's Governors, 1792–1985*, ed. Lowell H. Harrison (1985). Some of Brown's most significant political controversies are covered in John Edward Wilz, "The 1895 Election: A Watershed in Kentucky Politics," *Filson Club History Quarterly* 37 (Apr. 1963): 117–36; Nicholas C. Burckel, "William Goebel and the Campaign for Railroad Regulation in Kentucky, 1888–1900," *Filson Club History Quarterly* 48 (Jan. 1974): 43–60; and Franklin T. Lambert, "Free Silver and the Kentucky Democracy, 1891–1895," *Filson Club History Quarterly* 53 (Apr. 1979): 145–76. For an account of his record as governor, see John E. Kleber, ed., *The Kentucky Encyclopedia* (1992). The *Congressional Record* yields significant glimpses into his congressional experiences, and the *Congressional Globe* covers the first part of his congressional career. Obituaries are in the *Louisville Courier-Journal* and the *New York Times*, 12 Jan. 1904.

ROBERT M. IRELAND

BROWN, Joseph (3 Dec. 1733–3 Dec. 1785), businessman and scientist, was born in Providence, Rhode Island, the son of James Brown, a merchant and West Indies trader, and Hope Power. Little is known about Joseph Brown's upbringing, except that his father died when he was five; his education was limited; and his scientific bent may have been encouraged by his brother-in-law, John Vanderlight, who had a medical degree from the University of Leiden, offered anatomy lessons, and was the principal pharmacist in Providence. In 1759 Brown married Elizabeth Power, a cousin. The couple had five children. Brown worked first as an assistant and then as a partner in the family firm run by his uncle, Obadiah Brown. When his uncle died in 1762, Brown and his brothers—Nicholas, John, and Moses—continued the business under the name Nicholas Brown and Company. Although their mercantile ventures were enormously successful, Brown's heart was not in this trade. When the firm dissolved in 1774, he took the opportunity to pursue scientific studies at greater length. He maintained his interests, however, in the family's spermaceti candle works in Tockwotton, a district in Providence, having served as its production manager since the 1750s; and he remained a partner in and technical consultant to "Furnace Hope," the iron manufactory built by the Browns in 1765 in Scituate, Rhode Island.

Brown is best known for his role in making observations of the transit of Venus across the sun's face in 1769. Astronomers around the world collaborated in this venture. By comparing transit measurements made at distant sites, scientists were able to determine the parallax of the sun and from this, the dimensions of the solar system. (The results were published in 1771 and 1772.) A description by Professor John Winthrop of Harvard of an earlier transit in 1761 was the source of Brown's interest. Working from a list of necessary equipment drawn up by the American Philosophical Society, and seeking the advice of Benjamin West, the almanac compiler, Brown ordered a reflecting telescope and other apparatus from London. He spent close to £100 sterling and donated a month of his own time and that of his servants to the project. West donated his astronomical and mathematical expertise and published the observations in *An Account of the Observation of Venus upon the Sun* (1769). Aside from newspaper reports, West's *Account* was the first to be printed. The collaboration of Brown and West was not a happy one, however. Although West publicly praised Brown's mechanical skills and generosity in the *Account*, he privately let it be known that Brown had taken advantage of the difference in their financial circumstances and had refused to subsidize the publication until West had inserted the aforementioned compliments. In 1780 Brown used the same telescopic apparatus to observe a solar eclipse—again with the help of West—but this time authored the report himself and published it in 1785 in the *Memoirs* of the American Academy of Arts and Sciences. This very minor piece of work was Brown's only publication. Like his business papers, it shows him to be vacillating and indecisive—not good qualities for a man of science or commerce.

Aside from astronomy, Brown was interested in chemistry, electricity, and meteorology. West remarked that Brown had as complete a set of electrical apparatus as any in America and enjoyed performing experiments with it. In his parlor, Brown kept a barometer and thermometer, which he also used to entertain guests.

Brown's technological and architectural endeavors earned him further recognition from his contemporaries. In 1772 he supervised the assembly of a new fire engine for Providence; and in 1780 he constructed pumps and an improved, Newcomen, steam engine to raise water out of the ore mines that supplied Furnace Hope. Between 1770 and 1785 Brown also helped to design several notable buildings in Providence, including the College Edifice, the First Baptist Meeting House, the Market House, his own house on South Main Street, and his brother John's house on Power Street.

In patriotic activities during the American Revolution, Brown's mechanical skills and sense of civic duty came together. In 1775 he helped to erect a beacon to be used to warn people in the countryside of the approach of British vessels and was appointed "master of the beacon." The Rhode Island General Assembly also asked him to inspect and manufacture saltpeter for the colony; had him conduct a field study to determine where entrenchments, cannons, and fire ships were necessary to defend the colony; and empowered him to execute his recommendations. Beginning in 1776 cannons were cast and bored at Furnace Hope. Brown played a leading role in adapting the furnace to war needs. Moreover, Brown represented Providence in the general assembly in 1781 and was an assistant to the governor in council from 1782 to 1784.

From 1769 until 1785, Brown served as a trustee of Rhode-Island College (chartered in 1764 and renamed Brown University in 1804 in honor of the benefactions of his nephew, Nicholas Brown). The Brown family was instrumental in the relocation of the college from rural Warren to Providence in 1770, in part because they pledged a good deal of money toward the building of the College Edifice. In addition, Brown promised to donate philosophical apparatus valued at £100. As a trustee, Brown was not aloof from student activities. According to the diary of Solomon Drowne (class of 1773), Brown conversed with students about scientific matters and performed experiments for them at the candle works. In 1784, when the college struggled to resume activities after the war, he volunteered to serve as professor of experimental philosophy without pay. He did not long hold this post. In November 1784 Brown suffered a stroke from which he never fully recovered. He died in Providence. Before he died, Brown was elected a member of the American Academy of Arts and Sciences, presumably, in recognition of his patronage of science in Providence, his efforts to invigorate science studies at Rhode-Island College, and perhaps also his technological and architectural pursuits.

• Papers pertaining to Brown (and some by him) are preserved in the John Carter Brown Library and John Hay Library, Brown University. Brown's only publication was "An Observation of a Solar Eclipse, October 27, 1780, at Providence," *Memoirs of the American Academy of Arts and Sciences* 1 (1785): 149–50. For biographical and genealogical information, see J. Walter Wilson, "Joseph Brown, Scientist and Architect," *Rhode Island History* 4 (1945): 67–79, 121–28; and Abby Isabel Bulkley, ed., *The Chad Brown Memorial* (1888). The best study of his business activities is James B. Hedges, *The Browns of Providence Plantations: Colonial Years* (1952). For his wartime duties, see John Russell Bartlett, ed., *Records of the Colony of Rhode Island and Providence Plantations in New England* (10 vols., 1856–1865). For his connections with Rhode-Island College, see Donald Fleming, *Science and Technology in Providence, 1760–1914* (1952), and Reuben A. Guild, *Life, Times, and Correspondence of James Manning and the Early History of Brown University* (1864). An obituary is in the *Providence Gazette and Country Journal*, 10 Dec. 1785.

SARA SCHECHNER GENUTH

BROWN, Joseph Emerson (15 Apr. 1821–30 Nov. 1894), U.S. senator, governor, and entrepreneur, was born at Long Creek in the Pickens District of South Carolina, the son of Mackey Brown and Sally Rice, farmers. The family moved to Union County in northern Georgia, where Brown spent most of his childhood and adolescence on the family farm. His formal education was meager until, at the age of nineteen, he left home to attend an academy in the Anderson District of South Carolina. Returning to Georgia, he taught school for a time to repay tuition charges, and he subsequently read law and was admitted to the Georgia bar in August 1845. During 1845–1846 he attended the Yale Law School but did not receive a degree. In 1847 Brown married Elizabeth Grisham, daughter of a prominent Baptist minister. The marriage produced seven children. Moderate and controlled in his public actions, Brown has been characterized by his biographer as a traditional, occasionally even harsh, husband and father.

Sober, industrious, conscientious, and thorough, Brown became known in northern Georgia as a "working man's lawyer." The reputation was one he retained, even as he built his personal fortune by successful real estate investments and, later in his life, by investments in coal and iron mines and in railroad companies.

Brown was elected to the Georgia Senate as a Democrat in 1849 and used his single term in office to build valuable political contacts within the state party. Though he himself owned only a handful of slaves and though he represented an area of Georgia in which large plantations were few, Brown emerged as a strong defender of slavery and an advocate of slavery's extension into the territories added to the United States at the end of the Mexican War. Recognized by the term's end as a leader among Democrats in the Georgia Senate, Brown curiously declined to seek reelection for a second term in 1851 and returned to his law practice and his growing real estate interests in Canton. He retained his political ties, however, serving as a presidential elector in 1852. In 1855 he was elected judge of the Blue Ridge District, comprising eleven counties in Georgia.

In 1857 the state's divided Democratic party sought an acceptable compromise candidate for governor, and Brown was nominated. He went on to win the election later that year, defeating the American party candidate, Benjamin H. Hill. Reelected in 1859, 1861, and 1863, Brown remained in office until allowed by President Andrew Johnson to resign on 25 June 1865, more than two months after Appomattox. He was often at odds with his legislature over currency policy and over his extension of the patronage to the state-owned Western & Atlantic Railroad. A strong supporter of President James Buchanan, he played little role in the southern Democrats' walkout from the party convention at Charleston in 1860 and both publicly and privately worried what secession portended for Georgia and the South. He backed John C. Breckinridge for the presidency in 1860, however, as a more acceptable alternative than either John Bell or Stephen A. Douglas. Abraham Lincoln's election converted Brown to secession, and he moved far ahead of his legislature, Georgia's secession convention, and his longtime political allies to pledge support to South Carolina and to proclaim Georgia's allegiance to the Confederacy. Even before hostilities formally commenced, he directed Georgia's militia to seize Fort Pulaski (at Savannah) and the Federal arsenal at Augusta.

Once hostilities began and the Confederate government at Richmond asserted its authority, Brown clashed often with the Confederate regime. He denounced conscription as unconstitutional, opposed suspension of the writ of habeas corpus, and generally opposed war measures that asserted even temporarily the authority of the central government at Richmond over the administrations of the separate states. By 1863 he had joined his old political ally Linton Stephens and Confederate vice president Alexander H. Stephens in urging the removal of Jefferson Davis as Confederate president. Brown called for a convention of the Confederate states to discuss peace terms, and his apparent willingness to negotiate an end to hostilities was so widely known that, after the battle of Atlanta in 1864, unsuccessful overtures for peace negotiations were made indirectly to his administration by Union general William T. Sherman, in an effort to separate Georgia from the Confederacy.

Brown was less a political theorist than a pragmatist, and 1865 saw him willing, as he later put it, to "agree with thine adversary quickly." Arrested at the end of the war and briefly imprisoned by Federal forces, he was quickly allowed to return to Georgia, where he urged cooperation with Johnson's program of presidential Reconstruction. His efforts brought the gratitude of Lincoln's successor and a full presidential pardon for Brown's wartime activities in September 1865. Though he continued to maintain his political ties and to act as informal adviser to Georgia's provisional governor, James Johnson, Brown returned in the autumn of 1865 to his law practice and his business interests.

By 1866 the growing power of the northern Radical Republicans and the failure of Johnson's Reconstruction program were apparent. Brown traveled to Washington, met with Republican leaders, and returned to Georgia urging his fellow southerners to ratify the Fourteenth Amendment and to accept black suffrage. Denounced by his former allies as an opportunist and a traitor to his state and region, he stood virtually alone among prominent prewar and wartime Georgia politicians in allying himself with the Reconstruction Republican party and in supporting the election of Republican Rufus B. Bullock as governor in 1868. Bullock sought to reward Brown with one of Georgia's two U.S. Senate seats; when the general assembly balked, Bullock offered instead appointment as chief justice of the Georgia Supreme Court. Brown accepted the appointment in 1868.

Though politically linked with the Republican party during Reconstruction, Brown never wholeheartedly supported the Radical Bullock regime. In Ulysses S. Grant's failure to carry Georgia in the presidential balloting of 1868, Brown realized that Republicans could only build a viable, lasting coalition by winning over moderate Democrats to their camp. Resigning as chief justice in 1870, he sought through his participation in the lease of the state-owned Western & Atlantic Railroad that fall to combine old-line moderate Democrats (including his former political opponent Hill) with pragmatic Republicans in an alliance both economically and politically beneficial. Brown apparently viewed the lease as a bridge to the reconciliation of Georgia's warring political camps.

As Brown expected, the Bullock regime in Georgia crumbled with the withdrawal of federal military support after 1870, and when Governor Bullock resigned and fled the state in October 1871, Brown supported James M. Smith, the Speaker of the Georgia House of Representatives, as his successor. (Smith won the governorship, serving until 1877.) In 1872 he endorsed Horace Greeley as the Liberal Republican and Democratic candidate for president, and though still often vilified in state Democratic papers for his Reconstruction political course, Brown was by the mid-1870s generally recognized as back within the Democratic fold.

Throughout the post-Reconstruction years, Brown pursued an active and lucrative law practice and, with his sons, managed his growing iron, coal, railroad, and real estate interests. He spoke frequently on public issues, opposing efforts to force equality in public accommodations and, as chair of the Atlanta school board, supporting racially separate public education.

In 1880 he was appointed to the U.S. Senate to succeed John Brown Gordon, who resigned. Reelected on pledges to advance the industrial and commercial as well as the agricultural interests of Georgia and to advocate the improvement of public education, Brown served until his retirement in 1890. In self-described poor health, he retired to his home in Atlanta, where he died.

• Many of Brown's papers were burned by his descendants during the 1930s, but important correspondence and other materials have survived in the Felix Hargrett Collection at the University of Georgia Library, Athens. Correspondence from and concerning Brown is also scattered among the papers of important state and national leaders of the 1850–1890 period, including Andrew Johnson, Ulysses S. Grant, and William Chandler. The full biography of Brown by Joseph H. Parks, *Joseph E. Brown of Georgia* (1977), supersedes earlier studies. In its treatment of Brown's political activities, Parks's biography also largely supersedes the accounts in the standard histories of Georgia Reconstruction: C. Mildred Thompson, *Reconstruction in Georgia* (1915); Alan Conway, *The Reconstruction of Georgia* (1966); and Elizabeth Studley Nathans, *Losing the Peace: Georgia Republicans and Reconstruction, 1865–1871* (1968). An obituary is in the *Atlanta Daily Constitution*, 1 Dec. 1894.

ELIZABETH STUDLEY NATHANS

BROWN, Josephine Chapin (20 Oct. 1887–25 Oct. 1976), public welfare administrator and social work educator, was born in Ogdensburg, New York, the daughter of Silas Edgar Brown, a physician and surgeon, and Mary Chapin. Josephine received her primary and secondary education in private schools at Ogdensburg and Utica and entered Bryn Mawr College in 1906. Shortly thereafter, Brown's family, in financial difficulty, moved to St. Paul, Minnesota. She dropped out of college and taught school, but, after two years, aided by gifts through the college, Brown reentered Bryn Mawr. She graduated in June 1913 with a B.A. in physics and biology.

For seven years after graduation Brown worked at one thing and another—teaching at an exclusive school near Bryn Mawr, then at a girl's reform-farm school at Sauk Center, Minnesota. Interested in farming, she took an extension course from the University of Wisconsin's School of Agriculture. She and a friend then tried unsuccessfully to manage a large farm in Idaho. Persisting, they turned to chicken farming in Minnesota.

Although this venture was more successful, in 1920 Brown began a long career in social work, first with the United Charities of St. Paul, then as executive secretary—the top job—of the Dakota County, Minnesota, Welfare Association. She acquired some formal social work training along the way by attending the Social Casework Institute at the New York School of Social Work.

In 1923 Brown became the associate field director for family welfare agencies affiliated with the Family Welfare Association of America in eight southern states. Joining her firsthand knowledge of farm life to her social work training and experience, she rapidly became a pioneer in rural social work, which she maintained should be represented by generalists rather than psychologically oriented urban caseworkers. In 1929 she took a year's leave of absence from her job to represent social work among economists and sociologists who were studying problems peculiar to agricultural occupations at the Social Science Research Council (SSRC). There she compiled and edited the SSRC publication, *Research in Rural Social Work—Scope and Method* (1932). In 1933 the Family Welfare Association of America published her *Rural Community and Social Case Work*.

With the onset of the Great Depression in 1929, social welfare administrators became important policy advocates and government officials. In April 1933 President Franklin Roosevelt appointed former social worker Harry L. Hopkins to head the new Federal Emergency Relief Administration (FERA). Brown had known Hopkins and his deputy, Aubrey Williams, when all three worked in the South. In April 1934, following an outburst of charges that relief rolls were swollen with ineligible persons, Brown was asked to head a newly established social service section within FERA.

At age forty-seven—a career woman who never married—Brown was subdued in appearance and manner. She was friendly yet firm—virtues of considerable merit in one whose main duty was to supervise the twenty or so field-workers whose job was to keep the states in conformity with FERA rules and regulations.

Equally important, Brown was creative. In April 1935, backed by Hopkins and Williams and encouraged by the theories of the "functional" school of social casework, Brown made a sharp break with private agency practices. She pointed out that private welfare agencies dealt with "problem" families in which financial relief was deemed incidental. In public welfare agencies, she emphasized, "financial relief was the common problem." The proper function of the public welfare agency was, therefore, to determine eligibility for assistance—to conduct a means test. "In the administration of unemployment relief," she asserted, "we are creating a new type of social work and of public welfare . . . adapting whatever is applicable from the rest of social work and adding the results of our own experience in standards, methods, training, and terminology."

Despite her belief that public welfare agencies must develop their own priorities, Brown saw to it that large sums of FERA training money were channeled into special short-term institutes and courses that were offered by existing schools of social work. With the support of Katherine Lenroot, chief of the U.S. Children's Bureau, Brown also strongly endorsed both undergraduate and graduate study offered in sociology departments of state colleges and universities. Brown's separatist approach to public welfare service was resented and opposed by social work educators and some professional organizations. They argued that Brown was not an educator and therefore was not qualified to project her theories onto a profession in which relief-giving had been shunted aside in order to "treat" troubled families.

After certain public welfare programs (e.g., Old Age Assistance and Aid to Dependent Children) were incorporated into the Social Security Act of 1935 as a permanent federal-state function, Brown continued to work for the Works Progress Administration (WPA) until 1939. During 1937–1939, while the WPA was winding down, Brown wrote an important comprehensive history, *Public Relief: 1929–1939* (1940). Its continuing significance was indicated by a reprinting in 1971.

Meanwhile, in the 1930s Brown, a Presbyterian, converted to Catholicism. In 1939 she began to teach public welfare policy and administration at the School of Social Service, Catholic University of America, rising to associate professor. Her M.A. from Catholic University in 1943 was in sociology, which at that time served as a qualifying degree for professional social work practice in many colleges and universities.

During World War II, Brown was active in promoting day care centers for the care of children whose mothers had entered the labor force, and she served on committees such as the steering committee of the District of Columbia Draft Aid Center. Over the years she delivered scores of papers on public relief at meetings of social workers, many of which were published in the annual reports of the National Conference of Social Work or in journals such as *The Family*, *The Survey*, and *Catholic Charities Review*.

At age sixty-five Brown retired from Catholic University and left the Washington, D.C., area for Princeton, New Jersey, where Katherine Lenroot and other friends lived. Housekeeping, she reported to Bryn Mawr with an "!" in 1961, had become her chief occupation. Glaucoma and cataracts having appeared even before she retired, she was unable to continue her professional activities. Brown died in Princeton.

• Brown's papers during her tenure with FERA and WPA are in the National Archives. Records relating to her academic career are in the archives of the Catholic University of America and the School of Social Work at that institution. See also Brown's personal history statement for the WPA, filed in the Office of Personnel Management, Workforce Records Management Division, Washington, D.C., and the 1961 Bryn Mawr Alumnae Survey, Bryn Mawr College Archives. An evaluation of her contribution to rural social work is Joseph Davenport III and Judith A. Davenport, "Josephine Brown's Classic Book Still Guides Rural Social Work," *Social Casework* 65 (Sept. 1984): 413–19. See also Emilia E. Martinez-Brawley, "Josephine Chapin Brown," in the *Biographical Dictionary of Social Welfare in America*, ed. Walter I. Trattner (1983), which contains a complete bibliography; and Blanche D. Coll, *Safety Net: Welfare and Social Security, 1929–1979* (1995). A short obituary is in "Town Topics," filed with the 1961 Bryn Mawr Alumnae Survey, 16 Mar. 1961.

BLANCHE D. COLL

BROWN, Junius Flagg (3 Aug. 1902–14 Oct. 1970), psychologist, was born in Denver, Colorado, the son of Harry Kilbourne Brown, an investment banker, and Susan Gaylord. After receiving a B.S. from Yale University (1925), Brown spent two years at the University of Berlin working under Wolfgang Köhler, Max Wertheimer, and Kurt Lewin. Adopting the Gestalt perspective of his teachers, Brown discovered what he termed the transposition phenomenon—how changing the size of a moving object and its surroundings changes its perceived velocity. He also studied physics and the philosophy of science, which he used in promoting the Gestaltists' antimechanistic "field theory" as a philosophically superior approach to psychology.

From 1927 to 1929 Brown completed his graduate studies in psychology at Yale (Ph.D., 1929). While there, in 1928, he married Grace Higgins, a fellow student in Berlin who had accompanied him to New Haven; they had two children. In 1929–1930 a National Research Council fellowship helped Brown return with his wife to Berlin. There he again collaborated with Köhler in studies on the determinants of perceived velocity, which Brown reported in a series of articles in the Gestaltists' journal *Psychologische Forschung* between 1931 and 1933. Of equal significance, Brown introduced English-language readers to Kurt Lewin's research on motivation, and to the holistic epistemology upon which it was based.

Brown taught at the University of Colorado for two years (1930–1932) and moved to the University of Kansas after the depression led to the elimination of his position. At Kansas he was a renowned lecturer on abnormal and social psychology, having shifted the focus of his research to these subjects by 1932. Asserting that "the future of world civilization depends on obtaining a knowledge of social psychology," Brown's *Psychology and the Social Order* (1936) presented an all-encompassing analysis of social behavior based on Marxism, Freudianism, and Lewin's field theory. In this popular text, Brown used Gestalt principles to evaluate competing forms of government; for most citizens, he concluded, socialism was preferable to fascism and was likely to surpass capitalism as the depression wore on. He also analyzed the implicit psychology of various social philosophies and concluded that Marxism best represented the dynamics of social change.

Brown's interest in social psychology developed simultaneously with his political radicalization, aided by a summer 1933 trip to Berlin and Moscow. Following his return, the Communist Party USA advised him against formal membership, fearing he would be fired if state legislators launched an anti-Communist purge; instead he became a supporter, host for visiting Communist speakers, and contributor to antifascist causes and organizations—including the Society for the Psychological Study of Social Issues and the journal *Science and Society*.

Abnormal psychology provided Brown with another opportunity to demonstrate his skill at bridging intellectual disciplines and creating opportunities for himself at the boundaries of professions. He began in 1935 by attending a weekly psychiatry seminar at the Menninger Clinic, became a part-time research associate there, and by 1939 had become the clinic's first chief psychologist. Following Kurt Lewin, Brown embraced Freudian theory for its ability to be integrated with Gestalt psychology and spent a sabbatical year (1938–1939) undergoing psychoanalysis with Franz Alexander in Chicago and La Jolla, California. Soon Brown had established himself as a respected interpreter of Freud for psychologists and an interpreter of experimental psychology and Marxism for psychiatrists. He also brought news of the Menningers and neo-Freudianism to the readers of the *Nation* and the *New Republic* and wrote a popular college text from a Gestaltist-Freudian viewpoint (*The Psychodynamics of Abnormal Behavior* [1940]).

Throughout his life Brown was afflicted with alcoholism (at Kansas he was remembered for giving "better lectures while intoxicated than almost any other professor did while sober"). In 1942–1943, with a divorce pending, he was hospitalized for acute psychosis, first in La Jolla and then in Chicago, Kenilworth, England, and Topeka, Kansas. In January 1944 he moved to New York City, married Rosabel Velde (they divorced in 1946), and spent the following academic year teaching at Connecticut College. Moving to Los Angeles in 1945, Brown became a psychotherapist, with occasional work as a university lecturer and researcher (he contributed to the influential psychological analysis of fascism and authoritarianism, *The Authoritarian Personality*, ed. Theodore W. Adorno [1950]). He married Helene Sparling in 1948 and retired in 1959 because of poor health. He had no children with his second and third wives. He died in Beaumont, California.

In the 1930s and 1940s Brown exercised considerable influence in psychology, psychiatry, and among liberal intellectuals. Within psychology he was first known as an effective proponent of the Gestalt school. Later, his *Psychology and the Social Order* inspired many, such as Frank Fearing and Arthur Staats, to study social and political problems, while his clinical writing helped confer academic respectability to Freudianism. Within psychiatry, Brown was well received by liberal neo-Freudians such as Karl Menninger, who praised the "utter courage [and] fine spirit" of his 1936 text, calling it "immensely significant, not only to psychoanalysts, but to everyone who believes in the possibility of describing in a scientific way . . . the behavior of human beings" (*Psychoanalytic Quarterly* 6 [1937]: 131–32). Equally significant was Brown's participation (with David Rapaport) in the Menningers' midcentury transformation of the clinical psychologist's role—from a tester of intelligence to a coordinator of research and a full member of the clinical treatment team.

As Kurt Lewin noted in his review of *Psychology and the Social Order* (*American Journal of Psychology* 51 [1938]: 603–4), Brown's offering of a sweeping social analysis rather than a specific research agenda ultimately limited his influence on psychology; his abrupt departure from academics and his arrogance and bluntness also contributed. Replying to leftist critics of his work, for example, Brown wrote "I am sick to death of having 'marxists' tell me I am doing fine work as long as I preach 'party line' and am all sorts of a Jackass when I don't" (*Psychologists League Journal* [Mar. 1937]: 10). And as he explained in his autobiography, Brown spent the 1930s supported by his grandfather's trust fund, looking down on his academic colleagues for being "falsely convinced of their importance. . . . Most of the members of the American Psychological Association . . . originated in some jerkwater college [and were] rejected misfits there, who somehow got on to the state or private universities and became psychologists."

• Brown left no papers, but an unpublished autobiography and book prospectus are in private hands. The Yale University Alumni Office and Psychology Department have biographical records and correspondence, and the Wolfgang Köhler Papers at the American Philosophical Society contain a few relevant letters. Brown articulated his relationship to the work of Kurt Lewin in his two texts and in articles such as "The Methods of Kurt Lewin in the Psychology of Action and Affection," *Psychological Review* 36 (1929): 200–221; "The Field-Theoretical Approach in Social Psychology," *Social Forces* 15 (1937): 482–84; "Psychoanalysis, Topological Psychology and Experimental Psychopathology," *Psychoanalytic Quarterly* 6 (1937): 227–37; and "Individual, Group, and Social Field," *American Journal of Sociology* 44 (1939): 858–67. The increasing pessimism of Brown's amalgam of Marxism and Freudianism was reflected in his articles "Freud vs. Marx: Real and Pseudo-Problems Distinguished," *Psychiatry* 2 (1938): 249–55, and "Social Science and Psychiatry," *American Journal of Orthopsychiatry* 11 (1941): 628–34, and in an unfinished book, "Barriers to Utopia" (manuscript not preserved); his initial popularity with Marxist academics can be seen in his first book's review by Richard L. Schanck in *Science and Society* 1 (1937): 429. His skill at anticipating new, interdisciplinary trends can be seen in his having published articles in the inaugural volumes of the journals *Bulletin of the Menninger Clinic*, *Philosophy of Science*, *Psychometrika*, and *Science and Society*. For a modern appreciation of Brown's perceptual research, see Hans Wallach, *On Perception* (1976). Two recent appraisals of Brown's place in the history of psychology by Henry L. Minton are "J. F. Brown's Social Psychology of the 1930s: A Historical Antecedent to the Contemporary Crisis in Social Psychology," *Personality and Social Psychology Bulletin* 10 (1984): 31–42, and "J. F. Brown: Unsung Hero or Misguided Prophet in the History of Political Psychology?" *Political Psychology* 9 (1988): 165–73.

BENJAMIN HARRIS

BROWN, Lawrason (29 Sept. 1871–26 Dec. 1937), physician, was born in Baltimore, Maryland, the son of William Judson Brown, a prosperous commission merchant, and Mary Louise Lawrason. He attended the public schools of Baltimore, received his preparatory education at Baltimore City College, and graduated with an A.B. in 1895 from Johns Hopkins University, where he distinguished himself as both a student and an athlete. In the fall of 1895 he joined the third class at Johns Hopkins Medical School, which had set a new standard for excellence in medical education since it had opened two years earlier. Near the end of his third year in medical school, Brown was diagnosed with pulmonary tuberculosis and directed to a sanatorium established by Edward Livingston Trudeau in the Adirondack Mountains near Saranac Lake, New York.

Brown spent a year taking the open-air treatment for tuberculosis, which Trudeau had pioneered in the United States, and fell under the magnetic professional influence of the institution's founder. After Brown had restored his health sufficiently, he returned to Johns Hopkins to finish his last year of medical school, receiving an M.D. in 1900. He then left Baltimore and returned to Saranac Lake, which would be his home for the rest of his life. For his first year with Trudeau as a physician, Brown served as assistant resident physician in the sanatorium. He was then promoted to resident physician, holding this position from 1901 through 1912. In 1914 he married Martha Lewis Harris; they had no children.

During his twelve-year tenure as the chief physician in the Trudeau Sanatorium, Brown did much to bring efficient order and clear purpose to the activities of both staff and patients. He developed a system for keeping detailed records on all patients during their time at the sanatorium, and he also inaugurated a program of gathering follow-up data on patients who had left the institution. Brown made great use of the information he gleaned from these records; during his term as sanatorium resident he published more than forty articles based on careful study of data collected from systematic observation of tuberculosis patients. One of Brown's colleagues, David R. Lyman, offered the following assessment of this work:

> The work of collecting and making available to the world the wealth of information found in these medical histories was perhaps Lawrason Brown's greatest contribution to the welfare of mankind, for, in addition to helping to a clearer understanding of tuberculosis, he changed our whole conception of a sanatorium from that of a mere home where patients lived in the open air to that of a well organized centre where patients are given the highest type of medical and social aid, and where, through constant stimulation of its staff to clinical and laboratory research, the quality of this service is undergoing continual improvement. (p. 364)

Brown resigned from his full-time post at the Trudeau Sanatorium in 1912 and established a private practice in Saranac Lake, centered on the treatment of tuberculosis patients. He also remained a powerful presence at the Trudeau Sanatorium as a consulting and visiting physician until ill health forced him to give up even his part-time official position at the sanatorium in 1929. Even after he severed his formal ties, he maintained an active interest in the affairs of this institution. Throughout his career Brown struggled against poor health that arose primarily from tuberculosis but also included a skin affliction that often made it impossible for him to sleep—and forced him to avoid wearing shoes for long periods. His friend Lyman remembered, though, that Brown handled his medical difficulties with courage and good humor.

In addition to building a large private practice and consulting at the Trudeau Sanatorium, Brown remained a prolific scholar and author after 1912, building his bibliography to more than 150 entries. Perhaps his most important contribution as an author was a clearly written and widely read patient handbook, *Rules for Recovery from Pulmonary Tuberculosis*, which first appeared in 1915 and went through several editions. He was also among the early and influential proponents of the use of X-ray technology in the diagnosis of tuberculosis.

Brown was active in several professional societies and held the presidency of both the National Tuberculosis Association (1922–1923) and the American Sanatorium Association (1919–1923). He received numerous awards and honors in recognition of his achievements. In 1933 the National Tuberculosis Association conferred on him its highest award, the Trudeau Medal. Brown died at his home in Saranac Lake from complications associated with the disease against which he had battled both personally and professionally for almost four decades.

• Brown coauthored *Intestinal Tuberculosis*, with Homer L. Sampson (1926) and *The Lung and Tuberculosis*, with Fred H. Heise (1931). S. Adolphus Smith included a short biographical chapter on Brown in *A History of the National Tuberculosis Association: The Anti-Tuberculosis Movement in the United States* (1922), pp. 456–60, with a bibliography of Brown's writings through the early 1920s. David R. Lyman wrote a vivid biographical tribute on the occasion of Brown's death, *American Review of Tuberculosis* 37 (1938): 361–66. An obituary is in the *New York Times*, 27 Dec. 1937.

JON M. HARKNESS

BROWN, Lawrence (3 Aug. 1907–5 Sept. 1988), jazz trombonist, was born in Lawrence, Kansas, the son of John M. Brown, a minister in the African Methodist Episcopal church, and Maggie (maiden name unknown), who played pump organ for the church. When Brown was six the family moved to Oakland, California, where he learned piano; tuba, which he began to play in the Oakland public school system; and violin. He also briefly experimented with alto saxophone before taking up trombone, to which he became intensely devoted after the Browns relocated across the bay to San Francisco.

The family moved to Pasadena, and around 1924 Brown enrolled at Pasadena Junior College for music and premedical studies. Risking his father's disapproval, Brown dropped out of school, moved to North Pasadena on his own, and went into jazz as a member of Charlie Echols's seven-piece band at a dime-a-dance venue, the 401 Ballroom, around 1927. From 1928 to 1931 he worked with the bands of Paul Howard, Curtis Mosby, and Les Hite. The affiliation with Mosby included acting in and recording the soundtrack for director King Vidor's movie *Hallelujah!* (1929) and performing at Mosby's Apex clubs in Los Angeles (later renamed the Club Alabam) and San Francisco. But these affiliations were not continuous, because Brown and drummer (soon to be vibraphonist) Lionel Hampton were also contracted individually to Frank Sebastian's Cotton Club in Los Angeles, where they played under Mosby, Howard, and others, most notably Louis Armstrong with Hite's big band in 1931.

In the spring of 1932 Brown joined Duke Ellington's big band, with which he remained, except for a brief absence in 1943, for two decades. His career followed the leader's grueling schedule of far-ranging touring. In 1934 or 1935 Brown married Freddi Washington, an actress. They divorced, and at an unknown point he married Dorothea Bundrant, whom he also subsequently divorced. Obituaries do not mention children.

Brown became one of Ellington's principal soloists, featured on recordings of "The Sheik of Araby," "Ducky Wucky" (both 1932), "Slippery Horn" (1933), "Stompy Jones" (1934), "Braggin' in Brass," "Rose of the Rio Grande" (both 1938), "Across the Track Blues" (1940), "Come Sunday" on the *Black, Brown and Beige* suite (as premiered at Carnegie Hall in Jan. 1943), and his own compositions "Golden Cress" and "On a Turquoise Cloud" (both 1947). He may be seen and heard as a soloist in the film short *Salute to Duke Ellington* (1950).

In March 1951 Brown left Ellington to work in saxophonist Johnny Hodges's small band, with which he recorded the album *Used to Be Duke* (1954). In the spring of 1955 he began to work as a freelancer in New York City, but a year later, when trombonist Warren Covington resigned as a studio musician for CBS, Brown took his place. He rejoined Ellington in May 1960. Notable recordings include "The Mooche" on *Duke Ellington's Greatest Hits*, from a concert in Paris in 1963, and the album *Popular Duke Ellington* (1966). He also was featured again in a film short, *Playback: Duke Ellington* (1963).

Brown left Ellington and retired from music in 1970. Moving to Washington, D.C., he was appointed by President Richard Nixon to the advisory committee of the Kennedy Center. In 1974 he settled in the Los Angeles area and worked as a recording agent for Local 47 of the musicians' union. He had a stroke and not long afterward died in Los Angeles.

From writer Richard O. Boyer comes a description of a quiet and reserved personality that was not the norm for Ellington's band:

> Brown . . . used to play trombone for Aimee Semple McPherson in the Angelus Temple in Los Angeles, a fact which disturbs some of his admirers, who, with the reverse morality of jazz fanciers, would prefer that he had begun his career in a sporting house. While his mates riot in the dressing room, Brown may say with quiet pride, "I do not curse, drink, or smoke." Not long ago he said that if he couldn't become a doctor, he would be a dentist or an undertaker. (quoted in Tucker, p. 223)

Brown explained on several occasions that he wanted to play trombone in a pretty manner, as if it were a cello, not in the blustery sliding fashion popular in early New Orleans jazz. Hence in his first tenure with Ellington he was featured on romantic melodies, and he also favored clear-toned, nimble lines, as heard on "The Sheik of Araby." From 1961 to the end of his career he supplied a third type of solo for Ellington's orchestra, playing emotive, vocalized, plunger-muted melodies in the manner created by his predecessors Bubber Miley and Tricky Sam Nanton.

• A tape and transcript of an interview for the Smithsonian Institution taken by Patricia Willard in June 1976 are held at the Institute of Jazz Studies, Newark, N.J. Published interviews are by Valerie Wilmer, "Lawrence Brown," *Jazz Monthly*, Apr. 1965, pp. 18–21; Stanley Dance, *The World of Duke Ellington* (1970; repr. 1981), pp. 117–25; and Lowell D. Holmes and John W. Thomson, *Jazz Greats: Getting Better with Age* (1986). See also Duke Ellington, *Music Is My Mistress* (1973), p. 122; Albert McCarthy, *Big Band Jazz* (1974); Graham Colombé, "How Do They Age So Well?, no. 4: 'Lawrence, Dicky and Vic,'" *Jazz Journal*, Aug. 1976, pp. 4–6, 8; John Chilton, *Who's Who of Jazz: Storyville to Swing Street*, 4th ed. (1985); Gunther Schuller, *The Swing Era: The Development of Jazz, 1930–1945* (1989); Mark Tucker, ed., *The Duke Ellington Reader* (1993); and Kurt Dietrich, *Duke's Bones: Ellington's Great Trombonists* (1995). Obituaries are in the *New York Times*, 9 Sept. 1988, and *Jazz Journal International*, Nov. 1988, pp. 16–17.

BARRY KERNFELD

BROWN, Letitia Christine Woods (24 Oct. 1915–3 Aug. 1976), historian, was born in Tuskegee, Alabama, the daughter of Matthew Woods and Evadne Adams, professors. Her maternal grandfather, Lewis Adams, was born a slave and after the Civil War was instrumental in establishing the Tuskegee Normal School in 1881. Letitia's parents both taught at Tuskegee Institute, continuing the family's commitment to education. Letitia attended Tuskegee Institute High School and graduated with a B.S. from Tuskegee Institute in 1935. In 1937 she completed her M.A. at Ohio State University. While working on her advanced degree at Radcliffe College, she married Theodore E. Brown, a labor economist who later worked for the Agency for International Development in the U.S. Department of State. After raising two children and becoming involved in community projects in Mount Vernon, New York, she attended Harvard University, which awarded her a Ph.D. in 1966.

As a historian, Letitia Woods Brown sought to educate people, in a variety of forums, about the African-American experience and race relations. Her career as a teacher began in 1935 when she taught in the segregated Macon County school system in Alabama. She then returned to Tuskegee, where she taught from 1937 to 1940. From 1940 to 1945 she was an instructor at another black college, LeMoyne College in Memphis, and from 1961 to 1970 she taught at Howard

University, where she served on several committees, including the committee to establish the Department of Afro-American Studies. In 1968 she became a Fulbright professor in Australia at Monash University and Australia National University. After brief teaching stints at Georgetown University and Goucher College, in 1971 she became the only full-time black faculty member in the College of Arts and Sciences at George Washington University.

Throughout her career, she taught courses in U.S. history and African-American history. At George Washington University, she promoted interracial educational experiences by encouraging graduate students from George Washington and Howard Universities to take courses at both institutions. While at George Washington, Brown also helped develop a course on the history of the District of Columbia. Emphasizing local rather than federal history, the course was a model for other interdisciplinary classes within the university.

Brown also taught outside the traditional classroom setting. In 1961 she instructed the first group of Peace Corps volunteers, eventually assigned to Ghana. For teacher in-service projects in Maryland and Virginia, she helped develop educational materials on blacks and other minorities. In 1972–1973 she served as the only historian on the National Assessment of Educational Progress's panel that set objectives for congressionally mandated tests for precollegiate students in social studies. Brown also was a professor at the Federal Executive Institute (1970–1973), after which she conducted training programs for the Federal Executive Institute, including the Department of Agriculture.

Brown's writing reflected her interest in reaching audiences beyond academe and her commitment to studying the local history of the District of Columbia. With coauthor Elsie M. Lewis, Brown wrote *Washington from Banneker to Douglass, 1791–1870* and *Washington in the New Era, 1870–1970*, which accompanied a two-part exhibition on African Americans at the National Portrait Gallery, Smithsonian Institution, in Washington, D.C., 1971–1972. Her major work, *Free Negroes in the District of Columbia, 1790–1846*, was published in 1972. Historian Benjamin Quarles said of the work: "In language as concise and conclusive as the court records she has searched, Professor Brown traces the ways—many of them novel—in which blacks in the District moved from slavery to freedom." Brown's other writing included an essay on residential patterns of African Americans in the District of Columbia and an article entitled "Why and How the Negro in History," published in the fall 1969 issue of the *Journal of Negro Education*.

Brown also promoted awareness of African-American history and racial issues through her work in the local community, on public history projects, and at international history conferences. As vice chair of the Joint Committee on Landmarks of the National Capital, Brown broadened the committee's interpretation of its criteria for designating landmarks by promoting the recognition of sites important to the history of African-American residents, which had been ignored by previous committees. As consultant to the Capitol Historical Society, she advocated the inclusion of the contributions of many groups, including the slaves who built the structure, in the historical narrative of the Capitol. She served on the Advisory Board of the Schlesinger Library on the History of Women in America at Radcliffe College and helped the library initiate the Black Women Oral History Project, which eventually interviewed seventy-two African-American women and published the transcripts in ten volumes in 1990. Her work with the Bicentennial Committee on International Conferences of Americanists led to the African Regional American Studies Conference in Lagos, Nigeria, in 1976. She served on the Advisory Committee on Historical Research for the Columbia Historical Society, helping it become more knowledgeable of local African-American history, and was a cofounder of the annual conference on Washington, D.C., Historic Studies. Her other professional affiliations included membership on the executive board of the National Humanities Institute at Yale University; the National Archives Advisory Council; and the review board of the American Historical Association, which oversaw the restructuring of that organization in the early 1970s.

Brown died of cancer at her home in Washington, D.C. Throughout her life, she used her expertise as a historian both in academe and in public arenas to increase awareness of the history of African Americans in the United States. She encouraged the reinterpretation of U.S. history both locally and nationally to include the historical experience of blacks, and she helped redefine the ways in which that history was conceptualized. Brown saw herself as "both historian and futurist. I suppose I shall continue to grapple with it—with a growing awareness that the way we organize and present data helps shape the way people think, that how we teach is as important as what we teach."

• Some of Brown's papers are in the Special Collections at the Melvin Gelman Library, George Washington University, and the Radcliffe College Archives, which include an article by Brown, "Something for Me, My Family, the Race, and Mankind," *Radcliffe College Quarterly* (Mar. 1974): 17–19. For Roderick French's tribute at her memorial service, see "Letitia Woods Brown, 1915–1976," *Records of the Columbia Historical Society of Washington, D.C.* 50 (1980): 522–24. Obituaries are in the *New York Times* and the *Washington Post*, 5 August 1976.

NORALEE FRANKEL

BROWN, Lew (10 Dec. 1893–5 Feb. 1958), popular-song lyricist, was born Louis Brownstein in Odessa, in Ukraine (parents' names unknown). At the age of five he came to the United States with his family, settling first in New Haven, Connecticut. The family then moved to New York City, where Brown attended DeWitt Clinton High School. At sixteen, Brown worked briefly as a lifeguard at Rockaway Beach, at the same time scribbling out parodies of and original lyrics for popular songs. His first break came when a publisher paid him $7 for "Please Don't Take My Lovin' Man Away," which was first sung by Belle Baker. Soon, publishers were employing him to "improve" the new songs submitted to them. One of the songs on which Brown is said to have worked was the absurd ditty "Yes, We Have No Bananas," which Eddie Cantor made into a hit in 1923.

Brown began a collaboration with the composer Albert Von Tilzer, achieving his first popular triumph in 1912 with "I'm the Lonesomest Gal in Town," followed by "I May Be Gone for a Long, Long Time" (1917), which was interpolated into the show *Hitchy-Koo,* "Give Me the Moonlight, Give Me the Girl" (1917), "Oh, By Jingo" (1919), sung in *Linger Longer Letty,* and "Dapper Dan" (1921).

Brown entered a partnership with the songwriter Ray Henderson in 1922 and that same year achieved two successes: "Georgette" and "Humming." The two men teamed up with Buddy DeSylva in 1925, and until 1931 they formed an outstanding songwriting trio. The three men worked so closely with each other that one could not determine who contributed what to the music and lyrics. They wrote the scores for many noteworthy Broadway musicals, starting with *George White's Scandals of 1925.* "Black Bottom," in the *Scandals of 1926,* inaugurated a new dance craze. The same show included "The Birth of the Blues," which won phenomenal acclaim and popularity. *Good News* of 1927, a college musical, contained "The Varsity Drag," generator of another dance vogue, and "The Best Things in Life Are Free." One song hit after another followed, among them "You're the Cream in My Coffee" from *Hold Everything!* (1928), "Button Up Your Overcoat" and "My Lucky Star" from *Follow Thru* (1929), and "Good for You, Bad for Me" and "Wasn't It Beautiful While It Lasted?" from *Flying High* (1930), a show about airmail aviators. "Together," issued as an independent piece, remained popular for some years after its first publication in 1928. Their celebrated sentimental ballad "Sonny Boy" (1928) was a favorite of Al Jolson's. Around 1928–1929 Brown, Henderson, and DeSylva were responsible for five shows playing at the same time on Broadway: *Good News, Manhattan Mary, Three Cheers, Follow Thru,* and *George White's Scandals.* They also contributed songs to the motion pictures *Say It with Songs* (1929), *Follow the Leader* (1930), and *Just Imagine* (1930). A motion picture based on their professional lives, *The Best Things in Life Are Free,* was produced in 1956, featuring their most celebrated compositions. Fifteen years later, Stephen Sondheim imitated their style for the song "Broadway Baby," heard in *Follies.*

After DeSylva's departure, Brown and Henderson stayed together for some three more years, writing three Broadway successes: *Scandals of 1931, Hot-Cha* (1932), and *Strike Me Pink* (1933). *Scandals,* the most noteworthy of the three, included five smash hits. Two of these were "Life Is Just a Bowl of Cherries," performed by Ethel Merman, and "This Is the Missus," sung by Rudy Vallee. Recording history was made when Bing Crosby and the Boswell Sisters sang not just one or two, but all of the *Scandals* hits on a single 12-inch Brunswick disc.

Calling All Stars (1934), which Brown produced with Harry Akst, was a failure, and Brown quickly departed for Hollywood, where he worked as a film producer and wrote songs for movies, among them "Baby, Take a Bow" in *Stand Up and Cheer* (1934), a film that rocketed Shirley Temple to fame; "Life Begins When You're in Love" in *The Music Goes Round* (1936); "The Lady Dances" in *Strike Me Pink* (1936); "That Old Feeling" in *New Faces of 1937* (1937); and "Don't Sit under the Apple Tree" in *Private Buckaroo* (1942). Brown also supplied the lyrics in English for the "Beer Barrel Polka" (1934). The "Beer Barrel Polka" and "Don't Sit under the Apple Tree" were favored songs among U.S. soldiers during World War II.

Other of Brown's more noted song hits include "Last Night on the Back Porch I Loved Her Best of All" (1923), "Seven or Eleven (My Dixie Pair O' Dice)" (1923), "Then I'll Be Happy" (1925), and "I'd Climb the Highest Mountain" (1926). At the end of the 1930s Brown estimated that he had worked alone on or assisted in the writing of about 7,000 songs. In 1939 he returned to Broadway with the production of *Yokel Boy,* which contained the song "Comes Love." In 1941 he produced *Crazy with the Heat.* Twice married, he had two children by his first wife. He died of a heart attack in his New York City apartment.

Brown's most significant contributions to popular music were made in the 1920s when he, DeSylva, and Henderson were collaborators. During the years of their partnership no other songwriters produced more hits than they did. Although Henderson's music was rarely more than competent, the lyrics of Brown and DeSylva continue to be admired for their diversity of inventive phrase and rhyme schemes and their imaginative figures of speech. In 1963 "The Birth of the Blues" was one of sixteen songs that ASCAP named to the all-time hit parade for the first fifty years of its existence.

• The best of the skimpy sources for details on Brown's life and activities are David Ewen's *All the Years of American Popular Music* (1977); Philip Furia's *The Poets of Tin Pan Alley* (1990); and the obituary in the *New York Times,* 6 Feb. 1958. Facts about individual songs are supplied in David Ewen's *American Popular Songs: From the Revolutionary War to the Present* (1966). Also useful are Sigmund Spaeth's *A History of Popular Music in America* (1948) and Mark White's *"You Must Remember This . . . "* (1985).

NICHOLAS E. TAWA

BROWN, Lydia (July 1780–19 Nov. 1865), missionary to Hawaii and pioneer of textile production on the islands, was born in Wilton, New Hampshire. Nothing about her life is known before she became a member of the seventh company of missionaries sent to Hawaii by the American Board of Commissioners for Foreign Missions (ABCFM), arriving in Honolulu aboard the *Hellespont* on 6 June 1835. She was particularly connected to the family of Reverend Richard Armstrong and labored for thirty years in the islands, where she taught native Hawaiian women the arts and crafts of homemaking, concentrating on carding, spinning, weaving, and knitting Hawaiian-grown cotton and wool. When she arrived, she found fine, long staple cotton growing wild, perhaps part of a crop planted by Don Francisco Marin in 1812 or 1817. Pioneer missionary James Hunnewell had sent barrels of the best-grade cotton seed and two cotton gins to the islands in 1820, and later the Hawaiian government attempted to encourage the growing of cotton by granting liberal land leases and tax relief, so Brown's original sources of cotton simply had to be handpicked from plants then growing wild.

At Wailuku, Maui, Brown introduced her first classes to a loom and several spinning wheels, which she had brought with her. By that fall, her class of six young Hawaiian women had produced thirty-seven yards of cloth (by the end of the year eight pupils had produced ninety yards). Her letters from the islands to the ABCFM reported long hours spent demonstrating and supervising work on the spinning wheels and the loom as well as building additional spinning wheels and repairing old ones. As each of her classes became proficient in carding, spinning, and weaving, she dismissed them and trained another class. Each lesson was opened with a prayer, as Brown's efforts were directed toward molding Christian women trained in domestic crafts.

In August 1835 Brown was visited by Kuakini, governor of Hawaii and the most business oriented of the Hawaiian chiefs. He watched her classes and, convinced that native Hawaiians needed to have employment opportunities in industry, decided to develop a textile factory on the island of Hawaii. In the fall of 1837 he opened the first factory at Kailua-Kona, where he could provide land, labor, and political direction, and he tried to persuade Brown to come and teach his factory girls. She remained at her Maui mission post but sent three skilled Hawaiian women whom she had trained. Kuakini had two looms patterned after Brown's and employed a foreign artisan to craft a model spinning wheel, from which he had others fashioned. Brown's students were now teachers, and by January 1838 the factory in Kona utilized twenty-two spinning wheels and employed thirty Hawaiian women.

As early as December 1836 Brown proposed dyeing the yarn to be spun and woven with dyes similar to those that the Hawaiians used to color tapa cloth. Her experiment worked, and the local demand for the new cloth quickly outstripped the supply. One of her enterprising former students set up a textile business, and most of her students now made their own clothes at home. Brown sent "Sandwich Island Gingham" to the mission house in Honolulu, where it was distributed to the missionary women. At her suggestion, Levi Chamberlain, superintendent for secular affairs for the mission in the Islands, sent samples to the ABCFM in Boston in order to illustrate the work that was being accomplished at the mission and to secure additional financial support for the mission's work in teaching native Hawaiians how to weave. Kuakini's factory copied her ideas and produced twilled, striped, and plaid cotton cloth in 1838. Selling for fifty cents a yard, the cloth became the fashion of the day throughout the islands. Kuakini's factory closed for repairs, then was later abandoned in 1840, perhaps due to Kuakini's illness, from which he died in 1844. Because of competition from foreign imports, other factories did not spring up without royal patronage, but the missionary desire to offer Hawaiian girls a vocational trade (which also enabled them to clothe themselves more modestly) remained a priority. Most cloth produced was for home consumption, however, and did not advance beyond the cottage-industry level.

In 1840, seeking to spread weaving into the remote areas, Brown moved her school to Kaluaaha on the island of Molokai. The native Hawaiians on Molokai began planting cotton at Kalaupapa in order to supply Brown's classes long before lepers were sent to live there by the Hawaiian government beginning in 1866. Brown built a stone schoolhouse at her own expense and taught English to younger female students as well as classes in spinning and domestic arts to Hawaiian women. Reverend C. B. Andrews reported in 1842 that Brown's teaching had inspired every island girl to want to knit and that knitting needles were always in short supply. The Hawaiian government continued to encourage her enterprise with tax benefits and liberal leases of land for cotton planting. After 1850 the Hawaiian Agricultural Society presented an annual award for the best woven native cloth, and other community leaders continued to promote the cotton industry in the years that followed. Brown remained on Molokai, teaching until 1857, when she moved to Lahaina and then to Honolulu, where she died nearly a decade later.

Like other missionaries, Brown rejoiced at the emancipation of the slaves, but she also welcomed the demand for cotton and cotton cloth that was stimulated by the Civil War because it created new economic opportunities for Hawaii. She had learned Hawaiian and had taught young Hawaiians how to build schools and teach, training women in domestic duties and the fundamentals of right living while offering herself as moral exemplar.

• A brief biography of Brown appears in Bernice Judd, Audrey Sexton, Barbara Wilcox, and Elizabeth Alexander, *Missionary Album* (1969). An excellent account of the cotton spinning and weaving industry is offered by Rossie Moodie Frost, "King Cotton, the Spinning Wheel and Loom in the Sandwich Islands," *Hawaiian Journal of History* (1971): 110–22. Extracts from the translated *Journals of Don Francisco de Paulo Marin* in the State Archives of Hawaii offer primary references to the early cotton plantings in the islands. Additional primary material is found in Laura Fish Judd, *Honolu-*

lu, Sketches of the Life, Social, Political and Religious, in the Hawaiian Islands from 1828–1861 (1880; rev. ed., 1928), and Samuel M. Kamakau, *Ruling Chiefs of Hawaii* (1961), p. 278.

BARBARA BENNETT PETERSON
LENA LOW

BROWN, Margaret Wise (23 May 1910–13 Nov. 1952), author of children's books, was born in Brooklyn, New York, the daughter of Robert Bruce Brown, a business executive, and Maude Johnson. Brown attended private boarding schools in both New England and Switzerland to prepare for college. After receiving her B.A. in English literature from Hollins College in 1932, she enrolled briefly in a short-story writing course at Columbia University. Not long afterward, she became affiliated with the Writers Laboratory, part of the Bureau of Educational Experimentation (soon to be known as the Bank Street College of Education), where her interest in early childhood education resulted in her writing books for preschool children.

During Brown's years there, Bank Street was making its influence felt in the field of education for young children, as well as in the area of children's literature. Bank Street founder Lucy Sprague Mitchell herself experimented with imaginative literature for young children. Challenging the received wisdom of contemporary librarianship that only fantasy was appropriate for preschoolers, Mitchell published her *Here and Now Storybook* in 1921, furnishing her plots with the materials of children's immediate world and recognizing that, for the majority of them, that world had become an urban one. As the controversy over juvenile literature heated up, Brown, who became Mitchell's assistant in the Bank Street publication office, was at its center, supporting the realistic, "here and now" position.

Part of Brown's work at Bank Street involved the hand transcription of the stories narrated by young children themselves. Her notes provided primary source material for the study of children's language development, but, perhaps more important, they stood her in good stead as a writer for children. In contrast to her own early attempts at juvenile literature, she found that the nursery school children's stories were "truer in language, even though often incomplete. . . . The more I listened the more I learned and admired the accidental art of the descriptions and occasional flashes of words very near to real poetry and sometimes poetry itself." Brown's remarkable "ear" does not so much reflect children's ordinary speech as it does this narrative effort on the part of the very young.

Between 1937 and 1939 Brown published her first eight children's books, including *When the Wind Blew* (1937) and *Bumble Bugs and Elephants* (1938), and also contributed fourteen pieces to Mitchell's *Another Here and Now Story-book* (1937). At this time, in addition to her work for Bank Street, she was employed as the first children's book editor at Scott Publications, which published a few of her own books. The writers and educators who were interested in relating children's language to literature were very much attracted to the stylistic experimentation of modernist writers like Gertrude Stein and Virginia Woolf. During her time as an editor, Brown solicited and acquired Stein's children's book, *The World Is Round*, published by Scott in 1939.

Brown's breach with Bank Street, which was complete sometime in the 1940s, was occasioned by a change in her own perspective about the nature of children's imaginative lives. She had never embraced a "sweetness and light" version of the role of fairy tales in children's lives, but she could no longer accept the notion that the alternative was as down to earth and pragmatic as Mitchell maintained. Rather, she believed that children's literature should take account of the fact that fantasy, including grim and frightening fantasy, was part of children's inner lives and must be addressed in their literature.

In her best work, Brown brings the language lessons of her Bank Street days to bear on her own research into the inner life of memory and imagination. The result, as in her masterpiece, *Goodnight Moon* (1947), combines a sleepy repetitiveness of speech and ritual gesture with a sense of the imagination at play. Like *The Runaway Bunny* (1942) and its sequel, *Wait Till the Moon Is Full* (1948), *Goodnight Moon* uses a "child-animal" protagonist to embody the child's relationship to the experience of separation, first symbolically and then more directly.

Brown was a prolific writer and used several pseudonyms in addition to her own name, signing books as Golden MacDonald, Timothy Hay, and Juniper Sage, as well as other pen names for her magazine and anthology work. The passionate energy with which she wrote and the casual way she selected and used pseudonyms reflect her personality as others knew it. The number of her books, as well as their appeal, contributed to her enormous sales; by the end of 1946, well before her most successful works appeared, some 835,000 copies of her books had been sold. A number of them have been reprinted or have remained constantly in print. Ironically, Brown's productivity may have delayed formal recognition of her talent.

Brown, who never married, was engaged to be married when she died following an appendectomy in Nice, France, when an embolism in her leg dislodged and traveled to her brain.

• The Margaret Wise Brown Collection of books and papers is housed at the Memorial and Library Association of Westerly, R.I. In addition to the titles mentioned above, Brown published or contributed to more than 100 books, including *The Little Fireman* (1938), *The Noisy Book* (1939), *Country Noisy Book* (1940), *A Child's Good Night Book* (1943), *SHHhhh . . . BANG: A Whispering Book* (1943), *The Man in the Manhole and the Fix-it Men* (1946), *The Winter Noisy Book* (1947), *Five Little Firemen* (1948), *The Color Kittens* (1949), *The Dark Wood of the Golden Birds* (1950), *The Dream Book, First Comes the Dream* (1950), *The Little Fat Policeman* (1950), *The Summer Noisy Book* (1951), *The Train to Timbuc-*

too (1952), *A Child's Good Morning* (1952), and *The Dead Bird* (1958).

The most important biographical source is Leonard S. Marcus, *Margaret Wise Brown: Awakened by the Moon* (1992). See also Louise Seaman Bechtel, "Margaret Wise Brown: 'Laureate of the Nursery,'" *Horn Book Magazine*, June 1958, pp. 172–86; Bruce Bliven, Jr., "Child's Best Seller," *Life*, 2 Dec. 1946, pp. 59–66; and Lucy Sprague Mitchell, "Margaret Wise Brown, 1910–1952," *Children Here and Now: Notes from 69 Bank Street* 1, no. 1 (1953), pp. 18–20.

LILLIAN S. ROBINSON

BROWN, Mather (7 Oct. 1761–25 May 1831), painter, was born Mather Byles Brown in Boston, Massachusetts, the son of Gawen Brown, a clockmaker, and Elizabeth Byles. Through his mother, Mather Brown was directly descended from the esteemed Puritan divines John Cotton, Increase Mather, and Cotton Mather, and his maternal grandfather was the influential Congregational clergyman Mather Byles. Family portraits by Peter Pelham of Cotton Mather and of Mather Byles hung in the home of Brown's aunts, Mary and Catherine Byles. These portraits may have encouraged Brown to pursue a career in painting. Brown probably received his earliest lessons in drawing from his Aunt Catherine, who helped to raise him after his mother's death in 1763. She showed him how to copy pictures from Comenius' *Orbis Sensualium Pictus*, an illustrated encyclopedia for children. As a boy he also studied briefly with Gilbert Stuart, who worked in Boston between sojourns in Great Britain. Brown later recalled that Stuart gave him the first instruction that directly touched on his work as an artist.

Brown began his career as an itinerant miniature painter. His cousin Rebecca Byles wrote to Catherine and Mary Byles in 1781 about having seen a "very pretty" miniature of Mrs. Greenleafe that Brown had painted (Evans, *Mather Brown*, p. 12). The money Brown earned by painting miniatures enabled him to sail to Europe in 1780. He carried with him letters of introduction to Benjamin Franklin and John Singleton Copley provided by his grandfather. He traveled first to Paris, where he stayed with Franklin, at that time the chief American representative to the French court. Brown then moved on to England and, equipped with a letter of introduction from Franklin, sought out the American painter Benjamin West. Together with Gilbert Stuart, John Trumbull, and William Dunlap, Brown was among the "second generation" of West's students. Thanks to Franklin's letter of introduction, West took on his new pupil free of charge. West's interest in Brown helped the young artist to achieve early recognition in England.

In 1782 Brown exhibited the first of eighty paintings he would show at the Royal Academy during the course of his career. The following year he wrote home that four of his paintings were on exhibit at the Royal Academy and that he had spent three weeks as a guest at Windsor Castle, where he had hunted with King George III. In 1784 Brown established himself in a fashionable district in London, at 20 Cavendish Square, where he devoted himself exclusively to portraiture. He told his aunts that his objective was "to get my Name established and to get Commissions from America, to paint their Friends and Relations here" (quoted in Gardner and Feld, p. 109). Over the next five years, demand for Brown's work grew rapidly. In a letter of 1789 John Holmes informed Brown's father that his son was "in the highest state of success" and enjoyed a "great run of business," having "painted a great number of our nobility" (Evans, p. 84). Works from this period include *Joseph Holman and Anne Brunton as Romeo and Juliet* (1786, Mander and Mitchenson Theatre Collection, London), *Lady with a Dog* (1786, Metropolitan Museum of Art) and *Charles Bullfinch* (1785–1786, Harvard University Portrait Collection). It was also during this time that John Adams and Thomas Jefferson made a special point of having Brown paint their portraits, each statesman commissioning one for himself and one for the other diplomat; only one of these pairs survives (*John Adams* [1788], Boston Athenaeum, and *Thomas Jefferson* [1786], in the collection of Charles Francis Adams).

While portraying British aristocrats and American notables, Brown came to the attention of the royal family. A portrait of *George IV when Prince of Wales*, executed in 1789, now hangs in Buckingham Palace. The duke of York appointed Brown his official portrait painter in December 1788; in 1790 the duke of Clarence (later William IV) appointed Brown his official portrait painter as well. Two years later Brown apparently acquired the new title of historical painter to the duke and duchess of York. The promotion may have been linked to Brown's 1791 painting of *Richard II Resigning His Crown to Bolingbroke* (British Museum, London) for John Boydell's Shakespeare Gallery, a collection of scenes from Shakespeare's plays painted by highly acclaimed artists such as West and Joshua Reynolds. Boydell, its founder, intended that the gallery should help establish an English school of history painting, a highly regarded genre because it combined the erudition of historical knowledge with a morally compelling sensibility. In 1793 Brown created an acclaimed series of three paintings of the events surrounding the "Definitive Treaty" between the British and the vanquished Indian ruler, Tipu Sultan. In the same year Brown produced three celebrated versions of *Louis XVI Saying Farewell to His Family*. Both series were engraved.

Despite Brown's success in the 1780s and his recognition as a history painter during the early 1790s, he was denied membership in the Royal Academy on three successive occasions, in 1792, 1793, and 1794. This rejection, coupled with financial hardships imposed by the Napoleonic wars, contributed to a decline in Brown's fortunes after the mid-1790s. In ensuing years his reputation suffered, and his commissions diminished. In 1808 he left his London residence at Cavendish Square as his lease drew to a close and moved to Buckinghamshire, where he filled a temporary teaching position in a local school. Brown continued to exhibit his paintings in a rented room in London until 1813, but he remained in the English provinces, painting, exhibiting, and taking on students in towns such as Bath, Liverpool, and Manchester until 1824. He never married. His 1812 *Self-Portrait*, sent to his aunts, is now owned by and is part of the collection of the American Antiquarian Society in Worcester, Massachusetts.

Brown spent the last years of his life in London, living in a room in the house of Thomas Hofland, a landscape painter. Brown continued to paint portraits and history paintings, but by then they were no longer fashionable. Nonetheless, at the time of Brown's death in London, Hofland predicted that the artistic value of his paintings would, in time, be appreciated—an opinion that apparently was shared by several prominent artists, in particular, the recently deceased English painter Sir Thomas Lawrence.

Despite the difficulties Mather Brown suffered in the later years of his career, his accomplishments cannot be overlooked. Engravings of his work expanded the influence of history painting and affected his contemporaries' perception of the important political events of the day. His portraiture proved to be extremely compelling. Today his depictions of the events and figures of his era continue to shape our understanding of historical moments, such as the execution of Louis XVI, and our impression of historical leaders, such as Thomas Jefferson and John Adams.

• Brown's unpublished correspondence, 1777–1830, is housed at the Massachusetts Historical Society in Boston. The Byles papers and letterbooks are available also at the Massachusetts Historical Society and at the New England Historic Genealogical Society in Boston. Apart from his self-portrait, the only other known likeness of Brown is a drawing by J. T. Smith (c. 1824) owned by the Metropolitan Museum of Art in New York. Dorinda Evans, *Mather Brown: Early American Artist* (1982), the definitive biography of the artist, provides a catalogue raisonné of his work. Evans presents a valuable study of drawings by Brown in her article "Twenty-six Drawings Attributed to Mather Brown," *Burlington Magazine*, Aug. 1972, pp. 534–41. Frederick W. Coburn's entry on Brown in the *Dictionary of American Biography* and his "Mather Brown," *Art in America* 11 (Aug. 1923): 252–60, are valuable sources, although some of the information he presents must be revised in light of Evans's research. David Meschutt provides an intriguing account of the exchange of Brown portraits by John Adams and Thomas Jefferson in "The Adams-Jefferson Portrait Exchange," *American Art Journal* 14 (Spring 1982): 47–54. Albert Ten Eyck Gardner and Stuart P. Feld provide a useful account of Brown's career in *American Paintings: A Catalogue of the Collection of the Metropolitan Museum of Art*, vol. 1 (1965). Louisa Dresser, "Portraits Owned by the American Antiquarian Society," *Antiques* 96 (Nov. 1969): 717–27, discusses Brown's self-portrait as well as the paintings of Cotton Mather and Mather Byles once owned by Brown's aunts and now owned by the society.

ANNE F. COLLINS

BROWN, Milton (8 Sept. 1903–18 Apr. 1936), country music vocalist and bandleader, was born Willie Milton Brown in Stephenville, Texas, the son of Barty Lee Brown, a sharecropper, and Martha Annie Huxford. A bright child with an outgoing personality, Milton early on exhibited a love for singing and entertaining. In the summer of 1918 after the sudden death of Milton's older sister Era, the Browns moved to Fort Worth. There Milton attended West Side and then Arlington Heights High Schools, where he was active in school government, sports, and clubs, and where his singing abilities and sociable personality earned him the nickname "Harmony Boy." Because he had to work on the family farm, Milton didn't graduate from high school until age twenty-one, when he began to take various labor and sales jobs. At the same time he was singing at local functions in a variety of small vocal groups.

Shortly after the stock market crash in 1929, Brown was laid off from his sales job at Lowe Cigar. From that time on he supported himself entirely from music, in vocal groups and as a duo with his younger brother Derwood on guitar. At a house dance in 1930 in the Fort Worth area Milton and Derwood encountered the fiddle-guitar duo of James Robert "Bob" Wills and Herman Arnspiger. They immediately joined forces, and the quartet began performing locally under various names. In 1930 they played a weekly dance at the Eagles Hall in Fort Worth and performed on a weekly show on WBAP radio as the Aladdin Laddies, taking their name from the program's sponsor, the Aladdin Lamp Company. When this program ended in the fall, Milton arranged for them to play weekly dances at Crystal Springs recreation area just outside of Fort Worth, and the group began a daily program on KFJZ radio as the Light Crust Doughboys, a show sponsored by the Burrus Mill and Elevator Company, maker of Light Crust Flour. In early 1932 Victor sent a recording team to Dallas to record various local talent and in February the group (with Clifton "Sleepy" Johnson replacing Arnspiger) recorded two cuts as the Fort Worth Doughboys. After disagreements with the Burrus Mill general sales manager, Milton and Derwood resigned from the Doughboys in mid-September 1932 (as did Wills in 1933). Knowing that the parting was imminent, Brown had already begun to form his own group, including Ocie Stockard on banjo, Wanna Coffman on bass, Jesse Ashlock on fiddle, and Derwood. Milton Brown and his Musical Brownies began performing at the Crystal Springs dances and on a daily radio program on KTAT immediately after the brothers left the Doughboys.

Brown had already been leaning toward a sound that was new for string bands, one that incorporated jazz influences, featuring a bluesy vocal style and emphasizing rhythm and hot, "take-off" instrumental solos. Leading his own group, he was able to cultivate this sound further into a style that would later be called western swing, though the Brownies themselves remained essentially a pre-swing, non-"western" group. A major turning point came with the addition of jazz pianist Frederick E. "Papa" Calhoun in late fall of 1932. The sound of piano in a string band was unusual, and Calhoun brought a new jazz and dance band repertory to the group, further strengthened the rhythm section, and freed up Derwood and Stockard to experiment with solos.

In 1934 Brown married Mary Helen Hames; they had one son before divorcing in December 1935. On 4 April and again on 8 August 1934, the Brownies—with Cecil Brower replacing Ashlock at the first session and Theodore Grantham added on second fiddle at the second—took their sound to San Antonio to record for Bluebird, producing a total of eighteen sides. A second major step in the development of the Brownie sound came in late fall of 1934, when fiddler Grantham left the group and Robert Lee "Bob" Dunn on amplified steel guitar was hired. Dunn was also a jazz trombonist, which greatly influenced his steel playing style, and he delivered hot, single-note solos with wild abandon. When the Brownies recorded again in January 1935, Dunn had the distinction of being the first musician to play an amplified instrument on a phonograph record. This time they recorded a total of thirty-six sides in Chicago for Decca.

The Brownies were at the top of their form and working hard, playing Crystals Springs on Saturdays and out-of-town dances throughout Texas on the weeknights, and returning to Fort Worth each day for their regular radio program. As manager, treasurer, front man on stage, and booking agent, Milton worked hardest of all. In early 1936 big plans were in the making: a recording session for Decca in New Orleans in March (which produced forty-nine more sides), a Texas centennial celebration planned for the summer, and negotiations with Bob Wills for a possible joint tour in Oklahoma. But on the night of 12 April, Easter Sunday, misfortune struck when Milton fell asleep at the wheel driving back into Fort Worth. His vehicle veered off the road and slammed into a utility pole, instantly killing the young woman he was with. Brown was taken to the Methodist Hospital in Fort Worth, and while at first his chances for survival looked promising, pneumonia soon developed from a punctured lung, and he died the following Saturday morning. The Brownies continued for roughly another year under Derwood's leadership, recording fourteen more sides for Decca in February 1937. But with the loss of Milton as their musical, business, and personal leader, the group soon lost its momentum and disintegrated.

Because of his popular success in the 1940s and his longevity in the field, Bob Wills is generally regarded as the great figure of western swing music. In the formative years of this style, however, Brown was responsible, perhaps more than any figure, for fostering jazz influences. His innovations include the incorporation of a smooth yet bluesy vocal (his own); expanded instrumentation to include piano, twin fiddles, and amplified steel guitar; a repertory that included Tin Pan Alley pop songs, blues numbers, and jazz instrumentals; strong backbeat rhythm; and hot instrumental improvisation. Had he not been killed prematurely at the age of thirty-two, he would certainly have earned far greater recognition for his contributions.

• With the resurgence of interest in western swing since 1980 and the scholarly recognition of Brown's historical significance, many reissues of the Brownies' recordings have been undertaken, including *Milton Brown/Clayton McMichen* (Japan, 1976), *Taking Off: Hot Western Swing from the Thirties* (U.K., 1977), *Milton Brown and His Musical Brownies, 1934* (1982), *Pioneer Western Swing Band 1935–36* (1982), *Easy Ridin' Papa* (U.K., 1987), and *Milton Brown and the Musical Brownies: Complete Recordings 1932–37* (5 CDs, 1995). Also useful for gaining an overview of the western swing style and hearing the development of the Brownie sound from 1934 to 1937 is the series *Western Swing* (8 vols., 1966–1981).

The most comprehensive source of information on Brown and his group is Cary Ginell, with special assistance from Roy Lee Brown, *Milton Brown and the Founding of Western Swing* (1994), which offers a detailed account of Brown's career by weaving together recollections from surviving Brownie band members and other acquaintances with Ginell's extensive background research. It includes a complete discography of original recordings and a discussion of each cut. Extant primary source material is a scrapbook containing news clippings, photographs, and other memorabilia housed at Texas Tech University in Lubbock. Also useful for overviews of the development of western swing and the roles of Wills and Brown are Ginell, "The Development of Western Swing," *JEMF Quarterly* 20, no. 74 (Fall/Winter 1984): 58–67, and Charles Townsend, "A Brief History of Western Swing," *Southern Quarterly* 22, no. 3 (Spring 1984): 31–51.

DANIEL C. L. JONES

BROWN, Mordecai Peter Centennial (19 Oct. 1876–14 Feb. 1948), baseball player, was born in Nyesville, Indiana, a rural community near Terre Haute, the son of Peter P. Brown, a farmer, and Jane Marsh. At the age of seven, Brown caught his right hand in a feed cutter on his uncle's farm and lost the top joint of the index finger and use of the little finger. With the hand still in a cast, he broke the other two fingers, which remained permanently deformed. Brown's crippled hand enabled him to throw a natural sinker ball and a sharper-breaking curveball that batters found difficult to hit; the hand also earned him the nickname among fans of "Three Finger."

In the late 1890s Brown began his baseball career as a third baseman for a semiprofessional team from Coxville, Indiana. In 1901 he established himself as a pitcher with Terre Haute of the Three-I League, winning 23 games and losing 8. The following year, he pitched for Omaha of the Western League, where his record was 27 wins and 15 losses.

Brown signed with the St. Louis Cardinals in 1903 and began a 14-year major league career that included stints with the Cardinals (1903), the Chicago Cubs (1904–1912 and 1916), and the Cincinnati Reds (1913) of the National League, and with the St. Louis Terriers, Brooklyn Feds, and Chicago Whales of the short-lived Federal League in 1914 and 1915. During his career Brown won 239 games and lost 130 for a .648 winning percentage. His 2.06 earned run average is one of the very highest among all major league pitchers, and his 57 career shutouts in the National League add to his stature as one of the pitching elite. He won twenty or more games in six consecutive years (1906–1911), and his outstanding pitching helped the Cubs win National League pennants in 1906, 1907, 1908, and 1910. He won five World Series games, including two as a relief pitcher, and lost four. Three of his World Series victories were complete game shutouts—over the Chicago White Sox in 1906 and the Detroit Tigers in 1907 and 1908.

His best single seasons were 1909, when he led the National League with 27 wins, 32 complete games, 7 saves, and 343 innings pitched, and 1911, when he won 16 of 27 starts, completed 21 games, and led the National League with 26 relief appearances and 13 saves. Brown led the league in 1904 by allowing only 6.6 hits per game; in 1908 he performed the same feat with 6.2 hits per game. In 1906 he led the league with nine shutouts and a 1.04 earned run average, and in 1910 he set the pace in the National League with 8 shutouts and 27 complete games. Throughout his career, Brown had excellent control, walking an average of fewer than two batters per game.

Brown was also an excellent fielder. He set a National League record in 1908 by handling 108 chances without an error, and he shared with Christy Mathewson, the great New York Giants pitcher, a number of World Series fielding records.

Brown's most important victory may have been over the Giants and Mathewson in a makeup game played at the end of the 1908 season after the Cubs and Giants had finished the regular season in a tie. The game was necessary because of a notorious "boner" by Giants' utility player Fred Merkle, who failed to touch second base and nullified the potential winning run on the final play of an earlier game. In the makeup game, Brown came on in relief after the Giants had scored one first-inning run. He pitched a four-hitter the rest of the way, besting Mathewson, 4–2, for the pennant.

Brown's overall physical fitness during his career was much admired and doubtless contributed to his seldom missing a pitching turn. In 1914 his conditioning regimen was featured in an *American Monthly* article that included photographs of his bodybuilding exercises.

Following his major league career, Brown pitched for Columbus of the International League in 1917 and 1918 and served as player-manager for Terre Haute of the Three-I League in 1919 and 1920. He continued to live in Terre Haute, where he operated a filling station and managed a semiprofessional baseball team out of Lawrenceville, Indiana. He retired in 1945 and died in Terre Haute, survived by his wife, the former Sallie Burgham, whom he had married in 1903. They had no children. In 1949 he was elected to the National Baseball Hall of Fame.

• Material related to Brown's career may be found in his file at the National Baseball Hall of Fame, Cooperstown, N.Y. See also Ralph Hickok, *Who Was Who in American Sports* (1971); Warren Brown, *The Chicago Cubs* (1946); Lowell Reidenbaugh, *Cooperstown: Where Baseball's Legends Live Forever* (1983); David Porter, ed., *Biographical Dictionary of American Sports: Baseball* (1987); and Mike Shatzkin, *The Ballplayers* (1990). Obituaries are in the *Terre Haute Tribune*, 14 Feb. 1948, and the *New York Times*, 15 Feb. 1948.

JOHN E. FINDLING

BROWN, Morris (12 Feb. 1770–9 May 1849), African Methodist Episcopal minister and bishop, was born of mixed parentage in Charleston, South Carolina, where he spent his early and middle years. Apparently self-educated, he worked as a bootmaker and shoe repairman; he married Maria (maiden name unknown), with whom he had six children. Associated with the city's community of free people of color, Brown earned a reputation for assisting slaves to purchase their freedom and for teaching and advising both free and enslaved Africans in the region.

Soon after his religious conversion and joining the Methodist Episcopal (ME) church, Brown was licensed to preach. In that role he had greater access to the slave population as well as to groups of free African Americans. As their numbers grew, both generally and within the African church in Charleston, Brown emerged as their leader. In 1816, in a dispute over a burial ground, many African church members withdrew from their connection with the ME church. When the opportunity came later that year, Brown's congregation of about 1,400 members transferred to the new African Methodist Episcopal (AME) denomination, centered in Philadelphia and headed by Bishop Richard Allen. In that association Brown was ordained deacon in 1817 and elder the following year.

The Charleston African Church, by meeting independently of white authorities and supervision, ran afoul of local and state laws intended to control religious gatherings of slaves and free blacks. Consequently, Brown and other ministers of the church served prison sentences in 1818, while protesting the repression of the free exercise of religion. Brown also attended early AME annual and general conferences, where he reported both the difficulties of being harassed by the police and the spectacular growth of the Charleston congregation. It enrolled more than 2,000 members by 1822.

That year civil authorities uncovered a conspiracy to overthrow slavery associated with the initiative of Denmark Vesey, a lay class leader in the African church. Betrayed by slaves loyal to their masters, the plot involved six other class leaders from Brown's AME community; it ended with 131 arrests and thirty-five executions. Suspected of knowing about Vesey's plan (though there was no direct evidence), Brown, aided by some local white clergy who advised him to leave, saw his church forced to close. Before the year ended he went north; early in 1823 he was joined by his family in Philadelphia, where he served as an assistant at the Mother Bethel AME Church and as aide to the aging Bishop Allen. Occasionally he traveled as an itinerant preacher, also organizing new AME congregations. On 25 May 1828 the AME General Conference selected Brown as its second bishop. When Allen died in 1831, Brown became the sole bishop of the denomination, and its senior bishop in 1836. Never forgetting his southern experience, Brown was active in the Vigilance Committee of Philadelphia, a public arm of the underground railroad for fugitives from slavery.

During Brown's thirteen active years in the episcopacy, the AME church expanded westward. Brown organized the Pittsburgh Conference in Ohio in 1830 and the Indiana Conference ten years later. By the time of his death the church had congregations in fourteen states and Canada, organized into six annual conferences, and more than 17,000 members. In 1841 the denomination launched its first periodical, the *A. M. E. Church Magazine*, published until 1848; in it the initial debate was held about women's right to preach. The AME church also sent a representative to the 1846 international meeting of the Evangelical Alliance in London.

While in Toronto, Canada, in 1844, Brown suffered a paralytic stroke, from which he never regained mobility. He even lost his voice in his last months, though it returned briefly just before his death in Philadelphia. By that time his son, Morris, Jr., had become a well-known musician in Philadelphia, and the senior Brown had accumulated enough property to support his widow and their five other children.

Not known for literary productions or great preaching, Brown was a practical administrator and effective speaker who kept his message plain and pointed. His portrait shows him to have been a tall man with a large frame, a light complexion, and piercing eyes. His admirers named local churches after him in Philadelphia and Charleston, as well as a denominational college founded in Atlanta after the Civil War.

• Short biographical accounts of Brown include Richard R. Wright, ed., *The Centennial Encyclopedia of the African Methodist Episcopal Church* (1916), and Wright, *The Bishops of the African Methodist Episcopal Church* (1963). On Brown's relationship to the Vesey insurrection, see J. O. Killens, *The Trial Record of Denmark Vesey* (1970). On the emergence of the AME denomination, see Carol V. R. George, *Segregated Sabbaths: Richard Allen and the Rise of Independent Black Churches, 1760–1840* (1973).

WILL GRAVELY

BROWN, Moses (12 Sept. 1738–6 Sept. 1836), merchant and philanthropist, was born in Providence, Rhode Island, the son of James Brown, merchant, and Hope Power. The father died the next year, leaving a variety of properties and businesses, which indicates that his family was far from poor. Moses Brown had a few years of formal schooling before being apprenticed to his merchant uncle, Obadiah, to learn the intricacies of eighteenth-century commerce and to be adopted as a son and partner. After Obadiah died in 1762, Moses managed the business, and in 1774 married Obadiah's daughter Anna, who bore three children, two of whom lived to maturity. Moses joined his three surviving brothers in the firm of Nicholas Brown & Co. to operate the family businesses. The profits of trade were diversified by manufacturing and money-lending. The Brown brothers inherited profitable candle and chocolate works and started a plant to smelt and work iron. They also tried at least one ill-fated slaving voyage.

The whole family was in the Baptist church and the political party led by Stephen Hopkins. Moses Brown was elected as a deputy to the Rhode Island General Assembly from Providence first in 1764 and served until 1771 as fundraiser, organizer, and legislative captain for Hopkins. In the political battles the Hopkins side generally favored the northern part of the colony against the southern in appropriations for bridges and revision of tax assessments. More subtly, it sought management of the paper currency to avoid siphoning wealth from north to south, but its effort to put Rhode Island College (now Brown University) in Providence instead of Warren was quite blatant. The Browns helped get the college for their town by contributing land and money for it and persuading the other businessmen to donate. Hopkins and the Browns, who were temperate in their opposition to the unpopular British measures that led to the American Revolution, had a hard time steering through the political upheavals that began in 1764.

Moses Brown took an interest in projects that could increase knowledge, yield profit, and benefit society. He observed an inoculation clinic in New Jersey in 1760, was inoculated himself, encouraged the procedure in New England, and served for many years as supervisor of the pest house in Providence. In 1769 he helped his brother Joseph Brown and Benjamin West (1730–1813) observe the transit of Venus across the sun, a project to determine the size of the solar system and ascertain longitude in American locations. It was the first major international scientific collaboration that required precise coordination. Though the result did credit to the Providence men, there was no obvious practical benefit, and Moses Brown turned to the more useful arts of surveying and materia medica. He took the lead in various civic projects, notably building bridges, sometimes with success—but not in his efforts to get general support for creating public schools.

His life radically changed direction in 1773. His wife had given birth to their third child, a son named Obadiah, two years before and then contracted a fatal illness. Moses, too, was in poor health. Already drawn to Quakerism, he in his grief joined the Society of Friends in 1774. He thought he should cast aside all his worldly concerns, and he certainly did cut down his immersion in business and withdraw from public office. Brown avidly embraced Quakerism and the Quakers' efforts to promote educational and social reforms by working quietly behind the scenes and within the system.

Quite soon he became a leading figure in the Quaker ecclesiastical organization. When New England Yearly Meeting set up the Meeting for Sufferings, an executive arm to deal with emergencies created by the Revolution, Brown became its most active member. Over some opposition he turned its efforts to help Friends who faced hunger or destitution during the siege of Boston into a program to relieve the miseries of all noncombatants. Later attempts to alleviate the extreme deprivations of people in Nantucket were less successful.

As a conscientious Quaker, Brown firmly opposed slavery. He freed his own slaves on terms that were advantageous to them. He advocated Rhode Island's prohibition of the importation of slaves in 1774, its gradual manumission law ten years later, and its law of 1787 forbidding anybody to fit out slaving voyages in its ports. As he knew, the last of these laws was enforced loosely; his brother John violated it with impunity. Moses urged Quakers to oppose ratification of the Constitution because it countenanced slavery. Their opposition was a secondary element in Rhode Island's first vote against ratification. When he changed his mind and decided that the Constitution should be ratified because at least it allowed the stoppage of the slave trade after 1808 and could not be amended to rule out slavery until it had been adopted, he strenuously urged the Friends to help form a solid majority in favor of ratification in 1790. Soon thereafter, Brown's son Obadiah helped teach basic literacy to African Americans in Providence.

Moses Brown was married twice more, in 1779 to Mary Olney and in 1799 to Phebe Lockwood, both stalwart Quakers. Mary was in poor health and bore no children; Phebe had some from a previous marriage. She died in 1809, and Brown remained without a wife for many more years.

His conversion to Quakerism nearly ended his concern for public schools because he was determined to provide sectarian schools for Friends' children. Given the inability of some monthly meetings to underwrite the costs of day schools, he advocated a boarding school operated by the Yearly Meeting. He and others got one started in 1784, but it failed financially in 1788. He led the effort to gather an endowment, gave generously himself, and, in a change of heart, insisted that the Quaker school admit the children of the poor and other non-Friends who would abide by its rules. In 1819 he saw the opening of what is now Moses Brown School.

Throughout these years Brown often set aside his business concerns. He also launched businesses in new directions only to disengage himself from them once they were firmly established. The most important of his commercial endeavors was textile manufacturing. Brown wanted to follow the English lead and experimented with mechanizing spinning as early as 1788. His goals were characteristic: make money, reduce dependence on imported fabrics, and give employment to poor Quakers, especially women and children, both in the mills and in the homes or workshops of domestic handweavers. Investors would finance the whole system and market the fabrics. The machines were unsatisfactory until Samuel Slater arrived in 1790 with full knowledge of English designs and consented to work for Brown. Thereafter, Slater built the first water-powered Arkwright spinning mill in the United States, and with some Rhode Island men steadily improved the machinery and enlarged the profitable operations.

Although a silent partner in the textile business from 1790 onward, Moses Brown was an inspirational and a financial presence at the firm of Almy, [Smith] Brown & Slater (originally Brown & Almy). While William Almy and Smith Brown oversaw the day-to-day commercial side of the business, Slater was in charge of production. The investors and some former employees of the firm provided much of the capital that financed the rapid construction of additional mills in southern New England.

Still thinking of himself as retired, Moses Brown turned to other pursuits. He experimented with agricultural improvement on his extensive farm in Providence, where the soil was mediocre at best. He made meticulous natural observations and read up on the latest discoveries in science. He collected historical materials on Providence and Rhode Island as well as books on Quakerism. He promoted civic improvements and the establishment of a bank in Providence. Avoiding active direction, he promoted many projects and gave advice or encouragement to ingenious young people. He continued his philanthropy on an intimate personal scale as well as through institutional arrangements. His life grew steadily less eventful. Although he had kept out of the limelight since his turn to Quakerism, he became a legendary figure. Born in the reign of George II, he lived to receive a visit from President Andrew Jackson and Vice President Martin Van Buren. He died in Providence.

• Manuscript sources pertaining to Moses Brown, the Brown family, and Brown University are available in several Providence repositories. The Rhode Island Historical Society maintains the Moses Brown Papers and records of Brown & Almy; the John Carter Brown Library on the Brown University campus houses the Brown papers. The John Hay Library at the university has records pertaining to the founding of Rhode Island College. The Moses Brown School library maintains a collection of Moses Brown's correspondence in the Austin MSS. Additionally these resources are supplemented by the Almy, Brown & Slater business records at the Baker Library at Harvard University. The most pertinent secondary sources are Mack Thompson, *Moses Brown: Reluctant Reformer* (1962), and James Hedges, *The Browns of Providence Plantations* (2 vols., 1952; repr. 1968). Other studies of Moses Brown include Robert Morton Hazelton, *Let Freedom Ring!* (1957), and Augustine Jones, *Moses Brown: His Life and Services* (1892). Brown's obituary appears in the Providence *Manufacturers' and Farmers' Journal*, 7 Sept. 1836.

SYDNEY V. JAMES
GAIL FOWLER MOHANTY

BROWN, Nacio Herb (22 Feb. 1896–28 Sept. 1964), songwriter, was born Ignacio Herb Brown in Deming, New Mexico, the son of a clarinet-playing law enforcement officer and former Wells Fargo agent and his wife, who taught Brown to play the piano. In 1902 the family moved to Los Angeles. There Brown graduated from Manual Arts High School, where he learned tailoring.

In 1916 Brown opened a custom tailoring business in Los Angeles; among his clients were Rudolph Valentino and Charlie Chaplin. In 1921, while serving as accompanist to a vaudeville singer named Alice Doll, Brown met the amateur lyricist Arthur Freed in a Los

Angeles bookstore. They decided to collaborate, quickly evolving a modus operandi: first came the title, then the music, finally the lyrics. With the help of Doll's musician husband, they created "When Buddha Smiles" (1921). They traveled to New York City, where they sold it to Harms Publishers, and Paul Whiteman's orchestra recorded it. It sold one million copies and remained for many years a jazz standard.

Also in 1921 Brown's "Doll Dance" became popular in sheet music, recordings, and piano rolls. Other compositions were unsuccessful. At an unknown date Brown married Ruby Porter. They had one child and were divorced in 1932. Between 1920 and 1924 more than 100,000 new residents yearly moved into booming Los Angeles. An average of 700 new housing tracts were begun yearly. Brown closed his tailoring business; keeping songwriting as a hobby, he became a real estate entrepreneur and built a home for himself in Beverly Hills.

In the mid-1920s Freed was running the Orange Grove, a small theater in Hollywood, and writing songs for its annual *Hollywood Music Box Revue*. The 1927 edition included a melody written by Brown, which Freed called "a great tune for a coloratura soprano, full of classic trills." Freed added some lyrics of his own and changed the tempo. This song became "Singin' in the Rain," the most enduring of many Brown-Freed hits to follow.

In 1928, as the Los Angeles boom faded and sound swept into motion pictures, Irving Thalberg, the production chief for Metro-Goldwyn-Mayer, was looking for a musical project. Acquainted with Brown and Freed's work, he auditioned them at Los Angeles radio station KFI. The collaborators brought with them "The Broadway Melody," "The Wedding of the Painted Doll," and "You Were Meant for Me." Thalberg hired them for *The Broadway Melody*. Shot in twenty-six days, the film, which opened at Grauman's Chinese Theater in February 1929, incorporated these melodies and more. "Wedding of the Painted Doll" became the first musical sequence filmed in color. *Broadway Melody*, the first great movie musical, a tribute to a theatrical tradition it was doing its best to destroy, told a backstage story of broken hearts on Broadway. "You Were Meant for Me" was sung by Charles King to Anita Page, later to become Brown's third wife. Brown and Freed signed an M-G-M contract.

A few months later Brown and Freed took two hours to write a pseudo-Tahitian song for Ramon Novarro to sing in *The Pagan*. Reprised twenty-seven times in the film, "Pagan Love Song" sold 1.6 million copies. Still later, Brown and Freed wrote the score for M-G-M's *Hollywood Revue of 1929*, an all-star anthology. The film's foot-tapping finale was "Singin' in the Rain." Before the end of 1929 Brown-Freed songs were heard in four more musicals. Five of the top ten songs in the ASCAP (American Society of Composers, Authors and Publishers) rankings for 1929 were theirs.

Brown's melodies were never innovative. Some were simple and catchy and others were melodramatic; they were perfect for a medium that combined these qualities. With Freed he had another hit, "Should I?" in *Lord Byron of Broadway* (1930). When they were not writing for musicals, the collaborators turned out "title songs," which in those all-talking, all-singing days were somehow fitted into almost any story. "Singin' in the Rain" and "You Were Meant for Me" showed up in film after film.

Freed continued at M-G-M, where in the 1940s and 1950s he produced many of the studio's best musicals. Brown, however, left for a time, teaming with Gordon Clifford in 1932 on the languorous "Paradise," whose smoky lyrics as sung on screen by vamp Pola Negri in *A Woman Commands* brought a temporary broadcasting ban. In 1932 Brown married Jeanne Lochart. They had no children and were divorced in 1934. When movie musicals began to slump, Brown turned to Broadway. Collaborating with Richard Whiting and Buddy DeSylva, he wrote most of the score for *Take a Chance* (1932), called by theater historian Stanley Green "a good old-fashioned knockabout musical comedy with . . . some memorable songs." *Take a Chance* gave Ethel Merman and Jack Haley a nonchalant duet, "You're an Old Smoothie," and Merman the raucous "Eady Was a Lady," which theater critic Brooks Atkinson called "half-burlesque, half-jubilee."

When *Take a Chance* closed in mid-1933, movie musicals were reviving. Brown returned to M-G-M and again collaborated with Freed. Their "Sweetheart Darlin'," from *Peg o' My Heart* (1933), became the nation's bestseller, while the moody, throbbing "Temptation," from *Going Hollywood* (1933), became a dramatic staple for crooners. In *Sadie McKee* (1934) crooner Gene Austin and matinee idol Gene Raymond sang "All I Do Is Dream of You," a song that used so few notes practically anyone could sing it. As Latin dances swept film, Brown's "American Bolero" metamorphosed into "The Carlo" for *Student Tour* (1934). Brown married Anita Page in 1935. The marriage was annulled in the same year.

The Broadway Melody of 1936 (1935) contained several Brown-Freed hits, including two lilting songs, "You Are My Lucky Star" and "I've Got a Feelin' You're Foolin'," plus the driving "Broadway Rhythm." The Marx Brothers' *A Night at the Opera* (1935) included the songwriting team's histrionic "Alone." They wrote "Would You?" for *San Francisco* (1936) and "Smoke Dreams" for the nonmusical *After the Thin Man* (1936); "Smoke Dreams" became the theme song of Chesterfield cigarettes. Their rather defiant "Everybody Sing" (from *The Broadway Melody of 1938*, 1937) and the cheerful "Good Morning" was interpolated into *Babes in Arms* (1939). In 1939 Brown married Beffie Kellogg. They had no children and were divorced in 1941.

Brown's remaining film hit songs were with other collaborators—"You Stepped Out of a Dream" (*Ziegfeld Girl*, 1941), with Gus Kahn, and the operatic "Love Is Where You Find It" (*The Kissing Bandit*,

1948), with Earl Brent. In 1942 Brown married Georgeann Morris; they moved to New Mexico, had two children, and were divorced in 1953. *Singin' in the Rain* (1952), a witty and affectionate Freed-produced sendup of movies' transition to sound, revived in definitive versions nearly all of the Brown-Freed hits. Brown and Freed contributed one new song, the slapstick "Make 'em Laugh," and Brown teamed with librettists Adolph Comden and Betty Green for a knockout comedy dance song, "Moses Supposes."

Brown was the featured guest on the "This Is Your Life" television program in 1952. In 1960 a Nacio Herb Brown Day was held in Deming, New Mexico. Brown moved to San Francisco, where he lived quietly until his death there. Although never nominated for an Academy Award, Nacio Herb Brown proved himself a practical man and an adaptable composer. By providing the distinctive melodies of movie musicals' first decade, he gained immortality.

• The Deming Luna Mimbres Museum, Deming, N.Mex., holds letters, photographs, and articles relating to Nacio Herb Brown. Aside from the films in which his songs appeared, the many recordings of his songs, and the catalogs of the American Film Institute, discussion of the quality of Brown's songwriting can be glimpsed in Richard Fehr and Frederick Vogel, *Lullabies of Hollywood: Movie Music and the Movie Musical 1915–1992* (1993); Mark White, *You Must Remember This* (1983); and Warren Craig, *Sweet and Lowdown* (1978). Stanley Green, *Ring Bells, Sing Songs!* (1975), provides excellent coverage of the Broadway musical in the 1930s. See also Ian Whitcomb, *After the Ball: Pop Music from Rag to Rock* (1972). Brooks Atkinson's review of *Take a Chance* ran in the *New York Times*, 28 Nov. 1932. An obituary is in the same newspaper on 30 Sept. 1964.

JAMES ROSS MOORE

BROWN, Nicholas (28 July 1729–29 May 1791), merchant, was born in Providence, Rhode Island, the son of James Brown, a merchant, and Hope Tillinghast Power. He and his three brothers, after their father's death in 1739, were raised by their uncle Obadiah Brown and were brought by him into the family's mercantile firm then bearing his name. This introduced them to the network of kinship, business, and social connections established over the five generations since their family had settled in Providence. At the age of twenty-five Nicholas Brown was named clerk of the Providence County Court of Common Pleas, where he served from 1755 to 1760 under Chief Justice Daniel Jenckes, whose daughter Rhoda Jenckes he married in 1762. They had ten children together, two of whom survived childhood. While serving as clerk he also assumed duties as the founding librarian of the Providence Library, the forerunner of the present-day Providence Athenaeum, as all the while he undertook increasing responsibility in the family firm.

As Brown rose from assistant to partner, Obadiah Brown & Company progressed from a trade of coastal shipping and local shopkeeping to manufacturing and mercantile pursuits of international reputation. After the death of Obadiah Brown in 1762, the four nephews renamed the firm Nicholas Brown and Company. Under Brown's management the firm established trade across the Caribbean Sea to ports as distant as Surinam, including, during the Seven Years' War, a thriving illicit business with French colonies at Martinique and Hispaniola. In their search for goods to export from the meager Rhode Island hinterland, they found markets for locally grown tobacco and horses, but they soon came to rely on reexporting their imports and on manufacturing their own goods. Nicholas Brown and Company imported molasses from the Carribbean and built distilleries to produce rum, which it supplied to the African slave trade, the most important foreign trade in eighteenth-century Rhode Island. As early as 1735 the Brown family conducted or financed occasional ventures in the slave trade, though without conspicuous financial success, and after a severe financial loss in a slaving voyage in 1765, Nicholas Brown and Company abandoned that business in favor of more conservative enterprise. Although the family firm withdrew from the slave trade primarily because the economic risk had proved too great, Brown was remembered by his brother Moses, who later became an ardent abolitionist, as having regretted for moral reasons his early participation in slaving voyages.

Nicholas Brown and Company produced cordage from its own ropewalks and was especially noted for its candle manufactory, which made it the leading producer and wholesaler of spermaceti candles in the colonies. In 1765 the firm established an iron foundry to produce pig iron, which it exported to other manufacturers, and finished goods, which it retailed. Though his three brothers withdrew from Nicholas Brown and Company in the early 1770s, they all continued to engage in business with one another through their individual successor firms.

With the outset of the American Revolution, Brown supplied the Continental navy with cannon and anchors from the iron foundry, while at the same time provisioning his own ships, which he fitted out as privateers under a letter of marque from the Continental Congress. Through his merchant fleet he initiated trade directly with France and Holland, by which he was able to import and sell at great profit much-sought-after goods of English manufacture and at the same time to support the revolutionary cause by supplying the Continental army with clothing and munitions. With the conclusion of hostilities, Brown took George Benson, a former clerk in Nicholas Brown and Company, as a partner to replace his brothers, and the new firm of Brown and Benson began the large-scale importation of goods directly from British merchants. In the last years of his life, Brown also helped capitalize his brother John's trading voyages to Canton, the first China Trade ventures to set forth from Providence. So successful was his trading that by 1790 Brown held public securities worth $200,000, rendering him one of the wealthiest men in the state. He was opposed to the Continental Impost, a proposed amendment to the Articles of Confederation to levy duties on imports, and helped delay its acceptance until 1786, although he actively worked for Rhode Island's ratification of the U.S. Constitution.

With the Browns' ascendance as one of the leading families of Rhode Island, Brown accepted numerous civic and cultural responsibilities. In 1764 he was elected treasurer of the nascent College of Rhode Island, later named Brown University after his son Nicholas and in recognition of his family's contributions in its behalf. Six years later he was instrumental in the community's efforts to locate the college permanently in Providence, where the firm of Nicholas Brown and Company oversaw and managed the construction of the College Edifice, now the National Historic Landmark University Hall, on the height of land once owned by his ancestor. Brown successfully promoted a lottery to fund the construction of a public market building in the center of town, for which he laid the cornerstone in 1773. He was also a director of a lottery to fund the design by his brother Joseph and the construction by his brother John of what would be the outstanding architectural work of the colonial period in Providence, the 1774 First Baptist Meetinghouse. Brown contributed liberally to this and other appeals from the Baptist church, of which he was an ardent and lifelong member. The only one of the four Brown brothers not to be elected to public office, he was an active and longtime supporter of Stephen Hopkins, who for many years served as governor of the colony and represented Providence in its political struggles with Newport.

Throughout his adult life Brown lived, like his brothers, on land settled by his forebears in a prominent brick house that he furnished with the best of the china, silver, and furniture imported through his trading ventures. In 1989 the carved mahogany desk and bookcase made for him by the Newport, Rhode Island, cabinetmaker John Goddard was sold for $12.1 million, setting a world record for any piece of furniture ever to appear at auction. After the death of his first wife in 1783, he married Avis Binney in 1785. They had one child, who died in infancy. Brown died in Providence.

• Nicholas Brown's papers are at Brown University, in the John Carter Brown Library and in the John Nicholas Brown Center for the Study of American Civilization; and at the Rhode Island Historical Society. The most thorough study of Brown's economic activities is in James B. Hedges, *The Browns of Providence Plantations: The Colonial Years* (1952), and Hedges, *The Browns of Providence Plantations: The Nineteenth Century* (1968). See also Abby Isabel Brown Bulkley, comp., *The Chad Browne Memorial* (1888), for geneological and biographical notes on the Brown family, and Walter C. Bronson, *History of Brown University 1764–1914* (1914), for the relationship of the Browns to the university that bears their name.

ROBERT P. EMLEN

BROWN, Obadiah (15 July 1771–15 Oct. 1822), merchant and manufacturer, was born in Providence, Rhode Island, the son of Moses Brown, a merchant, and Anna Brown. He sometimes used the name Obadiah M. Brown to distinguish himself from other Browns with the same first name. Sickly as a child, he initially was educated at home and then attended the Friends New England Yearly Meeting School in Portsmouth, Rhode Island, between 1784 and 1788. This was followed by an informal apprenticeship with Almy and Brown, a Providence cotton textile manufactory established by his father, one of four brothers who were successful Providence merchants and manufacturers. The manufactory was initially managed by Obadiah's brother-in-law, William Almy, and a cousin, Smith Brown, although under the watchful eye of Moses Brown.

He formally joined Almy & Brown as a partner in 1793, replacing Smith Brown. At the same time he became a partner in Almy, Brown & Slater, a Pawtucket, Rhode Island, cotton spinning mill that the Browns and Almy had started with Englishman Samuel Slater in 1790. He also became a prominent member of the Society of Friends, following in the footsteps of his father, who was the leading New England Quaker and was well known nationally. In 1798 Brown married Dorcas Hadwen; they had no children.

During the cotton manufactory's seven-year existence, Brown supervised apprentices, assisted in putting out various tasks to outworkers, and frequently traveled throughout the Northeast to contact customers. These trips generally combined his business and religious interests. On one such occasion in 1795, he visited mills and potential customers in Connecticut, New York, Maryland, and Pennsylvania, attending local Friends meetings held in his honor along the way. Owing to nearly nonexistent roads and undependable sailing schedules, such journeys were extremely difficult. His most important early assignment within the partnership may have been to work with the sometimes skeptical and usually caustic Samuel Slater, whose expertise in building and operating waterpowered spinning machinery was crucial to their business. Slater's machines produced much of the yarn used by Almy & Brown's Providence-based cotton goods operation.

The cotton manufactory closed its doors in 1796, primarily owing to foreign competition. Brown then became the "outside" man as Almy & Brown constructed a new industry around Slater's yarn. Brown was primarily responsible for building the first national market for an American-made product. The resulting yarn market in turn convinced Almy & Brown to add three mills in Rhode Island, two at Warwick (1799, 1806) and one at Smithfield (1806), the latter with Samuel and John Slater as partners. For at least fifteen years, beginning in 1800, Almy & Brown, with Slater and his partners, controlled a majority of the cotton spindles in operation in the United States.

Once Almy & Brown established local and regional agents after 1808, the firm's correspondence shows that Brown stayed in Providence to supervise the "indoor business going from home." In spite of significant financial success, he described the partnership's position in 1814 as "somewhat precarious" due to increased domestic competition brought on by the Embargo of 1807 and the War of 1812. This perception caused Obadiah Brown and William Almy to limit the partnership's postwar activities and consequently to lose the leadership of the cotton textile industry to Massachusetts mills.

Brown's work with Almy & Brown reflected only one aspect of his life. He also was deeply involved in community service and fully aware of his personal obligations as a Quaker. In Providence he was treasurer of the Providence Mutual Fire Insurance Company, a director of the Providence Bank, and the treasurer of the Providence Library. He gave significant support to the local Abolition Society, the Peace Society, and the Rhode Island Bible Society. Probably Brown's greatest interest, however, was in assisting the Society of Friends and its young scholars. When the Friends New England Yearly Meeting Boarding School (renamed Moses Brown School in 1904) was established in Providence in 1814, he helped to oversee its construction, contributed to the building fund, and served as an active member of the school committee. At his death in Providence, while a partner in Almy & Brown, he left the Yearly Meeting School $100,000, probably the largest single donation made to an American educational institution to that time.

Brown's success as a businessman and his stature as a highly respected Providence citizen resulted from a remarkable strength and purpose of character. The *Providence Daily Journal* in 1859 recalled that he was "a munificent benefactor, an unsullied merchant, a thoughtful Christian . . . [who knew how to] reconcile commerce and conscience . . . " His ability to inspire confidence and trust was essential as Almy & Brown built a national market and then dominated the embryonic American yarn industry. His long and enduring friendship with Samuel Slater made it possible for the pioneer manufacturers to coordinate their technical and managerial talents for nearly thirty years. In his will Brown referred to Slater as "my esteemed friend" when he named him as his only nonfamily executor. As for Slater, once when discussing great difficulties experienced during a financial panic in 1829, he said that he "should not have been so tired, if Obadiah Brown had been living" (White, p. 266). This was a high compliment from the man generally accepted as "The Father of American Manufactures."

• Brown's correspondence can be found in the Obadiah M. Brown Papers, the Almy & Brown Papers, the Moses Brown Papers, and the Austin Collection, all located at the Rhode Island Historical Society Library, Providence. Published works mentioning Brown in the context of the cotton textile industry include James B. Hedges, *The Browns of Providence Plantations; the Nineteenth Century* (1968), and Caroline F. Ware, *The Early New England Cotton Manufacture: A Study in Industrial Beginnings* (1931). For additional references to Brown, see Mack Thompson, *Moses Brown: Reluctant Reformer* (1962), and George S. White, *Memoir of Samuel Slater* (1836).

JAMES L. CONRAD, JR.

BROWN, Olympia (5 Jan. 1835–23 Oct. 1926), Universalist minister and suffragist, was born in Prairie Ronde, Kalamazoo County, Michigan, the daughter of Asa B. Brown and Lephia Olympia, farmers. Her parents were Universalists with a strong commitment to education for their children. She first attended school with her two younger sisters and brother in a building on her family's farm and later in Schoolcraft, Michigan. In 1854 she went to Mount Holyoke Female Seminary in Massachusetts. She disliked the stultifying rules and religious orthodoxy there and transferred in 1856 to the newly organized coeducational Antioch College in Yellow Springs, Ohio.

For Brown, Antioch College was a formative experience. There the preaching of Antoinette Brown (later Blackwell) inspired her to enter the ministry. "It was the first time I had heard a woman preach," Brown wrote, "and the sense of victory lifted me up. . . . I felt as though the Kingdom of Heaven were at hand" ("Autobiography," pp. 24, 26).

After graduating in 1860, Brown remained in Ohio and began to write theological schools in an attempt to gain admission. After many rejections, and with mixed support from school officials, she was accepted at the Canton School of Theology at St. Lawrence University in Canton, New York. As a student Brown encountered deep prejudice against women ministers, which manifested itself when she applied for ordination. After considerable controversy, she was ordained by the Northern (St. Lawrence) Association of Universalists in Malone, New York, on 25 June 1863. She was the first woman ordained with full denominational approval in the United States. Because of her own struggles, Brown encouraged young women to enter the ministry, among them Phoebe A. Hanaford.

In April 1864 Brown was called to the Universalist church in Weymouth, Massachusetts, and in that year became the first woman to be installed by the denomination. She later served congregations in Bridgeport, Connecticut; Racine, Mukwanago, and Neenah, Wisconsin; and Columbus, Ohio. Later in her career Brown referred to her pastorate in Weymouth as "perhaps the most enjoyable part of my ministerial career" ("Autobiography," p. 33). While in Massachusetts, Brown took public speaking lessons and gained a reputation as a skilled orator. In 1866 she attended her first women's rights meeting with Susan B. Anthony and became a charter member of the American Equal Rights Association. A year later, at the urging of Lucy Stone and Henry Blackwell, Brown became active in the woman suffrage movement in Kansas. Although the campaign in Kansas failed to pass the amendment, Brown gained valuable experience and became a cofounder in 1868 of the New England Woman Suffrage Association.

Brown met and married businessman and publisher John Henry Willis in April 1873. Although the marriage went against the advice of her family, who feared for her career, Willis was her greatest supporter, and she continued to use her own name. They had two children, and the family moved in 1878 to Racine,

Wisconsin. She immediately became involved with the suffrage campaign in Wisconsin and in 1884 was elected president of the Wisconsin Woman Suffrage Association (WWSA), a position she held for the next twenty-eight years. While in Wisconsin, Brown advocated for a broad interpretation of a state statute allowing women to vote in school matters. She argued that all elections concerned school matters and urged women to vote in state and local elections as well. When her own ballot was refused in a Racine election in 1887, she became involved in a civil suit that almost bankrupted the Wisconsin movement.

Brown believed there was a continuity between spreading the principles of Universalism as a minister and promoting the struggle for equality and liberty as a suffrage reformer. After 1887 she resigned her pastorate and worked primarily within the suffrage movement, although she still continued to preach occasionally. Unlike some of her colleagues within the suffrage movement, Brown worked within the context of organized religion. Accused of opposing the extension of suffrage to immigrants, Brown actually sought a broader extension of the franchise, including immigrants after a residence period. Her Universalist beliefs in "the fatherhood of God, the brotherhood of man, and the liberty and equality of all" challenged her into action and were a source of solace in times of disappointment.

An indefatigable speaker, Brown once gave no fewer than 205 addresses while traveling in Kansas. She exhibited "great physical power of endurance, . . . speaking two or three times a day, in the hottest weather, travelling from twenty to fifty miles each day, with only an average of about four hours sleep, and her speeches from one to two hours in length, . . . and only weighing ninety-one pounds" (Miller, vol. 1, p. 545).

Brown came to believe that the only way to obtain the vote for women was through a constitutional amendment. In 1892 she founded the Federal Suffrage Association. But Brown suffered a deep disappointment when a second generation of suffragists in Wisconsin merged with the WWSA. Bitter at being ignored, she resigned her presidency of the WWSA in 1912. In 1913 she was elected to the advisory board of the Congressional Union (later National Woman's party), founded by Alice Paul and Lucy Burns. Nevertheless, she lived to see the passage of the Nineteenth Amendment in 1920 and to vote in an election. Beginning in 1914 she had begun to live for part of the year with her daughter in Baltimore, where she died.

Although she never obtained the prominence of some suffragists, Brown is an important figure because of her connections to organized religion. Moreover, she was a tireless advocate for women's education, temperance, crime prevention, and the repeal of capital punishment.

• Brown's papers are in the Schlesinger Library on the History of Women, Radcliffe College, Cambridge, Mass. Material related to her suffrage efforts are in the Wisconsin Woman Suffrage Association Papers and the Ada James Papers, State Historical Society of Wisconsin, along with an interview with her daughter, Gwendolyn Willis, recorded in 1959. The papers of the National Woman's party in the Library of Congress refer to Brown's later suffrage efforts. Her "Autobiography," published in a special issue of the *Annual Journal of the Universalist Historical Society* (1963), is an important source, as is her biography in Catherine F. Hitchings, *Universalist and Unitarian Women Ministers* (1975). A selection of her papers are published in *Suffrage and Religious Principle: Speeches and Writings of Olympia Brown*, ed. Dana Greene (1983). For her contributions to Universalism, see Russell E. Miller, *The Larger Hope: The First Century of the Universalist Church in America, 1770–1870*, vol. 1 (1979). The most comprehensive history of the suffrage movement is Elizabeth Cady Stanton et al., eds., *History of Woman Suffrage* (6 vols., 1881–1922). Obituaries are in the *Baltimore Sun* and the *New York Times*, both 24 Oct. 1926, and the *Racine Journal-News*, 25 Oct. 1926.

SHERYL A. KUJAWA

BROWN, Paul E. (7 Sept. 1908–5 Aug. 1991), football coach and executive, was born in Norwalk, Ohio, the son of Lester Brown, a railroad dispatcher, and Ida Sherwood. Both of his parents were of English descent. Brown's father, whose job required precise planning, instilled in him a love of organization. His mother enjoyed competing at games, particularly cards, and taught him the thrill of competition. Brown was given his first football when he was six years old; when the ball could no longer be inflated, he stuffed it with rags and leaves and continued playing with it.

When Brown was nine years old, he moved with his family to Massillon, Ohio, where he excelled in school and played several sports. As a sophomore at Massillon's Washington High School, Brown, undersized at 120 pounds, tried out for the football team. He impressed his coach, Dave Stewart, with his determination and understanding of the game, and he was the starting quarterback by his junior year. After graduating from high school, Brown enrolled at Ohio State University, but he was too small to play football at that level and unhappy on such a large campus. After one year he transferred to Miami University in Oxford, Ohio; there he performed well both on the football field and in the classroom. In 1929 he married Kathryn Kester; they had three sons.

After receiving a B.A. in education from Miami in 1930, Brown became the head football coach at Severn Middle Preparatory School in Severn, Maryland. Two years later, after considering a law career, he returned to Massillon as the head football and basketball coach of Washington High School. The success of the school's athletic program, particularly its football team, had been minimal since Stewart's departure some years earlier, and community interest had waned. Brown immediately began to reshape the program into a model of consistency and success that was unparalleled in Ohio high school athletics.

Brown's football philosophy, which never changed throughout his career, was based on his belief that the quality of a player is determined not just by his athletic ability but by his attitude and intelligence. Brown coveted players who worked hard, were disciplined in their technique, and were willing to make personal sacrifices for the benefit of the team. His players were always well conditioned, and each through endless repetition in practice developed a reflexive knowledge of football fundamentals. His Massillon teams went 80–8–2 over the next nine years, and their six straight state championships (1935–1940) brought immeasurable pride to a town devastated by the Great Depression.

In 1941 Brown became the head football coach at Ohio State University; a year earlier he had earned an M.A. in education from the school. He oversaw every facet of the program—including training facilities and equipment purchases—and molded a team that won the unofficial 1942 national championship. World War II enlistment ravaged his team's ranks, however, and in 1944 Brown himself was called to service in the U.S. Navy. He coached at the Great Lakes Naval Training Center near Chicago, Illinois, guiding his teams against major college programs such as Notre Dame, Illinois, and Ohio State. Brown's role as a lieutenant and battalion commander, however, often superceded his duties as coach during his tenure at Great Lakes.

At the end of the war, Brown—after having been convinced by Arch Ward, the influential sports editor of the *Chicago Tribune*, that pro football was the proper forum for his skills—accepted an offer to coach the Cleveland, Ohio, franchise of a new professional league, the All-America Football Conference (AAFC). He agreed to coach the new team for $25,000 per year and 5 percent ownership. More importantly to Brown, he also became the vice president and general manager, and his contract gave him total control over all football operations—including the hiring of coaches and the signing of players. Cleveland's fans were given the opportunity to vote on the team's name; they chose the Cleveland Browns, a reflection of the esteem in which they held their fellow Ohioan.

Because the league had not yet organized a college draft, Brown was able to handpick players he had already successfully coached or who he knew would thrive within his system. Many players, like Brown himself, were still serving in the military; the Browns had the finances to woo stars such as quarterback Otto Graham with generous monthly retainers until they were out of the service and able to devote their time to football. Brown chose his players without considering their race, unlike the leaders of the well-established National Football League (NFL), who had effectively barred blacks from playing since 1932. Two of Brown's signees, Bill Willis and Marion Motley, became the first African Americans to play professional football in the so-called modern era (both were later inducted into the Pro Football Hall of Fame).

The Cleveland Browns dominated the AAFC, compiling a 52–4–3 record between 1946 and 1949 and winning all four league championships. Brown's many innovations were renowned and widely imitated. Among other distinctions, he was the first to hire and train full-time assistant coaches; the first to give intelligence tests to players to determine their football aptitude; the first to grade player performances using game film; the first to teach his players through classroom studies as well as on-the-field training; and the first to call his team's offensive plays by using "messenger guards" to communicate with his quarterback. His emphasis on speed at every position, precise pass patterns, and a wide-open passing attack employing the T-formation (in which the quarterback stands directly behind the center instead of several yards in the backfield) revamped the game and made his teams nearly impossible to stop.

The great success of Brown's AAFC Cleveland teams brought him little personal satisfaction, however, as he began to realize that the league was doomed. In 1950, after much negotiation, the AAFC was disbanded and the Browns joined the NFL. Although considered by many NFL fans and players as upstarts, the Browns won the NFL crown in their first year in the league, beating the Los Angeles Rams 30–28 in the championship game. Brown's teams went on to win a string of Eastern Conference championships (1951–1953, 1957) and two more NFL championships (1954 and 1955).

In early 1961 Art Modell became the majority owner of the Cleveland Browns. Although he had no substantial football experience, he desired to take control of the football side of the organization. After two years of conflict that saw Brown's contractual powers as coach, vice president, and general manager consistently undermined by Modell, the owner fired Brown as head coach and demoted him to what Brown described as a "vice president in charge of I-don't-know-what" (*Philadelphia Enquirer*, 11 Jan. 1963). Brown, though embittered, remained a semiretired consultant to the Browns organization, spending most of his time with his wife and family.

Brown's mind and heart were never far from football, however, even after moving to La Jolla, California, in 1964. A new league, the American Football League (AFL), had been formed in 1959 and had successfully competed against the NFL; in 1966 the two leagues reached a merger agreement. As early as 1965 Brown had made clear his desire to form an expansion NFL franchise in Cincinnati, Ohio. In 1967 a group led by Brown paid $9 million for the new team, and the Cincinnati Bengals, with Brown as head coach and general manager, joined the league. That year Brown was also inducted into the Pro Football Hall of Fame.

Brown's Bengals won three games in 1968, setting the record for the most wins by an NFL or AFL expansion team in its first year. The team under Brown also managed to win three Central Division championships (1970, 1973, 1975). Perhaps Brown's greatest achievement as an owner of the Bengals was convincing other NFL owners to restructure the league into two equal conferences of thirteen teams. Brown argued that the change was necessary to ensure competitive balance and the financial health of all the franchises; the new scheme was adopted, and in 1969 the NFL was divided into the American Football Conference and the National Football Conference. That year Brown's wife died, and in 1973 he married Mary Rightsell, a widow with four grown children. After the 1975 season, Brown retired from coaching, although he remained active in the Bengals' operations.

Critics, including Hall of Fame running back Jim Brown, have suggested that Brown was an unfeeling disciplinarian and that his teams played with a robot-like consistency that somehow betrayed the emotional heart of the game. While his coaching style was markedly stern, he was a master teacher and motivator, and his passion for the intricacies of football translated into victories at every level of competition. Brown's organizational system set the standard for virtually all modern professional and college teams. Many of his former players and assistant coaches had highly successful coaching careers of their own, including all-time greats Weeb Eubank, Bud Grant, Chuck Noll, Bill Walsh, and Don Shula. As Walsh said, Brown was an "innovator who bridged the gap from the 1930s to the 1990s. No one, not [George] Halas, not [Vince] Lombardi, not [Pete] Rozelle, can make that claim on the history of modern pro football" (*New York Times*, 11 Aug. 1991). Brown died at his home in Cincinnati.

• Materials relating to Brown's life and career are held in the Paul Brown File at the Pro Football Hall of Fame in Canton, Ohio. His autobiography, *PB: The Paul Brown Story* (1979), written with Jack Clary, contains many player anecdotes as well as some harsh criticism of Modell. Other informative articles include Charles Heaton, "The Warm Side of Paul Brown," *Cleveland Plain Dealer*, 25 Sept. 1964; Ed Hershey, "That Old Brown Magic," *Newsday*, Nov. 1968, pp. 19–25; Jack Newcombe, "Paul Brown: Football's Licensed Genius," *Sport*, Dec. 1954, pp. 51–59; Ira Berkow, "At One Time Paul Brown Jumped for Joy, Too," *New York Times*, 7 Aug. 1991; and Bill Walsh, "Paul Brown: Sixty Years of Quiet, Innovative Football," *New York Times*, 11 Aug. 1991. An obituary is in the *New York Times*, 6 Aug. 1991.

JAY MAZZOCCHI

BROWN, Phoebe Hinsdale (1 May 1783–10 Aug. 1861), hymnist and religious writer, was born in Canaan, New York, the daughter of George Hinsdale (profession unrecorded) and Phoebe Allen. Brown's father died ten months after she was born, and her mother died shortly before her eighth birthday. Brown and her sister Lydia spent the year after their mother's death in the home of their maternal grandparents in Norwich, Connecticut, where Brown's grandmother treated her kindly and instructed her in reading and religion. During this period Brown demonstrated her piety, her aptitude for learning, and her desire for education by reading the Bible through three times. From the ages of nine to eighteen, however, Brown lived with her married sister Chloe and Chloe's tyrannical and brutish husband William Noyes, Jr., in Claverack, New York. Brown was miserable during these years not only because William Noyes overworked her and treated her like a servant, but also because he forbade her to attend church and to read books.

Soon after coming of age, Brown left the Noyeses' household and attended the Claverack district school with local children. Here she learned to write and immediately began composing her own verses and prose pieces. In 1801 Brown returned to Canaan where she lived with the family of William and Amy Whiting, joined the Congregational church, and participated in a religious revival.

On 1 June 1805 she married Timothy H. Brown, a carpenter, painter, cabinetmaker, glazier, and paper-hanger. In November the couple moved to East Windsor, Connecticut, where they spent the next eight years and where her two eldest children were born. Always poor but never destitute, the family moved in 1813 to nearby Ellington to secure Timothy Brown more dependable employment in construction. During the five years the family lived in Ellington, Brown gave birth to two more children, became avidly interested in foreign and Indian missionary endeavors, and began publishing poems and stories in weekly papers, including the New Haven *Religious Intelligencer* edited by Nathan Whiting. Following the prospect of steadier work, the Browns moved to Monson, Massachusetts, in 1818. Always devout, Brown was initially alarmed at the dismal spiritual condition of the Monson congregation, a concern reflected in her hymn "Prayer for a Revival." Fortunately, the Monson community was soon rejuvenated, and Brown founded and headed the school, an experience that led to the publication of her school lessons by the Massachusetts Sunday School Society. She resided in Monson until Timothy Brown's death in 1853.

Brown had earned local renown as a poet and hymnist before New York evangelist Asahel Nettleton collected, adapted, and published four of her works in *Village Hymns* (1824), the finest evangelical hymnbook produced in America to that date. The best-loved of these, "My Apology for My Twilight Rambles, Addressed to a Lady," begins "I love to steal awhile away / From every cumbering care." Two tunes were written in its honor, "Monson" by Brown's son Samuel Robbins Brown, and "Brown" by William B. Bradbury. Although this hymn is the only one of Brown's widely known in the twentieth century, hymns by her appeared in many of the most popular collections of her own day, including Thomas Hastings and Lowell Mason's *Spiritual Songs* (1832), James Linsley and Gustavus Davis's *Select Hymns* (1836), and Elias Nason's *Congregational Hymn Book* (1857).

Brown also wrote religious fiction and poetry, a selection of which can be found in the weekly Boston magazine *The Pearl* (1831–1836). Brown's most widely read fictional works are *The Village School* (1836) and *The Tree and Its Fruits* (1836; 2d ed., 1838). Designed both to instruct children and to engage their emotions, *The Village School* teaches the Ten Commandments and righteous behavior by embedding its lessons in two children's conversion narratives. Aimed at a more mature audience, *The Tree and Its Fruits* relies on realistic narrative techniques to paint the wretched consequences of gambling, drinking, and impious reading. Like that of many Calvinist prose writers of the 1830s and 1840s, Brown's fiction emphasizes the efficacy of personal ministrations rather than the potency of reform movements and a sentimental ethic of feeling right and doing good rather than theological exhortations or arguments. Her fiction focuses on the social environment of sin, sometimes equating sin with bad habits and conversion with the reform of those habits.

After her husband's death, Brown lived with her surviving children in various locations, including Owasco Outlet, New York, and Henry, Illinois, where she died. Although her work is seldom read or sung any longer, Brown overcame nearly insurmountable personal, economic, and cultural deprivations to achieve success as a hymnist and author.

• Biographical accounts of Brown are found in Herbert C. Andrews, *Hinsdale Genealogy* (1906); Edwin F. Hatfield, *Poets of the Church* (1884), pp. 96–101; Edward S. Ninde, *The Story of the American Hymn* (1921), pp. 176–87; and William E. Griffis, *A Maker of the Orient: Samuel Robbins Brown* (1902), passim. Many commentators report that Brown wrote an unpublished autobiography of over 400 pages in the late 1840s at the request of her children. A manuscript volume of similar length containing her poems was compiled by Charles Hammond before his death. If these manuscripts survive, they are probably in the hands of family members. For discussions of her hymns and fiction, see Henry Wilder Foote, *Three Centuries of American Hymnody* (1968); Samuel Willoughby Duffield, *English Hymns: Their Authors and History* (1886); and David S. Reynolds, *Faith in Fiction: The Emergence of Religious Literature in America* (1981), pp. 86–90.

JEANNE M. MALLOY

BROWN, Rachel Fuller (23 Nov. 1898–14 Jan. 1980), biochemist, was born in Springfield, Massachusetts, the daughter of George Hamilton Brown, a real estate and insurance agent, and Annie Fuller, a director of religious education for various Episcopal churches. They moved to Missouri, where in Brown's last year of elementary school her father left the family in poverty. On the family's return to Springfield, Rachel enrolled in Commercial High School to become a wage earner, but her mother insisted she transfer to Central High School for a classical education.

Brown's yearnings to go to college were fulfilled by a woman friend of her grandmother's, who paid her way through Mount Holyoke College. During her life Brown repaid that kindness both with gifts to her alma mater and scholarships to high school and college women who planned to become scientists. Although Brown initially chose history for her major at Mount Holyoke, she was required to take a science course. She came to love chemistry, a strong field at Mount Holyoke since the days of its founder Mary Lyon. Brown earned her A.B. in chemistry and history in 1920. She worked as a laboratory assistant until she began graduate work at the University of Chicago, from which she earned an M.S. in organic chemistry in 1921. She then taught at the Frances Shimer School near Chicago, a girls' preparatory school and junior college, but three years was enough to convince her that teaching was not her career.

After taking courses in languages and chemistry at Harvard University in the summer of 1924, she returned to Chicago for further graduate work in organic chemistry with a minor in bacteriology. She successfully completed her research projects and course work in 1926 and submitted her Ph.D. thesis, but there was some difficulty in scheduling her committee members for her oral exam. She rapidly exhausted her meager savings, and in desperate need of a job she left Chicago without her Ph.D. for a job at the Division of Laboratories and Research in Albany, New York. The division, a major arm of the New York Department of Health, was famous for its laboratory identification of human disease-causing agents and preparation of antisera and vaccines. Brown was immediately immersed in research, and for seven years she worked without her Ph.D. until division director Augustus Wadsworth personally arranged for her to take her orals when she was in Chicago for a meeting. She finally received her Ph.D. in 1933 and was elected to Sigma Xi.

On arriving in Albany, Brown became a member of St. Peter's Episcopal Church, where she met Dorothy Wakerley, a woman who became her lifetime friend and companion. They soon shared a house, and following a common pattern for unmarried women they cared for an extended family over the years. Along with Brown's grandmother and mother, the house was rarely empty of various nieces and nephews and a succession of visiting women scientists from China.

At the division's laboratory Brown worked on research to develop a pneumonia vaccine and on improving tests for syphilis. The antibacterial and antifungal work for which she is most noted began in 1948 in collaboration with Elizabeth Lee Hazen, a microbiologist also with the division but working in New York City. Fungal diseases were a little recognized yet serious source of sickness and death, and there were no antifungal agents safe for human use. In fact, the increasing use of antibiotics following World War II had led to a dramatic increase in opportunistic fungal infections. Hazen cultured soil samples for possible antifungal organisms and sent promising ones to Brown to purify and find the particular chemical agents having the property of arresting or killing fungal growth.

Microorganism no. 48240, collected by Hazen from some soil on a friend's farm, yielded two antifungal substances called Fractions N and AN. The women tested it against two common pathogenic fungi, *Cryptococcus neoformans*, a fungus responsible for the chronic disease cryptococcosis, which affects lungs, skin, and other body parts like the central nervous system, and *Candida albicans*, which causes candidiasis, a serious systemic infection in patients treated with broad-spectrum antibiotics. Fraction N was too toxic, but Fraction AN proved effective not only against the initial two fungi but fourteen others, and they gave it the scientific name *Streptomyces noursei*, after the owners of the farm on which Hazen had dug the soil sample. They first named the drug "fungicidin," but because they discovered that that name was already in use, they changed the name to "nystatin" in honor of the New York State Division of Laboratories and Research.

Brown presented their work at the National Academy of Sciences regional meeting in 1950, and the report by the *New York Times* started a flurry of calls from pharmaceutical companies excited by its commercial possibilities. The pharmaceutical industry had the manufacturing capabilities and ability to test the compound in humans. But to license the substance, control the purity, and protect the financial interests of a commercial development company, Gilbert Dalldorf, Wadsworth's successor, assigned patent royalties to the Research Corporation of New York, a nonprofit foundation for the advancement of science. The production license was awarded to E. R. Squibb & Sons who produced the first sale of tablets for human use in 1954. Nystatin was the first antifungal antibiotic to be safe and effective in treating human diseases. Over the years it proved effective in more than human disorders and was used to stop fungal growth on flood-damaged works of art in Florence, Italy, and showed limited help in slowing Dutch elm disease. Royalties reached a total of $13.4 million. As Brown and Hazen wanted no financial returns for themselves, the philanthropic Research Corporation used half for grants to further scientific research and the other half to support what became known as the Brown-Hazen Fund. Between 1957 and 1978 the Brown-Hazen Fund supported training and research in biomedical sciences and encouraged women to take up careers in science. For several years the fund was the largest single source of nonfederal funds for medical mycology in the United States.

Both Brown and Hazen received many awards for their collaborative work, the first major prize being the Squibb Award in Chemotherapy (1955). Brown was elected a fellow of the New York Academy of Sciences in 1957. In 1972 she was given the Rhoda Benham Award of the Medical Mycological Society of the Americas. Brown and Hazen were the first women ever to receive, in 1975, the American Institute of Chemists' Chemical Pioneer Award. On Brown's retirement in 1968 she received the Distinguished Service Award of the New York Department of Health. For more than fifty years Brown was an active member of the American Association of University Women and strongly supported the participation of women in science. She died in Albany, New York.

Brown, a meticulous organic chemist, made a major scientific and medical contribution to society as the codiscoverer of the fungicide nystatin, the first effective antibiotic against fungal disease in humans. Brown and Hazen's project highlighted the fruitfulness of scientific collaboration and philanthropy, which they continued with the later discovery of two other antibiotics, phalamycin and capacidin. Brown actively worked to create a sense of shared purpose and achievement in both her scientific and community work.

• Brown's papers are at the Schlesinger Library, Radcliffe College. Richard S. Baldwin, *The Fungus Fighters: Two Women Scientists and Their Discovery* (1981), has provided a well-crafted tale of Brown's scientific collaboration with Elizabeth Lee Hazen. Details of Brown's life and accomplishments have been included in Edna Yost, *Women of Modern Science* (1959), and Louis Haber, *Women Pioneers of Science* (1979).

SARA F. TJOSSEM

BROWN, Ralph Hall (12 Jan. 1898–23 Feb. 1948), geographer, was born in Ayer, Massachusetts, the son of William Brown, a pharmacist, and Nellie Eliza Leavitt. He attended Massachusetts State College from 1915 to 1917 and graduated in 1921 from the Wharton School of Finance and Commerce, University of Pennsylvania, with a B.S. in economics. In 1925 he received a Ph.D. in geography and economics from the University of Wisconsin. In 1924 Brown married Eunice Rasmussen; three of their four children survived to maturity.

After graduation in 1925 Brown became an instructor of geography at the University of Colorado, where in 1927 he was promoted to assistant professor. In 1929 he moved to the new Department of Geography at the University of Minnesota, where he served first as an assistant professor, from 1938 as an associate professor, and from 1945 as a full professor.

In teaching at both Colorado and Minnesota, Brown stressed the need to understand how the settlers in specific regions, like the Great Plains, adjusted to the region's geographical conditions. But his perceptions altered in the late 1920s and 1930s, when he became interested in studying how people not only interacted with the geographic environment but how they changed it. In doing so, he became an advocate of historical geography, an area in which English and German geographers and the Americans Ellen Churchill Semple and Albert Perry Brigham were already active. Their work had been preceded by that of Frederick Jackson Turner in providing descriptions of the land that the settlers found. Brown gave details of how people had settled it with charts, documentary evidence, and maps.

Brown's innovations were recognized early in his career. In 1928 he was elected a fellow in the Council of the American Geographical Society. In 1933 he was chosen for a three-year term as one of the nine councillors in the Association of American Geographers. Elevation to this post indicated that Brown, at the age of thirty-five, had arrived as a geographer in the eyes of his colleagues. His chairman at Minnesota, Darnell Davis, noted that Brown was "one of the most promising of the younger geographers in the United States" (Miles, p. 56).

In 1941 Brown was elected secretary of the Association of American Geographers. When he resigned that position in 1945, he was chosen the following year as the editor of the *Annals* of the Association of American Geographers, and his wife served as his assistant. His first article in the *Annals* was a report of his study, funded by the Rockefeller Foundation in 1932, of the landscape changes in the Great Plains that resulted from irrigation. His article "Belle Fourche Valley and Uplands" appeared in the *Annals* in 1933.

Brown, in his two major works, *Mirror for Americans: Likeness of the Eastern Seaboard* (1943) and *Historical Geography of the United States* (1948), stressed the personal reactions of and changes made by the settlers. Historical geography, he wrote in *Historical Geography*, depends "on original eyewitness accounts and contemporary maps" (pp. iii, iv), which unfortunately were not always available. In addition, Brown used field work to enhance his understanding of the environmental changes that had occurred.

Brown's *Mirror for Americans* won immediate praise from his colleagues and reviewers. A review in the *Journal of Geography* (1944) called the work "a milestone in American geographical literature." A Canadian reviewer found the study "thoroughly readable and instructive" (*Canadian Geographical Journal* [1943]). An American historian reviewing the book found it "an achievement of the first rank; indeed, it is a pioneer work in the field of historical geography" (*Mississippi Valley Historical Review* [1944]).

The author of the *Historical Geography of the United States* did not live to see the reviews of this book, which was landed by the colonial historian Lawrence Gipson and a reviewer in the *New York Times* (22 Aug. 1948). The book received the Chicago Geographical Society's William S. Monroe Award as the best geographical publication of 1948. In 1954 Columbia University presented to Brown's wife the prestigious Laubat Prize, recognizing Brown's *Historical Geography* as one of the two outstanding studies to have appeared in the past five years. It carried a stipend of $5,000.

Before Brown's death in Minneapolis, Minnesota, he had received copies of his *Historical Geography* and was distressed at a number of misprints in the text. He was also disturbed by the failure of the printer of the *Annals* to perform tasks as Brown, a perfectionist, thought they should be done. His body was found slumped over the wheel of his car in his garage. The death was ruled accidental, the result of a heart attack, but rumors persisted that he had committed suicide. A subsequent investigation by the University of Minnesota ruled the death accidental.

Brown became known as the father of American historical geography. Historian Robin A. Butler observed that historical geography in the United States was "conditioned by a small group of highly influential individual scholars, conspicuously Harlan Barrows, Ralph Brown, and Carl Sauer" and labels Brown as a major figure in historical geography. Another observer, Henry C. Darby, has described *Mirror for Americans* as "a magnificent tour de force and an intellectual exercise that throws light upon some of the problems involved in the creation of the 'historic present'" (Butler, p. 37).

Brown's influence can be discerned in the work of Eric Ross, for whose *Beyond the River and the Bay* (1970), a study of early Manitoba, Canada, Brown's *Mirror for Americans* served as a model, and in Donald Meinig's prize-winning study, *The Great Columbia Plain* (1963).

• Brown's letters (1929–1948) are available in the Ralph Hall Brown Collection, University of Minnesota Geography Department. Other letters are housed in the Archives of the American Geographical Society, New York City, and the Association of the American Geographer Archives (1942–1945), Washington, D.C. There are also a small number of Brown letters in the Ellsworth Huntington Papers, Yale University Library. A good portrait of Brown is Jeanne Linda Miles, "Ralph Hall Brown: Gentlescholar of Historical Geography" (Ph.D. diss., Univ. of Oklahoma, 1982). A list of Brown's fifty-two articles and hundreds of reviews can be found in Miles's dissertation and in Stanley D. Dodge, "Ralph Hall Brown, 1898–1948," *Annals of the Association of American Geographers* 38 (1948): 305–9. Secondary sources include Andrew Clark, "Ralph Brown's Contribution to Historical Geography," *Die Erde* 5 (1952–1953): 148–52; and D. McManis, "A Prism to the Past: The Historical Geography of Ralph Hall Brown," *Social Science History* 3 (1978): 72–86. See also Robin A. Butler, *Historical Geography: Through the Gates of Space and Time* (1993), pp. 35–39; Donald W. Meinig, *The Shaping of America: A Geographical Perspective on 500 Years of History*, vol. 1, *Atlantic American, 1492–1800* (1986), pp. 438–39; Michael Pacione, ed., *Historical Geography: Progress and Prospect* (1987), p. 284; and David Hawke, *The Colonial Experience* (1966).

THOMAS J. CURRAN

BROWN, Roy James (10 Sept. 1925–25 May 1981), blues singer and piano player, was born in New Orleans, Louisiana, the son of Yancy Brown, a brick mason and plasterer, and Tru-Love Warren, a schoolteacher. At the age of five, Roy began learning piano from his mother, a professional music teacher who also directed a church choir. After the family moved to a farming community in Eunice, Louisiana, Roy attended elementary school, sang in the local church, and later formed a gospel quartet. By his own account, he once earned a whipping by "jazzing up" a spiritual in a church performance.

When he was fourteen, Brown's mother died of pneumonia. He moved to Houston, Texas, and then, in 1942, to Los Angeles, California, where he attended high school. He became interested in the music of crooner Bing Crosby, whose songs and movies he studied carefully in hopes of becoming a pop singer. In 1945 Brown won first prize in an amateur talent contest at the Million Dollar Theater with two cowboy pop selections, "San Antonio Rose" and "I Got Spurs That Jingle Jangle Jingle."

In the mid-1940s, by now married to his lifelong companion Gertrude (maiden name unknown), Brown returned to Louisiana and landed a job as a vocalist and master of ceremonies at a Shreveport club, soon branching out to other clubs in Louisiana and East Texas. Eventually, he joined a vocal group called the Melodeers from Galveston, Texas. Through 1946 and early 1947, the Melodeers worked with a band at the Club Grenada, broadcasting a local radio program over KGBC. While entertaining in Galveston, Brown came up with the suggestive rhythm and blues vehicle "Good Rockin' Tonight," a racy title since the word "rocking" carried sexual connotations at that time. Because Brown was still a crooner of pop material, the song was initially sung by his band's trumpet player. When the trumpeter was sick one night, Brown sang the number, and it became a hit with local club patrons and radio listeners. In 1947 Brown cut his first record for the Gold Star label.

After an altercation with a club owner in Galveston, which was then a notoriously open seaport, Brown left town and went home to New Orleans, where he tried to sell "Good Rockin' Tonight" to popular blues shouter Wynonie Harris. Rebuffed, he offered it to another popular recording artist, Cecil Gant, who saw potential in both the song and in Brown. Gant telephoned Deluxe Records executive Jules Braun, who listened to an over-the-phone, middle-of-the-night audition and promptly arranged to sign and record Brown, who was then only twenty-two. In July 1947 he cut "Good Rockin' Tonight" in New Orleans with Bob Ogden's Orchestra. Issued in September, the record rose to number thirteen on the charts the following spring, launching Brown on a tour with his own band, the Mighty Men.

In the late 1940s and early 1950s Brown returned for at least fifteen recording sessions with DeLuxe, producing more than a dozen top-ten rhythm and blues hits, including "Long about Midnight," number one in 1948; "Boogie at Midnight," number three in 1949; "Cadillac Baby," number six in 1950; and "Hard Luck Blues," a number-one hit that remained on the charts for eighteen weeks in 1950.

At the peak of his popularity in the early 1950s, Brown's contract was sold to Sid Nathen's Cincinnati-based King Records. He recorded for King through 1955, but his relationship with the label became strained after he discovered that both Deluxe and King had withheld royalties from him. With the help of the musicians' union, bandleader Dave Bartholomew, and Broadcast Music Incorporated, Brown finally began to receive royalties, although his victory came too late; the hit wagon had stopped. After brief and unsuccessful stints with three record labels and trouble with the Internal Revenue Service, which was allegedly resolved with the help of Elvis Presley, Brown moved with his wife and daughter to Los Angeles in the early 1960s.

Living in the San Fernando Valley, Brown continued to record for various labels: Chess, D.R.A., Gert, Connie, and his own labels, Tru-Love and Friendship. Except for occasional club dates, he worked outside of music, selling encyclopedias while Gertrude ran a nursery school. In the late 1960s he began to work with Johnny Otis, a rhythm and blues bandleader whose revue featured several West Coast blues shouters who were trying to jump start their careers. Brown's own comeback was sparked by a 1968 Bluesway album and a 1970 appearance with Otis at the Monterey Jazz Festival. Popular once more, Brown played an extended engagement at the Parisian Room in Los Angeles in the mid-1970s and a successful European tour in 1978. He also had bookings in various U.S. clubs and at many festivals, including the 1981 Jazz and Heritage Festival in his hometown, New Orleans. Not long after that appearance, however, Brown returned to California, where he suffered a fatal heart attack in San Fernando.

Although he was often typecast as a tragic figure, a prime example of exploitation and hard luck, Brown had a long and relatively successful career by R&B standards. He was a major star in the late 1940s and early 1950s, recording more than 120 sides and producing a remarkable string of hits. Brown could handle rhythm and blues or pop material with equal facility, and with his gospel training he was also considered one of the first soul singers. "Good Rockin' Tonight," his signature song, became a rock and roll classic, recorded by Elvis Presley, among others.

Because Brown's hits came early in his career, he missed out on the high volume record buying of the rock and roll era, and there is little doubt he was cheated out of royalties—an all-too-common practice at the time. Nevertheless, he was a pioneering vocalist who influenced a range of blues, rock, and soul artists, including Junior Parker, Jackie Wilson, B. B. King, James Brown, and Presley. He was a solid professional performer who enjoyed a 35-year career. He was inducted into the Blues Foundation's Hall of Fame in Memphis in 1981.

• For additional information on Brown, see Jason Berry et al., *Up from the Cradle of Jazz: New Orleans Music since World War II* (1986); John Broven, *Walking to New Orleans: The Story of New Orleans Rhythm and Blues* (1974); and Sheldon Harris, *Blues Who's Who: A Biographical Dictionary of Blues Singers* (1979; rev. ed., 1989). For a discography, see Mike Leadbitter and Neil Slaven, *Blues Records 1943–1970: A Selective Discography*, vol. 1: *A–K* (1987).

BILL MCCULLOCH
BARRY LEE PEARSON

BROWN, R. R. (19 Oct. 1885–20 Feb. 1964), pastor and radio evangelist, was born Robert Roger Brown in Dagus Falls, Pennsylvania, the son of Scottish immigrants William Murray Brown, a miner, and Mary Elizabeth Rogers. One of fourteen children, he was raised as a Presbyterian but had little interest in religion until he was converted at the age of eighteen during a revival in a Presbyterian church. At a subsequent meeting at a local nondenominational church, Brown encountered a representative of A. B. Simpson's Christian and Missionary Alliance (CMA), an association of ministers and churches founded in 1881 to promote greater missionary activity both in the United States and abroad. Impressed by the movement's organization, dedication to missions, and nonpartisan tone, he decided to train for the ministry in the CMA. In 1906 he entered Alliance College at Nyack, New York, earning a B.A. in 1910. After serving as an interim pastor for a Baptist church on Long Island, Brown was ordained on 19 August 1911. He then accepted the pastorate of an Alliance church in Beaver

Falls, Pennsylvania, and during his nine years there became friends with leading CMA figures, such as Simpson, E. D. Whiteside, and Paul Rader. Soon after his arrival at the church, Brown met and, in 1912, married a member of his congregation, Mary Edith Swihart; the couple had three children.

In 1920, at the invitation of new Alliance president Paul Rader, Brown moved to Chicago and became the district superintendent for seven midwestern states. After establishing a new CMA congregation in Chicago, he went on the road, conducting a series of revivals in his new territory. In July 1922 Brown went to Omaha, where he erected a temporary tabernacle for what he thought would be a short evangelistic campaign. The meetings were so successful, however, that he decided to make the tabernacle a permanent congregation, the Gospel Tabernacle, and relocated his base of operations to Omaha.

In April 1923 Brown was asked by officials at local radio station WOAW (later WOW) to conduct a service for the station's first Sunday on the air. He was asked to return the following week but agreed only at the urging of a local Congregational pastor, who said he had been praying that God would "get an advantage" over the air. Though hesitant in the beginning, Brown continued to broadcast his "World Radio Chapel" program over WOAW/WOW for the next forty-one years, becoming a fundamentalist broadcasting fixture in the Plains states with one of the longest-running religious broadcasts of its time.

Especially in the early years, Brown had a tendency to attack the microphone—literally shouting out his sermons—but he always acted as if he were addressing the individual. The effectiveness of his style is evident in a letter sent by one repentant listener who wrote that he was lying on his couch smoking a pipe when he heard Brown say, "You mossback, ungrateful creature of God! If you would think of what God's done for you, you'd take that pipe out of your mouth and get down on your knees and give thanks to God," whereupon, convinced that Brown could see him, he claimed to have jumped up.

Brown's broadcast differed in three major ways from those of most fundamentalist radio preachers of that period. First, aside from an occasional foray into dispensational prophetic speculation, he rarely strayed from an individualist, evangelistic appeal and thereby avoided the stigma of intolerance that marked some fundamentalist preachers, such as the controversial "Fighting Bob" Shuller of Los Angeles. Largely for this reason, his radio ministry made Brown something of a civic institution; as a result, his broadcasts, unlike most others of his ilk, received free air time, and thus he did not need to solicit funds to sustain the ministry. The third distinguishing feature was Brown's strategy of dubbing his program the "World Radio Congregation" and issuing official certificates of membership to interested listeners. At the peak of his popularity in the mid-1930s, Brown's World Radio Congregation boasted as many as 200,000 "members" in the Plains and Midwest. Despite the success of this concept, however, Brown did not see it as a new ecclesiastical vision but rather as a publicity strategy, which he used only in the 1920s and 1930s, dropping it once the novelty had outlived its usefulness.

Brown's broadcast ministry afforded him great visibility, and in his later years he was a prominent figure at Alliance conventions, where he developed the "Preacher's Chorus" and orchestrated the missionary rally that closed each meeting. He was made a member of the CMA Board of Managers in 1925 and held the position until 1960. In 1933 he founded the Bible and Missionary Conference Center at Okoboji Lakes, Iowa, an important ecumenical gathering spot for midwestern fundamentalists as well as an Alliance campground. He also made several well-publicized world missionary tours, and his Omaha congregation was directly responsible for raising more than $1 million for Alliance missions. After several months of failing health, Brown died in Omaha. His congregation continued the radio broadcast—renamed "The Radio Chapel Service"—over a small network of about a dozen stations until 1977. He was elected to the National Religious Broadcasters' Hall of Fame posthumously in 1976.

R. R. Brown's efforts in early fundamentalist radio, along with those of evangelists Aimee Semple McPherson and Paul Rader, showed skeptical fundamentalists that radio could be an effective tool for evangelization. Brown's World Radio Congregation gained him his greatest notoriety, but his limited use of the strategy is suggestive of the primary importance that fundamentalists placed on traditional notions of local church polity and congregational life. Brown's broadcasts and his Omaha congregation served primarily as rallying points for the CMA and—more importantly—for fundamentalist activity in general in the Midwest and Plains states after 1925, during the post–Scopes trial period of retrenchment and institution-building that insured fundamentalism's post–World War II reemergence.

• There is no collection of R. R. Brown Papers; such materials as exist are largely in the possession of family members and the Christ Community Church (formerly the Omaha Gospel Tabernacle) in Omaha, Neb. A small amount of material on Brown is in the archives of the Christian and Missionary Alliance at Alliance headquarters in Colorado Springs, Colo. Brown's personal style lent itself to the pulpit and the radio ministry, and as a result he did not leave a prolific written legacy. Now-hard-to-find pamphlets from his radio sermons, such as, "Did Jesus Know Our Times? Dictatorship" (1933), typify the sorts of things he sent to his listeners. Brown did occasionally pen devotional articles and sermons for Alliance organs; representative of them is "Intellectualism vs. The Illuminated Mind," *Alliance Weekly*, 9 Oct. 1957, pp. 3–4. There has been no attempt at a scholarly examination of Brown's life and career, but his involvement with the CMA is covered succinctly in an obituary tribute by William F. Smalley, "Dr. R. R. Brown: His Contribution to the Christian and Missionary Alliance," *Alliance Weekly*, 1 Apr. 1964, pp. 6–7, 13. Brown also receives some attention in Robert L. Niklaus, John S. Sawin, and Samuel J. Stoesz's general history of the CMA, *All for Jesus* (1986). Brown's radio work is examined somewhat by Dennis Voskuil in "The Power of the Air: Evangelicals and the Rise of Religious Broadcasting," in *American Evangelicals and the Mass Media*, ed. Quentin J. Schultze (1990), and by Mark Ward, Sr., in *Air of Salvation: The Story of Christian Broadcasting* (1994).

LARRY ESKRIDGE

BROWN, Samuel (30 Jan. 1769–12 Jan. 1830), physician, was born in Timber Ridge, near Lexington, Virginia, the son of John Brown, a Presbyterian minister, and Margaret Preston. After attending his father's grammar school and the Reverend James Waddell's seminary in Louisa County, he entered Dickinson College in Carlisle, Pennsylvania, as a junior and there was active in the "Belles Lettres Society," a student debating society. He graduated in 1789 with a B.A. and then studied medicine with his brother-in-law, Alexander Humphreys, of Staunton, Virginia. In the fall of 1792 Brown went to Philadelphia and is said to have been a private pupil of Benjamin Rush. For two years, 1793–1794, he attended the University of Edinburgh in Scotland, which at that time had the world's leading medical school. Because he did not study at Edinburgh the three years required to receive an M.D. from that institution, he arranged, through letters attesting to the completeness of his medical education, to have his M.D. awarded in 1794 by Marischal College of the University of Aberdeen.

On his return, Brown practiced medicine in Bladensburg, Maryland, and in 1797 he moved to Lexington, Kentucky, where he practiced medicine and surgery and accepted private pupils. In June 1799 he published the first medical paper by a Kentucky physician: a report in the *Medical Repository* of a patient who had lost sensation but retained movement. Brown was to publish several other case reports and a few articles on scientific subjects. In 1799 he was appointed professor of chemistry, anatomy, and surgery at Transylvania University in Lexington and was allocated funds for the purchase of books for the library and chemical supplies for the laboratory.

In 1800 Brown was elected a member of the American Philosophical Society, reportedly having been sponsored by Benjamin Rush and Thomas Jefferson. Over the years he contributed many fossils and minerals to the society.

In May 1801 Brown and Transylvania University professor Frederick Ridgely vaccinated two young men against smallpox, and by August of the following year they had vaccinated more than 500 persons, far more than had been vaccinated in any other American city up to that time.

The French botanist François-André Michaux traveled to Lexington in 1802 in order to meet Brown, and Michaux wrote in his *Travels to the West of the Alleghany Mountains, in the States of Ohio, Kentucky, and Tennessea* [sic] . . . (2d ed., 1805) that Brown was "in the first rank of physicians settled in that part of the country," that he subscribed to the scientific journals from London, and that he was "always in the channel of new discoveries, and turns them to the advantage of his fellow-citizens" (pp. 130–31).

On 8 July 1803 Brown, together with Edward and Thomas West, received a patent for "distillation by steam in wooden or other stills." This new still improved the quality of Kentucky bourbon, and Brown derived some income by licensing its manufacture.

In 1804 Brown, along with Thomas Hart, Jr., a merchant, purchased what is now known as the Great Saltpeter Cave in Rockcastle County. Brown's account of it, titled "A Description of a Cave on Crooked Creek, with Remarks and Observations on Nitre and Gunpowder," in the *Transactions of the American Philosophical Society* (6 [1809]: 235–47) was the first scientific study of an American cave. Brown mined saltpeter from this cave and sent the fossils he found in it to the American Philosophical Society.

In October 1804 Brown began to practice medicine and surgery in partnership with Elisha Warfield in Lexington, Kentucky. They opened an apothecary shop and sold surgical instruments.

In 1805 Brown's brother James Brown, an attorney, moved to New Orleans, and early in 1806 Samuel Brown followed him and established a medical practice there. He spent the summers in the Mississippi Territory, where he met Catherine Percy, the daughter of a wealthy plantation owner. They were married near Natchez in September 1808. Brown acquired a plantation near Fort Adams and in December 1811 began to practice medicine in Natchez.

After the death of his wife in 1813, not long after the birth of their third child, who soon also died, Brown moved to Huntsville, Alabama, to be near his wife's brother, Thomas G. Percy. There Brown acquired a plantation, established a medical practice, and remained until late in 1819, although he often traveled, especially to Philadelphia.

During a visit to Philadelphia in the spring of 1819, Brown borrowed a lithographic stone from the American Philosophical Society, experimented with it, and persuaded the artist, Bass Otis, to make a drawing on it. Thus were printed what are considered to be the first American lithographs. He also tried to find an American source of lithographic stone. That summer Brown visited New Haven, Connecticut, where he and his brother Preston helped to found the American Geological Society.

In November 1819 Brown returned to Transylvania University as professor of theory and practice of medicine. In accepting the position, he reneged on an earlier agreement to become the first professor of anatomy at a medical school in Cincinnati established by Daniel Drake.

In 1822 Brown founded a secret medical society, the Kappa Lambda Society of Hippocrates, to promote medical ethics and professional relations among physicians. It was the first Greek-letter professional society, and, since there would soon be chapters in other cities, it was also the first medical society of national importance. At Brown's suggestion, the Philadelphia chapter started a medical journal, the *North American Medical and Surgical Journal*, in 1825.

In 1823 Brown's brother James became American minister to France, and in the summer of 1824 Brown visited him in Paris and attended lectures by the great physicians and scientists of the day. He was impressed by Jean Civiale's new method of removing bladder stones by crushing them with an instrument he invented. Brown bought one of these instruments and on his return gave lectures on its use in Philadelphia, Baltimore, and Washington, D.C. He then went back to Transylvania University, but not long afterward, for unknown reasons, he retired to his plantation near Huntsville.

In 1826, while traveling in the western states, Brown suffered the first of several strokes. He spent the winter of 1827–1828 in Philadelphia and in May 1828 sailed to France again, returning in September. He had another stroke in December 1829 and died three weeks later at the home of Thomas G. Percy, his brother-in-law.

Brown's reputation as a physician rests on his being a pioneer vaccinator and medical educator in the West and the founder of a national medical society. As a scientist he is best known for his paper on the Great Saltpeter Cave. Although he has received little recognition for helping introduce lithography to the United States, this achievement may have been his most important.

• The Filson Club, Louisville, Ky., has a large collection of Brown's letters. Smaller collections are in the Historical Society of Pennsylvania, the Library of Congress, the University of Kentucky, and Yale University. James Padgett published some of Brown's letters in "The Letters of Dr. Samuel Brown to President Jefferson and James Brown," *Register of the Kentucky State Historical Society* 35 (Apr. 1937): 99–130. Three letters on lithography were published in Philip J. Weimerskirch, "Lithographic Stone in America," *Printing History* 11 (1989): 2–15. In 1816 Brown published a 32-page pamphlet attacking George Poindexter, *To the Public. Address on the Conduct of Colonel Poindexter*, which is quoted in part in Mack Buckley Swearingen, *The Early Life of George Poindexter* (1934). On Brown's family, see Bertram Wyatt-Brown, *The House of Percy* (1994), Rebecca K. Pruett, *The Browns of Liberty Hall* (1966), and Bayless Hardin, "Dr. Samuel Brown, 1769–1830: His Family and Descendants," *Filson Club History Quarterly* 26 (1952): 3–27. Brown's involvement with saltpeter is described in Angelo I. George, "Miscellaneous Notes on Two Prominent New Athens Salt Merchants. Part Two: Samuel Brown and His 1806 Memoir on Saltpeter and Gunpowder," *Journal of Spelean History* 19 (Jan.–Mar. 1985): 20–24, and Fred A. Coy et al., "Samuel Brown on Saltpeter from Sandstone Cliffs in Eastern Kentucky in 1806," *Tennessee Anthropologist* 9 (1984): 48–65.

PHILIP J. WEIMERSKIRCH

BROWN, Samuel Robbins (1810–26 June 1880), missionary and educator, was born in East Windsor, Connecticut, the son of Timothy Hill Brown, a carpenter and painter, and Phoebe Hinsdale. His parents had strong religious convictions, and his mother was the author of several hymns published in Protestant hymnals. The family moved to Monson, Massachusetts, when Brown was a young child, and he attended the Monson Academy before going to Yale. While in college, he supported himself by sawing wood, instructing fellow students in music, and ringing the college bell. After graduating in 1832, he applied to the American Board of Commissioners for Foreign Missions for appointment as a foreign missionary; but as no post was immediately forthcoming, he became a teacher of the deaf in New York City. In 1835 he began a two-year course of study first at Columbia Theological Seminary in Columbia, South Carolina, then at Union Seminary in New York.

Though his acceptance by the American Board finally came through in 1838, Brown chose to go to China under different circumstances. He was hired as a teacher for the Morrison Education Society, named after Dr. Robert Morrison, the first missionary to China. Before setting sail for China, he married Elizabeth Bartlett in October 1838; they had no children. Four days after his marriage he was ordained by the Third Presbytery of New York.

The Browns boarded the *Morrison* via the Cape of Good Hope and arrived in Macao, China, on 19 February 1839. Brown established the Morrison School in Macao, which provided a secular education combined with religious instruction for young Chinese men. The classes, mostly taught in English, introduced the Chinese students to Western liberal education primarily through literature and science. After Hong Kong was ceded to the British in 1842 by the treaty of Nanking, which ended the Opium War, the school was moved there. The school was then much enlarged with three additional classes of new students, bringing the total enrollment to more than forty. At that time, Brown was the sole teacher. One of his students was Yung Wing, who became the first Chinese person to graduate from an American college. Later, because of Yung's influence, the Chinese Educational Commission sent more than a hundred boys to the United States. Of Brown, Yung wrote, "He found no difficulty in endearing himself to his pupils, because he sympathized with them in their efforts to master their studies, and entered heart and soul into his work" (Yung, p. 16).

After eight successful years as head of the Morrison School, Brown returned to the United States due to his wife's failing health. Four months before leaving, he told his students he would like to take a few of them with him to finish their education in the United States. This was a great opportunity for these young men, and Yung Wing and two classmates were the three selected to go. According to Yung, "[I]f it had depended on our own resources, we never could have come to America to finish our education, for we were all poor. . . . It was also through [Brown's] influence that due provision was made for the support of our parents for at least two years, during our absence in America" (Yung, p. 19).

In addition to Yung Wing another of Brown's students, Wong Fun, received funding from foreign patrons to go abroad to study medicine at the University of Edinburgh. He was probably the first Chinese person to acquire medical training in the Occident. Brown's influence on his Chinese students was great; and in part because of the work he did at the Morrison School, Robert Morrison's dreams for Christian education were realized.

Brown's work in education and religion continued after his return to the United States. From 1848 to 1851 he conducted a school in Rome, New York. Then from 1851 to 1859, while pastor of the Reformed Dutch Church in Owasco Outlet, New York, he was an active founder and director of Elmira College.

He returned to the Far East in 1859 at the age of fifty, arriving in Japan as one of the first three members of the Dutch Reformed Mission. He learned to speak and write Japanese, and taught first at Kanagawa, then Yokohama. According to a colleague, Brown's students were always readily identifiable by the correctness and purity of the English they spoke.

Brown worked on a translation of the Bible into Japanese even before the Protestant missionaries to Japan decided in 1872 to work jointly on that task. He was chairman of the committee that translated the New Testament into Japanese, himself contributing first drafts of the translations of Acts, Philippians, Philemon, and Revelation. Despite poor health, he continued to work on the Japanese version of the New Testament until it was published in 1879. He published other works, including a translation of *Prendergast's Mastery System Adapted to the Japanese* (1875), and biographies written in Japanese on Yung Wing, Wong Fun, and Wong Shin, intending to share the success stories of his former students with young Japanese men to inspire them to become benefactors of their country. Brown was a founder and president of the Asiatic Society of Japan and the Japan branch of the Evangelical Alliance.

Brown's health forced him to return to the United States in 1879, and the following year he died in Monson, Massachusetts, after visiting the graves of his parents. His success as a missionary to China and Japan is evident through the many lives that he influenced. As Yung Wing wrote, "He had an innate faculty of making things clear to the pupils . . . with great directness and facility. . . . [He] was a fine teacher and one eminently fitted from inborn tact and temperament to be a successful school master" (Wing, p. 17).

• Brown's life is the subject of William E. Griffis, *A Maker of the New Orient* (1903). Additional information can be found in Edward T. Corwin, *A Manual of the Reformed Church in America* (1902); Evarts B. Greene, *A New Englander in Japan, Daniel Crosby Greene* (1927); Yung Wing, *My Life in China and America* (1909); and Kenneth S. Latourette, *A History of Christian Missions in China* (1929). In addition to Brown's publications mentioned in the text, he wrote *Colloquial Japanese* (1863). An obituary appears in *Record of Graduates, Yale College* (2d series, 1870–1880).

KATHLEEN L. LODWICK
LISABETH G. SVENDSGAARD

BROWN, Sterling Allen (1 May 1901–13 Jan. 1989), professor of English, poet, and essayist, was born in Washington, D.C., the son of Sterling Nelson Brown, a minister and divinity school professor, and Adelaide Allen. After graduating as valedictorian from Dunbar High School in 1918, Brown matriculated at Williams College, where he studied French and English literature and won the Graves Prize for an essay on Molière and Shakespeare. He was graduated from Williams in 1922, with Phi Beta Kappa honors and a Clark fellowship for graduate studies in English at Harvard University. Once at Harvard, Brown studied with Bliss Perry and notably with George Lyman Kittredge, the distinguished scholar of Shakespeare and the ballad. Kittredge's example as a scholar of both formal and vernacular forms of literature doubtlessly encouraged Brown to contemplate a similar professorial career, though for Brown the focus would be less on the British Isles than on the United States and on African-American culture in particular. Brown received his M.A. in English from Harvard in 1923 and went south to his first teaching job at Virginia Seminary and College at Lynchburg.

Brown's three years at Virginia Seminary represent much more than the beginning of his teaching career, for it was there that he began to immerse himself in the folkways of rural black people, absorbing their stories, music, and idioms. In this regard, Brown is usefully likened to two of his most famous contemporaries, Zora Neale Hurston and Jean Toomer (with whom Brown attended high school). Like Hurston, Brown conducted a kind of iconoclastic ethnographic fieldwork among southern black people in the 1920s (she in Florida, he in Virginia) and subsequently produced a series of important essays on black folkways. Like Hurston and Toomer, Brown drew on his observations to produce a written vernacular literature that venerated black people of the rural South instead of championing the new order of black life being created in cities and the North. And like Toomer in particular, Brown's wanderings in the South represented not just a quest for literary material, but also an odyssey in search of roots more meaningful than what seemed to be provided by college in the North and black bourgeois culture in Washington. After Virginia Seminary, Brown taught briefly at Lincoln University in Missouri and Fisk University before beginning his forty-year career at Howard University in 1929.

Brown's first published poems, frequently "portraitures" of Virginia rural black folk such as Sister Lou and Big Boy Davis, appeared in the 1920s in *Opportunity* magazine and in celebrated anthologies including Countee Cullen's *Caroling Dusk* (1927) and James Weldon Johnson's *The Book of American Negro Poetry* (1922); 2d ed., 1931). When Brown's first book of poems, *Southern Road* was published in 1932, Johnson's introduction praised Brown for having, in effect, discovered how to write a black vernacular poetry that was not fraught with the limitations of the "dialect verse" of the Paul Laurance Dunbar era thirty years earlier. Johnson wrote that Brown "has made more than mere transcriptions of folk poetry, and he has done more than bring to it mere artistry; he has deepened its meanings and multiplied its implications." Johnson also showed his respect for Brown by inviting him to write the *Outline for the Study of the Poetry of American Negroes* (1931), a teacher's guide to accompany Johnson's poetry anthology.

The 1930s were productive and exciting years for Brown. In addition to settling into teaching at Howard and publishing *Southern Road*, he wrote a regular column for *Opportunity* ("The Literary Scene: Chronicle and Comment"), reviewing plays and films as well as novels, biographies, and scholarship by black and white Americans alike. From 1936 to 1939 Brown was the Editor on Negro Affairs for the Federal Writers' Project. In that capacity he oversaw virtually everything written about African Americans and wrote large sections of *The Negro in Virginia* (1940), a work that led to his being named a researcher on the Carnegie-Myrdal Study of the Negro, which generated the data for Gunnar Myrdal's classic study, *An American Dilemma: The Negro Problem and Modern Democracy* (1944). In 1937 Brown was awarded a Guggenheim Fellowship, which afforded him the opportunity to complete *The Negro in American Fiction* and *Negro Poetry and Drama*, both published in 1937. *The Negro Caravan: Writings by American Negroes* (1941), a massive anthology of African-American writing, edited by Brown with Ulysses Lee and Arthur P. Davis, continues to be the model for bringing song, folktale, mother wit, and written literature together in a comprehensive collection.

From the 1940s into the 1960s Brown was no longer an active poet, in part because his second book, "No Hidin' Place," was rejected by his publisher. Even though many of his poems were published in the *Crisis*, the *New Republic*, and the *Nation*, Brown found little solace and turned instead to teaching and writing essays. In the 1950s Brown published such major essays as "Negro Folk Expression," "The Blues," and "Negro Folk Expression: Spirituals, Seculars, Ballads and Work Songs," all in the Atlanta journal, *Phylon*. Also in this period Brown wrote "The New Negro in Literature (1925–1955)" (1955). In this essay he argued that the Harlem Renaissance was in fact a New Negro Renaissance, not a Harlem Renaissance, because few of the significant participants, including himself, lived in Harlem or wrote about it. He concluded that the Harlem Renaissance was the publishing industry's hype, an idea that gained renewed attention when publishers once again hyped the Harlem Renaissance in the 1970s.

The 1970s and 1980s were a period of recognition and perhaps of subtle vindication for Sterling Brown. While enduring what was for him the melancholy of retirement from Howard in 1969, he found himself suddenly in the limelight as a rediscovered poet and as a pioneering teacher and founder of the new field of Afro-American studies. Numerous invitations followed for poetry readings, lectures, tributes, and for fourteen honorary degrees. In 1974, *Southern Road* was reissued. In 1975 Brown's ballad poems were collected and published under the title *The Last Ride of Wild Bill and Eleven Narrative Poems*. In 1980 Brown's *Collected Poems*, edited by Michael S. Harper, were published in the National Poetry Series. Brown was named Poet Laureate of the District of Columbia in 1984.

Brown had married Daisy Turnbull in 1927, possibly in Lynchburg, where they had met. They had one child. Brown was very close to his two sisters, who lived next door in Washington. They cared for him after Daisy's death in 1979 until Brown entered a health center in Tacoma Park, Maryland, where he died.

Brown returned to Williams College for the first time in fifty-one years on 22 September 1973 to give an autobiographical address and again in June 1974 to receive an honorary degree. The address, "A Son's Return: 'Oh Didn't He Ramble'" (*Berkshire Review* 10 [Summer 1974]: 9–30; repr. in Harper and Stepto, eds., *Chant of Saints* [1979]), offers much of Brown's philosophy for living a productive American life. At one point he declares, "I am an integrationist . . . because I know what segregation really was. And by integration, I do not mean assimilation. I believe what the word means—an integer is a whole number. I want to be in the best American traditions. I want to be accepted as a whole man. My standards are not white. My standards are not black. My standards are human." Brown largely achieved these goals and standards. His poetry, for example, along with that of Langston Hughes, forever put to rest the question of whether a black vernacular-based written art could be resilient, substantial, and read through the generations. Despite his various careers, Brown saw himself primarily as a teacher, and it was as a professor at Howard that he felt he had made his mark, training hundreds of students, pioneering those changes in the curriculum that would lead to increasing appreciation and scrutiny of vernacular American and African-American art forms. In short, Brown was one of the scholar-teachers whose work before 1950 enabled the creation and development of American studies and African-American studies programs in colleges and universities in the decades to follow.

• Brown's papers are housed at Howard University, chiefly in the Moorland-Spingard Collection. Joanne Gabbin, *Sterling A. Brown: Building the Black Aesthetic Tradition* (1985), is the sole book-length study of his work to date. Robert G. O'Meally's "Annotated Bibliography of the Works of Sterling Brown" appears in Brown's *Collected Poems* (1980) and in *Callaloo* 14/15 (1982): 90–105, an issue with a special section devoted to Brown. Robert Stepto assesses Brown in "'When de Saints go Ma'chin' Home:' Sterling Brown's Blueprint for a New Negro Poetry," *Kunapipi* 4, no. 1 (1982): 94–105, and in "Sterling Brown: Outsider in the Renaissance," in *Harlem Renaissance Revaluations*, ed. Amritjit Singh et al. (1989). See also Henry Louis Gates, Jr., *Figures in Black: Words, Signs, and the "Racial" Self* (1987). A later discussion is in Gayl

Jones, *Liberating Voices: Oral Tradition in African American Literature* (1991). An obituary is in the *New York Times*, 17 Jan. 1989.

ROBERT STEPTO

BROWN, Thomas (27 May 1750–3 Aug. 1825), revolutionary war soldier and superintendent of the Southern Indian Department, was born in Whitby, England, the son of Jonas Brown, a shipowner and alum manufacturer, and Margaret Jackson. Captain Cook, the celebrated explorer, was a near neighbor during Thomas Brown's youth. After several voyages to America on his father's ships, Brown decided to seek his fortune on Georgia's newly ceded lands above Augusta in 1773. With the financial support of his father, Brown recruited seventy-four indentured servants in Yorkshire and in the Orkney Islands and sailed for Georgia in August 1774. A second contingent of the same number followed a year later.

Governor James Wright greeted Brown on his arrival in November 1774, granted him an extensive tract in St. Paul Parish, and appointed him a justice of the peace. Brown's settlement on Kiokee Creek was called Brownsborough. Many of his backcountry neighbors, who professed loyalty to the king during an Indian scare in 1774, were disappointed that Governor Wright failed to obtain an additional land cession in the peace treaty of 20 October 1774. Radical leaders in South Carolina spread the rumor that the king's agents intended to instigate an Indian war in order to terrorize people into subjection. Some whispered that Brown was the illegitimate son of Lord North, come to spy on them.

The news of the battles of Lexington and Concord prompted the Georgia Provincial Congress to join the continental association against trade with Britain and to appoint local committees to enforce the ban. Brown, the most conspicuous opponent of the association, drew the wrath of the Augusta Sons of Liberty, and they made an example of him. They scalped him, fractured his skull, burned his feet, and hauled him around town in a cart, more dead than alive. The incident, on 2 August 1775, marked the beginning of the American Revolution in the Georgia backcountry.

When he recovered from his injuries, Brown attempted to rally supporters in South Carolina. Many were loyal to the king but unwilling to take up arms in the absence of British troops. In cooperation with South Carolina governor Lord William Campbell and other Loyalists, Brown concocted a plan calculated to turn the worst fears of his opponents into reality. They urged the British commander in America to use Indians against rebellious Americans in concert with the landing of troops on the coast.

Banished from Carolina, Brown gained an enthusiastic sponsor for the plan in Governor Patrick Tonyn of Florida. John Stuart, the Indian superintendent and a refugee like Brown, cooperated less enthusiastically. Although totally inexperienced in Indian affairs, Brown plunged into the Creek country seeking Indian allies and recruiting a corps of rangers. His commission as lieutenant colonel of the East Florida Rangers, known after 1780 as the King's Rangers, dated from 1 June 1776. By the end of that year Rangers and Indians harassed the southern Georgia frontier. Georgia launched three expeditions in successive years in a vain effort to put a stop to Brown's raids.

As the war slowed to a stalemate in the North, the British ministry yielded to the lobbying of Governors Tonyn, Wright, and Campbell and dispatched troops from New York under the command of Lieutenant Colonel Archibald Campbell. Savannah fell quickly on 28 December 1778, and Campbell marched to Augusta, with Brown's Rangers in the van. Along the way, Brown was wounded in a skirmish at Burke County Courthouse. This test of the southern strategy failed, partly because an army of North Carolina Whigs appeared along the Savannah River before the expected Indians arrived at Augusta. The British retreated as far as Brier Creek and there turned on their pursuers and routed them on 3 March 1779. After Brier Creek, Brown's Rangers helped defend Savannah against a combined French and American assault on 9 October 1779. The partial success of the southern strategy prompted General Sir Henry Clinton to bring his army from New York, disembark near Savannah, and besiege Charleston. When General Benjamin Lincoln surrendered Charleston on 12 May 1780 Whig resistance in Georgia and the Carolinas collapsed.

In 1779, following the death of John Stuart, Brown was appointed to the superintendency of the southeastern Indians and the supervision of the war-related activities of the Creek and Cherokee nations. For the second time Brown returned to Augusta. He denied allegations that he was motivated by revenge, indeed some of the leading liberty boys walked the streets of Augusta freely after taking loyalty oaths. Brown established an elaborate communications network throughout the Indian country; his Indian allies brought prisoners from the Ohio and Mississippi rivers to Augusta.

On 14 September 1780 Whig lieutenant colonel Elijah Clark attacked Augusta and besieged Brown's Rangers in the Mackay House for four days. British reinforcements from Ninety-six, South Carolina, rescued Brown and forced Clark to retreat to the Carolina mountains. Clark's friends from the mountain settlements answered his call for help and defeated a British detachment at Kings Mountain. Brown was accused of excessive cruelty when thirteen of Clark's raiders were hanged in Augusta. All had violated their paroles and suffered punishment under the standing orders of General Charles Cornwallis.

Anticipating a second attack, Brown constructed Fort Cornwallis on the Savannah River. General Nathanael Greene dispatched Lieutenant Colonel Henry "Light-Horse Harry" Lee to Augusta with orders to cooperate with Brigadier General Andrew Pickens of South Carolina. Lee, Pickens, and Elijah Clark began a siege of Fort Cornwallis on 22 May 1781. After two weeks of fierce fighting, Brown surrendered on 6 June 1781.

When he was exchanged for an American officer and free to fight again Brown raised another corps of rangers and defended Savannah until that town surrendered to General Anthony Wayne on 11 July 1781. Brown escorted the Georgia Loyalists to Florida and helped them settle on the St. Johns River. He continued to act as Indian superintendent until the British turned Florida over to Spain under terms of the Treaty of 1783.

Brown was compensated for his losses in Georgia by extensive grants in the Bahamas. He was an acknowledged leader of the refugees and was elected to the Bahamian assembly. At age thirty-nine Brown married Esther Farr, age sixteen, and with her had five children. In 1802 Brown returned to Whitby, where he was regarded as a celebrity. In 1805 he was granted 6,000 acres on St. Vincent Island; however the governor of that island refused to honor the grant. Frustrated by legal entanglements, Brown secured deeds of ownership from government officials that proved to be fraudulent. Brown was blamed for the forgery and, despite his denials, was sentenced to a two-year prison term. After his release he returned to St. Vincent and cultivated a reduced but still substantial estate. He ended his years there as a wealthy planter.

Brown's importance in the American Revolution can be credited to his conspicuous loyalty to the king, which made him the target of the Georgia Whigs; his energetic promotion of the strategy that was adopted by the British military; and finally his allying of the Creek Indians with the Spanish in Florida, after the British evacuation. Brown's memory lingered long in Georgia as the personification of a Tory.

• Manuscript collections are the Waddington papers, Literary and Philosophical Society, Whitby, England, and the Thomas Alexander Browne Collection, private collection of Heather Lancaster, London, England; a microfilm copy of the latter collection is in the Georgia Department of Archives and History, Atlanta. (Thomas Alexander Browne was the son of Thomas Brown.) The most complete treatment of Brown's career is Edward J. Cashin, *The King's Ranger: Thomas Brown and the American Revolution on the Southern Frontier* (1989). The bibliography is reasonably complete. Martha Condray Searcy, *The Georgia-Florida Contest in the American Revolution, 1776–1778* (1985), is a thorough review of Brown's border warfare. Gary Olsen wrote about Brown's activities in South Carolina in "Loyalists and the American Revolution: Thomas Brown and the South Carolina Backcountry, 1775–1776," *South Carolina Historical Magazine* 68 (1967): 201–19, and 69 (1968): 44–56. Olsen treated Brown's Georgia career in "Thomas Brown, Partisan, and the Revolutionary War in Georgia, 1777–1782," *Georgia Historical Quarterly* 44 (1970): 1–19, 183–208.

EDWARD J. CASHIN

BROWN, Thomas Allston (16 Jan. 1836–2 Apr. 1918), theatrical agent and historian, was born in Newburyport, Massachusetts, the son of Thomas Brown, an innkeeper, and Lucretia H. Milton. He was educated in Newburyport until 1852, when he became an advance agent for traveling circuses. From then until 1857, he said, he traveled "from Maine to California" and gathered theatrical information and history at every chance along his routes.

In 1858, settling in Philadelphia, he started a theatrical weekly, the *Tatler*, wrote for the drama department of the Philadelphia *Daily Item*, and supplied theatrical news of his city to the New York *Clipper*, a weekly covering the American entertainment world. His first effort at theatrical history, a history of the American stage, was serialized in the *Clipper* from 1858 through 1861. In 1860 he also became advance agent for the Henry Cooper English Opera Company and then treasurer for Gardner & Madigan's Circus. One of the circus attractions was the famous tightrope walker Blondin. The climax of Blondin's appearance at a Baltimore theater was to walk a tightrope from the stage upward 100 feet to the top balcony, carrying a man on his back. When that man failed to appear one night, the 24-year-old Brown volunteered at the last moment to replace him. For the daring of his exploit, Brown was dubbed "Colonel" by his friends, and the honorary rank would cling to his name the rest of his life.

In 1863 Brown moved to New York City to become drama editor of the *Clipper*, a post he held until 1870. His *Showman's Guide*, a listing of distances and routes, available halls with their seating capacity and rentals per night, plus local hotels, bill posters, and newspapermen, was published in 1868 and reached a third edition in 1874. When he left his position at the *Clipper* in 1870, the New York theater managers and the editors of two newspapers staged a benefit for him, which took in more than $1,800.

Brown's *History of the American Stage . . . from 1733 to 1870*, comprising the biographical section of his *Clipper* serial, was published as a book in 1870. He continued to amass theatrical playbills, programs, and clippings in pursuit of his historical interests. That same year he became a partner of Morris Simmonds in the theatrical agency Simmonds and Brown. It was an early example of a new type of agency, which not only secured parts for actors but also was able to book routes for entire companies on national tours owing to the newly completed network of railroads across the United States. Brown and Simmonds scored their own success as managers in 1881, when they gained the American rights to the spectacular French "vaudeville, pantomime, musical, and dramatic composition" titled *Le Voyage en Suisse*, with all its "properties, tricks, scenery, and . . . mechanical arrangements" imported from Europe (*History of the New York Stage*, vol. 3, p. 204). Brown later called it a "Parisian absurdity." Starring the Hanlon-Lees acrobatic troupe, the Simmonds and Brown production played until 1884 in New York and gave 574 performances on the road.

During his years with Simmonds Brown also took on outside assignments. For the 1874–1875 season he managed New York's Theatre Comique, and during the 1877–1878 season he managed a tour for Dion Boucicault in *The Shaughraun*, leaving his agency work to his younger brother John Alexander Brown. At other times he managed tours for theatrical figures such as Marie Aimée, a star of Parisian light opera, and Mrs. General Tom Thumb, P. T. Barnum's tiny star. His final managerial efforts were for Charles Arnold in a tour of *Hans the Boatman* (1891–1892). Meanwhile he wrote his most ambitious work, a history of the New York theaters, beginning with the first recorded dramatic performance in 1732. This work was serialized in the *Clipper* from 1888 to 1892. After he brought the work up to date, it was published in book form in 1903 as the three-volume *A History of the New York Stage . . . 1732 to 1901*.

Brown and Simmonds worked together until Simmonds's death in 1896. From 1896 to 1906 Brown ran his agency alone. Known as "the oldest dramatic agent in the world," the Colonel was a fount of advice to young hopefuls and of historical lore to information seekers. On his retirement, the *New York Times* (11 Nov. 1906) described him as "a fit subject for the pen of Dickens" in an office full of theatrical volumes, scrapbooks, and canaries in cages, but noted that his agency had "not been too flourishing" in recent years. Brown was quoted as saying he had decided to leave the business "'because I do not like the manner in which it is now conducted . . . the methods now in vogue,'" an apparent reference to the monopolistic Theatrical Syndicate. Brown retired to Philadelphia, where he lived his last years with a niece and where he died. *Who's Who in America* (1903) lists him as "widower," but no other details of his marriage are recorded in biographical sources.

Today Brown's theatrical histories have been superseded and their errors corrected by later historians. His enduring place in theatrical history is as a pioneer booking agent whose knowledge of "the road" helped create the system of touring entire theatrical productions across America. The man himself remains a colorful figure of the nineteenth-century entertainment world, from circus to New York stage.

• Brown's collected volumes of programs, playbills, and clippings (interspersed with his handwritten notes), which were the basis for his historical works, are at the University of Pennsylvania. The *Clipper* serial version of his *History of the New York Stage* is available as mounted clippings in the Boston Public Library and the Harvard Library. For a short essay Brown wrote on "the origins of negro minstrelsy," see C. H. Day, *Fun in Black* (1874). A valuable biographical sketch is found in the unsigned article "A Theatrical Antiquarian," *Theatre Magazine*, Dec. 1904, p. ii. Other details are in M. B. Leavitt, *Fifty Years in Theatrical Management* (1909), in the *New York Times* interview on his retirement (11 Nov. 1906), in scattered personal references in Brown's *History of the New York Stage* (1903), and in the *New York Times* obituary of Morris Simmonds (22 May 1896). A small portrait of Brown heads the *Theatre Magazine* biographical sketch, and a photograph of him in his theatrical office is in the Aug. 1902 issue of the magazine. His obituary is in the *New York Times*, 4 Apr. 1918.

WILLIAM STEPHENSON

BROWN, Three Finger. *See* Brown, Mordecai Peter Centennial.

BROWN, Walter A. (10 Feb. 1905–7 Sept. 1964), sports promoter and coach, was born in Hopkinton, Massachusetts, the son of George Victory Brown, a sports promoter and athletic director at Boston University, and Elizabeth Gallagher. Brown attended Boston Latin School and graduated from Phillips Exeter Academy in 1926. After brief stints in the business world and an apprenticeship under his father, who was general manager of Boston Arena and president of Boston Garden, Brown turned to coaching amateur hockey. From 1931 to 1936 he toured Europe with a team of handpicked players, making history in 1933 when the team defeated Toronto 2–1 in Prague for the world's amateur title—the first non-Canadian team to win the championship. In 1932 he founded the Boston Olympics hockey team of the Amateur Hockey Association of America; he coached the team for four years before moving to the front office in 1936. During the next decade the Olympics won five U.S. national titles.

On his father's death in 1937, Brown became vice president and general manager of Boston Garden. At the 1938 Boston Marathon he succeeded his father as starter, a position he retained until passing along the antique gun in 1942. Brown's acumen as a promoter brought rodeos, boxing matches, circuses, and ski jumping to Boston Garden. A major success occurred in 1940 when he helped organize, finance, and promote the Ice Capades. That August he married Marjorie Hall of Arlington; they had one child. In 1941, a year before entering military service, he was elected president of the Boston Garden-Arena Corporation. During World War II he was attached to the army's general staff corps, becoming a lieutenant colonel before his discharge in 1945.

After the war Brown embarked on ventures that would propel him to the forefront of the sports promotion world. He astutely recognized the pent-up demand for entertainment and the incredible popularity of college basketball—insights that led him to promote professional basketball. In 1946 Brown, Edwin Trish, and Al Sutphin met in New York City and organized the Basketball Association of America. At that time Brown, as president of the Garden-Arena Corporation, helped found the Boston Celtics, the team he would run until his death. In 1949 the BAA merged with the National Basketball League to form the National Basketball Association. During this hectic postwar period, Brown also coached AHA teams in the world championship matches at Prague, St. Moritz, and Stockholm.

After four years, professional basketball was foundering, and Brown was on his way to losing $500,000 with the Celtics. But 1950 proved to be fortuitous for both the team and the league. First, Brown shrewdly hired Arnold "Red" Auerbach as the Celtics' new head coach. He then formed a new corporation and, along with Lou Pieri, purchased the Celtics for an estimated $30,000. Marjorie Brown recalled: "By 1950 Walter had sold most of the stock and remortgaged the house. . . . The Celtics were Walter's idea from the very beginning and he just never stopped believing in them." The whole league would reap incalculable benefits because of Brown's precedent-setting selection of Chuck Cooper in 1950, the first black player ever drafted into the NBA. The Celtics' imminent rise to the top ranks of professional basketball was solidified through a major stroke of luck. Five of the seventeen teams in the league folded before the 1950–1951 season, leading to the distribution of many players to the remaining teams. On 6 October 1950 Brown drew the name of Bob Cousy out of a hat. With Auerbach on the bench and Cousy running the team on the court, the stage was set for basketball dominance. Nearly a decade later, Brown would be asked by John Gillooly of the *Boston Record American* to name his top ten entertainers, and he responded, "No. 1 would be Cousy, bar none. Nobody close."

Brown initiated another significant innovation in 1951 when he proposed the first NBA all-star game. Unanimous opposition from other owners failed to deter him, and he personally shouldered financial obligations for the game. Held at Boston Garden on 2 March, the event barely met expenses during its first two years, but eventually it became a crowd favorite and a major financial success on television.

Throughout the 1950s Brown worked tirelessly in a wide variety of roles. He was president and general manager of the Boston Garden, president of the Boston Bruins, president and half-owner of the Boston Celtics, vice president of the Ice Capades, and president of the International Hockey Federation. Also, he was an official of the Arena Managers' Association and of the American Hockey Association, while serving as a member of the National Hockey League's board of governors. He remained active in amateur sports as well. He served as president of the Boston Athletic Association, promoting track meets at the Garden while maintaining his efforts on behalf of the Boston Marathon. When hockey coach Fred Metcalfe of the Boston Olympics resigned in January 1950, Brown became the team's bench coach once again. In 1952 he was chosen to be the chairman of the selection committee of the U.S. Olympic hockey team that traveled to Finland.

In the last decade of his life Brown saw his efforts on behalf of the Boston Celtics pay impressive athletic dividends. Beginning in 1957, the Celtics, led by stars such as Cousy, Bill Sharman, Bill Russell, and Tom Heinsohn, reeled off the first of nine successive Eastern Conference championships and from 1959 through 1966, eight straight NBA titles. Brown received substantial recognition for his work in sports and fundraising. In 1961 he served as chairman of the board of trustees of the Basketball Hall of Fame. Two years later, he served as the AHA's representative to the U.S. Olympic Association for the 1964 Winter Olympic Games; he subsequently was named chairman of the U.S. Olympic ice hockey committee and a member of the board of directors of the U.S. Olympic committee. Simultaneously, he also received awards and recognition for his work with charitable and voluntary organizations.

Brown died of a heart attack in Hyannis, Massachusetts. His life and achievements immediately received an outpouring of praise from prominent figures in sports, politics, and business. Bill Russell said, "I have lost one of my best friends. Walter was the real world champion, not the Celtics." And Senator Edward M. Kennedy lamented, "We have lost a champion as well as a civic leader." In June 1962 Brown had been elected to the NHL Hall of Fame in Montreal, and in 1965 he was inducted into the Naismith Memorial Basketball Hall of Fame.

For nearly two decades Brown was one of the most prominent figures in the world of sports. His memory is honored by the Walter Brown trophy, which is awarded to the NBA champions each year. As a promoter, visionary, and innovator, he established Boston as the center of amateur and professional sports activity in New England and as one of the leading sports cities in the United States.

• The most comprehensive sources of information on Brown are files of the *Boston Record American*, the *Boston Globe*, and the Sports Museum of New England. Each newspaper printed an extensive tribute to Brown, which appeared following his death. Obituaries were carried in both Boston newspapers and in the *New York Times*, 8 Sept. 1964. Secondary works with extensive information on Brown are Red Auerbach, *On and Off the Court* (1985); Harvey Araton and Filip Bondy, *The Selling of the Green* (1992); and Dan Shaughnessy, *Ever Green* (1990). Good secondary sources are Frederick Lewis and Dick Johnson, *Young at Heart* (1992), on the BAA, and Joe Falls, *The Boston Marathon* (1977), on the marathon as well as the Brown family. See also George Sullivan, *The Picture History of the Boston Celtics* (1982); Bob Ryan, *The Boston Celtics* (1990); and Leonard Koppett, *24 Seconds to Shoot: An Informal History of the NBA* (1968).

DANIEL FRIO

BROWN, Walter Folger (31 May 1869–26 Jan. 1961), lawyer, politician, and government official, was born in Massillon, Ohio, the son of James Marshall Brown, a lawyer, and Lavinia Folger. Reared in comfortable circumstances, Brown graduated from Western Reserve Academy in 1888 and Harvard University in 1892, worked briefly for the *Toledo Blade*, and then attended Harvard Law School. He passed the bar examination and joined his father's law firm in Toledo in 1894. In 1903 he married Katherine Hafer. The couple had no children. After his father's retirement, Brown founded Brown, Hahn, and Sanger and was a member of that firm from 1905 to 1927.

While building a successful law practice, primarily as a representative of utility companies, Brown also acquired business interests and became involved in managing such firms as the Toledo Trust Company, the Cleveland Automatic Machine Company, and the National Can Company. In addition, he early became involved in Ohio politics. In 1897, as chair of the Toledo Republican Central Committee, he helped elect Samuel "Golden Rule" Jones as the city's reform mayor.

Subsequently he became a leader in the Mark Hanna faction of the party, gained recognition as the "boss" of Toledo, and while chairing the Ohio Republican Central Committee (1906–1912) strongly supported party regularity and William Howard Taft. By 1912, however, he had broken with Taft over patronage and antitrust issues, joined Theodore Roosevelt's Progressive party, and become head of the Progressive organization in Ohio. After Roosevelt's defeat, Brown continued to head the state's Progressive party, but in 1916 he returned to the Republican fold. In 1920 he became a supporter of Warren G. Harding and acted as Harding's floor manager at the Republican National Convention. Brown also ran for a seat in the U.S. Senate in 1920 but lost in the Republican primary.

In 1921 Brown turned down Harding's offer to appoint him ambassador to Japan but did accept an appointment as the president's representative on and chair of the Congressional Joint Committee on Reorganization. In this position, he became an expert on public administration, embraced the period's efficiency mystique, and by 1924 had worked out a reorganization plan that, among other things, called for a unified Department of Defense, a new Department of Health, Education, and Welfare, and extensive restructuring of the Commerce and Interior departments. The plan was never adopted, but it foreshadowed future developments. Consideration of Brown's plan brought him into a close association with Secretary of Commerce Herbert Hoover, who had also become an advocate of reorganization and who credited Brown with having "a greater knowledge of the federal mechanism and its duties than any other man in the United States." In 1927 Hoover made Brown his assistant secretary of commerce, and in 1928 Brown played a leading role in shaping the organization and strategy of Hoover's presidential campaign, including responsibility for a new Colored Voters Division. In 1929 Brown joined the new president's cabinet as postmaster general and chief patronage adviser.

As head of the postal system, Brown tried to make it more businesslike and profit oriented but could not secure the higher postage rates regarded as necessary for this purpose. He also continued to play an important role in party affairs, especially in efforts to reform and gain respectability for the Republican party in the South and in Hoover's reelection bid in 1932. His actions receiving the greatest attention were those intended to rationalize the aviation industry through changes in the airmail subsidies. Under the McNary-Watres Act of 1930, a measure that failed to give Brown the kind of negotiating power he desired, he shaped bidding procedures and rules in such a way as to encourage large, well-financed, and well-equipped companies flying long routes, connecting major cities, and carrying express and passengers as well as mail. The result was a movement toward a modern air transportation system comparable to the one eventually realized under the Civil Aeronautics Act of 1938. Politically, however, Brown's reforms proved unsustainable. They were severely criticized by the smaller airline operators and their government allies, who claimed that Brown was promoting monopoly, playing favorites, and subverting the law's competitive bidding requirements. In 1934 his critics took their case to a Senate investigating committee chaired by Senator Hugo Black, and in response the Franklin D. Roosevelt administration canceled the contracts and eventually secured legislation undoing Brown's achievements. Brown strongly defended his actions as being in the public interest, but he had stretched the law. He lost the public relations battle with Black, especially after first denying knowledge about missing documents and then finding them among his personal papers.

After leaving government in 1933, Brown moved to New York, where he became chairman of the board and subsequently president of the Hudson and Manhattan Railroad. He retired from the company in 1946 and returned to Toledo, where he continued to be active in philanthropic endeavors, especially the Toledo Humane Society and the Lucas County Child Welfare Board.

In his unobtrusive but complex personality, Brown combined the interpersonal skills and shrewd judgment of a political operator with the calculating demeanor of an efficiency expert, the earnestness of a reformer, and the deferential confidence of a general staff official. Solidly built with a square brow, thin lips, thick dark hair, gold-edged spectacles, polished speech, and an air of quiet assurance, he could distance himself from those with whom he dealt. Yet he was also capable of generating an attractive human interest, as when he insisted upon an automobile that would accommodate his top hat or when he installed a kitchen in his government office to indulge his interest in practicing the culinary arts. His place in history is clouded by the fallout from the airmail controversy, but he was a true visionary in the aviation field, a political strategist of remarkable acumen, and an interesting illustration of how reformism, business, and bossism could sometimes be interwoven. He died in Toledo.

• The Brown papers are at the Ohio Historical Society in Columbus. Relevant materials are also in the Herbert Hoover and William P. MacCracken papers at the Hoover Presidential Library, the Post Office Department records at the National Archives, and the Warren G. Harding Papers at the Ohio Historical Society. Useful biographical information is in Harvey Ford, "Walter Folger Brown," *Northwest Ohio Quarterly* 26 (Summer 1954), 200–209; David D. Lee, "Walter Folger Brown," in *The Encyclopedia of American Business History and Biography: The Airline Industry*, ed. William M. Leary (1992); Theodore G. Joslin, "Postmaster General Brown: His Past and Yours," *World's Work* 59 (Aug. 1930): 38–40ff; and Anne Hard, "Uncle Sam's New Mail Man," *New York Herald Tribune*, 7 Apr. 1929. Also useful for various aspects of Brown's career are Henry Ladd Smith, *Airways: The History of Commercial Aviation in the United States* (1942); Nick A. Komons, *Bonfires to Beacons: Federal Civil Aviation Policy under the Air Commerce Act, 1926–1938* (1978); David D. Lee, "Senator Black's Investigation of the Airmail, 1933–34," *Historian* 53 (Spring 1991): 423–42; and

Donald J. Lisio, *Hoover, Blacks, and Lily-Whites: A Study of Southern Strategies* (1985). An obituary is in the *New York Times*, 27 Jan. 1961.

ELLIS W. HAWLEY

BROWN, Warner (2 Feb. 1882–6 Feb. 1956), experimental psychologist, was born in Greensboro, Georgia, the son of Jacob Conklin Brown and Alida Robins Warner. His early education consisted of informal tutoring. In his teenage years "he read the Greek classics in Greek, the Latin classics in Latin, French literature in French, and had a wide acquaintance with English literature." He was also well informed about botany and the law.

Brown and his parents moved to California. He enrolled in the University of California, Berkeley, in 1901, graduating in 1904 with an A.B. As an undergraduate, he studied philosophy with Josiah Royce and experimental psychology with George M. Stratton. He pursued graduate study and served as assistant in psychology from 1904 to 1906 when he received his A.M. He continued his education in psychology at Columbia University under Robert S. Woodworth and also studied with the philosopher John Dewey and the psychologist James McKeen Cattell, earning his Ph.D. in 1908. In that year he married Jessie Milliken, a botanist, and returned to Berkeley to begin his academic career as an instructor in psychology. He and his wife had two children. At Berkeley, Brown was promoted to assistant professor in 1913, associate professor in 1920, and professor in 1923. He served as dean of the College of Letters and Science from 1926 to 1927 and again in 1929.

Brown's research contributions were modest in number. His publications were characterized by precision of experimental design and reluctance to engage in premature theorizing. He published on a wide range of topics in the *University of California Publications in Psychology* and in journals of the American Psychological Association. His research reflected the active areas of experimental psychological investigation across the decades. A 1910 publication, "The Judgement of Difference," examined the perception of a difference at the psychophysical threshold; sensory discrimination and the assessment of psychophysical laws constituted an early focus of psychological research. Brown's research demonstrated "that even small differences are discriminated with a certain frequency while large ones are sometimes not" (p. 71). An early interest in hypnosis resulted in a monograph on suggestibility (1916).

Memory was a common topic of research in the 1920s. Brown published experiments on the reminiscence effect in memory; he examined conditions under which the number of words recalled was greater after a delay than when tested immediately after the words were presented. Brown utilized multiple recall tests and assessed the effect on reminiscence of primacy and recency, the tendencies to recall more words from the first and last parts of a list than were recalled from the middle of a list. In the 1930s the study of learning became a significant arena for psychological research. Brown conducted and published studies of variables influencing maze learning in rats and humans, particularly on the effects of punishment in the elimination of incorrect responses.

Brown was well regarded by his colleagues in psychology. The esteem in which he and his research were held is indicated by his inclusion as a charter member in the select Society of Experimental Psychologists. He was elected to serve as secretary-treasurer of the Western Psychological Association (founded in 1921) for three terms, from 1926 to 1929. He was also elected president of the association for the year 1929–1930.

In 1949 Brown published, with H. C. Gilhousen, an introductory textbook, *College Psychology*. The text emphasized facts over theory, with experimental illustrations of the historical foundations of psychology to demonstrate the relevance of past research. While it was written to appeal to students, with clear language and an absence of a single theoretical perspective, it was judged to have mixed, but not avoided, theory; and the historical examples made the text less representative of postwar contemporary psychology than texts that used current experiments to illustrate psychological principles.

Brown's students saw him as an individual of independent thought, a psychologist who loved to teach, who was "more interested in making dedicated psychologists than in his own scientific achievements" (Gilhousen and Macfarlane, p. 496). His modest number of published papers reflects what students saw as his greater interest in "investigation than in communication" and his unwillingness to contribute to the proliferation of published research that failed to meet his high standards for experimental design. He was generous with his time and advice to his students and his colleagues. He encouraged students in their pursuit of careers in psychology, exemplifying to them the high standards of experimental design and clarity of thought to which psychology as science aspired. He died in Berkeley.

• The Archives of the University of California-Berkeely contain information related to Brown's career there. Information about his life and career may be found in H. C. Gilhousen and Jean Macfarlane, *American Journal of Psychology* 69 (1956): 495–97. A brief history of the Western Psychological Association is in Donald B. Lindsley and Thomas W. Harrell, "History of the Western Psychological Association," *American Psychologist* 19 (1964): 290–91. An account of the founding of the Society of Experimentalist Psychologists is in E. G. Boring, "The Society of Experimentalist Psychologists—1904–1938," *American Journal of Psychology* 51 (1938): 410–23. For a review of Brown and H. C. Gilhousen's *College Psychology*, see R. C. Davis, *American Journal of Psychology* 48 (1951): 366–67. Published papers that exemplify Brown's research interests include "The Judgement of Difference with Special Reference to the Doctrine of the Threshold, in the Case of Lifted Weights," *University of California Publications in Psychology* 1, no. 1 (1910): p. 71; "Individual and Sex Differences in Suggestibility," *University of California Publications in Psychology* 2, no. 6 (1916): 291–430; "Effects of Interval on Recall," *Journal of Experimental Psychology* 7 (1924): 469–75; and "The Positive Effect of Punishment," *Journal of Comparative Psychology* 28 (1939): 17–22.

ALFRED H. FUCHS

BROWN, William (1748–11 Jan. 1792), physician, was born in Haddington, near Edinburgh, Scotland, the son of Richard Brown and Helen Bailey of Maryland, who were living with relatives in Scotland while Richard studied for the ministry. Although the family went back to Maryland, William returned to Scotland for his professional education. In 1770 he earned an M.D. at Edinburgh, then the leading medical school in the English-speaking world. On his thesis about detecting contagions in the air, *De viribus atmosphaerae sentienti obviis*, he identified himself as "Americanus." After opening a medical practice in Alexandria, Virginia, Brown married his first cousin Catherine Scott and had "many children."

In the fall of 1775 he enlisted as surgeon in the Second Virginia Regiment. In September 1776, Dr. William Shippen, Jr., recruited him to be assistant surgeon, Shippen's deputy, at the Continental army's Flying Camp field hospital, and three months later Brown was assigned to the military hospital in Bethlehem, Pennsylvania. Like other Continental army hospitals, it was overcrowded, inefficient, and so filthy that he had to requisition brooms from local homes to clean it. When Congress reorganized the army hospital service in May 1777, Brown was elected Surgeon General of the Middle Department (from the Hudson to the Potomac), perhaps because of his successful efforts at Bethlehem. He probably spent the winter of 1777–1778 with General George Washington's army at Valley Forge. In February 1778 he was promoted to Physician General of the Middle Department to replace the eminent Dr. Benjamin Rush, who had been implicated in the so-called "Conway Cabal" of disgruntled commanders and politicians who wished to have Washington replaced.

Brown established his headquarters near the general hospital that had been opened in December 1777 at Lititz, in Lancaster County, Pennsylvania. It was as crowded as the Bethlehem hospital had been, and in his new, essentially administrative, position he cleaned up the hospital and developed an emergency list of drugs suitable for military use. The result was the thirty-two-page *Pharmacopoeia simpliciorum et efficaciorum in usum nosocomii militaris (Pharmacopoeia of Simple and Effective Drugs for the Use of Military Hospitals)*, now commonly known as the "Lititz Pharmacopoeia." The first pharmacopoeia printed in America, it was published at Philadelphia soon after the British evacuated the city in June 1778. Brown's name did not appear on the title page, but it did in the 1781 reprint, which was also advertised in the public press. The compendium of eighty-four remedies for internal use and sixteen for external application was based on recent editions of the pharmacopoeias of Edinburgh and London, although it contained a few additional medicines. Brown designed it as a collection of formulas for drugs that could be made with cheap ingredients not affected by the British blockade of American ports.

When the hospital at Lititz closed in August 1778, Brown moved to central New Jersey with the main army. In February 1779 General Washington prevailed on him to give a series of lectures on anatomy for army surgeons stationed around his headquarters at Middlebrook. A year later Brown resigned from the army in order to resume his practice in Alexandria, where he died of unknown causes. Although nothing is known of his private or social life, he must have been held in high regard in Virginia, since in 1782 that state overrode its usual rules by awarding him a land grant although he had not been on continuous service with Virginia troops throughout the war.

• Bessie Wilmarth Gahn, "Dr. William Brown, Physician-General to the American Army," *Journal of the American Pharmacy Association* 16 (1927): 1090–91; Wyndham B. Blanton, *Medicine in Virginia in the Eighteenth Century* (1931), pp. 130–34; Edward Kremers, "The Lititz Pharmacopoeia," *The Badger Pharmacist*, nos. 22–25 (June–Dec. 1938); Mary C. Gillett, *The Army Medical Department 1775–1818* (1981), pp. 50–128.

J. WORTH ESTES

BROWN, William (30 May 1784–3 Mar. 1864), **George Brown** (17 Apr. 1787–26 Aug. 1859), **John A. Brown** (21 May 1788–31 Dec. 1872), and **James Brown** (4 Feb. 1791–1 Nov. 1877), merchant bankers, were born in Ballymena, Northern Ireland, the sons of Alexander Brown, a linen auctioneer in Belfast, and Grace Davison. Alexander Brown was sufficiently wealthy to send his four sons to school in England at Catterick in Yorkshire. All the boys were at first backward until their bad eyesight—a Brown genetic trait—was corrected by strong eyeglasses. Late in life William admitted he was fonder of play than of work at school, but each acquired a good education. About 1798 their father decided to emigrate to Baltimore, Maryland. Relatives were already there, Baltimore was evidently prosperous, and he had been involved in some way in the contemporary Irish troubles. Hence he took William from school in 1800 and almost immediately sailed to Baltimore. His wife and the other boys followed in July 1802.

In Baltimore, Alexander soon became a successful merchant and took the boys into his own firm. As soon as possible he sent them to represent the house in the other leading commercial cities. William, the oldest and most forceful son, tried Philadelphia in 1806 but then returned to Europe in 1809. In 1810 he married Sarah Gihon, daughter of Andrew Gihon of Ballymena, Alexander's main linen supplier, and settled in Liverpool. William was the senior partner in Liverpool of William and James Brown from 1814 to 1839 and of the successor firm, Brown Shipley, from 1839 until he died in 1864. The other brothers also had short periods in Britain from 1810 to 1814. They did not altogether escape the wars. William narrowly avoided capture by a French privateer in the English Channel, John was captured returning to the United

States, and George enrolled as a private to fight the British. Alexander's plan was completed after the war when John settled in Philadelphia in 1818 and James in New York in 1825. In addition he established lasting contacts with efficient agents, usually fellow Ulstermen, in all the major cotton ports.

All the brothers were partners in Alexander Brown's Baltimore house and the New York, Liverpool, and Philadelphia houses, but Alexander was not a partner in the Liverpool house. George Brown became senior partner in Baltimore from 1834, after Alexander's death, until he retired in 1839. John A. Brown was the senior partner of the Philadelphia branch from 1818 until he retired in 1837. The middle "A" in his name stood for nothing at all. He adopted it while in Baltimore to distinguish his mail from that of another John Brown. James Brown was senior partner in Brown Brothers, New York, from 1825 until he died in 1877. In each house there were usually one or two junior partners to help with the routine. The younger brothers' marriages, like William's, to a certain extent mirrored their interest in trade. John, in 1813, married Isabella Patrick, the daughter of John Patrick of Ballymena, who, like Andrew Gihon, was a large linen supplier. She died in 1820, and in 1823 he married Grace Brown, the daughter of George Brown, a Baltimore doctor. James, in 1817, married Louisa Kirkland Benedict, the daughter of the Reverend Joel Benedict. Louisa died in 1829, and in 1831 he married Eliza Maria Coe, the daughter of the Reverend Jonas Coe of New York. George, in 1818, married Isabella McClanahan, the sister of Johnston McClanahan, a dry goods importer who was John A. Brown's partner in Philadelphia from 1818 to 1839.

The firms traded so successfully during and after the war that by 1820 they were worth nearly $1 million and by 1830 nearly $3 million. Initially Alexander Brown imported Irish linen into Baltimore, but after 1820 Baltimore declined relative to Philadelphia and New York. Hence he relied increasingly on his sons and the southern agents to export American cotton, tobacco, and other products to Liverpool and British manufactures to the United States. Cotton was the most important new staple, and in the 1820s and 1830s William was frequently the largest Liverpool importer. In 1827, when total American exports to Britain were worth about $26 million, he imported 65,000 bales, worth about $3 million. In the 1830s his share fell, but in 1838, after the 1837 panic, he imported 178,000 bales worth about $7 million. This was probably more than Biddle and Humphreys, the Liverpool agents of Nicholas Biddle's Second Bank of the United States (BUS). In 1839 he received about 74,000 bales, nearly twice as much as Biddle. After 1840 his cotton imports fell.

Close family cooperation was essential to manage this huge trade. In the early 1820s William regularly took orders from Lancashire cotton spinners and brokers. Alexander transmitted the orders to the southern agents and managed their purchases. He also regularly transferred his capital to Liverpool to enable William to borrow cheaply or finance British manufactured exports. Alexander, John, and James made large advances to carefully chosen southern bankers and factors for consignments to William. Usually the firms handled the goods in return for commission and interest, but sometimes they purchased on their own account to speculate or fill their ships. They were sufficiently well informed and decisive to time and balance their separate interlocked houses successfully and earn very good profits. Many transatlantic firms broke down over similar complex distributions of burdens, risks, and rewards, compounded by slow communications. In the Brown firms, Alexander was "the head that thought for all," and his decisive orders are revealed in his letter books. Unfortunately, William and James's replies have mostly been lost. William clearly had a mind of his own, but not to the extent of disrupting the firms' organization.

In the 1820s the Browns' interest in trade gradually extended into finance. Growing international and intersectional trade inevitably necessitated corresponding financial movements. The Browns had the necessary information to handle the great variety of bills and currency presented for payment and during the 1830s became the largest operators in transatlantic exchange. However, the internal American market was controlled by the BUS. The Browns were both competitors with and involved in the bank. At this time banks were often strongly influenced by the merchants who directed them. Alexander had purchased large holdings of BUS stock between 1816 and 1820, was a director of the Baltimore branch, and ensured that the southern agents were directors of their local branches. This role was continued by his sons. John was a director of the bank's central board in Philadelphia, and in 1828 Biddle complained to Dr. John Campbell White, cashier of the Baltimore branch, that John saw too much of the bank's business. James was a director of the Bank of Manhattan. William was the first chairman of the Bank of Liverpool from 1831 to 1835. His excellent relationship with the leading London private bankers, Denisons, saved the firms in 1837.

Alexander Brown purchased the firms' first ship, the *Armata*, in 1811 and in the 1820s built up a small fleet that was mostly used in the cotton trade. However, the highest returns came from the scheduled transatlantic packet service between New York and Liverpool, including in the 1830s at least two New York lines—Robert Kermit's Red Star Line and E. K. Collins's Dramatic Line. In New York they were managed by their American owners, but in Liverpool they were handled by W&J Brown. The only long-lasting Philadelphia-Liverpool line—the Cope line—was started in 1822 by the Browns and Thomas Cope. Cope managed the line, but the Browns contributed two ships until 1844. Brown Shipley remained Cope's Liverpool agents until the 1870s. Baltimore's transatlantic trade was too small to mount a packet line in the 1820s, but Alexander attempted to appease the importers by providing "regular ships." George managed these ships after Alexander's death.

The Browns were responsible more than any other merchant house for introducing railroads into the United States. William was a substantial shareholder in the first great British railway, the Liverpool and Manchester; Alexander and George organized the Baltimore and Ohio, the first large American railroad; and their Charleston agent, James Adger, was a leading organizer of the South Carolina Railway. Alexander hoped the Baltimore and Ohio would reverse the relative decline of Baltimore. The organizing meeting was held in George's house. William sent detailed technical information from Liverpool and introduced B&O and SCRR engineers to the pioneer British engine builder George Stephenson. George actually directed engineering work on the B&O. The Brown family rode in the first public trials of both the L&M and B&O. In the mid-1830s the firm assisted Maryland to raise loans in Britain and imported railroad iron.

By the early 1830s the Browns had become the largest and most efficient merchant house in Anglo-American trade. When Alexander died in Baltimore in 1834 he was probably the richest active merchant in the United States, and his sons were among the wealthiest merchants in Baltimore, Liverpool, New York, and Philadelphia. His death so shook George that he resigned from the treasurership of the B&O and asked his brothers to reduce their activities. However, the Browns' Liverpool–New York business boomed in the mid-1830s along with the general Anglo-American economy. The collapse began in late 1836 when the Bank of England, concerned about British gold flows to the United States, tightened credit by refusing the bills of the leading Anglo-American houses, including the Browns. By January 1837 the Browns themselves had curtailed their advances, and by April there was widespread financial panic in the United States that soon spread to Britain. American firms could not repay former credits, and the value of cotton remittances halved.

By late May W&J Brown and most other Anglo-American houses were desperate. William, however, supported by the Bank of Liverpool and Denisons, approached the Bank of England and secured an unprecedentedly large loan of £2 million ($9.8 million). Joseph Shipley, William's partner, rather than William, who was ill, conducted the negotiations in London and impressed the Bank with the Browns' solidity and the danger of widespread failure. The Browns therefore survived the panic and the renewed pressure in 1839 and even gained at the expense of weaker firms. However, the shock confirmed John and George's determination to retire in 1837 and 1839, respectively, and forced William and James to change the firm's strategy.

Hence, after about 1840 William and James gradually specialized in finance. The opportunity to expand the firms' financial interests came when the BUS collapsed in the early 1840s, enabling the Browns to become the leading American domestic as well as international exchange dealers. In the mid-1830s the Browns had already been handling nearly $11 million worth of sterling exchange annually (when American exports to Britain were about $50 million). In 1839 they established their own branches in the main cotton ports, and by the late 1840s were transmitting huge flows of exchange between the South, New York, and Liverpool. They also provided credits or arranged exchange for American and British merchants importing goods into the United States from all over the world. The business became increasingly competitive and efficient. In 1859, when total American exports to Britain were $126 million, the Browns calculated they handled $45 million of sterling remittances at a profit of only about one-eighth percent.

The Browns' specialization in finance made them increasingly sensitive to the danger of "lock ups" in other areas. The first casualty was their dry goods trade. The linen trade had never been strong after 1818 either in Baltimore or Philadelphia, but the American branches had successfully solicited very large general consignments from Britain (1831–1837). British exports to the United States fell drastically in the early 1840s, and the Browns apparently sacrificed their share to free resources for finance. The cotton consignment business lasted longer, but, except when crises removed the weaker houses, had become dangerously competitive. Overgenerous advances during the boom obliged the Browns to manage several bankrupt southern plantations until the mid-1850s, and William's advice thereafter was to stick to legitimate business and to avoid southern commitments. The firms' cotton business therefore declined in the 1840s and 1850s, but its assets in the South were still substantial in 1861.

The Browns' interest in ships persisted until almost 1860, but not without internal controversy. Their most important venture was the Collins line (1848–1858). Collins conceived his "Steam Scheme"—an American New York–Liverpool steamship line to rival Cunard's in 1841. Initially the Browns, especially William, opposed the scheme, but in 1848 Collins won over James by securing a $385,000 annual federal government subsidy to carry the mails, and James committed the firm to finance four 2,000-ton wooden side wheel steamers, convertible into war steamers. The line began running against Cunard in 1850, generating great public interest. However, despite the subsidy, which was increased to $858,000 in 1852 when the *Baltic* was taken to Washington to entertain congressmen, and a secret pooling agreement with Cunard, the ships seldom made profits. The capital costs were far over estimate—about $2.8 million instead of $1.2 million—and the engines, made at James's Novelty Iron Works in New York, frequently broke down. Finally after two ships sank—the first, the *Arctic* in 1854 with 250 passengers, including six of James's family—the subsidy was withdrawn, and the remaining ships were sold in 1858.

William and James appointed able juniors to handle routine matters in Liverpool and New York, but they retained control of strategic decisions and held most of the capital. Arrangements were made for handling the residual business in Philadelphia and Baltimore. The firms had been worth nearly $6 million in December 1836. George and John's retirement and the effects of the 1837–1839 crises reduced the residual to $3 million by December 1840, but by 1850 and 1855 this had recovered to $5.1 million and $7 million, respectively. In 1853 the credit rating agency R. G. Dun, with some exaggeration and no doubt also including George and John's assets, described the Brown firms as "the richest house doing business in America, reported to be worth . . . about twelve to fourteen million dollars." The firms easily survived the financial crises of 1847 and 1857, but the English partners continually worried that heavy lock ups plus the potential dispersal of William and James's capital might damage the firms' credit. Hence William reacted angrily to James's investments in the Collins steamers and various railroad stocks. In 1862 he argued that the partners' primary duty was to the firms' future and that James should resist government and popular pressures to invest in U.S. stock.

William made good use of the simplification of the firms' business. He had entered Liverpool politics in the 1820s and served on the council in the 1830s. Election squibs of 1830 describe him as "an Irish American settled down here" with grand social ambitions and too great a preference for "Yankee shipping." In the early 1840s the Free Trade movement enabled him to embody these interests in a high moral cause, and in 1846 he entered Parliament. At Westminster he consistently supported liberal and Anglo-American causes. For instance, in the mid-1850s he successfully mediated between Prime Minister Lord Palmerston and American ambassador George Mifflin Dallas over the foreign recruitment incident and at British government request attempted to promote the Interoceanic Railway across Honduras. He entertained and attempted to influence each American ambassador to Britain and consul to Liverpool. He supported the extension of the uniform cheap Penny Post principle to transatlantic mail and was president of the first Atlantic Cable Company. He secured an abortive Royal Commission investigation into the creation of a British decimal coinage. His final and longest-lasting bequest to Liverpool was the gift of the impressive Liverpool Public Library for which he was made a baronet. He died in Liverpool, but despite his many contributions to the city, his obituaries imply that he earned the respect of his townsmen but not their love.

The three Brown brothers in the United States were never politically prominent but did aid their communities in many other ways. James was shy and reticent in speech but clear and forceful on paper. For many years he was an active member of the New York Chamber of Commerce and a director of several banks, insurance companies, and railroads. He was a founder of the New York Association for Improving the Condition of the Poor and its president from 1843 to 1875. He was a devout Presbyterian, served as an elder in his church, and gave $300,000 to the Union Theological Seminary. George was similarly modest and retiring but served on many Baltimore institutions and gave generously to the House of Refuge for Juvenile Offenders, the Baltimore Association for Improving the Condition of the Poor, and the Presbyterian church. John speculated successfully in railroads and amassed a large fortune. Like the others he supported causes such as the American Sunday School Union, gave liberally to the Presbyterian church, and donated $300,000 to the Presbyterian hospital. George died in Baltimore, John in Philadelphia, and James in New York.

The brothers were worthy in the Presbyterian tradition but never became central figures in the British or American establishment. However, they were all able businessmen, and William and James were clearly exceptional. First, as general merchants they grasped all the interlocking opportunities of early nineteenth-century trade. Then, when the Atlantic environment changed after 1837, they seized the central specialization in trade finance. Finally, they successfully passed on viable firms to the next generation of partners. This was not easy, and they did not transfer their essential health and longevity. None of William's eight children survived him, and his grandchildren were still young when he died. Similarly, although James had six children with his first wife Louisa, of whom three survived him, and five children with his second wife Eliza, of whom two survived him, only one of his five sons, John Crosby Brown, became an active leading partner. Hence succession required complicated negotiations among William and James, their "juniors," who included several very experienced businessmen, and their families.

Nevertheless, satisfactory agreements were eventually made, and during and after the Civil War the firms remained the leaders of transatlantic trade finance. As the largest organization at the time they gained from the wartime uncertainties and the dramatic postwar recovery. However, possibly due to the brothers' North British provincial background—so helpful in early nineteenth-century trade—they never developed strong interests in mainland Europe or in investment banking, and in the later nineteenth century they were eventually overshadowed by better-placed rivals. Hence Brown Shipley did not open a London branch until 1863, and the Liverpool branch was retained until 1888 despite declining business.

Brown Brothers and Brown Shipley operated as essentially one firm with common partners until 1914. Inevitably the war and rising taxation caused difficulties, and although each remained agents for the other, the houses split in 1918. Since the 1920s Brown Shipley has continued as one of the leading London merchant banks, but Brown Brothers merged in 1931 with W. A. Harriman & Co., the private bank of the Harriman family. As part of the financial establishment in London and New York the firms continued to attract partners whose general aims included values dear to the Browns, such as financial stability and transatlantic comity. Brown Shipley, for instance, produced two governors of the Bank of England, Mark Collet (1887–1889) and his far more influential grandson, Montagu Norman (1920–1944). Similarly, two of Brown Brothers' leading partners, Averell Harriman and Robert Lovett, with of course many characteristics and interests of their own, articulated in modern form some of the brothers' main concerns.

• Nearly all of Alexander and George Brown's (Baltimore) letter copy and account books from 1800 on are in the Library of Congress, but the collection loses centrality after 1839. John's (Philadelphia) letter copy and account books were destroyed. James's (New York) account books are in the New York Public Library, but nearly all his letter copy books were destroyed. William's (Liverpool) office letter copy books and account books were mostly destroyed, although the Liverpool Public Library holds some general items. However, William's private letter copy books from 1846, when he entered Parliament, are at Brown Shipley, London. John Crosby Brown, James's son, collected many of the partners' private letters and other materials and wrote a thorough survey of the firms in *A Hundred Years of Merchant Banking: A History of Brown Brothers and Company, Brown Shipley and Co. and the Allied Firms* (1909). The collection was preserved at Brown Brothers and cataloged by John A. Kouwenhoven, whose wide-ranging pictorial survey, *Partners in Banking: An Historical Portrait of a Great Private Bank: Brown Brothers Harriman & Co., 1818–1968* (1968), was commissioned for Brown Brothers' 150th anniversary. This collection is now at the New-York Historical Society. Successive anniversaries of the other branches have been celebrated in Brown Brothers and Company, *Experiences of a Century, 1818–1918* (Philadelphia, 1919), probably written earlier by J. C. Brown, who died in 1909, and by Frank R. Kent, *The Story of Alexander Brown and Sons* (Baltimore, 1925), and Aytoun Ellis, *Heir of Adventure: The Story of Brown, Shipley & Co.: Merchant Bankers* (London, 1960). Edwin J. Perkins, *Financing Anglo-American Trade: The House of Brown, 1800–1880* (1975), a book-length modern academic study, concentrates on the firms' financial and managerial innovations. See also J. R. Killick, "Risk, Specialisation and Profit in the Mercantile Sector of the Nineteenth Century Cotton Trade, Alexander Brown and Sons, 1820–1880," *Business History* 16 (1974): 1–16, and Killick, "The Cotton Operations of Alexander Brown and Sons in the Deep South, 1820–1860," *Journal of Southern History* 53 (1977): 169–94. More detailed bibliographies are in Kouwenhoven, pp. 236–67, and Perkins, pp. 301–11.

J. R. KILLICK

BROWN, William Adams (29 Dec. 1865–15 Dec. 1943), Presbyterian theologian, educator, and activist, was born in New York City, the son of John Crosby Brown, the head of Brown Brothers and Company, a large New York banking firm, and Mary Elizabeth Adams, the daughter of William Adams, pastor of the Central (later Madison Square) Presbyterian Church. Both the Brown and Adams families were active in New York philanthropy and, in particular, supported Union Theological Seminary. Brown was educated at Yale University (B.A. 1886, M.A. 1888), Union Theological Seminary (B.D. 1890), and the University of Berlin (1890–1892). Union Seminary appointed Brown to teach church history in 1892; however, one year later the school transferred him to the Department of Theology. He earned a Ph.D. from Yale in 1901. Brown served as professor of theology until 1930, when Union appointed him research professor in applied Christianity. In 1892 he had married Helen Gilman Noyes; they had four children.

Brown had studied with Adolf von Harnack at the University of Berlin, and throughout his career his theological work reflected Harnack's influence. As Brown interpreted Christianity, the essence of the faith was in Jesus' teachings about the parental character of God, the familial character of humanity, the need for service and sacrifice, and God's dominion. This did not mean that other Christian teachings lacked contemporary meaning. Largely through his work in the ecumenical movement, Brown came to appreciate classical Christian doctrines, especially the historical expressions of the doctrine of the church. He first gave expression to these ideas in his *Christian Theology in Outline* (1906).

In *Church: Catholic and Protestant* (1935), Brown argued that the church had two aspects. First, he believed that the church in a democracy ought to unify the society and provide it with a moral vision. Therefore, he urged the churches to join for common practical purposes. Such federation did not require that a denomination surrender or compromise its own religious teachings. Brown realized that, as valuable as federation was, it was no theological answer to Christian division. Eventually all churches, he believed, would discover their common affirmations and cooperate to create a rich, new form of Christianity.

Brown considered himself primarily a theologian, and his advanced students included such important American theologians as Henry Pitney "Pitt" Van Dusen, Walter Horton, Marion Bradshaw, and John C. Bennett. As an educator, Brown helped to pioneer field education for ministers. In 1893 the Alumni Club of Union Seminary appointed him a member of the board of directors for a proposed Union Settlement House, which would provide a place for university students and social workers to live in the poorer sections of town. The hope was that settlement houses might serve as centers for both teaching and research. He remained a member of the settlement's board until 1930, and he was also active in the City Mission Council, which employed many Union students. Brown was also a member of the board of the Labor Temple (New York) and of the Presbyterian Home Mission Board. In 1912 he organized the American Theological Society and served as its first president.

Brown served on the Yale Corporation from 1917 to 1934 and as chair of the corporation's Educational Policy Committee from 1919 to 1930. In that office he discerned the need for a provost to coordinate the various educational programs of the university and served from 1919 to 1920 as acting provost. He also served in 1925 as acting president of Union Seminary.

In 1930 Brown went to India as a member of the Commission on Christian Higher Education in India (the Lindsey commission). The commission studied the various schools maintained by the American Protestant missionaries. Its report, *The Christian College in India* (1931), helped direct schools on the subcontinent for the next two decades.

In 1929 Brown and Mark A. May launched their survey of American theological schools. Working under the auspices of the Institute of Social and Religious Research, they asked the schools for information about their enrollments, the percentage of college graduates in their student bodies, and their curriculum. In 1934 Brown and May published their results as *The Education of American Ministers*. The four-volume work was the most comprehensive study of seminaries to date, and it highlighted the need for seminaries to form an accrediting agency. Two years later the nation's leading divinity schools formed the American Association of Theological Schools to accredit the schools and monitor their progress.

Brown was an important participant in the ecumenical movement. During the First World War, he served as the executive secretary of the Federal Council of Churches' General War-Time Commission. The General Commission secured chaplains for the armed services and coordinated the various churches' ministries to the troops.

Since Brown was sufficiently fluent in German and French to preach in those languages, Presbyterian church leaders often invited him to represent that church in early ecumenical meetings. Brown participated in the most important world Christian meetings. He was a member of the planning group for the Universal Christian Conference on Life and Work in Stockholm in 1925, and he was a leader at the second Life and Work Conference held in Oxford in 1937. Similarly, he was a member of the first Faith and Order meeting held at Lausanne in 1937, and he helped to plan the Faith and Order meeting in Oxford in 1937. His hard work in these preliminary meetings helped frame the constitution and theology of the World Council of Churches, which held its first official meeting in 1948, five years after Brown's death.

Brown retired from Union Seminary in 1936 and published his autobiography, *A Teacher and His Times*, in 1940. He continued an active career of writing until his death in New York City. Brown was perhaps the most important representative of American theological liberalism in the United States in the first half of the twentieth century. His application of theological principles to such widely varying areas as war and peace, interchurch cooperation, and education was an important example of how theology was relevant to the modern world.

• Brown told the story of his life in two works. The first was "Seeking Beliefs That Matter," in *Contemporary American Theology*, 2d ser., ed. Vergilius Ferm (1932–1933); the second was his autobiography, *A Teacher and His Times* (1940). Other important information is in Henry Pitney Van Dusen and Samuel McCrea Cavert, *The Church through Half a Century: Essays in Honor of William Adams Brown* (1936). Kenneth Cauthen, *The Impact of American Religious Liberalism* (1962), contains an important theological assessment of Brown's work in chap. 3, "The Old Gospel and the New Theology: William Adams Brown." An obituary is in the *New York Times*, 16 Dec. 1943.

GLENN T. MILLER

BROWN, William Alexander (fl. 1817–1823), theater manager and playwright, was born in the West Indies, probably on St. Vincent, before 1780. Little is known about Brown's early life. He worked for some years as steward on passenger ships, then left the sea and settled in New York City, where he worked as a tailor. The 1820 census shows him as a middle-aged free black man, living on Thomas Street with his wife and daughter. At about this time he opened a public garden in the grounds behind the house in which he lived on Thomas Street, between West Broadway and Hudson Street. This was a sort of open-air cabaret, offering light refreshments and music. The "African Grove," as he called it, served the city's African-American population, which was excluded from the other, larger public gardens in the city.

The African Grove presumably opened in the spring of 1821, but our only knowledge of it comes from a story in the *National Advocate* of August of that year. A few weeks later, another story reported that the Grove had been forced to close because of complaints from its neighbors. Brown proceeded to move his entertainment indoors—the season for an open-air resort was coming to an end anyway—and formed a company of actors to present an abridged production of Shakespeare's *Richard III* in an upper floor of his house. The first performance was given on 17 September. Evidently the complaints continued, as the company's second performance a week later, also of *Richard III*, was in a house on Mercer Street at Bleecker, then an undeveloped part of town. By the end of the year Brown attempted to move his theater back to the center of the city, arranging to present plays in Hampton's Hotel, a porter house next door to the Park Theatre, the only other theater in New York. Unfortunately, the Park's manager, Stephen Price, was intolerant of competition and entirely unscrupulous. He caused a performance on 7 January 1822 to be raided by the police and the actors to be hauled from the stage and arrested.

Brown issued a defiant handbill, excerpts from which appeared in the *Commercial Advertiser*, and returned to finish the season at Mercer Street. Early in 1822 Brown leased a lot on the east side of Mercer Street above Houston and had a theater built on the property. The theater opened in early August with productions of *The Poor Soldier* and *Don Juan*. A few days later a band of white hooligans broke up a performance and assaulted Brown and the actors, destroying costumes, scenery, and props. The police responded promptly and the ringleaders were arrested, but damage was done that affected subsequent performances. This gang may have been acting out of motiveless malignity, but they may also have been instigated by Price.

The repertory of the African Company included Shakespeare's *Richard III*, *Othello*, and *Macbeth*; other standards like John Home's *Douglas* and Kotzebue's *Pizarro*; and current hits like *Tom and Jerry* and Mordecai Noah's *The Fortress of Sorrento*. In addition, Brown wrote a play called *The Drama of King Shotaway*, which the company presented in January 1822 and again in June 1823. The play, which Brown described as "written from experience," dealt with an insurrection on St. Vincent against the British in 1795, led by Chatoyer, the paramount chief of the Caribs. The plot of the play and Brown's presentation of Chatoyer are unknown. The play was never printed, and its text has been lost. Indeed, the play may never have been written down as there is evidence that suggests that Brown was illiterate. He may have dictated the play in detail, or he may have simply outlined the plot and the content of each scene and allowed his actors to improvise the dialog. His company seems in fact to have relied on improvisation to a great extent even when presenting published plays, Shakespeare excepted. The playbill of their production of *Tom and Jerry* shows only a general similarity with the then-popular play by W. T. Moncrieff, and a notice of their production of *The Poor Soldier* ironically but uncomprehendingly praised the company for presenting "this familiar play . . . so artfully, that . . . I found it impossible to tell what would come next."

Brown had originally intended that the African Company, like the African Grove, would serve New York's black community, which was then only allowed into an upper balcony at the Park Theatre. Playbills from September and October of 1821 had been addressed to "Ladies and Gentlemen of Colour." But before long, as reports in the *National Advocate* drew the attention of white New Yorkers to the company, whites came to outnumber the blacks in the audience, and Brown began addressing his bills to "The Public." In late October 1821 he had announced that a section at the back of his theater would be reserved for whites; by the fall of 1822, it was the black members of the audience for whom a section of the house was being set aside. Nonetheless, Brown and his company presented plays dealing with controversial issues. *Pizarro*, a standard play from the Anglo-American repertory, and Brown's own *Shotaway*, concerned armed resistance to colonial domination. The Theatre's interpretation of *Tom and Jerry* included a scene set in a southern slave market, and the company also offered a short play based on the exploits of the Jamaican folk hero Three-Finger'd Jack, a rebel against slavery.

In July 1823 a man named William Brown filed for bankruptcy. This is likely to have been Brown, although records of the bankruptcy proceeding have been lost and the 1824 tax records show him to have been still responsible for the taxes on the land on which his theater stood. The theater must have represented a heavy investment, and its demise was probably hastened by the vandalism spree and by a citywide epidemic of yellow fever that forced Brown to close the theater in early October 1822 and take his company on a tour. In any event, during the 1823–1824 season, the African Company was under the direction of James Hewlett, its leading actor. This was to be the Company's last season. In March 1825 the land on which the building stood was sold, and its new owner assumed responsibility for the taxes.

Nothing more is known of Brown's life, his commonplace name making him impossible to trace. A notice published in 1880 says that on 19 December 1823, a man named Brown presented an African theatrical company in Albany, but this has not been confirmed in contemporary sources.

The African Company was the first theater company in the United States to be managed and staffed by African Americans; Brown's *Shotaway* was the first play to have been written by an African-American; its Mercer Street theater was the first building to have been erected for use by an African-American theater company. In addition to James Hewlett, Ira Aldridge began his career with the African Company (though the only reference during the years when the African Company was active that connects Aldridge to the company is a criminal complaint that he filed for assault against one of the louts involved in the vandalism spree of 1822).

• Information about Brown must be pieced together from scattered sources. Several playbills from his company are available in the Harvard Theater Collection, Harvard University. Others are reprinted in Laurence Hutton, *Curiosities of the American Stage* (1891), and George Odell, *Annals of the New York Stage*, vol. 3 (1928). Information about Brown is also available in the *National Advocate*, 3 Aug. 21 and 25 Sept., and 27 Oct. 1821; 9 Jan. and 12 Oct. 1822; and 26 May 1823; and in the *Commercial Advertiser*, 16 Jan. and 10 and 17 Aug. 1822. See also Simon Snipe, *The Sports of New York* (1823, 1824), and H. P. Phelps, *Players of a Century: A Record of the Albany Stage* (1880). Information regarding the police raid on Brown's theater, and the vandalism by white hooligans, is contained in the records of the New York County District Attorney, 1821–1822, and the Cases Dismissed records of the New York City Police Court. For a more recent work that discusses Brown, see George A. Thompson, Jr., *The African Theatre and James Hewlett: A Documentary Study* (1997).

GEORGE A. THOMPSON, JR.

BROWN, William Carlos (29 July 1853–6 Dec. 1924), railroad executive, was born in Norway, Herkimer County, New York, the son of Charles E. Brown, a Baptist minister, and Frances Lyon. The family moved to Vernon Springs, Iowa, in 1857. Brown attended public schools briefly and was then tutored at home. In 1869 he joined a section gang on the Chicago, Milwaukee & St. Paul Railway (St. Paul Road) in Illinois. He advanced to fireman and telegrapher, and in 1876 he was hired by the Chicago, Burlington & Quincy Railroad. During the next twenty-five years Brown moved up through the ranks of the CB&Q, which served as a training ground for several generations of railroad leaders. Ambitious and hardworking, Brown was noticed by CB&Q executives when, in the midst of a blizzard, he completed his telegrapher's shift and then voluntarily helped to unload cattle trapped in stockcars. Determined to find better methods of operating the railroad, Brown offered many suggestions and initiatives, leading to his promotion in 1896 to general manager at Chicago, where he served for five years.

When William Henry Newman, president of the Lake Shore & Michigan Southern Railway, became president of its parent company, the New York Central, in 1901, he made Brown vice president and general manager of the LS&MS. Thus Brown entered the orbit of the New York Central, which, along with the Pennsylvania Railroad, was the most important railroad in the eastern United States. Advancing rapidly at the Central, Brown became the carrier's vice president in 1905. When Newman retired four years later, Brown was named president over many long-time Central executives.

Brown overcame his lack of formal education through self-discipline and a wide-ranging reading program. He studied finance, government, and economics. While with the CB&Q he asked his secretary to help him learn proper grammar, and after becoming a leading railroad manager Brown contributed articles to trade and popular journals and gave numerous well-received addresses to civic and business groups. In New York his world broadened, and he moved in the highest levels of commerce. There he used his considerable talents to argue against railroad regulations that precluded legitimate profits. He was convinced that the carriers needed substantial funds for modernization and that strict regulations denied railways access to capital. Brown believed, however, that shippers and consumers were correct in opposing free passes, rebates, and discriminatory rates. Regulation appeared inevitable to him, but he argued that in setting maximum rates the Interstate Commerce Commission should establish "fair" rates that would provide profit levels to support modernization. Along with other railway executives, Brown watched in dismay as rising prices and wages drove expenses higher, while the ICC refused nearly all rate increase requests. Declining profits slowed his efforts to modernize the New York Central on the eve of World War I.

As an executive at the Central, Brown advocated larger and more efficient locomotives, steel passenger cars, freight equipment with greater capacities, an extended signaling system, more double-track mainlines, and the electrification of trackage into New York City. The enormous cost of the Grand Central Terminal, in addition to noise and pollution abatement projects, provided a dramatic example of the need to issue additional securities, which meant raising the profit level of the railroads. When Brown argued widely for a 10 percent increase in freight rates in 1908, President Theodore Roosevelt told him that it was a lost cause in an election year.

Throughout the Progressive Era Brown led the rail industry in seeking fair rates. He and other railroad presidents sought to win President William Howard Taft's support in 1910 but to no avail. Brown then created a major public relations campaign to explain to consumers the costs of betterment programs and the need for additional resources. The political leaders in Washington sensed, however, that the public wanted greater regulation, not less. Brown's efforts were defeated when the Mann-Elkins Act, passed in 1910, expanded the powers of the ICC. Brown pleaded with the ICC for adequate rates to help fund a $230 million improvement program for his railroad. When progressive lawyer Louis Brandeis told Brown to cut dividends and hire efficiency experts, the railroad president replied that experts who could solve the problems of the Central could find immediate employment with the railroad.

Brown's efforts to obtain fair treatment of the railroads continued until his retirement. He stepped up public relations efforts and helped form the Bureau of Railway Economics, a private agency that gathered statistical evidence for the carriers. Despite rebuffs from the ICC, Brown continued the modernization campaign, and during his presidency revenues and traffic doubled, but not the profits that would have paid for additional improvements. Plagued by increasing deafness, Brown resigned the presidency in 1914. The railroad missed his capacity for organization, talent in selecting subordinates, and ability to maintain harmony.

Brown retired to a farm near Lime Springs, Iowa, with his wife, Mary Ella Hewitt, whom he had married in 1874. He thereafter devoted himself to his family of three daughters and to scientific agriculture. He promoted soil conservation and experimental farms. Brown lived in Pasadena, California, in the winter and was in residence there when he died.

• No papers of William Carlos Brown are known to exist. Brown published two articles on his business philosophy, "The Remedy for the High Cost of Living," *Independent* 68 (30 June 1910): 1424–28, and "Relations of the Railroads to the Public—Co-operative, Not Antagonistic," *Scientific American*, 17 June 1911, pp. 587, 607–8. See also Brown's *Freight Rates and Railway Conditions: Addresses and Correspondence* (1990). Contemporary articles about him include two written anonymously, "A Back-to-the-Lander's Vision," *Literary Digest* 47 (13 Dec. 1913): 1192–93, and "The Footprints of William C. Brown," *Current Literature* 51 (Dec. 1911): 618–20; and John Kimberly Mumford, "This Land of Opportunity: The Story of a Man Who Stayed 'On His Job,'" *Harper's Weekly*, 20 June 1900, pp. 11–14. Obituaries are in *Railway Age*, 13 Dec. 1924, p. 1104, and the *New York Times*, 7 Dec. 1924.

KEITH L. BRYANT, JR.

BROWN, William Hill (late Nov.? 1765–2 Sept. 1793), writer, was born in Boston, Massachusetts, the son of Gawen Brown, an English-born clockmaker of repute, and his third wife, Elizabeth Hill Adams. He attended a Boston boys' school and assisted in his father's shop during vacation periods. In his lifetime Brown's writings appeared under various initials or names such as "Pollio" or "Columbus." His work reveals a broad acquaintance with classical and British literature and a keen awareness of contemporary American writers. His first published poems were witty treatments of political topics. "Shays to Shattuck: An Epistle" (*Massachusetts Centinel*, 5 Sept. 1787), in the form of twenty-six tetrameter couplets and a closing triplet, is presented as a letter from Daniel Shays to his jailed colleague Job Shattuck, ruefully reflecting on their mistaken action in leading an armed uprising in western Massachusetts in 1786 to protest high taxation and subsequent mortgage foreclosures. Brown's "Yankee Song," celebrating Massachusetts's ratification of the federal Constitution, appeared in the *Pennsylvania Mercury* on 21 February 1788 and later that year was reprinted in the *Massachusetts Centinel* (Boston) and the *Worcester Magazine*. As part of an eight-page pamphlet published in New York City titled *Four Excellent Songs*, the poem was renamed "Yankee Doodle." One of the many versions of the marching song that had been popular since the American Revolution, it closes with a cheerful toast:

So here I end my fed'ral song
  Compos'd of thirteen verses.
May agriculture flourish long,
  And commerce fill our purses.
    Yankee doodle, keep it up!
    Yankee doodle dandy . . .

In 1789 the two books published by Brown in his lifetime appeared anonymously; according to their title pages, both were "Printed at Boston by Isaiah Thomas and Company." *The Power of Sympathy; or, The Triumph of Nature* was announced in the *Massachusetts Centinel* as "the first American novel *this day published*." Although several other books have been proposed, the consensus of literary historians is that Brown's is indeed the first American novel. In the introduction to his definitive edition of *The Power of Sympathy* (1969), William S. Kable notes that "the novel is thoroughly American" and "the fictional world of the book is consistently that of the young Republic" (p. xiv). In the form of an epistolary novel, a popular genre of the time, *The Power of Sympathy* dramatizes the theme identified in the title by portraying a rake's pursuit of a woman who, unbeknownst to either of them, is his sister. They are intuitively drawn to each other, but once their blood relationship is revealed to them their love cannot be consummated. In deep despair, the sister pines away unto death; the brother then commits suicide, with his parting note placed beside a copy of the era's most sensational fictional account of self-destructive romantic love, Goethe's *Sorrows of Young Werther* (originally published, in German, in 1774). As viewed by late twentieth-century feminist critics, the novel offers a significant portrayal of the vulnerability of women within a patriarchal society. According to Cathy N. Davidson, "The real model for this portion of the novel is not the already established epistolary novel but the even more established format of the collected sermons of some respected divine. . . . Side by side with the didactic epistles, however, are quite different letters which, taken together, give us a salacious, sexually charged novel" (pp. 98–99).

Brown's second book, a play titled *The Better Sort; or, The Girl of Spirit: An Operatical, Comical Farce*, could not be more different in kind and spirit. The speaker of the prologue assures the audience that the author, "a warm good fed'ralist at heart," believes "'tis vice awakes the muse's rage, / Her pow'rs satirick but reform the age." With its lighthearted satire presented in dialogue and in eighteen "airs, songs, duets, etc." sung to familiar tunes, the farce resembles the English playwright John Gay's enormously popular *The Beggar's Opera* (1724).

Brown next appeared in print as an essayist. In February 1790 the *Massachusetts Magazine* carried the first essay in a series called "The Reformer," and from September to December the semiweekly *Columbian Centinel* published twenty-two "Yankee" essays by Brown. His last published essay appeared in North Carolina, where he had gone to visit his younger sister, Eliza, and her new husband at their plantation home near the town of Murfreesboro. Brown stayed on to study law under General William Richardson Davie in Halifax, a town in the vicinity. On 10 July 1793 the *North-Carolina Journal* (Halifax) carried an essay by "Columbus," a pen name of Brown. Simply titled "Education," the piece champions the University of North Carolina, which had been chartered in 1789 and was founded under Davie's guiding spirit. When an epidemic struck a month later, Brown died, probably of malaria, in Murfreesboro, North Carolina.

Brown's literary career entered a new phase after his death. His authorship of some pieces became publicly known; for instance, when reprinting "Shays to Shattuck" in the *Massachusetts Mercury* (13 Dec. 1797) the editor identified it as the work of "Mr. William Brown, a person who was much celebrated for poetic genius and general erudition." By that time Brown was recognized as a playwright as well, for his *West Point Preserved; or, The Treason of Arnold: An Historical Tragedy in Five Acts* had been performed seven times by professionals at Boston's Haymarket Theatre in April 1797 and had been favorably reviewed by critics. Thanks to members of Brown's family, works left in manuscript form, including verse fables and other poems, appeared in the *Boston Magazine* and the *Emerald* between 1805 and 1807. Brown's second novel, *Ira and Isabella; or, The Natural Children: A Novel, Founded in Fiction*, also was published in 1807, identified as "A Posthumous Work. By the late William H. Brown, of Boston." Robert D. Arner, noting its similarities with *The Power of Sympathy*, regards *Ira and Isabella* as "a hasty work instead of a deliberate parody" (p. 83), in which, however, the purported sibling relationship turns out happily not to be the case. In Anne Dalke's view, the title characters, both of them offspring of their fathers' illicit affairs, are allowed to marry "only because both are illegitimate and so unworthy of concern. They share the same lowly class" (p. 194).

No collection of the poems appeared until 1982, when Richard Walser published *William Hill Brown: Selected Poems and Verse Fables, 1784–1793*. Although the slender volume includes "only about half the poetry definitely identified as Brown's" (p. 85), it amply demonstrates that Brown was a versatile writer in love with his craft, at home in a variety of forms suited to the thoughtful or humorous subjects treated. Taken together with his novels, plays, and essays, they suggest that when he died Brown was a true man of letters in the making.

• Some of Brown's letters are in the Bancroft Library at the University of California, Berkeley, and at the Massachusetts Historical Society. The text of *West Point Preserved,* said to have been published in 1797 and certainly produced in that year, has been lost. Good brief accounts of Brown's life are included in Kable's edition of *The Power of Sympathy* and Walser's *Selected Poems.* Robert D. Arner's illuminating essay on Brown in the *Dictionary of Literary Biography,* vol. 37 (1985) includes a useful selective bibliography. In *Philenia: The Life and Works of Mrs. Sarah Wentworth Morton, 1759–1846* (written with Emily Pendleton, 1931), Milton Ellis first made his case against the possibility of Morton's authorship of *The Power of Sympathy.* He proposed Brown in "The Author of the First American Novel," *American Literature* 4 (1932–1933): 359–68. Brown's novels are considered in Herbert Ross Brown, *The Sentimental Novel in America, 1789–1860* (1940, repr. 1977); Leslie Fiedler, *Love and Death in the American Novel* (1960; rev. ed., 1966); Henri Petter, *The Early American Novel* (1971); and in later studies influenced by feminist criticism, such as Cathy N. Davidson, *Revolution and the Word: The Rise of the Novel in America* (1986), and Anne Dalke, "Original Vice: The Political Implications of Incest in the Early American Novel," *Early American Literature* 23 (1988): 188–201.

VINCENT FREIMARCK

BROWN, William Wells (1814?–6 Nov. 1884), author and reformer, was born near Lexington, Kentucky, the son of George Higgins, a relative of his master, and Elizabeth, a slave. Dr. John Young, Brown's master, migrated with his family from Kentucky to the Missouri Territory in 1816. Eleven years later the Youngs moved to St. Louis. Although Brown never experienced the hardship of plantation slavery, he was hired out regularly and separated from his family. He worked for a while in the printing office of abolitionist Elijah Lovejoy's *St. Louis Times.* He was also hired out to a slave trader who took coffles of slaves down the Mississippi River for sale in New Orleans. Brown's task was to prepare the slaves for sale, making sure that they all appeared to be in good health. Among other things, that meant dyeing the hair of the older slaves black to remove any trace of gray. At the end of one of these trips to New Orleans, Brown discovered that his master, short of cash, had sold his sister and had plans to sell him. Brown decided to escape with his mother, and they crossed into Illinois sometime in the spring in 1833. They were soon captured, however, and brought back to St. Louis. Young sold Brown to a local tailor and his mother to a slave trader, who took her south. In January 1834 Brown made another, this time successful, attempt to escape, crossing the Ohio River to Cincinnati and on to Cleveland.

Soon after settling in Cleveland, Brown met and married Elizabeth Schooner; they had three children. The couple had a strained and difficult relationship, and the marriage finally ended in an acrimonious separation in 1847. Brown married Annie Elizabeth Gray of Cambridgeport, Massachusetts in 1860. During his years in Cleveland, Brown worked as a boatman on Lake Erie and was an active member of the local Underground Railroad, ferrying fugitives across the lake to Canada. He was also active in local and regional abolitionist associations and the Negro Convention Movement. He was employed as a lecturing agent by the Western New York Anti-Slavery Society in 1843 and later in a similar position by the Massachusetts Anti-Slavery Society. These agencies aimed to spread the abolitionist message throughout the state, in small towns and hamlets, in an attempt to persuade their listeners to join the anti-slavery cause. By the latter part of the decade, he had become a major figure in the American abolitionist movement.

Brown's *Narrative of William W. Brown, a Fugitive Slave, Written by Himself* was published in 1847 and became an immediate bestseller; 3,000 copies of the first edition were sold in six months. The book went through four editions in two years with sales of 10,000 copies. Brown's rise to prominence in abolitionist circles and the success of his book led to his appointment as a delegate to the Peace Congress in Paris in 1849. Presided over by French author Victor Hugo, the congress was attended by 800 delegates. The twenty delegates from the United States included two other African Americans, J. W. C. Pennington and Alexander Crummell. After the meeting, Brown went to London, where he spent the next five years working to win British support for the American abolitionist movement.

During his stay in Britain, Brown claimed to have traveled 25,000 miles and given 1,000 lectures, the majority of which were on abolition. He also found time to write. The first British edition of his *Narrative* appeared in 1849. Three years later he published *Three Years in Europe; or, Places I Have Seen and People I Have Met,* an account of his travels in Europe. His novel *Clotel; of the President's Daughter: A Narrative of Slave Life in the United States* was published in 1853, the first novel published by an African American. A tragic story of a mulatto mother and her quadroon daughter, Clotel, who was fathered by Thomas Jefferson, the novel paints a lurid and sometimes moving picture of the devastating impact of slavery and racism. All of these publications were generally well received.

Brown's successes in Britain were crowned by the decision of British friends to raise sufficient money to purchase his freedom in 1854. Like so many of his contemporaries who had campaigned in Britain, Brown returned to the United States that year fortified by his successes and recommitted to the struggle against slavery and racial discrimination at home. But these were dark and uncertain times for African Americans in the wake of the Fugitive Slave Law (1850), the Kansas-Nebraska Act (1854), and the *Dred Scott* decision (1857), in which the U.S. Supreme Court ruled that blacks were not citizens and as such had no constitutionally protected rights. This period of uncertainty prompted many African Americans to renew the debate over the wisdom of remaining in the United States. Although he had formerly opposed colonization and emigration, Brown became an active promoter of Haitian emigration during this period and regularly contributed to the *Pine and Palm*, the movement's newspaper. He lectured throughout the Northeast and Canada West in 1861–1862 as an agent of the Haytian Emigration Bureau, promoting the black independent nation as a future home for African Americans.

While the outbreak of the Civil War dampened emigrationist enthusiasm and raised expectations of a brighter future among some African Americans, Brown counciled caution, insisting that the United States first commit itself to emancipation and full equality for all before blacks would volunteer their services. President Abraham Lincoln's Emancipation Proclamation and the decision of Massachusetts governor John Andrew to raise two black regiments finally brought Brown into the fold as a recruiter and supporter of the Union.

During the war Brown renewed his interest in medicine, an interest first developed while he was a slave and later encouraged by Dr. John Bishop Estlin, the British surgeon and abolitionist who was one of Brown's mentors. Brown conducted a relatively successful practice as a "Dermapathic and Practical Physician" in Boston for almost nineteen years. He also continued to publish. *The Black Man, His Antecedents, His Genius and His Achievements*, a compendium of biographical vignettes of people of African descent, appeared in 1863. Four years later Brown published *The Negro in the American Rebellion: His Heroism and his Fidelity*. The first history of black involvement in the Civil War, it was set in the context of black contributions to the American Revolution and the War of 1812. Brown's final historical study, *The Rising Son; or, The Antecedents and Advancement of the Colored Race*, appeared in 1873. A general history of the African experience in the New World, it contains ethnographic analysis, biographical sketches, and brief accounts of blacks in Haiti, the United States, South America, and the Caribbean. Brown's final publication, *My Southern Home; or, The South and Its People*, an account of slave life and his travels through the South in 1879–1880, appeared in 1880. He died in Chelsea, Massachusetts.

The Irish abolitionist Richard Webb wrote of Brown in 1851: he is "excellent company, full of anecdotes, has graphic and dramatic powers of no mean order, and a keen appreciation of character. . . . He and I get on so pleasantly together, and he is so much beloved by his friends that I naturally look to him as a perfect rock of sense." As these comments and those of other abolitionists suggest, Brown epitomized the true potential of the enslaved once freed from the shackles of oppression. A universal reformer, Brown worked not only for emancipation and the removal of racial restrictions, but also for the promotion of peace and temperance. His publications, together with his reform efforts, are a substantial legacy.

• A number of letters by or about Brown can be found in the Anti-Slavery Collection, Boston Public Library; the Gerrit Smith Papers, Syracuse University; the British and Foreign Anti-Slavery Society Papers, Rhodes House Library, Oxford University; the Leon Gardiner Collection, Pennsylvania Historical Society; and the Estlin Papers, Dr. Williams' Library, London. Additional letters can be found in C. Peter Ripley, ed., *The Black Abolitionists Papers*, microfilm. The definitive biography of Brown is William Edward Farrison, *William Wells Brown: Author and Reformer* (1969). Also useful is Josephine Brown, *Biography of an American Bondman, by His Daughter* (1856). An obituary is in the *Boston Daily Globe*, 10 Nov. 1884.

R. J. M. BLACKETT

BROWNE, Benjamin Frederick (17 July 1793–23 Nov. 1873), druggist and author, was born in Salem, Massachusetts, the son of Benjamin Browne and Elizabeth Andrew, occupations unknown. Browne attended classes beginning in 1797 in a school run by Madame Babbidge. He served as apprentice to apothecary E. S. Lang for five years (1807–1812), immediately after which the outbreak of the War of 1812 destroyed all commerce moving through the port of Salem.

In September 1812 Browne signed aboard the privateer *Alfred* as a surgeon's assistant. The *Alfred* met with success at first by capturing two enemy brigs and their valuable cargo. But then the captain grew cautious and soon docked at Portsmouth, New Hampshire. Browne shipped aboard the *Frolic* and served as captain's clerk, purser, and sergeant of marines until the boat was captured in January 1814 by the *Heron*, an English man-of-war. The American crew was imprisoned at Barbados until August, at which time the men were shipped to Plymouth, England, marched to Dartmoor prison, and jailed until May 1815. When freed, Browne weighed only ninety-four pounds. He made his way to New York, Providence, and finally Salem again. His family and friends had heard nothing from or about him since his capture by the British. He had written letters that never arrived in America.

In 1816 "Doctor" Browne, as his profession entitled him to be addressed, went into business with a fellow apothecary named William Stearns in the corner store of Salem's Union Street building. In 1823 Browne established his own drugstore on the corner of Essex and Washington streets. In 1825 he married Sally Bott; the couple evidently had no children. In 1833 he moved to a store on Essex Street, opposite the First Church. Ever a loyal member of the Democratic party, he was elected in 1831 as a representative of the General Court of Massachusetts. Twelve years later he became a state senator and gained fame as a skillful and witty debater. He was appointed by Presidents John Tyler and James K. Polk to be postmaster of Salem (1845–1849). On a few occasions he was an unsuccessful candidate for mayor of Salem.

Browne led a quiet life during his last decades. He regularly attended the Independent Congregational Church in Salem. In 1860 he retired, giving over his practice to Charles H. Price, his partner of ten years. He made it his habit, however, to visit the old store daily, to sit at his old desk, to watch his former partner at work, and to gossip with anyone—old or, preferably, young—who came by. In September 1873 he suffered a paralytic stroke, was comforted by his strong religious faith, and soon died in Salem.

One of the most significant experiences of Browne's life was his association with Nathaniel Hawthorne. In 1840 a mutual friend showed Hawthorne a narrative that Browne had written about his life at sea and his imprisonment at Dartmoor. Hawthorne read it and reported that he thought it could easily be made publishable, but nothing happened for several years. Then, as soon as Polk was elected president, Hawthorne wrote (Nov. 1844) to urge his close friend Horatio Bridge, an influential naval officer then in Washington, D.C., to recommend that Browne, by that time appointed Salem's postmaster but not yet confirmed, be removed and replaced by Hawthorne himself. The plan failed. In the winter of 1845–1846 Hawthorne edited Browne's narrative for anonymous, abridged publication as "Papers of an Old Dartmoor Prisoner" in the *United States Magazine and Democratic Review* (Jan.–Sept. 1846). Hawthorne was motivated less by the money he would be paid than by his wanting Browne, still the influential postmaster, to recommend his appointment as surveyor of the Salem Custom House. Browne did so, and the two men remained good friends ever after.

Browne's major claim to fame now is his "Papers of an Old Dartmoor Prisoner." It proved popular when it was published in 1846, but its authorship was not widely known for eighty years. In the 1920s Hawthorne's daughter Rose Hawthorne Lathrop (Mother Alphonsa) gave the unsigned manuscript to Clifford Smyth, who prepared it for republication as *The Yarn of a Yankee Privateer* (1926), with the addition of four chapters concerning Barbados omitted by Hawthorne. At this time the new publishers, still not knowing who had written the work, offered a $500 reward to anyone who could identify him. Within a year, Browne was named. His full account is in twenty chapters. The fourth chapter ends with the capture of the *Frolic*. The next six chapters concern life at Barbados, where the Americans were accorded limited freedom. By the end of the tenth chapter, however, they are on their way to England. The last half of the book recounts their life at Dartmoor prison. Conditions were deplorable. The place was wet and gloomy. The men wore prison garb, slung hammocks, and had wooden spoons and tin pots. Food consisted mainly of beef and bread, and occasionally herring, cod, potatoes, turnips, and onions. For sanitary purposes every six men had one bucket. The U.S. government gave each prisoner about $3 a month, to spend in a makeshift market the prisoners set up to buy daintier food items, and even brandy, that made their way past the stone walls. Even so, one in thirteen of the 4,000 prisoners died while Browne was there. On 6 April 1815 the brutalized men mutinied, since by then peace had been declared. The British authorities responded by ordering 700 or more soldiers to enter and attack. Browne details what followed in chapter 19, "The Massacre." The soldiers fired on the prisoners for ten minutes, killing and wounding many. The last chapter tells of their release and long voyage home. Browne's narrative is straightforward, detailed, graphic, occasionally humorous, and most readable.

• Many of Browne's personal papers were destroyed when his store burned in 1862. "Memoir of Benjamin Frederick Browne," *Historical Collections of the Essex Institute* 13 (Apr. 1875): 81–89, is the best source of biographical information. Two essays on Browne's prison papers and the "discovery" of their authorship are, respectively, "The True 'Yarn' of a Yankee Privateer," *Literary Digest*, 22 May 1926, pp. 34, 36, 38, 40, with illustrations, and "Hawthorne's 'Privateer' Revealed at Last," *Literary Digest*, 9 Apr. 1927, pp. 44, 49. Letters by Hawthorne concerning Browne are in Nathaniel Hawthorne, *The Letters, 1813–1843* (1984) and *The Letters, 1843–1853* (1985), both ed. Thomas Woodson et al. Among many discussions of Browne's friendship with Hawthorne, the best is in Arlin Turner, *Nathaniel Hawthorne: A Biography* (1980). Two essays providing information on Dartmoor prison are Reginald Horsman, "The Paradox of Dartmoor Prison," *American Heritage* 26 (Feb. 1975): 12–17, 85; and Robin F. A. Fabel, "Self-help in Dartmoor: Black and White Prisoners in the War of 1812," *Journal of the Early Republic* 9 (Summer 1989): 165–90.

ROBERT L. GALE

BROWNE, Carl (1846–16 Jan. 1914), political agitator, reform journalist, and organizer of "Coxey's Army," was born in Springfield, Illinois. (The date and place of his birth are sometimes less reliably given as 4 July 1849 in Newton, Iowa). Browne was working as a sign painter in western Iowa in 1869 when he suddenly decided to move to California. At that time he desired more than anything else to paint a gargantuan panorama of the Yosemite Valley. He later exhibited this painting up and down the Pacific Coast, such panoramas being a popular form of folk art in the nineteenth century. One unfriendly critic observed, "As an artist Carl Browne belongs to a distinct school. In fact, he constitutes the entire school." Browne's response to critics was to affirm that as a young man he had apprenticed with a carriage and house painter (an experience that probably accounted for his love of huge panoramic images and garish colors such as might adorn a circus wagon).

Browne's cartoons lampooning wealthy San Francisco citizens first attracted notice in the late 1870s when they appeared in a radical newspaper called the *Open Letter*. The art so amused Denis Kearney, leader of the workingmen's movement to rid California of Chinese, that he made the caricaturist his personal secretary. In 1878 the two crossed the continent together to take the cause of Chinese exclusion to Boston's workingmen in historic Faneuil Hall and to instruct President Rutherford B. Hayes during an interview at the White House. Some contemporaries even claimed that Browne was the brains behind the Kearney movement, but that was surely an exaggeration. It was true that during the Kearneyite agitation Browne first toyed with the idea of organizing a march of the unemployed to demand jobs from lawmakers. He also honed his skills as a stump orator for various causes.

It was in California that Browne perfected the technique of wearing a variety of outlandish costumes to grab attention during public orations. On occasion he might give a street-corner lecture dressed in silver armor as the Labor Knight; later he might appear as Daniel Boone or Davy Crockett. He most often imitated the popular showman Buffalo Bill Cody by dressing in buckskin and sporting a large white sombrero. Browne, who first met Jacob S. Coxey in Chicago at the World's Columbian Exposition in 1893, later claimed that a San Francisco business newspaper commissioned him to attend the fair as its artist and correspondent and provided the "Buffalo Bill suit" so he could join an exhibit labeled the "wild and wooly West." In fact, Browne, who was forever reinventing his public persona and his past, conveniently forgot that he had earlier used the frontiersman's garb to attract notice during a series of street-corner lectures in Los Angeles.

It was in Los Angeles in the 1880s that Browne stumbled into trouble when he gave one of his public lectures dressed in a heavy overcoat, corduroy pantaloons, top boots, and a skull cap. Publicity-sensitive officials interpreted his garb as libeling the much-advertised ideal climate of Los Angeles and had him committed briefly to the state mental hospital at Napa, or so his many detractors claimed. Browne himself boasted that he had been in more jails than any other living agitator for labor's cause.

In many ways Browne, an eccentric, energetic, flamboyant man, was a parody of the Gilded Age promoter, forever dabbling in agriculture, patent medicine, panoramic art, journalism, and political nostrums. As an orator he was noted not so much for what he said or how he said it, but for sheer stamina on the stump. For example, when he toured Nebraska in 1892 on behalf of Populist candidates, he once lectured for three hours in a raging windstorm. The same heroic quality characterized everything else he did. When he concocted a patent medicine in 1896, Browne advertised it as "Carl's California Cure" made by "Carl Browne, man's mightiest microbe master."

Browne married Alice Courier in 1872. Little is known of their relationship except that they met in California and lived for a time in Berkeley. In the early 1890s Alice suddenly exhibited signs of severe mental illness. For a year Browne remained at her bedside in their mountain retreat near Napa and attempted to nurse her back to health. Alice's sudden death from pneumonia late in 1892 plunged him into a period of prolonged grief and intense study of metaphysics and death. He apparently adopted the tenets of Theosophy, a mystical faith prominent in southern California that professed reincarnation. It was Browne's religious bent that caused him officially to label Coxey's crusaders the "Commonweal of Christ." The name shocked Victorian sensibilities but increased popular interest in the protest.

After Browne and Coxey met in Chicago, their shared interest in monetary reform made the two men increasingly close friends. Coxey, a wealthy businessman, invited the peripatetic Californian to spend the following winter at his home in Massillon, Ohio. It was there that Browne perfected his idea of a marching "petition in boots" to Congress to demand public-works jobs to alleviate the depression and unemployment then sweeping the country. During preparations for the march, Browne promulgated numerous manifestos that inspired other contingents to form, the largest in California and the Far West. More than anyone else, it was Browne who made "Coxey's Army" a household word in the spring of 1894, attracting unprecedented nationwide newspaper attention.

The six-week march from Massillon to Washington in March and April 1894 ended with the arrest and jailing of Coxey and Browne. During their three weeks in prison the two leaders planned an even larger march for the following year, but these plans collapsed when the press leaked word that Browne had secretly courted Coxey's eighteen-year-old daughter Mamie. Coxey disowned Mamie and disavowed Browne shortly after they were married in mid-1895. At the turn of the century the couple was living at Browne's "Commonweal Castle," a modest retreat near Calistoga, California, where Mamie bore a son. They split up a short time thereafter.

Browne occasionally mounted a soap box on the streets of San Francisco during the early years of the twentieth century to champion radical causes, primarily those of the Industrial Workers of the World and the Socialist party. He could be counted on to attend every radical gathering open to the public. During a 24-hour anti–capital punishment rally in San Francisco in 1912, Browne turned up to issue hourly "extras" throughout the day and evening. He reported the speeches, illustrated them with his cartoons, and sold the finished products on the spot.

Beginning about 1910, Browne also devoted time to planning and promoting an airplane of his own design, one that boasted eight engines and seemed the aviation counterpart to his gargantuan paintings. During a trip to Capitol Hill to promote various causes, including his "octo plane," Browne suffered an apparent heart attack and died. Members of the Socialist party, his only real family in the later years of his life, conducted the funeral. A few months earlier, Browne had at least had the satisfaction of speaking from the Capitol steps, a privilege the police had denied him during the Coxey crusade.

A close friend once called Browne the "Don Quixote of California"; his numerous detractors called him much worse names. One of his most fervid critics was Ambrose Bierce, who, when accused of libeling Browne, retorted that the worst possible libel was simply to call him Carl Browne. Browne himself proudly summed up his life by quoting a San Francisco journalist who wrote of him, "Carl Browne has spent his life championing the cause of the underdog."

• Browne left no known body of papers, although some examples of his highly idiosyncratic journalism and artwork are preserved at the Bancroft Library, University of California, Berkeley. He figures prominently in two books that detail the history of the Coxey movement, Donald L. McMurry, *Coxey's Army: A Study of the Industrial Army Movement of 1894* (1929), and Carlos A. Schwantes, *Coxey's Army: An American Odyssey* (1985). He receives sympathetic treatment in Henry Vincent's contemporary account of the march, *The Story of the Commonweal* (1894). See also William McDevitt's edited version of Carl Browne, *When Coxey's "Army" Marcht* (1944).

CARLOS A. SCHWANTES

BROWNE, Charles Farrar (26 Apr. 1834–6 Mar. 1867), author and lecturer, known by the pseudonym Artemus Ward, was born in Waterford, Maine, the son of Levi Brown, a surveyor, farmer, and justice of the peace, and Caroline Farrar. (Charles added the *e* to his surname about 1861.) He seems to have been educated in local schools until 1847, when his father died and he went to work as a printer. In 1851 he was in Boston, setting type for the *Carpet-Bag*, which published in its 1 May 1852 issue "The Dandy Frightening the Squatter," the earliest-known piece by Samuel Langhorne Clemens (Mark Twain). A decade or so later the lives and writings of Browne and Clemens would become inextricably entangled. Browne wrote a number of pieces for the *Carpet-Bag*, usually under the pen name "Chub," or "Lt. Chubb."

After the *Carpet-Bag* went out of business in March 1853, Browne found employment in Cincinnati, Dayton, Springfield, Sandusky, and Tiffin, Ohio. He acquired more opportunity to write, however, as local editor of the Toledo *Commercial* and soon established a regional reputation as an entertaining writer. On 29 October 1857 he became local editor of the Cleveland *Plain Dealer* and before long found the writing formula that brought him the fame his name still possesses. It lay in a bogus letter to the editor, which read:

Pitsburg, Jan. 27, 18&58

The Plane Deeler:
Sir:

i write to no how about the show bisnes in Cleeveland i have a show consisting in part of a Calforny Bare two snakes tame foxies &c also wax works my wax works is hard to beat, all say they is life and nateral curiosities among my wax works is Our Saveyer Gen taylor and Docktor Webster in the ackt of killing Parkman. now mr. Editor scratch off few lines and tel me how is the show bisnes in your good city i shal have hanbils printed at your offis you scratch my back i will scratch your back, also git up a grate blow in the paper about my show don't forgit the wax works.

yours truly,
ARTEMUS WARD
Pitsburg, Penny

p S pitsburg is a l horse town. A. W.

Thus the itinerant showman Artemus Ward was born, complete with menagerie, waxworks of famous and infamous people, handbills, and wryly humorous comments about the places or personalities he visited. The spelling became even more adventurous, and the showman added a "moral bare" or so and a "Cangeroo," but the pattern was established that allowed Browne to travel imaginatively in his columns and later physically as a lecturer throughout the United States and England, where he achieved his greatest success and died at the height of his fame. The name "Artemus Ward," so spelled, belonged to one of the figures in a Maine land dispute that called on the surveying services of at least three generations of Browne's forebears. The Ward letters to the *Plain Dealer* kept coming, from "Wheeling, va"; "Kolumbus, ohio"; "Tiffin"; "Toledo"; "Sandusty"; and, after a time, his putative home in "Baldingsville, Indianny," where he claimed to live with his wife Betsy Jane, a daughter, and twin sons.

In 1861 Browne moved to New York and a connection with *Vanity Fair* that brought him the managing editor's chair in May. There he assumed a position among the nation's principal humorists and showed his mettle with wide-ranging interviews and reports signed by Artemus Ward and with a number of conventionally spelled satires on current romantic drama and fiction. Then, late in 1861, he took to the road with comic lectures that were parodies of the serious lectures so popular at the time. The title of the first was "The Children of the Wood," which ultimately became celebrated as "The Babes in the Wood." The form of Browne's lectures was similar to what the American public of a century later would call "standup comedy": disconnected jokes of all kinds, seldom even close to the advertised topic, deriving extra force from the lecturer's deadpan delivery. Browne resigned from his position with *Vanity Fair* in April 1862 but continued to publish occasionally in that periodical until it ceased publication in 1863.

The best-selling collection entitled *Artemus Ward: His Book*, which came out in May 1862, gave immediate solace to a troubled president. Abraham Lincoln led off an extraordinary meeting of his cabinet by reading the piece entitled "High-handed Outrage at Utica." It described an event that had taken place purportedly in "the Faul of 1856," which caused Ward "skorn & disgust to see a big burly feller walk up to the cage containin my wax figgers of the Lord's Last Supper, and cease Judas Iscarrot by the feet and drag him out on the ground. He then commenced fur to pound him as hard as he could." After finishing his reading of this short piece, Lincoln read to his not entirely appreciative audience—almost as anticlimax—his first draft of the Emancipation Proclamation.

Late in 1863 Browne set out for San Francisco and a successful speaking tour in California, Nevada, and Utah, managed by the celebrated promoter E. P. Hingston. Audiences loved him, even in Salt Lake City, where Brigham Young, whom he had satirized, was reported to be in the audience. Much of his week in Virginia City, Nevada, was spent with his new friend Mark Twain, whose first important story, "Jim Smiley and His Frog," was addressed to Artemus Ward when it first appeared in 1865. The Ward influence may be seen in that piece and in Clemens's lecturing style. In fact, the raft journey down the Mississippi in Twain's *Adventures of Huckleberry Finn* is, in many ways, a ride through the fictional world of Artemus Ward. The Duke and the Dauphin, for instance, follow a showman's itinerary much like that of the fictitious Artemus, with visits to printers and the preparation of handbills, and their histrionics on stage are much like those of Ward's Edwin Forrest, doing Shakespeare in the Ward style. Twain's Duke, also, has much in common with Ward's Duke in "Moses the Sassy; or, the Disguised Duke," as do both the Duke and the Dauphin with Ward's "Prints of Wales" and "Prints Napoleon." And when Jim complains that the French don't speak like men, he is echoing Ward's complaint that opera singers "orter sing in the Inglish tung." The Widder's effort to sober up Pap Finn, furthermore, is not far from the Oberlin "Perfesser's" effort to treat Ward's "kangeroo" humanely, in spite of his "little excentrissities." Ward's "dawter execootin' ballads" like "Hark, I hear a angel singin, a angel now is onto the wing . . . " has much in common with the obituary lyrics of Twain's Emmeline Grangerford. There are many other examples of satire on sentimental poetry in Browne's writings.

Browne returned from the West and began a successful tour of New York, Cincinnati, and cities of the reconstructing South as "Artemus Ward among the Mormons," using panoramic backdrops. In June 1866 he set out for England, where he was a great success, lecturing and also writing a number of pieces for *Punch*. Unfortunately the strain of his busy public and private life was too much for him; he died of tuberculosis at Southampton as he prepared to sail home.

• Little of Browne's correspondence and papers survives. Two sources, however, reproduce some: *Letters of Artemus Ward to Charles E. Wilson, 1858–61* (1900) and Don C. Seitz, ed., "Artemus Ward Letters," *American Collector* 3 (Feb. 1927): 195–98. The most recent biography, furthermore, lists a number of repositories of letters: see John J. Pullen, *Comic Relief: The Life and Laughter of Artemus Ward, 1834–67* (1983). *The Complete Works of Artemus Ward* (1862–1898) is by far the most complete edition and includes reproductions of the panoramas used in the lectures. Other biographies are James C. Austin, *Artemus Ward* (1964); Don C. Seitz, *Artemus Ward: A Biography and Bibliography* (1919); and Edward P. Hingston, *The Genial Showman: Being Reminiscences of the Life of Artemus Ward* (1870). John Q. Reed, who has published a number of valuable articles on Browne, completed a Ph.D. dissertation at the State University of Iowa in 1955 entitled *Artemus Ward: A Critical Study*. All biographies mentioned above, save that by Hingston, include useful bibliographies of works primary and secondary.

The techniques and content of Browne's lectures are shown best in T. W. Robertson and E. P. Hingston, *Artemus Ward's Lecture* (As delivered at the Egyptian Hall, London) [also titled *Artemus Ward's Panorama*] (1869); Curtis Dahl, "Artemus Ward: Comic Panoramist," *New England Quarterly* 32 (Dec. 1959): 476–85; and Edgar M. Branch, "The Babes in the Woods: Artemus Ward's 'Double Health' to Mark Twain," *PMLA*, 93 (Oct. 1978): 955–72.

ALFRED H. MARKS

BROWNE, Dik (11 Aug. 1917–4 June 1989), cartoonist, was born Richard Arthur Allan Browne in New York City, the son of William Joseph Browne, a cost accountant, and Mary Slattery, a theatrical wardrobe mistress. Browne had early dreams of being a sculptor, and after finishing high school in 1934 he enrolled in the Cooper Union art school in New York. A year later, family finances required that he get a job, and in 1936 he became a copyboy for the *New York Journal*. A career as a journalist attracted him, but he found himself unable to remember phone numbers and too shy to ask questions. During his spare time, he collaborated with a fellow copyboy on a comic strip called "Muttle the Gonif" ("Muttle the Thief"), retelling stories by Sholem Aleichem translated to the streets of New York, but he was never able to sell it. His amusing drawings and caricatures soon came to the attention of his editors, however, and he was sent to do courtroom sketches at the Lucky Luciano trial, from which photographers and newspaper artists were banned. Unrecognized as a reporter, young Browne made the only drawings of the case to appear in the papers. The feat earned him a promotion to the *Journal's* art department, where he spent the next five years drawing maps, charts, and weather cartoons.

In 1941 *Newsweek* hired Browne away for three times what he was making at the *Journal*, and he celebrated his newfound solvency by marrying Joan Marie Therese Hosey Haggerty Kelly, his childhood sweetheart. They had two children and adopted a third. The next year he was drafted. Assigned to the Army Engineering Corps, where he attained the rank of technical sergeant, he continued drawing maps and charts, adding to his output an occasional poster warning about venereal diseases. He also wrote and drew a comic strip about a WAC, "Ginny Jeep," for the Third Air Force newspaper and created another, "Rembrandt," which he tried unsuccessfully to place with the *New York Journal-American*.

When Browne returned to civilian life in 1946 he accepted a job with the prominent New York advertising agency of Johnstone & Cushing and soon became one of the top comic artists in advertising. He stayed with Johnstone & Cushing for eight years, during which he redesigned the Campbell Soup kids, created the Birdseye bird symbol and United Fruit Company's Chiquita Banana, and produced the art for several candy companies.

Browne never gave up his ambition to be an independent cartoonist, and he took on numerous projects outside the agency office. From 1950 to 1954 he drew clever illustrations for Bishop Fulton J. Sheen's seven-book series *Life Is Worth Living* and from 1952 to 1957 created the blackboard sketches for Sheen's television series. From 1950 to 1960 he also drew the humorous adventure strip "The Tracy Twins," written by Al

Stenzel, for *Boy's Life*. His work for this feature, and an ad he had drawn for the Peter/Paul candy bar Mounds, brought him to the attention of both a King Features Syndicate editor and the cartoonist Mort Walker in 1954. Together they invited him to work on a spinoff from Walker's popular army strip "Beetle Bailey." The new feature, a warm domestic humor strip called "Hi & Lois," began on 18 October 1954 in thirty-two newspapers and was to become one of the most popular comic strips in the history of the medium, appearing in more than 1,100 papers and in fifty countries by the time of the artist's death. A wholesome family strip about the daily lives of a likable suburban couple and their children, "Hi & Lois" was neither satiric nor sentimental but made its points with insight and gentle humor. Browne's clean, economical line and graceful compositions contributed greatly to the strip's popularity.

In 1973 Browne suffered a detached retina and, concerned about the financial security of his family, determined to create a strip of his own. For a year he had been thinking of developing a daily gag strip about a viking named Hägar the Horrible. Debuting on 4 February 1973, "Hägar" became the fastest-growing strip in the history of the comics. Its broad visual humor struck a responsive chord worldwide almost at once. In its first two years it was sold to some 600 papers, and by 1989 it was appearing in more than 1,800, in fifty-eight countries and thirteen languages. An engagingly childlike barbarian, the shaggy, bearded Hägar represented a universal anarchic spirit, the Natural Person we all secretly recognize within ourselves, and the strip was drawn in an appropriately loose, vigorous style. "In 'Hi & Lois,'" Browne reported to *Contemporary Graphic Artists*, "the line is clean and round, and that suits a clean, round, tight, warm family. . . . When you get to someone as raunchy as Hägar, I like the line a lot cruder and bolder" (p. 51). Browne's ability to create a pictorial style harmonious with his various subject matter earned him the title of a cartoonist's cartoonist and brought him an unprecedented number of awards from the industry. The only artist to win the National Cartoonists Society's (NCS) top prize, the Reuben, for two different strips, he received the Best Humor Strip of the Year award for both "Hi & Lois" (1962) and "Hägar" (1973), as well as honors from German and English cartoonist societies. During Browne's lifetime more than forty collections of the two strips were published, and his readership was estimated at more than 100 million internationally.

A large, convivial man resembling his burly, bearded viking creation, Browne was described by his son Chris (in *Something about the Author*) as "an imp and a gentle giant." Browne was much loved by his colleagues and served as NCS president from 1963 to 1965. A devoted family man, Browne engaged his two sons, Chris and Bob, in his work, creating what he liked to call "a cottage industry." After his death in Sarasota, Florida, his sons successfully carried on his work with "Hi & Lois" and "Hägar."

• Most of Browne's manuscripts, original art, and personal papers are in the possession of his family. Informative entries on the life and work of Dik Browne are in all contemporary histories and encyclopedias of cartoons, the most notable of which are Maurice Horn, ed., *World Encyclopedia of Comics* (1976); Horn, ed., *Contemporary Graphic Artists*, vol. 1 (1985); and Ron Goulart, ed., *The Encyclopedia of American Comics* (1995). For extensive articles on Browne, see also *Cartoonist Profiles* 41 (Mar. 1979): 12–27, and 83 (Sept. 1989): 43–45, and the *Hartford (Conn.) Courant*, 11 Nov. 1974, repr. in *Authors in the News*, vol. 1 (1976). Obituaries are in the *New York Times*, 5 June 1989; the *Washington Post*, 6 June 1989; and *Comics Journal*, July 1989.

DENNIS WEPMAN

BROWNE, Herbert Wheildon Cotton (22 Nov. 1860–29 Apr. 1946), architect, was born in Boston, Massachusetts, the son of T. Quincy Browne, a merchant, banker, and mill owner, and Juliet Frances Wheildon. He was raised in Boston and at "Elmwood," his father's Roxbury country house, a Federal-style mansion built in 1806 by Peter Banner. Browne was educated at Noble's Private School, and in 1879 he entered the School of Drawing and Painting at the Boston Museum of Fine Arts. In the early 1880s he studied at the Académie Julian in Paris and with Fabio Fabbi, a sculptor and painter, in Florence. Back in Boston he apprenticed as a draftsman with Andrews, Jaques and Rantoul. Browne, his fellow apprentice Ogden Codman, Jr., and Arthur Little, already a well-known architect, were known as the "Colonial Trinity" for their interest in early New England houses. Measuring and drawing them became their passion.

When and where Browne and Little first met is not known. Their fathers were in the same business and they moved in similar social circles. They were working together by 1887 while Browne was still an apprentice. In April 1890 Little, Browne, and a third partner, George A. Moore, signed a contract forming their own architectural firm. Important members of the firm were Lester Couch, the head draftsman and later business manager, and George Porter Fernald, a draftsman, designer, and decorative painter.

In 1892 Browne, with his Italian manservant, moved into a bachelor flat at 66 Beacon Street, where he lived for the rest of his life. He never owned property, and, unlike Little, he did not have the capital for speculative building. He never married.

Browne brought to the firm his considerable abilities as an artist, renderer, draftsman, and designer. He possessed a knowledge and love of European classical architecture and decoration, especially that of Italy, and during the 1890s grandeur and formality began to overtake the shingled New England vernacular in their work. Their first commissions for remodeling and redecorating houses, with the occasional new house in town or country, came from friends and family, Boston's social elite. Browne expanded and remodeled "Glen Magna Farm" in Danvers, Massachusetts (1893), into a formal, colonnaded neocolonial manor house for William Crowninshield Endicott, and in 1894 he began work in "Faulkner Farm" in Brookline, creating a symmetrical, white clapboarded mansion with French period interiors for Charles F. Sprague, said to be then the richest member of Congress. Seven years later Browne returned to add a third story, enclosing the whole in brick and limestone. A new ballroom wing housed neoclassical plasterwork and Gobelin tapestries.

In 1898 a branch office of Little and Browne was opened in New York at 11 Broadway, and in 1899, its busiest year, the firm handled forty jobs, including sixteen new buildings. In 1902, after a European trip, Browne began one of the firm's largest commissions, a Washington, D.C., house for the diplomat Larz Anderson and his heiress wife Isabel, a cousin of Mrs. Charles Sprague. This white limestone, English Palladian mansion, at 2118 Massachusetts Avenue, took more than three years to build and cost $727,000. The interior was decorated with true Browne bravura-paneled salons and a second-story dining room floored in polychrome marble like a Roman palazzo.

This first decade of the 1900s saw the deepening of Browne's interest in garden design. In 1906 he compiled for his own use a glossary of Italian gardening terms that he surely made use of when planning the gardens at "Hawthorne Hill," in Lancaster, Massachusetts (1906–1908, for Bayard Thayer), a series of outdoor rooms descending a gentle slope away from the house. They depended, like classic Italian gardens, on strong architecture, greenery, and water.

The passage of income tax in 1913 led to a decline in work for the firm. Browne was in Italy in 1912 and again in 1914. In August 1914 he was caught by the outbreak of the war, and he was briefly detained as an Austrian spy. When he arrived home in November a major job awaited him, again for Larz Anderson, at "Weld" in Brookline. He added two wings to the house and during the next three years gradually wrapped its stone and shingle exterior in a classical stucco skin.

Work largely ceased for the duration of the war. During the 1920s the firm continued to show photos at the yearly Massachusetts Institute of Technology exhibits, but they were often of work done fifteen or twenty years earlier. Arthur Little died in 1925, and Browne made Lester Couch a full partner. Couch's Danvers connections brought much civic and commercial work from that town.

In 1925 Brown was retained by William Summer Appleton, director of the Society for the Preservation of New England Antiquities, to move its headquarters, the first Harrison Gray Otis house (1796, Bulfinch), during the widening of Cambridge Street. The work took two years and cost $65,000. Browne was deeply committed to the society and its aims: he was a trustee for sixteen years, a friend of Appleton's, and an adviser on the acquisition of properties. After 1930, large scale commissions largely vanished. The firm continued to repair and alter its earlier houses and to install elevators for an aging clientele.

In 1937 Doll and Richards Gallery mounted a show of Browne's watercolors. Browne reported to Ogden Codman in France that critical response was favorable and sales brisk. When Lester Couch died in 1939, Browne closed the office. He spent his last years in retirement and died at 66 Beacon Street. Browne was a fellow of the American Institute of Architects, a member of the Boston Society of Architects, and the Somerset Club. An avid book collector and bibliophile, he was a proprietor of the Boston Athenaeum for twenty years.

That Browne's professional years coincided with a period of great prosperity and expansion was fortuitous. He was given a rich clientele and almost limitless resources to realize his designs, and his capabilities were recognized and valued in the circles that he served. The role that he and his partner played in carrying the colonial revival into the twentieth century and in awakening their clients to European classical design and gardening makes him a pivotal figure in the history of architecture.

• In 1939 Browne gave job account books, scrapbooks, photo albums, and drawings—the major archives of the firm—to the Society for the Preservation of New England Antiquities (SPNEA), where they remain. Letters between Browne and Ogden Codman survive in the Codman Family Papers there and at the Boston Athenaeum, which also owns Browne's personal scrapbook of photos of the firm's work. Four further scrapbooks, compiled either by Browne or Couch, are in the Avery Architectural Library, Columbia University. Correspondence between the office and W. C. Endicott is owned by the Danvers Historical Society, now owner of Glen Magna Farm, and is on deposit at the Danvers Public Library, Danvers, Mass. The Frick Museum and Archive in Pittsburgh, Pa., preserves correspondence between H. C. Frick and the firm concerning the building of "Eagle Rock" in Prides Crossing, Mass. (1904–1908). On the "Colonial Trinity" see Christopher Monkhouse, "The Making of a Colonial Revival Architect," in *Ogden Codman and the Decoration of Houses*, ed. Pauline C. Metcalf (1988); and concerning Browne's work for Mrs. George Tyson at South Berwick, Maine, see Sarah Giffen and Kevin D. Murphy, eds., *A Noble and Dignified Stream: The Piscataqua Region in the Colonial Revival 1860–1930*. For an analysis of 2118 Massachusetts Avenue, Washington, D.C., see *Massachusetts Avenue Architecture*, vol. 1 (1973), pp. 148–86. Browne's role in the design of the Weld garden is discussed in Richard G. Kenworthy, "Bringing the World to Brookline: The Gardens of Larz and Isabel Anderson," *Journal of Garden History* 2, no. 4 (1991): 224–41. James O'Gorman reproduces a Browne drawing in *On the Boards: Drawings by Nineteenth Century Boston Architects* (1989), pp. 116–17. Finally, Browne's treasured library, left intact to the Society for the Preservation of New England Antiquities is analyzed by Elizabeth C. Leuthner in a paper done for the American Studies Program at Boston University in 1991 titled *A Small Archs. Library: The Herbert W. C. Brown Collection*; copies are at Boston University and in the SPNEA archives in Boston. An obituary is in the *Boston Herald*, 30 Apr. 1946.

STUART A. DRAKE

BROWNE, John Ross (11 Feb. 1821–8 Dec. 1875), writer, world traveler, and government agent, was born in Beggars Bush, near Dublin, Ireland, the son of Thomas Egerton Browne and Elana Buck. His father was a refugee from British rule. As the editor of three publications, Thomas Browne satirized British tithing measures and earned the enmity of the Crown, a fine, and a jail sentence for "seditious libel."

J. Ross Browne, as he would always be known publicly, arrived with his parents in America in 1833. He spent his early years in Louisville, Kentucky, where his father ran a seminary for young women, which Ross attended along with a handful of young boys. Aside from a few dead-end months at the Louisville Medical Institute, Browne enjoyed no higher education. But, thanks to the intellectual environment of his home and his native intelligence, self-education served him well through life. His early interests were writing, drawing, and traveling. He found writing to be a gift, to which he added a modest talent in sketching. His art, mainly light caricature, remained that of an amateur, but his sketches were so clever and humorous that, when properly enhanced by professional artists and engravers, formed the illustrations for many of his magazine articles and books of later years.

Especially important to Browne was travel. He would spend a quarter-century of his prime in this activity. He started out before he was seventeen by making a 600-mile "ramble" by land, followed by one of 1,600 miles by water, working as a deckhand on a flatboat between Louisville and New Orleans.

After three years as a police reporter for the *Louisville Advertiser* and as a correspondent for Cincinnati and Columbus papers, Browne became determined to have a career that would permit him to travel in reasonable comfort. He chose stenography and shorthand and worked as a reporter in Washington (1841–1842) for the *Congressional Globe*. He also contributed a few stories to *Graham's Lady's and Gentleman's Magazine*, edited by Edgar Allan Poe. Browne planned to sail to Europe but, lacking funds, had to ship out instead as an ordinary seaman on a New Bedford whaler. His passage to the Indian Ocean was ruined by the bark's bully of a captain, and Browne bought his freedom on the island of Zanzibar.

Browne used humor to expose the abuses of whaleship crews and illustrated his account with his own sketches. The articles were published in *Harper's Monthly Magazine* and later became chapters of his book *Etchings of a Whaling Cruise* (1846), a sequence that would be repeated several times in his long association with the magazine and Harper & Bros. Reviews were flattering and that of the *American Review* compared Browne favorably with Richard Henry Dana of *Two Years Before the Mast*. Herman Melville reviewed *Etchings* for *Literary World* in 1847, and the book influenced his writing of *Moby Dick*.

In 1844 Browne married Lucy Anna Mitchell; the couple had ten children, of whom eight lived to maturity. Although his work in the Senate had given him a jaundiced view of Washington politics, common sense led Browne to accept in 1845 a position as clerk in the Treasury Department. His intelligence and uncompromising honesty led to his being given the post of private secretary to Robert J. Walker, secretary of the Treasury. However, when the California gold rush attracted his attention, Browne persuaded Walker to appoint him as a third lieutenant in the U.S. Revenue Service with the assignment of trying to prevent the mass desertion of American merchant seamen in San Francisco's harbor. He arrived in San Francisco on 5 August 1849 after a voyage made interesting by a mutiny and a stopover at Juan Fernández Island, off Chile. His adventures led again to articles in *Harper's Monthly* followed by chapters, this time in his popular book *Crusoe's Island* (1864). The revenue cutter *Lawrence*, which would have been his "base," was delayed getting to San Francisco, and Browne took a temporary commission as inspector of postal services, with instructions to establish post offices between San Francisco and San Luis Obispo. The only post office that he founded, however, was in San Jose.

Because Browne was believed to be the only man on the West Coast skilled in shorthand, he was appointed official reporter, or recording secretary, of the first California Constitutional Convention, held in Monterey in 1849, and was paid the princely sum of $10,000. The official document he compiled, *Report of the Debates in the Convention . . .* (1850), was published in a Spanish-language edition the following year. Browne also made good use of his experiences on the trail to Monterey and San Luis Obispo, embroidering them with fictional touches for "A Dangerous Journey," published in *Harper's* in 1862 and two years later as part of *Crusoe's Island*. *A Dangerous Journey* was reprinted as a book in 1950, the same year that the Book Club of California published Browne's letters of the period as *Muleback to the Convention*.

Thanks to his convention windfall, Browne was finally able to become a world traveler. He made a base for his family in Florence and roamed Europe and the Near East. Out of these travels came his book *Yusef* (1853). Joaquin Miller wrote of it, "If there had been no *Yusef*, there would have been no *Innocents Abroad*" by Mark Twain.

When he returned to California, Browne settled his family permanently in Oakland, then accepted an appointment as a confidential (secret) agent for the Treasury Department. From 1853 to 1860 he uncovered much incompetence, waste, corruption, and fraud in customhouses, the San Francisco mint, and *rancherias* (Indian reservations) in California. In 1857 he was asked to investigate and report on the Indian wars in Oregon and Washington territories. In 1860 he visited the mines of Washoe (Nev.).

After another European sojourn, this time in Frankfurt, which led to two books, Browne tried lecturing (1862) but found it disappointing. He was pleased when his former boss, Walker, got him a commission in the Indian Service. Browne's combined interests in Indians and mining led him to accompany Charles D. Poston to Arizona Territory in 1863. He later revisited both Nevada and Arizona and wrote articles and perhaps his best book, *Adventures in the Apache Country* (1869). Having become an expert on minerals, Browne had a post created for him, U.S. commissioner of mines and mining. As commissioner, he compiled two major reports that stressed the mineral resources of the states and territories west of the Rockies.

In 1868 Browne was honored with appointment as minister to China, but as usual, he vigorously stated his opinions—which were not those of the State Department—and was recalled less than a year later. Back home, he entered the real estate business and represented mining interests in London and an English syndicate interested in the reclamation of overflowed (intermittently flooded) lands in the Sacramento Valley, but he was less successful as a businessman than as a writer or government agent. Returning by ferry from his San Francisco office, he was stricken with appendicitis and died in the Oakland home of a friend, unable to make it to his home, "Pagoda Hill."

Browne has been relegated to the secondary rank of American authors, well to the rear of Twain, yet his humorous travel essays and even his hard-hitting government reports are far more readable today than are the once-popular works of most of his peers. Many of the books by this generous and very well liked adventurer have been reprinted in recent years.

• Several volumes of Browne's government reports are on microfilm at the National Archives, and his personal correspondence has been ably edited by Lina Fergusson Browne as *J. Ross Browne: His Letters, Journals and Writings* (1969). The best early sketch of Browne was published in *Harper's Weekly*, 22 Feb. 1868. Francis J. Rock's biography, *J. Ross Browne* (1929), has been superseded by David M. Goodman's *A Western Panorama: The Travels, Writings and Influence of J. Ross Browne . . .* (1966) and by Richard H. Dillon's *J. Ross Browne: Confidential Agent in Old California* (1965). Obituaries are in the *Oakland Daily Evening Tribune* and the *San Francisco Evening Bulletin*, both 8 Dec. 1875, the *San Francisco Chronicle* and the *Sacramento Daily Record-Union*, both 9 Dec. 1875, and the *Daily Alta California*, 9 and 12 Dec. 1875.

RICHARD H. DILLON

BROWNE, Mary Kendall (3 June 1891–19 Aug. 1971), tennis player and golfer, was born in Ventura County, California, the daughter of Albert William Browne, a rancher and Spanish-American War captain, and Neotia Rice. She attended Los Angeles (Calif.) Polytechnic High School. Her older brother Nathaniel Borrodail Browne, an excellent tennis competitor, taught Mary a sound all-court style and sharpened her volleying and smashing skills in practice by stationing her at the net to parry his hardest drives.

Browne began her tournament career at the 1908 Southern California championship by losing in the preliminary round to Elizabeth "Bunny" Ryan, later famous as the winner of nineteen women's and mixed doubles championships at Wimbledon. At the 1909 tournament in Ojai, California, Browne defeated Ryan and Florence Sutton but lost the final to May Sutton, her persistent nemesis. Browne finally captured a singles title in 1911—the Washington State championship, which lacked the presence of her formidable California rivals, Ryan, the Sutton sisters, and Hazel Hotchkiss.

In 1912 Browne traveled east alone to enter the U.S. women's championship at the Philadelphia (Penn.) Cricket Club. Homesick and playing on grass for the first time, the slight, 5′2½″ righthander barely survived a semifinal struggle with Adelaide Browning, 6–4, 3–6, 9–7. On finals day she beat Eleonora Sears for the singles title and teamed with Dorothy Green and Dick Williams to take the women's and mixed doubles crowns, equalling the triple win feat of Hotchkiss three years earlier. Before returning to California, Browne played in a circuit of Eastern, Midwestern, and Canadian tournaments, winning four singles events and losing four finals to May Sutton.

During the next two years "Brownie" scored triple U.S. championship victories, vanquishing Green and Marie Wagner in singles challenge rounds and, with Louise Riddell Williams and Bill Tilden, won the women's and mixed doubles titles, equalling Hotchkiss's record of three consecutive sweeps and bringing Tilden the earliest of his many national championships. During this time Browne lost only one singles tournament match, the 1913 Niagara-on-the-Lake, Ontario, Canada, final to Louise Williams, 6–8, 6–3, 4–6. Women's U.S. rankings began in 1913, and Browne ranked first in 1913 and 1914.

Having nothing left to conquer in tennis, Browne divided her attention between her job as superintendent of the Los Angeles Humane Society and golf, which she mastered with characteristic intensity. Nevertheless, she did win the 1916 Ojai tennis singles. During World War II, in 1917, she toured with Molla Bjurstedt, the 1915 and 1916 U.S. champion, playing exhibitions for the benefit of the Ambulance Fund. The rusty Browne lost the first three contests, but by the end of the tour she had sixteen victories to Bjurstedt's eleven. Now at the top of her game, Browne had eliminated the erratic spells that formerly plagued her. Nevertheless, she again disappeared from competition for several years.

In 1921 Browne won the Southern California women's golf championship, and in tennis she won the Ojai tournament and the Crescent Athletic Club invitation, defeating May Sutton Bundy in the latter, before losing in finals to Eleanor Goss at the Seabright (N.J.) invitation and to Molla Bjurstedt Mallory in the U.S. nationals. Browne and Louise Williams again won the U.S. doubles crown. In singles Browne ranked second nationally, behind Mallory.

In 1924, following another layoff from national competition, Browne won at Seabright and reached the U.S. semifinals. In the latter tournament her brilliant net play finally succumbed to Helen Wills's backcourt strength, 4–6, 6–4, 3–6. Three weeks later she played for the first time in the U.S. women's golf championship, barely qualifying for the event but then upsetting four favorites to reach the final. In her semifinal match she defeated the medalist and 1922 champion Glenna Collett on the 19th hole by sinking a 15-foot putt which caromed off Collett's ball. Dorothy Campbell Hurd, however, defeated Browne, 7 and 6, in the final. Browne's tennis national ranking that year rose to second.

In 1925 Browne enjoyed greater success in tennis doubles than in singles, winning the U.S. women's title with Wills plus other women's and mixed events. In singles she lost to Mallory and Goss twice, to Ryan, and, in the nationals, to Englishwoman Joan Fry. Browne also captained the U.S. Wightman Cup team which lost to Great Britain, 3–4, as she and Wills lost a key doubles match. That year she ranked sixth nationally. In golf she won the Southern California woman's title again and reached the U.S. women's championship quarterfinals.

Abroad in 1926, Browne scored impressive victories in the French championship over Kitty McKane Godfree and Kea Bouman, but Suzanne Lenglen routed her in the final, 1–6, 0–6. The U.S. won back the Wightman Cup as Browne, the captain of the U.S. team, and Ryan captured a decisive doubles point. Browne lost a U.S. nationals quarterfinal to Ryan in her amateur finale. That year sports promoter Charles C. Pyle organized a professional tennis tour starring Lenglen and featuring Browne and Vincent Richards. The tour opened on 9 October 1926 at Madison Square Garden in New York City, and it closed in mid-February 1927. Lenglen defeated Browne in all 38 of their tour matches, with Browne winning only two sets; however, Browne reputedly received $25,000 for participating. As a result, the U.S. tennis and golf associations revoked her amateur status in both sports. Immediately she applied to the golf authorities for reinstatement, which they granted in 1930 following a customary three-year waiting period.

Browne subsequently worked for a Cleveland, Ohio, sporting goods firm. From 1930 to 1941 she served as a part-time tennis instructor at Lake Erie College in Painesville, Ohio. Representing the Kirtland (Ohio) Country Club, she won the Cleveland city women's golf title four times from 1931 to 1935 and the 1931 Ohio crown. She also played in five U.S. women's amateur championships between 1932 and 1939.

During World War II Browne worked for the American Red Cross in Australia for twenty months as supervisor of canteen services in the South and Southwest Pacific and one year in the Mediterranean Theater. From 1945 to 1951 she worked as an instructor in physical education at Lake Erie College, after which she moved to California, where she learned painting and became a successful portrait artist. In 1957 she was inducted into the National Lawn (later International) Tennis Hall of Fame. The following year she married Kenneth Kenneth-Smith, a high school classmate, in Honolulu, Hawaii. The marriage dissolved five years later.

Browne wrote four books: *Top-Flite Tennis* (1928), *Streamlined Tennis* (1940), *Design for Tennis* (1949), and, with James Weaver, *Victorious* (1949), about historical personages who overcame handicaps.

During 1966 and 1967 she shared a house in Palm Desert, California, with Alice Marble, another former tennis champion. On her seventy-fifth birthday, she shot a golf score of 78. On the day she died in Laguna Hills, California, following a stroke, she was packed to play golf with Marble.

• Browne described her championship tennis in "Net Play Continues to Win," and "Doubles Play" in U.S. Lawn Tennis Association, *Fifty Years of Lawn Tennis in the United States* (1931). She also shared her experiences playing Lenglen in "What I Learned from Suzanne," *Colliers*, 7 May 1927, pp. 14, 43. Reports of her key tennis events appear in *American Lawn Tennis*, 15 Aug. 1917, p. 213; 1 Aug. 1921, pp. 273, 296; 15 Oct. 1924, p. 448; and, for her time in Australia, Apr. 1944, pp. 16–17. Her play in the 1924 U.S. women's golf championship is covered in the *New York Times*, 2–7 Sept. 1924; her opponent's perspective is presented in Glenna Collett, *Ladies in the Rough* (1928), pp. 72–77. *Lake Erie College Bulletin* (1972) outlines her accomplishments as an artist.

FRANK V. PHELPS

BROWNE, Maurice (12 Feb. 1881–21 Jan. 1955), actor, director, and producer, was born in Reading, England, the son of Frederick Herbert Browne, a distinguished teacher, and Francis-Anna "Marsie" Neligan, the founder of a number of successful private schools. Educated at the private schools of Ipswich, Temple Grove, and Winchester, Browne later attended Eastbourne College and received his B.A. from Cambridge University.

Traveling extensively as a young man, Browne acted as a schoolmaster in Darjeeling, India, journeyed to Capri and Sicily, and worked as a tutor in Florence. While in Florence in 1910 Browne met Ellen Van Volkenburg, an American woman from Chicago. When she returned to the United States, Browne followed. There he was engaged to lecture on modern poets at the University of Chicago, the Lincoln Center, and elsewhere around Chicago. Browne and Van Volkenburg, an aspiring actress, were married in 1911; they had no children. After a conversation with Lady Gregory of the Abbey Theatre, the two decided to start a "little" theater, believing a little theater would cost less to operate than a big one. Engaging amateur performers and renting the fourth floor of the Fine Arts Building in Chicago, the Brownes founded the Chicago Little Theatre (CLT).

The 91-seat converted storage room opened to the public in November 1912 with Wilfrid Wilson Gibson's *Womenkind* and William Butler Yeats's *On Brailes Strand.* The CLT was one of the first public theaters to operate on a subscription basis. A lifetime membership cost $100 and a yearly membership $10. Reviews of the CLT were mixed. A production of Arthur Schnitzler's *Anatol* and an adaptation of Euripides's *The Trojan Women* followed, and although most critics did not consider the latter a particularly notable production, theater critic Oliver Saylor listed *The Trojan Women* as one of the important productions on the American stage between 1908 and 1923, based on its innovative staging.

Letters from all over the country began to arrive in Chicago asking how to start a little theater. The CLT company toured to cities interested in starting their own theater, and Browne became known as the "father of the little theater movement," although he gave that credit to one who inspired him—Laura Pelnam, the director of the successful Hull House Players. In Chicago Browne produced plays, out of necessity, for a fraction of the cost of other theaters. The survival of the theater was due in part to his frugal production. The CLT moved briefly from the Fine Arts Building to the Playhouse in 1915, but after disputes with the lessor, the company moved back to its original home. In their fifth season, they suspended productions during parts of the First World War. They were unable to recover fully thereafter, and after subscriptions dropped in 1917, the theater closed. In its five years of existence the CLT had produced forty-four plays, eighteen for the first time on any stage and seven for the first time in America.

The mainstream commercial theater of the period was primarily concerned with commercial success. For Browne, the purpose of the CLT was to present theater not promoted by the commercial theater. He believed that drama was an art, not a commodity, the theater a "temple," not an "amusement-house." Browne stayed away from realistic plays, preferring a more poetic style and what he called "rhythmic drama—a rhythmic fusion of light, movement, and sound." Under Browne, CLT's innovations included its emphasis on noncommercial dramatic literature, its use of nonprofessionals, the unity of its product, and its deployment of the new stagecraft. A number of distinguished artists worked with CLT as performers or guest artists, including Ralph Roeder, Mme. August Strindberg, Frank Lloyd Wright, Carl Sandburg, Jane Addams, Floyd Dell, John Barrymore, Harley Granville Barker, and Amy Lowell.

In 1921 Browne produced and directed *Medea* on Broadway, followed in the same year by *Iphigenia at Aulis* and *Joan of Arc* for Margaret Anglin. Browne spent the next few years touring in the Northwest. In 1927, after divorcing Van Volkenburg and marrying Ellen Janson, with whom he had one son, Browne returned to England to direct and produce shows for the Arts Theatre Club. The next five years would be a time of intense creative activity for Browne. He produced and performed in Strindberg's *The Creditors*, the first play by the author to be seen in England; it was followed by George Bernard Shaw's *The Glimpse of Reality* and Susan Glaspell's *Women's Honor*. After acting in *The Unknown Warrior* at the Arts Theatre in 1928, Browne's popularity as an actor grew, and he collaborated with Robert Nichols on the play *Wings over Europe*, first performed by New York Theatre Guild during the 1928–1929 season. With financial backing from friends, he formed his own production company, Maurice Browne, Ltd., and bought the rights to *Journey's End*, which he produced at the Savoy Theatre in 1929. The play proved to be a huge hit and was soon moved to the Prince of Wales Theatre. Within one year the play was being performed by seventy-six companies in twenty-five different languages, including every European language and Japanese. With this success came financial security. Maurice Browne, Ltd., rented the Globe Theatre and the Queens Theatre and in 1930 produced the racially controversial *Othello* with Paul Robeson in the title role, Sybil Thorndike, Peggy Ashcroft, Ralph Richardson, and Browne, who played Iago. At one time during these successful years, Browne had shows running in six West End theaters simultaneously.

After a number of bad business deals left him with little money, Browne took an acting role in Manchester out of desperation. He then produced his own verse drama, *The Wife of William Flavy*. He continued to write verse drama, including *The King of the Jews*, *The Mother of Gregory*, *The Strange Case of God and Miss Sipps* (banned by the British censor), *What Men Call Themselves*, and *Dr. Job*. Before retiring from the theater in 1939 he produced, most notably *Viceroy Sarah* (1935), starring Edith Evans; Ester McCracken's *Quiet Wedding* (1939); and two motion pictures, *Doomsday England* (1934) and *The Improper Duchess* (1936). He also served as artist in residence at the University of California at Los Angeles. After his retirement in 1939 Browne periodically returned to direct and act. He died in London.

Although Browne was an important director, producer, and actor in England, his contribution to the American theater cannot be denied. When introducing Browne at the Malvern Festival, George Bernard Shaw said, "You all know Maurice Brown. You all know that he is running six West End theatres simultaneously and putting on grand shows there. You have all heard and read how he presented Journey's End all over the world. Well, I'm here to tell you that none of those things matters a tupenny damn. The work this man sitting behind me did twenty years ago on a fourth-floor-back in Chicago—that is what matters." The Chicago Little Theatre was at the forefront of a movement to improve the American theater, to bring the theater to places outside New York, and to create a new producible dramaturgy not seen in the popular American theater. In establishing the Chicago Little Theatre as an art theater, Browne helped begin a process in regionalizing theater that continues to the present day.

• The primary resources on Browne's life are his own writings, including his autobiography, *Too Late to Lament* (1955), and a number of articles that outline his philosophy of theater: "The Nature and Function of Poetry," *Theatre Arts Magazine*, 1908, pp. 12–17; "The Temple of a Living Art," *Drama*, 1913, pp. 36–38; and "The New Rhythmic Drama," *Drama*, 1914, pp. 16–23. Other important sources on the Chicago Little Theatre are Bernard F. Dukore, "Maurice Browne and the Chicago Little Theatre" (Ph.D. diss., Univ. of Illinois, 1957); Rachel Whitfield, "A History of the Chicago Little Theatre from 1912–1917" (master's thesis, Northwestern Univ., 1937); and Kendra A. Chopcian, "An Analysis of Maurice Browne's Directing Theories and Practices with the Chicago Little Theatre" (Ph.D. diss., Univ. of

Michigan, 1989). Browne is also included in *Who Was Who*, vol. 3, and the *Enciclopedia dello Spettacolo*. An obituary is in the *New York Times*, 22 Jan. 1955.

MELISSA VICKERY-BAREFORD

BROWNE, William (27 Feb. 1737–13 Feb. 1802), Massachusetts Superior Court judge and Loyalist, was born in Salem, Massachusetts, the son of Samuel Browne, Jr., a merchant, and Catherine Winthrop. Both families had lived in Salem for five generations. On the matrilineal side William could trace his lineage back to four colonial governors, the Winthrops and the Dudleys. On the patrilineal side one of William's great-grandfathers was Gilbert Burnet, bishop of Salisbury, England. When William was only five years old, his father died, and when William was seven, his mother married Colonel Epes Sargent. Because the Browne family was the most distinguished and popular in Salem, when William entered Harvard at age fourteen, he was ranked third in his class. He lived in Massachusetts Hall, held a scholarship, and was noted as "an excellent scholar." He graduated in 1755 as valedictorian of his class. Classmate John Adams recalled his friend Browne as "a solid, judicious character." For a number of years he studied law with Edmund Trowbridge, but he never practiced, since the management of his large inheritance, 104,000 acres and £5,000 cash from his father, was a full-time task.

After receiving his M.A. from Harvard, Browne spent the rest of his life in business and politics. In 1761 Governor Francis Bernard appointed him justice of the peace of the quorum, the most important justice of the peace for Essex County; in 1762 his fellow townsmen elected him to the first of six consecutive terms as Salem's representative; and in 1764 the Crown appointed him customs collector for the port of Salem and the townsmen elected him one of their selectmen. He lived in Salem's most opulent house, a mansion built in 1740 by his grandfather, Colonel Samuel Browne, that was three stories high and contained seventeen large rooms. Surrounding the mansion were extensive gardens, orchards, offices, and stables. The house, worth at least £2,000 sterling, was lavishly furnished and staffed by eleven black slaves. Browne was active in town and church affairs. Originally a member of the First Church of Salem (Congregational), he left in 1770 in a dispute over the selection of a new pastor. Browne then became a charter member of Salem's North Church (Unitarian) and owned several pews. He also rented a pew in St. Peter's Church (Episcopalian). He was active in a literary club made up of the leading gentlemen of Salem, many of whom became Loyalists.

As Salem's representative in the legislature, Browne opposed the Sugar Act and the Stamp Act. Because of this, he fell into disfavor with Governor Bernard and was dismissed from his customs position in 1766. Possibly prompted by this disciplinary action, Browne voted in the legislature as one of a minority of seventeen in favor of rescinding the Massachusetts Circular Letter against the Townshend Acts. For this pro-British vote, he was labeled a "Rescinder," burned in effigy on the Boston Common, censured in a July 1768 Salem town meeting, denied reelection to the legislature in 1769, and named as an accessory in the September 1769 beating of the patriot James Otis, Jr., by customs commissioner John Robinson. After losing the people's support, Browne increasingly found himself wedded to the king's party through appointive offices: judge of the Court of Common Pleas of Essex County (1770), colonel of the Essex militia (1771), and judge of the superior court (1774).

When Governor Thomas Hutchinson paid his last official visit to Salem in April 1774, he stayed in Browne's house. The next day Hutchinson reviewed the First Essex Regiment, since Browne was still its commander. In the evening Browne gave a very elaborate ball and served some taxed East India Company tea. In early June 1774 newly appointed Governor Thomas Gage shifted the site of the legislature from Boston to Salem, and upon his arrival, Governor Gage stayed in the Browne mansion. In August 1774, when he established martial law, Governor Gage appointed Browne to one of thirty-six seats on the new council by a writ of mandamus or executive order. Since this method bypassed the Massachusetts Charter method of election by the lower house in conjunction with the outgoing council, only ten appointees, Browne among them, took the required oath.

Shortly after Browne's council appointment, a committee from the Essex County Convention, led by Elbridge Gerry, demanded he resign all his appointive offices. Browne boldly declined, citing "fidelity, . . . honor and integrity." The Salem Committee of Safety hoped to induce this wealthy man to enlist in their cause and offered to nominate him for the governorship of Massachusetts, but again he refused. In August the Salem Committee of Correspondence called for a town meeting, an action that was illegal under recently revised laws. Governor Gage held a meeting with the committee in Browne's home, had the members jailed briefly, and then returned to Boston. In late fall 1774 a committee from the Ipswich Convention pressured Browne to resign as mandamus councilor, but he again refused. In October 1774 all the officers of his militia regiment resigned their commissions and refused to serve under his command.

Shortly thereafter Judge Browne slipped into British-occupied Boston. His wife, Ruth Wanton, daughter of Governor Joseph Wanton of Rhode Island, remained briefly in Salem but then moved in with relatives in Rhode Island. She lived there for two years before she and her daughter Catherine joined Browne in exile. (Browne and his wife had one son and two daughters during their marriage.) The family took china and linen with them, but mobs pillaged £500 worth of furniture from the Salem mansion and removed a library worth £150. Mobs repeatedly broke the mansion's windows, drove the tenants off Browne's farms, and burned down some of his buildings. All the while he remained in Boston, serving on the council and helping form Loyalist militia units. He sailed for England on 26 March 1776 with his son William on the *Lord Hyde*, bearing confidential dispatches to British authorities from Lord William Howe.

In exile the Brownes lived briefly in London on the continuation of Browne's £200 salary as a councilor but soon moved to inexpensive Cowbridge, South Wales. He was cheerful and serene in exile, enjoying the company of his fellow refugees. However, Massachusetts wanted revenge and in 1778 included Browne in the Banishment Act. The next year he was condemned as one of twenty-nine "notorious conspirators" who immediately forfeited all property and rights without a hearing or trial. In Browne's case the confiscated property was extensive. Massachusetts sold his Salem mansion to Elias Derby for £6,050 in state bonds. The state also seized his other properties in Salem, including a 200-foot wharf, stores, lands, and various leased farms. In addition, Browne forfeited 4,000 acres in Massachusetts, primarily holdings in the towns of Ashley, Charlton, Fitchburg, Hadley, Marblehead, Springfield, and Yarmouth. He lost 2,500 acres in Maine and his land around Hartford and New London, Connecticut, which included fourteen confiscated farms and timberland totaling 9,663 acres. His slaves received their freedom, since Massachusetts had "doubts about the legality of such sale." Further plunder of his assets followed as Massachusetts allowed £2,674 (27 percent of the net proceeds) in debt claims against Browne, although he claimed that only £700 were legitimate. In addition, Captain Samuel Flagg, agent for the sale of Browne's confiscated property, spent 12 percent of the proceeds in administrative costs. After the war Judge Browne unsuccessfully tried to recover money from his Massachusetts debtors. After years of effort, he also failed to recover debts from his own nephews and from the state of Rhode Island, which had confiscated the Wanton estate.

In 1781, because of the intercession of Benjamin Thompson, the king appointed Browne governor of Bermuda at a salary of £750 per year. For six years he ruled Bermuda and in the process revived its whale fishery, encouraged cotton cultivation, promoted shipbuilding, and stimulated the economy. He was a popular governor, owing in part to his wisdom and nonpartisan spirit. In his own words, "I am the advocate of no man, the patron of no party, at the head of no cabal." In October 1784 and again in 1788 the Brownes visited friends in Massachusetts and Rhode Island. He filed claims totaling £32,256 with the Commissioners on American Loyalists, a board appointed by Parliament to reimburse American Loyalists, and received £7,658. After his retirement as Bermuda's governor, Browne moved to Percy Street, Westminster, London, where he lived with his wife, who preceded him in death by three years. After his death there, an old Salem friend remembered Browne as short, overweight, and possessed of remarkably large legs.

• A number of Browne's letters and letter books are in the Massachusetts Historical Society in Boston. For his claims for losses, see the American Loyalists Claims, Audit Office 12/10/220; 12/61/34; 12/109; 13/43/639; 13/50; 13/90, Public Record Office, London. His exile letters are published as "Letters of William Browne, American Loyalist," ed. Sydney W. Jackman, *Essex Institute Historical Collections* 96 (Jan. 1960): 1–46. Extracts of his letter book as governor of Bermuda are in *Bermuda Historical Quarterly* 13 (Spring 1956): 11–20, 62–179. For a printed version of his American Loyalist Claim, see "Essex County Loyalists," *Historical Collections of the Essex Institute* 43 (Oct. 1907): 289–316. For short biographies, see James H. Stark, *The Loyalists of Massachusetts and the Other Side of the American Revolution* (1907); E. Alfred Jones, *The Loyalists of Massachusetts: Their Memorials, Petitions and Claims* (1930); and Clifford Shipton, *Sibley's Harvard Graduates*, vol. 13 (1965).

DAVID E. MAAS

BROWNE, William Washington (20 Oct. 1849–21 Dec. 1897), fraternal society leader and banker, was born in Habersham County, Georgia, the son of Joseph Browne and Mariah (maiden name unknown), field slaves. As a young child he was called Ben Browne and was chosen to be the companion of his owner's son. A subsequent owner who lived near Memphis trained Browne as a jockey for race circuits in Tennessee and Mississippi. During the Civil War he plotted an escape with fellow slaves. When his owner learned about the conspiracy, he transferred Browne to a plantation in Mississippi. Despite the difficulties of tramping fifty miles without a compass, Browne persuaded three other young slaves to join him in a successful escape to the Union army at Memphis. After learning that his owner could demand his return, Browne fled upriver as a stowaway.

Browne later worked as a saloon servant in Illinois, where his barroom experiences made him a teetotaler, and as a farm laborer in Wisconsin, where he attended school for the first time. He also was a servant aboard a navy gunboat on the Mississippi and a paid substitute in an infantry regiment. In 1869 he left Wisconsin to return to Georgia, where he taught school and studied for the ministry in Atlanta at what later became the Gammon Seminary. In 1871 he moved to Alabama to teach in the public schools. Two years later he married Mary A. "Molly" Graham. Childless, they adopted two children. In 1876 he was ordained a minister in the Colored (later Christian) Methodist church at Piedmont, Alabama.

Browne believed that alcoholic drink stood in the way of the uplift of his race. Blacks convicted of the crime of public intoxication were disenfranchised. More important to Browne, money used to buy alcohol was money unavailable to buy land. To promote temperance among their people, Browne and two other black reformers asked the Good Templars in Alabama, a white fraternal temperance society, to let blacks organize Templar lodges. Refusing, the Good Templars offered instead to help Browne and company organize the United Order of True Reformers in Alabama, a fraternal temperance society for blacks created by the Good Templars of Kentucky in 1873. In 1874 Browne became a full-time worker for the True Reformers; presumably the Good Templars paid his salary. In 1875 the True Reformers of Alabama organized the Grand Fountain, a statewide lodge, and became independent of the Good Templars. Browne was the first Grand Worthy Secretary and in 1877–1880 served as Grand Worthy Master. Browne cared little about ritual and regalia but a great deal about black people saving money, buying land, and helping one another. He wanted his organization to acquire the power to issue life insurance and operate a bank. Rivals in the African-American community, fearing that Browne would overshadow them, persuaded the Alabama legislature to reject his request for the charter he needed.

At the end of 1880, disillusioned with Alabama, Browne moved to Virginia, the birthplace of his parents. The True Reformers there had invited him to take charge of their organization, which had lost most of its members to a rival society. From 1881 to his death he served as Grand Worthy Master of this Grand Fountain, with headquarters at Richmond, Virginia. Overcoming internal dissension, Browne made the True Reformers the dominant black fraternal society in Virginia and also established fountains in other states. Perhaps as early as 1881, members of the True Reformer society ceased to be pledged to abstinence. Although Browne briefly served as pastor of a Colored Methodist church at Richmond, he resigned when the local bishop insisted that he abandon his True Reformer work. The African Methodist Episcopal church recognized Browne as a minister, but he never had his own church again.

Emphasizing economic progress, the True Reformers became a mutual insurance organization with many auxiliary businesses. To supplement the modest life insurance that all members of the lodge paid for, the True Reformers offered larger policies that Browne called the Classes. In addition, Browne's order pioneered for black insurance enterprises the practice of charging older members more because of the greater likelihood of their imminent death. In 1888 the Virginia legislature chartered a True Reformer savings bank, which opened for business in 1889 with Browne as its president. Although another black bank in Washington, D.C., was the first one to conduct business, the True Reformer bank was the first black-controlled financial institution to receive a charter. The order constructed a large headquarters building at Richmond in 1891 and later operated general stores, a hotel, a weekly newspaper, and a printing plant, and it also acquired farms and other real estate. Browne raised money and purchased land for an old-age home that was established after his death.

W. E. B. Du Bois, ordinarily critical of African Americans who made economic improvement their priority, characterized the True Reformers as "probably the most remarkable Negro organization in the country." This tribute, in *Economic Co-Operation among Negro Americans* (1907), no doubt owed much to Du Bois's belief in the African origins of the True Reformer strategy of economic cooperation.

Unlike many large black fraternal societies, the True Reformers accepted women as members. Women had special responsibility for a juvenile auxiliary, the Rosebuds. Like the adult order, the children's society stressed the importance of saving, investment, and mutual assistance, all grounded in self-respect.

Always a controversial figure whose domineering personality occasioned many quarrels, Browne acquired new enemies in the mid-1890s. In 1894 he asked the order to pay him for what he called his "plans," the conception of a business-oriented fraternal society he had brought to Virginia from Alabama. In 1895 the order promised $50,000 (and turned over more than half that amount to his widow before a court order to prevent the loss of money meant for insurance purposes stopped further payments). In the same year two black men—John R. Mitchell, Jr., editor of the *Richmond Planet*, and Massachusetts legislator Robert Teamoh—visited the Virginia governor's mansion in the company of the white members of a Massachusetts delegation. Worried that blacks in general would suffer the consequences of this violation of social segregation, Browne denounced Mitchell and Teamoh in a letter to a white newspaper. In response, most black newspapers accused him of being subservient to white supremacists. (In fact, Browne possessed great racial pride, boasting that he was of pure African descent unlike most black leaders.) Browne also quarreled with members of his True Reformer inner circle during his last years. In 1897 he denounced his protégé, W. P. Burrell, the Grand Worthy Secretary, and passed over his best-known lieutenants in designating an Acting Grand Worthy Master to serve while he battled cancer. After wandering from physician to physician in search of a cure, he died in Washington, D.C.

Browne's Grand Fountain prospered for a decade or so after his death, eventually attaining an adult membership of around 60,000. After the bank collapsed in 1910, the order lost most of its members and disappeared during the depression of the 1930s. Browne's renown faded with that of the Grand Fountain and of other African-American fraternal societies.

• Neither Browne's personal nor business papers survive. Commissioned by Browne's widow, Daniel Webster Davis wrote *The Life and Public Services of Rev. Wm. Washington Browne, Founder of the Grand Fountain, U[nited]. O[rder]. of True Reformers and Organizer of the First Distinctive Negro Bank in America* (1910); in 1994 it was reprinted, with editorial notes and an introductory essay by David M. Fahey, under the title *The Black Lodge in White America: "True Reformer" Browne and His Economic Strategy*. Browne dominates the official history by W. P. Burrell and D. E. Johnson, Sr., *Twenty-Five Years History of the Grand Fountain of the United Order of True Reformers, 1881–1905* (1909). See also James D. Watkinson, "William Washington Browne and the True Reformers of Richmond, Virginia," *Virginia Magazine of History* 97 (July 1989): 375–98. For a picture of the True Reformer bank, see Abram L. Harris, *The Negro as Capitalist: A Study of Banking and Business among American Negroes* (1936).

DAVID M. FAHEY

BROWNELL, Henry Howard (6 Feb. 1820–31 Oct. 1872), author and naval officer, was born in Providence, Rhode Island, the son of Pardon Brownell, a physician, and Lucia de Wolf. His father's brother Thomas Church Brownell was bishop of the Episcopal diocese of Connecticut and also president of Washington (later Trinity) College, in Hartford, Connecticut. After attending public schools in Providence and East Hartford, Brownell enrolled in Washington College, graduating in 1841. He moved to the South in order to improve his health and taught school in Mobile, Alabama. Brownell returned to Hartford, where he read for the law. He was admitted to the bar in 1844, practiced for a short time, and then returned to teaching. He joined his brother in literary pursuits, contributing to magazines and publishing *Poems* (1847), the contents of which were devoted to such topics as love, beauty, and a young poet's struggles against difficult odds. The book never achieved a great popularity.

Brownell's enormous books *The People's Book of Ancient and Modern History* . . . (1851) and *The Discoverers, Pioneers, and Settlers of North and South America* . . . (1853) are strictly hack work and, though conscientiously composed, are derivative and prolix. Created for subscription house publishers, the books were updated and retitled—as, respectively, *The Eastern, or Old World, Embracing Ancient and Modern History* (1855) and *The Pioneer Heroes of the New World* . . . (1856)—went through many editions, and sold well, presumably because of their praise of Anglo-Saxon and Anglo-American expansionist and colonial successes. Brownell also enjoyed sailing on Narragansett Bay and taking sea voyages.

Soon after the beginning of the Civil War, an event occurred that changed Brownell's life. Always an abolitionist, he was so thrilled when he read U.S. Navy captain David Glasgow Farragut's 20 April 1862 orders to the fleet—to carry the fight to rebel waters vigorously—that he wrote and published a rhymed version as "General Orders," published in the *Hartford Evening Press* a few days later. Farragut liked the verses and wrote to Brownell to compliment him. When Brownell replied that he longed to observe a naval battle, Farragut swore him into the navy, appointed him his personal secretary, and made him a master's mate and then an ensign. Serving on Farragut's flagship, the *Hartford*, Brownell witnessed considerable action, most memorably the attack at Mobile Bay on 5 August 1864. Ordered to take notes during combat, he astounded the more experienced officers with his nerve; it was even said that some of his jottings were in verse. In official dispatches Farragut cited Brownell for his "coolness and accuracy."

Brownell published *Lyrics of a Day, or Newspaper-poetry*, including "General Orders," in 1863. To commemorate Farragut's bombardment of Confederate forts on the Mississippi River southeast of New Orleans, resulting in the surrender of that city on 25 April 1862, Brownell composed "The River Fight" (1864), which incorporates his famous "General Orders." After the battle of Mobile Bay, he wrote "The Bay Fight." Soon after the war had ended, Brownell was invited by James T. Fields, editor of the *Atlantic Monthly*, to attend a meeting of the Saturday Club, the literary dining association in Boston, in order to meet some ecstatic admirers of his war poetry. On 29 April 1865 the modest poet was introduced to such eminent men as John Sullivan Dwight, Ralph Waldo Emerson, Frederic Henry Hedge, Oliver Wendell Holmes, James Russell Lowell, and Edwin P. Whipple. Brownell's *War-lyrics and Other Poems* followed in 1866; it contains his violently antisouthern poem "Down!" in which he compares the defeated South to a sinking "Ship of Hell." In 1867–1868 Brownell accompanied Farragut, by then the nation's first admiral, when he commanded a goodwill squadron on a visit to various Continental seaports. Upon the completion of this spectacular tour Brownell resigned from the navy and returned to Hartford. Also during this period he valiantly fought a losing battle against cancer of the face. Brownell, who never married, died in Hartford.

Thomas Bailey Aldrich eulogized Brownell in two poems published in the *Atlantic Monthly* (May 1873, Apr. 1888). Emerson included two of Brownell's poems, "The Old Cove" and "The Bay Fight," in an anthology he edited titled *Parnassus* (1875). Edmund Clarence Stedman, editor of *An American Anthology, 1787–1900* (1900), included Brownell's "The Burial of the Dane," "The Sphinx," and parts of "The Bay Fight" in the collection. Since the beginning of the twentieth century, however, Brownell has been an almost forgotten figure.

A representative example of Brownell's stilted prose is his description of the response of Christopher Columbus and his men upon first seeing "Hayti." It is taken from *North and South America Illustrated* . . . (2 vols., 1859), a revision of his 1853 history book: "The voyagers were enchanted at the beauty of the island, the delicious mildness of the climate, and the gentle manners of the kindly inhabitants. . . . The mildness of the air and the exuberant fertility of the earth freed them from the first evils of barbarism, and their mild and gentle temperament of character allayed the usual ferocity of savage enmity." Far better is Brownell's war verse, which is regularly vigorous and realistic, if unmelodic. "The River Fight" begins by calling the South "the dreary Land" with "unclean" pelicans and "rebel mud" and ends, after a violent but indecisive naval engagement, by expressing the hope that the "Lord of mercy and scorn" will provide another opportunity for "black ships [to] bear down / On tyrant foe and town." In "Bury Them," commemorating Colonel Robert Gould Shaw's ill-conceived but brave attack on Fort Wagner in South Carolina on 18 July 1863, Brownell remarks that the Union dead, flung into a "horrible Pit," will—like fabled "Dragon's Teeth"—emerge a "crop of steel." In "The Bay Fight" he praises his fellow sailors:

Fear? A forgotten form!
Death? A dream of the eyes!
We were atoms in God's great storm
That roared through the angry skies.

He reviles "our devilish Foe," with his "cursèd craft," and exults when at last "Down comes the traitor Blue, / And up goes the captive White!"

• Brownell's papers are at the Huntington Library in San Marino, Calif. Oliver Wendell Holmes, in an anonymous essay titled "Our Battle-Laureate," *Atlantic Monthly*, May 1865, pp. 589–91, praises Brownell's war poetry for its combination of realistic detail and skillful poetic technique. John Townsend Trowbridge, "An Early Contributor's Recollections," *Atlantic Monthly*, Nov. 1907, pp. 582–93, describes a meeting between Brownell and Trowbridge at the Saturday Club and praises Brownell and his poetry. Will D. Howe, "Poets of the Civil War I: The North," in *The Cambridge History of American Literature*, ed. William Peterfield Trent et al. (4 vols., 1918), places Brownell's war poems in the context of mid-century poets concentrating almost exclusively on the Civil War. Edmund Wilson, *Patriotic Gore: Studies in the Literature of the American Civil War* (1966), comments, mostly in a derogatory manner, on Brownell's Civil War poetry. Daniel Aaron, *The Unwritten War: American Writers and the Civil War* (1973), admires the "graphic power" of Brownell's war poetry. An obituary is in the *Hartford Courant*, 9 Nov. 1872.

ROBERT L. GALE

BROWNELL, Thomas Church (19 Oct. 1779–13 Jan. 1865), Episcopal bishop and college president, was born in Westport, Massachusetts, the son of Sylvester Brownell and Nancy Church, farmers. After studying at Bristol Academy in Taunton, Massachusetts, he entered the College of Rhode Island at Providence (now Brown University) in 1800. In 1802 the president of the college, Jonathan Maxcy, moved to Schenectady, New York, to become the president of Union College, and young Brownell went with him. He graduated in 1804 at the top of his class.

In his autobiography Brownell said, "It had been for some time, my intention to devote myself to the study of theology, at the conclusion of my collegiate course; and it was the earnest wish of my parents that I should do so." He had been raised a Presbyterian, but he had some reservations about Calvinism, especially the doctrine of predestination. Eliphalet Nott, a Presbyterian pastor in Albany who later became the president of Union College, helped Brownell appreciate the doctrines of Calvinism by presenting them, as Brownell reported, in a "somewhat mitigated form." Nott gave him books that helped him realize that his problems were more with the polity of the Presbyterian church than with its theology. Brownell told Nott that the "first generation of the Christian Church must have been more like that of the Episcopal communion, than either the Presbyterian or Congregational denominations." Another clergyman, Frederic Beasley, gave Brownell a copy of John Potter's *Discourse on Church Government* (1707); Brownell said later, "It unfolded to me a new aspect of Christianity. The survey afforded to me unspeakable relief; but it was attended with many regrets. I had no near relation, and no intimate friend belonging to the Episcopal Church."

In 1805 Brownell began duties as tutor in Latin and Greek at Union College, and after two years he was made professor of belles lettres and moral philosophy. In 1808 he was named professor of chemistry and mineralogy; the following year he traveled in England, Scotland, and Ireland, where he met distinguished scientists, visited their laboratories, and gathered specimens to take back to the United States to prepare him for his new position. He returned to Union in 1810 and before long met Charlotte Dickinson of Lansingburgh, New York, whom he married in 1811. They had no children. An ardent member of the Episcopal church, she helped him with his religious dilemma.

Brownell was convinced of the historical and scriptural grounds for episcopacy, and with his wife's support and encouragement he decided to join the Episcopal church. On 5 September 1813 he was baptized in St. George's Church, Schenectady, and soon after confirmed. He studied theology on his own, and on 11 April 1816 he was ordained deacon, and on 4 August 1816, priest. Brownell began his duties as assistant minister at Trinity Church in New York City on 11 August 1818, but he did not remain there long. Connecticut had been without a bishop since 1813 and had had difficulty electing one, and on 2 June 1819 the diocese elected Brownell to the position. On 27 October 1819 he was consecrated the third Bishop of Connecticut, remaining so until his death. His rapid promotion was without parallel in the history of the Episcopal church—baptized in 1813 and consecrated a bishop in 1819.

Brownell's predecessor had lived in New Haven, but he decided to make Hartford his see, and while there he served as the rector of Christ Church. The General Theological Seminary had opened in New York City in 1819, but the general convention of May 1820 voted to move it to New Haven, and later that year it opened at its new location. Brownell felt obligated to move to New Haven to support the school, and he assisted its one professor, Samuel Hulbeart Turner, by teaching pastoral theology. When the special general convention of 1821 voted to move the seminary back to New York, Brownell felt keen disappointment, and he decided to establish an educational institution in Connecticut. Through his efforts, the Connecticut legislature granted a charter for Washington College in 1823, and the school opened at Hartford the following year. Brownell served as president until 1831. In 1845 the name was changed to Trinity College.

At the general convention of 1829 Brownell preached the opening sermon, urging support of the Domestic and Foreign Missionary Society. The directors of the society were eager for a bishop to visit the South and Southwest, and since Brownell was one of the younger bishops, they asked him to undertake the arduous trip. In November he left Hartford and visited Kentucky, Mississippi, Louisiana, and Alabama.

On this tour he administered thirty-four baptisms, confirmed 142 persons, consecrated six churches, and ordained one priest. He made a similar tour in 1834. From 1852 to 1865 Brownell served as the seventh presiding bishop of the Episcopal church, the senior bishop who presided when the House of Bishops met.

Brownell was the author of several books. Probably his most significant was *The Family Prayer Book; or, The Book of Common Prayer, and Administration of the Sacraments, and Other Rites and Ceremonies of the Church, According to the Use of the Protestant Episcopal Church in the United States of America; Accompanied by a General Commentary, Historical, Explanatory, Doctrinal, and Practical* (1823), one of the earliest commentaries on the 1789 *Prayer Book*; in it he argued for set forms of prayer. Two other publications were *Errors of Times* (1843) and *New Englandism Not the Religion of the Bible* (1844). *Errors* was an address to the clergy of Connecticut and criticized the romanism and puritanism of the time. *New Englandism* was a criticism of New England Congregationalism and a defense of episcopacy.

Brownell, like other Connecticut Episcopalians, followed "high church" practices, but he was not attracted by the Oxford Movement to reunite the Anglican and Episcopal churches with Roman Catholicism and did not involve himself in that important nineteenth-century controversy. He died in Hartford, having been bishop of a significant diocese for forty-five years.

• Brownell's papers are in the archives of the Diocese of Connecticut at Hartford. Studies of his life and ministry include William Agur Beardsley, "Thomas Church Brownell, Third Bishop of Connecticut," *Historical Magazine of the Protestant Episcopal Church* 6 (1937): 350–69; "The Rev. Thomas C. Brownell, D.D., L.L.D." *Church Review* 17 (1865–1866): 261–73; and "Thomas Church Brownell: 1819–1865," in Nelson R. Burr, *The Story of the Diocese of Connecticut* (1962), 449–53. His missionary tours are documented in "Bishop Thomas C. Brownell's Journal of His Missionary Tours, 1829 and 1834," ed. William A. Beardsley, *Historical Magazine of the Protestant Episcopal Church* 7 (1938): 303–22. Brownell edited *The Religion of the Heart and Life, Compiled from the Works of the Best Writers on Experimental and Practical Piety, with an Introductory Chapter Prefixed to Each Volume* (5 vols., 1840).

DON S. ARMENTROUT

BROWNELL, William Crary (30 Aug. 1851–22 July 1928), literary critic, was born in New York City, the son of Isaac Wilbour Brownell, a commission merchant, and Lucia Emilie Brown. When William was five, the family moved to Buffalo and remained there for five years. After his mother died, he was sent to Adamsville, Rhode Island, where he lived with her parents. In 1867, at sixteen, he entered Amherst College. Upon graduating, he became a reporter and, two years later, the city editor for the *New York World*. From 1879 to 1881, he wrote for the *Nation*, contributing many literary essays, including perceptive and influential articles on Matthew Arnold, Henry James, Nathaniel Hawthorne, George Eliot, and William Wordsworth. In January 1878, he married Virginia Shields Swinburne. The young couple traveled abroad extensively, spending most of their time in Paris. They returned to America in 1884. Brownell then took a position with the *Philadelphia Press*, where he worked for the next four years. In January 1888, he became editor and literary adviser for Charles Scribner's Sons, a position he retained until his death over forty years later. In January 1921, ten years after the death of his first wife, he married Gertrude Hall, a poet and translator of the French writers Verlaine and Rostand.

Brownell worked with Scribner's most important late nineteenth- and early twentieth-century authors. Little evidence remains to document his editorial capabilities. Brownell's surviving correspondence, however, shows that he was "helpful, restrained, and impartial—but rarely specific" (West, p. 50). His most notable author was Edith Wharton, and his greatest achievement as editor was to encourage and guide her during the early and middle years of her career. After Brownell's death, Wharton eulogized in *Scribner's* (Nov. 1928): "In his spoken counsels the eagerest openmindedness was combined with an unwavering perception of final values. Rarely as I saw him—alas, too rarely!—the sense of his wisdom and sympathy was always with me, like a guiding touch on my shoulder."

While at Scribner's, Brownell wrote critically on art and literature and insightfully compared European and American social values, contributing to the major periodicals and publishing separate volumes of criticism. His first two books were products of his sojourn in France with his first wife. *French Traits: An Essay in Comparative Criticism* (1889), clearly indebted to Ralph Waldo Emerson's *English Traits* (1856), presented reflective sketches concerning Paris life and culture. In his next book, *French Art* (1892), Brownell described how the French national character overshadowed the personal quality of French art. He thus signaled the direction his subsequent criticism would take. The significance of personality in artistic and literary creation would become Brownell's central critical principle, a perspective he derived largely from Charles Augustin Sainte-Beuve, who pioneered the idea. In 1896, Brownell published *Newport* (1896), a fond description of the Rhode Island city.

Brownell's criticism reached its high-water mark during the first decade of the twentieth century. When published, *Victorian Prose Masters: Thackeray, Carlyle, George Eliot, Matthew Arnold, Ruskin, George Meredith* (1901) was recognized for its "intellectual quality . . . of a very high order" (*Outlook*, 14 Dec. 1901). Brownell's discussion of Arnold's critical principles in *Victorian Prose Masters* reveals his scholarly indebtedness. Following Arnold, Brownell believed that great literature should both embody time-honored artistic standards and have an ethical basis.

Brownell's most important critical work, *American Prose Masters: Cooper, Hawthorne, Emerson, Poe, Lowell, Henry James* (1909), is remarkably different from the American literary criticism that was being published during the late nineteenth and early twentieth centuries. Avoiding impressionistic criticism, pedantry, and chest-beating nationalism, Brownell forced his readers to reexamine the critical basis of America's most revered authors. At a time when much American criticism offered little more than "a holiday excursion to the homes of popular authors with biographical anecdotes," Brownell analyzed representative American writing with "penetrating force" and "intellectual integrity" (*Outlook*, 27 Nov. 1909). In *American Prose Masters*, as in *Victorian Prose Masters*, Brownell analyzes his subjects by examining how their individual personalities evoked their ideas rather than viewing the biographical aspects of the creative process. One reviewer, calling him "the most admired American critic now living," explained that he "sets up Cooper, knocks down Hawthorne, pats Emerson on the back, turns Poe out-of-doors entirely, and is consistently and temperamentally on the offensive toward Mr. James" (*North American Review*, Jan. 1910).

Brownell wrote several other works during the next two decades, but his critical principles changed little. His literary conservatism, however, made his work increasingly out-of-date. Brownell refused to accept the critical tenets of the burgeoning modernist movement. Literature, he believed, must adhere to traditional standards. Experiments with form and structure were not to be encouraged. Stuart P. Sherman essentially called Brownell's *Criticism* (1914) an old man's book: "It should be pointed out that a critic of his standards will hardly enter upon his task before the age of forty. He must outlive so much emotional ferment and acquire so much intellectual culture before he can attain the high rational disinterestedness, poise, and serenity proper to criticism" (*Nation*, 31 Dec. 1914). Brownell's conservative stance prevented him from acknowledging the work of important writers who came to the forefront during the early decades of the twentieth century. *Standards* appeared in 1917 and *The Genius of Style* in 1924. Reviewing the latter work, Mark Van Doren clearly hinted that Brownell's critical principles were on the wane: "Members of the generation will perhaps share with him his desire to see prose today grow into a richer, more beautiful instrument. As censor and counselor, however, they will feel that he has laid a hand upon them quite as dead as it is shapely" (*Nation*, 11 Feb. 1925). Brownell's last work, *Democratic Distinction in America* (1927), appeared the year before his death in Williamstown, Massachusetts.

• Brownell's editorial correspondence is preserved in the Scribner Archive at Princeton University. Other manuscript material can be found at Amherst College, the American Academy of Arts and Letters, and the University of Virginia. An anthology of Brownell's works along with much biographical information can be found in *William Crary Brownell: An Anthology*, ed. Gertrude Hall Brownell (1933). *American Prose Masters* (1963) has been edited and meticulously annotated by Howard Mumford Jones. For a primary and secondary bibliography of Brownell's work, see Frank Fletcher, "A Bibliography of William Crary Brownell," *Bulletin of Bibliography* 20 (1953): 242–44, but be aware that Fletcher's bibliography contains several errors. Fletcher does not identify Brownell's contributions to the *Nation*, but those articles can be easily found using Daniel C. Haskell, *The Nation: Indexes of Titles and Contributors, Volumes 1–105, New York, 1865–1917*, vol. 2 (1953), pp. 60–63. Edith Wharton's fond remembrance of Brownell appeared in *Scribner's*, Nov. 1928, pp. 596–602. A good estimate of Brownell's critical principles can be found in Robert E. Spiller, *Literary History of the United States* (1947). For a brief but excellent appreciation of Brownell's editorial responsibilities, see James L. W. West III, *American Authors and the Literary Marketplace since 1900* (1988), pp. 49–51.

KEVIN J. HAYES

BROWNING, Orville Hickman (10 Feb. 1806–10 Aug. 1881), lawyer and politician, was born near Cynthiana, Kentucky, the son of Micajah Browning, a prosperous farmer and merchant, and Sally Brown. He attended Augusta College in Kentucky from 1825 through 1829 then read law in his uncle William Brown's office in Cynthiana. In 1831 he was admitted to the bar and moved permanently to Quincy, Illinois. Browning served five weeks in the Illinois militia in the 1832 Black Hawk War. In 1836 he married Eliza Caldwell; the couple adopted a five-year-old daughter in 1853. In 1837 Browning and Nehemiah Bushnell formed a law partnership that lasted until Bushnell's death in 1873.

Browning soon entered politics and was elected as a Whig to the state senate in 1836, serving until 1840. While supporting a state bank and protective tariffs, Browning opposed funding extensive internal improvements, such as the Illinois and Michigan Canal and railroads. In 1842 Browning was elected to the Illinois House, then Stephen A. Douglas defeated him for a new congressional seat in 1843. William Alexander Richardson bested Browning for that same seat in both 1850 and 1852.

Browning was against the extension of slavery into the territories and thus strongly opposed the 1854 Kansas-Nebraska Act, but he also criticized abolitionists as extremists and advocated colonization of blacks. By 1856 Browning had become a Republican, and he wrote the platform resolutions for the 1856 and 1858 Illinois Republican conventions. He favored Edward Bates for the 1860 Republican presidential nomination but helped garner support for Abraham Lincoln at the Chicago convention. Lincoln and Browning had become friends in the 1830s and occasionally collaborated on legal cases. Lincoln submitted a draft of his first inaugural address to Browning, who softened the tone of the speech a bit by deleting the more strident idea of reclaiming the public property in favor of a pledge to "hold, occupy and possess" this property. Browning's ambition in 1861 was a place on the U.S. Supreme Court. He wrote to Lincoln that it was "an office peculiarly adapted to my tastes" and that "there is nothing in your power to do for me which would gratify me so much as this" (9 Apr. 1861; Lincoln papers). Instead, Illinois governor Richard Yates appointed Browning to the U.S. Senate seat left vacant after Douglas's death in June.

Browning advocated vigorous prosecution of the war in its early stages. He supported Lincoln's call for troops, voted for the First Confiscation Act, and even supported John C. Frémont's proclamation freeing slaves in Missouri. However, early in 1862 he broke with the radicals in Congress over the Second Confiscation Act, which he felt unconstitutionally deprived southern slaveholders of their property. Regarding emancipation, Browning adhered to Lincoln's earlier formulation of compensated emancipation and colonization and felt slavery was entirely a matter for the individual states to decide. Thus he opposed the issuance of the Emancipation Proclamation, and even at the end of December 1862 he was still trying to convince Lincoln not to put it into effect. Browning also criticized the suppression of the Chicago *Times*, arbitrary arrests of civilians, and the vilification of southerners in the press and Congress. Many fellow Republicans viewed him as hopelessly conservative. While Browning remained true to the Union cause, he felt the war effort was being controlled by radical elements with dangerous views, and he gave no support to Lincoln in the 1864 election. In fact, he never again supported a Republican candidate for president.

Upon leaving the Senate in early 1863, Browning remained in the capital and continued to lobby Lincoln and administration officials for appointments, pardons, passes, and contracts. He formed a law partnership with fellow conservatives Thomas Ewing, Sr., Edgar Cowan, and Britton Hall. In January 1865 Browning was involved in a failed scheme to sell a large amount of Confederate commodities, "which will make us rich if we can only get it out" (Browning, *Diary*, vol. 2, p. 4).

Browning became a strong supporter of Andrew Johnson and lauded Johnson's vetoes of the Freedman's Bureau and civil rights bills because he felt they made a privileged class of blacks and infringed on states' powers. He condemned the 1867 Reconstruction Act as a "military despotism bill" (Browning, *Diary*, vol. 2, p. 135). Browning strongly opposed the Fifteenth Amendment, arguing that suffrage was purely a state matter and that the interests of all classes were better served by "retaining the government in the hands of the Anglo Saxon race . . . than they would [be] if we permitted African and Asiatic races to share political power and privileges with us" (Browning, *Diary*, vol. 2, pp. 258–59). He also dismissed female suffrage as a "silly clamor" (Browning, *Diary*, vol. 2, p. 272). Johnson appointed Browning secretary of the interior in 1866. In his two and a half years in that office, Browning advocated stricter government inspections of Union Pacific Railroad construction and urged timely congressional subsistence appropriations to help quell Indian unrest. Opposed to War Department control of Indian policy, he felt Indians should hold land individually on reservations and learn agriculture—"the only policy that can be pursued to preserve them from extinction" (Report of the Secretary of the Interior, 1866, pp. 7–8). He firmly supported Johnson against his congressional impeachers, and when Henry Stanbery resigned as attorney general to aid in Johnson's defense, Browning served in that office from March to July 1868.

Browning resumed his law practice in Quincy upon leaving office in 1869 and became one of the leading attorneys of the Chicago, Burlington & Quincy Railroad. He argued one of the Granger cases, *Chicago, Burlington & Quincy v. Iowa*, before the U.S. Supreme Court and other railroad cases in Illinois and Iowa. He thought state regulation of railroads unconstitutional and bemoaned the "popular prejudice against Rail Roads" that made it "impracticable to get justice at the hands of the juries" (Browning, *Diary*, vol. 2, p. 279). He also served as a delegate to the 1869 Illinois constitutional convention, where he argued against black suffrage. Later in life Browning tended to take political sides with Democrats, yet he wrote in 1872, "I am outside all political organizations, not being able to cooperate with either the radicals or the democrats" (18 Sept. 1872; William Seward papers).

Browning died in Quincy. His ill-considered financial dealings with his unscrupulous son-in-law, Orrin Skinner, resulted in creditors plundering his estate, leaving his wife penniless. Browning was an able and prominent lawyer, and a thoroughgoing conservative, especially on matters of race, property, and civil rights.

• Browning's diary and personal papers are held by the Illinois State Historical Library. The diary, published as *The Diary of Orville Hickman Browning*, ed. Theodore Calvin Pease and James G. Randall (2 vols., 1925; repr. 1933), is a major source for the Civil War and Reconstruction period. The introductions give a good overview of his life. Suppressed passages of the diary referring to Mary Todd Lincoln were officially opened to scholars in 1994. The Illinois Historical Survey, University of Illinois at Urbana-Champaign, holds transcripts of Browning's papers as well as additional materials gathered by Pease and Randall. The sole but solid biography is Maurice Baxter, *Orville H. Browning, Lincoln's Friend and Critic* (1957). An obituary is in the *Chicago Tribune*, 12 Aug. 1881.

BRIAN J. KENNY

BROWNING, Pete (17 June 1861–10 Sept. 1905), baseball player, was born Lewis Rogers Browning in Louisville, Kentucky. Very little is known of his parents and early years. As a child Browning contracted mastoiditis, a middle ear infection. Because the illness was never properly diagnosed or treated, Browning suffered from it his entire life. Periodically his ear filled with fluid, rendering him totally deaf. His condition embarrassed him, and he missed so much school because of it that he never attained literacy. Nonetheless he developed athletic prowess in shooting marbles, ice skating, and playing baseball. The pain from his condition led Browning to drink heavily from an early age, though very few people ever knew of his medical problems, and many criticized what they perceived as Browning's moral weakness.

Browning began his baseball career in 1878 with a local semiprofessional team formed by his friend John

Reccius. He was first tried as a pitcher and then as an infielder, but his hearing problems made him a defensive liability. His poor fielding was overlooked because Browning was a formidable hitter. He was particularly renowned for his prodigious blasts in the era of the "dead ball," which lacked corked centers. In 1882 Browning signed a professional contract with the Louisville Eclipse in the American Association, which at the time was a legitimate major league rival to the officially sanctioned National League and routinely drew larger crowds.

Browning paid immediate dividends for Louisville as he captured the batting title with a .378 average and compiled a .510 slugging percentage in his rookie year. He also committed 63 errors while playing three infield positions. Because he could not hear runners bearing down on him, Browning planted one leg and extended the other toward the base runner, a position that made fielding quite difficult. In 1885 Louisville moved Browning permanently to the outfield, where it was thought he would cause the least damage as a fielder. Even then he had problems. Since he could hear neither the bat striking the ball nor his teammates calling instructions, Browning suffered numerous collisions with both outfield fences and fellow players. His battles with fly balls and his nicked and scarred body led fans to dub him "The Old Gladiator." But Browning hit above .300 for seven consecutive seasons.

Early in the 1884 season Browning broke his favorite bat. A woodworker, John A. "Bud" Hillerich, offered to produce a custom-made bat in his father's shop. In his next game Browning got three hits in three at-bats and finished the season with a .336 average using the barrel-shaped bat. The firm of Hillerich and Bradsby was soon flooded with requests for this new kind of bat, which became known as the "Louisville Slugger." Browning was said to have owned 200 of the bats, each one named for a biblical character. He won his second batting title in 1885 with a .362 average. In 1887, his best year, he hit .402 and stole 103 bases but lost the batting title to Tip O'Neill, who hit .435 that year. Louisville fans honored "Line-em-out Pete" Browning's efforts by buying him a diamond-encrusted watch.

Browning was known as much for his quirkiness as for his hitting. He insisted on touching third base each inning for good luck, and he feared getting his feet wet. He once was fined for refusing to chase a ball that rolled into a puddle. Browning attributed his keen batting eye to a ritual of staring into the full sun, a practice he called "filling the lamps with sunshine," and he was known to deeply inhale a cigarette before batting in the belief that smoke was good for his eyes. He was also rumored to be drunk much of the time he played, a legend to which he contributed by remarking, "I can't hit the ball until I hit the bottle." His batting average slipped to .256 in 1889, a year in which he was fined $600 for missing a game on account of drunkenness. Unaware of the pain in which he played, fans and sportswriters promptly blamed Browning's decline on alcohol, and thus Browning felt betrayed by them.

In 1890 unionized National League players resisting an owner-imposed salary cap formed the Players' League, and Browning signed with the league's Cleveland entry. In what would be the league's only season, he won the batting title with a .373 average. After the league folded, Browning spent the next three years in the National League with clubs in Pittsburgh, Cincinnati, and Louisville. Although he hit well, he began the 1894 season in the minor leagues with Allentown in the Pennsylvania State League, before playing in his final three major league games with St. Louis and Brooklyn. There is no record of Browning playing baseball in 1895, though in 1896 he appeared with Columbus in the Western League where he hit .333 in 26 games. Browning finished his major league career with a .341 batting average and three batting championships.

Browning's life turned more tragic after he retired from baseball. He tried his hand as a saloonkeeper, but the business failed because Browning proved more adroit at sampling his wares than selling them. Other ventures proved equally unsuccessful. On 7 June 1905 he was declared a lunatic by a Kentucky circuit court and committed to an insane asylum in Lakeland, Kentucky. Three weeks later a sister assumed custody of him, but Browning spent the next few months in and out of treatment at Louisville's City Hospital. He died from the results of brain damage due to heavy drinking and two unsuccessful operations for mastoiditis in Louisville. An alcoholic loner, it is unlikely he ever married, and his gravesite was marked by a misspelled tombstone.

• For more information, see the Lewis R. Browning Folder in the National Baseball Library in Cooperstown, N.Y. Browning's career statistics are in *The Baseball Encyclopedia*, 8th ed. (1990). Other sources include Hy Turkin and Sherley Clark Thompson, *The Official Encyclopedia of Baseball* (1951); Microsoft Corporation, *Complete Baseball* (CD-Rom, 1994); Robert Smith, *Baseball* (1947); Harold Seymour, *Baseball: The Early Years* (1960); David Quentin Voigt, *American Baseball*, vol. 1: *From Gentlemen's Sport to the Commissioner System* (1966); and Geoffrey M. Ward and Ken Burns, eds., *Baseball: An Illustrated History* (1994). An obituary is in *Sporting Times*, 16 Sept. 1905.

ROBERT E. WEIR

BROWNING, Tod (12 July 1882–6 Oct. 1962), film director, was born Charles Albert Browning in Louisville, Kentucky. Nothing is known of his parents. He attended school in Churchill Downs and went to the Louisville Male High School before running away from home to join a touring carnival in 1898. He worked as a contortionist and a clown on the carnival circuit for a few years before moving up to burlesque and vaudeville where he became known as an expert in blackface comic performing. He toured the United States as the principal burlesque comic in *The Whirl of Mirth* before he signed on at Hollywood's Biograph Studios as a comic actor in 1913. He appeared in several Biograph films, including D. W. Griffith's *The Mother and the Law* (1916). He began directing in 1915 with *The Lucky Transfer* and continued as a screen director, occasional actor, and story contributor until his retirement in 1942.

Browning married actress Alice Rae Wilson (her name at birth was Houghton) in 1918; they did not have children. A rumor persists that early in his filmmaking career at Biograph Browning was castrated in an auto accident that resulted in the death of actor Elmer Booth, a passenger in his vehicle. Browning, who struggled with alcoholism throughout his life, was behind the wheel when the accident occurred. Whether he was indeed castrated is speculative, but the dark tones in his films and his interest in the horror genre may result, in part, from this accident.

Browning directed nearly fifty feature films during the silent era. He worked with screen pioneer D. W. Griffith, acting and serving as an assistant director for crowd scenes on Griffith's masterpiece, *Intolerance* (1916). He also directed silent star Priscilla Dean in *The Virgin of Stanboul* (1920) and gave an early break to actor Wallace Beery.

Browning's best pictures were made when he joined Universal Studios and formed a close working relationship with actor Lon Chaney. Widely credited as being the first to recognize Chaney's superior talents, Browning helped the actor find his niche in extreme character roles and horror films. Browning directed Chaney in classics such as *Outside the Law*, which also starred Dean (1921), *The Unholy Three* (1925), *The Blackbird* (1926), *The Unknown* (1927), *The Big City* (1928), *West of Zanzibar* (1928), and *Where East Meets West* (1929). In all these films, Browning placed the emphasis on Chaney's adeptness with makeup and as a character actor. Several of the films featured Chaney in multiple roles and usually as a fiend or villain. Although Browning directed features on various subjects, the teaming with Chaney established him as the premiere director of the horror genre.

During the 1920s Browning directed twenty-three features. At the end of the decade he made a comfortable transition to sound, although many of his contemporaries from the silent film days were defeated by the new medium. In fact, the two movies for which Browning is most remembered were "talkies." He planned to make a screen version starring Chaney of the popular Hamilton Deane stage play *Dracula*, which was based on Bram Stoker's Victorian gothic novel about a Transylvanian vampire on the loose in London. When he was unable to obtain the rights, he wrote his own vampire film for Chaney, *London after Midnight* (1927), but continued to try to obtain the rights to *Dracula*. He finally succeeded, but before *Dracula* was ready to go before the cameras in 1931, Chaney died, and Browning replaced him with little-known Hungarian actor Bela Lugosi, who had appeared successfully in the stage version of *Dracula*. Despite Lugosi's thick accent, the film made him a star, and it brought in a fortune for Universal. And in a rare return to acting, Browning himself supplied the voice for the harbormaster in the film.

Dracula also spawned numerous sequels, but none were directed by Browning, whose career faltered the following year when he made *Freaks*, which he also produced. *Freaks* was a frighteningly realistic portrait of the revenge visited on a self-centered trapeze artist, played memorably by Russian actress Olga Baclanova, by the maimed and deformed performers of a tawdry touring carnival. Using real sideshow performers (from bearded ladies to armless, legless men) and employing a stark realism in the visual elements, Browning's macabre *Freaks* was too far ahead of its time for audiences, and it failed at the box office. At one preview in San Diego, California, a woman fled the theater screaming, and Browning was forced by studio executives to cut some of the movie's more grotesque moments. Although it has become a cult classic to subsequent generations, the failure of *Freaks* in 1932 significantly damaged Browning's career. He only directed four more features, *Fast Workers* (1933), *Mark of the Vampire* (1935), *The Devil-Doll* (1936), and the lackluster *Miracles for Sale* (1942). Browning later contributed the story to *Inside Job* (1946), but he did not direct it.

Following the release of *Miracles for Sale*, Browning retired bitterly from directing, although he was awarded an honorary life membership in the Directors Guild of America, and for the remaining years of his life he refused to discuss his screen work. Browning, a quiet and self-effacing man in contrast with his image as a master of horror, retired quietly to his home in Santa Monica, California, where he died.

• For information on Browning, see Joan Dickey, "A Maker of Mystery," *Motion Picture Classic*, Mar. 1928; A. Garsault, "Tod Browning: à la recherche de la réalité," *Positif*, July–Aug. 1978; George Geltzer, "Tod Browning," *Film in Review*, Oct. 1953; Rory Guy, "The Browning Version," *Cinema*, June–July 1963; James Hoberman, "Tod Browning's Side Show," *Village Voice*, 17 Sept. 1979; Ephraim Katz, *The Film Encyclopedia* (1994); John McCarty, *The Fearmakers* (1994); Jean-Claude Romer, "Tod Browning," *Bizarre*, no. 3 (1962); Stuart Rosenthal, "Tod Browning," *The Hollywood Professionals* (1975); Eli Savada, "Tod Browning," *Photon*, no. 23 (1973); and David J. Skal and Elias Savada, *Dark Carnival* (1995). Obituaries are in the *New York Times*, 10 Oct. 1962, and *Variety*, 17 Oct. 1962.

JAMES FISHER

BROWNLOW, William Gannaway (29 Aug. 1805–29 Apr. 1877), minister, newspaper editor, and governor of Tennessee, was born in Wytheville, Virginia, the son of Joseph A. Brownlow and Catherine Gannaway, farmers. Born into a moderately comfortable, slaveholding family, Brownlow was taken in by a maternal uncle after both parents died in 1816. From ages eleven through eighteen he worked on his uncle's farm and attended the local common schools when possible, although most of his education came through his own private reading. In 1823 he moved to Abingdon, Virginia, to learn the carpentry trade from another uncle.

His work as a carpenter ended abruptly when he experienced a religious conversion at a Methodist camp meeting in nearby Sulphur Springs in 1825. Following this meeting, he completed his current carpentry jobs and moved back to Wytheville to study for the ministry with William Horne. After a year of training, he was licensed for the ministry by the church's Holston Conference and began a career as an itinerant preacher.

Through the early to mid-1830s Brownlow traversed the hills of southern Appalachia, proclaiming the Methodist message and provoking bitter conflicts with Baptist and Presbyterian rivals. His sharp wit and biting vituperation quickly brought him the reputation of a hardheaded, controversial, and uncompromising adversary. He ended his itinerancy in 1836 when he married Eliza Ann O'Brien, with whom he had seven children, but he continued to preach and advocate Methodism throughout his life. Settling first in Elizabethton, Tennessee, Brownlow at this time also became a champion of the new Whig party, which organized in the 1830s in opposition to Andrew Jackson and the Democratic party. In 1839 Brownlow established his first newspaper, the *Tennessee Whig*, to defend both religious and political truth. Published with the motto "Cry Aloud and Spare Not," the paper soon became one of Tennessee's leading Whig organs while sustaining its editor's reputation as a reckless incendiary. He relocated the paper to nearby Jonesborough (later Jonesboro) in 1840 before finally settling in 1849 in Knoxville, which became his permanent home.

Brownlow's Whiggery expressed itself most clearly in his advocacy of Henry Clay's presidential prospects. His son later recalled that the only time he saw his father weep was after he learned of Clay's defeat in the presidential election of 1844. When in 1848 the Whig National Convention bypassed Clay, Brownlow refused to support the party nominee Zachary Taylor. His recalcitrance continued into the 1852 election when he promoted Daniel Webster instead of Winfield Scott, whom the Whigs nominated in place of Millard Fillmore, the president who had signed into law the national compromise over slavery's expansion that Clay had proposed in 1850. After the demise of the national Whig party, Brownlow became one of the leading Southern advocates of the nativist Know Nothing movement. As the question of slavery's expansion became the nation's most pressing issue, he championed the preservation of both slavery and the Union. A slaveowner himself, he defended slavery on biblical grounds, but at the same time he condemned advocates of secession as radical fanatics who sought to dissolve the Union merely for personal gain. With the onset of the Civil War, Brownlow, despite his devotion to slavery, chose to remain loyal to the Union. Ultimately, he accepted emancipation as a means to help to defeat the Confederacy, though he also advocated removing the freed slaves to a territory away from the white population.

Despite Tennessee's withdrawal from the Union, Brownlow continued to publish his paper and condemn the Confederacy until he was arrested and briefly imprisoned in late 1861. Released on condition that he leave the state, he in March 1862 began a speaking tour of several northern cities. This tour earned him a small fortune while making him a national symbol of Southern loyalty to the Union. On a break from this tour, Brownlow stayed at Crosswicks, New Jersey, and composed *Sketches of the Rise, Progress, and Decline of Secession* (1862). Better known as *Parson Brownlow's Book*, this publication brought him greater renown by popularizing even further his acrimonious denunciation of Confederate leaders. He returned to East Tennessee as an agent for the U.S. Treasury following the region's occupation by Federal troops in December 1863. After he had also revived his paper, he took a leading role in the movement to reestablish civil government in Tennessee in 1865. Despite the absence of any previous officeholding experience, Brownlow, as the state's second most prominent Unionist behind Andrew Johnson, became the Unionists' candidate for governor. Because Johnson, as the state's military governor, had effectively disfranchised supporters of the Confederacy, Brownlow won the election by a virtually unanimous vote.

With the support of only a minority faction of Unionists, Brownlow's governorship was characterized by his desire to suppress Tennessee's pro-Confederate majority. At his urging, the general assembly formally disfranchised all but those who had been unconditional Unionists during the war while enfranchising the state's freedmen and giving the governor the authority to appoint local election officials. Brownlow meanwhile appointed Unionists to state judgeships before elections could be held to fill these posts. He frequently requested federal troops to intervene in state affairs and approved the creation of a state army under his command. The legislature's excessive granting of state bonds to railroad companies, many of which received approval through bribery, joined salary increases, extravant expenditures, a dramatic increase in the state debt and tax burden to give his administration a reputation for corruption. Brownlow himself appears to have been innocent of any plundering, though he often displayed poor judgment in managing the state's funds.

Brownlow's vehemence toward former Confederates divided Tennessee's Unionists into a Radical faction, led by the governor, and a Conservative faction that advocated reconciliation. At Brownlow's direction, the legislature rejected the policy of President Andrew Johnson and ratified the fourteenth amendment. Tennessee thus became the only former Confederate state to accept the terms of reunion designed by Congress and to avoid the occupation prescribed by the Military Reconstruction Act of 1867. With the state's electoral machinery under his control, Brownlow easily defeated Conservative candidate Emerson Etheridge for reelection in 1867, and shortly after his inauguration the legislature acted upon Brownlow's request and elected him to the U.S. Senate. His term did not begin until 1869, however, and before leaving for Washington the governor invited federal troops to occupy twenty-one counties to counter the activities of the Ku Klux Klan. When these troops were denied, Brownlow attempted to suppress the Klan by calling out the state militia and declaring martial law in nine counties. No conviction of any Klan member resulted from this action, but these counties remained under military rule until the Conservative victory in the state elections in the following August.

Brownlow's health had long been in decline, and he served only one unexceptional term in the Senate. At the conclusion of this term in 1875, he returned to Knoxville and briefly resumed his editorial career, but poor health kept him largely inactive until his death there. Despite his acerbity and his controversial public image, Brownlow in private life was known to be mild-mannered, polite, generous, and honest. Historians long vilified him as one of the most vicious of the Radical Republicans. In retrospect, he seems less a villain than a tragic figure who was unsuited for public office but whose career reflected the difficulty of the challenges facing the South during Reconstruction.

• A few letters are scattered in a variety of collections, the most substantive of which are the David Campbell Papers, Duke University, and the Thomas Amis Rogers Nelson Papers, McClung Collection, East Tennessee Historical Center. Brownlow published his newspaper under several titles, but all titles included the label *Whig*; most issues are extant. His other books and pamphlets include *Helps to the Study of Presbyterianism* (1834), *A Political Register, Setting forth the Principles of the Whig and Locofoco Parties in the United States* (1844), *Americanism Contrasted with Foreignism, Romanism, and Bogus Democracy* (1856), *The Great Iron Wheel Examined* (1856), *A Sermon on Slavery* (1857), and *Irreligious Character of the Rebellion* (1862). The standard biographical treatment is E. Merton Coulter, *William G. Brownlow: Fighting Parson of the Southern Highlands* (1937). More recent are Steve Humphrey, *"That D——d Brownlow"* (1978), and James C. Kelly, "William Gannaway Brownlow," *Tennessee Historical Quarterly* 43 (Spring 1984): 25–43 and (Summer 1984): 155–72. Biographical sketches are in Kenneth McKellar, *Tennessee Senators as seen by one of their successors* (1942), and Margaret I. Phillips, *The Governors of Tennessee* (1978). Brownlow's governorship is well covered in Robert H. White, ed., *Messages of the Governors of Tennessee*, vol. 5 (1959), and Thomas B. Alexander, *Political Reconstruction in Tennessee* (1950), though use of these works should be tempered by more recent treatments of the Reconstruction Era. See also William G. Miscamble, "Andrew Johnson and the Election of William G. ('Parson') Brownlow as Governor of Tennessee," *Tennessee Historical Quarterly* 37 (Fall 1978): 308–20; Thomas B. Alexander, "Strange Bedfellows: The Interlocking Careers of T. A. R. Nelson, Andrew Johnson, and W. G. (Parson) Brownlow," *East Tennessee Historical Society's Publications* 51 (1979): 54–77; and Forrest Conklin and John W. Wittig, "Religious Warfare in the Southern Highlands: Brownlow versus Ross," *Journal of East Tennessee History* 63 (1991): 33–50. Obituaries are in the Memphis *Public Ledger*, 1 May 1877, and the *New York Times*, 30 Apr. 1877.

JONATHAN M. ATKINS

BROWN-POTTER, Cora Urquhart (15 May 1857–12 Feb. 1936), actress, was born in New Orleans, Louisiana, the daughter of Colonel David Urquhart, a banker and plantation owner, and Augusta Slocomb. Some sources list the year of her birth as 1859. Her childhood was spent in the gardens and drawing rooms of a prosperous, cultured New Orleans society. Cora displayed a talent for the stage at an early age and, encouraged by her French-born father, she often recited passages by writers such as Racine, Corneille, and Victor Hugo for family and friends. As a child Cora did not attend school but was educated both at home, benefiting from her parents' extensive library, and through travel abroad. The family lived in Paris for two years during the unsettled period immediately following the Civil War. Cora later accompanied her grandmother on summer trips to Scotland, England, Norway, and Sweden.

In 1877 Cora married James Brown-Potter of New York, and after a year of honeymooning in Europe the couple settled in New York City. They had one child. In an article for *International Cosmopolitan*, Brown-Potter looked back on her New York life as "one round of balls, dinners, operas and receptions. Everywhere, I was asked to recite, which I always did, and that helped to make me popular" (Mar. 1933).

From 1883 to 1886 Brown-Potter was the "belle of New York" according to the *Illustrated American* (7 Jan. 1893), which describes her as "an exceptional woman whose individuality asserts itself . . . a combination of beauty . . . vivacity, genuineness . . . freedom from conventional constraints."

Brown-Potter's recitations evolved into amateur theatricals and charity benefits. She became more skillful and successful and eventually decided to become a professional actress—an extraordinary and, in some quarters, unacceptable undertaking for a New York society matron of the 1880s. Undaunted, she set out for London in 1886 to pursue a stage career, forsaking her disapproving husband, young daughter, wealth, and social position. The Potters divorced in 1903.

Brown-Potter made her London theatrical debut on 29 March 1887 as Anne Sylvester in Wilkie Collins's *Man and Wife* at the Haymarket Theatre. Collins praised her performance, claiming that she had played Anne "as he had dreamed it," but critics deemed the role beyond her capacity. Nonetheless she persevered, and in association with actor-director Kyrle Bellew also in 1887 performed in *Civil War*, an Anglicized production of Albert Delpit's *Mademoiselle de Bressier* that they later brought to New York, opening to much fanfare and anticipation on 31 October 1887 at the Fifth Avenue Theatre. The *New York Times* reported, "Mrs. Potter began her new career . . . as a full fledged actress before a fashionable society audience of which she had been a leader. . . . she has much to learn, but has learned much . . . her first triumph . . . she charmed a large and critical audience by force of personal loveliness aided by artistic ability" (1 Nov. 1887).

Returning to England and continuing in partnership with Bellew, Brown-Potter played a variety of strong roles, including Juliet, Kate Hardcastle in *She Stoops to Conquer*, Cleopatra, Rosalind in J. M. Barrie's *Rosalind*, Camille, and Charlotte Corday. She performed in India, Australia, Japan, and the United States. In 1898 Brown-Potter was engaged by London manager Beerbohm Tree. Her roles under his management included Miladi in Alexandre Dumas's *The Three Musketeers*, in honor of which Londoners created a new drink called Miladi's Smile. Her career in London continued with appearances in Herman Heyermans, Jr.'s *The Ghetto*, Frank Stayton's *Mrs. Willoughby's Kiss*, Stephen Phillips's *Ulysses*, Russell Vaun's *Nicandra*, and Herman Merivale and F. C. Grove's *Forget-Me-Not*, among others. Brown-Potter continued to declaim poetry and poetic prose, and she tried her hand at managing the Savoy Theatre in London. The latter venture proved a financial fiasco. In 1906 Brown-Potter toured the music hall circuit in her own version of *Mary Queen of Scots*. After playing *La Belle Marseillaise* in 1907 in South Africa she toured the English provinces during 1908. An interview in the *Chicago Daily Journal* (15 Jan. 1904) revealed what Brown-Potter's life in the theater meant to her: "My real happiness is in my work. . . . I go on the principle that life is made up of tears and laughter, and that by giving a little of both I can touch the human side of an audience."

Over the two decades during which she lived in England (from 1886 to about 1912), Brown-Potter enjoyed a life of celebrity and counted among her friends the Prince of Wales (later King Edward VII); Field Marshal Horatio Herbert Kitchener, earl of Kitchener, who expressed a desire to become her husband; writer Oscar Wilde, whose "Happy Prince" she recited often (but she turned down his request to star in his drama *Salome* because she was "not at all in sympathy with her"); poet Robert Browning, to whom she dedicated her book *My Recitations*; and painter James McNeill Whistler.

In 1912 Brown-Potter retired from the theater to live in Guernsey, England, in the house where Victor Hugo had died. She gave her last performance, a benefit at St. Julian's, Guernsey, in February 1919. Brown-Potter became a French citizen (date unknown). She died at her home, "Villa des Bambou," in Beaulieu-sur-Mer, France. The *London Times* (13 Feb. 1936) summarized Brown-Potter's career: "Though not entitled to a place in the front rank of actresses, she was always earnest, intelligent and refined . . . "

• The Players Collection and the Robinson Locke Collection of the New York Public Library for the Performing Arts provide valuable historical material. An extensive source of information by Brown-Potter on her life, travels, and career is "The Age of Innocence—and I," published in the Mar., Apr., and May 1933 issues of *Hearst's International Cosmopolitan*. Two nonautobiographical manuscripts by Brown-Potter are helpful, "My Recitations" (1887) and "The Secrets of Beauty and Mysteries of Health" (1908), both available at the New York Public Library Center for the Humanities. Information regarding Brown-Potter's first professional appearance in the United States is in the *New York Times*, 10, 12, 23, 30 Oct. and 1 Nov. 1887. Detailed obituaries are in the *New York Times* and the *Times* (London), both 13 Feb. 1936. See other obituaries in *Variety*, 19 Feb. 1936, and the *Stage*, 20 Feb. 1936.

ADELE S. PARONI

BROWNSON, Henry Francis (7 Aug. 1835–19 Dec. 1913), editor and publisher, was born in Canton, Massachusetts, the son of Orestes Augustus Brownson, a philosopher and publisher, and Sarah Healy. Handicapped somewhat in youth by poor health, Brownson nonetheless excelled in school. He attended Holy Cross College from 1844 until 1848, when he was thirteen. On 18 November 1844, a month after his father's conditional baptism into the church, he was baptized into the Roman Catholic church. He was joined at the college chapel font by his brother William Brownson; by James Healy, the future bishop of Portland, Maine; and by Healy's brothers.

Brownson spent two years at the Jesuit novitiate in Frederick, Maryland (1848–1850), and then studied philosophy at Georgetown (1850–1851). For the next two years he studied theology at the Sulpician Seminaire de Saint Sulpice in Paris (1851–1853), followed by studies at the University of Munich (1853–1855), where he met John Acton and Johann Joseph Ignaz von Döllinger. During this time in Europe Brownson studied many languages, including Italian, French, Spanish, Portuguese, German, Swedish, Danish, Flemish, and Dutch. He returned to the United States and studied law, and he was admitted to the New York bar in 1856. He also utilized his language skills to translate Jamie Balmes's *Fundamental Philosophy* (2 vols., 1856) and Francesco Tarducci's *Life of Christopher Columbus* (1890) and *John and Sebastian Cabot* (1893). In addition, he authored *The History of Waterbury* (1858), chronicling the Brownson genealogy in Connecticut.

During the Civil War, sharing the patriotic fervor of his father, Brownson joined the Union army with the rank of second lieutenant. He was wounded in the head and right hand at Chancellorsville (May 1863), and because he assisted others rather than retreating, he was captured and held at City Point for several weeks. He remained in the army after the war, being stationed at Fort Wayne, near Detroit. He retired in 1871 with the rank of major. In January 1868 he married Josephine "Fifine" Van Dyke; they had seven children. After his retirement from the army he opened a law practice in Detroit with his brother-in-law, Philip Van Dyke. His father noted that this marriage dissipated a certain melancholy that had overhung Henry. Perhaps it was this quality that caused Isaac Hecker in 1887 to describe Henry as the "Cub of the 'Old Bear' in crossness and brightness."

Beginning in June 1866 Brownson's father invited him several times to help revive *Brownson's Quarterly Review* and to serve as the proprietor and editor, allowing the father to focus on writing articles. Instead, Henry contributed articles to the journal once his father began to publish it. Henry's mother died in 1872, and his father moved into Henry's Detroit residence in October 1875, bringing with him all his papers and books. The elder Brownson died on 17 April 1876. From that time, Henry dedicated his family's money to republishing his father's works in twenty volumes (1882–1887). This collection, *The Works of Orestes A. Brownson*, contains nearly all of his father's articles written as a Catholic and a selection of articles prior to 1844. Brownson, speaking at a historical society gathering in 1891, disagreed with the notion "that biographers so identify themselves with the men whose lives they are writing, that they can see no fault in their heroes" (*Records of the American Catholic Historical Society of Philadelphia*, vol. 3, p. 70). He demonstrated this with his critical and thorough three-volume *Life of Orestes A. Brownson* (1898–1900), which is a fair and complete account of his father's life but a bit pedantic and disjointed. His other works include *The Religion of Ancient Craft Masonry* (1890); *Faith and Science* (1895), mostly a repetition of his father's philosophical thought; and *The Proof of Miracles* (1898), an apologetic pamphlet.

The American Catholic hierarchy planned a celebration in Baltimore for November 1889 to remember the naming of the first bishop in the United States in 1789 and to dedicate the new Catholic University of America. Brownson decided in the winter of 1888 to use that occasion to hold a Catholic congress for the laity. He believed that the United States was "destined to be a Catholic land," and this congress would further that prospect. After initial encouragement from some bishops and in spite of Cardinal James Gibbons's initial coolness, Brownson held two planning meetings in Chicago, May 1889 and Detroit, June 1889, attended by some clergy and leading Catholic laity. The purposes of the congress were a closer union of Catholics, encouragement of lay assistance to the clergy, reaction to the major issues of the day, and assistance to the poor. The congress was held in Baltimore on 11–12 November 1889 with many laity and clergy in attendance, and thirteen major papers were delivered. Brownson's paper, "Lay Action in the Church," encouraged Catholic political involvement in order to affect the tone of public opinion and to purify the politics of corruption. He promoted temperance, care for the poor, and the examination of social problems. He urged an expression of Catholic loyalty and a protection of Catholic rights. He also called for the clergy to provide the laity with enough scope and freedom to think and act.

In 1897 Brownson was awarded Notre Dame's Laetare Medal, delivering the impressive address *Equality and Democracy*, which was published that year. Brownson's last thirty years were spent almost entirely at home, editing, writing, and influencing his children. He enjoyed being addressed as "Major" and living the life of a gentleman of leisure, funded by his mother-in-law. His youngest daughter, Josephine Van Dyke Brownson, was an author and catechist who received the Laetare Medal in 1939. He died in Detroit, reputed among Catholics as "perhaps the most learned man in America" (C. E. McGuire, ed., *Catholic Builders of the Nation* [1923], vol. 5, p. 262).

• Brownson's papers are at the University of Notre Dame. His sketch, "Major Henry F. Brownson," is in *Some Roads to Rome*, 2d ed., ed. Georgina Pell Curtis (1910). See Thomas Ryan, *Orestes A. Brownson: A Definitive Biography* (1976); Walter Romig, *Josephine Van Dyke Brownson* (1955); and William H. Hughes, pub., *Three Great Events in the History of the Catholic Church in the United States: The Centenary Celebration, Proceedings of the First American Catholic Congress, Dedication of the Catholic University* (1889). An obituary is in *America* 10 (10 Jan. 1914): 333.

EARL BOYEA

BROWNSON, Nathan (14 May 1742–18 Oct. 1796), physician and politician, was born in Woodbury, Connecticut, the son of Timothy Brownson and Abigail Jenner. He graduated from Yale College in 1761 and practiced medicine in his hometown. In 1769 he married Elizabeth Lewis. The couple moved to St. John Parish, Georgia, in 1774 and began working a 500-acre plantation. Brownson's wife died in 1775, and the following year he married Elizabeth McLean, with whom he had two children.

In 1774 St. John was a hotbed of revolutionary activity; many of its people were New England Congregationalists by way of Dorchester, South Carolina, a settlement on the Ashley River above Charlestown that had been founded by Puritans from Massachusetts. Brownson and another transplanted Connecticut physician, Lyman Hall, were among the eleven delegates chosen to represent the parish at the provincial congress, which met in Savannah in July 1775. Both men were elected to represent Georgia in the Continental Congress. Brownson served from January to May 1777 and again from late August to early October of the same year.

Brownson's absence from Georgia in 1777 was a political advantage. He remained above the factional strife that divided the state in the aftermath of Button Gwinnett's fatal duel with Lachlan McIntosh. Gwinnett's radical Whig followers regarded conservative Georgians as no better than Tories.

The British invasion of Georgia in the final days of 1778 put a temporary stop to the internal dissension, but with the expulsion of the king's troops from Augusta in June 1781, factional disputes threatened to spoil the victory. At this critical moment Brownson, then acting as deputy purveyor of hospitals in the South, was dispatched to Georgia with a brigadier's commission from Congress. A compromise was worked out whereby Brownson became governor and John Twiggs was promoted to brigadier general.

Brownson served as governor for the last four and a half months in 1781. He seems to have held his office in greater regard than the impecunious and helpless condition of his state warranted. The lower half of Georgia was still in British hands; hostile American Indians and bands of Tories haunted the countryside.

In one brush with British guerrillas Brownson's lieutenant governor, Myrick Davies, was killed. Despite the weakness of his position, Brownson sent emissaries to the American Indians telling them to stop fighting and admonished General Nathanael Greene for communicating with General Twiggs directly instead of through him. Brownson sent Greene a copy of the Georgia Constitution, which specified that the governor was commander in chief of the state militia. Georgians who had fled the state were warned that they must return within four months or face a threefold increase of taxes on their property. Brownson's administration resorted to desperate measures to feed the starving. Provisions were confiscated from Loyalists and impressed from patriots. After his short stint as governor, Brownson returned to his hospital duties until the Georgia lowcountry was liberated in 1782, permitting him to return with his family to their plantation.

During the decade following the war, Brownson served the public almost continuously as justice of the peace, as a commissioner for erecting a new capital in Louisville, as a member of the convention that ratified the federal constitution, as a delegate to the convention that drafted the state constitution in 1788, and as the first president of the Georgia Senate. He was one of the trustees for the establishment of the University of Georgia. Brownson died at his plantation. Although his career was not as distinguished as some others of Georgia's founding fathers, Brownson's service at crucial periods helped the state transcend factional bickering and focus on the improvement of society.

• Correspondence with Nathanael Greene is in the Greene papers, Perkins Library, Duke University. There are sketches of Brownson's life in James F. Cook, *Governors of Georgia* (1979), and Kenneth Coleman and Charles Stephen Gurr, eds., *Dictionary of Georgia Biography* (2 vols., 1983). His dealings with Greene are related in Edward J. Cashin, "Nathanael Greene's Campaign for Georgia in 1781," *Georgia Historical Quarterly* 61 (Spring 1977): 43–58. Official dispatches are in Allen D. Candler, ed., *The Revolutionary Records of the State of Georgia* (3 vols., 1908).

EDWARD J. CASHIN

BROWNSON, Orestes Augustus (16 Sept. 1803–17 Apr. 1876), educator and philosopher, was born in Stockbridge, Vermont, the son of Sylvester Augustus Brownson and Relief Metcalf, farmers. His father died when Brownson was two, and he was placed with a nearby family. The couple reared him in strict Calvinist Congregationalism. At fourteen he rejoined his mother and twin sister in Ballston Spa in upstate New York, where he studied briefly in an academy before going to work in a printer's office. He had no more formal education. In 1827 he married Sally Healy of Elbridge, New York; they had eight children.

Brownson's intellectual career falls dramatically into two periods, marked by his conversion to Roman Catholicism, on 19 October 1844. Until that date his spiritual quests took him in several directions. He joined the Presbyterian church in 1822, and in 1826, after teaching in Michigan and New York, he was ordained a Universalist preacher in Jaffey, New Hampshire. He would later refer to his years in this fold as "the most anti-Christian period of my life." For the time, however, he committed himself to the ideas of Hosea Ballou, who preached that all would be saved, for God's plan for humanity embraced universal salvation. Brownson edited a Universalist journal, the *Gospel Advocate and Impartial Investigator*, and took an interest in radical social causes, particularly the socialism of Robert Owen and Fanny Wright. He denounced organized religion and the priesthood and generally considered established religion an ally of political despotism. He also spoke against capital punishment, imprisonment for debt, and slavery, while endorsing women's rights and education.

In 1832 Brownson became a Unitarian minister and both edited and published the *Philanthropist* in Walpole, New Hampshire. At this time he became interested in Transcendentalism. He published his first book, *New Views of Christianity, Society, and the Church* (1836). He sojourned at Brook Farm near Boston and maintained his allegiance to working-class causes, now as a staunch Jacksonian Democrat. In 1838 he established the *Boston Quarterly Review*, to enlist "literature, religion, and philosophy on the side of democracy," he wrote. One of his most famous essays, "The Laboring Classes," appeared in the journal in 1840.

A few key issues prepared Brownson for his conversion in 1844. For one, he dissented from other Democratic intellectuals who espoused radical individualism and anti-statism. Not adhering to the maxim vox populi, vox dei, he stressed the organic unity of society and located its collective soul in the state, which, he believed, must be more than the sum of its individuals. He soon concluded that Catholicism underscored such an ideal in a way that Protestantism could not. Also, the election of 1840 had left him bitterly disillusioned. The defeat of the Democratic incumbent Martin Van Buren, in the famous "log cabin and hard cider" presidential campaign, led him to distrust the political wisdom of the masses. He saw how easily people were humbugged by slogans, symbols, and songs.

Brownson sought a principle of order amid the disintegration of the modern world. He saw that Protestantism legitimized individualism and thus promoted capitalism. To this extent, he believed that Transcendentalism signified the logical culmination of the Reformation, a purely spiritual and individualistic religion with no corporate structure and no organic relationship to the larger society.

After his conversion Brownson undertook an extensive study of Catholic literature under the direction of a Sulpician-trained priest. His new commitment was unyielding, and he became a brilliant Catholic polemicist. In the year of his conversion he founded *Brownson's Quarterly Review*, which he continued until 1864, stopped publishing for reasons of ill health, and resumed in 1873. This journal brought to the public his Catholic views on a wide array of subjects, mostly social and political in nature; he was sharp and often acerbic in stating his Catholic analysis. When asked what might have happened had he died before 19 October 1844, Brownson replied, "I should have gone straight to hell." A Protestant who worked for him at the *Quarterly* once tweaked him by asking if God would give the worker a reward for his efforts. Brownson replied that he would get a reward: every million years, he said, for one-millionth of a second he would be allowed to place his foot on the coolest spot in hell.

Brownson devoted the rest of his life to creating a vision of a Catholic America. His intellectual legacy was this effort. He wrote deductive essays that followed logically from one point to another, always placing him on the side of a supreme sovereign authority, God the lawgiver, and on the side of the institutional location of Christianity. Only Roman Catholicism, he believed, could impose on an undisciplined and impulsive people the restraint necessary to make democracy workable. A strong thematic perspective emerged in Brownson's essays, a Catholic eschatology. Derived perhaps from his own Puritan background, the idea of an American mission to the world showed up in his Catholic understanding of his country. Furthermore, Brownson linked Catholicism specifically to the American political experiment. At a time when the papacy adhered to a strict social and economic conservatism, Brownson continued his commitments to social reform. Against the charge that Catholicism stood for reactionism, he tried to show that the natural rights philosophy in the American founding derived directly from the Catholic natural law intellectual tradition.

The doctrine of the Incarnation became critical for Brownson's linking of religion and social reform. Christ's mediating activity, he insisted, could not take place apart from the universal, institutional church. He broke from his earlier liberal faith in progress and placed no hope in unaided humanity to effect its own salvation. Without the corporate life and discipline of the church, such effort would invariably succumb to anarchic individualism and its destructive tendencies, he said. Only the Catholic church could supply the need, he believed, because Protestantism could not repair what it had created.

Brownson did not achieve the intellectual influence that he so badly wanted in his own time. Literary critic Van Wyck Brooks said of him that he was too Yankee for the Catholics and too Catholic for the Yankees. Brownson often did not see eye-to-eye with the American Catholic leadership, and some considered him too politically radical. In addition his references to the "miserable rabble" of Irish immigrants, though misconstrued, lost him support. In the twentieth century, however, Brownson acquired a place of great prestige among academic scholars and Catholic intellectuals. Nor should one ignore his contributions to American intellectual conservatism. Much of what he said of politics and religion is in the tradition of Edmund Burke and successor conservatives such as Irving Babbitt, Paul Elmer More, and Russell Kirk. Brownson showed that one can be a friend and supporter of democracy while faulting its weaknesses and shortcomings. He died in Detroit, Michigan.

• The Brownson papers at the University of Notre Dame, carefully cataloged, contain hundreds of letters and articles of his and many letters sent to him. One should consult H. F. Brownson, ed., *The Works of Orestes A. Brownson*, 20 vols. (1882–1887), which includes the essays in *Brownson's Quarterly Review* and his major book, *The American Republic: Its Constitution, Tendencies, and Destiny* (1865). See also Alvin S. Ryan, ed., *The Brownson Reader* (1955).

Brownson has been the subject of several useful books. Arthur M. Schlesinger, Jr., *Orestes Brownson: A Pilgrim's Progress* (1939), looks mostly at his social and political thought. Theodore Maynard, *Orestes Brownson: Yankee, Radical, Catholic* (1943), is more personal, and Americo D. Lapati, *Orestes A. Brownson* (1965), is an approving study. Hugh Marshall, *Orestes Brownson and the American Republic* (1971), focuses on Brownson's political thought. Leonard Gilhooley's *Contradiction and Dilemma: Orestes Brownson and the American Idea* (1972) considers Brownson's place in American intellectual history. See also the essays Gilhooley edited for *No Divided Allegiance: Essays in Brownson's Thought* (1980).

Helpful academic essays on Brownson include Allen Guttman, "From Brownson to Eliot: The Conservative Theory of Church and State," *American Quarterly* 17 (1965): 484–99; Richard M. Leliaert, "The Religious Significance of Democracy in the Thought of Orestes A. Brownson," *Review of Politics* 38 (1976): 3–26; Patrick W. Carey, "American Catholic Romanticism, 1830–1888," *Catholic Historical Review* 74 (1988): 590–606; and Mark S. Burrows, "The Catholic Revision of an American Myth: The Eschatology of Orestes Brownson as an Apology of American Catholicism," *Catholic Historical Review* 76 (1990): 18–43.

J. DAVID HOEVELER, JR.

BRUCE, Archibald (Feb. 1777–22 Feb. 1818), physician, mineralogist, and editor, was born in New York City, the son of William Bruce, a British army medical officer, and Judith Bayard Van Rensselaer. Despite his father's expressed wish, Bruce pursued medical education and practice. After taking an A.B. at Columbia College in 1797, he continued his studies in New York and then moved on to Edinburgh (M.D., 1800). As was common in this period, his medical education included exposure to the natural sciences, and Bruce developed a lifelong interest in mineralogy. After completing his M.D., he extended his European stay with travels on the Continent to study mineralogy and collect materials for his own mineralogical cabinet.

On his return to America in 1803 Bruce began medical practice. He was one of the founders of the College of Physicians and Surgeons of New York, serving at various times during his tenure there (1807–1811) as registrar, professor of mineralogy, and professor of materia medica. Moving to Queen's College in New Jersey (later Rutgers), he again served as professor of mineralogy and materia medica (1812–1818).

Bruce made important contributions to the development of the science of mineralogy in America. He described two new mineral species, one of which was named brucite in his honor. He was among the first professors of mineralogy in the United States and made his large collection of specimens available to other workers. In 1810 he founded the *American Mineralogical Journal*, frequently known as *Bruce's Journal*. Although medical periodicals of the time also published papers on the natural sciences, *Bruce's* was the first specialized scientific periodical in the United States. Friends and contemporaries, including Parker Cleaveland, George Gibbs, and Benjamin Silliman, contributed to *Bruce's Journal* and lauded it. It was well known in European scientific circles and was often cited or quoted. After the appearance of the second number, Bruce wrote to Silliman that he had "within a very short time since received orders for its being sent to France, Germany, England, Scotland, and Ireland."

Owing to declining health, Bruce was able to produce only one volume, consisting of four numbers, the last number appearing in 1814. As it became increasingly clear in 1817 that Bruce might never produce a second volume, Cleaveland expressed his frustration in a letter to Silliman, concluding, "This Journal *must not* be discontinued—the honor of our country and more especially the interests of mineralogy forbid" (29 Sept. 1817, Silliman Family Papers). With encouragement from Cleaveland and Gibbs, Silliman subsequently sought and received Bruce's blessing to found a journal of his own to carry on the ideal of an American scientific journal. Silliman's journal, the *American Journal of Science and the Arts*, was founded in 1818, the year of Bruce's death. In the introductory remarks of his first number, Silliman gave a contemporary evaluation of Bruce's journal: "No future historian of American science will fail to commemorate this work as our earliest *purely scientific* Journal, supported by *original American communications*. Both in this country and in Europe, it was received in a very flattering manner; it excited, *at home*, great zeal and effort in support of the sciences which it fostered, and, *abroad*, it was hailed as the harbinger of our future exertions" (emphases in original; *American Journal of Science and the Arts* 1 [1818]: 3).

Bruce married in London in 1803, just before his return to the United States, but no information is available on his spouse or any children. He died of apoplexy in New York City.

• Bruce's letters to Benjamin Silliman are part of the Silliman Family Papers at Yale University. His scientific papers, including the two describing new mineral species, were published in his own *Journal. Bruce's Journal* was reprinted as volume 1 (1968) in Hafner's Contributions to the History of Geology series. The earliest source of information on Bruce's life is Benjamin Silliman, "Biographical Notice," *American Journal of Science and the Arts* 1 (1818): 299–304.

JULIE R. NEWELL

BRUCE, Blanche Kelso (1 Mar. 1841–17 Mar. 1898), black political leader and U.S. senator during the Reconstruction era, was born in Farmville, Virginia, the son of Polly (surname unknown), a slave. The identity of his father is unknown, but he took the surname of the man who owned his mother before he was born. His childhood as a slave on a small plantation, first in Virginia, then briefly in Mississippi, and finally in Missouri did not significantly differ, as he later recalled, from that of the sons of whites. This relatively benign experience in slavery perhaps owed a great deal to the fact that he was a light-skinned mulatto and the favorite of a benevolent master and mistress. He shared a tutor with his master's son and thus obtained the education that prepared him for later success. During the Civil War, despite the benevolence of his owner, he fled to freedom in Kansas, but after slavery was abolished he returned to Missouri where he reportedly established the first school in the state for blacks, at Hannibal.

After the war Bruce briefly attended Oberlin College; but following the passage of the Reconstruction Acts of 1867, which provided for black political equality in the former Confederate states, he moved to Bolivar County in the Mississippi Delta. Soon after his arrival the district commander appointed him a voter registrar in neighboring Tallahatchie County. He also organized plantation blacks into the new Republican party and soon attracted the attention of state party leaders.

When the first Mississippi legislature under the new order met, Bruce was elected sergeant-at-arms of the state senate. A man of magnificent physique, handsome countenance, and possessed of impeccable manners, Bruce won the support of white Republicans like Governor James Lusk Alcorn as well as blacks. In 1871 he won election to the joint office of sheriff and tax collector of Bolivar County. The Republican state board of education also appointed him county superintendent of education. He virtually created the biracial but segregated system of education in the county and secured the support of whites for it. In all of these positions he gained a reputation for financial integrity.

Bruce also invested in land and within a decade had attained the status of planter. In 1872 he was named to the board of levee commissioners for a three-county district—a group with the power to raise revenue and build embankments in the Delta region. Bruce's political and financial success and his promotion of labor stability among black workers had the effect of moderating the opposition of conservative planters to Republican control in Bolivar County.

By 1874 Bruce's fame had spread beyond the Delta. His political skill and his moderation had won him support from all factions of the Mississippi Republican party. In February the legislature elected him to the U.S. Senate by a nearly unanimous vote, which included the support of a few conservative Democrats. In March 1875 Bruce took his seat in the Senate, becoming the nation's second black senator and the first black to be elected to a full term.

In the Senate he served on four committees, including the important select committees on Mississippi River improvements and on the Freedmen's Bank. As chairman of the latter committee, he led the effort to reform the management of the institution and provide relief for depositors. But a Bruce-sponsored Senate bill to obtain congressional reimbursement for black victims of the bank's failure did not pass. He also spoke out against a Chinese exclusion bill and for a more humane Indian policy. Bruce took these positions, primarily because of the harsh implications that such racist, exclusionist policy had for blacks.

Bruce's main interest in the Senate was the defense of black rights in the South when state and local Republican governments were replaced by hostile conservative ones. Although he was usually unobtrusive in attempting to persuade Congress, and specifically its Republican members, to enforce the Reconstruction amendments to the Constitution, he became passionate in denouncing the violence and intimidation that characterized the Mississippi election of 1875 overthrowing Republican rule.

Despite bitter setbacks for blacks during this period, Bruce remained committed to the Reconstruction goal of black assimilation into American society with all of the rights of whites. He opposed both organized efforts at black migration of the late 1870s: the Kansas Exodus and the Back-to-Africa movement. He did so on the grounds that neither destination had much to offer blacks and that the rights of the race could yet be achieved in white America. His prestige among blacks suffered considerably because of his opposition to emigration. In 1878 he married Josephine B. Wilson, the daughter of a prominent black dentist of Cleveland, Ohio; they had one son. After their marriage and the couple's acceptance into white Washingtonian society, Bruce became largely insulated from the black masses.

During his last years in the Senate he devoted much of his time to Republican party affairs and black education. In Mississippi he combined with two other black leaders, John R. Lynch and James Hill, to dominate the state Republican organization, gaining important federal patronage for his supporters. In promoting black education, he advanced the self-help doctrine, which ultimately became associated with Booker T. Washington.

With the Democrats in control of the state legislature, Bruce made no effort to obtain reelection to the U.S. Senate. After the expiration of his term in 1881 he continued to live in Washington but retained his plantation in Mississippi. He also continued to participate in national Republican politics and was a popular speaker on behalf of black education. In 1881 President Garfield appointed Bruce register of the treasury, and he continued to hold the office in Chester A. Arthur's administration. In 1884–1885 he served as director of the black exhibits in the Industrial Cotton Centennial Exposition held in New Orleans. These exhibits focused on the material progress that blacks had made since emancipation. In 1896 he received strong support for a seat in William McKinley's cabinet, but he had to settle for his previous position of register of the treasury. Bruce died of diabetes in Washington, D.C., and was buried there.

• Letters from Bruce can be found in the Blanche K. Bruce Papers, Rutherford B. Hayes Presidential Center Library, Fremont, Ohio, and in the Bruce papers, Howard University Library, Washington, D.C. Two biographical accounts are Sadie Daniel St. Clair, "The National Career of Blanche Kelso Bruce" (Ph.D. diss., New York Univ., 1947), and William C. Harris, "Blanche K. Bruce of Mississippi: Conservative Assimilationist," in *Southern Black Leaders of the Reconstruction Era*, ed. Howard N. Rabinowitz (1982).

WILLIAM C. HARRIS

BRUCE, Catherine Wolfe (22 Jan. 1816–13 Mar. 1900), benefactor of astronomers and philanthropist, was born in New York City, the daughter of George Bruce, the country's leading typographer, and Catherine Wolfe. Privately educated in New York City, Catherine Bruce resided there all her life, except for periods of travel in Europe. Besides pursuing what might be considered the traditional interests of a wealthy young woman of her time—painting, collecting art and antiquities, touring and learning languages (Latin, French, German, and Italian)—she shared her father's interest in printing and in books, collecting fine typography along with other art.

When Bruce's father died in 1866, he left an estate of over half a million dollars to his three surviving children, of whom Bruce was the oldest. As a memorial to him, she donated $50,000 in 1887 to create the George Bruce Free Library, a branch of the New York Free-Circulating Library (later the New York Public Library). Bruce also provided $10,000 to purchase books for this library. In 1890 she translated and published an edition of the *Dies Irae* of Tommaso da Celano.

Although both Catherine Bruce and her sister Matilda contributed portions of their wealth to museums, parks, and libraries, Catherine distinguished herself, from about 1889 until her death, by regularly donating money for equipment and research to the world's most active astronomers and astrophysicists. She also studied astronomy for her own enjoyment and corresponded with some of the most eminent scientists of her time, including Edward C. Pickering and Simon Newcomb, two of America's most famous astronomers. As a benefactor, Bruce is associated with a number of important projects, including the manufacture of a 24-inch photographic telescope known as the Bruce Telescope, a purchase made possible by her 1889 contribution of $50,000 to the Harvard College Observatory, then directed by Pickering. Also endowed by and named for her was the Bruce Medal, an award presented annually by the Astronomical Society of the Pacific. The first Bruce Medal recipient was Newcomb.

Evidence of her personal enthusiasm for astronomy appears in her correspondence. On 6 November 1890, writing to thank Newcomb for a copy of a technical article he had sent her, she declared herself, at age seventy-four, unable to follow the mathematics. She went on in the same letter to contradict an assertion he had made in another article that astronomers may "be fast approaching the limits of our knowledge." She responded with a show of dismay and also amusement: "My hair stood on end. Such a blow from a friend! I think we are [just] beginning. . . . Think of the great mechanical improvements—think of the double stars rotating around a common centre, of the variable stars . . . you laugh at being as it were lectured by me. The world is young and is probably yet to go through a few more solar cycles." Her dismay at Newcomb's prognosis may have inspired her to continue funding astronomers for the whole of the next decade.

Catherine Bruce's many smaller grants of money provided salaries, bought equipment, paid for travel, and subsidized the publications of many astronomers. In appreciation of her contributions, she received on different occasions two unusual tributes: a gold medal was presented to her by the grand duke of Baden for her support of the Heidelberg Observatory, and, perhaps closer to her heart, a newly discovered asteroid was named after her.

In her later years, Catherine Bruce, who did not marry and whom illness made a recluse, lived with her sister Matilda. In a letter to Newcomb, dated 10 November 1898, Matilda told him that Catherine "has been an invalid for more than five years . . . at times a great sufferer." At her death in New York City, the *Astrophysical Journal* remembered Bruce as "one of the most sympathetic and generous patrons astronomy has ever known," who aided "as perhaps no other has done the progress of research" (Mar. 1900).

• No collection of Bruce's letters or papers is known to exist, although some of her correspondence with prominent astronomers is in the Simon Newcomb Papers at the Library of Congress and the Edward C. Pickering Papers in the archives at Harvard University. The most thorough overview of her life appears in the *New York Tribune*, 23 Mar. 1900, in a letter to the editor in the women's section. See also Solon I. Bailey, *The History and Work of Harvard Observatory* (1931). An obituary of George Bruce appears in the *New York Times*, 8 July 1866, and a description of the Bruce Free Library can be found in the *New York Tribune*, 5 Jan. 1888. See also a notice referring to Catherine Bruce's gifts for research in *Science* 16 (18 July 1890): 34. The most complete list of her philanthropic gifts to astronomers is printed at the end of an obituary in *Popular Astronomy* 8 (May 1900): 235–38.

LYNETTE FLANDERS MOYER

BRUCE, David Kirkpatrick Este (12 Feb. 1898–5 Dec. 1977), diplomat, was born in Baltimore, Maryland, the son of William Cabell Bruce, a writer and U.S. senator, and Louise Este Fisher. Bruce grew up with the internationalist outlook of the southern landed gentry. In April 1917, when the United States entered World War I, he cut short his second year at Princeton University to join the National Guard and was sent to France; before he saw combat, however, the war ended. After the armistice he spent the better part of a year studying at two French universities and serving as a U.S. diplomatic courier, an exposure to European culture that he was later to regard as crucial to his adult mindset. In 1921, after law studies at the Universities of Virginia and Maryland, he entered private legal practice. Three years later, elected from a working-class Baltimore district, he served a term in Maryland's House of Delegates.

In 1926 Bruce married Alisa Mellon, the daughter of Andrew W. Mellon, the wealthy industrialist who was then secretary of the treasury. They had one child. The marriage ended in divorce in 1945. Bruce nevertheless remained a lifelong friend of Alisa and of her brother, Paul Mellon.

Bruce's introduction to diplomatic service came in 1926, when he served briefly in Rome as vice consul. Soon, however, he returned to the United States to help manage the Mellon interests. He spent the years before World War II in business activities, mostly with the Mellons and with W. Averell Harriman, who also became his close friend, and in the management of his 500-acre tobacco plantation in Virginia. At one point he sat on the boards of more than two dozen leading American corporations. Throughout his life he was a connoisseur of fine art, furniture, rare books, and wine. In the late 1930s he helped the Mellons create the National Gallery of Art in Washington and served as its president.

In 1939 Bruce was elected to Virginia's House of Delegates. By then, however, World War II had broken out in Europe. A year later, anticipating U.S. entry into the war, he went to London as chief representative of the American Red Cross. He was soon recruited by William J. Donovan to help set up the Office of Strategic Services (OSS), forerunner of the postwar Central Intelligence Agency (CIA). From 1943 until the end of the war, with the nominal rank of colonel in the U.S. Army Air Corps, Bruce commanded all OSS operations in Europe. He accompanied the first Free French division when it entered Paris to liberate the city in 1944. In 1945 he married Evangeline Bell, herself a diplomat's daughter who had worked with Bruce during the war. A brilliant hostess, she was regarded as a perfect foil for her husband. They had three children.

Bruce's next assignment came in 1947, when Harriman, then commerce secretary, chose him as assistant secretary. A year later, when Harriman became chief of the organization set up to administer Marshall Plan aid, he put Bruce in charge of its Paris office. In 1949 President Harry Truman appointed him ambassador to France, a post to which his knowledge of French language and culture perfectly suited him. Secretary of State Dean Acheson called him back to Washington to serve as under secretary in 1952.

The following year, President Dwight D. Eisenhower sent Bruce back to Paris to observe the committee planning the European Defense Community and to serve as special representative to the newborn European Coal and Steel Community, from which grew the Common Market. Bruce had long admired Jean Monnet, a French businessman who was the leading architect of European integration, and during this time they became daily collaborators. He fully shared Monnet's disappointment when the French National Assembly failed to ratify the Defense Community treaty in 1954.

Bruce returned to private life in Georgetown, District of Columbia, until 1957, when Eisenhower made him ambassador to the Federal Republic of Germany. There he forged a close relationship with Chancellor Konrad Adenauer. However, he resigned at the start of the 1960 election campaign to serve as foreign policy adviser to the Democratic presidential candidate, John F. Kennedy. After the election, President Kennedy appointed Bruce ambassador to London, a post he held for a record eight years, serving three presidents. He enjoyed immense influence with both Conservative and Labor governments and was popular with the British public as well.

Health problems led Bruce to retire temporarily from ambassadorial service in 1969. He returned to service when President Richard M. Nixon appointed him chief negotiator at the Paris peace talks on Vietnam in July 1970. A year later, disappointed at the lack of progress, Bruce resigned. Nixon called him out of retirement again in March 1973 to head the new U.S. liaison office in the People's Republic of China. In September 1974, President Gerald R. Ford gave him his last assignment, ambassador to the North Atlantic Treaty Organization. Suffering from a heart ailment, Bruce retired for the last time in January 1976. He died in Washington, D.C.

Bruce was one of America's premier diplomats. His record of six major ambassadorial assignments under six presidents will surely never be equaled. He was a negotiator and conciliator of legendary skill, a draftsman of brilliantly acute reports, and a consummate host who freely used his own wealth to make his embassies focal points of political and intellectual discourse.

His diaries, reports, and telegrams, and the memoirs of the presidents and secretaries of state he served, all attest to his humane, civilizing influence on foreign policy. A loyal subordinate, he nevertheless did not hesitate to make his chiefs know his personal views. He was an early and constant advocate of European integration, of nuclear arms control, and of severe restraints on the covert operations of the CIA. Although an intensely private man, he operated with unfailing effectiveness in the public arena. A lifelong student of the presidency—the subject of his only book, *Revolution to Reconstruction: A History of American Presidents* (1939)—Bruce saw himself as an aristocratic servant of the Republic willing to accept presidential assignments long after normal retirement age.

• From World War II onward, Bruce kept a copious typescript diary of his official activities. The original is still held by the Department of State; a photocopy, with minor excisions, is in the Virginia Historical Society, Richmond, which also holds Bruce personal papers not yet open to the public. Some of Bruce's letters are available in his mother's papers, also in the Virginia Historical Society. Those of Bruce's diplomatic communications (memoranda, dispatches, telegrams, etc.) thus far declassified may be found in the National Archives and in the official libraries of the presidents he served. Many have been published in the ongoing State Department series, *Foreign Relations of the United States.* Bruce's wartime diaries have been published, with a biographical sketch, in Nelson D. Lankford, ed., *OSS against the Reich* (1991). Information about Bruce and his family is in Joan Mellen's account of the circumstances surrounding his daughter's death, *Privilege: The Enigma of Sasha Bruce* (1982). Detailed obituaries are in the *New York Times* and the *Washington Post*, 6 Dec. 1977.

RICHARD H. ULLMAN

BRUCE, John Edward (22 Feb. 1856–7 Aug. 1924), journalist and historian, was born in Piscataway, Maryland, the son of Martha Allen Clark and Robert Bruce, who were both enslaved Africans. In 1859 Major Harvey Griffin, Robert Bruce's slaveholder, sold him to a Georgia slaveholder. Raised by his mother, Bruce lived in Maryland until 1861 when Union troops marching through Maryland freed him and his mother, taking them to Washington, D.C., where Bruce lived until 1892. In 1865 Bruce's mother worked as a domestic in Stratford, Connecticut, where Bruce received his early education in an integrated school. One year later they returned to Washington, where Bruce continued his education. Although he did not complete high school, he enrolled in a course at Howard University in 1872. Bruce married Lucy Pinkwood, an opera singer from Washington, D.C. They had no children. In 1895 Bruce married Florence Adelaide Bishop, with whom he had one child.

Bruce began his journalistic career at eighteen as a general helper to the Washington correspondent of the *New York Times*. He was also employed as correspondent in New York for John Freeman's *Progressive American*, which published his first article, "The Distillation of Coal Tar." Between 1879 and 1884 Bruce, under the pen name "Rising Sun," started three newspapers: the *Argus* (1879), the *Sunday Item* (1880), which was the first African-American daily, and the *Washington Grit* (1884). Following the publication of the *Grit*, which was known for its frank style, T. Thomas Fortune, editor of the *New York Freeman*, referred to Bruce as "Bruce Grit." In order to maintain financial stability as a journalist, Bruce worked the majority of his life as a messenger in the federal customs house in Westchester, New York, retiring in 1922.

Throughout his life Bruce was an active proponent of African-American civil rights. In 1890 Fortune founded the Afro American League (AAL), a pioneer civil rights organization that supported African-American suffrage. Recognized as a talented speaker, Bruce addressed delegates at the AAL inaugural convention in Washington, D.C. Citing the Constitution, Bruce examined the legal justification of African-American citizenship; he contended that the federal government had failed to protect African-American civil rights, and as long as white violence and African-American disfranchisement continued, "a blot will remain on the escutcheon."

Between 1896 and 1901 Bruce served as an associate editor of *Howard's American Magazine*, for which he published an influential pamphlet, *The Blood Red*

Record. The pamphlet, which was advertised in a number of African-American newspapers, was a condemnation of lynching and racism in the American justice system. Bruce listed the names and "alleged" crimes of more than a hundred African-American men who were killed by white mobs. According to Bruce, whites denied African Americans an opportunity to receive a fair trial. Whites, he argued, received a trial by jury even if they "assassinate the President of the United States." Bruce's scathing remarks on American justice revealed its historical legacy of racism.

After serving as associate editor of *Howard's American Magazine*, Bruce moved to Albany, New York, and worked as a journalist for the *Albany Evening Journal* and the *Times Union*. He also contributed articles to the *New York Age*, the *Cleveland Gazette*, and the *Washington Colored American*, three prominent African-American newspapers. In Albany, Bruce continued to work for African-American civil rights. In 1898 he joined the Afro American Council, founded by Bishop Alexander Walters of the African Methodist Episcopal church. In "Concentration of Energy," Bruce insisted that the only way for African Americans to obtain political and economic power is "with intelligent organization." He urged African Americans to invest in banks owned by African Americans, and he encouraged African-American cooperative economics. In July 1905 W. E. B. Du Bois organized the Niagara Conference to protest Booker T. Washington's accommodationist philosophy and segregation in the South. Bruce, a proponent of African-American civil rights, was invited by Du Bois to attend the conference, but Bruce did not have the money to travel to the historic meeting.

Bruce was an active member in a number of African-American literary societies, such as the American Negro Academy founded by Alexander Crummell, an intellectual and scholar. Bruce believed that African Americans must engage in the realm of ideas because, as he said on the occasion of becoming president of the literary Phalanx Club, "The battle of this race is an intellectual one" and "anybody of earnest and clear-thinking, clear headed men is a potent and powerful force." Moreover, he said, the "secret of power is knowledge" and whites aspire to "repress black men who are seeking this power" ("An Intellectual Battle," 25 Nov. 1915).

Another major interest for Bruce was history. On 18 April 1911 Bruce, along with Arthur Schomburg, a renowned bibliophile, founded the Negro Society for Historical Research (NSHR), which was a precursor of Carter G. Woodson's Association for the Study of African American Life and History. The NSHR sought to "teach, enlighten, and instruct our people in Negro history and achievement" (Ferris, p. 863). Bruce viewed history as a medium to combat intellectual racism and promote racial pride. Before the founding of the NSHR, Bruce published *Short Biographical Sketches of Eminent Negro Men and Women in Europe and the United States* (1910). Designed for children, the text contained short biographies of prominent African-American leaders in order to "awaken race pride."

In addition to his historical and political tracts, Bruce wrote short stories, poems, plays, and one novel, *The Awakening of Hezekiah Jones* (1916). The novel described the life of Jones, an African-American official elected in a southern city. At the end of the novel, Jones experiences an "awakening" and recognizes the political necessity of racial unity. Because Bruce's literary activities mirrored his ideology, his art served a political function.

After World War I Bruce became increasingly disenchanted with the pace of African-American progress. Following the war race riots, lynchings, and racial inequality intensified throughout the nation, and in 1919 Bruce became a major figure in the largest black nationalist organization for people of African descent, Marcus Garvey's Universal Negro Improvement Association (UNIA). Between 1921 and 1923 Bruce served as a contributing editor of Garvey's *Negro World*, his opinions appearing as "Bruce Grit's Column." Five years after joining the UNIA in 1919, Bruce died in Bellevue Hospital in New York City.

Unlike Booker T. Washington, W. E. B. Du Bois, and Marcus Garvey, John Edward Bruce has not received a great deal of scholarly attention despite the fact that he was so well known that 5,000 people attended his funeral. As a distinguished African-American journalist, Bruce's articles were read not only in the United States but throughout the African diaspora. His tenacity and political participation became a model for African-American journalists, historians, and political activists.

• Bruce's papers, including his two books on microfilm, and a brief but informative autobiographical sketch are in the Schomburg Center for Research and Black Culture, New York Public Library. See also *The Selected Writings of John Edward Bruce: Militant Black Journalist*, ed. Peter Gilbert (1971), and Robert Hill, ed., *The Marcus Garvey and Universal Negro Improvement Association Papers* (1983). For biographical information, see I. Garland Penn, *The Afro American Press and Its Editors* (1891), and William H. Ferris, *The African Abroad and His Evolution in Western Civilization* (1913). For a modern assessment of Bruce's life and his influence on black nationalism, see Ralph Crowder, "John Edward Bruce: Pioneer Black Nationalist," *Afro Americans in New York Life and History* 2 (1978): 47–65. On his contribution to pan-Africanism, see George Shepperson, "Notes on Negro American Influences on the Emergence of African Nationalism," *Journal of African History* 1 (1960): 299–312; Tony Martin, *The Pan-African Connection: From Slavery to Garvey and Beyond* (1984); and Milfred C. Fierce, *The Pan African Idea in the United States 1900–1919: African American Interest in Africa and Interaction with West Africa* (1993). Alfred Moss covers Bruce's participation in the American Negro Academy in *The American Negro Academy: The Voice of the Talented Tenth* (1981). On the Niagara Movement, see David Levering Lewis, *W. E. B. Du Bois: A Biography of Race, 1868–1919* (1993). On his contribution to the modern African-American history movement, see Earl Thorpe, *Black Historians: A Critique* (1971); Ralph Crowder, "Self-Taught Street Scholars," *Black Collegian* 9 (1979): 2–22; and Elinor

Des Virney Sinnette et al., *Black Bibliophiles and Collectors: Preservers of Black History* (1990). An obituary is in the *New York Times*, 11 Aug. 1924.

DAVID ALVIN CANTON

BRUCE, Lenny (13 Oct. 1925–3 Aug. 1966), comedian, was born Leonard Alfred Schneider in Mineola, New York, the son of Myron Schneider and Sadie Kitchenburg. Because his father sought a professional occupation, throughout more than twenty years of shoe-clerking he also pursued various other tracks, including law and pharmacy. After World War II Myron Schneider used the GI Bill to complete his education and qualified in California as a physiotherapist, which he combined with his vocation of fitting orthopedic shoes.

Lenny's father often doted on him and imparted a love of reading and knowledge. His mother was a dreamer. She was entranced with the world of show business and sought to become a dancer, eventually changing her name to Sally Marr. Over time she honed her talents on stage as a comedian and performed as Boots Malloy, doing stand-up routines and serving as a master of ceremonies. Her energies and aspirations influenced Lenny's comedic sensibilities, and they were devoted to each other. "I really love her," he acknowledged, "and the reason I dig her is I realize . . . I got a lot of humor from her. She exposed me to many areas that I never would have been hip to." Lenny's parents divorced when he was still a child, and he bounced between them over the years, frequently being shunted off to sets of relatives. "My childhood," he wrote in his autobiography, "seemed like an endless exodus from aunts and uncles and grandmothers. Their dialog still rings in my ears. . . . The plan was I would stay with relatives till my parents 'could get straightened out.'"

A high school dropout at age sixteen, Bruce joined the U.S. Navy early in World War II, but in 1946 he was given a dishonorable discharge when he falsely claimed to possess homosexual obsessions. He then worked at a string of various jobs until he arrived in Hollywood to study acting under the GI Bill. His first stint as a comedian came in a Brooklyn, New York, nightclub, and he performed in burlesque clubs along the eastern seaboard introducing strippers, silencing inebriated customers, and demanding attention from inattentive audiences. In 1949 he achieved recognition winning on Arthur Godfrey's "Talent Scouts," a top-rated television show, by impersonating such Hollywood stars as James Cagney, Edgar G. Robinson, and Peter Lorre. Bruce's nightclub routines, however, were evolving an outlaw style that reflected and vastly extended the new forms of humor that were being created by a younger set of stand-up and stage comedians in the mid-1950s and early 1960s.

In Baltimore in 1951 Bruce met and married Honey Harlowe, a stripper who had been twice-divorced, and subordinated his work to manage her new singing career. To raise money, Bruce fraudulently impersonated a priest, "Father Mathias," claiming himself to be the director of a charitable foundation supporting an African leper colony. He was arrested and charged but received no sentence. Returning to Los Angeles, for several years he performed at various nightclubs, notably the Crescendo, a favorite Sunset Strip nightspot where he developed a following as an ultrahip comic. Harlowe and Bruce had one child, a daughter, Brandie Kathleen. Shortly after their 1957 divorce, however, Bruce moved to eliminate the child's first name because he thought it connoted a stripper's image.

In January 1958 Bruce trekked to Ann's 440, a lesbian club, in North Beach, San Francisco, and later at other popular places such as Fack's No. 2 and the hungry i, where his reputation as an extraordinary comic was solidified. When he appeared the next year at a new Chicago club, the Cloister, he was singled out as the most controversial comedian in the country. He appeared at the Den in the Duane in New York City to similar strife over the nature of his comedic technique. Long-playing records and word-of-mouth spread his particular approach across the country. By the early 1960s Bruce had attained a special place in American comedy, labeled either as a "hipster comic," the most radical of the social satirists, or as the "sickest of the sick" of the new comics. Bruce disputed the label "sick" to describe his or anyone's comedy, arguing that the media-devised term obscured the complexities of contemporary comedy.

Bruce's career coincided with the social rebellions of the 1950s and 1960s, the Beat Generation, and the Counterculture, and he was as controversial as the movements he reflected. In spontaneously crafted routines, he assaulted the barriers of conventional public comedy, expanding its language to include the scatalogical and widening its subject matter. By doing so he incurred the wrath of both religious and civil constituencies. Consequently, Bruce was constantly hounded by law-enforcement officials who frequented his shows and arrested him on charges of obscenity and possession of narcotics. Judges in various cities admonished him for his "lewd" language and religious spoofs. By 1964 many clubs throughout the country refused to book him. In the aftermath of his arrest and subsequent conviction for obscenity in a Greenwich Village nightclub in 1964, however, nearly 100 figures prominent in the arts and intellectual life—mobilized by the Beat poet Allen Ginsberg—came to his defense. They signed a statement describing Bruce as "a popular and controversial performer in the field of social satire in the tradition of Swift, Rabelais and Twain. Although Bruce makes use of the vernacular in his nightclub performances, he does so within the context of his satirical intent and not to arouse the prurient interests of his listeners."

Just short of his forty-first birthday, Bruce was found dead of a heroin overdose in his Hollywood Hills home. The obscenity conviction was overturned eighteen months after his death.

A lean, intense figure on stage, Bruce regarded the nightclub setting of his forays as "the last frontier" of uninhibited entertainment. He brilliantly prodded his audiences in a Socratic, stream-of-consciousness style that ranged widely over the social landscape, unearthing taboos and mining them for their absurdities and contradictions. He contended that "satire is tragedy plus time" and regarded humor as a means of confrontation. He rarely wrote out his routines in advance, relying instead on his own set of experiences and intuitions, particularly his sense of the pulse of American culture. "I never sit down and write anything out," Bruce said. "I've never sat down and typed out a satire. What I will do, is I will *ad lib* a line on the stage. It'll be funny. Then the next night I'll do another line, or I'll be thinking about it, like in a cab, and it'll get some form, and I will work into a bit. Everything I do on the stage I create myself."

The result was either free-form rambling or a highly crafted seriocomedic scenario, improvised like a theme in jazz, changing from one show to another but always fueled with a sense of purpose. Bruce aimed his barbs at organized religion, racial hypocrisy, cultural myths, and the law and during his discourses openly spotlighted stereotypical and taboo terms. In this connection he thought of himself as a neologist, one who either invents new words or discovers new meanings for old ones.

Although Bruce seemed antagonistic toward his audiences, his questioning of society's mores and values was not malicious. He possessed a defined sense of morality undergirded by introspection, and he was acutely aware that he was not innocent of abetting social irrationality. "Sometimes I look at life in the fun mirror at a carnival," Bruce said. "I see myself as a profound, incisive wit, concerned with man's humanity to man. Then I stroll to the next mirror and I see a pompous, subjective ass whose humor is hardly spiritual. I see traces of Mephistopheles. All my humor is based on destruction and despair." As is characteristic of American humor in general, his came from the culture's deeply ingrained irreverence toward authority. His autobiography, published a year before his death, was whimsically titled *How to Talk Dirty and Influence People*, a satirical dig at Dale Carnegie's perennial bestseller *How to Win Friends and Influence People* (1926), which preaches the virtues and power of ingratiating oneself in order to be a social success.

Perhaps paradoxically, Bruce was a quintessential American optimist. What he desired was a democratic order that would be open to a wide range of cultural outlooks. Along with his contemporary Mort Sahl, whose forte was political satire, Bruce transformed the character of publicly performed comedy by bringing into clubs and coffeehouses, as well as incorporating into his records and autobiography, language and subject matter generally considered offensive. His immense influence has been acknowledged by comedians who reached prominence in the later decades of the twentieth century, such as George Carlin, Richard Pryor, and David Steinberg.

A comedic shaman, Lenny Bruce used humor to confront taboos. The laughter that he elicited had a cathartic effect and contributed to the widening range of socially acceptable beliefs and practices. Toward the end of the twentieth century, the shock of his humor—its transgressions of the permissible—no longer sounded dangerously out of bounds. For stand-up comics, his way of expressing himself and his slant on life had become commonplace.

• Bruce's thoughts and observations are in his autobiography, *How to Talk Dirty and Influence People* (1965). John Cohen, ed., *The Essential Lenny Bruce* (1968), is an excellent compilation of the comedian's diverse routines. A substantial biography is Albert Goldman with Lawrence Schiller, *Ladies and Gentlemen, Lenny Bruce!* (1974), but it lacks sources and an index. Frank Kofsky, *Lenny Bruce: The Comedian as Social Critic and Secular Moralist* (1974), is highly thoughtful but limited. Essential interpretations of Bruce's place in American comedy are Tony Hendra, *Going Too Far* (1987), pp. 114–45, and Joseph Dorinson, "Lenny Bruce: A Jewish Humorist in Babylon," *Jewish Currents* (Feb. 1981), pp. 14–32. See also Phil Berger, *The Last Laugh: The World of the Stand-up Comics* (1975). Bruce was the subject of a Broadway play, *Lenny* (1971), by Julian Barry, and a film, *Lenny* (1974), starring Dustin Hoffman. An obituary is in the *New York Times*, 4 Aug. 1966.

JOSEPH BOSKIN

BRUCE, Philip Alexander (7 Mar. 1856–16 Aug. 1933), historian, was born at the Staunton Hill plantation in Charlotte County, Virginia, the sixth child of Charles Bruce and Sarah Alexander Seddon. Among his earliest recollections, he wrote in 1911, were the plantation, the plantation home, and slaves. Although his antebellum years were but five, he was eminently proud of that heritage throughout his life. Bruce received his education at the University of Virginia, where he studied English and history, graduating in 1876, and Harvard Law School. He graduated with the LL.B. in 1878.

Steeped in the glorious tradition of the Old South, Bruce was disillusioned as a young man by the mounting problems that faced the post–Civil War South. Convinced that industrialization was the only cure for the South's economic woes, he devoted much of his early work to the dissemination of the New South gospel of Henry W. Grady and others. To Bruce, the free black seemed to be a major stumbling block for a region beginning the long climb back. His study of this "obstacle" led to his first book, *The Plantation Negro as a Freeman* (1889). At the time, Bruce maintained that blacks constituted a permanently inferior race, which could fill the need for unskilled labor when supervised by whites. By the 1920s, however, Bruce—perhaps simply reporting what he observed—held that blacks could rise to the level of whites if given education and sympathetic treatment.

By the mid-1880s, Bruce found that he lacked a strong inclination toward the practice of law. In 1887 he became the secretary-treasurer of his brother's Vulcan Iron Works in Richmond. In 1890 he moved on to join the editorial staff of the Richmond *Times*, where his work ran the gamut from commentary against women in the pulpit to editorials on the "Negro problem." All the while, Bruce found himself slowly drifting from the active life into scholarly pursuits. He left the *Times* in 1892 and became the corresponding secretary of the Virginia Historical Society. The following year he helped found the society's *Virginia Magazine of History and Biography* and became its first editor. He held both positions until 1898.

In his own historical research, Bruce quickly concluded that the basis of the society he had known in his youth lay in the seventeenth century. The result of years of intensive research and writing, his *Economic History of Virginia in the Seventeenth Century* was published in two volumes in 1895 and 1896; it examined Seventeenth-century history through the lens of late–nineteenth-century New South optimism. The work met a mixed reception from critics, yet Bruce was happy. In the course of his research, he had developed a taste for history that was never to leave him.

In October of 1896 Bruce married Elizabeth Tunstall Taylor Newton of Norfolk, Virginia. The couple had one child. In 1898 Bruce took a research trip to Great Britain. While there he wrote articles explaining the New South and the "Negro problem" to British readers. In 1905 Bruce published *The Rise of the New South*, which was well received. Marked by rampant optimism, it reads like an industrial gazetteer of the South, foretelling further southern progress and prosperity based on economic, social, and political accomplishments since 1877. The book established Bruce as a pioneer of the New South school of historians and stands as the capstone of the New South crusade.

In 1907 Bruce and his family returned to the United States, taking up residence in Norfolk, Virginia. His mother had died early that year, and upon division of the Staunton Hill estate he received 1,402 acres of hill and lowland and a modest personal income. Coupled with his earnings from writing, editing, and reviewing, this inheritance was to provide Bruce with his long-sought sense of financial security. Bruce's straightforward *Robert E. Lee* was published in 1907, as was the second part of his trilogy, *Social Life of Virginia in the Seventeenth Century*, in which he traced the origin of Virginia's planters to the squirearchy and the mercantile class.

The years 1903 through 1907 can be seen as marking a major change in Bruce's scholarly interests. He became more and more preoccupied with the glories of the southern and Virginian past—with the myth of the Old South. Work on the Virginia trilogy continued. In 1910 the third part was completed and published as the two-volume *Institutional History of Virginia in the Seventeenth Century*, in which he treated many facets of early Virginian life: religion and morals, education, legal administration, the military system, and political conditions. Considering all five of Bruce's volumes on seventeenth-century Virginia together, the *American Historical Review* cited the "flood of enlightenment" resulting from the author's "hard work and erudition."

In 1916 Bruce took up residence in Charlottesville, having accepted the position as centennial historian of the University of Virginia. Soon after his arrival, his *Brave Deeds of Confederate Soldiers* (1916) was published. This work unmistakably reflects his allegiance to the mythology and symbolism of the Old South and the Lost Cause. After four years of research and writing, Bruce published the first two volumes of his history of the University of Virginia in 1920. Three more volumes followed, the last appearing in January of 1922. Bruce dealt with the university as an institution of culture and learning about which centered much of Virginia's history. His subtitle for the work, "The Lengthened Shadow of One Man," summed up his belief that Thomas Jefferson's influence had been pervasive throughout the university's history. Published in two volumes in 1929, Bruce's last major work, *The Virginia Plutarch*, consists of sketches of those individuals he considered most important in Virginia's history. From 1930 until his death, Bruce was ill for extended periods. He died at his home in Charlottesville and was buried in the University of Virginia cemetery.

Though much of Bruce's writing was ephemeral, and though his racial and class theories are now outmoded, he holds an important place among writers of the history of the United States. His five volumes on the economic, institutional, and social history of seventeenth-century Virginia are still cited as standard references because Bruce was painstaking in his research and a pioneer in the use of colonial court records as a source of historical interpretation. If for no other reason, Bruce's Virginia trilogy earned him the respect and admiration of his profession.

• Bruce's papers are at the Alderman Library, University of Virginia, Charlottesville, and the Virginia Historical Society, Richmond. Materials dealing with Bruce and his writings can be found in L. Moody Simms, Jr., "Philip Alexander Bruce: His Life and Works" (Ph.D. diss., Univ. of Virginia, 1966), "A Childhood at Staunton Hill," *Virginia Cavalcade* 16 (Autumn 1966): 23–8, "Philip Alexander Bruce and the New South," *Mississippi Quarterly* 19 (Fall 1966): 171–83, "Philip Alexander Bruce and the Negro Problem, 1884–1930," *Virginia Magazine of History and Biography* 75 (July 1967): 349–62, "History as Inspiration: Philip Alexander Bruce and the Old South Mystique," *McNeese Review* 18 (1967): 3–10, and "Philip Alexander Bruce: The Charlottesville Years," *Magazine of Albemarle County History* 29 (1971): 69–79.

L. MOODY SIMMS, JR.

BRUCE, William Cabell (12 Mar. 1860–9 May 1946), author, municipal politician, reformer, and U.S. senator, was born at "Staunton Hill," his father's plantation, in Charlotte County, Virginia, the son of Charles Bruce, a planter, Virginia state senator, and captain during the Civil War, and Sarah Alexander Seddon, both members of established, affluent families in Virginia. Although the Bruce family lost much of their wealth during the Civil War, William still grew up surrounded by maids, servants, tailors, and tutors. Bruce's mother, a devout Christian, instilled in William strong religious beliefs that influenced his character throughout his formative years.

After William finished private school in the local community—King William and Nelson counties—he enrolled in 1879 at the University of Virginia but left the next year to study law at the University of Maryland Law School, in Baltimore. During his brief time at the University of Virginia, he was awarded the Jefferson Society Medal and another award for the best essay in the university's magazine. Among those who competed with Bruce for these awards was Woodrow Wilson, a fellow student at Virginia.

In 1882 Bruce received his LL.B. from the University of Maryland School of Law and began to practice law in Baltimore. He and William A. Fisher, a local municipal judge, in 1887 formed the law firm of Fisher, Bruce and Fisher. In October 1887 Bruce married Louise Este Fisher, the daughter of his senior partner. They had three sons, two of whom survived to maturity.

Politically, Bruce characterized himself as a Jeffersonian Republican and a moderate Democrat. He became active in local politics as the spirit of governmental reform emerged throughout both the city of Baltimore and the state of Maryland. Moreover, in the late 1880s, he joined the Baltimore Reform League. In 1893 Bruce initiated a political challenge to the local Democratic machine of Arthur Pue Gorman. This challenge propelled him into the Maryland State Senate and eventually led to his election as its president. As senate president Bruce helped to pass into law several major reform bills in the areas of civil service and election law. However, when the Democratic machine regained control of the General Assembly in 1897, Bruce decided not to seek reelection. Instead, he returned to his local law practice.

In 1901 Bruce became the general counsel for the local gas and utility company of Baltimore. In 1903 Robert McLane, the newly elected reformist mayor, appointed Bruce head of the Baltimore City Law Department and city solicitor. During the next five years, Bruce wrote several statutes that introduced a plan to sell city bonds for municipal improvements. In 1909 Bruce was appointed one of nine commissioners selected to draft a proposal to strengthen the power of the city government, to increase governmental efficiency, to enhance city services, and to eliminate the influence of upper-class citizens on municipal affairs. These proposals, however, were not fully adopted. One of the proposals that was enacted sought to separate and balance the political functions and governing powers of the city council and the Boards of Estimates and Awards. Another enacted proposal enhanced the power of the city council. In the following year, Governor Austin L. Crothers named Bruce the first general counsel for the newly formed Public Service Commission, created to regulate the rates charged by public utilities companies to the citizens of the state of Maryland. Bruce held this position until 1922.

In 1922 Bruce was elected to the U.S. Senate. During his single term as a Democratic senator from Maryland, Bruce won national acclaim as a reformer and an advocate of progressivism. He argued against the expansion of powers from the federal government. He also fought against Prohibition, became an intense opponent of the Ku Klux Klan, and advocated an antilynching bill. Bruce asserted that both Prohibition and the Klan were characteristics of a nation based on bigotry and immorality.

Bruce's hopes for a second term in the Senate ended in 1928 when he was defeated by a nationwide Republican landslide. Returning to his Baltimore law practice, Bruce gradually moved away from the Democratic party. In 1936 he opposed the reelection of Franklin D. Roosevelt.

In between his political appointments and elections, Bruce engaged in historical writing. His biography *Benjamin Franklin, Self-Revealed* (1917) won the Pulitzer Prize for its depth and critical insight. His other writings included *Below the James* (1918) and *John Randolph of Roanoke* (1922).

Bruce was a member of the Baltimore, the Maryland, and the American bar associations and of the Maryland Historical Society and several other historical associations throughout the state. In 1937 Bruce retired from his law practice. He spent his retirement years working on a biography of Thomas Jefferson that he never completed. He died in Baltimore.

• The Bruce papers are at the Alderman Library of the University of Virginia. Kent State University Library has several of Bruce's little-known addresses, political writings, and speeches. Genealogical information is in Alexander Brown, *The Cabells and Their Kin* (1805). The most complete assessment of Bruce's life and work is his own book *Recollections* (1931). An analysis of the early political career of Bruce is James B. Crooks, *Politics and Progress: The Rise of Urban Progressivism in Baltimore, 1895 to 1911* (1968). His record as a U.S. senator can be found in the *New York Times* and Congressional Record indexes. An obituary is in the *New York Times*, 10 May 1946.

ERIC R. JACKSON

BRUCKER, Herbert (4 Oct. 1898–5 Apr. 1977), newspaper editor, syndicated columnist, and teacher, was born in Passaic, New Jersey, the son of Carl Brucker, the head of Fritzsche Bros., U.S. division of Schimmel & Cie., a German chemical company, and Adele Balthasar. After graduating from Williams College, Williamstown, Massachusetts, in 1921, Brucker reported for the *Springfield* (Mass.) *Union* and then studied journalism at Columbia University, earning a bachelor of letters degree in 1924.

Following a year in Europe on a Pulitzer Fellowship, he joined the *New York World* as a reporter and then worked on the editorial staffs of two national magazines, the *World's Work* (1926–1927) and the *Review of Reviews* (1927–1932). He returned to Columbia in 1932 as assistant to the dean of the journalism school. He added teaching duties as assistant professor (1933–1935), associate professor (1935–1942), and full professor (1942–1944). On leave from 1942 to 1944, he served as chief of the Media Division and associate chief of the Bureau of Overseas Publications of the Office of War Information. He assumed the associate editorship of the *Hartford* (Conn.) *Courant* in 1944 and served as editor from 1947 to 1966.

Brucker was one of journalism's most outspoken defenders of press freedom and the "precious right" of the people to have access to the truth. In his editorials, syndicated column, and four books on the press, he emphasized the interdependence of democracy, press freedom, and open government. "We can't have government by the people and for the people," he said, "unless the people know what the government is doing." From 1956 to 1959 Brucker chaired the Freedom of Information Committee of the American Society of Newspaper Editors, and in 1963–1964 he served as ASNE's president. He also presided over the American Council on Education for Journalism (1959–1962). He had a reputation for leadership and, as a *Courant* editorial noted, for "physical, intellectual and moral courage."

In 1956 Brucker fought the ban by the Eisenhower administration on travel to China by U.S. journalists, verbally confronting Secretary of State John Foster Dulles. In a 1951 *Courant* editorial, he was among the first editors in the nation to call for Senator Joseph R. McCarthy's resignation. Brucker wrote that "political life in this country would be healthier were Mr. McCarthy to leave it." Brucker believed in writing strong editorials, and he criticized editorial pages that were "so much boiled watermelon."

Despite heavy opposition from the Catholic church, he editorialized against Connecticut's ban on birth control, helping eventually to repeal that law. He also led successful fights against the sale of fireworks in Connecticut and for fluoridation of the public water supply. A liberal Republican, he lamented the *Courant*'s decision to go "to ridiculous lengths to pussyfoot on Nixon and Watergate." In a 30 May 1974 column he criticized the sleaziness of Richard M. Nixon's oval office conversations. "It is made of hatred and meanness and vengeance" Brucker wrote, "of a conspiratorial air, an imperviousness to moral standards, a readiness to corrupt the integrity of government to maintain personal power."

From his first book, *The Changing American Newspaper* (1937), to his last, *Communication Is Power* (1973), Brucker questioned the newspaper establishment of which he was a member. He worried that the concentration in ownership of the news media meant increasingly that "money controls journalism." And he cautioned against the news media turning into the "mob media whenever a spectacular event comes along." To Brucker every event should be presented factually and with "dignity and decorum." In 1974, when he critiqued a half-dozen newspapers as part of the book-length New England Daily Newspaper Survey, he argued that other evaluators' critiques were burdened by "a supercilious and disdainful attitude." He preferred dignified dissection to "snotty denunciation."

After retirement, Brucker wrote a weekly syndicated column and spent three years organizing and operating the Stanford University Fellowships for Professional Journalists program. He worked almost nonstop during his so-called retirement years despite several eye operations and a seven-year bout with cancer. In 1975 Governor Ella Grasso named him the first chairman of Connecticut's pioneering Freedom of Information Commission. He resigned only two weeks before his death in Hartford Hospital, explaining that he was terminally ill with cancer. He went public about his cancer, he said, to encourage openness toward the disease.

Friends labeled Brucker an intellectual, more a philosophy professor (which he once aspired to be) than a *Front Page*–style, tough-talking newsman. Dwight E. Sargent, editorial editor of the defunct *New York Herald Tribune*, described Brucker as having the "bearing of a Senator, the conscience of a Congregational minister, the literacy of a college president and the restless mind of a good lawyer." A *Courant* writer capsulized Brucker as "a six-footer, lean as hickory, with a craggy look, laconic in speech, urbane in manner, whose interests ranged from the Federalist Papers to fast sports cars and fast ski slopes."

Brucker married Sydney Seabury Cook in 1926; they had three children. She died in 1950. He married his second wife, Elizabeth Spock Dominick, in 1951.

• Brucker's papers are stored in the Archive of Contemporary History at the library of the University of Wyoming, Laramie. His other books are *Freedom of Information* (1948) and *Journalist: Eyewitness to History* (1962). The most detailed obituary is in the *Hartford* (Conn.) *Courant*, 6 Apr. 1977.

LOREN GHIGLIONE

BRUCKER, Wilber Marion (23 June 1894–28 Oct. 1968), governor of Michigan and secretary of the army, was born in Saginaw, Michigan, the son of Ferdinand Brucker, a lawyer and politician, and Roberta Hawn. Brucker attended local public schools and then enrolled at the University of Michigan, where he excelled in debating and graduated with the LL.B. in 1916. He passed his Michigan bar exams that same year.

After graduation Brucker enlisted in the Michigan National Guard in 1916. While a member of the guard, he participated in the American expedition against the forces of Pancho Villa along the United States–Mexico border. During World War I Brucker served in the U.S. Army and saw combat in the major Allied offensives at Aisne-Marne, Saint-Mihiel, and Meuse-Argonne. He received the Silver Star in recognition of his bravery in combat.

Brucker returned to Saginaw after the war and resumed his law practice. He also chose to enter Republican politics and, beginning in 1922, was elected to a number of local and state offices. In 1923 Brucker married Clara Hantel; they had one child. In 1928 Brucker won election as Michigan's attorney general and began establishing a record in the field of law enforcement.

By this time, Brucker's political ambitions went well beyond the attorney general's office, and in 1930 he won the Republican nomination for governor. In the fall campaign Brucker defeated his Democratic opponent, William A. Comstock, by a comfortable margin of 126,236 votes (483,900 to 357,664). His victory margin, however, was the smallest of any Republican candidate for governor since 1918 and signified a weakening of the GOP's political stronghold on the state of Michigan. Nevertheless, Brucker had managed to become the governor of a major industrial state at the young age of thirty-six, and he appeared to have a bright political future ahead.

Brucker became governor just as Michigan was being gripped by the Great Depression. Between 1929 and 1933 automobile production in the state declined from five million units to two million. By 1932 unemployment in the nonagricultural sector of the workforce stood at 43 percent. Bank failures threatened the entire state economy. By 1932 50 percent of Michiganites was receiving some sort of public assistance.

Like President Herbert Hoover, Brucker was criticized by his opponents for failing to understand the severity of the economic crisis and then failing to develop effective measures to deal with it. Between 1930 and 1932 Michigan spent more than $30 million to provide assistance to unemployed workers, but about 80 percent of those funds came from local government. When Brucker stood for reelection in 1932, he lost convincingly to Comstock, his rival from 1930, by a margin of more than 190,000 votes (887,672 to 696,935). Brucker thereby became the first Michigan Republican since 1852 to lose a race for governor. The depression had broken the Republican stronghold on state government.

After he failed to win reelection Brucker moved to Detroit and resumed practicing law. He maintained his interest and involvement in Michigan politics, however. Brucker returned to the political scene in 1936 as the Republican candidate for the U.S. Senate, but he lost to Congressman Prentiss Brown, a strong Democrat from northern Michigan. Following that defeat, Brucker confined his political activity to fundraising, candidate recruitment, and party organization for the next sixteen years.

In 1954 Brucker returned once again to full-time politics but this time at the national level. After Dwight D. Eisenhower won the presidency in 1952, he had nominated Charles E. Wilson, president of General Motors from 1941 to 1952, as secretary of defense. In 1954 Wilson appointed Brucker, whom he had known from his years in Detroit, as general counsel of the Defense Department. Brucker soon discovered that he had walked into a hornet's nest. The Army-McCarthy hearings were under way, and Brucker faced the challenge of preparing the defense of the service against the claims of Senator Joseph R. McCarthy (R.-Wisc.) that it was "coddling Communists." Brucker proved to be an effective member of Wilson's team, nevertheless, and earned the respect of the army's military leadership for his defense strategy and for his work in strengthening the service's security program.

In 1955, on Wilson's recommendation, President Eisenhower nominated Brucker for the post of secretary of the army; the nomination was greeted skeptically by some in the army leadership. As General Maxwell D. Taylor, army chief of staff from 1955 to 1959, later explained: "My first reaction to [Brucker's] appointment was negative, as it appeared that Secretary of Defense Wilson had reached into the ranks of his official family to get a safe man to run the Army in accordance with Wilson's predilections. Experience soon proved, however, that whatever the motive behind the appointment the consequences feared did not ensue. Brucker was too honorable a man to yield to unjustified pressure and developed into a stalwart defender of the Army's role in national security" (Taylor, p. 167).

Brucker's tenure as secretary of the army lasted from 1955 to 1961. In the words of Thomas S. Gates, who served both as secretary of the navy and secretary of defense while Brucker led the army, Brucker "could always be counted upon to fight to the last penny for the Army in budget meetings" (Gates interview with author, 25 Jan. 1982). John S. D. Eisenhower, still in uniform during the 1950s and a member of the president's staff toward the end of the administration, also commented that the army leadership "wished the rest of the Administration would pay more attention to [Brucker]" (Eisenhower interview with author, 11 Feb. 1982).

Unfortunately for both Brucker and the army, however, the Eisenhower administration's "New Look" defense policy placed a higher priority on a tight federal budget and a greater reliance on strategic capability than it did on the army's traditional emphasis on preparedness for conventional war. Eisenhower and his secretaries of defense as well as the chairmen of the Joint Chiefs of Staff pursued "more bang for the buck." As a consequence, on Brucker's watch the army's role in national security policy diminished, in terms of both its levels of manpower and percentage of funding and the attractiveness of its military doctrine of "Flexible Response." Between 1954 and 1959 Eisenhower's New Look defense budget reduced the army's manpower by almost 150,000 men, and the service received only limited funding to modernize its aging weapons and equipment.

Occasionally Brucker broke ranks with the administration when he believed that the army was being short-changed in its funding requests. For example, in 1956 Brucker testified before the Senate Subcommittee on Defense Appropriations that the administration's proposed budget left the service seriously deficient in its ability to airlift troops to trouble spots in certain key areas around the world, such as the Middle East. Also, in 1960 he provoked a bitter dispute with Secretary Gates by failing to support publicly the administration's decision to remove army dependents from American posts in Europe, an action that led Gates to reprimand him.

Despite the budget constraints under which the army operated during Brucker's tenure as its secretary, the service nevertheless made progress in the late 1950s. The army developed its own successful ballistic missile program, it reorganized its combat divisions to develop a capability for contributing to America's strategic (nuclear) arsenal as well as participating in conventional wars, and it strengthened its Ready Reserve force as a supplement to the loss of several permanent divisions. In 1957 Brucker also won approval for the army's role in keeping the peace during the desegregation of the public schools in Little Rock, Arkansas.

Brucker returned to Detroit after the end of the Eisenhower administration. He remained active in his law practice and also participated in numerous civic and philanthropic programs. Brucker, who died in Detroit, proved himself to be an energetic public official whose success was limited by the difficult circumstances that he encountered on taking office, first as governor of Michigan during the Great Depression and later as secretary of the army during the New Look days of the Pentagon in the 1950s.

• Brucker's papers are at the University of Michigan library. For additional information on Brucker, see F. Cleaver Bald, *Michigan in Four Centuries* (1954); James Gavin, *War and Peace in the Space Age* (1958); Willis F. Dunbar, *Michigan: A History of the Wolverine State* (1965); Dwight D. Eisenhower, *Waging Peace: The White House Years, 1956–1960* (1965); Maxwell D. Taylor, *Swords and Plowshares* (1972); Richard A. Aliano, *American Defense Policy from Eisenhower to Kennedy* (1975); Robert Sohel and John Raino, eds., "Wilbur M. Brucker," in *Biographical Directory of Governors of the United States* (1978); and E. Bruce Geelhoed, *Charles E. Wilson and Controversy at the Pentagon, 1953–1957* (1979).

E. BRUCE GEELHOED

BRUHN, Erik (3 Oct 1928–1 Apr. 1986), ballet dancer and ballet director, was born Erik Belton Evers Bruhn in Copenhagen, Denmark, the son of Ernst Bruhn and Ellen Evers. His mother owned and operated an exclusive hairdressing establishment, Evers Hairdressing Salon, at Kobmagergade 16; his father, originally an irrigation engineer, failed at a number of business ventures after suffering ill effects from malaria contracted while working in Russia before the Revolution, and for much of his adult life he was essentially without a profession. The couple separated when their son was five years old.

Bruhn was accepted by the famed Royal Danish Ballet School, which provided academic as well as dance education, in the fall of 1937. Ten years later he was taken into the parent company, the Royal Danish Ballet, but soon began a pattern of extended guest appearances with other troupes, punctuated by return engagements with his home company. This behavior was unprecedented in Denmark, where absolute loyalty to the system was a prerequisite to entering the company (dancers wishing to perform elsewhere had to resign from the Royal Danish Ballet and give up lifetime security). Bruhn's extraordinary talent permitted him leaves of absence denied others. Over the course of his career, in addition to the Royal Danish Ballet, he performed with the Metropolitan Ballet, London (1947–1949); American Ballet Theatre (1949–late 1970s); New York City Ballet (1959–1960); Royal Ballet, London (1962); Stuttgart Ballet (1962); Australian Ballet (1962); La Scala Ballet (1962); Harkness Ballet (1964); and the National Ballet of Canada (off and on from 1965), among others.

Bruhn's finely chiseled blond looks, nobility of bearing, and pure, highly polished classical dance technique made him the epitome of the Prince figure. Although his reputation was mostly based on a fairly conservative repertory—the standard classics such as *Swan Lake*, *Giselle*, and *La Sylphide*—his restless (and unconservative) desire to dance with many companies and ballerinas led to worldwide exposure. With hindsight, he can be recognized as the first genuine male superstar in the classical dance field to emerge after World War II, although his stature in this regard was somewhat overshadowed for a time when, starting in the 1960s, the Soviet defectors Rudolf Nureyev, Natalia Makarova, and Mikhail Baryshnikov made headlines around the world. A large touring company such as American Ballet Theatre, with which he performed off and on for almost thirty years (his longest tenure anywhere), provided an ideal venue for his talents, as the company regularly mounted lavish productions of the classics, performed in large and gilded theaters and opera houses, and attracted other dancers of the highest caliber, thus projecting an image of glamor as well as respect for tradition. In Bruhn's opinion, "My real breakthrough as a dancer took place in America. . . . It was a revelation because I was exposed to so many kinds of dancing. . . . I must admit, however, that as much as I wanted to join in some . . . modern classes, I didn't dare, because I did not wish to break the classical discipline" (Gruen, *Private World*, p. 270).

Bruhn's partners were some of the most renowned ballerinas of the age and included Alicia Markova, Alicia Alonso, Natalia Makarova, and Maria Tallchief. His partnership with the Italian ballerina Carla Fracci was the most celebrated: her dark coloring and delicate manner contrasted with his Nordic bearing and natural elegance and made them ideally suited for leads in Romantic ballets, notably *Giselle* and *La Sylphide*. As he told *New York Times* dance critic Anna Kisselgoff (27 Dec. 1968), "It is Carla who keeps me alive as a dancer. I don't hold back. I'm dancing for [her]."

Bruhn had a moody streak and confessed that the pressure to be the "perfect" princely figure at every performance was enormous; in 1972 he abruptly retired, citing the strain, but three years later, after treatment for an ulcer, he returned to the stage and proved himself a brilliant dance-actor in such ballets as *Petrouchka* and *The Moor's Pavane*. Until the end of his life he continued to appear on stage as Madge the Witch in *La Sylphide*, a character role.

Bruhn choreographed a few works, but his talents lay rather in restaging the classics, which he did for companies around the world. His production of *Swan Lake* for the National Ballet of Canada in 1967 was particularly controversial, as he greatly enlarged the role of the Prince (foreshadowing Nureyev's reworking of a number of classics to give greater emphasis to the male) and changed von Rothbart the sorcerer from a man into a woman, the alter ego of the Prince's mother. As director, Bruhn endured a stormy tenure with the Royal Swedish Ballet (1967–1971), then found his true artistic home with the National Ballet of Canada, where he was resident producer from 1973 to 1976 and a much-loved artistic director from 1983 until his death.

Bruhn was an exceptionally tasteful and thoughtful performer, qualities reflected in his important monograph, *Beyond Technique* (Dance Perspectives no. 36 [1968]), in which he eloquently discussed aspects of artistic performance that transcend technical proficiency, or in his own case, technical perfection. With the dance historian Lillian Moore he also wrote *Bournonville and Ballet Technique* (1961), a study of the chief architect of Danish ballet technique and repertory, August Bournonville. Bruhn received numerous awards, including the title Knight of Dannebrog in his native land; the Literis et Artibus Medal, Stockholm; and the *Dance Magazine* Award, New York. Bruhn, who never married, died in Toronto of lung cancer.

• Assessments of Bruhn as a performer and artistic director can be found in newspaper reviews, magazines, and journals covering his and his companies' appearances throughout Europe and the United States during the period of his long career, 1947 to 1986. Bruhn also gave numerous interviews. Two books containing interviews are John Gruen, *The Private World of Ballet* (1975) and *People Who Dance* (1988). For a biography consult Gruen, *Erik Bruhn: Danseur Noble* (1979). An assessment of Bruhn's place among the great male ballet dancers of the twentieth century can be found in Alexander Bland and John Percival, *Men Dancing: Performers and Performing* (1984). Although Bruhn's performing career occurred mainly before the age of video, footage of his dancing in *La Sylphide* (with Fracci), *Giselle* (with Fracci), and *Swan Lake*, as well as of his stagings of *Swan Lake* (1967) and *Napoli* (1965), is housed in the Dance Collection, New York Public Library for the Performing Arts, Lincoln Center. He was also the subject of a Danish television feature, *Erik Bruhn: Artist of the Ballet* (1971).

NANCY REYNOLDS

BRUMIDI, Constantino (26 July 1805–19 Feb. 1880), mural painter, was born in Rome, Italy, the son of Stauros Brumidi, a coffee shop owner from Greece, and Anna Bianchini. Beginning at age thirteen, Brumidi studied for fourteen years, at the Accademia di San Luca under sculptors Bertel Thorwaldsen and Antonio Canova and painters Vincenzo Camuccini and Filippo Agricola. Trained in the full range of painting mediums, including true fresco, he gained a mastery of the human figure and of using light, shadow, and color to create forms that appear three-dimensional. He also developed a repertory of poses and allegorical symbols. He made sculptures for the Clifford-Weld Chapel in the Church of San Marcello al Corso in 1837 and for Count Maxwell in England.

In Rome, Brumidi was part of the team that decorated Prince Alessandro Torlonia's palace on the Palazzo Venezia beginning in 1836. From 1842 to 1844 he created paintings for the Gothic-style family chapel in the palace (unfortunately demolished in 1900). At the Villa Torlonia on the Via Nomentana, Brumidi is thought to have been in charge of decorating the new theater, where murals he signed and dated in 1844 and 1845 have recently been discovered. The walls of the theater's numerous rooms are lavishly covered with trompe l'oeil architectural forms and classical motifs that he later adapted for the U.S. Capitol.

Brumidi also worked extensively for the church. From 1840 to 1842 he restored for Pope Gregory XVI, one bay of the third loggia, painted by followers of Raphael, in the Vatican Palace. He also painted the portrait of Pope Pius IX, worked in the papal residence, and was commissioned to create portraits of fifteen popes as models for mosaics at Saint Paul's Outside the Walls. His last commission in Rome was for the murals in the tiny Church of the Madonna dell'Archetto dedicated in 1851.

Brumidi was made captain in the civic guard created by Pius IX in 1847. The following year in the midst of an uprising the pope fled the city and in 1849 a republic was declared. During the turmoil, Brumidi moved valuable objects (art and furniture) from a monastery for protection. After the pope was restored to power, Brumidi was among many arrested and accused by the pope's tribunal of larceny, extortion, and other serious crimes. Despite many testimonies in his favor, he was sentenced to eighteen years in prison. He was pardoned on condition that he leave Rome for America, where he was already promised a commission for St. Stephen's Church in New York City.

Arriving in New York City in September 1852, Brumidi immediately applied for citizenship, which was granted in 1857. His first of many important New World Catholic church commissions was an altarpiece for the Mexico City cathedral, painted in 1854. The next year, he painted an altarpiece for the new building of St. Stephen's Church, where he worked again between 1866 and 1872. He created altarpieces for the Church of St. Ignatius in Baltimore, Maryland (1856), and the Church of St. Aloysius in Washington, D.C. (1859), as well as frescoes in the Cathedral of Saints Peter and Paul in Philadelphia, Pennsylvania, dedicated in 1864. He worked in the cathedral in Havana, Cuba, in 1867.

Brumidi's work at the Capitol began with his 1854 introduction to Captain Montgomery C. Meigs, who superintended construction and decoration of the Capitol extensions and dome designed by Thomas U. Walter. Meigs allowed Brumidi to paint a sample fresco in his Capitol office (now room H-144). This work was well received, and Meigs hired Brumidi to complete the decoration of the room in fresco and to make designs for the most important of the other new rooms. Brumidi worked with teams of artists of varied national origins to carry out his designs, executing all of the true frescoes himself. His murals throughout the building combine classical and allegorical subjects with portraits and scenes from American history and tributes to American inventions. He also created and executed designs for the Hall of the House of Representatives, the Senate Library (S-211), the Senate Military Affairs Committee room (S-128), the office of the Senate Sergeant at Arms (S-212), and the President's Room (S-216).

Because of scheduling and financial constraints, Brumidi was never allowed to complete his designs in many rooms. Blank spaces still remain, for example, in the room for the Senate Committee on Naval Affairs (S-127), the Senate first-floor corridors, and the Senate Reception Room (S-213), one of the most lavishly decorated spaces in the Capitol.

Brumidi had married twice while in Rome during the 1830s, to Maria Covaluzzi in 1832 and to Anna Rovelli in 1838; he had one child from each of these marriages. He also had one son, painter Laurence S. Brumidi, with Lola Germon. It is believed, although not certain, that Brumidi and Germon married around 1860.

Brumidi worked intensively at the Capitol through the early 1860s into the 1870s. His major contributions are the monumental canopy and frieze of the new cast-iron Capitol dome. The canopy over the rotunda comprises *The Apotheosis of Washington*, which he painted in fresco in 1865. He began painting the frieze depicting major events in American history in 1878; it was less than half finished when he died in Washington, D.C. His designs were carried out by Filippo Costaggini between 1881 and 1889, although the entire frieze was not completed until 1953.

In 1985 the Architect of the Capitol established a program to systematically clean Brumidi's murals of grime, discolored coatings, and heavy-handed overpainting. The conservation efforts revealed the beauty and quality of Brumidi's work. He was a master in the academic tradition grounded in ancient Roman art and Raphael. He was also an expert in a wide range of mural techniques and in creating the illusion of three-dimensional forms on a flat surface through his understanding of light and color. In the Capitol, he created a unique synthesis of classical symbols with American history.

• Correspondence and official transactions with Brumidi are preserved in the Records of the Architect of the Capitol and the National Archives and Records Administration, Washington, D.C., as well as in the Journals of Montgomery C. Meigs, Manuscript Division, Library of Congress, as transcribed by William Mohr for the United States Senate Bicentennial Commission. Early books describing his work include Samuel D. Wyeth, *The Federal City* (1865); B. Randolph Keim, *Keim's Capitol Interior and Diagrams* (1875); George Hazelton, Jr., *The National Capitol* (1897); and Charles E. Fairman, *Art and Artists of the Capitol of the United States of America* (1927). The pioneering monograph on the artist is Myrtle Cheney Murdock, *Constantino Brumidi: Michelangelo of the United States Capitol* (1950). Research on Brumidi in Italy is summarized by Alberta Campitelli and Barbara Steindl in "Costantino Brumidi da Roma a Washington: Vicende e opere di un artist romano," *Richerche di Storia Dell'Arte: Pittori fra Rivoluzione e Restaurazione* (1992). See also Barbara A. Wolanin, *Constantino Brumidi: Artist of the Capitol* (1998). An obituary is in the *Washington Post*, 20 Feb. 1880.

BARBARA A. WOLANIN

BRUNAUER, Esther (7 July 1901–26 June 1959), international affairs specialist and State Department official, was born Esther Delia Caukin near Jackson, California, the daughter of Ray Oakheart Caukin, an electrician, and Grace Elizabeth Blackwell, a suffragist and, later, a federal employee. Esther attended Mills College where she earned an A.B. in 1924. Three years later she received a Ph.D. in modern European history and international politics from Stanford University.

Immediately upon graduating, she took a position in Washington, D.C., with the American Association of University Women (AAUW) as a research associate in international education, a post that afforded her the opportunity to develop the AAUW's program on world affairs. Soon she was addressing AAUW chapters on European politics, focusing particularly on the dangers of totalitarianism. Additionally, she served as secretary to the Committee on International Relations of the AAUW, an assignment that took her to Europe annually. In 1931 she married Stephen Brunauer, a Hungarian chemist who had immigrated to the United States in 1921; they had two daughters and a son (who died in 1937).

In 1933 Esther Brunauer spent a year in Germany as a fellow of the Carl Schurz Foundation, studying the rise of the National Socialists. She attended the University of Berlin, interviewed party officials, pored over newspapers and documents in the Reichstag library, and attended mass meetings, parades, and films. She was received by Adolf Hitler for a short interview, and by the end of her stay she had reaffirmed the need to alert democratic countries to the dangers of Nazism and fascism. Her experience in Germany became the basis of her writings and lectures, and they took on an urgency, especially after war broke out in Europe. The chief of naval operations, Admiral W. H. Standley, lauded Brunauer's report *National Defense, Institutions, Concepts, and Policies* (1937) for being "largely responsible for converting various pacifistic organizations in this country and thus making possible an immediate program of rearmament" (*Department of State Bulletin*, 10 Apr. 1950). In *Has America Forgotten? Myths and Facts about World Wars I and II* (1941), Brunauer wrote, "Yet the conflict comes home to us, and we are gradually realizing that our own destiny depends on who wins this war. This is the moment when we need to know thoroughly and accurately what happened to us during the last great war" (p. 15).

Brunauer addressed AAUW chapters and women's clubs across the country. In October 1940, for example, she visited twenty-nine AAUW chapters in Illinois alone, speaking on the importance of preparedness and rejecting isolationism. In 1941 Brunauer played a key role in convincing the AAUW to support the Allies unconditionally. During the war she helped found the Committee to Defend America by Aiding the Allies and chaired a committee that created the Women's Action Committee for Victory and Lasting Peace.

In March 1944 Brunauer resigned from the AAUW to take a post in the State Department as a divisional assistant in the Division of International Security and Organization. Her dedication and experience helped her advance rapidly, and later she served as a technical expert to the U.S. delegations at the San Francisco conference at the founding of the United Nations. In February 1946 Brunauer became only the third woman in American history to hold the diplomatic rank of minister when she was appointed as the U.S. representative to the Preparatory Commission to the United Nations Educational, Scientific, and Cultural Organizations (UNESCO).

Whether because of her association with the United Nations and UNESCO, her Hungarian husband, or the fact that she was a high-ranking woman in the field of foreign affairs, Brunauer soon found herself under attack by critics questioning her loyalty. Her troubles began in 1947 when Illinois congressman Fred Busby accused her of making a disloyal radio broadcast on behalf of UNESCO. In fact, one of Brunauer's superiors had made the broadcast, and Busby's speculations were quickly dismissed. One year later Brunauer was targeted as a Communist sympathizer because of her membership in the American Friends of the Soviet Union some thirteen years before. After a full inquiry, she was cleared of all charges.

As the Cold War heated up, Brunauer's predicament worsened. In February 1950 she was named by Wisconsin senator Joseph McCarthy as one of "57 card-carrying Communists" in the State Department. Later listed as case 47 out of 81, by mid-March she was one of nine State Department employees charged with harboring Communist sympathies. Individuals such as Milton Eisenhower came to Brunauer's defense, citing her views during the 1947 Mexico City UNESCO conference as "counteracting the efforts of the Russian-dominated Polish delegation to pin the tag of 'war-monger' on the Western democracies, and especially on the United States." Brunauer's able responses to the attacks and the credibility of those who sided with her resulted in the charges being dropped.

Unfortunately for Brunauer, the ordeal was far from over. On 10 April 1951 the Department of the Navy suspended her husband on charges (among others) of being a "security risk," causing the State Department to suspend Brunauer as well. After learning that the secretary of the navy was intent on firing him, her husband resigned in June. Brunauer, however, continued to fight. The most serious charges, those of "close and habitual association" with her husband, raised a xenophobic specter. Some detractors believed that since Stephen Brunauer was Hungarian, Esther Brunauer was a logical suspect, or that she had married her husband to rehabilitate him. On 14 April 1952 Brunauer was declared by both the State Department and the Tydings Subcommittee of the Senate Committee on Foreign Relations to be a loyal American but was nevertheless deemed a security risk. She appealed the decision, but on 16 June the State Department dismissed her.

After working briefly at the Library of Congress, Brunauer followed her husband to Evanston, Illinois, where she worked first as an associate director of the Film Council of America, then as an editor for Rand McNally, and finally as a textbook editor for the Follett Publishing Company. She died in Evanston of a heart condition.

Esther Brunauer was a pioneering woman in the field of pre- and postwar international relations, teaching women about their roles in the world community and everyone about the dangers of totalitarianism. Brunauer's writings and speeches of the 1930s and 1940s helped garner support for American involvement abroad, promoting her conviction that organizations like the United Nations and UNESCO were vital to peaceful coexistence. She will probably be remembered best, however, for her struggle against the anti-Communist witch hunts of the late 1940s and early 1950s. For all of her expertise and commitment, Brunauer became the victim of a time when one's actions and loyalties were little protection against the political ambitions of a powerful few.

• The Mills College Alumnae Office and Special Collections Department has papers pertaining to Brunauer's college days and after. The AAUW in Washington, D.C., has numerous files on her time there and with the State Department, and the FBI has about 100 pages of material available through the Freedom of Information Act. Writings by Brunauer include her master's thesis, "The Rhineland Policy of Napoleon III, 1848–1870" (1925), and her doctoral dissertation, "The Peace Proposals of Germany and Austria-Hungary, 1914–1918" (1927), both available at Stanford University. Among Brunauer's many published books are *The Foreign Policy of the United States: A Study Course* (1931), *Reparations and War Debts: A Study Course and Bibliography* (1932), *The National Revolution in Germany, 1933* (1933), *Germany, the National Socialist State* (1934), and *Building the New World Order* (1939). Among Brunauer's articles are "National Socialist Youth in Germany," the *English Journal* 24 (Mar. 1935): 196–98; "The Peace Proposals of December, 1916–January, 1917," *Journal of Modern History* 4, no. 4 (Dec. 1932): 544–71; and "A Member of the Audience Looks at the Mass Media Program of UNESCO," *Mills Quarterly* 32, no. 4 (May 1950): 103–5. An important assessment of Brunauer is in Richard M. Fried, *Nightmare in Red* (1990). For contemporary portraits see "Brunauer Enigma," *Newsweek*, 23 Apr. 1951, and William F. Buckley, Jr., and L. Brent Bozell, *McCarthy and His Enemies* (1954). An obituary is in the *New York Times*, 27 June 1959, and an article in memoriam of Brunauer is in the *AAUW Journal* 53 (Jan. 1960): 122.

JONATHAN M. SCHOENWALD

BRUNDAGE, Avery (28 Sept. 1887–8 May 1975), athlete, businessman, and sports administrator, was born in Detroit, Michigan, the son of Charles Brundage, a stonecutter, and Amelia "Minnie" Lloyd. After a move to Chicago, Charles Brundage deserted his family, leaving the five-year-old Avery and his brother Chester to be reared by their mother. Thanks to some fairly affluent uncles, the Brundages endured genteel rather than desperate poverty. Brundage worked his way through the University of Illinois, earning a B.A. in engineering in 1909. In college and after, he was a dedicated and successful track-and-field athlete. His participation in the 1912 Olympic Games in Stockholm, Sweden, in the decathlon and pentathlon, was a defining experience. In an unpublished autobiography he wrote that his "conversion, along with many others, to [founder Pierre de] Coubertin's religion, the Olympic Movement, was complete." The choice of the word "religion" was deliberate. For Brundage, the Olympic Games were a utopian contrast to the sordid worlds of business and politics.

Brundage's energy and determination enabled him to amass a fortune in the construction business and, simultaneously, to continue as a nationally ranked athlete for another seven years. Never having had an athletic scholarship or any other kind of sports-related financial support, he was a fanatical believer in the nineteenth-century concept of amateur sports.

In 1927 Brundage married the socially prominant Elizabeth Dunlap. His only children, two sons whom he never publicly acknowledged, were the result of a later liaison, in the fifties, with Lilian Wahamaki Dresden. Paternal instincts suppressed at home were sublimated into a career in sports administration. In 1928 he became president of the Amateur Athletic Association, a post he held—with only a one-year break—until 1935. More than anyone else he deserves credit for resolving some of the bitter jurisdictional disputes between the Amateur Athletic Union and the National Collegiate Athletic Association (which controlled intercollegiate sports). More than anyone else, he deserves credit—or blame—for averting a United States boycott of the 1936 Olympics.

The venue of the 1936 games, unproblematic when Berlin was chosen in 1931, occasioned a crisis in 1933 when Adolf Hitler became Germany's chancellor. As Hitler began to fulfill his promise to eliminate Jews from German society, the International Olympic Committee, (IOC), led by Belgium's Comte Henri de Baillet-Latour, realized that National Socialist doctrines were incompatible with the Olympic Charter. But the IOC was assured by its German members that Jews would be allowed to compete for places on the German team. With mounting evidence that this was not the case, Jeremiah T. Mahoney and other influential American sports administrators urged that the United States boycott the games. Brundage, sent to Europe to investigate, consulted with his friend Carl Diem, secretary of Berlin's Olympic organizing commitee, and reported that there was no evidence of discrimination against Jewish athletes. Brundage dismissed as propaganda any testimony to the contrary. Returning home, he fought fiercely to defeat the boycott campaign, which he misleadingly described as a Communist and Jewish cabal. His reward was election to the IOC to replace Ernest Lee Jahncke, an American member who was expelled from the committee for questioning the decision to accept Hitler's promises at face value. To the day of his death, Brundage denied that Jews had been excluded from the German team and that the games had been a propaganda coup for the Nazis.

In another controversial move, Brundage joined with Charles Lindbergh and other isolationists in an attempt to block American involvement in the European war that broke out in 1939. The obverse of Brundage's appeal to keep the United States out of war was his desire to keep war from interfering with the Olympic Games. Like most of the IOC, Brundage thought that the Olympics—scheduled for Tokyo in 1940—should continue despite Japan's invasion of China. When the Japanese government informed the IOC that it was unable to host the games, Brundage redirected his energies to Latin America and campaigned for the establishment of Pan-American Games. When the United States entered the war, Brundage was forced to abandon these plans.

As soon as the war ended in August 1945, Brundage—an IOC executive board member since 1937—sailed to London, where he met with Sigfrid Edstrøm, the Swedish industrialist who had become acting IOC president in 1942 after the death of Baillet-Latour. Discounting the pessimism of Britain's Lord Aberdare, the only other member at the meeting, Brundage and Edstrøm were determined to revive the interrupted games as quickly as possible. A mail ballot of the IOC chose London as the site for the 1948 Olympics. At the first postwar meeting of the IOC, at Lausanne, Switzerland, in September 1946, Edstrøm was elected president and Brundage was elected first vice president.

At its postwar sessions, the committee had to deal with a more awkward question than the administrative succession. What was to be done about the IOC members who had represented Nazi Germany and Fascist Italy? (One of them, Karl Ritter von Halt, was a close friend of Brundage.) Despite the fervent appeals of members whose homelands had been occupied by Axis armies, Edstrøm and Brundage insisted that the German and Italian members not be expelled. By fiat, Edstrøm simply welcomed them back.

Judging from his role in this controversy and in the boycott controversy of 1933–1936, one might conclude that Brundage's detractors were right to label him a "proto-Nazi," but the truth is more complicated. Brundage's belief in the Olympic Games as a "modern, exciting, virile, dynamic religion" did indeed blind him to the horrors of the prewar Nazi dictatorship, but his fanatic belief in "Olympism" enabled him to overcome his prejudices against left-wing totalitarianism as well. He worked for the admission of the Soviet Union to the IOC and to the games as he had worked against the boycott of the "Nazi Olympics" because he believed—no doubt naively—that the games really were what Coubertin had intended them to be: a means to bring the people of the world together in the spirit of fair play and good sportsmanship. To Brundage, if the games were to be a truly universal force for international reconciliation, the USSR and the other nations of the Soviet bloc had to be included. When journalists asked him why he did not protest against government support of Soviet athletes, Brundage remarked ingenuously that Comrade Aleksi Romanov, a Russian member of the OIC, had assured him that the USSR's athletes were all amateurs.

In 1952, after Edstrøm's term, Brundage was elected IOC president. Among the challenges he faced were the controversies over how Germany and China were to be represented in the games. Brundage's solution to the first divided-nation problem was to insist that the Federal Republic of Germany and the German Democratic Republic field a single German team. Years of complicated negotiations were necessary before this occurred. (Forced unity lasted from 1956 to 1972.) The Chinese dilemma proved to be more intractable. The Communists on the mainland and the Nationalists on Taiwan both claimed to be the legitimate rulers of all China. Neither government wanted to send a team to the Olympic Games if the other's athletes also were invited to participate. Attempting vainly to find a compromise, Brundage was vilified by the Communists as "a faithful menial of the U.S. imperialists" and by right-wing Americans as a dupe of international communism. He never found a solution to the Chinese puzzle.

Elected in 1960 to a second eight-year term as IOC president, Brundage sought to integrate into the "Olympic family" the newly independent nations of Africa and Asia. This meant not only that more athletes from the Third World participated in the games but also that Asians and Africans were named to the IOC. In 1963, for instance, Nigeria's Adetokunbo Ademola became the first black African to sit on the committee. In another effort to widen the scope of "Olympism," Tokyo was selected as the site of the 1964 games.

With the movement to broaden the Olympics came additional political problems. One was precipitated by Indonesia's refusal to allow Israeli or Nationalist Chinese athletes to participate in the IOC-sanctioned Asian Games of 1963, which were held in Jakarta. When the IOC suspended the Indonesian National Olympic Committee for refusing to protest its government's decision, Indonesia's dictator, Sukarno, created a short-lived rival to the Olympics named the Games of the New Emerging Forces. These games failed to win significant support, and a promise by the Indonesians to obey Olympic rules enabled them to return to the Olympic fold for the 1964 games in Tokyo.

A more serious crisis was occasioned by South Africa's policy of apartheid, unquestionably a violation of the Olympic Charter. After prolonged negotiations, the South African National Olympic Committee agreed, in 1967, to field a racially mixed team. But years of stubborn resistance had created such a reservoir of resentment that black African countries were not satisfied with this concession. Supported by the Communist bloc, they threatened to boycott the 1968 games if South Africa participated. Against Brundage's angry opposition, the IOC acquiesced and voted to rescind South Africa's invitation to Mexico City. (In 1970 the IOC decided by a vote of 35–28 to withdraw recognition from the South African National Olympic Committee, a move Brundage opposed.) Barring South Africa did not end controversy; on the victory stand, 200-meter champion Tommy Smith and third-place runner John Carlos raised their gloved fists in the "black power" salute.

Economic realities also intruded upon Brundage's fantasy of "Olympism" wholly apart from mundane affairs. After years of indigence, during which IOC members paid dues to finance the committee's work, the sale of television rights—which began in 1960—brought sudden wealth to the IOC. Brundage feared, correctly, that the committee's rush into the world of commerce would mean the demise of the amateur ideal. By the seventies, amateur athletes could no longer compete sucessfully against subsidized full-time Olympians for whom sports were a way of life. The latter, amateurs in name only, watched as hundreds of millions of dollars flowed from network television into Olympic coffers. Dissatisfied with traditional athletic scholarships or token payments from the government, top athletes now demanded (and received) a share of the new wealth. Brundage, despite his fulminations, was unable to resist the interrelated forces of commercialization and professionalization.

Although many of his colleagues resented Brundage's authoritarian style and increasingly anachronistic views, challenges to his leadership from France's Comte Jean de Beaumont and Italy's Giulio Onesti failed, and Brundage was reelected in 1968 to a final four-year term as IOC president. The opposition was able, however, in the late sixties and early seventies to force him to pay more attention to their opinions and to those of national Olympic committees.

Brundage's last days in office were the most dramatic. When the games opened in Munich in 1972, the German organizers hoped to erase memories of the "Nazi Olympics" of 1936. However, in the predawn hours of 5 September, Palestinian terrorists infiltrated the Olympic Village, made their way to the quarters of the Israeli team, murdered several of the athletes, and took others hostage. At Fürstenfeldbruck airfield, where the terrorists expected to make their escape, they were attacked by German sharpshooters in a bungled assault. All of the hostages and three of their captors were killed. With the approval of the Israeli government, the IOC decided to interrupt but not to abort the games. At a memorial service held in the Olympic Stadium on 6 September, Brundage said what he always said whenever political crisis threatened the Olympic movement: "The Games must go on."

In retirement, Brundage grumbled at the weak leadership of his successor, Ireland's amiable Lord Killanin. He found some comfort in a second marriage (in 1973) to Princess Mariann von Reuss. (His first wife had died in 1971.) Always fond of Garmisch in what was then West Germany, Brundage bought a house there, where he died.

An embattled, controversial figure, Brundage has been praised by his admirers for his obdurate defense of "Olympism" and condemned by his detractors for his stubborn refusal to accept political and economic realities. Neither group, however, disputes his importance as an international sports administrator.

• Brundage's papers, including his manuscript autobiography, are in the archives of the University of Illinois, Champaign-Urbana. Microfilmed copies are accessible in Cologne, Lausanne, and a number of other cities. Although Brundage's activities were headline news for decades, historians have paid him scant attention. Aside from a number of scholarly articles, mostly critical, surprisingly little has been published. Heinz Schöbel's *The Four Dimensions of Avery Brundage* (1968) is a collection of photographs introduced by an uncritical biographical sketch. Similarly uncritical is Hans Klein, *Avery Brundage: Die Herausforderung* (1972), which consists mostly of photographs from the Brundage archives and excerpts from the unpublished autobiography. The most complete account of Brundage's life is Allen Guttmann, *The Games Must Go On: Avery Brundage and the Olympic Movement* (1984).

ALLEN GUTTMANN

BRUNS, Henriette (28 Oct. 1813–7 Nov. 1899), writer and political observer, was born Anna Elizabeth Henriette Bernadine Geisberg in Stromberg in the Prussian province of Westphalia, Germany, the oldest child of Maximilian Friedrich Geisberg, the mayor and tax collector of Oelde, and Johanna Hüffer. Both the Geisbergs and the Hüffers were old respected Catholic families in the area, constituting, as Bruns later wrote, the "so-called distinguished people" of the provincial society. The Geisbergs had held the Stromberg office of tax collector for the prince bishop of Münster since 1625, and the Hüffers were successful linen merchants and bankers.

Called "Jette" by her family, who moved to nearby Oelde shortly after her birth, Bruns enjoyed the advantages of a family devoted to books, received an excellent early education, and participated in a rich community musical life. She sang with her mother, became a member of the church choir, and attended meetings of the local singing society. From her mother Bruns also learned gardening and grafting, as well as household skills. Accompanying her father on his monthly tax collecting circuit, she widened her intellectual horizons by visits with relatives and family friends at Liesborn Monastery. There were also occasional vacation trips to Münster, where her father's younger brothers were canons, archivists, and court counselors.

These happy childhood days ended in 1827 with the sudden death after childbirth of her 31-year-old mother. Although Bruns wanted to assume the responsibilities of her father's household and the care of her six younger brothers and sisters, she was sent to live with her father's family in Münster to continue her education. She received practical training from her aunt in cooking and sewing, and formal instruction at the rectorate of St. Aegidi in world history, geography, music, and composition. Her two years of study concluded with a trip by special coach with her uncle through the Wupper Valley to Cologne and then up the Rhine past Bingen, Rüdesheim, and Mainz and up the Main River to Frankfurt. There, at the annual trade fair, they heard a concert by Niccolò Paganini before traveling back to Westphalia.

Returning to Oelde, Bruns kept house for her father, sewed for her little sisters, and participated in a lively social life with cousins and former schoolmates, going to house balls, sheep-shearing parties, choral practice, music-club events, and Mardi Gras festivities. When relatives in Münster heard that sixteen-year-old Bruns was receiving the attention of the local doctor, they invited her to spend the winter season with them "to see something of the world." Her father insisted she go, and after a stay in Münster, she was sent to her mother's relatives in Stromberg to learn more about housekeeping.

In November 1831 Bruns's father died suddenly of a stroke, leaving seven orphaned children. Hoping to keep her siblings together, Bruns defied family opposition and on 24 May 1832 married Johann Bernard Bruns, who had trained as a medical doctor and surgeon in Berlin and Münster. A son was born to them on 20 October 1833. Despite his good medical practice, Dr. Bruns soon caught the prevailing emigration fever and persuaded his wife that their son's future would be brighter in the United States. To select a location for his family in the new land Dr. Bruns and a younger brother sailed for the United States in June 1835. After traveling to St. Louis, they bought land on the Maries River in Gasconade County, Missouri, an isolated area where a few Germans had already settled. Returning to Germany to get his wife and son, Dr. Bruns gathered a family party that included his wife's two brothers, another of his brothers, and a maid and her child. Joining approximately fifty other emigrants from Oelde and neighboring towns, they sailed from Bremen, landing at Baltimore sixty-six days later, on 16 September 1836. Their long overland trip to Missouri ended on All Souls Day, 2 November, when Bruns and her family reached their one-room log cabin in the small frontier settlement that was to be their new home.

For the next fifteen years letters from Bruns to her brother Heinrich Geisberg and other relatives in Münster document the struggles, hardships, joys, and successes of the German immigrants in the Westphalia Settlement. Her second child was born in the log cabin in February 1837, but in December of that year the family moved into their new half-timbered house, reminiscent of the sturdy dwellings in their home country. During the next sixteen years nine more children were born to Bruns, but five died in childhood, three within two weeks in 1841.

Bruns epitomized the experience of many educated, middle-class immigrant women on the early frontier, taking care of her children and a large household and garden and always on call for sick relatives and neighbors who needed help. She struggled for a number of years to save a brother suffering from mental illness, but he eventually returned to Germany and had to be institutionalized. She dispensed medicine when her husband was away visiting patients and entertained travelers and clergymen who periodically visited the settlement. Writing in 1846, she reported:

> This past week we had the visit from our bishop that had been promised us for a long time. Since he, as well as the superior, stayed with us, you can understand that we had a great deal on our minds. The bishop confirmed and dedicated the new cemetery. He is a very fine and kind gentleman, Irish by birth, perhaps of high birth, and was called Lordship. Mrs. Bruns participated in the conversation in English, which amazed the gentlemen. (Schroeder and Schulz-Geisberg, p. 136)

In 1853, after sixteen years at Westphalia and nearby Shipley's Ferry on the Osage River, Bruns and her family moved to Jefferson City, the capital of Missouri, which offered better educational opportunities for her children and a more stimulating social and intellectual life for her. From a large house across from the capitol she wrote of political events and family tragedies. Her brother died in 1858, and she took his three children into her household. Besides reports on family matters, her letters reflect political conflicts as the Civil War approached, the growing threat of sudden evacuation, her husband's involvement in political and military affairs, and the departure of her son and a nephew to join the Union forces. In 1862 her mortally wounded nephew returned to her home to die, and a year later her son was killed in battle at Iuka, Mississippi. After a long illness Dr. Bruns died in 1864, leaving his financial affairs in disarray. Left alone with debts her husband had incurred on both sides of the Atlantic, Bruns opened a boarding house to support her family. Catering to legislators, mostly German Radical Republicans, Bruns managed to take care of her family and send her daughters to private schools and academies.

In her seventies Bruns tried farming with her youngest son. Intending to raise silkworms, they planted over 150 mulberry trees; but their efforts were unsuccessful, and she moved into her youngest daughter's home in Jefferson City. Her failing eyesight made reading difficult, and even gardening became impossible when she could no longer differentiate between flowers and weeds. However, as she wrote, she maintained a cheerful attitude: "I really should be much more serious, and I tell myself every day that in the late fall I shall be eighty years old. In the morning I begin by singing the school song, 'Let my first feeling be praise and thanks.' But soon thereafter all kinds of gay and worldly thoughts occur. I live for the present, but even more I enjoy reminiscing" (Schroeder and Schulz-Geisberg, p. 281). She wrote that she was rereading Thomas à Kempis, the book she had received as an award from her pastor as an eleven-year-old.

For the rest of her life Bruns continued to comment in letters home on the national and international news, which her daughter regularly read to her. Still interested in local and state affairs, she reported on the construction of the Missouri River bridge, the attempts to move the capital from Jefferson City to Sedalia, and the coming of electricity to the city.

Over 270 letters, mostly written to relatives in Germany, and an unfinished autobiography ending in 1868 document the life of this remarkable woman, who grew up in post-Napoleonic Germany and was transplanted to the American West. Enduring the life of a pioneer woman, Bruns became a keen observer of one of the most exciting periods in American history.

• Copies of the original letters and translations by A. E. Schroeder are deposited in the Western Historical Manuscript Collection of the University of Missouri in Columbia, Missouri. For more on Bruns, see Adolf E. Schroeder and Carla Schulz-Geisberg, eds., *Hold Dear, as Always: Jette, a German Immigrant Life in Letters* (1988); Silke Schütter and Carla Schulz-Geisberg, eds., *Ein Auswanderinnenschicksal in Briefen und Dokumenten* (1989); and Walter D. Kamphoefner et al., eds., *News from the Land of Freedom: German Immigrants Write Home* (1991).

ADOLF E. SCHROEDER

BRUNSWICK, Ruth Jane Mack (17 Feb. 1897–24 Jan. 1946), psychoanalyst, was born in Chicago, Illinois, the daughter of Julian Mack, a judge and prominent Jewish philanthropist, and Jessie Fox. Julian Mack helped found the *Harvard Law Review* and later served as a Harvard overseer. Ruth Mack attended Radcliffe College during World War I and graduated from Tufts Medical School in 1922. In 1917 she had married Herrman Blumgart, who later pursued an extraordinarily successful medical career in Boston as an expert in heart disease; his brother Leonard had gone to Vienna for a short analysis with Sigmund Freud after the end of World War I.

Ruth Mack Blumgart had completed her psychiatric residency when she decided, at the age of twenty-five, to be analyzed by Freud. By 1922 she was seeking help with personal problems as well as going to Freud for training. Her marriage was already troubled; her husband saw Freud in Vienna in an unsuccessful effort to salvage the marriage, but Freud evidently decided that the relationship between Herrman and Ruth was hopelessly compromised. The couple divorced in 1924. Ruth had fallen in love with an American music student five years younger than she, Mark Brunswick, a distant relative. She was in analysis with Freud in 1924 when Mark, twenty-two years old, himself went into analysis with Freud. According to Mark, Freud later admitted to him that it had been a mistake at the time for Freud and Ruth to have discussed Mark's case in complete detail.

In the meantime Ruth was teaching at the Vienna Psychoanalytic Training Institute; her specialty was in extending psychoanalytic knowledge to the psychoses, an area that Freud personally had avoided. She was also a practicing analyst, and Freud sent her a number of well-paying patients.

Ruth Mack and Mark Brunswick were married at the town hall in Vienna in 1928; it was one of the few wedding ceremonies Freud ever attended. He was one of the official witnesses; the second witness was Oscar Rie, Freud's old friend and the father of Ruth's best friend in Vienna, Marianne Kris, also an analyst. Martin Freud, Freud's eldest son, drew up the marriage papers, and Mark's brother David was also present, since he too was at the time in analysis with Freud. In those days Freud had five regular analytic cases, so Ruth, Mark, and David made up 60 percent of Freud's analytic time. Mark's youngest sister, who was in analysis then with Herman Nunberg in Vienna, was also present at the wedding.

Ruth Brunswick's access to Freud seemed unique; she came to meals at his apartment, visited him in summers, and was on excellent terms with his children. Anna Freud, the only child to follow him in his profession, was both fond of Brunswick and also considered her a rival. Freud's oldest daughter Mathilda Hollitscher was a special friend, and Mark and Ruth Brunswick's only child, a daughter, was named for Mathilda. Ruth Brunswick was considered a member of Freud's extended family. It is generally agreed that she was, during this last phase in Freud's career, the most important of his female followers; he treated her virtually as an adopted daughter.

Brunswick also played a special role in mediating between the American analysts and Freud's circle in Vienna. She was a member of both the New York and Vienna Psychoanalytic societies. She became an important channel through which wealthy American patients arranged to undergo analyses with Freud; she undertook also to look after all the American analytic patients who were in Vienna. In recognition of her special standing, Brunswick became one of the few women who received a ring, signifying she was a designated apostle, from Freud. Freud trusted her to see that his work was correctly communicated to his followers in the United States.

Brunswick played a notable part in supervising Freud's precarious health. Her own patient in analysis, Max Schur, became Freud's personal physician. Brunswick and the Princess Marie Bonaparte, who were close friends, once arranged for a famous Harvard professor to make a new prosthesis for Freud's mouth. She and Marie paid the expensive bill; Brunswick even watched over Freud's diet.

Brunswick's central contribution to psychoanalytic thinking concerned the child's earliest relationship to the mother; in 1929 she was the first in print to use the term "pre-oedipal," and Freud himself adopted it two years later. Brunswick, however, was increasingly bothered by medical symptoms that resisted clear diagnosis; she could prescribe drugs for herself, and at one point was hospitalized to overcome her dependency.

The Brunswicks left Vienna in 1928, and their one child was born in the United States; they returned to Europe in 1929 and remained in Vienna until 1938. Around the end of 1933 or early 1934 Mark Brunswick, who felt his own neurotic symptoms had remained uncured, went back into analysis with Freud. Ruth was more or less continuously in analysis with Freud throughout these years. Ruth and Mark were divorced in 1937, and then—against Freud's advice—they remarried within six months.

In these years the Brunswicks were disappointed in Freud politically; when the socialists in Vienna were violently suppressed in 1934, they thought Freud betrayed himself by arguing on behalf of the Dollfuss regime. Freud was irritated because Ruth and Mark constantly urged him to leave Vienna because of their fears about the Austrian political future.

The cloudy circumstances associated with Brunswick's medical troubles, and in particular her early death in 1946, has obscured both her scientific contributions as well as her immense personal standing with Freud. She will always be remembered as the Wolf-Man's second analyst; Freud had himself treated this patient between 1910 and 1914 and had written one of his most famous case histories about him. When in 1926 Freud had referred the Wolf-Man to Brunswick for treatment, Freud was paying her a high compliment. He knew that anything she published would become famous in the clinical literature. She wrote an article about the Wolf-Man in close collaboration with Freud, and, after the Wolf-Man had again returned to her for analysis, she composed the notes for a second case history, which has remained unpublished; her own inhibitions, amounting to a work block, have combined with the secrecy of the Freud Archives to keep her stature relatively minimized.

In Vienna Brunswick, whatever her emotional problems may have been, continued to give a seminar on psychosis for her colleagues in the Vienna Psychoanalytic Society. She had a special talent for manipulating Freud's theoretical concepts and used them to set forth new ideas of her own. She was tactful enough to be able to emphasize the importance of the mother in the development of the child without rebelling against his basic ideas. By stressing the significance of what she called the "pre-oedipal" layer, she meant that an early emotional relationship preceded the triangular conflict commonly associated with the arrival of what Freud had named the Oedipus complex. The pre-oedipal had to be in principle a far more archaic and primitive emotional bond than the oedipal, and she conjectured that it lay at the root of the psychotic problems she was studying.

Freud publicly included Brunswick among those women analysts who had been able to discover, in their female patients, an early exclusive attachment to the mother that he himself had not been able to discern. Freud wrote in 1932 that she had been "the first to describe a case of neurosis which went back to a fixation to the pre-Oedipus stage and had never reached the Oedipus situation at all" ("New Introductory Lectures on Psychoanalysis," *Standard Edition*, ed. James Strachey [1964], vol. 22, p. 130).

Brunswick's analytic time with Freud was arranged whenever his schedule permitted. In the meantime she trained some famous future analysts. She analyzed Muriel Gardiner, Diana Trilling, Max and Helen

Schur, and Robert Fliess, the son of Freud's former friend Wilhelm. Her most famous student was Karl Menninger, who saw her later in the United States. She continued to have health problems that her doctors could not diagnose as unquestionably organic. She used morphine to cope with gallbladder attacks. She also suffered from neuritis. She took sleeping pills and painkillers; at least by 1933–1934 she had a serious drug problem, and by 1937 she had become an addict.

Yet in Vienna Brunswick did not seem outwardly disturbed. Given Freud's own general intolerance of addictions, however, her drug difficulties may have been especially hard for him to accept. Freud recognized her addiction as an illness to be understood and treated rather than criticized, but he found it personally distasteful. Her failure to overcome her difficulties was probably the main reason for his final disappointment in her, which coincided with his own succumbing to cancer in 1939.

Brunswick's analysis with Freud can be said to have stretched, with some interruptions, from 1922 until 1939. Such a long treatment was in itself an addiction. Unwittingly Freud had helped bring about the very dependency that it ideally should have been the task of analysis to dissipate. Perhaps Freud had liked working with her too much; Mark Brunswick certainly thought that Freud's feelings for her had interfered with her cure. The worst of Brunswick's drug addiction occurred in the United States. Her mother died in 1940, her father in 1943. Mark Brunswick finally divorced her in 1945, and she went to Herman Nunberg in New York City for analysis while she was still a prominent analyst.

Brunswick's death in New York City was the end result of a pattern of self-destructive behavior. She had been drinking paregoric the way an alcoholic consumes whiskey. Her health was undermined, and the federal authorities had taken note of her drug taking. She caught pneumonia, recovered, and then died of too many opiates combined with a fall in the bathroom; she had hit her head and fractured her skull. The full story was not publicly known for many years.

To insiders within the psychoanalytic movement, Brunswick's addictions and death were proof that analytic treatment could not be counted on to prevent human tragedy. Although Freud's intentions toward Brunswick may have been the best, in the end he collaborated in her undoing. The secrecy associated with her difficulties, however, and the length of time it may be before her surviving papers become publicly accessible, should not obscure the outstanding role she played in the history of psychoanalysis. Others, such as Otto Rank and Melanie Klein, for example, went on to make "pre-oedipal" problems the center of their respective systems of thought.

• Brunswick's papers are held by the Freud Archives, Library of Congress, and will not be available until sometime in the twenty-first century. Her three best-known articles are "The Analysis of a Case of Paranoia (Delusions of Jealousy)," *Journal of Nervous and Mental Disease* 70 (1929): 1–22, 155–78; "The Preoedipal Phase of the Libido Development," *Psychoanalytic Quarterly* 9 (1940): 293–319; and "A Supplement to Freud's *History of an Infantile Neurosis*," *International Journal of Psychoanalysis* 9 (1928): 439–76. For secondary literature, see Paul Roazen, *Freud and His Followers* (1975; repr. 1992) and "Freud's Patients: First-Person Accounts," in *Freud and the History of Psychoanalysis*, ed. Toby Gelfand and John Kerr (1992). There are some important references to Ruth Mack Brunswick in Roazen, *How Freud Worked* (1995). An obituary appears in the *New York Times*, 26 Jan. 1946.

PAUL ROAZEN

BRUNTON, David William (11 June 1849–20 Dec. 1927), mining engineer, was born in Ayr, Ontario, Canada, the son of James Brunton, an engineer, and Agnes Dickie. After attending grammar school he went to Toronto, Canada, and apprenticed under civil engineer Edmund Wragge, chief engineer of the Toronto, Gray and Bruce Railway in 1870, and under J. C. Bailey, chief engineer of the Toronto and Nipissing Railroad in 1871. He emigrated to the United States in 1873 to take a special course in geology, chemistry, and metallurgy at the University of Michigan in 1874–1875. Major Charles H. McIntyre, president of the newly organized Dakota and San Juan Mining Co., recruited him to take charge of the engineering department in 1875. He and McIntyre traveled to Denver, Colorado, to hire miners and organize equipment. Brunton then set out with the miners and equipment for Mineral Point, in the San Juan Mountains, 230 miles from the nearest railroad and 11,700 feet above sea level. He traveled by narrow-gauge railroad to Pueblo, Colorado, and thereafter by pack train. Inadequate supplies forced the crew to leave Mineral Point before snow blocked the passes, and Brunton walked about 75 miles to the San Luis Valley in the fall of 1875. Brunton then became superintendent of the Stewart Mill at Georgetown, Colorado, resolving severe chemical problems in treating their ore. Here he formed a lasting association with James Douglas and Thomas Sterry Hunt, partners in the metallurgical firm of Hunt, Douglas, and Stewart, for whom Brunton worked. Thereafter H. Augustus Taylor, owner of the Clear Creek works at Georgetown, offered him a much higher salary to construct a similar, efficient reduction works to recover silver associated with iron pyrite and zinc blende. After a year and a half he moved to the Native Silver Mining Company at Caribou, Colorado. After one winter there, he joined the Silver Peak Mining Company in Nevada. The principal owner attempted to force out minority stockholders by closing the mines in 1879, and Brunton returned to Colorado. Reaching Leadville by sled in 1879, he opened the first of a chain of sampling works and custom mills in partnership with Frank M. Taylor, son of H. Augustus Taylor, in 1880. In 1885 he married Katherine Kemble; they had three sons and a daughter. That same year, he took over management of the Colonel Sellars mine, designing a mill to treat its complex ore. He also designed a mill for Benjamin

Guggenheim's adjacent A. Y. and Minnie Mine. In 1886 he went to Aspen, Colorado, as an expert in a protracted series of apex suits. Under the apex concept, the party holding the claim including the topographically highest exposure owns all of a mineral vein, including portions beneath the surface property of others. Complex geological conditions thereby produce conflicts, such as who owns the lower portion of a vein that divides into two.

Brunton became manager of the Della S., J. C. Johnson, and Free Silver mines at Aspen in 1887. He became famous for driving the 2½-mile Cowenhaven Tunnel, a deep drainage and access tunnel. He also was one of the first to adopt electrical machinery in mining, installing what was then the largest electric hoist in the world at the Free Silver Mine. From 1887 to 1905, while continuing Colorado work, he consulted on apex litigation with the Anaconda Mining Company and the Consolidated Mining Company at Butte, Montana. In 1905 he formed a consulting partnership with F. M. Taylor, Taylor and Brunton, in Denver. Important contracts included the Roosevelt Drainage Tunnel at Cripple Creek and the Laramie-Poudre Tunnel (water diversion) in northern Colorado in 1910. During World War I he was an advisory member of the U.S. Army General Staff inventions section. He was chairman of the board of consulting engineers for the Moffet Tunnel in 1922–1927.

Brunton was active during the time when professional engineers and geologists replaced practical miners in mine management. Brunton invented many machines and processes for mining and ore dressing. His pocket transit, a hand-held sighting compass and inclinometer patented in 1894, became the standard for American geologists and, also, was adopted by the U.S. Army for field use in World War I. His participation in apex litigation at Butte included some of the earliest intensive underground geological mapping. His maps, made for litigation, also led to economical control of mining and the discovery of extensive additional ore bodies. Through assembling a corps of expert geologists and engineers, Brunton not only helped make the Anaconda Copper Company one of the world's largest mining concerns but also firmly established the place of mining geologists in the industry. Brunton's Cowenhoven Tunnel won the Telford Premium of the (British) Institution of Engineers in 1898. Subsequently, his Cripple Creek deep drainage tunnel, Laramie-Poudre water diversion tunnel, and Moffet railroad tunnels became technological landmarks. The 6½-mile Moffet Tunnel, the world's longest tunnel at the time, reduced rail mileage from Denver to Salt Lake City by 173 miles. Brunton was author of *Safety and Efficiency in Mine Tunneling* (1914) and *Modern Tunneling* (1914). He was president of the American Institute of Mining Engineers in 1909–1910 and president of the American Mining Congress in 1912–1913, and he was awarded the William Laurence Saunders mining medal of the American Institute of Mining and Metallurgical Engineers in 1926.

• "Engineering Record, 1870–1920" (c. 1920), Brunton's personal memoir and diary, is held in the Denver Public Library, Western History Division. Brunton's "Technical Reminiscences," *Mining and Scientific Press* 111 (17 Nov. 1915): 811–18, is his own account of his career. T. A. Rickard, "David W. Brunton: Consulting Engineer," *Mining and Scientific Press* 122 (28 May 1921): 745–66, reports an interview with Brunton on the highlights of his career. P. H. Von Bitter, "The Brunton Pocket Transit: A One Hundred Year Old North American Invention," *Earth Sciences History* 14, no. 1 (1995): 98–102, recounts the development of the standard American geological field surveying instrument.

R. L. LANGENHEIM, JR.

BRUSH, Charles Francis (17 Mar. 1849–15 June 1929), inventor, was born in Euclid, near Cleveland, Ohio, the son of Isaac Elbert Brush, a woolens manufacturer and farmer, and Delia Williams Phillips. The youngest of nine children, he was spared many of the farm chores and spent much of his youth reading about astronomy, chemistry, and physics or working with microscopes, telescopes, and photographic equipment in a small workshop. At Cleveland's Central High School he built his own battery-powered arc lighting system. At the University of Michigan he earned a bachelor's degree (1869) in mining engineering in just two years.

In 1869 Brush set up shop as an analytical and consulting chemist, and in 1873 he became a partner in an iron ore marketing firm. That provided sufficient income and spare time to undertake electrical research. In the early 1870s a long-time friend, George Stockly, general manager of the Telegraph Supply Company in Cleveland, asked Brush for help with electrical experiments. At this time, the commercial practicality of electric arc lighting was beginning to emerge in Europe. In 1875, with Stockly's encouragement and assistance in the form of materials and facilities, Brush began his own efforts to develop a practical arc lighting system.

The electric arc is essentially a very powerful continuous spark capable of producing light in large quantities for such purposes as outdoor illumination, but it is too bright to use inside houses. Success in the technology and business of arc lighting depended on inventiveness, tinkering, and "systems thinking"—putting together the most reliable, affordable, and efficient combination of up to a few dozen large lamps, a generator of electricity, regulating equipment, and a circuit of wire.

Brush began by improving the generator, starting with the best existing device, the Gramme dynamo, and constructing one that was lighter, smaller, more efficient, and less expensive. In 1877 it won a competition at the Franklin Institute of Philadelphia against a dozen or so rival machines submitted by all the leading manufacturers in the United States and Europe. He proceeded to sell a dynamo to the Franklin Institute and five more, each powering four lights, to the Philadelphia store owner John Wanamaker, and his career as a manufacturer was launched. In 1879 he operated the first electric street lighting system in the United States, in Cleveland.

Over the next three years Brush developed a steady stream of improvements to meet the practical problems of arc lighting that trials such as the Cleveland installation had revealed. Lamps burned out in a few hours, cost too much, and flickered unpleasantly, and generators provided a varying current. Brush's key inventions for solving these problems, completed between 1878 and 1880, included the double carbon arc lamp, which gave light for sixteen hours; the automatic regulator that kept the current from his generator constant no matter how many lamps were burning; improved carbon compositions and the practice of copper plating the arc carbons, which helped eliminate the flickering; better materials and processes for lowering the cost of the carbons while improving the quality of the light; and an electromagnetically actuated feedback device for keeping the gap between the arc carbons constant, an essential element in maintaining the illumination and current use of the arc lamp uniform over time. By 1880 Brush had developed the basic arc lighting system that would dominate the market for the next decade, and he had installed the first commercially successful outdoor arc lighting system in the United States: fifty lamps illuminating the streets of San Francisco for $10 per lamp per week.

He and Stockly incorporated the Brush Electric Company in 1880. It led the nation, installing systems in New York, Philadelphia, Boston, and many other cities. Production grew from 250 arc lamps per month in 1880 to 1,500 a month in 1885, and sales passed the $1 million mark. But the company was not able to hold its lead. After 1885 Brush Electric was eclipsed by the Thomson-Houston Company of Lynn, Massachusetts, which drew on larger stores of capital and a larger team of technologists. In 1889 Thomson-Houston purchased the British Electric Company, a sale that left Brush independently wealthy and able to devote the rest of his life to science and invention.

One of Brush's early interests had been the development of an improved storage battery. He believed that a battery with long life and relatively short charging time could give his company a competitive advantage in the arc lighting industry by allowing the use of smaller and therefore less expensive generators. So in 1880 he invented a battery based on a combination of lead plates and sulfuric acid with the required characteristics. The same system was simultaneously and independently invented by Camille Fauré of France. Its usefulness in electric lighting was short-lived, but in the form of the modern lead-acid battery it now supplies the starting energy for automobiles.

Brush also provided both technical consultation and financial backing to the Linde Air Products Company, an American pioneering venture in the use of low-temperature apparatus to separate the gases of the air for use in chemical manufacturing. A building block of the later Union Carbide Company, Linde's success further increased Brush's financial independence. He lived out his life in comfort in Cleveland, where he had married Mary E. Morris in 1875; they had three children.

He later built a giant windmill (1888) to produce electricity, developed a kinetic theory of gravitation that earned the disapproval of the scientific community, and tried to prove the existence of the luminiferous ether as a medium for carrying electromagnetic waves. Science and invention were Brush's only real hobbies.

Throughout his life he worked alone or with only a few associates, remaining outside the giant companies that came to dominate the electrical industry, in part with the aid of his patents. He did form a small independent research laboratory, the Brush Laboratories, and a research foundation in the field of eugenics. He died in Cleveland, leaving behind a legacy of two giant leaps in electrical technology: the arc lighting system, which had been one of the world's first successful large-scale applications of electricity, and the lead-acid battery, which became one of the world's most widely used forms of energy storage.

• Brush's papers are in the Special Collections Department, Case Western Reserve University. The most complete summary of his life is Harry J. Eisenman III, "Charles F. Brush: Pioneer Innovator in Electrical Technology" (Ph.D. diss., Case Institute of Technology, 1967). The best sources of perspective on his work are Harold Passer, *The Electrical Manufacturers, 1875–1900* (1953), and W. Bernard Carlson, *Innovation as a Social Process* (1991).

GEORGE WISE

BRUSH, George de Forest (28 Sept. 1855–24 Apr. 1941), painter, was born in Shelbyville, Tennessee, the son of Alfred Clark Brush, at the time a practicing dentist, and Nancy Douglas. One year after his birth, the family moved to Danbury, Connecticut, where his father pursued a number of professions, eventually becoming a prosperous hat manufacturer in New York City. His mother was a self-taught artist who encouraged her son's creative interests.

At the age of fifteen Brush enrolled at the National Academy of Design in New York, where his principal instructor was Lemuel E. Wilmarth. He studied there for three years, then in 1874 moved to Paris to continue his artistic education at the École des Beaux-Arts under Jean Léon Gérôme, a favorite teacher of the many American art students then flocking to France. Gérôme's instruction and example were to have a lasting impact on Brush's art. From Gérôme, Brush acquired a lifelong commitment to craftsmanship and good design, a respect for the old masters, and a marked preference for figural subjects and historical themes.

In 1880 Brush returned to New York. The following summer he traveled west with his brother Alfred, a trip that was to have a significant impact on the development of George's career. The two men spent a number of months on American Indian reservations in Wyoming and Montana, where Brush amassed sketches, memories, and artifacts. For the next decade he specialized in paintings of Native Americans, producing romanticized images of men and women hunting, canoeing, weaving, carving, making headdresses, and mourning their dead, the men's beautiful, perfectly proportioned bodies recalling the classical statuary that had been at the heart of Brush's academic education. Typical of these carefully designed and meticulously painted images is *The Indian and the Lily* (1887), showing a man, clad only in a belt and leggings, kneeling by the edge of a swamp to pluck a water lily. These pictures established Brush's reputation; they were greeted with ready buyers and considerable critical acclaim, garnering the Hallgarten Prize at the National Academy of Design in 1888 and a gold medal at the World's Columbian Exposition in Chicago in 1893.

During the 1880s Brush also launched his teaching career in New York City. In 1880 he taught at the Workingman's School (a free school for working-class men), a position indicative of his lifelong interest in progressive social reform. From 1882 to 1883 he was an instructor at the Woman's Art School of the Cooper Union, and in 1883 he took a position at the Art Students' League, where he continued to teach on and off until 1898. Among his students at the league was Mary Taylor "Mittie" Whelpley, with whom he eloped in 1886. The couple had eight children, three of whom died young.

In 1890 Brush moved to Paris for two years, the first of many long European sojourns he undertook with his family. During this Parisian interlude, Brush's art underwent a marked change as he shifted his attention from Indian subjects to images of mothers and children cast in the guise of Renaissance Madonnas. His wife and children usually served as models for these works. An 1898 trip to Florence strengthened the Renaissance flavor of his art, as did six further trips to Italy between 1903 and 1928. The paintings he produced from the 1890s onward, such as *Mother and Child* (c. 1897, Pennsylvania Academy of Fine Arts) and *Mother and Child: A Modern Madonna* (1919, Brooklyn Museum), evoke Renaissance prototypes in format, technique, and style, as well as in the poses and dress of the figures. During his years in Florence, Brush became deeply interested in Renaissance painting techniques, sometimes working with egg tempera on panel.

Brush's work from this period placed him in the forefront of the American Renaissance, an artistic, critical, and historical rediscovery of the Renaissance in the United States at the turn of the century. Artistically, this movement embraced the architecture of Richard Morris Hunt and McKim, Mead, and White, the sculpture of Augustus Saint-Gaudens, and the paintings of Abbot H. Thayer and Thomas W. Dewing. Brush had strong links with this group of artists. He had been friends with Thayer since his student days, and beginning in 1887 he spent a number of summers at artists' colonies in Cornish and Dublin, New Hampshire, with Saint-Gaudens, Thayer, Dewing, and other conservative, academically trained artists. In 1901 Brush purchased a farm in Dublin that eventually became the family's permanent home.

Brush's Renaissance-inspired works won many awards, including a gold medal at the Paris Exposition of 1900, and were snapped up soon after completion by public institutions and private collectors. Among the purchasers were the Metropolitan Museum of Art, the Museum of Fine Arts in Boston, the Corcoran Gallery of Art in Washington, D.C., and the Chicago businessman Potter Palmer. Brush was also in demand as a portraitist during these years, charging as much as $12,000 for a full-length portrait. Among his sitters was Henry George (National Portrait Gallery, Washington, D.C.), whom Brush greatly admired. In 1932 Sadakichi Hartman, in his *History of American Art*, described Brush as "standing now at the head of 'modern scholarly art' in America." Yet by 1930 the American Renaissance was over, and during that decade Brush virtually stopped painting. In 1937 a fire swept through his Dublin studio, destroying many of his works. He died in Hanover, New Hampshire.

Brush's career spanned the period when modern art was in ascendancy, yet he remained adamantly opposed to modernist ideas. In 1919 he told a reporter for the *New York Times*, "Artists are producing works today for which they ought to be arrested" (quoted in Morgan, p. 41). In his own art, Brush remained true to the academic ideals of his youth. His works embody his respect for tradition, his love of family, and his longing for stability and beauty in a world that seemed to him to have far too little of both.

• Brush's major works in public collections include *The Moose Chase* (1888, National Museum of American Art, Washington, D.C.), *In the Garden* (1906, Metropolitan Museum of Art), and *A Family Group* (1907, Art Institute of Chicago). Brush's papers are available on microfilm through the Archives of American Art, Smithsonian Institution. Nancy Douglas Bowditch, *George de Forest Brush: Recollections of a Joyous Painter* (1970), is an affectionate, anecdotal biography by the artist's daughter. Art-historical treatments include Joan B. Morgan, *George de Forest Brush: Master of the American Renaissance* (1985), and Mary Ann Lublin, "The Religion of Maternity: The Mother-and-Child Paintings of George de Forest Brush" (Ph.D. diss., Columbia Univ., 1989), which examines the intersection of Brush's political and artistic ideals; both contain extensive bibliographies. See also the Metropolitan Museum of Art's *Catalogue of American Paintings*, vol. 3 (1980), pp. 193–94. An obituary is in the *New York Times*, 25 Apr. 1941.

REBECCA BEDELL

BRUSH, George Jarvis (15 Dec. 1831–6 Feb. 1912), geologist and administrator, was born in Brooklyn, New York, the son of Jarvis Brush, an importing merchant, and Sarah Keeler. When Brush was about four, his father retired from business, and the family moved to Danbury, Connecticut, for six years, then returned to Brooklyn. In each place Brush's education was in private schools. When he was fifteen, he attended for six months a school in West Cornwall, Connecticut, conducted by Theodore S. Gold, who was keenly interested in mineralogy and natural history. These subjects appealed to Brush, but he was expected by his family to go into business. He worked in a mercantile house in New York City for about two years from 1847, occasionally finding time to collect minerals.

When he became seriously ill in 1848, Brush left his job, and "it was decided that he should devote himself to farming," presumably by his family. To prepare for that, Brush entered Yale College in 1848 in the second class of its School of Applied Chemistry, where John Pitkin Norton and Benjamin Silliman, Jr., were teaching agriculture and practical chemistry.

While a student, in 1850 Brush became assistant to Silliman in the chemistry and toxicology program in the medical department of the University of Louisville in Kentucky. During the spring and summer of 1851 he traveled throughout Europe in a group with the senior Benjamin Silliman. He completed his work at Yale, partly by a special examination because of his absences, and received the newly established degree of Ph.B. in 1852.

In the fall of 1852 Brush became assistant in chemistry at the University of Virginia in Charlottesville. He began researches in minerals with colleague J. Lawrence Smith, and they published together several chemical analyses of various minerals that clarified obscure points in their classification. During the summer of 1853 he was in charge of the exhibit of mineralogy at the International Exposition in New York. That fall he went to Europe to study mineralogy in greater detail at the University of Munich with Justus von Liebig, Franz von Kobell, and Max Joseph von Pettenkofer. He followed that with time at the mining school at Freiburg, Saxony.

In 1855 Brush was appointed to the newly established professorship of metallurgy at Yale in its Scientific School, the successor name of the unit from which he had graduated. He continued his studies abroad at the Royal School of Mines in London and with visits to mining regions in Great Britain and Europe, then began his new appointment in January 1857. He did considerable teaching and was said to be inspiring to students. From 1864 he primarily taught mineralogy. Brush married Harriet Silliman Trumbull in 1864; they had three daughters.

Edward Salisbury Dana noted that Brush "developed early a remarkably keen eye for recognizing mineral species, even those which were a puzzle to an ordinary mineralogist" (p. 393). James Dwight Dana found Brush's ability helpful while constantly updating the *Manual of Mineralogy*, which had become the standard in the field. Brush contributed information to the eighth, ninth, and tenth supplements of that book from 1860 to 1862 and to the fifth edition in 1868. He published *Manual of Determinative Mineralogy* (1874 and later editions to 1898), in which techniques of determining minerals were well explained. He also wrote about fifty scientific papers, including several with Edward S. Dana that described distinctive minerals from Branchville, Connecticut, in a region that had just come to the attention of geologists. Brush assembled a personal collection of about 15,000 minerals, by purchase and exchange. Carefully annotated for each specimen's history and locality, "this collection was especially notable for its completeness for the purposes of scientific study and the type specimens which it contained," said E. S. Dana (p. 393).

Because of generous donations by philanthropist Joseph Earl Sheffield, the school was renamed Sheffield Scientific School in 1860. Brush was appointed its director in 1872, having already served as its secretary and treasurer. He was especially responsible for maintaining Sheffield's continuing interest and financial support, and he ably managed its finances. The school increased considerably in faculty and students during his tenure. E. S. Dana noted:

> The successive steps by which the Sheffield Scientific School grew under his guidance, from 1857 on, show at every stage his ability and his strong hand. . . . It would be difficult, without detailed historical discussion, to give any adequate idea of the complexity and difficulty of the problems of the growing school and of the skill and wisdom with which they were met and solved by Mr. Brush. (Pp. 394–95)

Peabody Museum of Natural History, named for major donor George Peabody, was built in 1876, under the careful financial management of Yale professors Brush, James Dwight Dana, and Othniel Charles Marsh. Brush served effectively on the board of trustees of the museum for many years.

From 1863 to 1879 Brush was an associate editor of the *American Journal of Science*, the highly respected scientific journal established at Yale by Benjamin Silliman, Sr., in 1818. His own papers were published entirely in that journal.

When Brush retired as professor and director of Sheffield Scientific School in 1898, he continued as one of its trustees, and from 1900 he served as president of its board until his death. Brush donated his mineral collection and its associated library to the school in 1904, with a generous fund for its increase and maintenance, and he was gratified by the care that it received there.

Brush was elected to the National Academy of Sciences in 1868 and was president of the American Association for the Advancement of Science in 1881. He died in New Haven, Connecticut.

• Brush's archival papers are in the Yale University Library Manuscripts and Archives (George Jarvis Brush Family Papers). Biographies include William E. Ford, "George Jarvis Brush," *Science* 35 (1912): 409–11, with bibliography; and Edward S. Dana, "George Jarvis Brush," *American Journal of Science*, 4th ser., 33 (1912): 389–96, which was "reprinted with unessential changes" in National Academy of Sciences, *Memoirs* 17 (1924): 107–12, with bibliography.

ELIZABETH NOBLE SHOR

BRUTÉ DE RÉMUR, Simon William Gabriel (20 Mar. 1779–26 June 1839), first Catholic bishop of Vincennes, Indiana, was born in Rennes, France, the son of Simon Gabriel, the superintendent of royal domains in Brittany, France, and Jeanne Renée le Saulnier, an owner and manager of a printing business. Simon William Gabriel Bruté was born into a prerevolutionary bourgeois family that had influential associations in both the church and the state. When Bruté was seven his father died and his mother—who had inherited a printing business from her first husband, François Vatar, printer to the king and the Parliament at Rennes—became the primary source of support for the two Bruté sons, Simon and Alexander. When Bruté was ten years old the Bastille was stormed, and in 1791 his college at Rennes was forced to close because the clergy there refused to take the constitutional oath. During the Reign of Terror, the Brutés harbored various clergy.

In 1794, after the Terror, Bruté began studying medicine at Rennes and in 1799 went to the College of Medicine in Paris, graduating in 1803. He never practiced medicine, however, because immediately after graduation he entered the Seminary of St. Sulpice in Paris where he studied for the priesthood and thereafter joined the Society of Saint Sulpice, a religious order devoted exclusively to the education and training of the clergy.

After ordination to the priesthood in 1808 he became a professor of theology at the diocesan seminary in Rennes where he befriended fellow Briton Jean de Lamennais and his brother Félicité. In 1810, because of an invitation from the newly elected Bishop of Bardstown, Kentucky, Benedict Joseph Flaget, Bruté emigrated to the United States where numerous French clergy, fleeing the Revolution, had become missionaries. In 1791 the French Sulpicians had established Baltimore St. Mary's, the first Catholic seminary, where Bruté became a professor of philosophy until 1812. From 1812 to 1814 he taught philosophy and theology at the newly established Mount Saint Mary's College in Emmitsburg, Maryland. While at Mount Saint Mary's he met and became the spiritual director of Mother Elizabeth Seton, the foundress and superior of the Sisters of Charity, one of the first native orders of women religious in the United States. As spiritual director he was responsible for providing Mother Seton and members of her order with spiritual guidance in the confessional and for helping them appropriate in their lives the directives of their community's religious rule.

In the spring of 1815 Bruté went to France to visit his mother and to report to Sulpician superiors on the role of the Sulpicians in the United States. In late 1815 he returned to Baltimore, where he became president of St. Mary's College, a school established by the Sulpician Louis William Valentine DuBourg to provide a classical education for Protestant and Catholic young men and to serve as a preparatory school for the Baltimore seminary. Bruté, however, soon discovered that he was more at home at Mount Saint Mary's in Emmitsburg and returned there in 1818 to continue teaching theology. From 1818 until his ordination to the episcopacy of Vincennes, Indiana, in 1834, he taught theology, served as spiritual director of the Sisters of Charity, and became a theological consultant to Bishop John England of Charleston and other bishops in the fledgling American episcopal sees. His theological education, his knowledge of the newly educated clergy in the United States, and his awareness of the practical problems of lay trusteeism in American Catholicism made him an apt candidate for an episcopal see.

At the time of his appointment to Vincennes, a diocese that comprised the entire state of Indiana and part of eastern Illinois, there were only about 25,000 Catholics and two priests in the territory. The town of Vincennes had been established by the French in the early eighteenth century and still had a strong contingent of French Catholics in the early nineteenth century. German, Irish, and, until their removal in 1837, Potawatomi were also part of the Catholic community in the diocese. In 1835 Bruté, like many other French émigré bishops, went to France to secure financial support and to recruit priests, seminarians, and women religious for his new diocese. By the time of his death, he had increased the number of clergy to twenty-five (most of whom were from France), brought the Sisters of Charity to Vincennes, established twenty-seven new churches, an episcopal house-seminary, a college for young men, and a girls' academy.

Shy and retiring, Bruté was more comfortable in his library and behind his teaching desk than he was in ecclesiastical affairs. He preferred the spirituality of the inner life to the activity of ecclesiastical politics and institution-building. After a trip to the Third Provincial Council of Baltimore in 1837, he developed tuberculosis and never recovered his health. He died at Vincennes.

• Bruté's letters and unpublished papers are located primarily in the Archives of the Diocese of Vincennes (now Indianapolis), the Archdiocese of Baltimore, Propaganda Fide (Rome), the Sulpicians (Baltimore), and the University of Notre Dame. There is no adequate critical biography of Bruté, but Theodore Maynard, *The Reed and the Rock: Portrait of Simon Bruté* (1942), provides basic biographical information. See also Leo F. Ruskowski, *French Émigré Priests in the United States, 1791–1815* (1940), and Christopher J. Kauffman, *Tradition and Transformation in Catholic Culture: The Priests of Saint Sulpice in the United States from 1791 to the Present* (1987).

PATRICK W. CAREY

BRYAN, Andrew (1737–6 Oct. 1812), clergyman, was born at Goose Creek, South Carolina, about sixteen miles from Charleston. His slave parents' names are unknown. George Liele, the itinerant African-American Baptist minister from Savannah, Georgia, baptized Bryan in 1782. Bryan married Hannah (maiden name unknown) about nine years after his conversion. Jonathan Bryan, Andrew's master and a New Light Presbyterian sympathetic to the evangelical movement in the South, allowed him to exhort both blacks and whites. About 1790 a white landowner allowed Bryan to build a wooden shed on the outskirts of Savannah at Yamacraw. Here Bryan held religious meetings for African Americans, both slave and free, between sunrise and sunset. When white opposition arose, Bryan and his hearers retreated to the nearby swamp to conduct their religious activities.

The evangelical revivals fostered by the Second Great Awakening drew blacks and whites together into common religious circles. In 1788 Abraham Marshall, a white Baptist clergyman, ordained Bryan, baptized about fifty of his followers, and organized them into a congregation known as the Ethiopian Church of Jesus Christ. By strict Baptist rules, the constitution of the church was an irregular act, since a council of Baptist clergy was not involved. Nevertheless, the Ethiopian Church of Jesus Christ became a center of Baptist activity among African Americans in the Savannah region.

During the British occupation of Savannah, whites, fearful of slave insurrection, imprisoned Andrew and his brother Sampson. While defending himself before the city magistrates, Andrew Bryan, according to a report in the *Baptist Annual Register*, "told his persecutors that he rejoiced not only to be whipped, but *would freely suffer death for the cause of Jesus Christ*." Jonathan Bryan arranged for the release of Andrew and Sampson and allowed Andrew to resume worship services in a barn on his estate at Brampton. A Savannah court ruled that the congregation could hold meetings between sunrise and sunset, which it did without significant opposition during the next two years. By 1790 Bryan's church had 225 full communicants and about 350 converts. Renamed the first African Baptist Church, it was now a member of the predominantly white Georgia Baptist Association, which had decided that Marshall's irregular action in organizing the congregation was justifiable given the circumstances.

In 1794, with financial assistance from influential whites, Bryan purchased a plot of land in Savannah for a permanent church building. In 1795 Jonathan Bryan died, and his heirs allowed Andrew to purchase his freedom for £50 sterling. Bryan's congregation prospered, growing to over 700 members in 1800. In that year Bryan wrote the English Baptist John Rippon, publisher of the *Baptist Annual Register*: "With much pleasure, I inform you, dear Sir, that I enjoy good health, and am strong in body, at the age of sixty-three years, and am blessed with a pious wife, whose freedom I have obtained and an only daughter and child who is married to a free man, tho' she, and consequently under our laws, her seven children, five sons and two daughters, are slaves. By a kind Providence I am well provided for, as to worldly comforts, (tho' I have had very little given me as a minister) having a house and lot in this city, besides the land on which several buildings stand, for which I receive a small rent, and a fifty-six acre tract of land, with all necessary buildings, four miles in the country, and eight slaves; for whose education and happiness, I am enabled thro' mercy to provide."

First African Baptist Church sponsored the formation of a daughter congregation, Second African Baptist Church, in 1799. Second African eventually sponsored the organization of the Ogeechee or Third African Baptist Church. At the time of Bryan's death, First African Baptist had 1,458 members. Andrew Marshall, Bryan's nephew, succeeded him as pastor. First African Baptist Church, with its roots in the work of Liele and Bryan in the Savannah region and the preaching of David George on the Galphin plantation at Silver Bluff, Georgia, has been called the first independent African-American Baptist church in North America. Recent research has uncovered earlier Baptist slave congregations, but Bryan and First African remain important in early black Baptist history. When Bryan died in Savannah, the white Savannah Baptist Association eulogized him, declaring, "This son of Africa, after suffering inexpressible persecutions in the cause of his divine Master, was at length permitted to discharge the duties of the ministry among his colored friends in peace and quiet, hundreds of whom, through his instrumentality, were brought to a knowledge of the truth as 'it is in Jesus.'"

Andrew Bryan pioneered in efforts to plant the Christian faith under the Baptist banner among fellow blacks in the postrevolutionary era. Though not without opposition, he enjoyed a surprising degree of religious freedom during the evangelical renaissance in the South. After the insurrections led by Denmark Vesey in 1822 and Nat Turner, a fellow Baptist, in 1831, the white South severely restricted black preaching. Nevertheless, the seeds sown by Bryan and others during the earlier decades matured. Historically, more African Americans, slave and free, have belonged to Baptist churches in the South than to any other denomination.

• The principal sources of information on Bryan are the occasional Baptist almanacs, known as *The Baptist Annual Register*, edited and published by John Rippon, the English Baptist, in the early 1790s. They have been republished in "Letters Showing the Rise and Progress of the Early Negro Churches of Georgia and the West Indies," *Journal of Negro History* 1 (Jan. 1916): 69–92. John W. Davis drew heavily on these materials in his "George Liele and Andrew Bryan, Pioneer Negro Baptist Preachers," *Journal of Negro History* 3 (Apr. 1918): 119–27. There are two competing histories of Savannah's First African Baptist Church, due to a split in the congregation in the 1820s over doctrinal teachings. One is by James M. Simms, *The First Colored Baptist Church in North America, Constituted at Savannah, Georgia, January 20, A.D. 1788* (1888); the other is by Emmanual K. Love, *History of the First African Baptist Church from Its Organization, January 20th 1788 to July 1st 1888* (1888). See also Edgar G. Thomas, *The First African Baptist Church of North America* (1925). Walter H. Brooks sought to resolve the question of preeminence by tracing the roots of the black Baptists of Savannah back to the slave congregation at Silver Bluff, Georgia, in "The Priority of Silver Bluff Church and Its Promoters," *Journal of Negro History* 7 (Apr. 1922): 172–96. More contemporary accounts of the origin and evolution of black Baptist churches are Mechal Sobel, *Trabelin' On: The Slave Journey to an Afro-Baptist Faith* (1979), and James M. Washington, Jr., *Frustrated Fellowship: The Black Baptist Quest for Social Power* (1986).

MILTON C. SERNETT

BRYAN, Anna E. (July 1858–21 Feb. 1901), kindergarten educator, was born in Louisville, Kentucky, the daughter of Parish G. Bryan, a piano maker, and Eliza H. Belle Richard. She graduated from Louisville's

Girls High School in 1878. While visiting with friends in Chicago she heard about the idea of the kindergarten, which had been introduced to the United States in the late 1850s by German immigrants, and enrolled in a training school run by the Chicago Free Kindergarten Association. In 1884, after completing what was apparently a rather minimal course, she began teaching at the Marie Chapel Charity Kindergarten in Chicago. In 1887 she returned to Louisville to direct a training school being organized by the Louisville Free Kindergarten Association.

Bryan became a leader of the "free" kindergarten movement, as the charity organizations that provided kindergarten education at little or no cost to poor children in the 1880s and 1890s were called. She became well known for advocating modification of Friedrich Froebel's formalistic pedagogy, which required kindergarten teachers to have young children play in prearranged ways with the sets of small wooden blocks and other materials that Froebel called "gifts" and to do complicated arts and crafts activities he called "occupations." Rather than insisting on strict adherence to Froebelian orthodoxy, as was the norm in the early decades of the American kindergarten movement, Bryan experimented with different educational approaches and encouraged other kindergarten teachers to do likewise. In 1890 she was asked to describe her innovative practices to the kindergarten department of the National Education Association. In her published speech, "The Letter Killeth," she expressed strong opposition to kindergarten educators who followed Froebel's methods to the letter rather than thinking independently about what was best for young children. An advocate of "creative spontaneity," she favored "free play" over "dictation play," a radical departure from the rigidly sequenced approach of early, German-trained Froebelians who taught children to copy Froebel's games and activities in an exact, unvarying order.

Bryan's intellectual independence, warm personal manner, and great energy attracted able young women to train under her. Her best-known pupil, Patty Smith Hill, aided in her experimentation and went on to become a professor of kindergarten education at Columbia University's Teachers College in New York City and the leader of the younger generation that took over the kindergarten movement in the twentieth century. Like Bryan, Hill encouraged her trainees to incorporate aspects of children's actual daily home life into their kindergarten teaching rather than relying solely on the songs, games, and finger plays Froebel had taken from German folklore.

Bryan's work with the Louisville Free Kindergarten Association was successful; after seven years the program had expanded from one to eight kindergartens and from five trainees to more than forty. Taking a kind of sabbatical leave, she spent the winter of 1893–1894 in New York City, studying art and design and attending science lectures. In 1894 she was asked to become director of kindergarten training at the Armour Institute in Chicago. She accepted, leaving Hill in charge of the kindergartens in Louisville.

While in Chicago, Bryan worked with Francis Parker, John Dewey, and others in the progressive educational reform movement centered in that city. Dewey consulted her when he started a kindergarten at his University of Chicago Laboratory School and found her flexible approach a welcome change from the rigidity of many in the kindergarten movement. Bryan also became allied with psychologist G. Stanley Hall, founder of the child study movement, an early variant of developmental psychology, which relied in part on data collected from teachers and mothers in formulating its theoretical principles. She attended Hall's summer sessions on child study at Clark University in Worcester, Massachusetts, in 1894, stayed to listen to Hall when other kindergarten educators walked out of a presentation he gave criticizing Froebelian orthodoxy in Chicago in 1895, and in 1896 helped Hall design a questionnaire to be distributed to kindergarten teachers, which solicited information about their use of experimental practices. Bryan chaired the International Kindergarten Union's committee on child study from 1897 to 1901, served on its teacher-training committee, and sided with Patty Smith Hill and other younger kindergarten leaders in the debates over curricular reform that divided the movement at the turn of the century, when older and younger kindergarten advocates split into factions over whether or not to adapt Froebel's ideas in the light of modern psychological theories.

Bryan's leavening influence was important in the adaptation of Froebelian kindergarten methods to American culture. Though her career was cut short by her death in Chicago of heart disease, her innovativeness and impact on younger kindergarten educators did much to transform the kindergarten from a formalistic, philosophically based, German pedagogical method to a more experimental, psychologically oriented, modern, American educational reform. Bryan's ideas on the importance of teachers incorporating children's own interests and themes from their home life into classroom curricula prevailed and shaped the practice of kindergarten teaching for years to come.

• The papers of Patty Smith Hill, held at the Filson Club Library in Louisville, contain references to Bryan. See also Anna E. Bryan, "The Letter Killeth," National Education Association, *Journal of Proceedings and Addresses* (1890), pp. 573–81. There are memorial articles on Bryan in the *Kindergarten Magazine* 13 (Apr. 1901): 433–41, and a biographical entry by Patty Smith Hill in Committee of Nineteen, *Pioneers of the Kindergarten in America* (1924). Bryan's work is discussed in Cora L. Stockton, "A Glimpse of the Louisville Kindergartens," *Kindergarten Magazine* 2 (Apr. 1890): 383–86; Ilse Forest, *Preschool Education: A Historical and Critical Study* (1924); and Michael Steven Shapiro, *Child's Garden: The Kindergarten Movement from Froebel to Dewey* (1983).

BARBARA BEATTY

BRYAN, Charles Wayland (10 Feb. 1867–4 Mar. 1945), political adviser, governor of Nebraska, and vice presidential nominee, was born in Salem, Illinois, the son of Silas Lillard Bryan, a lawyer and farmer, and Mariah Elizabeth Jennings. He was the brother of William Jennings Bryan. Bryan's father was active in Democratic politics and served as an Illinois state senator and circuit judge. A well-educated and deeply religious man, Silas Bryan died in 1880 when Charles was just thirteen years old. An undistinguished student, Charles entered the University of Chicago in 1885 but dropped out his first year. For a short time he farmed and raised livestock. In 1891, at the urging of his brother William, who was then serving his first term as a U.S. congressman from Nebraska, Charles moved to Lincoln, where he worked for the Purity Extract Company selling products such as soap, tobacco, flavoring extracts, and baking powder. In 1892 Charles Bryan returned to Salem to marry his childhood girlfriend, Bessie Louis Brokaw. They would have three children, one of whom, Silas Millard Bryan, would serve as lieutenant governor of Minnesota.

Charles Bryan's political career began in 1896 when he became his older brother's secretary. William, who was nominated as the Democratic presidential nominee in 1896, 1900, and 1908, depended heavily on Charles to handle his personal correspondence, schedule speaking engagements, maintain political files, recommend patronage appointments, organize supporters, and develop campaign strategies. Bryan also managed his brother's personal finances and from 1901 until 1923 published his nationally known newspaper, the *Commoner*. The publication promoted William's career and provided an important voice for progressive, midwestern causes that the Bryans supported. Although Charles and William's careers would remain inextricably intertwined, Charles launched his own political career when he was elected to serve a two-year term on the Lincoln City Commission in 1915. Bryan not only won election to the city commission, but he was chosen by his fellow commissioners to be mayor of the city. While serving the city Bryan supported the municipal ownership of utilities, challenged the power of large corporations, and expanded legal services and welfare programs for the poor.

In 1916 and again in 1918 Bryan failed in his bid to win his party's nomination for governor, but in 1921 he was elected to serve another term as city commissioner. Bryan also served as superintendent of streets and public improvements. In 1922, after receiving the Democratic party's nomination, he was elected governor, serving in office from 1923 to 1925. As governor Bryan supported a state income tax, Prohibition, the expansion of farm credit programs, and reduced government expenditures. He was nominated to run for governor again in 1924 but withdrew to accept the Democratic party's vice presidential nomination.

In 1924 a badly divided Democratic party chose John W. Davis, a conservative, as its nominee. To balance the ticket and placate the Bryan wing of the party, Charles Bryan was nominated for the vice presidency. Bryan and Davis were soundly defeated in the campaign by Republicans Calvin Coolidge and Charles G. Dawes. Though they campaigned hard, outpolling Robert La Follette of the Progressive party, Bryan and Davis won only 28.8 percent of the popular vote, failing even to carry Nebraska. Following William Bryan's death in 1925, Bryan again ran for governor in 1926 and 1928 but lost both elections. Undaunted, Bryan was again nominated by the Democrats to run for governor in 1930. He won the election and was reelected for a second term in 1932. From 1931 to 1935, as governor of Nebraska, Bryan championed relief for depression- and drought-stricken farmers, old-age assistance, tariff reductions on manufactured goods, and assistance for bank depositors who had lost their money following the collapse of the financial system. In 1934 Bryan sought national office, running for the U.S. Senate, but was defeated in the primaries. In 1935, however, he was elected to serve another two-year term as mayor of Lincoln. In 1938 he ran unsuccessfully for governor as an independent. In 1940 Bryan again ran for national office, this time for the U.S. Congress, but went down to defeat. Bryan made his last attempt, his ninth, to win the governorship in 1942 but again lost in the general election.

Charles Bryan will forever live in the shadow of his more famous brother, William Jennings Bryan. He served his brother well but was himself a major political force in Nebraska for nearly thirty years. Charles Bryan failed in his efforts to gain national office but gained national fame when he was chosen as the vice presidential nominee of the Democratic party in 1924. While Bryan was considered abrasive, egotistical, and authoritarian by many of his contemporaries, he worked hard, as a populist and a progressive, to maintain the people's voice in government. Bryan died at his home in Lincoln.

• The Charles W. Bryan Papers, which cover his years as governor, are located at the Nebraska State Historical Society in Lincoln. The most important secondary source available is Larry G. Osnes, "Charles W. Bryan: 'His Brother's Keeper'," *Nebraska History* 48 (Spring 1967): 45–67. Major studies of William Jennings Bryan, including books by Leroy Ashby, Robert W. Cherny, Paolo E. Coletta, Louis W. Koening, Paul W. Glad, Lawrence W. Levine, Wayne Williams, and Charles M. Wilson, contain useful information about the Bryan family. See also James Olson, *History of Nebraska* (1955) and *The Memoirs of William Jennings Bryan* (1925). For contemporary accounts of Charles Bryan see in particular Albert Shaw, "Nine Governors of the Middle West," *American Review of Reviews* 67 (Mar. 1923): 275–86; Chester H. Rowell, "Brookhart, Howell, and 'Brother Charley' Bryan," *World's Work* 46 (Sept. 1923): 478–85; and William Jennings Bryan, "My Brother Charles," *World's Work* 48 (Sept. 1924): 553.

MICHAEL W. SCHUYLER

BRYAN, George (11 Aug. 1731–27 Jan. 1791), politician and jurist, was born in Dublin, Ireland, the son of Samuel Bryan, a merchant, and Sarah Dennis. Little is known about his first twenty years in Dublin other than that he was reared in a Presbyterian household while his father developed trade connections in the colonies. Apparently self-educated, Bryan clearly learned much about his father's commercial activities. Samuel Bryan arranged a partnership for his son with Philadelphia merchant and fellow Presbyterian James Wallace in 1752. George Bryan then migrated to America, but his joint venture lasted only three years.

As an independent merchant, Bryan developed an extensive commercial network that encompassed most of the major trade marts in the British Isles, Europe, and the West Indies. Beyond a lucrative import and export trade and investment in several ships, Bryan established a successful retail business in Philadelphia. He profited substantially from war contracts in the French and Indian War and speculated in land from Canada to New Jersey.

Bryan married Elizabeth Smith in 1757, and the increasingly prosperous couple had ten children. While his family and business grew, Bryan became a lay leader in the Presbyterian church. Serving the church in a variety of capacities, he sought to heal the schism that had developed during the Great Awakening. This religious movement had split the denomination between the New Side faction, which embraced the new emotional, revivalist style of worship, and the Old Side faction, which remained skeptical of the innovations.

Bryan's involvement in church governance led him into provincial politics, where he became a Presbyterian activist in the struggle against the dominant Quaker antiproprietary faction. Angered by the failure of the government to defend predominantly Presbyterian frontier settlers and the Quaker faction's effort to transform Pennsylvania into a royal colony, Bryan and fellow Presbyterian Thomas Willing joined other opponents of Benjamin Franklin and Joseph Galloway and replaced Franklin and Galloway as assemblymen from Philadelphia in the 1764 elections. The same year Governor John Penn appointed Bryan to the courts of common pleas and quarter sessions.

In 1765 imperial concerns intruded into provincial politics with Parliament's passage of the Stamp Act. Eager to prevent the implementation of direct taxation on the colonies, Bryan not only helped write the instructions for his colony's delegation to the Stamp Act Congress in New York but was also one of its four delegates. While there, he lost his seat in the assembly in the 1765 elections. Although defeated in legislative politics, Bryan continued his budding judicial career.

While not a leader in the resistance movement against British rule, Bryan nonetheless joined John Dickinson in writing the "Centinel" essays, which opposed the establishment of an Anglican bishop in America and the English government's expansion of admiralty courts. He also joined other Philadelphia merchants in supporting the nonimportation agreements organized in response to the Stamp Act and the 1767 Townshend duties, a decision that may have contributed to his declaring bankruptcy in 1771.

Bryan's economic difficulties and an illness kept him out of the resistance movement against England in the early 1770s. Yet, after the Second Continental Congress declared America independent of England and the state of Pennsylvania approved a constitution, Bryan became a leader in state politics, a role he would play until his death. Although he did not attend the convention that wrote the state constitution, he became one of the strongest supporters of this radical document. Almost immediately opponents denounced its creation of a unicameral legislature and an elected administrative council rather than a governor. In 1777 Bryan, writing as "Whitlocke," penned a series of essays defending the document and rejecting the concept of bicameralism because, in his view, upper houses only served as bastions for the wealthy. Elected to the Supreme Executive Council in the same year, he served for three years. For most of that time he was vice president of the council, but when President Thomas Wharton died in May 1778, Bryan carried out the role of chief executive for the state until the election of Joseph Reed in December of that year.

Throughout his years on the council, Bryan led the struggle to mobilize the state's resources to meet threats on the frontier posed by American Indians and Tories and to help provision the Continental army. He also actively supported restrictions on prices and exports to deal with inflation and profiteering merchants who, he believed, were hoarding and driving up the prices of basic commodities.

When his council term ended in 1779, Bryan won election to the assembly, where he supported the seizure of proprietary land and pushed through an act for the gradual emancipation of slaves in Pennsylvania, a model for other northern states. Perhaps Bryan's greatest legacy, the abolition of slavery, he believed, was an essential act of justice and morality. In a new nation committed to the natural rights of man, Bryan argued that slavery was a disgrace.

A key figure in the creation of state government in Pennsylvania, Bryan gained an opportunity to enforce and interpret its laws. In 1780 Reed appointed him to the state's supreme court, a position he held until his death. Four years later Pennsylvanians elected him to the Council of Censors, which had been charged by the state constitution to meet every seven years and recommend the repeal of laws contrary to the charter's provisions and was empowered to call a constitutional convention to amend the document. While on the council, Bryan played a key role in stopping those who advocated a constitutional convention to replace the state's radical government with a bicameral legislature and governor.

Although Bryan acknowledged that the Articles of Confederation, adopted in 1781, were in need of revision, he vigorously opposed the 1787 Constitution and the centralization of power it portended. Believing that the majority of Pennsylvanians opposed the new framework for a national government, he worked hard to rally anti-Federalist forces. His son Samuel Bryan, probably in collaboration with his father, wrote a series of essays that borrowed the pseudonym George Bryan had used two decades earlier. In "Centinel," Samuel warned of the threat the new document posed to state sovereignty and individual liberties, particularly with its power to tax citizens directly, its standing army, and its omission of a bill of rights. Once Pennsylvania ratified the document, Bryan worked with anti-Federalists throughout the nation in a vain effort to call a second constitutional convention to offer amendments to the document.

Bryan was on the losing side not only in the ratification struggle but also in the battle to preserve the state constitution. Since the late 1770s the conflict over the constitution had become institutionalized with the emergence of two parties. Bryan led the Constitutionalist party against the attacks of a faction known initially as the Anticonstitutionalists and later the Republican party. In 1790 the latter gained the ultimate victory with the approval of a new state constitution that included a bicameral legislature and a governor. Bryan argued that the opposition triumphed because Pennsylvania's elite had deluded the voters. In reality the Constitutionalist party, with its base of Scots-Irish Presbyterian and German Reformed voters, gradually lost power to a stronger, better-organized ethno-religious coalition of Quakers, Lutherans, Anglicans, and Baptists.

Bryan led a long life of public service. In addition to his work for the Presbyterian church, in the assembly, on the executive council, and on the bench, he was named port officer for Philadelphia early in the revolutionary war and for many years served as a trustee of the University of Pennsylvania. Throughout his public life, he acted from a consistent core of principles. He believed that government should be responsible directly to the citizens, and as a consequence, it should be simple in structure. Always believing that the rich sought special privilege from government and that they tended to abuse the power given them, he saw himself as an advocate for the poor and the powerless. Although his position was apparent in his fight against the 1787 Constitution and efforts to replace the state constitution, it was most evident in his opposition to the Bank of North America. He viewed this financial institution, chartered in Pennsylvania, as a monopoly devised for the benefit of the wealthy at the expense of the masses.

This able statesman, jurist, political organizer, and essayist had lost his struggle for simple, decentralized government responsive to the people by the time he died in Philadelphia. Yet his determined opposition to slavery contributed to the ultimate demise of an institution that denied the freedoms he had struggled to maintain.

• Many of Bryan's letters are in the Historical Society of Pennsylvania, and his diary is in the Library of Congress. Some Bryan letters are also in the Joseph Reed Papers in the New-York Historical Society. His activity with the Presbyterian church can be followed in the First Presbyterian Church Minutes in the Presbyterian Historical Society in Philadelphia. Some of Bryan's letters are published in William B. Reed, *Life and Correspondence of Joseph Reed* (1847). Two biographies are Burton Alva Konkle, *George Bryan and the Constitution of Pennsylvania 1731–1791* (1922), and Joseph S. Foster, *In Pursuit of Equal Liberty: George Bryan and the Revolution in Pennsylvania* (1994).

LARRY GRAGG

BRYAN, Hugh (1699–31 Dec. 1753), planter, assemblyman, and evangelical Christian, was born near Beaufort in South Carolina, the son of Joseph Bryan, an Indian trader and farmer, and Janet Cochran. Bryan's father was an early settler on South Carolina's southern frontier, and it was there that Hugh Bryan spent most of his life. As a boy he was taken prisoner by Indians during the Yamasee War (1715) and was carried to St. Augustine, where he was eventually released. According to tradition, Bryan "met with a Bible among the *Indians*," which sustained him through the ordeal and gave him a concern for things spiritual that lasted his whole life. Married to Catherine Barnwell, a member of one of the region's most important families, he rose rapidly both socially and economically and by the late 1730s Bryan was the largest cattle raiser in St. Helena's Parish. He was also a substantial rice planter and slaveholder.

His wife's conversion to evangelical Christianity led to the family's association with English evangelist George Whitefield, and Bryan and his brother Jonathan became enthusiastic followers. They contributed financially to Bethesda, Whitefield's orphanage near Savannah; and in 1742 when a Spanish attack on Georgia seemed imminent, the brothers offered their plantations as a haven for Whitefield's community. Under Whitefield's influence, Bryan began intensely studying religious writings and applying what he read to contemporary events. He concluded that a series of misfortunes that had befallen South Carolina (slave rebellion, a fire in Charleston, drought, and epidemic diseases) were signs of God's displeasure. Communication with what he called an "Angel of Light" convinced him that if the colony did not repent, it would be destroyed by "African Hosts" who would be the instruments of God's vengeance. Because Bryan's evangelical activities had included assembling "great Bodies of Negroes" for religious instruction, he was already being watched, and in 1742, when he sent the Commons House of Assembly his predictions, orders were issued for his arrest. Amid the uproar that followed, Bryan wandered into the woods and, according to witnesses, tried to part the waters of a creek with a staff and walk across. Pulled from the stream before he drowned, he blamed what had taken place on "a Delusion of Satan" and repented for the "Disquiet which I may have occasioned to Country." Bryan married Mary Prioleau in 1744. It is not known what happened to his first wife, and there is no record of children from either marriage.

Bryan returned to his plantation in St. Helena and did not trouble the colony again. He did not reject evangelicalism, however, nor did he stop teaching religion to slaves, and in this regard he represents an early example of what would become the "Christian master." He also helped to found the Stoney Creek Independent Presbyterian Church, one of the oldest dissenter congregations in the province, and one that allowed a significant degree of slave participation. Thus Bryan's career offers insight into the impact that Whitefieldian revivalism had on southern slaveholders. Bryan's "enthusiastic Prophecies" of slave rebellion as a punishment for Carolina's sins may have retarded the evangelical movement in the colony, for supporters of the established church now argued that if carried to its extreme, Whitefield's crusade threatened the racial relations on which slavery rested. Meanwhile Bryan, no longer the center of attention, lived out his days as he believed Whitefield, and God, would have him live. He apparently died at his plantation in St. Helena, for his grave is nearby.

• The largest single body of primary material relating to Bryan's career can be found in Hugh Bryan and Mary Hutson, *Living Christianity Delineated* . . . (1760). See also Harvey H. Jackson, "Hugh Bryan and the Evangelical Movement in Colonial South Carolina," *William and Mary Quarterly*, 3d ser., 43 (1986): 594–614, and "Prophecy and Community: Hugh Bryan, George Whitefield, and the Stoney Creek Independent Presbyterian Church," *American Presbyterians: Journal of Presbyterian History* 49 (1991): 11–20; Leigh Eric Schmidt, "The 'Grand Prophet', Hugh Bryan: Early Evangelicalism's Challenge to the Establishment and Slavery in the Colonial South," *South Carolina Historical and Genealogical Magazine* 88 (1986): 238–50; Alan Gallay, "The Great Awakening in the Deep South: George Whitefield, the Bryan Family, and the Origins of Slaveholders' Paternalism," *Journal of Southern History* 53 (1987): 369–94; and Gallay, *The Formation of a Planter Elite: Jonathan Bryan and the Southern Colonial Frontier* (1989).

HARVEY H. JACKSON

BRYAN, John Stewart (23 Oct. 1871–16 Oct. 1944), newspaper publisher and college president, was born at Brook Hill, Henrico County, Virginia, the son of Joseph Bryan, a newspaper publisher, and Isobel Lamont Stewart. Bryan grew up at "Brook Hill" and "Laburnum," his family's ancestral estates near Richmond, Virginia. Among his ancestors were Virginia's first families, including the Byrds and the Blands, as well as many leaders of the Confederacy; General Robert E. Lee visited Bryan's home on several occasions. These connections proved important in shaping his sense of Virginia's place in history and his stubborn resistance to perceived intrusions into its affairs by northerners. He graduated from the University of Virginia in 1893 with an M.A. and earned his LL.B. from the Harvard Law School in 1897.

After practicing law briefly in New York and in Richmond, in 1900 Bryan joined his father as an associate at the *Richmond Times* and the *Richmond Dispatch* (formerly the *Evening Leader*), the family newspapers. In 1903, the newspapers were consolidated into the *Richmond Times-Dispatch*; in 1908, at his father's death, he became publisher, a position he held for thirty-six unbroken years. Bryan worked closely with the journalistic community during World War I, helping to establish camp newspapers for troops and working to provide more complete coverage of the war for the reading public. He enjoyed mentoring young editors, many of whom became managing editors at major southern newspapers, including those at most of Virginia's important dailies. He was a charter member of the Associated Press at its reorganization in 1900 and served as president of the American Newspaper Publishers Association in 1926–1928. Bryan published two books privately, one on his father, *Joseph Bryan: His Times, His Family, His Friends* (1935), and one on his grandfather, John Randolph Bryan, *Diary of John Randolph Bryan* (1941). His other business activities included a term as the director of the Southern Railway.

Following an active role as a member of the school board of Henrico County, Bryan served on the boards of visitors of the University of Virginia (1920–1922) and the College of William and Mary (1926–1934); his service with William and Mary included a term as vice rector of the board (he assumed the duties of rector during the extended incapacitation of J. Dillard). He also served on the board of overseers of Harvard University from 1937 to 1943. In 1934 the board at William and Mary selected Bryan as the successor to J. A. C. Chandler. His selection was a watershed event in the history of William and Mary, signaling the future direction of the college away from teacher education to a more traditional liberal arts program. Bryan's administration was noted for its genial profaculty tenor, a marked contrast from the previous administration. During his presidency, student admission standards were tightened, and the student body became a female majority for the first time in its history. He retired from this position in 1942, when the trustees named him chancellor, a title originally assigned to George Washington.

Bryan participated in a number of civic activities. He sponsored the Richmond Young Men's Christian Association and was president of the Confederate Memorial Institute, the Virginia Historical Society, and, in 1933, the Community Chests and Councils. He served on the International Education Board, the National Council of the Protestant Episcopal Church, and the board of the Richmond Public Library, and he held membership in the Southern Historical Society, the Society of the Cincinnati in Virginia, the Society of Colonial Wars, the Sons of the American Revolution, the Sons of Confederate Veterans, the American Antiquarian Society, and the New England Historical Genealogical Society. Bryan represented Virginia at the Democratic National Convention several times. In 1943 the Virginia Chamber of Commerce named him First Citizen of the state.

In 1903 Bryan married Anne Eliza Tennant, and the couple had three children.

Bryan will be remembered for his role in making the College of William and Mary a preeminent liberal arts college. His efforts saw the school through the effects of the Great Depression and set the stage for its rapid expansion following World War II. At his death, he was eulogized by many important figures, including Franklin D. Roosevelt. He died in Richmond.

• Bryan's personal papers are in the archives at the College of William and Mary. For a detailed account of his administration at William and Mary, see Susan H. Godson et al., *The College of William & Mary: A History*, vol. 2: *1888–1993* (1993). An extensive obituary is in his newspaper, the *Richmond Times-Dispatch*, 17 Oct. 1944, and one is in the [Williamsburg] *Virginia Gazette*, 20 Oct. 1944.

GENE C. FANT, JR.

BRYAN, Kirk (22 July 1888–21 Aug. 1950), geologist, was born in Albuquerque, New Mexico, the son of Richard William Dickinson Bryan, a teacher and lawyer, and Suzannah Hunter Patten, a teacher. Bryan lived to early manhood in Albuquerque, where he earned one of the first bachelor's degrees (1909) in geology granted by the University of New Mexico. His first two years at the university were devoted to the classics, at the wish of his father, who had been alienated by a dictatorial German scientist, Emil Bessels, while on the Arctic Polaris Expedition (1871–1873) and did not wish his son to pursue his interests in science. Having exhausted the classics curriculum, however, Kirk turned to geology; after graduation, he continued his study of the subject at Yale. He received a Ph.D. in geology there in 1920. In 1923 he married Mary MacArthur; they had four children.

During World War I Kirk was drafted as a private and served with the U.S. Expeditionary Forces in Europe (1918–1919) in the Corps of Engineering. He received a field citation and promotion to second lieutenant for block diagrams he constructed of battlefield terrains. This military service created an enduring interest in engineering geology, which he subsequently used in evaluating dam and reservoir sites for the Republic of Mexico.

Bryan's professional life began in 1912 as an aide in the U.S. Geological Survey, where he rose to senior geologist by 1926. He served as visiting lecturer in physiography at Harvard University in 1924–1925, was appointed assistant professor in 1926, and rose to full professor by 1943. He continued teaching and research at Harvard until his death.

Kirk's scientific reputation is based primarily on his research on arid-region landforms and processes, conducted largely in the southwestern United States. He was also a noted leader in the geology and dating of archeological sites. Early in his career he became a recognized authority on the evolution of mountain slopes, especially of pediments, the smooth, gently-sloping, erosional rock surfaces at the foot of rugged mountains in arid regions. The recognition that low-relief surfaces could form within rugged mountainous terrain without reducing the whole to a marine-controlled baselevel (a peneplain) was a major contribution to geological thinking. Kirk argued that pediments were formed by mountain-front recession under the attack of rock weathering, rainwash, and rill erosion, contrary to the widely held opinion that they were carved by lateral stream erosion.

At Harvard, Kirk's interests and research were strongly interdisciplinary, ranging from geology to botany, soil science, cryopedology (frozen ground), paleoclimatology, hydrology, and aspects of engineering. A latent interest in archeology blossomed and led to his participation in the education of archeologists and research on the geology and age of archeological sites. Archeologists greatly appreciated his interest in their problems.

As a review editor for the *Zeitschrift für Geomorphologie*, Bryan wrote many pithy critical reviews of geomorphological papers. He had a knack for penetrating succinctly to the core of a subject and revealing errors in an author's thinking. Bryan wrote fluently and gracefully; his USGS mentor, Oscar E. Meinzer, described one of Kirk's government publications as so interesting that it has the fascination of a good novel.

Bryan's benchmark papers on arid landforms and processes became the basis of later research by others. His studies on archeological geology were almost unique within the discipline. However, his greatest contribution involved personal relationships, largely teaching, advising, and supporting students and working with colleagues. He had an uncanny ability for recognizing talent in students, whom he then helped to capitalize on their abilities. He was friendly, warm, humorous, infectiously enthusiastic, and constructively critical. Personal relationships with many former students extended far beyond their graduation. He was affectionately known to many as "Uncle Kirk" and occasionally referred to himself that way. Only seven scientists whose work might generously be classed as related to the earth sciences were awarded the National Medal of Science between 1952 and 1994, and two were Bryan's students.

Despite many years of residence in New England, Kirk remained a New Mexican to the core and returned frequently to his home state for fieldwork, especially on the Rio Grande rift. He was entirely a field geologist, not an armchair theoretician. Appropriately, he died in Cody, Wyoming, while engaged in archeological research. After Bryan's death, an upwelling of respect and affection led to the institution of the prestigious Kirk Bryan Award of the Geological Society of America, given to a young geologist for a recently-published paper of special note on Quaternary geology.

• Much of Bryan's most seminal early work on mountain slopes, pediments, and other arid-region landscape features is in publications on the geology of the Papago Reservation in southern Arizona: *U.S. Geological Survey Bulletin* 730 (1922): 19–90; and *USGS Water Supply Paper* 499 (1925): 436. The most complete list and discussion of his contributions to archeology are in C. V. Haynes, *Geological Society of America Special Paper* 242 (1900): 55–67. Informative memorial articles are in *Harvard University Gazette*, 16 Dec. 1950; see also E. S. Larsen, "Memorial to Kirk Bryan," *Proceedings of the Geological Society of America Annual Report* (1951), pp.

91–96; and L. L. Ray, *Geographical Review* 41 (Jan. 1951): 165–66. The Larsen article contains a nearly complete list of Bryan's 117 published papers.

ROBERT P. SHARP

BRYAN, William Jennings (19 Mar. 1860–26 July 1925), Democratic party leader, was born in Salem, Illinois, the son of Silas Bryan, a lawyer and judge, and Mariah Jennings. Bryan received strong values from his parents. His father was a Baptist, and his mother was a Methodist; church took a central place in the family's life. William, at age fourteen, avoided choosing between his parents' churches by becoming a Presbyterian during a revival meeting. Although he was a devout and active Presbyterian throughout his life, he felt comfortable worshiping with any of the major Protestant denominations. Silas Bryan was also a staunch Jacksonian Democrat, and William enthusiastically embraced his father's party.

Valedictorian at Illinois College (Jacksonville) in 1881, Bryan graduated from Union College of Law (Chicago) in 1883. He established a practice in Jacksonville and, in 1884, married his college sweetheart, Mary Baird. Between 1885 and 1891, they had three children. Unlike most women of the time, Mary continued her education after their marriage.

Seeing little future for a young lawyer and would-be Democratic politician in central Illinois, Bryan in 1887 chose Lincoln, Nebraska, as a new home. Once the family was settled there, Mary completed her legal studies and was admitted to the bar. In Nebraska, Bryan's eloquence quickly attracted local Democrats, whose hapless organization rarely won elections.

In 1890 Bryan accepted the Democratic nomination for the U.S. House of Representatives in a district that included Lincoln and Omaha. That year witnessed a state referendum to prohibit alcohol and the debut of Nebraska's Independent (Populist) party. Born of the economic distress of agriculture, the Populist party called for government ownership of railroads, currency inflation (to counter the prevailing deflation that disadvantaged debtors, including many farmers), and greater popular control of government. Although he focused his campaign against the tariff, Bryan endorsed some Populist proposals, including direct election of U.S. senators and limited currency inflation through coinage of both silver and gold (i.e., a bimetallic standard). He won, by 6,713 votes, through both his effectiveness as a campaigner and the disruption of state politics created by Populism and prohibition. In the Fifty-second Congress, Bryan secured a seat on the influential Ways and Means Committee. He and Mary became a highly effective working team, and he won wide attention for his speaking.

The realities of Nebraska politics pushed Bryan toward accommodation with the Populists. In 1892 he faced reelection in a reapportioned district without Omaha's Democratic strongholds. By courting the Populists, he eked out a tiny plurality. In 1893, as the nation entered a serious depression, he played the key role in convincing Democrats in the Nebraska legislature to help elect William V. Allen, a Populist, to the U.S. Senate. In Congress, Bryan captured national attention when he defended a proposed income tax. He also took a leading role in opposing President Grover Cleveland's call to repeal the Sherman Silver Purchase Act (1890). Support for silver drew a popular response from many debtor farmers in the South and West and from many western miners (both important sources of support for the Populist party), as well as from western silver mining interests.

Bryan led Nebraska Democrats (who, since 1890, usually finished in third place in state elections) to support some Populists in the state elections of 1894. The Republican gubernatorial candidate that year had close ties to the anti-Catholic American Protective Association (APA). Bryan fused opposition to the APA with support for silver to forge an organization that captured the state Democratic party and gave Democratic nominations to several Populist candidates, including Silas Holcomb, candidate for governor. Instead of seeking a third term in Congress, Bryan ran in a nonbinding poll for U.S. Senate; half the voters ignored the senatorial popularity contest, but Bryan received three-fourths of the votes cast. Holcomb won the governorship, but Republicans dashed Bryan's senatorial hopes by capturing the legislature.

Beginning in 1895, Bryan traveled the country, sometimes as a journalist for the Omaha *World-Herald* and sometimes as a silver advocate. By the opening gavel of the 1896 Democratic convention, a majority of the delegates favored silver, and Bryan had made himself well known to most of them. A delegate from Nebraska and not a declared candidate for the presidential nomination, Bryan served on the platform committee; the committee named him to present the closing argument on behalf of silver before the convention.

Bryan's speech has become the standard example for capturing a convention through oratory. He claimed later that he only "put into words the sentiments of a majority of the delegates," but his address electrified the convention, especially its dramatic conclusion: "we will answer their demand for a gold standard by saying to them: You shall not press down upon the brow of labor this crown of thorns. You shall not crucify mankind upon a cross of gold." The Cross of Gold speech gave Bryan the presidential nomination on the fifth ballot. The convention picked Arthur Sewall of Maine, a successful businessman who supported silver, for its vice presidential candidate.

Dubbed the "Boy Orator of the Platte," Bryan now faced the Republican candidate, William McKinley, nominated earlier on a platform that endorsed the gold standard. Leading western Republicans bolted their party when it rejected silver, and Bryan hoped to unite all silver advocates behind his banner. A convention of Silver Republicans enthusiastically endorsed Bryan and Sewall. Many Populists, however, feared they would lose their identity if they did the same. In the end, the Populist convention named their own vice presidential candidate, Thomas Edward Watson of

Georgia, hoping Sewall would withdraw; then the convention endorsed Bryan.

Public interest in the election was high, and the campaign was closely fought. The McKinley campaign raised $10–16 million, but Bryan collected only $300,000. Republican campaigners deluged the nation with pamphlets and political gewgaws—including the first campaign buttons—but McKinley ran a traditional campaign by remaining at home and delivering speeches from his front porch. Bryan reasoned that his only hope was to ignore the precedent that candidates did not aggressively campaign and to take his cause directly to the voters. He traveled 18,000 miles and delivered as many as 600 speeches, especially in the crucial Middle West; en route he earned the nickname "the Great Commoner" for his unassuming ways.

The campaign focused on federal economic policy. McKinley defended the gold standard but concentrated especially on the protective tariff as the best means to restore prosperity. Bryan emphasized silver but did not ignore the tariff, income tax, and other reforms. "There are two ideas of government," he maintained. "There are those who believe that, if you will only legislate to make the well-to-do prosperous, their prosperity will leak through on those below. The Democratic idea, however, has been that if you legislate to make the masses prosperous, their prosperity will find its way up through every class which rests upon them."

Voters turned out in extraordinary proportions—up to 95 percent of those eligible in some states. In the end, Republican tariff arguments and fears of inflation gave McKinley the edge among voters in urban and industrial areas (especially among the middle class but including many workers) and among more prosperous farmers in the eastern Middle West and Northeast. Bryan took 6.5 million votes and McKinley took 7.1 million.

Bryan supporters pointed to fraud and intimidation in some areas and claimed the election was stolen, but McKinley's victory actually marked a significant, long-term shift in voter loyalties. From 1880 through 1892, the two major parties were so evenly matched in national elections that neither could achieve a majority. After the mid-1890s, the Republicans usually held an unquestioned national majority until the early 1930s.

War with Spain in 1898 presented new political issues when Bryan sought the presidency a second time in 1900. When the war began, Governor Holcomb named Bryan as colonel of the Third Nebraska Volunteer Regiment; the regiment spent the war in Florida, however, devastated by typhoid and other illness. Bryan resigned his commission as soon as the peace treaty was signed. Proclaiming his opposition to imperialism, Bryan urged the Senate to ratify the treaty promptly so that the United States alone could determine the future of the Philippine Islands. In 1900 he faced no opposition for the Democratic and Silver Republican presidential nominations. The Populists, however, divided; one faction supported Bryan, and the other ran a separate candidate. The three parties that nominated Bryan all accepted the Democrats' choice for vice president, Adlai Stevenson.

Bryan's platform condemned imperialism, promised independence to the Philippines, attacked big business, and reaffirmed support for silver. Republicans repeated arguments from 1896 that election of Bryan would endanger prosperity by bringing inflation and ending the protective tariff, and they added a flag-waving defense of territorial acquisition. McKinley won by a larger margin in 1900 than he had in 1896 and carried most western states, including Nebraska. Bryan took 6.4 million votes to McKinley's 7.2 million.

Twice defeated, Bryan nonetheless remained the Democratic party's most significant leader, speaking frequently throughout the country on behalf of Democratic candidates and organizations. After his 1896 defeat, he quickly wrote *The First Battle*, a popular account of the election; thereafter he earned his income by speaking and writing. His many books and, after 1901, a weekly newspaper, the *Commoner*, carried his views into thousands of homes. Bryan spent every summer on the Chautauqua circuit, speaking in hundreds of towns. In the winter he often appeared on the lyceum lecturing circuit. His lectures were sometimes political but more often addressed social, religious, or educational topics. One prominent Democrat claimed that Bryan's constant traveling made him personally acquainted with more people than anyone else in the nation.

This constant contact with ordinary citizens did more to shape Bryan's thinking than did exhaustive research or formal analysis. Committed to the people and devoted to equality and self-government, Bryan nonetheless accepted the arguments of southern Democrats that African Americans should not participate in the political process in the South. With that significant exception, Bryan believed that all citizens should share as equally as possible in the process of governing themselves. Toward that end, he championed greater public participation in politics through direct election of senators, the initiative and referendum, and, eventually, woman suffrage. On similar grounds, he advocated independence for the Philippines and India. His sincere, unshakable confidence in the ability of the people to govern themselves was reciprocated by a popular following with few parallels in American politics.

Bryan launched a third presidential campaign in 1908. He mobilized his supporters early and had the nomination in hand when the convention opened. He declared the major issue to be "Shall the people rule?" The platform he wrote reflected his own long-standing commitment to economic opportunity and popular democracy by advocating regulation of corporations, tariff reform, an income tax, an insurance fund to protect bank depositors, direct election of senators, and other reforms. He fully supported the political program of the American Federation of Labor, and unions gave him unprecedented support. For the vice presidential nomination, Bryan approved John Kern of Indiana.

President Theodore Roosevelt (1858–1919) selected William Howard Taft as his successor, but Bryan found himself running, in fact, against the enormously popular Roosevelt. Taft took 7.7 million votes to 6.4 million for Bryan. Soon after the results were known, Bryan announced he would not seek another presidential nomination; he kept his word, although he left the door open to a draft that never came.

During the years that Bryan led the Democratic party, it largely rejected the belief in minimal government characteristic of both Andrew Jackson and Grover Cleveland. Instead, Bryan and his allies fused the antimonopolism of Jackson to a commitment to governmental intervention on behalf of "the people" and against powerful economic interests. In 1900, 1904, 1908, 1912, and 1924, he wrote into Democratic platforms his conviction that "a private monopoly is indefensible and intolerable." Toward that end, he sought regulation, and sometimes even government ownership, "to make it impossible for a private monopoly to exist."

Through the 1912 primaries, Bryan expressed no preference between Woodrow Wilson and James Beauchamp Clark, the two Democrats he considered closest to his own views, and he promised to support the winner of the Nebraska primary, who proved to be Clark. Bryan wrote much of the Democratic platform; when the convention headed toward deadlock, Bryan swung his support from Clark to Wilson. Not decisive, the action nonetheless put Bryan on the side of the eventual victor. Wilson faced a divided opposition when Taft was renominated by the Republicans and former president Roosevelt ran as a Progressive. Bryan campaigned extensively for Wilson, who won with 6.3 million votes—fewer than Bryan had secured in any of his defeats.

Wilson acknowledged Bryan's stature as the nation's leading Democrat by naming him secretary of state, even though diplomats sniggered when the Bryans, lifelong teetotalers, served grape juice rather than wine at state dinners. Beyond foreign affairs, Bryan enjoyed finding patronage positions for his many loyal supporters, and he took a strong interest in the course of domestic economic policy. When the Federal Reserve proposal divided congressional Democrats, Bryan pushed strongly for significant government controls over banking and threatened to resign if Wilson sided with the conservatives.

As secretary of state, Bryan hoped to make a major contribution to world peace by promoting bilateral conciliation treaties through which the participating nations agreed, in event of a dispute, to observe a "cooling off" period when they would seek outside fact-finding instead of going to war. Eventually Bryan negotiated such treaties with thirty nations. Bryan failed, however, to apply his anti-imperialist principles to circumstances in Central America; he reluctantly supported a treaty that compromised the independence of Nicaragua (the Bryan-Chamorro Treaty) and approved a naval occupation of Vera Cruz, Mexico's chief port, both in 1914. For so long as he was secretary, Bryan held off those who wanted to occupy Haiti; eventually, however, Wilson directed more interventions in Latin America than during any other presidential administration.

Bryan's commitment to peace met its greatest challenge when Europe plunged into war in August 1914. Initially Bryan and Wilson agreed to maintain strict neutrality; their interpretations of neutrality soon diverged, however. For Bryan, avoiding war took precedence over all other considerations. Wilson, however, and Robert Lansing, the State Department counselor, increasingly leaned toward the Allies, Bryan thought, as they insisted on maintaining traditional neutral rights even at the risk of war with Germany. After a German submarine sank the *Lusitania* in 1915, Wilson composed a protest note so strong that Bryan feared it would bring war; he resigned rather than sign it.

Still a popular public figure, Bryan then resumed his role as a leading Democrat, Chautauqua lecturer, reformer, and political critic. In 1916, he spoke for Wilson's reelection throughout the nation, especially in the West, which provided Wilson's margin of victory. He continued to demand neutrality and opposed preparedness, which, he said, "provokes war." When war came in 1917, he gave the government full support, to bring victory and peace as soon as possible. Pleased with federal operation of the railroads during the war, he urged permanent government ownership. He supported the League of Nations in 1919; when it was blocked in the Senate, he recommended compromise in 1920 to save it.

After 1915, however, Bryan turned increasingly to social issues. He spoke extensively on behalf of woman suffrage and prohibition, embracing the latter after concluding that the liquor industry had contributed to his defeat in 1908. The National Dry Federation named him as its president in 1918, and opponents and supporters of prohibition alike credited him with having done more than any other single individual to enact the Eighteenth Amendment. He rejected the presidential nomination of the Prohibition party in 1920 but had little influence on that year's Democratic platform or campaign.

Bryan's last appearance at a Democratic convention was as a delegate from Florida. The Bryans moved there in 1921, in part because the Nebraska climate seemed to provoke Mary's arthritis. (Bryan, too, had health problems including diabetes, first diagnosed in 1914.) Elected to the 1924 Democratic convention, Bryan took his usual prominent role in platform discussions. Successful in proposing several planks on economic reform, he addressed the convention in support of the majority report, just as in 1896. This time, however, the debate was on a proposal to condemn the Ku Klux Klan by name. Bryan stood opposed, arguing that party unity for economic reform took precedence over condemning the KKK; Bryan's side won by a tiny margin. When the deeply divided delegates finally compromised on John William Davis as their presidential candidate, Davis chose Bryan's brother, Charles Bryan (elected governor of Nebraska in 1922), for the vice presidential nomination, and Bryan spoke widely in support of the ticket.

During his final years, more than anything else, Bryan focused on evolution, which he believed undermined religious faith and thus threatened society. Increasingly aligned with the growing fundamentalist movement, he opposed evolution less from a reasoned analysis of evidence than from its social impact. Never a deep thinker, he often turned to simple-minded but euphonious metaphors. "It is better to trust in the Rock of Ages," he often proclaimed, "than to know the age of rocks." He attacked evolution on the lecture circuit, and he urged his political allies in state governments to pass laws requiring teachers to treat evolution as hypothesis and not fact.

In 1925 the Tennessee legislature set the stage for Bryan's final battle when it prohibited any teaching of evolution. John Scopes, a biology teacher in Dayton, accepted an offer from the American Civil Liberties Union to defend any teacher willing to test the constitutionality of the law. When Bryan agreed to assist the prosecution, the trial captured national attention, for it pitted Clarence Darrow, the nation's most prominent trial lawyer, against Bryan, the nation's best-known orator. Toward the trial's end, Darrow called Bryan to the witness stand as an expert on the Bible and revealed him to be woefully ignorant of science and archaeology. The jury found Scopes guilty, although the state supreme court later overturned the verdict on technical grounds. Bryan died in Dayton soon after the trial there.

The most prominent leader of the Democratic party from 1896 to 1912, Bryan defined for himself a role as a political crusader. "Clad in the armor of a righteous cause" (a metaphor from his Cross of Gold speech), he fought zealously and tirelessly throughout his career for one issue after another. By reviving the antimonopolism of Andrew Jackson but interring Jackson's belief in minimal government, Bryan played a pivotal role in the development of the Democratic party, laying the basis for the Democratic progressivism of Woodrow Wilson's administration. Some of Bryan's concerns—guarantee of bank deposits, federal rather than banker control of the Federal Reserve Board, and even silver coinage—also found echoes in New Deal measures. Early in Bryan's career, his faith in the people and his willingness to use the powers of government led him to advocate the right of the majority to place limitations on the property rights of the privileged few; late in his career, the same combination, together with his religious faith, led him to argue for the right of the majority to prohibit alcohol and to dictate how to teach biology.

• The largest collection of Bryan papers is at the Library of Congress; smaller collections are at Occidental College, the Nebraska State Historical Society, and the Illinois State Historical Society. Bryan's *Memoirs* (1925) draw heavily upon earlier speeches and writings and were completed by his wife. The most thorough biographies are Paolo E. Coletta, *William Jennings Bryan* (3 vols., 1964–1969), and Louis W. Koenig, *Bryan: A Political Biography* (1971); Coletta's bibliographies contain the most complete list of Bryan's writings, and Koenig's bibliography includes the most complete list of Bryan's letters. Other important treatments include Paul W. Glad, *The Trumpet Soundeth: William Jennings Bryan and His Democracy, 1896–1912* (1960); Lawrence W. Levine, *Defender of the Faith: William Jennings Bryan, The Last Decade, 1915–1925* (1965); Kendrick A. Clements, *William Jennings Bryan: Missionary Isolationist* (1982); Robert W. Cherny, *A Righteous Cause: The Life of William Jennings Bryan* (1985); and Leroy Ashby, *William Jennings Bryan: Champion of Democracy* (1987).

ROBERT W. CHERNY

BRYAN, William Lowe (11 Nov. 1860–21 Nov. 1955), philosopher, psychologist, and educator, was born William Julian Bryan on a farm near Bloomington, Indiana, the son of John Bryan, a Presbyterian minister, and Eliza Jane Philips. In 1876 he entered the preparatory department of Indiana University in Bloomington, which served as the local high school, and the next year he matriculated as a university student. As an undergraduate he developed his skills in public speaking and helped to revive the *Indiana Student* newspaper in 1882. He became a member of the Specialists' Club organized by David Starr Jordan, professor of natural sciences, to encourage promising students to pursue research careers. Bryan was graduated in 1884 with a bachelor's degree in ancient classics.

After graduation Bryan was hired as an English instructor in the preparatory department. Within a few months he received an unexpected opportunity to join the regular faculty when the president of the university, Baptist minister Lemuel Moss, and Katherine Graydon, the professor of Greek, were caught up in a romantic scandal and left the university. Bryan was hired as Graydon's replacement, and in early 1885 Jordan was appointed president. Jordan, a noted ichthyologist, placed science at the center of his ideas on educational reform and stressed that "the highest function of the real university is that of instruction by investigation." Working with limited financial support from the state he relied heavily on local talent to fill the ranks of the faculty.

Although Bryan earned a master's degree in philosophy at Indiana in 1886 with a thesis on ancient Greek logic, his interests shifted toward the "new psychology" that promised to revolutionize the study of human nature through laboratory experimentation and other empirical techniques. He went to Germany, the center of scientific psychology, in 1886–1887 to study at the University of Berlin; after returning he was promoted to full professor and granted $100 to purchase a Hipp chronoscope for experimental studies of human reaction times. In January 1888 Bryan opened the Indiana University Psychological Laboratory, the second such facility established in the United States.

Bryan married Charlotte Augusta Lowe in 1889 and in her honor replaced his given middle name with her last name. His wife was a graduate of Indiana University, having earned a bachelor's degree (1888) and a master's degree (1889) in Greek. They collaborated on two books, *Plato the Teacher: Selections from Plato* (1897) and *Studies in Plato's Republic for Teachers* (1898). They had no children.

Bryan carried a heavy teaching load, and at first the psychological laboratory was used mainly for classroom demonstrations rather than original research. In 1891 he went to Clark University to pursue a doctorate under G. Stanley Hall, a prominent advocate of the new psychology. Bryan received his Ph.D. in psychology in 1892 for a dissertation on the development of voluntary motor abilities in children. He was also recruited by Hall to help organize the American Psychological Association, founded in July 1892, and became one of its twenty-six charter members.

After returning to Indiana University, Bryan expanded the psychological laboratory and was appointed vice president of the institution. He resisted repeated offers by Jordan, who had become president of Stanford University in 1891, to join the faculty of the California school. Bryan also became involved in the child-study movement, an effort to develop a scientific foundation for pedagogical techniques. He served as an officer in several national organizations, including the secretary of the National Association for the Study of Children (1893) and the president of the Child-Study Section of the National Educational Association (1894).

In the 1890s Bryan conducted pioneering psychological experiments. He investigated the process of learning to send and receive messages in Morse code on the telegraph. The research, published in the *Psychological Review* (1897, 1899), was among the first such studies to graphically represent its data in the form of "learning curves" and became a classic in the study of human learning. Because of Bryan's efforts, during this period Indiana University became an undergraduate training ground for notable future psychologists, including Edwin D. Starbuck, Ernest H. Lindley, and Lewis M. Terman.

In 1902 Bryan was appointed the tenth president of Indiana University. The next year he was elected president of the American Psychological Association and delivered his presidential address on the problem of "Theory and Practice" (repr., *Psychological Review* 11 [1904]: 71–82). His remark that "the scholar may at great price become a statesman" suggested his ambivalence about leaving the laboratory for administration.

Pious and scholarly, Bryan presided over the transformation of Indiana University from a small, traditional liberal arts college into a modern research university. He led the institution for thirty-five years and oversaw an era of enormous growth in student enrollments, physical facilities, and curricular offerings. He considered administration an exercise in practical psychology and viewed the university as a key institution for the transmission of cultural values as well as specialized knowledge. His most notable accomplishment was the expansion of graduate and professional training. During his administration, schools of medicine, education, nursing, business, music, and dentistry were established, along with many graduate programs and several satellite campuses around the state. By the time Bryan retired at the age of seventy-six, Indiana University had significantly broadened access to its programs and had dramatically increased the quality of graduate and professional education.

Bryan was known as a pithy orator, and his speeches were highly moralistic. His strong belief in the scientific study of human nature was tempered by an equally powerful conviction that it was not sufficient to provide moral and spiritual guidance. Hence he maintained an interest in ethics and metaphysics throughout his life. In 1940 Bryan published *Wars of Families of Minds*, a book that reflected on the consequences of different ways of knowing the world. A colleague once called him "a philosopher tamed by science"—a characterization that could have easily been applied to Bryan's intellectual hero, William James.

After retirement Bryan continued to live on campus in the president's house, and he remained a familiar sight walking along its wooded paths. He died in Bloomington. The institution he developed commemorated his work with many memorials, including the William Lowe Bryan Hall, the main administration building at Indiana University, and his hometown also named in his honor Bryan Park, a large municipal park.

• Bryan's papers are in the Indiana University Archives. On his university administration, see Thomas D. Clark, *Indiana University: Midwestern Pioneer*, vol. 2 (1973), and Burton Dorr Myers, *History of Indiana University, 1902–1937, the Bryan Administration* (1952). Bryan's career as a psychologist is described in Eliot Hearst and James H. Capshew, eds., *Psychology at Indiana University: A Centennial Review and Compendium* (1988), which also contains a comprehensive bibliography of his writings. Additional biographical material can be found in Manfred Wolfe Deputy, "The Philosophical Ideas and Related Achievements of William Lowe Bryan" (Ph.D. diss., Indiana Univ., 1947). Major obituaries are in the *American Journal of Psychology* 69 (1956): 325–27; *Science* 123 (1956): 214; and the *New York Times*, 22 Nov. 1955.

JAMES H. CAPSHEW

BRYANT, Bear (11 Sept. 1913–26 Jan. 1983), football coach, was born Paul William Bryant in Moro Bottom, Arkansas, the son of Wilson Monroe Bryant and Ida Kilgore, truck farmers. The eleventh of twelve children, Bryant worked hard as a boy to contribute to the family's meager income. As a teenager, he is said to have accepted a challenge to wrestle a bear at a traveling carnival show in nearby Fordyce in order to collect the one-dollar-a-minute prize money. Bryant later claimed that he easily wrestled the skinny bear to the floor, but the promoters left town before he could collect his money. All he got out of the experience, he said, was the nickname "Bear," which he retained all his life. Bryant, who at age sixteen was 6′3″, 190 pounds, and still growing, was a star athlete at Fordyce High School and played tackle on the 1929 and 1930 state championship football teams.

After the 1930 season, Bryant was recruited to play football at the University of Alabama in Tuscaloosa. Although provided a scholarship by the university, he had to attend a local high school during 1931 in order to obtain admission. In 1934, Bryant played end on the unbeaten, untied Alabama team that included All-America end Don Hutson and tailback Millard "Dixie" Howell. He participated in the team's 29-13 upset victory over Stanford in the 1935 Rose Bowl. In 1935, he married Mary Harmon Black. They had two children. When his athletic eligibility expired following the 1935 season, Bryant became an assistant coach at Alabama, a post he held for four seasons. He graduated from Alabama in 1939.

In 1940, Bryant accepted an assistant coaching position at Vanderbilt, but soon after the United States entered World War II he resigned to join the navy and was commissioned as an officer. After service in the Atlantic, Bryant coached the North Carolina Pre-Flight School football team in 1943–1944. In the fall of 1945, he became head coach at the University of Maryland, beginning a career as a Division I college head coach that spanned thirty-eight years. Recruiting many of his former navy players, Bryant had a 6-2-1 record at Maryland. He resigned after one season, however, because of a dispute with university president H. C. "Curly" Byrd, who, he said, interfered with the football program by reinstating a player whom Bryant had dropped from the team. It was the first of many controversies that marked Bryant's career. Bryant was a strict, and some thought brutal, disciplinarian who tolerated little interference from university officials. He became head coach at the University of Kentucky in 1946 and revived the school's ailing football program. In eight years at Kentucky, Bryant had a record of 60-23-5, including a victory over Oklahoma in the 1951 Sugar Bowl.

After the 1953 season, Bryant abruptly resigned and took over as head coach at Texas A&M. He later explained that he was jealous of Kentucky basketball coach Adolph Rupp and that one of them had to go. After his first season at A&M, in which the team won only one game, the National Collegiate Athletic Association put the Aggie football program on probation because recruits were offered money. Bryant later admitted that some of his recruits at both Kentucky and Texas A&M were paid by alumni and friends of the teams. Despite the NCAA penalties, Bryant turned out winning teams at A&M. In 1956, the Aggies won the Southwest Conference championship with a 9-0-1 record. At both Kentucky and A&M, Bryant was known as a hard-nosed taskmaster who imposed a rigorous, if not torturous, training and practice regimen on the players. In 1958, Bryant broke a long-term contract with Texas A&M to become head coach and athletic director at his alma mater, Alabama. He explained the controversial move to reporters by saying "Mama called."

Controversy continued to swirl around Bryant at Alabama. In 1962, he sued sportswriter Furman Bisher and the Curtis Publishing Company, publisher of the *Saturday Evening Post*, for printing a story accusing him of being cruel to his players. The following year the same magazine ran a story by syndicated sports writer Frank Graham, Jr., alleging that Bryant and former Georgia coach Wally Butts conspired to "fix" a football game played between the two schools in 1962. Both coaches denied the allegation, and each sued Curtis Publishing for $10 million. In 1963, Butts won his suit and after appeal received damages of about $300,000. Bryant settled out of court for a slightly higher sum.

The Butts trial, at which Bryant testified, and the criticism of his coaching techniques heightened by Bisher's 1962 *Saturday Evening Post* article marked a turning point in Bryant's career. Thereafter he tried to improve his public image, became more flexible in dealing with his players, and moderated his win-at-all-costs philosophy. But he continued to devote almost every waking moment to football, recruited top-quality players, and won football games. On 28 November 1981, against Auburn, he surpassed Amos Alonzo Stagg as the winningest coach in college football history, with 315 wins. Before retiring, Bryant increased his total to 323 victories. Although Eddie Robinson of Grambling University broke that record in 1985, Bryant continued to hold the record for the most victories by a Division I coach. Bryant coached at Alabama from 1958 to 1982. His teams won six national championships (1961, 1964, 1965, 1973, 1978, 1979), and the American Football Coaches Association voted him coach of the year three times (1961, 1971, 1973).

During his last decade at Alabama, Bryant became a venerable figure. Slowly pacing the sidelines in his familiar houndstooth check hat, he was widely regarded as the dean of the coaching fraternity. More than forty of his former players became head coaches in either college or professional football. He coached some of the finest players of the post–World War II era, including George Blanda, John David Crow, Lee Roy Jordan, Joe Namath, and Kenny Stabler. Eddie Robinson credited him with hastening the integration of football teams at predominantly white southern universities in the early 1970s. A self-made millionaire who invested shrewdly throughout his coaching career, Bryant donated more than $300,000 to the University of Alabama. Thirty-seven days after retiring as head coach at his alma mater, Bryant died of a heart attack in Tuscaloosa.

• Bryant described his coaching philosophy in *Building a Championship Football Team* (1960), and his autobiography, co-authored with John Underwood, is *Bear: The Hard Life and Good Times of Alabama's Coach Bryant* (1975). Two biographies are John A. Peterson and Bill Cromartie, *Bear Bryant: Count Down to Glory* (1983), and Mickey Herskowitz, *The Legend of Bear Bryant* (1987). Also see Clyde Bolton, *The Crimson Tide: A Story of Alabama Football* (1973). The college football "fix" controversy is analyzed in James Kirby, *Fumble: Bear Bryant, Wally Butts, and the Great College Football Scandal* (1986). An obituary is in the *New York Times*, 27 Jan. 1983.

JOHN M. CARROLL

BRYANT, Boudleaux (13 Feb. 1920–25 June 1987), songwriter, was born Diadorius Boudleaux Bryant in Shellman, Georgia, the son of Daniel Green Bryant, a lawyer and amateur musician, and Louise Farham. Boudleaux was the name of a man who had saved Daniel Bryant's life in the First World War. When Bryant was young, his father moved the family to Moultrie, Georgia, where he practiced law. Bryant studied violin under a member of the Boston Symphony who had retired to Moultrie. He moved to Atlanta in 1937 and worked for both the Atlanta Symphony and for local rural string bands, as well as on Works Progress Administration projects.

Bryant moved to Memphis, working there on radio station WMC with country guitarists Smitty Smith and Hank Penny (recording with the latter in Memphis in 1939). In 1940 he moved to Detroit, where he worked for Ford and played for CIO (Congress of Industrial Organizations) bands. He did not stay long in one place, though, and returned frequently to Moultrie, where he played with a local band called the Mills Brothers. In 1945 he moved to Chicago, then on to Milwaukee. While in Milwaukee, he met Felice Scaduto, then an elevator operator at the Schroeder Hotel. They were wed within a week and would eventually have two children. Initially, the Bryants did not write songs together; Felice, who set words to Italian melodies she had learned as a child, termed herself a closet poet. Once they started writing together, though, they generated more than eighty songs within a few weeks. They wrote to all the music publishers listed in *Billboard* magazine but could not place their material. Rome Johnson, a country singer, recommended that the Bryants contact Fred Rose, a music publisher who in 1942 had set up the Acuff-Rose music publishing company in Nashville. Rose took "Country Boy" from the Bryants and placed it with country singer Little Jimmy Dickens, who scored a hit with it in 1949.

To that point, there had been few—if any—full-time songwriters in country music. Sales of country recordings were sufficiently low that no one, no matter how successful, could earn a living from publishing royalties alone. That had begun to change in the years after the Second World War, though, and Rose invited the Bryants to Nashville in 1950 and arranged for them to represent Tannen Music locally for $35 a week while they wrote for Acuff-Rose. Rose also arranged for the Bryants to record for MGM, a company for which he was a producer; they did so as "Bud and Betty Bryant."

Acuff-Rose used a number of the Bryants' songs through the early to mid-1950s, such as "Midnight" (co-written by Bryant and guitarist/record producer Chet Atkins, and a number one hit for country star Red Foley), and "How's the World Treating You?" (another Bryant-Atkins composition that singer Eddy Arnold and, later, Elvis Presley recorded). However, the Bryants' songs, which had always had the potential to be recorded by either country or pop artists, found their niche during the rock 'n' roll era. The first copyright that proved successful for them was "Bye, Bye Love," which the Everly Brothers recorded in March 1957. From that point, the Bryants were virtually the Everly Brothers' exclusive songwriters until the Everlys broke with Acuff-Rose in 1961. Among the Bryants' songs that the Everlys recorded were "Wake up Little Susie," "Problems," "Bird Dog," "Love Hurts," "Sleepless Nights," and "All I Have to Do Is Dream." The Everlys eventually began to write their own material, but they credited Bryant with helping them establish their writing style and define their work ethic. A resident of Gatlinburg, Tennessee, for the last years of his life, Bryant died in Knoxville.

The Bryants were the first in the country market to learn how to write to order and the first to earn a living at it. They proved especially adept at identifying with the teenage themes that populated country music and especially pop music from the mid-1950s onward. It was not unknown for the Bryants to write a song for a client on the way to a session. The Bryants were prolific; they kept their songs in 500-page law ledgers, of which there were twelve at the time of his death. Of those, 710 had been registered with the performing-rights organization BMI (Broadcast Music, Inc.) as copyrights that had been recorded. They won nineteen BMI country awards and three BMI rhythm 'n' blues awards, and five songs were honored for sales of one million copies.

Under the contract that Bryant negotiated with Acuff-Rose in 1955, their copyrights returned to them after ten years, so virtually all of the Bryants' most lucrative copyrights reside with the Bryants' own House of Bryant publishing company.

A number of the Bryants' songs have proved to be remarkably durable; these include "All I Have to Do Is Dream," "Love Hurts," "Raining in My Heart," and "Rocky Top." "Rocky Top" was first recorded by the bluegrass group the Osborne Brothers in 1967, but it was a bigger hit for country-pop singer Lynn Anderson in 1970 and has since become a bluegrass standard; it is also one of Tennessee's state songs. It epitomized the deceptive simplicity that was the Bryants' hallmark. By 1975 their compositions had sold more than 200 million records.

• An article by Boudleaux Bryant is "Country Is What You Make It," *Nashville Sound*, Sept. 1975. The Bryants' career is covered in various articles in *American Songwriter*, Nov.–Dec. 1992. The 26 Jan. 1974 issue of *Billboard*, "Twenty-five Years of Harmony," is dedicated to the Bryants. See also "The Whole Nation Sings Their Songs," *Nashville Tennessean Showcase*, 8 Jan. 1956.

COLIN ESCOTT

BRYANT, Charles Grandison (1803–12 Jan. 1850), architect, was born in Belfast, Maine, the son of Charles Bryant, a shipwright, and Elizabeth Lowden. His grandfather was a shipwright as well, his uncle was a joiner, and as a youth Charles was well trained in carpentry. With the death of his father during the War of 1812, his mother was left with eight children to support. The family relocated from Belfast to Bangor, a town on the Penobscot River that was soon to become Maine's second city. Bangor's proximity to the north woods and its location on one of the state's major rivers led to an extraordinary period of growth, fueled primarily by the lumber industry. Hundreds of buildings were constructed in the 1830s, providing great opportunities for those in the building trades.

Bryant was established as a Bangor housewright by 1825. In 1827 he married Sarah Getchell; they had seven children. When, by 1830, Bryant had declared himself an architect, he was the first in the state to do so. His earliest documented project dates from 1831, and over the next six years he designed many substantial Greek Revival–style buildings in Bangor. Particularly elegant and sophisticated examples of his work are the Kent-Cutting Double House (1833), the Merchantile Bank (1833–1834), the Pine Street Methodist Church (1836–1837), and the Poor-Appleton Double House (1836–1837). In addition, he was the local architect supervising the construction of the palatial Bangor House hotel in 1833–1834, designed by Isaiah Rogers. Bryant also prepared plans for streets and developments in Bangor and designed the grounds of Mount Hope Cemetery in 1834. Inspired by Mount Auburn Cemetery in Cambridge, Mount Hope was one of the earliest garden cemeteries in America.

Bryant's public service included command of the local militia to suppress riots and involvement in politics as a Jacksonian Democrat. This promising career came to an end when land speculation ruined him financially in the Panic of 1837. For the next two years he participated in clandestine military adventures, beginning with organizing American volunteers to assist Robert Nelson in fomenting rebellion for the independence of Canada. With no popular support among the Canadians, the uprising was quickly crushed. The fiasco of this enterprise was followed by Bryant's efforts to become militarily involved in border controversies with Great Britain on the Maine frontier. In this instance, disagreement over the location of the border between Maine and Canada led to warlike preparations on both sides. Bryant was a leading figure in the efforts to raise volunteers in defense of Maine's boundary claims. Evidence suggests that Bryant's participation in these events had less to do with idealistic freedom fighting than with a search for adventure and personal glory.

With the failure of his architectural, political, and military careers in Maine, Bryant emigrated to the Republic of Texas in 1839. He lived there for the remaining decade of his life, engaging in architecture, speculative development, and Indian fighting. Taking up an architectural practice again, Bryant worked mostly in Galveston, where he designed St. Mary's Catholic Church (1847–1848) and a county jail (1847–1848). Shortly thereafter, as a major in the Texas Rangers, Bryant served as a mustering and commissary officer. It was while acting in that capacity that he was killed by a party of Lipan Indians at Wood's Rancho.

Bryant practiced as an architect in Bangor, Maine, and Galveston, Texas, when both cities were undergoing their formative years of development. As a designer, Bryant produced some of the most original Greek Revival architecture in Maine.

• The only account of Bryant's life is James H. Mundy and Earle G. Shettleworth, Jr., *The Flight of the Grand Eagle* (1977). Additional information on Bryant's architectural career in Bangor can be found in Deborah Thompson, *Bangor, Maine, 1796–1914: An Architectural History* (1988).

EARLE G. SHETTLEWORTH, JR.

BRYANT, Dan (9 May 1833–10 Apr. 1875), actor and musician, was born Daniel Webster O'Brien in Troy, New York, the son of Timothy O'Brien, a wood craftsman, and Margaret Duggan, a fiddlemaker. The youngest of three brothers, all blackface minstrels, Bryant made his debut in 1845 carried onstage in a sack at his eldest brother Jerry's benefit at the Vauxhall Gardens in New York City. He appeared as a jig dancer in 1848 at the Pantheon Theatre in New York and at Thalian Hall a year later in the same city. In the early 1850s he performed with several minstrel troupes, including Charley White's, Woods and Fellows, and Morris and Campbell's. By 1856 he was comanaging the company known as Bryant and Mallory's Campbell's Minstrels.

In February 1857 Bryant and his two brothers, Jerry and Neil, joined forces and established Bryant's Minstrels. This was the beginning of an extraordinary nine-year run at Mechanics' Hall, the former home of the popular E. P. Christy's Minstrels. The reaction to the Bryants' brand of minstrelsy clearly placed them as the front-runners in a very crowded field. The *New York Clipper*, a contemporary entertainment weekly, commented that "the different bands of Minstrels, in this city, have experienced a wonderful falling off in patronage since the advent among us of the Bryants." Dan excelled as a musician and dancer. Like his brothers, he played the banjo, tambourine, and bones. Part of his troupe's popularity can be attributed to Dan Bryant's decision to present minstrel shows in the manner of the late 1840s—that is, with more emphasis on so-called plantation material. Such a policy was the impetus for the showcasing of the song "Dixie" in 1859, on the eve of the Civil War. It was written expressly for Bryant's Minstrels by Dan Emmett as a walkaround, and it very quickly swept the nation. Bryant was equally renowned for another plantation entertainment, a dance called the "Essence of Old Virginny," in which it was said that Bryant outshone all others.

In 1860, the same year his mother died, Bryant married Ellen Fitzgibbon of St. Louis. They had five children. A year later his brother Jerry died, but the troupe continued to come up with new musical novelties. Bryant provided the words to "Turkey in the Straw" (1861) and also made a hit out of the song "Shoo Fly." As performed by Bryant and Dave Reed, "Shoo Fly" was sung more than 250 consecutive nights in New York in 1869, being declared a "public necessity."

While Bryant was celebrated for his musical and dancing talents, he was also recognized for his fine comedic and acting abilities. *Galaxy* magazine wrote of him that "there is no doubt that he has given to more people the good gift of after-dinner laughter than any one man we have had among us for a long time." Bryant's ability to bring a richness and a verisimilitude to even the broadest comic sketch set his minstrelsy apart from the usual one-dimensional portrayals of the time. His acting was appreciated by the great American actor Edwin Forrest. Speaking of Bryant in the role of a hungry black man in the comic sketch "Old Times Rock," Forrest declared that there was not a finer bit of tragic acting to be seen in America. *Harper's* magazine wrote of this same performance that "tears were constantly checking laughter in this little scene of the black man's suffering through hunger," and that "one's sympathies were irresistably wrung by the pathos of the minstrel's voice, when, on being questioned as to when he had eaten a square meal, he answered, humbly, 'I had a peanut last week.' It was side-splitting—It was heartbreaking."

Bryant proved his comedic talents not only in blackface but also in a series of Irish comedies. He first appeared as an Irishman in a benefit for W. R. Floyd in *Handy Andy* in 1863; then, in the summer of 1864, after the winter minstrel season, he appeared at Wallack's in *The Irish Immigrant* and *The Colleen Bawn*. In 1865 he made a tour of England and Ireland, impressing the Dublin critics with his comic performances. Of his *Handy Andy*, the *Dublin Freeman's Journal* commented, "a better Irishman has not been seen on the boards of the Theatre Royal for a long time." After a season playing in San Francisco, Bryant and his minstrels returned to New York to play at Tammany Hall in 1868. Two years later Bryant opened up his own opera house on Twenty-third Street in New York, which caused the *Spirit of the Times* to rave that "Dan Bryant's name has become a household word, and a visit to his opera house once a week is essential to the health and happiness of every well-regulated family." The theater continued to attract audiences including the elite of New York and "the foremost men of the nation" for the next five years until Bryant's death from pneumonia. Bryant was well loved not only by his public but by the New York theater community as well; after his death, eleven major New York City theaters held benefit performances for Bryant's family.

• Clippings on Bryant can be found in the Billy Rose Theatre Collection of the New York Public Library for the Performing Arts, Lincoln Center. See also Edward LeRoy Rice, *Monarchs of Minstrelsy* (1911); Carl Wittke, *Tambo and Bones* (1930); Hans Nathan, *Dan Emmett and the Rise of Early Negro Minstrelsy* (1962); Robert Toll, *Blacking Up* (1974); and Eric Lott, *Love and Theft* (1993). An obituary is in the *New York Times*, 11 Apr. 1875.

JACK SHALOM

BRYANT, John Emory (13 Oct. 1836–27 Feb. 1900), editor and politician, was born in Wayne, Maine, the son of Benjamin Franklin Bryant, a Methodist minister and (later) physician, and Lucy Ford French. Bryant was born into a family with firm religious convictions but limited financial resources. During his childhood, the family lived in several different Maine communities where his father was minister. His first profession was teaching. By offering "subscription" or "rate schools," in which the teacher advertised for scholars and "subscribed" students for a short term, Bryant earned money to pay for his own education. In 1859 he received a college certificate from Maine Wesleyan Seminary.

During the Civil War, as captain in the Eighth Maine Infantry, Bryant served in the Department of the South, in the Sea Islands of Georgia and South Carolina. There he worked with General Rufus Saxton and commanded African-American troops, leading raids to rescue slaves from nearby plantations. In 1864 he married Emma Frances Spaulding, a strong, well-educated, and devout woman who shared and supported his work. They had two children, one of whom died in infancy. After leaving the army in September 1864, Bryant returned to Maine, studied law, and was accepted into the bar.

On 1 May 1865, General Saxton, assistant commissioner for Georgia, South Carolina, and Florida, appointed Bryant general superintendent of the Freedmen's Bureau in Augusta, Georgia. He served until 1866, when a new head of the bureau in Georgia cut him from the rolls because of his association with Saxton. In the same month in which he received his notice, Bryant was a primary organizer for the Georgia Equal Rights Association (GERA), which first met in January 1866, bringing together African Americans from all over the state. The GERA elected Bryant its first president. He also began editing a Republican newspaper, the *Augusta Loyal Georgian*, the first of several newspapers he would try unsuccessfully to make solvent during and after Reconstruction. By definition, a carpetbagger was a northerner engaged in southern politics. Although the term was not widely used until 1867, Bryant's activities in 1866 made him a candidate for the epithet. Throughout the year, he continued to practice law as well.

After the Reconstruction Acts of 1867, Bryant assisted in the formation of the Republican party in Georgia, and served in the state's constitutional convention in the fall of that year. In spring 1868 Georgia voters ratified the state's new constitution and elected Republican Rufus Bullock as governor. As a member of the state central committee, Bryant had been instrumental in choosing Bullock as the party's nominee. Bryant himself was elected from Richmond County as a member of the Georgia House of Representatives, where he served on the manufacturers and judiciary committees, and as chairman of the Public Education Committee.

Bryant had expected that he would be a part of the inner circle and that the *Loyal Georgian* would be the official paper of the Republican administration. Soon after the election he became disillusioned with Bullock's blueprint for Georgia, which he feared encased the primary goal of self-aggrandisement and wealth for the governor and his fast friend Foster Blodgett, for whom Bryant had no respect at all. Bullock, on the other hand, saw Bryant as a disappointed office seeker who turned on the governor in revenge. The vicious feud between the two men became a part of the debilitating divisions of the Republicans that contributed to the shattering of party goals for reform during the Reconstruction years. When the governor fled the state in October 1871 to avoid impeachment on charges of corruption, Bryant took major credit for Bullock's exposure and fall. In May 1872, President Ulysses S. Grant appointed Bryant deputy collector of customs in Savannah, a position he held until January 1877. This post allowed him to continue editing a Republican newspaper, the *Savannah Journal.*

In 1874 and again in 1876, Bryant was the Republican nominee for Congress from Georgia's First Congressional District, where he ran on a platform of public education for all, internal improvements, and cooperation between black and white laborers for higher wages. The bickering of Republicans and unsubstantiated charges of corruption against Bryant, as well as Democratic fraud, marred the campaigns and rendered his bids unsuccessful. Exonerated in the eyes of a majority of the party through investigation of the charges against him, from 1876 to 1880 Bryant served as Republican state party chairman. Unable to prevent them, he watched the meager remaining party strength in the state further eroded by the policies of the incoming U.S. president, Rutherford B. Hayes. With the Republican party losing ground, Bryant spent more time traveling through the North, lecturing on conditions in the South, and raising money for his Republican newspapers, the last of which was published in Atlanta in 1879 under the name the *Georgia Republican.*

In the 1880s Bryant turned once again to education as a remedy for racism and directed a portion of the money solicited in his lectures to a school for poor white children in Atlanta. He worked closely with Methodist minister Erasmus Q. Fuller in this effort and enlisted the assistance of the Methodist church at its annual conference in 1883. Bryant was convinced that racism was so engrained in white southerners that only careful education in American "nationalism" and equal rights could overcome the generations of hate. In his view, radical Republican reforms had been thwarted by white intransigence; therefore, changing white attitudes was the only way, in the long run, to change conditions for blacks. From 1882 to 1884, Bryant was secretary of the Republican state central committee, and for less than a year during 1884–1885, he was U.S. marshal for northern Georgia.

By the late 1880s, Bryant confined himself to the speakers circuit, particularly at meetings of the national Union League, in which he was an officeholder. First organized in the North during the Civil War, the Union League was an agent of support for President Abraham Lincoln and the entire northern war effort. During Reconstruction it served as an agent of Republicanism in the South as well, especially before the formation of the Republican party in southern states. In the 1880s, the national Union League, particularly strong in the Northeast, continued its support for equal rights and education. In the 1890s Bryant turned to business and local politics in New York. His last project, between 1891 and 1895, was a Methodist mission in Mount Vernon, New York, where he and his wife dispensed food and sermons on temperance and equal rights. It was in Mount Vernon that he died.

By the usual definitions of success, the political career of John Emory Bryant would be deemed less than outstanding. After one term in the Reconstruction legislature, he never again held elective office in Georgia. Enemies frequently assailed his character. On the other hand, religious and reform leaders were among those who admired and respected him. One must be careful in evaluating the role of any particular carpetbagger such as Bryant. Because of the unproven charges against him, many of them doubtlessly unfounded, it is difficult to assess his true character. As a reformer Bryant worked tirelessly and spoke for the aspirations and hopes of the freed slaves. Faced with the impossible task of changing generations-old racism, he sought to establish a new sense of social justice in the state and to educate both blacks and poor white children. Bryant's goals were unacceptable to most white Georgians, and his personality was abrasive to their sensibilities. He was energetic, self-righteous, arrogant, and totally committed to change occurring through the political process and by the instrument of the Republican party.

• Bryant's papers, including manuscripts of his speeches, are in the Manuscript Department of Perkins Library, Duke University, Durham, N.C. Other collections that contain some letters and papers are the Maine State Archives, Augusta, Maine; American Missionary Association Archives, Amistad Research Center, New Orleans; Henry P. Farrow Papers, Special Collections, University of Georgia, Athens; William E. Chandler Papers, Library of Congress; and O. O. Howard Papers, Bowdoin College, Brunswick, Maine. There are very few extant copies of Bryant's newspapers. Scattered issues of the *Loyal Georgian* are in the Perkins Library at Duke University, the University of Georgia Library, and Widener Library of Harvard University. Ruth Currie-McDaniel, *Carpetbagger of Conscience: A Biography of John Emory Bryant* (1987), is the most complete record and assessment of his career. Also see Olive Hall Shadgett, *The Republican Party in Georgia from Reconstruction through 1900* (1964), Elizabeth Studley Nathans, *Losing the Peace: Georgia Republicans and Reconstruction, 1865–1871* (1968), and Russell Duncan, *Entrepreneur for Equality: Governor Rufus Bullock, Commerce, and Race in Post-Civil War Georgia* (1994).

RUTH CURRIE-MCDANIEL

BRYANT, Joseph Decatur (12 Mar. 1845–7 Apr. 1914), surgeon and medical educator, was born in East Troy, Wisconsin, the son of Alonzo Ambrose Bryant and Harriet Atkins, farmers. He completed his early education in the local public schools and received his secondary education at a private academy in Norwich, New York, near his father's boyhood home. He then moved to New York City to study medicine with George W. Avery, a local physician, and attend Bellevue Hospital Medical College, where he received an M.D. in 1868.

After spending the next three years at Bellevue Hospital as a surgical intern, Bryant in 1871 joined the college's anatomy department as assistant to the chairman and lecturer on surgical anatomy. In 1872 he took on the additional duties of attending physician at the West Side Dispensary. Two years later he married Annette Amelia Crum, with whom he had one child. He was promoted by the college to demonstrator of anatomy in 1875, lecturer on general descriptive and surgical anatomy in 1877, and professor of anatomy in 1878. In 1883 he also assumed the position of associate professor of orthopedic surgery. During this period he authored *Manual of Operative Surgery* (2 vols., 1884; 4th ed., 1905), one of the day's more important surgical textbooks. In 1897 he served on the committee that arranged to merge the college with the New York University Medical College. After the merger he was appointed professor of the principles and practice of surgery as well as professor of operative and clinical surgery, positions he held for the next seventeen years. In 1906 he coedited with Albert H. Buck *American Practice of Surgery* (8 vols., 1906–1911), an important series of surgical textbooks.

Bryant played a prominent role in New York's public health affairs. As sanitary inspector of the city health department from 1873 to 1879 and commissioner of both that department and the state board of health from 1887 to 1893, he campaigned assiduously in an effort to eradicate pulmonary tuberculosis, spurred the appropriate authorities to reduce the overcrowding in tenements, and helped to effect improvements in the removal of raw sewage. In 1892, when shipborne cholera threatened to engulf the city, he greatly exceeded his authority and outraged New York's powerful shipping interests by quarantining every vessel that entered the harbor until it could be inspected, thus nullifying the threat of a deadly epidemic.

For many years Bryant was a confidant, fishing companion, and personal physician to U.S. president Grover Cleveland, whom he had come to know well while Cleveland was governor of New York. In 1893 he saved the president's life by excising a malignant growth from his mouth and jaw, a procedure that necessitated the removal of a considerable portion of the left upper jawbone. At the time the United States stood on the brink of economic depression, following a wave of bank failures a few months earlier. This situation was exacerbated by the depletion of the nation's gold reserves via the provisions of the Sherman Silver Purchase Act, and Cleveland faced a bitter battle in Congress over its repeal. He feared that a public announcement of his medical condition would serve only to panic the nation's already shaky investors and that a temporary abatement of his duties would undermine the chances of repeal because the reins of power would pass for the duration to Vice President Adlai E. Stevenson, a staunch supporter of the act. Therefore, Cleveland insisted that the operation take place secretly. Aided only by a dentist and an anesthetist, Bryant performed the delicate operation aboard a private yacht sailing up the East River while Cleveland sat in a chair on deck. So skillfully did Bryant do his work that for several months afterward no one but those connected with the logistics of the operation even suspected that it had occurred.

For many years Bryant was actively involved in the affairs of the American Medical Association (AMA). In 1903 he was a member of the committee on medical ethics that recommended that the state medical associations and not the national organization be responsible for determining the guidelines for ethical behavior; the acceptance of this recommendation ended much rancorous debate at national meetings. He also chaired the committee on national incorporation that unsuccessfully sought official recognition for the AMA by the U.S. Congress and served as its president in 1907–1908.

Bryant presided over the New York Academy of Medicine from 1895 to 1897, the New York State Medical Association in 1898–1899, and the Medical Society of the State of New York in 1905–1906. As a member of the New York National Guard, he served as surgeon of the Seventy-first Regiment from 1873 to 1882 and as surgeon general with the rank of brigadier general from 1882 to 1894. At the time of his death he was also a lieutenant in the U.S. Army Medical Reserve Corps. At various times he was visiting or consulting surgeon for nine New York hospitals and medical institutions besides Bellevue; several of these facilities specialized in treating the destitute, and at these he dispensed his services at no charge. He died in New York City.

Bryant contributed to the advance of American medicine in two ways. As an educator and author he imparted his operative expertise to a great number of students. As a public health official he helped to make New York City a healthier place in which to live.

• Bryant's papers have not been located. His relationship with Cleveland is discussed in Allan Nevins, *Grover Cleveland: A Study in Courage* (1934). Obituaries are in the *New York Times*, 8 Apr. 1914, and the *New York State Journal of Medicine* 14, no. 5 (May 1914): 229–30.

CHARLES W. CAREY, JR.

BRYANT, Louise (5 Dec. 1885–6 Jan. 1936), journalist, was born Anna Louise Mohan in San Francisco, California, the daughter of Hugh Mohan and Louisa Flick. Her father, a writer, worked in government jobs and for newspapers in the West until shortly after Louise's birth, when the family moved to Reno, Nevada. After Hugh Mohan abandoned the family, her mother filed for divorce in 1889, but Louise, always prone to romanticizing and exaggerating her childhood years, held that her father had died when she was four. Not long after the divorce, Louise's mother married Sheridan Bryant, who gave Louise her name, and the Bryants moved to Wadsworth, Nevada. Sheridan Bryant, a freight train conductor, kept his family on the move, and Louise was educated at schools in both Wadsworth and Reno. In 1905 she entered Nevada State University (now the University of Nevada).

Moving to Eugene, Oregon, in 1906, the twenty-year-old Bryant, who habitually lied about her age throughout her life, registered as an eighteen-year-old history student at the University of Oregon. She acquired a reputation at Oregon of being "fast"—she wore makeup, dated men she did not intend to marry, and dressed unconventionally. She was awarded a B.A. in January 1909 and relocated to Portland, where, after unsuccessfully trying to find a position on the daily *Oregonian*, she was hired by the weekly *Spectator* as an illustrator and society editor. In November 1909 she married Paul Trullinger, a dentist, but kept her small studio apartment in her own name. The couple had a happy marriage and led a somewhat unorthodox social life, highlighted by Friday afternoon martini and ether parties in Trullinger's dental suite. In 1912 Bryant joined the College Equal Suffrage League and began to tour the state speaking on behalf of woman suffrage.

In the summer of 1914 Bryant met the Portland-born journalist John Reed, whose passionate, radical articles she devoutly read in the socialist publication *The Masses*. They became lovers, and his stories of life in Greenwich Village and travels around the world enthralled her. Resolved to experience the life he led, she shocked Portland by leaving for New York City on New Year's Eve 1915 and moving into Reed's Washington Square apartment. Like many of the freethinkers populating the Village in the 1910s, Reed and Bryant had an "open relationship," and Reed's frequent absences allowed Bryant (and Reed) to engage in numerous affairs. In April 1916 Bryant's sympathetic article about two liberal Portland judges appeared in *The Masses*. In July her divorce from Trullinger was finalized.

Provincetown, Massachusetts, was a summer home to many who inhabited the Village, and in the summer of 1916 Reed and Bryant joined the annual migration. The couple, along with playwrights George Cram Cook and Eugene O'Neill (with whom Bryant began an affair), founded the Provincetown Players, a group some consider the precursor of modern American drama. The Players wrote, directed, and acted in their own plays, which were shown nightly for local residents. Playbills included Bryant's *The Game* alongside O'Neill's *Bound East for Cardiff*. In November Reed was to have life-threatening kidney surgery and wanted Bryant to become his legal heir. Though both Bryant and Reed opposed marriage in theory, they married a few days before he entered the hospital.

The United States had entered World War I in April 1917, and Reed's antiwar writings were making him less marketable to the commercial press. Money was tight, and the couple's relationship was strained because of both partners' continued extramarital activities. To ease the marital and financial strain, Bryant secured press credentials with the Bell Syndicate and set sail in June to cover the war in France.

Feeling independent and confident in her journalistic aptitude, Bryant returned home on 13 August. Reed met her boat and announced that they were off to Russia in just four days to cover the impending revolution. Bryant secured assignments from both Bell Syndicate and *Metropolitan* magazine. Despite the arduous journey, they arrived at an auspicious time. While there, they interviewed Alexander Kerensky, the leader of the provisional government, and Leon Trotsky, the head of the Petrograd Soviet; met Lenin; and witnessed what turned out to be a virtually bloodless revolution on 6 and 7 November. Eager to return, Bryant left in January 1918 and began compiling her articles into the book *Six Red Months in Russia*, which was published that October. Written hurriedly, *Six Red Months* differs from Reed's electric *Ten Days That Shook the World* (1919) in that it is less a historical record than her interpretation of the events of the revolution. Reviews of her work were mixed, with some critics deeming it biased and hastily done. Capitalizing on the attention she had received, Bryant spent the balance of 1918 and 1919 touring the country and speaking about her experiences in Russia and for the cause of woman suffrage.

Reed had returned to Russia in late 1919 as a delegate of the Communist Labor party, of which he had been a founder, and was imprisoned on smuggling charges on his way home. In early 1920 the United States brought charges of anarchy against him, and he realized it was impossible for him to return. In September 1920 Bryant joined him in Russia, but their time together was short. He died of typhus the next month in Moscow. Though devastated, Bryant remained in Russia and concentrated on writing, filing an exhaustive number of stories with the International News Service.

In July 1921 Bryant was back in the United States with the intent of putting Reed's papers in order and perhaps writing his biography. William Randolph Hearst hired her to write an article series on Russia for his newspapers, and she traveled the world as a correspondent. She perhaps reached her journalistic pinnacle in January 1923 with the publication in Hearst newspapers of an exclusive interview with the Italian fascist leader Benito Mussolini. That same year her second book on Russia, *Mirrors of Moscow*, appeared.

Bryant's life changed dramatically in 1921, when she met former assistant secretary of state and future U.S. ambassador to the Soviet Union William Christian Bullitt, Jr., an arrogant and charming man who some likened to John Reed. In July 1923 she became pregnant with her only child, and five months later Bullitt and Bryant married. Bullitt was wealthy (a fact that led to the severance of all of Bryant's former connections to Greenwich Village) but disillusioned with government work, and the couple spent their time socializing and traveling, dividing their time between Paris, New York City, and Massachusetts. They also sponsored young artists, including the painter Marsden Hartley and the poet Claude McKay. Perhaps at Bullitt's request, Bryant retired from journalism; her last article appeared in *The Nation* in August 1925.

In the late 1920s Bryant's life began to deteriorate. She was diagnosed with Dercum's disease, a rare disfiguring condition whose symptoms include the appearance of fatty deposits all over the body and mental confusion. During this period she also began to drink voraciously, often embarrassing herself with public episodes of drunkenness. Citing her drinking and a lesbian affair with the American sculptor Gwen Le Gallienne, Bullitt filed for divorce without her knowledge in 1930 and was given custody of their child (Bryant claimed never to have seen her daughter again). Bryant spent the last years of her life in Paris, gathering Reed's papers and trying but failing to complete a book on his life. Continuing to drink and becoming increasingly paranoid, she ended her relationship with Le Gallienne after suspecting the sculptor of poisoning her. She died of a cerebral hemorrhage outside of the squalid hotel in Paris in which she had been staying.

Bryant is remembered not as a widely read journalist but as the wife of the heroic revolutionary John Reed. Emma Goldman, the celebrated leftist, said after Bryant's death, "Louise was never a communist, she only slept with a communist." Never wholeheartedly espousing Reed's political views and never fitting in with the Greenwich Village radicals, Bryant was above all a journalist, a writer with a mind and a will of her own.

• Information on Bryant is in the John Reed Papers, Houghton Library, Harvard University. (Bryant had loaned Reed's papers to Harvard for a biography of Reed by Granville Hicks, a faculty member. Harvard saw the papers as a gift, not a loan, and they became part of the Louise Bryant Collection. Just nine months after her death, however, Harvard officials voted to change the title to the John Reed Collection.) Also see an unpublished memoir by Bryant, written in the last year of her life, in the Granville Hicks Papers in the Department of Special Collections, Syracuse University Library. A sympathetic biography is Mary V. Dearborn, *Queen of Bohemia: The Life of Louise Bryant* (1996). For Bryant and Reed's relationship, see Barbara Gelb, *So Short a Time: A Biography of John Reed and Louise Bryant* (1973). *Reds* (1981), a widely acclaimed motion picture, was based on the relationship between Reed and Bryant; directed by Warren Beatty, it starred Beatty as Reed and Diane Keaton as Bryant.

STACEY HAMILTON

BRYANT, Louise Frances Stevens (19 Sept. 1885–29 Aug. 1959), social statistician and medical editor, was born in Paris, France, the daughter of Charles E. Stevens, a civil engineer, and Miriam Collins Nicholson. She spent her first three years touring Europe with her mother and sister while her father led government-sponsored prospecting operations in South America. In 1888 he died, leaving a sizable inheritance, and they settled in New York City. The inheritance dissipated in unfortunate investments, and in 1910 she moved with her family to Rahway, New Jersey. After attending Hunter College and the Normal College of the City of New York for a year, she matriculated in 1904 at Smith College, where she studied philosophy and zoology and received her B.A. in 1908. Later that year she married Arthur A. Bryant; they had no children.

Bryant and her husband returned to New York City, where she worked as a laboratory assistant in the American Museum of Natural History's Department of Physiology and Osteology. In 1909 she became a special agent in the Russell Sage Foundation's Department of Education and conducted a statistical survey of school feeding programs in Europe and the United States that demonstrated that a significant percentage of American schoolchildren suffered from malnutrition. Because her report concluded that this condition correlated to the poverty of a child's family and advocated the establishment of an inexpensive, publically subsidized school lunch program in every school, it was rejected for publication by the foundation on the grounds that it smacked of socialism. Undaunted, Bryant publicized her findings in a syndicated article in 125 Sunday newspapers in 1911; while serving as the chairman of the school feeding section of the International Conference on School Hygiene in Buffalo, New York, in 1913; and as secretary of the American Home Economics Association's school lunch committee. Published commercially as *School Feeding: Its Organization and Planning at Home and Abroad* (1913), her report stimulated the establishment of school lunch programs in a number of schools.

In 1911, the year before she divorced her husband, Bryant moved to Philadelphia to enroll in the University of Pennsylvania's Department of Medical Science and to take charge of the social service department of the university's psychological clinic. In the latter capacity, she taught courses to social workers that emphasized disease, neglect, and child abuse rather than genetics as the primary causes of behavioral problems in young people. In 1914 she received her Ph.D. in medical science and became an instructor of psychology at the Pennsylvania School for Social Service and Health as well as the chief of the Philadelphia municipal court's women's division. Her primary responsibility in the latter capacity involved gathering data pertinent to the court's cases and presenting it during hearings; to this end, she created a department of statistics and research, one of the first of its kind to be affiliated with a court. Bryant also served as a champion for the legal rights of unmarried and incarcerated women and their children at a time when society regarded such people with disdain.

During World War I, Bryant served as a statistician with the U.S. Army Chief of Staff and the War Industries Board. She returned to New York in 1919 to become the educational and publications secretary of the Girl Scouts of America. Four years later she became the secretary of publications and the coordinator of research for the Committee on Dispensary Development, a joint effort of the United Hospital Fund and the New York Academy of Medicine designed to identify ways to provide health care to city residents who could not afford it. In *Better Doctoring, Less Dependency* (1927), Bryant concluded that the different ways in which hospitals and social agencies relate to clients resulted in the waste of about 20 percent of the available public and charitable funds, a problem that could be solved only by better cooperation between clinic personnel and welfare agents. In 1924 she and her mother, whom she had lived with and supported since her divorce, began sharing a house in Bronxville, New York, with Lura Beam, a medical writer and editor, and Beam's mother; Bryant and Beam lived together for the next thirty-five years.

In 1927 Bryant became the executive secretary of the National Committee on Maternal Health (NCMH), an organization that was founded three years earlier by the gynecologist Robert L. Dickinson to conduct ground-breaking statistical research concerning the medical aspects of human sex behavior. Between 1930 and 1935 she supervised the research and writing of ten monographs and forty-two articles concerning such topics as the sex life of women, the control of conception, the medico-chemical aspects of contraception, human sex anatomy and sterility, spontaneous and induced abortion, and maternal mortality. She also helped Havelock Ellis, the English essayist and physician, find a new publisher for his seven-volume *Studies in the Psychology of Sex* (1935). Although these topics were considered to be scandalous by organizations such as the Society for the Suppression of Vice, she avoided legal difficulties by refusing to popularize any of the finished manuscripts and by submitting them for publication to reputable medical publishers only. Because she was also responsible for raising enough money to permit the publication of NCMH manuscripts, her professional relationship with Dickinson grew increasingly difficult after he began insisting on using donations for purposes different from the donor's original intent. Bryant resigned in 1935, partly because Dickinson attempted to fund a project on homosexuality with a Rockefeller Foundation grant intended for a study of marriage counseling and partly because she had developed a heart condition that impaired her ability to handle the stress of her position.

After a year's rest, Bryant served as Mabel E. Todd's ghostwriter on a book about structural anatomy. In 1938 she joined the American Association of University Women's art department as a clerk, and for the next fifteen years she supervised its circulating exhibitions. Bryant died in Bronxville.

• Bryant's papers are located in the Sophia Smith Collection at Smith College. A biography is Lura Beam, *Bequest from a Life: A Biography of Louise Stevens Bryant* (1963).

CHARLES W. CAREY, JR.

BRYANT, Paul William. *See* Bryant, Bear.

BRYANT, William Cullen (3 Nov. 1794–12 June 1878), poet and journalist, was born in Cummington, Massachusetts, the son of Peter Bryant, a physician, and Sarah Snell, daughter of one of the first settlers. Young Cullen, as he was called, was a precocious child of poor health and nervous temperament. His mother taught him the alphabet at sixteen months. At twelve he was tutored in Latin by an uncle, Rev. Thomas Snell, and in Greek by Rev. Moses Halleck. His father, himself well versed in the classics as well as British poetry, shared his sizable personal library with his son and encouraged him to write poetry. Bryant's mother kept a diary of observations on local events. Thus, the environment of his boyhood was not only conducive to an appreciation of culture and the disciplined development of his literary skills, but also to the nurture of spiritual and moral qualities. In particular, Bryant retained through his life vivid memories of long hours spent at the Congregational church, with its biblical orientation and rigorous Calvinism.

Bryant was composing simple rhymes at the age of seven and, under his father's guidance, became adept at versification in the contemporary neoclassic style. By the age of thirteen he had published a poem in the *Hampshire Gazette* in Northampton, Massachusetts, and a pamphlet in verse in Boston. In 1808 he published a satirical treatment of national politics, which he called *The Embargo; or, Sketches of the Times*. It appeared as a pamphlet, reflective of the orthodox views of New England Federalists smarting under the trade restrictions imposed by President Thomas Jefferson.

At the age of sixteen Bryant attended Williams College in western Massachusetts for one year. He wished to pursue his studies at Yale, but his family was unable to support him financially. Instead he studied law under attorneys at Worthington and later at Bridgewater while continuing to write poetry. After admission to the bar in 1815, Bryant practiced law for ten years, first in Plainfield and then in Great Barrington. He became progressively disenchanted with a life of petty wrangles and litigation among tradesmen and farmers, however, and sought respite in his writing.

During these years Bryant took long walks through the rural countryside, and his meditations on the natural scenery of the Berkshires fed directly into his poetry. His reading of the *Lyrical Ballads* of William Wordsworth gave confirmation to his own responses to natural beauty. An early draft of "Thanatopsis" was composed during this time and published, in 1817, in the *North American Review*. Outstanding among his poems of this period were "The Yellow Violet" (1814), "To a Waterfowl" (1815), and "Inscription for the Entrance to a Wood" (1817).

In 1818 Bryant published his *Essay on American Poetry*. Subsequently he was invited to deliver the Phi Beta Kappa poem at the Harvard College commencement of 1821. For this occasion Bryant composed "The Ages," a long poem in Spenserian stanzas. Praising the progress toward human liberty from the distant past to his own day, Bryant's theme owed more to the spirit of the Enlightenment than to the religious and political orthodoxy in which he had been raised.

In 1821 Bryant married Frances Fairchild, by whom he was to have two children. His first collection of verse, simply titled *Poems*, also appeared in 1821. This was the first of many collections of his work. It contained the enlarged and revised version of "Thanatopsis," Bryant's major work in blank verse. The poem addresses the plight of those individuals who are anxious and fearful about death: "When thoughts / Of the last bitter hour come like a blight / Over thy spirit." Nature, however, has powers to console in a "still voice." Arguing that "All that breathe / shall share thy destiny," it bids a calm and stoic acceptance of death: "sustained and soothed / By an unfaltering trust, approach thy grave, / Like one who wraps the drapery of his couch / About him, and lies down to pleasant dreams." The poem is without reference to rewards or punishments in the afterlife. Bryant's later poetry alluded to an afterlife, but in "Thanatopsis" he made a clean break with his religious upbringing. In his maturity he attended various Protestant churches and composed the lyrics of about two dozen hymns expressing the sentiments of the liberalized religious community of his day.

Bryant's place in American letters was largely established through this early poetry. While evoking the natural beauty of the American landscape by naming specific places and species of wildlife, his contemplations held to a solemn piety and serious moralism, which prepared the way for the poetry of Ralph Waldo Emerson and Walt Whitman, both of whom would later pay tribute to his role in American letters. His poems of natural scenery have often been compared with the landscape painting of the Hudson River School. There is, in fact, a well-known painting, *Kindred Spirits* (1848), by Asher B. Durand, which portrays from a distance the relatively small figures of the poet and Thomas Cole standing on a promontory in the Catskills while they solemnly survey the wild scenery about them.

Bryant's success in belles lettres led him, at the age of thirty-one, to seek a career in this field rather than in law. To this end he moved his family to New York City. At first he edited a literary journal, the *New York Review and Atheneum Magazine,* and his reputation was further enhanced by public lectures to the Athenaeum Society and the American Academy of Art. He became a member of the Sketch Club, a society of New York literati, whose meetings he attended for over forty years.

In 1827 Bryant joined the editorial staff of the *New York Evening Post,* and within two years he had become part owner and editor in chief of the paper. This position, while making strenuous demands on his time and energy to the detriment of his poetry, gave him for the first time the financial resources to provide for his family and made possible, in the long run, the continuation of his literary efforts. Under Bryant, the *Evening Post* increased its circulation and developed a faithful readership. While other New York daily papers were beginning to attract mass appeal through low prices and sensationalism, the *Evening Post* directed its appeal to readers who were willing and able to pay for an authoritative source of news and opinion.

The editorial positions of Bryant's newspaper led it to assume a position of leadership in many of the progressive causes of the day. In its editorial columns it advocated free trade, more humane conditions for prison inmates, the enactment of copyright laws, and the eventual abolition of slavery. Bryant endorsed Andrew Jackson and Martin Van Buren in their presidential campaigns, opposed the annexation of Texas, denounced the Dred Scott decision, and extolled John Brown as a martyr to the cause of abolition. In respect to local New York political affairs, Bryant spoke for the improvement of the public schools, and he was among the first to propose the establishment of a city park. In his later years he took a personal interest in the building of Central Park.

While forcefully addressing the issues of the day, Bryant and the *Post* spoke in a moderate voice, seeking to convince through solid reasoning and eloquence. In the years before the Civil War, Bryant supported the new Republican party and its Free Soil platform. Indeed, it was Bryant who introduced Abraham Lincoln when he gave his famous speech at Cooper Union in 1860. When Lincoln became president, the *Evening Post,* while being generally supportive of the administration, urged more decisiveness and vigor in the waging of the war. Bryant not only corresponded with Lincoln, but, in 1862, also joined a delegation pressing for greater military action. Upon the assassination of Lincoln, Bryant read to the bereaved New Yorkers gathered in Union Square his poem "The Death of Lincoln" (1865), which began, "Oh, slow to smite and swift to spare, / Gentle and merciful and just!"

Of medium height, clean shaven, and of upright stature, Bryant was ordinarily reserved and aloof in his personal demeanor. The only person with whom he maintained a longstanding and friendly relationship was Richard Henry Dana, Sr. However, Bryant had a wide range of acquaintances and conducted a voluminous correspondence. He impressed people with his good sense and quiet manner. An attentive listener, inquisitive, well informed, shrewd in professional matters, Bryant did not conform to any of the stereotypes of the "poet" of his day. Among his many avocational interests was the practice of homeopathic medicine, and for many years he was active in the Homeopathic Society of New York.

Even while pursuing his responsibilities as an editor and publisher, Bryant continued to write poetry. In addition to descriptions of and meditations on nature, he wrote verses idealizing the freedom fighters of Greece, Italy, and other lands; poems of romantic and tragic passion, such as "Monument Mountain" (1824); and tributes to Native Americans. While visiting Germany in 1835 he was fascinated by German Romanticism and wove its folk themes into his own work. Bryant was a proficient linguist, well read in the poetry of other cultures, and he translated poetry from medieval and modern French, German, Italian, Spanish, and Portuguese.

Bryant associated with many of the literary figures of his time and, as they passed from the scene, delivered "memorial orations" upon them, most notably for Washington Irving and James Fenimore Cooper.

He also composed poetic tributes to prominent public figures such as Thomas Cole and William Ellery Channing (1780–1842).

Bryant had been able to leave the daily management of the *Evening Post* to capable associates, John Bigelow and later his son-in-law, Parke Godwin, in order to pursue his literary and other interests as well as travel. His poem "The Prairies" (1833) was written after a trip to Illinois. He continued to publish poetry in newspapers and journals, both his original work and translations from European writers. He had ventured to Europe for the first time in 1834 and sent back to the newspaper graphic and detailed accounts of his travels. These were subsequently collected into two volumes. In all he made six voyages abroad. During an 1852–1853 trip to Egypt and the Near East, where he traveled on camelback hundreds of miles, Bryant was quarantined by Turkish soldiers and acquired the full, gray beard that he wore during his later years. His final trip, to Spain, was undertaken at the age of seventy-two.

In 1843 Bryant purchased property on Long Island, New York, at Roslyn, where he was not only free to write, but also able to pursue his botanical interests, planting and nurturing specimens of trees and shrubs from around the world. The house and grounds of Roslyn have been preserved and are open to the public.

Bryant devoted much of his later life to the translation from the Greek of Homer's *Iliad* and *Odyssey*. Beginning in 1863, he worked on these translations over nine years, taking the materials with him on his travels. The two volumes appeared in 1871 and 1873 to favorable reviews.

Bryant died as a result of head injuries sustained in a fall outside of his New York home. He was returning from delivering a speech in honor of the Italian political leader Mazzini. His estate amounted to $1 million. His son-in-law, Parke Godwin, continued to publish the *Evening Post* and edited the posthumous *Life and Writings of William Cullen Bryant* (1883, 1884).

• There are collections of Bryant material in libraries throughout the nation. Foremost is the Goddard-Roslyn Collection in the custody of a descendant, Mr. Conrad G. Goddard of New York City. These substantial materials, including diaries, letters, and manuscripts of poetry, may be studied from microfilmed copies on eight reels at the New York Public Library. The most recent descriptive guide to materials is Herman E. Spivey, "Manuscript Resources for the Study of William Cullen Bryant," *Bibliographical Society of American Papers* 44 (3d Quarter, 1950): 254–68. Bryant's correspondence through 1857 has been collected by William Cullen Bryant II and Thomas G. Voss, eds., *The Letters of William Cullen Bryant* (4 vols., 1975–1984). The best biography is Charles H. Brown, *William Cullen Bryant: A Biography* (1971), which contains a bibliographic essay as well as notes. The only collections of Bryant's writings are those edited by his son-in-law, Parke Godwin: *The Poetical Works* (2 vols., 1883), published as vols. 3 and 4 of *The Life and Writings*, and *The Prose Writings* (2 vols., 1884), published as vols. 1 and 2 of *The Life and Writings*. See also Tremaine McDowell, *William Cullen Bryant* (1935); Albert F. McLean, *William Cullen Bryant* (1989); and Allan Nevins, *The Evening Post: A Century of Journalism* (1922).

ALBERT F. MCLEAN

BRYCE, James (10 May 1838–22 Jan. 1922), author and statesman, was born in Belfast, Ireland, the son of James Bryce, a schoolmaster, and Margaret Young. The family moved to Glasgow, Scotland, when James was eight. His father instilled in Bryce a wide-ranging interest in the arts and sciences, and after attending Glasgow University he matriculated at Oxford. His entry there was a landmark event: he was the first student to be admitted without having to subscribe to the Thirty-nine Articles of the Anglican Church. Bryce distinguished himself as a scholar at Oxford, producing as his entry for the Arnold Historical Essay Prize a treatise that would be expanded for publication in 1864 as *The Holy Roman Empire*.

After taking his B.A. at Oxford, Bryce studied law in Heidelberg, Germany; he was admitted to the bar in 1867 and in that year completed his service on the nation's Schools Enquiry Commission, the first of what was to be a series of political appointments that would extend throughout his life. Three years later, he was appointed Regius Professor of Civil Law at Oxford; more significantly, in the same year he embarked on the first of his many visits to the United States.

Bryce made a second visit to America in 1881 and a third in 1883. During each of these three excursions, he made a special effort to get to know both the laws and customs of the people. Even after he was elected to Parliament in 1880, he maintained his keen interest in the United States. In 1883, feeling confident in his knowledge of that vast new nation, he began composing the work that would make his reputation as a writer and link him inevitably to the country that had captured his imagination. Five years later, he brought forth the first edition of *The American Commonwealth*.

Modeling his work on Alexis de Tocqueville's influential study of America done half a century earlier, Bryce set out to describe the government and the life of the nation. With the skill of a political scientist and a sociologist, he directed his trained eye at federal, state, and local government structures, summarizing their common traits and highlighting the strengths and weaknesses he found in the various methods Americans had developed to govern themselves. The original edition was published in three volumes. The first two focused on government structures. Bryce's summary of the national government was most useful to his readers; his description of state government was authoritative. The third volume was particularly valuable as a record of the American character; readers on both sides of the Atlantic developed a sympathetic appreciation for the customs and values of the citizens of England's former colony. The work was praised by future U.S. presidents Theodore Roosevelt (1858–1919) and Woodrow Wilson and by U.S. Supreme Court Associate Justice Oliver Wendell Holmes (1841–1935).

In 1889 Bryce married Marion Ashton; they had no children. Marriage did little to restrict his traveling, however; during the next quarter century he went with his wife or with other friends to more than four dozen countries on six continents. The observations made on these treks found their way into several books that further established Bryce's reputation as one of the era's premier political and sociological thinkers. During the same period, Bryce made several revisions to the various reprintings and new editions of *The American Commonwealth*, providing readers even sharper insights into the unique qualities of the citizens of the United States.

At the same time, capitalizing on the success of *The American Commonwealth* and other writings, Bryce continued his political career in British governments controlled by the Liberal party, serving in a variety of posts for Prime Ministers William E. Gladstone and Lord Roseberry. When his party was not in power, Bryce was a vocal back-bencher, criticizing the conservative governments for their handling of numerous foreign policy issues. In 1905 Prime Minister Henry Campbell-Bannerman appointed him chief secretary for Ireland and two years later offered him the crowning appointment of his diplomatic career: British ambassador to the United States. For the next six years, Bryce made use of the knowledge he had gained in numerous visits to America, and the friendships he had made there, to solidify Anglo-American relationship during a period when such ties were to prove crucial.

Bryce was an activist ambassador. He spent considerable time working to strengthen U.S.-Canadian relations, traveling extensively in both countries, where his immense popularity gave him entree to boardrooms and barrooms. Relying on his firsthand knowledge of Americans' character, he was able to negotiate effectively a series of treaties between the countries that settled disputes about boundaries and territorial waters and improved trade relations between the two countries. The Boundary Waters Treaty of 1909 and the Pecuniary Claims Agreement of 1910 were brought to fruition largely through his efforts. Bryce traveled extensively to all parts of the nation during these years, turning up in such places as Madison, Wisconsin; Lake Champlain, New York; Raleigh, North Carolina; Tampa, Florida; and the California coast. Bryce also involved himself in the improvement of black colleges. He visited Tuskegee Institute, where he was a guest of college president Booker T. Washington, and he participated in the 1910 founder's day celebration at Hampton Normal Institute in Virginia. He also contributed financially to black colleges in America.

During the years that Bryce served as his country's chief emissary to the United States, he was a frequent speaker on college campuses and at political gatherings. A common theme of his addresses was the similarity he found between his country and the new nation founded by Britain's onetime colonials. He became a confidant of the rich and powerful, too. His personal friendships with Theodore Roosevelt (with whom he had stayed at the White House in 1904), William Howard Taft, and Woodrow Wilson (who entertained him at Princeton in 1908) made him an important adviser to these men who shaped American foreign and domestic policy during the first decades of the twentieth century. It may be argued that his efforts had a significant, if subtle, impact on the decision of the United States to side with England rather than Germany in the world war that erupted less than a year after Bryce left his post to return to England.

Though he had been offered a peerage before going to the United States as Britain's chief ambassador, Bryce had declined the honor, believing that Americans would respond more favorably to an emissary who was, like them, without title. Upon his return to England, however, he agreed to accept the honor of a peerage, and in 1914 entered the House of Lords as Viscount Bryce of Dechemont.

The final years of Bryce's life were far from quiet. He continued in an advisory capacity to the government, serving the war effort as chair of the Inquiry into Alleged German Outrages in Belgium. He was also active on the committee that developed the proposal for the League of Nations. He remained an active author, completing *Modern Democracies* only a year before his death. He died in Sidmouth.

• A substantial collection of letters, papers, and miscellaneous correspondence is in the Western Manuscripts Collection, Bodleian Library, Oxford University. A more limited collection of personal and official correspondence is in the Library of Congress. The most comprehensive biography is H. A. L. Fisher, *James Bryce* (2 vols., 1927). Additional biographical information and an analysis of Bryce's contributions to American political thought can be found in Robert C. Brooks, ed., *Bryce's American Commonwealth Fiftieth Anniversary* (1939), and Edmund Ions, *James Bryce and American Democracy* (1968). A lengthy obituary is in the *New York Times*, 23 Jan. 1922.

LAURENCE W. MAZZENO

BRYCE, Peter (5 Mar. 1834–14 Aug. 1892), psychiatrist and mental hospital superintendent, was born in Columbia, South Carolina, the son of Peter Bryce and Martha Smith. His father died before Bryce had finished preparatory school. In 1852 Bryce enrolled at the Citadel in South Carolina, from which he graduated with distinction in 1855. In 1857 he entered the medical school of the University of New York (now New York University), from which he graduated in 1859. As was common in medical schools of that era, there were no courses that prepared him for a career in mental health care. In the summer following his graduation, however, he traveled to Europe, where he toured psychiatric hospitals. After his return to the United States, he served briefly at a psychiatric hospital in Trenton, New Jersey; shortly thereafter he returned to Columbia, where he took a position as assistant physician at the South Carolina Lunatic Asylum.

Bryce became acquainted with Dorothea Dix, a leader in the reform of mental health care, who recommended him for the position of superintendent of the

Alabama Insane Hospital, then being built at Tuscaloosa. Bryce formally applied for the position and, after some intense lobbying by a local politician, was selected. The Alabama legislature had specified that the superintendent be a physician, be married, and agree to live in quarters at the hospital. Although Bryce was unmarried at the time of his appointment, he married Marie Ellen Clarkson, also of Columbia, prior to assuming the position in October 1860. The newly married couple moved immediately into the hospital and lived there until Bryce's death. They had no children, so the activities at the hospital became the focus of her attention as well as his. Shortly after Bryce's burial on the hospital grounds, it was renamed the Bryce Hospital, the name it has now.

Bryce developed the policies and procedures by which the new institution was to be governed for the remainder of his tenure. As a state institution, the hospital was required to serve as a military hospital during the Civil War; it lacked funding during the Civil War and for decades thereafter. In the postwar years it teetered on the verge of bankruptcy, and this did much to demonstrate Bryce's exceptional management capabilities.

Like many of his contemporaries, Bryce believed that insanity was caused by the interplay of predisposing and precipitating causes and that the most effective treatment was one that minimized the presence or influence of precipitating causes while allowing the mind to heal itself. A therapy known as "moral treatment" had been devised and advocated widely as a means of minimizing antagonistic events in patients' lives while allowing their minds to heal. Psychiatrists and mental hospital superintendents praised moral treatment and reported extraordinary successes using it. Bryce advocated it initially and continued to employ it long after its successes had been discredited and it had been discarded by most American psychiatrists.

As employed by Bryce, moral treatment included a normalized environment characterized by kind treatment, absence of restraints, and regular work by all patients who were able. During his tenure the hospital population averaged 87 percent indigents. Bryce extolled the therapeutic value of work—arguing that idle hands allowed mental patients too much time to focus on their condition—and, at the same time, he recognized its importance to the hospital's economic survival. Whether this treatment policy was maintained because of its therapeutic successes or its economic benefits, it was unquestionably a key method by which the hospital was able to survive on its ever-decreasing state funds and its dearth of patients who could contribute financially to their own care.

Although Bryce was influenced by national professional organizations and literature, he attended national meetings infrequently. Illness prevented him from being able to serve when he was elected in 1892 as president of the Medico-Psychological Association (formerly the Association of Medical Superintendents of American Institutions for the Insane, and later the American Psychiatric Association). At the time of his death in Tuscaloosa, Alabama, he was at the center of a lively debate among mental hospital superintendents concerning nonrestraint of patients; many believed Bryce had advocated nonrestraint too widely. As a superintendent, he was interested in the management side of hospital care. He was also a strong advocate of advanced methods of farming, which he employed on the hospital's farm.

As a physician and leader of one of the state's largest institutions, he was highly respected in Alabama, serving as president of both the state medical and state historical associations. As a mental hospital superintendent whose longevity at one hospital exceeded that of most of his contemporaries, a steady advocate of moral treatment, and a persistent proponent of nonrestraint of patients, he was an important figure in both psychiatry and mental hospital management. Ironically, charges of abuse of patient labor by subsequent superintendents caused the hospital to become the focus of nationwide investigation in the 1970s that ultimately led to outright release of many patients and removal of others to less restricted environments.

• Information on Bryce's philosophy of mental illness and mental health care can be found in his annual and biennial reports located at the Bryce Hospital, in a small collection of letters located at the Alabama Department of Archives and History in Montgomery, and in his articles, "State Aid to Hospitals," *Transactions of the Medical Association of the State of Alabama* (1874): 256–76; "The Mind and How to Preserve It," *Transactions of the Medical Association of the State of Alabama* (1880): 243–91; "A Short Study of Some of the Phenomena of the Mind," *Transactions of the Medical Association of the State of Alabama* (1882): 291–316; "Report of a Clinic Held Before the State Medical Association by the Superintendent and Staff of the Alabama Insane Hospital," *Transactions of the Medical Association of the State of Alabama* (1887): 83–91; "Moral and Criminal Responsibility," *The Alienist and Neurologist* (1888): 428–48; and "A Case of Mania Transitoria," *American Journal of Insanity* 45 (1889): 442–45. Biographical information on Bryce can be found in Thomas M. Owen, "Peter Bryce," *Dictionary of Alabama Biography*, vol. 3 (1921), pp. 244–45; Emmett B. Carmichael, "Peter Bryce," *The American Surgeon* 26 (1960): 750–55; and Henderson M. Somerville, "In Memoriam: Peter Bryce, M.D.," *American Journal of Insanity* 49 (1892): 545–54. Two tributes to Bryce are James T. Searcy, "The Annual Message of the President," *Transactions of the Medical Association of the State of Alabama* (1893), and Henderson M. Somerville, "Memorial of the Late Peter Bryce," *Biennial Report* of the Alabama Insane Hospital (1892).

BILL WEAVER

BRYNNER, Yul (11 July 1920?–10 Oct. 1985), actor, was born in Vladivostok, Russia, the son of Boris Bryner, a mining engineer, and Marousia Blagavidova, an actress. Brynner first attended school in Harbin, China, where he lived with his mother from age four after his parents separated. In 1934 his mother moved to Paris, where he learned to sing and play the seven-stringed gypsy guitar, and, encouraged by the large community of Russian gypsies there, he began his stage career by singing cabaret in 1935.

Physically strong, Brynner joined the Cirque d'Hiver as a flying acrobat about this time, but his career was cut short by severe injuries sustained in a fall. During his recovery, he became addicted to opium, through which he became friends with certain members of the French intelligentsia: Jean Cocteau, Colette, Marcel Marceau, and Jean Marais. He also met Michael Chekhov, who interested him in an acting career. His addiction forced him to retreat in 1937 to Switzerland, where he was cured. Returning to Paris, he became an unpaid apprentice to the repertory company of Georges and Ludmilla Pitoeff. In 1939 he returned to Dalian, China, with his mother, briefly traveled with his father, then brought his mother to New York in 1941 to seek treatment for her leukemia and to study acting with Chekhov, who directed a traveling theater company based in Ridgefield, Connecticut.

Brynner's acting career formally began with his association with Chekhov, whom he later counted as the most important artistic influence on his career. In 1943 he worked for the U.S. Office of War Information as a foreign-language radio broadcaster and made many contacts in the broadcasting business. That same year he married Virginia Gilmore, a film actress, and had one child by her.

After the war Brynner won the part of the poet Tsai-Yong in the Broadway musical *Lute Song* (1946), which starred Mary Martin, and in 1948 he began directing television shows for CBS. Highly regarded by his colleagues, he earned credits for directing programs on "Studio One" and "Omnibus," among others. In 1949 he made his screen debut, his first of more than forty career films, acting as a villain in *Port of New York*.

At Mary Martin's suggestion, Richard Rodgers and Oscar Hammerstein II cast Brynner as one of the leads in their musical *The King and I* in 1951. Brynner shaved his head for the role, a highly unusual practice at the time and one that he never abandoned. The part made Brynner nationally famous; he won many of the major New York theater awards, including the Antoinette Perry and the New York Drama Critics' Circle Award. The role remains his best known. He played the King of Siam for 4,625 performances, including the initial Broadway run of 1,246 from 1951 until 1954, the national tour that immediately followed, and numerous revivals beginning in 1977 and lasting until 1985.

Brynner's film career was firmly established by his appearing in director Cecil B. DeMille's *The Ten Commandments* and by the film version of *The King and I*, for which Brynner won an Oscar as best actor. Both films, released in 1956, were box-office successes and made him a leading Hollywood star for several years. Other films soon followed: *Anastasia* (1956), *The Brothers Karamazov* (1958), *The Buccaneer* (1958), *The Journey* (1958), and *The Sound and the Fury* (1959). While *The Journey* was being filmed in Austria, he fathered a daughter by an Austrian woman, one of many love affairs during his life.

Brynner became separated from his first wife when he moved to Switzerland to avoid paying U.S. income taxes. He suddenly became interested in the United Nations World Refugee Year of 1959–1960, writing a book, *Bring Forth the Children* (1960), and producing a television special, "Rescue—with Yul Brynner." He also was appointed a special consultant to the UN High Commissioner for Refugees in 1959–1960. In 1960 he married Doris Kleiner; the couple had one child.

About the same time, his film career began to decline. Of the more than thirty remaining films he was to make, only *The Magnificent Seven* (1960) and *Westworld* (1973) received critical and box-office acclaim, and he was severely disappointed in the failure of the adaptation of Nicolai Gogol's *Taras Bulba* (1962). He became seriously interested in art, investing in works by Cézanne, Picasso, and a large collection of drawings by Cocteau as well as others. In 1965 he became a Swiss citizen, and in 1971 he divorced his second wife and married a third, Jacqueline de Croisset. They moved to Normandy and adopted two Vietnamese refugee children.

Brynner revived his career by returning to the role that had established him, King Mongut of Siam. In May 1977 *The King and I* opened on Broadway, and Brynner played a grueling eight performances per week, in New York and on the road, with few breaks, until his last year, often with excruciating pain from cracked vertebrae and developing lung cancer. The constant touring ruined his third marriage, and he was divorced for a third time in 1982 (?). In April 1983 he married a dancer in the company, Kathy Lee (née Kathy Yam Choo). He played his last performance on 30 June 1985. Brynner died in New York City.

By the accounts of critical review and his colleagues, Brynner the actor was an extremely powerful artist. Believing that every movement of the body contributed to characterization, he took pride in his excellent physique and insisted on doing his own stunt work in films, driving the chariot in *The Ten Commandments* and leaping from a mast in *The Buccaneer*. Deborah Kerr, his opposite in the film *The King and I*, credited Brynner alone with making it much better than the typical Hollywood musical adaptation: "He had a wonderful way of handling actors—got things out of them they never realized they possessed." Despite such talent, Brynner did not leave a legacy of artistically important films, and since he never touched the classical repertory, he did not influence the acting profession in any lasting way. Only in the film version of *The King and I* will any sense of his acting be felt by future re-creaters of that role.

• A critically documented biography of Brynner has yet to be published. One can consult, with caution, Jhan Robbins's popular biography, *Yul Brynner: The Inscrutable King* (1987), and Rock Brynner's biographical memoir, *Yul: The Man Who Would Be King* (1989). Because much of the information in these two books comes from their subject, who was famous for fabricating stories about himself, there are numerous discrepancies between them. Cover articles on Brynner appear in *Life*, 10 Mar. 1958, and *Newsweek*, 19 May 1958. An obituary is in the *New York Times*, 10 and 11 Oct. 1985.

JOSEPH P. SWAIN

BUADE, Louis de (22 May 1622–28 Nov. 1698), French soldier and courtier, was born at Saint-Germain-en-Laye, the son of Henri de Buade and Anne Phélypeaux de Pontchartrain, aristocrats. On his father's side he was descended from the old nobility of the sword and on his mother's from the ascending nobility of the robe. His father, comte de Frontenanc, baron (later comte) de Palluau, and colonel of the Régiment de Navarre, was highly regarded by Louis XIII, who stood as godfather to the infant Louis at his baptism.

Louis de Buade received a good education, likely at a Jesuit college, which may explain his hostility to that order later in life. He entered the army in his teens, served in campaigns in the Thirty Years' War, and in 1643 acquired the colonelcy of the Régiment de Normandie. When not in active service he resided at the royal court and was always more the courtier than the soldier. There he lived extravagantly and incurred huge debts that he never honored. At his father's death, Louis inherited his titles and became known as the comte de Frontenac.

In 1648 Frontenac married clandestinely Anne de la Grange, a tempestuous beauty and daughter of a wealthy judge who deemed him to be a fortune hunter and who succeeded in preventing him, or his wife, from garnering a penny from her inheritance. To evade his exasperated creditors Frontenac acquired a commission as lieutenant general with the Venetian army defending Crete against the Turks. It did not serve him long. He quarreled with everyone and was summarily dismissed by the Venetian captain general, Francesco Morosini. In 1672, his creditors pressing him hard, he somehow obtained the appointment as governor general of New France, thereby bilking them. He arrived in Quebec in the autumn of 1672, unaccompanied by his wife.

The intendant, Jean Talon, had been recalled to France and was not replaced until 1675. An intendant had charge of civil administration (*police*), justice, and finance. Frontenac assumed that, in the absence of this official, authority devolved to him, and he set about governing despotically. He quarreled violently with the members of the Sovereign Council who opposed him, the governor of Montreal, senior members of the clergy, and Jacques Duchesneau when he arrived to assume his duties and powers as intendant. Frontenac could not comprehend how a lowly member of the *noblesse de robe*, as was Duchesneau, or petty colonial notables, such as the judges and attorney general of the Sovereign Council, could presume to oppose him, could dare to protest when he had those who defied him thrown into prison or shipped to France to answer to the king for their lèse majesté.

The members of the Sovereign Council thus sent into exile, along with the detailed written protests of others, crossed the Atlantic and were presented to Jean-Baptiste Colbert, the secretary of state responsible for the colonies. Exiling them had been a stupid move on Frontenac's part. He was not Louis XIV, and Colbert minced no words in warning him to mend his ways or be recalled in disgrace. Colbert then defined Frontenac's powers stringently, but Frontenac took no heed; instead he took counsel from the sycophants, such as Robert Cavelier de La Salle, with whom he had surrounded himself.

The main source of wealth in the colony was the fur trade, and Frontenac and his coterie were determined to reap most of it. Colbert wanted the colony's meager manpower employed in farming and such industries as timber and shipbuilding in order to establish a firmly based, compact, defensible colony. Frontenac wanted none of that; he persisted in having fur trade posts established through the Great Lakes basin and down the Mississippi. There, with Cavelier de La Salle and Henri Tonty to the fore, the adventurers clashed head on with the powerful Iroquois Confederacy, who challenged the French for control of the Ohio Valley.

In the face of this threat, Frontenac proved to be pusillanimous. In 1682, before the storm burst on the French, he was recalled to France, dismissed from office. Ironically, he was not recalled for his failure to cope with the Iroquois menace but for his having reduced the colony's civil administration to virtual chaos. On arrival in France he asserted endlessly that he had subdued the Iroquois and left the colony secure. Nothing could have been further from the truth.

Stripped of his properties by his creditors, Frontenac was nothing but an embarrassment to the members of his wife's powerful family, the Pontchartrains. Thus it was that he eventually received a reappointment as governor general of New France in 1689, although he claimed that he deserved a much more prestigious post.

When he arrived back in Quebec, France and England were at war and the Iroquois had just delivered a devastating attack on the French settlement at Lachine, near Montreal. This dire situation Frontenac blamed on the ineptitude of the two governors general who had succeeded him after his dismissal from office. The Canadian military had been planning an assault on the Iroquois supply base, Albany. Frontenac rejected that as being too risky. Instead, in January 1690 he launched three war parties to attack two frontier settlements in New England and a village in New York, Schenectady. All three were destroyed.

These raids had an unforeseen result. The fractious English colonies united for once and that same year, 1690, mustered an expedition to conquer Canada, once and for all. Under the leadership of Sir William Phips, a magistrate in the provincial government of Massachusetts, the campaign was a total disaster. When the American fleet arrived at Quebec, Phips's emissary called on Frontenac to surrender the town, whereupon he gave his resounding response, "I have no reply to make to your general other than from the mouths of my cannon and muskets." Phips and his inept militiamen were quickly seen off, suffering humiliating losses. From then on the Anglo-Americans left the fighting to the disgruntled Iroquois, who eventually were ground down by disease and heavy casualties inflicted by the Canadians and their Indian allies, the Ottawas, Ojibwas, Nipissing, Abenaquis, and Mission Iroquois. Yet Frontenac, despite urging from the Canadians and the minister of marine, was most reluctant to invade Iroquois territory with his entire forces and quell them completely. By 1696 he had to give way to pressure from his subordinates Hector de Callières and Philippe de Rigaud de Vaudreuil, both of whom had powerful friends at Versailles. Despite his advanced age of seventy-four, he insisted on accompanying the expedition that destroyed the Onondaga and Oneida villages and crops. The following year the war in Europe ended, and the English colonies abandoned their Iroquois allies to their fate. They were now forced to treat for peace.

Frontenac took little part in the final act of the drama. His health failed, and he made a graceful exit from this life, greeting death the way Louis XIV would have greeted an emissary from the pope, with condescension. A gallant courtier to the last, he made his peace with those who had opposed his grandiose plans for western expansion and his feeble response to the Iroquois challenge. He had flouted the ministry's policy of curbing the fur trade, thereby glutting the market for beaver, which bankrupted that part of the trade for two decades. Yet two years later French policy changed dramatically, now to establish French dominance in the west. This imperialist policy then built on what Frontenac had created.

As governor general of New France, Frontenac was one of the more flamboyant figures in the history of North America. A charismatic personage, he strutted across the North American scene during exciting times. An arrogant, overbearing aristocrat, undoubtedly possessed of great charm, he was a romantic product of a past age, born a generation too late.

• The bulk of the correspondence exchanged between Frontenac and Versailles has been printed in the *Rapport de l'archiviste de la Province de Québec pour 1926–1927* and the *Rapport* for 1927–1928. A photocopy of his will is contained in the *Rapport de l'archiviste* for 1920–1921. Several biographies of Frontenac have been written, the first significant one by Francis Parkman, *Count Frontenac and New France under Louis XIV* (1877). It is more a historical novel than scholarly history. Henri Lorin, *Le comte de Frontenac* (1895), is an anticlerical panegyric of its subject, written at the time of the Dreyfus case, wherein liberties are taken with the evidence. Jean Delanglez, *Frontenac and the Jesuits* (1939), is an antidote, by a Jesuit historian, to the rabid anticlericalism of Parkman and Lorin, but it deals with only one aspect of Frontenac's career. The biographies by W. Lesueur, *Count Frontenac* (1906), and C. W. Colby, *The Fighting Governor* (1922), are merely potted Parkman and worthless. A more recent critical study of Frontenac and his life and times is W. J. Eccles, *Frontenac: The Courtier Governor* (1959).

W. J. Eccles

BUBBLES, John (19 Feb. 1902–18 May 1986), tap dancer and vaudevillian, was born John William Sublett in Louisville, Kentucky, where he attended grammar and high school. His parents' names are unknown. He began entertaining in his neighborhood as a singer beginning when he was about seven. For a time, he worked in vaudeville in Louisville and on the road. While working as a pin setter at a local bowling alley, Sublett met Ford Lee Washington. They formed a vaudeville act called "Buck and Bubbles" in 1915, with Sublett taking the name of "Bubbles" while Washington became "Buck." Until Washington's death on 31 January 1955, they worked together to become one of vaudeville's legendary acts.

Buck and Bubbles were not an instantaneous success, but within four years they were part of the bill at B. F. Keith's Mary Anderson Theatre in Louisville, an engagement that was noteworthy since they were the first African Americans to play there. Bubbles later recalled that he and Buck were working as ushers in the theater when they were invited to perform. Unfortunately, as was typical of the time, the team was required to wear burnt cork on their faces and to cover their hands with white gloves so that the audience would not know that they were black. Bubbles later noted that this Louisville performance was the only time they were forced to "black up." Their act included their singing and dancing to "The Curse of an Aching Heart" and "Somebody Loves Me."

In September 1919 Buck and Bubbles appeared in New York City at the Columbia Theatre before moving on to vaudeville's mecca, the Palace Theatre, only three weeks later. They subsequently toured the Keith vaudeville circuit with great success, and in 1923 they headlined their own revue at New York's City Theatre. At the time, *Variety*'s critic noted that "the revue has plenty of entertainment" (26 July, 1923).

Buck and Bubbles headlined at the Palace again in September 1928 and December 1929 and played one of their last vaudeville engagements at Loew's State Theatre in July 1932. By this time, the team had switched to Broadway. As with their vaudeville success, their popularity and talent permitted them to cross color lines and perform with both white and black artists of the first rank, including Al Jolson, Eddie Cantor, George Burns and Gracie Allen, Kate Smith, and Danny Kaye. Bubbles later remembered his vaudeville experience fondly, recalling, "Vaudeville was wonderful. You can see it was good to us. Sure, it was hard sometimes. But nothing was easy" (quoted in Smith, p. 62).

Buck and Bubbles were featured in Broadway revues like Lew Leslie's *Blackbirds* of 1930 and the 1931 edition of Florenz Ziegfeld's *Follies*. George Gershwin admired Bubbles and conceived the role of Sportin' Life in *Porgy and Bess* for the dancer. This first great American folk opera opened at Boston's Colonial Theatre on 30 September 1935, before moving to Broadway. In *Porgy and Bess*, Bubbles introduced Gershwin's "It Ain't Necessarily So" and "There's a Boat

Dat's Leavin' for New York" and scored a personal triumph.

In 1936 Buck and Bubbles appeared successfully in the London revue *Transatlantic Rhythm*, costarring with Ruth Etting, Lou Holtz, and Lupe Velez. During this same era, Buck and Bubbles made their first screen appearances, with sporadic returns to the movies throughout the remainder of their partnership. Their films include *Variety Show* (1937), *Cabin in the Sky* (1943), *Atlantic City* (1944), and *A Song Is Born* (1948), as well as some short subjects for Pathé.

Bubbles is credited with originating the rhythm style of tap dancing. Hollywood tap dancer Eleanor Powell, who appeared in vaudeville at New York's Paramount Theatre with Buck and Bubbles, admired his innovations. She recalled that Bubbles "is fantastic. He did things with his feet. . . . When Bubbles was on, I'd be in the wings, on my stomach, watching the feet, and it got so he was playing to me, not the audience. And I'm doing the same thing when he's on. And after the show, we'd go down to the basement and knock our brains out jamming around" (quoted in Slide, *Encyclopedia of Vaudeville*, p. 71). Improvisation was a key to Bubble's dancing. He recalled that he studied steps performed by both white and black performers, stating, "I'd just listen to the music and feel what I could do with it. Then I'd put it together in my head. I didn't often get up and dance without planning it first; that's a waste of energy. When I figure I've got it, I get up and do it. Then it's all synchronized together" (quoted in Slide, *Encyclopedia of Vaudeville*, p. 71).

After Buck's death, Bubble's career waned for about ten years, although he made periodic appearances on television's "The Tonight Show," "The Lucy Show," and "The Perry Como Show." He made United Service Organizations tours with Bob Hope and enjoyed a popular nightclub pairing with Anna Maria Alberghetti. He also made a highly publicized return to the stage as Judy Garland's opening act during her final Palace Theatre engagement in the summer of 1967. He and Garland, along with her children Lorna and Joey Luft, joined forces onstage to perform "Me and My Shadow." Bubbles also recreated routines associated with Buck and Bubbles, as well as his *Porgy and Bess* numbers. Between 1962 and 1980 Bubbles recorded several albums.

Shortly after his stint with Garland, Bubbles suffered a stroke that left him partially paralyzed. Despite this setback, he continued to make occasional appearances and was seen in the 1979 documentary film *No Maps on My Taps*. Among his final performances were a 1979 appearance at the Newport Jazz Festival, a Gershwin tribute at the Hollywood Bowl in 1980 (during which he sang his two *Porgy and Bess* songs), and a performance at the Library of Congress in 1984. He also appeared in the short-lived 1980 Broadway revue *Black Broadway*, leading the audience in singing "It Ain't Necessarily So" and closing the performance with a touching rendition of Eubie Blake's "Memories of You." Bubbles died at his Baldwin Hills, California, home.

• For additional information, see "Bubbles," *New Yorker*, 26 Aug. 1967, pp. 21–23; Jane Goldberg, "John Bubbles: A Hoofer's Homage," *Village Voice*, 4 Dec. 1978, p. 112; Anthony Slide, *The Encyclopedia of Vaudeville* (1994); Slide, *The Vaudevillians* (1981); Bill Smith, "John Bubbles," *The Vaudevillians* (1976); and Julie Wheelock, "Bubbles: The Rhythm Tap King," *Los Angeles Times Calendar*, 19 Dec. 1982, pp. 82–83. Obituaries are in the *New York Times*, 20 May 1986, and *Variety*, 21 May 1986.

James Fisher

BUCHANAN, Franklin (13 Sept. 1800–11 May 1874), U.S. and Confederate naval officer, was born in Baltimore, Maryland, the son of George Buchanan, a prominent doctor and abolitionist, and Laetitia McKean. He entered the U.S. Navy as a midshipman in 1815, a few months after the end of the War of 1812, and was ordered to the new frigate *Java*, which shortly afterward sailed for the Mediterranean. Buchanan's early career as a junior naval officer was marked by the slow promotion and lengthy sea service interspersed with brief tours of shore duty characteristic of the antebellum navy. He served on virtually every distant station, making four Mediterranean cruises, three cruises in the Gulf of Mexico and the Caribbean, a cruise on the Asiatic station, and a cruise to Brazil. In 1825 he was promoted to lieutenant and sixteen years later to commander. In 1835 he married Anne Catherine Lloyd, with whom he had three children. Buchanan assumed his first command, the sloop *Vincennes*, in 1842.

In 1845, when the U.S. Naval Academy was established at Annapolis, Maryland, Buchanan was named its first superintendent. In this capacity, he is credited with creating high standards of scholarship and service at the academy that remain in effect today. He served as superintendent until 1847, when he was detached for sea duty upon the outbreak of the Mexican War, commanding the sloop *Germantown*. He distinguished himself in a number of amphibious operations and engagements against Mexican forts. The war's end led to an extended period of inactivity, until his appointment in 1852 to command the steam frigate *Susquehanna* in Matthew C. Perry's expedition to Japan. He remained in Asian waters for nearly two years before relinquishing his command. This was his last active sea command as a U.S. naval officer. Promoted to captain in 1855, he languished until ordered to command the Washington Navy Yard in 1859. He was in command of the yard when Fort Sumter was fired on and the Civil War began.

Buchanan, convinced that Maryland would secede, resigned his commission on 22 April 1861. But when his native state failed to secede, he tried in vain to withdraw his resignation. Secretary of the Navy Gideon Welles informed him that his name had been "stricken from the rolls of the Navy." Commissioned a captain in the Confederate States Navy, he became head of the Office of Orders and Detail. In February 1862 he was appointed flag officer in command of the James River naval defenses. His command included several wooden gunboats and the ironclad *Virginia*, converted from the U.S. steam sloop *Merrimack*. On 8 March 1862 his small force attacked units of the North Atlantic Blockading Squadron in Hampton Roads. Taking personal command of the *Virginia*, he attacked and destroyed the wooden frigates *Congress* and *Cumberland*. Buchanan was wounded in the engagement and had to relinquish command before the battle with the *Monitor* the following day.

He remained inactive while convalescing until August 1862, when he was promoted to admiral and appointed to command the naval defenses of Mobile Bay. For two years Buchanan concentrated on strengthening his force in preparation for a Union attack. However, when the attack came, only one out of four ironclads under construction, the *Tennessee*, was completed and in the bay. On 5 August 1864 a Union squadron under Admiral David G. Farragut penetrated the confederate mine field and entered Mobile Bay. Buchanan, with three small wooden gunboats and the ironclad *Tennessee*, fought until his force was destroyed. Only one of the small wooden vessels escaped. On his flagship *Tennessee*, Buchanan surrendered after the vessel was heavily damaged and he was once again wounded.

Buchanan remained a prisoner until he was exchanged in February 1865. He never resumed an active command and was still on convalescent leave when the war ended. After the war, he returned to Maryland. He later went to Mobile, where he engaged briefly in business before returning in 1870 to Maryland, where he died.

"Old Buck" was the most respected naval officer in Confederate service. He was recognized as an aggressive commander, willing to challenge an enemy force regardless of its strength. Throughout his career, both as a U.S. and as a Confederate naval officer, he was considered a strict disciplinarian, ambitious, highly opinionated, and principled. Personally, he had unusual physical strength and stamina. As one officer who served under him in the Confederate navy declared, he was "a man and a Commander."

• Few of Buchanan's personal papers have survived. Typed copies of his official letterbooks from the time when he was in Mobile are in the Southern Historical Collection at the University of North Carolina at Chapel Hill. The Maryland Historical Society has a Buchanan scrapbook. The most complete biography is Charles Lee Lewis, *Admiral Franklin Buchanan: Fearless Man of Action* (1929). The best brief account is Charles M. Todorich, "Franklin Buchanan: Symbol for Two Navies," in *Captains of the Old Steam Navy*, ed. James C. Bradford (1986).

WILLIAM N. STILL, JR.

BUCHANAN, Herbert Earle (4 Oct. 1881–17 Jan. 1974), mathematician, astronomer, and educator, was born in Cane Hill, Arkansas, the son of James A. Buchanan, farmer, surveyor, and Presbyterian minister, and Susan Clark Williamson. Until he was fourteen, he was educated at home and in a local "subscription" school (in other words, several families got up a "subscription" to hire a teacher for several months of the year). Then he moved to Fayetteville to attend the University of Arkansas's Preparatory School. There Buchanan discovered his love and talent for mathematics. However, lack of money eventually sent him back to the family farm for more than a year before he was able to finish the preparatory school and enter the university in 1898. He took an A.B. with honors in mathematics in 1902. During his senior year the sudden death of one of his professors gave Buchanan the opportunity to teach mathematics, launching a career that spanned fifty-two years of service.

His finances buoyed by a dramatic upturn in his father's apple business, Buchanan was able to begin graduate study at the University of Chicago in 1902. There he quickly came under the influence of the distinguished German mathematician Heinrich Maschke, with whom he studied advanced integral calculus and plane geometry, and Forest R. Moulton, who introduced him to mechanics and astronomy. Buchanan finished his A.M. at Chicago within a year, and in 1903 he took up his first regular teaching position, at Kentucky Military Institute. At KMI he taught mathematics and military drill, and because there were no eligibility rules he even joined the varsity football team for its entire season.

In 1904 Buchanan moved to Lincoln College in Lincoln, Illinois, and married Ada Tilley, his longtime sweetheart and the daughter of a prosperous Arkansas farmer. They had four children. After a second year at Lincoln, Buchanan returned to Chicago to continue his studies. F. R. Moulton soon encouraged his interest in astronomy. In 1908 he was elected by the faculty to Sigma Xi (the national fraternity for excellence in research) and afterward—again encouraged by Moulton—he moved on to the Yerkes Observatory in Williams Bay, Wisconsin, to learn more about observational astronomy. Buchanan used much of his time at Yerkes and most of the next year to solve the problem assigned as his doctoral thesis. These researches were later published by the University of Chicago as *Periodic Oscillations of Three Finite Masses about the Lagrangian Circular Solutions* (1909 and 1923).

Buchanan's important scholarship lay in the field of celestial mechanics and focused on the stability of the orbits of heavenly bodies. In large part, his work advanced a mathematical understanding of what was called "the three-bodies problem." The issue was whether an orbiting body, if disturbed, would merely oscillate in its orbit or go away and never return.

After receiving his Ph.D. in June 1909, Buchanan moved directly to the University of Wisconsin at Madison. But after two years at Wisconsin he accepted a position at the University of Tennessee that promised greater responsibility; he became a full professor after only one year.

At Tennessee Buchanan not only honed his talents as a teacher, he also gave full vent to his enthusiasm and energy as an academic citizen, the two aspects of his character that were to mark his distinguished career. Shortly after arriving at Knoxville, the president of the university appointed him chairman of the athletic committee, charged with the task of cleaning up a considerable mess in the program's finances and administration. Buchanan put both on such a firm footing and in so short a time that his reputation spread well beyond Tennessee. He was quickly elected southeastern vice president of the newly formed National Collegiate Athletic Association, and in this capacity he joined with UT president Brown Ayres and Tom Bragg of Auburn to found just before World War I the Southern Athletic Conference—forerunner of the Southeastern Athletic Conference. Buchanan was later reelected regional vice president of the NCAA. It was Buchanan who introduced the "one-year rule," which precluded students from playing varsity athletics until their second year.

In 1915 Buchanan joined with several other noted mathematicians to form the Mathematical Association of America, which he later served as vice president (1935–1936). Remarkably, four of Buchanan's students served as presidents of the MAA over the next fifty years.

World War I soon emptied Buchanan's classroom of conscription-age men, so characteristically he followed his students into the military, directing the YMCA program in Atlanta, Georgia, that offered basic education to American soldiers awaiting transport to France in 1917–1918. Teaming up with A. I. Roehm, he even wrote a remarkably lucid primer entitled *Camp Arithmetic for American Soldiers* (1917). In 1918, the YMCA sent him to investigate some irregularities in its program in France; once the war ended he remained as professor of mathematics in the American Expeditionary Force University at Beaune. There he taught mostly young artillery officers who were preparing to return to university in the United States. After the war Buchanan returned to Tennessee for yet another year, during which he sent E. P. Lane, one of his brightest students, on scholarship to Chicago. Lane distinguished himself and eventually became head of the Chicago mathematics department.

This established a pattern of mentoring that Buchanan followed his entire career in teaching. Moving to head the mathematics department at Tulane University in 1920, he ultimately sent more than twenty of his protégés to Chicago, all of whom later became heads of university departments. Among these, Edward J. McShane went on to a stellar career as one of the world's dozen leading mathematicians.

Soon after arriving at Tulane, Buchanan also wrote the first of seven highly successful textbooks. These, combined with his growing reputation as a teacher, soon won the recognition of his old university. In 1932 he was inducted retroactively into the University of Arkansas's new chapter of Phi Beta Kappa. During his first years at Tulane, Buchanan's dry wit, devotion to his students, and reputation as author of some classic campus pranks (some even reported in the national media) won him the affectional sobriquet "Dr. Buck." During this time as well, his accumulating textbooks—among them, *A Brief Course in Advanced Algebra* (1925), *The Elements of Analytic Geometry* (1937), and *Plane Trigonometry* (1926)—were increasingly adopted in American colleges. At the same time, moreover, Buchanan published the remainder of the twenty-five research papers that formed the basis of his reputation as a brilliant scholar as well as a distinguished teacher. Not surprisingly, Buchanan himself became Tulane's first Distinguished Professor in 1937.

Buchanan twice retired, once in 1947 and again in 1949; the second time, he later said, "finally took." Although he looked forward to retirement on his farm near the small Arkansas village where he was born, his devotion to the Presbyterian church led him to accept in 1951 the post of interim president of the College of the Ozarks in Clarksville, Arkansas, where he spent two years restoring the institution's financial and academic foundations.

During his long retirement Buchanan devoted himself to writing his memoirs and to restoring the farm and antebellum house that were the legacy of his wife's family. He remained active in Rotary International, in the Presbyterian church, and on the boards of several institutions and was a lifelong member of the Round Table Club of New Orleans. He maintained an active correspondence with former students and participated in experimental projects of the University of Arkansas's College of Agriculture. Buchanan once said he regretted that the many activities of his retirement made it impossible for him to keep up with the fast-paced developments in mathematics. He died in Fayetteville.

• Buchanan's papers are in the Library of the John Tilley House, Prairie Grove, Arkansas. In addition to his autobiography, *My Life Story* (1974), the following articles are important sources: "The Saga of Dr. Buck," *Newsweek*, 6 June 1949, p. 78; *Arkansas Alumnus*, Sept. 1949, pp. 12–13; *Tulanian*, June 1949, p. 4; and Thomas Rothrock, "Dr. Buck from Cane Hill," *Arkansas Historical Quarterly* 22 (Winter 1963): 332–37.

EDWARD A. ALLEN

BUCHANAN, James (23 Apr. 1791–1 June 1868), fifteenth president of the United States, was born near Mercersburg, Pennsylvania, the son of James Buchanan, a storekeeper, and Elizabeth Speer. He was educated at a local academy and then at Dickinson College, where he graduated in 1809. He then studied law in Lancaster and was admitted to the bar in 1812. He prospered in his profession and through shrewd investments acquired considerable wealth. In 1819, for obscure reasons, his fiancée broke off their engagement, and when she died shortly thereafter, he vowed never to marry. Though he subsequently carried on many flirtations, he remained a bachelor throughout his life. Henceforth, he found his deepest friendships in the world of politics, while his family interests increasingly centered on his many nephews and nieces.

Buchanan's interest in oratory soon drew him to politics. A moderate Federalist, he served in the Pennsylvania legislature (1814–1816) and then was elected to the U.S. House of Representatives (1821–1831). In Washington he initially gravitated to Henry Clay, but after 1824 he supported Andrew Jackson, who appointed him minister to Russia, where he served from 1832 to 1833. Upon his return, Buchanan won election as a Democrat to the U.S. Senate, where he served from 1834 to 1845. A party loyalist, he increasingly adopted a strict constructionist outlook and supported the policies of Jackson and then Martin Van Buren.

As a member of Congress, Buchanan was notable for his prosouthern views. Although he considered slavery wrong, he lacked strong moral feelings about the institution, saw no practical solution to its existence, and opposed any outside interference in the South's internal affairs. Buchanan's closest friends in Congress were southerners, and he increasingly sided with the South in sectional controversies. Strongly denouncing the abolitionist movement, he backed southern leaders' demand that abolitionist literature be excluded from the mails, upheld the gag rule tabling antislavery petitions, and supported the annexation of Texas. Buchanan sought the 1844 Democratic presidential nomination and was instrumental in Van Buren's defeat at the national convention, although James K. Polk obtained the nomination. Polk selected Buchanan as his secretary of state but found him too indecisive and largely conducted foreign affairs himself. Buchanan waffled on Polk's demand for all of the Oregon country, and during the Mexican War he wavered on how much territory should be annexed from Mexico. Polk confided in his diary, "Mr. Buchanan is an able man, but in small matters without judgment and sometimes acts like an old maid." Buchanan's most decisive act was taking the lead in the cabinet in urging the acquisition of Cuba, a goal he consistently pursued for the rest of his public career. He opposed the Wilmot Proviso, which sought to prohibit slavery from any territory acquired from Mexico, and advocated the extension of the Missouri Compromise line to the Pacific to settle the question of slavery's status in the territories.

After unsuccessfully seeking the Democratic presidential nomination in 1848, Buchanan retired to private life at the end of the Polk administration. He made another unsuccessful bid for the nomination in 1852, losing to Franklin Pierce, who was elected. He hoped to become secretary of state again, but Pierce instead named him minister to Great Britain. The most notable development during his tenure was the Ostend Manifesto, which he drew up with two other American ministers. This document declared that Cuba was vital to American interests and, if Spain would not sell the island, it should be forcibly seized. The ensuing outcry in the northern press helped block the Pierce administration's efforts to acquire Cuba.

Buchanan resigned in early 1856 and returned to the United States to once again seek the Democratic presidential nomination. His two main rivals, Pierce and Stephen A. Douglas, were both hurt by their connections to the Kansas-Nebraska Act (1854) and the ensuing turmoil in Kansas, which had badly weakened the Democratic party in the free states. As a result, the convention turned to Buchanan, who had the good fortune to be out of the country in 1854 and was thus not associated with the Kansas controversy. In addition, Buchanan's extensive experience and conservative outlook encouraged the belief that he would dampen sectional tensions. Aided by very strong support in the South, Buchanan was elected in November in a three-way race, but he managed to win only a plurality of the vote. Indeed, the strength of the antislavery Republican party, which finished first in the northern states, was the most significant feature of the election.

During the campaign, southerners threatened to secede if the Republicans were victorious, and unlike many northerners, Buchanan recognized that the Union was in serious danger. Therefore, he took office determined to defuse the sectional crisis by settling the Kansas controversy, reassuring public opinion in both sections, and checking the growth of the Republican party. Rarely has a president pursued policies, however, that so consistently defeated his larger purposes. Under his leadership, sectional animosities deepened, popular fears in both the North and the South intensified, and the Republican party steadily gained strength.

Buchanan carefully balanced the two sections in selecting his cabinet, but rather than include diverse viewpoints, he appointed advisers he was comfortable with personally and who agreed with him ideologically. As a result, his cabinet, while providing him with crucial emotional support, was excessively prosouthern in its orientation. Contrary to the view that Buchanan was controlled by a cabinet "directory," he was in fundamental agreement with his advisers, and indeed his cabinet was unusually harmonious until the final months of his term. Excluded from the cabinet was any supporter of Douglas, the most popular and influential northern Democrat. Buchanan heartily disliked the Illinois senator and, in an ill-fated decision, ignored him in patronage matters.

The most explosive issue confronting the country was the status of slavery in the territories. The 1856 Democratic platform endorsed the principle of popular sovereignty, which declared that the residents of a territory and not Congress should determine the status of slavery there. Northern and southern Democrats disagreed, however, on the meaning of this principle. Northern Democrats, led by Douglas, argued that this decision could be made at any time during the settlement of a territory, whereas southern Democrats generally insisted that it could be made only when its residents drafted a state constitution. Buchanan looked to the Supreme Court to settle this question in the *Dred Scott* case (1857), and prior to his inauguration he improperly intervened to get a northern justice to join the Court's southern majority in issuing a broad prosouthern decision. The Court's opinion, announced two days after Buchanan's inauguration, declared that, since the U.S. Constitution protected slave property, Congress could not prohibit slavery from any territory. Buchanan naively believed that this decision would settle the territorial controversy. But the decision, which reversed a number of political and judicial precedents, strengthened the growing northern belief in the existence of a "slave power," determined to spread slavery everywhere, at the same time that it weakened northern Democrats by calling into question the constitutionality of popular sovereignty. Republicans, who refused to accept the ruling, now took up the cry that slavery threatened the free states as well.

Buchanan's political position was further undermined by an economic depression that began in the fall of 1857 and continued for the duration of his presidency. The administration failed to respond effectively to this economic downturn, which revitalized economic issues in national politics and increasingly pitted northerners against southerners in votes in Congress. Buchanan hurt his party in the North by vetoing bills to finance agricultural colleges, improve navigation on the Great Lakes, and provide free homesteads to western farmers, actions that drove many conservative northerners into the Republican ranks.

Buchanan's greatest challenge, however, was to settle the Kansas controversy and remove the issue of slavery's expansion from national politics. Since Kansas was opened to white settlement in 1854, chaos and disorder had plagued it as antislavery and proslavery forces battled for control of the territory. By 1857 a majority of the residents opposed slavery, but proslavery elements managed to win control of a convention to draft a state constitution when free state men refused to participate in the election. The resulting Lecompton constitution recognized slavery and prohibited any amendments until 1865. Unwilling to submit the constitution to the electorate for approval, proslavery leaders in the convention provided for a limited submission, allowing voters to decide only if new slaves could be brought into the state. With antislavery voters again abstaining, the constitution with additional slaves won approval.

Under heavy southern pressure, Buchanan ignored his earlier pledge that the people of Kansas would be allowed to vote on the proposed constitution as well as the warning of the territorial governor that a decided majority of the residents of Kansas opposed the Lecompton constitution. Buchanan endorsed admitting Kansas under this constitution. Following a stormy personal meeting on 3 December 1857, Douglas broke with Buchanan on this issue, declaring that the Lecompton constitution made a mockery of the principle of popular sovereignty. Despite Douglas's opposition, the Senate approved the Lecompton constitution, with most Democrats following Buchanan. The president then pulled out all the stops to get the Lecompton constitution through the House, authorizing various inducements, including cash, to congressmen for their support. Nevertheless, after an extremely bitter debate, the House rejected it. Democratic leaders eventually fashioned a compromise that by indirect means provided for a new vote in Kansas. With both factions participating this time, the constitution was defeated by an overwhelming margin. Buchanan's defeat was obvious.

The Lecompton struggle embittered southerners, strengthened the northern fear of the slave power, and ruptured the Democratic party. Southerners bitterly assailed Douglas and vowed that they would never accept him as the party's presidential nominee in 1860. Buchanan systematically removed anti-Lecompton Democrats from federal office and tried unsuccessfully to defeat Douglas's reelection in Illinois. The Republican party made significant gains in the 1858 fall elections in the North, yet Buchanan stubbornly refused to heal the breach with Douglas and instead aided southern party leaders intent on politically destroying the northern Democratic leader.

As president, Buchanan aggressively promoted American expansion. He tried to buy Alaska from Russia, secured groundbreaking treaties with China and Japan, and sought to limit British influence in Central America. While more vigilant than his predecessor, he failed to prevent several southern filibustering expeditions. Congressional opposition, however, stymied his expansionist schemes. His main goal continued to be Cuba, but a bill introduced by one of his associates appropriating $30 million to purchase Cuba garnered only limited support. Thus he increasingly refocused his expansionist policy on Mexico. Congress ignored his proposal to establish a protectorate in northern Mexico, fearing it was a pretext to annex the region, and in 1860 the Senate rejected a treaty he submitted that gave the United States two perpetual transit routes in Mexico from the Atlantic to the Pacific along with the right to protect them militarily. By adding credence to Republican charges of a conspiracy to expand slavery, these policies further inflamed sectional tensions.

Democratic prospects were further damaged by a series of scandals that wracked the Buchanan administration, which was one of the most corrupt in American history. A congressional investigation revealed that postal funds had been diverted to Democratic candidates, naval contracts were dispensed in exchange for campaign contributions, public printing contracts involved kickbacks and bribes, and Secretary of War John Floyd sold public lands at minimal prices to friends of the administration and covered up the embezzlement of federal funds by a kinsman. While he had not profited personally from these misdeeds, Buchanan displayed little interest in ferreting out or preventing such wrongdoing.

The rupture in the Democratic party that developed during Buchanan's presidency came to a climax at the 1860 national convention in Charleston, South Carolina. Southern radicals, aided by Buchanan's closest advisers, were determined to prevent Douglas's nomination. They demanded adoption of the "Alabama Platform," which called for a congressional slave code to protect slavery in the territories. Northern delegates retorted that this platform would destroy the party in the free states and refused to accept it. When the convention finally rejected the southern platform, the delegates from eight southern states walked out. All efforts to heal the breach failed, and eventually two Democratic candidates were nominated. Northern Democrats put forward Douglas on a platform endorsing popular sovereignty, while southern Democrats, joined by Buchanan's northern followers, selected Vice President John C. Breckinridge on the minority southern platform. With the Democratic party hopelessly divided, Abraham Lincoln, the Republican nominee, swept to victory in November. Buchanan's misguided sectional policies and his continuing personal war against Douglas had played a major role in producing this outcome—precisely what he had set out to avoid when he assumed office.

In response to Lincoln's election, the seven states of the Deep South began the process of seceding from the Union. Buchanan traced this crisis entirely to the northern antislavery movement, and in his annual message singled out for condemnation "the long-continued and intemperate interference of the Northern people with the question of slavery in the Southern states." He denied any right of secession but insisted that under the Constitution he had no power to prevent it. He also urged that a constitutional convention be called to devise amendments to protect slavery in the territories, overturn northern laws that interfered with the rendition of fugitive slaves, and safeguard slavery in the southern states. This one-sided message destroyed the little remaining prestige Buchanan had in the North.

Still, Buchanan's devotion to the Union was unshakable. He steadfastly refused to recognize the legality of secession or to negotiate the surrender of federal forts in the South. The most precarious situation existed at Fort Sumter in Charleston Harbor. Still under construction and manned by only a small garrison, it could easily be attacked or isolated by batteries ringing the harbor. After some indecision, Buchanan refused to abandon the fort. In response his cabinet, which contained several secessionists, dissolved. Eventually a majority of its members, including all who favored secession, resigned, and the cabinet was reorganized on a firm Unionist basis. Bolstered by his Unionist advisers, Buchanan on the last day of the year dispatched the unarmed merchant vessel, the *Star of the West*, to reinforce Fort Sumter, but fire from the shore batteries prevented it from accomplishing its mission. In his last weeks in office Buchanan avoided any similar action that might precipitate a war, but he announced his determination to use force to protect federal property in the South. He goal was to get through his term without starting a war, and it was with considerable relief that he turned the crisis over to Lincoln in March.

Returning to his estate, "Wheatland," near Lancaster, Pennsylvania, Buchanan found little peace in retirement. Partisan critics hounded him, blaming him for failing to deal decisively with secession, for allegedly arming the South, and for not preparing the North for war. Buchanan bore these unfair charges with his accustomed dignity. While no longer politically active, he supported the Union war effort, although he believed the policy of emancipation mistaken and hoped to restore the Union as it had existed before the war. His memoirs vindicating his conduct as president were published in 1866. Shortly before his death at Wheatland he declared: "I have always felt and still feel that I discharged every public duty imposed on me constitutionally. I have no regret for any public act of my life."

Tall and stout, with an imposing physique and flowing white hair, the meticulously dressed Buchanan presented a distinguished appearance that was reinforced by his courtly manners. Fussy and legalistic, he had a passion for precision, displayed great diligence, and was an indefatigable correspondent. Although he enjoyed society and dancing and brought a festive air to the White House, he did not make friends easily and was unusually dependent emotionally on his closest associates. He enjoyed good liquor and cigars and spent long evenings conversing with friends. Plodding and unimaginative, he was a useful subordinate but an unsuccessful leader. He lacked a brilliant mind and had no gift for writing memorable words or uttering striking phrases and thus was ineffective at rallying popular support. Acquaintances were struck by his exceedingly cautious nature, and his closest friends found him very timid about voicing his own opinions on controversial issues, even in private. He was sincere and well-intentioned, but his presidential term was largely a disaster. He isolated himself from dissenting views, disliked confrontation, never understood northern feelings against slavery, and was excessively prosouthern in his views, qualities that eventually destroyed his political influence and wrecked his presidency.

• Buchanan's voluminous papers are in the Historical Society of Pennsylvania, with a smaller collection in the Library of Congress. His memoirs, *Mr. Buchanan's Administration on the Eve of the Rebellion* (1866), are self-serving but informative. Many of his important letters and documents are published in John B. Moore, ed., *The Works of James Buchanan* (12 vols., 1908–1910). See also George T. Curtis, *Life of James Buchanan* (2 vols., 1883). The fullest modern biography, defensive in tone, is Philip S. Klein, *President James Buchanan* (1962). Elbert B. Smith, *The Presidency of James Buchanan* (1975), is briefer and more critical. Allan Nevins, *The Emergence of Lincoln* (2 vols., 1950), presents a full account of Buchanan's presidency but is weakened by its view of Buchanan as merely a tool of his cabinet. David M. Potter, *The Impending Crisis* (1976), completed and edited by Don E. Fehrenbacher, is a magisterial history of these years that provides a particularly penetrating analysis of Buchanan's presidency. Roy F. Nichols, *The Disruption of American Democracy* (1948), is a brilliant examination of the Democratic party's worsening internal divisions under Buchanan's leadership. Valuable specialized studies include Fehrenbacher's authoritative *The Dred Scott Case* (1978); Kenneth M. Stampp, *America in 1857* (1990); James Huston, *The Panic of 1857 and the Coming of the Civil War* (1987); Mark W. Summers, *The Plundering Generation* (1987), which details the extensive corruption of Buchanan's administration; and Stampp, *And the*

War Came (1950), an astute study of the secession crisis. Michael J. Birkner, ed., *James Buchanan and the Political Crisis of the 1850s* (1996), contains important essays evaluating Buchanan's leadership and presidency from the perspective of recent scholarship.

WILLIAM E. GIENAPP

BUCHANAN, John (1772–6 Nov. 1844), jurist, was born in Prince George's County, Maryland, the son of Thomas Buchanan, a well-to-do landowner, and Mary Cook. Orphaned at an early age, he received his only formal education at Charlotte Hall Academy, the leading educational institution in southern Maryland. Thereafter he began the study of law under Judge Robert White of Winchester, Virginia, but soon returned to Maryland to enter the office of a prominent Hagerstown attorney, John Thomson Mason. Admitted to the local bar in 1794, he became a Jeffersonian Republican in politics and served in the lower house of the state legislature from 1797 to 1799. In 1808 he married Sophia Williams, the daughter of a Maryland judge; they had two children.

On Mason's recommendation, Governor Robert Wright appointed Buchanan chief judge of Maryland's fifth judicial district in 1806. Pursuant to the state constitution, he thus became ex officio an associate judge of the Maryland Court of Appeals. On 27 July 1824 he succeeded Jeremiah Townley Chase as chief judge of the appellate court and continued to fill that position until his death twenty years later. Only one brief period of state service interrupted his long judicial tenure, when in 1837 he joined two other Maryland commissioners on an unsuccessful mission to sell state-secured railroad and canal stock in England.

As an appellate judge, Buchanan sought to reconcile the customary and anticompetitive features of eighteenth-century jurisprudence with the needs of a rapidly developing commercial society. Like his contemporary John Marshall on the federal level, he espoused an expansive theory of judicial review and occasionally struck down state legislation on constitutional grounds. In economic cases he relied upon natural-law principles, as well as constitutional construction, to limit legislative control of private corporations. His most controversial decision, *Chesapeake and Ohio Canal Company v. Baltimore and Ohio Rail Road Company* (1832), involved the charter rights of two competing agencies of transportation, each of which wanted to build along the same narrow route. The canal company, which won the case, based its claim upon the survey rights granted to a predecessor corporation, although that company had never exercised its franchise. Buchanan ruled that a right once granted by the legislature becomes permanently vested in a corporation and can only be forfeited through a judicial proceeding. He employed similar reasoning in *Regents of the University of Maryland v. Williams* (1838) to overturn a state law of 1825 that attempted to restructure a major educational institution. State interference with the university's charter, he affirmed, violated both the contract clause of the U.S. Constitution and a "fundamental principle of right and justice" that restrained legislatures from invading property rights, even in the absence of express constitutional prohibitions. By reducing public charters to the status of private contracts, he ensured that the judiciary, and not the legislature, would retain ultimate supervision of the state's economic development.

Buchanan's judicial activism did not extend to slave cases, however. A slaveholding farmer himself, he made no effort to challenge the state's harsh slave code by appealing to natural-law principles or to the common-law rights of the individual.

Buchanan died in Williamsport, Maryland. Urbane and erudite, he was widely regarded by contemporaries as one of Maryland's foremost jurists.

• For useful appraisals of Buchanan's judicial career, see William McSherry, "The Former Chief Justices of the Court of Appeals of Maryland," in *Maryland State Bar Association Report* (1904), and Carroll T. Bond, *The Court of Appeals of Maryland: A History* (1928). An obituary is in the *Baltimore Clipper*, 8 Nov. 1844.

MAXWELL BLOOMFIELD

BUCHANAN, John Alexander (7 Oct. 1843–2 Sept. 1921), lawyer and judge, was born near the village of Groseclose in Smyth County, Virginia, the son of James Augustus Buchanan and Mary Glenn Thomas, farmers. He attended local schools and was still enrolled at the Marion Male Academy when, at the age of seventeen, he joined the Confederate army. He enlisted in July 1861 as a private in the Smyth County Blues, which became Company D of the Fourth Virginia Infantry, part of the Stonewall Brigade. Though home on sick leave for several months beginning in October 1861 and again beginning in September 1862 (he was certified as suffering from asthma), he saw action in various capacities before being wounded and captured at Gettysburg, Pennsylvania, in July 1863. He was sent successively to Fort McHenry, Fort Delaware, and then Point Lookout, all in Maryland, where he remained from September 1863 until February 1865, when he was released in a prisoner exchange.

After the war Buchanan enrolled at Emory and Henry College as a preparatory student in 1865 and as a freshman a year later; he graduated as valedictorian in 1870. He studied law at the University of Virginia in 1870–1871 and in April 1872 gained admission to the bar in Washington County. He practiced law in southwest Virginia during the next two decades, and he represented Washington County in the Virginia House of Delegates for one term from 1885 to 1887.

Buchanan never lost an election. After he declined a second term in the legislature, the Democratic party nominated him for the Ninth District seat in the U.S. House of Representatives. The "Fighting Ninth," in southwestern Virginia, was one of the state's few competitive Congressional districts, where Republicans won as often as Democrats did. In 1888 Buchanan defeated the Republican incumbent, Henry Bowen, and he won again in 1890, over George H. Mills, but he declined nomination in 1892. Like Virginia's other Democratic congressmen, but unlike the two Republicans, he opposed the 1890 Federal Elections Bill, which his fellow Democrats dubbed the Force Bill. The measure, had it passed, would have directed the national government to intervene in federal elections in the South to ensure that black men had the right to vote. Buchanan gave a forceful speech against the bill on 30 June 1890.

In 1894, with the twelve-year terms of the five judges on the Virginia Supreme Court of Appeals due to expire at the end of the year, the state legislature elected Buchanan to that court. The state constitution had once required, and practice continued to suggest, that each major section of the state have one seat on the court. Ensuring that the southwest get a judge took strong maneuvering, however, and then Buchanan won out over four other nominees from that section. Buchanan's kinsman and law partner, Benjamin F. Buchanan, spearheaded the campaign to secure his election to the court. The new judge's predecessors had all been elected by the Readjusters in 1882, during the brief period when the Democratic party was out of power in postwar Virginia, and now the Democrats had reclaimed all three branches of state government.

On some matters, the new court soon made a difference. The old court had decided in 1894 to permit a woman lawyer from out of state, Belva Lockwood, to be admitted to practice law in Virginia. In 1895, however, Judge Buchanan joined with his colleagues on the new court to refuse to let her argue a case before it. The legislature then made the exclusion of women explicit under state law, and not until 1920 did it enact a statute to permit women to practice the legal profession in Virginia. Another change concerned the application of Virginia's Sunday Closing laws to freight trains. The old court ruled that trains engaged in interstate commerce were exempt from the Sunday Closing law. Writing for a unanimous court in *Norfolk & Western Railroad Company v. Commonwealth* (1896), however, Judge Buchanan insisted that a westbound Norfolk and Western train, hauling only empty coal cars on its way to West Virginia, carried nothing in "interstate commerce." That decision, in according greater deference to the state legislature and the police power and less to Congress and the Commerce Clause, reflected the political culture of late nineteenth-century Virginia.

Because the court usually reported unanimous decisions, Judge Buchanan's vote did not so much affect the outcome as confirm the court's approach to the questions that came before it. Among the more significant questions, some related to the Virginia constitution of 1902. In *Taylor v. Commonwealth* (1903), a unanimous court ruled the new constitution valid even though it had never been submitted to the electorate for ratification. In *Winchester and Strasburg Railroad Company v. Commonwealth* (1906), the court upheld the constitutionality of the State Corporation Commission, a powerful regulatory body established under the new constitution. Unyielding in support of the legislature's authority under the police power, the court upheld a 1908 prohibition law against challenges to its constitutionality in such cases as *Commonwealth v. Henry* (1909).

Judge Buchanan served on the state's highest court from January 1895 until January 1915. He then became the court's first member to take advantage of a 1914 law permitting a judge to retire at 60 percent of his salary after reaching the age of seventy and completing twelve years of service. Among his civic and religious activities, Buchanan was a ruling elder in the Presbyterian church, and from 1878 to 1920 he served on the board of trustees of his alma mater, Emory and Henry College. He also served on the board of trustees of Stonewall Jackson College, a school for young white women in Abingdon, and he was a major contributor to the school. Never married, he lived alone on his farm near Emory, where he died.

Buchanan was reputed to be a superior lawyer, legislator, and judge. High ability, achievement, performance, and character aside, he was a representative lawyer-politician of the late nineteenth-century American South. As a young man he fought for the Confederacy and was wounded and captured. In the difficult early postwar years he secured an education and became a lawyer. He entered public life as a Democrat, represented his southwestern Virginia constituency in the state legislature and in Congress, and served twenty years on the Virginia Supreme Court of Appeals.

• The history of Judge Buchanan's family is traced in David Buchanan Trimble, *Southwest Virginia Families* (1974). Obituaries are in the *Richmond Times-Dispatch*, 3 Sept. 1921; *Confederate Veteran* 29 (Oct. 1921): 391; and *Virginia Reports* 179 (1942): vii–x, also published in Virginia State Bar Association *Proceedings* 54 (1942): 111–13.

PETER WALLENSTEIN

BUCHANAN, Joseph Rodes (11 Dec. 1814–26 Dec. 1899), physician and author, was born in Frankfort, Kentucky, the son of Joseph Buchanan, a physician, and Nancy Rodes Garth. His father had a varied career as a physician and journalist and was one of the first faculty members at Transylvania University in Lexington. Upon his father's death in 1829, Buchanan worked as both a printer and schoolteacher in Lexington. In 1835 he became acquainted with the "science" of phrenology formulated by the European investigators, Franz Joseph Gall and Johann Gaspar Spurzheim. Buchanan found phrenology to be a promising technique for investigating humanity's moral and intellectual capacities and resolved to further his studies by entering medical school at the University of Louisville.

Disappointed by how little attention was given to brain physiology in his medical curriculum, he began his own independent set of experiments, which were designed to improve upon Gall's and Spurzheim's phrenological studies of the location of various mental capacities. He used techniques drawn from mesmerism, or the science of animal magnetism, to put his subjects into a light trance, which he termed the "impressible state." He argued that by first putting subjects into this state he could more directly and reliably excite specific regions on the skull and discern the specific cognitive or moral faculties that were located there. Buchanan's research led him to conclude that the brain has the capacity to be affected not only by the physical impressions made upon the senses, but also by purely mental or nonphysical sensations, which he termed the "nervaura." The latter, he maintained, is a purely mental or spiritual energy through which humans are psychically connected to the wider, spiritual reaches of the universe. Heightened receptivity to these spiritual sensations afford us the mental capacity for clairvoyance, telepathy, religious inspiration, and nonmedical healing. These findings served as the foundation for two new medical theories. The first, which Buchanan called "psychometry," explained how the human brain can receive sensations directly from another person's aura, and the second, "sarcognomy," described the rapport between the human body and the indwelling soul. He presented his theories to the faculty of the medical school and received support from just one professor, Charles Caldwell, who was himself a mesmeric researcher and author of books championing progressive intellectual causes of the day. With Caldwell's support, Buchanan received his M.D. in 1842 and continued in his investigation and advocacy of unconventional medical and physiological research. The previous year he had married Anne Rowan, with whom he had four children.

Upon graduation from medical school, Buchanan began a lengthy career of writing and speaking about his research on the nature and highest potentials of the human brain. In 1845 he joined with several other physicians to establish the Eclectic Medical Institute in Cincinnati, Ohio, which was dedicated to independent and innovative thinking about the human constitution. Buchanan served there as professor of physiology from 1846 to 1856 and as dean of the faculty from 1851 to 1856. Turmoil within the college prompted him to retire in 1856 and to devote more time to the promotion of his nontraditional views concerning brain physiology, medical treatment, and philosophy. His *Outlines of Lectures on the Neurological System of Anthropology* (1854), for example, included summaries of the era's most advanced neurophysiological studies, phrenological charts, testimonies concerning the reality of extrasensory phenomena among those subjects who could be placed into the "impressible state," and impassioned advocacy of the belief that a suitably enlarged scientific method could demonstrate humanity's true spiritual nature and provide the empirical foundations for a new, nondogmatic religious philosophy. Beginning in 1849 he also published and edited the *Journal of Man*, which for several years carried articles on mesmerism, Swedenborgianism, abolition, women's rights, and metaphysical interpretations of Christianity. In 1877 he became an instructor at the Eclectic Medical College in New York City, while simultaneously operating a college of therapeutics in Boston, at which he taught his views on innovative approaches to medical treatment and his own philosophy of the human condition from 1883 to 1892. His first wife having died in 1873, in 1881 he married Cornelia H. Decker, who died in 1891. In 1892 he moved to Kansas City, Missouri, and then a year later to San Jose, California. In 1894 he married a third time, Elizabeth S. Worthington. He died in San Jose.

Buchanan's importance in the history of American thought is threefold. First, his writings helped create popular awareness of the dawning field of psychology (which emerged in American universities in the 1880s). His books popularized current neurophysiological knowledge, and his belief in the existence of extraordinary mental powers for clairvoyance and telepathy whetted Americans' appetite for continued investigation into humanity's psychological constitution. Second, Buchanan stands as an important figure in the tradition of alternative medicine in the United States. During the very years that scientific medicine was becoming institutionalized in American universities and hospitals, Buchanan's teaching and publications contributed to the continuation of metaphysical approaches to healing. Finally, Buchanan's eclectic use of phrenology, mesmerism, and mystical spirituality locates him squarely amid the nineteenth-century "metaphysical movements" that eventually would spawn the New Thought movement, spiritualism (with which he became involved midway through his career), Theosophy, and sundry twentieth-century New Age fascinations.

• Buchanan's publications that have not already been mentioned in the text include *Eclectic Practice of Medicine and Surgery* (1850), *Moral Education* (1882), *Therapeutic Sarcognomy* (1884), *Manual of Psychometry* (1885), and *Primitive Christianity* (1898). Works that locate his life and thought in American intellectual history are Robert C. Fuller's *Mesmerism and the American Cure of Souls* (1982) and *Alternative Medicine and American Religious Life* (1989).

ROBERT C. FULLER

BUCHANAN, Scott Milross (17 Mar. 1895–25 Mar. 1968), educator and scholar, was born in Sprague, Washington, the son of William Duncan, a physician, and Lillian Elizabeth Bagg, a milliner and dressmaker. Buchanan received his A.B. in Greek and mathematics from Amherst College in 1916. He was influenced by Alexander Meiklejohn, president of the college, from whom, he later claimed, the "living Socratic method became clear." He taught Greek for a year at Amherst and then in 1917, inspired in part by a patriotic poem, he joined the navy, rising to the rank of ensign in 1918 before the end of World War I. As a committed pacifist, Buchanan felt conflicted about his military service and decided that he should have himself arrested for being a conscientious objector. Ultimately, he chose not to proceed with his protest, but the incident demonstrates the depth of his convictions.

From 1919 to 1921 Buchanan studied philosophy as a Rhodes scholar at Balliol College, Oxford, during which time he married Mariam Thomas in 1921; they had one child. He received his doctorate in 1925 from

Harvard, where he also taught. He then went to New York City, where he was assistant director of the People's Institute. In 1929 he became a professor of philosophy at the University of Virginia in Charlottesville. Buchanan also spent a year at the Johns Hopkins Medical School, probably in 1934, attending classes and studying medicine's relation to modern science. Later he published the results in *The Doctrine of Signatures: A Defense of Theory in Medicine* (1938). Buchanan left Virginia when Robert Hutchins asked him in 1936 to assist in revising the curriculum at the University of Chicago. There, as chairman of the Liberal Arts Committee, he helped (with Hutchins and Mortimer Adler) to institute what became known as the "Great Books Program," which emphasizes a core list of great books from the Western world. These works are called "great" because of their clarity and beauty and because they raise perennial human questions, which thereby bear directly on contemporary problems.

In 1937 Stringfellow Barr, then president of St. John's College in Annapolis, appointed Buchanan dean of St. John's. Together they created a curriculum centered around small seminars in which students discuss questions put to them by "tutors" and the conversation is allowed to wander wherever reasoned argument might take it. Their implementation of a new program of liberal arts and the Great Books approach resulted in a rebirth for St. John's, which became one of the premier liberal arts colleges in the nation. Still regarded as the father of St. John's College, Buchanan is often credited with having infused the college with the spirit of Socratic inquiry—love of good questions, good conversations, and good books.

After ten years at St. John's, Buchanan left to become director of Liberal Arts, Inc., of Pittsfield, Massachusetts, and later as consultant and secretary of the Foundation for World Government. He served as chairman of the religion and philosophy department at Fisk University in Nashville, Tennessee, from 1956 to 1957 and then as a consultant and fellow of the Center for the Study of Democratic Institutions, in Santa Barbara, until his death.

In his written work Buchanan combined an intimate knowledge of political theory, literature, medicine, mathematics, and the natural sciences in novel formulations to reveal, for example, the scientist in Dante and the poet in Newton. When he examined such connections in works like *Poetry and Mathematics* (1929), *Symbolic Distance in Relation to Analogy and Fiction* (1932), and *Truth in the Sciences* (1972), his mind roved over often esoteric topics with his thoughts fixed all the more on the nature of philosophical inquiry and its application to a myriad of human concerns. While he wrote on subjects as seemingly disparate as the theory of the scientific method and political responsibility, a number of these concerns are reflected throughout his work. Among them are his desire to make good citizens and his belief that the good citizen, the one capable of truly living a free life, is one who knows what are the proper ends of human action. Since a liberal education contributes to the discovery of those ends, the life of freedom will be a life of learning. "In the end," he explains, "a democracy demands that its government shall be educational," that is, "that everybody in it can learn."

For Buchanan, an education for freedom implied responsibility. Discussing this proposition in *Tragedy and the New Politics* (1960), he proposed the following as postulates: that "the human individual is responsible for injustice anywhere in the universe"; that "within a given community, politics is the means for discharging this responsibility"; and that "law is the essential part of politics; it is therefore the principal means for discharging the citizen's responsibility for injustice." According to Buchanan, the mechanisms by which this responsibility is discharged, whether theological, familial, or otherwise, were taken for granted by the Founding Fathers who assumed that they would be maintained with little formal support in the kind of rational self-government they envisioned. Such eighteenth-century idealism may have assumed too much in this regard, not forseeing the tension between acknowledging the indispensability of these informal mechanisms and rejecting the traditional natural and common law order in favor of a new rational one.

Those who knew Buchanan often spoke of his ability to enchant his listeners and interlocutors and to turn almost any sentence into a question open for discussion. Frequently compared with Socrates, he has been described as a man "who believes the truth must be found and yet may not be found," as Mark Van Doren put it, and who, in a manner of speaking, corrupts the youth by compelling them to follow intellectual paths that may be too perilous for them. This danger Buchanan admitted—for bold and thoughtful students are sometimes misfits for a time—but thought necessary since the problems of the world would only be tackled after gaining enough intellectual distance to come to new and even revolutionary understandings.

• The Buchanan papers, including photographs, a large number of unpublished papers, and more than 3,000 letters to and from Mortimer Adler, Mark Van Doren, Alexander Meiklejohn, Robert Hutchins, and others are in the Houghton Library at Harvard University. Works by Buchanan include *Possibility* (1927), *Essay in Politics* (1953), *The Corporation and the Republic* (1958), and *Rediscovering Natural Law* (1962). Charles A. Nelson has compiled recollections and sketches of Buchanan, along with the most complete bibliography of Buchanan's works, in *Scott Buchanan: A Centennial Appreciation of His Life and Work, 1895–1968* (1995). See also Harris Wofford, Jr.'s "Introduction" to *Embers of the World: Conversations with Scott Buchanan* (1970) and Edwin J. Delattre's "Introduction" to Buchanan's *So Reason Can Rule* (1982), on Buchanan's life, writings, and influence on a generation of educators. Obituaries are in the *New York Times*, 29 Mar. 1968, and *Publishers Weekly*, 13 May 1968.

DOMOKOS HAJDO

BUCHMAN, Frank Nathan Daniel (4 June 1878–7 Aug. 1961), founder of Moral Re-Armament, was born in Pennsburg, Pennsylvania, to Franklin Buchman, a small-town businessman, and Sarah Anna Greenwalt.

He graduated from Muhlenburg College (B.A., 1899) and Lutheran Theological Seminary in Philadelphia (1902), and later attended Westminster College, Cambridge (1921–1922). Following his seminary training, Buchman served as pastor of a church in Overbrook, Pennsylvania. He also started a hospice for young men and became its full-time head in 1905. He clashed repeatedly with the Lutheran Board of Inner Mission, which had ultimate authority over the hospice. He resigned in 1908. The conflict left Buchman with a deep sense of failure, but later in 1908, during a trip to England, he had a profound religious experience that recharged him with new purpose. Buchman felt he had *experienced* truth—the truth that before he had known only intellectually. After returning from Europe, Buchman became secretary of the YMCA at Pennsylvania State College. Later, in 1916, he took a position as an extension lecturer at Hartford Theological Seminary. During this period he undertook campaigns at home and abroad, gradually perfecting his personal approach to evangelism.

Feeling that his efforts to promote transforming religious experiences were more effective in intimate gatherings than in large meetings, Buchman developed what came to be known as "house parties," the first of which was held in Kuling, China, in 1918. Beyond this technique, his message was not new. Rather than trying to establish a new sect, he was attempting a kind of Christian renaissance that would cross denominational boundaries and, he hoped, bring the world back to God. In 1921 Buchman initiated a cycle of evangelical work at Oxford University. Following one of his house parties that year, a group touched by his ministry established the First Century Christian Fellowship. During a visit to South Africa in 1929 with a group of followers, some of whom had come from Oxford, a train porter wrote "Oxford Group" on their reserved compartments. The press picked up the name, and Buchman's movement became known as the Oxford Group Movement. The fellowship continued to grow and in 1938 changed its name to Moral Re-Armament.

Buchman's evangelical methods included "sharing," a kind of public confession, and "quiet time," a process of listening for the Holy Spirit to disclose the will of God. He considered such techniques to be alternatives to war. (The MRA's slogan during these years was "guidance or guns.") In the pattern of the biblical prophets, Buchman felt that the holocaust of a world war could be prevented if nations returned to God through moral reformation. To this end, he increasingly focused his evangelical efforts on the aristocratic, politically influential levels of society. When war broke out, a disappointed Buchman returned to the United States, where he suffered a severe stroke. Following the war, he reorganized and continued to preach his message of saving the world through a return to God. Buchman's organization was strongly anticommunist during the Cold War era, but it never recovered the strength it enjoyed before World War II. He traveled so much that he never really settled, though the conference center at Caux, Switzerland, served him as a home toward the end of his life. He died in Freudenstadt, Germany.

• A collection of Buchman's speeches was published in Frank Buchman, *Remaking the World* (1949). Other primary materials can be found in the archives of Moral Re-Armament centers around the world, including MRA's international headquarters in Caux, Switzerland and the organization's national headquarters in Washington, D.C. Easily the best available biography is Garth Lean, *Frank Buchman* (1985). A critical examination of Buchman and the MRA can be found in Tom Driberg, *The Mystery of Moral Re-Armament: A Study of Frank Buchman and His Movement* (1965). Also useful are the various books by Peter Howard, such as *Frank Buchman's Secret* (1961). A good short introduction to Buchman can be found in J. Gordon Melton, *Religious Leaders of America* (1991).

JAMES R. LEWIS

BUCHTEL, John Richards (18 Jan. 1820–23 May 1892), businessman and philanthropist, was born in Green Township in Summit County, Ohio, the son of John Buchtel and Catherine Richards, farmers. His early years were spent on his father's farm, during which time he received a rudimentary education. In later years Buchtel regretted his lack of formal schooling and donated most of his fortune to educate others. While still a young man, Buchtel acquired a 100-acre farm from his father by paying a $700 encumbrance on the property. In 1844 he married Elizabeth Davidson, whose parents had recently moved to Summit County from Pennsylvania. The Buchtels had no children.

Buchtel worked farms in the Akron region, where he was admired for his profitable, progressive methods. He sold his most successful Akron farm, expecting to move to LaPorte, Indiana, but he remained in the Akron area to accept a position in 1854 as sales agent for a farm machinery manufacturing concern, C. Aultman & Company of Canton. He left the firm in 1856 but returned in 1864 to lead in the construction of a new branch operation in Akron. Locally this venture was known as the Buckeye Reaper and Mower Works, although the official name was Aultman, Miller and Company. Both the company and Buchtel prospered as their machines, incorporating improvements devised by inventor Lewis Miller, became a force in the industry.

Buchtel did not serve in the Union armies during the Civil War. He bought a substitute, but he expended great energy in securing bounty money to encourage enlistments, and he worked diligently in support of the Union cause.

As president of the Buckeye Company, Buchtel was soon involved in many new industrial enterprises in rapidly growing Akron. He led in developing new mineral lands in Ohio's Hocking Valley for the Akron Iron and Rolling Mill Company. By 1882 the company was operating Ohio's largest blast furnace, using local coal and iron ore. Buchtel directed the development of a town for newly arrived immigrant Europeans who worked for the Akron Iron and Rolling Mill Company; he provided decent housing at fair prices and donated land for a church, an opera house, and other amenities. In gratitude, the workers named their town for him; Buchtel, Ohio, still exists.

Throughout his career, Buchtel donated generously to nearly every church and good cause in Akron. Although he was probably raised in the German Evangelical church, be became a staunch Universalist, and as such he provided major financing for a new Universalist college in Akron. Buchtel College, named in his honor, was chartered in 1870, admitting students two years later. With his whole-hearted support, the college admitted students without distinctions regarding gender, race or ethnic origins. Buchtel was president of the board of trustees from the college's inception until his death twenty-two years later. He took an active part in every aspect of college life.

His experience in starting Buchtel College may have influenced Governor Rutherford B. Hayes to appoint him in 1870 as a trustee of the newly chartered Ohio Agricultural and Mechanical College, now the Ohio State University. He served in this capacity until 1892. As an executive committee member, Buchtel selected the campus site, secured the architect for the first college building, and supported a comprehensive curriculum in contrast to the narrow agricultural curriculum favored by some trustees. At this time he also contributed money to a new college being promoted in Indiana by his friend John Purdue.

Buchtel served his community as township trustee and secretary of the county agricultural society; he led the move for a free public library and supported Republican politics. In 1872 he was an elector for President Ulysses S. Grant, and in 1874 he ran unsuccessfully for the secretary of state's office on the Prohibition ticket.

Although Buchtel and his wife were both confined to wheelchairs in their last years, they continued supporting Buchtel College activities. Having expended their entire fortune on the public good, with an estimated one-half million dollars going to Buchtel College, the Buchtels died, Elizabeth in 1891 and John the following year in Akron. On Buchtel's death, J. Park Alexander, a prominent Akron businessman, said of him: "To John R. Buchtel is due full credit for what Akron is today. He neither lagged nor shirked from his full share of any enterprise to build up Akron." To his associates "he never said 'Go!' It was always the hearty 'Come on, boys' " (quoted in Spanton, pp. 28–29).

Buchtel's memory is perpetuated in Akron; his name is found on a high school, on a major street, and in numerous places on the campus of the University of Akron, the large, state university that grew from its solid Buchtel College core.

• Scattered letters are in the University of Akron Archives and in the Rutherford B. Hayes Memorial Library, Fremont, Ohio. Samuel A. Lane, *Fifty Years and Over of Akron and Summit County* (1892), contains a brief biographical sketch and also details Buchtel's contributions to various aspects of Akron's life and development. His connections with Buchtel College (now The University of Akron) are described in Albert I. Spanton, ed., *Fifty Years of Buchtel* (1922). More extended accounts are in George W. Knepper, *New Lamps for Old: One Hundred Years of Urban Higher Education at the University of Akron* (1970), and in Knepper, *Summit's Glory: Sketches of Buchtel College and The University of Akron* (1990).

GEORGE W. KNEPPER

BUCK, Carl Darling (2 Oct. 1866–8 Feb. 1955), linguist and educator, was born in Orlando, Maine, the son of Edward Buck and Emeline Darling. Buck's father was involved in lumbering and shipbuilding. Like his father, Buck attended Yale College, passing the entrance examination before his sixteenth birthday. His undergraduate and graduate studies (interrupted by a year's stay in Italy and Greece) culminated in 1889 by his receiving the Ph.D.; the title of his thesis was "The Choregia in Athens and at Ikaria," partly published in the *American Journal of Archaeology* (5 [1889]: 18–33). In his studies he concentrated on Greek and Latin, but he studied Old French, Old English, and other languages as well; in his senior year he studied Sanskrit under William Dwight Whitney, the leading Sanskritist, whose *Sanskrit Grammar* (1879) continues to be used and reprinted.

In 1889, immediately after his marriage, Buck left for study in Germany, where he spent three years, mostly in Leipzig and partly in Berlin. He enlarged the scope of his linguistic studies, becoming one of the leading Indo-European scholars of the day. The neogrammarian school of comparative historical linguistics had its center in Leipzig; Buck studied there mostly with the leaders of the school, Karl Brugmann and August Leskien (Slavic languages), but also with Ernst Windisch (Sanskrit and Celtic languages) and other scholars. In Berlin, Buck came into contact with Johannes Schmidt, the Indo-European scholar largely opposed to the neogrammarian doctrines. During a shorter visit to Münster, Buck also studied the Old Iranian languages with Christian Bartholomae. A complete enumeration of his teachers contains practically the whole galaxy of the leading Indo-European scholars of the day. During this stay in Germany, Buck embraced the neogrammarian doctrine. Even in his later days, he preferred to indicate Indo-European roots and reconstructed forms without modifications deemed necessary by the adherents of the laryngeal theory in its various forms.

Returning from Germany in 1892, Buck became assistant professor of Sanskrit and comparative philology of the newly founded University of Chicago; he remained at Chicago for his full career, up to a named distinguished service professorship in 1930. He retired in 1933 but lived with his daughter close to the campus, daily visiting his office, up to his death. (His wife and two sons predeceased him.) Buck's two most important students were Leonard Bloomfield, who started his career as a successful comparativist in the area of Germanic languages before turning to general linguistics, and Edgar H. Sturtevant, who fully integrated Hittite into Indo-European studies.

Buck's most important works include *Grammar of Oscan and Umbrian* (1928), first published in German as *Elementarbuch der oskisch-umbrischen Dialekte* (1905); *Introduction to the Study of the Greek Dialects* (1910; 2d ed., 1928), the standard textbook and book of reference for many years; *Comparative Grammar of Greek and Latin* (1933), reprinted several times; and *Reverse Index of Greek Nouns and Adjectives*, written with Walter Petersen (1945). His last masterpiece was *Dictionary of Selected Synonyms in the Principal Indo-European Languages* (1949), a thesaurus of nearly 1,500 notions with the indication of how they are expressed in more than 30 languages; the etymology of each word is given, and the motivation, or the reason for the naming, is discussed. For the study of historical semantics the work is of unequaled value.

Buck was one of the Signers of the Call that led to the founding of the Linguistic Society of America. He served twice as the society's president and received many outstanding honors. He educated a whole generation of Indo-European students in the United States; they described him as the teacher of the future researcher, not just the normal undergraduate's teacher by whom to be judged "satisfactory" was a huge success. A writer with clear, elegant style, he was a man of few but witty words. Many anecdotes are told about his dry humor. When his wife's tongue was wounded because she talked while the denist was drilling in her mouth, he is reported to have said, "That could never have happened to me."

Buck died in Chicago.

• Buck's main works are listed above. The best biography is George S. Lane, "Carl Darling Buck," in *Portraits of Linguists*, ed. Thomas A. Sebeok, vol. 2 (1966), pp. 266–77. For a bibliography of Buck's writings, see Vittorio Mondolfo, *Language* 32 (1956): 603–7.

LADISLAV ZGUSTA

BUCK, Carrick Hume (5 July 1900–18 Oct. 1959), lawyer, was born in Las Vegas, New Mexico, the daughter of Arthur Perry Buck, a sheep and cattle rancher, and Henrietta Hume Pettijohn, a lawyer. Buck decided on a legal career after watching defense lawyer Earl Rogers during a trial. Buck's mother may have also influenced her decision to pursue law. Henrietta Hume Buck is distinguished as the first woman admitted to the New Mexico bar. In 1920 Carrick Buck completed her legal education at the University of Southern California, the same institution from which she had received her undergraduate degree. At age twenty-one Buck began her career as the youngest woman admitted to the California bar, one year after women received the right to vote.

In 1923, with two years of legal practice in Los Angeles, Buck and her sister moved from southern California to Hawaii. Buck became only the third woman to practice law in Hawaii and the first woman assistant U.S. attorney. In the era of Prohibition, Buck and her female co-worker organized raids to confiscate liquor and paraphernalia. The success of these raids established Buck's reputation as an aggressive and thorough law enforcer. Buck left the U.S. district attorney's office after five months and joined the Honolulu City & County (C&C) attorney's office, where she became its first female city attorney. Two years later, in 1927, Buck left the C&C to pursue private practice. Throughout these years, Buck garnered a well-earned reputation in government service as a hard-working, competent lawyer. Consequently, in 1928 she decided to enter the political arena by running for the territorial house of representatives as a Democrat. Buck's bid for a seat in the house proved unsuccessful against the well-financed Republican incumbents. During that period the Republican party maintained a dominant hold in Hawaiian politics primarily through the ownership of all major businesses, especially the newspapers. Despite continuing encouragement from fellow Democrats, Buck never again ran for political office.

President Franklin D. Roosevelt appointed Buck to the bench of the Fifth Circuit Court on the island of Kauai. Hawaii's territorial status accounted for federal appointment of even county court positions. Buck's appointment shocked many in the predominantly Republican, conservative Hawaii community, since Buck was appointed before a man. The kind of success attained by Buck was previously unknown for a woman during this period in U.S. history, when gender bias barred almost all women from positions of influence or power, including male-dominated professions such as the law. Buck not only gained entry but achieved success. She viewed her continuing achievements, however, with a parallel sense of responsibility. Buck's awareness of limited court funds motivated her to place the Kauai court on a strict budget. Her plan met with success. She was able to return $1,500 to the county treasury and was even able to satisfy a $700 debt to the court library.

Recognizing Buck's reputation as a judge and skilled financial manager, President Roosevelt in March 1942 appointed her to the First Circuit Court on Oahu. With this position came the power to approve all court finances and another "first" for Buck as she became the first woman judge on Oahu. She handled the most criminal cases by a First Circuit judge in the history of the court to date. Buck saw her role as a judge as a protector of the community and regarded objectivity as furthering that commitment: "If a judge gets overly sentimental, it just encourages further crime" (*Honolulu Advertiser*, 11 Oct. 1949). Her beliefs proved steadfast, and threats to her safety did not scare her into resignation. Judge Buck's meticulous research also became her benchmark, especially evident in only nine reversals out of 4,000 judgments. Accordingly, she easily won reappointment in 1946 and 1950. However, President Dwight D. Eisenhower, a Republican, replaced her in 1958 with a fellow Republican, concluding Buck's twenty-four years on the bench.

In 1958 the Business and Professional Women awarded Buck the title of "First Lady of the Year" for her exemplary service, leadership, and integrity in the territorial courts. Buck believed that law was a satisfying career choice for women, a view consistent with her career success as a judge and lawyer. She never married or had children. One year after opening her own law office, Judge Buck, the public servant who broke all gender stereotypes of her day, died in Honolulu, Hawaii, from pneumonia complicated by a leaky heart valve.

• For biographies of Buck see Barbara Bennett Peterson, ed., *Notable Women of Hawaii* (1984), and Mari Matsuda, ed., *Called from Within: Early Women Lawyers of Hawaii* (1992). An obituary is in the *Honolulu Advertiser*, 20 Oct. 1959.

TERRI ANN M. K. MOTOSUE

BUCK, Dudley (10 Mar. 1839–6 Oct. 1909), organist and composer, was born in Hartford, Connecticut, the son of Dudley Buck and Martha Church Adams. He grew up in the nineteenth-century small-town culture he would serve and develop. Unlike many masters of keyboard instruments, Buck began piano study relatively late (at age sixteen), and indeed his playing, while always solid, was never considered spectacular. His contributions lay in composition and, even more, in the organizational and entrepreneurial aspects of music making.

Like many aspiring American musicians of the mid-nineteenth century, Buck went to Europe for much of his musical training, studying composition, harmony, counterpoint, orchestration, and organ in Leipzig (1857–1860), where he played on the very spot where but a little over a century before J. S. Bach had been organist and Kappelmeister. He also studied in Dresden (1860–1861) and in Paris (1861–1862). Buck returned to Hartford in 1862 and spent the Civil War years teaching music and playing organ at the city's largest Congregational church.

Buck married Mary Elizabeth van Wegener in October 1865, and in 1869 they ventured westward, settling in Chicago. There he played concerts in the city and toured many midwestern towns. The concerts helped prompt some town benefactors to fund the construction of larger and more sophisticated organs in their churches. In the nineteenth century only the very largest American cities could support and patronize full symphony orchestras and opera companies. In the small towns that were the mainstay of much nineteenth-century American culture, an organ, usually housed in a local church, was central to the musical life of the community. The organ's stylistic and dynamic range eclipsed all other instruments of the day, and organ concerts were major cultural events. Within this now long eclipsed and historically neglected corner of American cultural history, Buck was an important figure. Before the Civil War, however, the situation had been different. There had been little grand organ building in the United States and equally little high-quality composing for the instrument; what was constructed and written in Europe had little impact beyond the large cities in the East. Buck's musical performances helped demonstrate to small-town audiences the musical potential of these instruments. Thanks in large part to Buck's efforts, in the generation after the war literally hundreds of midwestern towns installed large organs in their churches. Buck also made significant contributions during these years as a composer. He was the first American to compose sophisticated works for the organ, and his *Grand Sonata in E Flat* (1868) remains a standard in organ repertory.

Buck's years in Chicago were quite successful, financially as well as artistically. Unfortunately, the Chicago fire of 1871 literally and figuratively burned him out. In an era before property insurance was the norm, Buck lost everything—home, possessions, money, a valuable library, manuscripts of his compositions, even the recital hall where he performed. He returned to the East, settling in Boston for a few years. In 1875 he moved to Brooklyn, where he became choirmaster and organist at Holy Trinity Church. During the 1870s Buck also took up conducting. As with his earlier organ concerts, Buck helped to pioneer concert touring by major orchestras, bringing yet another aspect of American musical culture to small towns and expanding it in cities where it had been growing. Along with Theodore Thomas, Buck helped organize and conduct the first Central Park Garden Concerts in 1874.

In addition to the *Grand Sonata*, Buck wrote several notable compositions for choir, orchestra, and organ. In 1876 the U.S. Centennial Commission engaged Buck to collaborate with the poet Sidney Lanier on a piece to commemorate the nation's hundredth anniversary. With the memories of the Civil War painfully fresh, the collaboration of a Georgia poet and a Yankee composer symbolized reconciliation, and their *Centennial Meditation of Columbia* enjoyed immense success at the celebration in Philadelphia. This piece was a hymn that captured the meditative postwar solemnity, the stirring patriotism, and the Victorian propriety of the age. Buck's *Light of Asia* and *The Golden Legend* were popular at both American and European festivals in the 1880s. Like most of his organ music, the works are full of trills and flourishes, often climaxing in a grand fugue. *The Golden Legend*, based on a Henry Wadsworth Longfellow poem, won a prize at the 1886 Cincinnati Festival. Boston's prestigious Handel and Haydn Society performed his *Forty-Sixth Psalm*, their first performance of a work by an American composer. Buck continued to write and perform until his retirement in 1903, when he settled in the New Jersey countryside, where he died.

Like the organ concert tradition Buck led, nineteenth-century secular organ music has fallen into neglect. Yet, beyond its aesthetic value, its fervor and quality remain a window onto the culture of an older, more sentimental but culturally vibrant era.

• Buck's papers, consisting largely of his organ compositions, are housed in the Library of Congress. There are no published biographies of Buck. There is one work on his life and music by William Gallo, "The Life and Church Music of Dudley Buck" (Ph.D. diss., Catholic Univ. of America, 1968).

ALAN LEVY

BUCK, Gurdon (4 May 1807–6 Mar. 1877), surgeon, was born in New York City, the son of Gurdon Buck, a merchant, and Susannah Manwaring. After completing his secondary education at the Nelson Classical School, he reluctantly went to work as a clerk for G. and D. Buck, his father's mercantile establishment. Evidently he demonstrated little business acumen, for shortly thereafter he began studying medicine with Thomas Cock, a city physician. He later enrolled in New York's College of Physicians and Surgeons, from which he received an M.D. in 1830. After spending the next eighteen months as an intern at New York Hospital, he went to Europe to study medicine in clinics in Paris, Berlin, and Vienna.

In 1834 Buck became an attending physician at the newly opened New York Dispensary, where he increasingly developed an interest in surgery. He returned to Europe the next year, presumably to study the latest surgical techniques, and in 1836 he married Henriette Elizabeth Wolff, a native of Geneva, Switzerland; they had one child. In 1837 he returned to New York City, where he opened a general medical practice and became a visiting surgeon at New York Hospital, situations in which he continued for the next forty years. In 1846 he became an adviser to the managing board working to establish St. Luke's Hospital, and when it opened twelve years later he became a visiting surgeon there as well. During this period he devoted much effort to the surgical correction of throat disorders, such as croup and laryngitis caused by swelling, and by 1860 he had performed several innovative operations on the epiglottis and trachea.

Although Buck remained interested in surgery involving the larynx throughout his career, he is best remembered for his contributions to orthopedic procedures involving the lower extremities. In 1845 he became the first surgeon to restore a knee joint to a straight position by removing the patella, a small knee bone, and its connections with the calf and shin bones, a procedure that became known as Buck's operation. In 1860 he developed Buck's extension, the modern method for treating fractured femurs or thighbones. A decade earlier all broken bones had been set by means of splints, a method that sufficiently stabilized short bones but did not always provide the necessary stability for long bones, such as the femur. Moreover, because an adult femur can take up to six months to heal, the patient's inability to flex the leg during convalescence frequently resulted in muscle shortening. In the late 1850s New York surgeon Henry Gassett Davis developed a method for treating bone deformities and joint irritations, such as ulcerated vertebrae, by using weights and pulleys to apply vertical traction to the bone or joint in question and adapted it for use in treating fractures. In 1860 Buck improved on Davis's method by using longitudinally positioned lengths of adhesive tape to attach one end of a rope to the length of the thigh; the other end was attached to a weight-and-pulley apparatus. By adjusting the amount of weight, elevating the foot of the bed, and securing the lower torso by means of a long strap attached to the head of the bed, he employed the patient's body as a counterweight. This method of applying longitudinal traction to the femur provides greater stability for the fracture, keeps the muscles stretched, and permits the patient a slightly greater range of motion. He tested and modified this method at New York Hospital and, as a member of the New York auxiliary corps of volunteer surgeons, during the Civil War in the city's military hospitals before publicizing it in 1867. Although his apparatus has been modified over the years, the basic principle of setting long bones by placing them in traction remains unchanged.

During the Civil War, Buck began experimenting with plastic surgery of the face. Although reconstruction of the nose had been performed successfully by ancient Hindu surgeons, such procedures remained a rarity in the United States. By reshaping muscle, cartilage, and skin, in 1864 he successfully restored the right half of a patient's upper lip and the adjacent portions of the cheek and nose. In 1871 he used the same techniques to close an opening in a patient's right upper nasal cavity. He reported on these and similar procedures in *Contributions to Reparative Surgery* (1876). This work was so well received by his surgical colleagues that it was quickly translated into three languages.

In 1872 Buck severed his ties with St. Luke's to become a visiting surgeon at the newly opened Presbyterian Hospital. Four years later, when failing health greatly diminished his ability to operate, he was made consulting surgeon at Presbyterian.

Buck became a charter member of the New York Academy of Medicine in 1847 and served two terms as vice president. He was a visiting surgeon at the New York Eye and Ear Infirmary from 1852 to 1862 and served as a trustee of that institution as well as of the New York Ophthalmic and Aural Institute, the New York Dispensary, and the College of Physicians and Surgeons. He also served as president of the New York Pathological Society. He died in New York City.

Buck is remembered for his role in the development of the modern method of setting broken bones by means of traction and for performing a number of the first operations involving laryngology and plastic surgery in the United States.

• Buck's papers have not been located. A biography, which includes a bibliography, is F. A. Castle, "Biographical Sketch of Gurdon Buck, M.D.," *Transactions of the Medical Society of the State of New York* (1877): 367–74. An obituary is in the *New York Times*, 9 Mar. 1877.

CHARLES W. CAREY, JR.

BUCK, Paul Herman (25 Aug. 1899–23 Dec. 1978), historian and university administrator, was born in Columbus, Ohio, the son of Henry John Buck and Adele

Kreppelt. Buck took his A.B. in 1921 and his A.M. in 1922 at Ohio State University in Columbus. His master's thesis, "The Evolution of the National Park System," was published by the Government Printing Office in 1946, after he had achieved some scholarly distinction.

In 1924 Buck earned a second A.M., at Harvard University, where for the next ten years he taught history while working on his doctoral dissertation under the direction of Arthur M. Schlesinger, Sr. He completed the Ph.D. in 1935. Buck's scholarly interests and intellectual inclinations placed him within the New History movement, of which Schlesinger was a major proponent. The historian James Harvey Robinson had given New History its name in 1898, and his followers, influenced by the emerging social sciences and the Progressive Era, believed that present needs and interests ought to determine the central concerns and research agendas of historians, that recent history ought to be privileged over older eras, and that the scope of history ought to be broadened beyond politics and leadership to include social and cultural forces as well as everyday life.

These influences were reflected in Buck's dissertation, which became his principal scholarly book, the Pulitzer Prize–winning *Road to Reunion, 1865–1900* (1937). Integrating political and cultural history, *Road to Reunion* analyzes and celebrates the sectional reconciliation of the North and South in the late nineteenth century. Blaming Republican bloody shirt politicians in the North for keeping sectional animosity alive longer than necessary, Buck was sympathetic to the South's bitterness over the alleged excesses and failures of Reconstruction. Driven by an impulse to nationalism and uninterested in the racial and civil rights legacies of Reconstruction, Buck made his major contribution by analyzing how white southern writers—in fiction and journalism—had transformed their bitter memories of war into an enduring pathos, which proved especially effective among northern readers: it became a means of evading conflict and of forging reconciliation.

The irony of this process, by which black Americans became the forgotten presence in the nation's reunification, was not the focus of Buck's widely acclaimed book. Implicit in Buck's analysis was the regrettable, and now supplanted, claim that the freedpeople had been unfit for the experiment in racial equality, if not for freedom itself. The "Negro Problem" ran headlong into the spirit of the "New Nationalism" of the 1890s, and in Buck's summation, "Once a people admits that a problem is insoluble they have taken the first step in learning how to live with it." Buck used the new approaches of cultural and social history, and he wrote engaging narrative, making his book accessible to a wide audience. But an overriding assumption lay at the root of the work: "The central theme of American life after the war," Buck wrote, "even in the years of political radicalism, is not to be found in a narrative of sectional divergence. It was national integration . . . that marked every important development." Many reviews of *Road to Reunion* lauded its scope, its model of American cohesion, and its evident links to Margaret M. Mitchell's enormously popular novel *Gone with the Wind*, published the previous year in 1936. Mitchell's epic story of a defeated but revitalized South, personified in Scarlett O'Hara's struggle against poverty, defeat, and gender conventions, may indeed have helped create the wide audience for Buck's story of energetic businessmen, New South entrepreneurs, editors, veterans, and writers who buried animosities and tried to render race invisible in a Jim Crow society, in favor of nationalism and progress.

Buck remained at Harvard for the rest of his life, becoming Frances Lee Higginson Professor of History in 1955 and the first Carl H. Pforzheimer University Professor in 1958. At the same time, he held a series of administrative posts. In 1942 he was appointed dean of the faculty of arts and sciences, and in 1945 he became provost; he served in both posts until 1953. During World War II and the early Cold War years, while Harvard president James B. Conant was absent from campus on government service, Buck served, for all practical purposes, as the university's chief executive officer, steering its considerable research and training contribution to the war effort and effectively defending academic freedom against McCarthyite attacks during the early 1950s. Buck chaired the committee that wrote *General Education in a Free Society* (1945), a landmark study that led to the creation of a core curriculum for Harvard undergraduates and that had great influence on national trends in liberal education in the post–World War II era. As provost he also played an important role in developing Harvard's faculty structure, especially what he called the "five-year term . . . up or out principle" of the assistant professorship, whereby junior faculty at Harvard are appointed for terminal periods and only rarely given tenure.

From 1955 to 1964 Buck served as director of the university library at Harvard. When he left that post, he published a collection of his essays and lectures on the function and meaning of libraries, *Libraries and Universities: Addresses and Reports* (1964), edited by Edwin E. Williams. In 1965 Buck edited a collection of essays by former students in his seminars, *Social Sciences at Harvard, 1860–1920: From Inculcation to the Open Mind.* Buck became a professor emeritus in 1969, and during the latter stage of his career he served on numerous educational commissions as well as the boards of learned societies and journals. He died in Cambridge, Massachusetts.

• Correspondence, records of Buck's administrative career, and reviews of *Road to Reunion* are in the Paul Buck Papers, Harvard University Archives. Useful secondary sources include John Higham, with Leonard Krieger and Felix Gilbert, *History: The Development of Historical Studies in the United States* (1965); E. J. Kahn, Jr., *Harvard: Through Change and*

Through Storm (1969); and Ellen Schrecker, *No Ivory Tower: McCarthyism and the Universities* (1986). An obituary is in the *New York Times*, 24 Dec. 1978.

DAVID W. BLIGHT

BUCK, Pearl S. (26 June 1892–6 Mar. 1973), author and humanitarian, was born Pearl Sydenstricker in Hillsboro, West Virginia, the daughter of Absalom Sydenstricker and Caroline Stulting, missionaries who were on furlough from their Presbyterian missionary activities in China when Pearl, their first daughter, was born in the United States. Three months later the infant was taken to China when her parents returned to their duties. Educated by her mother at home and then by a Chinese tutor, Buck later attributed much of her knowledge to the influence of her Chinese amah who, together with Chinese playmates, gave her many insights into her exotic surroundings and developed imaginative outlets. Indeed Buck claimed that in her early years she was more fluent in Chinese than in English. She received additional training at a mission school and in 1909 was sent to board for a year at Miss Jewell's School in Shanghai. Her parents insisted that she attend college in the United States, so in 1910 she enrolled in Randolph-Macon Woman's College in Lynchburg, Virginia, where she won several academic honors and graduated four years later with a bachelor of arts degree. She received a teaching assistantship at Randolph-Macon, but upon learning that her mother was seriously ill she returned to China to care for her.

As her mother's health improved and demanded less attention, she accepted a position teaching English to high school students. In 1917 she married John Lossing Buck, an agricultural expert who was employed by the Presbyterian Mission Board to teach American farming methods. She and her husband moved to North China, where he researched farming procedures and she mingled constantly with Chinese peasant families and familiarized herself with their lives. In 1921 the Bucks moved to Nanking, where John taught agricultural techniques as a professor at the city's university and Pearl began a career of teaching English at several Chinese colleges. At this time Pearl began to write nonfiction articles of Chinese life, which were published in several American magazines.

The Bucks' only child, Carol, was born in 1921 and very soon thereafter evinced distressing signs of abnormality. In 1925 the mission board granted the Bucks a year's leave of absence, during which they sought medical treatment for their daughter in the United States. There it was confirmed that the child was mentally retarded and would never improve. To help themselves cope with this diagnosis, the Bucks enrolled in graduate school; Pearl received an M.A. degree in English from Cornell University in 1926.

Returning to China, the family escaped death only by being secretly hidden by Chinese friends when a revolutionary army uprising against Western imperialism occured in Nanking in 1927. Convinced that Carol needed more specialized care than she could be given at home, Buck enrolled her daughter in the famous Training School in Vineland, New Jersey, in 1929. She also devoted herself to the cause of helping mentally retarded children. After deciding in 1934 to take up permanent residence in the United States, she joined various committees for this purpose and worked with state and local groups; much later she wrote a book about Carol's condition, *The Child Who Never Grew* (1950).

Financial necessity along with a compulsion toward *furor scribendi* spurred Buck to continue writing, and she produced two long short stories of Chinese life and sent them to an agent. Richard Walsh, president of the John Day Company, became interested and suggested that the stories be published in one volume under the title *East Wind: West Wind*. This book, issued in 1930, went through three printings in less than a year, gave Buck confidence in her narrative ability, and demonstrated that there was a market for Chinese themes and material. On 2 March 1931, Buck's novel *The Good Earth* was published. It immediately became an international bestseller, won the Pulitzer Prize in 1932, and made Pearl Buck's name a household word.

The Good Earth portrays a Chinese peasant family whose husband and wife struggle with the harsh farming realities of northern China. Through laborious effort and dedication they struggle to more financially secure conditions but are never free from the various difficulties and disappointments that are the lot of humankind. By vividness of character portrayal and authenticity of setting, Buck was able to convey her material so that people the world over could identify closely with the events and characters presented. In addition to its universal themes, *The Good Earth* appealed to readers because its style was influenced by the King James version of the Bible. The writing only occasionally captures the mellifluousness and imaginative coloring of the Old and New testaments, but it has a simple, archaic, and quietly stately quality that effectively fits her saga of struggle and triumph. Chinese critics denounced *The Good Earth* for giving an unflattering portrait of Chinese life and for several alleged inaccuracies. Yet in a striking and persuasive essay in the *New York Times*, Buck refuted these charges and demonstrated that the critics were distressed because they felt that any picture of Chinese life should focus on the intellectuals and the well educated and that the harsh realities of peasant life should be ignored.

After the publication of *The Good Earth*, a steady stream of books flowed from Buck's pen. *Sons* (1932) and *A House Divided* (1935) were sequels to *The Good Earth* and formed a trilogy titled *House of Earth* which was published in one volume in 1935. Her novel *The Mother* (1934) was popular, and biographies of her mother and father—*The Exile* and *Fighting Angel* (both 1936)—attracted considerable worldwide attention. In recognition primarily of *The Good Earth* and the two biographies, Buck was awarded the Nobel Prize in Literature in 1938. She divorced her first husband in 1935 and married Walsh that same year.

Although Buck continued to write prolifically, after the Nobel award she became more involved in humanitarian concerns. In 1941 she founded the East-West Association, a nonprofit group designed to promote understanding and harmony by sponsoring visits and discussions between Americans and Asians.

When World War II commenced, she began to write radio plays and scripts for the Office of War Information. These productions, which were broadcast to China by short wave, encouraged home front support for the Chinese, and she took a very active role in working for United China Relief. She also authored numerous magazine articles and letters to editors and gave many speeches supporting the American war effort, emphasizing that the war should be fought to guarantee freedom for people of all races. Although she denounced the horrors of Nazism, her familiarity with Asian countries persuaded her to concentrate more on the war in the Orient. Two of her most popular wartime novels, *Dragon Seed* (1942) and *The Promise* (1943), trumpeted the cause of China against Japanese aggression.

Throughout her life Buck campaigned against all forms of racism. As early as the early 1930s she worked actively to eliminate prejudice against blacks. She gave speeches against prejudice; wrote articles for *Opportunity*, a journal published in Harlem; and coauthored, with Pulitzer Prize–winning Filipino author and noted diplomat Carlos Romulo, *Friend to Friend* (1958), which discussed colonialism and demonstrated its blight on the image of America. She reiterated this theme in several additional books, speeches, and articles. She was outraged over the dropping of the atomic bomb, not only because of the horrible desolation and suffering it wrought but also because it seemed to further demonstrate prejudice against nonwhite races.

Buck's unceasing energy moved her into another area of writing. Because she felt she was being labeled as a novelist of Asian themes, and because her publishers worried that her prolificness would be detrimental to financial success, she adopted the pseudonym "John Sedges," under which she wrote five novels focusing on American scenes and characters. The most successful of these books was *The Townsman* (1945), a perceptive and convincing study of pioneer life in Kansas.

After the war Buck continued to be a popular author. While novels such as *Pavilion of Women* (1946), *Kinfolk* (1949), and *Imperial Woman* (1956) sold thousands of copies, Buck's altruistic concerns never ceased. She became particularly interested in the plight of children of mixed races, whom she knew faced constant prejudice. In 1949 she founded Welcome House, an agency designed to find adoptive homes for part-Asian children who were born in the United States. As Welcome House became successful, she sought to expand the program to include children of American servicemen in Korea, Japan, and other countries who had been abandoned by their fathers and were ostracized in their own countries.

In 1960 Walsh died after a long illness. In the same year Buck proposed the formation of the Pearl S. Buck Foundation for the assistance of overseas children, which she hoped would become a unit of Welcome House. The Welcome House Board of Directors found the additional task of handling overseas children too overwhelming, so in 1964 the Pearl S. Buck Foundation was established as a separate, independent organization to help half-American children who for various reasons had to remain in their native lands. The foundation sought financial support for food, clothing, and education. Centers in foreign countries were set up, and advisers and counselors were hired to work with these children in their own countries. Buck gave the foundation considerable financial assistance.

Soon, however, the foundation was involved in a personal scandal that almost destroyed its credibility. In 1963 Buck had met a 32-year-old suave and handsome Arthur Murray Dance Studio instructor named Theodore Harris. He convinced her that a vast amount of money could be raised for the foundation by producing several benefit balls in various U.S. cities; Buck would move about the country and personally meet the donors. Harris's idea was adopted and became enormously successful. He was put in charge of the foundation and was lavished with expensive gifts by the infatuated Buck. Rumors of his homosexuality circulated and eventually proved to be true. In addition, with Buck's support, Harris lived extravagantly. Charges of financial irregularities were made in 1968, and the following year Harris resigned as director of the foundation. It barely survived but eventually was reorganized with dedicated medical and social workers in charge. It has since continued as one of the most successful world humanitarian groups bringing educational opportunities to thousands of Amerasian children in Korea, Japan, Taiwan, Vietnam, and Thailand.

During the Harris scandal, Buck denied any impropriety on his part and fiercely supported him. Harris moved with Buck to Danby, Vermont, although Buck kept her Green Hills Farm in Bucks County, Pennsylvania. In 1970 Harris set up Creativity, Inc., a corporation designed to manage many of Buck's later publications.

The scandal had no effect on the success of Buck's books. While many of her last efforts were mere potboilers, competent bestsellers such as *The Living Reed* (1963), *The Three Daughters of Madame Liang* (1969), and *Mandala* (1970) demonstrated that while Harris may have overwhelmed her heart, her mind and her narrative ability never lost their strength and never failed to attract an avid reading public. She died in Danby.

Professional literary critics have tended to denigrate Buck's writing as too facile, as the work of a mere storyteller. Her bestseller status automatically aroused ire from serious literary critics, and the fact that her generally optimistic view of life did not square with the pessimistic, angst-ridden emphasis of much contemporary literature also lowered her reputation in critical circles.

Although there is no question that she possessed considerable narrative ability and always focused on significant topics, it is clear that her post–Nobel Prize work was uneven. She also wrote much too much, lowering the quality of most of her later novels. Characters were not as well-developed as they could have been, and narrative occurrences sometimes became improbable or unconvincing. Further, she allowed a too obvious and often-labored didacticism to dominate and make her writing less artistic.

In addition to her bestselling American status, it should be noted that Buck's works have been immensely popular abroad. Her writings have been translated into every major language, and she and Mark Twain have generally ranked as the most popular American writers in countries overseas. In retrospect, Buck's abilities and energies were astonishing. She wrote more than 100 books and thousands of nonfiction articles, gave countless speeches, and was personally active on many committees and devoted to many altruistic causes. Although the climate was not receptive at the time, she wrote numerous magazine articles in the 1940s and 1950s that planted the seeds of feminism. She worked unceasingly for universal understanding among people of all races and creeds. Her preaching was always supported by practice. She remains an inspiration to those who would not merely hope for a better world but who will work with inspired dedication to bring about such a goal.

• The Pearl S. Buck Birthplace Foundation in Hillsboro, W. Va., which operates Buck's ancestral home as a museum, holds many of the author's manuscripts. Several of her letters are available at the libraries of Yale University and Randolph-Macon Woman's College. Theordore F. Harris's two-volume biography, *Pearl S. Buck* (1969, 1971), is eclectic and sycophantic. The second volume is a selected compilation of speeches, essays, and letters. Cornelia Spencer, Buck's sister, wrote *The Exile's Daughter: A Biography of Pearl S. Buck* (1944) covering her life somewhat sketchily up to the World War II period. Nora Stirling's biography, *Pearl Buck: A Woman in Conflict* (1983), gives the most frank, intimate picture, with an effective emphasis on the last years. A chronology of her career, a literary analysis, and a detailed annotated bibliography of the most significant articles and studies can be found in Paul A. Doyle, *Pearl S. Buck* (1980). The most complete listing of primary material is contained in Lucille S. Zinn, "The Works of Pearl S. Buck: A Bibliography," *Bulletin of Bibliography* 36 (Oct.–Dec. 1979): 194–208. An obituary is in the *New York Times*, 7 Mar. 1973.

PAUL A. DOYLE

BUCKALEW, Charles Rollin (28 Dec. 1821–19 May 1899), senator, was born at Fishing Creek, Columbia County, Pennsylvania, the son of John McKinney Buckalew and Martha Funston, farmers. Buckalew was educated at Hartford Academy, Hartford, Pennsylvania, then taught school and clerked in a grocery store for a few years before beginning a systematic study of law with a local attorney. He was admitted to the bar at the age of twenty-two and after two years' experience entered the Bloomsburg district prosecuting attorney's office for Columbia County, where he practiced until 1847. In 1849 he married Permelia S. Wadsworth, with whom he had two children. At the age of twenty-nine, he was elected as a Democrat to the state senate, where he served from 1850 to 1858. In 1854 he was appointed one of the commissioners sent to negotiate a treaty with Paraguay. He became chairman of the state Democratic committee in 1857 and was elected again a state senator.

In the state legislature Buckalew was committed to reducing the state debt. In 1857 Governor Asa Packer appointed him to serve as a member of a commission to reform the state penal code. Buckalew also headed the effort to sell the state's transportation facilities to private corporations.

President James Buchanan appointed Buckalew as minister to Ecuador, where he served from 1858 to 1861. When the Civil War broke out, he returned to the United States and ran successfully for the U.S. Senate in 1863. He won the election by a majority of one vote in the legislature against Simon Cameron after a particularly bitter and vindictive contest. Democrats openly threatened that any Democrat voting for Cameron rather than Buckalew "would be carried feet first from the House chamber." He distinguished himself in the Senate chiefly by adhering to his convictions, against open and sometimes vehement party criticism. He felt that it was his duty to cooperate with the administration's war effort; consequently, he came under fire from Democrats for not opposing the more stringent Republican war measures more energetically and from Republicans for opposing emancipation. Indeed, one Republican newspaper criticized him as a "true slave-loving demagogue."

Although Buckalew took a prominent part in some of the more contentious Senate debates, he also served on many committees, including those on Indian affairs, post offices and post roads, pensions, mines and mining, and foreign relations. Throughout his congressional career he toiled on various important but less contentious matters, such as improvements in Congressional buildings. Buckalew vigorously opposed extreme war powers, the Freedman's Bureau, the Military Reconstruction Bill, and President Andrew Johnson's impeachment. He argued against harsh reconstruction measures, which he opposed as unconstitutional. He was criticized, throughout his service in Congress, by both the Democratic and Republican parties for his moderate views. He served in the Senate until 1869.

After leaving Washington in 1869 Buckalew was again elected to the Pennsylvania State Senate and while there began the movement for a state constitutional convention, to be held in 1872–1873. Widespread corruption and dishonesty in the state legislature had prompted a statewide call for constitutional reform. As a former senator, Buckalew was considered one of the most distinguished leaders of a convention otherwise populated by the wealthiest businessmen of the state. Buckalew believed that reforming the method of representation would remove the worst offenses of gerrymandering and vote buying, but he was ultimately unable to get his ideas adopted. Partly in response to this failure, he published *Examination of the Constitution of Pennsylvania* (1883). He also wrote a treatise on proportional representation, long a deeply held conviction, in which he espoused the cause of minority representation. Buckalew considered the lack of representation of minority views to amount to a disfranchisement of voters and argued that a system that took into account minority views would "impart health, vigor and endurance to our political institutions." Although he had, while in the Senate, vigorously opposed the Freedman's Bureau, he felt that his plan of representation would be fairer to the black people of the South and to their "white allies."

During Buckalew's 1872 race for governor, Republicans accused him of having encouraged resistance to the federal government during his wartime service as senator. Stung by this criticism and his subsequent defeat, he left public office until 1887.

In 1887 Buckalew was returned to Congress, to serve in the House of Representatives. When his second term expired in 1891, he retired from politics and returned to Bloomsburg, Columbia County, where he died. In his memoirs, George W. Julian wrote that Buckalew was "one of the really sterling men of his party, but he was a modest man, and only appreciated by those who knew him intimately."

• Buckalew's papers are in the collections of the Wyoming Historical and Geological Society in Wilkes-Barre, Pennsylvania. Some of his letters are also located in various collections in the Library of Congress, Manuscripts Division. Buckalew also wrote *Proportional Representation* (1872). His work in the Pennsylvania State Senate is recorded in the proceedings of the state senate. For his work during the Pennsylvania state constitutional convention, see A. D. Harland, *Pennsylvania Constitutional Convention* (1873). Erwin Stanley Bradley, *The Triumph of Militant Republicanism* (1964), contains an assessment of Buckalew's political career. An obituary is in the *New York Times*, 20 May 1899.

SILVANA SIDDALI

BUCKE, Richard Maurice (18 Mar. 1837–19 Feb. 1902), psychiatrist and biographer, was born in Methwold, County of Norfolk, England, the son of Reverend Horatio Walpole Bucke, a Church of England curate and a direct descendant of Sir Robert Walpole, the renowned prime minister of England. (His mother's name has been recorded as Clarissa Andrews, but that cannot be confirmed.) Within a year of his birth, Bucke's parents emigrated to Upper Canada, settling on a farm near London, Ontario. His father, a classical scholar and linguist, brought to Canada a library of five or six thousand books in English, French, Italian, Spanish, Latin, Greek, and Hebrew. Bucke and his six siblings received their schooling at home.

Following the death of his parents in the mid-1850s, Bucke left home and worked as a laborer in the Ohio and Mississippi valleys and the cypress swamps of Louisiana and as a deckhand on a Mississippi River steamboat. His travels took him west, where he took part in a deadly fight between white settlers and a band of Shoshone Indians near Salt Lake City. In California he joined Alan and Hosea Grosh, discoverers of the famous Comstock Lode. In 1856 they became lost in a snowstorm in the Sierras for five days and four nights. Alan Grosh lost his life, and Bucke lost one foot and part of the other as the result of frostbite.

After life on an adventurer's trail, Bucke turned to a more sedentary venture. He enrolled in Canada's McGill University as a medical student in 1858. Upon his graduation in 1862, he was awarded the Governor's Prize and the Professor's Prize in Clinical Medicine for his thesis, "The Correlation of the Vital and Physical Forces." This work, published in the *British American Journal* the same year, anticipated Bucke's interest in the relationship between the physical and the spiritual that eventually led him to the study of Theosophy and mysticism. Although Bucke had been raised in a Christian household, he was never able to accept the doctrines of Christianity and regarded Christ as "a man—great and good no doubt—but a man." Following his graduation from McGill, he spent two years as a postdoctoral student in England and France. Bucke returned to Canada, married a woman named Jessie (reported elsewhere as Jesse Maria Gurd), and began practicing medicine in Sarnia, Ontario. In 1876 he was appointed superintendent of the newly opened mental hospital in Hamilton, Ontario, but within the year he became superintendent of the Asylum for the Insane in London, Ontario, a position he held throughout his professional life. Although not the first "alienist" (then the term for psychiatrist) to introduce what was called the moral treatment of the insane, Bucke became best known for putting this concept into practice at his asylum, abolishing both the use of restraints and the use of distilled alcohol as a sedative. He was, however, later criticized by the medical community for "meddlesome gynecology" and "mutilating helpless patients."

Bucke viewed mental illness as the result of man's inadequately developed ability to adapt to change, not merely lifetime alterations but evolution. His first book, *Man's Moral Nature* (1879), adapted Ralph Waldo Emerson's idea that the source of knowledge is both intellectual and moral (meaning "emotional") and argued that the intellectual nature, having its origin in the cerebrospinal system, had kept up with evolutionary change. On the other hand the moral nature, having its foundation in the sympathetic nervous system, had failed to develop adequately its aesthetic appreciation of nature, which rightly seen revealed the true nature of the universe (love instead of hate). The book was dedicated "to the man who of all men past and present that I have known has the most exalted moral nature—to WALT WHITMAN."

Bucke credited Whitman with inspiring this first book, and the poet was to inspire everything else Bucke published. Introduced to Whitman's poetry in 1867, Bucke wrote to him that year, sending money to cover the purchase of various editions of *Leaves of Grass*, but he received no answer. The men finally met in Camden, New Jersey, on 18 October 1877. They became friends instantly, and soon afterward Bucke planned to write a biography of the poet. During the summer of 1880 Whitman was a guest of the Buckes on the grounds of the London asylum so that Bucke could gather information for his book. *Walt Whitman*, which with Whitman's heavy revisions virtually became a joint project, was published in 1883. Although it is regarded as the first Whitman biography, it is more a sourcebook—with more than half of its 236 pages devoted to testimonies by others. Bucke, who considered Whitman more important as a prophet than as a poet, attempted to develop his theory of "cosmic consciousness" in the portrait, but Whitman deleted most of that material before publication. Many literary scholars have regarded Bucke's biography as "Whitman's book," or autobiography.

Bucke became one of Whitman's three literary executors and is still considered one of his most ardent disciples. When the poet died in 1892, Bucke conducted a grandiose funeral that he had been planning for three years. Afterward he set about publishing Whitman's literary remains. Either alone or with the other executors, he edited *In Re Walt Whitman* (1893), *Calamus: A Series of Letters Written during the Years 1863–1880, by Walt Whitman to a Young Friend* (1897), *The Wound Dresser: Letters Written to His Mother from the Hospitals in Washington during the Civil War* (1898), *Notes & Fragments* (1899), and *The Complete Writings* (1902) in ten volumes.

Bucke also wrote and published *Cosmic Consciousness: A Study in the Evolution of the Human Mind* in 1901. Unlike *Walt Whitman*, which has been reprinted only once, in 1970, *Cosmic Consciousness* has gone through many editions and is said to have never been out of print, possibly because of its utopian appeal. Essentially a eugenicist and a protosocialist, Bucke argues that human mental development evolved from higher animals' "simple consciousness" through "self consciousness" to a moral nature that has prepared human beings for "cosmic consciousness," or mysticism. This experience produces, as most mystical experiences are supposed to do, not a "knowledge" of the cosmos but a "consciousness" of its life-force and order. As more and more humans develop this capacity, "National boundaries, tariffs, and perhaps distinctions in language will fade out. Great cities will have no longer reason for being and will melt away" as a worldwide utopia comes into existence. The most notable examples of cosmic consciousness, in Bucke's estimation, were Christ and Whitman. He placed Whitman as possibly superior to Christ because the poet saw more clearly that the mystical faculty is "no more supernatural" than any of the senses. Bucke died from a cerebral concussion suffered in a fall while contemplating the stars on his icy London, Ontario, veranda.

• For additional information see James H. Coyne, *Richard Maurice Bucke: A Sketch* (1923); Arthur R. Ford, "The Amazing Dr. Bucke," *London* (Ontario) *Free Press*, 9 Apr. 1960; Stephen Railton, ed., *Walt Whitman's Autograph Revision of the Analysis of "Leaves of Grass" (For Dr. R. M. Bucke's "Walt Whitman")* (1974); Artem Lozynsky, ed., *Richard Maurice Bucke, Medical Mystic: [Selected] Letters of Dr. Bucke to Walt Whitman and His Friends* (1977) and *Letters of Dr. Richard Maurice Bucke to Walt Whitman* (1977; published on demand by Univ. of Michigan Microfilm); Mary Ann Jameson, ed., *Richard Maurice Bucke: A Catalogue Based upon the Collections at the University of Western Ontario Libraries* (1978); and Cyril Greenland and John Robert Colombo, eds., *Walt Whitman's Canada* (1992). *Beautiful Dreamers*, a 1990 video, dramatizes Whitman's summer 1880 stay with the Buckes in London.

JEROME LOVING

BUCKEL, C. Annette (25 Aug. 1833–17 Aug. 1912), physician, Civil War nurse, and mental health activist, was born Cloe Annette Buckel in Warsaw, New York, the daughter of Thomas Buckel and his wife (given name unknown), whose surname was Bartlett. Both parents died when Buckel, an only child, was three months old. Until the age of four she lived with her grandparents, and after they died she lived with two young aunts, neither of whom exhibited much warmth toward her. By age four Buckel had learned to read and write. Quickly outgrowing the local district school, she moved on to a more advanced one in a neighboring town. At age fourteen she started teaching school, boarding with her students' parents, both in New York State and in Canada. While a youth she decided to become a physician. Financially unable to immediately begin formal medical school, she worked in a burnishing factory in Connecticut, living with her employer's family, and studied Latin as she worked. By living simply and borrowing on a life insurance policy she had purchased, Buckel was able to enter the Women's Medical College of Pennsylvania in 1856. She later demonstrated the high regard she felt for the school by leaving it a bequest in her will.

After graduation in 1858, Buckel worked for a year at the New York Infirmary and Dispensary with Elizabeth Blackwell and Emily Blackwell and then, in 1859, opened a medical practice in Chicago, where she and another woman physician founded a dispensary for women and children. In 1863, because women were not recognized as physicians, she volunteered as a nurse to the Union army and served in military hospitals in the Southwest until the end of the war.

After practicing briefly in Evansville, Indiana, Buckel accepted a position at the New England Hospital for Women and Children in Boston in 1866. As a resident physician, she taught medical students her specialty, diseases of the chest. Her health began to fail, however, and in 1872 she left on a leave of absence for Vienna and Paris for convalescence and further study. Buckel returned to the New England Hospital in 1875, but her health continued to decline, so she moved to California, drawn to the state's mild climate as well as to the San Francisco Bay area, where Washington Bartlett, a cousin on her mother's side, was a well-known politician.

Buckel opened a practice in Oakland in 1877, was a consulting physician at the Pacific Dispensary for

Women and Children in San Francisco, and was the first woman to be admitted to the Alemeda County Medical Association. She became very active in addressing the needs of children, particularly their health and well-being. Her focus on the prevention of illness rather than its cure was ahead of her time. She helped found Oakland's Milk Commission, the first in the state, which rejected the use of tubercular cows. The cooking school she opened in her own home led to the introduction of vocational training in the Oakland public schools, and Buckel was one of the first directors of the Mary R. Smith Trust, which provided care and housing for orphan and delinquent girls. Interested in the welfare of mentally retarded and developmentally delayed children, in her later years she provided in her will that her estate be held in trust for the benefit of such children. (In 1914 a grant from the trust established the C. Annette Buckel Foundation Research Fellowship at Stanford University for the study of child psychology.)

Buckel was also active in the community. Interested in nature, literature, music, and astronomy, she helped found the Home Club (a women's association interested in public health issues) and a local Agassiz society and a Chautauqua group, and she was active in the Oakland Ebell Society (a women's cultural and study group). She never married. About fifteen years before her death, in Piedmont, California, Buckel had a log cabin built on one and a half acres in the Piedmont Hills above Oakland for her own use as well as for use by friends. She later built a home on the site and retired there with a friend and former patient, Charlotte Playter. Even in retirement Buckel was active in advocating appropriate educational programs for scholastically handicapped children. Throughout her life she was known for her broad intellectual interests and for her eagerness to share her knowledge—and her life—with those around her.

• The California Historical Society has a small collection of papers concerning Brown's Civil War work, and five of her letters are at the Indiana State Library, Indianapolis. The most complete biographical source is Joan Jensen's sketch in *Notable American Women*, vol. 1 (1971), but also useful are Eliza M. Mosher's article in *Medical Woman's Journal* 31 (Jan. 1924): 14–16; Margaret Elizabeth Martin, "Dr. C. Annette Buckel, the 'Little Major,'" *California Historical Society Quarterly* 19 (Mar. 1940): 74–76; and Adelaide Brown, "The History of the Development of Women in Medicine in California," *California and Western Medicine* 23 (May 1925): 579–82. For Buckel's Civil War work see Elvira J. Powers, *Hospital Pencillings* (1866), pp. 95, 129, 141, 194, 197, 200–201. On her Boston and New York work see Annie S. Daniel, "A Cautious Experiment," *Medical Woman's Journal* 46 (Oct. 1939): 295–99, 309, and Agnes C. Vietor, *A Woman's Quest: The Life of Marie E. Zakrzewska* (1924). Also see the *Annual Reports* of the New England Hospital for Women and Children (1866–1877) and those of the Pacific Dispensary for Women and Children (1881–1888); *A Sketch of the Origin and Work of the Home Club Milk Commission in Oakland, California* (pamphlet, c. 1905); and the *San Francisco Call*, 4 May 1894. On the Buckel Foundation see Stanford University, *Annual Report of the President* (1915), pp. 50–51. A death notice is in the *San Francisco Call*, 18 Aug. 1912.

SANDRA VARNEY MACMAHON

BUCKHAM, John Wright (5 Nov. 1864–30 Mar. 1945), theologian, was born in Burlington, Vermont, the son of Matthew Henry Buckham, a president of the University of Vermont, and Elizabeth Wright. Buckham studied at the University of Vermont where he was influenced by Kantian professor Henry A. P. Torrey. Following his graduation in 1885, Buckham enrolled in Andover Theological Seminary where he absorbed "Progressive Orthodoxy," the distinctive trinitarian theology emphasizing divine immanence and religious experience that was then being expounded by the Andover Liberals, the faculty who had recently wrested control of the institution away from the previous generation of Edwardsean traditionalists. Buckham graduated from Andover in 1888 and accepted a call to the Second Congregational Church in Conway, New Hampshire; it was a tiny, mountainous parish still supported by denominational home mission funds. Buckham's ordination there in August 1888 was controversial; his endorsement of universal rather than limited salvation led to a split vote in the ordination council, and one neighboring pastor refused him the right hand of fellowship. The parishioners, however, embraced him proudly. On New Year's Day 1889 he married Helen E. Willard; they had three children.

In 1890 he moved to the Crombie Street Church in Salem, Massachusetts. There he enlarged his philosophical idealism and theological liberalism by studying the writings of Josiah Royce, F. D. Maurice, and Edward Caird. His early theological articles led the Pacific School of Religion in Berkeley, California, to offer him its Chair of Christian Theology in 1903. He accepted with the understanding that he would have "entire liberty of thought and utterance" (Ferm, p. 94). Buckham found the school's broad, progressive outlook congenial, and he remained there until his retirement in 1937.

Buckham's California years were productive ones as his reputation and publications increased together. His first important theological work, *Christ and the Eternal Order*, appeared in 1906. In it, he pondered how Christianity could center on a single, historical Jesus and still speak to all human cultures. Starting from the Johannine concept of *logos*, or Word, Buckham argued that because the eternal Word had become flesh in Jesus of Nazareth, it was possible to claim universal significance. Buckham also benefited from the intellectual bonds he established with philosophers at the University of California, Berkeley. George H. Howison, in particular, was important to his choice of personalism as a philosophical starting point. Buckham's admiration of personalism, a form of idealism that made personality or selfhood the basis of ultimate reality, increased as he pursued the concept in the works of George Herbert Palmer, Borden Bowne, Hermann Lotze, James Seth, and Josiah

Royce. Thereafter, personality became the central concept in Buckham's publications. His well-received *Personality and the Christian Ideal* (1909) and his Taylor Lectures at Yale in 1914 each advanced personality as a resolution of the problem of reality. God was the "Supreme Person," each human being was a "developing person," and Jesus was the "ideal divine-human person." Buckham made personality the precondition of religious experience in his *Mysticism and Modern Life* (1915).

In anticipation of the tercentenary of the Plymouth Colony, Buckham undertook a history of New England theology. Published in 1919, *Progressive Religious Thought in America* recounted the freeing of theology from "the somber shades" of Edwardsean Calvinism by innovators like Horace Bushnell and the Andover Liberals. Now, in the aftermath of World War I, Buckham admitted that the liberals had underestimated the "flinty factuality" of evil and sin. "Not only did the New Theology allow its optimism to obscure the enormity of existing evils," he wrote, "but it did not recognize to the full the patient effort and suffering necessary for their eradication" (p. 318). He called, therefore, for "a *new* New Theology" that would study "religion as a whole," focus on religious experience, incorporate the results of religious psychology, develop links between personality and community, and articulate the ethical demands of Christianity. This was a reevaluation of his liberal idealism, not an abandonment; he remained convinced that "Pure Personality is the conception of God toward which theology is tending" (p. 334). Buckham continued to explore the theological dimensions of personalism in *Religion as Experience* (1922). Although he generally considered the insights of psychology helpful, and found William James's views on religious experience particularly valuable, in *Personality and Psychology* (1924) he challenged the radical empiricism of behaviorism and psychoanalysis, which he believed undermined personality.

During the late 1920s and 1930s, Buckham's goal was "to reinterpret the Christian conception of God as Supreme Personality under the analogy that Jesus made the central and supremely vital symbol for God—Divine Fatherhood" (Ferm, p. 99), and he explored this theme in *The Humanity of God* (1928) and in *Christianity and Personality* (1936). Reflecting on his accomplishments in a 1932 autobiography, Buckham argued that personalism held two advantages. First, it was "a refutation of Naturalism." By promoting a spiritual interpretation of Nature, it permitted humans to "resist dehumanization" and allowed Nature to become "the plastic medium of Divine revelation." Second, personalism was "a furtherer and purifier of Humanism." It strengthened the social ideals that were implicit in humanism while clarifying humanity's need for a "Source transcending itself" and a "moral Perfection infinitely above its own" (Ferm, pp. 100–101).

After he retired from teaching, Buckham served as president of the John Muir Society, a group committed to wilderness preservation, and continued to write theology. A final book, *The Inner World*, appeared in 1941. At one level, it was a recapitulation of all he had written and a reaffirmation of the theological liberalism and philosophical idealism he had championed since the 1880s. At another level, it was very much a book for the moment, illustrating how world events and the neo-orthodox theology of the Swiss theologian Karl Barth had reshaped, but not replaced, that earlier liberalism. As he watched Nazism and war spread over Europe, Buckham had a more vivid "sense of the reality of racial and individual *sinfulness*," and he was grateful to Barthian theology for its "wholesome rebuke to the easygoing humanistic liberalism of recent theology" (pp. 63–64). Unlike the Barthians, however, he refused to support war, primarily because of his supreme confidence in the spiritual power of "victorious love," love that "goes out to meet and vanquish man's relentless foes—one and all" (pp. 268–69). More than anything else, the European crisis convinced Buckham that the need to value personality and to affirm the worth and freedom of the individual had never been greater. Sobered, saddened by a world at war, Buckham nevertheless remained, at the time of his death in Berkeley, California, what he had been throughout his life, a leading exponent of the philosophical idealism and Christocentric theology that dominated American liberal Protestantism at the end of the nineteenth and the beginning of the twentieth centuries.

• One portfolio of Buckham papers, relating to his publication, with G. M. Stratton, of *George Holmes Howison, Philosopher and Teacher: A Selection from His Writings* (1934), is in the Bancroft Library, University of California, Berkeley. An autobiography, "From Philosophy to Theology," is in vol. 1 of Vergilius Ferm, ed., *Contemporary American Theology: Theological Autobiographies* (1932). Buckham's works also include a devotional aid, *Whence Cometh Help* (1902), as well as *John Knox McLean, a Biography* (1914). His inaugural lecture at the Pacific School of Religion came out as a small booklet, *An Estimate of Evolution Theology* (1905). With J. G. Goodrich he compiled his father's discourses as *The Very Elect: Baccalaureate Sermons and Occasional Addresses of Matthew Henry Buckham, President of the University of Vermont* (1912).

CHARLES D. CASHDOLLAR

BUCKINGHAM, Joseph Tinker (21 Dec. 1779–11 Apr. 1861), editor and publisher, was born in Windham, Connecticut, the son of Nehemiah Tinker and Mary Huntington, tavernkeepers. For reasons that remain obscure, he was baptized "Joseph Buckingham" after his maternal grandmother but in 1804 legally made "Tinker" his middle name. Although Buckingham faced early poverty, owing to the death of his father in 1783 and to lingering revolutionary war debts against the estate, he acquired a scant but serviceable education. He occasionally attended the local district school while his mother unsuccessfully struggled to keep the tavern and to support the family as a seamstress. He received his principal instruction, however, from her. After the winter of 1785–1786, during which the family had to rely on charity, Buckingham was indentured by the overseers of the poor to a farmer on the outskirts of town. He tried to get to the village school, but, according to his own calculations, only managed to do so from about twelve days to a few months a year. He attributed most of his education in this period to self-study and to the encouragement given to devotional reading by the farmer's family, who like his mother, stressed the fundamentals of Congregationalism.

With the expiration of his indenture in 1795, Buckingham embarked on a career as a printer. His appetite for the trade was whetted while watching a Windham compositor at work, and he secured an apprenticeship in Walpole, New Hampshire, in 1796. He became dissatisfied with the leisurely work rhythms of the shop and transferred the next year to the Greenfield, Massachusetts, *Gazette*, and then, for a few months in 1799, to the Northampton firms of Andrew Wright and, subsequently, William Butler. He left for Boston in early 1800; after a three-week stint at Manning & Loring, he moved to Thomas & Andrews, the city's principal book printing establishment, where he remained until 1803.

Buckingham acquired an interest in drama in the summer of 1803 when, because of ill health, he became a prompter at theaters in Salem, Massachusetts, and Providence, Rhode Island. On his return to printing work, Thomas & Andrews gave him a five-year contract to run the shop, with the stipulation that he could use the facilities for his own projects. The first of these reflected his experiences in the theater: the *Polyanthos* (Dec. 1805–Sept. 1807; Feb. 1812–Sept. 1814), a pioneering monthly of dramatic criticism and biography (mostly written by him).

Another abortive effort, the *Ordeal*, a Federalist weekly (7 Jan. 1809–1 July 1809), ushered in financially difficult times for Buckingham. Having married Melinda Alvord in 1805, shortly after his promotion to manager at Thomas & Andrews, and having a young family to support (he and his wife would have thirteen children), Buckingham jumped at his employers' offer to sell him the printing office. Lack of work and too much speculative publishing, however, caused him to lose everything. After teaching school briefly (c. 1814–1815), he became an overseer—"nothing more than a journeyman, except in responsibility," according to him—in the printing firm of West & Richardson. The partners allowed him to use their equipment to publish Noah Worcester's monthly *Christian Disciple* (May 1813–Dec. 1818) and quarterly *Friend of Peace* (1815–1827).

With backing from prominent Freemasons, including Samuel L. Knapp, Buckingham published the weekly *New-England Galaxy* (10 Oct. 1817–14 Nov. 1828), "chiefly of a literary and miscellaneous character, eschewing entirely all partizanship [sic]." (For a time the weekly was called the *New-England Galaxy and Masonic Magazine*.) Enlisting prominent Boston writers like Susanna Rowson, Edward Everett, and William Austin, the *Galaxy* became known for its editorial independence and bold opinions.

The latter led to several lawsuits for libel. The most important of these was brought by the Methodist minister John N. Maffitt, accused by the paper of obscuring his origins, plagiarizing sermons, sexually harassing women, declaring his infidelity (disbelief in Christianity), ridiculing congregants, fomenting family quarrels, and other transgressions. Buckingham spoke in his own defense at the 1822 trial, presided over by Josiah Quincy (1772–1864), who admitted as evidence the truth of the charges—"a doctrine, which however novel in the practice of the courts," Buckingham declaimed, "is the one which corresponds with the wishes, the feelings, and the good sense of every man in the nation."

Shortly after his court victory, Buckingham founded and edited the daily *Courier* (2 Mar. 1824–24 June 1848). He devoted the paper to the American system, especially to the protective tariff, and even served for a time as Washington correspondent. The *Courier*, a liberal Whig newspaper, first published such important works as James Russell Lowell's "The Present Crisis" and the first series of the "Biglow Papers." In 1848, after several lean years, Buckingham left the newspaper because he could not support the Whig presidential candidate, Zachary Taylor.

Before Buckingham's retirement from journalism, he and his son Edwin launched the *New England Magazine*, a literary monthly (July 1831–Dec. 1834). Joseph Story, Richard Hildreth, Oliver Wendell Holmes, Henry Wadsworth Longfellow, among other local luminaries, graced its pages. With the death of his son at sea in 1833, Buckingham took over full editorship but found the task so onerous that he sold out to Samuel Gridley Howe and John O. Sargent a year later.

Buckingham's activities extended beyond the editorial office. In 1810 he became a member of the Massachusetts Charitable Mechanics Association and served in varying capacities, including three years as president. He also held high offices in the Bunker Hill Monument Association, Middlesex Agricultural Society, and the Anniversary Cattle Show and Fair. He was elected state representative from Boston in 1828 and 1831–1833, Cambridge in 1836 and 1838–1839, and senator from Middlesex County in 1847–1848, 1850–1851. During the course of his political life, Buckingham moved from Federalist, to Whig, to Native American, and finally, as senator, to the Free Soil and Democratic parties. Throughout the last decade of his life he wrote occasional pieces for journals; his homage to the early press, *Specimens of Newspaper Literature* (1850); and his classic *Personal Memoirs and Recollections of Editorial Life* (1852). He died in Cambridge, Massachusetts.

"Hypocrisy and cant in all their forms, were always objects of my supreme and immitigable hatred," Buckingham concluded, looking back over his life. "Man-worship and party discipline were alike objects of ineffable contempt." In his vigorous espousal of

First Amendment rights, his commitment to objectivity and nonpartisan editorializing, and his inclusion of cultural and economic criticism in periodicals, Buckingham helped set the direction for future American journalism.

• Scattered letters from Buckingham are housed at the Massachusetts Historical Society in Boston. Also see Gary John Kornblith, *From Artisans to Businessmen: Master Mechanics in New England, 1789–1850*, vol. 2 (1983), pp. 291–349. Buckingham's writings also appear in his *Trial: Commonwealth versus J. T. Buckingham* (1822 and subsequent editions), *Devotional Exercises for Common Schools* (1842), and various pamphlet versions of his addresses, such as *Book for the Times* (1844) and the Free Soil *Speeches of Hon. Joseph T. Buckingham, Charles M. Ellis, Esq., Hon. Anson Burlingame* (1852). Richardson Wright, "Buckingham of the Galaxy," American Lodge of Research Free and Accepted Masons *Transactions* 3 (1938–1939): 647–49, is the only biography that adds details to Buckingham's own reminiscences. For a rich characterization, see Frederic Hudson, *Journalism in the United States, 1690–1872* (1873). On music criticism in his theater columns, see Nicholas Tawa, "Buckingham's Musical Commentaries in Boston," *New England Quarterly* 51 (1978): 333–47, and "Musical Criticism and the Terrible Mr. Buckingham," *New England Galaxy* 20 (1978): 3–11. Obituaries are in the Boston *Transcript*, 11 Apr. 1861, and the Boston *Courier*, 12 Apr. 1861.

RONALD J. ZBORAY

BUCKINGHAM, William Alfred (28 May 1804–5 Feb. 1875), governor and U.S. senator, was born in Lebanon, Connecticut, the son of Samuel Buckingham, a prosperous farmer, and Joanna Matson. After a common school education and labor on his father's farm, Buckingham entered his uncle's dry goods store in Norwich, Connecticut, where he developed a strong aptitude for business in its managerial and marketing aspects. In 1830 he married Eliza Ripley; they had one child. Encouraged by his family, Buckingham established his own dry goods firm in Norwich, and under his careful management, it became the most successful enterprise of its kind in southeastern Connecticut.

Always on the outlook for profitable ventures, Buckingham invested his surplus capital in the manufacture and sale of ingrain carpets in 1830 and in 1848 in the manufacture of rubber products, a new industry that sprang up after Charles Goodyear's discovery of vulcanizing raw rubber. The major organizer of the Hayward Rubber Company in nearby Colchester, Buckingham soon devoted himself entirely to this enterprise. In half a dozen years he had become a rich man, who could spare some of his time for nonbusiness pursuits.

Politics had always interested Buckingham. A strong advocate of Henry Clay's American system, with its tariff protection for manufacturers and its emphasis on internal improvements, he joined the Whig party in 1836. He was elected mayor of Norwich in 1849 and again in 1856. Although a leading figure in Connecticut's Whig organization, he was never associated with its nativist tilt. Thus he did not follow many of his associates into Know Nothing ranks when the Whig party began to break up after the Compromise of 1850.

An earnest opponent of slavery and especially of its extension into the territories, Buckingham joined the Republican party in 1855. He served as an elector for John C. Frémont, who received Connecticut's vote for president in 1856. Two years later Buckingham was nominated for governor on the Republican ticket. Cast as a moderate on the slavery issue and trusted as an honest businessman, Buckingham won the election with a substantial majority. In 1860 he again ran for governor in an election that was closely watched as a bellwether of political trends, with the Lower South threatening secession if the Republicans triumphed in the presidential campaign. Buckingham was elected by the slender majority of 541 votes.

After the Lower South seceded during the early winter of 1860–1861, Buckingham proclaimed a state of emergency in Connecticut. At the same time he ordered his state's quartermaster general to begin purchasing equipment for 5,000 men, subject to approval of the legislature. Hampered by constitutional provisions that gave the legislature sole power over the militia and its pay, rations, and equipment, Buckingham could do little to put the militia in any state of immediate readiness.

When the war began with the attack on Fort Sumter, Connecticut's arsenals were virtually empty, and what equipment they contained was obsolete. On his account, Buckingham borrowed funds for the procurement of military supplies. He directed the recruitment, equipment, and organization of three ninety-day regiments to meet Lincoln's call for 75,000 men. Less than a month after Fort Sumter, the First Connecticut Regiment, fully equipped, was en route to Washington. Thereafter, the state enlisted a volunteer force equivalent to more than 48,000 three-year enlistees out of a total population of less than half a million.

Primarily concerned with raising and transporting troops, Buckingham's staff, acting under revised militia laws, provided uniforms, muskets, and other related supplies. The federal government would reimburse at a later date a part of the state's outlays. Both the Norwich *Bulletin* and the *New York Times* obituaries (6 Feb. 1875) judged Buckingham's wartime administration to be one of the best in the Union. Secretary of the Navy Gideon Welles, more acerbic than not in his estimate of public people, wrote that Buckingham "made an excellent chief magistrate for the period." Lincoln said of his wartime role, "The Connecticut regiments give me no trouble. Governor Buckingham sends them fully equipped for any emergency." A moderate to radical Republican in politics during the war, he headed what was known as the state faction that opposed the more conservative congressional group. In the forefront of those politicians who urged the total abolition of slavery, he supported unrestricted male suffrage for former slaves and Congressional Reconstruction.

In 1866 Buckingham declined renomination for governor, and two years later he was elected to the

U.S. Senate. His term in Washington was an undistinguished one. Generally supportive of Ulysses S. Grant's administration, Buckingham differed, however, with the president on his efforts to acquire Santo Domingo. Buckingham was not involved in the scandals that surrounded postwar Washington, yet he did not take a firm stand against corruption in the federal government. As chairman of a special committee to investigate abuses in the New York Customs House and as a party loyalist, he turned in a majority report that found no evidence of graft.

It was as governor that Buckingham established his reputation as a gifted executive and administrator. He served for eight years as chief executive of Connecticut, longer than any of his predecessors except the revolutionary war governor Jonathan Trumbull (1710–1785), to whom he was often compared. He died at his home in Norwich, Connecticut.

• Unfortunately, few of Buckingham's personal papers have survived. His official correspondence is in the Connecticut State Library. Some letters crop up in the papers of Mark Howard, Joseph R. Hawley, and Gideon Welles at the Connecticut Historical Society and the Library of Congress. Rev. Samuel G. Buckingham, *The Life of William A. Buckingham, the War Governor of Connecticut* (1894), contains some pertinent information but casts little light on the governor's career. For Connecticut politics before and during the Civil War, the best works are Richard Purcell, *Connecticut in Transition* (1918); Carroll J. Noonan, *Nativism in Connecticut 1829–1860* (1938); and J. Robert Lane, *Political History of Connecticut during the Civil War* (1941). A contemporary study is William A. Croffut and John M. Morris, *Military and Civil History of Connecticut* (1868), but most of this work concerns itself with the state's military contributions rather than the governor's role. For more attention to Buckingham's leadership and his concerns about the impact of the war effort on the civilian population, see John Niven, *Connecticut for the Union* (1965) and *Gideon Welles, Lincoln's Secretary of the Navy* (1974).

JOHN NIVEN

BUCKLAND, William (14 Aug. 1734–Nov. or Dec. 1774), craftsman, designer, and architect, was born in Oxford, England, the son of Francis Buckland, a small property-owning farmer, and Mary Dunsdown. On 5 April 1748 he was apprenticed for a term of seven years to a London joiner, James Buckland, who may have been his uncle. Joinery, the craft of smoothly fitting together small pieces of wood, was taught according to rules and standards established by a trade organization, which was organized along the lines of a traditional medieval guild. In eighteenth-century England formal academic architectural training was absent, and it was primarily out of the ranks of the building trades that ambitious men, armed with drawing skills, rose to claim the title of architect.

William Buckland's first chance to follow this path occurred in 1755. On 4 August of that year Buckland signed an indenture with Thomson Mason, brother of the prominent Virginia plantation owner George Mason. Thomson Mason was then building a large dwelling called "Gunston Hall" in Fairfax County. Although the exterior of the house was already erected, Mason required the services of a skilled artisan to ornament the interior according to prevailing London architectural taste, which scholars now refer to as English Palladianism. During his four years of service at Gunston Hall Buckland designed and supervised the construction of two exterior porches, the interior woodwork, and the relocation of doorways and an ancillary stair. The most important interior space of Gunston Hall, Buckland's Palladian formal parlor, is composed of a lively combination of classical details. The Chinese dining room, with its fish-scale and strapwork carving, demonstrates a mid-eighteenth-century fascination with the decorative styles of oriental cultures. Influenced by the published designs of Thomas Chippendale, the ornamental scheme of the dining room may be the first extensive use of *chinoiserie* in the North American British colonies. Buckland's role at Gunston Hall appears to have been one of directing and designing; the carving was executed by another indentured servant from England, William Bernard Sears.

In 1983, during investigation of Gunston Hall's structural fabric, a set of very small sketches of courthouses was discovered behind some paneling. Convincingly attributed to Buckland, these pencil drawings demonstrate the immigrant's ability to combine cosmopolitan architectural features with the requirements and traditions of colonial Virginia courthouse design. Upon Buckland's completion of his term of service in 1759, Mason wrote on the back of the indenture that Buckland was a master of both the theory and the practice of carpentry and joinery. A year later Buckland was paid by the Truro Parish vestry, of which Mason was a member, for completing a house for their minister. Around 1760 Buckland married Mary Moore; they had three children.

In 1761 Buckland moved to Richmond County, Virginia, and established himself as a successful independent builder and designer. By assembling a workshop of capable indentured servants, by training apprentices, and by obtaining the patronage of wealthy landowners, he was able to secure commissions ranging from elegant private interiors to utilitarian public projects, pigeon houses, mantlepieces, and furniture. Unfortunately, little of his work from this period survives. Based on documentary evidence and a small portion of a cornice, it is believed that Buckland was responsible for the design of the now lost interior ornamentation of "Mount Airy," John Tayloe's Palladian villa complex near the Rappahannock River. Academic style was less of a priority in Buckland's public work, which included alterations to a prison and construction of a workhouse, both for the Richmond County authorities, and the erection of a minister's dwelling for Lunenburg Parish, completed by July of 1767.

Buckland's move to Annapolis, Maryland, in 1771 can be seen as a continuation of earlier patronage and as a search for new opportunities in an urban environment. Here Buckland first began to call himself an architect. The move was likely prompted by Edward Lloyd IV, John Tayloe's son-in-law, who engaged Buckland to finish a three-story house purchased from Samuel Chase in July 1771. Buckland was responsible for most of the decorative scheme including the entrance frontispiece, in the form of *serliana*, and the columnar screen in the entrance salon, a device that was inspired by Palladio's drawings of the Roman baths. Beyond the screen is an elaborate imperial, or double cantilevered, staircase illuminated by another *serliana*.

The Hammond-Harwood House, begun in 1774 for Mathias Hammond, demonstrated Buckland's ability as a designer of fashionable exterior architecture. The five-part massing of the dwelling reveals a knowledge of the small Palladian villa form as interpreted from the mid-eighteenth-century publications of Robert Morris. The polygonal projecting walls of the end units, also from Morris, were novel features in the colonies; Thomas Jefferson drew them when he visited Annapolis. Buckland died before the Hammond House was complete, and it is believed that his craftsmen finished the interior ornamentation. Buckland's Annapolis workshop also produced furniture and contributed to the creation of the State House, but the precise nature of his role in the latter is undetermined. In early November 1774 he had prepared plans and elevations for the Caroline County, Maryland, courthouse and was in the process of accepting bids for its construction. By mid-December Buckland's estate was in probate. The exact date, cause, and place of his death are not known.

Despite an accusation made by a contemporary that he was financially careless, Buckland was able to accumulate a respectable amount of real and personal property during the course of his career. The inventory taken after his death shows that in addition to two city lots with houses, outbuildings, and comfortable furnishings, he owned six indentured servants, five slaves, four chests of carpenter's and carver's tools, and fifteen architecture books from which he had derived many of his designs. Charles Willson Peale's portrait of the architect, showing Buckland drawing the plan and elevation of Hammond House, was begun in 1774 but not finished until 1787. The painting, now at Yale University, is clear evidence of Buckland's own view of his rising stature within colonial society.

Buckland's worldly success as a designer and architect was the result of his combination of business acumen and artistic talent. By organizing a labor force of skilled craftsmen, some of whom went on to achieve independent careers in their own right, he was able to undertake major colonial building projects and establish a reputation among the monied class. Buckland, however, was not the only reliable builder in the Tidewater; his particular advantage lay in his London training. By carrying cosmopolitan English Palladian motifs to the colonies and adapting them to provincial circumstances, Buckland could cater to the vanities of wealthy clients who were eager to display their fashionable taste and their own relatively new high status.

• Only one of Buckland's letters, which includes a solicitation for work, survives and is located at the Virginia Historical Society. The standard biography of Buckland remains Rosamond R. Beirne and John H. Scarff, *William Buckland, 1734–1774: Architect of Virginia and Maryland* (1958), which provides transcriptions of important documents but erroneously attributes many buildings to the builder. Barbara Allston Brand, "William Buckland: Architect in Annapolis," *Building by the Book* 2 (1986): 65–100, corrects those attributions and also examines Buckland's design sources. A specialized study of Buckland's workshop and carvers is found in two articles by Luke Beckerdite, "William Buckland and William Bernard Sears: The Designer and the Carver," and "William Buckland Reconsidered: Architectural Carving in Chesapeake Maryland, 1771–1774," both in the *Journal of Early Southern Decorative Arts* 8 (1982): 6–41, 42–89. The Gunston Hall sketches are analyzed by Carl R. Lounsbury in "'An Elegant and Commodious Building': William Buckland and the Design of the Prince William County Courthouse," *Journal of the Society of Architectural Historians* 46 (1987): 228–40.

BARBARA BURLISON MOONEY

BUCKLEY, James Monroe (16 Dec. 1836–8 Feb. 1920), Methodist clergyman and journalist, was born in Rahway, New Jersey, the son of John Buckley, a Methodist clergyman, and Abbie Lonsdale Monroe. When Buckley was five years old his father died, and the family went to live with his maternal grandfather. The boy was plagued with ill health, suffering from the same pulmonary consumption that claimed his father. Aware of this genetic frailty, he took steps to strengthen his physical condition, especially with breathing exercises and long walks in the open air. Slender financial resources did not provide much formal education, but as a teenager Buckley studied for a few years at a New Jersey academy known as the Pennington Seminary. In 1856 he entered Wesleyan University, but college discipline apparently had little attraction for him; he spent much of the year campaigning for John C. Frémont, presidential candidate nominated by the newly organized Republican party. Still, experience in public speaking showed that he had talent in that direction, and by 1858 he decided to enter the ministry.

Buckley's first pastorate was a small Methodist congregation in Exeter, New Hampshire, where he preached, led the singing, gave doctrinal instruction, and kept the financial records. During that year he also read theology and classical literature with private tutors who lived nearby. In 1859 the New Hampshire Conference ordained him as elder and moved his post to Dover, then in 1861 to Manchester. During these early assignments Buckley gained a reputation for sound executive abilities and effective preaching. In 1863 he transferred to a large parish in Detroit, Michigan. There he married Eliza A. Burns in 1864; she died two years later. In 1874 he married Sarah Isabella French Staples; they had two children. In 1883 Sarah died, and three years later Buckley married Adelaide Shackford Hill.

Buckley and his family moved to Brooklyn, New York, where he occupied a pulpit from 1866 to 1869, then to Stamford, Connecticut (1869–1872), and back to Brooklyn (1878–1880). This progression of successful parish assignments might have continued indefinitely, but in 1880 the General Conference, meeting at Cincinnati, Ohio, elected him editor of the *Christian Advocate*, largest and oldest weekly publication of the Methodist church. Over the next thirty-two years he wielded a great deal of influence both in his own church and with the general populace through editorials in this the best known of all religious journals. In an early issue (3 June 1880) he announced that as a Christian advocate he would vindicate Christian principles against the misrepresentations of infidelity; as a Protestant advocate he would vindicate the refusal to accept the claims of the Roman Catholic church to be the only true, legitimate form of Christianity; as a Methodist advocate he could vindicate the doctrines and discipline of his church, its institutions and ceremonies, demonstrating the benefits of their use. Buckley produced a phenomenal amount of material over the years, furnishing not only religious news but addressing social, intellectual, and moral questions of the day. One of his devices for keeping readers' interest was to publish articles on a single subject in a series. Some of his more notable efforts along that line were dozens of essays on temperance, education, labor-management struggles, Mormons, health and exercise, Christian Science, and travelogs.

While pursuing his vocation in New York City, Buckley traveled extensively. Some of his articles related a panoply of sights and impressions that he collected in Europe, Africa, and Asia. Such wide and varied knowledge, together with a retentive memory and voracious reading habits, stood him in good stead as commentator and critic. He attended every General Conference from 1872 to 1912 and came to exercise great power at those national conventions. His influence as denominational statesman became such that one of his honorific nicknames was "bishop maker." He also attended ecumenical conferences in London, England (1881), Washington, D.C. (1891), and Toronto, Ontario, Canada (1911). He also complemented decades of journalistic writing with scholarly treatments of his church's history, writing the fifth volume of the American Church History Series (1896). He retired as editor of the *Christian Advocate* in 1912. He died in Morristown, New Jersey. As editor, historian, and parliamentarian Buckley embodied American Methodism in his day as much as anyone could outside the episcopacy.

• Buckley's publications include *Oats or Wild Oats? Common Sense for Young Men* (1885), *Travels in Three Continents* (1895), *A History of the Methodists in the United States* (1896), *Extemporaneous Oratory for Professional and Amateur Speakers* (1898), *The Wrong and Peril of Woman Suffrage* (1909), *Theory and Practice of Foreign Missions* (1911), and *Constitutional and Parliamentary History of the Methodist Episcopal Church* (1912). Biographical information can be found in George Preston Mains, *James Monroe Buckley* (1917). An obituary is in the *New York Times*, 9 Feb. 1920.

HENRY WARNER BOWDEN

BUCKLEY, Oliver Ellsworth (8 Aug. 1887–14 Dec. 1959), telecommunications engineer, was born in Sloan, Iowa, the son of William Doubleday Buckley, a lawyer and school superintendent, and Sarah Elizabeth Jeffrey, secretary to her husband. Buckley's introduction to telecommunications came in 1903 when he went to work as a maintenance man for the local telephone exchange while completing high school. He studied mathematics and physics at Grinnell College and received his B.S. degree in 1909. He then taught physics at Grinnell for a year before enrolling in the graduate physics program at Cornell University; in 1914 he received his Ph.D. in physics. He married Clara Louise Lane that year; they had four children. On completing his Ph.D. Buckley joined the research department of the Western Electric Company, a subsidiary of the American Telephone and Telegraph Company (AT&T).

Buckley's first engineering projects involved thermionic vacuum tubes, electronic devices that amplified signals in the radio-telephone systems of the day. He invented the mercury-vapor diffusion pump, which evacuated air from a vacuum tube faster and more completely than previous means, and the ionization manometer, a device that measures the degree of vacuum in a vacuum tube. When the United States entered World War I in 1917, Buckley concentrated on developing a means to track German submarines by detecting the noise of their engines and propellors. Later that year he joined the U.S. Army as a first lieutenant; in September, as part of the American Expeditionary Force, he was promoted to major and assigned to the Signal Corps' Division of Research and Inspection in Paris, France. He quickly realized that the existing transatlantic telegraph cables, laid in 1865, could no longer handle the ever-increasing communications traffic between the Old World and the New. When he returned to Western Electric in late 1918, he convinced his superiors to let him try to solve this problem.

Buckley reasoned that transmission speeds were slowed in submarine cables because capacitance in the cables' wires caused them to store some of the electric charge being fed to them rather than transmitting it. Therefore, if he could "load" or increase inductance, which has an effect opposite to that of capacitance, he could speed up transmission significantly. In 1920 he discovered that wrapping a cable's wires with a thin ribbon of heat-treated Permalloy, an iron-nickel alloy invented by Western Electric's Gustav Elmen, provided a continuous source of magnetic loading, thereby increasing transmission speed fourfold. Over the next four years Buckley supervised the successful testing of the loaded cable and invented several pieces of terminal equipment to optimize its performance. In 1924 the first transatlantic loaded submarine telegraph cable was laid between New York City and the Azores Islands.

In 1925 Buckley became associated with Bell Telephone Laboratories (BTL) when the research operations of AT&T and Western Electric were consolidated, and in 1927 he was promoted to assistant director of research. Having completed the telegraph cable project, he turned his attention to developing a transatlantic telephone cable. He devised a method for seeding a single-channel cable with vacuum tube amplifiers in order to boost the signal from one side of the Atlantic Ocean to the other; however, the project was deemed economically infeasible and dropped. Undaunted, Buckley concentrated on adapting the multichannel carrier transmission system AT&T used on land for service in a much shorter submarine cable. In 1930 he oversaw the installation of a six-channel telephone cable with terminal amplifiers linking Havana, Cuba, and Key West, Florida. Buoyed by this success, he returned to the development of an economically feasible transatlantic telephone cable. The biggest challenge was satisfying AT&T's requirements that the system carry multiple channels and that its mid-ocean components operate virtually maintenance-free for the first twenty years. Despite the ever-increasing load of management responsibility that accompanied his promotions to director of research in 1933, executive vice president in 1936, and president and chief executive officer in 1940, Buckley spent a portion of almost every day working on these problems; at last, the first transatlantic submarine telephone cable was installed between the United States and England in 1956.

Buckley took charge of BTL on the eve of the United States's entry into World War II. He devoted almost 80 percent of the company's manpower to designing new weapons systems, particularly radar, for the U.S. Office of Scientific Research and Development. His expertise in administering BTL's defense contracts earned him a presidential citation and the U.S. Medal for Merit in 1946. Although BTL continued to do military work after the war, Buckley's insistence that its research concentrate on peacetime applications resulted in important telecommunications developments such as the transistor, the microwave radio relay system, and long-distance direct dialing. In 1951, during the Korean War, Buckley resigned as BTL's president to become its chairman of the board and to accept positions as chairman of the Science Advisory Committee and science advisor to the Office of Defense Mobilization. Poor health forced him to retire from all three positions in 1952; however, he continued to serve as a board member or trustee of several charitable organizations, including the Thomas Alva Edison Foundation and the National Multiple Sclerosis Society. He died in Newark, New Jersey.

Buckley was elected to the National Academy of Sciences in 1937. He was chairman of the Engineering Foundation Board from 1939 to 1942 and vice president of the American Institute of Electrical Engineers from 1946 to 1948. He received the American Institute of Electrical Engineers' Edison Medal in 1954. He was a member of the American Physical Society's policy and finance committees and was honored annually between 1952 and 1977 by the presentation of its Oliver E. Buckley Solid State Physics Prize.

Buckley contributed to American society in two ways. As a telecommunications engineer he was the driving force behind the invention of submarine cables for telegraphy and telephony. As an administrator he oversaw the emergence of BTL as a major research center for telecommunications and defense technology.

• A good biography of Buckley, including a complete bibliography of his works and a list of his patents, is Mervin J. Kelly, "Oliver Ellsworth Buckley," National Academy of Sciences, *Biographical Memoirs* 37 (1964): 1–32. Obituaries are in the *New York Times*, 15 Dec. 1959, and in *Newsweek* and *Time*, both 28 Dec. 1959.

CHARLES W. CAREY, JR.

BUCKMASTER, Henrietta (c. 1909–26 Apr. 1983), writer and editor, was born Henrietta Henkle in Cleveland, Ohio, the daughter of Rae D. Henkle, a newspaperman, and Pearl Wintermute. Her father moved with his family to New York City to become foreign editor of the *New York Herald*. She attended private schools there—the Friends Seminary and the Brearley School—and in Europe. She refused to give her precise birthdate, but she claimed that she published her first short story at the age of twelve, and in her twenties she began publishing books. Her father had become a book editor, and his publishing house brought out her first two novels: *Tomorrow Is Another Day* (1934), about a young woman who runs off to New York to achieve literary recognition, and *His End Was His Beginning* (1936), set in Vienna during the era of World War I. She wrote her many novels and historical works under the pseudonym Henrietta Buckmaster. She was married to Peter John Stephens, an Englishman, during the 1940s.

In 1945–1946 Buckmaster went to Paris as a representative of *Woman's Day* to attend the International Women's Conference, sponsored by the Comité d'Initiative Internationale. There she was one of about eight hundred women from forty-five countries, meeting in the ruins of World War II to promote world peace and to improve the lives of women and children around the globe. While in Europe she went to Germany to write articles on the survivors of concentration camps. These activities were consistent with her commitment to the downtrodden, past and present, as was her involvement with the Committee for Equal Justice for Mrs. Recy Taylor in 1944–1945. A black woman from Alabama, Taylor was raped by three young white men who escaped prosecution, and Buckmaster, a co-chair on the committee, wrote a preface to a pamphlet on the case, authored by her kindred spirit Earl Conrad.

By the early 1940s, indeed, Buckmaster displayed a particular interest in African Americans in slavery and freedom. *Let My People Go: The Story of the Underground Railroad and the Growth of the Abolition Movement* (1941) was the first of her books to explore relations of race and class in the nineteenth century. In it she contrasted the colonists and later immigrants from England, Germany, Ireland, and Italy, who came to

America "to escape oppression," with the Africans, who came "to be oppressed" (p. 1). She took the story to Emancipation and then glanced ahead to the post–Civil War Exodusters, who continued the tradition of escaping oppression by leaving the South. She resumed the story, or filled in the final chapter of her earlier history of African Americans, with *Freedom Bound* (1965), which, relying to a considerable extent on freedmen's sources to depict the Reconstruction era in the South, celebrated the successful accomplishments and failed efforts to forge a biracial democracy in the world that followed slavery.

A 1959 reprint edition of *Let My People Go* occasioned Buckmaster's comment that her book had "tended to fulfill the only valid function of history: the illumination of the present experience." At the high tide of the Civil Rights movement, she picked up that theme in the introduction to *Freedom Bound* when she declared, "This is not an objective book," nor had there ever been an objective book about an era that "demands friends or enemies." History, she claimed, must be "concerned with living" (p. 3).

Buckmaster's books more typically used a novelist's approach to depict historical events and people. *Deep River* (1944), set in Georgia on the eve of secession and the Civil War, focuses on an abolitionist from the mountain South who is married to the daughter of a plantation owner. The man, Simon Bliss, is portrayed as a state legislator who reckons that "the poor black man and the poor white man are held down by the same hand," the slave power (p. 274). Reviewers said that *Deep River* was "full of vitality as well as scholarly research," a historical novel "in which events have moral values"; the book gained wide distribution in an Armed Services edition and won Buckmaster the 1945 Ohioana Award for fiction. *Fire in the Heart* (1948) tells the story of the English actress Fanny Kemble, her marriage to Pierce Butler, a wealthy Georgia planter, and her "fire in the heart" to see slaves set free.

Buckmaster's later books often took other themes and were set in other times and places. Some focused on Elizabethan England, as in *All the Living: A Novel of One Year in the Life of William Shakespeare* (1962). Others took religious themes, including her critically acclaimed *And Walk in Love: A Novel Based on the Life of the Apostle Paul* (1956), which took place in the time of the New Testament and reflected her wish, as she put it, to understand "the metamorphosis of Sauls into Pauls." *Bread from Heaven* (1952) depicts the prejudice a woman encounters when she takes her maimed child to a New England town. Buckmaster also wrote children's books that reflected her major interests and concerns and her desire to reach a younger audience. These include *Flight to Freedom: The Story of the Underground Railroad* (1958); *Walter Raleigh, Man of Two Worlds* (1964); *The Seminole Wars* (1966); and *Women Who Shaped History* (1966).

Most of Buckmaster's novels and historical works reflected her commitment to social change. Even her first publication displayed her central concern that writing exemplify "some particular love of freedom." Despite her many trips to Europe (chiefly Great Britain) and her marriage, she called herself "indisputably American." During her last ten years she lived in Boston and worked as editor of the *Home Forum* or editor of the fine arts and literary page of the *Christian Science Monitor*. She died in a nursing home in Chestnut Hills, Massachusetts.

• The New York Public Library's Schomburg Center for Research in Black Culture has some of Buckmaster's typescripts and correspondence. Darlene Clark Hine supplies an account of Buckmaster's life and an analysis of perhaps her most notable book in an introduction to a reprint of *Let My People Go* (1992). An obituary is in the *New York Times*, 27 Apr. 1983.

PETER WALLENSTEIN

BUCKMINSTER, Joseph Stevens (26 May 1784–9 June 1812), Unitarian minister, was born in Portsmouth, New Hampshire, the son of Joseph Buckminster, a Congregationalist minister, and Sarah Stevens. Buckminster completed his A.B. at Harvard in 1800 and became pastor of the Brattle Street Church in Boston in 1804. Young, passionately eloquent in his preaching, and committed to a more rigorous form of biblical scholarship influenced by the German "higher criticism," Buckminster soon made an enormous impact on Boston intellectual culture.

The extraordinary fervor with which Buckminster was revered in Boston partly resulted from his personal qualities: an emotional intensity—which verged on fragility and manifested itself in an aesthetic turn—combined with piety, a searching intelligence, and a sharp wit. These qualities, which seemed so precociously developed, accorded well with Buckminster's preaching and pastoral duties, and during his short pastorate he cultivated an aura of aesthetic spirituality that marked the Unitarian ministry for decades. But his impact is also explained by the way these qualities embodied his culture's self-conceptions and aspirations, for he was perceived to have enacted the cultural myth of New England's liberals in his establishment of a religion based on human potential and endeavor. Buckminster's rejection of the orthodox Calvinism of his father, and his embracing of the liberal or Arminian theology that had taken a foothold at Harvard College and in eastern Massachusetts, gave dramatic form to the theological shift underlying the establishment of New England Unitarianism. That he came to liberalism despite the consternation of his more conservative father dramatized the sense in which liberalism was for many the result of generational change and sometimes conflict.

The Brattle Street Church, a fashionable and privileged congregation, provided Buckminster with the institutional base to advance the liberal cause on several fronts in the next eight years, before his early death. His sermons, noted for their literary polish and delivered with an extraordinary rhetorical brilliance, presented religion as "an active and progressive principle" that was to be pursued in a life of spiritual self-culture. This vision of the strenuous but harmonious development of the divine capacity of the soul was central to the Unitarian movement and constituted the vision with which Buckminster and other religious liberals countered the Calvinist emphasis on innate depravity. The notion of instantaneous regeneration or salvation became increasingly suspect among the liberals, and Buckminster argued for a demystified view of salvation, presenting it as a gradual process of spiritual development. The process of self-culture as Buckminster and other early Unitarians conceived it included the development of an intense devotionalist piety, a rigorous emphasis on moral action, and a broadened sensibility that included both aesthetic and intellectual development.

Buckminster's commitment to biblical scholarship suggests the importance that he attached to intellectual pursuits as an element of the spiritual life. He explained that recent advances in research rendered the Bible less a single book than a collection of books, each of which had to be assessed within its historical framework, as were the texts of classical antiquity. This represented a serious challenge to the orthodox Calvinists, who were concerned about the undermining of biblical authority by such scholarship. The debate over the limits of intellectual inquiry into the Bible represented one of the central aspects of the Unitarian controversy with Calvinism.

Buckminster's aesthetic and literary sensibilities, traits that had to some extent been held in suspicion by New England's theological establishment, nurtured the Unitarian transformation of the sermon from a form based in doctrinal argument to one that stressed moral principles and concrete applications. Preaching thus began to become a quasi-aesthetic form. Buckminster was an important contributor to the *Monthly Anthology and Boston Review*, one of New England's first intellectual journals, where he published key essays on the new biblical scholarship. His leadership in literary and scholarly causes signified in part the shifting authority of the New England ministry and its correspondingly widening range of cultural activities in an increasingly diverse and complex culture. This transformation of the role of the liberal ministry helps explain the heavy influence of Unitarianism on the formation of American literature in the early nineteenth century.

Actively engaged in his scholarly and ministerial work in Boston, Buckminster succumbed to an acute epileptic attack.

• Buckminster's papers, including his manuscript sermons, are in the Boston Athenaeum. His sister Eliza Buckminster Lee's biography of him and his father is an important source of information: *Memoirs of Rev. Joseph Buckminster, D.D., and of His Son, Rev. Joseph Stevens Buckminster* (1849). The most complete modern assessment is Lawrence Buell, "Joseph Stevens Buckminster: The Making of a New England Saint," *Canadian Review of American Studies* 10 (1979): 1–29. Other important modern assessments include Daniel Walker Howe, *The Unitarian Conscience: Harvard Moral Philosophy, 1805–1861* (1970), and Lewis P. Simpson, *The Man of Letters in New England and the South* (1973), on Buckminster's identity as a man of letters; Jerry Wayne Brown, *The Rise of Biblical Criticism in America, 1810–1870* (1969), on his biblical scholarship; and David Robinson, *The Unitarians and the Universalists* (1985), on his theological identity and contribution to the formation of American Unitarianism.

DAVID M. ROBINSON

BUCKNER, Emory Roy (7 Aug. 1877–11 Mar. 1941), lawyer, was born in Pottawattamie County, Iowa, the son of James Monroe Dysant Buckner, a minister, and Sarah Addie Ellis. In 1883 his father was assigned to his first Methodist parish, and the family moved to Hebron, Nebraska. Despite this commission, the Buckners remained extremely poor, and at the urging of his father Emory spent the summer of 1892 in Lincoln studying shorthand at a business college in hopes of learning a marketable trade. Upon graduating from high school in 1894, Buckner briefly attended a teachers' institute. He taught one year near Hebron and another in Guthrie, Oklahoma Territory. While in Oklahoma, Buckner also spent three years as a circuit court reporter, during which time he decided to become a lawyer. In the fall of 1900 he enrolled at the University of Nebraska as an undergraduate, along with fellow Guthrie teacher Wilhelmina Kathryn Keach; the couple was married during their freshman year on 4 April 1901. They had three children.

In college Buckner was a Phi Beta Kappa, and by the time he graduated in 1904 he had established a close relationship with the dean of the law school, Roscoe Pound, who raised tuition funds for Buckner to enter Harvard Law School that fall. At Harvard, Buckner supported his family by freelancing as a stenographer, one of his clients being author Henry James. He also forged a lasting friendship with future Supreme Court justice Felix Frankfurter.

One of only two married students, Buckner graduated third in his class of about 190 in the spring of 1907. In October of that same year he reported for work at Cravath, Henderson & de Gersdorff in New York City. Buckner found the "Cravath system" of breaking in law clerks juvenile, and he left after five months to join Frankfurter and a young staff of reformers at the U.S. Attorney's Office in New York under the leadership of Henry Stimson.

Buckner soon became involved in Stimson's battle with the American Sugar Refining Company over customs frauds. In a case involving weights at the company's Brooklyn docks that had been rigged to cheat the government out of duties, Buckner suggested that the weights be brought into court as exhibits and that a model scale be built in front of the jury box. Such use of physical evidence helped the team prosecute the case successfully; eventually, civil suits against the company recovered more than $2 million for the government and resulted in several criminal convictions.

In 1910 Buckner joined the staff of Charles Whitman, recently elected anti-Tammany district attorney of New York County. While there Buckner prosecuted two major cases: the *People v. O'Reilly*, a case charging a former assistant district attorney with criminally receiving stolen property; and a sensational case involving the prosecution of chorus girls Lillian Graham and Ethel Conrad, who allegedly shot W. E. D. Stokes in a histrionic showdown, later reenacted during Oscar Hammerstein's *The Shooting Showgirls*. Buckner won the first case, generating a precedent that lawyers can be held accountable for their involvement in bond thefts, but lost the second. In 1912, disheartened by the defeat and dissatisfied with the district attorney's office, Buckner left public office to become counsel to an aldermanic committee investigating the New York Police Department.

After establishing a partnership with former classmate Silas Howland, Buckner focused his attention on reforming the police department's internal organizational structure. The highly-publicized hearings ended on 27 March 1913, and the committee came up with fifty-two recommendations for reform that centered on basic questions of administration rather than social vices. While thirty-seven of the recommendations were eventually approved by the board of aldermen and many later adopted, the tangible results were less immediate than Buckner would have liked.

Meanwhile, Buckner & Howland flourished, and with the additions of Elihu Root, Jr., and Grenville Clark in September 1913, it became the prototype of a successful Wall Street firm. Although Buckner was possibly the highest-priced trial lawyer in New York by the late 1920s, he presided over the firm's daily operations, spending much of his time honing the skills of his young assistants.

In 1925 Buckner accepted appointment as U.S. attorney in the Southern District of New York. Struggling under allegations of wrongdoing in the Justice Department, the Calvin Coolidge administration was looking for an apolitical appointee; Buckner accepted the position under the conditions that he would be free to decide which cases to prosecute and to recruit a competent staff. It was in this post that Buckner made a name for himself; rather than futilely prosecuting countless Prohibition offenders each year, Buckner padlocked dozens of establishments that served or distributed liquor. Ironically, Buckner, long an avid anti-Prohibitionist, had often violated the law himself, but he remained a teetotaler throughout his stint as a public servant, demanding that his staff do likewise.

While Buckner's efforts to dry up the city met with moderate success, his most significant accomplishment as U.S. attorney was the prosecution of former attorney general Harry M. Daugherty and alien property custodian Thomas W. Miller, both accused of taking bribes in 1921. The defendants were shielded by a three-year statue of limitations; consequently, both men were brought to trial in 1926 on charges of "conspiracy to deprive the government of honest services." The first trial resulted in a hung jury, but in 1927 Miller was convicted and Daughtery saved by the vote of a single juror.

Buckner resigned from public office on 7 April 1927 and returned to private practice; however, in 1928 he was appointed independent prosecutor by Governor Alfred Smith in the case against Queens Borough president Maurice E. Connolly for his role in sewer construction fraud. Smith was a Democrat seeking the presidency, and he knew that Buckner, a lifelong Republican, was one of a few men who would not exploit the appointment. Once again exhibiting his penchant for concrete evidence, Buckner convicted Connolly largely with the help of an enormous chart that depicted various sewer transactions of Queens and personal indiscretions of Connolly. In an article on Buckner in the *New Yorker* (19 Mar. 1932), Alva Johnston wrote, "Nothing else could have brought an encyclopedia of suspicious circumstances to a focus." In that same year Buckner suffered the first of a series of strokes, but he continued to play an active role in his firm. He died nine years later at his home in New York City.

In addition to his success at the bar, Buckner is remembered for his zealous pursuit of "the facts" and his unrelenting commitment to young lawyers, many of whom became judges, congressmen, and deans of prestigious law schools. One of those men, Justice John Marshall Harlan, wrote that Buckner's "influence was not of the pedantic sort, but was born of the human and professional stuff that sticks with those who were exposed to it" (Mayer, p. ix). Although his cases rarely made law, Emory Buckner remained an ethically uncompromising trial lawyer capable of bringing even the most indecipherable cases into focus. Frankfurter once remarked, "He would have made a great governor—he would have made a wonderful President, would have done what Jack Kennedy could never do, lay out these problems so people would understand them" (Mayer, p. 1). Beyond his eye for talent and his capacity to explain, however, Buckner also cherished the law, prompting Bethuel Webster to say, "He made people feel that the law was a great calling, not just an occupation" (Mayer, p. 293).

• Letters between Buckner and Frankfurter as well as correspondence between Buckner and both Learned Hand and Roscoe Pound are on deposit at the Harvard Law School Library. Buckner's life and career are discussed extensively in Martin Mayer, *Emory Buckner* (1968). Several other articles have been written featuring Buckner, including an unsigned tribute by Felix Frankfurter, "The Investigator of the N.Y. Police," *Outlook*, 28 Sept. 1912. A series of two profiles entitled "Courtroom Warrior" by Alva Johnston also appeared in the *New Yorker*, 12 and 19 Mar. 1932, respectively. See also the *New York Times* editorial following Buckner's death printed on 13 Mar. 1941 and Felix Frankfurter's letter to the editor, which was published the following day in the *Times*. Finally, Buckner's involvement with the aldermanic investigation of the New York Police Department was described in various New York newspapers from Sept. 1912 through June 1913 and, likewise, during his stint as U.S. attorney, from Apr. 1925 through Mar. 1927. An obituary is in the *New York Times*, 12 Mar. 1941.

DONNA GREAR PARKER

BUCKNER, Milt (10 July 1915–27 July 1977), jazz pianist, organist, and arranger, was born Milton Brent Buckner in St. Louis, Missouri. Details of his parentage are unknown. His brother Ted was a jazz saxophonist who became a member of Jimmie Lunceford's big band (the brothers were not related to jazz trumpeter Teddy Buckner).

Buckner's mother died when he was eight years old and his father died the following year. He went to live with a foster father, trombonist John Tobias, in Detroit, Michigan; Ted also moved there and lived in the home of Fred Kewley, a saxophonist who worked with Tobias in Earl Walton's Orchestra. Buckner took up piano at age ten, and he reported that Tobias made him practice six hours a day. After Tobias and his wife separated, Buckner was raised by drummer George Robinson, also a member of Walton's band. Ted's foster father Kewley owned a record shop and music studio where Buckner heard the latest jazz and played with Ted in a rehearsal band.

By his mid-teens, Buckner was playing professionally. He dropped out of high school before graduating. After hearing Cab Calloway's ensemble, he was inspired to teach himself to write scores for big bands. Impressed by the effort, Walton's band members sent him to the Detroit Institute of Arts, where he studied arranging, composition, and harmony for two years while continuing to perform locally.

Around 1932, while with drummer Don Cox, Buckner developed the "locked-hands" or "block-chord" style later popularized by pianist George Shearing. Derived from an effort to evoke in Cox's five-piece band a sound reminiscent of a big band with massed brass and reed sections, the locked-hands technique involved moving about the keyboard with the hands striking in rhythmic unison. In this manner Buckner played a melody in octaves and harmonized that melody with the other fingers in an essentially fixed position, allowing for small adjustments to make the harmonies work the right way.

Cox's band played at Wood's Dancing School and was broadcast nightly on WXYZ. Buckner left to serve briefly as a staff arranger for McKinney's Cotton Pickers in 1934, but he was back in Cox's band after a few months, resuming the dance and broadcasting work. In 1935 he toured with Jimmy Raschell's band, in which he once again played alongside his brother Ted. That year he met Gladys (maiden name unknown), whom he married in 1936.

Buckner left Raschell in January 1937 to settle in Detroit before the birth of his daughter. He worked with Cox once again, until rejoining Raschell in 1940, at which point he resumed touring with his family. He returned to Detroit, where he remained until November 1941, when he sat in with vibraphonist Lionel Hampton's big band and was immediately asked to join.

Through much of the decade, Buckner toured nationally with Hampton. He explained to interviewer Max Jones, "I was known as an arranger with Hamp more than as a pianist." Among his recorded arrangements were "Nola" (1941); "Hamp's Boogie Woogie," "The Lamplighter," and "Overtime" (1944); "Slide, Hamp, Slide" (1945) (the last four titles were also composed or cocomposed by Buckner); "He-ba-ba-rebop" (1945); "Rockin' in Rhythm" (1946); and "Goldwyn Stomp" and "Hawk's Nest" (1947). Additionally, although the original arrangement of the band's biggest hit, "Flying Home" (1942), was credited to Hampton, Buckner told Jones, "I guess I made about 15 arrangements of that tune."

After leaving Hampton in September 1948, Buckner attempted to establish a big band. In March and June 1949, before the endeavor failed completely, the big band made a few recordings, including "M. B. Blues." He rejoined Hampton from July 1950 to August 1952, during which time he gradually switched from piano to organ, initially playing a theater instrument at an engagement in Los Angeles, California, before purchasing a Hammond electronic organ. Buckner participated in a number of Hampton's "soundies" (film shorts for video jukeboxes), including those for the songs "Air Mail Special" (1950) and "Slide, Hamp, Slide" (1951). He also appeared with Hampton in the movie *Harlem Jazz Festival* (1955).

Apart from recordings—including a session under his own name in 1953—nothing is known of Buckner's activities from 1952 to 1955, when he formed an organ trio with drummer Sam Woodyard and saxophonist Danny Turner, both heard on the quintet album *Rockin' with Milt* from that same year. Woodyard soon left to join Duke Ellington, but Turner remained with Buckner for four years, during which time Buckner had modest hits with "Count's Basement" and "Mighty Low" from the album *Rockin' Hammond* (1956). After further changes in membership, the trio disbanded in 1964. Buckner then performed as a soloist at Playboy clubs and worked thereafter as a freelance musician.

Buckner performed at Lennie's-on-the-Turnpike in Boston, Massachusetts, with tenor saxophonist Illinois Jacquet and drummer Alan Dawson, and from 1966 onward he played in Europe once or twice annually, often with Jacquet and drummer Jo Jones. On the first of these tours he played piano, but otherwise he continued to focus mainly on the Hammond organ. Buckner and Jones performed in the film *L'Adventure [sic] de jazz* (1969–1970), and the two men accompanied the reunited duo of Slim and Slam—guitarist and singer Slim Gaillard and vocalizing bassist Slam Stewart—at the 1970 Monterey Jazz Festival. Buckner also took part from time to time in reunions with Hampton, including performances at the Newport–New York Jazz Festival in 1973 and an engagement at the Rainbow Grill in New York City.

Buckner's recordings in Europe included the albums *Buddy Tate Featuring Milt Buckner* (1967) and *Crazy Rhythm* (1967–1968), both under tenor saxophonist Tate's coleadership; his own *More Chords* (1969); Jacquet's *Genius at Work* (1971) and *Jacquet's Street* (1976); and Hampton's *Blues in Toulouse* (1977). Buckner also played in the documentary movie *Swingmen in Europe* (1977). Hampton's session in Toulouse was recorded shortly before Buckner's death of heart failure while setting up his instrument for a job with Jacquet at a nightclub in Chicago, Illinois.

Buckner was among a number of leading keyboard players and arrangers who carried on the swing style from the late swing era into the 1970s. His delightfully unpretentious personality was epitomized by his reaction to questions about his principal contribution to jazz. Asked repeatedly, he expressed no bitterness over Shearing's having popularized the locked-hands style. He asserted that everyone copied: he had taken ideas from Earl Hines and would have imitated Art Tatum had his style not been so impossibly difficult, and he saw no reason why Shearing should not have also benefited in this way.

• Buckner recalls a disappointment with Hampton in "Big Night at Carnegie Hall," *Tan*, Mar. 1955, pp. 22–23. Surveys and interviews are by Sharon Pease, "Hamp's Pianist Reared by Band," *Down Beat* 10 (1 Oct. 1943): 14, which includes a detailed notated musical example of his locked-hands style; Bob Fulford, "Milt Buckner," *Down Beat* 22 (15 June 1955): 13; Max Jones, "The Spirit of St. Louis Swings On," *Melody Maker* (24 May 1969): 8; Peter Vacher, "The Milt Buckner Story," *Jazz and Blues* 2 (Dec. 1972): 15–18, which gives the fullest details of his upbringing; Les Tomkins, "Milt Buckner," *Crescendo International* 11 (Apr. 1973): 8, 10; and Alan Offstein, "The Milt Buckner Interview," *Coda* no. 154 (Mar.–Apr. 1977): 2–3, 5–8. See also Gunther Schuller, *The Swing Era: The Development of Jazz, 1930–1945* (1989). An obituary is in the *New York Times*, 30 July 1977.

BARRY KERNFELD

BUCKNER, Simon Bolivar (1 Apr. 1823–8 Jan. 1914), Confederate lieutenant general and governor of Kentucky (1887–1891), was born at his family's home, "Glen Lily," in Hart County, Kentucky, the son of Aylett H. Buckner, a planter and iron manufacturer, and Elizabeth Ann Morehead. He graduated from the U.S. Military Academy at West Point in 1844. For gallant and meritorious conduct during the Mexican War Buckner was breveted captain. Before and after that war he served as a tactical officer at West Point and in other military posts.

In 1850 Buckner married Mary Jane Kingsbury, daughter of Major Julius B. Kingsbury. Kingsbury owned property in Chicago, and failing health led him to ask Buckner to manage it. Though Buckner continued his interest in military affairs, he resigned his commission in 1855.

While Buckner managed Kingsbury's properties he maintained an office in Chicago; however, he finally settled in Louisville, Kentucky. In March 1860, as the Civil War approached, Governor Beriah Magoffin appointed Buckner inspector general of the state militia. Buckner supported Magoffin's efforts to maintain Kentucky neutrality and several times served as his agent to Washington.

Both Union and Confederate forces entered Kentucky in 1861, effectively ending any hope of neutrality. When the largely Unionist Kentucky Military Board ended funding for state military encampments in July 1861, Buckner resigned. More than a month later President Abraham Lincoln tendered him a commission as brigadier general. Buckner turned that down, as he had earlier been offered a major generalship by U.S. General Winfield Scott.

Buckner considered Union actions in Kentucky to be violations of the U.S. Constitution and of states' rights, so in September 1861 he went to Nashville, where he accepted Confederate General Albert Sidney Johnston's offer of a brigadier generalship. Johnston ordered Buckner to Fort Donelson, where a terribly confused situation left him in command. The Union forces enveloped that position, and in February 1862 Buckner surrendered the fort on the now-famous "unconditional surrender" terms of General Ulysses S. Grant. Buckner remained a prisoner for more than five months. After being exchanged he was promoted to major general and served capably in a number of battles, notably Perryville and Chickamauga. In 1864 Buckner joined the trans-Mississippi forces of General E. Kirby Smith and in September received promotion to lieutenant general. After Appomattox, Buckner negotiated the surrender of troops in that command late in 1865.

The U.S. War Department forbade Buckner to return to Kentucky. He remained in New Orleans until 1868, working as an editorial writer, as commission merchant, and in the insurance business. When he was allowed to return to Kentucky in 1868, he filed suits to recover his confiscated Kentucky property and the Kingsbury property of his wife in Chicago. While awaiting judgment, Buckner continued his insurance business and, for a few months, edited the *Louisville Courier*. He won the case involving his Kentucky property, and when the Kingsbury case was settled in 1871 the Buckners became moderately wealthy.

Buckner's wife died in 1874, leaving him and their only daughter, Lily. They left Louisville in 1877 for Glen Lily, from which place the general traveled often, filling speaking engagements. He married Delia Claiborne of Richmond, Virginia, in 1885. Their only child, Simon Bolivar Buckner, Jr., served with distinction in World War II. The commanding general in charge of the invasion of Okinawa, he was killed in action in 1945.

The Democrats nominated Buckner for governor in 1887, and he won. His administration proved honest and would have been outstanding had not the lobby-controlled legislature killed his programs for educational and prison reform, trust and railroad regulation, and conservation. He dealt with such now-famous feuds as the Hatfield-McCoy and the French-Eversole. The defalcation of the state treasurer drew widespread attention. As Hart County delegate, Buckner also played an active role in the state constitutional convention of 1890–1891, where he fought the railroad lobby that had blocked regulatory legislation.

After serving as governor, Buckner returned to Glen Lily. He retained his interest in politics, generally supporting the Conservative Democrats. The silver-gold controversy became a major political issue in the 1890s. Buckner believed in the gold standard, and when the party nominated silver champion William Jennings Bryan in 1896, Buckner joined the gold

Democrats and was nominated for vice president on that ticket. Both Democratic factions lost. After that election Buckner traveled a great deal. He died at Glen Lily.

• There is no major collection of Buckner materials; however, the libraries of the University of Kentucky (Lexington) and Western Kentucky University (Bowling Green) have some papers, as does the Kentucky State Historical Society (Frankfort). The best source on Buckner remains Arndt M. Stickles, *Simon Bolivar Buckner: Borderland Knight* (1940). *The Military History of Kentucky* (1939) has much detail on Buckner's role during the neutrality crisis of 1860–1861 and, as governor, dealing with clan-type feuds in Eastern Kentucky. Hambleton Tapp and James C. Klotter, *Kentucky: Decades of Discord, 1865–1900* (1977), covers the Buckner administration (1887–1891). E. Merton Coulter, *The Civil War and Readjustment in Kentucky* (1926), is the best source on that subject. For the circumstances leading to Buckner's surrender of Fort Donelson, see U.S. Grant, *Personal Memoirs* (2 vols., 1885–1886), and Bruce Catton, *Grant Moves South* (1960). W. S. McFeely, *Grant: A Biography* (1981), explains well the Buckner-Grant relationship. Lowell H. Harrison, ed., *Kentucky Governors, 1792–1985* (1985), includes a brief sketch of Buckner as governor.

BENNETT H. WALL

BUCKNER, Simon Bolivar, Jr. (18 July 1886–18 June 1945), the highest-ranking American general killed in combat during World War II, was born in Munfordville, Kentucky, the son of Simon Bolivar Buckner (1823–1914) and his second wife, Delia Hayes Claiborne. Buckner's father, a distinguished Confederate officer, editor of the Louisville *Courier,* and governor of Kentucky (1887–1891), is best remembered as the recipient of Union major general Ulysses S. Grant's famous "unconditional surrender" ultimatum at the siege of Fort Donelson on the Tennessee River in February 1862.

Buckner attended the Virginia Military Institute for two years before entering the U.S. Military Academy at West Point in 1904, graduating fifty-eighth in a class of 108 in 1908. Commissioned in the infantry, he spent the early part of his army career in Panama, the Philippines, and Washington, D.C. He married Adele Blanc of New Orleans in 1916; the couple had three children.

Although he did not see combat in the First World War, Buckner gained a solid reputation as a trainer of army air service units after joining the Signal Corps Aviation Section in 1917. During the interwar years, Buckner spent most of his time as either a student or instructor in a variety of army schools, including the Infantry School, the Command and General Staff School (from which he was a distinguished graduate), and the Army War College. The highlight of his mid-career service was a three-year stint as commandant of cadets at West Point from 1933 to 1936. Buckner was viewed as a harsh taskmaster who tempered his severity with profound common sense and justice. Camp Buckner, the cadet summer training area at the military academy, is named in his honor.

In July 1940 Buckner was ordered to take over the Alaskan Defense Command at Fort Richardson and was promoted to brigadier general in September, making him the first member of his West Point class to wear a star. Within a year he had earned his second star, and troops under his command defeated the Japanese attempt to gain a strong foothold in the Aleutian Islands in 1942–1943.

Buckner's efforts in Alaska earned him a promotion to lieutenant general, and in June 1944 he was made Tenth Army commander. He spent most of the next year whipping his new command into shape for the invasion of Okinawa, the last stop in the U.S. military's island-hopping campaign against the Japanese. The campaign, one of the bloodiest of the Second World War, began 1 April 1945 with virtually unopposed landings by the army's Twenty-fourth Corps and the Third Marine Corps. After quickly driving across the center of the island, the Twenty-fourth Corps swung south, running into some of the strongest defenses encountered by American forces during the entire war. Throughout the attack, Buckner regularly toured the front, spurring his troops forward in the face of stiff Japanese opposition. On 18 June, while observing an attack from a battalion observation post within 300 yards of the front line, Buckner was struck by fragments from a Japanese shell and died in less than ten minutes. Within just a few hours of his death the fighting on Okinawa ended. He was posthumously awarded the Distinguished Service Cross for his "outstanding leadership, tactical genius, and personal courage."

The Buckner family has left a proud legacy of leadership and service to the nation. Simon Sr. graduated from West Point in 1844; Simon Jr. in 1908; and William Buckner in 1948—a span of 104 years represented by only three generations; a unique page in the annals of West Point.

• A small collection of Buckner's papers is maintained in the U.S. Military Academy Library Special Collections, and the Association of Graduates at West Point maintains a Buckner file containing numerous press clippings spanning his career. An article titled "Lieutenant General Simon Bolivar Buckner," by David G. Wittels, appears in *These Are the Generals* (1943). An excellent obituary is in the U.S. Military Academy Association of Graduates's *Assembly,* July 1946.

DALE E. WILSON

BUCKONGAHELAS (1725?–May 1805), Delaware war leader of the Wolf phratry, was possibly the son of Wyondochella, whose village was situated on the Walhonding River (Ohio) at the beginning of the American Revolution. His name, sometimes given as Pakandgihiles, has been variously translated but in a Delaware message of 1794 appears as "Giver of Presents."

Buckongahelas and Wyondochella attracted notice in 1776 when they broke with the Delaware leadership of White Eyes and Killbuck of the senior Turtle phratry, who advocated neutrality in the war between Britain and its colonies, and threw in their lot with those Indians the British were directing against the American frontiers. In August and September 1777 they joined the Wyandot chief Half King's assault on Wheeling. Neither Buckongahelas nor Wyondochella was a phratry chief, for the head of the Wolf division was Pipe. Initially the pair had only a handful of followers, with whom they withdrew westward and established a town on the headwaters of the Great Miami, about three miles north of present Bellefontaine (Ohio). Buckongahelas found support for his militant stand from the neighboring Shawnee villages.

Throughout the revolutionary war Buckongahelas led parties against American settlements. At the end of 1781, for example, he presented sixteen scalps at Detroit and requested additional resources from the British there to enable him to prosecute the war. He regularly decried the neutrality policy, referring to its advocates as "a few drunken people," and he warned them of the dangers of retaliation from American frontiersmen angered by British-Indian raids. Time proved him right, and such events as the murder of White Eyes, the attack on the Delaware town of Coshocton on the Muskingum in 1781, and the massacre of Delaware Moravian converts at Gnadenhutten in 1782 enhanced his credibility. As the peace faction crumbled, refugees joined Buckongahelas's village, and in 1781 he could muster about 240 warriors.

After the war the United States claimed Indian land in Ohio on the basis of conquest, and the Delawares under Pipe, Buckongahelas's principal rival, were party to the treaties of Fort McIntosh (1785) and Fort Harmar (1789) acceding to these pretensions. Buckongahelas and the civil chief of his village, Big Cat, were also desirous of peace after the insecurities of several years of warfare and witnessed another such treaty at Fort Finney (1786), but they did not put their marks to the agreements and probably increased their prestige thereby. Encouraged by British supplies shipped through Detroit, some Indians resisted American encroachments, and in 1786 a Kentuckian army destroyed the Shawnee towns at the head of the Great Miami. Remarkably, Buckongahelas's town escaped attack, but the inhabitants decided to move with the displaced Shawnees, and it was apparently they who joined the multitribal complex situated at the head of the Maumee near present-day Fort Wayne (Ind.). There Buckongahelas supported Shawnee attempts to form an anti-American confederacy, and he probably led the Delawares in the multitribal defeat of the U.S. army of Josiah Harmar when it attacked the Indians in October 1790.

In November 1791 Buckongahelas commanded the Delawares in the confederacy's annihilation of Arthur St. Clair's army on the Wabash. During war the Delaware war chiefs took precedence over their civil chiefs, and although neither the tribal nor a phratry chief, Buckongahelas's standing was unquestionably the highest in the nation. As one observer later remarked, he was regarded "a man among them as General Washington was among the white people." In 1791–1792 he reestablished his town on the Auglaize River, Ohio, just above its junction with the Maumee, close to allied Shawnee and Miami villages, and drew Pipe's faction from the Sandusky to the Maumee to join the victorious confederacy. Buckongahelas favored peace but on the basis of Shawnee demands for an Indian boundary along the Ohio, and he was one of the chiefs chosen to meet the American commissioners on the Detroit River in July–August 1793 during abortive negotiations. He was prominent in the final military campaigns of the Indian confederacy. Although he arrived too late to participate in the attack on Fort Recovery in June 1794, he was among the Indians defeated by Major General Anthony Wayne's army at Fallen Timbers on 20 August.

Wayne's advance to the Maumee caused Buckongahelas and other Indians to abandon their towns at the junction of the Auglaize and the Maumee and withdraw to the mouth of the latter, where they were protected and provisioned by the British. In September the war chief had more than 1,100 of his people there. But during the winter the Indians lost faith in Britain's support, and Buckongahelas joined the Shawnee chief Blue Jacket's peace initiatives. In May 1795 he led his followers back to their old homes about the Auglaize to plant corn with American permission, and on 3 August 1795 he signed the treaty of Greenville, releasing most of modern Ohio to the United States. Buckongahelas then appears to have joined Blue Jacket in the region of Fort Wayne, where he received the first Delaware annuities under the treaty in 1796.

About 1797 Buckongahelas joined his tribesmen on the White River, establishing himself as the preeminent leader in the town of Woapicamikunk, three miles southeast of present-day Muncie, Indiana. While Tetepachsit was the principal chief on the White, Hackinkpomska led the Wolf phratry. Buckongahelas surrendered his war chieftainship in 1802, but he retained enormous influence. His final years, however, were marred by regrets. In an effort to consolidate the Delawares on the White, he and others invited the Moravian Delawares to settle with them and unwittingly encouraged the establishment of a mission there in 1801. While he did not harass the missionaries, Buckongahelas disapproved of their influence. He was, they said at the time of his death, "ever an enemy of the word of God and . . . continually urged the Indians never to forsake their ancient customs but to live as did their fathers before him" (quoted in Gipson, pp. 357–58). Worse, despite opposing land cessions—in 1802 he visited Washington, D.C., to complain about white encroachments—he was induced to sign the treaties at Fort Wayne (June 1803) and Vincennes (August 1804) ceding tracts on the Wabash and Ohio. The Delaware chiefs were so ashamed of their part in the latter that they did not report it to their people on the White, and when the story leaked out, they tried to deflect criticism by claiming they had been misled. One signatory, Tetepachsit, was executed by the Delawares in 1806 for this and other reasons. Buckongahelas was spared undue criticism. He fell ill of the "bilious fever" sweeping the area and died. Nothing is known of his marriages or children, if any.

Buckongahelas was about five feet, ten inches in height, and in later years his appearance was marked by a split ear lobe that fell on his shoulder "like a long worm" and which he chewed on during conversation. Richard Butler, one of the American peace commissioners at Fort Finney in 1786, referred to him as "the strange chief" (quoted in Craig, p. 517). Strong-willed and remarkably brave, he was yet affable, mild-mannered, and humane.

During the American Revolution and after Buckongahelas occupied lands directly in the path of U.S. expansion north of the Ohio, and he shared with his neighbors, the Shawnees, a militant determination to defend Indian territory and culture. He was one of the most important architects of the pan-tribal confederacy that resisted the United States prior to 1795, and his influence was felt equally around the council fire and on the battlefield. He died before his role in the treaties of 1803 and 1804 had become sufficiently known to detract from his powerful reputation, and his death produced a veritable revolution on the White because it was believed to have been caused by witchcraft. In efforts to punish the supposed witches, the Delawares executed several of their people in 1806, a purge that first brought to widespread notice the witchfinder, Tenskwatawa, the Shawnee Prophet.

• Buckongahelas's life is sketched in Benjamin B. Thatcher, *Indian Biography*, vol. 2 (1832), pp. 172–80, but he has attracted no modern biographer. References to him are scattered throughout both American and British records of the period, but notable sources are John Heckewelder, *A Narrative of the Mission of the United Brethren among the Delaware and Mohegan Indians* (1907); Richard Butler's journal in *The Olden Time*, vol. 2, ed. Neville B. Craig (1848), pp. 433–64, 481–531; B. H. Coates, ed., "A Narrative of an Embassy to the Western Tribes, from the Original Manuscript of Hendrick Aupaumut," *Memoirs of the Historical Society of Pennsylvania* 2 (1827): 61–131; and Lawrence Henry Gipson, ed., *The Moravian Indian Mission on White River* (1938). For contextual information, see C. A. Weslager, *The Delaware Indians: A History* (1972), and Helen Hornbeck Tanner, ed., *Atlas of Great Lakes Indian History* (1986). Recent comments about Buckongahelas are contained in Richard White, *The Middle Ground* (1991).

JOHN SUGDEN

BUDD, Ralph (20 Aug. 1879–2 Feb. 1962), railroad president, was born near Washburn, Iowa, the son of Charles Wesley Budd and Mary Ann Warner, farmers. After living and working on the family farm until the age of thirteen, he relocated with his family to Des Moines, Iowa, where he finished high school. He completed his education at nearby Highland Park College, graduating in 1899 at age nineteen with a degree in civil engineering.

Determined to follow an older brother into railroading, he went to work as a draftsman at the Chicago Great Western Railway following graduation. Having made a favorable impression on his superiors, he became an assistant engineer in the following year and, with his career on the rise, married Georgia A. Marshall in 1900; the marriage produced three children. A voracious reader, Budd spent hours pouring over A. N. Talbot's classic treatise on railroads, *Talbot's Railway Transition Spiral* (1909), and in search of advancement moved to the Chicago, Rock Island & Pacific Railway in 1902. He became a division engineer in 1903, involved in extending that firm's line between St. Louis and Kansas City. While working in that capacity he met the road's vice president, John F. Stevens, who would have an enormous influence on his career. In 1906 Stevens had successfully argued against U.S. efforts to build a sea-level canal across the Panamanian Isthmus; when the decision had been made to construct a facility with a series of locks, the need for efficient earth removal became apparent, as did the inadequacy of the existing Panama Railroad for the task. Stevens recruited Budd to Panama in 1906, where he spent the next three years relocating and extending the existing road under horrific conditions; the project was nevertheless completed ahead of schedule.

In 1909 Budd returned to the United States, where his mentor Stevens had taken a position in the Pacific Northwest with James J. Hill's Northern Pacific and Great Northern Railroads. Locked as the two lines were in mortal combat with Edward H. Harriman and the Union Pacific, Hill sought a direct route from the Northwest in San Francisco. Budd became chief engineer on the projected Oregon Trunk Railroad, where he was in charge of surveying the route between Bend, Oregon, and Keddie, California. By 1912 Budd held the same position with the affiliated Spokane, Portland & Seattle Railroad and, with his star clearly on the rise, in the same year moved to St. Paul, Minnesota, to serve as assistant to the president of the Great Northern. He became executive vice president in 1918, while simultaneously serving as assistant regional director of the U.S. Railroad Administration (during the federal government takeover of the railroads during World War I).

In 1919 Budd replaced Hill as president of Great Northern. Although he shared Hill's dream of building a low-cost, high-efficiency line through Washington State's Cascade Mountains, he faced a number of challenges. Most railroads suffered from the deferred maintenance that had accrued while the lines were under federal control, and all firms faced resentment on the part of railworker unions, which had prospered under federal rule and did not view a return to private ownership with favor. In addition, recent legislation had given the Interstate Commerce Commission (ICC) increased regulatory powers. Finally, the Great Northern faced the particular challenge of realigning its infrastructure in its western routes in order to maintain cost competitiveness.

Budd faced these challenges head on. Perhaps his greatest achievement while president was the building of the Cascade Tunnel. Initiated in 1926, the 7.79-mile-long bore was completed amid great fanfare in 1929. The new structure proved to be a bonanza;

the longest tunnel in the world for nearly sixty years, the bore eliminated nine miles from Great Northern's route as well as ten miles of curvature and 1,000 feet in elevation change. Another notable construction feat that occurred under Budd's leadership was the 1931 completion of an interior route (the Bend-Bieber line) that he had surveyed nearly two decades before. Ever interested in the bottom line, Budd increased the efficiency of Great Northern's freight hauling by substituting seventy-ton net capacity iron ore cars for the standard fifty-ton models. Although he realized that freight hauling would always pay Great Northern's bills, Budd did not share his predecessor's disdain for passenger traffic. In 1929 he introduced a new service, the "Empire Builder," which cut an entire day from the trip between Chicago and Seattle as it ran through Glacier National Park.

With his reputation for innovation within the industry spreading, Budd accepted an additional task in the summer of 1930—that of consultant. He journeyed to the Soviet Union as part of a five-man team to inspect current transportation conditions in that country, which were then in a state of turmoil. The 376-page report issued by the group recommended that the Soviet Union realign its rail system along American (rather than European) lines.

By 1932 the railroads, along with the rest of American industry, were feeling the full effects of the Great Depression. In early 1932 Budd assumed the presidency of the Chicago, Burlington & Quincy, which was jointly owned by the Great Northern and the Northern Pacific. Although the line had been a profitable source of dividend income for Great Northern and Northern Pacific for years, as a major transporter of agricultural produce the line suffered terribly with the collapse of the farm economy. Budd quickly restructured the CB&Q, reducing the number of its divisions (with a corresponding reduction in the ranks of middle management) from seventeen to eleven. Wall Street took due notice of this action, as well as his debt reduction plan, which cut the railroad's payments on fixed interest by over 37 percent between 1940 and 1945. Budd's conservative money management paid off during his presidency, as the line often had to refinance maturing bonds in the depressed financial markets of the depression years.

Not content with cost-cutting alone, Budd brought the CB&Q through the depression with operational innovations as well. He built the Dotsero Cutoff in Colorado, which eliminated 175 miles from the Denver–Salt Lake City run of the Denver & Rio Grande Western Railroad (the CB&Q's western connection) and resulted in a quadrupling of transcontinental traffic. Budd also remained committed to passenger traffic and was a pioneer in the utilization of diesel engines for passenger trains. After obtaining new, streamlined stainless steel passenger cars from the Edward G. Budd Company, he commissioned the Electro-Motive Division of General Motors to build a new diesel-powered locomotive. His first diesel train, the "Pioneer Zephyr," made a spectacular debut at Chicago's Century of Progress Exposition in May 1934, and by the time Budd retired as CB&Q president in 1949, over 80 percent of passenger trains (and 50 percent of freight trains) used diesel locomotives exclusively.

Budd reentered federal service in May 1940, when he agreed to serve as transportation commissioner on the Advisory Commission to the Council of National Defense. He remained on the commission until December 1941 and during his tenure argued successfully that the ICC was fully equipped to manage the nation's railroad affairs in wartime. This advocacy, combined with his skill in matching shippers' demands with available rolling stock, helped to forestall another government wartime takeover of the nation's rail system.

Budd retired as president of the Chicago, Burlington & Quincy in 1949. He remained in Chicago to assist newly elected mayor Martin Kennelly as the first head of the new Chicago Transit Authority. After five years in the position, which required as much political skill as it did technical knowledge, Budd presided over the creation of a fully integrated municipal transportation system (including a new subway). During the course of his career he received numerous awards in recognition of his innovative service, including the Franklin Institute's Henderson medal (1939) and the John Fritz medal (1941). Having also served as a director of Equitable Life Assurance Society, the International Harvester Company, and the First National Bank of Chicago, he retired to Santa Barbara, California, in 1954 but remained a senior statesman of the railroad industry until his death in Santa Barbara.

Ralph Budd's career was illustrative of the transitions that the railroad industry was undergoing at that point in history. He entered the field during the last great phase of line building and remained in the business long enough to guide two major carriers through both wartime and peace, prosperity and depression, government control and a return to free enterprise. His legacy is the growth and prosperity of the lines that he ran, as well as the formation and initial success of the Chicago Transit Authority.

• Budd's professional activities can be traced through the papers of the Chicago, Burlington & Quincy Railroad at the Newberry Library in Chicago, and in the papers of the Great Northern Railway, which are held at the Minnesota Historical Society, St. Paul. Excellent secondary sources include Richard C. Overton, *Burlington Route: A History of the Burlington Lines* (1965), Ralph W. Hidy et al., *A History of the Great Northern Railway* (1988), and Albro Martin, *James J. Hill and the Opening of the Northwest* (1976). An obituary is in the *New York Times*, 3 Feb. 1962.

EDWARD L. LACH, JR.

BUDDINGTON, Arthur Francis (29 Nov. 1890–25 Dec. 1980), geologist, was born in Wilmington, Delaware, the son of Osmer Gilbert Buddington, a Baptist minister, and Mary Salina Wheeler. When Buddington was thirteen, the family moved to Poquonnock Bridge (near Mystic), Connecticut, where his father also raised vegetables and poultry to supplement his ministerial income. Buddington attended high school in Mystic and had a final year in Westerly, Rhode Island. During high school and college summers he worked on an uncle's farm and did some lobster fishing. He entered Brown University in 1908. Because he disliked the Latin and Greek required in the liberal arts curriculum, he turned to the scientific program in botany, chemistry, and finally geology. His degree in 1912 was in chemistry. In 1913 he went on to receive an M.S., for which he wrote a thesis on fossil plants in Carboniferous shales from a new tunnel on the college campus.

Awarded a graduate fellowship at Princeton in 1913, Buddington joined a field party of that college in Newfoundland for the summer, where his experience in small boats from lobstering proved useful. His dissertation was a description of the metamorphosed rocks from the area of Conception Bay, Newfoundland, for which he received a Ph.D. in geology in 1916. He held a postdoctoral position at Princeton for a year and briefly began geologic studies in the Adirondack Mountains for the New York State Museum. He spent part of 1917 teaching at Brown University, returned to Princeton to teach a course, and in April 1918 enlisted in the U.S. Army Signal Corps. He was transferred to the Chemical Warfare Service and mustered out at the rank of sergeant when World War I ended. He returned to Brown University as an instructor.

For fifteen months in 1919–1920 Buddington was at the Geophysical Laboratory of the Carnegie Institution of Washington, where he was associated with excellent geochemists. This affiliation contributed to his interest in the chemical nature of rocks and minerals and his ability to analyze them. Buddington accepted a position in 1920 as assistant professor in geology at Princeton University. In 1924 he married Jene Elizabeth Muntz; they had one child.

Buddington advanced to professor and from 1936 to 1950 was chair of the geology department. In that role, he expanded the department from its earlier emphasis on vertebrate paleontology to researches in economic geology and in the chemical processes involved in the formation of rocks. He encouraged the establishment of a laboratory using high-temperature and high-pressure equipment on rock samples. Increasing numbers of graduate students were attracted to this department. They and his colleagues considered Buddington a very effective teacher and a congenial and modest man of high integrity. He became emeritus in 1959 and continued his research at Princeton for some years.

Buddington was an "ardent and expert field geologist," according to biographer Harry H. Hess. From 1921, simultaneously with his Princeton work, he held an appointment with the U.S. Geological Survey (USGS) for summer studies that emphasized economic mineral resources. His first assignment was in southeastern Alaska, where, over five summers, he participated in mapping 4,000 miles of its rugged coastline, much of it by using small boats in fjords as he had in Newfoundland. In the 1920s and early 1930s he described this work in several papers, of which the most extensive was "Geology and Mineral Deposits of Southeastern Alaska" (*USGS Bulletin* 800 [1929]: 1–398), written with T. Chapin. The program was responsible for identifying some low-grade magnetite iron ore prospects. Buddington recognized a succession from east to west of the placement of deep igneous rocks in the Coast Range batholith of southeastern Alaska, on which he published in 1927.

Also for the USGS, Buddington spent the summer of 1930 mapping mining regions of the Cascade Mountains in Oregon. This study was published as "Metalliferous Mineral Deposits of the Cascade Range in Oregon" (*USGS Bulletin* 893 [1938]: 1–141), with Eugene Callaghan.

Buddington's most extensive program for the USGS concerned iron ores in the region of the Adirondack Mountains of the northeastern United States, which lasted for seventeen years, beginning in 1943. Several commercially successful ore bodies were located through the use of an airborne magnetometer developed during World War II by geophysicist Victor Vacquier for magnetic mines and for detecting submarines. Buddington enjoyed participating in the low-level flights in the Adirondacks in 1944, and with coauthors he described various mineralized areas in the Adirondack Mountains in the Professional Papers series of the USGS. He personally mapped thirteen geologic quadrangles in the Adirondacks.

Beyond the descriptive regional papers, Buddington wrote significant ones in which he presented his theories on geologic processes. In 1935 he published "High-Temperature Mineral Associations at Shallow to Moderate Depths" (*Economic Geologist* 30: 205–22), which refuted the concept that the depth of emplacement of ores was associated with the temperature of formation. His point of view was derived from his fieldwork in Oregon, where he had found shallow intrusive rocks associated with ore deposits. Buddington's 1939 publication "Adirondack Igneous Rocks and Their Metamorphism" (*Geological Society of America Memoir* 7:1–354) was said by his biographer Harold L. James to be "a monumental work. . . . With few exceptions the petrologic concepts expressed in the Memoir—many of which were expanded or further developed in later papers—have proved remarkably sound." In 1959 Buddington presented an account of the differences in igneous intrusive rocks as related to their depth in "Granite Emplacement with Special Reference to North America" (*Bulletin of Geological Society of America* 70: 671–747).

During studies in the northeastern United States, Buddington and colleagues discovered relationships between the minerals in rocks and magnetic anomalies. For example, titanium-bearing iron ore was characterized by remanent magnetism reversed from normal. Buddington's 1964 summary, with D. H. Lindsley of the Geophysical Laboratory of the Carnegie Institution of Washington, "Iron-Titanium Oxide Minerals and Synthetic Equivalents" (*Journal of Pe-*

trology 5: 310–57), was widely acknowledged and led to further researches by others.

Buddington served as a temporary geologist for the New York State Museum for many years, and he published descriptions of some of the geologic quadrangles of that state in the museum's bulletins. Among the many honors and awards Buddington received were election to the National Academy of Sciences (1943), the Penrose Medal of the Geological Society of America (1954), the Roebling Medal of the Mineralogical Society of America (1956), the Distinguished Service Award of the Department of the Interior for his service to the USGS (1963), and the naming of a complex mineral as "buddingtonite" (1964). He died in Cohasset, Massachusetts, where he had lived with his daughter after his wife died in 1975.

• The location of Buddington's archival records is not known. Biographical accounts are Harry H. Hess, "An Appreciation," *Petrologic Studies: A Volume to Honor A. F. Buddington*, ed. A. E. J. Engel et al. (1962), pp. vii–xi; R. B. Hargraves, "Memorial to Arthur Francis Buddington, 1890–1980," *Geological Society of America* (1984), and Harold L. James, National Academy of Sciences, *Biographical Memoirs* 57 (1987): 3–24, which includes a bibliography.

ELIZABETH NOBLE SHOR

BUDENZ, Louis (17 July 1891–27 Apr. 1972), labor organizer and anti-Communist government witness, was born in Indianapolis, Indiana, the son of Henry Joseph Budenz, a bank cashier, and Mamie Gertrude Sullivan. Both parents were devout Catholics. After graduating from Indianapolis Law School in 1912, Budenz served as national organizer for the Catholic Young Men's Institute. Although he was admitted to the bar, he never worked as a lawyer. A brief stint as editor of the Carpenters' Union journal from 1912 to 1913 ended with his move to St. Louis to work for the Central Bureau of the Catholic Central Verein, where his main task was to try to secure passage of state workmen's compensation laws. During his stay in St. Louis, Budenz, an independent radical, helped lead a strike of 4,000 women working in department stores and fought for public ownership of utilities.

In 1920 Budenz moved to New York to become the national publicity director of the American Civil Liberties Union. The following year he launched a new journal, *Labor Age*, devoted to industrial unionism and remained its editor until 1933. For the next decade he crisscrossed the United States to report on strikes, oppose company-dominated unions, encourage industrial unions, and sell subscriptions. He was arrested nearly two dozen times but never convicted of any crimes.

Budenz was a delegate to the Conference for Progressive Political Action in 1924 at which Senator Robert La Follette was nominated for president. He served as the Progressive party campaign manager in New Jersey, where he then lived. In the late 1920s he joined A. J. Muste's Conference for Progressive Labor Action and became national secretary. In 1933 he was a founder of Muste's American Workers Party (AWP) and was active during a bitter strike at the Auto-Lite plant in Toledo, Ohio. However, when Muste agreed to let Trotskyists (American followers of Leon Trotsky, the dissident Soviet communist) into the AWP in 1934, Budenz balked and resigned.

For several years Budenz had been calling for alliances with Communists. Prior to 1935 the Communist Party of the United States of America (CPUSA) had viewed other radical groups, such as the followers of A. J. Muste, with suspicion and scorn. That August, however, the Seventh World Congress of the Communist International, meeting in Moscow, proclaimed a new policy of a popular front against fascism. Enthusiastic about the new line, Budenz secretly joined the Communist party in August, the secrecy enabling him to recruit several of his old Musteite comrades, and he publicly announced his conversion in October.

Most of his party career was spent in journalism. After writing for the *Daily Worker*, the Communist newspaper, he became its labor editor. In November 1937 he was appointed editor of the *Midwest Daily Record*, a regional version of the *Daily Worker* designed to appeal to a non-Communist audience. He remained in that post until the *Record* folded in February 1940, when he became president of Freedom of the Press, Inc., a dummy corporation, controlled by the CPUSA, that owned the *Daily Worker*. In 1941 Budenz was appointed managing editor of the *Daily Worker*, a position he held until he resigned from the CPUSA in 1945. During this period he also served on the party's National Trade Union Commission and National Committee.

Budenz later testified that J(osef) Peters, head of the CPUSA's underground apparatus, informed him about conspiratorial activities in 1935. In succeeding years, Budenz had numerous contacts with Jacob Golos, a veteran agent of the Communist International, and several Soviet intelligence officials anxious to infiltrate the American Trotskyists. Budenz introduced Ruby Weil, an old friend, to the Russians; by manipulating her, a Soviet agent was able to gain entrée to Trotsky's home in Mexico and assassinate him in 1940. (Budenz was unaware of this plot.)

Although Budenz was unhappy with the party's abandonment of the Popular Front following the Nazi-Soviet Pact in 1939, he swallowed his objections. By 1943, however, he decided to return to the Catholic church, although he still hoped he could be both a Catholic and a Communist. Within two years Budenz concluded that such a combination was impossible. Budenz had married a divorced woman, Gizella (last name unknown), in 1916 and been excommunicated. The childless couple had separated in 1931 and divorced in 1938. Since 1933 he had been living with Margaret Rogers in a common-law relationship. In August 1945 he wrote to Monsignor Fulton J. Sheen, with whom he had corresponded during the Popular Front years. Rogers and their four children were baptized, she and Budenz were married at St. Patrick's Cathedral in New York by Sheen, and Budenz's resignation from the Communist party was announced on 10 October 1945.

The family moved to Notre Dame University, where Budenz lived in seclusion for one year, although he met frequently with Federal Bureau of Investigation agents. In 1946 he joined the faculty of Fordham University and began speaking to Catholic groups and giving interviews to newspapers. He identified Gerhart Eisler as a Communist International (Comintern) agent in the United States; before he could be deported, Eisler fled to East Germany. By 1947 Budenz began to testify as a government witness in deportation cases brought by the Immigration and Naturalization Service.

In 1949 he was one of the chief government witnesses at the first trial of Communist party leaders for violating the Smith Act, which made it a crime to conspire to teach and advocate the overthrow of the government by force and violence. Budenz testified that Communists used "Aesopian language" to disguise their revolutionary intent. In 1950 he testified that Owen Lattimore, a prominent Sinologist accused of being a Soviet agent by Senator Joseph McCarthy, was in fact a Communist. Budenz's credibility was sharply challenged, since he had never mentioned Lattimore to FBI agents or in public articles during the preceding five years.

In 1955 he suffered a stroke. Following a heart attack in 1957 he remained an invalid until he died in Newport, Rhode Island.

By the mid-1950s Budenz had testified in at least sixty proceedings. As one of the foremost ex-Communist witnesses against his old comrades, he was subjected to withering attacks. While historians have disparaged his evidence for the charge that Lattimore was a Communist, recent revelations from Russian archives have substantiated many of his claims about the Communist underground in the United States and its links to Soviet intelligence.

• Budenz wrote four books: *This Is My Story* (1947), *Men without Faces* (1950), *The Cry Is Peace* (1952), and *The Techniques of Communism* (1954). His widow, Margaret Budenz, also wrote a reminiscence, *Our Sunday Visitor* (1979). A critical assessment of his testimony can be found in Herbert Packer, *Ex-Communist Witnesses* (1962). Material from Russian archives is found in Harvey Klehr et al., *The Secret World of American Communism: Documents from the Soviet Archives* (1995). An obituary is in the *New York Times*, 28 Apr. 1972.

HARVEY KLEHR

BUECHE, Arthur Maynard (14 Nov. 1920–22 Oct. 1981), chemist and industrialist, was born in Flushing, Michigan, the son of Bernard P. Bueche, a merchant, and Margaret Rekart. He grew up in Flushing, where he worked in the family store, played football, and was school valedictorian and class poet at Flushing High School. He earned the associate degree in science from Flint Junior College in Michigan in 1941 and a B.S. in chemistry from the University of Michigan in 1943. He began graduate school in chemistry at Ohio State University in 1943 and then transferred to Cornell, where he did his thesis work under Nobel laureate Peter Debye on the topic "The Diffusion and Sedimentation Constants of Polymers," earning the Ph.D. degree in physical chemistry in 1947.

From 1945 through 1950 Bueche carried out graduate and postdoctoral research sponsored by the Reconstruction Finance Corporation's Office of Rubber Reserve, investigating the structure of polymers, inhomogeneities in solids, adsorption of polymers, and other areas of polymer and colloid chemistry. In 1945 he married Margaret Bassler, with whom he had four children.

In 1950 Bueche joined the General Electric (GE) Research Laboratory in Schenectady, New York, as a research associate. GE was then entering such chemical businesses as silicones and plastics. He carried out studies of crystalline polymers, did pioneering work on radiation chemistry leading to the cross-linking of polymers using electron beams, studied the curing and filling of silicone elastomers, and the surface properties of particulate solids.

In 1956 Bueche became manager of the Polymer and Interface Studies Unit of the GE Research Lab. He directed the work of a dozen researchers on the fracture of plastics and elastomers, the structure of polymers, the use of fillers in elastomers, and the chemistry and physics of surfaces. The most notable research achievement of the group was a breakthrough in the understanding of friction, carried out under his leadership by Richard Roberts, Robert Klint, and Robert Owens. This led to the invention of the first practical lubricants for aluminum, a material notoriously difficult to lubricate.

In 1961 Bueche became manager of the chemical laboratory of the GE Research Lab, where he directed some two hundred scientists and engineers helping GE's plastics business with its introduction of such major new products as Lexan polycarbonate resin and Noryl resin, plastics today widely used in applications ranging from computer housings to automobile components to compact disks. Most notable of his management achievements in this period was the forging of effective bonds of teamwork between the research lab and GE Plastics, the manufacturing operation, at a time when standard practice was for industrial research laboratories to operate as "ivory towers" unfettered by links with business operations.

This success made Bueche the logical candidate to head a new organization formed by GE in 1965, the GE Research and Development Center. It combined the Research Lab with GE's Advanced Technology Laboratories, with the specific purpose of narrowing the gulf between research and application and speeding new ideas into commercialization. During Bueche's tenure as vice president of research and development and director of the Research and Development (R&D) Center between 1965 and 1978, GE achieved major innovations from its research in such fields as plastics and other engineered materials, medical technology, lighting, and energy. In addition, Bueche pioneered methods of managing technical ventures within a corporation (a spin-off company formed by this means, Intermagnetics General, is today a world leader in the field of superconductivity) and created a division of technology application in GE's decentralized businesses. He became recognized as a major innovator in the planning and management of research and development and as an internationally known spokesman in the fields of research management and energy policy. He emphasized the desirability of developing known energy sources, such as nuclear power and coal, rather than relying on energy conservation or the development of wholly new sources.

Again, Bueche emphasized close ties among research, development, engineering, and manufacturing and used business priorities to guide research. These ideas were ahead of their time in the United States, though more widespread in Japan. For example, the GE R&D Center was organized to support GE's investments in the 1960s and 1970s in the areas of plastics, nuclear power, aircraft engines, and the coal-based generation of electric power. Under his guidance the staff of the GE R&D Center grew from 1,500 people in 1965 to 2,100 in 1978.

In 1978 Bueche was appointed GE's senior vice president of corporate technology, the company's chief technology officer at GE corporate headquarters in Fairfield, Connecticut. In early 1981 he also served as chief science adviser to the transition team of the incoming administration of President Ronald Reagan. He was offered the position of presidential science adviser by Reagan in April 1981, but he declined. He was still active as chief technologist of GE when he was suddenly stricken with a heart attack and died after a short illness at St. Vincent's Hospital in Bridgeport, Connecticut.

Bueche was considered a "tough minded" colleague who appreciated—in his own frequently used phrase—"good new ideas." A champion of innovation, he nevertheless subjected R&D initiatives to tough business scrutiny and reality checks and harnessed science to business strategies and national priorities such as energy and the environment. It was for his management skills and public advocacy that he earned membership in both the National Academy of Sciences and the National Academy of Engineering, as well as numerous awards, such as the Delmer F. Fahrney Award of the Franklin Institute and the Industrial Research Institute Medal.

• Some of Bueche's papers are at the Hall of History, Schenectady, N.Y. The best biographical sketch is Roland W. Schmitt, National Academy of Sciences, *Biographical Memoirs* 56 (1987): 53. An obituary is in the *New York Times*, 23 Oct. 1981.

GEORGE WISE

BUEL, Jesse (4 Jan. 1778–6 Oct. 1839), agriculturist, was born in Coventry, Connecticut, the son of Elias Buel and Sarah (maiden name unknown), farmers. In 1790 the family moved to Rutland, Vermont. The youngest of fourteen children, Jesse Buel had little formal education. In 1792 he was apprenticed to a local printer and learned his trade quickly; by the age of eighteen he had finished his apprenticeship and moved to New York City as a journeyman printer. During the next few years he worked there and in the Albany-Troy region, first as a journeyman and later as a master printer. After marrying Susan Pierce of Troy in 1801, he moved to Poughkeepsie where an attempt to establish a weekly paper ended in bankruptcy. The couple would have four children.

Between 1803 and 1813 Buel's fortunes changed as he moved to Kingston and became the editor and owner of an Antifederalist paper, the *Ulster Plebeian*. He also began aggressively buying up land that was sold for taxes and in this way accumulated a substantial personal fortune. Buel secured an appointment as judge of the Court of Common Pleas for Ulster County. In 1813 he moved again, this time to Albany, where he founded the *Argus*, which became a partisan organ of the Democrats; two years later he secured the lucrative post of printer to the state. His career as a newspaper editor continued until 1821, when he relinquished the state printership, probably under political pressure. He continued to be a leading Albany citizen, helping to organize the Albany Savings Bank and serving as a regent of the state university.

Except for a brief interlude as Whig candidate for governor—he ran as a loyal party member in a futile campaign against William Marcy in 1836—Buel gave up his publishing interests in the early 1820s and acquired a farm outside of Albany, where he embarked on the work for which he is best remembered. Even as a newspaper editor Buel had evinced an interest in agricultural issues; now he acted upon those interests and in the process became a key figure in the mid-century agricultural reform movement. His work in agriculture can be divided roughly into two categories. During the twenties, Buel developed his farm, which was located in an area called the "Sandy Barrens." He was an agricultural experimenter, undertaking to drain some of the land, to rotate crops, to apply manure, and to prepare the soil thoroughly by careful harrowing and planting. He advocated a "scientific" approach to farming, and he was remarkably successful in revitalizing a previously unproductive farm. He gained a wide reputation for his accomplishments.

Buel's practical experience lent him credibility as he pursued the second phase of his agricultural reform work—his efforts to establish agricultural societies, agricultural education, and journals to disseminate new knowledge about farming. He became a founder and active member of various agricultural societies, such as the New York State Board of Agriculture and the New York State Agricultural Society. Buel also worked, though less successfully in the short run, to get the state to sponsor agricultural schools; eventually his efforts would influence the shape of the land-grant system set up during the Civil War. But perhaps his most important accomplishment was to establish a career as an influential agricultural writer. He set the Albany *Cultivator* on a firm footing as one of the leading journals of its day. After the journal barely survived its first year (1834) under the sponsorship of the state agricultural society, Buel took it over and, through his able editorship, soon increased its circulation substantially. He included many original contributions in its pages, enlisting the knowledge of hundreds of agents and correspondents for the magazine. He himself wrote extensively for the *Cultivator* and for other agricultural journals. He was also in popular demand as a lecturer. His ideas were compiled in *The Farmer's Companion*, first published in 1839 and appearing thereafter in ten or more additional editions. For his accomplishments, Buel was made an honorary member of many agricultural and scientific societies, including the Massachusetts Agricultural Society and the Charleston (S.C.) Horticultural Society, and a corresponding member of the London Horticultural Society.

Buel's ideas and career illustrate well the strengths and weaknesses of nineteenth-century agricultural reform. He successfully pointed to the shortcomings of American agriculture—wastefulness, declining soil fertility, erosion—and demonstrated ways of remedying those problems. However, his faith in science was somewhat premature and occasionally misplaced, since agricultural science was as yet unable to make direct contributions to everyday farming, and some "scientific" procedures turned out to be inappropriate or even destructive. Buel represented the course that American agriculture was to take, however, in the years to come. Moreover, the fact that he commanded wide respect—his modesty, piety, and hard-working nature were well known—aided the cause of reform in agriculture. He died in Danbury, Connecticut.

• A compilation of Buel's writings from the *Cultivator* is in *The Farmer's Companion* (1839). With John Armstrong, he wrote *A Treatise on Agriculture* (1839). Published versions of his lectures include *Address before the Berkshire Agricultural Society* (1837) and *Address Delivered before the Agricultural and Horticultural Society of New Haven County, Connecticut* (1839). Harry J. Carman, ed., *Jesse Buel: Agricultural Reformer* (1947), contains a brief biographical sketch and many reprinted essays and addresses.

SALLY MCMURRY

BUELL, Don Carlos (23 Mar. 1818–19 Nov. 1898), soldier and businessman, was born near Marietta, Ohio, the son of Salmon D. Buell and Eliza (maiden name unknown), farmers. After his father's death in 1823, the boy lived mostly in Lawrenceburg, Indiana, with an uncle, George P. Buell, who got him an appointment to West Point in 1837. Graduating in the lower half of his 1841 class, Buell was commissioned a second lieutenant in the Third Infantry. He served in the Seminole War and was promoted to first lieutenant on 18 June 1846. In November 1851 he married Margaret Hunter Mason, a widow. They had no children.

During the Mexican War Buell served with both Zachary Taylor and Winfield Scott and earned brevet promotions to captain and major for his services at Monterrey, Contreras, and Churubusco, where he suffered a severe shoulder wound. After the war Buell transferred to the adjutant general's department. Capable and diligent in carrying out his duties, he went to the office of the Secretary of War in 1859. In the spring of 1861 Lieutenant Colonel Buell was ordered to the West Coast, but he was recalled in August. Buell was ninth on the 17 May 1861 list of Union brigadier generals for the volunteer army, and he trained a division for the Army of the Potomac.

In November Buell was sent west to command the Army of the Ohio, with particular orders to train the army in Kentucky and to liberate strongly unionist East Tennessee. Of average height but possessed of a compact, powerful body, Buell wore a full beard that was already touched with gray. An able organizer and administrator, he did a commendable job of building up the army, but he insisted stubbornly that inadequate transportation facilities and the presence of a large Confederate force at Bowling Green made the East Tennessee mission impossible. A segment of his army under the command of George Henry Thomas won the battle of Mill Springs on 19 January 1862, but Buell continued to advocate an advance up the Cumberland and Tennessee rivers with Nashville as its immediate object. That was much the plan followed by Ulysses S. Grant in early 1862, and Buell was told to support him. His supply line threatened by Grant, Albert Sidney Johnston, the Confederate commander in Kentucky, abandoned Bowling Green and Nashville and withdrew south of the Tennessee River.

After occupying Nashville Buell moved unhurriedly toward Grant's position on the Tennessee River. His lead division reached the Shiloh battlefield late on 6 April 1862 in time to help prevent a Confederate victory. Two other divisions crossed the river that night, and Buell's attack on 7 April helped secure the Union victory. Promoted to major general as of 21 March 1862, Buell accompanied Henry Halleck's glacial advance on Corinth, Mississippi. On 10 June he was given four divisions and ordered to repair the Memphis and Charleston Railroad on his way to occupy Chattanooga. Confederate raiders cut the rebuilt line so often that Braxton Bragg's Confederate army reached the city first. Buell then withdrew his troops to the vicinity of Murfreesboro.

In the late summer, when Edmund Kirby Smith and Bragg invaded Kentucky, Buell left a holding force in Nashville but followed Bragg with most of his army and secured Louisville before the Confederates could occupy it. Then, moving with unusual rapidity, Buell launched a multipronged attack against the scattered Confederates. At Perryville on 8 October, neither side employed all of its strength. The Confederates made gains in savage fighting but then withdrew from the state. Unable to bring the Confederates to another battle, Buell soon gave up the pursuit. President Abraham Lincoln and Secretary of War Edwin M. Stanton blamed Buell for not forcing a decisive battle and crushing the Confederate forces. Buell's belief that a conciliatory policy would hasten the reconstruction of the Union displeased the Radicals, who were demanding total war with significant changes in the postwar South. At least in part, Buell was sacrificed to the imminent November elections. Removed from command on 24 October 1862, he was replaced by William S. Rosecrans. In late 1862–early 1863 Buell ably defended his conduct before a commission that included several hostile critics, and no recommendations were made as to his future. Although Grant recommended that he be reinstated, Buell did not get another assignment, and on 23 May 1864 he was separated from the volunteer army. On 1 June Buell resigned his regular army commission. A contemporary called him "perfect in manner, bearing, coolness, courage, energy—physically and mentally a perfect soldier," but he lacked the imagination and spark that might have lifted him to conspicuous success. His talents for discipline, logistics, and administration did not fully compensate for his perceived deficiencies in aggressive and decisive leadership.

In his postwar years Buell managed extensive coal and iron operations and dabbled in oil production in Muhlenburg County, Kentucky. A Democrat, he was the federal pension agent in Kentucky (1885–1889). He wrote three Civil War articles for the *Century Magazine* and was active in civic activities. Perhaps his favorite service was on the Shiloh Park Commission. He died at his Airdrie estate near Rockport, Kentucky, and was buried in St. Louis.

• The major collection of Buell papers is at Rice University; others are at the University of Notre Dame and the National Archives. His Civil War articles are most easily located in Robert U. Johnson and Clarence C. Buel, eds., *Battles and Leaders of the Civil War* (4 vols., 1887–1888). Neglected by biographers, the fullest account of his military career is James Robert Chumney, Jr., "Don Carlos Buell, Gentleman General" (Ph.D. diss., Rice Univ., 1964). *The War of the Rebellion: A Compilation of the Official Records of the Union and Confederate Armies* (128 vols., 1880–1901) contains a great deal of information, including the 1862–1863 commission hearing on his conduct. Buell is a major figure in any work dealing with the western theater of operations in 1861–1862. See especially James B. Fry, *Operations of the Army under Buell . . . and the Buell Commission* (1884); Henry M. Cist, *The Army of the Cumberland* (1882); and Kenneth A. Hafendorfer, *Perryville: Battle for Kentucky* (rev. ed., 1991). An extended obituary is in the Louisville *Courier-Journal*, 20 Nov. 1898.

LOWELL H. HARRISON

BUFFALO (1759?–7 Sept. 1855), traditional chief of the Lake Superior bands of Chippewa, was born along the southern shore of Lake Superior to Chippewa parents whose names did not come down to us. Reared in the traditional ways of the Anishinabe or Chippewa or Ojibway, Buffalo, who also was known as Ke Che Waish Ke or Bezhike, lived a rigorous, healthy life while acquiring a thorough knowledge of the history of the tribe and traditions of his culture. Early in life his marked ability to use the expressive Chippewa language distinguished him in councils. He rose to become the principal chief of the several bands of Chippewa inhabiting 19 million acres of the forests and lakes from the upper peninsula of Michigan across the northern third of Wisconsin into the eastern portion of Minnesota, a region of beauty as well as great wealth in timber and natural resources.

A peace chief, he kept his lodge at Madeleine Island (La Pointe), near present-day Bayfield, Wisconsin, a communication and trade center of the north country, a region primarily dependent on water routes. He consistently worked with tribal warriors and leaders to soften the harshness of the Chippewa wars with the Sioux. Around 1500 the Chippewa had drifted into the Lake Superior basin and established themselves at Madeleine Island. For 250 years they had slowly pushed inland against the Sioux, eventually to shove them into southern Minnesota.

In the treaties of 1837 and 1842 the Chippewa bands of Lake Superior ceded their lands in Michigan and Wisconsin to the United States, reserving the right to remain if they were peaceful, a condition they carefully fulfilled. Almost immediately, white traders and speculators began to press the government to remove them. In 1849 President Zachary Taylor issued an order to remove them from Wisconsin. The Chippewa and their white friends, missionaries, teachers, traders, and Wisconsin citizens tried to have the order negated. To facilitate their removal, major officials in the Indian bureaucracy connived to pay their annuity payments, money the Chippewa used to purchase necessary supplies, in distant Sandy Lake in central Minnesota. They then deliberately withheld payment until early November when the snows began, hoping the fierce winter would lock the Chippewa in Minnesota. With rivers frozen, canoes crushed, disease rife, and the weather fierce, the Chippewa attempted to carry their provisions overland to their Wisconsin homes to feed their destitute families. Perhaps 500 Chippewas, mostly young men, perished from disease and the cold in the government's diabolical trap, an estimated 12 percent of the tribe.

Having exhausted local remedies and after the federal bureaucracy callously thwarted their pleadings, the 92-year-old Chief Buffalo resorted to the only move he felt was left to save the tribe. He decided to journey to Washington to make a personal appeal to President Millard Fillmore. The bureaucracy refused to release travel money from the Chippewa's own funds; whereupon, with his small group of assistants and interpreter Benjamin Armstrong, Buffalo canoed to the nearest steamboat town. There they danced and performed on the streets to beg sufficient money to take them to the next town and by this means traveled to the national capital. When the group reached Washington, the government supported them. By persistence Buffalo finally saw Fillmore and convinced him of the justness of the Chippewa request. Fillmore canceled the removal order and ordered a new treaty to define homes for them in Wisconsin. In the treaty of 1854 the bands of Lake Superior Chippewa of Wisconsin, Michigan, and Minnesota each obtained a reservation.

Revered by Chippewa bands of Lake Superior, Buffalo rightly is regarded as their exemplary leader whose courage in the face of overwhelming odds, coupled with the wisdom to penetrate the white man's governmental structure, saved them from expulsion and a grim fate. He enabled the Chippewa to keep their homes around the southern end of the great lake. He accomplished this by adhering to the principles of the traditional Chippewa and utilizing the peace path, a testament to the strength of a culture and to the abilities of an aged honorable man.

When he died in his lodge on Madeleine Island, Buffalo left a widow, his fifth wife. None of the names of his wives was recorded, and nothing is known of his immediate family, who were numerous. Two busts of Chief Buffalo are in the Capitol in Washington, D.C. In 1855 a marble bust by Francis Vincenti was placed in the Senate gallery, and in 1858 Joseph Lassalle made a bronze replica for the west staircase of the House of Representatives.

• Buffalo left no papers; he was illiterate. A few of his translated speeches delivered during negotiations with whites appear in various federal records and are discussed in Ronald N. Satz, *Chippewa Treaty Rights* (1991). The pipe that Buffalo carried to Washington, with the historical ideographs he scratched on it depicting his journey and his meeting with the president, is a record of his success, which he gave to his honest interpreter Benjamin Armstrong. It survives in the private possession of Armstrong's great-grandson in Stevens Point, Wis. The primary source for the journey to Washington is in the memoirs of Benjamin Armstrong, *Early Life among the Indians: Reminiscences of Benj. G. Armstrong* (1892). Richard F. Morse, "The Chippewa of Lake Superior," State Historical Society of Wisconsin, *Collections* 3 (1904): 365–69, contains an obituary. William Warren, *History of the Ojibway People* (1885), p. 464, mentions Buffalo, while Hamilton Nelson Ross, *La Pointe: Village Outpost* (1960), contains scattered references. His badly damaged tombstone still stands in the Madeleine Island cemetery (La Pointe). A description and discussion of the Buffalo bust in the Capitol building is in John O. Holtzhueter, "Chief Buffalo and Other Wisconsin Related Art in the National Capitol," *Wisconsin Magazine of History* 56 (1973–1974): 284–88. James A. Clifton, "Wisconsin Death March: Explaining the Extremes in Old Northwest Indian Removal," Wisconsin Academy of Sciences, Arts and Letters, *Transactions* 75 (1987): 1–39, provides a picture of the forced removal of the Chippewa that contains numerous weaknesses, some of which are corrected in Satz, *Chippewa Treaty Rights*. Satz's discussion of the period is excellent.

DAVID R. WRONE

BUFFALO BILL. *See* Cody, William Frederick.

BUFORD, Abraham (31 July 1749–30 June 1833), revolutionary war officer, was born in Culpeper County, Virginia, the son of John Buford and Judith Early. Although his father was one of the largest landholders in the area, little is known about Abraham until 1775, when he commanded a company in one of the fifteen battalions of minutemen established by the revolutionary Virginia Convention. His unit was involved in the military actions against the last royal governor, Lord Dunmore, which culminated in the battle of Great Bridge on 9 December and Dunmore's withdrawal from Virginia. On 13 November 1776 Buford became a major in the Fourteenth Virginia Regiment of the Continental Line. Promoted to lieutenant colonel on 1 April 1777, he joined the Fifth Virginia Regiment, of which he became the commanding colonel on 15 May 1778. Serving in the northern states during the first three years of the war, he joined with other Continental army officers in staging a play in Brunswick, New Jersey, to raise money for the relief of army camp followers. Buford also spent the winter of 1777–1778 with Washington's forces at Valley Forge. But late in 1778 British forces captured Savannah, Georgia, and thereafter much of the military action took place in the South. Buford assumed command of the Eleventh Virginia Regiment on 14 September 1778, and the following spring he received orders to South Carolina. Marching approximately 400 recruits and returning veterans to reinforce the garrison at Charleston, Buford had reached the Santee River, about thirty miles from the city, when he learned that the American forces there had surrendered to the British on 12 May 1780. Joined by the remnants of the Third Continental Dragoons, which had been badly mauled by the British several days earlier, Buford retreated to Camden, South Carolina, and then toward Salisbury, North Carolina. Lieutenant Colonel Banastre Tarleton, in command of a mounted legion of Loyalist troops and some regulars, pursued him. The two forces met at the Waxhaws, a small settlement less than ten miles east of Lancaster, South Carolina.

The exact details of the encounter on 29 May 1780 will probably never be known, but firsthand accounts from the British and American sides agree on some particulars about the early part of the action; the discrepancies mainly concerned events in the final phase while Americans were trying to surrender. Although the Americans outnumbered him, by about 350 men to 270, Tarleton demanded that the Americans surrender. After consulting with his officers, Buford refused, and the British promptly attacked. Surprised by such celerity, the Americans nevertheless held their fire—as ordered, Tarleton believed—until the enemy was within ten paces. But at that range the momentum of the British horsemen brought them into the American ranks before the latter could reload for a second volley. The American lines collapsed, and many of Buford's men soon attempted to surrender. The result was a complete British victory. At the cost of only nineteen casualties, Tarleton killed or captured more than 300 Americans. Few Whigs actually engaged in the battle escaped; Buford was among the lucky ones. American survivors believed that Tarleton's men deliberately slaughtered men who were trying to capitulate. Tarleton, whose horse had been shot, went so far as to admit that restraining his men, who thought their commander had been killed, was difficult. Charles Stedman, a Loyalist historian who served in South Carolina, summed up the matter more bluntly, "the virtue of humanity was totally forgot." Tarleton emerged from the affair with a fearsome reputation. But if British commanders believed that such ruthlessness would intimidate Americans, they erred. Vowing vengeance and shouting "Remember Buford" and "Tarleton's Quarter," Whig forces massacred Loyalists at Kings Mountain and elsewhere. Tarleton's defeat of Buford, in the words of David Ramsay, a Whig contemporary, "gave a more sanguinary turn to the war."

Buford's subsequent career was less dramatic. Joining Continental forces under General Horatio Gates during the summer of 1780, Buford served throughout the remainder of the war. After a brief period as commander of the Third Virginia Regiment, he—like a number of other Virginia officers—retired on 1 January 1783. He joined the Virginia Society of the Cincinnati, composed of ex-Continental officers, including Washington. Becoming deputy surveyor for Lincoln County and receiving land for his Revolutionary War service, Buford soon moved to Kentucky, where he first located in the Danville area. Later, he moved to Scott County, near Georgetown. Meanwhile, in 1788 he married Martha McDowell, the daughter of a local judge; they eventually had six children. Buford also became a member of the Political Club of Danville. During the 1780s, the membership of this club, which was composed of many of the leading men of the area, favored the immediate separation of Kentucky from Virginia and the adoption of a state constitution that, among other things, would restrict suffrage to property holders. Such an elitist position suggests that Buford was one of the more conservative members of the Virginia-Kentucky gentry, but he remains a relatively shadowy figure for a man of his prominence. During the latter part of his life, he appears to have devoted most of his attention to domestic concerns and improving his property. He died in Scott County. "Tarleton's Quarter" and "Buford's Play" ensured his place in history, however, and the battlefield at the Waxhaws joined the register of National Historic Places in 1990.

• No important collection of Buford papers is known to have survived, though some of his letters are scattered through the correspondence of Generals Benjamin Lincoln and George Washington. The minutes of the Political Club of Danville are also available at the Filson Club, Louisville, Ky. Contemporary opinion about the battle at the Waxhaws can be found in David Ramsay, *The History of South Carolina* (1858; repr. 1959–1962); Charles Stedman, *The History of the Origin, Progress, and Termination of the American War* (1794); and Banastre Tarleton, *A History of the Campaigns of 1780 and 1781 in the Southern Provinces of North America* (1781). The best modern summary is J. Tracy Power, "'The Virtue of Humanity Was Totally Forgot': Buford's Massacre, May 29, 1780," *South Carolina Historical Magazine* 93 (1992): 5–14. See also Marcus Bainbridge Buford, *History and Genealogy of the Buford Family in America*, revised and enlarged edition by George Washington Buford and Mildred Buford Minter (1924).

ROBERT M. WEIR

BUFORD, Abraham (18 Jan. 1820–9 June 1884), horseman and soldier, was born in Woodford County, Kentucky, the son of William Buford, a stockman, and Frances Walker Kirtley. The youth left Centre College in 1837 to accept an appointment to West Point, where he graduated in 1841 next to last in a class of fifty-two. Brevetted a second lieutenant in the First Dragoons, he received his regular commission on 12 April 1842. Satisfactory service on the western frontier brought promotion to first lieutenant on 6 December 1846. The previous year he had married Amanda Harris; they had one child.

Gallantry in action at Buena Vista earned Buford a brevet captaincy as of 23 February 1847. Promotion to captain came on 15 July 1853. Advancement was slow in the peacetime army, and Buford resigned on 22 October 1854. His father was a noted breeder of thoroughbreds and shorthorn cattle, and Buford purchased a large bluegrass farm, "Bosque Bonita," in Woodford County. He was soon known for the horses and cattle produced there.

Although Buford was a slaveholder and a staunch believer in states' rights, he loved the Union and opposed secession during the 1860–1861 crisis. Well aware of Kentucky's divided sentiment, he approved the state's neutrality policy. When it ended in September 1861 and Kentucky remained in the Union, Buford chafed under Federal constraints and regulations. When Braxton Bragg and Edmund Kirby Smith led a Confederate invasion of the state during the late summer of 1862, Buford decided to join the Confederate army. He was commissioned a brigadier general to rank from 2 September 1862. More than six feet tall and weighing in excess of 300 pounds, he had a powerful physical appearance that was reinforced by a forceful personality.

During the Stones River (Murfreesboro) campaign in late 1862 and early 1863, Buford commanded three new cavalry regiments. On 30 January 1863 he was transferred to the Mississippi command of Lieutenant General John C. Pemberton. No command suitable to his rank being available, Buford was passed by Pemberton on to Major General Franklin Gardner at Port Hudson, Louisiana, who organized an infantry brigade for the Kentuckian. Buford declined an assignment to the Trans-Mississippi theater, and he and his brigade joined Major General William W. Loring at Jackson, Mississippi. Buford was shifted to Meridian to help check the Union raiders of Colonel Benjamin Grierson, then was ordered to join the garrison at Vicksburg. At the Battle of Champion's Hill on 16 May 1863, his brigade was among the Confederate units cut off from Pemberton's army as it retired within its fortifications.

Buford then participated in Joseph E. Johnston's futile efforts to relieve the Vicksburg siege. After the city fell, Buford and his brigade served in Mississippi under Lieutenant Generals William J. Hardee and Leonidas Polk. The most active portion of Buford's Confederate career came after 2 March 1864, when he was assigned to Major General Nathan B. Forrest's command. Given a cavalry division, Buford participated actively in the spring campaign in West Tennessee and Kentucky. Some of his troops were involved in the slaughter of black Union soldiers at Fort Pillow on 12 April 1864, but Buford was leading the rest of his command on a raid into western Kentucky. One of Buford's best performances was at Brice's Crossroads (Tishomingo Creek) on 10 June 1864, when Forrest routed a Union force double the size of his own. "He was prompt in obeying orders and exhibited great energy in assaulting and pursuing the enemy," Forrest wrote in his battle report. Buford also displayed initiative, an essential trait when working with Forrest. Buford often exercised independent command, as he did on his April 1864 raid against Paducah, Kentucky, and in his capture of several Union boats on the Tennessee River near the end of October 1864.

During the Atlanta campaign, as the Army of Tennessee was forced back toward that city, Buford was almost constantly engaged in skirmishes and scouting activities as Forrest tried to cut the Union supply line in northern Alabama and Tennessee. The Kentuckian's most unusual operation of the war came in October-November 1864, when Forrest moved to stop Union traffic on the Tennessee River and to destroy the huge Union supply depot at Jacksonville, Tennessee. In addition to blocking the river traffic and destroying some steamers and gunboats, Buford found himself for a few days commanding a small Confederate naval force on the river. The Jacksonville supplies that could not be removed were burned.

Buford was actively involved in John B. Hood's ill-advised Nashville campaign, for Forrest then commanded the army's cavalry. Buford's dismounted men fought well at Spring Hill on 29 November 1864, but he missed the disastrous battle of Nashville because he was helping raid Murfreesboro. When he rejoined the remnants of the Army of Tennessee, Buford helped cover the retreat. He was seriously wounded on 24 December at Richland Creek, south of Columbia, Tennessee, when Forrest made a stand to halt the Federal pursuit. After his return to duty on 18 February 1865, Buford was given command of the Confederate cavalry remaining in Alabama. With dwindling forces he fought in several small engagements, notably at Selma, which fell to Federal troops on 2 April 1865. Buford surrendered at Gainesville, Alabama, on 9 May 1865 with what was left of Forrest's command.

Buford returned to Bosque Bonita and resumed breeding thoroughbreds and shorthorn cattle. He owned some of the outstanding horses in the country, such as Leamington, Enquirer, and McWhirter, in the post-war years, and his home became famous among horsemen for his lavish hospitality. He accepted the results of the war, advocated a swift reunification of the nation, and was persuaded to serve one term (1877–1879) in the state house of representatives. The deaths of his son in 1872 and his wife in 1879 depressed Buford, and financial reverses cost him his beloved farm and horses. "I have no home to go to," he wrote in his suicide note to a nephew he was visiting in Danville, Indiana, before shooting himself.

• Buford has received little biographical treatment. Brief sketches are found in William C. Davis, ed., *The Confederate General*, vol. 1 (6 vols., 1991–1992; J. M. Armstrong, ed., *Biographical Encyclopedia of Kentucky* (1878); Marcus Bainbridge Buford, *A Genealogy of the Buford Family in America . . .* (1903); and Clement A. Evans, *Confederate Military History*, vol. 9 (12 vols., 1899). *The War of the Rebellion: A Compilation of the Official Records of the Union and Confederate Armies* (128 vols., 1880–1901) is essential for the details of his Civil War experiences. All of the biographies of Forrest make frequent reference to Buford. See especially Brian Steel Wills, *A Battle from the Start: The Life of Nathan Bedford Forrest* (1992), and John Allan Wyeth, *Life of General Nathan Bedford Forrest* (1899). An obituary is in the Louisville *Courier-Journal*, 10 June 1884.

LOWELL H. HARRISON

BUFORD, John (4 Mar. 1826–16 Dec. 1863), soldier, was born in Woodford County, Kentucky, the son of John Buford, a planter and politician, and Anne Bannister Watson. After moving with his family to Rock Island, Illinois, Buford followed the example of his older half-brother, Napoleon Bonaparte Buford, and entered the U.S. Military Academy. He graduated sixteenth out of thirty-eight in the class of 1848 and was brevetted second lieutenant of dragoons. His regular commission came on 17 February 1849; promotion to first lieutenant, on 9 July 1853. In May 1854 he married Martha Duke; the marriage produced two children, neither of whom reached adulthood.

As regimental quartermaster of the Second Dragoons from 1855 to 1858, Buford served at various posts, principally on the Great Plains. He first saw combat during a campaign against the Sioux in Nebraska. His performance at the Battle of Blue Water on 3 September 1855 impressed his commanding officer, who complimented Buford in his campaign report. In 1856–1857 Buford saw duty in Kansas, where his unit was interposed between battling free state and proslavery settlers. In 1857 the Second Dragoons were ordered to assert federal authority over the Mormons in Utah. Colonel Philip St. George Cooke, the regimental commander, lavishly praised Buford for his efficient handling of the quartermaster department during the unit's grueling winter march to Fort Bridger. Buford remained in Utah until August, when he was granted leave to visit his family in Kentucky. While in Kentucky, Buford received word of his promotion to captain, dated 9 March 1859. He returned to Utah in early 1860 to assume command of Company B, Second Dragoons, but saw no combat with that unit.

Unlike many Kentuckians, Buford firmly cast his lot with the Union in 1861. Though desirous of a field command, Buford lacked political influence and was only able to attain promotion to major and transfer to the Inspector General's department. In the spring of 1862 he was assigned to the staff of Major General

John Pope (1822–1892), commander of the newly organized Army of Virginia. Pope sympathized with Buford's predicament and successfully petitioned the War Department on his behalf. Buford was commissioned brigadier general of volunteers on 27 July 1862 and given command of a cavalry brigade in Pope's army.

Throughout August 1862 his units conducted scouting missions in northern Virginia. In a surprise attack on Verdiersville on 17 August one of Buford's regiments barely missed capturing Confederate major general J. E. B. Stuart but managed to come away with the general's cloak and plumed hat as well as orders signed by General Robert E. Lee, which revealed a concentration of Confederate forces along the Rappahannock River against Pope's army. On 28 and 29 August Buford's dismounted troopers fought a stubborn rearguard action west of Thoroughfare Gap against an overwhelming Confederate force. Though forced to fall back, Buford relayed precise information on the strength of the approaching enemy column. Through no fault of Buford's, this intelligence failed to reach General Pope, and the Federal army was swept from the field in the second battle of Manassas. On 30 August Buford sustained a minor wound during a rearguard action at Bull Run Creek and then proceeded to cover the army's retreat to Washington.

Reorganization of the Federal army in September resulted in Buford's appointment as chief of cavalry in the Army of the Potomac, but the piecemeal dispersion of cavalry units made Buford's office primarily an administrative one that offered no opportunity to distinguish himself.

Consolidation of Union cavalry into a single corps came in the spring of 1863. Buford assumed command of the Reserve Cavalry Brigade and took part in George Stoneman's unproductive raid against Confederate lines of communication during the Chancellorsville campaign in May. On 9 June, Buford performed well in command of a division at the battle of Brandy Station, which, although essentially a tactical draw, demonstrated that the qualitative gap between Confederate and Federal cavalry had closed considerably.

In the Gettysburg campaign, Buford's division struck northward across the Potomac on 27 June and covered the western flank of the Federal First Corps as it marched through Maryland. On 30 June 1863 Buford encountered enemy infantry about four miles west of Gettysburg. The next morning Buford's dismounted cavalry held its position against a considerably larger Confederate force, giving the Federal army time to concentrate on the heights south and east of Gettysburg. Buford's division was not significantly involved during the remaining two days of the battle. In pursuit of the retreating Confederate army on 6 July, Buford engaged, but was unable to penetrate, the enemy defenses at Williamsport, Maryland.

During the waning months of 1863, as the opposing armies attempted to outmaneuver each other in northern Virginia, their movements necessitated the constant use of cavalry. The wet weather and hard service took a severe toll on Buford's health. Suffering from typhoid fever, he retired to Washington, D.C., on sick leave. At the personal request of President Lincoln, he was promoted to major general, receiving news of his promotion only hours before his death at the home of Major General Stoneman.

Buford did not possess the flamboyant cavalier image traditionally associated with Civil War cavalry commanders. After the war, Pope remarked on Buford's "quiet dignity . . . presence and manner," which held "an influence over men as remarkable as it was useful." Buford probably has received more praise for his action in the opening hours of Gettysburg than the situation warranted. What often has been represented as a determined stand of more than two hours by precariously placed dismounted troopers, most notably in the movie *Gettysburg* (1993) and Michael Sharra's prize-winning novel *The Killer Angels* (1974), upon which the movie was based, was by other accounts a steady withdrawal lasting perhaps forty minutes. In truth, much of the two hours' fighting that Buford described in his postbattle report was consumed by the enemy in deploying infantry for battle and carried over past the arrival of the First Corps. Buford's more lasting contribution was his recognition of defensible ground in the Gettysburg vicinity. For this reason he made the stand, however brief, in the face of overwhelming force.

• There is no known extant collection of Buford papers. Buford's several reports and battlefield dispatches are published in *The War of the Rebellion: A Compilation of the Official Records of the Union and Confederate Armies* (128 vols., 1881–1901). Pope's brief eulogy is in *Battles and Leaders of the Civil War*, ed. Robert U. Johnson and Clarence C. Buell (1884–1887). Edward G. Longacre's *General John Buford* (1995) is the only full-length scholarly study of Buford's life and career. See also Russell F. Weigley, "John Buford," *Civil War Times Illustrated* 5 (1966): 14–23, and Michael Phipps and John S. Peterson, *"The Devil's To Pay": General John Buford* (1995). Fletcher Pratt, *Eleven Generals* (1949), presents Buford as an astute innovator who was the first to fight with dismounted cavalry; the antebellum record of American dragoons, however, debunks this myth. Buford and his role in the fighting on 1 July 1863 are most dramatically depicted, with some artistic license, in Michael Sharra's *The Killer Angels* (1974) and the movie *Gettysburg* (1993).

HERMAN HATTAWAY
ETHAN S. RAFUSE

BUGBEE, Emma (19 May 1888–6 Oct. 1981), journalist, was born in Shippensburg, Pennsylvania, the daughter of Edward Howard Bugbee and Emma A. J. Bugbee, high school teachers. Although her mother's maiden name was Bugbee, her parents apparently were not related. Her mother traced her family back to Edward Bugbee, who arrived in Massachusetts in 1634. Her father was a grandson of Howard Bugbee, who appeared in Cornish, New Hampshire, in 1811 but never revealed his parents or his birthplace. Her mother refused to wear a wedding ring, which she considered a symbol of female servitude.

When Bugbee was eleven years old, her father died while the family was living in Port Jervis, New York. Her mother took his place as a teacher to finish out the school year. She then returned to her parents' hometown of Methuen, Massachusetts, where she taught French at the public high school to support her family.

After graduating from the school at which her mother taught, Bugbee entered Barnard College, where she got a taste of journalism by joining the college press club and becoming the campus correspondent for the *New York Tribune*. She was graduated from Barnard in 1909 and returned to Methuen to teach Greek for one year at the high school that she had attended. Bugbee disliked teaching, however, and was delighted when asked to be a summer substitute on the *Tribune* in 1910 for a Barnard friend, Eva vom Baur Hamsl, who wanted to travel to Germany. Hamsl, later women's editor of the *New York Sun*, failed to return on schedule, and Bugbee's temporary job turned into a reporting career that lasted for a record fifty-five years on the *Tribune*, which merged into the *Herald Tribune* in 1924.

As a reporter in New York, Bugbee encountered the customary prejudice against women journalists of her day. For decades she was a token woman on her newspaper's general assignment staff. She usually was limited to stories on women and their activities, but Bugbee did not complain. "There were some situations I just took for granted: that I was covering famous women of the period and not particularly famous men," she explained in later years.

Bugbee's spirit and determination to be a reporter showed in her coverage of the woman suffrage campaign, her first important assignment. In 1911 she marched for three weeks with a group of suffragists from New York to Albany during the day, hitchhiking in the evening to telegraph offices to file her stories. Three years later she received her first by-line (an uncommon achievement for reporters in that era), when she posed as a Salvation Army bellringer, collecting money for the poor at Christmas.

She was best known, however, for her coverage of Eleanor Roosevelt, which included reports on Mrs. Roosevelt's White House press conferences for women only and ended with a reminiscence of the former first lady at her death in 1962. Sent to Washington, D.C., to cover Mrs. Roosevelt's first press conference in 1933, Bugbee stayed on in the capital for weeks after Mrs. Roosevelt invited her to lunch at the White House, a notable event because previous first ladies had not developed close relationships with journalists. Bugbee was one of a handful of women reporters who accompanied Mrs. Roosevelt on a tour of Puerto Rico and the Virgin Islands in 1934. The two women became close friends, even though the *Herald Tribune* was a Republican newspaper and the Roosevelts were Democrats. Bugbee admired Mrs. Roosevelt and helped in developing her positive public image. She pictured Mrs. Roosevelt as a warm, caring individual whose ceaseless activity on behalf of worthy causes reflected her interest in bettering conditions for women and society as a whole.

Over the years Bugbee covered fourteen Republican and Democratic conventions, concentrating on the women's angle. Known as a competent but not particularly clever or rapid writer, she interviewed hundreds of outstanding women, including Alice Paul, founder of the National Woman's party; Lady Nancy Astor, the first woman to serve in the British Parliament; and Marie Curie, winner of Nobel prizes in physics and chemistry. Before her retirement in 1966 she served as religion editor. She enjoyed the friendship of Helen Rogers Reid, who succeeded her husband, Ogden Reid, as president of the *Herald Tribune* corporation in 1947.

Bugbee's last story for the *Herald Tribune* appeared in the final edition of the newspaper before it ceased publication in 1966. It described the dedication of a memorial bench to Mrs. Roosevelt at the United Nations. The newspaper paid tribute to Bugbee by running a picture of her seated on the bench along with a story on her retirement the previous day that was headlined "A Parting Salute to a Great Lady."

A warm, motherly figure who never lost her small-town air, Bugbee worked tirelessly to open the world of journalism to other women. She was a founder of the Newspaper Women's Club of New York and served three terms as its president. In addition, she was the author of the "Peggy" books, *Peggy Covers the News* (1936), *Peggy Covers Washington* (1937), *Peggy Covers London* (1939), *Peggy Covers the Clipper* (1941), and *Peggy Goes Overseas* (1945), a series of five fictional books for young women that dramatized newspaper reporting. With royalties from the series she built a country house in Bethel, Connecticut, where she spent her weekends. She never married.

Bugbee died in a nursing home in Warwick, Rhode Island, where she spent the last eleven years of her life. Bugbee showed that it was possible for a woman to succeed in the highly competitive world of New York journalism without giving up the personal characteristics of unselfishness, kindness, and caring for others typically associated with women's roles in family life. A beloved figure treated like a favorite aunt by her male counterparts, she worked ceaselessly to bring other women into journalism, but she sidestepped controversy. She was a feminist but not an outspoken one. With her quiet manner and sunny disposition, she bridged the gap between the assertiveness expected of journalists and the image of middle-class women as ladies. She helped make journalism a respectable occupation for women.

• Bugbee left no papers. A biographical article appeared in the final issue of the New York *Herald Tribune*, 24 Apr. 1966. An interview with Bugbee is in Jean E. Collins, *She Was There: Stories of Pioneering Women Journalists* (1980). See also Collins, "Two of Barnard's Nellie Blys," *Barnard Alumnae* 65 (Winter 1976): 2–5; Richard Kluger, *The Paper: The Life and Death of the New York Herald Tribune* (1986); and Ishbel Ross, *Ladies of the Press* (1936). Bugbee's niece, Norma

Starr, Cranston, R.I., has considerable information on her aunt. Obituaries are in the *New York Times*, 10 Oct. 1981, and the *Barnard Alumnae* 71 (Winter 1982).

MAURINE BEASLEY

BÜHLER, Charlotte (20 Dec. 1893–3 Feb. 1974), psychologist and psychotherapist, was born Charlotte Bertha Malachowski in Berlin, Germany, the daughter of Hermann Malachowski, a successful architect, and Rose Kristeller, a former opera singer. Born into an assimilated Jewish family, she attended school in Berlin and then studied psychology and philosophy at the Universities of Freiburg, Berlin, and Munich, completing her doctorate at the latter institution with research on thought experiments in 1918. She met Karl Bühler, an authority on her research topic, shortly after coming to Munich in 1915. They married the next year in a Protestant church (her husband was Catholic); they had two children, both of whom were included in the couple's research in developmental psychology.

In 1919 Bühler moved with her husband to Dresden, where he had received an associate professorship. There she became the first woman university teacher in Saxony in 1920; the same year she published a study on psychology and aesthetics titled "Discovery and Invention in Literature and Art." When her husband became a professor of philosophy and the director of the Psychological Institute at the University of Vienna in 1922, she joined him there, beginning as an unpaid assistant and eventually overcoming sexist and anti-Semitic prejudice to become an associate professor in 1929. From 1925 she also taught at the city of Vienna's Pedagogical Academy. After coming to the United States as a Rockefeller fellow in the 1923–1924 academic year and visiting leading developmental psychologists such as Edward Thorndike at Columbia and Arnold Gesell at Yale, Bühler brought objective assessment methods, including intelligence and behavioral tests, to Vienna. These she combined creatively with her own humanistic research style based, for example, on interpretive studies of word choice and semantic patterns in the diaries of young girls.

As the head of the Psychological Institute's Department of Child and Youth Psychology, sponsored by and located in the city of Vienna's adoption center, Bühler and her associates Hildegard Hetzer and Lotte Schenck-Danziger organized and directed a multifaceted body of research in child and youth development, with dozens of doctoral students from eighteen countries. In *Der menschliche Lebenslauf als psychologisches Problem* (The course of human life as a psychological problem, 1933), Bühler extended the study of development from childhood and youth into adulthood. She thus became a pioneer of what is now called lifespan developmental psychology, which is the effort to discover behavioral and attitudinal patterns particular to all stages of life.

After an authoritarian regime came to power in Austria in 1934, the Vienna school reformers who had supported Bühler's work were dismissed, but she and her husband elected to remain in Vienna and were able to continue working much as before. In this period she and her students extended their work from development to family studies and clinical diagnostics, publishing a book on practical child psychology. When Nazi Germany invaded Austria in March 1938, Bühler was in England on a research visit. In April, while she was in Norway on a visiting professorship, she learned that her husband had been arrested and was being held by the Gestapo. After his release, he joined his wife in Norway; they then emigrated via Great Britain to the United States. When her husband obtained a position at St. Thomas College in Minneapolis, Minnesota, in 1940, Bühler took a position at the College of St. Catherine in St. Paul. In 1943 she accepted a visiting professorship at Clark University in Massachusetts, thinking that it would become a permanent position; she attempted at the same time to establish herself as a therapist in New York City but was not successful. When the position at Clark was not renewed for financial reasons, she returned to Minnesota and became a full-time clinical psychologist at Minneapolis General Hospital, immersing herself in psychoanalytic diagnostics and therapy. In 1945 Bühler moved to California, where she became a clinical psychologist at Los Angeles County General Hospital.

While her much older husband lost contact with the American scientific community, Bühler blossomed in California. She published studies on Rorschach diagnostics as well as the World Test—a diagnostic tool based on play therapy techniques created in Vienna—and established a successful practice in Beverly Hills. She later became a leader of the emerging humanistic psychology movement, which presented itself as an alternative to the two predominant approaches in American psychology, behaviorism and Freudian psychoanalysis. She was a cofounder in 1962 and later president of the Association for Humanistic Psychology. Her most important later books are *Values in Psychotherapy* (1962), an attempt to bring together psychoanalytic and humanistic approaches; *The Course of Human Life* (1969), edited with Fred Masarik, a revised and updated version of her earlier work extending developmental psychology from childhood and youth into the adult years; and *Introduction to Humanistic Psychology* (1972), with Melanie Allen, a wide-ranging survey text. Bühler also published new German editions of her earlier work in developmental psychology as well as German translations of the World Test and other diagnostic works. She also brought out two popular German-language books, *Psychologie im Leben unserer Zeit* (Psychology in the life of our time, 1962), a survey text, and *Wenn das Leben gelingen soll* (If life is to succeed, 1969), a distillation of her work in adult development and humanistic psychotherapy. These works were widely read in Europe but never translated into English.

After her husband's death in 1963, Bühler became increasingly lonely and despondent. Eventually, she joined her son in Stuttgart, where she died. She is recognized today as a pioneer in developmental and humanistic psychology and as one of the most successful women professionals of her generation.

• Bühler's papers are in the possession of Achim Eschbach at the Max Planck Institute for Psycholinguistics in Nijmegen, Netherlands. Records of her career in Vienna are in the archives of the University of Vienna and the Austrian National Archives. Rockefeller Foundation support of the Vienna Psychological Institute is documented in the Rockefeller Family Archive Center in North Tarrytown, N.Y. Records relating to the Bühlers' emigration to the United States are in the Willard Olsen Papers at the Archives for the History of American Psychology in Akron, Ohio. Correspondence is in the Lawrence Frank Papers at the National Library of Medicine in Bethesda, Md., and the Gordon Allport Papers at the Harvard University Archives. Bühler's autobiography, "Charlotte Bühler," in *Psychologie in Selbstdarstellungen*, vol. 1, ed. Ludwig Pongratz and E. G. Wehner (1972), is valuable in many respects but not entirely reliable. The most extensive biography, which includes a full bibliography of Bühler's works, is Ilse Bürmann and Leonie Herwartz-Emden, "Charlotte Bühler: Leben und Werk einer selbstbewussten Wissenschaftlerin des 20. Jahrhunderts," *Psychologische Rundschau* 44 (1993): 205–25. On the founding and development of the Vienna Psychological Institute see Mitchell G. Ash, "Psychology and Politics in Interwar Vienna: The Vienna Psychological Institute, 1922–1942," in *Psychology in Twentieth-century Thought and Society*, ed. Ash and William R. Woodward (1987); and Gerhard Benetka, *Psychologie in Wien: Sozial- und Theoriegeschichte des Wiener Psychologischen Instituts, 1922–1938* (1995). On Bühler's emigration and career in America see Lewis A. Coser, *Refugee Scholars in America: Their Impact and Their Experiences* (1984); and Ash, "Women Émigré Psychologists and Psychoanalysts in the United States," in *Between Sorrow and Strength: Women Refugees of the Nazi Period*, ed. Sybille Quack and Daniel S. Mattern (1995).

MITCHELL G. ASH

BÜHLER, Karl (27 May 1879–24 Oct. 1963), psychologist and theorist of language, was born in Meckesheim, in the state of Baden, Germany. Both his parents, whose names are unknown, were of peasant stock; his father was a railway official. After attending school in Meckesheim and in nearby Tauberbischofsheim, he studied natural sciences and medicine at the University of Freiburg, receiving a medical degree in 1903 for research on the physiology of vision. After further study at the University of Strasbourg, he earned a doctorate in philosophy in 1904. Accounts of the following months differ. Some sources state that Bühler worked briefly as a ship's physician; others say that he studied under psychologists Carl Stumpf in Berlin and Benno Erdmann in Bonn.

Bühler began his research career as a psychologist in 1906, when he became Oswald Külpe's assistant at the psychological institute of the University of Würzburg. Between 1907 and 1909 he published experimental studies of thinking that clearly identify him as a member of the so-called Würzburg school. He argued on the basis of extensive introspective reports that thought is a continuous, dynamic, goal-directed process and that there are conscious contents, such as the awareness of a rule, that cannot be described as reproductions of or associations from sensory contents. His work helped introduce concepts from Edmund Husserl's phenomenological philosophy into cognitive psychology. However, the method that Bühler used in these studies led to a sharp controversy with Wilhelm Wundt and others on the limits of experimental method in psychology. In 1909 he moved with Külpe to Bonn, where he carried out pioneering experimental studies of form and proportion perception (*Die Gestaltwahrnehmung*, 1913) and published on child psychology.

Shortly after following Külpe to Munich, in 1916 Bühler married one of his students, Charlotte Malachowski. Research with their two children is reported in Bühler's major survey of developmental psychology, *The Mental Development of the Child* (1918; trans. 1929). The book, which posited a three-stage evolutionary schema from instinctive behavior to training to behavior guided by intellect, soon became a standard text in the field. After teaching as associate professor at the Technical Academy in Dresden from 1918 to 1922, Bühler became professor of philosophy and director of the Psychological Institute at the University of Vienna in 1922. From 1925 he and his wife also taught at the city's Pedagogical Academy. The couple, with the help of associates Egon Brunswik, Hildegard Hetzer, and Paul Lazarsfeld, soon made the Vienna institute one of the leading centers of basic and applied psychological research in Europe. In *Die Krise der Psychologie* (The crisis of psychology, 1927), Bühler attempted to overcome conflicts among competing psychological schools.

In the early 1930s Bühler published a full-scale theory of language in three works: *Ausdruckstheorie: Das System an der Geschichte aufgezeigt* (A theory of expression: The system as shown by history, 1933); "Die Axiomatik der Sprachwissenschaften" (The axiomatization of the language sciences, 1933; repr. 1969); and *Theory of Language: The Expressive Function of Language* (1934; trans. 1990). The theory considers the expressive and representational functions of language, deriving both from the biological concept of signal; it also includes a systematic "axiomatics" of symbol systems, the foundations of what would later be called semiotics. Bühler's interest in formal symbol systems and the theory of knowledge linked him to his colleague Moritz Schlick and the "Vienna circle" of logical empiricist philosophy. His theory of language appears to have been received with interest at the time, especially by the so-called Prague school of linguistics headed by Roman Jakobson.

Bühler first came to the United States in 1927–1928 to give lectures at Stanford, Harvard, and Johns Hopkins universities; he returned in 1929 to attend the International Congress of Psychology at Yale University. In the same year he was elected chair of the German Society for Psychology. He was offered a professorship at Harvard in 1930 but decided to reject it. After an authoritarian regime came to power in Austria in 1934, he and his wife elected to remain and were able to continue working much as before despite a 1936 police raid on the Research Center for Economic Psychology and the forced exile of Marie Jahoda and other politically active institute members.

After Nazi Germany invaded Austria in March 1938, Bühler was arrested and held briefly by the Gestapo. Released after signing a spurious "confession," he joined his wife, who was then a visiting professor in Norway, and emigrated with her via Great Britain to the United States in 1940. In the United States his age, his poor command of English, and the growing dominance of neobehaviorism in American psychology proved to be serious handicaps. With the help of the Emergency Committee in Aid of Displaced Foreign Psychologists of the American Psychological Association, he obtained positions at St. Scholastica College in Duluth, Minnesota, and then at St. Thomas College in Minneapolis in 1940; his wife found a position at the College of St. Catherine in St. Paul. In 1945 the Bühlers moved to Los Angeles, where Karl Bühler became a clinical psychologist at Cedars of Lebanon Hospital, retiring in 1955.

After 1945 Bühler published essays in German on biological topics such as animal navigation, which were collected in *Das Gestaltprinzip im Leben der Menschen und der Tiere* (The Gestalt principle in the life of humans and animals, 1960), and produced extensive manuscripts elaborating his theory of language. But he published nothing in the United States after his immigration, and none of his works on language was translated into English in his lifetime. Belated recognition came from German-speaking colleagues when he was named honorary president of the Sixteenth International Congress of Psychology in Bonn in 1960. He died three years later in Los Angeles.

Despite the lack of recognition accorded to him in the United States after his immigration, Bühler is acknowledged today as a significant contributor to many fields of psychology. His studies of form perception helped establish the basis for Gestalt psychology by providing evidence that certain formal relationships, such as the relative lengths of lines, could be perceived directly. His research on thinking is noted more favorably now that introspection is again a topic in cognition research. His theory of language had a formative influence on the Prague school of linguistics, and he is recognized in America as a founder of modern semiotics.

• Bühler's papers are in the possession of Achim Eschbach at the Max Planck Institute for Psycholinguistics, Nijmegen, Netherlands. Records of his career in Vienna are in the archives of the University of Vienna and the Austrian National Archives. Rockefeller Foundation support of the Vienna Psychological Institute is documented in the Rockefeller Family Archive Center, North Tarrytown, N.Y. Records relating to Bühler's emigration to the United States are in the Willard Olsen Papers at the Archives for the History of American Psychology, Akron, Ohio. Informative biographies are Gustav Lebzeltern, "Karl Bühler—Leben und Werk," in Bühler, *Die Uhren der Lebewesen und Fragmente aus dem Nachlaß* (1969); and Achim Eschbach and Gabi Willenberg, "Karl Bühler," in *Vertriebene Vernunft II: Emigration und Exil österreichischer Wissenschaft*, ed. Friedrich Stadler (1988). On the founding and development of the Vienna Psychological Institute see Mitchell G. Ash, "Psychology and Politics in Interwar Vienna: The Vienna Psychological Institute, 1922–1942," in *Psychology in Twentieth-century Thought and Society*, ed. Ash and William R. Woodward (1987); Gerhard Benetka, *Zur Geschichte der Institutionalisierung der Psychologie in Österreich* (1990); and Benetka, *Psychologie in Wien: Sozial- und Theoriegeschichte des Wiener Psychologischen Instituts, 1922–1938* (1995). On Bühler's emigration and career in America see Lewis A. Coser, *Refugee Scholars in America: Their Impact and Their Experiences* (1984). Sources for Bühler's influence are Robert E. Innis, ed., *Karl Bühler: Semiotic Foundations of Language Theory* (1982); and Eschbach, ed., *Karl Bühler's Theory of Language* (1988).

MITCHELL G. ASH

BUICK, David Dunbar (17 Sept. 1854–6 Mar. 1929), inventor and businessman, was born in Arbroath, Scotland, the son of Alexander Buick and Jane Roger. The family emigrated from Scotland to Detroit, Michigan, two years after Buick was born; his father died three years later. Buick attended elementary school, but the poverty of his single-parent family forced him to find full-time employment when he was just eleven years old. By the time he was fifteen, he had delivered newspapers, worked on a farm, and served as a machinist's apprentice at the James Flower & Brothers Machine Shop (the same firm where Henry Ford apprenticed in 1880).

In 1869 Buick went to work for the Alexander Manufacturing Company, a plumbing supply company in Detroit, where his mechanical skills helped him rise to foreman. In 1878 he married Catherine Schwinck. They had four children; Thomas, the eldest, eventually worked with his father in the automotive business.

When the Alexander Manufacturing Company failed in 1882, Buick and William S. Sherwood took over its assets and founded the Buick & Sherwood Plumbing and Supply Company. With Sherwood managing business affairs and Buick directing product development and production, the new company prospered. By 1889 Buick had been granted thirteen patents. Buick's patented process for bonding porcelain to metal was widely used on the plumbing fixtures that were then becoming a standard feature of everyday life.

Sometime after 1895 Buick became interested in the gasoline-powered internal combustion engine. In December 1899 he and Sherwood sold their plumbing supply company for $100,000. Although Buick continued to serve as president of the company until 1901, he devoted most of his time to experimentation on engines. Initially he worked to increase the power of marine engines and the type of stationary engines that were widely used to run farming and lumbering equipment. Working with Walter L. Marr and Eugene C. Richard, Buick developed a new "L-head" design. In 1901 he established the Buick Auto-Vim and Power Company to produce and sell this new type of engine.

The subsequent failure of the L-head engine in the marketplace did not discourage the inventor in Buick, but it did put him in financial straits. In 1902 he reorganized his business and renamed it the Buick Manufacturing Company. He now directed the effort to develop a "valve-in-head" engine for what he hoped would be a commercially successful automobile. In September 1902 Benjamin and Frank Briscoe, owners of a company that supplied metal parts to Detroit's fledgling automobile industry, agreed to advance Buick $650 in return for the car that he was developing.

The first Buick automobile was successfully road tested in early 1903, but Buick needed additional capital to set up manufacturing operations. Again the Briscoe brothers came to the rescue, but their intervention cost Buick his independence. In return for a $3,500 loan, the reorganized Buick Motor Company was recapitalized at $100,000 with the Briscoes holding $99,700 of its stock, and Buick just $300 worth. Moreover, the Briscoes gave Buick just six months to repay his debt to them or they would assume complete control of the company.

In the summer of 1903 the Briscoes lost all confidence in Buick. They sold the Buick Motor Company to a group of Flint, Michigan, businessmen led by James H. Whiting, president of the Flint Wagon Works. A reorganized Buick Motor Company began operations in Flint in January 1904. Buick was named secretary of the company, but he acted as its general manager and was barred from actually owning the stock assigned to him until the debts he had accumulated (which Whiting and his partners now owned) were cleared.

Working again with Walter Marr, Buick was able to produce a two-cylinder Model B that Marr and Thomas Buick drove without mishap to Detroit and back in July 1904 in just three hours and thirty-seven minutes. The next month the company began to produce a commercially successful Model B. By the end of the year, thirty-seven cars had been produced and sold. Nonetheless, James Whiting was not pleased with Buick's business performance. Buick had borrowed heavily from Flint banks to finance commercial operations, but he had not developed systematic marketing efforts for his car. As a consequence, Whiting turned to Flint's marketing genius, William C. Durant, president of the Durant-Dort Carriage Company, for assistance.

Durant personally tested Buick's car, liked it, and decided to move into the automobile industry. The Buick Motor Company was recapitalized at $300,000 in November 1904, and William C. Durant became its president and guiding force. Durant rapidly made the company into the automobile industry's first successful mass producer (8,820 Buicks were produced in 1908, more than Ford and Cadillac combined), but he also forced Buick out of the company.

In late 1905 Buick was removed from production management and put in charge of the company's "experimental room." At the time he owned 110 shares of stock, but he still owed the company far more than the value of his shares. Buick was never able to repay the debt, so he forfeited his stock when he finally resigned from the company in 1908. At that time, Durant gave him at least $100,000 in severance pay.

During the next ten years Buick lost most of his money in an oil-company venture in California and real estate speculation in Florida. The rest disappeared in a failed carburetor company and an unsuccessful automobile manufacturing firm he and his son tried to establish in Grand Rapids, Michigan. In the last few years of his life, Buick taught classes in mechanics at the Young Men's Christian Association in Detroit, where he died. He and his wife were so poor they could not afford a telephone, and of course they could not afford an automobile.

• Buick's papers have not been preserved; a few relevant documents are located in the William C. Durant Papers and the Daniel Wilkerson Files in the GMI Alumni Foundation Collection at the GMI Engineering and Management Institute, Flint, Mich. For additional information see Terry B. Dunham and Lawrence R. Gustin, *The Buick: A Complete History* (1985); George Humphrey Maines, *Men, a City, and a Buick* (1953); and George S. May, *A Most Unique Machine: The Michigan Origins of the American Automobile Industry* (1975). An obituary is in the *New York Times*, 27 Mar. 1929.

RONALD EDSFORTH

BUKOWSKI, Charles (16 Aug. 1920–9 Mar. 1994), poet and novelist, was born Henry Charles Bukowski, Jr., in Andernach, Germany, the son of Henry Charles Bukowski, an American soldier, and Katherine Fett. His father moved the family to Los Angeles when Bukowski, an only child, was two years old. Henry, Sr., held various jobs, including delivering milk and working as a museum guard, though he was often unemployed. Katherine Bukowski supplemented the family income by working as a housecleaner. Bukowski attended local public schools, including Mount Vernon Junior High School and Los Angeles High School on Olympic Boulevard. His early years were made difficult by his strict and overbearing father, who frequently beat him with a razor strop for minor infractions such as poor performance in school or failure to mow the front lawn with precision. To make matters worse, not long after starting high school, Bukowski developed a severe case of acne, which covered his face, neck, and body. It became so serious that he was briefly removed from school and taken to Los Angeles County Hospital, where doctors treated him with ultraviolet light and drained his boils with electric needles. With few close friends, Bukowski began a life of hard drinking while still in his teens. He found solace in the local public libraries, where he discovered Ernest Hemingway, James Thurber, and other writers he enjoyed.

Except for two years at Los Angeles City College (1940–1941) studying journalism, Bukowski spent the three decades after high school as a self-described "factotum." Traveling to New Orleans, San Francisco, St. Louis, and Philadelphia, Bukowski found work in a clothing warehouse, a dog biscuit factory, a print shop, and a slaughterhouse. In 1942 he was arrested in Philadelphia for avoiding the draft. He passed his army physical but failed a psychiatric exam and was released. In 1952 he began one of his most notable jobs, working for the post office delivering mail during the Christmas rush. He stayed on for three years, leaving after his hospitalization for a bleeding ulcer in 1955. He returned to the post office in 1958, however, and remained there for twelve years, working as a mail sorter in Los Angeles's Terminal Annex.

Throughout these years Bukowski was turning his experiences into fiction. After submitting a number of short stories, he got his first acceptance with "Aftermath of a Lengthy Rejection Slip," which appeared in the March–April 1944 edition of *Story* magazine. This early success was not repeated, however, and Bukowski published only sporadically in minor magazines. In his mid-thirties he turned to poetry. In lean and clear verse, Bukowski described his drinking, womanizing, horse-track gambling, and evenings spent at the typewriter listening to classical music on the radio. He mailed one batch of poems to the small Texas magazine *Harlequin*, edited by Barbara Frye. Frye not only published the poems but traveled to Los Angeles to meet the poet. Shortly after her arrival in 1955, the two were married, though the marriage ended in divorce less than three years later.

From the 1960s to the 1990s Bukowski was enormously productive, writing more than forty volumes of poetry and prose. His first book of poems, *Flower, Fist and Bestial Wail*, appeared in 1960. His success was facilitated by a number of loyal supporters, often editors of small magazines, who recognized Bukowski's talent. One was *Outsider* editor Jon Edgar Webb, who published several volumes of Bukowski's poetry in elaborately colored and illustrated editions, including *Crucifix in a Death Hand* (1965). Another backer was Douglas Blazek, editor of *Ole* magazine, who helped increase Bukowski's audience by printing poems in mimeographed editions. Most important, however, was John Martin, who set up Black Sparrow Press in Santa Rosa, California, largely to publish Bukowski. Martin first published Bukowski's poetry in 1966 in broadsides and, later, in more substantial volumes, including *Mockingbird Wish Me Luck* (1972), *Love Is a Dog from Hell* (1977), *Hot Water Music* (1983), and *The Roominghouse Madrigals* (1988). Bukowski also began writing a weekly column, "Notes of a Dirty Old Man," for the local magazine *Open City* in May 1967. With Neeli Cherkovski he founded a short-lived poetry magazine, *Laugh Literary and Man the Humping Guns*, which ran from 1969 to 1971. Already an underground favorite, Bukowski achieved acceptance from established circles with his inclusion in the Penguin Modern Poets series in 1969. His reputation grew further through his raucous live readings. At the 1972 City Lights Poet's Theater in San Francisco, Bukowski taunted his audience while he read and pulled beers out of a refrigerator onstage.

On 2 January 1970 Bukowski quit his job sorting mail and, with the aid of a small salary from John Martin, concentrated on writing full time. His first novel, *Post Office* (1971), was finished in less than a month. Bukowski became the subject of a documentary by Taylor Hackford, *Bukowski*, which aired on television in Los Angeles in 1973. Other novels followed under the Black Sparrow imprint: *Factotum* (1975), *Women* (1978), and *Ham on Rye* (1982). The protagonist of his novels was Bukowski's alter ego, Henry Chinaski. Together, the novels follow Chinaski through the childhood beatings, the disfiguring acne, and the endless jobs with their absurd and contradictory regulations. The novels sold fairly well in the United States but were far more popular in Europe. Carl Weissner, an editor based in Heidelberg, Germany, helped to win Bukowski a European audience, translating some of Bukowski's work himself. Bukowski acknowledged his German and French readers by visiting both countries in 1978 and giving a reading in Hamburg.

In 1976 Bukowski married again, this time to Linda Lee Beighle, owner of a health food restaurant. She turned him away from hard liquor to wine and got him in the habit of taking vitamin pills. Bukowski's work became the subject of films. Marco Ferreri directed *Tales of Ordinary Madness* (1983), which met with little success. Far better was Barbet Schroeder's *Barfly* (1987), for which Bukowski himself wrote the screenplay. Like all else, Bukowski incorporated his experiences on the movie set into a novel, *Hollywood* (1989). In it, Bukowski poked fun at himself, now quite wealthy, living in a big house in San Pedro, California, and driving a black BMW. The last books were *Septuagenarian Stew* (1990) and *Pulp* (1994), a detective story.

Bukowski's writings presented a vision of America starkly different from other celebratory accounts of post–World War II prosperity. Barflies, whores, and vengeful managers populated his pages. But at the same time, he made the down-and-out, crapulous life seem romantic. In *Ham on Rye*, Henry Chinaski remarks, "The life of the sane, average man was dull, worse than death."

Bukowski, called Hank by friends, died in the San Pedro Peninsula Hospital in Los Angeles. He had one child, a daughter, born to Frances Smith in 1964.

• Some Bukowski papers are at the University of California, Santa Barbara; in the American Literature Collection at the University of Southern California; and in Special Collections at Temple University. A biography by Neeli Cherkovski, *Hank: The Life of Charles Bukowski* (1991), recounts many of the incidents Bukowski himself described in his thinly veiled novels, adding accurate names and dates. More revealing are collections of Bukowski's letters, such as *Screams from the Balcony: Selected Letters, 1960–1970* (1993), *Living on Luck: Selected Letters, 1960s–1970s* (1995), and his correspondence with Canadian poet Al Purdy, *The Bukowski/Purdy Letters: A Decade of Dialog, 1964–1974* (1983). There are several critical discussions of his work, including Russell Harrison, *Against the American Dream: Essays on Charles Bukowski* (1994). Also useful is Sanford Dorbin, *A Bibliography of Charles Bukowski* (1969), which lists all of Bukowski's early publications. Obituaries are in the *Los Angeles Times*, 10 Mar. 1994, and in the *New York Times* and the *Chicago Tribune*, both 11 Mar. 1994.

A lengthy article about Bukowski's life is Suzanne Lummis, "Charles Bukowski," *Los Angeles Times Book Review*, 10 Apr. 1994, p. 15.

WALTER A. FRIEDMAN

BULEY, Roscoe Carlyle (8 July 1893–25 Apr. 1968), historian, was born in Georgetown, Indiana, the son of David Marion Buley, a physician, and Nora Keithley. He graduated from Vincennes High School and entered Indiana University in 1910, earning a B.A. in 1914 with a major in history and minors in government and economics. After teaching high school for a year at Delphi, Indiana, he returned to Bloomington as a research fellow and in 1916 received an A.M. in history with a master's thesis titled "Indiana in the Mexican War." He taught high school for two more years, at Muncie, Indiana, before serving in the U.S. Army in 1918–1919. He then returned to high school teaching, in Springfield, Illinois, and in 1923 began work on his doctorate in history at the University of Wisconsin, Madison. He wrote his dissertation, "The Political Balance in the Old Northwest, 1820–1860," under the direction of Frederic Paxson.

After receiving his Ph.D. in 1925, Buley returned for the rest of his career to Indiana University, where he served as instructor of history until 1929, assistant professor to 1937, associate professor until 1945, and professor until his retirement in 1964. In 1919 he married Esther Giles, who died two years later. In 1926 he married Evelyn Barnett. He had no children from either marriage.

Buley was a popular classroom teacher, and his courses, mostly surveys and post–Civil War U.S. history, demonstrated his interest in the ordinary experiences of "just folks, doing their day's work, and caring little for the verdict of history" (Buley, "Glimpses," p. 510), presented in a provocative and often humorous manner. They did not, however, provide a window onto his life as a scholar, where his focus was primarily on the Old Northwest (particularly Indiana) and on business history (especially insurance companies). His research took the form of three major two-volume works: *The Old Northwest: Pioneer Period, 1815–1840* (1951), which was awarded the Pulitzer Prize in history; *The American Life Convention, 1906–1952: A Study in the History of Life Insurance* (1953); and *The Equitable Life Assurance Society of the United States, 1859–1964* (1967).

To some extent, all of these writings share the same virtues and defects. All are massive compendiums of data, demonstrating enormous energy in gathering information from archival sources. *The Old Northwest*, in particular, seemed to set new standards in the way in which the frontier society was portrayed in a rich and detailed recounting of the tastes and smells, beliefs and habits, life and death of the pioneers—mostly male, mostly white, mostly successful subduers of the wilderness. Yet the volumes also tax the reader's patience, for they fall short in analytical arguments and provide far fewer generalizations from the evidence presented than did the works of most mid-twentieth-century historians. Reviewers termed Buley's life insurance studies, which were commissioned works and were handsomely printed and bound, "unduly discursive, bogged down in routine and inconsequential detail" and, more critically, unfortunately cast in an ultraconservative mode that suggested close affinity in outlook between author and subject.

By the standards of his times, a period when social and cultural history were in their infancy, Buley's methods of stacking evidence of all human activities into impressive "wholes" seemed unique and intriguing. Human history could contain everything one could document (or remember from one's own experiences) about how people were born, grew up, married, parented, worked, played, and died.

Among Buley's other writings was a 1943 edited version of *The Indiana Home* by Logan Esarey, who had been his teacher and friend. Two years later he and Madge E. Pickard joined as authors of *The Midwest Pioneer—His Ills, Cures and Doctors*, anticipating some of the topics that Buley would emphasize in his later publications about the Old Northwest. In 1959, eight years before his two volumes on the Equitable Life Assurance Society of the United States appeared, he wrote a shorter centennial history of and for the insurance company. In 1961 he published *The Romantic Appeal of the New West, 1815–1840*. He also produced eleven essays and twenty-five book reviews in historical journals.

In his writings Buley emphasized individual initiative and achievement; he lamented what he saw as panaceas for society's ills being proposed by progressives or New Dealers. He once described progressives "as piebald a conglomerate of balmy idealists, hero worshipers, out-faction city bosses, office seekers, pro-tariff anti-trusters, anti-tariff pro-trusters, egotists, puzzlewits, 'apostates,' revivalists, 'honeyfuglers,' and 'reformers' as ever staged a pitch on the American scene" (*Mississippi Valley Historical Review* 33 [1946]: 328). His basic conservatism sometimes intruding into the historical past he recreated, he found highest value in the lives of ordinary frontier settlers and in the entrepreneurship of insurance company executives. Yet he was a careful scholar who followed the professional mandates for documenting the sources of information from archival research, stressed accuracy and precision in his historical writing, and was always generous in his appreciation of others' monographs, if they were well written. He died in Indianapolis four years after retiring.

His most notable legacy is his prize-winning history of *The Old Northwest*. Social history has evolved in many ways since Buley's time, and his focus on white males on the frontier seems limited in a time when victims as well as victors are included, and class, gender, and race necessitate a wider angled lens when viewing the past. Yet Buley's experience and interest in an agricultural past—his affectionate descriptions of farm and small-town styles and manners—preserve for our understanding aspects of the past that would otherwise be lost.

• Scattered fragments of Buley's personal papers are at the Indiana University archives and the Indiana Historical Society. Buley's methods of historical recreations are examined in Fulmer Mood, "The Theory of the History of an American Section and the Practice of R. Carlyle Buley," *Indiana Magazine of History* 48 (1952): 1–22; see also Buley, "Glimpses of Pioneer Mid-West Social and Cultural History," *Mississippi Valley Historical Review* 23, no. 4 (Mar. 1937): 481–510. Carl Ubbelohde, "R. Carlyle Buley," in *Historians of the American Frontier: A Bio-bibliographical Sourcebook*, ed. John R. Wunder (1988), pp. 161–70, contains a listing of Buley's writings and writings about him and his work.

CARL UBBELOHDE

BULFINCH, Charles (8 Aug. 1763–15 Apr. 1844), civil servant and architect, was born in Boston, Massachusetts, the son of Thomas Bulfinch, a physician, and Susan Apthorp. Scion of long-established and wealthy colonial families, some members of which had been recognized amateur architects whose books were available to him, Bulfinch graduated from Harvard College in 1781. Apparently it was at Harvard that he learned drafting and the geometrical construction of linear perspective. After a period in the counting house of Joseph Barrell, where, as he later wrote, the "unsettled state of the time" produced "leisure to cultivate a taste for Architecture," he spent the period from June 1785 to January 1787 on a grand tour of England, France, and Italy, "observing . . . the wonders of Architecture, & the kindred arts of painting and sculpture." Described by Louis XVI's director general of gardens and buildings as "un gentilhomme américain" who was already "plein de goût et de connaissance dan [*sic*] les arts" (full of taste and familiarity with the arts), Bulfinch while in Paris made contact with, and was perhaps guided in his studies by, Thomas Jefferson. After his return home he finished his education with a journey to New York City, where he witnessed George Washington's inauguration and sketched its setting, Pierre Charles L'Enfant's Federal Hall, and Philadelphia, where the sumptuous new residence of William Bingham (1752–1804) in particular caught his eye.

In November 1787 Bulfinch married his cousin, Hannah Apthorp; of their seven surviving children, one, Thomas Bulfinch, achieved lasting fame as the author of the *Mythology*. His public life as gentleman-amateur architect in the tradition of the eighteenth-century dilettante began in the same year. The period just after Bulfinch's return to Boston was, in his own words, a "season of leisure, pursuing no business, but giving gratuitous advice in Architecture." This was advice derived from his European and American sojourns, and the large library he had begun to accumulate abroad and continued to enlarge from London booksellers, I. & J. Taylor, through transatlantic orders. He began his architectural career in 1787 with a project for the Massachusetts State House (not actually erected until the mid-1790s and since greatly expanded) and the Hollis Street Church (since demolished). In publishing a perspective view of the recently erected church in the next year, and thus providing Bulfinch with national exposure for his first design (Albany's Philip Hooker adapted it for his own North Dutch Church about 1796), the *Columbian Magazine* of Philadelphia mentioned "with pleasure" the name of the young architect, "whose genius aided by a liberal education, and improved by a tour through Europe, has rendered him an ornament to the place of his nativity." For that brief moment, at least, there were few designers in the new country to rival him.

For all the "improving" aspects of his continental tour, however, Bulfinch relied almost exclusively on English inspiration in these as in most of his early works. The plan and interior spatial organization of the Hollis Street Church depends on Christopher Wren's St. Stephen, Walbrook. The State House borrows its exterior *parti*, an axial stacking of arcade, colonnade, pediment, and dome, from William Chambers's recent front to Somerset House in London—appropriately enough, for that too was a government building; the decoration of its Senate Chamber from the designs of Robert Adam; and, perhaps not quite so appropriately, the interior of its House of Representatives from James Wyatt's pleasure dome, the London Pantheon. The English connection was to be expected, of course, in the works of an architect whose patrons, such as Harrison Gray Otis (1765–1848), espoused the politics of Federalism and who worked in a place with continuing strong ties to the mother country. Bulfinch was the architect of anglophile New England just as Thomas Jefferson was in architectural matters the representative of the francophile South. Bulfinch in the North worked for the urban Federal aristocracy while Jefferson embellished the Virginia countryside of his agrarian democracy.

In 1791 Bulfinch was elected for the first time to the Boston Board of Selectmen, and with the financial failure of his Tontine Crescent (1793–1795; demolished), a curve of sixteen urban townhouses modeled on fashionable English designs by Adam and others in London, Bath, and Buxten, the period of his leisure came to an abrupt end, and the period of his ceaseless toil began. Although his wife was to write that "Architecture [became] his business, as it had been his pleasure," in fact, civil administration became his business and architecture a second—and, perhaps, less income-producing—endeavor. His chairmanship of the selectmen—a board he headed from 1799 to 1817 and a position that included the superintendence of public schools—and his concurrent position as superintendent of police made him the chief administrator of the town, and his responsibilities occupied most of his time. It is a mystery where he found the energy also to design and oversee the erection of the many buildings—public and private, churches, jails, schools, hospitals, a theater, city and country houses, warehouses, civic buildings, and many more—with which he is credited.

The town of Boston doubled its population, from 20,000 to 40,000, during Bulfinch's tenure as chairman of the selectmen and superintendent of police. One of his successors as head of Boston government,

Mayor Josiah Quincy (1772–1864), in his history of the city (1852), summed up Bulfinch's accomplishments: "During the many years he presided over the town government, he improved its finances, executed the laws with firmness, and was distinguished for gentleness and urbanity, . . . integrity and purity." New construction, better streets, revamped wharfage, the filling of coves to increase the constricted land mass of the Shawmut Peninsula upon which Boston rests, services such as lighting and sewage; all these civic necessities captured the administrator's attention. These activities, of course, also gave him ample opportunity to exercise his architectural and engineering skills. Kirker has written (1963), concerning Bulfinch's duties as superintendent of police, that he "not only discharged . . . [them] with rectitude but designed the State House in which law was promulgated, the Court House in which it was administered, and the town, county, and state jails in which the guilty were incarcerated. It can also be said he designed many of the buildings and houses, streets and wharves, in which the crimes were committed." To have managed all that he did in the administration of Boston in an era of political turmoil and without lingering criticism represents a major accomplishment in itself.

Bulfinch and Boston are names forever linked. Despite the demolitions of time and man, the city to this day, in street patterns as well as isolated architectural monuments, bears the imprint of this busy architect and administrator. The present pattern of streets south of the Boston Garden reflects his triangular 1808 project for filling the Mill Pond. This was one of his several designs for large sections of the city. The curve of present-day Franklin Street recalls his Tontine Crescent; where Arch Street intersects with Franklin the central pavilion of the crescent once spanned that side street. The Tontine disappeared long ago, as did the Colonnade on Tremont Street, and, in effect, the Mason Houses, Park Row, and other altered streets of townhouses, but the original portion of the State House, New North Church (1802; now St. Stephen's), the remodeled Faneuil Hall (1805), all three of his houses for Harrison Gray Otis, and many other public and private works in and around Boston survive to demonstrate Bulfinch's refined, anglophile, and bookish neoclassicism.

All three Otis houses remain as witness to Bulfinch's early accomplishment. Designed between 1795 and 1805 for the Federalist lawyer and politician who moved often in order to keep abreast of changes in fashionable address, the Otis houses are paradigms of the Federal urban dwelling. All are formal and frontal variations of the Adam style. The first, its principal facade adapted from that of the Bingham house in Philadelphia, sits on a plan centered on a stairhall. The three-story brick facade on Cambridge Street is balanced about a central axis marked by a fan-lighted entrance, an elegant Palladian window above, and a semicircular window in the attic. The second faces Mt. Vernon Street near the top of Beacon Hill. Its principal facade is thinly articulated with shallow segmental arches at the ground level and colossal Corinthian pilasters embracing the main and attic floors. A balustrade crowns the whole. The third is on Beacon Street facing the Common; it is the largest and most elaborate of the three, a four-story brick rectangle topped with a balustrade and enriched by an Ionic portico at the entrance and triple-hung second-story windows with headers on consoles. It is clear that in all this Otis and Bulfinch sought to emulate their London peers.

It has been said that Bulfinch found Boston a town of wood and left it a city of stone. To some extent revised fire codes enforced by Bulfinch-the-administrator drove Bulfinch-the-architect to design for fire-resistant materials. The brick buildings of his earlier career, of the 1790s, with their axial and hierarchical designs, elegantly elongated Roman classical details, and delicate Adamesque ornament, gradually gave way after 1800 to more robust buildings of Chelmsford granite. In these late works the earlier axial and hierarchical arrangement continued, but the density of the stone called for works of monumental proportions and little decorative detail. As Bulfinch himself wrote in 1817, concerning his project for the Massachusetts General Hospital, "the building must consist as usual, of a centre & wings" while "public sentiment seems to require that all new buildings for general purposes should be of stone. . . . It will be more costly at the beginning, but will be more durable & require fewer repairs; and [the] richness of the material, will allow of a less decorated stile of ornament." Bulfinch's building still stands, as later enlarged, at Massachusetts General, a gray Chelmsford granite neoclassical block with central, octastyle, Ionic portico surmounted by a dome and flanked by symmetrical wings.

In the late Boston commissions, such as the Suffolk County Court House (1810; demolished), University Hall at Harvard (1813; altered), New South Church (1814; demolished), as well as the Massachusetts General Hospital, Bulfinch laid the groundwork for the "Boston Granite Style," the works of the next generation, of Alexander Parris and others, that gave special character to the city's buildings through mid-century. He also recognized the international architectural development toward larger, simpler, and bolder forms that would eventually lead to the use of Greek as well as Roman precedent. Only in some projects and buildings of the 1820s, however—such as the 1825 drawing for a monument, perhaps for Bunker Hill, now in the Library of Congress, and the Maine State House of 1829, his last work—did Bulfinch himself turn to orders of Grecian derivation.

Greek forms were introduced to the young United States by Benjamin Henry Latrobe (1764–1820), an Englishman who arrived in 1796 as a fully trained and experienced architect. It was Latrobe who set architecture in this country on its path toward professionalism. He was a skilled designer, an accomplished engineer, and a gifted artist. He established a new standard of architectural draftsmanship that far exceeded the labored efforts of Bulfinch and his peers. Bulfinch's drawings were adequate by eighteenth-century standards, and his use of perspective in all stages of the design process, from initial concept to presentation drawing, was rare in the era, but his best efforts could not hold a candle to Latrobe's gifted graphics. When Bulfinch first laid eyes on Latrobe's drawings, he wrote his wife, "my courage almost failed me—they are beautifully executed and the design is in the boldest stile." In his draftsmanship, as in his Boston practice, Bulfinch stood somewhere between the eighteenth-century amateur Thomas Jefferson and the nineteenth-century professional Latrobe.

Bulfinch examined Latrobe's drawings when, in 1818, having been appointed by President James Monroe to the post of architect of the United States Capitol, and having accepted the job because he needed the income, despite the inconvenience of moving himself and family to an unfamiliar city, he replaced Latrobe, who had been in charge of the building since early in the century. It was Bulfinch's first full-time, paid position as architect; at the age of fifty-five, after thirty years of part-time Boston practice, he had finally become a professional. During the twelve years of his residence at Washington, Bulfinch designed a Unitarian church, a federal prison, and a few other projects, but his primary attention was directed toward the nation's Capitol.

The original design of the Capitol had been given in 1792 by the amateur William Thornton. After many false starts Latrobe had taken over during the Jefferson administration. With the burning of the unfinished building by British troops in 1814, and the subsequent inability of Latrobe to get on with his superiors, the task of finishing Thornton's project fell to Bulfinch. In the years between his appointment in January 1818 and his dismissal in June 1829, Bulfinch completed the Senate and House wings, redesigned and constructed the central rotunda and its elevated dome, and added the Library of Congress and western front. He also planned the planting and fencing of the grounds. He had in hand, and was expected to follow where possible, Latrobe's drawings, so his contribution to the final result was more executive than creative, and in the present building largely buried beneath the later additions of Thomas U. Walter. It was nonetheless Bulfinch who by the end of the 1820s brought to completion the long process of adequately and expressively housing the legislative branch of federal government.

Bulfinch returned to Boston in 1830 at the age of sixty-seven. We know little of his life during his last fourteen years, although he seems not to have designed after the Maine State House, a work finished in 1832. By 1837 he was writing that he is "fully done with active business." The scanty sources available depict him as living quietly until his death in the next decade.

Bulfinch's labors as urban administrator laid the groundwork for the incorporation of the city of Boston in 1822, just five years after his departure. Bulfinch's architectural career exemplifies that transition from amateur to professional, and brick to stone, from English neoclassicism to the international Greek revival, that characterizes his age. His works also expanded from regional to national in scope, from the design of the Massachusetts State House to the completion of the federal Capitol, but this was not just because of his move from Boston to Washington. His work first reshaped architecture throughout New England, influencing the careers of designers such as Samuel McIntire, who followed Bulfinch's lead in giving Salem, Massachusetts, its Federal character; and then spread across the country, into the Western Reserve and near South, by means of the early publications of his prolific follower, Asher Benjamin. Bulfinch's influence did not end with his death, for his works continued to inspire Bostonian, or rather American, architects well into the twentieth century.

• Bulfinch's papers are scattered among many New England collections; the largest collection of his architectural drawings is in the Library of Congress. The basic source is his granddaughter, Ellen Susan Bulfinch, *The Life and Letters of Charles Bulfinch, Architect* (1896); some of the documents she cites are now in the Boston Athenaeum. Charles A. Place, *Charles Bulfinch, Architect and Citizen* (1925), is dated but contains information not found elsewhere. For Bulfinch's work as a civil servant, see Harold Kirker, "Charles Bulfinch: Architect as Administrator," *Journal of the Society of Architectural Historians* 22 (Mar. 1963): 29–35. Harold Kirker and James Kirker, *Bulfinch's Boston 1787–1817* (1964), places the man in the context of his time and place, while Harold Kirker, *The Architecture of Charles Bulfinch* (1969), is a catalog of his buildings. See also the chapter on Bulfinch in William H. Pierson, Jr., *American Buildings and Their Architects, vol. 1, The Colonial and Neoclassical Styles* (1970).

JAMES O'GORMAN

BULFINCH, Thomas (15 July 1796–27 May 1867), man of letters famous for a popularizing book on mythology, was born in Newton, Massachusetts, the son of Charles Bulfinch, an architect, and Hannah Apthorp. Although he was born at the height of an extended period of financial difficulties for his father, he was able to enroll at Harvard in 1811 and graduate in 1814. Upon graduation he taught for one year at Boston Latin School. He was a devoted and successful teacher, but at the end of the year he decided to pursue a career in business and became a salesman in his brother Charles's hardware firm. In 1818 he followed his family to Washington where he worked as a salesman of construction materials. In 1825 he returned to Boston and was a partner in a textile firm but, owing to his temperament and a self-confessed lack of business acumen, had little success. In 1837 he withdrew from private business and became collection clerk at the Merchants' Bank of Boston.

Bulfinch never married, and he lived with his mother and father, looking after them until their deaths. All of his literary work was the product of the hours outside his employment at the Merchants' Bank. Although his father's misfortunes meant that Bulfinch's financial situation never matched his family's social position, the family's connections did associate Bulfinch with both the literary and the scientific elite of

Boston, and from 1842 to 1848 Bulfinch was recording secretary of the Boston Society of Natural History. As late as 1850 he seems still to have been debating whether to concentrate his studies on science or literature when work on a revision of the prayer book for his family's church, King's Chapel, decided him for the latter. In 1853 he published his *Hebrew Lyrical History; or, Select Psalms, Arranged in the Order of the Events to Which They Relate*. In 1855 followed *The Age of Fable; or, Stories of Gods and Heroes*, which made Bulfinch's name synonymous with mythology. *The Age of Fable* was not meant to be a reference work for classical mythology but rather a retelling of the most important myths that would make them accessible to contemporary readers of English and American poets. The sources Bulfinch used were the best-known versions of the stories, most often those of Homer, Virgil, or Ovid. He made no attempt to reconcile versions and no attempt at completeness. His stories are not translations, but fresh narrations of the myths conforming to the contemporary taste for charming anecdote and absence of brutal physical detail. There are occasional attempts at etiological or psychological interpretation. Thus Ariadne's marriage crown becomes a constellation; Echo's responses continue to this day; and Hyacinthus and Narcissus are immortalized as flowers. Orpheus loses Eurydice because of hesitation, while jealousy undoes Daedalus and Deianara.

The Age of Fable was an instant success, which made Bulfinch's financial situation much more comfortable, with new printings of the book almost every year until his death. In 1858 he published a sequel, *The Age of Chivalry; or, Legends of King Arthur*, and in 1863 he published a third volume devoted to myth, *Legends of Charlemagne; or, Romance of the Middle Ages*. The title *Bulfinch's Mythology*, first used much later, sometimes refers to *The Age of Fable* alone and sometimes to all three of these volumes together. *Poetry of the Age of Fable* (1857) is Bulfinch's anthology of English and American poetry based on classical texts. Bulfinch's compendium was of immense importance at the time because it made classical mythology accessible to readers who had not learned Latin and Greek, and it remained for decades the principal source through which the general American public learned the Greek and Roman myths. In the twentieth century the impact of anthropology on the study of myth, the influence of myth theory, and Bulfinch's suppression of the sexuality and brutality of many of the myths have left *Bulfinch's Mythology* useful largely only for younger readers.

In 1858 Bulfinch became acquainted with a young English immigrant and would-be inventor named Matthew Edwards, who quickly became a surrogate son to him. Edwards died within a year, and his death moved Bulfinch to write an idealizing biography, *The Boy Inventor: A Memoir of Matthew Edwards, Mathematical-Instrument Maker* (1860). Bulfinch ended his literary career with two collaborations with his brother Stephen: *Shakespeare Adapted for Reading Classes and for the Family Circle* (1865) and *Oregon and Eldorado; or, Romance of the Rivers Columbia and Amazon* (1866), which popularized stories associated with the discovery and exploration of the two rivers. Bulfinch died in Boston, while still employed at the Merchants' Bank and still active in his writing.

• Bulfinch's major papers are at the Massachusetts Historical Society in Boston. For the location of other papers, see the work by Cleary, cited below. Andrew P. Peabody, *Voices of the Dead: A Sermon Preached at King's Chapel, Boston, June 2, 1867, Being the Sunday Following the Decease of Mr. Thomas Bulfinch* (1867), contains the text of the eulogistic sermon, reminiscences by friends, and a short autobiography by Bulfinch. Ellen S. Bulfinch, *The Life and Letters of Charles Bulfinch, Architect, with Other Family Papers* (1896), offers a personal view of the family. Indispensable is Marie Sally Cleary, *The Bulfinch Solution: Teaching the Ancient Classics in American Schools* (1989), particularly the chapter "Bulfinch's Life as a Matrix for *The Age of Fable*" (pp. 57–93), the source for the biographical material in this article. Obituaries, brief and lacking in substantial information, are in the *New York Times*, 31 May 1867, and the *Commonwealth* (Boston), 1 and 8 June 1867.

TIMOTHY LONG

BULKELEY, Gershom (Dec. 1636?–2 Dec. 1713), minister, physician, and author, was born in Concord, Massachusetts, the son of Peter Bulkeley, a founder and the first minister of Concord and a graduate of St. John's College, Cambridge, and Grace Chetwoode. Gershom Bulkeley received bachelor's (1655) and master's (1658) degrees from Harvard College, where he served for three years as a fellow and tutor. He was married in 1659 to Sarah Chauncy, the daughter of Harvard president Charles Chauncy (1592–1672); they had seven children. Bulkeley served as minister to the Congregational church in New London, Connecticut, from 1661 to late 1666 or early 1667, when he answered a call from the Congregational church in Wethersfield, Connecticut. More receptive to his emerging Presbyterian views regarding greater ministerial authority, as well as his support of inclusive church membership and the Half-Way Covenant, the Wethersfield church retained Bulkeley until he retired from the pulpit in 1677, claiming a "weak voice."

Bulkeley's learning and wide interests are indicated by an inventory of his personal library. While just over half of the 300-odd works are theological in nature, approximately 40 percent are concerned with scientific and medical subjects, with the remainder treating primarily legal topics. Recognition of Bulkeley's medical capabilities led to his service as a "chyrurgion to our army" in King Philip's War (1675–1676), during which he was wounded. Until his death he practiced medicine throughout the Connecticut River valley, traveling north into Massachusetts and south to Long Island. His library and his voluminous medical notebooks and account books demonstrate that Bulkeley both knew and practiced the latest advances in iatrochemistry, or chemical medicine. Familiar with the work of Robert Boyle, Paracelsus, and Johann Baptist van Helmont, Bulkeley preferred proven recipes and medicines to the mystical alchemical elements suggested by these scientific revolutionaries.

Bulkeley's historical reputation rests mainly on his staunch support of King James II's effort to centralize English imperial control by combining the colonies from New Jersey to Maine into the Dominion of New England (1685–1689). With the apparent surrender of the colony's charter to the dominion's governor-general, Sir Edmund Andros, in October 1687, Connecticut became part of this new and unwieldy dominion. In recognition of his developing legal talents and interests, Bulkeley was named a justice of the peace for Hartford County. With the overthrow of Andros's regime in the spring of 1689 and the concurrent reestablishment of Connecticut's charter government, Bulkeley made his principled royalism evident in a letter sent first to Connecticut's political leaders and then published as *The People's Right to Election, Or Alteration of Government in Connecticut, Argued In a Letter* (1689).

In the letter Bulkeley contended that the Connecticut corporation had ceased to exist in October 1687, that the colony's inhabitants should now continue in their loyalty to the supreme power in the empire, which was located in London, and that the colony should maintain its dominion-appointed government until it received from England an official notice of how to proceed. Unsuccessful in his initial effort to prevent a reversion to Connecticut's charter government, Bulkeley maintained his opposition to the proceedings in his colony for the next five years, an opposition that featured participation in a short-lived tax protest in Wethersfield. In addition, Bulkeley's resistance to Connecticut's government during this period inspired two more manuscripts, the first written in 1692 and published in 1895, the other published in 1694.

The first manuscript, "Will and Doom, Or the Miseries of Connecticut by and under an Usurped and Arbitrary Power," a royalist tour de force, was described by Perry Miller as "a minor masterpiece" and "the first explicitly anti-democratic utterance in our literature, . . . and one of the most vigorous and best written productions of the era." Samuel Eliot Morison considered it "unquestionably the ablest colonial writing that came out of the 'Glorious Revolution'; and one of the ablest of colonial political tracts prior to the American Revolution." An indictment of Connecticut's history and government with specifics concerning the colony's indigenous legal system, "Will and Doom" is fired by Bulkeley's contention that an English corporation could not legally or morally exercise a fundamental sovereignty, a charge he leveled emphatically at his adopted colony. While the royalist tract is flavored with the traditional scriptural citations and principles concerning properly constituted (monarchical) authority and the obedience due it, his argument is strongly influenced by an appreciation of the limitations on such authority imposed both by the law of nature and the English common law. For example, Bulkeley believed that the proper response to the unlawful demands of lawful authority was passive resistance. In short, while he held a pronounced attachment to order, monarchy, and English imperial authority, he was no political absolutist.

His other work, *Some Seasonable Considerations for the Good People of Connecticut* (1694), was an argument counseling his audience to acquiesce in the royal appointment of Benjamin Fletcher, governor of New York, as commander in chief of New England's military forces. Connecticut's government continued to resist inclusion in Fletcher's commission, however, and Bulkeley's pamphlet was briskly answered by two members of the Connecticut government, Secretary John Allyn and William Pitkin (1635–1694), the senior member of the governor's council, in *Their Majesties Colony of Connecticut in New-England Vindicated* (1694). By the autumn of 1694, word had arrived in Connecticut of the success of Governor Fitz-John Winthrop's mission to England: royal authority had officially recognized the revived Connecticut charter government. A perplexed Bulkeley returned to his books and his medical practice.

History is not often kind to apparent losers, and Gershom Bulkeley, royalist, Anglophile, and nondemocrat, mostly chose the losing side politically and socially in colonial Connecticut. Nevertheless, his principles included a passionate allegiance to the limitations on authority imposed by England's common law, and his intellectual achievements in science and medicine indicate that he was not completely out of step with his time. A man of singular accomplishments, he was memorialized in his epitaph as a "Jurist, Divine, and Med'cines Votary."

• Bulkeley materials are located in several depositories: over twenty volumes of his medical notebooks and account books are at the Hartford Medical Society Library, with a similar but smaller collection at the Watkinson Library at Trinity College, Hartford. A small number of Bulkeley letters and other manuscripts are at the Connecticut Historical Society and the Connecticut State Library, both in Hartford, and the Massachusetts Historical Society, Boston. Several important petitions and letters are located at the Public Record Office, London. Two of his works, *The People's Right* (1689) and "Will and Doom" (1692) may be found in volumes 1 (1860) and 3 (1895), respectively, of the Connecticut Historical Society, *Collections*. *Some Seasonable Considerations* (1694) is available only in its original printing. Thomas W. Jodziewicz has reproduced Bulkeley's 1699 diary in the American Philosophical Society, *Proceedings* 131 (1987): 425–41 and his 1710 diary in the Connecticut Historical Society, *Bulletin*, 56 (1991): 57–88; see also *A Stranger in the Land: Gershom Bulkeley of Connecticut* in the American Philosophical Society, *Transactions* 78 (1988), which includes a lengthy bibliography and an appendix identifying the books in Bulkeley's library. Also helpful for Bulkeley and his historical moment are Richard S. Dunn, *Puritans and Yankees: The Winthrop Dynasty of New England, 1630–1717* (1962), and Richard R. Johnson, *Adjustment to Empire: The New England Colonies, 1675–1715* (1981).

THOMAS W. JODZIEWICZ

BULKELEY, Morgan Gardner (26 Dec. 1837–6 Nov. 1922), president of the Aetna Life Insurance Company, governor of Connecticut, and U.S. senator from Connecticut, was born in East Haddam, Connecticut, the son of Eliphalet Adams Bulkeley, a public official, Republican party leader, and founder of the Aetna Life Insurance Company, and Lydia S. Morgan Gardner.

Morgan Bulkeley, who claimed direct descent from the Puritan founders of the Massachusetts Bay Colony, benefited from his Yankee heritage. It provided him with social status and instilled a respect for hard work, honesty, and public service. Somewhat surprising for a lad from the upper middle class, Bulkeley received only a modest formal education, leaving school in Hartford, Connecticut, at fifteen to work as an errand boy in an uncle's store in Brooklyn, New York. There he learned the world of business firsthand.

Bulkeley interrupted his labors during the Civil War when he rallied to the colors. He enlisted in the Thirteenth New York Regiment, serving with General George McClellan in the bloody Peninsular campaign. After the war Bulkeley returned to Brooklyn, but moved to Hartford in 1872 after the death of his father. Soon Bulkeley helped to establish the U.S. Bank with family money and became its first president. Seven years later he assumed the presidency of the growing local firm his father had created in 1853, the Aetna Life Insurance Company.

It was with Aetna that Bulkeley made his greatest mark. The life insurance industry experienced unparalleled growth after the Civil War, and Aetna benefited from this trend. Under Morgan Bulkeley's leadership the firm became one of the nation's largest and most secure financial institutions; assets soared from $25 million in 1880 to more than $200 million in 1900, and the number of employees rose from twenty-nine to more than 1,500 during this time period. As an insurance executive Bulkeley represented the less speculative and less flamboyant element within the industry; he lacked the anticonsumer tendencies of a Frederick Burnham, James Hazen Hyde, or John A. McCall. Bulkeley's responses to the sensational revelations of the New York State Armstrong Committee hearings in 1905 were like those of managers of conservative, consumer-sensitive companies.

While some life insurance firms attempted to seek federal protection from pro-policyholder state legislation, especially measures passed by New York lawmakers in 1906, Bulkeley refused to turn to Washington for assistance. He represented the sentiments of his home state companies and several of the small, regional life insurance concerns that feared domination of the federal regulatory machinery by the giant and politically powerful New York–based firms. These companies, as Bulkeley and his supporters privately surmised, would surely exploit their economic and political advantages.

Bulkeley also had an extensive political career. An enthusiastic member of the Republican party, influenced by his father's early work for the GOP and his own wartime and business attitudes, Bulkeley had entered grassroots politics when a resident of Brooklyn. Later in Hartford he won election as alderman, president of the court of common council, and mayor; he served four successive terms as mayor between 1880 and 1888. In 1885 Bulkeley married Frances Briggs Haughton, with whom he had three children.

In 1888 Bulkeley became the Republican candidate for governor of Connecticut. His opponent, Luzon Morris, received 1,505 more votes than did Bulkeley but fell short of a majority because of several thousand votes that went to minor candidates. The matter was sent to the state legislature, where the Republican majority voted to seat Bulkeley. A more chaotic election for the governorship, however, occurred two years later. In 1890 neither the Democratic candidate (Morris) nor the Republican one (Samuel Merwin) obtained a majority of votes. But the matter was not easily resolved; Democrats controlled the senate and Republicans led the house, and they failed to agree on a candidate. This caused Bulkeley to remain the de facto governor for the next two years. Although the Connecticut Supreme Court approved Bulkeley's tenure, his inability to work with a politically divided general assembly meant that he was forced to finance state government from his own pocketbook in 1891 and 1892. The state later reimbursed him.

Bulkeley concluded his involvement in electoral politics as U.S. senator from 1905 to 1911. He was a vocal critic of President Theodore Roosevelt's expansion of the central government's powers, and he successfully opposed efforts in the Senate to institute federal regulation of the insurance industry. Bulkeley also opposed Roosevelt on the Philippine tariff, arguing that the importation of cheap Philippine tobacco would hurt tobacco farmers in Connecticut.

Bulkeley sought diversion from the insurance industry and public life through sports, mainly baseball and horse racing. He served as the first president of the National Baseball League in 1876 and for three decades actively backed the work of the National Trotting Association. He died in Hartford.

• Some letters and related materials on the business and political career of Morgan Gardner Bulkeley are housed in the Connecticut Historical Society in Hartford. Also in Hartford are the corporate records of the Aetna Life Insurance Company, which include numerous documents relating to Bulkeley's long reign. Obituaries are in the *Hartford Courant*, the *Hartford Times*, and the *New York Times*, all on 7 Nov. 1922.

H. ROGER GRANT

BULKELEY, Peter (31 Jan. 1583–9 Mar. 1659), Puritan clergyman, was born in Odell, Bedfordshire, England, the son of Edward Bulkeley, the rector of Odell, and Olyff Irby, of Lincolnshire. At about age sixteen he entered the Puritan-inclined St. John's College, Cambridge, becoming fellow in 1605 and receiving his M.A. in 1608. In the same year he was ordained at Ely and in 1610 became university preacher. On the death of his father in 1620 he succeeded to the rectory of Odell and to his father's sizable estate. A Nonconformist like his father, he was overlooked by John Williams, the bishop of Lincoln, until after the accession of Archbishop Laud (1633). His first wife, Jane Allen (marriage date unknown), of Goldington, Bedfordshire, with whom he had eleven children, died in 1626. In 1634 he married Grace Chetwode, of Odell, who had four children. Complained against in 1635 for his nonconformity, he was silenced by Laud's vicar-general, Nathaniel Brent.

That year Bulkeley sold his estate and removed to Massachusetts, sending part of his family over first to mislead the authorities. He stopped for a time in Newtown (now Cambridge), where he was made freeman. Shortly thereafter he led a group of planters to the Musketequid (now Concord) River, where he directed the founding of Concord under a grant from the General Court of September 1635. In July 1636 he gathered the twelfth church in the colony, being installed the following April as principal minister ("teacher"). Among the most prosperous of the original settlers, he invested extensively in the town, setting up a grist mill, for which he received acreage in the town center. From these and other lands he provided farms for his servants. In 1642 friction with his cominister, John Jones (the "pastor"), and unhappiness about the cost of supporting two elders, occasioned a meeting of ministers at Concord, which advised patience and cooperation. This tension and the general difficulty of farming there prompted a substantial exodus to Connecticut in 1644, led by Jones. Bulkeley remained a leading man of Concord in both temporal and spiritual affairs. It has been said that in 1676, during King Philip's War, his reputation saved Concord from Indian attack because "'Big Pray' had lived there" (Hudson, p. 331).

Bulkeley was a strict and conscientious Puritan in dress, conduct, and piety, and a scholarly, industrious, and winning minister. Prevented by infirmity from visiting his people to instruct them, he introduced the practice of catechizing the young on Sundays in the presence of the congregation, using as his text William Perkins's *The Foundation of the Christian Religion* (1591). He preached regularly upon the chief heads of Puritan divinity, especially on the nature, person, and work of Christ. His fellow ministers considered him learned and judicious. In the Antinomian controversy (1636–1638) he played a leading part with Thomas Shepard, minister at Newtown, in opposing the views of Anne Hutchinson and John Wheelwright, with whom John Cotton, minister at Boston, was briefly associated. In August 1637 he was chosen comoderator with Thomas Hooker, founder of Connecticut, of the ministerial synod that dealt with the doctrinal errors and disruptive practices of the Antinomians.

Shortly after arriving in New England, Bulkeley began a sermon series, on Zech. 9:11, on the covenant of grace, which he considered the central topic in divinity. In these sermons he addressed the chief theological issues in the Antinomian controversy: the relation between the covenants of works and grace, the relation of faith and justification, and assurance of salvation. He offered a characteristic Reformed Protestant statement of the roles, in Christian experience, of divine grace and created human nature as articulated by the English Puritan divines William Perkins, John Preston, and William Ames. Bulkeley represented the covenant of grace as the great medium through which God's decree of election is made effectual in the conversion of individuals and God's benevolence toward them is manifested. God's covenant of grace through Christ accomplishes salvation, which God's covenant of works with Adam had failed to do. Its condition is not obedience to the moral law, as in the covenant of works, but the act of faithful acceptance of Christ as savior, which springs from grace implanted by God in the soul. By this gracious act, individuals enter covenant with God. This active faith does not cause justification in God's sight—justification results from Christ's work—but applies that result to persons. Faith thus objectively justifies and is not, as the Antinomians held, merely subjective belief that a person is already justified. Grace, further, produces a real change in the soul, sanctifying it by turning it toward God in loving obedience. The covenant of grace frees from obedience to the moral law as the condition of salvation but not from the law as Christians' rule and guide, and the sanctified are truly motivated to obey it. In the rational soul, conscience is naturally privy to motives, and the sanctified, by introspection, can know whether they obey willingly. In this way people whose faith is real but weak may nonetheless perceive in themselves gracious motives, and therefrom have assurance of salvation. They need not, as the Antinomians argued, wait for a special revelation from the Holy Spirit to "prove" their justification and sanctification. This covenant, in which God by grace provides the required condition and restores the soul, is the foundation of Christian confidence. Bulkeley's conception of Puritan "covenant theology" maintained both the graciousness of salvation and the created autonomy of the rational soul. Because he and his colleagues made "active faith" the condition of the covenant of grace and allowed assurance to be concluded from sanctification properly discerned, the Antinomians regarded them as "mere legal preachers" and "under a covenant of works."

Bulkeley's sermon series was published in England in the context of a similar controversy during the civil war as *The Gospel Covenant, or the Covenant of Grace Opened* (1646; 2d enlarged ed., 1651, 1674), dedicated to Oliver St. John, an important figure on the parliamentary side, with whom Bulkeley stood in close personal relation. This was his only published work, besides some unremarkable Latin and English verses printed by Cotton Mather and Nathaniel Morton.

Little is known about Bulkeley's later life. He died in Concord, and was succeeded as principal minister there by his son Edward. He bequeathed part of his library to Harvard College.

• Material pertaining to Bulkeley's biography may be found in Cotton Mather, *Magnalia Christi Americana*, bk. 3 (1702); Edward Johnson, *The Wonder-working Providence of Zion's Saviour* (1654); William Sprague, *Annals of the American Pulpit*, vol. 1 (1856); Edward Hudson, *A History of Concord Massachusetts*, vol. 1 (1904); *The New England Historical and Ge-*

nealogical Register, vol. 10 (1856), pp. 167–70; J. Venn and J. A. Venn, *Alumni Cantabrigiensis*, pt. 1 (1922); and the prefaces to *The Gospel Covenant*. Michael McGiffert, "The Problem of the Covenant in Puritan Thought: Peter Bulkeley's *Cospel-Covenant*," *New England Historical and Genealogical Register* 130 (1976): 107–29, closely analyzes Bulkeley's text. Bulkeley's theological position is treated in William Stoever, *'A Faire and Easie Way to Heaven': Covenant Theology and Antinomianism in Early Massachusetts* (1978). John von Rohr, *The Covenant of Grace in Puritan Thought* (1986), offers an overview of Puritan covenant doctrine.

WILLIAM K. B. STOEVER

BULKLEY, John Williams (3 Nov. 1802–19 June 1888), teacher, administrator, and educational reformer, was born in Fairfield, Connecticut. The identities of his parents are unknown. Bulkley's father arranged for his son's common school education with an eye to mechanical pursuits, but young Bulkley's inclinations gravitated toward more intellectual endeavors. About 1820 he moved to Clinton, New York, to prepare himself for Hamilton College. Focusing on the study of mathematics and the classics, he hoped to enter Hamilton as a sophomore. His health failed, however, and he was compelled to disrupt his educational ambitions and embark on a recuperative sea voyage. Bulkley never did return to college, but he had the satisfaction in 1853 of receiving an honorary master of arts from his intended alma mater.

In 1825 Bulkley began a career pattern that was characteristic of intellectually oriented youth in the early nineteenth century. He took up "school-keeping," presumably as a temporary occupation, hoping eventually to become a minister. At this time, the public was demanding and newspaper editorials were calling for the creation of state-supported public school systems. Bulkley's home state of Connecticut authorized a common school system in 1837, the second state to do so. This reform ferment persuaded many young men to think of schoolteaching as a permanent occupation, one that might be developed into a bona fide profession, akin to the ministry. Bulkley's hometown of Fairfield offered him his first teaching position (1825–1831) in a local district school. He was then called to be the principal of a private academy in Troy, New York (1831–1838), and later (1838–1850) of the public grammar schools of Albany, New York. Earning favorable reputations in these cities, he became a leader in the educational reform movement at the state and national levels.

During the 1840s, Bulkley's activism focused on two principal goals, maintaining the public's commitment to public education and elevating the teaching profession. In his view, formal tax support from the state of New York was insufficient to sustain schools without supportive public opinion. At the same time, he did not think a school system could survive merely by selecting candidates from available pools. The aspiring professional teacher, he believed, must educate both pupils and parents. Before teaching was firmly established as a profession, the teacher was viewed less as an educational specialist and more as a general evangelist for the social benefits of instruction.

In an effort to professionalize schoolteaching, Bulkley advocated the development of a major organizational structure whose methods were rooted in the highly effective revival organizations. He looked to establish organizations that, though voluntary and officially nonpolitical, nevertheless would be capable of bettering the situation for teachers as well as "converting" both potential teachers and public school critics. First, at the local level, Bulkley founded the Troy Teachers' Society in 1836 and later the Albany County Teachers Association, which in 1845 called for the creation of the New York State Teachers Association, the first of its kind in the United States. Bulkley served as its first president and was named to a second term in 1851. Also at its 1845 meeting, the Albany association founded the *Teacher's Advocate*, the first teachers' journal in the country. Bulkley later served on the editorial board of the *New York Teacher*, founded in 1850. In 1857 he was one of eleven founding members of the National Teachers' Association, which in 1870 became the National Education Association. Bulkley held the office of secretary in 1856 and became the national organization's fourth president in 1860. His principal lifetime achievement, after schoolteaching itself, was his constant contributions to this hierarchical network of teachers' organizations.

Bulkley worked and preached in behalf of an expansive professional network that integrated local, county, state, and national educational organizations. In writing and in speeches he exuded the extraordinary confidence that mid-nineteenth-century Americans placed in the genteel force of voluntary associations. "In the first place, let the effort be informal and social," he said in a speech at the the 1864 National Teachers' Association meeting, "in the spirit of the learner rather than that of the teacher, who should be ever ready to receive while endeavoring to communicate truth. Thus confidence will be inspired, interest enlisted, a healthy public sentiment created, and hearty cooperation secured in the work of reform. Then the way may be prepared for the public movement of the town."

In 1850 Bulkley joined the American Institute of Instruction (founded in 1830), which put him in contact with every major educator in the country, and he used this broad forum to promote educational reform in New York as well as broader educational concerns. In his speeches before the American Institute of Instruction, he distilled the interpretive stance that he took in compiling his many school reports and in talking about educational reform to organizations both large and small. At the institute's meetings, Bulkley participated in professional discussions or lectured on such broad issues as "The Moral Office of the Teacher" (1855), "The Means of Awakening in the Minds of Parents a Deeper Interest in Educational Welfare" (1856), "Self-Culture and Self-Reliance" (1857), "The Education of Both Sexes Together" (1857), "Ought Military Instruction to Be Generally Introduced into

Our Schools?" (1863), and "To What Extent Should Oral Instruction Take the Place of Textbooks in Schools?" (1869). In these presentations he stressed his belief that books, pedagogical techniques, and even organizations were insufficient if either teacher or student depended on them uncritically. He endorsed coeducational classrooms, minimal homework (no more than two hours), graded schools (but without military regimentation), and promotion by examination; yet at the same time, he continually stressed the centrality of self-culture, a pan-Christian notion of initiative guided by a sense of the public good. Bulkley repeated his quasi-evangelical statements before the councils of the American Association for the Advancement of Education as well as at educational conventions in other states.

In 1850 Bulkley became the principal of a large public school in Williamsburg, New York. Associated with this work was his creation of a Saturday Normal School class as well as teachers' institutes held twice a year for those interested in professional study. When the towns of Williamsburg, Bushwick, and Brooklyn merged in 1855 to form the fourth largest city in the United States, Bulkley became the first superintendent of the expanded Brooklyn educational system. He continued in that office until 1873, when, due to advanced age, he accepted the position of assistant superintendent; he served in that office until 1885. Bulkley died at his home at 167 South Elliott Place in Brooklyn.

It appears that Bulkley was married more than once; his wife at the time of his death was Abby Isobel. He was survived by two daughters.

• Bulkley's most polished and representative speech before the American Institute of Instruction was "Self-Culture and Self-Reliance," delivered in 1857. Variations on these bedrock themes resonate throughout his official reports to the Brooklyn Board of Education and in his published remarks in the *Lectures and Proceedings of the American Institute of Instruction*, especially between 1855 and 1871. See also his rationale for a hierarchical organizational network for teachers in *American Journal of Education*, vol. 15 (1864): 185–88. His sketch in the *Dictionary of American Biography* synthesizes the basic information from *U.S. Commissioner of Education's Report* (1887–1888) and the *NEA Proceedings* (1888). David Tyack, *The One Best System* (1974), explores the broader dynamics that produced a bureaucratized public school system, and Paul H. Mattingly, *The Classless Profession: American Schoolmen in the Nineteenth Century* (1975), analyzes the development of teaching as a profession and its evangelical roots. An obituary is in the *New York Times*, 21 June 1888.

PAUL H. MATTINGLY

BULL, Ole (5 Feb. 1810–17 Aug. 1880), concert violinist, composer, and patriot, was born Ole Bornemann Bull in Bergen, Norway, the son of Johan Storm Bull, an apothecary, and Anna Dorothea Geelmuyden. Musically precocious by age three, he was encouraged by his mother and his uncle, a good amateur cellist, who bought the child his first violin and persuaded the parents to engage an instructor, the closest brush Bull would have with formal violin study. Two years were spent with Johan H. Paulson, followed in 1822 by a six-year stint with Mathias Lundholm. Beyond this early foundation, Bull remained almost entirely self-taught, although he sometimes sought informal help from artists like Torgeir Augundson, the legendary Norwegian folk fiddler.

Bull's family had the means to fill his youth with pleasure as well as education and culture. He roamed the family estate near Bergen and learned to use his violin to imitate sounds in nature. He also absorbed, in contacts with local farmers, the style of Norwegian hardanger fiddle music native to the area. These elements he would later blend and shape into a unique music vocabulary that became immensely popular.

As a child, Bull was emotional and temperamental. All forms of formal education, other than music, met with rebellious indifference. He was dispatched to the University of Christiania at age eighteen to prepare for a career in theology but failed the entrance exams. Reacting instinctively, he secured a position as violinist with the local orchestra and, a few months later, became its leader.

With his new friend Henrik Wergeland, a rising poet and patriot, Bull joined the National Revival movement to promote native Norwegian culture. In 1828 the two were in a demonstration that was broken up by police, and Bull fled to Germany, where he hoped to study with Louis Spohr. There is some question whether he actually met with Spohr at that time. Later Spohr would, in his autobiography, comment on Bull's style and technique, but there is no evidence that he ever accepted the younger man as a student.

With little direction and no funds, Bull went in 1831 to Paris, where romantic stories about the headstrong young violinist grew. Paris offered little encouragement, however, for Bull was inexperienced and musically unrefined, and although he met important people, notably Rossini and Chopin (he shared a concert with Chopin), he failed to make use of such contacts to further his career. He worked seriously with Paganini's Violin Method and, dabbling with composition, began to study music theory and orchestration.

In 1833 Bull left Paris to tour Switzerland and Italy, where he enjoyed his first success. He traveled and performed, placing more emphasis on his own compositions, like *Polacca Guerriera*, which mixed dazzling technique with folk melody. He had learned showmanship, and his stage presence projected warmth, modesty, and congeniality. One Norwegian critic wrote, "There is no need of musical knowledge to admire Bull. . . . He speaks a language all understand" (Haugen and Cai, p. 54).

Musically Bull was unique. His prodigious natural talent made him fluent in any style. His skill in improvisation, which stemmed from hardanger fiddle tradition, was combined with the free forms of Italian opera to produce a spontaneous, emotional musical language that communicated readily with most any audience.

As a technician he excelled. His method of holding the instrument, balancing rather than constricting, was original. He perfected, with a longer, heavier bow and a flattened bridge, a quadruple stopping technique that enabled him to play four parts at once. He was adept at harmonics, and his intonation was superb. Scales and position changes were executed effortlessly, and he could trill flawlessly with any two fingers. All these skills, coupled with intense powers of concentration and memory, enabled him to digest new pieces quickly and seemingly without effort. It made him a worthy successor to his idol, Paganini.

Bull's audiences grew, and the next nine years were a blur of tours, interrupted only by his marriage to Alexandrine Félicité Villeminot in 1836. In 1840 he met the great pianist Liszt in London. They formed a firm friendship and performed together numerous times. Bull worked furiously, at one point giving 274 concerts in fourteen months. A German critic described his "incomparable virtuosity . . . geniality, enrapturing grace . . . elegance, warmth, strength and clarity . . . it bears the stamp of perfection" (Haugen and Cai, pp. 48, 50). Despite his success, he was always on the brink of financial crisis because of lavish entertaining, excessive generosity, careless purchases, and gambling. Félicité, living alternately in Norway and Paris, felt the strain, for she was tied increasingly to home and children, of whom four would live to adulthood.

On his first tour to the United States in 1843, Bull established a bond between himself and the audience that depended as much on showmanship as on musical skills. As in Europe, some critics branded him a charlatan, but in answer, George William Curtis later wrote in the *New York Tribune* in 1852,

> Like Paganini, he is an exceptional person. . . . He is his own standard; he makes his own rules. . . . He uses music as color, and it matters nothing to him if the treatment be more or less elaborate, or rhythmical, or detailed, if it succeed in striking the hearer with the vivid impression sought. It is unavoidable, therefore, that he is called a charletan. . . . The artist magnetizes them and they can think and dream as he chooses. (quoted in Sara Bull, pp. 217–18)

Bull returned to Norway in 1848. His objective was to establish a national theater, and in 1850 he produced a working company but soon wearied of administration and appointed others to succeed him. Among them was an aspiring young playwright, Henrik Ibsen, who would later borrow from the personality of Bull to fashion the central character of his *Peer Gynt*.

The national theater represented a turning point for Bull. His patriotism and compassion for the common folk of Norway had broadened his ambitions. Facing increased competition in Europe, he returned to America in 1852 with a dual mission: he would reestablish his successful concert work and he would start a colony for Norwegians. As in all his projects, Bull commenced with a frenzy of activity, bought 11,000 acres of forested mountain land in Pennsylvania, received the first group of immigrants, and began building a community, Oleana, in September of 1852. The land, however, was poorly chosen, isolated, and infertile for agriculture. Within a year Oleana failed. He sold the land back to his American partners, using the proceeds and more of his own money to assist the immigrants in resettling elsewhere. In 1920 the Commonwealth of Pennsylvania established Ole Bull State Park at the site.

An abortive effort at starting an opera company in New York, a bout of yellow fever contracted in Panama, and the depletion of his fortunes sent Bull back in 1857 to Norway, where he found further trouble. The failure of Oleana had put off his countrymen, and after five years of separation his wife was in ill humor. He resumed touring, and in 1862 Félicité died in Norway while he was away.

Bull devoted the next several years to activities at home and tours in the United States, where he felt increasingly at home. Early in 1870, in Madison, Wisconsin, he met twenty-year-old Sara Thorp, the daughter of Joseph G. Thorp, a lumber tycoon and Wisconsin state senator. With her mother, Sara accompanied Bull on his next tour in Norway, and they were married that summer in Christiania. They had one child.

The union had a turbulent beginning. In 1874 an open quarrel erupted between Bull and the conservative Thorps, and Sara left with her parents. Both sides, Bull and at least Sara, who had extricated herself from the influence of her dominating mother, sought reconciliation in 1876. Sara was now a social and intellectual figure in her own right and became Bull's guardian, accompanist, and manager, giving strong, loyal direction to his affairs and bringing him a period of order and tranquility. He continued to tour, at a reduced pace, mostly in America but occasionally abroad, and on his sixty-sixth birthday he fulfilled a promise to the king of Sweden by playing his "Et Saeterbesog" from atop an Egyptian pyramid, the kind of flamboyant gesture that magnified his reputation long after his death.

Bull's final performances were in Chicago in May 1880. He was tired and ill with cancer and returned with Sara to Norway, where he died at his island estate, Lysöen.

To evaluate Bull as a composer is difficult. Few of his works were published, many manuscripts were lost, some were reworked or renamed, and he frequently did not play his music as written because he drew so heavily on his skill in improvisation. There have been some commendable efforts to recreate his music, but they remain somewhat speculative.

Bull molded his style with a fervent, personal nationalism that exceeded the role of performer. To his followers he was artist, storyteller, and spokesman for the common folk, and he was loved and admired throughout the world he had touched. A funeral tribute summed up his career: "Our great artist, ardently loving his native land, saw with clear, penetrating vision the influence of art on the development of a people" (Sara Bull, p. 324).

• Because he so often revised or renamed his compositions, Bull seldom submitted them for publication. For a sample from his few published works, see *Fantasie et variations de bravure sur un theme de Bellini pour violin avec orchestre ou piano*, Opus 3 (1843). A compact disc recording of this work, together with "Adagio" from the *Violin Concerto in E minor*, *Adagio religioso*, *Pollacca Guerriera*, *Et Saeterbesog*, and *I Ensomme Stunde*, is available in a realization of Bull's music by Arve Tellefsen, violin, and the Bergen Symphony Orchestra, conducted by Karsten Anderson under the title *Ole Bull: A Festival of Violin Works*, Norsk Kulturr Åds Klaffikerserie, NKFCD 50008-2 (1988). A thorough biography, with good bibliographic appendices, is Einar Haugen and Camilla Cai, *Ole Bull: Norway's Romantic Musician and Cosmopolitan Patriot* (1993). A less detailed but very readable treatment is Mortimer B. Smith, *The Life of Ole Bull* (1943; repr. 1947). Sara C. Bull, *Ole Bull: A Memoir* (1882), is a personal, anecdotal account by his second wife, subjective but with useful insights. Vera Brodsky Lawrence, *Strong on Music* (1988), has numerous references to Bull's New York appearances with critical reactions. The colony of Oleana is described in Norman B. Wilkinson et al., "Ole Bull's New Norway," in *Historic Pennsylvania Leaflet*, no. 14, ed. Harold L. Myers (1988). An obituary in the *New York Times*, 19 Aug. 1880, contains some inaccuracies.

RUSSELL C. NELSON

BULL, William (Apr. 1683–21 Mar. 1755), lieutenant governor and acting governor of South Carolina, was born at "Ashley Hall," South Carolina, the son of Colonel Stephen Bull, a deputy of the lords proprietors and member of the proprietary council. His mother's name is not known. A planter and surveyor, William Bull held numerous government offices. He was elected to the assembly in 1706, 1707, and 1716. During the Yemassee Indian war of 1715, Bull and his brother John served as militia captains on an expedition into the western mountains of the Cherokee Indians that was famed in colonial South Carolina history for the heroism of those involved and for its important consequences. In 1716 they participated in the Convention of Tugaloo, which served as a cornerstone of Carolina Indian policy and a foundation of peace with the Cherokees for almost half a century.

As a supporter of the lords proprietors, Bull was appointed a member of their last council in 1719. Later that year, local dissatisfaction with proprietary government led to a successful revolt against the proprietors. Partly in an attempt to conciliate their faction, the Crown then reappointed Bull to the council under the new royal government in 1720; he remained a member of this body until 1737. Also named as one of three Indian commissioners, he became known as an authority on Indian affairs.

Bull's success as a rice planter enabled him to greatly expand his landholdings at Sheldon in the southern part of the colony. A surveyor, Bull's prominence and experience in establishing new settlements led to his participation with General James Oglethorpe in the founding of Georgia in 1733. He and his family contributed time and slave labor to the settlement of Savannah, and he remained an important supporter of Georgia, which he regarded as a buffer between Carolina and Spanish Florida.

In 1737, after the death of Lieutenant Governor Thomas Broughton, Bull, as the senior member of the council, became acting governor, a post he held until the arrival of Governor James Glen from England in 1743. As acting governor, Bull in 1739 suppressed a major slave revolt known as the Stono Rebellion, directed the reconstruction of Charleston after a disastrous fire in 1740, and reorganized the militia. He also raised a regiment of militia for an expedition against St. Augustine led by General Oglethorpe in 1740. The expedition failed, South Carolinians believed, because of Oglethorpe's bungling and mishandling of his Indian allies.

In local political affairs, Bull not only achieved relative harmony after years of political turbulence but also promoted what local leaders considered to be a properly balanced constitution by recognizing a distinction between the legislative and advisory functions of the council. During the latter part of his tenure as acting governor, he cooperated closely with his son William Bull II, who served as speaker of the Commons. From 1743 until his death, the elder Bull continued to exercise an important role in Indian affairs and political life, where he headed a loose coalition of Carolina planters and merchants who successfully opposed Governor Glen when his actions appeared to be inimical to local interests. Bull was married to Mary Quintyne; the couple had five children. She died in 1939. Bull died in Sheldon, Prince William County, South Carolina.

Primarily a conciliator, Bull displeased a few individuals who considered him to be a "weak person" devoid of "resolution." Many South Carolinians, however, believed him to be an unusually successful political figure.

• The principal accounts of the life of William Bull are contained in M. Eugene Sirmans, "Masters of Ashley Hall: A Biographical Study of the Bull Family of Colonial South Carolina, 1670–1737" (Ph.D. diss., Princeton Univ., 1959); Kinloch Bull, Jr., *The Oligarchs in Colonial and Revolutionary Charleston: Lieutenant Governor William Bull II and His Family* (1991); and Geraldine M. Meroney, *Inseparable Loyalty: A Biography of William Bull* (1991). Other sources are Edward McCrady, *History of South Carolina under the Proprietary Government, 1670–1719* (1969), and *History of South Carolina under the Royal Government, 1719–1776* (1969).

KINLOCH BULL, JR.

BULL, William, II (24 Sept. 1710–4 July 1791), lieutenant governor and acting governor of South Carolina, was born at "Ashley Hall," near Charleston, South Carolina, the son of William Bull, later lieutenant governor of South Carolina, and Mary Quintyne. He was educated at Westminster School in London and at Leyden University, where in 1734 he became the first native-born American to receive a degree of doctor of medicine.

On returning to America, Bull began what was to be a successful career as a planter and, until at least 1745, a practicing physician. In 1746 he married Hannah Beale, daughter of Othniel Beale, who was president of the royal council, 1761–1773. He also joined the militia as a cavalry officer and in 1751 became a brigadier general and senior officer of the colonial militia. His public service was as diverse as it was lengthy, and he served as an assistant justice in the courts during the 1740s and 1750s. Elected to the Commons House of Assembly in 1736, he was its speaker in 1740–1742, 1744–1747, and 1748; he also acted as floor manager for his father, the lieutenant governor. In 1749 he joined the royal council, where he served until the end of the colonial period when not acting as governor.

Preoccupied, like his father, with Indian affairs, in 1751 Bull represented South Carolina in Albany, New York, at a conference designed to establish peace between the Iroquois Confederation and the Indian tribes of the South. Numerous family connections with other members strengthened his position on the council, and he proved to be a forceful and articulate exponent of the preeminent position of South Carolina in Indian affairs and matters of defense. In 1759 he opposed Governor William Henry Lyttelton's war against the Cherokee Indians; Bull became acting governor the following year and concluded the war with moderate peace terms in 1761.

While acting governor in 1768, and again in 1769–1771, Bull advocated leniency in dealing with local vigilantes (the Regulators) in the lawless backcountry, for which he recommended establishing courts, parishes, and schools. He also pardoned many leaders of the Regulator movement, whom he restored to office. During his more than eight years as acting governor, including a term from 1773 to 1775, South Carolina flourished, partly through his efforts to broaden and improve its agricultural base. His political astuteness and compassion contributed to his popularity among the people.

With the rise of revolutionary sentiment in the late 1760s, he sympathized with legitimate American grievances but believed that the best interests of the province lay within the British empire. Despite the ineptness of several royal governors from 1760 to 1775, Bull strengthened the hand of the moderate revolutionaries as the province moved toward rebellion. His efforts were not assisted, however, by his more revolutionary relatives—his brother-in-law Henry Middleton, president of the Continental Congress in 1774, and his radical revolutionary nephews William Henry Drayton and General Stephen Bull of Sheldon. Bull retired from public office in 1775 and departed for England in 1777 rather than abjure his loyalty to the British crown. He returned to British-occupied Charleston in 1781 as intendant general of the Board of Police, a quasi-judicial body advisory to the British military authorities, but went into exile again in 1782. Bull kept the love and respect of his countrymen and was exempted from the Confiscation Act that was applied to other Loyalists. He died in London.

• Large collections of Bull's official correspondence are in the British Public Record Office, London, and in the Gage papers at the William L. Clements Library, University of Michigan, Ann Arbor. His only known personal letters are in the Peters papers at the Historical Society of Pennsylvania. The principal work on William Bull II is Kinloch Bull, Jr., *The Oligarchs in Colonial and Revolutionary Charleston: Lieutenant Governor William Bull II and His Family* (1991). See also Geraldine M. Meroney, *Inseparable Loyalty: A Biography of William Bull* (1991). Edward McCrady, *South Carolina under the Royal Government* (1899), and W. R. Smith, *South Carolina as a Royal Province* (1903), give accounts and assessments of his public life prior to the Revolution.

KINLOCH BULL, JR.

BULLARD, Arthur (8 Dec. 1879–10 Sept. 1929), writer and government official, was born in St. Joseph, Missouri, the son of Henry Bullard, a prominent Presbyterian minister, and Helen Nelson. After graduating in 1899 from Blair Academy in Blairstown, New Jersey, Bullard enrolled at Hamilton College in Clinton, New York. Two years later his growing social consciousness led him to leave college to join New York City's burgeoning reform community. In 1903 he became a probation officer for the New York Prison Association and a resident worker at the University Settlement on New York's Lower East Side.

With the start of the 1905 revolution in Russia, Bullard served briefly as secretary-treasurer of the Friends of Russian Freedom and soon followed his settlement colleagues William English Walling and Ernest Poole to Europe. In Geneva, Switzerland, Bullard managed Walling's pro-revolution news bureau and met prominent Russian exiles such as Lenin. Late in 1905 he joined Walling in the Russian capital, St. Petersburg. The bureau sent him to Moscow to cover an uprising in the factories and then to the Baltic states and the Ukraine to report on czarist military repression. Concealing his name from Russian authorities with the pen name Albert Edwards, he provided vivid accounts to American magazines such as *Harper's Weekly* and *Collier's Weekly*.

Bullard remained in Russia more than a year. When he returned to the United States from Europe late in 1908, he wrote for a new socialist daily, the New York *Call*, and produced articles and books based on his travels to the Caribbean and Panama. Still using the Albert Edwards name, he wrote a novel, a semiautobiographical narrative that appeared in 1912 as *A Man's World*. His highly regarded second novel, *Comrade Yetta*, published in 1913, was a panorama of the era's reform movements and socialist politics. *Comrade Yetta* was also notable in its era for acknowledging women's sexuality.

His promising career as a novelist soon yielded to his journalist's fascination with war. In 1912 and 1913 he covered conflicts in the Balkans for *Outlook* magazine. At the outbreak of World War I in August 1914 he was in New York and for a time compiled a war summary for *Outlook*, but he left for Europe at the end of the year to work as a freelance correspondent. In addition to writing articles and a book on wartime diplomacy, he sent analyses on an unofficial basis to President Woodrow Wilson's chief aide, Colonel E. M. House. Such contacts led him into a substantial policy role as the United States neared entry into the war. In 1916 Bullard successfully challenged—both in a memorandum to House and in an article—a plan presented by General Douglas MacArthur for military rather than civilian control of wartime information.

Early in 1917 Bullard completed a short book, *Mobilising America*, which proposed methods for arousing public opinion, relying on output of information rather than censorship. Historians credit Bullard with laying the foundation for the Committee on Public Information (CPI), the official U.S. propaganda agency created immediately after the American declaration of war in April 1917. With other socialist intellectuals, Bullard abandoned the Socialist party's antiwar position and supported Wilson's war policies. He aided the CPI in its first months, most notably producing *How the War Came to America*, a compilation of documents that was distributed by the millions.

Eager to return to Russia with the overthrow of the czar, Bullard and Ernest Poole arrived there in July 1917 as journalists, without official standing. Bullard worked as a volunteer press aide at the American consulate in Moscow, and when the CPI opened an office in Petrograd after the Bolsheviks took power in October 1917 he was drafted as second in command. Despite dubious health—his associates noted that he was often afflicted with unspecified illnesses—he organized campaigns to make American war aims known to the Russian public and wrote a widely distributed pamphlet, *Letters to a Russian Friend*.

At the same time, Bullard was thrown into the angry dispute among Americans in Russia over U.S. policy toward the new Russian government and Bolshevik efforts to withdraw Russia from the war by making a separate peace with Germany. Never a supporter of the Bolsheviks, Bullard advocated moderation and realism in dealing with the new regime and was stung when his old colleague Walling mistakenly charged in January 1918 that CPI representatives in Russia—meaning Bullard—were responsible for advocating pro-Bolshevik and pro-German policies. However, Bullard did not reply publicly at the time. He also managed to steer clear of the controversy created when his superior, Edgar Sisson, acquired documents, later shown to be suspect, purporting to substantiate that Bolshevik leaders had been bribed by the Germans to make peace.

In March 1918 Bullard became head of all CPI activities in Russia, but the next month Washington ordered him to leave Bolshevik-dominated western Russia, lest he and his American assistants be taken hostage. Protesting his "ignominious flight," he sailed from Archangel on a British vessel disguised as a British sailor. Back in the United States, he paused in Washington, where he married Ethel Mather in July, and then traveled with her to the new CPI headquarters in Russian Manchuria. After the war ended in November 1918, Bullard was reassigned to the peace conference in Paris but en route was afflicted with mastoiditis; an emergency operation in San Francisco narrowly saved his life. While convalescing he gained permission from his superiors to publicize his views and wrote *The Russian Pendulum* (1919), an incisive review of Russia's transition from czarism to communism. In it he supported diplomatic recognition of the new Soviet Union, which did not happen until 1933.

In the last months of the Wilson administration, Bullard was appointed head of the State Department's Russian Division, but he resigned when Warren G. Harding took office. While continuing to write on diplomatic issues, he also edited a short-lived magazine, *Our World*, devoted to international affairs. In 1925 he went to Geneva representing the American League of Nations Non-Partisan Association and became a member of the league secretariat. He died in Geneva just short of his fiftieth birthday, after a final illness that his friend Poole attributed to the weakening effects of his time in Russia. He and his wife were childless.

Having performed his most useful work behind the scenes, Bullard never became a well-known public figure. Nonetheless, he is credited not only with being the key founder of the Committee on Public Information, but he is also held responsible in part for the zeal with which the CPI sought to dominate public opinion. In his history of America's role in Russia in 1917 and 1918, George F. Kennan praised Bullard's diplomacy and found his analyses alone among U.S. official views in achieving "independent literary and historical distinction." Bullard's career as a writer and journalist, even less well known than his brief government career, evinced the same qualities of facility and acuity.

• Arthur Bullard's papers are in the Seeley G. Mudd Manuscript Library, Princeton University. Material relating to his writing career is in the Macmillan Company records, New York Public Library. Under the name Albert Edwards, Bullard wrote *Panama* (1911) and *The Barbary Coast* (1913). Under his own name he wrote *The Diplomacy of the Great War* (1916); a novel, *The Stranger* (1920); *The ABC's of Disarmament* (1921); *American Diplomacy in the Modern World* (1929); and *The Volcano* (1930), also a novel. Bullard's work for the 1905 revolution is described in Arthur W. Thompson and Robert A. Hart, *The Uncertain Crusade* (1970). Bullard's fiction is dealt with in Peter Conn, *The Divided Mind* (1983), pp. 98–103, and Mari Jo Buhle, *Women and American Socialism* (1983), pp. 264–65. Material relating to his role in the Wilson administration includes correspondence in Arthur S. Link, ed., *The Papers of Woodrow Wilson*, vols. 37, 42, 45, and 47 (1981–1984); *Report of the Chairman of the Committee on Public Information* (1919), republished as *The Creel Report* (1972); and Edgar Sisson, *One Hundred Red Days* (1931). Histories dealing with Bullard's work during World War I include James R. Mock and Cedric Larson, *Words That Won the War* (1939); George F. Kennan's authoritative *Soviet-American Relations, 1917–1920: Russia Leaves the War* (1956) and *The Decision to Intervene* (1958); Christopher Lasch, *The American Liberals and the Russian Revolution* (1962); Stephen Vaughn, *Holding Fast the Inner Lines* (1980) and "Arthur Bullard and the Creation of the Committee on Public Information," *New Jersey History* 97 (Spring 1979): 45–53. An obituary is in the *New York Times*, 11 Sept. 1929.

JAMES BOYLAN

BULLARD, Robert Lee (5 Jan. 1861–11 Sept. 1947), U.S. Army officer, was born William Robert Bullard in Russell County, Alabama, the son of Daniel Bullard, a cotton gin salesman and farmer, and Susan Mizell. Born into the Civil War, Bullard grew to manhood in a family reduced in wealth by the war but rich in the military memories of kinfolk and the glories of the "Lost Cause." As a boy Bullard changed his name to Robert Lee. He tried school teaching and attended the Agricultural and Mechanical College of Alabama and later Auburn University before winning an appointment in 1881 to the U.S. Military Academy, West Point, through competitive examination from the Third Congressional District, Alabama. Not averse to serving in the national army but more interested in a complete college education, Bullard accepted the appointment.

Bullard graduated in 1885 twenty-seventh in a class of thirty-nine. He then served as a lieutenant in the Tenth Infantry Regiment at various posts in the New Mexico and Oklahoma territories, Texas, and Kansas. In 1888 he married Rose Douglass Brabson; before her death in 1921 the Bullards had four children. As a junior officer Bullard participated in one campaign against the Apaches (but saw no combat), developed a reputation for attention to duty, studied military affairs when such activity was not fashionable, and yearned for some duty that would take him and his family away from the harsh life of frontier posts. He received one teaching assignment in Georgia and earned an appointment to the new Infantry and Cavalry School at Fort Leavenworth, but eyesight problems, sinus headaches, and a long-sought transfer (and promotion to captain) to the Commissary Department seemed to doom his chances for any special distinction in the army.

The war with Spain (1898) and the subsequent Filipino-American War (1899–1902) brought Bullard the opportunities for combat experience and professional identity that had thus far eluded him. He became colonel of the Third Alabama Volunteer Infantry, an African-American regiment that earned a reputation for steadiness and skill in the military camps of the South in 1898. Although the regiment did not go overseas, it remained cohesive in the face of racist pressure, much to the credit of its commanding officer, who treated his men fairly. His work with the Third Alabama won Bullard appointment as colonel of the Thirty-ninth U.S. Volunteer Infantry Regiment. In his first combat experience in conventional and guerrilla warfare in southern Luzon, Bullard demonstrated skill, tenacity, intelligence, and a rare ability to deal with difficult superiors while he retained the confidence and admiration of his officers and men.

Promoted to major in the Commissary Department in the expansion of the army in 1901, Bullard persuaded Secretary of War Elihu Root to approve his return to the infantry at the same rank, which enabled Bullard to reach colonel in 1912, well before his other classmates in the line. Bullard spent most of the years between 1901 and 1916 in the field. As a major in the Twenty-eighth Infantry he commanded a battalion and a district in the Moro province of Mindanao (1902–1904), served in the provisional government of Cuba during the Second Intervention (1906–1909) as a lieutenant colonel, and commanded in the field twice during the border troubles spawned by the Mexican Revolution. After a short tour on the California-Mexico border, Bullard attended the Army War College (class of 1912) then took command of the Twenty-sixth Infantry just before it deployed to the southeastern tip of Texas in 1915. In two years of watch on the Rio Grande, Bullard reestablished himself as one of the sturdiest regimental commanders in the army. After the mobilization of the National Guard in 1916 for border service, he assumed command of a brigade that included his own regiment and regiments from Louisiana, South Dakota, and Oklahoma. In all his field assignments Bullard received high praise from his superior officers.

Two months after the nation's entry into World War I in April 1917, Bullard reached a personal goal, appointment as a brigadier general and command of the Second Brigade (the Twenty-sixth and Twenty-eighth Infantry) of the newly formed First Division, a formation of regulars and wartime volunteers that sailed for France as the token vanguard of the American Expeditionary Forces (AEF). Aware of Bullard's skill as an organizer and driving commander, General John J. Pershing, commander in chief of the AEF, detached Bullard from the division and placed him in charge of the AEF schools for infantry officer training. In December 1917, however, Bullard returned to the elite First Division as its second commanding general, following the relief of William L. Sibert. As a major general Bullard led the division, blessed with superior officers and men, through a defensive campaign in Picardy during the early stages of the German major offensive of 1918. The division's most noted feat was the seizure and defense of Cantigny (28–31 May 1918), a set-piece attack designed to prove the offensive ability of an American division to the French and Germans. The feat ensured the reputation of Bullard and his division operations officer, Lieutenant Colonel George C. Marshall, Jr.

Meeting Pershing's demanding standards as an active, firm, and tactically sound division commander, Bullard advanced to the position of III Corps commanding general in July 1918 and participated in two major engagements, the Aisne-Marne counteroffensive (18 July–31 Aug. 1918) and the Meuse-Argonne offensive (26 Sept.–11 Nov. 1918). Second only to Major General Hunter Liggett in Pershing's esteem, Bullard ended the war as the commanding general, Second Army, which opened a new offensive toward the fortified city of Metz two days before the armistice. For his wartime service Bullard received the Distinguished Service Medal and several foreign decorations.

For most of the period between his return to the United States in 1919 until his retirement in 1925, Bullard commanded the II Corps Area with headquarters at Governor's Island, New York. He did not contribute much to the army's postwar reorganization, but he performed his public relations duties as a spokesman for the National Defense Act of 1920 with gusto and established a reputation as an interesting and forceful writer on military affairs. He eventually wrote three books on his service in World War I, became a magazine and newspaper columnist, and spoke often to military and patriotic groups. From 1925 until 1942 he served as president of the National Security League, a propreparedness lobby. In 1927 he married Ella Reiff Wall, a widow from Philadelphia high society, and the Bullards enjoyed the best New York City social circles until the general's death there in 1947.

Clean-shaven and thin in a generation of generals given to girth and mustaches, Bullard looked the part of a modern major general, and he proved professionally adept enough to perform as one in World War I. Like Pershing and others, he made the transition from an army shaped by its duties in the American West and in Asia into an industrialized bloodletting on the Western Front, 1917–1918. His generation shaped the next, which led the United States to victory in World War II.

• Letters, diaries, and official papers are held in the General Robert L. Bullard Papers in the Library of Congress with assorted correspondence in the papers of Generals Pershing, Leonard Wood, and James G. Harbord, also in the Library of Congress. Bullard himself wrote *Personalities and Reminiscences of the War* (1925), *American Soldiers Also Fought* (1936), and *Fighting Generals* (1944). A biography is Allan R. Millett, *The General: Robert L. Bullard and Officership in the U.S. Army, 1881–1925* (1975). His life, career, and character are described in two lengthy obituaries: Irving J. Palmer, "Robert Lee Bullard," *Assembly*, July 1948, pp. 3–4; and "Robert L. Bullard," *New York Times*, 12 Sept. 1947.

ALLAN R. MILLETT

BULLITT, Alexander Scott (1762–13 Apr. 1816), lieutenant governor of Kentucky, was born in Dumfries, Prince William County, Virginia, the son of Cuthbert Bullitt, a lawyer and judge, and Helen Scott. The particulars of Bullitt's early education are not known. He studied law but did not become a practicing attorney. Serving two terms in the Virginia House of Delegates, from 5 May 1783 to 7 January 1785, he was not an active member of the legislature and did not attend in late 1784. He was also a major in the Prince William County militia.

Bullitt went to Kentucky in 1784, settling first at Bullskin Creek (in present Shelby County). Because of the vulnerability of the location to American Indian attacks and a desire to be closer to the falls of the Ohio River, after a few months he moved to a 1,000-acre plantation he had purchased on Beargrass Creek, east of Louisville. Bullitt named his new estate "Oxmoor," from Laurence Sterne's *Tristram Shandy* (1761–1767) novels. In 1786 he married Priscilla Christian, a niece of Patrick Henry. They had four children. Priscilla died on 11 November 1806, and in 1807 Bullitt married Mary Churchill Prather. They had three children.

In Kentucky Bullitt contented himself with running his plantation, where he raised tobacco and had various farm industries. By 1793 only fourteen (eight men and six women) of his forty-five slaves were common laborers. Reputed to be a heavy drinker during the early Kentucky years, Bullitt only slowly emerged as a political leader. On 2 May 1786 he was appointed county lieutenant for Jefferson County. In that capacity he presided over a court-martial on 21 March 1787 that tried Colonel Hugh McGary, who had killed a captive Shawnee chief, Moluntha. Convicted of murder, McGary was sentenced to a one-year suspension from the militia. In 1787 Bullitt was named a trustee of Louisville.

It is not known whether Bullitt was involved to any large degree in the so-called "Spanish Conspiracy" (1796–1805), as were other prominent Kentuckians, or whether his name was simply used by the conspirators. The scheme meant to bring Kentucky into a close relation with Spanish Louisiana, even to the point of separation from the United States. James Wilkinson wrote Esteban Rodríguez Miró, Spanish governor of Louisiana, in May 1788 that if anything should happen to him Bullitt was one of two men that Miró could count on to further the Spanish interest. On 18 September 1789 Wilkinson wrote Miró that Bullitt was "a man of ability and fortune, but very changeable; still he will be of use to our cause." Wilkinson estimated that Bullitt could be bribed for $1,000.

Bullitt was a delegate from Jefferson County to the Kentucky statehood conventions of July and November 1788 and July 1790. The latter meeting voted by a surprisingly narrow margin of 24–18 to accept Virginia's offer for statehood, to be effected on 1 June 1792. Bullitt was one of a select committee of eleven that drafted addresses to the Virginia General Assembly and to Congress pertaining to the implementation of statehood.

In December 1791 Bullitt was elected to the Tenth Convention, which met in April 1792, and he served on a ten-member committee that drafted a constitution for the new state. Under the Kentucky constitution, Bullitt was chosen one of forty electors whose duty was to name senators and the governor, and he was elected one of eleven state senators. At the first meeting of the legislature in Lexington, on 4 June 1792, he was named Speaker of the state senate, a position he held until 1800.

As president of the second Kentucky constitutional convention, which met 22 July–17 August 1799, Bullitt favored legislative supremacy, saying, "Departments [were] distinct in theory; but impossible in practice" (Coward, p. 157). Under the revised constitution of 1799, the governor and lieutenant governor each were elected for one four-year term by the voters directly. In the election of 5–7 May 1800, Bullitt won the lieutenant governorship by a plurality of 2,400 votes. As Kentucky's first lieutenant governor, he presided over the state senate, just as he had as Speaker. After leaving executive office, he served one more term in the senate, 1804–1808.

Bullitt died at Oxmoor. Bullitt County, Kentucky, established in 1796, is named for him. Oxmoor, in Louisville, was placed on the National Register of Historic Places.

• The Bullitt family papers are deposited at the Filson Club, Louisville, Ky. Notice of Bullitt's political career is in *Journal of the House of Delegates of the Commonwealth of Virginia*, sessions 1783, 1784, 1785 (1828); *Journal of the Senate of the Commonwealth of Kentucky*, issued according to sessions, 1792–1808; and *Journal of the First Constitutional Convention of Kentucky* (1942). Recollections of life at Oxmoor during Bullitt's time and afterward are in Thomas W. Bullitt, *My Life at Oxmoor, Life on a Farm in Kentucky before the War* (1911), and Ella H. Ellwanger, "Oxmoor—Its Builder and Its Historian," *Register of the Kentucky State Historical Society* 17 (1919): 9–21. A Spanish Conspiracy connection is suggested in "Papers Bearing on James Wilkinson's Relations with Spain, 1787–1789," *American Historical Review* 9 (1903–1904): 748–66. Bullitt's role in the formation of the Ky. government is referred to in J. D. Barnhart, "Frontiersmen and Planters in the Formation of Kentucky," *Journal of Southern History* 7 (1941): 19–36; Lowell H. Harrison, *Kentucky's Road to Statehood* (1992); Patricia Watlington, *The Partisan Spirit: Kentucky Politics, 1779–1792* (1972); Joan W. Coward, *Kentucky in the New Republic: The Process of Constitution Making* (1979); Charles G. Talbert, *Benjamin Logan: Kentucky Frontiersman* (1962); and Lewis Collins with revision by Richard H. Collins, *History of Kentucky* (2 vols., 1874; repr. 1966).

HARRY M. WARD

BULLITT, William Christian (25 Jan. 1891–15 Feb. 1967), diplomat, was born in Philadelphia, Pennsylvania, the son of William Christian Bullitt, a lawyer, and Louisa Gross Horwitz, the granddaughter of Samuel Gross, a leading medical researcher and surgeon. His father had made a fortune from investments in coal operations in West Virginia and Virginia. After graduating from DeLancey preparatory school, he entered Yale in 1908. In the summer of 1911, he became very ill, with symptoms of exhaustion, intestinal pain, and diminished sight and hearing. At first doctors attributed the illness to overwork, but when several months' rest produced no improvement, exploratory surgery revealed adhesions left over from a childhood appendectomy. He was treated with X-rays, a new technique. His health was restored, but the treatment may have caused the leukemia that killed him many years later. As a result of his illness, he graduated from Yale a year late, in 1913.

In the fall of 1913 Bullitt entered Harvard Law School at the insistence of his father. When his father died the next year, however, he dropped out and returned to Philadelphia, determined to pursue a career in government service. He visited Russia and Western Europe with his mother in the summer of 1914. The outbreak of World War I found them in Paris, where they had gone to retrieve his late grandmother's jewelry from a wall safe in her apartment. That fall he went to work as a foreign correspondent for the *Public Ledger* in Philadelphia. One of his early assignments was to cover Henry Ford's ill-fated peace voyage in 1915. His articles were syndicated in more than 230 newspapers and won him a promotion to associate editor.

In 1916 Bullitt married Ernesta Drinker, the daughter of the president of Lehigh University and the older sister of writer Catherine Drinker Bowen. They had no children. That year they traveled extensively in Europe, spending much of their time in Germany and Austria. Partly because of his familiarity with those countries, the next year he was appointed chief of the State Department's Bureau of Central European Information. There he prepared reports, especially on the Russian revolution, for President Woodrow Wilson and his adviser Colonel Edward M. House.

In December 1918 Bullitt went to Paris as a member of the United States peace delegation. Early the next year he led a secret mission to the Soviet Union, apparently to negotiate an end to the civil war there. He met with V. I. Lenin in March and obtained very favorable terms. When he returned to Paris, however, Wilson refused even to meet with him; negotiations had bogged down over personal differences between the president and British prime minister David Lloyd George, pressure by interventionists led by French prime minister George Clemenceau, and a popular proposal by Norwegian explorer Fridtjof Nansen to provide food to the Soviet Union in return for more modest terms. Frustrated, Bullitt resigned and returned to the United States. Before the Senate Foreign Relations Committee that fall he provided testimony that contributed to the Senate's refusal to ratify the Treaty of Versailles.

In the following years Bullitt traveled and edited scripts as managing editor for the Famous Players–Lasky Corporation, a forerunner of Paramount Pictures. In 1921 he met Louise Bryant, the widow of John Reed, who had come to him to discuss a film version of Reed's *Ten Days That Shook the World*. By this time he had separated from his wife, and after they divorced in 1923 he married Bryant. In 1925 he may have become a patient of Sigmund Freud, who apparently was also treating Bryant. In any case, Bullitt and Freud developed a close relationship that would last the rest of the psychoanalyst's life. In 1931 Bullitt completed *Thomas Woodrow Wilson: 28th President, a Psychological Study*, which he wrote in consultation with Freud, but his friends persuaded him not to publish it by pointing out that it would ruin his future in the Democratic party. He finally published the book in 1967, after the death of Mrs. Wilson. It received devastating reviews from both historians and Freud scholars, who saw little but vindictiveness in Bullitt's characterization of Wilson as a man driven by an obsession with his father.

In 1926 Bullitt published an autobiographical novel, *It's Not Done*, which satirized high society in Philadelphia and dealt frankly with sexual themes. Meanwhile, his marriage to Bryant deteriorated, partly because she contracted Dercum's disease, a rare and disfiguring ailment that also causes emotional distress. They divorced in 1930, and Bullitt received custody of their daughter.

Bullitt had met Franklin Delano Roosevelt during World War I, when Roosevelt was an assistant secretary of the navy, and became an early supporter when Roosevelt ran for president in 1932. After his victory the president-elect sent Bullitt on two secret (and possibly illegal) missions to Europe to look into the issue of war debts and to make political observations. After the inauguration he became special assistant to Secretary of State Cordell Hull. At the London Monetary and Economic Conference of 1933 he served as executive officer of the U.S. delegation. Although the conference failed in its economic objectives, he met Soviet diplomat Maxim Litvinov, and that fall he played a significant role in negotiating the opening of formal diplomatic relations under the Roosevelt-Litvinov Agreements. Roosevelt immediately appointed him ambassador to Moscow.

The Soviets greeted Bullitt warmly when he arrived in December 1933, and he began his tenure on a note of high idealism. However, he soon found himself shut off from diplomatic contacts, harassed by bureaucratic complexities, and faced with maintaining security in a hostile environment. By all accounts he ran the embassy capably, but he gradually became convinced that Stalin was violating the terms of the Roosevelt-Litvinov Agreements. The embassy staff supported his increasingly critical reports to Washington, but they displeased Roosevelt, who began to shun his advice. Bullitt's disappointment with the Soviet experiment would gradually evolve into a strident anticommunist stance.

Despite disagreements over Soviet policy, Bullitt's personal relationship with the president remained cordial, and in 1936 he was appointed ambassador to France. During his four years in Paris he won the confidence of French leaders, as well as the president's trust as an adviser on European affairs. Particularly valuable were his predictions of German maneuvers leading up to World War II, including the advances into Austria, the Sudetenland, and finally the rest of Czechoslovakia. Some critics charged that he overstepped his authority by pledging American intervention in support of the French should war break out. There is, however, no written evidence to support these allegations. He returned to the United States after the surrender of France in June 1940.

Back home Bullitt sought a significant wartime post in the administration. He spoke widely in favor of an all-out effort, short of U.S. intervention, to support Britain, loyally supported the president, and went on a brief fact-finding mission to North Africa and the Middle East in preparation for the North African campaign of 1942. He was no longer welcome in the president's inner circle, however, because of his longstanding feud with Undersecretary of State Sumner Welles. Bullitt had advised Roosevelt to fire Welles, alleging that the undersecretary was a latent homosexual and thus vulnerable to blackmail. The president had high regard for Welles, and when the matter leaked to the press, he blamed Bullitt for the leak and never forgave him.

Frustrated again, Bullitt returned to France in May 1944. There he became an infantry commandant in the French Free Forces under General Jean de Lattre de Tassigny. He participated in the liberation of Paris that August, and remained in the infantry until he returned home the following year. He spent the rest of his life speaking and writing, often in the cause of anticommunism. In 1946 he published *The Great Globe Itself*, an attack on Roosevelt's foreign policy and Soviet postwar assertiveness. The book was not well received by critics. He also wrote frequently for *Life* on foreign topics ranging from France to the Far East. He visited Vietnam in 1947 as a guest of the French government and advocated Emperor Bao Dai as the most likely anticommunist to serve as a French surrogate leader. Later he also supported Chiang Kai-shek's ambitions to return to mainland China. After a lifetime as a Democrat, he switched to the Republican party.

Bullitt's extensive experience in Europe, his fluency in French and German, and his bright and charming manner made him a valuable contributor to U.S. diplomacy, especially during the 1930s. But his idealism, intellectual arrogance, and scorn for the capabilities of most of those who worked around him undermined his achievements and ultimately prevented him from moving into higher government office. Cast away from the center of government power at what should have been the peak of his career, he spent his last twenty years with few friends, less influence, and virtually no public notice. He lived in France much of the time and devoted his last years arranging for the publication of the Wilson book. He died in Neuilly, France.

• Most of Bullitt's papers and his unpublished autobiography are in private hands. A copy of his diary is at Yale University. Information relating to Bullitt is in the Edward M. House Papers at the Library of Congress, the Louise Bryant Papers at Syracuse University, and at the Franklin D. Roosevelt Library. See also Orville H. Bullitt, ed., *"For the President: Personal and Secret": Correspondence between Franklin D. Roosevelt and William C. Bullitt* (1972). Secondary sources include Janet Flanner, "Mr. Ambassador," in *Modern Short Biographies and Autobiographies*, ed. M. Balch (1940), pp. 338–58; Beatrice Farnsworth, *William C. Bullitt and the Soviet Union* (1967); Lloyd C. Gardner, *Architects of Illusion: Men and Ideas in American Policy, 1941–1949* (1970); Robert Dallek, *Franklin D. Roosevelt and American Foreign Policy, 1932–1945* (1979); and Will Brownell and Richard N. Billings, *So Close to Greatness: A Biography of William C. Bullitt* (1987). An obituary is in the *New York Times*, 16 Feb. 1967.

JOHN E. FINDLING

BULLOCH, Archibald (1730–1777), lawyer and revolutionary war leader, was born in Charleston, South Carolina, the son of James Bulloch, a clergyman, member of the South Carolina Assembly, merchant, and Colleton County planter, and Jean Stobo. Although little is known about his early years, it is believed that he received a liberal education and studied law. Prior to his move to Georgia in 1758, he was admitted to the bar and acquired a rice plantation near Purrysburg on the Savannah River. In 1764 he married Mary De Veaux; they had four children. President Theodore Roosevelt was a great-great-grandson of Bulloch.

Bulloch began his political career in 1768, when he was elected to represent Christ Church Parish in the assembly. In his first term he was appointed to a committee to correspond with Benjamin Franklin, Georgia's agent in London. The next year Bulloch was named to a commission to choose vestrymen for the respective parishes. When, in 1771 and 1772, respectively, Governor James Wright and his surrogate James Habersham disapproved the election to the Speakership of Noble W. Jones, a leader in the opposition to British measures, Bulloch became Speaker of the assembly both years.

Bulloch was, from its inception, associated with the Liberty party, a faction of Whigs mainly from Christ Church and St. John's parishes that challenged Governor Wright and the new imperial policy that implemented the revenue acts. This faction formed the nucleus of the revolutionary movement in the colony and gained control of the assembly by 1768.

In 1774, after the enactment of the Intolerable Acts that closed the port of Boston, an invitation signed by Jones, Bulloch, John Houston, and George Walton appeared in the *Georgia Gazette* on 14 July. It issued a call for all Georgians to meet in Savannah on 27 July to consider the critical situation caused by the punitive measures and the parliamentary acts for raising revenue in the colonies. Owing to poor representation from the outlying parishes, however, they planned to reassemble on 5 August. The main work of this meeting was the adoption of eight resolutions that denounced British measures against Massachusetts and parliamentary taxation. In spite of the urgent demands of delegates from St. John's Parish, they decided not to send delegates to the First Continental Congress. Governor Wright attempted to sabotage the meeting, which undoubtedly diminished attendance.

On 18 January 1775 a provincial congress representing five parishes convened in Savannah at the same time that the Commons House of Assembly was in session. This de facto body elected Bulloch, Jones, and Houstoun delegates to the Second Continental Congress, which was to convene at Philadelphia in May. The assembled delegates also entered into a nonimportation, nonconsumption, and nonexportation agreement and approved the guidelines for its enforcement. In a letter to Congress dated 6 April 1775, the Georgia delegates explained that they had decided not to come to Philadelphia, since they had not been elected by a majority of the parishes. The prevailing mood in Georgia still vacillated between a passion for liberty and a desire for economic security.

Ten parishes, however, sent representatives to a second provincial congress that met on 4 July 1775. This body selected Bulloch president and Walton secretary, and on 6 July they ended Georgia's policy of hesitation and endorsed the actions of the Continental Congress. They publicly approved the American declaration of a "Bill of Rights" and vowed not to import goods from Great Britain, Ireland, or any colony in North America that did not accede to the Continental Association. The following day the provincial congress chose Bulloch, Houstoun, Jones, and John Zubly to join Lyman Hall, who was already in Philadelphia, to represent Georgia for the first time in the Continental Congress. On 14 July 1775 Bulloch, by order of the provincial congress, signed an emotional petition to King George III, informing him that Georgia now stood resolutely with the other colonies. Again in February 1776 Bulloch, Houstoun, and Hall, along with Button Gwinnett and Walton, were nominated as the Georgia delegation to the Continental Congress.

Until his death Bulloch was president of the provincial congress and an occasional delegate to the Continental Congress. Although he was not present during the debate and signing of the Declaration of Independence, he did sign the secret pact of 9 November 1775, whereby eighty-seven delegates of the Congress pledged not to divulge any matter debated under penalty of expulsion. After Governor Wright fled Georgia on 11 February 1776, Bulloch was elected president and commander in chief under the "Rules and Regulations," a preliminary constitution, that went into effect on 1 May 1776.

Besides running the government, on 25 March 1776 Bulloch led a detachment to evict the Tory refugees and king's officers who had fled to Tybee Island. He supervised the confiscation of estates of prominent Tories, the arrest of "harmful" persons, and the disbursement of funds for arms and provisions. He also issued a proclamation against swearing on the streets of Savannah and set aside a day of prayer to restore the enemy to reason and justice and to relieve the country from the distresses of war.

When the Declaration of Independence arrived in Savannah on 8 August 1776, Bulloch read the document publicly at a meeting of the legislative assembly, the liberty pole, and the battery. Subsequently President Bulloch, with the consent of his council, ordered the several parishes to send delegates to a constitutional convention in early October. The convention that drafted Georgia's constitution of 1777 finished its work on 5 February 1777.

In the meantime, since a council of safety could not be assembled, Bulloch was granted broad executive powers on 22 February 1777. Before elections could be held and a government launched under the new constitution, President Bulloch died in late February of unknown causes at his residence in Savannah. The inscription on his monument reads "Georgians! Let the memory of Archibald Bulloch live in your breasts, tell your children of him and let them tell another generation."

Bulloch was in the vanguard of the Revolution in Georgia during the crucial years 1768–1777, when patriots were few and timid. As president and commander in chief, he grappled with the problems that confronted the infant commonwealth and managed to hold in check the factions and ambitious rivalries that later fractured the patriot cause. Bulloch was honored in 1796, when his name was given to a new county created in Southeast Georgia.

• Archibald Bulloch's career as an early Whig leader is covered in Allen D. Candler et al., eds., *The Colonial Records of Georgia* (1904), and Candler, comp., *The Revolutionary Records of the State of Georgia* (1908). Further material on Bulloch can be found in Kenneth Coleman, *The American Revolution in Georgia, 1763–1789* (1958); Charles C. Jones, Jr., *Biographical Sketches of the Delegates from Georgia to the Continental Congress* (1891); and Joseph G. B. Bulloch, "A Biographical Sketch of Hon. Archibald Bulloch, President of Georgia, 1776–1777" (1900). For information on the Bulloch family, see Emma H. Bulloch, "The Blood of Theodore Roosevelt," *Journal of American History* 2 (1908): 225–34; and Elizabeth A. Ford, "The Bullochs of Georgia," *Georgia Review* 6 (Fall 1952): 318–31.

R. F. SAUNDERS, JR.

BULLOCK, Georgia Philipps (18 Nov. 1878–29 Aug. 1957), state trial judge, was born in Chicago, Illinois, the daughter of Thomas Herbert Morgan, a manufacturer, and Mary Potwin Judd. She attended a number of public and private schools, including girls' schools in Wales (England) and Indiana. When she received a contract offer for concert singing in her late teens, her parents discouraged a career in music because they disapproved of public performances by women. She married William Wingfield Bullock in 1899 and divorced him ten years later. In 1910 she moved with her parents and two children to Pasadena, California, where she always characterized herself as a widow. Her children became important icons in her efforts to assure California voters and politicians of her feminine credentials for serving on the women's court.

Although she had a private income and parental support for a conventional domestic life, Bullock wanted independence and responsibility. She wrote later, "My decision to work really grew out of a dislike for inactivity and a resentment for the way women were supposed to be seen and not heard. . . . I didn't think it right that the feminine brain should be underrated." She took shorthand and typing courses at night; her daytime work at a law firm suggested to her that she was competent to handle a legal practice. In 1912 she registered for night classes at Trojan law school (University of Southern California) in Los Angeles and volunteered as a probation officer for women convicted in police court. Even before receiving her LL.B. in June 1914, Bullock passed the California bar and represented criminal defendants in court.

Her judicial career began in 1914 as the unpaid adviser who sat next to the police judge on the experimental women's court bench. Court business proceeded behind closed doors to protect the feelings and safety of the female defendants. All court officers were women, except for the male judge who legitimized Bullock's disposition of each case. At the end of her first day performing as "judge" she announced to the press that "the salvation of women must be through women." Professional and club women generated favorable publicity for the new court, supplied facilities for homeless convicted defendants who were given suspended sentences, and provided the salaries for the court's female probation officers.

Bullock's judicial career was closely tied to women's organizations and Republican politics. She belonged to Eastern Star, Business and Professional Women, Zonta International, and the Friday Morning Club, and she invested in her political future by speaking regularly to local ethnic, religious, and other clubs. She was a founding member of Phi Delta Delta, a national sorority of law students, and with Clara S. Foltz and others established the Women Lawyers Club of Los Angeles. Through the National Association of Women Lawyers (NAWL), which she joined in 1913 and served as vice president in 1932, she became acquainted with women judges in other states. She attended national conventions of the American Bar Association as a NAWL delegate. Bullock was one of the first women members of the Los Angeles County Bar Association.

From her law school days until the New Deal she was a loyal and active Republican party member, joining the local study club and attending county central committee meetings and national conventions. She made an effort to put male politicians in her debt, with the idea of running for state assembly or judge, by campaigning for Republican candidates for local office and the U.S. presidency.

In 1917 Bullock left her volunteer judgeship and accepted the salaried position set aside for women of deputy district attorney. She handled a heavy caseload of prostitution charges during World War I. Under pressure from the public defender, Mabel W. Willebrandt, Bullock prosecuted the clients as well as the prostitutes and refused to allow police entrapment. After the war she returned to private practice. In 1924 the county supervisors selected her for a vacant seat on the police court, where the presiding judge immediately assigned her to the woman's department. Bullock thus became the first woman judge in California above the level of justice of the peace.

When the U.S. attorney general charged in 1925 that women who chose political life necessarily neglected their private obligations, she responded, "It is not fair to condemn all women in public life. . . . The intelligent woman who hears the call to politics . . . will work out her career without in any way neglecting her family or her home." Yet Bullock made a conscious decision not to remarry; she did not want to be criticized for neglecting private duties or taking a family man's job.

The state judiciary was reorganized in 1926, and her title was changed to municipal judge. In 1927 she defeated a male opponent for her position, and in 1929 she faced no opposition. As the "woman judge" on municipal court, Bullock dealt with female prostitutes, drug addicts, and disturbers of the peace, and with men who failed to support their families. She held women fully responsible for their behavior, deserving of the same penalties and rewards as men. However, she would not allow men to victimize women. When a woman beaten by her partner and hospitalized failed to appear, Bullock ordered her brought to court to testify, grumbling that the maximum sentence was "unfortunately . . . only 90 days." She studied criminology hoping to uncover the causes of criminal behavior so that she could combine strict law enforcement with scientifically based rehabilitation.

Bullock ran for superior court in 1928 but lost after the local bar association plebiscite rated her as unqualified. Republican governor James Rolph, Jr., appointed her to a vacant seat in 1931, however, making her the second woman in the nation to serve on a court of general jurisdiction. Some opponents to her elevation argued that no one could replace her on the women's court. One local attorney praised her "uncanny instinct, keen intuition, and . . . personal knowledge of feminine psychology." On superior court Bullock was still the "woman judge," assigned to psychopathic and domestic relations branches and later to adoption court. She retained her position in the 1932, 1938, 1944, and 1950 elections.

Bullock sought appointments to the federal bench from Presidents Herbert Hoover and Franklin D. Roosevelt. There are, however, no indications that the U.S. senators from California treated her candidacy seriously. Bullock had earned a Republican appointment, but Democrats had a political reason to reject her: she did not switch parties until 1934.

Bullock retired in October 1955 at age 76. She moved to a rest home in Monterey County, where she died, and was buried in Los Angeles in her judicial robes. Even her obituary took notice of her attractiveness, which the media had emphasized throughout her career. Commentators never separated her judicial achievements from her looks, clothes, and feminine demeanor.

Between the two world wars she was a newspaper personality and a public role model for professional women in Los Angeles. Bullock encouraged women to work for public policies such as prohibition, which she believed would protect traditional family life, and to take public office if they could carry the double burden. Her own public role was rooted in the cultural belief in distinctive female characteristics. She approved of the segregated treatment of women who were vulnerable to male aggression. Because she was convinced of the equal mental capacity of the sexes, she insisted that public institutions would benefit from the sex integration of policymaking bodies. Within the chauvinistic legal and political culture of her time, her ability, energy, and sociability carried her only one rung above her starting place in the judicial hierarchy, but for over forty years she held open the door in California for the women judges who followed her.

• Bullock's papers, which consist of newspaper clippings, letters, diaries, and memorabilia, are in the manuscript collection of the University Research Library, University of California at Los Angeles. Her campaign strategies for judicial office are covered in Beverly B. Cook, "Moral Authority and Gender Difference: Georgia Bullock and the Los Angeles Women's Court," *Judicature* 77 (Nov.–Dec. 1993): 144–55. A list of names and dates of the first women judges on courts of general jurisdiction and on supreme courts can be found in Cook, "Women on the State Bench: Correlates of Success," in *Political Women*, ed. Janet A. Flammang (1984). Obituaries (not entirely accurate ones) appear in the *Los Angeles Times*, 30 Aug. 1957, and the *New York Times*, 31 Aug. 1957.

BEVERLY B. COOK

BULLOCK, Rufus Brown (28 Mar. 1834–27 Apr. 1907), businessman and Reconstruction governor of Georgia, was born in Bethlehem, New York, the son of Volckert Veeder Bullock, a foundry operator and early promoter of the telegraph through his House Printing Telegraph Company, and Jane Eliza Brown. The family moved to Albion, New York, in 1840; Bullock was educated at Albion Academy.

Bullock became an expert in telegraphy and spent his early working years managing the construction of telegraph lines in Buffalo, New York City, Albany, and Philadelphia. In 1857 he moved to Augusta, Georgia, where he worked with the Adams Express Company and its successor, the Southern Express Company. In 1860 he married Marie Salisbury, originally from Pawtucket, Rhode Island; they had two sons and a daughter. When Georgia seceded, he volunteered for Confederate service and worked to extend telegraph and railroad lines in the lower tier of the Confederacy.

Returning to Augusta in 1865, Bullock helped secure northern financial backing for the First National Bank of Augusta. By 1867 he was president of the Macon and Augusta Railroad. The railroad's finances had been depleted, and its track and rolling stock had been devastated by the Civil War. Unable to secure the northern backing he sought to rebuild the road, Bullock apparently recognized that northern investment in the South would be limited until the southern states were readmitted to the Union and their loyalty and political stability assured. His desire to guarantee a political climate in Georgia attractive to northern investors quite likely motivated Bullock's entry into Republican politics in 1867.

Bullock served as a delegate to the Georgia Constitutional Convention of 1867–1868. A large and florid man, outgoing and approachable, he emerged as a leader of the "Augusta Ring" that dominated the state's newly organized Republican party. Nominated for governor in the spring of 1868 and supported by a coalition of newly enfranchised black voters, declared Republicans, and working-class whites burdened by postwar debts, Bullock defeated Democratic candidate John Brown Gordon by a margin of approximately 13,000 votes. Installed as governor on 4 July, he was formally inaugurated on 22 July 1868.

Bullock's tenure as governor was marked by controversy and charges of malfeasance and corruption. The Republican coalition was never stable, and Bullock proved unable to control either his party or the general assembly. He was defeated in his efforts to expel from the assembly those he believed ineligible under the terms of the federal Test Oath and thwarted in his wish that Georgia's wartime governor Joseph E. Brown and his Augusta political crony Foster Blodgett fill Georgia's U.S. Senate seats. Bullock was often opposed by moderate members of his own party, as well as by the state's old-line Democratic establishment. His standing was temporarily bolstered when the Georgia General Assembly expelled its black members and refused to ratify the Fifteenth Amendment and Congress accordingly remanded Georgia to a "Second Military Reconstruction" in March 1869. The legislature's actions, along with a bloody race riot at Camilla and Georgia's failure to deliver a Republican majority in the 1868 presidential election, enabled Bullock to prolong the Federal presence in the state and to protect his own administration.

When the general assembly reinstated its black members and ratified the Fifteenth Amendment, both early in 1870, the pretext for continued Federal military intervention in Georgia vanished. More than a year elapsed between Georgia's formal readmission to the Union in the summer of 1870 and the end of Republican rule in the state in 1871, but Bullock's political fate was sealed when military support for his administration ended.

With the moderate Republicans ascendant and his own political coalition crumbling, Bullock tried in 1870–1871 to preserve his political influence through economic agreements that transcended political allegiances. Most notable was the lease in December 1870 of the state-owned Western & Atlantic Railroad to a group of twenty-three named directors, including prominent national investors, prominent Georgia Reconstruction Republicans such as Brown (who resigned as the state's chief justice to bid for the lease), and longtime Democratic leader Benjamin H. Hill. Bullock himself, it was alleged, was promised a share of the lease profits, the funds to be paid to him after his term as governor ended; the allegation was never proved.

Widespread charges of fraud and corruption in the management and lease of the Western & Atlantic Railroad led to repeated investigations, while other allegations of fraud and malfeasance were raised against Bullock and his political allies. The state debt increased by nearly $5 million during Bullock's term; Bullock's administration stood accused of selling pardons to convicted offenders; and Bullock and his allies allegedly profited personally from the sale of state bonds. By 1870–1871 these charges obscured the unquestioned contributions of Bullock's regime, which included successful rebuilding of state railroad beds destroyed during the Civil War and the extension of new lines into southern and western Georgia, the successful discharge of a major share of the state's war debt, and moving the state capital from Milledgeville to Atlanta.

By 1871 Federal support for Bullock's administration had ended, and the governor feared impeachment when the legislature convened in the fall. On 23 October 1871 he resigned and fled the state, returning to his prewar home in Albion, New York. There he apparently encountered financial difficulties. Through correspondence and emissaries, he kept in touch with Brown and other Georgia notables, soliciting their support in his efforts to gain employment.

In 1876, when he was under indictment for alleged fraud and embezzlement during his gubernatorial regime, Bullock was arrested in New York City and, without fighting extradition, readily agreed to return to Georgia for trial. By the time his trial took place in 1878, testimony against Bullock was conflicting and equivocal, and many seemed disinclined to reopen old issues. Bullock was acquitted on all charges and, remarkably, remained in Atlanta after his trial. Eschewing further political involvement, he turned again to the business ventures that had brought him prewar and wartime success. He became president of the Atlanta Cotton Mills and a director of the Union Pacific Railroad, was active in social and civic clubs, and was a respected warden and vestryman in his Episcopal parish. He was elected president of the Atlanta Chamber of Commerce in 1892 and 1893 and was chosen to open the Cotton States and International Exhibition at Atlanta in 1895.

Bullock moved back to Albion in 1903. Ill, reportedly suffering locomotor ataxia secondary to a syphilitic infection, he lived in Albion until his death there. The *Atlanta Constitution*'s obituary came closer than have Reconstruction historians to a balanced appraisal of Bullock's career. Historians of Georgia Reconstruction have understandably focused on Bullock's political machinations and on his apparently questionable political and financial dealings. In so doing they may have obscured both Bullock's personal contributions to the building of a new economic climate in Georgia and his regime's contributions (however temporary) to the inclusion of blacks in Georgia politics. The *Constitution*'s obituary, as well as the only extant full biography of Bullock, offer important correctives by balancing Bullock's activities as a businessman and entrepreneur against his better-known but vastly more controversial public career.

• No major collection of Bullock's papers is known to exist, and remarkably few records of Bullock's gubernatorial administration survive. Still, the political record is more voluminous than that of his business and personal involvements. Letters from and about Bullock are scattered among the papers of national and state Republican leaders of the period (see, especially, the William Chandler Papers and the Joseph E. Brown Papers), in sources cited in the bibliographies to the standard secondary studies of Georgia Reconstruction. Bullock's political career is treated in detail in C. Mildred Thompson, *Reconstruction in Georgia: Economic, Social, Political, 1865–1872* (1915); Alan Conway, *The Reconstruction of Georgia* (1966); Elizabeth Studley Nathans, *Losing the Peace: Georgia Republicans and Reconstruction 1865–1871* (1968); and Joseph H. Parks, *Joseph E. Brown of Georgia* (1977). A full and favorable study, Russell Duncan, *Entrepreneur for Equality: Governor Rufus Bullock, Commerce, and Race in Post–Civil War Georgia* (1994), attempts to correct earlier accounts by stressing Bullock's contributions to Georgia's economic development and his forward-looking ideas on racial equality. A laudatory obituary is in the *Atlanta Constitution*, 28 Apr. 1907.

ELIZABETH STUDLEY NATHANS

BULOVA, Arde (24 Oct. 1889–19 Mar. 1958), businessman, was born in New York City, the son of Joseph Bulova and Bertha Eisner. His father emigrated to New York from Bohemia and in 1873 started a small jewelry manufacturing business that eventually became the Bulova Watch Company. Bulova attended school in New York and in 1905 began working as a salesman for his father's company. The family business prospered and in 1911 was incorporated, with the father as president and the son as vice president and treasurer. The firm was reincorporated in 1923 as the Bulova Watch Company, Inc. Bulova became chairman of the board in 1930, a position he held until his death in 1958.

Bulova helped pioneer several technical innovations and offered new consumer products. In 1919 the company began selling the first full line of men's jeweled wristwatches and two years later came out with the first complete line of women's watches. In 1928 it began selling the first clock radio.

Bulova's most important technical contribution was the mass production of watches using standardized parts. His inventions were used to make special gauges and tools needed to produce watches with almost no variation in quality. After importing many of its watch parts from Switzerland, the company factory at Woodside, New York, was able to make all needed parts except jewel bearings by the late 1940s. When Bulova died, standard features on company watches included shock resistance, waterproofing, unbreakable mainsprings, and self-winding mechanisms.

The firm under Bulova also made products for military use. In World War II the company made a major contribution to national defense by producing precision aviation instruments and fire control devices. Such high-tech advances were stimulated by the creation of the Bulova Research and Development Laboratories in 1950. In the postwar period the firm provided parts needed for guided missiles, infrared sensors, and other electronic systems. In 1951 the company was authorized to run the Rolla, North Dakota, ordnance plant, the nation's only domestic source of synthetic sapphire jewel bearings for military instruments. The next year Bulova opened a new electronics manufacturing division to produce military parts. Also in that year he married Ileana Marie Kerciu; they had no children.

Bulova also made important contributions in the areas of advertising and distribution. With company vice president John Ballard, he produced the nation's first spot radio ads in 1926. In 1941 the company aired the first TV commercial, with the theme "America Runs on Bulova Time," broadcast live from a Brooklyn Dodgers game. Originally the firm distributed its products only through retail jewelers, but during the Great Depression it extended credit to its customers by many months. This led to the establishment of credit jewelry stores, which numbered approximately 18,000 by 1957. At the end of Bulova's career, the firm employed approximately 5,000 workers and had assets of $41.8 million and annual sales of $63.8 million.

Bulova was not only a hard-nosed businessman; he also assisted the nation's handicapped persons years before it was popular to do so. He initiated preferential hiring practices for the disabled at the Bulova Watch Company. On 14 August 1945 the Joseph Bulova School of Watchmaking, chartered by the New York State Board of Regents, was opened in Woodside to train handicapped veterans to make and repair watches. By 1958 it had trained 578 persons. Supported by hundreds of jewelers who committed to hire the trainees, the school was financed entirely by the Bulova Foundation. Howard Beehler, dean of the Bulova School, also began similar training programs at eastern hospitals.

Bulova's efforts to help disabled veterans led to his 1955 appointment as the first chairman of the president's Committee on the Employment of the Physically Handicapped. In that position he promoted training programs in several American industries. As the director of the World Rehabilitation Fund, he extended these efforts to other nations.

Bulova's other civic activities included serving on the steering committee of the United Negro College Fund and on the mayor's Committee for a Quiet New York City. A member of the Jewish faith, Bulova contributed to several Jewish charities. In World War II he assisted hundreds of refugees in escaping from Fascist and Communist oppression.

Bulova was an assertive and decisive man, a deductive thinker who had many answers but few questions. His nephew Harry B. Henshel characterized Bulova as an outspoken and "take-charge person." He had a sense of humor, but rarely did he ever poke fun at himself. Bulova attended many social functions and traveled widely. He collected antiques, played golf, and enjoyed music. After being ill for several months, Bulova died in Encino, California.

• Bulova did not write an autobiography or leave a collection of personal papers. Bulova's Public Relations Office has on file a two-page undocumented corporate history. Many of the firm's records were destroyed when it became a subsidiary of Loews Corporation. The Bulova School of Watchmaking was featured in "School Days at Bulova," *Newsweek*, 22 Oct. 1945, p. 76; and Laura Haddock, "Training Disabled Veterans," *Christian Science Monitor Weekly*, 29 Dec. 1945, p. 5. John H. Ballard, president of Bulova Watch Company, wrote "Arde Bulova—Industry Pioneer," *National Jeweler*, May 1958, pp. 50–51. For information on the company and its place in the watch industry, see "Corporations: 5 Billion Time Signals," *Time*, 28 Dec. 1954, pp. 48–49. Bulova's widow, Ileana, was featured in "The Lap of Luxury," *Cosmopolitan*, Oct. 1959, pp. 50–51. Bulova's death and funeral were covered in the *New York Times*, 20 Mar. 1958, and 24 Mar. 1958.

DAVID M. WALDEN

BUMGARNER, Samantha (30 Oct. 1878–24 Dec. 1960), folksinger and instrumentalist, was born Samantha Biddix in Jackson County, North Carolina, the daughter of Has Biddix, a well-known local fiddler. (Her mother's name is unknown.) She grew up in the hilly area southeast of Asheville, a region rich in fiddle and banjo music and in old ballads. Her father could, she recalled, make his fiddle "croon like a lovin' woman," but at first he would not let his daughter touch his instrument. She persisted and became adept at the fiddle; she also, like many mountain musicians of the time, developed skill on the banjo. Her first banjo was "a gourd with cat's hide stretched over it and strings made of cotton thread and waxed with beeswax," but by the time she was fifteen she had learned to play it so well that her father bought her a "real" store-made banjo. She began to travel with her father as he went around the region playing for dances and fiddling contests. (Before the turn of the century, the guitar was rare in the Appalachians, and a mountain "string band" often consisted of a fiddle and banjo.)

Shortly before the turn of the century, Samantha married Carse Bumgarner, who was living in the community of Love Field, North Carolina. Far from being jealous of her musical talent, her husband seemed to encourage it and soon bought his new wife her first fiddle. Shortly after, though, the couple watched their house burn and Bumgarner's instruments go up in flames. Struggling to recover financially, she was able to replace only her banjo with what she called "a ten-cent banjo." She continued to hone her skills, and with her cheap instrument she entered a fiddle and banjo contest at nearby Canton; to her surprise, she won the contest and continued to win contests for some time afterward. Her efforts to start a family were not as successful; she never had any children.

As a result of Bumgarner's growing reputation as a musician and the efforts of a talent scout for Columbia Records, in 1924 she journeyed to New York to make records. The country music recording industry was barely a year old, but the companies producing Victrola Records were excited about recording authentic practitioners of what they were calling "old time music." Though Bumgarner would not become the first artist to record (an honor that is shared by fiddlers Eck Robertson and John Carson), she was one of the first women to make records and emerged as the leader of one of the first southern string bands to record.

With Bumgarner when she appeared at the Columbia studios on the top floor of the Gotham National Bank Building was a younger woman who introduced herself as Eva Davis. Eva was a young banjoist and fiddler who lived in Gastonia, North Carolina, and had been married only a short time before the 22 April 1924 recording session. Once the recording horn began (the records were still made in the old acoustic method), the pair began to play an old dance tune, "Cindy in the Meadows." Bumgarner played the fiddle and Davis accompanied, playing straightforward chords on the banjo.

The Columbia producers, though still inexperienced with the sound of mountain music, let the pair record ten selections. On five of these, including "I Am My Mama's Darling Child" and "Big-Eyed Rabbit," Bumgarner played fiddle. On other tunes, such as "John Hardy" and "Wild Bill Jones," Davis played banjo and Bumgarner sang. At the end, Bumgarner picked up the banjo and played and sang several solos, including "Shout Lou," "Fly around My Pretty Little Miss," and "Georgia Blues." The records that would create their reputation having been completed, the two boarded the train for Asheville, and waited. As early as June Columbia began advertising the new records, describing Bumgarner and Davis as "quaint musicians" who were "famed for their skill with fiddle and banjo." The records were soon selling so well that the company took out full-page ads that included photographs of the artists. Bumgarner and Davis continued to perform as a duo for some years, but Davis later dropped from sight.

During the late 1920s record talent scouts scoured the mountains looking for more musicians, but for some reason neither Bumgarner nor Davis recorded any more. By 1928 a local lawyer-musician, Bascom Lamar Lunsford, had started the Mountain Dance and Folk Festival at Asheville; one of the first of such festivals, it would soon became one of the most important. Bumgarner became a charter member of the roster of musicians and never missed a year through 1959. In the 1940s, when she was in her sixties, she often appeared with fiddler Bill Hensley and frequently won the clog-dancing championship in addition to winning the prize in the banjo category. Lunsford later recalled that so many fans looked forward to the appearances of "Aunt Samantha" at the festival that she was given a regular spot, just about sundown, every year.

By the 1950s Bumgarner's fame increased considerably as the "folk revival" swept the country. In August 1955 she was the subject of an article in *Life* magazine and was recorded by folklorist Kenneth Goldstein for an album called *Banjo Songs of the Southern Mountains*. She also recorded some of her later music for the Library of Congress's Archive of American Folk Music. During these later years, after her husband's death, she lived alone in a white bungalow at Love Field and attended festivals dressed in an old-fashioned frilled dress; her famous banjo featured flowers painted on its head. She wrote a few songs, including the protest song "The Last Gold Dollar," referring to "when the government took up the gold" (in 1934).

Bumgarner's death on Christmas Eve in Asheville was preceded by a debilitating case of arthritis and a broken hip. Her regional fame was such that her obituary on 26 December 1960 in the *Asheville Citizen-Times* was the occasion for a full-length editorial. Her death, it noted, "marked the passing of one of this mountain region's most colorful and picturesque individuals." Known as the "fiddlin' ballad-woman," she had been an inspiration to younger women musicians and, as historians began to document the role of women in traditional and country music, Samantha Bumgarner's reputation grew.

• A detailed account of Bumgarner's life is Charles K. Wolfe, "Samantha Bumgarner: The Original Banjo Pickin' Girl," *Devil's Box* 12, no. 1 (May 1978): 19–22. She has a prominent place in Robert Oerman and Mary Bufwack's *Singing Her Song* (1993), a history of women in country music, and in 1978 some of her records were reissued on the Rounder album *Banjo Pickin' Girl.* Bumgarner was the subject of numerous newspaper features during her lifetime; see various collections of columns by Asheville writer John Parris, especially *Mountain Bred* (1967).

CHARLES K. WOLFE

BUMSTEAD, Henry Andrews (12 Mar. 1870–31 Dec. 1920), physicist, was born in Pekin, Illinois, the son of Samuel Josiah Bumstead, a physician, and Sarah Ellen Seiwell. The young Bumstead attended high school in Decatur, Illinois, before entering the Johns Hopkins University in 1887 with the intention of becoming a physician. There, under the influence of the mathematician Fabian Franklin and the physicist Henry A. Rowland, he decided to study physics. He received his A.B. in 1891 and remained at Hopkins as an assistant in physics from 1891 to 1893; he then entered graduate school at Yale. There he was instructor in physics at the Sheffield Scientific School (1893–1900), and in 1897 he was awarded his Ph.D. with a dissertation, "A Comparison of Electrodynamic Theories," written under the direction of J. Willard Gibbs. Bumstead stayed at Yale as assistant professor (1900–1906) and later professor and director of the Sloane Physical Laboratory (1906–1920).

Bumstead spent the academic year 1904–1905 at the Cavendish Laboratory of Cambridge University, where he worked with Joseph J. Thomson. In 1917 he was a member of a national committee to examine proposals for antisubmarine devices for the U.S. Navy, and in February 1918 he became the scientific attaché to the U.S. embassy in London. There he was to function as liaison with the British Board of Invention and Research and to facilitate the exchange of information useful for the war effort. In this capacity he had close contact with Sir Joseph Larmor, Sir Oliver Lodge, Lord Rayleigh, and Sir Joseph J. Thomson.

Bumstead returned to Yale in February 1919 and was subsequently elected chairman of the National Research Council. He had been elected a member of the National Academy of Science in 1913 and had served as a member of the board of editors of the *Physical Review* (1914–1916). He was a fellow of the American Physical Society and served as its president (1918–1919). In 1920 he was awarded an honorary doctorate by the University of Toronto.

Bumstead was probably Gibbs's most gifted student, but because of his heavy teaching and administrative duties at Yale and his government service, he published fewer than two dozen papers, most of them on experimental topics. Those on theoretical physics reveal a remarkable grasp of situation and its evolutionary character. He explained an anomaly in the reflection of electric waves on the basis of Maxwell's equations (1902), and he gave a critical assessment of the work of Einstein and Lorentz on special relativity (1908). The latter was one of the earliest papers in English dealing with relativity, and one of the first on the topic by an American physicist. In experimental physics, Bumstead's most significant work was concerned with the delta rays (named by Thomson), which are emitted by metals bombarded by alpha rays (1911, 1913, 1916). Bumstead was one of the editors of the two-volume *Scientific Papers of J. Willard Gibbs* (1906). Despite his rather sparse publication record, Bumstead was one of the most esteemed and influential physicists of his era. He had a brilliant analytical mind that, coupled with his broad scholarship and excellent judgment, made him the man of the moment at scientific meetings. Gibbs is alleged to have remarked that some things came easier to Bumstead than to most men. He had an engaging personality and natural modesty, which made him a valued friend to both his students and fellow physicists. Had he lived longer, he might well have hastened American acceptance of relativity and quantum theory. Nevertheless, Bumstead made a significant contribution to Yale, his government, and the American physical community.

Bumstead married Luetta Ullrich of Decatur in 1896; they had two children. Never physically robust, Bumstead had frequent health problems. He died of heart failure on a train returning from the annual meeting of the American Physical Society in Chicago.

• Bumstead's critical acumen and felicity of style are displayed in his papers, "Present Tendencies in Theoretical Physics," *Science* 47 (Jan. 1918): 51–62, and "The History of Physics," *Scientific Monthly* 21 (Apr. 1921): 289–309, which also exhibit his remarkable insight on the changes then occurring in physics. Leigh Page, National Academy of Sciences, *Biographical Memoirs* 13 (1929): 103–24, contains a portrait and a list of publications. There are also noteworthy obituaries by Robert A. Millikan in *Science* 53 (Jan. 1921): 84–85, and by Sir Joseph J. Thomson in *Nature* 106 (Feb. 1921): 734–35.

JOSEPH D. ZUND

BUNCHE, Ralph Johnson (7 Aug. 1904–9 Dec. 1971), scholar and diplomat, was born in Detroit, Michigan, the son of Fred Bunch, a barber, and Olive Agnes Johnson. His grandmother added an "e" to the family's last name following a move to Los Angeles, California. Because his family moved frequently, Bunche attended a number of public schools before graduating first in his class from Jefferson High School in Los Angeles in 1922. He majored in political science at the University of California, Southern Branch (now University of California at Los Angeles or UCLA). He graduated summa cum laude and served as class valedictorian in 1927. He continued his studies in political science at Harvard, receiving his M.A. in 1928, then taught at Howard University in Washington, D.C., while working toward his Ph.D. at Harvard. In 1930 he married Ruth Ethel Harris; they had three children. Bunche traveled to Europe and Africa researching his dissertation and received his Ph.D. from Harvard in February 1934.

Concerned with the problems facing African Americans in the United States, Bunche published numerous articles on racial issues and the monograph *A World View of Race* (1936). He and his colleague John P. Davis organized a 1935 conference called "The Status of the Negro under the New Deal," at which Bunche criticized the Franklin D. Roosevelt administration and the New Deal. He was also involved in the creation of the National Negro Congress, an attempt to bring white Americans and African Americans of different social and economic backgrounds together to discuss race matters. In the final years of the decade Bunche contributed research and reports to a Carnegie study on American race relations headed by sociologist Gunnar Myrdal. The resulting work, *An American Dilemma: The Negro Problem and Modern Democracy*, published in 1944, was a landmark study of racial conflicts in the United States.

The rise of totalitarianism in Europe and the outbreak of war in 1939 worried Bunche, who feared that a Nazi victory in Europe would spur the growth of fascism in the United States, with disastrous consequences for African Americans. In 1941 he entered public service, accepting a position as a senior analyst in the Office of the Coordinator of Information (later the Office of Strategic Services). As head of the Africa Section, Bunche urged his superiors to approach the problem of postwar decolonization of European holdings in Africa. His proposal was rejected, and he transferred to the Department of State in 1944.

Bunche served as an adviser to the American delegations at the conferences in Dumbarton Oaks and San Francisco concerning the creation of the United Nations (UN). Recognized for his contributions on colonial and trusteeship policies, he was appointed a member of the U.S. delegation to the 1945 meeting of the Preparatory Commission of the UN and the first session of the UN General Assembly in 1946. In April 1946 Bunche took a temporary position on the United Nations Secretariat as director of the trusteeship position. The temporary position became permanent, and he served on the UN Secretariat for the remainder of his life.

In 1947 Bunche was appointed to the United Nations Special Committee on Palestine. He drafted both the majority report, which recommended a partition of the territory between Palestinians and Jews, and the minority report, which called for the creation of a federal state. The UN General Assembly accepted the partition plan, and Bunche was named the principal secretary for a commission designed to oversee its implementation. With the outbreak of war in 1948, Bunche was appointed as an assistant to the UN mediator, Count Folke Bernadotte. Following Bernadotte's assassination in September of that year, Bunche became the acting mediator. He successfully negotiated armistice agreements between Israel and several Arab states and was awarded the 1950 Nobel Peace Prize for his efforts.

Bunche's commitment to the United Nations did not prevent him from speaking out against racial discrimination in the United States. In 1949 he turned down a position as assistant secretary of state, noting that he did not want to experience the blatant discrimination against African Americans that existed in the nation's capital.

Bunche was appointed an undersecretary-general for special political affairs in 1954. With the outbreak of the Suez crisis in 1956, he was again called upon to use his diplomatic skills in a Middle Eastern conflict, and he organized the UN Emergency Force that was responsible for peacekeeping activities in the region. His Middle East experience prepared him for the difficulties he faced in 1960, when he organized and commanded both the military and civilian branches of the UN peacekeeping force sent to the Congo. He again directed a peacekeeping force when conflicts erupted on the island of Cyprus in 1964.

Bunche continued to press for the civil rights of African Americans. Though he still hoped for a society free from racial division, the civil rights conflicts of the late 1960s troubled him greatly. He participated in the 1965 march from Selma to Montgomery with Martin Luther King, Jr. However, Bunche found himself under attack from leaders, such as Stokely Carmichael and Malcolm X, who argued that he had served white society and abandoned his African heritage. In turn, Bunche denounced the separatist agenda of the Black Power movement. Health problems, many related to his diabetes, slowed him in the final years of his life. He died in New York City.

During his lifetime Bunche garnered international recognition and numerous rewards for his United Nations service, including the U.S. Medal of Freedom in 1963. Though his position earned him the derision of many civil rights leaders in the 1960s, he was dedicated to the cause of African-American civil rights throughout his career. By using his diplomatic skills in the service of the United Nations, he promoted the cause of peace in a world that sorely needed men of dedication and ability in this area.

• Bunche's papers are at the Library of the University of California at Los Angeles and the United Nations Archives in New York City. A smaller collection is at the Schomburg Center for Research in Black Culture. Bunche wrote numerous articles, including "A Critique of the New Deal Social Planning as It Affects Negroes," *Journal of Negro Education* 4 (Jan. 1936): 59–65; and "The Programs of Organizations Devoted to the Improvement of the Status of the American Negro," *Journal of Negro Education* 8 (July 1939): 539–50. A monograph he wrote for the Carnegie study was posthumously published as *The Political Status of the Negro in the Age of FDR* (1973). Scholarly works on Bunche include Brian Urquhart, *Ralph Bunche: An American Life* (1993), written by an associate of Bunche; Benjamin Rivlin, ed., *Ralph Bunche: The Man and His Times* (1990), a collection of essays; and Ben Keppel, *The Work of Democracy: Ralph Bunche, Kenneth B.*

Clark, Lorraine Hansberry, and the Cultural Politics of Race (1995), which assesses Bunche's status as a symbol of racial equality in the United States.

THOMAS CLARKIN

BUNDESEN, Herman Niels (27 Apr. 1882–15 Aug. 1960), physician, author, and politician, was born in Berlin, Germany, the son of a Danish father and a German mother whose identities are unknown. Brought to Chicago at an early age by his impoverished, widowed mother, he graduated from Northwestern University Medical School in 1909. Also in 1909 he married Rega Russell; they had six children.

Following his service in the U.S. Army during the First World War, Bundesen returned to Chicago to practice medicine. Because of his dedicated efforts to battle a local typhoid epidemic, he was appointed Chicago health commissioner in 1922. By 1926 he had persuaded dairy farmers in Illinois to destroy approximately 400,000 diseased cows and milk processors to install better pasteurizing equipment, thereby virtually eliminating bone tuberculosis as a major health problem in Chicago. He also waged successful campaigns to reduce rates of diphtheria, syphilis, and infant and maternal mortality in the city. In 1927 he was discharged by Mayor William Hale Thompson for refusing to send political materials along with the maternity care pamphlets he mailed to new mothers. The following year, running as a Democrat, Bundesen was elected Cook County coroner, receiving more than one million votes. In 1931 Mayor Anton Cermak reappointed him Chicago health commissioner, and two years later he was elected president of the Chicago Board of Health, a position he retained until his death. In 1933 he won national acclaim for identifying and eradicating an outbreak of amoebic dysentery in Chicago, which was then hosting the Century of Progress Exposition.

Bundesen became widely renowned as an expert on infant care and wrote a syndicated column on the topic that appeared in more than 500 newspapers. He also wrote three books—*Our Babies* (1925), *Before the Baby Comes* (1926), and *The Growing Child* (1927)—that became bestselling texts in the 1920s and 1930s. Consulting city birth records, the board of health mailed complimentary copies of Bundesen's books to all new Chicago mothers and sold them to insurance companies. The flamboyant administrator frequently referred to himself in public appearances and interviews as the "savior of babies, friend of mothers, builder of health" (Biles, p. 53).

Capitalizing on the high visibility provided by his books and the great following he enjoyed in the German-American communities in Chicago and elsewhere, Bundesen agreed to seek the Democratic gubernatorial nomination in 1936. He received the endorsement of Chicago's Kelly-Nash political machine against the Democratic incumbent, Henry Horner, an irascible independent who had clashed often with Boss Edward J. Kelly. Closely allying with the Democratic machine, the health commissioner conducted an energetic—if unorthodox—primary campaign. He toured Illinois in spats and a monocle, handing out copies of his books, urging voters to drink several glasses of milk each day, and pounding on his own abdomen to demonstrate his fitness. His reputation tarnished because of the association with Chicago's corrupt political machine and unable to convince the voters that he was a serious candidate, Bundesen lost to Horner by 161,092 votes.

After his ill-fated run for statewide political office, Bundesen spent the rest of his life administering the Chicago Board of Health. During a 1956 poliomyelitis epidemic, he made national headlines by campaigning for comprehensive inoculation of all children. Having personally inspected the areas of Chicago with the highest incidence of the disease, he argued that children not given the entire series of shots ran the greatest risk of illness and death. Highly respected within the medical community, he served as president of the American Public Health Association and was a senior surgeon in the U.S. Public Health Service.

His frequently eccentric behavior notwithstanding, Bundesen was credited with reducing a number of health hazards in Chicago, and many of his innovations were copied in other U.S. cities. His reforms were in the vanguard of the post–World War I public health movement, and his unorthodox promotions drew attention to new programs and techniques. He died in Chicago.

• Bundesen's political career is discussed in Roger Biles, *Big City Boss in Depression and War: Mayor Edward J. Kelly of Chicago* (1984), and Thomas B. Littlewood, *Horner of Illinois* (1969). Obituaries are in the *New York Times*, 26 Aug. 1960, and the *Chicago Tribune*, 25 Aug. 1960.

ROGER BILES

BUNDY, Elroy Lorraine (1920–1975), professor of classics, was born in Fergus Falls, Minnesota, the son of Arthur C. Bundy, a farmer, and Sybil F. Tarkett, a seamstress. His family soon after moved to Duluth, where Bundy's father found intermittent employment as a security guard and county sheriff while also serving as a lay minister of the Reorganized Church of Jesus Christ of Latter-Day Saints. Bundy always attributed his intellect to his father, his artistic skills to his mother. In 1942 military service took him to California, where he returned four years later to enroll at the University of California at Berkeley. There he soon changed his major from English, which he had chosen as the best preparation for a career as a poet, to classics, finding the ancient poets particularly challenging and stimulating. He received his B.A. in 1948 and then spent a year at Princeton on a Woodrow Wilson Fellowship. He taught briefly at the University of Washington (1952–1953) before being appointed to the Department of Classics at Berkeley in 1953. He received his Ph.D. in classics there in 1954 and remained on the faculty until his death.

His doctoral thesis, "Hesychia in Pindar," concerned one of antiquity's most celebrated and influential—yet supposedly most obscure—authors, the Greek choral poet Pindar, best remembered for his epinician odes (choral songs in praise of victors at Olympia, Delphi, and other venues of athletic competition). Bundy's work benefited from the direction of Ivan Linforth, whose influence on his intellectual development, together with that of Harold Cherniss, Bundy always acknowledged. But his thesis sprang from his own insights, which in time revolutionized scholarly interpretations of Pindar's work.

The University of California Press accepted for publication in 1959 a revised version of his doctoral dissertation. So rapidly were his ideas on Pindar maturing, however, that Bundy withdrew the book. As a consequence, his major scholarly output consists of only two short monographs, *Studia Pindarica*, I–II (1962). By his own admission these deal with two of Pindar's least problematic odes, the *Eleventh Olympian* and the *First Isthmian*, respectively. Bundy believed that the critical methodology he established for and the provisional conclusions he advanced about Pindar's art as a eulogist would in future studies unlock the secrets of the more difficult odes.

Those studies never materialized. Disappointed by the initially cool, at times even frosty, reception of his ideas by traditional Hellenists, who accused him of reducing Pindar's poetry to mere sequences of rhetorical conventions at the expense of the fiery heart of its complex genius, and beset by marital and other personal difficulties, Bundy fell victim to alcohol and drugs for more than a decade; suicide seemed always a possibility. By the early 1970s, however, he had recovered well, buoyed not least by the international reputation he was now slowly acquiring, as a new generation of scholars applied his methods both to Pindaric praise rhetoric and to other genres of ancient poetry, with persuasive results.

In 1972 Bundy published "The 'Quarrel between Kallimachos and Apollonius,'" part 1, "The Epilogue of Kallimachos' *Hymn to Apollo*." In it he argues that scholars who find in *Hymn to Apollo* an implicit reference to personal enmity between Kallimachos and Apollonius, Kallimachos's "rival," are mistaken; there is no personal allusion in the passage in question, only the kind of rhetoric by which ancient poets insist on the trustworthiness of their accounts. At the time of Bundy's death from a heart attack, he was working with great energy and enthusiasm on two books: a history of Pindaric scholarship, particularly in the Middle Ages and Renaissance, the time he believed when modern misconceptions about Pindar took root; and the long-promised critical study of Pindaric eulogy.

In his published work on Pindar, Bundy argues that the received wisdom about the poet, consolidated in the nineteenth century, is riddled with misconceptions. The conventional critics argued that much of Pindar's epinician poetry is an uncoordinated jumble of abrupt transitions, passages of "gorgeous irrelevance," and expressions of personal preoccupations. The result is brilliant but often incoherent, even perplexing, poetry. Bundy suggested instead that one master organizing principle obtains in the art of Pindar and of all ancient eulogists: the primary function of every ode, in part and in whole, is to persuade a skeptical audience that the subject of the poet's praise deserves his high acclaim. It is an end fraught with pitfalls, for we are suspicious of praise that goes either too far or not far enough. Pindar succeeds with distinction by an unusually skillful deployment of the conventional "thematic and motivational grammar of choral composition" in which the original audience was well versed but which moderns must strive to rediscover. Bundy, himself a poet, saw his analysis of praise rhetoric not as a final word on Pindar but as a necessary introduction to that poet's many virtues.

Bundy's fame rests primarily on his seminal study of Pindar. In addition he was no mean athlete, a sensitive poet and translator of poetry, and he read widely outside his professional area (he was an expert on, among other things, California butterflies). He was also recognized as one of the superior university teachers of his day: he thought deeply about the goals and methods of education; his commitment to bold yet precise research was infectious; and he was a dynamic and inspiring presence in the classroom. Students came from far afield to learn from him. So did many a professor, for Bundy was essentially a shy, introverted man, who shunned the limelight of national and international gatherings of scholars.

• Bundy's *Studia Pindarica*, I–II, first appeared in University of California Publications in Classical Philology, vol. 18 (1962), nos. 1–2. His "'Quarrel between Kallimachos and Apollonius'" is in *California Studies in Classical Antiquity* 5 (1972): 39–94. For more on Pindaric criticism, see E. Christian Kopff, "American Pindaric Criticism after Bundy," in *Aischylos und Pindar*, ed. Ernst Günther Schmidt (1981), and David C. Young, "Pindaric Criticism," in *Pindaros und Bukchyliddes*, ed. William C. Calder III and Jacob Stern (1970).

HUGH PARRY

BUNDY, Harvey Hollister (30 Mar. 1888–7 Oct. 1963), lawyer, assistant secretary of state, and special assistant to the secretary of war, was born in Grand Rapids, Michigan, the son of McGeorge Bundy, a lawyer, and Mary Goodhue Hollister. Bundy attended private school in his hometown and Hackley School in Tarrytown, New York. He graduated from Yale University in 1909 with a degree in psychology. Unsure about a career in law, he accepted a one-year teaching position at St. Mark's Boys Preparatory School in Southboro, Massachusetts. The following year he served as a traveling companion for a "wayward" boy on a trip around much of the world, which seems to have shaped Bundy's love for international affairs. Upon his return he entered Harvard University Law School, and following graduation in 1914, he worked as a stenographic clerk, legal aide, and traveling companion for U.S. Supreme Court justice Oliver Wendell Holmes. In 1915 Bundy was admitted to the Massachusetts bar and began a legal practice in Boston. That year he married Katherine L. Putnam. They had five children, two of whom, William Bundy and McGeorge Bundy, would become prominent in government service.

Bundy frequently interrupted his successful legal practice to perform government service, earning a reputation as an effective administrator. He worked as a junior partner with the firm of Hale and Grinell for about eleven months before joining his father-in-law's firm of Putnam, Putnam and Bell. Specializing in wills and trusts, Bundy chaired the Boston Personal Property Trust. He relished his work with major banking interests, believing he was "greasing the wheels of this industrial enterprise system" (Hodgson, p. 247). Unfit for military service during World War I because of poor eyesight, he served in several war agencies under the direction of Herbert Hoover. Bundy was assistant counsel for the U.S. Food Administration from 1917 to 1919 and secretary of the U.S. Sugar Equalization Board from 1919 to 1925 before returning to Boston to resume his private legal practice, which dealt primarily with brokerage bankruptcies.

In July 1931 Secretary of State Henry L. Stimson, who needed an aide with experience in finance, noticed Bundy's background in corporate law and government service. Stimson appointed Bundy assistant secretary of state for economic and financial affairs, and during Bundy's 22-month tenure they became good friends. Bundy accompanied Stimson to Germany several times, helped initiate the successful Foreign Bondholders' Protective Council, and was a State Department contact with President-elect Franklin D. Roosevelt during the final months of the Hoover administration.

In 1933 Bundy returned to Boston to resume his law practice at Choate, Hall and Stewart, where he had become a senior partner in 1929. He was also a special legal adviser to the secretary of the U.S. Department of the Treasury, chairman of the Foreign Policy Association, and president of the World Peace Foundation. These activities kept him engaged in governmental affairs. In April 1941 Secretary of War Stimson appointed Bundy his special assistant. Stimson was looking for "another pair of eyes and ears," and Bundy served as confidential adviser, liaison officer, and troubleshooter. Bundy had no official job title but justifiably claimed to have the "Secretary's initials in my pocket." Only General George C. Marshall enjoyed greater access to the secretary than Bundy, whose quiet, cautious advice Stimson sought on every critical issue. Bundy often traveled with Stimson to conferences in Europe and on tours of combat areas, and he prepared the secretary for cabinet meetings and press conferences. He also played an instrumental role in getting the Selective Service Act passed in Congress.

After the American entry into World War II, Bundy learned from James B. Conant, a prominent scientist and president of Harvard University, of concern among the nation's scientists that German scientists might develop nuclear weapons that could be decisive in defeating the United States. Soon Bundy was assigned to oversee scientific projects, and in this role he worked closely with Conant and Vannevar "Van" Bush, a former dean of engineering at the Massachusetts Institute of Technology and the president of the Carnegie Institution, who headed the Office of Scientific Research and Development. Bundy, Bush, and representatives of the military created a committee whose purpose was advise the Joint Chiefs of Staff on scientific developments, and in 1942, upon Bundy and Bush's recommendations, the General Staff's new-weapons section was established as an independent body. In 1942 knowledge about the development of the atomic bomb was restricted to a few top officials, and Bundy served as the secretary's contact with the critical Manhattan Project. Bundy coordinated his work with General Leslie R. Groves, the director of the top-secret project, and apprised Stimson regularly on matters related to the bomb's construction and issues concerning its deployment. In 1945 Secretary Stimson established an Interim Committee, which Bundy helped chair, that met to consider recommendations from the Manhattan Project scientists concerning the military use of atomic weapons. As the war progressed, a rift developed between Roosevelt and the project's scientific coordinators, Bush and Conant, over the use of atomic weaponry, and Bundy became an intermediary between the scientists, the secretary of war, and the president. On 5 March 1945 Bundy and Stimson had what the secretary considered "a most thorough and searching talk" on the strategic uses of atomic weapons. Bundy convinced Stimson to urge President Harry S. Truman and Secretary of State James F. Byrnes to share the secrets of nuclear energy with the Allies and to warn the Japanese leaders prior to dropping the atomic bomb. Meanwhile, following meetings with British prime minister Winston Churchill and his aides in 1940 to discuss collaboration with the British in the development of atomic weapons, Bundy served as the American secretary for the high-level Combined Policy Committee, which reviewed nuclear interchange between the two Allies. Attending the Potsdam Conference with Stimson in the summer of 1945, Bundy participated behind the scenes in talks regarding strategic uses of atomic energy.

Upon Secretary Stimson's retirement in 1945, Bundy left the War Department and returned once more to Boston, where he rejoined Choate, Hall and Stewart and remained active in public service. He encouraged Stimson to write his memoirs, which the elder statesman completed with the assistance of Bundy's son McGeorge Bundy. Reacting to criticism over the use of nuclear weapons against Japan, Bundy helped Stimson write "The Decision to Use the Atomic Bomb," which appeared in *Harper's Magazine* in February 1947 and sought to justify the use of atomic weapons to bring World War II to a close. In January 1948 Truman appointed Bundy along with his old friend and colleague James Grafton Rogers, former assistant secretary of state and deputy director of the Office of Strategic Services, to a special task force to study American foreign policy. In January 1949 they presented their report, *Task Force Report on Foreign Affairs*, to the Congressional Commission of the Organization of the Executive Branch of the Government. Bundy also was chairman of the Foreign Bondholders' Protective Council (1946–1952), chairman of the Boston Chapter of the American Red Cross (1952–1963), and chairman of the Carnegie Endowment for International Peace (1952–1958). He died in Boston.

• Bundy's 319-page transcript, "The Reminiscences of Harvey H. Bundy" (1961), is in the Oral History Research Office, Columbia University. His correspondence (1942–1963) is in the James Grafton Rogers Papers, Colorado Historical Society, Denver. Also see Henry L. Stimson and McGeorge Bundy, *On Active Service in Peace and War* (1948); Elting E. Morison, *Turmoil and Tradition: A Study of the Life and Times of Henry L. Stimson* (1960); Godfrey Hodgson, *The Colonel: The Life and Wars of Henry Stimson, 1867–1950* (1990); Herbert Feis, *1933: Characters in Crisis* (1966); and James Hershberg, *James B. Conant: Harvard to Hiroshima and the Making of the Nuclear Age* (1993). Obituaries are in the *New York Times* and the *Boston Herald*, 8 Oct. 1963.

MICHAEL J. DEVINE
ELIZABETH E. CURRAN

BUNDY, May Godfray Sutton (25 Sept. 1887–4 Oct. 1975), tennis player, was born in Plymouth, England, the daughter of Adolphus Ade G. Sutton, an English navy captain, and Adelina E. Godfray. Her family immigrated to the United States when she was six. On the clay court built by one of her two older brothers and a sister on the family ranch near Pasadena, California, Bundy at age ten followed in the footsteps of three of her four older sisters by becoming a tennis enthusiast. Beginning tournament play in 1898, Bundy won the prestigious Southern California Women's Singles Championship in 1899 at age twelve. Because she was the strongest, quickest, and most determined of the sisters, by 1901 she emerged as the best of the quartet, leading to the often-heard quip in California that it took a Sutton to beat a Sutton.

In 1901–1903 Bundy won the Southern California and Pacific Coast Women's Singles championships. As the best female player in the West, she traveled east in 1904 to play in the United States Women's Championships. She totally dominated the field there, losing only ten games and defeating Elisabeth Moore 6–1, 6–2 in the finals. Bundy also teamed with Miriam Hall to win the 1904 United States Women's Doubles Championship.

Bundy's greatest weapon was her lethal forehand. The bulldozer power of this stroke was matched only by her consistency in hitting it. Although primarily a baseliner, her quickness and speed enabled her occasionally to advance to the net for volleys. She also demonstrated a stronger serve than her opponents, while her backhand was mostly a defensive stroke. This sixteen-year-old American champion, the youngest to capture a title at the time, possessed an indomitable spirit, leading reporters to maintain that she had no peer in the United States and was the greatest player ever.

Instead of defending her title in 1905, Bundy traveled to England to enter the All-England Singles Championship at Wimbledon. Defeating England's best, former champion Dorothea Douglas, Bundy became the first American—man or woman—to win at Wimbledon. She lost the Wimbledon crown to Douglas in 1906 but regained it in 1907. Bundy also won Welsh championships in 1905–1907. Among the other singles titles won by Bundy were the Pacific Coast Championships (eight years) and the Southern California Championships (seven years).

Tennis for women around the turn of the century was characterized primarily by baseline play and little stroke versatility. Most women players were self-taught, and the serve was often their weakest stroke. The fact that few ventured to the net could be partially attributed to the constraints of their clothing. Typical attire included an undershirt, drawers, petticoats, a linen corset cover, a duck skirt, shirtwaist, and long, white silk stockings. Bundy, allergic to these heavy, confining items, wore shorter skirts and fewer petticoats and rolled up her sleeves, while eschewing high-collared shirtwaists. Her youth when she became champion probably allowed her this freedom, as she led in the emancipation of women from restrictive tennis clothing.

In 1912, in the first wedding of national tennis champions, she married Thomas Clark Bundy, a real estate developer who earlier that year had teamed with Maurice McLoughlin to win the United States Men's Doubles Championship. Before being divorced in 1940, they had three children, including perennial tennis champion Dorothy Bundy Cheney. Although never a winner of the United States or Wimbledon crowns, "Dodo" adopted her mother's western grip and determination. A Santa Monica resident, Cheney won over 130 national tennis titles, most after the age of forty.

Following the birth of her children, Bundy returned to national level competition in the 1920s, earning national rankings of fourth in 1921 and fifth in 1925 and 1928. She advanced to the national singles semifinals in 1921 and 1922, the national doubles semifinals in 1922 and 1928, and the national doubles finals in 1925. She played for the United States in the Wightman Cup matches in 1925, and in 1929 at age forty-one she reached the quarterfinals at Wimbledon. Bundy taught tennis in the 1930s through the 1950s and continued to play until she was eighty-five. She died in Santa Monica, California.

As a tribute to her trailblazing, international championship career and her domination of California tennis for decades, in 1956 she became the first woman enshrined in the International Tennis Hall of Fame.

• Bundy wrote "My Career as a Lawn Tennis Player," *American Lawn Tennis*, 15 May 1912, pp. 40–41. Articles that describe significant times of her life include Jeane Hoffman, "The Sutton Sisters," *Racquet*, Aug. 1953, pp. 7, 27; (unsigned) "A Wedding of Champions," *American Lawn Tennis*, 15 Dec. 1912, p. 379; and (unsigned) "Mother and Daughter," *American Lawn Tennis*, 5 Sept. 1936, p. 25. A few of the books that chronicle Bundy's tennis career are Bud Collins and Zander Hollander, *Bud Collins' Modern Encyclopedia of Tennis* (1980); Billie Jean King and Cynthia Starr, *We Have Come a Long Way* (1988); and Angela Lumpkin, *Women's Tennis: A Historical Documentary of the Players and Their Game* (1981). *May Sutton* is the title of the Wimbledon Lawn Tennis Museum booklet #5 (1984). An obituary is in the *New York Times*, 7 Oct. 1975.

ANGELA LUMPKIN

BUNDY, Ted (24 Nov. 1946–24 Jan. 1989), serial murderer, was born Theodore Robert Cowell at the Elizabeth Lund Home for Unwed Mothers in Burlington, Vermont, the son of Louise Cowell. (His father's name is unknown.) About two months after Ted's birth, Louise Cowell returned with her son to her parents' house in Philadelphia, Pennsylvania. When Ted was about five, his mother took him to Tacoma, Washington, where she met Johnnie Bundy, a cook at a military hospital. They were married in 1951. For the first few years of Ted's life he apparently was led to believe that his mother was his sister and that his grandparents were his parents. Despite this somewhat nontraditional upbringing, by most accounts he experienced a happy and normal childhood and adolescence, albeit a frugal one, as the family did not have much money. A good-looking and serious young man, Bundy earned above-average grades and graduated from high school in 1965. That same year he entered the University of Puget Sound, where he felt uncomfortable around the predominantly affluent student body. He transferred to the University of Washington for his sophomore year and finally earned his bachelor's degree in psychology in 1972. During his college years Bundy became involved with Republican party politics, serving on the Nelson Rockefeller presidential campaign in 1968. After graduation he was a crisis counselor and worked on Washington governor Dan Evans's successful reelection campaign. As a reward for his diligent service on behalf of Evans, Bundy was appointed to the Seattle Crime Prevention Advisory Committee and later did some contractual work, compiling a criminal justice survey for King County. In 1973 Bundy became assistant to Ross Davis, the chairman of the Washington State Republican party. Most people who worked with Bundy during this time believed he had a promising political future.

In early 1974, beginning with 21-year-old Lynda Healy, several attractive young women vanished from college campuses and surrounding areas in Washington State and Oregon. In one instance eighteen-year-old Georgann Hawkins disappeared while walking the 200-foot distance from her boyfriend's fraternity house to her home. In July 1974 two women at a state park outside Seattle told police that a handsome man named Ted had approached them, soliciting their help with his sailboat. Suspicious, they refused, but two other women at the park that day accompanied him to his car and were never seen alive again.

In the fall of 1974 Bundy moved to Salt Lake City, Utah, where he enrolled in law school at the University of Utah. In November Carol DaRonch was lured away from a mall in a Salt Lake City suburb and was attacked by a man dressed as a police officer, but she escaped. That same evening, seventeen-year-old Debbie Kent disappeared from a local school. About this time hikers in the dense forests of Washington found human bones that were later identified as those of the missing women from Washington and Oregon. The murders remained unsolved, and police had few clues to work with.

In August 1975 Bundy, recently baptized into the Mormon church, was stopped by police for driving erratically. A search of his vehicle produced handcuffs, pantyhose cut with eyeholes, and an ice pick, among other suspicious items. Later, DaRonch, whose assailant had tried to handcuff her, identified Bundy as her attacker, and he was subsequently charged with attempted kidnapping. At his trial in February 1976 Bundy, who took the stand in his own defense and waived his right to a jury trial, was found guilty of attempted kidnapping and was sentenced to one to fifteen years in prison.

Meanwhile, police were investigating Bundy's visits to Colorado, which were made, according to charge card receipts, in early 1975, a time when several women had disappeared there. In October 1976 officials presented Bundy, who was serving his time in the Utah penitentiary, with a warrant charging him in the murder of Caryn Campbell, who had been abducted from a ski resort in Aspen and murdered in early 1975. Bundy was soon extradited to Glenwood Springs, Colorado, where the murder trial was to take place. Dissatisfied with his appointed public counsel, he served as his own attorney and began writing a flurry of legal briefs, requesting better prison food, vitamin supplements, and the privilege of appearing in court in street clothes without leg irons, among other demands. In a television interview before the trial, Bundy proclaimed, "More than ever, I am convinced of my innocence." In June 1977, at one of many pretrial hearings, he escaped by leaping from the courthouse window. Though apprehended within a week, Bundy became something of a celebrity around Glenwood Springs, foretelling his future notoriety. On the night of 30 December 1977 Bundy escaped again, this time by crawling through a loose fixture in the ceiling, and by January 1978 he was living in a small apartment in Tallahassee, Florida.

On the early morning of 15 January 1978 Bundy raped, bludgeoned, and strangled to death two women at Florida State University's Chi Omega sorority house. He also assaulted two others, leading authorities to believe that, had he not been surprised and forced to flee by a resident coming home late that night, he would have murdered every woman sleeping in the house. On 9 February Bundy abducted twelve-year-old Kimberly Diane Leach from her school in Lake City, Florida, and brutally murdered her. Six days later Bundy was arrested in Pensacola for driving a stolen vehicle. On 7 April Leach's mutilated body was found in a deserted hog pen near Florida's Suwanee State Park. By this time, compelling clues, including an eyewitness's account that placed Bundy at a disco where the Chi Omegas had gone the night of the murders, made him the prime suspect in the sorority house massacre. In addition, the woman who had startled Bundy on 15 January identified him as the man she saw leaving the house. He was indicted for the Chi Omega killings when, in late April, a mold of his teeth matched bite marks found on the body of one of the victims. In July testimony and evidence connecting Bundy to Lake City and the disappearance of Leach led a grand jury to indict him for her murder also.

After brazenly turning down a plea bargain whereby he would plead guilty to all three Florida killings in exchange for three 25-year sentences, Bundy went on trial in June 1979 for the murders of the two sorority women. In the nationally televised trial, in which he occasionally acted as his own attorney, Bundy was convicted of both murders and was sentenced to die in the electric chair.

In early 1980 Bundy was given his third sentence of death after being found guilty in Leach's slaying. During his sentencing hearing a couple of days after his conviction, Bundy surprised court onlookers when he married Carole Boone, whom he had called to the stand as a character witness. They had been close since his time in Utah, and she was convinced of his innocence. He spent the last nine years of his life uncharacteristically avoiding interviews, filing appeals, and dodging three signed death warrants. His appeals finally ran out in January 1989, and Bundy, his usual cocky demeanor more subdued, was electrocuted at the Florida state prison in Starke, while a carnival-like atmosphere prevailed outside. A few days before his death Bundy, who until that time professed his innocence, told details of murders of more than fifty other women, citing his obsession with, and early exposure to, pornography as a primary motive. While some speculate the figure could be as high as 100, the true number of his victims will never be known.

Bundy has the dubious distinction of making the term "serial killer" a household word. What caused the handsome, intelligent Bundy to begin the grisly killing spree that made him one of the most notorious mass murderers in American history remains unknown. Using his charm and good looks, he lured trusting strangers to certain death and, once caught for his crimes, mocked the legal system, filing appeal after appeal, costing the state of Florida at least $5 million to execute him. In addition to the sheer number of his victims and the frighteningly random nature of his crimes, Bundy became so infamous because his seemingly "normal" exterior masked evil within, compelling people to question the intentions of those around them and causing them not to take polite, handsome strangers at face value. In 1986 Bundy told the *New York Times*, "If anyone considers me a monster, that's just something they'll have to confront in themselves. . . . To dehumanize someone like me is . . . a[n] understandable way of dealing with a fear and a threat that is incomprehensible."

• Several books have been written about Bundy, the least sensational of which is Richard W. Larsen, *Bundy: The Deliberate Stranger* (1980); a television miniseries based on the book was released in 1986. Other accounts of Bundy include crime writer Ann Rule's *The Stranger beside Me* (1980; rev. ed., 1989), and Robert D. Keppel, *The Riverman: Ted Bundy and I Hunt for the Green River Killer* (1995), in which Keppel publishes excerpts of his conversations with Bundy and broaches the subject of Bundy's necrophilia. A transcript of Bundy's 23 Jan. 1989 interview with Christian broadcaster James Dobson in which Bundy rails against pornography is in the *St. Louis Post-Dispatch*, 25 Jan. 1989. Accounts of his execution are in the *New York Times*, the *Los Angeles Times*, and the *St. Petersburg (Fla.) Times*, all 25 Jan. 1989.

STACEY HAMILTON

BUNKER, Dennis Miller (5 Nov. 1861–28 Dec. 1890), painter, was born in New York, New York, the son of Matthew Bunker, the secretary-treasurer of the Union Ferry Company, and Mary Anne Eytinge. Bunker began his artistic training at age fifteen, when he enrolled concurrently at New York's National Academy of Design and at the Art Students League. For the next several years he spent his winters in school, mastering the art of figure painting, and his summers painting outdoors, first in upstate New York and later along the north shore of Long Island.

Bunker first exhibited his work at the National Academy of Design in 1880; for the next two years he showed frequently there and at the Society of American Artists, the Brooklyn Art Association, and the Boston Art Club. Bunker's early pictures are devoted primarily to nostalgic images of beached boats such as *Saltmarsh Landscape with Two Children Near a Beached Sailboat and Dory* (1881, Museum of Fine Arts, Boston), paintings that were quickly sold and for which he began to receive favorable critical attention.

Like most young artists of his generation, however, Bunker felt compelled to travel to Paris to complete his education. He left New York late in September 1882 to enroll at the École des Beaux-Arts in Paris, the most prestigious art school of the late nineteenth century. Bunker studied at the École for two years under the instruction of Jean-Léon Gérôme and perfected his ability to draw and to paint the human figure. During the summers, Bunker, usually in the company of fellow American art students Kenneth Cranford and Charles Platt, painted landscapes in the French countryside, working in Lacroix-St. Ouen (Oise) in 1883 and in Larmor (Brittany) in 1884.

Bunker returned to New York in the fall of 1884, taking a studio at 140 West Fifty-fifth Street. That winter he completed his figural composition *A Bohemian* (Fine Arts Museums of San Francisco), for which he received the prestigious Hallgarten prize at the National Academy of Design's 1885 exhibition. Bunker was elected to the Society of American Artists that spring, and in the fall he moved to Boston, Massachusetts, to accept a position as chief instructor of painting at the newly formed Cowles Art School. Bunker, now living above the school at 145 Dartmouth Street, had his first solo exhibition at the Noyes and

Blakeslee Gallery in Boston in late October 1885. In November he became a member of the St. Botolph Club and the Tavern Club, two Boston institutions that fostered friendships among the city's leading artists, musicians, and patrons.

Bunker continued his habit of painting one major figural composition during the winter months, completing the mysterious *A Winter's Tale of Sprites and Goblins* (Simmons College) in 1885–1886 and the ethereal *Portrait of Anne Page* (private collection) in 1886–1887. During the summer he proceeded with his exploration of rural landscape subjects, working in South Woodstock, Connecticut, with painter Abbott Thayer in 1886 and in Newburyport, Massachusetts, with Charles Platt in 1887. During the fall of 1887, either through his connections at the Tavern Club or his friendships with the art collectors Isabella Stewart Gardner and Sarah Choate Sears, Bunker met John Singer Sargent, who traveled to Boston in November during his first working visit to America. Sargent and Bunker became close friends and spent the summer of 1888 painting together in Calcot Mill, near London.

During his time with Sargent, Bunker faced the challenge that the spontaneity of the new impressionist style posed against the strict standards of his academic training. Perhaps unwilling to reconcile the two, Bunker now divided his painting method, using a loosely brushed, brightly colored technique for his landscapes and a darker, more tightly rendered approach for portraits. His first extant impressionist picture, *Chrysanthemums* (1888, Isabella Stewart Gardner Museum, Boston), representing the floral display in Gardner's Brookline greenhouse, is among the earliest paintings in the impressionist style to be crafted in the United States by an American artist. Bunker continued experimenting with the modern French style during the summers of 1889 and 1890 in Medfield, Massachusetts, where he created a series of meadow views. These were exhibited, along with Sargent's impressionist figure studies, to mixed reviews in Boston and New York; the critic for the *Boston Transcript* described them as "interesting freaks of painting [that] may be classified as bold and original experiments" (28 Jan. 1890).

In October 1889 Bunker moved to New York, taking rooms at 3 North Washington Square. He concentrated on figure painting during the 1889–1890 winter season, creating two pictures of women, *Jessica* (Museum of Fine Arts, Boston) and *The Mirror* (Terra Museum of American Art), that relate to the aristocratic and ethereal figure pieces of his friend and neighbor Thomas Wilmer Dewing. As Bunker explained to his fiancée, "[I] strive to work towards something distinguished that goes by the name of Beauty." *The Mirror* won several prizes at various exhibitions over the following months. After a year's engagement, Bunker married Eleanor Hardy, the daughter of a prominent Boston businessman, in October 1890, and the couple settled into rooms at the Sherwood Studio Building in New York. Bunker died unexpectedly three months later from meningitis during a Christmas visit to Boston; he was twenty-nine years old. His friends the painter and designer Charles Platt and the architect Stanford White organized a memorial exhibition of Bunker's work at the St. Botolph Club in Boston in January 1891. White and the sculptor Augustus Saint-Gaudens, also a friend of Bunker's, later collaborated on the design of Bunker's tombstone.

• Bunker's surviving papers are held by the Archives of American Art, Smithsonian Institution; they include both scattered early correspondence and letters to Eleanor Hardy, an intimate and complete record of Bunker's last year. Correspondence between Bunker and Isabella Stewart Gardner is in the collection of the archives of the Isabella Stewart Gardner Museum. Published sources include R. H. Ives Gammell, *Dennis Miller Bunker* (1953); the exhibition catalog prepared by Charles B. Ferguson for the New Britain Museum of American Art, *Dennis Miller Bunker (1861–1890) Rediscovered* (1978); Jared I. Edwards, "Dennis Miller Bunker (1861–1890) Rediscovered," *Nineteenth Century* 4 (Spring 1978): 70–75; and Erica E. Hirshler, *Dennis Miller Bunker: American Impressionist* (1994), which includes a complete bibliography and a checklist of Bunker's extant work.

ERICA E. HIRSHLER

BUNKER, Ellsworth (11 May 1894–27 Sept. 1984), businessman and diplomat, was born in Yonkers, New York, the son of George R. Bunker, a founder of the National Sugar Refining Company, and Jean Polhemus Cobb. Bunker was educated in private schools in Dobbs Ferry, New York, and attended Yale University, where he majored in history and economics. After graduating in 1916, he entered the family business as a dockworker. In 1920 he married Harriet Allen Butler, with whom he was to have three children. Bunker advanced quickly in the National Sugar Refining Company and was named a director of the company in 1927. He went on to become secretary, treasurer, president, and chairman of the board, retiring in 1950. He remained a member of the board of directors until 1966.

During his business career, Bunker organized the Cane Sugar Research Foundation in New York, became chairman of the United States Cane Sugar Refiners Association, and, during World War II, headed the Cane Sugar Refiners War Committee, a governmental advisory agency. Having interests in the sugar industry outside the United States, Bunker served in the early 1940s as president of the Portrero Sugar Company of Mexico and as a director of the Guantánamo Sugar Company of Cuba and of Central Aguirre Associates of Puerto Rico.

Bunker's government service began in 1951 when President Harry S. Truman named him ambassador to Argentina, then under the rule of Juan Domingo Perón. Dean Acheson, Truman's secretary of state, was a former Yale classmate of Bunker; when the post of ambassador became available, Acheson recommended Bunker for the job. Although he had no previous diplomatic experience, Bunker's extensive business experience in Latin America made him in fact an excellent candidate. He accounted himself well in Argentina and won the trust of Perón, who described him as "our country's good friend." He went on to other ambassadorial posts in Italy (1952–1953), India (1956–1961), and South Vietnam (1967–1973). Between the Italy and India posts, he served as the first salaried president of the American Red Cross and as a U.S. delegate to the Eleventh General Assembly of the United Nations (1956). In 1962, at the request of the United Nations, he mediated a dispute between the Netherlands and Indonesia over what was then known as Dutch New Guinea (later West Irian). The two countries had been at loggerheads over the area for the previous twelve years, and war seemed inevitable. After several months of negotiations, the "Bunker plan" that emerged was accepted on all sides, and the area was surrendered to Indonesia. A year later, at the request of President John F. Kennedy, Bunker traveled to the Middle East to mediate a dispute between Prince Faisal, the prime minister of Saudi Arabia, and President Gamal Abdel Nasser of Egypt over the future of the emerging Republic of Yemen. The two countries were interfering in the Yemeni civil war on opposite sides, but Bunker was able to convince both men to withdraw their troops from the conflict. Although the disengagement agreement and subsequent truce lasted only days, Bunker earned the reputation of being one of the country's most skilled negotiators.

In January 1964 President Lyndon B. Johnson appointed Bunker U.S. representative to the Organization of American States (OAS); by November of that year, he was elected chairman of the council. As part of a three-man OAS team, he was sent in 1965 to the Dominican Republic to confront an internal government crisis following the assassination of the country's dictator, Rafael Trujillo. Again, Bunker's negotiation skills impressed both factions, and he was able to arrange the appointment of a provisional civilian president.

Following the death of his first wife in 1964, Bunker in 1967 married Carol C. Laise, a career foreign service officer and, at the time, U.S. ambassador to Nepal. He was now of retirement age, but President Johnson fatefully called on him again: to serve as ambassador to South Vietnam, replacing Henry Cabot Lodge. Bunker accepted the post, which was initially expected to be a short stint; Johnson was hopeful that American involvement in the Vietnam crisis was coming to an end. The war, however, escalated after Bunker arrived, and he spent six years in Vietnam, the longest tour served by an American ambassador there.

Saigon was the largest and, in some ways, the most important American embassy in the world at that time. During his tenure Bunker was more than simply an ambassador. As chief of mission he was chief adviser to the government of Vietnam. He was in effect American proconsul to the U.S. military, dispensing millions of dollars in economic assistance funds. His responsibilities extended into the intelligence community, the pacification sector, psychological warfare activity, and military affairs outside the battlefield.

While Bunker early on reported progress in South Vietnam, specifically in regard to political reform, his efforts there were subject to criticism. In the 1967 election he persuaded Premier Nguyen Cao Ky, who had been accused of illegal campaign practices, to withdraw from the presidential race. Bunker's open support of Nguyen Van Thieu in that election as well as the one in 1971, when Thieu ran unopposed, led some Americans to dub the ambassador "soft" and under Thieu's thumb. Nonetheless, Bunker defended his position, stating that it was part of his obligation to work with our ally and halt the incursions of the North Vietnam army.

Throughout his tenure in Vietnam, Bunker's constant objective was to reach a negotiated settlement that would allow the South Vietnamese to determine their own future. His efforts were thwarted to an extent by Thieu's refusal to participate in the Paris peace talks, which began in November 1968. Bunker supported President Richard M. Nixon's "Vietnamization" of the war—that is, the phasing out of American troops—which began in earnest in 1972. That same year, Bunker persuaded Thieu to agree to a cease-fire with North Vietnam, and by October Hanoi dropped all of its political demands for the dismantling of the South Vietnamese government. Despite his initial unease, Thieu signed the Paris Agreement of January 1973. With a negotiated settlement accomplished, Bunker resigned his position on 30 March 1973 and left Saigon in May on his seventy-ninth birthday. Commenting about his extended service, Bunker said, "The tunnel was longer and the light was dimmer and farther away than any of us realized at the time I came here" (qtd. in *New York Times*, 28 Sept. 1984).

Bunker returned to Washington with the rank of ambassador-at-large and, despite his advanced age, accepted two major assignments from the president. He headed the American delegation to the first Geneva peace conference on the Middle East between the Arab nations and Israel, and he became chief negotiator to the secretive Panama Canal treaty negotiations. For the next three and a half years, Bunker diligently worked toward an agreement that was finally signed by President Jimmy Carter and Panamanian general Omar Torrijos Herrera on 7 September 1977. Once again, his patient negotiations involving highly complex issues earned him quiet praise.

Bunker retired from government service permanently in 1978. His appearance even later in life was striking: tall and imperiously slim, with a ramrod-straight back and silver-gray hair. His manner, that of a courtly patrician, invariably caused journalists writing of him to use the term "gentleman." To the South Vietnamese he had been "this blue-eyed sorcerer," and in some diplomatic circles he was known as "the refrigerator" because of his ability to remain cool under pressure.

Bunker died in Putney, Vermont. At the requiem his friends and associates said of him that he represented the best of old-school diplomacy, that of a saner era when honor counted for more and opportunistic success for less.

• Source materials, including Bunker's collected speeches and interviews, are available at the University of California's Indochina Archive in Berkeley. One of Bunker's conditions in accepting the Saigon assignment was direct access to President Lyndon B. Johnson at all times; it was agreed he would send Johnson a "back channel" cable weekly (later, each month) setting before the president matters Bunker thought important. There were seventy-six of these cables in all, and they amount to an autobiography of his Saigon years; once declassified, they were published in three volumes: Douglas Pike, ed., *The Bunker Papers: Report to the President from Vietnam, 1967–1973* (1990). A brief Bunker biography can be found in the *Department of State Newsletter*, Apr. 1967, and an obituary appears in the *New York Times*, 28 Sept. 1984.

DOUGLAS PIKE
LISABETH G. SVENDSGAARD

BUNNER, Henry Cuyler (3 Aug. 1855–11 May 1896), author, was born in Oswego, New York, the son of Rudolph Bunner, a lawyer and editor, and Ruth Tuckerman. Bunner had a nomadic boyhood; his family moved frequently, living in several places in and around New York City, which became the locus of his literary works. Educated with the intent of attending Columbia College, he was unable to enroll because of his father's financial difficulties. After a brief, unhappy stint with L. E. Amsinck & Company, a wine importing firm, he turned to journalism. He contributed several pieces to the short-lived *Arcadian* before joining the staff of *Puck*, the first long-lived American comic weekly, where he remained from 1877 until his death.

Hired as an assistant editor, Bunner contributed to the publication also as a story writer and versifier. A year later he was promoted to editor, and under his leadership the English language edition of *Puck* surpassed its German language originator, both in circulation and in longevity. Bunner clearly foresaw the possibilities for the comic paper in America, and he wrote straightforward, commonsensical editorials "waging war" against sham in politics and the church and against snobbery in general. He is also credited with originating the idea for the destructive political cartoon characterizing James G. Blaine as the Tattooed Man during the presidential campaign of 1884. Brander Matthews, a critic and friend, considered Bunner "one of the great parodists of the nineteenth century."

Bunner experimented with several different forms of literary expression. A poet as well as a short-story writer, he also wrote plays, comic operas, and stories and operettas for children. According to his biographer, Gerard Jensen, Bunner's contemporaries consistently commented on "his amazing celerity of composition, . . . his fecundity, and . . . the scrupulous care which he gave his serious work." His most successful lyrics were in the style of French *vers de société*, or familiar verse; these include pieces such as "Forfeits," "Candor," and "Just a Love-Letter." *Airs from Arcady and Elsewhere*, his first volume of poems, mostly light lyrical pieces, appeared in 1884, followed by *Rowen: Second-Crop Songs* in 1892. The second collection, comprising mostly occasional verse, was not as well received as the first, general opinion holding that the subject matter was not nearly as interesting. Augmented by later lyrics and "Ballads of the Town," his verse was collected posthumously as *The Poems of H. C. Bunner* (1896).

Bunner's prose reputation outlasted his poetic reputation. Influenced by a number of important authors, including Guy de Maupassant, Giovanni Boccaccio, and Nathaniel Hawthorne, his most famous fiction collection, *Short Sixes* (1890), is characterized by humor, variety, and keen observations of life in New York City, his most common subject. Bunner is remembered as among the first writers to set his works in the American city and suburbs. For him, New York City remained evocative and rich in material, a place congenial to the needs of his imagination. *Zadoc Pine and Other Stories* (1891), *More Short Sixes* (1894), and *Jersey Street and Jersey Lane* (1896) contain many of the same elements of *Short Sixes*, but reviewers complained that some of the stories lacked the spirited jocularity of his earlier pieces. Although they are rarely read today, "Zenobia's Infidelity" from *Short Sixes* and "The Zadoc Pine Labor Union" from *Zadoc Pine and Other Stories* were considered to be among his finest efforts. Four volumes of Bunner's short stories were published posthumously as *The Stories of H. C. Bunner* (1916–1917).

In addition to writing his own short stories, Bunner adapted a collection of de Maupassant's tales, published as *Made in France: French Tales Retold with a United States Twist* (1893). Unknown to many, one of the ten tales, "The Joke on M. Peptonneau," was actually a Bunner original masquerading as a translation/adaptation of a story written by the French master. Bunner's imitative ability was such that the story's true authorship went undetected for many years.

In 1886 Bunner married Alice Learned, and they had five children, two of whom died in infancy. In the 1890s he became ill, often complaining of malaria. After an attack of the grippe and a trip South for his health, he died at home in Nutley, New Jersey.

• Bunner's letters and manuscripts are scattered but appear in numerous collections, usually of other writers. Several letters and some manuscripts are in the Columbia University Library; a few others are in the libraries at Princeton, Yale, Harvard, the University of Virginia, and the Huntington Library. In 1939, when Gerard E. Jensen's critical biography, *The Life and Letters of Henry Cuyler Bunner*, was published, about fifty letters along with other correspondence and literary effects remained in the Bunners' home in New London, Conn. Since then, the house has been torn down, and the whereabouts of those materials are no longer known.

Bunner's other published works include *In Partnership* (1884), a collection of short stories by Bunner and Brander Matthews, two of which they collaborated on; two additional posthumously published collections of short stories, *Love in Old Cloathes and Other Stories* (1896) and *The Suburban Sage*

(1896); three novelettes, *The Midge* (1887), *The Runaway Browns: A Story of Small Stories* (1892), and *The Story of a New York House* (1887); one not very well received novel, *A Woman of Honor* (1883), which Bunner came to despise and that led him to focus on short-story writing; *Three Operettas* (1897), written for children; and a nonfiction work, *The Modern Poster* (1895), a collection of essays on posters.

Additional information can be found in Laurence Hutton, "Henry Cuyler Bunner," *Bookman* 4 (July 1896): 398–402, a reminiscence; Brander Matthews, "H. C. Bunner," *Scribner's Magazine*, Sept. 1896, pp. 287–94, an extended obituary later published in Brander's *The Historical Novel and Other Essays* (1901), and "The Uncollected Poems of H. C. Bunner," in Brander's *The Recreations of an Anthropologist* (1904), a brief article that preserves nine of Bunner's more broadly comic pieces; (unsigned) "Henry Cuyler Bunner," *Scribner's Magazine*, July 1896, p. 124, a brief editorial notice of Bunner's death; and Benjamin W. Wells, "Henry Cuyler Bunner," *Sewanee Review* 5 (Jan. 1897): 17–32, an obituary and tribute.

ROBERT LEE LYNCH

BUNSHAFT, Gordon (9 May 1909–6 Aug. 1990), architect, was born in Buffalo, New York, the son of David Bunshaft, an egg merchant, and Yetta (maiden name unknown). Inspired by a high school manual training teacher to become an architect, Bunshaft earned bachelor's and master's degrees (1933, 1935) from the Massachusetts Institute of Technology. He won MIT's Rotch Travelling Fellowship, for which he became eligible after nearly a year's work in Boston for Harold Field Kellogg. Following his travels in western and southern Europe, he returned briefly to Buffalo but moved to New York where he was for short periods in the offices of Edward Durell Stone and Raymond Loewy. By the end of 1937 Bunshaft was working for Skidmore & Owings (soon to become SOM with the addition of a third partner), where he became a senior designer and, after serving as a major in the U.S. Army Corps of Engineers (1942–1946), an associate (1946) and, later, full partner (1949–1979). In 1943 he married Nina Elizabeth Wayler, a dancer; they did not have children. Also in 1943 he was sent to London and Paris. In France he became well acquainted with Auguste Perret and Le Corbusier.

SOM became the nation's largest architectural firm, in part because of the distinguished designs that Bunshaft created or supervised. In 1988 he received the Pritzker Architecture Prize in recognition of his achievements, having earlier been elected to the American Academy and Institute of Arts and Letters, which had awarded him its gold medal in 1984. He was also honored by being asked to serve on the Fine Arts Commission for Washington, D.C., in the 1960s.

Bunshaft's buildings are distinguished by simple and logical contours, clean-lined modernism resulting from attention to current technology and to precision of detail, contemporary materials, attentiveness to complementary landscaping when that was possible, and an increasing sensitivity to climatic conditions and to the needs of building users. In the hands of SOM, and thanks largely to Bunshaft's early urban and suburban business headquarters, what had begun in Europe as socially oriented modernism directed especially at working-class housing conditions became the vernacular of American, and eventually worldwide, corporate architecture.

SOM's reputation was made by Lever House on Park Avenue in midtown Manhattan, completed in 1952. Until then, that broad thoroughfare had been lined almost entirely by limestone-trimmed and massive brick buildings that covered their lots. Because Lever's officers wanted a conspicuous monument, but one to house only their relatively few employees, Bunshaft had the freedom to execute a slender slab sheathed in green glass. Twenty-four stories high (low by the standards of Manhattan's skyscrapers), it covers only a quarter of its site. A one-story lateral extension supported by thin metal-clad piers surrounds an open space with a bed of plants in the center. Visitors cross the court to enter the building, which looks transparent and accessible because plate glass walls cover the ground floor. The contrast between this building and its older neighbors drew widespread attention in the Americas and Europe, giving the Lever company the publicity it wanted and offering ideas to other architects and corporate executives who were searching for a distinctive and progressive postwar image. As Lever House was a contemporary of the United Nations Secretariat, another structure partly clad in glass, the public was persuaded that technologically oriented modern architecture suited both idealistic and capitalist objectives.

During the next decade Bunshaft created and supervised other moderately sized urban corporate buildings using similar materials and pure geometric forms. These included New York City's first glass-walled bank, for the Manufacturers' Trust Company on Fifth Avenue (1954), and the Pepsi-Cola Company headquarters a few blocks north of Lever House (1960). Other clients, who demanded space in their new buildings for rental to other tenants, led Bunshaft to design the huge high-rise buildings for Chase Manhattan Bank (1961) and the Union Carbide Corporation (1960). The bulk of the former is mitigated by a plaza created adjacent to it by SOM's intelligent interpretation of possibilities in the city's zoning regulations that govern the height and extent of buildings and by the presence of sculpture and trees, which are welcome in the densely packed Wall Street area. Union Carbide, however, became a model for many other glass-walled, prismatic structures of excessive size that give modernism a reputation for insensitivity.

In suburbs and at city edges, both of which grew rapidly after the Second World War, Bunshaft had the opportunity to create office buildings in expansive, carefully designed landscape settings. These buildings, too, became prototypes for thousands of others. Corporate officials often wish to remove themselves and their employees from urban stresses and diversions while working in progressive and rational structures identified by twentieth century materials and smooth, machine-made forms. Connecticut General (1957); Reynolds Metals (1958); Emhart (1963); offices for IBM in Armonk, New York (1964); American

Can Company in Greenwich, Connecticut (1970); and the H. J. Heinz Company, Ltd., in suburban London (1965) all exemplify this aspect of Bunshaft's work. The last of these was initially resented by a number of British architects and critics for exceeding the competitive abilities of British technology and architectural practice at the time, but it provided a model widely adopted by the end of the decade. After the mid-1950s, Bunshaft found ways to disguise employee parking facilities, sometimes by tucking the parking places into accommodating landscape features, as at American Can or Emhart. He also became known for his ability to persuade corporate executives to include works of art in and near their buildings.

Perhaps the most remarkable of Bunshaft's low-rise designs is a factory rather than a corporate headquarters. The Philip Morris Cigarette Manufacturing Plant (1974), at the edge of Richmond, Virginia, has been praised by its corporate owners, and by Wallace Merghler, head of its 5,000 unionized workers, who called it "the Taj Mahal of Industry." The reinforced concrete building is almost 1,000 feet long and thus potentially formidable. It consists of a low entrance wing housing offices, a manufacturing wing punctuated by five towers behind it, and a low wing behind that for the machine shop and various services. To relieve the mass and monotony, garden courts open between the towers so that greenery and flowers can be seen by the workers. Employee lounges overlook the gardens.

From the late 1960s onward, SOM's clients commissioned buildings with so much square footage that inevitably the structures became obtrusive within their urban settings, giving corporate modernism a low reputation among urbanists and postmodern architects of the latter part of the twentieth century. Bunshaft designed and supervised a number of these, some with surrounding public open spaces intended to counteract the buildings' bulk and the forcefulness of the reinforced concrete, which, by then, often replaced glass curtain walls. In two cases, by building precisely within the limitations of New York City's zoning regulations, he produced dramatic tall office buildings with curved sloping contours. One of these, 9 West 57th Street, faced with black glass contrasting with huge white reinforced concrete structural elements visible on the narrow sides of the building, captures the interest of tourists but is disliked by New Yorkers who want buildings to fit into an existing urban pattern. When a client required a smaller building that could fit its context, as at American Republic Life Insurance Company in Des Moines (1965), or when a building had to be inserted into a difficult site, as at the Library and Museum of the Performing Arts at Lincoln Center in New York (1965), Bunshaft welcomed the chance to use his ingenuity to satisfy these needs.

Bunshaft is best known for his buildings for business, but he was equally proud of his institutional designs. An extension to the prismatic neoclassical Albright-Knox Art Gallery in Buffalo (1962) is widely admired for its reference to the older gallery's forms in modern materials. His black glass prism contrasts with the original white-colored wing but defers to the larger size of the older part. Interior spaces are refined, comfortable, and well suited to the display of art, especially twentieth-century art, which Bunshaft and his wife collected with discernment.

The architect believed that his enduring monument would be the Beinecke Rare Book and Manuscript Library at Yale (1963), a marble-clad box sustained by low supports joined to the box by minute joints. The structural drama is echoed inside the building, where a six-level, glass-covered book stack in the center displays the library's precious holdings and where the perimeter walls allow softened daylight to enter through "windows" made of thin slabs of veined marble. The Lyndon B. Johnson Library and Museum (1971) on the campus of the University of Texas at Austin has a simpler exterior but a comparable plan, with archival boxes illuminated in the center of the building. Fewer people admire his ring-shaped Hirshhorn Museum and Sculpture Garden (1974) in Washington, D.C., but its almost windowless exterior was intended to mediate between the visually incompatible buildings on either side of it.

Before his retirement at age seventy, Bunshaft was in charge of the design of two extraordinary buildings in Jeddah, Saudi Arabia. He was inventive in responding to the fierce heat and dry air of the region, employing both natural and artificial means of climate control, while designing handsome and functional works of architecture. One, the National Commercial Bank (1983) on a site near but separated from much of the then lower-rise city, is a triangular structure with reinforced concrete walls pierced by three openings, two of them near the top and bottom of one side. These openings allow staff in offices on the other two sides to see outdoors, but they do not let sunlight reach the air-conditioned offices. A central air funnel, created by the alternation of sides on which offices are located, produces an updraft that also helps cool the interior. The exterior appears formidable in scale, but with the sea immediately adjacent it need not be seen as destructive to the cityscape, which continues to change in any case.

The other structure, the Haj Terminal (1981), designed with SOM's great engineer Fazlur Khan, uses the reflective capacity of Teflon-covered glass fiber to create soaring, softly lit tents 150 by 150 feet, arranged in ten modules of 450 by 1,050 feet. Beneath them it is up to forty degrees (Fahrenheit) cooler than the surrounding air. The tents shade thousands of Muslim pilgrims in transit between jet planes and buses to nearby Mecca, many of whom are not dressed for air-conditioned interior spaces. The design of the tents was also influenced by considerations of maintenance and of user acceptance of the architectural forms.

At his best, then, Bunshaft was sensitive to the needs of both corporate managers and those who worked in and used his buildings. He also was concerned with the building in its setting, even if today's idea of the proper context is not the same as his. His crisp, geometric aesthetic, his use of clearly revealed industrial and luxurious materials, and his reluctance to embrace any theory beyond that of rationally produced beauty separate him from many architects of the post–World War Two era and from brilliant predecessors such as artist-architect Ludwig Mies van der Rohe or Le Corbusier and Frank Lloyd Wright, the latter two having been advocates of artistic and social change. Nevertheless, Bunshaft's aesthetic and technical standards exceeded those of any architect in commercial practice within his own generation. He died in New York City.

• Bunshaft, little given to writing, donated some papers and his few remaining drawings to Avery Library at Columbia University, while other papers remain in the care of SOM's New York office. This firm commissioned the following books about its own architecture, in which Bunshaft's work is prominently represented: Ernst Danz, *Architecture of Skidmore, Owings & Merrill, 1950–1962* (1963); Axel Menges, *Architecture of Skidmore, Owings & Merrill, 1963–1972* (1974); and Albert Bush-Brown, *Skidmore, Owings & Merrill: Architecture and Urbanism, 1973–1983* (1983). Carol Herselle Krinsky, *Gordon Bunshaft of Skidmore, Owings & Merrill* (1988), is the only book-length account of Bunshaft's work.

CAROL HERSELLE KRINSKY

BUNTLINE, Ned. *See* Judson, Edward Zane Carroll.

BURBANK, Albert (25 Mar. 1902–15 Aug. 1976), jazz clarinetist and singer, was born in New Orleans, Louisiana. His father was a painter, but the names of his parents are unknown. Unusually for a New Orleans jazzman, Burbank was not from a musical family. Burbank first attended a private school; however, other details of his upbringing and schooling are unknown.

Burbank loved to listen to clarinet players at local picnics, and at age seventeen he acquired his own instrument. He took lessons for a few months from Walter Duvernay and then from Big Eye Louis Nelson, and soon he was performing professionally. While working as a stock-cutter in a shoe factory during the 1920s, he served as a substitute in cornetist Isaiah Morgan's band at Artisan Hall (c. 1920) and as a substitute for clarinetists Barney Bigard and Adolphe Alexander, Jr., in various bands.

Burbank married in 1923. He had at least three children—he mentioned them in an interview—and he remained deeply devoted to his wife, whose name is unknown. Toward the end of the decade he joined the band of cornetist Buddy Petit for performances in Bogalusa, Louisiana, and in Mississippi and also worked with trumpeter Leonard Parker's band in Slidell, Louisiana, and in Mississippi. He then became a member of the Olympia Band, led by drummer Arnold DePass, and he took some further lessons from Lionel Dupart, the godfather of one of his fellow bandsmen.

Around 1930 Burbank left DePass to become a member of trumpeter Willie Pajeaud's band at the Alamo, a "jitney" (dime-a-dance) hall in New Orleans. At some point, perhaps during the 1930s, he worked for a year with trumpeter Kid Thomas Valentine. He led a four-piece band at the Dandy Inn until it closed sometime after 1938. Perhaps at this time, or in the mid-1940s, he formed a trio, the Three Als, with drummer Albert Jiles, Jr., and a guitarist whose name is unknown. He also worked with guitarist Johnny St. Cyr.

All these jobs were of note only regionally or locally. But in 1943, after serving in the navy, Burbank was discovered by New Orleans jazz scholar and producer Bill Russell, who rated him nearly the equal of clarinetist George Lewis. Burbank performed with the Eureka Brass Band from around 1944 to 1945, and in the latter year he recorded a now-classic session of New Orleans jazz revival music with trumpeter Wooden Joe Nicholas, including versions of "Shake It and Break It," "Careless Love," and "Eh la bas," with Burbank singing in Creole patois on the last title. Over the next few years in New Orleans, he worked with Jiles (1946), pianist Billie Pierce and trumpeter De De Pierce (1947), trumpeter Herb Morand (1949–1950), drummer Paul Barbarin (1950–1952), and trumpeters Kid Clayton and Percy Humphrey.

Early in 1954 Burbank traveled with pianist Octave Crosby's band to Los Angeles, where trombonist Kid Ory heard him and hired him to work for about three months in a band that included trumpeter Alvin Alcorn, pianist Don Ewell, bassist Ed Garland, and drummer Ram Hall. Burbank then returned home and worked regularly with Crosby at the Paddock Lounge until 1966. He made his finest albums apart from Crosby: *Percy Humphrey's Crescent City Joy Makers*, *Kid Thomas and His Algiers Stompers*, and *Kid Howard's Olympia Band: The Heart and Bowels of New Orleans Jazz, Featuring Albert Burbank, "the Clarinet Wizard"* (1962).

Burbank suffered a heart attack in 1965 but recovered. From 1968 to 1969 he worked at Dixieland Hall with banjoist Albert French. He also recorded his own album *Albert Burbank* (1969). From 1969 to 1973 he performed at Preservation Hall in Valentine's band, in which he also toured to Australia and Europe in 1971 and recorded a further album *Kid Thomas' Jazzband* (1972). In 1973 he joined Humphrey's band, but from fall 1973 to spring 1974 his career was stopped by severe burns from an accident with hot pitch and by a stroke that left one arm temporarily limp. In 1974 he rejoined Humphrey. Late in 1975 another stroke ended his playing career, but he continued singing at Preservation Hall. He died in New Orleans.

The intensity of Burbank's playing was not mirrored by his personality, which was quiet and shy, except on the subject of incompetent drummers. Once he jokingly suggested that he might take an inept drummer fishing so he could drown him. Like a number of New Orleans jazz clarinetists, Burbank played an Albert system instrument that lacked the intricate keywork of the now-standard Boehm system clarinet but offered, he felt, a louder sound and fuller tone than the Boehm. The hallmarks of his playing were a preference for passionately swooping melodies and a wonderfully outrageous sense of tuning.

• Interviews taped 18 Mar. 1959 by William Russell and Ralph Collins and 4 Jan. 1962 by Richard B. Allen and Herb Friedwald are at Tulane University; a transcript summary is published in microform as *New York Times Oral History Program: New Orleans Jazz Oral History Collection of Tulane University* (1978). See also Max Jones, "Albert Memorial," *Melody Maker*, 27 Nov. 1971, p. 18; and Kenny Davern, "Memories of Albert Burbank," *Footnote* 9 (Oct.–Nov. 1977): 16–21. Surveys of his recordings are by J. C. Hillman: "Albert Burbank: The Clarinet Wizard," *Jazz Journal* 21 (May 1968): 26–27, 29; and Alan Barrell, "Albert Burbank: Some Significant Recordings," *Footnote* 7 (June–July 1976): 4–7. Obituaries are in the *New Orleans Times-Picayune*, 19 Aug. 1976; and the *Mississippi Rag* 3 (Oct. 1976): 1–3.

BARRY KERNFELD

BURBANK, Elbridge Ayer (10 Aug. 1858–21 Mar. 1949), painter, was born in Harvard, Illinois, the son of Abner Jewett Burbank, a station agent for the Chicago and Northwestern Railroad Company, and Annie Ayer. In 1874 he began art studies at the Academy of Design in Chicago. By 1880 he had opened a small portrait studio in St. Paul, Minnesota, and in November of that year he married Alice Blanche Wheeler. He first traveled west in 1885 when he was hired by Eugene V. Smalley, editor of the *North-West* magazine, to sketch scenes along the Northern Pacific Railroad route. After returning in 1886, he left for Munich, Germany, where he studied under Toby Rosenthal and Paul Nauen. He opened a portrait studio upon his return to Chicago in 1892, winning several awards and becoming well known for his figure and genre studies of African-American subjects.

Although most of the financial responsibility for his studio fell to his wife, Burbank began to feel overwhelmed by the pressures of "society life," as he called it, in Chicago. Eventually diagnosed as manic-depressive, he had the first of a series of mental breakdowns that would plague him throughout his career. In a sense, his next extended trip west, in 1897, seems as much to have been a respite from Chicago and all he felt it required of him as it was a chance to return to the area he had found so invigorating in 1885. The trip was conceived of and sponsored by his uncle Edward Ayer, first president of the Field Museum in Chicago and avid collector of Native American artifacts. Burbank painted a portrait of the Apache Geronimo, with whom he formed a lasting friendship, as well as portraits of other Indians. That June he had his first of many annual exhibitions of Native American portraits at Thurber's Art Galleries in Chicago, and several eastern periodicals carried stories about his travels, illustrated with his portraits.

Burbank returned to the West after only a few weeks and never really lived again in Chicago except for an extended stay in 1910. During this trip he met A. J. Hubbell, owner of the Hubbell Trading Post in Ganado, Arizona, who allowed him as well as other artists, anthropologists, and surveyors working in the area to stay gratis. Here Burbank found the social and financial freedom that he required in order to paint, and during the next six years he produced the best of his portraits. He had a generous sponsor, easy access to subjects, and successful exhibition and sale of his work in the East. He traveled extensively throughout these years in order to obtain portraits, including those of the Nez Perce chief Joseph and the Sioux chief Red Cloud. His portraits are typically bust-length, in frontal or three-quarter view, and rarely larger than 24 by 18 inches. His sitters' features are highly detailed, although the patterns of their dress are often flattened in a manner reminiscent of Indian designs. Burbank's conception of his work, which eventually included nearly a thousand portraits, was as a comprehensive collection that could be studied as ethnographic material. He viewed his oil portraits as historical documents. He, like ethnographers of the time, often felt pressed to obtain images of important Indians before they were gone.

In 1904 Hubbell commissioned Burbank to make red chalk drawings of two Indians from every tribe in the United States. Soon Burbank was also doing this for other patrons, including Ayer and the Smithsonian Institution. Burbank's patronage for his oil portraits had been dwindling as most of the Indians well known in the East died and as the wars with the Native Americans faded from public memory. He could produce the drawings with a smaller investment of time and money and still achieve a clear and specific likeness. Consequently, he began to concentrate his energies on drawing and produced fewer oil paintings.

Around 1907 Burbank began working on Indian genre scenes, showing them in galleries on the West Coast. Because he was not traveling as much and did not have access to subjects, he began using photographs that he had taken earlier for his paintings and also began to make multiple copies of his more successful oil portraits.

In 1907 Burbank and his wife were divorced. Two years later he married Nettie Taber in San Francisco, but after financial difficulties that included a short attempt to work in his home town of Harvard, this marriage also ended in divorce in 1916. He had no children. After an extended mental breakdown he was admitted in 1917 to the Napa State Hospital, from which he often contributed illustrations for the *San Francisco Chronicle*. In 1934 he moved into the Manx Hotel in San Francisco, where he lived until his death.

Burbank's portraiture was not particularly well known in his time, and he has not received much scholarly attention. However, in its comprehensiveness, visual specificity, and psychological sensitivity, Burbank's Native American portraits are some of the most articulate productions of their kind.

• Most of Burbank's works are in the collections of the National Museum of American Art, Washington, D.C.; the Newberry Library, Chicago, Ill.; the Butler Institute of American Art, Youngstown, Ohio; and the Hubbell Trading Post National Historic Site, Ganado, Ariz. Letters between

Ayer and Burbank are in the Ayer Collection at the Newberry Library. Letters between Hubbell and Burbank are in the Hubbell papers, Rare Collections Library, Southern Arizona State Univ., Tucson. Two contemporary reviews of Burbank's work are Charles Francis Browne, "Elbridge Ayer Burbank," *Brush and Pencil* 3 (1898), and Everett Maxwell, "The Art of Elbridge A. Burbank," *Fine Arts Journal* 22, no. 1 (Jan. 1910). Burbank's experiences are recounted in a series by Herb Hamlin, "Burbank the Great Contributor," *Pony Express Courier*, Nov. 1942, pp. 3–4; Dec. 1942, pp. 3–4; Mar. 1943, pp. 5–7; and Apr. 1943, pp. 3–7; and in his autobiography, *Burbank among the Indians, as Told by Ernest Royce*, ed. Frank J. Taylor (1944). However, both of these works are nostalgic and romanticized. An obituary is in the *New York Times*, 22 Mar. 1949.

M. MELISSA WOLFE

BURBANK, Luther (7 Mar. 1849–11 Apr. 1926), horticulturist, was born in Lancaster, Massachusetts, the son of Samuel Walton Burbank, a farmer and brickmaker, and Olive Ross. Although Burbank's family was of comfortable middle-class means, his formal schooling was modest, consisting of public school attendance until the age of fifteen, supplemented by part-time study during the next four winters at the Lancaster Academy. An important influence in his early life was his cousin Levi Sumner Burbank, who had been curator of geology at the Boston Society of Natural History and often took the youngster with him on local natural history excursions.

During the summers the young Burbank worked at the Ames Plow Works in Worcester, where he displayed an inventive bent with machines; he abandoned this line of work, however, and began studying medicine with a local physician. After his father's death in 1868, Burbank used his inheritance to buy a seventeen-acre farm in Lancaster in 1871, setting up as a market gardener. Here he had his first striking success as a horticulturist, the Burbank potato, which became one of the most widely grown varieties in the United States. In 1875 he set out for California, where he would become internationally famous as an inventor of new plant varieties, achieve the status of a sage, and ultimately emerge as a figure of controversy within the scientific community.

Burbank settled in Santa Rosa, north of San Francisco in Sonoma County. Although his success in the nursery business was earning him an income of more than $10,000 a year by the 1880s, he had a larger enterprise in view: to cease cultivating standard varieties in favor of experimenting with the production of new forms of plant life. In 1888 he purchased additional farmland in nearby Sebastopol and began experimenting with cross-fertilization and artificial selection, raising hundreds of thousands of individual plants in his quest for novelties. Burbank's massive entrepreneurial production efforts were matched by his promotional flair, displayed in a series of catalogs titled *New Creations in Fruits and Flowers*; the first was published in 1893.

Burbank soon found his personal promotion efforts significantly augmented by those of the public press, who dubbed him a "plant wizard" for his seemingly boundless ability to produce startling new plants. Heralding Burbank as an apostle of progress, newspapers and magazines featured his most dramatic hybrids—a white blackberry, a stoneless prune, a plumcot (a hybrid of plum and apricot), and a spineless cactus. They also conveyed Burbank's philosophical musings on the nature of the universe, "the training of the human plant," religion, and other topics. Burbank's most commercially successful products included the Burbank potato (from which the Idaho russet is descended), the Shasta daisy, and a variety of plums, including the Burbank, the Formosa, the Santa Rosa, and the Wickson. The best estimates of his plant introductions place the number between 800 and 1,000.

Burbank's career in experimental horticulture also attracted attention from the professional scientific community, especially biologists, who were debating rival claims concerning evolutionary theory. In 1904 and 1906 Burbank was visited by European experimentalist Hugo de Vries, who challenged the view that new species originate through the slow accumulation of variations by natural selection, positing instead that the emergence of new species was induced by mutation. De Vries believed that Burbank's results could be used to buttress his mutation theory; other scientists, notably biologists David Starr Jordan and Vernon Kellogg, argued the opposite. Appropriated by members of the warring camps, Burbank's results could be used to support diverse interpretations but offered no definitive evidence for any.

Seeking to throw more light on the question, the newly established Carnegie Institution of Washington (CIW) awarded a multiyear grant of $10,000 annually to Burbank in 1905 to further his "experimental investigations in the evolution of plants." Because Burbank did not keep accurate, detailed records, the CIW also appointed a young geneticist, George Harrison Shull, to closely observe Burbank at work, analyze his procedures, and report any findings of scientific value. Both Shull and Burbank found the arrangement frustrating. Burbank wished that Shull, "when he asks a question . . . could wait for me to reply before giving me a half hour lecture on the subject of his question," and Shull remarked that while Burbank's observations were no doubt "of great practical value to other breeders," they must be regarded by scientists "in many cases simply as suggestions" (Glass, pp. 136, 138).

Whether to count these suggestions as scientific contributions became a matter of heated debate among professionals. Jordan declared in 1909 that if Burbank's "place is outside the temple of science, there are not many of the rest of us who will be found fit to enter" (p. 81). Where Jordan spied a "scientific man" belonging among "the class of Faraday and the long array of self-taught great men" (p. 79), others saw nothing more than a presumptuous nurseryman. The CIW terminated its grants to Burbank in 1910, and Shull's final report on Burbank's work was never produced.

A popular, laudatory account of Burbank's work was published in 1914 and 1915 by his local boosters. *Luther Burbank: His Methods and Discoveries and Their Practical Application*, a lavishly illustrated 12-volume set, was funded by subscribers. Soon after publication, however, the Luther Burbank Society publishing venture collapsed. Other money-making schemes with which Burbank was either directly or tangentially involved during this period also ended badly, tarnishing his reputation for benevolence. Despite such negative publicity, however, his image persisted. Burbank's residence and experimental grounds were a popular attraction to visitors.

Burbank's popular appeal owed as much to his social philosophy as to his plant breeding. He affirmed that, unlike the materialists, he believed in a higher power: "All my investigations have led me away from the idea of a dead, material universe, tossed about by various forces, to that of a universe which is absolutely all force, life, soul, thought, or whatever name we may choose to call it" (Harwood, p. 837). Burbank believed that the human species could be improved by controlling the hereditary process, but he differed from the majority of those in the eugenics movement on how such improvement could be achieved, because he believed in the inheritance of acquired characteristics. He emphasized the transformative power of the environment rather than granting sole deterministic control to the "germ plasm."

Such thoughts were encapsulated in his treatise on child rearing, *The Training of the Human Plant* (1907). Burbank emphasized the child's sensitivity to the environment and objected to the institutional regimentation of schooling, arguing against the "absurdity, not to call it by a harsher term, of running children through the same mill in a lot, with absolutely no real reference to their individuality" (p. 19). Burbank had no children of his own, although he was twice married, first in 1890 to Helen A. Coleman, whom he divorced in 1896, and in 1916 to Elizabeth Waters.

Burbank's name became prominent in the press again in 1926, when a newspaper reported that he had called himself an "infidel." Burbank felt compelled to deliver a public address, "In Tune with the Infinite," to clarify his remarks. Declaring himself "a lover of man and Christ, as a man and his work, and all things that help humanity," Burbank nevertheless insisted that damnation was nothing more than "superstition gone to seed" and argued for "the right to worship the Infinite, Everlasting, Almighty God of His vast Universe as revealed to us gradually step by step by the demonstrable truths of our Saviour Science" (reprinted in *My Beliefs* [c. 1927], pp. 58–59). He died soon after this episode at his Santa Rosa home.

Burbank's name symbolized turn-of-the-century American ingenuity and progress, much as did Thomas Edison's. He was also considered by many to be a latter-day Ralph Waldo Emerson, a "partner of nature." After his death Burbank was held up as an exemplar of humanitarian values to several generations of schoolchildren. The scientific community, however, judged Burbank as representing only a footnote to the advance of the biological sciences. In an age of tension over the professionalization and commercialization of the scientific enterprise, Burbank stood in both the scientific and the public realms, a hybrid like one of his own creations.

• Original material is in the Luther Burbank Papers in the Library of Congress; the Walter Howard Papers, Bancroft Library, University of California at Berkeley; the George Harrison Shull Papers, American Philosophical Society; the Edward Wickson Papers, University of California at Davis; and the Carnegie Institution of Washington archives. The most comprehensive discussion of Burbank is Peter Dreyer, *A Gardener Touched with Genius: The Life of Luther Burbank*, rev. ed. (1985). An early retrospective assessment is Walter L. Howard, "Luther Burbank: A Victim of Hero Worship," *Chronica Botanica* 9, nos. 5–6 (Winter 1945–1946): 300–506. Texts presented as autobiographical include Luther Burbank, with Wilbur Hall, *The Harvest of the Years* (1927), and Burbank, *Partner of Nature*, ed. Hall (1939). Burbank wrote little himself, preferring to give interviews, reported in E. J. Wickson, *Luther Burbank, Man, Methods and Achievements: An Appreciation* (1902), and William S. Harwood, "A Wonder-Worker of Science: An Authoritative Account of Luther Burbank's Unique Work in Creating New Forms of Plant Life," *Century Magazine*, Apr. 1905, pp. 821–37. Evaluations of Burbank's work by scientists include Hugo de Vries, *Plant-Breeding: Comments on the Experiments of Nilsson and Burbank* (1907), and David Starr Jordan and Vernon Kellogg, *The Scientific Aspects of Luther Burbank's Work* (1909). For modern assessments of Burbank within the history of science, see Nathan Reingold, "National Science Policy in a Private Foundation: The Carnegie Institution of Washington," in *The Organization of Knowledge in Modern America, 1860–1920*, ed. Alexandra Oleson and John Voss (1979); Bentley Glass, "The Strange Encounter of Luther Burbank and George Harrison Shull," *Proceedings of the American Philosophical Society* 124 (1980): 133–53; and Sharon E. Kingsland, "The Battling Botanist: Daniel Trembly MacDougal, Mutation Theory, and the Rise of Experimental Evolutionary Biology in America, 1900–1912," *Isis* 82 (1991): 479–509.

KATHERINE PANDORA

BURCHFIELD, Charles Ephraim (9 Apr. 1893–10 Jan. 1967), painter, was born in Ashtabula Harbor, Ohio, the son of William Charles Burchfield, a merchant-tailor, and Alice Murphy, a former schoolteacher. The fifth of six children, Burchfield was only five when his father's sudden death at the age of thirty-eight left the family impoverished. His mother moved the family to her hometown of Salem, Ohio, where her brothers purchased a home for them; Burchfield's fifteen-year-old brother went to work full time to enable the family to stay together. Burchfield himself worked after school and on Saturdays beginning in the seventh grade, first at a drugstore and then at W. H. Mullins Co., a metal-fabricating plant. A small manufacturing town, Salem provided Burchfield with what he always considered an idyllic American boyhood. Vivid memories of his childhood exerted a powerful influence on his art.

A shy, sensitive youth, Burchfield was drawn to nature at an early age, spending countless hours collecting wildflowers and wandering the fields and woods that surrounded Salem. He began drawing when he was very young and in 1911 began the journal that he kept throughout his life, ultimately filling more than 10,000 pages with thoughts on life and art. Burchfield graduated in 1911 as valedictorian of his high school class, with a scholarship to continue his education.

After working full time for a year at Mullins to supplement his modest scholarship, Burchfield entered the Cleveland School (now Institute) of Art in the fall of 1912. He was strongly influenced by his teachers Henry G. Keller, Frank Wilcox, and William J. Eastman, all of whom encouraged their students to paint out-of-doors and to use bold, often arbitrary color. Burchfield excelled in his courses in design and decorative illustration, but he developed little interest in the human figure. Torn between his love for writing and for the visual arts, Burchfield initially planned a career as an illustrator; he hoped to write and illustrate his own books on nature. With youthful enthusiasm he proclaimed in his journal, "I hereby dedicate my life and soul to the study and love of nature, with the purpose to bring it before the mass of uninterested public" (cited in Baur, p. 27).

Although by his third year in art school Burchfield had decided to devote himself solely to painting, he remained committed to his original dedication to nature, leading him to complain in his journal years later that "the great difficulty of my whole career as a painter is that what I love most . . . holds little interest for most people. . . . I love the approach of winter, the change from snow to rain and vice-versa; the decay of vegetation and the resurgence of plant life in the spring . . . but . . . the mass of humanity remains either bored or indifferent or actually hostile" (cited in Baur, pp. 224–25).

Burchfield always considered the year 1915 as the true beginning of his career as an artist. That summer, according to an autobiographical manuscript, he "began to seriously paint outdoors, trying to record my personal reactions to nature" (cited in Baur, p. 31). He also began to fill his journal notebooks with aesthetic and technical challenges that would carry him beyond his formal training. For example, he set out to "study solutions of how sun hurls itself headlong thru the clouds" and to learn how to paint "lightning across the moon" (cited in Baur, p. 31). Burchfield's preferred medium was watercolor and gouache, and he developed a highly individual style. His love of music, including that of Wagner, Beethoven, and Sibelius, influenced his early development as an artist and deepened as he matured.

Burchfield graduated from the Cleveland School of Art in June 1916 and received a scholarship to the National Academy of Design in New York for that fall. One day of classes at the academy, however, convinced him that he did not wish to continue formal study. He remained in New York through the fall, making several important contacts within the New York art establishment. Most significant among these was Mary Mowbray-Clarke of the Sunwise Turn Bookshop, who encouraged his artistic development and who later arranged Burchfield's first New York exhibitions. Burchfield returned to Salem (and his old job in the cost department at Mullins) in late November, determined to develop independently as an artist by painting in his spare time.

Except for a brief tour of duty in the army at Camp Jackson, South Carolina, during World War I, Burchfield lived and worked in Salem through the fall of 1921. His first eighteen months back in Salem were ones of remarkable artistic achievement that proved to be the most prolific of his career. Burchfield believed 1917 to have been his "golden year." He later recollected, "I was back home in the town and countryside where I had grown up, which were now transformed by the magic of an awakened art outlook. Memories of my boyhood crowded in upon me to make that time also a dream world of the imagination" (Burchfield, 1965, p. 20). The stylistic directions Burchfield had been exploring came to their fullest expression during this period. The decorative, flat patterning that had characterized his work to date gave way to greater breadth and complexity as he moved toward the romantic expressionism that became identified with Burchfield's work and that led Alfred Barr, director of New York's Museum of Modern Art, to declare Burchfield's 1916 to 1918 watercolors some "of the most isolated and original phenomena in American art." Burchfield's sensitivity to nature's moods and the way they mirrored his own increased, and he searched for ways to visualize sound and to express the emotions of childhood. In a notable stylistic innovation he developed a series of graphic symbols to represent various emotions and states of being, such as fear, dangerous brooding, and imbecility, which he then weaved into his paintings. Significant works that reveal these concerns are *Church Bells Ringing, Rainy Winter Night* (1917, Cleveland Museum of Art) and *The Insect Chorus* (1917, Munson-Williams-Proctor Institute, Utica, N.Y.).

Burchfield's service in the army from July 1918 to January 1919 disrupted the carefully guarded isolation he had enjoyed in Salem. He became estranged from his painting and, when he returned from his stint of duty, struggled to recapture his earlier intimacy with nature and his own childhood. In a fit of despair, he later destroyed much of his 1919 work. Similar periods of dark, emotional turmoil, alternating with periods of intense euphoria, characterized Burchfield's temperament throughout his life.

By early 1920 Burchfield had recovered from his artistic crisis and had begun to explore the American scene subjects that would occupy him for the next twenty years. In the spring of 1921 Burchfield lost his job at Mullins. Unable to find other work in Salem, and in love with his future bride, Bertha Kenreich, Burchfield accepted a position as assistant designer in the wallpaper firm of M. H. Birge and Sons in Buffalo, New York, in November 1921. He married the following May and by April 1925 had bought the house in the Buffalo suburb of Gardenville in which he would live for the rest of his life. All five of his children had been born by 1929. Montross Gallery in New York became his dealer in 1924, followed by the Frank K. M. Rehn Gallery in 1929, which continued to represent Burchfield's work until his death.

In 1920, influenced by the fiction of Sherwood Anderson, Willa Cather, Sinclair Lewis, and Zona Gale, Burchfield began to move away from romantic expressionism toward realism. Images of the villages, towns, and cities of Ohio and western New York supplanted nature as the dominant subject of his work through the early 1940s. Characteristic works of this period include *Old Tavern At Hammondsville, Ohio* (1926–1928, Addison Gallery of American Art, Andover, Mass.), *Rainy Night* (1929–1930, Fine Arts Society of San Diego), *End of Day* (1936–1938, Pennsylvania Academy of the Fine Arts, Philadelphia), and scenes of industrial America, such as *Black Iron* (1935, collection of Mr. and Mrs. John D. Rockefeller III). Human figures appear on occasion in these works, but Burchfield preferred to paint the buildings in which people lived and worked and the machines they used as a way to reveal American life through a sense of place.

Throughout his career Burchfield pushed the boundaries of watercolor technique. Ignoring the luminous washes of traditional watercolor, he increasingly worked with heavy opaque strokes of color, which gave his watercolors weight and solidity. Beginning in the 1920s he increased the size and scale of his watercolors significantly, commonly working on a scale of 30″ by 40″; his early watercolors had rarely exceeded 14″ by 20″. The traditional belief that a serious artist should work in oil prompted Burchfield to experiment with that medium. In the 1930s he made a concerted effort to master oil painting, and he produced a handful of notable canvases, such as *November Evening* (1931–1934, Metropolitan Museum of Art). Burchfield abandoned oil painting entirely in 1938.

Burchfield received his first critical and popular acclaim for his American scenes of the 1920s and 1930s, in which he embraced what he called "the great epic poetry of midwest American life." By 1930 critics typically referred to him, along with his friend Edward Hopper, as a "pioneer of the American scene." One critic heralded Burchfield as a "100 per cent American recorder of the American scene," who had "taken the obvious and familiar Main Street, the desolute urban landscape, and our mongrel architecture as subject for his art and transformed it into something epic and universal" (*Art Digest*, 1 Apr. 1930, p. 16). Another critic (*Art Digest*, 15 Nov. 1931, pp. 18–24) described him as a "thoroughly American artist not only because he paints the American scene, but because he combines realism and romance in a characteristically American manner." Burchfield described himself during these years as a "romantic-realist." By 1929 he was confident enough in his success as an artist that he quit his job at M. H. Birge and devoted himself full time to painting. Though he later taught an occasional painting class, he always remained a reluctant teacher.

At the height of his career as a painter of the American scene in the late 1930s, critical support for the American scene movement began to erode. By then Burchfield himself had begun to feel dissatisfied with his work, writing in a letter in 1934 that he longed for "those rapturous headlong days of 1916 and 1917" (quoted in Baur, p. 192). Determined "to learn to establish the same relation to nature as an adult as he had when a child," Burchfield began working on unfinished watercolors that he had begun around 1917, enlarging and finishing them to create what he referred to as "reconstructions." Working with reconstructions, such as *The Coming of Spring* (1917/1943, Metropolitan Museum of Art), signaled Burchfield's transition from realism back to fantasy and foreshadowed the triumph of his personal expressionism in the 1950s. Burchfield also began to explore his renewed penchant for fantasy in new works, such as *Midsummer Caprice* (1945, Columbus Museum of Art).

The last two decades of Burchfield's life were dominated by his work on monumental expressionist landscapes, such as *The Sphinx and the Milky Way* (1946, Munson-Williams-Proctor), *Night of the Equinox* (1917/1955, the Sara Roby Foundation), and *Orion in Winter* (1962, the Thyssen-Bornemisza Collection); these works earned him acclaim from critics and scholars as the last great exponent of American pantheism. The source of much of his late work lay in memory and imagination: "I find myself being drawn almost inexorably into a dream world," he wrote in a letter in 1960. "It is not that I am trying to escape real life, but that the realm of fantasy offers the true solution of truly evaluating an experience" (quoted in Baur, p. 239). As in his early paintings, radical distortions and exaggerations of natural forms characterize many of Burchfield's later works, and the scale increased yet again. His technical mastery of watercolor, which had been perfected during the middle period of his career, became the foundation for a mature assurance and inventiveness.

By 1955 Burchfield had begun to suffer from failing health. Although this caused periods of artistic inactivity, he continued to paint without any apparent loss of creative power. His last years were filled with a growing number of honors and major retrospectives. He died in West Seneca, New York.

• Burchfield's journals and certain papers are held by the Charles E. Burchfield Foundation. The journals are housed at the Burchfield Art Center (State University of New York at Buffalo), which also owns additional papers and letters by Burchfield. Other papers, particularly those related to Burchfield's association with the Rehn Gallery, are at the Archives of American Art, Washington, D.C. Burchfield published several statements about his own work and that of friends and teachers. Important essays by Burchfield include "On the Middle Border," *Creative Art* 3 (Sept. 1928): xxv–xxxii; "Edward Hopper—Classicist," *Edward Hopper Retrospective Exhibition* (Museum of Modern Art, 1933); and "Fifty Years as a Painter," *CB: His Golden Year: A Retrospective Exhibition of Watercolors, Oils and Graphics* (University of Arizona, 1965). Two important monographs exist: John I. H.

Baur, *The Inlander: Life and Work of Charles Burchfield 1893–1967* (1982), and Matthew Baigell, *Charles Burchfield* (1976). A catalogue raisonné of Burchfield was compiled by Joseph Trovato, *Charles Burchfield: Catalogue of Paintings in Public and Private Collections* (1970). J. Benjamin Townsend, ed., *Charles Burchfield's Journals: The Poetry of Place* (1993), is a volume of annotated selections from Burchfield's journals arranged thematically. Extensive bibliographies are included in the works by Baur, Trovato, and Townsend. Significant recent exhibition catalogs are Nancy Weekly, *Charles E. Burchfield: The Sacred Woods* (Burchfield Art Center, 1993); Ruth Osgood Trovato, *Extending the Golden Year: Charles Burchfield Centennial* (Emerson Gallery, Hamilton College, Clinton, N.Y., 1993); and Nannette V. Maciejunes et al., *On the Middle Border: The Art of Charles E. Burchfield* (Columbus Museum of Art, 1997). Obituaries are in the *New York Times*, 11 Jan. 1967, and *American Artist* 31 (June 1967): 4.

NANNETTE MACIEJUNES

BURDEN, Henry (22 Apr. 1791–19 Jan. 1871), inventor and ironmaster, was born in Dunblane, Stirlingshire, Scotland, the son of Peter Burden and Elizabeth Abercrombie, farmers. Burden discovered his talent for invention as a youth on his family's modest farm, where with few tools and no models he constructed a threshing machine, several gristmills, and various farm implements. Encouraged by these successes he enrolled in a course of drawing, engineering, and mathematics at the University of Edinburgh (he received no degree).

In 1819 Burden followed a well-worn path of European engineers, mechanics, and artisans to the United States, drawn by the new nation's insatiable demand for European scientific, technological, and manufacturing skills. He found work immediately with Townsend & Corning, a small agricultural implement manufacturer in Albany, New York, on the strength of a letter from the American minister in London to the influential New York magnate Stephen Van Rensselaer. Within two years at this company Burden had designed one of the first practicable cultivators in the United States, won the top prize for an improved plow at several country fairs, and received his first patent for a hemp and flax machine. In the summer of 1821 Burden married Helen McOuat, to whom he had been engaged before leaving Scotland. They had seven children, two of whom predeceased Burden.

Burden and his family moved in 1822 to Woodside, a village just outside Troy, New York, where he became superintendent of a small, ramshackle plant, the Troy Iron and Nail Factory. From this inauspicious beginning, Burden took better advantage than most mechanics of the country's national patent system, its abundant natural resources, and, in particular, its crash development of waterpower and steampower. Burden acted quickly to correct the physical defects of his new charge. He ordered his men to dredge the Wynantskill Creek to increase the volume of water flowing by his plant and to build dams for a fourteen-acre reservoir to ensure year-round power. With sufficient water guaranteed, Burden constructed an enormous and locally celebrated waterwheel—fully sixty feet in diameter—capable of powering an unprecedented number of machines. Dissatisfied with current iron manufacturing technology, Burden devoted most of his time to inventing machines, many of which quickly became standard equipment for the industry. With astonishing speed his inventions transformed the Troy Iron and Nail Factory into one of the nation's largest iron manufacturers and earned Burden sufficient revenues to become majority stockholder by 1835 and sole owner by 1848. That year he renamed the enterprise H. Burden & Sons.

Burden's earliest and perhaps most remunerative inventions capitalized on the explosive growth of railroads after 1820. In 1825 Burden patented a machine to make wrought-iron spikes for ships and the flat rails then used by railroads. On a trip to England in 1835–1836, he noted that superior T- and I-shaped rails were coming into use there and quickly modified his machine (later patented in 1840) to produce the necessary hook-headed spike. The Albany Iron Works contested his patent for two decades (failing before the U.S. Supreme Court), but in the meantime Burden became the largest supplier of such spikes to American railroads. Burden also patented in 1840 a "rotary concentric squeezer" that rendered unnecessary the laborious hand hammering of puddled iron into bars. The commissioner of patents called it the single most important invention in iron manufacturing ever to come through his office. A number of Pittsburgh iron manufacturers also testified that in the short time since they had installed Burden's machine it had saved them collectively more than $350,000.

Burden's best-known invention, a self-acting machine to make horseshoes (patented in 1835), found a new, inexhaustible market during the Civil War. He improved his machine in 1843, 1857, and 1862. In its final form it could produce sixty horseshoes per minute, each equal to, if not of better quality than, hand-forged shoes. After 1862 Burden became the sole supplier of horseshoes to the northern army and the target of a celebrated but unsuccessful Confederate attempt near the end of the war to steal the pattern for his labor-saving machine. The machine alone earned Burden & Sons $2 million in annual sales and catapulted the company into the ranks of the largest and most profitable iron manufacturers.

Burden was less successful as an inventor and promoter of steamboats but hardly less prolific—spurred no doubt by Troy's location at the navigational headwaters of the Hudson River. In 1825 the Troy Steamboat Association built the *Hendrick Hudson* based on a number of Burden's design suggestions, such as placing passenger berths above the waterline. Burden himself built a 300-foot, cigar-shaped steamboat with a thirty-foot paddle wheel in its center in 1833; the next year a mistake by the pilot destroyed the craft on its second trial run. Chastened but not discouraged by this loss, Burden traveled to England twice in the 1830s and 1840s to advocate transatlantic steamers of an unprecedented length and tonnage, propelled by side wheels instead of screw blades. In 1846 Burden and several Glasgow capitalists printed a long and detailed prospectus for "Burden's Atlantic Steam Ferry Company." While the company never produced any boats, its vision of an enormous line of steamers anticipated by a number of years the highly successful Great Eastern line.

Burden made no more significant inventions in his final years but continued to supervise his expanding enterprise with help from his two sons, William and Townsend. In contrast to his fellow Trojan ironmasters, Burden showed little interest in local, state, or national politics. He was active in his community's Second Presbyterian Church and built at his own expense the elegant, gray, stone Woodside Presbyterian Church. Like many other iron factories, after the Civil War Burden & Sons endured an unprecedented wave of strikes by the powerful Iron Molder's International Union. By all accounts, however, the elder Burden enjoyed an unusual level of respect from his workers. After his death in his elegant Woodside mansion overlooking the ironworks, a memorial from his men upheld him as a model for industrious and ambitious craftsmen. It also lauded his mechanical abilities, frequent walks through the hot and dangerous plant, and fairness toward his employees. Two thousand men joined in his funeral procession. By the time of his death the company comprised an upper and lower works, employed 1,400 people, and paid total annual wages of $500,000.

Burden was one of America's leading inventors and entrepreneurs. His career spanned the golden age of iron before the introduction of Bessemer steel and the heyday of independent inventors before the proliferation of corporate laboratories modeled on Edison's Menlo Park (1876) and university laboratories such as Johns Hopkins (1876). Burden also exemplified a significant minority of early industrial capitalists who came from modest roots, possessed extraordinary skills, and earned their wealth as much from their inventiveness as from their connections and timing. The successors of these early industrialists were rarely able to emulate them. Burden's sons, for example, renamed the firm the Burden Iron Company and reorganized it several times but proved unable to halt its slow decline in the face of competition from Bessemer steel and national conglomerates. They closed the upper works in 1900 and in 1940 sold the remaining assets of Burden & Sons to Republic Steel.

• No collections of Burden's personal papers or manuscripts are known to exist. A short biographical essay, reprints of numerous obituaries and memorials, and descriptions and diagrams of his inventions are in Margaret Burden Proudfit, *Henry Burden: His Life and a History of His Inventions* (1904). Additional family information can be found in *A Memorial of Mrs. Henry Burden* (1860). For a history of Burden's businesses see Samuel Rezneck, "Burden Iron Company, Troy," *A Report of the Mohawk Area Survey*, ed. Robert M. Vogel (1973). Burden and his business also figure largely in a contemporary municipal history, Arthur James Weise, *The City of Troy and Vicinity* (1886). Burden's treatment of and difficulties with workers are detailed in Daniel J. Walkowitz, *Worker City, Company Town: Iron and Cotton-Worker Protests in Troy and Cohoes, New York, 1855–1884* (1978). Obituaries are in the *Troy Daily Times*, 19 and 20 Jan. 1871, *Troy Press*, 19 Jan. 1871, *Troy Daily Whig*, 21 Jan. 1871, and *Phrenological Journal*, Apr. 1871.

CHARLES B. FORCEY

BURDEN, William Douglas (24 Sept. 1898–14 Nov. 1978), naturalist and explorer, was born in Troy, New York, the son of James Abercrombie Burden, an iron manufacturer, and Florence Adele Sloane. Burden received his A.B. in 1922 from Harvard College. He received his M.A. (in geology) in 1926 from Columbia University. After graduating from Harvard he traveled in the Orient studying oriental civilizations and collecting specimens of local fauna for the American Museum of Natural History.

Burden led expeditions to tropical islands and to the Arctic, but his most famous expedition was one he led in 1926 to the Indonesian island of Komodo in the Dutch East Indies in search of the Komodo dragon (*Varanus komodoensis*). These are the largest lizards on earth, reaching a length of 10 feet and a weight of 300 pounds. The purpose of the expedition, sponsored by the American Museum of Natural History, was to bring back the first Komodo dragons (both dead and alive) to the West. The president of the museum, Henry Fairfield Osborn, also requested the first live film footage of the Komodo dragon in its native habitat.

Since the lizards prefer carrion, Burden would leash a dead boar to a stake and film the lizards feeding. The lizards were slow moving and therefore easy to kill. Capturing them, however, was a more difficult task. A dead boar was used for bait; this was surrounded by a stockade with a narrow entrance where a noose was placed. When a large lizard stepped into the noose, it was captured, and a lasso was placed over the lizard's head and another around its tail. Burden captured two live Komodo dragons and shot twelve others. The two live dragons were given to the Bronx Zoo. Three of the dragons and one skeleton are on display in the Hall of Amphibians and Reptiles at the American Museum of Natural History. A detailed account of this expedition may be found in Burden's first book, *Dragon Lizards of Komodo: An Expedition to the Lost World of the Dutch East Indies* (1927).

In 1928 Burden filmed the daily life of the Native American tribe the Chippewa. This resulted in the film *The Silent Enemy* (1928). Realizing the importance of motion pictures in education, in 1931 Burden formed Beacon Films. The company was dissolved in 1933 when Burden realized he was ahead of the times.

In 1928 Burden also founded the Department of Experimental Biology (later the Department of Animal Behavior) at the American Museum of Natural History. Burden was a trustee of the museum from 1926 to 1961.

In 1937 Burden organized a $600,000 aquarium at Marineland, Florida. The aquarium was specially designed for underwater photography, containing the only two large oceanariums in the world at that time.

One was circular with a 75-foot diameter; the second was polygonal and 100 feet at its widest point. These underwater studios were opened to the public in 1938. Burden served as president of Marineland from 1937–1961.

From 1938 to 1941 he was a trustee of the New York Zoological Society. During World War II Burden developed a shark repellent for the U.S. Navy. He published his second book, *Look to the Wilderness*, in 1960. From 1966 to 1978 he served as chairman of the board of the Vermont Wildland Foundation.

Burden was married three times. His first marriage was in 1924 to Katherine Sage White, with whom he had three children. They divorced in 1939. The second marriage was in 1940 to Elizabeth Chace Gammack, with whom he had one child. After they divorced (year unknown) he married Jeanne Wight Booth in 1971.

He held memberships in Sigma Xi (the scientific research society) and the Harvard Travelers and was an honorary member of the Explorer's Club. He died in Charlotte, Vermont.

• There are no collections of Burden's papers, but his scientific work "Results of the Douglas Burden Expedition to the Island of Komodo" is in *American Museum Novitates*, no. 316, 18 May 1928. A popular account of this expedition may be found in *Natural History* 27, no. 1 (1927): 3–18, and in Burden's book *Dragon Lizards of Komodo*. Another account of the expedition may be found in Douglas Preston, *Dinosaurs in the Attic* (1986), pp. 163–66. A photograph of Burden may be found in the *National Cyclopedia of American Biography*, vol. F, p. 224. His obituary is in the *New York Times*, 16 Nov. 1978.

WALTER KANZLER

BURDICK, Usher Lloyd (21 Feb. 1879–19 Aug. 1960), author, educator, and legislator, was born in Owatonna, Minnesota, the son of Ozias Burdick and Lucy Farnum, farmers. In 1882 the family settled in Graham's Island in the Dakota Territory, where Burdick attended local public schools and learned the Sioux Indian language and customs. Following his graduation from the State Normal School at Mayville, North Dakota, in 1900, he worked for two years as deputy superintendent of schools in Benson County, North Dakota. In 1901 he married Emma Rassmussen, and they had two sons and a daughter. Frustrated by local politics, Burdick changed career objectives and moved to Minneapolis, Minnesota, where he taught in a business college while attending the University of Minnesota's law program, from which he graduated in 1904. He also played football at the university, which won the Big Ten championships in 1903 and 1904. After graduating he returned to Munich, North Dakota, where he was admitted to the bar and began practicing law.

From 1907 until 1932 Burdick served the state of North Dakota in many capacities, including in the state house of representatives (1907–1911), as lieutenant governor (1911–1913), as state's attorney for Williams County (1913–1915), as special prosecutor (1915–1920), and as assistant U.S. district attorney (1929–1932). In 1917, as a Progressive Republican, Burdick made a try for the governorship but withdrew his candidacy after only two weeks in favor of Arthur Townley's Nonpartisan League. Burdick endorsed the league's platform to improve farm business conditions through legislation.

Between 1920 and 1929 Burdick engaged in livestock breeding, farming, and writing. His study of General George A. Custer's battle against the Sioux Indians, *The Last Battle of the Sioux Nation*, appeared in 1929 and was the first of some twenty-two pieces on western history that Burdick authored.

Burdick failed in his first attempt as a Republican to win election to U.S. Congress in 1932, a time when his advocacy of repealing Prohibition and supporting Franklin D. Roosevelt over Herbert Hoover were not popular in North Dakota. Burdick was successful in 1934 with the support of the Nonpartisan League, and thereafter he was reelected for five successive terms. He chose not to seek renomination to the House in 1944, instead opting to seek the party's senatorial nomination. When that failed, he unsuccessfully ran as an independent candidate. He returned to Congress in 1948 and was reelected for four consecutive terms until 1958, when he was not a candidate for renomination but instead supported his son Quentin Burdick, who was also endorsed by the Nonpartisan League.

While in Congress Burdick served on the Indian Affairs, Pensions, and Territories committees, but he became known as a maverick because of his independent voting habits. For example, he supported New Deal programs such as President Roosevelt's work relief legislation, the Wagner Housing Act, and the Supreme Court Retirement Bill, yet he voted against the establishment of Social Security, banking laws that restricted institutional freedoms, and laws that authorized federal investigations of sit-down strikes. In 1939 he stood in opposition to his Republican colleagues when he supported the nomination of liberal Frank Murphy as attorney general.

Beginning in 1940 Burdick, suspicious of Democratic corruption and graft, championed placing limitations on outside pay and honorariums for congressmen, federal judges, and appointed executive officers. He continued the crusade when he returned to Congress after World War II. In 1950 he wanted a special investigating committee to examine charges of congressional payroll padding and a year later proposed that congressmen publish all their income sources.

In foreign affairs Burdick, like many of his colleagues from the prairie states, was an isolationist before Pearl Harbor. He supported the 1937 embargo on peacetime munitions exports and opposed naval expansion in 1939, military conscription in 1940, and lend-lease in 1941. After Pearl Harbor he supported Roosevelt's wartime policies, including the proposal to establish the United Nations.

When Burdick returned to Congress in January 1948 he continued his independent voting habits on federal government programs. He supported portions of President Harry S. Truman's Fair Deal, including rent control, long-range public housing, and rollbacks on federal subsidies for cattle producers, but he opposed repeal of federal taxes on oleomargarine. After the war Burdick returned to his isolationist position and voted against arms aid to Europe, loans to Great Britain, and the European Recovery Program (popularly known as the Marshall Plan). He described each as a waste of taxpayer monies in the belief that the Europeans would never repay their loans. Burdick also often expressed opposition to United Nations declarations that infringed on human rights issues, asserting that no international organization had the right to interfere with national customs and practices. In 1956 he married Edna Bryant Sierson, who died the same year. At the time of his death in Washington, D.C, he was survived by his third wife, Jean Rodgers.

• Burdick's papers are in the University of North Dakota Library, Grand Forks. Related material is in the State Historical Society of North Dakota in Bismark. A good discussion of Burdick's career through World War II is in his "Recollections and Reminiscences of Graham's Island," *North Dakota History*, July 1949, pp. 165–91. Other significant works by Burdick include *The Life of George Sperry Loftus* (1939) and *History of the Farmers' Political Action in North Dakota* (1944). A good account of Roosevelt's domestic program is Kenneth M. Davis, *FDR: The New Deal Years* (1986). For a discussion of the postwar domestic issues see Alonzo B. Hamby, *Harry S. Truman and the Fair Deal* (1974). An excellent analysis of Roosevelt's foreign policy is in Frederick W. Marks III, *Wind over Sand: The Diplomacy of Franklin Roosevelt* (1988). A recent study of the Cold War that encompasses Burdick's time in Congress is John Lewis Gaddis, *The Long Peace: Inquiries into the History of the Cold War* (1987). An obituary is in the *New York Times*, 20 Aug. 1960.

THOMAS M. LEONARD

BURGER, Nelle Gilham Lemon (27 July 1869–24 Dec. 1957), temperance leader, was born Nelle Gilham Lemons in St. Louis, Missouri, the daughter of Charles J. Lemons and Irene C. Jacobs. Their occupations are unknown. When Nelle was ten the family moved to Roodhouse, Illinois, where she began attending public schools and graduated from high school with honors. She then began teaching in area public schools. Two years later, on 1 September 1886, she married Charles A. Burger, an engineer.

Not long after her marriage a tragic accident changed the course of Burger's life. A former schoolmate had taken part in a drunken brawl and was sent to jail, where he died in a fire. Distressed by the incident, Burger made an "inward pledge" to help curtail the public use of alcohol so as to prevent other deaths. An active member of the Methodist church, she joined the Woman's Christian Temperance Union (WCTU) in 1890 and served as president of both the local and county organizations. Six years later she attended a national WCTU convention in St. Louis. There she met and received great inspiration from the national president, Frances E. Willard.

Later that year the Burgers moved to Clark, Missouri, and Burger immediately began to organize a temperance union. Clara C. Hoffman, longtime president of the Missouri WCTU, visited the county in 1897 and stayed in the Burger home. Burger's devotion to the cause and her organizing abilities were apparent to Hoffman. She encouraged Burger to speak and to organize local unions. Burger felt inadequate to the task, but her husband convinced her to try. Hoffman appointed her state organizer, and reluctantly she set out on her reform mission.

Burger worked successfully until 1899, when delegates at the national convention in Seattle elected her national lecturer. In this important work she traveled all over the United States and much of Canada speaking on the ill effects of liquor and encouraging the formation of local temperance unions.

Burger's other WCTU offices during those early years included secretary of the Young Woman's Branch of Missouri, 1897–1901, and the WCTU state recording secretary, 1907–1908. In 1910 the Mexican government requested an American worker to come to that country and organize a national WCTU. Burger spent two years there as a missionary, speaking on temperance, recruiting workers to the cause, and perfecting a national organization. During 1910–1913 she also served as corresponding secretary for the Missouri WCTU. After twenty-five years as president of the Missouri WCTU, Clara Hoffman announced her retirement in 1913. Meeting in convention that year at the University of Missouri, delegates elected Nelle Burger to succeed her as Missouri's state president.

Burger served thirty-four years as president of the Missouri WCTU. During her term of office she successfully directed the organization and presented bills to the Missouri legislature. She witnessed major developments in the temperance movement, including the beginning and end of prohibition. Important early events during her tenure included a large prohibition rally in Kansas City in 1914 and on 28 March of that year a National Constitutional Poster Day. In 1915 Burger urged the unions to work toward the National Constitution Prohibition Amendment.

In Moberly, Missouri, during a local option campaign just before passage of the prohibition law, Burger faced one of her most frightening challenges. Saloon men had threatened her life if she returned to that city. Nevertheless when local ministers asked for her assistance, she attended a gathering in front of one of the largest saloons the night before the vote. She stood on a wagon between the ministers and gave what she regarded as the best speech of her life. An excellent speaker, she used humor, drama, logic, and spiritual fervor to sway her audience.

Activities increased for Burger in 1918 as voting drew near for the state prohibition law. William Jennings Bryan delivered three addresses at a statewide temperance rally in Jefferson City the day the prohibition referendum was submitted to the Missouri legislature. Despite wet voters in St. Louis City and County, it finally passed. Union members then attempted to educate their congressmen on the benefits of prohibition. They sent petitions to Washington showing support for the Eighteenth Amendment, which became law in 1919.

While performing her duties as president, Burger also held the national office of recording secretary (1926–1944) and edited the *Missouri Counselor*. This state publication of the WCTU kept members informed on current events and temperance issues and helped bind together a tight-knit organization. After the Eighteenth Amendment passed, Burger pointed out in the *Missouri Counselor* other WCTU concerns: woman suffrage, working and neglected children, mothers' pensions, and juvenile courts. She also found it necessary to continually present the benefits of prohibition to help combat organizations that sought to repeal the Eighteenth Amendment.

When repeal of the amendment eventually did occur in 1933, Burger said that the "wet vote brought sorrow to our hearts." In order to carry on the cause, Burger urged temperance teaching in public and Sunday schools and temperance organizations for children and youth. She also influenced members to defeat campaigns for Sunday liquor sales and to support local options in liquor-by-the-drink elections.

Because of a heart condition, Burger announced her retirement as WCTU state president in 1947. Tributes to her many accomplishments and effective administration poured in from friends and foes alike. Meeting in Moberly at their annual convention in 1953, Missouri WCTU members honored their leader by launching the Nelle G. Burger Anniversary Fund.

The Burgers moved to Springfield, Missouri, in 1918. There Burger helped organize the Springfield Community Chest and worked for city improvement. She also served on the State Board of Charities and Corrections (1917–1925). Burger's husband died in the late 1930s. The couple had no children. By the time of Nelle Burger's death in Springfield, the cause for which she worked during her life had lost its prestige and power.

• The major reference work on the Woman's Christian Temperance Union in Missouri and the role of Nelle Burger in the union is B. Blanche Butts-Runion, *"Through the Years": A History of the First Seventy-five Years of the Woman's Christian Temperance Union in Missouri (1882–1957)* (n.d.). A biographical sketch appears in Mary K. Dains, ed., *Show Me Missouri Women: Selected Biographies* (1989). An obituary is in the *Springfield Leader and Press*, 24 Dec. 1957.

MARY K. DAINS

BURGER, Warren Earl (17 Sept. 1907–25 June 1995), chief justice of the United States, was born in St. Paul, Minnesota, the son of Charles Joseph Burger, a rail cargo inspector and sometime traveling salesman, and Katharine Schnittger. Burger spent his childhood in St. Paul. He worked his way through college, selling insurance. After attending the University of Minnesota from 1925 to 1927, he earned an LL.B., magna cum laude, from St. Paul College of Law (now William Mitchell College of Law) in 1931; he was admitted that same year to the Minnesota bar. He married Elvera Stromber in 1933; they had two children.

After graduation, Burger was appointed to the adjunct faculty of his law school and taught there for twenty-two years. From 1931 to 1953, he practiced law with Boyesen, Otis & Faricy, one of the oldest firms in the state. He soon became a partner in the firm, which in 1935 was renamed Faricy, Burger, Moore & Costello. He handled probate, real estate, and corporate matters and did trial and appellate work, arguing more than a dozen cases before the U.S. Supreme Court. An active member of the Republican party, he involved himself in civic and political concerns. He participated in Harold E. Stassen's campaign for governor in 1938 and was Stassen's floor manager at the 1952 Republican National Convention, when Minnesota's switch from supporting its "favorite son" supplied the necessary votes for Dwight D. Eisenhower's presidential nomination.

As a reward, in 1953 Burger was appointed assistant attorney general of the Claims Division (now the Civil Division) of the Department of Justice, which put him in charge of the government's civil litigation. Two years later, he was named to the U.S. Court of Appeals in Washington, D.C., where he developed a reputation as a conservative, particularly in criminal cases. But he also rendered several important opinions aimed at protecting individual rights: in one instance, he held that a contractor could not be excluded from government contracts without notice and a hearing; in another, he validated the right of television viewers to challenge an FCC decision renewing a broadcaster's license.

President Richard M. Nixon named Burger chief justice of the United States on Earl Warren's retirement in June 1969. The choice was made because of Burger's reputation as a conservative opponent of the Warren Court jurisprudence, notably its criminal law decisions. As the *New York Times* columnist Anthony Lewis later remarked, "It was often said [that] the Warren Court had made a constitutional revolution. Now a counter-revolution was seemingly at hand." To be sure, Burger began his tenure with a definite program to overrule the principal Warren Court decisions. According to Justice William O. Douglas's *Autobiography*, the new chief justice "announced in Conference . . . the precedents we should overrule. . . . many [Warren Court decisions] were on the list." Although, as Douglas put it, "Burger worked hard on it," he was nevertheless unable to secure the drastic rollback that headed his agenda.

In fact, no important Warren Court decision was overruled while Burger was chief justice. It is true that some of them were narrowed by Burger Court decisions; others were, however, fully applied and even expanded. The area where Burger was most eager to disown the Warren heritage was criminal law, and Nixon had in his presidential campaign emphasized that he wished to see the Supreme Court return to a viewpoint sympathetic to the state and its police powers as opposed to the rights of alleged criminals. Ironically, the right to counsel secured by *Gideon v. Wainright* (1963), the most famous and controversial

Warren Court ruling with regard to criminal law, was substantially broadened under Burger. Related Warren decisions protecting criminal defendants were also followed by the Burger Court.

The Warren Court landmarks in other areas of the law were similarly left to stand. *Brown v. Board of Education* (1954), for example, was consistently applied in the Burger era with the view that the courts possessed broad remedial power to bring about desegregation. When Burger spoke for the Supreme Court in *Swann v. Charlotte-Mecklenburg Board of Education* (1970), he upheld extensive busing as a means to desegregate schools. The antidiscrimination premise that underlay *Brown* was never questioned; it was even extended to uphold affirmative action programs to aid minorities. Burger himself wrote the opinion in *Fullilove v. Klutznick* (1980) sustaining congressional power to mandate that 10 percent of government construction contracts should be awarded to minority business enterprises. At the end of Burger's tenure, an opinion rendered in his Court concluded that "we have reached a common destination in sustaining affirmative action against constitutional attack."

Despite Burger's determination to reverse the trend of judicial activism, he presided over the creation of new constitutional doctrine with regard to sexual equality, the right to privacy, and due process. The chief justice himself wrote the opinion in *Reed v. Reed* (1971), the first Supreme Court decision striking down a law because of discrimination on the basis of sex. Other important Burger opinions invalidated the "legislative veto" used by Congress to annul executive action and compelled President Nixon to turn over the Watergate tapes. The impact of judicial review was dramatically demonstrated by these opinions concerning the separation of powers in the federal government. If Nixon had prevailed in claiming executive privilege with regard to the secret tape recordings made in the White House, he probably would not have faced the choice of being impeached or resigning; one of the tapes released to the special prosecutor became the "smoking gun" that revealed the president's willingness to engage in the obstruction of justice. Burger, however, did not play a significant part in his Court's most controversial decision: *Roe v. Wade* (1973), which ruled that the constitutional right of privacy protected a woman's right to secure an abortion. Although he had indicated a contrary view at the conference at which the justices discussed the case, he ultimately joined in the decision.

In one particular area, Burger was opposed to giving much latitude to the exercise of constitutional rights. Personally and as a jurist, he was not sympathetic to what he perceived to be the intrusiveness of the press. Once, when asked what he thought of reporters, he replied, "I admire those who do a good job, and I have sympathy for the rest, who are in the majority." In *New York Times v. United States* (1971)—the so-called Pentagon Papers case—he sharply dissented from the majority, who refused to prohibit the *Times* and the *Washington Post* from publishing a top-secret history of American involvement in Vietnam prepared within the Defense Department. "To me," Burger wrote, "it is hardly believable that a newspaper long regarded as a great institution in American life would fail to perform one of the basic and simple duties of every citizen with respect to the discovery or possession of . . . secret government documents." Yet he also wrote some significant Court opinions protecting First Amendment free speech and free press rights. The decisions that he articulated upheld the televising of criminal trials; invalidated "gag orders" prohibiting the press from publishing information about a criminal trial; struck down a law requiring a newspaper to give free reply space to a political candidate attacked by the paper; and held that a First Amendment right of access to the courts barred the exclusion of the public and press from a criminal trial. In *Miller v. California* (1973), Burger also wrote the opinion that finally resolved the legal definition of obscenity, shifting the emphasis to local community standards on the matter.

Burger had what amounted to an adversarial relationship with the news media. According to one reporter, "He fostered an atmosphere of secrecy around the court that left some employees terrified of being caught chatting with us." When a network asked permission to carry live radio coverage of the arguments in what promised to be a landmark case, Burger replied with a one-sentence letter: "It is not possible to arrange for any broadcast of any Supreme Court proceeding." Handwritten at the bottom was a postscript: "When you get the Cabinet meetings on the air, call me!" Burger was especially concerned about leaks to the press. He once circulated a memorandum to the other justices headed "CONFIDENTIAL" because a reporter had attempted to interview law clerks. "I have categorically directed," Burger declared, "that none of my staff have any conversation on any subject with any reporter. . . . I know of no one who is skilled enough to expose himself to any conversation with a reporter without getting into 'forbidden territory.' The reporter will inevitably extract information on the internal mechanisms of the Court, one way or another, to our embarrassment." Burger was deeply hurt by derogatory press accounts about his performance and was outraged by the attempt to reveal the Court's inner workings in Bob Woodward and Scott Armstrong's bestselling book *The Brethren* (1979). With undisguised glee, the chief justice told people that copies of the book were remaindered at ninety-eight cents in a Washington bookstore.

Burger's opinions are full of statements on the virtue of judicial restraint. A typical one reads: "The Constitution does not constitute us as 'Platonic Guardians' nor does it vest in this Court the authority to strike down laws because they do not meet our standards of desirable social policy, 'wisdom,' or 'common sense.'" If one measure of restraint is a hesitancy to intervene in the exercise of legislative power, Burger did not effectively rein in the impulse to do otherwise. Whereas the Warren Court invalidated 21 federal and 150 state statutes, the Burger Court struck down 31 federal and 288 state laws. The federal statutes that failed to pass constitutional muster in the Burger years were at least as significant as those ruled unconstitutional by the Warren Court. They included laws governing election financing and judicial salaries, granting eighteen-year-olds the vote in state elections, and establishing bankruptcy courts, as well as laws based on gender classifications in the military and in various social security programs, and a law designed to deal with the endemic budget deficit. Conservative opponents of the Warren Court saw its activism in the extension of established rights and recognition of "new" rights; by that gauge, however, the Burger Court was only rhetorically less inclined to engage in the "rights explosion." Few decisions were more far-reaching in their recognition of new rights than *Roe v. Wade*. Indeed, the *Roe* decision was the very archetype of the activist decision: one based not on legal principles and precedents but on "policy judgments."

As chief justice, Burger was administrative head of the federal judicial system, and he may have been more effective as an administrator than as a jurist. (The *New York Times* termed him "an innovator in administration.") Under Burger's leadership, a number of organizations designed to improve court administration were set up, including the Institute for Court Management, the National Center for State Courts, and the National Institute of Corrections. He also expanded the Federal Judicial Center for State Courts into a major resource for court research and education.

Burger stepped down from the position of chief justice in 1986. In retirement, he headed the Commission on the Bicentennial of the U.S. Constitution from 1986 to 1992 and served as chancellor of the College of William and Mary from 1986 to 1993. He died in Washington, D.C.

Burger was probably miscast in the role of leader of the U.S. Supreme Court—a harsh but fair judgment of a man who devoted so much of his life to the bench and worked as hard as he could to improve the judicial system. His personality was, in many ways, contradictory; a reporter characterized the chief justice as "at once gracious and petty, unselfish and self-serving, arrogant and insecure, politically shrewd yet stupid and heavyhanded at dealing with people." Burger has a place in judicial history as head of the Court that consolidated, often against the chief justice's wishes, what Justice Abe Fortas termed "the most profound and pervasive revolution ever achieved by substantially peaceful means," the revolution brought about by the Warren Court.

• Burger's papers were left to the College of William and Mary. He published *Delivery of Justice: Proposals for Changes to Improve the Administration of Justice* (1990), a collection of articles and addresses; and *It Is So Ordered* (1995), an account of fourteen important constitutional cases. The work of the Burger Court is covered in Bernard Schwartz, *The Ascent of Pragmatism: The Burger Court in Action* (1990), and Vincent Blasi, ed., *The Burger Court: The Counter-Revolution That Wasn't* (1983).

BERNARD SCHWARTZ

BURGESS, Ernest Watson (16 May 1886–27 Dec. 1966), sociologist, was born in Tilbury, Ontario, Canada, the son of Edmund James Burgess, an Anglican minister and teacher, and Mary Ann Jane Wilson. Having moved to the United States as a young child, Burgess grew up in a conventional middle-class family in small towns in Michigan and Oklahoma. Early in life he appeared destined for an academic career; his first grade teacher nicknamed him "the little professor." He attended public schools through tenth grade, completed high school at a private academy near his home, and earned a bachelor's degree from Kingfisher College in Oklahoma in 1908. One of the first sociologists to complete his advanced education in the United States, Burgess received his Ph.D. from the University of Chicago in 1913.

Burgess began his professional career as an instructor at the University of Toledo in 1912, then continued as an assistant professor at the University of Kansas from 1913 to 1915 and Ohio State University from 1915 to 1916. He returned to the University of Chicago as an assistant professor in 1916 during the major period of development of American sociology. He was promoted to associate professor in 1921 and to full professor in 1927.

On returning to Chicago, Burgess shared an office with his senior colleague, Robert Ezra Park. This office assignment proved to be fortunate, as Park and Burgess formed a productive, long-lasting partnership. Park was the charismatic one with a creative mind who attracted able students, while Burgess was quiet and retiring, yet intensely curious about and sensitive to other people. The collaboration benefited from Burgess's grant-writing skills, organizational abilities, and meticulous attention to details.

Team-teaching responsibilities for introductory sociology classes were assigned to Burgess and Park. Because of a scarcity of appropriate texts, they wrote their own. Their text evolved from conversations between them about the scope of sociology and included their own essays, focusing on the sociological treatment of human nature, group formation, interaction patterns, social organization, and social change, as well as works by Auguste Comte, Georg Simmel, Emile Durkheim, Herbert Spencer, and other contemporary social scientists. *Introduction to the Science of Sociology* was originally distributed to students in mimeographed form and later published in 1921. This text standardized the subject matter of sociology and became known as the "Green Bible" (the color of the cover was green), demonstrating its importance as the first introductory text in the history of the discipline.

Although often underrated because of Park's influence, Burgess's contributions to sociology are substantial. He was a prodigious sociologist who contributed significantly to research on community, criminology, family, and aging. He introduced an ecological model for studying communities, was the first sociologist to utilize a Thurstone scale for empirical research, and identified factors predicting marital adjustment. Burgess's reserved, judicious nature earned him the respect of his colleagues; and throughout his career, he was a leader in professional organizations. Appointed secretary-treasurer of the American Sociological Society in 1921, he remained in the position until 1930 and served as president of the society in 1934.

Burgess's early scholarship focused on urban analysis. *The City* (1925), a book Burgess co-edited with Park and Roderick McKenzie, detailed his concentric zone model of city development. This model suggests cities do not grow only at the periphery but expand radially from the center in a pattern of concentric zones. Burgess, Park, and McKenzie also contributed to the development of urban sociology in the United States and the ecological perspective for community study by illustrating the social importance of the spatial distribution of cities and utilizing the community as a laboratory for study. Burgess was first to use the conceptual terminology of human ecology in scientific research, a perspective that dominated early American sociology.

Interest in community led Burgess to the study of juvenile delinquency and the social control of crime. He was a key figure in the Chicago Area Project, a local program designed to control crime and restructure the community. He used scientific methods to study crime and reported his most significant predictive research in "Factors Making for Success or Failure on Parole" (*Journal of Criminal Law and Criminology* 19, no. 2 [1928]: 239–306).

In the 1930s Burgess turned his attention to the dynamics of marital and family relationships in a community context. His *The Family: From Institution to Companionship* (1945) focused on how the family changed in form and function in the early twentieth century and quickly became the leading textbook on sociology of the family. Burgess also furthered the scientific study of the family by helping found the National Council on Family Relations and serving as its fourth president in 1942

Toward the end of his career, Burgess studied aging. He researched adjustment to retirement in Florida communities, coined the term "roleless role" (a role for which society holds poorly defined behavioral expectations), and edited a special issue of the *American Journal of Sociology* on aging (1954). In addition, Burgess assisted in gaining recognition for the field of gerontology. As chair of the Social Science Research Council's Committee on Social Adjustment in 1941, he formed a committee on Social Adjustment in Old Age, and in the mid-1940s he helped organize the Gerontological Society, an interdisciplinary organization studying aging. In 1952 he served as president of this body.

A lifelong bachelor, Burgess lived with his sister and an elderly woman friend in a home near the University of Chicago campus. He remained active professionally for several years after his retirement until a series of illnesses and despondency over the death of his sister made it impossible to continue. He lived in a nursing home near campus until his death there from pneumonia. He willed his property to the University of Chicago, with proceeds to be used to promote social science research.

Burgess devoted his career to the development of sociology as a science. Society was his laboratory, and he believed empirical data integrated into a theoretical framework could be used to solve social problems. Although an expert in the case study method, Burgess used large-scale quantitative analysis when necessary. Because of the lack of systematic social research before Burgess, he is considered a pioneer in studying community, crime and delinquency, family, and aging.

• Leonard S. Cottrell, Jr., et al., eds., *Ernest W. Burgess, On Community Family and Delinquency* (1973), is a collection of articles recognizing his contributions to sociology. For more on Burgess, see Donald Joseph Bogue, *The Writings of Ernest W. Burgess* (1974), and Robert E. L. Faris, *Chicago Sociology 1920–1932* (1967). See also Leonard S. Cottrell, Jr., "Ernest Watson Burgess, 1886–1966: Contributions in the Field of Marriage and the Family Life," *American Sociologist* 2, no. 3 (Aug. 1967): 145–48. Obituaries are in *American Sociologist* 2, no. 2 (1967): 103–4, and the *New York Times*, 28 Dec. 1966.

BARBARA E. JOHNSON

BURGESS, Gelett (30 Jan. 1866–18 Sept. 1951), author, editor, and illustrator, was born Frank Gelett Burgess in Boston, Massachusetts, the son of Thomas Harvey Burgess, a well-to-do painting contractor, and Caroline Matilda Brooks, a genteel Unitarian. After graduating from the English High School in Boston, Burgess attended the Massachusetts Institute of Technology, where he earned his B.S. in 1887. To avoid perceived restrictions of life in New England, he became a draftsman on survey work with the Southern Pacific Railroad (1888–1891), hiked and sketched his way through France and Spain, and instructed topographical drawing at the University of California at Berkeley (1891–1894). He was dismissed from his academic post for pulling down a cast-iron statue of Henry Cogswell, a prominent local dentist revered as a philanthropic teetotaler. Burgess designed furniture for a San Francisco firm at minimal pay, lived on Russian Hill, and puzzled his neighbors by appearing at odd hours with his 5′4″ frame draped in vivid capes.

Then Burgess began his real career. He served as an editor (part of the time with Frank Norris) of *The Wave*, a San Francisco literary and society magazine (1894) and cofounded and edited *The Lark* (1895–1897). His avant-garde pals there included illustrator Ernest Peixotto and muralist Bruce Porter. The three were part of a rollicking group that called themselves Les Jeunes and included calligrapher-printer Porter Garnett, artist Florence Lundborg, architect Willis Polk, and writers Yone Noguchi, Carolyn Wells, and Juliet Wilbor Tomkins. Although Burgess also founded other little magazines, his fame came mainly from *The Lark*, which lasted for twenty-four numbers until he deliberately killed it despite a circulation of 5,000. Each issue was hand-set in beautiful type, with unjustified lines, and printed on one side of thin, yellow-brown bamboo paper bought in Chinatown. *The Lark* was the most original, brilliant, and significant "fada-zine" of its time and helped make San Francisco the literary center of the Pacific Coast. In it Burgess published many of his nonsense poems and illustrations.

After returning to the East in 1897 and to writing in Boston and New York for a couple of years, Burgess went to London (1899–1900), borrowing money for a lavish wardrobe, and pretended he was not seeking work. The pretense was a success, and he was besieged by editors and spent a year as a member of *The Sketch* staff. He returned to San Francisco (1900–1904), then moved back east again. In 1914 he married Estelle Loomis, formerly an actress and later a writer of stories and articles. They passed the World War I years in France as nonparticipants. The couple had no children. After many years back in the eastern United States, Burgess returned in 1949 to his beloved California, where he died in Carmel.

Obviously fun-loving and gregarious, even while serious in the pursuit of humor, Burgess was a welcome member of the Bohemian Club in San Francisco and the Players' Club in New York. When he was not socializing, he was busy as an energetic and prolific writer and illustrator. His first book was *Some Experiences with Hashish* (1886). It is possible that the use of narcotics inspired some of his wild written and pictorial effects. At any rate, forty-eight more books poured out, including eleven novels and additional items, among them essays, parodies, poetry, and short stories—many with his illustrations. Burgess's writings have evoked comparisons with some of the work of Woody Allen, Art Buchwald, Lewis Carroll, the Dadaists, W. C. Fields, Edward Lear, and Andy Rooney. His illustrations and writings are akin to Al Capp's Shmoos, to Caspar the friendly ghost, and to the work of Gary Larson, James Thurber, and Garry Trudeau. Critics have called Burgess's work absurd, antic, ebullient, flippant, iconoclastic, rebellious, wild, and zany. Burgess was a unique comic spirit.

His first *Lark* poem is unfortunately the one by which Burgess is best known:

> I never saw a purple cow
> I never hope to see one
> But I can tell you anyhow
> I'd rather see than be one. (1895)

The poor fellow grew so tired of its notoriety that he penned this in mock despair:

> Ah, yes, I wrote the "Purple Cow,"
> I'm Sorry, now, I wrote it;
> But I can tell you Anyhow
> I'll kill you if you Quote it! (1897)

He is also known for poems about characters called "Goops," boneless, oval-headed, portly little humanoids. Burgess divided his Goops into two groups. Sulphites are independent thinkers, whereas bromides—this neologism has survived—are dull, platitudinous bores. His Goop books were designed to teach children good manners in a funny way. Here is the start of a typical Goop poem:

> The Goops, they lick their fingers;
> The Goops, they lick their knives.
> They spill their broth on the table cloth—
> They lead disgusting lives!" (1900)

Goop poems are collected in popular books such as *Goops and How to Be Them* (1900), *More Goops and How Not to Be Them* (1903), *Blue Goops and Red* (1909), *The Goop Directory of Juvenile Offenders* (1913), and *New Goops and How to Know Them* (1951).

It would be goopish to say anything about the novels of Burgess except to indicate that they are all forgotten. Many of his other books have also lost their appeal. His *Burgess Unabridged: A New Dictionary of Words You Have Always Needed* (1914) can still evoke a smile, as the clever man invents word after word to be used instead of tedious circumlocutions. Examples include "tashivate," reply without attention, speak aimlessly, as to a child; and "huzzlecoo," intimate conversation, confidential chat, flirtation. Burgess had high hopes for "spuzz," aggressive, spicy mental energy. These words all failed. But his "blurb," meaning flamboyant, fulsome ad, caught on (as did his "bromide"). *Have You an Educated Heart?* (1923) beseeches readers to be nicer to others than rational evaluations of relationships might dictate, even though *Why Men Hate Women* (1927) may not seem very educated to the modern reader. In *Look Eleven Years Younger* (1937) Burgess tells readers how to achieve mental and physical well-being. Late in life (1948–1949) he became embroiled in the perennial controversy over who wrote the plays of William Shakespeare, whom Burgess called an impostor. Most sadly, however, it is for his purple cow and his Goops that Gelett Burgess will be remembered.

• General studies that describe Burgess's role in the San Francisco Bohemian scene are: Albert Parry, *Garrets and Pretenders: A History of Bohemianism in America* (1933); and Oscar Lewis, *Bay Window Bohemia: An Account of the Brilliant Artistic World of Gaslit San Francisco* (1956). Lawrence Ferlinghetti and Nancy J. Peters, *Literary San Francisco: A Pictorial History from Its Beginnings to the Present Day* (1980), devote pictures and text to Burgess. *Behind the Scenes: Glimpses of Fin de Siècle San Francisco* (1968) collects Burgess's best *Lark* pieces and includes useful editorial commentary by Joseph M. Backus. Robert A. Morace discusses *The Lark* in *American Literary Magazines: The Eighteenth and Nineteenth Centuries*, ed. Edward E. Chielens (1986), pp. 208–13. In *America's Humor: From Poor Richard to Doonesbury* (1978), Walter Blair and Hamlin Hill provide expert criticism of Burgess as humorist. The following include reminiscences by four of Burgess's acquaintances: Claude Bragdon, "The Purple Cow Period: The 'Dinky Magazines' That Caught the Spirit of the 'Nineties," *Bookman* 69 (July 1929): 475–78; Carolyn Wells, "What a Lark!" *Colophon* 22 (1931): pt. 8; S. J. Woolf, "Still No Purple Cow," *New York Times Magazine*, 8 June 1941, pp. 16–17; and Charles Hanson Towne, "The One-Man Magazines," *American Mercury* 63 (July 1946): 104–8. In a foreword to a reprint of *Burgess Unabridged: A New Dictionary of Words You Have Always Needed*

(1986), Paul Dickson offers lively, well-documented praise of Burgess. An obituary is in the *New York Times*, 19 Sept. 1951.

ROBERT L. GALE

BURGESS, George Kimball (4 Jan. 1874–2 July 1932), physicist and director of the National Bureau of Standards, was born in Newton, Massachusetts, the son of Charles A. Burgess and Addie Louise Kimball. Burgess attended the public schools of Newton, graduating from Newton High School in 1892, and the Massachusetts Institute of Technology (MIT), graduating in 1896 with a B.S. degree in physics. He remained at MIT for two additional years as an assistant instructor in physics and won an MIT traveling fellowship to do graduate study abroad. He chose the Sorbonne, a choice that had two major consequences for him. First, as a student of physics there (1898–1900) he came to know such leading French scientists as Henri Le Chatelier, Gabriel Lippmann, and Henri Poincaré. During his two years in Paris, Burgess completed his course work, performed high-temperature measurements, and translated Le Chatelier's book on temperature measurement into English. After spending the academic year 1900–1901 as an instructor in physics at the University of Michigan, Burgess returned to Paris to defend his doctoral thesis, a redetermination of the gravitational constant by means of a redesigned torsion balance. The second major consequence of his Paris sojourn was that he met Suzanne Babut, whom he married in 1901; they had no children.

After spending the next two academic years (1901–1903) as a physics instructor at the University of California, Burgess ended his brief teaching career by joining the recently established (1901) National Bureau of Standards in Washington, D.C. At the heart of the bureau's mission stood the establishment of the scientific foundations of physical measurement, the development of new instruments, the determination of the properties of materials, and strong support for American industry. That mission perfectly matched Burgess's training as a measuring physicist. He spent the remainder of his career there.

Burgess's career at the bureau assumed three phases: staff physicist (1903–1913), founding head of the Division of Metallurgy (1913–1923), and director (1923–1932). As an assistant (1903–1905), later associate staff physicist (1905–1913), Burgess pursued high-temperature measurements and metallurgy, above all developing optical pyrometers. He conducted research in the thermal analysis of metals and their alloys, determining their physical constants, properties, and behavior. With Charles W. Waidner he developed a light standard that eventually became the international standard. His pyrometric and metallurgical work in setting temperature standards helped lay scientific foundations for the American metallurgical industry.

In 1913 the bureau established the Division of Metallurgy with Burgess as its first chief. He developed close contacts with, and did research for, the iron, steel, and other metallurgical industries. His own research centered on improving railway materials. At the urging of railway experts and manufacturers, he analyzed metals used in railways and developed tests and specifications aimed at reducing railway accidents. Above all, he used his optical pyrometers to measure the precise temperatures at which steel was treated in furnaces and rails rolled through hot presses. Moreover, he developed new methods for creating nonfissured ingots on steel rails, thereby eliminating the fatal accidents due to fissured ingots; and he discovered the metallurgical causes of wheel and axle breakages, work that led to a marked decrease in railroad accidents. During this second phase of his career, Burgess devoted himself exclusively to applied science.

Burgess also built close ties with the American metallurgical industry by training many of its future leaders. He initiated a research association plan that brought industrial technologists to the bureau to do research on problems confronting their industry. Moreover, he established a regular series of bureau conferences on metallurgical research that brought academic and industrial representatives together, and his division systematically collected and published the latest technical information on metals and metallurgy. Under Burgess, the division did much work on light alloys, a topic of keen importance to the new airplane and automobile industries. Burgess himself became a leading expert on aircraft standards.

Burgess created an outstandingly effective and efficient division that demonstrated his skillful managerial abilities. When he started it in 1913, he had a staff of one; by the time he left in 1923, his staff had grown to fifty-three. Under his leadership, the division had developed into one of the world's premier metallurgical laboratories.

During World War I, Burgess and his division served the Allied war effort. The division helped develop and test aeronautical instruments and radio communications, and Burgess served as the American representative on the Allied International Aircraft Standards Board. In addition, in 1917 he became an American scientific attaché; he toured laboratories and manufacturing plants in the United States, Britain, and France and visited the Allied forces in France to assess potential research needs for their metal equipment and weaponry. He became one of Washington's foremost experts on the applications of science to warfare. After the war Burgess argued publicly for increased support for industrial research, lecturing on such topics as "Science and the After-War Period," "Governmental Research," and "The Government Laboratory and Industrial Research." In 1921 he was appointed the bureau's chief physicist and was considered one of the foremost American metallurgists.

Burgess began the third phase of his bureau career in 1923 when President Warren G. Harding appointed him the bureau's new director. His administrative style was marked by a delegation of authority that boosted staff morale. He promoted staff efficiency and work conditions and gave individuals full credit for work done in groups. The staff found ready access to him, discussion with him open and friendly, and his decision-making ability prompt and fair. Yet few knew him personally. By 1931 the bureau under Burgess had grown twofold in appropriations (to some $4 million) and by 25 percent in personnel (to more than 1,000 employees). As bureau director, Burgess sat on dozens of committees. For example, he served as chairman of the Federal Specifications Board, the National Screw Thread Commission, and the National Research Council; as president of the American Society for Testing Materials; as director of the American Standards Association; as a member of the National Academy of Sciences, the National Advisory Committee for Aeronautics, and the American Engineering Standards Committee; and as a representative to the International Committee on Weights and Measures. He was a great committeeman, constantly demonstrating diplomacy and an ability to work with others.

Budgetary problems occasioned by the depression worried him greatly. While working with his staff to meet a congressional mandate to dismiss about 100 bureau employees, he was stricken with a fatal cerebral hemorrhage and died in Washington.

• Larger collections of Burgess's papers are his personnel file at the U.S. Office of Personnel Management, Federal Records Center, St. Louis; some 133 letters in the William F. Meggers Papers and seven letters in the Max Mason Papers, American Institute of Physics, College Park, Md.; and some twenty-five pieces of correspondence in the Herbert Hoover Presidential Library, West Branch, Iowa. Very small collections are his correspondence with Robert Millikan and George Ellery Hale (California Institute of Technology, Institute Archives, Pasadena); Raymond T. Birge (Birge papers, University of California Archives, Bancroft Library, Berkeley); Gano Dunn (Oswald Veblen Papers, Library of Congress, Washington, D.C.); and Arthur O. Lovejoy (Lovejoy papers, Johns Hopkins University, Baltimore). One item is at the National Institute of Standards and Technology, MC51, Box 31 (Gaithersburg, Md). Official records of Burgess's administration of the bureau are in Record Group 167 at the National Archives and Records Administration in Washington, D.C.

Burgess's books are *Recherches sur la constante de gravitation* (1901), *Experimental Physics—A Laboratory Course for Freshmen* (1902), and (with Henri Le Chatelier) *The Measurement of High Temperatures* (1912). His translations are of Chatelier, *High Temperature Measurements* (1901; 2d ed., 1904), and Pierre Duhem, *Thermodynamics and Chemistry* (1903). Burgess published more than 100 scientific and technical articles, which are listed in the best biographical account, Lyman J. Briggs and Wallace R. Brode, "George Kimball Burgess, 1874–1932," National Academy of Sciences, *Biographical Memoirs* 30 (1957): 57–72, and in *J. C. Poggendorffs biographisch-literarisches Handwörterbuch für Mathematik, Astronomie, Physik, Chemie und verwandte Wissenschaftsgebiete*, vol. 5 (1926), pp. 189–90, and vol. 6 (1936), p. 373.

No scholarly books or articles on Burgess have been published. In addition to the standard biographical references, see Samuel J. Rosenberg, "George K. Burgess: 'A Human Being'," *NBS Standard*, 17 July 1974, p. 3. Obituaries are in *Science* 76 (1932): 46–47; the *New York Times*, 2 July 1932; the *Washington Star*, 3 July 1932; *Engineering News-Record* 109 (1932): 24; the *Iron Age* 130, no. 1 (1932): 22; *Technical News Bulletin of the Bureau of Standards* 183 (July 1932): 63–64; *Scientific Monthly* 35 (1932): 182–84; and *Journal of the Franklin Institute* 214 (1932): 237–39.

DAVID CAHAN

BURGESS, John William (26 Aug. 1844–13 Jan. 1931), political theorist, historian, and university dean, was born in Cornersville, Giles County, Tennessee, the son of Thomas T. Burgess, a planter, and Mary Judith Edwards. He was a descendant of Thomas Burgess, who landed in Massachusetts in 1630. Raised in Tennessee in a slaveholding, pro-Union southern Whig family, Burgess became interested in politics early in life upon hearing the orations and debates of Henry Clay, Andrew Johnson, and Alexander Stephens. During the Civil War he served as a federal scout and quartermaster, having barely escaped impressment into the Confederate army. Burgess took away from the war a deepened commitment to American nationalism and an avowed devotion to teaching politics as a matter of reason and compromise.

Burgess attended Amherst College, graduating in 1867; there he was influenced by the Hegelian Julius Seelye. Typhoid fever prevented him from realizing his plans for postgraduate study with Francis Lieber at Columbia College in New York City. Instead he studied law in a firm in Springfield, Massachusetts, passing the bar in 1869. That year he married Augusta Thayer Jones; they had no children. Within a year of her death in 1884, Burgess married Ruth Payne Jewett; they had one son.

From 1871 to 1873 Burgess studied law, history, and political science at the Universities of Göttingen, Leibzig, and Berlin under Theodore Mommsen, Heinrich von Treitschke, Wilhelm Roscher, Georg Waitz, Gustav Droysen, and Rudolf von Gneist. As a result of their broadly Hegelian teachings, Burgess became firmly attached to the philosophy of the modern state and an advocate of Germany and German-American alliances. Before completing his doctoral thesis he returned to Amherst to accept a professorship in 1873. Three years later he accepted a professorship in history, political science, and international law at Columbia. In 1880 Burgess succeeded in establishing the School of Political Science at Columbia. Taking as its models the German university with its emphasis on advanced research, and the École Libre des Science Politiques at Paris with its emphasis on the preparation of men for public service, the school provided the first graduate training in political science and related studies in the United States. As the dean, Burgess drew around him several distinguished colleagues and students-turned-colleagues, including Edmund Munroe Smith, Richmond Mayo-Smith, E. R. A. Seligman, John Bates Clark, Franklin Giddings, Herbert L. Osgood, Frank J. Goodnow, William A. Dunning, Daniel De Leon, and Charles A. Beard. Under Burgess the school published the *Political Science Quarterly* beginning in 1886, organized the Academy of Political Science, and sponsored an influential series of research monographs.

In 1890–1891 Burgess published his most important and ambitious theoretical work, *Political Science and Comparative Constitutional Law*. This two-volume treatise became a standard in political theory at the turn of the century. With related works by Woodrow Wilson and W. W. Willoughby, it identified political science as the science of the state: "The national popular state alone furnishes the objective reality upon which political science can rest in the construction of a truly scientific political system." This conception of political science (and the related studies of law and history) was to dominate American higher education until Progressive-era political scientists directed attention to administration, policy, and the realities of governmental practice. Reflecting the Hegelian influences of his teachers, Burgess developed a theory of the modern state as the progressive realization of human reason through history. He based the state on the nation, which he understood as a body of people unified by language, custom, and culture. The defining characteristic of the state was its sovereignty, giving it a higher legal status than church, corporation, or government.

Burgess rejected what he took to be the fictions of "dual sovereignty" in America and of natural rights anywhere. In the United States there was a single sovereign state founded on popular will despite the existence of several levels of government that administered law and policy. So-called "natural rights" were socially defined immunities against the government granted by the state—that is, by the people in their sovereign capacity. In short, the state was to be distinguished from the government and to limit it. Burgess also thought that the nation-state was the highest form of political life and that it had only been realized in Europe and the United States. The European and American state had a duty to "civilize" other nations and races in the ways of individual liberty. Thus one finds in Burgess not only nationalism and liberal individualism, but imperialism and Teutonic racialism, as well as an elitism that sought to continue restrictions on the franchise.

Burgess historicized his theory of the state in the course of writing histories of American institutions, especially *The Middle Period, 1817–1858* (1896), *The Civil War and the Constitution* (1901), and *Reconstruction and the Constitution* (1902). Besides their nationalism and institutionalism, these works sought in his words "a more complete reconciliation of North and South," a task more fully realized by William Dunning and the historiographical school of Reconstruction studies that formed around him. Burgess's commitment to the ideal of a national state that protected individual liberty—as well as his devotion to German-American relations—was made clear in his inaugural address as the first Roosevelt Professor of American History and Institutions at the Friedrich Wilhelms University in Berlin in 1906, in addresses before the Germanistic Society of America in 1908, in pamphlets for the German-American Literary Defense Committee in 1914, and in two book-length studies of the causes of World War I, *The European War of 1914* (1915) and *America's Relation to the Great War* (1916). Burgess was extremely distressed by the war, particularly by American and British involvement in it against Germany.

Burgess became dean of the entire Graduate Faculties of Political Science, Philosophy, and Pure Science at Columbia in 1909, holding that position until his formal retirement in 1912. He spent his remaining nineteen years in Newport, Rhode Island. Columbia celebrated Burgess as guest of honor in 1930 on the fiftieth anniversary of the founding of the School of Political Science just a few months before his death in Brookline, Massachusetts. His *Foundations of Political Science* (1933) was published posthumously, as was *Reminiscences of an American Scholar* (1934), an uncompleted autobiography that selectively traced his life until 1907.

• The principal collection of Burgess's lectures, correspondence, and manuscripts resides in the Columbia University libraries, including the Law School Library. Burgess also wrote *The American University: When Shall It Be? Where Shall It Be?* (1884); *The Reconciliation of Government with Liberty* (1915); *The Administration of President Hayes* (1916); *The Russian Revolution and the Soviet Constitution* (1919); *The Transformation of the Constitutional Law of the United States between 1898 and 1920* (1921); *Recent Changes in American Constitutional Theory* (1923); and *The Sanctity of the Law: In What Does It Consist?* (1928). A general bibliography of his writings is in *A Bibliography of the Faculty of Political Science of Columbia University, 1880–1930* (1931). R. Gordon Hoxie, "John W. Burgess: American Scholar" (Ph.D. diss., Columbia Univ., 1950), contains biographical information. Burgess figures prominently in various studies of Columbia University, especially Hoxie et al., *A History of the Faculty of Political Science, Columbia University* (1955). A snapshot of his metropolitan intellectual profile may be found in Thomas Bender, *New York Intellect* (1987). Burgess's political theory is treated exegetically in Bernard E. Brown, *American Conservatives: The Political Thought of Francis Lieber and John W. Burgess* (1951). Shorter but perceptive accounts of his contributions to political science and political theory may be found in Dorothy Ross, *The Origins of American Social Science* (1991), and John G. Gunnell, *The Descent of Political Theory: The Genealogy of an American Vocation* (1993).

JAMES FARR

BURGESS, Neil (29 June 1846?–19 Feb. 1910), actor, was born in Boston, Massachusetts, the son of a man whose last name was Burgess and Ellen A. Lunt. Nothing else is known of his parents. He was educated in public schools in Cambridge, Massachusetts, and for several years ran an art store on Tremont Street in Boston. According to many accounts, he debuted in Boston in 1865, playing minor roles in a burlesque with Spalding's Bell Ringers. However, the manager, M. B. Leavitt, claimed that these often-repeated statements concerning Burgess's debut are incorrect; in his version, Burgess was working in a photography gallery in Cort Square in 1870 when he was tutored in the song "Nicodemus Johnson" by the minstrel "Cool"

Burgess (no relation). Burgess consequently performed the selection in Leavitt's minstrel show in Springfield, Massachusetts, imitating "Cool's" Yankee twang and black dialect. According to Leavitt, Burgess joined Spalding's Bell Ringers some time later.

Burgess played in vaudeville and toured with minstrel troupes on the New England circuit until his career took an unexpected turn in Providence, Rhode Island. An actress in the stock company took ill, and Burgess, who also served as stage manager, was pressed into assuming the role of Mrs. Barnaby Bibbs in R. W. Suter's comedy *The Quiet Family* (1857). Improvising simpering expressions, he was such a hit that he was compelled to repeat the performance. He later claimed that he was disgusted by this relegation to "dame" parts and resigned in disgust, but the fact appears to be that he capitalized on his abrupt popularity by elaborating the character sketch of a finicky matron.

From 1872 to 1879 Burgess appeared in "drag" in New York variety shows in sketches such as "The Coming Woman" and as Hebe in *T. P. S. Canal Boat Pinafore*. Meanwhile, he sought full-length plays that would allow him the chance to star in female impersonations. One of these, an 1872 burlesque of the melodrama *Kenilworth* (in which he played Queen Elizabeth), proved unsuitable.

Burgess had better luck with *Josiah Allen's Wife* (1878), in which he was featured as Tryphena "Betsy" Puffy. While touring with the production in Toledo, Ohio, he attracted the attention of the humorist David R. Locke (Petroleum V. Nasby), who some time previously had dramatized Alice B. Neal's *The Widow Bedott Papers*. On 28 March 1879, after a week's rehearsal, Burgess produced his adaptation, *Widow Bedott; or, A Hunt for a Husband*, at Low's Opera House in Providence. This tale of a poor "widdy woman" wooed by seedy Deacon Sniffles enjoyed immediate success; despite the farce inherent in the story, Burgess's movements, gestures, and facial expressions, all based on his observation of New England village life, were considered natural. He continued to present these plays for nine seasons; *Josiah Allen's Wife*, now rechristened *Vim; or, A Visit to Puffy Farm* (1879), reopened at the St. Louis Opera House in an improved version and made an even bigger hit, owing to a treadmill device Burgess introduced to present a climactic horse race.

On 7 September 1880 Burgess married a member of his *Widow Bedott* company, Mary E. Stoddart, a niece of actor James H. Stoddart. They had one son and resided in a handsome home in Atlantic Highlands, New Jersey. During a fire there in the summer of 1889 Burgess was so seriously burned that many feared he would be disfigured for life; nevertheless, he recovered fully.

Burgess's next new production, *The County Fair*, was a rural play by Charles Barnard. With his wife playing Sallie Greenway, the play opened in Burlington, New Jersey, on 6 October 1888. It was then transferred to New York City to inaugurate Proctor's Twenty-third Street Theatre (5 Mar. 1889), where it ran for the rest of the season. The comedy then moved to the Union Square Theatre for four years, also playing twenty-nine weeks at the Park Theatre in Boston in 1891. Eventually, it celebrated its 5,000th performance at the Park Theatre, fourteen years after its original debut. *The County Fair* was seen in almost every American town that boasted a theater, and it made Burgess several fortunes. The story could not have been simpler: an elderly spinster is about to lose her home to wicked creditors when her horse wins a race and enough money to redeem the farm. Burgess's interpretation of "Aunt Abby" Prue became a classic in stage history and one of the biggest personal successes of any actor of his time, on a par with Joseph Jefferson's Rip van Winkle and Maggie Mitchell's Fanchon. *The County Fair* was followed by a failure, an elaboration of *Vim* titled *Neil Burgess's Circus*.

Although his comic vehicles made Burgess one of America's richest actors, his fortune evaporated in ill-advised speculations. He lost a great deal of money in his investment in New York City's Star Theatre, which he outfitted expensively, going so far as to install an innovative electric lighting system. It opened on 2 November 1895 with *The Year One* by Charles Barnard, a farce in which a vestal virgin disguises herself as Caesar to be near her beloved, a charioteer in the dictator's employ. Burgess played both the heroine and Caesar. *The County Fair*'s treadmill racetrack was enlarged to accommodate four-horse chariots, an improvement that eventually enabled *Ben Hur* to be successfully adapted for the stage. Public disinterest in *The Year One* forced it to close after one month, however, and the theater reopened on 9 December with *The County Fair*. Another novelty, *The Odd Miss Podd*, also failed, and Burgess, as always, revived *The County Fair*. Unfortunately, even that perennial went unappreciated during an 1897 tour of England.

After a brief retirement, Burgess returned to the American stage in 1899 in a one-act version of *Widow Bedott*, which he took on the vaudeville circuit. Another resuscitation of *The County Fair* (1899–1900) was welcomed but not enthusiastically enough to recuperate Burgess's fortune. When his wife died in 1905, he declared bankruptcy, and a court in Trenton, New Jersey, disclosed that he had liabilities of $21,113 and assets of two suits of clothes worth $25. He retired on the advice of Mrs. Nellie Bingham, a spiritualist whose counsel he had followed closely for some years, but in 1909 he returned to the vaudeville stage in a tabloid version of *The County Fair*. By this time Burgess was suffering from diabetes, which led to his death at his home in New York City. (According to some accounts, he died at his country home in Atlantic Highlands, New Jersey.)

Like so many nineteenth-century stars, Burgess's reputation and career were based on a single character, in his case a strong-minded, warm-hearted, tart-tongued New England spinster. When he first created the role, female impersonation was known on the American stage chiefly through the blackface "wench" of the minstrel show. Although the long-standing tradition of the dame, an elderly woman played by a man, survived in burlesque comedy, Burgess assimilated it to the legitimate stage through his realism and avoidance of the suggestive. Contemporary praise pointed out that "his personations have been very artistic and quite free from vulgarity, and he has the extreme happy gift of being able to talk very rapidly, and at the same time be distinct in utterance" (William F. Sage, "Impersonators of Women," *Theatre* 13 [May 1889]: 286). The only adverse criticism Burgess received was for having Aunt Abby don a tutu and parody a ballerina in his *Circus*, which was considered indecently out of character. Tall, pop-eyed Burgess, described by George Odell as "that king of impersonators of eccentric old maids or widows" and "always excruciatingly funny" (Odell, vol. 10, pp. 265, 455), powerfully influenced not only imitators such as Harry Lamarr, but also George Monroe's Aunt Bridget in musical comedy and Gilbert Sarony's Giddy Gusher in vaudeville; Aunt Abby even recurred as a leading character in the comic strip "Abbie 'n' Slats" by Al Capp and Raeburn Van Buren, looking much the way Burgess had created her.

• Clippings concerning Burgess's career can be found in the Billy Rose Theatre Collection at the New York Public Library for the Performing Arts, Lincoln Center; the Harvard Theatre Collection; and the Hoblitzelle Theatre Collection at the University of Texas, Austin. Useful articles about Burgess are in the *New York Clipper*, 2 Oct. 1880 and 18 Jan. 1890; the *Boston Morning Journal*, 2 Apr. 1892 and 13 Feb 1893; the *Illustrated American*, 14 Jan. 1893; and the *Providence Daily Journal*, 16 Feb. 1903. Specifics about his New York appearances to 1898 can be found in G. C. Odell, *Annals of the New York Stage*, vols. 9–15 (1937–1949). There are also entries on Burgess in Johnson Briscoe, *The Actors' Birthday Book* (1907); J. B. Clapp and E. F. Edgett, *Players of the Present* (1899–1901); and A. D. Storms, ed., *The Players Blue Book* (c. 1901). Obituaries are in the *New York Dramatic Mirror* and the *New York Clipper*, both 26 Feb. 1910, and the *Boston Evening Transcript*, 19 Feb. 1910.

LAURENCE SENELICK

BURGESS, Thornton Waldo (14 Jan. 1874–5 June 1965), writer, was born in Sandwich, Massachusetts, the son of Thornton Waldo Burgess, Sr., a traveling salesman, and Caroline F. Haywood, a confectioner. Before Burgess was a year old, his father died. Despite the fact that he began working as soon as he was able, he recalled his childhood as one of idealized simplicity woven through with innocence. During his early years in Massachusetts, he wandered the marshes and beaches, unaware that he was building a familiarity with nature and an appreciation of animal life that would later boost him to popularity.

After high school, Burgess moved to Boston in 1892. Following two tedious years of employment at a shoe store, he took the first step toward his publishing career. He wrote a jingle promoting his work as a copywriter and ran it in *Brains*, a trade publication for advertisers. Work began coming his way: a parody of "The Courtship of Miles Standish," advertising copy for dog biscuits, and a short piece for Shredded Wheat. Burgess supported himself with other occasional work, but he was led back to the world of publishing. In 1895 he was hired by the Phelps Publishing Company in Springfield, Massachusetts, cleaning offices and running errands. He soon worked his way up to a new post at the firm: reporter for the weekly paper, the *Springfield Homestead*.

Soon Burgess expanded into magazine publishing, writing for *Collier's*, *Country Life*, and *Good Housekeeping*. He married Nina E. Osborne in 1905 and soon published a collection called *A Bride's Primer*. There was nothing in this small volume of domestic humor to indicate what was forthcoming with his career. A year after his marriage, his wife died, leaving him with an infant. Once, while his son was visiting relatives in Chicago, Burgess wrote down the bedtime stories he usually told the boy at night and sent them to be read to the child. Friends and relatives urged Burgess to share the stories with others. These animal stories appeared first in *Good Housekeeping*. Later he augmented them with more tales of Peter Rabbit and his friends from the Green Forest and the Green Meadow and called the collection *Old Mother West Wind*, published in 1910. This collection was followed in 1911 by *Mother West Wind's Children*, and in 1913 by *Mother West Wind's Neighbors*.

The first volume of a series about Boy Scouts was published in 1912: *The Boy Scouts of Woodcraft Camp*. This series was destined not to be as successful as Burgess's animal stories, and only four volumes were published between 1912 and 1915.

Burgess married Fannie P. Johnson in 1911, and his family grew with the addition of two stepchildren. He had been working for *Good Housekeeping*, but the magazine was sold and Burgess was out of work. In 1912 he began writing children's stories based on animal characters for a newspaper syndicate, first the Associated Newspaper Syndicate and then the New York Tribune Syndicate. It was at this time that he initially worked with the illustrator Harrison Cady, beginning a partnership that would extend throughout their careers, as Cady's trademark illustrations appeared in most of Burgess's work.

Burgess proved himself to be a prolific and rapid writer. His books appeared quickly. In 1915, for example, nine volumes of his work were published. During his career, he wrote more than 170 junior novels and other books, and at least 15,000 "Bedtime Stories" for newspapers. Additionally, his articles, stories, poems, and advertising work add to his oeuvre. Burgess did not limit his concern about the natural world to his writing. He was a staunch supporter of conservation efforts and a believer in the potential of all creatures to live in harmony. He began the Green Meadow Clubs through newspapers and the Radio Nature League on the radio to reach children with the message of the importance of the preservation of wildlife. The Green Meadow Clubs saw an ultimate membership of 200,000, and the Radio Nature League, out of Springfield, Massachusetts, had a membership of 50,000.

Burgess's animal books are marked by a close mixture of personification and natural science. The characters wear clothes, as did most animal characters in children's books of the day, and they have relationships of family and friends that parallel those of human children; they have similar problems, and resolve them as children might. Yet Burgess strives to keep Jerry Muskrat a muskrat, Billy Mink a mink, Reddy Fox a fox, and so on. This propels Burgess into a conflict that, in its existence, assured his success: the balance of moral education and scientific training. He accomplishes this in part by admitting humans into the story only as vicarious participants: as readers. Very rarely does a human intrude into the world of the Green Meadow. This closed environment enables Burgess to control the influences on the characters, limiting what can exist in the fictional structure and allowing him dominion over their environment.

In 1960 Burgess wrote *Now I Remember*, which, as he pointed out, is not an autobiography as such but a remembrance. It stops short of examining his personal family relationships, dwelling instead on his writing and his readers. Yet it is, nevertheless, an interesting and thought-provoking glimpse inside the mind of the man who brought the Green Meadow to life. Burgess died in Hampden, Massachusetts.

• The Thornton W. Burgess Society in Sandwich, Mass., is the primary informative and historical source of Burgess material. Burgess's autobiography, *Now I Remember: Autobiography of an Amateur Naturalist* (1960), contains the author's personal reminiscences. See also his "The Gold Mine I Discovered When I Was 35," *American Magazine*, May 1919, pp. 36–37, 80, 83, 86, 89, 92, 93, for the author's personal perspective on his rise to popularity and its relationship to his early industriousness. J. Bryan III, "Mother Nature's Brother," *Saturday Review Gallery* (1959), is based on a 1940 interview with Burgess. Wayne W. Wright, *Thornton W. Burgess: A Descriptive Book Bibliography* (1979), is the definitive listing of Burgess's books by series and includes a publishing chronology and bibliography. Russell A. Lovell, Jr., *The Cape Cod Story of Thornton W. Burgess* (1974), is strong on aspects of Burgess's early life. Michael W. Dowhan, Jr., *Thornton W. Burgess, Harrison Cady: A Book, Magazine and Newspaper Bibliography* (1988), includes a catalog of the works of Harrison Cady, the man who illustrated most of Burgess's books. An obituary is in the *New York Times*, 6 May 1965.

JANET SPAETH

BURGOS, Julia de (17 Feb. 1914–4 Aug. 1953), poet and activist, was born in Carolina, Puerto Rico, the daughter of Francisco Burgos Hans, a member of the National Guard, and Paula García. The family was extremely poor, which may explain the death of six of the twelve siblings. Despite their poverty, for Julia, a bright and studious child, the Burgos family found the means for an education. In 1933 she received a teaching degree from the University of Puerto Rico.

It was during Burgos's college years that she became a member of the Nationalist party, a leftist group that proposed the independence of Puerto Rico by guerrilla force. She befriended Pedro Albizu Campos, a Harvard-educated lawyer and president of the party, who on several occasions invited Burgos to join him in addressing crowds during political rallies. Eventually, she fully accepted nationalism and became an effective political speaker and activist. During the Spanish Civil War (1936–1939), she sided with the Republican faction. It has been suggested that her first poems were inspired by that fratricidal war, but none of her work from those years survived.

Burgos's commitment to social causes led to her first job in 1934, when she worked briefly for the Puerto Rico Emergency Relief Administration (PRERA). That same year she married Ruben Rodriguez Beauchamp, a journalist. In 1935 she served as a teacher in an isolated country town. In 1936 and 1937 Burgos took part in educational radio programs organized by the Department of Education for the Universidad del Aire, but because of her political involvement she was dismissed and marked as a "revolutionary." During this period she wrote several plays for children, and in 1937 she published a collection of poetry entitled, *Poemas exactos a mí misma* (Poems like myself). A second collection, *Poemas en veinte surcos* (Poems in twenty furrows), followed the next year. These early collections establish her favorite literary motifs: nature and love as sources of the poetic inspiration.

Economic hard times persisted, and the young poet was forced to hand-sell her privately printed work to help pay her mother's medical bills. Burgos's efforts to make her poetry known paid off, and in 1939 the Instituto de Literatura Puertorriqueña awarded her a prize for her next poetry collection, *Canción de la verdad sencilla* (A song of simple truth). This collection develops a strong feminist self and includes love poems with a highly erotic discourse. Recognition of her literary talent came fast as she was introduced to important local figures like poets Luis Palés Matos and Luis Lloréns Torres.

Burgos's marriage ended in divorce in 1937 because of her inability to bear children. Her infertility left a feeling of emptiness that haunted her for life and shaped her feminist and erotic poetry. In 1939 Burgos met a wealthy Dominican, Dr. Juan Isidoro Jiménez Grullón, who took her as his mistress. She made a short trip to New York City in 1940; there she was well received by the Hispanic intelligentsia but also experienced racial and sexual discrimination by the elitist intellectual community of New York.

In 1940 her lover's career took Burgos to Cuba. During her two-year stay she furthered her college education at the University of Havana. There she met experimental surrealist poets and political activists. She produced another poetry collection, *El mar y tú* (The sea and you), published posthumously in 1954. Politically, Burgos continued her involvement in the cause for Puerto Rican independence by organizing public rallies.

Burgos's personal life was in trouble, however. Her relationship with Grullón was rapidly deteriorating. Reluctant to acknowledge his relationship with a beautiful mulatto of humble upbringing, he refused to get married. In her later poetry there is a clear tendency toward feminism marked by eroticism as a weapon against male chauvinism.

Burgos left Cuba for New York City in 1942. The 1940s marked the beginning of heavy Puerto Rican migration to industrial American cities, as thousands of unemployed laborers tried to escape harsh poverty in Puerto Rico. Burgos hoped to find work as a journalist or a teacher. Instead, she found herself trapped in several odd or low-paying jobs such as those of office clerk or saleswoman.

In 1943 Burgos married Armando Marín, and the next year she and her husband moved to Washington, D.C. Back in New York in 1945, she continued writing, and in 1946 she received a prize from the Instituto de Cultura Puertorriqueña. Burgos's continued involvement with the cause for Puerto Rican independence became more painful with the defeat of a nationalist revolt in 1950. Deeply distressed, and socially isolated by her inability to become part of American society, Burgos resorted to alcohol to cope with acute depression. In March 1949 she began treatment for alcoholism at Loeb Memorial Home for Convalescents, a process that was to continue in various institutions. Finally, during the early months of 1953 she was hospitalized in Goldwater Memorial Hospital, where she produced two poems in English, "Farewell in Welfare Island" and "The Sun in Welfare Island." These poems reflect her loneliness in a foreign land and her inability to cope with feelings of isolation.

Suffering from pneumonia, Burgos collapsed on a New York City street corner and was dead on arrival at Harlem Hospital. Her identity was unknown, and Burgos was buried in Potter's Field, a cemetery for the indigent. A month later relatives identified her from a photograph taken at the morgue, exhumed her body, and buried Burgos in her beloved Puerto Rico.

Julia de Burgos has become a major figure of the Hispanic-American movement. Along with other women activists, such as Puerto Rican nationalist Lolita Lebrón, Burgos adds a feminist dimension to the Hispanic cause for social and ethnic equality. Above all, her poetry and her feminist voice, challenging traditional sexual taboos, act as a connecting force between Hispanic women and women everywhere fighting for equal rights.

• A complete collection of Julia de Burgos's poems has yet to be published. An undetermined number of poems are still scattered in journals and newspapers in Puerto Rico, Cuba, and New York. Most of her poems have not been translated into English. For a complete biography consult Yvette Jiménez de Báez, *Julia de Burgos: vida y poesía* (1966), and *Spanish American Women Writers*, ed. Diane E. Marting (1990).

RAFAEL OCASIO

BURGOYNE, John (24 Feb. 1723–4 Aug. 1792), British soldier and dramatist, was born in London, England, the son of Captain John Burgoyne, a soldier, and Anna Maria Burneston. The popular belief that he was the natural son of Robert Benson, Lord Bingley, may have been true, but legally he was the son of Burgoyne. Educated at Westminster School, he entered the army at the age of fifteen, joining the Third Regiment of Horse Guards. Three years later he became a cornet in the Thirteenth Regiment of Light Dragoons and was promoted to lieutenant in 1741. In 1743 Burgoyne eloped with fifteen-year-old Lady Charlotte Stanley, daughter of Edward Stanley, earl of Derby; they had one child, who died at the age of ten. Lord Derby disapproved of the marriage; he gave his daughter only a small dowry and refused to see her or her husband. With Lady Charlotte's money, Burgoyne purchased a captaincy in the Thirteenth Dragoons, and for three years the couple lived in London. After that time gambling debts forced Burgoyne to sell his commission. He and his wife retired to a quiet life in the French countryside near Chanteloup, where they lived for seven years on Lady Charlotte's money and the proceeds from the sale of Burgoyne's captaincy.

With Anglo-French political rivalries rapidly building toward war by 1755, the Burgoynes decided to return to England, family difficulties or no. To their delight, Lady Charlotte's father welcomed them home, providing his daughter with an annuity of £400 and a promise of £25,000 upon his death. Additionally, he secured for his son-in-law a captaincy in the Eleventh Regiment of Dragoons, which Burgoyne two years later exchanged for a lieutenant colonelcy in the Coldstream Regiment of Foot, commonly known as the Coldstream Guards. Actively engaging in the Seven Years' War, Burgoyne participated in expeditions to Cherbourg and St. Malo in 1758 and 1759, then raised the Sixteenth Regiment of Light Dragoons, subsequently called "Burgoyne's Light-Horse." In 1762 Burgoyne was elected to Parliament, but before he began service he participated in a British harassing raid against Belle Ile on the coast of Brittany. The following year he was sent to Portugal as a brigadier general under Count la Lippe. In July he attacked Valencia d'Alcantara, capturing a general, and in October he stormed the fortified camp of Villa Velha to end the campaign. Thus ending the war with a brilliant record for military daring, Burgoyne was promoted in late 1762 to a colonelcy. In the following decade he served as a parliamentary spokesman for the ministry, violently criticizing and coming close to impeaching Robert, Lord Clive, who was suspected of plundering India while pretending to act for the India Company. Meanwhile, Burgoyne frequented fashionable clubs, acted on an amateur level, and gambled heavily. In 1774 he wrote a play, *Maid of the Oaks*, which David Garrick, an outstanding theater manager, staged at Drury Lane. Reportedly it ran for several nights, but critics considered it dull and tedious.

In May 1775 Major General Burgoyne (he had been promoted two years before) joined the British in attempts to suppress rebelling American colonists. After spending the summer at Boston bitterly complaining about his enforced inactivity, Burgoyne went home in disgust. The following year he reluctantly left his wife, who died a month later, and returned to the United States with the local rank of lieutenant general, second in command to Canadian governor Guy Carleton. After suffering another summer of frustration as Carleton managed to drive only a short way south into New York, Burgoyne returned once more to England. That winter, at the request of the ministry of Frederick, Lord North, Burgoyne drew up a plan of campaign for 1777, which was accepted. According to the plan, a large army under his command would advance to Albany by way of Lake Champlain. Simultaneously, a division from General William Howe's forces in New York would move northward and effect a junction, isolating New England from the other American colonies. A third body of men, under Barry St. Leger, would act as a diversion at Oswego on the Mohawk River. Following his program, Burgoyne in May advanced up Lake Champlain and quickly seized Fort Ticonderoga. Then, however, he inexplicably wasted much time plodding overland to Fort Edward, instead of going by water up Lake George. Burgoyne also impeded the mission by bringing along his mistress, a splendid wardrobe, and many cartloads of champagne. Thus, the Americans were given time to collect their forces at Bennington and Bemis Heights. After suffering a serious check at Bennington, Burgoyne arrived at Bemis Heights in September. In two major battles on 19 September and 7 October, he was first halted in his advance and then forced to retreat to Saratoga. Cut off from succor to the northward by John Stark's militia, Burgoyne surrendered to General Horatio Gates on 17 October. The decisive defeat hastened French recognition of the United States.

Given leave by the Americans to return to England in 1778, Burgoyne arrived home to face cold anger from the king, ministry, and people. Vainly demanding a court-martial, he managed to have his case heard in Parliament and also published a vindication of his actions. Nevertheless, in 1779 he was stripped of all military offices except his rank. Thereupon he joined the parliamentary opposition, and when Lord Rockingham came to power in 1782 Burgoyne was appointed commander in chief in Ireland and colonel of the Fourth Regiment of Foot, and was made an Irish privy councillor. After only a year the ministry fell and he was removed from power. He then distanced himself from politics—except to help manage the impeachment of Warren Hastings in 1787 for malpractice as governor of India—and instead cultivated a literary career. He wrote a number of comedies that were staged in the 1780s. One, *The Heiress*, was a great success; it went through ten editions in a year and was translated into French, German, Italian, and Spanish. All of Burgoyne's plays were published in 1808. Burgoyne formed a liaison with actress Susan Caulfield, and they had four children, the eldest of whom was Sir John Burgoyne, of Crimean War fame. Burgoyne died in London and was buried in Westminster Abbey.

• Burgoyne's personal papers have disappeared, but large numbers of his official letters are in the British Library, the William L. Clements Library in Ann Arbor, Mich., and the Public Record Office. Burgoyne's vindication is *A State of the Expedition from Canada, as Laid before the House of Commons . . .* (1780), and his literary efforts are in *The Dramatic and Poetical Works of the Late Lieutenant-general John Burgoyne* (2 vols., 1808). The finest biography is Richard J. Hargrove, *General John Burgoyne* (1983). Other recent monographs are James Lunt, *John Burgoyne of Saratoga* (1976), and Michael Glover, *General Burgoyne in Canada and America: Scapegoat for a System* (1976). An older work, important primarily because the author had access to Burgoyne's private correspondence, is Edward B. DeFonblanque, *Political and Military Episodes . . . from the Life and Correspondence of the Rt. Hon. John Burgoyne, General, Statesman, Dramatist* (1876). A short sketch is George A. Billias, "John Burgoyne: Ambitious General," in *George Washington's Opponents*, ed. Billias (1969). Useful treatments of Burgoyne's role in the Saratoga campaign are Charles Neilson, *An Original, Compiled, and Corrected Account of Burgoyne's Campaign, and the Memorable Battles of Bemis Heights* (1844); Max M. Mintz, *The Generals of Saratoga: John Burgoyne & Horatio Gates* (1990); Harrison Bird, *March to Saratoga: General Burgoyne and the American Campaign, 1777* (1963); and John S. Pancake, *1777: The Year of the Hangman* (1977).

PAUL DAVID NELSON

BURK, John Daly (1776?–?11 Apr. 1808), editor, historian, and dramatist, was born in Ireland, arriving in America at the age of twenty. His parents' names are unknown. He was a student at Trinity College in Dublin, but he was dismissed for "deism and republicanism" and eventually forced to leave Ireland, presumably because of political difficulties. Legend has it that a woman named Miss Daly gave him her female attire to help him escape from the British, hence the use of Daly in his name.

On this side of the Atlantic, Burk quickly became known as a strongly opinionated, hot-tempered individual whose passion was freedom. He came to Boston in 1796, where he founded and edited the *Polar Star and Boston Daily Advertiser*, an anti-British newspaper. Editions appeared from 6 October 1796 to 2 February 1797. In February 1797 Burk's play *Bunker-Hill; or, The Death of General Warren* was brought out at Boston's Haymarket Theatre. *Bunker-Hill*, for which he is best known, is a patriotic piece couched in a story of ill-fated love between a British officer and an American woman, climaxing with the smoky spectacle of the taking of Bunker Hill and concluding with "a grand procession in honor of General Warren." "American music only" was played at its debut between the acts. Burk made $2,000 from the play's seven performances in Boston. It was then presented at the John Street Theatre in New York in September 1797, where President John Adams saw the play and reportedly stated, "My friend, General Warren, was a scholar and a gentleman, but your author has made him a bully and a blackguard" (Clapp, p. 55). Nevertheless, the play was very popular and for many years was standard fare for both Fourth of July and Evacuation Day performances.

Having moved to New York City, Burk edited another newspaper, *Time-Piece*, but ceased this activity when he was arrested for "publishing a libel contrary to the provisions of the Sedition Law of 1798" (Clapp,

p. 54), an infraction that almost forced him to leave the country. He brought out another play in 1798, *Female Patriotism; or, The Death of Joan D'Arc*, which played twice at the Park Theatre in April of that year. Burk also undertook writing histories, and in 1799 his *History of the Late War in Ireland, with an Account of the United Irish Association, from the First Meeting at Belfast, to the Landing of the French at Kilala* was published in Philadelphia. Around 1800 Burk moved to Petersburg, Virginia, where he married, worked with an amateur "Thespian Company," and wrote a three-volume *History of Virginia* (1804–1805). (Another volume, completed by others, was published in 1816.) His republican fervor soon turned to the sentiments of Jefferson, and he became an enthusiastic Jeffersonian. His third major play, a melodrama filled with Gothic conventions titled *Bethlem Gabor, Lord of Transylvania; or The Man-Hating Palatine*, was performed in Petersburg with Burk directing and acting the lead in 1803. *Bethlem* was also performed in Richmond, Virginia, by a professional company and published in 1807. Burk's last argument took place in a pub in Petersburg, Virginia, where he denounced the French as a "pack of rascals" while a Monsieur Coquebert was present. A duel ensued in which Burk was shot through the heart. His *Historical Essay on the Character and Antiquity of Irish Songs* was published posthumously in the *Richmond Enquirer* in May 1808. Although William Dunlap attributes three other plays to Burk—*The Death of General Montgomery in Storming the City of Quebec*, *The Innkeeper of Abbeville*, and *Which Do You Like Best, the Poor Man or the Lord?*—Meserve and Arthur Hobson Quinn doubt their authorship.

Burk is remembered for his work as a playwright and for his passionate diatribes on freedom, equality, and the evils of tyranny, which he presented in print and on the stage. Although his play, *Bunker-Hill*, met with much critical disdain and he was never granted any substantial literary status, Burk has been considered notable for his powerful characterization of Joan of Arc in *Female Patriotism*. His Joan is not a saint, nor does she claim divine guidance, but still she has a desire and a talent to inspire the love of liberty in her soldiers. Both Quinn and Meserve rank the play highly and place Burk with Royall Tyler, William Dunlap, and Susanna Rowson as an important postrevolutionary playwright who asserted an American presence in what was still a British-based theater. Throughout his career Burk promoted a sense of nationalism, bringing local scenes of excitement and republican sentiments to the stage of a fledgling country.

• Of importance to theater historians is Burk's letter to the New York manager, John Hodgkinson, detailing at length how the battle scene on Bunker Hill was staged in Boston, which appears in William Dunlap, *History of the American Theatre* (1797; repr. 1963), and is reproduced by Richard Moody in his introduction to the play in *Dramas from the American Theatre, 1762–1909* (1966). The first playbill of *Bunker-Hill* can be found in William Clapp, *Record of the Boston Stage* (1853; repr. 1968). Walter Meserve has the most recent account and consideration of Burk in his *An Emerging Entertainment* (1977). Besides the stage chronicles of Clapp and Dunlap, the most contemporaneous, although written sixty years after Burk's life, is Charles Campbell, ed., *Some Materials to Serve for a Brief Memoir of John Daly Burk* (1868). Other secondary sources include Arthur Hobson Quinn, *A History of the American Drama: From the Beginning to the Civil War*, 2d ed. (1951); Joseph I. Shulim, "John Daly Burk: Playwright of Libertarianism," *Bulletin of the New York Public Library* 65 (Sept. 1961): 451–63; Edward Avery Wyatt, *John Daly Burk* (1936); and Oscar Wegelin, *Early American Plays* (1900). Moody's edition of *Bunker-Hill* includes its dedication to Aaron Burr.

SALLY L. JONES

BURK, Martha Cannary. *See* Calamity Jane.

BURKE, Aedanus (16 June 1743–30 Mar. 1802), congressman and judge, was born in County Galway, Ireland. His parentage is unknown, although he acknowledged that his grandfather served in the Irish army of James II. Burke attended a Jesuit seminary in St. Omer, France, and had he completed his studies there would have been destined for the priesthood. Never renouncing Catholicism or affiliating with any religious denomination in America, Burke, in order to be eligible to hold public office in South Carolina, became a nominal Protestant. After a brief stay in Bermuda, Burke showed up in 1766 at John Mercer's "Marlborough" plantation, near Fredericksburg, Virginia; what employment he had is not known, but Burke availed himself of Mercer's large law library for legal study. Leaving Virginia in early 1770, his activities until 1775, when he appeared in Charleston, South Carolina, were not recorded.

In August of that year Burke joined the second regiment of the South Carolina militia, and a year later began service in the South Carolina Continental Line, rising to the rank of lieutenant. He resigned from the army in February 1778 to accept election as a judge of the state's Court of Common Pleas and General Sessions. With the state overrun by the British army in 1780 and the courts unable to function, Burke reentered military service as a captain in the South Carolina militia. Captured along with the rest of General Benjamin Lincoln's army in Charleston on 12 May 1780, Burke remained a prisoner of war for sixteen months. After his exchange in mid-1781, he became an aide to General Arthur St. Clair and arrived in Yorktown, Virginia, just in time to witness the surrender of Cornwallis's army.

Burke retained his judgeship while in his latter military service, as well as a seat in the state's House of Representatives. He was a member of the legislature during 1779 to 1786 and 1787 to 1789, representing the parishes of St. Philip and St. Michael. After his captivity and his subsequent brief military service, Burke returned to South Carolina in time to sit in the Assembly convening at Jacksonborough, near Charleston, in January 1782. He was already indignant over Governor John Rutledge's proclamation of 27 September 1781 that pardoned certain Tories but excluded others. The Jacksonborough Assembly passed two laws in the same vein, the Confiscation and the Amercement Acts, which selected individual South Carolinians who were to be punished by banishment, confiscation of property, or amercement. Burke objected to these measures because he thought they were divisive of the people, excessive punishment, and no more than bills of attainder and ex post facto laws. In advocating leniency toward Tories, Burke went against the grain of much of public opinion. "My idea of managing internal enemies, or seditious revolters," he wrote Arthur Middleton on 14 May 1782, "is this, either drive them out of the State altogether . . . or make them our Friends by Pardoning."

A man of modest means and a champion of backcountry settlers, Burke disdained anything that smacked of aristocracy. The formation in 1783 of the Society of the Cincinnati, a hereditary order of Continental army officers, infuriated him. In a pamphlet, *Considerations on the Society or Order of the Cincinnati* (1783), and in successive editions in England, France, and Germany, Burke warned that the organization sought to widen the division between "the patricians or nobles and the rabble," and if it succeeded it "would give a fatal wound to civil liberty through the world" (Meleney, p. 85).

At the end of the war Burke delayed the reopening of the Court of Common Pleas as long as he could to keep away British creditors. While sympathetic to Loyalists, he opposed British merchants emigrating to South Carolina, fearing they would join ranks with wealthy South Carolinians to form an oligarchy. To sound this warning he published his third pamphlet, *A Few Salutary Hints Pointing Out the Policy and Consequences of Admitting British Subjects* . . . (1786).

The South Carolina legislature, in 1785, appointed Burke one of three commissioners to form a digest-revision of the state's laws. Although only some of the recommendations made by Burke and John F. Grimké (the other commissioner; Henry Pendleton died) were adopted, their work influenced the writing of a new South Carolina constitution in 1790. Representing the district between the Broad and Saluda Rivers, Burke served in the state convention for ratification of the U.S. Constitution. In the vote of 23 May 1788 he opposed ratification, chiefly on the grounds that amendments were needed and that an unlimited number of terms for the president might lead to a hereditary monarch.

Burke was elected to the first federal Congress (4 Mar. 1789–3 Mar. 1793), representing the Beaufort and Orangeburg districts, and was active in supporting the interests of his state and opposing nondemocratic tendencies. The *New York Morning Post*, 21 July 1790, said that Burke engaged in "scrutinizing the conduct of a dangerous Aristocratic faction . . . and GUARDING THE LIBERTIES OF MANKIND." He hoped that a delay in adopting the Bill of Rights would make possible the holding of a second constitutional convention. He favored more amendments and thought those proposed were too vague.

Burke served on thirty-eight congressional committees, reporting for nine. He sought exemption from import duties on articles consumed in South Carolina while asking for a protective duty on hemp produced in the state. He opposed a high tonnage rate, discrimination in payment of interest between original holders of U.S. securities and their assignees, chartering a national bank, and an excise tax. He voted for the United States to assume state debts and for patent and copyright legislation.

Displaying his outspokenness, Burke condemned Quakers, who had sent three petitions to Congress for abolishing the slave trade, "for sowing the seeds of insurrection and public calamity" (De Pauw et al., eds., vol. 12, p. 749). In the debate regarding the petitions, Burke said, "I do not rise . . . to advocate the cause of slavery. I am on the contrary a friend to civil liberty, but I rise as an advocate for the protection of the property, the order, and the tranquility of the state to which I belong." Arguing that South Carolinians treated their slaves with "humanity," Burke extended his remarks to state that emancipation "would be not only impolitic and mischievous to the public interest, but would carry along with it the greatest cruelty to these very Africans" (De Pauw et al., eds., vol. 12, pp. 746–47, 749). Burke shocked congressmen when in a speech he defended the revolutionary war militia, who "sacrificed lives at the holy altar of liberty. On their account I give the lie to Colonel Hamilton." The Treasury secretary, who was in the gallery at the time, had denigrated the militia as "small fugitive bodies" in a eulogy to Nathanael Greene at St. Paul's Church, New York (De Pauw et al., eds., vol. 12, p. 890). A duel between Alexander Hamilton and Burke was narrowly averted. One observer recorded that Burke "blazes against the Attentions shewed to General Washington, which he calls Idolatry, and that a Party wish as much to make him a King" (De Pauw et al., eds., vol. 9, p. 348).

Burke refused to run for a second term in Congress and left New York. Although Burke was a lifelong bachelor, while a congressman in New York City, he fathered a son by Isabella Murphy, and he made provision for the youth in his will. Having been on a leave of absence as a judge, he returned to the common law bench in South Carolina. Many humorous anecdotes were told about Burke as judge. One commentator mentioned that Burke "was thought to be a good Judge of law, but so fond of fun, as to forget very often the awfulness of the place which he filled and turned the whole proceedings into a farce" (Meleney, p. 17).

In February 1791 John Rutledge defeated Burke for chief justice by a vote of 70 to 51 in the legislature. Burke declined election to the Senate in 1798 and the following year was elected a judge on the Court of Chancery, a position he held until his death. Burke made extended visits to the North in 1792, 1794, 1797, and 1799, during which he consulted with Democratic-Republican leaders, and during the latter trip he served as a second to Aaron Burr in a duel with John B. Church (brother-in-law of Alexander Hamilton).

Burke lived modestly in Charleston; he owned two small tracts of land in the interior of the state. He was a member of the Charleston Library Society, the Palmetto Society (an organization of Charleston mechanics), and the Mount Zion Society, which established schools in the backcountry; he was also a director of the Santee-Cooper Canal Company.

A die-hard Democratic-Republican and too independent to be included in the inner circle of South Carolina's power elite, Burke brought a fresh perspective to politics and to the judiciary. In politics, however, he often seemed to be an oppositionist and rarely pursued well-defined goals. Burke died at his home in Charleston.

• Burke's personal papers, in accordance with his will, were destroyed after his death. Linda G. De Pauw et al., eds., *Documentary History of the First Federal Congress*, vols. 3, 9, and 10–14 (1977–1995), cover fully Burke's service as congressman, with a biographical sketch in Volume 14, pp. 836–43. Revealing Burke letters from 1781 to 1782 are in Joseph W. Barnwell, ed., "Correspondence of Hon. Arthur Middleton, Signer of the Declaration of Independence," *South Carolina Historical and Genealogical Magazine* 26 (1925): 183–206. John C. Meleney, *The Public Life of Aedanus Burke: Revolutionary Republican in Post-Revolutionary South Carolina* (1989), thoroughly examines Burke's political and judicial careers. Two sketches that emphasize humorous anecdotes relating to Burke are U. R. Brooks, *The South Carolina Bench and Bar* (1908), and John B. O'Neall, *Biographical Sketches of the Bench and Bar of South Carolina* (1859). See also George C. Rogers, Jr., "Aedanus Burke, Nathanael Greene, Anthony Wayne, and the British Merchants of Charleston" and Michael E. Stevens, "'Wealth, Influence or Powerful Connections: Aedanus Burke and the Case of Hezekiah Maham," *South Carolina Historical Magazine* 67 (1966): 75–83 and 81 (1980): 163–68, respectively. Information on Burke in the context of war and politics is in Jerome J. Nadelhaft, *The Disorders of War: The Revolution in South Carolina* (1981); Raymond G. Starr, "The Conservative Revolution: South Carolina Public Affairs, 1775–1790" (Ph.D. diss., Univ. of Texas, 1964); Rachel N. Klein, *The Rise of the Planter Class in the South Carolina Backcountry, 1760–1808* (1990); and George C. Rogers, Jr., *Evolution of a Federalist: William Loughton Smith of Charleston* (1962). A long obituary is in *City-Gazette and Daily Advertiser* (Charleston), 2 Apr. 1802. Much of this item is reproduced in *South Carolina Historical and Genealogical Magazine* 27 (1926): 45–48.

HARRY M. WARD

BURKE, James Anthony (30 Mar. 1910–13 Oct. 1983), congressman, was born in Boston, Massachusetts, the son of Joseph E. Burke, a railway clerk, and Bridget Collins. Burke grew up in the Mattapan and Hyde Park sections of Boston. His father died when Burke was young. He attended Suffolk University Law School but did not receive a degree. In 1934 he married Margaret Ethel Grant, who died in 1964. He married Aileen McDonald in 1968. There were no children by either marriage.

Burke worked as an accountant before his election as a Democrat to the Massachusetts state legislature in 1936, where he served for two years. While Burke was in the legislature in 1938, Boston mayor Maurice J. Tobin appointed him registrar of vital statistics for the city, and he held that post until 1941.

Burke served in World War II for four years, working for two years as a special agent in army counterintelligence attached to the Seventy-seventh Infantry Division in the South Pacific. Returning to Boston after the war, he was again elected from his Hyde Park district to the Massachusetts House of Representatives, serving from 1947 to 1954. For four of those years, 1949–1952, he was the Democratic assistant majority leader. After running unsuccessfully for lieutenant governor in 1954, he spent several years in the real estate business.

In 1958 Republican congressman Richard B. Wigglesworth, who had served the Massachusetts Thirteenth District for thirty years, announced his retirement. After World War II many Democrats, particularly those of Irish ancestry, had moved from Boston to the southern suburbs that comprised the bulk of the Thirteenth District. Burke himself had moved to suburban Milton and well understood the political implications of this migration. He won the seat handily, serving two terms. In 1962 his hometown of Milton was redistricted to the Eleventh District, and Burke easily won election there. For the rest of his career, he would represent the Eleventh District, which extended from the Hyde Park and Dorchester sections of Boston through the southern suburbs to the industrial city of Brockton.

Early in Burke's congressional career, in January 1961, the Democrats chose him for the powerful Ways and Means Committee, attributable at least in part to the patronage of Democratic majority leader John W. McCormack, who represented an adjacent Massachusetts congressional district. Burke was already seen in his own right as a loyal supporter of the House leadership, and his selection maintained the ratio of northern liberals to southern conservatives among the Democrats on the committee.

By the mid-1960s Burke was focusing on issues of concern to the elderly, which would characterize the rest of his career. Colleagues increasingly looked to him to shepherd legislation for the elderly through the critical Ways and Means Committee. In 1966 he offered the Democratic proposal in the Ways and Means Committee for a cost of living increase for Social Security recipients. Burke's social proposal provided a basis for the changes in the Social Security program enacted by Congress in 1967. Burke later stated that his work on the passage of the Medicare program in 1965, providing medical services to the elderly, was his most important legacy.

In 1968 President Lyndon B. Johnson credited Burke with playing a crucial role in the passage of a 10 percent tax surcharge that Johnson felt was necessary to deal with inflation. Burke offered a compromise motion on budget cuts that conservatives were demanding in return for support for the surcharge. The compromise failed, but President Johnson later wrote that Burke's motion allowed liberals to save face by voting for a smaller budget cut than the one Congress eventually approved.

By the early 1970s Burke was a senior member of the Ways and Means Committee and a close associate of its chairperson, Wilbur Mills. He was also one of the first supporters of Representative Thomas P. "Tip" O'Neill, Jr., in his quest for the position of House majority leader. Burke and O'Neill had been close friends since serving together in the Massachusetts legislature.

Burke continued his work with Social Security, playing a major role in the passage of the 1972 law indexing Social Security payments to inflation. He also fought that year for the successful passage of the Supplementary Security Income program that gave poor Americans who were aged, blind, or disabled additional income beyond that provided by Social Security. In 1975, as chairperson of the new Social Security Subcommittee of Ways and Means, he was the leading proponent of a proposal to change the basis of payments of Social Security taxes. Under the existing system, employers and employees each paid one-half of the tax; to lower the burden on workers, Burke argued that, as in many other industrial nations, the employer, the employee, and the general revenue account of the federal government should each pay one-third of the tax. Burke later considered his inability to bring about this change the major disappointment of his career.

During the early 1970s Burke became gravely concerned over the loss of American jobs to foreign competition. His interest in this issue grew in large part from the loss of jobs in the shoe factories clustered in the Brockton area of his district. With Senator Vance Hartke of Indiana, he cosponsored the Hartke-Burke Trade Bill, which would have limited imports to the annual levels of the 1965–1969 period and would have restricted the tax credits and incentives American companies received for foreign investments and operations. The bill did not pass, being widely viewed as too protectionist.

Until 1976 Burke had no significant opposition in his election campaigns and often ran unopposed. In that year, however, a young, transplanted Californian, Patrick H. McCarthy, opposed Burke in the Democratic primary, running on a platform of "New Blood, Old Values." Burke ran in his usual low-key manner, accepting only $1,300 in contributions during the whole campaign. He prevailed, but McCarthy received 43 percent of the vote, confronting Burke with the first real electoral challenge in his congressional career. At the same time, Burke was weakened by the effects of diabetes, which had required the amputation of a leg, confined him to a wheelchair, and seriously impaired his vision. In 1978 he announced he would not run for reelection. He retired to Milton and died in Boston.

Burke was a key member of the exceptionally powerful Massachusetts congressional delegation of the 1960s and 1970s. Together the members of this delegation were almost always able to hold their seats as long as they wished and accordingly built up considerable seniority. Burke, in particular, benefited from his close friendships with McCormack and O'Neill, each of whom served in this period as majority leader and then as Speaker of the House.

Burke always called himself a "bread and butter" congressman, indicating he was a traditional Democrat whose focus was on domestic issues and the economic concerns of his constituents. He had limited interest in broad ideological matters or foreign affairs. For example, he only opposed the Vietnam War after the Democrats lost the presidency in 1968. Yet within the areas he chose to concentrate upon, he had considerable influence. He played a central role in the dramatic improvement in the economic status of the elderly in the United States in the late 1960s and 1970s. He was one of the first political figures to draw attention to what would later be called the deindustrialization of the United States, the dramatic decrease in the percentage of Americans holding manufacturing jobs and the increased dependence on foreign imports that occurred after 1970. The alarm raised in the early 1970s by Burke and others also presaged America's tougher stand in trade negotiations in later years. A kindly man with a wry wit, he was an archetypical congressional insider of his period.

• Burke's congressional papers are in the John F. Kennedy Library at Columbia Point in Boston. An interview with Burke, mainly dealing with his relations with President Kennedy, is in the oral history collection of the Kennedy Library. Burke reflected on his congressional career in an interview in the *Milton (Mass.) Record-Transcript*, 17 Sept. 1981. For reminiscences and tributes from Burke's colleagues in Congress, see *Memorial Addresses and Other Tributes in the Congress of the United States on the Life and Contributions of James A. Burke* (1984). Burke's career in the 1970s is charted in Michael Barone et al., *The Almanac of American Politics: The Senators, the Representatives—Their Records, States and Districts 1974, 1976, 1978, 1980* (1973, 1975, 1977, 1979). See also *Congress and the Nation*, vols. 2, 4 (1969, 1977). For insights on Burke in particular and the Mass. congressional delegation in general, see Thomas P. O'Neill, Jr., with William Novak, *Man of the House: The Life and Political Memoirs of Speaker Tip O'Neill* (1987). The most complete obituary for Burke appears in the *Boston Globe*, 14 Oct. 1983. See also the *Milton Record-Transcript*, 21 Oct. 1983, and the *Enterprise* (Brockton, Mass.), 14 and 18 Oct. 1983.

THOMAS A. MCMULLIN

BURKE, John Joseph (6 June 1875–30 Oct. 1936), national Catholic leader, was born in New York City, the son of Patrick Burke, a blacksmith, and Mary Regan. Burke received his secondary and college courses from the Jesuits at St. Xavier in New York and then entered the Missionary Congregation of St. Paul the Apostle (Paulists) to prepare for the priesthood. He studied theology at the Paulist seminary on the campus of the Catholic University of America in Washington, D.C., was ordained in 1899, and received the degree of licenciate in sacred theology in 1901. In 1903 he joined the staff of the Paulist journal *Catholic World* and as its editor from 1904 to 1922 published notable material on issues of ecclesiology and social reform. He helped organize the Catholic Press Association in 1911 and continued to support the development of the Catholic press in the United States by introducing the National Catholic News wire service after World War I.

His Paulist-inspired vision of American Catholicism eventually led Burke to involve himself in national ecclesiastical organization. During World War I he founded the National Catholic War Council to direct Catholic participation in the war effort, served as chair of the ecumenical Committee of Six to advise the secretary of war on war-related religious concerns, and was awarded the Distinguished Service Medal for his efforts in 1919. He subsequently played a major role in transforming the War Council into a permanent national organization of the American hierarchy, the National Catholic Welfare Conference. As the general secretary of the Welfare Conference from 1919 to 1936, Burke, convinced that national Catholic organization was essential if the church was to make a strong contribution to public life, pursued his commitments to the welfare of both church and country. Under his leadership, the conference developed a staff of laity and clergy and launched a series of policy and organizational initiatives. Staffers developed positions on the economy, the family, public education, immigration, Prohibition, rural life, and even the movies. They testified before Congress as representatives of the conference, issued policy statements in the name of the Catholic bishops, and organized regional and local Catholic initiatives—activities that were publicized nationally by the conference press service. Burke's leadership of the conference was characterized by his loyalty to the wishes of the bishops and to the cause of national Catholic organization. These two commitments did not always coexist smoothly, and Burke was skilled at negotiating between them. At one point, his success in this area even led him to become involved in international diplomacy. In 1928, at the insistence of the Vatican and with the approval of the U.S. State Department, Burke carried out a secret mission to Mexico to mediate the dispute between the Vatican and the Calles government over the rights of Catholics in Mexico.

In addition to organizing the hierarchy on a national basis, Burke developed twin national federations for the laity. His success in this area was mixed. When the National Council of Catholic Men was organized in 1920, it drew a lukewarm response from existing societies of Catholic men. On the other hand, the National Council of Catholic Women drew dedicated responses from thousands of women in support of conference initiatives.

During his time as general secretary, Burke made his home at the National Catholic School of Social Service in Washington. The NCSSS was an institution created and sustained by the efforts of the National Council of Catholic Women to provide Catholic social workers for the welfare activities of the church. Burke made the school his special preserve. He was the chairman of the board of managers and the chaplain of the school until his death in Washington.

In addition to these major organizational efforts, Burke sustained a lifelong interest in spiritual direction and was especially successful as a spiritual adviser for women. Many of the women who sought his advice on spiritual matters also made significant contributions to his public work through the National Council of Catholic Women and the National Catholic School of Social Service as well as on the staff of the National Catholic Welfare Conference.

The importance of Burke's contribution can be seen in the subsequent development of his initiatives for national Catholic organization. In the wake of Vatican II (1962–1965), the National Catholic Welfare Conference became, under conciliar mandate, the National Conference of Catholic Bishops. The NCCB and its public policy arm, the United States Catholic Conference, have been significantly involved in the internal renewal of the American church and in public welfare and justice issues ranging from the economy and the family to the use of nuclear weapons. The National Council of Catholic Women has weathered dramatic changes in the status of women in both church and culture and continues to offer women a forum for national participation. Although Burke would have been very unhappy to see his beloved National Catholic School of Social Service lose its independent status and become absorbed by the School of Social Work at Catholic University in 1947, he would have found great satisfaction in the Second Vatican Council's imprimatur on his dream of national church organization.

• John Burke's papers, including his extensive correspondence with women, are housed in the archives of the College of St. Paul in Washington, D.C. He has been the subject of a biography by fellow Paulist John B. Sheerin, *Never Look Back: The Career and Concerns of John J. Burke, C.S.P.* (1975), and his contribution to national Catholic organization is detailed by Douglas Slawson, *The Foundation and First Decade of the National Catholic Welfare Council* (1992).

ELIZABETH MCKEOWN

BURKE, Kenneth (5 May 1897–19 Nov. 1993), writer and critic, was born Kenneth Duva Burke in Pittsburgh, Pennsylvania, the son of James Leslie Burke and Lillyan May Duva. He attended Ohio State University from 1916 to 1917 and Columbia University from 1917 to 1918 but quit college to concentrate on his writing. He imposed on himself a rigorous and systematic study of literature, beginning with Virgil and Homer and working through Milton, Keats, Shelley, Dostoyevsky, Mann, and Flaubert. Burke was a member of an informal group of avant-garde writers that included his high school friend Malcolm Cowley, Allen Tate, Matthew Josephson, Slater Brown, Hart Crane, and Gorham B. Munson. His marriage in 1919 to Lily Batterham produced three children but ended in divorce in 1933. With his second wife, Elizabeth Batterham Burke, Lily's sister, whom he married in 1933, Burke had two children. A number of Burke's short pieces of fiction were published in the magazine *Secession*, which he coedited for a short time. A collection of these and other stories was published as *The White Oxen and Other Stories* (1924). His translation of Thomas Mann's *Death in Venice* (1925) was the first English translation of the novel. Supporting himself by working as the music critic for *The Dial* from 1927 to 1929 and for *The Nation* from 1934 to 1936, Burke wrote the initial two scholarly studies and the collection of essays that were to bring him academic recognition.

Burke's first major scholarly publication was a book of essays titled *Counter-Statement* (1931). It included his essay "Psychology and Form," first published in *The Dial* (1925), which sets out a conception of poetry as a means to evoke emotional response through technical devices. Accordingly, a good author must understand his audience's psychological triggers. Burke's theory focuses on the writing of poetry as the active side, seeing its reading and interpretation as essentially passive. The later essays in *Counter-Statement* focus less on literary form and more on the relationship between art and ideology. Although Burke's *Towards a Better Life* (1932) is identified as a novel, it does not fit the genre in the conventional sense of plot, action, or scenes but develops instead through a series of detailed descriptions of emotional states, set forth in letters written by the protagonist, John Neal. In the correspondence he gives the impression of a man increasingly speaking only to himself, and in fact the letters are never mailed.

With *Permanence and Change: An Anatomy of Purpose* (1935), Burke turned to a sociological look at the way language is used. From the premise that motives arise in and through language, he contends here that in a stable, homogeneous society each member's motivations are relatively clear to the others. But when a culture becomes politically or socially unstable, motives and, by extension, language, symbolism, and literature come into question and convey ambiguities. Burke cites the political instability of Renaissance Italy as an example of a culture whose tensions produced rich literature. His subsequent *Attitudes toward History* (1937) examines the methods through which an individual conforms to a social system, and it treats history and historical change in terms of a poetic catalog, corresponding to the literary terms of epic, tragedy, comedy, elegy, satiric burlesque, the grotesque, and the didactic. All of Western history is presented as a five-act drama. Following the publication of *Attitudes toward History*, Burke was hired by Bennington College as a lecturer in literary criticism.

Burke's stature as a theorist grew with the publication of the widely acclaimed *The Philosophy of Literary Form: Studies in Symbolic Action* (1941), which examines the implications of a literary work's formal structure and explores the ways that these structures create meaning. *A Grammar of Motives* (1945) attempts to outline a methodology and a vocabulary with which to discuss motivation, attempting to situate the discussion within the great philosophical systems in the history of thought; the text introduces five key elements of motivation: Act, Scene, Agent, Agency, and Purpose. A companion volume, *A Rhetoric of Motives* (1950), analyzes how society is structured around the sharing of motivation that rhetoric facilitates. *The Rhetoric of Religion* (1961) considers the structure of Christian stories as rhetorical pieces, arguing that the remarkable emotional power of biblical stories is caused by man's dependence on language and his inherent nature as a symbol-using thinker. Continuing in that vein, *Language as Symbolic Action: Essays on Life, Literature and Method* (1966) focuses on the relationship between thought and the action of articulation.

Burke remained at Bennington until 1962, teaching and lecturing on literary criticism and literature. He was also a visiting professor or lecturer at several prestigious institutions, including Princeton (1949) and Kenyon (1950). Among his many honors, he was elected to National Institute of Arts and Letters in 1951 and to the American Academy of Arts and Sciences in 1966. Burke died in Andover, New Jersey.

A principal figure of the New Criticism, Burke was one of the most controversial literary figures of his time. The poet W. H. Auden called him "unquestionably, the most brilliant and suggestive critic now writing in America." He was innovative in employing techniques and insights from psychology, anthropology, sociology, and Marxist economics in his analysis. His work and his eclectic methodology have always been controversial: supporters claim his methods to be brilliant and original, while detractors claim that his use of methods from other fields is simply inappropriate and irrelevant. He has also been criticized for sophistry and a slippery use of language. A major tenet of Burke's work related to the contextually dependent nature of truth. He argued that often the converse of obviously true statements is also true. Burke was interested in Communist economic theory and, for a time in the 1930s, expressed sympathies with the movement, but the Communist party itself felt Burke was not closely enough aligned with their ideas and consequently disavowed the ideological correctness of his writings. Construing writing in anthropological and religious terms, Burke was interested in analyzing literary works in terms of ritual drama and seeing writers in the cultural roles of medicine men or priests. His philosophy of art was one in which the aesthetic and the ethical merge, where the moral life is characterized by the presence of intensive aesthetic moments.

• Burke's papers are scattered throughout twenty-eight publicly held collections. The largest of these are at the Newberry Library, Chicago; the Beinecke Library, Yale University; the Morris Library, Southern Illinois State University, Carbondale; Washington University, St. Louis; the Fred Lewis Patee Library, Pennsylvania State University; and the Suzallo Library, University of Washington, Seattle. *The Collected Criticism of Kenneth Burke*, ed. William H. Rueckert (1969), is an excellent primary source. Further information on Burke can be found in Rueckert, *Kenneth Burke and the Drama of Human Relations* (1963), George Know, *Critical Moments: Kenneth Burke's Categories and Critiques* (1957), Merle E. Brown, *Kenneth Burke* (1969), and Laura Virginia Holland,

Counterpoint: Kenneth Burke and Aristotle's Theories of Rhetoric (1959). An obituary is in the *New York Times*, 21 Nov. 1993.

ELIZABETH ZOE VICARY

BURKE, Michael (8 June 1918–5 Feb. 1987), intelligence operative and sports executive, was born in Enfield, Connecticut, the son of Patrick Burke, an attorney, and Mary Fleming. After Patrick Burke graduated from the Yale University Law School, the family moved to County Galway, Ireland, where they lived from 1918 to 1925. Each side of the family claimed ancestry as far back as the Norman invasion of 1169.

The family returned to the United States, to Hartford, Connecticut, when Burke was nine. After starring in sports in prep school, he won an athletic scholarship to the University of Pennsylvania where he played halfback on the football team and also played basketball. Graduating in 1939, he had a chance to play professional football with the Philadelphia Eagles, but recently married to a New York model, Faith Long, and with an infant daughter, he chose instead to become a marine insurance salesman in New York.

With the outbreak of World War II, Burke joined the nascent Office of Strategic Services (OSS) in Europe under William J. Donovan, a former Columbia University quarterback whom Burke knew from stories of and a movie about Donovan's leadership during World War I of the "Fighting 69th Regiment." Burke landed behind enemy lines in France and Italy several times during World War II; he also was a member of the Jedburghs, a three-man team of operatives, nearly always including a Frenchman, that helped to plan the D-Day invasion of France. The Jedburghs were known for their daring, engaging, for instance, in paratrooping maneuvers with only three days of preparation compared to the six weeks that was the norm for the regular military. Burke was decorated with a Navy Cross, a Silver Star, and the French Médaille de la Résistance.

In 1945 he divorced his first wife and the following year married Timothy Campbell, with whom he would have three children. From 1946 until 1950 he lived in Hollywood where he first served as an adviser on the film *Cloak and Dagger,* starring Gary Cooper, which was based on many of Burke's war experiences. Burke recalled that he spent the rest of his Hollywood years writing subtitles in English for terrible Italian movies. Late in 1949, however, he participated in an aborted attempt to train Albanian émigrés based in Italy for an overthrow of the newly formed Communist Albanian government.

From 1951 to 1954 Burke worked in Europe as special adviser to John J. McCloy and the U.S. High Commission in Germany. Burke worked on projects exploring the overthrow of Communist governments in Czechoslovakia and Poland, but the plans were never carried out. He believed the anti-Communist exiles lacked grassroots support in their homelands and that the American government did not have the will to overthrow the Communist regimes. But he looked back at his spy work fondly. "The covert world demanded that you find more within yourself—in your head and in your stomach—than the conventional world did," he wrote in his memoirs.

Returning to the United States in 1954, he went to work for Henry North, a former OSS colleague, as chief executive of the North/Ringling Brothers circus. A Teamsters-led strike precipitated the demise of the circus in mid-1956, but Burke quickly found work as an executive for the Columbia Broadcasting System (CBS). From June 1957 to the autumn of 1962, Burke was based in London as head of the network's European branch. In 1962 he returned to New York City to become CBS vice president in charge of American development and acquisition. In December 1964 CBS bought 80 percent of the New York Yankees baseball club from Dan Topping and Del Webb, and Burke became an active member of the Yankee board of directors. In September 1966 CBS bought the remaining 20 percent of the team—the total purchase price being approximately $14 million—and named Burke president and chairman of the board, positions he held through the 1972 season.

Burke presided over Yankees teams that finished in last place in 1966 and rose as high as second only once. "We bought a pig in a poke," he said later, admitting that CBS had not known that the Yankees' pipeline of farm system talent had run dry. Burke did succeed in sprucing up the Yankees' stodgy image. He courted fans from all boroughs of New York and all social classes. He moved the team's offices from Manhattan to Yankee Stadium itself and was a visible presence in both the office and the seats of the ballpark. In "'B' as in Baseball," an eloquent article he wrote for the *Saturday Evening Post,* Burke rhapsodized about how at a ballpark "communal juices flow through an event which is part sporting competition, part picnic and part town meeting." Under Burke's leadership the Yankees arranged with the city government for a renovation of Yankee Stadium, which assured that the team stayed in the Bronx.

In 1967 Burke was considered as a possible replacement for baseball commissioner William Eckert (who was fired after the 1968 season). Burke wrote a memo to high officials hoping "to break baseball out of the prison of traditional attitudes, to change archaic states of mind." But he was too much an outsider to receive serious consideration.

In January 1973 CBS sold the Yankees to a consortium headed by George M. Steinbrenner, a Cleveland shipping executive. Burke stayed on as president and 10 percent owner, but after three months he resigned, realizing that Steinbrenner did not want to share power. "He careens through life," Burke said of Steinbrenner in his memoirs. "No brakes, loose steering apparatus."

Later that year Burke reemerged as the chief executive of the Madison Square Garden Corporation. Among his duties was overseeing the affairs of the New York Knickerbockers basketball team and the

New York Rangers hockey team. Neither team won a championship during Burke's tenure. In 1975 the National Basketball Association fined the Knicks $250,000 and the loss of a first-round draft choice because Burke approved improper negotiations with a star basketball player. Burke did preside over the second Muhammad Ali–Joe Frazier heavyweight bout at the Garden in 1976, and he initiated successful and continuing indoor tennis tournaments there.

With the return to the Madison Square Garden hierarchy of David "Sonny" Werblin, another strong-minded sports executive, Burke retired in November 1981, eighteen months before the end of his contract. He had served the Garden for eight years, the longest job tenure of his career. He moved back to Ireland to a 500-acre farm in Aughrim, thirty-five miles east of Galway. He died in Dublin.

Burke was a rare sports executive who also competed on the playing field and had an eloquent regard for the spiritual nature of sports. "Rest your eyes, ease the tensions from your body, recover your human equilibrium and refresh your spirit," he wrote of watching a baseball game. "And don't bother to bring your watch." Although his tenure as a New York City sports executive coincided with organizations in decline, he exuded an affection for the teams and the fans that was unusual in high places. Asked once for a self-description, he replied, "Just say that I was a jocko who read a book."

• Burke's autobiography, *Outrageous Good Fortune* (1984), has its eloquent moments, especially when he writes about his sports involvements (see his chapter on the Yankees). His essay, "'B' as in Baseball," *Saturday Evening Post,* Summer 1971, pp. 76–78, is memorable. Sportswriters, usually a crusty lot, genuinely seemed to like him. See two articles by George Vecsey in the *New York Times,* "The Gentleman," 7 Nov. 1981, and "Well, I'm a Gentleman," 11 Feb. 1987; also Roger Kahn's sports column, *Esquire,* Aug. 1971. Predictably differing views have been offered on the merits of the attempt to make Burke commissioner of baseball. A positive view can be found in players' union leader Marvin Miller's *A Whole Different Ball Game: The Sport and Business of Baseball* (1991). Former commissioner Bowie Kuhn takes the opposite view of the limitations of this "circus guy" in *Hardball: The Education of a Baseball Commissioner* (1987). Jack Mann, *The Decline and Fall of the New York Yankees* (1967), contains an excellent analysis of the Yankees of the Burke era. For assessments of Burke's role in the intelligence community, see Charles D. Ameringer, *U.S. Foreign Intelligence: The Secret Side of American History* (1990); Corey Ford, *Donovan of OSS* (1970); and Burton Hersh, *The Old Boys: The American Elite and the Origins of the C.I.A.* (1992).

LEE LOWENFISH

BURKE, Thomas (c. 1747–2 Dec. 1783), congressman and governor, was born in County Galway, Ireland, the son of Ulick Burke and Letitia Ould. The family apparently fell on hard times. Burke wrote John Bloomfield on 25 April 1782 that "misfortunes reduced me to the alternative of domestic indolent dependence or an enterprising peregrination, and I very early made choice of the latter." At an early age Burke was blinded in one eye (the circumstances are unknown). As a youth he lived with an uncle, Fielding Ould, a "man-midwife," who had a practice in Dublin. Burke had university training, probably at the University of Dublin, and some medical education. Having quarreled with his uncle, he went to America in 1763. After a few months in Philadelphia he resided in Accomac County on Virginia's Eastern Shore for a year and then in Norfolk, Virginia. Burke had several essays and poems published in the *Virginia Gazette.* He wrote an ode celebrating the repeal of the Stamp Act.

Burke first worked as a physician in Virginia, but finding this vocation not lucrative enough he studied law "for a few months" and was licensed to practice. Burke prospered as a lawyer, specializing in commercial law, often with agents of British mercantile firms as his clients. Burke was an attorney for the Transylvania (Kentucky land) company. He married Mary Freeman of Norfolk in 1770; they had one child.

Witty and congenial, the talented Irishman quickly made friends among the elite in Virginia and then in North Carolina. Raised a Catholic, Burke disavowed that faith and became a deist. Seeking a more healthful abode, Burke moved to central North Carolina in 1772, acquiring a plantation near Hillsboro (now Hillsborough), which he named "Tyaquin," after the Burke family homestead in Ireland. He was immediately licensed to practice law before the Superior Court of Orange County.

Burke was a delegate, 1775–1776, from Orange County at the North Carolina Provincial Congress that sat at New Bern, Hillsborough, and Halifax. A radical, he served on a committee of seven that persuaded the provincial congress to instruct its delegates to the Continental Congress in Philadelphia to vote for independence. Burke wanted North Carolina to establish a purely democratic government; the constitution of 1777, however, provided for property requirements for voting and officeholding. He favored popular ratification of the constitution.

Burke was elected to the Continental Congress on 20 December 1776 and arrived in Philadelphia to take his seat on 4 February 1777. In Congress Burke acted as a watchdog over military affairs. He served on the marine and military supply committees and the Board of War. Among his many assignments in Congress he also served on the committee on Indian affairs and the Board of Treasury. Believing that "power breeds power," Burke resisted any attempts by Congress to expand military authority. He wanted the states to have exclusive power to apprehend and punish deserters. He worked for reform in the quartermaster department of the Continental army.

As an observer at the battle of Brandywine on 11 September 1777, Burke rode among the troops attempting to stem the retreat. He prodded Congress unsuccessfully to remove General John Sullivan, whom he regarded as grossly incompetent, and almost fought a duel with Sullivan and later also with Major Henry Lee. Burke refused to vote for a censorious congressional letter to George Washington in April 1778. Since his presence was required for a quorum, he simply walked out of Congress, stating that he was not obligated to attend when Congress was acting unreasonably. The action, which led to rebukes on the floor by many congressmen, opened up a bitter rift between Burke and Henry Laurens, the president of Congress. Burke declared that he was responsible only to his state and that he would not be tyrannized by Congress. Ironically, at the time he was passed over for reelection to Congress because he supported the appointment of General Edward Hand, a Pennsylvanian, to command the North Carolina brigade. After his return home, however, North Carolinians showed their appreciation for his strong states' right stand in Congress and reinstated him as a delegate to Congress.

As Congress prepared the Articles of Confederation, Burke argued the position that Congress should have no powers over the states other than to declare war and peace and to conduct foreign relations. He was largely responsible for the provision in the Articles of Confederation that powers not delegated to Congress were reserved to the states. Burke even advocated dispensing with Congress at the war's end.

A sound money man, Burke opposed congressional paper money, half-pay-for-life pensions for army officers, and the issuance of loan office certificates, which he felt would primarily benefit speculators. Thomas Rodney of Delaware in March 1781 sized up Burke's role in Congress. Burke "may Justly be Stiled the ablest And Most useful Member there at present," said Rodney. Though not eloquent, Burke was "correct and pointed in his debates, possesses the Honest integrity of a republican and is for preserving inviolable the rights of the people." Yet "he is Some times not fully guarded from Dictatorial language" and "Confines himself Too Much To particular Objects." Toward the end of his congressional career Burke veered away from states' rights to become a nationalist. He proposed a bicameral Congress: a "General House" chosen proportionately according to population and a "Council of State" consisting of one person from each state. Burke favored giving Congress the power to levy impost duties.

Granted a leave of absence from Congress on 12 April 1781, Burke returned to North Carolina, where he was elected by the general assembly on 25 June 1781 to a one-year term as the third governor of North Carolina. As governor Burke showed ability for organization and handling specific problems. Now less the democratic idealist, he advocated a state government controlled by "the few who have wealth and leisure." Burke condoned a policy of retaliation against Tories and persuaded the legislature to confer on him the authority to establish courts of oyer and terminer to try treason cases. Unfortunately for Burke, North Carolina during 1781 was a virtual anarchy; the southern army of Nathanael Greene was in South Carolina, and the partisan war between patriots and Tories had heated up.

A Loyalist guerrilla band under David Fanning, on 12 September 1781, raided Hillsboro, capturing Burke and many state officials. Turned over to the British army, Burke was confined in the Wilmington jail and then at the fort on Sullivan's Island off Charleston, South Carolina. On 6 November 1781 he gained parole but was restricted to the limits of James Island, also off Charleston. Burke's status was "prisoner of the State," meaning that he was regarded as a hostage should Fanning or other Tory military leaders fall into American hands. Burke felt that his life was in danger on James Island, where North Carolina Tories had taken refuge, and one assassination attempt was made on his life. Burke regarded his hostage status and the endangerment of his life as violations of his parole on the part of the British. On 16 January 1782 he escaped and fled to Nathanael Greene's headquarters in South Carolina. Burke offered to return to his parole if he would be treated as a captured Continental army officer, but the request was not granted by the British. Burke returned to the governorship. General Greene held a military court of inquiry, which refused to vindicate Burke's escape from his parole. Burke was formally exchanged on 23 October 1783.

Burke refused to announce for reelection when the North Carolina General Assembly met in April 1782 but expected a draft. Instead Alexander Martin was elected governor. Many North Carolinians, especially the army officers, thought that Burke had dishonored himself by violating his parole. Burke went back to Orange County, in bad health and separated from his wife. He was embittered that the state and the army had deserted him. He died at his estate, Tyaquin.

Although Burke was impetuous, obstinate, and idealistic, few men of his time had greater impact on the evolving political developments. Burke wrote about two dozen poems, mostly love lyrics, and three of his poems were published in his lifetime. One of his first poems was "Hymn to Spring by a Physician." Burke County, North Carolina, created 1 May 1777, was named for Burke while he was serving in Congress.

• Burke's papers are in the Southern Historical Collection, University of North Carolina, Chapel Hill, and also at the North Carolina State Department of Archives and History, Raleigh. Important published collections that contain Burke's papers and correspondence are Walter Clark, ed., *The State Records of North Carolina*, vols. 11–26 (1895–1914), *The Papers of James Iredell*, ed. Don Higginbotham (2 vols., 1976), which covers mainly Burke's activities for 1781, and *The Papers of Thomas Jefferson*, ed. Julian P. Boyd, vol. 1 (1950), which sheds light on Burke's early law practice. For the congressional career, see *Journals of the Continental Congress*, vols. 7–21 (1907–1912); Paul H. Smith, ed., *Letters of Delegates to Congress*, vols. 5–18 (1979–1991); Jennings B. Sanders, "Thomas Burke in the Continental Congress," *North Carolina Historical Review* 9 (1932): 22–37; and Jack N. Rakove, *The Beginnings of National Politics: An Interpretive History of the Continental Congress* (1979). A full biography is John S. Watterson III, *Thomas Burke: Restless Revolutionary* (1980); also useful is Elisha P. Douglass, "Thomas Burke, Disillusioned Democrat," *North Carolina Historical Review* 26 (1949): 150–86. Hugh F. Rankin, *The North Caro-*

lina Continentals (1971), notes Burke's relationship to the North Carolina military effort, and John S. Watterson III, "The Ordeal of Governor Burke," *North Carolina Historical Review* 48 (1971): 95–117, discusses his captivity. Edward W. Phifer, Jr., *Burke: The History of a North Carolina County, 1777–1920* (1977), has some interesting comments on Burke. All the extant poems are published in *The Poems of Governor Thomas Burke of North Carolina*, ed. Richard Walser (1961).

HARRY M. WARD

BURKE, Thomas (22 Dec. 1849–4 Dec. 1925), lawyer, was born in Clinton County, New York, the son of James Burke and Delia Bridget Ryan, farmers. After his mother's death in 1861, eleven-year-old Thomas left the farm and struck out on his own. He secured a position in a grocery store and then as a water carrier for railroad crews while boarding in Marion, Iowa. Later, while working part-time, he attended Ypsilanti Seminary in Michigan. Although slight of build and with a partially crippled arm, Thomas soon gained the respect of his classmates with his quick wit, unbounded energy, deep resonant voice, and eloquent speech—talents he would later use to great advantage in court and at public forums.

Following completion of his seminary course at Ypsilanti, in 1870 Thomas enrolled in the University of Michigan, paying the cost of tuition and books by teaching school between terms. In 1871 he entered the university's Department of Law but, for financial reasons, withdrew after a year to study law with an attorney in Jackson County, Michigan. In December 1873 he gained admission to the bar and embarked on a legal career as city attorney for Marshall, Michigan. Discouraged by the lack of opportunities in Marshall, Burke took a train to San Francisco, California, and then a steamer to Seattle, Washington, arriving in May 1875 in what was then a small but bustling mill town. There law practice, politics, and business interests soon thrust Burke into the limelight, resulting eventually in his identification as the person "Who Built Seattle."

Burke quickly formed a partnership with John J. McGilvra, a former U.S. attorney and Burke's future father-in-law. Burke married Caroline McGilvra in 1876; they had no children. Typical of struggling lawyers in the new settlement, the partners worked primarily for small businesses and individuals. On rare occasions they did legal work for a San Francisco company, a lumber mill, or the city of Seattle. However, debt collections, foreclosures, and loggers' litigation against the mill companies filled much of their calendar.

Within two years of his arrival, Burke was elected probate judge; he was reelected in 1878. In that post he settled issues concerning wills, estates, guardianships, and breaches of the peace. Although a minor judicial office, it helped bring Burke into prominence throughout the area and attracted clients to his private practice. He refused in 1880 to run for a third term. Over the course of the decade, Burke's legal business prospered. His books showed that in 1888 his firm had taken in over $27,000, an impressive sum for those days.

Because of the reputation Burke had earned as probate judge and as an attorney, the local bar urged President Grover Cleveland to appoint him chief justice of the Territorial Supreme Court, specifically to clear up the dockets of the high court and the Third District trial bench, which, by 1888, had accumulated nearly impossible backlogs. He accepted the appointment with the understanding that as soon as the dockets were cleared he would resign. By March 1889, the task was completed, and Burke returned to his private legal, business, and civic concerns.

Early in his career, Burke had become a leading figure in the Democratic party, which remained the minority party throughout most of the territorial years. In 1880 the state Democratic convention nominated Burke as its candidate for delegate to Congress, the only elected national representative of the territory. Although a strong campaigner, Burke lost the race to his Republican opponent 8,814 to 7,014. In 1882 he was renominated; he again lost, this time by nearly 3,000 votes.

The Judge, as he was known, was drawn back into partisan politics after statehood, but now as a Republican. He had become disillusioned with the Democrats because of their failure to repudiate the anti-Chinese riots, their lack of support for the ultimately successful Lake Washington canal through Lake Union to Puget Sound (one of Burke's many civic and business successes), and the party's fusion with Populists and its support of William Jennings Bryan in 1896. In 1910 Republicans persuaded Burke to run for the U.S. Senate. Although direct election of senators was not yet a requirement of the U.S. Constitution, the legislature had agreed to follow the results of a preferential primary. Again, victory eluded Burke. His conservative politics, railroad connections, and ties to out-of-state corporations were liabilities too strong for the voters. After his defeat, Burke turned his attention to civic affairs and promotion of Seattle and the state.

Burke's business interests nearly always dictated his politics. He was the driving force behind a direct railroad connection between Seattle and the East, rather than first going through Tacoma and Portland. The connection was essential to the development of Seattle. He and other Seattle leaders formed their own railroad company, hoping either to complete a line from Seattle to the East to connect with transcontinental railroads or to persuade the Northern Pacific or Great Northern companies to purchase the fledgling line and complete the project. In 1890, largely as a result of Burke's efforts, the Great Northern, which Burke served as counsel, chose Seattle as its western terminus. The railroad connections proved to be "the greatest single factor in the city's growth and subsequent prosperity" (Nesbit, p. 243). Burke's real estate developments, mining, smeltering, and transportation ventures and his successes in luring outside capital to Seattle helped the Emerald City to grow during his lifetime from a small settlement to a bustling metropolis of nearly a third of a million inhabitants.

Burke's activities to promote and develop Seattle involved leadership in the Chamber of Commerce, membership in the Board of Trustees of the University of Washington and in territorial and Seattle school boards, and service as overseer of Whitman College and founder of a number of service clubs and the Washington Historical Society. He also moved easily among national figures, including presidents, secretaries of state, senators, and business leaders, such as oil magnate John D. Rockefeller. In 1910 industrialist and philanthropist Andrew Carnegie appointed Burke a trustee of the Carnegie Endowment for International Peace, providing Burke with an opportunity to promote Washington State ties with the Far East. During a speech in New York City at a gathering of the board of trustees of the endowment on 4 December 1925, Burke hesitated, stumbled, and fell dead. Historians generally agree that Burke's business, political, and legal leadership played a vital role in the growth of Seattle from a small settlement to a thriving metropolis.

• The Thomas Burke Papers, 1875–1925, are at the University of Washington Library. Robert Nesbit, *He Built Seattle: A Biography of Judge Thomas Burke* (1962), contains an extensive bibliography. An earlier source is Charles T. Conover, *Thomas Burke: 1849–1925* (1926). An obituary is in the *New York Times*, 5 Dec. 1925.

CHARLES H. SHELDON

BURKETT, Jesse Cail (12 Feb. 1870?–27 May 1953), baseball player, was born in Wheeling, West Virginia. His parents' names are unknown, and little is known of his youth; Burkett never knew his actual birthdate. Some sources list it as 4 December 1868. Burkett stood 5′8″ inches, weighed around 150 pounds, and threw and batted left-handed. He began his professional baseball career as a pitcher and showed tremendous promise, winning 27 games at Scranton, Pennsylvania (Central League), in 1888 and 39 games at Worcester, Massachusetts (Atlantic Association), in 1889. His major league debut came the following season with the New York Giants. Control problems sent him reeling to 10 defeats in 13 decisions with a lone victory in 12 starting assignments. That was the downside. However, Burkett's biggest break also occurred that year when Giants manager Jim Mutrie began playing him in right field between pitching turns. Burkett answered with a .309 batting average, the second best on the team. Although his fielding needed polish, his good speed and strong arm promised better defense ahead.

Sold to the Cleveland Spiders of the National League in 1891, Burkett was sent to Lincoln, Nebraska, to play every day in the outfield. By August he had been recalled by the Spiders. Not a power hitter, Burkett made his way in the major leagues as a line drive hitter, an extraordinarily good bunter, and an intelligent baserunner. His speed enabled him to get to almost everything hit to left field in the cozy confines of Cleveland's League Park. He meshed well with the Spiders, who were an aggressive and scrappy team. He was tagged "the Crab" for his short temper on the ballfield. No one was exempt from his ire. He argued calls with the umpires and hurled barbs and insults at opposing managers, players, and fans. In 1896 he was thrown out of both ends of a doubleheader with Louisville and fined in court for causing a riot. He was fined for punching Washington manager Tom Loftus in the face during a game in 1903. Fans and players would taunt Burkett by asking him if he was Jack Glasscock's son. Glasscock was a longtime National League shortstop and Burkett's teammate on the 1890 Giants. Like Burkett, Glasscock hailed from Wheeling, West Virginia, and was a terror on the basepaths. At a distance the two could be confused for each other. Why Burkett went into tirades at the comparison is unclear. Despite his behavior on the field, in his private life he did not drink or smoke and loved to spend time with young baseball fans. He married Nellie McGrath in 1890, and they made her hometown of Worcester their lifelong residence.

From 1893 through 1898 Burkett paced the Spiders every season in batting, never dipping below a .345 average. In 1895 and 1896 he led the National League with .423 and .410 batting averages. His speed and excellent bunting contributed greatly to his lofty averages. Brothers Frank and Stanley Robison owned the Cleveland Spiders and through an attorney bought another National League franchise, the St. Louis Browns, in 1898. Cleveland experienced poor attendance despite having good ball clubs. Therefore, for the 1899 campaign the Robison brothers traded the Spiders' stars, including Burkett, to their St. Louis Browns franchise, which they outfitted in red-trimmed uniforms and red socks instead of the traditional brown. This led to a new team name, the Cardinals. Burkett continued his hitting heroics with a .402 batting average, making him the first player to bat .400 three times. He won a third National League batting title in 1901 with a .382 average. Between 1892 and 1901 Burkett scored 115 or more runs in a season nine times, including league highs of 160 in 1896 and 139 in 1901. His 225 hits topped the league in 1895, as did his 240 hits the following year and his 228 hits in 1901.

When the Milwaukee Brewers of the American League moved to St. Louis for the 1902 season, they made Burkett's former teammate Jim McAleer the manager. Burkett was persuaded by his old friend to abandon the Cardinals for the new St. Louis Browns. For three seasons he was everyday left fielder for the Browns. Traded for outfielder George Stone, he finished his major league career with the Boston Red Sox in 1905. In 2,072 games Burkett batted .341 on 2,873 hits.

The sweat and spit of the ball diamond had flowed in Burkett's veins too long to allow him to be away from the game he loved. Therefore, in 1906 he purchased the Worcester, Massachusetts, team in the New England League, managed it, played the outfield, and won a minor league batting title with a .344

average. He continued to play and manage the club through 1913 and won four pennants. Unable to stay away from the game, he returned to managing in 1916 in the Eastern League at Lawrence, Massachusetts. He then managed teams at Hartford, Connecticut, and Lowell, Massachusetts, at Worcester again in 1923 and 1924, at Lewiston, Maine, in 1928 and 1929, and finally returned to Lowell for the 1933 campaign. In between his managerial stints he was baseball coach at Holy Cross College and a scout and coach for the New York Giants. Burkett was hired as a special assignment coach in 1921 by the Giants' field boss, John McGraw. His on-the-field disposition caused the players to refuse to vote Burkett a World Series share. Although he was one of the greatest hitters in the history of the game, his nineteenth-century heroics were dimmed by the passage of time. Burkett was not elected to the National Baseball Hall of Fame until 1946. He died in Worcester.

• The Jesse Cail Burkett File is available at the National Baseball Hall of Fame Library, Cooperstown, N.Y. Complete statistical coverage of Burkett's major league career is in MacMillan's *The Baseball Encyclopedia*, 8th ed. (1990). Short biographies are in Martin Appel and Burt Goldblatt, *Baseball's Best: The Hall of Fame Gallery* (1977); David L. Porter, *Biographical Dictionary of American Sports: Baseball* (1987); and Lowell Reidenbaugh, *Cooperstown: Where Baseball Legends Live Forever* (1983). See also John Thorn and Peter Palmer, eds., *Total Baseball* (1989). An obituary is in the *New York Times*, 28 May 1953.

FRANK J. OLMSTED

BURKHOLDER, Paul Rufus (1 Feb. 1903–11 Aug. 1972), microbiologist, was born in Orrstown, Pennsylvania, the son of William Rankin Burkholder, a minister of the United Brethren church, and Mary Ellen Schubert. He attended high school in nearby Chambersburg and in 1920 matriculated at Dickinson College in Carlisle, Pennsylvania. Coming from a family of modest means, he paid for his education by working in the campus library when school was in session and as a farm laborer in the summer. After receiving his A.B. in 1924, he enrolled in Cornell University and studied plant physiology. He supported himself by surveying phytoplankton in the Cayuga Lake basin as part of a geographical and biological study of New York's watersheds for the State Conservation Department; he received his Ph.D. in botany in 1929.

Burkholder then became a curator at the Buffalo (New York) Museum of Natural Sciences. In 1930 he married Lillian Miller, with whom he had three children. At the museum he taught and mounted exhibits on heredity and the environment, while continuing his phytoplankton studies, now a joint project of the museum and the state of New York. He conducted microplankton studies on Lake Erie, several lakes in northern New York, and Frenchman's and Penobscot bays near Bar Harbor, Maine, while affiliated with the museum. In 1932 he was awarded a National Research Council Fellowship in botany and spent the next two years at Harvard and Columbia Universities, studying the effect of changes in hydrogen ion concentration in water on the movement of blue-green algae, primitive photosynthetic organisms that at the time were considered to occupy a middle ground between bacteria and higher plants.

In 1934 Burkholder accepted an appointment as assistant professor of botany at Connecticut College for Women; he was promoted to associate professor three years later. While at Connecticut College, he conducted research on the role of light in the life of plants and on the relationship between plant hormones and mineral nutrition. He collaborated in the latter area with George S. Avery, a fellow teacher at the college; in 1936 they published the textbook *Growth Hormones in Plants*.

In 1938 Burkholder became associate professor of botany and plant physiologist at the University of Missouri, where he continued his research on plant nutrition. He was especially curious about the relationship of the vitamin B complex, particularly pyridoxine and thiamine, to the growth and development of plants. In 1940 he left Missouri to join the faculty of botany at Yale University, where he was named Eaton Professor of Botany in 1944.

The creation in 1940 of an injectable agent of penicillin, an antibiotic drug derived from certain fungal molds, inspired Burkholder to search for other useful antibiotics by investigating the antimicrobial activity of lower forms of plant life. He began by studying lichens, symbiotic unions between fungi and algae, and proceeded to the study of fungus colonies. After Selman A. Waksman in 1944 discovered that certain actinomycetes, or soil bacteria, produce the antibiotic streptomycin, Burkholder refocused his research efforts on these microorganisms. He studied and rejected sixty-four different species of soil bacteria before discovering in 1947 that a Venezuelan actinomycete produces chloramphenicol, an antibiotic substance that interferes with protein synthesis in many disease-causing bacteria. Chloramphenicol, the fifth antibiotic to be discovered, was synthesized in 1949 and brought to market under the trade name Chloromycetin. It quickly became the preferred treatment for epidemic typhus, scrub typhus, and typhoid fever, and it was used to save the lives of many American combat troops during the Korean War.

While searching for new antibiotics, Burkholder also devoted much attention to the study of vitamins, especially the vitamin B complex. In 1952, after extensive experimentation with hog and human stomachs, he developed a method of administering vitamin B_{12} orally in the hope that patients with pernicious anemia, who had been required to take the vitamin intravenously, could be treated with greater ease. The method failed to be effective, however, because pernicious anemia inhibits the body's production of intrinsic factor, a substance that must combine with vitamin B_{12} before the stomach can absorb it, and today the vitamin is still administered by injection.

Burkholder became the chairman of Yale's Department of Plant Science in 1950. Although a brilliant researcher, he had no interest in the politics of science and proved to be a poor administrator, and several of the department's faculty members responded by transferring to other departments or leaving Yale. Burkholder himself soon departed, in 1953 becoming head of the Department of Bacteriology at the University of Georgia. When things worked out no better for him there, in 1956 he accepted an offer from his old friend Avery, now director of the Brooklyn Botanic Garden, to become that institution's director of research. This move suited Burkholder well because it allowed him to work night and day on research. He supervised investigations of tissue culture, the physiology of lower plants, and experimental horticulture while continuing his own search for new antibiotics. He was especially interested in finding an antibiotic that could destroy cancer cells; to this end he collaborated with the research staff at the Sloan-Kettering Institute for Cancer Research, sending them specimens he believed to hold potential for use in chemotherapy. His most promising discoveries in this line came from various strains of the same bacteria that produce streptomycin, but none of the antibiotics produced by these strains were developed into effective chemotherapeutic agents. By his own calculation, he experimented with more than 100,000 different soil samples before abandoning his quest to find a cure for cancer among the actinomycetes.

While at the Botanic Garden, Burkholder renewed his interest in marine life; in addition to his work with soil bacteria, he began to seek antimicrobial activity among such aquatic creatures as horny corals and the marine life of shallow waters. In 1961 he became chairman of the marine biology program at Columbia University's Lamont Geological Observatory (later called the Lamont-Doherty Earth Observatory), continuing his search for new antibiotics by investigating phytoplankton, corals, sponges, and seaweeds. His search led him to the waters of Antarctica, the Gaspé Peninsula, Puerto Rico, the Philippines, and Australia's Great Barrier Reef. He retired in 1969, later holding appointments as visiting professor at the University of Puerto Rico, the College of the Virgin Islands, and the University of Wisconsin. He died in Madison, Wisconsin.

Burkholder received several honors for his contributions, including election to the National Academy of Sciences (1949), and Dickinson's Joseph Priestley Memorial Award (1953). He served as secretary of the Biological Society of America (1940–1945) and as president of the American Society of Naturalists (1948).

Burkholder's major contribution to science was his discovery of chloramphenicol. Although this antibiotic has been used to treat eye, ear, and skin infections as well as meningitis, rickettsial diseases, and brain abscess, its greatest value is its exceptional effectiveness against the killers typhus and typhoid fever.

• A good biography of Burkholder and a complete bibliography of his work appear in James G. Horsfall, "Paul Rufus Burkholder," National Academy of Sciences, *Biographical Memoirs* 47 (1975): 3–25. His obituary is in the *New York Times*, 13 Aug. 1972.

CHARLES W. CAREY, JR.

BURLEIGH, Charles Calistus (3 Nov. 1810–13 June 1878), antislavery lecturer and reformer, was born in Plainfield, Connecticut, the son of Rinaldo Burleigh, a farmer and educator, and Lydia Bradford. Burleigh came from a family that was passionately committed to antislavery and other moral reforms. His father was the first president of the Windham County Antislavery Society, his sister taught at Prudence Crandall's school for African-American girls, and, of his five brothers, no less than three (Cyrus M., George S., and William H.) were committed abolitionists.

Burleigh's active involvement in the antislavery cause began in 1833 while he was working on his father's farm and reading law. By that time Prudence Crandall's decision to open a school for African-American girls had provoked the Connecticut legislature to enact a law prohibiting anyone who operated a school for African Americans from admitting out-of-state students without the consent of the local authorities. In an article in *The Genius of Temperance* Burleigh attacked the statute. As Crandall's school became a cause célèbre within the early abolition movement, Arthur Tappan counselled Crandall's supporters to put out a newspaper to publicize their cause, and he promised to pay all of its expenses. Thus it was that Samuel J. May came to invite Burleigh to edit a new paper, *The Unionist*. Burleigh put out the paper for the next year and a half, all the while preparing himself for a career in the law.

In January 1835 Burleigh took the examination for admission to the Windham County Bar and won the praise of his examiners as the most knowledgeable candidate in memory. At this time Samuel J. May approached Burleigh again, asking if he would take the post of general agent of the Middlesex (Connecticut) Antislavery Society. As May described it, Burleigh agonized over the decision for about an hour, weighing hopes for professional prestige and wealth against the difficulties of life as an antislavery agent. Then he told May, "This is not what I expected or intended, but it is what I ought to do."

After this, Burleigh devoted his life to lecturing on behalf of abolition and other reforms. He was with William Lloyd Garrison in October 1835 when the latter was led through the streets of Boston by an antiabolitionist mob, and he wrote the first abolitionist account of that event. By mid-1836 both Burleigh and his brother William were members of Theodore Dwight Weld's "Band of Seventy" antislavery agents.

In 1836 the American Antislavery Society sent Burleigh and nine of his fellow agents to Philadelphia, and for more than a year he was part of an intense campaign to spread the gospel of abolition throughout eastern Pennsylvania. As a probable consequence of this work, the number of antislavery societies in the state grew within a two year period from thirty-two to ninety-three. Exhausted and ill from his labors, Burleigh temporarily retired from lecturing in December 1837. Hoping that a warm climate might restore his health, he joined L. C. Gunn on a visit to Haiti to gather evidence that blacks could successfully govern themselves. Unfortunately, Haiti was under the brutal rule of Jean Pierre Boyer at this time, and the two came home without the material they sought.

On 15 May 1838, just two days before the burning of Philadelphia's Pennsylvania Hall, Burleigh spoke in that meetinghouse on the mistreatment of Native Americans. His choice of topic reflected the growing breadth of his reform interests. An enthusiastic follower of William Lloyd Garrison, Burleigh supported women's rights and pacifism, opposed government as an institution, and came to believe that the U.S. Constitution was little more than a covenant with slaveholders.

In 1840 John Greenleaf Whittier stepped down as editor of the *Pennsylvania Freeman*, the official newspaper of the state antislavery society, and Burleigh stepped in to take his place. Over the next six years the editorship of the *Freeman* underwent a variety of changes, but, whether as sole editor, coeditor, or occasional editor, Burleigh was usually somewhere in the picture. Burleigh married Gertrude Kimber in 1842; they had three children.

In 1845 Burleigh published an attack on capital punishment titled *Thoughts on the Death Penalty*. In this tract he argued that "humanity forbids, and the spirit of Christ condemns, all punishment aimed at retribution merely." Burleigh was equally passionate in his opposition to legal enforcement of the sabbath, and early in 1847 the authorities in West Chester, Pennsylvania, arrested him for selling books on Sunday. Unrepentant, he was among the participants in an Anti-Sabbath Convention held in Boston in 1848.

From the 1830s on Burleigh was deeply committed to the cause of women's rights. Speaking at the Cleveland Women's Rights Convention of 1853, he summed up his views by saying that the question was not about defining the proper sphere of women but rather about "whether one human being . . . is to fix for another human being . . . the proper field of action and the proper mode of employing the faculties which God has given them" (Stanton, p. 148).

In 1859 Burleigh published a lecture titled *No Slave Hunting in the Old Bay State*. Chosen as corresponding secretary of the American Antislavery Society in the same year, Burleigh wrote the society's annual reports for the next three years. The 1860 report was titled *The Antislavery History of the John Brown Year* (1861) and was considered something of a classic within its genre.

To the displeasure of some of his coworkers, Burleigh cut a strikingly unusual figure on the lecture circuit. He had a flowing beard, hair that came down to his shoulders in ringlets, and a robe reminiscent of an Old Testament prophet. He spent his later years in Florence, Massachusetts, where he died in a railroad accident.

Charles C. Burleigh was a deeply committed reformer and Garrisonian abolitionist. Unlike many of the early antislavery advocates who traveled the lecture circuit, he was not trained as a minister, but even so, there is no doubt that the wellsprings of his commitment to reform are to be found in the Second Great Awakening. He was an incisive thinker with a widely recognized talent for debate, but Garrison, among others, expressed concern that the unconventionality of his appearance had the effect of "subtracting from his usefulness as a public lecturer" (quoted in Aileen S. Kraditor, *Means and Ends in American Abolitionism* [1967], p. 224). It appears, however, that after he became a Garrisonian abolitionist his beliefs did not significantly change.

• Manuscript materials pertaining to Charles C. Burleigh are scattered and scant, the richest sources being the Edward M. Davis Collection at the Houghton Library, Harvard University and the William Lloyd Garrison Collection of the Boston Public Library. The Historical Society of Pennsylvania has a good collection of pamphlets and tracts written by Burleigh in the years before 1857. Samuel J. May, *Some Recollections of Our Antislavery Conflict* (1869) provides an eyewitness account of Burleigh's entrance into the antislavery movement. Ira V. Brown, "An Antislavery Agent: C. C. Burleigh in Pennsylvania, 1836–1837," *Pennsylvania Magazine of History and Biography*, 105 (1981): 66–84, focuses on Burleigh's first labors as a lecturer in Pennsylvania but also provides valuable material on his career both before and after 1836–1837. For genealogical information see Charles Burleigh, *Genealogy of the Burley or Burleigh Family of America* (1880). See also brief references in Wendell Phillips Garrison and Francis Jackson Garrison, *William Lloyd Garrison* (1885–1889), Elizabeth Cady Stanton et al., *History of Woman Suffrage*, vol. 1 (1881), Dwight L. Dumond, *Antislavery* (1966), Seth Hunt, "Charles C. Burleigh," in Charles A. Sheffield, ed., *The History of Florence, Massachusetts* (1895), and Ellen Larned, *History of Windham County, Connecticut*, vol. 2 (1880). Burleigh's obituary is in the *Boston Evening Transcript*, 14 June 1878.

WILLIAM COHEN

BURLEIGH, Henry Thacker (2 Dec. 1866–12 Sept. 1949), composer and spiritual singer, was born in Erie, Pennsylvania. Nothing is known about his parentage. When he was a little boy his excellent singing voice made him a sought-after performer in churches and synagogues in and around his hometown. In 1892, having decided on a career in music, Burleigh won a scholarship to the National Conservatory of Music in New York. His matriculation coincided with the arrival of the Czech composer Antonín Dvořák, who taught there for four years. Dvořák, who desired exposure to indigenous American musical materials, found a valuable resource in the young Burleigh, who sang for him various African-American spirituals. From Burleigh, Dvořák first heard "Go Down, Moses," "Roll, Jordan, Roll," "Were You There," "Swing Low," and "Deep River." When Dvořák set an arrangement of Stephen Foster's "Old Folks at Home," he dedicated it to Burleigh.

Buoyed by Dvořák's interest, Burleigh was further encouraged by what he interpreted to be fragments of these spirituals in Dvořák's famous *New World Symphony*. Some analysts agreed, but others took exception to this interpretation. An aesthetic dispute quickly took on political overtones. "Nothing could be more ridiculous than the attempts that have been made to find anything black . . . in the glorious soulful melody which opens the symphony," opined one New York critic. "Nothing could be more white. . . . Only a genius could have written it." While a few figures in the outwardly refined world of concert music had expressed some appreciation of African-American traditions, Burleigh saw how readily this attitude could yield to prejudices that were ultimately no different from the racism so obvious elsewhere in his life. Burleigh never forgot the lesson. Indeed, when his own compositions first came before the same New York critics in the late 1890s, the composer encountered the same perverse efforts to reduce art to racial categories. One critic, admitting Burleigh's quality, proclaimed that "in his excellent songs [Burleigh was] more white than black."

Torn between the sincere appreciation he received from such a luminary as Dvořák and the racism of others, Burleigh was wary of the white-dominated music world, but he was also leery of racially based separatism, which for him was equally dispiriting. He was uncomfortable with the growing popularity of minstrelsy and jazz in the early twentieth century, for he feared that African-American musical traditions could too easily be caricatured and mocked. Minstrel songs, he declared, "are gay and attractive. They have a certain rhythm, but they are not really music. The mistake [in capitalizing on their appeal] was partly the fault of the Negroes, partly the result of economic pressure."

Burleigh would never sell out his art, as he was sensitive to how easily it could be miscast and distorted. At the same time, though, he never abandoned the ideal that the cultural store he could bring forth in his singing and songwriting had a universality and hence a potential to reach out to all. The spiritual, he felt, provided "the accent that is needed, a warm personal feeling which goes directly to the heart of the people." It had meaning as an articulation not only of African-American culture but of the general human experience, particularly of the great human yearnings for freedom and universality, illustrated by what Burleigh believed to be the two most profound stories in scripture—those of Moses and of the Resurrection. To Burleigh the spirituals embodied these profound sentiments. Dvořák's response to them revealed how they could resonate in the soul of another musically sensitive person who was as yet unacquainted with any component of American culture. During World War I Burleigh found this point further underscored when a song he wrote called "The Young Warrior" became a popular marching tune among troops in the Italian army.

While working as a notator and editor in a New York publishing house, Burleigh continued to compose, almost exclusively as a songwriter, and throughout his life he sang. He became a celebrated performer of spirituals in several New York churches and compiled and published the first full anthology of African-American religious music. He died in New York City.

• The only biography of Burleigh is Anne K. Simpson, *Hard Trials: The Life and Music of Henry T. Burleigh* (1990). Eileen Southern's noted work, *The Music of Black Americans: A History* (1971), is also a useful reference on Burleigh.

ALAN LEVY

BURLEIGH, William Henry (2 Feb. 1812–18 Mar. 1871), abolitionist and editor, was born in Woodstock, Connecticut, the son of Rinaldo Burleigh, a schoolmaster and farmer, and Lydia Bradford. Most of Burleigh's boyhood was spent on his father's Plainfield, Connecticut, farm, and like many Yankee farm boys, his seasonal labors were punctuated by episodes of formal education. He and his five brothers enjoyed the instruction of their father, a Yale graduate and director of the local Plainfield Academy until 1823. While a young man Burleigh was apprenticed, first to a clothing dyer and later to a printer, and by 1830 had risen to journeyman in the printing office of the Stonington *Phenix*, where some of his earliest articles appeared. Two years later he joined the Schenectady (N.Y.) *Cabinet* as a printer and contributor. He married twice, the first time around 1833 to Harriet Adelia Frink of Stonington, Connecticut, with whom he had seven children. Following her death in 1864, he married Celia Burr of Troy, New York, in 1865. There is no evidence that they had any children together.

In 1833 Burleigh went to work for his older brother Charles, a law student and recently appointed editor of the Brooklyn (Conn.) *Unionist*. The *Unionist* began publication in July to support Prudence Crandall, a local Quaker schoolmistress, who won attention throughout the North in 1833 after her arrest for violating a state statute against the "instruction of colored persons." Crandall's efforts on behalf of black education won the respect of northern reformers. One admirer, Arthur Tappan, was a wealthy New York merchant who bankrolled the publication of the *Unionist* on behalf of Crandall and appointed the Burleigh brothers as editors. While assisting Charles, William Burleigh also taught in Crandall's school and thus joined the growing circle of reformers dedicated to abolitionism.

From the Crandall affair Burleigh earned a reputation as an able advocate of abolitionism and soon won another editorial position with the Schenectady *Literary Journal*. Abolitionist leader Theodore Dwight Weld described Burleigh as a "powerful lecturer" and in August 1836 recommended him as a paid agent to the American Anti-Slavery Society, a position Burleigh accepted. Most likely he served primarily as a lecturer, though he no doubt also solicited subscriptions to abolitionist newspapers, such as the *Liberator*. The young reformer moved west from New England to Pittsburgh, Pennsylvania, in 1837 and for the next three years took up editorial duties for the *Christian*

Witness (later named the *Temperance Banner*), an organ of the Pennsylvania State Anti-Slavery Society. Although he was one of many abolitionist editors who decried the 1837 murder of Elijah Lovejoy in Illinois at the hands of an anti-abolitionist mob, Burleigh was one of the few who approved of Lovejoy's resort to violence. He was also one of the few individuals welcomed in the rival abolition circles of New England's William Lloyd Garrison and New York's Tappan brothers, both Arthur and Lewis. Abolitionists were ambivalent about the issue of violence, and for a younger man like Burleigh it was easier to move between groups without rigidly declaring a single personal allegiance.

In 1841 Burleigh's first volume of poetry was published in Philadelphia by fellow abolitionist J. Miller McKim. His works exalted the "abolitionists of America" and sang praises to the martyred Lovejoy and to the fortitude of moral reformers: "Unmoved, unswerving, in the thickest fight, / Though scoffs, and jeers, and curses from the vile, / And hate, be poured upon his head the while, / The fearless champion of the True and Right." Although earnest in his reform interests, Burleigh was also self-effacing, and once claimed that only the dullest critics could find nothing to condemn in his poetry. Enlarged reprinted editions of his work appeared in 1845, 1850, and at the time of his death.

By 1843 Burleigh was on his way back to New England, where he edited the Hartford (Conn.) *Christian Freeman* (later known as the *Charter Oak*), which was the principal publication of Connecticut abolitionists. During the decade William joined his brother George in championing the temperance cause and, true to form, traveled in 1849 to Syracuse and then Albany, New York, to become corresponding secretary and lecturer for the New York State Temperance Society and to edit its publication, the *Prohibitionist.* He long remained associated with the temperance cause and contributed to the large body of temperance literature a volume entitled *The Rum Fiend and Other Poems* (1871).

Burleigh had once shared with other abolitionists a distrust of mainstream politics, and in 1841 he had denounced the "Party Spirit—heartless—blind with rage." With the growth of antislavery politics in the 1850s, however, Burleigh overcame his antiparty scruples. He joined a small circle of politically minded abolitionists, including Henry Stanton, Thomas Wentworth Higginson, and Elizur Wright, to work for the Republican party presidential ticket in 1860 and 1864. He also edited the *Republican Pocket Pistol*, a monthly campaign tract in support of Abraham Lincoln, and improvised a volume of partisan sing-alongs called the *Republican Campaign Songster* ("And the hour hastens when the right shall prevail / And the banner of freedom triumphantly wave / O'er the land of the free and the home of the brave"). Burleigh's work in New York reform circles and his willingness to embrace partisan politics landed him the appointment of harbor master in 1855 and later warden for the port of New York, positions he held until displaced by a Democrat in 1870. Throughout the last half-decade of his life he remained politically active and in demand as a lyceum lecturer. He died in Brooklyn, New York.

During a career that spanned six decades, Burleigh contributed scores of newspaper articles, editorials, tracts, campaign propaganda, and poetry to the most important reform movements of his day. He joined the modern abolitionist movement in its infancy and encouraged its evolution into a political force, and he proved versatile enough to reconcile the often contradictory impulses of moral reform and practical politics.

• The best sources for Burleigh's reform sentiments are the many newspapers he edited and the poetry he published, but a number of more recently edited or secondary sources help place him in the context of antebellum reform. These include Gilbert H. Barnes and Dwight L. Dumond, eds., *Letters of Theodore Dwight Weld, Angelina Grimke Weld, and Sarah Grimke, 1822–1844* (1934; repr. 1965); Alma Lutz, *Crusade for Freedom: Women of the Anti-Slavery Movement* (1968); James M. McPherson, *The Struggle for Equality: Abolitionists and the Negro in the Civil War and Reconstruction* (1964); and Lawrence J. Friedman, *Gregarious Saints: Self and Community in American Abolitionism* (1982). The facts of his life are recounted in an obituary in the *New York Tribune*, 20 Mar. 1871, as well as in a memoir written by his wife for the 1871 edition of his *Poems*.

CHRIS PADGETT

BURLESON, Albert Sidney (7 June 1863–24 Nov. 1937), congressman and postmaster general, was born in San Marcos, Hays County, Texas, the son of Edward Burleson, Jr., and Emma Kyle, farmers. His paternal grandfather was a general in the Texas Revolution, a member of the First Texas Congress, and in 1841 vice president of the Texas Republic. His mother's father was a colonel in the Confederate army, and his own father served in the Mexican War, with the Texas Rangers, and in the Confederate army.

Burleson lost both parents early in life, but a substantial inheritance made his broad education possible. He attended the public schools in San Marcos, the Coronal Institute in that city, Texas Agricultural and Mechanical College, and graduated from Baylor University in Waco in 1881. In 1884 he received a law degree from the Department of Law at the University of Texas in Austin and began a law practice there the following year. In 1889 he married Adele Steiner, with whom he had three children.

Burleson was the assistant city attorney in Austin from 1885 to 1891 and district attorney for the Twenty-sixth District from 1891 to 1898, when he was elected as a Democratic congressman to the Fifty-sixth Congress. Returned to office through seven succeeding Congresses, he served in the House until 1913, when Woodrow Wilson appointed him postmaster general.

Burleson was an early supporter of Wilson and worked diligently for his presidential nomination at Baltimore in 1912 and for his election. Although publicly disclaiming interest in a cabinet appointment, he vigorously pursued such a post behind the scenes, using powerful friends to help overcome Wilson's obvious reluctance to appoint him. The president initially did not want someone from Congress in his cabinet, and Burleson had, he thought, pushed too hard for the job. Also, William Jennings Bryan had questioned Burleson's progressivism. But among those who urged his appointment were leading Democrats in Congress, who trusted him to protect their patronage, and his longtime friend, fellow Texan, and confidential adviser to the president, Colonel Edward M. House. Wilson resisted this pressure until February 1913, when he made the appointment that gave Burleson the first cabinet seat held by a Texan.

Burleson was an ambivalent progressive. Too conservative to join the Populist party in the 1890s, he was, nevertheless, attracted to certain Populist proposals, including free silver. He supported Bryan through three presidential campaigns. In Congress, however, he proved to be a fiscal conservative. As a well-off landowner, he was always interested in agriculture, backing, for example, a bill to tax oleomargerine and introducing relatively unimportant legislation to protect cotton growers, including the Cotton Futures Act to regulate speculation in cotton prices. But he spoke very little, and it was suggestive of both his fiscal conservatism and undistinguished role as congressman that one of the few congressional debates in which he vigorously participated centered upon his effort to persuade the House to reduce the budget for Washington, D.C., in 1912 (*Congressional Record*, 62d Cong., 2d sess.). Burleson was, however, highly esteemed by his fellow Democrats for his partisanship, party loyalty, and astute political sense, and he was elected chairman of the Democratic caucus in 1910.

Burleson's conservatism was displayed in his management of the U.S. Post Office. He opposed postal workers' unions, separated black and white workers in the postal service, and was quick to refuse mailing rights to publications critical of America's wartime policies. Acting under the Espionage Act (1917) Burleson forbade the mailing of printed matter he considered to be German propaganda or disloyal. Among the socialist papers refused admittance to the mails was *the American Socialist*. Moreover, his effort to make the U.S. Post Office self-sustaining, thereby reversing the traditional postal policy, wreaked havoc in the rural mail service. Certain that this service was needlessly extravagant, he first proposed letting the rural routes out to the lowest bidder and eliminating the salaried mail carriers, most of whom were Republican. When Congress refused to adopt this, he and his fourth assistant postmaster general began a massive revision of the service. They lengthened the carriers' rural routes, eliminated many, and rerouted others. In the turmoil a number of rural carriers lost their jobs, farmers were inconvenienced, and businesspeople in small towns were infuriated when rural routes no longer emanated from their towns. Moreover, Burleson refused to spend all the money Congress appropriated to extend the service even when indirectly ordered to do so by Congress.

On the other hand, Burleson brought helpful changes to the U.S. Post Office. He established the airmail service and substantially reduced the cost of transporting the mails by rail. Other changes revealed his agrarian inclinations. He placed in operation the nation's present parcel post system and readily enlarged its usefulness to farmers by increasing the size of mailable parcels. He also entered on a short-lived farm-to-table experiment, in which the Washington post office became a store where urbanites purchased farm products brought directly from farms by postal trucks.

Although in 1910 he voted against the Republican version of the postal savings bank, as postmaster general Burleson encouraged its use. In his first and succeeding reports he also recommended the creation of a publicly owned postal telegraph and telephone enterprise, which, like the postal savings bank, had been a Populist proposal in 1892. Congress resisted this effort until 1918, when it permitted the Post Office to seize these lines of communication as a means of controlling information in wartime. Burleson thereby became chairman of the U.S. Telegraph and Telephone Administration. The success of his management of this venture was much disputed, but the argument became moot when Congress returned these businesses to their owners at the close of the war. By that time Burleson's policies and arrogant manner had made him one of the most disliked postmasters general in the nation's history.

Blunt and somewhat pompous, Burleson habitually dressed in a high wing collar and dark suit and was often referred to as "the Cardinal." Such eccentricities did not, however, mar his usefulness to the president. Though often at odds with Wilson's progressive programs, he helped push some of them through Congress and loyally served the president as his liaison with Congress and principal dispenser of patronage. Following the election of 1920, he returned to Austin, where he engaged in banking, farming, and ranching. He died in Austin.

• Important primary materials relating to Burleson include his papers and the papers of Ray Stannard Baker, both in the Library of Congress. Significant published sources are Arthur Link, ed., *The Papers of Woodrow Wilson* (1966–1993); Ray Stannard Baker, *The Intimate Papers of Colonel House: Behind the Political Curtain* (1926); and Josephus Daniels, *The Cabinet Diaries of Josephus Daniels*, ed. E. David Cronon (1963). The *Congressional Record*, 56th to 62d Congresses, is essential for Burleson's legislative career, as are the *Postmaster General Reports, 1913–1920* and *Postal Records*, Record Group 28, in the National Archives, for his management of the U.S. Post Office. The most detailed study of Burleson is Adrian N. Anderson, "Albert Sidney Burleson: A Southern Politician in the Progressive Era" (Ph.D. diss., Texas Tech Univ., 1967), a segment of which appeared in Anderson, "Albert Sidney Burleson: Wilson's Politician," *Southwestern Historical Quarterly* 77 (Jan. 1974): 339–54. Link, *The New Freedom* (1956), The New American Nation Series, ed. Henry Steele Commager and Richard B. Norris; and John Blum,

Joe Tumulty and the Wilson Era (1951), cast light on Burleson's role in the administration, as does Baker, *Woodrow Wilson: President, 1913–1914* (1931). Burleson's change in postal policy is noted in Melville Clyde Kelly, *The United States Postal Policy* (1931). The obituary in the *New York Times*, 25 Nov. 1937, has a summary of his life, and a eulogy by Lyndon Johnson is in the *Congressional Record*, 75th Cong., 2d sess., pp. 353–54.

WAYNE E. FULLER

BURLESON, Edward (15 Dec. 1798–26 Dec. 1851), frontiersman and vice president of the Republic of Texas, was born in Buncombe County, North Carolina, the son of James Burleson and Elizabeth Shipman, a couple who never lived in the same place for more than ten years and never settled on cleared land. During Burleson's youth, his family gained a reputation as American Indian fighters in eastern Tennessee and northern Alabama, and he became part of that tradition by serving as a fifteen-year-old volunteer with Andrew Jackson's army at the battle of Horseshoe Bend in March 1814. He received only an informal and rudimentary education.

Burleson married Sarah Owen in Madison County, Alabama, in 1816; they had nine children, six of whom survived infancy. In 1817 the couple moved to the Missouri Territory, where Burleson was soon elected a lieutenant colonel in the Missouri Territorial Militia. Six or seven years later, Burleson recrossed the Mississippi River to Tennessee, settling briefly in Tipton County and then moving to Hardeman County. In 1827 he was elected a colonel in the Tennessee militia.

Burleson went to Texas in 1830 and on 4 April 1831 received title from Stephen F. Austin to a league of land on the Colorado River in present-day Bastrop County. Once again a frontier settler, Burleson resumed his family's American Indian fighting tradition, in this case against the Comanches.

When conflict between the government of Mexico and Anglo settlers developed during the early 1830s, Burleson's abilities and reputation as a soldier made him a leader in the Texas Revolution. He represented his community at the San Felipe Convention in April 1833 and endorsed the Convention's call for separating Texas from Coahuila and giving it greater self-government within the Mexican federation. Burleson participated in the first fight of the revolution at Gonzales in October 1835 and remained with the Texan volunteer army commanded by Austin that besieged San Antonio. First elected a lieutenant colonel, Burleson became commander in chief on 24 November 1835, when Austin was sent as a commissioner to the United States. San Antonio fell to the Texans on 10 December, and Burleson soon went home to be with his father, who died in January 1836. He was fortunate to escape involvement with ill-fated plans for a Texan attack on Matamoros and was not at the Alamo when General Antonio López de Santa Anna's army arrived on 23 February 1836.

In early March Burleson was waiting at Gonzales as a volunteer when Sam Houston, newly appointed commander in chief of all Texan forces, arrived almost simultaneously with news of the fall of the Alamo. Elected colonel, Burleson commanded an infantry regiment during the five-week retreat that concluded with the battle of San Jacinto on 21 April 1836. His unit occupied the center in Houston's successful attack on Santa Anna's army, and he commanded the force that followed the remaining Mexican army under General Vicente Filisola as it retreated across the Rio Grande. Throughout the campaign, Burleson accepted Houston's leadership and did not become part of the group that threatened to remove the commander in chief. Burleson was discharged from the army on 22 December 1836.

During the years of the Republic of Texas, politics and town building as well as military activity occupied Burleson. He served in the house of representatives of the Second Congress of the Republic (1837–1838) and in the senate of the Third Congress (1838–1839). In 1838 he surveyed a townsite called Waterloo on land he owned about thirty miles up the Colorado River from Bastrop. In October of the following year, his town, renamed Austin, became the capital of Texas. Burleson returned to active military duty in January 1839, when he resigned from the senate and was appointed by President Mirabeau B. Lamar as colonel of a regular army regiment created to protect the frontier against the Comanches. The following summer Burleson's command went into East Texas and participated in the campaign culminating in the battle of the Neches on 15–16 July 1839, which drove the Cherokee Indians from the republic. He resigned from the army on 29 January 1840 but saw action again on 12 August of that year at the battle of Plum Creek. A force of Comanches numbering more than 500 left their usual home to the west of San Antonio and raided all the way to the Gulf Coast, destroying the town of Linnville on Matagorda Bay. On their return west, the American Indians were met by Texans, including volunteers under Burleson, at Plum Creek near present-day Lockhart. The battle that followed resulted in a serious defeat for the Comanches and ended the threat of similar raids in the future.

On 6 September 1841 Burleson was elected vice president of the Republic of Texas. Taking office in December, he served with President Houston for three years, an administration made difficult by his disagreement with the president's pacifistic policies toward American Indians and Mexico. Mexican forces invaded Texas and took San Antonio twice during 1842 (in March and again in September), and in both cases Burleson called for volunteers to punish the invaders by pursuing them across the Rio Grande if necessary. Houston responded by appointing a less aggressive commander of Texan forces and preventing any serious troubles with Mexico. Burleson acquiesced in the president's decision.

Burleson ran for the presidency of the Republic of Texas in September 1844 but was defeated by Anson Jones, who had the support of Houston. Following the annexation of Texas to the United States, which Burleson supported, he served in the senate of the first two state legislatures from 1846 to 1848. He volunteered for the Mexican War immediately upon its outbreak in May 1846, serving as an aide with the rank of major on the staff of General James Pinckney Henderson. Burleson's unit fought in the taking of Monterrey in September, a fight that proved to be his last military action as he was mustered out and returned to Texas in November 1846.

True to his frontier heritage, Burleson moved again in 1847 or 1848, settling a new home at San Marcos in Hays County. He joined the Methodist church in 1848. Elected to the state senate in 1849 and reelected in 1851, Burleson served in the third and fourth legislatures. He was in Austin attending the legislature when he became ill with pneumonia and died. Burleson was the first Texas leader to be buried in the newly created Texas State Cemetery in Austin.

• There is no major body of Burleson papers. Small manuscript collections are located in the Texas Collection at Baylor University and the Center for American History at the University of Texas at Austin. The only full-scale biography is John H. Jenkins and Kenneth Kesselus, *Edward Burleson: Texas Frontier Leader* (1990). A useful sketch of Burleson's life, written only a few years after his death, appeared in the *Texas Almanac for 1859* (1858).

RANDOLPH B. CAMPBELL

BURLIN, Natalie Curtis. *See* Curtis, Natalie.

BURLINGAME, Anson (14 Nov. 1820–23 Feb. 1870), congressman and diplomat, was born in New Berlin, New York, the son of Joel Burlingame, a farmer and Methodist lay preacher, and Freelove Angell. During his childhood, Burlingame's family moved to Seneca County, Ohio, and then to Detroit, Michigan. He entered the Detroit branch of the University of Michigan in 1837 and graduated in 1841, having excelled in rhetoric and oratory. He began the study of law at Harvard University in 1843 and received a law degree there in 1846. Thereafter, he made his home in Cambridge, Massachusetts. He became a junior partner in the Boston law firm of George P. Briggs, son of former governor George Nixon Briggs, and in 1847 he married Jane Cornelia Livermore. Burlingame and his wife had three children.

Friends later recalled Burlingame as possessing "a frank, noble disposition, habits of industry, a charming and persuasive manner, and promising talents as an orator." With these skills, he embarked upon a career in politics. In 1848 he campaigned for Free Soil presidential candidate Martin Van Buren. After passage of the Fugitive Slave Act in 1850, he took to the stump frequently to denounce that controversial legislation. In 1852 Burlingame won election to the Massachusetts Senate and helped host Hungarian revolutionary Louis Kossuth's visit to the state. After participating in the state constitutional convention in 1853, Burlingame joined several other Free Soilers in a temporary alliance with the Know Nothing party. The virtual Know Nothing sweep of the Massachusetts elections in 1854 carried Burlingame to the U.S. House of Representatives.

Congressman Burlingame served his Cambridge constituents well for three terms, but he became nationally known as an antislavery orator and campaigner for the newly formed Republican party. In June 1856, after Congressman Preston Brooks of South Carolina caned Massachusetts senator Charles Sumner in the Senate chamber, Burlingame delivered a powerful "Defense of Massachusetts" in the House. He declared that he would defend his state and free speech "on any field," and Brooks promptly challenged him to a duel. An expert marksman, Burlingame proposed rifles as weapons and the Canadian side of Niagara Falls as the place. There was no duel because Brooks refused the arrangements, believing he could not safely travel to Canada, but the incident transformed Burlingame into a northern regional hero. Large and enthusiastic crowds came to hear him denounce slavery and urge the election in 1856 of Republican presidential nominee John C. Frémont. In 1860 Burlingame spent so much time campaigning in the critical Great Lakes states for Abraham Lincoln that he neglected his own reelection effort in Cambridge and fell to defeat. Lincoln rewarded Burlingame's efforts with a diplomatic appointment to Austria.

Secretary of State William H. Seward sent Burlingame to China when the Austrian monarchy objected to Burlingame's association with Kossuth and expressions of support for Sardinian independence. Burlingame reached Beijing in the summer of 1862. He was the first American diplomatic minister to reside in China's capital, and he faced a sensitive assignment. The so-called unequal treaty system, which Britain and France had forced upon China, gave foreigners economic and legal privileges—such as extraterritoriality and control over China's tariffs—that undermined Chinese sovereignty. Through its own treaties with China, the United States enjoyed the advantages of this system, although it had not joined in the wars that secured them.

With the Civil War eliminating any U.S. naval presence on the China coast, Seward instructed Burlingame to cooperate with Britain and France and simply follow their lead. Burlingame embraced the concept of cooperation, but he extended it to include the Chinese government. His antislavery rhetoric had always proclaimed respect for human dignity and had condemned oppression. In China he began a new reform effort to convert the Western approach toward China from force to forbearance. In 1863 he gained agreement from the ministers of Britain, France, and Russia to abide by a "cooperative policy" that treated the government in Beijing as a sovereign authority. This self-denying pledge did not eliminate the unequal treaties, but it was a marked change in Western diplomatic attitudes.

Burlingame resigned as U.S. minister to China in November 1867 and accepted a commission as China's first official envoy to the West. With an impressive entourage that included two Chinese co-envoys and several Western and Chinese secretaries, he traveled to the United States, Britain, France, Germany, and Russia seeking formal agreements that would ensure continuation of the cooperative policy. Many Western observers characterized the effort to bridge the material and cultural gap between East and West as hopelessly idealistic. Burlingame achieved a notable success in the United States, when he and Seward signed an agreement on 28 July 1868. The Burlingame Treaty, as it became known, was in effect China's first equal treaty, because it explicitly recognized China's rights and sovereignty as a nation. One provision of this convention provided for the free immigration of Chinese into the United States, which Seward sought as a means of providing labor for work on the transcontinental railroad. A decade later this immigration guarantee came under sharp attack in California and elsewhere in the western United States, as American workers demanded the exclusion of Chinese laborers.

Burlingame's only achievement in Europe was to obtain a vaguely worded letter from Lord Clarendon, the British foreign secretary, in December 1868 pledging that China could "count upon the forbearance of foreign nations." He obtained an even more modest assurance in Berlin and nothing in Paris. He traveled finally to St. Petersburg for discussions with the Russian government. While there, Burlingame developed pneumonia and died. He had intended to move to California after completing his Chinese mission, and the town of Burlingame eventually developed on land that he had purchased there.

No other American minister to China matched Burlingame's zeal and optimism. He was absolutely sincere in his belief that mutual friendship could only benefit both China and the West. In one of his most widely reported speeches during his mission on China's behalf, he informed an audience of New York merchants, "The imagination kindles at the future which may be and which will be if you will be fair and just to China."

• The principal collection of Burlingame family papers is in the Library of Congress, Washington, D.C. There is also a collection of Burlingame family papers in the Syracuse University Library, Syracuse, N.Y. Burlingame's diplomatic correspondence is in the General Records of the Department of State, National Archives, Washington, D.C. Some of his congressional speeches are in the *Congressional Globe*, and some of his campaign speeches are in the Massachusetts State Library, Boston.

There is no biography of Burlingame, but one of the most thorough studies of the man and his work is Frederick Wells Williams, *Anson Burlingame and the First Chinese Mission to Foreign Powers* (1912). On Burlingame's career as an antislavery politician, see David L. Anderson, "Anson Burlingame: Reformer and Diplomat," *Civil War History* 25 (1979): 293–308. Some older examinations of his diplomacy include Knight Biggerstaff, "The Official Chinese Attitude toward the Burlingame Mission," *American Historical Review* 41 (1936): 682–702; and Tyler Dennett, *Americans in Eastern Asia* (1922). For a modern analysis see David L. Anderson, *Imperialism and Idealism: American Diplomats in China, 1861–1898* (1985). An obituary is in the *New York Times*, 24 Feb. 1870.

DAVID L. ANDERSON

BURLINGHAM, Charles Culp (31 Aug. 1858–6 June 1959), attorney, civic leader, and social and political reformer, was born in Plainfield, New Jersey, the son of the Reverend Aaron Hale Burlingham, a Baptist minister, and Emma Starr. Reverend Burlingham was a minister in New York City. C. C. B., as he was known by friends, lived in France for a time, after his father became minister of the American Chapel in Paris in 1863. In 1866 the family returned to the United States, and Charles's father accepted a position as a pastor in St. Louis, Missouri, where Charles lived until he enrolled in Harvard University in 1875. He graduated in 1879 with an A.B. He then entered Columbia Law School, from which he received an LL.B. in 1881, the same year he was admitted to the New York bar. Two years later he married Louisa W. Lawrence; they had two sons and a daughter.

In 1883 Burlingham joined what years later became the law firm of Burlingham, Veeder, Clark and Hupper. He became head of the firm in 1910 and practiced law into his nineties, specializing in admiralty law. He served as lead attorney in the United States for litigation resulting from the sinking of the *Titanic* in 1912, since his firm was the legal counsel for the White Star Line. The official reports of the U.S. Supreme Court contain decisions of several important admiralty cases on which Burlingham worked, including *The Styria* (1902); *The Titanic* (1914); *United States v. Hamburg-American Co.* (1916); and *Standard Oil Co. v. Southern Pacific Co.* (1925).

From 1929 to 1931 Burlingham was president of the Association of the Bar of the City of New York. In 1953 he was awarded a medal by that body for "exceptional Contributions to the Honor and Standing of the Bar in this Community." In 1897 he became a member of the board of the New York (City) Board of Education, serving as board president in 1902–1903. Within the framework of his admiralty law specialty, he served in 1909–1910 as a member of the American Delegation to the Brussels Conferences on Maritime Law, which drafted treaties relating to collisions and salvage, two international maritime issues. Also he was a founder of the American Law Institute, an important body of legal scholars, judges, and political scientists that seeks to direct the law in an orderly and meaningful fashion and that issues model legislation in various legal disciplines.

Burlingham had a strong interest in improving the quality of the judiciary, seeing that judges remained independent of outside influences and that unqualified persons were not appointed to the bench. He supported the careers of many important judges, including Learned Hand, Augustus Hand, Benjamin N. Cardozo, and many others of less lasting fame. He viewed the judiciary and the courts as having a central place in our society. He once said, "Our Government, indeed our civilization, rests on the integrity of the courts." He corresponded with influential figures in the United States and Britain. In one instance, he wrote to Supreme Court justice Felix Frankfurter to tease him about the inordinate number of concurring opinions he was writing.

Burlingham also took great pride in working to improve the quality of administration of New York City and in advancing the election of two important reform mayors, John Purroy Mitchel and Fiorello H. La Guardia. Burlingham's efforts in support of the Fusion ticket in 1913 resulted in the nomination and election of Cardozo as judge and the election of Mitchel as mayor. In 1933 his support of the progressive coalition helped elect La Guardia mayor.

Burlingham worked both openly and behind the scenes for many social causes. He helped steer Cardozo's application for membership in the Century Club through residuals of anti-Semitism, played a part in persuading Harvard to award honorary degrees to women, and worked to open the American Bar Association to African Americans. He also helped to allow female students the opportunity to attend Columbia and Harvard law schools.

Burlingham remained a deeply religious man, serving as a vestryman for many years and then as junior and senior warden of St. George's (Episcopal) Church in New York City. He died in New York City.

Burlingham was so influential because of his personality, competence, good judgment, and the quality of the persons and causes that he supported. Andrew L. Kaufman of Harvard Law School wrote of his "wisdom . . . capacity for friendship . . . zest for life, and boundless good humor."

• Information on Burlingham can be found in a catalog at the Harvard Law School Library, "Charles C. Burlingham: Twentieth-century Crusader," with an introduction by Andrew L. Kaufman. See also "Nonagenarian," *New Yorker*, 27 Sept. 1952, pp. 21–22; and "A Legal Triptych: Charles Culp Burlingham," *Harvard Law Review* 74, no. 3 (Jan. 1961): 433–40. The obituary in the *New York Times*, 8 June 1959, contains a front-page photograph. A short editorial can be found in the same newspaper, 9 June 1959.

PAUL BRICKNER

BURNELLI, Vincent Justus (22 Nov. 1895–22 June 1964), aircraft designer, was born Vincent Justus Buranelli in Temple, Texas, the son of Vincent Justus Buranelli and Margaret Myers. His parents' occupations are unknown, as is the reason for the changed spelling of his last name. Burnelli attended local schools in Temple; in Monterey, Mexico; and, after 1907, in the New York City area. He studied mechanical engineering for three years at St. Peter's College in New Jersey but apparently did not earn a degree.

Burnelli, who had been fascinated with aviation ever since he had learned about the exploits of the Wright brothers, found employment in 1915 as a draftsman with the ABC Exhibition Company, which was converting a Bleriot monoplane for exhibition flying. The following year he spent eight months at the Washington Navy Yard, conducting wind tunnel tests for the International Aircraft Company. In 1917 he became chief engineer and factory superintendent for the Continental Aircraft Company of Amityville, Long Island. Burnelli designed and built several airplanes during the next two years, including the Continental Pusher, a two-seat biplane. The machines proved to be a technical, if not commercial, success.

In 1919 Burnelli joined the Lawson Aircraft Corporation of Green Bay, Wisconsin, where he designed the Lawson C-2, a 26-passenger biplane that was powered by two Liberty-12 engines. As aviation historian Richard P. Hallion has pointed out, "This was the first multiengine passenger airplane ever designed in the United States, and it was a historic milestone on the road to the commercial airliner" (*Legacy of Flight: The Guggenheim Contribution to American Aviation* [1977], p. 9). Unfortunately, there was no market for the transport.

Burnelli took little pride in his accomplishment. The C-2, he commented, looked like "a street car with wings." He had become convinced that the future lay with a "lifting body" design for aircraft. That is, instead of the traditional cylindrical fuselage, Burnelli envisioned a fuselage with an airfoil shape that would provide 40 percent of the total lifting surface of the airplane. This configuration, he believed, would be both more efficient and safer than existing designs. What started out as a new idea soon became a lifelong passion. Obtaining financial support from George C. T. Remington, Burnelli set out to realize his dream. In July 1921 the RB-1 (Remington Burnelli-1) appeared. A twin-engine biplane of lifting body design, it featured an airfoil fuselage that could hold twenty-five passengers. Although successfully flight tested, the airplane attracted no customers. By 1924 the initial design had evolved into the RB-2, a slightly larger aircraft with more powerful engines. Intended as a freight carrier, it performed well but did not sell.

In 1927 Burnelli found a new patron for his aeronautical experiments. He joined with Inglis M. Uppercu—a wealthy automobile dealer, wartime manufacturer of flying boats, and pioneer airline operator—to form the Uppercu-Burnelli Aircraft Corporation of Keyport, New Jersey. Obtaining a contract from banker Paul W. Chapman for an executive transport, Burnelli in 1928 designed and built the innovative CB-16 (Chapman Burnelli-16). This sixteen-passenger, all-metal, twin-engine monoplane of lifting body design featured a retractable landing gear (first to be installed on a multiengine aircraft) and high lift flaps. Able to climb on a single (windmilling) engine with a full passenger load, the $230,000 aircraft won high praise from test pilot Leigh Wade. During routine maintenance work, however, the aileron cables became crossed, causing the handsome CB-16 to crash.

In 1931 Burnelli married Hazel M. Goodwin; the union produced two children. Burnelli remained with the Uppercu-Burnelli Aircraft Corporation until 1934. Thereafter he was more or less an independent designer (Burnelli Aircraft Corporation) associated with a variety of companies.

Burnelli built other aircraft on the lifting body principle, notably the UB-20 in 1930 and the CBY-3 in 1946. At one point, it appeared that he would obtain a military contract, leading to mass production, but he was disappointed. Burnelli believed that President Franklin D. Roosevelt had ordered the War Department not to do business with him after FDR learned that one of Burnelli's financial backers was a wealthy supporter of Wendell L. Willkie, Roosevelt's Republican opponent in the election of 1940. Over the years, Burnelli's supporters would point to a conspiracy against him that involved the military-industrial complex. General H. H. Arnold, who considered Burnelli to be "a real pioneer," denied that there had been anything sinister involved. There simply was no demand for Burnelli's aircraft, Arnold explained. The designer, he concluded, "deserves nothing but the highest praise even though he has been unfortunate and unlucky" (quoted in Colonel Albert L. Barbero to John F. Seiberling, 13 July 1983, in Burnelli Biographical File, National Air and Space Museum).

Burnelli supported himself by working as an aeronautical engineer for a number of companies, but he never lost sight of his dream, and he used his own funds to develop plans for innovative lifting body designs. He died in Southampton, Long Island. Heartbroken and nearly penniless at the time of his demise, he left plans for a giant, four-engine, turbojet flying wing transport that would carry a payload of 100,000 pounds at speeds over 600 miles per hour.

• Significant collections of Burnelli papers are in the History of Aviation Collection at the University of Texas at Dallas and at the Connecticut Aeronautical Historical Association, Windsor Locks. The biographical files of the National Air and Space Museum, Washington, D.C., also contain important material. An obituary is in the *New York Times*, 23 June 1964.

WILLIAM M. LEARY

BURNET, David Gouverneur (4 Apr. 1788–5 Dec. 1870), political leader in Texas, was born in Newark, New Jersey, the son of William Burnet, a physician and a member of the Continental Congress, and Gertrude Gouverneur. Both of his parents died while Burnet was still a child, and his upbringing and education were overseen by his older half brothers, one of whom, Jacob Burnet, eventually became a U.S. senator from Ohio, while another became mayor of Cincinnati.

After a brief and unsuccessful stint in a New York counting house, Burnet, aged eighteen, joined the ill-fated expeditions led by Francisco de Miranda for the purpose of liberating Venezuela from Spanish rule in 1806 and 1808. In 1813 he joined his brothers in Ohio. In 1817 he moved to Louisiana and, after contracting tuberculosis, moved to the Mexican province of Texas and lived among the Comanche Indians. After recovering his health he returned to Ohio, where he studied law, but the seeds of his interest in Texas had been planted.

Bearing letters from Secretary of State Henry Clay and Stephen Austin, Burnet returned to Texas in 1826 and obtained an *empresario* contract to settle some three hundred families near Nacogdoches. In this he was ultimately unsuccessful, but Burnet nonetheless remained an enthusiastic booster of American settlement in Texas, warning Secretary of State Martin Van Buren in 1829 that the acquisition of the territory between the Sabine and the Trinity rivers "seems absolutely necessary to the compleat rounding-off of the southwestern frontier."

In 1830 Burnet returned to New York City, where with the help of a new acquaintance, Sam Houston, he was able to sell his contract for settlement to a group of investors calling themselves the Galveston Bay and Texas Land Company. In recruiting settlers the company turned out to be less than completely honest about prospects in Texas, issuing worthless land scrip as a means of encouraging settlement. Burnet never completely escaped the taint of his association with this group. While in New York Burnet married Hannah Este. Little else is known about their marriage other than that they had several children. Burnet returned to Texas with his wife in 1831 and settled on the San Jacinto River.

In time Burnet became involved in the increasingly strained relations between the province and the Mexican government. Along with Houston, Austin, and Mirabeau B. Lamar, Burnet was a member of the convention that met at San Felipe in 1833, seeking greater autonomy for Texas within the Mexican federation. He was the principal author of the *Memorial al Congreso General de los Estados Unidos Mexicanos* (Memorandum to the general congress of the United States of Mexico), which called for the separation of Texas from the Mexican state of Coahuila but which was rejected by the Mexican government. Initially Burnet did not favor Texas independence, but gradually he was drawn into the movement, along with most North American–born Texans. Perhaps because of his earlier conservatism, Burnet was chosen as provisional president after Texans declared their independence from Mexico in 1836, while Houston was named to lead the army. Burnet's relationship with Houston proceeded to deteriorate, in spite of Houston's earlier assistance in the sale of Burnet's contract in 1830.

Following the annihilation of the Texas garrison at the Alamo in March 1836, the army under Antonio López de Santa Anna moved northward toward the Galveston area. Burnet wrote Houston an insulting letter, calling on him to stand and fight. This Houston proceeded to do at the battle of San Jacinto on 21 April, resulting in an unexpected American victory and Santa Anna's capture. Burnet, however, remained critical of Houston and negotiated a treaty that resulted in Santa Anna's return to Mexico.

Burnet's term as provisional president was less than successful. The Texan army was largely untrained and restless, especially after Houston's departure to New

Orleans for treatment of a wound received at San Jacinto. Burnet attempted to appoint Lamar as head of the army, but the army rejected him. Before his repatriation, Santa Anna was nearly seized from captivity by an element of the army intent on executing him as a reprisal for the Texans' defeats at the Alamo and Goliad, and some even talked of kidnapping Burnet himself. Following his return in the summer, Houston was elected president of Texas. Burnet stepped down immediately.

Along with Lamar, Burnet became part of the anti-Houston element in Texas. With Houston unable to succeed himself under the Texas constitution, Lamar was elected president in 1838, with Burnet as vice president. Both Lamar and Burnet, who stepped in as acting president in December 1840 when Lamar became ill, pursued an aggressive and expansionist policy toward both Mexico and the Indians, which proved to be both expensive and controversial. Indeed, while vice president Burnet participated in the removal of the Cherokees from the republic in 1839. As acting president he also tried to ally Texas with the secessionist-minded Mexican province of Yucatan and sent an expedition across the Rio Grande that was captured and executed.

Burnet and Houston confronted one another as candidates for the presidency of Texas in 1841. The campaign featured extraordinarily venomous attacks on both sides, Burnet accusing Houston of being a half Indian and an alcoholic. Houston replied that Burnet's middle initial "G" stood for "Grog" and that the vice president was a hog thief. Two years before, Burnet had challenged Houston to a duel, which Houston had declined, saying, "The people are equally disgusted with both of us."

The Lamar administration's reputation for fiscal extravagance and military adventurism cost Burnet the election; Houston won by better than a 2–1 margin. From that time on Burnet's political career was in decline. He initially opposed annexation to the United States in 1844, but he eventually changed his mind and served as secretary of state under Texas's first governor, J. P. Henderson. Time did not abate his animosity toward Houston. For the next fifteen years Burnet continued his attacks, accusing Houston of intoxication, cowardice at San Jacinto, and partiality toward the Indians.

In the 1850s Burnet's life was marked by personal tragedy, including the loss of all but one of his children and the death of his wife in 1858. He opposed the secession of Texas from the Union, yet his only surviving son died in the Confederate army during the last weeks of the Civil War. Following the end of the war, Burnet was elected to the U.S. Senate but was denied his seat by the Radical Republicans. In 1868 he journeyed again to New York as a delegate to the Democratic National Convention and served as a presidential elector. Increasing ill health prevented him from further activity, and he retired to Galveston, where he died.

• Burnet's papers are in the University of Texas library. For official papers by and about him, see William C. Binkley, ed., *Official Correspondence of the Texas Revolution* (2 vols., 1936), and George P. Garrison, ed., "Diplomatic Correspondence of Republic of Texas," *American Historical Association Report for 1907–1908* (1908–1911).

Burnet is the subject of A. M. Hobby, *Life and Times of David G. Burnet, First President of the Republic of Texas* (1871). See also Conn D. Catterton, "The Political Campaigns of the Republic of Texas of 1841 and 1844" (M.A. thesis, Univ. of Texas, 1935), and Sallie Sloane, "The Presidential Administration of David G. Burnet" (M.A. thesis, Univ. of Texas, 1918). Burnet is also discussed in several works about Texas history, including Binkley, *The Expansionist Movement in Texas, 1836–1850* (1925; repr. 1970); Joseph Milton Nance, *After San Jacinto: The Texas-Mexican Frontier, 1836–1841* (1963); Stanley Siegel, *A Political History of the Texas Republic* (1956); and Justin H. Smith, *The Annexation of Texas*, corrected ed. (1941). Burnet's disputes with Houston are discussed in *The Autobiography of Sam Houston*, ed. Donald Day and Harry Herbert Ullom (1954); Marshall de Bruhl, *Sword of San Jacinto* (1993); Llerena Friend, *Sam Houston: The Great Designer* (1954); Marquis James, *The Raven: A Biography of Sam Houston* (1929); and John Hoyt Williams, *Sam Houston* (1993).

LYNN HUDSON PARSONS

BURNET, Jacob (22 Feb. 1770–10 May 1853), Ohio lawmaker and U.S. senator, was born in Newark, New Jersey, the son of William Burnet, a doctor and farmer, and Mary Camp. His father was the son of Scottish Presbyterian immigrants and served in the Continental Congress and as surgeon general in the Continental army. Jacob Burnet graduated from Nassau Hall in September 1791, studied law, and gained admittance to the New Jersey bar in spring 1796. He promptly moved to Cincinnati in the Northwest Territory, where he married Rebecca Wallace, daughter of a former pastor of the Presbyterian church, in 1800. They had seven children.

Within four years of his arrival, Burnet was "at the head of the Bar and the popular, intelligent and efficient leader of the legislature" (Este, p. 9). He represented both small and large claimants against the legally dubious sale of Miami Company lands by John Cleves Symmes, and despite all hazards attended every session of the peripatetic general court of the far-flung territory. Failing in 1798 to win election to the new territorial House of Delegates, he was named by President John Adams to the legislative council. There he devised a system of laws for the territory, preparing and reporting sixteen bills in the first session alone. A staunch Federalist, Burnet opposed the statehood movement in Ohio on the grounds that it was premature and designed to serve only narrow partisan interests. In a bitter contest Burnet showed himself willing to accept party discipline and campaign among the people, but the popular demand for an early end to the territory's colonial status ensured Federalist defeat and Burnet's exclusion from the constitutional convention of 1802.

Though willing to cooperate with dissident Republicans, Burnet remained an irreconcilable Federalist.

In 1807 he attacked a local Republican editor "with a *large* bludgeon," for which he was convicted of assault and battery (Cincinnati *Liberty Hall*, 3 Nov. 1807, 13 Aug. 1808). The *Chesapeake* incident, however, saw Burnet publicly supporting Jefferson's government against Britain, and in 1812 he even advanced his own money to help recruit and furnish troops. His active support of the war resulted in his election, on the Republican ticket, to the state legislature in 1814 and 1815, where he was even spoken of for the U.S. Senate.

In 1816 Burnet retired from both the legislature and the bar and became a more conspicuously active member of the Cincinnati economic elite, founding local industrial and commercial enterprises, fostering internal improvements, and encouraging educational institutions. In 1817 he was appointed president of the Cincinnati branch of the new Bank of the United States. The parent bank ordered the branch first to overissue paper money; then, in 1818, to curtail drastically; and finally, in 1820, to close. These financial shocks crippled Cincinnati and its vicinity for many years, and Burnet was the greatest single sufferer. All his industrial and commercial enterprises were total losses, and he claimed to have lost nearly $80,000 in public enterprises.

During this depression, which persisted in southwestern Ohio until at least 1823, Burnet shared the popular local resentment against dictation by "selfish" eastern interests. Aware that many settlers who were buying federal land on credit were likely to lose their purchases, he devised a scheme of relief and mobilized so much support throughout the West that Congress implemented his plan in the relief act of 1821. Similarly Burnet sympathized with the state in its confrontation with the national bank in 1819–1822 and questioned claims of federal judicial supremacy. Accordingly Governor Ethan Allen Brown appointed him to the state supreme court in July 1821, with the overwhelming approval of the legislature. Serving until 1828, Burnet displayed "great acuteness of intellect" in his judgments, but, according to an associate, he also often "gave dissenting opinions, which manifested more of his own opinions than of law. No man ever questioned his integrity, but no man ever knew him swerve from his own side" (Mansfield, p. 159). Regarded by many as self-centered, Burnet was to restore his fortune after 1825, since he still owned many outlots that became prime sites for city development.

Burnet's active support of his friend Henry Clay, the American System, and the administration of John Quincy Adams earned him election to the U.S. Senate in December 1828. Though embarrassed during his two years in Washington by the loss of two front teeth, Burnet spoke up for western measures, securing for Ohio the renewal, on improved terms, of a land grant for the extension of the Miami Canal as well as the right to raise money for the repair of the National Road by erecting tollgates. In 1834 Burnet joined the new Whig party, though he still bore the name "Federalist" with pride. According to one contemporary, "no man was a stronger Whig, and few men a stronger partisan" (Mansfield, p. 160). At the party's national convention at Harrisburg in 1839 he nominated his friend William Henry Harrison for president and then served as one of the candidate's "conscience-keepers" during the campaign.

In his later years Burnet was notable for his commitment to intellectual and moral improvement. At various times he was president of Cincinnati College, the Medical College of Ohio, and the local colonization, astronomical, and historical societies. On Lafayette's recommendation he was elected a corresponding member of the French Academy of Science. A staunch Presbyterian of "quickened religious sensibility," he believed in the literal truth of the Bible and was concerned to reconcile the latest scientific observations with it. He produced his recollections for the local historical society, later transforming them into book form, partly to do justice to "that abused, persecuted, misunderstood party," the Federalists (*Notes*, p. 299). A former colleague compared Burnet's *Notes* with Jefferson's *Notes on Virginia*, declaring the book "remarkable for his habit of condensation and succinctness of expression, as . . . for the correctness and purity of his style" (Worth, pp. 60–61).

The Burnet of 1845 was remembered as "a thorough gentleman of the old school, of Scotch descent, his complexion very dark, swarthy; eyes black, and general expression forbidding, and manner reserved and dignified. He walked with a cane, his hair in a queue, and we think he wore a ruffled shirt" (Howe, p. 817). Symbol of an older generation, he was revered in his last years as the "first citizen" of Cincinnati, though his severity gave him the nickname "Cato the Censor." Widely praised on his death in Cincinnati for his constructive services to western development, his career compares with those of his distinguished brothers—the physician William Burnet, Jr., Major Ichabod Burnet, and David Gouverneur Burnet, the ad interim president of the Republic of Texas.

• The main sources are the semiautobiographical "Letters Relating to the Early Settlement of the North-Western Territory, Contained in a Series of Letters Addressed to J. Delafield, Esq., during the Years 1837–38," Historical and Philosophical Society of Ohio, *Transactions*, Part Second, 1 (1839): 9–180, which were later revised as *Notes on the Early Settlement of the North-Western Territory* (1847). Cincinnati Historical Society possesses one box of rather diffuse Jacob Burnet Papers, but his letters may be found in small numbers in the papers of his contemporaries. For personal recollections, see Gorham A. Worth, *Recollections of Cincinnati, from a Residence of Five Years, 1817 to 1821* (1851), pp. 60–61; Edward D. Mansfield, *Personal Memories, Social, Political, and Literary, 1803–1843* (1879), pp. 155–61; Clement L. Martzolff, "The Autobiography of Thomas Ewing," Ohio Archaeological and Historical Society, *Publications* 22 (1933): 162; and Henry Howe, *Historical Collections of Ohio* (1896), vol. 1, pp. 816–17. Burnet's religious and intellectual life is interestingly assessed in Samuel W. Fisher, *History, the Unfolding of God's Providence; A Discourse Occasioned by the Death of Hon. Jacob Burnet, Ll.D.* (1853), and a lawyer's appreciation is given in D[avid] K. Este, *Discourse on the Life and Public Services of the Late Jacob Burnet* (1853). Obituaries are in the *Daily Cincinnati Commercial*, 11 May 1853, and the *Daily Cincinnati Gazette*, 12 May 1853.

DONALD J. RATCLIFFE

BURNET, William (?Mar. 1688–7 Sept. 1729), attorney and royal governor of New York and New Jersey and of Massachusetts and New Hampshire, was born in the Hague, the Netherlands, the son of Gilbert Burnet, a bishop of Salisbury, and his second wife, Mary Scott. William was named for his godfather William of Orange, who became William III of England after the 1688 Glorious Revolution. William entered Trinity College, Cambridge, was expelled, and was then privately instructed by tutors. He was admitted to the bar and in May 1712 married a daughter of Dean Stanhope (her first name and the number of their children is unknown). His wife died three years later. In 1722 Burnet married Anna Maria Van Horne, who died in 1728; the couple had three children.

Burnet's Whig connections served him well after the 1714 ascension of George I to the English throne when Burnet was named comptroller of customs. In 1720 Burnet incurred heavy losses in the South Sea Bubble. In need of money, he exchanged posts with Robert Hunter, governor of New York and New Jersey. When he assumed control of New York's government on 17 September 1720, Burnet allied with Chief Justice Lewis Morris and Speaker of the House Robert Livingston, both large landowners who formed the nucleus of Hunter's court party. Burnet's opposition, like Hunter's, was the "country" party, composed predominantly of merchants. This faction, irritated at being on the sidelines of power, severely criticized the governor shortly after his arrival. The issue concerned assembly elections. On Hunter's advice, Burnet decided to break with custom and not call new assembly elections on his arrival. The existing assembly, which Hunter had earlier packed, promptly voted another five-year revenue.

Controversy between landowners and merchants escalated when Burnet and the landowner-dominated assembly attempted to reduce the influence of the French in Canada. The western Indians were bringing their furs to the French in Montreal, rather than to Albany, and there exchanging them for English-made trade goods that the French obtained through purchase from Albany traders. Imperial-minded English officials disliked seeing the western Indians under the hegemony and exposed to the influence of the French rather than the English. The French intent seemed to be to use this influence as a wedge to establish themselves in the heart of the North American continent, confining the English to a narrow coastal strip. To prevent the spread of French influence, the New York assembly, at Burnet's urging, passed a law banning the Albany-Montreal trade in the expectation that this measure would draw the Indians and the fur trade to Albany. New York's merchants resented this curtailment of their business. To encourage western Indians to trade with New York Burnet then decided in 1722 to establish a trading post at Oswego at the head of the Onondaga River.

Dissension in New York also increased over control of the colony's revenue. Hunter, to obtain funds, had permitted the colony's treasurer rather than the Crown's agent to control the disbursement of revenue. Shortly after Burnet's installation, the colony's treasurer received a letter from the treasury demanding that he give an accounting of the colony's revenue to England's auditor general Horatio Walpole or his New York deputy George Clarke and that 5 percent of New York's revenue be paid to the auditor general, including the arrears unpaid since 1715. The letter was considered by the assembly, where both court and country factions were furious at this threat to provincial autonomy and the provincial pocketbook. The representatives asserted that no such accounting would be made and that the assembly alone would control New York's funds. Walpole was equally furious at the blatant defiance shown by the New York assembly. Burnet, a placeman of Prime Minister Robert Walpole, Horatio's brother, had no choice but to support the auditor general's demands, and the governor's stand was reluctantly supported by the landowner court party. The assembly remained defiant until 1722 but finally acquiesced to the demands in 1723 and agreed to pay the 5 percent fee by the imposition of a land tax.

Burnet encountered steadier opposition from his council, dominated by merchants Adeolph Philipse and Peter Schuyler. When Burnet expelled both from the council, they ran for and won assembly seats. Irritated with the election of his enemies to the assembly, Burnet refused to administer the oath of office to merchant Stephen DeLancey, on the grounds he was an alien, having emigrated from France after the 1685 revocation of the Edict of Nantes. DeLancey and all other foreign-born New Yorkers had been naturalized by a 1715 act, but Burnet chose to ignore this. Instead, the governor asked his ally, Chief Justice Morris, to rule on DeLancey's qualifications. The assembly, indignant that the chief justice and the governor should presume to judge the qualifications of its members, unanimously voted in September 1725 that DeLancey was eligible to serve. Burnet's actions caused formerly neutral assemblymen to swing away from the governor to the Philipse-DeLancey side. The results of this alienation were soon apparent as the assembly that year voted only a two-year instead of a five-year revenue.

In New Jersey Burnet met opposition primarily in the assembly. As in New York, Burnet in New Jersey favored the interests of the large landowners, the proprietary party. His opposition came mostly from antiproprietary interests, the Nicolls patentees, who had received their patents from New York governor Richard Nicolls, not the Crown. The antiproprietary party dominated Burnet's first assembly. Burnet dissolved the assembly in 1722 and achieved a more agreeable body that twice provided five-year support for the government. The colony's economy also benefited when the assembly in 1723 passed the Loan Act, providing for a new issue of paper money to be put into circulation by loans to New Jersey farmers.

In 1727 Burnet was transferred from the governorship of New York and New Jersey to that of Massachusetts and New Hampshire. His transfer was primarily to make way in New York for the appointment of the king's placeman, John Montgomery. It may also have been the result of rising opposition in New York and England to Burnet's antimercantile policies, which conflicted with Robert Walpole's commitment to trade. To the complaints of New York merchants were added those of English merchants, who brought pressure on Walpole and King George II, and Burnet was dismissed, giving the ministry a temporary respite. Two years later the act concerning the Albany-Montreal trade was overturned by the Crown.

Burnet arrived in Boston on 13 July 1728 and called his first assembly. He immediately met opposition when, on the question of his salary, the assembly refused to commit itself to paying him a fixed sum. Burnet consequently refused to accept any salary from the assembly and remained unpaid. In an effort to remove the assembly from the influence of urban radicals, Burnet moved it to Salem and then to Cambridge, but the change of location had no effect. Burnet was further criticized when, desperate for money and living off the charity of friends, he tried to impose a fee on shipping. At Burnet's suggestion, the ministry asked for parliamentary intervention. Before the Massachusetts issue was considered, the governor contracted a fatal fever following a carriage accident and died in Massachusetts. His will stipulated that he be buried next to his wife in New York City.

Although Burnet's struggles with the Massachusetts assembly centered on his salary, and although he came to America primarily to repair his ruined fortune, he was not considered a particularly avaricious or greedy governor by colonials. In fact he was regarded as one of the few governors who was not overly concerned with making money. This attitude, along with his competence, intelligence, and honesty, won him the respect of most provincials, as did his commitment to protecting the royal prerogative and to furthering England's imperial interests. His administrations in New York and New Jersey are generally not considered as successful as those of his predecessor Robert Hunter, but Hunter's longer tenure gave him more time to solve problems; his conciliatory nature also made him a more effective governor. Burnet himself admitted that he was stubborn and inflexible. A committed Whig in England who was devoted to republican principles of government, Burnet, like all other royal governors, did not apply Whig theories of government to the colonies and could not condone rising republican tendencies in England's provinces.

• Personal and official correspondence and addresses to and from William Burnet are in Additional Manuscripts, British Library; Privy Council Register, Admiralty Papers, and Colonial Office papers in the Public Record Office, London; Colonial Documents, New York State Library; Livingston Family Papers, 1664–1780, Franklin Delano Roosevelt Library, Hyde Park, N.Y.

Published correspondence is in William Nelson, ed., *Original Documents Relating to the Life and Administrations of William Burnet, Governor of New York and New Jersey, 1720–1728* (1897); E. B. O'Callaghan, ed., *Documents Relative to the Colonial History of New York* (15 vols., 1856–1887), and *Documentary History of the State of New York* (4 vols., 1849–1851); Charles Z. Lincoln, ed., *Messages from the Governors, 1683–1776* (1909); *The Colonial Laws of New York from the Year 1664 to the Revolution* (5 vols., 1894); *Calendar of State Papers Colonial Series, America and West Indies* (1916); William Adee Whitehead, ed., *Documents Relating to the Colonial History of the State of New Jersey* (10 vols., 1880); *Minutes of the Common Council of the City of New York, 1675–1776* (1905). See also Cadwallader Colden, "The Colden Letters on Smith's History," vol. 1, New-York Historical Society, *Collections* (1868) and "The Letters and Papers of Cadwallader Colden," vol. 1, New-York Historical Society, *Collections* (1918–1937).

For an eighteenth-century account of Burnet's New York administration see William Smith, Jr., *The History of the Province of New York*, ed. Michael Kammen (2 vols., 1972); for an eighteenth-century account of Burnet's Massachusetts administration see Thomas Hutchinson, *The History of the Colony and Province of Massachusetts-Bay*, ed. Lawrence Shaw Mayo (3 vols., 1970). For a modern interpretation of Burnet's New Jersey administration see E. Peter Ellertsen, "Prosperity and Paper Money: The Loan Office Act of 1723," *New Jersey History* 85 (1967): 47–57.

MARY LOU LUSTIG

BURNET, William (2 Dec. 1730–7 Oct. 1791), physician, judge, and member of the Continental Congress, was born in Lyon's Farms, a town located between Newark and Elizabethtown, New Jersey, the son of Ichabod Burnet, a physician who emigrated from Scotland, and Hannah (maiden name unknown). He was educated at the College of New Jersey (now Princeton University) when it was located in Newark under Rev. Aaron Burr. Burnet received his A.B. in 1749, graduating at the head of what was the institution's second class, and was awarded his A.M. in 1752. He studied medicine in New York City under Dr. Staats and then probably continued working with his father in New Jersey until he established his own medical practice in Newark.

In 1754 Burnet married Mary Camp, who died in 1781. In 1783 he married Gertrude Gouverneur Rutgers. The eleven children from his first marriage include William Burnet and Ichabod Burnet, both physicians who served with the patriot forces during the revolutionary war, and Jacob Burnet, who became an Ohio judge and was the author of *Notes on the Early Settlement of the Northwestern Territory* (1847). The three children from his second marriage include Isaac G. Burnet, an early mayor of Cincinnati, and David G. Burnet, who in 1836 became the first president of the Republic of Texas, under the *ad interim* government (before the first constitution was written).

Burnet was one of seventeen doctors who met in New Brunswick in 1766 and started the New Jersey Medical Society, the first such group in the colonies. The society's constitution stated that it was established "to discourage and discountenance all quacks, mountebanks, impostors, or other ignorant pretenders to medicine" while supporting "those who have been regularly initiated into medicine, either at some university, or under the direction of some able master or masters" (Wickes, p. 48). Burnet served as president of the society in 1767 and again in 1786. During a speech to the members in 1787, he said that patients had "often received benefit . . . from the frequent meetings, the friendly conferences, and learned consultations of this Society." He urged the members "to assist in raising the noble, God-like art of healing to the highest pitch of possible perfection" (Rogers and Reasoner-Sayre, pp. 45, 48). In addition to consulting about cases, the Medical Society established a schedule of fees and a committee, which included Burnet, to ask the legislature for a law regulating medicine. In 1772 the colony passed a law requiring that physicians be examined and licensed, thus enabling Burnet and other members of the Medical Society to exclude those they considered uneducated and incompetent.

During his terms as president Burnet presented at least two formal speeches. The first was "An Essay in Latin on the Use of the Lancet in Pleurisy," and the second was a "Dissertation on the Nature and Importance of Our Indefatigable Researches after Medical Knowledge, Together with a Few Observations on the Effects of Opium in the Cure of Dysentery." They indicate that as a physician Burnet was involved in early efforts both to professionalize medicine and to nurture medical research.

Like many of his contemporaries, Burnet was also caught up in the politics of the period. Most, but not all, physicians in New Jersey sided with the patriots. He was a member of the Committees of Safety of both Newark and Essex County in 1775; involved in the arrest of the royal governor, William Franklin, in 1776; and selected to serve in the Continental Congress in 1776–1777 and again in 1780–1781. He was appointed to two committees to consider and reply to petitions and letters, 18 Dec. 1780 and 22 Feb. 1781, and to a standing committee, called the Medical Committee, 16 Feb. 1781. During the war he was active in raising troops and served with the militia and later the Continental army as a doctor. When 1,000 soldiers wounded in the battle of Long Island were removed to New Jersey in September and October 1776, Burnet helped establish two hospitals, one in Newark, which utilized two local churches, the courthouse, and academy, and another in Hackensack.

When Congress divided the country into four military districts in 1777, Burnet was appointed physician and surgeon for the Eastern District. With another reorganization of the medical department in 1781, he became chief hospital physician and surgeon. The medical service, run by three different directors dismissed for treason, corruption, and inability to work with others, was troubled with charges of inefficiency and scandal. Matters were complicated by congressional incompetence and political interference. Serving through this difficult period, Burnet received his promotion as chief when his colleague from New Jersey, John Cochran, was appointed the fourth and final wartime director.

During the war Burnet also served as an Essex County judge, 1776–1786, and then as judge of the court of common pleas. He was active against the Loyalists, and in retaliation, the British reportedly took his medical library and cattle during a raid. After the war ended Burnet continued his practice as a physician in Newark while also farming and serving as a judge. He died in Newark, leaving his large family with substantial property, which included a number of slaves.

Burnet was an active patriot and physician. He successfully helped establish medicine as a profession and the United States as an independent country.

• Details about Burnet's life are in Joseph P. Bradley, "Biographical Sketch of William Burnet M.D.," *Pennsylvania Magazine of History and Biography* 3 (1879): 308–14, by the husband of one of Burnet's granddaughters; James Henry Clark, *The Medical Men of New Jersey* (1867); Irving Kull, *New Jersey: A History, Biographical and Genealogical Records*, vol. 5 (1930); James McLachlan, *Princetonians, 1748–1768: A Biographical Dictionary* (1976); and Stephen Wickes, *History of Medicine in New Jersey* (1879). Information on Burnet's connections to the Medical Society and the military are in Howard Applegate, "The American Revolutionary War Hospital Departments," *Military Medicine* 126 (1961): 296–306, 616–18; David L. Cowen, *Medicine and Health in New Jersey: A History* (1964); Cowen, *Medicine in Revolutionary New Jersey* (1975); Fred B. Rogers and A. Reasoner-Sayre, *The Healing Art: A History of the Medical Society of New Jersey* (1966); Morris H. Saffron, *Surgeon to Washington, Dr. John Cochran, 1730–1807* (1977); and Saffron, "A Sketch of Medicine in New Jersey to 1825," *Journal of the Medical Society of New Jersey* 81, no. 9 (Sept. 1984): 10–15.

MAXINE N. LURIE